Auditing Standards 2020

Standards examinable in 2020 ACA exams

Auditing Standards 2020

Standards examinable in 2020 ACA exams

Croner-i
HR · Tax · H&S · Audit & Accounting

Disclaimer

This publication is sold with the understanding that neither the publisher nor ICAEW nor the authors, with regard to this publication, are engaged in rendering legal or professional services. The material contained in this publication neither purports, nor is intended to be, advice on any particular matter.

Although this publication incorporates a considerable degree of standardisation, subjective judgment by the user, based on individual circumstances, is indispensable. This publication is an 'aid' and cannot be expected to replace such judgment.

Neither the publisher nor ICAEW nor the authors can accept any responsibility or liability to any person, whether a purchaser of this publication or not, in respect of anything done or omitted to be done by any such person in reliance, whether sole or partial, upon the whole or any part of the contents of this publication.

© 2019 Croner-i Ltd

Published by Croner-i Ltd
240 Blackfriars Road
London SE1 8NW
United Kingdom
Telephone: 0800 231 5199
E-mail: client.experience@croneri.co.uk
Website: croneri.co.uk

ISBN 978-1-78887-292-8

Documents in Parts One, Nine, Eleven and the Glossary of Terms reproduced with the permission of the Financial Reporting Council (FRC) and the International Federation of Accountants (IFAC).

Documents in Parts Two to Four, Six, Seven and Ten are copyright July 2014 and August 2016 by the International Federation of Accountants (IFAC). All rights reserved. Used with permission of IFAC. Contact permissions@ifac.org for permission to reproduce, store or transmit, or to make other similar uses of this document.

Documents in Part Ten are Institute of Chartered Accountants of England and Wales copyright and should not be reproduced without their permission.

No responsibility for loss occasioned to any person acting or refraining from action as a result of any material in this publication can be accepted by the ICAEW, the author or publisher.

Material is contained in this publication for which copyright is acknowledged. Permission to reproduce such material cannot be granted by the publisher and application must be made to the copyright holder.

ICAEW guidance is reproduced with the permission of the Institute of Chartered Accountants in England and Wales.

European Communities Copyright material is reproduced with permission.

Crown copyright is reproduced with the permission of the Controller of Her Majesty's Stationery Office.

British Library Cataloguing-in-Publication Data.

A catalogue record for this book is available from the British Library.

Typeset by Innodata Inc., India.

Printed and bound by L.E.G.O. S.p.A. – Italy.

Auditing Standards 2020

Standards examinable in 2020 ICAEW ACA exams

This publication is recommended for students sitting all Audit and Assurance and Business Planning: Banking exams in 2020.

For Audit and Assurance exams, the text may be annotated ONLY to the extent of underlining, sidelining and highlighting. Page tabs may be used, but must not be written on.

For more information on suggested texts and exam regulations, please visit icaew.com/exams.

Preface

Welcome to ICAEW

I'd like to personally welcome you to ICAEW.

In a fast-changing and volatile world, the role of the accountancy profession has never been more important.

As an ICAEW Chartered Accountant, you'll make decisions that will define the future of global business.

By choosing our world-leading chartered accountancy qualification, the ACA, you'll acquire world-leading knowledge and skills – with technology and ethics at the heart of your learning. A focus on capabilities such as judgement and scepticism will enable you to make the right decisions in diverse and often complex environments.

You'll be equipped to flourish and to lead, to embrace technological change and to be adaptable and agile in your work – all within a set of values fundamental to trust and transparency and which set you apart from others.

As the future professional, you're a force for positive change, investing in your own future and contributing to wider economic progress.

Joining over 180,000 ICAEW Chartered Accountants and students worldwide, you are now part of a global community. This unique network of talented and diverse professionals work in the public interest to build economies that are sustainable, accountable and fair.

You'll also join a community of 1.7 million chartered accountants and students as part of Chartered Accountants Worldwide – a family of leading institutes, of which we are a founder member.

ICAEW will support you through your studies and throughout your career: this is the start of a lifetime relationship, and we'll be with you every step of the way to ensure you are ready to face the challenges of the global economy.

With our training, guidance and support, you'll join our members in realising your career ambitions, developing world-leading insights and maintaining a competitive edge.

We'll create a world of strong economies, together.

I wish you the best of luck with your studies.

Michael Izza
Chief Executive
ICAEW

The ICAEW faculties, which include the Audit and Assurance Faculty, provide additional specialised support to faculty members in key areas and invaluable networking opportunities. Support and first-hand knowledge has never been more valuable to the audit profession and the Audit and Assurance Faculty is at the cutting edge of all audit and assurance developments. The faculty provides a comprehensive and accessible package of essential and timely guidance and technical advice which enables its members to stay ahead of the rest.

What do you get from the faculty?

Adding value to your career – the faculty will give you access to expert, exclusive and unbiased information.

Providing a single, authoritative source of information on audit and assurance – via impeccable sources from leading technical experts, a team of dedicated technical managers as well as influential volunteers working in the profession.

Staying ahead of the rest – faculty publications will provide perspectives on wider issues affecting the profession and will give you competitive advantage in the workplace.

Your voice will be heard – the faculty is ICAEW's voice on all audit and assurance related matters. In addition to its proactive work, the faculty responds to consultations, giving you the opportunity to input into developments affecting the profession.

Networking opportunities – as well as providing timely and practical guidance, our regional events can also be a useful networking opportunity.

To find out more, visit www.icaew.com/aaf.

Contents

Part One

International Standards on Auditing (UK)

International Standard on Auditing (UK) 200 (Revised June 2016)

Overall objectives of the independent auditor and the conduct of an audit in accordance with International Standards on Auditing (UK)

(Effective for audits of financial statements for periods commencing on or after 17 June 2016)

Contents

Introduction

Scope of this ISA (UK)

1 This International Standard on Auditing (UK) (ISA (UK)) deals with the independent auditor's overall responsibilities when conducting an audit of financial statements in accordance with ISAs (UK). Specifically, it sets out the overall objectives of the independent auditor, and explains the nature and scope of an audit designed to enable the independent auditor to meet those objectives. It also explains the scope, authority and structure of the ISAs (UK), and includes requirements establishing the general responsibilities of the independent auditor applicable in all audits, including the obligation to comply with the ISAs (UK). The independent auditor is referred to as 'the auditor' hereafter.

2 ISAs (UK) are written in the context of an audit of financial statements by an auditor. They are to be adapted as necessary in the circumstances when applied to audits of other historical financial information. ISAs (UK) do not address the responsibilities of the auditor that may exist in legislation, regulation or otherwise in connection with, for example, the offering of securities to the public.[1a] Such responsibilities may differ from those established in the ISAs (UK). Accordingly, while the auditor may find aspects of the ISAs (UK) helpful in such circumstances, it is the responsibility of the auditor to ensure compliance with all relevant legal, regulatory or professional obligations.

An Audit of Financial Statements

3 The purpose of an audit is to enhance the degree of confidence of intended users in the financial statements. This is achieved by the expression of an opinion by the auditor on whether the financial statements are prepared, in all material respects, in accordance with an applicable financial reporting framework. In the case of most general purpose frameworks, that opinion is on whether the financial statements are presented fairly, in all material respects, or give a true and fair view in accordance with the framework. An audit conducted in accordance with ISAs (UK) and relevant ethical requirements enables the auditor to form that opinion. (Ref: Para. A1b)

> The scope of an audit does not, however, constitute an assurance engagement with respect to the future viability of the audited entity or on the efficiency or effectiveness with which the management or administrative body has conducted or will conduct the affairs of the entity. When conducting an audit, the auditor may identify or be required to consider related matters and, where applicable, may be required to report or to communicate with management or those charged with governance or other parties on such matters in accordance with applicable laws or regulations, the ISAs (UK) or relevant ethical requirements.

4 The financial statements subject to audit are those of the entity, prepared by management of the entity with oversight from those charged with governance.[1b] ISAs (UK) do not impose responsibilities on management or those charged with governance and do not override laws and regulations that govern their responsibilities. However, an audit in

---

[1a] *In the UK, standards and guidance for accountants undertaking engagements in connection with an investment circular are set out in the FRC's Standards for Investment Reporting (SIRS).*

[1b] *In the UK, those charged with governance are responsible for the preparation of the financial statements. For corporate entities, directors have a collective responsibility; those charged with governance of other types of entity may also have a collective responsibility established in applicable law or regulation or under the terms of their appointment.*

accordance with ISAs (UK) is conducted on the premise that management and, where appropriate, those charged with governance have acknowledged certain responsibilities that are fundamental to the conduct of the audit. The audit of the financial statements does not relieve management or those charged with governance of their responsibilities. (Ref: Para. A2–A11)

As the basis for the auditor's opinion, ISAs (UK) require the auditor to obtain reasonable **5** assurance about whether the financial statements as a whole are free from material misstatement, whether due to fraud or error. Reasonable assurance is a high level of assurance. It is obtained when the auditor has obtained sufficient appropriate audit evidence to reduce audit risk (that is, the risk that the auditor expresses an inappropriate opinion when the financial statements are materially misstated) to an acceptably low level. However, reasonable assurance is not an absolute level of assurance, because there are inherent limitations of an audit which result in most of the audit evidence on which the auditor draws conclusions and bases the auditor's opinion being persuasive rather than conclusive. (Ref: Para. A28–A52)

The concept of materiality is applied by the auditor both in planning and performing the **6** audit, and in evaluating the effect of identified misstatements on the audit and of uncorrected misstatements, if any, on the financial statements.[1] In general, misstatements, including omissions, are considered to be material if, individually or in the aggregate, they could reasonably be expected to influence the economic decisions of users taken on the basis of the financial statements. Judgments about materiality are made in the light of surrounding circumstances, and are affected by the auditor's perception of the financial information needs of users of the financial statements, and by the size or nature of a misstatement, or a combination of both. The auditor's opinion deals with the financial statements as a whole and therefore the auditor is not responsible for the detection of misstatements that are not material to the financial statements as a whole.

The ISAs (UK) contain objectives, requirements and application and other explanatory **7** material that are designed to support the auditor in obtaining reasonable assurance. The ISAs (UK) require that the auditor exercise professional judgment and maintain professional skepticism throughout the planning and performance of the audit and, among other things:

- Identify and assess risks of material misstatement, whether due to fraud or error, based on an understanding of the entity and its environment, including the entity's internal control.
- Obtain sufficient appropriate audit evidence about whether material misstatements exist, through designing and implementing appropriate responses to the assessed risks.
- Form an opinion on the financial statements based on conclusions drawn from the audit evidence obtained.

The form of opinion expressed by the auditor will depend upon the applicable financial **8** reporting framework and any applicable law or regulation. (Ref: Para. A12–A13)

The auditor may also have certain other communication and reporting responsibilities **9** to users, management, those charged with governance, or parties outside the entity, in relation to matters arising from the audit. These may be established by the ISAs (UK) or by applicable law or regulation.[2]

---

[1] *ISA (UK) 320 (Revised June 2016)*, Materiality in Planning and Performing an Audit *and ISA (UK) 450 (Revised June 2016)*, Evaluation of Misstatements Identified during the Audit.

[2] *See, for example, ISA (UK) 260 (Revised June 2016)*, Communication with Those Charged with Governance; *and paragraph 43 of ISA (UK) 240 (Revised June 2016)*, The Auditor's Responsibilities Relating to Fraud in an Audit of Financial Statements.

Effective Date

10   This ISA (UK) is effective for audits of financial statements for periods commencing on or after 17 June 2016. Earlier adoption is permitted.

Overall Objectives of the Auditor

11   In conducting an audit of financial statements, the overall objectives of the auditor are:

(a)   To obtain reasonable assurance about whether the financial statements as a whole are free from material misstatement, whether due to fraud or error, thereby enabling the auditor to express an opinion on whether the financial statements are prepared, in all material respects, in accordance with an applicable financial reporting framework; and

(b)   To report on the financial statements, and communicate as required by the ISAs (UK), in accordance with the auditor's findings.

12   In all cases when reasonable assurance cannot be obtained and a qualified opinion in the auditor's report is insufficient in the circumstances for purposes of reporting to the intended users of the financial statements, the ISAs (UK) require that the auditor disclaim an opinion or withdraw (or resign)[3] from the engagement, where withdrawal is possible under applicable law or regulation.

Definitions

13   For purposes of the ISAs (UK), the following terms have the meanings attributed below:

(a)   Applicable financial reporting framework – The financial reporting framework adopted by management and, where appropriate, those charged with governance in the preparation of the financial statements that is acceptable in view of the nature of the entity and the objective of the financial statements, or that is required by law or regulation.

The term 'fair presentation framework' is used to refer to a financial reporting framework that requires compliance with the requirements of the framework and:

(i)   Acknowledges explicitly or implicitly that, to achieve fair presentation of the financial statements, it may be necessary for management to provide disclosures beyond those specifically required by the framework; or

(ii)   Acknowledges explicitly that it may be necessary for management to depart from a requirement of the framework to achieve fair presentation of the financial statements. Such departures are expected to be necessary only in extremely rare circumstances.

The term 'compliance framework' is used to refer to a financial reporting framework that requires compliance with the requirements of the framework, but does not contain the acknowledgements in (i) or (ii) above.

In the UK, the applicable financial reporting framework includes the requirements of applicable law.

(b)   Audit evidence – Information used by the auditor in arriving at the conclusions on which the auditor's opinion is based. Audit evidence includes both information contained in the accounting records underlying the financial statements and other information. For purposes of the ISAs (UK):

(i)   Sufficiency of audit evidence is the measure of the quantity of audit evidence. The quantity of the audit evidence needed is affected by the auditor's assessment of the risks of material misstatement and also by the quality of such audit evidence.

---

[3]   *In the ISAs (UK), only the term 'withdrawal' is used.*

(ii) Appropriateness of audit evidence is the measure of the quality of audit evidence; that is, its relevance and its reliability in providing support for the conclusions on which the auditor's opinion is based.

(c) Audit risk – The risk that the auditor expresses an inappropriate audit opinion when the financial statements are materially misstated. Audit risk is a function of the risks of material misstatement and detection risk.

(d) Auditor – 'Auditor' is used to refer to the person or persons conducting the audit, usually the engagement partner or other members of the engagement team,[3a] or, as applicable, the firm. Where an ISA (UK) expressly intends that a requirement or responsibility be fulfilled by the engagement partner, the term 'engagement partner' rather than 'auditor' is used. 'Engagement partner' and 'firm' are to be read as referring to their public sector equivalents where relevant.

(e) Detection risk – The risk that the procedures performed by the auditor to reduce audit risk to an acceptably low level will not detect a misstatement that exists and that could be material, either individually or when aggregated with other misstatements.

(f) Financial statements – A structured representation of historical financial information, including disclosures, intended to communicate an entity's economic resources or obligations at a point in time or the changes therein for a period of time in accordance with a financial reporting framework. The term 'financial statements' ordinarily refers to a complete set of financial statements as determined by the requirements of the applicable financial reporting framework, but can also refer to a single financial statement. Disclosures comprise explanatory or descriptive information, set out as required, expressly permitted or otherwise allowed by the applicable financial reporting framework, on the face of a financial statement, or in the notes, or incorporated therein by cross-reference. (Ref: Para. A1–A1a)

(g) Historical financial information – Information expressed in financial terms in relation to a particular entity, derived primarily from that entity's accounting system, about economic events occurring in past time periods or about economic conditions or circumstances at points in time in the past.

(h) Management – The person(s) with executive responsibility for the conduct of the entity's operations. For some entities in some jurisdictions, management includes some or all of those charged with governance, for example, executive members of a governance board, or an owner-manager.

In the UK, management will not normally include non-executive directors.

(i) Misstatement – A difference between the amount, classification, presentation, or disclosure of a reported financial statement item and the amount, classification, presentation, or disclosure that is required for the item to be in accordance with the applicable financial reporting framework. Misstatements can arise from error or fraud.

Where the auditor expresses an opinion on whether the financial statements are presented fairly, in all material respects, or give a true and fair view, misstatements also include those adjustments of amounts, classifications, presentation, or disclosures that, in the auditor's judgment, are necessary for the financial statements to be presented fairly, in all material respects, or to give a true and fair view.

(j) Premise, relating to the responsibilities of management and, where appropriate, those charged with governance, on which an audit is conducted – That management and, where appropriate, those charged with governance have acknowledged and understand that they have the following responsibilities that are fundamental to the conduct of an audit in accordance with ISAs (UK). That is, responsibility:

[3a] *In the UK, this includes the key audit partner as defined in ISA (UK) 220 (Revised June 2016),* Quality Control for an Audit of Financial Statements, *paragraph 7D-1(d).*

     (i)   For the preparation of the financial statements in accordance with the applicable financial reporting framework, including where relevant their fair presentation;

    (ii)   For such internal control as management and, where appropriate, those charged with governance determine is necessary to enable the preparation of financial statements that are free from material misstatement, whether due to fraud or error; and

   (iii) To provide the auditor with:

       a.   Access to all information of which management and, where appropriate, those charged with governance are aware that is relevant to the preparation of the financial statements such as records, documentation and other matters;

       b.   Additional information that the auditor may request from management and, where appropriate, those charged with governance for the purpose of the audit; and

       c.   Unrestricted access to persons within the entity from whom the auditor determines it necessary to obtain audit evidence.

In the case of a fair presentation framework, (i) above may be restated as 'for the preparation and *fair* presentation of the financial statements in accordance with the financial reporting framework,' or 'for the preparation of financial statements *that give a true and fair view* in accordance with the financial reporting framework.'

The 'premise, relating to the responsibilities of management and, where appropriate, those charged with governance, on which an audit is conducted' may also be referred to as the 'premise.'

(k) Professional judgment – The application of relevant training, knowledge and experience, within the context provided by auditing, accounting and ethical standards, in making informed decisions about the courses of action that are appropriate in the circumstances of the audit engagement.

(l) Professional skepticism – An attitude that includes a questioning mind, being alert to conditions which may indicate possible misstatement due to error or fraud, and a critical assessment of audit evidence.

(m) Reasonable assurance – In the context of an audit of financial statements, a high, but not absolute, level of assurance.

(n) Risk of material misstatement – The risk that the financial statements are materially misstated prior to audit. This consists of two components, described as follows at the assertion level:

     (i)   Inherent risk – The susceptibility of an assertion about a class of transaction, account balance or disclosure to a misstatement that could be material, either individually or when aggregated with other misstatements, before consideration of any related controls.

    (ii)   Control risk – The risk that a misstatement that could occur in an assertion about a class of transaction, account balance or disclosure and that could be material, either individually or when aggregated with other misstatements, will not be prevented, or detected and corrected, on a timely basis by the entity's internal control.

(o) Those charged with governance – The person(s) or organization(s) (for example, a corporate trustee) with responsibility for overseeing the strategic direction of the entity and obligations related to the accountability of the entity. This includes overseeing the financial reporting process. For some entities in some jurisdictions, those charged with governance may include management personnel, for example, executive members of a governance board of a private or public sector entity, or an owner-manager.

In the UK, those charged with governance include the directors (executive and non-executive) of a company and the members of an audit committee where one exists. For other types of entity it usually includes equivalent persons such as the partners, proprietors, committee of management or trustees.

Requirements

Ethical Requirements Relating to an Audit of Financial Statements

The auditor shall comply with relevant ethical requirements, including those pertaining to **14** independence, relating to financial statement audit engagements. (Ref: Para. A14–A17)

Professional Skepticism

The auditor shall plan and perform an audit with professional skepticism recognizing that **15** circumstances may exist that cause the financial statements to be materially misstated. (Ref: Para. A18–A22)

In the UK, the auditor shall maintain professional skepticism throughout the audit, recognising the possibility of a material misstatement due to facts or behaviour indicating irregularities, including fraud, or error, notwithstanding the auditor's past experience of the honesty and integrity of the entity's management and of those charged with governance.

Professional Judgment

The auditor shall exercise professional judgment in planning and performing an audit of **16** financial statements. (Ref: Para. A23–A27)

Sufficient Appropriate Audit Evidence and Audit Risk

To obtain reasonable assurance, the auditor shall obtain sufficient appropriate audit **17** evidence to reduce audit risk to an acceptably low level and thereby enable the auditor to draw reasonable conclusions on which to base the auditor's opinion. (Ref: Para. A28–A52)

Conduct of an Audit in Accordance with ISAs (UK)

Complying with ISAs (UK) Relevant to the Audit

The auditor shall comply with all ISAs (UK) relevant to the audit. An ISA (UK) is relevant **18** to the audit when the ISA (UK) is in effect and the circumstances addressed by the ISA (UK) exist. (Ref: Para. A53–A57)

The auditor shall have an understanding of the entire text of an ISA (UK), including its **19** application and other explanatory material, to understand its objectives and to apply its requirements properly. (Ref: Para. A58–A66)

The auditor shall not represent compliance with ISAs (UK) in the auditor's report unless **20** the auditor has complied with the requirements of this ISA (UK) and all other ISAs (UK) relevant to the audit.

Objectives Stated in Individual ISAs (UK)

21   To achieve the overall objectives of the auditor, the auditor shall use the objectives stated in relevant ISAs (UK) in planning and performing the audit, having regard to the interrelationships among the ISAs (UK), to: (Ref: Para. A67–A69)

   (a)   Determine whether any audit procedures in addition to those required by the ISAs (UK) are necessary in pursuance of the objectives stated in the ISAs (UK); and (Ref: Para. A70)

   (b)   Evaluate whether sufficient appropriate audit evidence has been obtained. (Ref: Para. A71)

Complying with Relevant Requirements

22   Subject to paragraph 23, the auditor shall comply with each requirement of an ISA (UK) unless, in the circumstances of the audit:

   (a)   The entire ISA (UK) is not relevant; or

   (b)   The requirement is not relevant because it is conditional and the condition does not exist. (Ref: Para. A72–A73)

23   In exceptional circumstances, the auditor may judge it necessary to depart from a relevant requirement in an ISA (UK). In such circumstances, the auditor shall perform alternative audit procedures to achieve the aim of that requirement. The need for the auditor to depart from a relevant requirement is expected to arise only where the requirement is for a specific procedure to be performed and, in the specific circumstances of the audit, that procedure would be ineffective in achieving the aim of the requirement. (Ref: Para. A74)

Failure to Achieve an Objective

24   If an objective in a relevant ISA (UK) cannot be achieved, the auditor shall evaluate whether this prevents the auditor from achieving the overall objectives of the auditor and thereby requires the auditor, in accordance with the ISAs (UK), to modify the auditor's opinion or withdraw from the engagement (where withdrawal is possible under applicable law or regulation). Failure to achieve an objective represents a significant matter requiring documentation in accordance with ISA (UK) 230 (Revised June 2016).[4] (Ref: Para. A75–A76)

***

Application and Other Explanatory Material

Definitions

Financial Statements (Ref: Para. 13(f))

A1   Some financial reporting frameworks may refer to an entity's economic resources or obligations in other terms. For example, these may be referred to as the entity's assets and liabilities, and the residual difference between them may be referred to as equity or equity interests.

---

[4] *ISA (UK) 230 (Revised June 2016)*, Audit Documentation, *paragraph 8(c)*.

Explanatory or descriptive information required to be included in the financial statements **A1a**
by the applicable financial reporting framework may be incorporated therein by cross-
reference to information in another document, such as a management report or a risk
report. 'Incorporated therein by cross-reference' means cross-referenced from the financial
statements to the other document, but not from the other document to the financial
statements, Where the applicable financial reporting framework does not expressly
prohibit the cross-referencing of where explanatory or descriptive information may be
found, and the information has been appropriately cross-referenced, the information will
form part of the financial statements.

An Audit of Financial Statements

Scope of the Audit (Ref: Para. 3)

The auditor's opinion on the financial statements deals with whether the financial **A1b**
statements are prepared, in all material respects, in accordance with the applicable financial
reporting framework. Such an opinion is common to all audits of financial statements. The
auditor's opinion therefore does not assure, for example, the future viability of the entity
nor the efficiency or effectiveness with which management has conducted the affairs of the
entity. In some jurisdictions, however, applicable law or regulation may require auditors to
provide opinions on other specific matters, such as the effectiveness of internal control, or
the consistency of a separate management report with the financial statements. While the
ISAs (UK) include requirements and guidance in relation to such matters to the extent that
they are relevant to forming an opinion on the financial statements, the auditor would be
required to undertake further work if the auditor had additional responsibilities to provide
such opinions.

Preparation of the Financial Statements (Ref: Para. 4)

Law or regulation may establish the responsibilities of management and, where **A2**
appropriate, those charged with governance in relation to financial reporting. However,
the extent of these responsibilities, or the way in which they are described, may differ
across jurisdictions. Despite these differences, an audit in accordance with ISAs (UK) is
conducted on the premise that management and, where appropriate, those charged with
governance have acknowledged and understand that they have responsibility:

(a) For the preparation of the financial statements in accordance with the applicable
     financial reporting framework, including where relevant their fair presentation;
(b) For such internal control as management and, where appropriate, those charged with
     governance determine is necessary to enable the preparation of financial statements
     that are free from material misstatement, whether due to fraud or error; and
(c) To provide the auditor with:
     (i)   Access to all information of which management and, where appropriate, those
           charged with governance are aware that is relevant to the preparation of the
           financial statements such as records, documentation and other matters;
     (ii) Additional information that the auditor may request from management and,
           where appropriate, those charged with governance for the purpose of the audit;
           and
     (iii) Unrestricted access to persons within the entity from whom the auditor
           determines it necessary to obtain audit evidence.

The preparation of the financial statements by management and, where appropriate, those **A3**
charged with governance requires:

- The identification of the applicable financial reporting framework, in the context of any relevant laws or regulations.
- The preparation of the financial statements in accordance with that framework.
- The inclusion of an adequate description of that framework in the financial statements.

The preparation of the financial statements requires management to exercise judgment in making accounting estimates that are reasonable in the circumstances, as well as to select and apply appropriate accounting policies. These judgments are made in the context of the applicable financial reporting framework.

A4   The financial statements may be prepared in accordance with a financial reporting framework designed to meet:

- The common financial information needs of a wide range of users (that is, 'general purpose financial statements'); or
- The financial information needs of specific users (that is, 'special purpose financial statements').

A5   The applicable financial reporting framework often encompasses financial reporting standards established by an authorized or recognized standards setting organization, or legislative or regulatory requirements. In some cases, the financial reporting framework may encompass both financial reporting standards established by an authorized or recognized standards setting organization and legislative or regulatory requirements. Other sources may provide direction on the application of the applicable financial reporting framework. In some cases, the applicable financial reporting framework may encompass such other sources, or may even consist only of such sources. Such other sources may include:

- The legal and ethical environment, including statutes, regulations, court decisions, and professional ethical obligations in relation to accounting matters;
- Published accounting interpretations of varying authority issued by standards setting, professional or regulatory organizations;
- Published views of varying authority on emerging accounting issues issued by standards setting, professional or regulatory organizations;
- General and industry practices widely recognized and prevalent; and
- Accounting literature.

Where conflicts exist between the financial reporting framework and the sources from which direction on its application may be obtained, or among the sources that encompass the financial reporting framework, the source with the highest authority prevails.

A6   The requirements of the applicable financial reporting framework determine the form and content of the financial statements. Although the framework may not specify how to account for or disclose all transactions or events, it ordinarily embodies sufficient broad principles that can serve as a basis for developing and applying accounting policies that are consistent with the concepts underlying the requirements of the framework.

A7   Some financial reporting frameworks are fair presentation frameworks, while others are compliance frameworks. Financial reporting frameworks that encompass primarily the financial reporting standards established by an organization that is authorized or recognized to promulgate standards to be used by entities for preparing general purpose financial statements are often designed to achieve fair presentation, for example, International Financial Reporting Standards (IFRSs) issued by the International Accounting Standards Board (IASB).

The requirements of the applicable financial reporting framework also determine what **A8** constitutes a complete set of financial statements. In the case of many frameworks, financial statements are intended to provide information about the financial position, financial performance and cash flows of an entity. For such frameworks, a complete set of financial statements would include a balance sheet; an income statement; a statement of changes in equity; a cash flow statement; and related notes. For some other financial reporting frameworks, a single financial statement and the related notes might constitute a complete set of financial statements:

- For example, the International Public Sector Accounting Standard (IPSAS), 'Financial Reporting Under the Cash Basis of Accounting' issued by the International Public Sector Accounting Standards Board states that the primary financial statement is a statement of cash receipts and payments when a public sector entity prepares its financial statements in accordance with that IPSAS.
- Other examples of a single financial statement, each of which would include related notes, are:
  - Balance sheet.
  - Statement of income or statement of operations.
  - Statement of retained earnings.
  - Statement of cash flows.
  - Statement of assets and liabilities that does not include owner's equity.
  - Statement of changes in owners' equity.
  - Statement of revenue and expenses.
  - Statement of operations by product lines.

ISA (UK) 210 (Revised June 2016) establishes requirements and provides guidance on **A9** determining the acceptability of the applicable financial reporting framework.[5] ISA 800 deals with special considerations when financial statements are prepared in accordance with a special purpose framework.[6]

Because of the significance of the premise to the conduct of an audit, the auditor is **A10** required to obtain the agreement of management and, where appropriate, those charged with governance that they acknowledge and understand that they have the responsibilities set out in paragraph A2 as a precondition for accepting the audit engagement.[7]

Considerations Specific to Audits in the Public Sector

The mandates for audits of the financial statements of public sector entities may be **A11** broader than those of other entities. As a result, the premise, relating to management's responsibilities, on which an audit of the financial statements of a public sector entity is conducted may include additional responsibilities, such as the responsibility for the execution of transactions and events in accordance with law, regulation or other authority.[8]

---

[5] *ISA (UK) 210 (Revised June 2016)*, Agreeing the Terms of Audit Engagements, *paragraph 6(a)*.

[6] *ISA 800*, Special Considerations—Audits of Financial Statements Prepared in Accordance with Special Purpose Frameworks, *paragraph 8*.
ISA 800 has not been promulgated by the FRC for application in the UK.

[7] *ISA (UK) 210 (Revised June 2016), paragraph 6(b).*

[8] *See paragraph A57.*

Form of the Auditor's Opinion (Ref: Para. 8)

A12   The opinion expressed by the auditor is on whether the financial statements are prepared, in all material respects, in accordance with the applicable financial reporting framework. The form of the auditor's opinion, however, will depend upon the applicable financial reporting framework and any applicable law or regulation. Most financial reporting frameworks include requirements relating to the presentation of the financial statements; for such frameworks, *preparation* of the financial statements in accordance with the applicable financial reporting framework includes *presentation*.

A13   Where the financial reporting framework is a fair presentation framework, as is generally the case for general purpose financial statements, the opinion required by the ISAs (UK) is on whether the financial statements are presented fairly, in all material respects, or give a true and fair view. Where the financial reporting framework is a compliance framework, the opinion required is on whether the financial statements are prepared, in all material respects, in accordance with the framework. Unless specifically stated otherwise, references in the ISAs (UK) to the auditor's opinion cover both forms of opinion.

Ethical Requirements Relating to an Audit of Financial Statements
(Ref: Para. 14)

A14   The auditor is subject to relevant ethical requirements, including those pertaining to independence, relating to financial statement audit engagements. Relevant ethical requirements ordinarily comprise Parts A and B of the International Ethics Standards Board of Accountants' *Code of Ethics for Professional Accountants* (the IESBA Code) related to an audit of financial statements together with national requirements that are more restrictive.

A14-1   In the UK, auditors are subject to ethical requirements from two sources: the FRC's Ethical Standard concerning the integrity, objectivity and independence of the auditor, and the ethical pronouncements established by the auditor's relevant professional body.

A15   Part A of the IESBA Code establishes the fundamental principles of professional ethics relevant to the auditor when conducting an audit of financial statements and provides a conceptual framework for applying those principles. The fundamental principles with which the auditor is required to comply by the IESBA Code are:

(a)   Integrity;
(b)   Objectivity;
(c)   Professional competence and due care;
(d)   Confidentiality; and
(e)   Professional behavior.

Part B of the IESBA Code illustrates how the conceptual framework is to be applied in specific situations.

A16   In the case of an audit engagement it is in the public interest and, therefore, required by the IESBA Code, that the auditor be independent of the entity subject to the audit. The IESBA Code describes independence as comprising both independence of mind and independence in appearance. The auditor's independence from the entity safeguards the auditor's ability to form an audit opinion without being affected by influences that might compromise that opinion. Independence enhances the auditor's ability to act with integrity, to be objective and to maintain an attitude of professional skepticism.

International Standard on Quality Control (ISQC) (UK) 1 (Revised June 2016)[9], or **A17**
national requirements that are at least as demanding,[10] deal with the firm's responsibilities
to establish and maintain its system of quality control for audit engagements. ISQC (UK)
1 (Revised June 2016) sets out the responsibilities of the firm for establishing policies and
procedures designed to provide it with reasonable assurance that the firm and its personnel
comply with relevant ethical requirements, including those pertaining to independence.[11]
ISA (UK) 220 (Revised June 2016) sets out the engagement partner's responsibilities
with respect to relevant ethical requirements. These include remaining alert, through
observation and making inquiries as necessary, for evidence of non-compliance with
relevant ethical requirements by members of the engagement team, determining the
appropriate action if matters come to the engagement partner's attention that indicate that
members of the engagement team have not complied with relevant ethical requirements,
and forming a conclusion on compliance with independence requirements that apply to the
audit engagement.[12] ISA (UK) 220 (Revised June 2016) recognizes that the engagement
team is entitled to rely on a firm's system of quality control in meeting its responsibilities
with respect to quality control procedures applicable to the individual audit engagement,
unless information provided by the firm or other parties suggests otherwise.

Professional Skepticism (Ref: Para. 15)

Professional skepticism includes being alert to, for example: **A18**

- Audit evidence that contradicts other audit evidence obtained.
- Information that brings into question the reliability of documents and responses to
  inquiries to be used as audit evidence.
- Conditions that may indicate possible fraud.
- Circumstances that suggest the need for audit procedures in addition to those required
  by the ISAs (UK).

Maintaining professional skepticism throughout the audit is necessary if the auditor is, for   **A19**
example, to reduce the risks of:

- Overlooking unusual circumstances.
- Over generalizing when drawing conclusions from audit observations.
- Using inappropriate assumptions in determining the nature, timing, and extent of the
  audit procedures and evaluating the results thereof.

Professional skepticism is necessary to the critical assessment of audit evidence. This   **A20**
includes questioning contradictory audit evidence and the reliability of documents and
responses to inquiries and other information obtained from management and those charged
with governance. It also includes consideration of the sufficiency and appropriateness of
audit evidence obtained in the light of the circumstances, for example in the case where
fraud risk factors exist and a single document, of a nature that is susceptible to fraud, is the
sole supporting evidence for a material financial statement amount.

The auditor may accept records and documents as genuine unless the auditor has reason   **A21**
to believe the contrary. Nevertheless, the auditor is required to consider the reliability

---

[9] *International Standard on Quality Control (ISQC) (UK) 1 (Revised June 2016)*, Quality Control for Firms that
Perform Audits and Reviews of Financial Statements, and Other Assurance and Related Services Engagements.

[10] *ISA (UK) 220 (Revised June 2016)*, Quality Control for an Audit of Financial Statements, *paragraph 2.*

[11] *ISQC (UK) 1 (Revised June 2016)*, *paragraphs 20–25.*

[12] *ISA (UK) 220 (Revised June 2016)*, *paragraphs 9–11.*

of information to be used as audit evidence.[13] In cases of doubt about the reliability of information or indications of possible fraud (for example, if conditions identified during the audit cause the auditor to believe that a document may not be authentic or that terms in a document may have been falsified), the ISAs (UK) require that the auditor investigate further and determine what modifications or additions to audit procedures are necessary to resolve the matter.[14]

A22   The auditor cannot be expected to disregard past experience of the honesty and integrity of the entity's management and those charged with governance. Nevertheless, a belief that management and those charged with governance are honest and have integrity does not relieve the auditor of the need to maintain professional skepticism or allow the auditor to be satisfied with less-than-persuasive audit evidence when obtaining reasonable assurance.

Professional Judgment (Ref: Para. 16)

A23   Professional judgment is essential to the proper conduct of an audit. This is because interpretation of relevant ethical requirements and the ISAs (UK) and the informed decisions required throughout the audit cannot be made without the application of relevant knowledge and experience to the facts and circumstances. Professional judgment is necessary in particular regarding decisions about:

- Materiality and audit risk.
- The nature, timing, and extent of audit procedures used to meet the requirements of the ISAs (UK) and gather audit evidence.
- Evaluating whether sufficient appropriate audit evidence has been obtained, and whether more needs to be done to achieve the objectives of the ISAs (UK) and thereby, the overall objectives of the auditor.
- The evaluation of management's judgments in applying the entity's applicable financial reporting framework.
- The drawing of conclusions based on the audit evidence obtained, for example, assessing the reasonableness of the estimates made by management in preparing the financial statements.

A24   The distinguishing feature of the professional judgment expected of an auditor is that it is exercised by an auditor whose training, knowledge and experience have assisted in developing the necessary competencies to achieve reasonable judgments.

A25   The exercise of professional judgment in any particular case is based on the facts and circumstances that are known by the auditor. Consultation on difficult or contentious matters during the course of the audit, both within the engagement team and between the engagement team and others at the appropriate level within or outside the firm, such as that required by ISA (UK) 220 (Revised June 2016),[15] assist the auditor in making informed and reasonable judgments.

A26   Professional judgment can be evaluated based on whether the judgment reached reflects a competent application of auditing and accounting principles and is appropriate in the light of, and consistent with, the facts and circumstances that were known to the auditor up to the date of the auditor's report.

---

[13] *ISA (UK) 500, Audit Evidence, paragraphs 7–9.*

[14] *ISA (UK) 240 (Revised June 2016), paragraph 13; ISA (UK) 500, paragraph 11; ISA (UK) 505,* External Confirmations, *paragraphs 10–11, and 16.*

[15] *ISA (UK) 220 (Revised June 2016), paragraph 18.*

Professional judgment needs to be exercised throughout the audit. It also needs to be appropriately documented. In this regard, the auditor is required to prepare audit documentation sufficient to enable an experienced auditor, having no previous connection with the audit, to understand the significant professional judgments made in reaching conclusions on significant matters arising during the audit.[16] Professional judgment is not to be used as the justification for decisions that are not otherwise supported by the facts and circumstances of the engagement or sufficient appropriate audit evidence. A27

Sufficient Appropriate Audit Evidence and Audit Risk (Ref: Para. 5 and 17)

Sufficiency and Appropriateness of Audit Evidence

Audit evidence is necessary to support the auditor's opinion and report. It is cumulative in nature and is primarily obtained from audit procedures performed during the course of the audit. It may, however, also include information obtained from other sources such as previous audits (provided the auditor has determined whether changes have occurred since the previous audit that may affect its relevance to the current audit[17]) or a firm's quality control procedures for client acceptance and continuance. In addition to other sources inside and outside the entity, the entity's accounting records are an important source of audit evidence. Also, information that may be used as audit evidence may have been prepared by an expert employed or engaged by the entity. Audit evidence comprises both information that supports and corroborates management's assertions, and any information that contradicts such assertions. In addition, in some cases, the absence of information (for example, management's refusal to provide a requested representation) is used by the auditor, and therefore, also constitutes audit evidence. Most of the auditor's work in forming the auditor's opinion consists of obtaining and evaluating audit evidence. A28

The sufficiency and appropriateness of audit evidence are interrelated. Sufficiency is the measure of the quantity of audit evidence. The quantity of audit evidence needed is affected by the auditor's assessment of the risks of misstatement (the higher the assessed risks, the more audit evidence is likely to be required) and also by the quality of such audit evidence (the higher the quality, the less may be required). Obtaining more audit evidence, however, may not compensate for its poor quality. A29

Appropriateness is the measure of the quality of audit evidence; that is, its relevance and its reliability in providing support for the conclusions on which the auditor's opinion is based. The reliability of evidence is influenced by its source and by its nature, and is dependent on the individual circumstances under which it is obtained. A30

Whether sufficient appropriate audit evidence has been obtained to reduce audit risk to an acceptably low level, and thereby enable the auditor to draw reasonable conclusions on which to base the auditor's opinion, is a matter of professional judgment. ISA (UK) 500 and other relevant ISAs (UK) establish additional requirements and provide further guidance applicable throughout the audit regarding the auditor's considerations in obtaining sufficient appropriate audit evidence. A31

---

[16] *ISA (UK) 230 (Revised June 2016), paragraph 8.*

[17] *ISA (UK) 315 (Revised June 2016),* Identifying and Assessing the Risks of Material Misstatement through Understanding the Entity and Its Environment, *paragraph 9.*

Audit Risk

A32   Audit risk is a function of the risks of material misstatement and detection risk. The assessment of risks is based on audit procedures to obtain information necessary for that purpose and evidence obtained throughout the audit. The assessment of risks is a matter of professional judgment, rather than a matter capable of precise measurement.

A33   For purposes of the ISAs (UK), audit risk does not include the risk that the auditor might express an opinion that the financial statements are materially misstated when they are not. This risk is ordinarily insignificant. Further, audit risk is a technical term related to the process of auditing; it does not refer to the auditor's business risks such as loss from litigation, adverse publicity, or other events arising in connection with the audit of financial statements.

Risks of Material Misstatement

A34   The risks of material misstatement may exist at two levels:

- The overall financial statement level; and
- The assertion level for classes of transactions, account balances, and disclosures.

A35   Risks of material misstatement at the overall financial statement level refer to risks of material misstatement that relate pervasively to the financial statements as a whole and potentially affect many assertions.

A36   Risks of material misstatement at the assertion level are assessed in order to determine the nature, timing, and extent of further audit procedures necessary to obtain sufficient appropriate audit evidence. This evidence enables the auditor to express an opinion on the financial statements at an acceptably low level of audit risk. Auditors use various approaches to accomplish the objective of assessing the risks of material misstatement. For example, the auditor may make use of a model that expresses the general relationship of the components of audit risk in mathematical terms to arrive at an acceptable level of detection risk. Some auditors find such a model to be useful when planning audit procedures.

A37   The risks of material misstatement at the assertion level consist of two components: inherent risk and control risk. Inherent risk and control risk are the entity's risks; they exist independently of the audit of the financial statements.

A38   Inherent risk is higher for some assertions and related classes of transactions, account balances, and disclosures than for others. For example, it may be higher for complex calculations or for accounts consisting of amounts derived from accounting estimates that are subject to significant estimation uncertainty. External circumstances giving rise to business risks may also influence inherent risk. For example, technological developments might make a particular product obsolete, thereby causing inventory to be more susceptible to overstatement. Factors in the entity and its environment that relate to several or all of the classes of transactions, account balances, or disclosures may also influence the inherent risk related to a specific assertion. Such factors may include, for example, a lack of sufficient working capital to continue operations or a declining industry characterized by a large number of business failures.

A39   Control risk is a function of the effectiveness of the design, implementation and maintenance of internal control by management to address identified risks that threaten the achievement of the entity's objectives relevant to preparation of the entity's financial statements. However, internal control, no matter how well designed and operated, can only reduce, but not eliminate, risks of material misstatement in the financial statements, because of the inherent limitations of internal control. These include, for example, the possibility of human errors or mistakes, or of controls being circumvented by collusion or inappropriate management override. Accordingly, some control risk will always exist. The ISAs (UK) provide the conditions under which the auditor is required to, or may choose to, test the operating effectiveness of controls in determining the nature, timing and extent of substantive procedures to be performed.[18]

The ISAs (UK) do not ordinarily refer to inherent risk and control risk separately, but rather to a combined assessment of the 'risks of material misstatement.' However, the auditor may make separate or combined assessments of inherent and control risk depending on preferred audit techniques or methodologies and practical considerations. The assessment of the risks of material misstatement may be expressed in quantitative terms, such as in percentages, or in non-quantitative terms. In any case, the need for the auditor to make appropriate risk assessments is more important than the different approaches by which they may be made.   **A40**

ISA (UK) 315 (Revised June 2016) establishes requirements and provides guidance on identifying and assessing the risks of material misstatement at the financial statement and assertion levels.   **A41**

Detection Risk

For a given level of audit risk, the acceptable level of detection risk bears an inverse relationship to the assessed risks of material misstatement at the assertion level. For example, the greater the risks of material misstatement the auditor believes exists, the less the detection risk that can be accepted and, accordingly, the more persuasive the audit evidence required by the auditor.   **A42**

Detection risk relates to the nature, timing, and extent of the auditor's procedures that are determined by the auditor to reduce audit risk to an acceptably low level. It is therefore a function of the effectiveness of an audit procedure and of its application by the auditor. Matters such as: **A43**

- adequate planning;
- proper assignment of personnel to the engagement team;
- the application of professional scepticism; and
- supervision and review of the audit work performed,

assist to enhance the effectiveness of an audit procedure and of its application and reduce the possibility that an auditor might select an inappropriate audit procedure, misapply an appropriate audit procedure, or misinterpret the audit results.

ISA (UK) 300 (Revised June 2016)[19] and ISA (UK) 330 (Revised June 2016) establish requirements and provide guidance on planning an audit of financial statements and the auditor's responses to assessed risks. Detection risk, however, can only be reduced, not eliminated, because of the inherent limitations of an audit. Accordingly, some detection risk will always exist.   **A44**

---

[18] *ISA (UK) 330 (Revised June 2016)*, The Auditor's Reponses to Assessed Risks, *paragraphs 7–17.*

[19] *ISA (UK) 300 (Revised June 2016)*, Planning an Audit of Financial Statements.

Inherent Limitations of an Audit

A45   The auditor is not expected to, and cannot, reduce audit risk to zero and cannot therefore obtain absolute assurance that the financial statements are free from material misstatement due to fraud or error. This is because there are inherent limitations of an audit, which result in most of the audit evidence on which the auditor draws conclusions and bases the auditor's opinion being persuasive rather than conclusive. The inherent limitations of an audit arise from:

- The nature of financial reporting;
- The nature of audit procedures; and
- The need for the audit to be conducted within a reasonable period of time and at a reasonable cost.

The Nature of Financial Reporting

A46   The preparation of financial statements involves judgment by management in applying the requirements of the entity's applicable financial reporting framework to the facts and circumstances of the entity. In addition, many financial statement items involve subjective decisions or assessments or a degree of uncertainty, and there may be a range of acceptable interpretations or judgments that may be made. Consequently, some financial statement items are subject to an inherent level of variability which cannot be eliminated by the application of additional auditing procedures. For example, this is often the case with respect to certain accounting estimates. Nevertheless, the ISAs (UK) require the auditor to give specific consideration to whether accounting estimates are reasonable in the context of the applicable financial reporting framework and related disclosures, and to the qualitative aspects of the entity's accounting practices, including indicators of possible bias in management's judgments.[20]

The Nature of Audit Procedures

A47   There are practical and legal limitations on the auditor's ability to obtain audit evidence. For example:

- There is the possibility that management or others may not provide, intentionally or unintentionally, the complete information that is relevant to the preparation of the financial statements or that has been requested by the auditor. Accordingly, the auditor cannot be certain of the completeness of information, even though the auditor has performed audit procedures to obtain assurance that all relevant information has been obtained.
- Fraud may involve sophisticated and carefully organized schemes designed to conceal it. Therefore, audit procedures used to gather audit evidence may be ineffective for detecting an intentional misstatement that involves, for example, collusion to falsify documentation which may cause the auditor to believe that audit evidence is valid when it is not. The auditor is neither trained as nor expected to be an expert in the authentication of documents.
- An audit is not an official investigation into alleged wrongdoing. Accordingly, the auditor is not given specific legal powers, such as the power of search, which may be necessary for such an investigation.

---

[20] *ISA (UK) 540 (Revised June 2016)*, Auditing Accounting Estimates, Including Fair Value Accounting Estimates, and Related Disclosures, *and ISA (UK) 700 (Revised June 2016)*, Forming an Opinion and Reporting on Financial Statements, *paragraph 13.*

Timeliness of Financial Reporting and the Balance between Benefit and Cost

The matter of difficulty, time, or cost involved is not in itself a valid basis for the auditor **A48** to omit an audit procedure for which there is no alternative or to be satisfied with audit evidence that is less than persuasive. Appropriate planning assists in making sufficient time and resources available for the conduct of the audit. Notwithstanding this, the relevance of information, and thereby its value, tends to diminish over time, and there is a balance to be struck between the reliability of information and its cost. This is recognized in certain financial reporting frameworks (see, for example, the IASB's 'Framework for the Preparation and Presentation of Financial Statements'). Therefore, there is an expectation by users of financial statements that the auditor will form an opinion on the financial statements within a reasonable period of time and at a reasonable cost, recognizing that it is impracticable to address all information that may exist or to pursue every matter exhaustively on the assumption that information is in error or fraudulent until proved otherwise.

Consequently, it is necessary for the auditor to: **A49**

- Plan the audit so that it will be performed in an effective manner;
- Direct audit effort to areas most expected to contain risks of material misstatement, whether due to fraud or error, with correspondingly less effort directed at other areas; and
- Use testing and other means of examining populations for misstatements.

In light of the approaches described in paragraph A49, the ISAs (UK) contain requirements **A50** for the planning and performance of the audit and require the auditor, among other things, to:

- Have a basis for the identification and assessment of risks of material misstatement at the financial statement and assertion levels by performing risk assessment procedures and related activities;[21] and
- Use testing and other means of examining populations in a manner that provides a reasonable basis for the auditor to draw conclusions about the population.[22]

Other Matters that Affect the Inherent Limitations of an Audit

In the case of certain assertions or subject matters, the potential effects of the inherent **A51** limitations on the auditor's ability to detect material misstatements are particularly significant. Such assertions or subject matters include:

- Fraud, particularly fraud involving senior management or collusion. See ISA (UK) 240 (Revised June 2016) for further discussion.
- The existence and completeness of related party relationships and transactions. See ISA (UK) 550[23] for further discussion.
- The occurrence of non-compliance with laws and regulations. See ISA (UK) 250 (Revised June 2016)[24] for further discussion.
- Future events or conditions that may cause an entity to cease to continue as a going concern. See ISA (UK) 570 (Revised June 2016)[25] for further discussion.

---

[21] *ISA (UK) 315 (Revised June 2016), paragraphs 5–10.*

[22] *ISA (UK) 330 (Revised June 2016); ISA (UK) 500; ISA (UK) 520,* Analytical Procedures; *ISA (UK) 530,* Audit Sampling.

[23] *ISA (UK) 550,* Related Parties.

[24] *ISA (UK) 250 (Revised June 2016),* Consideration of Laws and Regulations in an Audit of Financial Statements.

[25] *ISA (UK) 570 (Revised June 2016),* Going Concern.

Relevant ISAs (UK) identify specific audit procedures to assist in mitigating the effect of the inherent limitations.

A52   Because of the inherent limitations of an audit, there is an unavoidable risk that some material misstatements of the financial statements may not be detected, even though the audit is properly planned and performed in accordance with ISAs (UK). Accordingly, the subsequent discovery of a material misstatement of the financial statements resulting from fraud or error does not by itself indicate a failure to conduct an audit in accordance with ISAs (UK). However, the inherent limitations of an audit are not a justification for the auditor to be satisfied with less-than-persuasive audit evidence. Whether the auditor has performed an audit in accordance with ISAs (UK) is determined by the audit procedures performed in the circumstances, the sufficiency and appropriateness of the audit evidence obtained as a result thereof and the suitability of the auditor's report based on an evaluation of that evidence in light of the overall objectives of the auditor.

Conduct of an Audit in Accordance with ISAs (UK)

Nature of the ISAs (UK) (Ref: Para. 18)

A53   The ISAs (UK), taken together, provide the standards for the auditor's work in fulfilling the overall objectives of the auditor. The ISAs (UK) deal with the general responsibilities of the auditor, as well as the auditor's further considerations relevant to the application of those responsibilities to specific topics.

A54   The scope, effective date and any specific limitation of the applicability of a specific ISA (UK) is made clear in the ISA (UK). Unless otherwise stated in the ISA (UK), the auditor is permitted to apply an ISA (UK) before the effective date specified therein.

A55   In performing an audit, the auditor may be required to comply with legal or regulatory requirements in addition to the ISAs (UK). The ISAs (UK) do not override law or regulation that governs an audit of financial statements. In the event that such law or regulation differs from the ISAs (UK), an audit conducted only in accordance with law or regulation will not automatically comply with ISAs (UK).

A56   The auditor may also conduct the audit in accordance with both ISAs (UK) and auditing standards of a specific jurisdiction or country. In such cases, in addition to complying with each of the ISAs (UK) relevant to the audit, it may be necessary for the auditor to perform additional audit procedures in order to comply with the relevant standards of that jurisdiction or country.

Considerations Specific to Audits in the Public Sector

A57   The ISAs (UK) are relevant to engagements in the public sector. The public sector auditor's responsibilities, however, may be affected by the audit mandate, or by obligations on public sector entities arising from law, regulation or other authority (such as ministerial directives, government policy requirements, or resolutions of the legislature), which may encompass a broader scope than an audit of financial statements in accordance with the ISAs (UK). These additional responsibilities are not dealt with in the ISAs (UK). They may be dealt with in the pronouncements of the International Organization of Supreme Audit Institutions or national standard setters, or in guidance developed by government audit agencies.

Contents of the ISAs (UK) (Ref: Para. 19)

In addition to objectives and requirements (requirements are expressed in the ISAs (UK)   **A58**
using 'shall'), an ISA (UK) contains related guidance in the form of application and
other explanatory material. It may also contain introductory material that provides context
relevant to a proper understanding of the ISA (UK), and definitions. The entire text of an
ISA (UK), therefore, is relevant to an understanding of the objectives stated in an ISA
(UK) and the proper application of the requirements of an ISA (UK).

Where necessary, the application and other explanatory material provides further   **A59**
explanation of the requirements of an ISA (UK) and guidance for carrying them out. In
particular, it may:

● Explain more precisely what a requirement means or is intended to cover.
● Include examples of procedures that may be appropriate in the circumstances.

While such guidance does not in itself impose a requirement, it is relevant to the proper
application of the requirements of an ISA (UK). The application and other explanatory
material may also provide background information on matters addressed in an ISA (UK).

Appendices form part of the application and other explanatory material. The purpose and   **A60**
intended use of an appendix are explained in the body of the related ISA (UK) or within
the title and introduction of the appendix itself.

Introductory material may include, as needed, such matters as explanation of: **A61**

● The purpose and scope of the ISA (UK), including how the ISA (UK) relates to
  other ISAs (UK).
● The subject matter of the ISA (UK).
● The respective responsibilities of the auditor and others in relation to the subject
  matter of the ISA (UK).
● The context in which the ISA (UK) is set.

An ISA (UK) may include, in a separate section under the heading 'Definitions,' a   **A62**
description of the meanings attributed to certain terms for purposes of the ISAs (UK). These
are provided to assist in the consistent application and interpretation of the ISAs (UK), and
are not intended to override definitions that may be established for other purposes, whether
in law, regulation or otherwise. Unless otherwise indicated, those terms will carry the
same meanings throughout the ISAs (UK). The Glossary of Terms relating to International
Standards issued by the International Auditing and Assurance Standards Board in the
*Handbook of International Quality Control, Auditing, Review, Other Assurance, and
Related Services Pronouncements* published by IFAC contains a complete listing of terms
defined in the ISAs (UK). It also includes descriptions of other terms found in ISAs (UK)
to assist in common and consistent interpretation and translation.

When appropriate, additional considerations specific to audits of smaller entities and   **A63**
public sector entities are included within the application and other explanatory material of
an ISA (UK). These additional considerations assist in the application of the requirements
of the ISA (UK) in the audit of such entities. They do not, however, limit or reduce the
responsibility of the auditor to apply and comply with the requirements of the ISAs (UK).

Considerations Specific to Smaller Entities

For purposes of specifying additional considerations to audits of smaller entities, a 'smaller   **A64**
entity' refers to an entity which typically possesses qualitative characteristics such as:

(a) Concentration of ownership and management in a small number of individuals (often a single individual – either a natural person or another enterprise that owns the entity provided the owner exhibits the relevant qualitative characteristics); and

(b) One or more of the following:

  (i)   Straightforward or uncomplicated transactions;

  (ii) Simple record-keeping;

  (iii) Few lines of business and few products within business lines;

  (iv) Few internal controls;

  (v)   Few levels of management with responsibility for a broad range of controls; or

  (vi) Few personnel, many having a wide range of duties.

These qualitative characteristics are not exhaustive, they are not exclusive to smaller entities, and smaller entities do not necessarily display all of these characteristics.

A65 The considerations specific to smaller entities included in the ISAs (UK) have been developed primarily with unlisted entities in mind. Some of the considerations, however, may be helpful in audits of smaller listed entities.

A66 The ISAs (UK) refer to the proprietor of a smaller entity who is involved in running the entity on a day-to-day basis as the 'owner-manager.'

Objectives Stated in Individual ISAs (UK) (Ref: Para. 21)

A67 Each ISA (UK) contains one or more objectives which provide a link between the requirements and the overall objectives of the auditor. The objectives in individual ISAs (UK) serve to focus the auditor on the desired outcome of the ISA (UK), while being specific enough to assist the auditor in:

- Understanding what needs to be accomplished and, where necessary, the appropriate means of doing so; and
- Deciding whether more needs to be done to achieve them in the particular circumstances of the audit.

A68 Objectives are to be understood in the context of the overall objectives of the auditor stated in paragraph 11 of this ISA (UK). As with the overall objectives of the auditor, the ability to achieve an individual objective is equally subject to the inherent limitations of an audit.

A69 In using the objectives, the auditor is required to have regard to the interrelationships among the ISAs (UK). This is because, as indicated in paragraph A53, the ISAs (UK) deal in some cases with general responsibilities and in others with the application of those responsibilities to specific topics. For example, this ISA (UK) requires the auditor to adopt an attitude of professional skepticism; this is necessary in all aspects of planning and performing an audit but is not repeated as a requirement of each ISA (UK). At a more detailed level, ISA (UK) 315 (Revised June 2016) and ISA (UK) 330 (Revised June 2016) contain, among other things, objectives and requirements that deal with the auditor's responsibilities to identify and assess the risks of material misstatement and to design and perform further audit procedures to respond to those assessed risks, respectively; these objectives and requirements apply throughout the audit. An ISA (UK) dealing with specific aspects of the audit (for example, ISA (UK) 540 (Revised June 2016)) may expand on how the objectives and requirements of such ISAs (UK) as ISA (UK) 315 (Revised June 2016) and ISA (UK) 330 (Revised June 2016) are to be applied in relation to the subject of the ISA (UK) but does not repeat them. Thus, in achieving the objective stated in ISA (UK) 540 (Revised June 2016), the auditor has regard to the objectives and requirements of other relevant ISAs (UK).

Use of Objectives to Determine Need for Additional Audit Procedures (Ref: Para. 21(a))

The requirements of the ISAs (UK) are designed to enable the auditor to achieve the **A70** objectives specified in the ISAs (UK), and thereby the overall objectives of the auditor. The proper application of the requirements of the ISAs (UK) by the auditor is therefore expected to provide a sufficient basis for the auditor's achievement of the objectives. However, because the circumstances of audit engagements vary widely and all such circumstances cannot be anticipated in the ISAs (UK), the auditor is responsible for determining the audit procedures necessary to fulfill the requirements of the ISAs (UK) and to achieve the objectives. In the circumstances of an engagement, there may be particular matters that require the auditor to perform audit procedures in addition to those required by the ISAs (UK) to meet the objectives specified in the ISAs (UK).

Use of Objectives to Evaluate Whether Sufficient Appropriate Audit Evidence Has Been Obtained (Ref: Para. 21(b))

The auditor is required to use the objectives to evaluate whether sufficient appropriate **A71** audit evidence has been obtained in the context of the overall objectives of the auditor. If as a result the auditor concludes that the audit evidence is not sufficient and appropriate, then the auditor may follow one or more of the following approaches to meeting the requirement of paragraph 21(b):

● Evaluate whether further relevant audit evidence has been, or will be, obtained as a result of complying with other ISAs (UK);
● Extend the work performed in applying one or more requirements; or
● Perform other procedures judged by the auditor to be necessary in the circumstances.

Where none of the above is expected to be practical or possible in the circumstances, the auditor will not be able to obtain sufficient appropriate audit evidence and is required by the ISAs (UK) to determine the effect on the auditor's report or on the auditor's ability to complete the engagement.

Complying with Relevant Requirements

Relevant Requirements (Ref: Para. 22)

In some cases, an ISA (UK) (and therefore all of its requirements) may not be relevant **A72** in the circumstances. For example, if an entity does not have an internal audit function, nothing in ISA (UK) 610 (Revised June 2013)[26] is relevant.

Within a relevant ISA (UK), there may be conditional requirements. Such a requirement **A73** is relevant when the circumstances envisioned in the requirement apply and the condition exists. In general, the conditionality of a requirement will either be explicit or implicit, for example:

● The requirement to modify the auditor's opinion if there is a limitation of scope[27] represents an explicit conditional requirement.

---

[26] *ISA (UK) 610 (Revised June 2013)*, Using the Work of Internal Auditors, *Paragraph 2.*

[27] *ISA (UK) 705 (Revised June 2016)*, Modifications to the Opinion in the Independent Auditor's Report, *paragraph 13.*

- The requirement to communicate significant deficiencies in internal control identified during the audit to those charged with governance,[28] which depends on the existence of such identified significant deficiencies; and the requirement to obtain sufficient appropriate audit evidence regarding the presentation and disclosure of segment information in accordance with the applicable financial reporting framework,[29] which depends on that framework requiring or permitting such disclosure, represent implicit conditional requirements.

In some cases, a requirement may be expressed as being conditional on applicable law or regulation. For example, the auditor may be required to withdraw from the audit engagement, *where withdrawal is possible under applicable law or regulation*, or the auditor may be required to do something, *unless prohibited by law or regulation*. Depending on the jurisdiction, the legal or regulatory permission or prohibition may be explicit or implicit.

Departure from a Requirement (Ref: Para. 23)

A74   ISA (UK) 230 (Revised June 2016) establishes documentation requirements in those exceptional circumstances where the auditor departs from a relevant requirement.[30] The ISAs (UK) do not call for compliance with a requirement that is not relevant in the circumstances of the audit.

Failure to Achieve an Objective (Ref: Para. 24)

A75   Whether an objective has been achieved is a matter for the auditor's professional judgment. That judgment takes account of the results of audit procedures performed in complying with the requirements of the ISAs (UK), and the auditor's evaluation of whether sufficient appropriate audit evidence has been obtained and whether more needs to be done in the particular circumstances of the audit to achieve the objectives stated in the ISAs (UK). Accordingly, circumstances that may give rise to a failure to achieve an objective include those that:

- Prevent the auditor from complying with the relevant requirements of an ISA (UK).
- Result in its not being practicable or possible for the auditor to carry out the additional audit procedures or obtain further audit evidence as determined necessary from the use of the objectives in accordance with paragraph 21, for example due to a limitation in the available audit evidence.

A76   Audit documentation that meets the requirements of ISA (UK) 230 (Revised June 2016) and the specific documentation requirements of other relevant ISAs (UK) provides evidence of the auditor's basis for a conclusion about the achievement of the overall objectives of the auditor. While it is unnecessary for the auditor to document separately (as in a checklist, for example) that individual objectives have been achieved, the documentation of a failure to achieve an objective assists the auditor's evaluation of whether such a failure has prevented the auditor from achieving the overall objectives of the auditor.

---

[28] *ISA (UK) 265*, Communicating Deficiencies in Internal Control to Those Charged with Governance and Management, *paragraph 9.*

[29] *ISA (UK) 501*, Audit Evidence—Specific Considerations for Selected Items, *paragraph 13.*

[30] *ISA (UK) 230 (Revised June 2016), paragraph 12.*

International Standard on Auditing (UK) 210 (Revised June 2016) (Updated July 2017)
Agreeing the terms of audit engagements

(Effective for audits of financial statements for periods commencing on or after 17 June 2016)[0]

Contents

International Standard on Auditing (UK) (ISA (UK)) 210 (Revised June 2016), *Agreeing the Terms of Audit Engagements* should be read in conjunction with ISA (UK) 200 (Revised June 2016), *Overall Objectives of the Independent Auditor and the Conduct of an Audit in Accordance with International Standards on Auditing (UK).*

---

[0] *Conforming amendments to this standard as a result of ISA (UK) 250 (Revised July 2017), Section A—Consideration of Laws and Regulations in an Audit of Financial Statements, are included that are effective for audits of financial statements for periods commencing on or after 15 December 2017. Details of the amendments are given in the Annexure to ISA (UK) 250 (Revised December 2017) Section A.*

Introduction

Scope of this ISA (UK)

1   This International Standard on Auditing (UK) (ISA (UK)) deals with the auditor's responsibilities in agreeing the terms of the audit engagement with management and, where appropriate, those charged with governance. This includes establishing that certain preconditions for an audit, responsibility for which rests with management and, where appropriate, those charged with governance, are present. ISA (UK) 220 (Revised June 2016)[1] deals with those aspects of engagement acceptance that are within the control of the auditor. (Ref: Para. A1)

Effective Date

2   This ISA (UK) is effective for audits of financial statements for periods commencing on or after 17 June 2016. Earlier adoption is permitted.

Objective

3   The objective of the auditor is to accept or continue an audit engagement only when the basis upon which it is to be performed has been agreed, through:

   (a)   Establishing whether the preconditions for an audit are present; and

   (b)   Confirming that there is a common understanding between the auditor and management and, where appropriate, those charged with governance of the terms of the audit engagement.

Definitions

4   For purposes of the ISAs (UK), the following term has the meaning attributed below:

   Preconditions for an audit – The use by management[1a] of an acceptable financial reporting framework in the preparation of the financial statements and the agreement of management and, where appropriate, those charged with governance to the premise[2] on which an audit is conducted.

5   For the purposes of this ISA (UK), references to 'management' should be read hereafter as 'management and, where appropriate, those charged with governance.'

Requirements

Preconditions for an Audit

6   In order to establish whether the preconditions for an audit are present, the auditor shall:

   (a)   Determine whether the financial reporting framework to be applied in the preparation of the financial statements is acceptable; and (Ref: Para. A2–A10)

---

[1] *ISA (UK) 220 (Revised June 2016),* Quality Control for an Audit of Financial Statements.

[1a] *In the UK those charged with governance are responsible for the preparation of the financial statements.*

[2] *ISA (UK) 200 (Revised June 2016),* Overall Objectives of the Independent Auditor and the Conduct of an Audit in Accordance with International Standards on Auditing (UK), *paragraph 13.*

(b) Obtain the agreement of management that it acknowledges and understands its responsibility: (Ref: Para. A11–A14, A21)

    (i) For the preparation of the financial statements in accordance with the applicable financial reporting framework, including where relevant their fair presentation; (Ref: Para. A15–A15-2)

    (ii) For such internal control as management determines is necessary to enable the preparation of financial statements that are free from material misstatement, whether due to fraud or error; and (Ref: Para. A16–A19)

    (iii) To provide the auditor with:[2a]

        (a) Access to all information of which management is aware that is relevant to the preparation of the financial statements such as records, documentation and other matters;

        (b) Additional information that the auditor may request from management for the purpose of the audit; and

        (c) Unrestricted access to persons within the entity from whom the auditor determines it necessary to obtain audit evidence.

Limitation on Scope Prior to Audit Engagement Acceptance

If management or those charged with governance impose a limitation on the scope of the auditor's work in the terms of a proposed audit engagement such that the auditor believes the limitation will result in the auditor disclaiming an opinion on the financial statements, the auditor shall not accept such a limited engagement as an audit engagement, unless required by law or regulation to do so.   **7**

Other Factors Affecting Audit Engagement Acceptance

If the preconditions for an audit are not present, the auditor shall discuss the matter with management. Unless required by law or regulation to do so, the auditor shall not accept the proposed audit engagement: **8**

(a) If the auditor has determined that the financial reporting framework to be applied in the preparation of the financial statements is unacceptable, except as provided in paragraph 19; or

(b) If the agreement referred to in paragraph 6(b) has not been obtained.

Agreement on Audit Engagement Terms

The auditor shall agree the terms of the audit engagement with management or those charged with governance, as appropriate. (Ref: Para. A22)   **9**

Subject to paragraph 11, the agreed terms of the audit engagement shall be recorded in an audit engagement letter or other suitable form of written agreement and shall include: (Ref: Para. A23–A27)   **10**

(a) The objective and scope of the audit of the financial statements;

(b) The responsibilities of the auditor;

(c) The responsibilities of management;[2b]

(d) Identification of the applicable financial reporting framework for the preparation of the financial statements; and

---

[2a] *Sections 499 and 500 of the Companies Act 2006 set legal requirements in relation to the auditor's right to obtain information.*

[2b] *In the UK, the engagement letter sets out the responsibilities of those charged with governance.*

(e)   Reference to the expected form and content of any reports to be issued by the auditor; and (Ref: Para. A24)

(f)   A statement that there may be circumstances in which a report may differ from its expected form and content.

11   If law or regulation prescribes in sufficient detail the terms of the audit engagement referred to in paragraph 10, the auditor need not record them in a written agreement, except for the fact that such law or regulation applies and that management acknowledges and understands its responsibilities as set out in paragraph 6(b). (Ref: Para. A23, A28–A29)

12   If law or regulation prescribes responsibilities of management similar to those described in paragraph 6(b), the auditor may determine that the law or regulation includes responsibilities that, in the auditor's judgment, are equivalent in effect to those set out in that paragraph. For such responsibilities that are equivalent, the auditor may use the wording of the law or regulation to describe them in the written agreement. For those responsibilities that are not prescribed by law or regulation such that their effect is equivalent, the written agreement shall use the description in paragraph 6(b). (Ref: Para. A28)

Recurring Audits

13   On recurring audits, the auditor shall assess whether circumstances require the terms of the audit engagement to be revised and whether there is a need to remind the entity of the existing terms of the audit engagement. (Ref: Para. A30)

Acceptance of a Change in the Terms of the Audit Engagement

14   The auditor shall not agree to a change in the terms of the audit engagement where there is no reasonable justification for doing so. (Ref: Para. A31–A33)

15   If, prior to completing the audit engagement, the auditor is requested to change the audit engagement to an engagement that conveys a lower level of assurance, the auditor shall determine whether there is reasonable justification for doing so. (Ref: Para. A34–A35)

16   If the terms of the audit engagement are changed, the auditor and management shall agree on and record the new terms of the engagement in an engagement letter or other suitable form of written agreement.

17   If the auditor is unable to agree to a change of the terms of the audit engagement and is not permitted by management to continue the original audit engagement, the auditor shall:

(a)   Withdraw from the audit engagement where possible under applicable law or regulation; and

(b)   Determine whether there is any obligation, either contractual or otherwise, to report the circumstances to other parties, such as those charged with governance, owners or regulators. (Ref: Para. A35-1)

Additional Considerations in Engagement Acceptance

Financial Reporting Standards Supplemented by Law or Regulation

18   If financial reporting standards established by an authorized or recognized standards setting organization are supplemented by law or regulation, the auditor shall determine whether there are any conflicts between the financial reporting standards and the additional

requirements. If such conflicts exist, the auditor shall discuss with management the nature of the additional requirements and shall agree whether:

(a) The additional requirements can be met through additional disclosures in the financial statements; or

(b) The description of the applicable financial reporting framework in the financial statements can be amended accordingly.

If neither of the above actions is possible, the auditor shall determine whether it will be necessary to modify the auditor's opinion in accordance with ISA (UK) 705 (Revised June 2016).[3] (Ref: Para. A36)

Financial Reporting Framework Prescribed by Law or Regulation—Other Matters Affecting Acceptance

If the auditor has determined that the financial reporting framework prescribed by law or regulation would be unacceptable but for the fact that it is prescribed by law or regulation, the auditor shall accept the audit engagement only if the following conditions are present: (Ref: Para. A37)   **19**

(a) Management agrees to provide additional disclosures in the financial statements required to avoid the financial statements being misleading; and

(b) It is recognized in the terms of the audit engagement that:

(i) The auditor's report on the financial statements will incorporate an Emphasis of Matter paragraph, drawing users' attention to the additional disclosures, in accordance with ISA (UK) 706 (Revised June 2016);[4] and

(ii) Unless the auditor is required by law or regulation to express the auditor's opinion on the financial statements by using the phrases 'present fairly, in all material respects,' or 'give a true and fair view' in accordance with the applicable financial reporting framework, the auditor's opinion on the financial statements will not include such phrases.

If the conditions outlined in paragraph 19 are not present and the auditor is required by law or regulation to undertake the audit engagement, the auditor shall: **20**

(a) Evaluate the effect of the misleading nature of the financial statements on the auditor's report; and

(b) Include appropriate reference to this matter in the terms of the audit engagement.

Auditor's Report Prescribed by Law or Regulation

In some cases, law or regulation of the relevant jurisdiction prescribes the layout or wording of the auditor's report in a form or in terms that are significantly different from the requirements of ISAs (UK). In these circumstances, the auditor shall evaluate: **21**

(a) Whether users might misunderstand the assurance obtained from the audit of the financial statements and, if so,

(b) Whether additional explanation in the auditor's report can mitigate possible misunderstanding.[5]

---

[3] *ISA (UK) 705 (Revised June 2016),* Modifications to the Opinion in the Independent Auditor's Report.

[4] *ISA (UK) 706 (Revised June 2016),* Emphasis of Matter Paragraphs and Other Matter Paragraphs in the Independent Auditor's Report.

[5] *ISA (UK) 706 (Revised June 2016).*

If the auditor concludes that additional explanation in the auditor's report cannot mitigate possible misunderstanding, the auditor shall not accept the audit engagement, unless required by law or regulation to do so. An audit conducted in accordance with such law or regulation does not comply with ISAs (UK). Accordingly, the auditor shall not include any reference within the auditor's report to the audit having been conducted in accordance with ISAs (UK).[6] (Ref: Para. A38–A39)

***

Application and Other Explanatory Material

Scope of this ISA (UK) (Ref: Para. 1)

A1 Assurance engagements, which include audit engagements, may only be accepted when the practitioner considers that relevant ethical requirements such as independence and professional competence will be satisfied, and when the engagement exhibits certain characteristics.[7] The auditor's responsibilities in respect of ethical requirements in the context of the acceptance of an audit engagement and in so far as they are within the control of the auditor are dealt with in ISA (UK) 220 (Revised June 2016).[8] This ISA (UK) deals with those matters (or preconditions) that are within the control of the entity and upon which it is necessary for the auditor and the entity's management to agree.

Preconditions for an Audit

The Financial Reporting Framework (Ref: Para. 6(a))

A2 A condition for acceptance of an assurance engagement is that the criteria referred to in the definition of an assurance engagement are suitable and available to intended users.[9] Criteria are the benchmarks used to evaluate or measure the subject matter including, where relevant, benchmarks for presentation and disclosure. Suitable criteria enable reasonably consistent evaluation or measurement of a subject matter within the context of professional judgment. For purposes of the ISAs (UK), the applicable financial reporting framework provides the criteria the auditor uses to audit the financial statements, including where relevant their fair presentation.

A3 Without an acceptable financial reporting framework, management does not have an appropriate basis for the preparation of the financial statements and the auditor does not have suitable criteria for auditing the financial statements. In many cases the auditor may presume that the applicable financial reporting framework is acceptable, as described in paragraphs A8–A9.

---

[6] *See also ISA (UK) 700 (Revised June 2016)*, Forming an Opinion and Reporting on Financial Statements, *paragraph 43.*

[7] International Framework for Assurance Engagements, *paragraph 17.*
The International Framework for Assurance Engagements *has not been promulgated by the FRC for application in the UK.*

[8] *ISA (UK) 220 (Revised June 2016), paragraphs 9–11.*

[9] International Framework for Assurance Engagements, *paragraph 17(b)(ii).*
The International Framework for Assurance Engagements *has not been promulgated by the FRC for application in the UK.*

Determining the Acceptability of the Financial Reporting Framework

Factors that are relevant to the auditor's determination of the acceptability of the financial   **A4**
reporting framework to be applied in the preparation of the financial statements include:

- The nature of the entity (for example, whether it is a business enterprise, a public
  sector entity or a not for profit organization);
- The purpose of the financial statements (for example, whether they are prepared
  to meet the common financial information needs of a wide range of users or the
  financial information needs of specific users);
- The nature of the financial statements (for example, whether the financial statements
  are a complete set of financial statements or a single financial statement); and
- Whether law or regulation prescribes the applicable financial reporting framework.

Many users of financial statements are not in a position to demand financial statements   **A5**
tailored to meet their specific information needs. While all the information needs of
specific users cannot be met, there are financial information needs that are common to a
wide range of users. Financial statements prepared in accordance with a financial reporting
framework designed to meet the common financial information needs of a wide range of
users are referred to as general purpose financial statements.

In some cases, the financial statements will be prepared in accordance with a financial   **A6**
reporting framework designed to meet the financial information needs of specific users.
Such financial statements are referred to as special purpose financial statements. The
financial information needs of the intended users will determine the applicable financial
reporting framework in these circumstances. ISA 800 discusses the acceptability of
financial reporting frameworks designed to meet the financial information needs of
specific users.[10]

Deficiencies in the applicable financial reporting framework that indicate that the framework   **A7**
is not acceptable may be encountered after the audit engagement has been accepted. When use
of that framework is prescribed by law or regulation, the requirements of paragraphs 19–20
apply. When use of that framework is not prescribed by law or regulation, management
may decide to adopt another framework that is acceptable. When management does so,
as required by paragraph 16, new terms of the audit engagement are agreed to reflect the
change in the framework as the previously agreed terms will no longer be accurate.

General purpose frameworks

At present, there is no objective and authoritative basis that has been generally recognized   **A8**
globally for judging the acceptability of general purpose frameworks. In the absence of such
a basis, financial reporting standards established by organizations that are authorized or
recognized to promulgate standards to be used by certain types of entities are presumed to
be acceptable for general purpose financial statements prepared by such entities, provided
the organizations follow an established and transparent process involving deliberation and
consideration of the views of a wide range of stakeholders. Examples of such financial
reporting standards include:

- International Financial Reporting Standards (IFRSs) promulgated by the International
  Accounting Standards Board;
- International Public Sector Accounting Standards (IPSASs) promulgated by the
  International Public Sector Accounting Standards Board; and

---

[10] *ISA 800,* Special Considerations—Audits of Financial Statements Prepared in Accordance with Special Purpose
Frameworks, *paragraph 8.*

- Accounting principles promulgated by an authorized or recognized standards setting organization in a particular jurisdiction, provided the organization follows an established and transparent process involving deliberation and consideration of the views of a wide range of stakeholders.

These financial reporting standards are often identified as the applicable financial reporting framework in law or regulation governing the preparation of general purpose financial statements.

Financial reporting frameworks prescribed by law or regulation

A9   In accordance with paragraph 6(a), the auditor is required to determine whether the financial reporting framework, to be applied in the preparation of the financial statements, is acceptable. In some jurisdictions, law or regulation may prescribe the financial reporting framework to be used in the preparation of general purpose financial statements for certain types of entities. In the absence of indications to the contrary, such a financial reporting framework is presumed to be acceptable for general purpose financial statements prepared by such entities. In the event that the framework is not considered to be acceptable, paragraphs 19–20 apply.

Jurisdictions that do not have standards setting organizations or prescribed financial reporting frameworks

A10   When an entity is registered or operating in a jurisdiction that does not have an authorized or recognized standards setting organization, or where use of the financial reporting framework is not prescribed by law or regulation, management identifies a financial reporting framework to be applied in the preparation of the financial statements. Appendix 2 contains guidance on determining the acceptability of financial reporting frameworks in such circumstances.

Agreement of the Responsibilities of Management (Ref: Para. 6(b))

A11   An audit in accordance with ISAs (UK) is conducted on the premise that management has acknowledged and understands that it has the responsibilities set out in paragraph 6(b).[11] In certain jurisdictions, such responsibilities may be specified in law or regulation. In others, there may be little or no legal or regulatory definition of such responsibilities. ISAs (UK) do not override law or regulation in such matters. However, the concept of an independent audit requires that the auditor's role does not involve taking responsibility for the preparation of the financial statements or for the entity's related internal control, and that the auditor has a reasonable expectation of obtaining the information necessary for the audit (including information obtained from outside of the general and subsidiary ledgers) in so far as management is able to provide or procure it. Accordingly, the premise is fundamental to the conduct of an independent audit. To avoid misunderstanding, agreement is reached with management that it acknowledges and understands that it has such responsibilities as part of agreeing and recording the terms of the audit engagement in paragraphs 9–12.

A12   The way in which the responsibilities for financial reporting are divided between management and those charged with governance will vary according to the resources and structure of the entity and any relevant law or regulation, and the respective roles of management and those charged with governance within the entity. In most cases, management is responsible for execution while those charged with governance have oversight of management. In some cases, those charged with governance will have, or will

---

[11] *ISA (UK) 200 (Revised June 2016), paragraph A4.*

assume, responsibility for approving the financial statements or monitoring the entity's internal control related to financial reporting. In larger or public entities, a subgroup of those charged with governance, such as an audit committee, may be charged with certain oversight responsibilities.

ISA (UK) 580 requires the auditor to request management to provide written representations **A13** that it has fulfilled certain of its responsibilities.[12] It may therefore be appropriate to make management aware that receipt of such written representations will be expected, together with written representations required by other ISAs (UK) and, where necessary, written representations to support other audit evidence relevant to the financial statements or one or more specific assertions in the financial statements.

Where management will not acknowledge its responsibilities, or agree to provide the **A14** written representations, the auditor will be unable to obtain sufficient appropriate audit evidence.[13] In such circumstances, it would not be appropriate for the auditor to accept the audit engagement, unless law or regulation requires the auditor to do so. In cases where the auditor is required to accept the audit engagement, the auditor may need to explain to management the importance of these matters, and the implications for the auditor's report.

Preparation of the Financial Statements (Ref: Para. 6(b)(i))

Most financial reporting frameworks include requirements relating to the presentation of **A15** the financial statements; for such frameworks, *preparation* of the financial statements in accordance with the financial reporting framework includes *presentation*. In the case of a fair presentation framework the importance of the reporting objective of fair presentation is such that the premise agreed with management includes specific reference to fair presentation, or to the responsibility to ensure that the financial statements will 'give a true and fair view' in accordance with the financial reporting framework.

In the UK, accounting standards relating to the small companies regime are prohibited **A15-1** by EU law from specifying disclosure requirements in addition to the limited number of disclosures set out in the Accounting Directive, even though the financial statements of those small entities are required by law to give a true and fair view.[13a] Further, it is not sufficient for the auditor to conclude that the financial statements give a true and fair view solely on the basis that the financial statements were prepared in accordance with accounting standards and any other applicable legal requirements.[13b] The auditor therefore considers whether additional disclosures will be necessary in the financial statements when compliance with an accounting standard is insufficient to give a true and fair view.

Where the auditor determines that the financial statements do not provide the additional **A15-2** disclosures necessary to achieve fair presentation, ISA (UK) 450 (Revised June 2016)[13c] and ISA (UK) 700 (Revised June 2016)[13d] establish requirements and provide guidance

---

[12] *ISA (UK) 580,* Written Representations, *paragraphs 10–11.*

[13] *ISA (UK) 580, paragraph A26.*

[13a] *In the United Kingdom, the Companies Act 2006 establishes this requirement.*

[13b] *ISA (UK) 700 (Revised June 2016), paragraph 16.*

[13c] *ISA (UK) 450 (Revised June 2016),* Evaluation of Misstatements Identified During the Audit.

[13d] *ISA (UK) 700 (Revised June 2016).*

on the evaluation and disposition of misstatements and the effect on the auditor's opinion in the auditor's report.

Internal Control (Ref: Para. 6(b)(ii))

A16   Management maintains such internal control as it determines is necessary to enable the preparation of financial statements that are free from material misstatement, whether due to fraud or error. Internal control, no matter how effective, can provide an entity with only reasonable assurance about achieving the entity's financial reporting objectives due to the inherent limitations of internal control.[14]

A17   An independent audit conducted in accordance with the ISAs (UK) does not act as a substitute for the maintenance of internal control necessary for the preparation of financial statements by management. Accordingly, the auditor is required to obtain the agreement of management that it acknowledges and understands its responsibility for internal control. However, the agreement required by paragraph 6(b)(ii) does not imply that the auditor will find that internal control maintained by management has achieved its purpose or will be free of deficiencies.

A18   It is for management to determine what internal control is necessary to enable the preparation of the financial statements. The term 'internal control' encompasses a wide range of activities within components that may be described as the control environment; the entity's risk assessment process; the information system, including the related business processes relevant to financial reporting, and communication; control activities; and monitoring of controls. This division, however, does not necessarily reflect how a particular entity may design, implement and maintain its internal control, or how it may classify any particular component.[15] An entity's internal control (in particular, its accounting books and records, or accounting systems) will reflect the needs of management, the complexity of the business, the nature of the risks to which the entity is subject, and relevant laws or regulation.

A19   In some jurisdictions, law or regulation may refer to the responsibility of management for the adequacy of accounting books and records, or accounting systems. In some cases, general practice may assume a distinction between accounting books and records or accounting systems on the one hand, and internal control or controls on the other. As accounting books and records, or accounting systems, are an integral part of internal control as referred to in paragraph A18, no specific reference is made to them in paragraph 6(b)(ii) for the description of the responsibility of management. To avoid misunderstanding, it may be appropriate for the auditor to explain to management the scope of this responsibility.

Additional Information (Ref: Para. 6(b)(iii)b)

A20   Additional information that the auditor may request from management for the purpose of the audit may include when applicable, matters related to other information in accordance with ISA (UK) 720 (Revised June 2016). When the auditor expects to obtain other information after the date of the auditor's report, the terms of the audit engagement may also acknowledge the auditor's responsibilities relating to such other information including, if applicable, the actions that may be appropriate or necessary if the auditor

---

[14] *ISA (UK) 315 (Revised June 2016),* Identifying and Assessing the Risks of Material Misstatement through Understanding the Entity and Its Environment, *paragraph A54.*

[15] *ISA (UK) 315 (Revised June 2016), paragraph A59 and Appendix 1.*

concludes that a material misstatement of the other information exists in other information obtained after the date of the auditor's report.[15a]

Considerations Relevant to Smaller Entities (Ref: Para. 6(b))

One of the purposes of agreeing the terms of the audit engagement is to avoid   **A21** misunderstanding about the respective responsibilities of management and the auditor. For example, when a third party has assisted with the preparation of the financial statements, it may be useful to remind management that the preparation of the financial statements in accordance with the applicable financial reporting framework remains its responsibility.

Agreement on Audit Engagement Terms

Agreeing the Terms of the Audit Engagement (Ref: Para. 9)

The roles of management and those charged with governance in agreeing the terms of   **A22** the audit engagement for the entity depend on the governance structure of the entity and relevant law or regulation.

Audit Engagement Letter or Other Form of Written Agreement[16] (Ref: Para. 10–11)

It is in the interests of both the entity and the auditor that the auditor sends an audit   **A23** engagement letter before the commencement of the audit to help avoid misunderstandings with respect to the audit. In some countries, however, the objective and scope of an audit and the responsibilities of management and of the auditor may be sufficiently established by law, that is, they prescribe the matters described in paragraph 10. Although in these circumstances paragraph 11 permits the auditor to include in the engagement letter only reference to the fact that relevant law or regulation applies and that management acknowledges and understands its responsibilities as set out in paragraph 6(b), the auditor may nevertheless consider it appropriate to include the matters described in paragraph 10 in an engagement letter for the information of management.

Form and Content of the Audit Engagement Letter

The form and content of the audit engagement letter may vary for each entity. Information   **A24** included in the audit engagement letter on the auditor's responsibilities may be based on ISA (UK) 200 (Revised June 2016).[17] Paragraphs 6(b) and 12 of this ISA (UK) deal with the description of the responsibilities of management. In addition to including the matters required by paragraph 10, an audit engagement letter may make reference to, for example:

- Elaboration of the scope of the audit, including reference to applicable legislation, regulations, ISAs (UK), and ethical and other pronouncements of professional bodies to which the auditor adheres.
- The form of any other communication of results of the audit engagement.

[15a] *ISA (UK) 700 (Revised June 2016) requires that 'The auditor shall not sign, and hence date, the auditor's report earlier than the date on which all the other information contained in the annual report has been approved by those charged with governance and the auditor has considered all necessary available evidence.'*

[16] *In the paragraphs that follow, any reference to an audit engagement letter is to be taken as a reference to an audit engagement letter or other suitable form of written agreement.*

[17] *ISA (UK) 200 (Revised June 2016), paragraphs 3–9.*

- The requirement for the auditor to communicate key audit matters in the auditor's report in accordance with ISA (UK) 701.[18]
- The fact that because of the inherent limitations of an audit, together with the inherent limitations of internal control, there is an unavoidable risk that some material misstatements may not be detected, even though the audit is properly planned and performed in accordance with ISAs (UK).
- Arrangements regarding the planning and performance of the audit, including the composition of the audit team.
- The expectation that management will provide written representations (see also paragraph A13).
- The expectation that management will provide access to all information of which management is aware that is relevant to the preparation of the financial statements, including an expectation that management will provide access to information relevant to disclosures.
- The agreement of management to make available to the auditor draft financial statements, including all information relevant to their preparation, whether obtained from within or outside of the general and subsidiary ledgers (including all information relevant to the preparation of disclosures), and the other information,[19] if any, in time to allow the auditor to complete the audit in accordance with the proposed timetable.
- The agreement of management to inform the auditor of facts that may affect the financial statements, of which management may become aware during the period from the date of the auditor's report to the date the financial statements are issued.
- The basis on which fees are computed and any billing arrangements.
- A request for management to acknowledge receipt of the audit engagement letter and to agree to the terms of the engagement outlined therein.

A25   When the auditor is not required to communicate key audit matters, it may be helpful for the auditor to make reference in the terms of the audit engagement to the possibility of communicating key audit matters in the auditor's report and, in certain jurisdictions, it may be necessary for the auditor to include a reference to such possibility in order to retain the ability to do so.

A26   When relevant, the following points could also be made in the audit engagement letter:

- Arrangements concerning the involvement of other auditors and experts in some aspects of the audit.
- Arrangements concerning the involvement of internal auditors and other staff of the entity.
- Arrangements to be made with the predecessor auditor, if any, in the case of an initial audit.
- A reference to, and description of, the auditor's responsibilities under law, regulation or relevant ethical requirements that address reporting identified or suspected non-compliance with laws and regulations to an appropriate authority outside the entity.
- Any restriction of the auditor's liability when such possibility exists.
- A reference to any further agreements between the auditor and the entity.
- Any obligations to provide audit working papers to other parties.

An example of an audit engagement letter is set out in Appendix 1.[19a]

---

[18] *ISA (UK) 701*, Communicating Key Audit Matters in the Independent Auditor's Report.

[19] *As defined in ISA (UK) 720 (Revised June 2016)*, The Auditor's Responsibilities Relating to Other Information.

[19a] *The example letter in Appendix 1 has not been tailored for the UK.*

Audits of Components

When the auditor of a parent entity is also the auditor of a component, the factors that may **A27** influence the decision whether to send a separate audit engagement letter to the component include the following:

- Who appoints the component auditor;
- Whether a separate auditor's report is to be issued on the component;
- Legal requirements in relation to audit appointments;
- Degree of ownership by parent; and
- Degree of independence of the component management from the parent entity.

Responsibilities of Management Prescribed by Law or Regulation (Ref: Para. 11–12)

If, in the circumstances described in paragraphs A23 and A29, the auditor concludes that **A28** it is not necessary to record certain terms of the audit engagement in an audit engagement letter, the auditor is still required by paragraph 11 to seek the written agreement from management that it acknowledges and understands that it has the responsibilities set out in paragraph 6(b). However, in accordance with paragraph 12, such written agreement may use the wording of the law or regulation if such law or regulation establishes responsibilities for management that are equivalent in effect to those described in paragraph 6(b). The accounting profession, audit standards setter, or audit regulator in a jurisdiction may have provided guidance as to whether the description in law or regulation is equivalent.

Considerations specific to public sector entities

Law or regulation governing the operations of public sector audits generally mandate the **A29** appointment of a public sector auditor and commonly set out the public sector auditor's responsibilities and powers, including the power to access an entity's records and other information. When law or regulation prescribes in sufficient detail the terms of the audit engagement, the public sector auditor may nonetheless consider that there are benefits in issuing a fuller audit engagement letter than permitted by paragraph 11.

Recurring Audits (Ref: Para. 13)

The auditor may decide not to send a new audit engagement letter or other written **A30** agreement each period. However, the following factors may make it appropriate to revise the terms of the audit engagement or to remind the entity of existing terms:

- Any indication that the entity misunderstands the objective and scope of the audit.
- Any revised or special terms of the audit engagement.
- A recent change of senior management.
- A significant change in ownership.
- A significant change in nature or size of the entity's business.
- A change in legal or regulatory requirements.
- A change in the financial reporting framework adopted in the preparation of the financial statements.
- A change in other reporting requirements.

Acceptance of a Change in the Terms of the Audit Engagement

Request to Change the Terms of the Audit Engagement (Ref: Para. 14)

A31   A request from the entity for the auditor to change the terms of the audit engagement may result from a change in circumstances affecting the need for the service, a misunderstanding as to the nature of an audit as originally requested or a restriction on the scope of the audit engagement, whether imposed by management or caused by other circumstances. The auditor, as required by paragraph 14, considers the justification given for the request, particularly the implications of a restriction on the scope of the audit engagement.

A32   A change in circumstances that affects the entity's requirements or a misunderstanding concerning the nature of the service originally requested may be considered a reasonable basis for requesting a change in the audit engagement.

A33   In contrast, a change may not be considered reasonable if it appears that the change relates to information that is incorrect, incomplete or otherwise unsatisfactory. An example might be where the auditor is unable to obtain sufficient appropriate audit evidence regarding receivables and the entity asks for the audit engagement to be changed to a review engagement to avoid a qualified opinion or a disclaimer of opinion.

Request to Change to a Review or a Related Service (Ref: Para. 15)

A34   Before agreeing to change an audit engagement to a review or a related service, an auditor who was engaged to perform an audit in accordance with ISAs (UK) may need to assess, in addition to the matters referred to in paragraphs A31–A33 above, any legal or contractual implications of the change.

A35   If the auditor concludes that there is reasonable justification to change the audit engagement to a review or a related service, the audit work performed to the date of change may be relevant to the changed engagement; however, the work required to be performed and the report to be issued would be those appropriate to the revised engagement. In order to avoid confusing the reader, the report on the related service would not include reference to:

(a)   The original audit engagement; or

(b)   Any procedures that may have been performed in the original audit engagement, except where the audit engagement is changed to an engagement to undertake agreed-upon procedures and thus reference to the procedures performed is a normal part of the report.

Statement by Auditor on Ceasing to Hold Office (Ref: Para. 17)

A35-1   The auwditor of a limited company in the UK who ceases to hold office as auditor is required to comply with the requirements of Sections 519 and 521 of the Companies Act 2006 regarding the statement to be made by the auditor in relation to ceasing to hold office.

Additional Considerations in Engagement Acceptance

Financial Reporting Standards Supplemented by Law or Regulation (Ref: Para. 18)

A36   In some jurisdictions, law or regulation may supplement the financial reporting standards established by an authorized or recognized standards setting organization with additional requirements relating to the preparation of financial statements. In those jurisdictions, the applicable financial reporting framework for the purposes of applying the ISAs (UK) encompasses both the identified financial reporting framework and such additional requirements provided they do not conflict with the identified financial reporting framework. This may, for example, be the case when law or regulation prescribes disclosures in addition to those required by the financial reporting standards or when they narrow the range of acceptable choices that can be made within the financial reporting standards.[20]

Financial Reporting Framework Prescribed by Law or Regulation—Other Matters Affecting Acceptance (Ref: Para. 19)

Law or regulation may prescribe that the wording of the auditor's opinion use the phrases 'present fairly, in all material respects' or 'give a true and fair view' in a case where the auditor concludes that the applicable financial reporting framework prescribed by law or regulation would otherwise have been unacceptable. In this case, the terms of the prescribed wording of the auditor's report are significantly different from the requirements of ISAs (UK) (see paragraph 21).

A37

Auditor's Report Prescribed by Law or Regulation (Ref: Para. 21)

ISAs (UK) require that the auditor shall not represent compliance with ISAs (UK) unless the auditor has complied with all of the ISAs (UK) relevant to the audit.[21] When law or regulation prescribes the layout or wording of the auditor's report in a form or in terms that are significantly different from the requirements of ISAs (UK) and the auditor concludes that additional explanation in the auditor's report cannot mitigate possible misunderstanding, the auditor may consider including a statement in the auditor's report that the audit is not conducted in accordance with ISAs (UK). The auditor is, however, encouraged to apply ISAs (UK), including the ISAs (UK) that address the auditor's report, to the extent practicable, notwithstanding that the auditor is not permitted to refer to the audit being conducted in accordance with ISAs (UK).

A38

In the UK, certain small companies are permitted by law to prepare their financial statements in accordance with the micro-entities regime[21a] in which those financial statements are presumed in law to give a true and fair view of the micro-entity's assets, liabilities, financial position and profit or loss. This financial reporting framework is not considered to be a fair presentation framework as defined in ISA (UK) 200 (Revised June 2016)[21b] as it does not explicitly or implicitly acknowledge that to achieve fair presentation of the financial statements it may be necessary for management to either provide additional disclosures beyond those required by the framework or to depart from a requirement of the framework. Accordingly, this financial reporting framework is a compliance framework.

A38-1

---

[20] *ISA (UK) 700 (Revised June 2016), paragraph 15, includes a requirement regarding the evaluation of whether the financial statements adequately refer to or describe the applicable financial reporting framework.*

[21] *ISA (UK) 200 (Revised June 2016), paragraph 20.*

[21a] *The micro-entities regime consists of FRS 105* The Financial Reporting Standard applicable to the Micro-entities Regime *and* The Small Companies and Groups (Accounts and Directors' Report) Regulations 2008 *(SI 2008/409) amended by* The Small Companies (Micro-Entities' Accounts) Regulations 2013 *(SI 2013/3008) and* The Companies, Partnerships and Groups (Accounts and Reports) Regulations 2015 *(SI 2015/980).*

[21b] *ISA (UK) 200 (Revised June 2016), paragraph 13(a).*

A38-2   Whilst entities eligible to prepare financial statements in accordance with the micro-entities regime are not required by UK legislation to have those financial statements audited, in the rare circumstances that such an audit of financial statements is requested, the auditor is required by law to state whether the financial statements give a true and fair view. In accordance with paragraphs 25 and 26 of ISA (UK) 700 (Revised June 2016) expressing an unmodified opinion in terms of a true and fair view is reserved for financial statements prepared in accordance with a fair presentation framework. Accordingly, there is a risk that the auditor's report may be misunderstood by users as implying that the micro-entities regime is a fair presentation framework. The auditor therefore considers this requirement in light of paragraph 21 of this ISA (UK). It may be possible for the auditor to mitigate the potential misunderstanding through the prominent inclusion of an other matter paragraph addressing this in the auditor's report in accordance with ISA (UK) 706 (Revised June 2016).

Considerations Specific to Public Sector Entities

A39   In the public sector, specific requirements may exist within the legislation governing the audit mandate; for example, the auditor may be required to report directly to a minister, the legislature or the public if the entity attempts to limit the scope of the audit.

Appendix 1   (Ref: Para. A24–26)

Example of an Audit Engagement Letter

The example letter in this Appendix has not been tailored for the UK.

The following is an example of an audit engagement letter for an audit of general purpose financial statements prepared in accordance with International Financial Reporting Standards. This letter is not authoritative but is intended only to be a guide that may be used in conjunction with the considerations outlined in this ISA. It will need to be varied according to individual requirements and circumstances. It is drafted to refer to the audit of financial statements for a single reporting period and would require adaptation if intended or expected to apply to recurring audits (see paragraph 13 of this ISA). It may be appropriate to seek legal advice that any proposed letter is suitable.

***

To the appropriate representative of management or those charged with governance of ABC Company:[1]

[The objective and scope of the audit]

You[2] have requested that we audit the financial statements of ABC Company, which comprise the statement of financial position as at December 31, 20X1, and the statement of

---

[1] *The addressees and references in the letter would be those that are appropriate in the circumstances of the engagement, including the relevant jurisdiction. It is important to refer to the appropriate persons – see paragraph A22.*

[2] *Throughout this letter, references to 'you,' 'we,' 'us,' 'management,' 'those charged with governance' and 'auditor' would be used or amended as appropriate in the circumstances.*

comprehensive income, statement of changes in equity and statement of cash flows for the year then ended, and notes to the financial statements, including a summary of significant accounting policies. We are pleased to confirm our acceptance and our understanding of this audit engagement by means of this letter.

The objectives of our audit are to obtain reasonable assurance about whether the financial statements as a whole are free from material misstatement, whether due to fraud or error, and to issue an auditor's report that includes our opinion. Reasonable assurance is a high level of assurance, but is not a guarantee that an audit conducted in accordance with International Standards on Auditing (ISAs) will always detect a material misstatement when it exists. Misstatements can arise from fraud or error and are considered material if, individually or in the aggregate, they could reasonably be expected to influence the economic decisions of users taken on the basis of these financial statements.

[*The responsibilities of the auditor*]

We will conduct our audit in accordance with ISAs. Those standards require that we comply with ethical requirements. As part of an audit in accordance with ISAs, we exercise professional judgment and maintain professional skepticism throughout the audit. We also:

- Identify and assess the risks of material misstatement of the financial statements, whether due to fraud or error, design and perform audit procedures responsive to those risks, and obtain audit evidence that is sufficient and appropriate to provide a basis for our opinion. The risk of not detecting a material misstatement resulting from fraud is higher than for one resulting from error, as fraud may involve collusion, forgery, intentional omissions, misrepresentations, or the override of internal control.
- Obtain an understanding of internal control relevant to the audit in order to design audit procedures that are appropriate in the circumstances, but not for the purpose of expressing an opinion on the effectiveness of the entity's internal control.[3] However, we will communicate to you in writing concerning any significant deficiencies in internal control relevant to the audit of the financial statements that we have identified during the audit.
- Evaluate the appropriateness of accounting policies used and the reasonableness of accounting estimates and related disclosures made by management
- Conclude on the appropriateness of management's use of the going concern basis of accounting and, based on the audit evidence obtained, whether a material uncertainty exists related to events or conditions that may cast significant doubt on the Company's ability to continue as a going concern. If we conclude that a material uncertainty exists, we are required to draw attention in our auditor's report to the related disclosures in the financial statements or, if such disclosures are inadequate, to modify our opinion. Our conclusions are based on the audit evidence obtained up to the date of our auditor's report. However, future events or conditions may cause the Company to cease to continue as a going concern.
- Evaluate the overall presentation, structure and content of the financial statements, including the disclosures, and whether the financial statements represent the underlying transactions and events in a manner that achieves fair presentation.

Because of the inherent limitations of an audit, together with the inherent limitations of internal control, there is an unavoidable risk that some material misstatements may not be detected, even though the audit is properly planned and performed in accordance with ISAs.

[*The responsibilities of management and identification of the applicable financial reporting framework (for purposes of this example it is assumed that the auditor has not determined*

---

[3] *This sentence would be modified, as appropriate, in circumstances when the auditor also has responsibility to issue an opinion on the effectiveness of internal control in conjunction with the audit of the financial statements.*

that the law or regulation prescribes those responsibilities in appropriate terms; the descriptions in paragraph 6(b) of this ISA are therefore used).]

Our audit will be conducted on the basis that [management and, where appropriate, those charged with governance][4] acknowledge and understand that they have responsibility:

(a)   For the preparation and fair presentation of the financial statements in accordance with International Financial Reporting Standards;[5]

(b)   For such internal control as [management] determines is necessary to enable the preparation of financial statements that are free from material misstatement, whether due to fraud or error; and

(c)   To provide us with:[6]

(i)   Access to all information of which [management] is aware that is relevant to the preparation of the financial statements such as records, documentation and other matters;

(ii)   Additional information that we may request from [management] for the purpose of the audit; and

(iii)   Unrestricted access to persons within the entity from whom we determine it necessary to obtain audit evidence.

As part of our audit process, we will request from [management and, where appropriate, those charged with governance], written confirmation concerning representations made to us in connection with the audit.

We look forward to full cooperation from your staff during our audit.

[*Other relevant information*]

[*Insert other information, such as fee arrangements, billings and other specific terms, as appropriate.*]

[*Reporting*]

[*Insert appropriate reference to the expected form and content of the auditor's report including, if applicable, the reporting on other information in accordance with ISA 720 (Revised).*]

The form and content of our report may need to be amended in the light of our audit findings.

Please sign and return the attached copy of this letter to indicate your acknowledgement of, and agreement with, the arrangements for our audit of the financial statements including our respective responsibilities.

XYZ & Co.

Acknowledged and agreed on behalf of ABC Company by

(signed)

....

Name and Title

Date

---

[4] *Use terminology as appropriate in the circumstances.*

[5] *Or, if appropriate, 'For the preparation of financial statements that give a true and fair view in accordance with International Financial Reporting Standards.'*

[6] *See paragraph A23 for examples of other matters relating to management's responsibilities that may be included.*

Appendix 2

(Ref: Para. A10)

Determining the Acceptability of General Purpose Frameworks

Jurisdictions that Do Not Have Authorized or Recognized Standards Setting Organizations or Financial Reporting Frameworks Prescribed by Law or Regulation

As explained in paragraph A10 of this ISA (UK), when an entity is registered or operating in   **1**
a jurisdiction that does not have an authorized or recognized standards setting organization,
or where use of the financial reporting framework is not prescribed by law or regulation,
management identifies an applicable financial reporting framework. Practice in such
jurisdictions is often to use the financial reporting standards established by one of the
organizations described in paragraph A8 of this ISA (UK).

Alternatively, there may be established accounting conventions in a particular jurisdiction that   **2**
are generally recognized as the financial reporting framework for general purpose financial
statements prepared by certain specified entities operating in that jurisdiction. When such a
financial reporting framework is adopted, the auditor is required by paragraph 6(a) of this
ISA (UK) to determine whether the accounting conventions collectively can be considered
to constitute an acceptable financial reporting framework for general purpose financial
statements. When the accounting conventions are widely used in a particular jurisdiction,
the accounting profession in that jurisdiction may have considered the acceptability of the
financial reporting framework on behalf of the auditors. Alternatively, the auditor may make
this determination by considering whether the accounting conventions exhibit attributes
normally exhibited by acceptable financial reporting frameworks (see paragraph 3 below),
or by comparing the accounting conventions to the requirements of an existing financial
reporting framework considered to be acceptable (see paragraph 4 below).

Acceptable financial reporting frameworks normally exhibit the following attributes that   **3**
result in information provided in financial statements that is useful to the intended users:
(a) Relevance, in that the information provided in the financial statements is relevant to
    the nature of the entity and the purpose of the financial statements. For example, in
    the case of a business enterprise that prepares general purpose financial statements,
    relevance is assessed in terms of the information necessary to meet the common
    financial information needs of a wide range of users in making economic decisions.
    These needs are ordinarily met by presenting the financial position, financial
    performance and cash flows of the business enterprise.
(b) Completeness, in that transactions and events, account balances and disclosures that
    could affect conclusions based on the financial statements are not omitted.
(c) Reliability, in that the information provided in the financial statements:
    (i) Where applicable, reflects the economic substance of events and transactions
         and not merely their legal form; and
    (ii) Results in reasonably consistent evaluation, measurement, presentation and
         disclosure, when used in similar circumstances.
(d) Neutrality, in that it contributes to information in the financial statements that is free
    from bias.
(e) Understandability, in that the information in the financial statements is clear and
    comprehensive and not subject to significantly different interpretation.

The auditor may decide to compare the accounting conventions to the requirements of   **4**
an existing financial reporting framework considered to be acceptable. For example,
the auditor may compare the accounting conventions to IFRSs. For an audit of a small
entity, the auditor may decide to compare the accounting conventions to a financial

reporting framework specifically developed for such entities by an authorized or recognized standards setting organization. When the auditor makes such a comparison and differences are identified, the decision as to whether the accounting conventions adopted in the preparation of the financial statements constitute an acceptable financial reporting framework includes considering the reasons for the differences and whether application of the accounting conventions, or the description of the financial reporting framework in the financial statements, could result in financial statements that are misleading.

5   A conglomeration of accounting conventions devised to suit individual preferences is not an acceptable financial reporting framework for general purpose financial statements. Similarly, a compliance framework will not be an acceptable financial reporting framework, unless it is generally accepted in the particular jurisdictions by preparers and users.

International Standard on Auditing (UK) 220 (Revised June 2016) (Updated July 2017)

Quality control for an audit of financial statements

(Effective for audits of financial statements for periods commencing on or after 17 June 2016)[0]

Contents

International Standard on Auditing (UK) (ISA (UK)) 220 (Revised June 2016), *Quality Control for an Audit of Financial Statements*, should be read in conjunction with ISA (UK) 200 (Revised June 2016), *Overall Objectives of the Independent Auditor and the Conduct of an Audit in Accordance with International Standards on Auditing (UK)*.

[0] *Conforming amendments to this standard as a result of ISA (UK) 250 (Revised July 2017),* Section A—Consideration of Laws and Regulations in an Audit of Financial Statements, *are included that are effective for audits of financial statements for periods commencing on or after 15 December 2017. Details of the amendments are given in the Annexure to ISA (UK) 250 (Revised December 2017) Section A.*

Introduction

Scope of this ISA (UK)

1   This International Standard on Auditing (UK) (ISA (UK)) deals with the specific responsibilities of the auditor regarding quality control procedures for an audit of financial statements. It also addresses, where applicable, the responsibilities of the engagement quality control reviewer. This ISA (UK) is to be read in conjunction with relevant ethical requirements.

System of Quality Control and Role of Engagement Teams

2   Quality control systems, policies and procedures are the responsibility of the audit firm. Under ISQC (UK) 1 (Revised June 2016), the firm has an obligation to establish and maintain a system of quality control to provide it with reasonable assurance that:

(a)   The firm and its personnel comply with professional standards and applicable legal and regulatory requirements; and

(b)   The reports issued by the firm or engagement partners are appropriate in the circumstances.[1]

This ISA (UK) is premised on the basis that the firm is subject to ISQC (UK) 1 (Revised June 2016) or to national requirements that are at least as demanding. (Ref: Para. A1)

3   Within the context of the firm's system of quality control, engagement teams have a responsibility to implement quality control procedures that are applicable to the audit engagement and provide the firm with relevant information to enable the functioning of that part of the firm's system of quality control relating to independence.

4   Engagement teams are entitled to rely on the firm's system of quality control, unless information provided by the firm or other parties suggests otherwise. (Ref: Para. A2)

Effective Date

5   This ISA (UK) is effective for audits of financial statements for periods commencing on or after 17 June 2016. Earlier adoption is permitted.

Objective

6   The objective of the auditor is to implement quality control procedures at the engagement level that provide the auditor with reasonable assurance that:

(a)   The audit complies with professional standards and applicable legal and regulatory requirements; and

(b)   The auditor's report issued is appropriate in the circumstances.

Definitions

7   For purposes of the ISAs (UK), the following terms have the meanings attributed below:

(a)   Engagement partner[2] – The partner or other person in the firm who is responsible for the audit engagement and its performance, and for the auditor's report that is issued

---

[1] *ISQC (UK) 1 (Revised June 2016),* Quality Control for Firms that Perform Audits and Reviews of Financial Statements, and Other Assurance and Related Services Engagements, *paragraph 11.*

[2] *'Engagement partner,' 'partner,' and 'firm' should be read as referring to their public sector equivalents where relevant.*

on behalf of the firm, and who, where required, has the appropriate authority from a professional, legal or regulatory body.

(b)   Engagement quality control review – A process designed to provide an objective evaluation, on or before the date of the auditor's report, of the significant judgments the engagement team made and the conclusions it reached in formulating the auditor's report. The engagement quality control review process is only for audits of financial statements of listed entities and those other audit engagements, if any, for which the firm has determined an engagement quality control review is required.

(c)   Engagement quality control reviewer – A partner, other person in the firm, suitably qualified external person, or a team made up of such individuals, none of whom is part of the engagement team, with sufficient and appropriate experience and authority to objectively evaluate the significant judgments the engagement team made and the conclusions it reached in formulating the auditor's report.

(d)   Engagement team – All partners and staff performing the engagement, and any individuals engaged by the firm or a network firm who perform audit procedures on the engagement. This excludes an auditor's external expert engaged by the firm or by a network firm.[3] The term 'engagement team' also excludes individuals within the client's internal audit function who provide direct assistance on an audit engagement when the external auditor complies with the requirements of ISA (UK) 610 (Revised June 2013).[4]

(e)   Firm – A sole practitioner, partnership or corporation or other entity of professional accountants.

(f)   Inspection – In relation to completed audit engagements, procedures designed to provide evidence of compliance by engagement teams with the firm's quality control policies and procedures.

(f)-1   Key audit partner – Is defined in UK legislation[4a] as:

(i)   The statutory auditor designated by an audit firm for a particular audit engagement as being primarily responsible for carrying out the statutory audit on behalf of the audit firm; or

(ii)   In the case of a group audit, the statutory auditor designated by an audit firm as being primarily responsible for carrying out the statutory audit at the level of the group and the statutory auditor designated at the level of material subsidiaries; or

(iii)   The statutory auditor who signs the audit report.

(g)   Listed entity – An entity whose shares, stock or debt are quoted or listed on a recognized stock exchange, or are marketed under the regulations of a recognized stock exchange or other equivalent body.

In the UK, this includes any company in which the public can trade shares, stock or debt on the open market, such as those listed on the London Stock Exchange (including those admitted to trading on the Alternative Investments Market) and ISDX Markets. It does not include entities whose quoted or listed shares, stock or debt are in substance not freely transferable or cannot be traded freely by the public or the entity.

---

[3] *ISA (UK) 620 (Revised June 2016),* Using the Work of an Auditor's Expert, *paragraph 6(a), defines the term 'auditor's expert.'*

[4] *ISA 610 (Revised June 2013),* Using the Work of Internal Auditors, *establishes limits on the use of direct assistance. It also acknowledges that the external auditor may be prohibited by law or regulation from obtaining direct assistance from internal auditors. Therefore, the use of direct assistance is restricted to situations where it is permitted.*
The use of internal auditors to provide direct assistance is prohibited in an audit conducted in accordance with ISAs (UK) – see ISA (UK) 610 (Revised June 2013), paragraph 5-1.

[4a] *In the UK, Schedule 10 to the Companies Act 2006.*

(h)   Monitoring – A process comprising an ongoing consideration and evaluation of the firm's system of quality control, including a periodic inspection of a selection of completed engagements, designed to provide the firm with reasonable assurance that its system of quality control is operating effectively.

(i)   Network firm – A firm or entity that belongs to a network.

(j)   Network – A larger structure:

    (i)   That is aimed at cooperation, and

    (ii)   That is clearly aimed at profit or cost-sharing or shares common ownership, control or management, common quality control policies and procedures, common business strategy, the use of a common brand name, or a significant part of professional resources.

(k)   Partner – Any individual with authority to bind the firm with respect to the performance of a professional services engagement.

(l)   Personnel – Partners and staff.

(m)   Professional standards – International Standards on Auditing (UK) (ISAs (UK)) and relevant ethical requirements.

(m)-1 Public interest entity – Is defined in UK legislation[4b] as:

    (i)   An issuer whose transferable securities are admitted to trading on a regulated market;[4c]

    (ii)   A credit institution within the meaning given by Article 4(1)(1) of Regulation (EU) No. 575/2013 of the European Parliament and of the Council, other than one listed in Article 2 of Directive 2013/36/EU of the European Parliament and of the Council on access to the activity of credit institutions and investment firms;

    (iii)   An insurance undertaking within the meaning given by Article 2(1) of Council Directive 1991/674/EEC of the European Parliament and of the Council on the annual accounts and consolidated accounts of insurance undertakings.

(n)   Relevant ethical requirements – Ethical requirements to which the engagement team and engagement quality control reviewer are subject, which ordinarily comprise Parts A and B of the International Ethics Standards Board for Accountants' *Code of Ethics for Professional Accountants* (IESBA Code) related to an audit of financial statements together with national requirements that are more restrictive.

Auditors in the UK are subject to ethical requirements from two sources: the FRC's Ethical Standard concerning the integrity, objectivity and independence of the auditor, and the ethical pronouncements established by the auditor's relevant professional body.

(o)   Staff – Professionals, other than partners, including any experts the firm employs.

(p)   Suitably qualified external person – An individual outside the firm with the competence and capabilities to act as an engagement partner, for example a partner of another firm, or an employee (with appropriate experience) of either a professional accountancy body whose members may perform audits of historical financial information or of an organization that provides relevant quality control services.

[4b] *In the UK, Section 494A of the Companies Act 2006.*

[4c] *In the UK, 'issuer' and 'regulated market' have the same meaning as in Part 6 of the Financial Services and Markets Act 2000.*

Requirements

Leadership Responsibilities for Quality on Audits

The engagement partner shall take responsibility for the overall quality on each audit   **8** engagement to which that partner is assigned. (Ref: Para. A3)

Relevant Ethical Requirements

Throughout the audit engagement, the engagement partner shall remain alert, through   **9** observation and making inquiries as necessary, for evidence of non-compliance with relevant ethical requirements by members of the engagement team. (Ref: Para. A4–A5)

If matters come to the engagement partner's attention through the firm's system of quality   **10** control or otherwise that indicate that members of the engagement team have not complied with relevant ethical requirements, the engagement partner, in consultation with others in the firm, shall determine the appropriate action. (Ref: Para. A5)

Independence

The engagement partner shall form a conclusion on compliance with independence   **11** requirements that apply to the audit engagement. In doing so, the engagement partner shall: (Ref: Para. A5)

(a) Obtain relevant information from the firm and, where applicable, network firms, to identify and evaluate circumstances and relationships that create threats to independence;

(b) Evaluate information on identified breaches, if any, of the firm's independence policies and procedures to determine whether they create a threat to independence for the audit engagement; and

(c) Take appropriate action to eliminate such threats or reduce them to an acceptable level by applying safeguards, or, if considered appropriate, to withdraw from the audit engagement, where withdrawal is possible under applicable law or regulation. The engagement partner shall promptly report to the firm any inability to resolve the matter for appropriate action. (Ref: Para. A6–A7)

Acceptance and Continuance of Client Relationships and Audit Engagements

The engagement partner shall be satisfied that appropriate procedures regarding the   **12** acceptance and continuance of client relationships and audit engagements have been followed, and shall determine that conclusions reached in this regard are appropriate. (Ref: Para. A8–A9)

If the engagement partner obtains information that would have caused the firm to decline   **13** the audit engagement had that information been available earlier, the engagement partner shall communicate that information promptly to the firm, so that the firm and the engagement partner can take the necessary action. (Ref: Para. A9)

Assignment of Engagement Teams

The engagement partner shall be satisfied that the engagement team, and any auditor's   **14** experts who are not part of the engagement team, collectively have the appropriate competence and capabilities to:

(a) Perform the audit engagement in accordance with professional standards and applicable legal and regulatory requirements; and

(b) Enable an auditor's report that is appropriate in the circumstances to be issued. (Ref: Para. A10–A12)

Engagement Performance

Direction, Supervision and Performance

15 The engagement partner shall take responsibility for:

(a) The direction, supervision and performance of the audit engagement in compliance with professional standards and applicable legal and regulatory requirements; and (Ref: Para. A13–A15, A20)

(b) The auditor's report being appropriate in the circumstances.

Reviews

16 The engagement partner shall take responsibility for reviews being performed in accordance with the firm's review policies and procedures. (Ref: Para. A16–A17, A20)

17 On or before the date of the auditor's report, the engagement partner shall, through a review of the audit documentation and discussion with the engagement team, be satisfied that sufficient appropriate audit evidence has been obtained to support the conclusions reached and for the auditor's report to be issued. (Ref: Para. A18–A20)

Consultation

18 The engagement partner shall:

(a) Take responsibility for the engagement team undertaking appropriate consultation on difficult or contentious matters;

(b) Be satisfied that members of the engagement team have undertaken appropriate consultation during the course of the engagement, both within the engagement team and between the engagement team and others at the appropriate level within or outside the firm;

(c) Be satisfied that the nature and scope of, and conclusions resulting from, such consultations are agreed with the party consulted; and

(d) Determine that conclusions resulting from such consultations have been implemented. (Ref: Para. A21–A22)

Engagement Quality Control Review

19 For audits of financial statements of listed entities, and those other audit engagements, if any, for which the firm has determined that an engagement quality control review is required, the engagement partner shall:

(a) Determine that an engagement quality control reviewer has been appointed;

(b) Discuss significant matters arising during the audit engagement, including those identified during the engagement quality control review, with the engagement quality control reviewer; and

(c) Not date the auditor's report until the completion of the engagement quality control review. (Ref: Para. A23–A25)

The engagement quality control reviewer shall perform an objective evaluation of the **20** significant judgments made by the engagement team, and the conclusions reached in formulating the auditor's report. This evaluation shall involve:

(a) Discussion of significant matters with the engagement partner;
(b) Review of the financial statements and the proposed auditor's report;
(c) Review of selected audit documentation relating to the significant judgments the engagement team made and the conclusions it reached; and
(d) Evaluation of the conclusions reached in formulating the auditor's report and consideration of whether the proposed auditor's report is appropriate. (Ref: Para. A26–A28, A30–A32)

For audits of financial statements of listed entities, the engagement quality control reviewer, **21** on performing an engagement quality control review, shall also consider the following:

(a) The engagement team's evaluation of the firm's independence in relation to the audit engagement;
(b) Whether appropriate consultation has taken place on matters involving differences of opinion or other difficult or contentious matters, and the conclusions arising from those consultations; and
(c) Whether audit documentation selected for review reflects the work performed in relation to the significant judgments and supports the conclusions reached. (Ref: Para. A29–A32)

For audits of financial statements of public interest entities, the engagement quality **21R-1** control reviewer, on performing an engagement quality control review,[4d] shall also consider the following elements:

(a) The independence of the firm from the entity;
(b) The significant risks which are relevant to the audit and which the key audit partner(s) has identified during the performance of the audit and the measures that the key audit partner(s) has taken to adequately manage those risks;
(c) The reasoning of the key audit partner(s), in particular with regard to the level of materiality and the significant risks referred to in paragraph 21R-1(b);
(d) Any request for advice to external experts and the implementation of such advice;
(e) The nature and scope of the corrected and uncorrected misstatements in the financial statements that were identified during the carrying out of the audit;
(f) The subjects discussed with the audit committee and management and/or supervisory bodies of the entity;
(g) The subjects discussed with competent authorities[4e] and, where applicable, with other third parties; and
(h) Whether the documents and information selected from the file by the engagement quality control reviewer support the opinion of the key audit partner(s) as expressed in the draft of the auditor's report and the additional report to the audit committee.[4f]

The engagement quality control reviewer shall discuss the results of the review, **21R-2** including the elements assessed in paragraph 21R-1, with the key audit partner(s).

[4d] *The requirement for an engagement quality control review is established in ISQC (UK) 1 (Revised June 2016), paragraph 36R-1.*

[4e] *In the UK, the competent authority designated by law is the Financial Reporting Council.*

[4f] *The requirements for these reports are set out respectively in ISA (UK) 700 (Revised June 2016),* Forming an Opinion and Reporting on Financial Statements *and ISA (UK) 260 (Revised June 2016),* Communication with Those Charged with Governance.

Differences of Opinion

22   If differences of opinion arise within the engagement team, with those consulted or, where applicable, between the engagement partner and the engagement quality control reviewer, the engagement team shall follow the firm's policies and procedures for dealing with and resolving differences of opinion.

Monitoring

23   An effective system of quality control includes a monitoring process designed to provide the firm with reasonable assurance that its policies and procedures relating to the system of quality control are relevant, adequate, and operating effectively. The engagement partner shall consider the results of the firm's monitoring process as evidenced in the latest information circulated by the firm and, if applicable, other network firms and whether deficiencies noted in that information may affect the audit engagement. (Ref: Para A33–A35)

Documentation

24   The auditor shall include in the audit documentation:[5]

(a)   Issues identified with respect to compliance with relevant ethical requirements and how they were resolved.

(b)   Conclusions on compliance with independence requirements that apply to the audit engagement, and any relevant discussions with the firm that support these conclusions.

(c)   Conclusions reached regarding the acceptance and continuance of client relationships and audit engagements.

(d)   The nature and scope of, and conclusions resulting from, consultations undertaken during the course of the audit engagement. (Ref: Para. A35)

24D-1   The auditor shall include in the audit documentation:

(a)   All significant threats to the firm's independence as well as the safeguards applied to mitigate those threats; and

(b)   Those matters it is required to assess before accepting or continuing a statutory audit engagement in accordance with ISQC (UK) 1 (Revised June 2016).

25   The engagement quality control reviewer shall document, for the audit engagement reviewed, that:

(a)   The procedures required by the firm's policies on engagement quality control review have been performed;

(b)   The engagement quality control review has been completed on or before the date of the auditor's report; and

(c)   The reviewer is not aware of any unresolved matters that would cause the reviewer to believe that the significant judgments the engagement team made and the conclusions it reached were not appropriate.

25R-1   For audits of financial statements of public interest entities, the engagement quality control reviewer shall also record:

(a)   The oral and written information provided by the key audit partner(s) to support the significant judgments as well as the main findings of the audit procedures

---

[5] ISA (UK) 230 (Revised June 2016), Audit Documentation, *paragraphs 8–11, and A6.*

carried out and the conclusions drawn from those findings, whether or not at the request of the engagement quality control reviewer; and

(b) The opinions of the key audit partner(s), as expressed in the draft of the reports required by ISA (UK) 260 (Revised June 2016) and ISA (UK) 700 (Revised June 2016).

For audits of financial statements of public interest entities, the auditor and the engagement quality control reviewer shall keep a record of the results of the engagement quality control review, together with the considerations underlying those results, in the audit documentation.

25R-2

***

Application and Other Explanatory Material

System of Quality Control and Role of Engagement Teams (Ref: Para. 2)

ISQC (UK) 1 (Revised June 2016), or national requirements that are at least as demanding, deals with the firm's responsibilities to establish and maintain its system of quality control for audit engagements. The system of quality control includes policies and procedures that address each of the following elements:

A1

- Leadership responsibilities for quality within the firm;
- Relevant ethical requirements;
- Acceptance and continuance of client relationships and specific engagements;
- Human resources;
- Engagement performance; and
- Monitoring.

National requirements that deal with the firm's responsibilities to establish and maintain a system of quality control are at least as demanding as ISQC (UK) 1 (Revised June 2016) when they address all the elements referred to in this paragraph and impose obligations on the firm that achieve the aims of the requirements set out in ISQC (UK) 1 (Revised June 2016).

Reliance on the Firm's System of Quality Control (Ref: Para. 4)

Unless information provided by the firm or other parties suggest otherwise, the engagement team may rely on the firm's system of quality control in relation to, for example:

A2

- Competence of personnel through their recruitment and formal training.
- Independence through the accumulation and communication of relevant independence information.
- Maintenance of client relationships through acceptance and continuance systems.
- Adherence to applicable legal and regulatory requirements through the monitoring process.

Leadership Responsibilities for Quality on Audits (Ref: Para. 8)

The actions of the engagement partner and appropriate messages to the other members of the engagement team, in taking responsibility for the overall quality on each audit engagement, emphasize:

A3

(a) The importance to audit quality of:
   (i)   Performing work that complies with professional standards and applicable legal and regulatory requirements;
   (ii) Complying with the firm's quality control policies and procedures as applicable;
   (iii) Issuing auditor's reports that are appropriate in the circumstances; and
   (iv) The engagement team's ability to raise concerns without fear of reprisals; and

(b) The fact that quality is essential in performing audit engagements.

A3-1   ISQC (UK) 1 (Revised June 2016)[5a] sets out requirements to ensure that securing audit quality, independence and competence are the main criteria used by the firm to select the engagement partner or key audit partner(s).

Relevant Ethical Requirements

Compliance with Relevant Ethical Requirements (Ref: Para. 9)

A4   The IESBA Code[5b] establishes the fundamental principles of professional ethics, which include:
(a) Integrity;
(b) Objectivity;
(c) Professional competence and due care;
(d) Confidentiality; and
(e) Professional behavior.

Definition of 'Firm,' 'Network' and 'Network Firm' (Ref: Para. 9–11)

A5   The definitions of 'firm,' 'network' or 'network firm' in relevant ethical requirements may differ from those set out in this ISA (UK). For example, the IESBA Code[5b] defines the 'firm' as:
(a) A sole practitioner, partnership or corporation of professional accountants;
(b) An entity that controls such parties through ownership, management or other means; and
(c) An entity controlled by such parties through ownership, management or other means.

The IESBA Code also provides guidance in relation to the terms 'network' and 'network firm.'

In complying with the requirements in paragraphs 9–11, the definitions used in the relevant ethical requirements apply in so far as is necessary to interpret those ethical requirements.

Threats to Independence (Ref: Para. 11(c))

A6   The engagement partner may identify a threat to independence regarding the audit engagement that safeguards may not be able to eliminate or reduce to an acceptable level. In that case, as required by paragraph 11(c), the engagement partner reports to the relevant person(s) within the firm to determine appropriate action, which may include eliminating the activity or interest that creates the threat, or withdrawing from the audit engagement, where withdrawal is possible under applicable law or regulation.

[5a] *ISQC (UK) 1 (Revised June 2016), paragraph 30D-1.*

[5b] *In the UK, auditors are subject to ethical requirements from two sources: the FRC's Ethical Standard concerning the integrity, objectivity and independence of the auditor, and the ethical pronouncements established by the auditor's relevant professional body.*

Considerations Specific to Public Sector Entities

Statutory measures may provide safeguards for the independence of public sector auditors.   **A7**
However, public sector auditors or audit firms carrying out public sector audits on behalf
of the statutory auditor may, depending on the terms of the mandate in a particular
jurisdiction, need to adapt their approach in order to promote compliance with the spirit of
paragraph 11. This may include, where the public sector auditor's mandate does not permit
withdrawal from the engagement, disclosure through a public report, of circumstances
that have arisen that would, if they were in the private sector, lead the auditor to withdraw.

Acceptance and Continuance of Client Relationships and Audit Engagements (Ref: Para. 12)

ISQC (UK) 1 (Revised June 2016) requires the firm to obtain information considered   **A8**
necessary in the circumstances before accepting an engagement with a new client, when
deciding whether to continue an existing engagement, and when considering acceptance
of a new engagement with an existing client.[6] Information such as the following assists
the engagement partner in determining whether the conclusions reached regarding the
acceptance and continuance of client relationships and audit engagements are appropriate:

- The integrity of the principal owners, key management and those charged with
  governance of the entity;
- Whether the engagement team is competent to perform the audit engagement and has
  the necessary capabilities, including time and resources;
- Whether the firm and the engagement team can comply with relevant ethical
  requirements; and
- Significant matters that have arisen during the current or previous audit engagement,
  and their implications for continuing the relationship.

Law, regulation, or relevant ethical requirements[7] may require the auditor to request, prior to   **A8a**
accepting the engagement, the predecessor auditor to provide known information regarding
any facts or circumstances that, in the predecessor auditor's judgment, the auditor needs
to be aware of before deciding whether to accept the engagement. In some circumstances,
the predecessor auditor may be required, on request by the proposed successor auditor,
to provide information regarding identified or suspected non-compliance with laws and
regulations to the proposed successor auditor.[7a] For example, where the predecessor auditor
has withdrawn from the engagement as a result of identified or suspected non-compliance
with laws and regulations, the IESBA Code requires that the predecessor auditor, on request
by a proposed successor auditor, provides all such facts and other information concerning
such non-compliance that, in the predecessor auditor's opinion, the proposed successor
auditor needs to be aware of before deciding whether to accept the audit appointment.[8]

---

[6] *ISQC (UK) 1 (Revised June 2016), paragraph 27(a).*

[7] *See, for example, Sections 210.14 of the IESBA Code.*
*In the UK, the relevant guidance on proposed communications with a predecessor auditor is provided by the
pronouncements relating to the work of auditors issued by the auditor's relevant professional body.*

[7a] *In the UK, the predecessor auditor is required to provide the successor statutory auditor with access to all relevant
information concerning the entity, including information concerning the most recent audit. This would include
non-compliance with laws and regulations. See ISQC (UK) 1 (Revised June 2016),* Quality Control for Firms that
Perform Audits and Reviews of Financial Statements, *and other Assurance and Related Services Engagements,
paragraph 28D-1.*

[8] *See, for example, Sections 225.31 of the IESBA Code.*
In the UK, the auditor has regard to any specific requirements of the auditor's relevant professional body.

Considerations Specific to Public Sector Entities (Ref: Para. 12–13)

A9   In the public sector, auditors may be appointed in accordance with statutory procedures. Accordingly, certain of the requirements and considerations regarding the acceptance and continuance of client relationships and audit engagements as set out in paragraphs 12, 13 and A8 may not be relevant. Nonetheless, information gathered as a result of the process described may be valuable to public sector auditors in performing risk assessments and in carrying out reporting responsibilities.

Assignment of Engagement Teams (Ref: Para. 14)

A10   An engagement team includes a person using expertise in a specialized area of accounting or auditing, whether engaged or employed by the firm, if any, who performs audit procedures on the engagement. However, a person with such expertise is not a member of the engagement team if that person's involvement with the engagement is only consultation. Consultations are addressed in paragraph 18, and paragraph A21–A22.

A11   When considering the appropriate competence and capabilities expected of the engagement team as a whole, the engagement partner may take into consideration such matters as the team's:

- Understanding of, and practical experience with, audit engagements of a similar nature and complexity through appropriate training and participation.
- Understanding of professional standards and applicable legal and regulatory requirements.
- Technical expertise, including expertise with relevant information technology and specialized areas of accounting or auditing.
- Knowledge of relevant industries in which the client operates.
- Ability to apply professional judgment.
- Understanding of the firm's quality control policies and procedures.

Considerations Specific to Public Sector Entities

A12   In the public sector, additional appropriate competence may include skills that are necessary to discharge the terms of the audit mandate in a particular jurisdiction. Such competence may include an understanding of the applicable reporting arrangements, including reporting to the legislature or other governing body or in the public interest. The wider scope of a public sector audit may include, for example, some aspects of performance auditing or a comprehensive assessment of compliance with law, regulation or other authority and preventing and detecting fraud and corruption.

Engagement Performance

Direction, Supervision and Performance (Ref: Para. 15(a))

A13   Direction of the engagement team involves informing the members of the engagement team of matters such as:

- Their responsibilities, including the need to comply with relevant ethical requirements, and to plan and perform an audit with professional skepticism as required by ISA (UK) 200 (Revised June 2016).[9]

---

[9] *ISA (UK) 200 (Revised June 2016)*, Overall Objectives of the Independent Auditor and the Conduct of an Audit in Accordance with International Standards on Auditing (UK), *paragraph 15*.

- Responsibilities of respective partners where more than one partner is involved in the conduct of an audit engagement.
- The objectives of the work to be performed.
- The nature of the entity's business.
- Risk-related issues.
- Problems that may arise.
- The detailed approach to the performance of the engagement.

Discussion among members of the engagement team allows less experienced team members to raise questions with more experienced team members so that appropriate communication can occur within the engagement team.

Appropriate teamwork and training assist less experienced members of the engagement team to clearly understand the objectives of the assigned work.
A14

Supervision includes matters such as:
A15

- Tracking the progress of the audit engagement.
- Considering the competence and capabilities of individual members of the engagement team, including whether they have sufficient time to carry out their work, whether they understand their instructions, and whether the work is being carried out in accordance with the planned approach to the audit engagement.
- Addressing significant matters arising during the audit engagement, considering their significance and modifying the planned approach appropriately.
- Identifying matters for consultation or consideration by more experienced engagement team members during the audit engagement.

Reviews

Review Responsibilities (Ref: Para. 16)

Under ISQC (UK) 1 (Revised June 2016), the firm's review responsibility policies and procedures are determined on the basis that work of less experienced team members is reviewed by more experienced team members.[10]
A16

A review consists of consideration whether, for example:
A17

- The work has been performed in accordance with professional standards and applicable legal and regulatory requirements;
- Significant matters have been raised for further consideration;
- Appropriate consultations have taken place and the resulting conclusions have been documented and implemented;
- There is a need to revise the nature, timing and extent of work performed;
- The work performed supports the conclusions reached and is appropriately documented;
- The evidence obtained is sufficient and appropriate to support the auditor's report; and
- The objectives of the engagement procedures have been achieved.

The Engagement Partner's Review of Work Performed (Ref: Para. 17)

Timely reviews of the following by the engagement partner at appropriate stages during the engagement allow significant matters to be resolved on a timely basis to the engagement partner's satisfaction on or before the date of the auditor's report:
A18

---

[10] *ISQC (UK) 1 (Revised June 2016), paragraph 33.*

- Critical areas of judgment, especially those relating to difficult or contentious matters identified during the course of the engagement;
- Significant risks; and
- Other areas the engagement partner considers important.

The engagement partner need not review all audit documentation, but may do so. However, as required by ISA (UK) 230 (Revised June 2016), the partner documents the extent and timing of the reviews.[11]

A19 An engagement partner taking over an audit during the engagement may apply the review procedures as described in paragraph A18 to review the work performed to the date of a change in order to assume the responsibilities of an engagement partner.

Considerations Relevant Where a Member of the Engagement Team with Expertise in a Specialized Area of Accounting or Auditing Is Used (Ref: Para. 15–17)

A20 Where a member of the engagement team with expertise in a specialized area of accounting or auditing is used, direction, supervision and review of that engagement team member's work may include matters such as:

- Agreeing with that member the nature, scope and objectives of that member's work; and the respective roles of, and the nature, timing and extent of communication between that member and other members of the engagement team.
- Evaluating the adequacy of that member's work including the relevance and reasonableness of that member's findings or conclusions and their consistency with other audit evidence.

Consultation (Ref: Para. 18)

A21 Effective consultation on significant technical, ethical, and other matters within the firm or, where applicable, outside the firm can be achieved when those consulted:

- Are given all the relevant facts that will enable them to provide informed advice; and
- Have appropriate knowledge, seniority and experience.

A22 It may be appropriate for the engagement team to consult outside the firm, for example, where the firm lacks appropriate internal resources. They may take advantage of advisory services provided by other firms, professional and regulatory bodies, or commercial organizations that provide relevant quality control services.

Engagement Quality Control Review

Completion of the Engagement Quality Control Review before Dating of the Auditor's Report (Ref: Para. 19(c))

A23 ISA (UK) 700 (Revised June 2016) requires the auditor's report to be dated no earlier than the date on which the auditor has obtained sufficient appropriate evidence on which to base the auditor's opinion on the financial statements.[12] In cases of an audit of financial statements of listed entities or when an engagement meets the criteria for an engagement quality control review, such a review assists the auditor in determining whether sufficient appropriate evidence has been obtained.

---

[11] *ISA (UK) 230 (Revised June 2016), paragraph 9(c).*

[12] *ISA (UK) 700 (Revised June 2016),* Forming an Opinion and Reporting on Financial Statements, *paragraph 4911.*

Conducting the engagement quality control review in a timely manner at appropriate   **A24**
stages during the engagement allows significant matters to be promptly resolved to the
engagement quality control reviewer's satisfaction on or before the date of the auditor's
report.

Completion of the engagement quality control review means the completion by the   **A25**
engagement quality control reviewer of the requirements in paragraphs 20–21, and where
applicable, compliance with paragraph 22. Documentation of the engagement quality
control review may be completed after the date of the auditor's report as part of the assembly
of the final audit file. ISA (UK) 230 (Revised June 2016) establishes requirements and
provides guidance in this regard.[13]

Nature, Extent and Timing of Engagement Quality Control Review (Ref: Para. 20)

Remaining alert for changes in circumstances allows the engagement partner to identify   **A26**
situations in which an engagement quality control review is necessary, even though at the
start of the engagement, such a review was not required.

The extent of the engagement quality control review may depend, among other things, on   **A27**
the complexity of the audit engagement, whether the entity is a listed entity, and the risk that
the auditor's report might not be appropriate in the circumstances. The performance of an
engagement quality control review does not reduce the responsibilities of the engagement
partner for the audit engagement and its performance.

When ISA (UK) 701[14] applies, the conclusions reached by the engagement team in   **A28**
formulating the auditor's report include determining:

- The key audit matters to be included in the auditor's report;
- The key audit matters that will not be communicated in the auditor's report in
  accordance with paragraph 14 of ISA (UK) 701, if any; and
- If applicable, depending on the facts and circumstances of the entity and the audit,
  that there are no key audit matters to communicate in the auditor's report.

In addition, the review of the proposed auditor's report in accordance with paragraph 20(b)
includes consideration of the proposed wording to be included in the Key Audit Matters
section.

Engagement Quality Control Review of Listed Entities (Ref: Para. 21)

Other matters relevant to evaluating the significant judgments made by the engagement   **A29**
team that may be considered in an engagement quality control review of a listed entity
include:

- Significant risks identified during the engagement in accordance with ISA (UK)
  315 (Revised June 2016),[15] and the responses to those risks in accordance with ISA

---

[13] *ISA (UK) 230 (Revised June 2016), paragraphs 14–16.*

[14] *ISA (UK) 701*, Communicating Key Audit Matters in the Auditor's Report.

[15] *ISA (UK) 315 (Revised June 2016)*, Identifying and Assessing the Risks of Material Misstatement through Understanding the Entity and Its Environment.

(UK) 330 (Revised July 2017),[16] including the engagement team's assessment of, and response to, the risk of fraud in accordance with ISA (UK) 240 (Revised June 2016).[17]

- Judgments made, particularly with respect to materiality and significant risks.
- The significance and disposition of corrected and uncorrected misstatements identified during the audit.
- The matters to be communicated to management and those charged with governance and, where applicable, other parties such as regulatory bodies.

These other matters, depending on the circumstances, may also be applicable for engagement quality control reviews for audits of financial statements of other entities.

Considerations Specific to Smaller Entities (Ref: Para. 20–21)

A30   In addition to the audits of financial statements of listed entities, an engagement quality control review is required for audit engagements that meet the criteria established by the firm that subjects engagements to an engagement quality control review. In some cases, none of the firm's audit engagements may meet the criteria that would subject them to such a review.

Considerations Specific to Public Sector Entities (Ref: Para. 20–21)

A31   In the public sector, a statutorily appointed auditor (for example, an Auditor General, or other suitably qualified person appointed on behalf of the Auditor General), may act in a role equivalent to that of engagement partner with overall responsibility for public sector audits. In such circumstances, where applicable, the selection of the engagement quality control reviewer includes consideration of the need for independence from the audited entity and the ability of the engagement quality control reviewer to provide an objective evaluation.

A32   Listed entities as referred to in paragraphs 21 and A29 are not common in the public sector. However, there may be other public sector entities that are significant due to size, complexity or public interest aspects, and which consequently have a wide range of stakeholders. Examples include state owned corporations and public utilities. Ongoing transformations within the public sector may also give rise to new types of significant entities. There are no fixed objective criteria on which the determination of significance is based. Nonetheless, public sector auditors evaluate which entities may be of sufficient significance to warrant performance of an engagement quality control review.

Monitoring (Ref: Para. 23)

A33   ISQC (UK) 1 (Revised June 2016) requires the firm to establish a monitoring process designed to provide it with reasonable assurance that the policies and procedures relating to the system of quality control are relevant, adequate and operating effectively.[18]

A34   In considering deficiencies that may affect the audit engagement, the engagement partner may have regard to measures the firm took to rectify the situation that the engagement partner considers are sufficient in the context of that audit.

---

[16] *ISA (UK) 330 (Revised July 2017)*, The Auditor's Responses to Assessed Risks.

[17] *ISA (UK) 240 (Revised June 2016)*, The Auditor's Responsibilities Relating to Fraud in an Audit of Financial Statements.

[18] *ISQC (UK) 1 (Revised June 2016), paragraph 48.*

A deficiency in the firm's system of quality control does not necessarily indicate that a **A35** particular audit engagement was not performed in accordance with professional standards and applicable legal and regulatory requirements, or that the auditor's report was not appropriate.

Documentation

Documentation of Consultations (Ref: Para. 24(d))

Documentation of consultations with other professionals that involve difficult or contentious **A36** matters that is sufficiently complete and detailed contributes to an understanding of:

- The issue on which consultation was sought; and
- The results of the consultation, including any decisions taken, the basis for those decisions and how they were implemented.

International Standard on Auditing (UK) 230 (Revised June 2016)

Audit documentation

(Effective for audits of financial statements for periods commencing on or after 17 June 2016)

Contents

International Standard on Auditing (UK) (ISA (UK)) 230 (Revised June 2016), *Audit Documentation*, should be read in conjunction with ISA (UK) 200 (Revised June 2016), *Overall Objectives of the Independent Auditor and the Conduct of an Audit in Accordance with International Standards on Auditing (UK)*.

Introduction

Scope of this ISA (UK)

This International Standard on Auditing (UK) (ISA (UK)) deals with the auditor's **1** responsibility to prepare audit documentation for an audit of financial statements. The Appendix lists other ISAs (UK) that contain specific documentation requirements and guidance. The specific documentation requirements of other ISAs (UK) do not limit the application of this ISA (UK). Law or regulation may establish additional documentation requirements.

Nature and Purposes of Audit Documentation

Audit documentation that meets the requirements of this ISA (UK) and the specific **2** documentation requirements of other relevant ISAs (UK) provides:

(a) Evidence of the auditor's basis for a conclusion about the achievement of the overall objectives of the auditor;[1] and
(b) Evidence that the audit was planned and performed in accordance with ISAs (UK) and applicable legal and regulatory requirements.

Audit documentation serves a number of additional purposes, including the following: **3**

- Assisting the engagement team to plan and perform the audit.
- Assisting members of the engagement team responsible for supervision to direct and supervise the audit work, and to discharge their review responsibilities in accordance with ISA (UK) 220 (Revised June 2016).[2]
- Enabling the engagement team to be accountable for its work.
- Retaining a record of matters of continuing significance to future audits.
- Enabling the conduct of quality control reviews and inspections in accordance with ISQC (UK) 1 (Revised June 2016)[3] or national requirements that are at least as demanding.[4]
- Enabling the conduct of external inspections in accordance with applicable legal, regulatory or other requirements.

Effective Date

This ISA (UK) is effective for audits of financial statements for periods commencing on **4** or after 17 June 2016. Earlier adoption is permitted.

---

[1] *ISA (UK) 200 (Revised June 2016)*, Overall Objectives of the Independent Auditor and the Conduct of an Audit in Accordance with International Standards on Auditing (UK), *paragraph 11.*

[2] *ISA (UK) 220 (Revised June 2016)*, Quality Control for an Audit of Financial Statements, *paragraphs 15–17.*

[3] *ISQC (UK) 1 (Revised June 2016)*, Quality Control for Firms that Perform Audits and Reviews of Financial Statements, and Other Assurance and Related Services Engagements, *paragraphs 32– 33, 35–38, and 48.*

[4] *ISA (UK) 220 (Revised June 2016), paragraph 2.*

Objective

5 The objective of the auditor is to prepare documentation that provides:

(a) A sufficient and appropriate record of the basis for the auditor's report; and

(b) Evidence that the audit was planned and performed in accordance with ISAs (UK) and applicable legal and regulatory requirements.

Definitions

6 For purposes of the ISAs (UK), the following terms have the meanings attributed below:

(a) Audit documentation – The record of audit procedures performed, relevant audit evidence obtained, and conclusions the auditor reached (terms such as 'working papers' or 'workpapers' are also sometimes used).

> In the UK, audit documentation shall include all documents, information, records and other data required by ISQC (UK) 1 (Revised June 2016), ISAs (UK) and applicable legal and regulatory requirements.

(b) Audit file – One or more folders or other storage media, in physical or electronic form, containing the records that comprise the audit documentation for a specific engagement.

(c) Experienced auditor – An individual (whether internal or external to the firm) who has practical audit experience, and a reasonable understanding of:

(i) Audit processes;

(ii) ISAs (UK) and applicable legal and regulatory requirements;

(iii) The business environment in which the entity operates; and

(iv) Auditing and financial reporting issues relevant to the entity's industry.

Requirements

Timely Preparation of Audit Documentation

7 The auditor shall prepare audit documentation on a timely basis. (Ref: Para. A1)

Documentation of the Audit Procedures Performed and Audit Evidence Obtained

Form, Content and Extent of Audit Documentation

8 The auditor shall prepare audit documentation that is sufficient to enable an experienced auditor, having no previous connection with the audit, to understand: (Ref: Para. A2–A5, A16–A17)

(a) The nature, timing and extent of the audit procedures performed to comply with the ISAs (UK) and applicable legal and regulatory requirements; (Ref: Para. A6–A7)

(b) The results of the audit procedures performed, and the audit evidence obtained; and

(c) Significant matters arising during the audit, the conclusions reached thereon, and significant professional judgments made in reaching those conclusions. (Ref: Para. A8–A11)

8D-1 The auditor shall retain any other data and documents that are important in supporting the auditor's report as part of the audit documentation.

In documenting the nature, timing and extent of audit procedures performed, the auditor **9** shall record:

(a) The identifying characteristics of the specific items or matters tested; (Ref: Para. A12)
(b) Who performed the audit work and the date such work was completed; and
(c) Who reviewed the audit work performed and the date and extent of such review. (Ref: Para. A13)

The auditor shall document discussions of significant matters with management, those **10** charged with governance, and others, including the nature of the significant matters discussed and when and with whom the discussions took place. (Ref: Para. A14)

If the auditor identified information that is inconsistent with the auditor's final conclusion **11** regarding a significant matter, the auditor shall document how the auditor addressed the inconsistency. (Ref: Para. A15)

Departure from a Relevant Requirement

If, in exceptional circumstances, the auditor judges it necessary to depart from a **12** relevant requirement in an ISA (UK), the auditor shall document how the alternative audit procedures performed achieve the aim of that requirement, and the reasons for the departure. (Ref: Para. A18–A19)

Matters Arising after the Date of the Auditor's Report

If, in exceptional circumstances, the auditor performs new or additional audit procedures **13** or draws new conclusions after the date of the auditor's report, the auditor shall document: (Ref: Para. A20)

(a) The circumstances encountered;
(b) The new or additional audit procedures performed, audit evidence obtained, and conclusions reached, and their effect on the auditor's report; and
(c) When and by whom the resulting changes to audit documentation were made and reviewed.

Assembly of the Final Audit File

The auditor shall assemble the audit documentation in an audit file and complete the **14** administrative process of assembling the final audit file on a timely basis after the date of the auditor's report. (Ref: Para. A21–A22)

In the UK, the assembly of the final audit file shall be completed no later than 60 days from the date of the auditor's report.

The auditor shall retain audit documentation that is important for monitoring compliance **14D-1** with ISAs (UK) and other applicable legal requirements.

After the assembly of the final audit file has been completed, the auditor shall not delete **15** or discard audit documentation of any nature before the end of its retention period. (Ref: Para. A23)

In circumstances other than those envisaged in paragraph 13 where the auditor finds it **16** necessary to modify existing audit documentation or add new audit documentation after the assembly of the final audit file has been completed, the auditor shall, regardless of the nature of the modifications or additions, document: (Ref: Para. A24)

(a)   The specific reasons for making them; and

(b)   When and by whom they were made and reviewed.

***

Application and Other Explanatory Material

Timely Preparation of Audit Documentation (Ref: Para. 7)

A1   Preparing sufficient and appropriate audit documentation on a timely basis helps to enhance the quality of the audit and facilitates the effective review and evaluation of the audit evidence obtained and conclusions reached before the auditor's report is finalized. Documentation prepared after the audit work has been performed is likely to be less accurate than documentation prepared at the time such work is performed.

Documentation of the Audit Procedures Performed and Audit Evidence Obtained

Form, Content and Extent of Audit Documentation (Ref: Para. 8)

A2   The form, content and extent of audit documentation depend on factors such as:

- The size and complexity of the entity.
- The nature of the audit procedures to be performed.
- The identified risks of material misstatement.
- The significance of the audit evidence obtained.
- The nature and extent of exceptions identified.
- The need to document a conclusion or the basis for a conclusion not readily determinable from the documentation of the work performed or audit evidence obtained.
- The audit methodology and tools used.

A3   Audit documentation may be recorded on paper or on electronic or other media. Examples of audit documentation include:

- Audit programs.
- Analyses.
- Issues memoranda.
- Summaries of significant matters.
- Letters of confirmation and representation.
- Checklists.
- Correspondence (including e-mail) concerning significant matters.

The auditor may include abstracts or copies of the entity's records (for example, significant and specific contracts and agreements) as part of audit documentation. Audit documentation, however, is not a substitute for the entity's accounting records.

A4   The auditor need not include in audit documentation superseded drafts of working papers and financial statements, notes that reflect incomplete or preliminary thinking, previous copies of documents corrected for typographical or other errors, and duplicates of documents.

A5   Oral explanations by the auditor, on their own, do not represent adequate support for the work the auditor performed or conclusions the auditor reached, but may be used to explain or clarify information contained in the audit documentation.

Documentation of Compliance with ISAs (UK) (Ref: Para. 8(a))

In principle, compliance with the requirements of this ISA (UK) will result in the audit **A6** documentation being sufficient and appropriate in the circumstances. Other ISAs (UK) contain specific documentation requirements that are intended to clarify the application of this ISA (UK) in the particular circumstances of those other ISAs (UK). The specific documentation requirements of other ISAs (UK) do not limit the application of this ISA (UK). Furthermore, the absence of a documentation requirement in any particular ISA (UK) is not intended to suggest that there is no documentation that will be prepared as a result of complying with that ISA (UK).

Audit documentation provides evidence that the audit complies with the ISAs (UK). **A7** However, it is neither necessary nor practicable for the auditor to document every matter considered, or professional judgment made, in an audit. Further, it is unnecessary for the auditor to document separately (as in a checklist, for example) compliance with matters for which compliance is demonstrated by documents included within the audit file. For example:

- The existence of an adequately documented audit plan demonstrates that the auditor has planned the audit.
- The existence of a signed engagement letter in the audit file demonstrates that the auditor has agreed the terms of the audit engagement with management or, where appropriate, those charged with governance.
- An auditor's report containing an appropriately qualified opinion on the financial statements demonstrates that the auditor has complied with the requirement to express a qualified opinion under the circumstances specified in the ISAs (UK).
- In relation to requirements that apply generally throughout the audit, there may be a number of ways in which compliance with them may be demonstrated within the audit file:

  o For example, there may be no single way in which the auditor's professional skepticism is documented. But the audit documentation may nevertheless provide evidence of the auditor's exercise of professional skepticism in accordance with the ISAs (UK). Such evidence may include specific procedures performed to corroborate management's responses to the auditor's inquiries.
  o Similarly, that the engagement partner has taken responsibility for the direction, supervision and performance of the audit in compliance with the ISAs (UK) may be evidenced in a number of ways within the audit documentation. This may include documentation of the engagement partner's timely involvement in aspects of the audit, such as participation in the team discussions required by ISA (UK) 315 (Revised June 2016).[5]

Documentation of Significant Matters and Related Significant Professional Judgments (Ref: Para. 8(c))

Judging the significance of a matter requires an objective analysis of the facts and **A8** circumstances. Examples of significant matters include:

- Matters that give rise to significant risks (as defined in ISA (UK) 315 (Revised June 2016)).[6]
- Results of audit procedures indicating (a) that the financial statements could be materially misstated, or (b) a need to revise the auditor's previous assessment of the risks of material misstatement and the auditor's responses to those risks.
- Circumstances that cause the auditor significant difficulty in applying necessary audit procedures.

[5] *ISA (UK) 315 (Revised June 2016),* Identifying and Assessing the Risks of Material Misstatement through Understanding the Entity and Its Environment, *paragraph 10.*

[6] *ISA (UK) 315 (Revised June 2016), paragraph 4(e).*

- Findings that could result in a modification to the audit opinion or the inclusion of an Emphasis of Matter paragraph in the auditor's report.
- Concerns about the entity's ability to continue as a going concern.

A9   An important factor in determining the form, content and extent of audit documentation of significant matters is the extent of professional judgment exercised in performing the work and evaluating the results. Documentation of the professional judgments made, where significant, serves to explain the auditor's conclusions and to reinforce the quality of the judgment. Such matters are of particular interest to those responsible for reviewing audit documentation, including those carrying out subsequent audits when reviewing matters of continuing significance (for example, when performing a retrospective review of accounting estimates).

A10 Some examples of circumstances in which, in accordance with paragraph 8, it is appropriate to prepare audit documentation relating to the use of professional judgment include, where the matters and judgments are significant:

- The rationale for the auditor's conclusion when a requirement provides that the auditor 'shall consider' certain information or factors, and that consideration is significant in the context of the particular engagement.
- The basis for the auditor's conclusion on the reasonableness of areas of subjective judgments (for example, the reasonableness of significant accounting estimates).
- The basis for the auditor's conclusions about the authenticity of a document when further investigation (such as making appropriate use of an expert or of confirmation procedures) is undertaken in response to conditions identified during the audit that caused the auditor to believe that the document may not be authentic.
- When ISA (UK) 701 applies,77 the auditor's determination of the key audit matters or the determination that there are no key audit matters to be communicated.

A11 The auditor may consider it helpful to prepare and retain as part of the audit documentation a summary (sometimes known as a completion memorandum) that describes the significant matters identified during the audit and how they were addressed, or that includes cross-references to other relevant supporting audit documentation that provides such information. Such a summary may facilitate effective and efficient reviews and inspections of the audit documentation, particularly for large and complex audits. Further, the preparation of such a summary may assist the auditor's consideration of the significant matters. It may also help the auditor to consider whether, in light of the audit procedures performed and conclusions reached, there is any individual relevant ISA (UK) objective that the auditor cannot achieve that would prevent the auditor from achieving the overall objectives of the auditor.

Identification of Specific Items or Matters Tested, and of the Preparer and Reviewer (Ref: Para. 9)

A12 Recording the identifying characteristics serves a number of purposes. For example, it enables the engagement team to be accountable for its work and facilitates the investigation of exceptions or inconsistencies. Identifying characteristics will vary with the nature of the audit procedure and the item or matter tested. For example:

- For a detailed test of entity-generated purchase orders, the auditor may identify the documents selected for testing by their dates and unique purchase order numbers.
- For a procedure requiring selection or review of all items over a specific amount from a given population, the auditor may record the scope of the procedure and identify the population (for example, all journal entries over a specified amount from the journal register).

---

7 *ISA (UK) 701,* Communicating Key Audit Matters in the Independent Auditor's Report.

- For a procedure requiring systematic sampling from a population of documents, the auditor may identify the documents selected by recording their source, the starting point and the sampling interval (for example, a systematic sample of shipping reports selected from the shipping log for the period from April 1 to September 30, starting with report number 12345 and selecting every 125th report).
- For a procedure requiring inquiries of specific entity personnel, the auditor may record the dates of the inquiries and the names and job designations of the entity personnel.
- For an observation procedure, the auditor may record the process or matter being observed, the relevant individuals, their respective responsibilities, and where and when the observation was carried out.

ISA (UK) 220 (Revised June 2016) requires the auditor to review the audit work performed **A13** through review of the audit documentation.[8] The requirement to document who reviewed the audit work performed does not imply a need for each specific working paper to include evidence of review. The requirement, however, means documenting what audit work was reviewed, who reviewed such work, and when it was reviewed.

Documentation of Discussions of Significant Matters with Management, Those Charged with Governance, and Others (Ref: Para. 10)

The documentation is not limited to records prepared by the auditor but may include **A14** other appropriate records such as minutes of meetings prepared by the entity's personnel and agreed by the auditor. Others with whom the auditor may discuss significant matters may include other personnel within the entity, and external parties, such as persons providing professional advice to the entity.

Documentation of How Inconsistencies have been Addressed (Ref: Para. 11)

The requirement to document how the auditor addressed inconsistencies in information **A15** does not imply that the auditor needs to retain documentation that is incorrect or superseded.

Considerations Specific to Smaller Entities (Ref: Para. 8)

The audit documentation for the audit of a smaller entity is generally less extensive than **A16** that for the audit of a larger entity. Further, in the case of an audit where the engagement partner performs all the audit work, the documentation will not include matters that might have to be documented solely to inform or instruct members of an engagement team, or to provide evidence of review by other members of the team (for example, there will be no matters to document relating to team discussions or supervision). Nevertheless, the engagement partner complies with the overriding requirement in paragraph 8 to prepare audit documentation that can be understood by an experienced auditor, as the audit documentation may be subject to review by external parties for regulatory or other purposes.

When preparing audit documentation, the auditor of a smaller entity may also find it **A17** helpful and efficient to record various aspects of the audit together in a single document, with cross-references to supporting working papers as appropriate. Examples of matters that may be documented together in the audit of a smaller entity include the understanding of the entity and its internal control, the overall audit strategy and audit plan, materiality

---

[8] *ISA (UK) 220 (Revised June 2016), paragraph 17.*

determined in accordance with ISA (UK) 320 (Revised June 2016),[9] assessed risks, significant matters noted during the audit, and conclusions reached.

Departure from a Relevant Requirement (Ref: Para. 12)

A18   The requirements of the ISAs (UK) are designed to enable the auditor to achieve the objectives specified in the ISAs (UK), and thereby the overall objectives of the auditor. Accordingly, other than in exceptional circumstances, the ISAs (UK) call for compliance with each requirement that is relevant in the circumstances of the audit.

A19   The documentation requirement applies only to requirements that are relevant in the circumstances. A requirement is not relevant[10] only in the cases where:

(a)   The entire ISA (UK) is not relevant (for example, if an entity does not have an internal audit function, nothing in ISA (UK) 610 (Revised June 2013)[11] is relevant); or

(b)   The requirement is conditional and the condition does not exist (for example, the requirement to modify the auditor's opinion where there is an inability to obtain sufficient appropriate audit evidence, and there is no such inability).

Matters Arising after the Date of the Auditor's Report (Ref: Para. 13)

A20   Examples of exceptional circumstances include facts which become known to the auditor after the date of the auditor's report but which existed at that date and which, if known at that date, might have caused the financial statements to be amended or the auditor to modify the opinion in the auditor's report.[12] The resulting changes to the audit documentation are reviewed in accordance with the review responsibilities set out in ISA (UK) 220 (Revised June 2016),[13] with the engagement partner taking final responsibility for the changes.

Assembly of the Final Audit File (Ref: Para. 14–16)

A21   ISQC (UK) 1 (Revised June 2016) (or national requirements that are at least as demanding) requires firms to establish policies and procedures for the timely completion of the assembly of audit files.[14] An appropriate time limit within which to complete the assembly of the final audit file is ordinarily not more than 60 days after the date of the auditor's report.[15]

A22   The completion of the assembly of the final audit file after the date of the auditor's report is an administrative process that does not involve the performance of new audit procedures or the drawing of new conclusions. Changes may, however, be made to the audit documentation during the final assembly process if they are administrative in nature. Examples of such changes include:

---

[9] *ISA (UK) 320 (Revised June 2016),* Materiality in Planning and Performing an Audit.

[10] *ISA (UK) 200 (Revised June 2016), paragraph 22.*

[11] *ISA (UK) 610 (Revised June 2013),* Using the Work of Internal Auditors, *paragraph 2.*

[12] *ISA (UK) 560,* Subsequent Events, *paragraph 14.*

[13] *ISA (UK) 220 (Revised June 2016), paragraph 16.*

[14] *ISQC (UK) 1 (Revised June 2016), paragraph 45.*

[15] *ISQC (UK) 1 (Revised June 2016), paragraph A54.*

- Deleting or discarding superseded documentation.
- Sorting, collating and cross-referencing working papers.
- Signing off on completion checklists relating to the file assembly process.
- Documenting audit evidence that the auditor has obtained, discussed and agreed with the relevant members of the engagement team before the date of the auditor's report.

ISQC (UK) 1 (Revised June 2016) (or national requirements that are at least as demanding)   **A23**
requires firms to establish policies and procedures for the retention of engagement
documentation.[16] The retention period for audit engagements ordinarily is no shorter than
five years from the date of the auditor's report, or, if later, the date of the group auditor's
report.[17]

An example of a circumstance in which the auditor may find it necessary to modify   **A24**
existing audit documentation or add new audit documentation after file assembly has
been completed is the need to clarify existing audit documentation arising from comments
received during monitoring inspections performed by internal or external parties.

---

[16] *ISQC (UK) 1 (Revised June 2016), paragraph 47.*

[17] *ISQC (UK) 1 (Revised June 2016), paragraph A61.*
    In the UK, the auditor has regard to specific requirements of the auditor's relevant professional body.

Appendix

(Ref: Para. 1)

Specific Audit Documentation Requirements in Other ISAs (UK)

This appendix identifies paragraphs in other ISAs (UK) that contain specific documentation requirements. The list is not a substitute for considering the requirements and related application and other explanatory material in ISAs (UK).

- ISA (UK) 210 (Revised June 2016), *Agreeing the Terms of Audit Engagements* – paragraphs 10–12
- ISA (UK) 220 (Revised June 2016), *Quality Control for an Audit of Financial Statements* – paragraphs 24–25R-2
- ISA (UK) 240 (Revised June 2016), *The Auditor's Responsibilities Relating to Fraud in an Audit of Financial Statements* – paragraphs 44–47
- ISA (UK) 250 (Revised June 2016), Section A—*Consideration of Laws and Regulations in an Audit of Financial Statements* – paragraph 29
- ISA (UK) 260 (Revised June 2016), Communication with Those Charged with Governance – paragraphs 23 and 23D-1
- ISA (UK) 300 (Revised June 2016), *Planning an Audit of Financial Statements* – paragraph 12
- ISA (UK) 315 (Revised June 2016), *Identifying and Assessing the Risks of Material Misstatement through Understanding the Entity and Its Environment* – paragraph 32
- ISA (UK) 320 (Revised June 2016), *Materiality in Planning and Performing an Audit* – paragraph 14
- ISA (UK) 330 (Revised June 2016), *The Auditor's Responses to Assessed Risks* – paragraphs 28–30
- ISA (UK) 450 (Revised June 2016), *Evaluation of Misstatements Identified During the Audit* – paragraph 15
- ISA (UK) 540 (Revised June 2016), *Auditing Accounting Estimates, Including Fair Value Accounting Estimates, and Related Disclosures* – paragraph 23
- ISA (UK) 550, *Related Parties* – paragraph 28
- ISA (UK) 600 (Revised June 2016), *Special Considerations—Audits of Group Financial Statements (Including the Work of Component Auditors)* – paragraphs 50–50D-3
- ISA (UK) 610 (Revised June 2013), *Using the Work of Internal Auditors* – paragraphs 36 and 37
- ISA (UK) 620 (Revised June 2016), Using the Work of an Auditor's Expert – paragraph 15D-1
- ISA (UK) 701, Communicating Key Audit Matters in the Independent Auditor's Report – paragraph 18
- ISA (UK) 720 (Revised June 2016), *The Auditor's Responsibilities Relating to Other Information* – paragraph 25

International Standard on Auditing (UK) 240 (Revised June 2016) (Updated July 2017)

The auditor's responsibilities relating to fraud in an audit of financial statements

(Effective for audits of financial statements for periods commencing on or after 17 June 2016)[0]

Contents

---

[0] *Conforming amendments to this standard as a result of ISA (UK) 250 (Revised July 2017), Section A—Consideration of Laws and Regulations in an Audit of Financial Statements, are included that are effective for audits of financial statements for periods commencing on or after 15 December 2017. Details of the amendments are given in the Annexure to ISA (UK) 250 (Revised December 2017) Section A.*

International Standard on Auditing (UK) (ISA (UK)) 240 (Revised June 2016), *The Auditor's Responsibilities Relating to Fraud in an Audit of Financial Statements* should be read in conjunction with ISA (UK) 200 (Revised June 2016), *Overall Objectives of the Independent Auditor and the Conduct of an Audit in Accordance with International Standards on Auditing (UK).*

Introduction

Scope of this ISA (UK)

This International Standard on Auditing (UK) (ISA (UK)) deals with the auditor's **1**
responsibilities relating to fraud in an audit of financial statements. Specifically, it expands
on how ISA (UK) 315 (Revised June 2016)[1] and ISA (UK) 330 (Revised July 2017)[2] are
to be applied in relation to risks of material misstatement due to fraud.

Characteristics of Fraud

Misstatements in the financial statements can arise from either fraud or error. The **2**
distinguishing factor between fraud and error is whether the underlying action that results
in the misstatement of the financial statements is intentional or unintentional.

Although fraud is a broad legal concept, for the purposes of the ISAs (UK), the auditor is **3**
concerned with fraud that causes a material misstatement in the financial statements. Two
types of intentional misstatements are relevant to the auditor – misstatements resulting
from fraudulent financial reporting and misstatements resulting from misappropriation
of assets. Although the auditor may suspect or, in rare cases, identify the occurrence
of fraud, the auditor does not make legal determinations of whether fraud has actually
occurred. (Ref: Para. A1–A6)

Responsibility for the Prevention and Detection of Fraud

The primary responsibility for the prevention and detection of fraud rests with both those **4**
charged with governance of the entity and management. It is important that management,
with the oversight of those charged with governance, place a strong emphasis on fraud
prevention, which may reduce opportunities for fraud to take place, and fraud deterrence,
which could persuade individuals not to commit fraud because of the likelihood of
detection and punishment. This involves a commitment to creating a culture of honesty
and ethical behavior which can be reinforced by an active oversight by those charged
with governance. Oversight by those charged with governance includes considering
the potential for override of controls or other inappropriate influence over the financial
reporting process, such as efforts by management to manage earnings in order to influence
the perceptions of analysts as to the entity's performance and profitability.

Responsibilities of the Auditor

An auditor conducting an audit in accordance with ISAs (UK) is responsible for obtaining **5**
reasonable assurance that the financial statements taken as a whole are free from material
misstatement, whether caused by fraud or error. Owing to the inherent limitations of
an audit, there is an unavoidable risk that some material misstatements of the financial
statements may not be detected, even though the audit is properly planned and performed
in accordance with the ISAs (UK).[3]

---

[1] *ISA (UK) 315 (Revised June 2016)*, Identifying and Assessing the Risks of Material Misstatement through
Understanding the Entity and Its Environment.

[2] *ISA (UK) 330 (Revised July 2017)*, The Auditor's Responses to Assessed Risks.

[3] *ISA (UK) 200 (Revised June 2016)*, Overall Objectives of the Independent Auditor and the Conduct of an Audit in
Accordance with International Standards on Auditing (UK), *paragraph A53–A54.*

6   As described in ISA (UK) 200 (Revised June 2016),[4] the potential effects of inherent limitations are particularly significant in the case of misstatement resulting from fraud. The risk of not detecting a material misstatement resulting from fraud is higher than the risk of not detecting one resulting from error. This is because fraud may involve sophisticated and carefully organized schemes designed to conceal it, such as forgery, deliberate failure to record transactions, or intentional misrepresentations being made to the auditor. Such attempts at concealment may be even more difficult to detect when accompanied by collusion. Collusion may cause the auditor to believe that audit evidence is persuasive when it is, in fact, false. The auditor's ability to detect a fraud depends on factors such as the skillfulness of the perpetrator, the frequency and extent of manipulation, the degree of collusion involved, the relative size of individual amounts manipulated, and the seniority of those individuals involved. While the auditor may be able to identify potential opportunities for fraud to be perpetrated, it is difficult for the auditor to determine whether misstatements in judgment areas such as accounting estimates are caused by fraud or error.

7   Furthermore, the risk of the auditor not detecting a material misstatement resulting from management fraud is greater than for employee fraud, because management is frequently in a position to directly or indirectly manipulate accounting records, present fraudulent financial information or override control procedures designed to prevent similar frauds by other employees.

8   When obtaining reasonable assurance, the auditor is responsible for maintaining professional skepticism throughout the audit, considering the potential for management override of controls and recognizing the fact that audit procedures that are effective for detecting error may not be effective in detecting fraud. The requirements in this ISA (UK) are designed to assist the auditor in identifying and assessing the risks of material misstatement due to fraud and in designing procedures to detect such misstatement.

8a   The auditor may have additional responsibilities under law, regulation or relevant ethical requirements regarding an entity's non-compliance with laws and regulations, including fraud, which may differ from or go beyond this and other ISAs (UK), such as: (Ref: Para. A5a)

   (a) Responding to identified or suspected non-compliance with laws and regulations, including requirements in relation to specific communications with management and those charged with governance, assessing the appropriateness of their response to non-compliance and determining whether further action is needed;

   (b) Communicating identified or suspected non-compliance with laws and regulations to other auditors (e.g., in an audit of group financial statements); and

   (c) Documentation requirements regarding identified or suspected non-compliance with laws and regulations.

Complying with any additional responsibilities may provide further information that is relevant to the auditor's work in accordance with this and other ISAs (UK) (e.g., regarding the integrity of management or, where appropriate, those charged with governance).

Effective Date

9   This ISA (UK) is effective for audits of financial statements for periods commencing on or after 17 June 2016. Earlier adoption is permitted.

---

[4] *ISA (UK) 200 (Revised June 2016), paragraph A53.*

Objectives

The objectives of the auditor are:
      10

(a) To identify and assess the risks of material misstatement of the financial statements due to fraud;

(b) To obtain sufficient appropriate audit evidence regarding the assessed risks of material misstatement due to fraud, through designing and implementing appropriate responses; and

(c) To respond appropriately to fraud or suspected fraud identified during the audit.

Definitions

For purposes of the ISAs (UK), the following terms have the meanings attributed below: **11**

(a) Fraud – An intentional act by one or more individuals among management, those charged with governance, employees, or third parties, involving the use of deception to obtain an unjust or illegal advantage.

(b) Fraud risk factors – Events or conditions that indicate an incentive or pressure to commit fraud or provide an opportunity to commit fraud.

Requirements

Professional Skepticism

In accordance with ISA (UK) 200 (Revised June 2016),[5] the auditor shall maintain   **12** professional skepticism throughout the audit, recognizing the possibility that a material misstatement due to fraud could exist, notwithstanding the auditor's past experience of the honesty and integrity of the entity's management and those charged with governance. (Ref: Para. A7–A8)

Unless the auditor has reason to believe the contrary, the auditor may accept records and   **13** documents as genuine. If conditions identified during the audit cause the auditor to believe that a document may not be authentic or that terms in a document have been modified but not disclosed to the auditor, the auditor shall investigate further. (Ref: Para. A9)

Where responses to inquiries of management or those charged with governance are   **14** inconsistent, the auditor shall investigate the inconsistencies.

Discussion among the Engagement Team

ISA (UK) 315 (Revised June 2016) requires a discussion among the engagement team   **15** members and a determination by the engagement partner of which matters are to be communicated to those team members not involved in the discussion.[6] This discussion shall place particular emphasis on how and where the entity's financial statements may be susceptible to material misstatement due to fraud, including how fraud might occur. The discussion shall occur setting aside beliefs that the engagement team members may have that management and those charged with governance are honest and have integrity. (Ref: Para. A10–A11)

---

[5] *ISA (UK) 200 (Revised June 2016), paragraph 15.*

[6] *ISA (UK) 315 (Revised June 2016), paragraph 10.*

Risk Assessment Procedures and Related Activities

16   When performing risk assessment procedures and related activities to obtain an understanding of the entity and its environment, including the entity's internal control, required by ISA (UK) 315 (Revised June 2016),[7] the auditor shall perform the procedures in paragraphs 17–24 to obtain information for use in identifying the risks of material misstatement due to fraud.

Management and Others within the Entity

17   The auditor shall make inquiries of management regarding:
   (a)   Management's assessment of the risk that the financial statements may be materially misstated due to fraud, including the nature, extent and frequency of such assessments; (Ref: Para. A12–A13)
   (b)   Management's process for identifying and responding to the risks of fraud in the entity, including any specific risks of fraud that management has identified or that have been brought to its attention, or classes of transactions, account balances, or disclosures for which a risk of fraud is likely to exist; (Ref: Para. A14)
   (c)   Management's communication, if any, to those charged with governance regarding its processes for identifying and responding to the risks of fraud in the entity; and
   (d)   Management's communication, if any, to employees regarding its views on business practices and ethical behavior.

18   The auditor shall make inquiries of management, and others within the entity as appropriate, to determine whether they have knowledge of any actual, suspected or alleged fraud affecting the entity. (Ref: Para. A15–A17)

19   For those entities that have an internal audit function, the auditor shall make inquiries of appropriate individuals within the function to determine whether they have knowledge of any actual, suspected or alleged fraud affecting the entity, and to obtain its views about the risks of fraud. (Ref: Para. A18)

Those Charged with Governance

20   Unless all of those charged with governance are involved in managing the entity,[8] the auditor shall obtain an understanding of how those charged with governance exercise oversight of management's processes for identifying and responding to the risks of fraud in the entity and the internal control that management has established to mitigate these risks. (Ref: Para. A19–A21)

21   Unless all of those charged with governance are involved in managing the entity, the auditor shall make inquiries of those charged with governance to determine whether they have knowledge of any actual, suspected or alleged fraud affecting the entity. These inquiries are made in part to corroborate the responses to the inquiries of management.

Unusual or Unexpected Relationships Identified

22   The auditor shall evaluate whether unusual or unexpected relationships that have been identified in performing analytical procedures, including those related to revenue accounts, may indicate risks of material misstatement due to fraud.

---

[7] *ISA (UK) 315 (Revised June 2016), paragraphs 5–24.*

[8] *ISA (UK) 260 (Revised June 2016),* Communication with Those Charged with Governance, *paragraph 13.*

Other Information

The auditor shall consider whether other information obtained by the auditor indicates   **23**
risks of material misstatement due to fraud. (Ref: Para. A22)

Evaluation of Fraud Risk Factors

The auditor shall evaluate whether the information obtained from the other risk assessment   **24**
procedures and related activities performed indicates that one or more fraud risk factors are
present. While fraud risk factors may not necessarily indicate the existence of fraud, they
have often been present in circumstances where frauds have occurred and therefore may
indicate risks of material misstatement due to fraud. (Ref: Para. A23–A27)

Identification and Assessment of the Risks of Material Misstatement Due to Fraud

In accordance with ISA (UK) 315 (Revised June 2016), the auditor shall identify and   **25**
assess the risks of material misstatement due to fraud at the financial statement level, and
at the assertion level for classes of transactions, account balances and disclosures.[9]

When identifying and assessing the risks of material misstatement due to fraud, the auditor   **26**
shall, based on a presumption that there are risks of fraud in revenue recognition, evaluate
which types of revenue, revenue transactions or assertions give rise to such risks. Paragraph 47
specifies the documentation required where the auditor concludes that the presumption is
not applicable in the circumstances of the engagement and, accordingly, has not identified
revenue recognition as a risk of material misstatement due to fraud. (Ref: Para. A28–A30)

The auditor shall treat those assessed risks of material misstatement due to fraud as   **27**
significant risks and accordingly, to the extent not already done so, the auditor shall obtain
an understanding of the entity's related controls, including control activities, relevant to
such risks. (Ref: Para. A31–A32)

Responses to the Assessed Risks of Material Misstatement Due to Fraud

Overall Responses

In accordance with ISA (UK) 330 (Revised July 2017), the auditor shall determine overall   **28**
responses to address the assessed risks of material misstatement due to fraud at the financial
statement level.[10] (Ref: Para. A33)

In determining overall responses to address the assessed risks of material misstatement due   **29**
to fraud at the financial statement level, the auditor shall:
(a) Assign and supervise personnel taking account of the knowledge, skill and ability of
     the individuals to be given significant engagement responsibilities and the auditor's
     assessment of the risks of material misstatement due to fraud for the engagement;
     (Ref: Para. A34–A35)
(b) Evaluate whether the selection and application of accounting policies by the entity,
     particularly those related to subjective measurements and complex transactions, may
     be indicative of fraudulent financial reporting resulting from management's effort to
     manage earnings; and

---

[9] *ISA (UK) 315 (Revised June 2016), paragraph 25.*

[10] *ISA (UK) 330 (Revised July 2017), paragraph 5.*

(c)   Incorporate an element of unpredictability in the selection of the nature, timing and extent of audit procedures. (Ref: Para. A36)

Audit Procedures Responsive to Assessed Risks of Material Misstatement Due to Fraud at the Assertion Level

30   In accordance with ISA (UK) 330 (Revised July 2017), the auditor shall design and perform further audit procedures whose nature, timing and extent are responsive to the assessed risks of material misstatement due to fraud at the assertion level.[11] (Ref: Para. A37–A40)

Audit Procedures Responsive to Risks Related to Management Override of Controls

31   Management is in a unique position to perpetrate fraud because of management's ability to manipulate accounting records and prepare fraudulent financial statements by overriding controls that otherwise appear to be operating effectively. Although the level of risk of management override of controls will vary from entity to entity, the risk is nevertheless present in all entities. Due to the unpredictable way in which such override could occur, it is a risk of material misstatement due to fraud and thus a significant risk.

32   Irrespective of the auditor's assessment of the risks of management override of controls, the auditor shall design and perform audit procedures to:

(a)   Test the appropriateness of journal entries recorded in the general ledger and other adjustments made in the preparation of the financial statements. In designing and performing audit procedures for such tests, the auditor shall:

(i)   Make inquiries of individuals involved in the financial reporting process about inappropriate or unusual activity relating to the processing of journal entries and other adjustments;

(ii)   Select journal entries and other adjustments made at the end of a reporting period; and

(iii)   Consider the need to test journal entries and other adjustments throughout the period. (Ref: Para. A41–A44)

(b)   Review accounting estimates for biases and evaluate whether the circumstances producing the bias, if any, represent a risk of material misstatement due to fraud. In performing this review, the auditor shall:

(i)   Evaluate whether the judgments and decisions made by management in making the accounting estimates included in the financial statements, even if they are individually reasonable, indicate a possible bias on the part of the entity's management that may represent a risk of material misstatement due to fraud. If so, the auditor shall reevaluate the accounting estimates taken as a whole; and

(ii)   Perform a retrospective review of management judgments and assumptions related to significant accounting estimates reflected in the financial statements of the prior year. (Ref: Para. A45–A47)

(c)   For significant transactions that are outside the normal course of business for the entity, or that otherwise appear to be unusual given the auditor's understanding of the entity and its environment and other information obtained during the audit, the auditor shall evaluate whether the business rationale (or the lack thereof) of the transactions suggests that they may have been entered into to engage in fraudulent financial reporting or to conceal misappropriation of assets. (Ref: Para. A48)

33   The auditor shall determine whether, in order to respond to the identified risks of management override of controls, the auditor needs to perform other audit procedures in

---

[11] *ISA (UK) 330 (Revised July 2017), paragraph 6.*

addition to those specifically referred to above (that is, where there are specific additional risks of management override that are not covered as part of the procedures performed to address the requirements in paragraph 32).

Evaluation of Audit Evidence (Ref: Para. A49)

The auditor shall evaluate whether analytical procedures that are performed near the end **34** of the audit, when forming an overall conclusion as to whether the financial statements are consistent with the auditor's understanding of the entity, indicate a previously unrecognized risk of material misstatement due to fraud. (Ref: Para. A50)

If the auditor identifies a misstatement, the auditor shall evaluate whether such a **35** misstatement is indicative of fraud. If there is such an indication, the auditor shall evaluate the implications of the misstatement in relation to other aspects of the audit, particularly the reliability of management representations, recognizing that an instance of fraud is unlikely to be an isolated occurrence. (Ref: Para. A51)

If the auditor identifies a misstatement, whether material or not, and the auditor has reason **36** to believe that it is or may be the result of fraud and that management (in particular, senior management) is involved, the auditor shall reevaluate the assessment of the risks of material misstatement due to fraud and its resulting impact on the nature, timing and extent of audit procedures to respond to the assessed risks. The auditor shall also consider whether circumstances or conditions indicate possible collusion involving employees, management or third parties when reconsidering the reliability of evidence previously obtained. (Ref: Para. A52)

If the auditor confirms that, or is unable to conclude whether, the financial statements are **37** materially misstated as a result of fraud the auditor shall evaluate the implications for the audit. (Ref: Para. A53)

Auditor Unable to Continue the Engagement

If, as a result of a misstatement resulting from fraud or suspected fraud, the auditor **38** encounters exceptional circumstances that bring into question the auditor's ability to continue performing the audit, the auditor shall:
(a) Determine the professional and legal responsibilities applicable in the circumstances, including whether there is a requirement for the auditor to report to the person or persons who made the audit appointment or, in some cases, to regulatory authorities;
(b) Consider whether it is appropriate to withdraw from the engagement, where withdrawal is possible under applicable law or regulation; and
(c) If the auditor withdraws:
   (i) Discuss with the appropriate level of management and those charged with governance the auditor's withdrawal from the engagement and the reasons for the withdrawal; and
   (ii) Determine whether there is a professional or legal requirement to report to the person or persons who made the audit appointment or, in some cases, to regulatory authorities, the auditor's withdrawal from the engagement and the reasons for the withdrawal. (Ref: Para. A54–A57)

Written Representations

39   The auditor shall obtain written representations from management and, where appropriate, those charged with governance that:

(a)   They acknowledge their responsibility for the design, implementation and maintenance of internal control to prevent and detect fraud;

(b)   They have disclosed to the auditor the results of management's assessment of the risk that the financial statements may be materially misstated as a result of fraud;

(c)   They have disclosed to the auditor their knowledge of fraud or suspected fraud affecting the entity involving:

(i)   Management;

(ii)   Employees who have significant roles in internal control; or

(iii)   Others where the fraud could have a material effect on the financial statements; and

(d)   They have disclosed to the auditor their knowledge of any allegations of fraud, or suspected fraud, affecting the entity's financial statements communicated by employees, former employees, analysts, regulators or others. (Ref: Para. A58–A59)

Communications to Management and with Those Charged with Governance

40   If the auditor has identified a fraud or has obtained information that indicates that a fraud may exist, the auditor shall communicate these matters, unless prohibited by law or regulation, on a timely basis with the appropriate level of management in order to inform those with primary responsibility for the prevention and detection of fraud of matters relevant to their responsibilities. (Ref: Para. A59a–A60)

41   Unless all of those charged with governance are involved in managing the entity, if the auditor has identified or suspects fraud involving:

(a)   management;

(b)   employees who have significant roles in internal control; or

(c)   others where the fraud results in a material misstatement in the financial statements,

the auditor shall communicate these matters with those charged with governance on a timely basis. If the auditor suspects fraud involving management, the auditor shall communicate these suspicions with those charged with governance and discuss with them the nature, timing and extent of audit procedures necessary to complete the audit. Such communications with those charged with governance are required unless the communication is prohibited by law or regulation. (Ref: Para. A59a, A61–A63)

41R-1   For audits of financial statements of public interest entities, when an auditor suspects or has reasonable grounds to suspect that irregularities, including fraud with regard to the financial statements of the entity, may occur or has occurred, the auditor shall, unless prohibited by law or regulation, inform the entity and invite it to investigate the matter and take appropriate measures to deal with such irregularities and to prevent any recurrence of such irregularities in the future. (Ref: Para. A63-1–A63-2)

42   The auditor shall communicate, unless prohibited by law or regulation, with those charged with governance any other matters related to fraud that are, in the auditor's judgment, relevant to their responsibilities. (Ref: Para. A59a, A64)

Reporting Fraud to an Appropriate Authority Outside the Entity

If the auditor has identified or suspects a fraud, the auditor shall determine whether law, regulation or relevant ethical requirements: (Ref: Para. A65–A67)   **43**

(a)   Require the auditor to report to an appropriate authority outside the entity.

(b)   Establish responsibilities under which reporting to an appropriate authority outside the entity may be appropriate in the circumstances.

> For audits of financial statements of public interest entities, where the entity does not investigate the matter referred to in paragraph 41R-1, the auditor shall inform the authorities responsible for investigating such irregularities. (Ref: Para. A66-1–A66-2)   **43R-1**

Documentation

The auditor shall include the following in the audit documentation[12] of the auditor's understanding of the entity and its environment and the assessment of the risks of material misstatement required by ISA (UK) 315 (Revised June 2016):[13]   **44**

(a)   The significant decisions reached during the discussion among the engagement team regarding the susceptibility of the entity's financial statements to material misstatement due to fraud; and

(b)   The identified and assessed risks of material misstatement due to fraud at the financial statement level and at the assertion level.

The auditor shall include the following in the audit documentation of the auditor's responses to the assessed risks of material misstatement required by ISA (UK) 330 (Revised July 2017):[14]   **45**

(a)   The overall responses to the assessed risks of material misstatement due to fraud at the financial statement level and the nature, timing and extent of audit procedures, and the linkage of those procedures with the assessed risks of material misstatement due to fraud at the assertion level; and

(b)   The results of the audit procedures, including those designed to address the risk of management override of controls.

The auditor shall include in the audit documentation communications about fraud made to management, those charged with governance, regulators and others.   **46**

If the auditor has concluded that the presumption that there is a risk of material misstatement due to fraud related to revenue recognition is not applicable in the circumstances of the engagement, the auditor shall include in the audit documentation the reasons for that conclusion.   **47**

***

---

[12] *ISA (UK) 230 (Revised June 2016)*, Audit Documentation, *paragraphs 8–11, and paragraph A6.*

[13] *ISA (UK) 315 (Revised June 2016), paragraph 32.*

[14] *ISA (UK) 330 (Revised July 2017), paragraph 28.*

Application and Other Explanatory Material

Characteristics of Fraud (Ref: Para. 3)

A1   Fraud, whether fraudulent financial reporting or misappropriation of assets, involves incentive or pressure to commit fraud, a perceived opportunity to do so and some rationalization of the act. For example:

- Incentive or pressure to commit fraudulent financial reporting may exist when management is under pressure, from sources outside or inside the entity, to achieve an expected (and perhaps unrealistic) earnings target or financial outcome – particularly since the consequences to management for failing to meet financial goals can be significant. Similarly, individuals may have an incentive to misappropriate assets, for example, because the individuals are living beyond their means.
- A perceived opportunity to commit fraud may exist when an individual believes internal control can be overridden, for example, because the individual is in a position of trust or has knowledge of specific deficiencies in internal control.
- Individuals may be able to rationalize committing a fraudulent act. Some individuals possess an attitude, character or set of ethical values that allow them knowingly and intentionally to commit a dishonest act. However, even otherwise honest individuals can commit fraud in an environment that imposes sufficient pressure on them.

A2   Fraudulent financial reporting involves intentional misstatements including omissions of amounts or disclosures in financial statements to deceive financial statement users. It can be caused by the efforts of management to manage earnings in order to deceive financial statement users by influencing their perceptions as to the entity's performance and profitability. Such earnings management may start out with small actions or inappropriate adjustment of assumptions and changes in judgments by management. Pressures and incentives may lead these actions to increase to the extent that they result in fraudulent financial reporting. Such a situation could occur when, due to pressures to meet market expectations or a desire to maximize compensation based on performance, management intentionally takes positions that lead to fraudulent financial reporting by materially misstating the financial statements. In some entities, management may be motivated to reduce earnings by a material amount to minimize tax or to inflate earnings to secure bank financing.

A3   Fraudulent financial reporting may be accomplished by the following:

- Manipulation, falsification (including forgery), or alteration of accounting records or supporting documentation from which the financial statements are prepared.
- Misrepresentation in, or intentional omission from, the financial statements of events, transactions or other significant information.

A4   Fraudulent financial reporting often involves management override of controls that otherwise may appear to be operating effectively. Fraud can be committed by management overriding controls using such techniques as intentionally:

- Recording fictitious journal entries, particularly close to the end of an accounting period, to manipulate operating results or achieve other objectives.
- Inappropriately adjusting assumptions and changing judgments used to estimate account balances.
- Omitting, advancing or delaying recognition in the financial statements of events and transactions that have occurred during the reporting period.

- Omitting, obscuring or misstating disclosures required by the applicable financial reporting framework, or disclosures that are necessary to achieve fair presentation.
- Concealing facts that could affect the amounts recorded in the financial statements.
- Engaging in complex transactions that are structured to misrepresent the financial position or financial performance of the entity.
- Altering records and terms related to significant and unusual transactions.

Misappropriation of assets involves the theft of an entity's assets and is often perpetrated **A5** by employees in relatively small and immaterial amounts. However, it can also involve management who are usually more able to disguise or conceal misappropriations in ways that are difficult to detect. Misappropriation of assets can be accomplished in a variety of ways including:

(a) Embezzling receipts (for example, misappropriating collections on accounts receivable or diverting receipts in respect of written-off accounts to personal bank accounts).

(b) Stealing physical assets or intellectual property (for example, stealing inventory for personal use or for sale, stealing scrap for resale, colluding with a competitor by disclosing technological data in return for payment).

(c) Causing an entity to pay for goods and services not received (for example, payments to fictitious vendors, kickbacks paid by vendors to the entity's purchasing agents in return for inflating prices, payments to fictitious employees).

(d) Using an entity's assets for personal use (for example, using the entity's assets as collateral for a personal loan or a loan to a related party).

Misappropriation of assets is often accompanied by false or misleading records or documents in order to conceal the fact that the assets are missing or have been pledged without proper authorization.

Responsibility for the Prevention and Detection of Fraud

Responsibilities of the Auditor (Ref: Para. 8a)

Law, regulation or relevant ethical requirements may require the auditor to perform **A5a** additional procedures and take further actions. For example, the Code of Ethics for Professional Accountants issued by the International Ethics Standards Board for Accountants (IESBA Code) requires the auditor to take steps to respond to identified or suspected non-compliance with laws and regulations and determine whether further action is needed. Such steps may include the communication of identified or suspected non-compliance with laws and regulations to other auditors within a group, including a group engagement partner, component auditors or other auditors performing work at components of a group for purposes other than the audit of the group financial statements.[15]

Considerations Specific to Public Sector Entities

The public sector auditor's responsibilities relating to fraud may be a result of law, **A6** regulation or other authority applicable to public sector entities or separately covered by the auditor's mandate. Consequently, the public sector auditor's responsibilities may not be limited to consideration of risks of material misstatement of the financial statements, but may also include a broader responsibility to consider risks of fraud.

---

[15] *See Sections 225.21–225.22 of the IESBA Code.*
In the UK, the auditor has regard to any specific requirements of the auditor's relevant professional body.

Professional Skepticism (Ref: Para. 12–14)

A7   Maintaining professional skepticism requires an ongoing questioning of whether the information and audit evidence obtained suggests that a material misstatement due to fraud may exist. It includes considering the reliability of the information to be used as audit evidence and the controls over its preparation and maintenance where relevant. Due to the characteristics of fraud, the auditor's professional skepticism is particularly important when considering the risks of material misstatement due to fraud.

A8   Although the auditor cannot be expected to disregard past experience of the honesty and integrity of the entity's management and those charged with governance, the auditor's professional skepticism is particularly important in considering the risks of material misstatement due to fraud because there may have been changes in circumstances.

A9   An audit performed in accordance with ISAs (UK) rarely involves the authentication of documents, nor is the auditor trained as or expected to be an expert in such authentication.[16] However, when the auditor identifies conditions that cause the auditor to believe that a document may not be authentic or that terms in a document have been modified but not disclosed to the auditor, possible procedures to investigate further may include:

- Confirming directly with the third party.
- Using the work of an expert to assess the document's authenticity.

Discussion among the Engagement Team (Ref: Para. 15)

A10   Discussing the susceptibility of the entity's financial statements to material misstatement due to fraud with the engagement team:

- Provides an opportunity for more experienced engagement team members to share their insights about how and where the financial statements may be susceptible to material misstatement due to fraud.
- Enables the auditor to consider an appropriate response to such susceptibility and to determine which members of the engagement team will conduct certain audit procedures.
- Permits the auditor to determine how the results of audit procedures will be shared among the engagement team and how to deal with any allegations of fraud that may come to the auditor's attention.

A11   The discussion may include such matters as:

- An exchange of ideas among engagement team members about how and where they believe the entity's financial statements (including the individual financial statements and the disclosures) may be susceptible to material misstatement due to fraud, how management could perpetrate and conceal fraudulent financial reporting, and how assets of the entity could be misappropriated.
- A consideration of circumstances that might be indicative of earnings management and the practices that might be followed by management to manage earnings that could lead to fraudulent financial reporting.
- A consideration of the risk that management may attempt to present disclosures in a manner that may obscure a proper understanding of the matters disclosed (for example, by including too much immaterial information or by using unclear or ambiguous language).

---

[16] *ISA (UK) 200 (Revised June 2016), paragraph A49.*

- A consideration of the known external and internal factors affecting the entity that may create an incentive or pressure for management or others to commit fraud, provide the opportunity for fraud to be perpetrated, and indicate a culture or environment that enables management or others to rationalize committing fraud.
- A consideration of management's involvement in overseeing employees with access to cash or other assets susceptible to misappropriation.
- A consideration of any unusual or unexplained changes in behavior or lifestyle of management or employees which have come to the attention of the engagement team.
- An emphasis on the importance of maintaining a proper state of mind throughout the audit regarding the potential for material misstatement due to fraud.
- A consideration of the types of circumstances that, if encountered, might indicate the possibility of fraud.
- A consideration of how an element of unpredictability will be incorporated into the nature, timing and extent of the audit procedures to be performed.
- A consideration of the audit procedures that might be selected to respond to the susceptibility of the entity's financial statement to material misstatement due to fraud and whether certain types of audit procedures are more effective than others.
- A consideration of any allegations of fraud that have come to the auditor's attention.
- A consideration of the risk of management override of controls.

Risk Assessment Procedures and Related Activities

Inquiries of Management

Management's Assessment of the Risk of Material Misstatement Due to Fraud
(Ref: Para. 17(a))

Management[16a] accepts responsibility for the entity's internal control and for the preparation of the entity's financial statements. Accordingly, it is appropriate for the auditor to make inquiries of management regarding management's own assessment of the risk of fraud and the controls in place to prevent and detect it. The nature, extent and frequency of management's assessment of such risk and controls may vary from entity to entity. In some entities, management may make detailed assessments on an annual basis or as part of continuous monitoring. In other entities, management's assessment may be less structured and less frequent. The nature, extent and frequency of management's assessment are relevant to the auditor's understanding of the entity's control environment. For example, the fact that management has not made an assessment of the risk of fraud may in some circumstances be indicative of the lack of importance that management places on internal control. **A12**

Considerations specific to smaller entities

In some entities, particularly smaller entities, the focus of management's assessment may be on the risks of employee fraud or misappropriation of assets. **A13**

Management's Process for Identifying and Responding to the Risks of Fraud (Ref: Para. 17(b))

In the case of entities with multiple locations management's processes may include different levels of monitoring of operating locations, or business segments. Management may also have identified particular operating locations or business segments for which a risk of fraud may be more likely to exist. **A14**

[16a] *In the UK, those charged with governance are responsible for the preparation of the financial statements.*

Inquiry of Management and Others within the Entity (Ref: Para. 18)

A15   The auditor's inquiries of management may provide useful information concerning the risks of material misstatements in the financial statements resulting from employee fraud. However, such inquiries are unlikely to provide useful information regarding the risks of material misstatement in the financial statements resulting from management fraud. Making inquiries of others within the entity may provide individuals with an opportunity to convey information to the auditor that may not otherwise be communicated.

A16   Examples of others within the entity to whom the auditor may direct inquiries about the existence or suspicion of fraud include:

- Operating personnel not directly involved in the financial reporting process.
- Employees with different levels of authority.
- Employees involved in initiating, processing or recording complex or unusual transactions and those who supervise or monitor such employees.
- In-house legal counsel.
- Chief ethics officer or equivalent person.
- The person or persons charged with dealing with allegations of fraud.

A17   Management is often in the best position to perpetrate fraud. Accordingly, when evaluating management's responses to inquiries with an attitude of professional skepticism, the auditor may judge it necessary to corroborate responses to inquiries with other information.

Inquiries of the Internal Audit Function (Ref: Para. 19)

A18   ISA (UK) 315 (Revised June 2016) and ISA (UK) 610 (Revised June 2013) establish requirements and provide guidance relevant to audits of those entities that have an internal audit function.[17] In carrying out the requirements of those ISAs (UK) in the context of fraud, the auditor may inquire about specific activities of the function including, for example:

- The procedures performed, if any, by the internal audit function during the year to detect fraud.
- Whether management has satisfactorily responded to any findings resulting from those procedures.

Obtaining an Understanding of Oversight Exercised by Those Charged with Governance (Ref: Para. 20)

A19   Those charged with governance of an entity oversee the entity's systems for monitoring risk, financial control and compliance with the law. In many countries, corporate governance practices are well developed and those charged with governance play an active role in oversight of the entity's assessment of the risks of fraud and of the relevant internal control. Since the responsibilities of those charged with governance and management may vary by entity and by country, it is important that the auditor understands their respective responsibilities to enable the auditor to obtain an understanding of the oversight exercised by the appropriate individuals.[18]

---

[17] *ISA (UK) 315 (Revised June 2016), paragraphs 6(a) and 23, and ISA (UK) 610 (Revised June 2013), Using the Work of Internal Auditors.*

[18] *ISA (UK) 260 (Revised June 2016), paragraphs A1–A8, discuss with whom the auditor communicates when the entity's governance structure is not well defined.*

An understanding of the oversight exercised by those charged with governance may provide **A20** insights regarding the susceptibility of the entity to management fraud, the adequacy of internal control over risks of fraud, and the competency and integrity of management. The auditor may obtain this understanding in a number of ways, such as by attending meetings where such discussions take place, reading the minutes from such meetings or making inquiries of those charged with governance.

Considerations Specific to Smaller Entities

In some cases, all of those charged with governance are involved in managing the entity. **A21** This may be the case in a small entity where a single owner manages the entity and no one else has a governance role. In these cases, there is ordinarily no action on the part of the auditor because there is no oversight separate from management.

Consideration of Other Information (Ref: Para. 23)

In addition to information obtained from applying analytical procedures, other information **A22** obtained about the entity and its environment may be helpful in identifying the risks of material misstatement due to fraud. The discussion among team members may provide information that is helpful in identifying such risks. In addition, information obtained from the auditor's client acceptance and retention processes, and experience gained on other engagements performed for the entity, for example engagements to review interim financial information, may be relevant in the identification of the risks of material misstatement due to fraud.

Evaluation of Fraud Risk Factors (Ref: Para. 24)

The fact that fraud is usually concealed can make it very difficult to detect. Nevertheless, **A23** the auditor may identify events or conditions that indicate an incentive or pressure to commit fraud or provide an opportunity to commit fraud (fraud risk factors). For example:

- The need to meet expectations of third parties to obtain additional equity financing may create pressure to commit fraud;
- The granting of significant bonuses if unrealistic profit targets are met may create an incentive to commit fraud; and
- A control environment that is not effective may create an opportunity to commit fraud.

Fraud risk factors cannot easily be ranked in order of importance. The significance of **A24** fraud risk factors varies widely. Some of these factors will be present in entities where the specific conditions do not present risks of material misstatement. Accordingly, the determination of whether a fraud risk factor is present and whether it is to be considered in assessing the risks of material misstatement of the financial statements due to fraud requires the exercise of professional judgment.

Examples of fraud risk factors related to fraudulent financial reporting and misappropriation **A25** of assets are presented in Appendix 1. These illustrative risk factors are classified based on the three conditions that are generally present when fraud exists:

- An incentive or pressure to commit fraud;
- A perceived opportunity to commit fraud; and
- An ability to rationalize the fraudulent action.

Risk factors reflective of an attitude that permits rationalization of the fraudulent action may not be susceptible to observation by the auditor. Nevertheless, the auditor may become aware of the existence of such information. Although the fraud risk factors described in Appendix 1 cover a broad range of situations that may be faced by auditors, they are only examples and other risk factors may exist.

A26   The size, complexity, and ownership characteristics of the entity have a significant influence on the consideration of relevant fraud risk factors. For example, in the case of a large entity, there may be factors that generally constrain improper conduct by management, such as:

●   Effective oversight by those charged with governance.
●   An effective internal audit function.
●   The existence and enforcement of a written code of conduct.

Furthermore, fraud risk factors considered at a business segment operating level may provide different insights when compared with those obtained when considered at an entity-wide level.

Considerations Specific to Smaller Entities

A27   In the case of a small entity, some or all of these considerations may be inapplicable or less relevant. For example, a smaller entity may not have a written code of conduct but, instead, may have developed a culture that emphasizes the importance of integrity and ethical behavior through oral communication and by management example. Domination of management by a single individual in a small entity does not generally, in and of itself, indicate a failure by management to display and communicate an appropriate attitude regarding internal control and the financial reporting process. In some entities, the need for management authorization can compensate for otherwise deficient controls and reduce the risk of employee fraud. However, domination of management by a single individual can be a potential deficiency in internal control since there is an opportunity for management override of controls.

Identification and Assessment of the Risks of Material Misstatement Due to Fraud

Risks of Fraud in Revenue Recognition (Ref: Para. 26)

A28   Material misstatement due to fraudulent financial reporting relating to revenue recognition often results from an overstatement of revenues through, for example, premature revenue recognition or recording fictitious revenues. It may result also from an understatement of revenues through, for example, improperly shifting revenues to a later period.

A29   The risks of fraud in revenue recognition may be greater in some entities than others. For example, there may be pressures or incentives on management to commit fraudulent financial reporting through inappropriate revenue recognition in the case of listed entities when, for example, performance is measured in terms of year-over-year revenue growth or profit. Similarly, for example, there may be greater risks of fraud in revenue recognition in the case of entities that generate a substantial portion of revenues through cash sales.

A30   The presumption that there are risks of fraud in revenue recognition may be rebutted. For example, the auditor may conclude that there is no risk of material misstatement due to fraud relating to revenue recognition in the case where a there is a single type of simple revenue transaction, for example, leasehold revenue from a single unit rental property.

Identifying and Assessing the Risks of Material Misstatement Due to Fraud and Understanding the Entity's Related Controls (Ref: Para. 27)

Management may make judgments on the nature and extent of the controls it chooses to implement, and the nature and extent of the risks it chooses to assume.[19] In determining which controls to implement to prevent and detect fraud, management considers the risks that the financial statements may be materially misstated as a result of fraud. As part of this consideration, management may conclude that it is not cost effective to implement and maintain a particular control in relation to the reduction in the risks of material misstatement due to fraud to be achieved.   **A31**

It is therefore important for the auditor to obtain an understanding of the controls that management has designed, implemented and maintained to prevent and detect fraud. In doing so, the auditor may learn, for example, that management has consciously chosen to accept the risks associated with a lack of segregation of duties. Information from obtaining this understanding may also be useful in identifying fraud risks factors that may affect the auditor's assessment of the risks that the financial statements may contain material misstatement due to fraud.   **A32**

Responses to the Assessed Risks of Material Misstatement Due to Fraud

Overall Responses (Ref: Para. 28)

Determining overall responses to address the assessed risks of material misstatement due to fraud generally includes the consideration of how the overall conduct of the audit can reflect increased professional skepticism, for example, through: **A33**

- Increased sensitivity in the selection of the nature and extent of documentation to be examined in support of material transactions.
- Increased recognition of the need to corroborate management explanations or representations concerning material matters.

It also involves more general considerations apart from the specific procedures otherwise planned; these considerations include the matters listed in paragraph 29, which are discussed below.

Assignment and Supervision of Personnel (Ref: Para. 29(a))

The auditor may respond to identified risks of material misstatement due to fraud by, for example, assigning additional individuals with specialized skill and knowledge, such as forensic and IT experts, or by assigning more experienced individuals to the engagement.   **A34**

The extent of supervision reflects the auditor's assessment of risks of material misstatement due to fraud and the competencies of the engagement team members performing the work.   **A35**

Unpredictability in the Selection of Audit Procedures (Ref: Para. 29(c))

Incorporating an element of unpredictability in the selection of the nature, timing and extent of audit procedures to be performed is important as individuals within the entity who are familiar with the audit procedures normally performed on engagements may be more able to conceal fraudulent financial reporting. This can be achieved by, for example: **A36**

---

[19] *ISA (UK) 315 (Revised June 2016), paragraph A56.*

- Performing substantive procedures on selected account balances and assertions not otherwise tested due to their materiality or risk.
- Adjusting the timing of audit procedures from that otherwise expected.
- Using different sampling methods.
- Performing audit procedures at different locations or at locations on an unannounced basis.

Audit Procedures Responsive to Assessed Risks of Material Misstatement Due to Fraud at the Assertion Level (Ref: Para. 30)

A37   The auditor's responses to address the assessed risks of material misstatement due to fraud at the assertion level may include changing the nature, timing and extent of audit procedures in the following ways:

- The nature of audit procedures to be performed may need to be changed to obtain audit evidence that is more reliable and relevant or to obtain additional corroborative information. This may affect both the type of audit procedures to be performed and their combination. For example:
  - o   Physical observation or inspection of certain assets may become more important or the auditor may choose to use computer-assisted audit techniques to gather more evidence about data contained in significant accounts or electronic transaction files.
  - o   The auditor may design procedures to obtain additional corroborative information. For example, if the auditor identifies that management is under pressure to meet earnings expectations, there may be a related risk that management is inflating sales by entering into sales agreements that include terms that preclude revenue recognition or by invoicing sales before delivery. In these circumstances, the auditor may, for example, design external confirmations not only to confirm outstanding amounts, but also to confirm the details of the sales agreements, including date, any rights of return and delivery terms. In addition, the auditor might find it effective to supplement such external confirmations with inquiries of non-financial personnel in the entity regarding any changes in sales agreements and delivery terms.

- The timing of substantive procedures may need to be modified. The auditor may conclude that performing substantive testing at or near the period end better addresses an assessed risk of material misstatement due to fraud. The auditor may conclude that, given the assessed risks of intentional misstatement or manipulation, audit procedures to extend audit conclusions from an interim date to the period end would not be effective. In contrast, because an intentional misstatement – for example, a misstatement involving improper revenue recognition – may have been initiated in an interim period, the auditor may elect to apply substantive procedures to transactions occurring earlier in or throughout the reporting period.
- The extent of the procedures applied reflects the assessment of the risks of material misstatement due to fraud. For example, increasing sample sizes or performing analytical procedures at a more detailed level may be appropriate. Also, computer-assisted audit techniques may enable more extensive testing of electronic transactions and account files. Such techniques can be used to select sample transactions from key electronic files, to sort transactions with specific characteristics, or to test an entire population instead of a sample.

A38   If the auditor identifies a risk of material misstatement due to fraud that affects inventory quantities, examining the entity's inventory records may help to identify locations or items that require specific attention during or after the physical inventory count. Such a review may lead to a decision to observe inventory counts at certain locations on an unannounced basis or to conduct inventory counts at all locations on the same date.

The auditor may identify a risk of material misstatement due to fraud affecting a number of   **A39**
accounts and assertions. These may include asset valuation, estimates relating to specific
transactions (such as acquisitions, restructurings, or disposals of a segment of the business),
and other significant accrued liabilities (such as pension and other post-employment
benefit obligations, or environmental remediation liabilities). The risk may also relate to
significant changes in assumptions relating to recurring estimates. Information gathered
through obtaining an understanding of the entity and its environment may assist the
auditor in evaluating the reasonableness of such management estimates and underlying
judgments and assumptions. A retrospective review of similar management judgments and
assumptions applied in prior periods may also provide insight about the reasonableness of
judgments and assumptions supporting management estimates.

Examples of possible audit procedures to address the assessed risks of material   **A40**
misstatement due to fraud, including those that illustrate the incorporation of an element
of unpredictability, are presented in Appendix 2. The appendix includes examples of
responses to the auditor's assessment of the risks of material misstatement resulting from
both fraudulent financial reporting, including fraudulent financial reporting resulting from
revenue recognition, and misappropriation of assets.

Audit Procedures Responsive to Risks Related to Management Override of Controls

Journal Entries and Other Adjustments (Ref: Para. 32(a))

Material misstatement of financial statements due to fraud often involve the manipulation   **A41**
of the financial reporting process by recording inappropriate or unauthorized journal
entries. This may occur throughout the year or at period end, or by management making
adjustments to amounts reported in the financial statements that are not reflected in journal
entries, such as through consolidating adjustments and reclassifications.

Further, the auditor's consideration of the risks of material misstatement associated with   **A42**
inappropriate override of controls over journal entries is important since automated
processes and controls may reduce the risk of inadvertent error but do not overcome the risk
that individuals may inappropriately override such automated processes, for example, by
changing the amounts being automatically passed to the general ledger or to the financial
reporting system. Furthermore, where IT is used to transfer information automatically,
there may be little or no visible evidence of such intervention in the information systems.

When identifying and selecting journal entries and other adjustments for testing and   **A43**
determining the appropriate method of examining the underlying support for the items
selected, the following matters are of relevance:

- *The assessment of the risks of material misstatement due to fraud* – the presence
  of fraud risk factors and other information obtained during the auditor's assessment
  of the risks of material misstatement due to fraud may assist the auditor to identify
  specific classes of journal entries and other adjustments for testing.
- *Controls that have been implemented over journal entries and other adjustments*
  – effective controls over the preparation and posting of journal entries and other
  adjustments may reduce the extent of substantive testing necessary, provided that the
  auditor has tested the operating effectiveness of the controls.
- *The entity's financial reporting process and the nature of evidence that can be
  obtained* – for many entities routine processing of transactions involves a combination
  of manual and automated steps and procedures. Similarly, the processing of journal
  entries and other adjustments may involve both manual and automated procedures
  and controls. Where information technology is used in the financial reporting process,
  journal entries and other adjustments may exist only in electronic form.

- *The characteristics of fraudulent journal entries or other adjustments* – inappropriate journal entries or other adjustments often have unique identifying characteristics. Such characteristics may include entries (a) made to unrelated, unusual, or seldom-used accounts, (b) made by individuals who typically do not make journal entries, (c) recorded at the end of the period or as post-closing entries that have little or no explanation or description, (d) made either before or during the preparation of the financial statements that do not have account numbers, or (e) containing round numbers or consistent ending numbers.

- *The nature and complexity of the accounts* – inappropriate journal entries or adjustments may be applied to accounts that (a) contain transactions that are complex or unusual in nature, (b) contain significant estimates and period-end adjustments, (c) have been prone to misstatements in the past, (d) have not been reconciled on a timely basis or contain unreconciled differences, (e) contain intercompany transactions, or (f) are otherwise associated with an identified risk of material misstatement due to fraud. In audits of entities that have several locations or components, consideration is given to the need to select journal entries from multiple locations.

- *Journal entries or other adjustments processed outside the normal course of business* – non standard journal entries may not be subject to the same level of internal control as those journal entries used on a recurring basis to record transactions such as monthly sales, purchases and cash disbursements.

A44   The auditor uses professional judgment in determining the nature, timing and extent of testing of journal entries and other adjustments. However, because fraudulent journal entries and other adjustments are often made at the end of a reporting period, paragraph 32(a)(ii) requires the auditor to select the journal entries and other adjustments made at that time. Further, because material misstatements in financial statements due to fraud can occur throughout the period and may involve extensive efforts to conceal how the fraud is accomplished, paragraph 32(a)(iii) requires the auditor to consider whether there is also a need to test journal entries and other adjustments throughout the period.

Accounting Estimates (Ref: Para. 32(b))

A45   The preparation of the financial statements requires management[14a] to make a number of judgments or assumptions that affect significant accounting estimates and to monitor the reasonableness of such estimates on an ongoing basis. Fraudulent financial reporting is often accomplished through intentional misstatement of accounting estimates. This may be achieved by, for example, understating or overstating all provisions or reserves in the same fashion so as to be designed either to smooth earnings over two or more accounting periods, or to achieve a designated earnings level in order to deceive financial statement users by influencing their perceptions as to the entity's performance and profitability.

A46   The purpose of performing a retrospective review of management judgments and assumptions related to significant accounting estimates reflected in the financial statements of the prior year is to determine whether there is an indication of a possible bias on the part of management. It is not intended to call into question the auditor's professional judgments made in the prior year that were based on information available at the time.

A47   A retrospective review is also required by ISA (UK) 540 (Revised June 2016).[20] That review is conducted as a risk assessment procedure to obtain information regarding the effectiveness of management's prior period estimation process, audit evidence about the outcome, or where applicable, the subsequent re-estimation of prior period accounting estimates that is pertinent to making current period accounting estimates, and audit evidence of matters, such as estimation uncertainty, that may be required to be disclosed

---

[20] *ISA (UK) 540 (Revised June 2016)*, Auditing Accounting Estimates, Including Fair Value Accounting Estimates, and Related Disclosures, *paragraph 9.*

in the financial statements. As a practical matter, the auditor's review of management judgments and assumptions for biases that could represent a risk of material misstatement due to fraud in accordance with this ISA (UK) may be carried out in conjunction with the review required by ISA (UK) 540 (Revised June 2016).

Business Rationale for Significant Transactions (Ref: Para. 32(c))

Indicators that may suggest that significant transactions that are outside the normal course of business for the entity, or that otherwise appear to be unusual, may have been entered into to engage in fraudulent financial reporting or to conceal misappropriation of assets include: **A48**

- The form of such transactions appears overly complex (for example, the transaction involves multiple entities within a consolidated group or multiple unrelated third parties).
- Management has not discussed the nature of and accounting for such transactions with those charged with governance of the entity, and there is inadequate documentation.
- Management is placing more emphasis on the need for a particular accounting treatment than on the underlying economics of the transaction.
- Transactions that involve non-consolidated related parties, including special purpose entities, have not been properly reviewed or approved by those charged with governance of the entity.
- The transactions involve previously unidentified related parties or parties that do not have the substance or the financial strength to support the transaction without assistance from the entity under audit.

Evaluation of Audit Evidence (Ref: Para. 34–37)

ISA (UK) 330 (Revised July 2017) requires the auditor, based on the audit procedures performed and the audit evidence obtained, to evaluate whether the assessments of the risks of material misstatement at the assertion level remain appropriate.[21] This evaluation is primarily a qualitative matter based on the auditor's judgment. Such an evaluation may provide further insight about the risks of material misstatement due to fraud and whether there is a need to perform additional or different audit procedures. Appendix 3 contains examples of circumstances that may indicate the possibility of fraud. **A49**

Analytical Procedures Performed Near the End of the Audit in Forming an Overall Conclusion (Ref: Para. 34)

Determining which particular trends and relationships may indicate a risk of material misstatement due to fraud requires professional judgment. Unusual relationships involving year-end revenue and income are particularly relevant. These might include, for example: uncharacteristically large amounts of income being reported in the last few weeks of the reporting period or unusual transactions; or income that is inconsistent with trends in cash flow from operations. **A50**

Consideration of Identified Misstatements (Ref: Para. 35–37)

Since fraud involves incentive or pressure to commit fraud, a perceived opportunity to do so or some rationalization of the act, an instance of fraud is unlikely to be an isolated occurrence. Accordingly, misstatements, such as numerous misstatements at a specific location even though the cumulative effect is not material, may be indicative of a risk of material misstatement due to fraud. **A51**

---

[21] *ISA (UK) 330 (Revised July 2017), paragraph 25.*

A52   The implications of identified fraud depend on the circumstances. For example, an otherwise insignificant fraud may be significant if it involves senior management. In such circumstances, the reliability of evidence previously obtained may be called into question, since there may be doubts about the completeness and truthfulness of representations made and about the genuineness of accounting records and documentation. There may also be a possibility of collusion involving employees, management or third parties.

A53   ISA (UK) 450 (Revised June 2016)[22] and ISA (UK) 700 (Revised June 2016)[23] establish requirements and provide guidance on the evaluation and disposition of misstatements and the effect on the auditor's opinion in the auditor's report.

Auditor Unable to Continue the Engagement (Ref: Para. 38)

A54   Examples of exceptional circumstances that may arise and that may bring into question the auditor's ability to continue performing the audit include:

- The entity does not take the appropriate action regarding fraud that the auditor considers necessary in the circumstances, even where the fraud is not material to the financial statements;
- The auditor's consideration of the risks of material misstatement due to fraud and the results of audit tests indicate a significant risk of material and pervasive fraud; or
- The auditor has significant concern about the competence or integrity of management or those charged with governance.

A55   Because of the variety of the circumstances that may arise, it is not possible to describe definitively when withdrawal from an engagement is appropriate. Factors that affect the auditor's conclusion include the implications of the involvement of a member of management or of those charged with governance (which may affect the reliability of management representations) and the effects on the auditor of a continuing association with the entity.

A56   The auditor has professional and legal responsibilities in such circumstances and these responsibilities may vary by country. In some countries, for example, the auditor may be entitled to, or required to, make a statement or report to the person or persons who made the audit appointment or, in some cases, to regulatory authorities. Given the exceptional nature of the circumstances and the need to consider the legal requirements, the auditor may consider it appropriate to seek legal advice when deciding whether to withdraw from an engagement and in determining an appropriate course of action, including the possibility of reporting to shareholders, regulators or others.[24]

Considerations Specific to Public Sector Entities

A57   In many cases in the public sector, the option of withdrawing from the engagement may not be available to the auditor due to the nature of the mandate or public interest considerations.

---

[22] *ISA (UK) 450 (Revised June 2016)*, Evaluation of Misstatements Identified during the Audit.

[23] *ISA (UK) 700 (Revised June 2016)*, Forming an Opinion and Reporting on Financial Statements.

[24] *The IESBA* Code of Ethics for Professional Accountants *provides guidance on communications with an auditor replacing the existing auditor.*
In the UK, the relevant ethical guidance on proposed communications with a successor auditor is provided by the ethical pronouncements relating to the work of auditors issued by the auditor's relevant professional body.

Written Representations (Ref: Para. 39)

ISA (UK) 580[25] establishes requirements and provides guidance on obtaining appropriate **A58** representations from management and, where appropriate, those charged with governance in the audit. In addition to acknowledging that they have fulfilled their responsibility for the preparation of the financial statements, it is important that, irrespective of the size of the entity, management and, where appropriate, those charged with governance acknowledge their responsibility for internal control designed, implemented and maintained to prevent and detect fraud.

Because of the nature of fraud and the difficulties encountered by auditors in detecting **A59** material misstatements in the financial statements resulting from fraud, it is important that the auditor obtain a written representation from management and, where appropriate, those charged with governance confirming that they have disclosed to the auditor:

(a)   The results of management's assessment of the risk that the financial statements may be materially misstated as a result of fraud; and
(b)   Their knowledge of actual, suspected or alleged fraud affecting the entity.

Communications to Management and with Those Charged with Governance (Ref: Para. 40–42)

In some jurisdictions, law or regulation may restrict the auditor's communication of certain **A59a** matters with management and those charged with governance. Law or regulation may specifically prohibit a communication, or other action, that might prejudice an investigation by an appropriate authority into an actual, or suspected, illegal act, including alerting the entity, for example, when the auditor is required to report the fraud to an appropriate authority pursuant to anti-money laundering legislation. In these circumstances, the issues considered by the auditor may be complex and the auditor may consider it appropriate to obtain legal advice.

Communication to Management (Ref: Para. 40)

When the auditor has obtained evidence that fraud exists or may exist, it is important that **A60** the matter be brought to the attention of the appropriate level of management as soon as practicable. This is so even if the matter might be considered inconsequential (for example, a minor defalcation by an employee at a low level in the entity's organization). The determination of which level of management is the appropriate one is a matter of professional judgment and is affected by such factors as the likelihood of collusion and the nature and magnitude of the suspected fraud. Ordinarily, the appropriate level of management is at least one level above the persons who appear to be involved with the suspected fraud.

Communication with Those Charged with Governance (Ref: Para. 41)

The auditor's communication with those charged with governance may be made orally or **A61** in writing. ISA (UK) 260 (Revised June 2016) identifies factors the auditor considers in determining whether to communicate orally or in writing.[26] Due to the nature and sensitivity of fraud involving senior management, or fraud that results in a material misstatement in the financial statements, the auditor reports such matters on a timely basis and may consider it necessary to also report such matters in writing.

---

[25] *ISA (UK) 580,* Written Representations.

[26] *ISA (UK) 260 (Revised June 2016), paragraph A38.*

A62 In some cases, the auditor may consider it appropriate to communicate with those charged with governance when the auditor becomes aware of fraud involving employees other than management that does not result in a material misstatement. Similarly, those charged with governance may wish to be informed of such circumstances. The communication process is assisted if the auditor and those charged with governance agree at an early stage in the audit about the nature and extent of the auditor's communications in this regard.

A63 In the exceptional circumstances where the auditor has doubts about the integrity or honesty of management or those charged with governance, the auditor may consider it appropriate to obtain legal advice to assist in determining the appropriate course of action.

> ### Communication with Those Charged with Governance of Public Interest Entities (Ref: Para. 41R-1)
>
> **A63-1** For audits of financial statements of public interest entities, ISA (UK) 260 (Revised June 2016)[26a] requires the auditor to communicate in the additional report to the audit committee any significant matters involving actual or suspected non-compliance with laws and regulations, including from fraud or suspected fraud, which were identified in the course of the audit.
>
> **A63-2** In the UK, laws or regulations may prohibit alerting ('tipping off') the entity when, for example, the auditor is required to report the non-compliance to an appropriate authority pursuant to anti-money laundering legislation.

Other Matters Related to Fraud (Ref: Para. 42)

A64 Other matters related to fraud to be discussed with those charged with governance of the entity may include, for example:

- Concerns about the nature, extent and frequency of management's assessments of the controls in place to prevent and detect fraud and of the risk that the financial statements may be misstated.
- A failure by management to appropriately address identified significant deficiencies in internal control, or to appropriately respond to an identified fraud.
- The auditor's evaluation of the entity's control environment, including questions regarding the competence and integrity of management.
- Actions by management that may be indicative of fraudulent financial reporting, such as management's selection and application of accounting policies that may be indicative of management's effort to manage earnings in order to deceive financial statement users by influencing their perceptions as to the entity's performance and profitability.
- Concerns about the adequacy and completeness of the authorization of transactions that appear to be outside the normal course of business.

Reporting Fraud to an Appropriate Authority outside the Entity (Ref: Para. 43)

A65 ISA (UK) 250 (Revised July 2017)[27] provides further guidance with respect to the auditor's determination of whether reporting identified or suspected non-compliance with laws or

---

[26a] *ISA (UK) 260 (Revised June 2016),* Communication with Those Charged with Governance, *paragraph 16R-2(k).*

[27] *ISA (UK) 250 (Revised December 2017),* Section A—Consideration of Laws and Regulations in an Audit of Financial Statements, *paragraphs A28–A34.*

regulations to an appropriate authority outside the entity is required or appropriate in the circumstances, including consideration of the auditor's duty of confidentiality.

The determination required by paragraph 43 may involve complex considerations and professional judgments. Accordingly, the auditor may consider consulting internally (e.g., within the firm or a network firm) or on a confidential basis with a regulator or professional body (unless doing so is prohibited by law or regulation or would breach the duty of confidentiality). The auditor may also consider obtaining legal advice to understand the auditor's options and the professional or legal implications of taking any particular course of action. **A66**

Reporting to Authorities of Public Interest Entities (Ref: Para. 43R-1)

The disclosure in good faith to the authorities responsible for investigating such irregularities, by the auditor, of any irregularities referred to in paragraph 43R-1 shall not constitute a breach of any contractual or legal restriction on disclosure of information in accordance with the Audit Regulation.[27a] **A66-1**

The auditor considers whether to take further action when the entity investigates the matter referred to in paragraph 41R-1 but where the measures taken by management or those charged with governance, in the auditor's professional judgement, were not appropriate to deal with the actual or potential risks of fraud identified or would fail to prevent future occurrences of fraud. **A66-2**

Considerations Specific to Public Sector Entities

In the public sector, requirements for reporting fraud, whether or not discovered through the audit process, may be subject to specific provisions of the audit mandate or related law, regulation or other authority. **A67**

Appendix 1 (Ref: Para. A25)

Examples of Fraud Risk Factors

The fraud risk factors identified in this Appendix are examples of such factors that may be faced by auditors in a broad range of situations. Separately presented are examples relating to the two types of fraud relevant to the auditor's consideration – that is, fraudulent financial reporting and misappropriation of assets. For each of these types of fraud, the risk factors are further classified based on the three conditions generally present when material misstatements due to fraud occur: (a) incentives/pressures, (b) opportunities, and (c) attitudes/rationalizations. Although the risk factors cover a broad range of situations, they are only examples and, accordingly, the auditor may identify additional or different risk factors. Not all of these examples are relevant in all circumstances, and some may be of greater or lesser significance in entities of different size or with different ownership characteristics or circumstances. Also, the order of the examples of risk factors provided is not intended to reflect their relative importance or frequency of occurrence.

[27a] *Article 7 of Regulation (EU) No 537/2014 of the European Parliament and of the Council of 16 April 2014.*

Risk Factors Relating to Misstatements Arising from Fraudulent Financial Reporting

The following are examples of risk factors relating to misstatements arising from fraudulent financial reporting.

Incentives/Pressures

Financial stability or profitability is threatened by economic, industry, or entity operating conditions, such as (or as indicated by):

- High degree of competition or market saturation, accompanied by declining margins.
- High vulnerability to rapid changes, such as changes in technology, product obsolescence, or interest rates.
- Significant declines in customer demand and increasing business failures in either the industry or overall economy.
- Operating losses making the threat of bankruptcy, foreclosure, or hostile takeover imminent.
- Recurring negative cash flows from operations or an inability to generate cash flows from operations while reporting earnings and earnings growth.
- Rapid growth or unusual profitability especially compared to that of other companies in the same industry.
- New accounting, statutory, or regulatory requirements.

Excessive pressure exists for management to meet the requirements or expectations of third parties due to the following:

- Profitability or trend level expectations of investment analysts, institutional investors, significant creditors, or other external parties (particularly expectations that are unduly aggressive or unrealistic), including expectations created by management in, for example, overly optimistic press releases or annual report messages.
- Need to obtain additional debt or equity financing to stay competitive – including financing of major research and development or capital expenditures.
- Marginal ability to meet exchange listing requirements or debt repayment or other debt covenant requirements.
- Perceived or real adverse effects of reporting poor financial results on significant pending transactions, such as business combinations or contract awards.

Information available indicates that the personal financial situation of management or those charged with governance is threatened by the entity's financial performance arising from the following:

- Significant financial interests in the entity.
- Significant portions of their compensation (for example, bonuses, stock options, and earn-out arrangements) being contingent upon achieving aggressive targets for stock price, operating results, financial position, or cash flow.[1a]
- Personal guarantees of debts of the entity.

There is excessive pressure on management or operating personnel to meet financial targets established by those charged with governance, including sales or profitability incentive goals.

[1a] *Management incentive plans may be contingent upon achieving targets relating only to certain accounts or selected activities of the entity, even though the related accounts or activities may not be material to the entity as a whole.*

Opportunities

The nature of the industry or the entity's operations provides opportunities to engage in fraudulent financial reporting that can arise from the following:

- Significant related-party transactions not in the ordinary course of business or with related entities not audited or audited by another firm.
- A strong financial presence or ability to dominate a certain industry sector that allows the entity to dictate terms or conditions to suppliers or customers that may result in inappropriate or non-arm's-length transactions.
- Assets, liabilities, revenues, or expenses based on significant estimates that involve subjective judgments or uncertainties that are difficult to corroborate.
- Significant, unusual, or highly complex transactions, especially those close to period end that pose difficult 'substance over form' questions.
- Significant operations located or conducted across international borders in jurisdictions where differing business environments and cultures exist.
- Use of business intermediaries for which there appears to be no clear business justification.
- Significant bank accounts or subsidiary or branch operations in tax-haven jurisdictions for which there appears to be no clear business justification.

The monitoring of management is not effective as a result of the following:

- Domination of management by a single person or small group (in a non owner-managed business) without compensating controls.
- Oversight by those charged with governance over the financial reporting process and internal control is not effective.

There is a complex or unstable organizational structure, as evidenced by the following:

- Difficulty in determining the organization or individuals that have controlling interest in the entity.
- Overly complex organizational structure involving unusual legal entities or managerial lines of authority.
- High turnover of senior management, legal counsel, or those charged with governance.

Internal control components are deficient as a result of the following:

- Inadequate monitoring of controls, including automated controls and controls over interim financial reporting (where external reporting is required).
- High turnover rates or employment of staff in accounting, information technology, or the internal audit function that are not effective.
- Accounting and information systems that are not effective, including situations involving significant deficiencies in internal control.

Attitudes/Rationalizations

- Communication, implementation, support, or enforcement of the entity's values or ethical standards by management, or the communication of inappropriate values or ethical standards, that are not effective.
- Nonfinancial management's excessive participation in or preoccupation with the selection of accounting policies or the determination of significant estimates.
- Known history of violations of securities laws or other laws and regulations, or claims against the entity, its senior management, or those charged with governance alleging fraud or violations of laws and regulations.

- Excessive interest by management in maintaining or increasing the entity's stock price or earnings trend.
- The practice by management of committing to analysts, creditors, and other third parties to achieve aggressive or unrealistic forecasts.
- Management failing to remedy known significant deficiencies in internal control on a timely basis.
- An interest by management in employing inappropriate means to minimize reported earnings for tax-motivated reasons.
- Low morale among senior management.
- The owner-manager makes no distinction between personal and business transactions.
- Dispute between shareholders in a closely held entity.
- Recurring attempts by management to justify marginal or inappropriate accounting on the basis of materiality.
- The relationship between management and the current or predecessor auditor is strained, as exhibited by the following:
  - Frequent disputes with the current or predecessor auditor on accounting, auditing, or reporting matters.
  - Unreasonable demands on the auditor, such as unrealistic time constraints regarding the completion of the audit or the issuance of the auditor's report.
  - Restrictions on the auditor that inappropriately limit access to people or information or the ability to communicate effectively with those charged with governance.
  - Domineering management behavior in dealing with the auditor, especially involving attempts to influence the scope of the auditor's work or the selection or continuance of personnel assigned to or consulted on the audit engagement.

Risk Factors Arising from Misstatements Arising from Misappropriation of Assets

Risk factors that relate to misstatements arising from misappropriation of assets are also classified according to the three conditions generally present when fraud exists: incentives/pressures, opportunities, and attitudes/rationalization. Some of the risk factors related to misstatements arising from fraudulent financial reporting also may be present when misstatements arising from misappropriation of assets occur. For example, ineffective monitoring of management and other deficiencies in internal control may be present when misstatements due to either fraudulent financial reporting or misappropriation of assets exist. The following are examples of risk factors related to misstatements arising from misappropriation of assets.

Incentives/Pressures

Personal financial obligations may create pressure on management or employees with access to cash or other assets susceptible to theft to misappropriate those assets.

Adverse relationships between the entity and employees with access to cash or other assets susceptible to theft may motivate those employees to misappropriate those assets. For example, adverse relationships may be created by the following:

- Known or anticipated future employee layoffs.
- Recent or anticipated changes to employee compensation or benefit plans.
- Promotions, compensation, or other rewards inconsistent with expectations.

Opportunities

Certain characteristics or circumstances may increase the susceptibility of assets to misappropriation. For example, opportunities to misappropriate assets increase when there are the following:

- Large amounts of cash on hand or processed.
- Inventory items that are small in size, of high value, or in high demand.
- Easily convertible assets, such as bearer bonds, diamonds, or computer chips.
- Fixed assets which are small in size, marketable, or lacking observable identification of ownership.

Inadequate internal control over assets may increase the susceptibility of misappropriation of those assets. For example, misappropriation of assets may occur because there is the following:

- Inadequate segregation of duties or independent checks.
- Inadequate oversight of senior management expenditures, such as travel and other reimbursements.
- Inadequate management oversight of employees responsible for assets, for example, inadequate supervision or monitoring of remote locations.
- Inadequate job applicant screening of employees with access to assets.
- Inadequate record keeping with respect to assets.
- Inadequate system of authorization and approval of transactions (for example, in purchasing).
- Inadequate physical safeguards over cash, investments, inventory, or fixed assets.
- Lack of complete and timely reconciliations of assets.
- Lack of timely and appropriate documentation of transactions, for example, credits for merchandise returns.
- Lack of mandatory vacations for employees performing key control functions.
- Inadequate management understanding of information technology, which enables information technology employees to perpetrate a misappropriation.
- Inadequate access controls over automated records, including controls over and review of computer systems event logs.

Attitudes/Rationalizations

- Disregard for the need for monitoring or reducing risks related to misappropriations of assets.
- Disregard for internal control over misappropriation of assets by overriding existing controls or by failing to take appropriate remedial action on known deficiencies in internal control.
- Behavior indicating displeasure or dissatisfaction with the entity or its treatment of the employee.
- Changes in behavior or lifestyle that may indicate assets have been misappropriated.
- Tolerance of petty theft.

Appendix 2

Examples of Possible Audit Procedures to Address the Assessed Risks of Material Misstatement Due to Fraud

The following are examples of possible audit procedures to address the assessed risks of material misstatement due to fraud resulting from both fraudulent financial reporting and misappropriation of assets. Although these procedures cover a broad range of situations, they are only examples and, accordingly they may not be the most appropriate nor necessary in each circumstance. Also the order of the procedures provided is not intended to reflect their relative importance.

Consideration at the Assertion Level

Specific responses to the auditor's assessment of the risks of material misstatement due to fraud will vary depending upon the types or combinations of fraud risk factors or conditions identified, and the classes of transactions, account balances, disclosures and assertions they may affect.

The following are specific examples of responses:

- Visiting locations or performing certain tests on a surprise or unannounced basis. For example, observing inventory at locations where auditor attendance has not been previously announced or counting cash at a particular date on a surprise basis.
- Requesting that inventories be counted at the end of the reporting period or on a date closer to period end to minimize the risk of manipulation of balances in the period between the date of completion of the count and the end of the reporting period.
- Altering the audit approach in the current year. For example, contacting major customers and suppliers orally in addition to sending written confirmation, sending confirmation requests to a specific party within an organization, or seeking more or different information.
- Performing a detailed review of the entity's quarter-end or year-end adjusting entries and investigating any that appear unusual as to nature or amount.
- For significant and unusual transactions, particularly those occurring at or near year-end, investigating the possibility of related parties and the sources of financial resources supporting the transactions.
- Performing substantive analytical procedures using disaggregated data. For example, comparing sales and cost of sales by location, line of business or month to expectations developed by the auditor.
- Conducting interviews of personnel involved in areas where a risk of material misstatement due to fraud has been identified, to obtain their insights about the risk and whether, or how, controls address the risk.
- When other independent auditors are auditing the financial statements of one or more subsidiaries, divisions or branches, discussing with them the extent of work necessary to be performed to address the assessed risk of material misstatement due to fraud resulting from transactions and activities among these components.
- If the work of an expert becomes particularly significant with respect to a financial statement item for which the assessed risk of misstatement due to fraud is high, performing additional procedures relating to some or all of the expert's assumptions, methods or findings to determine that the findings are not unreasonable, or engaging another expert for that purpose.
- Performing audit procedures to analyze selected opening balance sheet accounts of previously audited financial statements to assess how certain issues involving accounting estimates and judgments, for example, an allowance for sales returns, were resolved with the benefit of hindsight.

- Performing procedures on account or other reconciliations prepared by the entity, including considering reconciliations performed at interim periods.
- Performing computer-assisted techniques, such as data mining to test for anomalies in a population.
- Testing the integrity of computer-produced records and transactions.
- Seeking additional audit evidence from sources outside of the entity being audited.

Specific Responses—Misstatement Resulting from Fraudulent Financial Reporting

Examples of responses to the auditor's assessment of the risks of material misstatement due to fraudulent financial reporting are as follows:

Revenue Recognition

- Performing substantive analytical procedures relating to revenue using disaggregated data, for example, comparing revenue reported by month and by product line or business segment during the current reporting period with comparable prior periods. Computer-assisted audit techniques may be useful in identifying unusual or unexpected revenue relationships or transactions.
- Confirming with customers certain relevant contract terms and the absence of side agreements, because the appropriate accounting often is influenced by such terms or agreements and basis for rebates or the period to which they relate are often poorly documented. For example, acceptance criteria, delivery and payment terms, the absence of future or continuing vendor obligations, the right to return the product, guaranteed resale amounts, and cancellation or refund provisions often are relevant in such circumstances.
- Inquiring of the entity's sales and marketing personnel or in-house legal counsel regarding sales or shipments near the end of the period and their knowledge of any unusual terms or conditions associated with these transactions.
- Being physically present at one or more locations at period end to observe goods being shipped or being readied for shipment (or returns awaiting processing) and performing other appropriate sales and inventory cutoff procedures.
- For those situations for which revenue transactions are electronically initiated, processed, and recorded, testing controls to determine whether they provide assurance that recorded revenue transactions occurred and are properly recorded.

Inventory Quantities

- Examining the entity's inventory records to identify locations or items that require specific attention during or after the physical inventory count.
- Observing inventory counts at certain locations on an unannounced basis or conducting inventory counts at all locations on the same date.
- Conducting inventory counts at or near the end of the reporting period to minimize the risk of inappropriate manipulation during the period between the count and the end of the reporting period.
- Performing additional procedures during the observation of the count, for example, more rigorously examining the contents of boxed items, the manner in which the goods are stacked (for example, hollow squares) or labeled, and the quality (that is, purity, grade, or concentration) of liquid substances such as perfumes or specialty chemicals. Using the work of an expert may be helpful in this regard.
- Comparing the quantities for the current period with prior periods by class or category of inventory, location or other criteria, or comparison of quantities counted with perpetual records.

- Using computer-assisted audit techniques to further test the compilation of the physical inventory counts – for example, sorting by tag number to test tag controls or by item serial number to test the possibility of item omission or duplication.

Management Estimates

- Using an expert to develop an independent estimate for comparison to management's estimate.
- Extending inquiries to individuals outside of management and the accounting department to corroborate management's ability and intent to carry out plans that are relevant to developing the estimate.

Specific Responses—Misstatements Due to Misappropriation of Assets

Differing circumstances would necessarily dictate different responses. Ordinarily, the audit response to an assessed risk of material misstatement due to fraud relating to misappropriation of assets will be directed toward certain account balances and classes of transactions. Although some of the audit responses noted in the two categories above may apply in such circumstances, the scope of the work is to be linked to the specific information about the misappropriation risk that has been identified.

Examples of responses to the auditor's assessment of the risk of material misstatements due to misappropriation of assets are as follows:

- Counting cash or securities at or near year-end.
- Confirming directly with customers the account activity (including credit memo and sales return activity as well as dates payments were made) for the period under audit.
- Analyzing recoveries of written-off accounts.
- Analyzing inventory shortages by location or product type.
- Comparing key inventory ratios to industry norm.
- Reviewing supporting documentation for reductions to the perpetual inventory records.
- Performing a computerized match of the vendor list with a list of employees to identify matches of addresses or phone numbers.
- Performing a computerized search of payroll records to identify duplicate addresses, employee identification or taxing authority numbers or bank accounts.
- Reviewing personnel files for those that contain little or no evidence of activity, for example, lack of performance evaluations.
- Analyzing sales discounts and returns for unusual patterns or trends.
- Confirming specific terms of contracts with third parties.
- Obtaining evidence that contracts are being carried out in accordance with their terms.
- Reviewing the propriety of large and unusual expenses.
- Reviewing the authorization and carrying value of senior management and related party loans.
- Reviewing the level and propriety of expense reports submitted by senior management.

Appendix 3

(Ref: Para. A49)

Examples of Circumstances that Indicate the Possibility of Fraud

The following are examples of circumstances that may indicate the possibility that the financial statements may contain a material misstatement resulting from fraud.

Discrepancies in the accounting records, including:

- Transactions that are not recorded in a complete or timely manner or are improperly recorded as to amount, accounting period, classification, or entity policy.
- Unsupported or unauthorized balances or transactions.
- Last-minute adjustments that significantly affect financial results.
- Evidence of employees' access to systems and records inconsistent with that necessary to perform their authorized duties.
- Tips or complaints to the auditor about alleged fraud.

Conflicting or missing evidence, including:

- Missing documents.
- Documents that appear to have been altered.
- Unavailability of other than photocopied or electronically transmitted documents when documents in original form are expected to exist.
- Significant unexplained items on reconciliations.
- Unusual balance sheet changes, or changes in trends or important financial statement ratios or relationships – for example, receivables growing faster than revenues.
- Inconsistent, vague, or implausible responses from management or employees arising from inquiries or analytical procedures.
- Unusual discrepancies between the entity's records and confirmation replies.
- Large numbers of credit entries and other adjustments made to accounts receivable records.
- Unexplained or inadequately explained differences between the accounts receivable sub-ledger and the control account, or between the customer statements and the accounts receivable sub-ledger.
- Missing or non-existent cancelled checks in circumstances where cancelled checks are ordinarily returned to the entity with the bank statement.
- Missing inventory or physical assets of significant magnitude.
- Unavailable or missing electronic evidence, inconsistent with the entity's record retention practices or policies.
- Fewer responses to confirmations than anticipated or a greater number of responses than anticipated.
- Inability to produce evidence of key systems development and program change testing and implementation activities for current-year system changes and deployments.

Problematic or unusual relationships between the auditor and management, including:

- Denial of access to records, facilities, certain employees, customers, vendors, or others from whom audit evidence might be sought.
- Undue time pressures imposed by management to resolve complex or contentious issues.
- Complaints by management about the conduct of the audit or management intimidation of engagement team members, particularly in connection with the auditor's critical assessment of audit evidence or in the resolution of potential disagreements with management.

- Unusual delays by the entity in providing requested information.
- Unwillingness to facilitate auditor access to key electronic files for testing through the use of computer-assisted audit techniques.
- Denial of access to key IT operations staff and facilities, including security, operations, and systems development personnel.
- An unwillingness to add or revise disclosures in the financial statements to make them more complete and understandable.
- An unwillingness to address identified deficiencies in internal control on a timely basis.

Other

- Unwillingness by management to permit the auditor to meet privately with those charged with governance.
- Accounting policies that appear to be at variance with industry norms.
- Frequent changes in accounting estimates that do not appear to result from changed circumstances.
- Tolerance of violations of the entity's code of conduct.

International Standard on Auditing (UK) 250 (Revised December 2017)

Section A – Consideration of laws and regulations in an audit of financial statements

(Effective for audits of financial statements for periods commencing on or after 15 December 2017)

Contents

International Standard on Auditing (UK) (ISA (UK)) 250 (Revised December 2017), *Section A – Consideration of Laws and Regulations in an Audit of Financial Statements*, should be read in conjunction with ISA (UK) 200 (Revised June 2016), *Overall Objectives of the Independent Auditor and the Conduct of an Audit in Accordance with International Standards on Auditing (UK)*.

Introduction

Scope of this ISA (UK)

1   This International Standard on Auditing (UK) (ISA (UK)) deals with the auditor's responsibility to consider laws and regulations in an audit of financial statements. This ISA (UK) does not apply to other assurance engagements in which the auditor is specifically engaged to test and report separately on compliance with specific laws or regulations.

1-1   Guidance on the auditor's responsibility to report direct to regulators of public interest entities and regulators of other entities in the financial sector is provided in Section B of this ISA (UK).[1a]

Effect of Laws and Regulations

2   The effect on financial statements of laws and regulations varies considerably. Those laws and regulations to which an entity is subject constitute the legal and regulatory framework. The provisions of some laws or regulations have a direct effect on the financial statements in that they determine the reported amounts and disclosures in an entity's financial statements. Other laws or regulations are to be complied with by management or set the provisions under which the entity is allowed to conduct its business but do not have a direct effect on an entity's financial statements. Some entities operate in heavily regulated industries (such as banks and chemical companies). Others are subject only to the many laws and regulations that relate generally to the operating aspects of the business (such as those related to occupational safety and health, and equal employment opportunity). Noncompliance with laws and regulations may result in fines, litigation or other consequences for the entity that may have a material effect on the financial statements.

Responsibility for Compliance with Laws and Regulations
(Ref: Para. A1–A8)

3   It is the responsibility of management, with the oversight of those charged with governance, to ensure that the entity's operations are conducted in accordance with the provisions of laws and regulations, including compliance with the provisions of laws and regulations that determine the reported amounts and disclosures in an entity's financial statements.[1b]

Responsibility of the Auditor

4   The requirements in this ISA (UK) are designed to assist the auditor in identifying material misstatement of the financial statements due to non-compliance with laws and regulations. However, the auditor is not responsible for preventing non-compliance and cannot be expected to detect non-compliance with all laws and regulations.

5   The auditor is responsible for obtaining reasonable assurance that the financial statements, taken as a whole, are free from material misstatement, whether due to fraud or error.[1] In

---

[1a] *ISA (UK) 250 (Revised June 2016)*, Section B – *The Auditor's Statutory Right and Duty to Report to Regulators of Public Interest Entities and Regulators of Other Entities in the Financial Sector.*

[1b] *In the UK, those charged with governance are responsible for the preparation of the financial statements.*

[1] *ISA (UK) 200 (Revised June 2016)*, Overall Objectives of the Independent Auditor and the Conduct of an Audit in Accordance with International Standards on Auditing (UK), *paragraph 5.*

conducting an audit of financial statements, the auditor takes into account the applicable legal and regulatory framework. Owing to the inherent limitations of an audit, there is an unavoidable risk that some material misstatements in the financial statements may not be detected, even though the audit is properly planned and performed in accordance with the ISAs (UK).[2] In the context of laws and regulations, the potential effects of inherent limitations on the auditor's ability to detect material misstatements are greater for such reasons as the following:

- There are many laws and regulations, relating principally to the operating aspects of an entity, that typically do not affect the financial statements and are not captured by the entity's information systems relevant to financial reporting.
- Non-compliance may involve conduct designed to conceal it, such as collusion, forgery, deliberate failure to record transactions, management override of controls or intentional misrepresentations being made to the auditor.
- Whether an act constitutes non-compliance is ultimately a matter to be determined by a court or other appropriate adjudicative body.

Ordinarily, the further removed non-compliance is from the events and transactions reflected in the financial statements, the less likely the auditor is to become aware of it or to recognize the non-compliance.

This ISA (UK) distinguishes the auditor's responsibilities in relation to compliance with two different categories of laws and regulations as follows: (Ref: Para. A6, A12–A13)   **6**

(a) The provisions of those laws and regulations generally recognized to have a direct effect on the determination of material amounts and disclosures in the financial statements such as tax and pension laws and regulations (see paragraph 14) (Ref: Para. A12); and

(b) Other laws and regulations that do not have a direct effect on the determination of the amounts and disclosures in the financial statements, but compliance with which may be fundamental to the operating aspects of the business, to an entity's ability to continue its business, or to avoid material penalties (e.g., compliance with the terms of an operating license, compliance with regulatory solvency requirements, or compliance with environmental regulations); non-compliance with such laws and regulations may therefore have a material effect on the financial statements (see paragraph 15) (Ref: Para. A13).

In this ISA (UK), differing requirements are specified for each of the above categories of laws and regulations. For the category referred to in paragraph 6(a), the auditor's responsibility is to obtain sufficient appropriate audit evidence regarding compliance with the provisions of those laws and regulations. For the category referred to in paragraph 6(b), the auditor's responsibility is limited to undertaking specified audit procedures to help identify non-compliance with those laws and regulations that may have a material effect on the financial statements.   **7**

The auditor is required by this ISA (UK) to remain alert to the possibility that other audit procedures applied for the purpose of forming an opinion on financial statements may bring instances of non-compliance to the auditor's attention. Maintaining professional skepticism throughout the audit, as required by ISA (UK) 200 (Revised June 2016),[3] is important in this context, given the extent of laws and regulations that affect the entity.   **8**

---

[2] *ISA (UK) 200 (Revised June 2016), paragraph A51.*

[3] *ISA (UK) 200 (Revised June 2016), paragraph 15.*

9   The auditor may have additional responsibilities under law, regulation or relevant ethical requirements regarding an entity's non-compliance with laws and regulations, which may differ from or go beyond this ISA (UK), such as: (Ref: Para. A8)

   (a)   Responding to identified or suspected non-compliance with laws and regulations, including requirements in relation to specific communications with management and those charged with governance, assessing the appropriateness of their response to non-compliance and determining whether further action is needed;

   (b)   Communicating identified or suspected non-compliance with laws and regulations to other auditors (e.g., in an audit of group financial statements); and

   (c)   Documentation requirements regarding identified or suspected non-compliance with laws and regulations.

Complying with any additional responsibilities may provide further information that is relevant to the auditor's work in accordance with this and other ISAs (UK) (e.g., regarding the integrity of management or, where appropriate, those charged with governance).

Effective Date

10   This ISA (UK) is effective for audits of financial statements for periods commencing on or after 15 December 2017.

Objectives

11   The objectives of the auditor are:

   (a)   To obtain sufficient appropriate audit evidence regarding compliance with the provisions of those laws and regulations generally recognized to have a direct effect on the determination of material amounts and disclosures in the financial statements;

   (b)   To perform specified audit procedures to help identify instances of non-compliance with other laws and regulations that may have a material effect on the financial statements; and

   (c)   To respond appropriately to identified or suspected non-compliance with laws and regulations identified during the audit.

Definition

12   For the purposes of this ISA (UK), the following term has the meaning attributed below:

   Non-compliance – Acts of omission or commission intentional or unintentional, committed by the entity, or by those charged with governance, by management or by other individuals working for or under the direction of the entity, which are contrary to the prevailing laws or regulations. Non-compliance does not include personal misconduct unrelated to the business activities of the entity. (Ref: Para. A9–A10)

Requirements

The Auditor's Consideration of Compliance with Laws and Regulations

13   As part of obtaining an understanding of the entity and its environment in accordance with ISA (UK) 315 (Revised June 2016),[4] the auditor shall obtain a general understanding of:

---

[4] *ISA (UK) 315 (Revised June 2016)*, Identifying and Assessing the Risks of Material Misstatement through Understanding the Entity and Its Environment, *paragraph 11.*

(a)   The legal and regulatory framework applicable to the entity and the industry or sector in which the entity operates; and

(b)   How the entity is complying with that framework. (Ref: Para. A11)

The auditor shall obtain sufficient appropriate audit evidence regarding compliance with the provisions of those laws and regulations generally recognized to have a direct effect on the determination of material amounts and disclosures in the financial statements. (Ref: Para. A12–A12-1)   **14**

The auditor shall perform the following audit procedures to help identify instances of non-compliance with other laws and regulations that may have a material effect on the financial statements: (Ref: Para. A13–A14-1)   **15**

(a)   Inquiring of management and, where appropriate, those charged with governance, as to whether the entity is in compliance with such laws and regulations; and

(b)   Inspecting correspondence, if any, with the relevant licensing or regulatory authorities.

During the audit, the auditor shall remain alert to the possibility that other audit procedures applied may bring instances of non-compliance or suspected non-compliance with laws and regulations to the auditor's attention. (Ref: Para. A15)   **16**

The auditor shall request management and, where appropriate, those charged with governance to provide written representations that all known instances of non-compliance or suspected non-compliance with laws and regulations whose effects should be considered when preparing financial statements have been disclosed to the auditor. (Ref: Para. A16)   **17**

In the absence of identified or suspected non-compliance, the auditor is not required to perform audit procedures regarding the entity's compliance with laws and regulations, other than those set out in paragraphs 13–17.   **18**

Audit Procedures When Non-Compliance Is Identified or Suspected

If the auditor becomes aware of information concerning an instance of non-compliance or suspected non-compliance with laws and regulations, the auditor shall obtain: (Ref: Para. A17–A18)   **19**

(a)   An understanding of the nature of the act and the circumstances in which it has occurred; and

(b)   Further information to evaluate the possible effect on the financial statements. (Ref: Para. A19)

If the auditor suspects there may be non-compliance, the auditor shall discuss the matter, unless prohibited by law or regulation, with the appropriate level of management and, where appropriate, those charged with governance. If management or, as appropriate, those charged with governance do not provide sufficient information that supports that the entity is in compliance with laws and regulations and, in the auditor's judgment, the effect of the suspected non-compliance may be material to the financial statements, the auditor shall consider the need to obtain legal advice. (Ref: Para. A20–A22)   **20**

If sufficient information about suspected non-compliance cannot be obtained, the auditor shall evaluate the effect of the lack of sufficient appropriate audit evidence on the auditor's opinion.   **21**

The auditor shall evaluate the implications of identified or suspected non-compliance in relation to other aspects of the audit, including the auditor's risk assessment and the reliability of written representations, and take appropriate action. (Ref: Para. A23–A25-2)   **22**

Communicating and Reporting Identified or Suspected Non-Compliance

Communicating Identified or Suspected Non-Compliance with Those Charged with Governance

23   Unless all of those charged with governance are involved in management of the entity, and therefore are aware of matters involving identified or suspected non-compliance already communicated by the auditor,[5] the auditor shall communicate, unless prohibited by law or regulation, with those charged with governance matters involving non-compliance with laws and regulations that come to the auditor's attention during the course of the audit, other than when the matters are clearly inconsequential.

23R-1   For audits of financial statements of public interest entities, when an auditor suspects or has reasonable grounds to suspect that irregularities, including fraud with regard to the financial statements of the entity, may occur or have occurred, the auditor shall, unless prohibited by law or regulation, inform the entity and invite it to investigate the matter and take appropriate measures to deal with such irregularities and to prevent any recurrence of such irregularities in the future. (Ref: Para. A25-3–A25-4)

24   If, in the auditor's judgment, the non-compliance referred to in paragraph 23 is believed to be intentional and material, the auditor shall communicate the matter with those charged with governance as soon as practicable. (Ref: Para. A25-5)

25   If the auditor suspects that management or those charged with governance are involved in non-compliance, the auditor shall communicate the matter to the next higher level of authority at the entity, if it exists, such as an audit committee or supervisory board. Where no higher authority exists, or if the auditor believes that the communication may not be acted upon or is unsure as to the person to whom to report, the auditor shall consider the need to obtain legal advice. (Ref: Para. A25-6)

Potential Implications of Identified or Suspected Non-Compliance for the Auditor's Report on the Financial Statements (Ref: Para. A26–27-1)

26   If the auditor concludes that the identified or suspected non-compliance has a material effect on the financial statements, and has not been adequately reflected in the financial statements, the auditor shall, in accordance with ISA (UK) 705 (Revised June 2016), express a qualified opinion or an adverse opinion on the financial statements.[6]

27   If the auditor is precluded by management or those charged with governance from obtaining sufficient appropriate audit evidence to evaluate whether non-compliance that may be material to the financial statements has, or is likely to have, occurred, the auditor shall express a qualified opinion or disclaim an opinion on the financial statements on the basis of a limitation on the scope of the audit in accordance with ISA (UK) 705 (Revised June 2016).[7]

28   If the auditor is unable to determine whether non-compliance has occurred because of limitations imposed by the circumstances rather than by management or those charged

---

[5] *ISA (UK) 260 (Revised June 2016),* Communication with Those Charged with Governance, *paragraph 13.*

[6] *ISA (UK) 705 (Revised June 2016),* Modifications to the Opinion in the Independent Auditor's Report, *paragraphs 7–8.*

[7] *ISA (UK) 705 (Revised June 2016), paragraphs 7 and 9.*

with governance, the auditor shall evaluate the effect on the auditor's opinion in accordance with ISA (UK) 705 (Revised June 2016). (Ref: Para. A27-1)

Reporting Identified or Suspected Non-Compliance to an Appropriate Authority Outside the Entity

If the auditor has identified or suspects non-compliance with laws and regulations, **29** the auditor shall determine whether law, regulation or relevant ethical requirements: (Ref: Para. A28–A34-1)

(a) Require the auditor to report to an appropriate authority outside the entity.

(b) Establish responsibilities under which reporting to an appropriate authority outside the entity may be appropriate in the circumstances.

For audits of financial statements of public interest entities, where the entity does **29R-1** not investigate the matter referred to in paragraph 23R-1, the auditor shall inform the authorities responsible for investigating such irregularities. (Ref: Para. A34-2–A34-3)

Documentation

The auditor shall include in the audit documentation[8] identified or suspected non- **30** compliance with laws and regulations and: (Ref: Para. A35–A36)

(a) The audit procedures performed, the significant professional judgments made and the conclusions reached thereon; and

(b) The discussions of significant matters related to the non-compliance with management, those charged with governance and others, including how management and, where applicable, those charged with governance have responded to the matter.

***

Application and Other Explanatory Material

Responsibility for Compliance with Laws and Regulations (Ref: Para. 3–9)

It is the responsibility of management, with the oversight of those charged with governance, **A1** to ensure that the entity's operations are conducted in accordance with laws and regulations. Laws and regulations may affect an entity's financial statements in different ways: for example, most directly, they may affect specific disclosures required of the entity in the financial statements or they may prescribe the applicable financial reporting framework. They may also establish certain legal rights and obligations of the entity, some of which will be recognized in the entity's financial statements. In addition, laws and regulations may impose penalties in cases of non

The following are examples of the types of policies and procedures an entity may implement **A2** to assist in the prevention and detection of non-compliance with laws and regulations:

● Monitoring legal requirements and ensuring that operating procedures are designed to meet these requirements.

● Instituting and operating appropriate systems of internal control.

● Developing, publicizing and following a code of conduct.

● Ensuring employees are properly trained and understand the code of conduct.

---

[8] *ISA (UK) 230 (Revised June 2016),* Audit Documentation, *paragraphs 8–11, and A6.*

- Monitoring compliance with the code of conduct and acting appropriately to discipline employees who fail to comply with it.
- Engaging legal advisors to assist in monitoring legal requirements.
- Maintaining a register of significant laws and regulations with which the entity has to comply within its particular industry and a record of complaints.

In larger entities, these policies and procedures may be supplemented by assigning appropriate responsibilities to the following:

- An internal audit function.
- An audit committee.
- A compliance function.

A2-1   In the UK, in certain sectors or activities (e.g., financial services), there are detailed laws and regulations that specifically require directors to have systems to ensure compliance. Non-compliance with these laws and regulations could have a material effect on the financial statements.

A2-2   In the UK, the directors are responsible for the preparation of financial statements that give a true and fair view. Accordingly it is necessary, where identified or suspected non-compliance with laws and regulations has occurred which may result in a material misstatement in the financial statements, for the directors to ensure that the matter is appropriately reflected and/or disclosed in the financial statements.

A2-3   In the UK, directors and officers of companies have responsibility to provide information required by the auditor, to which they have a legal right of access.[8a] Such legislation also provides that it is a criminal offence to give to the auditor information or explanations which are misleading, false or deceptive.

Responsibility of the Auditor

A3   Non-compliance by the entity with laws and regulations may result in a material misstatement of the financial statements. Detection of non-compliance, regardless of materiality, may affect other aspects of the audit including, for example, the auditor's consideration of the integrity of management, those charged with governance or employees.

A4   Whether an act constitutes non-compliance with laws and regulations is a matter to be determined by a court or other appropriate adjudicative body, which is ordinarily beyond the auditor's professional competence to determine. Nevertheless, the auditor's training, experience and understanding of the entity and its industry or sector may provide a basis to recognize that some acts, coming to the auditor's attention, may constitute non-compliance with laws and regulations.

A5   In accordance with specific statutory requirements, the auditor may be specifically required to report, as part of the audit of the financial statements, on whether the entity complies with certain provisions of laws or regulations. In these circumstances, ISA (UK) 700 (Revised June 2016)[9] or ISA (UK) 800 (Revised)[10] deal with how these audit responsibilities are

---

[8a] *In the UK, under Section 499 of the Companies Act 2006.*

[9] *ISA (UK) 700 (Revised June 2016),* Forming an Opinion and Reporting on Financial Statements, *paragraph 43.*

[10] *ISA (UK) 800 (Revised)* Special Considerations – Audits of Financial Statements Prepared in Accordance with Special Purpose Frameworks, *paragraph 11.*

addressed in the auditor's report. Furthermore, where there are specific statutory reporting requirements, it may be necessary for the audit plan to include appropriate tests for compliance with these provisions of the laws and regulations.

Categories of Laws and Regulations (Ref: Para. 6)

The nature and circumstances of the entity may impact whether relevant laws and regulations are within the categories of laws and regulations described in paragraphs 6(a) or 6(b). Examples of laws and regulations that may be included in the categories described in paragraph 6 include those that deal with: **A6**

- Fraud, corruption and bribery.
- Money laundering,[10a] terrorist financing and proceeds of crime.
- Securities markets and trading.
- Banking and other financial products and services.
- Data protection.
- Tax and pension liabilities and payments.
- Environmental protection.
- Public health and safety.

In the UK, legislation relating to money laundering, terrorist financing and proceeds of crime imposes additional responsibilities on the auditor. The Appendix contains further guidance on these responsibilities. **A6-1**

Considerations Specific to Public Sector Entities

In the public sector, there may be additional audit responsibilities with respect to the consideration of laws and regulations which may relate to the audit of financial statements or may extend to other aspects of the entity's operations. **A7**

Additional Responsibilities Established by Law, Regulation or Relevant Ethical Requirements (Ref: Para. 9)

Law, regulation or relevant ethical requirements may require the auditor to perform additional procedures and take further actions. For example, the Code of Ethics for Professional Accountants issued by the International Ethics Standards Board for Accountants (IESBA Code) requires the auditor to take steps to respond to identified or suspected non-compliance with laws and regulations and determine whether further action is needed. Such steps may include the communication of identified or suspected non-compliance with laws and regulations to other auditors within a group, including a group engagement partner, component auditors or other auditors performing work at components of a group for purposes other than the audit of the group financial statements.[11] **A8**

Definition (Ref: Para. 12)

Acts of non-compliance with laws and regulations include transactions entered into by, or in the name of, the entity, or on its behalf, by those charged with governance, by management or by other individuals working for or under the direction of the entity. **A9**

[10a] *'Money laundering' is defined in UK legislation and in general terms involves an act which conceals, disguises, converts, transfers, removes, uses, acquires or possesses property resulting from criminal conduct.*

[11] *See Sections 225.21–225.22 of the IESBA Code.*
In the UK, the auditor has regard to any specific requirements of the auditor's relevant professional body.

A10 Non-compliance also includes personal misconduct related to the business activities of the entity, for example, in circumstances where an individual in a key management position, in a personal capacity, has accepted a bribe from a supplier of the entity and in return secures the appointment of the supplier to provide services or contracts to the entity.

The Auditor's Consideration of Compliance with Laws and Regulations

Obtaining an Understanding of the Legal and Regulatory Framework (Ref: Para. 13)

A11 To obtain a general understanding of the legal and regulatory framework, and how the entity complies with that framework, the auditor may, for example:

- Use the auditor's existing understanding of the entity's industry, regulatory and other external factors;
- Update the understanding of those laws and regulations that directly determine the reported amounts and disclosures in the financial statements;
- Inquire of management as to other laws or regulations that may be expected to have a fundamental effect on the operations of the entity;
- Inquire of management concerning the entity's policies and procedures regarding compliance with laws and regulations; and
- Inquire of management regarding the policies or procedures adopted for identifying, evaluating and accounting for litigation claims.

Laws and Regulations Generally Recognized to Have a Direct Effect on the Determination of Material Amounts and Disclosures in the Financial Statements (Ref: Para. 6, 14)

A12 Certain laws and regulations are well-established, known to the entity and within the entity's industry or sector, and relevant to the entity's financial statements (as described in paragraph 6(a)). They could include those that relate to, for example:

- The form and content of financial statements;[11a]
- Industry-specific financial reporting issues;
- Accounting for transactions under government contracts; or
- The accrual or recognition of expenses for income tax or pension costs.

> In the UK, these laws and regulations include those which:
>
> - Determine the circumstances under which a company is prohibited from making a distribution except out of profits available for the purpose.[11b]
> - Require auditors expressly to report non-compliance, such as the requirements relating to the maintenance of adequate accounting records[11c] or the disclosure of particulars of directors' remuneration in a company's financial statements.[11d]

[11a] *In the UK, under The Small Companies and Groups (Accounts and Directors' Report) Regulations 2008 (SI 2008 No. 409) and The Large and Medium-sized Companies and Groups (Accounts and Reports) Regulations 2008 (SI 2008 No. 410).*

[11b] *In the UK, under Section 830 of the Companies Act 2006.*

[11c] *In the UK, under Section 498 of the Companies Act 2006.*

[11d] *In the UK, under Section 497 of the Companies Act 2006.*

Some provisions in those laws and regulations may be directly relevant to specific assertions in the financial statements (e.g., the completeness of income tax provisions), while others may be directly relevant to the financial statements as a whole (e.g., the required statements constituting a complete set of financial statements). The aim of the requirement in paragraph 14 is for the auditor to obtain sufficient appropriate audit evidence regarding the determination of amounts and disclosures in the financial statements in compliance with the relevant provisions of those laws and regulations.

Non-compliance with other provisions of such laws and regulations and other laws and regulations may result in fines, litigation or other consequences for the entity, the costs of which may need to be provided for in the financial statements, but are not considered to have a direct effect on the financial statements as described in paragraph 6(a).

In the UK, the auditor's responsibility to express an opinion on an entity's financial statements does not extend to determining whether the entity has complied in every respect with applicable tax legislation. The auditor needs to obtain sufficient appropriate evidence to give reasonable assurance that the amounts included in the financial statements in respect of taxation are not materially misstated. This will usually include making appropriate enquiries of those advising the entity on taxation matters (whether within the firm or elsewhere). If the auditor becomes aware that the entity has failed to comply with the requirements of tax legislation, the auditor considers whether to report the matter to an appropriate authority outside the entity.   **A12-1**

Procedures to Identify Instances of Non-Compliance – Other Laws and Regulations
(Ref: Para. 6, 15)

Certain other laws and regulations may need particular attention by the auditor because they have a fundamental effect on the operations of the entity (as described in paragraph 6(b)). Non-compliance with laws and regulations that have a fundamental effect on the operations of the entity may cause the entity to cease operations, or call into question the entity's continuance as a going concern.[12] For example, non-compliance with the requirements of the entity's license or other entitlement to perform its operations could have such an impact (e.g., for a bank, non-compliance with capital or investment requirements).[12a] There are also many laws and regulations relating principally to the operating aspects of the entity that typically do not affect the financial statements and are not captured by the entity's information systems relevant to financial reporting.   **A13**

As the financial reporting consequences of other laws and regulations can vary depending on the entity's operations, the audit procedures required by paragraph 15 are directed to bringing to the auditor's attention instances of non-compliance with laws and regulations that may have a material effect on the financial statements.   **A14**

When determining the type of procedures necessary in a particular instance the auditor takes account of the particular entity concerned and the complexity of the law and regulations with which it is required to comply. In general, a small entity which does not operate in a regulated area will require few specific procedures compared with a large multinational corporation carrying on complex, regulated business.   **A14-1**

---

[12] *See ISA (UK) 570 (Revised June 2016),* Going Concern.

[12a] *Such requirements exist in the UK under the Financial Services and Markets Act 2000.*

Non-Compliance Brought to the Auditor's Attention by Other Audit Procedures
(Ref: Para. 16)

A15   Audit procedures applied to form an opinion on the financial statements may bring instances of non-compliance or suspected non-compliance with laws and regulations to the auditor's attention. For example, such audit procedures may include:

- Reading minutes;
- Inquiring of the entity's management and in-house legal counsel or external legal counsel concerning litigation, claims and assessments; and
- Performing substantive tests of details of classes of transactions, account balances or disclosures.

Written Representations (Ref: Para. 17)

A16   Because the effect on financial statements of laws and regulations can vary considerably, written representations provide necessary audit evidence about management's knowledge of identified or suspected non-compliance with laws and regulations, whose effects may have a material effect on the financial statements. However, written representations do not provide sufficient appropriate audit evidence on their own and, accordingly, do not affect the nature and extent of other audit evidence that is to be obtained by the auditor.[13]

Audit Procedures When Non-Compliance Is Identified or Suspected

Indications of Non-Compliance with Laws and Regulations (Ref: Para. 19)

A17   The auditor may become aware of information concerning an instance of non-compliance with laws and regulations other than as a result of performing the procedures in paragraphs 13–17 (e.g., when the auditor is alerted to non-compliance by a whistle blower).

A18   The following matters may be an indication of non-compliance with laws and regulations:

- Investigations by regulatory organizations and government departments or payment of fines or penalties.
- Payments for unspecified services or loans to consultants, related parties, employees or government employees.
- Sales commissions or agent's fees that appear excessive in relation to those ordinarily paid by the entity or in its industry or to the services actually received.
- Purchasing at prices significantly above or below market price.
- Unusual payments in cash, purchases in the form of cashiers' cheques payable to bearer or transfers to numbered bank accounts.
- Unusual transactions with companies registered in tax havens.
- Payments for goods or services made other than to the country from which the goods or services originated.
- Payments without proper exchange control documentation.
- Existence of an information system which fails, whether by design or by accident, to provide an adequate audit trail or sufficient evidence.
- Unauthorized transactions or improperly recorded transactions.
- Adverse media comment.

---

[13] *ISA (UK) 580*, Written Representations, *paragraph 4.*

Matters Relevant to the Auditor's Evaluation (Ref: Para. 19(b))

Matters relevant to the auditor's evaluation[13a] of the possible effect on the financial   **A19**
statements include:

- The potential financial consequences of identified or suspected non-compliance with laws and regulations on the financial statements including, for example, the imposition of fines, penalties, damages, threat of expropriation of assets,[13b] enforced discontinuation of operations, and litigation.
- Whether the potential financial consequences require disclosure.
- Whether the potential financial consequences are so serious as to call into question the fair presentation of the financial statements, or otherwise make the financial statements misleading.

Audit Procedures and Communicating Identified or Suspected Non-Compliance with Management and Those Charged with Governance (Ref: Para. 20)

The auditor is required to discuss the suspected non-compliance with the appropriate   **A20**
level of management and, where appropriate, with those charged with governance, as they may be able to provide additional audit evidence. For example, the auditor may confirm that management and, where appropriate, those charged with governance have the same understanding of the facts and circumstances relevant to transactions or events that have led to the suspected non-compliance with laws and regulations.

However, in some jurisdictions, law or regulation may restrict the auditor's communication   **A21**
of certain matters with management and those charged with governance. Law or regulation may specifically prohibit a communication, or other action, that might prejudice an investigation by an appropriate authority into an actual, or suspected, illegal act, including alerting the entity, for example, when the auditor is required to report the identified or suspected non-compliance to an appropriate authority pursuant to anti-money laundering legislation. In these circumstances, the issues considered by the auditor may be complex and the auditor may consider it appropriate to obtain legal advice.

In the UK, the auditor is subject to compliance with legislation relating to 'tipping off'.   **A21-1**
'Tipping off' is an offence under Section 333A of the Proceeds of Crime Act 2002 (POCA). It arises when an individual discloses that:

(a) A report (internal or external) has already been made where the disclosure by the individual is likely to prejudice an investigation which might be conducted following the internal or external report that has been made; or

(b) An investigation is being contemplated or is being carried out into allegations that a money laundering offence has been committed and the disclosure by the individual is likely to prejudice that investigation.

Whilst 'tipping off' requires a person to have knowledge or suspicion that a report has been or will be made, a further offence of prejudicing an investigation is included in Section 342 of the POCA. Under this provision, it is an offence to make any disclosure which may prejudice an investigation of which a person has knowledge or suspicion, or

---

[13a] *ISA (UK) 620 (Revised June 2016),* Using the Work of an Auditor's Expert *applies if the auditor judges it necessary to obtain appropriate expert advice in connection with the evaluation of the possible effect of legal matters on the financial statements.*

[13b] *In the UK, the Proceeds of Crime Act 2002 provides procedures to enable the authorities to confiscate in criminal proceedings or bring an action for civil recovery of assets which represent the benefits of criminal conduct.*

to falsify, conceal, destroy or otherwise dispose of, or cause or permit the falsification, concealment, destruction or disposal of, documents relevant to such an investigation.

The disclosure offences under Sections 333A and 342 of the POCA are not committed if the person disclosing does not know or suspect that it is likely to prejudice an investigation.

A22   If management or, as appropriate, those charged with governance do not provide sufficient information to the auditor that the entity is in fact in compliance with laws and regulations, the auditor may consider it appropriate to consult with the entity's in-house or external legal counsel about the application of the laws and regulations to the circumstances, including the possibility of fraud, and the possible effects on the financial statements. If it is not considered appropriate to consult with the entity's legal counsel or if the auditor is not satisfied with the legal counsel's opinion, the auditor may consider it appropriate to consult on a confidential basis with others within the firm, a network firm, a professional body, or with the auditor's legal counsel as to whether a contravention of a law or regulation is involved, including the possibility of fraud, the possible legal consequences, and what further action, if any, the auditor would take.

Evaluating the Implications of Identified or Suspected Non-Compliance (Ref: Para. 22)

A23   As required by paragraph 22, the auditor evaluates the implications of identified or suspected non-compliance in relation to other aspects of the audit, including the auditor's risk assessment and the reliability of written representations. The implications of particular identified or suspected non-compliance will depend on the relationship of the perpetration and concealment, if any, of the act to specific control activities and the level of management or individuals working for, or under the direction of, the entity involved, especially implications arising from the involvement of the highest authority within the entity. As noted in paragraph 9, the auditor's compliance with law, regulation or relevant ethical requirements may provide further information that is relevant to the auditor's responsibilities in accordance with paragraph 22.

A24   Examples of circumstances that may cause the auditor to evaluate the implications of identified or suspected non-compliance on the reliability of written representations received from management and, where applicable, those charged with governance include when:

- The auditor suspects or has evidence of the involvement or intended involvement of management and, where applicable, those charged with governance in any identified or suspected non-compliance.
- The auditor is aware that management and, where applicable, those charged with governance have knowledge of such non-compliance and, contrary to legal or regulatory requirements, have not reported, or authorized reporting of, the matter to an appropriate authority within a reasonable period.

A25   In certain circumstances, the auditor may consider withdrawing from the engagement, where permitted by law or regulation, for example when management or those charged with governance do not take the remedial action that the auditor considers appropriate in the circumstances or the identified or suspected non-compliance raises questions regarding the integrity of management or those charged with governance, even when the non-compliance is not material to the financial statements. The auditor may consider it appropriate to obtain legal advice to determine whether withdrawal from the engagement is appropriate. When the auditor determines that withdrawing from the engagement would be appropriate, doing so would not be a substitute for complying with other responsibilities under law, regulation or relevant ethical requirements to respond to identified or suspected non-compliance. Furthermore, paragraph A8a of ISA (UK) 220 (Revised June 2016)[14] indicates that some ethical requirements may require the predecessor auditor, upon request by the proposed successor auditor, to provide information regarding non-compliance with laws and regulations to the successor auditor.

Withdrawal from the engagement by the auditor is a step of last resort. It is normally preferable for the auditor to remain in office to fulfil the auditor's statutory duties, particularly where minority interests are involved. However, there are circumstances where there may be no alternative to withdrawal, for example, where the directors of a company refuse to issue its financial statements or the auditor wishes to inform the shareholders or creditors of the company of the auditor's concerns and there is no immediate occasion to do so.   **A25-1**

If the auditor determines that continued holding of office is untenable or the auditor is removed from office by the entity, the auditor will be mindful of the auditor's reporting duties.[14a]   **A25-2**

Communicating and Reporting Identified or Suspected Non-Compliance

Communicating Identified or Suspected Non-Compliance with Those Charged with Governance (Ref: Para. 23R-1–24)

For audits of financial statements of public interest entities, ISA (UK) 260 (Revised June 2016)[14b] requires the auditor to communicate in the additional report to the audit committee any significant matters involving actual or suspected non-compliance with laws and regulations or articles of association which were identified in the course of the audit.   **A25-3**

In the UK, laws or regulations may prohibit alerting ('tipping off') the entity when, for example, the auditor is required to report the identified or suspected non-compliance with laws and regulations to an appropriate authority outside the entity pursuant to anti-money laundering legislation.   **A25-4**

If non-compliance with laws and regulations is intentional but not material the auditor considers whether the nature and circumstances make it appropriate to communicate the matter with those charged with governance as soon as practicable.   **A25-5**

Suspicion that Management or Those Charged with Governance are Involved in Non-Compliance (Ref: Para. 25)

In the case of suspected money laundering it may be appropriate to report the matter direct to an appropriate authority outside the entity (see paragraph A28).   **A25-6**

---

[14] *ISA (UK) 220 (Revised June 2016)*, Quality Control for an Audit of Financial Statements.

[14a] *In the UK, under Part 16 of the Companies Act 2006.*

[14b] *ISA (UK) 260 (Revised June 2016), paragraph 16R-2(k).*

Potential Implications of Identified or Suspected Non-Compliance for the Auditor's Report (Ref: Para. 26–28)

A26   Identified or suspected non-compliance with laws and regulation is communicated in the auditor's report when the auditor modifies the opinion in accordance with paragraphs 26–28. In certain other circumstances, the auditor may communicate identified or suspected non-compliance in the auditor's report, for example:

- When the auditor has other reporting responsibilities, in addition to the auditor's responsibilities under the ISAs (UK), as contemplated by paragraph 43 of ISA (UK) 700 (Revised June 2016);
- When the auditor determines that the identified or suspected non-compliance is a key audit matter and accordingly communicates the matter in accordance with ISA (UK) 701,[15] unless paragraph 14 of that ISA (UK) applies; or
- In exceptional cases when management or those charged with governance do not take the remedial action that the auditor considers appropriate in the circumstances and withdrawal from the engagement is not possible (see paragraph A25), the auditor may consider describing the identified or suspected non-compliance in an Other Matter paragraph in accordance with ISA (UK) 706 (Revised June 2016).[16]

A26-1   In the UK, if the auditor concludes that the view given by the financial statements could be affected by a level of uncertainty concerning the consequences of identified or suspected non-compliance with laws and regulations which, in the auditor's professional judgment, is significant, the auditor, subject to a consideration of 'tipping off' (see paragraph A21-1), includes an explanatory paragraph referring to the matter in the auditor's report.

A27   Law or regulation may preclude public disclosure by either management, those charged with governance or the auditor about a specific matter. For example, law or regulation may specifically prohibit a communication, or other action, that might prejudice an investigation by an appropriate authority into an actual, or suspected, illegal act, including a prohibition on alerting the entity. When the auditor intends to communicate identified or suspected non-compliance in the auditor's report under the circumstances set out in paragraph A26 or otherwise, such law or regulation may have implications for the auditor's ability to describe the matter in the auditor's report, or in some circumstances to issue the auditor's report. In such cases, the auditor may consider obtaining legal advice to determine the appropriate course of action.

A27-1   In the UK, when considering whether the financial statements reflect the possible consequences of any identified or suspected non-compliance with laws and regulations, the auditor has regard to the requirements of the applicable financial reporting framework. Identified or suspected non-compliance with laws and regulations may require disclosure in the financial statements because, although the immediate financial effect on the entity may not be material,[16a] there could be future material consequences such as fines, litigation or other consequences for the entity. For example, an illegal payment may not itself be material but may result in criminal proceedings against the

---

[15] *ISA (UK) 701*, Communicating Key Audit Matters in the Independent Auditor's Report.

[16] *ISA (UK) 706 (Revised June 2016)*, Emphasis of Matter Paragraphs and Other Matter Paragraphs in the Independent Auditor's Report.

[16a] *As discussed in ISA (UK) 320 (Revised June 2016)*, Materiality in Planning and Performing an Audit, *judgments about materiality are made in light of surrounding circumstances and are affected by the size or nature of a matter or a combination of both.*

entity or loss of business which could have a material effect on the true and fair view given by the financial statements.

Reporting Identified or Suspected Non-Compliance to an Appropriate Authority Outside the Entity (Ref: Para. 29)

Reporting identified or suspected non-compliance with laws and regulations to an appropriate authority outside the entity may be required or appropriate in the circumstances because:

(a) Law, regulation or relevant ethical requirements require the auditor to report (see paragraph A29–A29-3);

(b) The auditor has determined reporting is an appropriate action to respond to identified or suspected non-compliance in accordance with relevant ethical requirements (see paragraph A30); or

(c) Law, regulation or relevant ethical requirements provide the auditor with the right to do so (see paragraph A31).

A28

In some jurisdictions, the auditor may be required by law, regulation or relevant ethical requirements to report identified or suspected non-compliance with laws and regulations to an appropriate authority outside the entity. For example, in some jurisdictions, statutory requirements exist for the auditor of a financial institution to report the occurrence, or suspected occurrence, of non-compliance with laws and regulations to a supervisory authority. Also, misstatements may arise from non-compliance with laws or regulations and, in some jurisdictions, the auditor may be required to report misstatements to an appropriate authority in cases where management or those charged with governance fail to take corrective action.

A29

Anti-money laundering legislation in the UK imposes a duty on the auditor to report suspected money laundering activity. There are similar laws and regulations relating to financing terrorist offences.[16b] The impact on the auditor of this legislation can broadly be summarized as follows:

● Partners and staff in the firm are required to report suspicions of conduct which would constitute a criminal offence which gives rise to direct or indirect benefit; and

● Partners and staff in the firm need to be alert to the dangers of 'tipping off' as this will constitute a criminal offence under the anti-money laundering legislation.

The Appendix contains further guidance on the auditor's responsibilities in respect of money laundering, terrorist financing and proceeds of crime legislation in the UK.

A29-1

For auditors of certain entities subject to statutory regulation,[16c] laws and regulations establish separate responsibilities for the auditor to report certain information direct to an appropriate authority outside the entity. Standards and guidance on these responsibilities is given in Section B of this ISA (UK)[1a] and relevant FRC Practice Notes.

A29-2

[16b] *In the UK, the Terrorism Act 2000 contains reporting requirements for the laundering of terrorist funds which include any funds that are likely to be used for the financing of terrorism.*

[16c] *Auditors of public interest entities and other entities in the financial sector, pension schemes and charities have a statutory responsibility, subject to compliance with legislation relating to 'tipping off' (see paragraph A21-1), to report matters that are likely to be of material significance to the regulator.*

A29-3 The procedures and guidance in Section B of this ISA (UK)[1a] can be adapted to circumstances in which the auditor of other types of entity identifies or suspects non-compliance with laws and regulations which the auditor is under a statutory duty to report.

A30 In other cases, the relevant ethical requirements may require the auditor to determine whether reporting identified or suspected non-compliance with laws and regulations to an appropriate authority outside the entity is an appropriate action in the circumstances. For example, the IESBA Code requires the auditor to take steps to respond to identified or suspected non-compliance with laws and regulations and determine whether further action is needed, which may include reporting to an appropriate authority outside the entity.[17] The IESBA Code explains that such reporting would not be considered a breach of the duty of confidentiality under the IESBA Code.[18]

A31 Even if law, regulation or relevant ethical requirements do not include requirements that address reporting identified or suspected non-compliance, they may provide the auditor with the right to report identified or suspected non-compliance to an appropriate authority outside the entity. For example, when auditing the financial statements of financial institutions, the auditor may have the right under law or regulation to discuss matters such as identified or suspected non-compliance with laws and regulations with a supervisory authority.

A32 In other circumstances, the reporting of identified or suspected non-compliance with laws and regulations to an appropriate authority outside the entity may be precluded by the auditor's duty of confidentiality under law, regulation or relevant ethical requirements.

A33 The determination required by paragraph 29 may involve complex considerations and professional judgments. Accordingly the auditor may consider consulting internally (e.g., within the firm or a network firm) or on a confidential basis with a regulator or professional body (unless doing so is prohibited by law or regulation or would breach the duty of confidentiality). The auditor may also consider obtaining legal advice to understand the auditor's options and the professional or legal implications of taking any particular course of action.

Reporting in the Public Interest

A33-1 Where the auditor has identified or suspects non-compliance with laws and regulations which does not give rise to a responsibility under law, regulation or relevant ethical requirements to report to an appropriate authority outside the entity, the auditor considers whether the matter may be one that ought to be reported in the public interest to an appropriate authority outside the entity and, where this is the case, except in the circumstances covered in paragraph A33-3 below, discusses the matter with those charged with governance, including any audit committee.[18a]

---

[17] *See, for example, Section 225.29 and Sections 225.33–225.36 of the IESBA Code.*
In the UK, the auditor has regard to paragraphs A33-1–A33-8 of this ISA (UK) and any specific requirements of the auditor's relevant professional body.

[18] *See, for example, Section 140.7 and Section 225.35 of the IESBA Code.*
In the UK, the auditor has regard to any specific requirements of the auditor's relevant professional body.

[18a] *In rare circumstances, according to common law, disclosure might also be justified in the public interest where there is no instance of non-compliance with laws and regulations, e.g. where the public is being misled or their financial interests are being damaged; where a miscarriage of justice has occurred; where the health and safety of members of the public or the environment is being endangered – although such events may well constitute breaches of laws and regulations.*

If, having considered any views expressed on behalf of the entity and in the light of any legal advice obtained, the auditor concludes that the matter ought to be reported in the public interest to an appropriate authority outside the entity, the auditor notifies those charged with governance in writing of the auditor's conclusion and, if the entity does not voluntarily do so itself or is unable to provide evidence that the matter has been reported, the auditor reports the matter direct to an appropriate authority outside the entity. **A33-2**

The auditor reports in the public interest a matter direct to an appropriate authority outside the entity and without discussing the matter with the entity if the auditor concludes that the identified or suspected non-compliance with laws and regulations has caused the auditor no longer to have confidence in the integrity of those charged with governance. Such a conclusion may arise in the circumstances identified in paragraph A24 or as a result of other audit procedures. **A33-3**

Determination of where the balance of public interest lies requires careful consideration. An auditor whose suspicions have been aroused uses professional judgment to determine whether the auditor's misgivings justify the auditor in carrying the matter further or are too insubstantial to deserve reporting. The auditor is protected from the risk of liability for breach of confidence or defamation provided that: **A33-4**

- In the case of breach of confidence, disclosure is made in the public interest, and such disclosure is made to an appropriate body or person,[18b] and there is no malice motivating the disclosure; and
- In the case of defamation, disclosure is made in the auditor's capacity as auditor of the entity concerned, and there is no malice motivating the disclosure.

In addition, the auditor is protected from such risks where the auditor is expressly permitted or required by legislation to disclose information.[18c]

'Public interest' is a concept that is not capable of general definition. Each situation must be considered individually. In the UK, legal precedent indicates that matters to be taken into account when considering whether disclosure is justified in the public interest may include: **A33-5**

- The extent to which the identified or suspected non-compliance with laws and regulations is likely to affect members of the public.
- Whether those charged with governance have rectified the matter or are taking, or are likely to take, effective corrective action.
- The extent to which non-disclosure is likely to enable the identified or suspected non-compliance with laws and regulations to recur with impunity.
- The gravity of the matter.

[18b] *In the UK, appropriate authorities outside the entity could include the Serious Fraud Office, the Crown Prosecution Service, police forces, the Financial Conduct Authority, the Prudential Regulation Authority, the Panel on Takeovers and Mergers, the Society of Lloyd's, local authorities, the Charity Commission for England and Wales, the Office of the Scottish Charity Regulator, the Charity Commission for Northern Ireland, HM Revenue and Customs, the Department of Business, Energy and Industrial Strategy and the Health and Safety Executive.*

[18c] *In the UK, the Employments Rights Act 1996 would give similar protection to an individual member of the engagement team who made an appropriate report in the public interest. However, ordinarily a member of the engagement team who believed there was a reportable matter would follow the firm's policies and procedures to address such matters. ISA (UK) 220 (Revised June 2016), Quality Control for an Audit of Financial Statements, paragraph 18(a), requires that the engagement partner shall take responsibility for the engagement team undertaking appropriate consultation on difficult or contentious matters. If differences of opinion arise within the engagement team, ISA (UK) 220 (Revised June 2016) paragraph 22, requires that the engagement team shall follow the firm's policies and procedures for dealing with and resolving differences of opinion.*

- Whether there is a general ethos within the entity of disregarding laws and regulations.
- The weight of evidence and the degree of the auditor's suspicion that there has been non-compliance with laws and regulations.

A33-6   An auditor who can demonstrate having acted reasonably and in good faith in informing an appropriate authority of non-compliance with laws and regulations which the auditor suspects has been committed would not be held by the court to be in breach of duty to the client even if, an investigation or prosecution having occurred, it were found that there had been no offence.

A33-7   The auditor needs to remember that the auditor's decision as to whether to report, and if so to whom, may be called into question at a future date, for example on the basis of:
- What the auditor knew at the time;
- What the auditor ought to have known in the course of the audit;
- What the auditor ought to have concluded; and
- What the auditor ought to have done.

The auditor may also wish to consider the possible consequences if financial loss is occasioned by non-compliance with laws and regulations which the auditor suspects (or ought to suspect) has occurred but decided not to report.

A33-8   The auditor may need to take legal advice before making a decision on whether identified or suspected non-compliance with laws and regulations needs to be reported to an appropriate authority in the public interest.

Considerations Specific to Public Sector Entities

A34   A public sector auditor may be obliged to report on identified or suspected non-compliance to the legislature or other governing body or to report them in the auditor's report.

Timing of Reports

A34-1   Laws and regulations may stipulate a period within which reports are to be made. If the auditor becomes aware of a suspected or actual non-compliance with laws and regulations which gives rise to a statutory duty to report, the auditor complies with any such stipulated periods for reporting. Ordinarily the auditor makes a report to an appropriate authority outside the entity as soon as practicable.

Reporting to Authorities of Public Interest Entities (Ref: Para. 29R-1)

A34-2   The disclosure in good faith to the authorities responsible for investigating such irregularities, by the auditor, of any irregularities referred to in paragraph 29R-1 shall not constitute a breach of any contractual or legal restriction on disclosure of information in accordance with the Audit Regulation.[18d]

A34-3   The auditor considers whether to take further action when the entity investigates the matter referred to in paragraph 23R-1 but where the measures taken by management or those charged with governance, in the auditor's professional judgement, were not

---

[18d] *Article 7 of Regulation (EU) No 537/2014 of the European Parliament and of the Council of 16 April 2014.*

appropriate to deal with the irregularities identified or would fail to prevent future occurrences.

Documentation (Ref: Para. 30)

The auditor's documentation of findings regarding identified or suspected non-compliance   **A35**
with laws and regulations may include, for example:

- Copies of records or documents.
- Minutes of discussions held with management, those charged with governance or parties outside the entity.

Law, regulation or relevant ethical requirements may also set out additional documentation   **A36**
requirements regarding identified or suspected non-compliance with laws and regulations.[19]

---

[19] *See, for example, Section 225.37 of the IESBA Code.*
In the UK, the auditor has regard to any specific requirements of the auditor's relevant professional body.

Appendix   (Ref: Para. A6-1, A29-1)

Money Laundering, Terrorist Financing and Proceeds of Crime Legislation in the United Kingdom[1]

1   In the UK, the auditor has additional responsibilities that arise as a result of money laundering, terrorist financing and proceeds of crime legislation, including:[2]
   - Proceeds of Crime Act 2002 (POCA) (as subsequently amended by the Serious and Organised Crime and Police Act 2005 (SOCPA)).
   - Terrorism Act 2000 (TACT) (as amended).
   - Crime and Courts Act 2013.
   - Money Laundering, Terrorist Financing and Transfer of Funds (Information on the Payer) Regulations 2017 (SI 692/2017).
   - Criminal Finances Act 2017.

   Hereafter known collectively as the 'Anti-Money Laundering Legislation'.

2   The Anti-Money Laundering Legislation is complex and this Appendix focuses on the impact of the Anti-Money Laundering Legislation on the auditor's responsibilities when auditing and reporting on financial statements, and should be read in conjunction with the more detailed updated guidance, which includes a series of practical examples, issued by the Consultative Committee of Accountancy Bodies (CCAB).[3] To obtain a full understanding of the legal requirements auditors will need to refer to the relevant provisions of the legislation and, if necessary, obtain legal advice.[4]

Changes Under the Money Laundering, Terrorist Financing and Transfer of Funds (Information on the Payer) Regulations 2017

3   The Money Laundering, Terrorist Financing and Transfer of Funds (Information on the Payer) Regulations 2017 ('2017 Regulations') replace the Money Laundering Regulations 2007. The 2017 Regulations apply to persons acting in the course of business as a statutory auditor within the meaning of Part 42 of the Companies Act 2006, when carrying out statutory audit work within the meaning of Section 1210 of the Companies Act 2006.[5] The 2017 Regulations amend POCA and TACT to make them applicable to those persons carrying out audits in accordance with Section 4(1) of the Local Audit and Accountability Act 2014. Regulation 100(1) also provides an updated list of public bodies and persons who are obliged to report where they know or suspect money laundering has taken place, or have reasonable ground for suspicion thereof, to the National Crime Agency (NCA). For the purposes of this Appendix, 'person' is interpreted as referring to a UK firm (or sole practitioner) that is designated

---

[1] *The revised guidance in this Appendix has been shared with HM Treasury, HM Revenue and Customs and the National Crime Agency (NCA) before being finalised.*

[2] *This Appendix reflects the legislation effective at 26 June 2017. Auditors need to be alert to subsequent changes in legislative requirements.*

[3] *The CCAB has issued revised 'Anti-Money Laundering Guidance for the Accountancy Sector' ('CCAB Guidance') which provides detailed guidance on the legislation for all entities providing audit, accountancy, tax advisory or insolvency related services. This is available on the CCAB website at http://www.ccab.org.uk/documents.php The CCAB Guidance is approved by HM Treasury.*

[4] *Detailed guidance by the NCA is available at: http://www.nationalcrimeagency.gov.uk/publications/725-sar-glossary-code-and-reporting-routes/file*

[5] *Regulation 11(1) of the 2017 Regulations.*

as a 'Registered Auditor' to which the 2017 Regulations apply. The 2017 Regulations also set out a series of key changes in respect of:

- More prescriptive risk assessments.
- Policies and procedures to mitigate money laundering and terrorist financing risks.
- Enhanced transparency over beneficial owners.
- Customer due diligence.
- Changes to extend the definition of Politically Exposed Persons.
- A person responsible for compliance at Board level.
- Enhanced training requirements.

Where a Registered Auditor is not carrying out statutory audit work, the 2017 Regulations will nevertheless often apply as they also cover a firm or sole practitioner who provides accountancy services to, or advice about the tax affairs of, other persons.[6] The 2017 Regulations impose requirements on businesses in the regulated sector relating to systems, procedures and training to prevent money laundering, provide identification procedures for clients, maintaining records, and internal reporting.   **4**

To Whom Does the Anti-Money Laundering Legislation Apply?

The requirement to make a report under Sections 330 and 331 of POCA applies to information which comes to a person in the course of a business, or a Money Laundering Reporting Officer ('MLRO'), in the regulated sector. That information may relate to money laundering by persons or businesses inside or outside the regulated sector. The offence of failing to report that another person is engaged in money laundering applies to all money laundering, including conduct taking place overseas that would be an offence if it took place in the UK. For that reason, there may be an obligation to report information arising from the audit of non-UK companies or their subsidiaries.   **5**

Sections 45 and 46 of the Criminal Finances Act 2017 create criminal offences for failing to prevent the facilitation of tax evasion. These offences apply to Companies, Partnerships and Limited Liability Partnerships (LLPs) where: **6**

- Criminal tax evasion takes place under UK or foreign law;
- It is facilitated by the business' employee, agent or those performing services for the business; and
- The business, by virtue of failing to put in place reasonable prevention methods, has failed to prevent that person from enabling the crime.

When is an Auditor in the UK Regulated Sector?

The regulated sector includes any firm or individual who acts in the course of a business carried on in the UK as an auditor. This is set out in more detail in paragraphs 8–10 of this Appendix.   **7**

A person is eligible for appointment as an auditor if the person is a member of a Recognised Supervisory Body[7] and is eligible for appointment under the rules of that Body. A person will fall within the regulated sector in their capacity as an auditor when carrying out statutory audit work within the meaning of Section 1210 of the Companies Act 2006. In summary, this comprises the audit of UK private or public companies,   **8**

---

[6] *Regulations 11(3) and 11(4) of the 2017 Regulations.*

[7] *A Recognised Supervisory Body is a body established in the UK which maintains and enforces rules as to the eligibility of persons to seek appointment as an auditor and the conduct of audit work, and which is recognised by the Secretary of State by Order.*

building societies, friendly societies, Lloyds syndicate aggregate accounts, insurance undertakings, LLPs, qualifying partnerships, those carrying out audits in accordance with Section 4(1) of the Local Audit and Accountability Act 2014 and any other such bodies as the Secretary of State may prescribe by Order.

9   The Anti-Money Laundering Legislation applies to all partners and staff within a UK firm who are involved in providing audit services in relation to statutory audit work in the UK. Where they become involved in audit work in the UK, such persons may include experts from other disciplines within the UK firm and employees (both audit partners and staff and experts from other disciplines) of non-UK firms, including contractors.

10   Where they are not involved in audit work in the UK such persons may fall within other parts of the regulated sector. For example, the provision of accountancy services to other persons by way of business is within the regulated sector regardless of whether the person providing the services is or is not a member of a UK Recognised Supervisory Body.

11   It is unlikely that it will be practicable or desirable for a UK firm which is within the regulated sector to distinguish for reporting purposes between partners and staff who are providing services in the regulated sector and those who are not. Accordingly, UK firms may choose to impose procedures across the firm requiring all partners and staff to report to the firm's MLRO.[8]

12   The use of the term 'auditor' in this Appendix means anyone who is part of the engagement team as defined in ISA (UK) 220 (Revised June 2016).[9] For audits carried out in accordance with the FRC Ethical Standard, the audit team comprises all persons who are directly involved in the acceptance and performance of a particular audit. This includes the audit team (including audit professionals contracted by the firm), professional personnel from other disciplines involved in the audit engagement, and those who provide quality control or direct oversight of the audit engagement, but it does not include experts contracted by the firm.

Key Legal Requirements

13   The Anti-Money Laundering Legislation establishes the following auditor's responsibilities:
- The Anti-Money Laundering Legislation does not extend the scope of the audit, but the auditor is within the regulated sector and is required to report where:
  - The auditor knows or suspects, or has reasonable grounds to know or suspect, that another person is engaged in money laundering; and
  - The auditor can identify the other person or the whereabouts of any of the laundered property, or that the auditor believes, or it is reasonable to expect the auditor to believe, that information that the auditor has obtained will or may assist in identifying that other person or the whereabouts of the laundered property; and
  - The information has come to the auditor in the course of the auditor's 'regulated' business.

---

[8] *Persons outside the regulated sector are not obliged to report to their MLRO under Sections 330 and 331 of POCA (the 'failure to report' offence), but can make voluntary reports under Section 337.*

[9] *ISA (UK) 220 (Revised June 2016),* Quality Control for an Audit of Financial Statements, *paragraph 7(d).*

- POCA defines both the money laundering offences and the auditor's reporting responsibilities. The Anti-Money Laundering Legislation imposes a duty to report money laundering in respect of all criminal property.[10]
- Failure by an auditor to report knowledge or suspicion of, or reasonable grounds to know or suspect, money laundering in relation to the proceeds of any crime is a criminal offence.[11] Auditors (partners and staff) will face criminal penalties[12] if they breach the requirements.
- The requirement to report is not just related to matters that might be considered material to the financial statements; the auditor has to report knowledge or suspicion, or reasonable grounds for knowledge or suspicion, of crimes that potentially have no material financial statement impact. The Anti-Money Laundering Legislation does not contain de minimis concessions.
- A very wide range of offences (e.g., bribery and corruption both in and outside of the UK, and therefore also subject to the provisions of the Bribery Act 2010) may give rise to a responsibility to report money laundering suspicions.
- Where an auditor knows or suspects that the auditor themselves are involved in money laundering, the auditor is required to report this in order that appropriate consent can be obtained.
- The firm must take appropriate measures so that partners and staff are made aware of the provisions of the Anti-Money Laundering Legislation and are given training in how to recognise and deal with actual or suspected money laundering activities.
- The firm is required to adopt rigorous client identification procedures and appropriate anti-money laundering procedures.

Money Laundering Offences

There are three principal money laundering offences in POCA which define money laundering to encompass offences relating to: **14**
- The concealment (Section 327);
- Becoming involved in arrangements which facilitate the creation (Section 328); and
- Acquisition, use, and possession (Section 329)

of criminal property and involvement in arrangements relating to criminal property. These principal offences apply to all persons and businesses whether or not they are within the regulated sector.

Under Section 330 of POCA, persons working in the regulated sector are   **15**
required to report knowledge or suspicion, or reasonable grounds for knowledge or suspicion, that another person is engaged in money laundering to a nominated officer where that knowledge or suspicion, or reasonable grounds for knowledge or suspicion, came to those persons in the course of their business or employment in the regulated sector. In a firm, the nominated officer is usually known as a

---

[10] *Property is criminal property if: (i) it constitutes a person's benefit from criminal conduct or it represents such a benefit (in whole or in part and whether directly or indirectly); and (ii) the alleged offender knows or suspects that it constitutes or represents such a benefit.*

[11] *Subject to the provisions of Section 330(6) of POCA relating to information coming to a legal adviser or relevant professional adviser in 'privileged circumstances' and Section 330(7A) relating to offences committed overseas.*

[12] *Criminal penalties are covered under Sections 334 and 336(6) of POCA. The maximum penalty for the three principal money laundering offences on conviction on indictment is fourteen years imprisonment. The maximum penalty on conviction on indictment is five years imprisonment. In all cases, an unlimited fine can be imposed.*

Money Laundering Reporting Officer[13] ('MLRO') and is referred to as such in this Appendix (see paragraphs 22–24 of this Appendix).[14] If, as a result of that report, the MLRO has knowledge or suspicion of, or reasonable grounds to know or suspect money laundering, the MLRO then has a responsibility to report to the Financial Intelligence Unit of the NCA.

16   Auditors who consider that the actions they plan to take, or may be asked to take, will result in themselves committing a principal money laundering offence are required to obtain prior consent to those actions from their MLRO and the MLRO is required to seek appropriate prior consent from the NCA (see paragraphs 49–51 of this Appendix). Auditors could also commit a principal offence through acts of omission.

Firm-wide Practices

17   The Anti-Money Laundering Legislation requires the firm to establish risk-sensitive policies and procedures[15] relating to:
- Customer identification and ongoing monitoring of business relationships.
- Reporting internally and to the NCA.[16]
- Record keeping.
- Internal control, risk assessment and management.
- Training for all relevant employees.
- Monitoring and management of compliance with a firm's policies and procedures.
- The internal communication of such policies and procedures throughout the firm.

In addition, the firm needs to ensure sufficient senior management oversight of the systems used for monitoring compliance with these procedures. It may be helpful for this to be coordinated with the responsibility for the firm's quality control systems under ISQC (UK) 1 (Revised June 2016).[17]

Client Identification and Ongoing Monitoring of Business Relationships

18   Appropriate identification procedures,[18] as required by the Anti-Money Laundering Legislation, are mandatory when accepting appointment as auditor. The extent of information collected about the client and verification of identity undertaken will depend on the client risk assessment.

---

[13] *The 2017 legislation creates a new role of 'officer responsible for compliance'; however, for the purposes of this guidance the term MLRO should be deemed to cover both roles. More detailed explanation is provided in Section 3 of the CCAB Guidance.*

[14] *Requirements relating to internal reporting procedures do not apply to sole practitioners; however, a sole practitioner is still subject to external reporting obligations under POCA. Where a sole practitioner has knowledge or suspicion of, or reasonable grounds to know or suspect, money laundering they have a responsibility to report to the NCA (see paragraph 23 of this Appendix).*

[15] *Detailed guidance on developing and applying a risk based approach is given in Section 4 of the CCAB Guidance.*

[16] *Whilst a risk based approach is appropriate when devising policies and procedures, the auditor does not adopt a risk based approach to making reports either internally or to the NCA.*

[17] *International Standard on Quality Control (UK) 1 (Revised June 2016),* Quality Control for Firms that Perform Audits and Reviews of Financial Statements, and other Assurance and Related Services Engagements.

[18] *Guidance on identification procedures, including references to financial restrictions regimes (i.e., sanctions), is given in Section 5 of the CCAB Guidance.*

Auditing standards on quality control require the firm to consider the integrity of the client. This involves the firm making appropriate enquiries and may involve discussions with third parties, the obtaining of written references and searches of relevant databases. These procedures may provide some of the relevant client identification information, but may need to be extended to comply with the Anti-Money Laundering Legislation. **19**

It may be helpful for the auditor to explain to the client the reason for requiring evidence of identity and this can be achieved by including this matter in pre-engagement letter communications with the potential client. It may also be helpful to inform clients of the auditor's responsibilities under the Anti-Money Laundering Legislation to report knowledge or suspicion, or reasonable grounds to know or suspect, that a money laundering offence has been committed and the restrictions created by the 'tipping off' rules on the auditor's ability to discuss such matters with management and those charged with governance. Such wording could be included in the auditor's engagement letter.[19] **20**

The activities of and the relationship with the client are monitored by the firm on an ongoing basis. For example, if there has been a change in the client's circumstances, such as changes in beneficial ownership, control or directors, and this information was relied upon originally as part of the client identification procedures, then, depending on the auditor's assessment of risk, the procedures may need to be re-performed and documented. However, annual reappointment as auditor does not, in itself, require the client identification procedures to be re-performed. **21**

Money Laundering Reporting Officer

The Anti-Money Laundering Legislation requires relevant entities to appoint a nominated officer (usually known as the MLRO[13]). The auditor is required to report to the MLRO where the auditor knows or suspects, or has reasonable grounds to know or suspect, that another person is engaged in money laundering or, for the purposes of obtaining consent, where the auditor knows or suspects that the auditor themselves are involved in money laundering. The Anti-Money Laundering Legislation does not contain de minimis concessions that affect the reporting requirements with the result that reports need to be made irrespective of the quantum of the benefits derived from, or the seriousness of, the offence. **22**

A sole practitioner is not required to appoint a MLRO; however, the external reporting obligations under the Anti-Money Laundering Legislation remain, and where a sole practitioner has knowledge or suspicion of, or reasonable grounds to know or suspect, money laundering they have a responsibility to report to the NCA. References in this Appendix to reporting matters to the MLRO should be read as making a report directly to the NCA in the case of a sole practitioner. **23**

Partners and staff in a firm discharge their responsibilities by reporting to the firm's MLRO and, where appropriate, by obtaining consent from the MLRO or the NCA to continue with any prohibited activities. The MLRO is responsible for deciding, on the basis of the information provided by the partners and staff, whether further inquiry is required, whether the matter should be reported to the NCA and for making the report. Partners and staff may seek advice from the MLRO who will often act as the main source of guidance and, if necessary, act as the liaison point for communication with the firm's own legal counsel, the NCA and the relevant law enforcement agency. When a report has been made to the NCA, partners and staff need to be alert to the **24**

---

[19] *ISA (UK) 210 (Revised June 2016),* Agreeing the Terms of Audit Engagements.

dangers of disseminating information that is likely to 'tip off' a money launderer or prejudice an investigation as this may constitute a criminal offence under the Anti-Money Laundering Legislation.

Training

25   Firms are required to take appropriate measures so that partners and staff are made aware of the relevant provisions of the Anti-Money Laundering Legislation and are given training in how to recognise and deal with activities which may be related to money laundering and terrorist financing.[20] The level of training provided to partners and staff needs to be appropriate to both the level of exposure of the individual to money laundering and terrorist financing risk and the individual's role and seniority within the firm. Senior members of the firm whatever their role need to understand the requirements of the Anti-Money Laundering Legislation. Additional training or expertise in criminal law is not required under the Anti-Money Laundering Legislation. However, ISA (UK) 250 (Revised December 2017)[21] requires the auditor to obtain a general understanding of the legal and regulatory framework applicable to the entity and the industry or sector in which the entity operates and how the entity is complying with that framework.

Impact of Anti-Money Laundering Legislation on Audit Procedures

Identification of Knowledge or Suspicions

26   ISA (UK) 250 (Revised December 2017) establishes standards and provides guidance on the auditor's responsibility to consider laws and regulations in an audit of financial statements. The Anti-Money Laundering Legislation does not require the auditor to extend the scope of the audit, save as referred to in paragraph 35 of this Appendix, but during the course of the audit, knowledge or suspicion, or reasonable grounds for knowledge or suspicion, relating to money laundering activities may arise that will need to be reported.

27   ISA (UK) 250 (Revised December 2017) requires the auditor to obtain:
- A general understanding of the legal and regulatory framework applicable to the entity and the industry or sector in which the entity operates and how the entity is complying with that framework;[22] and
- Sufficient appropriate audit evidence regarding compliance with the provisions of those laws and regulations generally recognised to have a direct effect on the determination of material amounts and disclosures in the financial statements.[23]

This may cause the auditor to be suspicious that, for example, breaches of the Companies Act 2006 or tax offences have taken place, which may be criminal offences resulting in criminal property.

---

[20] *Guidance on training is given in Section 3 of the CCAB Guidance and in Regulation 24 of the 2017 Regulations.*

[21] *ISA (UK) 250 (Revised December 2017),* Section A—Consideration of Laws and Regulations in an Audit of Financial Statements, *paragraph 13.*

[22] *ISA (UK) 250 (Revised December 2017) Section A, paragraph 13.*

[23] *ISA (UK) 250 (Revised December 2017) Section A, paragraph 14.*

ISA (UK) 250 (Revised December 2017) also requires the auditor to perform procedures to help identify instances of non-compliance with other laws and regulations which may have a material effect on the financial statements.[24] These procedures may include:
- Enquiring of management and, where appropriate, those charged with governance as to whether the entity is in compliance with such laws and regulations.
- Inspecting correspondence, if any, with the relevant licensing or regulatory authorities.

These procedures may give the auditor grounds to suspect that criminal offences have been committed.

For entities within the regulated sector[25] or public interest entities, other laws and regulations that may have a material effect on the financial statements will include Anti-Money Laundering Legislation. When auditing the financial statements of entities within the regulated sector, the auditor reviews the steps taken by the entity to comply with the Anti-Money Laundering Legislation, assesses their effectiveness and obtains management representations concerning compliance with that legislation. If the auditor assesses the entity's internal control as ineffective, the auditor considers whether there is a statutory responsibility to report 'a matter of material significance' to the regulator in accordance with ISA (UK) 250 (Revised June 2016).[26]

Where the entity's business is outside the regulated sector, although the auditor's reporting responsibilities under the Anti-Money Laundering Legislation are unchanged, the entity's management is not required to implement the Anti-Money Laundering Legislation. Whilst the principal money laundering offences apply to these entities, the laws relating to money laundering are unlikely to be considered by the auditor to be other laws and regulations that may have a material effect on the financial statements for the purposes of ISA (UK) 250 (Revised December 2017), unless there are other indicators that may lead to a risk of material misstatement of the financial statements.

ISA (UK) 250 (Revised December 2017) requires the auditor to be alert to the possibility that audit procedures applied for the purpose of forming an opinion on the financial statements may bring instances of possible non-compliance with other laws and regulations to the auditor's attention.[27] This includes non-compliance that might incur obligations for the auditor to report to an appropriate authority outside the entity.

The auditor also gives consideration to whether any contingent liabilities might arise in this area. For example, there may be regulatory or criminal fines for offences under the Anti-Money Laundering Legislation. Even where no offence under the Anti-Money Laundering Legislation has been committed, civil recovery actions under POCA (Part 5) or other civil claims may give rise to contingent liabilities. The auditor remains

28

29

30

31

32

---

[24] *ISA (UK) 250 (Revised December 2017) Section A, paragraph 15.*

[25] *For the purposes of this Appendix this includes (but is not restricted to) the following persons acting in the course of business in the UK: credit institutions; financial institutions (including money service operators); auditors; insolvency practitioners, external accountants and tax advisers; independent legal professionals; trust or company service providers; estate agents; high value dealers when dealing in goods of any description which involves accepting a total cash payment of 10,000 or more; and casinos. More detail is provided in Part 2 of the 2017 Regulations.*

[26] *ISA (UK) 250 (Revised June 2016)*, Section B – The Auditor's Statutory Right and Duty to Report to Regulators of Public interest Entities and Regulators of Other Entities in the Financial Sector.

[27] *ISA (UK) 250, (Revised December 2017) Section A, paragraph 16.*

alert to the fact that discussions with the entity on such matters may give rise to a risk of 'tipping off' (see paragraphs 45–48 of this Appendix).

33   In some situations the entity may have obtained legal advice to the effect that certain actions or circumstances do not give rise to criminal conduct and therefore cannot give rise to criminal property. Whether an act constitutes non-compliance with laws and regulations may involve consideration of matters beyond the auditor's professional competence to determine. Provided that the auditor considers that the advice has been obtained from a suitably qualified and independent solicitor and that the solicitor was made aware of all relevant circumstances known to the auditor, the auditor may rely on such advice, provided the auditor has complied with the requirements of ISA (UK) 500[28] and ISA (UK) 620 (Revised June 2016).[29]

34   The Anti-Money Laundering Legislation requires the auditor to report the laundering of the proceeds of conduct which takes place overseas if that conduct would constitute an offence in any part of the UK, subject to certain exceptions. The Anti-Money Laundering Legislation does not change the scope of the audit and does not therefore impose any requirement for the group engagement team to change or add to the normal instructions to component auditors of overseas subsidiaries. However, when considering non-UK parts of the group audit, the group engagement team should consider whether information obtained as part of the group audit procedures (e.g., reports made by non-UK component auditors, discussions with non-UK component auditors or discussions with UK and non-UK management and those charged with governance) gives rise to knowledge or suspicion, or reasonable grounds for knowledge or suspicion, such that there is a requirement for the auditor to report to the NCA. The auditor also considers whether such conduct constitutes an offence under Section 6 of the Bribery Act 2010.

Further Inquiry

35   Once the auditor identifies or suspects non-compliance with laws and regulations, the auditor makes further enquiries to assess the implications of this for the audit of the financial statements. ISA (UK) 250 (Revised December 2017) requires that when the auditor becomes aware of information concerning a possible instance of non-compliance, the auditor should obtain an understanding of the nature of the act and the circumstances in which it has occurred, and sufficient other information to evaluate the possible effect on the financial statements.[30] Where the auditor knows or suspects, or has reasonable grounds to know or suspect, that another person is engaged in money laundering, a disclosure must be made to the firm's MLRO. The Anti-Money Laundering Legislation does not require the auditor to undertake any additional enquiries to determine further details of the criminal offence. Where the auditor is uncertain as to whether or not there are grounds to make a disclosure, the engagement partner may wish to seek advice from the firm's MLRO.

36   In performing any further enquiries in the context of the audit of the financial statements, the auditor takes care not to alert a money launderer to the possibility that a report will be or has been made, especially if management and, where applicable, those charged with governance are themselves involved in the suspected criminal activity.

---

[28] *ISA (UK) 500,* Audit Evidence.

[29] *ISA (UK) 620 (Revised June 2016),* Using the Work of an Auditor's Expert.

[30] *ISA (UK) 250 (Revised July 2017) Section A, paragraph 19.*

Reporting to the MLRO and to the NCA

The auditor reports to the firm's MLRO where the auditor knows or suspects, or has **37** reasonable grounds to know or suspect, that another person is engaged in money laundering. Money laundering reports need to be made irrespective of the quantum of the benefits derived from, or the seriousness of, the offence. There is no provision for the auditor not to make a report even where the auditor considers that the matter has already been reported, unless the auditor:

- Does not have the information to identify the money launderer and the whereabouts of any of the laundered property; or
- Does not believe, and it is unreasonable to expect the auditor to believe, that any information held by the auditor will or may assist in identifying the money launderer or the whereabouts of any of the laundered property.

Where suspected money laundering occurs wholly or partially overseas in relation to **38** conduct that is lawful in the country where it occurred the position is more complicated, and the auditor needs to be careful to ensure that the strict requirements of the Anti-Money Laundering Legislation have been satisfied if no report is to be made to the MLRO or to the NCA. In these circumstances, the auditor considers two questions:

- Where the client or third party's money laundering is occurring wholly overseas, is the money laundering lawful there? If it is, a report is not required. However, the auditor needs to be careful to ensure that no consequences of the criminal conduct are, in fact, occurring in the UK;
- Where the client or third party's money laundering is occurring in the UK in relation to underlying conduct which occurred overseas and was lawful there, would the conduct amount to a 'serious offence' under UK law[31] if it had occurred here? If it would have amounted to such an offence, a report is required. The auditor should also consider whether such conduct would be an offence under Section 6 of the Bribery Act 2010.

The duties to report on overseas money laundering activity are complex as they rely on knowledge of both overseas and UK law. In practice, the auditor may choose to report all overseas money laundering activity to the firm's MLRO, subject to the auditor having the information set out in paragraph 37 of this Appendix.

During the course of the audit, the auditor may obtain knowledge or form a suspicion **39** about a prohibited act that would be a criminal offence under the Anti-Money Laundering Legislation but has yet to occur. Because attempting or conspiring to commit a money laundering offence is in itself a money laundering offence, a report might need to be made.

The format of the internal report made to the MLRO is not specified by the Anti-Money Laundering Legislation. MLROs determine the form in which partners and **40** staff report knowledge or suspicion of, or reasonable grounds to know or suspect, money laundering offences. The form and content of these reports will need to provide the MLRO with sufficient information to enable a report to be made to the NCA if necessary, and it may be helpful, therefore, for the reports to use the NCA templates

---

[31] *A 'serious offence' is conduct that would constitute an offence punishable by imprisonment for a maximum term in excess of 12 months if it occurred in any part of the UK, with the exception of an offence under:*

(a)   *The Gaming Act 1968;*

(b)   *The Lotteries and Amusements Act 1976; or*

(c)   *Section 23 or 25 of the Financial Services and Markets Act 2000.*

available online for the purposes of gathering information.[32] The auditor follows the firm's internal documentation procedures when considering whether to include documentation relating to money laundering reporting in the audit working papers. In order to prevent 'tipping off' where another auditor or professional advisor has access to the audit file, the auditor may wish to exclude from the audit file all details of internal reports held by the MLRO. Reporting as soon as is practicable to the MLRO is the responsibility of the auditor and, although suspicions would normally be discussed within the engagement team before deciding whether or not to make an internal report to the MLRO, this should not delay the report.

41   The MLRO makes the decision as to whether a report is made by the firm to the NCA. Suspicious Activity Reports may be made using one of the NCA's manual or on-line forms.[32]

42   The timing of reporting by the MLRO is governed by the Anti-Money Laundering Legislation which requires the disclosure to be made 'as soon as is practicable' after the information or other matter comes to the attention of the MLRO.[33] Where the information includes time sensitive information (e.g., that may allow the recovery of proceeds of crime if communicated immediately) the report will need to be made quickly.

43   Where the auditor has made a report to the MLRO and the MLRO has decided that further inquiry is necessary, the auditor will need to be made aware of the outcome of the inquiry to determine whether there are any implications for the auditor's report or the decision to accept reappointment as auditor.

Legal Privilege

44   Legal privilege can provide a defence for a professional legal adviser to a charge of failing to report knowledge or suspicion of money laundering and is generally available to the legal profession when giving legal advice to a client or acting in relation to litigation.[34] If the auditor is given access to client information over which legal professional privilege may be asserted (e.g., correspondence between clients and solicitors in relation to legal advice or litigation) and that information gives grounds to suspect money laundering, the auditor considers whether the auditor is nevertheless obliged to report to the MLRO. There is some ambiguity about how the issue of legal privilege is interpreted and a prudent approach is to assume that legal privilege does not extend to the auditor. Where the auditor is in possession of client information which is clearly privileged (e.g., a solicitor's advice to an entity), the auditor seeks legal advice.

'Tipping Off' and Prejudicing an Investigation

45   In the UK, 'tipping off' is an offence for individuals in the regulated sector under the Anti-Money Laundering Legislation. This offence arises:

---

[32] *http://www.nationalcrimeagency.gov.uk/about-us/what-we-do/economic-crime/ukfiu/how-to-report-sars*

[33] *Guidance on the reporting of knowledge and suspicions by the MLRO to the NCA is given in Section 7 of the CCAB Guidance.*

[34] *The Proceeds of Crime Act 2002 and Money Laundering Regulations 2003 (Amendment) Order 2006 (SI 2006/308) extended this defence to accountants, auditors or tax advisers who satisfy certain conditions where the information on which their suspicion of money laundering is based comes to their attention in privileged circumstances. In such circumstances, the auditor may discuss their suspicions with the MLRO without requiring a disclosure to the NCA.*

(a) When an individual discloses that a report (either internal or external) has been made based on information that came to that individual in the course of a business in the regulated sector and the disclosure by the individual is likely to prejudice an investigation which might be conducted; or

(b) When an individual discloses that an investigation is being contemplated or is being carried out into allegations that a money laundering offence has been committed and the disclosure by the individual is likely to prejudice that investigation and the information on which the report is based came to a person in the course of a business in the regulated sector.

There are a number of exceptions to this offence under the Anti-Money Laundering Legislation, including where disclosures are made: **46**

- To a fellow auditor employed by a firm that shares common ownership, management or control with the firm;[35]
- To an auditor in another firm in the EEA (or an equivalent jurisdiction for money laundering purposes, where both are subject to equivalent confidentiality and data protection obligations), in relation to the same entity and a transaction or service involving them both, for the purpose of preventing a money laundering offence;
- To a supervisory authority for the person making the disclosure;
- For the purpose of the detection, investigation or prosecution of a criminal offence (whether in the UK or elsewhere);
- Where the auditor is acting as a relevant professional adviser to the client, for the purpose of dissuading the client from engaging in an offence; or
- In circumstances where the person making the disclosure does not know or suspect that the disclosure is likely to prejudice an investigation.

A further offence of prejudicing an investigation is included in the Anti-Money   **47**
Laundering Legislation. Under this provision,[36] it is an offence to make any disclosure which is likely to prejudice an investigation of which a person has knowledge or suspicion, or to falsify, conceal, destroy or otherwise dispose of, or cause or permit the falsification, concealment, destruction or disposal of, documents relevant to such an investigation.

ISA (UK) 260 (Revised June 2016),[37] requires the auditor to communicate significant   **48**
findings from the audit with those charged with governance of an entity. The auditor considers whether there is a need to communicate suspicions of money laundering to those charged with governance of an entity. Under the Anti-Money Laundering Legislation a 'tipping off' offence is not committed by an auditor where a disclosure is made to the entity in order to dissuade the entity from engaging in a money laundering offence (e.g., where an employee is engaged in money laundering using the entity's financial systems, the auditor may inform management, or, where applicable, those charged with governance of the situation in order to prevent the entity from committing a money laundering offence). However, care should be taken as to whom the disclosure is made where management or those charged with governance are, or are suspected to be, involved in the money laundering activity or complicit with it.

---

[35] *Some network firms may not meet these criteria.*

[36] *Section 342 of POCA.*

[37] *ISA (UK) 260 (Revised June 2016),* Communication with Those Charged with Governance, *paragraph 16.*

Reporting to Obtain Appropriate Consent

49   In addition to the auditor's duty to report knowledge or suspicion of, or reasonable grounds to know or suspect, money laundering under the Anti-Money Laundering Legislation, the auditor may need to obtain appropriate consent to perform an act which could otherwise constitute a principal money laundering offence.[38] For example, if the auditor suspected that the auditor's report was necessary in order for financial statements to be issued in connection with a transaction involving the proceeds of crime, or if the auditor was to issue an auditor's report on financial statements for an entity that was a front for illegal activity, the auditor might be involved in an arrangement which facilitated the acquisition, retention, use or control of criminal property under the Anti-Money Laundering Legislation. In these circumstances, in addition to the normal procedures, the auditor would generally need to obtain appropriate consent from the NCA via the MLRO as soon as is practicable. Consent may be given expressly or may be deemed to have been given following the expiry of certain time limits specified in the Anti-Money Laundering Legislation.[39]

50   The auditor also needs to consider whether continuing to act for the entity could itself constitute money laundering, for example, if it amounted to aiding or abetting the commission of one of the principal money laundering offences, or if it amounted to one of the principal money laundering offences itself, in particular the offence of becoming involved in an arrangement under the Anti-Money Laundering Legislation. In those circumstances, the auditor may want to consider whether to resign, but should firstly contact the MLRO, both to report the suspicions and to seek guidance in respect of 'tipping off'. If the auditor wishes to continue the engagement the auditor may need to seek NCA consent for such an action to be taken.

51   Appropriate consent from the NCA will protect the auditor from committing a principal money laundering offence but will not relieve the auditor from any civil liability or other professional, legal or ethical obligations. As an alternative to seeking appropriate consent, the auditor may wish to consider resignation from the audit but, in such circumstances, is still required to disclose suspicions to the MLRO. Further guidance on resignation is given in paragraphs 58–62 of this Appendix.

Reporting to Regulators

52   Reporting to the NCA does not relieve the auditor from other statutory duties. Examples of statutory reporting responsibilities include:
- *Audits of financial statements of public interest entities and other entities in the financial sector*: the auditor has a statutory duty to report matters of 'material significance' to the FCA or PRA (or other appropriate authority outside the entity) which come to the auditor's attention in the course of the audit.
- *Audits of financial statements of entities in the public sector*: the auditor of some public sector entities may be required to report on the entity's compliance with

---

[38] *Subject to the SOCPA amendments to Sections 327, 328 and 329 for overseas activities which state that it is not a money laundering offence for a person to deal with the proceeds of conduct which that person knows, or believes on reasonable grounds, occurred in a particular country or territory outside the UK, and which was known to be lawful, at the time it occurred, under the criminal law then applying in that country or territory, and does not constitute a 'serious offence' under UK law (see footnote 31).*

[39] *Further guidance on seeking appropriate consent is given in the NCA publication:* Requesting a Defence from the NCA under POCA and TACT *which can be downloaded from: http://www.nationalcrimeagency.gov.uk/ publications/713-requesting-a-defence-under-poca-tact/file*

requirements to ensure the regularity and propriety of financial transactions. Activity connected with money laundering may be a breach of those requirements.

- *Audits of financial statements of other types of entity*: the auditor of some other entities are also required to report matters of 'material significance' to regulators (e.g., charities and occupational pension schemes).

Knowledge or suspicion, or reasonable grounds for knowledge or suspicion, of involvement of the entity's management or those charged with governance in money laundering, or of a failure of a regulated business to comply with the Anti-Money Laundering Legislation would normally be regarded as being of material significance to a regulator, and so give rise to a statutory duty to report to the regulator, in addition to the requirement to report to the NCA. A 'tipping off' offence is not committed when a report is made to that entity's supervisory authority and where a disclosure is not likely to prejudice an investigation.

    53

The Auditor's Report on Financial Statements

Where money laundering has been identified or is suspected, the auditor evaluates the possible effect, both in quantitative and qualitative terms, on the financial statements, taking into account whether:

- The crime itself has a material effect on the financial statements;
- The consequences of the crime have a material effect on the financial statements; or
- The outcome of any subsequent investigation by the police or other investigatory body may have a material effect on the financial statements.

    54

If it is known that money laundering has occurred and that management or those charged with governance were knowingly involved, the auditor needs to consider whether the auditor's report should:

- Be modified in accordance with ISA (UK) 705 (Revised June 2016);[40] or
- Incorporate an Emphasis of Matter paragraph in accordance with ISA (UK) 706 (Revised June 2016).[41]

    55

However, the auditor also needs to consider whether including information in the auditor's report about any identified or suspected money laundering activities, for example, through modifying the auditor's opinion or communicating key audit matters,[42] could alert a money launderer.

    56

Timing may be the crucial factor. Any delay in issuing the auditor's report pending the outcome of an investigation is likely to be impracticable and could in itself alert a money launderer. The auditor seeks advice from the MLRO who acts as the main source of guidance and if necessary is the liaison point for communication with the firm's own legal counsel, the NCA and the relevant law enforcement agency.

    57

---

[40] *ISA (UK) 705 (Revised June 2016),* Modifications to the Opinion in the Independent Auditor's Report.

[41] *ISA (UK) 706 (Revised June 2016),* Emphasis of Matter Paragraphs and Other Matter Paragraphs in the Independent Auditor's Report.

[42] *Paragraph A24 of ISA (UK) 260 (Revised June 2016) describes the circumstances in which the auditor is required, or may otherwise consider it necessary, to include additional information in the auditor's report in accordance with the ISAs (UK).*

Resignation and Communication With Successor Auditors[43]

58   The auditor may wish to resign from the position as auditor if the auditor believes that the entity or an employee of that entity is engaged in money laundering or any other illegal act, particularly where a normal relationship of trust can no longer be maintained. Where the auditor intends to cease to hold office there may be a conflict between the requirements under Section 519 of the Companies Act 2006 for the auditor to deposit a statement at a company's registered office of any circumstances that the auditor believes should be brought to the attention of members or creditors and the risk of 'tipping off'. This may arise if, for example, the circumstances connected with the resignation of the auditor include knowledge or suspicion of money laundering and an internal or external disclosure being made.

59   Where such disclosure of circumstances may amount to 'tipping off', the auditor seeks to agree the wording of the Section 519 statement with the relevant law enforcement agency and, failing that, seeks legal advice. The auditor seeks advice from the MLRO who acts as the main source of guidance, including from the firm's own legal counsel, the NCA and the relevant law enforcement agency. The auditor may as a last resort need to apply to the court for direction as to what is included in the Section 519 statement.

60   The offence of 'tipping off' may also cause a conflict with the need to communicate with the prospective successor auditor in accordance with legal and ethical requirements relating to changes in professional appointment. For example, the existing auditor might feel obliged to mention knowledge or suspicion regarding suspected money laundering and any external disclosure made to the NCA. Under the Anti-Money Laundering Legislation this would not constitute 'tipping off' if it was done to prevent the successor auditor from committing a money laundering offence.

61   If information about internal and external reports made by the auditor is considered relevant information for the purposes of Paragraph 9 of Schedule 10 of the Companies Act 2006,[44] the auditor considers whether the disclosure of that information would constitute a 'tipping off' offence under the Anti-Money Laundering Legislation as it may prejudice an investigation. If the auditor considers a 'tipping off' offence might be committed, the auditor speaks to the NCA to see if they are content that disclosure in those circumstances would not prejudice any investigation. The auditor may, as a last resort, need to apply to the Court for directions as to what is disclosed to the successor auditor.

62   Where the only information which needs to be disclosed is the underlying circumstances which gave rise to the disclosure, there are two scenarios to consider:
- Where the auditor only wishes to disclose the suspicions about the underlying criminal conduct and the basis for those suspicions, the auditor will not commit an offence under the Anti-Money Laundering Legislation if that information only is disclosed. For example, if audit files are made available to the successor auditor which detail circumstances which have lead the audit team to suspect management of a fraud, this will not constitute a 'tipping off' offence.[45]

---

[43] *Section 9 of the CCAB Guidance provides more general guidance on cessation of work and resignation.*

[44] *The Statutory Auditors and Third Country Auditors Regulations 2016 (SI 2016/649) came into force on 15 June 2016 and amended the Companies Act 2006 requiring auditors to make available all relevant information held in relation to holding the office as auditor to a successor auditor.*

[45] *Where the auditor knows or suspects that a confiscation, civil recovery, detained cash or money laundering investigation is being or is about to be conducted, the auditor also considers Section 342 of POCA. If the auditor suspects that the disclosure of the working papers would be likely to prejudice that investigation, the auditor takes the approach described in paragraphs 56 and 57 of this Appendix in relation to the Section 519 statement.*

- If the auditor wishes to disclose any suspicions specifically about money laundering (e.g., if the working papers in the example above indicated that the suspected fraud also constituted a suspicion of money laundering), then as a matter of prudence, the approach adopted follows that described in paragraphs 58–59 of this Appendix in relation to the Section 519 statement.

Annexure

CONFORMING AMENDMENTS TO OTHER ISAs (UK)

In July 2017, the FRC issued ISA (UK) 250 (Revised July 2017), *Section A— Consideration of Laws and Regulations in an Audit of Financial Statements*, which reflects the amendments made by the International Auditing and Standards Board (IAASB) to the corresponding international standard.[1]

This Annexure shows the conforming amendments to other ISAs (UK) as a result of ISA (UK) 250 (Revised July 2017). These amendments are effective for audits of financial statements for periods commencing on or after 15 December 2017, and are shown with marked changes from the latest published versions of the ISAs (UK). The footnote numbers within these amendments do not align with the ISAs (UK) that are amended, and reference should be made to those ISAs (UK).

ISQC (UK) 1 (Revised June 2016), Quality Control for Firms that Perform Audits and Reviews of Financial Statements, and Other Assurance and Related Services Engagements

Application and Other Explanatory Material

Confidentiality, Safe Custody, Integrity, Accessibility and Retrievability of Engagement Documentation (Ref: Para. 46)

A56   Relevant ethical requirements establish an obligation for the firm's personnel to observe at all times the confidentiality of information contained in engagement documentation, unless specific client authority has been given to disclose information, or there <u>are responsibilities under law, regulation or relevant ethical requirements</u> is a legal or professional duty to do so.[2] Specific laws or regulations may impose additional obligations on the firm's personnel to maintain client confidentiality, particularly where data of a personal nature are concerned.

ISA (UK) 210 (Revised June 2016), Agreeing the Terms of Audit Engagements

Application and Other Explanatory Material

Agreement on Audit Engagement Terms

A24   When relevant, the following points could also be made in the audit engagement letter:

- Arrangements concerning the involvement of other auditors and experts in some aspects of the audit.
- Arrangements concerning the involvement of internal auditors and other staff of the entity.

---

[1] *ISA 250 (Revised),* Consideration of Laws and Regulations in an Audit of Financial Statements *published in July 2016.*

[2] *See, for example, Section 140.7 and Section 225.35 of the IESBA Code.*
In the UK, the auditor has regard to paragraph 46D-1 of this ISQC (UK) and any specific requirements of the auditor's relevant professional body.

- Arrangements to be made with the predecessor auditor, if any, in the case of an initial audit.
- A reference to, and description of, the auditor's responsibilities under law, regulation or relevant ethical requirements that address reporting identified or suspected non-compliance with laws and regulations to an appropriate authority outside the entity.
- Any restriction of the auditor's liability when such possibility exists.
- A reference to any further agreements between the auditor and the entity.
- Any obligations to provide audit working papers to other parties.

An example of an audit engagement letter is set out in Appendix 1.

ISA (UK) 220 (Revised June 2016), Quality Control for an Audit of Financial Statements

Application and Other Explanatory Material

Acceptance and Continuance of Client Relationships and Audit Engagements
(Ref: Para. 12)

Law, regulation, or relevant ethical requirements[3] may require the auditor to request, prior to accepting the engagement, the predecessor auditor to provide known information regarding any facts or circumstances that, in the predecessor auditor's judgment, the auditor needs to be aware of before deciding whether to accept the engagement. In some circumstances, the predecessor auditor may be required, on request by the proposed successor auditor, to provide information regarding identified or suspected non-compliance with laws and regulations to the proposed successor auditor.[3a] For example, where the predecessor auditor has withdrawn from the engagement as a result of identified or suspected non-compliance with laws and regulations, the IESBA Code requires that the predecessor auditor, on request by a proposed successor auditor, provides all such facts and other information concerning such non-compliance that, in the predecessor auditor's opinion, the proposed successor auditor needs to be aware of before deciding whether to accept the audit appointment.[4]   **A8a**

ISA (UK) 240 (Revised June 2016), The Auditor's Responsibilities Relating to Fraud in an Audit of Financial Statements

Introduction

Responsibility for the Prevention and Detection of Fraud

Responsibilities of the Auditor

The auditor may have additional responsibilities under law, regulation or relevant ethical requirements regarding an entity's non-compliance with laws and regulations,   **8a**

---

[3] *See, for example, Sections 210.14 of the IESBA Code.*
In the UK, the relevant guidance on proposed communications with a predecessor auditor is provided by the pronouncements relating to the work of auditors issued by the auditor's relevant professional body.

[3a] *In the UK, the predecessor auditor is required to provide the successor statutory auditor with access to all relevant information concerning the entity, including information concerning the most recent audit. This would include non-compliance with laws and regulations. See ISQC (UK) 1 (Revised June 2016), Quality Control for Firms that Perform Audits and Reviews of Financial Statements, and other Assurance and Related Services Engagements, paragraph 28D-1.*

[4] *See, for example, Sections 225.31 of the IESBA Code.*
In the UK, the auditor has regard to any specific requirements of the auditor's relevant professional body.

including fraud, which may differ from or go beyond this and other ISAs (UK), such as: (Ref: Para. A5a)

(a) Responding to identified or suspected non-compliance with laws and regulations, including requirements in relation to specific communications with management and those charged with governance, assessing the appropriateness of their response to non-compliance and determining whether further action is needed;

(b) Communicating identified or suspected non-compliance with laws and regulations to other auditors (e.g., in an audit of group financial statements); and

(c) Documentation requirements regarding identified or suspected non-compliance with laws and regulations.

Complying with any additional responsibilities may provide further information that is relevant to the auditor's work in accordance with this and other ISAs (UK) (e.g., regarding the integrity of management or, where appropriate, those charged with governance).

Requirements

Communications to Management and with Those Charged with Governance

40   If the auditor has identified a fraud or has obtained information that indicates that a fraud may exist, the auditor shall communicate these matters, unless prohibited by law or regulation, on a timely basis with ~~to~~ the appropriate level of management in order to inform those with primary responsibility for the prevention and detection of fraud of matters relevant to their responsibilities. (Ref: Para. A59a–A60)

41   Unless all of those charged with governance are involved in managing the entity, if the auditor has identified or suspects fraud involving:

(a)   management;

(b)   employees who have significant roles in internal control; or

(c)   others where the fraud results in a material misstatement in the financial statements,

the auditor shall communicate these matters with ~~to~~ those charged with governance on a timely basis. If the auditor suspects fraud involving management, the auditor shall communicate these suspicions with ~~to~~ those charged with governance and discuss with them the nature, timing and extent of audit procedures necessary to complete the audit. Such communications with those charged with governance are required unless the communication is prohibited by law or regulation. (Ref: Para. A59a, A61–A63)

42   The auditor shall communicate, unless prohibited by law or regulation, with those charged with governance any other matters related to fraud that are, in the auditor's judgment, relevant to their responsibilities. (Ref: Para. A59a, A64)

Reporting Fraud to an Appropriate Authority Outside the Entity ~~Communications to Regulatory and Enforcement Authorities~~

43   If the auditor has identified or suspects a fraud, the auditor shall determine whether law, regulation or relevant ethical requirements: ~~there is a responsibility to report the occurrence or suspicion to a party outside the entity. Although the auditor's professional duty to maintain the confidentiality of client information may preclude such reporting, the auditor's legal responsibilities may override the duty of confidentiality in some circumstances.~~ (Ref: Para. A65–A67)

(a)   Require the auditor to report to an appropriate authority outside the entity.

(b)   Establish responsibilities under which reporting to an appropriate authority outside the entity may be appropriate in the circumstances.

Application and Other Explanatory Material

Responsibility for the Prevention and Detection of Fraud

Responsibilities of the Auditor (Ref: Para. 8a)

Law, regulation or relevant ethical requirements may require the auditor to perform additional procedures and take further actions. For example, the *Code of Ethics for Professional Accountants* issued by the International Ethics Standards Board for Accountants (IESBA Code) requires the auditor to take steps to respond to identified or suspected non-compliance with laws and regulations and determine whether further action is needed. Such steps may include the communication of identified or suspected non-compliance with laws and regulations to other auditors within a group, including a group engagement partner, component auditors or other auditors performing work at components of a group for purposes other than the audit of the group financial statements.[5]   **A5a**

Communications to Management and with Those Charged with Governance (Ref: Para. 40–42)

In some jurisdictions, law or regulation may restrict the auditor's communication of certain matters with management and those charged with governance. Law or regulation may specifically prohibit a communication, or other action, that might prejudice an investigation by an appropriate authority into an actual, or suspected, illegal act, including alerting the entity, for example, when the auditor is required to report the fraud to an appropriate authority pursuant to anti-money laundering legislation. In these circumstances, the issues considered by the auditor may be complex and the auditor may consider it appropriate to obtain legal advice.   **A59a**

Reporting Fraud to an Appropriate Authority outside the Entity ~~Communications to Regulatory and Enforcement Authorities~~ (Ref: Para. 43)

ISA (UK) 250 (Revised June 2016)[6] provides further guidance with respect to the auditor's determination of whether reporting identified or suspected non-compliance with laws or regulations to an appropriate authority outside the entity is required or appropriate in the circumstances, including consideration of the auditor's duty of confidentiality. ~~The auditor's professional duty to maintain the confidentiality of client information may preclude reporting fraud to a party outside the client entity. However, the auditor's legal responsibilities vary by country and, in certain circumstances, the duty of confidentiality may be overridden by statute, the law or courts of law. In some countries, the auditor of a financial institution has a statutory duty to report the occurrence of fraud to supervisory authorities. Also, in some countries the auditor has a duty to report misstatements to authorities in those cases where management and those charged with governance fail to take corrective action.~~   **A65**

The determination required by paragraph 43 may involve complex considerations and professional judgments. Accordingly, ~~t~~The auditor may consider consulting internally (e.g., within the firm or a network firm) or on a confidential basis with a regulator or professional body (unless doing so is prohibited by law or regulation or would breach the duty of confidentiality). The auditor may also consider ~~it appropriate to~~ obtaining legal   **A66**

[5] *See Sections 225.21–225.22 of the IESBA Code.*
In the UK, the auditor has regard to any specific requirements of the auditor's relevant professional body.

[6] *ISA (UK) 250 (Revised July 2017),* Consideration of Laws and Regulations in an Audit of Financial Statements, *paragraphs A28–A34.*

advice to <u>understand the auditor's options and the professional or legal implications of taking any particular</u> ~~determine the appropriate~~ course of action ~~in the circumstances, the purpose of which is to ascertain the steps necessary in considering the public interest aspects of identified fraud~~.

ISA (UK) 260 (Revised June 2016), Communication with Those Charged with Governance

Introduction

The Role of Communication

7   In some jurisdictions, ~~L~~law or regulation may restrict the auditor's communication of certain matters with those charged with governance. ~~For example, l~~Laws or regulations may specifically prohibit a communication, or other action, that might prejudice an investigation by an appropriate authority into an actual, or suspected, illegal act<u>, including alerting the entity, for example, when the auditor is required to report identified or suspected non-compliance with laws and regulations to an appropriate authority pursuant to anti-money laundering legislation</u>. In ~~some~~ <u>these</u> circumstances<u>, the issues considered by the auditor</u> ~~potential conflicts between the auditor's obligations of confidentiality and obligations to communicate~~ may be complex.~~ In such cases,~~ <u>and</u> the auditor may consider <u>it appropriate</u> to obtain~~ing~~ legal advice.

ISA (UK) 450 (Revised June 2016), Evaluation of Misstatements Identified During the Audit

Requirements

Communication and Correction of Misstatements

8   The auditor shall communicate<u>, unless prohibited by law or regulation,</u> on a timely basis all misstatements accumulated during the audit with the appropriate level of management~~, unless prohibited by law or regulation~~.[7] The auditor shall request management to correct those misstatements. (Ref: Para. A7–A9)

Application and Other Explanatory Material

Communication and Correction of Misstatements (Ref: Para. 8–9)

A8   In some jurisdictions, ~~l~~Law or regulation may restrict the auditor's communication of certain misstatements to management, or others, within the entity. ~~For example, L~~<u>l</u>aws or regulations may specifically prohibit a communication, or other action, that might prejudice an investigation by an appropriate authority into an actual, or suspected, illegal act<u>, including alerting the entity, for example, when the auditor is required to report identified or suspected non-compliance with law or regulation to an appropriate authority pursuant to anti-money laundering legislation</u>. In ~~some~~ <u>these</u> circumstances, ~~potential conflicts between the auditor's obligations of confidentiality and obligations to communicate may be complex. In such cases,~~ <u>the issues considered by</u> the auditor may <u>be complex and the auditor may</u> consider ~~seeking~~ <u>it appropriate to obtain</u> legal advice.

---

[7] *ISA (UK) 260 (Revised June 2016),* Communication with Those Charged with Governance, *paragraph 7.*

ISA (UK) 500, Audit Evidence

Requirements

Information to Be Used as Audit Evidence

When designing and performing audit procedures, the auditor shall consider the relevance
and reliability of the information to be used as audit evidence. (Ref: Para. A26–A33<u>a</u>)   **7**

Application and Other Explanatory Material

Information to Be Used as Audit Evidence

Relevance and Reliability (Ref: Para. 7)

As noted in paragraph A1, while audit evidence is primarily obtained from audit procedures   **A26**
performed during the course of the audit, it may also include information obtained from
other sources such as, for example, previous audits, in certain circumstances, ~~and a~~ firm's
quality control procedures for client acceptance and continuance <u>and complying with
certain additional responsibilities under law, regulation or relevant ethical requirements
(e.g., regarding an entity's non-compliance with laws and regulations)</u>. The quality of all
audit evidence is affected by the relevance and reliability of the information upon which
it is based.

<u>ISA (UK) 250 (Revised July 2017)[8] provides further guidance with respect to the auditor   **A33a**
complying with any additional responsibilities under law, regulation or relevant ethical
requirements regarding an entity's identified or suspected non-compliance with laws and
regulations that may provide further information that is relevant to the auditor's work in
accordance with ISAs (UK) and evaluating the implications of such non-compliance in
relation to other aspects of the audit.</u>

---

[8] <u>*ISA (UK) 250 (Revised July 2017)*, Consideration of Laws and Regulations in an Audit of Financial Statements,
paragraph 9.</u>

154

International Standard on Auditing (UK) 250 (Revised June 2016)
Section B – The auditor's statutory right and duty to report to regulators of public interest entities and regulators of other entities in the financial sector

(Effective for audits of financial statements for periods commencing on or after 17 June 2016)

Contents

International Standard on Auditing (UK) (ISA (UK)) 250 (Revised June 2016), *Consideration of Laws and Regulations in an Audit of Financial Statements*, should be read in conjunction with ISA (UK) 200 (Revised June 2016), *Overall Objectives of the Independent Auditor and the Conduct of an Audit in Accordance with International Standards on Auditing (UK)*.

Introduction

Scope of this Section

This Section of ISA (UK) 250 deals with the circumstances in which the auditor of an entity subject to statutory regulation (a 'regulated entity') is required to report direct to a regulator information which comes to the auditor's attention in the course of the work undertaken in the auditor's capacity as auditor of the regulated entity. This may include work undertaken to express an opinion on the entity's financial statements, other financial information or on other matters specified by legislation or by a regulator.   **1**

The Auditor's Responsibilities (Ref: Para. A1–A8)

The auditor of a regulated entity generally has special reporting responsibilities in addition to the responsibility to report on financial statements. These special reporting responsibilities take two forms: **2**

(a) *A responsibility to provide a report on matters specified in legislation or by a regulator.* This form of report is often made on an annual or other routine basis and does not derive from another set of reporting responsibilities. The auditor is required to carry out appropriate procedures sufficient to form an opinion on the matters concerned. These procedures may be in addition to those carried out to form an opinion on the financial statements; and

(b) *A statutory duty to report certain information, relevant to the regulators' functions, that come to the auditor's attention in the course of the audit work.* The auditor has no responsibility to carry out procedures to search out the information relevant to the regulator. This form of report is derivative in nature, arising only in the context of another set of reporting responsibilities, and is initiated by the auditor on discovery of a reportable matter.

This Section of this ISA (UK) deals with both forms of direct reports. Guidance on the auditor's responsibility to provide special reports on a routine basis on other matters specified in legislation or by a regulator is given in the Practice Notes dealing with regulated business, for example banks, building societies, investment businesses and insurers.   **3**

The statutory duty to report to a regulator applies to information which comes to the attention of the auditor in the auditor's capacity as auditor. In determining whether information is obtained in that capacity, two criteria in particular need to be considered: first, whether the person who obtained the information also undertook the audit work; and if so, whether it was obtained in the course of or as a result of undertaking the audit work. Appendix 2 to this Section of this ISA (UK) sets out guidance on the application of these criteria.   **4**

The auditor may have a statutory right to bring information to the attention of the regulator in particular circumstances which lie outside those giving rise to a statutory duty to initiate a direct report. Where this is so, the auditor may use that right to make a direct report relevant to the regulator on a specific matter which comes to the auditor's attention when the auditor concludes that doing so is necessary to protect the interests of those for whose benefit the regulator is required to act.   **5**

The requirements and explanatory material in this section of this ISA (UK) complement but do not replace the legal and regulatory requirements applicable to each regulated entity. Where the application of those legal and regulatory requirements, taking into   **6** account any published interpretations, is insufficiently clear for the auditor to determine whether a particular circumstance results in a legal duty to make a report to a regulator, or a right to make such a report, it may be appropriate to take legal advice.

Effective Date

7   This Section of ISA (UK) 250 (Revised June 2016) is effective for audits of financial statements for periods commencing on or after 17 June 2016. Earlier adoption is permitted.

Objective

8   The objective of the auditor of a regulated entity is to bring information of which the auditor has become aware in the ordinary course of performing work undertaken to fulfil the auditor's audit responsibilities to the attention of the appropriate regulator as soon as practicable when:

(a) The auditor concludes that it is relevant to the regulator's functions having regard to such matters as may be specified in statute or any related regulations; and

(b) In the auditor's opinion there is reasonable cause to believe it is or may be of material significance to the regulator.

Definitions

9   For purposes of this Section of this ISA (UK), the following terms have the meanings attributed below:

(a) **The Act(s)** – Means those Acts that give rise to a duty to report to a regulator. For example, in the UK, this includes the Audit Regulation,[1] the Financial Services and Markets Act 2000, the Financial Services Act 2012 and regulations made under those Acts, and any future legislation including provisions relating to the duties of auditors similar to those contained in that statute.

(b) **Audit** – For the purpose of this Section of this ISA (UK), the term 'audit' refers both to an engagement to report on the financial statements of a regulated entity and to an engagement to provide a report on other matters specified by statute or by a regulator undertaken in the capacity of auditor.

(c) **Auditor** – The term 'auditor' should be interpreted in accordance with the requirements of the Acts. Guidance on its interpretation is contained in Practice Notes relating to each area of the financial sector to which the duty applies.

(d) **Material significance** – The term 'material significance' requires interpretation in the context of the specific legislation applicable to the regulated entity. A matter or group of matters is normally of material significance to a regulator's functions when, due either to its nature or its potential financial impact, it is likely of itself to require investigation by the regulator. Further guidance on the interpretation of the term in the context of specific legislation is contained in Practice Notes dealing with the rights and duties of auditors of regulated entities to report direct to regulators.

(e) **Regulated entity** – An individual, company or other type of entity which is:

(i) Authorized to carry on business in the financial sector which is subject to statutory regulation; or

(ii) A public interest entity.[2]

---

[1]   *Regulation (EU) No 537/2014 of the European Parliament and of the Council of 16 April 2014.*

[2]   *ISA (UK) 220 (Revised June 2016), Quality Control for an Audit of Financial Statements, paragraph 7(m)-1 defines public interest entity.*

(f) **Regulator** – Such persons as are empowered by the Act(s) to regulate the entity. The term includes the Financial Conduct Authority, the Prudential Regulation Authority, and such other bodies as may be so empowered in future legislation.

(g) **'Tipping off'** – Involves a disclosure that is likely to prejudice any investigation into suspected money laundering which might arise from a report being made to a regulatory authority.[3] Money laundering involves an act which conceals, disguises, converts, transfers, removes, uses, acquires or possesses property which constitutes or represents a benefit from criminal conduct.

Requirements

Conduct of the Audit

Planning

When obtaining an understanding of the business for the purpose of the audit, the auditor of a regulated entity shall obtain an understanding of its current activities, the scope of its authorization and the effectiveness of its control environment. (Ref: Para. A9–A16)

10

Supervision and Control

The auditor shall ensure that all staff involved in the audit of a regulated entity have an understanding of:

11

(a) The provisions of applicable legislation;
(b) The regulator's rules and any guidance issued by the regulator; and
(c) Any specific requirements which apply to the particular regulated entity,

appropriate to their role in the audit and sufficient (in the context of that role) to enable them to identify situations which may give reasonable cause to believe that a matter should be reported to the regulator. (Ref: Para. A17–A23)

Identifying Matters Requiring a Report Direct to Regulators

Where an apparent breach of statutory or regulatory requirements comes to the auditor's attention, the auditor shall:

12

(a) Obtain such evidence as is available to assess its implications for the auditor's reporting responsibilities;
(b) Determine whether, in the auditor's opinion, there is reasonable cause to believe that the breach is of material significance to the regulator; and
(c) Consider whether the apparent breach is criminal conduct that gives rise to criminal property and, as such, should be reported to the specified authorities. (Ref: Para. A24–A30)

---

[3] *More detail is provided in the definition contained in Section A of ISA (UK) 250 (Revised June 2016).*

Reporting (Ref: Para. A31–A46)

The Auditor's Statutory Duty to Report Direct to Regulators

13   When the auditor concludes, after appropriate discussion and investigations, that a matter which has come to the auditor's attention gives rise to a statutory duty to make a report the auditor shall[4] bring the matter to the attention of the regulator as soon as practicable in a form and manner which will facilitate appropriate action by the regulator. When the initial report is made orally, the auditor shall make a contemporaneous written record of the oral report and shall confirm the matter in writing to the regulator. (Ref: Para. A31–A35)

13R-1   For audits of financial statements of public interest entities, the auditor shall:

(a) Report promptly to the regulator any information concerning that public interest entity of which the auditor has become aware while carrying out the audit and which may bring about any of the following:

(i) A material breach of the laws, regulations or administrative provisions which lay down, where appropriate, the conditions governing authorization or which specifically govern pursuit of the activities of such public interest entity; or

(ii) A material threat or doubt concerning the continuous functioning of the public interest entity; or

(iii) A refusal to issue an audit opinion on the financial statements or the issuing of an adverse or qualified opinion.

(b) Report any information referred to in paragraph 13R-1(a)(i)–(iii) of which the auditor becomes aware in the course of carrying out the audit of an undertaking having close links[5] with the public interest entity for which they are also carrying out the audit.

14   When the matter giving rise to a statutory duty to make a report direct to a regulator casts doubt on the integrity of those charged with governance or their competence to conduct the business of the regulated entity, the auditor shall[4] make the report to the regulator as soon as practicable and without informing those charged with governance in advance. (Ref: Para. A35)

The Auditor's Right to Report Direct to Regulators

15   When a matter comes to the auditor's attention which the auditor concludes does not give rise to a statutory duty to report but nevertheless may be relevant to the regulator's exercise of its functions, the auditor shall[2]:

(a) Consider whether the matter should be brought to the attention of the regulator under the terms of the appropriate legal provisions enabling the auditor to report direct to the regulator; and, if so

(b) Advise those charged with governance that in the auditor's opinion the matter should be drawn to the regulators' attention.

---

[4] *In the UK, subject to compliance with legislation relating to 'tipping off'.*

[5] *'Close links' is defined in point (38) of Article 4(1) of Regulation (EU) No 575/2013 of the European Parliament and of the Council of 26 June 2013.*

Where the auditor is unable to obtain, within a reasonable period, adequate evidence that those charged with governance have properly informed the regulator of the matter, the auditor shall[4] make a report direct to the regulator as soon as practicable. (Ref: Para. A36–A37)

Contents of a Report Initiated by the Auditor

When making or confirming in writing a report direct to a regulator, the auditor shall: **16**

(a) State the name of the regulated entity concerned;
(b) State the statutory power under which the report is made;
(c) State that the report has been prepared in accordance with ISA (UK) 250, *Section B—The Auditor's Statutory Right and Duty to Report to Regulators of Public Interest Entities and Regulators of Other Entities in the Financial Sector*;
(d) Describe the context in which the report is given;
(e) Describe the matter giving rise to the report;
(f) Request the regulator to confirm that the report has been received; and
(g) State the name of the auditor, the date of the written report and, where appropriate, the date on which an oral report was made to the regulator and the name and title of the individual to whom the oral report was made. (Ref: Para. A38–A39)

Relationship With Other Reporting Responsibilities

When issuing a report expressing an opinion on a regulated entity's financial statements or on other matters specified by legislation or a regulator, the auditor: **17**

(a) Shall consider whether there are consequential reporting issues affecting the auditor's opinion which arise from any report previously made direct to the regulator in the course of the auditor's appointment; and
(b) Shall assess whether any matters encountered in the course of the audit indicate a need for a further direct report. (Ref: Para. A40–A43)

***

Application and Other Explanatory Material

The Auditor's Responsibilities (Ref: Para. 2–6)

Before accepting appointment, the auditor follows the procedures identified in the FRC's Ethical Standard and the ethical pronouncements and Audit Regulations issued by the auditor's relevant professional body.   **A1**

In the case of regulated entities, the auditor would in particular obtain an understanding of the appropriate statutory and regulatory requirements and a preliminary knowledge of the management and operations of the entity, so as to enable the auditor to determine whether a level of knowledge of the business adequate to perform the audit can be obtained. The procedures carried out by the auditor in seeking to obtain this preliminary understanding may include discussion with the previous auditor and, in some circumstances, with the regulator.   **A2**

On ceasing to hold office, the auditor may be required by statute or by regulation to make specific reports concerning the circumstances relating to that event, and would also follow the procedures identified in the ethical guidance issued by the relevant professional body.   **A3**

A4   In addition, the auditor of a regulated entity would assess whether it is appropriate to bring any matters of which the auditor is then aware to the notice of the regulator. Under legislation in the UK, this may be done either before or after ceasing to hold office, as the auditor's statutory right to disclose to a regulator information obtained in the course of the auditor's appointment is not affected by the auditor's removal, resignation or otherwise ceasing to hold office.

A5   The duty to make a report direct to a regulator does not impose upon the auditor a duty to carry out specific work: it arises solely in the context of work carried out to fulfil other reporting responsibilities. Accordingly, no auditing procedures in addition to those carried out in the normal course of auditing the financial statements, or for the purpose of making any other specified report, are necessary for the fulfilment of the auditor's responsibilities.

A6   It will, however, be necessary for the auditor to take additional time in carrying out a financial statement audit or other engagement to assess whether matters which come to the auditor's attention should be included in a direct report and, where appropriate, to prepare and submit the report. These additional planning and follow-up procedures do not constitute an extension of the scope of the financial statement audit or of other work undertaken to provide a specified report relating to a regulated entity. They are necessary solely in order to understand and clarify the reporting responsibility and, where appropriate, to make a report.

A7   The circumstances in which the auditor is required by statute to make a report direct to a regulator include matters which are not considered as part of the audit of financial statements or of work undertaken to discharge other routine responsibilities. For example, the duty to report would apply to information of which the auditor became aware in the course of the auditor's work which is relevant to the Financial Conduct Authority's criteria for approved persons, although the auditor is not otherwise required to express an opinion on such matters. However, legislation imposing a duty to make reports direct to regulators does not require the auditor to change the scope of the audit work, nor does it place on the auditor an obligation to conduct the audit work in such a way that there is reasonable certainty that the auditor will discover all matters which regulators might consider as being of material significance. Therefore, whilst the auditor of a regulated entity is required to be alert to matters which may require a report, the auditor is not expected to be aware of all circumstances which, had the auditor known of them, would have led the auditor to make such a report. It is only when the auditor becomes aware of such a matter during the conduct of the normal audit work that the auditor has an obligation to determine whether a report to the regulator is required by statute or appropriate for other reasons.

A8   Similarly, the auditor is not responsible for reporting on a regulated entity's overall compliance with rules with which it is required to comply nor is the auditor required to conduct the audit work in such a way that there is reasonable certainty that the auditor will discover breaches. Nevertheless, breaches of rules with which a regulated entity is required to comply may have implications for the financial statements and, accordingly, the auditor of a regulated entity needs to consider whether any actual or contingent liabilities may have arisen from breaches of regulatory requirements. Breaches of a regulator's requirements may also have consequences for other matters on which the auditor of a regulated entity is required to express an opinion and, if such breaches represent criminal conduct, could give rise to the need to report to specified authorities.

Conduct of the Audit

Planning (Ref: Para. 10)

ISAs (UK) require the auditor to obtain an understanding of the entity and its environment.[6]

A9

In the context of a regulated entity, the auditor's understanding of its environment needs to extend to the applicable statutory provisions, the rules of the regulator concerned and any guidance issued by the regulator on the interpretation of those rules, together with other guidance issued by relevant authorities, including the FRC.

A10

The auditor is also required to identify and assess the risks of material misstatements to provide a basis for designing and performing further audit procedures.[7] In making such an assessment the auditor takes into account the control environment, including the entity's higher level procedures for complying with the requirements of its regulator. Such a review gives an indication of the extent to which the general atmosphere and controls in the regulated entity are conducive to compliance, for example through consideration of *inter alia:*

A11

- The adequacy of procedures and training to inform staff of the requirements of relevant legislation and the rules or other regulations of the regulator.
- The adequacy of procedures for authorization of transactions.
- Procedures for internal review of the entity's compliance with regulatory or other requirements.
- The authority of, and any resources available to, the compliance officer/Money Laundering Reporting Officer (MLRO).
- Procedures to ensure that possible breaches of requirements are investigated by an appropriate person and are brought to the attention of senior management.

In some areas of the financial sector, conducting business outside the scope of the entity's authorization is a serious regulatory breach, and therefore of material significance to the regulator. In addition, it may result in fines, suspension or loss of authorization.

A12

Where the auditor's review of the reporting entity's activities indicates that published guidance by the regulator may not be sufficiently precise to enable the auditor to identify circumstances in which it is necessary to initiate a report, the auditor would consider whether it is necessary to discuss the matters specified in legislation with the appropriate regulator with a view to reaching agreement on its interpretation.

A13

Similarly, where a group includes two or more companies separately regulated by different regulators, there may be a need to clarify the regulators' requirements in any overlapping areas of activity. However, the statutory duty to make a report as presently defined arises only in respect of the legal entity subject to regulation. Therefore the auditor of an unregulated company in a group that includes one or more other companies which are authorized by regulators would not have a duty to report matters to the regulators of those companies.

A14

---

[6] *ISA (UK) 315 (Revised June 2016), Identifying and Assessing the Risks of Material Misstatement through Understanding the Entity and Its Environment, paragraph 11.*

[7] *ISA (UK) 315 (Revised June 2016), paragraph 25.*

A15 When a regulated entity is subject to provisions of two or more regulators, the auditor needs to take account of the separate reporting requirements in planning and conducting the audit work. Arrangements may exist for one regulatory body to rely on financial monitoring being carried out by another body (the 'lead regulator') and where this is the case, routine reports by the regulated entity's auditor may be made to the lead regulator alone.

A16 However, the auditor's statutory duty to report cannot be discharged by reliance on the lead regulator informing others. Therefore, where the auditor concludes that a matter is of material significance to one regulator, the auditor needs to assess the need for separate reports informing each regulator of matters which the auditor concludes are or may be of material significance to it.

Supervision and Control (Ref: Para. 11)

A17 ISAs (UK) require the engagement partner to take responsibility for the direction, supervision and performance of the audit engagement in compliance with professional standards and applicable legal and regulatory requirements.[8] Consequently, in planning and conducting the audit of a regulated entity the auditor needs to ensure that staff are alert to the possibility that a report to its regulator may be required.

A18 Auditing firms also need to establish adequate procedures to ensure that any matters which are discovered in the course of or as a result of audit work and may give rise to a duty to report are brought to the attention of the engagement partner responsible for the audit on a timely basis.

A19 The right and duty to report to a regulator applies to information of which the auditor becomes aware in the auditor's capacity as such. They do not extend automatically to any information obtained by a firm regardless of its source. Consequently partners and staff undertaking work in another capacity are not required to have detailed knowledge of the regulator's requirements (unless necessary for that other work) nor to bring information to the attention of the engagement partner responsible for the audit on a routine basis.

A20 However, as discussed further in Appendix 2, firms need to establish lines of communications, commensurate with their size and complexity, sufficient to ensure that non-audit work undertaken for a regulated entity which is likely to have an effect on the audit is brought to the attention of the engagement partner responsible for the audit, who will need to determine whether the results of non-audit work undertaken for a regulated entity ought to be assessed as part of the audit process.

Use of the Work of Other Auditors

A21 An auditor with responsibilities for reporting on financial statements including financial information of one or more components audited by other auditors is required to obtain sufficient appropriate audit evidence that the work of the other auditors is adequate for the purposes of the audit. The same principle applies to using the work of another auditor in a different type of engagement. The auditor of a regulated entity who uses the work undertaken by other auditors needs to establish reporting arrangements such that the other auditors bring to the attention of the auditor of the regulated entity matters arising from their work which may give rise to a duty to report to a regulator.

---

[8] *ISA (UK) 220 (Revised June 2016), Quality Control for an Audit of Financial Statements, paragraph 15.*

The nature of the reporting arrangements will depend on the nature of the work   **A22**
undertaken by the other auditors. For example, the statutory duty to make a report
relates to the legal entity subject to regulation rather than to the entire group to which
that entity may belong. Consequently, the auditor of a holding company authorized
by one regulator would not be expected to have knowledge of all matters which come
to the attention of a component auditor. The auditor of the regulated entity would,
however, have a duty to report, where appropriate, matters which arise from the audit of
the regulated entity's own financial statements and of the consolidated group figures.

Where the audit of a regulated entity is undertaken by joint auditors, knowledge obtained   **A23**
by one firm is likely to be deemed to be known by the other. Care will therefore be
needed in agreeing and implementing arrangements to exchange information relating
to matters which may give rise to a duty to report to a regulator.

Identifying Matters Requiring a Report Direct to Regulators (Ref: Para. 12)

The precise matters which give rise to a statutory duty on auditors to make a report to   **A24**
a regulator derive from the relevant Acts. Broadly, such matters fall into three general
categories:

(a) The financial position of the regulated entity;
(b) Its compliance with requirements for the management of its business; and
(c) The status of those charged with governance as fit and proper persons.

Further detailed guidance on the interpretation of these matters in the context of
specific legislation applicable to each type of regulated entity is contained in Practice
Notes dealing with the rights and duties of auditors of regulated entities to report direct
to regulators.

In assessing the effect of an apparent breach, the auditor takes into account the quantity   **A25**
and type of evidence concerning such a matter which may reasonably be expected to be
available. If the auditor concludes that the auditor has been prevented from obtaining all
such evidence concerning a matter which may give rise to a duty to report, the auditor
would normally make a report direct to the regulator as soon as practicable.

An apparent breach of statutory or regulatory requirements may not of itself give rise to   **A26**
a statutory duty to make a report to a regulator. There will normally be a need for some
further investigation and discussion of the circumstances surrounding the apparent
breach with the directors in order to obtain sufficient information to determine whether
it points to a matter which is or may be of material significance to the regulator. For
example, a minor breach which has been corrected by the regulated entity and reported
(if appropriate) to the regulator, and which from the evidence available to the auditor
appears to be an isolated occurrence, would not normally give the auditor reasonable
cause to believe that it is or may be of material significance to the regulator. However,
a minor breach that results in a criminal offence that gave rise to the criminal property
would be reportable to the specified authorities under the anti-money laundering
legislation.

When determining whether a breach of statutory or regulatory requirements gives rise   **A27**
to a statutory duty to make a report direct to a regulator, the auditor considers factors
such as:

● Whether the breach, though minor, is indicative of a general lack of compliance
with the regulator's requirements or otherwise casts doubt on the status of those
charged with governance as fit and proper persons.

- Whether a breach which occurred before the auditor's visit to the regulated entity was reported by the entity itself and has since been corrected, such that, at the date of the auditor's discovery, no breach exists.
- Whether the circumstances giving rise to a breach which occurred before the auditors visit to the regulated entity continue to exist, or those charged with governance have not taken corrective action, or the breach has re-occurred.
- Whether the circumstances suggest that an immediate report to the regulator is necessary in order to protect the interests of depositors, investors, policyholders, clients of the entity or others in whose interests the regulator is required to act.

A28   The auditor would normally seek evidence to assess the implications of a suspected breach before reporting a matter to the regulator. However, the auditor's responsibility to make a report does not require the auditor to determine the full implications of a matter before reporting: the auditor is required to exercise professional judgment as to whether or not there is reasonable cause to believe that a matter is or may be of material significance to the regulator. In forming that judgment, the auditor undertakes appropriate investigations to determine the circumstances but does not require the degree of evidence which would be a normal part of forming an opinion on financial statements. Such investigations would normally include:

- Enquiry of appropriate level of staff;
- Review of correspondence and documents relating to the transaction or event concerned; and
- Discussion with those charged with governance, or other senior management where appropriate.

In the case of a life company, it would also be appropriate to consult with the appointed actuary, who also has various statutory duties under insurance companies legislation.

A29   The potential gravity of some apparent breaches may be such that an immediate report to the regulator is essential in order to enable the regulator to take appropriate action: in particular, prompt reporting of a loss of client assets may be necessary to avoid further loss to investors or others in whose interests the regulator is required to act. The auditor is therefore required to balance the need for further investigation of the matter with the need for prompt reporting.

A30   On completion of the auditor's investigations, the auditor needs to ensure that the facts and the basis for the auditor's decision (whether to report or not) is adequately documented such that the reasons for that decision may be clearly demonstrated should the need to do so arise in future.

Reporting

The Auditor's Statutory Duty to Report Direct to Regulators (Ref: Para. 13–14)

A31   Except in the circumstances referred to in paragraph 14 the auditor seeks to reach agreement with those charged with governance on the circumstances giving rise to a report direct to the regulator. However, where a statutory duty to report arises, the auditor is required to make such a report regardless of:

(a) Whether the matter has been referred to the regulator by other parties (including the company, whether by those charged with governance or otherwise); and
(b) Any duty owed to other parties, including those charged with governance of the regulated entity and its shareholders (or equivalent persons).

Except in the circumstances set out in paragraph 14, the auditor sends a copy of the auditor's written report to those charged with governance and (where appropriate) audit committee of the regulated entity.

A32

In normal circumstances, the auditor would wish to communicate with the regulator with the knowledge and agreement of those charged with governance of the regulated entity. However, in some circumstances immediate notification of the discovery of a matter giving reasonable grounds to believe that a reportable matter exists will be necessary – for example, a phone call to alert the regulator followed by a meeting to discuss the circumstances.

A33

Speed of reporting is essential where the circumstances cause the auditor no longer to have confidence in the integrity of those charged with governance. In such circumstances, there may be a serious and immediate threat to the interests of depositors or other persons for whose protection the regulator is required to act; for example where the auditor believes that a fraud or other irregularity may have been committed by, or with the knowledge of, those charged with governance, or have evidence of the intention of those charged with governance to commit or condone a suspected fraud or other irregularity.

A34

In circumstances where the auditor no longer has confidence in the integrity of those charged with governance, it is not appropriate to provide those charged with governance with copies of the auditor's report. Since such circumstances will be exceptional and extreme, the auditor may wish to seek legal advice as to the auditor's responsibilities and the appropriate course of action.

A35

The Auditor's Right to Report Direct to Regulators (Ref: Para. 15)

The auditor may become aware of matters which the auditor concludes are relevant to the exercise of the regulator's functions even though they fall outside the statutory definition of matters which must be reported to a regulator. In such circumstances, the Acts in the UK provide the auditor with protection for making disclosure of the matter to the appropriate regulator.

A36

Where the auditor considers that a matter which does not give rise to a statutory duty to report is nevertheless, in the auditor's professional judgment, such that it should be brought to the attention of the regulator, it is normally appropriate for the auditor to request those charged with governance of the regulated entity in writing to draw it to the attention of the regulator.

A37

Contents of a Report Initiated by the Auditor (Ref: Para. 16)

Such a report is a by-product of other work undertaken by the auditor. As a result it is not possible for the auditor or the regulator to conclude that all matters relevant to the regulator were encountered in the course of the auditor's work. The auditor's report therefore sets out the context in which the information reported was identified and indicates the extent to which the matter has been investigated and discussed with those charged with governance.

A38

Matters to which the auditor may wish to refer when describing the context in which a report is made direct to a regulator include:

A39

- The nature of the appointment from which the report derives. For example, it may be appropriate to distinguish between a report made in the course of an audit of financial statements and one which arises in the course of a more limited engagement, such as an appointment to report on specified matters by the Financial Conduct Authority;

- The applicable legislative requirements and interpretations of those requirements which have informed the auditor's judgment;
- The extent to which the auditor has investigated the circumstances giving rise to the matter reported;
- Whether the matter reported has been discussed with those charged with governance;
- Whether steps to rectify the matter have been taken.

Relationship With Other Reporting Responsibilities (Ref: Para. 17)

A40　The circumstances which give rise to a report direct to a regulator may involve an uncertainty or other matter which requires disclosure in the financial statements. The auditor will therefore need to consider whether the disclosures made in the financial statements are adequate for the purposes of giving a true and fair view of the regulated entity's state of affairs and profit or loss. Where the auditor considers it necessary to draw users' attention to a matter presented or disclosed in the financial statements that, in the auditor's judgment, is of such importance that it is fundamental to users' understanding of the financial statements, the auditor is required to include an Emphasis of Matter paragraph in the auditor's report.[9]

A41　Similarly, circumstances giving rise to a report direct to a regulator may also require reflection in the auditor's reports on other matters required by legislation or another regulator.

A42　In fulfilling the responsibility to report direct to a regulator, it is important that the auditor not only assess the significance of individual transactions or events but also consider whether a combination of such items over the course of the work undertaken for the auditor's primary reporting responsibilities may give the auditor reasonable grounds to believe that they constitute a matter of material significance to the regulator, and so give rise to a statutory duty to make a report.

A43　As there is no requirement for the auditor to extend the scope of the audit work to search for matters which may give rise to a statutory duty to report, such an assessment of the cumulative effect of evidence obtained in the course of an audit would be made when reviewing the evidence in support of the opinions to be expressed in the reports the auditor has been appointed to make. Where such a review leads to the conclusion that the cumulative effect of matters noted in the course of the audit is of material significance to the regulator, it will be appropriate for a report to be made as set out in paragraph 16. However, reports indicating a 'nil return' are not appropriate.

Communication of Information by the Regulator

A44　The Acts provide that, in certain exceptional circumstances, regulators may pass confidential information to another party. The precise circumstances in which regulators may disclose information varies, but in general they may do so if considered necessary to fulfil their own obligations under the appropriate Act, or, in some cases, to enable the auditor to fulfil the auditor's duties either to the

---

[9] *ISA (UK) 706 (Revised June 2016), Emphasis of Matter Paragraphs and Other Matter Paragraphs in the Independent Auditor's Report, paragraph 6.*

regulated entity or, in other cases, to the regulator. Confidential information remains confidential in the hands of the recipient.

In so far as the law permits, regulators have confirmed that they will consider taking the initiative in bringing a matter to the attention of the auditor of a regulated entity in circumstances where:

A45

(a) They believe the matter is of such importance that the auditor's knowledge of it could significantly affect the form of the auditor's report on the entity's financial statements or other matters on which the auditor is required to report, or the way in which the auditor discharges the auditor's reporting responsibilities; and

(b) The disclosure is for the purpose of enabling or assisting the regulator to discharge its functions under the Acts.

The auditor needs to be aware that there may be circumstances in which the regulators are unable to disclose such information. Where the auditor of a regulated entity is not informed by the regulator of any matter, therefore, the auditor cannot assume that there are no matters known to the regulator which could affect the auditor's judgment as to whether information is of material significance. However, in the absence of disclosure by the regulator, the auditor can only form a judgment in the light of evidence to which the auditor has access.

A46

For audits of public interest entities, the Audit Regulation[10] requires an effective dialogue to be established between the supervising credit institutions and insurance undertakings, on the one hand, and the auditor carrying out the audit of those institutions and undertakings, on the other hand. The responsibility for compliance with this requirement of the Audit Regulation rests with both parties to the dialogue.

A47

---

[10] *Regulation (EU) No 537/2014 of the European Parliament and of the Council of 16 April 2014.*

Appendix 1

The Regulatory Framework in the Financial Sector

1   In the UK, legislation exists in the principal areas of financial services to protect the interests of investors, depositors in banks and other users of financial services. Regulated entities operating in the financial sector are required to comply with legal and regulatory requirements concerning the way their business is conducted. Compliance with those rules is monitored in four principal ways:

- Internal monitoring by those charged with governance of the regulated entity;
- Submission of regular returns by the regulated entity to the regulator;
- Monitoring and, in some cases, inspection of the entity by the regulator;
- Reports[4] by the reporting entity's auditor on its financial statements and other specified matters required by legislation or by the regulator.

Responsibility for Ensuring Compliance

2   Ensuring compliance with the requirements with which a regulated entity is required to comply in carrying out its business is the responsibility of those charged with governance of a regulated entity. It requires adequate organization and systems of controls. The regulatory framework provides that adequate procedures for compliance must be established and maintained. Those charged with governance of a regulated entity are also normally required to undertake regular reviews of compliance and to inform the regulator of any breach of the rules and regulations applicable to its regulated business. In addition, regulators may undertake compliance visits.

3   The auditor of a regulated entity normally has responsibilities for reporting[4] on particular aspects of its compliance with the regulator's requirements. However, the auditor has no direct responsibility for expressing an opinion on an entity's overall compliance with the requirements for the conduct of its business, nor does an audit provide any assurance that breaches of requirements which are not the subject of regular auditors' reports will be detected.

The Role of Auditors

4   Those charged with governance of regulated entities have primary responsibility for ensuring that all appropriate information is made available to regulators. Normal reporting procedures (including auditor's reports on records, systems and returns, and regular meetings with those charged with governance and/or management and auditors) supplemented by any inspection visits considered necessary by the regulators should provide the regulators with all the information they need to carry out their responsibilities under the relevant Act.

Routine Reporting by Auditors

5   Regulators' requirements for reports by auditors vary. In general terms, however, such reports may include opinions on:

- The regulated entity's annual financial statements;
- The regulated entity's compliance with requirements for financial resources; and

- The adequacy of the regulated entity's system of controls over its transactions and in particular over its clients' money and other property.

As a result of performing the work necessary to discharge their routine reporting responsibilities, or those arising from an appointment to provide a special report required by the regulator, the auditor of a regulated entity may become aware of matters which the auditor considers need to be brought to the regulator's attention sooner than would be achieved by routine reports by the entity or its auditor.   6

The auditor of a regulated entity normally has a right to communicate in good faith[4] information the auditor considers is relevant to the regulators' functions.   7

The Auditor's Statutory Duty to Report to the Regulator

In addition, the auditor is required by law to report[4] direct to a regulator when the auditor concludes that there is reasonable cause to believe that a matter is or may be of material significance to the regulator. The precise matters which result in a statutory duty to make such a report vary, depending upon the specific requirements of relevant legislation and the regulator's rules. In general, however, a duty to report to a regulator arises when the auditor becomes aware that: 8

- The regulated entity is in serious breach of:
  - Requirements to maintain adequate financial resources; or
  - Requirements for those charged with governance to conduct its business in a sound and prudent manner (including the maintenance of systems of control over transactions and over any clients' assets held by the business); or
- There are circumstances which give reason to doubt the status of those charged with governance or senior management as fit and proper persons.

Confidentiality

Confidentiality is an implied term of the auditor's contracts with client entities. However, in the circumstances leading to a right or duty to report,[4] the auditor is entitled to communicate to regulators in good faith information or opinions relating to the business or affairs of the entity or any associated body without contravening the duty of confidence owed to the entity and, in the case of a bank, building society and friendly society, its associated bodies.   9

The statutory provisions permitting the auditor to communicate information to regulators relate to information obtained in the auditor's capacity as auditor of the regulated entity concerned. Auditors and regulators therefore should be aware that confidential information obtained in other capacities may not normally be disclosed to another party.   10

Appendix 2

(Ref: Para. 4)

The Application of the Statutory Duty to Report to Regulators

Introduction

1   The statutory duty to report to a regulator[4] applies to information which comes to the attention of the auditor in the auditor's capacity as auditor. However, neither the term 'auditor' nor the phrase 'in the capacity of auditor' are defined in the legislation, nor has the court determined how these expressions should be construed.

2   As a result, it is not always clearly apparent when a firm should regard itself as having a duty to report to a regulator. For example, information about a regulated entity may be obtained when partners or staff of the firm which is appointed as its auditor carry out work for another client entity; or when the firm undertakes other work for the regulated entity. Auditors, regulated entities and regulators need to be clear as to when the normal duty of confidentiality will be overridden by the auditor's statutory duty to report to the regulator.

3   In order to clarify whether or not a firm should regard itself as bound by the duty, the FRC developed, in conjunction with HM Treasury and the regulators, guidance on the interpretation of the key conditions for the existence of that duty, namely that the firm is to be regarded as auditor of a regulated entity and that information is obtained in the capacity of auditor.

4   Guidance on the interpretation of the term 'auditor' in the context of each Act is contained in the separate Practice Notes dealing with each area affected by the legislation.

5   This appendix sets out guidance on the interpretation of the phrase 'in the capacity of auditor'. The Board nevertheless continues to hold the view that the meaning of the phrase should be clarified in legislation in the longer term.

In the Capacity of Auditor

6   In determining whether information is obtained in the capacity of auditor, two criteria in particular should be considered:

   (a) Whether the person who obtained the information also undertook the audit work; and if so
   (b) Whether it was obtained in the course of or as a result of undertaking the audit work.

7   It is then necessary to apply these criteria to information about a regulated entity which may become known from a number of sources, and by a number of different individuals within a firm. Within a large firm, for example, information may come to the attention of the partner responsible for the audit of a regulated entity, a partner in another office who undertakes a different type of work, or members of the firm's staff at any level. In the case of a sole practitioner who is the auditor of a regulated entity, information about a regulated entity may also be obtained by the practitioner in the course of work other than its audit.

Non-Audit Work Carried out in Relation to a Regulated Entity

Where partners or staff involved in the audit of a regulated entity carry out work other than its audit (non-audit work) information about the regulated entity will be known to them as individuals. In circumstances which suggest that a matter would otherwise give rise to a statutory duty to report[4] if obtained in the capacity of auditor, it will be prudent for them to make enquiries in the course of their audit work in order to establish whether this is the case from information obtained in that capacity.

8

However, where non-audit work is carried out by other partners or staff, neither of the criteria set out in paragraph 6 is met in respect of information which becomes known to them. Nevertheless the firm should take proper account of such information when it could affect the audit so that it is treated in a responsible manner, particularly since in partnership law the knowledge obtained by one partner in the course of the partnership business may be imputed to the entire partnership. In doing so, two types of work may be distinguished: first, work which could affect the firm's work as auditor and, secondly, work which is undertaken purely in an advisory capacity.

9

A firm appointed as auditor of a regulated entity needs to have in place appropriate procedures to ensure that the partner responsible for the audit function is made aware of any other relationship which exists between any department of the firm and the regulated entity when that relationship could affect the firm's work as auditor. Common examples of such work include accounting work, particularly for smaller entities, and provision of tax services to the regulated entity.

10

Prima facie, information obtained in the course of non-audit work is not covered by either the right or the duty to report to a regulator. However, the firm appointed as auditor needs to consider whether the results of other work undertaken for a regulated entity need to be assessed as part of the audit process. In principle, this is no different to seeking to review a report prepared by outside consultants on, say, the entity's accounting systems so as to ensure that the auditor makes a proper assessment of the risks of misstatement in the financial statements and of the work needed to form an opinion. Consequently, the partner responsible for the audit needs to make appropriate enquiries in the process of planning and completing the audit (see paragraph 17 above). Such enquiries would be directed to those aspects of the non-audit work which might reasonably be expected to be relevant to the audit. When, as a result of such enquiries, those involved in the audit become aware of issues which may be of material significance to a regulator such issues should be considered, and if appropriate reported[4] following the requirements set out in this Section of this ISA (UK).

11

Work which is undertaken in an advisory capacity, for example to assist the directors of a regulated entity to determine effective and efficient methods of discharging their duties, would not normally affect the work undertaken for the audit. Nevertheless, in rare instances, the partner responsible for such advisory work may conclude that steps considered necessary in order to comply with the regulator's requirements have not been taken by the directors or that the directors intend in some respect not to comply with the regulator's requirements. Such circumstances would require consideration in the course of work undertaken for the audit, both to consider the effect on the auditor's routine reports and to determine whether the possible non-compliance is or is likely to be of material significance to the regulator.

12

Work Relating to a Separate Entity

13   Information obtained in the course of work relating to another entity audited by the same firm (or the same practitioner) is confidential to that other entity. The auditor is not required, and has no right, to report to a regulator confidential information which arises from work undertaken by the same auditing firm for another client. However, as a matter of sound practice, individuals involved in the audit of a regulated entity who become aware (in a capacity other than that of auditor of a regulated entity) of a matter which could otherwise give rise to a statutory duty to report would normally make enquiries in the course of their audit of the regulated entity to establish whether the information concerned is substantiated.

14   In carrying out the audit work, the auditor is required to have due regard to whether disclosure of non-compliance with laws and regulations to a proper authority is appropriate in the public interest. standards and guidance on this general professional obligation is set out in Section A of this ISA (UK).

Conclusion

15   The phrase 'in his capacity as auditor' limits information subject to the duty to report to matters of which the auditor becomes aware in the auditor's capacity as such. Consequently, it is unlikely that a partnership can be said to be acting in its capacity as auditor of a particular regulated entity whenever any apparently unrelated material comes to the attention of a partner or member of staff not engaged in that audit, particularly if that material is confidential to another client.

16   The statutory duty to report to a regulator[4] therefore does not extend automatically to any information obtained by a firm regardless of its source. Firms undertaking audits of regulated entities need, however, to establish lines of communication, commensurate with their size and organizational structure, sufficient to ensure that non-audit work undertaken for a regulated entity which is likely to have an effect on the audit is brought to the attention of the partner responsible for the audit and to establish procedures for the partner responsible for the audit to make appropriate enquiries of those conducting such other work as part of the process of planning and completing the audit.

Appendix 3

Action by the Auditor on Discovery of a Breach of a Regulator's Requirements

1   This appendix sets out in the form of a flowchart the steps involved in assessing whether a report to a regulator is required when a breach of the regulator's requirements comes to the attention of the auditor.

2   The flowchart is intended to provide guidance to readers in understanding this Section of this ISA (UK). It does not form part of the auditing standards contained in the ISA (UK).

Action by the Auditor on Discovery of a Breach of a Regulator's Requirement

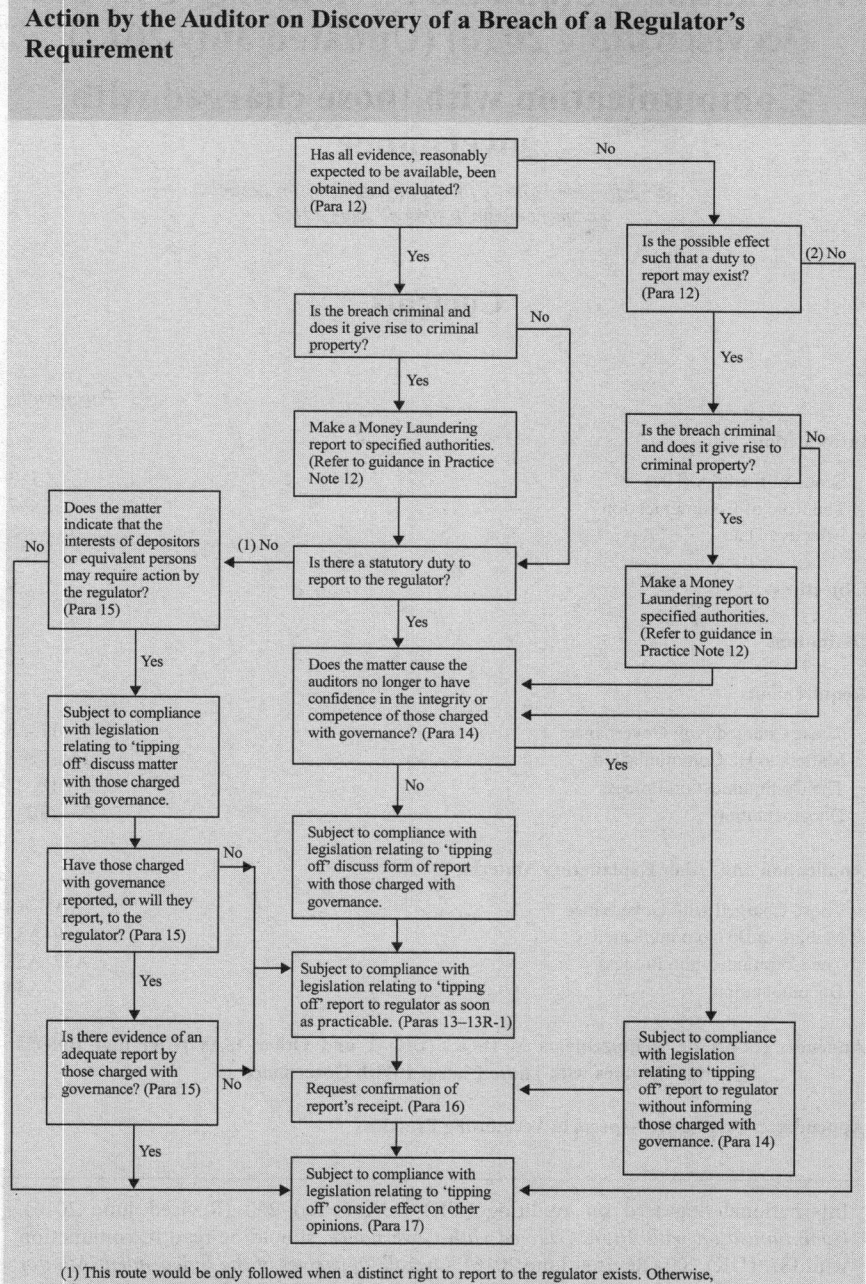

(1) This route would be only followed when a distinct right to report to the regulator exists. Otherwise, where no duty to report exists, the auditor would next consider the effect on other opinions.

(2) Where the auditor considers that a distinct right to report to the regulator exists, the auditor would next consider the question marked (1).

International Standard on Auditing (UK) 260 (Revised June 2016) (Updated July 2017) Communication with those charged with governance

(Effective for audits of financial statements for periods commencing on or after 17 June 2016)[0]

Contents

International Standard on Auditing (UK) (ISA (UK)) 260 (Revised June 2016), *Communication with Those Charged with Governance*, should be read in conjunction with ISA (UK) 200 (Revised June 2016), *Overall Objectives of the Independent Auditor and the Conduct of an Audit in Accordance with International Standards on Auditing (UK)*.

---

[0] *Conforming amendments to this standard as a result of ISA (UK) 250 (Revised July 2017)*, Section A—Consideration of Laws and Regulations in an Audit of Financial Statements, *are included that are effective for audits of financial statements for periods commencing on or after 15 December 2017. Details of the amendments are given in the Annexure to ISA (UK) 250 (Revised December 2017) Section A.*

Introduction

Scope of this ISA (UK)

This International Standard on Auditing (UK) (ISA (UK)) deals with the auditor's   1
responsibility to communicate with those charged with governance in an audit of financial
statements. Although this ISA (UK) applies irrespective of an entity's governance structure
or size, particular considerations apply where all of those charged with governance are
involved in managing an entity, and for listed entities. This ISA (UK) does not establish
requirements regarding the auditor's communication with an entity's management or
owners unless they are also charged with a governance role.

This ISA (UK) is written in the context of an audit of financial statements, but may also be   2
applicable, adapted as necessary in the circumstances, to audits of other historical financial
information when those charged with governance have a responsibility to oversee the
preparation of the other historical financial information.

Recognizing the importance of effective two-way communication in an audit of   3
financial statements, this ISA (UK) provides an overarching framework for the auditor's
communication with those charged with governance, and identifies some specific matters to
be communicated with them. Additional matters to be communicated, which complement
the requirements of this ISA (UK), are identified in other ISAs (UK) (see Appendix 1). In
addition, ISA (UK) 265[1] establishes specific requirements regarding the communication
of significant deficiencies in internal control the auditor has identified during the audit to
those charged with governance. Further matters, not required by this or other ISAs (UK),
may be required to be communicated by law or regulation, by agreement with the entity,
or by additional requirements applicable to the engagement, for example, the standards of
a national professional accountancy body. Nothing in this ISA (UK) precludes the auditor
from communicating any other matters to those charged with governance. (Ref: Para.
A33–A36)

The Role of Communication

This ISA (UK) focuses primarily on communications from the auditor to those charged   4
with governance. Nevertheless, effective two-way communication is important in assisting:
(a) The auditor and those charged with governance in understanding matters related
     to the audit in context, and in developing a constructive working relationship.
     This relationship is developed while maintaining the auditor's independence and
     objectivity;
(b) The auditor in obtaining from those charged with governance information relevant
     to the audit.[1a] For example, those charged with governance may assist the auditor in
     understanding the entity and its environment, in identifying appropriate sources of
     audit evidence, and in providing information about specific transactions or events;
     and
(c) Those charged with governance in fulfilling their responsibility to oversee the
     financial reporting process, thereby reducing the risks of material misstatement of the
     financial statements.

---

[1] *ISA (UK) 265,* Communicating Deficiencies in Internal Control to Those Charged with Governance and
Management.

[1a] *In the UK, Sections 499 and 500 of the Companies Act 2006 set legal requirements in relation to the auditor's right
to obtain information.*

5   Although the auditor is responsible for communicating matters required by this ISA (UK), management also has a responsibility to communicate matters of governance interest to those charged with governance. Communication by the auditor does not relieve management of this responsibility. Similarly, communication by management with those charged with governance of matters that the auditor is required to communicate does not relieve the auditor of the responsibility to also communicate them. Communication of these matters by management may, however, affect the form or timing of the auditor's communication with those charged with governance.

6   Clear communication of specific matters required to be communicated by ISAs (UK) is an integral part of every audit. ISAs (UK) do not, however, require the auditor to perform procedures specifically to identify any other matters to communicate with those charged with governance.

7   In some jurisdictions, law or regulation may restrict the auditor's communication of certain matters with those charged with governance. Law or regulation may specifically prohibit a communication, or other action, that might prejudice an investigation by an appropriate authority into an actual, or suspected, illegal act, including alerting the entity, for example, when the auditor is required to report identified or suspected non-compliance with law or regulation to an appropriate authority pursuant to anti-money laundering legislation. In these circumstances, the issues considered by the auditor may be complex and the auditor may consider it appropriate to obtain legal advice.

Effective Date

8   This ISA (UK) is effective for audits of financial statements for periods commencing on or after 17 June 2016. Earlier adoption is permitted.

Objectives

9   The objectives of the auditor are:
   (a) To communicate clearly with those charged with governance the responsibilities of the auditor in relation to the financial statement audit, and an overview of the planned scope and timing of the audit;
   (b) To obtain from those charged with governance information relevant to the audit;
   (c) To provide those charged with governance with timely observations arising from the audit that are significant and relevant to their responsibility to oversee the financial reporting process; and
   (d) To promote effective two-way communication between the auditor and those charged with governance.

Definitions

10   For purposes of the ISAs (UK), the following terms have the meanings attributed below:
   (a) Those charged with governance – The person(s) or organization(s) (e.g., a corporate trustee) with responsibility for overseeing the strategic direction of the entity and obligations related to the accountability of the entity. This includes overseeing the financial reporting process. For some entities in some jurisdictions, those charged with governance may include management personnel, for example, executive members of a governance board of a private or public sector entity, or an owner-manager. For discussion of the diversity of governance structures, see paragraphs A1–A8.

In the UK, those charged with governance include the directors (executive and non-executive) of a company and the members of an audit committee where one exists. For other types of entity it usually includes equivalent persons such as the partners, proprietors, committee of management or trustees.

(b) Management – The person(s) with executive responsibility for the conduct of the entity's operations. For some entities in some jurisdictions, management includes some or all of those charged with governance, for example, executive members of a governance board, or an owner-manager.

In the UK, management will not normally include non-executive directors.

Requirements

Those Charged with Governance

The auditor shall determine the appropriate person(s) within the entity's governance structure with whom to communicate. (Ref: Para. A1–A4-1) **11**

For audits of financial statements of public interest entities, if the entity does not have an audit committee, the additional report to the audit committee required by paragraph 16R-2 shall be submitted to the body performing equivalent functions within the entity. **11R-1**

Communication with a Subgroup of Those Charged with Governance

If the auditor communicates with a subgroup of those charged with governance, for example, an audit committee, or an individual, the auditor shall determine whether the auditor also needs to communicate with the governing body. (Ref: Para. A5–A7) **12**

When All of Those Charged with Governance Are Involved in Managing the Entity

In some cases, all of those charged with governance are involved in managing the entity, for example, a small business where a single owner manages the entity and no one else has a governance role. In these cases, if matters required by this ISA (UK) are communicated with person(s) with management responsibilities, and those person(s) also have governance responsibilities, the matters need not be communicated again with those same person(s) in their governance role. These matters are noted in paragraph 16(c). The auditor shall nonetheless be satisfied that communication with person(s) with management responsibilities adequately informs all of those with whom the auditor would otherwise communicate in their governance capacity. (Ref: Para. A8) **13**

Matters to Be Communicated

The Auditor's Responsibilities in Relation to the Financial Statement Audit

The auditor shall communicate with those charged with governance the responsibilities of the auditor in relation to the financial statement audit, including that: **14**

(a) The auditor is responsible for forming and expressing an opinion on the financial statements that have been prepared by management[1b] with the oversight of those charged with governance; and

(b) The audit of the financial statements does not relieve management or those charged with governance of their responsibilities. (Ref: Para. A9–A10)

Planned Scope and Timing of the Audit

15 The auditor shall communicate with those charged with governance an overview of the planned scope and timing of the audit, which includes communicating about the significant risks identified by the auditor. (Ref: Para. A11–A16)

> When the auditor is required or decides to communicate key audit matters in accordance with ISA (UK) 701,[1c] the overview of the planned scope and timing of the audit shall also include communicating about the most significant assessed risks of material misstatement (whether or not due to fraud) identified by the auditor, including those that had the greatest effect on: the overall audit strategy; the allocation of resources in the audit; and directing the efforts of the engagement team.

Significant Findings from the Audit

16 The auditor shall communicate with those charged with governance: (Ref: Para. A17–A18)

(a) The auditor's views about significant qualitative aspects of the entity's accounting practices, including accounting policies, accounting estimates and financial statement disclosures. When applicable, the auditor shall explain to those charged with governance why the auditor considers a significant accounting practice, that is acceptable under the applicable financial reporting framework, not to be most appropriate to the particular circumstances of the entity; (Ref: Para. A19–A20)

(b) Significant difficulties, if any, encountered during the audit; (Ref: Para. A21)

(c) Unless all of those charged with governance are involved in managing the entity:

    (i) Significant matters arising during the audit that were discussed, or subject to correspondence, with management; and (Ref: Para. A22)

    (ii) Written representations the auditor is requesting;

(d) Circumstances that affect the form and content of the auditor's report, if any; and (Ref: Para. A23–A25)

(e) Any other significant matters arising during the audit that, in the auditor's professional judgment, are relevant to the oversight of the financial reporting process. (Ref: Para. A26–A28)

[1b] *In the UK, those charged with governance are responsible for the preparation of the financial statements.*

[1c] *Paragraphs 30–31 of ISA (UK) 700 (Revised June 2016),* Forming an Opinion and Reporting on Financial Statements, *set out the requirements to apply ISA (UK) 701,* Communicating Key Audit Matters in the Independent Auditor's Report.

Entities that Report on Application of the UK Corporate Governance Code

In the case of entities that are required,[1d] and those that choose voluntarily, to report on how they have applied the UK Corporate Governance Code, or to explain why they have not, the auditor shall communicate to the audit committee the information that the auditor believes will be relevant to: (Ref: Para. A28-1)

16-1

- The board (in the context of fulfilling its responsibilities under Code provisions C.1.1, C.1.3, C.2.1, C.2.2 and C.2.3) and, where applicable, the audit committee (in the context of fulfilling its responsibilities under Code provision C.3.4); and
- The audit committee (in the context of fulfilling its responsibilities under Code provision C.3.2) in order to understand the rationale and the supporting evidence the auditor has relied on when making significant professional judgments in the course of the audit and in reaching an opinion on the financial statements.

If not already covered by communications under paragraphs 15, 16 and 16R-2 of this ISA (UK) and paragraph 25 of ISA (UK) 570 (Revised June 2016), this information shall include the auditor's views: (Ref: Para. A28-2–A28-5)

(a) About business risks relevant to financial reporting objectives, the application of materiality and the implications of their judgments in relation to these for the overall audit strategy, the audit plan and the evaluation of misstatements identified;

(b) On the significant accounting policies (both individually and in aggregate);

(c) On management's valuations of the entity's material assets and liabilities and the related disclosures provided by management;

(d) Without expressing an opinion on the effectiveness of the entity's system of internal control as a whole, and based solely on the audit procedures performed in the audit of the financial statements, about:
  (i) The effectiveness of the entity's system of internal control relevant to risks that may affect financial reporting; and
  (ii) Other risks arising from the entity's business model and the effectiveness of related internal controls to the extent, if any, the auditor has obtained an understanding of these matters;

(e) About the robustness of the directors' assessment of the principal risks facing the entity, including those that would threaten its business model, future performance, solvency or liquidity and its outcome, including the related disclosures in the annual report confirming that they have carried out such an assessment and describing those risks and explaining how they are being managed or mitigated (in accordance with Code provision C.2.1);

(f) About the directors' explanation in the annual report as to how they have assessed the prospects of the entity, over what period they have done so and why they consider that period to be appropriate (in accordance with Code provision C.2.2), and their statements:
  (i) in the financial statements, as to whether they considered it appropriate to adopt the going concern basis of accounting in preparing them, including any related disclosures identifying any material uncertainties to the entity's ability to continue to do so over a period of at least twelve months from the date of approval of the financial statements (in accordance with Code provision C.1.3); and
  (ii) in the annual report as to whether they have a reasonable expectation that the entity will be able to continue in operation and meet its liabilities as they fall due over the period of their assessment, including any related

---

[1d] *In the UK, these include companies with a premium listing of equity shares regardless of whether they are incorporated in the UK or elsewhere.*

disclosures drawing attention to any necessary qualifications or assumptions (in accordance with Code provision C.2.2); and

(g)   On any other matters identified in the course of the audit that the auditor believes will be relevant to the board or the audit committee in the context of fulfilling their responsibilities referred to above.

The auditor shall include with this communication sufficient explanation to enable the audit committee to understand the context within which the auditor's views relating to the matters in paragraph (d) above are expressed, including the extent to which the auditor has developed an understanding of these matters in the course of the audit and, if not already communicated to the audit committee, that the audit included consideration of internal control relevant to the preparation of the financial statements only in order to design audit procedures that are appropriate in the circumstances, and not for the purpose of expressing an opinion on the effectiveness of internal control.

Public Interest Entities

16R-2   For audits of financial statements of public interest entities, the auditor shall submit an additional report to the audit committee of the entity explaining the results of the audit carried out and shall at least:

(a)   Include the declaration of independence required by paragraph 17R-1(a);

(b)   Identify each key audit partner(s)[1e] involved in the audit;

(c)   Where the auditor has made arrangements for any of the auditor's activities to be conducted by another firm[1f] that is not a member of the same network, or has used the work of external experts, the report shall indicate that fact and shall confirm that the auditor received a confirmation from the other firm and/or the external expert regarding their independence;

(d)   Describe the nature, frequency and extent of communication with the audit committee or the body performing equivalent functions within the entity, the management body and the administrative or supervisory body of the entity, including the dates of meetings with those bodies;

(e)   Include a description of the scope and timing of the audit;

(f)   Where more than one auditor has been appointed, describe the distribution of tasks among the auditors;

(g)   Describe the methodology used, including which categories of the balance sheet have been directly verified and which categories have been verified based on system and compliance testing, including an explanation of any substantial variation in the weighting of system and compliance testing when compared to the previous year, even if the previous year's audit was carried out by another firm;

(h)   Disclose the quantitative level of materiality applied to perform the audit for the financial statements as a whole and where applicable the materiality level or levels for particular classes of transactions, account balances or disclosures, and disclose the qualitative factors which were considered when setting the level of materiality;

(i)   Report and explain judgments about events or conditions identified in the course of the audit that may cast significant doubt on the entity's ability to continue as a going concern and whether they constitute a material uncertainty, and provide a summary of all guarantees, comfort letters, undertakings of public intervention

---

[1e] *'Key audit partner' is defined in paragraph 7(f)-1 of ISA (UK) 220 (Revised June 2016),* Quality Control for an Audit of Financial Statements.

[1f] *'Firm' is defined in ISA (UK) 220 (Revised June 2016) as a sole practitioner, partnership or corporation or other entity of professional accountants.*

and other support measures that have been taken into account when making a going concern assessment;

(j) Report on any significant deficiencies in the entity's or, in the case of consolidated financial statements, the parent undertaking's internal financial control system, and/or in the accounting system. For each such significant deficiency, the additional report shall state whether or not the deficiency in question has been resolved by management;

(k) Report any significant matters involving actual or suspected non-compliance with laws and regulations or articles of association which were identified in the course of the audit, in so far as they are considered to be relevant in order to enable the audit committee to fulfil its tasks;

(l) Report the valuation methods[1g] applied to the various items in the annual or consolidated financial statements including any impact of changes of such methods;

(m) In the case of an audit of consolidated financial statements, explain the scope of consolidation and the exclusion criteria applied by the entity to the non-consolidated entities, if any, and whether those criteria applied are in accordance with the financial reporting framework;

(n) Where applicable, identify any audit work performed by component auditors in relation to an audit of consolidated financial statements other than by members of the same network to which the auditor of the consolidated financial statements belongs;

(o) Indicate whether all requested explanations and documents were provided by the entity;

(p) Report:
   (i) Any significant difficulties encountered in the course of the audit;
   (ii) Any significant matters arising from the audit that were discussed or were the subject of correspondence with management; and
   (iii) Any other matters arising from the audit that in the auditor's professional judgment, are significant to the oversight of the financial reporting process.

Where more than one auditor has been engaged simultaneously, and any disagreement has arisen between them on auditing procedures, accounting rules or any other issue regarding the conduct of the audit, the reasons for such disagreement shall be explained in the additional report to the audit committee.

Auditor Independence

In the case of listed entities, the auditor shall communicate with those charged with governance: **17**

(a) A statement that the engagement team and others in the firm as appropriate, the firm and, when applicable, network firms have complied with relevant ethical requirements regarding independence;[1h] and
   (i) All relationships and other matters between the firm, network firms, and the entity that, in the auditor's professional judgment, may reasonably be thought to bear on independence. This shall include total fees charged during the period

---

[1g] *ISA (UK) 330 (Revised July 2017)*, The Auditor's Responses to Assessed Risks, *paragraph 19R-1 deals with the auditor's responsibility to assess the valuation methods applied, including any impact of changes of such methods.*

[1h] *In the UK, auditors are subject to ethical requirements from two sources: the FRC's Ethical Standard concerning the integrity, objectivity and independence of the auditor and the ethical pronouncements established by the auditor's relevant professional body. In the case of listed companies, the FRC's Ethical Standard, Part B, Section 1 – General Requirements and Guidance, paragraphs 1.61 to 1.71 address communication with those charged with governance.*

covered by the financial statements for audit and non-audit services provided by the firm and network firms to the entity and components controlled by the entity. These fees shall be allocated to categories that are appropriate to assist those charged with governance in assessing the effect of services on the independence of the auditor; and

    (ii) The related safeguards that have been applied to eliminate identified threats to independence or reduce them to an acceptable level. (Ref: Para. A29–A32)

17R-1   For audits of financial statements of public interest entities, the auditor shall: (Ref: Para. A32-1)

    (a) Confirm annually in writing to the audit committee that the firm and partners, senior managers and managers, conducting the audit are independent from the audited entity; and

    (b) Discuss with the audit committee the threats to the auditor's independence and the safeguards applied to mitigate those threats.[li]

The Communication Process

Establishing the Communication Process

18   The auditor shall communicate with those charged with governance the form, timing and expected general content of communications. (Ref: Para. A37–A45)

Forms of Communication

19   The auditor shall communicate in writing with those charged with governance regarding significant findings from the audit if, in the auditor's professional judgment, oral communication would not be adequate. Written communications need not include all matters that arose during the course of the audit. (Ref: Para. A46–A48)

20   The auditor shall communicate in writing with those charged with governance regarding auditor independence when required by paragraph 17 and 17R-1.

20R-1   For audits of financial statements of public interest entities:

    (a) The additional report to the audit committee[lj] shall be in writing.

    (b) The additional report to the audit committee shall be signed and dated by the engagement partner.

    (c) Upon request by either the auditor or the audit committee, the auditor shall discuss key matters arising from the audit, referred to in the additional report to the audit committee, and in particular deficiencies communicated in accordance with paragraph 16R-2(j).

[li] *Paragraph 27R-2 of ISQC (UK) 1 (Revised June 2016),* Quality Control for Firms that Perform Audits and Reviews of Financial Statements, and Other Assurance and Related Services Engagements, *deals with the auditor's responsibility to assess such matters.*

[lj] *Paragraph 16R-2 deals with the auditor's responsibilities to prepare an additional report to the audit committee.*

Timing of Communications

The auditor shall communicate with those charged with governance on a timely basis.   **21**
(Ref: Para. A49–A50-1)

> For audits of financial statements of public interest entities, the auditor shall submit   **21R-1**
> the additional report to the audit committee not later than the date of submission of the
> auditor's report.[1k] (Ref: Para. A50-2)

Adequacy of the Communication Process

The auditor shall evaluate whether the two-way communication between the auditor and   **22**
those charged with governance has been adequate for the purpose of the audit. If it has
not, the auditor shall evaluate the effect, if any, on the auditor's assessment of the risks of
material misstatement and ability to obtain sufficient appropriate audit evidence, and shall
take appropriate action. (Ref: Para. A51–A53)

Documentation

Where matters required by this ISA (UK) to be communicated are communicated orally,   **23**
the auditor shall include them in the audit documentation, and when and to whom they
were communicated. Where matters have been communicated in writing, the auditor shall
retain a copy of the communication as part of the audit documentation.[2] (Ref: Para. A54)

> For audits of financial statements of public interest entities, the auditor shall retain any   **23D-1**
> other data and documents that are important in supporting the additional report to the
> audit committee[2a] as part of the audit documentation.

***

Application and Other Explanatory Material

Those Charged with Governance (Ref: Para. 11)

Governance structures vary by jurisdiction and by entity, reflecting influences such as   **A1**
different cultural and legal backgrounds, and size and ownership characteristics. For
example:

- In some jurisdictions a supervisory (wholly or mainly non-executive) board exists
  that is legally separate from an executive (management) board (a 'two-tier board'
  structure). In other jurisdictions, both the supervisory and executive functions are the
  legal responsibility of a single, or unitary, board (a 'one-tier board' structure).
- In some entities, those charged with governance hold positions that are an integral
  part of the entity's legal structure, for example, company directors. In others, for
  example, some government entities, a body that is not part of the entity is charged
  with governance.

[1k] *ISA (UK) 700 (Revised June 2016),* Forming an Opinion and Reporting on Financial Statements.

[2] *ISA (UK) 230 (Revised June 2016),* Audit Documentation, *paragraphs 8–11, and A6.*

[2a] *Paragraph 16R-2 deals with the auditor's responsibilities to prepare an additional report to the audit committee.*

- In some cases, some or all of those charged with governance are involved in managing the entity. In others, those charged with governance and management comprise different persons.
- In some cases, those charged with governance are responsible for approving[3] the entity's financial statements (in other cases management has this responsibility).

A2   In most entities, governance is the collective responsibility of a governing body, such as a board of directors, a supervisory board, partners, proprietors, a committee of management, a council of governors, trustees, or equivalent persons. In some smaller entities, however, one person may be charged with governance, for example, the owner-manager where there are no other owners, or a sole trustee. When governance is a collective responsibility, a subgroup such as an audit committee or even an individual, may be charged with specific tasks to assist the governing body in meeting its responsibilities. Alternatively, a subgroup or individual may have specific, legally identified responsibilities that differ from those of the governing body.

A3   Such diversity means that it is not possible for this ISA (UK) to specify for all audits the person(s) with whom the auditor is to communicate particular matters. Also, in some cases the appropriate person(s) with whom to communicate may not be clearly identifiable from the applicable legal framework or other engagement circumstances, for example, entities where the governance structure is not formally defined, such as some family-owned entities, some not-for-profit organizations, and some government entities. In such cases, the auditor may need to discuss and agree with the engaging party the relevant person(s) with whom to communicate. In deciding with whom to communicate, the auditor's understanding of an entity's governance structure and processes obtained in accordance with ISA (UK) 315 (Revised June 2016)[4] is relevant. The appropriate person(s) with whom to communicate may vary depending on the matter to be communicated.

A4   ISA (UK) 600 (Revised June 2016) includes specific matters to be communicated by group auditors with those charged with governance.[5] When the entity is a component of a group, the appropriate person(s) with whom the component auditor communicates depends on the engagement circumstances and the matter to be communicated. In some cases, a number of components may be conducting the same businesses within the same system of internal control and using the same accounting practices. Where those charged with governance of those components are the same (e.g., common board of directors), duplication may be avoided by dealing with these components concurrently for the purpose of communication.

A4-1   In the UK, there are statutory obligations on corporate subsidiary undertakings, and their auditors and other parties, to provide the auditor of a corporate parent undertaking with such information and explanations as that auditor may reasonably require for

---

[3] As described in paragraph A68 of ISA (UK) 700 (Revised June 2016), Forming an Opinion and Reporting on Financial Statements, *having responsibility for approving in this context means having the authority to conclude that all the statements that comprise the financial statements, including the related notes, have been prepared. In the UK, those charged with governance are responsible for the approval of the financial statements.*

[4] ISA (UK) 315 (Revised June 2016), Identifying and Assessing the Risks of Material Misstatement through Understanding the Entity and Its Environment.

[5] ISA (UK) 600 (Revised June 2016), Special Considerations—Audits of Group Financial Statements (Including the Work of Component Auditors), *paragraph 49.*

the purposes of the audit.[5a] Where there is no such statutory obligation (e.g., for non corporate entities), permission may be needed by the auditors of the subsidiary undertakings, from those charged with governance of the subsidiary undertakings, to disclose the contents of any communication to them to the auditor of the parent undertaking and also for the auditor of the parent undertaking to pass those disclosures onto those charged with governance of the parent undertaking. The auditor of the parent undertaking seeks to ensure that appropriate arrangements are made at the planning stage for these disclosures. Normally, such arrangements for groups are recorded in the instructions to the auditors of subsidiary undertakings and relevant engagement letters.

Communication with a Subgroup of Those Charged with Governance (Ref: Para. 12)

When considering communicating with a subgroup of those charged with governance, the auditor may take into account such matters as: **A5**

- The respective responsibilities of the subgroup and the governing body.
- The nature of the matter to be communicated.
- Relevant legal or regulatory requirements.
- Whether the subgroup has the authority to take action in relation to the information communicated, and can provide further information and explanations the auditor may need.

When deciding whether there is also a need to communicate information, in full or in summary form, with the governing body, the auditor may be influenced by the auditor's assessment of how effectively and appropriately the subgroup communicates relevant information with the governing body. The auditor may make explicit in agreeing the terms of engagement that, unless prohibited by law or regulation, the auditor retains the right to communicate directly with the governing body.   **A6**

Audit committees report to the board on various matters related to the discharge of their responsibilities, including those related to the financial statements, the annual report and the audit process (see paragraph A28-1 below). The auditor, when assessing whether there is a need to communicate with the full board regarding matters communicated by the auditor to the audit committee, takes into consideration the adequacy of the communications between the audit committee and the board, including whether they appropriately address relevant matters communicated to the audit committee by the auditor. This may be achieved in one or more ways including: where judged appropriate attending the relevant part of a board meeting where the audit committee reports to the board, holding discussions with individual board members, or reviewing any written reports from the audit committee to the board.   **A6-1**

[5a] *In the UK, Section 499 of the Companies Act 2006 specifies that the auditor of a company may require any subsidiary undertaking of the company which is a body corporate incorporated in the UK, and any officer, employee or auditor of any such subsidiary undertaking or any person holding or accountable for any books, accounts or vouchers of any such subsidiary undertaking, to provide him with such information or explanations as he thinks necessary for the performance of his duties as auditor. If a parent company has a subsidiary undertaking that is not a body corporate incorporated in the UK, Section 500 of the Companies Act 2006 specifies that the auditor of the parent company may require it to take all such steps as are reasonably open to it to obtain from the subsidiary undertaking, any officer, employee or auditor of the undertaking, or any person holding or accountable for any of the undertaking's books, accounts or vouchers, such information and explanations as he may reasonably require for the purposes of his duties as auditor.*

A7   Audit committees (or similar subgroups with different names) exist in many jurisdictions. Although their specific authority and functions may differ, communication with the audit committee, where one exists, has become a key element in the auditor's communication with those charged with governance. Good governance principles suggest that:

- The auditor will be invited to regularly attend meetings of the audit committee.
- The chair of the audit committee and, when relevant, the other members of the audit committee, will liaise with the auditor periodically.
- The audit committee will meet the auditor without management present at least annually.

When All of Those Charged with Governance Are Involved in Managing the Entity (Ref: Para.13)

A8   In some cases, all of those charged with governance are involved in managing the entity, and the application of communication requirements is modified to recognize this position. In such cases, communication with person(s) with management responsibilities may not adequately inform all of those with whom the auditor would otherwise communicate in their governance capacity. For example, in a company where all directors are involved in managing the entity, some of those directors (e.g., one responsible for marketing) may be unaware of significant matters discussed with another director (e.g., one responsible for the preparation of the financial statements).

Matters to Be Communicated

The Auditor's Responsibilities in Relation to the Financial Statement Audit (Ref: Para. 14)

A9   The auditor's responsibilities in relation to the financial statement audit are often included in the engagement letter or other suitable form of written agreement that records the agreed terms of the engagement.[6] Law, regulation or the governance structure of the entity may require those charged with governance to agree the terms of the engagement with the auditor. When this is not the case, providing those charged with governance with a copy of that engagement letter or other suitable form of written agreement may be an appropriate way to communicate with them regarding such matters as:

- The auditor's responsibility for performing the audit in accordance with ISAs (UK), which is directed towards the expression of an opinion on the financial statements. The matters that ISAs (UK) require to be communicated, therefore, include significant matters arising during the audit of the financial statements that are relevant to those charged with governance in overseeing the financial reporting process.
- The fact that ISAs (UK) do not require the auditor to design procedures for the purpose of identifying supplementary matters to communicate with those charged with governance.
- When ISA (UK) 701[7] applies, the auditor's responsibilities to determine and communicate key audit matters in the auditor's report.
- When applicable, the auditor's responsibility for communicating particular matters required by law or regulation, by agreement with the entity or by additional requirements applicable to the engagement, for example, the standards of a national professional accountancy body.

---

[6] *See paragraph 10 of ISA (UK) 210 (Revised June 2016),* Agreeing the Terms of Audit Engagements.

[7] *ISA (UK) 701,* Communicating Key Audit Matters in the Independent Auditor's Report.

The provision of copies of the audit engagement letter to the audit committees of listed companies facilitates their review and agreement of the audit engagement letter as recommended by the FRC Guidance on Audit Committees. As part of their review, the guidance further recommends the audit committee to consider whether the audit engagement letter has been updated to reflect changes in circumstances since the previous year.

A9-1

Law or regulation, an agreement with the entity or additional requirements applicable to the engagement may provide for broader communication with those charged with governance. For example, (a) an agreement with the entity may provide for particular matters to be communicated when they arise from services provided by a firm or network firm other than the financial statement audit; or (b) the mandate of a public sector auditor may provide for matters to be communicated that come to the auditor's attention as a result of other work, such as performance audits.

A10

Planned Scope and Timing of the Audit (Ref: Para. 15)

Communication regarding the planned scope and timing of the audit may:

A11

(a)   Assist those charged with governance to understand better the consequences of the auditor's work, to discuss issues of risk and the concept of materiality with the auditor, and to identify any areas in which they may request the auditor to undertake additional procedures;[7a] and

(b)   Assist the auditor to understand better the entity and its environment.

The communication of the planned scope of the audit includes, where relevant, any limitations on the work the auditor proposes to undertake (e.g., if limitations are imposed by management).[7b]

A11-1

Communicating significant risks identified by the auditor helps those charged with governance understand those matters and why they require special audit consideration. The communication about significant risks may assist those charged with governance in fulfilling their responsibility to oversee the financial reporting process.

A12

Matters communicated may include:

A13

- How the auditor plans to address the significant risks of material misstatement, whether due to fraud or error.
- How the auditor plans to address areas of higher assessed risks of material misstatement.
- The auditor's approach to internal control relevant to the audit.
- The application of the concept of materiality in the context of an audit.[8]

[7a] *The UK Corporate Governance Code and the FRC Guidance on Audit Committees contain, inter alia, recommendations about the audit committee's relationship with the auditor.*

[7b] *ISA (UK) 210 (Revised June 2016), paragraph 7 requires that if management or those charged with governance impose a limitation on the scope of the auditor's work in the terms of a proposed audit engagement such that the auditor believes the limitation will result in the auditor disclaiming an opinion on the financial statements, the auditor shall not accept such a limited engagement as an audit engagement, unless required by law or regulation to do so.*

[8] *ISA (UK) 320 (Revised June 2016),* Materiality in Planning and Performing an Audit.

- The nature and extent of specialized skill or knowledge needed to perform the planned audit procedures or evaluate the audit results, including the use of an auditor's expert.[9]
- When ISA (UK) 701 applies, the auditor's preliminary views about matters that may be areas of significant auditor attention in the audit and therefore may be key audit matters.
- The auditor's planned approach to addressing the implications on the individual statements and the disclosures of any significant changes within the applicable financial reporting framework or in the entity's environment, financial condition or activities.

A13-1   The nature and detail of the planning information communicated will reflect the size and nature of the entity and the manner in which those charged with governance operate.

A13-2   In any particular year, the auditor may decide that there are no significant changes in the planned scope and timing of the audit that have been communicated previously and judge that it is unnecessary to remind those charged with governance of all or part of that information. In these circumstances, the auditor need only make those charged with governance aware that the auditor has no new matters to communicate concerning the planned scope and timing of the audit. Matters that are included in the audit engagement letter need not be repeated.

A14   Other planning matters that it may be appropriate to discuss with those charged with governance include:

- Where the entity has an internal audit function, how the external and internal auditors can work together in a constructive and complementary manner, including any planned use of the work of the internal audit function, and the nature and extent of any planned use of internal auditors to provide direct assistance.[10]
- The views of those charged with governance about:
  - o   The appropriate person(s) in the entity's governance structure with whom to communicate.
  - o   The allocation of responsibilities between those charged with governance and management.
  - o   The entity's objectives and strategies, and the related business risks that may result in material misstatements.
  - o   Matters those charged with governance consider warrant particular attention during the audit, and any areas where they request additional procedures to be undertaken.
  - o   Significant communications between the entity and regulators.
  - o   Other matters those charged with governance consider may influence the audit of the financial statements.
- The attitudes, awareness, and actions of those charged with governance concerning (a) the entity's internal control and its importance in the entity, including how those charged with governance oversee the effectiveness of internal control, and (b) the detection or possibility of fraud.
- The actions of those charged with governance in response to developments in accounting standards, corporate governance practices, exchange listing rules, and

---

[9] *See ISA (UK) 620 (Revised June 2016)*, Using the Work of an Auditor's Expert.

[10] *ISA 610 (Revised June 2013)*, Using the Work of Internal Auditors, *paragraph 31.*
The use of internal auditors to provide direct assistance is prohibited in an audit in accordance with ISAs (UK) – see ISA (UK) 610 (Revised June 2013), paragraph 5-1.

related matters, and the effect of such developments on, for example, the overall presentation, structure and content of the financial statements, including:

- o The relevance, reliability, comparability and understandability of the information presented in the financial statements; and
- o Considering whether the financial statements are undermined by the inclusion of information that is not relevant or that obscures a proper understanding of the matters disclosed.

- The responses of those charged with governance to previous communications with the auditor.
- The documents comprising the other information (as defined in ISA (UK) 720 (Revised June 2016)) and the planned manner and timing of the issuance of such documents. When the auditor expects to obtain other information after the date of the auditor's report, the discussions with those charged with governance may also include the actions that may be appropriate or necessary if the auditor concludes that a material misstatement of the other information exists in other information obtained after the date of the auditor's report.[10a]

While communication with those charged with governance may assist the auditor to plan the scope and timing of the audit, it does not change the auditor's sole responsibility to establish the overall audit strategy and the audit plan, including the nature, timing and extent of procedures necessary to obtain sufficient appropriate audit evidence.   **A15**

Care is necessary when communicating with those charged with governance about the planned scope and timing of the audit so as not to compromise the effectiveness of the audit, particularly where some or all of those charged with governance are involved in managing the entity. For example, communicating the nature and timing of detailed audit procedures may reduce the effectiveness of those procedures by making them too predictable.   **A16**

Significant Findings from the Audit (Ref: Para. 16–16R-2)

The communication of findings from the audit may include requesting further information from those charged with governance in order to complete the audit evidence obtained. For example, the auditor may confirm that those charged with governance have the same understanding of the facts and circumstances relevant to specific transactions or events.   **A17**

When ISA (UK) 701 applies, the communications with those charged with governance required by paragraph 16, 16-1 and 16R-2, as well as the communication about the significant risks identified by the auditor required by paragraph 15, are particularly relevant to the auditor's determination of matters that required significant auditor attention and which therefore may be key audit matters.[11]   **A18**

Significant Qualitative Aspects of Accounting Practices (Ref: Para. 16(a))

Financial reporting frameworks ordinarily allow for the entity to make accounting estimates, and judgments about accounting policies and financial statement disclosures for example, in relation to the use of key assumptions in the development of accounting estimates for which there is significant measurement uncertainty. In addition, law, regulation or financial reporting frameworks may require disclosure of a summary of   **A19**

[10a] *ISA (UK) 700 (Revised June 2016) requires that 'The auditor shall not sign, and hence date, the auditor's report earlier than the date on which all the other information contained in the annual report has been approved by those charged with governance and the auditor has considered all necessary available evidence.'*

[11] *ISA (UK) 701, paragraphs 9–10.*

significant accounting policies or make reference to 'critical accounting estimates' or 'critical accounting policies and practices' to identify and provide additional information to users about the most difficult, subjective or complex judgments made by management in preparing the financial statements.

A20   As a result, the auditor's views on the subjective aspects of the financial statements may be particularly relevant to those charged with governance in discharging their responsibilities for oversight of the financial reporting process. For example, in relation to the matters described in paragraph A19, those charged with governance may be interested in the auditor's evaluation of the adequacy of disclosures of the estimation uncertainty relating to accounting estimates that give rise to significant risks. Open and constructive communication about significant qualitative aspects of the entity's accounting practices also may include comment on the acceptability of significant accounting practices, and the quality of the disclosures. Appendix 2 identifies matters that may be included in this communication.

Significant Difficulties Encountered during the Audit (Ref: Para. 16(b))

A21   Significant difficulties encountered during the audit may include such matters as:

- Significant delays by management, the unavailability of entity personnel, or an unwillingness by management to provide information necessary for the auditor to perform the auditor's procedures.
- An unreasonably brief time within which to complete the audit.
- Extensive unexpected effort required to obtain sufficient appropriate audit evidence.
- The unavailability of expected information.
- Restrictions imposed on the auditor by management.
- Management's unwillingness to make or extend its assessment of the entity's ability to continue as a going concern when requested.

In some circumstances, such difficulties may constitute a scope limitation that leads to a modification of the auditor's opinion.[12]

Significant Matters Discussed, or Subject to Correspondence with Management (Ref: Para. 16(c)(i))

A22   Significant matters discussed, or subject to correspondence with management may include such matters as:

- Significant events or transactions that occurred during the year.
- Business conditions affecting the entity, and business plans and strategies that may affect the risks of material misstatement.
- Concerns about management's consultations with other accountants on accounting or auditing matters.
- Discussions or correspondence in connection with the initial or recurring appointment of the auditor regarding accounting practices, the application of auditing standards, or fees for audit or other services.
- Significant matters on which there was disagreement with management, except for initial differences of opinion because of incomplete facts or preliminary information that are later resolved by the auditor obtaining additional relevant facts or information.

---

[12] *ISA (UK) 705 (Revised June 2016)*, Modifications to the Opinion in the Independent Auditor's Report.

Circumstances that Affect the Form and Content of the Auditor's Report (Ref: Para 16(d))

ISA (UK) 210 (Revised June 2016) requires the auditor to agree the terms of the audit   **A23**
engagement with management or those charged with governance, as appropriate.[13] The
agreed terms of the audit engagement are required to be recorded in an audit engagement
letter or other suitable form of written agreement and include, among other things, reference
to the expected form and content of the auditor's report.[14] As explained in paragraph
A9, if the terms of engagement are not agreed with those charged with governance, the
auditor may provide those charged with governance with a copy of the engagement letter
to communicate about matters relevant to the audit. The communication required by
paragraph 16(d) is intended to inform those charged with governance about circumstances
in which the auditor's report may differ from its expected form and content or may include
additional information about the audit that was performed.

Circumstances in which the auditor is required or may otherwise consider it necessary to   **A24**
include additional information in the auditor's report in accordance with the ISAs (UK),
and for which communication with those charged with governance is required, include
when:

- The auditor expects to modify the opinion in the auditor's report in accordance with
  ISA (UK) 705 (Revised June 2016).[15]
- A material uncertainty related to going concern is reported in accordance with ISA
  (UK) 570 (Revised June 2016).[16]
- Key audit matters are communicated in accordance with ISA (UK) 701.[17]
- The auditor considers it necessary to include an Emphasis of Matter paragraph or
  Other Matters paragraph in accordance with ISA (UK) 706 (Revised June 2016)[18] or
  is required to do so by other ISAs (UK).
- The auditor has concluded that there is an uncorrected material misstatement of the
  other information in accordance with ISA (UK) 720 (Revised June 2016).[19]

In such circumstances, the auditor may consider it useful to provide those charged with
governance with a draft of the auditor's report to facilitate a discussion of how such matters
will be addressed in the auditor's report.

In the rare circumstances that the auditor intends not to include the name of the engagement   **A25**
partner in the auditor's report in accordance with ISA (UK) 700 (Revised June 2016),
the auditor is required to discuss this intention with those charged with governance to
inform the auditor's assessment of the likelihood and severity of a significant personal
security threat.[20] The auditor also may communicate with those charged with governance

---

[13] *ISA (UK) 210 (Revised June 2016), paragraph 9.*

[14] *ISA (UK) 210 (Revised June 2016), paragraph 10.*

[15] *ISA (UK) 705 (Revised June 2016), paragraph 30.*

[16] *ISA (UK) 570 (Revised June 2016),* Going Concern, *paragraph 25(d).*

[17] *ISA (UK) 701, paragraph 17.*

[18] *ISA (UK) 706 (Revised June 2016),* Emphasis of Matter Paragraphs and Other Matter Paragraphs in the Independent Auditor's Report, *paragraph 12.*

[19] *ISA (UK) 720 (Revised June 2016),* The Auditor's Responsibilities Relating to Other Information, *paragraph 18(a).*

[20] *ISA (UK) 700 (Revised June 2016), paragraphs 46 and A63.*

in circumstances when the auditor elects not to include the description of the auditor's responsibilities in the body of the auditor's report as permitted by ISA (UK) 700 (Revised June 2016).[21]

Other Significant Matters Relevant to the Financial Reporting Process (Ref: Para. 16(e))

A26   ISA (UK) 300 (Revised June 2016)[22] notes that, as a result of unexpected events, changes in conditions, or the audit evidence obtained from the results of audit procedures, the auditor may need to modify the overall audit strategy and audit plan and thereby the resulting planned nature, timing and extent of further audit procedures, based on the revised consideration of assessed risks. The auditor may communicate with those charged with governance about such matters, for example, as an update to initial discussions about the planned scope and timing of the audit.

A27   Other significant matters arising during the audit that are directly relevant to those charged with governance in overseeing the financial reporting process may include such matters as material misstatements of the other information that have been corrected.

A28   To the extent not already addressed by the requirements in paragraphs 16(a)–(d) and related application material, the auditor may consider communicating about other matters discussed with, or considered by, the engagement quality control reviewer, if one has been appointed, in accordance with ISA (UK) 220 (Revised June 2016).[23]

Entities that Report on Application of the UK Corporate Governance Code (Ref: Para. 16-1)

A28-1   Under the UK Corporate Governance Code, the responsibilities of the directors under Code provision C.1.1 include making a statement that they consider the annual report and accounts taken as a whole is fair, balanced and understandable and provides the information necessary for shareholders to assess the entity's position and performance, business model and strategy. The responsibilities of the audit committee under Code provision C.3.4 include, where requested by the board, providing advice in relation to that statement.[23a] The responsibilities of the board under Code provision C.2.3 include monitoring the entity's risk management and internal control systems and, at least annually, carrying out a review of their effectiveness and reporting on that review in the annual report.[23b] The responsibilities of the board under Code provisions C.1.3, C.2.1 and C.2.2 are described in paragraphs 16-1 (e) and (f). The responsibilities of the audit committee under Code provision C.3.2 include: monitoring the integrity of the financial statements of the entity and any formal announcements relating to the entity's financial performance, reviewing significant financial reporting judgments contained in them; reviewing the entity's internal financial controls and, unless expressly addressed by a separate board risk committee composed of independent directors or by the board itself,

---

[21] *ISA (UK) 700 (Revised June 2016), paragraph 41.*

[22] *ISA (UK) 300 (Revised June 2016),* Planning an Audit of Financial Statements, *paragraph A15.*

[23] *See paragraphs 19–22 and A23–A33 of ISA (UK) 220 (Revised June 2016),* Quality Control for an Audit of Financial Statements.

[23a] *Responsibility for ensuring the annual report is fair, balanced and understandable rests with the board as a whole. The board may ask the audit committee to provide advice on this.*

[23b] *In addition, FCA Rule DTR 7.2.5 R requires companies to describe the main features of the internal control and risk management systems in relation to the financial reporting process.*

the entity's internal control and risk management systems,[23c] review and monitor the effectiveness of the audit process; and reporting to the board on how it has discharged its responsibilities. The supporting Guidance on Audit Committees indicates that the report to the board should include, inter alia:[23d]

- The significant issues that the audit committee considered in relation to the financial statements and how these issues were addressed; and
- The basis for its advice, where requested by the board, that the annual report and accounts taken as a whole is fair, balanced and understandable and provides the information necessary for shareholders to assess the entity's performance, business model and strategy.

In fulfilling these responsibilities, the audit committee and the board will be assisted by an understanding of:

A28-2

(a) Issues that involve significant judgment; and
(b) Other matters communicated to them by the auditor relevant to those responsibilities.

This will include an understanding of the rationale and supporting evidence for the auditor's significant professional judgments made in the course of the audit and in reaching the opinion on the financial statements, and of other matters communicated to the audit committee by the auditor in accordance with the requirements of paragraph 16-1, including relevant information communicated in accordance with the requirements of paragraphs 15 and 16. The auditor's communications include information regarding separate components of a group where relevant. In fulfilling its responsibilities set out above, the board will be assisted by the report from the audit committee on how the audit committee has discharged its responsibilities.

The audit procedures that the auditor designs as part of the audit of the financial statements are not designed for the purpose of expressing an opinion on the effectiveness of the entity's system of internal control as a whole and accordingly the auditor does not express such an opinion on the basis of those procedures. However, communication of the auditor's views about the effectiveness of elements of the entity's system of internal control, based on the audit procedures performed in the audit of the financial statements, may help the audit committee and the board fulfil their respective responsibilities with respect to the entity's internal control and risk management systems.

A28-3

The auditor's understanding of the entity includes the entity's objectives and strategies and those related business risks that may result in risks of material misstatement, obtained in compliance with ISA (UK) 315 (Revised June 2016),[23e] and may also include other risks arising from the entity's business model that are relevant to an understanding of that model and the entity's strategy. To the extent that the auditor has obtained an understanding of such risks and the effectiveness of the entity's system of internal control in addressing them, communicating its views on those matters may be

A28-4

helpful to the audit committee and the board in their evaluation of whether the annual report is fair, balanced and understandable and provides the information necessary for users to assess the entity's position and performance, business model and strategy. However, the auditor is not required to design and perform audit procedures expressly for the purpose of forming views about the effectiveness of the entity's internal control in addressing such risks. Accordingly, to the extent applicable, the auditor may communicate that they have not obtained an understanding of, and therefore are not able to express views about, such risks and related aspects of the entity's internal control.

A28-5   The auditor's communication of views about the effectiveness of the entity's internal control may include, or refer to, the communication of significant deficiencies in internal control, if any, that is required by ISA (UK) 265. However, views about effectiveness can go beyond just identifying such deficiencies. For example views they may include views about such matters as the entity's strategies for identifying and responding quickly to significant new financial or operational risks; the quality of the reports that the board receives to provide them with information about risks and the operation of internal control; or how the entity's systems compare in general terms with those of other relevant entities of which the auditor has knowledge, such as the impact on internal control effectiveness that may result from different approaches to maintaining an appropriate control environment. The auditor's communications include the auditor's views relating to separate components of a group where relevant.

Auditor Independence (Ref: Para. 17)

A29   The auditor is required to comply with relevant ethical requirements, including those pertaining to independence, relating to financial statement audit engagements.[24]

A29-1   In the UK, auditors are subject to ethical requirements from two sources: the FRC's Ethical Standard concerning the integrity, objectivity and independence of the auditor,[24a] and the ethical pronouncements established by the auditor's relevant professional body.

A30   The relationships and other matters, and safeguards to be communicated, vary with the circumstances of the engagement, but generally address:
(a)   Threats to independence, which may be categorized as: self-interest threats, self-review threats, advocacy threats, familiarity threats, and intimidation threats; and
(b)   Safeguards created by the profession, legislation or regulation, safeguards within the entity, and safeguards within the firm's own systems and procedures.

A31   Relevant ethical requirements or law or regulation may also specify particular communications to those charged with governance in circumstances where breaches of independence requirements have been identified. For example, the International Ethics Standards Board for Accountants' Code of Ethics for Professional Accountants (IESBA

---

[24] *ISA (UK) 200 (Revised June 2016),* Overall Objectives of the Independent Auditor and the Conduct of an Audit in Accordance with International Standards on Auditing (UK), *paragraph 14.*

[24a] *The FRC's Ethical Standard,* Part B, Section 1 – General Requirements and Guidance, *paragraphs 1.61 to 1.70 address communication with those charged with governance.*

Code) requires the auditor to communicate with those charged with governance in writing about any breach and the action the firm has taken or proposes to take.[25]

The communication requirements relating to auditor independence that apply in the case of listed entities and public interest entities[25a] may also be appropriate in the case of some other entities, including those that may be of significant public interest, for example because they have a large number and wide range of stakeholders and considering the nature and size of the business. Examples of such entities may include financial institutions (such as banks, insurance companies, and pension funds), and other entities such as charities. On the other hand, there may be situations where communications regarding independence may not be relevant, for example, where all of those charged with governance have been informed of relevant facts through their management activities. This is particularly likely where the entity is owner-managed, and the auditor's firm and network firms have little involvement with the entity beyond a financial statement audit.   **A32**

Auditor Independence for Public Interest Entities (Ref: Para. 17R-1)

As part of the auditor's annual confirmation to the audit committee, the auditor identifies the ethical requirements relevant to the group audit that are applicable to' component auditors in accordance with Supporting Ethical Provision 2.4 of the FRC's Ethical Standard.[25b]   **A32-1**

Supplementary Matters (Ref: Para. 3)

The oversight of management by those charged with governance includes ensuring that the entity designs, implements and maintains appropriate internal control with regard to reliability of financial reporting, effectiveness and efficiency of operations and compliance with applicable laws and regulations.   **A33**

The auditor may become aware of supplementary matters that do not necessarily relate to the oversight of the financial reporting process but which are, nevertheless, likely to be significant to the responsibilities of those charged with governance in overseeing the strategic direction of the entity or the entity's obligations related to accountability. Such matters may include, for example, significant issues regarding governance structures or processes, and significant decisions or actions by senior management that lack appropriate authorization.   **A34**

In determining whether to communicate supplementary matters with those charged with governance, the auditor may discuss matters of this kind of which the auditor has become aware with the appropriate level of management, unless it is inappropriate to do so in the circumstances.   **A35**

---

[25] *See Section 290.39–49 of the IESBA Code, which addresses breaches of independence.*
In the UK, the FRC's Ethical Standard, Part B, Section 1 – General Requirements and Guidance, paragraph 1.61 requires the audit partner to ensure that those charged with governance are 'informed on a timely basis of all significant facts and matters that may bear upon the integrity, objectivity and independence of the firm or covered persons.'

[25a] *A public interest entity is defined in ISA (UK) 220 (Revised June 2016), paragraph 7(m)-1 in accordance with Article 2(13) of the Audit Directive. These public interest entities are distinct from entities that may be of significant public interest.*

[25b] *FRC's Ethical Standard, Part A – Overarching Principles and Supporting Ethical Provisions, Supporting Ethical Provision 2.4.*

A36   If a supplementary matter is communicated, it may be appropriate for the auditor to make those charged with governance aware that:

(a)   Identification and communication of such matters is incidental to the purpose of the audit, which is to form an opinion on the financial statements;

(b)   No procedures were carried out with respect to the matter other than any that were necessary to form an opinion on the financial statements; and

(c)   No procedures were carried out to determine whether other such matters exist.

The Communication Process

Establishing the Communication Process (Ref: Para. 18)

A37   Clear communication of the auditor's responsibilities, the planned scope and timing of the audit, and the expected general content of communications helps establish the basis for effective two-way communication.

A38   Matters that may also contribute to effective two-way communication include discussion of:

● The purpose of communications. When the purpose is clear, the auditor and those charged with governance are better placed to have a mutual understanding of relevant issues and the expected actions arising from the communication process.

● The form in which communications will be made.

● The person(s) in the engagement team and amongst those charged with governance who will communicate regarding particular matters.

● The auditor's expectation that communication will be two-way, and that those charged with governance will communicate with the auditor matters they consider relevant to the audit, for example, strategic decisions that may significantly affect the nature, timing and extent of audit procedures, the suspicion or the detection of fraud, and concerns with the integrity or competence of senior management.

● The process for taking action and reporting back on matters communicated by the auditor.

● The process for taking action and reporting back on matters communicated by those charged with governance.

A39   The communication process will vary with the circumstances, including the size and governance structure of the entity, how those charged with governance operate, and the auditor's view of the significance of matters to be communicated. Difficulty in establishing effective two-way communication may indicate that the communication between the auditor and those charged with governance is not adequate for the purpose of the audit (see paragraph A52).

Considerations Specific to Smaller Entities

A40   In the case of audits of smaller entities, the auditor may communicate in a less structured manner with those charged with governance than in the case of listed or larger entities.

Communication with Management

A41   Many matters may be discussed with management in the ordinary course of an audit, including matters required by this ISA (UK) to be communicated with those charged with governance. Such discussions recognize management's executive responsibility for the conduct of the entity's operations and, in particular, management's responsibility for the preparation of the financial statements.

Before communicating matters with those charged with governance, the auditor may   **A42**
discuss them with management, unless that is inappropriate. For example, it may not
be appropriate to discuss questions of management's competence or integrity with
management. In addition to recognizing management's executive responsibility, these
initial discussions may clarify facts and issues, and give management an opportunity to
provide further information and explanations. Similarly, when the entity has an internal
audit function, the auditor may discuss matters with appropriate individuals within the
function before communicating with those charged with governance.

Communication with Third Parties

Those charged with governance may be required by law or regulation, or may wish to   **A43**
provide third parties, for example, bankers or certain regulatory authorities, with copies
of a written communication from the auditor. In some cases, disclosure to third parties
may be illegal or otherwise inappropriate. When a written communication prepared for
those charged with governance is provided to third parties, it may be important in the
circumstances that the third parties be informed that the communication was not prepared
with them in mind, for example, by stating in written communications with those charged
with governance:

(a) That the communication has been prepared for the sole use of those charged with
     governance and, where applicable, the group management and the group auditor, and
     should not be relied upon by third parties;
(b) That no responsibility is assumed by the auditor to third parties; and
(c) Any restrictions on disclosure or distribution to third parties.

In some jurisdictions the auditor may be required by law or regulation to, for example: **A44**

- Notify a regulatory or enforcement body of certain matters communicated with
  those charged with governance. For example, in some countries the auditor has a
  duty to report misstatements to authorities where management and those charged with
  governance fail to take corrective action;
- Submit copies of certain reports prepared for those charged with governance to
  relevant regulatory or funding bodies, or other bodies such as a central authority in
  the case of some public sector entities; or
- Make reports prepared for those charged with governance publicly available.

Unless required by law or regulation to provide a third party with a copy of the auditor's   **A45**
written communications with those charged with governance, the auditor may need the
prior consent of those charged with governance before doing so.

Forms of Communication (Ref: Para. 19)

Effective communication may involve structured presentations and written reports as well   **A46**
as less structured communications, including discussions. The auditor may communicate
matters other than those identified in paragraphs 19–20R-1 either orally or in writing.
Written communications may include an engagement letter that is provided to those
charged with governance.

The auditor discusses issues clearly and unequivocally with those charged with   **A46-1**
governance so that the implications of those issues are likely to be fully comprehended
by them.

A47   In addition to the significance of a particular matter, the form of communication (e.g., whether to communicate orally or in writing, the extent of detail or summarization in the communication, and whether to communicate in a structured or unstructured manner) may be affected by such factors as:

- Whether a discussion of the matter will be included in the auditor's report. For example, when key audit matters are communicated in the auditor's report, the auditor may consider it necessary to communicate in writing about the matters determined to be key audit matters.
- Whether the matter has been satisfactorily resolved.
- Whether management has previously communicated the matter.
- The size, operating structure, control environment, and legal structure of the entity.
- In the case of an audit of special purpose financial statements, whether the auditor also audits the entity's general purpose financial statements.
- Legal requirements. In some jurisdictions, a written communication with those charged with governance is required in a prescribed form by local law.
- The expectations of those charged with governance, including arrangements made for periodic meetings or communications with the auditor.
- The amount of ongoing contact and dialogue the auditor has with those charged with governance.
- Whether there have been significant changes in the membership of a governing body.

A47-1   The judgment of whether to communicate significant matters orally or in writing may also be affected by the evaluation, required by paragraph 22, of whether the two-way communication between the auditor and those charged with governance has been adequate for the purpose of the audit. The auditor may judge also that for effective communication a written communication is issued even if its content is limited to explaining that there is nothing the auditor wishes to draw to the attention of those charged with governance. To avoid doubt where there are no matters the auditor wishes to communicate in writing, the auditor may communicate that fact in writing to those charged with governance.

A48   When a significant matter is discussed with an individual member of those charged with governance, for example, the chair of an audit committee, it may be appropriate for the auditor to summarize the matter in later communications so that all of those charged with governance have full and balanced information.

Timing of Communications (Ref: Para. 21)

A49   Timely communication throughout the audit contributes to the achievement of robust two-way dialogue between those charged with governance and the auditor. However, the appropriate timing for communications will vary with the circumstances of the engagement. Relevant circumstances include the significance and nature of the matter, and the action expected to be taken by those charged with governance. For example:

- Communications regarding planning matters may often be made early in the audit engagement and, for an initial engagement, may be made as part of agreeing the terms of the engagement.
- It may be appropriate to communicate a significant difficulty encountered during the audit as soon as practicable if those charged with governance are able to assist the auditor to overcome the difficulty, or if it is likely to lead to a modified opinion. Similarly, the auditor may communicate orally to those charged with governance as soon as practicable significant deficiencies in internal control that the auditor has identified, prior to communicating these in writing as required by ISA (UK) 265.[26]

---

[26] *ISA (UK) 265, paragraphs 9 and A14.*

- When ISA (UK) 701 applies, the auditor may communicate preliminary views about key audit matters when discussing the planned scope and timing of the audit (see paragraph A13), and the auditor also may have more frequent communications to further discuss such matters when communicating about significant audit findings.
- Communications regarding independence may be appropriate whenever significant judgments are made about threats to independence and related safeguards, for example, when accepting an engagement to provide non-audit services, and at a concluding discussion.
- Communications regarding findings from the audit, including the auditor's views about the qualitative aspects of the entity's accounting practices, may also be made as part of the concluding discussion.
- When auditing both general purpose and special purpose financial statements, it may be appropriate to coordinate the timing of communications.

Other factors that may be relevant to the timing of communications include: **A50**

- The size, operating structure, control environment, and legal structure of the entity being audited.
- Any legal obligation to communicate certain matters within a specified timeframe.
- The expectations of those charged with governance, including arrangements made for periodic meetings or communications with the auditor.
- The time at which the auditor identifies certain matters, for example, the auditor may not identify a particular matter (e.g., non-compliance with a law) in time for preventive action to be taken, but communication of the matter may enable remedial action to be taken.

Findings from the audit that are relevant to the financial statements, including the auditor's views about the qualitative aspects of the entity's accounting and financial reporting, are ordinarily communicated to those charged with governance before they approve the financial statements.   **A50-1**

Public Interest Entities (Ref: Para. 21R-1)

Whilst the auditor is required to submit the additional report to the audit committee no later than the date of submission of the auditor's report, the auditor has regard to the requirement in paragraph 21 to communicate with those charged with governance on a timely basis and the requirement in 20R-1(c) which requires the auditor, where requested, to discuss key matters arising from the audit referred to in the additional report to the audit committee.   **A50-2**

Adequacy of the Communication Process (Ref: Para. 22)

The auditor need not design specific procedures to support the evaluation of the two-way communication between the auditor and those charged with governance; rather, that evaluation may be based on observations resulting from audit procedures performed for other purposes. Such observations may include: **A51**

- The appropriateness and timeliness of actions taken by those charged with governance in response to matters raised by the auditor. Where significant matters raised in previous communications have not been dealt with effectively, it may be appropriate for the auditor to inquire as to why appropriate action has not been taken, and to consider raising the point again. This avoids the risk of giving an impression that the auditor is satisfied that the matter has been adequately addressed or is no longer significant.

- The apparent openness of those charged with governance in their communications with the auditor.
- The willingness and capacity of those charged with governance to meet with the auditor without management present.
- The apparent ability of those charged with governance to fully comprehend matters raised by the auditor, for example, the extent to which those charged with governance probe issues, and question recommendations made to them.
- Difficulty in establishing with those charged with governance a mutual understanding of the form, timing and expected general content of communications.
- Where all or some of those charged with governance are involved in managing the entity, their apparent awareness of how matters discussed with the auditor affect their broader governance responsibilities, as well as their management responsibilities.
- Whether the two-way communication between the auditor and those charged with governance meets applicable legal and regulatory requirements.

A52   As noted in paragraph 4, effective two-way communication assists both the auditor and those charged with governance. Further, ISA (UK) 315 (Revised June 2016) identifies participation by those charged with governance, including their interaction with the internal audit function, if any, and external auditors, as an element of the entity's control environment.[27] Inadequate two-way communication may indicate an unsatisfactory control environment and influence the auditor's assessment of the risks of material misstatements. There is also a risk that the auditor may not have obtained sufficient appropriate audit evidence to form an opinion on the financial statements.

A53   If the two-way communication between the auditor and those charged with governance is not adequate and the situation cannot be resolved, the auditor may take such actions as:

- Modifying the auditor's opinion on the basis of a scope limitation.
- Obtaining legal advice about the consequences of different courses of action.
- Communicating with third parties (e.g., a regulator), or a higher authority in the governance structure that is outside the entity, such as the owners of a business (e.g., shareholders in a general meeting), or the responsible government minister or parliament in the public sector.
- Withdrawing from the engagement, where withdrawal is possible under applicable law or regulation.

Documentation (Ref: Para. 23)

A54   Documentation of oral communication may include a copy of minutes prepared by the entity retained as part of the audit documentation where those minutes are an appropriate record of the communication.

---

[27] *ISA (UK) 315 (Revised June 2016), paragraph A78.*

Appendix 1

(Ref: Para. 3)

Specific Requirements in ISQC (UK) 1 and Other ISAs (UK) that Refer to Communications with Those Charged With Governance

This appendix identifies paragraphs in ISQC (UK) 1[28] and other ISAs (UK) that require communication of specific matters with those charged with governance. The list is not a substitute for considering the requirements and related application and other explanatory material in ISAs (UK).

- ISQC (UK) 1 (Revised June 2016), *Quality Control for Firms that Perform Audits and Reviews of Financial Statements, and Other Assurance and Related Services Engagements* – paragraph 30(a)
- ISA (UK) 240 (Revised June 2016), *The Auditor's Responsibilities Relating to Fraud in an Audit of Financial Statements* – paragraphs 21, 38(c)(i) and 40–42
- ISA (UK) 250 (Revised July 2017), *Section A—Consideration of Laws and Regulations in an Audit of Financial Statements* – paragraphs 15, 20 and 26–28
- ISA (UK) 265, *Communicating Deficiencies in Internal Control to Those Charged with Governance and Management* – paragraph 9
- ISA (UK) 450 (Revised June 2016), *Evaluation of Misstatements Identified during the Audit* – paragraphs 12–13
- ISA (UK) 505, *External Confirmations* – paragraph 9
- ISA (UK) 510 (Revised June 2016), *Initial Audit Engagements—Opening Balances* – paragraph 7
- ISA (UK) 550, *Related Parties* – paragraph 27
- ISA (UK) 560, *Subsequent Events* – paragraphs 7(b)–(c), 10(a), 13(b), 14(a) and 17
- ISA (UK) 570 (Revised June 2016), *Going Concern* – paragraph 25
- ISA (UK) 600 (Revised June 2016), *Special Considerations—Audits of Group Financial Statements (Including the Work of Component Auditors)* – paragraph 49
- ISA (UK) 610 (Revised June 2013), *Using the Work of Internal Auditors* – paragraphs 20 and 31
- ISA (UK) 700 (Revised June 2016), *Forming an Opinion and Reporting on Financial Statements* – paragraph 46
- ISA (UK) 701, *Communicating Key Audit Matters in the Independent Auditor's Report* – paragraph 17
- ISA (UK) 705 (Revised June 2016), *Modifications to the Opinion in the Independent Auditor's Report* – paragraphs 12, 14, 23 and 30
- ISA (UK) 706 (Revised June 2016), *Emphasis of Matter Paragraphs and Other Matter Paragraphs in the Independent Auditor's Report* – paragraph 12
- ISA (UK) 710, *Comparative Information—Corresponding Figures and Comparative Financial Statements* – paragraph 18
- ISA (UK) 720 (Revised June 2016), *The Auditor's Responsibilities Relating to Other Information* – paragraphs 17–19

---

[28] *ISQC (UK) 1 (Revised June 2016)*, Quality Control for Firms that Perform Audits and Reviews of Financial Statements, and Other Assurance and Related Services Engagements.

Appendix 2   (Ref: Para. 16(a), A19–A20)

Qualitative Aspects of Accounting Practices

The communication required by paragraph 16(a), and discussed in paragraph A19–A20, may include such matters as:

Accounting Policies

- The appropriateness of the accounting policies to the particular circumstances of the entity, having regard to the need to balance the cost of providing information with the likely benefit to users of the entity's financial statements. Where acceptable alternative accounting policies exist, the communication may include identification of the financial statement items that are affected by the choice of significant accounting policies as well as information on accounting policies used by similar entities.
- The initial selection of, and changes in significant accounting policies, including the application of new accounting pronouncements. The communication may include: the effect of the timing and method of adoption of a change in accounting policy on the current and future earnings of the entity; and the timing of a change in accounting policies in relation to expected new accounting pronouncements.
- The effect of significant accounting policies in controversial or emerging areas (or those unique to an industry, particularly when there is a lack of authoritative guidance or consensus).
- The effect of the timing of transactions in relation to the period in which they are recorded.

Accounting Estimates

- For items for which estimates are significant, issues discussed in ISA (UK) 540 (Revised June 2016),[29] including, for example:
  - How management identifies those transactions, events and conditions that may give rise to the need for accounting estimates to be recognized or disclosed in the financial statements.
  - Changes in circumstances that may give rise to new, or the need to revise existing, accounting estimates.
  - Whether management's decision to recognize, or to not recognize, the accounting estimates in the financial statements is in accordance with the applicable financial reporting framework.
  - Whether there has been or ought to have been a change from the prior period in the methods for making the accounting estimates and, if so, why, as well as the outcome of accounting estimates in prior periods.
  - Management's process for making accounting estimates (e.g., when management has used a model), including whether the selected measurement basis for the accounting estimate is in accordance with the applicable financial reporting framework.
  - Whether the significant assumptions used by management in developing the accounting estimate are reasonable.
  - Where relevant to the reasonableness of the significant assumptions used by management or the appropriate application of the applicable financial reporting framework, management's intent to carry out specific courses of action and its ability to do so.

---

[29] *ISA (UK) 540 (Revised June 2016),* Auditing Accounting Estimates, Including Fair Value Accounting Estimates, and Related Disclosures.

o Risks of material misstatement.
o Indicators of possible management bias.
o How management has considered alternative assumptions or outcomes and why it has rejected them, or how management has otherwise addressed estimation uncertainty in making the accounting estimate.
o The adequacy of disclosure of estimation uncertainty in the financial statements.

Financial Statement Disclosures

- The issues involved, and related judgments made, in formulating particularly sensitive financial statement disclosures (e.g., disclosures related to revenue recognition, remuneration, going concern, subsequent events, and contingency issues).
- The overall neutrality, consistency and clarity of the disclosures in the financial statements.

Related Matters

- The potential effect on the financial statements of significant risks, exposures and uncertainties, such as pending litigation, that are disclosed in the financial statements.
- The extent to which the financial statements are affected by significant transactions, that are outside the normal course of business for the entity, or that otherwise appear to be unusual. This communication may highlight:
  o The non-recurring amounts recognized during the period.
  o The extent to which such transactions are separately disclosed in the financial statements.
  o Whether such transactions appear to have been designed to achieve a particular accounting or tax treatment, or a particular legal or regulatory objective.
  o Whether the form of such transactions appears overly complex or where extensive advice regarding the structuring of the transaction has been taken.
  o Where management is placing more emphasis on the need for a particular accounting treatment than on the underlying economics of the transaction.

- The factors affecting asset and liability carrying values, including the entity's bases for determining useful lives assigned to tangible and intangible assets. The communication may explain how factors affecting carrying values were selected and how alternative selections would have affected the financial statements.
- The selective correction of misstatements, for example, correcting misstatements with the effect of increasing reported earnings, but not those that have the effect of decreasing reported earnings.

International Standard on Auditing (UK) 265

Communicating deficiencies in internal control to those charged with governance and management

(Effective for audits of financial statements for periods ending on or after 15 December 2010)

Contents

Paragraphs

International Standard on Auditing (UK) (ISA (UK)) 265, *Communicating Deficiencies in Internal Control to Those Charged with Governance and Management*, should be read in conjunction with ISA (UK) 200 (Revised June 2016), *Overall Objectives of the Independent Auditor and the Conduct of an Audit in Accordance with International Standards on Auditing (UK)*.

Introduction

Scope of this ISA (UK)

This International Standard on Auditing (UK) (ISA (UK)) deals with the auditor's **1** responsibility to communicate appropriately to those charged with governance and management deficiencies in internal control[1] that the auditor has identified in an audit of financial statements. This ISA (UK) does not impose additional responsibilities on the auditor regarding obtaining an understanding of internal control and designing and performing tests of controls over and above the requirements of ISA (UK) 315 (Revised June 2016) and ISA (UK) 330 (Revised June 2016).[2] ISA (UK) 260 (Revised June 2016)[3] establishes further requirements and provides guidance regarding the auditor's responsibility to communicate with those charged with governance in relation to the audit.

The auditor is required to obtain an understanding of internal control relevant to the audit **2** when identifying and assessing the risks of material misstatement.[4] In making those risk assessments, the auditor considers internal control in order to design audit procedures that are appropriate in the circumstances, but not for the purpose of expressing an opinion on the effectiveness of internal control. The auditor may identify deficiencies in internal control not only during this risk assessment process but also at any other stage of the audit. This ISA (UK) specifies which identified deficiencies the auditor is required to communicate to those charged with governance and management.

Nothing in this ISA (UK) precludes the auditor from communicating to those charged with **3** governance and management other internal control matters that the auditor has identified during the audit.

Effective Date

This ISA (UK) is effective for audits of financial statements for periods ending on or after **4** 15 December 2010.

Objective

The objective of the auditor is to communicate appropriately to those charged with **5** governance and management deficiencies in internal control that the auditor has identified during the audit and that, in the auditor's professional judgment, are of sufficient importance to merit their respective attentions.

---

[1] *ISA (UK) 315 (Revised June 2016)*, Identifying and Assessing the Risks of Material Misstatement through Understanding the Entity and Its Environment, *paragraphs 4 and 12.*

[2] *ISA (UK) 330 (Revised June 2016)*, The Auditor's Responses to Assessed Risks.

[3] *ISA (UK) 260 (Revised June 2016)*, Communication with Those Charged with Governance.

[4] *ISA (UK) 315 (Revised June 2016), paragraph 12. Paragraphs A60–A65 provide guidance on controls relevant to the audit.*

Definitions

6   For purposes of the ISAs (UK), the following terms have the meanings attributed below:

   (a) Deficiency in internal control – This exists when:
      (i)   A control is designed, implemented or operated in such a way that it is unable to prevent, or detect and correct, misstatements in the financial statements on a timely basis; or
      (ii) A control necessary to prevent, or detect and correct, misstatements in the financial statements on a timely basis is missing.

   (b) Significant deficiency in internal control – A deficiency or combination of deficiencies in internal control that, in the auditor's professional judgment, is of sufficient importance to merit the attention of those charged with governance. (Ref: Para. A5)

Requirements

7   The auditor shall determine whether, on the basis of the audit work performed, the auditor has identified one or more deficiencies in internal control. (Ref: Para. A1–A4)

8   If the auditor has identified one or more deficiencies in internal control, the auditor shall determine, on the basis of the audit work performed, whether, individually or in combination, they constitute significant deficiencies. (Ref: Para. A5–A11)

9   The auditor shall communicate in writing significant deficiencies in internal control identified during the audit to those charged with governance on a timely basis. (Ref: Para. A12–A18, A27)

10   The auditor shall also communicate to management at an appropriate level of responsibility on a timely basis: (Ref: Para. A19, A27)

   (a) In writing, significant deficiencies in internal control that the auditor has communicated or intends to communicate to those charged with governance, unless it would be inappropriate to communicate directly to management in the circumstances; and (Ref: Para. A14, A20–A21)

   (b) Other deficiencies in internal control identified during the audit that have not been communicated to management by other parties and that, in the auditor's professional judgment, are of sufficient importance to merit management's attention. (Ref: Para. A22–A26)

11   The auditor shall include in the written communication of significant deficiencies in internal control:

   (a) A description of the deficiencies and an explanation of their potential effects; and (Ref: Para. A28)

   (b) Sufficient information to enable those charged with governance and management to understand the context of the communication. In particular, the auditor shall explain that: (Ref: Para. A29–A30)
      (i)   The purpose of the audit was for the auditor to express an opinion on the financial statements;
      (ii) The audit included consideration of internal control relevant to the preparation of the financial statements in order to design audit procedures that are appropriate in the circumstances, but not for the purpose of expressing an opinion on the effectiveness of internal control; and
      (iii) The matters being reported are limited to those deficiencies that the auditor has identified during the audit and that the auditor has concluded are of sufficient importance to merit being reported to those charged with governance.

***

Application and Other Explanatory Material

Determination of Whether Deficiencies in Internal Control Have Been Identified (Ref: Para. 7)

In determining whether the auditor has identified one or more deficiencies in internal control, the auditor may discuss the relevant facts and circumstances of the auditor's findings with the appropriate level of management. This discussion provides an opportunity for the auditor to alert management on a timely basis to the existence of deficiencies of which management may not have been previously aware. The level of management with whom it is appropriate to discuss the findings is one that is familiar with the internal control area concerned and that has the authority to take remedial action on any identified deficiencies in internal control. In some circumstances, it may not be appropriate for the auditor to discuss the auditor's findings directly with management, for example, if the findings appear to call management's integrity or competence into question (see paragraph A20). **A1**

In discussing the facts and circumstances of the auditor's findings with management, the auditor may obtain other relevant information for further consideration, such as: **A2**

- Management's understanding of the actual or suspected causes of the deficiencies.
- Exceptions arising from the deficiencies that management may have noted, for example, misstatements that were not prevented by the relevant information technology (IT) controls.
- A preliminary indication from management of its response to the findings.

Considerations Specific to Smaller Entities

While the concepts underlying control activities in smaller entities are likely to be similar to those in larger entities, the formality with which they operate will vary. Further, smaller entities may find that certain types of control activities are not necessary because of controls applied by management. For example, management's sole authority for granting credit to customers and approving significant purchases can provide effective control over important account balances and transactions, lessening or removing the need for more detailed control activities. **A3**

Also, smaller entities often have fewer employees which may limit the extent to which segregation of duties is practicable. However, in a small owner-managed entity, the owner-manager may be able to exercise more effective oversight than in a larger entity. This higher level of management oversight needs to be balanced against the greater potential for management override of controls. **A4**

Significant Deficiencies in Internal Control (Ref: Para. 6(b), 8)

The significance of a deficiency or a combination of deficiencies in internal control depends not only on whether a misstatement has actually occurred, but also on the likelihood that a misstatement could occur and the potential magnitude of the misstatement. Significant deficiencies may therefore exist even though the auditor has not identified misstatements during the audit. **A5**

Examples of matters that the auditor may consider in determining whether a deficiency or combination of deficiencies in internal control constitutes a significant deficiency include: **A6**

- The likelihood of the deficiencies leading to material misstatements in the financial statements in the future.
- The susceptibility to loss or fraud of the related asset or liability.

- The subjectivity and complexity of determining estimated amounts, such as fair value accounting estimates.
- The financial statement amounts exposed to the deficiencies.
- The volume of activity that has occurred or could occur in the account balance or class of transactions exposed to the deficiency or deficiencies.
- The importance of the controls to the financial reporting process; for example:
  - General monitoring controls (such as oversight of management).
  - Controls over the prevention and detection of fraud.
  - Controls over the selection and application of significant accounting policies.
  - Controls over significant transactions with related parties.
  - Controls over significant transactions outside the entity's normal course of business.
  - Controls over the period-end financial reporting process (such as controls over non-recurring journal entries).
- The cause and frequency of the exceptions detected as a result of the deficiencies in the controls.
- The interaction of the deficiency with other deficiencies in internal control.

A7   Indicators of significant deficiencies in internal control include, for example:

- Evidence of ineffective aspects of the control environment, such as:
  - Indications that significant transactions in which management is financially interested are not being appropriately scrutinized by those charged with governance.
  - Identification of management fraud, whether or not material, that was not prevented by the entity's internal control.
  - Management's failure to implement appropriate remedial action on significant deficiencies previously communicated.
- Absence of a risk assessment process within the entity where such a process would ordinarily be expected to have been established.
- Evidence of an ineffective entity risk assessment process, such as management's failure to identify a risk of material misstatement that the auditor would expect the entity's risk assessment process to have identified.
- Evidence of an ineffective response to identified significant risks (for example, absence of controls over such a risk).
- Misstatements detected by the auditor's procedures that were not prevented, or detected and corrected, by the entity's internal control.
- Restatement of previously issued financial statements to reflect the correction of a material misstatement due to error or fraud.
- Evidence of management's inability to oversee the preparation of the financial statements.

A8   Controls may be designed to operate individually or in combination to effectively prevent, or detect and correct, misstatements.[5] For example, controls over accounts receivable may consist of both automated and manual controls designed to operate together to prevent, or detect and correct, misstatements in the account balance. A deficiency in internal control on its own may not be sufficiently important to constitute a significant deficiency. However, a combination of deficiencies affecting the same account balance or disclosure, relevant assertion, or component of internal control may increase the risks of misstatement to such an extent as to give rise to a significant deficiency.

A9   Law or regulation in some jurisdictions may establish a requirement (particularly for audits of listed entities) for the auditor to communicate to those charged with governance or to

---

[5] *ISA (UK) 315 (Revised June 2016), paragraph A66.*

other relevant parties (such as regulators) one or more specific types of deficiency in internal control that the auditor has identified during the audit. Where law or regulation has established specific terms and definitions for these types of deficiency and requires the auditor to use these terms and definitions for the purpose of the communication, the auditor uses such terms and definitions when communicating in accordance with the legal or regulatory requirement.

Where the jurisdiction has established specific terms for the types of deficiency in internal control to be communicated but has not defined such terms, it may be necessary for the auditor to use judgment to determine the matters to be communicated further to the legal or regulatory requirement. In doing so, the auditor may consider it appropriate to have regard to the requirements and guidance in this ISA (UK). For example, if the purpose of the legal or regulatory requirement is to bring to the attention of those charged with governance certain internal control matters of which they should be aware, it may be appropriate to regard such matters as being generally equivalent to the significant deficiencies required by this ISA (UK) to be communicated to those charged with governance. **A10**

The requirements of this ISA (UK) remain applicable notwithstanding that law or regulation may require the auditor to use specific terms or definitions. **A11**

Communication of Deficiencies in Internal Control

Communication of Significant Deficiencies in Internal Control to Those Charged with Governance (Ref: Para. 9)

Communicating significant deficiencies in writing to those charged with governance reflects the importance of these matters, and assists those charged with governance in fulfilling their oversight responsibilities. ISA (UK) 260 (Revised June 2016) establishes relevant considerations regarding communication with those charged with governance when all of them are involved in managing the entity.[6] **A12**

In the UK, where applicable, timely communication of significant deficiencies, in writing, to directors of listed entities can assist them to comply with the provisions of the UK Corporate Governance Code relating to internal control and reporting to shareholders. **A12-1**

In determining when to issue the written communication, the auditor may consider whether receipt of such communication would be an important factor in enabling those charged with governance to discharge their oversight responsibilities. In addition, for listed entities in certain jurisdictions, those charged with governance may need to receive the auditor's written communication before the date of approval of the financial statements in order to discharge specific responsibilities in relation to internal control for regulatory or other purposes. For other entities, the auditor may issue the written communication at a later date. Nevertheless, in the latter case, as the auditor's written communication of significant deficiencies forms part of the final audit file, the written communication is subject to the overriding requirement[7] for the auditor to complete the assembly of the final audit file on a timely basis. ISA (UK) 230 (Revised June 2016) states that an appropriate **A13**

---

[6] *ISA (UK) 260 (Revised June 2016), paragraph 13.*

[7] *ISA (UK) 230 (Revised June 2016),* Audit Documentation, *paragraph 14.*

time limit within which to complete the assembly of the final audit file is ordinarily not more than 60 days after the date of the auditor's report.[8]

A13-1   For audits of financial statements of public interest entities, ISA (UK) 260 (Revised June 2016)[8a] requires the auditor to communicate in the additional report to the audit committee any significant deficiencies in the entity's internal financial control system or in the accounting system, and whether or not the deficiencies reported have been resolved by management.

A14   Regardless of the timing of the written communication of significant deficiencies, the auditor may communicate these orally in the first instance to management and, when appropriate, to those charged with governance to assist them in taking timely remedial action to minimize the risks of material misstatement. Doing so, however, does not relieve the auditor of the responsibility to communicate the significant deficiencies in writing, as this ISA (UK) requires.

A15   The level of detail at which to communicate significant deficiencies is a matter of the auditor's professional judgment in the circumstances. Factors that the auditor may consider in determining an appropriate level of detail for the communication include, for example:

● The nature of the entity. For instance, the communication required for a public interest entity may be different from that for a non-public interest entity.
● The size and complexity of the entity. For instance, the communication required for a complex entity may be different from that for an entity operating a simple business.
● The nature of significant deficiencies that the auditor has identified.
● The entity's governance composition. For instance, more detail may be needed if those charged with governance include members who do not have significant experience in the entity's industry or in the affected areas.
● Legal or regulatory requirements regarding the communication of specific types of deficiency in internal control.

A16   Management and those charged with governance may already be aware of significant deficiencies that the auditor has identified during the audit and may have chosen not to remedy them because of cost or other considerations. The responsibility for evaluating the costs and benefits of implementing remedial action rests with management and those charged with governance. Accordingly, the requirement in paragraph 9 applies regardless of cost or other considerations that management and those charged with governance may consider relevant in determining whether to remedy such deficiencies.

A17   The fact that the auditor communicated a significant deficiency to those charged with governance and management in a previous audit does not eliminate the need for the auditor to repeat the communication if remedial action has not yet been taken. If a previously communicated significant deficiency remains, the current year's communication may repeat the description from the previous communication, or simply reference the previous communication. The auditor may ask management or, where appropriate, those charged with governance, why the significant deficiency has not yet been remedied. A failure to act, in the absence of a rational explanation, may in itself represent a significant deficiency.

Considerations Specific to Smaller Entities

A18   In the case of audits of smaller entities, the auditor may communicate in a less structured manner with those charged with governance than in the case of larger entities.

---

[8]   *ISA (UK) 230 (Revised June 2016), paragraph A21.*

[8a]   *ISA (UK) 260 (Revised June 2016), paragraph 16R-2(j).*

Communication of Deficiencies in Internal Control to Management (Ref: Para. 10)

Ordinarily, the appropriate level of management is the one that has responsibility and **A19** authority to evaluate the deficiencies in internal control and to take the necessary remedial action. For significant deficiencies, the appropriate level is likely to be the chief executive officer or chief financial officer (or equivalent) as these matters are also required to be communicated to those charged with governance. For other deficiencies in internal control, the appropriate level may be operational management with more direct involvement in the control areas affected and with the authority to take appropriate remedial action.

Communication of Significant Deficiencies in Internal Control to Management (Ref: Para. 10(a))

Certain identified significant deficiencies in internal control may call into question the **A20** integrity or competence of management. For example, there may be evidence of fraud or intentional non-compliance with laws and regulations by management, or management may exhibit an inability to oversee the preparation of adequate financial statements that may raise doubt about management's competence. Accordingly, it may not be appropriate to communicate such deficiencies directly to management.

ISA (UK) 250 (Revised June 2016) establishes requirements and provides guidance on the **A21** reporting of identified or suspected non-compliance with laws and regulations, including when those charged with governance are themselves involved in such noncompliance.[9] ISA (UK) 240 (Revised June 2016) establishes requirements and provides guidance regarding communication to those charged with governance when the auditor has identified fraud or suspected fraud involving management.[10]

Communication of Other Deficiencies in Internal Control to Management (Ref: Para. 10(b))

During the audit, the auditor may identify other deficiencies in internal control that are not **A22** significant deficiencies but that may be of sufficient importance to merit management's attention. The determination as to which other deficiencies in internal control merit management's attention is a matter of professional judgment in the circumstances, taking into account the likelihood and potential magnitude of misstatements that may arise in the financial statements as a result of those deficiencies.

The communication of other deficiencies in internal control that merit management's **A23** attention need not be in writing but may be oral. Where the auditor has discussed the facts and circumstances of the auditor's findings with management, the auditor may consider an oral communication of the other deficiencies to have been made to management at the time of these discussions. Accordingly, a formal communication need not be made subsequently.

If the auditor has communicated deficiencies in internal control other than significant **A24** deficiencies to management in a prior period and management has chosen not to remedy them for cost or other reasons, the auditor need not repeat the communication in the current period. The auditor is also not required to repeat information about such deficiencies if it has been previously communicated to management by other parties, such as the internal audit function or regulators. It may, however, be appropriate for the auditor to re-communicate

---

[9] *ISA (UK) 250 (Revised June 2016),* Consideration of Laws and Regulations in an Audit of Financial Statements, *paragraphs 22–28.*

[10] *ISA (UK) 240 (Revised June 2016),* The Auditor's Responsibilities Relating to Fraud in an Audit of Financial Statements, *paragraph 41.*

these other deficiencies if there has been a change of management, or if new information has come to the auditor's attention that alters the prior understanding of the auditor and management regarding the deficiencies. Nevertheless, the failure of management to remedy other deficiencies in internal control that were previously communicated may become a significant deficiency requiring communication with those charged with governance. Whether this is the case depends on the auditor's judgment in the circumstances.

A25   In some circumstances, those charged with governance may wish to be made aware of the details of other deficiencies in internal control the auditor has communicated to management, or be briefly informed of the nature of the other deficiencies. Alternatively, the auditor may consider it appropriate to inform those charged with governance of the communication of the other deficiencies to management. In either case, the auditor may report orally or in writing to those charged with governance as appropriate.

A26   ISA (UK) 260 (Revised June 2016) establishes relevant considerations regarding communication with those charged with governance when all of them are involved in managing the entity.[11]

Considerations Specific to Public Sector Entities (Ref: Para. 9–10)

A27   Public sector auditors may have additional responsibilities to communicate deficiencies in internal control that the auditor has identified during the audit, in ways, at a level of detail and to parties not envisaged in this ISA (UK). For example, significant deficiencies may have to be communicated to the legislature or other governing body. Law, regulation or other authority may also mandate that public sector auditors report deficiencies in internal control, irrespective of the significance of the potential effects of those deficiencies. Further, legislation may require public sector auditors to report on broader internal control-related matters than the deficiencies in internal control required to be communicated by this ISA (UK), for example, controls related to compliance with legislative authorities, regulations, or provisions of contracts or grant agreements.

Content of Written Communication of Significant Deficiencies in Internal Control (Ref: Para. 11)

A28   In explaining the potential effects of the significant deficiencies, the auditor need not quantify those effects. The significant deficiencies may be grouped together for reporting purposes where it is appropriate to do so. The auditor may also include in the written communication suggestions for remedial action on the deficiencies, management's actual or proposed responses, and a statement as to whether or not the auditor has undertaken any steps to verify whether management's responses have been implemented.

A29   The auditor may consider it appropriate to include the following information as additional context for the communication:

- An indication that if the auditor had performed more extensive procedures on internal control, the auditor might have identified more deficiencies to be reported, or concluded that some of the reported deficiencies need not, in fact, have been reported.
- An indication that such communication has been provided for the purposes of those charged with governance, and that it may not be suitable for other purposes.

A30   Law or regulation may require the auditor or management to furnish a copy of the auditor's written communication on significant deficiencies to appropriate regulatory authorities. Where this is the case, the auditor's written communication may identify such regulatory authorities.

---

[11] *ISA (UK) 260 (Revised June 2016), paragraph 13.*

International Standard on Auditing (UK) 300 (Revised June 2016)

Planning an audit of financial statements

(Effective for audits of financial statements for periods commencing on or after 17 June 2016)

Contents

International Standard on Auditing (UK) (ISA (UK)) 300 (Revised June 2016), *Planning an Audit of Financial Statements*, should be read in conjunction with ISA (UK) 200 (Revised June 2016), *Overall Objectives of the Independent Auditor and the Conduct of an Audit in Accordance with International Standards on Auditing (UK)*.

Introduction

Scope of this ISA (UK)

1   This International Standard on Auditing (UK) (ISA (UK)) deals with the auditor's responsibility to plan an audit of financial statements. This ISA (UK) is written in the context of recurring audits. Additional considerations in an initial audit engagement are separately identified.

The Role and Timing of Planning

2   Planning an audit involves establishing the overall audit strategy for the engagement and developing an audit plan. Adequate planning benefits the audit of financial statements in several ways, including the following: (Ref: Para. A1–A3)

- Helping the auditor to devote appropriate attention to important areas of the audit.
- Helping the auditor identify and resolve potential problems on a timely basis.
- Helping the auditor properly organize and manage the audit engagement so that it is performed in an effective and efficient manner.
- Assisting in the selection of engagement team members with appropriate levels of capabilities and competence to respond to anticipated risks, and the proper assignment of work to them.
- Facilitating the direction and supervision of engagement team members and the review of their work.
- Assisting, where applicable, in coordination of work done by auditors of components and experts.

Effective Date

3   This ISA (UK) is effective for audits of financial statements for periods commencing on or after 17 June 2016. Earlier adoption is permitted.

Objective

4   The objective of the auditor is to plan the audit so that it will be performed in an effective manner.

Requirements

Involvement of Key Engagement Team Members

5   The engagement partner and other key members of the engagement team shall be involved in planning the audit, including planning and participating in the discussion among engagement team members. (Ref: Para. A4)

Preliminary Engagement Activities

6   The auditor shall undertake the following activities at the beginning of the current audit engagement:

  (a) Performing procedures required by ISA (UK) 220 (Revised June 2016) regarding the continuance of the client relationship and the specific audit engagement;[1]

---

[1] *ISA (UK) 220 (Revised June 2016)*, Quality Control for an Audit of Financial Statements, *paragraphs 12–13*.

(b) Evaluating compliance with relevant ethical requirements, including independence, in accordance with ISA (UK) 220 (Revised June 2016);[2] and

(c) Establishing an understanding of the terms of the engagement, as required by ISA (UK) 210 (Revised June 2016).[3] (Ref: Para. A5–A7)

Planning Activities

The auditor shall establish an overall audit strategy that sets the scope, timing and direction of the audit, and that guides the development of the audit plan.   **7**

In establishing the overall audit strategy, the auditor shall: **8**

(a) Identify the characteristics of the engagement that define its scope;

(b) Ascertain the reporting objectives of the engagement to plan the timing of the audit and the nature of the communications required;

(c) Consider the factors that, in the auditor's professional judgment, are significant in directing the engagement team's efforts;

(d) Consider the results of preliminary engagement activities and, where applicable, whether knowledge gained on other engagements performed by the engagement partner for the entity is relevant; and

(e) Ascertain the nature, timing and extent of resources necessary to perform the engagement. (Ref: Para. A8–A11)

The auditor shall develop an audit plan that shall include a description of: **9**

(a) The nature, timing and extent of planned risk assessment procedures, as determined under ISA (UK) 315 (Revised June 2016).[4]

(b) The nature, timing and extent of planned further audit procedures at the assertion level, as determined under ISA (UK) 330 (Revised June 2016).[5]

(c) Other planned audit procedures that are required to be carried out so that the engagement complies with ISAs (UK). (Ref: Para. A12–A12b)

The auditor shall update and change the overall audit strategy and the audit plan as necessary during the course of the audit. (Ref: Para. A13)   **10**

The auditor shall plan the nature, timing and extent of direction and supervision of engagement team members and the review of their work. (Ref: Para. A14–A15)   **11**

Documentation

The auditor shall include in the audit documentation:[6]   **12**

(a) The overall audit strategy;

(b) The audit plan; and

---

[2] *ISA (UK) 220 (Revised June 2016), paragraphs 9–11.*

[3] *ISA (UK) 210 (Revised June 2016),* Agreeing the Terms of Audit Engagements, *paragraphs 9–13.*

[4] *ISA (UK) 315 (Revised June 2016),* Identifying and Assessing the Risks of Material Misstatement through Understanding the Entity and Its Environment.

[5] *ISA (UK) 330 (Revised June 2016),* The Auditor's Responses to Assessed Risks.

[6] *ISA (UK) 230 (Revised June 2016),* Audit Documentation, *paragraphs 8–11, and paragraph A6.*

(c) Any significant changes made during the audit engagement to the overall audit strategy or the audit plan, and the reasons for such changes. (Ref: Para. A16–A19)

Additional Considerations in Initial Audit Engagements

13   The auditor shall undertake the following activities prior to starting an initial audit:

(a) Performing procedures required by ISA (UK) 220 (Revised June 2016) regarding the acceptance of the client relationship and the specific audit engagement;[7] and

(b) Communicating with the predecessor auditor, where there has been a change of auditors, in compliance with relevant ethical requirements. (Ref: Para. A20)

***

Application and Other Explanatory Material

The Role and Timing of Planning (Ref: Para. 2)

A1   The nature and extent of planning activities will vary according to the size and complexity of the entity, the key engagement team members' previous experience with the entity, and changes in circumstances that occur during the audit engagement.

A2   Planning is not a discrete phase of an audit, but rather a continual and iterative process that often begins shortly after (or in connection with) the completion of the previous audit and continues until the completion of the current audit engagement. Planning, however, includes consideration of the timing of certain activities and audit procedures that need to be completed prior to the performance of further audit procedures. For example, planning includes the need to consider, prior to the auditor's identification and assessment of the risks of material misstatement, such matters as:

- The analytical procedures to be applied as risk assessment procedures.
- Obtaining a general understanding of the legal and regulatory framework applicable to the entity and how the entity is complying with that framework.
- The determination of materiality.
- The involvement of experts.
- The performance of other risk assessment procedures.

A3   The auditor may decide to discuss elements of planning with the entity's management to facilitate the conduct and management of the audit engagement (for example, to coordinate some of the planned audit procedures with the work of the entity's personnel). Although these discussions often occur, the overall audit strategy and the audit plan remain the auditor's responsibility. When discussing matters included in the overall audit strategy or audit plan, care is required in order not to compromise the effectiveness of the audit. For example, discussing the nature and timing of detailed audit procedures with management may compromise the effectiveness of the audit by making the audit procedures too predictable.

---

[7] *ISA (UK) 220 (Revised June 2016), paragraphs 12–13.*

Involvement of Key Engagement Team Members (Ref: Para. 5)

The involvement of the engagement partner and other key members of the engagement team in planning the audit draws on their experience and insight, thereby enhancing the effectiveness and efficiency of the planning process.[8]   **A4**

Preliminary Engagement Activities (Ref: Para. 6)

Performing the preliminary engagement activities specified in paragraph 6 at the beginning of the current audit engagement assists the auditor in identifying and evaluating events or circumstances that may adversely affect the auditor's ability to plan and perform the audit engagement.   **A5**

Performing these preliminary engagement activities enables the auditor to plan an audit engagement for which, for example: **A6**

- The auditor maintains the necessary independence and ability to perform the engagement.
- There are no issues with management[8a] integrity that may affect the auditor's willingness to continue the engagement.
- There is no misunderstanding with the client as to the terms of the engagement.

The auditor's consideration of client continuance and relevant ethical requirements, including independence, occurs throughout the audit engagement as conditions and changes in circumstances occur. Performing initial procedures on both client continuance and evaluation of relevant ethical requirements (including independence) at the beginning of the current audit engagement means that they are completed prior to the performance of other significant activities for the current audit engagement. For continuing audit engagements, such initial procedures often occur shortly after (or in connection with) the completion of the previous audit.   **A7**

Planning Activities

The Overall Audit Strategy (Ref: Para. 7–8)

The process of establishing the overall audit strategy assists the auditor to determine, subject to the completion of the auditor's risk assessment procedures, such matters as: **A8**

- The resources to deploy for specific audit areas, such as the use of appropriately experienced team members for high risk areas or the involvement of experts on complex matters;
- The amount of resources to allocate to specific audit areas, such as the number of team members assigned to observe the inventory count at material locations, the extent of review of other auditors' work in the case of group audits, or the audit budget in hours to allocate to high risk areas;
- When these resources are to be deployed, such as whether at an interim audit stage or at key cutoff dates; and

---

[8] *ISA (UK) 315 (Revised June 2016), paragraph 10, establishes requirements and provides guidance on the engagement team's discussion of the susceptibility of the entity to material misstatements of the financial statements. ISA (UK) 240 (Revised June 2016),* The Auditor's Responsibilities Relating to Fraud in an Audit of Financial Statements, *paragraph 15, provides guidance on the emphasis given during this discussion to the susceptibility of the entity's financial statements to material misstatement due to fraud.*

[8a] *In the UK, the auditor is also concerned to establish that there are no issues with the integrity of those charged with governance that may affect the auditor's willingness to continue the engagement.*

- How such resources are managed, directed and supervised, such as when team briefing and debriefing meetings are expected to be held, how engagement partner and manager reviews are expected to take place (for example, on-site or off-site), and whether to complete engagement quality control reviews.

A9   The Appendix lists examples of considerations in establishing the overall audit strategy.

A10   Once the overall audit strategy has been established, an audit plan can be developed to address the various matters identified in the overall audit strategy, taking into account the need to achieve the audit objectives through the efficient use of the auditor's resources. The establishment of the overall audit strategy and the detailed audit plan are not necessarily discrete or sequential processes, but are closely inter-related since changes in one may result in consequential changes to the other.

Considerations Specific to Smaller Entities

A11   In audits of small entities, the entire audit may be conducted by a very small audit team. Many audits of small entities involve the engagement partner (who may be a sole practitioner) working with one engagement team member (or without any engagement team members). With a smaller team, coordination of, and communication between, team members are easier. Establishing the overall audit strategy for the audit of a small entity need not be a complex or time-consuming exercise; it varies according to the size of the entity, the complexity of the audit, and the size of the engagement team. For example, a brief memorandum prepared at the completion of the previous audit, based on a review of the working papers and highlighting issues identified in the audit just completed, updated in the current period based on discussions with the owner-manager, can serve as the documented audit strategy for the current audit engagement if it covers the matters noted in paragraph 8.

The Audit Plan (Ref: Para. 9)

A12   The audit plan is more detailed than the overall audit strategy in that it includes the nature, timing and extent of audit procedures to be performed by engagement team members. Planning for these audit procedures takes place over the course of the audit as the audit plan for the engagement develops. For example, planning of the auditor's risk assessment procedures occurs early in the audit process. However, planning the nature, timing and extent of specific further audit procedures depends on the outcome of those risk assessment procedures. In addition, the auditor may begin the execution of further audit procedures for some classes of transactions, account balances and disclosures before planning all remaining further audit procedures.

A12a   Determining the nature, timing and extent of planned risk assessment procedures, and the further audit procedures, as they relate to disclosures is important in light of both the wide range of information and the level of detail that may be encompassed in those disclosures. Further, certain disclosures may contain information that is obtained from outside of the general and subsidiary ledgers, which may also affect the assessed risks and the nature, timing and extent of audit procedures to address them.

A12b   Consideration of disclosures early in the audit assists the auditor in giving appropriate attention to, and planning adequate time for, addressing disclosures in the same way as classes of transactions, events and account balances. Early consideration may also help the auditor to determine the effects on the audit of:

- Significant new or revised disclosures required as a result of changes in the entity's environment, financial condition or activities (for example, a change in the required identification of segments and reporting of segment information arising from a significant business combination);

- Significant new or revised disclosures arising from changes in the applicable financial reporting framework;
- The need for the involvement of an auditor's expert to assist with audit procedures related to particular disclosures (for example, disclosures related to pension or other retirement benefit obligations); and
- Matters relating to disclosures that the auditor may wish to discuss with those charged with governance.[9]

Changes to Planning Decisions during the Course of the Audit (Ref: Para. 10)

As a result of unexpected events, changes in conditions, or the audit evidence obtained **A13** from the results of audit procedures, the auditor may need to modify the overall audit strategy and audit plan and thereby the resulting planned nature, timing and extent of further audit procedures, based on the revised consideration of assessed risks. This may be the case when information comes to the auditor's attention that differs significantly from the information available when the auditor planned the audit procedures. For example, audit evidence obtained through the performance of substantive procedures may contradict the audit evidence obtained through tests of controls.

Direction, Supervision and Review (Ref: Para. 11)

The nature, timing and extent of the direction and supervision of engagement team **A14** members and review of their work vary depending on many factors, including:

- The size and complexity of the entity.
- The area of the audit.
- The assessed risks of material misstatement (for example, an increase in the assessed risk of material misstatement for a given area of the audit ordinarily requires a corresponding increase in the extent and timeliness of direction and supervision of engagement team members, and a more detailed review of their work).
- The capabilities and competence of the individual team members performing the audit work.

ISA (UK) 220 (Revised June 2016) contains further guidance on the direction, supervision and review of audit work.[10]

Considerations Specific to Smaller Entities

If an audit is carried out entirely by the engagement partner, questions of direction and **A15** supervision of engagement team members and review of their work do not arise. In such cases, the engagement partner, having personally conducted all aspects of the work, will be aware of all material issues. Forming an objective view on the appropriateness of the judgments made in the course of the audit can present practical problems when the same individual also performs the entire audit. If particularly complex or unusual issues are involved, and the audit is performed by a sole practitioner, it may be desirable to consult with other suitably-experienced auditors or the auditor's professional body.

---

[9] *ISA (UK) 260 (Revised June 2016),* Communication with Those Charged With Governance, *paragraph A12.*

[10] *ISA (UK) 220 (Revised June 2016), paragraphs 15–17.*

Documentation (Ref: Para. 12)

A16   The documentation of the overall audit strategy is a record of the key decisions considered necessary to properly plan the audit and to communicate significant matters to the engagement team. For example, the auditor may summarize the overall audit strategy in the form of a memorandum that contains key decisions regarding the overall scope, timing and conduct of the audit.

A17   The documentation of the audit plan is a record of the planned nature, timing and extent of risk assessment procedures and further audit procedures at the assertion level in response to the assessed risks. It also serves as a record of the proper planning of the audit procedures that can be reviewed and approved prior to their performance. The auditor may use standard audit programs or audit completion checklists, tailored as needed to reflect the particular engagement circumstances.

A18   A record of the significant changes to the overall audit strategy and the audit plan, and resulting changes to the planned nature, timing and extent of audit procedures, explains why the significant changes were made, and the overall strategy and audit plan finally adopted for the audit. It also reflects the appropriate response to the significant changes occurring during the audit.

Considerations Specific to Smaller Entities

A19   As discussed in paragraph A11, a suitable, brief memorandum may serve as the documented strategy for the audit of a smaller entity. For the audit plan, standard audit programs or checklists (see paragraph A17) drawn up on the assumption of few relevant control activities, as is likely to be the case in a smaller entity, may be used provided that they are tailored to the circumstances of the engagement, including the auditor's risk assessments.

Additional Considerations in Initial Audit Engagements (Ref: Para. 13)

A20   The purpose and objective of planning the audit are the same whether the audit is an initial or recurring engagement. However, for an initial audit, the auditor may need to expand the planning activities because the auditor does not ordinarily have the previous experience with the entity that is considered when planning recurring engagements. For an initial audit engagement, additional matters the auditor may consider in establishing the overall audit strategy and audit plan include the following:

●   Unless prohibited by law or regulation, arrangements to be made with the predecessor auditor, for example, to review the predecessor auditor's working papers.

●   Any major issues (including the application of accounting principles or of auditing and reporting standards) discussed with management in connection with the initial selection as auditor, the communication of these matters to those charged with governance and how these matters affect the overall audit strategy and audit plan.

●   The audit procedures necessary to obtain sufficient appropriate audit evidence regarding opening balances.[11]

●   Other procedures required by the firm's system of quality control for initial audit engagements (for example, the firm's system of quality control may require the involvement of another partner or senior individual to review the overall audit strategy prior to commencing significant audit procedures or to review reports prior to their issuance).

---

[11]   *ISA (UK) 510 (Revised June 2016)*, Initial Audit Engagements—Opening Balances.

Appendix   (Ref: Para. 7–8, A8–A11)

Considerations in Establishing the Overall Audit Strategy

This appendix provides examples of matters the auditor may consider in establishing the overall audit strategy. Many of these matters will also influence the auditor's detailed audit plan. The examples provided cover a broad range of matters applicable to many engagements. While some of the matters referred to below may be required by other ISAs (UK), not all matters are relevant to every audit engagement and the list is not necessarily complete.

Characteristics of the Engagement

- The financial reporting framework on which the financial information to be audited has been prepared, including any need for reconciliations to another financial reporting framework.
- Industry-specific reporting requirements such as reports mandated by industry regulators.
- The expected audit coverage, including the number and locations of components to be included.
- The nature of the control relationships between a parent and its components that determine how the group is to be consolidated.
- The extent to which components are audited by other auditors.
- The nature of the business segments to be audited, including the need for specialized knowledge.
- The reporting currency to be used, including any need for currency translation for the financial information audited.
- The need for a statutory audit of standalone financial statements in addition to an audit for consolidation purposes.
- Whether the entity has an internal audit function and if so, whether, in which areas and to what extent, the work of the function can be used, or internal auditors can be used to provide direct assistance,[11a] for purposes of the audit.
- The availability of the work of internal auditors and the extent of the auditor's potential reliance on such work.
- The entity's use of service organizations and how the auditor may obtain evidence concerning the design or operation of controls performed by them.
- The expected use of audit evidence obtained in previous audits, for example, audit evidence related to risk assessment procedures and tests of controls.
- The effect of information technology on the audit procedures, including the availability of data and the expected use of computer-assisted audit techniques.
- The coordination of the expected coverage and timing of the audit work with any reviews of interim financial information and the effect on the audit of the information obtained during such reviews.
- The availability of client personnel and data.

Reporting Objectives, Timing of the Audit, and Nature of Communications

- The entity's timetable for reporting, such as at interim and final stages.
- The organization of meetings with management and those charged with governance to discuss the nature, timing and extent of the audit work.

[11a] *The use of internal auditors to provide direct assistance is prohibited in an audit conducted in accordance with ISAs (UK) – see ISA (UK) 610 (Revised June 2013), Using the Work of Internal Auditors, paragraph 5-1.*

- The discussion with management and those charged with governance regarding the expected type and timing of reports to be issued and other communications, both written and oral, including the auditor's report, management letters and communications to those charged with governance.
- The discussion with management regarding the expected communications on the status of audit work throughout the engagement.
- Communication with auditors of components regarding the expected types and timing of reports to be issued and other communications in connection with the audit of components.
- The expected nature and timing of communications among engagement team members, including the nature and timing of team meetings and timing of the review of work performed.
- Whether there are any other expected communications with third parties, including any statutory or contractual reporting responsibilities arising from the audit.

Significant Factors, Preliminary Engagement Activities, and Knowledge Gained on Other Engagements

- The determination of materiality in accordance with ISA (UK) 320 (Revised June 2016)[12] and, where applicable:

  o The determination of materiality for components and communication thereof to component auditors in accordance with ISA (UK) 600 (Revised June 2016).[13]
  o The preliminary identification of significant components and material classes of transactions, account balances and disclosures.

- Preliminary identification of areas where there may be a higher risk of material misstatement.
- The impact of the assessed risk of material misstatement at the overall financial statement level on direction, supervision and review.
- The manner in which the auditor emphasizes to engagement team members the need to maintain a questioning mind and to exercise professional skepticism in gathering and evaluating audit evidence.
- Results of previous audits that involved evaluating the operating effectiveness of internal control, including the nature of identified deficiencies and action taken to address them.
- The discussion of matters that may affect the audit with firm personnel responsible for performing other services to the entity.
- Evidence of management's[13a] commitment to the design, implementation and maintenance of sound internal control, including evidence of appropriate documentation of such internal control.
- Changes within the applicable financial reporting framework, such as changes in accounting standards, which may involve significant new or revised disclosures.
- Volume of transactions, which may determine whether it is more efficient for the auditor to rely on internal control.
- Importance attached to internal control throughout the entity to the successful operation of the business.

---

[12] *ISA (UK) 320 (Revised June 2016)*, Materiality in Planning and Performing an Audit.

[13] *ISA (UK) 600 (Revised June 2016)*, Special Considerations—Audits of Group Financial Statements (Including the Work of Component Auditors), *paragraphs 21–23 and 40(c)*.

[13a] *In the UK the auditor also considers evidence of the commitment of those charged with governance to the design and operation of sound internal control.*

- The process(es) management uses to identify and prepare the disclosures required by the applicable financial reporting framework, including disclosures containing information that is obtained from outside of the general and subsidiary ledgers.
- Significant business developments affecting the entity, including changes in information technology and business processes, changes in key management, and acquisitions, mergers and divestments.
- Significant industry developments such as changes in industry regulations and new reporting requirements.
- Other significant relevant developments, such as changes in the legal environment affecting the entity.

Nature, Timing and Extent of Resources

- The selection of the engagement team (including, where necessary, the engagement quality control reviewer) and the assignment of audit work to the team members, including the assignment of appropriately experienced team members to areas where there may be higher risks of material misstatement.
- Engagement budgeting, including considering the appropriate amount of time to set aside for areas where there may be higher risks of material misstatement.

International Standard on Auditing (UK) 315 (Revised June 2016)

Identifying and assessing the risks of material misstatement through understanding of the entity and its environment

(Effective for audits of financial statements for periods commencing on or after 17 June 2016)

Contents

International Standard on Auditing (UK) (ISA (UK)) 315 (Revised June 2016), *Identifying and Assessing the Risks of Material Misstatement through Understanding the Entity and Its Environment*, should be read in conjunction with ISA (UK) 200 (Revised June 2016), *Overall Objectives of the Independent Auditor and the Conduct of an Audit in Accordance with International Standards on Auditing (UK)*.

Introduction

Scope of this ISA (UK)

This International Standard on Auditing (UK) (ISA (UK)) deals with the auditor's **1** responsibility to identify and assess the risks of material misstatement in the financial statements, through understanding the entity and its environment, including the entity's internal control.

Effective Date

This ISA (UK) is effective for audits of financial statements for periods commencing on or **2** after 17 June 2016. Earlier adoption is permitted.

Objective

The objective of the auditor is to identify and assess the risks of material misstatement, **3** whether due to fraud or error, at the financial statement and assertion levels, through understanding the entity and its environment, including the entity's internal control, thereby providing a basis for designing and implementing responses to the assessed risks of material misstatement.

Definitions

For purposes of the ISAs (UK), the following terms have the meanings attributed below: **4**

(a) Assertions – Representations by management,[1a] explicit or otherwise, that are embodied in the financial statements, as used by the auditor to consider the different types of potential misstatements that may occur.

(b) Business risk – A risk resulting from significant conditions, events, circumstances, actions or inactions that could adversely affect an entity's ability to achieve its objectives and execute its strategies, or from the setting of inappropriate objectives and strategies.

(c) Internal control – The process designed, implemented and maintained by those charged with governance, management and other personnel to provide reasonable assurance about the achievement of an entity's objectives with regard to reliability of financial reporting, effectiveness and efficiency of operations, and compliance with applicable laws and regulations. The term 'controls' refers to any aspects of one or more of the components of internal control.

(d) Risk assessment procedures – The audit procedures performed to obtain an understanding of the entity and its environment, including the entity's internal control, to identify and assess the risks of material misstatement, whether due to fraud or error, at the financial statement and assertion levels.

(e) Significant risk – An identified and assessed risk of material misstatement that, in the auditor's judgment, requires special audit consideration.

[1a] *In the UK, those charged with governance are responsible for preparing the financial statements.*

Requirements

Risk Assessment Procedures and Related Activities

5   The auditor shall perform risk assessment procedures to provide a basis for the identification and assessment of risks of material misstatement at the financial statement and assertion levels. Risk assessment procedures by themselves, however, do not provide sufficient appropriate audit evidence on which to base the audit opinion. (Ref: Para. A1–A5)

6   The risk assessment procedures shall include the following:

(a) Inquiries of management, of appropriate individuals within the internal audit function (if the function exists), and of others within the entity who in the auditor's judgment may have information that is likely to assist in identifying risks of material misstatement due to fraud or error. (Ref: Para. A6–A13)

(b) Analytical procedures. (Ref: Para. A14–A17)

(c) Observation and inspection. (Ref: Para. A18)

7   The auditor shall consider whether information obtained from the auditor's client acceptance or continuance process is relevant to identifying risks of material misstatement.

8   If the engagement partner has performed other engagements for the entity, the engagement partner shall consider whether information obtained is relevant to identifying risks of material misstatement.

9   Where the auditor intends to use information obtained from the auditor's previous experience with the entity and from audit procedures performed in previous audits, the auditor shall determine whether changes have occurred since the previous audit that may affect its relevance to the current audit. (Ref: Para. A19–A20)

10   The engagement partner and other key engagement team members shall discuss the susceptibility of the entity's financial statements to material misstatement, and the application of the applicable financial reporting framework to the entity's facts and circumstances. The engagement partner shall determine which matters are to be communicated to engagement team members not involved in the discussion. (Ref: Para. A21–A23)

The Required Understanding of the Entity and Its Environment, Including the Entity's Internal Control

The Entity and Its Environment

11   The auditor shall obtain an understanding of the following:

(a) Relevant industry, regulatory, and other external factors including the applicable financial reporting framework. (Ref: Para. A24–A29)

(b) The nature of the entity, including:

(i)   its operations;

(ii)   its ownership and governance structures;

(iii) the types of investments that the entity is making and plans to make, including investments in special-purpose entities; and

(iv) the way that the entity is structured and how it is financed

to enable the auditor to understand the classes of transactions, account balances, and disclosures to be expected in the financial statements. (Ref: Para. A30–A34)

(c) The entity's selection and application of accounting policies, including the reasons for changes thereto. The auditor shall evaluate whether the entity's accounting policies are appropriate for its business and consistent with the applicable financial reporting framework and accounting policies used in the relevant industry. (Ref: Para. A35)

(d) The entity's objectives and strategies, and those related business risks that may result in risks of material misstatement. (Ref: Para. A36–A42)

(e) The measurement and review of the entity's financial performance. (Ref: Para. A43–A48)

The Entity's Internal Control

The auditor shall obtain an understanding of internal control relevant to the audit. Although most controls relevant to the audit are likely to relate to financial reporting, not all controls that relate to financial reporting are relevant to the audit. It is a matter of the auditor's professional judgment whether a control, individually or in combination with others, is relevant to the audit. (Ref: Para. A49–A72)   **12**

Nature and Extent of the Understanding of Relevant Controls

When obtaining an understanding of controls that are relevant to the audit, the auditor shall evaluate the design of those controls and determine whether they have been implemented, by performing procedures in addition to inquiry of the entity's personnel. (Ref: Para. A73–A75)   **13**

Components of Internal Control

Control environment

The auditor shall obtain an understanding of the control environment. As part of obtaining this understanding, the auditor shall evaluate whether: **14**

(a) Management, with the oversight of those charged with governance, has created and maintained a culture of honesty and ethical behavior; and

(b) The strengths in the control environment elements collectively provide an appropriate foundation for the other components of internal control, and whether those other components are not undermined by deficiencies in the control environment. (Ref: Para. A76–A86)

The entity's risk assessment process

The auditor shall obtain an understanding of whether the entity has a process for: **15**

(a) Identifying business risks relevant to financial reporting objectives;

(b) Estimating the significance of the risks;

(c) Assessing the likelihood of their occurrence; and

(d) Deciding about actions to address those risks. (Ref: Para. A87)

If the entity has established such a process (referred to hereafter as the 'entity's risk assessment process'), the auditor shall obtain an understanding of it, and the results thereof. If the auditor identifies risks of material misstatement that management failed to identify, the auditor shall evaluate whether there was an underlying risk of a kind that the auditor expects would have been identified by the entity's risk assessment process. If there is such a risk, the auditor shall obtain an understanding of why that process failed to identify it, and evaluate whether the process is appropriate to its circumstances or determine if there is a significant deficiency in internal control with regard to the entity's risk assessment process.   **16**

17   If the entity has not established such a process or has an ad hoc process, the auditor shall discuss with management whether business risks relevant to financial reporting objectives have been identified and how they have been addressed. The auditor shall evaluate whether the absence of a documented risk assessment process is appropriate in the circumstances, or determine whether it represents a significant deficiency in internal control. (Ref: Para. A88)

The information system, including the related business processes, relevant to financial reporting, and communication

18   The auditor shall obtain an understanding of the information system, including the related business processes, relevant to financial reporting, including the following areas: (Ref: Para. A89–A89a)

(a)   The classes of transactions in the entity's operations that are significant to the financial statements;

(b)   The procedures, within both information technology (IT) and manual systems, by which those transactions are initiated, recorded, processed, corrected as necessary, transferred to the general ledger and reported in the financial statements;

(c)   The related accounting records, supporting information and specific accounts in the financial statements that are used to initiate, record, process and report transactions; this includes the correction of incorrect information and how information is transferred to the general ledger. The records may be in either manual or electronic form;

(d)   How the information system captures events and conditions, other than transactions, that are significant to the financial statements;

(e)   The financial reporting process used to prepare the entity's financial statements, including significant accounting estimates and disclosures; and

(f)   Controls surrounding journal entries, including non-standard journal entries used to record non-recurring, unusual transactions or adjustments. (Ref: Para. A89–A93)

This understanding of the information system relevant to financial reporting shall include relevant aspects of that system relating to information disclosed in the financial statements that is obtained from within or outside of the general and subsidiary ledgers.

19   The auditor shall obtain an understanding of how the entity communicates financial reporting roles and responsibilities and significant matters relating to financial reporting, including: (Ref: Para. A94–A95)

(a)   Communications between management and those charged with governance; and

(b)   External communications, such as those with regulatory authorities.

Control activities relevant to the audit

20   The auditor shall obtain an understanding of control activities relevant to the audit, being those the auditor judges it necessary to understand in order to assess the risks of material misstatement at the assertion level and design further audit procedures responsive to assessed risks. An audit does not require an understanding of all the control activities related to each significant class of transactions, account balance, and disclosure in the financial statements or to every assertion relevant to them. (Ref: Para. A96–A102)

21   In understanding the entity's control activities, the auditor shall obtain an understanding of how the entity has responded to risks arising from IT. (Ref: Para. A103–A105)

Monitoring of controls

22   The auditor shall obtain an understanding of the major activities that the entity uses to monitor internal control relevant to financial reporting, including those related to those control activities relevant to the audit, and how the entity initiates remedial actions to deficiencies in its controls. (Ref: Para. A106–A108)

If the entity has an internal audit function,[1] the auditor shall obtain an understanding of the nature of the internal audit function's responsibilities, its organizational status, and the activities performed, or to be performed. (Ref: Para. A109–A116) **23**

The auditor shall obtain an understanding of the sources of the information used in the entity's monitoring activities, and the basis upon which management considers the information to be sufficiently reliable for the purpose. (Ref: Para. A117) **24**

Identifying and Assessing the Risks of Material Misstatement

The auditor shall identify and assess the risks of material misstatement at: **25**

(a) the financial statement level; and (Ref: Para. A118–A121)
(b) the assertion level for classes of transactions, account balances, and disclosures (Ref: Para. A122–A126)

to provide a basis for designing and performing further audit procedures.

For this purpose, the auditor shall: **26**

(a) Identify risks throughout the process of obtaining an understanding of the entity and its environment, including relevant controls that relate to the risks, and by considering the classes of transactions, account balances, and disclosures (including the quantitative or qualitative aspects of such disclosures) in the financial statements; (Ref: Para. A127–A128b)
(b) Assess the identified risks, and evaluate whether they relate more pervasively to the financial statements as a whole and potentially affect many assertions;
(c) Relate the identified risks to what can go wrong at the assertion level, taking account of relevant controls that the auditor intends to test; and (Ref: Para. A129–A131)
(d) Consider the likelihood of misstatement, including the possibility of multiple misstatements, and whether the potential misstatement could result in a material misstatement. (Ref: Para. A131a)

Risks That Require Special Audit Consideration

As part of the risk assessment as described in paragraph 25, the auditor shall determine whether any of the risks identified are, in the auditor's judgment, a significant risk. In exercising this judgment, the auditor shall exclude the effects of identified controls related to the risk. **27**

In exercising judgment as to which risks are significant risks, the auditor shall consider at least the following: **28**

(a) Whether the risk is a risk of fraud;
(b) Whether the risk is related to recent significant economic, accounting or other developments and, therefore, requires specific attention;
(c) The complexity of transactions;
(d) Whether the risk involves significant transactions with related parties;

---

[1] *ISA (UK) 610 (Revised June 2013),* Using the Work of Internal Auditors, *paragraph 14, defines the term 'internal audit function' for purposes of the ISAs (UK).*

(e) The degree of subjectivity in the measurement of financial information related to the risk, especially those measurements involving a wide range of measurement uncertainty; and

(f) Whether the risk involves significant transactions that are outside the normal course of business for the entity, or that otherwise appear to be unusual. (Ref: Para. A132–A136)

29   If the auditor has determined that a significant risk exists, the auditor shall obtain an understanding of the entity's controls, including control activities, relevant to that risk. (Ref: Para. A137–A139)

Risks for Which Substantive Procedures Alone Do Not Provide Sufficient Appropriate Audit Evidence

30   In respect of some risks, the auditor may judge that it is not possible or practicable to obtain sufficient appropriate audit evidence only from substantive procedures. Such risks may relate to the inaccurate or incomplete recording of routine and significant classes of transactions or account balances, the characteristics of which often permit highly automated processing with little or no manual intervention. In such cases, the entity's controls over such risks are relevant to the audit and the auditor shall obtain an understanding of them. (Ref: Para. A140–A142)

Revision of Risk Assessment

31   The auditor's assessment of the risks of material misstatement at the assertion level may change during the course of the audit as additional audit evidence is obtained. In circumstances where the auditor obtains audit evidence from performing further audit procedures, or if new information is obtained, either of which is inconsistent with the audit evidence on which the auditor originally based the assessment, the auditor shall revise the assessment and modify the further planned audit procedures accordingly. (Ref: Para. A143)

Documentation

32   The auditor shall include in the audit documentation:[2]

(a) The discussion among the engagement team where required by paragraph 10, and the significant decisions reached;

(b) Key elements of the understanding obtained regarding each of the aspects of the entity and its environment specified in paragraph 11 and of each of the internal control components specified in paragraphs 14–24; the sources of information from which the understanding was obtained; and the risk assessment procedures performed;

(c) The identified and assessed risks of material misstatement at the financial statement level and at the assertion level as required by paragraph 25; and

(d) The risks identified, and related controls about which the auditor has obtained an understanding, as a result of the requirements in paragraphs 27–30. (Ref: Para. A144–A147)

***

---

[2] *ISA (UK) 230 (Revised June 2016)*, Audit Documentation, *paragraphs 8–11, and A6.*

Application and Other Explanatory Material

Risk Assessment Procedures and Related Activities (Ref: Para. 5)

Obtaining an understanding of the entity and its environment, including the entity's   **A1**
internal control (referred to hereafter as an 'understanding of the entity'), is a continuous,
dynamic process of gathering, updating and analyzing information throughout the audit.
The understanding establishes a frame of reference within which the auditor plans the audit
and exercises professional judgment throughout the audit, for example, when:

- Assessing risks of material misstatement of the financial statements;
- Determining materiality in accordance with ISA (UK) 320 (Revised June 2016);[3]
- Considering the appropriateness of the selection and application of accounting policies, and the adequacy of financial statement disclosures;
- Identifying areas relating to amounts or disclosures in the financial statements where special audit consideration may be necessary, for example, related party transactions or management's assessment of the entity's ability to continue as a going concern, or when considering the business purpose of transactions;
- Developing expectations for use when performing analytical procedures;
- Responding to the assessed risks of material misstatement, including designing and performing further audit procedures to obtain sufficient appropriate audit evidence; and
- Evaluating the sufficiency and appropriateness of audit evidence obtained, such as the appropriateness of assumptions and of management's[3a] oral and written representations.

Information obtained by performing risk assessment procedures and related activities   **A2**
may be used by the auditor as audit evidence to support assessments of the risks of
material misstatement. In addition, the auditor may obtain audit evidence about classes
of transactions, account balances, or disclosures and related assertions and about the
operating effectiveness of controls, even though such procedures were not specifically
planned as substantive procedures or as tests of controls. The auditor also may choose
to perform substantive procedures or tests of controls concurrently with risk assessment
procedures because it is efficient to do so.

The auditor uses professional judgment to determine the extent of the understanding   **A3**
required. The auditor's primary consideration is whether the understanding that has been
obtained is sufficient to meet the objective stated in this ISA (UK). The depth of the overall
understanding that is required by the auditor is less than that possessed by management in
managing the entity.

The risks to be assessed include both those due to error and those due to fraud, and both   **A4**
are covered by this ISA (UK). However, the significance of fraud is such that further
requirements and guidance are included in ISA (UK) 240 (Revised June 2016) in relation
to risk assessment procedures and related activities to obtain information that is used to
identify the risks of material misstatement due to fraud.[4]

---

[3] *ISA (UK) 320 (Revised June 2016)*, Materiality in Planning and Performing an Audit.

[3a] *In the UK, as explained in paragraph A2-1 of ISA (UK) 580*, Written Representations, *it is appropriate for written representations that are critical to obtaining sufficient appropriate audit evidence to be provided by those charged with governance, rather than other levels of the entity's management.*

[4] *ISA (UK) 240 (Revised June 2016)*, The Auditor's Responsibilities Relating to Fraud in an Audit of Financial Statements, *paragraphs 12–24.*

A5   Although the auditor is required to perform all the risk assessment procedures described in paragraph 6 in the course of obtaining the required understanding of the entity (see paragraphs 11–24), the auditor is not required to perform all of them for each aspect of that understanding. Other procedures may be performed where the information to be obtained therefrom may be helpful in identifying risks of material misstatement. Examples of such procedures include:

- Reviewing information obtained from external sources such as trade and economic journals; reports by analysts, banks, or rating agencies; or regulatory or financial publications.
- Making inquiries of the entity's external legal counsel or of valuation experts that the entity has used.

Inquiries of Management, the Internal Audit Function and Others within the Entity (Ref: Para. 6(a))

A6   Much of the information obtained by the auditor's inquiries is obtained from management and those responsible for financial reporting. Information may also be obtained by the auditor through inquiries with the internal audit function, if the entity has such a function, and others within the entity.

A7   The auditor may also obtain information, or a different perspective in identifying risks of material misstatement, through inquiries of others within the entity and other employees with different levels of authority. For example:

- Inquiries directed towards those charged with governance may help the auditor understand the environment in which the financial statements are prepared. ISA (UK) 260 (Revised June 2016)[5] identifies the importance of effective two-way communication in assisting the auditor to obtain information from those charged with governance in this regard.
- Inquiries of employees involved in initiating, processing or recording complex or unusual transactions may help the auditor to evaluate the appropriateness of the selection and application of certain accounting policies.
- Inquiries directed toward in-house legal counsel may provide information about such matters as litigation, compliance with laws and regulations, knowledge of fraud or suspected fraud affecting the entity, warranties, post-sales obligations, arrangements (such as joint ventures) with business partners and the meaning of contract terms.
- Inquiries directed towards marketing or sales personnel may provide information about changes in the entity's marketing strategies, sales trends, or contractual arrangements with its customers.
- Inquiries directed to the risk management function (or those performing such roles) may provide information about operational and regulatory risks that may affect financial reporting.
- Inquiries directed to information systems personnel may provide information about system changes, system or control failures, or other information system-related risks.

A8   As obtaining an understanding of the entity and its environment is a continual, dynamic process, the auditor's inquiries may occur throughout the audit engagement.

Inquiries of the Internal Audit Function

A9   If an entity has an internal audit function, inquiries of the appropriate individuals within the function may provide information that is useful to the auditor in obtaining an

---

[5] *ISA (UK) 260 (Revised June 2016)*, Communication with Those Charged with Governance, *paragraph 4(b).*

understanding of the entity and its environment, and in identifying and assessing risks of material misstatement at the financial statement and assertion levels. In performing its work, the internal audit function is likely to have obtained insight into the entity's operations and business risks, and may have findings based on its work, such as identified control deficiencies or risks, that may provide valuable input into the auditor's understanding of the entity, the auditor's risk assessments or other aspects of the audit. The auditor's inquiries are therefore made whether or not the auditor expects to use the work of the internal audit function to modify the nature or timing, or reduce the extent, of audit procedures to be performed.[6] Inquiries of particular relevance may be about matters the internal audit function has raised with those charged with governance and the outcomes of the function's own risk assessment process.

If, based on responses to the auditor's inquiries, it appears that there are findings that may   **A10**
be relevant to the entity's financial reporting and the audit, the auditor may consider it appropriate to read related reports of the internal audit function. Examples of reports of the internal audit function that may be relevant include the function's strategy and planning documents and reports that have been prepared for management or those charged with governance describing the findings of the internal audit function's examinations.

In addition, in accordance with ISA (UK) 240 (Revised June 2016),[7] if the internal audit   **A11**
function provides information to the auditor regarding any actual, suspected or alleged fraud, the auditor takes this into account in the auditor's identification of risk of material misstatement due to fraud.

Appropriate individuals within the internal audit function with whom inquiries are made   **A12**
are those who, in the auditor's judgment, have the appropriate knowledge, experience and authority, such as the chief internal audit executive or, depending on the circumstances, other personnel within the function. The auditor may also consider it appropriate to have periodic meetings with these individuals.

Considerations specific to public sector entities (Ref: Para 6(a))

Auditors of public sector entities often have additional responsibilities with regard   **A13**
to internal control and compliance with applicable laws and regulations. Inquiries of appropriate individuals in the internal audit function can assist the auditors in identifying the risk of material noncompliance with applicable laws and regulations and the risk of deficiencies in internal control over financial reporting.

Analytical Procedures (Ref: Para. 6(b))

Analytical procedures performed as risk assessment procedures may identify aspects of the   **A14**
entity of which the auditor was unaware and may assist in assessing the risks of material misstatement in order to provide a basis for designing and implementing responses to the assessed risks. Analytical procedures performed as risk assessment procedures may include both financial and non-financial information, for example, the relationship between sales and square footage of selling space or volume of goods sold.

Analytical procedures may help identify the existence of unusual transactions or events,   **A15**
and amounts, ratios, and trends that might indicate matters that have audit implications. Unusual or unexpected relationships that are identified may assist the auditor in identifying risks of material misstatement, especially risks of material misstatement due to fraud.

---

[6] *The relevant requirements are contained in ISA (UK) 610 (Revised June 2013).*

[7] *ISA (UK) 240 (Revised June 2016), paragraph 19.*

A16   However, when such analytical procedures use data aggregated at a high level (which may be the situation with analytical procedures performed as risk assessment procedures), the results of those analytical procedures only provide a broad initial indication about whether a material misstatement may exist. Accordingly, in such cases, consideration of other information that has been gathered when identifying the risks of material misstatement together with the results of such analytical procedures may assist the auditor in understanding and evaluating the results of the analytical procedures.

Considerations Specific to Smaller Entities

A17   Some smaller entities may not have interim or monthly financial information that can be used for purposes of analytical procedures. In these circumstances, although the auditor may be able to perform limited analytical procedures for purposes of planning the audit or obtain some information through inquiry, the auditor may need to plan to perform analytical procedures to identify and assess the risks of material misstatement when an early draft of the entity's financial statements is available.

Observation and Inspection (Ref: Para. 6(c))

A18   Observation and inspection may support inquiries of management and others, and may also provide information about the entity and its environment. Examples of such audit procedures include observation or inspection of the following:

- The entity's operations.
- Documents (such as business plans and strategies), records, and internal control manuals.
- Reports prepared by management (such as quarterly management reports and interim financial statements) and those charged with governance (such as minutes of board of directors' meetings).
- The entity's premises and plant facilities.

Information Obtained in Prior Periods (Ref: Para. 9)

A19   The auditor's previous experience with the entity and audit procedures performed in previous audits may provide the auditor with information about such matters as:

- Past misstatements and whether they were corrected on a timely basis.
- The nature of the entity and its environment, and the entity's internal control (including deficiencies in internal control).
- Significant changes that the entity or its operations may have undergone since the prior financial period, which may assist the auditor in gaining a sufficient understanding of the entity to identify and assess risks of material misstatement.
- Those particular types of transactions and other events or account balances (and related disclosures) where the auditor experienced difficulty in performing the necessary audit procedures, for example due to their complexity.

A20   The auditor is required to determine whether information obtained in prior periods remains relevant, if the auditor intends to use that information for the purposes of the current audit. This is because changes in the control environment, for example, may affect the relevance of information obtained in the prior year. To determine whether changes have occurred that may affect the relevance of such information, the auditor may make inquiries and perform other appropriate audit procedures, such as walk-throughs of relevant systems.

Discussion among the Engagement Team (Ref: Para. 10)

The discussion among the engagement team about the susceptibility of the entity's financial   **A21**
statements to material misstatement:

- Provides an opportunity for more experienced engagement team members, including the engagement partner, to share their insights based on their knowledge of the entity.
- Allows the engagement team members to exchange information about the business risks to which the entity is subject and about how and where the financial statements might be susceptible to material misstatement due to fraud or error.
- Assists the engagement team members to gain a better understanding of the potential for material misstatement of the financial statements in the specific areas assigned to them, and to understand how the results of the audit procedures that they perform may affect other aspects of the audit including the decisions about the nature, timing, and extent of further audit procedures.
- Provides a basis upon which engagement team members communicate and share new information obtained throughout the audit that may affect the assessment of risks of material misstatement or the audit procedures performed to address these risks.

ISA (UK) 240 (Revised June 2016) provides further requirements and guidance in relation to the discussion among the engagement team about the risks of fraud.[8]

As part of the discussion among the engagement team required by paragraph 10,   **A21a**
consideration of the disclosure requirements of the applicable financial reporting framework
assists in identifying early in the audit where there may be risks of material misstatement
in relation to disclosures. Examples of matters the engagement team may discuss include:

- Changes in financial reporting requirements that may result in significant new or revised disclosures;
- Changes in the entity's environment, financial condition or activities that may result in significant new or revised disclosures, for example, a significant business combination in the period under audit;
- Disclosures for which obtaining sufficient appropriate audit evidence may have been difficult in the past; and
- Disclosures about complex matters, including those involving significant management judgment as to what information to disclose.

It is not always necessary or practical for the discussion to include all members in a single   **A22**
discussion (as, for example, in a multi-location audit), nor is it necessary for all of the members
of the engagement team to be informed of all of the decisions reached in the discussion.
The engagement partner may discuss matters with key members of the engagement team
including, if considered appropriate, those with specific skills or knowledge, and those
responsible for the audits of components, while delegating discussion with others, taking
account of the extent of communication considered necessary throughout the engagement
team. A communications plan, agreed by the engagement partner, may be useful.

Considerations Specific to Smaller Entities

Many small audits are carried out entirely by the engagement partner (who may be a   **A23**
sole practitioner). In such situations, it is the engagement partner who, having personally
conducted the planning of the audit, would be responsible for considering the susceptibility
of the entity's financial statements to material misstatement due to fraud or error.

---

[8] *ISA (UK) 240 (Revised June 2016), paragraph 15.*

The Required Understanding of the Entity and Its Environment, Including the Entity's Internal Control

The Entity and Its Environment

Industry, Regulatory and Other External Factors (Ref: Para. 11(a))

Industry Factors

A24   Relevant industry factors include industry conditions such as the competitive environment, supplier and customer relationships, and technological developments. Examples of matters the auditor may consider include:

- The market and competition, including demand, capacity, and price competition.
- Cyclical or seasonal activity.
- Product technology relating to the entity's products.
- Energy supply and cost.

A25   The industry in which the entity operates may give rise to specific risks of material misstatement arising from the nature of the business or the degree of regulation. For example, long-term contracts may involve significant estimates of revenues and expenses that give rise to risks of material misstatement. In such cases, it is important that the engagement team include members with sufficient relevant knowledge and experience.[9]

Regulatory Factors

A26   Relevant regulatory factors include the regulatory environment. The regulatory environment encompasses, among other matters, the applicable financial reporting framework and the legal and political environment. Examples of matters the auditor may consider include:

- Accounting principles and industry specific practices.
- Regulatory framework for a regulated industry, including requirements for disclosures.
- Legislation and regulation that significantly affect the entity's operations, including direct supervisory activities.
- Taxation (corporate and other).
- Government policies currently affecting the conduct of the entity's business, such as monetary, including foreign exchange controls, fiscal, financial incentives (for example, government aid programs), and tariffs or trade restrictions policies.
- Environmental requirements affecting the industry and the entity's business.

A27   ISA (UK) 250 (Revised June 2016) includes some specific requirements related to the legal and regulatory framework applicable to the entity and the industry or sector in which the entity operates.[10]

Considerations specific to public sector entities

A28   For the audits of public sector entities, law, regulation or other authority may affect the entity's operations. Such elements are essential to consider when obtaining an understanding of the entity and its environment.

---

[9] *ISA (UK) 220 (Revised June 2016),* Quality Control for an Audit of Financial Statements, *paragraph 14.*

[10] *ISA (UK) 250 (Revised June 2016),* Consideration of Laws and Regulations in an Audit of Financial Statements, *paragraph 12.*

Other External Factors

Examples of other external factors affecting the entity that the auditor may consider include the general economic conditions, interest rates and availability of financing, and inflation or currency revaluation.

A29

Nature of the Entity (Ref: Para. 11(b))

An understanding of the nature of an entity enables the auditor to understand such matters as:

A30

- Whether the entity has a complex structure, for example with subsidiaries or other components in multiple locations. Complex structures often introduce issues that may give rise to risks of material misstatement. Such issues may include whether goodwill, joint ventures, investments, or special-purpose entities are accounted for appropriately and whether adequate disclosure of such issues in the financial statements has been made.
- The ownership, and relationships between owners and other people or entities. This understanding assists in determining whether related party transactions have been appropriately identified, accounted for, and adequately disclosed in the financial statements. ISA (UK) 550[11] establishes requirements and provides guidance on the auditor's considerations relevant to related parties.

Examples of matters that the auditor may consider when obtaining an understanding of the nature of the entity include:

A31

- Business operations such as:
  - Nature of revenue sources, products or services, and markets, including involvement in electronic commerce such as Internet sales and marketing activities.
  - Conduct of operations (for example, stages and methods of production, or activities exposed to environmental risks).
  - Alliances, joint ventures, and outsourcing activities.
  - Geographic dispersion and industry segmentation.
  - Location of production facilities, warehouses, and offices, and location and quantities of inventories.
  - Key customers and important suppliers of goods and services, employment arrangements (including the existence of union contracts, pension and other post employment benefits, stock option or incentive bonus arrangements, and government regulation related to employment matters).
  - Research and development activities and expenditures.
  - Transactions with related parties.
- Investments and investment activities such as:
  - Planned or recently executed acquisitions or divestitures.
  - Investments and dispositions of securities and loans.
  - Capital investment activities.
  - Investments in non-consolidated entities, including partnerships, joint ventures and special-purpose entities.
- Financing and financing activities such as:
  - Major subsidiaries and associated entities, including consolidated and non-consolidated structures.
  - Debt structure and related terms, including off-balance-sheet financing arrangements and leasing arrangements.

---

[11] *ISA (UK) 550*, Related Parties.

- o Beneficial owners (local, foreign, business reputation and experience) and related parties.
- o Use of derivative financial instruments.

- Financial reporting practices such as:

- o Accounting principles and industry specific practices, including for industry-specific significant classes of transactions, account balances and related disclosures in the financial statements (for example, loans and investments for banks, or research and development for pharmaceuticals).
- o Revenue recognition.
- o Accounting for fair values.
- o Foreign currency assets, liabilities and transactions.
- o Accounting for unusual or complex transactions including those in controversial or emerging areas (for example, accounting for stock-based compensation).

A32 Significant changes in the entity from prior periods may give rise to, or change, risks of material misstatement.

Nature of Special-Purpose Entities

A33 A special-purpose entity (sometimes referred to as a special-purpose vehicle) is an entity that is generally established for a narrow and well-defined purpose, such as to effect a lease or a securitization of financial assets, or to carry out research and development activities. It may take the form of a corporation, trust, partnership or unincorporated entity. The entity on behalf of which the special-purpose entity has been created may often transfer assets to the latter (for example, as part of a derecognition transaction involving financial assets), obtain the right to use the latter's assets, or perform services for the latter, while other parties may provide the funding to the latter. As ISA (UK) 550 indicates, in some circumstances, a special-purpose entity may be a related party of the entity.[12]

A34 Financial reporting frameworks often specify detailed conditions that are deemed to amount to control, or circumstances under which the special-purpose entity should be considered for consolidation. The interpretation of the requirements of such frameworks often demands a detailed knowledge of the relevant agreements involving the special-purpose entity.

The Entity's Selection and Application of Accounting Policies (Ref: Para. 11(c))

A35 An understanding of the entity's selection and application of accounting policies may encompass such matters as:

- The methods the entity uses to account for significant and unusual transactions.
- The effect of significant accounting policies in controversial or emerging areas for which there is a lack of authoritative guidance or consensus.
- Changes in the entity's accounting policies.
- Financial reporting standards and laws and regulations that are new to the entity and when and how the entity will adopt such requirements.

Objectives and Strategies and Related Business Risks (Ref: Para. 11(d))

A36 The entity conducts its business in the context of industry, regulatory and other internal and external factors. To respond to these factors, the entity's management or those charged

---

[12] *ISA (UK) 550, paragraph A7.*

with governance define objectives, which are the overall plans for the entity. Strategies are the approaches by which management intends to achieve its objectives. The entity's objectives and strategies may change over time.

Business risk is broader than the risk of material misstatement of the financial statements, though it includes the latter. Business risk may arise from change or complexity. A failure to recognize the need for change may also give rise to business risk. Business risk may arise, for example, from: **A37**

- The development of new products or services that may fail;
- A market which, even if successfully developed, is inadequate to support a product or service; or
- Flaws in a product or service that may result in liabilities and reputational risk.

An understanding of the business risks facing the entity increases the likelihood of identifying risks of material misstatement, since most business risks will eventually have financial consequences and, therefore, an effect on the financial statements. However, the auditor does not have a responsibility to identify or assess all business risks because not all business risks give rise to risks of material misstatement. **A38**

Examples of matters that the auditor may consider when obtaining an understanding of the entity's objectives, strategies and related business risks that may result in a risk of material misstatement of the financial statements include: **A39**

- Industry developments (a potential related business risk might be, for example, that the entity does not have the personnel or expertise to deal with the changes in the industry).
- New products and services (a potential related business risk might be, for example, that there is increased product liability).
- Expansion of the business (a potential related business risk might be, for example, that the demand has not been accurately estimated).
- New accounting requirements (a potential related business risk might be, for example, incomplete or improper implementation, or increased costs).
- Regulatory requirements (a potential related business risk might be, for example, that there is increased legal exposure).
- Current and prospective financing requirements (a potential related business risk might be, for example, the loss of financing due to the entity's inability to meet requirements).
- Use of IT (a potential related business risk might be, for example, that systems and processes are incompatible).
- The effects of implementing a strategy, particularly any effects that will lead to new accounting requirements (a potential related business risk might be, for example, incomplete or improper implementation).

A business risk may have an immediate consequence for the risk of material misstatement for classes of transactions, account balances, and disclosures at the assertion level or the financial statement level. For example, the business risk arising from a contracting customer base may increase the risk of material misstatement associated with the valuation of receivables. However, the same risk, particularly in combination with a contracting economy, may also have a longer-term consequence, which the auditor considers when assessing the appropriateness of the going concern assumption. Whether a business risk may result in a risk of material misstatement is, therefore, considered in light of the entity's circumstances. Examples of conditions and events that may indicate risks of material misstatement are indicated in Appendix 2. **A40**

A41 Usually, management identifies business risks and develops approaches to address them. Such a risk assessment process is part of internal control and is discussed in paragraph 15 and paragraphs A87–A88.

Considerations Specific to Public Sector Entities

A42 For the audits of public sector entities, 'management objectives' may be influenced by concerns regarding public accountability and may include objectives which have their source in law, regulation or other authority.

Measurement and Review of the Entity's Financial Performance (Ref: Para.11(e))

A43 Management and others will measure and review those things they regard as important. Performance measures, whether external or internal, create pressures on the entity. These pressures, in turn, may motivate management to take action to improve the business performance or to misstate the financial statements. Accordingly, an understanding of the entity's performance measures assists the auditor in considering whether pressures to achieve performance targets may result in management actions that increase the risks of material misstatement, including those due to fraud. See ISA (UK) 240 (Revised June 2016) for requirements and guidance in relation to the risks of fraud.

A44 The measurement and review of financial performance is not the same as the monitoring of controls (discussed as a component of internal control in paragraphs A106–A117), though their purposes may overlap:

- The measurement and review of performance is directed at whether business performance is meeting the objectives set by management (or third parties).
- Monitoring of controls is specifically concerned with the effective operation of internal control.

In some cases, however, performance indicators also provide information that enables management to identify deficiencies in internal control.

A45 Examples of internally-generated information used by management for measuring and reviewing financial performance, and which the auditor may consider, include:

- Key performance indicators (financial and non-financial) and key ratios, trends and operating statistics.
- Period-on-period financial performance analyses.
- Budgets, forecasts, variance analyses, segment information and divisional, departmental or other level performance reports.
- Employee performance measures and incentive compensation policies.
- Comparisons of an entity's performance with that of competitors.

A46 External parties may also measure and review the entity's financial performance. For example, external information such as analysts' reports and credit rating agency reports may represent useful information for the auditor. Such reports can often be obtained from the entity being audited.

A47 Internal measures may highlight unexpected results or trends requiring management to determine their cause and take corrective action (including, in some cases, the detection and correction of misstatements on a timely basis). Performance measures may also indicate to the auditor that risks of misstatement of related financial statement information do exist. For example, performance measures may indicate that the entity has unusually rapid growth or profitability when compared to that of other entities in the same industry.

Such information, particularly if combined with other factors such as performance-based bonus or incentive remuneration, may indicate the potential risk of management bias in the preparation of the financial statements.

Considerations Specific to Smaller Entities

Smaller entities often do not have processes to measure and review financial performance. **A48** Inquiry of management may reveal that it relies on certain key indicators for evaluating financial performance and taking appropriate action. If such inquiry indicates an absence of performance measurement or review, there may be an increased risk of misstatements not being detected and corrected.

The Entity's Internal Control (Ref: Para. 12)

An understanding of internal control assists the auditor in identifying types of potential **A49** misstatements and factors that affect the risks of material misstatement, and in designing the nature, timing, and extent of further audit procedures.

The following application material on internal control is presented in four sections, as **A50** follows:

- General Nature and Characteristics of Internal Control.
- Controls Relevant to the Audit.
- Nature and Extent of the Understanding of Relevant Controls.
- Components of Internal Control.

General Nature and Characteristics of Internal Control

Purpose of Internal Control

Internal control is designed, implemented and maintained to address identified business **A51** risks that threaten the achievement of any of the entity's objectives that concern:

- The reliability of the entity's financial reporting;
- The effectiveness and efficiency of its operations; and
- Its compliance with applicable laws and regulations.

The way in which internal control is designed, implemented and maintained varies with an entity's size and complexity.

Considerations specific to smaller entities

Smaller entities may use less structured means and simpler processes and procedures to **A52** achieve their objectives.

Limitations of Internal Control

Internal control, no matter how effective, can provide an entity with only reasonable **A53** assurance about achieving the entity's financial reporting objectives. The likelihood of their achievement is affected by the inherent limitations of internal control. These include the realities that human judgment in decision-making can be faulty and that breakdowns in internal control can occur because of human error. For example, there may be an error in the design of, or in the change to, a control. Equally, the operation of a control may not be effective, such as where information produced for the purposes of internal control (for example, an exception report) is not effectively used because the individual responsible for reviewing the information does not understand its purpose or fails to take appropriate action.

A54   Additionally, controls can be circumvented by the collusion of two or more people or inappropriate management override of internal control. For example, management may enter into side agreements with customers that alter the terms and conditions of the entity's standard sales contracts, which may result in improper revenue recognition. Also, edit checks in a software program that are designed to identify and report transactions that exceed specified credit limits may be overridden or disabled.

A55   Further, in designing and implementing controls, management may make judgments on the nature and extent of the controls it chooses to implement, and the nature and extent of the risks it chooses to assume.

Considerations specific to smaller entities

A56   Smaller entities often have fewer employees which may limit the extent to which segregation of duties is practicable. However, in a small owner-managed entity, the owner-manager may be able to exercise more effective oversight than in a larger entity. This oversight may compensate for the generally more limited opportunities for segregation of duties.

A57   On the other hand, the owner-manager may be more able to override controls because the system of internal control is less structured. This is taken into account by the auditor when identifying the risks of material misstatement due to fraud.

Division of Internal Control into Components

A58   The division of internal control into the following five components, for purposes of the ISAs (UK), provides a useful framework for auditors to consider how different aspects of an entity's internal control may affect the audit:

   (a)   The control environment;
   (b)   The entity's risk assessment process;
   (c)   The information system, including the related business processes, relevant to financial reporting, and communication;
   (d)   Control activities; and
   (e)   Monitoring of controls.

The division does not necessarily reflect how an entity designs, implements and maintains internal control, or how it may classify any particular component. Auditors may use different terminology or frameworks to describe the various aspects of internal control, and their effect on the audit than those used in this ISA (UK), provided all the components described in this ISA (UK) are addressed.

A59   Application material relating to the five components of internal control as they relate to a financial statement audit is set out in paragraphs A76–A117 below. Appendix 1 provides further explanation of these components of internal control.

Characteristics of Manual and Automated Elements of Internal Control Relevant to the Auditor's Risk Assessment

A60   An entity's system of internal control contains manual elements and often contains automated elements. The characteristics of manual or automated elements are relevant to the auditor's risk assessment and further audit procedures based thereon.

The use of manual or automated elements in internal control also affects the manner in **A61**
which transactions are initiated, recorded, processed, and reported:

- Controls in a manual system may include such procedures as approvals and reviews of transactions, and reconciliations and follow-up of reconciling items. Alternatively, an entity may use automated procedures to initiate, record, process, and report transactions, in which case records in electronic format replace paper documents.
- Controls in IT systems consist of a combination of automated controls (for example, controls embedded in computer programs) and manual controls. Further, manual controls may be independent of IT, may use information produced by IT, or may be limited to monitoring the effective functioning of IT and of automated controls, and to handling exceptions. When IT is used to initiate, record, process or report transactions, or other financial data for inclusion in financial statements, the systems and programs may include controls related to the corresponding assertions for material accounts or may be critical to the effective functioning of manual controls that depend on IT.

An entity's mix of manual and automated elements in internal control varies with the nature and complexity of the entity's use of IT.

Generally, IT benefits an entity's internal control by enabling an entity to: **A62**

- Consistently apply predefined business rules and perform complex calculations in processing large volumes of transactions or data;
- Enhance the timeliness, availability, and accuracy of information;
- Facilitate the additional analysis of information;
- Enhance the ability to monitor the performance of the entity's activities and its policies and procedures;
- Reduce the risk that controls will be circumvented; and
- Enhance the ability to achieve effective segregation of duties by implementing security controls in applications, databases, and operating systems.

IT also poses specific risks to an entity's internal control, including, for example: **A63**

- Reliance on systems or programs that are inaccurately processing data, processing inaccurate data, or both.
- Unauthorized access to data that may result in destruction of data or improper changes to data, including the recording of unauthorized or non-existent transactions, or inaccurate recording of transactions. Particular risks may arise where multiple users access a common database.
- The possibility of IT personnel gaining access privileges beyond those necessary to perform their assigned duties thereby breaking down segregation of duties.
- Unauthorized changes to data in master files.
- Unauthorized changes to systems or programs.
- Failure to make necessary changes to systems or programs.
- Inappropriate manual intervention.
- Potential loss of data or inability to access data as required.

Manual elements in internal control may be more suitable where judgment and discretion **A64**
are required such as for the following circumstances:

- Large, unusual or non-recurring transactions.
- Circumstances where errors are difficult to define, anticipate or predict.
- In changing circumstances that require a control response outside the scope of an existing automated control.
- In monitoring the effectiveness of automated controls.

A65　Manual elements in internal control may be less reliable than automated elements because they can be more easily bypassed, ignored, or overridden and they are also more prone to simple errors and mistakes. Consistency of application of a manual control element cannot therefore be assumed. Manual control elements may be less suitable for the following circumstances:

- High volume or recurring transactions, or in situations where errors that can be anticipated or predicted can be prevented, or detected and corrected, by control parameters that are automated.
- Control activities where the specific ways to perform the control can be adequately designed and automated.

A66　The extent and nature of the risks to internal control vary depending on the nature and characteristics of the entity's information system. The entity responds to the risks arising from the use of IT or from use of manual elements in internal control by establishing effective controls in light of the characteristics of the entity's information system.

Controls Relevant to the Audit

A67　There is a direct relationship between an entity's objectives and the controls it implements to provide reasonable assurance about their achievement. The entity's objectives, and therefore controls, relate to financial reporting, operations and compliance; however, not all of these objectives and controls are relevant to the auditor's risk assessment.

A68　Factors relevant to the auditor's judgment about whether a control, individually or in combination with others, is relevant to the audit may include such matters as the following:

- Materiality.
- The significance of the related risk.
- The size of the entity.
- The nature of the entity's business, including its organization and ownership characteristics.
- The diversity and complexity of the entity's operations.
- Applicable legal and regulatory requirements.
- The circumstances and the applicable component of internal control.
- The nature and complexity of the systems that are part of the entity's internal control, including the use of service organizations.
- Whether, and how, a specific control, individually or in combination with others, prevents, or detects and corrects, material misstatement.

A69　Controls over the completeness and accuracy of information produced by the entity may be relevant to the audit if the auditor intends to make use of the information in designing and performing further procedures. Controls relating to operations and compliance objectives may also be relevant to an audit if they relate to data the auditor evaluates or uses in applying audit procedures.

A70　Internal control over safeguarding of assets against unauthorized acquisition, use, or disposition may include controls relating to both financial reporting and operations objectives. The auditor's consideration of such controls is generally limited to those relevant to the reliability of financial reporting.

A71　An entity generally has controls relating to objectives that are not relevant to an audit and therefore need not be considered. For example, an entity may rely on a sophisticated system of automated controls to provide efficient and effective operations (such as an airline's system of automated controls to maintain flight schedules), but these controls ordinarily would not be relevant to the audit. Further, although internal control applies to the entire entity or to any of its operating units or business processes, an understanding of internal control relating to each of the entity's operating units and business processes may not be relevant to the audit.

Considerations Specific to Public Sector Entities

Public sector auditors often have additional responsibilities with respect to internal control, for example to report on compliance with an established code of practice. Public sector auditors can also have responsibilities to report on compliance with law, regulation or other authority. As a result, their review of internal control may be broader and more detailed.   **A72**

Nature and Extent of the Understanding of Relevant Controls (Ref: Para. 13)

Evaluating the design of a control involves considering whether the control, individually or in combination with other controls, is capable of effectively preventing, or detecting and correcting, material misstatements. Implementation of a control means that the control exists and that the entity is using it. There is little point in assessing the implementation of a control that is not effective, and so the design of a control is considered first. An improperly designed control may represent a significant deficiency in internal control.   **A73**

Risk assessment procedures to obtain audit evidence about the design and implementation of relevant controls may include: **A74**

- Inquiring of entity personnel.
- Observing the application of specific controls.
- Inspecting documents and reports.
- Tracing transactions through the information system relevant to financial reporting.

Inquiry alone, however, is not sufficient for such purposes.

Obtaining an understanding of an entity's controls is not sufficient to test their operating effectiveness, unless there is some automation that provides for the consistent operation of the controls. For example, obtaining audit evidence about the implementation of a manual control at a point in time does not provide audit evidence about the operating effectiveness of the control at other times during the period under audit. However, because of the inherent consistency of IT processing (see paragraph A62), performing audit procedures to determine whether an automated control has been implemented may serve as a test of that control's operating effectiveness, depending on the auditor's assessment and testing of controls such as those over program changes. Tests of the operating effectiveness of controls are further described in ISA (UK) 330 (Revised June 2016).[13]   **A75**

Components of Internal Control—Control Environment (Ref: Para. 14)

The control environment includes the governance and management functions and the attitudes, awareness, and actions of those charged with governance and management concerning the entity's internal control and its importance in the entity. The control environment sets the tone of an organization, influencing the control consciousness of its people.   **A76**

---

[13] *ISA (UK) 330 (Revised June 2016),* The Auditor's Responses to Assessed Risks.

A77 Elements of the control environment that may be relevant when obtaining an understanding of the control environment include the following:

(a) *Communication and enforcement of integrity and ethical values* – These are essential elements that influence the effectiveness of the design, administration and monitoring of controls.

(b) *Commitment to competence* – Matters such as management's consideration of the competence levels for particular jobs and how those levels translate into requisite skills and knowledge.

(c) *Participation by those charged with governance* – Attributes of those charged with governance such as:

- Their independence from management.
- Their experience and stature.
- The extent of their involvement and the information they receive, and the scrutiny of activities.
- The appropriateness of their actions, including the degree to which difficult questions are raised and pursued with management, and their interaction with internal and external auditors.

(d) *Management's philosophy and operating style* – Characteristics such as management's:

- Approach to taking and managing business risks.
- Attitudes and actions toward financial reporting.
- Attitudes toward information processing and accounting functions and personnel.

(e) *Organizational structure* – The framework within which an entity's activities for achieving its objectives are planned, executed, controlled, and reviewed.

(f) *Assignment of authority and responsibility* – Matters such as how authority and responsibility for operating activities are assigned and how reporting relationships and authorization hierarchies are established.

(g) *Human resource policies and practices* – Policies and practices that relate to, for example, recruitment, orientation, training, evaluation, counselling, promotion, compensation, and remedial actions.

Audit Evidence for Elements of the Control Environment

A78 Relevant audit evidence may be obtained through a combination of inquiries and other risk assessment procedures such as corroborating inquiries through observation or inspection of documents. For example, through inquiries of management and employees, the auditor may obtain an understanding of how management communicates to employees its views on business practices and ethical behavior. The auditor may then determine whether relevant controls have been implemented by considering, for example, whether management has a written code of conduct and whether it acts in a manner that supports the code.

A79 The auditor may also consider how management has responded to the findings and recommendations of the internal audit function regarding identified deficiencies in internal control relevant to the audit, including whether and how such responses have been implemented, and whether they have been subsequently evaluated by the internal audit function.

Effect of the Control Environment on the Assessment of the Risks of Material Misstatement

A80 Some elements of an entity's control environment have a pervasive effect on assessing the risks of material misstatement. For example, an entity's control consciousness is influenced significantly by those charged with governance, because one of their roles is to counterbalance pressures on management in relation to financial reporting that may arise from market demands or remuneration schemes. The effectiveness of the design of the control environment in relation to participation by those charged with governance is therefore influenced by such matters as:

- Their independence from management and their ability to evaluate the actions of management.
- Whether they understand the entity's business transactions.
- The extent to which they evaluate whether the financial statements are prepared in accordance with the applicable financial reporting framework, including whether the financial statements include adequate disclosures.

An active and independent board of directors may influence the philosophy and operating style of senior management. However, other elements may be more limited in their effect. For example, although human resource policies and practices directed toward hiring competent financial, accounting, and IT personnel may reduce the risk of errors in processing financial information, they may not mitigate a strong bias by top management to overstate earnings.   **A81**

The existence of a satisfactory control environment can be a positive factor when the auditor assesses the risks of material misstatement. However, although it may help reduce the risk of fraud, a satisfactory control environment is not an absolute deterrent to fraud. Conversely, deficiencies in the control environment may undermine the effectiveness of controls, in particular in relation to fraud. For example, management's failure to commit sufficient resources to address IT security risks may adversely affect internal control by allowing improper changes to be made to computer programs or to data, or unauthorized transactions to be processed. As explained in ISA (UK) 330 (Revised June 2016), the control environment also influences the nature, timing, and extent of the auditor's further procedures.[14]   **A82**

The control environment in itself does not prevent, or detect and correct, a material misstatement. It may, however, influence the auditor's evaluation of the effectiveness of other controls (for example, the monitoring of controls and the operation of specific control activities) and thereby, the auditor's assessment of the risks of material misstatement.   **A83**

Considerations Specific to Smaller Entities

The control environment within small entities is likely to differ from larger entities. For example, those charged with governance in small entities may not include an independent or outside member, and the role of governance may be undertaken directly by the owner-manager where there are no other owners. The nature of the control environment may also influence the significance of other controls, or their absence. For example, the active involvement of an owner-manager may mitigate certain of the risks arising from a lack of segregation of duties in a small entity; it may, however, increase other risks, for example, the risk of override of controls.   **A84**

In addition, audit evidence for elements of the control environment in smaller entities may not be available in documentary form, in particular where communication between management and other personnel may be informal, yet effective. For example, small entities might not have a written code of conduct but, instead, develop a culture that emphasizes the importance of integrity and ethical behavior through oral communication and by management example.   **A85**

---

[14] *ISA (UK) 330 (Revised June 2016), paragraphs A2–A3.*

A86   Consequently, the attitudes, awareness and actions of management or the owner-manager are of particular importance to the auditor's understanding of a smaller entity's control environment.

Components of Internal Control—The Entity's Risk Assessment Process
(Ref: Para. 15)

A87   The entity's risk assessment process forms the basis for how management determines the risks to be managed. If that process is appropriate to the circumstances, including the nature, size and complexity of the entity, it assists the auditor in identifying risks of material misstatement. Whether the entity's risk assessment process is appropriate to the circumstances is a matter of judgment.

Considerations Specific to Smaller Entities (Ref: Para. 17)

A88   There is unlikely to be an established risk assessment process in a small entity. In such cases, it is likely that management will identify risks through direct personal involvement in the business. Irrespective of the circumstances, however, inquiry about identified risks and how they are addressed by management is still necessary.

Components of Internal Control—The Information System, Including Related Business Processes, Relevant to Financial Reporting, and Communication

The Information System, Including Related Business Processes, Relevant to Financial Reporting (Ref: Para. 18)

A89   The information system relevant to financial reporting objectives, which includes the accounting system, consists of the procedures and records designed and established to:

- Initiate, record, process, and report entity transactions (as well as events and conditions) and to maintain accountability for the related assets, liabilities, and equity;
- Resolve incorrect processing of transactions, for example, automated suspense files and procedures followed to clear suspense items out on a timely basis;
- Process and account for system overrides or bypasses to controls;
- Transfer information from transaction processing systems to the general ledger;
- Capture information relevant to financial reporting for events and conditions other than transactions, such as the depreciation and amortization of assets and changes in the recoverability of accounts receivables; and
- Ensure information required to be disclosed by the applicable financial reporting framework is accumulated, recorded, processed, summarized and appropriately reported in the financial statements.

A89a   Financial statements may contain information that is obtained from outside of the general and subsidiary ledgers. Examples of such information may include:

- Information obtained from lease agreements disclosed in the financial statements, such as renewal options or future lease payments.
- Information disclosed in the financial statements that is produced by an entity's risk management system.
- Fair value information produced by management's experts and disclosed in the financial statements.
- Information disclosed in the financial statements that has been obtained from models, or from other calculations used to develop estimates recognized or disclosed in the financial statements, including information relating to the underlying data and assumptions used in those models, such as:

   ○ Assumptions developed internally that may affect an asset's useful life; or
   ○ Data such as interest rates that are affected by factors outside the control of the entity.

● Information disclosed in the financial statements about sensitivity analyses derived from financial models that demonstrates that management has considered alternative assumptions.
● Information recognized or disclosed in the financial statements that has been obtained from an entity's tax returns and records.
● Information disclosed in the financial statements that has been obtained from analyses prepared to support management's assessment of the entity's ability to continue as a going concern, such as disclosures, if any, related to events or conditions that have been identified that may cast significant doubt on the entity's ability to continue as a going concern.[15]

The understanding of the information system relevant to financial reporting required by paragraph 18 of this ISA (UK) (including the understanding of relevant aspects of that system relating to information disclosed in the financial statements that is obtained from within or outside of the general and subsidiary ledgers) is a matter of the auditor's professional judgment. For example, certain amounts or disclosures in the entity's financial statements (such as disclosures about credit risk, liquidity risk, and market risk) may be based on information obtained from the entity's risk management system. However, the auditor is not required to understand all aspects of the risk management system, and uses professional judgment in determining the necessary understanding. **A89b**

Journal entries

An entity's information system typically includes the use of standard journal entries that are required on a recurring basis to record transactions. Examples might be journal entries to record sales, purchases, and cash disbursements in the general ledger, or to record accounting estimates that are periodically made by management, such as changes in the estimate of uncollectible accounts receivable. **A90**

An entity's financial reporting process also includes the use of non-standard journal entries to record non-recurring, unusual transactions or adjustments. Examples of such entries include consolidating adjustments and entries for a business combination or disposal or non-recurring estimates such as the impairment of an asset. In manual general ledger systems, non-standard journal entries may be identified through inspection of ledgers, journals, and supporting documentation. When automated procedures are used to maintain the general ledger and prepare financial statements, such entries may exist only in electronic form and may therefore be more easily identified through the use of computer-assisted audit techniques. **A91**

Related business processes

An entity's business processes are the activities designed to: **A92**

● Develop, purchase, produce, sell and distribute an entity's products and services;
● Ensure compliance with laws and regulations; and
● Record information, including accounting and financial reporting information.

Business processes result in the transactions that are recorded, processed and reported by the information system. Obtaining an understanding of the entity's business processes,

---

[15] *See paragraphs 19–20 of ISA (UK) 570 (Revised June 2016),* Going Concern.

which include how transactions are originated, assists the auditor obtain an understanding of the entity's information system relevant to financial reporting in a manner that is appropriate to the entity's circumstances.

Considerations specific to smaller entities

A93   The information system, and related business processes, relevant to financial reporting in small entities, including relevant aspects of that system relating to information disclosed in the financial statements that is obtained from within or outside of the general and subsidiary ledgers, is likely to be less sophisticated than in larger entities, but its role is just as significant. Small entities with active management involvement may not need extensive descriptions of accounting procedures, sophisticated accounting records, or written policies. Understanding the entity's information system relevant to financial reporting may therefore be easier in an audit of smaller entities, and may be more dependent on inquiry than on review of documentation. The need to obtain an understanding, however, remains important.

Communication (Ref: Para. 19)

A94   Communication by the entity of the financial reporting roles and responsibilities and of significant matters relating to financial reporting involves providing an understanding of individual roles and responsibilities pertaining to internal control over financial reporting. It includes such matters as the extent to which personnel understand how their activities in the financial reporting information system relate to the work of others and the means of reporting exceptions to an appropriate higher level within the entity. Communication may take such forms as policy manuals and financial reporting manuals. Open communication channels help ensure that exceptions are reported and acted on.

Considerations specific to smaller entities

A95   Communication may be less structured and easier to achieve in a small entity than in a larger entity due to fewer levels of responsibility and management's greater visibility and availability.

Components of Internal Control—Control Activities Relevant to the Audit
(Ref: Para. 20)

A96   Control activities are the policies and procedures that help ensure that management directives are carried out. Control activities, whether within IT or manual systems, have various objectives and are applied at various organizational and functional levels. Examples of specific control activities include those relating to the following:

- Authorization.
- Performance reviews.
- Information processing.
- Physical controls.
- Segregation of duties.

A97   Control activities that are relevant to the audit are:

- Those that are required to be treated as such, being control activities that relate to significant risks and those that relate to risks for which substantive procedures alone do not provide sufficient appropriate audit evidence, as required by paragraphs 29 and 30, respectively; or
- Those that are considered to be relevant in the judgment of the auditor.

The auditor's judgment about whether a control activity is relevant to the audit is influenced by the risk that the auditor has identified that may give rise to a material misstatement and whether the auditor thinks it is likely to be appropriate to test the operating effectiveness of the control in determining the extent of substantive testing.   **A98**

The auditor's emphasis may be on identifying and obtaining an understanding of control activities that address the areas where the auditor considers that risks of material misstatement are likely to be higher. When multiple control activities each achieve the same objective, it is unnecessary to obtain an understanding of each of the control activities related to such objective.   **A99**

Control activities relevant to the audit may include controls established by management that address risks of material misstatement related to disclosures not being prepared in accordance with the applicable financial reporting framework, in addition to controls that address risks related to account balances and transactions. Such control activities may relate to information included in the financial statements that is obtained from outside of the general and subsidiary ledgers.   **A99a**

The auditor's knowledge about the presence or absence of control activities obtained from the understanding of the other components of internal control assists the auditor in determining whether it is necessary to devote additional attention to obtaining an understanding of control activities.   **A100**

Considerations Specific to Smaller Entities

The concepts underlying control activities in small entities are likely to be similar to those in larger entities, but the formality with which they operate may vary. Further, small entities may find that certain types of control activities are not relevant because of controls applied by management. For example, management's sole authority for granting credit to customers and approving significant purchases can provide strong control over important account balances and transactions, lessening or removing the need for more detailed control activities.   **A101**

Control activities relevant to the audit of a smaller entity are likely to relate to the main transaction cycles such as revenues, purchases and employment expenses.   **A102**

Risks Arising from IT (Ref: Para. 21)

The use of IT affects the way that control activities are implemented. From the auditor's perspective, controls over IT systems are effective when they maintain the integrity of information and the security of the data such systems process, and include effective general IT controls and application controls.   **A103**

General IT controls are policies and procedures that relate to many applications and support the effective functioning of application controls. They apply to mainframe, miniframe, and end-user environments. General IT controls that maintain the integrity of information and security of data commonly include controls over the following: **A104**

- Data center and network operations.
- System software acquisition, change and maintenance.
- Program change.
- Access security.
- Application system acquisition, development, and maintenance.

They are generally implemented to deal with the risks referred to in paragraph A63 above.

A105   Application controls are manual or automated procedures that typically operate at a business process level and apply to the processing of transactions by individual applications. Application controls can be preventive or detective in nature and are designed to ensure the integrity of the accounting records. Accordingly, application controls relate to procedures used to initiate, record, process and report transactions or other financial data. These controls help ensure that transactions occurred, are authorized, and are completely and accurately recorded and processed. Examples include edit checks of input data, and numerical sequence checks with manual follow-up of exception reports or correction at the point of data entry.

Components of Internal Control—Monitoring of Controls (Ref: Para. 22)

A106   Monitoring of controls is a process to assess the effectiveness of internal control performance over time. It involves assessing the effectiveness of controls on a timely basis and taking necessary remedial actions. Management accomplishes monitoring of controls through ongoing activities, separate evaluations, or a combination of the two. Ongoing monitoring activities are often built into the normal recurring activities of an entity and include regular management and supervisory activities.

A107   Management's monitoring activities may include using information from communications from external parties such as customer complaints and regulator comments that may indicate problems or highlight areas in need of improvement.

Considerations Specific to Smaller Entities

A108   Management's monitoring of control is often accomplished by management's or the owner-manager's close involvement in operations. This involvement often will identify significant variances from expectations and inaccuracies in financial data leading to remedial action to the control.

The Entity's Internal Audit Function (Ref: Para. 23)

A109   If the entity has an internal audit function, obtaining an understanding of that function contributes to the auditor's understanding of the entity and its environment, including internal control, in particular the role that the function plays in the entity's monitoring of internal control over financial reporting. This understanding, together with the information obtained from the auditor's inquiries in paragraph 6(a) of this ISA (UK), may also provide information that is directly relevant to the auditor's identification and assessment of the risks of material misstatement.

A110   The objectives and scope of an internal audit function, the nature of its responsibilities and its status within the organization, including the function's authority and accountability, vary widely and depend on the size and structure of the entity and the requirements of management and, where applicable, those charged with governance. These matters may be set out in an internal audit charter or terms of reference.

A111   The responsibilities of an internal audit function may include performing procedures and evaluating the results to provide assurance to management and those charged with governance regarding the design and effectiveness of risk management, internal control and governance processes. If so, the internal audit function may play an important role in the entity's monitoring of internal control over financial reporting. However, the responsibilities of the internal audit function may be focused on evaluating the economy, efficiency and effectiveness of operations and, if so, the work of the function may not directly relate to the entity's financial reporting.

The auditor's inquiries of appropriate individuals within the internal audit function in accordance with paragraph 6(a) of this ISA (UK) help the auditor obtain an understanding of the nature of the internal audit function's responsibilities. If the auditor determines that the function's responsibilities are related to the entity's financial reporting, the auditor may obtain further understanding of the activities performed, or to be performed, by the internal audit function by reviewing the internal audit function's audit plan for the period, if any, and discussing that plan with the appropriate individuals within the function. **A112**

If the nature of the internal audit function's responsibilities and assurance activities are related to the entity's financial reporting, the auditor may also be able to use the work of the internal audit function to modify the nature or timing, or reduce the extent, of audit procedures to be performed directly by the auditor in obtaining audit evidence. Auditors may be more likely to be able to use the work of an entity's internal audit function when it appears, for example, based on experience in previous audits or the auditor's risk assessment procedures, that the entity has an internal audit function that is adequately and appropriately resourced relative to the size of the entity and the nature of its operations, and has a direct reporting relationship to those charged with governance. **A113**

If, based on the auditor's preliminary understanding of the internal audit function, the auditor expects to use the work of the internal audit function to modify the nature or timing, or reduce the extent, of audit procedures to be performed, ISA (UK) 610 (Revised June 2013) applies. **A114**

As is further discussed in ISA (UK) 610 (Revised June 2013), the activities of an internal audit function are distinct from other monitoring controls that may be relevant to financial reporting, such as reviews of management accounting information that are designed to contribute to how the entity prevents or detects misstatements. **A115**

Establishing communications with the appropriate individuals within an entity's internal audit function early in the engagement, and maintaining such communications throughout the engagement, can facilitate effective sharing of information. It creates an environment in which the auditor can be informed of significant matters that may come to the attention of the internal audit function when such matters may affect the work of the auditor. ISA (UK) 200 (Revised June 2016) discusses the importance of the auditor planning and performing the audit with professional skepticism, including being alert to information that brings into question the reliability of documents and responses to inquiries to be used as audit evidence. Accordingly, communication with the internal audit function throughout the engagement may provide opportunities for internal auditors to bring such information to the auditor's attention. The auditor is then able to take such information into account in the auditor's identification and assessment of risks of material misstatement. **A116**

Sources of Information (Ref: Para. 24)

Much of the information used in monitoring may be produced by the entity's information system. If management assumes that data used for monitoring are accurate without having a basis for that assumption, errors that may exist in the information could potentially lead management to incorrect conclusions from its monitoring activities. Accordingly, an understanding of: **A117**

- the sources of the information related to the entity's monitoring activities; and
- the basis upon which management considers the information to be sufficiently reliable for the purpose,

is required as part of the auditor's understanding of the entity's monitoring activities as a component of internal control.

Identifying and Assessing the Risks of Material Misstatement

Assessment of Risks of Material Misstatement at the Financial Statement Level (Ref: Para. 25 (a))

A118   Risks of material misstatement at the financial statement level refer to risks that relate pervasively to the financial statements as a whole and potentially affect many assertions. Risks of this nature are not necessarily risks identifiable with specific assertions at the class of transactions, account balance, or disclosure level. Rather, they represent circumstances that may increase the risks of material misstatement at the assertion level, for example, through management override of internal control. Financial statement level risks may be especially relevant to the auditor's consideration of the risks of material misstatement arising from fraud.

A119   Risks at the financial statement level may derive in particular from a deficient control environment (although these risks may also relate to other factors, such as declining economic conditions). For example, deficiencies such as a lack of management competence or lack of oversight over the preparation of the financial statements may have a more pervasive effect on the financial statements and may require an overall response by the auditor.

A120   The auditor's understanding of internal control may raise doubts about the auditability of an entity's financial statements. For example:

- Concerns about the integrity of the entity's management may be so serious as to cause the auditor to conclude that the risk of management misrepresentation in the financial statements is such that an audit cannot be conducted.
- Concerns about the condition and reliability of an entity's records may cause the auditor to conclude that it is unlikely that sufficient appropriate audit evidence will be available to support an unmodified opinion on the financial statements.

A121   ISA (UK) 705 (Revised June 2016)[16] establishes requirements and provides guidance in determining whether there is a need for the auditor to express a qualified opinion or disclaim an opinion or, as may be required in some cases, to withdraw from the engagement where withdrawal is possible under applicable law or regulation.

Assessment of Risks of Material Misstatement at the Assertion Level (Ref: Para. 25(b))

A122   Risks of material misstatement at the assertion level for classes of transactions, account balances, and disclosures need to be considered because such consideration directly assists in determining the nature, timing, and extent of further audit procedures at the assertion level necessary to obtain sufficient appropriate audit evidence. In identifying and assessing risks of material misstatement at the assertion level, the auditor may conclude that the identified risks relate more pervasively to the financial statements as a whole and potentially affect many assertions.

The Use of Assertions

A123   In representing that the financial statements are in accordance with the applicable financial reporting framework, management[1a] implicitly or explicitly makes assertions regarding recognition, measurement and presentation of classes of transactions and events, account balances and disclosures.

---

[16]   *ISA (UK) 705 (Revised June 2016)*, Modifications to the Opinion in the Independent Auditor's Report.

The auditor may use the assertions as described in paragraph A124 (a)–(b) below or may express them differently provided all aspects described below have been covered. For example, the auditor may choose to combine the assertions about classes of transactions and events, and related disclosures, with the assertions about account balances, and related disclosures.   **A123a**

Assertions about classes of transaction, account balances, and related disclosures

Assertions used by the auditor in considering the different types of potential misstatements that may occur may fall into the following categories: **A124**

(a) Assertions about classes of transactions and events, and related disclosures, for the period under audit:
    (i) Occurrence—transactions and events that have been recorded or disclosed, have occurred, and such transactions and events pertain to the entity.
    (ii) Completeness—all transactions and events that should have been recorded have been recorded, and all related disclosures that should have been included in the financial statements have been included.
    (iii) Accuracy—amounts and other data relating to recorded transactions and events have been recorded appropriately, and related disclosures have been appropriately measured and described.
    (iv) Cutoff—transactions and events have been recorded in the correct accounting period.
    (v) Classification—transactions and events have been recorded in the proper accounts.
    (vi) Presentation—transactions and events are appropriately aggregated or disaggregated and clearly described, and related disclosures are relevant and understandable in the context of the requirements of the applicable financial reporting framework.
(b) Assertions about account balances, and related disclosures, at the period end:
    (i) Existence—assets, liabilities, and equity interests exist.
    (ii) Rights and obligations—the entity holds or controls the rights to assets, and liabilities are the obligations of the entity.
    (iii) Completeness—all assets, liabilities and equity interests that should have been recorded have been recorded, and all related disclosures that should have been included in the financial statements have been included.
    (iv) Accuracy, valuation and allocation—assets, liabilities, and equity interests have been included in the financial statements at appropriate amounts and any resulting valuation or allocation adjustments have been appropriately recorded, and related disclosures have been appropriately measured and described.
    (v) Classification—assets, liabilities, and equity interests have been recorded in the proper accounts.
    (vi) Presentation—assets, liabilities, and equity interests are appropriately aggregated or disaggregated and clearly described, and related disclosures are relevant and understandable in the context of the requirements of the applicable financial reporting framework.

Assertions about other disclosures

The assertions described in paragraph A124(a)–(b) above, adapted as appropriate, may also be used by the auditor in considering the different types of potential misstatements that may occur in disclosures not directly related to recorded classes of transactions, events, or account balances. As an example of such a disclosure, the entity may be required to describe its exposure to risks arising from financial instruments, including how the risks   **A124a** arise; the objectives, policies and processes for managing the risks; and the methods used to measure the risks.

Considerations specific to public sector entities

A126   When making assertions about the financial statements of public sector entities, in addition to those assertions set out in paragraph A124, management[1a] may often assert that transactions and events have been carried out in accordance with law, regulation or other authority. Such assertions may fall within the scope of the financial statement audit.

Process of Identifying Risks of Material Misstatement (Ref: Para. 26(a))

A127   Information gathered by performing risk assessment procedures, including the audit evidence obtained in evaluating the design of controls and determining whether they have been implemented, is used as audit evidence to support the risk assessment. The risk assessment determines the nature, timing, and extent of further audit procedures to be performed. In identifying the risks of material misstatement in the financial statements, the auditor exercise professional skepticism in accordance with ISA (UK) 200 (Revised June 2016).[17]

A128   Appendix 2 provides examples of conditions and events that may indicate the existence of risks of material misstatement, including risks of material misstatement relating to disclosures.

A128a   As explained in ISA (UK) 320 (Revised June 2016),[18] materiality and audit risk are considered when identifying and assessing the risks of material misstatement in classes of transactions, account balances and disclosures. The auditor's determination of materiality is a matter of professional judgment, and is affected by the auditor's perception of the financial reporting needs of users of the financial statements.[19]

A128b   The auditor's consideration of disclosures in the financial statements when identifying risks includes quantitative and qualitative disclosures, the misstatement of which could be material (i.e., in general, misstatements are considered to be material if they could reasonably be expected to influence the economic decisions of users taken on the basis of the financial statements as a whole). Depending on the circumstances of the entity and the engagement, examples of disclosures that will have qualitative aspects and that may be relevant when assessing the risks of material misstatement include disclosures about:

- Liquidity and debt covenants of an entity in financial distress.
- Events or circumstances that have led to the recognition of an impairment loss.
- Key sources of estimation uncertainty, including assumptions about the future.
- The nature of a change in accounting policy, and other relevant disclosures required by the applicable financial reporting framework, where, for example, new financial reporting requirements are expected to have a significant impact on the financial position and financial performance of the entity.
- Share-based payment arrangements, including information about how any amounts recognized were determined, and other relevant disclosures.
- Related parties, and related party transactions.

---

[17] *ISA (UK) 200 (Revised June 2016)*, Overall Objectives of the Independent Auditor and the Conduct of an Audit in Accordance with International Standards on Auditing (UK), *paragraph 15.*

[18] *ISA (UK) 320 (Revised June 2016)*, Materiality in Planning and Performing an Audit, *paragraph A1.*

[19] *ISA (UK) 320 (Revised June 2016), paragraph 4.*

- Sensitivity analysis, including the effects of changes in assumptions used in the entity's valuation techniques intended to enable users to understand the underlying measurement uncertainty of a recorded or disclosed amount.

Considerations specific to smaller entities

Disclosures in the financial statements of smaller entities may be less detailed or less complex (e.g., some financial reporting frameworks allow smaller entities to provide fewer disclosures in the financial statements). However, this does not relieve the auditor of the responsibility to obtain an understanding of the entity and its environment, including internal control, as it relates to disclosures. **A128c**

Relating Controls to Assertions (Ref: Para. 26(c))

In making risk assessments, the auditor may identify the controls that are likely to prevent, or detect and correct, material misstatement in specific assertions. Generally, it is useful to obtain an understanding of controls and relate them to assertions in the context of processes and systems in which they exist because individual control activities often do not in themselves address a risk. Often, only multiple control activities, together with other components of internal control, will be sufficient to address a risk. **A129**

Conversely, some control activities may have a specific effect on an individual assertion embodied in a particular class of transactions or account balance. For example, the control activities that an entity established to ensure that its personnel are properly counting and recording the annual physical inventory relate directly to the existence and completeness assertions for the inventory account balance. **A130**

Controls can be either directly or indirectly related to an assertion. The more indirect the relationship, the less effective that control may be in preventing, or detecting and correcting, misstatements in that assertion. For example, a sales manager's review of a summary of sales activity for specific stores by region ordinarily is only indirectly related to the completeness assertion for sales revenue. Accordingly, it may be less effective in reducing risk for that assertion than controls more directly related to that assertion, such as matching shipping documents with billing documents. **A131**

Material Misstatements

Potential misstatements in individual statements and disclosures may be judged to be material due to size, nature or circumstances. (Ref: Para. 26(d)) **A131a**

Significant Risks

Identifying Significant Risks (Ref: Para. 28)

Significant risks often relate to significant non-routine transactions or judgmental matters. Non-routine transactions are transactions that are unusual, due to either size or nature, and that therefore occur infrequently. Judgmental matters may include the development of accounting estimates for which there is significant measurement uncertainty. Routine, **A132** non-complex transactions that are subject to systematic processing are less likely to give rise to significant risks.

A133   Risks of material misstatement may be greater for significant non-routine transactions arising from matters such as the following:

- Greater management intervention to specify the accounting treatment.
- Greater manual intervention for data collection and processing.
- Complex calculations or accounting principles.
- The nature of non-routine transactions, which may make it difficult for the entity to implement effective controls over the risks.

A134   Risks of material misstatement may be greater for significant judgmental matters that require the development of accounting estimates, arising from matters such as the following:

- Accounting principles for accounting estimates or revenue recognition may be subject to differing interpretation.
- Required judgment may be subjective or complex, or require assumptions about the effects of future events, for example, judgment about fair value.

A135   ISA (UK) 330 (Revised June 2016) describes the consequences for further audit procedures of identifying a risk as significant.[20]

Significant risks relating to the risks of material misstatement due to fraud

A136   ISA (UK) 240 (Revised June 2016) provides further requirements and guidance in relation to the identification and assessment of the risks of material misstatement due to fraud.[21]

Understanding Controls Related to Significant Risks (Ref: Para. 29)

A137   Although risks relating to significant non-routine or judgmental matters are often less likely to be subject to routine controls, management may have other responses intended to deal with such risks. Accordingly, the auditor's understanding of whether the entity has designed and implemented controls for significant risks arising from non-routine or judgmental matters includes whether and how management responds to the risks. Such responses might include:

- Control activities such as a review of assumptions by senior management or experts.
- Documented processes for estimations.
- Approval by those charged with governance.

A138   For example, where there are one-off events such as the receipt of notice of a significant lawsuit, consideration of the entity's response may include such matters as whether it has been referred to appropriate experts (such as internal or external legal counsel), whether an assessment has been made of the potential effect, and how it is proposed that the circumstances are to be disclosed in the financial statements.

A139   In some cases, management may not have appropriately responded to significant risks of material misstatement by implementing controls over these significant risks. Failure

---

[20]   *ISA (UK) 330 (Revised June 2016), paragraphs 15 and 21.*

[21]   *ISA (UK) 240 (Revised June 2016), paragraphs 25–27.*

by management to implement such controls is an indicator of a significant deficiency in internal control.[22]

Risks for Which Substantive Procedures Alone Do Not Provide Sufficient Appropriate Audit Evidence (Ref: Para. 30)

Risks of material misstatement may relate directly to the recording of routine classes of **A140** transactions or account balances, and the preparation of reliable financial statements. Such risks may include risks of inaccurate or incomplete processing for routine and significant classes of transactions such as an entity's revenue, purchases, and cash receipts or cash payments.

Where such routine business transactions are subject to highly automated processing **A141** with little or no manual intervention, it may not be possible to perform only substantive procedures in relation to the risk. For example, the auditor may consider this to be the case in circumstances where a significant amount of an entity's information is initiated, recorded, processed, or reported only in electronic form such as in an integrated system. In such cases:

- Audit evidence may be available only in electronic form, and its sufficiency and appropriateness usually depend on the effectiveness of controls over its accuracy and completeness.
- The potential for improper initiation or alteration of information to occur and not be detected may be greater if appropriate controls are not operating effectively.

The consequences for further audit procedures of identifying such risks are described in **A142** ISA (UK) 330 (Revised June 2016).[23]

Revision of Risk Assessment (Ref: Para. 31)

During the audit, information may come to the auditor's attention that differs significantly **A143** from the information on which the risk assessment was based. For example, the risk assessment may be based on an expectation that certain controls are operating effectively. In performing tests of those controls, the auditor may obtain audit evidence that they were not operating effectively at relevant times during the audit. Similarly, in performing substantive procedures the auditor may detect misstatements in amounts or frequency greater than is consistent with the auditor's risk assessments. In such circumstances, the risk assessment may not appropriately reflect the true circumstances of the entity and the further planned audit procedures may not be effective in detecting material misstatements. See ISA (UK) 330 (Revised June 2016) for further guidance.

Documentation (Ref: Para. 32)

The manner in which the requirements of paragraph 32 are documented is for the auditor **A144** to determine using professional judgment. For example, in audits of small entities the documentation may be incorporated in the auditor's documentation of the overall strategy and audit plan.[24] Similarly, for example, the results of the risk assessment may be documented separately, or may be documented as part of the auditor's documentation of

---

[22] *ISA (UK) 265,* Communicating Deficiencies in Internal Control to Those Charged with Governance and Management, *paragraph A7.*

[23] *ISA (UK) 330 (Revised June 2016), paragraph 8.*

[24] *ISA (UK) 300 (Revised June 2016),* Planning an Audit of Financial Statements, *paragraphs 7 and 9.*

further procedures.[25] The form and extent of the documentation is influenced by the nature, size and complexity of the entity and its internal control, availability of information from the entity and the audit methodology and technology used in the course of the audit.

A145   For entities that have uncomplicated businesses and processes relevant to financial reporting, the documentation may be simple in form and relatively brief. It is not necessary to document the entirety of the auditor's understanding of the entity and matters related to it. Key elements of understanding documented by the auditor include those on which the auditor based the assessment of the risks of material misstatement.

A146   The extent of documentation may also reflect the experience and capabilities of the members of the audit engagement team. Provided the requirements of ISA (UK) 230 (Revised June 2016) are always met, an audit undertaken by an engagement team comprising less experienced individuals may require more detailed documentation to assist them to obtain an appropriate understanding of the entity than one that includes experienced individuals.

A147   For recurring audits, certain documentation may be carried forward, updated as necessary to reflect changes in the entity's business or processes.

---

[25]   *ISA (UK) 330 (Revised June 2016), paragraph 28.*

Appendix 1   (Ref: Para. 4(c), 14–24, A76–A117)

Internal Control Components

This appendix further explains the components of internal control, as set out in   **1**
paragraphs 4(c), 14–24 and A76–A117, as they relate to a financial statement audit.

Control Environment

The control environment encompasses the following elements: **2**

(a) *Communication and enforcement of integrity and ethical values.* The effectiveness of controls cannot rise above the integrity and ethical values of the people who create, administer, and monitor them. Integrity and ethical behavior are the product of the entity's ethical and behavioral standards, how they are communicated, and how they are reinforced in practice. The enforcement of integrity and ethical values includes, for example, management actions to eliminate or mitigate incentives or temptations that might prompt personnel to engage in dishonest, illegal, or unethical acts. The communication of entity policies on integrity and ethical values may include the communication of behavioral standards to personnel through policy statements and codes of conduct and by example.

(b) *Commitment to competence.* Competence is the knowledge and skills necessary to accomplish tasks that define the individual's job.

(c) *Participation by those charged with governance.* An entity's control consciousness is influenced significantly by those charged with governance. The importance of the responsibilities of those charged with governance is recognized in codes of practice and other laws and regulations or guidance produced for the benefit of those charged with governance. Other responsibilities of those charged with governance include oversight of the design and effective operation of whistle blower procedures and the process for reviewing the effectiveness of the entity's internal control.

(d) *Management's philosophy and operating style.* Management's philosophy and operating style encompass a broad range of characteristics. For example, management's attitudes and actions toward financial reporting may manifest themselves through conservative or aggressive selection from available alternative accounting principles, or conscientiousness and conservatism with which accounting estimates are developed.

(e) *Organizational structure.* Establishing a relevant organizational structure includes considering key areas of authority and responsibility and appropriate lines of reporting. The appropriateness of an entity's organizational structure depends, in part, on its size and the nature of its activities.

(f) *Assignment of authority and responsibility.* The assignment of authority and responsibility may include policies relating to appropriate business practices, knowledge and experience of key personnel, and resources provided for carrying out duties. In addition, it may include policies and communications directed at ensuring that all personnel understand the entity's objectives, know how their individual actions interrelate and contribute to those objectives, and recognize how and for what they will be held accountable.

(g) *Human resource policies and practices.* Human resource policies and practices often demonstrate important matters in relation to the control consciousness of an entity. For example, standards for recruiting the most qualified individuals – with emphasis on educational background, prior work experience, past accomplishments, and evidence of integrity and ethical behavior – demonstrate an entity's commitment to competent and trustworthy people. Training policies that communicate prospective roles and responsibilities and include practices such as training schools and seminars illustrate expected levels of performance and behavior. Promotions driven by periodic performance appraisals demonstrate the entity's commitment to the advancement of qualified personnel to higher levels of responsibility.

Entity's Risk Assessment Process

3 For financial reporting purposes, the entity's risk assessment process includes how management identifies business risks relevant to the preparation of financial statements in accordance with the entity's applicable financial reporting framework, estimates their significance, assesses the likelihood of their occurrence, and decides upon actions to respond to and manage them and the results thereof. For example, the entity's risk assessment process may address how the entity considers the possibility of unrecorded transactions or identifies and analyzes significant estimates recorded in the financial statements.

4 Risks relevant to reliable financial reporting include external and internal events, transactions or circumstances that may occur and adversely affect an entity's ability to initiate, record, process, and report financial data consistent with the assertions of management[1a] in the financial statements. Management may initiate plans, programs, or actions to address specific risks or it may decide to accept a risk because of cost or other considerations. Risks can arise or change due to circumstances such as the following:

- *Changes in operating environment.* Changes in the regulatory or operating environment can result in changes in competitive pressures and significantly different risks.
- *New personnel.* New personnel may have a different focus on or understanding of internal control.
- *New or revamped information systems.* Significant and rapid changes in information systems can change the risk relating to internal control.
- *Rapid growth.* Significant and rapid expansion of operations can strain controls and increase the risk of a breakdown in controls.
- *New technology.* Incorporating new technologies into production processes or information systems may change the risk associated with internal control.
- *New business models, products, or activities.* Entering into business areas or transactions with which an entity has little experience may introduce new risks associated with internal control.
- *Corporate restructurings.* Restructurings may be accompanied by staff reductions and changes in supervision and segregation of duties that may change the risk associated with internal control.
- *Expanded foreign operations.* The expansion or acquisition of foreign operations carries new and often unique risks that may affect internal control, for example, additional or changed risks from foreign currency transactions.
- *New accounting pronouncements.* Adoption of new accounting principles or changing accounting principles may affect risks in preparing financial statements.

Information System, Including the Related Business Processes, Relevant to Financial Reporting, and Communication

5 An information system consists of infrastructure (physical and hardware components), software, people, procedures, and data. Many information systems make extensive use of information technology (IT).

The information system relevant to financial reporting objectives, which includes the   **6**
financial reporting system, encompasses methods and records that:

- Identify and record all valid transactions.
- Describe on a timely basis the transactions in sufficient detail to permit proper classification of transactions for financial reporting.
- Measure the value of transactions in a manner that permits recording their proper monetary value in the financial statements.
- Determine the time period in which transactions occurred to permit recording of transactions in the proper accounting period.
- Present properly the transactions and related disclosures in the financial statements.

The quality of system-generated information affects management's ability to make   **7**
appropriate decisions in managing and controlling the entity's activities and to prepare
reliable financial reports.

Communication, which involves providing an understanding of individual roles and   **8**
responsibilities pertaining to internal control over financial reporting, may take such
forms as policy manuals, accounting and financial reporting manuals, and memoranda.
Communication also can be made electronically, orally, and through the actions of
management.

Control Activities

Generally, control activities that may be relevant to an audit may be categorized as policies   **9**
and procedures that pertain to the following:

- *Performance reviews*. These control activities include reviews and analyses of actual performance versus budgets, forecasts, and prior period performance; relating different sets of data – operating or financial – to one another, together with analyses of the relationships and investigative and corrective actions; comparing internal data with external sources of information; and review of functional or activity performance.
- *Information processing*. The two broad groupings of information systems control activities are application controls, which apply to the processing of individual applications, and general IT controls, which are policies and procedures that relate to many applications and support the effective functioning of application controls by helping to ensure the continued proper operation of information systems. Examples of application controls include checking the arithmetical accuracy of records, maintaining and reviewing accounts and trial balances, automated controls such as edit checks of input data and numerical sequence checks, and manual follow-up of exception reports. Examples of general IT controls are program change controls, controls that restrict access to programs or data, controls over the implementation of new releases of packaged software applications, and controls over system software that restrict access to or monitor the use of system utilities that could change financial data or records without leaving an audit trail.
- *Physical controls*. Controls that encompass:
  - The physical security of assets, including adequate safeguards such as secured facilities over access to assets and records.
  - The authorization for access to computer programs and data files.
  - The periodic counting and comparison with amounts shown on control records (for example, comparing the results of cash, security and inventory counts with accounting records).

The extent to which physical controls intended to prevent theft of assets are relevant to the reliability of financial statement preparation, and therefore the audit, depends on circumstances such as when assets are highly susceptible to misappropriation.

- *Segregation of duties*. Assigning different people the responsibilities of authorizing transactions, recording transactions, and maintaining custody of assets. Segregation of duties is intended to reduce the opportunities to allow any person to be in a position to both perpetrate and conceal errors or fraud in the normal course of the person's duties.

10   Certain control activities may depend on the existence of appropriate higher level policies established by management or those charged with governance. For example, authorization controls may be delegated under established guidelines, such as investment criteria set by those charged with governance; alternatively, non-routine transactions such as major acquisitions or divestments may require specific high level approval, including in some cases that of shareholders.

Monitoring of Controls

11   An important management responsibility is to establish and maintain internal control on an ongoing basis. Management's monitoring of controls includes considering whether they are operating as intended and that they are modified as appropriate for changes in conditions. Monitoring of controls may include activities such as management's review of whether bank reconciliations are being prepared on a timely basis, internal auditors' evaluation of sales personnel's compliance with the entity's policies on terms of sales contracts, and a legal department's oversight of compliance with the entity's ethical or business practice policies. Monitoring is done also to ensure that controls continue to operate effectively over time. For example, if the timeliness and accuracy of bank reconciliations are not monitored, personnel are likely to stop preparing them.

12   Internal auditors or personnel performing similar functions may contribute to the monitoring of an entity's controls through separate evaluations. Ordinarily, they regularly provide information about the functioning of internal control, focusing considerable attention on evaluating the effectiveness of internal control, and communicate information about strengths and deficiencies in internal control and recommendations for improving internal control.

13   Monitoring activities may include using information from communications from external parties that may indicate problems or highlight areas in need of improvement. Customers implicitly corroborate billing data by paying their invoices or complaining about their charges. In addition, regulators may communicate with the entity concerning matters that affect the functioning of internal control, for example, communications concerning examinations by bank regulatory agencies. Also, management may consider communications relating to internal control from external auditors in performing monitoring activities.

Appendix 2

Conditions and Events That May Indicate Risks of Material Misstatement

The following are examples of conditions and events that may indicate the existence of risks of material misstatement in the financial statements. The examples provided cover a broad range of conditions and events; however, not all conditions and events are relevant to every audit engagement and the list of examples is not necessarily complete.

- Operations in regions that are economically unstable, for example, countries with significant currency devaluation or highly inflationary economies.
- Operations exposed to volatile markets, for example, futures trading.
- Operations that are subject to a high degree of complex regulation.
- Going concern and liquidity issues including loss of significant customers.
- Constraints on the availability of capital and credit.
- Changes in the industry in which the entity operates.
- Changes in the supply chain.
- Developing or offering new products or services, or moving into new lines of business.
- Expanding into new locations.
- Changes in the entity such as large acquisitions or reorganizations or other unusual events.
- Entities or business segments likely to be sold.
- The existence of complex alliances and joint ventures.
- Use of off balance sheet finance, special-purpose entities, and other complex financing arrangements.
- Significant transactions with related parties.
- Lack of personnel with appropriate accounting and financial reporting skills.
- Changes in key personnel including departure of key executives.
- Deficiencies in internal control, especially those not addressed by management.
- Incentives for management and employees to engage in fraudulent financial reporting.
- Inconsistencies between the entity's IT strategy and its business strategies.
- Changes in the IT environment.
- Installation of significant new IT systems related to financial reporting.
- Inquiries into the entity's operations or financial results by regulatory or government bodies.
- Past misstatements, history of errors or a significant amount of adjustments at period end.
- Significant amount of non-routine or non-systematic transactions including intercompany transactions and large revenue transactions at period end.
- Transactions that are recorded based on management's intent, for example, debt refinancing, assets to be sold and classification of marketable securities.
- Application of new accounting pronouncements.
- Accounting measurements that involve complex processes.
- Events or transactions that involve significant measurement uncertainty, including accounting estimates, and related disclosures.
- Omission, or obscuring, of significant information in disclosures.
- Pending litigation and contingent liabilities, for example, sales warranties, financial guarantees and environmental remediation.

International Standard on Auditing (UK) 320 (Revised June 2016)

Materiality in planning and performing an audit

(Effective for audits of financial statements for periods commencing on or after 17 June 2016)

Contents

International Standard on Auditing (UK) (ISA (UK)) 320 (Revised June 2016), *Materiality in Planning and Performing an Audit*, should be read in the context of ISA (UK) 200 (Revised June 2016), *Overall Objectives of the Independent Auditor and the Conduct of an Audit in Accordance with International Standards on Auditing (UK)*.

Introduction

Scope of this ISA (UK)

This International Standard on Auditing (UK) (ISA (UK)) deals with the auditor's **1**
responsibility to apply the concept of materiality in planning and performing an audit
of financial statements. ISA (UK) 450 (Revised June 2016)[1] explains how materiality is
applied in evaluating the effect of identified misstatements on the audit and of uncorrected
misstatements, if any, on the financial statements.

Materiality in the Context of an Audit

Financial reporting frameworks often discuss the concept of materiality in the context **2**
of the preparation and presentation of financial statements. Although financial reporting
frameworks may discuss materiality in different terms, they generally explain that:

- Misstatements, including omissions, are considered to be material if they, individually
  or in the aggregate, could reasonably be expected to influence the economic decisions
  of users taken on the basis of the financial statements;
- Judgments about materiality are made in light of surrounding circumstances, and are
  affected by the size or nature of a misstatement, or a combination of both; and
- Judgments about matters that are material to users of the financial statements are
  based on a consideration of the common financial information needs of users as a
  group.[2] The possible effect of misstatements on specific individual users, whose
  needs may vary widely, is not considered.

Such a discussion, if present in the applicable financial reporting framework, provides a **3**
frame of reference to the auditor in determining materiality for the audit. If the applicable
financial reporting framework does not include a discussion of the concept of materiality, the
characteristics referred to in paragraph 2 provide the auditor with such a frame of reference.

The auditor's determination of materiality is a matter of professional judgment, and is **4**
affected by the auditor's perception of the financial information needs of users of the
financial statements. In this context, it is reasonable for the auditor to assume that users:

(a) Have a reasonable knowledge of business and economic activities and accounting
    and a willingness to study the information in the financial statements with reasonable
    diligence;
(b) Understand that financial statements are prepared, presented and audited to levels of
    materiality;
(c) Recognize the uncertainties inherent in the measurement of amounts based on the use
    of estimates, judgment and the consideration of future events; and
(d) Make reasonable economic decisions on the basis of the information in the financial
    statements.

The concept of materiality is applied by the auditor both in planning and performing **5**
the audit, and in evaluating the effect of identified misstatements on the audit and of
uncorrected misstatements, if any, on the financial statements and in forming the opinion
in the auditor's report. (Ref: Para. A1)

---

[1] *ISA (UK) 450 (Revised June 2016)*, Evaluation of Misstatements Identified during the Audit.

[2] *For example, the* Framework for the Preparation and Presentation of Financial Statements, *adopted by
the International Accounting Standards Board in April 2001, indicates that, for a profit-oriented entity,
as investors are providers of risk capital to the enterprise, the provision of financial statements that
meet their needs will also meet most of the needs of other users that financial statements can satisfy.*
The Framework for the Preparation and Presentation of Financial Statements, has not been promulgated by the FRC
for application in the UK.

6   In planning the audit, the auditor makes judgments about misstatements that will be considered material. These judgments provide a basis for:

(a)   Determining the nature, timing and extent of risk assessment procedures;

(b)   Identifying and assessing the risks of material misstatement; and

(c)   Determining the nature, timing and extent of further audit procedures.

The materiality determined when planning the audit does not necessarily establish an amount below which uncorrected misstatements, individually or in the aggregate, will always be evaluated as immaterial. The circumstances related to some misstatements may cause the auditor to evaluate them as material even if they are below materiality. It is not practicable to design audit procedures to detect all misstatements that could be material solely because of their nature. However consideration of the nature of potential misstatements in disclosures is relevant to the design of audit procedures to address risks of material misstatement.[3] In addition, when evaluating the effect on the financial statements of all uncorrected misstatements, the auditor considers not only the size but also the nature of uncorrected misstatements, and the particular circumstances of their occurrence.[4] (Ref: Para. A1a)

Effective Date

7   This ISA (UK) is effective for audits of financial statements for periods commencing on or after 17 June 2016. Earlier adoption is permitted.

Objective

8   The objective of the auditor is to apply the concept of materiality appropriately in planning and performing the audit.

Definition

9   For purposes of the ISAs (UK), performance materiality means the amount or amounts set by the auditor at less than materiality for the financial statements as a whole to reduce to an appropriately low level the probability that the aggregate of uncorrected and undetected misstatements exceeds materiality for the financial statements as a whole. If applicable, performance materiality also refers to the amount or amounts set by the auditor at less than the materiality level or levels for particular classes of transactions, account balances or disclosures.

Requirements

Determining Materiality and Performance Materiality When Planning the Audit

10   When establishing the overall audit strategy, the auditor shall determine materiality for the financial statements as a whole. If, in the specific circumstances of the entity, there is one or more particular classes of transactions, account balances or disclosures for which misstatements of lesser amounts than materiality for the financial statements as a whole could reasonably be expected to influence the economic decisions of users taken on the

---

[3]   *See ISA (UK) 315 (Revised June 2016)*, Identifying and Assessing the Risks of Material Misstatement through Understanding the Entity and its Environment, *paragraphs A128a–A128b.*

[4]   *ISA (UK) 450 (Revised June 2016), paragraph A16.*

basis of the financial statements, the auditor shall also determine the materiality level or levels to be applied to those particular classes of transactions, account balances or disclosures. (Ref: Para. A2–A11)

The auditor shall determine performance materiality for purposes of assessing the risks of material misstatement and determining the nature, timing and extent of further audit procedures. (Ref: Para. A12)   **11**

Revision as the Audit Progresses

The auditor shall revise materiality for the financial statements as a whole (and, if applicable, the materiality level or levels for particular classes of transactions, account balances or disclosures) in the event of becoming aware of information during the audit that would have caused the auditor to have determined a different amount (or amounts) initially. (Ref: Para. A13)   **12**

If the auditor concludes that a lower materiality for the financial statements as a whole (and, if applicable, materiality level or levels for particular classes of transactions, account balances or disclosures) than that initially determined is appropriate, the auditor shall determine whether it is necessary to revise performance materiality, and whether the nature, timing and extent of the further audit procedures remain appropriate.   **13**

Documentation

The auditor shall include in the audit documentation the following amounts and the factors considered in their determination:[5]   **14**

(a) Materiality for the financial statements as a whole (see paragraph 10);
(b) If applicable, the materiality level or levels for particular classes of transactions, account balances or disclosures (see paragraph 10);
(c) Performance materiality (see paragraph 11); and
(d) Any revision of (a)–(c) as the audit progressed (see paragraphs 12–13).

Application and Other Explanatory Material

Materiality and Audit Risk (Ref: Para. 5)

In conducting an audit of financial statements, the overall objectives of the auditor are to obtain reasonable assurance about whether the financial statements as a whole are free from material misstatement, whether due to fraud or error, thereby enabling the auditor to express an opinion on whether the financial statements are prepared, in all material respects, in accordance with an applicable financial reporting framework; and to report on the financial statements, and communicate as required by the ISAs (UK), in accordance with the auditor's findings.[6] The auditor obtains reasonable assurance by obtaining sufficient appropriate audit evidence to reduce audit risk to an acceptably low level.[7] Audit risk is the risk that the auditor expresses an inappropriate audit opinion when the financial statements are materially misstated. Audit risk is a function of the risks of material   **A1**

---

[5] *ISA (UK) 230 (Revised June 2016)*, Audit Documentation, *paragraphs 8–11, and paragraph A6.*

[6] *ISA (UK) 200 (Revised June 2016)*, Overall Objectives of the Independent Auditor and the Conduct of an Audit in Accordance with International Standards on Auditing (UK), *paragraph 11.*

[7] *ISA (UK) 200 (Revised June 2016), paragraph 17.*

misstatement and detection risk.[8] Materiality and audit risk are considered throughout the audit, in particular, when:

(a) Identifying and assessing the risks of material misstatement;[9]

(b) Determining the nature, timing and extent of further audit procedures;[10] and

(c) Evaluating the effect of uncorrected misstatements, if any, on the financial statements[11] and in forming the opinion in the auditor's report.[12]

Materiality in the Context of an Audit (Ref: Para. 6)

A1a   Identifying and assessing the risks of material misstatement[13] involves the use of professional judgment to identify those classes of transactions, account balances and disclosures, including qualitative disclosures, the misstatement of which could be material (i.e., in general, misstatements are considered to be material if they could reasonably be expected to influence the economic decisions of users taken on the basis of the financial statements as a whole). When considering whether misstatements in qualitative disclosures could be material, the auditor may identify relevant factors such as:

- The circumstances of the entity for the period (for example, the entity may have undertaken a significant business combination during the period).
- The applicable financial reporting framework, including changes therein (for example, a new financial reporting standard may require new qualitative disclosures that are significant to the entity).
- Qualitative disclosures that are important to users of the financial statements because of the nature of an entity (for example, liquidity risk disclosures may be important to users of the financial statements for a financial institution).

Determining Materiality and Performance Materiality When Planning the Audit

Considerations Specific to Public Sector Entities (Ref: Para. 10)

A2   In the case of a public sector entity, legislators and regulators are often the primary users of its financial statements. Furthermore, the financial statements may be used to make decisions other than economic decisions. The determination of materiality for the financial statements as a whole (and, if applicable, materiality level or levels for particular classes of transactions, account balances or disclosures) in an audit of the financial statements of a public sector entity is therefore influenced by law, regulation or other authority, and by the financial information needs of legislators and the public in relation to public sector programs.

---

[8] *ISA (UK) 200 (Revised June 2016), paragraph 13(c).*

[9] *ISA (UK) 315 (Revised June 2016),* Identifying and Assessing the Risks of Material Misstatements through Understanding the Entity and Its Environment.

[10] *ISA (UK) 330 (Revised June 2016),* The Auditor's Responses to Assessed Risks.

[11] *ISA (UK) 450 (Revised June 2016).*

[12] *ISA (UK) 700 (Revised June 2016),* Forming an Opinion and Reporting on Financial Statements.

[13] *ISA (UK) 315 (Revised June 2016), paragraph 25, requires the auditor to identify and assess the risk of material misstatement at the financial statement and assertion level.*

Use of Benchmarks in Determining Materiality for the Financial Statements as a Whole (Ref: Para. 10)

Determining materiality involves the exercise of professional judgment. A percentage is often applied to a chosen benchmark as a starting point in determining materiality for the financial statements as a whole. Factors that may affect the identification of an appropriate benchmark include the following:

A3

- The elements of the financial statements (for example, assets, liabilities, equity, revenue, expenses);
- Whether there are items on which the attention of the users of the particular entity's financial statements tends to be focused (for example, for the purpose of evaluating financial performance users may tend to focus on profit, revenue or net assets);
- The nature of the entity, where the entity is in its life cycle, and the industry and economic environment in which the entity operates;
- The entity's ownership structure and the way it is financed (for example, if an entity is financed solely by debt rather than equity, users may put more emphasis on assets, and claims on them, than on the entity's earnings); and
- The relative volatility of the benchmark.

Examples of benchmarks that may be appropriate, depending on the circumstances of the entity, include categories of reported income such as profit before tax, total revenue, gross profit and total expenses, total equity or net asset value. Profit before tax from continuing operations is often used for profit-oriented entities. When profit before tax from continuing operations is volatile, other benchmarks may be more appropriate, such as gross profit or total revenues.

A4

In relation to the chosen benchmark, relevant financial data ordinarily includes prior periods' financial results and financial positions, the period-to-date financial results and financial position, and budgets or forecasts for the current period, adjusted for significant changes in the circumstances of the entity (for example, a significant business acquisition) and relevant changes of conditions in the industry or economic environment in which the entity operates. For example, when, as a starting point, materiality for the financial statements as a whole is determined for a particular entity based on a percentage of profit before tax from continuing operations, circumstances that give rise to an exceptional decrease or increase in such profit may lead the auditor to conclude that materiality for the financial statements as a whole is more appropriately determined using a normalized profit before tax from continuing operations figure based on past results.

A5

Materiality relates to the financial statements on which the auditor is reporting. Where the financial statements are prepared for a financial reporting period of more or less than twelve months, such as may be the case for a new entity or a change in the financial reporting period, materiality relates to the financial statements prepared for that financial reporting period.

A6

Determining a percentage to be applied to a chosen benchmark involves the exercise of professional judgment. There is a relationship between the percentage and the chosen benchmark, such that a percentage applied to profit before tax from continuing operations will normally be higher than a percentage applied to total revenue. For example, the auditor may consider five percent of profit before tax from continuing operations to be appropriate for a profit-oriented entity in a manufacturing industry, while the auditor may consider one percent of total revenue or total expenses to be appropriate for a not-for-profit entity. Higher or lower percentages, however, may be deemed appropriate in the circumstances.

A7

Considerations Specific to Small Entities

A8   When an entity's profit before tax from continuing operations is consistently nominal, as might be the case for an owner-managed business where the owner takes much of the profit before tax in the form of remuneration, a benchmark such as profit before remuneration and tax may be more relevant.

Considerations Specific to Public Sector Entities

A9   In an audit of a public sector entity, total cost or net cost (expenses less revenues or expenditure less receipts) may be appropriate benchmarks for program activities. Where a public sector entity has custody of public assets, assets may be an appropriate benchmark.

Materiality Level or Levels for Particular Classes of Transactions, Account Balances or Disclosures (Ref: Para. 10)

A10   Factors that may indicate the existence of one or more particular classes of transactions, account balances or disclosures for which misstatements of lesser amounts than materiality for the financial statements as a whole could reasonably be expected to influence the economic decisions of users taken on the basis of the financial statements include the following:

- Whether law, regulation or the applicable financial reporting framework affect users' expectations regarding the measurement or disclosure of certain items (for example, related party transactions, and the remuneration of management and those charged with governance, and sensitivity analysis for fair value accounting estimates with high estimation uncertainty).
- The key disclosures in relation to the industry in which the entity operates (for example, research and development costs for a pharmaceutical company).
- Whether attention is focused on a particular aspect of the entity's business that is separately disclosed in the financial statements (for example, disclosures about segments or a significant business combination).

A11   In considering whether, in the specific circumstances of the entity, such classes of transactions, account balances or disclosures exist, the auditor may find it useful to obtain an understanding of the views and expectations of those charged with governance and management.

Performance Materiality (Ref: Para. 11)

A12   Planning the audit solely to detect individually material misstatements overlooks the fact that the aggregate of individually immaterial misstatements may cause the financial statements to be materially misstated, and leaves no margin for possible undetected misstatements. Performance materiality (which, as defined, is one or more amounts) is set to reduce to an appropriately low level the probability that the aggregate of uncorrected and undetected misstatements in the financial statements exceeds materiality for the financial statements as a whole. Similarly, performance materiality relating to a materiality level determined for a particular class of transactions, account balance or disclosure is set to reduce to an appropriately low level the probability that the aggregate of uncorrected and undetected misstatements in that particular class of transactions, account balance or disclosure exceeds the materiality level for that particular class of transactions, account balance or disclosure. The determination of performance materiality is not a simple mechanical calculation and involves the exercise of professional judgment. It is affected by the auditor's understanding of the entity, updated during the performance of the risk assessment procedures; and the nature and extent of misstatements identified in previous audits and thereby the auditor's expectations in relation to misstatements in the current period.

Revision as the Audit Progresses (Ref: Para. 12)

Materiality for the financial statements as a whole (and, if applicable, the materiality level   A13
or levels for particular classes of transactions, account balances or disclosures) may need
to be revised as a result of a change in circumstances that occurred during the audit (for
example, a decision to dispose of a major part of the entity's business), new information,
or a change in the auditor's understanding of the entity and its operations as a result of
performing further audit procedures. For example, if during the audit it appears as though
actual financial results are likely to be substantially different from the anticipated period
end financial results that were used initially to determine materiality for the financial
statements as a whole, the auditor revises that materiality.

International Standard on Auditing (UK) 330 (Revised July 2017)

The auditor's responses to assessed risks

(Effective for audits of financial statements for periods commencing on or after 15 December 2017)

Contents

International Standard on Auditing (UK) (ISA (UK)) 330 (Revised July 2017), *The Auditor's Responses to Assessed Risks*, should be read in conjunction with ISA (UK) 200 (Revised June 2016), *Overall Objectives of the Independent Auditor and the Conduct of an Audit in Accordance with International Standards on Auditing (UK)*.

Introduction

Scope of this ISA (UK)

This International Standard on Auditing (UK) (ISA (UK)) deals with the auditor's 1
responsibility to design and implement responses to the risks of material misstatement
identified and assessed by the auditor in accordance with ISA (UK) 315 (Revised
June 2016)[1] in an audit of financial statements.

Effective Date

This ISA (UK) is effective for audits of financial statements for periods commencing on 2
or after 15 December 2017.

Objective

The objective of the auditor is to obtain sufficient appropriate audit evidence regarding the 3
assessed risks of material misstatement, through designing and implementing appropriate
responses to those risks.

Definitions

For purposes of the ISAs (UK), the following terms have the meanings attributed below: 4
(a) Substantive procedure – An audit procedure designed to detect material misstatements
at the assertion level. Substantive procedures comprise:
   (i) Tests of details (of classes of transactions, account balances, and disclosures);
   and
   (ii) Substantive analytical procedures.

(b) Test of controls – An audit procedure designed to evaluate the operating effectiveness
of controls in preventing, or detecting and correcting, material misstatements at the
assertion level.

Requirements

Overall Responses

The auditor shall design and implement overall responses to address the assessed risks of 5
material misstatement at the financial statement level. (Ref: Para. A1–A3)

Audit Procedures Responsive to the Assessed Risks of Material Misstatement at the Assertion Level

The auditor shall design and perform further audit procedures whose nature, timing, and 6
extent are based on and are responsive to the assessed risks of material misstatement at the
assertion level. (Ref: Para. A4–A8)

In designing the further audit procedures to be performed, the auditor shall: 7

---

[1] *ISA (UK) 315 (Revised June 2016)*, Identifying and Assessing the Risks of Material Misstatement through Understanding the Entity and Its Environment.

   (a) Consider the reasons for the assessment given to the risk of material misstatement at the assertion level for each class of transactions, account balance, and disclosure, including:

      (i) The likelihood of material misstatement due to the particular characteristics of the relevant class of transactions, account balance, or disclosure (that is, the inherent risk); and

      (ii) Whether the risk assessment takes account of relevant controls (that is, the control risk), thereby requiring the auditor to obtain audit evidence to determine whether the controls are operating effectively (that is, the auditor intends to rely on the operating effectiveness of controls in determining the nature, timing and extent of substantive procedures); and (Ref: Para. A9–A18)

   (b) Obtain more persuasive audit evidence the higher the auditor's assessment of risk. (Ref: Para. A19)

Tests of Controls

8   The auditor shall design and perform tests of controls to obtain sufficient appropriate audit evidence as to the operating effectiveness of relevant controls if:

   (a) The auditor's assessment of risks of material misstatement at the assertion level includes an expectation that the controls are operating effectively (that is, the auditor intends to rely on the operating effectiveness of controls in determining the nature, timing and extent of substantive procedures); or

   (b) Substantive procedures alone cannot provide sufficient appropriate audit evidence at the assertion level. (Ref: Para. A20–A24)

9   In designing and performing tests of controls, the auditor shall obtain more persuasive audit evidence the greater the reliance the auditor places on the effectiveness of a control. (Ref: Para. A25)

Nature and Extent of Tests of Controls

10   In designing and performing tests of controls, the auditor shall:

   (a) Perform other audit procedures in combination with inquiry to obtain audit evidence about the operating effectiveness of the controls, including:

      (i) How the controls were applied at relevant times during the period under audit;

      (ii) The consistency with which they were applied; and

      (iii) By whom or by what means they were applied. (Ref: Para. A26–29)

   (b) Determine whether the controls to be tested depend upon other controls (indirect controls) and, if so, whether it is necessary to obtain audit evidence supporting the effective operation of those indirect controls. (Ref: Para. A30–A31)

Timing of Tests of Controls

11   The auditor shall test controls for the particular time, or throughout the period, for which the auditor intends to rely on those controls, subject to paragraphs 12 and 15 below, in order to provide an appropriate basis for the auditor's intended reliance. (Ref: Para. A32)

Using audit evidence obtained during an interim period

12   If the auditor obtains audit evidence about the operating effectiveness of controls during an interim period, the auditor shall:

(a) Obtain audit evidence about significant changes to those controls subsequent to the interim period; and

(b) Determine the additional audit evidence to be obtained for the remaining period. (Ref: Para. A33–A34)

Using audit evidence obtained in previous audits

In determining whether it is appropriate to use audit evidence about the operating effectiveness of controls obtained in previous audits, and, if so, the length of the time period that may elapse before retesting a control, the auditor shall consider the following: **13**

(a) The effectiveness of other elements of internal control, including the control environment, the entity's monitoring of controls, and the entity's risk assessment process;

(b) The risks arising from the characteristics of the control, including whether it is manual or automated;

(c) The effectiveness of general IT controls;

(d) The effectiveness of the control and its application by the entity, including the nature and extent of deviations in the application of the control noted in previous audits, and whether there have been personnel changes that significantly affect the application of the control;

(e) Whether the lack of a change in a particular control poses a risk due to changing circumstances; and

(f) The risks of material misstatement and the extent of reliance on the control. (Ref: Para. A35)

If the auditor plans to use audit evidence from a previous audit about the operating effectiveness of specific controls, the auditor shall establish the continuing relevance of that evidence by obtaining audit evidence about whether significant changes in those controls have occurred subsequent to the previous audit. The auditor shall obtain this evidence by performing inquiry combined with observation or inspection, to confirm the understanding of those specific controls, and: **14**

(a) If there have been changes that affect the continuing relevance of the audit evidence from the previous audit, the auditor shall test the controls in the current audit. (Ref: Para. A36)

(b) If there have not been such changes, the auditor shall test the controls at least once in every third audit, and shall test some controls each audit to avoid the possibility of testing all the controls on which the auditor intends to rely in a single audit period with no testing of controls in the subsequent two audit periods. (Ref: Para. A37–A39)

Controls over significant risks

If the auditor plans to rely on controls over a risk the auditor has determined to be a significant risk, the auditor shall test those controls in the current period.   **15**

Evaluating the Operating Effectiveness of Controls

When evaluating the operating effectiveness of relevant controls, the auditor shall evaluate whether misstatements that have been detected by substantive procedures indicate that controls are not operating effectively. The absence of misstatements detected by substantive procedures, however, does not provide audit evidence that controls related to the assertion being tested are effective. (Ref: Para. A40)   **16**

17   If deviations from controls upon which the auditor intends to rely are detected, the auditor shall make specific inquiries to understand these matters and their potential consequences, and shall determine whether: (Ref: Para. A41)

(a)   The tests of controls that have been performed provide an appropriate basis for reliance on the controls;

(b)   Additional tests of controls are necessary; or

(c)   The potential risks of misstatement need to be addressed using substantive procedures.

Substantive Procedures

18   Irrespective of the assessed risks of material misstatement, the auditor shall design and perform substantive procedures for each material class of transactions, account balance, and disclosure. (Ref: Para. A42–A47)

19   The auditor shall consider whether external confirmation procedures are to be performed as substantive audit procedures. (Ref: Para. A48–A51)

19R-1   For audits of financial statements of public interest entities, the auditor shall assess the valuation methods applied to the various items in the financial statements including any impact of changes of such methods. (Ref: Para. A51-1)

Substantive Procedures Related to the Financial Statement Closing Process

20   The auditor's substantive procedures shall include the following audit procedures related to the financial statement closing process:

(a)   Agreeing or reconciling information in the financial statements with the underlying accounting records, including agreeing or reconciling information in disclosures, whether such information is obtained from within or outside of the general and subsidiary ledgers; and

(b)   Examining material journal entries and other adjustments made during the course of preparing the financial statements. (Ref: Para. A52)

Substantive Procedures Responsive to Significant Risks

21   If the auditor has determined that an assessed risk of material misstatement at the assertion level is a significant risk, the auditor shall perform substantive procedures that are specifically responsive to that risk. When the approach to a significant risk consists only of substantive procedures, those procedures shall include tests of details. (Ref: Para. A53)

Timing of Substantive Procedures

22   If substantive procedures are performed at an interim date, the auditor shall cover the remaining period by performing:

(a)   substantive procedures, combined with tests of controls for the intervening period; or

(b)   if the auditor determines that it is sufficient, further substantive procedures only

that provide a reasonable basis for extending the audit conclusions from the interim date to the period end. (Ref: Para. A54–A57)

23   If misstatements that the auditor did not expect when assessing the risks of material misstatement are detected at an interim date, the auditor shall evaluate whether the related

assessment of risk and the planned nature, timing, or extent of substantive procedures covering the remaining period need to be modified. (Ref: Para. A58)

Adequacy of Presentation of the Financial Statements

The auditor shall perform audit procedures to evaluate whether the overall presentation of   **24** the financial statements is in accordance with the applicable financial reporting framework. In making this evaluation, the auditor shall consider whether the financial statements are presented in a manner that reflects the appropriate:

- Classification and description of financial information and the underlying transactions, events and conditions; and
- Presentation, structure and content of the financial statements. (Ref: Para. A59)

Evaluating the Sufficiency and Appropriateness of Audit Evidence

Based on the audit procedures performed and the audit evidence obtained, the auditor shall   **25** evaluate before the conclusion of the audit whether the assessments of the risks of material misstatement at the assertion level remain appropriate. (Ref: Para. A60–A61)

The auditor shall conclude whether sufficient appropriate audit evidence has been obtained.   **26** In forming an opinion, the auditor shall consider all relevant audit evidence, regardless of whether it appears to corroborate or to contradict the assertions in the financial statements. (Ref: Para. A62)

If the auditor has not obtained sufficient appropriate audit evidence as to a material   **27** financial statement assertion, the auditor shall attempt to obtain further audit evidence. If the auditor is unable to obtain sufficient appropriate audit evidence, the auditor shall express a qualified opinion or disclaim an opinion on the financial statements.

Documentation

The auditor shall include in the audit documentation:[2]   **28**
(a) The overall responses to address the assessed risks of material misstatement at the financial statement level, and the nature, timing, and extent of the further audit procedures performed;
(b) The linkage of those procedures with the assessed risks at the assertion level; and
(c) The results of the audit procedures, including the conclusions where these are not otherwise clear. (Ref: Para. A63)

If the auditor plans to use audit evidence about the operating effectiveness of controls   **29** obtained in previous audits, the auditor shall include in the audit documentation the conclusions reached about relying on such controls that were tested in a previous audit.

The auditor's documentation shall demonstrate that information in the financial statements   **30** agrees or reconciles with the underlying accounting records, including agreeing or reconciling disclosures, whether such information is obtained from within or outside of the general and subsidiary ledgers.

***

---

[2] *ISA (UK) 230 (Revised June 2016)*, Audit Documentation, *paragraphs 8–11, and A6.*

Application and Other Explanatory Material

Overall Responses (Ref: Para. 5)

A1   Overall responses to address the assessed risks of material misstatement at the financial statement level may include:

- Emphasizing to the audit team the need to maintain professional skepticism.
- Assigning more experienced staff or those with special skills or using experts.
- Providing more supervision.
- Incorporating additional elements of unpredictability in the selection of further audit procedures to be performed.
- Making general changes to the nature, timing, or extent of audit procedures, for example: performing substantive procedures at the period end instead of at an interim date; or modifying the nature of audit procedures to obtain more persuasive audit evidence.

A2   The assessment of the risks of material misstatement at the financial statement level, and thereby the auditor's overall responses, is affected by the auditor's understanding of the control environment. An effective control environment may allow the auditor to have more confidence in internal control and the reliability of audit evidence generated internally within the entity and thus, for example, allow the auditor to conduct some audit procedures at an interim date rather than at the period end. Deficiencies in the control environment, however, have the opposite effect; for example, the auditor may respond to an ineffective control environment by:

- Conducting more audit procedures as of the period end rather than at an interim date.
- Obtaining more extensive audit evidence from substantive procedures.
- Increasing the number of locations to be included in the audit scope.

A3   Such considerations, therefore, have a significant bearing on the auditor's general approach, for example, an emphasis on substantive procedures (substantive approach), or an approach that uses tests of controls as well as substantive procedures (combined approach).

Audit Procedures Responsive to the Assessed Risks of Material Misstatement at the Assertion Level

The Nature, Timing, and Extent of Further Audit Procedures (Ref: Para. 6)

A4   The auditor's assessment of the identified risks at the assertion level provides a basis for considering the appropriate audit approach for designing and performing further audit procedures. For example, the auditor may determine that:

(a)   Only by performing tests of controls may the auditor achieve an effective response to the assessed risk of material misstatement for a particular assertion;

(b)   Performing only substantive procedures is appropriate for particular assertions and, therefore, the auditor excludes the effect of controls from the relevant risk assessment. This may be because the auditor's risk assessment procedures have not identified any effective controls relevant to the assertion, or because testing controls would be inefficient and therefore the auditor does not intend to rely on the operating effectiveness of controls in determining the nature, timing and extent of substantive procedures; or

(c)   A combined approach using both tests of controls and substantive procedures is an effective approach.

However, as required by paragraph 18, irrespective of the approach selected, the auditor designs and performs substantive procedures for each material class of transactions, account balance, and disclosure.

The nature of an audit procedure refers to its purpose (i.e., test of controls or substantive procedure) and its type (that is, inspection, observation, inquiry, confirmation, recalculation, reperformance, or analytical procedure). The nature of the audit procedures is of most importance in responding to the assessed risks. **A5**

Timing of an audit procedure refers to when it is performed, or the period or date to which the audit evidence applies. **A6**

Extent of an audit procedure refers to the quantity to be performed, for example, a sample size or the number of observations of a control activity. **A7**

Designing and performing further audit procedures whose nature, timing, and extent are based on and are responsive to the assessed risks of material misstatement at the assertion level provides a clear linkage between the auditor's further audit procedures and the risk assessment. **A8**

Responding to the Assessed Risks at the Assertion Level (Ref: Para. 7(a))

Nature

The auditor's assessed risks may affect both the types of audit procedures to be performed and their combination. For example, when an assessed risk is high, the auditor may confirm the completeness of the terms of a contract with the counterparty, in addition to inspecting the document. Further, certain audit procedures may be more appropriate for some assertions than others. For example, in relation to revenue, tests of controls may be most responsive to the assessed risk of misstatement of the completeness assertion, whereas substantive procedures may be most responsive to the assessed risk of misstatement of the occurrence assertion. **A9**

The reasons for the assessment given to a risk are relevant in determining the nature of audit procedures. For example, if an assessed risk is lower because of the particular characteristics of a class of transactions without consideration of the related controls, then the auditor may determine that substantive analytical procedures alone provide sufficient appropriate audit evidence. On the other hand, if the assessed risk is lower because of internal controls, and the auditor intends to base the substantive procedures on that low assessment, then the auditor performs tests of those controls, as required by paragraph 8(a). This may be the case, for example, for a class of transactions of reasonably uniform, non-complex characteristics that are routinely processed and controlled by the entity's information system. **A10**

Timing

The auditor may perform tests of controls or substantive procedures at an interim date or at the period end. The higher the risk of material misstatement, the more likely it is that the auditor may decide it is more effective to perform substantive procedures nearer to, or at, the period end rather than at an earlier date, or to perform audit procedures unannounced or at unpredictable times (for example, performing audit procedures at selected locations on an unannounced basis). This is particularly relevant when considering the response to the risks of fraud. For example, the auditor may conclude that, when the risks of intentional misstatement or manipulation have been identified, audit procedures to extend audit conclusions from interim date to the period end would not be effective. **A11**

A12   On the other hand, performing audit procedures before the period end may assist the auditor in identifying significant matters at an early stage of the audit, and consequently resolving them with the assistance of management or developing an effective audit approach to address such matters.

A13   In addition, certain audit procedures can be performed only at or after the period end, for example:

- Agreeing or reconciling information in the financial statements with the underlying accounting records, including agreeing or reconciling disclosures, whether such information is obtained from within or outside of the general and subsidiary ledgers;
- Examining adjustments made during the course of preparing the financial statements; and
- Procedures to respond to a risk that, at the period end, the entity may have entered into improper sales contracts, or transactions may not have been finalized.

A14   Further relevant factors that influence the auditor's consideration of when to perform audit procedures include the following:

- The control environment.
- When relevant information is available (for example, electronic files may subsequently be overwritten, or procedures to be observed may occur only at certain times).
- The nature of the risk (for example, if there is a risk of inflated revenues to meet earnings expectations by subsequent creation of false sales agreements, the auditor may wish to examine contracts available on the date of the period end).
- The period or date to which the audit evidence relates.
- The timing of the preparation of the financial statements, particularly for those disclosures that provide further explanation about amounts recorded in the statement of financial position, the statement of comprehensive income, the statement of changes in equity or the statement of cash flows.

Extent

A15   The extent of an audit procedure judged necessary is determined after considering the materiality, the assessed risk, and the degree of assurance the auditor plans to obtain. When a single purpose is met by a combination of procedures, the extent of each procedure is considered separately. In general, the extent of audit procedures increases as the risk of material misstatement increases. For example, in response to the assessed risk of material misstatement due to fraud, increasing sample sizes or performing substantive analytical procedures at a more detailed level may be appropriate. However, increasing the extent of an audit procedure is effective only if the audit procedure itself is relevant to the specific risk.

A16   The use of computer-assisted audit techniques (CAATs) may enable more extensive testing of electronic transactions and account files, which may be useful when the auditor decides to modify the extent of testing, for example, in responding to the risks of material misstatement due to fraud. Such techniques can be used to select sample transactions from key electronic files, to sort transactions with specific characteristics, or to test an entire population instead of a sample.

Considerations specific to public sector entities

A17   For the audits of public sector entities, the audit mandate and any other special auditing requirements may affect the auditor's consideration of the nature, timing and extent of further audit procedures.

Considerations specific to smaller entities

In the case of very small entities, there may not be many control activities that could be **A18** identified by the auditor, or the extent to which their existence or operation have been documented by the entity may be limited. In such cases, it may be more efficient for the auditor to perform further audit procedures that are primarily substantive procedures. In some rare cases, however, the absence of control activities or of other components of control may make it impossible to obtain sufficient appropriate audit evidence.

Higher Assessments of Risk (Ref: Para 7(b))

When obtaining more persuasive audit evidence because of a higher assessment of risk, the **A19** auditor may increase the quantity of the evidence, or obtain evidence that is more relevant or reliable, for example, by placing more emphasis on obtaining third party evidence or by obtaining corroborating evidence from a number of independent sources.

Tests of Controls

Designing and Performing Tests of Controls (Ref: Para. 8)

Tests of controls are performed only on those controls that the auditor has determined are **A20** suitably designed to prevent, or detect and correct, a material misstatement in an assertion. If substantially different controls were used at different times during the period under audit, each is considered separately.

Testing the operating effectiveness of controls is different from obtaining an understanding **A21** of and evaluating the design and implementation of controls. However, the same types of audit procedures are used. The auditor may, therefore, decide it is efficient to test the operating effectiveness of controls at the same time as evaluating their design and determining that they have been implemented.

Further, although some risk assessment procedures may not have been specifically **A22** designed as tests of controls, they may nevertheless provide audit evidence about the operating effectiveness of the controls and, consequently, serve as tests of controls. For example, the auditor's risk assessment procedures may have included:

- Inquiring about management's use of budgets.
- Observing management's comparison of monthly budgeted and actual expenses.
- Inspecting reports pertaining to the investigation of variances between budgeted and actual amounts.

These audit procedures provide knowledge about the design of the entity's budgeting policies and whether they have been implemented, but may also provide audit evidence about the effectiveness of the operation of budgeting policies in preventing or detecting material misstatements in the classification of expenses.

In addition, the auditor may design a test of controls to be performed concurrently with **A23** a test of details on the same transaction. Although the purpose of a test of controls is different from the purpose of a test of details, both may be accomplished concurrently by performing a test of controls and a test of details on the same transaction, also known as a dual-purpose test. For example, the auditor may design, and evaluate the results of, a test to examine an invoice to determine whether it has been approved and to provide substantive audit evidence of a transaction. A dual-purpose test is designed and evaluated by considering each purpose of the test separately.

A24   In some cases, the auditor may find it impossible to design effective substantive procedures that by themselves provide sufficient appropriate audit evidence at the assertion level.[3] This may occur when an entity conducts its business using IT and no documentation of transactions is produced or maintained, other than through the IT system. In such cases, paragraph 8(b) requires the auditor to perform tests of relevant controls.

Audit Evidence and Intended Reliance (Ref: Para. 9)

A25   A higher level of assurance may be sought about the operating effectiveness of controls when the approach adopted consists primarily of tests of controls, in particular where it is not possible or practicable to obtain sufficient appropriate audit evidence only from substantive procedures.

Nature and Extent of Tests of Controls

Other audit procedures in combination with inquiry (Ref: Para. 10(a))

A26   Inquiry alone is not sufficient to test the operating effectiveness of controls. Accordingly, other audit procedures are performed in combination with inquiry. In this regard, inquiry combined with inspection or reperformance may provide more assurance than inquiry and observation, since an observation is pertinent only at the point in time at which it is made.

A27   The nature of the particular control influences the type of procedure required to obtain audit evidence about whether the control was operating effectively. For example, if operating effectiveness is evidenced by documentation, the auditor may decide to inspect it to obtain audit evidence about operating effectiveness. For other controls, however, documentation may not be available or relevant. For example, documentation of operation may not exist for some factors in the control environment, such as assignment of authority and responsibility, or for some types of control activities, such as control activities performed by a computer. In such circumstances, audit evidence about operating effectiveness may be obtained through inquiry in combination with other audit procedures such as observation or the use of CAATs.

Extent of tests of controls

A28   When more persuasive audit evidence is needed regarding the effectiveness of a control, it may be appropriate to increase the extent of testing of the control. As well as the degree of reliance on controls, matters the auditor may consider in determining the extent of tests of controls include the following:

- The frequency of the performance of the control by the entity during the period.
- The length of time during the audit period that the auditor is relying on the operating effectiveness of the control.
- The expected rate of deviation from a control.
- The relevance and reliability of the audit evidence to be obtained regarding the operating effectiveness of the control at the assertion level.
- The extent to which audit evidence is obtained from tests of other controls related to the assertion.

ISA (UK) 530[4] contains further guidance on the extent of testing.

---

[3] *ISA (UK) 315 (Revised June 2016), paragraph 30.*

[4] *ISA (UK) 530,* Audit Sampling.

Because of the inherent consistency of IT processing, it may not be necessary to increase   **A29**
the extent of testing of an automated control. An automated control can be expected to
function consistently unless the program (including the tables, files, or other permanent
data used by the program) is changed. Once the auditor determines that an automated
control is functioning as intended (which could be done at the time the control is initially
implemented or at some other date), the auditor may consider performing tests to determine
that the control continues to function effectively. Such tests might include determining that:

- Changes to the program are not made without being subject to the appropriate
  program change controls;
- The authorized version of the program is used for processing transactions; and
- Other relevant general controls are effective.

Such tests also might include determining that changes to the programs have not been
made, as may be the case when the entity uses packaged software applications without
modifying or maintaining them. For example, the auditor may inspect the record of the
administration of IT security to obtain audit evidence that unauthorized access has not
occurred during the period.

Testing of indirect controls (Ref: Para. 10(b))

In some circumstances, it may be necessary to obtain audit evidence supporting the   **A30**
effective operation of indirect controls. For example, when the auditor decides to test the
effectiveness of a user review of exception reports detailing sales in excess of authorized
credit limits, the user review and related follow up is the control that is directly of relevance
to the auditor. Controls over the accuracy of the information in the reports (for example, the
general IT controls) are described as 'indirect' controls.

Because of the inherent consistency of IT processing, audit evidence about the   **A31**
implementation of an automated application control, when considered in combination
with audit evidence about the operating effectiveness of the entity's general controls (in
particular, change controls), may also provide substantial audit evidence about its operating
effectiveness.

Timing of Tests of Controls

Intended period of reliance (Ref: Para. 11)

Audit evidence pertaining only to a point in time may be sufficient for the auditor's   **A32**
purpose, for example, when testing controls over the entity's physical inventory counting
at the period end. If, on the other hand, the auditor intends to rely on a control over a period,
tests that are capable of providing audit evidence that the control operated effectively at
relevant times during that period are appropriate. Such tests may include tests of the entity's
monitoring of controls.

Using audit evidence obtained during an interim period (Ref: Para. 12b)

Relevant factors in determining what additional audit evidence to obtain about controls   **A33**
that were operating during the period remaining after an interim period, include:

- The significance of the assessed risks of material misstatement at the assertion level.
- The specific controls that were tested during the interim period, and significant
  changes to them since they were tested, including changes in the information system,
  processes, and personnel.

- The degree to which audit evidence about the operating effectiveness of those controls was obtained.
- The length of the remaining period.
- The extent to which the auditor intends to reduce further substantive procedures based on the reliance of controls.
- The control environment.

A34   Additional audit evidence may be obtained, for example, by extending tests of controls over the remaining period or testing the entity's monitoring of controls.

Using audit evidence obtained in previous audits (Ref: Para. 13)

A35   In certain circumstances, audit evidence obtained from previous audits may provide audit evidence where the auditor performs audit procedures to establish its continuing relevance. For example, in performing a previous audit, the auditor may have determined that an automated control was functioning as intended. The auditor may obtain audit evidence to determine whether changes to the automated control have been made that affect its continued effective functioning through, for example, inquiries of management and the inspection of logs to indicate what controls have been changed. Consideration of audit evidence about these changes may support either increasing or decreasing the expected audit evidence to be obtained in the current period about the operating effectiveness of the controls.

Controls that have changed from previous audits (Ref: Para. 14(a))

A36   Changes may affect the relevance of the audit evidence obtained in previous audits such that there may no longer be a basis for continued reliance. For example, changes in a system that enable an entity to receive a new report from the system probably do not affect the relevance of audit evidence from a previous audit; however, a change that causes data to be accumulated or calculated differently does affect it.

Controls that have not changed from previous audits (Ref: Para. 14(b))

A37   The auditor's decision on whether to rely on audit evidence obtained in previous audits for controls that:

(a)   have not changed since they were last tested; and

(b)   are not controls that mitigate a significant risk,

is a matter of professional judgment. In addition, the length of time between retesting such controls is also a matter of professional judgment, but is required by paragraph 14(b) to be at least once in every third year.

A38   In general, the higher the risk of material misstatement, or the greater the reliance on controls, the shorter the time period elapsed, if any, is likely to be. Factors that may decrease the period for retesting a control, or result in not relying on audit evidence obtained in previous audits at all, include the following:

- A deficient control environment.
- Deficient monitoring of controls.
- A significant manual element to the relevant controls.
- Personnel changes that significantly affect the application of the control.
- Changing circumstances that indicate the need for changes in the control.
- Deficient general IT controls.

When there are a number of controls for which the auditor intends to rely on audit evidence obtained in previous audits, testing some of those controls in each audit provides corroborating information about the continuing effectiveness of the control environment. This contributes to the auditor's decision about whether it is appropriate to rely on audit evidence obtained in previous audits. **A39**

Evaluating the Operating Effectiveness of Controls (Ref: Para. 16–17)

A material misstatement detected by the auditor's procedures is a strong indicator of the existence of a significant deficiency in internal control. **A40**

The concept of effectiveness of the operation of controls recognizes that some deviations in the way controls are applied by the entity may occur. Deviations from prescribed controls may be caused by such factors as changes in key personnel, significant seasonal fluctuations in volume of transactions and human error. The detected rate of deviation, in particular in comparison with the expected rate, may indicate that the control cannot be relied on to reduce risk at the assertion level to that assessed by the auditor. **A41**

Substantive Procedures (Ref: Para. 18)

Paragraph 18 requires the auditor to design and perform substantive procedures for each material class of transactions, account balance, and disclosure, irrespective of the assessed risks of material misstatement. This requirement reflects the facts that: **A42**
(a) the auditor's assessment of risk is judgmental and so may not identify all risks of material misstatement; and
(b) there are inherent limitations to internal control, including management override.

Nature and Extent of Substantive Procedures

Depending on the circumstances, the auditor may determine that: **A43**

- Performing only substantive analytical procedures will be sufficient to reduce audit risk to an acceptably low level. For example, where the auditor's assessment of risk is supported by audit evidence from tests of controls.
- Only tests of details are appropriate.
- A combination of substantive analytical procedures and tests of details are most responsive to the assessed risks.

Substantive analytical procedures are generally more applicable to large volumes of transactions that tend to be predictable over time. ISA (UK) 520[5] establishes requirements and provides guidance on the application of analytical procedures during an audit. **A44**

The nature of the risk and assertion is relevant to the design of tests of details. For example, tests of details related to the existence or occurrence assertion may involve selecting from items contained in a financial statement amount and obtaining the relevant audit evidence. On the other hand, tests of details related to the completeness assertion may involve selecting from items that are expected to be included in the relevant financial statement amount and investigating whether they are included. **A45**

Because the assessment of the risk of material misstatement takes account of internal control, the extent of substantive procedures may need to be increased when the results **A46**

---

[5] *ISA (UK) 520*, Analytical Procedures.

from tests of controls are unsatisfactory. However, increasing the extent of an audit procedure is appropriate only if the audit procedure itself is relevant to the specific risk.

A47   In designing tests of details, the extent of testing is ordinarily thought of in terms of the sample size. However, other matters are also relevant, including whether it is more effective to use other selective means of testing. See ISA (UK) 500.[6]

Considering Whether External Confirmation Procedures Are to Be Performed (Ref: Para. 19)

A48   External confirmation procedures frequently are relevant when addressing assertions associated with account balances and their elements, but need not be restricted to these items. For example, the auditor may request external confirmation of the terms of agreements, contracts, or transactions between an entity and other parties. External confirmation procedures also may be performed to obtain audit evidence about the absence of certain conditions. For example, a request may specifically seek confirmation that no 'side agreement' exists that may be relevant to an entity's revenue cutoff assertion. Other situations where external confirmation procedures may provide relevant audit evidence in responding to assessed risks of material misstatement include:

- Bank balances and other information relevant to banking relationships.
- Accounts receivable balances and terms.
- Inventories held by third parties at bonded warehouses for processing or on consignment.
- Property title deeds held by lawyers or financiers for safe custody or as security.
- Investments held for safekeeping by third parties, or purchased from stockbrokers but not delivered at the balance sheet date.
- Amounts due to lenders, including relevant terms of repayment and restrictive covenants.
- Accounts payable balances and terms.

A49   Although external confirmations may provide relevant audit evidence relating to certain assertions, there are some assertions for which external confirmations provide less relevant audit evidence. For example, external confirmations provide less relevant audit evidence relating to the recoverability of accounts receivable balances, than they do of their existence.

A50   The auditor may determine that external confirmation procedures performed for one purpose provide an opportunity to obtain audit evidence about other matters. For example, confirmation requests for bank balances often include requests for information relevant to other financial statement assertions. Such considerations may influence the auditor's decision about whether to perform external confirmation procedures.

> In the UK, depending on the auditor's risk assessment, the auditor considers whether confirmation is needed in relation to additional information such as trade finance transactions and balances or information about guarantees and other third party securities, in addition to the confirmation of balances and other banking arrangements usually provided in such a request.

A51   Factors that may assist the auditor in determining whether external confirmation procedures are to be performed as substantive audit procedures include:

---

[6] ISA (UK) 500, Audit Evidence, *paragraph 10.*

- The confirming party's knowledge of the subject matter – responses may be more reliable if provided by a person at the confirming party who has the requisite knowledge about the information being confirmed.
- The ability or willingness of the intended confirming party to respond – for example, the confirming party:
  o May not accept responsibility for responding to a confirmation request;
  o May consider responding too costly or time consuming;
  o May have concerns about the potential legal liability resulting from responding;
  o May account for transactions in different currencies; or
  O May operate in an environment where responding to confirmation requests is not a significant aspect of day-to-day operations.

  In such situations, confirming parties may not respond, may respond in a casual manner or may attempt to restrict the reliance placed on the response.
- The objectivity of the intended confirming party – if the confirming party is a related party of the entity, responses to confirmation requests may be less reliable.

Valuation Methods (Ref: Para. 19R-1)

For audits of financial statements of public interest entities, ISA (UK) 260 (Revised June 2016)[6a] requires the auditor to communicate in the additional report to the audit committee the auditor's assessment of the valuation methods applied to the various items in the annual or consolidated financial statements including any impact of changes of such methods.

A51-1

Substantive Procedures Related to the Financial Statement Closing Process (Ref: Para. 20(b))

The nature, and also the extent, of the auditor's substantive procedures related to the financial statement closing process depends on the nature and complexity of the entity's financial reporting process and the related risks of material misstatement.

A52

Substantive Procedures Responsive to Significant Risks (Ref: Para. 21)

Paragraph 21 of this ISA (UK) requires the auditor to perform substantive procedures that are specifically responsive to risks the auditor has determined to be significant risks. Audit evidence in the form of external confirmations received directly by the auditor from appropriate confirming parties may assist the auditor in obtaining audit evidence with the high level of reliability that the auditor requires to respond to significant risks of material misstatement, whether due to fraud or error. For example, if the auditor identifies that management is under pressure to meet earnings expectations, there may be a risk that management is inflating sales by improperly recognizing revenue related to sales agreements with terms that preclude revenue recognition or by invoicing sales before shipment. In these circumstances, the auditor may, for example, design external confirmation procedures not only to confirm outstanding amounts, but also to confirm the details of the sales agreements, including date, any rights of return and delivery terms. In addition, the auditor may find it effective to supplement such external confirmation procedures with inquiries of non-financial personnel in the entity regarding any changes in sales agreements and delivery terms.

A53

[6a] *ISA (UK) 260 (Revised June 2016)*, Communication with Those Charged With Governance, *paragraph 16R-2(l).*

Timing of Substantive Procedures (Ref: Para. 22–23)

A54   In most cases, audit evidence from a previous audit's substantive procedures provides little or no audit evidence for the current period. There are, however, exceptions, for example, a legal opinion obtained in a previous audit related to the structure of a securitization to which no changes have occurred, may be relevant in the current period. In such cases, it may be appropriate to use audit evidence from a previous audit's substantive procedures if that evidence and the related subject matter have not fundamentally changed, and audit procedures have been performed during the current period to establish its continuing relevance.

Using audit evidence obtained during an interim period (Ref: Para. 22)

A55   In some circumstances, the auditor may determine that it is effective to perform substantive procedures at an interim date, and to compare and reconcile information concerning the balance at the period end with the comparable information at the interim date to:

(a)   Identify amounts that appear unusual;

(b)   Investigate any such amounts; and

(c)   Perform substantive analytical procedures or tests of details to test the intervening period.

A56   Performing substantive procedures at an interim date without undertaking additional procedures at a later date increases the risk that the auditor will not detect misstatements that may exist at the period end. This risk increases as the remaining period is lengthened. Factors such as the following may influence whether to perform substantive procedures at an interim date:

●   The control environment and other relevant controls.

●   The availability at a later date of information necessary for the auditor's procedures.

●   The purpose of the substantive procedure.

●   The assessed risk of material misstatement.

●   The nature of the class of transactions or account balance and related assertions.

●   The ability of the auditor to perform appropriate substantive procedures or substantive procedures combined with tests of controls to cover the remaining period in order to reduce the risk that misstatements that may exist at the period end will not be detected.

A57   Factors such as the following may influence whether to perform substantive analytical procedures with respect to the period between the interim date and the period end:

●   Whether the period end balances of the particular classes of transactions or account balances are reasonably predictable with respect to amount, relative significance, and composition.

●   Whether the entity's procedures for analyzing and adjusting such classes of transactions or account balances at interim dates and for establishing proper accounting cutoffs are appropriate.

●   Whether the information system relevant to financial reporting will provide information concerning the balances at the period end and the transactions in the remaining period that is sufficient to permit investigation of:

(a)   Significant unusual transactions or entries (including those at or near the period end);

(b)   Other causes of significant fluctuations, or expected fluctuations that did not occur; and

(c)   Other causes of significant fluctuations, or expected fluctuations that did not occur; and

Misstatements detected at an interim date (Ref: Para. 23)

When the auditor concludes that the planned nature, timing, or extent of substantive procedures covering the remaining period need to be modified as a result of unexpected misstatements detected at an interim date, such modification may include extending or repeating the procedures performed at the interim date at the period end. **A58**

Adequacy of Presentation of the Financial Statements (Ref: Para. 24)

Evaluating the appropriate presentation, arrangement and content of the financial statements, includes, for example, consideration of the terminology used as required by the applicable financial reporting framework, the level of detail provided, the aggregation and disaggregation of amounts, and the bases of amounts set forth. **A59**

Evaluating the Sufficiency and Appropriateness of Audit Evidence
(Ref: Para. 25–27)

An audit of financial statements is a cumulative and iterative process. As the auditor performs planned audit procedures, the audit evidence obtained may cause the auditor to modify the nature, timing or extent of other planned audit procedures. Information may come to the auditor's attention that differs significantly from the information on which the risk assessment was based. For example: **A60**

- The extent of misstatements that the auditor detects by performing substantive procedures may alter the auditor's judgment about the risk assessments and may indicate a significant deficiency in internal control.
- The auditor may become aware of discrepancies in accounting records, or conflicting or missing evidence.
- Analytical procedures performed at the overall review stage of the audit may indicate a previously unrecognized risk of material misstatement.

In such circumstances, the auditor may need to reevaluate the planned audit procedures, based on the revised consideration of assessed risks for all or some of the classes of transactions, account balances, or disclosures and related assertions. ISA (UK) 315 (Revised June 2016) contains further guidance on revising the auditor's risk assessment.[7]

The auditor cannot assume that an instance of fraud or error is an isolated occurrence. Therefore, the consideration of how the detection of a misstatement affects the assessed risks of material misstatement is important in determining whether the assessment remains appropriate. **A61**

The auditor's judgment as to what constitutes sufficient appropriate audit evidence is influenced by such factors as the following: **A62**

- Significance of the potential misstatement in the assertion and the likelihood of its having a material effect, individually or aggregated with other potential misstatements, on the financial statements.
- Effectiveness of management's responses and controls to address the risks.
- Experience gained during previous audits with respect to similar potential misstatements.
- Results of audit procedures performed, including whether such audit procedures identified specific instances of fraud or error.

---

[7] *ISA (UK) 315 (Revised June 2016), paragraph 31.*

- Source and reliability of the available information.
- Persuasiveness of the audit evidence.
- Understanding of the entity and its environment, including the entity's internal control.

Documentation (Ref: Para. 28)

A63   The form and extent of audit documentation is a matter of professional judgment, and is influenced by the nature, size and complexity of the entity and its internal control, availability of information from the entity and the audit methodology and technology used in the audit.

Annexure

Conforming Amendments to Other ISAs (UK)

This annexure shows the conforming amendments to ISAs (UK) as a result of ISA (UK) 330 (Revised July 2017) *The Auditor's Responses to Assessed Risks*. These amendments are effective for audits of financial statements for periods commencing on or after 15 December 2017, and are shown with marked changes from the latest published version of the ISA (UK).

ISA (UK) 505 External Confirmations

Factors to consider when designing confirmation requests include:[13a]   **A4**

- The assertions being addressed.
- Specific identified risks of material misstatement, including fraud risks.
- The layout and presentation of the confirmation request.
- Prior experience on the audit or similar engagements.
- The method of communication (for example, in paper form, or by electronic or other medium).
- Management's authorization or encouragement to the confirming parties to respond to the auditor. Confirming parties may only be willing to respond to a confirmation request containing management's authorization.
- The ability of the intended confirming party to confirm or provide the requested information (for example, individual invoice amount versus total balance).

[13a] *Pro-forma templates to obtain bank confirmations in the United Kingdom which have been agreed with the British Bankers' Association on behalf of the industry can be found at: https://www.bba.org.uk/policy/financial-and-risk-policy/financial-reporting/audit/instructions-for-using-pn16-templates/*

International Standard on Auditing (UK) 402

Audit considerations relating to an entity using a service organisation

(Effective for audits of financial statements for periods ending on or after 15 December 2010)

Contents

International Standard on Auditing (UK) (ISA (UK)) 402, *Audit Considerations Relating to an Entity Using a Service Organization*, should be read in conjunction with ISA (UK) 200 (Revised June 2016), *Overall Objectives of the Independent Auditor and the Conduct of an Audit in Accordance with International Standards on Auditing (UK)*.

Introduction

Scope of this ISA (UK)

This International Standard on Auditing (UK) (ISA (UK)) deals with the user auditor's **1** responsibility to obtain sufficient appropriate audit evidence when a user entity uses the services of one or more service organizations. Specifically, it expands on how the user auditor applies ISA (UK) 315 (Revised June 2016)[1] and ISA (UK) 330 (Revised June 2016)[2] in obtaining an understanding of the user entity, including internal control relevant to the audit, sufficient to identify and assess the risks of material misstatement and in designing and performing further audit procedures responsive to those risks.

Many entities outsource aspects of their business to organizations that provide services **2** ranging from performing a specific task under the direction of an entity to replacing an entity's entire business units or functions, such as the tax compliance function. Many of the services provided by such organizations are integral to the entity's business operations; however, not all those services are relevant to the audit.

Services provided by a service organization are relevant to the audit of a user entity's **3** financial statements when those services, and the controls over them, are part of the user entity's information system, including related business processes, relevant to financial reporting. Although most controls at the service organization are likely to relate to financial reporting, there may be other controls that may also be relevant to the audit, such as controls over the safeguarding of assets. A service organization's services are part of a user entity's information system, including related business processes, relevant to financial reporting if these services affect any of the following:

(a) The classes of transactions in the user entity's operations that are significant to the user entity's financial statements;
(b) The procedures, within both information technology (IT) and manual systems, by which the user entity's transactions are initiated, recorded, processed, corrected as necessary, transferred to the general ledger and reported in the financial statements;
(c) The related accounting records, either in electronic or manual form, supporting information and specific accounts in the user entity's financial statements that are used to initiate, record, process and report the user entity's transactions; this includes the correction of incorrect information and how information is transferred to the general ledger;
(d) How the user entity's information system captures events and conditions, other than transactions, that are significant to the financial statements;
(e) The financial reporting process used to prepare the user entity's financial statements, including significant accounting estimates and disclosures; and
(f) Controls surrounding journal entries, including non-standard journal entries used to record non-recurring, unusual transactions or adjustments.

The nature and extent of work to be performed by the user auditor regarding the services **4** provided by a service organization depend on the nature and significance of those services to the user entity and the relevance of those services to the audit.

This ISA (UK) does not apply to services provided by financial institutions that are **5** limited to processing, for an entity's account held at the financial institution, transactions that are specifically authorized by the entity, such as the processing of checking account

---

[1] *ISA (UK) 315 (Revised June 2016)*, Identifying and Assessing the Risks of Material Misstatement through Understanding the Entity and Its Environment.

[2] *ISA (UK) 330 (Revised June 2016)*, The Auditor's Responses to Assessed Risks.

transactions by a bank or the processing of securities transactions by a broker. In addition, this ISA (UK) does not apply to the audit of transactions arising from proprietary financial interests in other entities, such as partnerships, corporations and joint ventures, when proprietary interests are accounted for and reported to interest holders.

Effective Date

6   This ISA (UK) is effective for audits of financial statements for periods ending on or after 15 December 2010.

Objectives

7   The objectives of the user auditor, when the user entity uses the services of a service organization, are:

(a)   To obtain an understanding of the nature and significance of the services provided by the service organization and their effect on the user entity's internal control relevant to the audit, sufficient to identify and assess the risks of material misstatement; and

(b)   To design and perform audit procedures responsive to those risks.

Definitions

8   For purposes of the ISAs (UK), the following terms have the meanings attributed below:

(a)   Complementary user entity controls – Controls that the service organization assumes, in the design of its service, will be implemented by user entities, and which, if necessary to achieve control objectives, are identified in the description of its system.

(b)   Report on the description and design of controls at a service organization (referred to in this ISA (UK) as a type 1 report) – A report that comprises:

(i)   A description, prepared by management of the service organization, of the service organization's system, control objectives and related controls that have been designed and implemented as at a specified date; and

(ii)   A report by the service auditor with the objective of conveying reasonable assurance that includes the service auditor's opinion on the description of the service organization's system, control objectives and related controls and the suitability of the design of the controls to achieve the specified control objectives.

(c)   Report on the description, design, and operating effectiveness of controls at a service organization (referred to in this ISA (UK) as a type 2 report) – A report that comprises:

(i)   A description, prepared by management of the service organization, of the service organization's system, control objectives and related controls, their design and implementation as at a specified date or throughout a specified period and, in some cases, their operating effectiveness throughout a specified period; and

(ii)   A report by the service auditor with the objective of conveying reasonable assurance that includes:

a.   The service auditor's opinion on the description of the service organization's system, control objectives and related controls, the suitability of the design of the controls to achieve the specified control objectives, and the operating effectiveness of the controls; and

b.   A description of the service auditor's tests of the controls and the results thereof.

(d) Service auditor – An auditor who, at the request of the service organization, provides an assurance report on the controls of a service organization.

(e) Service organization – A third-party organization (or segment of a third-party organization) that provides services to user entities that are part of those entities' information systems relevant to financial reporting.

(f) Service organization's system – The policies and procedures designed, implemented and maintained by the service organization to provide user entities with the services covered by the service auditor's report.

(g) Subservice organization – A service organization used by another service organization to perform some of the services provided to user entities that are part of those user entities' information systems relevant to financial reporting.

(h) User auditor – An auditor who audits and reports on the financial statements of a user entity.

(i) User entity – An entity that uses a service organization and whose financial statements are being audited.

Requirements

Obtaining an Understanding of the Services Provided by a Service Organization, Including Internal Control

When obtaining an understanding of the user entity in accordance with ISA (UK) 315   **9** (Revised June 2016),[3] the user auditor shall obtain an understanding of how a user entity uses the services of a service organization in the user entity's operations, including: (Ref: Para. A1–A2)

(a) The nature of the services provided by the service organization and the significance of those services to the user entity, including the effect thereof on the user entity's internal control; (Ref: Para. A3–A5)

(b) The nature and materiality of the transactions processed or accounts or financial reporting processes affected by the service organization; (Ref: Para. A6)

(c) The degree of interaction between the activities of the service organization and those of the user entity; and (Ref: Para. A7)

(d) The nature of the relationship between the user entity and the service organization, including the relevant contractual terms for the activities undertaken by the service organization. (Ref: Para. A8–A11)

(e) If the service organization maintains all or part of a user entity's accounting records, whether those arrangements impact the work the auditor performs to fulfil reporting responsibilities in relation to accounting records that are established in law or regulation. (Ref: Para. A11-1–A11-3)

When obtaining an understanding of internal control relevant to the audit in accordance   **10** with ISA (UK) 315 (Revised June 2016),[4] the user auditor shall evaluate the design and implementation of relevant controls at the user entity that relate to the services provided by the service organization, including those that are applied to the transactions processed by the service organization. (Ref: Para. A12–A14)

The user auditor shall determine whether a sufficient understanding of the nature and   **11** significance of the services provided by the service organization and their effect on the

---

[3] *ISA (UK) 315 (Revised June 2016), paragraph 11.*

[4] *ISA (UK) 315 (Revised June 2016), paragraph 12.*

user entity's internal control relevant to the audit has been obtained to provide a basis for the identification and assessment of risks of material misstatement.

12   If the user auditor is unable to obtain a sufficient understanding from the user entity, the user auditor shall obtain that understanding from one or more of the following procedures:

(a) Obtaining a type 1 or type 2 report, if available;
(b) Contacting the service organization, through the user entity, to obtain specific information;
(c) Visiting the service organization and performing procedures that will provide the necessary information about the relevant controls at the service organization; or
(d) Using another auditor to perform procedures that will provide the necessary information about the relevant controls at the service organization. (Ref: Para. A15–A20)

Using a Type 1 or Type 2 Report to Support the User Auditor's Understanding of the Service Organization

13   In determining the sufficiency and appropriateness of the audit evidence provided by a type 1 or type 2 report, the user auditor shall be satisfied as to:

(a) The service auditor's professional competence and independence from the service organization; and
(b) The adequacy of the standards under which the type 1 or type 2 report was issued. (Ref: Para. A21)

14   If the user auditor plans to use a type 1 or type 2 report as audit evidence to support the user auditor's understanding about the design and implementation of controls at the service organization, the user auditor shall:

(a) Evaluate whether the description and design of controls at the service organization is at a date or for a period that is appropriate for the user auditor's purposes;
(b) Evaluate the sufficiency and appropriateness of the evidence provided by the report for the understanding of the user entity's internal control relevant to the audit; and
(c) Determine whether complementary user entity controls identified by the service organization are relevant to the user entity and, if so, obtain an understanding of whether the user entity has designed and implemented such controls. (Ref: Para. A22–A23)

Responding to the Assessed Risks of Material Misstatement

15   In responding to assessed risks in accordance with ISA (UK) 330 (Revised June 2016), the user auditor shall:

(a) Determine whether sufficient appropriate audit evidence concerning the relevant financial statement assertions is available from records held at the user entity; and, if not,
(b) Perform further audit procedures to obtain sufficient appropriate audit evidence or use another auditor to perform those procedures at the service organization on the user auditor's behalf. (Ref: Para. A24–A28)

Tests of Controls

16   When the user auditor's risk assessment includes an expectation that controls at the service organization are operating effectively, the user auditor shall obtain audit evidence about the operating effectiveness of those controls from one or more of the following procedures:

(a) Obtaining a type 2 report, if available;
(b) Performing appropriate tests of controls at the service organization; or
(c) Using another auditor to perform tests of controls at the service organization on behalf of the user auditor. (Ref: Para. A29–A30)

Using a Type 2 Report as Audit Evidence that Controls at the Service Organization Are Operating Effectively

If, in accordance with paragraph 16(a), the user auditor plans to use a type 2 report as audit evidence that controls at the service organization are operating effectively, the user auditor shall determine whether the service auditor's report provides sufficient appropriate audit evidence about the effectiveness of the controls to support the user auditor's risk assessment by: **17**

(a) Evaluating whether the description, design and operating effectiveness of controls at the service organization is at a date or for a period that is appropriate for the user auditor's purposes;
(b) Determining whether complementary user entity controls identified by the service organization are relevant to the user entity and, if so, obtaining an understanding of whether the user entity has designed and implemented such controls and, if so, testing their operating effectiveness;
(c) Evaluating the adequacy of the time period covered by the tests of controls and the time elapsed since the performance of the tests of controls; and
(d) Evaluating whether the tests of controls performed by the service auditor and the results thereof, as described in the service auditor's report, are relevant to the assertions in the user entity's financial statements and provide sufficient appropriate audit evidence to support the user auditor's risk assessment. (Ref: Para. A31–A39)

Type 1 and Type 2 Reports that Exclude the Services of a Subservice Organization

If the user auditor plans to use a type 1 or a type 2 report that excludes the services provided by a subservice organization and those services are relevant to the audit of the user entity's financial statements, the user auditor shall apply the requirements of this ISA (UK) with respect to the services provided by the subservice organization. (Ref: Para. A40) **18**

Fraud, Non-Compliance with Laws and Regulations and Uncorrected Misstatements in Relation to Activities at the Service Organization

The user auditor shall inquire of management of the user entity whether the service organization has reported to the user entity, or whether the user entity is otherwise aware of, any fraud, non-compliance with laws and regulations or uncorrected misstatements affecting the financial statements of the user entity. The user auditor shall evaluate how such matters affect the nature, timing and extent of the user auditor's further audit procedures, including the effect on the user auditor's conclusions and user auditor's report. (Ref: Para. A41) **19**

Reporting by the User Auditor

The user auditor shall modify the opinion in the user auditor's report in accordance with ISA (UK) 705 (Revised June 2016)[5] if the user auditor is unable to obtain sufficient appropriate audit evidence regarding the services provided by the service organization relevant to the audit of the user entity's financial statements. (Ref: Para. A42) **20**

---

[5] *ISA (UK) 705 (Revised June 2016)*, Modifications to the Opinion in the Independent Auditor's Report, *paragraph 6*.

21   The user auditor shall not refer to the work of a service auditor in the user auditor's report containing an unmodified opinion unless required by law or regulation to do so. If such reference is required by law or regulation, the user auditor's report shall indicate that the reference does not diminish the user auditor's responsibility for the audit opinion. (Ref: Para. A43)

22   If reference to the work of a service auditor is relevant to an understanding of a modification to the user auditor's opinion, the user auditor's report shall indicate that such reference does not diminish the user auditor's responsibility for that opinion. (Ref: Para. A44)

Application and Other Explanatory Material

Obtaining an Understanding of the Services Provided by a Service Organization, Including Internal Control

Sources of Information (Ref: Para. 9)

A1   Information on the nature of the services provided by a service organization may be available from a wide variety of sources, such as:

- User manuals.
- System overviews.
- Technical manuals.
- The contract or service level agreement between the user entity and the service organization.
- Reports by service organizations, the internal audit function or regulatory authorities on controls at the service organization.
- Reports by the service auditor, including management letters, if available.

A2   Knowledge obtained through the user auditor's experience with the service organization, for example through experience with other audit engagements, may also be helpful in obtaining an understanding of the nature of the services provided by the service organization. This may be particularly helpful if the services and controls at the service organization over those services are highly standardized.

Nature of the Services Provided by the Service Organization (Ref: Para. 9(a))

A3   A user entity may use a service organization such as one that processes transactions and maintains related accountability, or records transactions and processes related data. Service organizations that provide such services include, for example, bank trust departments that invest and service assets for employee benefit plans or for others; mortgage bankers that service mortgages for others; and application service providers that provide packaged software applications and a technology environment that enables customers to process financial and operational transactions.

A4   Examples of service organization services that are relevant to the audit include:

- Maintenance of the user entity's accounting records.
- Management of assets.
- Initiating, recording or processing transactions as agent of the user entity.

Compliance with Law and Regulations

The user auditor considers whether the activities undertaken by the service organization are in an area in which the user entity is required to comply with requirements of law and regulations (for example, there are legal requirements relating to the maintenance of accounting records by companies – see paragraphs A11-1– A11-3). In such circumstances, non-compliance may have a significant effect on the financial statements. The user auditor therefore determines whether the law and regulations concerned are to be regarded as relevant to the audit[5a] in order to meet the requirements of ISA (UK) 250 (Revised June 2016) Section A 'Consideration of Laws and Regulations in an Audit of Financial Statements' and undertake procedures to assess the risk of a misstatement arising from non-compliance as set out in that ISA (UK). **A4-1**

Considerations Specific to Smaller Entities

Smaller entities may use external bookkeeping services ranging from the processing of certain transactions (for example, payment of payroll taxes) and maintenance of their accounting records to the preparation of their financial statements. The use of such a service organization for the preparation of its financial statements does not relieve management of the smaller entity and, where appropriate, those charged with governance of their responsibilities for the financial statements.[6] **A5**

Nature and Materiality of Transactions Processed by the Service Organization
(Ref: Para. 9(b))

A service organization may establish policies and procedures that affect the user entity's internal control. These policies and procedures are at least in part physically and operationally separate from the user entity. The significance of the controls of the service organization to those of the user entity depends on the nature of the services provided by the service organization, including the nature and materiality of the transactions it processes for the user entity. In certain situations, the transactions processed and the accounts affected by the service organization may not appear to be material to the user entity's financial statements, but the nature of the transactions processed may be significant and the user auditor may determine that an understanding of those controls is necessary in the circumstances. **A6**

The Degree of Interaction between the Activities of the Service Organization and the User Entity (Ref: Para. 9(c))

The significance of the controls of the service organization to those of the user entity also depends on the degree of interaction between its activities and those of the user entity. The degree of interaction refers to the extent to which a user entity is able to and elects to implement effective controls over the processing performed by the service organization. For example, a high degree of interaction exists between the activities of the user entity and those at the service organization when the user entity authorizes transactions and the service organization processes and does the accounting for those transactions. In these circumstances, it may be practicable for the user entity to implement effective controls **A7**

[5a] *Laws and regulations are relevant to the audit when they either relate directly to the preparation of the financial statements of the entity, or are fundamental to the operating aspects of its business (ISA (UK) 250 (Revised June 2016) Section A,* Consideration of Laws and Regulations in an Audit of Financial Statements, *paragraph 6).*

[6] *ISA (UK) 200 (Revised June 2016),* Overall Objectives of the Independent Auditor and the Conduct of an Audit in Accordance with International Standards on Auditing (UK), *paragraphs 4 and A2–A3.*

over those transactions. On the other hand, when the service organization initiates or initially records, processes, and does the accounting for the user entity's transactions, there is a lower degree of interaction between the two organizations. In these circumstances, the user entity may be unable to, or may elect not to, implement effective controls over these transactions at the user entity and may rely on controls at the service organization.

Nature of the Relationship between the User Entity and the Service Organization (Ref: Para. 9(d))

A8   The contract or service level agreement between the user entity and the service organization may provide for matters such as:

- The information to be provided to the user entity and responsibilities for initiating transactions relating to the activities undertaken by the service organization;
- The application of requirements of regulatory bodies concerning the form of records to be maintained, or access to them;
- The indemnification, if any, to be provided to the user entity in the event of a performance failure;
- Whether the service organization will provide a report on its controls and, if so, whether such report would be a type 1 or type 2 report;
- Whether the user auditor has rights of access to the accounting records of the user entity maintained by the service organization and other information necessary for the conduct of the audit; and
- Whether the agreement allows for direct communication between the user auditor and the service auditor.

A8-1   Other matters which the auditor may consider include:
- The way that accounting records relating to relevant activities are maintained.
- Whether the entity has rights of access to accounting records prepared by the service organization concerning the activities undertaken, and relevant underlying information held by it, and the conditions in which such access may be sought.
- The nature of relevant performance standards.
- The way in which the entity monitors performance of relevant activities and the extent to which its monitoring process relies on controls operated by the service organization.

A8-2   Agreement by a service organization to provide an indemnity does not provide information directly relevant to the user auditor's assessment of the risk of material misstatements relating to financial statement assertions. However, such agreements may help to inform the user auditor's judgment concerning the effect of performance failure on the user entity's financial statements: this may be relevant in instances of performance failure, when the existence of an indemnity may help to ensure that the user entity's status as a going concern is not threatened. Where the user auditor wishes to rely on the operation of the indemnity for this purpose, the resources available to the service organization also need to be considered.

A8-3   The financial standing of a service organization is relevant to the audit insofar as the user auditor considers it necessary to rely on the operation of an indemnity from the service organization in assessing the entity's status as a going concern (see paragraph A8-2). However, a service organization whose cash and/or capital resources are low in relation to the nature of services provided or the volume of its customers may be susceptible to pressures resulting in errors or deliberate misstatements in reporting to the entity, or fraud. If the user auditor considers that this factor may be relevant to the assessment of risk, the user auditor also takes into account the existence of binding arrangements to provide resources to the service organizations from a holding company or other group company, and the financial strength of the group as a whole.

There is a direct relationship between the service organization and the user entity and between the service organization and the service auditor. These relationships do not necessarily create a direct relationship between the user auditor and the service auditor. When there is no direct relationship between the user auditor and the service auditor, communications between the user auditor and the service auditor are usually conducted through the user entity and the service organization. A direct relationship may also be created between a user auditor and a service auditor, taking into account the relevant ethical and confidentiality considerations. A user auditor, for example, may use a service auditor to perform procedures on the user auditor's behalf, such as: **A9**

(a) Tests of controls at the service organization; or
(b) Substantive procedures on the user entity's financial statement transactions and balances maintained by a service organization.

Considerations Specific to Public Sector Entities

Public sector auditors generally have broad rights of access established by legislation. However, there may be situations where such rights of access are not available, for example when the service organization is located in a different jurisdiction. In such cases, a public sector auditor may need to obtain an understanding of the legislation applicable in the different jurisdiction to determine whether appropriate access rights can be obtained. A public sector auditor may also obtain or ask the user entity to incorporate rights of access in any contractual arrangements between the user entity and the service organization.   **A10**

Public sector auditors may also use another auditor to perform tests of controls or substantive procedures in relation to compliance with law, regulation or other authority.   **A11**

Accounting Records (Ref: Para. 9(e))

Use of a service organization does not diminish the ultimate responsibility of those charged with governance of a user entity for conducting its business in a manner which meets their legal responsibilities, including those of safeguarding the user entity's assets, maintaining adequate accounting records and preparing financial statements which provide information about its economic activities and financial position. Practical issues, including the way in which accounting records will be kept and the manner in which those charged with governance assess the quality of the service, need to be addressed.   **A11-1**

An auditor of an entity incorporated under company law has statutory reporting obligations relating to compliance with requirements for companies to maintain adequate accounting records. Where such an entity outsources the preparation of its accounting records to a service organization, issues relating to whether the arrangements with the service organization are such as to permit the user entity to meet its statutory obligations may require careful consideration, by both those charged with governance and the user auditor. Where there is doubt, the user auditor may wish to encourage those charged with governance to take legal advice before issuing the auditor's report on its financial statements.   **A11-2**

A particular issue arises in relation to companies incorporated in the UK. The wording of UK company law appears to be prescriptive and to require the company itself to keep accounting records. Consequently, whether a company 'keeps' records (as opposed to 'causes records to be kept') will depend upon the particular terms of the outsourcing arrangements and, in particular, the extent to which the company retains ownership of, has access to, or holds copies of, those records.   **A11-3**

Understanding the Controls Relating to Services Provided by the Service Organization (Ref: Para. 10)

A12   The user entity may establish controls over the service organization's services that may be tested by the user auditor and that may enable the user auditor to conclude that the user entity's controls are operating effectively for some or all of the related assertions, regardless of the controls in place at the service organization. If a user entity, for example, uses a service organization to process its payroll transactions, the user entity may establish controls over the submission and receipt of payroll information that could prevent or detect material misstatements. These controls may include:

- Comparing the data submitted to the service organization with reports of information received from the service organization after the data has been processed.
- Recomputing a sample of the payroll amounts for clerical accuracy and reviewing the total amount of the payroll for reasonableness.

A13   In this situation, the user auditor may perform tests of the user entity's controls over payroll processing that would provide a basis for the user auditor to conclude that the user entity's controls are operating effectively for the assertions related to payroll transactions.

A14   As noted in ISA (UK) 315 (Revised June 2016),[7] in respect of some risks, the user auditor may judge that it is not possible or practicable to obtain sufficient appropriate audit evidence only from substantive procedures. Such risks may relate to the inaccurate or incomplete recording of routine and significant classes of transactions and account balances, the characteristics of which often permit highly automated processing with little or no manual intervention. Such automated processing characteristics may be particularly present when the user entity uses service organizations. In such cases, the user entity's controls over such risks are relevant to the audit and the user auditor is required to obtain an understanding of, and to evaluate, such controls in accordance with paragraphs 9 and 10 of this ISA (UK).

Further Procedures When a Sufficient Understanding Cannot Be Obtained from the User Entity (Ref: Para. 12)

A15   The user auditor's decision as to which procedure, individually or in combination, in paragraph 12 to undertake, in order to obtain the information necessary to provide a basis for the identification and assessment of the risks of material misstatement in relation to the user entity's use of the service organization, may be influenced by such matters as:

- The size of both the user entity and the service organization;
- The complexity of the transactions at the user entity and the complexity of the services provided by the service organization;
- The location of the service organization (for example, the user auditor may decide to use another auditor to perform procedures at the service organization on the user auditor's behalf if the service organization is in a remote location);
- Whether the procedure(s) is expected to effectively provide the user auditor with sufficient appropriate audit evidence; and
- The nature of the relationship between the user entity and the service organization.

A16   A service organization may engage a service auditor to report on the description and design of its controls (type 1 report) or on the description and design of its controls and their operating effectiveness (type 2 report). Type 1 or type 2 reports may be issued under International Standard on Assurance Engagements (ISAE) 3402[8] or under standards

---

[7] *ISA (UK) 315 (Revised June 2016), paragraph 30.*

[8] *ISAE 3402*, Assurance Reports on Controls at a Third Party Service Organization.

established by an authorized or recognized standards setting organization (which may identify them by different names, such as Type A or Type B reports).

The availability of a type 1 or type 2 report will generally depend on whether the contract   **A17**
between a service organization and a user entity includes the provision of such a report by the service organization. A service organization may also elect, for practical reasons, to make a type 1 or type 2 report available to the user entities. However, in some cases, a type 1 or type 2 report may not be available to user entities.

In some circumstances, a user entity may outsource one or more significant business units   **A18**
or functions, such as its entire tax planning and compliance functions, or finance and accounting or the controllership function to one or more service organizations. As a report on controls at the service organization may not be available in these circumstances, visiting the service organization may be the most effective procedure for the user auditor to gain an understanding of controls at the service organization, as there is likely to be direct interaction of management of the user entity with management at the service organization.

Another auditor may be used to perform procedures that will provide the necessary   **A19**
information about the relevant controls at the service organization. If a type 1 or type 2 report has been issued, the user auditor may use the service auditor to perform these procedures as the service auditor has an existing relationship with the service organization. The user auditor using the work of another auditor may find the guidance in ISA (UK) 600 (Revised June 2016)[9] useful as it relates to understanding another auditor (including that auditor's independence and professional competence), involvement in the work of another auditor in planning the nature, extent and timing of such work, and in evaluating the sufficiency and appropriateness of the audit evidence obtained.

A user entity may use a service organization that in turn uses a subservice organization   **A20**
to provide some of the services provided to a user entity that are part of the user entity's information system relevant to financial reporting. The subservice organization may be a separate entity from the service organization or may be related to the service organization. A user auditor may need to consider controls at the subservice organization. In situations where one or more subservice organizations are used, the interaction between the activities of the user entity and those of the service organization is expanded to include the interaction between the user entity, the service organization and the subservice organizations. The degree of this interaction, as well as the nature and materiality of the transactions processed by the service organization and the subservice organizations are the most important factors for the user auditor to consider in determining the significance of the service organization's and subservice organization's controls to the user entity's controls.

Using a Type 1 or Type 2 Report to Support the User Auditor's Understanding of the Service Organization (Ref: Para. 13–14)

The user auditor may make inquiries about the service auditor to the service auditor's   **A21**
professional organization or other practitioners and inquire whether the service auditor is subject to regulatory oversight. The service auditor may be practicing in a jurisdiction where different standards are followed in respect of reports on controls at a service organization, and the user auditor may obtain information about the standards used by the service auditor from the standard setting organization.

---

[9] *ISA (UK) 600 (Revised June 2016)*, Special Considerations-Audits of Group Financial Statements (Including the Work of Component Auditors), *paragraph 2, states: 'An auditor may find this ISA (UK), adapted as necessary in the circumstances, useful when that auditor involves other auditors in the audit of financial statements that are not group financial statements…' See also paragraph 19 of ISA (UK) 600 (Revised June 2016).*

A22   A type 1 or type 2 report, along with information about the user entity, may assist the user auditor in obtaining an understanding of:

(a)   The aspects of controls at the service organization that may affect the processing of the user entity's transactions, including the use of subservice organizations;

(b)   The flow of significant transactions through the service organization to determine the points in the transaction flow where material misstatements in the user entity's financial statements could occur;

(c)   The control objectives at the service organization that are relevant to the user entity's financial statement assertions; and

(d)   Whether controls at the service organization are suitably designed and implemented to prevent or detect processing errors that could result in material misstatements in the user entity's financial statements.

A type 1 or type 2 report may assist the user auditor in obtaining a sufficient understanding to identify and assess the risks of material misstatement. A type 1 report, however, does not provide any evidence of the operating effectiveness of the relevant controls.

A23   A type 1 or type 2 report that is as of a date or for a period that is outside of the reporting period of a user entity may assist the user auditor in obtaining a preliminary understanding of the controls implemented at the service organization if the report is supplemented by additional current information from other sources. If the service organization's description of controls is as of a date or for a period that precedes the beginning of the period under audit, the user auditor may perform procedures to update the information in a type 1 or type 2 report, such as:

● Discussing the changes at the service organization with user entity personnel who would be in a position to know of such changes;

● Reviewing current documentation and correspondence issued by the service organization; or

● Discussing the changes with service organization personnel.

Responding to the Assessed Risks of Material Misstatement (Ref: Para. 15)

A24   Whether the use of a service organization increases a user entity's risk of material misstatement depends on the nature of the services provided and the controls over these services; in some cases, the use of a service organization may decrease a user entity's risk of material misstatement, particularly if the user entity itself does not possess the expertise necessary to undertake particular activities, such as initiating, processing, and recording transactions, or does not have adequate resources (for example, an IT system).

A25   When the service organization maintains material elements of the accounting records of the user entity, direct access to those records may be necessary in order for the user auditor to obtain sufficient appropriate audit evidence relating to the operations of controls over those records or to substantiate transactions and balances recorded in them, or both. Such access may involve either physical inspection of records at the service organization's premises or interrogation of records maintained electronically from the user entity or another location, or both. Where direct access is achieved electronically, the user auditor may thereby obtain evidence as to the adequacy of controls operated by the service organization over the completeness and integrity of the user entity's data for which the service organization is responsible.

A26   In determining the nature and extent of audit evidence to be obtained in relation to balances representing assets held or transactions undertaken by a service organization on behalf of the user entity, the following procedures may be considered by the user auditor:

(a) Inspecting records and documents held by the user entity: the reliability of this source of evidence is determined by the nature and extent of the accounting records and supporting documentation retained by the user entity. In some cases, the user entity may not maintain independent detailed records or documentation of specific transactions undertaken on its behalf.

(b) Inspecting records and documents held by the service organization: the user auditor's access to the records of the service organization may be established as part of the contractual arrangements between the user entity and the service organization. The user auditor may also use another auditor, on its behalf, to gain access to the user entity's records maintained by the service organization.

(c) Obtaining confirmations of balances and transactions from the service organization: where the user entity maintains independent records of balances and transactions, confirmation from the service organization corroborating the user entity's records may constitute reliable audit evidence concerning the existence of the transactions and assets concerned. For example, when multiple service organizations are used, such as an investment manager and a custodian, and these service organizations maintain independent records, the user auditor may confirm balances with these organizations in order to compare this information with the independent records of the user entity.

If the user entity does not maintain independent records, information obtained in confirmations from the service organization is merely a statement of what is reflected in the records maintained by the service organization. Therefore, such confirmations do not, taken alone, constitute reliable audit evidence. In these circumstances, the user auditor may consider whether an alternative source of independent evidence can be identified.

(d) Performing analytical procedures on the records maintained by the user entity or on the reports received from the service organization: the effectiveness of analytical procedures is likely to vary by assertion and will be affected by the extent and detail of information available.

Another auditor may perform procedures that are substantive in nature for the benefit **A27** of user auditors. Such an engagement may involve the performance, by another auditor, of procedures agreed upon by the user entity and its user auditor and by the service organization and its service auditor. The findings resulting from the procedures performed by another auditor are reviewed by the user auditor to determine whether they constitute sufficient appropriate audit evidence. In addition, there may be requirements imposed by governmental authorities or through contractual arrangements whereby a service auditor performs designated procedures that are substantive in nature. The results of the application of the required procedures to balances and transactions processed by the service organization may be used by user auditors as part of the evidence necessary to support their audit opinions. In these circumstances, it may be useful for the user auditor and the service auditor to agree, prior to the performance of the procedures, to the audit documentation or access to audit documentation that will be provided to the user auditor.

In certain circumstances, in particular when a user entity outsources some or all of its finance **A28** function to a service organization, the user auditor may face a situation where a significant portion of the audit evidence resides at the service organization. Substantive procedures may need to be performed at the service organization by the user auditor or another auditor on its behalf. A service auditor may provide a type 2 report and, in addition, may perform substantive procedures on behalf of the user auditor. The involvement of another auditor does not alter the user auditor's responsibility to obtain sufficient appropriate audit evidence to afford a reasonable basis to support the user auditor's opinion. Accordingly, the user auditor's consideration of whether sufficient appropriate audit evidence has been obtained and whether the user auditor needs to perform further substantive procedures includes the user auditor's involvement with, or evidence of, the direction, supervision and performance of the substantive procedures performed by another auditor.

Tests of Controls (Ref: Para. 16)

A29   The user auditor is required by ISA (UK) 330 (Revised June 2016)10 to design and perform tests of controls to obtain sufficient appropriate audit evidence as to the operating effectiveness of relevant controls in certain circumstances. In the context of a service organization, this requirement applies when:

(a) The user auditor's assessment of risks of material misstatement includes an expectation that the controls at the service organization are operating effectively (that is, the user auditor intends to rely on the operating effectiveness of controls at the service organization in determining the nature, timing and extent of substantive procedures); or

(b) Substantive procedures alone, or in combination with tests of the operating effectiveness of controls at the user entity, cannot provide sufficient appropriate audit evidence at the assertion level.

A30   If a type 2 report is not available, a user auditor may contact the service organization, through the user entity, to request that a service auditor be engaged to provide a type 2 report that includes tests of the operating effectiveness of the relevant controls or the user auditor may use another auditor to perform procedures at the service organization that test the operating effectiveness of those controls. A user auditor may also visit the service organization and perform tests of relevant controls if the service organization agrees to it. The user auditor's risk assessments are based on the combined evidence provided by the work of another auditor and the user auditor's own procedures.

Using a Type 2 Report as Audit Evidence that Controls at the Service Organization Are Operating Effectively (Ref: Para. 17)

A31   A type 2 report may be intended to satisfy the needs of several different user auditors; therefore tests of controls and results described in the service auditor's report may not be relevant to assertions that are significant in the user entity's financial statements. The relevant tests of controls and results are evaluated to determine that the service auditor's report provides sufficient appropriate audit evidence about the effectiveness of the controls to support the user auditor's risk assessment. In doing so, the user auditor may consider the following factors:

(a) The time period covered by the tests of controls and the time elapsed since the performance of the tests of controls;

(b) The scope of the service auditor's work and the services and processes covered, the controls tested and tests that were performed, and the way in which tested controls relate to the user entity's controls; and

(c) The results of those tests of controls and the service auditor's opinion on the operating effectiveness of the controls.

A32   For certain assertions, the shorter the period covered by a specific test and the longer the time elapsed since the performance of the test, the less audit evidence the test may provide. In comparing the period covered by the type 2 report to the user entity's financial reporting period, the user auditor may conclude that the type 2 report offers less audit evidence if there is little overlap between the period covered by the type 2 report and

---

[10] *ISA (UK) 330 (Revised June 2016), paragraph 8.*

the period for which the user auditor intends to rely on the report. When this is the case, a type 2 report covering a preceding or subsequent period may provide additional audit evidence. In other cases, the user auditor may determine it is necessary to perform, or use another auditor to perform, tests of controls at the service organization in order to obtain sufficient appropriate audit evidence about the operating effectiveness of those controls.

It may also be necessary for the user auditor to obtain additional evidence about significant changes to the relevant controls at the service organization outside of the period covered by the type 2 report or determine additional audit procedures to be performed. Relevant factors in determining what additional audit evidence to obtain about controls at the service organization that were operating outside of the period covered by the service auditor's report may include: **A33**

- The significance of the assessed risks of material misstatement at the assertion level;
- The specific controls that were tested during the interim period, and significant changes to them since they were tested, including changes in the information system, processes, and personnel;
- The degree to which audit evidence about the operating effectiveness of those controls was obtained;
- The length of the remaining period;
- The extent to which the user auditor intends to reduce further substantive procedures based on the reliance on controls; and
- The effectiveness of the control environment and monitoring of controls at the user entity.

Additional audit evidence may be obtained, for example, by extending tests of controls over the remaining period or testing the user entity's monitoring of controls. **A34**

If the service auditor's testing period is completely outside the user entity's financial reporting period, the user auditor will be unable to rely on such tests for the user auditor to conclude that the user entity's controls are operating effectively because they do not provide current audit period evidence of the effectiveness of the controls, unless other procedures are performed. **A35**

In certain circumstances, a service provided by the service organization may be designed with the assumption that certain controls will be implemented by the user entity. For example, the service may be designed with the assumption that the user entity will have controls in place for authorizing transactions before they are sent to the service organization for processing. In such a situation, the service organization's description of controls may include a description of those complementary user entity controls. The user auditor considers whether those complementary user entity controls are relevant to the service provided to the user entity. **A36**

If the user auditor believes that the service auditor's report may not provide sufficient appropriate audit evidence, for example, if a service auditor's report does not contain a description of the service auditor's tests of controls and results thereon, the user auditor may supplement the understanding of the service auditor's procedures and conclusions by contacting the service organization, through the user entity, to request a discussion with the service auditor about the scope and results of the service auditor's work. Also, if the user auditor believes it is necessary, the user auditor may contact the service organization, through the user entity, to request that the service auditor perform procedures at the service organization. Alternatively, the user auditor, or another auditor at the request of the user auditor, may perform such procedures. **A37**

The service auditor's type 2 report identifies results of tests, including exceptions and other information that could affect the user auditor's conclusions. Exceptions noted by **A38** the service auditor or a modified opinion in the service auditor's type 2 report do not automatically mean that the service auditor's type 2 report will not be useful for the audit of the user entity's financial statements in assessing the risks of material misstatement. Rather, the exceptions and the matter giving rise to a modified opinion in the service auditor's type 2 report are considered in the user auditor's assessment of the testing of controls performed by the service auditor. In considering the exceptions and matters giving rise to a modified opinion, the user auditor may discuss such matters with the service auditor. Such communication is dependent upon the user entity contacting the service organization, and obtaining the service organization's approval for the communication to take place.

Communication of deficiencies in internal control identified during the audit

A39   The user auditor is required to communicate in writing significant deficiencies identified during the audit to both management and those charged with governance on a timely basis.[11] The user auditor is also required to communicate to management at an appropriate level of responsibility on a timely basis other deficiencies in internal control identified during the audit that, in the user auditor's professional judgment, are of sufficient importance to merit management's attention.[12] Matters that the user auditor may identify during the audit and may communicate to management and those charged with governance of the user entity include:

- Any monitoring of controls that could be implemented by the user entity, including those identified as a result of obtaining a type 1 or type 2 report;
- Instances where complementary user entity controls are noted in the type 1 or type 2 report and are not implemented at the user entity; and
- Controls that may be needed at the service organization that do not appear to have been implemented or that are not specifically covered by a type 2 report.

Type 1 and Type 2 Reports that Exclude the Services of a Subservice Organization (Ref: Para. 18)

A40   If a service organization uses a subservice organization, the service auditor's report may either include or exclude the subservice organization's relevant control objectives and related controls in the service organization's description of its system and in the scope of the service auditor's engagement. These two methods of reporting are known as the inclusive method and the carve-out method, respectively. If the type 1 or type 2 report excludes the controls at a subservice organization, and the services provided by the subservice organization are relevant to the audit of the user entity's financial statements, the user auditor is required to apply the requirements of this ISA (UK) in respect of the subservice organization. The nature and extent of work to be performed by the user auditor regarding the services provided by a subservice organization depend on the nature and significance of those services to the user entity and the relevance of those services to the audit. The application of the requirement in paragraph 9 assists the user auditor in determining the effect of the subservice organization and the nature and extent of work to be performed.

---

[11] *ISA (UK) 265*, Communicating Deficiencies in Internal Control to Those Charged with Governance and Management, *paragraphs 9–10.*

[12] *ISA (UK) 265, paragraph 10.*

Fraud, Non-Compliance with Laws and Regulations and Uncorrected Misstatements in Relation to Activities at the Service Organization
(Ref: Para. 19)

A service organization may be required under the terms of the contract with user entities **A41** to disclose to affected user entities any fraud, non-compliance with laws and regulations or uncorrected misstatements attributable to the service organization's management or employees. As required by paragraph 19, the user auditor makes inquiries of the user entity management regarding whether the service organization has reported any such matters and evaluates whether any matters reported by the service organization affect the nature, timing and extent of the user auditor's further audit procedures. In certain circumstances, the user auditor may require additional information to perform this evaluation, and may request the user entity to contact the service organization to obtain the necessary information.

Reporting by the User Auditor (Ref: Para. 20)

When a user auditor is unable to obtain sufficient appropriate audit evidence regarding **A42** the services provided by the service organization relevant to the audit of the user entity's financial statements, a limitation on the scope of the audit exists. This may be the case when:

- The user auditor is unable to obtain a sufficient understanding of the services provided by the service organization and does not have a basis for the identification and assessment of the risks of material misstatement;
- A user auditor's risk assessment includes an expectation that controls at the service organization are operating effectively and the user auditor is unable to obtain sufficient appropriate audit evidence about the operating effectiveness of these controls; or
- Sufficient appropriate audit evidence is only available from records held at the service organization, and the user auditor is unable to obtain direct access to these records.

Whether the user auditor expresses a qualified opinion or disclaims an opinion depends on the user auditor's conclusion as to whether the possible effects on the financial statements are material or pervasive.

Reference to the Work of a Service Auditor (Ref: Para. 21–22)

In some cases, law or regulation may require a reference to the work of a service auditor in **A43** the user auditor's report, for example, for the purposes of transparency in the public sector. In such circumstances, the user auditor may need the consent of the service auditor before making such a reference.

The fact that a user entity uses a service organization does not alter the user auditor's **A44** responsibility under ISAs (UK) to obtain sufficient appropriate audit evidence to afford a reasonable basis to support the user auditor's opinion. Therefore, the user auditor does not make reference to the service auditor's report as a basis, in part, for the user auditor's opinion on the user entity's financial statements. However, when the user auditor expresses a modified opinion because of a modified opinion in a service auditor's report, the user auditor is not precluded from referring to the service auditor's report if such reference assists in explaining the reason for the user auditor's modified opinion. In such circumstances, the user auditor may need the consent of the service auditor before making such a reference.

International Standard on Auditing (UK) 450 (Revised June 2016) (Updated July 2017)

Evaluation of misstatements identified during the audit

(Effective for audits of financial statements for periods commencing on or after 17 June 2016)[0]

Contents

International Standard on Auditing (UK) (ISA (UK)) 450 (Revised June 2016), *Evaluation of Misstatements Identified during the Audit*, should be read in the context of ISA (UK) 200 (Revised June 2016), *Overall Objectives of the Independent Auditor and the Conduct of an Audit in Accordance with International Standards on Auditing (UK)*.

[0] *Conforming amendments to this standard as a result of ISA (UK) 250 (Revised July 2017), Section A—Consideration of Laws and Regulations in an Audit of Financial Statements, are included that are effective for audits of financial statements for periods commencing on or after 15 December 2017. Details of the amendments are given in the Annexure to ISA (UK) 250 (Revised December 2017) Section A.*

Introduction

Scope of this ISA (UK)

This International Standard on Auditing (UK) (ISA (UK)) deals with the auditor's **1** responsibility to evaluate the effect of identified misstatements on the audit and of uncorrected misstatements, if any, on the financial statements. ISA (UK) 700 (Revised June 2016) deals with the auditor's responsibility, in forming an opinion on the financial statements, to conclude whether reasonable assurance has been obtained about whether the financial statements as a whole are free from material misstatement. The auditor's conclusion required by ISA (UK) 700 (Revised June 2016) takes into account the auditor's evaluation of uncorrected misstatements, if any, on the financial statements, in accordance with this ISA (UK).[1] ISA (UK) 320 (Revised June 2016)[2] deals with the auditor's responsibility to apply the concept of materiality appropriately in planning and performing an audit of financial statements.

Effective Date

This ISA (UK) is effective for audits of financial statements for periods commencing on or **2** after 17 June 2016. Earlier adoption is permitted.

Objective

The objective of the auditor is to evaluate: **3**
(a) The effect of identified misstatements on the audit; and
(b) The effect of uncorrected misstatements, if any, on the financial statements.

Definitions

For purposes of the ISAs (UK), the following terms have the meanings attributed below: **4**
(a) Misstatement – A difference between the reported amount, classification, presentation, or disclosure of a financial statement item and the amount, classification, presentation, or disclosure that is required for the item to be in accordance with the applicable financial reporting framework. Misstatements can arise from error or fraud. (Ref: Para. A1)
      When the auditor expresses an opinion on whether the financial statements are presented fairly, in all material respects, or give a true and fair view, misstatements also include those adjustments of amounts, classifications, presentation, or disclosures that, in the auditor's judgment, are necessary for the financial statements to be presented fairly, in all material respects, or to give a true and fair view.
(b) Uncorrected misstatements – Misstatements that the auditor has accumulated during the audit and that have not been corrected.

Requirements

Accumulation of Identified Misstatements

The auditor shall accumulate misstatements identified during the audit, other than those **5** that are clearly trivial. (Ref: Para. A2–A6)

---

[1] *ISA (UK) 700 (Revised June 2016)*, Forming an Opinion and Reporting on Financial Statements, *paragraphs 10–11*.

[2] *ISA (UK) 320 (Revised June 2016)*, Materiality in Planning and Performing an Audit.

Consideration of Identified Misstatements as the Audit Progresses

6   The auditor shall determine whether the overall audit strategy and audit plan need to be revised if:

(a)   The nature of identified misstatements and the circumstances of their occurrence indicate that other misstatements may exist that, when aggregated with misstatements accumulated during the audit, could be material; or (Ref: Para. A7)

(b)   The aggregate of misstatements accumulated during the audit approaches materiality determined in accordance with ISA (UK) 320 (Revised June 2016). (Ref: Para. A8)

7   If, at the auditor's request, management has examined a class of transactions, account balance or disclosure and corrected misstatements that were detected, the auditor shall perform additional audit procedures to determine whether misstatements remain. (Ref: Para. A9)

Communication and Correction of Misstatements

8   The auditor shall communicate, unless prohibited by law or regulation, on a timely basis all misstatements accumulated during the audit with the appropriate level of management.[3] The auditor shall request management to correct those misstatements. (Ref: Para. A10–A12)

9   If management refuses to correct some or all of the misstatements communicated by the auditor, the auditor shall obtain an understanding of management's reasons for not making the corrections and shall take that understanding into account when evaluating whether the financial statements as a whole are free from material misstatement. (Ref: Para. A13)

Evaluating the Effect of Uncorrected Misstatements

10   Prior to evaluating the effect of uncorrected misstatements, the auditor shall reassess materiality determined in accordance with ISA (UK) 320 (Revised June 2016) to confirm whether it remains appropriate in the context of the entity's actual financial results. (Ref: Para. A14–A15)

11   The auditor shall determine whether uncorrected misstatements are material, individually or in aggregate. In making this determination, the auditor shall consider:

(a)   The size and nature of the misstatements, both in relation to particular classes of transactions, account balances or disclosures and the financial statements as a whole, and the particular circumstances of their occurrence; and (Ref: Para. A16–A22, A24–A25)

(b)   The effect of uncorrected misstatements related to prior periods on the relevant classes of transactions, account balances or disclosures, and the financial statements as a whole. (Ref: Para. A23)

Communication with Those Charged with Governance

12   The auditor shall communicate with those charged with governance uncorrected misstatements and the effect that they, individually or in aggregate, may have on the opinion in the auditor's report, unless prohibited by law or regulation.[4] The auditor's

---

[3] *ISA (UK) 260 (Revised June 2016),* Communication with Those Charged with Governance, *paragraph 7.*

[4] *See footnote 3.*

communication shall identify material uncorrected misstatements individually. The auditor shall request that uncorrected misstatements be corrected. (Ref: Para. A26–A28-1)

The auditor shall also communicate with those charged with governance the effect of uncorrected misstatements related to prior periods on the relevant classes of transactions, account balances or disclosures, and the financial statements as a whole.   **13**

Written Representation

The auditor shall request a written representation from management and, where appropriate, those charged with governance whether they believe the effects of uncorrected misstatements are immaterial, individually and in aggregate, to the financial statements as a whole. A summary of such items shall be included in or attached to the written representation. (Ref: Para. A29–A29-1)   **14**

Documentation

The auditor shall include in the audit documentation:[5] (Ref: Para. A30)   **15**

(a) The amount below which misstatements would be regarded as clearly trivial (paragraph 5);

(b) All misstatements accumulated during the audit and whether they have been corrected (paragraphs 5, 8 and 12); and

(c) The auditor's conclusion as to whether uncorrected misstatements are material, individually or in aggregate, and the basis for that conclusion (paragraph 11).

***

Application and Other Explanatory Material

Definition of Misstatement (Ref: Para. 4(a))

Misstatements may result from: **A1**

(a) An inaccuracy in gathering or processing data from which the financial statements are prepared;

(b) An omission of an amount or disclosure, including inadequate or incomplete disclosures, and those disclosures required to meet disclosure objectives of certain financial reporting frameworks as applicable;[6]

(c) An incorrect accounting estimate arising from overlooking, or clear misinterpretation of, facts;

(d) Judgments of management concerning accounting estimates that the auditor considers unreasonable or the selection and application of accounting policies that the auditor considers inappropriate.

(e) An inappropriate classification, aggregation or disaggregation, of information; and

---

[5] *ISA (UK) 230 (Revised June 2016)*, Audit Documentation, *paragraphs 8–11, and A6.*

[6] *For example, International Financial Reporting Standard 7 (IFRS)*, Financial Instruments: Disclosures, *paragraph 42H states that 'an entity shall disclose any additional information that it considers necessary to meet the disclosure objectives in paragraph …'*

(f)   For financial statements prepared in accordance with a fair presentation framework, the omission of a disclosure necessary for the financial statements to achieve fair presentation beyond disclosures specifically required by the framework.[7]

Examples of misstatements arising from fraud are provided in ISA (UK) 240 (Revised June 2016).[8]

Accumulation of Identified Misstatements (Ref: Para. 5)

"Clearly Trivial"

A2   Paragraph 5 of this ISA (UK) requires the auditor to accumulate misstatements identified during the audit other than those that are clearly trivial. 'Clearly trivial' is not another expression for 'not material.' Misstatements that are clearly trivial will be of a wholly different (smaller) order of magnitude, or of a wholly different nature than those that would be determined to be material, and will be misstatements that are clearly inconsequential, whether taken individually or in aggregate and whether judged by any criteria of size, nature or circumstances. When there is any uncertainty about whether one or more items are clearly trivial, the misstatement is considered not to be clearly trivial.

Misstatements in Individual Statements

A3   The auditor may designate an amount below which misstatements of amounts in the individual statements would be clearly trivial, and would not need to be accumulated because the auditor expects that the accumulation of such amounts clearly would not have a material effect on the financial statements. However, misstatements of amounts that are above the designated amount are accumulated as required by paragraph 5 of this ISA (UK). In addition, misstatements relating to amounts may not be clearly trivial when judged on criteria of nature or circumstances, and, if not, are accumulated as required by paragraph 5 of this ISA (UK).

Misstatements in Disclosures

A4   Misstatements in disclosures may also be clearly trivial whether taken individually or in aggregate, and whether judged by any criteria of size, nature or circumstances. Misstatements in disclosures that are not clearly trivial are also accumulated to assist the auditor in evaluating the effect of such misstatements on the relevant disclosures and the financial statements as a whole. Paragraph A17 of this ISA (UK) provides examples of where misstatements in qualitative disclosures may be material.

Accumulation of Misstatements

A5   Misstatements by nature or circumstances, accumulated as described in paragraphs A3–A4, cannot be added together as is possible in the case of misstatements of amounts. Nevertheless, the auditor is required by paragraph 11 of this ISA (UK) to evaluate those

---

[7] *For example, IFRS requires an entity to provide additional disclosures when compliance with the specific requirements in IFRSs is insufficient to enable users to understand the impact of particular transactions, other events and conditions on the entity's financial position and financial performance (International Accounting Standard 1, Presentation of Financial Statements, paragraph 17(c)).*

[8] *ISA (UK) 240 (Revised June 2016),* The Auditor's Responsibilities Relating to Fraud in an Audit of Financial Statements, *paragraphs A1–A6.*

misstatements individually and in aggregate (i.e., collectively with other misstatements) to determine whether they are material.

To assist the auditor in evaluating the effect of misstatements accumulated during the audit and in communicating misstatements to management and those charged with governance, it may be useful to distinguish between factual misstatements, judgmental misstatements and projected misstatements.   **A6**

- Factual misstatements are misstatements about which there is no doubt.
- Judgmental misstatements are differences arising from the judgments of management including those concerning recognition, measurement, presentation and disclosure in the financial statements (including the selection or application of accounting policies) that the auditor considers unreasonable or inappropriate.
- Projected misstatements are the auditor's best estimate of misstatements in populations, involving the projection of misstatements identified in audit samples to the entire populations from which the samples were drawn. Guidance on the determination of projected misstatements and evaluation of the results is set out in ISA (UK) 530.[9]

Consideration of Identified Misstatements as the Audit Progresses
(Ref: Para. 6–7)

A misstatement may not be an isolated occurrence. Evidence that other misstatements may exist include, for example, where the auditor identifies that a misstatement arose from a breakdown in internal control or from inappropriate assumptions or valuation methods that have been widely applied by the entity.   **A7**

If the aggregate of misstatements accumulated during the audit approaches materiality determined in accordance with ISA (UK) 320 (Revised June 2016), there may be a greater than acceptably low level of risk that possible undetected misstatements, when taken with the aggregate of misstatements accumulated during the audit, could exceed materiality. Undetected misstatements could exist because of the presence of sampling risk and non-sampling risk.[10]   **A8**

The auditor may request management to examine a class of transactions, account balance or disclosure in order for management to understand the cause of a misstatement identified by the auditor, perform procedures to determine the amount of the actual misstatement in the class of transactions, account balance or disclosure, and to make appropriate adjustments to the financial statements. Such a request may be made, for example, based on the auditor's projection of misstatements identified in an audit sample to the entire population from which it was drawn.   **A9**

Communication and Correction of Misstatements (Ref: Para. 8–9)

Timely communication of misstatements to the appropriate level of management is important as it enables management to evaluate whether the classes of transactions, account balances and disclosures are misstated, inform the auditor if it disagrees, and take action as necessary. Ordinarily, the appropriate level of management is the one that has responsibility and authority to evaluate the misstatements and to take the necessary action.   **A10**

---

[9] *ISA (UK) 530, Audit Sampling, paragraphs 14–15.*

[10] *ISA (UK) 530, paragraph 5(c)–(d).*

A11   In some jurisdictions, law or regulation may restrict the auditor's communication of certain misstatements to management, or others, within the entity. Law or regulation may specifically prohibit a communication, or other action, that might prejudice an investigation by an appropriate authority into an actual, or suspected, illegal act, including alerting the entity, for example, when the auditor is required to report identified or suspected non-compliance with law or regulation to an appropriate authority pursuant to anti-money laundering legislation. In these circumstances, the issues considered by the auditor may be complex and the auditor may consider it appropriate to obtain legal advice.

A12   The correction by management of all misstatements, including those communicated by the auditor, enables management to maintain accurate accounting books and records and reduces the risks of material misstatement of future financial statements because of the cumulative effect of immaterial uncorrected misstatements related to prior periods.

A13   ISA (UK) 700 (Revised June 2016) requires the auditor to evaluate whether the financial statements are prepared and presented, in all material respects, in accordance with the requirements of the applicable financial reporting framework. This evaluation includes consideration of the qualitative aspects of the entity's accounting practices, including indicators of possible bias in management's judgments,[11] which may be affected by the auditor's understanding of management's reasons for not making the corrections.

Evaluating the Effect of Uncorrected Misstatements (Ref: Para. 10–11)

A14   The auditor's determination of materiality in accordance with ISA (UK) 320 (Revised June 2016) is often based on estimates of the entity's financial results, because the actual financial results may not yet be known. Therefore, prior to the auditor's evaluation of the effect of uncorrected misstatements, it may be necessary to revise materiality determined in accordance with ISA (UK) 320 (Revised June 2016) based on the actual financial results.

A15   ISA (UK) 320 (Revised June 2016) explains that, as the audit progresses, materiality for the financial statements as a whole (and, if applicable, the materiality level or levels for particular classes of transactions, account balances or disclosures) is revised in the event of the auditor becoming aware of information during the audit that would have caused the auditor to have determined a different amount (or amounts) initially.[12] Thus, any significant revision is likely to have been made before the auditor evaluates the effect of uncorrected misstatements. However, if the auditor's reassessment of materiality determined in accordance with ISA (UK) 320 (Revised June 2016) (see paragraph 10 of this ISA (UK)) gives rise to a lower amount (or amounts), then performance materiality and the appropriateness of the nature, timing and extent of the further audit procedures are reconsidered so as to obtain sufficient appropriate audit evidence on which to base the audit opinion.

A16   Each individual misstatement of an amount is considered to evaluate its effect on the relevant classes of transactions, account balances or disclosures, including whether the materiality level for that particular class of transactions, account balance or disclosure, if any, has been exceeded.

A17   In addition, each individual misstatement of a qualitative disclosure is considered to evaluate its effect on the relevant disclosure(s), as well as its overall effect on the financial statements as a whole. The determination of whether a misstatement(s) in a qualitative disclosure is material, in the context of the applicable financial reporting framework and

---

[11] *ISA (UK) 700 (Revised June 2016), paragraph 12.*

[12] *ISA (UK) 320 (Revised June 2016), paragraph 12.*

the specific circumstances of the entity, is a matter that involves the exercise of professional judgment. Examples where such misstatements may be material include:

- Inaccurate or incomplete descriptions of information about the objectives, policies and processes for managing capital for entities with insurance and banking activities.
- The omission of information about the events or circumstances that have led to an impairment loss (e.g., a significant long-term decline in the demand for a metal or commodity) in an entity with mining operations.
- The incorrect description of an accounting policy relating to a significant item in the statement of financial position, the statement of comprehensive income, the statement of changes in equity or the statement of cash flows.
- The inadequate description of the sensitivity of an exchange rate in an entity that undertakes international trading activities.

In determining whether uncorrected misstatements by nature are material as required by paragraph 11 of this ISA (UK), the auditor considers uncorrected misstatements in amounts and disclosures. Such misstatements may be considered material either individually, or when taken in combination with other misstatements. For example, depending on the misstatements identified in disclosures, the auditor may consider whether: **A18**

(a) Identified errors are persistent or pervasive; or
(b) A number of identified misstatements are relevant to the same matter, and considered collectively may affect the users' understanding of that matter.

This consideration of accumulated misstatements is also helpful when evaluating the financial statements in accordance with paragraph 13(d) of ISA (UK) 700 (Revised June 2016),[13] which requires the auditor to consider whether the overall presentation of the financial statements has been undermined by including information that is not relevant or that obscures a proper understanding of the matters disclosed.

If an individual misstatement is judged to be material, it is unlikely that it can be offset by other misstatements. For example, if revenue has been materially overstated, the financial statements as a whole will be materially misstated, even if the effect of the misstatement on earnings is completely offset by an equivalent overstatement of expenses. It may be appropriate to offset misstatements within the same account balance or class of transactions; however, the risk that further undetected misstatements may exist is considered before concluding that offsetting even immaterial misstatements is appropriate.[14] **A19**

Determining whether a classification misstatement is material involves the evaluation of qualitative considerations, such as the effect of the classification misstatement on debt or other contractual covenants, the effect on individual line items or sub-totals, or the effect on key ratios. There may be circumstances where the auditor concludes that a classification misstatement is not material in the context of the financial statements as a whole, even though it may exceed the materiality level or levels applied in evaluating other misstatements. For example, a misclassification between balance sheet line items may not be considered material in the context of the financial statements as a whole when the amount of the misclassification is small in relation to the size of the related balance sheet line items and the misclassification does not affect the income statement or any key ratios. **A20**

The circumstances related to some misstatements may cause the auditor to evaluate them as material, individually or when considered together with other misstatements accumulated **A21**

---

[13] *ISA (UK) 700 (Revised June 2016)*, Forming an Opinion and Reporting on Financial Statements.

[14] *The identification of a number of immaterial misstatements within the same account balance or class of transactions may require the auditor to reassess the risk of material misstatement for that account balance or class of transactions.*

during the audit, even if they are lower than materiality for the financial statements as a whole. Circumstances that may affect the evaluation include the extent to which the misstatement:

- Affects compliance with regulatory requirements;
- Affects compliance with debt covenants or other contractual requirements;
- Relates to the incorrect selection or application of an accounting policy that has an immaterial effect on the current period's financial statements but is likely to have a material effect on future periods' financial statements;
- Masks a change in earnings or other trends, especially in the context of general economic and industry conditions;
- Affects ratios used to evaluate the entity's financial position, results of operations or cash flows;
- Affects segment information presented in the financial statements (for example, the significance of the matter to a segment or other portion of the entity's business that has been identified as playing a significant role in the entity's operations or profitability);
- Has the effect of increasing management compensation, for example, by ensuring that the requirements for the award of bonuses or other incentives are satisfied;
- Is significant having regard to the auditor's understanding of known previous communications to users, for example, in relation to forecast earnings;
- Relates to items involving particular parties (for example, whether external parties to the transaction are related to members of the entity's management);
- Is an omission of information not specifically required by the applicable financial reporting framework but which, in the judgment of the auditor, is important to the users' understanding of the financial position, financial performance or cash flows of the entity; or
- Affects other information to be included in the entity's annual report (for example, information to be included in a 'Management Discussion and Analysis' or an 'Operating and Financial Review') that may reasonably be expected to influence the economic decisions of the users of the financial statements. ISA (UK) 720 (Revised June 2016)[15] deals with the auditor's responsibilities relating to other information.

These circumstances are only examples; not all are likely to be present in all audits nor is the list necessarily complete. The existence of any circumstances such as these does not necessarily lead to a conclusion that the misstatement is material.

A22   ISA (UK) 240 (Revised June 2016)[16] explains how the implications of a misstatement that is, or may be, the result of fraud ought to be considered in relation to other aspects of the audit, even if the size of the misstatement is not material in relation to the financial statements. Depending on the circumstances, misstatements in disclosures could also be indicative of fraud, and, for example, may arise from:

- Misleading disclosures that have resulted from bias in management's judgments; or
- Extensive duplicative or uninformative disclosures that are intended to obscure a proper understanding of matters in the financial statements.

When considering the implications of misstatements in classes of transactions, account balances and disclosures, the auditor exercises professional skepticism in accordance with ISA (UK) 200 (Revised June 2016).[17]

---

[15] *ISA (UK) 720 (Revised June 2016),* The Auditor's Responsibilities Relating to Other Information.

[16] *ISA (UK) 240 (Revised June 2016), paragraph 35.*

[17] *ISA (UK) 200 (Revised June 2016), paragraph 15.*

The cumulative effect of immaterial uncorrected misstatements related to prior periods may have a material effect on the current period's financial statements. There are different acceptable approaches to the auditor's evaluation of such uncorrected misstatements on the current period's financial statements. Using the same evaluation approach provides consistency from period to period. **A23**

Considerations Specific to Public Sector Entities

In the case of an audit of a public sector entity, the evaluation whether a misstatement is material may also be affected by the auditor's responsibilities established by law, regulation or other authority to report specific matters, including, for example, fraud. **A24**

Furthermore, issues such as public interest, accountability, probity and ensuring effective legislative oversight, in particular, may affect the assessment whether an item is material by virtue of its nature. This is particularly so for items that relate to compliance with law, regulation or other authority. **A25**

Communication with Those Charged with Governance (Ref: Para. 12)

If uncorrected misstatements have been communicated with person(s) with management responsibilities, and those person(s) also have governance responsibilities, they need not be communicated again with those same person(s) in their governance role. The auditor nonetheless has to be satisfied that communication with person(s) with management responsibilities adequately informs all of those with whom the auditor would otherwise communicate in their governance capacity.[18] **A26**

Where there is a large number of individual immaterial uncorrected misstatements, the auditor may communicate the number and overall monetary effect of the uncorrected misstatements, rather than the details of each individual uncorrected misstatement. **A27**

ISA (UK) 260 (Revised June 2016) requires the auditor to communicate with those charged with governance the written representations the auditor is requesting (see paragraph 14 of this ISA (UK)).[19] The auditor may discuss with those charged with governance the reasons for, and the implications of, a failure to correct misstatements, having regard to the size and nature of the misstatement judged in the surrounding circumstances, and possible implications in relation to future financial statements. **A28**

If management have corrected material misstatements, communicating those corrections of which the auditor is aware to those charged with governance may assist them to fulfill their governance responsibilities, including reviewing the effectiveness of the system of internal control. **A28-1**

Written Representation (Ref: Para. 14)

Because the preparation of the financial statements requires management and, where appropriate, those charged with governance to adjust the financial statements to correct material misstatements, the auditor is required to request them to provide a written representation about uncorrected misstatements. In some circumstances, management and, where appropriate, those charged with governance may not believe that certain **A29**

---

[18] *ISA (UK) 260 (Revised June 2016), paragraph 13.*

[19] *ISA (UK) 260 (Revised June 2016), paragraph 16(c)(ii).*

uncorrected misstatements are misstatements. For that reason, they may want to add to their written representation words such as: 'We do not agree that items … and … constitute misstatements because [description of reasons].' Obtaining this representation does not, however, relieve the auditor of the need to form a conclusion on the effect of uncorrected misstatements.

A29-1 Requesting those charged with governance to provide written representations that set out their reasons for not correcting misstatements brought to their attention by the auditor may help focus the attention of those charged with governance on those misstatements and the circumstances giving rise to them.

Documentation (Ref: Para. 15)

A30 The auditor's documentation of uncorrected misstatements may take into account:

(a) The consideration of the aggregate effect of uncorrected misstatements;

(b) The evaluation of whether the materiality level or levels for particular classes of transactions, account balances or disclosures, if any, have been exceeded; and

(c) The evaluation of the effect of uncorrected misstatements on key ratios or trends, and compliance with legal, regulatory and contractual requirements (for example, debt covenants).

International Standard on Auditing (UK) 500 (Updated July 2017)
Audit evidence

(Effective for audits of financial statements for periods ending on or after 15 December 2010)[0]

Contents

International Standard on Auditing (UK) (ISA (UK)) 500, *Audit Evidence*, should be read in conjunction with ISA (UK) 200 (Revised June 2016), *Overall Objectives of the Independent Auditor and the Conduct of an Audit in Accordance with International Standards on Auditing (UK)*.

[0] *Conforming amendments to this standard as a result of ISA (UK) 250 (Revised July 2017), Section A—Consideration of Laws and Regulations in an Audit of Financial Statements, are included that are effective for audits of financial statements for periods commencing on or after 15 December 2017. Details of the amendments are given in the Annexure to ISA (UK) 250 (Revised December 2017) Section A.*

Introduction

Scope of this ISA (UK)

1   This International Standard on Auditing (UK) (ISA (UK)) explains what constitutes audit evidence in an audit of financial statements, and deals with the auditor's responsibility to design and perform audit procedures to obtain sufficient appropriate audit evidence to be able to draw reasonable conclusions on which to base the auditor's opinion.

2   This ISA (UK) is applicable to all the audit evidence obtained during the course of the audit. Other ISAs (UK) deal with specific aspects of the audit (for example, ISA (UK) 315 (Revised June 2016)[1]), the audit evidence to be obtained in relation to a particular topic (for example, ISA (UK) 570 (Revised June 2016)[2]), specific procedures to obtain audit evidence (for example, ISA (UK) 520[3]), and the evaluation of whether sufficient appropriate audit evidence has been obtained (ISA (UK) 200 (Revised June 2016)[4] and ISA (UK) 330 (Revised July 2017)[5]).

Effective Date

3   This ISA (UK) is effective for audits of financial statements for periods ending on or after 15 December 2010.

Objective

4   The objective of the auditor is to design and perform audit procedures in such a way as to enable the auditor to obtain sufficient appropriate audit evidence to be able to draw reasonable conclusions on which to base the auditor's opinion.

Definitions

5   For purposes of the ISAs (UK), the following terms have the meanings attributed below:
   (a)   Accounting records – The records of initial accounting entries and supporting records, such as checks and records of electronic fund transfers; invoices; contracts; the general and subsidiary ledgers, journal entries and other adjustments to the financial statements that are not reflected in journal entries; and records such as work sheets and spreadsheets supporting cost allocations, computations, reconciliations and disclosures.
   (b)   Appropriateness (of audit evidence) – The measure of the quality of audit evidence; that is, its relevance and its reliability in providing support for the conclusions on which the auditor's opinion is based.
   (c)   Audit evidence – Information used by the auditor in arriving at the conclusions on which the auditor's opinion is based. Audit evidence includes both information

---

[1] *ISA (UK) 315 (Revised June 2016)*, Identifying and Assessing the Risks of Material Misstatement through Understanding the Entity and Its Environment.

[2] *ISA (UK) 570 (Revised June 2016)*, Going Concern.

[3] *ISA (UK) 520*, Analytical Procedures.

[4] *ISA (UK) 200 (Revised June 2016)*, Overall Objectives of the Independent Auditor and the Conduct of an Audit in Accordance with International Standards on Auditing (UK).

[5] *ISA (UK) 330 (Revised July 2017)*, The Auditor's Responses to Assessed Risks.

contained in the accounting records underlying the financial statements and information obtained from other sources.

(d) Management's expert – An individual or organization possessing expertise in a field other than accounting or auditing, whose work in that field is used by the entity to assist the entity in preparing the financial statements.

(e) Sufficiency (of audit evidence) – The measure of the quantity of audit evidence. The quantity of the audit evidence needed is affected by the auditor's assessment of the risks of material misstatement and also by the quality of such audit evidence.

Requirements

Sufficient Appropriate Audit Evidence

The auditor shall design and perform audit procedures that are appropriate in the circumstances for the purpose of obtaining sufficient appropriate audit evidence. (Ref: Para. A1–A25)   **6**

Information to Be Used as Audit Evidence

When designing and performing audit procedures, the auditor shall consider the relevance and reliability of the information to be used as audit evidence. (Ref: Para. A26–A33a)   **7**

If information to be used as audit evidence has been prepared using the work of a management's expert, the auditor shall, to the extent necessary, having regard to the significance of that expert's work for the auditor's purposes,: (Ref: Para. A34–A36)   **8**

(a) Evaluate the competence, capabilities and objectivity of that expert; (Ref: Para. A37–A43)

(b) Obtain an understanding of the work of that expert; and (Ref: Para. A44–A47)

(c) Evaluate the appropriateness of that expert's work as audit evidence for the relevant assertion. (Ref: Para. A48)

When using information produced by the entity, the auditor shall evaluate whether the information is sufficiently reliable for the auditor's purposes, including as necessary in the circumstances: **9**

(a) Obtaining audit evidence about the accuracy and completeness of the information; and (Ref: Para. A49–A50)

(b) Evaluating whether the information is sufficiently precise and detailed for the auditor's purposes. (Ref: Para. A51)

Selecting Items for Testing to Obtain Audit Evidence

When designing tests of controls and tests of details, the auditor shall determine means of selecting items for testing that are effective in meeting the purpose of the audit procedure. (Ref: Para. A52–A56)   **10**

Inconsistency in, or Doubts over Reliability of, Audit Evidence

If: **11**

(a) audit evidence obtained from one source is inconsistent with that obtained from another; or

(b) the auditor has doubts over the reliability of information to be used as audit evidence, the auditor shall determine what modifications or additions to audit procedures are necessary to resolve the matter, and shall consider the effect of the matter, if any, on other aspects of the audit. (Ref: Para. A57)

***

Application and Other Explanatory Material

Sufficient Appropriate Audit Evidence (Ref: Para. 6)

A1   Audit evidence is necessary to support the auditor's opinion and report. It is cumulative in nature and is primarily obtained from audit procedures performed during the course of the audit. It may, however, also include information obtained from other sources such as previous audits (provided the auditor has determined whether changes have occurred since the previous audit that may affect its relevance to the current audit[6]) or a firm's quality control procedures for client acceptance and continuance. In addition to other sources inside and outside the entity, the entity's accounting records are an important source of audit evidence. Also, information that may be used as audit evidence may have been prepared using the work of a management's expert. Audit evidence comprises both information that supports and corroborates management's assertions, and any information that contradicts such assertions. In addition, in some cases the absence of information (for example, management's refusal to provide a requested representation) is used by the auditor, and therefore, also constitutes audit evidence.

A2   Most of the auditor's work in forming the auditor's opinion consists of obtaining and evaluating audit evidence. Audit procedures to obtain audit evidence can include inspection, observation, confirmation, recalculation, reperformance and analytical procedures, often in some combination, in addition to inquiry. Although inquiry may provide important audit evidence, and may even produce evidence of a misstatement, inquiry alone ordinarily does not provide sufficient audit evidence of the absence of a material misstatement at the assertion level, nor of the operating effectiveness of controls.

A3   As explained in ISA (UK) 200 (Revised June 2016),[7] reasonable assurance is obtained when the auditor has obtained sufficient appropriate audit evidence to reduce audit risk (that is, the risk that the auditor expresses an inappropriate opinion when the financial statements are materially misstated) to an acceptably low level.

A4   The sufficiency and appropriateness of audit evidence are interrelated. Sufficiency is the measure of the quantity of audit evidence. The quantity of audit evidence needed is affected by the auditor's assessment of the risks of misstatement (the higher the assessed risks, the more audit evidence is likely to be required) and also by the quality of such audit evidence (the higher the quality, the less may be required). Obtaining more audit evidence, however, may not compensate for its poor quality.

A5   Appropriateness is the measure of the quality of audit evidence; that is, its relevance and its reliability in providing support for the conclusions on which the auditor's opinion is based. The reliability of evidence is influenced by its source and by its nature, and is dependent on the individual circumstances under which it is obtained.

---

[6] *ISA (UK) 315 (Revised June 2016), paragraph 9.*

[7] *ISA (UK) 200 (Revised June 2016), paragraph 5.*

ISA (UK) 330 (Revised July 2017) requires the auditor to conclude whether sufficient **A6** appropriate audit evidence has been obtained.[8] Whether sufficient appropriate audit evidence has been obtained to reduce audit risk to an acceptably low level, and thereby enable the auditor to draw reasonable conclusions on which to base the auditor's opinion, is a matter of professional judgment. ISA (UK) 200 (Revised June 2016) contains discussion of such matters as the nature of audit procedures, the timeliness of financial reporting, and the balance between benefit and cost, which are relevant factors when the auditor exercises professional judgment regarding whether sufficient appropriate audit evidence has been obtained.

Sources of Audit Evidence

Some audit evidence is obtained by performing audit procedures to test the accounting **A7** records, for example, through analysis and review, reperforming procedures followed in the financial reporting process, and reconciling related types and applications of the same information. Through the performance of such audit procedures, the auditor may determine that the accounting records are internally consistent and agree to the financial statements.

More assurance is ordinarily obtained from consistent audit evidence obtained from **A8** different sources or of a different nature than from items of audit evidence considered individually. For example, corroborating information obtained from a source independent of the entity may increase the assurance the auditor obtains from audit evidence that is generated internally, such as evidence existing within the accounting records, minutes of meetings, or a management representation.

Information from sources independent of the entity that the auditor may use as audit **A9** evidence may include confirmations from third parties, analysts' reports, and comparable data about competitors (benchmarking data).

Audit Procedures for Obtaining Audit Evidence

As required by, and explained further in, ISA (UK) 315 (Revised June 2016) and ISA (UK) **A10** 330 (Revised July 2017), audit evidence to draw reasonable conclusions on which to base the auditor's opinion is obtained by performing:
(a) Risk assessment procedures; and
(b) Further audit procedures, which comprise:
   (i) Tests of controls, when required by the ISAs (UK) or when the auditor has chosen to do so; and
   (ii) Substantive procedures, including tests of details and substantive analytical procedures.

The audit procedures described in paragraphs A14–A25 below may be used as risk **A11** assessment procedures, tests of controls or substantive procedures, depending on the context in which they are applied by the auditor. As explained in ISA (UK) 330 (Revised July 2017), audit evidence obtained from previous audits may, in certain circumstances, provide appropriate audit evidence where the auditor performs audit procedures to establish its continuing relevance.[9]

The nature and timing of the audit procedures to be used may be affected by the fact that **A12** some of the accounting data and other information may be available only in electronic

[8] *ISA (UK) 330 (Revised July 2017), paragraph 26.*

[9] *ISA (UK) 330 (Revised July 2017), paragraph A35.*

form or only at certain points or periods in time. For example, source documents, such as purchase orders and invoices, may exist only in electronic form when an entity uses electronic commerce, or may be discarded after scanning when an entity uses image processing systems to facilitate storage and reference.

A13   Certain electronic information may not be retrievable after a specified period of time, for example, if files are changed and if backup files do not exist. Accordingly, the auditor may find it necessary as a result of an entity's data retention policies to request retention of some information for the auditor's review or to perform audit procedures at a time when the information is available.

Inspection

A14   Inspection involves examining records or documents, whether internal or external, in paper form, electronic form, or other media, or a physical examination of an asset. Inspection of records and documents provides audit evidence of varying degrees of reliability, depending on their nature and source and, in the case of internal records and documents, on the effectiveness of the controls over their production. An example of inspection used as a test of controls is inspection of records for evidence of authorization.

A15   Some documents represent direct audit evidence of the existence of an asset, for example, a document constituting a financial instrument such as a stock or bond. Inspection of such documents may not necessarily provide audit evidence about ownership or value. In addition, inspecting an executed contract may provide audit evidence relevant to the entity's application of accounting policies, such as revenue recognition.

A16   Inspection of tangible assets may provide reliable audit evidence with respect to their existence, but not necessarily about the entity's rights and obligations or the valuation of the assets. Inspection of individual inventory items may accompany the observation of inventory counting.

Observation

A17   Observation consists of looking at a process or procedure being performed by others, for example, the auditor's observation of inventory counting by the entity's personnel, or of the performance of control activities. Observation provides audit evidence about the performance of a process or procedure, but is limited to the point in time at which the observation takes place, and by the fact that the act of being observed may affect how the process or procedure is performed. See ISA (UK) 501 for further guidance on observation of the counting of inventory.[10]

External Confirmation

A18   An external confirmation represents audit evidence obtained by the auditor as a direct written response to the auditor from a third party (the confirming party), in paper form, or by electronic or other medium. External confirmation procedures frequently are relevant when addressing assertions associated with certain account balances and their elements. However, external confirmations need not be restricted to account balances only. For example, the auditor may request confirmation of the terms of agreements or transactions an entity has with third parties; the confirmation request may be designed to ask if any modifications have been made to the agreement and, if so, what the relevant details are.

---

[10] *ISA (UK) 501*, Audit Evidence—Specific Considerations for Selected Items.

External confirmation procedures also are used to obtain audit evidence about the absence of certain conditions, for example, the absence of a 'side agreement' that may influence revenue recognition. See ISA (UK) 505 for further guidance.[11]

Recalculation

Recalculation consists of checking the mathematical accuracy of documents or records. Recalculation may be performed manually or electronically. **A19**

Reperformance

Reperformance involves the auditor's independent execution of procedures or controls that were originally performed as part of the entity's internal control. **A20**

Analytical Procedures

Analytical procedures consist of evaluations of financial information through analysis of plausible relationships among both financial and non-financial data. Analytical procedures also encompass such investigation as is necessary of identified fluctuations or relationships that are inconsistent with other relevant information or that differ from expected values by a significant amount. See ISA (UK) 520 for further guidance. **A21**

Inquiry

Inquiry consists of seeking information of knowledgeable persons, both financial and non-financial, within the entity or outside the entity. Inquiry is used extensively throughout the audit in addition to other audit procedures. Inquiries may range from formal written inquiries to informal oral inquiries. Evaluating responses to inquiries is an integral part of the inquiry process. **A22**

Responses to inquiries may provide the auditor with information not previously possessed or with corroborative audit evidence. Alternatively, responses might provide information that differs significantly from other information that the auditor has obtained, for example, information regarding the possibility of management override of controls. In some cases, responses to inquiries provide a basis for the auditor to modify or perform additional audit procedures. **A23**

Although corroboration of evidence obtained through inquiry is often of particular importance, in the case of inquiries about management intent, the information available to support management's intent may be limited. In these cases, understanding management's past history of carrying out its stated intentions, management's stated reasons for choosing a particular course of action, and management's ability to pursue a specific course of action may provide relevant information to corroborate the evidence obtained through inquiry. **A24**

In respect of some matters, the auditor may consider it necessary to obtain written representations from management and, where appropriate, those charged with governance to confirm responses to oral inquiries. See ISA (UK) 580 for further guidance.[12] **A25**

[11] *ISA (UK) 505*, External Confirmations.

[12] *ISA (UK) 580*, Written Representations.

Information to Be Used as Audit Evidence

Relevance and Reliability (Ref: Para. 7)

A26   As noted in paragraph A1, while audit evidence is primarily obtained from audit procedures performed during the course of the audit, it may also include information obtained from other sources such as, for example, previous audits, in certain circumstances, firm's quality control procedures for client acceptance and continuance and complying with certain additional responsibilities under law, regulation or relevant ethical requirements (e.g., regarding an entity's non-compliance with laws and regulations). The quality of all audit evidence is affected by the relevance and reliability of the information upon which it is based.

Relevance

A27   Relevance deals with the logical connection with, or bearing upon, the purpose of the audit procedure and, where appropriate, the assertion under consideration. The relevance of information to be used as audit evidence may be affected by the direction of testing. For example, if the purpose of an audit procedure is to test for overstatement in the existence or valuation of accounts payable, testing the recorded accounts payable may be a relevant audit procedure. On the other hand, when testing for understatement in the existence or valuation of accounts payable, testing the recorded accounts payable would not be relevant, but testing such information as subsequent disbursements, unpaid invoices, suppliers' statements, and unmatched receiving reports may be relevant.

A28   A given set of audit procedures may provide audit evidence that is relevant to certain assertions, but not others. For example, inspection of documents related to the collection of receivables after the period end may provide audit evidence regarding existence and valuation, but not necessarily cutoff. Similarly, obtaining audit evidence regarding a particular assertion, for example, the existence of inventory, is not a substitute for obtaining audit evidence regarding another assertion, for example, the valuation of that inventory. On the other hand, audit evidence from different sources or of a different nature may often be relevant to the same assertion.

A29   Tests of controls are designed to evaluate the operating effectiveness of controls in preventing, or detecting and correcting, material misstatements at the assertion level. Designing tests of controls to obtain relevant audit evidence includes identifying conditions (characteristics or attributes) that indicate performance of a control, and deviation conditions which indicate departures from adequate performance. The presence or absence of those conditions can then be tested by the auditor.

A30   Substantive procedures are designed to detect material misstatements at the assertion level. They comprise tests of details and substantive analytical procedures. Designing substantive procedures includes identifying conditions relevant to the purpose of the test that constitute a misstatement in the relevant assertion.

Reliability

A31   The reliability of information to be used as audit evidence, and therefore of the audit evidence itself, is influenced by its source and its nature, and the circumstances under which it is obtained, including the controls over its preparation and maintenance where relevant. Therefore, generalizations about the reliability of various kinds of audit evidence are subject to important exceptions. Even when information to be used as audit evidence is obtained from sources external to the entity, circumstances may exist that could affect its reliability. For example, information obtained from an independent external source may not be reliable if the source is not knowledgeable, or a management's expert may lack objectivity. While recognizing that exceptions may exist, the following generalizations about the reliability of audit evidence may be useful:

- The reliability of audit evidence is increased when it is obtained from independent sources outside the entity.
- The reliability of audit evidence that is generated internally is increased when the related controls, including those over its preparation and maintenance, imposed by the entity are effective.
- Audit evidence obtained directly by the auditor (for example, observation of the application of a control) is more reliable than audit evidence obtained indirectly or by inference (for example, inquiry about the application of a control).
- Audit evidence in documentary form, whether paper, electronic, or other medium, is more reliable than evidence obtained orally (for example, a contemporaneously written record of a meeting is more reliable than a subsequent oral representation of the matters discussed).
- Audit evidence provided by original documents is more reliable than audit evidence provided by photocopies or facsimiles, or documents that have been filmed, digitized or otherwise transformed into electronic form, the reliability of which may depend on the controls over their preparation and maintenance.

ISA (UK) 520 provides further guidance regarding the reliability of data used for purposes of designing analytical procedures as substantive procedures.[13] **A32**

ISA (UK) 240 (Revised June 2016) deals with circumstances where the auditor has reason to believe that a document may not be authentic, or may have been modified without that modification having been disclosed to the auditor.[14] **A33**

ISA (UK) 250 (Revised July 2017)[15] provides further guidance with respect to the auditor complying with any additional responsibilities under law, regulation or relevant ethical requirements regarding an entity's identified or suspected non-compliance with laws and regulations that may provide further information that is relevant to the auditor's work in accordance with ISAs (UK) and evaluating the implications of such non-compliance in relation to other aspects of the audit. **A33a**

Reliability of Information Produced by a Management's Expert (Ref: Para. 8)

The preparation of an entity's financial statements may require expertise in a field other than accounting or auditing, such as actuarial calculations, valuations, or engineering data. The entity may employ or engage experts in these fields to obtain the needed expertise to prepare the financial statements. Failure to do so when such expertise is necessary increases the risks of material misstatement. **A34**

When information to be used as audit evidence has been prepared using the work of a management's expert, the requirement in paragraph 8 of this ISA (UK) applies. For example, an individual or organization may possess expertise in the application of models to estimate the fair value of securities for which there is no observable market. If the **A35**

---

[13] *ISA (UK) 520, paragraph 5(a).*

[14] *ISA (UK) 240 (Revised June 2016),* The Auditor's Responsibilities Relating to Fraud in an Audit of Financial Statements, *paragraph 13.*

[15] *ISA (UK) 250 (Revised December 2017),* Section A—Consideration of Laws and Regulations in an Audit of Financial Statements, *paragraph 9.*

individual or organization applies that expertise in making an estimate which the entity uses in preparing its financial statements, the individual or organization is a management's expert and paragraph 8 applies. If, on the other hand, that individual or organization merely provides price data regarding private transactions not otherwise available to the entity which the entity uses in its own estimation methods, such information, if used as audit evidence, is subject to paragraph 7 of this ISA (UK), but is not the use of a management's expert by the entity.

A36   The nature, timing and extent of audit procedures in relation to the requirement in paragraph 8 of this ISA (UK), may be affected by such matters as:

- The nature and complexity of the matter to which the management's expert relates.
- The risks of material misstatement in the matter.
- The availability of alternative sources of audit evidence.
- The nature, scope and objectives of the management's expert's work.
- Whether the management's expert is employed by the entity, or is a party engaged by it to provide relevant services.
- The extent to which management can exercise control or influence over the work of the management's expert.
- Whether the management's expert is subject to technical performance standards or other professional or industry requirements.
- The nature and extent of any controls within the entity over the management's expert's work.
- The auditor's knowledge and experience of the management's expert's field of expertise.
- The auditor's previous experience of the work of that expert.

The Competence, Capabilities and Objectivity of a Management's Expert (Ref: Para. 8(a))

A37   Competence relates to the nature and level of expertise of the management's expert. Capability relates the ability of the management's expert to exercise that competence in the circumstances. Factors that influence capability may include, for example, geographic location, and the availability of time and resources. Objectivity relates to the possible effects that bias, conflict of interest or the influence of others may have on the professional or business judgment of the management's expert. The competence, capabilities and objectivity of a management's expert, and any controls within the entity over that expert's work, are important factors in relation to the reliability of any information produced by a management's expert.

A38   Information regarding the competence, capabilities and objectivity of a management's expert may come from a variety of sources, such as:

- Personal experience with previous work of that expert.
- Discussions with that expert.
- Discussions with others who are familiar with that expert's work.
- Knowledge of that expert's qualifications, membership of a professional body or industry association, license to practice, or other forms of external recognition.
- Published papers or books written by that expert.
- An auditor's expert, if any, who assists the auditor in obtaining sufficient appropriate audit evidence with respect to information produced by the management's expert.

A39   Matters relevant to evaluating the competence, capabilities and objectivity of a management's expert include whether that expert's work is subject to technical performance standards or other professional or industry requirements, for example, ethical standards and other membership requirements of a professional body or industry association, accreditation standards of a licensing body, or requirements imposed by law or regulation.

Other matters that may be relevant include:

A40

- The relevance of the management's expert's competence to the matter for which that expert's work will be used, including any areas of specialty within that expert's field. For example, a particular actuary may specialize in property and casualty insurance, but have limited expertise regarding pension calculations.
- The management's expert's competence with respect to relevant accounting requirements, for example, knowledge of assumptions and methods, including models where applicable, that are consistent with the applicable financial reporting framework.
- Whether unexpected events, changes in conditions, or the audit evidence obtained from the results of audit procedures indicate that it may be necessary to reconsider the initial evaluation of the competence, capabilities and objectivity of the management's expert as the audit progresses.

A broad range of circumstances may threaten objectivity, for example, self-interest threats, advocacy threats, familiarity threats, self-review threats and intimidation threats. Safeguards may reduce such threats, and may be created either by external structures (for example, the management's expert's profession, legislation or regulation), or by the management's expert's work environment (for example, quality control policies and procedures).

A41

Although safeguards cannot eliminate all threats to a management's expert's objectivity, threats such as intimidation threats may be of less significance to an expert engaged by the entity than to an expert employed by the entity, and the effectiveness of safeguards such as quality control policies and procedures may be greater. Because the threat to objectivity created by being an employee of the entity will always be present, an expert employed by the entity cannot ordinarily be regarded as being more likely to be objective than other employees of the entity.

A42

When evaluating the objectivity of an expert engaged by the entity, it may be relevant to discuss with management and that expert any interests and relationships that may create threats to the expert's objectivity, and any applicable safeguards, including any professional requirements that apply to the expert; and to evaluate whether the safeguards are adequate. Interests and relationships creating threats may include:

A43

- Financial interests.
- Business and personal relationships.
- Provision of other services.

Obtaining an Understanding of the Work of the Management's Expert (Ref: Para. 8(b))

An understanding of the work of the management's expert includes an understanding of the relevant field of expertise. An understanding of the relevant field of expertise may be obtained in conjunction with the auditor's determination of whether the auditor has the expertise to evaluate the work of the management's expert, or whether the auditor needs an auditor's expert for this purpose.[16]

A44

Aspects of the management's expert's field relevant to the auditor's understanding may include:

A45

---

[16] *ISA (UK) 620 (Revised June 2016)*, Using the Work of an Auditor's Expert, *paragraph 7*.

- Whether that expert's field has areas of specialty within it that are relevant to the audit.
- Whether any professional or other standards, and regulatory or legal requirements apply.
- What assumptions and methods are used by the management's expert, and whether they are generally accepted within that expert's field and appropriate for financial reporting purposes.
- The nature of internal and external data or information the auditor's expert uses.

A46   In the case of a management's expert engaged by the entity, there will ordinarily be an engagement letter or other written form of agreement between the entity and that expert. Evaluating that agreement when obtaining an understanding of the work of the management's expert may assist the auditor in determining the appropriateness of the following for the auditor's purposes:

- The nature, scope and objectives of that expert's work;
- The respective roles and responsibilities of management and that expert; and
- The nature, timing and extent of communication between management and that expert, including the form of any report to be provided by that expert.

A47   In the case of a management's expert employed by the entity, it is less likely there will be a written agreement of this kind. Inquiry of the expert and other members of management may be the most appropriate way for the auditor to obtain the necessary understanding.

Evaluating the Appropriateness of the Management's Expert's Work (Ref: Para. 8(c))

A48   Considerations when evaluating the appropriateness of the management's expert's work as audit evidence for the relevant assertion may include:

- The relevance and reasonableness of that expert's findings or conclusions, their consistency with other audit evidence, and whether they have been appropriately reflected in the financial statements;
- If that expert's work involves use of significant assumptions and methods, the relevance and reasonableness of those assumptions and methods; and
- If that expert's work involves significant use of source data the relevance, completeness, and accuracy of that source data.

Information Produced by the Entity and Used for the Auditor's Purposes
(Ref: Para. 9(a)–(b))

A49   In order for the auditor to obtain reliable audit evidence, information produced by the entity that is used for performing audit procedures needs to be sufficiently complete and accurate. For example, the effectiveness of auditing revenue by applying standard prices to records of sales volume is affected by the accuracy of the price information and the completeness and accuracy of the sales volume data. Similarly, if the auditor intends to test a population (for example, payments) for a certain characteristic (for example, authorization), the results of the test will be less reliable if the population from which items are selected for testing is not complete.

A50   Obtaining audit evidence about the accuracy and completeness of such information may be performed concurrently with the actual audit procedure applied to the information when obtaining such audit evidence is an integral part of the audit procedure itself. In other situations, the auditor may have obtained audit evidence of the accuracy and completeness of such information by testing controls over the preparation and maintenance of the information. In some situations, however, the auditor may determine that additional audit procedures are needed.

In some cases, the auditor may intend to use information produced by the entity for other audit purposes. For example, the auditor may intend to make use of the entity's performance measures for the purpose of analytical procedures, or to make use of the entity's information produced for monitoring activities, such as reports of the internal audit function. In such cases, the appropriateness of the audit evidence obtained is affected by whether the information is sufficiently precise or detailed for the auditor's purposes. For example, performance measures used by management may not be precise enough to detect material misstatements.   **A51**

Selecting Items for Testing to Obtain Audit Evidence (Ref: Para. 10)

An effective test provides appropriate audit evidence to an extent that, taken with other audit evidence obtained or to be obtained, will be sufficient for the auditor's purposes. In selecting items for testing, the auditor is required by paragraph 7 to determine the relevance and reliability of information to be used as audit evidence; the other aspect of effectiveness (sufficiency) is an important consideration in selecting items to test. The means available to the auditor for selecting items for testing are: **A52**

(a)   Selecting all items (100% examination);
(b)   Selecting specific items; and
(c)   Audit sampling.

The application of any one or combination of these means may be appropriate depending on the particular circumstances, for example, the risks of material misstatement related to the assertion being tested, and the practicality and efficiency of the different means.

Selecting All Items

The auditor may decide that it will be most appropriate to examine the entire population of items that make up a class of transactions or account balance (or a stratum within that population). 100% examination is unlikely in the case of tests of controls; however, it is more common for tests of details. 100% examination may be appropriate when, for example: **A53**

- The population constitutes a small number of large value items;
- There is a significant risk and other means do not provide sufficient appropriate audit evidence; or
- The repetitive nature of a calculation or other process performed automatically by an information system makes a 100% examination cost effective.

Selecting Specific Items

The auditor may decide to select specific items from a population. In making this decision, factors that may be relevant include the auditor's understanding of the entity, the assessed risks of material misstatement, and the characteristics of the population being tested. The judgmental selection of specific items is subject to non-sampling risk. Specific items selected may include: **A54**

- *High value or key items.* The auditor may decide to select specific items within a population because they are of high value, or exhibit some other characteristic, for example, items that are suspicious, unusual, particularly risk-prone or that have a history of error.

- *All items over a certain amount.* The auditor may decide to examine items whose recorded values exceed a certain amount so as to verify a large proportion of the total amount of a class of transactions or account balance.
- *Items to obtain information.* The auditor may examine items to obtain information about matters such as the nature of the entity or the nature of transactions.

A55   While selective examination of specific items from a class of transactions or account balance will often be an efficient means of obtaining audit evidence, it does not constitute audit sampling. The results of audit procedures applied to items selected in this way cannot be projected to the entire population; accordingly, selective examination of specific items does not provide audit evidence concerning the remainder of the population.

Audit Sampling

A56   Audit sampling is designed to enable conclusions to be drawn about an entire population on the basis of testing a sample drawn from it. Audit sampling is discussed in ISA (UK) 530.[17]

Inconsistency in, or Doubts over Reliability of, Audit Evidence (Ref: Para. 11)

A57   Obtaining audit evidence from different sources or of a different nature may indicate that an individual item of audit evidence is not reliable, such as when audit evidence obtained from one source is inconsistent with that obtained from another. This may be the case when, for example, responses to inquiries of management, internal auditors, and others are inconsistent, or when responses to inquiries of those charged with governance made to corroborate the responses to inquiries of management are inconsistent with the response by management. ISA (UK) 230 (Revised June 2016) includes a specific documentation requirement if the auditor identified information that is inconsistent with the auditor's final conclusion regarding a significant matter.[18]

---

[17] *ISA (UK) 530*, Audit Sampling.

[18] *ISA (UK) 230 (Revised June 2016)*, Audit Documentation, *paragraph 11.*

International Standard on Auditing (UK) 501

Audit evidence – specific considerations for selected items

(Effective for audits of financial statements for periods ending on or after 15 December 2010)

Contents

International Standard on Auditing (UK) (ISA (UK)) 501, *Audit Evidence—Specific Considerations for Selected Items*, should be read in conjunction with ISA (UK) 200 (Revised June 2016), *Overall Objectives of the Independent Auditor and the Conduct of an Audit in Accordance with International Standards on Auditing (UK)*.

Introduction

Scope of this ISA (UK)

1   This International Standard on Auditing (UK) (ISA (UK)) deals with specific considerations by the auditor in obtaining sufficient appropriate audit evidence in accordance with ISA (UK) 330 (Revised June 2016),[1] ISA (UK) 500[2] and other relevant ISAs (UK), with respect to certain aspects of inventory, litigation and claims involving the entity, and segment information in an audit of financial statements.

Effective Date

2   This ISA (UK) is effective for audits of financial statements for periods ending on or after 15 December 2010.

Objective

3   The objective of the auditor is to obtain sufficient appropriate audit evidence regarding the:

(a) Existence and condition of inventory;

(b) Completeness of litigation and claims involving the entity; and

(c) Presentation and disclosure of segment information in accordance with the applicable financial reporting framework.

Requirements

Inventory

4   If inventory is material to the financial statements, the auditor shall obtain sufficient appropriate audit evidence regarding the existence and condition of inventory by:

(a) Attendance at physical inventory counting, unless impracticable, to: (Ref: Para. A1–A3)

    (i) Evaluate management's instructions and procedures for recording and controlling the results of the entity's physical inventory counting; (Ref: Para. A4)

    (ii) Observe the performance of management's count procedures; (Ref: Para. A5)

    (iii) Inspect the inventory; and (Ref: Para. A6)

    (iv) Perform test counts; and (Ref: Para. A7–A8)

(b) Performing audit procedures over the entity's final inventory records to determine whether they accurately reflect actual inventory count results.

5   If physical inventory counting is conducted at a date other than the date of the financial statements, the auditor shall, in addition to the procedures required by paragraph 4, perform audit procedures to obtain audit evidence about whether changes in inventory between the count date and the date of the financial statements are properly recorded. (Ref: Para. A9–A11)

---

[1] *ISA (UK) 330 (Revised June 2016)*, The Auditor's Responses to Assessed Risks.

[2] *ISA (UK) 500*, Audit Evidence.

If the auditor is unable to attend physical inventory counting due to unforeseen **6** circumstances, the auditor shall make or observe some physical counts on an alternative date, and perform audit procedures on intervening transactions.

If attendance at physical inventory counting is impracticable, the auditor shall perform **7** alternative audit procedures to obtain sufficient appropriate audit evidence regarding the existence and condition of inventory. If it is not possible to do so, the auditor shall modify the opinion in the auditor's report in accordance with ISA (UK) 705 (Revised June 2016).[3] (Ref: Para. A12–A14)

If inventory under the custody and control of a third party is material to the financial **8** statements, the auditor shall obtain sufficient appropriate audit evidence regarding the existence and condition of that inventory by performing one or both of the following:

(a) Request confirmation from the third party as to the quantities and condition of inventory held on behalf of the entity. (Ref: Para. A15)
(b) Perform inspection or other audit procedures appropriate in the circumstances. (Ref: Para. A16)

Litigation and Claims

The auditor shall design and perform audit procedures in order to identify litigation **9** and claims involving the entity which may give rise to a risk of material misstatement, including: (Ref: Para. A17–A19)

(a) Inquiry of management[3a] and, where applicable, others within the entity, including in-house legal counsel;
(b) Reviewing minutes of meetings of those charged with governance and correspondence between the entity and its external legal counsel; and
(c) Reviewing legal expense accounts. (Ref: Para. A20)

If the auditor assesses a risk of material misstatement regarding litigation or claims that **10** have been identified, or when audit procedures performed indicate that other material litigation or claims may exist, the auditor shall, in addition to the procedures required by other ISAs (UK), seek direct communication with the entity's external legal counsel. The auditor shall do so through a letter of inquiry, prepared by management[3b] and sent by the auditor, requesting the entity's external legal counsel to communicate directly with the auditor. If law, regulation or the respective legal professional body prohibits the entity's external legal counsel from communicating directly with the auditor, the auditor shall perform alternative audit procedures. (Ref: Para. A21–A25)

If: **11**

(a) management[3c] refuses to give the auditor permission to communicate or meet with the entity's external legal counsel, or the entity's external legal counsel refuses to respond appropriately to the letter of inquiry, or is prohibited from responding; and
(b) the auditor is unable to obtain sufficient appropriate audit evidence by performing alternative audit procedures,

---

[3] *ISA (UK) 705 (Revised June 2016),* Modifications to the Opinion in the Independent Auditor's Report.

[3a] *In the UK the auditor also makes appropriate inquiry of those charged with governance.*

[3b] *In the UK the letter may need to be prepared by those charged with governance.*

[3c] *In the UK permission may be denied by those charged with governance.*

the auditor shall modify the opinion in the auditor's report in accordance with ISA (UK) 705 (Revised June 2016).

Written Representations

12   The auditor shall request management and, where appropriate, those charged with governance to provide written representations that all known actual or possible litigation and claims whose effects should be considered when preparing the financial statements have been disclosed to the auditor and accounted for and disclosed in accordance with the applicable financial reporting framework.

Segment Information

13   The auditor shall obtain sufficient appropriate audit evidence regarding the presentation and disclosure of segment information in accordance with the applicable financial reporting framework by: (Ref: Para. A26)

(a)   Obtaining an understanding of the methods used by management in determining segment information, and: (Ref: Para. A27)

   (i)   Evaluating whether such methods are likely to result in disclosure in accordance with the applicable financial reporting framework; and

   (ii)   Where appropriate, testing the application of such methods; and

(b)   Performing analytical procedures or other audit procedures appropriate in the circumstances.

Application and Other Explanatory Material

Inventory[3d]

Attendance at Physical Inventory Counting (Ref: Para. 4(a))

A1   Management ordinarily establishes procedures under which inventory is physically counted at least once a year to serve as a basis for the preparation of the financial statements and, if applicable, to ascertain the reliability of the entity's perpetual inventory system.

A2   Attendance at physical inventory counting involves:

●   Inspecting the inventory to ascertain its existence and evaluate its condition, and performing test counts;

●   Observing compliance with management's instructions and the performance of procedures for recording and controlling the results of the physical inventory count; and

●   Obtaining audit evidence as to the reliability of management's count procedures.

These procedures may serve as test of controls or substantive procedures depending on the auditor's risk assessment, planned approach and the specific procedures carried out.

A3   Matters relevant in planning attendance at physical inventory counting (or in designing and performing audit procedures pursuant to paragraphs 4–8 of this ISA (UK)) include, for example:

[3d] *For auditors in the UK further guidance has been promulgated by the FRC in Practice Note 25, Attendance at Stocktaking.*

- The risks of material misstatement related to inventory.
- The nature of the internal control related to inventory.
- Whether adequate procedures are expected to be established and proper instructions issued for physical inventory counting.
- The timing of physical inventory counting.
- Whether the entity maintains a perpetual inventory system.
- The locations at which inventory is held, including the materiality of the inventory and the risks of material misstatement at different locations, in deciding at which locations attendance is appropriate. ISA (UK) 600 (Revised June 2016)[4] deals with the involvement of other auditors and accordingly may be relevant if such involvement is with regards to attendance of physical inventory counting at a remote location.
- Whether the assistance of an auditor's expert is needed. ISA (UK) 620 (Revised June 2016)[5] deals with the use of an auditor's expert to assist the auditor to obtain sufficient appropriate audit evidence.

Evaluate Management's Instructions and Procedures (Ref: Para. 4(a)(i))

Matters relevant in evaluating management's instructions and procedures for recording and controlling the physical inventory counting include whether they address, for example:

A4

- The application of appropriate control activities, for example, collection of used physical inventory count records, accounting for unused physical inventory count records, and count and re-count procedures.
- The accurate identification of the stage of completion of work in progress, of slow moving, obsolete or damaged items and of inventory owned by a third party, for example, on consignment.
- The procedures used to estimate physical quantities, where applicable, such as may be needed in estimating the physical quantity of a coal pile.
- Control over the movement of inventory between areas and the shipping and receipt of inventory before and after the cutoff date.

Observe the Performance of Management's Count Procedures (Ref: Para. 4(a)(ii))

Observing the performance of management's count procedures, for example those relating to control over the movement of inventory before, during and after the count, assists the auditor in obtaining audit evidence that management's instructions and count procedures are adequately designed and implemented. In addition, the auditor may obtain copies of cutoff information, such as details of the movement of inventory, to assist the auditor in performing audit procedures over the accounting for such movements at a later date.

A5

Inspect the Inventory (Ref: Para. 4(a)(iii))

Inspecting inventory when attending physical inventory counting assists the auditor in ascertaining the existence of the inventory (though not necessarily its ownership), and in identifying, for example, obsolete, damaged or ageing inventory.

A6

[4] *ISA (UK) 600 (Revised June 2016)*, Special Considerations—Audits of Group Financial Statements (Including the Work of Component Auditors).

[5] *ISA (UK) 620 (Revised June 2016)*, Using the Work of an Auditor's Expert.

Perform Test Counts (Ref: Para. 4(a)(iv))

A7   Performing test counts, for example by tracing items selected from management's count records to the physical inventory and tracing items selected from the physical inventory to management's count records, provides audit evidence about the completeness and the accuracy of those records.

A8   In addition to recording the auditor's test counts, obtaining copies of management's completed physical inventory count records assists the auditor in performing subsequent audit procedures to determine whether the entity's final inventory records accurately reflect actual inventory count results.

Physical Inventory Counting Conducted Other than At the Date of the Financial Statements (Ref: Para. 5)

A9   For practical reasons, the physical inventory counting may be conducted at a date, or dates, other than the date of the financial statements. This may be done irrespective of whether management determines inventory quantities by an annual physical inventory counting or maintains a perpetual inventory system. In either case, the effectiveness of the design, implementation and maintenance of controls over changes in inventory determines whether the conduct of physical inventory counting at a date, or dates, other than the date of the financial statements is appropriate for audit purposes. ISA (UK) 330 (Revised June 2016) establishes requirements and provides guidance on substantive procedures performed at an interim date.[6]

A10   Where a perpetual inventory system is maintained, management may perform physical counts or other tests to ascertain the reliability of inventory quantity information included in the entity's perpetual inventory records. In some cases, management or the auditor may identify differences between the perpetual inventory records and actual physical inventory quantities on hand; this may indicate that the controls over changes in inventory are not operating effectively.

A11   Relevant matters for consideration when designing audit procedures to obtain audit evidence about whether changes in inventory amounts between the count date, or dates, and the final inventory records are properly recorded include:

●   Whether the perpetual inventory records are properly adjusted.
●   Reliability of the entity's perpetual inventory records.
●   Reasons for significant differences between the information obtained during the physical count and the perpetual inventory records.

Attendance at Physical Inventory Counting Is Impracticable (Ref: Para. 7)

A12   In some cases, attendance at physical inventory counting may be impracticable. This may be due to factors such as the nature and location of the inventory, for example, where inventory is held in a location that may pose threats to the safety of the auditor. The matter of general inconvenience to the auditor, however, is not sufficient to support a decision by the auditor that attendance is impracticable. Further, as explained in ISA (UK) 200 (Revised June 2016),[7] the matter of difficulty, time, or cost involved is not in itself a valid

---

[6] *ISA (UK) 330 (Revised June 2016), paragraphs 22–23.*

[7] *ISA (UK) 200 (Revised June 2016),* Overall Objectives of the Independent Auditor and the Conduct of an Audit in Accordance with International Standards on Auditing (UK), *paragraph A48.*

basis for the auditor to omit an audit procedure for which there is no alternative or to be satisfied with audit evidence that is less than persuasive.

In some cases where attendance is impracticable, alternative audit procedures, for example   **A13** inspection of documentation of the subsequent sale of specific inventory items acquired or purchased prior to the physical inventory counting, may provide sufficient appropriate audit evidence about the existence and condition of inventory.

In other cases, however, it may not be possible to obtain sufficient appropriate audit   **A14** evidence regarding the existence and condition of inventory by performing alternative audit procedures. In such cases, ISA (UK) 705 (Revised June 2016) requires the auditor to modify the opinion in the auditor's report as a result of the scope limitation.[8]

Inventory under the Custody and Control of a Third Party

Confirmation (Ref: Para. 8(a))

ISA (UK) 505[9] establishes requirements and provides guidance for performing external   **A15** confirmation procedures.

Other Audit Procedures (Ref: Para. 8(b))

Depending on the circumstances, for example where information is obtained that raises   **A16** doubt about the integrity and objectivity of the third party, the auditor may consider it appropriate to perform other audit procedures instead of, or in addition to, confirmation with the third party. Examples of other audit procedures include:

- Attending, or arranging for another auditor to attend, the third party's physical counting of inventory, if practicable.
- Obtaining another auditor's report, or a service auditor's report, on the adequacy of the third party's internal control for ensuring that inventory is properly counted and adequately safeguarded.
- Inspecting documentation regarding inventory held by third parties, for example, warehouse receipts.
- Requesting confirmation from other parties when inventory has been pledged as collateral.

Litigation and Claims

Completeness of Litigations and Claims (Ref: Para. 9)

Litigation and claims involving the entity may have a material effect on the financial   **A17** statements and thus may be required to be disclosed or accounted for in the financial statements.

In addition to the procedures identified in paragraph 9, other relevant procedures include,   **A18** for example, using information obtained through risk assessment procedures carried out as part of obtaining an understanding of the entity and its environment to assist the auditor to become aware of litigation and claims involving the entity.

---

[8] *ISA (UK) 705 (Revised June 2016), paragraph 13.*

[9] *ISA (UK) 505,* External Confirmations.

A19 Audit evidence obtained for purposes of identifying litigation and claims that may give rise to a risk of material misstatement also may provide audit evidence regarding other relevant considerations, such as valuation or measurement, regarding litigation and claims. ISA (UK) 540 (Revised June 2016)[10] establishes requirements and provides guidance relevant to the auditor's consideration of litigation and claims requiring accounting estimates or related disclosures in the financial statements.

Reviewing Legal Expense Accounts (Ref: Para. 9(c))

A20 Depending on the circumstances, the auditor may judge it appropriate to examine related source documents, such as invoices for legal expenses, as part of the auditor's review of legal expense accounts.

Communication with the Entity's External Legal Counsel (Ref: Para. 10–11)

A21 Direct communication with the entity's external legal counsel assists the auditor in obtaining sufficient appropriate audit evidence as to whether potentially material litigation and claims are known and management's estimates of the financial implications, including costs, are reasonable.

A22 In some cases, the auditor may seek direct communication with the entity's external legal counsel through a letter of general inquiry. For this purpose, a letter of general inquiry requests the entity's external legal counsel to inform the auditor of any litigation and claims that the counsel is aware of, together with an assessment of the outcome of the litigation and claims, and an estimate of the financial implications, including costs involved.

A23 If it is considered unlikely that the entity's external legal counsel will respond appropriately to a letter of general inquiry, for example if the professional body to which the external legal counsel belongs prohibits response to such a letter[10a], the auditor may seek direct communication through a letter of specific inquiry. For this purpose, a letter of specific inquiry includes:

(a) A list of litigation and claims;

(b) Where available, management's assessment of the outcome of each of the identified litigation and claims and its estimate of the financial implications, including costs involved; and

(c) A request that the entity's external legal counsel confirm the reasonableness of management's assessments and provide the auditor with further information if the list is considered by the entity's external legal counsel to be incomplete or incorrect.

A24 In certain circumstances, the auditor also may judge it necessary to meet with the entity's external legal counsel to discuss the likely outcome of the litigation or claims. This may be the case, for example, where:

- The auditor determines that the matter is a significant risk.
- The matter is complex.
- There is disagreement between management and the entity's external legal counsel.

Ordinarily, such meetings require management's permission[3c] and are held with a representative of management in attendance.

---

[10] ISA (UK) 540 (Revised June 2016), Auditing Accounting Estimates, Including Fair Value Accounting Estimates, and Related Disclosures.

[10a] *In the UK, the Council of the Law Society has advised solicitors that it is unable to recommend them to comply with non-specific requests for information.*

In accordance with ISA (UK) 700 (Revised June 2016),[11] the auditor is required to date   **A25**
the auditor's report no earlier than the date on which the auditor has obtained sufficient
appropriate audit evidence on which to base the auditor's opinion on the financial
statements. Audit evidence about the status of litigation and claims up to the date of the
auditor's report may be obtained by inquiry of management[3a], including in-house legal
counsel, responsible for dealing with the relevant matters. In some instances, the auditor
may need to obtain updated information from the entity's external legal counsel.

Segment Information (Ref: Para. 13)

Depending on the applicable financial reporting framework, the entity may be required   **A26**
or permitted to disclose segment information in the financial statements. The auditor's
responsibility regarding the presentation and disclosure of segment information is in
relation to the financial statements taken as a whole. Accordingly, the auditor is not
required to perform audit procedures that would be necessary to express an opinion on the
segment information presented on a stand alone basis.

Understanding of the Methods Used by Management (Ref: Para. 13(a))

Depending on the circumstances, example of matters that may be relevant when obtaining   **A27**
an understanding of the methods used by management in determining segment information
and whether such methods are likely to result in disclosure in accordance with the
applicable financial reporting framework include:

- Sales, transfers and charges between segments, and elimination of intersegment
  amounts.
- Comparisons with budgets and other expected results, for example, operating profits
  as a percentage of sales.
- The allocation of assets and costs among segments.
- Consistency with prior periods, and the adequacy of the disclosures with respect to
  inconsistencies.

---

[11] *ISA (UK) 700 (Revise June 2016)*, Forming an Opinion and Reporting on Financial Statements, *paragraph 41.*

International Standard on Auditing (UK) 505 (Updated July 2017)
External confirmations

(Effective for audits of financial statements for periods ending on or after 15 December 2010)[0]

Contents

International Standard on Auditing (UK) (ISA (UK)) 505, *External Confirmations*, should be read in conjunction with ISA (UK) 200 (Revised June 2016), *Overall Objectives of the Independent Auditor and the Conduct of an Audit in Accordance with International Standards on Auditing (UK)*.

[0] *Conforming amendments to this standard as a result of ISA (UK) 330 (Revised July 2017), The Auditor's Responses to Assessed Risks, are included that are effective for audits of financial statements for periods commencing on or after 15 December 2017. Details of the amendments are given in the Annexure to ISA (UK) 330 (Revised July 2017).*

Introduction

Scope of this ISA (UK)

This International Standard on Auditing (UK) (ISA (UK)) deals with the auditor's use   **1**
of external confirmation procedures to obtain audit evidence in accordance with the
requirements of ISA (UK) 330 (Revised July 2017)[1] and ISA (UK) 500.[2] It does not
address inquiries regarding litigation and claims, which are dealt with in ISA (UK) 501.[3]

External Confirmation Procedures to Obtain Audit Evidence

ISA (UK) 500 indicates that the reliability of audit evidence is influenced by its source and   **2**
by its nature, and is dependent on the individual circumstances under which it is obtained.[4]
That ISA (UK) also includes the following generalizations applicable to audit evidence:[5]

- Audit evidence is more reliable when it is obtained from independent sources outside
  the entity.
- Audit evidence obtained directly by the auditor is more reliable than audit evidence
  obtained indirectly or by inference.
- Audit evidence is more reliable when it exists in documentary form, whether paper,
  electronic or other medium.

Accordingly, depending on the circumstances of the audit, audit evidence in the form of
external confirmations received directly by the auditor from confirming parties may be
more reliable than evidence generated internally by the entity. This ISA (UK) is intended to
assist the auditor in designing and performing external confirmation procedures to obtain
relevant and reliable audit evidence.

Other ISAs (UK) recognize the importance of external confirmations as audit evidence,   **3**
for example:

- ISA (UK) 330 (Revised July 2017) discusses the auditor's responsibility to design and
  implement overall responses to address the assessed risks of material misstatement
  at the financial statement level, and to design and perform further audit procedures
  whose nature, timing and extent are based on, and are responsive to, the assessed risks
  of material misstatement at the assertion level.[6] In addition, ISA (UK) 330 (Revised
  July 2017) requires that, irrespective of the assessed risks of material misstatement,
  the auditor designs and performs substantive procedures for each material class of
  transactions, account balance, and disclosure. The auditor is also required to consider
  whether external confirmation procedures are to be performed as substantive audit
  procedures.[7]

---

[1] *ISA (UK) 330 (Revised July 2017)*, The Auditor's Responses to Assessed Risks.

[2] *ISA (UK) 500*, Audit Evidence.

[3] *ISA (UK) 501*, Audit Evidence—Specific Considerations for Selected Items.

[4] *ISA (UK) 500, paragraph A5.*

[5] *ISA (UK) 500, paragraph A31.*

[6] *ISA (UK) 330 (Revised July 2017), paragraphs 5–6.*

[7] *ISA (UK) 330 (Revised July 2017), paragraphs 18–19.*

- ISA (UK) 330 (Revised July 2017) requires that the auditor obtain more persuasive audit evidence the higher the auditor's assessment of risk.[8] To do this, the auditor may increase the quantity of the evidence or obtain evidence that is more relevant or reliable, or both. For example, the auditor may place more emphasis on obtaining evidence directly from third parties or obtaining corroborating evidence from a number of independent sources. ISA (UK) 330 (Revised July 2017) also indicates that external confirmation procedures may assist the auditor in obtaining audit evidence with the high level of reliability that the auditor requires to respond to significant risks of material misstatement, whether due to fraud or error.[9]
- ISA (UK) 240 (Revised June 2016) indicates that the auditor may design confirmation requests to obtain additional corroborative information as a response to address the assessed risks of material misstatement due to fraud at the assertion level.[10]
- ISA (UK) 500 indicates that corroborating information obtained from a source independent of the entity, such as external confirmations, may increase the assurance the auditor obtains from evidence existing within the accounting records or from representations made by management.[11]

Effective Date

4   This ISA (UK) is effective for audits of financial statements for periods ending on or after 15 December 2010.

Objective

5   The objective of the auditor, when using external confirmation procedures, is to design and perform such procedures to obtain relevant and reliable audit evidence.

Definitions

6   For purposes of the ISAs (UK), the following terms have the meanings attributed below:
  - (a)   External confirmation – Audit evidence obtained as a direct written response to the auditor from a third party (the confirming party), in paper form, or by electronic or other medium.
  - (b)   Positive confirmation request – A request that the confirming party respond directly to the auditor indicating whether the confirming party agrees or disagrees with the information in the request, or providing the requested information.
  - (c)   Negative confirmation request – A request that the confirming party respond directly to the auditor only if the confirming party disagrees with the information provided in the request.
  - (d)   Non-response – A failure of the confirming party to respond, or fully respond, to a positive confirmation request, or a confirmation request returned undelivered.
  - (e)   Exception – A response that indicates a difference between information requested to be confirmed, or contained in the entity's records, and information provided by the confirming party.

---

[8] *ISA (UK) 330 (Revised July 2017), paragraph 7(b).*

[9] *ISA (UK) 330 (Revised July 2017), paragraph A53.*

[10] *ISA (UK) 240 (Revised June 2016),* The Auditor's Responsibilities Relating to Fraud in an Audit of Financial Statements, *paragraph A37.*

[11] *ISA (UK) 500, paragraph A8–A9.*

Requirements

External Confirmation Procedures

When using external confirmation procedures, the auditor shall maintain control over   **7**
external confirmation requests, including:
(a) Determining the information to be confirmed or requested; (Ref: Para. A1)
(b) Selecting the appropriate confirming party; (Ref: Para. A2)
(c) Designing the confirmation requests, including determining that requests are properly addressed and contain return information for responses to be sent directly to the auditor; and (Ref: Para. A3–A6)
(d) Sending the requests, including follow-up requests when applicable, to the confirming party. (Ref: Para. A7)

Management's Refusal to Allow the Auditor to Send a Confirmation Request

If management refuses to allow the auditor to send a confirmation request, the auditor   **8**
shall:
(a) Inquire as to management's reasons for the refusal, and seek audit evidence as to their validity and reasonableness; (Ref: Para. A8)
(b) Evaluate the implications of management's refusal on the auditor's assessment of the relevant risks of material misstatement, including the risk of fraud, and on the nature, timing and extent of other audit procedures; and (Ref: Para. A9)
(c) Perform alternative audit procedures designed to obtain relevant and reliable audit evidence. (Ref: Para. A10)

If the auditor concludes that management's refusal to allow the auditor to send a   **9**
confirmation request is unreasonable, or the auditor is unable to obtain relevant and reliable audit evidence from alternative audit procedures, the auditor shall communicate with those charged with governance in accordance with ISA (UK) 260 (Revised June 2016).[12] The auditor also shall determine the implications for the audit and the auditor's opinion in accordance with ISA (UK) 705 (Revised June 2016).[13]

Results of the External Confirmation Procedures

Reliability of Responses to Confirmation Requests

If the auditor identifies factors that give rise to doubts about the reliability of the response   **10**
to a confirmation request, the auditor shall obtain further audit evidence to resolve those doubts. (Ref: Para. A11–A16)

If the auditor determines that a response to a confirmation request is not reliable, the   **11**
auditor shall evaluate the implications on the assessment of the relevant risks of material misstatement, including the risk of fraud, and on the related nature, timing and extent of other audit procedures. (Ref: Para. A17)

[12] ISA (UK) 260 (Revised June 2016), Communication with Those Charged with Governance, *paragraph 16.*

[13] ISA (UK) 705 (Revised June 2016), Modifications to the Opinion in the Independent Auditor's Report.

Non-Responses

12   In the case of each non-response, the auditor shall perform alternative audit procedures to obtain relevant and reliable audit evidence. (Ref: Para A18–A19)

When a Response to a Positive Confirmation Request Is Necessary to Obtain Sufficient Appropriate Audit Evidence

13   If the auditor has determined that a response to a positive confirmation request is necessary to obtain sufficient appropriate audit evidence, alternative audit procedures will not provide the audit evidence the auditor requires. If the auditor does not obtain such confirmation, the auditor shall determine the implications for the audit and the auditor's opinion in accordance with ISA (UK) 705 (Revised June 2016). (Ref: Para A20)

Exceptions

14   The auditor shall investigate exceptions to determine whether or not they are indicative of misstatements. (Ref: Para. A21–A22)

Negative Confirmations

15   Negative confirmations provide less persuasive audit evidence than positive confirmations. Accordingly, the auditor shall not use negative confirmation requests as the sole substantive audit procedure to address an assessed risk of material misstatement at the assertion level unless all of the following are present: (Ref: Para. A23)

   (a)   The auditor has assessed the risk of material misstatement as low and has obtained sufficient appropriate audit evidence regarding the operating effectiveness of controls relevant to the assertion;
   (b)   The population of items subject to negative confirmation procedures comprises a large number of small, homogeneous, account balances, transactions or conditions;
   (c)   A very low exception rate is expected; and
   (d)   The auditor is not aware of circumstances or conditions that would cause recipients of negative confirmation requests to disregard such requests.

Evaluating the Evidence Obtained

16   The auditor shall evaluate whether the results of the external confirmation procedures provide relevant and reliable audit evidence, or whether further audit evidence is necessary. (Ref: Para A24–A25)

***

Application and Other Explanatory Material

External Confirmation Procedures

Determining the Information to Be Confirmed or Requested (Ref: Para. 7(a))

A1   External confirmation procedures frequently are performed to confirm or request information regarding account balances and their elements. They may also be used to confirm terms of agreements, contracts, or transactions between an entity and other parties, or to confirm the absence of certain conditions, such as a 'side agreement.'

Selecting the Appropriate Confirming Party (Ref: Para. 7(b))

Responses to confirmation requests provide more relevant and reliable audit evidence when confirmation requests are sent to a confirming party the auditor believes is knowledgeable about the information to be confirmed. For example, a financial institution official who is knowledgeable about the transactions or arrangements for which confirmation is requested may be the most appropriate person at the financial institution from whom to request confirmation.

A2

Designing Confirmation Requests (Ref: Para. 7(c))

The design of a confirmation request may directly affect the confirmation response rate, and the reliability and the nature of the audit evidence obtained from responses.

A3

Factors to consider when designing confirmation requests include:[13a]

A4

- The assertions being addressed.
- Specific identified risks of material misstatement, including fraud risks.
- The layout and presentation of the confirmation request.
- Prior experience on the audit or similar engagements.
- The method of communication (for example, in paper form, or by electronic or other medium).
- Management's authorization or encouragement to the confirming parties to respond to the auditor. Confirming parties may only be willing to respond to a confirmation request containing management's authorization.
- The ability of the intended confirming party to confirm or provide the requested information (for example, individual invoice amount versus total balance).

A positive external confirmation request asks the confirming party to reply to the auditor in all cases, either by indicating the confirming party's agreement with the given information, or by asking the confirming party to provide information. A response to a positive confirmation request ordinarily is expected to provide reliable audit evidence. There is a risk, however, that a confirming party may reply to the confirmation request without verifying that the information is correct. The auditor may reduce this risk by using positive confirmation requests that do not state the amount (or other information) on the confirmation request, and ask the confirming party to fill in the amount or furnish other information. On the other hand, use of this type of 'blank' confirmation request may result in lower response rates because additional effort is required of the confirming parties.

A5

Determining that requests are properly addressed includes testing the validity of some or all of the addresses on confirmation requests before they are sent out.

A6

Follow-Up on Confirmation Requests (Ref: Para. 7(d))

The auditor may send an additional confirmation request when a reply to a previous request has not been received within a reasonable time. For example, the auditor may, having re-verified the accuracy of the original address, send an additional or follow-up request.

A7

[13a] *Pro-forma templates to obtain bank confirmations in the United Kingdom which have been agreed with the British Bankers' Association on behalf of the industry can be found at: https://www.bba.org.uk/policy/financial-and-risk-policy/financial-reporting/audit/instructions-for-using-pn16-templates/*

Management's Refusal to Allow the Auditor to Send a Confirmation Request

Reasonableness of Management's Refusal (Ref: Para. 8(a))

A8   A refusal by management to allow the auditor to send a confirmation request is a limitation on the audit evidence the auditor may wish to obtain. The auditor is therefore required to inquire as to the reasons for the limitation. A common reason advanced is the existence of a legal dispute or ongoing negotiation with the intended confirming party, the resolution of which may be affected by an untimely confirmation request. The auditor is required to seek audit evidence as to the validity and reasonableness of the reasons because of the risk that management may be attempting to deny the auditor access to audit evidence that may reveal fraud or error.

Implications for the Assessment of Risks of Material Misstatement (Ref: Para. 8(b))

A9   The auditor may conclude from the evaluation in paragraph 8(b) that it would be appropriate to revise the assessment of the risks of material misstatement at the assertion level and modify planned audit procedures in accordance with ISA (UK) 315 (Revised June 2016).[14] For example, if management's request to not confirm is unreasonable, this may indicate a fraud risk factor that requires evaluation in accordance with ISA (UK) 240 (Revised June 2016).[15]

Alternative Audit Procedures (Ref: Para. 8(c))

A10   The alternative audit procedures performed may be similar to those appropriate for a non-response as set out in paragraphs A18–A19 of this ISA (UK). Such procedures also would take account of the results of the auditor's evaluation in paragraph 8(b) of this ISA (UK).

Results of the External Confirmation Procedures

Reliability of Responses to Confirmation Requests (Ref: Para. 10)

A11   ISA (UK) 500 indicates that even when audit evidence is obtained from sources external to the entity, circumstances may exist that affect its reliability.[16] All responses carry some risk of interception, alteration or fraud. Such risk exists regardless of whether a response is obtained in paper form, or by electronic or other medium. Factors that may indicate doubts about the reliability of a response include that it:

- Was received by the auditor indirectly; or
- Appeared not to come from the originally intended confirming party.

A12   Responses received electronically, for example by facsimile or electronic mail, involve risks as to reliability because proof of origin and authority of the respondent may be difficult to establish, and alterations may be difficult to detect. A process used by the auditor and the respondent that creates a secure environment for responses received electronically may mitigate these risks. If the auditor is satisfied that such a process is secure and properly

---

[14] *ISA (UK) 315 (Revised June 2016),* Identifying and Assessing the Risks of Material Misstatement through Understanding the Entity and Its Environment, *paragraph 31.*

[15] *ISA (UK) 240 (Revised June 2016), paragraph 24.*

[16] *ISA (UK) 500, paragraph A31.*

controlled, the reliability of the related responses is enhanced. An electronic confirmation process might incorporate various techniques for validating the identity of a sender of information in electronic form, for example, through the use of encryption, electronic digital signatures, and procedures to verify web site authenticity.

If a confirming party uses a third party to coordinate and provide responses to confirmation requests, the auditor may perform procedures to address the risks that: **A13**

(a) The response may not be from the proper source;
(b) A respondent may not be authorized to respond; and
(c) The integrity of the transmission may have been compromised.

The auditor is required by ISA (UK) 500 to determine whether to modify or add procedures to resolve doubts over the reliability of information to be used as audit evidence.[17] The auditor may choose to verify the source and contents of a response to a confirmation request by contacting the confirming party. For example, when a confirming party responds by electronic mail, the auditor may telephone the confirming party to determine whether the confirming party did, in fact, send the response. When a response has been returned to the auditor indirectly (for example, because the confirming party incorrectly addressed it to the entity rather than to the auditor), the auditor may request the confirming party to respond in writing directly to the auditor. **A14**

On its own, an oral response to a confirmation request does not meet the definition of an external confirmation because it is not a direct written response to the auditor. However, upon obtaining an oral response to a confirmation request, the auditor may, depending on the circumstances, request the confirming party to respond in writing directly to the auditor. If no such response is received, in accordance with paragraph 12, the auditor seeks other audit evidence to support the information in the oral response. **A15**

A response to a confirmation request may contain restrictive language regarding its use. Such restrictions do not necessarily invalidate the reliability of the response as audit evidence. **A16**

Unreliable Responses (Ref: Para. 11)

When the auditor concludes that a response is unreliable, the auditor may need to revise the assessment of the risks of material misstatement at the assertion level and modify planned audit procedures accordingly, in accordance with ISA (UK) 315 (Revised June 2016).[18] For example, an unreliable response may indicate a fraud risk factor that requires evaluation in accordance with ISA (UK) 240 (Revised June 2016).[19] **A17**

Non-Responses (Ref: Para. 12)

Examples of alternative audit procedures the auditor may perform include: **A18**

- For accounts receivable balances – examining specific subsequent cash receipts, shipping documentation, and sales near the period-end.
- For accounts payable balances – examining subsequent cash disbursements or correspondence from third parties, and other records, such as goods received notes.

---

[17] *ISA (UK) 500, paragraph 11.*

[18] *ISA (UK) 315 (Revised June 2016), paragraph 31.*

[19] *ISA (UK) 240 (Revised June 2016), paragraph 24.*

A19   The nature and extent of alternative audit procedures are affected by the account and assertion in question. A non-response to a confirmation request may indicate a previously unidentified risk of material misstatement. In such situations, the auditor may need to revise the assessed risk of material misstatement at the assertion level, and modify planned audit procedures, in accordance with ISA (UK) 315 (Revised June 2016).[20] For example, fewer responses to confirmation requests than anticipated, or a greater number of responses than anticipated, may indicate a previously unidentified fraud risk factor that requires evaluation in accordance with ISA (UK) 240 (Revised June 2016).[21]

When a Response to a Positive Confirmation Request Is Necessary to Obtain Sufficient Appropriate Audit Evidence (Ref. Para. 13)

A20   In certain circumstances, the auditor may identify an assessed risk of material misstatement at the assertion level for which a response to a positive confirmation request is necessary to obtain sufficient appropriate audit evidence. Such circumstances may include where:

- The information available to corroborate management's assertion(s) is only available outside the entity.
- Specific fraud risk factors, such as the risk of management override of controls, or the risk of collusion which can involve employee(s) and/or management, prevent the auditor from relying on evidence from the entity.

Exceptions (Ref: Para. 14)

A21   Exceptions noted in responses to confirmation requests may indicate misstatements or potential misstatements in the financial statements. When a misstatement is identified, the auditor is required by ISA (UK) 240 (Revised June 2016) to evaluate whether such misstatement is indicative of fraud.[22] Exceptions may provide a guide to the quality of responses from similar confirming parties or for similar accounts. Exceptions also may indicate a deficiency, or deficiencies, in the entity's internal control over financial reporting.

A22   Some exceptions do not represent misstatements. For example, the auditor may conclude that differences in responses to confirmation requests are due to timing, measurement, or clerical errors in the external confirmation procedures.

Negative Confirmations (Ref: Para. 15)

A23   The failure to receive a response to a negative confirmation request does not explicitly indicate receipt by the intended confirming party of the confirmation request or verification of the accuracy of the information contained in the request. Accordingly, a failure of a confirming party to respond to a negative confirmation request provides significantly less persuasive audit evidence than does a response to a positive confirmation request. Confirming parties also may be more likely to respond indicating their disagreement with a confirmation request when the information in the request is not in their favor, and less likely to respond otherwise. For example, holders of bank deposit accounts may be more likely to respond if they believe that the balance in their account is understated in the confirmation request, but may be less likely to respond when they believe the balance is overstated. Therefore, sending negative confirmation requests to holders of bank

---

[20] *ISA (UK) 315 (Revised June 2016), paragraph 31.*

[21] *ISA (UK) 240 (Revised June 2016), paragraph 24.*

[22] *ISA (UK) 240 (Revised June 2016), paragraph 35.*

deposit accounts may be a useful procedure in considering whether such balances may be understated, but is unlikely to be effective if the auditor is seeking evidence regarding overstatement.

Evaluating the Evidence Obtained (Ref: Para. 16)

When evaluating the results of individual external confirmation requests, the auditor may categorize such results as follows:

(a) A response by the appropriate confirming party indicating agreement with the information provided in the confirmation request, or providing requested information without exception;

(b) A response deemed unreliable;

(c) A non-response; or

(d) A response indicating an exception.

A24

The auditor's evaluation, when taken into account with other audit procedures the auditor may have performed, may assist the auditor in concluding whether sufficient appropriate audit evidence has been obtained or whether further audit evidence is necessary, as required by ISA (UK) 330 (Revised July 2017).[23]

A25

---

[23] *ISA (UK) 330 (Revised July 2017), paragraphs 26–27.*

International Standard on Auditing (UK) 510 (Revised June 2016)

Initial audit engagements – opening balances

(Effective for audits of financial statements for periods commencing on or after 17 June 2016)

Contents

International Standard on Auditing (UK) (ISA (UK)) 510 (Revised June 2016), *Initial Audit Engagements—Opening Balances*, should be read in conjunction with ISA (UK) 200 (Revised June 2016), *Overall Objectives of the Independent Auditor and the Conduct of an Audit in Accordance with International Standards on Auditing (UK)*.

Introduction

Scope of this ISA (UK)

This International Standard on Auditing (UK) (ISA (UK)) deals with the auditor's **1** responsibilities relating to opening balances in an initial audit engagement. In addition to financial statement amounts, opening balances include matters requiring disclosure that existed at the beginning of the period, such as contingencies and commitments. When the financial statements include comparative financial information, the requirements and guidance in ISA (UK) 710[1] also apply. ISA (UK) 300 (Revised June 2016)[2] includes additional requirements and guidance regarding activities prior to starting an initial audit.

Effective Date

This ISA (UK) is effective for audits of financial statements for periods commencing on or **2** after 17 June 2016. Earlier adoption is permitted.

Objective

In conducting an initial audit engagement, the objective of the auditor with respect to **3** opening balances is to obtain sufficient appropriate audit evidence about whether:

(a) Opening balances contain misstatements that materially affect the current period's financial statements; and

(b) Appropriate accounting policies reflected in the opening balances have been consistently applied in the current period's financial statements, or changes thereto are appropriately accounted for and adequately presented and disclosed in accordance with the applicable financial reporting framework.

Definitions

For the purposes of the ISAs (UK), the following terms have the meanings attributed **4** below:

(a) Initial audit engagement – An engagement in which either:
   (i) The financial statements for the prior period were not audited; or
   (ii) The financial statements for the prior period were audited by a predecessor auditor.

(b) Opening balances – Those account balances that exist at the beginning of the period. Opening balances are based upon the closing balances of the prior period and reflect the effects of transactions and events of prior periods and accounting policies applied in the prior period. Opening balances also include matters requiring disclosure that existed at the beginning of the period, such as contingencies and commitments.

(c) Predecessor auditor – The auditor from a different audit firm, who audited the financial statements of an entity in the prior period and who has been replaced by the current auditor.

---

[1] *ISA (UK) 710*, Comparative Information—Corresponding Figures and Comparative Financial Statements.

[2] *ISA (UK) 300 (Revised June 2016)*, Planning an Audit of Financial Statements.

Requirements

Audit Procedures

Opening Balances

5   The auditor shall read the most recent financial statements, if any, and the predecessor auditor's report thereon, if any, for information relevant to opening balances, including disclosures.

6   The auditor shall obtain sufficient appropriate audit evidence about whether the opening balances contain misstatements that materially affect the current period's financial statements by: (Ref: Para. A1–A2)

   (a) Determining whether the prior period's closing balances have been correctly brought forward to the current period or, when appropriate, have been restated;

   (b) Determining whether the opening balances reflect the application of appropriate accounting policies; and

   (c) Performing one or more of the following: (Ref: Para. A3–A7)

      (i)   Where the prior year financial statements were audited, reviewing the predecessor auditor's working papers to obtain evidence regarding the opening balances;

      (ii) Evaluating whether audit procedures performed in the current period provide evidence relevant to the opening balances; or

      (iii) Performing specific audit procedures to obtain evidence regarding the opening balances.

7   If the auditor obtains audit evidence that the opening balances contain misstatements that could materially affect the current period's financial statements, the auditor shall perform such additional audit procedures as are appropriate in the circumstances to determine the effect on the current period's financial statements. If the auditor concludes that such misstatements exist in the current period's financial statements, the auditor shall communicate the misstatements with the appropriate level of management and those charged with governance in accordance with ISA (UK) 450 (Revised June 2016).[3]

Consistency of Accounting Policies

8   The auditor shall obtain sufficient appropriate audit evidence about whether the accounting policies reflected in the opening balances have been consistently applied in the current period's financial statements, and whether changes in the accounting policies have been appropriately accounted for and adequately presented and disclosed in accordance with the applicable financial reporting framework.

Required Understanding of Prior Year Responses to Risks

8R-1   For audits of financial statements of public interest entities, the auditor shall obtain an understanding of the predecessor auditor's methodology used to carry out the audit, sufficient to enable the auditor to communicate with those charged with governance those matters required by paragraph 16R-2(g) of ISA (UK) 260 (Revised June 2016).[3a] (Ref: Para. A7-1)

---

[3] ISA (UK) 450 (Revised June 2016), Evaluation of Misstatements Identified during the Audit, *paragraphs 8 and 12.*

[3a] *ISA (UK) 260 (Revised June 2016), Communication with Those Charged with Governance.*

Relevant Information in the Predecessor Auditor's Report

If the prior period's financial statements were audited by a predecessor auditor and there **9** was a modification to the opinion, the auditor shall evaluate the effect of the matter giving rise to the modification in assessing the risks of material misstatement in the current period's financial statements in accordance with ISA (UK) 315 (Revised June 2016).[4]

Audit Conclusions and Reporting

Opening Balances

If the auditor is unable to obtain sufficient appropriate audit evidence regarding the **10** opening balances, the auditor shall express a qualified opinion or disclaim an opinion on the financial statements, as appropriate, in accordance with ISA (UK) 705 (Revised June 2016).[5] (Ref: Para. A8)

If the auditor concludes that the opening balances contain a misstatement that materially **11** affects the current period's financial statements, and the effect of the misstatement is not appropriately accounted for or not adequately presented or disclosed, the auditor shall express a qualified opinion or an adverse opinion, as appropriate, in accordance with ISA (UK) 705 (Revised June 2016).

Consistency of Accounting Policies

If the auditor concludes that:
12

(a) the current period's accounting policies are not consistently applied in relation to opening balances in accordance with the applicable financial reporting framework; or
(b) a change in accounting policies is not appropriately accounted for or not adequately presented or disclosed in accordance with the applicable financial reporting framework,

the auditor shall express a qualified opinion or an adverse opinion as appropriate in accordance with ISA (UK) 705 (Revised June 2016).

Modification to the Opinion in the Predecessor Auditor's Report

If the predecessor auditor's opinion regarding the prior period's financial statements **13** included a modification to the auditor's opinion that remains relevant and material to the current period's financial statements, the auditor shall modify the auditor's opinion on the current period's financial statements in accordance with ISA (UK) 705 (Revised June 2016) and ISA (UK) 710. (Ref: Para. A9)

---

[4] *ISA (UK) 315 (Revised June 2016)*, Identifying and Assessing the Risks of Material Misstatement through Understanding the Entity and Its Environment.

[5] *ISA (UK) 705 (Revised June 2016)*, Modifications to the Opinion in the Independent Auditor's Report.

Application and Other Explanatory Material

Audit Procedures

Considerations Specific to Public Sector Entities (Ref: Para. 6)

A1   In the public sector, there may be legal or regulatory limitations on the information that the current auditor can obtain from a predecessor auditor. For example, if a public sector entity that has previously been audited by a statutorily appointed auditor (for example, an Auditor General, or other suitably qualified person appointed on behalf of the Auditor General) is privatized, the amount of access to working papers or other information that the statutorily appointed auditor can provide a newly-appointed auditor that is in the private sector may be constrained by privacy or secrecy laws or regulations. In situations where such communications are constrained, audit evidence may need to be obtained through other means and, if sufficient appropriate audit evidence cannot be obtained, consideration given to the effect on the auditor's opinion.

A2   If the statutorily appointed auditor outsources an audit of a public sector entity to a private sector audit firm, and the statutorily appointed auditor appoints an audit firm other than the firm that audited the financial statements of the public sector entity in the prior period, this is not usually regarded as a change in auditors for the statutorily appointed auditor. Depending on the nature of the outsourcing arrangement, however, the audit engagement may be considered an initial audit engagement from the perspective of the private sector auditor in fulfilling their responsibilities, and therefore this ISA (UK) applies.

Opening Balances (Ref: Para. 6(c))

A3   The nature and extent of audit procedures necessary to obtain sufficient appropriate audit evidence regarding opening balances depend on such matters as:

*   The accounting policies followed by the entity.
*   The nature of the account balances, classes of transactions and disclosures and the risks of material misstatement in the current period's financial statements.
*   The significance of the opening balances relative to the current period's financial statements.
*   Whether the prior period's financial statements were audited and, if so, whether the predecessor auditor's opinion was modified.

A4   If the prior period's financial statements were audited by a predecessor auditor, the auditor may be able to obtain sufficient appropriate audit evidence regarding the opening balances by reviewing the predecessor auditor's working papers. Whether such a review provides sufficient appropriate audit evidence is influenced by the professional competence and independence of the predecessor auditor.

A4-1   In the UK, where a statutory auditor[5a] is replaced by another statutory auditor, the predecessor auditor is required by ISQC (UK) 1 (Revised June 2016) to provide the auditor with access to all relevant information concerning the entity, including information concerning the most recent audit.[5b]

[5a] *In the UK, eligibility for appointment as a statutory auditor is dealt with in sections 1212 to 1225 of the Companies Act 2006.*

[5b] *ISQC (UK) 1 (Revised June 2016), Quality Control for Firms that Perform Audits and Reviews of Financial Statements, and Other Assurance and Related Services Engagements, paragraph 28D-1.*

Relevant ethical and professional requirements guide the current auditor's communications   **A5**
with the predecessor auditor.

In the UK, the relevant ethical guidance on proposed communications with a   **A5-1**
predecessor auditor is provided by the ethical pronouncements relating to the work of
auditors issued by the auditor's relevant professional body.

For current assets and liabilities, some audit evidence about opening balances may be   **A6**
obtained as part of the current period's audit procedures. For example, the collection
(payment) of opening accounts receivable (accounts payable) during the current period
will provide some audit evidence of their existence, rights and obligations, completeness
and valuation at the beginning of the period. In the case of inventories, however, the current
period's audit procedures on the closing inventory balance provide little audit evidence
regarding inventory on hand at the beginning of the period. Therefore, additional audit
procedures may be necessary, and one or more of the following may provide sufficient
appropriate audit evidence:

- Observing a current physical inventory count and reconciling it to the opening
  inventory quantities.
- Performing audit procedures on the valuation of the opening inventory items.
- Performing audit procedures on gross profit and cutoff.

For non-current assets and liabilities, such as property plant and equipment, investments   **A7**
and long-term debt, some audit evidence may be obtained by examining the accounting
records and other information underlying the opening balances. In certain cases, the
auditor may be able to obtain some audit evidence regarding opening balances through
confirmation with third parties, for example, for long-term debt and investments. In
other cases, the auditor may need to carry out additional audit procedures.

Required Understanding of Prior Year Responses to Risks (Ref: Para. 8R-1)

For audits of financial statements of public interest entities, the Audit Regulation[5c]   **A7-1**
imposes a requirement on a predecessor auditor to grant the auditor access to the
additional report to the audit committee[5d] in respect of previous years.

Audit Conclusions and Reporting

Opening Balances (Ref: Para. 10)

ISA (UK) 705 (Revised June 2016) establishes requirements and provides guidance on   **A8**
circumstances that may result in a modification to the auditor's opinion on the financial
statements, the type of opinion appropriate in the circumstances, and the content of the
auditor's report when the auditor's opinion is modified. The inability of the auditor to
obtain sufficient appropriate audit evidence regarding opening balances may result in one
of the following modifications to the opinion in the auditor's report:

(a) A qualified opinion or a disclaimer of opinion, as is appropriate in the circumstances;
   or

[5c] *Regulation (EU) No 537/2014 of the European Parliament and of the Council of 16 April 2014.*

[5d] *ISA (UK) 260 (Revised June 2016), paragraph 16R-2 deals with the auditor's responsibilities to prepare an additional report to the audit committee.*

(b) Unless prohibited by law or regulation, an opinion which is qualified or disclaimed, as appropriate, regarding the results of operations, and cash flows, where relevant, and unmodified regarding financial position.

The Appendix includes illustrative auditors' reports.[5e]

Modification to the Opinion in the Predecessor Auditor's Report (Ref: Para. 13)

A9   In some situations, a modification to the predecessor auditor's opinion may not be relevant and material to the opinion on the current period's financial statements. This may be the case where, for example, there was a scope limitation in the prior period, but the matter giving rise to the scope limitation has been resolved in the current period.

[5e] *The examples in the Appendix have not been tailored for the UK. Illustrative auditor's reports tailored for use with audits conducted in accordance with ISAs (UK) are given in the current version of the FRC's Compendium of Illustrative Auditor's Reports.*

Appendix

Illustrations of Auditor's Reports with Modified Opinions

The examples in the Appendix have not been tailored for the UK. Illustrative auditor's reports tailored for use with audits conducted in accordance with ISAs (UK) are given in the current versions of the FRC's Compendium of Illustrative Auditor's Reports.

Note: Throughout these illustrative auditor's reports, the Opinion section has been positioned first in accordance with ISA (UK) 700 (Revised), and the Basis for Opinion section is positioned immediately after the Opinion section. Also, the first and last sentence that was included in the extant auditor's responsibilities section is now subsumed as part of the new Basis for Opinion section.

Illustration 1:

For purposes of this illustrative auditor's report, the following circumstances are assumed:

- Audit of a complete set of financial statements of an entity other than a listed entity using a fair presentation framework. The audit is not a group audit (i.e., ISA 600[6] does not apply).
- The financial statements are prepared by management of the entity in accordance with International Financial Reporting Standards (IFRSs) (a general purpose framework).
- The terms of the audit engagement reflect the description of management's responsibility for the financial statements in ISA 210.[7]
- The auditor did not observe the counting of the physical inventory at the beginning of the current period and was unable to obtain sufficient appropriate audit evidence regarding the opening balances of inventory.
- The possible effects of the inability to obtain sufficient appropriate audit evidence regarding opening balances of inventory are deemed to be material but not pervasive to the entity's financial performance and cash flows.[8]
- The financial position at year end is fairly presented.
- In this particular jurisdiction, law and regulation prohibit the auditor from giving an opinion which is qualified regarding the financial performance and cash flows and unmodified regarding financial position.
- The relevant ethical requirements that apply to the audit are those of the jurisdiction.
- Based on the audit evidence obtained, the auditor has concluded that a material uncertainty does not exist related to events or conditions that may cast significant doubt on the entity's ability to continue as a going concern in accordance with ISA (UK) 570 (Revised).[9] The auditor is not required, and has otherwise not decided, to communicate key audit matters in accordance with ISA 701.[10]

---

[6] *ISA 600*, Special Considerations—Audits of Group Financial Statements (Including the Work of Component Auditors).

[7] *ISA 210*, Agreeing the Terms of Audit Engagements.

[8] *If the possible effects, in the auditor's judgment, are considered to be material and pervasive to the entity's financial performance and cash flows, the auditor would disclaim an opinion on the financial performance and cash flows.*

[9] *ISA 570 (Revised)*, Going Concern.

[10] *ISA 701*, Communicating Key Audit Matters in the Independent Auditor's Report.

- The auditor has obtained all of the other information prior to the date of the auditor's report and has not identified a material misstatement of the other information.
- Corresponding figures are presented, and the prior period's financial statements were audited by a predecessor auditor. The auditor is not prohibited by law or regulation from referring to the predecessor auditor's report on the corresponding figures and has decided to do so.
- Those responsible for oversight of the financial statements differ from those responsible for the preparation of the financial statements.
- In addition to the audit of the financial statements, the auditor has other reporting responsibilities required under local law.

INDEPENDENT AUDITOR'S REPORT

To the Shareholders of ABC Company [or Other Appropriate Addressee]

Report on the Audit of the Financial Statements[11]

Qualified Opinion

We have audited the financial statements of ABC Company (the Company), which comprise the statement of financial position as at December 31, 20X1, and the statement of comprehensive income , statement of changes in equity and statement of cash flows for the year then ended, and notes to the financial statements, including a summary of significant accounting policies.

In our opinion, except for the possible effects of the matter described in the Basis for Qualified Opinion section of our report, the accompanying financial statements present fairly, in all material respects, (or *give a true and fair view of*) the financial position of the Company as at December 31, 20X1, and (*of*) its financial performance and its cash flows for the year then ended in accordance with International Financial Reporting Standards (IFRSs).

Basis for Qualified Opinion

We were appointed as auditors of the company on June 30, 20X1 and thus did not observe the counting of the physical inventories at the beginning of the year. We were unable to satisfy ourselves by alternative means concerning inventory quantities held at December 31, 20X0. Since opening inventories enter into the determination of the financial performance and cash flows, we were unable to determine whether adjustments might have been necessary in respect of the profit for the year reported in the statement of comprehensive income and the net cash flows from operating activities reported in the statement of cash flows.

We conducted our audit in accordance with International Standards on Auditing (ISAs). Our responsibilities under those standards are further described in the *Auditor's Responsibilities for the Audit of the Financial Statements* section of our report. We are independent of the Company in accordance with the ethical requirements that are relevant to our audit of the financial statements in [*jurisdiction*], and we have fulfilled our other ethical responsibilities in accordance with these requirements. We believe that the audit evidence we have obtained is sufficient and appropriate to provide a basis for our qualified audit opinion.

---

[11] *The sub-title 'Report on the Audit of the Financial Statements' is unnecessary in circumstances when the second sub-title 'Report on Other Legal and Regulatory Requirements' is not applicable.*

Other Matter

The financial statements of the Company for the year ended December 31, 20X0 were audited by another auditor who expressed an unmodified opinion on those statements on March 31, 20X1.

Other Information [or another title if appropriate such as 'Information Other than the Financial Statements and Auditor's Report Thereon']

[*Reporting in accordance with the reporting requirements in ISA 720 (Revised) – see Illustration 1 in Appendix 2 of ISA 720 (Revised).*]

Responsibilities of Management and Those Charged with Governance for the Financial Statements[12]

[*Reporting in accordance with ISA 700 (Revised)[13] – see Illustration 1 in ISA 700 (Revised).*]

Auditor's Responsibilities for the Audit of the Financial Statements

[*Reporting in accordance with ISA 700 (Revised) – see Illustration 1 in ISA 700 (Revised).*]

Report on Other Legal and Regulatory Requirements

[*Reporting in accordance with ISA 700 (Revised) – see Illustration 1 in ISA 700 (Revised).*]

[*Signature in the name of the audit firm, the personal name of the auditor, or both, as appropriate for the particular jurisdiction*]

[*Auditor Address*]

[*Date*]

Illustration 2:

For purposes of this illustrative auditor's report, the following circumstances are assumed:

- Audit of a complete set of financial statements of an entity other than a listed entity using a fair presentation framework. The audit is not a group audit (i.e., ISA 600 does not apply).
- The financial statements are prepared by management of the entity in accordance with IFRSs (a general purpose framework).
- The terms of the audit engagement reflect the description of management's responsibility for the financial statements in ISA 210.
- The auditor did not observe the counting of the physical inventory at the beginning of the current period and was unable to obtain sufficient appropriate audit evidence regarding the opening balances of inventory.

---

[12] *Throughout these illustrative auditor's reports, the terms management and those charged with governance may need to be replaced by another term that is appropriate in the context of the legal framework in the particular jurisdiction.*

[13] ISA 700 (Revised), Forming an Opinion and Reporting on Financial Statements.

- The possible effects of the inability to obtain sufficient appropriate audit evidence regarding opening balances of inventory are deemed to be material but not pervasive to the entity's financial performance and cash flows.[14]
- The financial position at year end is fairly presented.
- An opinion that is qualified regarding the financial performance and cash flows and unmodified regarding financial position is considered appropriate in the circumstances.
- The relevant ethical requirements that apply to the audit are those of the jurisdiction.
- Based on the audit evidence obtained, the auditor has concluded that a material uncertainty does not exist related to events or conditions that may cast significant doubt on the entity's ability to continue as a going concern in accordance with ISA 570 (Revised).
- The auditor is not required, and has otherwise not decided, to communicate key audit matters in accordance with ISA 701.
- The auditor has obtained all of the other information prior to the date of the auditor's report and has not identified a material misstatement of the other information
- Corresponding figures are presented, and the prior period's financial statements were audited by a predecessor auditor. The auditor is not prohibited by law or regulation from referring to the predecessor auditor's report on the corresponding figures and has decided to do so.
- Those responsible for oversight of the financial statements differ from those responsible for the preparation of the financial statements.
- In addition to the audit of the financial statements, the auditor has other reporting responsibilities required under local law.

INDEPENDENT AUDITOR'S REPORT

To the Shareholders of ABC Company [or Other Appropriate Addressee]

Report on the Audit of the Financial Statements[15]

Opinions

We have audited the financial statements of ABC Company (the Company), which comprise the statement of financial position as at December 31, 20X1, and the statement of comprehensive income, statement of changes in equity and statement of cash flows for the year then ended, and notes to the financial statements, including a summary of significant accounting policies.

Qualified Opinion on the Financial Performance and Cash Flows

In our opinion, except for the possible effects of the matter described in the Basis for Qualified Opinion section of our report, the accompanying statement of Comprehensive Income and Statement of Cash Flows present fairly, in all material respects (or give a true

---

[14] *If the possible effects, in the auditor's judgment, are considered to be material and pervasive to the entity's financial performance and cash flows, the auditor would disclaim the opinion on the financial performance and cash flows.*

[15] *The sub-title 'Report on the Audit of the Financial Statements' is unnecessary in circumstances when the second sub-title 'Report on Other Legal and Regulatory Requirements' is not applicable.*

and fair view of) the financial performance and cash flows of the Company for the year ended December 31, 20X1 in accordance with International Financial Reporting Standards (IFRSs).

Opinion on the Financial Position

In our opinion, the accompanying statement of financial position presents fairly, in all material respects (or *gives a true and fair view of*) the financial position of the Company as at December 31, 20X1 in accordance with IFRSs.

Basis for Opinions, including basis for qualified opinion on the Financial Performance and Cash Flows

We were appointed as auditors of the company on June 30, 20X1 and thus did not observe the counting of the physical inventories at the beginning of the year. We were unable to satisfy ourselves by alternative means concerning inventory quantities held at December 31, 20X0. Since opening inventories enter into the determination of the financial performance and cash flows, we were unable to determine whether adjustments might have been necessary in respect of the profit for the year reported in the statement of comprehensive income and the net cash flows from operating activities reported in the statement of cash flows.

We conducted our audit in accordance with International Standards on Auditing (ISAs). Our responsibilities under those standards are further described in the *Auditor's Responsibilities for the Audit of the Financial Statements* section of our report. We are independent of the Company in accordance with the ethical requirements that are relevant to our audit of the financial statements in [*jurisdiction*], and we have fulfilled our other ethical responsibilities in accordance with these requirements. We believe that the audit evidence we have obtained is sufficient and appropriate to provide a basis for our unmodified opinion on the financial position and our qualified audit opinion on the financial performance and cash flows.

Other Matter

The financial statements of the Company for the year ended December 31, 20X0 were audited by another auditor who expressed an unmodified opinion on those statements on March 31, 20X1.

Other Information [or another title if appropriate such as 'Information Other than the Financial Statements and Auditor's Report Thereon']

[*Reporting in accordance with the reporting requirements in ISA 720 (Revised) – see Illustration 2 in Appendix 2 of ISA 720 (Revised).*]

Responsibilities of Management and Those Charged With Governance for the Financial Statements[16]

[*Reporting in accordance with ISA (Revised) – see Illustration 1 in ISA 700 (Revised).*]

---

[16] *Or other terms that are appropriate in the context of the legal framework in the particular jurisdiction.*

Auditor's Responsibilities for the Audit of the Financial Statements

[*Reporting in accordance with ISA 700 (Revised) – see Illustration 1 in ISA 700 (Revised).*]

Report on Other Legal and Regulatory Requirements

[*Reporting in accordance with ISA 700 (Revised) – see Illustration 1 in ISA 700 (Revised).*]

[*Signature in the name of the audit firm, the personal name of the auditor, or both, as appropriate for the particular jurisdiction*]

[*Auditor Address*]

[*Date*]

International Standard on Auditing (UK) 520
Analytical procedures

(Effective for audits of financial statements for periods ending on or after 15 December 2010)

Contents

International Standard on Auditing (UK) (ISA (UK)) 520, *Analytical Procedures*, should be read in conjunction with ISA (UK) 200 (Revised June 2016), *Overall Objectives of the Independent Auditor and the Conduct of an Audit in Accordance with International Standards on Auditing (UK).*

Introduction

Scope of this ISA (UK)

1   This International Standard on Auditing (UK) (ISA (UK)) deals with the auditor's use of analytical procedures as substantive procedures ('substantive analytical procedures'). It also deals with the auditor's responsibility to perform analytical procedures near the end of the audit that assist the auditor when forming an overall conclusion on the financial statements. ISA (UK) 315 (Revised June 2016) [1] deals with the use of analytical procedures as risk assessment procedures. ISA (UK) 330 (Revised June 2016) includes requirements and guidance regarding the nature, timing and extent of audit procedures in response to assessed risks; these audit procedures may include substantive analytical procedures. [2]

Effective Date

2   This ISA (UK) is effective for audits of financial statements for periods ending on or after 15 December 2010.

Objectives

3   The objectives of the auditor are:

(a)   To obtain relevant and reliable audit evidence when using substantive analytical procedures; and

(b)   To design and perform analytical procedures near the end of the audit that assist the auditor when forming an overall conclusion as to whether the financial statements are consistent with the auditor's understanding of the entity.

Definition

4   For the purposes of the ISAs (UK), the term 'analytical procedures' means evaluations of financial information through analysis of plausible relationships among both financial and non-financial data. Analytical procedures also encompass such investigation as is necessary of identified fluctuations or relationships that are inconsistent with other relevant information or that differ from expected values by a significant amount. (Ref: Para. A1–A3)

Requirements

Substantive Analytical Procedures

5   When designing and performing substantive analytical procedures, either alone or in combination with tests of details, as substantive procedures in accordance with ISA (UK) 330 (Revised June 2016), [3] the auditor shall: (Ref: Para. A4–A5)

(a)   Determine the suitability of particular substantive analytical procedures for given assertions, taking account of the assessed risks of material misstatement and tests of details, if any, for these assertions; (Ref: Para. A6–A11)

---

[1]   *ISA (UK) 315 (Revised June 2016)*, Identifying and Assessing the Risks of Material Misstatement through Understanding the Entity and Its Environment, *paragraph 6(b).*

[2]   *ISA (UK) 330 (Revised June 2016)*, The Auditor's Reponses to Assessed Risks, *paragraphs 6 and 18.*

[3]   *ISA (UK) 330 (Revised June 2016), paragraph 18.*

(b) Evaluate the reliability of data from which the auditor's expectation of recorded amounts or ratios is developed, taking account of source, comparability, and nature and relevance of information available, and controls over preparation; (Ref: Para. A12–A14)

(c) Develop an expectation of recorded amounts or ratios and evaluate whether the expectation is sufficiently precise to identify a misstatement that, individually or when aggregated with other misstatements, may cause the financial statements to be materially misstated; and (Ref: Para. A15)

(d) Determine the amount of any difference of recorded amounts from expected values that is acceptable without further investigation as required by paragraph 7. (Ref: Para. A16)

Analytical Procedures that Assist When Forming an Overall Conclusion

The auditor shall design and perform analytical procedures near the end of the audit that **6** assist the auditor when forming an overall conclusion as to whether the financial statements are consistent with the auditor's understanding of the entity. (Ref: Para. A17–A19)

Investigating Results of Analytical Procedures

If analytical procedures performed in accordance with this ISA (UK) identify fluctuations **7** or relationships that are inconsistent with other relevant information or that differ from expected values by a significant amount, the auditor shall investigate such differences by:

(a) Inquiring of management and obtaining appropriate audit evidence relevant to management's responses; and

(b) Performing other audit procedures as necessary in the circumstances. (Ref: Para. A20–A21)

Application and Other Explanatory Material

Definition of Analytical Procedures (Ref: Para. 4)

Analytical procedures include the consideration of comparisons of the entity's financial **A1** information with, for example:

- Comparable information for prior periods.
- Anticipated results of the entity, such as budgets or forecasts, or expectations of the auditor, such as an estimation of depreciation.
- Similar industry information, such as a comparison of the entity's ratio of sales to accounts receivable with industry averages or with other entities of comparable size in the same industry.

Analytical procedures also include consideration of relationships, for example: **A2**

- Among elements of financial information that would be expected to conform to a predictable pattern based on the entity's experience, such as gross margin percentages.
- Between financial information and relevant non-financial information, such as payroll costs to number of employees.

Various methods may be used to perform analytical procedures. These methods range from **A3** performing simple comparisons to performing complex analyses using advanced statistical techniques. Analytical procedures may be applied to consolidated financial statements, components and individual elements of information.

Substantive Analytical Procedures (Ref: Para. 5)

A4   The auditor's substantive procedures at the assertion level may be tests of details, substantive analytical procedures, or a combination of both. The decision about which audit procedures to perform, including whether to use substantive analytical procedures, is based on the auditor's judgment about the expected effectiveness and efficiency of the available audit procedures to reduce audit risk at the assertion level to an acceptably low level.

A5   The auditor may inquire of management as to the availability and reliability of information needed to apply substantive analytical procedures, and the results of any such analytical procedures performed by the entity. It may be effective to use analytical data prepared by management, provided the auditor is satisfied that such data is properly prepared.

Suitability of Particular Analytical Procedures for Given Assertions (Ref: Para. 5(a))

A6   Substantive analytical procedures are generally more applicable to large volumes of transactions that tend to be predictable over time. The application of planned analytical procedures is based on the expectation that relationships among data exist and continue in the absence of known conditions to the contrary. However, the suitability of a particular analytical procedure will depend upon the auditor's assessment of how effective it will be in detecting a misstatement that, individually or when aggregated with other misstatements, may cause the financial statements to be materially misstated.

A7   In some cases, even an unsophisticated predictive model may be effective as an analytical procedure. For example, where an entity has a known number of employees at fixed rates of pay throughout the period, it may be possible for the auditor to use this data to estimate the total payroll costs for the period with a high degree of accuracy, thereby providing audit evidence for a significant item in the financial statements and reducing the need to perform tests of details on the payroll. The use of widely recognized trade ratios (such as profit margins for different types of retail entities) can often be used effectively in substantive analytical procedures to provide evidence to support the reasonableness of recorded amounts.

A8   Different types of analytical procedures provide different levels of assurance. Analytical procedures involving, for example, the prediction of total rental income on a building divided into apartments, taking the rental rates, the number of apartments and vacancy rates into consideration, can provide persuasive evidence and may eliminate the need for further verification by means of tests of details, provided the elements are appropriately verified. In contrast, calculation and comparison of gross margin percentages as a means of confirming a revenue figure may provide less persuasive evidence, but may provide useful corroboration if used in combination with other audit procedures.

A9   The determination of the suitability of particular substantive analytical procedures is influenced by the nature of the assertion and the auditor's assessment of the risk of material misstatement. For example, if controls over sales order processing are deficient, the auditor may place more reliance on tests of details rather than on substantive analytical procedures for assertions related to receivables.

A10   Particular substantive analytical procedures may also be considered suitable when tests of details are performed on the same assertion. For example, when obtaining audit evidence regarding the valuation assertion for accounts receivable balances, the auditor may apply analytical procedures to an aging of customers' accounts in addition to performing tests of details on subsequent cash receipts to determine the collectability of the receivables.

Considerations Specific to Public Sector Entities

The relationships between individual financial statement items traditionally considered   **A11**
in the audit of business entities may not always be relevant in the audit of governments
or other non-business public sector entities; for example, in many public sector entities
there may be little direct relationship between revenue and expenditure. In addition,
because expenditure on the acquisition of assets may not be capitalized, there may be
no relationship between expenditures on, for example, inventories and fixed assets and
the amount of those assets reported in the financial statements. Also, industry data or
statistics for comparative purposes may not be available in the public sector. However,
other relationships may be relevant, for example, variations in the cost per kilometer of
road construction or the number of vehicles acquired compared with vehicles retired.

The Reliability of the Data (Ref: Para. 5(b))

The reliability of data is influenced by its source and nature and is dependent on the   **A12**
circumstances under which it is obtained. Accordingly, the following are relevant when
determining whether data is reliable for purposes of designing substantive analytical
procedures:

(a) Source of the information available. For example, information may be more reliable
     when it is obtained from independent sources outside the entity;[4]
(b) Comparability of the information available. For example, broad industry data may
     need to be supplemented to be comparable to that of an entity that produces and sells
     specialized products;
(c) Nature and relevance of the information available. For example, whether budgets have
     been established as results to be expected rather than as goals to be achieved; and
(d) Controls over the preparation of the information that are designed to ensure its
     completeness, accuracy and validity. For example, controls over the preparation,
     review and maintenance of budgets.
(e) Prior year knowledge and understanding. For example, the knowledge gained during
     previous audits, together with the auditor's understanding of the effectiveness of the
     accounting and internal control systems and the types of problems that in prior periods
     have given rise to accounting adjustments.

The auditor may consider testing the operating effectiveness of controls, if any, over the   **A13**
entity's preparation of information used by the auditor in performing substantive analytical
procedures in response to assessed risks. When such controls are effective, the auditor
generally has greater confidence in the reliability of the information and, therefore,
in the results of analytical procedures. The operating effectiveness of controls over
non-financial information may often be tested in conjunction with other tests of controls.
For example, in establishing controls over the processing of sales invoices, an entity may
include controls over the recording of unit sales. In these circumstances, the auditor may
test the operating effectiveness of controls over the recording of unit sales in conjunction
with tests of the operating effectiveness of controls over the processing of sales invoices.
Alternatively, the auditor may consider whether the information was subjected to audit
testing. ISA (UK) 500 establishes requirements and provides guidance in determining the
audit procedures to be performed on the information to be used for substantive analytical
procedures.[5]

The matters discussed in paragraphs A12(a)–A12(d) are relevant irrespective of whether   **A14**
the auditor performs substantive analytical procedures on the entity's period end financial

---

[4] *ISA (UK) 500*, Audit Evidence, *paragraph A31.*

[5] *ISA (UK) 500, paragraph 10.*

statements, or at an interim date and plans to perform substantive analytical procedures for the remaining period. ISA (UK) 330 (Revised June 2016) establishes requirements and provides guidance on substantive procedures performed at an interim date.[6]

Evaluation Whether the Expectation Is Sufficiently Precise (Ref: Para. 5(c))

A15   Matters relevant to the auditor's evaluation of whether the expectation can be developed sufficiently precisely to identify a misstatement that, when aggregated with other misstatements, may cause the financial statements to be materially misstated, include:

- The accuracy with which the expected results of substantive analytical procedures can be predicted. For example, the auditor may expect greater consistency in comparing gross profit margins from one period to another than in comparing discretionary expenses, such as research or advertising.
- The degree to which information can be disaggregated. For example, substantive analytical procedures may be more effective when applied to financial information on individual sections of an operation or to financial statements of components of a diversified entity, than when applied to the financial statements of the entity as a whole.
- The availability of the information, both financial and non-financial. For example, the auditor may consider whether financial information, such as budgets or forecasts, and non-financial information, such as the number of units produced or sold, is available to design substantive analytical procedures. If the information is available, the auditor may also consider the reliability of the information as discussed in paragraphs A12–A13 above.

Amount of Difference of Recorded Amounts from Expected Values that Is Acceptable (Ref: Para. 5(d))

A16   The auditor's determination of the amount of difference from the expectation that can be accepted without further investigation is influenced by materiality [7] and the consistency with the desired level of assurance, taking account of the possibility that a misstatement, individually or when aggregated with other misstatements, may cause the financial statements to be materially misstated. ISA (UK) 330 (Revised June 2016) requires the auditor to obtain more persuasive audit evidence the higher the auditor's assessment of risk.[8] Accordingly, as the assessed risk increases, the amount of difference considered acceptable without investigation decreases in order to achieve the desired level of persuasive evidence.[9]

Analytical Procedures that Assist When Forming an Overall Conclusion (Ref: Para. 6)

A17   The conclusions drawn from the results of analytical procedures designed and performed in accordance with paragraph 6 are intended to corroborate conclusions formed during the audit of individual components or elements of the financial statements. This assists the auditor to draw reasonable conclusions on which to base the auditor's opinion.

---

[6] *ISA (UK) 330 (Revised June 2016), paragraphs 22–23.*

[7] *ISA (UK) 320 (Revised June 2016),* Materiality in Planning and Performing an Audit, *paragraph A13.*

[8] *ISA (UK) 330 (Revised June 2016), paragraph 7(b).*

[9] *ISA (UK) 330 (Revised June 2016), paragraph A19*

Considerations when carrying out such procedures may include:

(a) Whether the financial statements adequately reflect the information and explanations previously obtained and conclusions previously reached during the course of the audit;

(b) Whether the procedures reveal any new factors which may affect the presentation of, or disclosures in, the financial statements;

(c) Whether analytical procedures applied when completing the audit, such as comparing the information in the financial statements with other pertinent data, produce results which assist in arriving at the overall conclusion as to whether the financial statements as a whole are consistent with the auditor's knowledge of the entity's business;

(d) Whether the presentation adopted in the financial statements may have been unduly influenced by the desire of those charged with governance to present matters in a favorable or unfavorable light; and

(e) The potential impact on the financial statements of the aggregate of uncorrected misstatements (including those arising from bias in making accounting estimates) identified during the course of the audit and the preceding period's audit, if any.

A17-1

The results of such analytical procedures may identify a previously unrecognized risk of material misstatement. In such circumstances, ISA (UK) 315 (Revised June 2016) requires the auditor to revise the auditor's assessment of the risks of material misstatement and modify the further planned audit procedures accordingly.[10]

A18

The analytical procedures performed in accordance with paragraph 6 may be similar to those that would be used as risk assessment procedures.

A19

Investigating Results of Analytical Procedures (Ref: Para. 7)

Audit evidence relevant to management's responses may be obtained by evaluating those responses taking into account the auditor's understanding of the entity and its environment, and with other audit evidence obtained during the course of the audit.

A20

The need to perform other audit procedures may arise when, for example, management is unable to provide an explanation, or the explanation, together with the audit evidence obtained relevant to management's response, is not considered adequate.

A21

[10] *ISA (UK) 315 (Revised June 2016), paragraph 31.*

International Standard on Auditing (UK) 530
Audit sampling

*(Effective for audits of financial statements for periods
ending on or after 15 December 2010)*

Contents

International Standard on Auditing (UK) (ISA (UK)) 530, *Audit Sampling*, should be read in conjunction with ISA 200 (UK) (Revised June 2016), *Overall Objectives of the Independent Auditor and the Conduct of an Audit in Accordance with International Standards on Auditing (UK).*

Introduction

Scope of this ISA (UK)

This International Standard on Auditing (UK) (ISA (UK)) applies when the auditor has 1
decided to use audit sampling in performing audit procedures. It deals with the auditor's
use of statistical and non-statistical sampling when designing and selecting the audit
sample, performing tests of controls and tests of details, and evaluating the results from
the sample.

This ISA (UK) complements ISA (UK) 500,[1] which deals with the auditor's responsibility 2
to design and perform audit procedures to obtain sufficient appropriate audit evidence to
be able to draw reasonable conclusions on which to base the auditor's opinion. ISA (UK)
500 provides guidance on the means available to the auditor for selecting items for testing,
of which audit sampling is one means.

Effective Date

This ISA (UK) is effective for audits of financial statements for periods ending on or after 3
15 December 2010.

Objective

The objective of the auditor, when using audit sampling, is to provide a reasonable basis 4
for the auditor to draw conclusions about the population from which the sample is selected.

Definitions

For purposes of the ISAs (UK), the following terms have the meanings attributed below: 5

(a) Audit sampling (sampling) – The application of audit procedures to less than 100%
of items within a population of audit relevance such that all sampling units have a
chance of selection in order to provide the auditor with a reasonable basis on which to
draw conclusions about the entire population.

(b) Population – The entire set of data from which a sample is selected and about which
the auditor wishes to draw conclusions.

(c) Sampling risk – The risk that the auditor's conclusion based on a sample may be
different from the conclusion if the entire population were subjected to the same audit
procedure. Sampling risk can lead to two types of erroneous conclusions:

  (i) In the case of a test of controls, that controls are more effective than they
  actually are, or in the case of a test of details, that a material misstatement does
  not exist when in fact it does. The auditor is primarily concerned with this
  type of erroneous conclusion because it affects audit effectiveness and is more
  likely to lead to an inappropriate audit opinion.

  (ii) In the case of a test of controls, that controls are less effective than they actually
  are, or in the case of a test of details, that a material misstatement exists when
  in fact it does not. This type of erroneous conclusion affects audit efficiency
  as it would usually lead to additional work to establish that initial conclusions
  were incorrect.

(d) Non-sampling risk – The risk that the auditor reaches an erroneous conclusion for any
reason not related to sampling risk. (Ref: Para A1)

---

[1] *ISA (UK) 500,* Audit Evidence.

(e) Anomaly – A misstatement or deviation that is demonstrably not representative of misstatements or deviations in a population.

(f) Sampling unit – The individual items constituting a population. (Ref: Para A2)

(g) Statistical sampling – An approach to sampling that has the following characteristics:
   (i) Random selection of the sample items; and
   (ii) The use of probability theory to evaluate sample results, including measurement of sampling risk.
   A sampling approach that does not have characteristics (i) and (ii) is considered non-statistical sampling.

(h) Stratification – The process of dividing a population into sub-populations, each of which is a group of sampling units which have similar characteristics (often monetary value).

(i) Tolerable misstatement – A monetary amount set by the auditor in respect of which the auditor seeks to obtain an appropriate level of assurance that the monetary amount set by the auditor is not exceeded by the actual misstatement in the population. (Ref: Para A3)

(j) Tolerable rate of deviation – A rate of deviation from prescribed internal control procedures set by the auditor in respect of which the auditor seeks to obtain an appropriate level of assurance that the rate of deviation set by the auditor is not exceeded by the actual rate of deviation in the population.

Requirements

Sample Design, Size and Selection of Items for Testing

6   When designing an audit sample, the auditor shall consider the purpose of the audit procedure and the characteristics of the population from which the sample will be drawn. (Ref: Para. A4–A9)

7   The auditor shall determine a sample size sufficient to reduce sampling risk to an acceptably low level. (Ref: Para. A10–A11)

8   The auditor shall select items for the sample in such a way that each sampling unit in the population has a chance of selection. (Ref: Para. A12–A13)

Performing Audit Procedures

9   The auditor shall perform audit procedures, appropriate to the purpose, on each item selected.

10 If the audit procedure is not applicable to the selected item, the auditor shall perform the procedure on a replacement item. (Ref: Para. A14)

11 If the auditor is unable to apply the designed audit procedures, or suitable alternative procedures, to a selected item, the auditor shall treat that item as a deviation from the prescribed control, in the case of tests of controls, or a misstatement, in the case of tests of details. (Ref: Para. A15–A16)

Nature and Cause of Deviations and Misstatements

12 The auditor shall investigate the nature and cause of any deviations or misstatements identified, and evaluate their possible effect on the purpose of the audit procedure and on other areas of the audit. (Ref: Para. A17)

In the extremely rare circumstances when the auditor considers a misstatement or deviation discovered in a sample to be an anomaly, the auditor shall obtain a high degree of certainty that such misstatement or deviation is not representative of the population. The auditor shall obtain this degree of certainty by performing additional audit procedures to obtain sufficient appropriate audit evidence that the misstatement or deviation does not affect the remainder of the population.   **13**

Projecting Misstatements

For tests of details, the auditor shall project misstatements found in the sample to the population. (Ref: Para. A18–A20)   **14**

Evaluating Results of Audit Sampling

The auditor shall evaluate: **15**

(a)   The results of the sample; and (Ref: Para. A21–A22)
(b)   Whether the use of audit sampling has provided a reasonable basis for conclusions about the population that has been tested. (Ref: Para. A23)

Application and Other Explanatory Material

Definitions

Non-Sampling Risk (Ref: Para. 5(d))

Examples of non-sampling risk include use of inappropriate audit procedures, or misinterpretation of audit evidence and failure to recognize a misstatement or deviation.   **A1**

Sampling Unit (Ref: Para. 5(f))

The sampling units might be physical items (for example, checks listed on deposit slips, credit entries on bank statements, sales invoices or debtors' balances) or monetary units.   **A2**

Tolerable Misstatement (Ref: Para. 5(i))

When designing a sample, the auditor determines tolerable misstatement in order to address the risk that the aggregate of individually immaterial misstatements may cause the financial statements to be materially misstated and provide a margin for possible undetected misstatements. Tolerable misstatement is the application of performance materiality, as defined in ISA (UK) 320 (Revised June 2016),[2] to a particular sampling procedure. Tolerable misstatement may be the same amount or an amount lower than performance materiality.   **A3**

Sample Design, Size and Selection of Items for Testing

Sample Design (Ref: Para. 6)

Audit sampling enables the auditor to obtain and evaluate audit evidence about some characteristic of the items selected in order to form or assist in forming a conclusion   **A4**

---

[2] *ISA (UK) 320 (Revised June 2016),* Materiality in Planning and Performing an Audit, *paragraph 9.*

concerning the population from which the sample is drawn. Audit sampling can be applied using either non-statistical or statistical sampling approaches.

A5   When designing an audit sample, the auditor's consideration includes the specific purpose to be achieved and the combination of audit procedures that is likely to best achieve that purpose. Consideration of the nature of the audit evidence sought and possible deviation or misstatement conditions or other characteristics relating to that audit evidence will assist the auditor in defining what constitutes a deviation or misstatement and what population to use for sampling. In fulfilling the requirement of paragraph 10 of ISA (UK) 500, when performing audit sampling, the auditor performs audit procedures to obtain evidence that the population from which the audit sample is drawn is complete.

A6   The auditor's consideration of the purpose of the audit procedure, as required by paragraph 6, includes a clear understanding of what constitutes a deviation or misstatement so that all, and only, those conditions that are relevant to the purpose of the audit procedure are included in the evaluation of deviations or projection of misstatements. For example, in a test of details relating to the existence of accounts receivable, such as confirmation, payments made by the customer before the confirmation date but received shortly after that date by the client, are not considered a misstatement. Also, a misposting between customer accounts does not affect the total accounts receivable balance. Therefore, it may not be appropriate to consider this a misstatement in evaluating the sample results of this particular audit procedure, even though it may have an important effect on other areas of the audit, such as the assessment of the risk of fraud or the adequacy of the allowance for doubtful accounts.

A7   In considering the characteristics of a population, for tests of controls, the auditor makes an assessment of the expected rate of deviation based on the auditor's understanding of the relevant controls or on the examination of a small number of items from the population. This assessment is made in order to design an audit sample and to determine sample size. For example, if the expected rate of deviation is unacceptably high, the auditor will normally decide not to perform tests of controls. Similarly, for tests of details, the auditor makes an assessment of the expected misstatement in the population. If the expected misstatement is high, 100% examination or use of a large sample size may be appropriate when performing tests of details.

A8   In considering the characteristics of the population from which the sample will be drawn, the auditor may determine that stratification or value-weighted selection is appropriate. Appendix 1 provides further discussion on stratification and value-weighted selection.

A9   The decision whether to use a statistical or non-statistical sampling approach is a matter for the auditor's judgment; however, sample size is not a valid criterion to distinguish between statistical and non-statistical approaches.

Sample Size (Ref: Para. 7)

A10   The level of sampling risk that the auditor is willing to accept affects the sample size required. The lower the risk the auditor is willing to accept, the greater the sample size will need to be.

A11   The sample size can be determined by the application of a statistically-based formula or through the exercise of professional judgment. Appendices 2 and 3 indicate the influences that various factors typically have on the determination of sample size. When circumstances are similar, the effect on sample size of factors such as those identified in Appendices 2 and 3 will be similar regardless of whether a statistical or non-statistical approach is chosen.

Selection of Items for Testing (Ref: Para. 8)

With statistical sampling, sample items are selected in a way that each sampling unit has **A12** a known probability of being selected. With non-statistical sampling, judgment is used to select sample items. Because the purpose of sampling is to provide a reasonable basis for the auditor to draw conclusions about the population from which the sample is selected, it is important that the auditor selects a representative sample, so that bias is avoided, by choosing sample items which have characteristics typical of the population.

The principal methods of selecting samples are the use of random selection, systematic **A13** selection and haphazard selection. Each of these methods is discussed in Appendix 4.

Performing Audit Procedures (Ref: Para. 10–11)

An example of when it is necessary to perform the procedure on a replacement item is **A14** when a voided check is selected while testing for evidence of payment authorization. If the auditor is satisfied that the check has been properly voided such that it does not constitute a deviation, an appropriately chosen replacement is examined.

An example of when the auditor is unable to apply the designed audit procedures to a **A15** selected item is when documentation relating to that item has been lost.

An example of a suitable alternative procedure might be the examination of subsequent **A16** cash receipts together with evidence of their source and the items they are intended to settle when no reply has been received in response to a positive confirmation request.

Nature and Cause of Deviations and Misstatements (Ref: Para. 12)

In analyzing the deviations and misstatements identified, the auditor may observe that **A17** many have a common feature, for example, type of transaction, location, product line or period of time. In such circumstances, the auditor may decide to identify all items in the population that possess the common feature, and extend audit procedures to those items. In addition, such deviations or misstatements may be intentional, and may indicate the possibility of fraud.

Projecting Misstatements (Ref: Para. 14)

The auditor is required to project misstatements for the population to obtain a broad view **A18** of the scale of misstatement but this projection may not be sufficient to determine an amount to be recorded.

When a misstatement has been established as an anomaly, it may be excluded when **A19** projecting misstatements to the population. However, the effect of any such misstatement, if uncorrected, still needs to be considered in addition to the projection of the non-anomalous misstatements.

For tests of controls, no explicit projection of deviations is necessary since the sample **A20** deviation rate is also the projected deviation rate for the population as a whole. ISA (UK) 330 (Revised June 2016)[3] provides guidance when deviations from controls upon which the auditor intends to rely are detected.

---

[3] *ISA (UK) 330 (Revised June 2016)*, The Auditor's Responses to Assessed Risks, *paragraph 17.*

Evaluating Results of Audit Sampling (Ref: Para. 15)

A21   For tests of controls, an unexpectedly high sample deviation rate may lead to an increase in the assessed risk of material misstatement, unless further audit evidence substantiating the initial assessment is obtained. For tests of details, an unexpectedly high misstatement amount in a sample may cause the auditor to believe that a class of transactions or account balance is materially misstated, in the absence of further audit evidence that no material misstatement exists.

A22   In the case of tests of details, the projected misstatement plus anomalous misstatement, if any, is the auditor's best estimate of misstatement in the population. When the projected misstatement plus anomalous misstatement, if any, exceeds tolerable misstatement, the sample does not provide a reasonable basis for conclusions about the population that has been tested. The closer the projected misstatement plus anomalous misstatement is to tolerable misstatement, the more likely that actual misstatement in the population may exceed tolerable misstatement. Also if the projected misstatement is greater than the auditor's expectations of misstatement used to determine the sample size, the auditor may conclude that there is an unacceptable sampling risk that the actual misstatement in the population exceeds the tolerable misstatement. Considering the results of other audit procedures helps the auditor to assess the risk that actual misstatement in the population exceeds tolerable misstatement, and the risk may be reduced if additional audit evidence is obtained.

A23   If the auditor concludes that audit sampling has not provided a reasonable basis for conclusions about the population that has been tested, the auditor may:

- Request management to investigate misstatements that have been identified and the potential for further misstatements and to make any necessary adjustments;

or

- Tailor the nature, timing and extent of those further audit procedures to best achieve the required assurance. For example, in the case of tests of controls, the auditor might extend the sample size, test an alternative control or modify related substantive procedures.

Appendix 1

Stratification and Value-Weighted Selection

In considering the characteristics of the population from which the sample will be drawn, the auditor may determine that stratification or value-weighted selection is appropriate. This Appendix provides guidance to the auditor on the use of stratification and value-weighted sampling techniques.

Stratification

(1)　Audit efficiency may be improved if the auditor stratifies a population by dividing it into discrete sub-populations which have an identifying characteristic. The objective of stratification is to reduce the variability of items within each stratum and therefore allow sample size to be reduced without increasing sampling risk.

(2)　When performing tests of details, the population is often stratified by monetary value. This allows greater audit effort to be directed to the larger value items, as these items may contain the greatest potential misstatement in terms of overstatement. Similarly, a population may be stratified according to a particular characteristic that indicates a higher risk of misstatement, for example, when testing the allowance for doubtful accounts in the valuation of accounts receivable, balances may be stratified by age.

(3)　The results of audit procedures applied to a sample of items within a stratum can only be projected to the items that make up that stratum. To draw a conclusion on the entire population, the auditor will need to consider the risk of material misstatement in relation to whatever other strata make up the entire population. For example, 20% of the items in a population may make up 90% of the value of an account balance. The auditor may decide to examine a sample of these items. The auditor evaluates the results of this sample and reaches a conclusion on the 90% of value separately from the remaining 10% (on which a further sample or other means of gathering audit evidence will be used, or which may be considered immaterial).

(4)　If a class of transactions or account balance has been divided into strata, the misstatement is projected for each stratum separately. Projected misstatements for each stratum are then combined when considering the possible effect of misstatements on the total class of transactions or account balance.

Value-Weighted Selection

(5)　When performing tests of details it may be efficient to identify the sampling unit as the individual monetary units that make up the population. Having selected specific monetary units from within the population, for example, the accounts receivable balance, the auditor may then examine the particular items, for example, individual balances, that contain those monetary units. One benefit of this approach to defining the sampling unit is that audit effort is directed to the larger value items because they have a greater chance of selection, and can result in smaller sample sizes. This approach may be used in conjunction with the systematic method of sample selection (described in Appendix 4) and is most efficient when selecting items using random selection.

Appendix 2

Examples of Factors Influencing Sample Size for Tests of Controls

The following are factors that the auditor may consider when determining the sample size for tests of controls. These factors, which need to be considered together, assume the auditor does not modify the nature or timing of tests of controls or otherwise modify the approach to substantive procedures in response to assessed risks.

FACTOR	EFFECT ON SAMPLE SIZE	
1. An increase in the extent to which the auditor's risk assessment takes into account relevant controls	Increase	The more assurance the auditor intends to obtain from the operating effectiveness of controls, the lower the auditor's assessment of the risk of material misstatement will be, and the larger the sample size will need to be. When the auditor's assessment of the risk of material misstatement at the assertion level includes an expectation of the operating effectiveness of controls, the auditor is required to perform tests of controls. Other things being equal, the greater the reliance the auditor places on the operating effectiveness of controls in the risk assessment, the greater is the extent of the auditor's tests of controls (and therefore, the sample size is increased).
2. An increase in the tolerable rate of deviation	Decrease	The lower the tolerable rate of deviation, the larger the sample size needs to be.
3. An increase in the expected rate of deviation of the population to be tested	Increase	The higher the expected rate of deviation, the larger the sample size needs to be so that the auditor is in a position to make a reasonable estimate of the actual rate of deviation. Factors relevant to the auditor's consideration of the expected rate of deviation include the auditor's understanding of the business (in particular, risk assessment procedures undertaken to obtain an understanding of internal control), changes in personnel or in internal control, the results of audit procedures applied in prior periods and the results of other audit procedures. High expected control deviation rates ordinarily warrant little, if any, reduction of the assessed risk of material misstatement.

FACTOR	EFFECT ON SAMPLE SIZE	
4. An increase in the auditor's desired level of assurance that the tolerable rate of deviation is not exceeded by the actual rate of deviation in the population	Increase	The greater the level of assurance that the auditor desires that the results of the sample are in fact indicative of the actual incidence of deviation in the population, the larger the sample size needs to be.
5. An increase in the number of sampling units in the population	Negligible effect	For large populations, the actual size of the population has little, if any, effect on sample size. For small populations however, audit sampling may not be as efficient as alternative means of obtaining sufficient appropriate audit evidence.

Appendix 3

Examples of Factors Influencing Sample Size for Tests of Details

The following are factors that the auditor may consider when determining the sample size for tests of details. These factors, which need to be considered together, assume the auditor does not modify the approach to tests of controls or otherwise modify the nature or timing of substantive procedures in response to the assessed risks.

FACTOR	EFFECT ON SAMPLE SIZE	
1. An increase in the auditor's assessment of the risk of material misstatement	Increase	The higher the auditor's assessment of the risk of material misstatement, the larger the sample size needs to be. The auditor's assessment of the risk of material misstatement is affected by inherent risk and control risk. For example, if the auditor does not perform tests of controls, the auditor's risk assessment cannot be reduced for the effective operation of internal controls with respect to the particular assertion. Therefore, in order to reduce audit risk to an acceptably low level, the auditor needs a low detection risk and will rely more on substantive procedures. The more audit evidence that is obtained from tests of details (that is, the lower the detection risk), the larger the sample size will need to be.
2. An increase in the use of other substantive procedures directed at the same assertion	Decrease	The more the auditor is relying on other substantive procedures (tests of details or substantive analytical procedures) to reduce to an acceptable level the detection risk regarding a particular population, the less assurance the auditor will require from sampling and, therefore, the smaller the sample size can be.
3. An increase in the auditor's desired level of assurance that tolerable misstatement is not exceeded by actual misstatement in the population	Increase	The greater the level of assurance that the auditor requires that the results of the sample are in fact indicative of the actual amount of misstatement in the population, the larger the sample size needs to be.
4. An increase in tolerable misstatement	Decrease	The lower the tolerable misstatement, the larger the sample size needs to be.

FACTOR	EFFECT ON SAMPLE SIZE	
5. An increase in the amount of misstatement the auditor expects to find in the population	Increase	The greater the amount of misstatement the auditor expects to find in the population, the larger the sample size needs to be in order to make a reasonable estimate of the actual amount of misstatement in the population. Factors relevant to the auditor's consideration of the expected misstatement amount include the extent to which item values are determined subjectively, the results of risk assessment procedures, the results of tests of control, the results of audit procedures applied in prior periods, and the results of other substantive procedures.
6. Stratification of the population when appropriate	Decrease	When there is a wide range (variability) in the monetary size of items in the population, it may be useful to stratify the population. When a population can be appropriately stratified, the aggregate of the sample sizes from the strata generally will be less than the sample size that would have been required to attain a given level of sampling risk, had one sample been drawn from the whole population.
7. The number of sampling units in the population	Negligible effect	For large populations, the actual size of the population has little, if any, effect on sample size. Thus, for small populations, audit sampling is often not as efficient as alternative means of obtaining sufficient appropriate audit evidence. (However, when using monetary unit sampling, an increase in the monetary value of the population increases sample size, unless this is offset by a proportional increase in materiality for the financial statements as a whole [and, if applicable, materiality level or levels for particular classes of transactions, account balances or disclosures].)

Appendix 4   (Ref: Para. A13)

Sample Selection Methods

There are many methods of selecting samples. The principal methods are as follows:

(a) Random selection (applied through random number generators, for example, random number tables).

(b) Systematic selection, in which the number of sampling units in the population is divided by the sample size to give a sampling interval, for example 50, and having determined a starting point within the first 50, each 50th sampling unit thereafter is selected. Although the starting point may be determined haphazardly, the sample is more likely to be truly random if it is determined by use of a computerized random number generator or random number tables. When using systematic selection, the auditor would need to determine that sampling units within the population are not structured in such a way that the sampling interval corresponds with a particular pattern in the population.

(c) Monetary Unit Sampling is a type of value-weighted selection (as described in Appendix 1) in which sample size, selection and evaluation results in a conclusion in monetary amounts.

(d) Haphazard selection, in which the auditor selects the sample without following a structured technique. Although no structured technique is used, the auditor would nonetheless avoid any conscious bias or predictability (for example, avoiding difficult to locate items, or always choosing or avoiding the first or last entries on a page) and thus attempt to ensure that all items in the population have a chance of selection. Haphazard selection is not appropriate when using statistical sampling.

(e) Block selection involves selection of a block(s) of contiguous items from within the population. Block selection cannot ordinarily be used in audit sampling because most populations are structured such that items in a sequence can be expected to have similar characteristics to each other, but different characteristics from items elsewhere in the population. Although in some circumstances it may be an appropriate audit procedure to examine a block of items, it would rarely be an appropriate sample selection technique when the auditor intends to draw valid inferences about the entire population based on the sample.

International Standard on Auditing (UK) 540 (Revised June 2016)

Auditing accounting estimates, including fair value accounting estimates, and related disclosures

(Effective for audits of financial statements for periods commencing on or after 17 June 2016)

Contents

International Standard on Auditing (UK) (ISA (UK)) 540 (Revised June 2016), *Auditing Accounting Estimates, Including Fair Value Accounting Estimates, and Related Disclosures*, should be read in conjunction with ISA (UK) 200 (Revised June 2016), *Overall Objectives of the Independent Auditor and the Conduct of an Audit in Accordance with International Standards on Auditing (UK)*.

Introduction

Scope of this ISA (UK)

This International Standard on Auditing (UK) (ISA (UK)) deals with the auditor's **1** responsibilities relating to accounting estimates, including fair value accounting estimates, and related disclosures in an audit of financial statements. Specifically, it expands on how ISA (UK) 315 (Revised June 2016)[1] and ISA (UK) 330 (Revised June 2016)[2] and other relevant ISAs (UK) are to be applied in relation to accounting estimates. It also includes requirements and guidance on misstatements of individual accounting estimates, and indicators of possible management bias.

Nature of Accounting Estimates

Some financial statement items cannot be measured precisely, but can only be estimated. **2** For purposes of this ISA (UK), such financial statement items are referred to as accounting estimates. The nature and reliability of information available to management to support the making of an accounting estimate varies widely, which thereby affects the degree of estimation uncertainty associated with accounting estimates. The degree of estimation uncertainty affects, in turn, the risks of material misstatement of accounting estimates, including their susceptibility to unintentional or intentional management bias. (Ref: Para. A1–A11)

The measurement objective of accounting estimates can vary depending on the applicable **3** financial reporting framework and the financial item being reported. The measurement objective for some accounting estimates is to forecast the outcome of one or more transactions, events or conditions giving rise to the need for the accounting estimate. For other accounting estimates, including many fair value accounting estimates, the measurement objective is different, and is expressed in terms of the value of a current transaction or financial statement item based on conditions prevalent at the measurement date, such as estimated market price for a particular type of asset or liability. For example, the applicable financial reporting framework may require fair value measurement based on an assumed hypothetical current transaction between knowledgeable, willing parties (sometimes referred to as 'marketplace participants' or equivalent) in an arm's length transaction, rather than the settlement of a transaction at some past or future date.[3]

A difference between the outcome of an accounting estimate and the amount originally **4** recognized or disclosed in the financial statements does not necessarily represent a misstatement of the financial statements. This is particularly the case for fair value accounting estimates, as any observed outcome is invariably affected by events or conditions subsequent to the date at which the measurement is estimated for purposes of the financial statements.

Effective Date

This ISA (UK) is effective for audits of financial statements for periods commencing on or **5** after 17 June 2016. Earlier adoption is permitted.

---

[1] *ISA (UK) 315 (Revised June 2016)*, Identifying and Assessing the Risks of Material Misstatement through Understanding the Entity and Its Environment.

[2] *ISA (UK) 330 (Revised June 2016)*, The Auditor's Responses to Assessed Risks.

[3] *Different definitions of fair value may exist among financial reporting frameworks.*

Objective

6   The objective of the auditor is to obtain sufficient appropriate audit evidence about whether:

(a)   accounting estimates, including fair value accounting estimates, in the financial statements, whether recognized or disclosed, are reasonable; and

(b)   related disclosures in the financial statements are adequate,

in the context of the applicable financial reporting framework.

Definitions

7   For purposes of the ISAs (UK), the following terms have the meanings attributed below:

(a)   Accounting estimate – An approximation of a monetary amount in the absence of a precise means of measurement. This term is used for an amount measured at fair value where there is estimation uncertainty, as well as for other amounts that require estimation. Where this ISA (UK) addresses only accounting estimates involving measurement at fair value, the term 'fair value accounting estimates' is used.

(b)   Auditor's point estimate or auditor's range – The amount, or range of amounts, respectively, derived from audit evidence for use in evaluating management's point estimate.

(c)   Estimation uncertainty – The susceptibility of an accounting estimate and related disclosures to an inherent lack of precision in its measurement.

(d)   Management bias – A lack of neutrality by management in the preparation of information.

(e)   Management's point estimate – The amount selected by management for recognition or disclosure in the financial statements as an accounting estimate.

(f)   Outcome of an accounting estimate – The actual monetary amount which results from the resolution of the underlying transaction(s), event(s) or condition(s) addressed by the accounting estimate.

Requirements

Risk Assessment Procedures and Related Activities

8   When performing risk assessment procedures and related activities to obtain an understanding of the entity and its environment, including the entity's internal control, as required by ISA (UK) 315 (Revised June 2016),[4] the auditor shall obtain an understanding of the following in order to provide a basis for the identification and assessment of the risks of material misstatement for accounting estimates: (Ref: Para. A12)

(a)   The requirements of the applicable financial reporting framework relevant to accounting estimates, including related disclosures. (Ref: Para. A13–A15)

(b)   How management identifies those transactions, events and conditions that may give rise to the need for accounting estimates to be recognized or disclosed in the financial statements. In obtaining this understanding, the auditor shall make inquiries of management about changes in circumstances that may give rise to new, or the need to revise existing, accounting estimates. (Ref: Para. A16–A21)

(c)   How management makes the accounting estimates, and an understanding of the data on which they are based, including: (Ref: Para. A22–A23)

(i)   The method, including where applicable the model, used in making the accounting estimate; (Ref: Para. A24–A26-1)

---

[4] *ISA (UK) 315 (Revised June 2016), paragraphs 5–6 and 11–12.*

(ii)   Relevant controls; (Ref: Para. A27–A28)

(iii)   Whether management has used an expert; (Ref: Para. A29–A30)

(iv)   The assumptions underlying the accounting estimates; (Ref: Para. A31–A36)

(v)   Whether there has been or ought to have been a change from the prior period in the methods for making the accounting estimates, and if so, why; and (Ref: Para. A37)

(vi)   Whether and, if so, how management has assessed the effect of estimation uncertainty. (Ref: Para. A38)

The auditor shall review the outcome of accounting estimates included in the prior period   **9** financial statements, or, where applicable, their subsequent re-estimation for the purpose of the current period. The nature and extent of the auditor's review takes account of the nature of the accounting estimates, and whether the information obtained from the review would be relevant to identifying and assessing risks of material misstatement of accounting estimates made in the current period financial statements. However, the review is not intended to call into question the judgments made in the prior periods that were based on information available at the time. (Ref: Para. A39–A44)

Identifying and Assessing the Risks of Material Misstatement

In identifying and assessing the risks of material misstatement, as required by ISA (UK)   **10** 315 (Revised June 2016),[5] the auditor shall evaluate the degree of estimation uncertainty associated with an accounting estimate. (Ref: Para. A45–A46)

The auditor shall determine whether, in the auditor's judgment, any of those accounting   **11** estimates that have been identified as having high estimation uncertainty give rise to significant risks. (Ref: Para. A47–A51)

Responses to the Assessed Risks of Material Misstatement

Based on the assessed risks of material misstatement, the auditor shall determine: **12** (Ref: Para. A52)

(a)   Whether management has appropriately applied the requirements of the applicable financial reporting framework relevant to the accounting estimate; and (Ref: Para. A53–A56)

(b)   Whether the methods for making the accounting estimates are appropriate and have been applied consistently, and whether changes, if any, in accounting estimates or in the method for making them from the prior period are appropriate in the circumstances. (Ref: Para. A57–A58)

In responding to the assessed risks of material misstatement, as required by ISA (UK) 330   **13** (Revised June 2016),[6] the auditor shall undertake one or more of the following, taking account of the nature of the accounting estimate: (Ref: Para. A59–A61)

(a)   Determine whether events occurring up to the date of the auditor's report provide audit evidence regarding the accounting estimate. (Ref: Para. A62–A67)

(b)   Test how management made the accounting estimate and the data on which it is based. In doing so, the auditor shall evaluate whether: (Ref: Para. A68–A70)

   (i)   The method of measurement used is appropriate in the circumstances; and (Ref: Para. A71–A76)

---

[5]   *ISA (UK) 315 (Revised June 2016), paragraph 25.*

[6]   *ISA (UK) 330 (Revised June 2016), paragraph 5.*

     (ii)   The assumptions used by management are reasonable in light of the measurement objectives of the applicable financial reporting framework. (Ref: Para. A77–A83)

(c) Test the operating effectiveness of the controls over how management made the accounting estimate, together with appropriate substantive procedures. (Ref: Para. A84–A86)

(d) Develop a point estimate or a range to evaluate management's point estimate. For this purpose: (Ref: Para. A87–A91)

     (i)   If the auditor uses assumptions or methods that differ from management's, the auditor shall obtain an understanding of management's assumptions or methods sufficient to establish that the auditor's point estimate or range takes into account relevant variables and to evaluate any significant differences from management's point estimate. (Ref: Para. A92)

     (ii)   If the auditor concludes that it is appropriate to use a range, the auditor shall narrow the range, based on audit evidence available, until all outcomes within the range are considered reasonable. (Ref: Para. A93–A95)

14 In determining the matters identified in paragraph 12 or in responding to the assessed risks of material misstatement in accordance with paragraph 13, the auditor shall consider whether specialized skills or knowledge in relation to one or more aspects of the accounting estimates are required in order to obtain sufficient appropriate audit evidence. (Ref: Para. A96–A101)

Further Substantive Procedures to Respond to Significant Risks

Estimation Uncertainty

15 For accounting estimates that give rise to significant risks, in addition to other substantive procedures performed to meet the requirements of ISA (UK) 330 (Revised June 2016),[7] the auditor shall evaluate the following: (Ref: Para. A102)

(a) How management has considered alternative assumptions or outcomes, and why it has rejected them, or how management has otherwise addressed estimation uncertainty in making the accounting estimate. (Ref: Para. A103–A106)

(b) Whether the significant assumptions used by management are reasonable. (Ref: Para. A107–A109)

(c) Where relevant to the reasonableness of the significant assumptions used by management or the appropriate application of the applicable financial reporting framework, management's intent to carry out specific courses of action and its ability to do so. (Ref: Para. A110)

16 If, in the auditor's judgment, management has not adequately addressed the effects of estimation uncertainty on the accounting estimates that give rise to significant risks, the auditor shall, if considered necessary, develop a range with which to evaluate the reasonableness of the accounting estimate. (Ref: Para. A111–A112)

Recognition and Measurement Criteria

17 For accounting estimates that give rise to significant risks, the auditor shall obtain sufficient appropriate audit evidence about whether:

---

[7] *ISA (UK) 330 (Revised June 2016), paragraph 18.*

(a) management's decision to recognize, or to not recognize, the accounting estimates in the financial statements; and (Ref: Para. A113–A114)

(b) the selected measurement basis for the accounting estimates, (Ref: Para. A115)

are in accordance with the requirements of the applicable financial reporting framework.

Evaluating the Reasonableness of the Accounting Estimates, and Determining Misstatements

The auditor shall evaluate, based on the audit evidence, whether the accounting estimates in the financial statements are either reasonable in the context of the applicable financial reporting framework, or are misstated. (Ref: Para. A116–A119)   **18**

Disclosures Related to Accounting Estimates

The auditor shall obtain sufficient appropriate audit evidence about whether the disclosures in the financial statements related to accounting estimates are in accordance with the requirements of the applicable financial reporting framework. (Ref: Para. A120–A121)   **19**

For accounting estimates that give rise to significant risks, the auditor shall also evaluate the adequacy of the disclosure of their estimation uncertainty in the financial statements in the context of the applicable financial reporting framework. (Ref: Para. A122–A123)   **20**

Indicators of Possible Management Bias

The auditor shall review the judgments and decisions made by management in the making of accounting estimates to identify whether there are indicators of possible management bias. Indicators of possible management bias do not themselves constitute misstatements for the purposes of drawing conclusions on the reasonableness of individual accounting estimates. (Ref: Para. A124–A125)   **21**

In accordance with ISA (UK) 200 (Revised June 2016),[7a] the auditor shall maintain professional skepticism throughout the audit and in particular when reviewing management estimates relating to fair values, the impairment of assets and provisions.   **21D-1**

Written Representations

The auditor shall obtain written representations from management and, where appropriate, those charged with governance whether they believe significant assumptions used in making accounting estimates are reasonable. (Ref: Para. A126–A127)   **22**

Documentation

The auditor shall include in the audit documentation:[8]   **23**

(a) The basis for the auditor's conclusions about the reasonableness of accounting estimates and their disclosure that give rise to significant risks; and

(b) Indicators of possible management bias, if any. (Ref: Para. A128)

***

[7a] *ISA (UK) 200 (Revised June 2016)*, Overall Objectives of the Independent Auditor and the Conduct of an Audit in Accordance with International Standards on Auditing (UK), *paragraph 15.*

[8] *ISA (UK) 230 (Revised June 2016)*, Audit Documentation, *paragraphs 8–11, and paragraph A6.*

Application and Other Explanatory Material

Nature of Accounting Estimates (Ref: Para. 2)

A1   Because of the uncertainties inherent in business activities, some financial statement items can only be estimated. Further, the specific characteristics of an asset, liability or component of equity, or the basis of or method of measurement prescribed by the financial reporting framework, may give rise to the need to estimate a financial statement item. Some financial reporting frameworks prescribe specific methods of measurement and the disclosures that are required to be made in the financial statements, while other financial reporting frameworks are less specific. The Appendix to this ISA (UK) discusses fair value measurements and disclosures under different financial reporting frameworks.

A2   Some accounting estimates involve relatively low estimation uncertainty and may give rise to lower risks of material misstatements, for example:

- Accounting estimates arising in entities that engage in business activities that are not complex.
- Accounting estimates that are frequently made and updated because they relate to routine transactions.
- Accounting estimates derived from data that is readily available, such as published interest rate data or exchange-traded prices of securities. Such data may be referred to as 'observable' in the context of a fair value accounting estimate.
- Fair value accounting estimates where the method of measurement prescribed by the applicable financial reporting framework is simple and applied easily to the asset or liability requiring measurement at fair value.
- Fair value accounting estimates where the model used to measure the accounting estimate is well-known or generally accepted, provided that the assumptions or inputs to the model are observable.

A3   For some accounting estimates, however, there may be relatively high estimation uncertainty, particularly where they are based on significant assumptions, for example:

- Accounting estimates relating to the outcome of litigation.
- Fair value accounting estimates for derivative financial instruments not publicly traded.
- Fair value accounting estimates for which a highly specialized entity-developed model is used or for which there are assumptions or inputs that cannot be observed in the marketplace.

A4   The degree of estimation uncertainty varies based on the nature of the accounting estimate, the extent to which there is a generally accepted method or model used to make the accounting estimate, and the subjectivity of the assumptions used to make the accounting estimate. In some cases, estimation uncertainty associated with an accounting estimate may be so great that the recognition criteria in the applicable financial reporting framework are not met and the accounting estimate cannot be made.

A5   Not all financial statement items requiring measurement at fair value, involve estimation uncertainty. For example, this may be the case for some financial statement items where there is an active and open market that provides readily available and reliable information on the prices at which actual exchanges occur, in which case the existence of published price quotations ordinarily is the best audit evidence of fair value. However, estimation uncertainty may exist even when the valuation method and data are well defined. For example, valuation of securities quoted on an active and open market at the listed market price may require adjustment if the holding is significant in relation to the market or is subject to restrictions in marketability. In addition, general economic circumstances prevailing at the time, for example, illiquidity in a particular market, may impact estimation uncertainty.

Additional examples of situations where accounting estimates, other than fair value accounting estimates, may be required include: **A6**

- Allowance for doubtful accounts.
- Inventory obsolescence.
- Warranty obligations.
- Depreciation method or asset useful life.
- Provision against the carrying amount of an investment where there is uncertainty regarding its recoverability.
- Outcome of long term contracts.
- Costs arising from litigation settlements and judgments.

Additional examples of situations where fair value accounting estimates may be required include: **A7**

- Complex financial instruments, which are not traded in an active and open market.
- Share-based payments.
- Property or equipment held for disposal.
- Certain assets or liabilities acquired in a business combination, including goodwill and intangible assets.
- Transactions involving the exchange of assets or liabilities between independent parties without monetary consideration, for example, a non-monetary exchange of plant facilities in different lines of business.

Estimation involves judgments based on information available when the financial statements are prepared. For many accounting estimates, these include making assumptions about matters that are uncertain at the time of estimation. The auditor is not responsible for predicting future conditions, transactions or events that, if known at the time of the audit, might have significantly affected management's actions or the assumptions used by management. **A8**

Management Bias

Financial reporting frameworks often call for neutrality, that is, freedom from bias. Accounting estimates are imprecise, however, and can be influenced by management judgment. Such judgment may involve unintentional or intentional management bias (for example, as a result of motivation to achieve a desired result). The susceptibility of an accounting estimate to management bias increases with the subjectivity involved in making it. Unintentional management bias and the potential for intentional management bias are inherent in subjective decisions that are often required in making an accounting estimate. For continuing audits, indicators of possible management bias identified during the audit of the preceding periods influence the planning and risk identification and assessment activities of the auditor in the current period. **A9**

Management bias can be difficult to detect at an account level. It may only be identified when considered in the aggregate of groups of accounting estimates or all accounting estimates, or when observed over a number of accounting periods. Although some form of management bias is inherent in subjective decisions, in making such judgments there may be no intention by management to mislead the users of financial statements. Where, however, there is intention to mislead, management bias is fraudulent in nature. **A10**

Considerations Specific to Public Sector Entities

A11   Public sector entities may have significant holdings of specialized assets for which there are no readily available and reliable sources of information for purposes of measurement at fair value or other current value bases, or a combination of both. Often specialized assets held do not generate cash flows and do not have an active market. Measurement at fair value therefore ordinarily requires estimation and may be complex, and in some rare cases may not be possible at all.

Risk Assessment Procedures and Related Activities (Ref: Para. 8)

A12   The risk assessment procedures and related activities required by paragraph 8 of this ISA (UK) assist the auditor in developing an expectation of the nature and type of accounting estimates that an entity may have. The auditor's primary consideration is whether the understanding that has been obtained is sufficient to identify and assess the risks of material misstatement in relation to accounting estimates, and to plan the nature, timing and extent of further audit procedures.

Obtaining an Understanding of the Requirements of the Applicable Financial Reporting Framework (Ref: Para. 8(a))

A13   Obtaining an understanding of the requirements of the applicable financial reporting framework assists the auditor in determining whether it, for example:

- Prescribes certain conditions for the recognition,[9] or methods for the measurement, of accounting estimates.
- Specifies certain conditions that permit or require measurement at a fair value, for example, by referring to management's intentions to carry out certain courses of action with respect to an asset or liability.
- Specifies required or permitted disclosures.

Obtaining this understanding also provides the auditor with a basis for discussion with management about how management has applied those requirements relevant to the accounting estimate, and the auditor's determination of whether they have been applied appropriately.

A14   Financial reporting frameworks may provide guidance for management on determining point estimates where alternatives exist. Some financial reporting frameworks, for example, require that the point estimate selected be the alternative that reflects management's judgment of the most likely outcome.[10] Others may require, for example, use of a discounted probability-weighted expected value. In some cases, management may be able to make a point estimate directly. In other cases, management may be able to make a reliable point estimate only after considering alternative assumptions or outcomes from which it is able to determine a point estimate.

A15   Financial reporting frameworks may require the disclosure of information concerning the significant assumptions to which the accounting estimate is particularly sensitive. Furthermore, where there is a high degree of estimation uncertainty, some financial reporting frameworks do not permit an accounting estimate to be recognized in the

---

[9] *Most financial reporting frameworks require incorporation in the balance sheet or income statement of items that satisfy their criteria for recognition. Disclosure of accounting policies or adding notes to the financial statements does not rectify a failure to recognize such items, including accounting estimates.*

[10] *Different financial reporting frameworks may use different terminology to describe point estimates determined in this way.*

financial statements, but certain disclosures may be required in the notes to the financial statements.

Obtaining an Understanding of How Management Identifies the Need for Accounting Estimates (Ref: Para. 8(b))

The preparation of the financial statements requires management to determine whether a transaction, event or condition gives rise to the need to make an accounting estimate, and that all necessary accounting estimates have been recognized, measured and disclosed in the financial statements in accordance with the applicable financial reporting framework.   **A16**

Management's identification of transactions, events and conditions that give rise to the need for accounting estimates is likely to be based on: **A17**

- Management's knowledge of the entity's business and the industry in which it operates.
- Management's knowledge of the implementation of business strategies in the current period.
- Where applicable, management's cumulative experience of preparing the entity's financial statements in prior periods.

In such cases, the auditor may obtain an understanding of how management identifies the need for accounting estimates primarily through inquiry of management. In other cases, where management's process is more structured, for example, when management has a formal risk management function, the auditor may perform risk assessment procedures directed at the methods and practices followed by management for periodically reviewing the circumstances that give rise to the accounting estimates and re-estimating the accounting estimates as necessary. The completeness of accounting estimates is often an important consideration of the auditor, particularly accounting estimates relating to liabilities.

The auditor's understanding of the entity and its environment obtained during the performance of risk assessment procedures, together with other audit evidence obtained during the course of the audit, assist the auditor in identifying circumstances, or changes in circumstances, that may give rise to the need for an accounting estimate.   **A18**

Inquiries of management about changes in circumstances may include, for example, inquiries about whether: **A19**

- The entity has engaged in new types of transactions that may give rise to accounting estimates.
- Terms of transactions that gave rise to accounting estimates have changed.
- Accounting policies relating to accounting estimates have changed, as a result of changes within the requirements of the applicable financial reporting framework or otherwise.
- Regulatory or other changes outside the control of management have occurred that may require management to revise, or make new, accounting estimates.
- New conditions or events have occurred that may give rise to the need for new or revised accounting estimates.

During the audit, the auditor may identify transactions, events and conditions that give rise to the need for accounting estimates that management failed to identify. ISA (UK) 315 (Revised June 2016) deals with circumstances where the auditor identifies risks of material misstatement that management failed to identify, including determining whether there is a significant deficiency in internal control with regard to the entity's risk assessment processes.[11]   **A20**

---

[11] *ISA (UK) 315 (Revised June 2016), paragraph 16.*

Considerations Specific to Smaller Entities

A21   Obtaining this understanding for smaller entities is often less complex as their business activities are often limited and transactions are less complex. Further, often a single person, for example the owner-manager, identifies the need to make an accounting estimate and the auditor may focus inquiries accordingly.

Obtaining an Understanding of How Management Makes the Accounting Estimates
(Ref: Para. 8(c))

A22   The preparation of the financial statements also requires management to establish financial reporting processes for making accounting estimates, including adequate internal control. Such processes include the following:

- Selecting appropriate accounting policies and prescribing estimation processes, including appropriate estimation or valuation methods, including, where applicable, models.
- Developing or identifying relevant data and assumptions that affect accounting estimates.
- Periodically reviewing the circumstances that give rise to the accounting estimates and re-estimating the accounting estimates as necessary.

A23   Matters that the auditor may consider in obtaining an understanding of how management makes the accounting estimates include, for example:

- The types of accounts or transactions to which the accounting estimates relate (for example, whether the accounting estimates arise from the recording of routine and recurring transactions or whether they arise from non-recurring or unusual transactions).
- Whether and, if so, how management has used recognized measurement techniques for making particular accounting estimates.
- Whether the accounting estimates were made based on data available at an interim date and, if so, whether and how management has taken into account the effect of events, transactions and changes in circumstances occurring between that date and the period end.

Method of Measurement, Including the Use of Models (Ref: Para. 8(c)(i))

A24   In some cases, the applicable financial reporting framework may prescribe the method of measurement for an accounting estimate, for example, a particular model that is to be used in measuring a fair value estimate. In many cases, however, the applicable financial reporting framework does not prescribe the method of measurement, or may specify alternative methods for measurement.

A25   When the applicable financial reporting framework does not prescribe a particular method to be used in the circumstances, matters that the auditor may consider in obtaining an understanding of the method or, where applicable the model, used to make accounting estimates include, for example:

- How management considered the nature of the asset or liability being estimated when selecting a particular method.
- Whether the entity operates in a particular business, industry or environment in which there are methods commonly used to make the particular type of accounting estimate.

There may be greater risks of material misstatement, for example, in cases when management has internally developed a model to be used to make the accounting estimate or is departing from a method commonly used in a particular industry or environment.   **A26**

For audits of financial statements of public interest entities, the auditor's obligations for auditing accounting estimates, including fair value accounting estimates, and related disclosures set out in this ISA (UK) may inform the auditor's assessment[11a] and communication[11b] in the additional report to the audit committee of the valuation methods applied to the various items in the financial statements.   **A26-1**

Relevant Controls (Ref: Para. 8(c)(ii))

Matters that the auditor may consider in obtaining an understanding of relevant controls include, for example, the experience and competence of those who make the accounting estimates, and controls related to: **A27**

- How management determines the completeness, relevance and accuracy of the data used to develop accounting estimates.
- The review and approval of accounting estimates, including the assumptions or inputs used in their development, by appropriate levels of management and, where appropriate, those charged with governance.
- The segregation of duties between those committing the entity to the underlying transactions and those responsible for making the accounting estimates, including whether the assignment of responsibilities appropriately takes account of the nature of the entity and its products or services (for example, in the case of a large financial institution, relevant segregation of duties may include an independent function responsible for estimation and validation of fair value pricing of the entity's proprietary financial products staffed by individuals whose remuneration is not tied to such products).

Other controls may be relevant to making the accounting estimates depending on the circumstances. For example, if the entity uses specific models for making accounting estimates, management may put into place specific policies and procedures around such models. Relevant controls may include, for example, those established over: **A28**

- The design and development, or selection, of a particular model for a particular purpose.
- The use of the model.
- The maintenance and periodic validation of the integrity of the model.

Management's Use of Experts (Ref: Para. 8(c)(iii))

Management may have, or the entity may employ individuals with, the experience and competence necessary to make the required point estimates. In some cases, however, management may need to engage an expert to make, or assist in making, them. This need may arise because of, for example: **A29**

- The specialized nature of the matter requiring estimation, for example, the measurement of mineral or hydrocarbon reserves in extractive industries.
- The technical nature of the models required to meet the relevant requirements of the applicable financial reporting framework, as may be the case in certain measurements at fair value.

[11a] *ISA (UK) 330 (Revised June 2016), paragraph 19R-1.*

[11b] *ISA (UK) 260 (Revised June 2016),* Communication with Those Charged with Governance, *paragraph 16R-2(l).*

- The unusual or infrequent nature of the condition, transaction or event requiring an accounting estimate.

Considerations specific to smaller entities

A30   In smaller entities, the circumstances requiring an accounting estimate often are such that the owner-manager is capable of making the required point estimate. In some cases, however, an expert will be needed. Discussion with the owner-manager early in the audit process about the nature of any accounting estimates, the completeness of the required accounting estimates, and the adequacy of the estimating process may assist the owner-manager in determining the need to use an expert.

Assumptions (Ref: Para. 8(c)(iv))

A31   Assumptions are integral components of accounting estimates. Matters that the auditor may consider in obtaining an understanding of the assumptions underlying the accounting estimates include, for example:

- The nature of the assumptions, including which of the assumptions are likely to be significant assumptions.
- How management assesses whether the assumptions are relevant and complete (that is, that all relevant variables have been taken into account).
- Where applicable, how management determines that the assumptions used are internally consistent.
- Whether the assumptions relate to matters within the control of management (for example, assumptions about the maintenance programs that may affect the estimation of an asset's useful life), and how they conform to the entity's business plans and the external environment, or to matters that are outside its control (for example, assumptions about interest rates, mortality rates, potential judicial or regulatory actions, or the variability and the timing of future cash flows).
- The nature and extent of documentation, if any, supporting the assumptions.

Assumptions may be made or identified by an expert to assist management in making the accounting estimates. Such assumptions, when used by management, become management's assumptions.

A32   In some cases, assumptions may be referred to as inputs, for example, where management uses a model to make an accounting estimate, though the term inputs may also be used to refer to the underlying data to which specific assumptions are applied.

A33   Management may support assumptions with different types of information drawn from internal and external sources, the relevance and reliability of which will vary. In some cases, an assumption may be reliably based on applicable information from either external sources (for example, published interest rate or other statistical data) or internal sources (for example, historical information or previous conditions experienced by the entity). In other cases, an assumption may be more subjective, for example, where the entity has no experience or external sources from which to draw.

A34   In the case of fair value accounting estimates, assumptions reflect, or are consistent with, what knowledgeable, willing arm's length parties (sometimes referred to as 'marketplace participants' or equivalent) would use in determining fair value when exchanging an asset or settling a liability. Specific assumptions will also vary with the characteristics of the asset or liability being valued, the valuation method used (for example, a market approach, or an income approach) and the requirements of the applicable financial reporting framework.

With respect to fair value accounting estimates, assumptions or inputs vary in terms of their source and bases, as follows: **A35**

(a) Those that reflect what marketplace participants would use in pricing an asset or liability developed based on market data obtained from sources independent of the reporting entity (sometimes referred to as 'observable inputs' or equivalent).

(b) Those that reflect the entity's own judgments about what assumptions marketplace participants would use in pricing the asset or liability developed based on the best information available in the circumstances (sometimes referred to as 'unobservable inputs' or equivalent).

In practice, however, the distinction between (a) and (b) is not always apparent. Further, it may be necessary for management to select from a number of different assumptions used by different marketplace participants.

The extent of subjectivity, such as whether an assumption or input is observable, influences the degree of estimation uncertainty and thereby the auditor's assessment of the risks of material misstatement for a particular accounting estimate.   **A36**

Changes in Methods for Making Accounting Estimates (Ref: Para. 8(c)(v))

In evaluating how management makes the accounting estimates, the auditor is required to understand whether there has been or ought to have been a change from the prior period in the methods for making the accounting estimates. A specific estimation method may need to be changed in response to changes in the environment or circumstances affecting the entity or in the requirements of the applicable financial reporting framework. If management has changed the method for making an accounting estimate, it is important that management can demonstrate that the new method is more appropriate, or is itself a response to such changes. For example, if management changes the basis of making an accounting estimate from a mark-to-market approach to using a model, the auditor challenges whether management's assumptions about the marketplace are reasonable in light of economic circumstances.   **A37**

Estimation Uncertainty (Ref: Para. 8(c)(vi))

Matters that the auditor may consider in obtaining an understanding of whether and, if so, how management has assessed the effect of estimation uncertainty include, for example: **A38**

- Whether and, if so, how management has considered alternative assumptions or outcomes by, for example, performing a sensitivity analysis to determine the effect of changes in the assumptions on an accounting estimate.
- How management determines the accounting estimate when analysis indicates a number of outcome scenarios.
- Whether management monitors the outcome of accounting estimates made in the prior period, and whether management has appropriately responded to the outcome of that monitoring procedure.

Reviewing Prior Period Accounting Estimates (Ref: Para. 9)

The outcome of an accounting estimate will often differ from the accounting estimate recognized in the prior period financial statements. By performing risk assessment procedures to identify and understand the reasons for such differences, the auditor may obtain: **A39**

- Information regarding the effectiveness of management's prior period estimation process, from which the auditor can judge the likely effectiveness of management's current process.
- Audit evidence that is pertinent to the re-estimation, in the current period, of prior period accounting estimates.
- Audit evidence of matters, such as estimation uncertainty, that may be required to be disclosed in the financial statements.

A40   The review of prior period accounting estimates may also assist the auditor, in the current period, in identifying circumstances or conditions that increase the susceptibility of accounting estimates to, or indicate the presence of, possible management bias. The auditor's professional skepticism assists in identifying such circumstances or conditions and in determining the nature, timing and extent of further audit procedures.

A41   A retrospective review of management judgments and assumptions related to significant accounting estimates is also required by ISA (UK) 240.[12] That review is conducted as part of the requirement for the auditor to design and perform procedures to review accounting estimates for biases that could represent a risk of material misstatement due to fraud, in response to the risks of management override of controls. As a practical matter, the auditor's review of prior period accounting estimates as a risk assessment procedure in accordance with this ISA (UK) may be carried out in conjunction with the review required by ISA (UK) 240.

A42   The auditor may judge that a more detailed review is required for those accounting estimates that were identified during the prior period audit as having high estimation uncertainty, or for those accounting estimates that have changed significantly from the prior period. On the other hand, for example, for accounting estimates that arise from the recording of routine and recurring transactions, the auditor may judge that the application of analytical procedures as risk assessment procedures is sufficient for purposes of the review.

A43   For fair value accounting estimates and other accounting estimates based on current conditions at the measurement date, more variation may exist between the fair value amount recognized in the prior period financial statements and the outcome or the amount re-estimated for the purpose of the current period. This is because the measurement objective for such accounting estimates deals with perceptions about value at a point in time, which may change significantly and rapidly as the environment in which the entity operates changes. The auditor may therefore focus the review on obtaining information that would be relevant to identifying and assessing risks of material misstatement. For example, in some cases, obtaining an understanding of changes in marketplace participant assumptions which affected the outcome of a prior period fair value accounting estimate may be unlikely to provide relevant information for audit purposes. If so, then the auditor's consideration of the outcome of prior period fair value accounting estimates may be directed more towards understanding the effectiveness of management's prior estimation process, that is, management's track record, from which the auditor can judge the likely effectiveness of management's current process.

A44   A difference between the outcome of an accounting estimate and the amount recognized in the prior period financial statements does not necessarily represent a misstatement of the prior period financial statements. However, it may do so if, for example, the difference arises from information that was available to management when the prior period's financial statements were finalized, or that could reasonably be expected to have been obtained and taken into account in the preparation of those financial statements. Many financial

---

[12] *ISA (UK) 240 (Revised June 2016),* The Auditor's Responsibilities Relating to Fraud in an Audit of Financial Statements, *paragraph 32(b)(ii).*

reporting frameworks contain guidance on distinguishing between changes in accounting estimates that constitute misstatements and changes that do not, and the accounting treatment required to be followed.

Identifying and Assessing the Risks of Material Misstatement

Estimation Uncertainty (Ref: Para. 10)

The degree of estimation uncertainty associated with an accounting estimate may be influenced by factors such as: **A45**

- The extent to which the accounting estimate depends on judgment.
- The sensitivity of the accounting estimate to changes in assumptions.
- The existence of recognized measurement techniques that may mitigate the estimation uncertainty (though the subjectivity of the assumptions used as inputs may nevertheless give rise to estimation uncertainty).
- The length of the forecast period, and the relevance of data drawn from past events to forecast future events.
- The availability of reliable data from external sources.
- The extent to which the accounting estimate is based on observable or unobservable inputs.

The degree of estimation uncertainty associated with an accounting estimate may influence the estimate's susceptibility to bias.

Matters that the auditor considers in assessing the risks of material misstatement may also include: **A46**

- The actual or expected magnitude of an accounting estimate.
- The recorded amount of the accounting estimate (that is, management's point estimate) in relation to the amount expected by the auditor to be recorded.
- Whether management has used an expert in making the accounting estimate.
- The outcome of the review of prior period accounting estimates.

High Estimation Uncertainty and Significant Risks (Ref: Para. 11)

Examples of accounting estimates that may have high estimation uncertainty include the following: **A47**

- Accounting estimates that are highly dependent upon judgment, for example, judgments about the outcome of pending litigation or the amount and timing of future cash flows dependent on uncertain events many years in the future.
- Accounting estimates that are not calculated using recognized measurement techniques.
- Accounting estimates where the results of the auditor's review of similar accounting estimates made in the prior period financial statements indicate a substantial difference between the original accounting estimate and the actual outcome.
- Fair value accounting estimates for which a highly specialized entity-developed model is used or for which there are no observable inputs.

A seemingly immaterial accounting estimate may have the potential to result in a material misstatement due to the estimation uncertainty associated with the estimation; that is, the size of the amount recognized or disclosed in the financial statements for an accounting estimate may not be an indicator of its estimation uncertainty.   **A48**

A49   In some circumstances, the estimation uncertainty is so high that a reasonable accounting estimate cannot be made. The applicable financial reporting framework may, therefore, preclude recognition of the item in the financial statements, or its measurement at fair value. In such cases, the significant risks relate not only to whether an accounting estimate should be recognized, or whether it should be measured at fair value, but also to the adequacy of the disclosures. With respect to such accounting estimates, the applicable financial reporting framework may require disclosure of the accounting estimates and the high estimation uncertainty associated with them (see paragraphs A120–A123).

A50   If the auditor determines that an accounting estimate gives rise to a significant risk, the auditor is required to obtain an understanding of the entity's controls, including control activities.[13]

A51   In some cases, the estimation uncertainty of an accounting estimate may cast significant doubt about the entity's ability to continue as a going concern. ISA (UK) 570 (Revised June 2016)[14] establishes requirements and provides guidance in such circumstances.

Responses to the Assessed Risks of Material Misstatement (Ref: Para. 12)

A52   ISA (UK) 330 (Revised June 2016) requires the auditor to design and perform audit procedures whose nature, timing and extent are responsive to the assessed risks of material misstatement in relation to accounting estimates at both the financial statement and assertion levels.[15] Paragraphs A53–A115 focus on specific responses at the assertion level only.

Application of the Requirements of the Applicable Financial Reporting Framework (Ref: Para. 12(a))

A53   Many financial reporting frameworks prescribe certain conditions for the recognition of accounting estimates and specify the methods for making them and required disclosures. Such requirements may be complex and require the application of judgment. Based on the understanding obtained in performing risk assessment procedures, the requirements of the applicable financial reporting framework that may be susceptible to misapplication or differing interpretations become the focus of the auditor's attention.

A54   Determining whether management has appropriately applied the requirements of the applicable financial reporting framework is based, in part, on the auditor's understanding of the entity and its environment. For example, the measurement of the fair value of some items, such as intangible assets acquired in a business combination, may involve special considerations that are affected by the nature of the entity and its operations.

A55   In some situations, additional audit procedures, such as the inspection by the auditor of the current physical condition of an asset, may be necessary to determine whether management has appropriately applied the requirements of the applicable financial reporting framework.

A56   The application of the requirements of the applicable financial reporting framework requires management to consider changes in the environment or circumstances that affect the entity. For example, the introduction of an active market for a particular class of asset

---

[13]   *ISA (UK) 315 (Revised June 2016), paragraph 29.*

[14]   *ISA (UK) 570 (Revised June 2016),* Going Concern.

[15]   *ISA (UK) 330 (Revised June 2016), paragraphs 5–6.*

or liability may indicate that the use of discounted cash flows to estimate the fair value of such asset or liability is no longer appropriate.

Consistency in Methods and Basis for Changes (Ref: Para. 12(b))

The auditor's consideration of a change in an accounting estimate, or in the method for making it from the prior period, is important because a change that is not based on a change in circumstances or new information is considered arbitrary. Arbitrary changes in an accounting estimate result in inconsistent financial statements over time and may give rise to a financial statement misstatement or be an indicator of possible management bias.   **A57**

Management often is able to demonstrate good reason for a change in an accounting estimate or the method for making an accounting estimate from one period to another based on a change in circumstances. What constitutes a good reason, and the adequacy of support for management's contention that there has been a change in circumstances that warrants a change in an accounting estimate or the method for making an accounting estimate, are matters of judgment.   **A58**

Responses to the Assessed Risks of Material Misstatements (Ref: Para. 13)

The auditor's decision as to which response, individually or in combination, in paragraph 13 to undertake to respond to the risks of material misstatement may be influenced by such matters as: **A59**

- The nature of the accounting estimate, including whether it arises from routine or non routine transactions.
- Whether the procedure(s) is expected to effectively provide the auditor with sufficient appropriate audit evidence.
- The assessed risk of material misstatement, including whether the assessed risk is a significant risk.

For example, when evaluating the reasonableness of the allowance for doubtful accounts, an effective procedure for the auditor may be to review subsequent cash collections in combination with other procedures. Where the estimation uncertainty associated with an accounting estimate is high, for example, an accounting estimate based on a proprietary model for which there are unobservable inputs, it may be that a combination of the responses to assessed risks in paragraph 13 is necessary in order to obtain sufficient appropriate audit evidence.   **A60**

Additional guidance explaining the circumstances in which each of the responses may be appropriate is provided in paragraphs A62–A95.   **A61**

Events Occurring Up to the Date of the Auditor's Report (Ref: Para. 13(a))

Determining whether events occurring up to the date of the auditor's report provide audit evidence regarding the accounting estimate may be an appropriate response when such events are expected to: **A62**

- Occur; and
- Provide audit evidence that confirms or contradicts the accounting estimate.

Events occurring up to the date of the auditor's report may sometimes provide sufficient appropriate audit evidence about an accounting estimate. For example, sale of the complete inventory of a superseded product shortly after the period end may provide audit evidence relating to the estimate of its net realizable value. In such cases, there may be no need to   **A63** perform additional audit procedures on the accounting estimate, provided that sufficient appropriate evidence about the events is obtained.

A64   For some accounting estimates, events occurring up to the date of the auditor's report are unlikely to provide audit evidence regarding the accounting estimate. For example, the conditions or events relating to some accounting estimates develop only over an extended period. Also, because of the measurement objective of fair value accounting estimates, information after the period-end may not reflect the events or conditions existing at the balance sheet date and therefore may not be relevant to the measurement of the fair value accounting estimate. Paragraph 13 identifies other responses to the risks of material misstatement that the auditor may undertake.

A65   In some cases, events that contradict the accounting estimate may indicate that management has ineffective processes for making accounting estimates, or that there is management bias in the making of accounting estimates.

A66   Even though the auditor may decide not to undertake this approach in respect of specific accounting estimates, the auditor is required to comply with ISA (UK) 560.[16] The auditor is required to perform audit procedures designed to obtain sufficient appropriate audit evidence that all events occurring between the date of the financial statements and the date of the auditor's report that require adjustment of, or disclosure in, the financial statements have been identified[17] and appropriately reflected in the financial statements.[18] Because the measurement of many accounting estimates, other than fair value accounting estimates, usually depends on the outcome of future conditions, transactions or events, the auditor's work under ISA (UK) 560 is particularly relevant.

Considerations specific to smaller entities

A67   When there is a longer period between the balance sheet date and the date of the auditor's report, the auditor's review of events in this period may be an effective response for accounting estimates other than fair value accounting estimates. This may particularly be the case in some smaller owner-managed entities, especially when management does not have formalized control procedures over accounting estimates.

Testing How Management Made the Accounting Estimate (Ref: Para. 13(b))

A68   Testing how management made the accounting estimate and the data on which it is based may be an appropriate response when the accounting estimate is a fair value accounting estimate developed on a model that uses observable and unobservable inputs. It may also be appropriate when, for example:

- The accounting estimate is derived from the routine processing of data by the entity's accounting system.
- The auditor's review of similar accounting estimates made in the prior period financial statements suggests that management's current period process is likely to be effective.
- The accounting estimate is based on a large population of items of a similar nature that individually are not significant.

---

[16] *ISA (UK) 560*, Subsequent Events.

[17] *ISA (UK) 560, paragraph 6.*

[18] *ISA (UK) 560, paragraph 8.*

Testing how management made the accounting estimate may involve, for example: **A69**

- Testing the extent to which data on which the accounting estimate is based is accurate, complete and relevant, and whether the accounting estimate has been properly determined using such data and management assumptions.
- Considering the source, relevance and reliability of external data or information, including that received from external experts engaged by management to assist in making an accounting estimate.
- Recalculating the accounting estimate, and reviewing information about an accounting estimate for internal consistency.
- Considering management's review and approval processes.

Considerations specific to smaller entities

In smaller entities, the process for making accounting estimates is likely to be less   **A70** structured than in larger entities. Smaller entities with active management involvement may not have extensive descriptions of accounting procedures, sophisticated accounting records, or written policies. Even if the entity has no formal established process, it does not mean that management is not able to provide a basis upon which the auditor can test the accounting estimate.

Evaluating the method of measurement (Ref: Para. 13(b)(i))

When the applicable financial reporting framework does not prescribe the method of   **A71** measurement, evaluating whether the method used, including any applicable model, is appropriate in the circumstances is a matter of professional judgment.

For this purpose, matters that the auditor may consider include, for example, whether: **A72**

- Management's rationale for the method selected is reasonable.
- Management has sufficiently evaluated and appropriately applied the criteria, if any, provided in the applicable financial reporting framework to support the selected method.
- The method is appropriate in the circumstances given the nature of the asset or liability being estimated and the requirements of the applicable financial reporting framework relevant to accounting estimates.
- The method is appropriate in relation to the business, industry and environment in which the entity operates.

In some cases, management may have determined that different methods result in a range   **A73** of significantly different estimates. In such cases, obtaining an understanding of how the entity has investigated the reasons for these differences may assist the auditor in evaluating the appropriateness of the method selected.

Evaluating the use of models

In some cases, particularly when making fair value accounting estimates, management   **A74** may use a model. Whether the model used is appropriate in the circumstances may depend on a number of factors, such as the nature of the entity and its environment, including the industry in which it operates, and the specific asset or liability being measured.

The extent to which the following considerations are relevant depends on the circumstances,   **A75** including whether the model is one that is commercially available for use in a particular sector or industry, or a proprietary model. In some cases, an entity may use an expert to develop and test a model.

A76   Depending on the circumstances, matters that the auditor may also consider in testing the model include, for example, whether:

- The model is validated prior to usage, with periodic reviews to ensure it is still suitable for its intended use. The entity's validation process may include evaluation of:
  o   The model's theoretical soundness and mathematical integrity, including the appropriateness of model parameters.
  o   The consistency and completeness of the model's inputs with market practices.
  o   The model's output as compared to actual transactions.
- Appropriate change control policies and procedures exist.
- The model is periodically calibrated and tested for validity, particularly when inputs are subjective.
- Adjustments are made to the output of the model, including in the case of fair value accounting estimates, whether such adjustments reflect the assumptions marketplace participants would use in similar circumstances.
- The model is adequately documented, including the model's intended applications and limitations and its key parameters, required inputs, and results of any validation analysis performed.

Assumptions used by management (Ref: Para. 13(b)(ii))

A77   The auditor's evaluation of the assumptions used by management is based only on information available to the auditor at the time of the audit. Audit procedures dealing with management assumptions are performed in the context of the audit of the entity's financial statements, and not for the purpose of providing an opinion on assumptions themselves.

A78   Matters that the auditor may consider in evaluating the reasonableness of the assumptions used by management include, for example:

- Whether individual assumptions appear reasonable.
- Whether the assumptions are interdependent and internally consistent.
- Whether the assumptions appear reasonable when considered collectively or in conjunction with other assumptions, either for that accounting estimate or for other accounting estimates.
- In the case of fair value accounting estimates, whether the assumptions appropriately reflect observable marketplace assumptions.

A79   The assumptions on which accounting estimates are based may reflect what management expects will be the outcome of specific objectives and strategies. In such cases, the auditor may perform audit procedures to evaluate the reasonableness of such assumptions by considering, for example, whether the assumptions are consistent with:

- The general economic environment and the entity's economic circumstances.
- The plans of the entity.
- Assumptions made in prior periods, if relevant.
- Experience of, or previous conditions experienced by, the entity, to the extent this historical information may be considered representative of future conditions or events.
- Other assumptions used by management relating to the financial statements.

A80   The reasonableness of the assumptions used may depend on management's intent and ability to carry out certain courses of action. Management often documents plans and intentions relevant to specific assets or liabilities and the financial reporting framework may require it to do so. Although the extent of audit evidence to be obtained about management's intent and ability is a matter of professional judgment, the auditor's procedures may include the following:

- Review of management's history of carrying out its stated intentions.
- Review of written plans and other documentation, including, where applicable, formally approved budgets, authorizations or minutes.
- Inquiry of management about its reasons for a particular course of action.
- Review of events occurring subsequent to the date of the financial statements and up to the date of the auditor's report.
- Evaluation of the entity's ability to carry out a particular course of action given the entity's economic circumstances, including the implications of its existing commitments.

Certain financial reporting frameworks, however, may not permit management's intentions or plans to be taken into account when making an accounting estimate. This is often the case for fair value accounting estimates because their measurement objective requires that assumptions reflect those used by marketplace participants.

Matters that the auditor may consider in evaluating the reasonableness of assumptions used by management underlying fair value accounting estimates, in addition to those discussed above where applicable, may include, for example: **A81**

- Where relevant, whether and, if so, how management has incorporated market-specific inputs into the development of assumptions.
- Whether the assumptions are consistent with observable market conditions, and the characteristics of the asset or liability being measured at fair value.
- Whether the sources of market-participant assumptions are relevant and reliable, and how management has selected the assumptions to use when a number of different market participant assumptions exist.
- Where appropriate, whether and, if so, how management considered assumptions used in, or information about, comparable transactions, assets or liabilities.

Further, fair value accounting estimates may comprise observable inputs as well as unobservable inputs. Where fair value accounting estimates are based on unobservable inputs, matters that the auditor may consider include, for example, how management supports the following: **A82**

- The identification of the characteristics of marketplace participants relevant to the accounting estimate.
- Modifications it has made to its own assumptions to reflect its view of assumptions marketplace participants would use.
- Whether it has incorporated the best information available in the circumstances.
- Where applicable, how its assumptions take account of comparable transactions, assets or liabilities.

If there are unobservable inputs, it is more likely that the auditor's evaluation of the assumptions will need to be combined with other responses to assessed risks in paragraph 13 in order to obtain sufficient appropriate audit evidence. In such cases, it may be necessary for the auditor to perform other audit procedures, for example, examining documentation supporting the review and approval of the accounting estimate by appropriate levels of management and, where appropriate, by those charged with governance.

In evaluating the reasonableness of the assumptions supporting an accounting estimate, the auditor may identify one or more significant assumptions. If so, it may indicate that the accounting estimate has high estimation uncertainty and may, therefore, give rise to a significant risk. Additional responses to significant risks are described in paragraphs A102–A115.   **A83**

Testing the Operating Effectiveness of Controls (Ref: Para. 13(c))

A84   Testing the operating effectiveness of the controls over how management made the accounting estimate may be an appropriate response when management's process has been well-designed, implemented and maintained, for example:

- Controls exist for the review and approval of the accounting estimates by appropriate levels of management and, where appropriate, by those charged with governance.
- The accounting estimate is derived from the routine processing of data by the entity's accounting system.

A85   Testing the operating effectiveness of the controls is required when:

(a) The auditor's assessment of risks of material misstatement at the assertion level includes an expectation that controls over the process are operating effectively; or

(b) Substantive procedures alone do not provide sufficient appropriate audit evidence at the assertion level.[19]

Considerations specific to smaller entities

A86   Controls over the process to make an accounting estimate may exist in smaller entities, but the formality with which they operate varies. Further, smaller entities may determine that certain types of controls are not necessary because of active management involvement in the financial reporting process. In the case of very small entities, however, there may not be many controls that the auditor can identify. For this reason, the auditor's response to the assessed risks is likely to be substantive in nature, with the auditor performing one or more of the other responses in paragraph 13.

Developing a Point Estimate or Range (Ref: Para. 13(d))

A87   Developing a point estimate or a range to evaluate management's point estimate may be an appropriate response where, for example:

- An accounting estimate is not derived from the routine processing of data by the accounting system.
- The auditor's review of similar accounting estimates made in the prior period financial statements suggests that management's current period process is unlikely to be effective.
- The entity's controls within and over management's processes for determining accounting estimates are not well designed or properly implemented.
- Events or transactions between the period end and the date of the auditor's report contradict management's point estimate.
- There are alternative sources of relevant data available to the auditor which can be used in making a point estimate or a range.

A88   Even where the entity's controls are well designed and properly implemented, developing a point estimate or a range may be an effective or efficient response to the assessed risks. In other situations, the auditor may consider this approach as part of determining whether further procedures are necessary and, if so, their nature and extent.

A89   The approach taken by the auditor in developing either a point estimate or a range may vary based on what is considered most effective in the circumstances. For example, the auditor may initially develop a preliminary point estimate, and then assess its sensitivity to changes in assumptions to ascertain a range with which to evaluate management's point estimate.

---

[19]   *ISA (UK) 330 (Revised June 2016), paragraph 8.*

Alternatively, the auditor may begin by developing a range for purposes of determining, where possible, a point estimate.

The ability of the auditor to make a point estimate, as opposed to a range, depends on several factors, including the model used, the nature and extent of data available and the estimation uncertainty involved with the accounting estimate. Further, the decision to develop a point estimate or range may be influenced by the applicable financial reporting framework, which may prescribe the point estimate that is to be used after consideration of the alternative outcomes and assumptions, or prescribe a specific measurement method (for example, the use of a discounted probability-weighted expected value).   **A90**

The auditor may develop a point estimate or a range in a number of ways, for example, by: **A91**

- Using a model, for example, one that is commercially available for use in a particular sector or industry, or a proprietary or auditor-developed model.
- Further developing management's consideration of alternative assumptions or outcomes, for example, by introducing a different set of assumptions.
- Employing or engaging a person with specialized expertise to develop or execute the model, or to provide relevant assumptions.
- Making reference to other comparable conditions, transactions or events, or, where relevant, markets for comparable assets or liabilities.

Understanding Management's Assumptions or Method (Ref: Para. 13(d)(i))

When the auditor makes a point estimate or a range and uses assumptions or a method different from those used by management, paragraph 13(d)(i) requires the auditor to obtain a sufficient understanding of the assumptions or method used by management in making the accounting estimate. This understanding provides the auditor with information that may be relevant to the auditor's development of an appropriate point estimate or range. Further, it assists the auditor to understand and evaluate any significant differences from management's point estimate. For example, a difference may arise because the auditor used different, but equally valid, assumptions as compared with those used by management. This may reveal that the accounting estimate is highly sensitive to certain assumptions and therefore subject to high estimation uncertainty, indicating that the accounting estimate may be a significant risk. Alternatively, a difference may arise as a result of a factual error made by management. Depending on the circumstances, the auditor may find it helpful in drawing conclusions to discuss with management the basis for the assumptions used and their validity, and the difference, if any, in the approach taken to making the accounting estimate.   **A92**

Narrowing a Range (Ref: Para. 13(d)(ii))

When the auditor concludes that it is appropriate to use a range to evaluate the reasonableness of management's point estimate (the auditor's range), paragraph 13(d)(ii) requires that range to encompass all 'reasonable outcomes' rather than all possible outcomes. The range cannot be one that comprises all possible outcomes if it is to be useful, as such a range would be too wide to be effective for purposes of the audit. The auditor's range is useful and effective when it is sufficiently narrow to enable the auditor to conclude whether the accounting estimate is misstated.   **A93**

Ordinarily, a range that has been narrowed to be equal to or less than performance materiality is adequate for the purposes of evaluating the reasonableness of management's point estimate. However, particularly in certain industries, it may not be possible to narrow the range to below such an amount. This does not necessarily preclude recognition of the accounting estimate. It may indicate, however, that the estimation uncertainty associated   **A94** with the accounting estimate is such that it gives rise to a significant risk. Additional responses to significant risks are described in paragraphs A102–A115.

A95   Narrowing the range to a position where all outcomes within the range are considered reasonable may be achieved by:

(a) Eliminating from the range those outcomes at the extremities of the range judged by the auditor to be unlikely to occur; and

(b) Continuing to narrow the range, based on audit evidence available, until the auditor concludes that all outcomes within the range are considered reasonable. In some rare cases, the auditor may be able to narrow the range until the audit evidence indicates a point estimate.

Considering whether Specialized Skills or Knowledge Are Required (Ref: Para. 14)

A96   In planning the audit, the auditor is required to ascertain the nature, timing and extent of resources necessary to perform the audit engagement.[20] This may include, as necessary, the involvement of those with specialized skills or knowledge. In addition, ISA (UK) 220 (Revised June 2016) requires the engagement partner to be satisfied that the engagement team, and any auditor's external experts who are not part of the engagement team, collectively have the appropriate competence and capabilities to perform the audit engagement.[21] During the course of the audit of accounting estimates the auditor may identify, in light of the experience of the auditor and the circumstances of the engagement, the need for specialized skills or knowledge to be applied in relation to one or more aspects of the accounting estimates.

A97   Matters that may affect the auditor's consideration of whether specialized skills or knowledge is required include, for example:

● The nature of the underlying asset, liability or component of equity in a particular business or industry (for example, mineral deposits, agricultural assets, complex financial instruments).

● A high degree of estimation uncertainty.

● Complex calculations or specialized models are involved, for example, when estimating fair values when there is no observable market.

● The complexity of the requirements of the applicable financial reporting framework relevant to accounting estimates, including whether there are areas known to be subject to differing interpretation or practice is inconsistent or developing.

● The procedures the auditor intends to undertake in responding to assessed risks.

A98   For the majority of accounting estimates, even when there is estimation uncertainty, it is unlikely that specialized skills or knowledge will be required. For example, it is unlikely that specialized skills or knowledge would be necessary for an auditor to evaluate an allowance for doubtful accounts.

A99   However, the auditor may not possess the specialized skills or knowledge required when the matter involved is in a field other than accounting or auditing and may need to obtain it from an auditor's expert. ISA (UK) 620 (Revised June 2016)[22] establishes requirements and provides guidance in determining the need to employ or engage an auditor's expert and the auditor's responsibilities when using the work of an auditor's expert.

---

[20] *ISA (UK) 300 (Revised June 2016),* Planning an Audit of Financial Statements, *paragraph 8(e).*

[21] *ISA (UK) 220 (Revised June 2016),* Quality Control for an Audit of Financial Statements, *paragraph 14.*

[22] *ISA (UK) 620 (Revised June 2016),* Using the Work of an Auditor's Expert.

Further, in some cases, the auditor may conclude that it is necessary to obtain specialized **A100** skills or knowledge related to specific areas of accounting or auditing. Individuals with such skills or knowledge may be employed by the auditor's firm or engaged from an external organization outside of the auditor's firm. Where such individuals perform audit procedures on the engagement, they are part of the engagement team and accordingly, they are subject to the requirements in ISA (UK) 220 (Revised June 2016).

Depending on the auditor's understanding and experience of working with the auditor's **A101** expert or those other individuals with specialized skills or knowledge, the auditor may consider it appropriate to discuss matters such as the requirements of the applicable financial reporting framework with the individuals involved to establish that their work is relevant for audit purposes.

Further Substantive Procedures to Respond to Significant Risks
(Ref: Para. 15)

In auditing accounting estimates that give rise to significant risks, the auditor's further **A102** substantive procedures are focused on the evaluation of:

(a) How management has assessed the effect of estimation uncertainty on the accounting estimate, and the effect such uncertainty may have on the appropriateness of the recognition of the accounting estimate in the financial statements; and
(b) The adequacy of related disclosures.

Estimation Uncertainty

Management's Consideration of Estimation Uncertainty (Ref: Para. 15(a))

Management may evaluate alternative assumptions or outcomes of the accounting **A103** estimates through a number of methods, depending on the circumstances. One possible method used by management is to undertake a sensitivity analysis. This might involve determining how the monetary amount of an accounting estimate varies with different assumptions. Even for accounting estimates measured at fair value there can be variation because different market participants will use different assumptions. A sensitivity analysis could lead to the development of a number of outcome scenarios, sometimes characterized as a range of outcomes by management, such as 'pessimistic' and 'optimistic' scenarios.

A sensitivity analysis may demonstrate that an accounting estimate is not sensitive to **A104** changes in particular assumptions. Alternatively, it may demonstrate that the accounting estimate is sensitive to one or more assumptions that then become the focus of the auditor's attention.

This is not intended to suggest that one particular method of addressing estimation **A105** uncertainty (such as sensitivity analysis) is more suitable than another, or that management's consideration of alternative assumptions or outcomes needs to be conducted through a detailed process supported by extensive documentation. Rather, it is whether management has assessed how estimation uncertainty may affect the accounting estimate that is important, not the specific manner in which it is done. Accordingly, where management has not considered alternative assumptions or outcomes, it may be necessary for the auditor to discuss with management, and request support for, how it has addressed the effects of estimation uncertainty on the accounting estimate.

Considerations specific to smaller entities

A106   Smaller entities may use simple means to assess the estimation uncertainty. In addition to the auditor's review of available documentation, the auditor may obtain other audit evidence of management consideration of alternative assumptions or outcomes by inquiry of management. In addition, management may not have the expertise to consider alternative outcomes or otherwise address the estimation uncertainty of the accounting estimate. In such cases, the auditor may explain to management the process or the different methods available for doing so, and the documentation thereof. This would not, however, change the responsibilities of management for the preparation of the financial statements.

Significant Assumptions (Ref: Para. 15(b))

A107   An assumption used in making an accounting estimate may be deemed to be significant if a reasonable variation in the assumption would materially affect the measurement of the accounting estimate.

A108   Support for significant assumptions derived from management's knowledge may be obtained from management's continuing processes of strategic analysis and risk management. Even without formal established processes, such as may be the case in smaller entities, the auditor may be able to evaluate the assumptions through inquiries of and discussions with management, along with other audit procedures in order to obtain sufficient appropriate audit evidence.

A109   The auditor's considerations in evaluating assumptions made by management are described in paragraphs A77–A83.

Management Intent and Ability (Ref: Para. 15(c))

A110   The auditor's considerations in relation to assumptions made by management and management's intent and ability are described in paragraphs A13 and A80.

Development of a Range (Ref: Para. 16)

A111   In preparing the financial statements, management may be satisfied that it has adequately addressed the effects of estimation uncertainty on the accounting estimates that give rise to significant risks. In some circumstances, however, the auditor may view the efforts of management as inadequate. This may be the case, for example, where, in the auditor's judgment:

- Sufficient appropriate audit evidence could not be obtained through the auditor's evaluation of how management has addressed the effects of estimation uncertainty.
- It is necessary to explore further the degree of estimation uncertainty associated with an accounting estimate, for example, where the auditor is aware of wide variation in outcomes for similar accounting estimates in similar circumstances.
- It is unlikely that other audit evidence can be obtained, for example, through the review of events occurring up to the date of the auditor's report.
- Indicators of management bias in the making of accounting estimates may exist.

A112   The auditor's considerations in determining a range for this purpose are described in paragraphs A87–A95.

Recognition and Measurement Criteria

Recognition of the Accounting Estimates in the Financial Statements (Ref: Para. 17(a))

Where management has recognized an accounting estimate in the financial statements, the focus of the auditor's evaluation is on whether the measurement of the accounting estimate is sufficiently reliable to meet the recognition criteria of the applicable financial reporting framework.   **A113**

With respect to accounting estimates that have not been recognized, the focus of the auditor's evaluation is on whether the recognition criteria of the applicable financial reporting framework have in fact been met. Even where an accounting estimate has not been recognized, and the auditor concludes that this treatment is appropriate, there may be a need for disclosure of the circumstances in the notes to the financial statements. Where applicable, the auditor may also determine that an accounting estimate that has been identified as having a high estimation uncertainty is a key audit matter to be communicated in the auditor's report in accordance with ISA (UK) 701,[23] or may consider it necessary to include an Emphasis of Matter paragraph in the auditor's report (see ISA (UK) 706 (Revised June 2016)[24]). If the matter is determined to be a key audit matter, ISA (UK) 706 (Revised June 2016) prohibits the auditor from including an Emphasis of Matter paragraph in the auditor's report.[25]   **A114**

Measurement Basis for the Accounting Estimates (Ref: Para. 17(b))

With respect to fair value accounting estimates, some financial reporting frameworks presume that fair value can be measured reliably as a prerequisite to either requiring or permitting fair value measurements and disclosures. In some cases, this presumption may be overcome when, for example, there is no appropriate method or basis for measurement. In such cases, the focus of the auditor's evaluation is on whether management's basis for overcoming the presumption relating to the use of fair value set forth under the applicable financial reporting framework is appropriate.   **A115**

Evaluating the Reasonableness of the Accounting Estimates, and Determining Misstatements (Ref: Para. 18)

Based on the audit evidence obtained, the auditor may conclude that the evidence points to an accounting estimate that differs from management's point estimate. Where the audit evidence supports a point estimate, the difference between the auditor's point estimate and management's point estimate constitutes a misstatement. Where the auditor has concluded that using the auditor's range provides sufficient appropriate audit evidence, a management point estimate that lies outside the auditor's range would not be supported by audit evidence. In such cases, the misstatement is no less than the difference between management's point estimate and the nearest point of the auditor's range.   **A116**

Where management has changed an accounting estimate, or the method in making it, from the prior period based on a subjective assessment that there has been a change in circumstances, the auditor may conclude based on the audit evidence that the accounting   **A117**

---

[23] *ISA (UK) 701*, Communicating Key Audit Matters in the Independent Auditor's Report.

[24] *ISA (UK) 706 (Revised June 2016)*, Emphasis of Matter Paragraphs and Other Matter Paragraphs in the Independent Auditor's Report.

[25] *ISA (UK) 706 (Revised June 2016), paragraph 8(b).*

estimate is misstated as a result of an arbitrary change by management, or may regard it as an indicator of possible management bias (see paragraphs A124–A125).

A118   ISA (UK) 450 (Revised June 2016)[26] provides guidance on distinguishing misstatements for purposes of the auditor's evaluation of the effect of uncorrected misstatements on the financial statements. In relation to accounting estimates, a misstatement, whether caused by fraud or error, may arise as a result of:

- Misstatements about which there is no doubt (factual misstatements).
- Differences arising from management's judgments concerning accounting estimates that the auditor considers unreasonable, or the selection or application of accounting policies that the auditor considers inappropriate (judgmental misstatements).
- The auditor's best estimate of misstatements in populations, involving the projection of misstatements identified in audit samples to the entire populations from which the samples were drawn (projected misstatements).

In some cases involving accounting estimates, a misstatement could arise as a result of a combination of these circumstances, making separate identification difficult or impossible.

A119   Evaluating the reasonableness of accounting estimates and related disclosures included in the notes to the financial statements, whether required by the applicable financial reporting framework or disclosed voluntarily, involves essentially the same types of considerations applied when auditing an accounting estimate recognized in the financial statements.

Disclosures Related to Accounting Estimates

Disclosures in Accordance with the Applicable Financial Reporting Framework (Ref: Para. 19)

A120   The presentation of financial statements in accordance with the applicable financial reporting framework includes adequate disclosure of material matters. The applicable financial reporting framework may permit, or prescribe, disclosures related to accounting estimates, and some entities may disclose voluntarily additional information in the notes to the financial statements. These disclosures may include, for example:

- The assumptions used.
- The method of estimation used, including any applicable model.
- The basis for the selection of the method of estimation.
- The effect of any changes to the method of estimation from the prior period.
- The sources and implications of estimation uncertainty.

Such disclosures are relevant to users in understanding the accounting estimates recognized or disclosed in the financial statements, and sufficient appropriate audit evidence needs to be obtained about whether the disclosures are in accordance with the requirements of the applicable financial reporting framework.

A121   In some cases, the applicable financial reporting framework may require specific disclosures regarding uncertainties. For example, some financial reporting frameworks prescribe:

- The disclosure of key assumptions and other sources of estimation uncertainty that have a significant risk of causing a material adjustment to the carrying amounts of assets and liabilities. Such requirements may be described using terms such as 'Key Sources of Estimation Uncertainty' or 'Critical Accounting Estimates.'

---

[26] *ISA (UK) 450 (Revised June 2016)*, Evaluation of Misstatements Identified during the Audit.

- The disclosure of the range of possible outcomes, and the assumptions used in determining the range.
- The disclosure of information regarding the significance of fair value accounting estimates to the entity's financial position and performance.
- Qualitative disclosures such as the exposures to risk and how they arise, the entity's objectives, policies and procedures for managing the risk and the methods used to measure the risk and any changes from the previous period of these qualitative concepts.
- Quantitative disclosures such as the extent to which the entity is exposed to risk, based on information provided internally to the entity's key management personnel, including credit risk, liquidity risk and market risk.

Disclosures of Estimation Uncertainty for Accounting Estimates that Give Rise to Significant Risks (Ref: Para. 20)

In relation to accounting estimates having significant risk, even where the disclosures are   **A122** in accordance with the applicable financial reporting framework, the auditor may conclude that the disclosure of estimation uncertainty is inadequate in light of the circumstances and facts involved. The auditor's evaluation of the adequacy of disclosure of estimation uncertainty increases in importance the greater the range of possible outcomes of the accounting estimate is in relation to materiality (see related discussion in paragraph A94).

In some cases, the auditor may consider it appropriate to encourage management to   **A123** describe, in the notes to the financial statements, the circumstances relating to the estimation uncertainty. ISA (UK) 705 (Revised June 2016)[27] provides guidance on the implications for the auditor's opinion when the auditor believes that management's disclosure of estimation uncertainty in the financial statements is inadequate or misleading.

Indicators of Possible Management Bias (Ref: Para. 21)

During the audit, the auditor may become aware of judgments and decisions made by   **A124** management which give rise to indicators of possible management bias. Such indicators may affect the auditor's conclusion as to whether the auditor's risk assessment and related responses remain appropriate, and the auditor may need to consider the implications for the rest of the audit. Further, they may affect the auditor's evaluation of whether the financial statements as a whole are free from material misstatement, as discussed in ISA (UK) 700 (Revised June 2016).[28]

Examples of indicators of possible management bias with respect to accounting estimates   **A125** include:

- Changes in an accounting estimate, or the method for making it, where management has made a subjective assessment that there has been a change in circumstances.
- Use of an entity's own assumptions for fair value accounting estimates when they are inconsistent with observable marketplace assumptions.
- Selection or construction of significant assumptions that yield a point estimate favorable for management objectives.
- Selection of a point estimate that may indicate a pattern of optimism or pessimism.

---

[27] *ISA (UK) 705 (Revised June 2016)*, Modifications to the Opinion in the Independent Auditor's Report.

[28] *ISA (UK) 700 (Revised June 2016)*, Forming an Opinion and Reporting on Financial Statements.

Written Representations (Ref: Para. 22)

A126   ISA (UK) 580[29] discusses the use of written representations. Depending on the nature, materiality and extent of estimation uncertainty, written representations about accounting estimates recognized or disclosed in the financial statements may include representations:

- About the appropriateness of the measurement processes, including related assumptions and models, used by management in determining accounting estimates in the context of the applicable financial reporting framework, and the consistency in application of the processes.
- That the assumptions appropriately reflect management's intent and ability to carry out specific courses of action on behalf of the entity, where relevant to the accounting estimates and disclosures.
- That disclosures related to accounting estimates are complete and appropriate under the applicable financial reporting framework.
- That no subsequent event requires adjustment to the accounting estimates and disclosures included in the financial statements.

A127   For those accounting estimates not recognized or disclosed in the financial statements, written representations may also include representations about:

- The appropriateness of the basis used by management for determining that the recognition or disclosure criteria of the applicable financial reporting framework have not been met (see paragraph A114).
- The appropriateness of the basis used by management to overcome the presumption relating to the use of fair value set forth under the entity's applicable financial reporting framework, for those accounting estimates not measured or disclosed at fair value (see paragraph A115).

Documentation (Ref: Para. 23)

A128   Documentation of indicators of possible management bias identified during the audit assists the auditor in concluding whether the auditor's risk assessment and related responses remain appropriate, and in evaluating whether the financial statements as a whole are free from material misstatement. See paragraph A125 for examples of indicators of possible management bias.

---

[29] *ISA (UK) 580*, Written Representations.

Appendix

Fair Value Measurements and Disclosures under Different Financial Reporting Frameworks

The purpose of this appendix is only to provide a general discussion of fair value measurements and disclosures under different financial reporting frameworks, for background and context.

(1) Different financial reporting frameworks require or permit a variety of fair value measurements and disclosures in financial statements. They also vary in the level of guidance that they provide on the basis for measuring assets and liabilities or the related disclosures. Some financial reporting frameworks give prescriptive guidance, others give general guidance, and some give no guidance at all. In addition, certain industry-specific measurement and disclosure practices for fair values also exist.

(2) Definitions of fair value may differ among financial reporting frameworks, or for different assets, liabilities or disclosures within a particular framework. For example, International Accounting Standard (IAS) 39[1a] defines fair value as 'the amount for which an asset could be exchanged, or a liability settled, between knowledgeable, willing parties in an arm's length transaction.' The concept of fair value ordinarily assumes a current transaction, rather than settlement at some past or future date. Accordingly, the process of measuring fair value would be a search for the estimated price at which that transaction would occur. Additionally, different financial reporting frameworks may use such terms as 'entity-specific value,' 'value in use,' or similar terms, but may still fall within the concept of fair value in this ISA (UK).

(3) Financial reporting frameworks may treat changes in fair value measurements that occur over time in different ways. For example, a particular financial reporting framework may require that changes in fair value measurements of certain assets or liabilities be reflected directly in equity, while such changes might be reflected in income under another framework. In some frameworks, the determination of whether to use fair value accounting or how it is applied is influenced by management's intent to carry out certain courses of action with respect to the specific asset or liability.

(4) Different financial reporting frameworks may require certain specific fair value measurements and disclosures in financial statements and prescribe or permit them in varying degrees. The financial reporting frameworks may:

- Prescribe measurement, presentation and disclosure requirements for certain information included in the financial statements or for information disclosed in notes to financial statements or presented as supplementary information;
- Permit certain measurements using fair values at the option of an entity or only when certain criteria have been met;
- Prescribe a specific method for determining fair value, for example, through the use of an independent appraisal or specified ways of using discounted cash flows;
- Permit a choice of method for determining fair value from among several alternative methods (the criteria for selection may or may not be provided by the financial reporting framework); or
- Provide no guidance on the fair value measurements or disclosures of fair value other than their use being evident through custom or practice, for example, an industry practice.

(5) Some financial reporting frameworks presume that fair value can be measured reliably for assets or liabilities as a prerequisite to either requiring or permitting

---

[1a] *IAS 39*, Financial Instruments: Recognition and Measurement.

fair value measurements or disclosures. In some cases, this presumption may be overcome when an asset or liability does not have a quoted market price in an active market and for which other methods of reasonably estimating fair value are clearly inappropriate or unworkable. Some financial reporting frameworks may specify a fair value hierarchy that distinguishes inputs for use in arriving at fair values ranging from those that involve clearly 'observable inputs' based on quoted prices and active markets and those 'unobservable inputs' that involve an entity's own judgments about assumptions that marketplace participants would use.

(6)   Some financial reporting frameworks require certain specified adjustments or modifications to valuation information, or other considerations unique to a particular asset or liability. For example, accounting for investment properties may require adjustments to be made to an appraised market value, such as adjustments for estimated closing costs on sale, adjustments related to the property's condition and location, and other matters. Similarly, if the market for a particular asset is not an active market, published price quotations may have to be adjusted or modified to arrive at a more suitable measure of fair value. For example, quoted market prices may not be indicative of fair value if there is infrequent activity in the market, the market is not well established, or small volumes of units are traded relative to the aggregate number of trading units in existence. Accordingly, such market prices may have to be adjusted or modified. Alternative sources of market information may be needed to make such adjustments or modifications. Further, in some cases, collateral assigned (for example, when collateral is assigned for certain types of investment in debt) may need to be considered in determining the fair value or possible impairment of an asset or liability.

(7)   In most financial reporting frameworks, underlying the concept of fair value measurements is a presumption that the entity is a going concern without any intention or need to liquidate, curtail materially the scale of its operations, or undertake a transaction on adverse terms. Therefore, in this case, fair value would not be the amount that an entity would receive or pay in a forced transaction, involuntary liquidation, or distress sale. On the other hand, general economic conditions or economic conditions specific to certain industries may cause illiquidity in the marketplace and require fair values to be predicated upon depressed prices, potentially significantly depressed prices. An entity, however, may need to take its current economic or operating situation into account in determining the fair values of its assets and liabilities if prescribed or permitted to do so by its financial reporting framework and such framework may or may not specify how that is done. For example, management's plan to dispose of an asset on an accelerated basis to meet specific business objectives may be relevant to the determination of the fair value of that asset.

Prevalence of Fair Value Measurements

(8)   Measurements and disclosures based on fair value are becoming increasingly prevalent in financial reporting frameworks. Fair values may occur in, and affect the determination of, financial statements in a number of ways, including the measurement at fair value of the following:

- Specific assets or liabilities, such as marketable securities or liabilities to settle an obligation under a financial instrument, routinely or periodically 'marked-to-market.'
- Specific components of equity, for example when accounting for the recognition, measurement and presentation of certain financial instruments with equity features, such as a bond convertible by the holder into common shares of the issuer.
- Specific assets or liabilities acquired in a business combination. For example, the initial determination of goodwill arising on the purchase of an entity in a

business combination usually is based on the fair value measurement of the identifiable assets and liabilities acquired and the fair value of the consideration given.

- Specific assets or liabilities adjusted to fair value on a one-time basis. Some financial reporting frameworks may require the use of a fair value measurement to quantify an adjustment to an asset or a group of assets as part of an asset impairment determination, for example, a test of impairment of goodwill acquired in a business combination based on the fair value of a defined operating entity or reporting unit, the value of which is then allocated among the entity's or unit's group of assets and liabilities in order to derive an implied goodwill for comparison to the recorded goodwill.

- Aggregations of assets and liabilities. In some circumstances, the measurement of a class or group of assets or liabilities calls for an aggregation of fair values of some of the individual assets or liabilities in such class or group. For example, under an entity's applicable financial reporting framework, the measurement of a diversified loan portfolio might be determined based on the fair value of some categories of loans comprising the portfolio.

- Information disclosed in notes to financial statements or presented as supplementary information, but not recognized in the financial statements.

International Standard on Auditing (UK) 550
Related parties

(Effective for audits of financial statements for periods ending on or after 15 December 2010)

Contents

International Standard on Auditing (UK) (ISA (UK)) 550, *Related Parties*, should be read in conjunction with ISA (UK) 200 (Revised June 2016), *Overall Objectives of the Independent Auditor and the Conduct of an Audit in Accordance with International Standards on Auditing (UK)*.

Introduction

Scope of this ISA (UK)

This International Standard on Auditing (UK) (ISA (UK)) deals with the auditor's **1** responsibilities relating to related party relationships and transactions in an audit of financial statements. Specifically, it expands on how ISA (UK) 315 (Revised June 2016),[1] ISA (UK) 330 (Revised June 2016),[2] and ISA (UK) 240 (Revised June 2016)[3] are to be applied in relation to risks of material misstatement associated with related party relationships and transactions.

Nature of Related Party Relationships and Transactions

Many related party transactions are in the normal course of business. In such circumstances, **2** they may carry no higher risk of material misstatement of the financial statements than similar transactions with unrelated parties. However, the nature of related party relationships and transactions may, in some circumstances, give rise to higher risks of material misstatement of the financial statements than transactions with unrelated parties. For example:

- Related parties may operate through an extensive and complex range of relationships and structures, with a corresponding increase in the complexity of related party transactions.
- Information systems may be ineffective at identifying or summarizing transactions and outstanding balances between an entity and its related parties.
- Related party transactions may not be conducted under normal market terms and conditions; for example, some related party transactions may be conducted with no exchange of consideration.

Responsibilities of the Auditor

Because related parties are not independent of each other, many financial reporting **3** frameworks establish specific accounting and disclosure requirements for related party relationships, transactions and balances to enable users of the financial statements to understand their nature and actual or potential effects on the financial statements. Where the applicable financial reporting framework establishes such requirements[3a], the auditor has a responsibility to perform audit procedures to identify, assess and respond to the risks of material misstatement arising from the entity's failure to appropriately account for or disclose related party relationships, transactions or balances in accordance with the requirements of the framework.

Even if the applicable financial reporting framework establishes minimal or no related **4** party requirements, the auditor nevertheless needs to obtain an understanding of the entity's related party relationships and transactions sufficient to be able to conclude

---

[1] *ISA (UK) 315 (Revised June 2016),* Identifying and Assessing the Risks of Material Misstatement through Understanding the Entity and Its Environment.

[2] *ISA (UK) 330 (Revised June 2016),* The Auditor's Responses to Assessed Risks.

[3] *ISA (UK) 240 (Revised June 2016),* The Auditor's Responsibilities Relating to Fraud in an Audit of Financial Statements.

[3a] *In the UK, specific accounting and disclosure requirements for related party relationships, transactions and balances are established in accounting standards and in law and regulations.*

whether the financial statements, insofar as they are affected by those relationships and transactions: (Ref: Para. A1)

(a) Achieve fair presentation (for fair presentation frameworks); or (Ref: Para. A2)

(b) Are not misleading (for compliance frameworks). (Ref: Para. A3)

5   In addition, an understanding of the entity's related party relationships and transactions is relevant to the auditor's evaluation of whether one or more fraud risk factors are present as required by ISA (UK) 240 (Revised June 2016),[4] because fraud may be more easily committed through related parties.

6   Owing to the inherent limitations of an audit, there is an unavoidable risk that some material misstatements of the financial statements may not be detected, even though the audit is properly planned and performed in accordance with the ISAs (UK).[5] In the context of related parties, the potential effects of inherent limitations on the auditor's ability to detect material misstatements are greater for such reasons as the following:

- Management may be unaware of the existence of all related party relationships and transactions, particularly if the applicable financial reporting framework does not establish related party requirements.
- Related party relationships may present a greater opportunity for collusion, concealment or manipulation by management.

7   Planning and performing the audit with professional skepticism as required by ISA (UK) 200 (Revised June 2016)[6] is therefore particularly important in this context, given the potential for undisclosed related party relationships and transactions. The requirements in this ISA (UK) are designed to assist the auditor in identifying and assessing the risks of material misstatement associated with related party relationships and transactions, and in designing audit procedures to respond to the assessed risks.

Effective Date

8   This ISA (UK) is effective for audits of financial statements for periods ending on or after 15 December 2010.

Objectives

9   The objectives of the auditor are:

(a) Irrespective of whether the applicable financial reporting framework establishes related party requirements, to obtain an understanding of related party relationships and transactions sufficient to be able:

(i)   To recognize fraud risk factors, if any, arising from related party relationships and transactions that are relevant to the identification and assessment of the risks of material misstatement due to fraud; and

(ii) To conclude, based on the audit evidence obtained, whether the financial statements, insofar as they are affected by those relationships and transactions:

a.   Achieve fair presentation (for fair presentation frameworks); or

b.   Are not misleading (for compliance frameworks); and

---

[4] *ISA (UK) 240 (Revised June 2016), paragraph 24.*

[5] *ISA (UK) 200 (Revised June 2016)*, Overall Objectives of the Independent Auditor and the Conduct of an Audit in Accordance with International Standards on Auditing (UK), *paragraphs A51–A52.*

[6] *ISA (UK) 200 (Revised June 2016), paragraph 15.*

(b) In addition, where the applicable financial reporting framework establishes related party requirements, to obtain sufficient appropriate audit evidence about whether related party relationships and transactions have been appropriately identified, accounted for and disclosed in the financial statements in accordance with the framework.

Definitions

For purposes of the ISAs (UK), the following terms have the meanings attributed below: **10**

(a) Arm's length transaction – A transaction conducted on such terms and conditions as between a willing buyer and a willing seller who are unrelated and are acting independently of each other and pursuing their own best interests.

(b) Related party – A party that is either: (Ref: Para. A4–A7)

   (i) A related party as defined in the applicable financial reporting framework; or

   (ii) Where the applicable financial reporting framework establishes minimal or no related party requirements:

      a. A person or other entity that has control or significant influence, directly or indirectly through one or more intermediaries, over the reporting entity;

      b. Another entity over which the reporting entity has control or significant influence, directly or indirectly through one or more intermediaries; or

      c. Another entity that is under common control with the reporting entity through having:

         i. Common controlling ownership;

         ii. Owners who are close family members; or

         iii. Common key management.

However, entities that are under common control by a state (that is, a national, regional or local government) are not considered related unless they engage in significant transactions or share resources to a significant extent with one another.

Requirements

Risk Assessment Procedures and Related Activities

As part of the risk assessment procedures and related activities that ISA (UK) 315 (Revised **11** June 2016) and ISA (UK) 240 (Revised June 2016) require the auditor to perform during the audit,[7] the auditor shall perform the audit procedures and related activities set out in paragraphs 12–17 to obtain information relevant to identifying the risks of material misstatement associated with related party relationships and transactions. (Ref: Para. A8)

Understanding the Entity's Related Party Relationships and Transactions

The engagement team discussion that ISA (UK) 315 (Revised June 2016) and ISA (UK) **12** 240 (Revised June 2016) require[8] shall include specific consideration of the susceptibility of the financial statements to material misstatement due to fraud or error that could result from the entity's related party relationships and transactions. (Ref: Para. A9–A10)

---

[7] *ISA (UK) 315 (Revised June 2016), paragraph 5; ISA (UK) 240 (Revised June 2016), paragraph 16.*

[8] *ISA (UK) 315 (Revised June 2016), paragraph 10; ISA (UK) 240 (Revised June 2016), paragraph 15.*

13   The auditor shall inquire of management regarding:

(a)   The identity of the entity's related parties, including changes from the prior period; (Ref: Para. A11–A14)

(b)   The nature of the relationships between the entity and these related parties; and

(c)   Whether the entity entered into any transactions with these related parties during the period and, if so, the type and purpose of the transactions.

14   The auditor shall inquire of management and others within the entity, and perform other risk assessment procedures considered appropriate, to obtain an understanding of the controls, if any, that management has established to: (Ref: Para. A15–A20)

(a)   Identify, account for, and disclose related party relationships and transactions in accordance with the applicable financial reporting framework;

(b)   Authorize and approve significant transactions and arrangements with related parties; and (Ref: Para. A21)

(c)   Authorize and approve significant transactions and arrangements outside the normal course of business.

Maintaining Alertness for Related Party Information When Reviewing Records or Documents

15   During the audit, the auditor shall remain alert, when inspecting records or documents, for arrangements or other information that may indicate the existence of related party relationships or transactions that management has not previously identified or disclosed to the auditor. (Ref: Para. A22–A23)

In particular, the auditor shall inspect the following for indications of the existence of related party relationships or transactions that management has not previously identified or disclosed to the auditor:

(a)   Bank and legal confirmations obtained as part of the auditor's procedures;

(b)   Minutes of meetings of shareholders and of those charged with governance; and

(c)   Such other records or documents as the auditor considers necessary in the circumstances of the entity.

16   If the auditor identifies significant transactions outside the entity's normal course of business when performing the audit procedures required by paragraph 15 or through other audit procedures, the auditor shall inquire of management about: (Ref: Para. A24–A25)

(a)   The nature of these transactions; and (Ref: Para. A26)

(b)   Whether related parties could be involved. (Ref: Para. A27)

Sharing Related Party Information with the Engagement Team

17   The auditor shall share relevant information obtained about the entity's related parties with the other members of the engagement team. (Ref: Para. A28)

Identification and Assessment of the Risks of Material Misstatement Associated with Related Party Relationships and Transactions

18   In meeting the ISA (UK) 315 (Revised June 2016) requirement to identify and assess the risks of material misstatement,[9] the auditor shall identify and assess the risks of material misstatement associated with related party relationships and transactions and determine

---

[9]   *ISA (UK) 315 (Revised June 2016), paragraph 25.*

whether any of those risks are significant risks. In making this determination, the auditor shall treat identified significant related party transactions outside the entity's normal course of business as giving rise to significant risks.

If the auditor identifies fraud risk factors (including circumstances relating to the existence **19** of a related party with dominant influence) when performing the risk assessment procedures and related activities in connection with related parties, the auditor shall consider such information when identifying and assessing the risks of material misstatement due to fraud in accordance with ISA (UK) 240 (Revised June 2016). (Ref: Para. A6 and A29–A30)

Responses to the Risks of Material Misstatement Associated with Related Party Relationships and Transactions

As part of the ISA (UK) 330 (Revised June 2016) requirement that the auditor respond **20** to assessed risks,[10] the auditor designs and performs further audit procedures to obtain sufficient appropriate audit evidence about the assessed risks of material misstatement associated with related party relationships and transactions. These audit procedures shall include those required by paragraphs 21–24. (Ref: Para. A31–A34)

Identification of Previously Unidentified or Undisclosed Related Parties or Significant Related Party Transactions

If the auditor identifies arrangements or information that suggests the existence of related **21** party relationships or transactions that management has not previously identified or disclosed to the auditor, the auditor shall determine whether the underlying circumstances confirm the existence of those relationships or transactions.

If the auditor identifies related parties or significant related party transactions that **22** management has not previously identified or disclosed to the auditor, the auditor shall:

(a) Promptly communicate the relevant information to the other members of the engagement team; (Ref: Para. A35)
(b) Where the applicable financial reporting framework establishes related party requirements:
  (i) Request management to identify all transactions with the newly identified related parties for the auditor's further evaluation; and
  (ii) Inquire as to why the entity's controls over related party relationships and transactions failed to enable the identification or disclosure of the related party relationships or transactions;
(c) Perform appropriate substantive audit procedures relating to such newly identified related parties or significant related party transactions; (Ref: Para. A36)
(d) Reconsider the risk that other related parties or significant related party transactions may exist that management has not previously identified or disclosed to the auditor, and perform additional audit procedures as necessary; and
(e) If the non-disclosure by management appears intentional (and therefore indicative of a risk of material misstatement due to fraud), evaluate the implications for the audit. (Ref: Para. A37)

[10] *ISA (UK) 330 (Revised June 2016), paragraphs 5–6.*

Identified Significant Related Party Transactions outside the Entity's Normal Course of Business

23   For identified significant related party transactions outside the entity's normal course of business, the auditor shall:

(a) Inspect the underlying contracts or agreements, if any, and evaluate whether:

    (i)   The business rationale (or lack thereof) of the transactions suggests that they may have been entered into to engage in fraudulent financial reporting or to conceal misappropriation of assets;[11] (Ref: Para. A38–A39)

    (ii) The terms of the transactions are consistent with management's explanations; and

    (iii) The transactions have been appropriately accounted for and disclosed in accordance with the applicable financial reporting framework; and

(b) Obtain audit evidence that the transactions have been appropriately authorized and approved. (Ref: Para. A40–A41)

Assertions That Related Party Transactions Were Conducted on Terms Equivalent to Those Prevailing in an Arm's Length Transaction

24   If management has made an assertion in the financial statements to the effect that a related party transaction was conducted on terms equivalent to those prevailing in an arm's length transaction, the auditor shall obtain sufficient appropriate audit evidence about the assertion. (Ref: Para. A42–A45)

Evaluation of the Accounting for and Disclosure of Identified Related Party Relationships and Transactions

25   In forming an opinion on the financial statements in accordance with ISA (UK) 700 (Revised June 2016),[12] the auditor shall evaluate: (Ref: Para. A46)

(a) Whether the identified related party relationships and transactions have been appropriately accounted for and disclosed in accordance with the applicable financial reporting framework; and (Ref: Para. A47–A47-1)

(b) Whether the effects of the related party relationships and transactions:

    (i)   Prevent the financial statements from achieving fair presentation (for fair presentation frameworks); or

    (ii) Cause the financial statements to be misleading (for compliance frameworks).

Written Representations

26   Where the applicable financial reporting framework establishes related party requirements, the auditor shall obtain written representations from management and, where appropriate, those charged with governance that: (Ref: Para. A48–A49-1)

(a) They have disclosed to the auditor the identity of the entity's related parties and all the related party relationships and transactions of which they are aware; and

(b) They have appropriately accounted for and disclosed such relationships and transactions in accordance with the requirements of the framework.

---

[11] *ISA (UK) 240 (Revised June 2016), paragraph 32(c).*

[12] *ISA (UK) 700 (Revised June 2016),* Forming an Opinion and Reporting on Financial Statements, *paragraphs 10–15.*

Communication with Those Charged with Governance

Unless all of those charged with governance are involved in managing the entity,[13] the auditor shall communicate with those charged with governance significant matters arising during the audit in connection with the entity's related parties. (Ref: Para. A50) **27**

Documentation

The auditor shall include in the audit documentation the names of the identified related parties and the nature of the related party relationships.[14] **28**

Application and Other Explanatory Material

Responsibilities of the Auditor

Financial Reporting Frameworks That Establish Minimal Related Party Requirements (Ref: Para. 4)

An applicable financial reporting framework that establishes minimal related party requirements is one that defines the meaning of a related party but that definition has a substantially narrower scope than the definition set out in paragraph 10(b)(ii) of this ISA (UK), so that a requirement in the framework to disclose related party relationships and transactions would apply to substantially fewer related party relationships and transactions. **A1**

Fair Presentation Frameworks (Ref: Para. 4(a))

In the context of a fair presentation framework,[15] related party relationships and transactions may cause the financial statements to fail to achieve fair presentation if, for example, the economic reality of such relationships and transactions is not appropriately reflected in the financial statements. For instance, fair presentation may not be achieved if the sale of a property by the entity to a controlling shareholder at a price above or below fair market value has been accounted for as a transaction involving a profit or loss for the entity when it may constitute a contribution or return of capital or the payment of a dividend. **A2**

Compliance Frameworks (Ref: Para. 4(b))

In the context of a compliance framework, whether related party relationships and transactions cause the financial statements to be misleading as discussed in ISA (UK) 700 (Revised June 2016) depends upon the particular circumstances of the engagement. For example, even if non-disclosure of related party transactions in the financial statements is in compliance with the framework and applicable law or regulation, the financial statements could be misleading if the entity derives a very substantial portion of its revenue from transactions with related parties, and that fact is not disclosed. However, it will be extremely rare for the auditor to consider financial statements **A3**

---

[13] *ISA (UK) 260 (Revised June 2016),* Communication with Those Charged with Governance, *paragraph 13.*

[14] *ISA (UK) 230 (Revised June 2016),* Audit Documentation, *paragraphs 8–11, and paragraph A6.*

[15] *ISA (UK) 200 (Revised June 2016), paragraph 13(a), defines the meaning of fair presentation and compliance frameworks.*

that are prepared and presented in accordance with a compliance framework to be misleading if in accordance with ISA (UK) 210 (Revised June 2016)[16] the auditor determined that the framework is acceptable.[17]

Definition of a Related Party (Ref: Para. 10(b))

A4   Many financial reporting frameworks discuss the concepts of control and significant influence. Although they may discuss these concepts using different terms, they generally explain that:

(a) Control is the power to govern the financial and operating policies of an entity so as to obtain benefits from its activities; and

(b) Significant influence (which may be gained by share ownership, statute or agreement) is the power to participate in the financial and operating policy decisions of an entity, but is not control over those policies.

A5   The existence of the following relationships may indicate the presence of control or significant influence:

(a) Direct or indirect equity holdings or other financial interests in the entity.

(b) The entity's holdings of direct or indirect equity or other financial interests in other entities.

(c) Being part of those charged with governance or key management (that is, those members of management who have the authority and responsibility for planning, directing and controlling the activities of the entity).

(d) Being a close family member of any person referred to in subparagraph (c).

(e) Having a significant business relationship with any person referred to in subparagraph (c).

Related Parties with Dominant Influence

A6   Related parties, by virtue of their ability to exert control or significant influence, may be in a position to exert dominant influence over the entity or its management. Consideration of such behavior is relevant when identifying and assessing the risks of material misstatement due to fraud, as further explained in paragraphs A29–A30.

Special-Purpose Entities as Related Parties

A7   In some circumstances, a special-purpose entity[18] may be a related party of the entity because the entity may in substance control it, even if the entity owns little or none of the special-purpose entity's equity.

---

[16] *ISA (UK) 210 (Revised June 2016),* Agreeing the Terms of Audit Engagements, *paragraph 6(a).*

[17] *ISA (UK) 700 (Revised June 2016), paragraph A12.*

[18] *ISA (UK) 315 (Revised June 2016), paragraphs A26–A27, provides guidance regarding the nature of a special-purpose entity.*

Risk Assessment Procedures and Related Activities

Risks of Material Misstatement Associated with Related Party Relationships and Transactions (Ref: Para. 11)

Considerations Specific to Public Sector Entities

The public sector auditor's responsibilities regarding related party relationships and **A8**
transactions may be affected by the audit mandate, or by obligations on public sector
entities arising from law, regulation or other authority. Consequently, the public
sector auditor's responsibilities may not be limited to addressing the risks of material
misstatement associated with related party relationships and transactions, but may also
include a broader responsibility to address the risks of non-compliance with law, regulation
and other authority governing public sector bodies that lay down specific requirements in
the conduct of business with related parties. Further, the public sector auditor may need to
have regard to public sector financial reporting requirements for related party relationships
and transactions that may differ from those in the private sector.

Understanding the Entity's Related Party Relationships and Transactions

Discussion among the Engagement Team (Ref: Para. 12)

Matters that may be addressed in the discussion among the engagement team include: **A9**

- The nature and extent of the entity's relationships and transactions with related parties
  (using, for example, the auditor's record of identified related parties updated after
  each audit).
- An emphasis on the importance of maintaining professional skepticism throughout
  the audit regarding the potential for material misstatement associated with related
  party relationships and transactions.
- The circumstances or conditions of the entity that may indicate the existence of related
  party relationships or transactions that management has not identified or disclosed to
  the auditor for example, a complex organizational structure, use of special-purpose
  entities for off-balance sheet transactions, or an inadequate information system).
- The records or documents that may indicate the existence of related party relationships
  or transactions.
- The importance that management and those charged with governance attach to the
  identification, appropriate accounting for, and disclosure of related party relationships
  and transactions (if the applicable financial reporting framework establishes related
  party requirements), and the related risk of management override of relevant controls.

In addition, the discussion in the context of fraud may include specific consideration of   **A10**
how related parties may be involved in fraud. For example:

- How special-purpose entities controlled by management might be used to facilitate
  earnings management.
- How transactions between the entity and a known business partner of a key member
  of management could be arranged to facilitate misappropriation of the entity's assets.

The Identity of the Entity's Related Parties (Ref: Para. 13(a))

Where the applicable financial reporting framework establishes related party requirements,   **A11**
information regarding the identity of the entity's related parties is likely to be readily
available to management because the entity's information systems will need to record,

process and summarize related party relationships and transactions to enable the entity to meet the accounting and disclosure requirements of the framework. Management is therefore likely to have a comprehensive list of related parties and changes from the prior period. For recurring engagements, making the inquiries provides a basis for comparing the information supplied by management with the auditor's record of related parties noted in previous audits.

A12　However, where the framework does not establish related party requirements, the entity may not have such information systems in place. Under such circumstances, it is possible that management may not be aware of the existence of all related parties. Nevertheless, the requirement to make the inquiries specified by paragraph 13 still applies because management may be aware of parties that meet the related party definition set out in this ISA (UK). In such a case, however, the auditor's inquiries regarding the identity of the entity's related parties are likely to form part of the auditor's risk assessment procedures and related activities performed in accordance with ISA (UK) 315 (Revised June 2016) to obtain information regarding:

- The entity's ownership and governance structures;
- The types of investments that the entity is making and plans to make; and
- The way the entity is structured and how it is financed.

In the particular case of common control relationships, as management is more likely to be aware of such relationships if they have economic significance to the entity, the auditor's inquiries are likely to be more effective if they are focused on whether parties with which the entity engages in significant transactions, or shares resources to a significant degree, are related parties.

A13　In the context of a group audit, ISA (UK) 600 (Revised June 2016) requires the group engagement team to provide each component auditor with a list of related parties prepared by group management and any other related parties of which the group engagement team is aware.[19] Where the entity is a component within a group, this information provides a useful basis for the auditor's inquiries of management regarding the identity of the entity's related parties.

A14　The auditor may also obtain some information regarding the identity of the entity's related parties through inquiries of management during the engagement acceptance or continuance process.

The Entity's Controls over Related Party Relationships and Transactions (Ref: Para. 14)

A15　Others within the entity are those considered likely to have knowledge of the entity's related party relationships and transactions, and the entity's controls over such relationships and transactions. These may include, to the extent that they do not form part of management:

- Those charged with governance;
- Personnel in a position to initiate, process, or record transactions that are both significant and outside the entity's normal course of business, and those who supervise or monitor such personnel;
- The internal audit function;
- In-house legal counsel; and
- The chief ethics officer or equivalent person.

---

[19] *ISA (UK) 600 (Revised June 2016)*, Special Considerations—Audits of Group Financial Statements (Including the Work of Component Auditors), *paragraph 40(e)*.

The audit is conducted on the premise that management and, where appropriate, those **A16** charged with governance have acknowledged and understand that they have responsibility for the preparation of the financial statements in accordance with the applicable financial reporting framework, including where relevant their fair presentation, and for such internal control as management and, where appropriate, those charged with governance determine is necessary to enable the preparation of financial statements that are free from material misstatement, whether due to fraud or error.[20] Accordingly, where the framework establishes related party requirements, the preparation of the financial statements requires management, with oversight from those charged with governance, to design, implement and maintain adequate controls over related party relationships and transactions so that these are identified and appropriately accounted for and disclosed in accordance with the framework. In their oversight role, those charged with governance monitor how management is discharging its responsibility for such controls. Regardless of any related party requirements the framework may establish, those charged with governance may, in their oversight role, obtain information from management to enable them to understand the nature and business rationale of the entity's related party relationships and transactions.

In meeting the ISA (UK) 315 (Revised) requirement to obtain an understanding of the **A17** control environment,[21] the auditor may consider features of the control environment relevant to mitigating the risks of material misstatement associated with related party relationships and transactions, such as:

- Internal ethical codes, appropriately communicated to the entity's personnel and enforced, governing the circumstances in which the entity may enter into specific types of related party transactions.
- Policies and procedures for open and timely disclosure of the interests that management and those charged with governance have in related party transactions.
- The assignment of responsibilities within the entity for identifying, recording, summarizing, and disclosing related party transactions.
- Timely disclosure and discussion between management and those charged with governance of significant related party transactions outside the entity's normal course of business, including whether those charged with governance have appropriately challenged the business rationale of such transactions (for example, by seeking advice from external professional advisors).
- Clear guidelines for the approval of related party transactions involving actual or perceived conflicts of interest, such as approval by a subcommittee of those charged with governance comprising individuals independent of management.
- Periodic reviews by the internal audit function, where applicable.
- Proactive action taken by management to resolve related party disclosure issues, such as by seeking advice from the auditor or external legal counsel.
- The existence of whistle-blowing policies and procedures, where applicable.

Controls over related party relationships and transactions within some entities may be **A18** deficient or non-existent for a number of reasons, such as:

- The low importance attached by management to identifying and disclosing related party relationships and transactions.
- The lack of appropriate oversight by those charged with governance.
- An intentional disregard for such controls because related party disclosures may reveal information that management considers sensitive, for example, the existence of transactions involving family members of management.

---

[20] *ISA (UK) 200 (Revised June 2016), paragraph A2.*

[21] *ISA (UK) 315 (Revised June 2016), paragraph 14.*

- An insufficient understanding by management of the related party requirements of the applicable financial reporting framework.
- The absence of disclosure requirements under the applicable financial reporting framework.

Where such controls are ineffective or non-existent, the auditor may be unable to obtain sufficient appropriate audit evidence about related party relationships and transactions. If this were the case, the auditor would, in accordance with ISA (UK) 705 (Revised June 2016),[22] consider the implications for the audit, including the opinion in the auditor's report.

A19 Fraudulent financial reporting often involves management override of controls that otherwise may appear to be operating effectively.[23] The risk of management override of controls is higher if management has relationships that involve control or significant influence with parties with which the entity does business because these relationships may present management with greater incentives and opportunities to perpetrate fraud. For example, management's financial interests in certain related parties may provide incentives for management to override controls by (a) directing the entity, against its interests, to conclude transactions for the benefit of these parties, or (b) colluding with such parties or controlling their actions. Examples of possible fraud include:

- Creating fictitious terms of transactions with related parties designed to misrepresent the business rationale of these transactions.
- Fraudulently organizing the transfer of assets from or to management or others at amounts significantly above or below market value.
- Engaging in complex transactions with related parties, such as special-purpose entities, that are structured to misrepresent the financial position or financial performance of the entity.

Considerations specific to smaller entities

A20 Control activities in smaller entities are likely to be less formal and smaller entities may have no documented processes for dealing with related party relationships and transactions. An owner-manager may mitigate some of the risks arising from related party transactions, or potentially increase those risks, through active involvement in all the main aspects of the transactions. For such entities, the auditor may obtain an understanding of the related party relationships and transactions, and any controls that may exist over these, through inquiry of management combined with other procedures, such as observation of management's oversight and review activities, and inspection of available relevant documentation.

Authorization and approval of significant transactions and arrangements
(Ref: Para. 14(b))

A21 Authorization involves the granting of permission by a party or parties with the appropriate authority (whether management, those charged with governance or the entity's shareholders) for the entity to enter into specific transactions in accordance with pre-determined criteria, whether judgmental or not. Approval involves those parties' acceptance of the transactions the entity has entered into as having satisfied the criteria on which authorization was granted. Examples of controls the entity may have established to authorize and approve significant transactions and arrangements with related parties or significant transactions and arrangements outside the normal course of business include:

---

[22] *ISA (UK) 705 (Revised June 2016)*, Modifications to the Opinion in the Independent Auditor's Report.

[23] *ISA (UK) 240 (Revised June 2016), paragraphs 31 and A4.*

- Monitoring controls to identify such transactions and arrangements for authorization and approval.
- Approval of the terms and conditions of the transactions and arrangements by management, those charged with governance or, where applicable, shareholders.

Maintaining Alertness for Related Party Information When Reviewing Records or Documents

Records or Documents That the Auditor May Inspect (Ref: Para. 15)

During the audit, the auditor may inspect records or documents that may provide information about related party relationships and transactions, for example: **A22**

- Third-party confirmations obtained by the auditor (in addition to bank and legal confirmations).
- Entity income tax returns.
- Information supplied by the entity to regulatory authorities.
- Shareholder registers to identify the entity's principal shareholders.
- Statements of conflicts of interest from management and those charged with governance.
- Records of the entity's investments and those of its pension plans.
- Contracts and agreements with key management or those charged with governance.
- Significant contracts and agreements not in the entity's ordinary course of business.
- Specific invoices and correspondence from the entity's professional advisors.
- Life insurance policies acquired by the entity.
- Significant contracts re-negotiated by the entity during the period.
- Reports of the internal audit function.
- Documents associated with the entity's filings with a securities regulator (for example, prospectuses).

Arrangements that may indicate the existence of previously unidentified or undisclosed related party relationships or transactions

An arrangement involves a formal or informal agreement between the entity and one or more other parties for such purposes as: **A23**

- The establishment of a business relationship through appropriate vehicles or structures.
- The conduct of certain types of transactions under specific terms and conditions.
- The provision of designated services or financial support.

Examples of arrangements that may indicate the existence of related party relationships or transactions that management has not previously identified or disclosed to the auditor include:

- Participation in unincorporated partnerships with other parties.
- Agreements for the provision of services to certain parties under terms and conditions that are outside the entity's normal course of business.
- Guarantees and guarantor relationships.

Identification of Significant Transactions outside the Normal Course of Business (Ref: Para. 16)

Obtaining further information on significant transactions outside the entity's normal course of business enables the auditor to evaluate whether fraud risk factors, if any, are **A24** present and, where the applicable financial reporting framework establishes related party requirements, to identify the risks of material misstatement.

A25 Examples of transactions outside the entity's normal course of business may include:

- Complex equity transactions, such as corporate restructurings or acquisitions.
- Transactions with offshore entities in jurisdictions with weak corporate laws.
- The leasing of premises or the rendering of management services by the entity to another party if no consideration is exchanged.
- Sales transactions with unusually large discounts or returns.
- Transactions with circular arrangements, for example, sales with a commitment to repurchase.
- Transactions under contracts whose terms are changed before expiry.

Understanding the nature of significant transactions outside the normal course of business (Ref: Para. 16(a))

A26 Inquiring into the nature of the significant transactions outside the entity's normal course of business involves obtaining an understanding of the business rationale of the transactions, and the terms and conditions under which these have been entered into.

Inquiring into whether related parties could be involved (Ref: Para. 16(b))

A27 A related party could be involved in a significant transaction outside the entity's normal course of business not only by directly influencing the transaction through being a party to the transaction, but also by indirectly influencing it through an intermediary. Such influence may indicate the presence of a fraud risk factor.

Sharing Related Party Information with the Engagement Team (Ref: Para. 17)

A28 Relevant related party information that may be shared among the engagement team members includes, for example:

- The identity of the entity's related parties.
- The nature of the related party relationships and transactions.
- Significant or complex related party relationships or transactions that may require special audit consideration, in particular transactions in which management or those charged with governance are financially involved.

Identification and Assessment of the Risks of Material Misstatement Associated with Related Party Relationships and Transactions

Fraud Risk Factors Associated with a Related Party with Dominant Influence (Ref: Para. 19)

A29 Domination of management by a single person or small group of persons without compensating controls is a fraud risk factor.[24] Indicators of dominant influence exerted by a related party include:

- The related party has vetoed significant business decisions taken by management or those charged with governance.
- Significant transactions are referred to the related party for final approval.

---

[24] *ISA (UK) 240 (Revised June 2016), Appendix 1.*

- There is little or no debate among management and those charged with governance regarding business proposals initiated by the related party.
- Transactions involving the related party (or a close family member of the related party) are rarely independently reviewed and approved.

Dominant influence may also exist in some cases if the related party has played a leading role in founding the entity and continues to play a leading role in managing the entity.

In the presence of other risk factors, the existence of a related party with dominant influence may indicate significant risks of material misstatement due to fraud. For example: **A30**

- An unusually high turnover of senior management or professional advisors may suggest unethical or fraudulent business practices that serve the related party's purposes.
- The use of business intermediaries for significant transactions for which there appears to be no clear business justification may suggest that the related party could have an interest in such transactions through control of such intermediaries for fraudulent purposes.
- Evidence of the related party's excessive participation in or preoccupation with the selection of accounting policies or the determination of significant estimates may suggest the possibility of fraudulent financial reporting.

Responses to the Risks of Material Misstatement Associated with Related Party Relationships and Transactions (Ref: Para. 20)

The nature, timing and extent of the further audit procedures that the auditor may select to respond to the assessed risks of material misstatement associated with related party relationships and transactions depend upon the nature of those risks and the circumstances of the entity.[25] **A31**

Examples of substantive audit procedures that the auditor may perform when the auditor has assessed a significant risk that management has not appropriately accounted for or disclosed specific related party transactions in accordance with the applicable financial reporting framework (whether due to fraud or error) include: **A32**

- Confirming or discussing specific aspects of the transactions with intermediaries such as banks, law firms, guarantors, or agents, where practicable and not prohibited by law, regulation or ethical rules.
- Confirming the purposes, specific terms or amounts of the transactions with the related parties (this audit procedure may be less effective where the auditor judges that the entity is likely to influence the related parties in their responses to the auditor).
- Where applicable, reading the financial statements or other relevant financial information, if available, of the related parties for evidence of the accounting of the transactions in the related parties' accounting records.

If the auditor has assessed a significant risk of material misstatement due to fraud as a result of the presence of a related party with dominant influence, the auditor may, in addition to the general requirements of ISA (UK) 240 (Revised June 2016), perform audit procedures such as the following to obtain an understanding of the business relationships that such a related party may have established directly or indirectly with the entity and to determine the need for further appropriate substantive audit procedures: **A33**

---

[25] *ISA (UK) 330 (Revised June 2016) provides further guidance on considering the nature, timing and extent of further audit procedures. ISA (UK) 240 (Revised June 2016) establishes requirements and provides guidance on appropriate responses to assessed risks of material misstatement due to fraud.*

- Inquiries of, and discussion with, management and those charged with governance.
- Inquiries of the related party.
- Inspection of significant contracts with the related party.
- Appropriate background research, such as through the Internet or specific external business information databases.
- Review of employee whistle-blowing reports where these are retained.

A34 Depending upon the results of the auditor's risk assessment procedures, the auditor may consider it appropriate to obtain audit evidence without testing the entity's controls over related party relationships and transactions. In some circumstances, however, it may not be possible to obtain sufficient appropriate audit evidence from substantive audit procedures alone in relation to the risks of material misstatement associated with related party relationships and transactions. For example, where intra-group transactions between the entity and its components are numerous and a significant amount of information regarding these transactions is initiated, recorded, processed or reported electronically in an integrated system, the auditor may determine that it is not possible to design effective substantive audit procedures that by themselves would reduce the risks of material misstatement associated with these transactions to an acceptably low level. In such a case, in meeting the ISA (UK) 330 (Revised June 2016) requirement to obtain sufficient appropriate audit evidence as to the operating effectiveness of relevant controls,[26] the auditor is required to test the entity's controls over the completeness and accuracy of the recording of the related party relationships and transactions.

Identification of Previously Unidentified or Undisclosed Related Parties or Significant Related Party Transactions

Communicating Newly Identified Related Party Information to the Engagement Team (Ref: Para. 22(a))

A35 Communicating promptly any newly identified related parties to the other members of the engagement team assists them in determining whether this information affects the results of, and conclusions drawn from, risk assessment procedures already performed, including whether the risks of material misstatement need to be reassessed.

Substantive Procedures Relating to Newly Identified Related Parties or Significant Related Party Transactions (Ref: Para. 22(c))

A36 Examples of substantive audit procedures that the auditor may perform relating to newly identified related parties or significant related party transactions include:

- Making inquiries regarding the nature of the entity's relationships with the newly identified related parties, including (where appropriate and not prohibited by law, regulation or ethical rules) inquiring of parties outside the entity who are presumed to have significant knowledge of the entity and its business, such as legal counsel, principal agents, major representatives, consultants, guarantors, or other close business partners.
- Conducting an analysis of accounting records for transactions with the newly identified related parties. Such an analysis may be facilitated using computer-assisted audit techniques.
- Verifying the terms and conditions of the newly identified related party transactions, and evaluating whether the transactions have been appropriately accounted for and disclosed in accordance with the applicable financial reporting framework.

---

[26] *ISA (UK) 330 (Revised June 2016), paragraph 8(b).*

Intentional Non-Disclosure by Management (Ref: Para. 22(e))

The requirements and guidance in ISA (UK) 240 (Revised June 2016) regarding the **A37** auditor's responsibilities relating to fraud in an audit of financial statements are relevant where management appears to have intentionally failed to disclose related parties or significant related party transactions to the auditor. The auditor may also consider whether it is necessary to re-evaluate the reliability of management's responses to the auditor's inquiries and management's representations to the auditor.

Identified Significant Related Party Transactions outside the Entity's Normal Course of Business

Evaluating the Business Rationale of Significant Related Party Transactions (Ref: Para. 23)

In evaluating the business rationale of a significant related party transaction outside the **A38** entity's normal course of business, the auditor may consider the following:

- Whether the transaction:
  - Is overly complex (for example, it may involve multiple related parties within a consolidated group).
  - Has unusual terms of trade, such as unusual prices, interest rates, guarantees and repayment terms.
  - Lacks an apparent logical business reason for its occurrence.
  - Involves previously unidentified related parties.
  - Is processed in an unusual manner.
- Whether management has discussed the nature of, and accounting for, such a transaction with those charged with governance.
- Whether management is placing more emphasis on a particular accounting treatment rather than giving due regard to the underlying economics of the transaction.

If management's explanations are materially inconsistent with the terms of the related party transaction, the auditor is required, in accordance with ISA (UK) 500,[27] to consider the reliability of management's explanations and representations on other significant matters.

The auditor may also seek to understand the business rationale of such a transaction **A39** from the related party's perspective, as this may help the auditor to better understand the economic reality of the transaction and why it was carried out. A business rationale from the related party's perspective that appears inconsistent with the nature of its business may represent a fraud risk factor.

Authorization and Approval of Significant Related Party Transactions (Ref: Para. 23(b))

Authorization and approval by management, those charged with governance, or, where **A40** applicable, the shareholders of significant related party transactions outside the entity's normal course of business may provide audit evidence that these have been duly considered at the appropriate levels within the entity and that their terms and conditions have been appropriately reflected in the financial statements. The existence of transactions of this nature that were not subject to such authorization and approval, in the absence of rational explanations based on discussion with management or those charged with governance, may indicate risks of material misstatement due to error or fraud. In these circumstances, the auditor may need to be alert for other transactions of a similar nature. Authorization

---

[27] *ISA (UK) 500, Audit Evidence, paragraph 11.*

and approval alone, however, may not be sufficient in concluding whether risks of material misstatement due to fraud are absent because authorization and approval may be ineffective if there has been collusion between the related parties or if the entity is subject to the dominant influence of a related party.

Considerations specific to smaller entities

A41   A smaller entity may not have the same controls provided by different levels of authority and approval that may exist in a larger entity. Accordingly, when auditing a smaller entity, the auditor may rely to a lesser degree on authorization and approval for audit evidence regarding the validity of significant related party transactions outside the entity's normal course of business. Instead, the auditor may consider performing other audit procedures such as inspecting relevant documents, confirming specific aspects of the transactions with relevant parties, or observing the owner-manager's involvement with the transactions.

Assertions That Related Party Transactions Were Conducted on Terms Equivalent to Those Prevailing in an Arm's Length Transaction (Ref: Para. 24)

A42   Although audit evidence may be readily available regarding how the price of a related party transaction compares to that of a similar arm's length transaction, there are ordinarily practical difficulties that limit the auditor's ability to obtain audit evidence that all other aspects of the transaction are equivalent to those of the arm's length transaction. For example, although the auditor may be able to confirm that a related party transaction has been conducted at a market price, it may be impracticable to confirm whether other terms and conditions of the transaction (such as credit terms, contingencies and specific charges) are equivalent to those that would ordinarily be agreed between independent parties. Accordingly, there may be a risk that management's assertion that a related party transaction was conducted on terms equivalent to those prevailing in an arm's length transaction may be materially misstated.

A43   The preparation of the financial statements requires management to substantiate an assertion that a related party transaction was conducted on terms equivalent to those prevailing in an arm's length transaction. Management's support for the assertion may include:

- Comparing the terms of the related party transaction to those of an identical or similar transaction with one or more unrelated parties.
- Engaging an external expert to determine a market value and to confirm market terms and conditions for the transaction.
- Comparing the terms of the transaction to known market terms for broadly similar transactions on an open market.

A44   Evaluating management's support for this assertion may involve one or more of the following:

- Considering the appropriateness of management's process for supporting the assertion.
- Verifying the source of the internal or external data supporting the assertion, and testing the data to determine their accuracy, completeness and relevance.
- Evaluating the reasonableness of any significant assumptions on which the assertion is based.

A45   Some financial reporting frameworks require the disclosure of related party transactions not conducted on terms equivalent to those prevailing in arm's length transactions. In these circumstances, if management has not disclosed a related party transaction in the financial statements, there may be an implicit assertion that the transaction was conducted on terms equivalent to those prevailing in an arm's length transaction.

Evaluation of the Accounting for and Disclosure of Identified Related Party Relationships and Transactions

Materiality Considerations in Evaluating Misstatements (Ref: Para. 25)

ISA (UK) 450 (Revised June 2016) requires the auditor to consider both the size and the nature of a misstatement, and the particular circumstances of its occurrence, when evaluating whether the misstatement is material.[28] The significance of the transaction to the financial statement users may not depend solely on the recorded amount of the transaction but also on other specific relevant factors, such as the nature of the related party relationship.   **A46**

Evaluation of Related Party Disclosures (Ref: Para. 25(a))

Evaluating the related party disclosures in the context of the disclosure requirements of the applicable financial reporting framework means considering whether the facts and circumstances of the entity's related party relationships and transactions have been appropriately summarized and presented so that the disclosures are understandable. Disclosures of related party transactions may not be understandable if: **A47**

(a) The business rationale and the effects of the transactions on the financial statements are unclear or misstated; or

(b) Key terms, conditions, or other important elements of the transactions necessary for understanding them are not appropriately disclosed.

Accounting standards and corporate law applicable in the UK include requirements for many entities for disclosures relating to control of the entity. The auditor may only be able to determine the name of the entity's ultimate controlling party through specific inquiry of management or those charged with governance. When the auditor considers it necessary, the auditor obtains corroboration from the ultimate controlling party confirming representations received in this regard.   **A47-1**

Written Representations (Ref: Para. 26)

Circumstances in which it may be appropriate to obtain written representations from those charged with governance include: **A48**

- When they have approved specific related party transactions that (a) materially affect the financial statements, or (b) involve management.
- When they have made specific oral representations to the auditor on details of certain related party transactions.
- When they have financial or other interests in the related parties or the related party transactions.

The auditor may also decide to obtain written representations regarding specific assertions that management may have made, such as a representation that specific related party transactions do not involve undisclosed side agreements.   **A49**

---

[28] *ISA (UK) 450 (Revised June 2016)*, Evaluation of Misstatements Identified during the Audit, *paragraph 11(a)*. *Paragraph A16 of ISA (UK) 450 (Revised June 2016) provides guidance on the circumstances that may affect the evaluation of a misstatement.*

A49-1   An entity may require its management and those charged with governance to sign individual declarations in relation to related party matters. It may be helpful if any such declarations are addressed jointly to a designated official of the entity and also to the auditor. In other cases, the auditor may wish to obtain written representations directly from each of those charged with governance and from members of management.

Communication with Those Charged with Governance (Ref: Para. 27)

A50   Communicating significant matters arising during the audit[29] in connection with the entity's related parties helps the auditor to establish a common understanding with those charged with governance of the nature and resolution of these matters. Examples of significant related party matters include:

- Non-disclosure (whether intentional or not) by management to the auditor of related parties or significant related party transactions, which may alert those charged with governance to significant related party relationships and transactions of which they may not have been previously aware.
- The identification of significant related party transactions that have not been appropriately authorized and approved, which may give rise to suspected fraud.
- Disagreement with management regarding the accounting for and disclosure of significant related party transactions in accordance with the applicable financial reporting framework.
- Non-compliance with applicable law or regulations prohibiting or restricting specific types of related party transactions.
- Difficulties in identifying the party that ultimately controls the entity.

---

[29] *ISA (UK) 230 (Revised June 2016), paragraph A8, provides further guidance on the nature of significant matters arising during the audit.*

International Standard on Auditing (UK) 560
Subsequent events

(Effective for audits of financial statements for periods ending on or after 15 December 2010)

Contents

International Standard on Auditing (UK) (ISA (UK)) 560, *Subsequent Events*, should be read in conjunction with ISA (UK) 200 (Revised June 2016), *Overall Objectives of the Independent Auditor and the Conduct of an Audit in Accordance with International Standards on Auditing (UK)*.

Introduction

Scope of this ISA (UK)

1   This International Standard on Auditing (UK) (ISA (UK)) deals with the auditor's responsibilities relating to subsequent events in an audit of financial statements. It does not deal with matters relating to the auditor's responsibilities for other information obtained after the date of the auditor's report, which are addressed in ISA (UK) 720 (Revised June 2016).[1] However, such other information may bring to light a subsequent event that is within the scope of this ISA (UK). (Ref: Para. A1)

Subsequent Events

2   Financial statements may be affected by certain events that occur after the date of the financial statements. Many financial reporting frameworks specifically refer to such events.[2] Such financial reporting frameworks ordinarily identify two types of events:

   (a) Those that provide evidence of conditions that existed at the date of the financial statements; and
   (b) Those that provide evidence of conditions that arose after the date of the financial statements.

ISA (UK) 700 (Revised June 2016) explains that the date of the auditor's report informs the reader that the auditor has considered the effect of events and transactions of which the auditor becomes aware and that occurred up to that date.[3]

Effective Date

3   This ISA (UK) is effective for audits of financial statements for periods ending on or after 15 December 2010.

Objectives

4   The objectives of the auditor are:

   (a) To obtain sufficient appropriate audit evidence about whether events occurring between the date of the financial statements and the date of the auditor's report that require adjustment of, or disclosure in, the financial statements are appropriately reflected in those financial statements in accordance with the applicable financial reporting framework; and
   (b) To respond appropriately to facts that become known to the auditor after the date of the auditor's report, that, had they been known to the auditor at that date, may have caused the auditor to amend the auditor's report.

---

[1] *ISA (UK) 720 (Revised June 2016),* The Auditor's Responsibilities Relating to Other Information.

[2] *For example, International Accounting Standard (IAS) 10,* Events After the Reporting Period *deals with the treatment in financial statements of events, both favorable and unfavorable, that occur between the date of the financial statements (referred to as the 'end of the reporting period' in the IAS) and the date when the financial statements are authorized for issue.*

[3] *ISA (UK) 700 (Revised June 2016),* Forming an Opinion and Reporting on Financial Statements, *paragraph A61.*

Definitions

For purposes of the ISAs (UK), the following terms have the meanings attributed below: **5**

(a) Date of the financial statements – The date of the end of the latest period covered by the financial statements.
(b) Date of approval of the financial statements – The date on which all the statements that comprise the financial statements, including the related notes, have been prepared and those with the recognized authority have asserted that they have taken responsibility for those financial statements. (Ref: Para. A2)
(c) Date of the auditor's report – The date the auditor dates the report on the financial statements in accordance with ISA (UK) 700 (Revised June 2016). (Ref: Para. A3)
(d) Date the financial statements are issued – The date that the auditor's report and audited financial statements are made available to third parties. (Ref: Para. A4–A5)
(e) Subsequent events – Events occurring between the date of the financial statements and the date of the auditor's report, and facts that become known to the auditor after the date of the auditor's report.

Requirements

Events Occurring between the Date of the Financial Statements and the Date of the Auditor's Report

The auditor shall perform audit procedures designed to obtain sufficient appropriate audit   **6** evidence that all events occurring between the date of the financial statements and the date of the auditor's report that require adjustment of, or disclosure in, the financial statements have been identified. The auditor is not, however, expected to perform additional audit procedures on matters to which previously applied audit procedures have provided satisfactory conclusions. (Ref: Para. A6)

The auditor shall perform the procedures required by paragraph 6 so that they cover the   **7** period from the date of the financial statements to the date of the auditor's report, or as near as practicable thereto. The auditor shall take into account the auditor's risk assessment in determining the nature and extent of such audit procedures, which shall include the following: (Ref: Para. A7–A8)

(a) Obtaining an understanding of any procedures management has established to ensure that subsequent events are identified.
(b) Inquiring of management and, where appropriate, those charged with governance as to whether any subsequent events have occurred which might affect the financial statements. (Ref: Para. A9)
(c) Reading minutes, if any, of the meetings, of the entity's owners, management and those charged with governance, that have been held after the date of the financial statements and inquiring about matters discussed at any such meetings for which minutes are not yet available. (Ref: Para. A10)
(d) Reading the entity's latest subsequent interim financial statements, if any.

If, as a result of the procedures performed as required by paragraphs 6 and 7, the auditor   **8** identifies events that require adjustment of, or disclosure in, the financial statements, the auditor shall determine whether each such event is appropriately reflected in those financial statements in accordance with the applicable financial reporting framework.

Written Representations

9   The auditor shall request management and, where appropriate, those charged with governance, to provide a written representation in accordance with ISA (UK) 580[4] that all events occurring subsequent to the date of the financial statements and for which the applicable financial reporting framework requires adjustment or disclosure have been adjusted or disclosed.

Facts Which Become Known to the Auditor after the Date of the Auditor's Report but before the Date the Financial Statements Are Issued

10   The auditor has no obligation to perform any audit procedures regarding the financial statements after the date of the auditor's report. However, if, after the date of the auditor's report but before the date the financial statements are issued, a fact becomes known to the auditor that, had it been known to the auditor at the date of the auditor's report, may have caused the auditor to amend the auditor's report, the auditor shall: (Ref: Para. A11)

    (a) Discuss the matter with management and, where appropriate, those charged with governance.

    (b) Determine whether the financial statements need amendment and, if so,

    (c) Inquire how management intends to address the matter in the financial statements.

11   If management[4a] amends the financial statements, the auditor shall:

    (a) Carry out the audit procedures necessary in the circumstances on the amendment.

    (b) Unless the circumstances in paragraph 12 apply:

        (i)   Extend the audit procedures referred to in paragraphs 6 and 7 to the date of the new auditor's report; and

        (ii) Provide a new auditor's report on the amended financial statements. The new auditor's report shall not be dated earlier than the date of approval of the amended financial statements.

12   Where law, regulation or the financial reporting framework does not prohibit management from restricting the amendment of the financial statements to the effects of the subsequent event or events causing that amendment and those responsible for approving the financial statements are not prohibited from restricting their approval to that amendment, the auditor is permitted to restrict the audit procedures on subsequent events required in paragraph 11(b)(i) to that amendment. In such cases, the auditor shall either:

    (a) Amend the auditor's report to include an additional date restricted to that amendment that thereby indicates that the auditor's procedures on subsequent events are restricted solely to the amendment of the financial statements described in the relevant note to the financial statements; or (Ref: Para. A12)

    (b) Provide a new or amended auditor's report that includes a statement in an Emphasis of Matter paragraph[5] or Other Matter paragraph that conveys that the auditor's procedures on subsequent events are restricted solely to the amendment of the financial statements as described in the relevant note to the financial statements.

13   In some jurisdictions, management may not be required by law, regulation or the financial reporting framework to issue amended financial statements and, accordingly, the auditor

---

[4] *ISA (UK) 580*, Written Representations.

[4a] In the UK the responsibility for amending the financial statements rests with those charged with governance.

[5] See *ISA (UK) 706 (Revised June 2016)*, Emphasis of Matter Paragraphs and Other Matter Paragraphs in the Independent Auditor's Report.

need not provide an amended or new auditor's report. However, if management does not amend the financial statements in circumstances where the auditor believes they need to be amended, then: (Ref: Para. A13–A14)

(a) If the auditor's report has not yet been provided to the entity, the auditor shall modify the opinion as required by ISA (UK) 705 (Revised June 2016)[6] and then provide the auditor's report; or

(b) If the auditor's report has already been provided to the entity, the auditor shall notify management and, unless all of those charged with governance are involved in managing the entity, those charged with governance, not to issue the financial statements to third parties before the necessary amendments have been made. If the financial statements are nevertheless subsequently issued without the necessary amendments, the auditor shall take appropriate action, to seek to prevent reliance on the auditor's report. (Ref. Para: A15–A16)

Facts Which Become Known to the Auditor after the Financial Statements Have Been Issued

After the financial statements have been issued, the auditor has no obligation to perform any audit procedures regarding such financial statements. However, if, after the financial statements have been issued, a fact becomes known to the auditor that, had it been known to the auditor at the date of the auditor's report, may have caused the auditor to amend the auditor's report, the auditor shall: **14**

(a) Discuss the matter with management and, where appropriate, those charged with governance;

(b) Determine whether the financial statements need amendment; and, if so,

(c) Inquire how management intends to address the matter in the financial statements. (Ref: Para. A16-1–A16-3)

If management amends the financial statements,[6a] the auditor shall: (Ref: Para. A17)   **15**

(a) Carry out the audit procedures necessary in the circumstances on the amendment.

(b) Review the steps taken by management to ensure that anyone in receipt of the previously issued financial statements together with the auditor's report thereon is informed of the situation.

(c) Unless the circumstances in paragraph 12 apply:

  (i) Extend the audit procedures referred to in paragraphs 6 and 7 to the date of the new auditor's report, and date the new auditor's report no earlier than the date of approval of the amended financial statements; and

  (ii) Provide a new auditor's report on the amended financial statements.

(d) When the circumstances in paragraph 12 apply, amend the auditor's report, or provide a new auditor's report as required by paragraph 12.

The auditor shall include in the new or amended auditor's report an Emphasis of Matter paragraph or Other Matter(s) paragraph referring to a note to the financial statements that more extensively discusses the reason for the amendment of the previously issued financial statements and to the earlier report provided by the auditor.   **16**

---

[6] *ISA (UK) 705 (Revised June 2016),* Modifications to the Opinion in the Independent Auditor's Report.

[6a] *Detailed regulations governing revised financial statements and directors' reports, where the revision is voluntary, are set out in the UK in section 454 of the Companies Act 2006.*

17   If management[6b] does not take the necessary steps to ensure that anyone in receipt of the previously issued financial statements is informed of the situation and does not amend the financial statements in circumstances where the auditor believes they need to be amended, the auditor shall notify management and, unless all of those charged with governance are involved in managing the entity[7], those charged with governance, that the auditor will seek to prevent future reliance on the auditor's report. If, despite such notification, management or those charged with governance do not take these necessary steps, the auditor shall take appropriate action to seek to prevent reliance on the auditor's report. (Ref: Para. A18–A18-1)

Application and Other Explanatory Material

Scope of this ISA (UK) (Ref: Para. 1)

A1   When the audited financial statements are included in other documents subsequent to the issuance of the financial statements (other than annual reports that would be within the scope of ISA (UK) 720 (Revised June 2016)), the auditor may have additional responsibilities relating to subsequent events that the auditor may need to consider, such as legal or regulatory requirements involving the offering of securities to the public in jurisdictions in which the securities are being offered. For example, the auditor may be required to perform additional audit procedures to the date of the final offering document. These procedures may include those referred to in paragraphs 6 and 7 performed up to a date at or near the effective date of the final offering document, and reading the offering document to assess whether the other information in the offering document is consistent with the financial information with which the auditor is associated.[8]

Definitions

Date of Approval of the Financial Statements (Ref: Para. 5(b))

A2   In some jurisdictions, law or regulation identifies the individuals or bodies (for example, management or those charged with governance) that are responsible for concluding that all the statements that comprise the financial statements, including the related notes, have been prepared, and specifies the necessary approval process. In other jurisdictions, the approval process is not prescribed in law or regulation and the entity follows its own procedures in preparing and finalizing its financial statements in view of its management and governance structures. In some jurisdictions, final approval of the financial statements by shareholders is required. In these jurisdictions, final approval by shareholders is not necessary for the auditor to conclude that sufficient appropriate audit evidence on which to base the auditor's opinion on the financial statements has been obtained. The date of approval of the financial statements for purposes of the ISAs (UK) is the earlier date on which those with the recognized authority determine that all the statements that comprise the financial statements, including the related notes, have been prepared and that those

---

[6b] *In the UK, those charged with governance have responsibility for taking the steps referred to in paragraph 17.*

[7] *ISA (UK) 260 (Revised June 2016)*, Communication with Those Charged with Governance, *paragraph 13.*

[8] *See ISA (UK) 200 (Revised June 2016)*, Overall Objectives of the Independent Auditor and the Conduct of an Audit in Accordance with International Standards on Auditing (UK), *paragraph 2.*
In the UK, standards and guidance for accountants engaged to prepare a report and/or letter for inclusion in, or in connection with, an investment circular are set out in the FRC's Statements of Investment Circular Reporting Standards (SIRS).

with the recognized authority have asserted that they have taken responsibility for those financial statements.

Date of the Auditor's Report (Ref: Para. 5(c))

The auditor's report cannot be dated earlier than the date on which the auditor has obtained **A3** sufficient appropriate audit evidence on which to base the opinion on the financial statements including evidence that all the statements that comprise the financial statements, including the related notes, have been prepared and that those with the recognized authority have asserted that they have taken responsibility for those financial statements.[9] Consequently, the date of the auditor's report cannot be earlier than the date of approval of the financial statements as defined in paragraph 5(b). A time period may elapse due to administrative issues between the date of the auditor's report as defined in paragraph 5(c) and the date the auditor's report is provided to the entity.

Date the Financial Statements Are Issued (Ref: Para. 5(d))

The date the financial statements are issued generally depends on the regulatory environment **A4** of the entity. In some circumstances, the date the financial statements are issued may be the date that they are filed with a regulatory authority. Since audited financial statements cannot be issued without an auditor's report, the date that the audited financial statements are issued must not only be at or later than the date of the auditor's report, but must also be at or later than the date the auditor's report is provided to the entity.

Considerations Specific to Public Sector Entities

In the case of the public sector, the date the financial statements are issued may be the **A5** date the audited financial statements and the auditor's report thereon are presented to the legislature or otherwise made public.

Events Occurring between the Date of the Financial Statements and the Date of the Auditor's Report (Ref: Para. 6–9)

Depending on the auditor's risk assessment, the audit procedures required by paragraph 6 **A6** may include procedures, necessary to obtain sufficient appropriate audit evidence, involving the review or testing of accounting records or transactions occurring between the date of the financial statements and the date of the auditor's report. The audit procedures required by paragraphs 6 and 7 are in addition to procedures that the auditor may perform for other purposes that, nevertheless, may provide evidence about subsequent events (for example, to obtain audit evidence for account balances as at the date of the financial statements, such as cut-off procedures or procedures in relation to subsequent receipts of accounts receivable).

Paragraph 7 stipulates certain audit procedures in this context that the auditor is required **A7** to perform pursuant to paragraph 6. The subsequent events procedures that the auditor performs may, however, depend on the information that is available and, in particular, the extent to which the accounting records have been prepared since the date of the financial statements. Where the accounting records are not up-to-date, and accordingly no interim financial statements (whether for internal or external purposes) have been prepared, or minutes of meetings of management or those charged with governance have not been

---

[9] *ISA (UK) 700 (Revised June 2016), paragraph 41. In some cases, law or regulation also identifies the point in the financial statement reporting process at which the audit is expected to be complete.*

prepared, relevant audit procedures may take the form of inspection of available books and records, including bank statements. Paragraph A8 gives examples of some of the additional matters that the auditor may consider in the course of these inquiries.

A8   In addition to the audit procedures required by paragraph 7, the auditor may consider it necessary and appropriate to:

- Read the entity's latest available budgets, cash flow forecasts and other related management reports for periods after the date of the financial statements;
- Inquire, or extend previous oral or written inquiries, of the entity's legal counsel concerning litigation and claims; or
- Consider whether written representations covering particular subsequent events may be necessary to support other audit evidence and thereby obtain sufficient appropriate audit evidence.

Inquiry (Ref. Para. 7(b))

A9   In inquiring of management and, where appropriate, those charged with governance, as to whether any subsequent events have occurred that might affect the financial statements, the auditor may inquire as to the current status of items that were accounted for on the basis of preliminary or inconclusive data and may make specific inquiries about the following matters:

- Whether new commitments, borrowings or guarantees have been entered into.
- Whether sales or acquisitions of assets have occurred or are planned.
- Whether there have been increases in capital or issuance of debt instruments, such as the issue of new shares or debentures, or an agreement to merge or liquidate has been made or is planned.
- Whether any assets have been appropriated by government or destroyed, for example, by fire or flood.
- Whether there have been any developments regarding contingencies.
- Whether any unusual accounting adjustments have been made or are contemplated.
- Whether any events have occurred or are likely to occur that will bring into question the appropriateness of accounting policies used in the financial statements, as would be the case, for example, if such events call into question the validity of the going concern assumption.
- Whether any events have occurred that are relevant to the measurement of estimates or provisions made in the financial statements.
- Whether any events have occurred that are relevant to the recoverability of assets.

Reading Minutes (Ref. Para. 7(c))

Considerations Specific to Public Sector Entities

A10   In the public sector, the auditor may read the official records of relevant proceedings of the legislature and inquire about matters addressed in proceedings for which official records are not yet available.

Implications of Other Information Obtained after the Date of the Auditor's Report (Ref: Para. 10)

A10a   While the auditor has no obligation to perform any audit procedures regarding the financial statements after the date of the auditor's report but before the date the financial statements are issued, ISA (UK) 720 (Revised June 2016) contains requirements and guidance with respect to other information obtained after the date of the auditor's report, which might include other information obtained after the date of the auditor's report, but before the date the financial statements are issued.[9a]

Facts Which Become Known to the Auditor after the Date of the Auditor's Report but before the Date the Financial Statements Are Issued

Management Responsibility towards Auditor (Ref: Para. 10)

As explained in ISA (UK) 210 (Revised June 2016), the terms of the audit engagement include the agreement of management[9b] to inform the auditor of facts that may affect the financial statements, of which management may become aware during the period from the date of the auditor's report to the date the financial statements are issued.[10]   **A11**

Dual Dating (Ref: Para. 12(a))

When, in the circumstances described in paragraph 12(a), the auditor amends the auditor's report to include an additional date restricted to that amendment, the date of the auditor's report on the financial statements prior to their subsequent amendment by management[3a] remains unchanged because this date informs the reader as to when the audit work on those financial statements was completed. However, an additional date is included in the auditor's report to inform users that the auditor's procedures subsequent to that date were restricted to the subsequent amendment of the financial statements. The following is an illustration of such an additional date: **A12**

"(Date of auditor's report), except as to Note Y, which is as of (date of completion of audit procedures restricted to amendment described in Note Y)."

No Amendment of Financial Statements by Management (Ref: Para. 13)

In some jurisdictions, management[3a] may not be required by law, regulation or the financial reporting framework to issue amended financial statements. This is often the case when issuance of the financial statements for the following period is imminent, provided appropriate disclosures are made in such statements.   **A13**

Considerations Specific to Public Sector Entities

In the public sector, the actions taken in accordance with paragraph 13 when management does not amend the financial statements may also include reporting separately to the legislature, or other relevant body in the reporting hierarchy, on the implications of the subsequent event for the financial statements and the auditor's report.   **A14**

[9a] *ISA (UK) 700 (Revised June 2016) requires that 'The auditor shall not sign, and hence date, the auditor's report earlier than the date on which all the other information contained in the annual report has been approved by those charged with governance and the auditor has considered all necessary available evidence.'*

[9b] *In the UK, the responsibility to inform the auditor of facts which may affect the financial statements usually rests with those charged with governance.*

[10] *ISA (UK) 210 (Revised June 2016),* Agreeing the Terms of Audit Engagements, *paragraph A23.*

Auditor Action to Seek to Prevent Reliance on Auditor's Report (Ref: Para. 13(b))

A15   The auditor may need to fulfill additional legal obligations even when the auditor has notified management not to issue the financial statements and management has agreed to this request.

A16   Where management has issued the financial statements despite the auditor's notification not to issue the financial statements to third parties, the auditor's course of action to prevent reliance on the auditor's report on the financial statements depends upon the auditor's legal rights and obligations. Consequently, the auditor may consider it appropriate to seek legal advice.

Facts Which Become Known to the Auditor after the Financial Statements Have Been Issued

Implications of Other Information Received after the Financial Statements Have Been Issued (Ref: Para. 14)

A16a   The auditor's obligations regarding other information received after the date of the auditor's report are addressed in ISA (UK) 720 (Revised June 2016). While the auditor has no obligation to perform any audit procedures regarding the financial statements after the financial statements have been issued, ISA (UK) 720 (Revised June 2016) contains requirements and guidance with respect to other information obtained after the date of the auditor's report.[9a]

A16-1   When issuing a new report the auditor has regard to the regulations relating to reports on revised annual financial statements and directors' reports.[6a]

A16-2   Where the auditor becomes aware of a fact relevant to the audited financial statements which did not exist at the date of the auditor's report there are no statutory provisions for revising financial statements. The auditor discusses with those charged with governance whether they should withdraw the financial statements and where those charged with governance decide not to do so the auditor may wish to take advice on whether it might be possible to withdraw their report. In both cases, other possible courses of action include the making of a statement by those charged with governance or the auditor at the annual general meeting. In any event legal advice may be helpful.

A16-3   In the UK, the auditor of a company has a statutory right to attend the Annual General Meeting and be heard on any part of the business of the meeting which concerns them as auditor.[10a] This right could include making a statement about facts discovered after the date of the auditor's report and where subsequent events come to the attention of the auditor, the auditor needs to consider what to do in relation to them.

No Amendment of Financial Statements by Management (Ref: Para. 15)

Considerations Specific to Public Sector Entities

A17   In some jurisdictions, entities in the public sector may be prohibited from issuing amended financial statements by law or regulation. In such circumstances, the appropriate course of action for the auditor may be to report to the appropriate statutory body.

[10a] *In the UK, Section 502 of the Companies Act 2006 establishes this right.*

Auditor Action to Seek to Prevent Reliance on Auditor's Report (Ref: Para. 17)

Where the auditor believes that management, or those charged with governance, have **A18** failed to take the necessary steps to prevent reliance on the auditor's report on financial statements previously issued by the entity despite the auditor's prior notification that the auditor will take action to seek to prevent such reliance, the auditor's course of action depends upon the auditor's legal rights and obligations. Consequently, the auditor may consider it appropriate to seek legal advice.

Where the financial statements of companies are issued but have not yet been laid **A18-1** before the members or equivalent, or if those charged with governance do not intend to make an appropriate statement at the annual general meeting, then the auditor may consider making an appropriate statement at the annual general meeting. The auditor does not have a statutory right to communicate directly in writing with the members although, if the auditor resigns or is removed or is not reappointed, the auditor has, for example, various duties under company law.[10b]

[10b] *The auditor of a limited company in the UK who ceases to hold office as auditor is required to comply with the requirements of section 519 of the Companies Act 2006 regarding the statement to be made by the auditor in relation to ceasing to hold office.*

International Standard on Auditing (UK) 570
(Revised June 2016)
Going concern

(Effective for audits of financial statements for periods commencing on or after 17 June 2016)

Contents

International Standard on Auditing (UK) (ISA (UK)) 570 (Revised June 2016), *Going Concern*, should be read in conjunction with ISA (UK) 200 (Revised June 2016), *Overall Objectives of the Independent Auditor and the Conduct of an Audit in Accordance with International Standards on Auditing (UK)*.

Interpreting the term 'going concern' in this ISA (UK)

The financial reporting frameworks applicable in the UK generally require the adoption of the ***going concern basis of accounting*** in financial statements, except in circumstances where management intends to liquidate the entity or to cease trading, or has no realistic alternative to liquidation or cessation of operations. In effect, an entity that does not meet the threshold for that exception is described as a ***going concern***. This requirement applies even when there are uncertainties about events or conditions that may cast significant doubt upon the entity's ability to continue as a going concern in the future. Such uncertainties are required to be disclosed in the financial statements when they are material.

The term ***going concern assumption*** is the defining assumption about the condition of an entity for which adoption of the going concern basis of accounting is appropriate: that the entity is, and will be able to continue as, a going concern. Accordingly, as used in this ISA (UK):

A.　　The term 'going concern' applies to any entity unless its management intends to liquidate the entity or to cease trading, or has no realistic alternative to liquidation or cessation of operations; and

B.　　The term 'ability to continue as a going concern' is equivalent to the term 'ability to continue to adopt the going concern basis of accounting' in the future.

Introduction

Scope of this ISA (UK)

1   This International Standard on Auditing (UK) (ISA (UK)) deals with the auditor's responsibilities in the audit of financial statements relating to going concern and the implications for the auditor's report. (Ref: Para. A1)

Going Concern Basis of Accounting

2   Under the going concern basis of accounting, the financial statements are prepared on the assumption that the entity is a going concern and will continue its operations for the foreseeable future. General purpose financial statements are prepared on a going concern basis of accounting, unless management either intends to liquidate the entity or to cease operations, or has no realistic alternative but to do so. Special purpose financial statements may or may not be prepared in accordance with a financial reporting framework for which the going concern basis of accounting is relevant (e.g., the going concern basis is not relevant for some financial statements prepared on a tax basis in particular jurisdictions). When the use of the going concern basis of accounting is appropriate, assets and liabilities are recorded on the basis that the entity will be able to realize its assets and discharge its liabilities in the normal course of business. (Ref: Para. A2)

Responsibility for Assessment of the Entity's Ability to Continue as a Going Concern

3   Some financial reporting frameworks contain an explicit requirement for management[1a] to make a specific assessment of the entity's ability to continue as a going concern, and standards regarding matters to be considered and disclosures to be made in connection with going concern. For example, International Accounting Standard (IAS) 1 requires management to make an assessment of an entity's ability to continue as a going concern.[1] The detailed requirements regarding management's responsibility to assess the entity's ability to continue as a going concern and related financial statement disclosures may also be set out in law or regulation.

4   In other financial reporting frameworks, there may be no explicit requirement for management to make a specific assessment of the entity's ability to continue as a going concern. Nevertheless, where the going concern basis of accounting is a fundamental principle in the preparation of financial statements as discussed in paragraph 2, the preparation of the financial statements requires management to assess the entity's ability to continue as a going concern even if the financial reporting framework does not include an explicit requirement to do so.

5   Management's assessment of the entity's ability to continue as a going concern involves making a judgment, at a particular point in time, about inherently uncertain future outcomes of events or conditions. The following factors are relevant to that judgment:

- The degree of uncertainty associated with the outcome of an event or condition increases significantly the further into the future an event or condition or the outcome occurs. For that reason, most financial reporting frameworks that require an explicit

---

[1a] *In the UK, those charged with governance are responsible for the preparation of the financial statements and the assessment of the entity's ability to continue as a going concern.*

[1] *IAS 1,* Presentation of Financial Statements *as at 1 January 2009, paragraphs 25–26.*

management assessment specify the period for which management is required to take into account all available information.

- The size and complexity of the entity, the nature and condition of its business and the degree to which it is affected by external factors affect the judgment regarding the outcome of events or conditions.
- Any judgment about the future is based on information available at the time at which the judgment is made. Subsequent events may result in outcomes that are inconsistent with judgments that were reasonable at the time they were made.

Responsibilities of the Auditor

The auditor's responsibilities are to obtain sufficient appropriate audit evidence regarding, **6** and conclude on, the appropriateness of management's use of the going concern basis of accounting in the preparation of the financial statements, and to conclude, based on the audit evidence obtained, whether a material uncertainty exists about the entity's ability to continue as a going concern. These responsibilities exist even if the financial reporting framework used in the preparation of the financial statements does not include an explicit requirement for management to make a specific assessment of the entity's ability to continue as a going concern.

However, as described in ISA (UK) 200 (Revised June 2016),[2] the potential effects of **7** inherent limitations on the auditor's ability to detect material misstatements are greater for future events or conditions that may cause an entity to cease to continue as a going concern. The auditor cannot predict such future events or conditions. Accordingly, the absence of any reference to a material uncertainty about the entity's ability to continue as a going concern in an auditor's report cannot be viewed as a guarantee as to the entity's ability to continue as a going concern.

Effective Date

This ISA (UK) is effective for audits of financial statements for periods commencing on or **8** after 17 June 2016. Earlier adoption is permitted.

Objectives

The objectives of the auditor are: **9**

(a) To obtain sufficient appropriate audit evidence regarding, and conclude on, the appropriateness of management's use of the going concern basis of accounting in the preparation of the financial statements;

(b) To conclude, based on the audit evidence obtained, whether a material uncertainty exists related to events or conditions that may cast significant doubt on the entity's ability to continue as a going concern; and

(c) To report in accordance with this ISA (UK).

---

[2] *ISA (UK) 200 (Revised June 2016)*, Overall Objectives of the Independent Auditor and the Conduct of an Audit in Accordance with International Standards on Auditing (UK).

Requirements

Risk Assessment Procedures and Related Activities

10   When performing risk assessment procedures as required by ISA (UK) 315 (Revised June 2016),[3] the auditor shall consider whether events or conditions exist that may cast significant doubt on the entity's ability to continue as a going concern. In so doing, the auditor shall determine whether management has already performed a preliminary assessment of the entity's ability to continue as a going concern, and: (Ref: Para. A2–A6)

(a) If such an assessment has been performed, the auditor shall discuss the assessment with management and determine whether management has identified events or conditions that, individually or collectively, may cast significant doubt on the entity's ability to continue as a going concern and, if so, management's plans to address them; or

(b) If such an assessment has not yet been performed, the auditor shall discuss with management the basis for the intended use of the going concern basis of accounting, and inquire of management whether events or conditions exist that, individually or collectively, may cast significant doubt on the entity's ability to continue as a going concern.

11   The auditor shall remain alert throughout the audit for audit evidence of events or conditions that may cast significant doubt on the entity's ability to continue as a going concern. (Ref: Para. A7)

Evaluating Management's Assessment

12   The auditor shall evaluate management's assessment of the entity's ability to continue as a going concern. (Ref: Para. A8–A10; A12–A13)

12D-1   In accordance with ISA (UK) 200 (Revised June 2016),[3a] the auditor shall maintain professional skepticism throughout the audit and in particular when reviewing future cash flow relevant to the entity's ability to continue as a going concern.

13   In evaluating management's assessment of the entity's ability to continue as a going concern, the auditor shall cover the same period as that used by management to make its assessment as required by the applicable financial reporting framework, or by law or regulation if it specifies a longer period. If management's assessment of the entity's ability to continue as a going concern covers less than twelve months from the date of the financial statements as defined in ISA (UK) 560,[4] the auditor shall request management to extend its assessment period to at least twelve months from that date.[4a] (Ref: Para. A11–A13)

14   In evaluating management's assessment, the auditor shall consider whether management's assessment includes all relevant information of which the auditor is aware as a result of the audit.

---

[3] *ISA (UK) 315 (Revised June 2016),* Identifying and Assessing the Risks of Material Misstatement through Understanding the Entity and Its Environment, *paragraph 5.*

[3a] *ISA (UK) 200 (Revised June 2016), paragraph 15.*

[4] *ISA (UK) 560,* Subsequent Events, *paragraph 5(a).*

[4a] *In the UK, the period used by those charged with governance in making their assessment is usually at least one year from the date of approval of the financial statements.*

Period beyond Management's Assessment

The auditor shall inquire of management as to its knowledge of events or conditions **15** beyond the period of management's assessment that may cast significant doubt on the entity's ability to continue as a going concern. (Ref: Para. A14–A15)

Additional Audit Procedures When Events or Conditions Are Identified

If events or conditions have been identified that may cast significant doubt on the entity's **16** ability to continue as a going concern, the auditor shall obtain sufficient appropriate audit evidence to determine whether or not a material uncertainty exists related to events or conditions that may cast significant doubt on the entity's ability to continue as a going concern (hereinafter referred to as 'material uncertainty') through performing additional audit procedures, including consideration of mitigating factors. These procedures shall include: (Ref: Para. A16)

(a) Where management has not yet performed an assessment of the entity's ability to continue as a going concern, requesting management to make its assessment.
(b) Evaluating management's plans for future actions in relation to its going concern assessment, whether the outcome of these plans is likely to improve the situation and whether management's plans are feasible in the circumstances. (Ref: Para. A17)
(c) Where the entity has prepared a cash flow forecast, and analysis of the forecast is a significant factor in considering the future outcome of events or conditions in the evaluation of management's plans for future actions: (Ref: Para. A18–A19)
 (i) Evaluating the reliability of the underlying data generated to prepare the forecast; and
 (ii) Determining whether there is adequate support for the assumptions underlying the forecast.
(d) Considering whether any additional facts or information have become available since the date on which management made its assessment.
(e) Requesting written representations from management and, where appropriate, those charged with governance, regarding their plans for future actions and the feasibility of these plans. (Ref: Para A20)

Auditor Conclusions

The auditor shall evaluate whether sufficient appropriate audit evidence has been obtained **17** regarding, and shall conclude on, the appropriateness of management's use of the going concern basis of accounting in the preparation of the financial statements.

Based on the audit evidence obtained, the auditor shall conclude whether, in the auditor's **18** judgment, a material uncertainty exists related to events or conditions that, individually or collectively, may cast significant doubt on the entity's ability to continue as a going concern. A material uncertainty exists when the magnitude of its potential impact and likelihood of occurrence is such that, in the auditor's judgment, appropriate disclosure of the nature and implications of the uncertainty is necessary for: (Ref: Para. A21–A22)

(a) In the case of a fair presentation financial reporting framework, the fair presentation of the financial statements, or
(b) In the case of a compliance framework, the financial statements not to be misleading.

If the period to which those charged with governance have paid particular attention in **18-1** assessing going concern is less than one year from the date of approval of the financial statements, and those charged with governance have not disclosed that fact, the auditor shall do so within the auditor's report.[4b] (Ref: Para. A19-1)

18-2   For entities that are required,[4c] and those that choose voluntarily, to report on how they have applied the UK Corporate Governance Code, or to explain why they have not, the auditor shall read and consider in light of the auditor's knowledge obtained in the audit, including that obtained in the evaluation of management's assessment of the entity's ability to continue as a going concern:

(a)   The directors' confirmation in the annual report that they have carried out a robust assessment of the principal risks facing the entity, including those that would threaten its business model, future performance, solvency or liquidity;

(b)   The disclosures in the annual report that describe those risks and explain how they are being managed or mitigated;

(c)   The directors' statement in the financial statements about whether they considered it appropriate to adopt the going concern basis of accounting in preparing them, and their identification of any material uncertainties to the entity's ability to continue to do so over a period of at least twelve months from the date of approval of the financial statements; and

(d)   The director's explanation in the annual report as to how they have assessed the prospects of the entity, over what period they have done so and why they consider that period to be appropriate, and their statement as to whether they have a reasonable expectation that the entity will be able to continue in operation and meet its liabilities as they fall due over the period of their assessment, including any related disclosures drawing attention to any necessary qualifications or assumptions.

The auditor shall determine whether the auditor has anything material to add or to draw attention to in the auditor's report on the financial statements in relation to these disclosures, and shall report in accordance with the requirements of paragraph 21-2 and ISA (UK) 720 (Revised June 2016).[4d]

18-3   Matters the auditor considers when determining whether there is anything to add or to draw attention to in the auditor's report on the financial statements shall include, based on the auditor's knowledge obtained in the audit, including that obtained in the evaluation of management's assessment of the entity's ability to continue as a going concern:

●   Whether the auditor is aware of information that would indicate that the annual report and accounts taken as a whole are not fair, balanced and understandable in relation to the principal risks facing the entity including those that would threaten its business model, future performance, solvency or liquidity; and

●   Matters relating to the robustness of the directors' assessment of the principal risks facing the entity and its outcome, including the related disclosures in the annual report and accounts, that the auditor communicated to the audit committee[4e] and that are not appropriately addressed in the section of the annual report that describes the work of the audit committee.

[4b]   *If the non-disclosure of the fact in the financial statements is a departure from the requirements of the applicable financial reporting framework, the auditor would give a qualified opinion ('except for').*

[4c]   *In the UK, these include companies with a premium listing of equity shares regardless of whether they are incorporated in the UK or elsewhere.*

[4d]   *ISA (UK) 720 (Revised June 2016),* The Auditor's Responsibilities Relating to Other Information, *paragraph 22-4.*

[4e]   *ISA (UK) 260 (Revised June 2016),* Communication with Those Charged with Governance, *paragraph 16-1(e).*

Adequacy of Disclosures When Events or Conditions Have Been Identified and a Material Uncertainty Exists

If the auditor concludes that management's use of the going concern basis of accounting **19** is appropriate in the circumstances but a material uncertainty exists, the auditor shall determine whether the financial statements: (Ref: Para. A22–A23)

(a) Adequately disclose the principal events or conditions that may cast significant doubt on the entity's ability to continue as a going concern and management's plans to deal with these events or conditions; and

(b) Disclose clearly that there is a material uncertainty related to events or conditions that may cast significant doubt on the entity's ability to continue as a going concern and, therefore, that it may be unable to realize its assets and discharge its liabilities in the normal course of business.

Adequacy of Disclosures When Events or Conditions Have Been Identified but No Material Uncertainty Exists

If events or conditions have been identified that may cast significant doubt on the entity's **20** ability to continue as a going concern but, based on the audit evidence obtained the auditor concludes that no material uncertainty exists, the auditor shall evaluate whether, in view of the requirements of the applicable financial reporting framework, the financial statements provide adequate disclosures about these events or conditions. (Ref: Para. A24–A25)

Implications for the Auditor's Report

Use of Going Concern Basis of Accounting Is Inappropriate

If the financial statements have been prepared using the going concern basis of accounting **21** but, in the auditor's judgment, management's use of the going concern basis of accounting in the preparation of the financial statements is inappropriate, the auditor shall express an adverse opinion. (Ref: Para. A26–A27)

Use of Going Concern Basis of Accounting is Appropriate and no Material Uncertainty has been Identified

When the auditor is required[4f] or decides to communicate key audit matters in **21-1** accordance with ISA (UK) 701, where the auditor concludes that management's use of the going concern basis of accounting is appropriate in the circumstances and no material uncertainty has been identified, the auditor shall:

(a) Determine in accordance with ISA (UK) 701, in light of the audit evidence obtained and the conclusions reached in the audit and having particular regard to any evaluation the auditor undertakes in accordance with paragraph 20, whether a key audit matter relating to going concern exists that should be communicated in the auditor's report; and

(b) Where a key audit matter exists that should be communicated, communicate the key audit matter in the auditor's report in accordance with ISA (UK) 701.

Where the auditor concludes that management's use of the going concern basis of **21-2** accounting is appropriate in the circumstances and no material uncertainty has been

---

[4f] *ISA (UK) 700 (Revised June 2016),* Forming an Opinion and Reporting on Financial Statements, *paragraphs 30–31 set out the requirements to apply ISA (UK) 701,* Communicating Key Audit Matters in the Independent Auditor's Report.

identified, the auditor shall report by exception in accordance with paragraph 43-1 of ISA (UK) 700 (Revised June 2016) in a separate section in the auditor's report with the heading 'Conclusions relating to Going Concern', or other appropriate heading, as to whether: (Ref: Para A27-1–A27-2)

(a) For entities that are required, and those that choose voluntarily, to report on how they have applied the UK Corporate Governance Code, or to explain why they have not, the auditor has anything material to add or draw attention to in relation to the directors' statement in the financial statements about whether the directors considered it appropriate to adopt the going concern basis of accounting in preparing the financial statements, and the directors' identification of any material uncertainties to the entity's ability to continue to do so over a period of at least twelve months from the date of approval of the financial statements; or

(b) In other cases, the auditor concludes that:

(i) Management's use of the going concern basis of accounting in the preparation of the entity's financial statements is not appropriate; or

(ii) Management has not disclosed in the entity's financial statements any identified material uncertainties that may cast significant doubt about the entity's ability to continue to adopt the going concern basis of accounting for a period of at least twelve months from when the financial statements are authorized for issue.

Use of Going Concern Basis of Accounting Is Appropriate but a Material Uncertainty Exists

Adequate Disclosure of a Material Uncertainty Is Made in the Financial Statements

22 If adequate disclosure about the material uncertainty is made in the financial statements, the auditor shall express an unmodified opinion and the auditor's report shall include a separate section under the heading 'Material Uncertainty Related to Going Concern' to: (Ref: Para. A28–A31, A34)

(a) Draw attention to the note in the financial statements that discloses the matters set out in paragraph 19; and

(b) State that these events or conditions indicate that a material uncertainty exists that may cast significant doubt on the entity's ability to continue as a going concern and that the auditor's opinion is not modified in respect of the matter.

Adequate Disclosure of a Material Uncertainty Is Not Made in the Financial Statements

23 If adequate disclosure about the material uncertainty is not made in the financial statements, the auditor shall: (Ref: Para. A32–A34-1)

(a) Express a qualified opinion or adverse opinion, as appropriate, in accordance with ISA (UK) 705 (Revised June 2016)[5]; and

(b) In the Basis for Qualified (Adverse) Opinion section of the auditor's report, state that a material uncertainty exists that may cast significant doubt on the entity's ability to continue as a going concern and that the financial statements do not adequately disclose this matter.

---

[5] *ISA (UK) 705 (Revised June 2016)*, Modifications to the Opinion in the Independent Auditor's Report.

Management Unwilling to Make or Extend Its Assessment

If management is unwilling to make or extend its assessment when requested to do so by the auditor, the auditor shall consider the implications for the auditor's report. (Ref: Para. A35) **24**

Communication with Those Charged with Governance

Unless all those charged with governance are involved in managing the entity,[6] the auditor **25**
shall communicate with those charged with governance events or conditions identified that may cast significant doubt on the entity's ability to continue as a going concern. Such communication with those charged with governance shall include the following: (Ref: Para. A35-1)

(a) Whether the events or conditions constitute a material uncertainty;
(b) Whether management's use of the going concern basis of accounting is appropriate in the preparation of the financial statements;
(c) The adequacy of related disclosures in the financial statements; and
(d) Where applicable, the implications for the auditor's report.

Significant Delay in the Approval of Financial Statements

If there is significant delay in the approval of the financial statements by management **26**
or those charged with governance after the date of the financial statements, the auditor shall inquire as to the reasons for the delay. If the auditor believes that the delay could be related to events or conditions relating to the going concern assessment, the auditor shall perform those additional audit procedures necessary, as described in paragraph 16, as well as consider the effect on the auditor's conclusion regarding the existence of a material uncertainty, as described in paragraph 18.

***

Application and Other Explanatory Material

Scope of this ISA (UK) (Ref: Para 1)

ISA (UK) 701[7] deals with the auditor's responsibility to communicate key audit matters **A1**
in the auditor's report. That ISA (UK) acknowledges that, when ISA (UK) 701 applies, matters relating to going concern may be determined to be key audit matters, and explains that a material uncertainty related to events or conditions that may cast significant doubt on the entity's ability to continue as a going concern is, by its nature, a key audit matter.[8]

Going Concern Basis of Accounting (Ref: Para. 2)

Considerations Specific to Public Sector Entities

Management's use of the going concern basis of accounting is also relevant to public **A2**
sector entities. For example, International Public Sector Accounting Standard (IPSAS) 1

---

[6] *ISA (UK) 260 (Revised June 2016), Communication with Those Charged with Governance, paragraph 13.*

[7] *ISA (UK) 701, Communicating Key Audit Matters in the Independent Auditor's Report.*

[8] *See paragraphs 15 and A41 of ISA (UK) 701.*

addresses the issue of the ability of public sector entities to continue as going concerns.[9] Going concern risks may arise, but are not limited to, situations where public sector entities operate on a for-profit basis, where government support may be reduced or withdrawn, or in the case of privatization. Events or conditions that may cast significant doubt on an entity's ability to continue as a going concern in the public sector may include situations where the public sector entity lacks funding for its continued existence or when policy decisions are made that affect the services provided by the public sector entity.

Risk Assessment Procedures and Related Activities

Events or Conditions That May Cast Significant Doubt on the Entity's Ability to Continue as a Going Concern (Ref: Para. 10)

A3   The following are examples of events or conditions that, individually or collectively, may cast significant doubt on the entity's ability to continue as a going concern. This listing is not all-inclusive nor does the existence of one or more of the items always signify that a material uncertainty exists.

Financial

- Net liability or net current liability position.
- Fixed-term borrowings approaching maturity without realistic prospects of renewal or repayment; or excessive reliance on short-term borrowings to finance long-term assets.
- Indications of withdrawal of financial support by creditors.
- Negative operating cash flows indicated by historical or prospective financial statements.
- Adverse key financial ratios.
- Substantial operating losses or significant deterioration in the value of assets used to generate cash flows.
- Arrears or discontinuance of dividends.
- Inability to pay creditors on due dates.
- Inability to comply with the terms of loan agreements.
- Change from credit to cash-on-delivery transactions with suppliers.
- Inability to obtain financing for essential new product development or other essential investments.

Operating

- Management intentions to liquidate the entity or to cease operations.
- Loss of key management without replacement.
- Loss of a major market, key customer(s), franchise, license, or principal supplier(s).
- Labor difficulties.
- Shortages of important supplies.
- Emergence of a highly successful competitor.

Other

- Non-compliance with capital or other statutory or regulatory requirements, such as solvency or liquidity requirements for financial institutions.
- Pending legal or regulatory proceedings against the entity that may, if successful, result in claims that the entity is unlikely to be able to satisfy.
- Changes in law or regulation or government policy expected to adversely affect the entity.
- Uninsured or underinsured catastrophes when they occur.

[9] *IPSAS 1*, Presentation of Financial Statements *as at 1 January 2009, paragraphs 38–41.*

The significance of such events or conditions often can be mitigated by other factors. For example, the effect of an entity being unable to make its normal debt repayments may be counter-balanced by management's plans to maintain adequate cash flows by alternative means, such as by disposing of assets, rescheduling loan repayments, or obtaining additional capital. Similarly, the loss of a principal supplier may be mitigated by the availability of a suitable alternative source of supply.

The risk assessment procedures required by paragraph 10 help the auditor to determine **A4** whether management's use of the going concern basis of accounting is likely to be an important issue and its impact on planning the audit. These procedures also allow for more timely discussions with management, including a discussion of management's plans and resolution of any identified going concern issues.

Considerations Specific to Smaller Entities (Ref: Para. 10)

The size of an entity may affect its ability to withstand adverse conditions. Small entities **A5** may be able to respond quickly to exploit opportunities, but may lack reserves to sustain operations.

Conditions of particular relevance to small entities include the risk that banks and **A6** other lenders may cease to support the entity, as well as the possible loss of a principal supplier, major customer, key employee, or the right to operate under a license, franchise or other legal agreement.

Remaining Alert throughout the Audit for Audit Evidence about Events or Conditions (Ref: Para. 11)

ISA (UK) 315 (Revised June 2016) requires the auditor to revise the auditor's risk **A7** assessment and modify the further planned audit procedures accordingly when additional audit evidence is obtained during the course of the audit that affects the auditor's assessment of risk.[10] If events or conditions that may cast significant doubt on the entity's ability to continue as a going concern are identified after the auditor's risk assessments are made, in addition to performing the procedures in paragraph 16, the auditor's assessment of the risks of material misstatement may need to be revised. The existence of such events or conditions may also affect the nature, timing and extent of the auditor's further procedures in response to the assessed risks. ISA (UK) 330 (Revised June 2016)[11] establishes requirements and provides guidance on this issue.

Evaluating Management's Assessment

Management's Assessment and Supporting Analysis and the Auditor's Evaluation (Ref: Para. 12)

Management's assessment of the entity's ability to continue as a going concern is a key **A8** part of the auditor's consideration of management's use of the going concern basis of accounting.

---

[10] *ISA (UK) 315 (Revised June 2016), paragraph 31.*

[11] *ISA (UK) 330 (Revised June 2016),* The Auditor's Responses to Assessed Risks.

A8-1 In the UK, applicable financial reporting frameworks generally specify that management takes into account all available information about the future.[11a] In evaluating management's assessment of the entity's ability to continue as a going concern, it is likely to be relevant for the auditor: to inquire as to what information is available about the future to management and those charged with governance; and determine whether this has been appropriately considered as part of management's assessment. For example, relevant information may be available to management through business planning activities, risk management processes, and for regulated entities, through regulatory reporting, planning or communications with regulatory, enforcement or supervisory authorities. For entities that are required, and those that choose voluntarily, to report on how they have applied the UK Corporate Governance Code, or to explain why they have not, there may also be information available that has been developed to support reporting about the entity's business model, principal risks and the entity's longer term viability statement.

A9 It is not the auditor's responsibility to rectify the lack of analysis by management. In some circumstances, however, the lack of detailed analysis by management to support its assessment may not prevent the auditor from concluding whether management's use of the going concern basis of accounting is appropriate in the circumstances. For example, when there is a history of profitable operations and a ready access to financial resources, management may make its assessment without detailed analysis. In this case, the auditor's evaluation of the appropriateness of management's assessment may be made without performing detailed evaluation procedures if the auditor's other audit procedures are sufficient to enable the auditor to conclude whether management's use of the going concern basis of accounting in the preparation of the financial statements is appropriate in the circumstances.

A10 In other circumstances, evaluating management's assessment of the entity's ability to continue as a going concern, as required by paragraph 12, may include an evaluation of the process management followed to make its assessment, the assumptions on which the assessment is based and management's plans for future action and whether management's plans are feasible in the circumstances.

The Period of Management's Assessment (Ref: Para. 13)

A11 Most financial reporting frameworks requiring an explicit management assessment specify the period for which management is required to take into account all available information.[12]

A11-1 If the future period to which those charged with governance have paid particular attention has been limited, for example, to a period of less than one year from the date of approval of the financial statements, those charged with governance will have determined whether, in their opinion, the financial statements require any additional disclosures to explain adequately the assumptions that underlie the adoption of the going concern basis of accounting.

A11-2 If the future period to which those charged with governance have paid particular attention is less than the minimum required by the financial reporting framework, the

---

[11a] *For example, IAS 1, paragraph 26 and FRS 102, paragraph 3.8 both require that management takes into account all available information about the future.*

[12] *Accounting frameworks do not normally specify a maximum period that should be reviewed as part of the assessment of going concern. However, IAS 1 and FRS 102* The Financial Reporting Standard applicable in the UK and Republic of Ireland *both require that management takes into account all available information about the future.*

auditor considers whether to express a modified opinion in accordance with ISA (UK) 705 (Revised June 2016).[12a]

The auditor assesses whether to concur with the judgments of those charged with governance regarding the need for additional disclosures and their adequacy. Disclosure, however, does not eliminate the need to make appropriate judgments about the suitability of the future period as an adequate basis for assessing the going concern position. Paragraph 18-1 requires the auditor to disclose in the auditor's report if the period to which those charged with governance have paid particular attention in assessing going concern is less than one year from the date of approval of the financial statements, and those charged with governance have not disclosed that fact. The auditor through discussion with those charged with governance of their plans and expectations may be able to obtain satisfaction that those charged with governance have in fact paid particular attention to a period of one year from the date of approval of the financial statements.

A11-3

Procedures to Identify Material Matters Indicating Concern

Having regard to the future period to which those charged with governance have paid particular attention in assessing going concern, the auditor plans and performs procedures specifically designed to identify any material matters which could indicate concern about the entity's ability to continue as a going concern.

A11-4

The extent of the auditor's procedures is influenced primarily by the excess of the financial resources available to the entity over the financial resources that it requires. The entity's procedures (and the auditor's procedures) need not always be elaborate in order to provide sufficient appropriate audit evidence. A determination of the sufficiency of the evidence supplied to the auditor by those charged with governance will depend on the particular circumstances. For example, to be sufficient the evidence may not require formal cash flow forecasts and budgets to have been prepared for the period ending one year from the date of approval of the financial statements. Although such forecasts and budgets are likely to provide the most persuasive evidence, alternative sources of evidence may also be acceptable. This is particularly likely to be the case in respect of entities with uncomplicated circumstances. Many smaller companies fall into this category.

A11-5

Considerations Specific to Smaller Entities (Ref: Para. 12–13)

In many cases, the management of smaller entities may not have prepared a detailed assessment of the entity's ability to continue as a going concern, but instead may rely on in-depth knowledge of the business and anticipated future prospects. Nevertheless, in accordance with the requirements of this ISA (UK), the auditor needs to evaluate management's assessment of the entity's ability to continue as a going concern. For smaller entities, it may be appropriate to discuss the medium and long-term financing of the entity with management, provided that management's contentions can be corroborated by sufficient documentary evidence and are not inconsistent with the auditor's understanding of the entity. Therefore, the requirement in paragraph 13 for the auditor to request management to extend its assessment may, for example, be satisfied by discussion, inquiry and inspection of supporting documentation, for example, orders received for future supply, evaluated as to their feasibility or otherwise substantiated.

A12

Continued support by owner-managers is often important to smaller entities' ability to continue as a going concern. Where a small entity is largely financed by a loan from the owner-manager, it may be important that these funds are not withdrawn. For example,

A13

[12a] *ISA (UK) 705 (Revised June 2016)*, Modifications to the Opinion in the Independent Auditor's Report.

the continuance of a small entity in financial difficulty may be dependent on the owner-manager subordinating a loan to the entity in favor of banks or other creditors, or the owner-manager supporting a loan for the entity by providing a guarantee with his or her personal assets as collateral. In such circumstances, the auditor may obtain appropriate documentary evidence of the subordination of the owner-manager's loan or of the guarantee. Where an entity is dependent on additional support from the owner-manager, the auditor may evaluate the owner-manager's ability to meet the obligation under the support arrangement. In addition, the auditor may request written confirmation of the terms and conditions attaching to such support and the owner-manager's intention or understanding.

Period beyond Management's Assessment (Ref: Para. 15)

A14   As required by paragraph 11, the auditor remains alert to the possibility that there may be known events, scheduled or otherwise, or conditions that will occur beyond the period of assessment used by management that may bring into question the appropriateness of management's use of the going concern basis of accounting in preparing the financial statements. Since the degree of uncertainty associated with the outcome of an event or condition increases as the event or condition is further into the future, in considering events or conditions further in the future, the indications of going concern issues need to be significant before the auditor needs to consider taking further action. If such events or conditions are identified, the auditor may need to request management to evaluate the potential significance of the event or condition on its assessment of the entity's ability to continue as a going concern. In these circumstances the procedures in paragraph 16 apply.

A15   Other than inquiry of management, the auditor does not have a responsibility to perform any other audit procedures to identify events or conditions that may cast significant doubt on the entity's ability to continue as a going concern beyond the period assessed by management, which, as discussed in paragraph 13, would be at least twelve months from the date of the financial statements.

Additional Audit Procedures When Events or Conditions Are Identified (Ref: Para. 16)

A16   Audit procedures that are relevant to the requirement in paragraph 16 may include the following:

- Analyzing and discussing cash flow, profit and other relevant forecasts with management.
- Analyzing and discussing the entity's latest available interim financial statements.
- Reading the terms of debentures and loan agreements and determining whether any have been breached.
- Reading minutes of the meetings of shareholders, those charged with governance and relevant committees for reference to financing difficulties.
- Inquiring of the entity's legal counsel regarding the existence of litigation and claims and the reasonableness of management's assessments of their outcome and the estimate of their financial implications.
- Confirming the existence, legality and enforceability of arrangements to provide or maintain financial support with related and third parties and assessing the financial ability of such parties to provide additional funds.
- Evaluating the entity's plans to deal with unfilled customer orders.
- Performing audit procedures regarding subsequent events to identify those that either mitigate or otherwise affect the entity's ability to continue as a going concern.
- Confirming the existence, terms and adequacy of borrowing facilities.
- Obtaining and reviewing reports of regulatory actions.
- Determining the adequacy of support for any planned disposals of assets.

Evaluating Management's Plans for Future Actions (Ref: Para. 16(b))

Evaluating management's plans for future actions may include inquiries of management as to its plans for future action, including, for example, its plans to liquidate assets, borrow money or restructure debt, reduce or delay expenditures, or increase capital. **A17**

The Period of Management's Assessment (Ref: Para. 16(c))

In addition to the procedures required in paragraph 16(c), the auditor may compare: **A18**

- The prospective financial information for recent prior periods with historical results; and
- The prospective financial information for the current period with results achieved to date.

Where management's assumptions include continued support by third parties, whether through the subordination of loans, commitments to maintain or provide additional funding, or guarantees, and such support is important to an entity's ability to continue as a going concern, the auditor may need to consider requesting written confirmation (including of terms and conditions) from those third parties and to obtain evidence of their ability to provide such support. **A19**

Written Representations (Ref: Para. 16(e))

The auditor may consider it appropriate to obtain specific written representations beyond those required in paragraph 16 in support of audit evidence obtained regarding management's plans for future actions in relation to its going concern assessment and the feasibility of those plans. **A20**

Auditor Conclusions

Material Uncertainty Related to Events or Conditions that May Cast Significant Doubt on the Entity's Ability to Continue as a Going Concern (Ref: Para. 18–19)

The phrase 'material uncertainty' is used in IAS 1 in discussing the uncertainties related to events or conditions which may cast significant doubt on the entity's ability to continue as a going concern that should be disclosed in the financial statements. In some other financial reporting frameworks the phrase 'significant uncertainty' is used in similar circumstances. **A21**

Where, in forming their opinion, the auditor's assessment of going concern is based on a period to which those charged with governance have paid particular attention which is less than one year from the date of approval of the financial statements, it is appropriate for the auditor to disclose that fact within the basis of the audit opinion, unless it is disclosed in the financial statements or accompanying information (for example, a Corporate Governance Statement). In deciding whether to disclose the fact, the auditor assesses whether the evidence supplied by those charged with governance is sufficient to demonstrate that those charged with governance have, in assessing going concern, paid particular attention to a period of one year from the date of approval of the financial statements (see paragraph A11-3). **A21-1**

A21-2   In complying with the requirements of ISA (UK) 230 (Revised June 2016) to document significant matters arising during the audit,[12b] the auditor documents concerns (if any) about the entity's ability to continue as a going concern.

Adequacy of Disclosure when Events or Conditions Have Been Identified and a Material Uncertainty Exists

A22   Paragraph 18 explains that a material uncertainty exists when the magnitude of the potential impact of the events or conditions and the likelihood of occurrence is such that appropriate disclosure is necessary to achieve fair presentation (for fair presentation frameworks) or for the financial statements not to be misleading (for compliance frameworks). The auditor is required by paragraph 18 to conclude whether such a material uncertainty exists regardless of whether or how the applicable financial reporting framework defines a material uncertainty.

A23   Paragraph 19 requires the auditor to determine whether the financial statement disclosures address the matters set forth in that paragraph. This determination is in addition to the auditor determining whether disclosures about a material uncertainty, required by the applicable financial reporting framework, are adequate. Disclosures required by some financial reporting frameworks that are in addition to matters set forth in paragraph 19 may include disclosures about:

- Management's evaluation of the significance of the events or conditions relating to the entity's ability to meet its obligations; or
- Significant judgments made by management as part of its assessment of the entity's ability to continue as a going concern.

Some financial reporting frameworks may provide additional guidance regarding management's consideration of disclosures about the magnitude of the potential impact of the principal events or conditions, and the likelihood and timing of their occurrence.

Adequacy of Disclosures When Events or Conditions Have Been Identified but No Material Uncertainty Exists (Ref: Para. 20)

A24   Even when no material uncertainty exists, paragraph 20 requires the auditor to evaluate whether, in view of the requirements of the applicable financial reporting framework, the financial statements provide adequate disclosure about events or conditions that may cast significant doubt on the entity's ability to continue as a going concern. Some financial reporting frameworks may address disclosures about:

- Principal events or conditions;
- Management's evaluation of the significance of those events or conditions in relation to the entity's ability to meet its obligations;
- Management's plans that mitigate the effect of these events or conditions; or
- Significant judgments made by management as part of its assessment of the entity's ability to continue as a going concern.

A25   When the financial statements are prepared in accordance with a fair presentation framework, the auditor's evaluation as to whether the financial statements achieve fair presentation includes the consideration of the overall presentation, structure and content of the financial statements, and whether the financial statements, including the related notes, represent the underlying transactions and events in a manner that achieves fair

---

[12b]   *ISA (UK) 230 (Revised June 2016),* Audit Documentation, *paragraph 8(c).*

presentation.[13] Depending on the facts and circumstances, the auditor may determine that additional disclosures are necessary to achieve fair presentation. This may be the case, for example, when events or conditions have been identified that may cast significant doubt on the entity's ability to continue as a going concern but, based on the audit evidence obtained, the auditor concludes that no material uncertainty exists, and no disclosures are explicitly required by the applicable financial reporting framework regarding these circumstances.

Implications for the Auditor's Report

Use of Going Concern Basis of Accounting is Inappropriate (Ref: Para. 21)

If the financial statements have been prepared using the going concern basis of accounting   A26
but, in the auditor's judgment, management's use of the going concern basis of accounting in the financial statements is inappropriate, the requirement in paragraph 21 for the auditor to express an adverse opinion applies regardless of whether or not the financial statements include disclosure of the inappropriateness of management's use of the going concern basis of accounting.

When the use of the going concern basis of accounting is not appropriate in the   A27
circumstances, management may be required, or may elect, to prepare the financial statements on another basis (e.g., liquidation basis). The auditor may be able to perform an audit of those financial statements provided that the auditor determines that the other basis of accounting is acceptable in the circumstances. The auditor may be able to express an unmodified opinion on those financial statements, provided there is adequate disclosure therein about the basis of accounting on which the financial statements are prepared, but may consider it appropriate or necessary to include an Emphasis of Matter paragraph in accordance with ISA (UK) 706 (Revised June 2016)[14] in the auditor's report to draw the user's attention to that alternative basis and the reasons for its use.

Use of Going Concern Basis of Accounting is Appropriate and no Material Uncertainty has been Identified (Ref: Para. 21-2)

Paragraph 43-1 of ISA (UK) 700 (Revised June 2016) requires that if the auditor is   A27-1
required to report on certain matters by exception the auditor includes a description of the auditor's responsibilities with respect to those matters in the auditor's report. When describing the auditor's responsibilities relating to management's use of the going concern basis of accounting and the disclosure of material uncertainties, the auditor may choose to include this description either:

(a) in the Conclusions Relating to Going Concern section of the auditor's report; or
(b) in the Auditor's Responsibilities for the Audit of the Financial Statements section of the auditor's report,

and cross-refer from the respective section as appropriate.

Auditor's reports which include a description of the auditor's responsibilities relating   A27-2
to management's use of the going concern basis of accounting and the disclosure of material uncertainties in the Conclusions Relating to Going Concern section of the auditor's report will include the minimum elements of an auditor's report required by paragraph 50(k) of ISA 700 (Revised) and therefore the auditor is not precluded from

---

[13] ISA (UK) 700 (Revised June 2016), Forming an Opinion and Reporting on Financial Statements, *paragraph 14.*

[14] ISA (UK) 706 (Revised June 2016), Emphasis of Matter Paragraphs and Other Matter Paragraphs in the Independent Auditor's Report.

being able to assert compliance with International Standards on Auditing issued by the IAASB.

Use of Going Concern Basis of Accounting Is Appropriate but a Material Uncertainty Exists (Ref: Para. 22–23)

A28   The identification of a material uncertainty is a matter that is important to users' understanding of the financial statements. The use of a separate section with a heading that includes reference to the fact that a material uncertainty related to going concern exists alerts users to this circumstance.

A29   The Appendix[14a] to this ISA (UK) provides illustrations of the statements that are required to be included in the auditor's report on the financial statements when International Financial Reporting Standards (IFRSs) is the applicable financial reporting framework. If an applicable financial reporting framework other than IFRSs is used, the illustrative statements presented in the Appendix to this ISA may need to be adapted to reflect the application of the other financial reporting framework in the circumstances.

A30   Paragraph 22 establishes the minimum information required to be presented in the auditor's report in each of the circumstances described. The auditor may provide additional information to supplement the required statements, for example to explain:

● That the existence of a material uncertainty is fundamental to users' understanding of the financial statements;[15] or
● How the matter was addressed in the audit. (Ref: Para. A1)

A30-1   In the UK, the requirement in legislation[15a] to include a statement on any material uncertainty relating to events or conditions that may cast significant doubt about the entity's ability to continue as a going concern is met by the requirements of paragraph 22.

Adequate Disclosure of a Material Uncertainty Is Made in the Financial Statements (Ref: Para. 22)

A31   Illustration 1 of the Appendix[15b] to this ISA is an example of an auditor's report when the auditor has obtained sufficient appropriate audit evidence regarding the appropriateness of management's use of the going concern basis of accounting but a material uncertainty exists and disclosure is adequate in the financial statements. The Appendix of ISA (UK) 700 (Revised June 2016) also includes illustrative wording to be included in the auditor's report for all entities in relation to going concern to describe the respective responsibilities of those responsible for the financial statements and the auditor in relation to going concern.

[14a] *The examples in the Appendix have not been tailored for the UK. Illustrative auditor's reports tailored for use with audits conducted in accordance with ISAs (UK) are given in the current version of the FRC's Compendium of Illustrative Auditor's Reports.*

[15] *ISA (UK) 706 (Revised June 2016), paragraph A2.*

[15a] *In the UK, section 495(4) establishes this requirement.*

[15b] *The examples in the Appendix have not been tailored for the UK. Illustrative auditor's reports tailored for use with audits conducted in accordance with ISAs (UK) are given in the current version of the FRC's Compendium of Illustrative Auditor's Reports.*

Adequate Disclosure of a Material Uncertainty Is Not Made in the Financial Statements (Ref: Para. 23)

Illustrations 2 and 3 of the Appendix[15b] to this ISA (UK) are examples of auditor's reports containing qualified and adverse opinions, respectively, when the auditor has obtained sufficient appropriate audit evidence regarding the appropriateness of the management's use of the going concern basis of accounting but adequate disclosure of a material uncertainty is not made in the financial statements. **A32**

In situations involving multiple uncertainties that are significant to the financial statements as a whole, the auditor may consider it appropriate in extremely rare cases to express a disclaimer of opinion instead of including the statements required by paragraph 22. ISA (UK) 705 (Revised June 2016) provides guidance on this issue.[16] **A33**

Communication with Regulators (Ref: Para. 22–23)

When the auditor of a regulated entity considers that it may be necessary to include a reference to going concern matters in the auditor's report, the auditor may have a duty to communicate with the applicable regulatory, enforcement or supervisory authorities. **A34**

In the UK, in such cases the regulatory, enforcement or supervisory authority might, if it has not already done so, specify corrective action to be taken by the entity.

At the time at which the auditor formulates the audit report, the auditor takes account of matters such as: **A34-1**

- Any views expressed by the regulatory, enforcement or supervisory authority.
- Any legal advice obtained by those charged with governance.
- The actual and planned corrective action.

For audits of public interest entities, ISA (UK) 250 Section B (Revised June 2016)[16a] requires the auditor to report to the relevant regulatory, enforcement or supervisory authority any information about the public interest entity (or an undertaking having close links with the public interest entity) that may bring about a material threat or doubt concerning the continuous functioning of the entity. **A34-2**

Management Unwilling to Make or Extend Its Assessment (Ref: Para. 22)

In certain circumstances, the auditor may believe it necessary to request management to make or extend its assessment. If management is unwilling to do so, a qualified opinion or a disclaimer of opinion in the auditor's report may be appropriate, because it may not be possible for the auditor to obtain sufficient appropriate audit evidence regarding management's use of the going concern basis of accounting in the preparation of the financial statements, such as audit evidence regarding the existence of plans management has put in place or the existence of other mitigating factors. **A35**

---

[16] ISA (UK) 705 (Revised June 2016), paragraph 10.

[16a] ISA (UK) 250 Section B (Revised June 2016), The Auditor's Statutory Right and Duty to Report to Regulators of Public Interest Entities and Regulators of Other Entities in the Financial Sector, paragraph 13R-1(a)(ii).

Communication with Those Charged with Governance (Ref: Para. 25)

A35-1   For audits of financial statements of public interest entities, ISA (UK) 260 (Revised June 2016)[16b] requires the auditor to:

- explain the judgments about events or conditions identified in the course of the audit that may cast significant doubt on the entity's ability to continue as a going concern and whether they constitute a material uncertainty; and
- provide a summary of all guarantees, comfort letters, undertakings of public intervention and other support measures that have been taken into account when making a going concern assessment,

in the additional report to the audit committee.

[16b] *ISA (UK) 260 (Revised June 2016),* Communication with Those Charged with Governance, *paragraph 16R-2(i).*

Appendix (Ref: Para. A29, A31–A32)

Illustrations of Auditor's Reports Relating to Going Concern

> The examples in the Appendix have not been tailored for the UK. Illustrative auditor's reports tailored for use with audits conducted in accordance with ISAs (UK) are given in the current version of the FRC's Compendium of Illustrative Auditor's Reports.

- Illustration 1: An auditor's report containing an unmodified opinion when the auditor has concluded that a material uncertainty exists and disclosure in the financial statements is adequate.
- Illustration 2: An auditor's report containing a qualified opinion when the auditor has concluded that a material uncertainty exists and that the financial statements are materially misstated due to inadequate disclosure.
- Illustration 3: An auditor's report containing an adverse opinion when the auditor has concluded that a material uncertainty exists and the financial statements omit the required disclosures relating to a material uncertainty.

Illustration 1 – Unmodified Opinion When a Material Uncertainty Exists and Disclosure in the Financial Statements Is Adequate

For purposes of this illustrative auditor's report, the following circumstances are assumed:

- Audit of a complete set of financial statements of a listed entity using a fair presentation framework. The audit is not a group audit (i.e., ISA 600[17] does not apply).
- The financial statements are prepared by management of the entity in accordance with IFRSs (a general purpose framework).
- The terms of the audit engagement reflect the description of management's responsibility for the financial statements in ISA 210.[18]
- The auditor has concluded an unmodified (i.e., 'clean') opinion is appropriate based on the audit evidence obtained.
- The relevant ethical requirements that apply to the audit are those of the jurisdiction.
- Based on the audit evidence obtained, the auditor has concluded that a material uncertainty exists related to events or conditions that may cast significant doubt on the entity's ability to continue as a going concern. The disclosure of the material uncertainty in the financial statements is adequate.
- Key audit matters have been communicated in accordance with ISA 701.
- The auditor has obtained all of the other information prior to the date of the auditor's report and has not identified a material misstatement of the other information.
- Those responsible for oversight of the financial statements differ from those responsible for the preparation of the financial statements.
- In addition to the audit of the financial statements, the auditor has other reporting responsibilities required under local law.

---

[17] *ISA 600*, Special Considerations—Audits of Group Financial Statements (Including the Work of Component Auditors.

[18] *ISA 210*, Agreeing the Terms of Audit Engagements.

INDEPENDENT AUDITOR'S REPORT

To the Shareholders of ABC Company [or Other Appropriate Addressee]

Report on the Audit of the Financial Statements[19]

Opinion

We have audited the financial statements of ABC Company (the Company), which comprise the statement of financial position as at December 31, 20X1, and the statement of comprehensive income, statement of changes in equity and statement of cash flows for the year then ended, and notes to the financial statements, including a summary of significant accounting policies.

In our opinion, the accompanying financial statements present fairly, in all material respects, (or *give a true and fair view of*) the financial position of the Company as at December 31, 20X1, and (of) its financial performance and its cash flows for the year then ended in accordance with International Financial Reporting Standards (IFRSs).

Basis for Opinion

We conducted our audit in accordance with International Standards on Auditing (ISAs). Our responsibilities under those standards are further described in the *Auditor's Responsibilities for the Audit of the Financial Statements* section of our report. We are independent of the Company in accordance with the ethical requirements that are relevant to our audit of the financial statements in [*jurisdiction*], and we have fulfilled *our* other ethical responsibilities in accordance with these requirements. We believe that the audit evidence we have obtained is sufficient and appropriate to provide a basis for our opinion.

Material Uncertainty Related to Going Concern

We draw attention to Note 6 in the financial statements, which indicates that the Company incurred a net loss of ZZZ *during* the year ended December 31, 20X1 and, as of that date, the Company's current liabilities exceeded its total assets by YYY. As stated in Note 6, these events or conditions, along with other matters as set forth in Note 6, indicate that a material uncertainty exists that may cast significant doubt on the Company's ability to continue as a going concern. Our opinion is not modified in respect of this matter.

Key Audit Matters

Key audit matters are those matters that, in our professional judgment, were of most significance in our audit of the financial statements of the current period. These matters were addressed in the context of our audit of the financial statements as a whole, and in forming our opinion thereon, and we do not provide a separate *opinion* on these matters. In addition to the matter described in the *Material Uncertainty Related to Going Concern* section, we have determined the matters described below to be the key audit matters to be communicated in our report.

[*Description of each key audit matter in accordance with ISA 701.*]

---

[19] *The sub-title 'Report on the Audit of the Financial Statements' is unnecessary in circumstances when the second sub-title 'Report on Other Legal and Regulatory Requirements' is not applicable.*

Other Information [or another title if appropriate such as 'Information Other than the Financial Statements and Auditor's Report Thereon']

[*Reporting in accordance with the reporting requirements in ISA 720 (Revised) – see Illustration 1 in Appendix 2 of ISA 720 (Revised).*]

Responsibilities of Management and Those Charged with Governance for the Financial Statements[20]

[*Reporting in accordance with ISA 700 (Revised) – see Illustration 1 in ISA 700 (Revised).*[21]]

Auditor's Responsibilities for the Audit of the Financial Statements

[*Reporting in accordance with ISA 700 (Revised) – see Illustration 1 in ISA 700 (Revised).*]

Report on Other Legal and Regulatory Requirements

[*Reporting in accordance with ISA 700 (Revised) – see Illustration 1 in ISA 700 (Revised).*]

The engagement partner on the audit resulting in this independent auditor's report is [*name*].

[*Signature in the name of the audit firm, the personal name of the auditor, or both, as appropriate for the particular jurisdiction*]

[*Auditor Address*]

[*Date*]

---

[20] *Throughout these illustrative auditor's reports, the terms management and those charged with governance may need to be replaced by another term that is appropriate in the context of the legal framework in the particular jurisdiction.*

[21] *Paragraphs 34 and 39 of ISA 700 (Revised) require wording to be included in the auditor's report for all entities in relation to going concern to describe the respective responsibilities of those responsible for the financial statements and the auditor in relation to going concern.*

Illustration 2 – Qualified Opinion When a Material Uncertainty Exists and the Financial Statements Are Materially Misstated Due to Inadequate Disclosure

For purposes of this illustrative auditor's report, the following circumstances are assumed:

- Audit of a complete set of financial statements of a listed entity using a fair presentation framework. The audit is not a group audit (i.e., ISA 600 does not apply).
- The financial statements are prepared by management of the entity in accordance with IFRSs (a general purpose framework).
- The terms of the audit engagement reflect the description of management's responsibility for the financial statements in ISA 210.
- The relevant ethical requirements that apply to the audit are those of the jurisdiction.
- Based on the audit evidence obtained, the auditor has concluded that a material uncertainty exists related to events or conditions that may cast significant doubt on the entity's ability to continue as a going concern. Note yy to the financial statements discusses the magnitude of financing arrangements, the expiration and the total financing arrangements; however the financial statements do not include discussion on the impact or the availability of refinancing or characterize this situation as a material uncertainty.
- The financial statements are materially misstated due to the inadequate disclosure of the material uncertainty. A qualified opinion is being expressed because the auditor concluded that the effects on the financial statements of this inadequate disclosure are material but not pervasive to the financial statements.
- Key audit matters have been communicated in accordance with ISA 701.
- The auditor has obtained all of the other information prior to the date of the auditor's report and the matter giving rise to the qualified opinion on the financial statements also affects the other information
- Those responsible for oversight of the financial statements differ from those responsible for the preparation of the financial statements.
- In addition to the audit of the financial statements, the auditor has other reporting responsibilities required under local law.

INDEPENDENT AUDITOR'S REPORT

To the Shareholders of ABC Company [or Other Appropriate Addressee]

Report on the Audit of the Financial Statements[22]

Qualified Opinion

We have audited the financial statements of ABC Company (the Company), which comprise the statement of financial position as at December 31, 20X1, and the statement of comprehensive income, statement of changes in equity and statement of cash flows for the year then ended, and notes to the financial statements, including a summary of significant accounting policies.

In our opinion, except for the incomplete disclosure of the information referred to in the Basis for Qualified Opinion section of our report, the accompanying financial statements present fairly, in all material respects (or give a true and fair view of), the financial position

---

[22] *The sub-title 'Report on the Audit of the Financial Statements' is unnecessary in circumstances when the second sub-title 'Report on Other Legal and Regulatory Requirements' is not applicable.*

of the Company as at December 31, 20X1, and (of) its financial performance and its cash flows for the year then ended in accordance with International Financial Reporting Standards (IFRSs).

Basis for Qualified Opinion

As discussed in Note yy, the Company's financing arrangements expire and amounts outstanding are payable on March 19, 20X2. The Company has been unable to conclude renegotiations or obtain replacement financing. This situation indicates that a material uncertainty exists that may cast significant doubt on the Company's ability to continue as a going concern. The financial statements do not adequately disclose this matter.

We conducted our audit in accordance with International Standards on Auditing (ISAs). Our responsibilities under those standards are further described in the *Auditor's Responsibilities for the Audit of the Financial Statements* section of our report. We are independent of the Company in accordance with the ethical requirements that are relevant to our audit of the financial statements in [*jurisdiction*], and we have fulfilled our other ethical responsibilities in accordance with these requirements. We believe that the audit evidence we have obtained is sufficient and appropriate to provide a basis for our qualified opinion.

Other Information [or another title if appropriate such as 'Information Other than the Financial Statements and Auditor's Report Thereon']

[*Reporting in accordance with the reporting requirements in ISA 720 (Revised) – see Illustration 6 in Appendix 2 of ISA 720 (Revised). The last paragraph of the other information section in Illustration 6 would be customized to describe the specific matter giving rise to the qualified opinion that also affects the other information.*]

Key Audit Matters

Key audit matters are those matters that, in our professional judgment, were of most significance in our audit of the financial statements of the current period. These matters were addressed in the context of our audit of the financial statements as a whole, and in forming our opinion thereon, and we do not provide a separate opinion on these matters. In addition to the matter described in the Basis for Qualified Opinion section, we have determined the matters described below to be the key audit matters to be communicated in our report.

[*Descriptions of each key audit matter in accordance with ISA 701.*]

Responsibilities of Management and Those Charged with Governance for the Financial Statements[23]

[*Reporting in accordance with ISA 700 (Revised) – see Illustration 1 in ISA 700 (Revised).*[24]]

Auditor's Responsibilities for the Audit of the Financial Statements

[*Reporting in accordance with ISA 700 (Revised) – see Illustration 1 in ISA 700 (Revised).*]

---

[23] Or other terms that are appropriate in the context of the legal framework of the particular jurisdiction.

[24] Paragraphs 34 and 39 of ISA 700 (Revised) require wording to be included in the auditor's report for all entities in relation to going concern to describe the respective responsibilities of those responsible for the financial statements and the auditor in relation to going concern.

Report on Other Legal and Regulatory Requirements

[*Reporting in accordance with ISA 700 (Revised) – see Illustration 1 in ISA 700 (Revised).*]

The engagement partner on the audit resulting in this independent auditor's report is [*name*].

[*Signature in the name of the audit firm, the personal name of the auditor, or both, as appropriate for the particular jurisdiction*]

[*Auditor Address*]

[*Date*]

Illustration 3 – Adverse Opinion When a Material Uncertainty Exists and Is Not Disclosed in the Financial Statements

For purposes of the illustrative auditor's report, the following circumstances are assumed:

- Audit of a complete set of financial statements of an entity other than a listed entity using a fair presentation framework. The audit is not a group audit (i.e., ISA 600 does not apply).
- The financial statements are prepared by management of the entity in accordance with IFRSs (a general purpose framework).
- The terms of the audit engagement reflect the description of management's responsibility for the financial statements in ISA 210.
- The relevant ethical requirements that apply to the audit are those of the jurisdiction.
- Based on the audit evidence obtained, the auditor has concluded that a material uncertainty exists related to events or conditions that may cast significant doubt on the entity's ability to continue as a going concern, and the Company is considering bankruptcy. The financial statements omit the required disclosures relating to the material uncertainty. An adverse opinion is being expressed because the effects on the financial statements of such omission are material and pervasive.
- The auditor is not required, and has otherwise not decided, to communicate key audit matters in accordance with ISA 701.
- The auditor has obtained all of the other information prior to the date of the auditor's report and the matter giving rise to the qualified/adverse opinion on the consolidated financial statements also affects the other information.
- Those responsible for oversight of the financial statements differ from those responsible for the preparation of the financial statements.
- In addition to the audit of the financial statements, the auditor has other reporting responsibilities required under local law.

INDEPENDENT AUDITOR'S REPORT

To the Shareholders of ABC Company [or Other Appropriate Addressee]

Report on the Audit of the Financial Statements[25]

Adverse Opinion

We have audited the financial statements of ABC Company (the Company), which comprise the statement of financial position as at December 31, 20X1, and the statement of comprehensive income, statement of changes in equity and statement of cash flows for the year then ended, and notes to the financial statements, including a summary of significant accounting policies.

In our opinion, because of the omission of the information mentioned in the *Basis for Adverse Opinion* section of our report, the accompanying financial statements do not present fairly (or *do not give a true and fair view of*), the financial position of the Company as at December 31, 20X1, and of its financial performance and its cash flows for the year then ended in accordance with International Financial Reporting Standards (IFRSs).

---

[25] *The sub-title 'Report on the Audit of the Financial Statements' is unnecessary in circumstances when the second sub-title 'Report on Other Legal and Regulatory Requirements' is not applicable.*

Basis for Adverse Opinion

The Company's financing arrangements expired and the amount outstanding was payable on December 31, 20X1. The Company has been unable to conclude re-negotiations or obtain replacement financing and is considering filing for bankruptcy. This situation indicates that a material uncertainty exists that may cast significant doubt on the Company's ability to continue as a going concern. The financial statements do not adequately disclose this fact.

We conducted our audit in accordance with International Standards on Auditing (ISAs). Our responsibilities under those standards are further described in the *Auditor's Responsibilities for the Audit of the Financial Statements* section of our report. We are independent of the Company in accordance with the ethical requirements that are relevant to our audit of the financial statements in [*jurisdiction*], and we have fulfilled our ethical responsibilities in accordance with these requirements. We believe that the audit evidence we have obtained is sufficient and appropriate to provide a basis for our adverse opinion.

Other Information [or another title if appropriate such as 'Information Other than the Financial Statements and Auditor's Report Thereon']

[*Reporting in accordance with the reporting requirements in ISA 720 (Revised) – see Illustration 7 in Appendix 2 of ISA 720 (Revised). The last paragraph of the other information section in Illustration 7 would be customized to describe the specific matter giving rise to the qualified opinion that also affects the other information.*]

Responsibilities of Management and Those Charged with Governance for the Financial Statements[26]

[*Reporting in accordance with ISA 700 (Revised) – see Illustration 1 in ISA 700 (Revised).*[27]]

Auditor's Responsibilities for the Audit of the Financial Statements

[*Reporting in accordance with ISA 700 (Revised) – see Illustration 1 in ISA 700 (Revised).*]

Report on Other Legal and Regulatory Requirements

[*Reporting in accordance with ISA 700 (Revised) – see Illustration 1 in ISA 700 (Revised).*]

[*Signature in the name of the audit firm, the personal name of the auditor, or both, as appropriate for the particular jurisdiction*]

[*Auditor Address*]

[*Date*]

---

[26] *Or other terms that are appropriate in the context of the legal framework of the particular jurisdiction.*

[27] *Paragraphs 34 and 39 of ISA 700 (Revised) require wording to be included in the auditor's report for all entities in relation to going concern to describe the respective responsibilities of those responsible for the financial statements and the auditor in relation to going concern.*

International Standard on Auditing (UK) 580
Written representations

*(Effective for audits of financial statements for periods
ending on or after 15 December 2010)*

Contents

International Standard on Auditing (UK) (ISA (UK)) 580, *Written Representations*, should be read in conjunction with ISA (UK) 200 (Revised June 2016), *Overall Objectives of the Independent Auditor and the Conduct of an Audit in Accordance with International Standards on Auditing (UK)*.

Introduction

Scope of this ISA (UK)

1   This International Standard on Auditing (UK) (ISA (UK)) deals with the auditor's responsibility to obtain written representations from management and, where appropriate, those charged with governance in an audit of financial statements.

2   Appendix 1 lists other ISAs (UK) containing subject-matter specific requirements for written representations. The specific requirements for written representations of other ISAs (UK) do not limit the application of this ISA (UK).

Written Representations as Audit Evidence

3   Audit evidence is the information used by the auditor in arriving at the conclusions on which the auditor's opinion is based. [1] Written representations are necessary information that the auditor requires in connection with the audit of the entity's financial statements. Accordingly, similar to responses to inquiries, written representations are audit evidence. (Ref: Para. A1)

4   Although written representations provide necessary audit evidence, they do not provide sufficient appropriate audit evidence on their own about any of the matters with which they deal. Furthermore, the fact that management has provided reliable written representations does not affect the nature or extent of other audit evidence that the auditor obtains about the fulfillment of management's responsibilities, or about specific assertions.

Effective Date

5   This ISA (UK) is effective for audits of financial statements for periods ending on or after 15 December 2010.

Objectives

6   The objectives of the auditor are:
   (a) To obtain written representations from management and, where appropriate, those charged with governance that they believe that they have fulfilled their responsibility for the preparation of the financial statements and for the completeness of the information provided to the auditor;
   (b) To support other audit evidence relevant to the financial statements or specific assertions in the financial statements by means of written representations if determined necessary by the auditor or required by other ISAs (UK); and
   (c) To respond appropriately to written representations provided by management and, where appropriate, those charged with governance, or if management or, where appropriate, those charged with governance do not provide the written representations requested by the auditor.

Definitions

7   For purposes of the ISAs (UK), the following term has the meaning attributed below:

---

[1] *ISA (UK) 500*, Audit Evidence, *paragraph 5(c).*

Written representation – A written statement by management provided to the auditor to confirm certain matters or to support other audit evidence. Written representations in this context do not include financial statements, the assertions therein, or supporting books and records.

For purposes of this ISA (UK), references to 'management' should be read as 'management   **8**
and, where appropriate, those charged with governance.' Furthermore, in the case of a fair presentation framework, management is responsible for the preparation and *fair presentation* of the financial statements in accordance with the applicable financial reporting framework; or the preparation of financial statements *that give a true and fair view* in accordance with the applicable financial reporting framework.

Requirements

Management from whom Written Representations Requested

The auditor shall request written representations from management with appropriate   **9**
responsibilities for the financial statements and knowledge of the matters concerned. (Ref: Para. A2–A6)

Written Representations about Management's Responsibilities

Written Representations about Management's Responsibilities

The auditor shall request management to provide a written representation that it has fulfilled   **10**
its responsibility for the preparation of the financial statements in accordance with the applicable financial reporting framework, including where relevant their fair presentation, as set out in the terms of the audit engagement.[2] (Ref: Para. A7–A9, A14, A22)

Information Provided and Completeness of Transactions

The auditor shall request management to provide a written representation that: **11**

(a) It has provided the auditor with all relevant information and access as agreed in the terms of the audit engagement,[3] and
(b) All transactions have been recorded and are reflected in the financial statements. (Ref: Para. A7–A9, A14, A22–A22-1)

Management may include in the written representations required by paragraphs 10 and   **11-1**
11 qualifying language to the effect that the representations are made to the best of its knowledge and belief. Such qualifying language does not cause paragraph 20 to apply if, during the audit, the auditor found no evidence that the representations are incorrect. (Ref; Para A5, A8-1)

Description of Management's Responsibilities in the Written Representations

Management's responsibilities shall be described in the written representations required   **12**
by paragraphs 10 and 11 in the manner in which these responsibilities are described in the terms of the audit engagement.

---

[2] *ISA (UK) 210 (Revised June 2016),* Agreeing the Terms of Audit Engagements, *paragraph 6(b)(i).*

[3] *ISA (UK) 210 (Revised June 2016), paragraph 6(b)(iii).*

Other Written Representations

13   Other ISAs (UK) require the auditor to request written representations. If, in addition to such required representations, the auditor determines that it is necessary to obtain one or more written representations to support other audit evidence relevant to the financial statements or one or more specific assertions in the financial statements, the auditor shall request such other written representations. (Ref: Para. A10–A13, A14, A22–A22-1)

Date of and Period(s) Covered by Written Representations

14   The date of the written representations shall be as near as practicable to, but not after, the date of the auditor's report on the financial statements. The written representations shall be for all financial statements and period(s) referred to in the auditor's report. (Ref: Para. A15–A18)

Form of Written Representations

15   The written representations shall be in the form of a representation letter addressed to the auditor. If law or regulation requires management to make written public statements about its responsibilities, and the auditor determines that such statements provide some or all of the representations required by paragraphs 10 or 11, the relevant matters covered by such statements need not be included in the representation letter. (Ref: Para. A19–A21)

Doubt as to the Reliability of Written Representations and Requested Written Representations Not Provided

Doubt as to the Reliability of Written Representations

16   If the auditor has concerns about the competence, integrity, ethical values or diligence of management, or about its commitment to or enforcement of these, the auditor shall determine the effect that such concerns may have on the reliability of representations (oral or written) and audit evidence in general. (Ref: Para. A24–A25)

17   In particular, if written representations are inconsistent with other audit evidence, the auditor shall perform audit procedures to attempt to resolve the matter. If the matter remains unresolved, the auditor shall reconsider the assessment of the competence, integrity, ethical values or diligence of management, or of its commitment to or enforcement of these, and shall determine the effect that this may have on the reliability of representations (oral or written) and audit evidence in general. (Ref: Para. A23)

18   If the auditor concludes that the written representations are not reliable, the auditor shall take appropriate actions, including determining the possible effect on the opinion in the auditor's report in accordance with ISA (UK) 705 (Revised June 2016),[4] having regard to the requirement in paragraph 20 of this ISA (UK).

Requested Written Representations Not Provided

19   If management does not provide one or more of the requested written representations, the auditor shall:

---

[4] *ISA (UK) 705 (Revised June 2016)*, Modifications to the Opinion in the Independent Auditor's Report.

(a) Discuss the matter with management;

(b) Reevaluate the integrity of management and evaluate the effect that this may have on the reliability of representations (oral or written) and audit evidence in general; and

(c) Take appropriate actions, including determining the possible effect on the opinion in the auditor's report in accordance with ISA (UK) 705 (Revised June 2016), having regard to the requirement in paragraph 20 of this ISA (UK).

Written Representations about Management's Responsibilities

The auditor shall disclaim an opinion on the financial statements in accordance with ISA (UK) 705 (Revised June 2016) if: **20**

(a) The auditor concludes that there is sufficient doubt about the integrity of management such that the written representations required by paragraphs 10 and 11 are not reliable; or

(b) Management does not provide the written representations required by paragraphs 10 and 11. (Ref: Para. A26–A27)

Application and Other Explanatory Material

Written Representations as Audit Evidence (Ref: Para. 3)

Written representations are an important source of audit evidence. If management modifies   **A1**
or does not provide the requested written representations, it may alert the auditor to the possibility that one or more significant issues may exist. Further, a request for written, rather than oral, representations in many cases may prompt management to consider such matters more rigorously, thereby enhancing the quality of the representations.

Management from whom Written Representations Requested (Ref: Para. 9)

Written representations are requested from those responsible for the preparation of the   **A2**
financial statements. Those individuals may vary depending on the governance structure of the entity, and relevant law or regulation; however, management (rather than those charged with governance) is often the responsible party. Written representations may therefore be requested from the entity's chief executive officer and chief financial officer, or other equivalent persons in entities that do not use such titles. In some circumstances, however, other parties, such as those charged with governance, are also responsible for the preparation and presentation of the financial statements.[4a]

In view of their importance, it is appropriate for written representations that are critical   **A2-1**
to obtaining sufficient appropriate audit evidence to be provided by those charged with governance rather than the entity's management.

Due to its responsibility for the preparation of the financial statements, and its responsibilities   **A3**
for the conduct of the entity's business, management would be expected to have sufficient knowledge of the process followed by the entity in preparing and presenting the financial statements and the assertions therein on which to base the written representations.

In some cases, however, management may decide to make inquiries of others who   **A4**
participate in preparing and presenting the financial statements and assertions therein, including individuals who have specialized knowledge relating to the matters about which written representations are requested. Such individuals may include:

[4a] *In the UK, those charged with governance are responsible for the preparation of the financial statements.*

- An actuary responsible for actuarially determined accounting measurements.
- Staff engineers who may have responsibility for and specialized knowledge about environmental liability measurements.
- Internal counsel who may provide information essential to provisions for legal claims.

A5   In some cases, management may include in the written representations qualifying language to the effect that representations are made to the best of its knowledge and belief. It is reasonable for the auditor to accept such wording if the auditor is satisfied that the representations are being made by those with appropriate responsibilities and knowledge of the matters included in the representations.

A6   To reinforce the need for management to make informed representations, the auditor may request that management include in the written representations confirmation that it has made such inquiries as it considered appropriate to place it in the position to be able to make the requested written representations. It is not expected that such inquiries would usually require a formal internal process beyond those already established by the entity.

Written Representations about Management's Responsibilities
(Ref: Para. 10–11)

A7   Audit evidence obtained during the audit that management has fulfilled the responsibilities referred to in paragraphs 10 and 11 is not sufficient without obtaining confirmation from management that it believes that it has fulfilled those responsibilities. This is because the auditor is not able to judge solely on other audit evidence whether management has prepared and presented the financial statements and provided information to the auditor on the basis of the agreed acknowledgement and understanding of its responsibilities. For example, the auditor could not conclude that management has provided the auditor with all relevant information agreed in the terms of the audit engagement without asking it whether, and receiving confirmation that, such information has been provided.

A7-1   A signed copy of the financial statements for a company may be sufficient evidence of the directors' acknowledgement of their collective responsibility for the preparation of the financial statements where it incorporates a statement to that effect. A signed copy of the financial statements, however, is not, by itself, sufficient appropriate evidence to confirm other representations given to the auditor as it does not, ordinarily, clearly identify and explain the specific separate representations.

A8   The written representations required by paragraphs 10 and 11 draw on the agreed acknowledgement and understanding of management of its responsibilities in the terms of the audit engagement by requesting confirmation that it has fulfilled them. The auditor may also ask management to reconfirm its acknowledgement and understanding of those responsibilities in written representations. This is common in certain jurisdictions, but in any event may be particularly appropriate when:

- Those who signed the terms of the audit engagement on behalf of the entity no longer have the relevant responsibilities;
- The terms of the audit engagement were prepared in a previous year;
- There is any indication that management misunderstands those responsibilities; or
- Changes in circumstances make it appropriate to do so.

Consistent with the requirement of ISA (UK) 210 (Revised June 2016),[5] such reconfirmation of management's acknowledgement and understanding of its responsibilities is not made

---

[5] *ISA (UK) 210 (Revised June 2016), paragraph 6(b).*

subject to the best of management's knowledge and belief (as discussed in paragraph A5 of this ISA (UK)).

Although reconfirmation of management's acknowledgement and understanding of its responsibilities is not made subject to the best of management's knowledge and belief, as discussed in paragraph A8, this does not prevent management from stating that the written representations required by paragraphs 10 and 11 relating to the fulfillment of its responsibilities are given to the best of its knowledge and belief.	**A8-1**

Considerations Specific to Public Sector Entities

The mandates for audits of the financial statements of public sector entities may be broader than those of other entities. As a result, the premise, relating to management's responsibilities, on which an audit of the financial statements of a public sector entity is conducted may give rise to additional written representations. These may include written representations confirming that transactions and events have been carried out in accordance with law, regulation or other authority.

A9

Other Written Representations (Ref: Para. 13)

Additional Written Representations about the Financial Statements

In addition to the written representation required by paragraph 10, the auditor may consider it necessary to request other written representations about the financial statements. Such written representations may supplement, but do not form part of, the written representation required by paragraph 10. They may include representations about the following:

A10

- Whether the selection and application of accounting policies are appropriate; and
- Whether matters such as the following, where relevant under the applicable financial reporting framework, have been recognized, measured, presented or disclosed in accordance with that framework:
    - Plans or intentions that may affect the carrying value or classification of assets and liabilities;
    - Liabilities, both actual and contingent;
    - Title to, or control over, assets, the liens or encumbrances on assets, and assets pledged as collateral; and
    - Aspects of laws, regulations and contractual agreements that may affect the financial statements, including non-compliance.

Additional Written Representations about Information Provided to the Auditor

In addition to the written representation required by paragraph 11, the auditor may consider it necessary to request management to provide a written representation that it has communicated to the auditor all deficiencies in internal control of which management is aware.

A11

Written Representations about Specific Assertions

When obtaining evidence about, or evaluating, judgments and intentions, the auditor may consider one or more of the following:

A12

- The entity's past history in carrying out its stated intentions.
- The entity's reasons for choosing a particular course of action.
- The entity's ability to pursue a specific course of action.

- The existence or lack of any other information that might have been obtained during the course of the audit that may be inconsistent with management's judgment or intent.

A13   In addition, the auditor may consider it necessary to request management to provide written representations about specific assertions in the financial statements; in particular, to support an understanding that the auditor has obtained from other audit evidence of management's judgment or intent in relation to, or the completeness of, a specific assertion. For example, if the intent of management is important to the valuation basis for investments, it may not be possible to obtain sufficient appropriate audit evidence without a written representation from management about its intentions. Although such written representations provide necessary audit evidence, they do not provide sufficient appropriate audit evidence on their own for that assertion.

Communicating a Threshold Amount (Ref: Para. 10–11, 13)

A14   ISA (UK) 450 (Revised June 2016) requires the auditor to accumulate misstatements identified during the audit, other than those that are clearly trivial.[6] The auditor may determine a threshold above which misstatements cannot be regarded as clearly trivial. In the same way, the auditor may consider communicating to management a threshold for purposes of the requested written representations.

Date of and Period(s) Covered by Written Representations (Ref: Para. 14)

A15   Because written representations are necessary audit evidence, the auditor's opinion cannot be expressed, and the auditor's report cannot be dated, before the date of the written representations. Furthermore, because the auditor is concerned with events occurring up to the date of the auditor's report that may require adjustment to or disclosure in the financial statements, the written representations are dated as near as practicable to, but not after, the date of the auditor's report on the financial statements.

A16   In some circumstances it may be appropriate for the auditor to obtain a written representation about a specific assertion in the financial statements during the course of the audit. Where this is the case, it may be necessary to request an updated written representation.

A17   The written representations are for all periods referred to in the auditor's report because management needs to reaffirm that the written representations it previously made with respect to the prior periods remain appropriate. The auditor and management may agree to a form of written representation that updates written representations relating to the prior periods by addressing whether there are any changes to such written representations and, if so, what they are.

A18   Situations may arise where current management were not present during all periods referred to in the auditor's report. Such persons may assert that they are not in a position to provide some or all of the written representations because they were not in place during the period. This fact, however, does not diminish such persons' responsibilities for the financial statements as a whole. Accordingly, the requirement for the auditor to request from them written representations that cover the whole of the relevant period(s) still applies.

Form of Written Representations (Ref: Para. 15)

A19   Written representations are required to be included in a representation letter addressed to the auditor. In some jurisdictions, however, management may be required by law or regulation

---

[6] *ISA (UK) 450 (Revised June 2016),* Evaluation of Misstatements Identified during the Audit, *paragraph 5.*

to make a written public statement about its responsibilities. Although such statement is a representation to the users of the financial statements, or to relevant authorities, the auditor may determine that it is an appropriate form of written representation in respect of some or all of the representations required by paragraph 10 or 11. Consequently, the relevant matters covered by such statement need not be included in the representation letter. Factors that may affect the auditor's determination include:

- Whether the statement includes confirmation of the fulfillment of the responsibilities referred to in paragraphs 10 and 11.
- Whether the statement has been given or approved by those from whom the auditor requests the relevant written representations.
- Whether a copy of the statement is provided to the auditor as near as practicable to, but not after, the date of the auditor's report on the financial statements (see paragraph 14).

A formal statement of compliance with law or regulation, or of approval of the financial **A20** statements, would not contain sufficient information for the auditor to be satisfied that all necessary representations have been consciously made. The expression of management's responsibilities in law or regulation is also not a substitute for the requested written representations.

Appendix 2[6a] provides an illustrative example of a representation letter. **A21**

Communication with Those Charged with Governance (Ref: Para. 10–11, 13)

ISA (UK) 260 (Revised June 2016) requires the auditor to communicate with those **A22** charged with governance the written representations which the auditor has requested from management.[7]

In the UK, these communications are made before those charged with governance **A22-1** approve the financial statements, to ensure that they are aware of the representations on which the auditor intends to rely in expressing the auditor's opinion on those financial statements.

For audits of financial statements of public interest entities, the written representations **A22-2** requested from those charged with governance are relevant to the auditor's communications in the additional report to the audit committee that all requested explanations and documents were provided by the entity.[7a]

Doubt as to the Reliability of Written Representations and Requested Written Representations Not Provided

Doubt as to the Reliability of Written Representations (Ref: Para. 16–17)

In the case of identified inconsistencies between one or more written representations and **A23** audit evidence obtained from another source, the auditor may consider whether the risk assessment remains appropriate and, if not, revise the risk assessment and determine the nature, timing and extent of further audit procedures to respond to the assessed risks.

[6a] *The illustrative representation letter in Appendix 2 has not been tailored for the UK.*

[7] *ISA (UK) 260 (Revised June 2016)*, Communication with Those Charged with Governance, *paragraph 16(c)(ii)*.

[7a] *ISA (UK) 260 (Revised June 2016), paragraph 16R-2(o).*

A24   Concerns about the competence, integrity, ethical values or diligence of management, or about its commitment to or enforcement of these, may cause the auditor to conclude that the risk of management misrepresentation in the financial statements is such that an audit cannot be conducted. In such a case, the auditor may consider withdrawing from the engagement, where withdrawal is possible under applicable law or regulation, unless those charged with governance put in place appropriate corrective measures. Such measures, however, may not be sufficient to enable the auditor to issue an unmodified audit opinion.

A25   ISA (UK) 230 (Revised June 2016) requires the auditor to document significant matters arising during the audit, the conclusions reached thereon, and significant professional judgments made in reaching those conclusions.[8] The auditor may have identified significant issues relating to the competence, integrity, ethical values or diligence of management, or about its commitment to or enforcement of these, but concluded that the written representations are nevertheless reliable. In such a case, this significant matter is documented in accordance with ISA (UK) 230 (Revised June 2016).

Written Representations about Management's Responsibilities (Ref: Para. 20)

A26   As explained in paragraph A7, the auditor is not able to judge solely on other audit evidence whether management has fulfilled the responsibilities referred to in paragraphs 10 and 11. Therefore, if, as described in paragraph 20(a), the auditor concludes that the written representations about these matters are unreliable, or if management does not provide those written representations, the auditor is unable to obtain sufficient appropriate audit evidence. The possible effects on the financial statements of such inability are not confined to specific elements, accounts or items of the financial statements and are hence pervasive. ISA (UK) 705 (Revised June 2016) requires the auditor to disclaim an opinion on the financial statements in such circumstances.[9]

A27   A written representation that has been modified from that requested by the auditor does not necessarily mean that management did not provide the written representation. However, the underlying reason for such modification may affect the opinion in the auditor's report. For example:

- The written representation about management's fulfillment of its responsibility for the preparation of the financial statements may state that management believes that, except for material non-compliance with a particular requirement of the applicable financial reporting framework, the financial statements are prepared in accordance with that framework. The requirement in paragraph 20 does not apply because the auditor concluded that management has provided reliable written representations. However, the auditor is required to consider the effect of the non-compliance on the opinion in the auditor's report in accordance with ISA (UK) 705 (Revised June 2016).
- The written representation about the responsibility of management to provide the auditor with all relevant information agreed in the terms of the audit engagement may state that management believes that, except for information destroyed in a fire, it has provided the auditor with such information. The requirement in paragraph 20 does not apply because the auditor concluded that management has provided reliable written representations. However, the auditor is required to consider the effects of the pervasiveness of the information destroyed in the fire on the financial statements and the effect thereof on the opinion in the auditor's report in accordance with ISA (UK) 705 (Revised June 2016).

---

[8]   *ISA (UK) 230 (Revised June 2016),* Audit Documentation, *paragraphs 8(c) and 10.*

[9]   *ISA (UK) 705 (Revised June 2016), paragraph 9.*

- The written representation that all transactions have been recorded and are reflected in the financial statements may be modified, for example to refer a threshold amount agreed with the auditor (see paragraph A14) or to state that all transactions that may have a material effect on the financial statements have been recorded.

Appendix 1 (Ref: Para. 2)

List of ISAs (UK) Containing Requirements for Written Representations

This appendix identifies paragraphs in other ISAs (UK) that require subject-matter specific written representations. The list is not a substitute for considering the requirements and related application and other explanatory material in ISAs (UK).

- ISA (UK) 240 (Revised June 2016), *The Auditor's Responsibilities Relating to Fraud in an Audit of Financial Statements* – paragraph 39
- ISA (UK) 250 (Revised June 2016), *Consideration of Laws and Regulations in an Audit of Financial Statements* – paragraph 16
- ISA (UK) 450 (Revised June 2016), *Evaluation of Misstatements Identified during the Audit* – paragraph 14
- ISA (UK) 501, Audit Evidence—*Specific Considerations for Selected Items* – paragraph 12
- ISA (UK) 540 (Revised June 2016), *Auditing Accounting Estimates, Including Fair Value Accounting Estimates, and Related Disclosures* – paragraph 22
- ISA (UK) 550, *Related Parties* – paragraph 26
- ISA (UK) 560, *Subsequent Events* – paragraph 9
- ISA (UK) 570 (Revised June 2016), *Going Concern* – paragraph 16(e)
- ISA (UK) 710, *Comparative Information—Corresponding Figures and Comparative Financial Statements* – paragraph 9
- ISA (UK) 720 (Revised June 2016), *The Auditor's Responsibilities Relating to Other Information* – paragraph 13(c)

Appendix 2 (Ref: Para. A21)

Illustrative Representation Letter

This illustrative representation letter has not been tailored for the UK. For example, when describing the responsibilities of management and those charged with governance for the financial statements and providing information to the auditor, the auditor has regard to the manner in which those responsibilities are described in the terms of the audit engagement (see ISA (UK) 210 (Revised June 2016)).

The following illustrative letter includes written representations that are required by this and other ISAs. It is assumed in this illustration that the applicable financial reporting framework is International Financial Reporting Standards; the requirement of ISA 570 (Revised)[10] to obtain a written representation is not relevant; and that there are no exceptions to the requested written representations. If there were exceptions, the representations would need to be modified to reflect the exceptions.

[10] *ISA 570 (Revised)*, Going Concern.

(Entity Letterhead)

(To Auditor)   (Date)

This representation letter is provided in connection with your audit of the financial statements of ABC Company for the year ended December 31, 20XX[11] for the purpose of expressing an opinion as to whether the financial statements are presented fairly, in all material respects, (or *give a true and fair view*) in accordance with International Financial Reporting Standards.

We confirm that (, *to the best of our knowledge and belief, having made such inquiries as we considered necessary for the purpose of appropriately informing ourselves*):

Financial Statements

- We have fulfilled our responsibilities, as set out in the terms of the audit engagement dated [insert date], for the preparation of the financial statements in accordance with International Financial Reporting Standards; in particular the financial statements are fairly presented (or *give a true and fair view*) in accordance therewith.
- Significant assumptions used by us in making accounting estimates, including those measured at fair value, are reasonable. (ISA 540)
- Related party relationships and transactions have been appropriately accounted for and disclosed in accordance with the requirements of International Financial Reporting Standards. (ISA 550)
- All events subsequent to the date of the financial statements and for which International Financial Reporting Standards require adjustment or disclosure have been adjusted or disclosed. (ISA 560)
- The effects of uncorrected misstatements are immaterial, both individually and in the aggregate, to the financial statements as a whole. A list of the uncorrected misstatements is attached to the representation letter. (ISA 450)
- [Any other matters that the auditor may consider appropriate (see paragraph A10 of this ISA).]

Information Provided

- We have provided you with:[12]
  - Access to all information of which we are aware that is relevant to the preparation of the financial statements such as records, documentation and other matters;
  - Additional information that you have requested from us for the purpose of the audit; and
  - Unrestricted access to persons within the entity from whom you determined it necessary to obtain audit evidence.
- All transactions have been recorded in the accounting records and are reflected in the financial statements.
- We have disclosed to you the results of our assessment of the risk that the financial statements may be materially misstated as a result of fraud. (ISA 240)
- We have disclosed to you all information in relation to fraud or suspected fraud that we are aware of and that affects the entity and involves:

---

[11] *Where the auditor reports on more than one period, the auditor adjusts the date so that the letter pertains to all periods covered by the auditor's report.*

[12] *If the auditor has included other matters relating to management's responsibilities in the audit engagement letter in accordance with ISA 210,* Agreeing the Terms of Audit Engagements, *consideration may be given to including these matters in the written representations from management or those charged with governance.*

- o   Management;
- o   Employees who have significant roles in internal control; or
- o   Others where the fraud could have a material effect on the financial statements. (ISA 240)
- We have disclosed to you all information in relation to allegations of fraud, or suspected fraud, affecting the entity's financial statements communicated by employees, former employees, analysts, regulators or others. (ISA 240)
- We have disclosed to you all known instances of non-compliance or suspected noncompliance with laws and regulations whose effects should be considered when preparing financial statements. (ISA 250)
- We have disclosed to you the identity of the entity's related parties and all the related party relationships and transactions of which we are aware. (ISA 550)
- [Any other matters that the auditor may consider necessary (see paragraph A11 of this ISA).]

Management   Management

International Standard on Auditing (UK) 600 (Revised June 2016) Special considerations – audits of group financial statements (including the work of component auditors)

(Effective for audits of group financial statements for periods commencing on or after 17 June 2016)

Contents

Appendix 1: Illustration of Auditor's Report Where the Group Engagement Team Is Not Able to Obtain Sufficient Appropriate Audit Evidence on Which to Base the Group Audit Opinion

Appendix 2: Examples of Matters about Which the Group Engagement Team Obtains an Understanding

Appendix 3: Examples of Conditions or Events that May Indicate Risks of Material Misstatement of the Group Financial Statements

Appendix 4: Examples of a Component Auditor's Confirmations

Appendix 5: Required and Additional Matters Included in the Group Engagement Team's Letter of Instruction

International Standard on Auditing (UK) (ISA (UK)) 600 (Revised June 2016), *Special Considerations—Audits of Group Financial Statements (Including the Work of Component Auditors)*, should be read in conjunction with ISA (UK) 200 (Revised June 2016), *Overall Objectives of the Independent Auditor and the Conduct of an Audit in Accordance with International Standards on Auditing (UK).*

Introduction

Scope of this ISA (UK)

1   The International Standards on Auditing (UK) (ISAs (UK)) apply to group audits. This ISA (UK) deals with special considerations that apply to group audits, in particular those that involve component auditors.

2   An auditor may find this ISA (UK), adapted as necessary in the circumstances, useful when that auditor involves other auditors in the audit of financial statements that are not group financial statements. For example, an auditor may involve another auditor to observe the inventory count or inspect physical fixed assets at a remote location.

3   A component auditor may be required by statute, regulation or for another reason, to express an audit opinion on the financial statements of a component. The group engagement team may decide to use the audit evidence on which the audit opinion on the financial statements of the component is based to provide audit evidence for the group audit, but the requirements of this ISA (UK) nevertheless apply. (Ref: Para. A1)

4   In accordance with ISA (UK) 220 (Revised June 2016),[1] the group engagement partner is required to be satisfied that those performing the group audit engagement, including component auditors, collectively have the appropriate competence and capabilities. The group engagement partner is also responsible for the direction, supervision and performance of the group audit engagement.

5   The group engagement partner applies the requirements of ISA (UK) 220 (Revised June 2016) regardless of whether the group engagement team or a component auditor performs the work on the financial information of a component. This ISA (UK) assists the group engagement partner to meet the requirements of ISA (UK) 220 (Revised June 2016) where component auditors perform work on the financial information of components.

6   Audit risk is a function of the risk of material misstatement of the financial statements and the risk that the auditor will not detect such misstatements.[2] In a group audit, this includes the risk that the component auditor may not detect a misstatement in the financial information of the component that could cause a material misstatement of the group financial statements, and the risk that the group engagement team may not detect this misstatement. This ISA (UK) explains the matters that the group engagement team considers when determining the nature, timing and extent of its involvement in the risk assessment procedures and further audit procedures performed by the component auditors on the financial information of the components. The purpose of this involvement is to obtain sufficient appropriate audit evidence on which to base the audit opinion on the group financial statements.

Effective Date

7   This ISA (UK) is effective for audits of group financial statements for periods commencing on or after 17 June 2016. Earlier adoption is permitted.

---

[1] ISA (UK) 220 (Revised June 2016), Quality Control for an Audit of Financial Statements, *paragraphs 14 and 15.*

[2] ISA (UK) 200 (Revised June 2016), Overall Objectives of the Independent Auditor and the Conduct of an Audit in Accordance with International Standards on Auditing (UK), *paragraph A32.*

Objectives

The objectives of the auditor are:

(a) To determine whether to act as the auditor of the group financial statements; and

(b) If acting as the auditor of the group financial statements:

    (i) To communicate clearly with component auditors about the scope and timing of their work on financial information related to components and their findings; and

    (ii) To obtain sufficient appropriate audit evidence regarding the financial information of the components and the consolidation process to express an opinion on whether the group financial statements are prepared, in all material respects, in accordance with the applicable financial reporting framework.

Definitions

For purposes of the ISAs (UK), the following terms have the meanings attributed below:

(a) Component – An entity or business activity for which group or component management prepares financial information that should be included in the group financial statements. (Ref: Para. A2–A4)

(b) Component auditor – An auditor who, at the request of the group engagement team, performs work on financial information related to a component for the group audit. (Ref: Para. A7)

(c) Component management – Management responsible for the preparation of the financial information of a component.

(d) Component materiality – The materiality for a component determined by the group engagement team.

(e) Group – All the components whose financial information is included in the group financial statements. A group always has more than one component.

(f) Group audit – The audit of group financial statements.

(g) Group audit opinion – The audit opinion on the group financial statements.

(h) Group engagement partner – The partner or other person in the firm who is responsible for the group audit engagement and its performance, and for the auditor's report on the group financial statements that is issued on behalf of the firm. Where joint auditors conduct the group audit, the joint engagement partners and their engagement teams collectively constitute the group engagement partner and the group engagement team. This ISA (UK) does not, however, deal with the relationship between joint auditors or the work that one joint auditor performs in relation to the work of the other joint auditor.

(i) Group engagement team – Partners, including the group engagement partner, and staff who establish the overall group audit strategy, communicate with component auditors, perform work on the consolidation process, and evaluate the conclusions drawn from the audit evidence as the basis for forming an opinion on the group financial statements.

(j) Group financial statements – Financial statements that include the financial information of more than one component. The term 'group financial statements' also refers to combined financial statements aggregating the financial information prepared by components that have no parent but are under common control. (Ref: Para. A4-1)

(k) Group management – Management responsible for the preparation of the group financial statements.

(l) Group-wide controls – Controls designed, implemented and maintained by group management over group financial reporting.

(m) Significant component – A component identified by the group engagement team (i) that is of individual financial significance to the group, or (ii) that, due to its specific nature or circumstances, is likely to include significant risks of material misstatement of the group financial statements. (Ref: Para. A5–A6)

10 Reference to 'the applicable financial reporting framework' means the financial reporting framework that applies to the group financial statements. Reference to 'the consolidation process' includes:

(a) The recognition, measurement, presentation, and disclosure of the financial information of the components in the group financial statements by way of consolidation, proportionate consolidation, or the equity or cost methods of accounting; and

(b) The aggregation in combined financial statements of the financial information of components that have no parent but are under common control.

Requirements

Responsibility

11 The group engagement partner is responsible for the direction, supervision and performance of the group audit engagement in compliance with professional standards and applicable legal and regulatory requirements, and whether the auditor's report that is issued is appropriate in the circumstances.[3] As a result, the auditor's report on the group financial statements shall not refer to a component auditor, unless required by law or regulation to include such reference. If such reference is required by law or regulation, the auditor's report shall indicate that the reference does not diminish the group engagement partner's or the group engagement partner's firm's responsibility for the group audit opinion. (Ref: Para. A8–A9)

In the UK, the group engagement partner's firm bears the full responsibility for the auditor's report on the group financial statements.

Acceptance and Continuance

12 In applying ISA (UK) 220 (Revised June 2016), the group engagement partner shall determine whether sufficient appropriate audit evidence can reasonably be expected to be obtained in relation to the consolidation process and the financial information of the components on which to base the group audit opinion. For this purpose, the group engagement team shall obtain an understanding of the group, its components, and their environments that is sufficient to identify components that are likely to be significant components. Where component auditors will perform work on the financial information of such components, the group engagement partner shall evaluate whether the group engagement team will be able to be involved in the work of those component auditors to the extent necessary to obtain sufficient appropriate audit evidence. (Ref: Para. A10–A12)

13 If the group engagement partner concludes that:

(a) it will not be possible for the group engagement team to obtain sufficient appropriate audit evidence due to restrictions imposed by group management; and

(b) the possible effect of this inability will result in a disclaimer of opinion on the group financial statements),[4]

the group engagement partner shall either:

---

[3] *ISA (UK) 220 (Revised June 2016), paragraph 15.*

[4] *ISA (UK) 705 (Revised June 2016),* Modifications to the Opinion in the Independent Auditor's Report.

- in the case of a new engagement, not accept the engagement, or, in the case of a continuing engagement, withdraw from the engagement, where withdrawal is possible under applicable law or regulation; or
- where law or regulation prohibits an auditor from declining an engagement or where withdrawal from an engagement is not otherwise possible, having performed the audit of the group financial statements to the extent possible, disclaim an opinion on the group financial statements. (Ref: Para. A13–A19)

Terms of Engagement

The group engagement partner shall agree on the terms of the group audit engagement in accordance with ISA (UK) 210 (Revised June 2016).[5] (Ref: Para. A20–A21)   **14**

Overall Audit Strategy and Audit Plan

The group engagement team shall establish an overall group audit strategy and shall develop a group audit plan in accordance with ISA (UK) 300 (Revised June 2016).[6]   **15**

The group engagement partner shall review the overall group audit strategy and group audit plan. (Ref: Para. A22)   **16**

Understanding the Group, Its Components and Their Environments

The auditor is required to identify and assess the risks of material misstatement through obtaining an understanding of the entity and its environment.[7] The group engagement team shall: **17**

(a) Enhance its understanding of the group, its components, and their environments, including group-wide controls, obtained during the acceptance or continuance stage; and
(b) Obtain an understanding of the consolidation process, including the instructions issued by group management to components. (Ref: Para. A23–A29)

The group engagement team shall obtain an understanding that is sufficient to: **18**

(a) Confirm or revise its initial identification of components that are likely to be significant; and
(b) Assess the risks of material misstatement of the group financial statements, whether due to fraud or error.[8] (Ref: Para. A30–A31)

Understanding the Component Auditor

If the group engagement team plans to request a component auditor to perform work on the financial information of a component, the group engagement team shall obtain an understanding of the following: (Ref: Para. A32–A35)   **19**

---

[5] *ISA (UK) 210 (Revised June 2016)*, Agreeing the Terms of Audit Engagements.

[6] *ISA (UK) 300 (Revised June 2016)*, Planning an Audit of Financial Statements, *paragraphs 7–12*.

[7] *ISA (UK) 315 (Revised June 2016)*, Identifying and Assessing the Risks of Material Misstatement through Understanding the Entity and Its Environment.

[8] *ISA (UK) 315 (Revised June 2016)*.

(a) Whether the component auditor understands and will comply with the ethical requirements that are relevant to the group audit and, in particular, is independent. (Ref: Para. A37–A37-1)

(b) The component auditor's professional competence. (Ref: Para. A38)

(c) Whether the group engagement team will be able to be involved in the work of the component auditor to the extent necessary to obtain sufficient appropriate audit evidence.

(d) Whether the component auditor operates in a regulatory environment that actively oversees auditors. (Ref: Para. A36)

19D-1   The group engagement team shall request the agreement of the component auditor to the transfer of relevant documentation during the conduct of the group audit, as a condition of the use by the group engagement team of the work of the component auditor.

20   If a component auditor does not meet the independence requirements that are relevant to the group audit, or the group engagement team has serious concerns about the other matters listed in paragraph 19(a)–(c), the group engagement team shall obtain sufficient appropriate audit evidence relating to the financial information of the component without requesting that component auditor to perform work on the financial information of that component. (Ref: Para. A39–A41)

Materiality

21   The group engagement team shall determine the following: (Ref: Para. A42)

(a) Materiality for the group financial statements as a whole when establishing the overall group audit strategy.

(b) If, in the specific circumstances of the group, there are particular classes of transactions, account balances or disclosures in the group financial statements for which misstatements of lesser amounts than materiality for the group financial statements as a whole could reasonably be expected to influence the economic decisions of users taken on the basis of the group financial statements, the materiality level or levels to be applied to those particular classes of transactions, account balances or disclosures.

(c) Component materiality for those components where component auditors will perform an audit or a review for purposes of the group audit. To reduce to an appropriately low level the probability that the aggregate of uncorrected and undetected misstatements in the group financial statements exceeds materiality for the group financial statements as a whole, component materiality shall be lower than materiality for the group financial statements as a whole. (Ref: Para. A43–A44)

(d) The threshold above which misstatements cannot be regarded as clearly trivial to the group financial statements. (Ref: Para. A45)

22   Where component auditors will perform an audit for purposes of the group audit, the group engagement team shall evaluate the appropriateness of performance materiality determined at the component level. (Ref: Para. A46)

23   If a component is subject to audit by statute, regulation or other reason, and the group engagement team decides to use that audit to provide audit evidence for the group audit, the group engagement team shall determine whether:

(a) materiality for the component financial statements as a whole; and

(b) performance materiality at the component level

meet the requirements of this ISA (UK).

Responding to Assessed Risks

The auditor is required to design and implement appropriate responses to address the **24** assessed risks of material misstatement of the financial statements.[9] The group engagement team shall determine the type of work to be performed by the group engagement team, or the component auditors on its behalf, on the financial information of the components (see paragraphs 26–29). The group engagement team shall also determine the nature, timing and extent of its involvement in the work of the component auditors (see paragraphs 30–31).

If the nature, timing and extent of the work to be performed on the consolidation process **25** or the financial information of the components are based on an expectation that group-wide controls are operating effectively, or if substantive procedures alone cannot provide sufficient appropriate audit evidence at the assertion level, the group engagement team shall test, or request a component auditor to test, the operating effectiveness of those controls.

Determining the Type of Work to Be Performed on the Financial Information of Components (Ref: Para. A47)

Significant Components

For a component that is significant due to its individual financial significance to the group, **26** the group engagement team, or a component auditor on its behalf, shall perform an audit of the financial information of the component using component materiality.

For a component that is significant because it is likely to include significant risks of **27** material misstatement of the group financial statements due to its specific nature or circumstances, the group engagement team, or a component auditor on its behalf, shall perform one or more of the following:

(a) An audit of the financial information of the component using component materiality.
(b) An audit of one or more account balances, classes of transactions or disclosures relating to the likely significant risks of material misstatement of the group financial statements. (Ref: Para. A48)
(c) Specified audit procedures relating to the likely significant risks of material misstatement of the group financial statements. (Ref: Para. A49)

Components that Are Not Significant Components

For components that are not significant components, the group engagement team shall **28** perform analytical procedures at group level. (Ref: Para. A50)

If the group engagement team does not consider that sufficient appropriate audit evidence **29** on which to base the group audit opinion will be obtained from:

(a) the work performed on the financial information of significant components;
(b) the work performed on group-wide controls and the consolidation process; and
(c) the analytical procedures performed at group level,

the group engagement team shall select components that are not significant components and shall perform, or request a component auditor to perform, one or more of the following on the financial information of the individual components selected: (Ref: Para. A51–A53)

● An audit of the financial information of the component using component materiality.
● An audit of one or more account balances, classes of transactions or disclosures.

[9] *ISA (UK) 330*, The Auditor's Responses to Assessed Risks.

- A review of the financial information of the component using component materiality.
- Specified procedures.

The group engagement team shall vary the selection of components over a period of time.

Involvement in the Work Performed by Component Auditors (Ref: Para. A54–A55)

Significant Components—Risk Assessment

30 If a component auditor performs an audit of the financial information of a significant component, the group engagement team shall be involved in the component auditor's risk assessment to identify significant risks of material misstatement of the group financial statements. The nature, timing and extent of this involvement are affected by the group engagement team's understanding of the component auditor, but at a minimum shall include:

(a) Discussing with the component auditor or component management those of the component's business activities that are significant to the group;

(b) Discussing with the component auditor the susceptibility of the component to material misstatement of the financial information due to fraud or error; and

(c) Reviewing the component auditor's documentation of identified significant risks of material misstatement of the group financial statements. Such documentation may take the form of a memorandum that reflects the component auditor's conclusion with regard to the identified significant risks.

Identified Significant Risks of Material Misstatement of the Group Financial Statements— Further Audit Procedures

31 If significant risks of material misstatement of the group financial statements have been identified in a component on which a component auditor performs the work, the group engagement team shall evaluate the appropriateness of the further audit procedures to be performed to respond to the identified significant risks of material misstatement of the group financial statements. Based on its understanding of the component auditor, the group engagement team shall determine whether it is necessary to be involved in the further audit procedures.

Consolidation Process

32 In accordance with paragraph 17, the group engagement team obtains an understanding of group-wide controls and the consolidation process, including the instructions issued by group management to components. In accordance with paragraph 25, the group engagement team, or component auditor at the request of the group engagement team, tests the operating effectiveness of group-wide controls if the nature, timing and extent of the work to be performed on the consolidation process are based on an expectation that group-wide controls are operating effectively, or if substantive procedures alone cannot provide sufficient appropriate audit evidence at the assertion level.

33 The group engagement team shall design and perform further audit procedures on the consolidation process to respond to the assessed risks of material misstatement of the group financial statements arising from the consolidation process. This shall include evaluating whether all components have been included in the group financial statements.

34 The group engagement team shall evaluate the appropriateness, completeness and accuracy of consolidation adjustments and reclassifications, and shall evaluate whether any fraud risk factors or indicators of possible management bias exist. (Ref: Para. A56)

If the financial information of a component has not been prepared in accordance with the same accounting policies applied to the group financial statements, the group engagement team shall evaluate whether the financial information of that component has been appropriately adjusted for purposes of preparing and presenting the group financial statements.   **35**

The group engagement team shall determine whether the financial information identified in the component auditor's communication (see paragraph 41(c)) is the financial information that is incorporated in the group financial statements.   **36**

If the group financial statements include the financial statements of a component with a financial reporting period-end that differs from that of the group, the group engagement team shall evaluate whether appropriate adjustments have been made to those financial statements in accordance with the applicable financial reporting framework.   **37**

Subsequent Events

Where the group engagement team or component auditors perform audits on the financial information of components, the group engagement team or the component auditors shall perform procedures designed to identify events at those components that occur between the dates of the financial information of the components and the date of the auditor's report on the group financial statements, and that may require adjustment to or disclosure in the group financial statements.   **38**

Where component auditors perform work other than audits of the financial information of components, the group engagement team shall request the component auditors to notify the group engagement team if they become aware of subsequent events that may require an adjustment to or disclosure in the group financial statements.   **39**

Communication with the Component Auditor

The group engagement team shall communicate its requirements to the component auditor on a timely basis. This communication shall set out the work to be performed, the use to be made of that work, and the form and content of the component auditor's communication with the group engagement team. It shall also include the following: (Ref: Para. A57, A58, A60)   **40**

(a) A request that the component auditor, knowing the context in which the group engagement team will use the work of the component auditor, confirms that the component auditor will cooperate with the group engagement team. (Ref: Para. A59)

(b) The ethical requirements that are relevant to the group audit and, in particular, the independence requirements.

(c) In the case of an audit or review of the financial information of the component, component materiality (and, if applicable, the materiality level or levels for particular classes of transactions, account balances or disclosures) and the threshold above which misstatements cannot be regarded as clearly trivial to the group financial statements.

(d) Identified significant risks of material misstatement of the group financial statements, due to fraud or error, that are relevant to the work of the component auditor. The group engagement team shall request the component auditor to communicate on a timely basis any other identified significant risks of material misstatement of the group financial statements, due to fraud or error, in the component, and the component auditor's responses to such risks.

(e) A list of related parties prepared by group management, and any other related parties of which the group engagement team is aware. The group engagement team shall request the component auditor to communicate on a timely basis related parties not previously identified by group management or the group engagement team. The group engagement team shall determine whether to identify such additional related parties to other component auditors.

41   The group engagement team shall request the component auditor to communicate matters relevant to the group engagement team's conclusion with regard to the group audit. Such communication shall include: (Ref: Para. A60)

(a)   Whether the component auditor has complied with ethical requirements that are relevant to the group audit, including independence and professional competence;

(b)   Whether the component auditor has complied with the group engagement team's requirements;

(c)   Identification of the financial information of the component on which the component auditor is reporting;

(d)   Information on instances of non-compliance with laws or regulations that could give rise to a material misstatement of the group financial statements;

(e)   A list of uncorrected misstatements of the financial information of the component (the list need not include misstatements that are below the threshold for clearly trivial misstatements communicated by the group engagement team (see paragraph 40(c));

(f)   Indicators of possible management bias;

(g)   Description of any identified significant deficiencies in internal control at the component level;

(h)   Other significant matters that the component auditor communicated or expects to communicate to those charged with governance of the component, including fraud or suspected fraud involving component management, employees who have significant roles in internal control at the component level or others where the fraud resulted in a material misstatement of the financial information of the component;

(i)   Any other matters that may be relevant to the group audit, or that the component auditor wishes to draw to the attention of the group engagement team, including exceptions noted in the written representations that the component auditor requested from component management; and

(j)   The component auditor's overall findings, conclusions or opinion.

Evaluating the Sufficiency and Appropriateness of Audit Evidence Obtained

Evaluating the Component Auditor's Communication and Adequacy of their Work

42   The group engagement team shall evaluate the component auditor's communication (see paragraph 41). The group engagement team shall:

(a)   Discuss significant matters arising from that evaluation with the component auditor, component management or group management, as appropriate; and

(b)   Determine whether it is necessary to review other relevant parts of the component auditor's audit documentation. (Ref: Para. A61)

42D-1   The group engagement team shall:

(a)   Evaluate and review the work performed by the component auditor for the purpose of the group audit; or

(b)   Where the group engagement team is unable to request or secure the agreement required by paragraph 19D-1, take appropriate measures (including carrying out additional work, either directly or by outsourcing such tasks, in the relevant component) and inform the competent authority.[9a]

[9a] *In the UK, the competent authority designated by law is the FRC or the Recognised Supervisory Body to whom the FRC has delegated regulatory tasks, as applicable.*

If the group engagement team concludes that the work of the component auditor is **43** insufficient, the group engagement team shall determine what additional procedures are to be performed, and whether they are to be performed by the component auditor or by the group engagement team.

Sufficiency and Appropriateness of Audit Evidence

The auditor is required to obtain sufficient appropriate audit evidence to reduce audit risk **44** to an acceptably low level and thereby enable the auditor to draw reasonable conclusions on which to base the auditor's opinion.[10] The group engagement team shall evaluate whether sufficient appropriate audit evidence has been obtained from the audit procedures performed on the consolidation process and the work performed by the group engagement team and the component auditors on the financial information of the components, on which to base the group audit opinion. (Ref: Para. A62)

The group engagement partner shall evaluate the effect on the group audit opinion of **45** any uncorrected misstatements (either identified by the group engagement team or communicated by component auditors) and any instances where there has been an inability to obtain sufficient appropriate audit evidence. (Ref: Para. A63)

Communication with Group Management and Those Charged with Governance of the Group

Communication with Group Management

The group engagement team shall determine which identified deficiencies in internal **46** control to communicate to those charged with governance and group management in accordance with ISA (UK) 265.[11] In making this determination, the group engagement team shall consider:

(a) Deficiencies in group-wide internal control that the group engagement team has identified;
(b) Deficiencies in internal control that the group engagement team has identified in internal controls at components; and
(c) Deficiencies in internal control that component auditors have brought to the attention of the group engagement team.

If fraud has been identified by the group engagement team or brought to its attention by a **47** component auditor (see paragraph 41(h)), or information indicates that a fraud may exist, the group engagement team shall communicate this on a timely basis to the appropriate level of group management in order to inform those with primary responsibility for the prevention and detection of fraud of matters relevant to their responsibilities. (Ref. Para. A64)

A component auditor may be required by statute, regulation or for another reason, to **48** express an audit opinion on the financial statements of a component. In that case, the group engagement team shall request group management to inform component management of any matter of which the group engagement team becomes aware that may be significant to the financial statements of the component, but of which component management may be unaware. If group management refuses to communicate the matter to component

---

[10] *ISA (UK) 200 (Revised June 2016), paragraph 17.*

[11] *ISA (UK) 265*, Communicating Deficiencies in Internal Control to Those Charged with Governance and Management.

management, the group engagement team shall discuss the matter with those charged with governance of the group. If the matter remains unresolved, the group engagement team, subject to legal and professional confidentiality considerations, shall consider whether to advise the component auditor not to issue the auditor's report on the financial statements of the component until the matter is resolved. (Ref: Para. A65)

Communication with Those Charged with Governance of the Group

49   The group engagement team shall communicate the following matters with those charged with governance of the group, in addition to those required by ISA (UK) 260 (Revised June 2016)[12] and other ISAs (UK): (Ref: Para. A66)

(a)   An overview of the type of work to be performed on the financial information of the components.

(b)   An overview of the nature of the group engagement team's planned involvement in the work to be performed by the component auditors on the financial information of significant components.

(c)   Instances where the group engagement team's evaluation of the work of a component auditor gave rise to a concern about the quality of that auditor's work.

(d)   Any limitations on the group audit, for example, where the group engagement team's access to information may have been restricted.

(e)   Fraud or suspected fraud involving group management, component management, employees who have significant roles in group-wide controls or others where the fraud resulted in a material misstatement of the group financial statements.

49D-1   For audits of group financial statements of public interest entities, the group engagement partner's firm shall bear the full responsibility for the additional report to the audit committee.[12a]

Documentation

50   The group engagement team shall include in the audit documentation the following matters:[13]

(a)   An analysis of components, indicating those that are significant, and the type of work performed on the financial information of the components.

(b)   The nature, timing and extent of the group engagement team's involvement in the work performed by the component auditors on significant components including, where applicable, the group engagement team's review of relevant parts of the component auditors' audit documentation and conclusions thereon. (Ref: Para. A66-1)

(c)   Written communications between the group engagement team and the component auditors about the group engagement team's requirements.

50D-1   The group engagement team shall include in the audit documentation the nature, timing and extent of the work performed by the component auditor, including, where applicable, the group engagement team's review of relevant parts of the component auditor's audit documentation.

---

[12] *ISA (UK) 260 (Revised June 2016)*, Communication with Those Charged with Governance.

[12a] *ISA (UK) 260 (Revised June 2016), paragraph 16R-2 deals with the auditor's responsibilities to prepare an additional report to the audit committee.*

[13] *ISA (UK) 230 (Revised June 2016)*, Audit Documentation, *paragraphs 8–11, and paragraph A6.*

The group engagement team shall retain sufficient and appropriate audit documentation to enable the competent authority[9a] to review the work of the auditor of the group financial statements.

50D-2

Where:

50D-3

- the group engagement team is subject to a quality assurance review or an investigation concerning the group audit; and
- the competent authority[9a] is unable to obtain audit documentation of the work carried out by any component auditor from a non-EEA member state; and
- the competent authority requests delivery of any additional documentation of the work performed by that component auditor for the purpose of the group audit (including the component auditor's working papers relevant to the group audit),

the group engagement team shall, in order to properly deliver such documentation in accordance with such request, either:

(a) Retain copies of the documentation of the work carried out by the relevant component auditor for the purpose of the group audit (including the component auditor's working papers relevant to the group audit); or
(b) Obtain the agreement of the relevant component auditor that the group engagement team shall have unrestricted access to such documentation on request; or
(c) Retain documentation to show that the group engagement team has undertaken the appropriate procedures in order to gain access to the audit documentation, together with evidence supporting the existence of any impediments to such access; or
(d) Take any other appropriate action.

***

Application and Other Explanatory Material

Components Subject to Audit by Statute, Regulation or Other Reason (Ref: Para. 3)

Factors that may affect the group engagement team's decision whether to use an audit required by statute, regulation or for another reason to provide audit evidence for the group audit include the following:

A1

- Differences in the financial reporting framework applied in preparing the financial statements of the component and that applied in preparing the group financial statements.
- Differences in the auditing and other standards applied by the component auditor and those applied in the audit of the group financial statements.
- Whether the audit of the financial statements of the component will be completed in time to meet the group reporting timetable.

Considerations Specific to Public Sector Entities

In certain parts of the public sector where the responsibilities of principal and other auditors are governed by statutory provisions, these override the provisions of this ISA (UK).

A1-1

Definitions

Component (Ref: Para. 9(a))

A2   The structure of a group affects how components are identified. For example, the group financial reporting system may be based on an organizational structure that provides for financial information to be prepared by a parent and one or more subsidiaries, joint ventures, or investees accounted for by the equity or cost methods of accounting; by a head office and one or more divisions or branches; or by a combination of both. Some groups, however, may organize their financial reporting system by function, process, product or service (or by groups of products or services), or geographical locations. In these cases, the entity or business activity for which group or component management prepares financial information that is included in the group financial statements may be a function, process, product or service (or group of products or services), or geographical location.

A3   Various levels of components may exist within the group financial reporting system, in which case it may be more appropriate to identify components at certain levels of aggregation rather than individually.

A4   Components aggregated at a certain level may constitute a component for purposes of the group audit; however, such a component may also prepare group financial statements that incorporate the financial information of the components it encompasses (that is, a subgroup). This ISA (UK) may therefore be applied by different group engagement partners and teams for different subgroups within a larger group.

Group Financial Statements (Ref: Para 9(j))

A4-1   In the UK, law or regulation may use other terms to describe the group financial statements including 'group accounts', 'consolidated accounts' and 'consolidated financial statements'.

Significant Component (Ref: Para. 9(m))

A5   As the individual financial significance of a component increases, the risks of material misstatement of the group financial statements ordinarily increase. The group engagement team may apply a percentage to a chosen benchmark as an aid to identify components that are of individual financial significance. Identifying a benchmark and determining a percentage to be applied to it involve the exercise of professional judgment. Depending on the nature and circumstances of the group, appropriate benchmarks might include group assets, liabilities, cash flows, profit or turnover. For example, the group engagement team may consider that components exceeding 15% of the chosen benchmark are significant components. A higher or lower percentage may, however, be deemed appropriate in the circumstances.

A6   The group engagement team may also identify a component as likely to include significant risks of material misstatement of the group financial statements due to its specific nature or circumstances (that is, risks that require special audit consideration[14]). For example, a component could be responsible for foreign exchange trading and thus expose the group to a significant risk of material misstatement, even though the component is not otherwise of individual financial significance to the group.

---

[14] *ISA (UK) 315 (Revised June 2016), paragraphs 27–29.*

Component Auditor (Ref: Para. 9(b))

A member of the group engagement team may perform work on the financial information of a component for the group audit at the request of the group engagement team. Where this is the case, such a member of the engagement team is also a component auditor.   **A7**

Responsibility (Ref: Para. 11)

Although component auditors may perform work on the financial information of the components for the group audit and as such are responsible for their overall findings, conclusions or opinions, the group engagement partner or the group engagement partner's firm is responsible for the group audit opinion.   **A8**

When the group audit opinion is modified because the group engagement team was unable to obtain sufficient appropriate audit evidence in relation to the financial information of one or more components, the Basis for Modification paragraph in the auditor's report on the group financial statements describes the reasons for that inability without referring to the component auditor, unless such a reference is necessary for an adequate explanation of the circumstances.[15]   **A9**

Acceptance and Continuance

Obtaining an Understanding at the Acceptance or Continuance Stage (Ref: Para. 12)

In the case of a new engagement, the group engagement team's understanding of the group, its components, and their environments may be obtained from: **A10**

- Information provided by group management;
- Communication with group management; and
- Where applicable, communication with the previous group engagement team, component management, or component auditors.

The group engagement team's understanding may include matters such as the following: **A11**

- The group structure, including both the legal and organizational structure (that is, how the group financial reporting system is organized).
- Components' business activities that are significant to the group, including the industry and regulatory, economic and political environments in which those activities take place.
- The use of service organizations, including shared service centers.
- A description of group-wide controls.
- The complexity of the consolidation process.
- Whether component auditors that are not from the group engagement partner's firm or network will perform work on the financial information of any of the components, and group management's rationale for appointing more than one auditor.
- Whether the group engagement team:
  - Will have unrestricted access to those charged with governance of the group, group management, those charged with governance of the component, component management, component information, and the component auditors (including relevant audit documentation sought by the group engagement team); and
  - Will be able to perform necessary work on the financial information of the components.

---

[15] *ISA (UK) 705 (Revised June 2016), paragraph 20.*

A12   In the case of a continuing engagement, the group engagement team's ability to obtain sufficient appropriate audit evidence may be affected by significant changes, for example:

- Changes in the group structure (for example, acquisitions, disposals, reorganizations, or changes in how the group financial reporting system is organized).
- Changes in components' business activities that are significant to the group.
- Changes in the composition of those charged with governance of the group, group management, or key management of significant components.
- Concerns the group engagement team has with regard to the integrity and competence of group or component management.
- Changes in group-wide controls.
- Changes in the applicable financial reporting framework.

Expectation to Obtain Sufficient Appropriate Audit Evidence (Ref: Para. 13)

A13   A group may consist only of components not considered significant components. In these circumstances, the group engagement partner can reasonably expect to obtain sufficient appropriate audit evidence on which to base the group audit opinion if the group engagement team will be able to:

(a) Perform the work on the financial information of some of these components; and

(b) Be involved in the work performed by component auditors on the financial information of other components to the extent necessary to obtain sufficient appropriate audit evidence.

Access to Information (Ref: Para. 13)

A14   The group engagement team's access to information may be restricted by circumstances that cannot be overcome by group management, for example, laws relating to confidentiality and data privacy, or denial by the component auditor of access to relevant audit documentation sought by the group engagement team. It may also be restricted by group management.

A14-1   In the UK, there are statutory obligations on corporate subsidiary undertakings, and their auditors and other parties, to provide the auditor of a corporate parent undertaking with such information and explanations as that auditor may reasonably require for the purposes of the audit.[15a] Where there is no such statutory obligation (e.g. for non corporate entities and overseas subsidiary undertakings), permission may be needed by the auditors of the subsidiary undertakings, from those charged with governance of the subsidiary undertakings, to disclose information to the auditor of the parent undertaking. Permission may also be needed from those charged with governance of the subsidiary undertakings for the auditor of the parent undertaking to pass those disclosures on to those charged with governance of the parent undertaking. The auditor of the parent undertaking seeks to ensure that appropriate arrangements are made at the planning stage for these disclosures. Normally, such arrangements for groups are recorded in the instructions to the auditors of subsidiary undertakings and relevant engagement letters.

[15a] *In the UK, Section 499 of the Companies Act 2006 specifies that the auditor of a company may require any subsidiary undertaking of the company which is a body corporate incorporated in the UK, and any officer, employee or auditor of any such subsidiary undertaking or any person holding or accountable for any books, accounts or vouchers of any such subsidiary undertaking, to provide him with such information or explanations as he thinks necessary for the performance of his duties as auditor. If a parent company has a subsidiary undertaking that is not a body corporate incorporated in the UK, Section 500 of the Companies Act 2006 specifies that the auditor of the parent company may require it to take all such steps as are reasonably open to it to obtain from the subsidiary undertaking, any officer, employee or auditor of the undertaking, or any person holding or accountable for any of the undertaking's books, accounts or vouchers, such information and explanations as he may reasonably require for the purposes of his duties as auditor.*

Where access to information is restricted by circumstances, the group engagement **A15**
team may still be able to obtain sufficient appropriate audit evidence; however, this
is less likely as the significance of the component increases. For example, the group
engagement team may not have access to those charged with governance, management,
or the auditor (including relevant audit documentation sought by the group engagement
team) of a component that is accounted for by the equity method of accounting. If
the component is not a significant component, and the group engagement team has a
complete set of financial statements of the component, including the auditor's report
thereon, and has access to information kept by group management in relation to that
component, the group engagement team may conclude that this information constitutes
sufficient appropriate audit evidence in relation to that component. If the component
is a significant component, however, the group engagement team will not be able to
comply with the requirements of this ISA (UK) relevant in the circumstances of the
group audit. For example, the group engagement team will not be able to comply with the
requirement in paragraphs 30–31 to be involved in the work of the component auditor.
The group engagement team will not, therefore, be able to obtain sufficient appropriate
audit evidence in relation to that component. The effect of the group engagement team's
inability to obtain sufficient appropriate audit evidence is considered in terms of ISA
(UK) 705 (Revised June 2016).

The group engagement team will not be able to obtain sufficient appropriate audit evidence   **A16**
if group management restricts the access of the group engagement team or a component
auditor to the information of a significant component.

Although the group engagement team may be able to obtain sufficient appropriate audit   **A17**
evidence if such restriction relates to a component considered not a significant component,
the reason for the restriction may affect the group audit opinion. For example, it may affect
the reliability of group management's responses to the group engagement team's inquiries
and group management's representations to the group engagement team.

Law or regulation may prohibit the group engagement partner from declining or   **A18**
withdrawing from an engagement. For example, in some jurisdictions the auditor is
appointed for a specified period of time and is prohibited from withdrawing before the
end of that period. Also, in the public sector, the option of declining or withdrawing from
an engagement may not be available to the auditor due to the nature of the mandate or
public interest considerations. In these circumstances, this ISA (UK) still applies to the
group audit, and the effect of the group engagement team's inability to obtain sufficient
appropriate audit evidence is considered in terms of ISA (UK) 705 (Revised June 2016).

Appendix 1 contains an example of an auditor's report containing a qualified opinion based   **A19**
on the group engagement team's inability to obtain sufficient appropriate audit evidence in
relation to a significant component accounted for by the equity method of accounting, but
where, in the group engagement team's judgment, the effect is material but not pervasive.[15b]

Terms of Engagement (Ref: Para. 14)

The terms of engagement identify the applicable financial reporting framework.[16]   **A20**
Additional matters may be included in the terms of a group audit engagement, such as the
fact that:

---

[16] *ISA (UK) 210 (Revised June 2016), paragraph 8.*

- The communication between the group engagement team and the component auditors should be unrestricted to the extent possible under law or regulation;
- Important communications between the component auditors, those charged with governance of the component, and component management, including communications on significant deficiencies in internal control, should be communicated as well to the group engagement team;
- Important communications between regulatory authorities and components related to financial reporting matters should be communicated to the group engagement team; and
- To the extent the group engagement team considers necessary, it should be permitted:
  - Access to component information, those charged with governance of components, component management, and the component auditors (including relevant audit documentation sought by the group engagement team); and
  - To perform work or request a component auditor to perform work on the financial information of the components.

A21   Restrictions imposed on:

- the group engagement team's access to component information, those charged with governance of components, component management, or the component auditors (including relevant audit documentation sought by the group engagement team); or
- the work to be performed on the financial information of the components

after the group engagement partner's acceptance of the group audit engagement, constitute an inability to obtain sufficient appropriate audit evidence that may affect the group audit opinion. In exceptional circumstances it may even lead to withdrawal from the engagement where withdrawal is possible under applicable law or regulation.

Overall Audit Strategy and Audit Plan (Ref: Para. 16)

A22   The group engagement partner's review of the overall group audit strategy and group audit plan is an important part of fulfilling the group engagement partner's responsibility for the direction of the group audit engagement.

Understanding the Group, Its Components and Their Environments

Matters about Which the Group Engagement Team Obtains an Understanding (Ref: Para. 17)

A23   ISA (UK) 315 (Revised June 2016) contains guidance on matters the auditor may consider when obtaining an understanding of the industry, regulatory, and other external factors that affect the entity, including the applicable financial reporting framework; the nature of the entity; objectives and strategies and related business risks; and measurement and review of the entity's financial performance.[17] Appendix 2 of this ISA (UK) contains guidance on matters specific to a group, including the consolidation process.

Instructions Issued by Group Management to Components (Ref: Para. 17)

A24   To achieve uniformity and comparability of financial information, group management ordinarily issues instructions to components. Such instructions specify the requirements for financial information of the components to be included in the group financial statements and often include financial reporting procedures manuals and a reporting package.

---

[17] *ISA (UK) 315 (Revised June 2016), paragraphs A17–A41.*

A reporting package ordinarily consists of standard formats for providing financial information for incorporation in the group financial statements. Reporting packages generally do not, however, take the form of complete financial statements prepared and presented in accordance with the applicable financial reporting framework.

The instructions ordinarily cover: **A25**

- The accounting policies to be applied;
- Statutory and other disclosure requirements applicable to the group financial statements, including:
  - The identification and reporting of segments;
  - Related party relationships and transactions;
  - Intra-group transactions and unrealized profits;
  - Intra-group account balances; and
- A reporting timetable.

The group engagement team's understanding of the instructions may include the following: **A26**

- The clarity and practicality of the instructions for completing the reporting package.
- Whether the instructions:
  - Adequately describe the characteristics of the applicable financial reporting framework;
  - Provide for disclosures that are sufficient to comply with the requirements of the applicable financial reporting framework, for example, disclosure of related party relationships and transactions, and segment information;
  - Provide for the identification of consolidation adjustments, for example, intra-group transactions and unrealized profits, and intra-group account balances; and
  - Provide for the approval of the financial information by component management.

Fraud (Ref: Para. 17)

The auditor is required to identify and assess the risks of material misstatement of the   **A27**
financial statements due to fraud, and to design and implement appropriate responses to the assessed risks.[18] Information used to identify the risks of material misstatement of the group financial statements due to fraud may include the following:

- Group management's assessment of the risks that the group financial statements may be materially misstated as a result of fraud.
- Group management's process for identifying and responding to the risks of fraud in the group, including any specific fraud risks identified by group management, or account balances, classes of transactions, or disclosures for which a risk of fraud is likely.
- Whether there are particular components for which a risk of fraud is likely.
- How those charged with governance of the group monitor group management's processes for identifying and responding to the risks of fraud in the group, and the controls group management has established to mitigate these risks.
- Responses of those charged with governance of the group, group management, appropriate individuals within the internal audit function (and if considered appropriate, component management, the component auditors, and others) to the group engagement team's inquiry whether they have knowledge of any actual, suspected, or alleged fraud affecting a component or the group.

---

[18] *ISA (UK) 240 (Revised June 2016)*, The Auditor's Responsibilities Relating to Fraud in an Audit of Financial Statements.

Discussion among Group Engagement Team Members and Component Auditors Regarding the Risks of Material Misstatement of the Group Financial Statements, Including Risks of Fraud (Ref: Para. 17)

A28   The key members of the engagement team are required to discuss the susceptibility of an entity to material misstatement of the financial statements due to fraud or error, specifically emphasizing the risks due to fraud. In a group audit, these discussions may also include the component auditors.[19] The group engagement partner's determination of who to include in the discussions, how and when they occur, and their extent, is affected by factors such as prior experience with the group.

A29   The discussions provide an opportunity to:

- Share knowledge of the components and their environments, including group-wide controls.
- Exchange information about the business risks of the components or the group.
- Exchange ideas about how and where the group financial statements may be susceptible to material misstatement due to fraud or error, how group management and component management could perpetrate and conceal fraudulent financial reporting, and how assets of the components could be misappropriated.
- Identify practices followed by group or component management that may be biased or designed to manage earnings that could lead to fraudulent financial reporting, for example, revenue recognition practices that do not comply with the applicable financial reporting framework.
- Consider known external and internal factors affecting the group that may create an incentive or pressure for group management, component management, or others to commit fraud, provide the opportunity for fraud to be perpetrated, or indicate a culture or environment that enables group management, component management, or others to rationalize committing fraud.
- Consider the risk that group or component management may override controls.
- Consider whether uniform accounting policies are used to prepare the financial information of the components for the group financial statements and, where not, how differences in accounting policies are identified and adjusted (where required by the applicable financial reporting framework).
- Discuss fraud that has been identified in components, or information that indicates existence of a fraud in a component.
- Share information that may indicate non-compliance with national laws or regulations, for example, payments of bribes and improper transfer pricing practices.

Risk Factors (Ref: Para. 18)

A30   Appendix 3 sets out examples of conditions or events that, individually or together, may indicate risks of material misstatement of the group financial statements, including risks due to fraud.

Risk Assessment (Ref: Para. 18)

A31   The group engagement team's assessment at group level of the risks of material misstatement of the group financial statements is based on information such as the following:

- Information obtained from the understanding of the group, its components, and their environments, and of the consolidation process, including audit evidence obtained in evaluating the design and implementation of group-wide controls and controls that are relevant to the consolidation.
- Information obtained from the component auditors.

---

[19] *ISA (UK) 240 (Revised June 2016), paragraph 15, and ISA (UK) 315 (Revised June 2016), paragraph 10.*

Understanding the Component Auditor (Ref: Para. 19)

The group engagement team obtains an understanding of a component auditor only when **A32**
it plans to request the component auditor to perform work on the financial information
of a component for the group audit. For example, it will not be necessary to obtain an
understanding of the auditors of those components for which the group engagement team
plans to perform analytical procedures at group level only.

Group Engagement Team's Procedures to Obtain an Understanding of the Component Auditor and Sources of Audit Evidence (Ref: Para. 19)

The nature, timing and extent of the group engagement team's procedures to obtain **A33**
an understanding of the component auditor are affected by factors such as previous
experience with or knowledge of the component auditor, and the degree to which the
group engagement team and the component auditor are subject to common policies and
procedures, for example:

- Whether the group engagement team and a component auditor share:
  o   Common policies and procedures for performing the work (for example, audit
      methodologies);
  o   Common quality control policies and procedures; or
  o   Common monitoring policies and procedures.
- The consistency or similarity of:
  o   Laws and regulations or legal system;
  o   Professional oversight, discipline, and external quality assurance;
  o   Education and training;
  o   Professional organizations and standards; or
  o   Language and culture.

These factors interact and are not mutually exclusive. For example, the extent of the group **A34**
engagement team's procedures to obtain an understanding of Component Auditor A, who
consistently applies common quality control and monitoring policies and procedures and a
common audit methodology or operates in the same jurisdiction as the group engagement
partner, may be less than the extent of the group engagement team's procedures to obtain
an understanding of Component Auditor B, who is not consistently applying common
quality control and monitoring policies and procedures and a common audit methodology
or operates in a foreign jurisdiction. The nature of the procedures performed in relation to
Component Auditors A and B may also be different.

The group engagement team may obtain an understanding of the component auditor in a **A35**
number of ways. In the first year of involving a component auditor, the group engagement
team may, for example:

- Evaluate the results of the quality control monitoring system where the group
  engagement team and component auditor are from a firm or network that operates
  under and complies with common monitoring policies and procedures;[20]
- Visit the component auditor to discuss the matters in paragraph 19(a)–(c);
- Request the component auditor to confirm the matters referred to in paragraph 19(a)–(c)
  in writing. Appendix 4 contains an example of written confirmations by a component
  auditor;
- Request the component auditor to complete questionnaires about the matters in
  paragraph 19(a)–(c);

---

[20] *As required by ISQC (UK) 1 (Revised June 2016),* Quality Control for Firms that Perform Audits and Reviews
of Financial Statements, and Other Assurance and Related Services Engagements, *paragraph 54, or national
requirements that are at least as demanding.*

- Discuss the component auditor with colleagues in the group engagement partner's firm, or with a reputable third party that has knowledge of the component auditor; or
- Obtain confirmations from the professional body or bodies to which the component auditor belongs, the authorities by which the component auditor is licensed, or other third parties.

In subsequent years, the understanding of the component auditor may be based on the group engagement team's previous experience with the component auditor. The group engagement team may request the component auditor to confirm whether anything in relation to the matters listed in paragraph 19(a)–(c) has changed since the previous year.

A36   Where independent oversight bodies have been established to oversee the auditing profession and monitor the quality of audits, awareness of the regulatory environment may assist the group engagement team in evaluating the independence and competence of the component auditor. Information about the regulatory environment may be obtained from the component auditor or information provided by the independent oversight bodies.

Ethical Requirements that Are Relevant to the Group Audit (Ref: Para. 19(a))

A37   When performing work on the financial information of a component for a group audit, the component auditor is subject to ethical requirements that are relevant to the group audit. Such requirements may be different or in addition to those applying to the component auditor when performing a statutory audit in the component auditor's jurisdiction. The group engagement team therefore obtains an understanding whether the component auditor understands and will comply with the ethical requirements that are relevant to the group audit, sufficient to fulfill the component auditor's responsibilities in the group audit.

A37-1   As part of obtaining an understanding of whether the component auditor understands and will comply with the ethical requirements that are relevant to the group audit, the group engagement team considers the implications of Supporting Ethical Provision 2.4 of the FRC's Ethical Standard[20a] for the component auditor.

The Component Auditor's Professional Competence (Ref: Para. 19(b))

A38   The group engagement team's understanding of the component auditor's professional competence may include whether the component auditor:

- Possesses an understanding of auditing and other standards applicable to the group audit that is sufficient to fulfill the component auditor's responsibilities in the group audit;
- Has sufficient resources (e.g. personnel with the necessary capabilities) to perform the work on the financial information of the particular component;
- Possesses the special skills (for example, industry specific knowledge) necessary to perform the work on the financial information of the particular component; and
- Where relevant, possesses an understanding of the applicable financial reporting framework that is sufficient to fulfill the component auditor's responsibilities in the group audit (instructions issued by group management to components often describe the characteristics of the applicable financial reporting framework).

[20a] *FRC's Ethical Standard,* Part A – Overarching Principles and Supporting Ethical Provisions, *Supporting Ethical Provision 2.4.*

Application of the Group Engagement Team's Understanding of a Component Auditor
(Ref: Para. 20)

The group engagement team cannot overcome the fact that a component auditor is not independent by being involved in the work of the component auditor or by performing additional risk assessment or further audit procedures on the financial information of the component. **A39**

However, the group engagement team may be able to overcome less than serious concerns about the component auditor's professional competency (for example, lack of industry specific knowledge), or the fact that the component auditor does not operate in an environment that actively oversees auditors, by being involved in the work of the component auditor or by performing additional risk assessment or further audit procedures on the financial information of the component. **A40**

Where law or regulation prohibits access to relevant parts of the audit documentation of the component auditor, the group engagement team may request the component auditor to overcome this by preparing a memorandum that covers the relevant information. **A41**

Materiality (Ref: Para. 21–23)

The auditor is required:[21] **A42**

(a) When establishing the overall audit strategy, to determine:
 (i) Materiality for the financial statements as a whole; and
 (ii) If, in the specific circumstances of the entity, there are particular classes of transactions, account balances or disclosures for which misstatements of lesser amounts than materiality for the financial statements as a whole could reasonably be expected to influence the economic decisions of users taken on the basis of the financial statements, the materiality level or levels to be applied to those particular classes of transactions, account balances or disclosures; and
(b) To determine performance materiality.

In the context of a group audit, materiality is established for both the group financial statements as a whole, and for the financial information of the components. Materiality for the group financial statements as a whole is used when establishing the overall group audit strategy.

To reduce to an appropriately low level the probability that the aggregate of uncorrected and undetected misstatements in the group financial statements exceeds materiality for the group financial statements as a whole, component materiality is set lower than materiality for the group financial statements as a whole. Different component materiality may be established for different components. Component materiality need not be an arithmetical portion of the materiality for the group financial statements as a whole and, consequently, the aggregate of component materiality for the different components may exceed the materiality for the group financial statements as a whole. Component materiality is used when establishing the overall audit strategy for a component. **A43**

Component materiality is determined for those components whose financial information will be audited or reviewed as part of the group audit in accordance with paragraphs 26, 27(a) and 29. Component materiality is used by the component auditor to evaluate whether uncorrected detected misstatements are material, individually or in the aggregate. **A44**

---

[21] *ISA (UK) 320 (Revised June 2016), Materiality in Planning and Performing an Audit, paragraphs 10–11.*

A45   A threshold for misstatements is determined in addition to component materiality. Misstatements identified in the financial information of the component that are above the threshold for misstatements are communicated to the group engagement team.

A46   In the case of an audit of the financial information of a component, the component auditor (or group engagement team) determines performance materiality at the component level. This is necessary to reduce to an appropriately low level the probability that the aggregate of uncorrected and undetected misstatements in the financial information of the component exceeds component materiality. In practice, the group engagement team may set component materiality at this lower level. Where this is the case, the component auditor uses component materiality for purposes of assessing the risks of material misstatement of the financial information of the component and to design further audit procedures in response to assessed risks as well as for evaluating whether detected misstatements are material individually or in the aggregate.

Responding to Assessed Risks

Determining the Type of Work to Be Performed on the Financial Information of Components (Ref: Para. 26–27)

A47   The group engagement team's determination of the type of work to be performed on the financial information of a component and its involvement in the work of the component auditor is affected by:

(a) The significance of the component;
(b) The identified significant risks of material misstatement of the group financial statements;
(c) The group engagement team's evaluation of the design of group-wide controls and determination whether they have been implemented; and
(d) The group engagement team's understanding of the component auditor.

The diagram shows how the significance of the component affects the group engagement team's determination of the type of work to be performed on the financial information of the component.

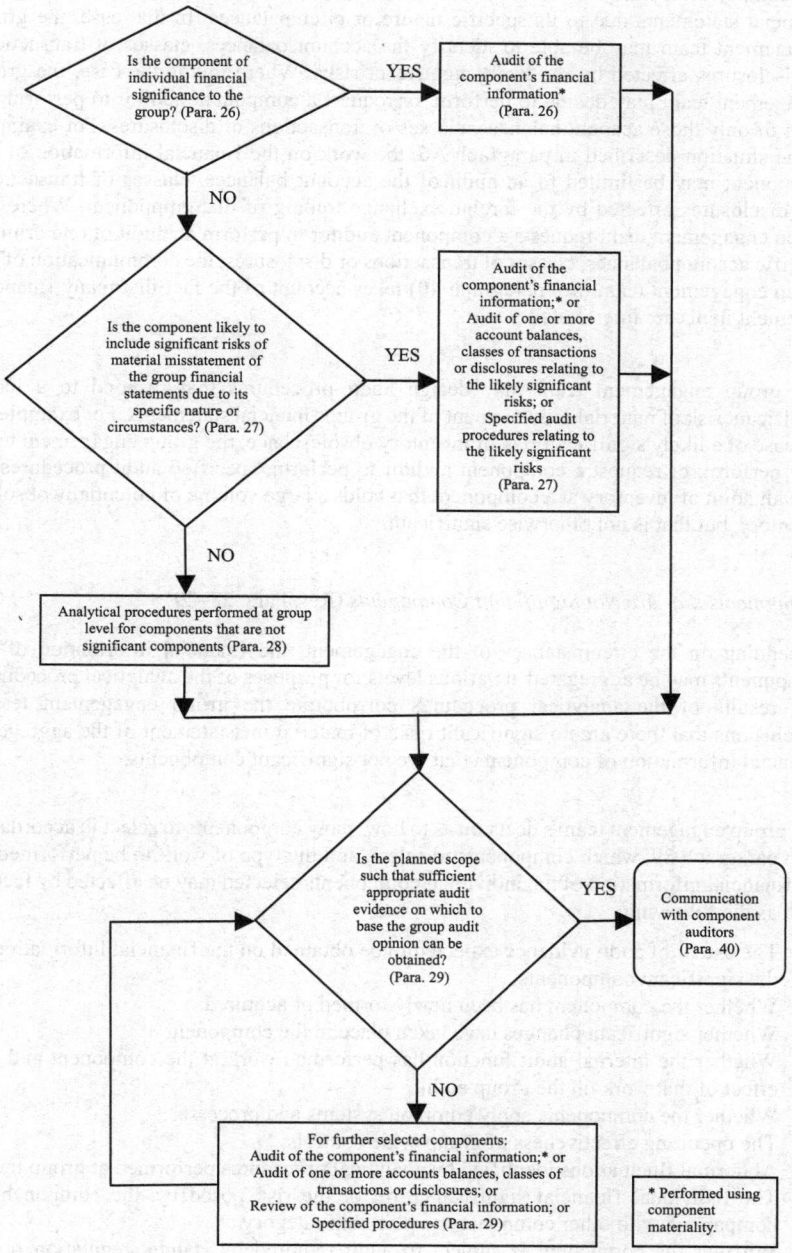

Is the component of individual financial significance to the group? (Para. 26)

YES → Audit of the component's financial information* (Para. 26)

NO ↓

Is the component likely to include significant risks of material misstatement of the group financial statements due to its specific nature or circumstances? (Para. 27)

YES → Audit of the component's financial information;* or Audit of one or more account balances, classes of transactions or disclosures relating to the likely significant risks; or Specified audit procedures relating to the likely significant risks (Para. 27)

NO ↓

Analytical procedures performed at group level for components that are not significant components (Para. 28)

Is the planned scope such that sufficient appropriate audit evidence on which to base the group audit opinion can be obtained? (Para. 29)

YES → Communication with component auditors (Para. 40)

NO ↓

For further selected components:
Audit of the component's financial information;* or
Audit of one or more accounts balances, classes of transactions or disclosures; or
Review of the component's financial information; or
Specified procedures (Para. 29)

* Performed using component materiality.

Significant Components (Ref: Para. 27(b)–(c))

A48   The group engagement team may identify a component as a significant component because that component is likely to include significant risks of material misstatement of the group financial statements due to its specific nature or circumstances. In that case, the group engagement team may be able to identify the account balances, classes of transactions or disclosures affected by the likely significant risks. Where this is the case, the group engagement team may decide to perform, or request a component auditor to perform, an audit of only those account balances, classes of transactions or disclosures. For example, in the situation described in paragraph A6, the work on the financial information of the component may be limited to an audit of the account balances, classes of transactions and disclosures affected by the foreign exchange trading of that component. Where the group engagement team requests a component auditor to perform an audit of one or more specific account balances, classes of transactions or disclosures, the communication of the group engagement team (see paragraph 40) takes account of the fact that many financial statement items are interrelated.

A49   The group engagement team may design audit procedures that respond to a likely significant risk of material misstatement of the group financial statements. For example, in the case of a likely significant risk of inventory obsolescence, the group engagement team may perform, or request a component auditor to perform, specified audit procedures on the valuation of inventory at a component that holds a large volume of potentially obsolete inventory, but that is not otherwise significant.

Components that Are Not Significant Components (Ref: Para. 28–29)

A50   Depending on the circumstances of the engagement, the financial information of the components may be aggregated at various levels for purposes of the analytical procedures. The results of the analytical procedures corroborate the group engagement team's conclusions that there are no significant risks of material misstatement of the aggregated financial information of components that are not significant components.

A51   The group engagement team's decision as to how many components to select in accordance with paragraph 29, which components to select, and the type of work to be performed on the financial information of the individual components selected may be affected by factors such as the following:

- The extent of audit evidence expected to be obtained on the financial information of the significant components.
- Whether the component has been newly formed or acquired.
- Whether significant changes have taken place in the component.
- Whether the internal audit function has performed work at the component and any effect of that work on the group audit.
- Whether the components apply common systems and processes.
- The operating effectiveness of group-wide controls.
- Abnormal fluctuations identified by analytical procedures performed at group level.
- The individual financial significance of, or the risk posed by, the component in comparison with other components within this category.
- Whether the component is subject to audit required by statute, regulation or for another reason.

Including an element of unpredictability in selecting components in this category may increase the likelihood of identifying material misstatement of the components' financial information. The selection of components is often varied on a cyclical basis.

A review of the financial information of a component may be performed in accordance **A52** with International Standard on Review Engagements (ISRE) 2400[22] or ISRE (UK and Ireland) 2410,[23] adapted as necessary in the circumstances. The group engagement team may also specify additional procedures to supplement this work.

As explained in paragraph A13, a group may consist only of components that are not **A53** significant components. In these circumstances, the group engagement team can obtain sufficient appropriate audit evidence on which to base the group audit opinion by determining the type of work to be performed on the financial information of the components in accordance with paragraph 29. It is unlikely that the group engagement team will obtain sufficient appropriate audit evidence on which to base the group audit opinion if the group engagement team, or a component auditor, only tests group-wide controls and performs analytical procedures on the financial information of the components.

Involvement in the Work Performed by Component Auditors (Ref: Para. 30–31)

Factors that may affect the group engagement team's involvement in the work of the **A54** component auditor include:

(a) The significance of the component;
(b) The identified significant risks of material misstatement of the group financial statements; and
(c) The group engagement team's understanding of the component auditor.

In the case of a significant component or identified significant risks, the group engagement team performs the procedures described in paragraphs 30–31. In the case of a component that is not a significant component, the nature, timing and extent of the group engagement team's involvement in the work of the component auditor will vary based on the group engagement team's understanding of that component auditor. The fact that the component is not a significant component becomes secondary. For example, even though a component is not considered a significant component, the group engagement team nevertheless may decide to be involved in the component auditor's risk assessment, because it has less than serious concerns about the component auditor's professional competency (for example, lack of industry specific knowledge), or the component auditor does not operate in an environment that actively oversees auditors.

Forms of involvement in the work of a component auditor other than those described in **A55** paragraphs 30–31 and 42 may, based on the group engagement team's understanding of the component auditor, include one or more of the following:

(a) Meeting with component management or the component auditors to obtain an understanding of the component and its environment.
(b) Reviewing the component auditors' overall audit strategy and audit plan.
(c) Performing risk assessment procedures to identify and assess the risks of material misstatement at the component level. These may be performed with the component auditors, or by the group engagement team.
(d) Designing and performing further audit procedures. These may be designed and performed with the component auditors, or by the group engagement team.

---

[22] *ISRE 2400*, Engagements to Review Financial Statements.
ISRE 2400 has not been promulgated by the FRC for application in the UK.

[23] *ISRE (UK and Ireland) 2410*, Review of Interim Financial Information Performed by the Independent Auditor of the Entity.

(e)   Participating in the closing and other key meetings between the component auditors and component management.

(f)   Reviewing other relevant parts of the component auditors' audit documentation.

Consolidation Process

Consolidation Adjustments and Reclassifications (Ref: Para. 34)

A56   The consolidation process may require adjustments to amounts reported in the group financial statements that do not pass through the usual transaction processing systems, and may not be subject to the same internal controls to which other financial information is subject. The group engagement team's evaluation of the appropriateness, completeness and accuracy of the adjustments may include:

- Evaluating whether significant adjustments appropriately reflect the events and transactions underlying them;
- Determining whether significant adjustments have been correctly calculated, processed and authorized by group management and, where applicable, by component management;
- Determining whether significant adjustments are properly supported and sufficiently documented; and
- Checking the reconciliation and elimination of intra-group transactions and unrealized profits, and intra-group account balances.

Communication with the Component Auditor (Ref: Para. 40–41)

A57   If effective two-way communication between the group engagement team and the component auditors does not exist, there is a risk that the group engagement team may not obtain sufficient appropriate audit evidence on which to base the group audit opinion. Clear and timely communication of the group engagement team's requirements forms the basis of effective two-way communication between the group engagement team and the component auditor.

A58   The group engagement team's requirements are often communicated in a letter of instruction. Appendix 5 contains guidance on required and additional matters that may be included in such a letter of instruction. The component auditor's communication with the group engagement team often takes the form of a memorandum or report of work performed. Communication between the group engagement team and the component auditor, however, may not necessarily be in writing. For example, the group engagement team may visit the component auditor to discuss identified significant risks or review relevant parts of the component auditor's audit documentation. Nevertheless, the documentation requirements of this and other ISAs (UK) apply.

A59   In cooperating with the group engagement team, the component auditor, for example, would provide the group engagement team with access to relevant audit documentation if not prohibited by law or regulation.

A60   Where a member of the group engagement team is also a component auditor, the objective for the group engagement team to communicate clearly with the component auditor can often be achieved by means other than specific written communication. For example:

- Access by the component auditor to the overall audit strategy and audit plan may be sufficient to communicate the group engagement team's requirements set out in paragraph 40; and

- A review of the component auditor's audit documentation by the group engagement team may be sufficient to communicate matters relevant to the group engagement team's conclusion set out in paragraph 41.

Evaluating the Sufficiency and Appropriateness of Audit Evidence Obtained

Reviewing the Component Auditor's Audit Documentation (Ref: Para. 42(b))

What parts of the audit documentation of the component auditor will be relevant to the group audit may vary depending on the circumstances. Often the focus is on audit documentation that is relevant to the significant risks of material misstatement of the group financial statements. The extent of the review may be affected by the fact that the component auditor's audit documentation has been subjected to the component auditor's firm's review procedures.   **A61**

Sufficiency and Appropriateness of Audit Evidence (Ref: Para. 44–45)

If the group engagement team concludes that sufficient appropriate audit evidence on which to base the group audit opinion has not been obtained, the group engagement team may request the component auditor to perform additional procedures. If this is not feasible, the group engagement team may perform its own procedures on the financial information of the component.   **A62**

The group engagement partner's evaluation of the aggregate effect of any misstatements (either identified by the group engagement team or communicated by component auditors) allows the group engagement partner to determine whether the group financial statements as a whole are materially misstated.   **A63**

Communication with Group Management and Those Charged with Governance of the Group

Communication with Group Management (Ref: Para. 46–48)

ISA (UK) 240 (Revised June 2016) contains requirements and guidance on communication of fraud to management and, where management may be involved in the fraud, to those charged with governance.[24]   **A64**

Group management may need to keep certain material sensitive information confidential. Examples of matters that may be significant to the financial statements of the component of which component management may be unaware include the following: **A65**

- Potential litigation.
- Plans for abandonment of material operating assets.
- Subsequent events.
- Significant legal agreements.

---

[24] *ISA (UK) 240 (Revised June 2016), paragraphs 40–42.*

A65-1   Information that group management has determined needs to be kept confidential would ordinarily be known to those charged with governance of the group.[24a]

Communication with Those Charged with Governance of the Group (Ref: Para. 49)

A66   The matters the group engagement team communicates to those charged with governance of the group may include those brought to the attention of the group engagement team by component auditors that the group engagement team judges to be significant to the responsibilities of those charged with governance of the group. Communication with those charged with governance of the group takes place at various times during the group audit. For example, the matters referred to in paragraph 49(a)–(b) may be communicated after the group engagement team has determined the work to be performed on the financial information of the components. On the other hand, the matter referred to in paragraph 49(c) may be communicated at the end of the audit, and the matters referred to in paragraph 49(d)–(e) may be communicated when they occur.

A66-1   For audits of group financial statements of public interest entities, ISA (UK) 260 (Revised June 2016)[24b] requires the group engagement team to:

- confirm that the group engagement team received a confirmation from the component auditor regarding the component auditor's independence;
- report on any significant deficiencies in the parent undertaking's internal financial control system and/or in the accounting system and state whether or not the deficiencies reported have been resolved by management;
- explain the scope of consolidation and the exclusion criteria applied to non-consolidated entities, and whether those criteria are in accordance with the applicable financial reporting framework; and
- identify any audit work performed by component auditors,

in the additional report to the audit committee.

[24a] *ISA (UK) 260 (Revised June 2016), paragraph 16(c), requires that, unless all of those charged with governance are involved in managing the entity, the auditor shall communicate with those charged with governance significant matters, if any, arising from the audit that were discussed, or subject to correspondence with management.*

[24b] *ISA (UK) 260 (Revised June 2016), paragraphs 16R-2 (c), (j), (m) and (n).*

Appendix 1

Illustration of Auditor's Report Where the Group Engagement Team Is Not Able to Obtain Sufficient Appropriate Audit Evidence on Which to Base the Group Audit Opinion

The example in this Appendix has not been tailored for the UK. Illustrative auditor's reports tailored for use with audits conducted in accordance with ISAs (UK) are given in the current version of the FRC's Compendium of Illustrative Auditor's Reports.

Note: Throughout this illustrative auditor's report, the Opinion section has been positioned first in accordance with ISA 700 (Revised), and the Basis for Opinion section is positioned immediately after the Opinion section. Also, the first and last sentence that was included in the extant auditor's responsibilities section is now subsumed as part of the new Basis for Opinion section.

Illustration – Example of a Qualified Opinion Where the Group Engagement Team Is Not Able to Obtain Sufficient Appropriate Audit Evidence on Which to Base the Group Audit Opinion

For purposes of this illustrative auditor's report, the following circumstances are assumed:

- Audit of a complete set of consolidated financial statements of an entity other than a listed entity using a fair presentation framework. The audit is a group audit (i.e., ISA 600 applies).
- The consolidated financial statements are prepared by management of the entity in accordance with IFRSs (a general purpose framework).
- The terms of the audit engagement reflect the description of management's responsibility for the consolidated financial statements in ISA 210 (Revised).
- The group engagement team is unable to obtain sufficient appropriate audit evidence relating to a significant component accounted for by the equity method (recognized at \$15 million in the balance sheet, which reflects total assets of \$60 million) because the group engagement team did not have access to the accounting records, management, or auditor of the component.
- The group engagement team has read the audited financial statements of the component as of December 31, 20X1, including the auditor's report thereon, and considered related financial information kept by group management in relation to the component.
- In the group engagement partner's judgment, the effect on the group financial statements of this inability to obtain sufficient appropriate audit evidence is material but not pervasive.[25]
- The International Ethics Standards Board for Accountants' Code of Ethics for Professional Accountants comprises all of the relevant ethical requirements that apply to the audit.

---

[25] *If, in the group engagement partner's judgment, the effect on the group financial statements of the inability to obtain sufficient appropriate audit evidence is material and pervasive, the group engagement partner would disclaim an opinion in accordance with ISA 705 (Revised).*

- Based on the audit evidence obtained, the auditor has concluded that a material uncertainty does not exist related to events or conditions that may cast significant doubt on the entity's ability to continue as a going concern in accordance with ISA 570 (Revised).
- The auditor is not required, and has otherwise not decided, to communicate key audit matters in accordance with ISA 701.
- The auditor has obtained all of the other information prior to the date of the auditor's report and the qualified opinion on the consolidated financial statements also affects the other information.
- Those responsible for oversight of the consolidated financial statements differ from those responsible for the preparation of the consolidated financial statements.
- In addition to the audit of the consolidated financial statements, the auditor has other reporting responsibilities required under local law.

INDEPENDENT AUDITOR'S REPORT

To the Shareholders of ABC Company [or Other Appropriate Addressee]

Report on the Audit of the Consolidated Financial Statements[26]

Qualified Opinion

We have audited the consolidated financial statements of ABC Company and its subsidiaries (the Group), which comprise the consolidated statement of financial position as at December 31, 20X1, and the consolidated statement of comprehensive income, the statement of changes in equity and the statement of cash flows for the year then ended, and notes to the financial statements, including a summary of significant accounting policies.

In our opinion, except for the possible effects of the matter described in the Basis for Qualified Opinion section of our report, the accompanying consolidated financial statements present fairly, in all material respects, (or *give a true and fair view of*) the financial position of the Group as at December 31, 20X1, and (*of*) their financial performance and cash flows for the year then ended in accordance with International Financial Reporting Standards (IFRSs).

Basis for Qualified Opinion

ABC Company's investment in XYZ Company, a foreign associate acquired during the year and accounted for by the equity method, is carried at $15 million on the consolidated balance sheet as at December 31, 20X1, and ABC's share of XYZ's net income of $1 million is included in the consolidated income statement for the year then ended. We were unable to obtain sufficient appropriate audit evidence about the carrying amount of ABC's investment in XYZ as at December 31, 20X1 and ABC's share of XYZ's net income for the year because we were denied access to the financial information, management, and the auditors of XYZ. Consequently, we were unable to determine whether any adjustments to these amounts were necessary.

We conducted our audit in accordance with International Standards on Auditing (ISAs). Our responsibilities under those standards are further described in the *Auditor's Responsibilities for the Audit of the Consolidated Financial Statements* section of our report. We are

---

[26] *The sub-title, 'Report on the Audit of the Consolidated Financial Statements' is unnecessary in circumstances when the second sub-title, 'Report on Other Legal and Regulatory Requirements' is not applicable.*

independent of the Group in accordance with the International Ethics Standards Board for Accountants' Code of Ethics for Professional Accountants (IESBA Code), and we have fulfilled our other ethical responsibilities in accordance with the IESBA Code. We believe that the audit evidence we have obtained is sufficient and appropriate to provide a basis for our qualified audit opinion.

Other Information [or another title if appropriate such as 'Information Other than the Financial Statements and Auditor's Report Thereon']

[*Reporting in accordance with the reporting requirements in ISA 720 (Revised) – see Illustration 6 in Appendix 2 of ISA 720 (Revised). The last paragraph of the other information section in Illustration 6 would be customized to describe the specific matter giving rise to the qualified opinion that also affects the other information.*]

Responsibilities of Management and Those Charged With Governance for the Consolidated Financial Statements[27]

[*Reporting in accordance with ISA 700 (Revised)[28] – see Illustration 2 in ISA 700 (Revised).*]

Auditor's Responsibilities for the Audit of the Consolidated Financial Statements

[*Reporting in accordance with ISA 700 (Revised) – see Illustration 2 in ISA 700 (Revised). The last two paragraphs which are applicable for audits of listed entities only would not be included.*]

Report on Other Legal and Regulatory Requirements

[*Reporting in accordance with ISA 700 (Revised) – see Illustration 2 in ISA 700 (Revised).*]

[*Signature in the name of the audit firm, the personal name of the auditor, or both, as appropriate for the particular jurisdiction*]

[*Auditor Address*]

[*Date*]

---

[27] *Throughout these illustrative auditor's reports, the terms management and those charged with governance may need to be replaced by another term that is appropriate in the context of the legal framework in the particular jurisdiction.*

[28] *ISA 700 (Revised),* Forming an Opinion and Reporting on Financial Statements.

Appendix 2

(Ref: Para. A23)

Examples of Matters about Which the Group Engagement Team Obtains an Understanding

The examples provided cover a broad range of matters; however, not all matters are relevant to every group audit engagement and the list of examples is not necessarily complete.

Group-Wide Controls

1 Group-wide controls may include a combination of the following:

- Regular meetings between group and component management to discuss business developments and to review performance.
- Monitoring of components' operations and their financial results, including regular reporting routines, which enables group management to monitor components' performance against budgets, and to take appropriate action.
- Group management's risk assessment process, that is, the process for identifying, analyzing and managing business risks, including the risk of fraud, that may result in material misstatement of the group financial statements.
- Monitoring, controlling, reconciling, and eliminating intra-group transactions and unrealized profits, and intra-group account balances at group level.
- A process for monitoring the timeliness and assessing the accuracy and completeness of financial information received from components.
- A central IT system controlled by the same general IT controls for all or part of the group.
- Control activities within an IT system that is common for all or some components.
- Monitoring of controls, including activities of internal audit and self-assessment programs.
- Consistent policies and procedures, including a group financial reporting procedures manual.
- Group-wide programs, such as codes of conduct and fraud prevention programs.
- Arrangements for assigning authority and responsibility to component management.

2 The internal audit function may be regarded as part of group-wide controls, for example, when the function is centralized. ISA (UK) 610 (Revised June 2013)[29] deals with the group engagement team's evaluation of whether the internal audit function's organizational status and relevant policies and procedures adequately supports the objectivity of internal auditors, the level of competence of the internal audit function, and whether the function applies a systematic and disciplined approach where the group engagement team expects to use the function's work.

Consolidation Process

3 The group engagement team's understanding of the consolidation process may include matters such as the following:

---

[29] *ISA (UK) 610 (Revised June 2013),* Using the Work of Internal Auditors, *paragraphs 15–16.*

Matters relating to the applicable financial reporting framework:

- The extent to which component management has an understanding of the applicable financial reporting framework.
- The process for identifying and accounting for components in accordance with the applicable financial reporting framework.
- The process for identifying reportable segments for segment reporting in accordance with the applicable financial reporting framework.
- The process for identifying related party relationships and related party transactions for reporting in accordance with the applicable financial reporting framework.
- The accounting policies applied to the group financial statements, changes from those of the previous financial year, and changes resulting from new or revised standards under the applicable financial reporting framework.
- The procedures for dealing with components with financial year-ends different from the group's year-end.

Matters relating to the consolidation process:

- Group management's process for obtaining an understanding of the accounting policies used by components, and, where applicable, ensuring that uniform accounting policies are used to prepare the financial information of the components for the group financial statements, and that differences in accounting policies are identified, and adjusted where required in terms of the applicable financial reporting framework. Uniform accounting policies are the specific principles, bases, conventions, rules, and practices adopted by the group, based on the applicable financial reporting framework, that the components use to report similar transactions consistently. These policies are ordinarily described in the financial reporting procedures manual and reporting package issued by group management.
- Group management's process for ensuring complete, accurate and timely financial reporting by the components for the consolidation.
- The process for translating the financial information of foreign components into the currency of the group financial statements.
- How IT is organized for the consolidation, including the manual and automated stages of the process, and the manual and programmed controls in place at various stages of the consolidation process.
- Group management's process for obtaining information on subsequent events.

Matters relating to consolidation adjustments:

- The process for recording consolidation adjustments, including the preparation, authorization and processing of related journal entries, and the experience of personnel responsible for the consolidation.
- The consolidation adjustments required by the applicable financial reporting framework.
- Business rationale for the events and transactions that gave rise to the consolidation adjustments.
- Frequency, nature and size of transactions between components.
- Procedures for monitoring, controlling, reconciling and eliminating intra-group transactions and unrealized profits, and intra-group account balances.
- Steps taken to arrive at the fair value of acquired assets and liabilities, procedures for amortizing goodwill (where applicable), and impairment testing of goodwill, in accordance with the applicable financial reporting framework.
- Arrangements with a majority owner or minority interests regarding losses incurred by a component (for example, an obligation of the minority interest to make good such losses).

Appendix 3 (Ref: Para. A30)

Examples of Conditions or Events that May Indicate Risks of Material Misstatement of the Group Financial Statements

The examples provided cover a broad range of conditions or events; however, not all conditions or events are relevant to every group audit engagement and the list of examples is not necessarily complete.

- A complex group structure, especially where there are frequent acquisitions, disposals or reorganizations.
- Poor corporate governance structures, including decision-making processes, that are not transparent.
- Non-existent or ineffective group-wide controls, including inadequate group management information on monitoring of components' operations and their results.
- Components operating in foreign jurisdictions that may be exposed to factors such as unusual government intervention in areas such as trade and fiscal policy, and restrictions on currency and dividend movements; and fluctuations in exchange rates.
- Business activities of components that involve high risk, such as long-term contracts or trading in innovative or complex financial instruments.
- Uncertainties regarding which components' financial information require incorporation in the group financial statements in accordance with the applicable financial reporting framework, for example, whether any special-purpose entities or non-trading entities exist and require incorporation.
- Unusual related party relationships and transactions.
- Prior occurrences of intra-group account balances that did not balance or reconcile on consolidation.
- The existence of complex transactions that are accounted for in more than one component.
- Components' application of accounting policies that differ from those applied to the group financial statements.
- Components with different financial year-ends, which may be utilized to manipulate the timing of transactions.
- Prior occurrences of unauthorized or incomplete consolidation adjustments.
- Aggressive tax planning within the group, or large cash transactions with entities in tax havens.
- Frequent changes of auditors engaged to audit the financial statements of components.

Appendix 4

(Ref: Para. A35)

Examples of a Component Auditor's Confirmations

The following is not intended to be a standard letter. Confirmations may vary from one component auditor to another and from one period to the next.

Confirmations often are obtained before work on the financial information of the component commences.

[Component Auditor Letterhead]

[Date]

[To Group Engagement Partner]

This letter is provided in connection with your audit of the group financial statements of [name of parent] for the year ended [date] for the purpose of expressing an opinion on whether the group financial statements present fairly, in all material respects (give a true and fair view of) the financial position of the group as of [date] and of its financial performance and cash flows for the year then ended in accordance with [indicate applicable financial reporting framework].

We acknowledge receipt of your instructions dated [date], requesting us to perform the specified work on the financial information of [name of component] for the year ended [date].

We confirm that:

1. We will be able to comply with the instructions. / We advise you that we will not be able to comply with the following instructions [specify instructions] for the following reasons [specify reasons].
2. The instructions are clear and we understand them. / We would appreciate it if you could clarify the following instructions [specify instructions].
3. We will cooperate with you and provide you with access to relevant audit documentation.

We acknowledge that:

1. The financial information of [name of component] will be included in the group financial statements of [name of parent].
2. You may consider it necessary to be involved in the work you have requested us to perform on the financial information of [name of component] for the year ended [date].
3. You intend to evaluate and, if considered appropriate, use our work for the audit of the group financial statements of [name of parent].

In connection with the work that we will perform on the financial information of [name of component], a [describe component, for example, wholly-owned subsidiary, subsidiary, joint venture, investee accounted for by the equity or cost methods of accounting] of [name of parent], we confirm the following:

1. We have an understanding of [indicate relevant ethical requirements] that is sufficient to fulfill our responsibilities in the audit of the group financial statements, and will comply therewith. In particular, and with respect to [name of parent] and the other components in the group, we are independent within the meaning of [indicate relevant ethical requirements] and comply with the applicable requirements of [refer to rules] promulgated by [name of regulatory agency].

2. We have an understanding of International Standards on Auditing and [indicate other national standards applicable to the audit of the group financial statements] that is sufficient to fulfill our responsibilities in the audit of the group financial statements and will conduct our work on the financial information of [name of component] for the year ended [date] in accordance with those standards.

3. We possess the special skills (for example, industry specific knowledge) necessary to perform the work on the financial information of the particular component.

4. We have an understanding of [indicate applicable financial reporting framework or group financial reporting procedures manual] that is sufficient to fulfill our responsibilities in the audit of the group financial statements.

We will inform you of any changes in the above representations during the course of our work on the financial information of [name of component].

[Auditor's signature]

[Date]

[Auditor's address]

Appendix 5

(Ref: Para. A58)

Required and Additional Matters Included in the Group Engagement Team's Letter of Instruction

Matters required by this ISA (UK) to be communicated to the component auditor are shown in italicized text.

Matters that are relevant to the planning of the work of the component auditor:

- *A request for the component auditor, knowing the context in which the group engagement team will use the work of the component auditor, to confirm that the component auditor will cooperate with the group engagement team.*
- The timetable for completing the audit.
- Dates of planned visits by group management and the group engagement team, and dates of planned meetings with component management and the component auditor.
- A list of key contacts.
- *The work to be performed by the component auditor, the use to be made of that work,* and arrangements for coordinating efforts at the initial stage of and during the audit, including the group engagement team's planned involvement in the work of the component auditor.
- *The ethical requirements that are relevant to the group audit and, in particular, the independence requirements,* for example, where the group auditor is prohibited by law or regulation from using internal auditors to provide direct assistance, it is relevant for the group auditor to consider whether the prohibition also extends to component auditors and, if so, to address this in the communication to the component auditors.[30]
- *In the case of an audit or review of the financial information of the component, component materiality (and, if applicable, the materiality level or levels for particular classes of transactions, account balances or disclosures), and the threshold above which misstatements cannot be regarded as clearly trivial to the group financial statements.*
- *A list of related parties prepared by group management, and any other related parties that the group engagement team is aware of, and a request that the component auditor communicates on a timely basis to the group engagement team related parties not previously identified by group management or the group engagement team.*
- Work to be performed on intra-group transactions and unrealized profits and intra-group account balances.
- Guidance on other statutory reporting responsibilities, for example, reporting on group management's assertion on the effectiveness of internal control.
- Where time lag between completion of the work on the financial information of the components and the group engagement team's conclusion on the group financial statements is likely, specific instructions for a subsequent events review.

---

[30] *ISA 610 (Revised June 2013),* Using the Work of Internal Auditors, *paragraph A31.*
The use of internal auditors to provide direct assistance is prohibited in an audit conducted in accordance with ISAs (UK). For a group audit this prohibition extends to the work of any component auditor which is relied upon by the group auditor, including for overseas components – see ISA (UK) 610 (Revised June 2013), paragraph 5-1.

Matters that are relevant to the conduct of the work of the component auditor

- The findings of the group engagement team's tests of control activities of a processing system that is common for all or some components, and tests of controls to be performed by the component auditor.
- *Identified significant risks of material misstatement of the group financial statements, due to fraud or error, that are relevant to the work of the component auditor, and a request that the component auditor communicates on a timely basis any other significant risks of material misstatement of the group financial statements, due to fraud or error, identified in the component and the component auditor's response to such risks.*
- The findings of the internal audit function, based on work performed on controls at or relevant to components.
- A request for timely communication of audit evidence obtained from performing work on the financial information of the components that contradicts the audit evidence on which the group engagement team originally based the risk assessment performed at group level.
- A request for a written representation on component management's compliance with the applicable financial reporting framework, or a statement that differences between the accounting policies applied to the financial information of the component and those applied to the group financial statements have been disclosed.
- Matters to be documented by the component auditor.

Other information

- A request that the following be reported to the group engagement team on a timely basis:
  o Significant accounting, financial reporting and auditing matters, including accounting estimates and related judgments.
  o Matters relating to the going concern status of the component.
  o Matters relating to litigation and claims.
  o Significant deficiencies in internal control that the component auditor has identified during the performance of the work on the financial information of the component, and information that indicates the existence of fraud.
- A request that the group engagement team be notified of any significant or unusual events as early as possible.
- *A request that the matters listed in paragraph 41 be communicated to the group engagement team when the work on the financial information of the component is completed.*

International Standard on Auditing (UK) 610 (Revised June 2013)

Using the work of internal auditors

(Effective for audits of financial statements for periods ending on or after 15 June 2014)

Contents

International Standard on Auditing (UK) (ISA (UK)) 610 (Revised June 2013), *Using the Work of Internal Auditors*, should be read in conjunction with ISA (UK) 200 (Revised June 2016), *Overall Objectives of the Independent Auditor and the Conduct of an Audit in Accordance with International Standards on Auditing (UK)*.

Introduction

Scope of this ISA (UK)

1   This International Standard on Auditing (UK) (ISA (UK)) deals with the external auditor's responsibilities if using the work of internal auditors. This includes (a) using the work of the internal audit function in obtaining audit evidence and (b) using internal auditors to provide direct assistance under the direction, supervision and review of the external auditor.

2   This ISA (UK) does not apply if the entity does not have an internal audit function. (Ref: Para. A2)

3   If the entity has an internal audit function, the requirements in this ISA (UK) relating to using the work of that function do not apply if:

(a)   The responsibilities and activities of the function are not relevant to the audit; or
(b)   Based on the auditor's preliminary understanding of the function obtained as a result of procedures performed under ISA (UK) 315 (Revised June 2016),[1] the external auditor does not expect to use the work of the function in obtaining audit evidence.

Nothing in this ISA (UK) requires the external auditor to use the work of the internal audit function to modify the nature or timing, or reduce the extent, of audit procedures to be performed directly by the external auditor; it remains a decision of the external auditor in establishing the overall audit strategy.

4   Furthermore, the requirements in this ISA (UK) relating to direct assistance do not apply if the external auditor does not plan to use internal auditors to provide direct assistance.

5   In some jurisdictions, the external auditor may be prohibited, or restricted to some extent, by law or regulation from using the work of the internal audit function or using internal auditors to provide direct assistance. The ISAs (UK) do not override laws or regulations that govern an audit of financial statements.[2] Such prohibitions or restrictions will therefore not prevent the external auditor from complying with the ISAs (UK). (Ref: Para. A31)

5-1   The use of internal auditors to provide direct assistance is prohibited in an audit conducted in accordance with ISAs (UK). For a group audit this prohibition extends to the work of any component auditor which is relied upon by the group auditor, including for overseas components. Accordingly, the requirements and related application material in this ISA (UK) relating to direct assistance are not applicable.[2a]

Relationship between ISA (UK) 315 (Revised June 2016) and ISA (UK) 610 (Revised June 2013)

6   Many entities establish internal audit functions as part of their internal control and governance structures. The objectives and scope of an internal audit function, the nature of its responsibilities and its organizational status, including the function's authority and

---

[1]   *ISA (UK) 315 (Revised June 2016)*, Identifying and Assessing the Risks of Material Misstatement through Understanding the Entity and Its Environment.

[2]   *ISA (UK) 200 (Revised June 2016)*, Overall Objectives of the Independent Auditor and the Conduct of an Audit in Accordance with International Standards on Auditing (UK), *paragraph A55.*

[2a]   *The non-applicable requirements are those set out in paragraphs 27–35 and 37. The non-applicable application material is that set out in paragraphs A32–A41.*

accountability, vary widely and depend on the size and structure of the entity and the requirements of management and, where applicable, those charged with governance.

ISA (UK) 315 (Revised June 2016) addresses how the knowledge and experience of the internal audit function can inform the external auditor's understanding of the entity and its environment and identification and assessment of risks of material misstatement. ISA (UK) 315 (Revised June 2016)[3] also explains how effective communication between the internal and external auditors also creates an environment in which the external auditor can be informed of significant matters that may affect the external auditor's work. **7**

Depending on whether the internal audit function's organizational status and relevant policies and procedures adequately support the objectivity of the internal auditors, the level of competency of the internal audit function, and whether the function applies a systematic and disciplined approach, the external auditor may also be able to use the work of the internal audit function in a constructive and complementary manner. This ISA (UK) addresses the external auditor's responsibilities when, based on the external auditor's preliminary understanding of the internal audit function obtained as a result of procedures performed under ISA (UK) 315 (Revised June 2016), the external auditor expects to use the work of the internal audit function as part of the audit evidence obtained.[4] Such use of that work modifies the nature or timing, or reduces the extent, of audit procedures to be performed directly by the external auditor. **8**

In addition, this ISA (UK) also addresses the external auditor's responsibilities if considering using internal auditors to provide direct assistance under the direction, supervision and review of the external auditor. **9**

There may be individuals in an entity that perform procedures similar to those performed by an internal audit function. However, unless performed by an objective and competent function that applies a systematic and disciplined approach, including quality control, such procedures would be considered internal controls and obtaining evidence regarding the effectiveness of such controls would be part of the auditor's responses to assessed risks in accordance with ISA (UK) 330 (Revised June 2016).[5] **10**

The External Auditor's Responsibility for the Audit

The external auditor has sole responsibility for the audit opinion expressed, and that responsibility is not reduced by the external auditor's use of the work of the internal audit function or internal auditors to provide direct assistance on the engagement. Although they may perform audit procedures similar to those performed by the external auditor, neither the internal audit function nor the internal auditors are independent of the entity as is required of the external auditor in an audit of financial statements in accordance with ISA (UK) 200 (Revised June 2016).[6] This ISA (UK), therefore, defines the conditions that are necessary for the external auditor to be able to use the work of internal auditors. It also defines the necessary work effort to obtain sufficient appropriate evidence that the work of the internal audit function, or internal auditors providing direct assistance, is adequate for the purposes of the audit. The requirements are designed to provide a framework for the **11**

---

[3] *ISA (UK) 315 (Revised June 2016), paragraph A116.*

[4] *See paragraphs 15–25.*

[5] *ISA (UK) 330 (Revised June 2016),* The Auditor's Responses to Assessed Risks.

[6] *ISA (UK) 200 (Revised June 2016), paragraph 14.*

external auditor's judgments regarding the use of the work of internal auditors to prevent over or undue use of such work.

Effective Date

12 This ISA (UK) is effective for audits of financial statements for periods ending on or after 15 June 2014.[6a]

Objectives

13 The objectives of the external auditor, where the entity has an internal audit function and the external auditor expects to use the work of the function to modify the nature or timing, or reduce the extent, of audit procedures to be performed directly by the external auditor, or to use internal auditors to provide direct assistance, are:

(a) To determine whether the work of the internal audit function or direct assistance from internal auditors can be used, and if so, in which areas and to what extent;

and having made that determination:

(b) If using the work of the internal audit function, to determine whether that work is adequate for purposes of the audit; and

(c) If using internal auditors to provide direct assistance, to appropriately direct, supervise and review their work.

Definitions

14 For purposes of the ISAs (UK), the following terms have the meanings attributed below:

(a) Internal audit function – A function of an entity that performs assurance and consulting activities designed to evaluate and improve the effectiveness of the entity's governance, risk management and internal control processes. (Ref: Para. A1–A4)

(b) Direct assistance – The use of internal auditors to perform audit procedures under the direction, supervision and review of the external auditor.

Requirements

Determining Whether, in Which Areas, and to What Extent the Work of the Internal Audit Function Can Be Used

Evaluating the Internal Audit Function

15 The external auditor shall determine whether the work of the internal audit function can be used for purposes of the audit by evaluating the following:

(a) The extent to which the internal audit function's organizational status and relevant policies and procedures support the objectivity of the internal auditors; (Ref: Para. A5–A9)

(b) The level of competence of the internal audit function; and (Ref: Para. A5–A9)

[6a] *For the purpose of audits under ISAs as issued by the IAASB, the material pertaining to the use of direct assistance has an effective date of audits of financial statements for periods ending on or after 15 December 2014. However, as stated in paragraph 5-1, the use of internal auditors to provide direct assistance is prohibited in an audit conducted in accordance with ISAs (UK) – such prohibition being effective from the effective date of this ISA (UK), audits of financial statements for periods ending on or after 15 June 2014.*

(c) Whether the internal audit function applies a systematic and disciplined approach, including quality control. (Ref: Para. A10–A11)

The external auditor shall not use the work of the internal audit function if the external auditor determines that: **16**

(a) The function's organizational status and relevant policies and procedures do not adequately support the objectivity of internal auditors;
(b) The function lacks sufficient competence; or
(c) The function does not apply a systematic and disciplined approach, including quality control. (Ref: Para. A12–A14)

Determining the Nature and Extent of Work of the Internal Audit Function that Can Be Used

As a basis for determining the areas and the extent to which the work of the internal audit function can be used, the external auditor shall consider the nature and scope of the work that has been performed, or is planned to be performed, by the internal audit function and its relevance to the external auditor's overall audit strategy and audit plan. (Ref: Para. A15–A17) **17**

The external auditor shall make all significant judgments in the audit engagement and, to prevent undue use of the work of the internal audit function, shall plan to use less of the work of the function and perform more of the work directly: (Ref: Para. A15–A17) **18**

(a) The more judgment is involved in:
　(i) Planning and performing relevant audit procedures; and
　(ii) Evaluating the audit evidence gathered; (Ref: Para. A18–A19)
(b) The higher the assessed risk of material misstatement at the assertion level, with special consideration given to risks identified as significant; (Ref: Para. A20–A22)
(c) The less the internal audit function's organizational status and relevant policies and procedures adequately support the objectivity of the internal auditors; and
(d) The lower the level of competence of the internal audit function.

The external auditor shall also evaluate whether, in aggregate, using the work of the internal audit function to the extent planned would still result in the external auditor being sufficiently involved in the audit, given the external auditor's sole responsibility for the audit opinion expressed. (Ref: Para. A15–A22) **19**

The external auditor shall, in communicating with those charged with governance an overview of the planned scope and timing of the audit in accordance with ISA (UK) 260 (Revised June 2016),[7] communicate how the external auditor has planned to use the work of the internal audit function. (Ref: Para. A23) **20**

Using the Work of the Internal Audit Function

If the external auditor plans to use the work of the internal audit function, the external auditor shall discuss the planned use of its work with the function as a basis for coordinating their respective activities. (Ref: Para. A24–A26) **21**

The external auditor shall read the reports of the internal audit function relating to the work of the function that the external auditor plans to use to obtain an understanding of the nature and extent of audit procedures it performed and the related findings. **22**

---

[7] *ISA (UK) 260 (Revised June 2016)*, Communication with Those Charged with Governance, *paragraph 15.*

23   The external auditor shall perform sufficient audit procedures on the body of work of the internal audit function as a whole that the external auditor plans to use to determine its adequacy for purposes of the audit, including evaluating whether:

(a) The work of the function had been properly planned, performed, supervised, reviewed and documented;

(b) Sufficient appropriate evidence had been obtained to enable the function to draw reasonable conclusions; and

(c) Conclusions reached are appropriate in the circumstances and the reports prepared by the function are consistent with the results of the work performed. (Ref: Para. A27–A30)

24   The nature and extent of the external auditor's audit procedures shall be responsive to the external auditor's evaluation of:

(a) The amount of judgment involved;

(b) The assessed risk of material misstatement;

(c) The extent to which the internal audit function's organizational status and relevant policies and procedures support the objectivity of the internal auditors; and

(d) The level of competence of the function;[8] (Ref: Para. A27–A29)

and shall include reperformance of some of the work. (Ref: Para. A30)

25   The external auditor shall also evaluate whether the external auditor's conclusions regarding the internal audit function in paragraph 15 of this ISA (UK) and the determination of the nature and extent of use of the work of the function for purposes of the audit in paragraphs 18–19 of this ISA (UK) remain appropriate.

Determining Whether, in Which Areas, and to What Extent Internal Auditors Can Be Used to Provide Direct Assistance

Determining Whether Internal Auditors Can Be Used to Provide Direct Assistance for Purposes of the Audit

26   The external auditor may be prohibited by law or regulation from obtaining direct assistance from internal auditors. If so, paragraphs 27–35 and 37 do not apply.[8a] (Ref: Para. A31)

27   If using internal auditors to provide direct assistance is not prohibited by law or regulation, and the external auditor plans to use internal auditors to provide direct assistance on the audit, the external auditor shall evaluate the existence and significance of threats to objectivity and the level of competence of the internal auditors who will be providing such assistance. The external auditor's evaluation of the existence and significance of threats to the internal auditors' objectivity shall include inquiry of the internal auditors regarding interests and relationships that may create a threat to their objectivity. (Ref: Para. A32–A34)

28   The external auditor shall not use an internal auditor to provide direct assistance if:

(a) There are significant threats to the objectivity of the internal auditor; or

(b) The internal auditor lacks sufficient competence to perform the proposed work. (Ref: Para. A32–A34)

---

[8] *See paragraph 18.*

[8a] *The use of internal auditors to provide direct assistance is prohibited in an audit conducted in accordance with ISAs (UK). See paragraph 5-1 above of this ISA (UK).*

Determining the Nature and Extent of Work that Can Be Assigned to Internal Auditors Providing Direct Assistance

In determining the nature and extent of work that may be assigned to internal auditors and the nature, timing and extent of direction, supervision and review that is appropriate in the circumstances, the external auditor shall consider: **29**

(a) The amount of judgment involved in:
  (i) Planning and performing relevant audit procedures; and
  (ii) Evaluating the audit evidence gathered;
(b) The assessed risk of material misstatement; and
(c) The external auditor's evaluation of the existence and significance of threats to the objectivity and level of competence of the internal auditors who will be providing such assistance. (Ref: Para. A35–A39)

The external auditor shall not use internal auditors to provide direct assistance to perform procedures that: **30**

(a) Involve making significant judgments in the audit; (Ref: Para. A19)
(b) Relate to higher assessed risks of material misstatement where the judgment required in performing the relevant audit procedures or evaluating the audit evidence gathered is more than limited; (Ref: Para. A38)
(c) Relate to work with which the internal auditors have been involved and which has already been, or will be, reported to management or those charged with governance by the internal audit function; or
(d) Relate to decisions the external auditor makes in accordance with this ISA (UK) regarding the internal audit function and the use of its work or direct assistance. (Ref: Para. A35–A39)

Having appropriately evaluated whether and, if so, to what extent internal auditors can be used to provide direct assistance on the audit, the external auditor shall, in communicating with those charged with governance an overview of the planned scope and timing of the audit in accordance with ISA (UK) 260 (Revised June 2016),[9] communicate the nature and extent of the planned use of internal auditors to provide direct assistance so as to reach a mutual understanding that such use is not excessive in the circumstances of the engagement. (Ref: Para. A39)   **31**

The external auditor shall evaluate whether, in aggregate, using internal auditors to provide direct assistance to the extent planned, together with the planned use of the work of the internal audit function, would still result in the external auditor being sufficiently involved in the audit, given the external auditor's sole responsibility for the audit opinion expressed.   **32**

Using Internal Auditors to Provide Direct Assistance

Prior to using internal auditors to provide direct assistance for purposes of the audit, the external auditor shall: **33**

(a) Obtain written agreement from an authorized representative of the entity that the internal auditors will be allowed to follow the external auditor's instructions, and that the entity will not intervene in the work the internal auditor performs for the external auditor; and
(b) Obtain written agreement from the internal auditors that they will keep confidential specific matters as instructed by the external auditor and inform the external auditor of any threat to their objectivity.

---

[9] *ISA (UK) 260 (Revised June 2016), paragraph 15.*

34   The external auditor shall direct, supervise and review the work performed by internal auditors on the engagement in accordance with ISA (UK) 220 (Revised June 2016).[10] In so doing:

(a)   The nature, timing and extent of direction, supervision, and review shall recognize that the internal auditors are not independent of the entity and be responsive to the outcome of the evaluation of the factors in paragraph 29 of this ISA (UK); and

(b)   The review procedures shall include the external auditor checking back to the underlying audit evidence for some of the work performed by the internal auditors.

The direction, supervision and review by the external auditor of the work performed by the internal auditors shall be sufficient in order for the external auditor to be satisfied that the internal auditors have obtained sufficient appropriate audit evidence to support the conclusions based on that work. (Ref: Para. A40–A41)

35   In directing, supervising and reviewing the work performed by internal auditors, the external auditor shall remain alert for indications that the external auditor's evaluations in paragraph 27 are no longer appropriate.

Documentation

36   If the external auditor uses the work of the internal audit function, the external auditor shall include in the audit documentation:

(a)   The evaluation of:
   (i)   Whether the function's organizational status and relevant policies and procedures adequately support the objectivity of the internal auditors;
   (ii)   The level of competence of the function; and
   (iii)   Whether the function applies a systematic and disciplined approach, including quality control;

(b)   The nature and extent of the work used and the basis for that decision; and

(c)   The audit procedures performed by the external auditor to evaluate the adequacy of the work used.

37   If the external auditor uses internal auditors to provide direct assistance on the audit, the external auditor shall include in the audit documentation:

(a)   The evaluation of the existence and significance of threats to the objectivity of the internal auditors, and the level of competence of the internal auditors used to provide direct assistance;

(b)   The basis for the decision regarding the nature and extent of the work performed by the internal auditors;

(c)   Who reviewed the work performed and the date and extent of that review in accordance with ISA (UK) 230 (Revised June 2016);[11]

(d)   The written agreements obtained from an authorized representative of the entity and the internal auditors under paragraph 33 of this ISA (UK); and

(e)   The working papers prepared by the internal auditors who provided direct assistance on the audit engagement.

---

[10]   *ISA (UK) 220 (Revised June 2016)*, Quality Control for an Audit of Financial Statements.

[11]   *ISA (UK) 230 (Revised June 2016)*, Audit Documentation.

Application and Other Explanatory Material

Definition of Internal Audit Function (Ref: Para. 2, 14(a))

The objectives and scope of internal audit functions typically include assurance and **A1** consulting activities designed to evaluate and improve the effectiveness of the entity's governance processes, risk management and internal control such as the following:

Activities Relating to Governance

- The internal audit function may assess the governance process in its accomplishment of objectives on ethics and values, performance management and accountability, communicating risk and control information to appropriate areas of the organization and effectiveness of communication among those charged with governance, external and internal auditors, and management.

Activities Relating to Risk Management

- The internal audit function may assist the entity by identifying and evaluating significant exposures to risk and contributing to the improvement of risk management and internal control (including effectiveness of the financial reporting process).
- The internal audit function may perform procedures to assist the entity in the detection of fraud.

Activities Relating to Internal Control

- Evaluation of internal control. The internal audit function may be assigned specific responsibility for reviewing controls, evaluating their operation and recommending improvements thereto. In doing so, the internal audit function provides assurance on the control. For example, the internal audit function might plan and perform tests or other procedures to provide assurance to management and those charged with governance regarding the design, implementation and operating effectiveness of internal control, including those controls that are relevant to the audit.
- Examination of financial and operating information. The internal audit function may be assigned to review the means used to identify, recognize, measure, classify and report financial and operating information, and to make specific inquiry into individual items, including detailed testing of transactions, balances and procedures.
- Review of operating activities. The internal audit function may be assigned to review the economy, efficiency and effectiveness of operating activities, including non-financial activities of an entity.
- Review of compliance with laws and regulations. The internal audit function may be assigned to review compliance with laws, regulations and other external requirements, and with management policies and directives and other internal requirements.

Activities similar to those performed by an internal audit function may be conducted by **A2** functions with other titles within an entity. Some or all of the activities of an internal audit function may also be outsourced to a third-party service provider. Neither the title of the function, nor whether it is performed by the entity or a third-party service provider, are sole determinants of whether or not the external auditor can use the work of the function. Rather, it is the nature of the activities; the extent to which the internal audit function's organizational status and relevant policies and procedures support the objectivity of the internal auditors; competence; and systematic and disciplined approach of the function that are relevant. References in this ISA (UK) to the work of the internal audit function include relevant activities of other functions or third-party providers that have these characteristics.

In addition, those in the entity with operational and managerial duties and responsibilities **A3** outside of the internal audit function would ordinarily face threats to their objectivity that would preclude them from being treated as part of an internal audit function for the purpose of this ISA (UK), although they may perform control activities that can be tested in accordance with ISA (UK) 330 (Revised June 2016).[12] For this reason, monitoring controls performed by an owner-manager would not be considered equivalent to an internal audit function.

A4   While the objectives of an entity's internal audit function and the external auditor differ, the function may perform audit procedures similar to those performed by the external auditor in an audit of financial statements. If so, the external auditor may make use of the function for purposes of the audit in one or more of the following ways:

- To obtain information that is relevant to the external auditor's assessments of the risks of material misstatement due to error or fraud. In this regard, ISA (UK) 315 (Revised June 2016)[13] requires the external auditor to obtain an understanding of the nature of the internal audit function's responsibilities, its status within the organization, and the activities performed, or to be performed, and make inquiries of appropriate individuals within the internal audit function (if the entity has such a function); or
- Unless prohibited, or restricted to some extent, by law or regulation, the external auditor, after appropriate evaluation, may decide to use work that has been performed by the internal audit function during the period in partial substitution for audit evidence to be obtained directly by the external auditor.[14]

In addition, unless prohibited, or restricted to some extent, by law or regulation, the external auditor may use internal auditors to perform audit procedures under the direction, supervision and review of the external auditor (referred to as 'direct assistance' in this ISA (UK)).[15]

Determining Whether, in Which Areas, and to What Extent the Work of the Internal Audit Function Can Be Used

Evaluating the Internal Audit Function

Objectivity and Competence (Ref: Para. 15(a)–(b))

A5   The external auditor exercises professional judgment in determining whether the work of the internal audit function can be used for purposes of the audit, and the nature and extent to which the work of the internal audit function can be used in the circumstances.

A6   The extent to which the internal audit function's organizational status and relevant policies and procedures support the objectivity of the internal auditors and the level of competence of the function are particularly important in determining whether to use and, if so, the nature and extent of the use of the work of the function that is appropriate in the circumstances.

A7   Objectivity refers to the ability to perform those tasks without allowing bias, conflict of interest or undue influence of others to override professional judgments. Factors that may affect the external auditor's evaluation include the following:

[12] *See paragraph 10.*

[13] *ISA (UK) 315 (Revised June 2016), paragraph 6(a).*

[14] *See paragraphs 15–25.*

[15] *See paragraphs 26–35.*
The use of internal auditors to provide direct assistance is prohibited in an audit conducted in accordance with ISAs (UK) – see paragraph 5-1.

- Whether the organizational status of the internal audit function, including the function's authority and accountability, supports the ability of the function to be free from bias, conflict of interest or undue influence of others to override professional judgments. For example, whether the internal audit function reports to those charged with governance or an officer with appropriate authority, or if the function reports to management, whether it has direct access to those charged with governance.
- Whether the internal audit function is free of any conflicting responsibilities, for example, having managerial or operational duties or responsibilities that are outside of the internal audit function.
- Whether those charged with governance oversee employment decisions related to the internal audit function, for example, determining the appropriate remuneration policy.
- Whether there are any constraints or restrictions placed on the internal audit function by management or those charged with governance, for example, in communicating the internal audit function's findings to the external auditor.
- Whether the internal auditors are members of relevant professional bodies and their memberships obligate their compliance with relevant professional standards relating to objectivity, or whether their internal policies achieve the same objectives.

Competence of the internal audit function refers to the attainment and maintenance of knowledge and skills of the function as a whole at the level required to enable assigned tasks to be performed diligently and in accordance with applicable professional standards. Factors that may affect the external auditor's determination include the following: **A8**

- Whether the internal audit function is adequately and appropriately resourced relative to the size of the entity and the nature of its operations.
- Whether there are established policies for hiring, training and assigning internal auditors to internal audit engagements.
- Whether the internal auditors have adequate technical training and proficiency in auditing. Relevant criteria that may be considered by the external auditor in making the assessment may include, for example, the internal auditors' possession of a relevant professional designation and experience.
- Whether the internal auditors possess the required knowledge relating to the entity's financial reporting and the applicable financial reporting framework and whether the internal audit function possesses the necessary skills (for example, industry-specific knowledge) to perform work related to the entity's financial statements.
- Whether the internal auditors are members of relevant professional bodies that oblige them to comply with the relevant professional standards including continuing professional development requirements.

Objectivity and competence may be viewed as a continuum. The more the internal audit function's organizational status and relevant policies and procedures adequately support the objectivity of the internal auditors and the higher the level of competence of the function, the more likely the external auditor may make use of the work of the function and in more areas. However, an organizational status and relevant policies and procedures that provide strong support for the objectivity of the internal auditors cannot compensate for the lack of sufficient competence of the internal audit function. Equally, a high level of competence of the internal audit function cannot compensate for an organizational status and policies and procedures that do not adequately support the objectivity of the internal auditors. **A9**

Application of a Systematic and Disciplined Approach (Ref: Para. 15(c))

The application of a systematic and disciplined approach to planning, performing, supervising, reviewing and documenting its activities distinguishes the activities of the internal audit function from other monitoring control activities that may be performed within the entity. **A10**

A11   Factors that may affect the external auditor's determination of whether the internal audit function applies a systematic and disciplined approach include the following:

- The existence, adequacy and use of documented internal audit procedures or guidance covering such areas as risk assessments, work programs, documentation and reporting, the nature and extent of which is commensurate with the size and circumstances of an entity.
- Whether the internal audit function has appropriate quality control policies and procedures, for example, such as those policies and procedures in ISQC (UK) 1 (Revised June 2016)[16] that would be applicable to an internal audit function (such as those relating to leadership, human resources and engagement performance) or quality control requirements in standards set by the relevant professional bodies for internal auditors. Such bodies may also establish other appropriate requirements such as conducting periodic external quality assessments.

Circumstances When Work of the Internal Audit Function Cannot Be Used (Ref: Para. 16)

A12   The external auditor's evaluation of whether the internal audit function's organizational status and relevant policies and procedures adequately support the objectivity of the internal auditors, the level of competence of the internal audit function, and whether it applies a systematic and disciplined approach may indicate that the risks to the quality of the work of the function are too significant and therefore it is not appropriate to use any of the work of the function as audit evidence.

A13   Consideration of the factors in paragraphs A7, A8 and A11 of this ISA (UK) individually and in aggregate is important because an individual factor is often not sufficient to conclude that the work of the internal audit function cannot be used for purposes of the audit. For example, the internal audit function's organizational status is particularly important in evaluating threats to the objectivity of the internal auditors. If the internal audit function reports to management, this would be considered a significant threat to the function's objectivity unless other factors such as those described in paragraph A7 of this ISA (UK) collectively provide sufficient safeguards to reduce the threat to an acceptable level.

A14   In addition, the IESBA Code[17] states that a self-review threat is created when the external auditor accepts an engagement to provide internal audit services to an audit client, and the results of those services will be used in conducting the audit. This is because of the possibility that the engagement team will use the results of the internal audit service without properly evaluating those results or without exercising the same level of professional skepticism as would be exercised when the internal audit work is performed by individuals who are not members of the firm. The IESBA Code[18] discusses the prohibitions that apply in certain circumstances and the threats and the safeguards that can be applied to reduce the threats to an acceptable level in other circumstances.

A14-1   Auditors in the UK are subject to ethical requirements from two sources: the FRC's Ethical Standard concerning the integrity, objectivity and independence of the auditor, and the ethical pronouncements established by the auditor's relevant professional

---

[16] *International Standard on Quality Control (ISQC) (UK) 1 (Revised June 2016)*, Quality Control for Firms that Perform Audits and Reviews of Financial Statements, and Other Assurance and Related Services Engagements.

[17] *The International Ethics Standards Board for Accountants' (IESBA)* Code of Ethics for Professional Accountants *(IESBA Code), Section 290.199.*

[18] *IESBA Code, Section 290.195–290.200.*

body. Requirements and guidance concerning the provision of internal audit services, including to address the self-review threat, are set out in the FRC's Ethical Standard.[18a]

Determining the Nature and Extent of Work of the Internal Audit Function that Can Be Used

Factors Affecting the Determination of the Nature and Extent of the Work of the Internal Audit Function that Can Be Used (Ref: Para. 17–19)

Once the external auditor has determined that the work of the internal audit function can be used for purposes of the audit, a first consideration is whether the planned nature and scope of the work of the internal audit function that has been performed, or is planned to be performed, is relevant to the overall audit strategy and audit plan that the external auditor has established in accordance with ISA (UK) 300 (Revised June 2016).[19]   **A15**

Examples of work of the internal audit function that can be used by the external auditor include the following: **A16**

- Testing of the operating effectiveness of controls.
- Substantive procedures involving limited judgment.
- Observations of inventory counts.
- Tracing transactions through the information system relevant to financial reporting.
- Testing of compliance with regulatory requirements.
- In some circumstances, audits or reviews of the financial information of subsidiaries that are not significant components to the group (where this does not conflict with the requirements of ISA (UK) 600 (Revised June 2016)).[20]

The external auditor's determination of the planned nature and extent of use of the work of the internal audit function will be influenced by the external auditor's evaluation of the extent to which the internal audit function's organizational status and relevant policies and procedures adequately support the objectivity of the internal auditors and the level of competence of the internal audit function in paragraph 18 of this ISA (UK). In addition, the amount of judgment needed in planning, performing and evaluating such work and the assessed risk of material misstatement at the assertion level are inputs to the external auditor's determination. Further, there are circumstances in which the external auditor cannot use the work of the internal audit function for purpose of the audit as described in paragraph 16 of this ISA (UK).   **A17**

Judgments in planning and performing audit procedures and evaluating results (Ref: Para. 18(a), 30(a))

The greater the judgment needed to be exercised in planning and performing the audit procedures and evaluating the audit evidence, the external auditor will need to perform more procedures directly in accordance with paragraph 18 of this ISA (UK), because using the work of the internal audit function alone will not provide the external auditor with sufficient appropriate audit evidence.   **A18**

[18a] *FRC's Ethical Standard, Section 5*, Non-audit/Additional Services.

[19] *ISA (UK) 300 (Revised June 2016)*, Planning an Audit of Financial Statements.

[20] *ISA (UK) 600 (Revised June 2016)*, Special Considerations—Audits of Group Financial Statements (Including the Work of Component Auditors).

A19   Since the external auditor has sole responsibility for the audit opinion expressed, the external auditor needs to make the significant judgments in the audit engagement in accordance with paragraph 18. Significant judgments include the following:

- Assessing the risks of material misstatement;
- Evaluating the sufficiency of tests performed;
- Evaluating the appropriateness of management's use of the going concern assumption;
- Evaluating significant accounting estimates; and
- Evaluating the adequacy of disclosures in the financial statements, and other matters affecting the auditor's report.

Assessed risk of material misstatement (Ref: Para. 18(b))

A20   For a particular account balance, class of transaction or disclosure, the higher an assessed risk of material misstatement at the assertion level, the more judgment is often involved in planning and performing the audit procedures and evaluating the results thereof. In such circumstances, the external auditor will need to perform more procedures directly in accordance with paragraph 18 of this ISA (UK), and accordingly, make less use of the work of the internal audit function in obtaining sufficient appropriate audit evidence. Furthermore, as explained in ISA (UK) 200 (Revised June 2016),[21] the higher the assessed risks of material misstatement, the more persuasive the audit evidence required by the external auditor will need to be, and, therefore, the external auditor will need to perform more of the work directly.

A21   As explained in ISA (UK) 315 (Revised June 2016),[22] significant risks require special audit consideration and therefore the external auditor's ability to use the work of the internal audit function in relation to significant risks will be restricted to procedures that involve limited judgment. In addition, where the risk of material misstatement is other than low, the use of the work of the internal audit function alone is unlikely to reduce audit risk to an acceptably low level and eliminate the need for the external auditor to perform some tests directly.

A22   Carrying out procedures in accordance with this ISA (UK) may cause the external auditor to reevaluate the external auditor's assessment of the risks of material misstatement. Consequently, this may affect the external auditor's determination of whether to use the work of the internal audit function and whether further application of this ISA (UK) is necessary.

Communication with Those Charged with Governance (Ref: Para. 20)

A23   In accordance with ISA (UK) 260 (Revised June 2016),[23] the external auditor is required to communicate with those charged with governance an overview of the planned scope and timing of the audit. The planned use of the work of the internal audit function is an integral part of the external auditor's overall audit strategy and is therefore relevant to those charged with governance for their understanding of the proposed audit approach.

---

[21]   *ISA (UK) 200 (Revised June 2016), paragraph A29.*

[22]   *ISA (UK) 315 (Revised June 2016), paragraph 4(e).*

[23]   *ISA (UK) 260 (Revised June 2016), paragraph 15.*

Using the Work of the Internal Audit Function

Discussion and Coordination with the Internal Audit Function (Ref: Para. 21)

In discussing the planned use of their work with the internal audit function as a basis for coordinating the respective activities, it may be useful to address the following: **A24**

- The timing of such work.
- The nature of the work performed.
- The extent of audit coverage.
- Materiality for the financial statements as a whole (and, if applicable, materiality level or levels for particular classes of transactions, account balances or disclosures), and performance materiality.
- Proposed methods of item selection and sample sizes.
- Documentation of the work performed.
- Review and reporting procedures.

Coordination between the external auditor and the internal audit function is effective when, for example: **A25**

- Discussions take place at appropriate intervals throughout the period.
- The external auditor informs the internal audit function of significant matters that may affect the function.
- The external auditor is advised of and has access to relevant reports of the internal audit function and is informed of any significant matters that come to the attention of the function when such matters may affect the work of the external auditor so that the external auditor is able to consider the implications of such matters for the audit engagement.

ISA (UK) 200 (Revised June 2016)[24] discusses the importance of the auditor planning and performing the audit with professional skepticism, including being alert to information that brings into question the reliability of documents and responses to inquiries to be used as audit evidence. Accordingly, communication with the internal audit function throughout the engagement may provide opportunities for internal auditors to bring matters that may affect the work of the external auditor to the external auditor's attention.[25] The external auditor is then able to take such information into account in the external auditor's identification and assessment of risks of material misstatement. In addition, if such information may be indicative of a heightened risk of a material misstatement of the financial statements or may be regarding any actual, suspected or alleged fraud, the external auditor can take this into account in the external auditor's identification of risk of material misstatement due to fraud in accordance with ISA (UK) 240 (Revised June 2016).[26] **A26**

Procedures to Determine the Adequacy of Work of the Internal Audit Function
(Ref: Para. 23– 24)

The external auditor's audit procedures on the body of work of the internal audit function as a whole that the external auditor plans to use provide a basis for evaluating the overall quality of the function's work and the objectivity with which it has been performed. **A27**

---

[24] *ISA (UK) 200 (Revised June 2016), paragraphs 15 and A18.*

[25] *ISA (UK) 315 (Revised June 2016), paragraph A116.*

[26] *ISA (UK) 315 (Revised June 2016), paragraph A11 in relation to ISA (UK) 240 (Revised June 2016),* The Auditor's Responsibilities Relating to Fraud in an Audit of Financial Statements.

A28 The procedures the external auditor may perform to evaluate the quality of the work performed and the conclusions reached by the internal audit function, in addition to reperformance in accordance with paragraph 24, include the following:

- Making inquiries of appropriate individuals within the internal audit function.
- Observing procedures performed by the internal audit function.
- Reviewing the internal audit function's work program and working papers.

A29 The more judgment involved, the higher the assessed risk of material misstatement, the less the internal audit function's organizational status and relevant policies and procedures adequately support the objectivity of the internal auditors, or the lower the level of competence of the internal audit function, the more audit procedures are needed to be performed by the external auditor on the overall body of work of the function to support the decision to use the work of the function in obtaining sufficient appropriate audit evidence on which to base the audit opinion.

Reperformance (Ref: Para. 24)

A30 For purposes of this ISA (UK), reperformance involves the external auditor's independent execution of procedures to validate the conclusions reached by the internal audit function. This objective may be accomplished by examining items already examined by the internal audit function, or where it is not possible to do so, the same objective may also be accomplished by examining sufficient other similar items not actually examined by the internal audit function. Reperformance provides more persuasive evidence regarding the adequacy of the work of the internal audit function compared to other procedures the external auditor may perform in paragraph A28. While it is not necessary for the external auditor to do reperformance in each area of work of the internal audit function that is being used, some reperformance is required on the body of work of the internal audit function as a whole that the external auditor plans to use in accordance with paragraph 24. The external auditor is more likely to focus reperformance in those areas where more judgment was exercised by the internal audit function in planning, performing and evaluating the results of the audit procedures and in areas of higher risk of material misstatement.

Determining Whether, in Which Areas and to What Extent Internal Auditors Can Be Used to Provide Direct Assistance

Determining Whether Internal Auditors Can Be Used to Provide Direct Assistance for Purposes of the Audit (Ref: Para. 5, 26–28)

A31 In jurisdictions where the external auditor is prohibited by law or regulation from using internal auditors to provide direct assistance, it is relevant for the group auditors to consider whether the prohibition also extends to component auditors and, if so, to address this in the communication to the component auditors.[27]

A32 As stated in paragraph A7 of this ISA (UK), objectivity refers to the ability to perform the proposed work without allowing bias, conflict of interest or undue influence of others to override professional judgments. In evaluating the existence and significance of threats to the objectivity of an internal auditor, the following factors may be relevant:

---

[27] *ISA (UK) 600 (Revised June 2016), paragraph 40(b).*

The use of internal auditors to provide direct assistance is prohibited in an audit conducted in accordance with ISAs (UK). For a group audit this prohibition extends to the work of any component auditor which is relied upon by the group auditor, including for overseas components – see paragraph 5-1 above of this ISA (UK).

- The extent to which the internal audit function's organizational status and relevant policies and procedures support the objectivity of the internal auditors.[28]
- Family and personal relationships with an individual working in, or responsible for, the aspect of the entity to which the work relates.
- Association with the division or department in the entity to which the work relates.
- Significant financial interests in the entity other than remuneration on terms consistent with those applicable to other employees at a similar level of seniority.

Material issued by relevant professional bodies for internal auditors may provide additional useful guidance.

There may also be some circumstances in which the significance of the threats to the objectivity of an internal auditor is such that there are no safeguards that could reduce them to an acceptable level. For example, because the adequacy of safeguards is influenced by the significance of the work in the context of the audit, paragraph 30 (a) and (b) prohibits the use of internal auditors to provide direct assistance in relation to performing procedures that involve making significant judgments in the audit or that relate to higher assessed risks of material misstatement where the judgment required in performing the relevant audit procedures or evaluating the audit evidence gathered is more than limited. This would also be the case where the work involved creates a self-review threat, which is why internal auditors are prohibited from performing procedures in the circumstances described in paragraph 30 (c) and (d).   **A33**

In evaluating the level of competence of an internal auditor, many of the factors in paragraph A8 of this ISA (UK) may also be relevant applied in the context of individual internal auditors and the work to which they may be assigned.   **A34**

Determining the Nature and Extent of Work that Can Be Assigned to Internal Auditors Providing Direct Assistance (Ref: Para. 29–31)

Paragraphs A15–A22 of this ISA (UK) provide relevant guidance in determining the nature and extent of work that may be assigned to internal auditors.   **A35**

In determining the nature of work that may be assigned to internal auditors, the external auditor is careful to limit such work to those areas that would be appropriate to be assigned. Examples of activities and tasks that would not be appropriate to use internal auditors to provide direct assistance include the following: **A36**

- Discussion of fraud risks. However, the external auditors may make inquiries of internal auditors about fraud risks in the organization in accordance with ISA (UK) 315 (Revised).[29]
- Determination of unannounced audit procedures as addressed in ISA (UK) 240 (Revised June 2016).

Similarly, since in accordance with ISA (UK) 505[30] the external auditor is required to maintain control over external confirmation requests and evaluate the results of external confirmation procedures, it would not be appropriate to assign these responsibilities to internal auditors. However, internal auditors may assist in assembling information necessary for the external auditor to resolve exceptions in confirmation responses.   **A37**

---

[28] *See paragraph A7.*

[29] *ISA (UK) 315 (Revised June 2016), paragraph 6(a).*

[30] *ISA (UK) 505,* External Confirmations, *paragraphs 7 and 16.*

A38   The amount of judgment involved and the risk of material misstatement are also relevant in determining the work that may be assigned to internal auditors providing direct assistance. For example, in circumstances where the valuation of accounts receivable is assessed as an area of higher risk, the external auditor could assign the checking of the accuracy of the aging to an internal auditor providing direct assistance. However, because the evaluation of the adequacy of the provision based on the aging would involve more than limited judgment, it would not be appropriate to assign that latter procedure to an internal auditor providing direct assistance.

A39   Notwithstanding the direction, supervision and review by the external auditor, excessive use of internal auditors to provide direct assistance may affect perceptions regarding the independence of the external audit engagement.

Using Internal Auditors to Provide Direct Assistance (Ref: Para. 34)

A40   As individuals in the internal audit function are not independent of the entity as is required of the external auditor when expressing an opinion on financial statements, the external auditor's direction, supervision and review of the work performed by internal auditors providing direct assistance will generally be of a different nature and more extensive than if members of the engagement team perform the work.

A41   In directing the internal auditors, the external auditor may for example, remind the internal auditors to bring accounting and auditing issues identified during the audit to the attention of the external auditor. In reviewing the work performed by the internal auditors, the external auditor's considerations include whether the evidence obtained is sufficient and appropriate in the circumstances, and that it supports the conclusions reached.

International Standard on Auditing (UK) 620 (Revised June 2016)

Using the work of an auditor's expert

(Effective for audits of financial statements for periods commencing on or after 17 June 2016)

Contents

International Standard on Auditing (UK) (ISA (UK)) 620 (Revised June 2016), *Using the Work of an Auditor's Expert*, should be read in conjunction with ISA (UK) 200 (Revised June 2016), *Overall Objectives of the Independent Auditor and the Conduct of an Audit in Accordance with International Standards on Auditing (UK)*.

Introduction

Scope of this ISA (UK)

1   This International Standard on Auditing (UK) (ISA (UK)) deals with the auditor's responsibilities relating to the work of an individual or organization in a field of expertise other than accounting or auditing, when that work is used to assist the auditor in obtaining sufficient appropriate audit evidence.

2   This ISA (UK) does not deal with:

(a) Situations where the engagement team includes a member, or consults an individual or organization, with expertise in a specialized area of accounting or auditing, which are dealt with in ISA (UK) 220 (Revised June 2016);[1] or

(b) The auditor's use of the work of an individual or organization possessing expertise in a field other than accounting or auditing, whose work in that field is used by the entity to assist the entity in preparing the financial statements (a management's expert), which is dealt with in ISA (UK) 500.[2]

The Auditor's Responsibility for the Audit Opinion

3   The auditor has sole responsibility for the audit opinion expressed, and that responsibility is not reduced by the auditor's use of the work of an auditor's expert. Nonetheless, if the auditor using the work of an auditor's expert, having followed this ISA (UK), concludes that the work of that expert is adequate for the auditor's purposes, the auditor may accept that expert's findings or conclusions in the expert's field as appropriate audit evidence.

Effective Date

4   This ISA (UK) is effective for audits of financial statements for periods commencing on or after 17 June 2016. Earlier adoption is permitted.

Objectives

5   The objectives of the auditor are:

(a) To determine whether to use the work of an auditor's expert; and

(b) If using the work of an auditor's expert, to determine whether that work is adequate for the auditor's purposes.

Definitions

6   For purposes of the ISAs (UK), the following terms have the meanings attributed below:

(a) Auditor's expert – An individual or organization possessing expertise in a field other than accounting or auditing, whose work in that field is used by the auditor to assist the auditor in obtaining sufficient appropriate audit evidence. An auditor's expert may be either an auditor's internal expert (who is a partner[3] or staff, including

---

[1] *ISA (UK) 220 (Revised June 2016)*, Quality Control for an Audit of Financial Statements, *paragraphs A10, A20–A22.*

[2] *ISA (UK) 500*, Audit Evidence, *paragraphs A34–A48.*

[3] *'Partner' and 'firm' should be read as referring to their public sector equivalents where relevant.*

temporary staff, of the auditor's firm or a network firm), or an auditor's external expert. (Ref: Para. A1–A3)

(b) Expertise – Skills, knowledge and experience in a particular field.

(c) Management's expert – An individual or organization possessing expertise in a field other than accounting or auditing, whose work in that field is used by the entity to assist the entity in preparing the financial statements.

Requirements

Determining the Need for an Auditor's Expert

If expertise in a field other than accounting or auditing is necessary to obtain sufficient appropriate audit evidence, the auditor shall determine whether to use the work of an auditor's expert. (Ref: Para. A4–A9)   **7**

Nature, Timing and Extent of Audit Procedures

The nature, timing and extent of the auditor's procedures with respect to the requirements in paragraphs 9–13 of this ISA (UK) will vary depending on the circumstances. In determining the nature, timing and extent of those procedures, the auditor shall consider matters including: (Ref: Para. A10)   **8**

(a) The nature of the matter to which that expert's work relates;

(b) The risks of material misstatement in the matter to which that expert's work relates;

(c) The significance of that expert's work in the context of the audit;

(d) The auditor's knowledge of and experience with previous work performed by that expert; and

(e) Whether that expert is subject to the auditor's firm's quality control policies and procedures. (Ref: Para. A11–A13)

The Competence, Capabilities and Objectivity of the Auditor's Expert

The auditor shall evaluate whether the auditor's expert has the necessary competence, capabilities and objectivity for the auditor's purposes. In the case of an auditor's external expert, the evaluation of objectivity shall include inquiry regarding interests and relationships that may create a threat to that expert's objectivity. (Ref: Para. A14–A20)   **9**

For audits of financial statements of public interest entities, where the auditor has used the work of an auditor's external expert, the auditor shall obtain a confirmation from the auditor's external expert regarding their independence. (Ref: Para. A20-1)   **9R-1**

Obtaining an Understanding of the Field of Expertise of the Auditor's Expert

The auditor shall obtain a sufficient understanding of the field of expertise of the auditor's expert to enable the auditor to: (Ref: Para. A21–A22)   **10**

(a) Determine the nature, scope and objectives of that expert's work for the auditor's purposes; and

(b) Evaluate the adequacy of that work for the auditor's purposes.

Agreement with the Auditor's Expert

11   The auditor shall agree, in writing when appropriate, on the following matters with the auditor's expert: (Ref: Para. A23–A26)

(a)   The nature, scope and objectives of that expert's work; (Ref: Para. A27)

(b)   The respective roles and responsibilities of the auditor and that expert; (Ref: Para. A28–A29)

(c)   The nature, timing and extent of communication between the auditor and that expert, including the form of any report to be provided by that expert; and (Ref: Para. A30)

(d)   The need for the auditor's expert to observe confidentiality requirements. (Ref: Para. A31)

Evaluating the Adequacy of the Auditor's Expert's Work

12   The auditor shall evaluate the adequacy of the auditor's expert's work for the auditor's purposes, including: (Ref: Para. A32)

(a)   The relevance and reasonableness of that expert's findings or conclusions, and their consistency with other audit evidence; (Ref: Para. A33–A34)

(b)   If that expert's work involves use of significant assumptions and methods, the relevance and reasonableness of those assumptions and methods in the circumstances; and (Ref: Para. A35–A37)

(c)   If that expert's work involves the use of source data that is significant to that expert's work, the relevance, completeness, and accuracy of that source data. (Ref: Para. A38–A39)

13   If the auditor determines that the work of the auditor's expert is not adequate for the auditor's purposes, the auditor shall: (Ref: Para. A40)

(a)   Agree with that expert on the nature and extent of further work to be performed by that expert; or

(b)   Perform additional audit procedures appropriate to the circumstances.

Reference to the Auditor's Expert in the Auditor's Report

14   The auditor shall not refer to the work of an auditor's expert in an auditor's report containing an unmodified opinion unless required by law or regulation to do so. If such reference is required by law or regulation, the auditor shall indicate in the auditor's report that the reference does not reduce the auditor's responsibility for the auditor's opinion. (Ref: Para. A41)

15   If the auditor makes reference to the work of an auditor's expert in the auditor's report because such reference is relevant to an understanding of a modification to the auditor's opinion, the auditor shall indicate in the auditor's report that such reference does not reduce the auditor's responsibility for that opinion. (Ref: Para. A42)

Documentation

15D-1   The auditor shall document any request for advice from an auditor's expert, together with the advice received.

Application and Other Explanatory Material

Definition of an Auditor's Expert (Ref: Para. 6(a))

Expertise in a field other than accounting or auditing may include expertise in relation to   **A1**
such matters as:

- The valuation of complex financial instruments, land and buildings, plant and machinery, jewelry, works of art, antiques, intangible assets, assets acquired and liabilities assumed in business combinations and assets that may have been impaired.
- The actuarial calculation of liabilities associated with insurance contracts or employee benefit plans.
- The estimation of oil and gas reserves.
- The valuation of environmental liabilities, and site clean-up costs.
- The interpretation of contracts, laws and regulations.
- The analysis of complex or unusual tax compliance issues.

In many cases, distinguishing between expertise in accounting or auditing, and expertise   **A2**
in another field, will be straightforward, even where this involves a specialized area of accounting or auditing. For example, an individual with expertise in applying methods of accounting for deferred income tax can often be easily distinguished from an expert in taxation law. The former is not an expert for the purposes of this ISA (UK) as this constitutes accounting expertise; the latter is an expert for the purposes of this ISA (UK) as this constitutes legal expertise. Similar distinctions may also be able to be made in other areas, for example, between expertise in methods of accounting for financial instruments, and expertise in complex modeling for the purpose of valuing financial instruments. In some cases, however, particularly those involving an emerging area of accounting or auditing expertise, distinguishing between specialized areas of accounting or auditing, and expertise in another field, will be a matter of professional judgment. Applicable professional rules and standards regarding education and competency requirements for accountants and auditors may assist the auditor in exercising that judgment.[4]

It is necessary to apply judgment when considering how the requirements of this ISA (UK)   **A3**
are affected by the fact that an auditor's expert may be either an individual or an organization. For example, when evaluating the competence, capabilities and objectivity of an auditor's expert, it may be that the expert is an organization the auditor has previously used, but the auditor has no prior experience of the individual expert assigned by the organization for the particular engagement; or it may be the reverse, that is, the auditor may be familiar with the work of an individual expert but not with the organization that expert has joined. In either case, both the personal attributes of the individual and the managerial attributes of the organization (such as systems of quality control the organization implements) may be relevant to the auditor's evaluation.

Determining the Need for an Auditor's Expert (Ref: Para. 7)

An auditor's expert may be needed to assist the auditor in one or more of the following: **A4**

- Obtaining an understanding of the entity and its environment, including its internal control.
- Identifying and assessing the risks of material misstatement.
- Determining and implementing overall responses to assessed risks at the financial statement level.

---

[4] *For example, International Education Standard 8,* Competence Requirements for Audit Professionals *may be of assistance.*

- Designing and performing further audit procedures to respond to assessed risks at the assertion level, comprising tests of controls or substantive procedures.
- Evaluating the sufficiency and appropriateness of audit evidence obtained in forming an opinion on the financial statements.

A5   The risks of material misstatement may increase when expertise in a field other than accounting is needed for management[4a] to prepare the financial statements, for example, because this may indicate some complexity, or because management may not possess knowledge of the field of expertise. If in preparing the financial statements management does not possess the necessary expertise, a management's expert may be used in addressing those risks. Relevant controls, including controls that relate to the work of a management's expert, if any, may also reduce the risks of material misstatement.

A6   If the preparation of the financial statements involves the use of expertise in a field other than accounting, the auditor, who is skilled in accounting and auditing, may not possess the necessary expertise to audit those financial statements. The engagement partner is required to be satisfied that the engagement team, and any auditor's experts who are not part of the engagement team, collectively have the appropriate competence and capabilities to perform the audit engagement.[5] Further, the auditor is required to ascertain the nature, timing and extent of resources necessary to perform the engagement.[6] The auditor's determination of whether to use the work of an auditor's expert, and if so when and to what extent, assists the auditor in meeting these requirements. As the audit progresses, or as circumstances change, the auditor may need to revise earlier decisions about using the work of an auditor's expert.

A7   An auditor who is not an expert in a relevant field other than accounting or auditing may nevertheless be able to obtain a sufficient understanding of that field to perform the audit without an auditor's expert. This understanding may be obtained through, for example:

- Experience in auditing entities that require such expertise in the preparation of their financial statements.
- Education or professional development in the particular field. This may include formal courses, or discussion with individuals possessing expertise in the relevant field for the purpose of enhancing the auditor's own capacity to deal with matters in that field. Such discussion differs from consultation with an auditor's expert regarding a specific set of circumstances encountered on the engagement where that expert is given all the relevant facts that will enable the expert to provide informed advice about the particular matter.[7]
- Discussion with auditors who have performed similar engagements.

A8   In other cases, however, the auditor may determine that it is necessary, or may choose, to use an auditor's expert to assist in obtaining sufficient appropriate audit evidence. Considerations when deciding whether to use an auditor's expert may include:

- Whether management[4a] has used a management's expert in preparing the financial statements (see paragraph A9).
- The nature and significance of the matter, including its complexity.
- The risks of material misstatement in the matter.

[4a] *In the UK, those charged with governance are responsible for the preparation of the financial statements.*

[5] *ISA (UK) 220 (Revised June 2016), paragraph 14.*

[6] *ISA (UK) 300 (Revised June 2016),* Planning an Audit of Financial Statements, *paragraph 8(e).*

[7] *ISA (UK) 220 (Revised June 2016), paragraph A21.*

- The expected nature of procedures to respond to identified risks, including: the auditor's knowledge of and experience with the work of experts in relation to such matters; and the availability of alternative sources of audit evidence.

When management has used a management's expert in preparing the financial statements,   **A9**
the auditor's decision on whether to use an auditor's expert may also be influenced by such factors as:

- The nature, scope and objectives of the management's expert's work.
- Whether the management's expert is employed by the entity, or is a party engaged by it to provide relevant services.
- The extent to which management can exercise control or influence over the work of the management's expert.
- The management's expert's competence and capabilities.
- Whether the management's expert is subject to technical performance standards or other professional or industry requirements.
- Any controls within the entity over the management's expert's work.

ISA (UK) 500[8] includes requirements and guidance regarding the effect of the competence, capabilities and objectivity of management's experts on the reliability of audit evidence.

Nature, Timing and Extent of Audit Procedures (Ref: Para. 8)

The nature, timing and extent of audit procedures with respect to the requirements in   **A10**
paragraphs 9–13 of this ISA (UK) will vary depending on the circumstances. For example, the following factors may suggest the need for different or more extensive procedures than would otherwise be the case:

- The work of the auditor's expert relates to a significant matter that involves subjective and complex judgments.
- The auditor has not previously used the work of the auditor's expert, and has no prior knowledge of that expert's competence, capabilities and objectivity.
- The auditor's expert is performing procedures that are integral to the audit, rather than being consulted to provide advice on an individual matter.
- The expert is an auditor's external expert and is not, therefore, subject to the firm's quality control policies and procedures.

The Auditor's Firm's Quality Control Policies and Procedures (Ref: Para. 8(e))

An auditor's internal expert may be a partner or staff, including temporary staff, of the   **A11**
auditor's firm, and therefore subject to the quality control policies and procedures of that firm in accordance with ISQC (UK) 1[9] or national requirements that are at least as demanding.[10] Alternatively, an auditor's internal expert may be a partner or staff, including temporary staff, of a network firm, which may share common quality control policies and procedures with the auditor's firm.

---

[8] *ISA (UK) 500, paragraph 8.*

[9] *ISQC (UK) 1 (Revised June 2016)*, Quality Control for Firms that Perform Audits and Reviews of Financial Statements, and Other Assurance and Related Services Engagements, *paragraph 12(f).*

[10] *ISA (UK) 220 (Revised June 2016), paragraph 2.*

A12   An auditor's external expert is not a member of the engagement team and is not subject to quality control policies and procedures in accordance with ISQC (UK) 1.[11] In some jurisdictions, however, law or regulation may require that an auditor's external expert be treated as a member of the engagement team, and may therefore be subject to relevant ethical requirements, including those pertaining to independence, and other professional requirements, as determined by that law or regulation.

A13   Engagement teams are entitled to rely on the firm's system of quality control, unless information provided by the firm or other parties suggests otherwise.[12] The extent of that reliance will vary with the circumstances, and may affect the nature, timing and extent of the auditor's procedures with respect to such matters as:

- Competence and capabilities, through recruitment and training programs.
- Objectivity. Auditor's internal experts are subject to relevant ethical requirements, including those pertaining to independence.
- The auditor's evaluation of the adequacy of the auditor's expert's work. For example, the firm's training programs may provide auditor's internal experts with an appropriate understanding of the interrelationship of their expertise with the audit process. Reliance on such training and other firm processes, such as protocols for scoping the work of auditor's internal experts, may affect the nature, timing and extent of the auditor's procedures to evaluate the adequacy of the auditor's expert's work.
- Adherence to regulatory and legal requirements, through monitoring processes.
- Agreement with the auditor's expert.

Such reliance does not reduce the auditor's responsibility to meet the requirements of this ISA (UK).

The Competence, Capabilities and Objectivity of the Auditor's Expert
(Ref: Para. 9)

A14   The competence, capabilities and objectivity of an auditor's expert are factors that significantly affect whether the work of the auditor's expert will be adequate for the auditor's purposes. Competence relates to the nature and level of expertise of the auditor's expert. Capability relates to the ability of the auditor's expert to exercise that competence in the circumstances of the engagement. Factors that influence capability may include, for example, geographic location, and the availability of time and resources. Objectivity relates to the possible effects that bias, conflict of interest, or the influence of others may have on the professional or business judgment of the auditor's expert.

A15   Information regarding the competence, capabilities and objectivity of an auditor's expert may come from a variety of sources, such as:

- Personal experience with previous work of that expert.
- Discussions with that expert.
- Discussions with other auditors or others who are familiar with that expert's work.
- Knowledge of that expert's qualifications, membership of a professional body or industry association, license to practice, or other forms of external recognition.
- Published papers or books written by that expert.
- The auditor's firm's quality control policies and procedures (see paragraphs A11–A13).

---

[11] *ISQC (UK) 1 (Revised June 2016), paragraph 12(f).*

[12] *ISA (UK) 220 (Revised June 2016), paragraph 4.*

Matters relevant to evaluating the competence, capabilities and objectivity of the auditor's expert include whether that expert's work is subject to technical performance standards or other professional or industry requirements, for example, ethical standards and other membership requirements of a professional body or industry association, accreditation standards of a licensing body, or requirements imposed by law or regulation. **A16**

Other matters that may be relevant include: **A17**

- The relevance of the auditor's expert's competence to the matter for which that expert's work will be used, including any areas of specialty within that expert's field. For example, a particular actuary may specialize in property and casualty insurance, but have limited expertise regarding pension calculations.
- The auditor's expert's competence with respect to relevant accounting and auditing requirements, for example, knowledge of assumptions and methods, including models where applicable, that are consistent with the applicable financial reporting framework.
- Whether unexpected events, changes in conditions, or the audit evidence obtained from the results of audit procedures indicate that it may be necessary to reconsider the initial evaluation of the competence, capabilities and objectivity of the auditor's expert as the audit progresses.

A broad range of circumstances may threaten objectivity, for example, self-interest threats, advocacy threats, familiarity threats, self-review threats, and intimidation threats. Safeguards may eliminate or reduce such threats, and may be created by external structures (for example, the auditor's expert's profession, legislation or regulation), or by the auditor's expert's work environment (for example, quality control policies and procedures). There may also be safeguards specific to the audit engagement. **A18**

The evaluation of the significance of threats to objectivity and of whether there is a need for safeguards may depend upon the role of the auditor's expert and the significance of the expert's work in the context of the audit. There may be some circumstances in which safeguards cannot reduce threats to an acceptable level, for example, if a proposed auditor's expert is an individual who has played a significant role in preparing the information that is being audited, that is, if the auditor's expert is a management's expert. **A19**

When evaluating the objectivity of an auditor's external expert, it may be relevant to: **A20**

(a) Inquire of the entity about any known interests or relationships that the entity has with the auditor's external expert that may affect that expert's objectivity.

(b) Discuss with that expert any applicable safeguards, including any professional requirements that apply to that expert; and evaluate whether the safeguards are adequate to reduce threats to an acceptable level. Interests and relationships that it may be relevant to discuss with the auditor's expert include:

- Financial interests.
- Business and personal relationships.
- Provision of other services by the expert, including by the organization in the case of an external expert that is an organization.

In some cases, it may also be appropriate for the auditor to obtain a written representation from the auditor's external expert about any interests or relationships with the entity of which that expert is aware.

Confirmation of Independence of an Auditor's External Expert (Ref: Para. 9R-1)

A20-1   For statutory audits of financial statements of public interest entities, ISA (UK) 260 (Revised June 2016)[12a] requires the auditor to communicate in the additional report to the audit committee when the auditor has used the work of an external expert and to confirm that the auditor obtained confirmation from the auditor's external expert regarding the external expert's independence.

Obtaining an Understanding of the Field of Expertise of the Auditor's Expert (Ref: Para. 10)

A21   The auditor may obtain an understanding of the auditor's expert's field of expertise through the means described in paragraph A7, or through discussion with that expert.

A22   Aspects of the auditor's expert's field relevant to the auditor's understanding may include:

- Whether that expert's field has areas of specialty within it that are relevant to the audit (see paragraph A17).
- Whether any professional or other standards, and regulatory or legal requirements apply.
- What assumptions and methods, including models where applicable, are used by the auditor's expert, and whether they are generally accepted within that expert's field and appropriate for financial reporting purposes.
- The nature of internal and external data or information the auditor's expert uses.

Agreement with the Auditor's Expert (Ref: Para. 11)

A23   The nature, scope and objectives of the auditor's expert's work may vary considerably with the circumstances, as may the respective roles and responsibilities of the auditor and the auditor's expert, and the nature, timing and extent of communication between the auditor and the auditor's expert. It is therefore required that these matters are agreed between the auditor and the auditor's expert regardless of whether the expert is an auditor's external expert or an auditor's internal expert.

A24   The matters noted in paragraph 8 may affect the level of detail and formality of the agreement between the auditor and the auditor's expert, including whether it is appropriate that the agreement be in writing. For example, the following factors may suggest the need for a more detailed agreement than would otherwise be the case, or for the agreement to be set out in writing:

- The auditor's expert will have access to sensitive or confidential entity information.
- The respective roles or responsibilities of the auditor and the auditor's expert are different from those normally expected.
- Multi-jurisdictional legal or regulatory requirements apply.
- The matter to which the auditor's expert's work relates is highly complex.
- The auditor has not previously used work performed by that expert.
- The greater the extent of the auditor's expert's work, and its significance in the context of the audit.

A25   The agreement between the auditor and an auditor's external expert is often in the form of an engagement letter. The Appendix lists matters that the auditor may consider for inclusion in such an engagement letter, or in any other form of agreement with an auditor's external expert.

[12a] *ISA (UK) 260 (Revised June 2016)*, Communication with Those Charged with Governance, *paragraph 16R-2(c)*.

When there is no written agreement between the auditor and the auditor's expert, evidence **A26** of the agreement may be included in, for example:

- Planning memoranda, or related working papers such as the audit program.
- The policies and procedures of the auditor's firm. In the case of an auditor's internal expert, the established policies and procedures to which that expert is subject may include particular policies and procedures in relation to that expert's work. The extent of documentation in the auditor's working papers depends on the nature of such policies and procedures. For example, no documentation may be required in the auditor's working papers if the auditor's firm has detailed protocols covering the circumstances in which the work of such an expert is used.

Nature, Scope and Objectives of Work (Ref: Para. 11(a))

It may often be relevant when agreeing on the nature, scope and objectives of the auditor's **A27** expert's work to include discussion of any relevant technical performance standards or other professional or industry requirements that the expert will follow.

Respective Roles and Responsibilities (Ref: Para. 11(b))

Agreement on the respective roles and responsibilities of the auditor and the auditor's **A28** expert may include:

- Whether the auditor or the auditor's expert will perform detailed testing of source data.
- Consent for the auditor to discuss the auditor's expert's findings or conclusions with the entity and others, and to include details of that expert's findings or conclusions in the basis for a modified opinion in the auditor's report, if necessary (see paragraph A42).
- Any agreement to inform the auditor's expert of the auditor's conclusions concerning that expert's work.

Working Papers

Agreement on the respective roles and responsibilities of the auditor and the auditor's **A29** expert may also include agreement about access to, and retention of, each other's working papers. When the auditor's expert is a member of the engagement team, that expert's working papers form part of the audit documentation. Subject to any agreement to the contrary, auditor's external experts' working papers are their own and do not form part of the audit documentation.

Communication (Ref: Para. 11(c))

Effective two-way communication facilitates the proper integration of the nature, timing **A30** and extent of the auditor's expert's procedures with other work on the audit, and appropriate modification of the auditor's expert's objectives during the course of the audit. For example, when the work of the auditor's expert relates to the auditor's conclusions regarding a significant risk, both a formal written report at the conclusion of that expert's work, and oral reports as the work progresses, may be appropriate. Identification of specific partners or staff who will liaise with the auditor's expert, and procedures for communication between that expert and the entity, assists timely and effective communication, particularly on larger engagements.

Confidentiality (Ref: Para. 11(d))

A31   It is necessary for the confidentiality provisions of relevant ethical requirements that apply to the auditor also to apply to the auditor's expert. Additional requirements may be imposed by law or regulation. The entity may also have requested that specific confidentiality provisions be agreed with auditor's external experts.

Evaluating the Adequacy of the Auditor's Expert's Work (Ref: Para. 12)

A32   The auditor's evaluation of the auditor's expert's competence, capabilities and objectivity, the auditor's familiarity with the auditor's expert's field of expertise, and the nature of the work performed by the auditor's expert affect the nature, timing and extent of audit procedures to evaluate the adequacy of that expert's work for the auditor's purposes.

The Findings and Conclusions of the Auditor's Expert (Ref: Para. 12(a))

A33   Specific procedures to evaluate the adequacy of the auditor's expert's work for the auditor's purposes may include:

- Inquiries of the auditor's expert.
- Reviewing the auditor's expert's working papers and reports.
- Corroborative procedures, such as:
  - Observing the auditor's expert's work;
  - Examining published data, such as statistical reports from reputable, authoritative sources;
  - Confirming relevant matters with third parties;
  - Performing detailed analytical procedures; and
  - Reperforming calculations.
- Discussion with another expert with relevant expertise when, for example, the findings or conclusions of the auditor's expert are not consistent with other audit evidence.
- Discussing the auditor's expert's report with management.

A34   Relevant factors when evaluating the relevance and reasonableness of the findings or conclusions of the auditor's expert, whether in a report or other form, may include whether they are:

- Presented in a manner that is consistent with any standards of the auditor's expert's profession or industry;
- Clearly expressed, including reference to the objectives agreed with the auditor, the scope of the work performed and standards applied;
- Based on an appropriate period and take into account subsequent events, where relevant;
- Subject to any reservation, limitation or restriction on use, and if so, whether this has implications for the auditor; and
- Based on appropriate consideration of errors or deviations encountered by the auditor's expert.

Assumptions, Methods and Source Data

Assumptions and Methods (Ref: Para. 12(b))

A35   When the auditor's expert's work is to evaluate underlying assumptions and methods, including models where applicable, used by management in developing an accounting estimate, the auditor's procedures are likely to be primarily directed to evaluating whether the auditor's expert has adequately reviewed those assumptions and methods. When the auditor's expert's work is to develop an auditor's point estimate or an auditor's range for comparison with management's point estimate, the auditor's procedures may be primarily directed to evaluating the assumptions and methods, including models where appropriate, used by the auditor's expert.

ISA (UK) 540 (Revised June 2016)[13] discusses the assumptions and methods used by management in making accounting estimates, including the use in some cases of highly specialized, entity-developed models. Although that discussion is written in the context of the auditor obtaining sufficient appropriate audit evidence regarding management's assumptions and methods, it may also assist the auditor when evaluating an auditor's expert's assumptions and methods.   **A36**

When an auditor's expert's work involves the use of significant assumptions and methods, factors relevant to the auditor's evaluation of those assumptions and methods include whether they are: **A37**

- Generally accepted within the auditor's expert's field;
- Consistent with the requirements of the applicable financial reporting framework;
- Dependent on the use of specialized models; and
- Consistent with those of management, and if not, the reason for, and effects of, the differences.

Source Data Used by the Auditor's Expert (Ref: Para. 12(c))

When an auditor's expert's work involves the use of source data that is significant to that expert's work, procedures such as the following may be used to test that data: **A38**

- Verifying the origin of the data, including obtaining an understanding of, and where applicable testing, the internal controls over the data and, where relevant, its transmission to the expert.
- Reviewing the data for completeness and internal consistency.

In many cases, the auditor may test source data. However, in other cases, when the nature of the source data used by an auditor's expert is highly technical in relation to the expert's field, that expert may test the source data. If the auditor's expert has tested the source data, inquiry of that expert by the auditor, or supervision or review of that expert's tests may be an appropriate way for the auditor to evaluate that data's relevance, completeness, and accuracy.   **A39**

Inadequate Work (Ref: Para. 13)

If the auditor concludes that the work of the auditor's expert is not adequate for the auditor's purposes and the auditor cannot resolve the matter through the additional audit procedures required by paragraph 13, which may involve further work being performed by both the expert and the auditor, or include employing or engaging another expert, it may be necessary to express a modified opinion in the auditor's report in accordance with ISA (UK) 705 (Revised June 2016) because the auditor has not obtained sufficient appropriate audit evidence.[14]   **A40**

---

[13] *ISA (UK) 540 (Revised June 2016)*, Auditing Accounting Estimates, Including Fair Value Accounting Estimates, and Related Disclosures, *paragraphs 8, 13 and 15.*

[14] *ISA (UK) 705 (Revised June 2016)*, Modifications to the Opinion in the Independent Auditor's Report, *paragraph 6(b).*

Reference to the Auditor's Expert in the Auditor's Report
(Ref: Para. 14–15)

A41   In some cases, law or regulation may require a reference to the work of an auditor's expert, for example, for the purposes of transparency in the public sector.

A42   It may be appropriate in some circumstances to refer to the auditor's expert in an auditor's report containing a modified opinion, to explain the nature of the modification. In such circumstances, the auditor may need the permission of the auditor's expert before making such a reference.

Appendix

(Ref: Para. A25)

Considerations for Agreement between the Auditor and an Auditor's External Expert

This Appendix lists matters that the auditor may consider for inclusion in any agreement with an auditor's external expert. The following list is illustrative and is not exhaustive; it is intended only to be a guide that may be used in conjunction with the considerations outlined in this ISA (UK). Whether to include particular matters in the agreement depends on the circumstances of the engagement. The list may also be of assistance in considering the matters to be included in an agreement with an auditor's internal expert.

Nature, Scope and Objectives of the Auditor's External Expert's Work

- The nature and scope of the procedures to be performed by the auditor's external expert.
- The objectives of the auditor's external expert's work in the context of materiality and risk considerations concerning the matter to which the auditor's external expert's work relates, and, when relevant, the applicable financial reporting framework.
- Any relevant technical performance standards or other professional or industry requirements the auditor's external expert will follow.
- The assumptions and methods, including models where applicable, the auditor's external expert will use, and their authority.
- The effective date of, or when applicable the testing period for, the subject matter of the auditor's external expert's work, and requirements regarding subsequent events.

The Respective Roles and Responsibilities of the Auditor and the Auditor's External Expert

- Relevant auditing and accounting standards, and relevant regulatory or legal requirements.
- The auditor's external expert's consent to the auditor's intended use of that expert's report, including any reference to it, or disclosure of it, to others, for example reference to it in the basis for a modified opinion in the auditor's report, if necessary, or disclosure of it to management or an audit committee.[14a]
- The nature and extent of the auditor's review of the auditor's external expert's work.
- Whether the auditor or the auditor's external expert will test source data.
- The auditor's external expert's access to the entity's records, files, personnel and to experts engaged by the entity.
- Procedures for communication between the auditor's external expert and the entity.
- The auditor's and the auditor's external expert's access to each other's working papers.
- Ownership and control of working papers during and after the engagement, including any file retention requirements.
- The auditor's external expert's responsibility to perform work with due skill and care.
- The auditor's external expert's competence and capability to perform the work.
- The expectation that the auditor's external expert will use all knowledge that expert has that is relevant to the audit or, if not, will inform the auditor.

[14a] *Auditors of public interest entities are required by paragraph 16R-1(c) of ISA (UK) 260 (Revised June 2016) to communicate matters relating to the use of the work of the auditor's external expert in the additional report to the audit committee.*

- Any restriction on the auditor's external expert's association with the auditor's report.
- Any agreement to inform the auditor's external expert of the auditor's conclusions concerning that expert's work

Communications and Reporting

- Methods and frequency of communications, including:
  - How the auditor's external expert's findings or conclusions will be reported (for example, written report, oral report, ongoing input to the engagement team).
  - Identification of specific persons within the engagement team who will liaise with the auditor's external expert.
- When the auditor's external expert will complete the work and report findings or conclusions to the auditor.
- The auditor's external expert's responsibility to communicate promptly any potential delay in completing the work, and any potential reservation or limitation on that expert's findings or conclusions.
- The auditor's external expert's responsibility to communicate promptly instances in which the entity restricts that expert's access to records, files, personnel or experts engaged by the entity.
- The auditor's external expert's responsibility to communicate to the auditor all information that expert believes may be relevant to the audit, including any changes in circumstances previously communicated.
- The auditor's external expert's responsibility to communicate circumstances that may create threats to that expert's objectivity, and any relevant safeguards that may eliminate or reduce such threats to an acceptable level.

Confidentiality

- The need for the auditor's expert to observe confidentiality requirements, including:
  - The confidentiality provisions of relevant ethical requirements that apply to the auditor.
  - Additional requirements that may be imposed by law or regulation, if any.
  - Specific confidentiality provisions requested by the entity, if any.

International Standard on Auditing (UK) 700 (Revised June 2016)

Forming an opinion and reporting on financial statements

(Effective for audits of financial statements for periods commencing on or after 17 June 2016)

Contents

International Standard on Auditing (ISA) (UK) 700 (Revised June 2016), *Forming an Opinion and Reporting on Financial Statements*, should be read in conjunction with ISA (UK) 200 (Revised June 2016), *Overall Objectives of the Independent Auditor and the Conduct of an Audit in Accordance with International Standards on Auditing (UK)*.

Introduction

Scope of this ISA (UK)

1   This International Standard on Auditing (UK) (ISA (UK)) deals with the auditor's responsibility to form an opinion on the financial statements. It also deals with the form and content of the auditor's report issued as a result of an audit of financial statements.

2   ISA (UK) 701[1] deals with the auditor's responsibility to communicate key audit matters in the auditor's report. ISA (UK) 705[2] (Revised June 2016) and ISA (UK) 706[3] (Revised June 2016) deal with how the form and content of the auditor's report are affected when the auditor expresses a modified opinion or includes an Emphasis of Matter paragraph or an Other Matter paragraph in the auditor's report. Other ISAs (UK) also contain reporting requirements that are applicable when issuing an auditor's report.

3   This ISA (UK) applies to an audit of a complete set of general purpose financial statements and is written in that context. ISA 800[4] deals with special considerations when financial statements are prepared in accordance with a special purpose framework. ISA 805[5] deals with special considerations relevant to an audit of a single financial statement or of a specific element, account or item of a financial statement. This ISA (UK) also applies to audits for which ISA 800 or ISA 805 apply.

4   The requirements of this ISA (UK) are aimed at addressing an appropriate balance between the need for consistency and comparability in auditor reporting globally and the need to increase the value of auditor reporting by making the information provided in the auditor's report more relevant to users. This ISA (UK) promotes consistency in the auditor's report, but recognizes the need for flexibility to accommodate particular circumstances of individual jurisdictions. Consistency in the auditor's report, when the audit has been conducted in accordance with ISAs (UK), promotes credibility in the global marketplace by making more readily identifiable those audits that have been conducted in accordance with globally recognized standards. It also helps to promote the user's understanding and to identify unusual circumstances when they occur.

Effective Date

5   This ISA (UK) is effective for audits of financial statements for periods commencing on or after 17 June 2016. Earlier adoption is permitted.

Objectives

6   The objectives of the auditor are:

---

[1] *ISA (UK) 701*, Communicating Key Audit Matters in the Independent Auditor's Report.

[2] *ISA (UK) 705 (Revised June 2016)*, Modifications to the Opinion in the Independent Auditor's Report.

[3] *ISA (UK) 706 (Revised June 2016)*, Emphasis of Matter Paragraphs and Other Matter Paragraphs in the Independent Auditor's Report.

[4] *ISA 800*, Special Considerations—Audits of Financial Statements Prepared in Accordance with Special Purpose Frameworks.
ISA 800 has not been promulgated by the FRC for application in the UK.

[5] *ISA 805*, Special Considerations—Audits of Single Financial Statements and Specific Elements, Accounts or Items of a Financial Statement.
ISA 805 has not been promulgated by the FRC for application in the UK.

(a) To form an opinion on the financial statements based on an evaluation of the conclusions drawn from the audit evidence obtained; and

(b) To express clearly that opinion through a written report.

Definitions

For purposes of the ISAs (UK), the following terms have the meanings attributed below: **7**

(a) General purpose financial statements – Financial statements prepared in accordance with a general purpose framework.

(b) General purpose framework – A financial reporting framework designed to meet the common financial information needs of a wide range of users. The financial reporting framework may be a fair presentation framework or a compliance framework.

   The term 'fair presentation framework' is used to refer to a financial reporting framework that requires compliance with the requirements of the framework and:

   (i) Acknowledges explicitly or implicitly that, to achieve fair presentation of the financial statements, it may be necessary for management to provide disclosures beyond those specifically required by the framework;[5a] or

   (ii) Acknowledges explicitly that it may be necessary for management to depart from a requirement of the framework to achieve fair presentation of the financial statements.[5b] Such departures are expected to be necessary only in extremely rare circumstances.

   The term 'compliance framework' is used to refer to a financial reporting framework that requires compliance with the requirements of the framework, but does not contain the acknowledgements in (i) or (ii) above.[6]

(c) Unmodified opinion – The opinion expressed by the auditor when the auditor concludes that the financial statements are prepared, in all material respects, in accordance with the applicable financial reporting framework.[7]

Reference to 'financial statements' in this ISA (UK) means 'a complete set of general **8** purpose financial statements.'[8] The requirements of the applicable financial reporting framework determine the presentation, structure and content of the financial statements, and what constitutes a complete set of financial statements.

Reference to 'International Financial Reporting Standards' in this ISA (UK) means **9** the International Financial Reporting Standards (IFRSs) issued by the International Accounting Standards Board, and reference to 'International Public Sector Accounting Standards' means the International Public Sector Accounting Standards (IPSASs) issued by the International Public Sector Accounting Standards Board.

[5a] *In the IFRS Framework this is acknowledged in paragraph 17(c) of IAS 1. In UK GAAP this is acknowledged in Sections 396(4) and 404(4) of the Companies Act 2006.*

[5b] *This is sometimes referred to as the 'true and fair override'. In the IFRS Framework this is acknowledged in paragraph 19 of IAS 1. In UK GAAP this is acknowledged in Sections 396(5) and 404(5) of the Companies Act 2006.*

[6] *ISA (UK) 200 (Revised June 2016)*, Overall Objectives of the Independent Auditor and the Conduct of an Audit in Accordance with International Standards on Auditing (UK), *paragraph 13(a)*.

[7] *Paragraphs 25–26 deal with the phrases used to express this opinion in the case of a fair presentation framework and a compliance framework respectively.*

[8] *ISA (UK) 200 (Revised June 2016)*, Overall Objectives of the Independent Auditor and the Conduct of an Audit in Accordance with International Standards on Auditing (UK), *paragraph 13(f) sets out the content of financial statements.*

Requirements

Forming an Opinion on the Financial Statements

10   The auditor shall form an opinion on whether the financial statements are prepared, in all material respects, in accordance with the applicable financial reporting framework.[9,10]

11   In order to form that opinion, the auditor shall conclude as to whether the auditor has obtained reasonable assurance about whether the financial statements as a whole are free from material misstatement, whether due to fraud or error. That conclusion shall take into account:

(a)   The auditor's conclusion, in accordance with ISA (UK) 330 (Revised June 2016), whether sufficient appropriate audit evidence has been obtained;[11]

(b)   The auditor's conclusion, in accordance with ISA (UK) 450 (Revised June 2016), whether uncorrected misstatements are material, individually or in aggregate;[12] and

(c)   The evaluations required by paragraphs 12–15.

12   The auditor shall evaluate whether the financial statements are prepared, in all material respects, in accordance with the requirements of the applicable financial reporting framework. This evaluation shall include consideration of the qualitative aspects of the entity's accounting practices, including indicators of possible bias in management's judgments. (Ref: Para. A1–A3)

13   In particular, the auditor shall evaluate whether, in view of the requirements of the applicable financial reporting framework:

(a)   The financial statements appropriately disclose the significant accounting policies selected and applied. In making this evaluation, the auditor shall consider the relevance of the accounting policies to the entity, and whether they have been presented in an understandable manner; (Ref: Para. A4)

(b)   The accounting policies selected and applied are consistent with the applicable financial reporting framework and are appropriate;

(c)   The accounting estimates made by management are reasonable;

(d)   The information presented in the financial statements is relevant, reliable, comparable, and understandable. In making this evaluation, the auditor shall consider whether:

- The information that should have been included has been included, and whether such information is appropriately classified, aggregated or disaggregated, and characterized.
- The overall presentation of the financial statements has been undermined by including information that is not relevant or that obscures a proper understanding of the matters disclosed. (Ref: Para. A5)

(e)   The financial statements provide adequate disclosures to enable the intended users to understand the effect of material transactions and events on the information conveyed in the financial statements; and (Ref: Para. A6)

(f)   The terminology used in the financial statements, including the title of each financial statement, is appropriate.

---

[9] *ISA (UK) 200 (Revised June 2016), paragraph 11.*

[10] *Paragraphs 25–26 deal with the phrases used to express this opinion in the case of a fair presentation framework and a compliance framework respectively.*

[11] *ISA (UK) 330 (Revised June 2016),* The Auditor's Responses to Assessed Risks, *paragraph 26.*

[12] *ISA (UK) 450 (Revised June 2016),* Evaluation of Misstatements Identified during the Audit, *paragraph 11.*

When the financial statements are prepared in accordance with a fair presentation **14** framework, the evaluation required by paragraphs 12–13 shall also include whether the financial statements achieve fair presentation. The auditor's evaluation as to whether the financial statements achieve fair presentation shall include consideration of: (Ref: Para A7–A9)

(a) The overall presentation, structure and content of the financial statements; and
(b) Whether the financial statements represent the underlying transactions and events in a manner that achieves fair presentation.

The auditor shall evaluate whether the financial statements adequately refer to or describe **15** the applicable financial reporting framework. (Ref: Para. A10–A15)

Form of Opinion

The auditor shall express an unmodified opinion when the auditor concludes that the **16** financial statements are prepared, in all material respects, in accordance with the applicable financial reporting framework.

In the UK, when expressing an unmodified opinion on financial statements prepared in accordance with a fair presentation framework it is not sufficient for the auditor to conclude that the financial statements give a true and fair view solely on the basis that the financial statements were prepared in accordance with accounting standards and any other applicable legal requirements. (Ref: Para. A15-1–A15-2)

If the auditor: **17**

(a) concludes that, based on the audit evidence obtained, the financial statements as a whole are not free from material misstatement; or
(b) is unable to obtain sufficient appropriate audit evidence to conclude that the financial statements as a whole are free from material misstatement,

the auditor shall modify the opinion in the auditor's report in accordance with ISA (UK) 705 (Revised June 2016).

If financial statements prepared in accordance with the requirements of a fair presentation **18** framework do not achieve fair presentation, the auditor shall discuss the matter with management and, depending on the requirements of the applicable financial reporting framework and how the matter is resolved, shall determine whether it is necessary to modify the opinion in the auditor's report in accordance with ISA (UK) 705 (Revised June 2016). (Ref: Para. A16)

When the financial statements are prepared in accordance with a compliance framework, **19** the auditor is not required to evaluate whether the financial statements achieve fair presentation. However, if in extremely rare circumstances the auditor concludes that such financial statements are misleading, the auditor shall discuss the matter with management and, depending on how it is resolved, shall determine whether, and how, to communicate it in the auditor's report. (Ref: Para. A17)

Auditor's Report

The auditor's report shall be in writing. (Ref: Para. A18–A19) **20**

The auditor's report shall be in clear and unambiguous language. **20-1**

Auditor's Report for Audits Conducted in Accordance with International Standards on Auditing (UK)

Title

21   The auditor's report shall have a title that clearly indicates that it is the report of an independent auditor. (Ref: Para. A20)

Addressee

22   The auditor's report shall be addressed, as appropriate, based on the circumstances of the engagement. (Ref: Para. A21–A21-1)

Auditor's Opinion

23   The first section of the auditor's report shall include the auditor's opinion, and shall have the heading 'Opinion.'

24   The Opinion section of the auditor's report shall also:

(a)   Identify the entity whose financial statements have been audited;
(b)   State that the financial statements have been audited;
(c)   Identify the title of each statement comprising the financial statements;
(d)   Refer to the notes, including the summary of significant accounting policies; and
(e)   Specify the date of, or period covered by, each financial statement comprising the financial statements. (Ref: Para. A22–A23)

25   When expressing an unmodified opinion on financial statements prepared in accordance with a fair presentation framework, the auditor's opinion shall, unless otherwise required by law or regulation, use one of the following phrases, which are regarded as being equivalent:

(a)   In our opinion, the accompanying financial statements present fairly, in all material respects, [...] in accordance with [the applicable financial reporting framework]; or
(b)   In our opinion, the accompanying financial statements give a true and fair view of [...] in accordance with [the applicable financial reporting framework]. (Ref: Para. A24–A31)

In the UK, when expressing an unmodified opinion on financial statements prepared in accordance with a fair presentation framework the opinion paragraph shall clearly state that the financial statements give a true and fair view. (Ref: Para. A24-1–A24-3)

26   When expressing an unmodified opinion on financial statements prepared in accordance with a compliance framework, the auditor's opinion shall be that the accompanying financial statements are prepared, in all material respects, in accordance with [the applicable financial reporting framework]. (Ref: Para. A26–A31-1)

27   If the reference to the applicable financial reporting framework in the auditor's opinion is not to IFRSs issued by the International Accounting Standards Board or IPSASs issued by the International Public Sector Accounting Standards Board, the auditor's opinion shall identify the jurisdiction of origin of the framework.

Basis for Opinion

28   The auditor's report shall include a section, directly following the Opinion section, with the heading 'Basis for Opinion', that: (Ref: Para. A32)

(a) States that the audit was conducted in accordance with International Standards on Auditing (UK) and applicable law; (Ref: Para. A33)
(b) Refers to the section of the auditor's report that describes the auditor's responsibilities under the ISAs (UK);
(c) Includes a statement that the auditor is independent of the entity in accordance with the relevant ethical requirements relating to the audit, and has fulfilled the auditor's other ethical responsibilities in accordance with these requirements. The statement shall identify the jurisdiction of origin of the relevant ethical requirements or refer to the International Ethics Standards Board for Accountants' *Code of Ethics for Professional Accountants* (IESBA Code); and (Ref: Para. A34–A39)

> In the UK, auditors are subject to ethical requirements from two sources: the FRC's Ethical Standard concerning the integrity, objectivity and independence of the auditor, and the ethical pronouncements established by the auditor's relevant professional body. When identifying the relevant ethical requirements in the auditor's report, the auditor indicates that these include the FRC's Ethical Standard, applied as required for the types of entity determined to be appropriate in the circumstances.

(d) States whether the auditor believes that the audit evidence the auditor has obtained is sufficient and appropriate to provide a basis for the auditor's opinion.

Going Concern

Where applicable, the auditor shall report in accordance with ISA (UK) 570 (Revised June 2016).[13]   **29**

Key Audit Matters

For audits of complete sets of general purpose financial statements of listed entities, the auditor shall communicate key audit matters in the auditor's report in accordance with ISA (UK) 701.   **30**

> For audits of complete sets of general purpose financial statements of public interest entities and other entities that are required, and those that choose voluntarily, to report on how they have applied the UK Corporate Governance Code, the auditor shall communicate in the auditor's report in accordance with ISA (UK) 701.   **30-1**

When the auditor is otherwise required by law or regulation or decides to communicate key audit matters in the auditor's report, the auditor shall do so in accordance with ISA (UK) 701. (Ref: Para. A40–A42)   **31**

Other Information

Where applicable, the auditor shall report in accordance with ISA (UK) 720 (Revised June 2016).   **32**

Responsibilities for the Financial Statements

The auditor's report shall include a section with a heading 'Responsibilities of Management for the Financial Statements.' The auditor's report shall use the term that is appropriate in the context of the legal framework in the particular jurisdiction and need not refer   **33**

---

[13] *ISA (UK) 570 (Revised June 2016)*, Going Concern, *paragraphs 21–23.*

specifically to 'management'. In some jurisdictions, the appropriate reference may be to those charged with governance.[13a] (Ref: Para. A44–A44-1)

34 This section of the auditor's report shall describe management's responsibility for: (Ref: Para. A45–A48)

(a) Preparing the financial statements in accordance with the applicable financial reporting framework, and for such internal control as management determines is necessary to enable the preparation of financial statements that are free from material misstatement, whether due to fraud or error; and

(b) Assessing the entity's ability to continue as a going concern[14] and whether the use of the going concern basis of accounting is appropriate as well as disclosing, if applicable, matters relating to going concern. The explanation of management's responsibility for this assessment shall include a description of when the use of the going concern basis of accounting is appropriate. (Ref: Para. A48)

35 This section of the auditor's report shall also identify those responsible for the oversight of the financial reporting process, when those responsible for such oversight are different from those who fulfill the responsibilities described in paragraph 33 above. In this case, the heading of this section shall also refer to 'Those Charged with Governance' or such term that is appropriate in the context of the legal framework in the particular jurisdiction. (Ref: Para. A49)

36 When the financial statements are prepared in accordance with a fair presentation framework, the description of responsibilities for the financial statements in the auditor's report shall refer to 'the preparation and fair presentation of these financial statements' or 'the preparation of financial statements that give a true and fair view' as appropriate in the circumstances.

> In the UK, the auditor's report shall include a statement that [those charged with governance] are responsible for the preparation of financial statements [that give a true and fair view].

Auditor's Responsibilities for the Audit of the Financial Statements

37 The auditor's report shall include a section with the heading 'Auditor's Responsibilities for the Audit of the Financial Statements.'

38 This section of the auditor's report shall: (Ref: Para. A50)

(a) State that the objectives of the auditor are to:
   (i) Obtain reasonable assurance about whether the financial statements as a whole are free from material misstatement, whether due to fraud or error; and
   (ii) Issue an auditor's report that includes the auditor's opinion. (Ref: Para. A51)

(b) State that reasonable assurance is a high level of assurance, but is not a guarantee that an audit conducted in accordance with ISAs (UK) will always detect a material misstatement when it exists; and

(c) State that misstatements can arise from fraud or error, and either:
   (i) Describe that they are considered material if, individually or in the aggregate, they could reasonably be expected to influence the economic decisions of users taken on the basis of these financial statements; or[15]

[13a] *In the UK, those charged with governance are responsible for the preparation of the financial statements.*

[14] *ISA (UK) 570 (Revised June 2016), paragraph 2.*

[15] *ISA (UK) 320 (Revised June 2016),* Materiality in Planning and Performing an Audit, *paragraph 2.*

(ii) Provide a definition or description of materiality in accordance with the applicable financial reporting framework. (Ref: Para. A52)

The Auditor's Responsibilities for the Audit of the Financial Statements section of the **39** auditor's report shall further: (Ref: Para. A50)

(a) State that, as part of an audit in accordance with ISAs (UK), the auditor exercises professional judgment and maintains professional skepticism throughout the audit; and

(b) Describe an audit by stating that the auditor's responsibilities are:

(i) To identify and assess the risks of material misstatement of the financial statements, whether due to fraud or error; to design and perform audit procedures responsive to those risks; and to obtain audit evidence that is sufficient and appropriate to provide a basis for the auditor's opinion. The risk of not detecting a material misstatement resulting from fraud is higher than for one resulting from error, as fraud may involve collusion, forgery, intentional omissions, misrepresentations, or the override of internal control.

(ii) To obtain an understanding of internal control relevant to the audit in order to design audit procedures that are appropriate in the circumstances, but not for the purpose of expressing an opinion on the effectiveness of the entity's internal control. In circumstances when the auditor also has a responsibility to express an opinion on the effectiveness of internal control in conjunction with the audit of the financial statements, the auditor shall omit the phrase that the auditor's consideration of internal control is not for the purpose of expressing an opinion on the effectiveness of the entity's internal control.

(iii) To evaluate the appropriateness of accounting policies used and the reasonableness of accounting estimates and related disclosures made by management.

(iv) To conclude on the appropriateness of management's use of the going concern basis of accounting and, based on the audit evidence obtained, whether a material uncertainty exists related to events or conditions that may cast significant doubt on the entity's ability to continue as a going concern. If the auditor concludes that a material uncertainty exists, the auditor is required to draw attention in the auditor's report to the related disclosures in the financial statements or, if such disclosures are inadequate, to modify the opinion. The auditor's conclusions are based on the audit evidence obtained up to the date of the auditor's report. However, future events or conditions may cause an entity to cease to continue as a going concern. (Ref: Para A50-1–A50-2)

(v) When the financial statements are prepared in accordance with a fair presentation framework, to evaluate the overall presentation, structure and content of the financial statements, including the disclosures, and whether the financial statements represent the underlying transactions and events in a manner that achieves fair presentation.

(c) When ISA (UK) 600 (Revised June 2016)[16] applies, further describe the auditor's responsibilities in a group audit engagement by stating that:

(i) The auditor's responsibilities are to obtain sufficient appropriate audit evidence regarding the financial information of the entities or business activities within the group to express an opinion on the group financial statements;

(ii) The auditor is responsible for the direction, supervision and performance of the group audit; and

(iii) The auditor remains solely responsible for the auditor's opinion.

---

[16] *ISA (UK) 600 (Revised June 2016)*, Special Considerations—Audits of Group Financial Statements (Including the Work of Component Auditors).

40   The Auditor's Responsibilities for the Audit of the Financial Statements section of the auditor's report also shall: (Ref: Para. A50)

(a)   State that the auditor communicates with those charged with governance regarding, among other matters, the planned scope and timing of the audit and significant audit findings, including any significant deficiencies in internal control that the auditor identifies during the audit;

(b)   For audits of financial statements of listed entities, state that the auditor provides those charged with governance with a statement that the auditor has complied with relevant ethical requirements regarding independence and communicate with them all relationships and other matters that may reasonably be thought to bear on the auditor's independence, and where applicable, related safeguards; and

(c)   For audits of financial statements of listed entities and any other entities for which key audit matters are communicated in accordance with ISA (UK) 701, state that, from the matters communicated with those charged with governance, the auditor determines those matters that were of most significance in the audit of the financial statements of the current period and are therefore the key audit matters. The auditor describes these matters in the auditor's report unless law or regulation precludes public disclosure about the matter or when, in extremely rare circumstances, the auditor determines that a matter should not be communicated in the auditor's report because the adverse consequences of doing so would reasonably be expected to outweigh the public interest benefits of such communication. (Ref: Para. A53)

Location of the Description of the Auditor's Responsibilities for the Audit of the Financial Statements

41   The description of the auditor's responsibilities for the audit of the financial statements required by paragraphs 39–40 shall be included: (Ref: Para. A54)

(a)   Within the body of the auditor's report;

(b)   Within an appendix to the auditor's report, in which case the auditor's report shall include a reference to the location of the appendix; or (Ref: Para. A54–A55)

(c)   By a specific reference within the auditor's report to the location of such a description on a website of an appropriate authority, where law, regulation or national auditing standards expressly permit the auditor to do so. (Ref: Para. A54, A56–A57-1)

In the UK, the auditor is permitted to cross-refer to the applicable version of a 'Description of the Auditor's Responsibilities for the Audit of the Financial Statements' that is maintained on the website of an appropriate authority.

42   When the auditor refers to a description of the auditor's responsibilities on a website of an appropriate authority, the auditor shall determine that such description addresses, and is not inconsistent with, the requirements in paragraphs 39–40 of this ISA (UK). (Ref: Para. A56)

Other Reporting Responsibilities

43   If the auditor addresses other reporting responsibilities in the auditor's report on the financial statements that are in addition to the auditor's responsibilities under the ISAs (UK), these other reporting responsibilities shall be addressed in a separate section in the auditor's report with a heading titled 'Report on Other Legal and Regulatory Requirements' or otherwise as appropriate to the content of the section, unless these other reporting responsibilities address the same topics as those presented under the reporting responsibilities required by the ISAs (UK) in which case the other reporting responsibilities may be presented in the same section as the related report elements required by the ISAs (UK). (Ref: Para. A58–A60)

If the auditor is required to report on certain matters by exception, the auditor shall   **43-1**
describe in the auditor's report the auditor's responsibilities for such matters and
incorporate a suitable conclusion in respect of such matters. (Ref: Para. A58-1–A58-3)

If other reporting responsibilities are presented in the same section as the related report   **44**
elements required by the ISAs (UK), the auditor's report shall clearly differentiate the
other reporting responsibilities from the reporting that is required by the ISAs (UK).
(Ref: Para. A60)

If the auditor's report contains a separate section that addresses other reporting   **45**
responsibilities, the requirements of paragraphs 20–40 of this ISA (UK) shall be included
under a section with a heading 'Report on the Audit of the Financial Statements.' The
'Report on Other Legal and Regulatory Requirements' shall follow the 'Report on the
Audit of the Financial Statements.' (Ref: Para. A60–A60-14)

For audits of financial statements of public interest entities, the auditor's report shall: **45R-1**
(a) State by whom or which body the auditor(s) was appointed;
(b) Indicate the date of the appointment and the period of total uninterrupted
    engagement including previous renewals and reappointments of the firm;
(c) Explain to what extent the audit was considered capable of detecting irregularities,
    including fraud;
(d) Confirm that the audit opinion is consistent with the additional report to the audit
    committee.[16a] Except as required by paragraph 45R-1(d), the auditor's report shall
    not contain any cross-references to the additional report to the audit committee;
(e) Declare that the non-audit services prohibited by the FRC's Ethical Standard were
    not provided and that the firm remained independent of the entity in conducting the
    audit; and
(f) Indicate any services, in addition to the audit, which were provided by the firm to
    the entity and its controlled undertaking(s), and which have not been disclosed in
    the annual report or financial statements.

Name of the Engagement Partner

The name of the engagement partner shall be included in the auditor's report on financial   **46**
statements of listed entities unless, in rare circumstances, such disclosure is reasonably
expected to lead to a significant personal security threat. In the rare circumstances that the
auditor intends not to include the name of the engagement partner in the auditor's report,
the auditor shall discuss this intention with those charged with governance to inform the
auditor's assessment of the likelihood and severity of a significant personal security threat.
(Ref: Para. A61–A63)

Signature of the Auditor

The auditor's report shall be signed. (Ref: Para. A64–A65)   **47**

Auditor's Address

The auditor's report shall name the location in the jurisdiction where the auditor practices.   **48**
(Ref: Para. A65-1)

[16a] *ISA (UK) 260 (Revised), Communication with Those Charged with Governance, paragraph 16R-2.*

Date of the Auditor's Report

49   The auditor's report shall be dated no earlier than the date on which the auditor has obtained sufficient appropriate audit evidence on which to base the auditor's opinion on the financial statements, including evidence that: (Ref: Para. A66–A69)

(a)   All the statements and disclosures that comprise the financial statements have been prepared; and

(b)   Those with the recognized authority have asserted that they have taken responsibility for those financial statements.

49-1   The date of an auditor's report on an entity's financial statements shall be the date on which the auditor signed the report expressing an opinion on those financial statements. (Ref: Para. A66)

49-2   The auditor shall not sign, and hence date, the auditor's report earlier than the date on which all the other information contained in the annual report has been approved by those charged with governance and the auditor has considered all necessary available evidence. (Ref: Para. A67-1–A67-4)

Auditor's Report Prescribed by Law or Regulation

50   If the auditor is required by law or regulation of a specific jurisdiction to use a specific layout, or wording of the auditor's report, the auditor's report shall refer to International Standards on Auditing only if the auditor's report includes, at a minimum, each of the following elements: (Ref: Para. A70–A71)

(a)   A title.

(b)   An addressee, as required by the circumstances of the engagement.

(c)   An Opinion section containing an expression of opinion on the financial statements and a reference to the applicable financial reporting framework used to prepare the financial statements (including identifying the jurisdiction of origin of the financial reporting framework that is not International Financial Reporting Standards or International Public Sector Accounting Standards, see paragraph 26).

(d)   An identification of the entity's financial statements that have been audited.

(e)   A statement that the auditor is independent of the entity in accordance with the relevant ethical requirements relating to the audit, and has fulfilled the auditor's other ethical responsibilities in accordance with these requirements. The statement shall identify the jurisdiction of origin of the relevant ethical requirements or refer to the IESBA Code.

(f)   Where applicable, a section that addresses, and is not inconsistent with, the reporting requirements in paragraph 22 of ISA 570 (Revised).

(g)   Where applicable, a Basis for Qualified (or Adverse) Opinion section that addresses, and is not inconsistent with, the reporting requirements in paragraph 23 of ISA 570 (Revised).

(h)   Where applicable, a section that includes the information required by ISA 701, or additional information about the audit that is prescribed by law or regulation and that addresses, and is not inconsistent with, the reporting requirements in that ISA.[17] (Ref: Para. A72–A75)

(i)   Where applicable, a section that addresses the reporting requirements in paragraph 24 of ISA 720 (Revised).

(j)   A description of management's responsibilities for the preparation of the financial statements and an identification of those responsible for the oversight of the financial

---

[17]   *ISA 701, paragraphs 11–16.*

reporting process that addresses, and is not inconsistent with, the requirements in paragraphs 33–36.

(k) A reference to International Standards on Auditing and the law or regulation, and a description of the auditor's responsibilities for an audit of the financial statements that addresses, and is not inconsistent with, the requirements in paragraphs 37–40. (Ref: Para. A50–A53)

(l) For audits of complete sets of general purpose financial statements of listed entities, the name of the engagement partner unless, in rare circumstances, such disclosure is reasonably expected to lead to a significant personal security threat.

(m) The auditor's signature.

(n) The auditor's address.

(o) The date of the auditor's report.

Auditor's Report for Audits Conducted in Accordance with Both Auditing Standards of a Specific Jurisdiction and International Standards on Auditing

An auditor may be required to conduct an audit in accordance with the auditing standards of a specific jurisdiction (the 'national auditing standards'), and has additionally complied with the ISAs in the conduct of the audit. If this is the case, the auditor's report may refer to International Standards on Auditing in addition to the national auditing standards, but the auditor shall do so only if: (Ref: Para. A76–A77)   **51**

(a) There is no conflict between the requirements in the national auditing standards and those in ISAs that would lead the auditor (i) to form a different opinion, or (ii) not to include an Emphasis of Matter paragraph or Other Matter paragraph that, in the particular circumstances, is required by ISAs; and

(b) The auditor's report includes, at a minimum, each of the elements set out in paragraphs 50(a)–(o) in ISA 700 (Revised) when the auditor uses the layout or wording specified by the national auditing standards. However, reference to 'law or regulation' in paragraph 50(k) shall be read as reference to the national auditing standards. The auditor's report shall thereby identify such national auditing standards.

When the auditor's report refers to both the national auditing standards and International Standards on Auditing, the auditor's report shall identify the jurisdiction of origin of the national auditing standards.   **52**

Supplementary Information Presented with the Financial Statements
(Ref: Para. A78– A84)

If supplementary information that is not required by the applicable financial reporting framework is presented with the audited financial statements, the auditor shall evaluate whether, in the auditor's professional judgment, supplementary information is nevertheless an integral part of the financial statements due to its nature or how it is presented. When it is an integral part of the financial statements, the supplementary information shall be covered by the auditor's opinion.   **53**

If supplementary information that is not required by the applicable financial reporting framework is not considered an integral part of the audited financial statements, the auditor shall evaluate whether such supplementary information is presented in a way that sufficiently and clearly differentiates it from the audited financial statements. If this is not the case, then the auditor shall ask management to change how the unaudited supplementary information is presented. If management refuses to do so, the auditor shall identify the unaudited supplementary information and explain in the auditor's report that such supplementary information has not been audited.   **54**

***

Application and Other Explanatory Material

Qualitative Aspects of the Entity's Accounting Practices (Ref: Para. 12)

A1   Management makes a number of judgments about the amounts and disclosures in the financial statements.

A2   ISA (UK) 260 (Revised June 2016) contains a discussion of the qualitative aspects of accounting practices.[18] In considering the qualitative aspects of the entity's accounting practices, the auditor may become aware of possible bias in management's judgments. The auditor may conclude that the cumulative effect of a lack of neutrality, together with the effect of uncorrected misstatements, causes the financial statements as a whole to be materially misstated. Indicators of a lack of neutrality that may affect the auditor's evaluation of whether the financial statements as a whole are materially misstated include the following:

- The selective correction of misstatements brought to management's attention during the audit (e.g., correcting misstatements with the effect of increasing reported earnings, but not correcting misstatements that have the effect of decreasing reported earnings).
- Possible management bias in the making of accounting estimates.

A3   ISA (UK) 540 (Revised June 2016) addresses possible management bias in making accounting estimates.[19] Indicators of possible management bias do not constitute misstatements for purposes of drawing conclusions on the reasonableness of individual accounting estimates. They may, however, affect the auditor's evaluation of whether the financial statements as a whole are free from material misstatement.

Accounting Policies Appropriately Disclosed in the Financial Statements (Ref: Para. 13(a))

A4   In evaluating whether the financial statements appropriately disclose the significant accounting policies selected and applied, the auditor's consideration includes matters such as:

- Whether all disclosures related to the significant accounting policies that are required to be included by the applicable financial reporting framework have been disclosed;
- Whether the information about the significant accounting policies that has been disclosed is relevant and therefore reflects how the recognition, measurement and presentation criteria in the applicable financial reporting framework have been applied to classes of transactions, account balances and disclosures in the financial statements in the particular circumstances of the entity's operations and its environment; and
- The clarity with which the significant accounting policies have been presented.

Information Presented in the Financial Statements Is Relevant, Reliable, Comparable and Understandable (Ref: Para. 13(d))

A5   Evaluating the understandability of the financial statements includes consideration of such matters as whether:

- The information in the financial statements is presented in a clear and concise manner.

---

[18] *ISA (UK) 260 (Revised June 2016),* Communication with Those Charged with Governance, *Appendix 2.*

[19] *ISA (UK) 540 (Revised June 2016),* Auditing Accounting Estimates, Including Fair Value Accounting Estimates, and Related Disclosures, *paragraph 21.*

• The placement of significant disclosures gives appropriate prominence to them (e.g., when there is perceived value of entity-specific information to users), and whether the disclosures are appropriately cross-referenced in a manner that would not give rise to significant challenges for users in identifying necessary information.

Disclosure of the Effect of Material Transactions and Events on the Information Conveyed in the Financial Statements (Ref: Para. 13(e))

It is common for financial statements prepared in accordance with a general purpose **A6** framework to present an entity's financial position, financial performance and cash flows. Evaluating whether, in view of the applicable financial reporting framework, the financial statements provide adequate disclosures to enable the intended users to understand the effect of material transactions and events on the entity's financial position, financial performance and cash flows includes consideration of such matters as

• The extent to which the information in the financial statements is relevant and specific to the circumstances of the entity; and
• Whether the disclosures are adequate to assist the intended users to understand:

   o The nature and extent of the entity's potential assets and liabilities arising from transactions or events that do not meet the criteria for recognition (or the criteria for derecognition) established by the applicable financial reporting framework.
   o The nature and extent of risks of material misstatement arising from transactions and events.
   o The methods used and the assumptions and judgments made, and changes to them, that affect amounts presented or otherwise disclosed, including relevant sensitivity analyses.

Evaluating Whether the Financial Statements Achieve Fair Presentation (Ref: Para. 14)

Some financial reporting frameworks acknowledge explicitly or implicitly the concept **A7** of fair presentation.[20] As noted in paragraph 7(b) of this ISA (UK), a fair presentation[21] financial reporting framework not only requires compliance with the requirements of the framework, but also acknowledges explicitly or implicitly that it may be necessary for management to provide disclosures beyond those specifically required by the framework.[22]

The auditor's evaluation about whether the financial statements achieve fair presentation, **A8** both in respect of presentation and disclosure, is a matter of professional judgment. This evaluation takes into account such matters as the facts and circumstances of the entity, including changes thereto, based on the auditor's understanding of the entity and the audit evidence obtained during the audit. The evaluation also includes consideration, for example, of the disclosures needed to achieve a fair presentation arising from matters that could be material (i.e., in general, misstatements are considered to be material if they could reasonably be expected to influence the economic decisions of the users taken on the basis

---

[20] *For example, International Financial Reporting Standards (IFRSs) note that fair presentation requires the faithful representation of the effects of transactions, other events and conditions in accordance with the definitions and recognition criteria for assets, liabilities, income and expenses.*

[21] *See ISA (UK) 200 (Revised June 2016), paragraph 13(a).*

[22] *For example, IFRSs require an entity to provide additional disclosures when compliance with the specific requirements in IFRSs is insufficient to enable users to understand the impact of particular transactions, other events and conditions on the entity's financial position and financial performance (International Accounting Standard 1, Presentation of Financial Statements, paragraph 17(c)).*

of the financial statements as a whole), such as the effect of evolving financial reporting requirements or the changing economic environment.

A9   Evaluating whether the financial statements achieve fair presentation may include, for example, discussions with management and those charged with governance about their views on why a particular presentation was chosen, as well as alternatives that may have been considered. The discussions may include, for example:

- The degree to which the amounts in the financial statements are aggregated or disaggregated, and whether the presentation of amounts or disclosures obscures useful information, or results in misleading information.
- Consistency with appropriate industry practice, or whether any departures are relevant to the entity's circumstances and therefore warranted.

Description of the Applicable Financial Reporting Framework
(Ref: Para. 15)

A10   As explained in ISA (UK) 200 (Revised June 2016), the preparation of the financial statements by management and, where appropriate, those charged with governance requires the inclusion of an adequate description of the applicable financial reporting framework in the financial statements.[23] That description advises users of the financial statements of the framework on which the financial statements are based.

A11   A description that the financial statements are prepared in accordance with a particular applicable financial reporting framework is appropriate only if the financial statements comply with all the requirements of that framework that are effective during the period covered by the financial statements.

A12   A description of the applicable financial reporting framework that contains imprecise qualifying or limiting language (e.g., 'the financial statements are in substantial compliance with International Financial Reporting Standards') is not an adequate description of that framework as it may mislead users of the financial statements.

Reference to More than One Financial Reporting Framework

A13   In some cases, the financial statements may represent that they are prepared in accordance with two financial reporting frameworks (e.g., the national framework and IFRSs). This may be because management is required, or has chosen, to prepare the financial statements in accordance with both frameworks, in which case both are applicable financial reporting frameworks. Such description is appropriate only if the financial statements comply with each of the frameworks individually. To be regarded as being prepared in accordance with both frameworks, the financial statements need to comply with both frameworks simultaneously and without any need for reconciling statements. In practice, simultaneous compliance is unlikely unless the jurisdiction has adopted the other framework (e.g., IFRSs) as its own national framework, or has eliminated all barriers to compliance with it.

A14   Financial statements that are prepared in accordance with one financial reporting framework and that contain a note or supplementary statement reconciling the results to those that would be shown under another framework are not prepared in accordance with that other framework. This is because the financial statements do not include all the information in the manner required by that other framework.

---

[23] *ISA (UK) 200 (Revised June 2016), paragraphs A2–A3.*

The financial statements may, however, be prepared in accordance with one applicable   **A15**
financial reporting framework and, in addition, describe in the notes to the financial
statements the extent to which the financial statements comply with another framework
(e.g., financial statements prepared in accordance with the national framework that also
describe the extent to which they comply with IFRSs). Such description may constitute
supplementary financial information as discussed in paragraph 53 and is covered by the
auditor's opinion if it cannot be clearly differentiated from the financial statements.

Form of Opinion (Ref: Para. 16, 18–19)

The 'true and fair' concept has been part of legislation and central to accounting and   **A15-1**
auditing practice in the UK for many years. However, there is no statutory definition of
'true and fair'. In 2008, the FRC published a legal opinion, that it had commissioned,
entitled 'The true and fair requirement revisited' (The Opinion).[23a] The Opinion confirms
the overarching nature of the true and fair requirement to the preparation of financial
statements in the UK, whether they are prepared in accordance with international or
national accounting standards. The Opinion states that 'The preparation of financial
statements is not a mechanical process where compliance with relevant accounting
standards will automatically ensure that those financial statements show a true and fair
view, or a fair presentation. Such compliance may be highly likely to produce such an
outcome; but it does not guarantee it.'

In addition to preparing the financial statements in accordance with a fair presentation   **A15-2**
framework, the directors are therefore required to consider whether the individual
accounting policies applied and the financial statements as a whole present a true
and fair view. Similarly, auditors are required to exercise professional judgment in
evaluating such matters before expressing an audit opinion. As a result, The Opinion
confirms that it will not be sufficient for either directors or auditors to reach such
conclusions solely because the financial statements were prepared in accordance with
applicable accounting standards.

There may be cases where the financial statements, although prepared in accordance with   **A16**
the requirements of a fair presentation framework, do not achieve fair presentation. Where
this is the case, it may be possible for management to include additional disclosures in the
financial statements beyond those specifically required by the framework or, in extremely
rare circumstances, to depart from a requirement in the framework in order to achieve fair
presentation of the financial statements. (Ref: Para. 18)

It will be extremely rare for the auditor to consider financial statements that are prepared   **A17**
in accordance with a compliance framework to be misleading if, in accordance with ISA
(UK) 210 (Revised June 2016), the auditor determined that the framework is acceptable.[24]
(Ref: Para. 19)

Auditor's Report (Ref: Para. 20)

A written report encompasses reports issued in hard copy and those using an electronic   **A18**
medium.

[23a] *The opinion can be downloaded from the FRC website at https://www.frc.org.uk/Our-Work/Codes-Standards/
Accounting-and-Reporting-Policy/True-and-Fair.aspx.*

[24] *ISA (UK) 210 (Revised June 2016),* Agreeing the Terms of Audit Engagements, *paragraph 6(a).*

A19   The Appendix to this ISA (UK)[24a] contains illustrations of auditor's reports on financial statements, incorporating the elements set out in paragraphs 20–49. With the exception of the Opinion and Basis for Opinion sections, this ISA (UK) does not establish requirements for ordering the elements of the auditor's report. However, this ISA (UK) requires the use of specific headings, which are intended to assist in making auditor's reports that refer to audits that have been conducted in accordance with ISAs (UK) more recognizable, particularly in situations where the elements of the auditor's report are presented in an order that differs from the illustrative auditor's reports in the Appendix to this ISA (UK).

Auditor's Report for Audits Conducted in Accordance with International Standards on Auditing (UK)

Title (Ref: Para. 21)

A20   A title indicating the report is the report of an independent auditor, for example, 'Independent Auditor's Report,' distinguishes the independent auditor's report from reports issued by others.

Addressee (Ref: Para. 22)

A21   Law, regulation or the terms of the engagement may specify to whom the auditor's report is to be addressed in that particular jurisdiction. The auditor's report is normally addressed to those for whom the report is prepared, often either to the shareholders or to those charged with governance of the entity whose financial statements are being audited.

A21-1   In the UK, for entities incorporated under the Companies Act,[24b] the auditor is required to report to the company's members because the audit is undertaken on their behalf. Such auditor's reports are, therefore, typically addressed to either the members or the shareholders of the company. The auditor's report on financial statements of other types of reporting entity is addressed to the appropriate person or persons, as defined by statute or by the terms of the individual engagement.

Auditor's Opinion (Ref. Para. 24–26)

Reference to the financial statements that have been audited

A22   The auditor's report states, for example, that the auditor has audited the financial statements of the entity, which comprise [state the title of each financial statement comprising the complete set of financial statements required by the applicable financial reporting framework, specifying the date or period covered by each financial statement] and notes to the financial statements, including a summary of significant accounting policies.

A23   When the auditor is aware that the audited financial statements will be included in a document that contains other information, such as an annual report, the auditor may consider, if the form of presentation allows, identifying the page numbers on which the audited financial statements are presented. This helps users to identify the financial statements to which the auditor's report relates.

[24a] *The examples in the Appendix have not been tailored for the UK. Illustrative auditor's reports tailored for use with audits conducted in accordance with ISAs (UK) are given in the current version of the FRC's Compendium of Illustrative Auditor's Reports.*

[24b] *In the UK, the Companies Act 2006 establishes this requirement.*

'Present fairly, in all material respects' or 'give a true and fair view'

The phrases 'present fairly, in all material respects,' and 'give a true and fair view' are   **A24**
regarded as being equivalent. Whether the phrase 'present fairly, in all material respects,' or
the phrase 'give a true and fair view' is used in any particular jurisdiction is determined by
the law or regulation governing the audit of financial statements in that jurisdiction, or by
generally accepted practice in that jurisdiction. Where law or regulation requires the use of
different wording, this does not affect the requirement in paragraph 14 of this ISA (UK) for
the auditor to evaluate the fair presentation of financial statements prepared in accordance
with a fair presentation framework.

For statutory audits of financial statements, the auditor's report is required by UK   **A24-1**
legislation[24c] to state clearly whether, in the auditor's opinion, the financial statements:
(a) Give a true and fair view:
   (i)   In the case of an individual balance sheet, of the state of affairs of the entity
      as at the end of the financial year;
   (ii) In the case of an individual profit and loss account, of the profit or loss of the
      entity for the financial year;
   (iii) In the case of group accounts, of the state of affairs as at the end of the
      financial year and of the profit or loss for the financial year of the undertakings
      included in the consolidation as a whole, so far as concerns members of the
      entity;
(b) Have been properly prepared in accordance with the relevant financial reporting
    framework; and
(c) Have been prepared in accordance with the requirements of the relevant legislation.

UK auditor's reports prepared in accordance with Section 495(3) of the Companies   **A24-2**
Act 2006 will meet the requirement in paragraph 25. This is supported by recital 10
of EU Directive 2003/51/EC which states 'The fundamental requirement that an audit
opinion states whether the annual or consolidated accounts give a true and fair view
in accordance with the relevant financial reporting framework does not represent a
restriction of the scope of that opinion but clarifies the context in which it is expressed'.

In the UK, 'relevant financial reporting framework' is used in legislation to refer to the   **A24-3**
applicable financial reporting framework.

When the auditor expresses an unmodified opinion, it is not appropriate to use phrases   **A25**
such as 'with the foregoing explanation' or 'subject to' in relation to the opinion, as these
suggest a conditional opinion or a weakening or modification of opinion.

Description of the financial statements and the matters they present

The auditor's opinion covers the complete set of financial statements as defined by the   **A26**
applicable financial reporting framework. For example, in the case of many general purpose
frameworks, the financial statements may include: a statement of financial position, a
statement of comprehensive income, a statement of changes in equity, a statement of cash
flows, and related notes, which ordinarily comprise a summary of significant accounting
policies and other explanatory information. In some jurisdictions, additional information
may also be considered to be an integral part of the financial statements.

In the case of financial statements prepared in accordance with a fair presentation   **A27**
framework, the auditor's opinion states that the financial statements present fairly, in all
material respects, or give a true and fair view of, the matters that the financial statements

---

[24c] *Section 495(3) of the Companies Act 2006.*

are designed to present. For example, in the case of financial statements prepared in accordance with IFRSs, these matters are *the financial position of the entity as at the end of the period and the entity's financial performance and cash flows for the period then ended.* Consequently, the [...] in paragraph 25 and elsewhere in this ISA (UK) is intended to be replaced by the words in italics in the preceding sentence when the applicable financial reporting framework is IFRSs or, in the case of other applicable financial reporting frameworks, be replaced with words that describe the matters that the financial statements are designed to present.

Description of the applicable financial reporting framework and how it may affect the auditor's opinion

A28   The identification of the applicable financial reporting framework in the auditor's opinion is intended to advise users of the auditor's report of the context in which the auditor's opinion is expressed; it is not intended to limit the evaluation required in paragraph 14. The applicable financial reporting framework is identified in such terms as:

'... in accordance with International Financial Reporting Standards' or
'... in accordance with accounting principles generally accepted in Jurisdiction X ...'

A28-1   In the UK, the financial reporting framework is normally one of:

- International Financial Reporting Standards (IFRSs) as adopted by the European Union, and the national law that is applicable when using IFRSs and, in the case of consolidated financial statements of publicly traded companies,[24d] Article 4 of the IAS Regulation (1606/2002/EC).

- UK Generally Accepted Accounting Practice, which comprises applicable UK law and UK Accounting Standards as issued by the FRC.

A29   When the applicable financial reporting framework encompasses financial reporting standards and legal or regulatory requirements, the framework is identified in such terms as '... in accordance with International Financial Reporting Standards and the requirements of Jurisdiction X Corporations Act.' ISA (UK) 210 (Revised June 2016) deals with circumstances where there are conflicts between the financial reporting standards and the legislative or regulatory requirements.[25]

A29-1   In the UK, certain small companies are permitted by law to prepare their financial statements in accordance with the micro-entities regime which is considered to be a compliance framework. Paragraph 26 sets out the form of opinion for a compliance framework, however, the auditor is required by law to state whether the financial statements give a true and fair view.[25a] ISA (UK) 210 (Revised June 2016) provides guidance to support the auditor's response in these circumstances.[25b]

A30   As indicated in paragraph A13, the financial statements may be prepared in accordance with two financial reporting frameworks, which are therefore both applicable financial reporting frameworks. Accordingly, each framework is considered separately when forming the auditor's opinion on the financial statements, and the auditor's opinion in accordance with paragraphs 25–27 refers to both frameworks as follows:

[24d] *A publicly traded company is one whose securities are admitted to trading on a regulated market in any Member State in the European Union.*

[25] *ISA (UK) 210 (Revised June 2016), paragraph 18.*

[25a] *Section 495(3A) of the Companies Act 2006.*

[25b] *ISA (UK) 210 (Revised June 2016), paragraphs A36-1–A36-2.*

(a) If the financial statements comply with each of the frameworks individually, two opinions are expressed: that is, that the financial statements are prepared in accordance with one of the applicable financial reporting frameworks (e.g., the national framework) and an opinion that the financial statements are prepared in accordance with the other applicable financial reporting framework (e.g., IFRSs). These opinions may be expressed separately or in a single sentence (e.g., the financial statements are presented fairly, in all material respects [...], in accordance with accounting principles generally accepted in Jurisdiction X and with IFRSs).

(b) If the financial statements comply with one of the frameworks but fail to comply with the other framework, an unmodified opinion can be given that the financial statements are prepared in accordance with the one framework (e.g., the national framework) but a modified opinion given with regard to the other framework (e.g., IFRSs) in accordance with ISA (UK) 705 (Revised June 2016).

As indicated in paragraph A13, the financial statements may represent compliance with the applicable financial reporting framework and, in addition, disclose the extent of compliance with another financial reporting framework. Such supplementary information is covered by the auditor's opinion if it cannot be clearly differentiated from the financial statements (see paragraphs 53–54 and related application material in paragraphs A78–A86). Accordingly,   **A31**

(a) If the disclosure as to the compliance with the other framework is misleading, a modified opinion is expressed in accordance with ISA (UK) 705 (Revised June 2016).

(b) If the disclosure is not misleading, but the auditor judges it to be of such importance that it is fundamental to the users' understanding of the financial statements, an Emphasis of Matter paragraph is added in accordance with ISA (UK) 706 (Revised June 2016), drawing attention to the disclosure.

Joint Audits

The Companies Act 2006 permits companies to appoint a sole auditor or joint auditors. Where a company appoints joint auditors each firm is required to agree on the results of the audit and submit a joint auditor's report and opinion. In the case of disagreement, each firm is required to submit the auditor's opinion in a separate paragraph of the auditor's report and state the reason for the disagreement.[25c]   **A31-1**

Basis for Opinion (Ref: Para. 28)

The Basis for Opinion section provides important context about the auditor's opinion. Accordingly, this ISA (UK) requires the Basis for Opinion section to directly follow the Opinion section in the auditor's report.   **A32**

The reference to the standards used conveys to the users of the auditor's report that the audit has been conducted in accordance with established standards.   **A33**

Relevant ethical requirements (Ref: Para. 28(c))

The identification of the jurisdiction of origin of relevant ethical requirements increases transparency about those requirements relating to the particular audit engagement. ISA (UK) 200 (Revised June 2016) explains that relevant ethical requirements ordinarily comprise Parts A and B of the IESBA Code related to an audit of financial statements   **A34**

[25c] *Section 495(5) of the Companies Act 2006.*

together with national requirements that are more restrictive.[26] When the relevant ethical requirements include those of the IESBA Code, the statement may also make reference to the IESBA Code. If the IESBA Code constitutes all of the ethical requirements relevant to the audit, the statement need not identify a jurisdiction of origin.

A35   In some jurisdictions, relevant ethical requirements may exist in several different sources, such as the ethical code(s) and additional rules and requirements within law and regulation. When the independence and other relevant ethical requirements are contained in a limited number of sources, the auditor may choose to name the relevant source(s) (e.g., the name of the code, rule or regulation applicable in the jurisdiction), or may refer to a term that is commonly understood and that appropriately summarizes those sources (e.g., independence requirements for audits of private entities in Jurisdiction X).

A35-1   The FRC's Ethical Standard applies to all audit engagements performed in compliance with ISAs (UK). For audit engagements of certain types of entities (Listed; SME Listed; Public Interest), it includes either additional, or less stringent, requirements that apply in certain circumstances.[26a]

A35-2   The firm is required to establish policies and procedures in accordance with the FRC's Ethical Standard[26b] that set out the circumstances in which the additional requirements, applicable to audit engagements for certain types of entities (Listed; SME Listed; Public Interest), apply to other audit engagements.

A35-3   When identifying the relevant ethical requirements in the auditor's report and indicating that these include the FRC's Ethical Standard, the auditor indicates that they were applied as required for each type of entity (Listed; SME Listed; Public Interest) for which the FRC Ethical Standard includes additional requirements:
   (a)   That is relevant in the case of the audited entity; and
   (b)   Where (having regard to the policies and procedures referred to in paragraph A30-2) the auditor determined it to be appropriate to apply to the audit engagement the additional requirements included in the FRC Ethical Standard applicable for that type of entity.

A35-4   Where the firm has taken advantage of an exemption provided in the FRC's Ethical Standard in relation to audits of small entities, the auditor's report discloses this fact.[26c]

A36   Law or regulation, national auditing standards or the terms of an audit engagement may require the auditor to provide in the auditor's report more specific information about the sources of the relevant ethical requirements, including those pertaining to independence, that applied to the audit of the financial statements.

A37   In determining the appropriate amount of information to include in the auditor's report when there are multiple sources of relevant ethical requirements relating to the audit of the financial statements, an important consideration is balancing transparency against the risk of obscuring other useful information in the auditor's report.

---

[26]   *ISA (UK) 200 (Revised June 2016), paragraph A14.*

[26a]   *FRC's Ethical Standard, Part B, Section 1 – General Requirements and Guidance, paragraph 1.48.*

[26b]   *FRC's Ethical Standard, Part B, Section 1 – General Requirements and Guidance, paragraph 1.49.*

[26c]   *FRC's Ethical Standard, Part B, Section 6 – Provisions Available for Audits of Small Entities, paragraph 6.15.*

Considerations specific to group audits

In group audits when there are multiple sources of relevant ethical requirements, including those pertaining to independence, the reference in the auditor's report to the jurisdiction ordinarily relates to the relevant ethical requirements that are applicable to the group engagement team. This is because, in a group audit, component auditors are also subject to ethical requirements that are relevant to the group audit.[27]   **A38**

The ISAs (UK) do not establish specific independence or ethical requirements for auditors, including component auditors, and thus do not extend, or otherwise override, the independence requirements of the IESBA Code or other ethical requirements to which the group engagement team is subject, nor do the ISAs (UK) require that the component auditor in all cases to be subject to the same specific independence requirements that are applicable to the group engagement team. As a result, relevant ethical requirements, including those pertaining to independence, in a group audit situation may be complex. ISA (UK) 600 (Revised June 2016)[28] provides guidance for auditors in performing work on the financial information of a component for a group audit, including those situations where the component auditor does not meet the independence requirements that are relevant to the group audit.   **A39**

Key Audit Matters (Ref: Para. 31)

Law or regulation may require communication of key audit matters for audits of entities other than listed entities, for example, entities characterized in such law or regulation as public interest entities.   **A40**

The auditor may also decide to communicate key audit matters for other entities, including those that may be of significant public interest, for example because they have a large number and wide range of stakeholders and considering the nature and size of the business. Examples of such entities may include financial institutions (such as banks, insurance companies, and pension funds), and other entities such as charities.   **A41**

ISA (UK) 210 (Revised June 2016) requires the auditor to agree the terms of the audit engagement with management and those charged with governance, as appropriate, and explains that the roles of management and those charged with governance in agreeing the terms of the audit engagement for the entity depend on the governance arrangements of the entity and relevant law or regulation.[29] ISA (UK) 210 (Revised June 2016) also requires the audit engagement letter or other suitable form of written agreement to include reference to the expected form and content of any reports to be issued by the auditor.[30] When the auditor is not otherwise required to communicate key audit matters, ISA (UK) 210 (Revised June 2016)[31] explains that it may be helpful for the auditor to make reference in the terms of the audit engagement to the possibility of communicating key audit matters in the auditor's report and, in certain jurisdictions, it may be necessary for the auditor to include a reference to such possibility in order to retain the ability to do so.   **A42**

---

[27] *ISA (UK) 600 (Revised June 2016), paragraph A37.*

[28] *ISA (UK) 600 (Revised June 2016), paragraphs 19–20.*

[29] *ISA (UK) 210 (Revised June 2016), paragraphs 9 and A21.*

[30] *ISA (UK) 210 (Revised June 2016), paragraph 10.*

[31] *ISA (UK) 210 (Revised June 2016), paragraph A23a.*

Considerations specific to public sector entities

A43   Listed entities are not common in the public sector. However, public sector entities may be significant due to size, complexity or public interest aspects. In such cases, an auditor of a public sector entity may be required by law or regulation or may otherwise decide to communicate key audit matters in the auditor's report.

Responsibilities for the Financial Statements (Ref: Para. 33–35)

A44   ISA (UK) 200 (Revised June 2016) explains the premise, relating to the responsibilities of management and, where appropriate, those charged with governance, on which an audit in accordance with ISAs (UK) is conducted.[32] Management and, where appropriate, those charged with governance accept responsibility for the preparation of the financial statements in accordance with the applicable financial reporting framework, including, where relevant, their fair presentation. Management also accepts responsibility for such internal control as it determines is necessary to enable the preparation of financial statements that are free from material misstatement, whether due to fraud or error. The description of management's responsibilities in the auditor's report includes reference to both responsibilities as it helps to explain to users the premise on which an audit is conducted. ISA (UK) 260 (Revised June 2016) uses the term those charged with governance to describe the person(s) or organization(s) with responsibility for overseeing the entity, and provides a discussion about the diversity of governance structures across jurisdictions and by entity.

A44-1   In the UK, the preparation of financial statements requires those charged with governance to make significant accounting estimates and judgments, as well as to determine the appropriate accounting principles and methods used in preparation of the financial statements. This determination will be made in the context of the financial reporting framework that those charged with governance choose, or are required, to use. In contrast, the auditor's responsibility is to audit the financial statements in order to express an opinion on them.

A45   There may be circumstances when it is appropriate for the auditor to add to the descriptions of the responsibilities of management and those charged with governance in paragraphs 34–35 to reflect additional responsibilities that are relevant to the preparation of the financial statements in the context of the particular jurisdiction or the nature of the entity.

A46   ISA (UK) 210 (Revised June 2016) requires the auditor to agree management's responsibilities in an engagement letter or other suitable form of written agreement.[33] ISA (UK) 210 (Revised June 2016) provides some flexibility in doing so, by explaining that, if law or regulation prescribes the responsibilities of management and, where appropriate, those charged with governance in relation to financial reporting, the auditor may determine that the law or regulation includes responsibilities that, in the auditor's judgment, are equivalent in effect to those set out in ISA (UK) 210 (Revised June 2016). For such responsibilities that are equivalent, the auditor may use the wording of the law or regulation to describe them in the engagement letter or other suitable form of written agreement. In such cases, this wording may also be used in the auditor's report to describe the responsibilities as required by paragraph 34(a) of this ISA (UK). In other circumstances, including where the auditor decides not to use the wording of law or regulation as incorporated in the engagement letter, the wording in paragraph 34(a) of this ISA (UK) is used. In addition

---

[32] *ISA (UK) 200 (Revised June 2016), paragraph 13(j).*

[33] *ISA (UK) 210 (Revised June 2016), paragraph 6(b)(i)–(ii).*

to including the description of management's responsibilities in the auditor's report as required by paragraph 34, the auditor may refer to a more detailed description of these responsibilities by including a reference to where such information may be obtained (e.g., in the annual report of the entity or a website of an appropriate authority).

In some jurisdictions, law or regulation prescribing management's responsibilities may **A47** specifically refer to a responsibility for the adequacy of accounting books and records, or accounting system. As books, records and systems are an integral part of internal control (as defined in ISA (UK) 315 (Revised June 2016)[34]), the descriptions in ISA (UK) 210 (Revised June 2016) and in paragraph 34 do not make specific reference to them.

The Appendix[34a] to this ISA (UK) provides illustrations of how the requirement in **A48** paragraph 34(b) would be applied when IFRSs is the applicable financial reporting framework. If an applicable financial reporting framework other than IFRSs is used, the illustrative statements featured in the Appendix to this ISA (UK) may need to be adapted to reflect the application of the other financial reporting framework in the circumstances.

Oversight of the financial reporting process (Ref: Para. 35)

When some, but not all, of the individuals involved in the oversight of the financial reporting **A49** process are also involved in preparing the financial statements, the description as required by paragraph 35 of this ISA (UK) may need to be modified to appropriately reflect the particular circumstances of the entity. When individuals responsible for the oversight of the financial reporting process are the same as those responsible for the preparation of the financial statements, no reference to oversight responsibilities is required.

Auditor's Responsibilities for the Audit of the Financial Statements (Ref: Para. 37–40)

The description of the auditor's responsibilities as required by paragraphs 37–40 of this **A50** ISA (UK) may be tailored to reflect the specific nature of the entity, for example, when the auditor's report addresses consolidated financial statements. Illustration 2 in the Appendix[34a] to this ISA (UK) includes an example of how this may be done.

Where the auditor is required to report by exception on certain matters relating to going **A50-1** concern, the auditor is required to include a description of the auditor's responsibilities with respect to those matters in the auditor's report. When describing the auditor's responsibilities relating to management's use of the going concern basis of accounting and the disclosure of material uncertainties, the auditor may choose to include this description either:
(a) in the Auditor's Responsibilities for the Audit of the Financial Statements section of the auditor's report; or
(b) in the Conclusions Relating to Going Concern section of the auditor's report,[34b]

and cross-refer from the respective section as appropriate.

---

[34] ISA (UK) 315 (Revised June 2016), Identifying and Assessing the Risks of Material Misstatement through Understanding the Entity and Its Environment, *paragraph 4(c).*

[34a] *The examples in the Appendix have not been tailored for the UK. Illustrative auditor's reports tailored for use with audits conducted in accordance with ISAs (UK) are given in the current version of the FRC's Compendium of Illustrative Auditor's Reports.*

[34b] *ISA (UK) 570 (Revised June 2016), paragraph 21-2 deals with the auditor's responsibilities to include such a section in the auditor's report.*

A50-2   Auditor's reports which include a description of the auditor's responsibilities relating to management's use of the going concern basis of accounting and the disclosure of material uncertainties in the Conclusions Relating to Going Concern section of the auditor's report will include the minimum elements of an auditor's report required by paragraph 50(k) of ISA 700 (Revised) and therefore the auditor is not precluded from being able to assert compliance with International Standards on Auditing issued by the IAASB.

Objectives of the auditor (Ref: Para. 38(a))

A51   The auditor's report explains that the objectives of the auditor are to obtain reasonable assurance about whether the financial statements as a whole are free from material misstatement, whether due to fraud or error, and to issue an auditor's report that includes the auditor's opinion. These are in contrast to management's responsibilities for the preparation for the financial statements.

Description of materiality (Ref: Para. 38(c))

A52   The Appendix to this ISA (UK) provides illustrations of how the requirement in paragraph 38(c), to provide a description of materiality, would be applied when IFRSs is the applicable financial reporting framework. If an applicable financial reporting framework other than IFRSs is used, the illustrative statements presented in the Appendix to this ISA (UK) may need to be adapted to reflect the application of the other financial reporting framework in the circumstances.

Auditor's responsibilities relating to ISA (UK) 701 (Ref: Para. 40(c))

A53   The auditor may also consider it useful to provide additional information in the description of the auditor's responsibilities beyond what is required by paragraph 40(c). For example, the auditor may make reference to the requirement in paragraph 9 of ISA (UK) 701 to determine the matters that required significant auditor attention in performing the audit, taking into account areas of higher assessed risk of material misstatement or significant risks identified in accordance with ISA (UK) 315 (Revised June 2016); significant auditor judgments relating to areas in the financial statements that involved significant management judgment, including accounting estimates that have been identified as having high estimation uncertainty; and the effects on the audit of significant events or transactions that occurred during the period.

Location of the description of the auditor's responsibilities for the audit of the financial statements (Ref: Para. 41, 50(k))

A54   Including the information required by paragraphs 39–40 of this ISA (UK) in an appendix to the auditor's report or, when law, regulation or national auditing standards expressly permit, referring to a website of an appropriate authority containing such information may be a useful way of streamlining the content of the auditor's report. However, because the description of the auditor's responsibilities contains information that is necessary to inform users' expectations of an audit conducted in accordance with ISAs (UK), a reference is required to be included in the auditor's report indicating where such information can be accessed.

Location in an appendix (Ref: Para. 41(b), 50(k))

A55   Paragraph 40 permits the auditor to include the statements required by paragraphs 39–40 describing the auditor's responsibilities for the audit of the financial statements in an appendix to the auditor's report, provided that appropriate reference is made within the body of the auditor's report to the location of the appendix. The following is an illustration of how such a reference to an appendix could be made in the auditor's report:

Auditor's Responsibilities for the Audit of the Financial Statements

Our objectives are to obtain reasonable assurance about whether the financial statements as a whole are free from material misstatement, whether due to fraud or error, and to issue an auditor's report that includes our opinion. Reasonable assurance is a high level of assurance, but is not a guarantee that an audit conducted in accordance with ISAs (UK) will always detect a material misstatement when it exists. Misstatements can arise from fraud or error and are considered material if, individually or in the aggregate, they could reasonably be expected to influence the economic decisions of users taken on the basis of these financial statements.

A further description of our responsibilities for the audit of the financial statements is included in appendix X of this auditor's report. This description, which is located at [*indicate page number or other specific reference to the location of the description*], forms part of our auditor's report.

Reference to a website of an appropriate authority (Ref: Para. 41(c), 42)

Paragraph 41 explains that the auditor may refer to a description of the auditor's responsibilities located on a website of an appropriate authority, only if expressly permitted by law, regulation or national auditing standards. The information on the website that is incorporated in the auditor's report by way of a specific reference to the website location where such information can be found may describe the auditor's work, or the audit in accordance with ISAs (UK) more broadly, but it cannot be inconsistent with the description required in paragraphs 39–40 of this ISA (UK). This means that the wording of the description of the auditor's responsibilities on the website may be more detailed, or may address other matters relating to an audit of financial statements, provided that such wording reflects and does not contradict the matters addressed in paragraphs 39–40.

A56

An appropriate authority could be a national auditing standard setter, regulator, or an audit oversight body. Such organizations are well-placed to ensure the accuracy, completeness and continued availability of the standardized information. It would not be appropriate for the auditor to maintain such a website. The following is an illustration of how such a reference to a website could be made in the auditor's report:

A57

Auditor's Responsibilities for the Audit of the Financial Statements

Our objectives are to obtain reasonable assurance about whether the financial statements as a whole are free from material misstatement, whether due to fraud or error, and to issue an auditor's report that includes our opinion. Reasonable assurance is a high level of assurance, but is not a guarantee that an audit conducted in accordance with ISAs (UK) will always detect a material misstatement when it exists. Misstatements can arise from fraud or error and are considered material if, individually or in the aggregate, they could reasonably be expected to influence the economic decisions of users taken on the basis of these financial statements.

A further description of our responsibilities for the audit of the financial statements is located at [*Organization's*] website at: [*website address*]. This description forms part of our auditor's report.

A57-1   The FRC maintains on its web-site a generic 'Description of the Auditor's Responsibilities for the Audit of the Financial Statements' of private sector entities.[34c] These descriptions address the auditor's responsibilities under ISAs (UK).

Other Reporting Responsibilities (Ref: Para. 43–45)

A58   In some jurisdictions, the auditor may have additional responsibilities to report on other matters that are supplementary to the auditor's responsibilities under the ISAs (UK). For example, the auditor may be asked to report certain matters if they come to the auditor's attention during the course of the audit of the financial statements. Alternatively, the auditor may be asked to perform and report on additional specified procedures, or to express an opinion on specific matters, such as the adequacy of accounting books and records, internal control over financial reporting or other information. Auditing standards in the specific jurisdiction often provide guidance on the auditor's responsibilities with respect to specific additional reporting responsibilities in that jurisdiction.

A58-1   In the UK, other reporting responsibilities may be determined by specific statutory requirements applicable to the reporting entity, or, in some circumstances, by the terms of the auditor's engagement. Such matters may be required to be dealt with by either:
(a)   A positive statement in the auditor's report; or
(b)   By exception.

An example of (b) arises in the UK where company legislation requires the auditor of a company to report when a company has not maintained adequate accounting records.[34d]

A58-2   Where the auditor is required to report by exception and has discharged the auditor's responsibilities and has nothing to report in respect of them, the conclusion could be expressed in the form of the following phrase: 'We have nothing to report in respect of the following.'

A58-3   Where the auditor expresses a modified conclusion in respect of other reporting responsibilities (including those on which they are required to report by exception), ISA (UK) 705 (Revised June 2016), adapted as necessary in the circumstances, may assist the auditor in considering the nature and form of the modification that is appropriate. Such a modification may also give rise to a modification of the auditor's opinion on the financial statements in accordance with ISA (UK) 705 (Revised June 2016). For example, if adequate accounting records have not been maintained and as a result it proves impracticable for the auditor to obtain sufficient appropriate evidence concerning material matters in the financial statements, the auditor's report on the financial statements includes a qualified opinion or disclaimer of opinion arising from that limitation in accordance with ISA (UK) 705 (Revised June 2016).

A59   In some cases, the relevant law or regulation may require or permit the auditor to report on these other responsibilities as part of their auditor's report on the financial statements. In other cases, the auditor may be required or permitted to report on them in a separate report.

A59-1   In the UK, for the audit of certain public sector entities the audit mandate may require the auditor to express an opinion on regularity. Regularity is the requirement that financial transactions are in accordance with the legislation authorizing them.

[34c] *The web-site reference relevant to the UK is www.frc.org.uk/auditscopeukprivate.*

[34d] *Section 498(2) of the Companies Act 2006.*

Paragraphs 43–45 of this ISA (UK) permit combined presentation of other reporting responsibilities and the auditor's responsibilities under the ISAs (UK) only when they address the same topics and the wording of the auditor's report clearly differentiates the other reporting responsibilities from those under the ISAs (UK). Such clear differentiation may make it necessary for the auditor's report to refer to the source of the other reporting responsibilities and to state that such responsibilities are beyond those required under the ISAs (UK). Otherwise, other reporting responsibilities are required to be addressed in a separate section in the auditor's report with a heading 'Report on Other Legal and Regulatory Requirements,' or otherwise as appropriate to the content of the section. In such cases, paragraph 45 requires the auditor to include reporting responsibilities under the ISAs (UK) under a heading titled 'Report on the Audit of the Financial Statements.' — **A60**

Auditor's responsibilities and duties for the directors' remuneration report in the UK

Section 420 of the Companies Act 2006 sets out the duty of directors of quoted companies[34e] to prepare a directors' remuneration report for each financial year of a company. — **A60-1**

Section 497 of the Companies Act 2006 requires in respect of quoted companies that the auditor in the auditor's report on the company's annual accounts for the financial year, must: — **A60-2**

(a) Report to the company's members on the auditable part of the directors' remuneration report, and
(b) State whether in the auditor's opinion that part of the directors' remuneration report has been properly prepared in accordance with this Act.

Section 498(2) of the Companies Act 2006 also requires the auditor of a quoted company to form an opinion as to whether the auditable part of the company's directors' remuneration report is in agreement with the accounting records and returns. If the auditor is of the opinion that the auditable part of the report is not in agreement with the accounting records and returns the auditor is required to state that fact in the auditor's report. — **A60-3**

Section 498(4) of the Companies Act 2006 further requires that if the requirements of regulations under Section 421 of the Companies Act 2006 as to information forming the auditable part of the directors' remuneration report are not complied with in that report the auditor is required to include in the auditor's report, so far as the auditor is reasonably able to do so, a statement giving the required particulars. — **A60-4**

Section 498(4) of the Companies Act 2006 has an identical requirement with respect to the disclosures made under Section 412 of the Companies Act 2006 (disclosure of directors' benefits: remuneration, pensions and compensation for loss of office in the notes to the accounts). These latter requirements are separate from the requirements relating to the directors' remuneration report. — **A60-5**

Provisions of the directors' remuneration report which are subject to audit

The information contained in the directors' remuneration report which is subject to audit is the information required by paragraphs 4–17 of Part 3 of Schedule 8 of The Large and Medium-sized Companies and Groups (Accounts and Reports) Regulations 2008. — **A60-6**

[34e] *A quoted company is defined in Section 385 of the Companies Act 2006.*

Reporting on the directors' remuneration report

A60-7   As the auditor is not required to audit all of the information contained in the directors' remuneration report the auditor will need, in the auditor's report, to describe accurately which elements of the directors' remuneration report the auditor has audited. The auditor, therefore, makes arrangements with the directors, well in advance of the year end, to ensure that the audited disclosures will be clearly distinguished from those that have not been audited.

A60-8   It would be unsatisfactory for an auditor, in the auditor's report, to describe what the auditor has audited in an uninformative manner such as 'the disclosures required by Part 3 of Schedule 8 to The Large and Medium-sized Companies and Groups (Accounts and Reports) Regulations' as this would require readers of the auditor's report to have a detailed knowledge of the requirements.

A60-9   The auditor assesses whether the scope of the audit will be capable of being clearly described. If this cannot be achieved to the auditor's satisfaction by cross-reference, the auditor sets out the particulars that have been audited within the auditor's report.

Difference between the disclosures required by Schedule 5 and Schedule 8 of The Large and Medium-sized Companies and Groups (Accounts and Reports) Regulations 2008

A60-10   Schedule 5 of the Regulations requires a company to provide certain information concerning directors' remuneration by way of the notes to the company's financial statements. The majority of the provisions of Schedule 5 apply only to unquoted companies (as the information required to be disclosed would be duplicated by disclosures in the directors' remuneration report). However, the provisions described as 'Total amount of directors' remuneration etc.' apply to both quoted and unquoted companies.

A60-11   A consequence of this may be that the financial statements of a quoted company disclose aggregate directors' remuneration that may differ from the aggregate directors' remuneration disclosed in the directors' remuneration report. This may arise because the definition of aggregate remuneration differs between the two Schedules.

A60-12   Both of these disclosures are reported on by the auditor. Where both disclosures have been prepared in accordance with the requirements of the Companies Act 2006 and the various Regulations any difference between the disclosures is, prima facie, an inconsistency. However, this inconsistency arises from complying with the law and it would, therefore, be inappropriate to 'correct' the inconsistency. However, as users may think the inconsistency is a mistake the auditor encourages the directors to provide an explanation of any difference within the annual report.

Issuing the directors' remuneration report as a separate document

A60-13   If a quoted company issues its directors' remuneration report as a separate document the scope of the auditor's report included in the annual report will, nevertheless, encompass the auditable part of the directors' remuneration report. For this reason the requirements of ISA (UK) 720 (Revised June 2016)[34f] apply to the content of a separate directors' remuneration report, notwithstanding the fact that the Report is not included in a document containing audited financial statements.

[34f] *ISA (UK) 720 (Revised June 2016), The Auditor's Responsibilities Relating to Other Information.*

When the directors' remuneration report is issued as a separate document, although not required by the Companies Act 2006, the auditor: **A60-14**

(a) When the auditor's report is unmodified, encourages the directors to indicate within the directors' remuneration report where the auditor's report, prepared in accordance with Section 495 of the Companies Act 2006, may be found; or

(b) When the auditor expresses either a qualified or adverse opinion or disclaims an opinion, which is relevant to the directors' remuneration report, requires the directors to reproduce the relevant parts of the auditor's report as part of the directors' remuneration report. In the event that the directors do not agree to do so, the auditor considers whether to resign.

Name of the Engagement Partner (Ref: Para. 46)

ISQC (UK) 1 (Revised June 2016)[35] requires that the firm establish policies and procedures to provide reasonable assurance that engagements are performed in accordance with professional standards and applicable legal and regulatory requirements. Notwithstanding these ISQC (UK) 1 (Revised June 2016) requirements, naming the engagement partner in the auditor's report is intended to provide further transparency to the users of the auditor's report on financial statements of a listed entity. **A61**

Law, regulation or national auditing standards may require that the auditor's report include the name of the engagement partner responsible for audits other than those of financial statements of listed entities. The auditor may also be required by law, regulation or national auditing standards, or may decide to include additional information beyond the engagement partner's name in the auditor's report to further identify the engagement partner, for example, the engagement partner's professional license number that is relevant to the jurisdiction where the auditor practices. **A62**

In rare circumstances, the auditor may identify information or be subject to experiences that indicate the likelihood of a personal security threat that, if the identity of the engagement partner is made public, may result in physical harm to the engagement partner, other engagement team members or other closely related individuals. However, such a threat does not include, for example, threats of legal liability or legal, regulatory or professional sanctions. Discussions with those charged with governance about circumstances that may result in physical harm may provide additional information about the likelihood or severity of the significant personal security threat. Law, regulation or national auditing standards may establish further requirements that are relevant to determining whether the disclosure of the name of the engagement partner may be omitted. **A63**

Signature of the Auditor (Ref: Para. 47)

The auditor's signature is either in the name of the audit firm, the personal name of the auditor or both, as appropriate for the particular jurisdiction. In addition to the auditor's signature, in certain jurisdictions, the auditor may be required to declare in the auditor's report the auditor's professional accountancy designation or the fact that the auditor or firm, as appropriate, has been recognized by the appropriate licensing authority in that jurisdiction. **A64**

---

[35] *ISQC (UK) 1 (Revised June 2016),* Quality Control for Firms that Perform Audits and Reviews of Financial Statements, and Other Assurance and Related Services Engagements, *paragraph 32.*

The 'Senior Statutory Auditor' under the UK Companies Act 2006[35a]

A64-1   Section 503(3) of the Companies Act 2006 requires, where the auditor is a firm, that the auditor's report must be signed by the 'senior statutory auditor in his or her own name for and on behalf of the auditor'.

A64-2   Sections 503 and 504 of the Companies Act 2006 address the signature of the auditor's report. The requirement for the senior statutory auditor to sign in his or her own name applies to auditor's reports:

(a) Prepared in accordance with the requirements of Sections 495, 496 and 497 of the Companies Act 2006; and

(b) In respect of voluntary revisions of annual accounts and reports made in accordance with Section 454 of the Companies Act 2006.

A64-3   The Companies Act 2006 sets out a number of requirements regarding the appointment of auditors. However, other than as described in paragraph A59-4, there are no legal requirements concerning eligibility for appointment as the senior statutory auditor. This is an internal matter for the firm as under Section 504(1) of the Companies Act 2006 it is the firm which is required to identify which individual is the senior statutory auditor.

Eligibility for appointment as senior statutory auditor in the UK

A64-4   Section 504(2) of the Companies Act 2006 requires that the person identified as senior statutory auditor of a company must be eligible for appointment as auditor of the company in question. Eligibility for appointment is dealt with in Sections 1212 to 1225 of the Companies Act 2006.

Meaning of 'Senior Statutory Auditor' in the UK

A64-5   Subject to meeting the Companies Act 2006 requirement described in paragraph A59-4, the term 'Senior Statutory Auditor' has the same meaning as the term 'Engagement Partner' when used in ISAs (UK).[35b]

Involvement of more than one partner in an audit engagement

A64-6   Where more than one partner is involved in the conduct of an audit engagement, it is important that the responsibilities of the respective partners are clearly defined and understood by the engagement team.[35c] In particular, it is necessary for it to be clearly understood which partner is designated as the engagement partner and is, therefore, the senior statutory auditor identified by the firm in accordance with Section 504(1) of the Companies Act 2006.

[35a] *The Secretary of State has appointed the Auditing Practices Board by virtue of Article 11 of the 'Statutory Auditors (Delegation of Functions etc) Order 2008'. SI 2008 No. 496 to issue guidance with respect to the meaning of the term 'senior statutory auditor'. This ISA (UK) constitutes that guidance.*

[35b] *ISA (UK) 220 (Revised June 2016), Quality Control for Audits of Historical Financial Information, paragraph 7(a).*

[35c] *ISA (UK) 220 (Revised June 2016), paragraph A13.*

Meaning of 'Signing' the Auditor's Report

Section 505(1) of the Companies Act 2006 requires that the name of the senior statutory auditor must be stated in copies of the auditor's report published by, or on behalf of, the company.

A64-7

In paragraph A59-7 references to the auditor's report is to the auditor's report provided to the company by the auditor upon completion of the audit. Such references do not refer to the authentication of the copy auditor's reports required to be delivered to the Registrar of Companies.[35d]

A64-8

Paragraphs 6–10 of Schedule 1 of 'The Companies Act 2006 (Commencement No.5, Transitional Provisions and Savings) Order 2007'[35e] address the authentication of accounts and reports filed with the Registrar. With effect from 6 April 2008 this order requires the copies of auditor's reports delivered to the Registrar to:

A64-9

(a) State the name of the auditor and (where the auditor is a firm) the name of the person who signed it as senior statutory auditor; and

(b) Be signed by the auditor or (where the auditor is a firm) in the name of the firm by a person authorized to sign on the firm's behalf.

The senior statutory auditor, therefore, does not necessarily need to sign copy auditor's reports that are required to be delivered to the Registrar.

Changing the senior statutory auditor during the reporting period

Where the firm changes the senior statutory auditor (ie the engagement partner) during the engagement the new senior statutory auditor reviews the audit work performed to the date of the change. The review procedures are sufficient to satisfy the new senior statutory auditor that the audit work performed to the date of the review had been planned and performed in accordance with professional standards and regulatory and legal requirements.[35f]

A64-10

Senior statutory auditor unable to be present to sign the auditor's report

Under Section 503(3) of the Companies Act 2006, the senior statutory auditor must sign the auditor's report. Another partner, or responsible individual, is not able to sign for and on behalf of the senior statutory auditor.

A64-11

In circumstances where the senior statutory auditor is unable to continue to take responsibility for the direction, supervision and performance of the audit, the firm appoints a replacement senior statutory auditor and the circumstances are treated in the same way as a change of engagement partner described in paragraph A19 of ISA (UK) 220 (Revised June 2016).

A64-12

In circumstances where the senior statutory auditor is absent but is still able to, and does, take responsibility for the direction, supervision and performance of the audit,

A64-13

[35d] *In the Companies Act 2006, the expressions 'the Registrar of Companies' and 'the Registrar' mean the registrar of companies for England & Wales, Scotland or Northern Ireland, as the case may require (Section 1060 (3) the Companies Act 2006).*

[35e] *SI 2007 No. 3495.*

[35f] *ISA (UK) 220 (Revised June 2016), Quality Control for Audits of Historical Financial Information, paragraph A19.*

the senior statutory auditor may sign the auditor's report using electronic means (eg e-mail or fax).

A64-14   In circumstances where the auditor's report needs to be signed by a certain date (eg listed entities and other public interest entities) it would be pragmatic for the firm to have a contingency plan as to who would succeed as senior statutory auditor in the event that the audit is at an advanced stage but the senior statutory auditor is unable to sign the auditor's report. If another audit partner is actively involved in the audit engagement, a suitable contingency plan may be for that other partner to work in parallel with the senior statutory auditor and be able to take over as senior statutory auditor if the need arises. Any contingency plan would also need to take into account the firm's plans for partner rotation in accordance with the requirements of the FRC's Ethical Standard.

A64-15   An audit is considered to be at an 'advanced stage' when it is complete subject only to the following:

(a) Clearing outstanding matters which are unlikely to have a material impact on the financial statements;

(b) Completing audit procedures on the detail of note disclosures on the financial statements that will not have a material impact on the primary financial statements and completing the auditor's reading of 'other information' in the annual report, in accordance with ISA (UK) 720 (Revised June 2016);

(c) Updating the subsequent events review covering the period to the date of the auditor's report on the financial statements; and

(d) Obtaining final written representations from management and establishing that the financial statements have been reviewed and approved by the directors.

A64-16   Circumstances may arise where another partner has not worked in parallel with the senior statutory auditor. In such exceptional circumstances it may be permissible for the engagement quality control reviewer[35g] to be appointed as the replacement senior statutory auditor[35h] where:

(a) the engagement quality control reviewer has completed his or her review; and

(b) the audit is at an 'advanced stage'.

However, once an engagement quality reviewer has been appointed as a replacement senior statutory auditor he or she can no longer act as the engagement quality control reviewer because his or her objectivity may have been impaired through assuming the role of senior statutory auditor.

Joint Audits

A64-17   As indicated in paragraph A26-1, where a company appoints joint auditors each firm appoints a senior statutory auditor both of which are required to sign the auditors' report in accordance with the requirements of Section 503 of the Companies Act 2006.

A65   In some cases, law or regulation may allow for the use of electronic signatures in the auditor's report.

[35g] *This is on the assumption that the engagement quality control reviewer is eligible to be appointed as the senior statutory auditor (see paragraph A59-4 for eligibility criterion).*

[35h] *ISA (UK) 220 (Revised June 2016) Quality Control for Audits of Historical Financial Information requires an engagement quality control reviewer to be appointed in respect of all listed entities and public interest entities.*

Auditor's Address (Ref: Para. 48)

In the UK, legislation[35i] requires the auditor's report to identify the auditor's place of establishment in addition to naming the location in the jurisdiction where the auditor practices as required by paragraph 48.

A65-1

Date of the Auditor's Report (Ref: Para. 49)

The date of the auditor's report informs the user of the auditor's report that the auditor has considered the effect of events and transactions of which the auditor became aware and that occurred up to that date. The auditor's responsibility for events and transactions after the date of the auditor's report is addressed in ISA (UK) 560.[36]

A66

Since the auditor's opinion is provided on the financial statements and the financial statements are the responsibility of management, the auditor is not in a position to conclude that sufficient appropriate audit evidence has been obtained until evidence is obtained that all the statements and disclosures that comprise the financial statements have been prepared and management has accepted responsibility for them.

A67

The auditor, therefore, plans the conduct of the audit to take account of the need to ensure, before expressing an opinion on financial statements, that those charged with governance have approved the financial statements and any accompanying other information and that the auditor has completed a sufficient review of post balance sheet events.

A67-1

The date of the auditor's report is, therefore, the date on which the auditor signs the auditor's report expressing an opinion on the financial statements for distribution with those financial statements, following:

(a) Receipt of the financial statements and accompanying documents in the form approved by those charged with governance for release;

(b) Review of all documents which the auditor is required to consider in addition to the financial statements (for example the directors' report, chairman's statement or other review of an entity's affairs which will form part of the annual report): and

(c) Completion of all procedures necessary to form an opinion on the financial statements (and any other opinions required by law or regulation) including a review of post balance sheet events.

A67-2

The form of the financial statements and other information approved by those charged with governance, and considered by the auditor when signing a report expressing the auditor's opinion, may be in the form of final drafts from which printed documents will be prepared. Subsequent production of printed copies of the financial statements and the auditor's report does not constitute the creation of a new document. Copies of the report produced for circulation to shareholders or others may, therefore, reproduce a printed version of the auditor's signature showing the date of actual signature.

A67-3

If the date on which the auditor signs the report is later than that on which those charged with governance approved the financial statements, the auditor takes such steps as are appropriate:

(a) To obtain assurance that those charged with governance would have approved the financial statements on that later date (for example, by obtaining confirmation from specified individual members of the board to whom authority has been delegated for this purpose); and

A67-4

[35i] *Section 495(4) of the Companies Act 2006.*

[36] *ISA (UK) 560, Subsequent Events, paragraphs 10–17.*

(b) To ensure that the auditor's procedures for reviewing subsequent events cover the period up to that date.

A68 In some jurisdictions, law or regulation identifies the individuals or bodies (e.g., the directors) that are responsible for concluding that all the statements and disclosures that comprise the financial statements have been prepared, and specifies the necessary approval process. In such cases, evidence is obtained of that approval before dating the report on the financial statements. In other jurisdictions, however, the approval process is not prescribed in law or regulation. In such cases, the procedures the entity follows in preparing and finalizing its financial statements in view of its management and governance structures are considered in order to identify the individuals or body with the authority to conclude that all the statements that comprise the financial statements, including the related notes, have been prepared. In some cases, law or regulation identifies the point in the financial statement reporting process at which the audit is expected to be complete.

A69 In some jurisdictions, final approval of the financial statements by shareholders is required before the financial statements are issued publicly. In these jurisdictions, final approval by shareholders is not necessary for the auditor to conclude that sufficient appropriate audit evidence has been obtained. The date of approval of the financial statements for purposes of ISAs (UK) is the earlier date on which those with the recognized authority determine that all the statements and disclosures that comprise the financial statements have been prepared and that those with the recognized authority have asserted that they have taken responsibility for them.

Auditor's Report Prescribed by Law or Regulation (Ref: Para. 50)

A70 ISA (UK) 200 (Revised June 2016) explains that the auditor may be required to comply with legal or regulatory requirements in addition to ISAs.[37] When the differences between the legal or regulatory requirements and ISAs relate only to the layout and wording of the auditor's report, the requirements in paragraph 50(a)–(o) set out the minimum elements to be included in the auditor's report to enable a reference to the International Standards on Auditing. In those circumstances, the requirements in paragraphs 21–49 that are not included in paragraph 50(a)–(o) do not need to be applied including, for example, the required ordering of the Opinion and Basis for Opinion sections.

A70-1 This ISA (UK) is consistent with ISA 700 (Revised) 'Forming an Opinion and Reporting on Financial Statements,' as issued by the IAASB. Auditor's reports prepared in compliance with the requirements of this ISA (UK) will include the minimum elements of an auditor's report required by paragraph 50(a)–(o) of ISA 700 (Revised) and does not therefore preclude the auditor from being able to assert compliance with International Standards on Auditing issued by the IAASB.

A71 Where specific requirements in a particular jurisdiction do not conflict with ISAs, the layout and wording required by paragraphs 21–48 of ISA 700 (Revised) assist users of the auditor's report in more readily recognizing the auditor's report as a report of an audit conducted in accordance with ISAs.

Information Required by ISA 701 (Ref: Para. 50(h))

A72 Law or regulation may require the auditor to provide additional information about the audit that was performed, which may include information that is consistent with the objectives of ISA 701, or may prescribe the nature and extent of communication about such matters.

---

[37] *ISA (UK) 200 (Revised June 2016), paragraph A55.*

The ISAs do not override law or regulation that governs an audit of financial statements. **A73** When ISA 701 is applicable, reference can only be made to ISAs in the auditor's report if, in applying the law or regulation, the section required by paragraph 50(h) of this ISA is not inconsistent with the reporting requirements in ISA 701. In such circumstances, the auditor may need to tailor certain aspects of the communication of key audit matters in the auditor's report required by ISA 701, for example by:

- Modifying the heading 'Key Audit Matters', if law or regulation prescribes a specific heading;
- Explaining why the information required by law or regulation is being provided in the auditor's report, for example by making a reference to the relevant law or regulation and describing how that information relates to the key audit matters;
- Where law or regulation prescribes the nature and extent of the description, supplementing the prescribed information to achieve an overall description of each key audit matter that is consistent with the requirement in paragraph 13 of ISA 701.

ISA 210 deals with circumstances where law or regulation of the relevant jurisdiction **A74** prescribes the layout or wording of the auditor's report in terms that are significantly different from the requirements of ISAs, which in particular includes the auditor's opinion. In these circumstances, ISA 210 requires the auditor to evaluate:

(a) Whether users might misunderstand the assurance obtained from the audit of the financial statements and, if so,
(b) Whether additional explanation in the auditor's report can mitigate possible misunderstanding.

If the auditor concludes that additional explanation in the auditor's report cannot mitigate possible misunderstanding, ISA 210 requires the auditor not to accept the audit engagement, unless required by law or regulation to do so. In accordance with ISA 210, an audit conducted in accordance with such law or regulation does not comply with ISAs. Accordingly, the auditor does not include any reference in the auditor's report to the audit having been conducted in accordance with International Standards on Auditing.[38]

Considerations specific to public sector entities

Auditors of public sector entities may also have the ability pursuant to law or regulation **A75** to report publicly on certain matters, either in the auditor's report or in a supplementary report, which may include information that is consistent with the objectives of ISA 701. In such circumstances, the auditor may need to tailor certain aspects of the communication of key audit matters in the auditor's report required by ISA 701 or include a reference in the auditor's report to a description of the matter in the supplementary report.

Auditor's Report for Audits Conducted in Accordance with Both Auditing Standards of a Specific Jurisdiction and International Standards on Auditing (Ref: Para. 51)

The auditor may refer in the auditor's report to the audit having been conducted in **A76** accordance with both International Standards on Auditing as well as the national auditing standards when, in addition to complying with the relevant national auditing standards, the auditor complies with each of the ISAs relevant to the audit.[39]

---

[38] *ISA 210, paragraph 21.*

[39] *ISA 200, paragraph A56.*

A77   A reference to both International Standards on Auditing and the national auditing standards is not appropriate if there is a conflict between the requirements in ISAs and those in the national auditing standards that would lead the auditor to form a different opinion or not to include an Emphasis of Matter or Other Matter paragraph that, in the particular circumstances, is required by ISAs. In such a case, the auditor's report refers only to the auditing standards (either International Standards on Auditing or the national auditing standards) in accordance with which the auditor's report has been prepared.

A77-1   ISAs (UK) are consistent with International Standards on Auditing as issued by the IAASB and the requirements of ISAs (UK) do not conflict with the requirements in ISAs. An audit conducted in accordance with ISAs (UK) does not therefore preclude the auditor from being able to assert compliance with International Standards on Auditing issued by the IAASB.

Supplementary Information Presented with the Financial Statements
(Ref: Para. 53–54)

A78   In some circumstances, the entity may be required by law, regulation or standards, or may voluntarily choose, to present together with the financial statements supplementary information that is not required by the applicable financial reporting framework. For example, supplementary information might be presented to enhance a user's understanding of the applicable financial reporting framework or to provide further explanation of specific financial statement items. Such information is normally presented in either supplementary schedules or as additional notes.

A79   Paragraph 53 of this ISA (UK) explains that the auditor's opinion covers supplementary information that is an integral part of the financial statements because of its nature or how it is presented. This evaluation is a matter of professional judgment. To illustrate:

- When the notes to the financial statements include an explanation or the reconciliation of the extent to which the financial statements comply with another financial reporting framework, the auditor may consider this to be supplementary information that cannot be clearly differentiated from the financial statements. The auditor's opinion would also cover notes or supplementary schedules that are cross-referenced from the financial statements.
- When an additional profit and loss account that discloses specific items of expenditure is disclosed as a separate schedule included as an Appendix to the financial statements, the auditor may consider this to be supplementary information that can be clearly differentiated from the financial statements.

A80   Supplementary information that is covered by the auditor's opinion does not need to be specifically referred to in the auditor's report when the reference to the notes in the description of the statements that comprise the financial statements in the auditor's report is sufficient.

A81   Law or regulation may not require that the supplementary information be audited, and management may decide to ask the auditor not to include the supplementary information within the scope of the audit of the financial statements.

A82   The auditor's evaluation whether unaudited supplementary information is presented in a manner that could be construed as being covered by the auditor's opinion includes, for example, where that information is presented in relation to the financial statements and any audited supplementary information, and whether it is clearly labeled as 'unaudited.'

Management could change the presentation of unaudited supplementary information that **A83** could be construed as being covered by the auditor's opinion, for example, by:

- Removing any cross-references from the financial statements to unaudited supplementary schedules or unaudited notes so that the demarcation between the audited and unaudited information is sufficiently clear.
- Placing the unaudited supplementary information outside of the financial statements or, if that is not possible in the circumstances, at a minimum placing the unaudited notes together at the end of the required notes to the financial statements and clearly labeling them as unaudited. Unaudited notes that are intermingled with the audited notes can be misinterpreted as being audited.

The fact that supplementary information is unaudited does not relieve the auditor of the **A84** responsibilities described in ISA (UK) 720 (Revised June 2016).[40]

---

[40] *ISA (UK) 720 (Revised June 2016),* The Auditor's Responsibilities Relating to Other Information.

Appendix   (Ref: Para. A19)

Illustrations of Independent Auditor's Reports on Financial Statements

The examples in the Appendix have not been tailored for the UK. Illustrative auditor's reports tailored for use with audits conducted in accordance with ISAs (UK) are given in the current version of the FRC's Compendium of Illustrative Auditor's Reports.

- Illustration 1: An auditor's report on financial statements of a listed entity prepared in accordance with a fair presentation framework
- Illustration 2: An auditor's report on consolidated financial statements of a listed entity prepared in accordance with a fair presentation framework
- Illustration 3: An auditor's report on financial statements of an entity other than a listed entity prepared in accordance with a fair presentation framework (where reference is made to material that is located on a website of an appropriate authority)
- Illustration 4: An auditor's report on financial statements of an entity other than a listed entity prepared in accordance with a general purpose compliance framework

---

Illustration 1 – Auditor's Report on Financial Statements of a Listed Entity Prepared in Accordance with a Fair Presentation Framework

For purposes of this illustrative auditor's report, the following circumstances are assumed:

- Audit of a complete set of financial statements of a listed entity using a fair presentation framework. The audit is not a group audit (i.e., ISA 600 does not apply).
- The financial statements are prepared by management of the entity in accordance with IFRSs (a general purpose framework).
- The terms of the audit engagement reflect the description of management's responsibility for the financial statements in ISA 210.
- The auditor has concluded an unmodified (i.e., 'clean') opinion is appropriate based on the audit evidence obtained.
- The relevant ethical requirements that apply to the audit comprise the International Ethics Standards Board for Accountants' *Code of Ethics for Professional Accountants* together with the ethical requirements relating to the audit in the jurisdiction, and the auditor refers to both.
- Based on the audit evidence obtained, the auditor has concluded that a material uncertainty does not exist related to events or conditions that may cast significant doubt on the entity's ability to continue as a going concern in accordance with ISA 570 (Revised).
- Key audit matters have been communicated in accordance with ISA 701.
- The auditor has obtained all of the other information prior to the date of the auditor's report and has not identified a material misstatement of the other information.
- Those responsible for oversight of the financial statements differ from those responsible for the preparation of the financial statements.
- In addition to the audit of the financial statements, the auditor has other reporting responsibilities required under local law.

INDEPENDENT AUDITOR'S REPORT

To the Shareholders of ABC Company [or Other Appropriate Addressee]

Report on the Audit of the Financial Statements[41]

Opinion

We have audited the financial statements of ABC Company (the Company), which comprise the statement of financial position as at December 31, 20X1, and the statement of comprehensive income, statement of changes in equity and statement of cash flows for the year then ended, and notes to the financial statements, including a summary of significant accounting policies.

In our opinion, the accompanying financial statements present fairly, in all material respects, (or *give a true and fair view of*) the financial position of the Company as at December 31, 20X1, and (*of*) its financial performance and its cash flows for the year then ended in accordance with International Financial Reporting Standards (IFRSs).

Basis for Opinion

We conducted our audit in accordance with International Standards on Auditing (ISAs). Our responsibilities under those standards are further described in the *Auditor's Responsibilities for the Audit of the Financial Statements* section of our report. We are independent of the Company in accordance with the International Ethics Standards Board for Accountants' *Code of Ethics for Professional Accountants (IESBA Code)* together with the ethical requirements that are relevant to our audit of the financial statements in [*jurisdiction*], and we have fulfilled our other ethical responsibilities in accordance with these requirements and the IESBA Code. We believe that the audit evidence we have obtained is sufficient and appropriate to provide a basis for our opinion.

Key Audit Matters

Key audit matters are those matters that, in our professional judgment, were of most significance in our audit of the financial statements of the current period. These matters were addressed in the context of our audit of the financial statements as a whole, and in forming our opinion thereon, and we do not provide a separate opinion on these matters.

[*Description of each key audit matter in accordance with ISA 701.*]

Other Information [or another title if appropriate such as 'Information Other than the Financial Statements and Auditor's Report Thereon']

[*Reporting in accordance with the reporting requirements in ISA 720 (Revised) – see Illustration 1 in Appendix 2 of ISA 720 (Revised).*]

---

[41] *The sub-title 'Report on the Audit of the Financial Statements' is unnecessary in circumstances when the second sub-title 'Report on Other Legal and Regulatory Requirements' is not applicable.*

Responsibilities of Management and Those Charged with Governance for the Financial Statements[42]

Management is responsible for the preparation and fair presentation of the financial statements in accordance with IFRSs,[43] and for such internal control as management determines is necessary to enable the preparation of financial statements that are free from material misstatement, whether due to fraud or error.

In preparing the financial statements, management is responsible for assessing the Company's ability to continue as a going concern, disclosing, as applicable, matters related to going concern and using the going concern basis of accounting unless management either intends to liquidate the Company or to cease operations, or has no realistic alternative but to do so.

Those charged with governance are responsible for overseeing the Company's financial reporting process.

Auditor's Responsibilities for the Audit of the Financial Statements

Our objectives are to obtain reasonable assurance about whether the financial statements as a whole are free from material misstatement, whether due to fraud or error, and to issue an auditor's report that includes our opinion. Reasonable assurance is a high level of assurance, but is not a guarantee that an audit conducted in accordance with ISAs will always detect a material misstatement when it exists. Misstatements can arise from fraud or error and are considered material if, individually or in the aggregate, they could reasonably be expected to influence the economic decisions of users taken on the basis of these financial statements.

Paragraph 41(b) of this ISA explains that the shaded material below can be located in an Appendix to the auditor's report. Paragraph 41(c) explains that when law, regulation or national auditing standards expressly permit, reference can be made to a website of an appropriate authority that contains the description of the auditor's responsibilities, rather than including this material in the auditor's report, provided that the description on the website addresses, and is not inconsistent with, the description of the auditor's responsibilities below.

As part of an audit in accordance with ISAs, we exercise professional judgment and maintain professional skepticism throughout the audit. We also:

- Identify and assess the risks of material misstatement of the financial statements, whether due to fraud or error, design and perform audit procedures responsive to those risks, and obtain audit evidence that is sufficient and appropriate to provide a basis for our opinion. The risk of not detecting a material misstatement resulting from fraud is higher than for one resulting from error, as fraud may involve collusion, forgery, intentional omissions, misrepresentations, or the override of internal control.

- Obtain an understanding of internal control relevant to the audit in order to design audit procedures that are appropriate in the circumstances, but not for the purpose of expressing an opinion on the effectiveness of the Company's internal control.[44]

---

[42] *Throughout these illustrative auditor's reports, the terms management and those charged with governance may need to be replaced by another term that is appropriate in the context of the legal framework in the particular jurisdiction.*

[43] *Where management's responsibility is to prepare financial statements that give a true and fair view, this may read: 'Management is responsible for the preparation of financial statements that give a true and fair view in accordance with International Financial Reporting Standards, and for such ...'*

[44] *This sentence would be modified, as appropriate, in circumstances when the auditor also has a responsibility to issue an opinion on the effectiveness of internal control in conjunction with the audit of the financial statements.*

- Evaluate the appropriateness of accounting policies used and the reasonableness of accounting estimates and related disclosures made by management.

- Conclude on the appropriateness of management's use of the going concern basis of accounting and, based on the audit evidence obtained, whether a material uncertainty exists related to events or conditions that may cast significant doubt on the Company's ability to continue as a going concern. If we conclude that a material uncertainty exists, we are required to draw attention in our auditor's report to the related disclosures in the financial statements or, if such disclosures are inadequate, to modify our opinion. Our conclusions are based on the audit evidence obtained up to the date of our auditor's report. However, future events or conditions may cause the Company to cease to continue as a going concern.

- Evaluate the overall presentation, structure and content of the financial statements, including the disclosures, and whether the financial statements represent the underlying transactions and events in a manner that achieves fair presentation.

We communicate with those charged with governance regarding, among other matters, the planned scope and timing of the audit and significant audit findings, including any significant deficiencies in internal control that we identify during our audit.

We also provide those charged with governance with a statement that we have complied with relevant ethical requirements regarding independence, and to communicate with them all relationships and other matters that may reasonably be thought to bear on our independence, and where applicable, related safeguards.

From the matters communicated with those charged with governance, we determine those matters that were of most significance in the audit of the financial statements of the current period and are therefore the key audit matters. We describe these matters in our auditor's report unless law or regulation precludes public disclosure about the matter or when, in extremely rare circumstances, we determine that a matter should not be communicated in our report because the adverse consequences of doing so would reasonably be expected to outweigh the public interest benefits of such communication.

Report on Other Legal and Regulatory Requirements

[*The form and content of this section of the auditor's report would vary depending on the nature of the auditor's other reporting responsibilities prescribed by local law, regulation, or national auditing standards. The matters addressed by other law, regulation or national auditing standards (referred to as 'other reporting responsibilities') shall be addressed within this section unless the other reporting responsibilities address the same topics as those presented under the reporting responsibilities required by the ISAs as part of the Report on the Audit of the Financial Statements section. The reporting of other reporting responsibilities that address the same topics as those required by the ISAs may be combined (i.e., included in the Report on the Audit of the Financial Statements section under the appropriate subheadings) provided that the wording in the auditor's report clearly differentiates the other reporting responsibilities from the reporting that is required by the ISAs where such a difference exists.*]

The engagement partner on the audit resulting in this independent auditor's report is [*name*].

[*Signature in the name of the audit firm, the personal name of the auditor, or both, as appropriate for the particular jurisdiction*]

[*Auditor Address*]

[*Date*]

Illustration 2 – Auditor's Report on Consolidated Financial Statements of a Listed Entity Prepared in Accordance with a Fair Presentation Framework

For purposes of this illustrative auditor's report, the following circumstances are assumed:

- Audit of a complete set of consolidated financial statements of a listed entity using a fair presentation framework. The audit is a group audit of an entity with subsidiaries (i.e., ISA 600 applies).
- The consolidated financial statements are prepared by management of the entity in accordance with IFRSs (a general purpose framework).
- The terms of the audit engagement reflect the description of management's responsibility for the consolidated financial statements in ISA 210.
- The auditor has concluded an unmodified (i.e., 'clean') opinion is appropriate based on the audit evidence obtained.
- The International Ethics Standards Board for Accountants' *Code of Ethics for Professional Accountants* comprises all of the relevant ethical requirements that apply to the audit.
- Based on the audit evidence obtained, the auditor has concluded that a material uncertainty does not exist related to events or conditions that may cast significant doubt on the entity's ability to continue as a going concern in accordance with ISA 570 (Revised).
- Key audit matters have been communicated in accordance with ISA 701.
- The auditor has obtained all of the other information prior to the date of the auditor's report and has not identified a material misstatement of the other information.
- Those responsible for oversight of the consolidated financial statements differ from those responsible for the preparation of the consolidated financial statements.
- In addition to the audit of the consolidated financial statements, the auditor has other reporting responsibilities required under local law.

INDEPENDENT AUDITOR'S REPORT

To the Shareholders of ABC Company [or Other Appropriate Addressee]

Report on the Audit of the Consolidated Financial Statements[45]

Opinion

We have audited the consolidated financial statements of ABC Company and its subsidiaries (the Group), which comprise the consolidated statement of financial position as at December 31, 20X1, and the consolidated statement of comprehensive income, consolidated statement of changes in equity and consolidated statement of cash flows for the year then ended, and notes to the consolidated financial statements, including a summary of significant accounting policies.

In our opinion, the accompanying consolidated financial statements present fairly, in all material respects, (or *give a true and fair view of*) the consolidated financial position of the Group as at December 31, 20X1, and (*of*) its consolidated financial performance and its consolidated cash flows for the year then ended in accordance with International Financial Reporting Standards (IFRSs).

---

[45] *The sub-title 'Report on the Audit of the Consolidated Financial Statements' is unnecessary in circumstances when the second sub-title 'Report on Other Legal and Regulatory Requirements' is not applicable.*

Basis for Opinion

We conducted our audit in accordance with International Standards on Auditing (ISAs). Our responsibilities under those standards are further described in the *Auditor's Responsibilities for the Audit of the Consolidated Financial Statements* section of our report. We are independent of the Group in accordance with the International Ethics Standards Board for Accountants' *Code of Ethics for Professional Accountants* (IESBA Code), and we have fulfilled our other ethical responsibilities in accordance with the IESBA Code. We believe that the audit evidence we have obtained is sufficient and appropriate to provide a basis for our opinion.

Key Audit Matters

Key audit matters are those matters that, in our professional judgment, were of most significance in our audit of the consolidated financial statements of the current period. These matters were addressed in the context of our audit of the consolidated financial statements as a whole, and in forming our opinion thereon, and we do not provide a separate opinion on these matters.

[*Description of each key audit matter in accordance with ISA 701.*]

Other Information [or another title if appropriate such as 'Information Other than the Financial Statements and Auditor's Report Thereon']

[*Reporting in accordance with the reporting requirements in ISA 720 (Revised) – see Illustration 1 in Appendix 2 of ISA 720 (Revised).*]

Responsibilities of Management and Those Charged with Governance for the Consolidated Financial Statements[46]

Management is responsible for the preparation and fair presentation of the consolidated financial statements in accordance with IFRSs,[47] and for such internal control as management determines is necessary to enable the preparation of consolidated financial statements that are free from material misstatement, whether due to fraud or error.

In preparing the consolidated financial statements, management is responsible for assessing the Group's ability to continue as a going concern, disclosing, as applicable, matters related to going concern and using the going concern basis of accounting unless management either intends to liquidate the Group or to cease operations, or has no realistic alternative but to do so.

Those charged with governance are responsible for overseeing the Group's financial reporting process.

Auditor's Responsibilities for the Audit of the Consolidated Financial Statements

Our objectives are to obtain reasonable assurance about whether the consolidated financial statements as a whole are free from material misstatement, whether due to fraud or error, and to issue an auditor's report that includes our opinion. Reasonable assurance is a high

---

[46] *Or other terms that are appropriate in the context of the legal framework of the particular jurisdiction.*

[47] *Where management's responsibility is to prepare financial statements that give a true and fair view, this may read: 'Management is responsible for the preparation of financial statements that give a true and fair view in accordance with International Financial Reporting Standards, and for such ...'*

level of assurance, but is not a guarantee that an audit conducted in accordance with ISAs will always detect a material misstatement when it exists. Misstatements can arise from fraud or error and are considered material if, individually or in the aggregate, they could reasonably be expected to influence the economic decisions of users taken on the basis of these consolidated financial statements.

Paragraph 41(b) of this ISA explains that the shaded material below can be located in an Appendix to the auditor's report. Paragraph 41(c) explains that when law, regulation or national auditing standards expressly permit, reference can be made to a website of an appropriate authority that contains the description of the auditor's responsibilities, rather than including this material in the auditor's report, provided that the description on the website addresses, and is not inconsistent with, the description of the auditor's responsibilities below.

As part of an audit in accordance with ISAs, we exercise professional judgment and maintain professional skepticism throughout the audit. We also:

- Identify and assess the risks of material misstatement of the consolidated financial statements, whether due to fraud or error, design and perform audit procedures responsive to those risks, and obtain audit evidence that is sufficient and appropriate to provide a basis for our opinion. The risk of not detecting a material misstatement resulting from fraud is higher than for one resulting from error, as fraud may involve collusion, forgery, intentional omissions, misrepresentations, or the override of internal control.

- Obtain an understanding of internal control relevant to the audit in order to design audit procedures that are appropriate in the circumstances, but not for the purpose of expressing an opinion on the effectiveness of the Group's internal control.[48]

- Evaluate the appropriateness of accounting policies used and the reasonableness of accounting estimates and related disclosures made by management.

- Conclude on the appropriateness of management's use of the going concern basis of accounting and, based on the audit evidence obtained, whether a material uncertainty exists related to events or conditions that may cast significant doubt on the Group's ability to continue as a going concern. If we conclude that a material uncertainty exists, we are required to draw attention in our auditor's report to the related disclosures in the consolidated financial statements or, if such disclosures are inadequate, to modify our opinion. Our conclusions are based on the audit evidence obtained up to the date of our auditor's report. However, future events or conditions may cause the Group to cease to continue as a going concern.

- Evaluate the overall presentation, structure and content of the consolidated financial statements, including the disclosures, and whether the consolidated financial statements represent the underlying transactions and events in a manner that achieves fair presentation.

- Obtain sufficient appropriate audit evidence regarding the financial information of the entities or business activities within the Group to express an opinion on the consolidated financial statements. We are responsible for the direction, supervision and performance of the group audit. We remain solely responsible for our audit opinion.

---

[48] *This sentence would be modified, as appropriate, in circumstances when the auditor also has a responsibility to issue an opinion on the effectiveness of internal control in conjunction with the audit of the consolidated financial statements.*

We communicate with those charged with governance regarding, among other matters, the planned scope and timing of the audit and significant audit findings, including any significant deficiencies in internal control that we identify during our audit.

We also provide those charged with governance with a statement that we have complied with relevant ethical requirements regarding independence, and to communicate with them all relationships and other matters that may reasonably be thought to bear on our independence, and where applicable, related safeguards.

From the matters communicated with those charged with governance, we determine those matters that were of most significance in the audit of the consolidated financial statements of the current period and are therefore the key audit matters. We describe these matters in our auditor's report unless law or regulation precludes public disclosure about the matter or when, in extremely rare circumstances, we determine that a matter should not be communicated in our report because the adverse consequences of doing so would reasonably be expected to outweigh the public interest benefits of such communication.

Report on Other Legal and Regulatory Requirements

[*The form and content of this section of the auditor's report would vary depending on the nature of the auditor's other reporting responsibilities prescribed by local law, regulation, or national auditing standards. The matters addressed by other law, regulation or national auditing standards (referred to as 'other reporting responsibilities') shall be addressed within this section unless the other reporting responsibilities address the same topics as those presented under the reporting responsibilities required by the ISAs as part of the Report on the Audit of the Consolidated Financial Statements section. The reporting of other reporting responsibilities that address the same topics as those required by the ISAs may be combined (i.e., included in the Report on the Audit of the Consolidated Financial Statements section under the appropriate subheadings) provided that the wording in the auditor's report clearly differentiates the other reporting responsibilities from the reporting that is required by the ISAs where such a difference exists.*]

The engagement partner on the audit resulting in this independent auditor's report is [*name*].

[*Signature in the name of the audit firm, the personal name of the auditor, or both, as appropriate for the particular jurisdiction*]

[*Auditor Address*]

[*Date*]

Illustration 3 – Auditor's Report on Financial Statements of an Entity Other than a Listed Entity Prepared in Accordance with a Fair Presentation Framework

For purposes of this illustrative auditor's report, the following circumstances are assumed:

- Audit of a complete set of financial statements of an entity other than a listed entity using a fair presentation framework. The audit is not a group audit (i.e., ISA 600 does not apply).
- The financial statements are prepared by management of the entity in accordance with IFRSs (a general purpose framework).

- The terms of the audit engagement reflect the description of management's responsibility for the financial statements in ISA 210.
- The auditor has concluded an unmodified (i.e., 'clean') opinion is appropriate based on the audit evidence obtained.
- The relevant ethical requirements that apply to the audit are those of the jurisdiction.
- Based on the audit evidence obtained, the auditor has concluded that a material uncertainty does not exist related to events or conditions that may cast significant doubt on the entity's ability to continue as a going concern in accordance with ISA 570 (Revised).
- The auditor is not required, and has otherwise not decided, to communicate key audit matters in accordance with ISA 701.
- The auditor has obtained all of the other information prior to the date of the auditor's report and has not identified a material misstatement of the other information.
- Those responsible for oversight of the financial statements differ from those responsible for the preparation of the financial statements.
- The auditor has no other reporting responsibilities required under local law.
- The auditor elects to refer to the description of the auditor's responsibility included on a website of an appropriate authority.

INDEPENDENT AUDITOR'S REPORT

To the Shareholders of ABC Company [or Other Appropriate Addressee]

Opinion

We have audited the financial statements of ABC Company (the Company), which comprise the statement of financial position as at December 31, 20X1, and the statement of comprehensive income, statement of changes in equity and statement of cash flows for the year then ended, and notes to the financial statements, including a summary of significant accounting policies.

In our opinion, the accompanying financial statements present fairly, in all material respects, (or *give a true and fair view of*) the financial position of the Company as at December 31, 20X1, and (*of*) its financial performance and its cash flows for the year then ended in accordance with International Financial Reporting Standards (IFRSs).

Basis for Opinion

We conducted our audit in accordance with International Standards on Auditing (ISAs). Our responsibilities under those standards are further described in the *Auditor's Responsibilities for the Audit of the Financial Statements* section of our report. We are independent of the Company in accordance with the ethical requirements that are relevant to our audit of the financial statements in [*jurisdiction*], and we have fulfilled our other ethical responsibilities in accordance with these requirements. We believe that the audit evidence we have obtained is sufficient and appropriate to provide a basis for our opinion.

Other Information [or another title if appropriate such as 'Information Other than the Financial Statements and Auditor's Report Thereon']

[*Reporting in accordance with the reporting requirements in ISA 720 (Revised) – see Illustration 1 in Appendix 2 of ISA 720 (Revised).*]

Responsibilities of Management and Those Charged with Governance for the Financial Statements[49]

Management is responsible for the preparation and fair presentation of the financial statements in accordance with IFRSs,[50] and for such internal control as management determines is necessary to enable the preparation of financial statements that are free from material misstatement, whether due to fraud or error.

In preparing the financial statements, management is responsible for assessing the Company's ability to continue as a going concern, disclosing, as applicable, matters related to going concern and using the going concern basis of accounting unless management either intends to liquidate the Company or to cease operations, or has no realistic alternative but to do so.

Those charged with governance are responsible for overseeing the Company's financial reporting process.

Auditor's Responsibilities for the Audit of the Financial Statements

Our objectives are to obtain reasonable assurance about whether the financial statements as a whole are free from material misstatement, whether due to fraud or error, and to issue an auditor's report that includes our opinion. Reasonable assurance is a high level of assurance, but is not a guarantee that an audit conducted in accordance with ISAs will always detect a material misstatement when it exists. Misstatements can arise from fraud or error and are considered material if, individually or in the aggregate, they could reasonably be expected to influence the economic decisions of users taken on the basis of these financial statements.

A further description of the auditor's responsibilities for the audit of the financial is located at [*Organization's*] website at: [*website link*]. This description forms part of our auditor's report.

[*Signature in the name of the audit firm, the personal name of the auditor, or both, as appropriate for the particular jurisdiction*]

[*Auditor Address*]

[*Date*]

Illustration 4 – Auditor's Report on Financial Statements of an Entity Other than a Listed Entity Prepared in Accordance with a General Purpose Compliance Framework

For purposes of this illustrative auditor's report, the following circumstances are assumed:
- Audit of a complete set of financial statements of an entity other than a listed entity required by law or regulation. The audit is not a group audit (i.e., ISA 600 does not apply).

---

[49] *Or other terms that are appropriate in the context of the legal framework of the particular jurisdiction.*

[50] *Where management's responsibility is to prepare financial statements that give a true and fair view, this may read: 'Management is responsible for the preparation of financial statements that give a true and fair view in accordance with International Financial Reporting Standards, and for such …'*

- The financial statements are prepared by management of the entity in accordance with the Financial Reporting Framework (XYZ Law) of Jurisdiction X (that is, a financial reporting framework, encompassing law or regulation, designed to meet the common financial information needs of a wide range of users, but which is not a fair presentation framework).

- The terms of the audit engagement reflect the description of management's responsibility for the financial statements in ISA 210.

- The auditor has concluded an unmodified (i.e., 'clean') opinion is appropriate based on the audit evidence obtained.

- The relevant ethical requirements that apply to the audit are those of the jurisdiction.

- Based on the audit evidence obtained, the auditor has concluded that a material uncertainty does not exist related to events or conditions that may cast significant doubt on the entity's ability to continue as a going concern in accordance with ISA 570 (Revised).

- The auditor is not required, and has otherwise not decided, to communicate key audit matters in accordance with ISA 701.

- The auditor has obtained all of the other information prior to the date of the auditor's report and has not identified a material misstatement of the other information.

- Those responsible for oversight of the financial statements differ from those responsible for the preparation of the financial statements.

- The auditor has no other reporting responsibilities required under local law.

INDEPENDENT AUDITOR'S REPORT

[Appropriate Addressee]

Opinion

We have audited the financial statements of ABC Company (the Company), which comprise the balance sheet as at December 31, 20X1, and the income statement, statement of changes in equity and cash flow statement for the year then ended, and notes to the financial statements, including a summary of significant accounting policies.

In our opinion, the accompanying financial statements of the Company are prepared, in all material respects, in accordance with XYZ Law of Jurisdiction X.

Basis for Opinion

We conducted our audit in accordance with International Standards on Auditing (ISAs). Our responsibilities under those standards are further described in the *Auditor's Responsibilities for the Audit of the Financial Statements* section of our report. We are independent of the Company in accordance with the ethical requirements that are relevant to our audit of the financial statements in [*jurisdiction*], and we have fulfilled our other responsibilities in accordance with these requirements. We believe that the audit evidence we have obtained is sufficient and appropriate to provide a basis for our opinion.

Other Information [or another title if appropriate such as 'Information Other than the Financial Statements and Auditor's Report Thereon']

[*Reporting in accordance with the reporting requirements in ISA 720 (Revised) – see Illustration 1 in Appendix 2 of ISA 720 (Revised).*]

Responsibilities of Management and Those Charged with Governance for the Financial Statements[51]

Management is responsible for the preparation of the financial statements in accordance with XYZ Law of Jurisdiction X,[52] and for such internal control as management determines is necessary to enable the preparation of financial statements that are free from material misstatement, whether due to fraud or error.

In preparing the financial statements, management is responsible for assessing the Company's ability to continue as a going concern, disclosing, as applicable, matters related to going concern and using the going concern basis of accounting unless management either intends to liquidate the Company or to cease operations, or has no realistic alternative but to do so.

Those charged with governance are responsible for overseeing the Company's financial reporting process.

Auditor's Responsibilities for the Audit of the Financial Statements

Our objectives are to obtain reasonable assurance about whether the financial statements as a whole are free from material misstatement, whether due to fraud or error, and to issue an auditor's report that includes our opinion. Reasonable assurance is a high level of assurance, but is not a guarantee that an audit conducted in accordance with ISAs will always detect a material misstatement when it exists. Misstatements can arise from fraud or error and are considered material if, individually or in the aggregate, they could reasonably be expected to influence the economic decisions of users taken on the basis of these financial statements.

Paragraph 41(b) of this ISA explains that the shaded material below can be located in an Appendix to the auditor's report. Paragraph 41(c) explains that when law, regulation or national auditing standards expressly permit, reference can be made to a website of an appropriate authority that contains the description of the auditor's responsibilities, rather than including this material in the auditor's report, provided that the description on the website addresses, and is not inconsistent with, the description of the auditor's responsibilities below.

As part of an audit in accordance with ISAs, we exercise professional judgment and maintain professional skepticism throughout the audit. We also:

- Identify and assess the risks of material misstatement of the financial statements, whether due to fraud or error, design and perform audit procedures responsive to those risks, and obtain audit evidence that is sufficient and appropriate to provide a basis for our opinion. The risk of not detecting a material misstatement resulting from fraud is higher than for one resulting from error, as fraud may involve collusion, forgery, intentional omissions, misrepresentations, or the override of internal control.

---

[51] *Or other terms that are appropriate in the context of the legal framework of the particular jurisdiction.*

[52] *Where management's responsibility is to prepare financial statements that give a true and fair view, this may read: 'Management is responsible for the preparation of financial statements that give a true and fair view in accordance with International Financial Reporting Standards, and for such …'*

- Obtain an understanding of internal control relevant to the audit in order to design audit procedures that are appropriate in the circumstances, but not for the purpose of expressing an opinion on the effectiveness of the Company's internal control.[53]

- Evaluate the appropriateness of accounting policies used and the reasonableness of accounting estimates and related disclosures made by management.

- Conclude on the appropriateness of management's use of the going concern basis of accounting and, based on the audit evidence obtained, whether a material uncertainty exists related to events or conditions that may cast significant doubt on the Company's ability to continue as a going concern. If we conclude that a material uncertainty exists, we are required to draw attention in our auditor's report to the related disclosures in the financial statements or, if such disclosures are inadequate, to modify our opinion. Our conclusions are based on the audit evidence obtained up to the date of our auditor's report. However, future events or conditions may cause the Company to cease to continue as a going concern.

We communicate with those charged with governance regarding, among other matters, the planned scope and timing of the audit and significant audit findings, including any significant deficiencies in internal control that we identify during our audit.

[*Signature in the name of the audit firm, the personal name of the auditor, or both, as appropriate for the particular jurisdiction*]

[*Auditor Address*]

[*Date*]

---

[53] *This sentence would be modified, as appropriate, in circumstances when the auditor also has responsibility to issue an opinion on the effectiveness of internal control in conjunction with the audit of the financial statements.*

International Standard on Auditing (UK) 701

Communicating key audit matters in the independent auditor's report

(Effective for audits of financial statements for periods commencing on or after 17 June 2016)

Contents

International Standard on Auditing (UK) (ISA (UK)) 701, *Communicating Key Audit Matters in the Independent Auditor's Report*, should be read in conjunction with ISA (UK) 200 (Revised June 2016), *Overall Objectives of the Independent Auditor and the Conduct of an Audit in Accordance with International Standards on Auditing (UK)*.

Introduction

Scope of this ISA (UK)

1 This International Standard on Auditing (UK) (ISA (UK)) deals with the auditor's responsibility to communicate key audit matters in the auditor's report. It is intended to address both the auditor's judgment as to what to communicate in the auditor's report and the form and content of such communication.

1-1 This ISA (UK) also deals with the auditor's responsibility to communicate other audit planning and scoping matters in the auditor's report.

2 The purpose of communicating key audit matters is to enhance the communicative value of the auditor's report by providing greater transparency about the audit that was performed. Communicating key audit matters provides additional information to intended users of the financial statements ('intended users') to assist them in understanding those matters that, in the auditor's professional judgment, were of most significance in the audit of the financial statements of the current period. Communicating key audit matters may also assist intended users in understanding the entity and areas of significant management judgment in the audited financial statements. (Ref: Para. A1–A4)

3 The communication of key audit matters in the auditor's report may also provide intended users a basis to further engage with management and those charged with governance about certain matters relating to the entity, the audited financial statements, or the audit that was performed.

4 Communicating key audit matters in the auditor's report is in the context of the auditor having formed an opinion on the financial statements as a whole. Communicating key audit matters in the auditor's report is not:

(a) A substitute for disclosures in the financial statements that the applicable financial reporting framework requires management to make, or that are otherwise necessary to achieve fair presentation;

(b) A substitute for the auditor expressing a modified opinion when required by the circumstances of a specific audit engagement in accordance with ISA (UK) 705 (Revised June 2016);[1]

(c) A substitute for reporting in accordance with ISA (UK) 570 (Revised June 2016)[2] when a material uncertainty exists relating to events or conditions that may cast significant doubt on an entity's ability to continue as a going concern; or

(d) A separate opinion on individual matters. (Ref: Para. A5–A8)

5 This ISA (UK) applies to audits of complete sets of general purpose financial statements of listed entities and circumstances when the auditor otherwise decides to communicate key audit matters in the auditor's report. This ISA (UK) also applies when the auditor is required by law or regulation to communicate key audit matters in the auditor's report.[3] However, ISA (UK) 705 (Revised June 2016) prohibits the auditor from communicating

---

[1] *ISA (UK) 705 (Revised June 2016)*, Modifications to the Opinion in the Independent Auditor's Report.

[2] *ISA (UK) 570 (Revised June 2016)*, Going Concern, *paragraphs 22–23*.

[3] *ISA (UK) 700 (Revised June 2016)*, Forming an Opinion and Reporting on Financial Statements, *paragraphs 30–31*.

key audit matters when the auditor disclaims an opinion on the financial statements, unless such reporting is required by law or regulation.[4]

> This ISA (UK) also applies to audits of complete sets of general purpose financial statements of other public interest entities and entities that are required, and those that choose voluntarily, to report on how they have applied the UK Corporate Governance Code.

Effective Date

This ISA (UK) is effective for audits of financial statements for periods commencing on or after 17 June 2016. Earlier adoption is permitted.   **6**

Objectives

The objectives of the auditor are to determine key audit matters and, having formed an opinion on the financial statements, communicate those matters by describing them in the auditor's report.   **7**

Definitions

For purposes of the ISAs (UK), the following term has the meaning attributed below: **8**

Key audit matters—Those matters that, in the auditor's professional judgment, were of most significance in the audit of the financial statements of the current period. Key audit matters are selected from matters communicated with those charged with governance. (Ref: Para. A8-1)

Requirements

Determining Key Audit Matters

The auditor shall determine, from the matters communicated with those charged with governance, those matters that required significant auditor attention in performing the audit. In making this determination, the auditor shall take into account the following: (Ref: Para. A9–A18)   **9**

(a) Areas of higher assessed risk of material misstatement, or significant risks identified in accordance with ISA (UK) 315 (Revised June 2016).[5] (Ref: Para. A19–A22)
(b) Significant auditor judgments relating to areas in the financial statements that involved significant management judgment, including accounting estimates that have been identified as having high estimation uncertainty. (Ref: Para. A23–A24)
(c) The effect on the audit of significant events or transactions that occurred during the period. (Ref: Para. A25–A26)

The auditor shall determine which of the matters determined in accordance with paragraph 9 were of most significance in the audit of the financial statements of the current period and therefore are the key audit matters. (Ref: Para. A9–A11, A27–A30-1)   **10**

---

[4] *ISA (UK) 705 (Revised June 2016), paragraph 29.*

[5] *ISA (UK) 315 (Revised June 2016),* Identifying and Assessing the Risks of Material Misstatement through Understanding the Entity and Its Environment.

Communicating Key Audit Matters

11   The auditor shall describe each key audit matter, using an appropriate subheading, in a separate section of the auditor's report under the heading 'Key Audit Matters,' unless the circumstances in paragraphs 14 or 15 apply. The introductory language in this section of the auditor's report shall state that:

(a)   Key audit matters are those matters that, in the auditor's professional judgment, were of most significance in the audit of the financial statements [of the current period] and include the most significant assessed risks of material misstatement (whether or not due to fraud) identified by the auditor, including those which had the greatest effect on: the overall audit strategy; the allocation of resources in the audit; and directing the efforts of the engagement team; and

(b)   These matters were addressed in the context of the audit of the financial statements as a whole, and in forming the auditor's opinion thereon, and the auditor does not provide a separate opinion on these matters. (Ref: Para. A31–A33)

Key Audit Matters Not a Substitute for Expressing a Modified Opinion

12   The auditor shall not communicate a matter in the Key Audit Matters section of the auditor's report when the auditor would be required to modify the opinion in accordance with ISA (UK) 705 (Revised June 2016) as a result of the matter. (Ref: Para. A5)

Descriptions of Individual Key Audit Matters

13   The description of each key audit matter in the Key Audit Matters section of the auditor's report shall include a reference to the related disclosure(s), if any, in the financial statements and shall address: (Ref: Para. A33-1–A41)

(a)   Why the matter was considered to be one of most significance in the audit and therefore determined to be a key audit matter; and (Ref: Para. A42–A45)

(b)   How the matter was addressed in the audit. (Ref: Para. A46–A51)

13R-1   In describing each of the key audit matters in accordance with paragraph 13, the auditor's report shall provide, in support of the audit opinion:

(a)   A description of the most significant assessed risks of material misstatement, (whether or not due to fraud);

(b)   A summary of the auditor's response to those risks; and

(c)   Where relevant, key observations arising with respect to those risks.

Where relevant to the above information provided in the auditor's report concerning each of the most significant assessed risks of material misstatement (whether or not due to fraud), the auditor's report shall include a clear reference to the relevant disclosures in the financial statements. (Ref: Para. A51-1)

13-2   In describing why the matter was determined to be a key audit matter in accordance with paragraph 13(a), the description shall indicate that the matter was one of the most significant assessed risks of material misstatement (whether or not due to fraud) identified by the auditor.

Circumstances in Which a Matter Determined to Be a Key Audit Matter Is Not Communicated in the Auditor's Report

14   The auditor shall describe each key audit matter in the auditor's report unless: (Ref: Para. A53–A56)

(a) Law or regulation precludes public disclosure about the matter; or (Ref: Para. A52)
(b) In extremely rare circumstances, the auditor determines that the matter should not be communicated in the auditor's report because the adverse consequences of doing so would reasonably be expected to outweigh the public interest benefits of such communication. This shall not apply if the entity has publicly disclosed information about the matter.

Interaction between Descriptions of Key Audit Matters and Other Elements Required to Be Included in the Auditor's Report

A matter giving rise to a modified opinion in accordance with ISA (UK) 705 (Revised June 2016), or a material uncertainty related to events or conditions that may cast significant doubt on the entity's ability to continue as a going concern in accordance with ISA (UK) 570 (Revised June 2016), are by their nature key audit matters. However, in such circumstances, these matters shall not be described in the Key Audit Matters section of the auditor's report and the requirements in paragraphs 13–14 do not apply. Rather, the auditor shall: **15**

(a) Report on these matter(s) in accordance with the applicable ISA(s) (UK); and
(b) Include a reference to the Basis for Qualified (Adverse) Opinion or the Material Uncertainty Related to Going Concern section(s) in the Key Audit Matters section. (Ref: Para. A6–A7)

Form and Content of the Key Audit Matters Section in Other Circumstances

If the auditor determines, depending on the facts and circumstances of the entity and the audit, that there are no key audit matters to communicate or that the only key audit matters communicated are those matters addressed by paragraph 15, the auditor shall include a statement to this effect in a separate section of the auditor's report under the heading 'Key Audit Matters.' (Ref: Para. A57–A59)   **16**

Communicating Other Audit Planning and Scoping Matters

The auditor's report shall provide: **16-1**

(a) An explanation of how the auditor applied the concept of materiality in planning and performing the audit. Such explanation shall specify the threshold used by the auditor as being materiality for the financial statements as a whole;[5a] and (Ref: Para. A59-1)
(b) An overview of the scope of the audit,[5b] including an explanation of how such scope:
    (i) Addressed each Key Audit Matter relating to one of the most significant risks of material misstatement disclosed in accordance with paragraph 13(b); and
    (ii) Was influenced by the auditor's application of materiality disclosed in accordance with paragraph 16-1(a). (Ref: Para. A59-2)

Communicating Key Audit Matters and Other Audit Planning and Scoping Matters

In order to be useful to users of the financial statements, the explanations of the matters required to be set out in the auditor's report in paragraphs 13 and 16-1 shall be described: **16-2**

[5a] *As required by paragraph 10 of ISA (UK) 320 (Revised June 2016),* Materiality in Planning and Performing an Audit.

[5b] *See also paragraphs 15 and A11 to A16 of ISA (UK) 260 (Revised June 2016),* Communication with Those Charged with Governance *and paragraph 49 of ISA (UK) 600 (Revised June 2016),* Special considerations – Audits of Group Financial Statements (Including the Work of Component Auditors).

(a) So as to enable a user to understand their significance in the context of the audit of the financial statements as a whole and not as discrete opinions on separate elements of the financial statements;

(b) In a way that enables them to be related directly to the specific circumstances of the entity and are not, therefore, generic or abstract matters expressed in standardized language; and

(c) In the case of entities that are required, and those that choose voluntarily, to report on how they have applied the UK Corporate Governance Code, or to explain why they have not, in a manner that complements the description of significant issues relating to the financial statements, required to be set out in the separate section of the annual report describing the work of the audit committee in discharging its responsibilities.[5c] The auditor seeks to coordinate descriptions of overlapping topics addressed in these communications, to avoid duplication of reporting about them, whilst having appropriate regard to the separate responsibilities of the auditor and the board for directly communicating information primarily in their respective domains.

Communication with Those Charged with Governance

17   The auditor shall communicate with those charged with governance:

(a) Those matters the auditor has determined to be the key audit matters; or

(b) If applicable, depending on the facts and circumstances of the entity and the audit, the auditor's determination that there are no key audit matters to communicate in the auditor's report. (Ref: Para. A60–A63)

Documentation

18   The auditor shall include in the audit documentation:[6] (Ref: Para. A64)

(a) The matters that required significant auditor attention as determined in accordance with paragraph 9, and the rationale for the auditor's determination as to whether or not each of these matters is a key audit matter in accordance with paragraph 10;

(b) Where applicable, the rationale for the auditor's determination that there are no key audit matters to communicate in the auditor's report or that the only key audit matters to communicate are those matters addressed by paragraph 15; and

(c) Where applicable, the rationale for the auditor's determination not to communicate in the auditor's report a matter determined to be a key audit matter.

***

Application and Other Explanatory Material

Scope of this ISA (UK) (Ref: Para. 2)

A1   Significance can be described as the relative importance of a matter, taken in context. The significance of a matter is judged by the auditor in the context in which it is being considered. Significance can be considered in the context of quantitative and qualitative factors, such as relative magnitude, the nature and effect on the subject matter and the expressed interests of intended users or recipients. This involves an objective analysis of the facts and circumstances, including the nature and extent of communication with those charged with governance.

[5c] *In accordance with provision C.3.8 of the UK Corporate Governance Code.*

[6] *ISA (UK) 230 (Revised June 2016), 'Audit Documentation,' paragraphs 8–11 and A6.*

Users of financial statements have expressed an interest in those matters about which   **A2**
the auditor had the most robust dialogue with those charged with governance as part of
the two-way communication required by ISA (UK) 260 (Revised June 2016)[7] and have
called for additional transparency about those communications. For example, users have
expressed particular interest in understanding significant judgments made by the auditor in
forming the opinion on the financial statements as a whole, because they are often related
to the areas of significant management judgment in preparing the financial statements.

Requiring auditors to communicate key audit matters in the auditor's report may also   **A3**
enhance communications between the auditor and those charged with governance about
those matters, and may increase attention by management and those charged with
governance to the disclosures in the financial statements to which reference is made in the
auditor's report.

ISA (UK) 320 (Revised June 2016)[8] explains that it is reasonable for the auditor to assume   **A4**
that users of the financial statements:

(a) Have a reasonable knowledge of business and economic activities and accounting
     and a willingness to study the information in the financial statements with reasonable
     diligence;
(b) Understand that the financial statements are prepared, presented and audited to levels
     of materiality;
(c) Recognize the uncertainties inherent in the measurement of amounts based on the use
     of estimates, judgment and the consideration of future events; and
(d) Make reasonable economic decisions on the basis of the information in the financial
     statements.

Because the auditor's report accompanies the audited financial statements, the users of
the auditor's report are considered to be the same as the intended users of the financial
statements.

***Relationship between Key Audit Matters, the Auditor's Opinion and Other Elements of
the Auditor's Report*** (Ref: Para. 4, 12, 15)

ISA (UK) 700 (Revised June 2016) establishes requirements and provides guidance on   **A5**
forming an opinion on the financial statements.[9] Communicating key audit matters is not a
substitute for disclosures in the financial statements that the applicable financial reporting
framework requires management to make, or that are otherwise necessary to achieve fair
presentation. ISA (UK) 705 (Revised June 2016) addresses circumstances in which the
auditor concludes that there is a material misstatement relating to the appropriateness or
adequacy of disclosures in the financial statements.[10]

When the auditor expresses a qualified or adverse opinion in accordance with ISA (UK)   **A6**
705 (Revised June 2016), presenting the description of a matter giving rise to a modified
opinion in the Basis for Qualified (Adverse) Opinion section helps to promote intended
users' understanding and to identify such circumstances when they occur. Separating the
communication of this matter from other key audit matters described in the Key Audit
Matters section therefore gives it the appropriate prominence in the auditor's report

---

[7] *ISA (UK) 260 (Revised June 2016)*, Communication with Those Charged with Governance.

[8] *ISA (UK) 320 (Revised June 2016)*, Materiality in Planning and Performing the Audit, *paragraph 4.*

[9] *ISA (UK) 700 (Revised June 2016), paragraphs 10–15 and A1–A10.*

[10] *See paragraph A7 of ISA (UK) 705 (Revised June 2016).*

(see paragraph 15). The Appendix in ISA (UK) 705 (Revised June 2016) includes illustrative examples of how the introductory language in the Key Audit Matters section is affected when the auditor expresses a qualified or adverse opinion and other key audit matters are communicated in the auditor's report. Paragraph A58 of this ISA (UK) illustrates how the Key Audit Matters section is presented when the auditor has determined that there are no other key audit matters to be communicated in the auditor's report beyond matters addressed in the Basis for Qualified (Adverse) Opinion section or Material Uncertainty Related to Going Concern section of the auditor's report.

A7   When the auditor expresses a qualified or adverse opinion, communicating other key audit matters would still be relevant to enhancing intended users' understanding of the audit, and therefore the requirements to determine key audit matters apply. However, as an adverse opinion is expressed in circumstances when the auditor has concluded that misstatements, individually or in the aggregate, are both material and pervasive to the financial statements:[11]

- Depending on the significance of the matter(s) giving rise to an adverse opinion, the auditor may determine that no other matters are key audit matters. In such circumstances, the requirement in paragraph 15 applies (see paragraph A58).
- If one or more matters other than the matter(s) giving rise to an adverse opinion are determined to be key audit matters, it is particularly important that the descriptions of such other key audit matters do not imply that the financial statements as a whole are more credible in relation to those matters than would be appropriate in the circumstances, in view of the adverse opinion (see paragraph A47).

A8   ISA (UK) 706 (Revised June 2016)[12] establishes mechanisms for auditors of financial statements of all entities to include additional communication in the auditor's report through the use of Emphasis of Matter paragraphs and Other Matter paragraphs when the auditor considers it necessary to do so. In such cases, these paragraphs are presented separately from the Key Audit Matters section in the auditor's report. When a matter has been determined to be a key audit matter, the use of such paragraphs is not a substitute for the description of the individual key audit matter in accordance with paragraph 13.[13] ISA (UK) 706 (Revised June 2016) provides further guidance on the relationship between key audit matters and Emphasis of Matter paragraphs in accordance with that ISA (UK).[14]

Definition

Key audit matters (Ref: Para. 8)

A8-1   In the UK, those matters that were of most significance in the audit of the financial statements of the current period include the most significant assessed risks of material misstatement (whether or not due to fraud) identified by the auditor, including those that had the greatest effect on: the overall audit strategy; the allocation of resources in the audit; and directing the efforts of the engagement team.

---

[11] *ISA (UK) 705 (Revised June 2016), paragraph 8.*

[12] *ISA (UK) 706 (Revised June 2016),* Emphasis of Matter Paragraphs and Other Matter Paragraphs in the Independent Auditor's Report.

[13] *See paragraphs 8(b) and 10(b) of ISA (UK) 706 (Revised June 2016).*

[14] *ISA (UK) 706 (Revised June 2016), paragraphs A1–A3.*

Determining Key Audit Matters (Ref: Para. 9–10)

The auditor's decision-making process in determining key audit matters is designed to **A9** select a smaller number of matters from the matters communicated with those charged with governance, based on the auditor's judgment about which matters were of most significance in the audit of the financial statements of the current period.

> In the UK, ISA (UK) 260 (Revised June 2016)[14a] requires the auditor to communicate **A9-1** with those charged with governance those matters that were of most significance in the audit of the financial statements of the current period include the most significant assessed risks of material misstatement (whether or not due to fraud) identified by the auditor, including those that had the greatest effect on: the overall audit strategy; the allocation of resources in the audit; and directing the efforts of the engagement team. Such matters are key audit matters as explained in paragraph A8-1.

The auditor's determination of key audit matters is limited to those matters of most **A10** significance in the audit of the financial statements of the current period, even when comparative financial statements are presented (i.e., even when the auditor's opinion refers to each period for which financial statements are presented).[15]

Notwithstanding that the auditor's determination of key audit matters is for the audit of the **A11** financial statements of the current period and this ISA (UK) does not require the auditor to update key audit matters included in the prior period's auditor's report, it may nevertheless be useful for the auditor to consider whether a matter that was a key audit matter in the audit of the financial statements of the prior period continues to be a key audit matter in the audit of the financial statements of the current period.

Matters that Required Significant Auditor Attention (Ref: Para. 9)

The concept of significant auditor attention recognizes that an audit is risk-based and **A12** focuses on identifying and assessing the risks of material misstatement of the financial statements, designing and performing audit procedures responsive to those risks, and obtaining audit evidence that is sufficient and appropriate to provide a basis for the auditor's opinion. For a particular account balance, class of transactions or disclosure, the higher an assessed risk of material misstatement at the assertion level, the more judgment is often involved in planning and performing the audit procedures and evaluating the results thereof. In designing further audit procedures, the auditor is required to obtain more persuasive audit evidence the higher the auditor's assessment of risk.[16] When obtaining more persuasive audit evidence because of a higher assessment of risk, the auditor may increase the quantity of the evidence, or obtain evidence that is more relevant or reliable, for example, by placing more emphasis on obtaining third party evidence or by obtaining corroborating evidence from a number of independent sources.[17]

Accordingly, matters that pose challenges to the auditor in obtaining sufficient appropriate **A13** audit evidence or pose challenges to the auditor in forming an opinion on the financial statements may be particularly relevant in the auditor's determination of key audit matters.

[14a] *ISA (UK) 260 (Revised June 2016)*, Communication with Those Charged with Governance, *paragraph 15.*

[15] *See ISA (UK) 710*, Comparative Information—Corresponding Figures and Comparative Financial Statements.

[16] *ISA (UK) 330 (Revised June 2016)*, The Auditor's Responses to Assessed Risks, *paragraph 7(b).*

[17] *ISA (UK) 330 (Revised June 2016), paragraph A19.*

A14   Areas of significant auditor attention often relate to areas of complexity and significant management judgment in the financial statements, and therefore often involve difficult or complex auditor judgments. In turn, this often affects the auditor's overall audit strategy, the allocation of resources and extent of audit effort in relation to such matters. These effects may include, for example, the extent of involvement of senior personnel on the audit engagement or the involvement of an auditor's expert or individuals with expertise in a specialized area of accounting or auditing, whether engaged or employed by the firm to address these areas.

A15   Various ISAs (UK) require specific communications with those charged with governance and others that may relate to areas of significant auditor attention. For example:

- ISA (UK) 260 (Revised June 2016) requires the auditor to communicate significant difficulties, if any, encountered during the audit with those charged with governance.[18] The ISAs (UK) acknowledge potential difficulties in relation to, for example:
  - Related party transactions,[19] in particular limitations on the auditor's ability to obtain audit evidence that all other aspects of a related party transaction (other than price) are equivalent to those of a similar arm's length transaction.
  - Limitations on the group audit, for example, where the group engagement team's access to information may have been restricted.[20]

- ISA (UK) 220 (Revised June 2016) establishes requirements for the engagement partner in relation to undertaking appropriate consultation on difficult or contentious matters.[21] For example, the auditor may have consulted with others within the firm or outside the firm on a significant technical matter, which may be an indicator that it is a key audit matter. The engagement partner is also required to discuss, among other things, significant matters arising during the audit engagement with the engagement quality control reviewer.[22]

Considerations in Determining Those Matters that Required Significant Auditor Attention (Ref: Para. 9)

A16   The auditor may develop a preliminary view at the planning stage about matters that are likely to be areas of significant auditor attention in the audit and therefore may be key audit matters. The auditor may communicate this with those charged with governance when discussing the planned scope and timing of the audit in accordance with ISA (UK) 260 (Revised June 2016). However, the auditor's determination of key audit matters is based on the results of the audit or evidence obtained throughout the audit.

A17   Paragraph 9 includes specific required considerations in the auditor's determination of those matters that required significant auditor attention. These considerations focus on the nature of matters communicated with those charged with governance that are often linked to matters disclosed in the financial statements, and are intended to reflect areas of the audit of the financial statements that may be of particular interest to intended users. The fact that these considerations are required is not intended to imply that matters related to them are always key audit matters; rather, matters related to such specific considerations

---

[18]   *ISA (UK) 260 (Revised June 2016), paragraphs 16(b) and A21.*

[19]   *ISA (UK) 550,* Related Parties, *paragraph A42.*

[20]   *ISA (UK) 600 (Revised June 2016),* Special Considerations—Audits of Group Financial Statements (Including the Work of Component Auditors), *paragraph 49(d).*

[21]   *ISA (UK) 220 (Revised June 2016),* Quality Control for an Audit of Financial Statements, *paragraph 18.*

[22]   *ISA (UK) 220 (Revised June 2016), paragraph 19.*

are key audit matters only if they are determined to be of most significance in the audit in accordance with paragraph 10. As the considerations may be interrelated (e.g., matters relating to the circumstances described in paragraphs 9(b)–(c) may also be identified as significant risks), the applicability of more than one of the considerations to a particular matter communicated with those charged with governance may increase the likelihood of the auditor identifying that matter as a key audit matter.

In addition to matters that relate to the specific required considerations in paragraphs 9, there may be other matters communicated with those charged with governance that required significant auditor attention and that therefore may be determined to be key audit matters in accordance with paragraph 10. Such matters may include, for example, matters relevant to the audit that was performed that may not be required to be disclosed in the financial statements. For example, the implementation of a new IT system (or significant changes to an existing IT system) during the period may be an area of significant auditor attention, in particular if such a change had a significant effect on the auditor's overall audit strategy or related to a significant risk (e.g., changes to a system affecting revenue recognition). **A18**

Areas of Higher Assessed Risk of Material Misstatement, or Significant Risks Identified in Accordance with ISA (UK) 315 (Revised June 2016) (Ref: Para. 9(a))

ISA (UK) 260 (Revised June 2016) requires the auditor to communicate with those charged with governance about the significant risks identified by the auditor.[23] Paragraph A13 of ISA (UK) 260 (Revised June 2016) explains that the auditor may also communicate with those charged with governance about how the auditor plans to address areas of higher assessed risks of material misstatement. **A19**

ISA (UK) 315 (Revised June 2016) defines a significant risk as an identified and assessed risk of material misstatement that, in the auditor's judgment, requires special audit consideration. Areas of significant management judgment and significant unusual transactions may often be identified as significant risks. Significant risks are therefore often areas that require significant auditor attention. **A20**

However, this may not be the case for all significant risks. For example, ISA (UK) 240 (Revised June 2016) presumes that there are risks of fraud in revenue recognition and requires the auditor to treat those assessed risks of material misstatement due to fraud as significant risks.[24] In addition, ISA (UK) 240 (Revised June 2016) indicates that, due to the unpredictable way in which management override of controls could occur, it is a risk of material misstatement due to fraud and thus a significant risk.[25] Depending on their nature, these risks may not require significant auditor attention, and therefore would not be considered in the auditor's determination of key audit matters in accordance with paragraph 10. **A21**

ISA (UK) 315 (Revised June 2016) explains that the auditor's assessment of the risks of material misstatement at the assertion level may change during the course of the audit as additional audit evidence is obtained.[26] Revision to the auditor's risk assessment and reevaluation of the planned audit procedures with respect to a particular area of the financial statements (i.e., a significant change in the audit approach, for example, if the **A22**

---

[23] *ISA (UK) 260 (Revised June 2016), paragraph 15.*

[24] *ISA (UK) 240 (Revised June 2016),* The Auditor's Responsibilities Relating to Fraud in an Audit of Financial Statements, *paragraphs 26–27.*

[25] *ISA (UK) 240 (Revised June 2016), paragraph 31.*

[26] *ISA (UK) 315 (Revised June 2016), paragraph 31.*

auditor's risk assessment was based on an expectation that certain controls were operating effectively and the auditor has obtained audit evidence that they were not operating effectively throughout the audit period, particularly in an area with higher assessed risk of material misstatement) may result in an area being determined as one requiring significant auditor attention.

Significant Auditor Judgments Relating to Areas in the Financial Statements that Involved Significant Management Judgment, Including Accounting Estimates that Have Been Identified as Having High Estimation Uncertainty (Ref: Para. 9(b))

A23   ISA (UK) 260 (Revised June 2016) requires the auditor to communicate with those charged with governance the auditor's views about significant qualitative aspects of the entity's accounting practices, including accounting policies, accounting estimates and financial statement disclosures.[27] In many cases, this relates to critical accounting estimates and related disclosures, which are likely to be areas of significant auditor attention, and also may be identified as significant risks.

A24   However, users of the financial statements have highlighted their interest in accounting estimates that have been identified as having high estimation uncertainty in accordance with ISA (UK) 540 (Revised June 2016)[28] that may have not been determined to be significant risks. Among other things, such estimates are highly dependent on management judgment and are often the most complex areas of the financial statements, and may require the involvement of both a management's expert and an auditor's expert. Users have also highlighted that accounting policies that have a significant effect on the financial statements (and significant changes to those policies) are relevant to their understanding of the financial statements, especially in circumstances where an entity's practices are not consistent with others in its industry.

The Effect on the Audit of Significant Events or Transactions that Occurred during the Period (Ref: Para. 9(c))

A25   Events or transactions that had a significant effect on the financial statements or the audit may be areas of significant auditor attention and may be identified as significant risks. For example, the auditor may have had extensive discussions with management and those charged with governance at various stages throughout the audit about the effect on the financial statements of significant transactions with related parties or significant transactions that are outside the normal course of business for the entity or that otherwise appear to be unusual.[29] Management may have made difficult or complex judgments in relation to recognition, measurement, presentation or disclosure of such transactions, which may have had a significant effect on the auditor's overall strategy.

A26   Significant economic, accounting, regulatory, industry, or other developments that affected management's assumptions or judgments may also affect the auditor's overall approach to the audit and result in a matter requiring significant auditor attention.

[27] *ISA (UK) 260 (Revised June 2016), paragraph 16(a).*

[28] *See paragraphs 10–11 of ISA (UK) 540 (Revised June 2016),* Auditing Accounting Estimates, Including Fair Value Accounting Estimates, and Related Disclosures.

[29] *See paragraphs 16(a), 16(c) and A22, and Appendix 2, of ISA (UK) 260 (Revised June 2016).*

Matters of Most Significance (Ref: Para. 10)

Matters that required significant auditor attention also may have resulted in significant   **A27**
interaction with those charged with governance. The nature and extent of communication
about such matters with those charged with governance often provides an indication of
which matters are of most significance in the audit. For example, the auditor may have had
more in-depth, frequent or robust interactions with those charged with governance on more
difficult and complex matters, such as the application of significant accounting policies
that were the subject of significant auditor or management judgment.

The concept of matters of most significance is applicable in the context of the entity and   **A28**
the audit that was performed. As such, the auditor's determination and communication of
key audit matters is intended to identify matters specific to the audit and to involve making
a judgment about their importance relative to other matters in the audit.

In the UK, the assessed risks of material misstatement which had the greatest effect   **A28-1**
on: the overall audit strategy; the allocation of resources in the audit; and directing
the efforts of the engagement team are likely to have been identified by the auditor in
meeting the requirements of ISA (UK) 315 (Revised June 2016),[29a] including those
relating to significant risks. However, the auditor uses its judgment to determine which,
if any, of the significant risks and which, if any, of the other identified risks meet the
criteria set out in paragraph 10 and are to be described in the auditor's report.

Other considerations that may be relevant to determining the relative significance of a   **A29**
matter communicated with those charged with governance and whether such a matter is a
key audit matter include:

- The importance of the matter to intended users' understanding of the financial
  statements as a whole, in particular, its materiality to the financial statements.
- The nature of the underlying accounting policy relating to the matter or the complexity
  or subjectivity involved in management's selection of an appropriate policy compared
  to other entities within its industry.
- The nature and materiality, quantitatively or qualitatively, of corrected and accumulated
  uncorrected misstatements due to fraud or error related to the matter, if any.
- The nature and extent of audit effort needed to address the matter, including:
  - The extent of specialized skill or knowledge needed to apply audit procedures to
    address the matter or evaluate the results of those procedures, if any.
  - The nature of consultations outside the engagement team regarding the matter.
- The nature and severity of difficulties in applying audit procedures, evaluating the
  results of those procedures, and obtaining relevant and reliable evidence on which
  to base the auditor's opinion, in particular as the auditor's judgments become more
  subjective.
- The severity of any control deficiencies identified relevant to the matter.
- Whether the matter involved a number of separate, but related, auditing considerations.
  For example, long-term contracts may involve significant auditor attention with
  respect to revenue recognition, litigation or other contingencies, and may have an
  effect on other accounting estimates.

Determining which, and how many, of those matters that required significant auditor   **A30**
attention were of most significance in the audit of the financial statements of the current
period is a matter of professional judgment. The number of key audit matters to be included
in the auditor's report may be affected by the size and complexity of the entity, the nature of
its business and environment, and the facts and circumstances of the audit engagement. In

---

[29a] *ISA (UK) 315 (Revised June 2016), paragraphs 25 to 31.*

general, the greater the number of matters initially determined to be key audit matters, the more the auditor may need to reconsider whether each of these matters meets the definition of a key audit matter. Lengthy lists of key audit matters may be contrary to the notion of such matters being those of most significance in the audit.

Communicating Key Audit Matters

Separate Key Audit Matters Section in the Auditor's Report (Ref: Para. 11)

A31 Placing the separate Key Audit Matters section in close proximity to the auditor's opinion may give prominence to such information and acknowledge the perceived value of engagement-specific information to intended users.

A32 The order of presentation of individual matters within the Key Audit Matters section is a matter of professional judgment. For example, such information may be organized in order of relative importance, based on the auditor's judgment, or may correspond to the manner in which matters are disclosed in the financial statements. The requirement in paragraph 11 to include subheadings is intended to further differentiate the matters.

A33 When comparative financial information is presented, the introductory language of the Key Audit Matters section is tailored to draw attention to the fact that the key audit matters described relate to only the audit of the financial statements of the current period, and may include reference to the specific period covered by those financial statements (e.g., 'for the year ended December 31, 20X1').

Communicating Key Audit Matters for Group and Parent Company Financial Statements

A33-1 An auditor's report for a group may include the auditor's report with respect to both the group and the parent company financial statements. This is typically the case where both sets of financial statements are presented in accordance with IFRSs as adopted in the European Union. However, where the financial statements of the group and the parent company are presented in accordance with different financial reporting frameworks, the financial statements might be presented separately within the annual report and in such circumstances separate auditor's reports in respect of the group and the parent company financial statements might be provided within the annual report.

A33-2 Most of the key audit matters communicated in the audit of the parent company would likely also be key audit matters in the audit of the group financial statements, subject to any differences in quantitative materiality considerations that may apply in those audits. However, there may be key audit matters that only arise in relation to the audit of the parent company financial statements (such as risks relating to investments in subsidiaries that could, for example, have implications for distributable reserves).

A33-3 An understanding of such key audit matters may be of interest to readers of auditor's reports. Readers may find such key audit matters to be of particular interest when their implications are relevant in the context of the parent company's reported distributable reserves. However, readers of the auditor's report(s) on the group and parent company financial statements will be assisted by avoiding unnecessary duplication or disaggregation of key audit matters arising from these audits in such report(s).

Application where there is a single auditor's report

Where the auditor's reports on both the group and parent company financial statements are combined within a single report, it may be appropriate for any relevant key audit matters and other information required by ISA (UK) 701 that are unique to the parent company audit to be separately identified but integrated within the disclosures in that report of corresponding matters arising from the audit of the group financial statements.   **A33-4**

Application where the auditor reports separately on the group and parent company financial statements

Where the auditor provides separate auditor's reports on the group and parent company financial statements, it may also be appropriate for any relevant key audit matters and other audit planning and scoping matters required by this ISA (UK) that are unique to the parent company audit to be separately identified but integrated within the disclosures within the group auditor's report of corresponding matters arising from the group audit. Except where such matters are required by law or regulation to be included in the auditor's report (as is the case, for example, in relation to an auditor's report on any financial statements of a public interest entity), the auditor could make reference in the other matter paragraph in the parent company auditor's report that refers to the separate auditor's report on the group financial statements to the fact that the key audit matters and other audit planning and scoping matters that relate to the parent company audit have been included in the group auditor's report, rather than repeating the information.   **A33-5**

Descriptions of Individual Key Audit Matters (Ref: Para. 13)

The adequacy of the description of a key audit matter is a matter of professional judgment. The description of a key audit matter is intended to provide a succinct and balanced explanation to enable intended users to understand why the matter was one of most significance in the audit and how the matter was addressed in the audit. Limiting the use of highly technical auditing terms also helps to enable intended users who do not have a reasonable knowledge of auditing to understand the basis for the auditor's focus on particular matters during the audit. The nature and extent of information provided by the auditor is intended to be balanced in the context of the responsibilities of the respective parties (i.e., for the auditor to provide useful information in a concise and understandable form, while not inappropriately being the provider of original information about the entity).   **A34**

Original information is any information about the entity that has not otherwise been made publicly available by the entity (e.g., has not been included in the financial statements or other information available at the date of the auditor's report, or addressed in other oral or written communications by management or those charged with governance, such as a preliminary announcement of financial information or investor briefings). Such information is the responsibility of the entity's management and those charged with governance.   **A35**

It is appropriate for the auditor to seek to avoid the description of a key audit matter inappropriately providing original information about the entity. The description of a key audit matter is not usually of itself original information about the entity, as it describes the matter in the context of the audit. However, the auditor may consider it necessary to include additional information to explain why the matter was considered to be one of most significance in the audit and therefore determined to be a key audit matter, and how the matter was addressed in the audit, provided that disclosure of such information is not precluded by law or regulation. When such information is determined to be necessary by the auditor, the auditor may encourage management or those charged with governance to disclose additional information, rather than the auditor providing original information in the auditor's report.   **A36**

A37   Management or those charged with governance may decide to include new or enhanced disclosures in the financial statements or elsewhere in the annual report relating to a key audit matter in light of the fact that the matter will be communicated in the auditor's report. Such new or enhanced disclosures, for example, may be included to provide more robust information about the sensitivity of key assumptions used in accounting estimates or the entity's rationale for a particular accounting practice or policy when acceptable alternatives exist under the applicable financial reporting framework.

A38   ISA (UK) 720 (Revised June 2016) defines the term annual report and explains that documents such as a management report, management commentary, or operating and financial review or similar reports by those charged with governance (e.g., a directors' report); a Chairman's statement; corporate governance statement; or internal control and risk assessment reports may form part of the annual report.[30] ISA (UK) 720 (Revised June 2016) addresses the auditor's responsibilities relating to other information included in the annual report. Although the auditor's opinion on the financial statements does not cover the other information, the auditor may consider this information, as well as other publicly available communications by the entity or other credible sources, in formulating the description of a key audit matter.

A39   Audit documentation prepared during the audit can also be useful to the auditor in formulating the description of a key audit matter. For example, written communications, or the auditor's documentation of oral communications, with those charged with governance and other audit documentation provides a useful basis for the auditor's communication in the auditor's report. This is because audit documentation in accordance with ISA (UK) 230 (Revised June 2016) is intended to address the significant matters arising during the audit, the conclusions reached thereon, and significant professional judgments made in reaching those conclusions, and serves as a record of the nature, timing and extent of the audit procedures performed, the results of those procedures, and the audit evidence obtained. Such documentation may assist the auditor in developing a description of key audit matters that explains the significance of the matter and also in applying the requirement in paragraph 18.

Reference to Where the Matter Is Disclosed in the Financial Statements (Ref: Para. 13)

A40   Paragraphs 13(a)–(b) requires the description of each key audit matter to address why the auditor considered the matter to be one of most significance in the audit and how the matter was addressed in the audit. Accordingly, the description of key audit matters is not a mere reiteration of what is disclosed in the financial statements. However, a reference to any related disclosures enables intended users to further understand how management has addressed the matter in preparing the financial statements.

A41   In addition to referring to related disclosure(s), the auditor may draw attention to key aspects of them. The extent of disclosure by management about specific aspects or factors in relation to how a particular matter is affecting the financial statements of the current period may help the auditor in pinpointing particular aspects of how the matter was addressed in the audit such that intended users can understand why the matter is a key audit matter. For example:

- When an entity includes robust disclosure about accounting estimates, the auditor may draw attention to the disclosure of key assumptions, the disclosure of the range of possible outcomes, and other qualitative and quantitative disclosures relating to key sources of estimation uncertainty or critical accounting estimates, as part of

---

[30] *ISA (UK) 720 (Revised June 2016)*, The Auditor's Responsibilities Relating to Other Information, *paragraphs 12(a) and A1–A3.*

addressing why the matter was one of most significance in the audit and how the matter was addressed in the audit.

- When the auditor concludes in accordance with ISA (UK) 570 (Revised June 2016) that no material uncertainty exists relating to events or conditions that may cast significant doubt on the entity's ability to continue as a going concern, the auditor may nevertheless determine that one or more matters relating to this conclusion arising from the auditor's work effort under ISA (UK) 570 (Revised June 2016) are key audit matters. In such circumstances, the auditor's description of such key audit matters in the auditor's report could include aspects of the identified events or conditions disclosed in the financial statements, such as substantial operating losses, available borrowing facilities and possible debt refinancing, or non-compliance with loan agreements, and related mitigating factors.[31]

Why the Auditor Considered the Matter to Be One of Most Significance in the Audit
(Ref: Para. 13(a))

The description of a key audit matter in the auditor's report is intended to provide insight as to why the matter was determined to be a key audit matter. Accordingly, the requirements in paragraphs 9–10 and the application material in paragraphs A12–A29 related to determining key audit matters may also be helpful for the auditor in considering how such matters are to be communicated in the auditor's report. For example, explaining the factors that led the auditor to conclude that a particular matter required significant auditor attention and was of most significance in the audit is likely to be of interest to intended users. **A42**

As indicated in paragraph A22, where the auditor significantly revises the auditor's assessment of the risks of material misstatement during the course of the audit, the auditor considers whether to disclose that fact and the circumstances giving rise to the changed assessment. **A42-1**

The relevance of the information for intended users is a consideration for the auditor in determining what to include in the description of a key audit matter. This may include whether the description would enable a better understanding of the audit and the auditor's judgments. **A43**

Relating a matter directly to the specific circumstances of the entity may also help to minimize the potential that such descriptions become overly standardized and less useful over time. For example, certain matters may be determined as key audit matters in a particular industry across a number of entities due to the circumstances of the industry or the underlying complexity in financial reporting. In describing why the auditor considered the matter to be one of most significance, it may be useful for the auditor to highlight aspects specific to the entity (e.g., circumstances that affected the underlying judgments made in the financial statements of the current period) in order to make the description more relevant for intended users. This also may be important in describing a key audit matter that recurs over periods. **A44**

The description may also make reference to the principal considerations that led the auditor, in the circumstances of the audit, to determine the matter to be one of most significance, for example: **A45**

- Economic conditions that affected the auditor's ability to obtain audit evidence, for example illiquid markets for certain financial instruments.
- New or emerging accounting policies, for example entity-specific or industry-specific matters on which the engagement team consulted within the firm.

---

[31] *See paragraph A3 of ISA (UK) 570 (Revised June 2016).*

- Changes in the entity's strategy or business model that had a material effect on the financial statements.

How the Matter Was Addressed in the Audit (Ref: Para. 13(b))

A46   The amount of detail to be provided in the auditor's report to describe how a key audit matter was addressed in the audit is a matter of professional judgment. In accordance with paragraph 13(b), the auditor may describe:

- Aspects of the auditor's response or approach that were most relevant to the matter or specific to the assessed risk of material misstatement;
- A brief overview of procedures performed;
- An indication of the outcome of the auditor's procedures; or
- Key observations with respect to the matter,

or some combination of these elements.

Law or regulation or national auditing standards may prescribe a specific form or content for the description of a key audit matter, or may specify the inclusion of one or more of these elements.

A47   In order for intended users to understand the significance of a key audit matter in the context of the audit of the financial statements as a whole, as well as the relationship between key audit matters and other elements of the auditor's report, including the auditor's opinion, care may be necessary so that language used in the description of a key audit matter:

- Does not imply that the matter has not been appropriately resolved by the auditor in forming the opinion on the financial statements.
- Relates the matter directly to the specific circumstances of the entity, while avoiding generic or standardized language.
- Takes into account how the matter is addressed in the related disclosure(s) in the financial statements, if any.
- Does not contain or imply discrete opinions on separate elements of the financial statements.

A48   Describing aspects of the auditor's response or approach to a matter, in particular when the audit approach required significant tailoring to the facts and circumstances of the entity, may assist intended users in understanding unusual circumstances and significant auditor judgment required to address the risk of material misstatement. In addition, the audit approach in a particular period may have been influenced by entity-specific circumstances, economic conditions, or industry developments. It may also be useful for the auditor to make reference to the nature and extent of communications with those charged with governance about the matter.

A49   For example, in describing the auditor's approach to an accounting estimate that has been identified as having high estimation uncertainty, such as the valuation of complex financial instruments, the auditor may wish to highlight that the auditor employed or engaged an auditor's expert. Such a reference to the use of an auditor's expert does not reduce the auditor's responsibility for the opinion on the financial statements and is therefore not inconsistent with paragraphs 14–15 of ISA (UK) 620 (Revised June 2016).[32]

A50   There may be challenges in describing the auditor's procedures, particularly in complex, judgmental areas of the audit. In particular, it may be difficult to summarize the procedures performed in a succinct way that adequately communicates the nature and extent of the auditor's response to the assessed risk of material misstatement, and the significant auditor judgments

---

[32] *ISA (UK) 620 (Revised June 2016)*, Using the Work of an Auditor's Expert.

involved. Nonetheless, the auditor may consider it necessary to describe certain procedures performed to communicate how the matter was addressed in the audit. Such description may typically be at a high level, rather than include a detailed description of procedures.

As noted in paragraph A46, the auditor may also provide an indication of the outcome   **A51**
of the auditor's response in the description of the key audit matter in the auditor's report. However, if this is done, care is needed to avoid the auditor giving the impression that the description is conveying a separate opinion on an individual key audit matter or that in any way may call into question the auditor's opinion on the financial statements as a whole.

***Circumstances in Which a Matter Determined to Be a Key Audit Matter Is Not
Communicated in the Auditor's Report*** (Ref: Para. 14)

Law or regulation may preclude public disclosure by either management or the auditor   **A52**
about a specific matter determined to be a key audit matter. For example, law or regulation may specifically prohibit any public communication that might prejudice an investigation by an appropriate authority into an actual, or suspected, illegal act (e.g., matters that are or appear to be related to money laundering).

As indicated by paragraph 14(b), it will be extremely rare for a matter determined to be a   **A53**
key audit matter not to be communicated in the auditor's report. This is because there is presumed to be a public interest benefit in providing greater transparency about the audit for intended users. Accordingly, the judgment not to communicate a key audit matter is appropriate only in cases when the adverse consequences to the entity or the public as a result of such communication are viewed as so significant that they would reasonably be expected to outweigh the public interest benefits of communicating about the matter.

The determination not to communicate a key audit matter takes into account the facts and   **A54**
circumstances related to the matter. Communication with management and those charged with governance helps the auditor understand management's views about the significance of the adverse consequences that may arise as a result of communicating about a matter. In particular, communication with management and those charged with governance helps to inform the auditor's judgment in determining whether to communicate the matter by:

- Assisting the auditor in understanding why the matter has not been publicly disclosed by the entity (e.g., if law, regulation or certain financial reporting frameworks permit delayed disclosure or non-disclosure of the matter) and management's views as to the adverse consequences, if any, of disclosure. Management may draw attention to certain aspects in law or regulation or other authoritative sources that may be relevant to the consideration of adverse consequences (e.g., such aspects may include harm to the entity's commercial negotiations or competitive position). However, management's views about the adverse consequences alone do not alleviate the need for the auditor to determine whether the adverse consequences would reasonably be expected to outweigh the public interest benefits of communication in accordance with paragraph 14(b).
- Highlighting whether there have been any communications with applicable regulatory, enforcement or supervisory authorities in relation to the matter, in particular whether such discussions would appear to support management's assertion as to why public disclosure about the matter is not appropriate.
- Enabling the auditor, where appropriate, to encourage management and those charged with governance to make public disclosure of relevant information about the matter. In particular, this may be possible if the concerns of management and those charged with governance about communicating are limited to specific aspects relating to the matter, such that certain information about the matter may be less sensitive and could be communicated.

The auditor also may consider it necessary to obtain a written representation from management as to why public disclosure about the matter is not appropriate, including management's view about the significance of the adverse consequences that may arise as a result of such communication.

A55 It may also be necessary for the auditor to consider the implications of communicating about a matter determined to be a key audit matter in light of relevant ethical requirements. In addition, the auditor may be required by law or regulation to communicate with applicable regulatory, enforcement or supervisory authorities in relation to the matter, regardless of whether the matter is communicated in the auditor's report. Such communication may also be useful to inform the auditor's consideration of the adverse consequences that may arise from communicating about the matter.

A56 The issues considered by the auditor regarding a decision to not communicate a matter are complex and involve significant auditor judgment. Accordingly, the auditor may consider it appropriate to obtain legal advice.

Form and Content of the Key Audit Matters Section in Other Circumstances
(Ref: Para. 16)

A57 The requirement in paragraph 16 applies in three circumstances:

(i)   The auditor determines in accordance with paragraph 10 that there are no key audit matters (seeparagraph A59).

(ii) The auditor determines in accordance with paragraph 14 that a key audit matter will not be communicated in the auditor's report and no other matters have been determined to be key audit matters.

(iii) The only matters determined to be key audit matters are those communicated in accordance with paragraph 15.

A58 The following illustrates the presentation in the auditor's report if the auditor has determined there are no key audit matters to communicate:

Key Audit Matters

[Except for the matter described in the *Basis for Qualified (Adverse) Opinion* section or *Material Uncertainty Related to Going Concern* section,] We have determined that there are no [other] key audit matters to communicate in our report.

A59 The determination of key audit matters involves making a judgment about the relative importance of matters that required significant auditor attention. Therefore, it may be rare that the auditor of a complete set of general purpose financial statements of a listed entity would not determine at least one key audit matter from the matters communicated with those charged with governance to be communicated in the auditor's report. However, in certain limited circumstances (e.g., for a listed entity that has very limited operations), the auditor may determine that there are no key audit matters in accordance with paragraph 10 because there are no matters that required significant auditor attention.

Communicating Other Audit Planning and Scoping Matters (Ref: Para. 16-1)

A59-1 The explanation, of how the auditor applied the concept of materiality in planning and performing the audit, is tailored to the particular circumstances and complexity of the audit and, in addition to specifying the threshold used by the auditor as being materiality for the financial statements as a whole, might include, for example:

- Materiality level or levels for those classes of transactions, account balances or disclosures where such materiality levels are lower than materiality for the financial statements as a whole (as described in paragraph 10 of ISA (UK) 320 (Revised June 2016)).
- Performance materiality (as described in paragraph 11 of ISA (UK) 320 (Revised June 2016)).
- Any significant revisions of materiality thresholds that were made as the audit progressed.
- The threshold used for reporting unadjusted differences to the audit committee.
- Significant qualitative considerations relating to the auditor's evaluation of materiality.

The content of the overview of the scope of the audit is tailored to the particular circumstances of the audit and how the scope was influenced by the auditor's application of materiality and addressed the key audit matters described in the auditor's report. Such a summary might also include, for example: **A59-2**

- The coverage of revenue, total assets and profit before tax achieved.
- The coverage of revenue, total assets and profit before tax of reportable segments achieved.
- The number of locations visited by the auditor as a proportion of the total number of locations, and the rationale underlying any program of visits.
- The effect of the group structure on the scope. The audit approach to a group consisting of autonomous subsidiary companies may differ from that applied to one which consists of a number of non-autonomous divisions.
- The nature and extent of the group auditor's involvement in the work of component auditors.

Communication with Those Charged with Governance (Ref: Para. 17)

ISA (UK) 260 (Revised June 2016) requires the auditor to communicate with those charged with governance on a timely basis.[33] The appropriate timing for communications about key audit matters will vary with the circumstances of the engagement. However, the auditor may communicate preliminary views about key audit matters when discussing the planned scope and timing of the audit, and may further discuss such matters when communicating about audit findings. Doing so may help to alleviate the practical challenges of attempting to have a robust two-way dialogue about key audit matters at the time the financial statements are being finalized for issuance.   **A60**

Communication with those charged with governance enables them to be made aware of the key audit matters that the auditor intends to communicate in the auditor's report, and provides them with an opportunity to obtain further clarification where necessary. The auditor may consider it useful to provide those charged with governance with a draft of the auditor's report to facilitate this discussion. Communication with those charged with governance recognizes their important role in overseeing the financial reporting process, and provides the opportunity for those charged with governance to understand the basis for the auditor's decisions in relation to key audit matters and how these matters will be described in the auditor's report. It also enables those charged with governance to consider whether new or enhanced disclosures may be useful in light of the fact that these matters will be communicated in the auditor's report.   **A61**

The communication with those charged with governance required by paragraph 17(a) also addresses the extremely rare circumstances in which a matter determined to be a key audit matter is not communicated in the auditor's report (see paragraphs 14 and A54).   **A62**

---

[33] *ISA (UK) 260 (Revised June 2016), paragraph 21.*

A63　The requirement in paragraph 17(b) to communicate with those charged with governance when the auditor has determined there are no key audit matters to communicate in the auditor's report may provide an opportunity for the auditor to have further discussion with others who are familiar with the audit and the significant matters that may have arisen (including the engagement quality control reviewer, where one has been appointed). These discussions may cause the auditor to re-evaluate the auditor's determination that there are no key audit matters.

Documentation (Ref: Para. 18)

A64　Paragraph 8 of ISA (UK) 230 (Revised June 2016) requires the auditor to prepare audit documentation that is sufficient to enable an experienced auditor, having no previous connection with the audit, to understand, among other things, significant professional judgments. In the context of key audit matters, these professional judgments include the determination, from the matters communicated with those charged with governance, of the matters that required significant auditor attention, as well as whether or not each of those matters is a key audit matter. The auditor's judgments in this regard are likely to be supported by the documentation of the auditor's communications with those charged with governance and the audit documentation relating to each individual matter (see paragraph A39), as well as certain other audit documentation of the significant matters arising during the audit (e.g., a completion memorandum). However, this ISA (UK) does not require the auditor to document why other matters communicated with those charged with governance were not matters that required significant auditor attention.

International Standard on Auditing (UK) 705 (Revised June 2016)

Modifications to the opinion in the independent auditor's report

(Effective for audits of financial statements for periods commencing on or after 17 June 2016)

Contents

International Standard on Auditing (UK) (ISA (UK)) 705 (Revised June 2016), *Modifications to the Opinion in the Independent Auditor's Report*, should be read in conjunction with ISA (UK) 200 (Revised June 2016), *Overall Objectives of the Independent Auditor and the Conduct of an Audit in Accordance with International Standards on Auditing (UK)*.

Introduction

Scope of this ISA (UK)

1   This International Standard on Auditing (UK) (ISA (UK)) deals with the auditor's responsibility to issue an appropriate report in circumstances when, in forming an opinion in accordance with ISA (UK) 700 (Revised June 2016),[1] the auditor concludes that a modification to the auditor's opinion on the financial statements is necessary. This ISA (UK) also deals with how the form and content of the auditor's report is affected when the auditor expresses a modified opinion. In all cases, the reporting requirements in ISA (UK) 700 (Revised June 2016) apply, and are not repeated in this ISA (UK) unless they are explicitly addressed or amended by the requirements of this ISA (UK).

Types of Modified Opinions

2   This ISA (UK) establishes three types of modified opinions, namely, a qualified opinion, an adverse opinion, and a disclaimer of opinion. The decision regarding which type of modified opinion is appropriate depends upon:

(a)   The nature of the matter giving rise to the modification, that is, whether the financial statements are materially misstated or, in the case of an inability to obtain sufficient appropriate audit evidence, may be materially misstated; and

(b)   The auditor's judgment about the pervasiveness of the effects or possible effects of the matter on the financial statements. (Ref: Para. A1)

Effective Date

3   This ISA (UK) is effective for audits of financial statements for periods commencing on or after 17 June 2016. Earlier adoption is permitted.

Objective

4   The objective of the auditor is to express clearly an appropriately modified opinion on the financial statements that is necessary when:

(a)   The auditor concludes, based on the audit evidence obtained, that the financial statements as a whole are not free from material misstatement; or

(b)   The auditor is unable to obtain sufficient appropriate audit evidence to conclude that the financial statements as a whole are free from material misstatement.

Definitions

5   For purposes of the ISAs (UK), the following terms have the meanings attributed below:

(a)   Pervasive – A term used, in the context of misstatements, to describe the effects on the financial statements of misstatements or the possible effects on the financial statements of misstatements, if any, that are undetected due to an inability to obtain sufficient appropriate audit evidence. Pervasive effects on the financial statements are those that, in the auditor's judgment:

(i)   Are not confined to specific elements, accounts or items of the financial statements;

(ii)   If so confined, represent or could represent a substantial proportion of the financial statements; or

---

[1]   *ISA (UK) 700 (Revised June 2016)*, Forming an Opinion and Reporting on Financial Statements.

    (iii) In relation to disclosures, are fundamental to users' understanding of the financial statements.
(b) Modified opinion – A qualified opinion, an adverse opinion or a disclaimer of opinion.

Requirements

Circumstances When a Modification to the Auditor's Opinion Is Required

The auditor shall modify the opinion in the auditor's report when: **6**

(a) The auditor concludes that, based on the audit evidence obtained, the financial statements as a whole are not free from material misstatement; or (Ref: Para. A2–A7)
(b) The auditor is unable to obtain sufficient appropriate audit evidence to conclude that the financial statements as a whole are free from material misstatement. (Ref: Para. A8–A12)

Determining the Type of Modification to the Auditor's Opinion

Qualified Opinion

The auditor shall express a qualified opinion when: **7**

(a) The auditor, having obtained sufficient appropriate audit evidence, concludes that misstatements, individually or in the aggregate, are material, but not pervasive, to the financial statements; or
(b) The auditor is unable to obtain sufficient appropriate audit evidence on which to base the opinion, but the auditor concludes that the possible effects on the financial statements of undetected misstatements, if any, could be material but not pervasive.

Adverse Opinion

The auditor shall express an adverse opinion when the auditor, having obtained sufficient   **8** appropriate audit evidence, concludes that misstatements, individually or in the aggregate, are both material and pervasive to the financial statements.

Disclaimer of Opinion

The auditor shall disclaim an opinion when the auditor is unable to obtain sufficient   **9** appropriate audit evidence on which to base the opinion, and the auditor concludes that the possible effects on the financial statements of undetected misstatements, if any, could be both material and pervasive.

The auditor shall disclaim an opinion when, in extremely rare circumstances involving   **10** multiple uncertainties, the auditor concludes that, notwithstanding having obtained sufficient appropriate audit evidence regarding each of the individual uncertainties, it is not possible to form an opinion on the financial statements due to the potential interaction of the uncertainties and their possible cumulative effect on the financial statements.

Consequence of an Inability to Obtain Sufficient Appropriate Audit Evidence Due to a Management-Imposed Limitation after the Auditor Has Accepted the Engagement

If, after accepting the engagement, the auditor becomes aware that management has   **11** imposed a limitation on the scope of the audit that the auditor considers likely to result in the need to express a qualified opinion or to disclaim an opinion on the financial statements, the auditor shall request that management remove the limitation.

12 If management refuses to remove the limitation referred to in paragraph 11 of this ISA (UK), the auditor shall communicate the matter to those charged with governance, unless all of those charged with governance are involved in managing the entity,[2] and determine whether it is possible to perform alternative procedures to obtain sufficient appropriate audit evidence.

13 If the auditor is unable to obtain sufficient appropriate audit evidence, the auditor shall determine the implications as follows:

(a) If the auditor concludes that the possible effects on the financial statements of undetected misstatements, if any, could be material but not pervasive, the auditor shall qualify the opinion; or

(b) If the auditor concludes that the possible effects on the financial statements of undetected misstatements, if any, could be both material and pervasive so that a qualification of the opinion would be inadequate to communicate the gravity of the situation, the auditor shall:

(i) Withdraw from the audit, where practicable and possible under applicable law or regulation; or (Ref: Para. A13)

(ii) If withdrawal from the audit before issuing the auditor's report is not practicable or possible, disclaim an opinion on the financial statements (Ref: Para. A14).

14 If the auditor withdraws as contemplated by paragraph 13(b)(i), before withdrawing, the auditor shall communicate to those charged with governance any matters regarding misstatements identified during the audit that would have given rise to a modification of the opinion. (Ref: Para. A15–A15-1)

Other Considerations Relating to an Adverse Opinion or Disclaimer of Opinion

15 When the auditor considers it necessary to express an adverse opinion or disclaim an opinion on the financial statements as a whole, the auditor's report shall not also include an unmodified opinion with respect to the same financial reporting framework on a single financial statement or one or more specific elements, accounts or items of a financial statement. To include such an unmodified opinion in the same report[3] in these circumstances would contradict the auditor's adverse opinion or disclaimer of opinion on the financial statements as a whole. (Ref: Para. A16)

Form and Content of the Auditor's Report When the Opinion Is Modified

Auditor's Opinion

16 When the auditor modifies the audit opinion, the auditor shall use the heading 'Qualified Opinion,' 'Adverse Opinion,' or 'Disclaimer of Opinion,' as appropriate, for the Opinion section. (Ref: Para. A17–A19)

---

[2] *ISA (UK) 260 (Revised June 2016)*, Communication with Those Charged with Governance, *paragraph 13*.

[3] *ISA 805*, Special Considerations—Audits of Single Financial Statements and Specific Elements, Accounts or Items of a Financial Statement, *deals with circumstances where the auditor is engaged to express a separate opinion on one or more specific elements, accounts or items of a financial statement.* ISA 805 has not been promulgated by the FRC for application in the UK.

Qualified Opinion

When the auditor expresses a qualified opinion due to a material misstatement in the   **17**
financial statements, the auditor shall state that, in the auditor's opinion, except for the
effects of the matter(s) described in the Basis for Qualified Opinion section:

(a) When reporting in accordance with a fair presentation framework, the accompanying
financial statements present fairly, in all material respects (or give a true and fair view
of) […] in accordance with [the applicable financial reporting framework]; or
(b) When reporting in accordance with a compliance framework, the accompanying
financial statements have been prepared, in all material respects, in accordance with
[the applicable financial reporting framework].

When the modification arises from an inability to obtain sufficient appropriate audit
evidence, the auditor shall use the corresponding phrase 'except for the possible effects of
the matter(s) …' for the modified opinion. (Ref: Para. A20)

Adverse Opinion

When the auditor expresses an adverse opinion, the auditor shall state that, in the auditor's   **18**
opinion, because of the significance of the matter(s) described in the Basis for Adverse
Opinion section:

(a) When reporting in accordance with a fair presentation framework, the accompanying
financial statements do not present fairly (or give a true and fair view of) […] in
accordance with [the applicable financial reporting framework]; or
(b) When reporting in accordance with a compliance framework, the accompanying
financial statements have not been prepared, in all material respects, in accordance
with [the applicable financial reporting framework].

Disclaimer of Opinion

When the auditor disclaims an opinion due to an inability to obtain sufficient appropriate   **19**
audit evidence, the auditor shall:

(a) State that the auditor does not express an opinion on the accompanying financial
statements;
(b) State that, because of the significance of the matter(s) described in the Basis for
Disclaimer of Opinion section, the auditor has not been able to obtain sufficient
appropriate audit evidence to provide a basis for an audit opinion on the financial
statements; and
(c) Amend the statement required by paragraph 24(b) of ISA (UK) 700 (Revised
June 2016), which indicates that the financial statements have been audited, to state
that the auditor was engaged to audit the financial statements.

Basis for Opinion

When the auditor modifies the opinion on the financial statements, the auditor shall, in   **20**
addition to the specific elements required by ISA (UK) 700 (Revised June 2016): (Ref:
Para. A21)

(a) Amend the heading 'Basis for Opinion' required by paragraph 28 of ISA (UK) 700
(Revised June 2016) to 'Basis for Qualified Opinion,' 'Basis for Adverse Opinion,' or
'Basis for Disclaimer of Opinion,' as appropriate; and
(b) Within this section, include a description of the matter giving rise to the modification.

21   If there is a material misstatement of the financial statements that relates to specific amounts in the financial statements (including quantitative disclosures), the auditor shall include in the Basis for Opinion section a description and quantification of the financial effects of the misstatement, unless impracticable. If it is not practicable to quantify the financial effects, the auditor shall so state in this section. (Ref: Para. A22)

22   If there is a material misstatement of the financial statements that relates to qualitative disclosures, the auditor shall include in the Basis for Opinion section an explanation of how the disclosures are misstated.

23   If there is a material misstatement of the financial statements that relates to the nondisclosure of information required to be disclosed, the auditor shall:

(a)   Discuss the non-disclosure with those charged with governance;

(b)   Describe in the Basis for Opinion section the nature of the omitted information; and

(c)   Unless prohibited by law or regulation, include the omitted disclosures, provided it is practicable to do so and the auditor has obtained sufficient appropriate audit evidence about the omitted information. (Ref: Para. A23)

24   If the modification results from an inability to obtain sufficient appropriate audit evidence, the auditor shall include in the Basis for Opinion section the reasons for that inability.

25   When the auditor expresses a qualified or adverse opinion, the auditor shall amend the statement about whether the audit evidence obtained is sufficient and appropriate to provide a basis for the auditor's opinion required by paragraph 28(d) of ISA (UK) 700 (Revised June 2016) to include the word 'qualified' or 'adverse', as appropriate.

26   When the auditor disclaims an opinion on the financial statements, the auditor's report shall not include the elements required by paragraphs 28(b) and 28(d) of ISA (UK) 700 (Revised June 2016). Those elements are:

(a)   A reference to the section of the auditor's report where the auditor's responsibilities are described; and

(b)   A statement about whether the audit evidence obtained is sufficient and appropriate to provide a basis for the auditor's opinion.

27   Even if the auditor has expressed an adverse opinion or disclaimed an opinion on the financial statements, the auditor shall describe in the Basis for Opinion section the reasons for any other matters of which the auditor is aware that would have required a modification to the opinion, and the effects thereof. (Ref: Para. A24)

Description of Auditor's Responsibilities for the Audit of the Financial Statements When the Auditor Disclaims an Opinion on the Financial Statements

28   When the auditor disclaims an opinion on the financial statements due to an inability to obtain sufficient appropriate audit evidence, the auditor shall amend the description of the auditor's responsibilities required by paragraphs 39–41 of ISA (UK) 700 (Revised June 2016) to include only the following: (Ref: Para. A25)

(a)   A statement that the auditor's responsibility is to conduct an audit of the entity's financial statements in accordance with International Standards on Auditing (UK) and to issue an auditor's report;

(b)   A statement that, however, because of the matter(s) described in the Basis for Disclaimer of Opinion section, the auditor was not able to obtain sufficient appropriate audit evidence to provide a basis for an audit opinion on the financial statements; and

(c) The statement about auditor independence and other ethical responsibilities required by paragraph 28(c) of ISA (UK) 700 (Revised June 2016).

Considerations When the Auditor Disclaims an Opinion on the Financial Statements

Unless required by law or regulation, when the auditor disclaims an opinion on the financial statements, the auditor's report shall not include a Key Audit Matters section in accordance with ISA (UK) 701[4] or an Other Information section in accordance with ISA (UK) 720 (Revised June 2016).[5] (Ref: Para. A26–A26-1)

29

Communication with Those Charged with Governance

When the auditor expects to modify the opinion in the auditor's report, the auditor shall communicate with those charged with governance the circumstances that led to the expected modification and the wording of the modification. (Ref: Para. A27)

30

***

Application and Other Explanatory Material

Types of Modified Opinions (Ref: Para. 2)

The table below illustrates how the auditor's judgment about the nature of the matter giving rise to the modification, and the pervasiveness of its effects or possible effects on the financial statements, affects the type of opinion to be expressed.

A1

Nature of Matter Giving Rise to the Modification	*Auditor's Judgment about the Pervasiveness of the Effects or Possible Effects on the Financial Statements*	
	Material but Not Pervasive	*Material and Pervasive*
Financial statements are materially misstated	Qualified opinion	Adverse opinion
Inability to obtain sufficient appropriate audit evidence	Qualified opinion	Disclaimer of opinion

Circumstances When a Modification to the Auditor's Opinion Is Required

Nature of Material Misstatements (Ref: Para. 6(a))

ISA (UK) 700 (Revised June 2016) requires the auditor, in order to form an opinion on the financial statements, to conclude as to whether reasonable assurance has been obtained about whether the financial statements as a whole are free from material misstatement.[6] This conclusion takes into account the auditor's evaluation of uncorrected misstatements, if any, on the financial statements in accordance with ISA (UK) 450 (Revised June 2016).[7]

A2

---

[4] *ISA (UK) 701*, Communicating Key Audit Matters in the Independent Auditor's Report, *paragraphs 11–13*.

[5] *ISA (UK) 720 (Revised June 2016)*, The Auditor's Responsibilities Relating to Other Information, *paragraph A54*.

[6] *ISA (UK) 700 (Revised June 2016), paragraph 11*.

[7] *ISA (UK) 450 (Revised June 2016)*, Evaluation of Misstatements Identified during the Audit, *paragraph 11*.

A3   ISA (UK) 450 (Revised June 2016) defines a misstatement as a difference between the reported amount, classification, presentation, or disclosure of a financial statement item and the amount, classification, presentation, or disclosure that is required for the item to be in accordance with the applicable financial reporting framework. Accordingly, a material misstatement of the financial statements may arise in relation to:

(a) The appropriateness of the selected accounting policies;

(b) The application of the selected accounting policies; or

(c) The appropriateness or adequacy of disclosures in the financial statements.

Appropriateness of the Selected Accounting Policies

A4   In relation to the appropriateness of the accounting policies management has selected, material misstatements of the financial statements may arise, for example, when:

(a) The selected accounting policies are not consistent with the applicable financial reporting framework;

(b) The financial statements do not correctly describe an accounting policy relating to a significant item in the statement of financial position, the statement of comprehensive income, the statement of changes in equity or the statement of cash flows; or

(c) The financial statements do not represent or disclose the underlying transactions and events in a manner that achieves fair presentation.

A5   Financial reporting frameworks often contain requirements for the accounting for, and disclosure of, changes in accounting policies. Where the entity has changed its selection of significant accounting policies, a material misstatement of the financial statements may arise when the entity has not complied with these requirements.

Application of the Selected Accounting Policies

A6   In relation to the application of the selected accounting policies, material misstatements of the financial statements may arise:

(a) When management has not applied the selected accounting policies consistently with the financial reporting framework, including when management has not applied the selected accounting policies consistently between periods or to similar transactions and events (consistency in application); or

(b) Due to the method of application of the selected accounting policies (such as an unintentional error in application).

Appropriateness or Adequacy of Disclosures in the Financial Statements

A7   In relation to the appropriateness or adequacy of disclosures in the financial statements, material misstatements of the financial statements may arise when:

(a) The financial statements do not include all of the disclosures required by the applicable financial reporting framework;

(b) The disclosures in the financial statements are not presented in accordance with the applicable financial reporting framework; or

(c) The financial statements do not provide the additional disclosures necessary to achieve fair presentation beyond disclosures specifically required by the applicable financial reporting framework.

Paragraph A13a of ISA (UK) 450 (Revised June 2016) provides further examples of material misstatements in qualitative disclosures that may arise.

Nature of an Inability to Obtain Sufficient Appropriate Audit Evidence
(Ref: Para. 6(b))

The auditor's inability to obtain sufficient appropriate audit evidence (also referred to as a   **A8**
limitation on the scope of the audit) may arise from:

(a)   Circumstances beyond the control of the entity;
(b)   Circumstances relating to the nature or timing of the auditor's work; or
(c)   Limitations imposed by management.

An inability to perform a specific procedure does not constitute a limitation on the scope of   **A9**
the audit if the auditor is able to obtain sufficient appropriate audit evidence by performing
alternative procedures. If this is not possible, the requirements of paragraphs 7(b) and 9–10
apply as appropriate. Limitations imposed by management may have other implications
for the audit, such as for the auditor's assessment of fraud risks and consideration of
engagement continuance.

Examples of circumstances beyond the control of the entity include when: **A10**

- The entity's accounting records have been destroyed.
- The accounting records of a significant component have been seized indefinitely by
  governmental authorities.

Examples of circumstances relating to the nature or timing of the auditor's work include   **A11**
when:

- The entity is required to use the equity method of accounting for an associated
  entity, and the auditor is unable to obtain sufficient appropriate audit evidence about
  the latter's financial information to evaluate whether the equity method has been
  appropriately applied.
- The timing of the auditor's appointment is such that the auditor is unable to observe
  the counting of the physical inventories.
- The auditor determines that performing substantive procedures alone is not sufficient,
  but the entity's controls are not effective.

Examples of an inability to obtain sufficient appropriate audit evidence arising from a   **A12**
limitation on the scope of the audit imposed by management include when:

- Management prevents the auditor from observing the counting of the physical
  inventory.
- Management prevents the auditor from requesting external confirmation of specific
  account balances.

Determining the Type of Modification to the Auditor's Opinion

*Consequence of an Inability to Obtain Sufficient Appropriate Audit Evidence Due to
a Management-Imposed Limitation after the Auditor Has Accepted the Engagement*
(Ref: Para. 13(b)(i)–14)

The practicality of withdrawing from the audit may depend on the stage of completion of   **A13**
the engagement at the time that management imposes the scope limitation. If the auditor
has substantially completed the audit, the auditor may decide to complete the audit to the
extent possible, disclaim an opinion and explain the scope limitation within the Basis for
Disclaimer of Opinion section prior to withdrawing.

A14   In certain circumstances, withdrawal from the audit may not be possible if the auditor is required by law or regulation to continue the audit engagement. This may be the case for an auditor that is appointed to audit the financial statements of public sector entities. It may also be the case in jurisdictions where the auditor is appointed to audit the financial statements covering a specific period, or appointed for a specific period and is prohibited from withdrawing before the completion of the audit of those financial statements or before the end of that period, respectively. The auditor may also consider it necessary to include an Other Matter paragraph in the auditor's report.[8]

A15   When the auditor concludes that withdrawal from the audit is necessary because of a scope limitation, there may be a professional, legal or regulatory requirement for the auditor to communicate matters relating to the withdrawal from the engagement to regulators or the entity's owners.

Statement by Auditor on Ceasing to Hold Office

A15-1   The auditor of a company in the UK who ceases to hold office as auditor is required to comply with the requirements of Sections 519 and 521 of the Companies Act 2006 regarding the statement to be made by the auditor in relation to ceasing to hold office. In addition, the auditor may need to notify the appropriate audit authority in accordance with Section 522 of the Companies Act 2006.

Other Considerations Relating to an Adverse Opinion or Disclaimer of Opinion
(Ref: Para. 15)

A16   The following are examples of reporting circumstances that would not contradict the auditor's adverse opinion or disclaimer of opinion:

- The expression of an unmodified opinion on financial statements prepared under a given financial reporting framework and, within the same report, the expression of an adverse opinion on the same financial statements under a different financial reporting framework.[9]
- The expression of a disclaimer of opinion regarding the results of operations, and cash flows, where relevant, and an unmodified opinion regarding the financial position (see ISA (UK) 510 (Revised June 2016)[10]). In this case, the auditor has not expressed a disclaimer of opinion on the financial statements as a whole.

Form and Content of the Auditor's Report When the Opinion Is Modified

Illustrative Auditors' Reports[10a] (Ref: Para. 16)

A17   Illustrations 1 and 2 in the Appendix contain auditor's reports with qualified and adverse opinions, respectively, as the financial statements are materially misstated.

---

[8] *ISA (UK) 706 (Revised June 2016)*, Emphasis of Matter Paragraphs and Other Matter Paragraphs in the Independent Auditor's Report, *paragraph A5.*

[9] *See paragraph A31 of ISA (UK) 700 (Revised June 2016) for a description of this circumstance.*

[10] *ISA (UK) 510 (Revised June 2016)*, Initial Audit Engagements—Opening Balances, *paragraph 10.*

[10a] *The examples in the Appendix have not been tailored for the UK. Illustrative auditor's reports tailored for use with audits conducted in accordance with ISAs (UK) are given in the current version of the FRC's Compendium of Illustrative Auditor's Reports.*

Illustration 3 in the Appendix contains an auditor's report with a qualified opinion as the   **A18**
auditor is unable to obtain sufficient appropriate audit evidence. Illustration 4 contains a
disclaimer of opinion due to an inability to obtain sufficient appropriate audit evidence
about a single element of the financial statements. Illustration 5 contains a disclaimer of
opinion due to an inability to obtain sufficient appropriate audit evidence about multiple
elements of the financial statements. In each of the latter two cases, the possible effects on
the financial statements of the inability are both material and pervasive. The Appendices
to other ISAs (UK) that include reporting requirements, including ISA (UK) 570 (Revised
June 2016),[11] also include illustrations of auditor's reports with modified opinions.

Auditor's Opinion (Ref: Para. 16)

Amending this heading makes it clear to the user that the auditor's opinion is modified and   **A19**
indicates the type of modification.

Qualified Opinion (Ref: Para. 17)

When the auditor expresses a qualified opinion, it would not be appropriate to use phrases   **A20**
such as 'with the foregoing explanation' or 'subject to' in the Opinion section as these are
not sufficiently clear or forceful.

Basis for Opinion (Ref: Para. 20, 21, 23, 27)

Consistency in the auditor's report helps to promote users' understanding and to identify   **A21**
unusual circumstances when they occur. Accordingly, although uniformity in the wording
of a modified opinion and in the description of the reasons for the modification may not
be possible, consistency in both the form and content of the auditor's report is desirable.

An example of the financial effects of material misstatements that the auditor may describe   **A22**
in the Basis for Opinion section in the auditor's report is the quantification of the effects on
income tax, income before taxes, net income and equity if inventory is overstated.

Disclosing the omitted information within the Basis for Opinion section would not be   **A23**
practicable if:

(a) The disclosures have not been prepared by management or the disclosures are
     otherwise not readily available to the auditor; or
(b) In the auditor's judgment, the disclosures would be unduly voluminous in relation to
     the auditor's report.

An adverse opinion or a disclaimer of opinion relating to a specific matter described   **A24**
within the Basis for Opinion section does not justify the omission of a description of
other identified matters that would have otherwise required a modification of the auditor's
opinion. In such cases, the disclosure of such other matters of which the auditor is aware
may be relevant to users of the financial statements.

Description of Auditor's Responsibilities for the Audit of the Financial Statements
When the Auditor Disclaims an Opinion on the Financial Statements (Ref: Para. 28)

When the auditor disclaims an opinion on the financial statements, the following statements   **A25**
are better positioned within the Auditor's Responsibilities for the Audit of the Financial

---

[11] *ISA (UK) 570 (Revised June 2016)*, Going Concern.

Statements section of the auditor's report, as illustrated in Illustrations 4–5 of the Appendix to this ISA (UK):[10a]

- The statement required by paragraph 28(a) of ISA (UK) 700 (Revised June 2016), amended to state that the auditor's responsibility is to conduct an audit of the entity's financial statements in accordance with ISAs (UK); and
- The statement required by paragraph 28(c) of ISA (UK) 700 (Revised June 2016) about independence and other ethical responsibilities.

Considerations When the Auditor Disclaims an Opinion on the Financial Statements (Ref: Para. 29)

A26   Providing the reasons for the auditor's inability to obtain sufficient appropriate audit evidence within the Basis for Disclaimer of Opinion section of the auditor's report provides useful information to users in understanding why the auditor has disclaimed an opinion on the financial statements and may further guard against inappropriate reliance on them. However, communication of any key audit matters other than the matter(s) giving rise to the disclaimer of opinion may suggest that the financial statements as a whole are more credible in relation to those matters than would be appropriate in the circumstances, and would be inconsistent with the disclaimer of opinion on the financial statements as a whole. Similarly, it would not be appropriate to include an Other Information section in accordance with ISA (UK) 720 (Revised June 2016) addressing the auditor's consideration of the consistency of the other information with the financial statements. Accordingly, paragraph 29 of this ISA (UK) prohibits a Key Audit Matters section or an Other Information section from being included in the auditor's report when the auditor disclaims an opinion on the financial statements, unless the auditor is otherwise required by law or regulation to communicate key audit matters or to report on other information.

A26-1   In the UK, the auditor is required by law or regulation to include a Key Audit Matters section or an Other Information section in the auditor's report, even when the auditor disclaims an opinion on the financial statements in the following circumstances:
- For audits of financial statements of public interest entities, the auditor is required to communicate certain key audit matters in accordance with ISA (UK) 701.[11a]
- For entities incorporated under the Companies Acts,[11b] the auditor is required to report in an Other Information section on the strategic report, the directors' report and, where one is prepared, the separate corporate governance statement in accordance with ISA (UK) 720 (Revised June 2016).[11c]
- For entities that are required, and those that choose voluntarily, to report on how they have applied the UK Corporate Governance Code, the auditor is required to report in an Other Information section on certain aspects of the entity's compliance with the UK Corporate Governance Code and the Listing Rules in accordance with ISA (UK) 720 (Revised June 2016).[11d]

Communication with Those Charged with Governance (Ref: Para. 30)

A27   Communicating with those charged with governance the circumstances that lead to an expected modification to the auditor's opinion and the proposed wording of the modification enables:

[11a] *ISA (UK) 701, paragraph 13R-1.*

[11b] *In the UK, the Companies Act 2006*

[11c] *ISA (UK) 720 (Revised June 2016), paragraphs 22D-1 and 22D-2.*

[11d] *ISA (UK) 720 (Revised June 2016), paragraphs 22-3 and 22-4.*

(a) The auditor to give notice to those charged with governance of the intended modification(s) and the reasons (or circumstances) for the modification(s);

(b) The auditor to seek the concurrence of those charged with governance regarding the facts of the matter(s) giving rise to the expected modification(s), or to confirm matters of disagreement with management as such; and

(c) Those charged with governance to have an opportunity, where appropriate, to provide the auditor with further information and explanations in respect of the matter(s) giving rise to the expected modification(s).

For audits of financial statements of public interest entities, ISA (UK) 250 (Revised June 2016) Section B[11e] requires the auditor to report to the relevant regulatory, enforcement or supervisory authority any information about the public interest entity (or an undertaking having close links with the public interest entity) that may bring about a refusal to issue an audit opinion on the financial statements or the issuing of an adverse or qualified opinion.

A27-1

Appendix   (Ref: Para. A17–A18, A25)

Illustrations of Auditor's Reports with Modifications to the Opinion

The examples in the Appendix have not been tailored for the UK. Illustrative auditor's reports tailored for use with audits conducted in accordance with ISAs (UK) are given in the current version of the FRC's Compendium of Illustrative Auditor's Reports.

- Illustration 1: An auditor's report containing a qualified opinion due to a material misstatement of the financial statements.
- Illustration 2: An auditor's report containing an adverse opinion due to a material misstatement of the consolidated financial statements.
- Illustration 3: An auditor's report containing a qualified opinion due to the auditor's inability to obtain sufficient appropriate audit evidence regarding a foreign associate.
- Illustration 4: An auditor's report containing a disclaimer of opinion due to the auditor's inability to obtain sufficient appropriate audit evidence about a single element of the consolidated financial statements.
- Illustration 5: An auditor's report containing a disclaimer of opinion due to the auditor's inability to obtain sufficient appropriate audit evidence about multiple elements of the financial statements.

Illustration 1 – Qualified Opinion due to a Material Misstatement of the Financial Statements

For purposes of this illustrative auditor's report, the following circumstances are assumed:

- Audit of a complete set of financial statements of a listed entity using a fair presentation framework. The audit is not a group audit (i.e., ISA 600[12] does not apply).
- The financial statements are prepared by management of the entity in accordance with IFRSs (a general purpose framework).
- The terms of the audit engagement reflect the description of management's responsibility for the financial statements in ISA 210.[13]
- Inventories are misstated. The misstatement is deemed to be material but not pervasive to the financial statements (i.e., a qualified opinion is appropriate).
- The relevant ethical requirements that apply to the audit are those of the jurisdiction.
- Based on the audit evidence obtained, the auditor has concluded that a material uncertainty does not exist related to events or conditions that may cast significant doubt on the entity's ability to continue as a going concern in accordance with ISA (UK) 570 (Revised).
- Key audit matters have been communicated in accordance with ISA 701.
- The auditor has obtained all of the other information prior to the date of the auditor's report and the matter giving rise to the qualified opinion on the consolidated financial statements also affects the other information.
- Those responsible for oversight of the financial statements differ from those responsible for the preparation of the financial statements.
- In addition to the audit of the financial statements, the auditor has other reporting responsibilities required under local law.

---

[12] *ISA 600*, Special Considerations—Audits of Group Financial Statements (Including the Work of Component Auditors).

[13] *ISA 210*, Agreeing the Terms of Audit Engagements.

INDEPENDENT AUDITOR'S REPORT

To the Shareholders of ABC Company [or Other Appropriate Addressee]

Report on the Audit of the Financial Statements[14]

Qualified Opinion

We have audited the financial statements of ABC Company (the Company), which comprise the statement of financial position as at December 31, 20X1, and the statement of comprehensive income, statement of changes in equity and statement of cash flows for the year then ended, and notes to the financial statements, including a summary of significant accounting policies.

In our opinion, except for the effects of the matter described in the *Basis for Qualified Opinion* section of our report, the accompanying financial statements present fairly, in all material respects, (or *give a true and fair view of*) the financial position of the Company as at December 31, 20X1, and (*of*) its financial performance and its cash flows for the year then ended in accordance with International Financial Reporting Standards (IFRSs).

Basis for Qualified Opinion

The Company's inventories are carried in the statement of financial position at xxx. Management has not stated the inventories at the lower of cost and net realizable value but has stated them solely at cost, which constitutes a departure from IFRSs. The Company's records indicate that, had management stated the inventories at the lower of cost and net realizable value, an amount of xxx would have been required to write the inventories down to their net realizable value. Accordingly, cost of sales would have been increased by xxx, and income tax, net income and shareholders' equity would have been reduced by xxx, xxx and xxx, respectively.

We conducted our audit in accordance with International Standards on Auditing (ISAs). Our responsibilities under those standards are further described in the *Auditor's Responsibilities for the Audit of the Financial Statements* section of our report. We are independent of the Company in accordance with the ethical requirements that are relevant to our audit of the financial statements in [jurisdiction], and we have fulfilled our other ethical responsibilities in accordance with these requirements. We believe that the audit evidence we have obtained is sufficient and appropriate to provide a basis for our qualified opinion.

Other Information [or another title if appropriate such as 'Information Other than the Financial Statements and Auditor's Report Thereon']

[*Reporting in accordance with the reporting requirements in ISA 720 (Revised) – see Illustration 6 in Appendix 2 of ISA 720 (Revised). The last paragraph of the other information section in Illustration 6 would be customized to describe the specific matter giving rise to the qualified opinion that also affects the other information.*]

---

[14] *The sub-title 'Report on the Audit of the Financial Statements' is unnecessary in circumstances when the second sub-title 'Report on Other Legal and Regulatory Requirements' is not applicable.*

Key Audit Matters

Key audit matters are those matters that, in our professional judgment, were of most significance in our audit of the financial statements of the current period. These matters were addressed in the context of our audit of the financial statements as a whole, and in forming our opinion thereon, and we do not provide a separate opinion on these matters. In addition to the matter described in the *Basis for Qualified Opinion* section we have determined the matters described below to be the key audit matters to be communicated in our report.

[*Description of each key audit matter in accordance with ISA 701.*]

Responsibilities of Management and Those Charged with Governance for the Financial Statements[15]

[*Reporting in accordance with ISA 700 (Revised) – see Illustration 1 in ISA 700 (Revised).*]

Auditor's Responsibilities for the Audit of the Financial Statements

[*Reporting in accordance with ISA 700 (Revised) – see Illustration 1 in ISA 700 (Revised).*]

Report on Other Legal and Regulatory Requirements

[*Reporting in accordance with ISA 700 (Revised) – see Illustration 1 in ISA 700 (Revised).*]

The engagement partner on the audit resulting in this independent auditor's report is [*name*].

[*Signature in the name of the audit firm, the personal name of the auditor, or both, as appropriate for the particular jurisdiction*]

[*Auditor Address*]

[*Date*]

Illustration 2 – Adverse Opinion due to a Material Misstatement of the Consolidated Financial Statements

For purposes of this illustrative auditor's report, the following circumstances are assumed:

- Audit of a complete set of consolidated financial statements of a listed entity using a fair presentation framework. The audit is a group audit of an entity with subsidiaries (i.e., ISA 600 applies).
- The consolidated financial statements are prepared by management of the entity in accordance with IFRSs (a general purpose framework).
- The terms of the audit engagement reflect the description of management's responsibility for the consolidated financial statements in ISA 210.
- The consolidated financial statements are materially misstated due to the non-consolidation of a subsidiary. The material misstatement is deemed to be pervasive to the consolidated financial statements. The effects of the misstatement on the consolidated financial statements have not been determined because it was not practicable to do so (i.e., an adverse opinion is appropriate).

---

[15] *Throughout the illustrative auditor's reports, the terms management and those charged with governance may need to be replaced by another term that is appropriate in the context of the legal framework in the particular jurisdiction.*

- The relevant ethical requirements that apply to the audit are those of the jurisdiction.
- Based on the audit evidence obtained, the auditor has concluded that a material uncertainty does not exist related to events or conditions that may cast significant doubt on the entity's ability to continue as a going concern in accordance with ISA 570 (Revised).
- ISA 701 applies; however, the auditor has determined that there are no key audit matters other than the matter described in the Basis for Adverse Opinion section.
- The auditor has obtained all of the other information prior to the date of the auditor's report and the matter giving rise to the adverse opinion on the consolidated financial statements also affects the other information.
- Those responsible for oversight of the consolidated financial statements differ from those responsible for the preparation of the consolidated financial statements.
- In addition to the audit of the consolidated financial statements, the auditor has other reporting responsibilities required under local law.

INDEPENDENT AUDITOR'S REPORT

To the Shareholders of ABC Company [or Other Appropriate Addressee]

Report on the Audit of the Consolidated Financial Statements[16]

Adverse Opinion

We have audited the consolidated financial statements of ABC Company and its subsidiaries (the Group), which comprise the consolidated statement of financial position as at December 31, 20X1, and the consolidated statement of comprehensive income, consolidated statement of changes in equity and consolidated statement of cash flows for the year then ended, and notes to the consolidated financial statements, including a summary of significant accounting policies.

In our opinion, because of the significance of the matter discussed in the *Basis for Adverse Opinion* section of our report, the accompanying consolidated financial statements do not present fairly (or *do not give a true and fair view of*) the consolidated financial position of the Group as at December 31, 20X1, and (*of*) its consolidated financial performance and its consolidated cash flows for the year then ended in accordance with International Financial Reporting Standards (IFRSs).

Basis for Adverse Opinion

As explained in Note X, the Group has not consolidated subsidiary XYZ Company that the Group acquired during 20X1 because it has not yet been able to determine the fair values of certain of the subsidiary's material assets and liabilities at the acquisition date. This investment is therefore accounted for on a cost basis. Under IFRSs, the Company should have consolidated this subsidiary and accounted for the acquisition based on provisional amounts. Had XYZ Company been consolidated, many elements in the accompanying consolidated financial statements would have been materially affected. The effects on the consolidated financial statements of the failure to consolidate have not been determined.

We conducted our audit in accordance with International Standards on Auditing (ISAs). Our responsibilities under those standards are further described in the *Auditor's*

---

[16] *The sub-title 'Report on the Audit of the Consolidated Financial Statements' is unnecessary in circumstances when the second sub-title 'Report on Other Legal and Regulatory Requirements' is not applicable.*

Responsibilities for the Audit of the Consolidated Financial Statements section of our report. We are independent of the Group in accordance with the ethical requirements that are relevant to our audit of the consolidated financial statements in [*jurisdiction*], and we have fulfilled our other ethical responsibilities in accordance with these requirements. We believe that the audit evidence we have obtained is sufficient and appropriate to provide a basis for our adverse opinion.

Other Information [or another title if appropriate such as 'Information Other than the Financial Statements and Auditor's Report Thereon']

[*Reporting in accordance with the reporting requirements in ISA 720 (Revised) – see Illustration 7 in Appendix 2 of ISA 720 (Revised). The last paragraph of the other information section in Illustration 7 would be customized to describe the specific matter giving rise to the qualified opinion that also affects the other information.*]

Key Audit Matters

Except for the matter described in the *Basis for Adverse Opinion* section, we have determined that there are no other key audit matters to communicate in our report.

Responsibilities of Management and Those Charged with Governance for the Consolidated Financial Statements[17]

[*Reporting in accordance with ISA 700 (Revised) – see Illustration 2 in ISA 700 (Revised).*]

Auditor's Responsibilities for the Audit of the Consolidated Financial Statements

[*Reporting in accordance with ISA 700 (Revised) – see Illustration 2 in ISA 700 (Revised).*]

Report on Other Legal and Regulatory Requirements

[*Reporting in accordance with ISA 700 (Revised) – see Illustration 2 in ISA 700 (Revised).*]

The engagement partner on the audit resulting in this independent auditor's report is [*name*].

[*Signature in the name of the audit firm, the personal name of the auditor, or both, as appropriate for the particular jurisdiction*]

[*Auditor Address*]

[*Date*]

Illustration 3 – Qualified Opinion due to the Auditor's Inability to Obtain Sufficient Audit Evidence Regarding a Foreign Associate

For purposes of this illustrative auditor's report, the following circumstances are assumed:
- Audit of a complete set of consolidated financial statements of a listed entity using a fair presentation framework. The audit is a group audit of an entity with subsidiaries (i.e., ISA 600 applies).

---

[17] *Or other terms that are appropriate in the context of the legal framework in the particular jurisdiction.*

- The consolidated financial statements are prepared by management of the entity in accordance with IFRSs (a general purpose framework).
- The terms of the audit engagement reflect the description of management's responsibility for the consolidated financial statements in ISA 210.
- The auditor was unable to obtain sufficient appropriate audit evidence regarding an investment in a foreign associate. The possible effects of the inability to obtain sufficient appropriate audit evidence are deemed to be material but not pervasive to the consolidated financial statements (i.e., a qualified opinion is appropriate).
- The relevant ethical requirements that apply to the audit are those of the jurisdiction.
- Based on the audit evidence obtained, the auditor has concluded that a material uncertainty does not exist related to events or conditions that may cast significant doubt on the entity's ability to continue as a going concern in accordance with ISA 570 (Revised).
- Key audit matters have been communicated in accordance with ISA 701.
- The auditor has obtained all of the other information prior to the date of the auditor's report and the matter giving rise to the qualified opinion on the consolidated financial statements also affects the other information.
- Those responsible for oversight of the consolidated financial statements differ from those responsible for the preparation of the consolidated financial statements.
- In addition to the audit of the consolidated financial statements, the auditor has other reporting responsibilities required under local law.

INDEPENDENT AUDITOR'S REPORT

To the Shareholders of ABC Company [or Other Appropriate Addressee]

Report on the Audit of the Consolidated Financial Statements[18]

Qualified Opinion

We have audited the consolidated financial statements of ABC Company and its subsidiaries (the Group), which comprise the consolidated statement of financial position as at December 31, 20X1, and the consolidated statement of comprehensive income, consolidated statement of changes in equity and consolidated statement of cash flows for the year then ended, and notes to the consolidated financial statements, including a summary of significant accounting policies.

In our opinion, except for the possible effects of the matter described in the *Basis for Qualified Opinion* section of our report, the accompanying consolidated financial statements present fairly, in all material respects, (or *give a true and fair view of*) the financial position of the Group as at December 31, 20X1, and (*of*) its consolidated financial performance and its consolidated cash flows for the year then ended in accordance with International Financial Reporting Standards (IFRSs).

Basis for Qualified Opinion

The Group's investment in XYZ Company, a foreign associate acquired during the year and accounted for by the equity method, is carried at xxx on the consolidated statement of financial position as at December 31, 20X1, and ABC's share of XYZ's net income of xxx is included in ABC's income for the year then ended. We were unable to obtain sufficient

---

[18] *The sub-title 'Report on the Audit of the Consolidated Financial Statements' is unnecessary in circumstances when the second sub-title 'Report on Other Legal and Regulatory Requirements' is not applicable.*

appropriate audit evidence about the carrying amount of ABC's investment in XYZ as at December 31, 20X1 and ABC's share of XYZ's net income for the year because we were denied access to the financial information, management, and the auditors of XYZ. Consequently, we were unable to determine whether any adjustments to these amounts were necessary.

We conducted our audit in accordance with International Standards on Auditing (ISAs). Our responsibilities under those standards are further described in the *Auditor's Responsibilities for the Audit of the Consolidated Financial Statements* section of our report. We are independent of the Group in accordance with the ethical requirements that are relevant to our audit of the consolidated financial statements in [*jurisdiction*], and we have fulfilled our other ethical responsibilities in accordance with these requirements. We believe that the audit evidence we have obtained is sufficient and appropriate to provide a basis for our qualified opinion.

Other Information [or another title if appropriate such as 'Information Other than the Financial Statements and Auditor's Report Thereon']

[*Reporting in accordance with the reporting requirements in ISA 720 (Revised) – see Illustration 6 in Appendix 2 of ISA 720 (Revised). The last paragraph of the other information section in Illustration 6 would be customized to describe the specific matter giving rise to the qualified opinion that also affects the other information.*]

Key Audit Matters

Key audit matters are those matters that, in our professional judgment, were of most significance in our audit of the consolidated financial statements of the current period. These matters were addressed in the context of our audit of the consolidated financial statements as a whole, and in forming our opinion thereon, and we do not provide a separate opinion on these matters. In addition to the matter described in the *Basis for Qualified Opinion* section, we have determined the matters described below to be the key audit matters to be communicated in our report.

[*Description of each key audit matter in accordance with ISA 701.*]

Responsibilities of Management and Those Charged with Governance for the Consolidated Financial Statements[19]

[*Reporting in accordance with ISA 700 (Revised) – see Illustration 2 in ISA 700 (Revised).*]

Auditor's Responsibilities for the Audit of the Consolidated Financial Statements

[*Reporting in accordance with ISA 700 (Revised) – see Illustration 2 in ISA 700 (Revised).*]

Report on Other Legal and Regulatory Requirements

[*Reporting in accordance with ISA 700 (Revised) – see Illustration 2 in ISA 700 (Revised).*]

The engagement partner on the audit resulting in this independent auditor's report is [*name*].

---

[19] *Or other terms that are appropriate in the context of the legal framework in the particular jurisdiction.*

[Signature in the name of the audit firm, the personal name of the auditor, or both, as appropriate for the particular jurisdiction]

[Auditor Address]

[Date]

Illustration 4 – Disclaimer of Opinion due to the Auditor's Inability to Obtain Sufficient Appropriate Audit Evidence about a Single Element of the Consolidated Financial Statements

For purposes of this illustrative auditor's report, the following circumstances are assumed:

- Audit of a complete set of consolidated financial statements of an entity other than a listed entity using a fair presentation framework. The audit is a group audit of an entity with subsidiaries (i.e., ISA 600 applies).
- The consolidated financial statements are prepared by management of the entity in accordance with IFRSs (a general purpose framework).
- The terms of the audit engagement reflect the description of management's responsibility for the consolidated financial statements in ISA 210.
- The auditor was unable to obtain sufficient appropriate audit evidence about a single element of the consolidated financial statements. That is, the auditor was also unable to obtain audit evidence about the financial information of a joint venture investment that represents over 90% of the entity's net assets. The possible effects of this inability to obtain sufficient appropriate audit evidence are deemed to be both material and pervasive to the consolidated financial statements (i.e., a disclaimer of opinion is appropriate).
- The relevant ethical requirements that apply to the audit are those of the jurisdiction.
- Those responsible for oversight of the consolidated financial statements differ from those responsible for the preparation of the consolidated financial statements.
- A more limited description of the auditor's responsibilities section is required.
- In addition to the audit of the consolidated financial statements, the auditor has other reporting responsibilities required under local law.

INDEPENDENT AUDITOR'S REPORT

To the Shareholders of ABC Company [or Other Appropriate Addressee]

Report on the Audit of the Consolidated Financial Statements[20]

Disclaimer of Opinion

We were engaged to audit the consolidated financial statements of ABC Company and its subsidiaries (the Group), which comprise the consolidated statement of financial position as at December 31, 20X1, and the consolidated statement of comprehensive income, consolidated statement of changes in equity and consolidated statement of cash flows for the year then ended, and notes to the consolidated financial statements, including a summary of significant accounting policies.

We do not express an opinion on the accompanying consolidated financial statements of the Group. Because of the significance of the matter described in the *Basis for Disclaimer*

---

[20] *The sub-title 'Report on the Audit of the Consolidated Financial Statements' is unnecessary in circumstances when the second sub-title 'Report on Other Legal and Regulatory Requirements' is not applicable.*

of Opinion section of our report, we have not been able to obtain sufficient appropriate audit evidence to provide a basis for an audit opinion on these consolidated financial statements.

Basis for Disclaimer of Opinion

The Group's investment in its joint venture XYZ Company is carried at xxx on the Group's consolidated statement of financial position, which represents over 90% of the Group's net assets as at December 31, 20X1. We were not allowed access to the management and the auditors of XYZ Company, including XYZ Company's auditors' audit documentation. As a result, we were unable to determine whether any adjustments were necessary in respect of the Group's proportional share of XYZ Company's assets that it controls jointly, its proportional share of XYZ Company's liabilities for which it is jointly responsible, its proportional share of XYZ's income and expenses for the year, and the elements making up the consolidated statement of changes in equity and the consolidated cash flow statement.

Responsibilities of Management and Those Charged with Governance for the Consolidated Financial Statements[21]

[*Reporting in accordance with ISA 700 (Revised) – see Illustration 2 in ISA 700 (Revised).*]

Auditor's Responsibilities for the Audit of the Consolidated Financial Statements

Our responsibility is to conduct an audit of the Group's consolidated financial statements in accordance with International Standards on Auditing and to issue an auditor's report. However, because of the matter described in the *Basis for Disclaimer of Opinion* section of our report, we were not able to obtain sufficient appropriate audit evidence to provide a basis for an audit opinion on these consolidated financial statements.

We are independent of the Group in accordance with the ethical requirements that are relevant to our audit of the financial statements in [*jurisdiction*], and we have fulfilled our other ethical responsibilities in accordance with these requirements.

Report on Other Legal and Regulatory Requirements

[*Reporting in accordance with ISA 700 (Revised) – see Illustration 2 in ISA 700 (Revised).*]

[*Signature in the name of the audit firm, the personal name of the auditor, or both, as appropriate for the particular jurisdiction*]

[*Auditor Address*]

[*Date*]

---

[21] *Or other terms that are appropriate in the context of the legal framework of the particular jurisdiction.*

Illustration 5 – Disclaimer of Opinion due to the Auditor's Inability to Obtain Sufficient Appropriate Audit Evidence about Multiple Elements of the Financial Statements

For purposes of this illustrative auditor's report, the following circumstances are assumed:

- Audit of a complete set of financial statements of an entity other than a listed entity using a fair presentation framework. The audit is not a group audit (i.e., ISA 600, does not apply).
- The financial statements are prepared by management of the entity in accordance with IFRSs (a general purpose framework).
- The terms of the audit engagement reflect the description of management's responsibility for the financial statements in ISA 210.
- The auditor was unable to obtain sufficient appropriate audit evidence about multiple elements of the financial statements, that is, the auditor was also unable to obtain audit evidence about the entity's inventories and accounts receivable. The possible effects of this inability to obtain sufficient appropriate audit evidence are deemed to be both material and pervasive to the financial statements.
- The relevant ethical requirements that apply to the audit are those of the jurisdiction.
- Those responsible for oversight of the financial statements differ from those responsible for the preparation of the financial statements.
- A more limited description of the auditor's responsibilities section is required.
- In addition to the audit of the financial statements, the auditor has other reporting responsibilities required under local law.

INDEPENDENT AUDITOR'S REPORT

To the Shareholders of ABC Company [or Other Appropriate Addressee]

Report on the Audit of the Financial Statements[22]

Disclaimer of Opinion

We were engaged to audit the financial statements of ABC Company (the Company), which comprise the statement of financial position as at December 31, 20X1, and the statement of comprehensive income, statement of changes in equity and statement of cash flows for the year then ended, and notes to the financial statements, including a summary of significant accounting policies.

We do not express an opinion on the accompanying financial statements of the Company. Because of the significance of the matters described in the *Basis for Disclaimer of Opinion* section of our report, we have not been able to obtain sufficient appropriate audit evidence to provide a basis for an audit opinion on these financial statements.

Basis for Disclaimer of Opinion

We were not appointed as auditors of the Company until after December 31, 20X1 and thus did not observe the counting of physical inventories at the beginning and end of the year. We were unable to satisfy ourselves by alternative means concerning the inventory quantities held at December 31, 20X0 and 20X1, which are stated in the statements of

---

[22] *The sub-title 'Report on the Audit of the Financial Statements' is unnecessary in circumstances when the second sub-title 'Report on Other Legal and Regulatory Requirements' is not applicable.*

financial position at xxx and xxx, respectively. In addition, the introduction of a new computerized accounts receivable system in September 20X1 resulted in numerous errors in accounts receivable. As of the date of our report, management was still in the process of rectifying the system deficiencies and correcting the errors. We were unable to confirm or verify by alternative means accounts receivable included in the statement of financial position at a total amount of xxx as at December 31, 20X1. As a result of these matters, we were unable to determine whether any adjustments might have been found necessary in respect of recorded or unrecorded inventories and accounts receivable, and the elements making up the statement of comprehensive income, statement of changes in equity and statement of cash flows.

Responsibilities of Management and Those Charged with Governance for the Financial Statements[23]

[*Reporting in accordance with ISA 700 (Revised) – see Illustration 1 in ISA 700 (Revised).*]

Auditor's Responsibilities for the Audit of the Financial Statements

Our responsibility is to conduct an audit of the Company's financial statements in accordance with International Standards on Auditing and to issue an auditor's report. However, because of the matters described in the *Basis for Disclaimer of Opinion* section of our report, we were not able to obtain sufficient appropriate audit evidence to provide a basis for an audit opinion on these financial statements.

We are independent of the Company in accordance with the ethical requirements that are relevant to our audit of the financial statements in [*jurisdiction*], and we have fulfilled our other ethical responsibilities in accordance with these requirements.

Report on Other Legal and Regulatory Requirements

[*Reporting in accordance with ISA 700 (Revised) – see Illustration 1 in ISA 700 (Revised).*]

[*Signature in the name of the audit firm, the personal name of the auditor, or both, as appropriate for the particular jurisdiction*]

[*Auditor Address*]

[*Date*]

---

[23] *Or other terms that are appropriate in the context of the legal framework of the particular jurisdiction.*

International Standard on Auditing (UK) 706 (Revised June 2016)

Emphasis of matter paragraphs and other matter paragraphs in the independent auditor's report

(Effective for audits of financial statements for periods commencing on or after 17 June 2016)

Contents

International Standard on Auditing (UK) (ISA (UK)) 706 (Revised June 2016), *Emphasis of Matter Paragraphs and Other Matter Paragraphs in the Independent Auditor's Report*, should be read in conjunction with ISA (UK) 200 (Revised June 2016), *Overall Objectives of the Independent Auditor and the Conduct of an Audit in Accordance with International Standards on Auditing (UK)*.

Introduction

Scope of this ISA (UK)

This International Standard on Auditing (UK) (ISA (UK)) deals with additional   **1**
communication in the auditor's report when the auditor considers it necessary to:

(a) Draw users' attention to a matter or matters presented or disclosed in the financial statements that are of such importance that they are fundamental to users' understanding of the financial statements; or
(b) Draw users' attention to any matter or matters other than those presented or disclosed in the financial statements that are relevant to users' understanding of the audit, the auditor's responsibilities or the auditor's report.

ISA (UK) 701[1] establishes requirements and provides guidance when the auditor   **2**
determines key audit matters and communicates them in the auditor's report. When
the auditor includes a Key Audit Matters section in the auditor's report, this ISA (UK)
addresses the relationship between key audit matters and any additional communication in
the auditor's report in accordance with this ISA (UK). (Ref: Para. A1–A3)

ISA (UK) 570 (Revised June 2016)[2] and ISA (UK) 720 (Revised June 2016)[3] establish   **3**
requirements and provide guidance about communication in the auditor's report relating to
going concern and other information respectively.

Appendices 1 and 2 identify ISAs (UK) that contain specific requirements for the auditor   **4**
to include Emphasis of Matter paragraphs or Other Matter paragraphs in the auditor's
report. In those circumstances, the requirements in this ISA (UK) regarding the form and
placement of such paragraphs apply. (Ref: Para. A4)

Effective Date

This ISA (UK) is effective for audits of financial statements for periods commencing on or   **5**
after 17 June 2016. Earlier adoption is permitted.

Objective

The objective of the auditor, having formed an opinion on the financial statements, is to   **6**
draw users' attention, when in the auditor's judgment it is necessary to do so, by way of
clear additional communication in the auditor's report, to:

(a) A matter, although appropriately presented or disclosed in the financial statements, that is of such importance that it is fundamental to users' understanding of the financial statements; or
(b) As appropriate, any other matter that is relevant to users' understanding of the audit, the auditor's responsibilities or the auditor's report.

---

[1] *ISA (UK) 701, Communicating Key Audit Matters in the Independent Auditor's Report.*

[2] *ISA (UK) 570 (Revised June 2016),* Going Concern.

[3] *ISA (UK) 720 (Revised June 2016),* The Auditor's Responsibilities Relating to Other Information.

Definitions

7   For the purposes of the ISAs (UK), the following terms have the meanings attributed below:

(a) Emphasis of Matter paragraph – A paragraph included in the auditor's report that refers to a matter appropriately presented or disclosed in the financial statements that, in the auditor's judgment, is of such importance that it is fundamental to users' understanding of the financial statements.

(b) Other Matter paragraph – A paragraph included in the auditor's report that refers to a matter other than those presented or disclosed in the financial statements that, in the auditor's judgment, is relevant to users' understanding of the audit, the auditor's responsibilities or the auditor's report.

Requirements

Emphasis of Matter Paragraphs in the Auditor's Report

8   If the auditor considers it necessary to draw users' attention to a matter presented or disclosed in the financial statements that, in the auditor's judgment, is of such importance that it is fundamental to users' understanding of the financial statements, the auditor shall include an Emphasis of Matter paragraph in the auditor's report provided: (Ref: Para. A5–A6)

(a) The auditor would not be required to modify the opinion in accordance with ISA (UK) 705 (Revised June 2016)[4] as a result of the matter; and

(b) When ISA (UK) 701 applies, the matter has not been determined to be a key audit matter to be communicated in the auditor's report. (Ref: Para. A1–A3)

9   When the auditor includes an Emphasis of Matter paragraph in the auditor's report, the auditor shall:

(a) Include the paragraph within a separate section of the auditor's report with an appropriate heading that includes the term 'Emphasis of Matter';

(b) Include in the paragraph a clear reference to the matter being emphasized and to where relevant disclosures that fully describe the matter can be found in the financial statements. The paragraph shall refer only to information presented or disclosed in the financial statements; and

(c) Indicate that the auditor's opinion is not modified in respect of the matter emphasized. (Ref: Para. A7–A8, A16–A17)

Other Matter Paragraphs in the Auditor's Report

10   If the auditor considers it necessary to communicate a matter other than those that are presented or disclosed in the financial statements that, in the auditor's judgment, is relevant to users' understanding of the audit, the auditor's responsibilities or the auditor's report, the auditor shall include an Other Matter paragraph in the auditor's report, provided:

(a) This is not prohibited by law or regulation; and

(b) When ISA (UK) 701 applies, the matter has not been determined to be a key audit matter to be communicated in the auditor's report. (Ref: Para. A9–A14)

---

[4] *ISA (UK) 705 (Revised June 2016)*, Modifications to the Opinion in the Independent Auditor's Report.

When the auditor includes an Other Matter paragraph in the auditor's report, the auditor shall include the paragraph within a separate section with the heading 'Other Matter,' or other appropriate heading. (Ref: Para. A15–A17) **11**

Communication with Those Charged with Governance

If the auditor expects to include an Emphasis of Matter or an Other Matter paragraph in the auditor's report, the auditor shall communicate with those charged with governance regarding this expectation and the proposed wording of this paragraph. (Ref: Para. A18) **12**

***

Application and Other Explanatory Material

The Relationship between Emphasis of Matter Paragraphs and Key Audit Matters in the Auditor's Report (Ref: Para. 2, 8(b))

Key audit matters are defined in ISA (UK) 701 as those matters that, in the auditor's professional judgment, were of most significance in the audit of the financial statements of the current period. Key audit matters are selected from matters communicated with those charged with governance, which include significant findings from the audit of the financial statements of the current period.[5] Communicating key audit matters provides additional information to intended users of the financial statements to assist them in understanding those matters that, in the auditor's professional judgment, were of most significance in the audit and may also assist them in understanding the entity and areas of significant management judgment in the audited financial statements. When ISA (UK) 701 applies, the use of Emphasis of Matter paragraphs is not a substitute for a description of individual key audit matters. **A1**

Matters that are determined to be key audit matters in accordance with ISA (UK) 701 may also be, in the auditor's judgment, fundamental to users' understanding of the financial statements. In such cases, in communicating the matter as a key audit matter in accordance with ISA (UK) 701, the auditor may wish to highlight or draw further attention to its relative importance. The auditor may do so by presenting the matter more prominently than other matters in the Key Audit Matters section (e.g., as the first matter) or by including additional information in the description of the key audit matter to indicate the importance of the matter to users' understanding of the financial statements. **A2**

In the UK, law or regulation may require a matter to be emphasized in the auditor's report in addition to communicating such a matter as a key audit matter in accordance with ISA (UK) 701. **A2-1**

There may be a matter that is not determined to be a key audit matter in accordance with ISA (UK) 701 (i.e., because it did not require significant auditor attention), but which, in the auditor's judgment, is fundamental to users' understanding of the financial statements (e.g., a subsequent event). If the auditor considers it necessary to draw users' attention to such a matter, the matter is included in an Emphasis of Matter paragraph in the auditor's report in accordance with this ISA (UK). **A3**

---

[5] *ISA (UK) 260 (Revised June 2016),* Communication with Those Charged with Governance, *paragraph 16.*

Circumstances in Which an Emphasis of Matter Paragraph May Be Necessary (Ref: Para. 4, 8)

A4   Appendix 1 identifies ISAs (UK) that contain specific requirements for the auditor to include Emphasis of Matter paragraphs in the auditor's report in certain circumstances. These circumstances include:

● When a financial reporting framework prescribed by law or regulation would be unacceptable but for the fact that it is prescribed by law or regulation.
● To alert users that the financial statements are prepared in accordance with a special purpose framework.
● When facts become known to the auditor after the date of the auditor's report and the auditor provides a new or amended auditor's report (i.e., subsequent events).[6]

A5   Examples of circumstances where the auditor may consider it necessary to include an Emphasis of Matter paragraph are:

● An uncertainty relating to the future outcome of exceptional litigation or regulatory action.
● A significant subsequent event that occurs between the date of the financial statements and the date of the auditor's report.[7]
● Early application (where permitted) of a new accounting standard that has a material effect on the financial statements.
● A major catastrophe that has had, or continues to have, a significant effect on the entity's financial position.

A5-1 In the UK, under legislation[7a] the auditor is required to include a reference to any matters to which the auditor wishes to draw attention by way of emphasis without modifying the audit opinion. Since it would be necessary for the auditor to do so, such a matter would be required to be included in the auditor's report in accordance with paragraph 8 of this ISA (UK).

A6   However, a widespread use of Emphasis of Matter paragraphs may diminish the effectiveness of the auditor's communication about such matters.

Including an Emphasis of Matter Paragraph in the Auditor's Report (Ref: Para. 9)

A7   The inclusion of an Emphasis of Matter paragraph in the auditor's report does not affect the auditor's opinion. An Emphasis of Matter paragraph is not a substitute for either:

(a) A modified opinion in accordance with ISA (UK) 705 (Revised June 2016) when required by the circumstances of a specific audit engagement;
(b) Disclosures in the financial statements that the applicable financial reporting framework requires management to make, or that are otherwise necessary to achieve fair presentation; or
(c) Reporting in accordance with ISA (UK) 705 (Revised June 2016)[8] when a material uncertainty exists relating to events or conditions that may cast significant doubt on an entity's ability to continue as a going concern.

---

[6] *ISA (UK) 560, paragraph 6.*

[7] *ISA (UK) 560, paragraph 6.*

[7a] *In the UK, Section 495(4) of the Companies Act 2006 establishes this requirement.*

[8] *ISA (UK) 705 (Revised June 2016), paragraphs 22–23.*

Paragraphs A16–A17 provide further guidance on the placement of Emphasis of Matter paragraphs in particular circumstances.   **A8**

Other Matter Paragraphs in the Auditor's Report (Ref: Para. 10–11)

Circumstances in Which an Other Matter Paragraph May Be Necessary

Relevant to Users' Understanding of the Audit

ISA (UK) 260 (Revised June 2016) requires the auditor to communicate with those charged with governance about the planned scope and timing of the audit, which includes communication about the significant risks identified by the auditor.[9] Although matters relating to significant risks may be determined to be key audit matters, other planning and scoping matters (e.g., the planned scope of the audit, or the application of materiality in the context of the audit) are unlikely to be key audit matters because of how key audit matters are defined in ISA (UK) 701. However, law or regulation may require the auditor to communicate about planning and scoping matters in the auditor's report, or the auditor may consider it necessary to communicate about such matters in an Other Matter paragraph.   **A9**

In the UK, when the auditor is required or decides to communicate key audit matters in accordance with ISA (UK) 701, the auditor communicates in the auditor's report other planning and scoping matters in accordance with paragraph 16-1 of ISA (UK) 701.   **A9-1**

In the rare circumstance where the auditor is unable to withdraw from an engagement even though the possible effect of an inability to obtain sufficient appropriate audit evidence due to a limitation on the scope of the audit imposed by management is pervasive,[10] the auditor may consider it necessary to include an Other Matter paragraph in the auditor's report to explain why it is not possible for the auditor to withdraw from the engagement.   **A10**

Relevant to Users' Understanding of the Auditor's Responsibilities or the Auditor's Report

Law, regulation or generally accepted practice in a jurisdiction may require or permit the auditor to elaborate on matters that provide further explanation of the auditor's responsibilities in the audit of the financial statements or of the auditor's report thereon. When the Other Matter section includes more than one matter that, in the auditor's judgment, is relevant to users' understanding of the audit, the auditor's responsibilities or the auditor's report, it may be helpful to use different sub-headings for each matter.   **A11**

An Other Matter paragraph does not deal with circumstances where the auditor has other reporting responsibilities that are in addition to the auditor's responsibility under the ISAs (UK) (see 'Other Reporting Responsibilities' section in ISA (UK) 700 (Revised June 2016)[11]), or where the auditor has been asked to perform and report on additional specified procedures, or to express an opinion on specific matters.   **A12**

---

[9] *ISA (UK) 260 (Revised June 2016), paragraph 15.*

[10] *See paragraph 13(b)(ii) of ISA (UK) 705 (Revised June 2016) for a discussion of this circumstance.*

[11] *ISA (UK) 700 (Revised June 2016),* Forming an Opinion and Reporting on Financial Statements, *paragraphs 42–44.*

Reporting on more than one set of financial statements

A13   An entity may prepare one set of financial statements in accordance with a general purpose framework (e.g., the national framework) and another set of financial statements in accordance with another general purpose framework (e.g., International Financial Reporting Standards), and engage the auditor to report on both sets of financial statements. If the auditor has determined that the frameworks are acceptable in the respective circumstances, the auditor may include an Other Matter paragraph in the auditor's report, referring to the fact that another set of financial statements has been prepared by the same entity in accordance with another general purpose framework and that the auditor has issued a report on those financial statements.

A13-1   The situation described in paragraph A13 is differentiated from the situation in paragraphs A8 and A25 of ISA (UK) 700 (Revised June 2016) in that, in the latter case, the auditor is engaged to express in the same auditor's report an opinion on the compliance of the financial statements with an additional financial reporting framework. This is only permissible if the auditor is satisfied that there are no differences between the two financial reporting frameworks that affect the financial statements being reported on.

Restriction on distribution or use of the auditor's report

A14   Financial statements prepared for a specific purpose may be prepared in accordance with a general purpose framework because the intended users have determined that such general purpose financial statements meet their financial information needs. Since the auditor's report is intended for specific users, the auditor may consider it necessary in the circumstances to include an Other Matter paragraph, stating that the auditor's report is intended solely for the intended users, and should not be distributed to or used by other parties.

Including an Other Matter Paragraph in the Auditor's Report

A15   The content of an Other Matter paragraph reflects clearly that such other matter is not required to be presented and disclosed in the financial statements. An Other Matter paragraph does not include information that the auditor is prohibited from providing by law, regulation or other professional standards, for example, ethical standards relating to confidentiality of information. An Other Matter paragraph also does not include information that is required to be provided by management.

Placement of Emphasis of Matter Paragraphs and Other Matter Paragraphs in the Auditor's Report (Ref: Para. 9, 11)

A16   The placement of an Emphasis of Matter paragraph or Other Matter paragraph in the auditor's report depends on the nature of the information to be communicated, and the auditor's judgment as to the relative significance of such information to intended users compared to other elements required to be reported in accordance with ISA (UK) 700 (Revised June 2016). For example:

Emphasis of Matter Paragraphs

- When the Emphasis of Matter paragraph relates to the applicable financial reporting framework, including circumstances where the auditor determines that the financial reporting framework prescribed by law or regulation would otherwise be unacceptable,[12] the auditor may consider it necessary to place the paragraph immediately following the Basis of Opinion section to provide appropriate context to the auditor's opinion.

- When a Key Audit Matters section is presented in the auditor's report, an Emphasis of Matter paragraph may be presented either directly before or after the Key Audit Matters section, based on the auditor's judgment as to the relative significance of the information included in the Emphasis of Matter paragraph. The auditor may also add further context to the heading 'Emphasis of Matter', such as 'Emphasis of Matter – Subsequent Event', to differentiate the Emphasis of Matter paragraph from the individual matters described in the Key Audit Matters section.

Other Matter Paragraphs

- When a Key Audit Matters section is presented in the auditor's report and an Other Matter paragraph is also considered necessary, the auditor may add further context to the heading 'Other Matter', such as 'Other Matter – Scope of the Audit', to differentiate the Other Matter paragraph from the individual matters described in the Key Audit Matters section.
- When an Other Matter paragraph is included to draw users' attention to a matter relating to Other Reporting Responsibilities addressed in the auditor's report, the paragraph may be included in the Report on Other Legal and Regulatory Requirements section.
- When relevant to all the auditor's responsibilities or users' understanding of the auditor's report, the Other Matter paragraph may be included as a separate section following the Report on the Audit of the Financial Statements and the Report on Other Legal and Regulatory Requirements.

Appendix 3[12a] is an illustration of the interaction between the Key Audit Matters section, an Emphasis of Matter paragraph and an Other Matter paragraph when all are presented in the auditor's report. The illustrative report in Appendix 4[13a] includes an Emphasis of Matter paragraph in an auditor's report for an entity other than a listed entity that contains a qualified opinion and for which key audit matters have not been communicated.

A17

Communication with Those Charged with Governance (Ref. Para. 12)

The communication required by paragraph 12 enables those charged with governance to be made aware of the nature of any specific matters that the auditor intends to highlight in the auditor's report, and provides them with an opportunity to obtain further clarification from the auditor where necessary. Where the inclusion of an Other Matter paragraph on a particular matter in the auditor's report recurs on each successive engagement, the auditor may determine that it is unnecessary to repeat the communication on each engagement, unless otherwise required to do so by law or regulation.

A18

---

[12] *For example, as required by ISA (UK) 210 (Revised June 2016),* Agreeing the Terms of Audit Engagements, *paragraph 19 and ISA 800,* Special Considerations—Audits of Financial Statements Prepared in Accordance with Special Purpose Frameworks, *paragraph 14.* ISA 800 has not been promulgated by the FRC for application in the UK.

[12a] *The examples in Appendices 3 and 4 have not been tailored for the UK. Illustrative auditor's reports tailored for use with audits conducted in accordance with ISAs (UK) are given in the current version of the FRC's Compendium of Illustrative Auditor's Reports.*

Appendix 1

List of ISAs (UK) Containing Requirements for Emphasis of Matter Paragraphs

This appendix identifies paragraphs in other ISAs (UK) that require the auditor to include an Emphasis of Matter paragraph in the auditor's report in certain circumstances. The list is not a substitute for considering the requirements and related application and other explanatory material in ISAs (UK).

- ISA (UK) 210 (Revised June 2016), *Agreeing the Terms of Audit Engagements* – paragraph 19(b)
- ISA (UK) 560, *Subsequent Events* – paragraphs 12(b) and 16
- ISA 800,[12b] *Special Considerations—Audits of Financial Statements Prepared in Accordance with Special Purpose Frameworks* – paragraph 14

[12b] *ISA 800 has not been promulgated by the FRC for application in the UK.*

Appendix 2

(Ref: Para. 4)

List of ISAs (UK) Containing Requirements for Other Matter Paragraphs

This appendix identifies paragraphs in other ISAs (UK) that require the auditor to include an Other Matter paragraph in the auditor's report in certain circumstances. The list is not a substitute for considering the requirements and related application and other explanatory material in ISAs (UK).

- ISA (UK) 560, *Subsequent Events* – paragraphs 12(b) and 16
- ISA (UK) 710, *Comparative Information—Corresponding Figures and Comparative Financial Statements* – paragraphs 13–14, 16–17 and 19
- ISA (UK) 720 (Revised June 2016), *The Auditor's Responsibilities Relating to Other Information* – paragraph 10(a)

Appendix 3

Illustration of an Auditor's Report that Includes a Key Audit Matters Section, an Emphasis of Matter Paragraph, and an Other Matter Paragraph

> The example in the Appendix has not been tailored for the UK. Illustrative auditor's reports tailored for use with audits conducted in accordance with ISAs (UK) are given in the current version of the FRC's Compendium of Illustrative Auditor's Reports.

For purposes of this illustrative auditor's report, the following circumstances are assumed:

- Audit of a complete set of financial statements of a listed entity using a fair presentation framework. The audit is not a group audit (i.e., ISA 600[13] does not apply).
- The financial statements are prepared by management of the entity in accordance with International Financial Reporting Standards (IFRSs) (a general purpose framework).
- The terms of the audit engagement reflect the description of management's responsibility for the financial statements in ISA 210.
- The auditor has concluded an unmodified (i.e., 'clean') opinion is appropriate based on the audit evidence obtained.
- The relevant ethical requirements that apply to the audit are those of the jurisdiction.
- Based on the audit evidence obtained, the auditor has concluded that a material uncertainty does not exist related to events or conditions that may cast significant doubt on the entity's ability to continue as a going concern in accordance with ISA 570 (Revised).
- Between the date of the financial statements and the date of the auditor's report, there was a fire in the entity's production facilities, which was disclosed by the entity as a subsequent event. In the auditor's judgment, the matter is of such importance that it is fundamental to users' understanding of the financial statements. The matter did not require significant auditor attention in the audit of the financial statements in the current period.
- Key audit matters have been communicated in accordance with ISA 701.
- The auditor has obtained all of the other information prior to the date of the auditor's report and has not identified a material misstatement of the other information.
- Corresponding figures are presented, and the prior period's financial statements were audited by a predecessor auditor. The auditor is not prohibited by law or regulation from referring to the predecessor auditor's report on the corresponding figures and has decided to do so.
- Those responsible for oversight of the financial statements differ from those responsible for the preparation of the financial statements.
- In addition to the audit of the financial statements, the auditor has other reporting responsibilities required under local law.

---

[13] ISA 600, Special Considerations—Audits of Group Financial Statements (Including the Work of Component Auditors).

INDEPENDENT AUDITOR'S REPORT

To the Shareholders of ABC Company [or Other Appropriate Addressee]

Report on the Audit of the Financial Statements[14]

Opinion

We have audited the financial statements of ABC Company (the Company), which comprise the statement of financial position as at December 31, 20X1, and the statement of comprehensive income, statement of changes in equity and statement of cash flows for the year then ended, and notes to the financial statements, including a summary of significant accounting policies.

In our opinion, the accompanying financial statements present fairly, in all material respects, (or *give a true and fair view of*) the financial position of the Company as at December 31, 20X1, and (*of*) its financial performance and its cash flows for the year then ended in accordance with International Financial Reporting Standards (IFRSs).

Basis for Opinion

We conducted our audit in accordance with International Standards on Auditing (ISAs). Our responsibilities under those standards are further described in the *Auditor's Responsibilities for the Audit of the Financial Statements* section of our report. We are independent of the Company in accordance with the ethical requirements that are relevant to our audit of the financial statements in [*jurisdiction*], and we have fulfilled our other ethical responsibilities in accordance with these requirements. We believe that the audit evidence we have obtained is sufficient and appropriate to provide a basis for our opinion.

Emphasis of Matter[15]

We draw attention to Note X of the financial statements, which describes the effects of a fire in the Company's production facilities. Our opinion is not modified in respect of this matter.

Key Audit Matters

Key audit matters are those matters that, in our professional judgment, were of most significance in our audit of the financial statements of the current period. These matters were addressed in the context of our audit of the financial statements as a whole, and in forming our opinion thereon, and we do not provide a separate opinion on these matters.

[*Description of each key audit matter in accordance with ISA 701.*]

---

[14] *The sub-title 'Report on the Audit of the Financial Statements' is unnecessary in circumstances when the second sub-title 'Report on Other Legal and Regulatory Requirements' is not applicable.*

[15] *As noted in paragraph A16, an Emphasis of Matter paragraph may be presented either directly before or after the Key Audit Matters section based on the auditor's judgment as to the relative significance of the information included in the Emphasis of Matter paragraph.*

Other Matter

The financial statements of ABC Company for the year ended December 31, 20X0, were audited by another auditor who expressed an unmodified opinion on those statements on March 31, 20X1.

Other Information [or another title if appropriate such as 'Information Other than the Financial Statements and Auditor's Report Thereon']

[Reporting in accordance with the reporting requirements in ISA 720 (Revised) – see Illustration 1 in Appendix 2 of ISA 720 (Revised).]

Responsibilities of Management and Those Charged with Governance for the Financial Statements[16]

[Reporting in accordance with ISA 700 (Revised) – see Illustration 1 in ISA 700 (Revised).]

Auditor's Responsibilities for the Audit of the Financial Statements

[Reporting in accordance with ISA 700 (Revised) – see Illustration 1 in ISA 700 (Revised).]

Report on Other Legal and Regulatory Requirements

[Reporting in accordance with ISA 700 (Revised) – see Illustration 1 in ISA 700 (Revised).]

The engagement partner on the audit resulting in this independent auditor's report is *[name]*.

[Signature in the name of the audit firm, the personal name of the auditor, or both, as appropriate for the particular jurisdiction]

[Auditor Address]

[Date]

---

[16] *Throughout these illustrative auditor's reports, the terms management and those charged with governance may need to be replaced by another term that is appropriate in the context of the legal framework in the particular jurisdiction.*

Appendix 4

Illustration of an Auditor's Report Containing a Qualified Opinion Due to a Departure from the Applicable Financial Reporting Framework and that Includes an Emphasis of Matter Paragraph

The example in the Appendix has not been tailored for the UK. Illustrative auditor's reports tailored for use with audits conducted in accordance with ISAs (UK) are given in the current version of the FRC's Compendium of Illustrative Auditor's Reports.

For purposes of this illustrative auditor's report, the following circumstances are assumed:

- Audit of a complete set of financial statements of an entity other than a listed entity using a fair presentation framework. The audit is not a group audit (i.e., ISA 600 does not apply).
- The financial statements are prepared by management of the entity in accordance with IFRSs (a general purpose framework).
- The terms of the audit engagement reflect the description of management's responsibility for the financial statements in ISA 210.
- A departure from the applicable financial reporting framework resulted in a qualified opinion.
- The relevant ethical requirements that apply to the audit are those of the jurisdiction.
- Based on the audit evidence obtained, the auditor has concluded that a material uncertainty does not exist related to events or conditions that may cast significant doubt on the entity's ability to continue as a going concern in accordance with ISA 570 (Revised).
- Between the date of the financial statements and the date of the auditor's report, there was a fire in the entity's production facilities, which was disclosed by the entity as a subsequent event. In the auditor's judgment, the matter is of such importance that it is fundamental to users' understanding of the financial statements. The matter did not require significant auditor attention in the audit of the financial statements in the current period.
- The auditor is not required, and has otherwise not decided, to communicate key audit matters in accordance with ISA 701.
- The auditor has not obtained any other information prior to the date of the auditor's report.Those responsible for oversight of the financial statements differ from those responsible for the preparation of the financial statements.
- Those responsible for oversight of the financial statements differ from those responsible for the preparation of the financial statements.
- In addition to the audit of the financial statements, the auditor has other reporting responsibilities required under local law.

INDEPENDENT AUDITOR'S REPORT

To the Shareholders of ABC Company [or Other Appropriate Addressee]

Report on the Audit of the Financial Statements[17]

Qualified Opinion

We have audited the financial statements of ABC Company (the Company), which comprise the statement of financial position as at December 31, 20X1, and the statement of comprehensive income, statement of changes in equity and statement of cash flows for the year then ended, and notes to the financial statements, including a summary of significant accounting policies.

In our opinion, except for the effects of the matter described in the Basis for Qualified Opinion section of our report, the accompanying financial statements present fairly, in all material respects, (or *give a true and fair view of*) the financial position of the Company as at December 31, 20X1, and (*of*) its financial performance and its cash flows for the year then ended in accordance with International Financial Reporting Standards (IFRSs).

Basis for Qualified Opinion

The Company's short-term marketable securities are carried in the statement of financial position at xxx. Management has not marked these securities to market but has instead stated them at cost, which constitutes a departure from IFRSs. The Company's records indicate that had management marked the marketable securities to market, the Company would have recognized an unrealized loss of xxx in the statement of comprehensive income for the year. The carrying amount of the securities in the statement of financial position would have been reduced by the same amount at December 31, 20X1, and income tax, net income and shareholders' equity would have been reduced by xxx, xxx and xxx, respectively.

We conducted our audit in accordance with International Standards on Auditing (ISAs). Our responsibilities under those standards are further described in the *Auditor's Responsibilities for the Audit of the Financial Statements* section of our report. We are independent of the Company in accordance with the ethical requirements that are relevant to our audit of the financial statements in [*jurisdiction*], and we have fulfilled our other ethical responsibilities in accordance with these requirements. We believe that the audit evidence we have obtained is sufficient and appropriate to provide a basis for our qualified opinion.

Emphasis of Matter – Effects of a Fire

We draw attention to Note X of the financial statements, which describes the effects of a fire in the Company's production facilities. Our opinion is not modified in respect of this matter.

---

[17] *The sub-title 'Report on the Audit of the Financial Statements' is unnecessary in circumstances when the second sub-title 'Report on Other Legal and Regulatory Requirements' is not applicable.*

Responsibilities of Management and Those Charged with Governance for the Financial Statements[18]

[*Reporting in accordance with ISA 700 (Revised) – see Illustration 1 in ISA 700 (Revised).*]

Auditor's Responsibilities for the Audit of the Financial Statements

[*Reporting in accordance with ISA 700 (Revised) – see Illustration 1 in ISA 700 (Revised).*]

Report on Other Legal and Regulatory Requirements

[*Reporting in accordance with ISA 700 (Revised) – see Illustration 1 in ISA 700 (Revised).*]

[*Signature in the name of the audit firm, the personal name of the auditor, or both, as appropriate for the particular jurisdiction*]

[*Auditor Address*]

[*Date*]

---

[18] *Or other terms that are appropriate in the context of the legal framework of the particular jurisdiction.*

International Standard on Auditing (UK) 710

Comparative information – corresponding figures and comparative financial statements

(Effective for audits of financial statements for periods ending on or after 15 December 2010)

Contents

International Standard on Auditing (UK) (ISA (UK)) 710, *Comparative Information—Corresponding Figures and Comparative Financial Statements*, should be read in conjunction with ISA (UK) 200 (Revised June 2016), *Overall Objectives of the Independent Auditor and the Conduct of an Audit in Accordance with International Standards on Auditing (UK)*.

Introduction

Scope of this ISA (UK)

This International Standard on Auditing (UK) (ISA (UK)) deals with the auditor's **1** responsibilities relating to comparative information in an audit of financial statements. When the financial statements of the prior period have been audited by a predecessor auditor or were not audited, the requirements and guidance in ISA (UK) 510 (Revised June 2016)[1] regarding opening balances also apply.

The Nature of Comparative Information

The nature of the comparative information that is presented in an entity's financial **2** statements depends on the requirements of the applicable financial reporting framework. There are two different broad approaches to the auditor's reporting responsibilities in respect of such comparative information: corresponding figures and comparative financial statements. The approach to be adopted is often specified by law or regulation but may also be specified in the terms of engagement.

In the UK, the corresponding figures method of presentation is usually required. **2-1**

The essential audit reporting differences between the approaches are: **3**

(a) For corresponding figures, the auditor's opinion on the financial statements refers to the current period only; whereas
(b) For comparative financial statements, the auditor's opinion refers to each period for which financial statements are presented.

This ISA (UK) addresses separately the auditor's reporting requirements for each approach.

Effective Date

This ISA (UK) is effective for audits of financial statements for periods ending on or after **4** 15 December 2010.

Objectives

The objectives of the auditor are: **5**

(a) To obtain sufficient appropriate audit evidence about whether the comparative information included in the financial statements has been presented, in all material respects, in accordance with the requirements for comparative information in the applicable financial reporting framework; and
(b) To report in accordance with the auditor's reporting responsibilities.

Definitions

For purposes of the ISAs (UK), the following terms have the meanings attributed below: **6**

(a) Comparative information – The amounts and disclosures included in the financial statements in respect of one or more prior periods in accordance with the applicable financial reporting framework.

---

[1] *ISA (UK) 510 (Revised June 2016)*, Initial Audit Engagements—Opening Balances.

(b) Corresponding figures – Comparative information where amounts and other disclosures for the prior period are included as an integral part of the current period financial statements, and are intended to be read only in relation to the amounts and other disclosures relating to the current period (referred to as 'current period figures'). The level of detail presented in the corresponding amounts and disclosures is dictated primarily by its relevance to the current period figures.

(c) Comparative financial statements – Comparative information where amounts and other disclosures for the prior period are included for comparison with the financial statements of the current period but, if audited, are referred to in the auditor's opinion. The level of information included in those comparative financial statements is comparable with that of the financial statements of the current period.

For purposes of this ISA (UK), references to 'prior period' should be read as 'prior periods' when the comparative information includes amounts and disclosures for more than one period.

Requirements

Audit Procedures

7   The auditor shall determine whether the financial statements include the comparative information required by the applicable financial reporting framework and whether such information is appropriately classified. For this purpose, the auditor shall evaluate whether:

(a) The comparative information agrees with the amounts and other disclosures presented in the prior period or, when appropriate, have been restated; (Ref: Para. A1-1) and

(b) The accounting policies reflected in the comparative information are consistent with those applied in the current period or, if there have been changes in accounting policies, whether those changes have been properly accounted for and adequately presented and disclosed.

8   If the auditor becomes aware of a possible material misstatement in the comparative information while performing the current period audit, the auditor shall perform such additional audit procedures as are necessary in the circumstances to obtain sufficient appropriate audit evidence to determine whether a material misstatement exists. If the auditor had audited the prior period's financial statements, the auditor shall also follow the relevant requirements of ISA (UK) 560.[2] If the prior period financial statements are amended, the auditor shall determine that the comparative information agrees with the amended financial statements.

9   As required by ISA (UK) 580,[3] the auditor shall request written representations for all periods referred to in the auditor's opinion. The auditor shall also obtain a specific written representation regarding any restatement made to correct a material misstatement in prior period financial statements that affect the comparative information. (Ref: Para. A1)

---

[2] *ISA (UK) 560, Subsequent Events, paragraphs 14–17.*

[3] *ISA (UK) 580, Written Representations, paragraph 14.*

Audit Reporting

Corresponding Figures

When corresponding figures are presented, the auditor's opinion shall not refer to the corresponding figures except in the circumstances described in paragraphs 11, 12, and 14. (Ref: Para. A2)   **10**

If the auditor's report on the prior period, as previously issued, included a qualified opinion, a disclaimer of opinion, or an adverse opinion and the matter which gave rise to the modification is unresolved, the auditor shall modify the auditor's opinion on the current period's financial statements. In the Basis for Modification paragraph in the auditor's report, the auditor shall either: **11**

(a) Refer to both the current period's figures and the corresponding figures in the description of the matter giving rise to the modification when the effects or possible effects of the matter on the current period's figures are material; or

(b) In other cases, explain that the audit opinion has been modified because of the effects or possible effects of the unresolved matter on the comparability of the current period's figures and the corresponding figures. (Ref: Para. A3–A5)

If the auditor obtains audit evidence that a material misstatement exists in the prior period financial statements on which an unmodified opinion has been previously issued, and the corresponding figures have not been properly restated or appropriate disclosures have not been made, the auditor shall express a qualified opinion or an adverse opinion in the auditor's report on the current period financial statements, modified with respect to the corresponding figures included therein. (Ref: Para. A6)   **12**

Prior Period Financial Statements Audited by a Predecessor Auditor

If the financial statements of the prior period were audited by a predecessor auditor and the auditor is not prohibited by law or regulation from referring to the predecessor auditor's report on the corresponding figures and decides to do so, the auditor shall state in an Other Matter paragraph in the auditor's report: **13**

(a) That the financial statements of the prior period were audited by the predecessor auditor;

(b) The type of opinion expressed by the predecessor auditor and, if the opinion was modified, the reasons therefore; and

(c) date of that report. (Ref: Para. A7 – A7-3)

Prior Period Financial Statements Not Audited

If the prior period financial statements were not audited, the auditor shall state in an Other Matter paragraph in the auditor's report that the corresponding figures are unaudited. Such a statement does not, however, relieve the auditor of the requirement to obtain sufficient appropriate audit evidence that the opening balances do not contain misstatements that materially affect the current period's financial statements.[4] (Ref: Para. A7a)   **14**

---

[4] *ISA (UK) 510 (Revised June 2016), paragraph 6.*

Comparative Financial Statements

15   When comparative financial statements are presented, the auditor's opinion shall refer to each period for which financial statements are presented and on which an audit opinion is expressed. (Ref: Para. A8–A9)

16   When reporting on prior period financial statements in connection with the current period's audit, if the auditor's opinion on such prior period financial statements differs from the opinion the auditor previously expressed, the auditor shall disclose the substantive reasons for the different opinion in an Other Matter paragraph in accordance with ISA (UK) 706 (Revised June 2016).[5] (Ref: Para. A10)

Prior Period Financial Statements Audited by a Predecessor Auditor

17   If the financial statements of the prior period were audited by a predecessor auditor, in addition to expressing an opinion on the current period's financial statements, the auditor shall state in an Other Matter paragraph:

    (a) that the financial statements of the prior period were audited by a predecessor auditor;

    (b) the type of opinion expressed by the predecessor auditor and, if the opinion was modified, the reasons therefore; and

    (c) the date of that report,

unless the predecessor auditor's report on the prior period's financial statements is reissued with the financial statements.

18   If the auditor concludes that a material misstatement exists that affects the prior period financial statements on which the predecessor auditor had previously reported without modification, the auditor shall communicate the misstatement with the appropriate level of management and, unless all of those charged with governance are involved in managing the entity,[6] those charged with governance and request that the predecessor auditor be informed. If the prior period financial statements are amended, and the predecessor auditor agrees to issue a new auditor's report on the amended financial statements of the prior period, the auditor shall report only on the current period. (Ref: Para. A11)

Prior Period Financial Statements Not Audited

19   If the prior period financial statements were not audited, the auditor shall state in an Other Matter paragraph that the comparative financial statements are unaudited. Such a statement does not, however, relieve the auditor of the requirement to obtain sufficient appropriate audit evidence that the opening balances do not contain misstatements that materially affect the current period's financial statements.[7] (Ref: Para. A12)

***

---

[5]   *ISA (UK) 706 (Revised June 2016)*, Emphasis of Matter Paragraphs and Other Matter Paragraphs in the Independent Auditor's Report, *paragraph 8.*

[6]   *ISA (UK) 260 (Revised June 2016)*, Communication with Those Charged with Governance, *paragraph 13.*

[7]   *ISA (UK) 510 (Revised June 2016), paragraph 6.*

Application and Other Explanatory Material

Audit Procedures (Ref: Para. 7(a))

When evaluating whether the comparative information agrees with the amounts and **A1-1** other disclosures presented in the prior period or, where appropriate, have been restated, the auditor's procedures include checking whether the related opening balances in the accounting records were appropriately brought forward.

Written Representations (Ref: Para. 9)

In the case of comparative financial statements, the written representations are requested **A1** for all periods referred to in the auditor's opinion because management needs to reaffirm that the written representations it previously made with respect to the prior period remain appropriate. In the case of corresponding figures, the written representations are requested for the financial statements of the current period only because the auditor's opinion is on those financial statements, which include the corresponding figures. However, the auditor requests a specific written representation regarding any restatement made to correct a material misstatement in the prior period financial statements that affect the comparative information.

Audit Reporting

Corresponding Figures

No Reference in Auditor's Opinion (Ref: Para. 10)

The auditor's opinion does not refer to the corresponding figures because the auditor's **A2** opinion is on the current period financial statements as a whole, including the corresponding figures.

Modification in Auditor's Report on the Prior Period Unresolved (Ref: Para. 11)

When the auditor's report on the prior period, as previously issued, included a qualified **A3** opinion, a disclaimer of opinion, or an adverse opinion and the matter which gave rise to the modified opinion is resolved and properly accounted for or disclosed in the financial statements in accordance with the applicable financial reporting framework, the auditor's opinion on the current period need not refer to the previous modification.

In some circumstances the auditor may consider it appropriate to qualify the audit **A3-1** opinion on the current period's financial statements. For example, if a provision which the auditor considered should have been made in the previous period is made in the current period.

When the auditor's opinion on the prior period, as previously expressed, was modified, **A4** the unresolved matter that gave rise to the modification may not be relevant to the current period figures. Nevertheless, a qualified opinion, a disclaimer of opinion, or an adverse opinion (as applicable) may be required on the current period's financial statements because of the effects or possible effects of the unresolved matter on the comparability of the current and corresponding figures.

A5   Illustrative examples of the auditor's report if the auditor's report on the prior period included a modified opinion and the matter giving rise to the modification is unresolved are contained in Illustrations 1 and 2 of the Appendix.[7a]

Misstatement in Prior Period Financial Statements (Ref: Para. 12)

A6   When the prior period financial statements that are misstated have not been amended and an auditor's report has not been reissued, but the corresponding figures have been properly restated or appropriate disclosures have been made in the current period financial statements, the auditor's report may include an Emphasis of Matter paragraph describing the circumstances and referring to where relevant disclosures that fully describe the matter can be found in the financial statements (see ISA (UK) 706 (Revised June 2016)).

Prior Period Financial Statements Audited by a Predecessor Auditor (Ref: Para. 13)

A7   An illustrative example of the auditor's report if the prior period financial statements were audited by a predecessor auditor and the auditor is not prohibited by law or regulation from referring to the predecessor auditor's report on the corresponding figures is contained in Illustration 3 of the Appendix.[7a]

A7-1   In the UK, the incoming auditor does not refer to the predecessor auditor's report on the corresponding figures in the incoming auditor's report for the current period. The incoming auditor assumes audit responsibility for the corresponding figures only in the context of the financial statements as a whole. The incoming auditor reads the preceding period's financial statements and, using the knowledge gained during the current audit, considers whether they have been properly reflected as corresponding figures in the current period's financial statements.

A7-2   Although the incoming auditor is not required to re-audit the financial statements of the preceding period, if the incoming auditor becomes aware of a possible material misstatement of corresponding figures, the requirement and guidance in paragraphs 12 and A6 apply.

A7-3   For audits of financial statements of public interest entities, the incoming auditor may become aware of a possible material misstatement of corresponding figures as part of the requirement in ISA (UK) 510 (Revised June 2016) to obtain an understanding of the methodology used to carry out the audit in the preceding period.[7b]

Prior Period Financial Statements Not Audited (Ref: Para. 14)

A7a   If the auditor is unable to obtain sufficient appropriate audit evidence regarding the opening balances, the auditor is required by ISA (UK) 705 (Revised June 2016)[8] to express a qualified opinion or disclaim an opinion on the financial statements, as appropriate, in accordance with ISA (UK) 705 (Revised June 2016). If the auditor encountered significant difficulty in obtaining sufficient appropriate audit evidence that the opening balances do

---

[7a] *The examples in the Appendix have not been tailored for the UK. Illustrative auditor's reports tailored for use with audits conducted in accordance with ISAs (UK) are given in the current version of the FRC's Compendium of Illustrative Auditor's Reports.*

[7b] *ISA (UK) 510 (Revised June 2016)*, Initial Audit Engagements—Opening Balances, *paragraph 8R-1.*

[8] *ISA (UK) 705 (Revised June 2016)*, Modifications to the Opinion in the Independent Auditor's Report.

not contain misstatements that materially affect the current period's financial statements, the auditor may determine this to be a key audit matter in accordance with ISA (UK) 701.[9]

Comparative Financial Statements

Reference in Auditor's Opinion (Ref: Para. 15)

Because the auditor's report on comparative financial statements applies to the financial statements for each of the periods presented, the auditor may express a qualified opinion or an adverse opinion, disclaim an opinion, or include an Emphasis of Matter paragraph with respect to one or more periods, while expressing a different auditor's opinion on the financial statements of the other period. **A8**

An illustrative example of the auditor's report if the auditor is required to report on both the current and the prior period financial statements in connection with the current year's audit and the prior period included a modified opinion and the matter giving rise to the modification is unresolved, is contained in Illustration 4 of the Appendix.[7a] **A9**

Opinion on Prior Period Financial Statements Different from Previous Opinion (Ref: Para. 16)

When reporting on the prior period financial statements in connection with the current period's audit, the opinion expressed on the prior period financial statements may be different from the opinion previously expressed if the auditor becomes aware of circumstances or events that materially affect the financial statements of a prior period during the course of the audit of the current period. In some jurisdictions, the auditor may have additional reporting responsibilities designed to prevent future reliance on the auditor's previously issued report on the prior period financial statements. **A10**

Prior Period Financial Statements Audited by a Predecessor Auditor (Ref: Para. 18)

The predecessor auditor may be unable or unwilling to reissue the auditor's report on the prior period financial statements. An Other Matter paragraph of the auditor's report may indicate that the predecessor auditor reported on the financial statements of the prior period before amendment. In addition, if the auditor is engaged to audit and obtains sufficient appropriate audit evidence to be satisfied as to the appropriateness of the amendment, the auditor's report may also include the following paragraph: **A11**

> "As part of our audit of the 20X2 financial statements, we also audited the adjustments described in Note X that were applied to amend the 20X1 financial statements. In our opinion, such adjustments are appropriate and have been properly applied. We were not engaged to audit, review, or apply any procedures to the 20X1 financial statements of the company other than with respect to the adjustments and, accordingly, we do not express an opinion or any other form of assurance on the 20X1 financial statements taken as a whole."

Prior Period Financial Statements Not Audited (Ref: Para. 19)

If the auditor is unable to obtain sufficient appropriate audit evidence regarding the opening balances, the auditor is required by ISA (UK) 705 (Revised June 2016) to express a qualified opinion or disclaim an opinion on the financial statements, as appropriate, in accordance with ISA (UK) 705 (Revised June 2016). If the auditor encountered significant difficulty in obtaining sufficient appropriate audit evidence that the opening balances do **A12**

---

[9] *ISA (UK) 701*, Communicating Key Audit Matters in the Independent Auditor's Report.

not contain misstatements that materially affect the current period's financial statements, the auditor may determine this to be a key audit matter in accordance with ISA (UK) 701.

Appendix

Illustrations of auditor's reports

The examples in the Appendix have not been tailored for the UK. Illustrative auditor's reports tailored for use with audits conducted in accordance with ISAs (UK) are given in the current version of the FRC's Compendium of Illustrative Auditor's Reports.

Note: Throughout these illustrative auditor's reports, the Opinion section has been positioned first in accordance with ISA 700 (Revised), and the Basis for Opinion section is positioned immediately after the Opinion section. Also, the first and last sentence that was included in the extant auditor's responsibilities section is now subsumed as part of the new Basis for Opinion section.

Illustration 1 - Corresponding Figures (Ref: Para. A5)

For purposes of this illustrative auditor's report, the following circumstances are assumed:
- Audit of a complete set of financial statements of an entity other than a listed entity using a fair presentation framework. The audit is not a group audit (i.e., ISA 600[10] does not apply).
- The financial statements are prepared by management of the entity in accordance with International Financial Reporting Standards (IFRSs) (a general purpose framework).
- The terms of the audit engagement reflect the description of management's responsibility for the financial statements in ISA 210.[11]
- The auditor's report on the prior period, as previously issued, included a qualified opinion.
- The matter giving rise to the modification is unresolved.
- The effects or possible effects of the matter on the current period's figures are material and require a modification to the auditor's opinion regarding the current period figures.
- The relevant ethical requirements that apply to the audit are those of the jurisdiction.
- Based on the audit evidence obtained, the auditor has concluded that a material uncertainty does not exist related to events or conditions that may cast significant doubt on the entity's ability to continue as a going concern in accordance with ISA 570 (Revised).[12]
- The auditor is not required, and has otherwise not decided, to communicate key audit matters in accordance with ISA 701.[13]
- The auditor has not obtained any other information prior to the date of the auditor's report.

---

[10] *ISA 600*, Special Considerations—Audits of Group Financial Statements (Including the Work of Component Auditors).

[11] *ISA 210*, Agreeing the Terms of Audit Engagements.

[12] *ISA 570 (Revised)*, Going Concern.

[13] *ISA 701*, Communicating Key Audit Matters in the Independent Auditor's Report.

- Those responsible for oversight of the financial statements differ from those responsible for the preparation of the financial statements.
- In addition to the audit of the financial statements, the auditor has other reporting responsibilities required under local law.

INDEPENDENT AUDITOR'S REPORT

To the Shareholders of ABC Company [or Other Appropriate Addressee]

Report on the Audit of the Financial Statements[14]

Qualified Opinion

We have audited the financial statements of ABC Company (the Company), which comprise the statement of financial position as at December 31, 20X1, and the statement of comprehensive income, statement of changes in equity and statement of cash flows for the year then ended, and notes to the financial statements, including a summary of significant accounting policies.

In our opinion, except for the effects of the matter described in the Basis for Qualified Opinion section of our report, the accompanying financial statements present fairly, in all material respects, (or give a true and fair view of) the financial position of the Company as at December 31, 20X1, and (of) its financial performance and its cash flows for the year then ended in accordance with International Financial Reporting Standards (IFRSs).

Basis for Qualified Opinion

As discussed in Note X to the financial statements, no depreciation has been provided in the financial statements, which constitutes a departure from IFRSs. This is the result of a decision taken by management at the start of the preceding financial year and caused us to qualify our audit opinion on the financial statements relating to that year. Based on the straight-line method of depreciation and annual rates of 5% for the building and 20% for the equipment, the loss for the year should be increased by xxx in 20X1 and xxx in 20X0, property, plant and equipment should be reduced by accumulated depreciation of xxx in 20X1 and xxx in 20X0, and the accumulated loss should be increased by xxx in 20X1 and xxx in 20X0.

We conducted our audit in accordance with International Standards on Auditing (ISAs). Our responsibilities under those standards are further described in the *Auditor's Responsibilities for the Audit of the Financial Statements* section of our report. We are independent of the Company in accordance with the ethical requirements that are relevant to our audit of the financial statements in [*jurisdiction*], and we have fulfilled our other ethical responsibilities in accordance with these requirements. We believe that the audit evidence we have obtained is sufficient and appropriate to provide a basis for our qualified audit opinion.

---

[14] *The sub-title 'Report on the Audit of the Financial Statements' is unnecessary in circumstances when the second sub-title 'Report on Other Legal and Regulatory Requirements' is not applicable.*

Responsibilities of Management and Those Charged With Governance for the Financial Statements[15]

[*Reporting in accordance with ISA 700 (Revised) – see Illustration 1 in ISA 700 (Revised).*]

Auditor's Responsibilities for the Audit of the Financial Statements

[*Reporting in accordance with ISA 700 (Revised) – see Illustration 1 in ISA 700 (Revised).*]

Report on Other Legal and Regulatory Requirements

[*Reporting in accordance with ISA 700 (Revised) – see Illustration 1 in ISA 700 (Revised).*]

[*Signature in the name of the audit firm, the personal name of the auditor, or both, as appropriate for the particular jurisdiction*]

[*Auditor Address*]

[*Date*]

Illustration 2 - Corresponding Figures (Ref: Para. A5)

For purposes of this illustrative auditor's report the following circumstances are assumed:
- Audit of a complete set of financial statements of an entity other than a listed entity using a fair presentation framework. The audit is not a group audit (i.e., ISA 600 does not apply).
- The financial statements are prepared by management of the entity in accordance with IFRSs (a general purpose framework).
- The terms of the audit engagement reflect the description of management's responsibility for the financial statements in ISA 210.
- The auditor's report on the prior period, as previously issued, included a qualified opinion.
- The matter giving rise to the modification is unresolved.
- The effects or possible effects of the matter on the current period's figures are immaterial but require a modification to the auditor's opinion because of the effects or possible effects of the unresolved matter on the comparability of the current period's figures and the corresponding figures.
- The relevant ethical requirements that apply to the audit are those of the jurisdiction.
- Based on the audit evidence obtained, the auditor has concluded that a material uncertainty does not exist related to events or conditions that may cast significant doubt on the entity's ability to continue as a going concern in accordance with ISA 570 (Revised).
- The auditor is not required, and has otherwise has not decided, to communicate key audit matters in accordance with ISA 701.
- The auditor has not obtained any other information prior to the date of the auditor's report.
- Those responsible for oversight of the financial statements differ from those responsible for the preparation of the financial statements.
- In addition to the audit of the financial statements, the auditor has other reporting responsibilities required under local law.

---

[15] *Throughout these illustrative auditor's reports, the terms management and those charged with governance may need to be replaced by another term that is appropriate in the context of the legal framework in the particular jurisdiction.*

INDEPENDENT AUDITOR'S REPORT

To the Shareholders of ABC Company [or Other Appropriate Addressee]

Report on the Audit of the Financial Statements[16]

Qualified Opinion

We have audited the financial statements of ABC Company (the Company), which comprise the statement of financial position as at December 31, 20X1, and the statement of comprehensive income, statement of changes in equity and statement of cash flows for the year then ended, and notes to the financial statements, including a summary of significant accounting policies.

In our opinion, except for the possible effects on the corresponding figures of the matter described in the Basis for Qualified Opinion section of our report, the accompanying financial statements present fairly, in all material respects, (or *give a true and fair view of*) the financial position of the Company as at December 31, 20X1, and (*of*) its financial performance and its cash flows for the year then ended in accordance with International Financial Reporting Standards (IFRSs).

Basis for Qualified Opinion

Because we were appointed auditors of the Company during 20X0, we were not able to observe the counting of the physical inventories at the beginning of that period or satisfy ourselves concerning those inventory quantities by alternative means. Since opening inventories affect the determination of the results of operations, we were unable to determine whether adjustments to the results of operations and opening retained earnings might be necessary for 20X0. Our audit opinion on the financial statements for the period ended December 31, 20X0 was modified accordingly. Our opinion on the current period's financial statements is also modified because of the possible effect of this matter on the comparability of the current period's figures and the corresponding figures.

We conducted our audit in accordance with International Standards on Auditing (ISAs). Our responsibilities under those standards are further described in the *Auditor's Responsibilities for the Audit of the Financial Statements* section of our report. We are independent of the Company in accordance with the ethical requirements that are relevant to our audit of the financial statements in [*jurisdiction*], and we have fulfilled our other ethical responsibilities in accordance with these requirements. We believe that the audit evidence we have obtained is sufficient and appropriate to provide a basis for our qualified audit opinion.

Responsibilities of Management and Those Charged With Governance for the Financial Statements[17]

[*Reporting in accordance with ISA 700 (Revised) – see Illustration 1 in ISA 700 (Revised).*]

---

[16] *The sub-title 'Report on the Audit of the Financial Statements' is unnecessary in circumstances when the second sub-title 'Report on Other Legal and Regulatory Requirements' is not applicable.*

[17] *Or other terms that are appropriate in the context of the legal framework in the particular jurisdiction.*

Auditor's Responsibilities for the Audit of the Financial Statements

[*Reporting in accordance with ISA 700 (Revised) – see Illustration 1 in ISA 700 (Revised).*]

Report on Other Legal and Regulatory Requirements

[*Reporting in accordance with ISA 700 (Revised) – see Illustration 1 in ISA 700 (Revised).*]

[*Signature in the name of the audit firm, the personal name of the auditor, or both, as appropriate for the particular jurisdiction*]

[*Auditor Address*]

[*Date*]

Illustration 3 - Corresponding Figures (Ref: Para. A7)

For purposes of this illustrative auditor's report the following circumstances are assumed:

- Audit of a complete set of financial statements of an entity other than a listed entity using a fair presentation framework. The audit is not a group audit (i.e., ISA 600 does not apply).
- The financial statements are prepared by management of the entity in accordance with IFRSs (a general purpose framework).
- The terms of the audit engagement reflect the description of management's responsibility for the financial statements in ISA 210.
- The auditor has concluded an unmodified (i.e., 'clean') opinion is appropriate based on the audit evidence obtained.
- The relevant ethical requirements that apply to the audit are those of the jurisdiction.
- Based on the audit evidence obtained, the auditor has concluded that a material uncertainty does not exist related to events or conditions that may cast significant doubt on the entity's ability to continue as a going concern in accordance with ISA 570 (Revised).
- The auditor is not required, and has otherwise has not decided, to communicate key audit matters in accordance with ISA 701.
- The auditor has obtained all of the other information prior to the date of the auditor's report and has not identified a material misstatement of the other information.
- Corresponding figures are presented, and the prior period's financial statements were audited by a predecessor auditor.
- The auditor is not prohibited by law or regulation from referring to the predecessor auditor's report on the corresponding figures and decides to do so.
- Those responsible for oversight of the financial statements differ from those responsible for the preparation of the financial statements.
- In addition to the audit of the financial statements, the auditor has other reporting responsibilities required under local law.

INDEPENDENT AUDITOR'S REPORT

To the Shareholders of ABC Company [or Other Appropriate Addressee]

Report on the Audit of the Financial Statements[18]

Opinion

We have audited the financial statements of ABC Company (the Company), which comprise the statement of financial position as at December 31, 20X1, and the statement of comprehensive income, statement of changes in equity and statement of cash flows for the year then ended, and notes to the financial statements, including a summary of significant accounting policies.

In our opinion, the accompanying financial statements present fairly, in all material respects, (or *give a true and fair view of*) the financial position of the Company as at December 31, 20X1, and (*of*) its financial performance and its cash flows for the year then ended in accordance with International Financial Reporting Standards (IFRSs).

Basis for Opinion

We conducted our audit in accordance with International Standards on Auditing (ISAs). Our responsibilities under those standards are further described in the *Auditor's Responsibilities for the Audit of the Financial Statements* section of our report. We are independent of the Company in accordance with the ethical requirements that are relevant to our audit of the financial statements in [*jurisdiction*], and we have fulfilled our other ethical responsibilities in accordance with these requirements. We believe that the audit evidence we have obtained is sufficient and appropriate to provide a basis for our audit opinion.

Other Matter

The financial statements of the Company for the year ended December 31, 20X0, were audited by another auditor who expressed an unmodified opinion on those statements on March 31, 20X1.

Other Information [or another title if appropriate such as 'Information Other than the Financial Statements and Auditor's Report Thereon']

[*Reporting in accordance with the reporting requirements in ISA 720 (Revised) – see Illustration 1 in Appendix 2 of ISA 720 (Revised).*]

Responsibilities of Management and Those Charged With Governance for the Financial Statements[19]

[*Reporting in accordance with ISA 700 (Revised) – see Illustration 1 in ISA 700 (Revised).*]

---

[18] *The sub-title 'Report on the Audit of the Financial Statements' is unnecessary in circumstances when the second sub-title 'Report on Other Legal and Regulatory Requirements' is not applicable.*

[19] *Or other terms that are appropriate in the context of the legal framework in the particular jurisdiction.*

Auditor's Responsibilities for the Audit of the Financial Statements

[*Reporting in accordance with ISA 700 (Revised) – see Illustration 1 in ISA 700 (Revised)*.]

Report on Other Legal and Regulatory Requirements

[*Reporting in accordance with ISA 700 (Revised) – see Illustration 1 in ISA 700 (Revised)*.]

[*Signature in the name of the audit firm, the personal name of the auditor, or both, as appropriate for the particular jurisdiction*]

[*Auditor Address*]

[*Date*]

Illustration 4 - Comparative Financial Statements (Ref: Para. A9)

For purposes of this illustrative auditor's report the following circumstances are assumed:

- Audit of a complete set of financial statements of an entity other than a listed entity using a fair presentation framework. The audit is not a group audit (i.e., ISA 600 does not apply).
- The financial statements are prepared by management of the entity in accordance with IFRSs (a general purpose framework).
- The terms of the audit engagement reflect the description of management's responsibility for the financial statements in ISA 210.
- The auditor is required to report on both the current period financial statements and the prior period financial statements in connection with the current year's audit.
- The auditor's report on the prior period, as previously issued, included a qualified opinion.
- The matter giving rise to the modification is unresolved.
- The effects or possible effects of the matter on the current period's figures are material to both the current period financial statements and prior period financial statements and require a modification to the auditor's opinion.
- The relevant ethical requirements that apply to the audit are those of the jurisdiction.
- Based on the audit evidence obtained, the auditor has concluded that a material uncertainty does not exist related to events or conditions that may cast significant doubt on the entity's ability to continue as a going concern in accordance with ISA 570 (Revised).
- The auditor is not required, and has otherwise has not decided, to communicate key audit matters in accordance with ISA 701.
- The auditor has not obtained any other information prior to the date of the auditor's report.
- Those responsible for oversight of the financial statements differ from those responsible for the preparation of the financial statements.
- In addition to the audit of the financial statements, the auditor has other reporting responsibilities required under local law.

INDEPENDENT AUDITOR'S REPORT

To the Shareholders of ABC Company [or Other Appropriate Addressee]

Report on the Audit of the Financial Statements[20]

Qualified Opinion

We have audited the financial statements of ABC Company (the Company), which comprise the statements of financial position as at December 31, 20X1 and 20X0, and the statements of comprehensive income, statements of changes in equity and statements of cash flows for the years then ended, and notes to the financial statements, including a summary of significant accounting policies.

In our opinion, except for the effects of the matter described in the Basis for Qualified Opinion paragraph, the accompanying financial statements present fairly, in all material respects, (or *give a true and fair view of*) the financial position of ABC Company as at December 31, 20X1 and 20X0 and (*of*) its financial performance and its cash flows for the years then ended in accordance with International Financial Reporting Standards (IFRSs).

Basis for Qualified Opinion

As discussed in Note X to the financial statements, no depreciation has been provided in the financial statements, which constitutes a departure from IFRSs. Based on the straight-line method of depreciation and annual rates of 5% for the building and 20% for the equipment, the loss for the year should be increased by xxx in 20X1 and xxx in 20X0, property, plant and equipment should be reduced by accumulated depreciation of xxx in 20X1 and xxx in 20X0, and the accumulated loss should be increased by xxx in 20X1 and xxx in 20X0.

We conducted our audit in accordance with International Standards on Auditing (ISAs). Our responsibilities under those standards are further described in the *Auditor's Responsibilities for the Audit of the Financial Statements* section of our report. We are independent of the Company in accordance with the ethical requirements that are relevant to our audit of the financial statements in [*jurisdiction*], and we have fulfilled our other ethical responsibilities in accordance with these requirements. We believe that the audit evidence we have obtained is sufficient and appropriate to provide a basis for our qualified audit opinion.

Responsibilities of Management and Those Charged with Governance for the Financial Statements[21]

[*Reporting in accordance with ISA 700 (Revised) – see Illustration 1 in ISA 700 (Revised).*]

Auditor's Responsibilities for the Audit of the Financial Statements

[*Reporting in accordance with ISA 700 (Revised) – see Illustration 1 in ISA 700 (Revised).*]

---

[20] *The sub-title 'Report on the Audit of the Financial Statements' is unnecessary in circumstances when the second sub-title 'Report on Other Legal and Regulatory Requirements' is not applicable.*

[21] *Or other terms that are appropriate in the context of the legal framework in the particular jurisdiction.*

Report on Other Legal and Regulatory Requirements

[Reporting in accordance with ISA 700 (Revised) – see Illustration 1 in ISA 700 (Revised).]

[Signature in the name of the audit firm, the personal name of the auditor, or both, as appropriate for the particular jurisdiction]

[Auditor Address]

[Date]

International Standard on Auditing (UK) 720
(Revised June 2016)
The auditor's responsibilities relating to other information

(Effective for audits of financial statements for periods commencing on or after 17 June 2016)

Contents

International Standard on Auditing (UK) (ISA (UK)) 720 (Revised June 2016), *The Auditor's Responsibilities Relating to Other Information*, should be read in conjunction with ISA (UK) 200 (Revised June 2016), *Overall Objectives of the Independent Auditor and the Conduct of an Audit in Accordance with International Standards on Auditing (UK)*.

Introduction

Scope of this ISA (UK)

This International Standard on Auditing (UK) (ISA (UK)) deals with the auditor's **1** responsibilities relating to other information, whether financial or non-financial information (other than financial statements and the auditor's report thereon), included in an entity's annual report. An entity's annual report may be a single document or a combination of documents that serve the same purpose.

This ISA (UK) also deals with certain additional obligations imposed by law or **1-1** regulation on the auditor to report on statutory other information, based on the work undertaken in the course of the audit.

This ISA (UK) is written in the context of an audit of financial statements by an independent **2** auditor. Accordingly, the objectives of the auditor in this ISA (UK) are to be understood in the context of the overall objectives of the auditor as stated in paragraph 11 of ISA (UK) 200 (Revised June 2016).[1] The requirements in the ISAs (UK) are designed to enable the auditor to achieve the objectives specified in the ISAs (UK), and thereby the overall objectives of the auditor. The auditor's opinion on the financial statements does not cover the other information, nor does this ISA (UK) require the auditor to obtain audit evidence beyond that required to form an opinion on the financial statements.

This ISA (UK) requires the auditor to read and consider the other information because **3** other information that is materially inconsistent with the financial statements or the auditor's knowledge obtained in the audit may indicate that there is a material misstatement of the financial statements or that a material misstatement of the other information exists, either of which may undermine the credibility of the financial statements and the auditor's report thereon. Such material misstatements may also inappropriately influence the economic decisions of the users for whom the auditor's report is prepared.

This ISA (UK) may also assist the auditor in complying with relevant ethical requirements[2] **4** that require the auditor to avoid being knowingly associated with information that the auditor believes contains a materially false or misleading statement, statements or information furnished recklessly, or omits or obscures information required to be included where such omission or obscurity would be misleading.

Other information may include amounts or other items that are intended to be the same as, **5** to summarize, or to provide greater detail, about amounts or other items in the financial statements, and other amounts or other items about which the auditor has obtained knowledge in the audit. Other information may also include other matters.

The auditor's responsibilities relating to other information (other than applicable reporting **6** responsibilities) apply regardless of whether the other information is obtained by the auditor prior to, or after, the date of the auditor's report.

This ISA (UK) does not apply to: **7**

(a) Preliminary announcements of financial information; or
(b) Securities offering documents, including prospectuses.

---

[1] *ISA (UK) 200 (Revised June 2016),* Overall Objectives of the Independent Auditor and the Conduct of an Audit in Accordance with International Standards on Auditing (UK).

[2] *International Ethics Standards Board for Accountants'* Code of Ethics for Professional Accountants *(IESBA Code), paragraph 110.2.*

8 The auditor's responsibilities under this ISA (UK) do not constitute an assurance engagement on other information or impose an obligation on the auditor to obtain assurance about the other information except in respect of the auditor's responsibilities to report in accordance with paragraphs 22D-1 and 22D-2.

9 Law or regulation may impose additional obligations on the auditor in relation to other information that are beyond the scope of this ISA (UK).

Effective Date

10 This ISA (UK) is effective for audits of financial statements for periods commencing on or after 17 June 2016. Earlier adoption is permitted.

Objectives

11 The objectives of the auditor, having read the other information, are:

(a) To consider whether there is a material inconsistency between the other information and the financial statements;

(b) To consider whether there is a material inconsistency between the other information and the auditor's knowledge obtained in the audit;

(c) To respond appropriately when the auditor identifies that such material inconsistencies appear to exist, or when the auditor otherwise becomes aware that other information appears to be materially misstated;

(c)-1 Where required by law or regulation, to form an opinion on whether the information given in the other information is consistent with the financial statements and the auditor's knowledge obtained in the audit; and

(d) To report in accordance with this ISA (UK).

Definitions

12 For purposes of the ISAs (UK), the following terms have the meanings attributed below:

(a) Annual report – A document, or combination of documents, prepared typically on an annual basis by management or those charged with governance in accordance with law, regulation or custom, the purpose of which is to provide owners (or similar stakeholders) with information on the entity's operations and the entity's financial results and financial position as set out in the financial statements. An annual report contains or accompanies the financial statements and the auditor's report thereon and usually includes information about the entity's developments, its future outlook and risks and uncertainties, a statement by the entity's governing body, and reports covering governance matters. (Ref: Para. A1–A5)

> In the UK, an annual report includes at least:
> (i) The statutory other information; and
> (ii) Any other documents that are incorporated by cross-reference in, or distributed to shareholders with, statutory other information either voluntarily or pursuant to law or regulation or the requirements of a stock exchange listing.

(b) Misstatement of the other information – A misstatement of the other information exists when the other information is incorrectly stated or otherwise misleading (including because it omits or obscures information necessary for a proper understanding of a matter disclosed in the other information). (Ref: Para. A6–A7)

> In the UK, a misstatement of the other information also exists when the statutory other information has not been prepared in accordance with the legal and regulatory requirements applicable to the statutory other information.

(c) Other information – Financial or non-financial information (other than financial statements and the auditor's report thereon) included in an entity's annual report. (Ref: Para. A8–A10)

(d) Statutory other information – For statutory audits of financial statements, Those documents or reports that are required to be prepared and issued by the entity (including any reports or documents that are incorporated by cross reference) in relation to which the auditor is required to report publicly in accordance with law or regulation. (Ref: Para. A10-1–A10-2)

In the UK, the statutory other information includes, where required to be prepared:
(i) The directors' report;
(ii) The strategic report;
(iii) The separate corporate governance statement.[2a]

Requirements

Obtaining an Understanding of the Entity and its Environment relating to Statutory Other Information

For entities that are required to prepare statutory other information, as part of obtaining an understanding of the entity and its environment in accordance with ISA (UK) 315 (Revised June 2016),[2b] the auditor shall obtain an understanding of: **12-1**

(a) The legal and regulatory requirements applicable to the statutory other information; and
(b) How the entity is complying with those legal and regulatory requirements.

Obtaining the Other Information

The auditor shall: (Ref: Para. A11–A22-1) **13**

(a) Determine, through discussion with management, which document(s) comprises the annual report, and the entity's planned manner and timing of the issuance of such document(s);
(b) Make appropriate arrangements with management to obtain in a timely manner and, if possible, prior to the date of the auditor's report, the final version of the document(s) comprising the annual report; and
(c) When some or all of the document(s) determined in (a) will not be available until after the date of the auditor's report, request management to provide a written representation that the final version of the document(s) will be provided to the auditor when available, and prior to its issuance by the entity, such that the auditor can complete the procedures required by this ISA (UK). (Ref: Para. A22)

Reading and Considering the Other Information

The auditor shall read the other information and, in doing so shall: (Ref: Para. A23–A24) **14**

(a) Consider whether there is a material inconsistency between the other information and the financial statements. As the basis for this consideration, the auditor shall, to evaluate their consistency, compare selected amounts or other items in the other information (that are intended to be the same as, to summarize, or to provide

---

[2a] *When the required information is not included within or incorporated by cross reference to the directors' report.*

[2b] *ISA (UK) 315 (Revised June 2016)*, Identifying and Assessing the Risks of Material Misstatement through Understanding the Entity and its Environment, *paragraph 11*.

greater detail about, the amounts or other items in the financial statements) with such amounts or other items in the financial statements; and (Ref: Para. A25–A29)

(b) Consider whether there is a material inconsistency between the other information and the auditor's knowledge obtained in the audit, in the context of audit evidence obtained and conclusions reached in the audit. (Ref: Para. A30–A36)

14-1   For entities that are required to prepare statutory other information, the auditor shall read the statutory other information and, in doing so shall consider, based on the work undertaken in the course of the audit, whether the statutory other information appears to be materially misstated in the context of the auditor's understanding of the legal and regulatory requirements applicable to the statutory other information. (Ref: Para. A36-1–A36-4)

14-2   For entities that are required to prepare statutory other information, as the basis for the consideration required by paragraphs 14(a), 14(b) and 14-1, the auditor shall perform such procedures as are necessary in the auditor's professional judgment to identify:

(a) Any material inconsistencies between the other information and the financial statements;

(b) Any material inconsistencies between the other information and the auditor's knowledge obtained in the audit, in the context of audit evidence obtained and conclusions reached in the audit; and

(c) Whether the statutory other information appears to be materially misstated in the context of the auditor's understanding of the legal and regulatory requirements applicable to the statutory other information.

15   While reading the other information in accordance with paragraph 14, the auditor shall remain alert for indications that the other information not related to the financial statements or the auditor's knowledge obtained in the audit appears to be materially misstated. (Ref: Para. A24, A37–A38)

Responding When a Material Inconsistency Appears to Exist or Other Information Appears to Be Materially Misstated

16   If the auditor identifies that a material inconsistency appears to exist (or becomes aware that the other information appears to be materially misstated), the auditor shall discuss the matter with management and, if necessary, perform other procedures to conclude whether: (Ref: Para. A39–A43)

(a) A material misstatement of the other information exists;

(b) A material misstatement of the financial statements exists; or

(c) The auditor's understanding of the entity and its environment needs to be updated.

Responding When the Auditor Concludes That a Material Misstatement of the Other Information Exists

17   If the auditor concludes that a material misstatement of the other information exists, the auditor shall request management to correct the other information. If management:

(a) Agrees to make the correction, the auditor shall determine that the correction has been made; or

(b) Refuses to make the correction, the auditor shall communicate the matter with those charged with governance and request that the correction be made.

18   If the auditor concludes that a material misstatement exists in other information obtained prior to the date of the auditor's report, and the other information is not corrected after communicating with those charged with governance, the auditor shall take appropriate action, including: (Ref: Para. A44–A44-2)

(a) Considering the implications for the auditor's report and communicating with those charged with governance about how the auditor plans to address the material misstatement in the auditor's report (see paragraph 22(e)(ii)); or (Ref: Para. A45)
(b) Withdrawing from the engagement, where withdrawal is possible under applicable law or regulation. (Ref: Para. A46–A47)

If the auditor concludes that a material misstatement exists in other information obtained **19** after the date of the auditor's report, the auditor shall:

(a) If the other information is corrected, perform the procedures necessary in the circumstances; or (Ref: Para. A48)
(b) If the other information is not corrected after communicating with those charged with governance, take appropriate action considering the auditor's legal rights and obligations, to seek to have the uncorrected material misstatement appropriately brought to the attention of users for whom the auditor's report is prepared. (Ref: Para. A49–A50)

Responding When a Material Misstatement in the Financial Statements Exists or the Auditor's Understanding of the Entity and Its Environment Needs to Be Updated

If, as a result of performing the procedures in paragraphs 14–15, the auditor concludes that **20** a material misstatement in the financial statements exists or the auditor's understanding of the entity and its environment needs to be updated, the auditor shall respond appropriately in accordance with the other ISAs (UK). (Ref: Para. A51)

Reporting

The auditor's report shall include a separate section with a heading 'Other Information', or **21** other appropriate heading, when, at the date of the auditor's report:

(a) For an audit of financial statements of a listed entity, the auditor has obtained, or expects to obtain, the other information; or
(b) For an audit of financial statements of an entity other than a listed entity, the auditor has obtained some or all of the other information. (Ref: Para. A52)

In the UK, the auditor's report shall always include a separate section with a heading 'Other Information', or other appropriate heading.[2c]

When the auditor's report is required to include an Other Information section in accordance **22** with paragraph 21, this section shall include: (Ref: Para. A53)

(a) A statement that management is responsible for the other information;
(b) An identification of:
  (i) Other information, if any, obtained by the auditor prior to the date of the auditor's report; and
  (ii) For an audit of financial statements of a listed entity, other information, if any, expected to be obtained after the date of the auditor's report;

[2c] *ISA (UK) 700 (Revised June 2016) requires that 'The auditor shall not sign, and hence date, the auditor's report earlier than the date on which all the other information has been approved by those charged with governance and the auditor has considered all necessary available evidence.'*

(c) A statement that the auditor's opinion does not cover the other information and, accordingly, that the auditor does not express (or will not express) an audit opinion or any form of assurance conclusion thereon;

> In the UK, where the auditor is required to express an opinion on some or all of the other information in accordance with paragraphs 22D-1 or 22D-2 or otherwise in accordance with law or regulation, the statement required by paragraph 22(c) shall be a modified statement that the auditor's opinion on the financial statements does not cover the other information and, accordingly, the auditor does not express an audit opinion or, except to the extent otherwise explicitly stated in the auditor's report, any form of assurance thereon.

(d) A description of the auditor's responsibilities relating to reading, considering and reporting on other information as required by this ISA (UK); and

> In the UK, the description of the auditor's responsibilities in relation to the other information required by paragraph 22(d) shall also include the auditor's responsibilities under paragraph 14-1, 22D-1, 22D-2, 22-3 and 22-4 where applicable.

(e) When other information has been obtained prior to the date of the auditor's report, either:
  (i)   A statement that the auditor has nothing to report; or
  (ii) If the auditor has concluded that there is an uncorrected material misstatement of the other information, a statement that describes the uncorrected material misstatement of the other information.

Strategic Report and Directors' Report

22D-1   For UK entities that are required to prepare statutory other information,[2d] the auditor shall in the auditor's report:

(a) State whether, in the auditor's opinion, based on the work undertaken in the course of the audit:
  (i)   The information given in the strategic report (if any) and the directors' report for the financial year for which the accounts are prepared is consistent with those accounts; and
  (ii) Any such strategic report and the directors' report have been prepared in accordance with applicable legal requirements;
(b) State whether, in the light of the knowledge and understanding of the company and its environment obtained in the course of the audit, the auditor has identified material misstatements in the strategic report (if any) and the directors' report; and
(c) If applicable, give an indication of the nature of each of the misstatements referred to in paragraph 22D-1(b).

Separate Corporate Governance Statement

22D-2   For UK entities that are required to prepare statutory other information,[2e] where the entity prepares a separate corporate governance statement in respect of a financial year, the auditor shall in the auditor's report: (Ref: Para. A53-1)

[2d] *In the UK, Section 496 of the Companies Act 2006 as amended by The Companies, Partnerships and Groups (Accounts and Reports) Regulations 2015.*

[2e] *In the UK, Section 497A of the Companies Act 2006 as amended by The Companies, Partnerships and Groups (Accounts and Reports) Regulations 2015.*

(a) State whether, in the auditor's opinion, based on the work undertaken in the course of the audit, the information given in the statement in compliance with rules 7.2.5 and 7.2.6 in the Disclosure Rules and Transparency Rules sourcebook made by the Financial Conduct Authority (information about internal control and risk management systems in relation to financial reporting processes and about share capital structures):

   (i) Is consistent with those accounts; and

   (ii) Has been prepared in accordance with applicable legal requirements;

(b) State whether, in the light of the knowledge and understanding of the company and its environment obtained in the course of the audit, the auditor has identified material misstatements in the information in the statement referred to in paragraph 22D-2(a);

(c) If applicable, give an indication of the nature of each of the misstatements referred to in paragraph 22D-2 (b), and

(d) State whether, in the auditor's opinion, based on the work undertaken in the course of the audit, rules 7.2.2, 7.2.3 and 7.2.7 in the Disclosure Rules and Transparency Rules sourcebook made by the Financial Conduct Authority (information about the company's corporate governance code and practices and about its administrative, management and supervisory bodies and their committees) have been complied with, if applicable.

UK Corporate Governance Code Reporting

For entities that are required, and those that choose voluntarily, to report on how they have applied the UK Corporate Governance Code or to explain why they have not, in meeting the auditor's responsibilities to report under paragraph 22(e), the auditor shall specifically address each of the following elements of the other information:

22-3

(a) The statement given by the directors that they consider the annual report and accounts taken as a whole is fair, balanced and understandable and provides the information necessary for shareholders to assess the entity's performance, business model and strategy, that is materially inconsistent with the auditor's knowledge obtained in the audit;

(b) The section describing the work of the audit committee that does not appropriately address matters communicated by the auditor to the audit committee;

(c) The explanation as to why the annual report does not include such a statement or section that is materially inconsistent with the auditor's knowledge obtained in the audit;

(d) The parts of the directors' statement required under the Listing Rules relating to the entity's compliance with the UK Corporate Governance Code containing provisions specified for review by the auditor in accordance with Listing Rule 9.8.10R(2) that do not properly disclose a departure from a relevant provision of the UK Corporate Governance Code; and

(e) The directors' statement relating to Going Concern required under the Listing Rules in accordance with Listing Rule 9.8.6R(3) that is materially inconsistent with the auditor's knowledge obtained in the audit.

In reporting under paragraph 22, the auditor shall describe the specific reporting responsibility relating to these matters in accordance with paragraph 22(d) and shall report on each of these matters by providing a statement in accordance with paragraph 22(e). (Ref: Para. A53-2–A53-3)

**UK Corporate Governance Code Reporting – Statement on the Directors'
Assessment of the Principal Risks that Would Threaten the Solvency or Liquidity of
the Entity**

22-4   For entities that are required, and those that choose voluntarily, to report on how they
have applied the UK Corporate Governance Code or to explain why they have not,
the auditor shall, having particular regard to the work performed in accordance with
paragraph 18-2 of ISA (UK) 570 (Revised June 2016), give a statement as to whether
the auditor has anything material to add or draw attention to in respect of:

(a)   The directors' confirmation in the annual report that they have carried out a robust
assessment of the principal risks facing the entity, including those that would
threaten its business model, future performance, solvency or liquidity;

(b)   The disclosures in the annual report that describe those risks and explain how they
are being managed or mitigated; and

(c)   The directors' explanation in the annual report as to how they have assessed the
prospects of the entity, over what period they have done so and why they consider
that period to be appropriate, and their statement as to whether they have a
reasonable expectation that the entity will be able to continue in operation and
meet its liabilities as they fall due over the period of their assessment, including
any related disclosures drawing attention to any necessary qualifications or
assumptions.

In reporting under paragraph 22, the description of the auditor's responsibilities in
relation to the other information required by paragraph 22(d) shall also include the
auditor's additional responsibilities under paragraph 18-2 of ISA (UK) 570 (Revised
June 2016) and the auditor's responsibility to report whether the auditor has anything
material to add or draw attention to in relation to each of the above elements of the
other information. In addition, where the auditor has identified anything material to
add or draw attention to in respect of these elements of the other information, the
auditor shall include in the auditor's report a statement that describes any other material
information that the auditor considers it appropriate to add or draw attention to.

23   When the auditor expresses a qualified or adverse opinion in accordance with ISA
(UK) 705 (Revised June 2016)[3], the auditor shall consider the implications of the matter
giving rise to the modification of opinion for the statement required in paragraph 22(e).
(Ref: Para. A54–A58)

Reporting Prescribed by Law or Regulation

24   If the auditor is required by law or regulation of a specific jurisdiction to refer to the
other information in the auditor's report using a specific layout or wording, the auditor's
report shall refer to International Standards on Auditing only if the auditor's report
includes, at a minimum: (Ref: Para. A59–A59-1)

(a)   Identification of the other information obtained by the auditor prior to the date of the
auditor's report;

(b)   A description of the auditor's responsibilities with respect to the other information;
and

(c)   An explicit statement addressing the outcome of the auditor's work for this purpose.

---

[3] *ISA (UK) 705 (Revised June 2016),* Modifications to the Opinion in the Independent Auditor's Report.

Documentation

In addressing the requirements of ISA (UK) 230 (Revised June 2016)[4] as it applies to this   **25**
ISA (UK), the auditor shall include in the audit documentation:

(a)   Documentation of the procedures performed under this ISA (UK); and
(b)   The final version of the other information on which the auditor has performed the
      work required under this ISA (UK).

***

Application and Other Explanatory Material

Definitions

Annual Report (Ref: Para. 12(a))

Law, regulation or custom may define the content of an annual report, and the name by   **A1**
which it is to be referred, for entities in a particular jurisdiction; however, the content and
the name may vary within a jurisdiction and from one jurisdiction to another.

An annual report is typically prepared on an annual basis. However, when the financial   **A2**
statements being audited are prepared for a period less than or more than a year, an annual
report may also be prepared that covers the same period as the financial statements.

In some cases, an entity's annual report may be a single document and referred to by the   **A3**
title 'annual report' or by some other title. In other cases, law, regulation or custom may
require the entity to report to owners (or similar stakeholders) information on the entity's
operations and the entity's financial results and financial position as set out in the financial
statements (i.e., an annual report) by way of a single document, or by way of two or more
separate documents that in combination serve the same purpose. For example, depending
on law, regulation or custom in a particular jurisdiction, one or more of the following
documents may form part of the annual report:

- Management report, management commentary, or operating and financial review or
  similar reports by those charged with governance (for example, a directors' report).
- Chairman's statement.
- Corporate governance statement.
- Internal control and risk assessment reports.

An annual report may be made available to users in printed form, or electronically,   **A4**
including on the entity's website. A document (or combination of documents) may meet
the definition of an annual report, irrespective of the manner in which it is made available
to users.

An annual report is different in nature, purpose and content from other reports, such as a   **A5**
report prepared to meet the information needs of a specific stakeholder group or a report
prepared to comply with a specific regulatory reporting objective (even when such a report
is required to be publicly available). Examples of reports that, when issued as standalone
documents, are not typically part of the combination of documents that comprise an annual
report (subject to law, regulation or custom), and that, therefore, are not other information
within the scope of this ISA (UK), include:

---

[4] *ISA (UK) 230 (Revised June 2016)*, Audit Documentation, *paragraphs 8–11.*

- Separate industry or regulatory reports (for example, capital adequacy reports), such as may be prepared in the banking, insurance, and pension industries.
- Corporate social responsibility reports.
- Sustainability reports.
- Diversity and equal opportunity reports.
- Product responsibility reports.
- Labor practices and working conditions reports.
- Human rights reports.

Misstatement of the Other Information (Ref: Para. 12(b))

A6 When a particular matter is disclosed in the other information, the other information may omit or obscure information that is necessary for a proper understanding of that matter. For example, if the other information purports to address the key performance indicators used by management, then omission of a key performance indicator used by management could indicate that the other information is misleading.

A7 The concept of materiality may be discussed in a framework applicable to the other information and, if so, such a framework may provide a frame of reference for the auditor in making judgments about materiality under this ISA (UK). In many cases, however, there may be no applicable framework that includes a discussion of the concept of materiality as it applies to the other information. In such circumstances, the following characteristics provide the auditor with a frame of reference in determining if a misstatement of the other information is material:

- Materiality is considered in the context of the common information needs of users as a group. The users of the other information are expected to be the same as the users of the financial statements as such users may be expected to read the other information to provide context to the financial statements.
- Judgments about materiality take into account the specific circumstances of the misstatement, considering whether users would be influenced by the effect of the uncorrected misstatement. Not all misstatements will influence the economic decisions of users.
- Judgments about materiality involve both qualitative and quantitative considerations. Accordingly, such judgments may take into account the nature or magnitude of the items that the other information addresses in the context of the entity's annual report.

Other Information (Ref: Para. 12(c))

A8 Appendix 1 contains examples of amounts or other items that may be included in the other information.

A9 In some cases, the applicable financial reporting framework may require specific disclosures but permit them to be located outside of the financial statements.[5] As such disclosures are required by the applicable financial reporting framework, they form part of the financial statements. Accordingly, they do not constitute other information for the purpose of this ISA (UK).

---

[5] *For example, International Financial Reporting Standards (IFRS) 7, 'Financial Instruments: Disclosures,' permits certain disclosures required by the IFRSs to either be given in the financial statements or incorporated by cross-reference from the financial statements to some other statement, such as a management commentary or risk report, that is available to users of the financial statements on the same terms as the financial statements and at the same time.*

eXtensible Business Reporting Language (XBRL) tags do not represent other information   **A10**
as defined in this ISA (UK).

Statutory Other Information (Ref: Para. 12(e))

Information given in the statutory other information includes information that is included   **A10-1**
by way of cross reference to other information presented separately from the statutory
other information. For example, a UK entity may decide to present a voluntary Operating
and Financial Review (OFR) which includes some or all of the matters required for the
business performance review section of the Strategic Report or the Directors' Report.
Rather than duplicate the information, the entity may cross refer from the Strategic
Report or the Directors' Report to the relevant information provided in the OFR.

Obtaining the Other Information (Ref: Para. 13)

Determining the document(s) that is or comprises the annual report is often clear based on   **A11**
law, regulation or custom. In many cases, management or those charged with governance
may have customarily issued a package of documents that together comprise the annual
report, or may have committed to do so. In some cases, however, it may not be clear which
document(s) is or comprises the annual report. In such cases, the timing and purpose of
the documents (and for whom they are intended) are matters that may be relevant to the
auditor's determination of which document(s) is or comprises the annual report.

When the annual report is translated into other languages pursuant to law or regulation   **A12**
(such as may occur when a jurisdiction has more than one official language), or when
multiple 'annual reports' are prepared under different legislation (for example, when an
entity is listed in more than one jurisdiction), consideration may need to be given as to
whether one, or more than one of the 'annual reports' form part of the other information.
Local law or regulation may provide further guidance in this respect.

Management, or those charged with governance, is responsible for preparing the annual   **A13**
report. The auditor may communicate with management or those charged with governance:

- The auditor's expectations in relation to obtaining the final version of the annual
  report (including a combination of documents that together comprise the annual
  report) in a timely manner prior to the date of the auditor's report such that the auditor
  can complete the procedures required by this ISA (UK) before the date of the auditor's
  report, or if that is not possible, as soon as practicable and in any case prior to the
  entity's issuance of such information.
- The possible implications when the other information is obtained after the date of the
  auditor's report.

The communications referred to in paragraph A13 may be particularly appropriate for   **A14**
example:

- In an initial audit engagement.
- When there has been a change in management or those charged with governance.
- When other information is expected to be obtained after the date of the auditor's
  report.

Where those charged with governance are to approve the other information prior to its   **A15**
issuance by the entity, the final version of such other information is the one that has been
approved by those charged with governance for issuance.

A16   In some cases, the entity's annual report may be a single document to be released, in accordance with law or regulation or the entity's reporting practice, shortly after the entity's financial reporting period such that it is available to the auditor prior to the date of the auditor's report. In other cases, such a document may not be required to be released until a later time, or at a time of the entity's choosing. There may also be circumstances when the entity's annual report is a combination of documents, each subject to different requirements or reporting practice by the entity with respect to the timing of their release.

A17   There may be circumstances when, at the date of the auditor's report, the entity is considering the development of a document that may be part of the entity's annual report (for example, a voluntary report to stakeholders) but management is unable to confirm to the auditor the purpose or timing of such a document. If the auditor is unable to ascertain the purpose or timing of such a document, the document is not considered other information for purposes of this ISA (UK).

A18   Obtaining the other information in a timely manner prior to the date of the auditor's report enables any revisions that are found to be necessary to be made to the financial statements, the auditor's report, or the other information prior to their issuance. The audit engagement letter[6] may make reference to an agreement with management to make available to the auditor the other information in a timely manner, and if possible prior to the date of the auditor's report.

A19   When other information is only made available to users via the entity's website, the version of the other information obtained from the entity, rather than directly from the entity's website, is the relevant document on which the auditor would perform procedures in accordance with this ISA (UK). The auditor has no responsibility under this ISA (UK) to search for other information, including other information that may be on the entity's website, nor to perform any procedures to confirm that other information is appropriately displayed on the entity's website or otherwise has been appropriately transmitted or displayed electronically.

A20   The auditor is not precluded from dating or issuing the auditor's report if the auditor has not obtained some or all of the other information.[6a]

A21   When the other information is obtained after the date of the auditor's report, the auditor is not required to update the procedures performed in accordance with paragraphs 6 and 7 of ISA (UK) 560.[7]

A22   ISA (UK) 580[8] establishes requirements and provides guidance on the use of written representations. The written representation required to be requested by paragraph 13(c) regarding other information that will be available only after the date of the auditor's report is intended to support the auditor's ability to complete the procedures required by this ISA (UK) with respect to such information. In addition, the auditor may find it useful to request other written representations, for example, that:

- Management has informed the auditor of all the documents that it expects to issue that may comprise other information;

[6] *ISA (UK) 210,* Agreeing the Terms of Audit Engagements, *paragraph A23.*

[6a] *ISA (UK) 700 (Revised June 2016) requires that 'The auditor shall not sign, and hence date, the auditor's report earlier than the date on which all the other information has been approved by those charged with governance and the auditor has considered all necessary available evidence.'*

[7] *ISA (UK) 560,* Subsequent Events.

[8] *ISA (UK) 580,* Written Representations.

- The financial statements and any other information obtained by the auditor prior to the date of the auditor's report are consistent with one another, and the other information does not contain any material misstatements; and
- With regard to other information that has not been obtained by the auditor prior to the date of the auditor's report, that management intends to prepare and issue such other information and the expected timing of such issuance.

Reading and Considering the Other Information (Ref: Para. 14–15)

The auditor is required by ISA (UK) 200 (Revised June 2016)[9] to plan and perform the audit with professional skepticism. Maintaining professional skepticism when reading and considering the other information includes, for example, recognizing that management may be overly optimistic about the success of its plans, and being alert to information that may be inconsistent with: **A23**

(a) The financial statements; or
(b) The auditor's knowledge obtained in the audit.

In accordance with ISA (UK) 220 (Revised June 2016),[10] the engagement partner is required to take responsibility for the direction, supervision and performance of the audit engagement in compliance with professional standards and applicable legal and regulatory requirements. In the context of this ISA (UK), factors that may be taken into account when determining the appropriate engagement team members to address the requirements of paragraphs 14–15, include: **A24**

- The relative experience of engagement team members.
- Whether the engagement team members to be assigned the tasks have the relevant knowledge obtained in the audit to identify inconsistencies between the other information and that knowledge.
- The degree of judgment involved in addressing the requirements of paragraph 14–15. For example, performing procedures to evaluate the consistency of amounts in the other information that are intended to be the same as amounts in the financial statements may be carried out by less experienced engagement team members.
- Whether, in the case of a group audit, it is necessary to make inquiries of a component auditor in addressing the other information related to that component.

Considering Whether There is a Material Inconsistency between the Other Information and the Financial Statements (Ref: Para. 14(a))

Other information may include amounts or other items that are intended to be the same as, to summarize, or to provide greater detail about, the amounts or other items in the financial statements. Examples of such amounts or other items may include: **A25**

- Tables, charts or graphs containing extracts of the financial statements.
- A disclosure providing greater detail about a balance or account shown in the financial statements, such as 'Revenue for 20X1 comprised XXX million from product X and YYY million from product Y.'
- Descriptions of the financial results, such as 'Total research and development expense was XXX in 20X1.'

In evaluating the consistency of selected amounts or other items in the other information with the financial statements, the auditor is not required to compare all amounts or   **A26**

---

[9] *ISA (UK) 200 (Revised June 2016), paragraph 15.*

[10] *ISA (UK) 220 (Revised June 2016),* Quality Control for an Audit of Financial Statements, *paragraph 15(a).*

other items in the other information that are intended to be the same as, to summarize, or to provide greater detail about, the amounts or other items in the financial statements, with such amounts or other items in the financial statements.

A27   Selecting the amounts or other items to compare is a matter of professional judgment. Factors relevant to this judgment include:

- The significance of the amount or other item in the context in which it is presented, which may affect the importance that users would attach to the amount or other item (for example, a key ratio or amount).
- If quantitative, the relative size of the amount compared with accounts or items in the financial statements or the other information to which they relate.
- The sensitivity of the particular amount or other item in the other information, for example, share based payments for senior management.

A28   Determining the nature and extent of procedures to address the requirement in paragraph 14(a) is a matter of professional judgment, recognizing that the auditor's responsibilities under this ISA (UK) do not constitute an assurance engagement on the other information or impose an obligation to obtain assurance about the other information. Examples of such procedures include:

- For information that is intended to be the same as information in the financial statements, comparing the information to the financial statements.
- For information intended to convey the same meaning as disclosures in the financial statements, comparing the words used and considering the significance of differences in wording used and whether such differences imply different meanings.
- Obtaining a reconciliation between an amount within the other information and the financial statements from management and:
  - Comparing items in the reconciliation to the financial statements and the other information; and
  - Checking whether the calculations within the reconciliation are arithmetically accurate.

A29   Evaluating the consistency of selected amounts or other items in the other information with the financial statements includes, when relevant given the nature of the other information, the manner of their presentation compared to the financial statements.

***Considering Whether There Is a Material Inconsistency between the Other
Information and the Auditor's Knowledge Obtained in the Audit*** (Ref: Para. 14(b))

A30   Other information may include amounts or items that are related to the auditor's knowledge obtained in the audit (other than those in paragraph 14(a)). Examples of such amounts or items may include:

- A disclosure of the units produced, or a table summarizing such production by geographical region.
- A statement that 'The company introduced product X and product Y during the year.'
- A summary of the locations of the entity's major operations, such as 'the entity's major center of operation is in country X, and there are also operations in countries Y and Z.'

A31   The auditor's knowledge obtained in the audit includes the auditor's understanding of the entity and its environment, including the entity's internal control, obtained in accordance with ISA (UK) 315 (Revised June 2016).[11] ISA (UK) 315 (Revised June 2016) sets out the auditor's required understanding, which includes such matters as obtaining an understanding of:

(a) The relevant industry, regulatory, and other external factors;
(b) The nature of the entity;
(c) The entity's selection and application of accounting policies;
(d) The entity's objectives and strategies;
(e) The measurement and review of the entity's financial performance; and
(f) The entity's internal control.

The auditor's knowledge obtained in the audit may also include matters that are prospective in nature. Such matters may include, for example, business prospects and future cash flows that the auditor considered when evaluating the assumptions used by management in performing impairment tests on intangible assets such as goodwill, or when evaluating management's assessment of the entity's ability to continue as a going concern. **A32**

In considering whether there is a material inconsistency between the other information and the auditor's knowledge obtained in the audit, the auditor may focus on those matters in the other information that are of sufficient importance that a misstatement of the other information in relation to that matter could be material. **A33**

In relation to many matters in the other information, the auditor's recollection of the audit evidence obtained and conclusions reached in the audit may be sufficient to enable the auditor to consider whether there is a material inconsistency between the other information and the auditor's knowledge obtained in the audit. The more experienced and the more familiar with the key aspects of the audit the auditor is, the more likely it is that the auditor's recollection of relevant matters will be sufficient. For example, the auditor may be able to consider whether there is a material inconsistency between the other information and the auditor's knowledge obtained in the audit in light of the auditor's recollection of discussions held with management or those charged with governance or findings from procedures carried out during the audit such as the reading of board minutes, without the need to take further action. **A34**

The auditor may determine that referring to relevant audit documentation or making inquiries of relevant members of the engagement team or relevant component auditors is appropriate as a basis for the auditor's consideration of whether a material inconsistency exists. For example: **A35**

- When the other information describes the planned cessation of a major product line and, although the auditor is aware of the planned cessation, the auditor may make inquiries of the relevant engagement team member who performed the audit procedures in this area to support the auditor's consideration of whether the description is materially inconsistent with the auditor's knowledge obtained during the audit.
- When the other information describes important details of a lawsuit addressed in the audit, but the auditor cannot recall them adequately, it may be necessary to refer to the audit documentation where such details are summarized to support the auditor's recollection.

Whether, and if so the extent to which, the auditor refers to relevant audit documentation, or makes inquiries of relevant members of the engagement team or relevant component auditors is a matter of professional judgment. However, it may not be necessary for the auditor to refer to relevant audit documentation, or to make inquiries of relevant members **A36**

---

[11] *ISA (UK) 315 (Revised June 2016)*, Identifying and Assessing the Risks of Material Misstatement through Understanding the Entity and Its Environment, *paragraphs 11–12*.

of the engagement team or relevant component auditors about any matter included in the other information.

Identifying Whether the Statutory Other Information Has Been Prepared in Accordance with the Applicable Legal and Regulatory Requirements (Ref: Para. 14D-1)

A36-1   As explained in paragraph 12(b), a misstatement of the other information also exists when the statutory other information has not been prepared in accordance with the legal and regulatory requirements applicable to the statutory other information.

A36-2   In considering whether the statutory other information has been prepared in accordance with the legal and regulatory requirements applicable to the statutory other information, the auditor identifies whether information that is required by law or regulation to be included in the statutory other information has been omitted. This includes situations where the required information is presented separately from the statutory other information without appropriate cross reference.

A36-3   If the auditor concludes that the statutory other information has not been prepared in accordance with the legal and regulatory requirements applicable to the statutory other information, the auditor determines whether non-compliance with the applicable legal or regulatory requirement has a material effect on the financial statements.[11a]

A36-4   For statutory audits of financial statements of public interest entities, the auditor considers whether to communicate any non-compliance with the applicable legal or regulatory requirement in the additional report to the audit committee.[11b]

Remaining Alert for Other Indications that the Other Information Appears to Be Materially Misstated (Ref: Para. 15)

A37   Other information may include discussion of matters that are not related to the financial statements and may also extend beyond the auditor's knowledge obtained in the audit. For example, the other information may include statements about the entity's greenhouse gas emissions.

A38   Remaining alert for other indications that the other information not related to the financial statements or the auditor's knowledge obtained in the audit appears to be materially misstated assists the auditor in complying with relevant ethical requirements that require the auditor to avoid being knowingly associated with other information that the auditor believes contains a materially false or misleading statement, a statement furnished recklessly, or omits or obscures necessary information such that the other information is misleading.[12] Remaining alert for other indications that the other information appears to be materially misstated could potentially result in the auditor identifying such matters as:

- Differences between the other information and the general knowledge, apart from the knowledge obtained in the audit, of the engagement team member reading the other information that lead the auditor to believe that the other information appears to be materially misstated; or

---

[11a] *ISA (UK) 250 (Revised June 2016)*, Consideration of Laws and Regulations in an Audit of Financial Statements.

[11b] *ISA (UK) 260 (Revised June 2016)*, Communication with Those Charged with Governance, *paragraph 16R-2(k).*

[12] *IESBA Code, paragraph 110.2.*
In the UK, the relevant ethical guidance on such matters is provided by the ethical pronouncements issued by the auditor's relevant professional body.

- An internal inconsistency in the other information that leads the auditor to believe that the other information appears to be materially misstated.

Responding When a Material Inconsistency Appears to Exist or Other Information Appears to Be Materially Misstated (Ref: Para. 16)

The auditor's discussion with management about a material inconsistency (or other information **A39** that appears to be materially misstated) may include requesting management to provide support for the basis of management's statements in the other information. Based on management's further information or explanations, the auditor may be satisfied that the other information is not materially misstated. For example, management explanations may indicate reasonable and sufficient grounds for valid differences of judgment.

Conversely, the discussion with management may provide further information that supports **A40** the auditor's conclusion that a material misstatement of the other information exists.

It may be more difficult for the auditor to challenge management on matters of judgment **A41** than on those of a more factual nature. However, there may be circumstances where the auditor concludes that the other information contains a statement that is not consistent with the financial statements or the auditor's knowledge obtained in the audit. These circumstances may raise doubt about the other information, the financial statements, or the auditor's knowledge obtained in the audit.

As there is a wide range of possible material misstatements of the other information, **A42** the nature and extent of other procedures the auditor may perform to conclude whether a material misstatement of the other information exists are matters of the auditor's professional judgment in the circumstances.

When a matter is unrelated to the financial statements or the auditor's knowledge **A43** obtained in the audit, the auditor may not be able to fully assess management's responses to the auditor's inquiries. Nevertheless, based on management's further information or explanations, or following changes made by management to the other information, the auditor may be satisfied that a material inconsistency no longer appears to exist or that the other information no longer appears to be materially misstated. When the auditor is unable to conclude that a material inconsistency no longer appears to exist or that the other information no longer appears to be materially misstated, the auditor may request management to consult with a qualified third party (for example, a management's expert or legal counsel). In certain cases, after considering the responses from management's consultation, the auditor may not be able to conclude whether or not a material misstatement of the other information exists. Actions the auditor may then take include one or more of the following:

- Obtaining advice from the auditor's legal counsel;
- Considering the implications for the auditor's report for example, whether to describe the circumstances when there is a limitation imposed by management; or
- Withdrawing from the audit, where withdrawal is possible under applicable law or regulation.

Responding When the Auditor Concludes That a Material Misstatement of the Other Information Exists

Responding When the Auditor Concludes That a Material Misstatement Exists in Other Information Obtained prior to the Date of the Auditor's Report (Ref: Para. 18)

A44   The actions the auditor takes if the other information is not corrected after communicating with those charged with governance are a matter of the auditor's professional judgment. The auditor may take into account whether the rationale given by management and those charged with governance for not making the correction raises doubt about the integrity or honesty of management or those charged with governance, such as when the auditor suspects an intention to mislead. The auditor may also consider it appropriate to seek legal advice. In some cases, the auditor may be required by law, regulation or other professional standards to communicate the matter to a regulator or relevant professional body.

A44-1   If the auditor concludes that a material misstatement of the other information exists, and the auditor is unable to resolve the matter through discussion with those charged with governance, the auditor considers requesting those charged with governance to consult with a qualified third party, such as the entity's legal counsel and considers the advice received.

Further Actions Available to the Auditor When a Material Inconsistency or Material Misstatement in Other Information is not Corrected

A44-2   In the UK, the auditor of a limited company may use the auditor's right to be heard at any general meeting of the members on any part of the business of the meeting which concerns the auditor as auditor.[12a]

Reporting Implications (Ref: Para. 18(a))

A45   In rare circumstances, a disclaimer of opinion on the financial statements may be appropriate when the refusal to correct the material misstatement of the other information casts such doubt on the integrity of management and those charged with governance as to call into question the reliability of audit evidence in general.

Withdrawal from the Engagement (Ref: Para. 18(b))

A46   Withdrawal from the engagement, where withdrawal is possible under applicable law or regulation, may be appropriate when the circumstances surrounding the refusal to correct the material misstatement of the other information cast such doubt on the integrity of management and those charged with governance as to call into question the reliability of representations obtained from them during the audit.

A46-1   In the case of auditors of limited companies in the UK, the requirements for the auditor to make a statement on ceasing to hold office as auditor apply.[12b] In addition, in the UK the auditor may need to notify the relevant audit authority.[12c]

[12a] *In the UK, Section 502 of the Companies Act 2006.*

[12b] *In the UK, Section 519 of the Companies Act 2006.*

[12c] *In the UK, Section 522 of the Companies Act 2006.*

Considerations specific to public sector entities (Ref: Para. 18(b))

In the public sector, withdrawal from the engagement may not be possible. In such cases, the auditor may issue a report to the legislature providing details of the matter or may take other appropriate actions.   **A47**

Responding When the Auditor Concludes That a Material Misstatement Exists in Other Information Obtained after the Date of the Auditor's Report (Ref: Para. 19)

If the auditor concludes that a material misstatement exists in other information obtained after the date of the auditor's report, and such a material misstatement has been corrected, the auditor's procedures necessary in the circumstances include determining that the correction has been made (in accordance with paragraph 17(a)) and may include reviewing the steps taken by management to communicate with those in receipt of the other information, if previously issued, to inform them of the revision.   **A48**

If those charged with governance do not agree to revise the other information, taking appropriate action to seek to have the uncorrected misstatement appropriately brought to the attention of users for whom the auditor's report is prepared requires the exercise of professional judgment, and may be affected by relevant law or regulation in the jurisdiction. Accordingly, the auditor may consider it appropriate to seek legal advice about the auditor's legal rights and obligations.   **A49**

When a material misstatement of the other information remains uncorrected, appropriate actions that the auditor may take to seek to have the uncorrected material misstatement appropriately brought to the attention of users for whom the auditor's report is prepared, when permitted by law or regulation, include, for example: **A50**

- Providing a new or amended auditor's report to management including a modified section in accordance with paragraph 22, and requesting management to provide this new or amended auditor's report to users for whom the auditor's report is prepared. In doing so, the auditor may need to consider the effect, if any, on the date of the new or amended auditor's report, in view of the requirements of the ISAs (UK) or applicable law or regulation. The auditor may also review the steps taken by management to provide the new or amended auditor's report to such users;
- Bringing the material misstatement of the other information to the attention of the users for whom the auditor's report is prepared (for example, by addressing the matter in a general meeting of shareholders);
- Communicating with a regulator or relevant professional body about the uncorrected material misstatement; or
- Considering the implications for engagement continuance (see also paragraph A46).

Responding When a Material Misstatement in the Financial Statements Exists or the Auditor's Understanding of the Entity and Its Environment Needs to Be Updated (Ref: Para. 20)

In reading the other information, the auditor may become aware of new information that has implications for: **A51**

- The auditor's understanding of the entity and its environment and, accordingly, may indicate the need to revise the auditor's risk assessment.[13]

---

[13] *ISA (UK) 315 (Revised June 2016), paragraphs 11, 31, and A1.*

- The auditor's responsibility to evaluate the effect of identified misstatements on the audit and of uncorrected misstatements, if any, on the financial statements.[14]
- The auditor's responsibilities relating to subsequent events.[15]

Reporting (Ref: Para. 21–24)

A52   For an audit of financial statements of an entity other than a listed entity, the auditor may consider that the identification in the auditor's report of other information that the auditor expects to obtain after the date of the auditor's report would be appropriate in order to provide additional transparency about the other information that is subject to the auditor's responsibilities under this ISA (UK). The auditor may consider it appropriate to do so, for example, when management is able to represent to the auditor that such other information will be issued after the date of the auditor's report.

Illustrative Statements (Ref: Para. 21–22)

A53   Illustrative examples of the 'Other Information' section of the auditor's report are included in Appendix 2.[15a]

Other Reporting Responsibilities for Entities Incorporated under the Companies Acts (Ref: Para. 22D-2)

A53-1   In the UK, under Section 497A of the Companies Act 2006 the auditor is required to consider whether the information given in the separate Corporate Governance Statement in compliance with rules 7.2.5 and 7.2.6 in the Disclosure Rules and Transparency Rules sourcebook made by the Financial Conduct Authority (information about internal control and risk management systems in relation to financial reporting processes and about share capital structures) is consistent with those accounts, and has been prepared in accordance with applicable legal requirements. The auditor is also required to consider whether rules 7.2.2, 7.2.3 and 7.2.7 in the Disclosure Rules and Transparency Rules sourcebook made by the Financial Conduct Authority (information about the company's corporate governance code and practices and about its administrative, management and supervisory bodies and their committees) have been complied with.

Other Reporting Responsibilities for Entities that Apply the UK Corporate Governance Code (Ref: Para. 22-3)

A53-2   For entities that apply the UK Corporate Governance Code, the directors are required to give a statement in the annual report that they consider the annual report and accounts taken as a whole is fair, balanced and understandable and provides the information necessary for shareholders to assess the entity's performance, business model and strategy. Such entities are also required to include a separate section of the annual report that describes the work of the audit committee in discharging its responsibilities. This should include, inter alia, the significant issues that the audit committee considered in relation to the financial statements, including appropriate matters considered that were communicated to it by the auditor, and how these issues were addressed.

---

[14] *ISA (UK) 450 (Revised June 2016),* Evaluation of Misstatements Identified during the Audit.

[15] *ISA (UK) 560, paragraphs 10 and 14.*

[15a] *The examples in Appendix 2 have not been tailored for the UK. Illustrative auditor's reports tailored for use with audits conducted in accordance with ISAs (UK) are given in the current version of the FRC's Compendium of Illustrative Auditor's Reports.*

Where applicable, the auditor includes a statements in accordance with paragraph 22(e)(ii) **A53-3** describing why the auditor believes that any such statement, section, or explanation or other information is materially inconsistent with the auditor's knowledge obtained in the audit or otherwise contains a material misstatement of the other information. If a section of the annual report describing the work of the audit committee does not appropriately disclose any matters communicated by the auditor to the audit committee that in the auditor's judgment should have been disclosed, or if the annual report does not contain such a section, the auditor's report shall also include any such information.

Reporting Implications When the Auditor's Opinion on the Financial Statements Is Qualified or Adverse (Ref: Para. 23)

A qualified or adverse auditor's opinion on the financial statements may not have an impact **A54** on the statement required by paragraph 22(e) if the matter in respect of which the auditor's opinion has been modified is not included or otherwise addressed in the other information and the matter does not affect any part of the other information. For example, a qualified opinion on the financial statements because of non-disclosure of directors' remuneration as required by the applicable financial reporting framework may have no implications for the reporting required under this ISA (UK). In other circumstances, there may be implications for such reporting as described in paragraphs A55–A58.

Qualified Opinion Due to a Material Misstatement in the Financial Statements

In circumstances when the auditor's opinion is qualified, consideration may be given as **A55** to whether the other information is also materially misstated for the same matter as, or a related matter to, the matter giving rise to the qualified opinion on the financial statements.

Qualified Opinion Due to Limitation of Scope

When there is a limitation of scope with respect to a material item in the financial **A56** statements, the auditor will not have obtained sufficient appropriate audit evidence about that matter. In these circumstances, the auditor may be unable to conclude whether or not the amounts or other items in the other information related to this matter result in a material misstatement of the other information. Accordingly, the auditor may need to modify the statement required by paragraph 22(e) to refer to the auditor's inability to consider management's description of the matter in the other information in respect of which the auditor's opinion on the financial statements has been qualified as explained in the Basis for Qualified Opinion paragraph. The auditor is nevertheless required to report any other uncorrected material misstatements of the other information that have been identified.

Adverse Opinion

An adverse opinion on the financial statements relating to a specific matter(s) described **A57** in the Basis for Adverse Opinion paragraph does not justify the omission of reporting of material misstatements of the other information that the auditor has identified in the auditor's report in accordance with paragraph 22(e)(ii). When an adverse opinion has been expressed on the financial statements, the auditor may need to appropriately modify the statement required by paragraph 22(e) for example, to indicate that amounts or items in the other information is materially misstated for the same matter as, or a related matter to, the matter giving rise to the adverse opinion on the financial statements.

Disclaimer of Opinion

A58   When the auditor disclaims an opinion on the financial statements, providing further details about the audit, including a section to address other information may overshadow the disclaimer of opinion on the financial statements as a whole. Accordingly, in those circumstances, as required by ISA (UK) 705 (Revised June 2016), the auditor's report does not include a section addressing the reporting requirements under this ISA (UK).

Reporting Prescribed by Law or Regulation (Ref: Para. 24)

A59   ISA (UK) 200 (Revised June 2016)[16] explains that the auditor may be required to comply with legal or regulatory requirements in addition to the ISAs (UK). Where this is the case, the auditor may be obliged to use a specific layout or wording in the auditor's report that differs from that described in this ISA (UK). Consistency in the auditor's report, when the audit has been conducted in accordance with ISAs (UK), promotes credibility in the global marketplace by making more readily identifiable those audits that have been conducted in accordance with globally recognized standards. When the differences between the legal or regulatory requirements to report with respect to the other information and this ISA (UK) relate only to the layout and wording in the auditor's report and, at a minimum, each of the elements identified in paragraph 24 is included in the auditor's report, the auditor's report may refer to International Standards on Auditing. Accordingly, in such circumstances the auditor is considered to have complied with the requirements of this ISA (UK), even when the layout and wording used in the auditor's report are specified by legal or regulatory reporting requirements.

---

[16] *ISA (UK) 200 (Revised June 2016), paragraph A55.*

Appendix 1   (Ref: Para. 14, A8)

Examples of Amounts or Other Items that May Be Included in the Other Information

The following are examples of amounts and other items that may be included in other information. This list is not intended to be exhaustive.

Amounts

- Items in a summary of key financial results, such as net income, earnings per share, dividends, sales and other operating revenues, and purchases and operating expenses.
- Selected operating data, such as income from continuing operations by major operating area, or sales by geographical segment or product line.
- Special items, such as asset dispositions, litigation provisions, asset impairments, tax adjustments, environmental remediation provisions, and restructuring and reorganization expenses.
- Liquidity and capital resource information, such as cash, cash equivalents and marketable securities; dividends; and debt, capital lease and minority interest obligations.
- Capital expenditures by segment or division.
- Amounts involved in, and related financial effects of, off-balance sheet arrangements.
- Amounts involved in guarantees, contractual obligations, legal or environmental claims, and other contingencies.
- Financial measures or ratios, such as gross margin, return on average capital employed, return on average shareholders' equity, current ratio, interest coverage ratio and debt ratio. Some of these may be directly reconcilable to the financial statements.

Other Items

- Explanations of critical accounting estimates and related assumptions.
- Identification of related parties and descriptions of transactions with them.
- Articulation of the entity's policies or approach to manage commodity, foreign exchange or interest rate risks, such as through the use of forward contracts, interest rate swaps, or other financial instruments.
- Descriptions of the nature of off-balance sheet arrangements.
- Descriptions of guarantees, indemnifications, contractual obligations, litigation or environmental liability cases, and other contingencies, including management's qualitative assessments of the entity's related exposures.
- Descriptions of changes in legal or regulatory requirements, such as new tax or environmental regulations, that have materially impacted the entity's operations or fiscal position, or will have a material impact on the entity's future financial prospects.
- Management's qualitative assessments of the impacts of new financial reporting standards that have come into effect during the period, or will come into effect in the following period, on the entity's financial results, financial position and cash flows.
- General descriptions of the business environment and outlook.
- Overview of strategy.
- Descriptions of trends in market prices of key commodities or raw materials.
- Contrasts of supply, demand and regulatory circumstances between geographic regions.
- Explanations of specific factors influencing the entity's profitability in specific segments.

Appendix 2   (Ref: Para. 21–22, A53)

Illustrations of Auditor's Reports Relating to Other Information

The examples in the Appendix have not been tailored for the UK. Illustrative auditor's reports tailored for use with audits conducted in accordance with ISAs (UK) are given in the current version of the FRC's Compendium of Illustrative Auditor's Reports.

Illustrations 2, 3 and 4 would not be relevant for audits of financial statements in the UK as the auditor is required to obtain all of the other information prior to the date of the auditor's report.

- Illustration 1: An auditor's report of any entity, whether listed or other than listed, containing an unmodified opinion when the auditor has obtained all of the other information prior to the date of the auditor's report and has not identified a material misstatement of the other information.
- Illustration 2: An auditor's report of a listed entity containing an unmodified opinion when the auditor has obtained part of the other information prior to the date of the auditor's report, has not identified a material misstatement of the other information, and expects to obtain other information after the date of the auditor's report.
- Illustration 3: An auditor's report of an entity other than a listed entity containing an unmodified opinion when the auditor has obtained part of the other information prior to the date of the auditor's report, has not identified a material misstatement of the other information, and expects to obtain other information after the date of the auditor's report.
- Illustration 4: An auditor's report of a listed entity containing an unmodified opinion when the auditor has obtained no other information prior to the date of the auditor's report but expects to obtain other information after the date of the auditor's report.
- Illustration 5: An auditor's report of any entity, whether listed or other than listed, containing an unmodified opinion when the auditor has obtained all of the other information prior to the date of the auditor's report and has concluded that a material misstatement of the other information exists.
- Illustration 6: An auditor's report of any entity, whether listed or other than listed, containing a qualified opinion when the auditor has obtained all of the other information prior to the date of the auditor's report and there is a limitation of scope with respect to a material item in the consolidated financial statements which also affects the other information.
- Illustration 7: An auditor's report of any entity, whether listed or other than listed, containing an adverse opinion when the auditor has obtained all of the other information prior to the date of the auditor's report and the adverse opinion on the consolidated financial statements also affects the other information.

Illustration 1 – An auditor's report of any entity, whether listed or other than listed, containing an unmodified opinion when the auditor has obtained all of the other information prior to the date of the auditor's report and has not identified a material misstatement of the other information.

For purposes of this illustrative auditor's report, the following circumstances are assumed:

- Audit of a complete set of financial statements of any entity, whether listed or other than listed, using a fair presentation framework. The audit is not a group audit (i.e., ISA 600[17] does not apply).
- The financial statements are prepared by management of the entity in accordance with IFRSs (a general purpose framework).
- The terms of the audit engagement reflect the description of management's responsibility for the financial statements in ISA 210.
- The auditor has concluded an unmodified (i.e., 'clean') opinion is appropriate based on the audit evidence obtained.
- The relevant ethical requirements that apply to the audit are those of the jurisdiction.
- Based on the audit evidence obtained, the auditor has concluded that a material uncertainty does not exist related to events or conditions that may cast significant doubt on the entity's ability to continue as a going concern in accordance with ISA 570 (Revised).[18]
- Key audit matters have been communicated in accordance with ISA 701.[19]
- The auditor has obtained all of the other information prior to the date of the auditor's report and has not identified a material misstatement of the other information.
- Those responsible for oversight of the financial statements differ from those responsible for the preparation of the financial statements.
- In addition to the audit of the financial statements, the auditor has other reporting responsibilities required under local law.

INDEPENDENT AUDITOR'S REPORT

To the Shareholders of ABC Company [or Other Appropriate Addressee]

Report on the Audit of the Financial Statements[20]

Opinion

We have audited the financial statements of ABC Company (the Company), which comprise the statement of financial position as at December 31, 20X1, and the statement of comprehensive income, statement of changes in equity and statement of cash flows for the year then ended, and notes to the financial statements, including a summary of significant accounting policies.

---

[17] *ISA 600*, Special Considerations–Audits of Group Financial Statements (Including the Work of Component Auditors).

[18] *ISA 570 (Revised)*, Going Concern.

[19] *ISA 701*, Communicating Key Audit Matters in the Independent Auditor's Report. *The Key Audit Matters section is required for listed entities only.*

[20] *The sub-title 'Report on the Audit of the Financial Statements' is unnecessary in circumstances when the second sub-title 'Report on Other Legal and Regulatory Requirements' is not applicable.*

In our opinion, the accompanying financial statements present fairly, in all material respects, (or *give a true and fair view of*) the financial position of the Company as at December 31, 20X1, and (*of*) its financial performance and its cash flows for the year then ended in accordance with International Financial Reporting Standards (IFRSs).

Basis for Opinion

We conducted our audit in accordance with International Standards on Auditing (ISAs). Our responsibilities under those standards are further described in the *Auditor's Responsibilities for the Audit of the Financial Statements* section of our report. We are independent of the Company in accordance with the ethical requirements that are relevant to our audit of the financial statements in [*jurisdiction*], and we have fulfilled our other ethical responsibilities in accordance with these requirements. We believe that the audit evidence we have obtained is sufficient and appropriate to provide a basis for our opinion.

[Key Audit Matters[21]

Key audit matters are those matters that, in our professional judgment, were of most significance in our audit of the financial statements of the current period. These matters were addressed in the context of our audit of the financial statements as a whole, and in forming our opinion thereon, and we do not provide a separate opinion on these matters.

[*Description of each key audit matter in accordance with ISA 701.*]]

Other Information [or another title if appropriate, such as 'Information Other than the Financial Statements and Auditor's Report Thereon']

Management[22] is responsible for the other information. The other information comprises the [information included in the X report,[23] but does not include the financial statements and our auditor's report thereon.]

Our opinion on the financial statements does not cover the other information and we do not express any form of assurance conclusion thereon.

In connection with our audit of the financial statements, our responsibility is to read the other information and, in doing so, consider whether the other information is materially inconsistent with the financial statements or our knowledge obtained in the audit or otherwise appears to be materially misstated. If, based on the work we have performed, we conclude that there is a material misstatement of this other information, we are required to report that fact. We have nothing to report in this regard.

---

[21] *The Key Audit Matters section is required for listed entities only.*

[22] *Or other terms that are appropriate in the context of the legal framework of the particular jurisdiction.*

[23] *A more specific description of the other information, such as 'the management report and chairman's statement,' may be used to identify the other information.*

Responsibilities of Management and Those Charged with Governance for the Financial Statements[24]

[*Reporting in accordance with ISA 700 (Revised)*[25] *– see Illustration 1 in ISA 700 (Revised).*]

Auditor's Responsibilities for the Audit of the Financial Statements

[*Reporting in accordance with ISA 700 (Revised) – see Illustration 1 in ISA 700 (Revised).*]

Report on Other Legal and Regulatory Requirements

[*Reporting in accordance with ISA 700 (Revised) – see Illustration 1 in ISA 700 (Revised).*]

[The engagement partner on the audit resulting in this independent auditor's report is [*name*].[26]]

[*Signature in the name of the audit firm, the personal name of the auditor, or both, as appropriate for the particular jurisdiction*]

[*Auditor Address*]

[*Date*]

---

[24] *Throughout these illustrative auditor's reports, the terms management and those charged with governance may need to be replaced by another term that is appropriate in the context of the legal framework in the particular jurisdiction.*

[25] *ISA 700 (Revised),* Forming an Opinion and Reporting on Financial Statements.

[26] *The name of the engagement partner is included in the auditor's report for audits of complete sets of general purpose financial statements of listed entities unless, in rare circumstances, such disclosure is reasonably expected to lead to a significant personal security threat (see ISA 700 (Revised), paragraph 46).*

Illustration 2 – An auditor's report of a listed entity containing an unmodified opinion when the auditor has obtained part of the other information prior to the date of the auditor 's report, has not identified a material misstatement of the other information, and expects to obtain other information after the date of the auditor's report.

For purposes of this illustrative auditor's report, the following circumstances are assumed:

- Audit of a complete set of financial statements of a listed entity using a fair presentation framework. The audit is not a group audit (i.e., ISA 600 does not apply).
- The financial statements are prepared by management of the entity in accordance with IFRSs (a general purpose framework).
- The terms of the audit engagement reflect the description of management's responsibility for the financial statements in ISA 210.
- The auditor has concluded an unmodified (i.e., 'clean') opinion is appropriate based on the audit evidence obtained.
- The relevant ethical requirements that apply to the audit are those of the jurisdiction.
- Based on the audit evidence obtained, the auditor has concluded that a material uncertainty does not exist related to events or conditions that may cast significant doubt on the entity's ability to continue as a going concern in accordance with ISA 570 (Revised).
- Key audit matters have been communicated in accordance with ISA 701.
- The auditor has obtained part of the other information prior to the date of the auditor's report, has not identified a material misstatement of the other information, and expects to obtain other information after the date of the auditor's report.
- Those responsible for oversight of the financial statements differ from those responsible for the preparation of the financial statements.
- In addition to the audit of the financial statements, the auditor has other reporting responsibilities required under local law.

INDEPENDENT AUDITOR'S REPORT

To the Shareholders of ABC Company [or Other Appropriate Addressee]

Report on the Audit of the Financial Statements[27]

Opinion

We have audited the financial statements of ABC Company (the Company), which comprise the statement of financial position as at December 31, 20X1, and the statement of comprehensive income, statement of changes in equity and statement of cash flows for the year then ended, and notes to the financial statements, including a summary of significant accounting policies.

In our opinion, the accompanying financial statements present fairly, in all material respects, (or *give a true and fair view of*) the financial position of the Company as at December 31, 20X1, and (*of*) its financial performance and its cash flows for the year then ended in accordance with International Financial Reporting Standards (IFRSs).

---

[27] *The sub-title 'Report on the Audit of the Financial Statements' is unnecessary in circumstances when the second sub-title 'Report on Other Legal and Regulatory Requirements' is not applicable.*

Basis for Opinion

We conducted our audit in accordance with International Standards on Auditing (ISAs). Our responsibilities under those standards are further described in the *Auditor's Responsibilities for the Audit of the Financial Statements* section of our report. We are independent of the Company in accordance with the ethical requirements that are relevant to our audit of the financial statements in [*jurisdiction*], and we have fulfilled our other ethical responsibilities in accordance with these requirements. We believe that the audit evidence we have obtained is sufficient and appropriate to provide a basis for our opinion.

Key Audit Matters

Key audit matters are those matters that, in our professional judgment, were of most significance in our audit of the financial statements of the current period. These matters were addressed in the context of our audit of the financial statements as a whole, and in forming our opinion thereon, and we do not provide a separate opinion on these matters.

[*Description of each key audit matter in accordance with ISA 701.*]

Other Information [or another title if appropriate, such as 'Information Other than the Financial Statements and Auditor's Report Thereon']

Management[28] is responsible for the other information. The other information comprises the X report[29] (but does not include the financial statements and our auditor's report thereon), which we obtained prior to the date of this auditor's report, and the Y report, which is expected to be made available to us after that date.

Our opinion on the financial statements does not cover the other information and we do not and will not express any form of assurance conclusion thereon.

In connection with our audit of the financial statements, our responsibility is to read the other information identified above and, in doing so, consider whether the other information is materially inconsistent with the financial statements or our knowledge obtained in the audit, or otherwise appears to be materially misstated.

If, based on the work we have performed on the other information that we obtained prior to the date of this auditor's report, we conclude that there is a material misstatement of this other information, we are required to report that fact. We have nothing to report in this regard.

[When we read the Y report, if we conclude that there is a material misstatement therein, we are required to communicate the matter to those charged with governance and [*describe actions applicable in the jurisdiction*].][30]

---

[28] *Or other terms that are appropriate in the context of the legal framework of the particular jurisdiction.*

[29] *A more specific description of the other information, such as 'the management report and chair's statement,' may be used to identify the other information.*

[30] *This additional paragraph may be useful when the auditor has identified an uncorrected material misstatement of the other information obtained after the date of the auditor's report and has a legal obligation to take specific action in response.*

Responsibilities of Management and Those Charged with Governance for the Financial Statements[31]

[*Reporting in accordance with ISA 700 (Revised) – see Illustration 1 in ISA 700 (Revised).*]

Auditor's Responsibilities for the Audit of the Financial Statements

[*Reporting in accordance with ISA 700 (Revised) – see Illustration 1 in ISA 700 (Revised).*]

Report on Other Legal and Regulatory Requirements

[*Reporting in accordance with ISA 700 (Revised) – see Illustration 1 in ISA 700 (Revised).*]

The engagement partner on the audit resulting in this independent auditor's report is [*name*].[32]

[*Signature in the name of the audit firm, the personal name of the auditor, or both, as appropriate for the particular jurisdiction*]

[*Auditor Address*]

[*Date*]

---

[31] *Or other terms that are appropriate in the context of the legal framework of the particular jurisdiction.*

[32] *The name of the engagement partner is included in the auditor's report for audits of complete sets of general purpose financial statements of listed entities unless, in rare circumstances, such disclosure is reasonably expected to lead to a significant personal security threat (see ISA 700 (Revised), paragraph 46).*

Illustration 3 – An auditor's report of an entity other than a listed entity containing an unmodified opinion when the auditor has obtained part of the other information prior to the date of the auditor's report, has not identified a material misstatement of the other information, and expects to obtain other information after the date of the auditor's report.

For purposes of this illustrative auditor's report, the following circumstances are assumed:

- Audit of a complete set of financial statements of an entity other than a listed entity using a fair presentation framework. The audit is not a group audit (i.e., ISA 600 does not apply).
- The financial statements are prepared by management of the entity in accordance with IFRSs (a general purpose framework).
- The terms of the audit engagement reflect the description of management's responsibility for the financial statements in ISA 210.
- The auditor has concluded an unmodified (i.e., 'clean') opinion is appropriate based on the audit evidence obtained.
- The relevant ethical requirements that apply to the audit are those of the jurisdiction.
- Based on the audit evidence obtained, the auditor has concluded that a material uncertainty does not exist related to events or conditions that may cast significant doubt on the entity's ability to continue as a going concern in accordance with ISA 570 (Revised).
- The auditor is not required, and has otherwise not decided, to communicate key audit matters in accordance with ISA 701.
- The auditor has obtained part of the other information prior to the date of the auditor's report, has not identified a material misstatement of the other information, and expects to obtain other information after the date of the auditor's report.
- Those responsible for oversight of the financial statements differ from those responsible for the preparation of the financial statements.
- The auditor has no other reporting responsibilities required under law or regulation.

INDEPENDENT AUDITOR'S REPORT

To the Shareholders of ABC Company [or Other Appropriate Addressee]

Opinion

We have audited the financial statements of ABC Company (the Company), which comprise the statement of financial position as at December 31, 20X1, and the statement of comprehensive income, statement of changes in equity and statement of cash flows for the year then ended, and notes to the financial statements, including a summary of significant accounting policies.

In our opinion, the accompanying financial statements present fairly, in all material respects, (or *give a true and fair view of*) the financial position of the Company as at December 31, 20X1, and (*of*) its financial performance and its cash flows for the year then ended in accordance with International Financial Reporting Standards (IFRSs).

Basis for Opinion

We conducted our audit in accordance with International Standards on Auditing (ISAs). Our responsibilities under those standards are further described in the *Auditor's Responsibilities for the Audit of the Financial Statements* section of our report. We are independent of the Company in accordance with the ethical requirements that are relevant to our audit of the financial statements in [*jurisdiction*], and we have fulfilled our other ethical responsibilities in accordance with these requirements. We believe that the audit evidence we have obtained is sufficient and appropriate to provide a basis for our opinion.

Other Information [or another title if appropriate, such as 'Information Other than the Financial Statements and Auditor's Report Thereon']

Management[33] is responsible for the other information. The other information obtained at the date of this auditor's report is [information included in the X report,[34] but does not include the financial statements and our auditor's report thereon].

Our opinion on the financial statements does not cover the other information and we do not express any form of assurance conclusion thereon.

In connection with our audit of the financial statements, our responsibility is to read the other information and, in doing so, consider whether the other information is materially inconsistent with the financial statements or our knowledge obtained in the audit, or otherwise appears to be materially misstated.

If, based on the work we have performed on the other information obtained prior to the date of this auditor's report, we conclude that there is a material misstatement of this other information, we are required to report that fact. We have nothing to report in this regard.

Responsibilities of Management and Those Charged with Governance for the Financial Statements[35]

[*Reporting in accordance with ISA 700 (Revised) – see Illustration 1 in ISA 700 (Revised).*]

Auditor's Responsibilities for the Audit of the Financial Statements

[*Reporting in accordance with ISA 700 (Revised) – see Illustration 1 in ISA 700 (Revised).*]

[*Signature in the name of the audit firm, the personal name of the auditor, or both, as appropriate for the particular jurisdiction*]

[*Auditor Address*]

[*Date*]

---

[33]   *Or other terms that are appropriate in the context of the legal framework of the particular jurisdiction.*

[34]   *A more specific description of the other information, such as 'the management report and chair's statement,' may be used to identify the other information.*

[35]   *Or other terms that are appropriate in the context of the legal framework of the particular jurisdiction.*

> **Illustration 4 – An auditor's report of a listed entity containing an unmodified opinion when the auditor has obtained no other information prior to the date of the auditor's report but expects to obtain other information after the date of the auditor's report.**
>
> For purposes of this illustrative auditor's report, the following circumstances are assumed:
>
> - Audit of a complete set of financial statements of a listed entity using a fair presentation framework. The audit is not a group audit (i.e., ISA 600 does not apply).
> - The financial statements are prepared by management of the entity in accordance with IFRSs (a general purpose framework).
> - The terms of the audit engagement reflect the description of management's responsibility for the financial statements in ISA 210.
> - The auditor has concluded an unmodified (i.e., 'clean') opinion is appropriate based on the audit evidence obtained.
> - The relevant ethical requirements that apply to the audit are those of the jurisdiction.
> - Based on the audit evidence obtained, the auditor has concluded that a material uncertainty does not exist related to events or conditions that may cast significant doubt on the entity's ability to continue as a going concern in accordance with ISA 570 (Revised).
> - Key audit matters have been communicated in accordance with ISA 701.
> - The auditor has obtained no other information prior to the date of the auditor's report but expects to obtain other information after the date of the auditor's report.
> - Those responsible for oversight of the financial statements differ from those responsible for the preparation of the financial statements.
> - In addition to the audit of the financial statements, the auditor has other reporting responsibilities required under local law.

INDEPENDENT AUDITOR'S REPORT

To the Shareholders of ABC Company [or Other Appropriate Addressee]

Report on the Audit of the Financial Statements[36]

Opinion

We have audited the financial statements of ABC Company (the Company), which comprise the statement of financial position as at December 31, 20X1, and the statement of comprehensive income, statement of changes in equity and statement of cash flows for the year then ended, and notes to the financial statements, including a summary of significant accounting policies.

In our opinion, the accompanying financial statements present fairly, in all material respects, (or *give a true and fair view of*) the financial position of the Company as at December 31, 20X1, and (*of*) its financial performance and its cash flows for the year then ended in accordance with International Financial Reporting Standards (IFRSs).

---

[36] *The sub-title 'Report on the Audit of the Financial Statements' is unnecessary in circumstances when the second sub-title 'Report on Other Legal and Regulatory Requirements' is not applicable.*

Basis for Opinion

We conducted our audit in accordance with International Standards on Auditing (ISAs). Our responsibilities under those standards are further described in the *Auditor's Responsibilities for the Audit of the Financial Statements* section of our report. We are independent of the Company in accordance with the ethical requirements that are relevant to our audit of the financial statements in [*jurisdiction*], and we have fulfilled our other ethical responsibilities in accordance with these requirements. We believe that the audit evidence we have obtained is sufficient and appropriate to provide a basis for our opinion.

Key Audit Matters

Key audit matters are those matters that, in our professional judgment, were of most significance in our audit of the financial statements of the current period. These matters were addressed in the context of our audit of the financial statements as a whole, and in forming our opinion thereon, and we do not provide a separate opinion on these matters.

[*Description of each key audit matter in accordance with ISA 701.*]

Other Information [or another title if appropriate, such as 'Information Other than the Financial Statements and Auditor's Report Thereon']

Management[37] is responsible for the other information. The other information comprises the [information included in the X report,[38] but does not include the financial statements and our auditor's report thereon]. The X report is expected to be made available to us after the date of this auditor's report.

Our opinion on the financial statements does not cover the other information and we will not express any form of assurance conclusion thereon.

In connection with our audit of the financial statements, our responsibility is to read the other information identified above when it becomes available and, in doing so, consider whether the other information is materially inconsistent with the financial statements or our knowledge obtained in the audit, or otherwise appears to be materially misstated.

[When we read the X report, if we conclude that there is a material misstatement therein, we are required to communicate the matter to those charged with governance and [*describe actions applicable in the jurisdiction*].][39]

Responsibilities of Management and Those Charged with Governance for the Financial Statements[40]

[*Reporting in accordance with ISA 700 (Revised) – see Illustration 1 in ISA 700 (Revised).*]

---

[37] *Or other terms that are appropriate in the context of the legal framework of the particular jurisdiction.*

[38] *A more specific description of the other information, such as 'the management report and chair's statement,' may be used to identify the other information.*

[39] *This additional paragraph may be useful when the auditor has identified an uncorrected material misstatement of the other information obtained after the date of the auditor's report and has a legal obligation to take specific action in response.*

[40] *Or other terms that are appropriate in the context of the legal framework of the particular jurisdiction.*

Auditor's Responsibilities for the Audit of the Financial Statements

[*Reporting in accordance with ISA 700 (Revised) – see Illustration 1 in ISA 700 (Revised).*]

Report on Other Legal and Regulatory Requirements

[*Reporting in accordance with ISA 700 (Revised) – see Illustration 1 in ISA 700 (Revised).*]

The engagement partner on the audit resulting in this independent auditor's report is [*name*].

[*Signature in the name of the audit firm, the personal name of the auditor, or both, as appropriate for the particular jurisdiction*]

[*Auditor Address*]

[*Date*]

Illustration 5 – An auditor's report of any entity, whether listed or other than listed, containing an unmodified opinion when the auditor has obtained all of the other information prior to the date of the auditor's report and has concluded that a material misstatement of the other information exists.

For purposes of this illustrative auditor's report, the following circumstances are assumed:

- Audit of a complete set of financial statements of any entity, whether listed or other than listed, using a fair presentation framework. The audit is not a group audit (i.e., ISA 600 does not apply).
- The financial statements are prepared by management of the entity in accordance with IFRSs (a general purpose framework).
- The terms of the audit engagement reflect the description of management's responsibility for the financial statements in ISA 210.
- The auditor has concluded an unmodified (i.e., 'clean') opinion is appropriate based on the audit evidence obtained.
- The relevant ethical requirements that apply to the audit are those of the jurisdiction.
- Based on the audit evidence obtained, the auditor has concluded that a material uncertainty does not exist related to events or conditions that may cast significant doubt on the entity's ability to continue as a going concern in accordance with ISA 570 (Revised).
- Key audit matters have been communicated in accordance with ISA 701.
- The auditor has obtained all of the other information prior to the date of the auditor's report and has concluded that a material misstatement of the other information exists
- Those responsible for oversight of the financial statements differ from those responsible for the preparation of the financial statements.
- The auditor has no other reporting responsibilities required under law or regulation.

INDEPENDENT AUDITOR'S REPORT

To the Shareholders of ABC Company [or Other Appropriate Addressee]

Opinion

We have audited the financial statements of ABC Company (the Company), which comprise the statement of financial position as at December 31, 20X1, and the statement of comprehensive income, statement of changes in equity and statement of cash flows for the year then ended, and notes to the financial statements, including a summary of significant accounting policies.

In our opinion, the accompanying financial statements present fairly, in all material respects, (or *give a true and fair view of*) the financial position of the Company as at December 31, 20X1, and (*of*) its financial performance and its cash flows for the year then ended in accordance with International Financial Reporting Standards (IFRSs).

Basis for Opinion

We conducted our audit in accordance with International Standards on Auditing (ISAs). Our responsibilities under those standards are further described in the *Auditor's Responsibilities for the Audit of the Financial Statements* section of our report. We are independent of the Company in accordance with the ethical requirements that are relevant to our audit of the financial statements in [*jurisdiction*], and we have fulfilled our other ethical responsibilities in accordance with these requirements. We believe that the audit evidence we have obtained is sufficient and appropriate to provide a basis for our opinion.

Other Information [or another title if appropriate, such as 'Information Other than the Financial Statements and Auditor's Report Thereon']

Management[41] is responsible for the other information. The other information comprises the [information included in the X report,[42] but does not include the financial statements and our auditor's report thereon.]

Our opinion on the financial statements does not cover the other information and we do not express any form of assurance conclusion thereon.

In connection with our audit of the financial statements, our responsibility is to read the other information and, in doing so, consider whether the other information is materially inconsistent with the financial statements or our knowledge obtained in the audit or otherwise appears to be materially misstated.

If, based on the work we have performed, we conclude that there is a material misstatement of this other information, we are required to report that fact. As described below, we have concluded that such a material misstatement of the other information exists.

[*Description of material misstatement of the other information*]

[Key Audit Matters[43]

Key audit matters are those matters that, in our professional judgment, were of most significance in our audit of the financial statements of the current period. These matters were addressed in the context of our audit of the financial statements as a whole, and in forming our opinion thereon, and we do not provide a separate opinion on these matters.

[*Description of each key audit matter in accordance with ISA 701.*]]

Responsibilities of Management and Those Charged with Governance for the Financial Statements[44]

[*Reporting in accordance with ISA 700 (Revised) – see Illustration 1 in ISA 700 (Revised).*]

Auditor's Responsibilities for the Audit of the Financial Statements

[*Reporting in accordance with ISA 700 (Revised) – see Illustration 1 in ISA 700 (Revised).*]

---

[41] *Or other terms that are appropriate in the context of the legal framework of the particular jurisdiction.*

[42] *A more specific description of the other information, such as 'the management report and chairman's statement,' may be used to identify the other information.*

[43] *The Key Audit Matters section is required for listed entities only.*

[44] *Or other terms that are appropriate in the context of the legal framework of the particular jurisdiction.*

[The engagement partner on the audit resulting in this independent auditor's report is [*name*].⁴⁵]

[*Signature in the name of the audit firm, the personal name of the auditor, or both, as appropriate for the particular jurisdiction*]

[*Auditor Address*]

[*Date*]

---

⁴⁵ *The name of the engagement partner is included in the auditor's report for audits of complete sets of general purpose financial statements of listed entities unless, in rare circumstances, such disclosure is reasonably expected to lead to a significant personal security threat (see ISA 700 (Revised), paragraph 46).*

Illustration 6 – An auditor's report of any entity, whether listed or other than listed, containing an qualified opinion when the auditor has obtained all of the other information prior to the date of the auditor's report and there is a limitation of scope with respect to a material item in the consolidated financial statements which also affects the other information.

For purposes of this illustrative auditor's report, the following circumstances are assumed:

● Audit of a complete set of consolidated financial statements of any entity, whether listed or other than listed, using a fair presentation framework. The audit is a group audit (i.e., ISA 600 applies).

● The consolidated financial statements are prepared by management of the entity in accordance with IFRSs (a general purpose framework).

● The terms of the audit engagement reflect the description of management's responsibility for the consolidated financial statements in ISA 210.

● The auditor was unable to obtain sufficient appropriate audit evidence regarding an investment in a foreign associate. The possible effects of the inability to obtain sufficient appropriate audit evidence are deemed to be material but not pervasive to the consolidated financial statements (i.e., a qualified opinion is appropriate).

● The relevant ethical requirements that apply to the audit are those of the jurisdiction.

● Based on the audit evidence obtained, the auditor has concluded that a material uncertainty does not exist related to events or conditions that may cast significant doubt on the entity's ability to continue as a going concern in accordance with ISA 570 (Revised).

● Key audit matters have been communicated in accordance with ISA 701.

● The auditor has obtained all of the other information prior to the date of the auditor's report and the matter giving rise to the qualified opinion on the consolidated financial statements also affects the other information

● Those responsible for oversight of the consolidated financial statements differ from those responsible for the preparation of the consolidated financial statements.

● The auditor has no other reporting responsibilities required under law or regulation.

INDEPENDENT AUDITOR'S REPORT

To the Shareholders of ABC Company [or Other Appropriate Addressee]

Qualified Opinion

We have audited the consolidated financial statements of ABC Company and its subsidiaries (the Group), which comprise the consolidated statement of financial position as at December 31, 20X1, and the consolidated statement of comprehensive income, consolidated statement of changes in equity and consolidated statement of cash flows for the year then ended, and notes to the consolidated financial statements, including a summary of significant accounting policies.

In our opinion, except for the possible effects of the matter described in the *Basis for Qualified Opinion* section of our report, the accompanying consolidated financial statements present fairly, in all material respects, (or *give a true and fair view of*) the financial position of the Group as at December 31, 20X1, and (*of*) its consolidated financial performance and its consolidated cash flows for the year then ended in accordance with International Financial Reporting Standards (IFRSs).

Basis for Qualified Opinion

The Group's investment in XYZ Company, a foreign associate acquired during the year and accounted for by the equity method, is carried at xxx on the consolidated statement of financial position as at December 31, 20X1, and ABC's share of XYZ's net income of xxx is included in ABC's income for the year then ended. We were unable to obtain sufficient appropriate audit evidence about the carrying amount of ABC's investment in XYZ as at December 31, 20X1 and ABC's share of XYZ's net income for the year because we were denied access to the financial information, management, and the auditors of XYZ. Consequently, we were unable to determine whether any adjustments to these amounts were necessary.

We conducted our audit in accordance with International Standards on Auditing (ISAs). Our responsibilities under those standards are further described in the *Auditor's Responsibilities for the Audit of the Consolidated Financial Statements* section of our report. We are independent of the Group in accordance with the ethical requirements that are relevant to our audit of the consolidated financial statements in [*jurisdiction*], and we have fulfilled our other ethical responsibilities in accordance with these requirements. We believe that the audit evidence we have obtained is sufficient and appropriate to provide a basis for our qualified opinion.

Other Information [or another title if appropriate, such as 'Information Other than the Financial Statements and Auditor's Report Thereon']

Management[46] is responsible for the other information. The other information comprises the [information included in the X report,[47] but does not include the consolidated financial statements and our auditor's report thereon.]

Our opinion on the consolidated financial statements does not cover the other information and we do not express any form of assurance conclusion thereon.

In connection with our audit of the consolidated financial statements, our responsibility is to read the other information and, in doing so, consider whether the other information is materially inconsistent with the consolidated financial statements or our knowledge obtained in the audit or otherwise appears to be materially misstated.

If, based on the work we have performed, we conclude that there is a material misstatement of this other information, we are required to report that fact. As described in the *Basis for Qualified Opinion* section above, we were unable to obtain sufficient appropriate evidence about the carrying amount of ABC's investment in XYZ as at December 31, 20X1 and ABC's share of XYZ's net income for the year. Accordingly, we are unable to conclude whether or not the other information is materially misstated with respect to this matter.

[Key Audit Matters[48]

Key audit matters are those matters that, in our professional judgment, were of most significance in our audit of the consolidated financial statements of the current period. These matters were addressed in the context of our audit of the consolidated financial

---

[46] *Or other terms that are appropriate in the context of the legal framework of the particular jurisdiction.*

[47] *A more specific description of the other information, such as 'the management report and chairman's statement,' may be used to identify the other information.*

[48] *The Key Audit Matters section is required for listed entities only.*

statements as a whole, and in forming our opinion thereon, and we do not provide a separate opinion on these matters. In addition to the matter described in the *Basis for Qualified Opinion* section we have determined the matters described below to be the key audit matters to be communicated in our report.

[*Description of each key audit matter in accordance with ISA 701.*]]

Responsibilities of Management and Those Charged with Governance for the Financial Statements[49]

[*Reporting in accordance with ISA 700 (Revised) – see Illustration 2 in ISA 700 (Revised).*]

Auditor's Responsibilities for the Audit of the Financial Statements

[*Reporting in accordance with ISA 700 (Revised) – see Illustration 2 in ISA 700 (Revised).*]

[The engagement partner on the audit resulting in this independent auditor's report is [*name*].[50]]

[*Signature in the name of the audit firm, the personal name of the auditor, or both, as appropriate for the particular jurisdiction*]

[*Auditor Address*]

[*Date*]

---

[49] *Or other terms that are appropriate in the context of the legal framework of the particular jurisdiction.*

[50] *The name of the engagement partner is included in the auditor's report for audits of complete sets of general purpose financial statements of listed entities unless, in rare circumstances, such disclosure is reasonably expected to lead to a significant personal security threat (see ISA 700 (Revised), paragraph 46).*

Illustration 7 – An auditor's report of any entity, whether listed or other than listed, containing an adverse opinion when the auditor has obtained all of the other information prior to the date of the auditor's report and the adverse opinion on the consolidated financial statements also affects the other information.

For purposes of this illustrative auditor's report, the following circumstances are assumed:
● Audit of a complete set of consolidated financial statements of any entity, whether listed or other than listed, using a fair presentation framework. The audit is a group audit (i.e., ISA 600 applies).
● The consolidated financial statements are prepared by management of the entity in accordance with IFRSs (a general purpose framework).
● The terms of the audit engagement reflect the description of management's responsibility for the consolidated financial statements in ISA 210.
● The consolidated financial statements are materially misstated due to the non-consolidation of a subsidiary. The material misstatement is deemed to be pervasive to the consolidated financial statements. The effects of the misstatement on the consolidated financial statements have not been determined because it was not practicable to do so (i.e., an adverse opinion is appropriate).
● The relevant ethical requirements that apply to the audit are those of the jurisdiction.
● Based on the audit evidence obtained, the auditor has concluded that a material uncertainty does not exist related to events or conditions that may cast significant doubt on the entity's ability to continue as a going concern in accordance with ISA 570 (Revised).
● Key audit matters have been communicated in accordance with ISA 701.
● The auditor has obtained all of the other information prior to the date of the auditor's report and the matter giving rise to the adverse opinion on the consolidated financial statements also affects the other information
● Those responsible for oversight of the consolidated financial statements differ from those responsible for the preparation of the consolidated financial statements.
● The auditor has no other reporting responsibilities required under law or regulation.

INDEPENDENT AUDITOR'S REPORT

To the Shareholders of ABC Company [or Other Appropriate Addressee]

Adverse Opinion

We have audited the consolidated financial statements of ABC Company and its subsidiaries (the Group), which comprise the consolidated statement of financial position as at December 31, 20X1, and the consolidated statement of comprehensive income, consolidated statement of changes in equity and consolidated statement of cash flows for the year then ended, and notes to the consolidated financial statements, including a summary of significant accounting policies.

In our opinion, because of the significance of the matter discussed in the *Basis for Adverse Opinion* section of our report, the accompanying consolidated financial statements do not present fairly (or *do not give a true and fair view of*) the consolidated financial position of the Group as at December 31, 20X1, and (*of*) its consolidated financial performance and its consolidated cash flows for the year then ended in accordance with International Financial Reporting Standards (IFRSs).

Basis for Adverse Opinion

As explained in Note X, the Group has not consolidated subsidiary XYZ Company that the Group acquired during 20X1 because it has not yet been able to determine the fair values of certain of the subsidiary's material assets and liabilities at the acquisition date. This investment is therefore accounted for on a cost basis. Under IFRSs, the Group should have consolidated this subsidiary and accounted for the acquisition based on provisional amounts. Had XYZ Company been consolidated, many elements in the accompanying consolidated financial statements would have been materially affected. The effects on the consolidated financial statements of the failure to consolidate have not been determined.

We conducted our audit in accordance with International Standards on Auditing (ISAs). Our responsibilities under those standards are further described in the *Auditor's Responsibilities for the Audit of the Consolidated Financial Statements* section of our report. We are independent of the Group in accordance with the ethical requirements that are relevant to our audit of the consolidated financial statements in [*jurisdiction*], and we have fulfilled our other ethical responsibilities in accordance with these requirements. We believe that the audit evidence we have obtained is sufficient and appropriate to provide a basis for our adverse opinion.

Other Information [or another title if appropriate, such as 'Information Other than the Financial Statements and Auditor's Report Thereon']

Management[51] is responsible for the other information. The other information comprises the [information included in the X report,[52] but does not include the consolidated financial statements and our auditor's report thereon.]

Our opinion on the consolidated financial statements does not cover the other information and we do not express any form of assurance conclusion thereon.

In connection with our audit of the consolidated financial statements, our responsibility is to read the other information and, in doing so, consider whether the other information is materially inconsistent with the consolidated financial statements or our knowledge obtained in the audit or otherwise appears to be materially misstated. If, based on the work we have performed, we conclude that there is a material misstatement of this other information, we are required to report that fact. As described in the *Basis for Adverse Opinion* section above, the Group should have consolidated XYZ Company and accounted for the acquisition based on provisional amounts. We have concluded that the other information is materially misstated for the same reason with respect to the amounts or other items in the X report affected by the failure to consolidate XYZ Company.

[Key Audit Matters[53]

Key audit matters are those matters that, in our professional judgment, were of most significance in our audit of the consolidated financial statements of the current period. These matters were addressed in the context of our audit of the consolidated financial statements as a whole, and in forming our opinion thereon, and we do not provide a separate opinion on these matters. In addition to the matter described in the *Basis for*

---

[51] *Or other terms that are appropriate in the context of the legal framework of the particular jurisdiction.*

[52] *A more specific description of the other information, such as 'the management report and chairman's statement,' may be used to identify the other information.*

[53] *The Key Audit Matters section is required for listed entities only.*

Adverse Opinion section we have determined the matters described below to be the key audit matters to be communicated in our report.

[Description of each key audit matter in accordance with ISA 701.]]

Responsibilities of Management and Those Charged with Governance for the Financial Statements[54]

[Reporting in accordance with ISA 700 (Revised) – see Illustration 2 in ISA 700 (Revised).]

Auditor's Responsibilities for the Audit of the Financial Statements

[Reporting in accordance with ISA 700 (Revised) – see Illustration 2 in ISA 700 (Revised).]

[The engagement partner on the audit resulting in this independent auditor's report is [*name*].[55]]

[Signature in the name of the audit firm, the personal name of the auditor, or both, as appropriate for the particular jurisdiction]

[Auditor Address]

[Date]

---

[54] *Or other terms that are appropriate in the context of the legal framework of the particular jurisdiction.*

[55] *The name of the engagement partner is included in the auditor's report for audits of complete sets of general purpose financial statements of listed entities unless, in rare circumstances, such disclosure is reasonably expected to lead to a significant personal security threat (see ISA 700 (Revised), paragraph 46).*

International Standard on Auditing (UK) 800 (October 2016)

Special considerations—audits of financial statements prepared in accordance with special purpose frameworks

(Effective for audits of financial statements for periods commencing on or after 1 January 2017)

Contents

International Standard on Auditing (UK) (ISA (UK)) 800 (Revised), *Special Considerations—Audits of Financial Statements Prepared in Accordance with Special Purpose Frameworks*, should be read in conjunction with ISA (UK) 200 (Revised June 2016), *Overall Objectives of the Independent Auditor and the Conduct of an Audit in Accordance with International Standards on Auditing (UK)*.

Introduction

Scope of this ISA (UK)

1   The International Standards on Auditing (UK) (ISAs (UK)) in the 100–700 series apply to an audit of financial statements. This ISA (UK) deals with special considerations in the application of those ISAs (UK) to an audit of financial statements prepared in accordance with a special purpose framework.

2   This ISA (UK) is written in the context of a complete set of financial statements prepared in accordance with a special purpose framework. ISA (UK) 805 (Revised)[1] deals with special considerations relevant to an audit of a single financial statement or of a specific element, account or item of a financial statement.

3   This ISA (UK) does not override the requirements of the other ISAs (UK); nor does it purport to deal with all special considerations that may be relevant in the circumstances of the engagement.

Effective Date

4   This ISA (UK) is effective for audits of financial statements for periods commencing on or after 1 January 2017. Early adoption is permitted[2].

Objective

5   The objective of the auditor, when applying ISAs (UK) in an audit of financial statements prepared in accordance with a special purpose framework, is to address appropriately the special considerations that are relevant to:

(a)   The acceptance of the engagement;
(b)   The planning and performance of that engagement; and
(c)   Forming an opinion and reporting on the financial statements.

Definitions

6   For purposes of the ISAs (UK), the following terms have the meanings attributed below:

(a)   Special purpose financial statements – Financial statements prepared in accordance with a special purpose framework. (Ref: Para. A4)
(b)   Special purpose framework – A financial reporting framework designed to meet the financial information needs of specific users. The financial reporting framework may be a fair presentation framework or a compliance framework.[3] (Ref: Para. A1–A4)

---

[1] *ISA (UK) 805 (Revised)*, Special Considerations—Audits of Single Financial Statements and Specific Elements, Accounts or Items of a Financial Statement.

[2] *Where ISA (UK) 800 (Revised) is adopted early for the audit of Solvency II Regulatory Returns for periods commencing prior to 1 January 2017 it may be used in conjunction with ISAs (UK and Ireland) where the audit of the statutory financial statements for the same period was conducted in accordance with ISAs (UK and Ireland).*

[3] *ISA (UK) 200 (Revised June 2016)*, Overall Objectives of the Independent Auditor and the Conduct of an Audit in Accordance with International Standards on Auditing (UK), *paragraph 13(a)*.

Reference to 'financial statements' in this ISA (UK) means 'a complete set of special 7 purpose financial statements'. The requirements of the applicable financial reporting framework determine the presentation, structure, and content of the financial statements, and what constitutes a complete set of financial statements. Reference to 'special purpose financial statements' includes the related disclosures.

Requirements

Considerations When Accepting the Engagement

Acceptability of the Financial Reporting Framework

ISA (UK) 210 (Revised June 2016) requires the auditor to determine the acceptability of 8 the financial reporting framework applied in the preparation of the financial statements.[4] In an audit of special purpose financial statements, the auditor shall obtain an understanding of: (Ref: Para. A5–A8)

(a) The purpose for which the financial statements are prepared;
(b) The intended users; and
(c) The steps taken by management to determine that the applicable financial reporting framework is acceptable in the circumstances.

Considerations When Planning and Performing the Audit

ISA (UK) 200 (Revised June 2016) requires the auditor to comply with all ISAs 9 (UK) relevant to the audit.[5] In planning and performing an audit of special purpose financial statements, the auditor shall determine whether application of the ISAs (UK) requires special consideration in the circumstances of the engagement. (Ref: Para. A9–A12)

ISA (UK) 315 (Revised June 2016) requires the auditor to obtain an understanding of 10 the entity's selection and application of accounting policies.[6] In the case of financial statements prepared in accordance with the provisions of a contract, the auditor shall obtain an understanding of any significant interpretations of the contract that management made in the preparation of those financial statements. An interpretation is significant when adoption of another reasonable interpretation would have produced a material difference in the information presented in the financial statements.

Forming an Opinion and Reporting Considerations

When forming an opinion and reporting on special purpose financial statements, the auditor 11 shall apply the requirements in ISA (UK) 700 (Revised June 2016).[7] (Ref: Para. A13–A19)

[4] *ISA (UK) 210 (Revised June 2016),* Agreeing the Terms of Audit Engagements, *paragraph 6(a).*

[5] *ISA (UK) 200 (Revised June 2016), paragraph 18.*

[6] *ISA (UK) 315 (Revised June 2016),* Identifying and Assessing the Risks of Material Misstatement through Understanding the Entity and Its Environment, *paragraph 11(c).*

[7] *ISA (UK) 700 (Revised June 2016),* Forming an Opinion and Reporting on Financial Statements.

Description of the Applicable Financial Reporting Framework

12   ISA (UK) 700 (Revised June 2016) requires the auditor to evaluate whether the financial statements adequately refer to or describe the applicable financial reporting framework.[8] In the case of financial statements prepared in accordance with the provisions of a contract, the auditor shall evaluate whether the financial statements adequately describe any significant interpretations of the contract on which the financial statements are based.

13   ISA (UK) 700 (Revised June 2016) deals with the form and content of the auditor's report, including the specific ordering for certain elements. In the case of an auditor's report on special purpose financial statements:

(a)   The auditor's report shall also describe the purpose for which the financial statements are prepared and, if necessary, the intended users, or refer to a note in the special purpose financial statements that contains that information; and

(b)   If management has a choice of financial reporting frameworks in the preparation of such financial statements, the explanation of management's[9] responsibility for the financial statements shall also make reference to its responsibility for determining that the applicable financial reporting framework is acceptable in the circumstances.

Alerting Readers that the Financial Statements Are Prepared in Accordance with a Special Purpose Framework

14   The auditor's report on special purpose financial statements shall include an Emphasis of Matter paragraph alerting users of the auditor's report that the financial statements are prepared in accordance with a special purpose framework and that, as a result, the financial statements may not be suitable for another purpose. (Ref: Para. A20–A21)

> In the UK, the auditor specifically describes the financial reporting framework as a special purpose framework in the auditor's report. The auditor also specifically states that the audit has been carried out in accordance with ISAs (UK), including ISA (UK) 800 and/or ISA (UK) 805.

***

Application and Other Explanatory Material

Definition of Special Purpose Framework (Ref: Para. 6)

A1   Examples of special purpose frameworks are:

- A tax basis of accounting for a set of financial statements that accompany an entity's tax return;
- The cash receipts and disbursements basis of accounting for cash flow information that an entity may be requested to prepare for creditors;
- The financial reporting provisions established by a regulator to meet the requirements of that regulator; or
- The financial reporting provisions of a contract, such as a bond indenture, a loan agreement, or a project grant.

---

[8] *ISA (UK) 700 (Revised June 2016), paragraph 15.*

[9] *Or other term that is appropriate in the context of the legal framework in the particular jurisdiction.*

There may be circumstances where a special purpose framework is based on a financial **A2** reporting framework established by an authorized or recognized standards setting organization or by law or regulation, but does not comply with all the requirements of that framework. An example is a contract that requires financial statements to be prepared in accordance with most, but not all, of the Financial Reporting Standards of Jurisdiction X. When this is acceptable in the circumstances of the engagement, it is inappropriate for the description of the applicable financial reporting framework in the special purpose financial statements to imply full compliance with the financial reporting framework established by the authorized or recognized standards setting organization or by law or regulation. In the above example of the contract, the description of the applicable financial reporting framework may refer to the financial reporting provisions of the contract, rather than make any reference to the Financial Reporting Standards of Jurisdiction X.

In the circumstances described in paragraph A2, the special purpose framework may not **A3** be a fair presentation framework even if the financial reporting framework on which it is based is a fair presentation framework. This is because the special purpose framework may not comply with all the requirements of the financial reporting framework established by the authorized or recognized standards setting organization or by law or regulation that are necessary to achieve fair presentation of the financial statements.

Financial statements prepared in accordance with a special purpose framework may be **A4** the only financial statements an entity prepares. In such circumstances, those financial statements may be used by users other than those for whom the financial reporting framework is designed. Despite the broad distribution of the financial statements in those circumstances, the financial statements are still considered to be special purpose financial statements for purposes of the ISAs (UK). The requirements in paragraphs 13–14 are designed to avoid misunderstandings about the purpose for which the financial statements are prepared. Disclosures comprise explanatory or descriptive information, set out as required, expressly permitted or otherwise allowed by the applicable financial reporting framework, on the face of financial statements, or in the notes, or incorporated therein by cross-reference.[10]

Considerations When Accepting the Engagement

Acceptability of the Financial Reporting Framework (Ref: Para. 8)

In the case of special purpose financial statements, the financial information needs of the **A5** intended users are a key factor in determining the acceptability of the financial reporting framework applied in the preparation of the financial statements.

The applicable financial reporting framework may encompass the financial reporting **A6** standards established by an organization that is authorized or recognized to promulgate standards for special purpose financial statements. In that case, those standards will be presumed acceptable for that purpose if the organization follows an established and transparent process involving deliberation and consideration of the views of relevant stakeholders. In some jurisdictions, law or regulation may prescribe the financial reporting framework to be used by management in the preparation of special purpose financial statements for a certain type of entity. For example, a regulator may establish financial reporting provisions to meet the requirements of that regulator. In the absence of indications to the contrary, such a financial reporting framework is presumed acceptable for special purpose financial statements prepared by such entity.

[10] *ISA (UK) 200 (Revised June 2016), paragraph 13(f).*

A7   Where the financial reporting standards referred to in paragraph A6 are supplemented by legislative or regulatory requirements, ISA (UK) 210 (Revised June 2016) requires the auditor to determine whether any conflicts between the financial reporting standards and the additional requirements exist, and prescribes actions to be taken by the auditor if such conflicts exist.[11]

A8   The applicable financial reporting framework may encompass the financial reporting provisions of a contract, or sources other than those described in paragraphs A6 and A7. In that case, the acceptability of the financial reporting framework in the circumstances of the engagement is determined by considering whether the framework exhibits attributes normally exhibited by acceptable financial reporting frameworks as described in Appendix 2 of ISA (UK) 210 (Revised June 2016). In the case of a special purpose framework, the relative importance to a particular engagement of each of the attributes normally exhibited by acceptable financial reporting frameworks is a matter of professional judgment. For example, for purposes of establishing the value of net assets of an entity at the date of its sale, the vendor and the purchaser may have agreed that very prudent estimates of allowances for uncollectible accounts receivable are appropriate for their needs, even though such financial information is not neutral when compared with financial information prepared in accordance with a general purpose framework.

Considerations When Planning and Performing the Audit (Ref: Para. 9)

A9   ISA (UK) 200 (Revised June 2016) requires the auditor to comply with (a) relevant ethical requirements, including those pertaining to independence, relating to financial statement audit engagements, and (b) all ISAs (UK) relevant to the audit. It also requires the auditor to comply with each requirement of an ISA (UK) unless, in the circumstances of the audit, the entire ISA (UK) is not relevant or the requirement is not relevant because it is conditional and the condition does not exist. In exceptional circumstances, the auditor may judge it necessary to depart from a relevant requirement in an ISA (UK) by performing alternative audit procedures to achieve the aim of that requirement.[12]

A10   Application of some of the requirements of the ISAs (UK) in an audit of special purpose financial statements may require special consideration by the auditor. For example, in ISA (UK) 320 (Revised June 2016), judgments about matters that are material to users of the financial statements are based on a consideration of the common financial information needs of users as a group.[13] In the case of an audit of special purpose financial statements, however, those judgments are based on a consideration of the financial information needs of the intended users.

A11   In the case of special purpose financial statements, such as those prepared in accordance with the requirements of a contract, management may agree with the intended users on a threshold below which misstatements identified during the audit will not be corrected or otherwise adjusted. The existence of such a threshold does not relieve the auditor from the requirement to determine materiality in accordance with ISA (UK) 320 (Revised June 2016) for purposes of planning and performing the audit of the special purpose financial statements.

---

[11] *ISA (UK) 210 (Revised June 2016), paragraph 18.*

[12] *ISA (UK) 200 (Revised June 2016), paragraphs 14, 18, and 22–23.*

[13] *ISA (UK) 320 (Revised June 2016),* Materiality in Planning and Performing an Audit, *paragraph 2.*

ISA (UK) 260 (Revised June 2016) requires the auditor to determine the appropriate   **A12**
person(s) within the entity's governance structure with whom to communicate.[14] ISA (UK)
260 (Revised June 2016) notes that, in some cases, all of those charged governance are
involved in managing the entity, and the application of the communication requirements
is modified to recognize this position.[15] When a complete set of general purpose financial
statements is also prepared by the entity, those person(s) responsible for the oversight of
the preparation of the special purpose financial statements may not be the same as those
charged with governance responsible for the oversight of the preparation of those general
purpose financial statements.

Forming an Opinion and Reporting Considerations (Ref: Para. 11)

The Appendix to this ISA (UK)[14a] contains illustrations of independent auditor's[2] reports   **A13**
on special purpose financial statements. Other illustrations of auditor's reports may
be relevant to reporting on special purpose financial statements (see for example, the
Appendices to ISA (UK) 700 (Revised June 2016), ISA (UK) 705 (Revised June 2016),[16]
ISA (UK) 570 (Revised June 2016),[17] ISA (UK) 720 (Revised June 2016), and ISA (UK)
706 (Revised June 2016)).[18]

Application of ISA (UK) 700 (Revised June 2016) When Reporting on Special Purpose Financial Statements

Paragraph 11 of this ISA (UK) explains that the auditor is required to apply ISA (UK) 700   **A14**
(Revised June 2016) when forming an opinion and reporting on special purpose financial
statements. In doing so, the auditor is also required to apply the reporting requirements in
other ISAs (UK) and may find the special considerations addressed in paragraphs A15–
A19 below helpful.

Going Concern

Special purpose financial statements may or may not be prepared in accordance with   **A15**
a financial reporting framework for which the going concern basis of accounting is relevant
(e.g., the going concern basis of accounting is not relevant for some financial statements
prepared on a tax basis in particular jurisdictions).[19] Depending on the applicable financial
reporting framework used in the preparation of the special purpose financial statements,
the description in the auditor's report of management's responsibilities[20] relating to going
concern may need to be adapted as necessary. The description in the auditor's report of

---

[14] *ISA (UK) 260 (Revised June 2016)*, Communication with Those Charged with Governance.

[15] *ISA (UK) 260 (Revised June 2016), paragraph A8.*

[14a] *The examples in the Appendix have not been tailored for the UK.*

[16] *ISA (UK) 705 (Revised June 2016)*, Modifications to the Opinion in the Independent Auditor's Report.

[17] *ISA (UK) 570 (Revised June 2016)*, Going Concern.

[18] *ISA (UK) 706 (Revised June 2016)*, Emphasis of Matter Paragraphs and Other Matter Paragraphs in the
Independent Auditor's Report.

[19] *ISA (UK) 570 (Revised June 2016)*, Going Concern, *paragraph 2.*

[20] *See ISA (UK) 700 (Revised June 2016), paragraphs 34(b) and A48.*

the auditor's responsibilities[21] may also need to be adapted as necessary depending on how ISA (UK) 570 (Revised June 2016) applies in the circumstances of the engagement.

Key Audit Matters

A16   ISA (UK) 700 (Revised June 2016) requires the auditor to communicate key audit matters in accordance with ISA (UK) 701[22] for audits of complete sets of general purpose financial statements of listed entities. For audits of special purpose financial statements, ISA (UK) 701 only applies when communication of key audit matters in the auditor's report on the special purpose financial statements is required by law or regulation or the auditor otherwise decides to communicate key audit matters. When key audit matters are communicated in the auditor's report on special purpose financial statements, ISA (UK) 701 applies in its entirety.[23]

Other Information

A17   ISA (UK) 720 (Revised June 2016)[24] deals with the auditor's responsibilities relating to other information. In the context of this ISA (UK), reports containing or accompanying the special purpose financial statements—the purpose of which is to provide owners (or similar stakeholders) with information on matters presented in the special purpose financial statements—are considered to be annual reports for the purpose of ISA (UK) 720 (Revised June 2016). In the case of financial statements prepared using a special purpose framework, the term 'similar stakeholders' includes the specific users whose financial information needs are met by the design of the special purpose framework used to prepare the special purpose financial statements. When the auditor determines that the entity plans to issue such a report, the requirements in ISA (UK) 720 (Revised June 2016) apply to the audit of the special purpose financial statements.

Name of the Engagement Partner

A18   The requirement in ISA (UK) 700 (Revised June 2016) for the auditor to include the name of the engagement partner in the auditor's report also applies to audits of special purpose financial statements of listed entities.[25] The auditor may be required by law or regulation to include the name of the engagement partner in the auditor's report or may otherwise decide to do so when reporting on special purpose financial statements of entities other than listed entities.

Inclusion of a Reference to the Auditor's Report on the Complete Set of General Purpose Financial Statements

A19   The auditor may deem it appropriate to refer, in an Other Matter paragraph in the auditor's report on the special purpose financial statements, to the auditor's report on the complete set of general purpose financial statements or to matter(s) reported therein (see ISA (UK)

---

[21] *See ISA (UK) 700 (Revised June 2016), paragraph 39(b)(iv).*

[22] *ISA (UK) 701, Communicating Key Audit Matters in the Independent Auditor's Report.*

[23] *ISA (UK) 700 (Revised June 2016), paragraph 31.*

[24] *ISA (UK) 720 (Revised June 2016), The Auditor's Responsibilities Relating to Other Information.*

[25] *See ISA (UK) 700 (Revised June 2016), paragraphs 45 and A56–A58.*

706 (Revised June 2016)).[26] For example, the auditor may consider it appropriate to refer in the auditor's report on the special purpose financial statements to a Material Uncertainty Related to Going Concern section included in the auditor's report on the complete set of general purpose financial statements.

Alerting Readers that the Financial Statements Are Prepared in Accordance with a Special Purpose Framework (Ref: Para. 14)

The special purpose financial statements may be used for purposes other than those for which they were intended. For example, a regulator may require certain entities to place the special purpose financial statements on public record. To avoid misunderstandings, the auditor alerts users of the auditor's report by including an Emphasis of Matter paragraph explaining that the financial statements are prepared in accordance with a special purpose framework and, therefore, may not be suitable for another purpose. ISA (UK) 706 (Revised June 2016) requires this paragraph to be included within a separate section of the auditor's report with an appropriate heading that includes the term 'Emphasis of Matter'.[27]   **A20**

Restriction on Distribution or Use (Ref: Para. 14)

In addition to the alert required by paragraph 14, the auditor may consider it appropriate to indicate that the auditor's report is intended solely for the specific users. Depending on the law or regulation of the particular jurisdiction, this may be achieved by restricting the distribution or use of the auditor's report. In these circumstances, the paragraph referred to in paragraph 14 may be expanded to include these other matters, and the heading modified accordingly (see illustrations in the Appendix to this ISA (UK)[26a]).   **A21**

---

[26] *See ISA (UK) 706 (Revised June 2016), paragraphs 10–11.*

[27] *See paragraph 9(a) of ISA (UK) 706 (Revised June 2016).*

[26a] *The examples in the Appendix have not been tailored for the UK.*

Appendix

Illustrations of Independent Auditor's Reports on Special Purpose Financial Statements

The examples in the Appendix have not been tailored for the UK.

- Illustration 1: An auditor's report on a complete set of financial statements of an entity other than a listed entity prepared in accordance with the financial reporting provisions of a contract (for purposes of this illustration, a compliance framework).
- Illustration 2: An auditor's report on a complete set of financial statements of an entity other than a listed entity prepared in accordance with the tax basis of accounting in Jurisdiction X (for purposes of this illustration, a compliance framework).
- Illustration 3: An auditor's report on a complete set of financial statements of a listed entity prepared in accordance with the financial reporting provisions established by a regulator (for purposes of this illustration, a fair presentation framework).

Illustration 1: An auditor's report on a complete set of financial statements of an entity other than a listed entity prepared in accordance with the financial reporting provisions of a contract (for purposes of this illustration, a compliance framework).

For purposes of this illustrative auditor's report, the following circumstances are assumed:
- The financial statements have been prepared by management of the entity in accordance with the financial reporting provisions of a contract (that is, a special purpose framework). Management does not have a choice of financial reporting frameworks.
- The applicable financial reporting framework is a compliance framework.
- An auditor's report on the complete set of general purpose financial statements was not issued.
- The terms of the audit engagement reflect the description of management's responsibility for the financial statements in ISA 210.
- The auditor has concluded an unmodified (i.e., 'clean') opinion is appropriate based on the audit evidence obtained.
- The relevant ethical requirements that apply to the audit are those of the jurisdiction.
- Based on the audit evidence obtained, the auditor has concluded that a material uncertainty does not exist related to events or conditions that may cast significant doubt on the entity's ability to continue as a going concern in accordance with ISA 570 (Revised).
- Distribution and use of the auditor's report are restricted.
- The auditor is not required, and has otherwise not decided, to communicate key audit matters in accordance with ISA 701.
- The auditor has determined that there is no other information (i.e., the requirements of ISA 720 (Revised) do not apply).
- Those responsible for oversight of the financial reporting process differ from those responsible for the preparation of the financial statements.
- The auditor has no other reporting responsibilities required under local law or regulation.

INDEPENDENT AUDITOR'S REPORT

[Appropriate Addressee]

Opinion

We have audited the financial statements of ABC Company (the Company), which comprise the balance sheet as at December 31, 20X1, and the income statement, statement of changes in equity and cash flow statement for the year then ended, and notes to the financial statements, including a summary of significant accounting policies.

In our opinion, the accompanying financial statements of the Company for the year ended December 31, 20X1 are prepared, in all material respects, in accordance with the financial reporting provisions of Section Z of the contract dated January 1, 20X1 between the Company and DEF Company ('the contract'). [Opinion section positioned first as required in ISA 700 (Revised)]

Basis for Opinion

We conducted our audit in accordance with International Standards on Auditing (ISAs). Our responsibilities under those standards are further described in the *Auditor's Responsibilities for the Audit of the Financial Statements* section of our report. We are independent of the Company in accordance with the ethical requirements that are relevant to our audit of the financial statements in [*jurisdiction*], and we have fulfilled our other ethical responsibilities in accordance with these requirements. We believe that the audit evidence we have obtained is sufficient and appropriate to provide a basis for our opinion. [The first and last sentences in this section used to be in the Auditor's Responsibility section. Also, the Basis for Opinion section is positioned immediately after the Opinion section as required in ISA 700 (Revised).]

Emphasis of Matter –Basis of Accounting and Restriction on Distribution and Use

We draw attention to Note X to the financial statements, which describes the basis of accounting. The financial statements are prepared to assist the Company in complying with the financial reporting provisions of the contract referred to above. As a result, the financial statements may not be suitable for another purpose. Our report is intended solely for the Company and DEF Company and should not be distributed to or used by parties other than the Company or DEF Company. Our opinion is not modified in respect of this matter.

Responsibilities of Management and Those Charged with Governance for the Financial Statements[28]

Management is responsible for the preparation of the financial statements in accordance with the financial reporting provisions of Section Z of the contract and for such internal control as management determines is necessary to enable the preparation of financial statements that are free from material misstatement, whether due to fraud or error.

---

[28] *Throughout these illustrative auditor's reports, the terms management and those charged with governance may need to be replaced by another term that is appropriate in the context of the legal framework in the particular jurisdiction.*

In preparing the financial statements, management is responsible for assessing the Company's ability to continue as a going concern, disclosing, as applicable, matters relating to going concern and using the going concern basis of accounting unless management either intends to liquidate the Company or to cease operations, or has no realistic alternative but to do so.

Those charged with governance are responsible for overseeing the Company's financial reporting process.

Auditor's Responsibilities for the Audit of the Financial Statements

Our objectives are to obtain reasonable assurance about whether the financial statements as a whole are free from material misstatement, whether due to fraud or error, and to issue an auditor's report that includes our opinion. Reasonable assurance is a high level of assurance, but is not a guarantee that an audit conducted in accordance with ISAs will always detect a material misstatement when it exists. Misstatements can arise from fraud or error and are considered material if, individually or in the aggregate, they could reasonably be expected to influence the economic decisions of users taken on the basis of these financial statements.

Paragraph 41(b) of ISA 700 (Revised) explains that the shaded material below can be located in an Appendix to the auditor's report. Paragraph 41(c) of ISA 700 (Revised) explains that when law, regulation or national auditing standards expressly permit, reference can be made to a website of an appropriate authority that contains the description of the auditor's responsibilities, rather than including this material in the auditor's report, provided that the description on the website addresses, and is not inconsistent with, the description of the auditor's responsibilities below.

As part of an audit in accordance with ISAs, we exercise professional judgment and maintain professional skepticism throughout the audit. We also:

- Identify and assess the risks of material misstatement of the financial statements, whether due to fraud or error, design and perform audit procedures responsive to those risks, and obtain audit evidence that is sufficient and appropriate to provide a basis for our opinion. The risk of not detecting a material misstatement resulting from fraud is higher than for one resulting from error, as fraud may involve collusion, forgery, intentional omissions, misrepresentations, or the override of internal control.
- Obtain an understanding of internal control relevant to the audit in order to design audit procedures that are appropriate in the circumstances, but not for the purpose of expressing an opinion on the effectiveness of the Company's internal control.[29]
- Evaluate the appropriateness of accounting policies used and the reasonableness of accounting estimates and related disclosures made by management.
- Conclude on the appropriateness of management's use of the going concern basis of accounting and, based on the audit evidence obtained, whether a material uncertainty exists related to events or conditions that may cast significant doubt on the Company's ability to continue as a going concern. If we conclude that a material uncertainty exists, we are required to draw attention in our auditor's report to the related disclosures in the financial statements or, if such disclosures are inadequate, to modify our opinion. Our conclusions are based on the audit evidence obtained up to the date of our auditor's report. However, future events or conditions may cause the Company to cease to continue as a going concern.

---

[29] *This sentence would be modified, as appropriate, in circumstances when the auditor also has responsibility to issue an opinion on the effectiveness of internal control in conjunction with the audit of the financial statements.*

We communicate with those charged with governance regarding, among other matters, the planned scope and timing of the audit and significant audit findings, including any significant deficiencies in internal control that we identify during our audit.

Signature in the name of the audit firm, the personal name of the auditor, or both, as appropriate for the particular jurisdiction]

[*Auditor address*] [Placement of date and address reversed)]

[*Date*]

Illustration 2: An auditor's report on a complete set of financial statements of an entity other than a listed entity prepared in accordance with the tax basis of accounting in Jurisdiction X (for purposes of this illustration, a compliance framework).

For purposes of this illustrative auditor's report, the following circumstances are assumed:

- Audit of a complete set of financial statements that have been prepared by management of a partnership in accordance with the tax basis of accounting in Jurisdiction X (that is, a special purpose framework) to assist the partners in preparing their individual income tax returns. Management does not have a choice of financial reporting frameworks.
- The applicable financial reporting framework is a compliance framework
- The terms of the audit engagement reflect the description of management's responsibility for the financial statements in ISA 210.
- The auditor has concluded an unmodified (i.e., 'clean') opinion is appropriate based on the audit evidence obtained.
- The relevant ethical requirements that apply to the audit are those of the jurisdiction.
- Based on the audit evidence obtained, the auditor has concluded that a material uncertainty does not exist related to events or conditions that may cast significant doubt on the entity's ability to continue as a going concern in accordance with ISA 570 (Revised).
- Distribution of the auditor's report is restricted.
- The auditor is not required, and has otherwise not decided, to communicate key audit matters in accordance with ISA 701.
- The auditor has determined that there is no other information (i.e., the requirements of ISA 720 (Revised) do not apply).
- Those responsible for oversight of the financial statements differ from those responsible for the preparation of the financial statements.
- The auditor has no other reporting responsibilities required under local law or regulation.

INDEPENDENT AUDITOR'S REPORT

[Appropriate Addressee]

Opinion

We have audited the financial statements of ABC Partnership (the Partnership), which comprise the balance sheet as at December 31, 20X1 and the income statement for the year then ended, and notes to the financial statements, including a summary of significant accounting policies.

In our opinion, the accompanying financial statements of the Partnership for the year ended December 31, 20X1 are prepared, in all material respects, in accordance with [*describe the applicable income tax law*] of Jurisdiction X. [Opinion section positioned first as required in ISA 700 (Revised)]

Basis for Opinion

We conducted our audit in accordance with International Standards on Auditing (ISAs). Our responsibilities under those standards are further described in the *Auditor's Responsibilities for the Audit of the Financial Statements* section of our report. We are independent of the Partnership in accordance with the ethical requirements that are relevant to our audit of the financial statements in [*jurisdiction*], and we have fulfilled our other ethical responsibilities in accordance with these requirements. We believe that the audit evidence we have obtained is sufficient and appropriate to provide a basis for our opinion. [The first and last sentences in this section used to be in the Auditor's Responsibility section. Also, the Basis for Opinion section is positioned immediately after the Opinion section as required in ISA 700 (Revised).]

Emphasis of Matter – Basis of Accounting and Restriction on Distribution

We draw attention to Note X to the financial statements, which describes the basis of accounting. The financial statements are prepared to assist the partners of the Partnership in preparing their individual income tax returns. As a result, the financial statements may not be suitable for another purpose. Our report is intended solely for the Partnership and its partners and should not be distributed to parties other than the Partnership or its partners. Our opinion is not modified in respect of this matter.

Responsibilities of Management and Those Charged with Governance for the Financial Statements[30]

Management is responsible for the preparation of the financial statements in accordance with the tax basis of accounting in Jurisdiction X and for such internal control as management determines is necessary to enable the preparation of financial statements that are free from material misstatement, whether due to fraud or error.

In preparing the financial statements, management is responsible for assessing the Company's ability to continue as a going concern, disclosing, as applicable, matters relating to going concern and using the going concern basis of accounting unless management either intends to liquidate the Company or to cease operations, or has no realistic alternative but to do so.

Those charged with governance are responsible for overseeing the Partnership's financial reporting process.

Auditor's Responsibilities for the Audit of the Financial Statements

Our objectives are to obtain reasonable assurance about whether the financial statements as a whole are free from material misstatement, whether due to fraud or error, and to

---

[30] *Or other terms that are appropriate in the context of the legal framework in the particular jurisdiction.*

issue an auditor's report that includes our opinion. Reasonable assurance is a high level of assurance, but is not a guarantee that an audit conducted in accordance with International Standards on Auditing (ISAs) will always detect a material misstatement when it exists. Misstatements can arise from fraud or error and are considered material if, individually or in the aggregate, they could reasonably be expected to influence the economic decisions of users taken on the basis of these financial statements.

Paragraph 41(b) of ISA 700 (Revised) explains that the shaded material below can be located in an Appendix to the auditor's report. Paragraph 41(c) of ISA 700 (Revised) explains that when law, regulation or national auditing standards expressly permit, reference can be made to a website of an appropriate authority that contains the description of the auditor's responsibilities, rather than including this material in the auditor's report, provided that the description on the website addresses, and is not inconsistent with, the description of the auditor's responsibilities below.

As part of an audit in accordance with ISAs, we exercise professional judgment and maintain professional skepticism throughout the audit. We also:

- Identify and assess the risks of material misstatement of the financial statements, whether due to fraud or error, design and perform audit procedures responsive to those risks, and obtain audit evidence that is sufficient and appropriate to provide a basis for our opinion. The risk of not detecting a material misstatement resulting from fraud is higher than for one resulting from error, as fraud may involve collusion, forgery, intentional omissions, misrepresentations, or the override of internal control.
- Obtain an understanding of internal control relevant to the audit in order to design audit procedures that are appropriate in the circumstances, but not for the purpose of expressing an opinion on the effectiveness of the Partnership's internal control.[31]
- Conclude on the appropriateness of management's use of the going concern basis of accounting and, based on the audit evidence obtained, whether a material uncertainty exists related to events or conditions that may cast significant doubt on the Company's ability to continue as a going concern. If we conclude that a material uncertainty exists, we are required to draw attention in our auditor's report to the related disclosures in the financial statements or, if such disclosures are inadequate, to modify our opinion. Our conclusions are based on the audit evidence obtained up to the date of our auditor's report. However, future events or conditions may cause the Company to cease to continue as a going concern.
- Evaluate the appropriateness of accounting policies used and the reasonableness of accounting estimates and related disclosures made by management.

We communicate with those charged with governance regarding, among other matters, the planned scope and timing of the audit and significant audit findings, including any significant deficiencies in internal control that we identify during our audit.

[*Signature in the name of the audit firm, the personal name of the auditor, or both, as appropriate for the particular jurisdiction*]

[*Auditor address*] [Placement of date and address reversed)]

[*Date*]

---

[31] *This sentence would be modified, as appropriate, in circumstances when the auditor also has responsibility to issue an opinion on the effectiveness of internal control in conjunction with the audit of the financial statements.*

Illustration 3: An auditor's report on a complete set of financial statements of a listed entity prepared in accordance with the financial reporting provisions established by a regulator (for purposes of this illustration, a fair presentation framework).

For purposes of this illustrative auditor's report, the following circumstances are assumed:

- Audit of a complete set of financial statements of a listed entity that have been prepared by management of the entity in accordance with the financial reporting provisions established by a regulator (that is, a special purpose framework) to meet the requirements of that regulator. Management does not have a choice of financial reporting frameworks.
- The applicable financial reporting framework is a fair presentation framework.
- The terms of the audit engagement reflect the description of management's responsibility for the financial statements in ISA 210.
- The auditor has concluded an unmodified (i.e., 'clean') opinion is appropriate based on the audit evidence obtained.
- The relevant ethical requirements that apply to the audit are those of the jurisdiction.
- Based on the audit evidence obtained, the auditor has concluded that a material uncertainty exists related to events or conditions that may cast significant doubt on the entity's ability to continue as a going concern in accordance with ISA 570 (Revised). The disclosure of the material uncertainty in the financial statements is adequate.
- Distribution or use of the auditor's report is not restricted.
- The auditor is required by the regulator to communicate key audit matters in accordance with ISA 701.
- The auditor has determined that there is no other information (i.e., the requirements of ISA 720 (Revised) do not apply).
- Those responsible for oversight of the financial statements differ from those responsible for the preparation of the financial statements.
- The auditor has no other reporting responsibilities required under local law or regulation.

INDEPENDENT AUDITOR'S REPORT

[To the Shareholders of ABC Company or Appropriate Addressee]

Opinion

We have audited the financial statements of ABC Company (the Company), which comprise the balance sheet as at December 31, 20X1, and the income statement, statement of changes in equity and cash flow statement for the year then ended, and notes to the financial statements, including a summary of significant accounting policies.

In our opinion, the accompanying financial statements present fairly, in all material respects, (or *give a true and fair view of*) the financial position of the Company as at December 31, 20X1, and (*of*) its financial performance and its cash flows for the year then ended in accordance with the financial reporting provisions of Section Y of Regulation Z.
[Opinion section positioned first as required in ISA 700 (Revised)]

Basis for Opinion

We conducted our audit in accordance with International Standards on Auditing (ISAs). Our responsibilities under those standards are further described in the *Auditor's Responsibilities for the Audit of the Financial Statements* section of our report. We are independent of the Company in accordance with the ethical requirements that are relevant to our audit of the financial statements in [*jurisdiction*], and we have fulfilled our other ethical responsibilities in accordance with these requirements. We believe that the audit evidence we have obtained is sufficient and appropriate to provide a basis for our opinion. [The first and last sentences in this section used to be in the Auditor's Responsibility section. Also, the Basis for Opinion section is positioned immediately after the Opinion section as required in ISA 700 (Revised).]

Emphasis of Matter – Basis of Accounting

We draw attention to Note X to the financial statements, which describes the basis of accounting. The financial statements are prepared to assist the Company to meet the requirements of Regulator DEF. As a result, the financial statements may not be suitable for another purpose. Our opinion is not modified in respect of this matter.

Material Uncertainty Related to Going Concern

We draw attention to Note 6 in the financial statements, which indicates that the Company incurred a net loss of ZZZ during the year ended December 31, 20X1 and, as of that date, the Company's current liabilities exceeded its total assets by YYY. As stated in Note 6, these events or conditions, along with other matters as set forth in Note 6, indicate that a material uncertainty exists that may cast significant doubt on the Company's ability to continue as a going concern. Our opinion is not modified in respect of this matter.

Key Audit Matters

Key audit matters are those matters that, in our professional judgment, were of most significance in our audit of the financial statements of the current period. These matters were addressed in the context of our audit of the financial statements as a whole, and in forming our opinion thereon, and we do not provide a separate opinion on these matters. In addition to the matter described in the Material Uncertainty Related to Going Concern section above, we have determined the matters described below to be key audit matters to be communicated in our report.

[*Description of each key audit matter in accordance with ISA 701 as applied to this audit.*]

Other Matter

The Company has prepared a separate set of financial statements for the year ended December 31, 20X1 in accordance with International Financial Reporting Standards on which we issued a separate auditor's report to the shareholders of the Company dated March 31, 20X2.

Responsibilities of Management and Those Charged with Governance for the Financial Statements[32]

Management is responsible for the preparation and fair presentation of the financial statements in accordance with the financial reporting provisions of Section Y of Regulation Z[33] and for such internal control as management determines is necessary to enable the preparation of financial statements that are free from material misstatement, whether due to fraud or error.

In preparing the financial statements, management is responsible for assessing the Company's ability to continue as a going concern, disclosing, as applicable, matters relating to going concern and using the going concern basis of accounting unless management either intends to liquidate the Company or to cease operations, or has no realistic alternative but to do so.

Those charged with governance are responsible for overseeing the Company's financial reporting process.

Auditor's Responsibilities for the Audit of the Financial Statements

Our objectives are to obtain reasonable assurance about whether the financial statements as a whole are free from material misstatement, whether due to fraud or error, and to issue an auditor's report that includes our opinion. Reasonable assurance is a high level of assurance, but is not a guarantee that an audit conducted in accordance with International Standards on Auditing (ISAs) will always detect a material misstatement when it exists. Misstatements can arise from fraud or error and are considered material if, individually or in the aggregate, they could reasonably be expected to influence the economic decisions of users taken on the basis of these financial statements.

Paragraph 41(b) of ISA 700 (Revised) explains that the shaded material below can be located in an Appendix to the auditor's report. Paragraph 41(c) of ISA 700 (Revised) explains that when law, regulation or national auditing standards expressly permit, reference can be made to a website of an appropriate authority that contains the description of the auditor's responsibilities, rather than including this material in the auditor's report, provided that the description on the website addresses, and is not inconsistent with, the description of the auditor's responsibilities below.

As part of an audit in accordance with ISAs, we exercise professional judgment and maintain professional skepticism throughout the audit. We also:

- Identify and assess the risks of material misstatement of the financial statements, whether due to fraud or error, design and perform audit procedures responsive to those risks, and obtain audit evidence that is sufficient and appropriate to provide a basis for our opinion. The risk of not detecting a material misstatement resulting from fraud is higher than for one resulting from error, as fraud may involve collusion, forgery, intentional omissions, misrepresentations, or the override of internal control.

---

[32] *Or other terms that are appropriate in the context of the legal framework in the particular jurisdiction.*

[33] *Where management's responsibility is to prepare financial statements that give a true and fair view, this may read: 'Management is responsible for the preparation of a financial statements that give a true and fair view in accordance with the financial reporting provisions of section Y of Regulation Z and for such ...'.*

- Obtain an understanding of internal control relevant to audit in order to design audit procedures that are appropriate in the circumstances, but not for the purpose of expressing an opinion on the effectiveness of the Company's internal control.[34]
- Evaluate the appropriateness of accounting policies used and the reasonableness of accounting estimates and related disclosures made by management.
- Conclude on the appropriateness of management's use of the going concern basis of accounting and, based on the audit evidence obtained, whether a material uncertainty exists related to events or conditions that may cast significant doubt on the Company's ability to continue as a going concern. If we conclude that a material uncertainty exists, we are required to draw attention in our auditor's report to the related disclosures in the financial statements or, if such disclosures are inadequate, to modify our opinion. Our conclusions are based on the audit evidence obtained up to the date of our auditor's report. However, future events or conditions may cause the Company to cease to continue as a going concern.
- Evaluate the overall presentation, structure and content of the financial statements, including the disclosures, and whether the financial statements represent the underlying transactions and events in a manner that achieves fair presentation.

We communicate with those charged with governance regarding, among other matters, the planned scope and timing of the audit and significant audit findings, including any significant deficiencies in internal control that we identify during our audit.

We also provide those charged with governance with a statement that we have complied with relevant ethical requirements regarding independence, and to communicate with them all relationships and other matters that may reasonably be thought to bear on our independence, and where applicable, related safeguards.

From the matters communicated with those charged with governance, we determine those matters that were of most significance in the audit of the financial statements of the current period and are therefore the key audit matters. We describe these matters in our auditor's report unless law or regulation precludes public disclosure about the matter or when, in extremely rare circumstances, we determine that a matter should not be communicated in our report because the adverse consequences of doing so would reasonably be expected to outweigh the public interest benefits of such communication.

The engagement partner on the audit resulting in this independent auditor's report is [*name*].

[*Signature in the name of the audit firm, the personal name of the auditor, or both, as appropriate for the particular jurisdiction*]

[*Auditor address*] [Placement of date and address reversed)]

[*Date*]

---

[34] *This sentence would be modified, as appropriate, in circumstances when the auditor also has responsibility to issue an opinion on the effectiveness of internal control in conjunction with the audit of the financial statements.*

International Standard on Auditing (UK) 805 (October 2016)

Special considerations—audits of single financial statements and specific elements, accounts or items of a financial statement

(Effective for audits for periods commencing on or after 1 January 2017)

Contents

International Standard on Auditing (UK) (ISA (UK)) 805 (Revised), *Special Considerations—Audits of Single Financial Statements and Specific Elements, Accounts or Items of a Financial Statement*, should be read in conjunction with ISA (UK) 200 (Revised June 2016), *Overall Objectives of the Independent Auditor and the Conduct of an Audit in Accordance with International Standards on Auditing (UK)*.

Introduction

Scope of this ISA (UK)

The International Standards on Auditing (UK) (ISAs (UK)) in the 100–700 series apply **1** to an audit of financial statements and are to be adapted as necessary in the circumstances when applied to audits of other historical financial information. This ISA (UK) deals with special considerations in the application of those ISAs (UK) to an audit of a single financial statement or of a specific element, account or item of a financial statement. The single financial statement or the specific element, account or item of a financial statement may be prepared in accordance with a general or special purpose framework. If prepared in accordance with a special purpose framework, ISA (UK) 800 (Revised)[1] also applies to the audit. (Ref: Para. A1–A4)

This ISA (UK) does not apply to the report of a component auditor, issued as a result of **2** work performed on the financial information of a component at the request of a group engagement team for purposes of an audit of group financial statements (see ISA (UK) 600 (Revised June 2016)).[2]

This ISA (UK) does not override the requirements of the other ISAs (UK); nor does it **3** purport to deal with all special considerations that may be relevant in the circumstances of the engagement.

Effective Date

This ISA (UK) is effective for audits of single financial statements or of specific elements, **4** accounts or items for periods commencing on or after 1 January 2017, early adoption is permitted[3]. In the case of audits of single financial statements or of specific elements, accounts or items of a financial statement as at a specific date, this ISA (UK) is effective for audits of such information as at a date on or after 1 January 2017, early adoption is permitted.[3]

Objective

The objective of the auditor, when applying ISAs (UK) in an audit of a single financial **5** statement or of a specific element, account or item of a financial statement, is to address appropriately the special considerations that are relevant to:

(a) The acceptance of the engagement;
(b) The planning and performance of that engagement; and
(c) Forming an opinion and reporting on the single financial statement or on the specific element, account or item of a financial statement.

---

[1] *ISA (UK) 800 (Revised)*, Special Considerations—Audits of Financial Statements Prepared in Accordance with Special Purpose Frameworks.

[2] *ISA (UK) 600 (Revised June 2016)*, Special Considerations—Audits of Group Financial Statements (Including the Work of Component Auditors).

[3] *Where ISA 805 (Revised) is adopted early for the audit of Solvency II Regulatory Returns for periods commencing prior to 1 January 2017 it may be used in conjunction with ISAs (UK and Ireland) where the audit of the statutory financial statements for the same period was conducted in accordance with ISAs (UK and Ireland).*

Definitions

6   For purposes of this ISA (UK), reference to:

(a)   'Element of a financial statement' or 'element' means an 'element, account or item of a financial statement;'

(b)   'International Financial Reporting Standards' means the International Financial Reporting Standards (IFRSs) issued by the International Accounting Standards Board; and

(c)   A single financial statement or to a specific element of a financial statement includes the related disclosures. (Ref: Para. A2)

Requirements

Considerations When Accepting the Engagement

Application of ISAs (UK)

7   ISA (UK) 200 (Revised June 2016) requires the auditor to comply with all ISAs (UK) relevant to the audit.[4] In the case of an audit of a single financial statement or of a specific element of a financial statement, this requirement applies irrespective of whether the auditor is also engaged to audit the entity's complete set of financial statements. If the auditor is not also engaged to audit the entity's complete set of financial statements, the auditor shall determine whether the audit of a single financial statement or of a specific element of those financial statements in accordance with ISAs (UK) is practicable. (Ref: Para. A5–A6)

Acceptability of the Financial Reporting Framework

8   ISA (UK) 210 (Revised June 2016) requires the auditor to determine the acceptability of the financial reporting framework applied in the preparation of the financial statements.[5] In the case of an audit of a single financial statement or of a specific element of a financial statement, this shall include whether application of the financial reporting framework will result in a presentation that provides adequate disclosures to enable the intended users to understand the information conveyed in the financial statement or the element, and the effect of material transactions and events on the information conveyed in the financial statement or the element. (Ref: Para. A7)

Form of Opinion

9   ISA (UK) 210 (Revised June 2016) requires that the agreed terms of the audit engagement include the expected form of any reports to be issued by the auditor.[6] In the case of an audit of a single financial statement or of a specific element of a financial statement, the auditor shall consider whether the expected form of opinion is appropriate in the circumstances. (Ref: Para. A8–A9)

---

[4] *ISA (UK) 200 (Revised June 2016)*, Overall Objectives of the Independent Auditor and the Conduct of an Audit in Accordance with International Standards on Auditing (UK), *paragraph 18*.

[5] *ISA (UK) 210 (Revised June 2016)*, Agreeing the Terms of Audit Engagements, *paragraph 6(a)*.

[6] *ISA (UK) 210 (Revised June 2016)*, *paragraph 10(e)*.

Considerations When Planning and Performing the Audit

ISA (UK) 200 (Revised June 2016) states that ISAs (UK) are written in the context of an **10** audit of financial statements; they are to be adapted as necessary in the circumstances when applied to audits of other historical financial information.[7],[8] In planning and performing the audit of a single financial statement or of a specific element of a financial statement, the auditor shall adapt all ISAs (UK) relevant to the audit as necessary in the circumstances of the engagement. (Ref: Para. A10–A15)

Forming an Opinion and Reporting Considerations

When forming an opinion and reporting on a single financial statement or on **11** a specific element of a financial statement, the auditor shall apply the requirements in ISA (UK) 700 (Revised June 2016),[9] and, when applicable, ISA (UK) 800 (Revised) adapted as necessary in the circumstances of the engagement. (Ref: Para. A16–A22)

Reporting on the Entity's Complete Set of Financial Statements and on a Single Financial Statement or on a Specific Element of Those Financial Statements

If the auditor undertakes an engagement to report on a single financial statement or on **12** a specific element of a financial statement in conjunction with an engagement to audit the entity's complete set of financial statements, the auditor shall express a separate opinion for each engagement.

The audited single financial statement or the audited specific element of a financial **13** statement may be published together with the entity's audited complete set of financial statements. If the auditor concludes that the presentation of the single financial statement or of the specific element of a financial statement does not differentiate it sufficiently from the complete set of financial statements, the auditor shall ask management to rectify the situation. Subject to paragraphs 15 and 16, the auditor shall also differentiate the opinion on the single financial statement or on the specific element of a financial statement from the opinion on the complete set of financial statements. The auditor shall not issue the auditor's report containing the opinion on the single financial statement or on the specific element of a financial statement until satisfied with the differentiation.

Considering the Implications of Certain Matters Included in the Auditor's Report on the Entity's Complete Set of Financial Statements for the Audit of the Single Financial Statement or the Specific Element of a Financial Statement and for the Auditor's Report Thereon

---

[7] *ISA (UK) 200 (Revised June 2016), paragraph 2.*

[8] *ISA (UK) 200 (Revised June 2016), paragraph 13(f), explains that the term 'financial statements' ordinarily refers to a complete set of financial statements as determined by the requirements of the applicable financial reporting framework.*

[9] *ISA (UK) 700 (Revised June 2016)*, Forming an Opinion and Reporting on Financial Statements.

14 If the auditor's report on an entity's complete set of financial statements includes:

(a) A modified opinion in accordance with ISA (UK) 705 (Revised June 2016);[10]

(b) An Emphasis of Matter paragraph or an Other Matter paragraph in accordance with ISA (UK) 706 (Revised June 2016),[11]

(c) A Material Uncertainty Related to Going Concern section in accordance with ISA (UK) 570 (Revised June 2016);[12]

(d) Communication of key audit matters in accordance with ISA (UK) 701;[13] or

(e) A statement that describes an uncorrected material misstatement of the other information in accordance with ISA (UK) 720 (Revised June 2016);[14]

the auditor shall consider the implications, if any, that these matters have for the audit of the single financial statement or of the specific element of a financial statement and for the auditor's report thereon. (Ref: Para. A23–A27)

Adverse Opinion or Disclaimer of Opinion in the Auditor's Report on the Entity's Complete Set of Financial Statements

15 If the auditor concludes that it is necessary to express an adverse opinion or disclaim an opinion on the entity's complete set of financial statements as a whole, ISA (UK) 705 (Revised June 2016) does not permit the auditor to include in the same auditor's report an unmodified opinion on a single financial statement that forms part of those financial statements or on a specific element of those financial statements.[15] This is because such an unmodified opinion would contradict the adverse opinion or disclaimer of opinion on the entity's complete set of financial statements as a whole. (Ref: Para. A28)

16 If the auditor concludes that it is necessary to express an adverse opinion or disclaim an opinion on the entity's complete set of financial statements as a whole but, in the context of a separate audit of a specific element of those financial statements, the auditor nevertheless considers it appropriate to express an unmodified opinion on that element, the auditor shall only do so if:

(a) The auditor is not prohibited by law or regulation from doing so;

(b) That opinion is expressed in an auditor's report that is not published together with the auditor's report containing the adverse opinion or disclaimer of opinion; and

(c) The element does not constitute a major portion of the entity's complete set of financial statements.

17 The auditor shall not express an unmodified opinion on a single financial statement of a complete set of financial statements if the auditor has expressed an adverse opinion or disclaimed an opinion on the complete set of financial statements as a whole. This is the case even if the auditor's report on the single financial statement is not published together with the auditor's report containing the adverse opinion or disclaimer of opinion. This

---

[10] *ISA (UK) 705 (Revised June 2016)*, Modifications to the Opinion in the Independent Auditor's Report.

[11] *ISA (UK) 706 (Revised June 2016)*, Emphasis of Matter Paragraphs and Other Matter Paragraphs in the Independent Auditor's Report.

[12] *ISA (UK) 570 (Revised June 2016)*, Going Concern, *paragraph 22*.

[13] *ISA (UK) 701*, Communicating Key Audit Matters in the Independent Auditor's Report, *paragraph 13*.

[14] *ISA (UK) 720 (Revised June 2016)*, The Auditor's Responsibilities Relating to Other Information, *paragraph 22(e)(ii)*.

[15] *ISA (UK) 705 (Revised June 2016), paragraph 15*.

is because a single financial statement is deemed to constitute a major portion of those financial statements.

***

Application and Other Explanatory Material

Scope of this ISA (UK) (Ref: Para. 1, 6(c))

ISA (UK) 200 (Revised June 2016) defines the term 'historical financial information' as information expressed in financial terms in relation to a particular entity, derived primarily from that entity's accounting system, about economic events occurring in past time periods or about economic conditions or circumstances at points in time in the past.[16]   **A1**

ISA (UK) 200 (Revised June 2016) defines the term 'financial statements' as a structured representation of historical financial information, including disclosures, intended to communicate an entity's economic resources or obligations at a point in time or the changes therein for a period of time in accordance with a financial reporting framework. The term 'financial statements' ordinarily refers to a complete set of financial statements as determined by the requirements of the applicable financial reporting framework, but can also refer to a single financial statement. Disclosures comprise explanatory or descriptive information, set out as required, expressly permitted or otherwise allowed by the applicable financial reporting framework, on the face of a financial statement, or in the notes, or incorporated therein by cross-reference.[17] As noted in paragraph 6(c), reference to a single financial statement or specific element of a financial statement includes the related disclosures.   **A2**

ISAs (UK) are written in the context of an audit of financial statements;[18] they are to be adapted as necessary in the circumstances when applied to an audit of other historical financial information, such as a single financial statement or a specific element of a financial statement. This ISA (UK) assists in this regard. (Appendix 1 lists examples of such other historical financial information.)   **A3**

A reasonable assurance engagement other than an audit of historical financial information is performed in accordance with International Standard on Assurance Engagements (ISAE) 3000 (Revised).[19]   **A4**

Considerations When Accepting the Engagement

Application of ISAs (UK) (Ref: Para. 7)

ISA (UK) 200 (Revised June 2016) requires the auditor to comply with (a) relevant ethical requirements, including those pertaining to independence, relating to financial statement audit engagements, and (b) all ISAs (UK) relevant to the audit. It also requires the auditor to comply with each requirement of an ISA (UK) unless, in the circumstances of the audit, the entire ISA (UK) is not relevant or the requirement is not relevant because it is conditional and the condition does not exist. In exceptional circumstances, the auditor may   **A5**

---

[16] *ISA (UK) 200 (Revised June 2016), paragraph 13(g).*

[17] *ISA (UK) 200 (Revised June 2016), paragraph 13(f).*

[18] *ISA (UK) 200 (Revised June 2016), paragraph 2.*

[19] *ISAE 3000 (Revised),* Assurance Engagements Other than Audits or Reviews of Historical Financial Information.

judge it necessary to depart from a relevant requirement in an ISA (UK) by performing alternative audit procedures to achieve the aim of that requirement.[20]

A6   Compliance with the requirements of ISAs (UK) relevant to the audit of a single financial statement or of a specific element of a financial statement may not be practicable when the auditor is not also engaged to audit the entity's complete set of financial statements. In such cases, the auditor often does not have the same understanding of the entity and its environment, including its internal control, as an auditor who also audits the entity's complete set of financial statements. The auditor also does not have the audit evidence about the general quality of the accounting records or other accounting information that would be acquired in an audit of the entity's complete set of financial statements. Accordingly, the auditor may need further evidence to corroborate audit evidence acquired from the accounting records. In the case of an audit of a specific element of a financial statement, certain ISAs (UK) require audit work that may be disproportionate to the element being audited. For example, although the requirements of ISA (UK) 570 (Revised June 2016) are likely to be relevant in the circumstances of an audit of a schedule of accounts receivable, complying with those requirements may not be practicable because of the audit effort required. If the auditor concludes that an audit of a single financial statement or of a specific element of a financial statement in accordance with ISAs (UK) may not be practicable, the auditor may discuss with management whether another type of engagement might be more practicable.

Acceptability of the Financial Reporting Framework (Ref: Para. 8)

A7   A single financial statement or a specific element of a financial statement may be prepared in accordance with an applicable financial reporting framework that is based on a financial reporting framework established by an authorized or recognized standards setting organization for the preparation of a complete set of financial statements (for example IFRSs). If this is the case, determination of the acceptability of the applicable framework may involve considering whether that framework includes all the requirements of the framework on which it is based that are relevant to the presentation of a single financial statement or of a specific element of a financial statement that provides adequate disclosures.

Form of Opinion (Ref: Para. 9)

A8   The form of opinion to be expressed by the auditor depends on the applicable financial reporting framework and any applicable laws or regulations.[21] In accordance with ISA (UK) 700 (Revised June 2016):[22]

(a)   When expressing an unmodified opinion on a complete set of financial statements prepared in accordance with a fair presentation framework, the auditor's opinion, unless otherwise required by law or regulation, uses one of the following phrases:

(i)   the financial statements present fairly, in all material respects, in accordance with [the applicable financial reporting framework]; or

(ii)   the financial statements give a true and fair view in accordance with [the applicable financial reporting framework]; and

---

[20] *ISA (UK) 200 (Revised June 2016), paragraphs 14, 18, and 22–23.*

[21] *ISA (UK) 200 (Revised June 2016), paragraph 8.*

[22] *ISA (UK) 700 (Revised June 2016), paragraphs 25–26.*

(b) When expressing an unmodified opinion on a complete set of financial statements prepared in accordance with a compliance framework, the auditor's opinion states that the financial statements are prepared, in all material respects, in accordance with [the applicable financial reporting framework].

In the case of a single financial statement or of a specific element of a financial statement, **A9** the applicable financial reporting framework may not explicitly address the presentation of the financial statement or of the specific element of the financial statement. This may be the case when the applicable financial reporting framework is based on a financial reporting framework established by an authorized or recognized standards setting organization for the preparation of a complete set of financial statements (for example, IFRSs). The auditor therefore considers whether the expected form of opinion is appropriate in the light of the applicable financial reporting framework. Factors that may affect the auditor's consideration as to whether to use the phrases 'presents fairly, in all material respects,' or 'gives a true and fair view' in the auditor's opinion include:

- Whether the applicable financial reporting framework is explicitly or implicitly restricted to the preparation of a complete set of financial statements.
- Whether the single financial statement or the specific element of a financial statement will:
  o Comply fully with each of those requirements of the framework relevant to the particular financial statement or the particular element, and the presentation of the financial statement or the specific element of a financial statement include the related disclosures.
  o If necessary to achieve fair presentation, provide disclosures beyond those specifically required by the framework or, in exceptional circumstances, depart from a requirement of the framework.

The auditor's decision as to the expected form of opinion is a matter of professional judgment. It may be affected by whether use of the phrases 'presents fairly, in all material respects,' or 'gives a true and fair view' in the auditor's opinion on a single financial statement or on a specific element of a financial statement prepared in accordance with a fair presentation framework is generally accepted in the particular jurisdiction.

Considerations When Planning and Performing the Audit (Ref: Para. 10)

The relevance of each of the ISAs (UK) requires careful consideration. Even when only **A10** a specific element of a financial statement is the subject of the audit, ISAs (UK) such as ISA (UK) 240 (Revised June 2016),[23] ISA (UK) 550[24] and ISA (UK) 570 (Revised June 2016) are, in principle, relevant. This is because the element could be misstated as a result of fraud, the effect of related party transactions, or the incorrect application of the going concern basis of accounting under the applicable financial reporting framework.

ISA (UK) 260 (Revised June 2016) requires the auditor to determine the appropriate **A11** person(s) within the entity's governance structure with whom to communicate.[25] ISA (UK) 260 (Revised June 2016) notes that, in some cases, all of those charged with governance are involved in managing the entity, and the application of communication requirements is

---

[23] *ISA (UK) 240 (Revised June 2016)*, The Auditor's Responsibilities Relating to Fraud in an Audit of Financial Statements.

[24] *ISA (UK) 550*, Related Parties.

[25] *ISA (UK) 260 (Revised June 2016)*, Communication with Those Charged with Governance, *paragraph 11*.

modified to recognize this position.[26] When a complete set of financial statements is also prepared by the entity, those person(s) responsible for the oversight of the preparation of the single financial statement or the element may not be the same as those charged with governance responsible for the oversight of the preparation of the complete set of financial statements.

A12   Furthermore, ISAs (UK) are written in the context of an audit of financial statements; they are to be adapted as necessary in the circumstances when applied to the audit of a single financial statement[27] or of a specific element of a financial statement.[28] For example, written representations from management about the complete set of financial statements would be replaced by written representations about the presentation of the financial statement or the element in accordance with the applicable financial reporting framework.

A13   Matters included in the auditor's report on the complete set of financial statements may have implications for the audit of a single financial statement or of an element of a financial statement (see paragraph 14). When planning and performing an audit of a single financial statement or a specific element of a financial statement in conjunction with the audit of the entity's complete set of financial statements, the auditor may be able to use audit evidence obtained as part of the audit of the entity's complete set of financial statements in the audit of the financial statement or the element. ISAs (UK), however, require the auditor to plan and perform the audit of the financial statement or element to obtain sufficient appropriate audit evidence on which to base the opinion on the financial statement or on the element.

A14   The individual financial statements that comprise a complete set of financial statements, and many of the specific elements of those financial statements, including their related disclosures, are interrelated. Accordingly, when auditing a single financial statement or a specific element of a financial statement, the auditor may not be able to consider the financial statement or the element in isolation. Consequently, the auditor may need to perform procedures in relation to the interrelated items to meet the objective of the audit.

A15   Furthermore, the materiality determined for a single financial statement or for a specific element of a financial statement may be lower than the materiality determined for the entity's complete set of financial statements; this will affect the nature, timing and extent of the audit procedures and the evaluation of uncorrected misstatements.

Forming an Opinion and Reporting Considerations (Ref: Para. 11)

A16   ISA (UK) 700 (Revised June 2016) requires the auditor, in forming an opinion, to evaluate whether the financial statements provide adequate disclosures to enable the intended users to understand the effect of material transactions and events on the information conveyed in the financial statements.[29] In the case of a single financial statement or of a specific element of a financial statement, it is important that the financial statement or the element, in view of the requirements of the applicable financial reporting framework, provides adequate disclosures to enable the intended users to understand the information conveyed in the financial statement or the element, and the effect of material transactions and events on the information conveyed in the financial statement or the element.

---

[26] *ISA (UK) 260 (Revised June 2016), paragraph 10(b), 13, A1 (third bullet), A2 and A8.*

[27] *ISA (UK) 200 (Revised June 2016), paragraph 2.*

[29] *ISA (UK) 700 (Revised June 2016), paragraph 13(e).*

Appendix 2[29a] contains illustrations of independent auditor's reports on a single financial statement and on a specific element of a financial statement. Other illustrations of auditor's reports may be relevant to reporting on a single financial statement or on a specific element of a financial statement (see, for example, the Appendices to ISA (UK) 700 (Revised June 2016), ISA (UK) 705 (Revised June 2016), ISA (UK) 570 (Revised June 2016), ISA (UK) 720 (Revised June 2016), and ISA (UK) 706 (Revised June 2016)). **A17**

Application of ISA (UK) 700 (Revised June 2016) When Reporting on a Single Financial Statement or on a Specific Element of a Financial Statement

Paragraph 11 of this ISA (UK) explains that the auditor is required to apply the requirements in ISA (UK) 700 (Revised June 2016), adapted as necessary in the circumstances of the engagement, when forming an opinion and reporting on a single financial statement or on a specific element of a financial statement. In doing so, the auditor is also required to apply the reporting requirements in other ISAs (UK) adapted as necessary in the circumstances of the engagement, and may find the considerations addressed in paragraphs A19–A21 below helpful. **A18**

Going Concern

Depending on the applicable financial reporting framework used in the preparation of the single financial statement or the specific element of a financial statement, the description in the auditor's report of management's responsibilities[30] relating to going concern may need to be adapted as necessary. The description in the auditor's report of the auditor's responsibilities[31] may also need to be adapted as necessary depending on how ISA (UK) 570 (Revised June 2016) applies in the circumstances of the engagement. **A19**

Key Audit Matters

ISA (UK) 700 (Revised June 2016) requires the auditor to communicate key audit matters in accordance with ISA (UK) 701 for audits of complete sets of general purpose financial statements of listed entities.[32] For audits of a single financial statement or a specific element of a financial statement, ISA (UK) 701 only applies when communication of key audit matters in the auditor's report on such financial statements or elements is required by law or regulation, or the auditor otherwise decides to communicate key audit matters. When key audit matters are communicated in the auditor's report on a single financial statement or a specific element of a financial statement, ISA (UK) 701 applies in its entirety.[33] **A20**

Other Information

ISA (UK) 720 (Revised June 2016) deals with the auditor's responsibilities relating to other information. In the context of this ISA (UK), reports containing or accompanying the single financial statement or specific element of a financial statement—the purpose of which is to provide owners (or similar stakeholders) with information on matters presented **A21**

[29a] *The examples in the Appendix have not been tailored for the UK.*

[30] *See ISA (UK) 700 (Revised June 2016), paragraphs 34(b) and A48.*

[31] *See ISA (UK) 700 (Revised June 2016), paragraphs 39(b)(iv).*

[32] *ISA (UK) 700 (Revised June 2016), paragraph 30.*

[33] *ISA (UK) 700 (Revised June 2016), paragraph 31.*

in the single financial statement or the specific element of a financial statement—are considered to be annual reports for purposes of ISA (UK) 720 (Revised June 2016). When the auditor determines that the entity plans to issue such a report, the requirements in ISA (UK) 720 (Revised June 2016) apply to the audit of the single financial statement or the element.

Name of the Engagement Partner

A22   The requirement in ISA (UK) 700 (Revised June 2016) for the auditor to include the name of the engagement partner in the auditor's report also applies to audits of single financial statements of listed entities or specific elements of financial statements of listed entities.[34] The auditor may be required by law or regulation to include the name of the engagement partner in the auditor's report or may otherwise decide to do so when reporting on a single financial statement or on an element of a financial statement of entities other than listed entities.

Reporting on the Entity's Complete Set of Financial Statements and on a Single Financial Statement or on a Specific Element of a Financial Statement (Ref: Para. 14)

Considering the Implications of Certain Matters Included in the Auditor's Report on the Entity's Complete Set of Financial Statements for the Audit of the Single Financial Statement or the Specific Element of a Financial Statement and for the Auditor's Report Thereon

A23   Paragraph 14 requires the auditor to consider the implications, if any, of certain matters included in the auditor's report on the complete set of financial statements for the audit of the single financial statement or the specific element of a financial statement and for the auditor's report thereon. Considering whether a matter included in the auditor's report on the complete set of financial statements is relevant in the context of an engagement to report on a single financial statement or a specific element of a financial statement involves professional judgment.

A24   Factors that may be relevant in considering those implications include:

- The nature of the matter(s) being described in the auditor's report on the complete set of financial statements and the extent to which it relates to what is included in the single financial statement or a specific element of a financial statement.
- The pervasiveness of the matter(s) described in the auditor's report on the complete set of financial statements.
- The nature and extent of the differences between the applicable financial reporting frameworks.
- The extent of the difference between the period(s) covered by the complete set of the financial statements compared to the period(s) or dates of the single financial statement or the element of a financial statement.
- The time elapsed since the date of the auditor's report on the complete set of the financial statements.

A25   For example, in the case when there is a qualification of the auditor's opinion in relation to accounts receivable in the auditor's report on the complete set of financial statements, and the single financial statement includes accounts receivable, or the specific element of a financial statement relates to accounts receivable, it is likely that there would be implications for the audit. On the other hand, if the qualification of the auditor's opinion on

---

[34] *See ISA (UK) 700 (Revised June 2016), paragraphs 46 and A61–A63.*

the complete set of financial statements relates to classification of long-term debt, then it is less likely that there would be implications for an audit of the single financial statement that is the income statement, or if the specific element of the financial statement relates to accounts receivable.

Key audit matters that are communicated in the auditor's report on the complete set of   **A26**
financial statements may have implications for an audit of a single financial statement or the specific element of the financial statement. The information included in the Key Audit Matters section about how the matter was addressed in the audit of the complete set of financial statements may be useful to the auditor's determination of how to address the matter when it is relevant to the audit of the single financial statement or the specific element of the financial statement.

Inclusion of a reference to the auditor's report on the complete set of financial statements

Even when certain matters included in the auditor's report on the complete set of financial   **A27**
statements do not have implications for the audit of, or for the auditor's report on, the single financial statement or the specific element of a financial statement, the auditor may deem it appropriate to refer to the matter(s) in an Other Matter paragraph in an auditor's report on the single financial statement or on the specific element of a financial statement (see ISA (UK) 706 Revised June 2016)).[35] For example, the auditor may consider it appropriate to refer in the auditor's report on the single financial statement or a specific element of the financial statement to a Material Uncertainty Related to Going Concern section included in the auditor's report on the complete set of financial statements.

Adverse Opinion or Disclaimer of Opinion in the Auditor's Report on the Entity's Complete Set of Financial Statements (Ref: Para. 15)

In the auditor's report on an entity's complete set of financial statements, the expression   **A28**
of a disclaimer of opinion regarding the results of operations and cash flows, where relevant, and an unmodified opinion regarding the financial position is permitted since the disclaimer of opinion is being issued in respect of the results of operations and cash flows only and not in respect of the financial statements as a whole.[36]

---

[35] *See ISA (UK) 706 (Revised June 2016), paragraphs 610–11.*

[36] *ISA (UK) 510 (Revised June 2016),* Initial Audit Engagements—Opening Balances, *paragraph A8, and ISA 705 (Revised), paragraph A16.*

Appendix 1

(Ref: Para. A3)

Examples of Specific Elements, Accounts or Items of a Financial Statement

- Accounts receivable, allowance for doubtful accounts receivable, inventory, the liability for accrued benefits of a private pension plan, the recorded value of identified intangible assets, or the liability for 'incurred but not reported' claims in an insurance portfolio, including related notes.
- A schedule of externally managed assets and income of a private pension plan, including related notes.
- A schedule of net tangible assets, including related notes.
- A schedule of disbursements in relation to a lease property, including explanatory notes.
- A schedule of profit participation or employee bonuses, including explanatory notes.

Appendix 2

Illustrations of Independent Auditor's Reports on a Single Financial Statement and on a Specific Element of a Financial Statement

The examples in the Appendix have not been tailored for the UK.

- Illustration 1: An auditor's report on a single financial statement of an entity other than a listed entity prepared in accordance with a general purpose framework (for purposes of this illustration, a fair presentation framework).
- Illustration 2: An auditor's report on a single financial statement of an entity other than a listed entity prepared in accordance with a special purpose framework (for purposes of this illustration, a fair presentation framework).
- Illustration 3: An auditor's report on a specific element of a financial statement of a listed entity prepared in accordance with a special purpose framework (for purposes of this illustration, a compliance framework).

Illustration 1: An auditor's report on a single financial statement of an entity other than a listed entity prepared in accordance with a general purpose framework (for purposes of this illustration, a fair presentation framework).

For purposes of this illustrative auditor's report, the following circumstances are assumed:

- Audit of a balance sheet (that is, a single financial statement) of an entity other than a listed entity.
- The balance sheet has been prepared by management of the entity in accordance with the requirements of the Financial Reporting Framework in Jurisdiction X relevant to preparing a balance sheet.
- The terms of the audit engagement reflect the description of management's responsibility for the financial statements in ISA 210.
- The applicable financial reporting framework is a fair presentation framework designed to meet the common financial information needs of a wide range of users.
- The auditor has determined that it is appropriate to use the phrase 'presents fairly, in all material respects,' in the auditor's opinion.
- The relevant ethical requirements that apply to the audit are those of the jurisdiction.
- Based on the audit evidence obtained, the auditor has concluded that a material uncertainty exists related to events or conditions that may cast significant doubt on the entity's ability to continue as a going concern in accordance with ISA 570 (Revised). The disclosure of the material uncertainty in the single financial statement is adequate.
- The auditor is not required, and has otherwise not decided, to communicate key audit matters in accordance with ISA 701 in the context of the audit of the balance sheet.
- The auditor has determined that there is no other information (i.e., the requirements of ISA 720 (Revised) do not apply).
- Those responsible for oversight of the financial statement differ from those responsible for the preparation of the financial statement.
- The auditor has no other reporting responsibilities required under local law or regulation.

INDEPENDENT AUDITOR'S REPORT

[Appropriate Addressee]

Opinion

We have audited the balance sheet of ABC Company (the Company) as at December 31, 20X1 and notes to the financial statement, including a summary of significant accounting policies (together 'the financial statement').

In our opinion, the accompanying financial statement presents fairly, in all material respects, the financial position of the Company as at December 31, 20X1 in accordance with those requirements of the Financial Reporting Framework in Jurisdiction X relevant to preparing such a financial statement. [Opinion section positioned first as required in ISA 700 (Revised)]

Basis for Opinion

We conducted our audit in accordance with International Standards on Auditing (ISAs). Our responsibilities under those standards are further described in the *Auditor's Responsibilities for the Audit of the Financial Statement* section of our report. We are independent of the Company in accordance with the ethical requirements that are relevant to our audit of the financial statement in [*jurisdiction*], and we have fulfilled our other ethical responsibilities in accordance with these requirements. We believe that the audit evidence we have obtained is sufficient and appropriate to provide a basis for our opinion. [The first and last sentences in this section used to be in the Auditor's Responsibility section. Also, the Basis for Opinion section is positioned immediately after the Opinion section as required in ISA 700 (Revised).]

Material Uncertainty Related to Going Concern

We draw attention to Note 6 in the financial statement, which indicates that the Company incurred a net loss of ZZZ during the year ended December 31, 20X1 and, as of that date, the Company's current liabilities exceeded its total assets by YYY. As stated in Note 6, these events or conditions, along with other matters as set forth in Note 6, indicate that a material uncertainty exists that may cast significant doubt on the Company's ability to continue as a going concern. Our opinion is not modified in respect of this matter.

Responsibilities of Management and Those Charged with Governance for the Financial Statement[37]

Management is responsible for the preparation and fair presentation of the financial statement in accordance with those requirements of the Financial Reporting Framework in Jurisdiction X relevant to preparing such a financial statement, and for such internal control as management determines is necessary to enable the preparation of a financial statement that is free from material misstatement, whether due to fraud or error.

In preparing the financial statement, management is responsible for assessing the Company's ability to continue as a going concern, disclosing, as applicable, matters relating to going

---

[37] *Throughout these illustrative auditor's reports, the terms management and those charged with governance may need to be replaced by another term that is appropriate in the context of the legal framework in the particular jurisdiction.*

concern and using the going concern basis of accounting unless management either intends to liquidate the Company or to cease operations, or has no realistic alternative but to do so.

Those charged with governance are responsible for overseeing the Company's financial reporting process.

Auditor's Responsibilities for the Audit of the Financial Statement

Our objectives are to obtain reasonable assurance about whether the financial statement as a whole is free from material misstatement, whether due to fraud or error, and to issue an auditor's report that includes our opinion. Reasonable assurance is a high level of assurance, but is not a guarantee that an audit conducted in accordance with ISAs will always detect a material misstatement when it exists. Misstatements can arise from fraud or error and are considered material if, individually or in the aggregate, they could reasonably be expected to influence the economic decisions of users taken on the basis of this financial statement.

Paragraph 41(b) of ISA 700 (Revised) explains that the shaded material below can be located in an Appendix to the auditor's report. Paragraph 41(c) of ISA 700 (Revised) explains that when law, regulation or national auditing standards expressly permit, reference can be made to a website of an appropriate authority that contains the description of the auditor's responsibilities, rather than including this material in the auditor's report, provided that the description on the website addresses, and is not inconsistent with, the description of the auditor's responsibilities below.

As part of an audit in accordance with ISAs, we exercise professional judgment and maintain professional skepticism throughout the audit. We also:

- Identify and assess the risks of material misstatement of the financial statement, whether due to fraud or error, design and perform audit procedures responsive to those risks, and obtain audit evidence that is sufficient and appropriate to provide a basis for our opinion. The risk of not detecting a material misstatement resulting from fraud is higher than for one resulting from error, as fraud may involve collusion, forgery, intentional omissions, misrepresentations, or the override of internal control.
- Obtain an understanding of internal control relevant to the audit in order to design audit procedures that are appropriate in the circumstances, but not for the purpose of expressing an opinion on the effectiveness of the Company's internal control.[38]
- Evaluate the appropriateness of accounting policies used and the reasonableness of accounting estimates, if any, and related disclosures made by management.;
- Conclude on the appropriateness of management's use of the going concern basis of accounting and, based on the audit evidence obtained, whether a material uncertainty exists related to events or conditions that may cast significant doubt on the Company's ability to continue as a going concern. If we conclude that a material uncertainty exists, we are required to draw attention in our auditor's report to the related disclosures in the financial statements or, if such disclosures are inadequate, to modify our opinion. Our conclusions are based on the audit evidence obtained up to the date of our auditor's report. However, future events or conditions may cause the Company to cease to continue as a going concern.
- Evaluate the overall presentation, structure and content of the financial statement, including the disclosures, and whether the financial statement represents the underlying transactions and events in a manner that achieves fair presentation.

---

[38] *This sentence would be modified, as appropriate, in circumstances when the auditor also has responsibility to issue an opinion on the effectiveness of internal control in conjunction with the audit of the financial statement.*

We communicate with those charged with governance regarding, among other matters, the planned scope and timing of the audit and significant audit findings, including any significant deficiencies in internal control that we identify during our audit.

[Signature in the name of the audit firm, the personal name of the auditor, or both, as appropriate for the particular jurisdiction]

[Auditor address] [Placement of date and address reversed)]

[Date]

Illustration 2: An auditor's report on a single financial statement of an entity other than a listed entity prepared in accordance with a special purpose framework.

For purposes of this illustrative auditor's report, the following Circumstances are assumed:

- Audit of a statement of cash receipts and disbursements (that is, a single financial statement) of an entity other than a listed entity.
- An auditor's report on the complete set of financial statements was not issued.
- The financial statement has been prepared by management of the entity in accordance with the cash receipts and disbursements basis of accounting to respond to a request for cash flow information received from a creditor. Management has a choice of financial reporting frameworks.
- The applicable financial reporting framework is a fair presentation framework designed to meet the financial information needs of specific users.[39]
- The auditor has concluded an unmodified (i.e., 'clean') opinion is appropriate based on the audit evidence obtained.
- The auditor has determined that it is appropriate to use the phrase 'presents fairly, in all material respects,' in the auditor's opinion.
- The relevant ethical requirements that apply to the audit are those of the jurisdiction.
- Distribution or use of the auditor's report is not restricted.
- Based on the audit evidence obtained, the auditor has concluded that a material uncertainty does not exist related to events or conditions that may cast significant doubt on the entity's ability to continue as a going concern in accordance with ISA 570 (Revised).
- The auditor is not required, and has otherwise not decided, to communicate key audit matters in accordance with ISA 701 in the context of the audit of the statement of cash receipts and disbursements.
- The auditor has determined that there is no other information (i.e., the requirements of ISA 720 (Revised) do not apply).
- Management is responsible for the preparation of the financial statement and oversight of the financial reporting process to prepare this financial statement.
- The auditor has no other reporting responsibilities required under local law or regulation.

---

[39] *ISA 800 (Revised) contains requirements and guidance on the form and content of financial statements prepared in accordance with a special purpose framework.*

INDEPENDENT AUDITOR'S REPORT

[Appropriate Addressee]

Opinion

We have audited the statement of cash receipts and disbursements of ABC Company (the Company) for the year ended December 31, 20X1 and notes to the statement of cash receipts and disbursements, including a summary of significant accounting policies (together 'the financial statement').

In our opinion, the accompanying financial statement presents fairly, in all material respects, the cash receipts and disbursements of the Company for the year ended December 31, 20X1 in accordance with the cash receipts and disbursements basis of accounting described in Note X. [Opinion section positioned first as required in ISA 700 (Revised)]

Basis for Opinion

We conducted our audit in accordance with International Standards on Auditing (ISAs). Our responsibilities under those standards are further described in the *Auditor's Responsibilities for the Audit of the Financial Statement* section of our report. We are independent of the Company in accordance with the ethical requirements that are relevant to our audit of the financial statement in [*jurisdiction*], and we have fulfilled our other ethical responsibilities in accordance with these requirements. We believe that the audit evidence we have obtained is sufficient and appropriate to provide a basis for our opinion. [The first and last sentences in this section used to be in the Auditor's Responsibility section. Also, the Basis for Opinion section is positioned immediately after the Opinion section as required in ISA 700 (Revised).]

Emphasis of Matter – Basis of Accounting

We draw attention to Note X to the financial statement, which describes the basis of accounting. The financial statement is prepared to provide information to XYZ Creditor. As a result, the statement may not be suitable for another purpose. Our opinion is not modified in respect of this matter.

Responsibilities of Management and Those Charged with Governance for the Financial Statement[40]

Management is responsible for preparation and fair presentation of the financial statement in accordance with the cash receipts and disbursements basis of accounting described in Note X; this includes determining that the cash receipts and disbursements basis of accounting is an acceptable basis for the preparation of the financial statement in the circumstances, and for such internal control as management determines is necessary to enable the preparation of a financial statement that is free from material misstatement, whether due to fraud or error.

In preparing the financial statement, management is responsible for assessing the Company's ability to continue as a going concern, disclosing, as applicable, matters relating to going concern and using the going concern basis of accounting unless management either intends to liquidate the Company or to cease operations, or has no realistic alternative but to do so.

---

[40] *Or other terms that are appropriate in the context of the legal framework in the particular jurisdiction.*

Auditor's Responsibilities for the Audit of the Financial Statement

Our objectives are to obtain reasonable assurance about whether the financial statement as a whole is free from material misstatement, whether due to fraud or error, and to issue an auditor's report that includes our opinion. Reasonable assurance is a high level of assurance, but is not a guarantee that an audit conducted in accordance with ISAs will always detect a material misstatement when it exists. Misstatements can arise from fraud or error and are considered material if, individually or in the aggregate, they could reasonably be expected to influence the economic decisions of users taken on the basis of this financial statement.

Paragraph 41(b) of ISA 700 (Revised) explains that the shaded material below can be located in an Appendix to the auditor's report. Paragraph 41(c) of ISA 700 (Revised) explains that when law, regulation or national auditing standards expressly permit, reference can be made to a website of an appropriate authority that contains the description of the auditor's responsibilities, rather than including this material in the auditor's report, provided that the description on the website addresses, and is not inconsistent with, the description of the auditor's responsibilities below.

As part of an audit in accordance with ISAs, we exercise professional judgment and maintain professional skepticism throughout the audit. We also:

- Identify and assess the risks of material misstatement of the financial statement, whether due to fraud or error, design and perform audit procedures responsive to those risks, and obtain audit evidence that is sufficient and appropriate to provide a basis for our opinion. The risk of not detecting a material misstatement resulting from fraud is higher than for one resulting from error, as fraud may involve collusion, forgery, intentional omissions, misrepresentations, or the override of internal control.
- Obtain an understanding of internal control relevant to the audit in order to design audit procedures that are appropriate in the circumstances, but not for the purpose of expressing an opinion on the effectiveness of the Company's internal control.[41]
- Conclude on the appropriateness of management's use of the going concern basis of accounting and based on the audit evidence obtained, whether a material uncertainty exists related to events or conditions that may cast significant doubt on the Company's ability to continue as a going concern. If we conclude that a material uncertainty exists, we are required to draw attention in our auditor's report to the related disclosures in the financial statement or, if such disclosures are inadequate, to modify our opinion. Our conclusions are based on the audit evidence obtained up to the date of our auditor's report. However, future events or conditions may cause the Company to cease to continue as a going concern.
- Evaluate the appropriateness of accounting policies used and the reasonableness of accounting estimates, if any, and related disclosures made by management.;
- Evaluate the overall presentation, structure and content of the financial statement, including the disclosures, and whether the financial statement represents the underlying transactions and events in a manner that achieves fair presentation.

We communicate with those charged with governance regarding, among other matters, the planned scope and timing of the audit and significant audit findings, including any significant deficiencies in internal control that we identify during our audit.

---

[41] *This sentence would be modified, as appropriate, in circumstances when the auditor also has responsibility to issue an opinion on the effectiveness of internal control in conjunction with the audit of the financial statement.*

[*Signature in the name of the audit firm, the personal name of the auditor, or both, as appropriate for the particular jurisdiction*]

[*Auditor address*] [Placement of date and address reversed)]

[*Date*]

Illustration 3: An auditor's report on a specific element of a financial statement of a listed entity prepared in accordance with a special purpose framework.

For purposes of this illustrative auditor's report, the following circumstances are assumed:

- Audit of an accounts receivable schedule (that is, element, account or item of a financial statement).
- The financial information has been prepared by management of the entity in accordance with the financial reporting provisions established by a regulator to meet the requirements of that regulator. Management does not have a choice of financial reporting frameworks.
- The applicable financial reporting framework is a compliance framework designed to meet the financial information needs of specific users.[42]
- The terms of the audit engagement reflect the description of management's responsibility for the financial statements in ISA 210.
- The auditor has concluded an unmodified (i.e., 'clean') opinion is appropriate based on the audit evidence obtained.
- The relevant ethical requirements that apply to the audit are those of the jurisdiction.
- Distribution of the auditor's report is restricted.
- Based on the audit evidence obtained, the auditor has concluded that a material uncertainty does not exist related to events or conditions that may cast significant doubt on the entity's ability to continue as a going concern in accordance with ISA 570 (Revised).
- The auditor is not required, and has otherwise not decided to communicate key audit matters in accordance with ISA 701 in the context of the audit of the accounts receivable schedule.
- The auditor has determined that there is no other information (i.e., the requirements of ISA 720 (Revised) do not apply).
- Those responsible for oversight of the financial statement differ from those responsible for the preparation of the financial statement.
- The auditor has no other reporting responsibilities required under local law or regulation.

---

[42] *ISA 800 (Revised) contains requirements and guidance on the form and content of financial statements prepared in accordance with a special purpose framework.*

INDEPENDENT AUDITOR'S REPORT

[To the Shareholders of ABC Company or Other Appropriate Addressee]

Opinion

We have audited the accounts receivable schedule of ABC Company (the Company) as at December 31, 20X1 ('the schedule').

In our opinion, the financial information in the schedule the Company as at December 31, 20X1 is prepared, in all material respects, in accordance with [describe the financial reporting provisions established by the regulator]. [Opinion section positioned first as required ISA 700 (Revised)]

Basis for Opinion

We conducted our audit in accordance with International Standards on Auditing (ISAs). Our responsibilities under those standards are further described in the *Auditor's Responsibilities for the Audit of the Schedule* section of our report. We are independent of the Company in accordance with the ethical requirements that are relevant to our audit of the schedule in [*jurisdiction*], and we have fulfilled our other ethical responsibilities in accordance with these requirements. We believe that the audit evidence we have obtained is sufficient and appropriate to provide a basis for our opinion. [The first and last sentences in this section used to be in the Auditor's Responsibility section. Also, the Basis for Opinion section is positioned immediately after opinion section as required in ISA 700 (Revised).]

Emphasis of Matter –Basis of Accounting and Restriction on Distribution

We draw attention to Note X to the schedule, which describes the basis of accounting. The schedule is prepared to assist the Company to meet the requirements of Regulator DEF. As a result, the schedule may not be suitable for another purpose. Our report is intended solely for the Company and Regulator DEF and should not be distributed to parties other than the Company or Regulator DEF. Our opinion is not modified in respect of this matter.

Responsibilities of Management and Those Charged with Governance for the Schedule[43]

Management is responsible for the preparation of the schedule in accordance with [describe the financial reporting provisions established by the regulator], and for such internal control as management determines is necessary to enable the preparation of the schedule that is free from material misstatement, whether due to fraud or error.

In preparing the schedule, management is responsible for assessing the Company's ability to continue as a going concern, disclosing, as applicable, matters relating to going concern and using the going concern basis of accounting unless management either intends to liquidate the Company or to cease operations, or has no realistic alternative but to do so.

Those charged with governance are responsible for overseeing the Company's financial reporting process.

---

[43] *Or other terms that are appropriate in the context of the legal framework in the particular jurisdiction.*

Auditor's Responsibilities for the Audit of the Schedule

Our objectives are to obtain reasonable assurance about whether the schedule is free from material misstatement, whether due to fraud or error, and to issue an auditor's report that includes our opinion. Reasonable assurance is a high level of assurance, but is not a guarantee that an audit conducted in accordance with ISAs will always detect a material misstatement when it exists. Misstatements can arise from fraud or error and are considered material if, individually or in the aggregate, they could reasonably be expected to influence the economic decisions of users taken on the basis of this schedule.

Paragraph 41(b) of ISA 700 (Revised) explains that the shaded material below can be located in an Appendix to the auditor's report. Paragraph 41(c) of ISA 700 (Revised) explains that when law, regulation or national auditing standards expressly permit, reference can be made to a website of an appropriate authority that contains the description of the auditor's responsibilities, rather than including this material in the auditor's report, provided that the description on the website addresses, and is not inconsistent with, the description of the auditor's responsibilities below.

As part of an audit in accordance with ISAs, we exercise professional judgment and maintain professional skepticism throughout the audit. We also:

- Identify and assess the risks of material misstatement of the schedule, whether due to fraud or error, design and perform audit procedures responsive to those risks, and obtain audit evidence that is sufficient and appropriate to provide a basis for our opinion. The risk of not detecting a material misstatement resulting from fraud is higher than for one resulting from error, as fraud may involve collusion, forgery, intentional omissions, misrepresentations, or the override of internal control.[44]
- Obtain an understanding of internal control relevant to the audit in order to design audit procedures that are appropriate in the circumstances, but not for the purpose of expressing an opinion on the effectiveness of the Company's internal control.
- Conclude on the appropriateness of management's use of the going concern basis of accounting and, based on the audit evidence obtained, whether a material uncertainty exists related to events or conditions that may cast significant doubt on the Company's ability to continue as a going concern. If we conclude that a material uncertainty exists, we are required to draw attention in our auditor's report to the related disclosures in the schedule or, if such disclosures are inadequate, to modify our opinion. Our conclusions are based on the audit evidence obtained up to the date of our auditor's report. However, future events or conditions may cause the Company to cease to continue as a going concern.
- Evaluate the appropriateness of accounting policies used and the reasonableness of accounting estimates, if any, and related disclosures made by management.

We communicate with those charged with governance regarding, among other matters, the planned scope and timing of the audit and significant audit findings, including any significant deficiencies in internal control that we identify during our audit.

We also provide those charged with governance with a statement that we have complied with relevant ethical requirements regarding independence, and to communicate with them all relationships and other matters that may reasonably be thought to bear on our independence, and where applicable, related safeguards.

---

[44] *This sentence would be modified, as appropriate, in circumstances when the auditor also has responsibility to issue an opinion on the effectiveness of internal control in conjunction with the audit of the schedule.*

The engagement partner on the audit resulting in this independent auditor's report is [*name*].

[*Signature in the name of the audit firm, the personal name of the auditor, or both, as appropriate for the particular jurisdiction*]

[*Auditor address*] [Placement of date and address reversed)]

[Date]

Part Two

International Standards on Auditing

International Standard on Auditing 810
Engagements to report on summary financial statements

(*Effective for engagements for periods
beginning on or after December 15, 2009*)

Contents

International Standard on Auditing (ISA) 810, "Engagements to Report on Summary Financial Statements" should be read in conjunction with ISA 200, "Overall Objectives of the Independent Auditor and the Conduct of an Audit in Accordance with International Standards on Auditing."

Introduction

Scope of this ISA

1   This International Standard on Auditing (ISA) deals with the auditor's responsibilities relating to an engagement to report on summary financial statements derived from financial statements audited in accordance with ISAs by that same auditor.

Effective Date

2   This ISA is effective for engagements for periods beginning on or after December 15, 2009.

Objectives

3   The objectives of the auditor are:

   (a) To determine whether it is appropriate to accept the engagement to report on summary financial statements; and
   (b) If engaged to report on summary financial statements:
      (i)   To form an opinion on the summary financial statements based on an evaluation of the conclusions drawn from the evidence obtained; and
      (ii) To express clearly that opinion through a written report that also describes the basis for that opinion.

Definitions

4   For purposes of this ISA, the following terms have the meanings attributed below:

   (a) Applied criteria – The criteria applied by management in the preparation of the summary financial statements.
   (b) Audited financial statements – Financial statements[1] audited by the auditor in accordance with ISAs, and from which the summary financial statements are derived.
   (c) Summary financial statements – Historical financial information that is derived from financial statements but that contains less detail than the financial statements, while still providing a structured representation consistent with that provided by the financial statements of the entity's economic resources or obligations at a point in time or the changes therein for a period of time.[2] Different jurisdictions may use different terminology to describe such historical financial information.

Requirements

Engagement Acceptance

5   The auditor shall accept an engagement to report on summary financial statements in accordance with this ISA only when the auditor has been engaged to conduct an

---

[1] *ISA 200, Overall Objectives of the Independent Auditor and the Conduct of an Audit in Accordance with International Standards on Auditing, paragraph 13(f), defines the term "financial statements."*

[2] *ISA 200, paragraph 13(f).*

audit in accordance with ISAs of the financial statements from which the summary financial statements are derived. (Ref: Para. A1)

Before accepting an engagement to report on summary financial statements, the **6** auditor shall: (Ref: Para. A2)

(a) Determine whether the applied criteria are acceptable; (Ref: Para. A3-A7)
(b) Obtain the agreement of management that it acknowledges and understands its responsibility:
   (i) For the preparation of the summary financial statements in accordance with the applied criteria;
   (ii) To make the audited financial statements available to the intended users of the summary financial statements without undue difficulty (or, if law or regulation provides that the audited financial statements need not be made available to the intended users of the summary financial statements and establishes the criteria for the preparation of the summary financial statements, to describe that law or regulation in the summary financial statements); and
   (iii) To include the auditor's report on the summary financial statements in any document that contains the summary financial statements and that indicates that the auditor has reported on them.
(c) Agree with management the form of opinion to be expressed on the summary financial statements (see paragraphs 9-11).

If the auditor concludes that the applied criteria are unacceptable or is unable to **7** obtain the agreement of management set out in paragraph 6(b), the auditor shall not accept the engagement to report on the summary financial statements, unless required by law or regulation to do so. An engagement conducted in accordance with such law or regulation does not comply with this ISA. Accordingly, the auditor's report on the summary financial statements shall not indicate that the engagement was conducted in accordance with this ISA. The auditor shall include appropriate reference to this fact in the terms of the engagement. The auditor shall also determine the effect that this may have on the engagement to audit the financial statements from which the summary financial statements are derived.

Nature of Procedures

The auditor shall perform the following procedures, and any other procedures that **8** the auditor may consider necessary, as the basis for the auditor's opinion on the summary financial statements:

(a) Evaluate whether the summary financial statements adequately disclose their summarized nature and identify the audited financial statements.
(b) When summary financial statements are not accompanied by the audited financial statements, evaluate whether they describe clearly:
   (i) From whom or where the audited financial statements are available; or
   (ii) The law or regulation that specifies that the audited financial statements need not be made available to the intended users of the summary financial statements and establishes the criteria for the preparation of the summary financial statements.
(c) Evaluate whether the summary financial statements adequately disclose the applied criteria.
(d) Compare the summary financial statements with the related information in the audited financial statements to determine whether the summary financial statements agree with or can be recalculated from the related information in the audited financial statements.

(e)   Evaluate whether the summary financial statements are prepared in accordance with the applied criteria.

(f)   Evaluate, in view of the purpose of the summary financial statements, whether the summary financial statements contain the information necessary, and are at an appropriate level of aggregation, so as not to be misleading in the circumstances.

(g)   Evaluate whether the audited financial statements are available to the intended users of the summary financial statements without undue difficulty, unless law or regulation provides that they need not be made available and establishes the criteria for the preparation of the summary financial statements. (Ref: Para. A8)

Form of Opinion

9   When the auditor has concluded that an unmodified opinion on the summary financial statements is appropriate, the auditor's opinion shall, unless otherwise required by law or regulation, use one of the following phrases: (Ref: Para. A9)

(a)   The summary financial statements are consistent, in all material respects, with the audited financial statements, in accordance with [the applied criteria]; or

(b)   The summary financial statements are a fair summary of the audited financial statements, in accordance with [the applied criteria].

10   If law or regulation prescribes the wording of the opinion on summary financial statements in terms that are different from those described in paragraph 9, the auditor shall:

(a)   Apply the procedures described in paragraph 8 and any further procedures necessary to enable the auditor to express the prescribed opinion; and

(b)   Evaluate whether users of the summary financial statements might misunderstand the auditor's opinion on the summary financial statements and, if so, whether additional explanation in the auditor's report on the summary financial statements can mitigate possible misunderstanding.

11   If, in the case of paragraph 10(b), the auditor concludes that additional explanation in the auditor's report on the summary financial statements cannot mitigate possible misunderstanding, the auditor shall not accept the engagement, unless required by law or regulation to do so. An engagement conducted in accordance with such law or regulation does not comply with this ISA. Accordingly, the auditor's report on the summary financial statements shall not indicate that the engagement was conducted in accordance with this ISA.

Timing of Work and Events Subsequent to the Date of the Auditor's Report on the Audited Financial Statements

12   The auditor's report on the summary financial statements may be dated later than the date of the auditor's report on the audited financial statements. In such cases, the auditor's report on the summary financial statements shall state that the summary financial statements and audited financial statements do not reflect the effects of events that occurred subsequent to the date of the auditor's report on the audited financial statements that may require adjustment of, or disclosure in, the audited financial statements. (Ref: Para. A10)

13   The auditor may become aware of facts that existed at the date of the auditor's report on the audited financial statements, but of which the auditor previously was unaware. In such cases, the auditor shall not issue the auditor's report on the summary financial statements until the auditor's consideration of such facts in

relation to the audited financial statements in accordance with ISA 560[3] has been completed.

Auditor's Report on Summary Financial Statements

Elements of the Auditor's Report

The auditor's report on summary financial statements shall include the following   **14**
elements:[4] (Ref: Para. A15)

(a)   A title clearly indicating it as the report of an independent auditor. (Ref: Para. A11)
(b)   An addressee. (Ref: Para. A12)
(c)   An introductory paragraph that:
   (i)   Identifies the summary financial statements on which the auditor is reporting, including the title of each statement included in the summary financial statements; (Ref: Para. A13)
   (ii)   Identifies the audited financial statements;
   (iii)   Refers to the auditor's report on the audited financial statements, the date of that report, and, subject to paragraphs 17-18, the fact that an unmodified opinion is expressed on the audited financial statements;
   (iv)   If the date of the auditor's report on the summary financial statements is later than the date of the auditor's report on the audited financial statements, states that the summary financial statements and the audited financial statements do not reflect the effects of events that occurred subsequent to the date of the auditor's report on the audited financial statements; and
   (v)   A statement indicating that the summary financial statements do not contain all the disclosures required by the financial reporting framework applied in the preparation of the audited financial statements, and that reading the summary financial statements is not a substitute for reading the audited financial statements.
(d)   A description of management's[5] responsibility for the summary financial statements, explaining that management[6] is responsible for the preparation of the summary financial statements in accordance with the applied criteria.
(e)   A statement that the auditor is responsible for expressing an opinion on the summary financial statements based on the procedures required by this ISA.
(f)   A paragraph clearly expressing an opinion (see paragraphs 9-11).
(g)   The auditor's signature.
(h)   The date of the auditor's report. (Ref: Para. A14)
(i)   The auditor's address.

If the addressee of the summary financial statements is not the same as the addressee   **15**
of the auditor's report on the audited financial statements, the auditor shall evaluate
the appropriateness of using a different addressee. (Ref: Para. A12)

The auditor shall date the auditor's report on the summary financial statements no   **16**
earlier than: (Ref: Para. A14)

---

[3] *ISA 560,* Subsequent Events.

[4] *Paragraphs 17-18, which deal with circumstances where the auditor's report on the audited financial statements has been modified, require additional elements to those listed in this paragraph.*

[5] *Or other term that is appropriate in the context of the legal framework in the particular jurisdiction.*

[6] *Or other term that is appropriate in the context of the legal framework in the particular jurisdiction.*

(a) The date on which the auditor has obtained sufficient appropriate evidence on which to base the opinion, including evidence that the summary financial statements have been prepared and those with the recognized authority have asserted that they have taken responsibility for them; and

(b) The date of the auditor's report on the audited financial statements.

Modifications to the Opinion, Emphasis of Matter Paragraph or Other Matter Paragraph in the Auditor's Report on the Audited Financial Statements (Ref: Para. A15)

17 When the auditor's report on the audited financial statements contains a qualified opinion, an Emphasis of Matter paragraph, or an Other Matter paragraph, but the auditor is satisfied that the summary financial statements are consistent, in all material respects, with or are a fair summary of the audited financial statements, in accordance with the applied criteria, the auditor's report on the summary financial statements shall, in addition to the elements in paragraph 14:

(a) State that the auditor's report on the audited financial statements contains a qualified opinion, an Emphasis of Matter paragraph, or an Other Matter paragraph; and

(b) Describe:
    (i) The basis for the qualified opinion on the audited financial statements, and that qualified opinion; or the Emphasis of Matter or the Other Matter paragraph in the auditor's report on the audited financial statements; and
    (ii) The effect thereof on the summary financial statements, if any.

18 When the auditor's report on the audited financial statements contains an adverse opinion or a disclaimer of opinion, the auditor's report on the summary financial statements shall, in addition to the elements in paragraph 14:

(a) State that the auditor's report on the audited financial statements contains an adverse opinion or disclaimer of opinion;

(b) Describe the basis for that adverse opinion or disclaimer of opinion; and

(c) State that, as a result of the adverse opinion or disclaimer of opinion, it is inappropriate to express an opinion on the summary financial statements.

Modified Opinion on the Summary Financial Statements

19 If the summary financial statements are not consistent, in all material respects, with or are not a fair summary of the audited financial statements, in accordance with the applied criteria, and management does not agree to make the necessary changes, the auditor shall express an adverse opinion on the summary financial statements. (Ref: Para. A15)

Restriction on Distribution or Use or Alerting Readers to the Basis of Accounting

20 When distribution or use of the auditor's report on the audited financial statements is restricted, or the auditor's report on the audited financial statements alerts readers that the audited financial statements are prepared in accordance with a special purpose framework, the auditor shall include a similar restriction or alert in the auditor's report on the summary financial statements.

Comparatives

If the audited financial statements contain comparatives, but the summary financial   **21**
statements do not, the auditor shall determine whether such omission is reasonable in
the circumstances of the engagement. The auditor shall determine the effect of an
unreasonable omission on the auditor's report on the summary financial statements.
(Ref: Para. A16)

If the summary financial statements contain comparatives that were reported on by   **22**
another auditor, the auditor's report on the summary financial statements shall also
contain the matters that ISA 710) requires the auditor to include in the auditor's
report on the audited financial statements.[7] (Ref: Para. A17)

Unaudited Supplementary Information Presented with Summary Financial Statements

The auditor shall evaluate whether any unaudited supplementary information pre-   **23**
sented with the summary financial statements is clearly differentiated from the
summary financial statements. If the auditor concludes that the entity's presentation
of the unaudited supplementary information is not clearly differentiated from the
summary financial statements, the auditor shall ask management to change the
presentation of the unaudited supplementary information. If management refuses to
do so, the auditor shall explain in the auditor's report on the summary financial
statements that such information is not covered by that report. (Ref: Para. A18)

Other Information in Documents Containing Summary Financial Statements

The auditor shall read other information included in a document containing the   **24**
summary financial statements and related auditor's report to identify material
inconsistencies, if any, with the summary financial statements. If, on reading the
other information, the auditor identifies a material inconsistency, the auditor shall
determine whether the summary financial statements or the other information needs
to be revised. If, on reading the other information, the auditor becomes aware of an
apparent material misstatement of fact, the auditor shall discuss the matter with
management. (Ref: Para. A19)

Auditor Association

If the auditor becomes aware that the entity plans to state that the auditor has   **25**
reported on summary financial statements in a document containing the summary
financial statements, but does not plan to include the related auditor's report, the
auditor shall request management to include the auditor's report in the document. If
management does not do so, the auditor shall determine and carry out other
appropriate actions designed to prevent management from inappropriately asso-
ciating the auditor with the summary financial statements in that document. (Ref:
Para. A20)

The auditor may be engaged to report on the financial statements of an entity, while   **26**
not engaged to report on the summary financial statements. If, in this case, the
auditor becomes aware that the entity plans to make a statement in a document that
refers to the auditor and the fact that summary financial statements are derived from
the financial statements audited by the auditor, the auditor shall be satisfied that:

[7] *ISA 710*, Comparative Information—Corresponding Figures and Comparative Financial Statements.

(a)　The reference to the auditor is made in the context of the auditor's report on the audited financial statements; and

(b)　The statement does not give the impression that the auditor has reported on the summary financial statements.

If (a) or (b) are not met, the auditor shall request management to change the statement to meet them, or not to refer to the auditor in the document. Alternatively, the entity may engage the auditor to report on the summary financial statements and include the related auditor's report in the document. If management does not change the statement, delete the reference to the auditor, or include an auditor's report on the summary financial statements in the document containing the summary financial statements, the auditor shall advise management that the auditor disagrees with the reference to the auditor, and the auditor shall determine and carry out other appropriate actions designed to prevent management from inappropriately referring to the auditor. (Ref: Para. A20)

***

Application and Other Explanatory Material

Engagement Acceptance (Ref: Para. 5-6)

A1　The audit of the financial statements from which the summary financial statements are derived provides the auditor with the necessary knowledge to discharge the auditor's responsibilities in relation to the summary financial statements in accordance with this ISA. Application of this ISA will not provide sufficient appropriate evidence on which to base the opinion on the summary financial statements if the auditor has not also audited the financial statements from which the summary financial statements are derived.

A2　Management's agreement with the matters described in paragraph 6 may be evidenced by its written acceptance of the terms of the engagement.

Criteria (Ref: Para. 6(a))

A3　The preparation of summary financial statements requires management to determine the information that needs to be reflected in the summary financial statements so that they are consistent, in all material respects, with or represent a fair summary of the audited financial statements. Because summary financial statements by their nature contain aggregated information and limited disclosure, there is an increased risk that they may not contain the information necessary so as not to be misleading in the circumstances. This risk increases when established criteria for the preparation of summary financial statements do not exist.

A4　Factors that may affect the auditor's determination of the acceptability of the applied criteria include:

- The nature of the entity;
- The purpose of the summary financial statements;
- The information needs of the intended users of the summary financial statements; and
- Whether the applied criteria will result in summary financial statements that are not misleading in the circumstances.

The criteria for the preparation of summary financial statements may be established   **A5** by an authorized or recognized standards setting organization or by law or regulation. Similar to the case of financial statements, as explained in ISA 210,[8] in many such cases, the auditor may presume that such criteria are acceptable.

Where established criteria for the preparation of summary financial statements do   **A6** not exist, criteria may be developed by management, for example, based on practice in a particular industry. Criteria that are acceptable in the circumstances will result in summary financial statements that:

(a) Adequately disclose their summarized nature and identify the audited financial statements;

(b) Clearly describe from whom or where the audited financial statements are available or, if law or regulation provides that the audited financial statements need not be made available to the intended users of the summary financial statements and establishes the criteria for the preparation of the summary financial statements, that law or regulation;

(c) Adequately disclose the applied criteria;

(d) Agree with or can be recalculated from the related information in the audited financial statements; and

(e) In view of the purpose of the summary financial statements, contain the information necessary, and are at an appropriate level of aggregation, so as not to be misleading in the circumstances.

Adequate disclosure of the summarized nature of the summary financial statements   **A7** and the identity of the audited financial statements, as referred to in paragraph A6(a), may, for example, be provided by a title such as "Summary Financial Statements Prepared from the Audited Financial Statements for the Year Ended December 31, 20X1."

Evaluating the Availability of the Audited Financial Statements (Ref: Para. 8(g))

The auditor's evaluation whether the audited financial statements are available to the   **A8** intended users of the summary financial statements without undue difficulty is affected by factors such as whether:

- The summary financial statements describe clearly from whom or where the audited financial statements are available;
- The audited financial statements are on public record; or
- Management has established a process by which the intended users of the summary financial statements can obtain ready access to the audited financial statements.

Form of Opinion (Ref: Para. 9)

A conclusion, based on an evaluation of the evidence obtained by performing the   **A9** procedures in paragraph 8, that an unmodified opinion on the summary financial statements is appropriate enables the auditor to express an opinion containing one of the phrases in paragraph 9. The auditor's decision as to which of the phrases to use may be affected by generally accepted practice in the particular jurisdiction.

---

[8] *ISA 210, Agreeing the Terms of Audit Engagements, paragraphs A3 and A8-A9.*

Timing of Work and Events Subsequent to the Date of the Auditor's Report on the Audited Financial Statements (Ref: Para. 12)

A10 The procedures described in paragraph 8 are often performed during or immediately after the audit of the financial statements. When the auditor reports on the summary financial statements after the completion of the audit of the financial statements, the auditor is not required to obtain additional audit evidence on the audited financial statements, or report on the effects of events that occurred subsequent to the date of the auditor's report on the audited financial statements since the summary financial statements are derived from the audited financial statements and do not update them.

Auditor's Report on Summary Financial Statements

Elements of the Auditor's Report

Title (Ref: Para. 14(a))

A11 A title indicating the report is the report of an independent auditor, for example, "Report of the Independent Auditor," affirms that the auditor has met all of the relevant ethical requirements regarding independence. This distinguishes the report of the independent auditor from reports issued by others.

Addressee (Ref: Para. 14(b), 15)

A12 Factors that may affect the auditor's evaluation of the appropriateness of the addressee of the summary financial statements include the terms of the engagement, the nature of the entity, and the purpose of the summary financial statements.

Introductory Paragraph (Ref: Para. 14(c)(i))

A13 When the auditor is aware that the summary financial statements will be included in a document that contains other information, the auditor may consider, if the form of presentation allows, identifying the page numbers on which the summary financial statements are presented. This helps readers to identify the summary financial statements to which the auditor's report relates.

Date of the Auditor's Report (Ref: Para. 14(h), 16)

A14 The person or persons with recognized authority to conclude that the summary financial statements have been prepared and take responsibility for them depend on the terms of the engagement, the nature of the entity, and the purpose of the summary financial statements.

Illustrations (Ref: Para.14. 17-18, 19)

A15 The Appendix to this ISA contains illustrations of auditors' reports on summary financial statements that:

(a) Contain unmodified opinions;

(b) Are derived from audited financial statements on which the auditor issued modified opinions; and

(c) Contain a modified opinion.

Comparatives (Ref: Para. 21-22)

If the audited financial statements contain comparatives, there is a presumption that   **A16**
the summary financial statements also would contain comparatives. Comparatives in
the audited financial statements may be regarded as corresponding figures or as
comparative financial information. ISA 710 describes how this difference affects the
auditor's report on the financial statements, including, in particular, reference to
other auditors who audited the financial statements for the prior period.

Circumstances that may affect the auditor's determination whether an omission of   **A17**
comparatives is reasonable include the nature and objective of the summary financial
statements, the applied criteria, and the information needs of the intended users of
the summary financial statements.

**Unaudited Supplementary Information Presented with Summary Financial
Statements** (Ref: Para. 23)

ISA 700[9] contains requirements and guidance to be applied when unaudited sup-   **A18**
plementary information is presented with audited financial statements that, adapted
as necessary in the circumstances, may be helpful in applying the requirement in
paragraph 23.

Other Information in Documents Containing Summary Financial Statements
(Ref: Para. 24)

ISA 720[10] contains requirements and guidance relating to reading other information   **A19**
included in a document containing the audited financial statements and related
auditor's report, and responding to material inconsistencies and material misstatements of fact. Adapted as necessary in the circumstances, they may be helpful in
applying the requirement in paragraph 24.

Auditor Association (Ref: Para. 25-26)

Other appropriate actions the auditor may take when management does not take the   **A20**
requested action may include informing the intended users and other known third-
party users of the inappropriate reference to the auditor. The auditor's course of
action depends on the auditor's legal rights and obligations. Consequently, the
auditor may consider it appropriate to seek legal advice.

Appendix   (Ref: Para. A15)

Illustrations of Reports on Summary Financial Statements

- Illustration 1: An auditor's report on summary financial statements prepared in
  accordance with established criteria. An unmodified opinion is expressed on the
  audited financial statements. The auditor's report on the summary financial
  statements is dated later than the date of the auditor's report on the financial
  statements from which summary financial statements are derived.

[9] *ISA 700*, Forming an Opinion and Reporting on Financial Statements, *paragraphs 46-47*.

[10] *ISA 720*, The Auditor's Responsibilities Relating to Other Information in Documents Containing Audited
Financial Statements.

- Illustration 2: An auditor's report on summary financial statements prepared in accordance with criteria developed by management and adequately disclosed in the summary financial statements. The auditor has determined that the applied criteria are acceptable in the circumstances. An unmodified opinion is expressed on the audited financial statements.
- Illustration 3: An auditor's report on summary financial statements prepared in accordance with criteria developed by management and adequately disclosed in the summary financial statements. The auditor has determined that the applied criteria are acceptable in the circumstances. A qualified opinion is expressed on the audited financial statements.
- Illustration 4: An auditor's report on summary financial statements prepared in accordance with criteria developed by management and adequately disclosed in the summary financial statements. The auditor has determined that the applied criteria are acceptable in the circumstances. An adverse opinion is expressed on the audited financial statements.
- Illustration 5: An auditor's report on summary financial statements prepared in accordance with established criteria. An unmodified opinion is expressed on the audited financial statements. The auditor concludes that it is not possible to express an unmodified opinion on the summary financial statements.

Illustration 1:

Circumstances include the following:

- **An unmodified opinion is expressed on the audited financial statements.**

- **Established criteria for the preparation of summary financial statements exist.**

- **The auditor's report on the summary financial statements is dated later than the date of the auditor's report on the financial statements from which the summary financial statements are derived.**

REPORT OF THE INDEPENDENT AUDITOR ON THE SUMMARY FINANCIAL STATEMENTS

[Appropriate Addressee]

The accompanying summary financial statements, which comprise the summary balance sheet as at December 31, 20X1, the summary income statement, summary statement of changes in equity and summary cash flow statement for the year then ended, and related notes, are derived from the audited financial statements of ABC Company for the year ended December 31, 20X1. We expressed an unmodified audit opinion on those financial statements in our report dated February 15, 20X2. Those financial statements, and the summary financial statements, do not reflect the effects of events that occurred subsequent to the date of our report on those financial statements.

The summary financial statements do not contain all the disclosures required by [describe financial reporting framework applied in the preparation of the audited financial statements of ABC Company]. Reading the summary financial statements, therefore, is not a substitute for reading the audited financial statements of ABC Company.

Management's[11] Responsibility for the Summary Financial Statements

Management is responsible for the preparation of a summary of the audited financial statements in accordance with [describe established criteria].

Auditor's Responsibility

Our responsibility is to express an opinion on the summary financial statements based on our procedures, which were conducted in accordance with International Standard on Auditing (ISA) 810, "Engagements to Report on Summary Financial Statements."

Opinion

In our opinion, the summary financial statements derived from the audited financial statements of ABC Company for the year ended December 31, 20X1 are consistent, in all material respects, with (or *a fair summary of*) those financial statements, in accordance with [describe established criteria].

[Auditor's signature]

[Date of the auditor's report]

[Auditor's address]

---

[11] *Or other term that is appropriate in the context of the legal framework in the particular jurisdiction.*

> **Illustration 2:**
>
> **Circumstances include the following:**
>
> - **An unmodified opinion is expressed on the audited financial statements.**
>
> - **Criteria are developed by management and adequately disclosed in Note X. The auditor has determined that the criteria are acceptable in the circumstances.**

REPORT OF THE INDEPENDENT AUDITOR ON THE SUMMARY FINANCIAL STATEMENTS

[Appropriate Addressee]

The accompanying summary financial statements, which comprise the summary balance sheet as at December 31, 20X1, the summary income statement, summary statement of changes in equity and summary cash flow statement for the year then ended, and related notes, are derived from the audited financial statements of ABC Company for the year ended December 31, 20X1. We expressed an unmodified audit opinion on those financial statements in our report dated February 15, 20X2.[12]

The summary financial statements do not contain all the disclosures required by [describe financial reporting framework applied in the preparation of the audited financial statements of ABC Company]. Reading the summary financial statements, therefore, is not a substitute for reading the audited financial statements of ABC Company.

Management's[13] Responsibility for the Summary Financial Statements

Management is responsible for the preparation of a summary of the audited financial statements on the basis described in Note X.

Auditor's Responsibility

Our responsibility is to express an opinion on the summary financial statements based on our procedures, which were conducted in accordance with International Standard on Auditing (ISA) 810, "Engagements to Report on Summary Financial Statements."

Opinion

In our opinion, the summary financial statements derived from the audited financial statements of ABC Company for the year ended December 31, 20X1 are consistent, in all material respects, with (or *a fair summary of*) those financial statements, on the basis described in Note X.

[Auditor's signature]

[Date of the auditor's report]

[Auditor's address]

---

[12] *When the auditor's report on the summary financial statements is dated later than the date of the auditor's report on the audited financial statements from which it is derived, the following sentence is added to this paragraph: "Those financial statements, and the summary financial statements, do not reflect the effects of events that occurred subsequent to the date of our report on those financial statements."*

[13] *Or other term that is appropriate in the context of the legal framework in the particular jurisdiction.*

Illustration 3:

Circumstances include the following:

- **A qualified opinion is expressed on the audited financial statements.**

- **Criteria are developed by management and adequately disclosed in Note X. The auditor has determined that the criteria are acceptable in the circumstances.**

REPORT OF THE INDEPENDENT AUDITOR ON THE SUMMARY FINANCIAL STATEMENTS

[Appropriate Addressee]

The accompanying summary financial statements, which comprise the summary balance sheet as at December 31, 20X1, the summary income statement, summary statement of changes in equity and summary cash flow statement for the year then ended, and related notes, are derived from the audited financial statements of ABC Company for the year ended December 31, 20X1.[14] We expressed a qualified audit opinion on those financial statements in our report dated February 15, 20X2 (see below).

The summary financial statements do not contain all the disclosures required by [describe financial reporting framework applied in the preparation of the audited financial statements of ABC Company]. Reading the summary financial statements, therefore, is not a substitute for reading the audited financial statements of ABC Company.

Management's[15] Responsibility for the Summary Financial Statements

Management is responsible for the preparation of a summary of the audited financial statements on the basis described in Note X.

Auditor's Responsibility

Our responsibility is to express an opinion on the summary financial statements based on our procedures, which were conducted in accordance with International Standard on Auditing (ISA) 810, "Engagements to Report on Summary Financial Statements."

Opinion

In our opinion, the summary financial statements derived from the audited financial statements of ABC Company for the year ended December 31, 20X1 are consistent, in all material respects, with (or *a fair summary of*) those financial statements, on the basis described in Note X. However, the summary financial statements are misstated to the equivalent extent as the audited financial statements of ABC Company for the year ended December 31, 20X1.

---

[14] *When the auditor's report on the summary financial statements is dated later than the date of the auditor's report on the audited financial statements from which it is derived, the following sentence is added to this paragraph: "Those financial statements, and the summary financial statements, do not reflect the effects of events that occurred subsequent to the date of our report on those financial statements."*

[15] *Or other term that is appropriate in the context of the legal framework in the particular jurisdiction.*

The misstatement of the audited financial statements is described in our qualified audit opinion in our report dated February 15, 20X2. Our qualified audit opinion is based on the fact that the company's inventories are carried in the balance sheet in those financial statements at xxx. Management has not stated the inventories at the lower of cost and net realizable value but has stated them solely at cost, which constitutes a departure from International Financial Reporting Standards. The company's records indicate that had management stated the inventories at the lower of cost and net realizable value, an amount of xxx would have been required to write the inventories down to their net realizable value. Accordingly, cost of sales would have been increased by xxx, and income tax, net income and shareholders' equity would have been reduced by xxx, xxx and xxx, respectively. Our qualified audit opinion states that, except for the effects of the described matter, those financial statements present fairly, in all material respects, (or *give a true and fair view of*) the financial position of ABC Company as at December 31, 20X1, and (*of*) its financial performance and its cash flows for the year then ended in accordance with International Financial Reporting Standards.

[Auditor's signature]

[Date of the auditor's report]

[Auditor's address]

> **Illustration 4:**
>
> **Circumstances include the following:**
>
> - **An adverse opinion is expressed on the audited financial statements.**
>
> - **Criteria are developed by management and adequately disclosed in Note X. The auditor has determined that the criteria are acceptable in the circumstances.**

REPORT OF THE INDEPENDENT AUDITOR ON THE SUMMARY FINANCIAL STATEMENTS

[Appropriate Addressee]

The accompanying summary financial statements, which comprise the summary balance sheet as at December 31, 20X1, the summary income statement, summary statement of changes in equity and summary cash flow statement for the year then ended, and related notes, are derived from the audited financial statements of ABC Company for the year ended December 31, 20X1.[16]

The summary financial statements do not contain all the disclosures required by [describe financial reporting framework applied in the preparation of the audited financial statements of ABC Company]. Reading the summary financial statements, therefore, is not a substitute for reading the audited financial statements of ABC Company.

Management's[17] Responsibility for the Summary Financial Statements

Management is responsible for the preparation of a summary of the audited financial statements on the basis described in Note X.

Auditor's Responsibility

Our responsibility is to express an opinion on the summary financial statements based on our procedures, which were conducted in accordance with International Standard on Auditing (ISA) 810, "Engagements to Report on Summary Financial Statements."

Denial of Opinion

In our report dated February 15, 20X2, we expressed an adverse audit opinion on the financial statements of ABC Company for the year ended December 31, 20X1. The basis for our adverse audit opinion was [describe basis for adverse audit opinion]. Our adverse audit opinion stated that [describe adverse audit opinion].

Because of the significance of the matter discussed above, it is inappropriate to express an opinion on the summary financial statements of ABC Company for the year ended December 31, 20X1.

---

[16] *When the auditor's report on the summary financial statements is dated later than the date of the auditor's report on the audited financial statements from which it is derived, the following sentence is added to this paragraph: "Those financial statements, and the summary financial statements, do not reflect the effects of events that occurred subsequent to the date of our report on those financial statements."*

[17] *Or other term that is appropriate in the context of the legal framework in the particular jurisdiction.*

[Auditor's signature]

[Date of the auditor's report]

[Auditor's address]

Illustration 5:

Circumstances include the following:

- An unmodified opinion is expressed on the audited financial statements.

- Established criteria for the preparation of summary financial statements exist.

- The auditor concludes that it is not possible to express an unmodified opinion on the summary financial statements.

REPORT OF THE INDEPENDENT AUDITOR ON THE SUMMARY FINANCIAL STATEMENTS

[Appropriate Addressee]

The accompanying summary financial statements, which comprise the summary balance sheet as at December 31, 20X1, the summary income statement, summary statement of changes in equity and summary cash flow statement for the year then ended, and related notes, are derived from the audited financial statements of ABC Company for the year ended December 31, 20X1. We expressed an unmodified audit opinion on those financial statements in our report dated February 15, 20X2.[18]

The summary financial statements do not contain all the disclosures required by [describe financial reporting framework applied in the preparation of the audited financial statements of ABC Company]. Reading the summary financial statements, therefore, is not a substitute for reading the audited financial statements of ABC Company.

Management's[19] Responsibility for the Summary Audited Financial Statements

Management is responsible for the preparation of a summary of the audited financial statements in accordance with [describe established criteria].

Auditor's Responsibility

Our responsibility is to express an opinion on the summary financial statements based on our procedures, which were conducted in accordance with International Standard on Auditing (ISA) 810, "Engagements to Report on Summary Financial Statements."

Basis for Adverse Opinion

[Describe matter that caused the summary financial statements not to be consistent, in all material respects, with (or *a fair summary of*) the audited financial statements, in accordance with the applied criteria.]

---

[18] *When the auditor's report on the summary financial statements is dated later than the date of the auditor's report on the audited financial statements from which it is derived, the following sentence is added to this paragraph: "Those financial statements, and the summary financial statements, do not reflect the effects of events that occurred subsequent to the date of our report on those financial statements."*

[19] *Or other term that is appropriate in the context of the legal framework in the particular jurisdiction.*

Adverse Opinion

In our opinion, because of the significance of the matter discussed in the Basis for Adverse Opinion paragraph, the summary financial statements referred to above are not consistent with (or *a fair summary of*) the audited financial statements of ABC Company for the year ended December 31, 20X1, in accordance with [describe established criteria].

[Auditor's signature]

[Date of the auditor's report]

[Auditor's address]

Part Three

International Auditing Practice Note (IAPN)

International Auditing Practice Note 1000

Special considerations in auditing financial instruments

Contents

International Auditing Practice Note (IAPN) 1000, *Special Considerations in Auditing Financial Instruments*, should be read in conjunction with the *Preface to the International Quality Control, Auditing, Review, Other Assurance, and Related Services Pronouncements*. IAPNs do not impose additional requirements on auditors beyond those included in the International Standards on Auditing (ISAs), nor do they change the auditor's responsibility to comply with all ISAs relevant to the audit. IAPNs provide practical assistance to auditors. They are intended to be disseminated by those responsible for national standards, or used in developing corresponding national material. They also provide material that firms can use in developing their training programs and internal guidance.

Introduction

Financial instruments may be used by financial and non-financial entities of all sizes   **1**
for a variety of purposes. Some entities have large holdings and transaction volumes
while other entities may only engage in a few financial instrument transactions. Some
entities may take positions in financial instruments to assume and benefit from risk
while other entities may use financial instruments to reduce certain risks by hedging
or managing exposures. This International Auditing Practice Note (IAPN) is relevant to all of these situations.

The following International Standards on Auditing (ISAs) are particularly relevant   **2**
to audits of financial instruments:

(a)   ISA 540[1] deals with the auditor's responsibilities relating to auditing accounting
      estimates, including accounting estimates related to financial instruments mea-
      sured at fair value;
(b)   ISA 315[2] and ISA 330[3] deal with identifying and assessing risks of material
      misstatement and responding to those risks; and
(c)   ISA 500[4] explains what constitutes audit evidence and deals with the auditor's
      responsibility to design and perform audit procedures to obtain sufficient
      appropriate audit evidence to be able to draw reasonable conclusions on which
      to base the auditor's opinion.

The purpose of this IAPN is to provide: **3**

(a)   Background information about financial instruments (Section I); and
(b)   Discussion of audit considerations relating to financial instruments (Section II).

IAPNs provide practical assistance to auditors. They are intended to be disseminated
by those responsible for national standards, or used in developing corresponding
national material. They also provide material that firms can use in developing their
training programs and internal guidance.

This IAPN is relevant to entities of all sizes, as all entities may be subject to risks of   **4**
material misstatement when using financial instruments.

The guidance on valuation[5] in this IAPN is likely to be more relevant for financial   **5**
instruments measured or disclosed at fair value, while the guidance on areas other
than valuation applies equally to financial instruments either measured at fair value
or amortized cost. This IAPN is also applicable to both financial assets and financial
liabilities. This IAPN does not deal with instruments such as:

(a)   The simplest financial instruments such as cash, simple loans, trade accounts
      receivable and trade accounts payable;
(b)   Investments in unlisted equity instruments; or
(c)   Insurance contracts.

[1] *ISA 540, Auditing Accounting Estimates, Including Fair Value Accounting Estimates, and Related Disclosures*

[2] *ISA 315, Identifying and Assessing the Risks of Material Misstatement through Understanding the Entity and Its Environment*

[3] *ISA 330, The Auditor's Responses to Assessed Risks*

[4] *ISA 500, Audit Evidence*

[5] *In this IAPN, the terms "valuation" and "measurement" are used interchangeably.*

6   Also, this IAPN does not deal with specific accounting issues relevant to financial instruments, such as hedge accounting, profit or loss on inception (often known as "Day 1" profit or loss), offsetting, risk transfers or impairment, including loan loss provisioning. Although these subject matters can relate to an entity's accounting for financial instruments, a discussion of the auditor's consideration regarding how to address specific accounting requirements is beyond the scope of this IAPN.

7   An audit in accordance with ISAs is conducted on the premise that management and, where appropriate, those charged with governance have acknowledged certain responsibilities. Such responsibilities subsume making fair value measurements. This IAPN does not impose responsibilities on management or those charged with governance nor override laws and regulation that govern their responsibilities.

8   This IAPN has been written in the context of general purpose fair presentation financial reporting frameworks, but may also be useful, as appropriate in the circumstance, in other financial reporting frameworks such as special purpose financial reporting frameworks.

9   This IAPN focuses on the assertions of valuation, and presentation and disclosure, but also covers, in less detail, completeness, accuracy, existence, and rights and obligations.

10   Financial instruments are susceptible to estimation uncertainty, which is defined in ISA 540 as "the susceptibility of an accounting estimate and related disclosures to an inherent lack of precision in its measurement."[6] Estimation uncertainty is affected by the complexity of financial instruments, among other factors. The nature and reliability of information available to support the measurement of financial instruments varies widely, which affects the estimation uncertainty associated with their measurement. This IAPN uses the term "measurement uncertainty" to refer to the estimation uncertainty associated with fair value measurements.

Section I—Background Information about Financial Instruments

11   Different definitions of financial instruments may exist among financial reporting frameworks. For example, International Financial Reporting Standards (IFRS) define a financial instrument as any contract that gives rise to a financial asset of one entity and a financial liability or equity instrument of another entity.[7] Financial instruments may be cash, the equity of another entity, the contractual right or obligation to receive or deliver cash or exchange financial assets or liabilities, certain contracts settled in an entity's own equity instruments, certain contracts on non-financial items, or certain contracts issued by insurers that do not meet the definition of an insurance contract. This definition encompasses a wide range of financial instruments from simple loans and deposits to complex derivatives, structured products, and some commodity contracts.

12   Financial instruments vary in complexity, though the complexity of the financial instrument can come from difference sources, such as:

- A very high volume of individual cash flows, where a lack of homogeneity requires analysis of each one or a large number of grouped cash flows to

---

[6] *ISA 540, paragraph 7(c)*

[7] *International Accounting Standard (IAS) 32, Financial Instruments: Presentation*, paragraph 11

evaluate, for example, credit risk (for example, collateralized debt obligations (CDOs)).
- Complex formulae for determining the cash flows.
- Uncertainty or variability of future cash flows, such as that arising from credit risk, option contracts or financial instruments with lengthy contractual terms.

The higher the variability of cash flows to changes in market conditions, the more complex and uncertain the fair value measurement of the financial instrument is likely to be. In addition, sometimes financial instruments that, ordinarily, are relatively easy to value become complex to value because of particular circumstances, for example, instruments for which the market has become inactive or which have lengthy contractual terms. Derivatives and structured products become more complex when they are a combination of individual financial instruments. In addition, the accounting for financial instruments under certain financial reporting frameworks or certain market conditions may be complex.

Another source of complexity is the volume of financial instruments held or traded. **13** While a "plain vanilla" interest rate swap may not be complex, an entity holding a large number of them may use a sophisticated information system to identify, value and transact these instruments.

Purpose and Risks of Using Financial Instruments

Financial instruments are used for: **14**
- Hedging purposes (that is, to change an existing risk profile to which an entity is exposed). This includes:
  - The forward purchase or sale of currency to fix a future exchange rate;
  - Converting future interest rates to fixed rates or floating rates through the use of swaps; and
  - The purchase of option contracts to provide an entity with protection against a particular price movement, including contracts which may contain embedded derivatives;
- Trading purposes (for example, to enable an entity to take a risk position to benefit from short term market movements); and
- Investment purposes (for example, to enable an entity to benefit from long term investment returns).

The use of financial instruments can reduce exposures to certain business risks, for **15** example changes in exchange rates, interest rates and commodity prices, or a combination of those risks. On the other hand, the inherent complexities of some financial instruments also may result in increased risk.

Business risk and the risk of material misstatement increase when management and **16** those charged with governance:
- Do not fully understand the risks of using financial instruments and have insufficient skills and experience to manage those risks;
- Do not have the expertise to value them appropriately in accordance with the applicable financial reporting framework;
- Do not have sufficient controls in place over financial instrument activities; or
- Inappropriately hedge risks or speculate.

Management's failure to fully understand the risks inherent in a financial instrument **17** can have a direct effect on management's ability to manage these risks appropriately, and may ultimately threaten the viability of the entity.

18   The principal types of risk applicable to financial instruments are listed below. This list is not meant to be exhaustive and different terminology may be used to describe these risks or classify the components of individual risks.

(a)   Credit (or counterparty) risk is the risk that one party to a financial instrument will cause a financial loss to another party by failing to discharge an obligation and is often associated with default. Credit risk includes settlement risk, which is the risk that one side of a transaction will be settled without consideration being received from the customer or counterparty.

(b)   Market risk is the risk that the fair value or future cash flows of a financial instrument will fluctuate because of changes in market prices. Examples of market risk include currency risk, interest rate risk, commodity and equity price risk.

(c)   Liquidity risk includes the risk of not being able to buy or sell a financial instrument at an appropriate price in a timely manner due to a lack of marketability for that financial instrument.

(d)   Operational risk relates to the specific processing required for financial instruments. Operational risk may increase as the complexity of a financial instrument increases, and poor management of operational risk may increase other types of risk. Operational risk includes:

(i)   The risk that confirmation and reconciliation controls are inadequate resulting in incomplete or inaccurate recording of financial instruments;

(ii)   The risks that there is inappropriate documentation of transactions and insufficient monitoring of these transactions;

(iii)   The risk that transactions are incorrectly recorded, processed or risk managed and, therefore, do not reflect the economics of the overall trade;

(iv)   The risk that undue reliance is placed by staff on the accuracy of valuation techniques, without adequate review, and transactions are therefore incorrectly valued or their risk is improperly measured;

(v)   The risk that the use of financial instruments is not adequately incorporated into the entity's risk management policies and procedures;

(vi)   The risk of loss resulting from inadequate or failed internal processes and systems, or from external events, including the risk of fraud from both internal and external sources;

(vii)   The risk that there is inadequate or non-timely maintenance of valuation techniques used to measure financial instruments; and

(viii)   Legal risk, which is a component of operational risk, and relates to losses resulting from a legal or regulatory action that invalidates or otherwise precludes performance by the end user or its counterparty under the terms of the contract or related netting arrangements. For example, legal risk could arise from insufficient or incorrect documentation for the contract, an inability to enforce a netting arrangement in bankruptcy, adverse changes in tax laws, or statutes that prohibit entities from investing in certain types of financial instruments.

19   Other considerations relevant to risks of using financial instruments include:

- The risk of fraud that may be increased if, for example, an employee in a position to perpetrate a financial fraud understands both the financial instruments and the processes for accounting for them, but management and those charged with governance have a lesser degree of understanding.
- The risk that master netting arrangements[8] may not be properly reflected in the financial statements.

---

[8] *An entity that undertakes a number of financial instrument transactions with a single counterparty may enter into a master netting arrangement with that counterparty. Such an agreement provides for a single net settlement of all financial instruments covered by the agreement in the event of default of any one contract.*

- The risk that some financial instruments may change between being assets or liabilities during their term and that such change may occur rapidly.

Controls Relating to Financial Instruments

The extent of an entity's use of financial instruments and the degree of complexity of the instruments are important determinants of the necessary level of sophistication of the entity's internal control. For example, smaller entities may use less structured products and simple processes and procedures to achieve their objectives.   **20**

Often, it is the role of those charged with governance to set the tone regarding, and approve and oversee the extent of use of, financial instruments while it is management's role to manage and monitor the entity's exposures to those risks. Management and, where appropriate, those charged with governance are also responsible for designing and implementing a system of internal control to enable the preparation of financial statements in accordance with the applicable financial reporting framework. An entity's internal control over financial instruments is more likely to be effective when management and those charged with governance have: **21**

(a) Established an appropriate control environment, active participation by those charged with governance in controlling the use of financial instruments, a logical organizational structure with clear assignment of authority and responsibility, and appropriate human resource policies and procedures. In particular, clear rules are needed on the extent to which those responsible for financial instrument activities are permitted to act. Such rules have regard to any legal or regulatory restrictions on using financial instruments. For example, certain public sector entities may not have the power to conduct business using derivatives;

(b) Established a risk management process relative to the size of the entity and the complexity of its financial instruments (for example, in some entities a formal risk management function may exist);

(c) Established information systems that provide those charged with governance with an understanding of the nature of the financial instrument activities and the associated risks, including adequate documentation of transactions;

(d) Designed, implemented and documented a system of internal control to:
   o   Provide reasonable assurance that the entity's use of financial instruments is within its risk management policies;
   o   Properly present financial instruments in the financial statements;
   o   Ensure that the entity is in compliance with applicable laws and regulations; and
   o   Monitor risk.
   The Appendix provides examples of controls that may exist in an entity that deals in a high volume of financial instrument transactions; and

(e) Established appropriate accounting policies, including valuation policies, in accordance with the applicable financial reporting framework.

Key elements of risk management processes and internal control relating to an entity's financial instruments include: **22**

- Setting an approach to define the amount of risk exposure that the entity is willing to accept when engaging in financial instrument transactions (this may be referred to as its "risk appetite"), including policies for investing in financial instruments, and the control framework in which the financial instrument activities are conducted;

- Establishing processes for the documentation and authorization of new types of financial instrument transactions which consider the accounting, regulatory, legal, financial and operational risks that are associated with such instruments;
- Processing financial instrument transactions, including confirmation and reconciliation of cash and asset holdings to external statements, and the payments process;
- Segregation of duties between those investing or trading in the financial instruments and those responsible for processing, valuing and confirming such instruments. For example, a model development function that is involved in assisting in pricing deals is less objective than one that is functionally and organizationally separate from the front office;
- Valuation processes and controls, including controls over data obtained from third-party pricing sources; and
- Monitoring of controls.

23   The nature of risks often differs between entities with a high volume and variety of financial instruments and those with only a few financial instrument transactions. This results in different approaches to internal control. For example:

- Typically, an institution with high volumes of financial instruments will have a dealing room type environment in which there are specialist traders and segregation of duties between those traders and the back office (which refers to the operations function that data-checks trades that have been conducted, ensuring that they are not erroneous, and transacting the required transfers). In such environments, the traders will typically initiate contracts verbally over the phone or via an electronic trading platform. Capturing relevant transactions and accurately recording financial instruments in such an environment is significantly more challenging than for an entity with only a few financial instruments, whose existence and completeness often can be confirmed with a bank confirmation to a few banks.
- On the other hand, entities with only a small number of financial instruments often do not have segregation of duties, and access to the market is limited. In such cases, although it may be easier to identify financial instrument transactions, there is a risk that management may rely on a limited number of personnel, which may increase the risk that unauthorized transactions may be initiated or transactions may not be recorded.

Completeness, Accuracy, and Existence

24   Paragraphs 25–33 describe controls and processes which may be in place in entities with a high volume of financial instrument transactions, including those with trading rooms. By contrast, an entity that does not have a high volume of financial instrument transactions may not have these controls and processes but may instead confirm their transactions with the counterparty or clearing house. Doing so may be relatively straightforward in that the entity may only transact with one or two counterparties.

Trade Confirmations and Clearing Houses

25   Generally, for transactions undertaken by financial institutions, the terms of financial instruments are documented in confirmations exchanged between counterparties and legal agreements. Clearing houses serve to monitor the exchange of confirmations by matching trades and settling them. A central clearing house is associated with an exchange and entities that clear through clearing houses typically have processes to manage the information delivered to the clearing house.

Not all transactions are settled through such an exchange. In many other markets **26**
there is an established practice of agreeing the terms of transactions before settlement
begins. To be effective, this process needs to be run separately from those who trade
the financial instruments to minimize the risk of fraud. In other markets, transactions are confirmed after settlement has begun and sometimes confirmation backlogs
result in settlement beginning before all terms have been fully agreed. This presents
additional risk because the transacting entities need to rely on alternative means of
agreeing trades. These may include:

- Enforcing rigorous reconciliations between the records of those trading the
  financial instruments and those settling them (strong segregation of duties
  between the two are important), combined with strong supervisory controls over
  those trading the financial instruments to ensure the integrity of the
  transactions;
- Reviewing summary documentation from counterparties that highlights the key
  terms even if the full terms have not been agreed; and
- Thorough review of traders' profits and losses to ensure that they reconcile to
  what the back office has calculated.

Reconciliations with Banks and Custodians

Some components of financial instruments, such as bonds and shares, may be held in **27**
separate depositories. In addition, most financial instruments result in payments of
cash at some point and often these cash flows begin early in the contract's life. These
cash payments and receipts will pass through an entity's bank account. Regular
reconciliation of the entity's records to external banks' and custodians' records
enables the entity to ensure transactions are properly recorded.

It should be noted that not all financial instruments result in a cash flow in the early **28**
stages of the contract's life or are capable of being recorded with an exchange or
custodian. Where this is the case, reconciliation processes will not identify an omitted
or inaccurately recorded trade and confirmation controls are more important. Even
where such a cash flow is accurately recorded in the early stages of an instrument's
life, this does not ensure that all characteristics or terms of the instrument (for
example, the maturity or an early termination option) have been recorded accurately.

In addition, cash movements may be quite small in the context of the overall size of **29**
the trade or the entity's own balance sheet and may therefore be difficult to identify.
The value of reconciliations is enhanced when finance, or other back office staff,
review entries in all general ledger accounts to ensure that they are valid and sup-
portable. This process will help identify if the other side to cash entries relating to
financial instruments has not been properly recorded. Reviewing suspense and
clearing accounts is important regardless of the account balance, as there may be
offsetting reconciling items in the account.

In entities with a high volume of financial instrument transactions, reconciliation and **30**
confirmation controls may be automated and, if so, adequate IT controls need to be
in place to support them. In particular, controls are needed to ensure that data is
completely and accurately picked up from external sources (such as banks and
custodians) and from the entity's records and is not tampered with before or during
reconciliation. Controls are also needed to ensure that the criteria on which entries
are matched are sufficiently restrictive to prevent inaccurate clearance of reconciling
items.

Other Controls over Completeness, Accuracy, and Existence

31   The complexity inherent in some financial instruments means that it will not always be obvious how they should be recorded in the entity's systems. In such cases, management may set up control processes to monitor policies that prescribe how particular types of transactions are measured, recorded and accounted for. These policies are typically established and reviewed in advance by suitably qualified personnel who are capable of understanding the full effects of the financial instruments being booked.

32   Some transactions may be cancelled or amended after initial execution. Application of appropriate controls relating to cancellation or amendment can mitigate the risks of material misstatement due to fraud or error. In addition, an entity may have a process in place to reconfirm trades that are cancelled or amended.

33   In financial institutions with a high volume of trading, a senior employee typically reviews daily profits and losses on individual traders' books to evaluate whether they are reasonable based on the employee's knowledge of the market. Doing so may enable management to determine that particular trades were not completely or accurately recorded, or may identify fraud by a particular trader. It is important that there are transaction authorization procedures that support the more senior review.

Valuation of Financial Instruments

Financial Reporting Requirements

34   In many financial reporting frameworks, financial instruments, including embedded derivatives, are often measured at fair value for the purpose of balance sheet presentation, calculating profit or loss, and/or disclosure. In general, the objective of fair value measurement is to arrive at the price at which an orderly transaction would take place between market participants at the measurement date under current market conditions; that is, it is not the transaction price for a forced liquidation or distressed sale. In meeting this objective, all relevant available market information is taken into account.

35   Fair value measurements of financial assets and financial liabilities may arise both at the initial recording of transactions and later when there are changes in value. Changes in fair value measurements that occur over time may be treated in different ways under different financial reporting frameworks. For example, such changes may be recorded as profit or loss, or may be recorded in the other comprehensive income. Also, depending on the applicable financial reporting framework, the whole financial instrument or only a component of it (for example, an embedded derivative when it is separately accounted for) may be required to be measured at fair value.

36   Some financial reporting frameworks establish a fair value hierarchy to develop increased consistency and comparability in fair value measurements and related disclosures. The inputs may be classified into different levels such as:

- Level 1 inputs—Quoted prices (unadjusted) in active markets for identical financial assets or financial liabilities that the entity can access at the measurement date.
- Level 2 inputs—Inputs other than quoted prices included within level 1 that are observable for the financial asset or financial liability, either directly or indirectly. If the financial asset or financial liability has a specified (contractual) term, a level 2 input must be observable for substantially the full term of the financial asset or financial liability. Level 2 inputs include the following:

- o   Quoted prices for similar financial assets or financial liabilities in active markets.
- o   Quoted prices for identical or similar financial assets or financial liabilities in markets that are not active.
- o   Inputs other than quoted prices that are observable for the financial asset or financial liability (for example, interest rates and yield curves observable at commonly quoted intervals, implied volatilities and credit spreads).
- o   Inputs that are derived principally from, or corroborated by, observable market data by correlation or other means (market-corroborated inputs).
- Level 3 inputs—Unobservable inputs for the financial asset or financial liability. Unobservable inputs are used to measure fair value to the extent that relevant observable inputs are not available, thereby allowing for situations in which there is little, if any, market activity for the financial asset or financial liability at the measurement date.

In general, measurement uncertainty increases as a financial instrument moves from level 1 to level 2, or level 2 to level 3. Also, within level 2 there may be a wide range of measurement uncertainty depending on the observability of inputs, the complexity of the financial instrument, its valuation, and other factors.

Certain financial reporting frameworks may require or permit the entity to adjust for   **37** measurement uncertainties, in order to adjust for risks that a market participant would make in the pricing to take account of the uncertainties of the risks associated with the pricing or cash flows of the financial instrument. For example:

- Model adjustments. Some models may have a known deficiency or the result of calibration may highlight the deficiency for the fair value measurement in accordance with the financial reporting framework.
- Credit-risk adjustments. Some models do not take into account credit risk, including counterparty risk or own credit risk.
- Liquidity adjustments. Some models calculate a mid-market price, even though the financial reporting framework may require use of a liquidity adjusted amount such as a bid/offer spread. Another, more judgmental, liquidity adjustment recognizes that some financial instruments are illiquid which affects the valuation.
- Other risk adjustments. A value measured using a model that does not take into account all other factors that market participants would consider in pricing the financial instrument may not represent fair value on the measurement date, and therefore may need to be adjusted separately to comply with the applicable financial reporting framework.

Adjustments are not appropriate if they adjust the measurement and valuation of the financial instrument away from fair value as defined by the applicable financial reporting framework, for example for conservatism.

Observable and Unobservable Inputs

As mentioned above, financial reporting frameworks often categorize inputs   **38** according to the degree of observability. As activity in a market for financial instruments declines and the observability of inputs declines, measurement uncertainty increases. The nature and reliability of information available to support valuation of financial instruments varies depending on the observability of inputs to its measurement, which is influenced by the nature of the market (for example, the level of market activity and whether it is through an exchange or over-the-counter (OTC)). Accordingly, there is a continuum of the nature and reliability of evidence used to support valuation, and it becomes more difficult for management to obtain information to support a valuation when markets become inactive and inputs become less observable.

39 When observable inputs are not available, an entity uses unobservable inputs (level 3 inputs) that reflect the assumption that market participants would use when pricing the financial asset or the financial liability, including assumptions about risk. Unobservable inputs are developed using the best information available in the circumstances. In developing unobservable inputs, an entity may begin with its own data, which is adjusted if reasonably available information indicates that (a) other market participants would use different data or (b) there is something particular to the entity that is not available to other market participants (for example, an entity-specific synergy).

Effects of Inactive Markets

40 Measurement uncertainty increases and valuation is more complicated when the markets in which financial instruments or their component parts are traded become inactive. There is no clear point at which an active market becomes inactive, though financial reporting frameworks may provide guidance on this issue. Characteristics of an inactive market include a significant decline in the volume and level of trading activity, available prices vary significantly over time or among market participants or the prices are not current. However, assessing whether a market is inactive requires judgment.

41 When markets are inactive, prices quoted may be stale (that is, out of date), may not represent prices at which market participants may trade or may represent forced transactions (such as when a seller is required to sell an asset to meet regulatory or legal requirements, needs to dispose of an asset immediately to create liquidity or the existence of a single potential buyer as a result of the legal or time restrictions imposed). Accordingly, valuations are developed based on level 2 and level 3 inputs. Under such circumstances, entities may have:

- A valuation policy that includes a process for determining whether level 1 inputs are available;
- An understanding of how particular prices or inputs from external sources used as inputs to valuation techniques were calculated in order to assess their reliability. For example, in an active market, a broker quote on a financial instrument that has not traded is likely to reflect actual transactions on a similar financial instrument, but, as the market becomes less active, the broker quote may rely more on proprietary valuation techniques to determine prices;
- An understanding of how deteriorating business conditions affect the counterparty, as well as whether deteriorating business conditions in entities similar to the counterparty may indicate that the counterparty may not fulfill its obligations (that is, non-performance risk);
- Policies for adjusting for measurement uncertainties. Such adjustments can include model adjustments, lack of liquidity adjustments, credit risk adjustments, and other risk adjustments;
- The capability to calculate the range of realistic outcomes given the uncertainties involved, for example by performing a sensitivity analysis; and
- Policies for identifying when a fair value measurement input moves to a different level of the fair value hierarchy.

42 Particular difficulties may develop where there is severe curtailment or even cessation of trading in particular financial instruments. In these circumstances, financial instruments that have previously been valued using market prices may need to be valued using a model.

Management's Valuation Process

Techniques that management may use to value their financial instruments include **43** observable prices, recent transactions, and models that use observable or unobservable inputs. Management may also make use of:

(a) A third-party pricing source, such as a pricing service or broker quote; or
(b) A valuation expert.

Third-party pricing sources and valuation experts may use one or more of these valuation techniques.

In many financial reporting frameworks, the best evidence of a financial instrument's **44** fair value is found in contemporaneous transactions in an active market (that is, level 1 inputs). In such cases, the valuation of a financial instrument may be relatively simple. Quoted prices for financial instruments that are listed on exchanges or traded in liquid over-the-counter markets may be available from sources such as financial publications, the exchanges themselves or third-party pricing sources. When using quoted prices, it is important that management understand the basis on which the quote is given to ensure that the price reflects market conditions at the measurement date. Quoted prices obtained from publications or exchanges may provide sufficient evidence of fair value when, for example:

(a) The prices are not out of date or "stale" (for example, if the quote is based on the last traded price and the trade occurred some time ago); and
(b) The quotes are prices at which dealers would actually trade the financial instrument with sufficient frequency and volume.

Where there is no current observable market price for the financial instrument (that **45** is, a level 1 input), it will be necessary for the entity to gather other price indicators to use in a valuation technique to value the financial instrument. Price indicators may include:

● Recent transactions, including transactions after the date of the financial statements in the same instrument. Consideration is given to whether an adjustment needs to be made for changes in market conditions between the measurement date and the date the transaction was made, as these transactions are not necessarily indicative of the market conditions that existed at the date of the financial statements. In addition it is possible that the transaction represents a forced transaction and is therefore not indicative of a price in an orderly trade.
● Current or recent transactions in similar instruments, often known as "proxy pricing." Adjustments will need to be made to the price of the proxy to reflect the differences between them and the instrument being priced, for example, to take account of differences in liquidity or credit risk between the two instruments.
● Indices for similar instruments. As with transactions in similar instruments, adjustments will need to be made to reflect the difference between the instrument being priced and the instrument(s) from which the index used is derived.

It is expected that management will document its valuation policies and model used **46** to value a particular financial instrument, including the rationale for the model(s) used, the selection of assumptions in the valuation methodology, and the entity's consideration of whether adjustments for measurement uncertainty are necessary.

Models

Models may be used to value financial instruments when the price cannot be directly **47** observed in the market. Models can be as simple as a commonly used bond pricing formula or involve complex, specifically developed software tools to value financial instruments with level 3 inputs. Many models are based on discounted cash flow calculations.

48 Models comprise a methodology, assumptions and data. The methodology describes rules or principles governing the relationship between the variables in the valuation. Assumptions include estimates of uncertain variables which are used in the model. Data may comprise actual or hypothetical information about the financial instrument, or other inputs to the financial instrument.

49 Depending on the circumstances, matters that the entity may address when establishing or validating a model for a financial instrument include whether:

- The model is validated prior to usage, with periodic reviews to ensure it is still suitable for its intended use. The entity's validation process may include evaluation of:
  - The methodology's theoretical soundness and mathematical integrity, including the appropriateness of parameters and sensitivities.
  - The consistency and completeness of the model's inputs with market practices, and whether the appropriate inputs are available for use in the model.
- There are appropriate change control policies, procedures and security controls over the model.
- The model is appropriately changed or adjusted on a timely basis for changes in market conditions.
- The model is periodically calibrated, reviewed and tested for validity by a separate and objective function. Doing so is a means of ensuring that the model's output is a fair representation of the value that marketplace participants would ascribe to a financial instrument.
- The model maximizes the use of relevant observable inputs and minimizes the use of unobservable inputs.
- Adjustments are made to the output of the model to reflect the assumptions marketplace participants would use in similar circumstances.
- The model is adequately documented, including the model's intended applications and limitations and its key parameters, required data, results of any validation analysis performed and any adjustments made to the output of the model.

An Example of a Common Financial Instrument

50 The following describes how models may be applied to value a common financial instrument, known as an asset backed security.[9] Because asset backed securities are often valued based on level 2 or 3 inputs, they are frequently valued using models and involve:

- Understanding the type of security—considering (a) the underlying collateral; and (b) the terms of the security. The underlying collateral is used to estimate the timing and amounts of cash flows such as mortgage or credit card interest and principal payments.
- Understanding the terms of the security—this includes evaluating contractual cash flow rights, such as the order of repayment, and any default events. The order of repayment, often known as seniority, refers to terms which require that some classes of security holders (senior debt) are repaid before others

---

[9] *An asset backed security is a financial instrument which is backed by a pool of underlying assets (known as the collateral, such as credit card receivables or vehicle loans) and derives value and income from those underlying assets.*

(subordinated debt). The rights of each class of security holder to the cash flows, frequently referred to as the cash flow "waterfall," together with assumptions of the timing and amount of cash flows are used to derive a set of estimated cash flows for each class of security holder. The expected cash flows are then discounted to derive an estimated fair value.

The cash flows of an asset backed security may be affected by prepayments of the **51** underlying collateral and by potential default risk and resulting estimated loss severities. Prepayment assumptions, if applicable, are generally based on evaluating market interest rates for similar collateral to the rates on the collateral underlying the security. For example, if market interest rates for mortgages have declined then the underlying mortgages in a security may experience higher prepayment rates than originally expected. Estimating potential default and loss severity involves close evaluation of the underlying collateral and borrowers to estimate default rates. For example, when the underlying collateral comprises residential mortgages, loss severities may be affected by estimates of residential housing prices over the term of the security.

Third-Party Pricing Sources

Entities may use third-party pricing sources in order to obtain fair value information. **52** The preparation of an entity's financial statements, including the valuation of financial instruments and the preparation of financial statement disclosures relating to these instruments, may require expertise that management does not possess. Entities may not be able to develop appropriate valuation techniques, including models that may be used in a valuation, and may use a third-party pricing source to arrive at a valuation or to provide disclosures for the financial statements. This may particularly be the case in smaller entities or in entities that do not engage in a high volume of financial instruments transactions (for example, non-financial institutions with treasury departments). Even though management has used a third-party pricing source, management is ultimately responsible for the valuation.

Third-party pricing sources may also be used because the volume of securities to **53** price over a short timeframe may not be possible by the entity. This is often the case for traded investment funds that must determine a net asset value each day. In other cases, management may have their own pricing process but use third-party pricing sources to corroborate their own valuations.

For one or more of these reasons most entities use third-party pricing sources when **54** valuing securities either as a primary source or as a source of corroboration for their own valuations. Third-party pricing sources generally fall into the following categories:

● Pricing services, including consensus pricing services; and
● Brokers proving broker quotes.

Pricing services

Pricing services provide entities with prices and price-related data for a variety of **55** financial instruments, often performing daily valuations of large numbers of financial instruments. These valuations may be made by collecting market data and prices from a wide variety of sources, including market makers, and, in certain instances, using internal valuations techniques to derive estimated fair values. Pricing services may combine a number of approaches to arrive at a price. Pricing services are often used as a source of prices based on level 2 inputs. Pricing services may have strong controls around how prices are developed and their customers often include a wide variety of parties, including buy and sell side investors, back and middle office functions, auditors and others.

56   Pricing services often have a formalized process for customers to challenge the prices received from the pricing services. These challenge processes usually require the customer to provide evidence to support an alternative price, with challenges categorized based on the quality of evidence provided. For example, a challenge based on a recent sale of that instrument that the pricing service was not aware of may be upheld, whereas a challenge based on a customer's own valuation technique may be more heavily scrutinized. In this way, a pricing service with a large number of leading participants, both buy and sell side, may be able to constantly correct prices to more fully reflect the information available to market participants.

Consensus pricing services

57   Some entities may use pricing data from consensus pricing services which differ from other pricing services. Consensus pricing services obtain pricing information about an instrument from several participating entities (subscribers). Each subscriber submits prices to the pricing service. The pricing service treats this information confidentially and returns to each subscriber the consensus price, which is usually an arithmetical average of the data after a data cleansing routine has been employed to eliminate outliers. For some markets, such as for exotic derivatives, consensus prices might constitute the best available data. However, many factors are considered when assessing the representational faithfulness of the consensus prices including, for example:

- Whether the prices submitted by the subscribers reflect actual transactions or just indicative prices based on their own valuation techniques.
- The number of sources from which prices have been obtained.
- The quality of the sources used by the consensus pricing service.
- Whether participants include leading market participants

58   Typically consensus prices are only available to subscribers who have submitted their own prices to the service. Accordingly not all entities will have direct access to consensus prices. Because a subscriber generally cannot know how the prices submitted were estimated, other sources of evidence in addition to information from consensus pricing services may be needed for management to support their valuation. In particular, this may be the case if the sources are providing indicative prices based on their own valuation techniques and management is unable to obtain an understanding of how these sources calculated their prices.

Brokers providing broker quotes

59   As brokers provide quotes only as an incidental service for their clients, quotes they provide differ in many respects from prices obtained in pricing services. Brokers may be unwilling to provide information about the process used to develop their quote, but may have access to information on transactions about which a pricing service may not be aware. Broker quotes may be executable or indicative. Indicative quotes are a broker's best estimate of fair value, whereas an executable quote shows that the broker is willing to transact at this price. Executable quotes are strong evidence of fair value. Indicative quotes are less so because of the lack of transparency into the methods used by the broker to establish the quote. In addition the rigor of controls over the brokers' quote often will differ depending on whether the broker also holds the same security in its own portfolio. Broker quotes are often used for securities with level 3 inputs and sometimes may be the only external information available.

Further considerations relating to third-party pricing sources

Understanding how the pricing sources calculated a price enables management to **60** determine whether such information is suitable for use in its valuation, including as an input to a valuation technique and in what level of inputs the security should be categorized for disclosure purposes. For example, third-party pricing sources may value financial instruments using proprietary models, and it is important that management understands the methodology, assumptions and data used.

If fair value measurements obtained from third-party pricing sources are not based **61** on the current prices of an active market, it will be necessary for management to evaluate whether the fair value measurements were derived in a manner that is consistent with the applicable financial reporting framework. Management's understanding of the fair value measurement includes:

- How the fair value measurement was determined—for example, whether the fair value measurement was determined by a valuation technique, in order to assess whether it is consistent with the fair value measurement objective;
- Whether the quotes are indicative prices, indicative spread, or binding offers; and
- How frequently the fair value measurement is estimated by the third-party pricing sources—in order to assess whether it reflects market conditions at the measurement date.

Understanding the bases on which third-party pricing sources have determined their quotes in the context of the particular financial instruments held by the entity assists management in evaluating the relevance and reliability of this evidence to support its valuations.

It is possible that there will be disparities between price indicators from different **62** sources. Understanding how the price indicators were derived, and investigating these disparities, assists management in corroborating the evidence used in developing its valuation of financial instruments in order to evaluate whether the valuation is reasonable. Simply taking the average of the quotes provided, without doing further research, may not be appropriate, because one price in the range may be the most representative of fair value and this may not be the average. To evaluate whether its valuations of financial instruments are reasonable, management may:

- Consider whether actual transactions represent forced transactions rather than transactions between willing buyers and willing sellers. This may invalidate the price as a comparison;
- Analyze the expected future cash flows of the instrument. This could be performed as an indicator of the most relevant pricing data;
- Depending on the nature of what is unobservable, extrapolate from observed prices to unobserved ones (for example, there may be observed prices for maturities up to ten years but not longer, but the ten year price curve may be capable of being extrapolated beyond ten years as an indicator). Care is needed to ensure that extrapolation is not carried so far beyond the observable curve that its link to observable prices becomes too tenuous to be reliable;
- Compare prices within a portfolio of financial instruments to each other to make sure that they are consistent among similar financial instruments;
- Use more than one model to corroborate the results from each one, having regard to the data and assumptions used in each; or
- Evaluate movements in the prices for related hedging instruments and collateral.

In coming to its judgment as to its valuation, an entity may also consider other factors that may be specific to the entity's circumstances.

Use of Valuation Experts

63 Management may engage a valuation expert from an investment bank, broker, or other valuation firm to value some or all of its securities. Unlike pricing services and broker quotes, generally the methodology and data used are more readily available to management when they have engaged an expert to perform a valuation on their behalf. Even though management has engaged an expert, management is ultimately responsible for the valuation used.

Issues Related to Financial Liabilities

64 Understanding the effect of credit risk is an important aspect of valuing both financial assets and financial liabilities. This valuation reflects the credit quality and financial strength of both the issuer and any credit support providers. In some financial reporting frameworks, the measurement of a financial liability assumes that it is transferred to a market participant at the measurement date. Where there is not an observable market price for a financial liability, its value is typically measured using the same method as a counterparty would use to measure the value of the corresponding asset, unless there are factors specific to the liability (such as third-party credit enhancement). In particular, the entity's own credit riskto the liability (such as third-party credit enhancement). In particular, the entity's own credit riskto the liability (such as third-party credit enhancement). In particular, the entity's own credit risk[10] can often be difficult to measure.

Presentation and Disclosure about Financial Instruments

65 Most financial reporting frameworks require disclosures in the financial statements to enable users of the financial statements to make meaningful assessments of the effects of the entity's financial instrument activities, including the risks and uncertainties associated with financial instruments.

66 Most frameworks require the disclosure of quantitative and qualitative information (including accounting policies) relating to financial instruments. The accounting requirements for fair value measurements in financial statement presentation and disclosures are extensive in most financial reporting frameworks and encompass more than just valuation of the financial instruments. For example, qualitative disclosures about financial instruments provide important contextual information about the characteristics of the financial instruments and their future cash flows that may help inform investors about the risks to which entities are exposed.

Categories of Disclosures

67 Disclosure requirements include:

(a) Quantitative disclosures that are derived from the amounts included in the financial statements—for example, categories of financial assets and liabilities;

(b) Quantitative disclosures that require significant judgment—for example, sensitivity analysis for each type of market risk to which the entity is exposed; and

(c) Qualitative disclosures—for example, those that describe the entity's governance over financial instruments; objectives; controls, policies and processes for managing each type of risk arising from financial instruments; and the methods used to measure the risks.

---

[10] *Own credit risk is the amount of change in fair value that is not attributable to changes in market conditions.*

The more sensitive the valuation is to movements in a particular variable, the more **68** likely it is that disclosure will be necessary to indicate the uncertainties surrounding the valuation. Certain financial reporting frameworks may also require disclosure of sensitivity analyses, including the effects of changes in assumptions used in the entity's valuation techniques. For example, the additional disclosures required for financial instruments with fair value measurements that are categorized within level 3 inputs of the fair value hierarchy are aimed at informing users of financial statements about the effects of those fair value measurements that use the most subjective inputs.

Some financial reporting frameworks require disclosure of information that enables **69** users of the financial statements to evaluate the nature and extent of the risks arising from financial instruments to which the entity is exposed at the reporting date. This disclosure may be contained in the notes to the financial statements, or in management's discussion and analysis within its annual report cross-referenced from the audited financial statements. The extent of disclosure depends on the extent of the entity's exposure to risks arising from financial instruments. This includes qualitative disclosures about:

- The exposures to risk and how they arise, including the possible effects on an entity's future liquidity and collateral requirements;
- The entity's objectives, policies and processes for managing the risk and the methods used to measure the risk; and
- Any changes in exposures to risk or objectives, policies or processes for managing risk from the previous period.

Section II—Audit Considerations Relating to Financial Instruments

Certain factors may make auditing financial instruments particularly challenging. **70** For example:

- It may be difficult for both management and the auditor to understand the nature of financial instruments and what they are used for, and the risks to which the entity is exposed.
- Market sentiment and liquidity can change quickly, placing pressure on management to manage their exposures effectively.
- Evidence supporting valuation may be difficult to obtain.
- Individual payments associated with certain financial instruments may be significant, which may increase the risk of misappropriation of assets.
- The amounts recorded in the financial statements relating to financial instruments may not be significant, but there may be significant risks and exposures associated with these financial instruments.
- A few employees may exert significant influence on the entity's financial instruments transactions, in particular where their compensation arrangements are tied to revenue from financial instruments, and there may be possible undue reliance on these individuals by others within the entity.

These factors may cause risks and relevant facts to be obscured, which may affect the auditor's assessment of the risks of material misstatement, and latent risks can emerge rapidly, especially in adverse market conditions.

Professional Skepticism[11]

71   Professional skepticism is necessary to the critical assessment of audit evidence and assists the auditor in remaining alert for possible indications of management bias. This includes questioning contradictory audit evidence and the reliability of documents, responses to inquiries and other information obtained from management and those charged with governance. It also includes being alert to conditions that may indicate possible misstatement due to error or fraud and considering the sufficiency and appropriateness of audit evidence obtained in light of the circumstances.

72   Application of professional skepticism is required in all circumstances, and the need for professional skepticism increases with the complexity of financial instruments, for example with regard to:

- Evaluating whether sufficient appropriate audit evidence has been obtained, which can be particularly challenging when models are used or in determining if markets are inactive.
- Evaluating management's judgments, and the potential for management bias, in applying the entity's applicable financial reporting framework, in particular management's choice of valuation techniques, use of assumptions in valuation techniques, and addressing circumstances in which the auditor's judgments and management's judgments differ.
- Drawing conclusions based on the audit evidence obtained, for example assessing the reasonableness of valuations prepared by management's experts and evaluating whether disclosures in the financial statements achieve fair presentation.

Planning Considerations[12]

73   The auditor's focus in planning the audit is particularly on:

- Understanding the accounting and disclosure requirements;
- Understanding the financial instruments to which the entity is exposed, and their purpose and risks;
- Determining whether specialized skills and knowledge are needed in the audit;
- Understanding and evaluating the system of internal control in light of the entity's financial instrument transactions and the information systems that fall within the scope of the audit;
- Understanding the nature, role and activities of the internal audit function;
- Understanding management's process for valuing financial instruments, including whether management has used an expert or a service organization; and
- Assessing and responding to the risk of material misstatement.

Understanding the Accounting and Disclosure Requirements

74   ISA 540 requires the auditor to obtain an understanding of the requirements of the applicable financial reporting framework relevant to accounting estimates, including related disclosures and any regulatory requirements.[13] The requirements of the

---

[11] *ISA 200, paragraph 15*

[12] *ISA 300, Planning an Audit of Financial Statements*, deals with the auditor's responsibility to plan an audit of financial statements.

[13] *ISA 540, paragraph 8(a)*

applicable financial reporting framework regarding financial instruments may themselves be complex and require extensive disclosures. Reading this IAPN is not a substitute for a full understanding of all the requirements of the applicable financial reporting framework. Certain financial reporting frameworks require consideration of areas such as:

- Hedge accounting;
- Accounting for "Day 1" profits or losses;
- Recognition and derecognition of financial instrument transactions;
- Own credit risk; and
- Risk transfer and derecognition, in particular where the entity has been involved in the origination and structuring of complex financial instruments.

Understanding the Financial Instruments

The characteristics of financial instruments may obscure certain elements of risk and   **75**
exposure. Obtaining an understanding of the instruments in which the entity has invested or to which it is exposed, including the characteristics of the instruments, helps the auditor to identify whether:

- Important aspects of a transaction are missing or inaccurately recorded;
- A valuation appears appropriate;
- The risks inherent in them are fully understood and managed by the entity; and
- The financial instruments are appropriately classified into current and non-current assets and liabilities.

Examples of matters that the auditor may consider when obtaining an understanding   **76**
of the entity's financial instruments include:

- To which types of financial instruments the entity is exposed.
- The use to which they are put.
- Management's and, where appropriate, those charged with governance's understanding of the financial instruments, their use and the accounting requirements.
- Their exact terms and characteristics so that their implications can be fully understood and, in particular where transactions are linked, the overall impact of the financial instrument transactions.
- How they fit into the entity's overall risk management strategy.

Inquiries of the internal audit function, the risk management function, if such functions exist, and discussions with those charged with governance may inform the auditor's understanding.

In some cases, a contract, including a contract for a non-financial instrument may   **77**
contain a derivative. Some financial reporting frameworks permit or require such "embedded" derivatives to be separated from the host contract in some circumstances. Understanding management's process for identifying, and accounting for, embedded derivatives will assist the auditor in understanding the risks to which the entity is exposed.

Using Those with Specialized Skills and Knowledge in the Audit[14]

78   A key consideration in audits involving financial instruments, particularly complex financial instruments, is the competence of the auditor. ISA 220[15] requires the engagement partner to be satisfied that the engagement team, and any auditor's experts who are not part of the engagement team, collectively have the appropriate competence and capabilities to perform the audit engagement in accordance with professional standards and applicable legal and regulatory requirements and to enable an auditor's report that is appropriate in the circumstances to be issued. Further, relevant ethical requirementsrequires the engagement partner to be satisfied that the engagement team, and any auditor's experts who are not part of the engagement team, collectively have the appropriate competence and capabilities to perform the audit engagement in accordance with professional standards and applicable legal and regulatory requirements and to enable an auditor's report that is appropriate in the circumstances to be issued. Further, relevant ethical requirements requires the engagement partner to be satisfied that the engagement team, and any auditor's experts who are not part of the engagement team, collectively have the appropriate competence and capabilities to perform the audit engagement in accordance with professional standards and applicable legal and regulatory requirements and to enable an auditor's report that is appropriate in the circumstances to be issued. Further, relevant ethical requirements[16] require the auditor to determine whether acceptance of the engagement would create any threats to compliance with the fundamental principles, including the professional competence and due care. Paragraph 79 below provides examples of the types of matters that may be relevant to the auditor's considerations in the context of financial instruments.

79   Accordingly, auditing financial instruments may require the involvement of one or more experts or specialists, for example, in the areas of:

- Understanding the financial instruments used by the entity and their characteristics, including their level of complexity. Using specialized skills and knowledge may be needed in checking whether all aspects of the financial instrument and related considerations have been captured in the financial statements, and evaluating whether adequate disclosure in accordance with the applicable financial reporting framework has been made where disclosure of risks is required.
- Understanding the applicable financial reporting framework, especially when there are areas known to be subject to differing interpretations, or practice is inconsistent or developing.
- Understanding the legal, regulatory, and tax implications resulting from the financial instruments, including whether the contracts are enforceable by the entity (for example, reviewing the underlying contracts), may require specialized skills and knowledge.
- Assessing the risks inherent in a financial instrument.

---

[14] *When such a person's expertise is in auditing and accounting, regardless of whether the person is from within or external to the firm, this person is considered to be part of the engagement team and is subject to the requirements of ISA 220, Quality Control for an Audit of Financial Statements.* When such a person's expertise is in a field other than accounting or auditing, such person is considered to be an auditor's expert, and the provisions of ISA 620, *Using the Work of an Auditor's Expert*, apply. ISA 620 explains that distinguishing between specialized areas of accounting or auditing, and expertise in another field, will be a matter of professional judgment, but notes the distinction may be made between expertise in methods of accounting for financial instruments (accounting and auditing expertise) and expertise in complex valuation techniques for financial instruments (expertise in a field other than accounting or auditing).

[15] *ISA 220, paragraph 14*

[16] *IESBA Code of Ethics for Professional Accountants* paragraphs 210.1 and 210.6

- Assisting the engagement team gather evidence to support management's valuations or to develop a point estimate or range, especially when fair value is determined by a complex model; when markets are inactive and data and assumptions are difficult to obtain; when unobservable inputs are used; or when management has used an expert.
- Evaluating information technology controls, especially in entities with a high volume of financial instruments. In such entities information technology may be highly complex, for example when significant information about those financial instruments is transmitted, processed, maintained or accessed electronically. In addition, it may include relevant services provided by a service organization.

The nature and use of particular types of financial instruments, the complexities **80** associated with accounting requirements, and market conditions may lead to a need for the engagement team to consult[17] with other accounting and audit professionals, from within or outside the firm, with relevant technical accounting or auditing expertise and experience, taking into account factors such as:

- The capabilities and competence of the engagement team, including the experience of the members of the engagement team.
- The attributes of the financial instruments used by the entity.
- The identification of unusual circumstances or risks in the engagement, as well as the need for professional judgment, particularly with respect to materiality and significant risks.
- Market conditions.

Understanding Internal Control

ISA 315 establishes requirements for the auditor to understand the entity and its **81** environment, including its internal control. Obtaining an understanding of the entity and its environment, including the entity's internal control, is a continuous, dynamic process of gathering, updating and analyzing information throughout the audit. The understanding obtained enables the auditor to identify and assess the risks of material misstatement at the financial statement and assertion levels, thereby providing a basis for designing and implementing responses to the assessed risks of material misstatement. The volume and variety of the financial instrument transactions of an entity typically determines the nature and extent of controls that may exist at an entity. An understanding of how financial instruments are monitored and controlled assists the auditor in determining the nature, timing and extent of audit procedures. The Appendix describes controls that may exist in an entity that deals in a high volume of financial instrument transactions.

Understanding the Nature, Role and Activities of the Internal Audit Function

In many large entities, the internal audit function may perform work that enables **82** senior management and those charged with governance to review and evaluate the entity's controls relating to the use of financial instruments. The internal audit function may assist in identifying the risks of material misstatement due to fraud or error. However, the knowledge and skills required of an internal audit function to understand and perform procedures to provide assurance to management or those charged with governance on the entity's use of financial instruments are generally quite different from those needed for other parts of the business. The extent to which

---

[17] *ISA 220, paragraph 18(b), requires the engagement partner to be satisfied that members of the engagement team have undertaken appropriate consultation during the course of the engagement, both within the engagement team and between the engagement team and others at the appropriate level within or outside the firm.*

the internal audit function has the knowledge and skill to cover, and has in fact covered, the entity's financial instrument activities, as well as the competence and objectivity of the internal audit function, is a relevant consideration in the external auditor's determination of whether the internal audit function is likely to be relevant to the overall audit strategy and audit plan.

83   Areas where the work of the internal audit function may be particularly relevant are:[18]

- Developing a general overview of the extent of use of financial instruments;
- Evaluating the appropriateness of policies and procedures and management's compliance with them;
- Evaluating the operating effectiveness of financial instrument control activities;
- Evaluating systems relevant to financial instrument activities; and
- Assessing whether new risks relating to financial instruments are identified, assessed and managed.

Understanding Management's Methodology for Valuing Financial Instruments

84   Management's responsibility for the preparation of the financial statements includes applying the requirements of the applicable financial reporting framework to the valuation of financial instruments. ISA 540 requires the auditor to obtain an understanding of how management makes accounting estimates and the data on which accounting estimates are based.[19] Management's approach to valuation also takes into account the selection of an appropriate valuation methodology and the level of the evidence expected to be available. To meet the objective of a fair value measurement, an entity develops a valuation methodology to measure the fair value of financial instruments that considers all relevant market information that is available. A thorough understanding of the financial instrument being valued allows an entity to identify and evaluate the relevant market information available about identical or similar instruments that should be incorporated into the valuation methodology.

Assessing and Responding to the Risks of Material Misstatement

Overall Considerations Relating to Financial Instruments

85   ISA 540[20] explains that the degree of estimation uncertainty affects the risk of material misstatement of accounting estimates. The use of more complex financial instruments, such as those that have a high level of uncertainty and variability of future cash flows, may lead to an increased risk of material misstatement, particularly regarding valuation. Other matters affecting the risk of material misstatement include:

- The volume of financial instruments to which the entity is exposed.
- The terms of the financial instrument, including whether the financial instrument itself includes other financial instruments.
- The nature of the financial instruments.

---

[18] *Work performed by functions such as the risk management function, model review functions, and product control, may also be relevant.*

[19] *ISA 540, paragraph 8(c)*

[20] *ISA 540, paragraph 2*

Fraud Risk Factors[21]

Incentives for fraudulent financial reporting by employees may exist where com-   **86**
pensation schemes are dependent on returns made from the use of financial
instruments. Understanding how an entity's compensation policies interact with its
risk appetite, and the incentives that this may create for its management and traders,
may be important in assessing the risk of fraud.

Difficult financial market conditions may give rise to increased incentives for man-   **87**
agement or employees to engage in fraudulent financial reporting: to protect
personal bonuses, to hide employee or management fraud or error, to avoid
breaching regulatory, liquidity or borrowing limits or to avoid reporting losses. For
example, at times of market instability, unexpected losses may arise from extreme
fluctuations in market prices, from unanticipated weakness in asset prices, through
trading misjudgments, or for other reasons. In addition, financing difficulties create
pressures on management concerned about the solvency of the business.

Misappropriation of assets and fraudulent financial reporting may often involve   **88**
override of controls that otherwise may appear to be operating effectively. This may
include override of controls over data, assumptions and detailed process controls
that allow losses and theft to be hidden. For example, difficult market conditions
may increase pressure to conceal or offset trades as they attempt to recover losses.

Assessing the Risk of Material Misstatement

The auditor's assessment of the identified risks at the assertion level in accordance   **89**
with ISA 315 includes evaluating the design and implementation of internal control.
It provides a basis for considering the appropriate audit approach for designing and
performing further audit procedures in accordance with ISA 330, including both
substantive procedures and tests of controls. The approach taken is influenced by the
auditor's understanding of internal control relevant to the audit, including the
strength of the control environment and any risk management function, the size and
complexity of the entity's operations and whether the auditor's assessment of the
risks of material misstatement include an expectation that controls are operating
effectively.

The auditor's assessment of the risk of material misstatement at the assertion level   **90**
may change during the course of the audit as additional information is obtained.
Remaining alert during the audit, for example, when inspecting records or documents may assist the auditor in identifying arrangements or other information that
may indicate the existence of financial instruments that management has not previously identified or disclosed to the auditor. Such records and documents may
include, for example:

- Minutes of meetings of those charged with governance; and
- Specific invoices from, and correspondence with, the entity's professional
  advisors.

---

[21] *See ISA 240, The Auditor's Responsibilities Relating to Fraud in an Audit of Financial Statements*, for
requirements and guidance dealing with fraud risk factors.

Factors to Consider in Determining Whether, and to What Extent, to Test the Operating Effectiveness of Controls

91   An expectation that controls are operating effectively may be more common when dealing with a financial institution with well-established controls, and therefore controls testing may be an effective means of obtaining audit evidence. When an entity has a trading function, substantive tests alone may not provide sufficient appropriate audit evidence due to the volume of contracts and the different systems used. Tests of controls, however, will not be sufficient on their own as the auditor is required by ISA 330 to design and perform substantive procedures for each material class of transactions, account balance and disclosure.[22]

92   Entities with a high volume of trading and use of financial instruments may have more sophisticated controls, and an effective risk management function, and therefore the auditor may be more likely to test controls in obtaining evidence about:

● The occurrence, completeness, accuracy, and cutoff of the transactions; and

● The existence, rights and obligations, and completeness of account balances.

93   In those entities with relatively few financial instrument transactions:

● Management and those charged with governance may have only a limited understanding of financial instruments and how they affect the business;

● The entity may only have a few different types of instruments with little or no interaction between them;

● There is unlikely to be a complex control environment (for example, the controls described in the Appendix may not be in place at the entity);

● Management may use pricing information from third-party pricing sources to value their instruments; and

● Controls over the use of pricing information from third-party pricing sources may be less sophisticated.

94   When an entity has relatively few transactions involving financial instruments, it may be relatively easy for the auditor to obtain an understanding of the entity's objectives for using the financial instruments and the characteristics of the instruments. In such circumstances, much of the audit evidence is likely to be substantive in nature, the auditor may perform the majority of the audit work at year-end, and third-party confirmations are likely to provide evidence in relation to the completeness, accuracy, and existence of the transactions.

95   In reaching a decision on the nature, timing and extent of testing of controls, the auditor may consider factors such as:

● The nature, frequency and volume of financial instrument transactions;

● The strength of controls, including whether controls are appropriately designed to respond to the risks associated with an entity's volume of financial instrument transactions and whether there is a governance framework over the entity's financial instrument activities;

● The importance of particular controls to the overall control objectives and processes in place at the entity, including the sophistication of the information systems to support financial instrument transactions;

● The monitoring of controls and identified deficiencies in control procedures;

● The issues the controls are intended to address, for example, controls related to the exercise of judgments compared with controls over supporting data.

[22] *ISA 330, paragraph 18*

Substantive tests are more likely to be effective than relying on controls related to the exercise of judgment;

- The competency of those involved in the control activities, for example whether the entity has adequate capacity, including during periods of stress, and ability to establish and verify valuations for the financial instruments to which it is exposed;
- The frequency of performance of these control activities;
- The level of precision the controls are intended to achieve;
- The evidence of performance of control activities; and
- The timing of key financial instrument transactions, for example, whether they are close to the period end.

Substantive Procedures

Designing substantive procedures includes consideration of: **96**

- The use of analytical procedures[23]—While analytical procedures undertaken by the auditor can be effective as risk assessment procedures to provide the auditor with information about an entity's business, they may be less effective as substantive procedures when performed alone. This is because the complex interplay of the drivers of the valuation often mask any unusual trends that might arise.
- Non-routine transactions—Many financial transactions are negotiated contracts between an entity and its counterparty (often known as "over the counter" or OTC.) To the extent that financial instrument transactions are not routine and outside an entity's normal activities, a substantive audit approach may be the most effective means of achieving the planned audit objectives. In instances where financial instrument transactions are not undertaken routinely, the auditor's responses to assessed risk, including designing and performing audit procedures, have regard to the entity's possible lack of experience in this area.
- Availability of evidence—For example, when the entity uses a third-party pricing source, evidence concerning the relevant financial statement assertions may not be available from the entity.
- Procedures performed in other audit areas—Procedures performed in other financial statement areas may provide evidence about the completeness of financial instrument transactions. These procedures may include tests of subsequent cash receipts and payments, and the search for unrecorded liabilities.
- Selection of items for testing—In some cases, the financial instrument portfolio will comprise instruments with varying complexity and risk. In such cases, judgmental sampling may be useful.

For example, in the case of an asset-backed security, in responding to the risks of   **97**
material misstatement for such a security, the auditor may consider performing some
of the following audit procedures:

- Examining contractual documentation to understand the terms of the security, the underlying collateral and the rights of each class of security holder.
- Inquiring about management's process of estimating cash flows.
- Evaluating the reasonableness of assumptions, such as prepayment rates, default rates and loss severities.

---

[23] *ISA 315, paragraph 6(b), requires the auditor to apply analytical procedures as risk assessment procedures to assist in assessing the risks of material misstatement in order to provide a basis for designing and implementing responses to the assessed risks. ISA 520, Analytical Procedures, paragraph 6, requires the auditor to use analytical procedures in forming an overall conclusion on the financial statements. Analytical procedures may also be applied at other stages of the audit.*

- Obtaining an understanding of the method used to determine the cash flow waterfall.
- Comparing the results of the fair value measurement with the valuations of other securities with similar underlying collateral and terms.
- Reperforming calculations.

Dual-Purpose Tests

98   Although the purpose of a test of controls is different from the purpose of a test of details, it may be efficient to perform both at the same time by, for example:

- Performing a test of controls and a test of details on the same transaction (for example, testing whether a signed contract has been maintained and whether the details of the financial instrument have been appropriately captured in a summary sheet; or
- Testing controls when testing management's process of making valuation estimates.

Timing of the Auditor's Procedures[24]

99   After assessing the risks associated with financial instruments, the engagement team determines the timing of planned tests of controls and substantive audit procedures. The timing of planned audit procedures varies depending on a number of factors, including the frequency of the control operation, the significance of the activity being controlled, and the related risk of material misstatement.

100   While it is necessary to undertake most of the audit procedures in relation to valuation and presentation at the period end, audit procedures in relation to other assertions such as completeness and existence can usefully be tested at an interim period. For example tests of controls may be performed at an interim period for more routine controls, such as IT controls and authorizations for new products. Also, it may be effective to test the operating effectiveness of controls over new product approval by gathering evidence of the appropriate level of management sign-off on a new financial instrument for an interim period.

101   Auditors may perform some tests on models as of an interim date, for example, by comparing the output of the model to market transactions. Another possible interim procedure for instruments with observable inputs is to test the reasonableness of the pricing information provided by a third-party pricing source.

102   Areas of more significant judgment are often tested close to, or at, the period end as:

- Valuations can change significantly in a short period of time, making it difficult to compare and reconcile interim balances with comparable information at the balance sheet date;
- An entity may engage in an increased volume of financial instrument transactions between an interim period and year-end;
- Manual journal entries may only be made after the end of the accounting period; and
- Non-routine or significant transactions may take place late in the accounting period.

---

[24] *Paragraphs 11–12 and 22–23 of ISA 330 establish requirements when the auditor performs procedures at an interim period and explains how such audit evidence can be used.*

Procedures Relating to Completeness, Accuracy, Existence, Occurrence and Rights and Obligations

Many of the auditor's procedures can be used to address a number of assertions. For **103** example, procedures to address the existence of an account balance at period end will also address the occurrence of a class of transactions, and may also assist in establishing proper cut-off. This is because financial instruments arise from legal contracts and, by verifying the accuracy of the recording of the transaction, the auditor can also verify its existence, and obtain evidence to support the occurrence and rights and obligations assertions at the same time, and confirm that transactions are recorded in the correct accounting period.

Procedures that may provide audit evidence to support the completeness, accuracy, **104** and existence assertions include:

- External confirmation[25] of bank accounts, trades, and custodian statements. This can be done by direct confirmation with the counterparty (including the use of bank confirmations), where a reply is sent to the auditor directly. Alternatively this information may be obtained from the counterparty's systems through a data feed. Where this is done, controls to prevent tampering with the computer systems through which the information is transmitted may be considered by the auditor in evaluating the reliability of the evidence from the confirmation. If confirmations are not received, the auditor may be able to obtain evidence by reviewing contracts and testing relevant controls. External confirmations, however, often do not provide adequate audit evidence with respect to the valuation assertion though they may assist in identifying any side agreements.
- Reviewing reconciliations of statements or data feeds from custodians with the entity's own records. This may necessitate evaluating IT controls around and within automated reconciliation processes and to evaluate whether reconciling items are properly understood and resolved.
- Reviewing journal entries and the controls over the recording of such entries. This may assist in, for example:
  - Determining if entries have been made by employees other than those authorized to do so.
  - Identifying unusual or inappropriate end-of-period journal entries, which may be relevant to fraud risk.
- Reading individual contracts and reviewing supporting documentation of the entity's financial instrument transactions, including accounting records, thereby verifying existence and rights and obligations. For example, an auditor may read individual contracts associated with financial instruments and review supporting documentation, including the accounting entries made when the contract was initially recorded, and may also subsequently review accounting entries made for valuation purposes. Doing so allows the auditor to evaluate whether the complexities inherent in a transaction have been fully identified and reflected in the accounts. Legal arrangements and their associated risks need to be considered by those with suitable expertise to ensure that rights exist.
- Testing controls, for example by reperforming controls.
- Reviewing the entity's complaints management systems. Unrecorded transactions may result in the entity's failure to make a cash payment to a counterparty, and may be detected by reviewing complaints received.
- Reviewing master netting arrangements to identify unrecorded instruments.

---

[25] *ISA 505, External Confirmations*, deals with the auditor's use of external confirmation procedures to obtain audit evidence in accordance with the requirements of ISA 330 and ISA 500, *Audit Evidence*. See also the Staff Audit Practice Alert, *Emerging Practice Issues Regarding the Use of External Confirmations in an Audit of Financial Statements*, issued in November 2009.

105   These procedures are particularly important for some financial instruments, such as derivatives or guarantees. This is because they may not have a large initial investment, meaning it may be hard to identify their existence. For example, embedded derivatives are often contained in contracts for non-financial instruments which may not be included in confirmation procedures.

Valuation of Financial Instruments

Financial Reporting Requirements

106   Fair presentation financial reporting frameworks often use fair value hierarchies, for example those used in IFRS and U.S. GAAP. This usually means that the volume and detail of the required disclosures increases as the level of measurement uncertainty increases. The distinction between the levels in the hierarchy may require judgment.

107   The auditor may find it useful to obtain an understanding of how the financial instruments relate to the fair value hierarchy. Ordinarily, the risk of material misstatement, and the level of audit procedures to be applied, increases as the level of measurement uncertainty increases. The use of level 3, and some level 2, inputs from the fair value hierarchy may be a useful guide to the level of measurement uncertainty. Level 2 inputs vary from those which are easily obtained to those which are closer to level 3 inputs. The auditor evaluates available evidence and understands both the fair value hierarchy and the risk of management bias in management's categorization of financial instruments in the fair value hierarchy.

108   In accordance with ISA 540,[26] the auditor considers the entity's valuation policies and methodology for data and assumptions used in the valuation methodology. In many cases, the applicable financial reporting framework does not prescribe the valuation methodology. When this is the case, matters that may be relevant to the auditor's understanding of how management values financial instruments include, for example:

- Whether management has a formal valuation policy and, if so, whether the valuation technique used for a financial instrument is appropriately documented in accordance with that policy;
- Which models may give rise to the greatest risk of material misstatement;
- How management considered the complexity of the valuation of the financial instrument when selecting a particular valuation technique;
- Whether there is a greater risk of material misstatement because management has internally developed a model to be used to value financial instruments or is departing from a valuation technique commonly used to value the particular financial instrument;
- Whether management made use of a third-party pricing source;
- Whether those involved in developing and applying the valuation technique have the appropriate skills and expertise to do so, including whether a management's expert has been used; and
- Whether there are indicators of management bias in selecting the valuation technique to be used.

[26] *ISA 540, paragraph 8(c)*

Assessing the Risk of Material Misstatement Related to Valuation

When evaluating whether the valuation techniques used by an entity are appropriate **109** in the circumstances, and whether controls over valuation techniques are in place, the factors considered by the auditor may include:

- Whether the valuation techniques are commonly used by other market participants and have been previously demonstrated to provide a reliable estimate of prices obtained from market transactions;
- Whether the valuation techniques operate as intended and there are no flaws in their design, particularly under extreme conditions, and whether they have been objectively validated. Indicators of flaws include inconsistent movements relative to benchmarks;
- Whether the valuation techniques take account of the risks inherent in the financial instrument being valued, including counterparty creditworthiness, and own credit risk in the case of valuation techniques used to measure financial liabilities;
- How the valuation techniques are calibrated to the market, including the sensitivity of the valuation techniques to changes in variables;
- Whether market variables and assumptions are used consistently and whether new conditions justify a change in the valuation techniques, market variables or assumptions used;
- Whether sensitivity analyses indicate that valuations would change significantly with only small or moderate changes in assumptions;
- The organizational structure, such as the existence of an internal department responsible for developing models to value certain instruments, particularly where level 3 inputs are involved. For example, a model development function that is involved in assisting in pricing deals is less objective than one which is functionally and organizationally segregated from the front office; and
- The competence and objectivity of those responsible for the development and application of the valuation techniques, including management's relative experience with particular models that may be newly developed.

The auditor (or auditor's expert) may also independently develop one or more valuation techniques to compare its output with that of the valuation techniques used by management.

Significant Risks

The auditor's risk assessment process may lead the auditor to identify one or more **110** significant risks relating to the valuation of financial instruments, when any of the following circumstances exist:

- High measurement uncertainty related to the valuation of financial instruments (for example, those with unobservable inputs).[27]
- Lack of sufficient evidence to support management's valuation of its financial instruments.
- Lack of management understanding of its financial instruments or expertise necessary to value such instruments properly, including the ability to determine whether valuation adjustments are needed.
- Lack of management understanding of complex requirements in the applicable financial reporting framework relating to measurement and disclosure of

---

[27] *Where the auditor determines that the high estimation uncertainty related to the valuation of complex financial instruments gives rise to a significant risk, ISA 540 requires the auditor to perform substantive procedures and evaluate the adequacy of the disclosure of their estimation uncertainty. See ISA 540, paragraphs 11, 15 and 20.*

financial instruments, and inability of management to make the judgments required to properly apply those requirements.

- The significance of valuation adjustments made to valuation technique outputs when the applicable financial reporting framework requires or permits such adjustments.

111   For accounting estimates that give rise to significant risks, in addition to other substantive procedures performed to meet the requirements of ISA 330, ISA 540[28] requires the auditor to evaluate the following:

(a)   How management has considered alternative assumptions or outcomes, and why it has rejected them, or how management has otherwise addressed measurement uncertainty in making the accounting estimate;

(b)   Whether the significant assumptions used by management are reasonable; and

(c)   Where relevant to the reasonableness of the significant assumptions used by management, or the appropriate application of the applicable financial reporting framework, management's intent to carry out specific courses of action and its ability to do so.

112   As markets become inactive, the change in circumstances may lead to a move from valuation by market price to valuation by model, or may result in a change from one particular model to another. Reacting to changes in market conditions may be difficult if management does not have policies in place prior to their occurrence. Management may also not possess the expertise necessary to develop a model on an urgent basis, or select the valuation technique that may be appropriate in the circumstances. Even where valuation techniques have been consistently used, there is a need for management to examine the continuing appropriateness of the valuation techniques and assumptions used for determining valuation of financial instruments. Further, valuation techniques may have been selected in times where reasonable market information was available, but may not provide reasonable valuations in times of unanticipated stress.

113   The susceptibility to management bias, whether intentional or unintentional, increases with the subjectivity of the valuation and the degree of measurement uncertainty. For example, management may tend to ignore observable marketplace assumptions or data and instead use their own internally-developed model if the model yields more favorable results. Even without fraudulent intent, there may be a natural temptation to bias judgments towards the most favorable end of what may be a wide spectrum, rather than the point in the spectrum that might be considered to be most consistent with the applicable financial reporting framework. Changing the valuation technique from period to period without a clear and appropriate reason for doing so may also be an indicator of management bias. Although some form of management bias is inherent in subjective decisions relating to the valuation of financial instruments, when there is intention to mislead, management bias is fraudulent in nature.

Developing an Audit Approach

114   In testing how management values the financial instrument and in responding to the assessed risks of material misstatement in accordance with ISA 540,[29] the auditor undertakes one or more of the following procedures, taking account of the nature of the accounting estimates:

---

[28] *ISA 540, paragraph 15(a)-(b)*

[29] *ISA 540, paragraphs 12–14*

(a) Test how management made the accounting estimate and the data on which it is based (including valuation techniques used by the entity in its valuations).
(b) Test the operating effectiveness of the controls over how management made the accounting estimate, together with appropriate substantive procedures.
(c) Develop a point estimate or a range to evaluate management's point estimate.
(d) Determine whether events occurring up to the date of the auditor's report provide audit evidence regarding the accounting estimate.

Many auditors find that a combination of testing how management valued the financial instrument, and the data on which it is based, and testing the operating effectiveness of controls, will be an effective and efficient audit approach. While subsequent events may provide some evidence about the valuation of financial instruments, other factors may need to be taken into account to address any changes in market conditions subsequent to the balance sheet date.[30] If the auditor is unable to test how management made the estimate, the auditor may choose to develop a point estimate or range.

As described in Section I, to estimate the fair value of financial instruments management may: **115**

- Utilize information from third-party pricing sources;
- Gather data to develop their own estimate using various techniques including models; and
- Engage an expert to develop an estimate.

Management often may use a combination of these approaches. For example, management may have their own pricing process but use third-party pricing sources to corroborate their own values.

Audit Considerations When Management Uses a Third-Party Pricing Source

Management may make use of a third-party pricing source, such as a pricing service   **116**
or broker, in valuing the entity's financial instruments. Understanding how management uses the information and how the pricing service operates assists the auditor in determining the nature and extent of audit procedures needed.

The following matters may be relevant where management uses a third-party pricing   **117**
source:

- *The type of third-party pricing source*—Some third-party pricing sources make more information available about their process. For example, a pricing service often provides information about their methodology, assumptions and data in valuing financial instruments at the asset class level. By contrast, brokers often provide no, or only limited, information about the inputs and assumptions used in developing the quote.
- *The nature of inputs used and the complexity of the valuation technique*—The reliability of prices from third-party pricing sources varies depending on the observability of inputs (and accordingly, the level of inputs in the fair value hierarchy), and the complexity of the methodology for valuing a specific security or asset class. For example, the reliability of a price for an equity investment actively traded in a liquid market is higher than that of a corporate bond traded in a liquid market that has not traded on the measurement date, which, in turn, is more reliable than that of an asset-backed security that is valued using a discounted cash flow model.

---

[30] *Paragraphs A63–A66 of ISA 540 provide examples of some of the factors that may be relevant.*

- *The reputation and experience of the third-party pricing source*—For example, a third-party pricing source may be experienced in a certain type of financial instrument, and be recognized as such, but may not be similarly experienced in other types of financial instruments. The auditor's past experience with the third-party pricing source may also be relevant in this regard.
- *The objectivity of the third-party pricing source*—For example, if a price obtained by management comes from a counterparty such as the broker who sold the financial instrument to the entity, or an entity with a close relationship with the entity being audited, the price may not be reliable.
- *The entity's controls over the use of third-party pricing sources*—The degree to which management has controls in place to assess the reliability of information from third-party pricing sources affects the reliability of the fair value measurement. For example, management may have controls in place to:
  - Review and approve the use of the third-party pricing source, including consideration of the reputation, experience and objectivity of the third-party pricing source.
  - Determine the completeness, relevance and accuracy of the prices and pricing-related data.
- *The third-party pricing source's controls*—The controls and processes over valuations for the asset classes of interest to the auditor. For example, a third-party pricing source may have strong controls around how prices are developed, including the use of a formalized process for customers, both buy and sell side, to challenge the prices received from the pricing service, when supported by appropriate evidence, which may enable the third-party pricing source to constantly correct prices to more fully reflect the information available to market participants.

118   Possible approaches to gathering evidence regarding information from third-party pricing sources may include the following:

- For level 1 inputs, comparing the information from third-party pricing sources with observable market prices.
- Reviewing disclosures provided by third-party pricing sources about their controls and processes, valuation techniques, inputs and assumptions.
- Testing the controls management has in place to assess the reliability of information from third-party pricing sources.
- Performing procedures at the third-party pricing source to understand and test the controls and processes, valuation techniques, inputs and assumptions used for asset classes or specific financial instruments of interest.
- Evaluating whether the prices obtained from third-party pricing sources are reasonable in relation to prices from other third-party pricing sources, the entity's estimate or the auditor's own estimate.
- Evaluating the reasonableness of valuation techniques, assumptions and inputs.
- Developing a point estimate or a range for some financial instruments priced by the third-party pricing source and evaluating whether the results are within a reasonable range of each other.
- Obtaining a service auditor's report that covers the controls over validation of the prices.[31]

119   Obtaining prices from multiple third-party pricing sources may also provide useful information about measurement uncertainty. A wide range of prices may indicate

---

[31] *Some pricing services may provide reports for users of its data to explain their controls over pricing data, that is, a report prepared in accordance with International Standard on Assurance Engagements (ISAE) 3402, Assurance Reports on Controls at a Service Organization.* Management may request, and the auditor may consider obtaining, such a report to develop an understanding of how the pricing data is prepared and evaluate whether the controls at the pricing service can be relied upon.

higher measurement uncertainty and may suggest that the financial instrument is sensitive to small changes in data and assumptions. A narrow range may indicate lower measurement uncertainty and may suggest less sensitivity to changes in data and assumptions. Although obtaining prices from multiple sources may be useful, when considering financial instruments that have inputs categorized at levels 2 or 3 of the fair value hierarchy, in particular, obtaining prices from multiple sources is unlikely to provide sufficient appropriate audit evidence on its own. This is because:

(a) What appear to be multiple sources of pricing information may be utilizing the same underlying pricing source; and

(b) Understanding the inputs used by the third-party pricing source in determining the price may be necessary in order to categorize the financial instrument in the fair value hierarchy.

In some situations, the auditor may be unable to gain an understanding of the **120** process used to generate the price, including any controls over the process of how reliably the price is determined, or may not have access to the model, including the assumptions and other inputs used. In such cases, the auditor may decide to undertake to develop a point estimate or a range to evaluate management's point estimate in responding to the assessed risk.

Audit Considerations When Management Estimates Fair Values Using a Model

Paragraph 13(b) of ISA 540 requires the auditor, if testing management's process of **121** making the accounting estimate, to evaluate whether the method of measurement used is appropriate in the circumstances and the assumptions used by management are reasonable in light of the measurement objectives of the applicable financial reporting framework.

Whether management has used a third-party pricing source, or is undertaking its **122** own valuation, models are often used to value financial instruments, particularly when using inputs at levels 2 and 3 of the fair value hierarchy. In determining the nature, timing and extent of audit procedures on models, the auditor may consider the methodology, assumptions and data used in the model. When considering more complex financial instruments such as those using level 3 inputs, testing all three may be a useful source of audit evidence. However, when the model is both simple and generally accepted, such as some bond price calculations, audit evidence obtained from focusing on the assumptions and data used in the model may be a more useful source of evidence.

Testing a model can be accomplished by two main approaches: **123**

(a) The auditor can test management's model, by considering the appropriateness of the model used by management, the reasonableness of the assumptions and data used, and the mathematical accuracy; or

(b) The auditor can develop their own estimate, and then compare the auditor's valuation with that of the entity.

Where valuation of financial instruments is based on unobservable inputs (that is, **124** level 3 inputs), matters that the auditor may consider include, for example, how management supports the following:

- The identification and characteristics of marketplace participants relevant to the financial instrument.
- How unobservable inputs are determined on initial recognition.
- Modifications it has made to its own assumptions to reflect its view of assumptions marketplace participants would use.

- Whether it has incorporated the best input information available in the circumstances.
- Where applicable, how its assumptions take account of comparable transactions.
- Sensitivity analysis of models when unobservable inputs are used and whether adjustments have been made to address measurement uncertainty.

125   In addition, the auditor's industry knowledge, knowledge of market trends, understanding of other entities' valuations (having regard to confidentiality) and other relevant price indicators informs the auditor's testing of the valuations and the consideration of whether the valuations appear reasonable overall. If the valuations appear to be consistently overly aggressive or conservative, this may be an indicator of possible management bias.

126   Where there is a lack of observable external evidence, it is particularly important that those charged with governance have been appropriately engaged to understand the subjectivity of management's valuations and the evidence that has been obtained to support these valuations. In such cases, it may be necessary for the auditor to evaluate whether there has been a thorough review and consideration of the issues, including any documentation, at all appropriate management levels within the entity, including with those charged with governance.

127   When markets become inactive or dislocated, or inputs are unobservable, management's valuations may be more judgmental and less verifiable and, as result, may be less reliable. In such circumstances, the auditor may test the model by a combination of testing controls operated by the entity, evaluating the design and operation of the model, testing the assumptions and data used in the model, and comparing its output to a point estimate or range developed by the auditor or to other third-party valuation techniques.[32]

128   It is likely that in testing the inputs used in an entity's valuation methodology,[33] for example, where such inputs are categorized in the fair value hierarchy, the auditor will also be obtaining evidence to support the disclosures required by the applicable financial reporting framework. For example, the auditor's substantive procedures to evaluate whether the inputs used in an entity's valuation technique (that is, level 1, level 2 and level 3 inputs) are appropriate, and tests of an entity's sensitivity analysis, will be relevant to the auditor's evaluation of whether the disclosures achieve fair presentation.

Evaluating Whether the Assumptions Used by Management Are Reasonable

129   An assumption used in a model may be deemed to be significant if a reasonable variation in the assumption would materially affect the measurement of the financial instrument.[34] Management may have considered alternative assumptions or outcomes by performing a sensitivity analysis. The extent of subjectivity associated with assumptions influences the degree of measurement uncertainty and may lead the auditor to conclude there is a significant risk, for example in the case of level 3 inputs.

---

[32] *ISA 540, paragraph 13(d) describes requirements when the auditor develops a range to evaluate management's point estimate. Valuation techniques developed by third parties and used by the auditor may, in some circumstances be considered the work of an auditor's expert and subject to the requirements in ISA 620.*

[33] *See, for example, paragraph 15 of ISA 540 for requirements relative to the auditor's evaluation of management's assumption regarding significant risks.*

[34] *See ISA 540, paragraph A107.*

Audit procedures to test the assumptions used by management, including those used   **130**
as inputs to models, may include evaluating:

- Whether, and if so, how, management has incorporated market inputs into the development of assumptions, as it is generally preferable to seek to maximize the use of relevant observable inputs and minimize unobservable inputs;
- Whether the assumptions are consistent with observable market conditions, and the characteristics of the financial asset or financial liability;
- Whether the sources of market-participant assumptions are relevant and reliable, and how management has selected the assumptions to use when a number of different marketplace assumptions exist; and
- Whether sensitivity analyses indicate that valuations would change significantly with only small or moderate changes in assumptions.

See paragraphs A77 to A83 of ISA 540 for further considerations relative to evaluating the assumptions used by management.

The auditor's consideration of judgments about the future is based on information   **131**
available at the time at which the judgment is made. Subsequent events may result in
outcomes that are inconsistent with judgments that were reasonable at the time they
were made.

In some cases, the discount rate in a present value calculation may be adjusted to   **132**
account for the uncertainties in the valuation, rather than adjusting each assumption.
In such cases, an auditor's procedures may focus on the discount rate, by looking at
an observable trade on a similar security to compare the discount rates used or
developing an independent model to calculate the discount rate and compare with
that used by management.

Audit Considerations When a Management's Expert Is Used by the Entity

As discussed in Section I, management may engage a valuation expert to value some   **133**
or all of their securities. Such experts may be brokers, investment bankers, pricing
services that also provide expert valuation services, or other specialized valuation
firms.

Paragraph 8 of ISA 500 contains requirements for the auditor when evaluating   **134**
evidence from an expert engaged by management. The extent of the auditor's procedures in relation to a management's expert and that expert's work depend on the
significance of the expert's work for the auditor's purposes. Evaluating the appropriateness of management's expert's work assists the auditor in assessing whether the
prices or valuations supplied by a management's expert provide sufficient appropriate audit evidence to support the valuations. Examples of procedures the auditor
may perform include:

- Evaluating the competence, capabilities and objectivity of management's expert for example: their relationship with the entity; their reputation and standing in the market; their experience with the particular types of instruments; and their understanding of the relevant financial reporting framework applicable to the valuations;
- Obtaining an understanding of the work of the management's expert, for example by assessing the appropriateness of the valuation technique(s) used and the key market variables and assumptions used in the valuation technique(s);
- Evaluating the appropriateness of that expert's work as audit evidence. At this point, the focus is on the appropriateness of the expert's work at the level of the individual financial instrument. For a sample of the relevant instruments, it may

be appropriate to develop an estimate independently (see paragraphs 136 to 137 on developing a point estimate or range), using different data and assumptions, then compare that estimate to that of the management's expert; and

● Other procedures may include:
  ○ Modeling different assumptions to derive assumptions in another model, then considering the reasonableness of those derived assumptions.
  ○ Comparing management's point estimates with the auditor's point estimates to determine if management's estimates are consistently higher or lower.

135   Assumptions may be made or identified by a management's expert to assist management in valuing its financial instruments. Such assumptions, when used by management, become management's assumptions that the auditor needs to consider in the same manner as management's other assumptions.

Developing a Point Estimate or Range

136   An auditor may develop a valuation technique and adjust the inputs and assumptions used in the valuation technique to develop a range for use in evaluating the reasonableness of management's valuation. Paragraphs 106 to 135 of this IAPN may assist the auditor in developing a point estimate or range. In accordance with ISA 540,[35] if the auditor uses assumptions, or methodologies that differ from management's, the auditor shall obtain an understanding of management's assumptions or methodologies sufficient to establish that the auditor's range takes into account relevant variables and to evaluate any significant differences from management's valuation. The auditor may find it useful to use the work of an auditor's expert to evaluate the reasonableness of management's valuation.

137   In some cases, the auditor may conclude that sufficient evidence cannot be obtained from the auditor's attempts to obtain an understanding of management's assumptions or methodology, for example when a third-party pricing source uses internally developed models and software and does not allow access to relevant information. In such cases, the auditor may not be able to obtain sufficient appropriate audit evidence about the valuation if the auditor is unable to perform other procedures to respond to the risks of material misstatement, such as developing a point estimate or a range to evaluate management's point estimate.[36] ISA 705[37] describes the implications of the auditor's inability to obtain sufficient appropriate audit evidence.

Presentation and Disclosure of Financial Instruments

138   Management's responsibilities include the preparation of the financial statements in accordance with the applicable financial reporting framework.[38] Financial reporting frameworks often require disclosures in the financial statements to enable users of the financial statements to make meaningful assessments of the effects of the entity's financial instrument activities, including the risks and uncertainties associated with these financial instruments. The importance of disclosures regarding the basis of

---

[35] *ISA 540, paragraph 13(c)*

[36] *ISA 540, paragraph 13(d)*

[37] *ISA 705, Modifications to the Opinion in the Independent Auditor's Report*

[38] *See paragraphs 4 and A2 of ISA 200.*

measurement increases as the measurement uncertainty of the financial instruments increases and is also affected by the level of the fair value hierarchy.

In representing that the financial statements are in accordance with the applicable **139** financial reporting framework, management implicitly or explicitly makes assertions regarding the presentation and disclosure of the various elements of financial statements and related disclosures. Assertions about presentation and disclosure encompass:

(a) Occurrence and rights and obligations—disclosed events, transactions, and other matters have occurred and pertain to the entity.
(b) Completeness—all disclosures that should have been included in the financial statements have been included.
(c) Classification and understandability—financial information is appropriately presented and described, and disclosures are clearly expressed.
(d) Accuracy and valuation—financial and other information are disclosed fairly and at appropriate amounts.

The auditor's procedures around auditing disclosures are designed in consideration of these assertions.

Procedures Relating to the Presentation and Disclosure of Financial Instruments

In relation to the presentation and disclosures of financial instruments, areas of **140** particular importance include:

- Financial reporting frameworks generally require additional disclosures regarding estimates, and related risks and uncertainties, to supplement and explain assets, liabilities, income, and expenses. The auditor's focus may need to be on the disclosures relating to risks and sensitivity analysis. Information obtained during the auditor's risk assessment procedures and testing of control activities may provide evidence in order for the auditor to conclude about whether the disclosures in the financial statements are in accordance with the requirements of the applicable financial reporting framework, for example about:
  o The entity's objectives and strategies for using financial instruments, including the entity's stated accounting policies;
  o The entity's control framework for managing its risks associated with financial instruments; and
  o The risks and uncertainties associated with the financial instruments.
- Information may come from systems outside traditional financial reporting systems, such as risk systems. Examples of procedures that the auditor may choose to perform in responding to assessed risks relative to disclosures include testing:
  o The process used to derive the disclosed information; and
  o The operating effectiveness of the controls over the data used in the preparation of disclosures.
- In relation to financial instruments having significant risk,[39] even where the disclosures are in accordance with the applicable financial reporting framework, the auditor may conclude that the disclosure of estimation uncertainty is inadequate in light of the circumstances and facts involved and, accordingly, the financial statements may not achieve fair presentation. ISA 705 provides

---

[39] *ISA 540, paragraph 20, requires the auditor to perform further procedures on disclosures relating to accounting estimates that give rise to significant risks to evaluate the adequacy of the disclosure of their estimation uncertainty in the financial statements in the context of the applicable financial reporting framework.*

guidance on the implications for the auditor's opinion when the auditor believes that management's disclosures in the financial statements are inadequate or misleading.

- Auditors may also consider whether the disclosures are complete and understandable, for example, all relevant information may be included in the financial statements (or accompanying reports) but it may be insufficiently drawn together to enable users of the financial statements to obtain an understanding of the position or there may not be enough qualitative disclosure to give context to the amounts recorded in the financial statements. For example, even when an entity has included sensitivity analysis disclosures, the disclosure may not fully describe the risks and uncertainties that may arise because of changes in valuation, possible effects on debt covenants, collateral requirements, and the entity's liquidity. ISA 260[40] contains requirements and guidance about communicating with those charged with governance, including the auditor's views about significant qualitative aspects of the entity's accounting practices, including accounting policies, accounting estimates and financial statement disclosures.

141   Consideration of the appropriateness of presentation, for example on short-term and long-term classification, in substantive testing of financial instruments is relevant to the auditor's evaluation of the presentation and disclosure.

Other Relevant Audit Considerations

Written Representations

142   ISA 540 requires the auditor to obtain written representations from management and, where appropriate, those charged with governance whether they believe significant assumptions used in making accounting estimates are reasonable.[41] ISA 580[42] requires that if, in addition to such required representations, the auditor determines that it is necessary to obtain one or more written representations to support other audit evidence relevant to the financial statements or one or more specific assertions in the financial statements, the auditor shall request such other written representations. Depending on the volume and degree of complexity of financial instrument activities, written representations to support other evidence obtained about financial instruments may also include:

- Management's objectives with respect to financial instruments, for example, whether they are used for hedging, asset/liability management or investment purposes;
- Representations about the appropriateness of presentation of the financial statements, for example the recording of financial instrument transactions as sales or financing transactions;
- Representations about the financial statement disclosures concerning financial instruments, for example that:
  - The records reflect all financial instrument transactions; and
  - All embedded derivative instruments have been identified;

---

[40] *ISA 260, Communication with Those Charged with Governance*

[41] *ISA 540, paragraph 22. Paragraph 4 of ISA 580, Written Representations*, states that written representations from management do not provide sufficient appropriate audit evidence on their own about any of the matters with which they deal. If the auditor is otherwise unable to obtain sufficient appropriate audit evidence, this may constitute a limitation on the scope of the audit that may have implications for the auditor's report (see ISA 705, *Modification to the Opinion in the Independent Auditor's Report*).

[42] *ISA 580, paragraph 13*

- Whether all transactions have been conducted at arm's length and at market value;
- The terms of transactions;
- The appropriateness of the valuations of financial instruments;
- Whether there are any side agreements associated with any financial instruments;
- Whether the entity has entered into any written options;
- Management's intent and ability to carry out certain actions;[43] and
- Whether subsequent events require adjustment to the valuations and disclosures included in the financial statements.

Communication with Those Charged with Governance and Others

Because of the uncertainties associated with the valuation of financial instruments, the potential effects on the financial statements of any significant risks are likely to be of governance interest. The auditor may communicate the nature and consequences of significant assumptions used in fair value measurements, the degree of subjectivity involved in the development of the assumptions, and the relative materiality of the items being measured at fair value to the financial statements as a whole. In addition, the need for appropriate controls over commitments to enter into financial instrument contracts and over the subsequent measurement processes are matters that may give rise to the need for communication with those charged with governance.   **143**

ISA 260 deals with the auditor's responsibility to communicate with those charged with governance in an audit of financial statements. With respect to financial instruments, matters to be communicated to those charged with governance may include: **144**

- A lack of management understanding of the nature or extent of the financial instrument activities or the risks associated with such activities;
- Significant deficiencies in the design or operation of the systems of internal control or risk management relating to the entity's financial instrument activities that the auditor has identified during the audit;[44]
- Significant difficulties encountered when obtaining sufficient appropriate audit evidence relating to valuations performed by management or a management's expert, for example, where management is unable to obtain an understanding of the valuation methodology, assumptions and data used by the management's experts, and such information is not made available to the auditor by management' s expert;
- Significant differences in judgments between the auditor and management or a management's expert regarding valuations;
- The potential effects on the entity's financial statements of material risks and exposures required to be disclosed in the financial statements, including the measurement uncertainty associated with financial instruments;
- The auditor's views about the appropriateness of the selection of accounting policies and presentation of financial instrument transactions in the financial statements;

---

[43] *Paragraph A80 of ISA 540 provides examples of procedures that may be appropriate in the circumstances.*

[44] *ISA 265, Communicating Deficiencies in Internal Control to Those Charged with Governance and Management,* establishes requirements and provides guidance on communicating deficiencies in internal control to management, and communicating significant deficiencies in internal control to those charged with governance. It explains that deficiencies in internal control may be identified during the auditor's risk assessment procedures in accordance with ISA 315 or at any other stage of the audit.

- The auditor's views about the qualitative aspects of the entity's accounting practices and financial reporting for financial instruments; or
- A lack of comprehensive and clearly stated policies for the purchase, sale and holding of financial instruments, including operational controls, procedures for designating financial instruments as hedges, and monitoring exposures.

The appropriate timing for communications will vary with the circumstances of the engagement; however, it may be appropriate to communicate significant difficulties encountered during the audit as soon as practicable if those charged with governance are able to assist the auditor to overcome the difficulty, or if it is likely to lead to a modified opinion.

Communications with Regulators and Others

145   In some cases, auditors may be required,[45] or may consider it appropriate, to communicate directly with regulators or prudential supervisors, in addition to those charged with governance, regarding matters relating to financial instruments. Such communication may be useful throughout the audit. For example, in some jurisdictions, banking regulators seek to cooperate with auditors to share information about the operation and application of controls over financial instrument activities, challenges in valuing financial instruments in inactive markets, and compliance with regulations. This coordination may be helpful to the auditor in identifying risks of material misstatement.

---

[45] For example, ISA 250, *Consideration of Laws and Regulations in an Audit of Financial Statements*, requires auditors to determine whether there is a responsibility to report identified or suspected non-compliance with laws and regulations to parties outside the entity. In addition, requirements concerning the auditor's communication to banking supervisors and others may be established in many countries either by law, by supervisory requirement or by formal agreement or protocol.

Appendix

Examples of Controls Relating to Financial Instruments

1. The following provides background information and examples of controls that may exist in an entity that deals in a high volume of financial instrument transactions, whether for trading or investing purposes. The examples are not meant to be exhaustive and entities may establish different control environments and processes depending on their size, the industry in which they operate, and the extent of their financial instrument transactions. Further information on the use of trade confirmations and clearing houses is contained in paragraphs 25–26.
2. As in any control system, it is sometimes necessary to duplicate controls at different control levels (for example, preventative, detective and monitoring) to avoid the risk of material misstatement.

The Entity's Control Environment

Commitment to Competent Use of Financial Instruments

3. The degree of complexity of some financial instrument activities may mean that only a few individuals within the entity fully understand those activities or have the expertise necessary to value the instruments on an ongoing basis. Use of financial instruments without relevant expertise within the entity increases the risk of material misstatement.

Participation by Those Charged with Governance

4. Those charged with governance oversee and concur with management's establishment of the entity's overall risk appetite and provide oversight over the entity's financial instrument activities. An entity's policies for the purchase, sale and holding of financial instruments are aligned with its attitude toward risk and the expertise of those involved in financial instrument activities. In addition, an entity may establish governance structures and control processes aimed at:
   (a) Communicating investment decisions and assessments of all material measurement uncertainty to those charged with governance; and
   (b) Evaluating the entity's overall risk appetite when engaging in financial instrument transactions.

Organizational Structure

5. Financial instrument activities may be run on either a centralized or a decentralized basis. Such activities and related decision making depend heavily on the flow of accurate, reliable, and timely management information. The difficulty of collecting and aggregating such information increases with the number of locations and businesses in which an entity is involved. The risks of material misstatement associated with financial instrument activities may increase with greater decentralization of control activities. This may especially be true where an entity is based in different locations, some perhaps in other countries.

Assignment of Authority and Responsibility

Investment and Valuation Policies

6.　Providing direction, through clearly stated policies approved by those charged with governance for the purchase, sale, and holding of financial instruments enables management to establish an effective approach to taking and managing business risks. These policies are most clear when they state the entity's objectives with regard to its risk management activities, and the investment and hedging alternatives available to meet these objectives, and reflect the:
　(a)　Level of management's expertise;
　(b)　Sophistication of the entity's internal control and monitoring systems;
　(c)　Entity's asset/liability structure;
　(d)　Entity's capacity to maintain liquidity and absorb losses of capital;
　(e)　Types of financial instruments that management believes will meet its objectives; and
　(f)　Uses of financial instruments that management believes will meet its objectives, for example, whether derivatives may be used for speculative purposes or only for hedging purposes.

7.　Management may design policies aligned with its valuation capabilities and may establish controls to ensure that these policies are adhered to by those employees responsible for the entity's valuation. These may include:
　(a)　Processes for the design and validation of methodologies used to produce valuations, including how measurement uncertainty is addressed; and
　(b)　Policies regarding maximizing the use of observable inputs and the types of information to be gathered to support valuations of financial instruments.

8.　In smaller entities, dealing in financial instruments may be rare and management's knowledge and experience limited. Nevertheless, establishing policies over financial instruments helps an entity to determine its risk appetite and consider whether investing in particular financial instruments achieves a stated objective.

Human Resource Policies and Practices

9.　Entities may establish policies requiring key employees, both front office and back office, to take mandatory time off from their duties. This type of control is used as a means of preventing and detecting fraud, in particular if those engaged in trading activities are creating false trades or inaccurately recording transactions.

Use of Service Organizations

10.　Entities may also use service organizations (for example asset managers) to initiate the purchase or sale of financial instruments, to maintain records of transactions for the entity or to value financial instruments. Some entities may be dependent on these service organizations to provide the basis of reporting for the financial instruments held. However, if management does not have an understanding about the controls in place at a service organization, the auditor may not be able to obtain sufficient appropriate audit evidence to rely on controls at that service organization. See ISA 402,[46] which establishes requirements for the auditor to obtain sufficient appropriate audit evidence when an entity uses the services of one or more service organizations.

---

[46] *ISA 402, Audit Considerations Relating to an Entity Using a Service Organization*

11. The use of service organizations may strengthen or weaken the control environment for financial instruments. For example, a service organization's personnel may have more experience with financial instruments than the entity's management or may have more robust internal control over financial reporting. The use of the service organization also may allow for greater segregation of duties. On the other hand, the service organization may have a poor control environment.

The Entity's Risk Assessment Process

12. An entity's risk assessment process exists to establish how management identifies business risks that derive from its use of financial instruments, including how management estimates the significance of the risks, assesses the likelihood of their occurrence and decides upon actions to manage them.
13. The entity's risk assessment process forms the basis for how management determines the risks to be managed. Risk assessment processes exist with the objective of ensuring that management:
    (a) Understands the risks inherent in a financial instrument before management enters into it, including the objective of entering into the transaction and its structure (for example, the economics and business purpose of the entity's financial instrument activities);
    (b) Performs adequate due diligence commensurate with the risks associated with particular financial instruments;
    (c) Monitors the entity's outstanding positions to understand how market conditions are affecting the entity's exposures;
    (d) Has procedures in place to reduce or change risk exposure if necessary and for managing reputational risk; and
    (e) Subjects these processes to rigorous supervision and review.
14. The structure implemented to monitor and manage exposure to risks should:
    (a) Be appropriate and consistent with the entity's attitude toward risk as determined by those charged with governance;
    (b) Specify the approval levels for the authorization of different types of financial instruments and transactions that may be entered into and for what purposes. The permitted instruments and approval levels should reflect the expertise of those involved in financial instrument activities, demonstrating management's commitment to competence;
    (c) Set appropriate limits for the maximum allowable exposure to each type of risk (including approved counterparties). Levels of allowable exposure may vary depending on the type of risk, or counterparty;
    (d) Provide for the objective and timely monitoring of the financial risks and control activities;
    (e) Provide for the objective and timely reporting of exposures, risks and the results of financial instrument activities in managing risk; and
    (f) Evaluate management's track record for assessing the risks of particular financial instruments.
15. The types and levels of risks an entity faces are directly related to the types of financial instruments with which it deals, including the complexity of these instruments and the volume of financial instruments transacted.

Risk Management Function

16. Some entities, for example large financial institutions with a high volume of financial instrument transactions, may be required by law or regulation, or may choose, to establish a formal risk management function. This function is separated from those responsible for undertaking and managing financial

instrument transactions. The function is responsible for reporting on and monitoring financial instrument activities, and may include a formal risk committee established by those charged with governance. Examples of key responsibilities in this area may include:

(a) Implementing the risk management policy set by those charged with governance (including analyses of the risks to which an entity may be exposed);

(b) Designing risk limit structures and ensuring these risk limits are implemented in practice;

(c) Developing stress scenarios and subjecting open position portfolios to sensitivity analysis, including reviews of unusual movements in positions; and

(d) Reviewing and analyzing new financial instrument products.

17. Financial instruments may have the associated risk that a loss might exceed the amount, if any, of the value of the financial instrument recognized on the balance sheet. For example, a sudden fall in the market price of a commodity may force an entity to realize losses to close a forward position in that commodity due to collateral, or margin, requirements. In some cases, the potential losses may be enough to cast significant doubt on the entity's ability to continue as a going concern. The entity may perform sensitivity analyses or value-at-risk analyses to assess the future hypothetical effects on financial instruments subject to market risks. However, value-at-risk analysis does not fully reflect the extent of the risks that may affect the entity; sensitivity and scenario analyses also may be subject to limitations.

18. The volume and sophistication of financial instrument activity and relevant regulatory requirements will influence the entity's consideration whether to establish a formal risk management function and how the function may be structured. In entities that have not established a separate risk management function, for example entities with relatively few financial instruments or financial instruments that are less complex, reporting on and monitoring financial instrument activities may be a component of the accounting or finance function's responsibility or management's overall responsibility, and may include a formal risk committee established by those charged with governance

The Entity's Information Systems

19. The key objective of an entity's information system is that it is capable of capturing and recording all the transactions accurately, settling them, valuing them, and producing information to enable the financial instruments to be risk managed and for controls to be monitored. Difficulties can arise in entities that engage in a high volume of financial instruments, in particular if there is a multiplicity of systems that are poorly integrated and have manual interfaces without adequate controls.

20. Certain financial instruments may require a large number of accounting entries. As the sophistication or level of the financial instrument activities increases, it is necessary for the sophistication of the information system to also increase. Specific issues which can arise with respect to financial instruments include:

(a) Information systems, in particular for smaller entities, not having the capability or not being appropriately configured to process financial instrument transactions, especially when the entity does not have any prior experience in dealing with financial instruments. This may result in an increased number of manual transactions which may further increase the risk of error;

(b) The potential diversity of systems required to process more complex transactions, and the need for regular reconciliations between them, in particular when the systems are not interfaced or may be subject to manual intervention;

(c) The potential that more complex transactions, if they are only traded by a small number of individuals, may be valued or risk managed on spreadsheets rather than on main processing systems, and for the physical and logical password security around those spreadsheets to be more easily compromised;

(d) A lack of review of systems exception logs, external confirmations and broker quotes, where available, to validate the entries generated by the systems;

(e) Difficulties in controlling and evaluating the key inputs to systems for valuation of financial instruments, particularly where those systems are maintained by the group of traders known as the front office or a third-party service provider and/or the transactions in question are non-routine or thinly traded;

(f) Failure to evaluate the design and calibration of complex models used to process these transactions initially and on a periodic basis;

(g) The potential that management has not set up a library of models, with controls around access, change and maintenance of individual models, in order to maintain a strong audit trail of the accredited versions of models and in order to prevent unauthorized access or amendments to those models;

(h) The disproportionate investment that may be required in risk management and control systems, where an entity only undertakes a limited number of financial instrument transactions, and the potential for misunderstanding of the output by management if they are not used to these types of transactions;

(i) The potential requirement for third-party systems provision, for example from a service organization, to record, process, account for or risk manage appropriately financial instrument transactions, and the need to reconcile appropriately and challenge the output from those providers; and

(j) Additional security and control considerations relevant to the use of an electronic network when an entity uses electronic commerce for financial instrument transactions.

21. Information systems relevant to financial reporting serve as an important source of information for the quantitative disclosures in the financial statements. However, entities may also develop and maintain non-financial systems used for internal reporting and to generate information included in qualitative disclosures, for example regarding risks and uncertainties or sensitivity analyses.

The Entity's Control Activities

22. Control activities over financial instrument transactions are designed to prevent or detect problems that hinder an entity from achieving its objectives. These objectives may be either operational, financial reporting, or compliance in nature. Control activities over financial instruments are designed relative to the complexity and volume of transactions of financial instruments and will generally include an appropriate authorization process, adequate segregation of duties, and other policies and procedures designed to ensure that the entity's control objectives are met. Process flow charts may assist in identifying an entity's controls and lack of controls. This IAPN focuses on control activities related to completeness, accuracy and existence, valuation, and presentation and disclosure.

Authorization

23. Authorization can affect the financial statement assertions both directly and indirectly. For example, even if a transaction is executed outside an entity's policies, it nonetheless may be recorded and accounted for accurately. However, unauthorized transactions could significantly increase risk to the entity, thereby significantly increasing the risk of material misstatement since they would be undertaken outside the system of internal control. To mitigate this risk, an entity will often establish a clear policy as to what transactions can be traded by whom and adherence to this policy will then be monitored by an entity's back office. Monitoring trading activities of individuals, for example by reviewing unusually high volumes or significant gains or losses incurred, will assist management in ensuring compliance with the entity's policies, including the authorization of new types of transactions, and evaluating whether fraud has occurred.

24. The function of an entity's deal initiation records is to identify clearly the nature and purpose of individual transactions and the rights and obligations arising under each financial instrument contract, including the enforceability of the contracts. In addition to the basic financial information, such as a notional amount, complete and accurate records at a minimum typically include:
    (a) The identity of the dealer;
    (b) The identity of the person recording the transaction (if not the dealer), when the transaction was initiated (including the date and time of the transaction), and how it was recorded in the entity's information systems; and
    (c) The nature and purpose of the transaction, including whether or not it is intended to hedge an underlying commercial exposure.

Segregation of Duties

25. Segregation of duties and the assignment of personnel is an important control activity, particularly when exposed to financial instruments. Financial instrument activities may be segregated into a number of functions, including:
    (a) Executing the transaction (dealing). In entities with a high volume of financial instrument transactions, this may be done by the front office;
    (b) Initiating cash payments and accepting cash receipts (settlements);
    (c) Sending out trade confirmations and reconciling the differences between the entity's records and replies from counterparties, if any;
    (d) Recording of all transactions correctly in the accounting records;
    (e) Monitoring risk limits. In entities with a high volume of financial instrument transactions, this may be performed by the risk management function; and
    (f) Monitoring positions and valuing financial instruments.

26. Many organizations choose to segregate the duties of those investing in financial instruments, those valuing financial instruments, those settling financial instruments and those accounting/recording financial instruments.

27. Where an entity is too small to achieve proper segregation of duties, the role of management and those charged with governance in monitoring financial instrument activities is of particular importance.

28. A feature of some entities' internal control is an independent price verification (IPV) function. This department is responsible for separately verifying the price of some financial instruments, and may use alternative data sources, methodologies and assumptions. The IPV provides an objective look at the pricing that has been developed in another part of the entity.

29. Ordinarily, the middle or back office is responsible for establishing policies on valuation and ensuring adherence to the policy. Entities with a greater use of financial instruments may perform daily valuations of their financial instrument portfolio and examine the contribution to profit or loss of individual financial instrument valuations as a test of the reasonableness of valuations.

Completeness, Accuracy, and Existence

30. Regular reconciliation of the entity's records to external banks' and custodians' records enables the entity to ensure transactions are properly recorded. Appropriate segregation of duties between those transacting the trades and those reconciling them is important, as is a rigorous process for reviewing reconciliations and clearing reconciling items.

31. Controls may also be established that require traders to identify whether a complex financial instrument may have unique features, for example embedded derivatives. In such circumstances, there may be a separate function that evaluates complex financial instrument transactions at their initiation (which may be known as a product control group), working in connection with an accounting policy group to ensure the transaction is accurately recorded. While smaller entities may not have product control groups, an entity may have a process in place relating to the review of complex financial instrument contracts at the point of origination in order to ensure they are accounted for appropriately in accordance with the applicable financial reporting framework.

Monitoring of Controls

32. The entity's ongoing monitoring activities are designed to detect and correct any deficiencies in the effectiveness of controls over transactions for financial instruments and their valuation. It is important that there is adequate supervision and review of financial instrument activity within the entity. This includes:
    (a) All controls being subject to review, for example, the monitoring of operational statistics such as the number of reconciling items or the difference between internal pricing and external pricing sources;
    (b) The need for robust information technology (IT) controls and monitoring and validating their application; and
    (c) The need to ensure that information resulting from different processes and systems is adequately reconciled. For example, there is little benefit in a valuation process if the output from it is not reconciled properly into the general ledger.

33. In larger entities, sophisticated computer information systems generally keep track of financial instrument activities, and are designed to ensure that settlements occur when due. More complex computer systems may generate automatic postings to clearing accounts to monitor cash movements, and controls over processing are put in place with the objective of ensuring that financial instrument activities are correctly reflected in the entity's records. Computer systems may be designed to produce exception reports to alert management to situations where financial instruments have not been used within authorized limits or where transactions undertaken were not within the limits established for the chosen counterparties. However, even a sophisticated computer system may not ensure the completeness of the recording of financial instrument transactions. Accordingly, management frequently puts additional procedures in place to increase the likelihood that all transactions will be recorded.

Part Four

International Standards on Review Engagements (ISREs)

International Standard on Review Engagements 2400 (Revised September 2012) Engagements to review historical financial statements

(Effective for reviews of financial statements for periods ending on or after December 31, 2013)

Contents

International Standard on Review Engagements (ISRE) 2400 (Revised), *Engagements to Review Historical Financial Statements*, should be read in conjunction with the *Preface to the International Standards on Quality Control, Auditing, Review, Other Assurance, and Related Services Pronouncements.*

Introduction

Scope of this ISRE

This International Standard on Review Engagements (ISRE) deals with: (Ref: Para. **1** A1)

(a) The practitioner's responsibilities when engaged to perform a review of historical financial statements, when the practitioner is not the auditor of the entity's financial statements; and

(b) The form and content of the practitioner's report on the financial statements.

This ISRE does not address a review of an entity's financial statements or interim **2** financial information performed by a practitioner who is the independent auditor of the entity's financial statements (Ref: Para. A2)

This ISRE is to be applied, adapted as necessary, to reviews of other historical **3** financial information. Limited assurance engagements other than reviews of historical financial information are performed under ISAE 3000.[1]

Relationship with ISQC 1[2]

Quality control systems, policies and procedures are the responsibility of the firm. **4** ISQC 1 applies to firms of professional accountants in respect of a firm's engagements to review financial statements.[3] The provisions of this ISRE regarding quality control at the level of individual review engagements are premised on the basis that the firm is subject to ISQC 1 or requirements that are at least as demanding. (Ref: Para. A3–A5)

The Engagement to Review Historical Financial Statements

The review of historical financial statements is a limited assurance engagement, as **5** described in the *International Framework for Assurance Engagements* (the Assurance Framework).[4] (Ref: Para. A6–A7)

In a review of financial statements, the practitioner expresses a conclusion that is **6** designed to enhance the degree of confidence of intended users regarding the preparation of an entity's financial statements in accordance with an applicable financial reporting framework. The practitioner's conclusion is based on the practitioner obtaining limited assurance. The practitioner's report includes a description of the nature of a review engagement as context for the readers of the report to be able to understand the conclusion.

The practitioner performs primarily inquiry and analytical procedures to obtain **7** sufficient appropriate evidence as the basis for a conclusion on the financial statements as a whole, expressed in accordance with the requirements of this ISRE.

---

[1] *International Standard on Assurance Engagements (ISAE) 3000,* Assurance Engagements Other than Audits or Reviews of Historical Financial Information.

[2] *International Standard on Quality Control (ISQC) 1,* Quality Control for Firms that Perform Audits and Reviews of Financial Statements, and Other Assurance and Related Services Engagements.

[3] *ISQC 1, paragraph 4.*

[4] *Assurance Framework, paragraphs 7 and 11*

8   If the practitioner becomes aware of a matter that causes the practitioner to believe the financial statements may be materially misstated, the practitioner designs and performs additional procedures, as the practitioner considers necessary in the circumstances, to be able to conclude on the financial statements in accordance with this ISRE.

Authority of this ISRE

9   This ISRE contains the objectives of the practitioner in following the ISRE which provide the context in which the requirements of this ISRE are set, and are intended to assist the practitioner in understanding what needs to be accomplished in a review engagement.

10   The ISRE contains requirements, expressed using "shall," that are designed to enable the practitioner to meet the stated objectives.

11   In addition, this ISRE contains introductory material, definitions, and application and other explanatory material, that provide context relevant to a proper understanding of the ISRE.

12   The application and other explanatory material provides further explanation of the requirements and guidance for carrying them out. While such guidance does not itself impose a requirement, it is relevant to the proper application of the requirements. The application and other explanatory material may also provide background information on matters addressed in this ISRE that assists in the application of the requirements.

Effective Date

13   This ISRE is effective for reviews of financial statements for periods ending on or after December 31, 2013.

Objectives

14   The practitioner's objectives in a review of financial statements under this ISRE are to:

(a) Obtain limited assurance, primarily by performing inquiry and analytical procedures, about whether the financial statements as a whole are free from material misstatement, thereby enabling the practitioner to express a conclusion on whether anything has come to the practitioner's attention that causes the practitioner to believe the financial statements are not prepared, in all material respects, in accordance with an applicable financial reporting framework; and

(b) Report on the financial statements as a whole and communicate, as required by this ISRE.

15   In all cases when limited assurance cannot be obtained and a qualified conclusion in the practitioner's report is insufficient in the circumstances, this ISRE requires that the practitioner either disclaim a conclusion in the report issued for the engagement or, where appropriate, withdraw from the engagement if withdrawal is possible under applicable law or regulation. (Ref. Para. A8–A10, A115–A116)

Definitions

The Handbook's Glossary of Terms[5] (the Glossary) includes the terms defined in this ISRE as well as descriptions of other terms used in this ISRE, to assist in consistent application and interpretation. For example, the terms "management" and "those charged with governance" used throughout this ISRE are as defined in the Glossary. (Ref: Para. A11–A12) **16**

For purposes of this ISRE, the following terms have the meanings attributed below: **17**

(a) *Analytical procedures*—Evaluations of financial information through analysis of plausible relationships among both financial and non-financial data. Analytical procedures also encompass such investigation as is necessary of identified fluctuations or relationships that are inconsistent with other relevant information or that differ from expected values by a significant amount.

(b) *Engagement risk*—The risk that the practitioner expresses an inappropriate conclusion when the financial statements are materially misstated.

(c) *General purpose financial statements*—Financial statements prepared in accordance with a general purpose framework.

(d) *General purpose framework*—A financial reporting framework designed to meet the common financial needs of a wide range of users. The financial reporting framework may be a fair presentation framework or a compliance framework.

(e) *Inquiry*—Inquiry consists of seeking information of knowledgeable persons from within or outside the entity.

(f) *Limited assurance*—The level of assurance obtained where engagement risk is reduced to a level that is acceptable in the circumstances of the engagement, but where that risk is greater than for a reasonable assurance engagement, as the basis for expressing a conclusion in accordance with this ISRE. The combination of the nature, timing and extent of evidence gathering procedures is at least sufficient for the practitioner to obtain a meaningful level of assurance. To be meaningful, the level of assurance obtained by the practitioner is likely to enhance the intended users' confidence about the financial statements. (Ref: Para. A13)

(g) *Practitioner*—A professional accountant in public practice. The term includes the engagement partner or other members of the engagement team, or, as applicable, the firm. Where this ISRE expressly intends that a requirement or responsibility be fulfilled by the engagement partner, the term "engagement partner" rather than "practitioner" is used. "Engagement partner" and "firm" are to be read as referring to their public sector equivalents where relevant.

(h) *Professional judgment*—The application of relevant training, knowledge and experience, within the context provided by assurance, accounting and ethical standards, in making informed decisions about the courses of action that are appropriate in the circumstances of the review engagement.

(i) *Relevant ethical requirements*—Ethical requirements the engagement team is subject to when undertaking review engagements. These requirements ordinarily comprise Parts A and B of the International Ethics Standards Board for Accountants' *Code of Ethics for Professional Accountants* (IESBA Code), together with national requirements that are more restrictive.

(j) *Special purpose financial statements*—Financial statements prepared in accordance with a special purpose framework.

---

[5] *The Glossary of Terms relating to International Standards issued by the IAASB in the* Handbook of International Quality Control, Auditing, Review, Other Assurance and Related Services Pronouncements *(the* Handbook*), published by IFAC.*

(k) *Special purpose framework*—A financial reporting framework designed to meet the financial information needs of specific users. The financial reporting framework may be a fair presentation framework or a compliance framework.

Requirements

Conduct of a Review Engagement in Accordance with this ISRE

18 The practitioner shall have an understanding of the entire text of this ISRE, including its application and other explanatory material, to understand its objectives and to apply its requirements properly. (Ref: Para. A14)

Complying with Relevant Requirements

19 The practitioner shall comply with each requirement of this ISRE, unless a requirement is not relevant to the review engagement. A requirement is relevant to the review engagement when the circumstances addressed by the requirement exist.

20 The practitioner shall not represent compliance with this ISRE in the practitioner's report unless the practitioner has complied with all the requirements of this ISRE relevant to the review engagement.

Ethical Requirements

21 The practitioner shall comply with relevant ethical requirements, including those pertaining to independence. (Ref: Para. A15–A16)

Professional Skepticism and Professional Judgment

22 The practitioner shall plan and perform the engagement with professional skepticism recognizing that circumstances may exist that cause the financial statements to be materially misstated. (Ref: Para. A17–A20)

23 The practitioner shall exercise professional judgment in conducting a review engagement. (Ref: Para. A21–A25)

Engagement Level Quality Control

24 The engagement partner shall possess competence in assurance skills and techniques, and competence in financial reporting, appropriate to the engagement circumstances. (Ref: Para. A26)

25 The engagement partner shall take responsibility for: (Ref: Para. A27–A30)

(a) The overall quality of each review engagement to which that partner is assigned;
(b) The direction, supervision, planning and performance of the review engagement in compliance with professional standards and applicable legal and regulatory requirements; (Ref: Para. A31)
(c) The practitioner's report being appropriate in the circumstances; and
(d) The engagement being performed in accordance with the firm's quality control policies, including the following:
  (i) Being satisfied that appropriate procedures regarding the acceptance and continuance of client relationships and engagements have been followed,

and that conclusions reached are appropriate, including considering whether there is information that would lead the engagement partner to
conclude that management lacks integrity; (Ref: Para. A32–A33)
(ii) Being satisfied that the engagement team collectively has the appropriate
competence and capabilities, including assurance skills and techniques and
expertise in financial reporting, to:
a. Perform the review engagement in accordance with professional
standards and applicable legal and regulatory requirements; and
b. Enable a report that is appropriate in the circumstances to be issued;
and
(iii) Taking responsibility for appropriate engagement documentation being
maintained.

Relevant Considerations after Engagement Acceptance

If the engagement partner obtains information that would have caused the firm to **26**
decline the engagement had that information been available earlier, the engagement
partner shall communicate that information promptly to the firm, so that the firm
and the engagement partner can take the necessary action.

Compliance with Relevant Ethical Requirements

Throughout the engagement, the engagement partner shall remain alert, through **27**
observation and making inquiries as necessary, for evidence of non-compliance with
relevant ethical requirements by members of the engagement team. If matters come
to the engagement partner's attention through the firm's system of quality control or
otherwise that indicate that members of the engagement team have not complied
with relevant ethical requirements, the engagement partner, in consultation with
others in the firm, shall determine the appropriate action.

Monitoring

An effective system of quality control for a firm includes a monitoring process **28**
designed to provide the firm with reasonable assurance that the firm's policies and
procedures relating to the system of quality control are relevant, adequate and
operate effectively. The engagement partner shall consider the results of the firm's
monitoring process as evidenced in the latest information circulated by the firm and,
if applicable, other network firms and whether deficiencies noted in that information
may affect the review engagement.

Acceptance and Continuance of Client Relationships and Review Engagements

Factors Affecting Acceptance and Continuance of Client Relationships and Review Engagements

Unless required by law or regulation, the practitioner shall not accept a review **29**
engagement if: (Ref: Para. A34–A35)

(a) The practitioner is not satisfied:
(i) That there is a rational purpose for the engagement; or (Ref: Para. A36)
(ii) That a review engagement would be appropriate in the circumstances; (Ref:
Para. A37)
(b) The practitioner has reason to believe that relevant ethical requirements,
including independence, will not be satisfied;

(c) The practitioner's preliminary understanding of the engagement circumstances indicates that information needed to perform the review engagement is likely to be unavailable or unreliable; (Ref: Para. A38)

(d) The practitioner has cause to doubt management's integrity such that it is likely to affect proper performance of the review; or (Ref: Para. A37(b))

(e) Management or those charged with governance impose a limitation on the scope of the practitioner's work in the terms of a proposed review engagement such that the practitioner believes the limitation will result in the practitioner disclaiming a conclusion on the financial statements.

Preconditions for Accepting a Review Engagement

30 Prior to accepting a review engagement, the practitioner shall: (Ref: Para. A39)

(a) Determine whether the financial reporting framework applied in the preparation of the financial statements is acceptable including, in the case of special purpose financial statements, obtaining an understanding of the purpose for which the financial statements are prepared and of the intended users; and (Ref: Para. A40–A46)

(b) Obtain the agreement of management that it acknowledges and understands its responsibilities: (Ref: Para. A47–A50)

   (i) For preparation of the financial statements in accordance with the applicable financial reporting framework, including, where relevant, their fair presentation;

   (ii) For such internal control as management determines is necessary to enable the preparation of financial statements that are free from material misstatement, whether due to fraud or error; and

   (iii) To provide the practitioner with:

      a. Access to all information of which management is aware that is relevant to the preparation of the financial statements, such as records, documentation and other matters;

      b. Additional information that the practitioner may request from management for the purpose of the review; and

      c. Unrestricted access to persons within the entity from whom the practitioner determines it necessary to obtain evidence.

31 If the practitioner is not satisfied as to any of the matters set out above as preconditions for accepting a review engagement, the practitioner shall discuss the matter with management or those charged with governance. If changes cannot be made to satisfy the practitioner as to those matters, the practitioner shall not accept the proposed engagement unless required by law or regulation to do so. However, an engagement conducted under such circumstances does not comply with this ISRE. Accordingly, the practitioner shall not include any reference within the practitioner's report to the review having been conducted in accordance with this ISRE.

32 If it is discovered after the engagement has been accepted that the practitioner is not satisfied as to any of the above preconditions, the practitioner shall discuss the matter with management or those charged with governance, and shall determine:

(a) Whether the matter can be resolved;

(b) Whether it is appropriate to continue with the engagement; and

(c) Whether and, if so, how to communicate the matter in the practitioner's report.

Additional Considerations When the Wording of the Practitioner's Report Is Prescribed by Law or Regulation

The practitioner's report issued for the review engagement shall refer to this ISRE only if the report complies with the requirements of paragraph 86.   **33**

In some cases, when the review is performed pursuant to applicable law or regulation   **34**
of a jurisdiction, the relevant law or regulation may prescribe the layout or wording of the practitioner's report in a form or in terms that are significantly different from the requirements of this ISRE. In those circumstances, the practitioner shall evaluate whether users might misunderstand the assurance obtained from the review of the financial statements and, if so, whether additional explanation in the practitioner's report can mitigate possible misunderstanding. (Ref: Para. A51, A142)

If the practitioner concludes that additional explanation in the practitioner's report   **35**
cannot mitigate possible misunderstanding, the practitioner shall not accept the review engagement unless required by law or regulation to do so. A review conducted in accordance with such law or regulation does not comply with this ISRE. Accordingly, the practitioner shall not include any reference within the practitioner's report to the review having been conducted in accordance with this ISRE. (Ref: Para. A51, A142)

Agreeing the Terms of Engagement

The practitioner shall agree the terms of the engagement with management or those   **36**
charged with governance, as appropriate, prior to performing the engagement.

The agreed terms of engagement shall be recorded in an engagement letter or other   **37**
suitable form of written agreement, and shall include: (Ref: Para. A52–A54, A56)

(a)   The intended use and distribution of the financial statements, and any restrictions on use or distribution where applicable;
(b)   Identification of the applicable financial reporting framework;
(c)   The objective and scope of the review engagement;
(d)   The responsibilities of the practitioner;
(e)   The responsibilities of management, including those in paragraph 30(b); (Ref: Para. A47–A50, A55)
(f)   A statement that the engagement is not an audit, and that the practitioner will not express an audit opinion on the financial statements; and
(g)   Reference to the expected form and content of the report to be issued by the practitioner, and a statement that there may be circumstances in which the report may differ from its expected form and content.

Recurring Engagements

On recurring review engagements, the practitioner shall evaluate whether circum-   **38**
stances, including changes in the engagement acceptance considerations, require the terms of engagement to be revised and whether there is a need to remind management or those charged with governance, as appropriate, of the existing terms of engagement. (Ref: Para. A57)

Acceptance of a Change in the Terms of the Review Engagement

The practitioner shall not agree to a change in the terms of the engagement where   **39**
there is no reasonable justification for doing so. (Ref: Para. A58–A60)

40   If, prior to completing the review engagement, the practitioner is requested to change the engagement to an engagement for which no assurance is obtained, the practitioner shall determine whether there is reasonable justification for doing so. (Ref: Para. A61–A62)

41   If the terms of engagement are changed during the course of the engagement, the practitioner and management or those charged with governance, as appropriate, shall agree on and record the new terms of the engagement in an engagement letter or other suitable form of written agreement.

Communication with Management and Those Charged with Governance

42   The practitioner shall communicate with management or those charged with governance, as appropriate, on a timely basis during the course of the review engagement, all matters concerning the review engagement that, in the practitioner's professional judgment, are of sufficient importance to merit the attention of management or those charged with governance, as appropriate. (Ref: Para. A63–A69)

Performing the Engagement

Materiality in a Review of Financial Statements

43   The practitioner shall determine materiality for the financial statements as a whole, and apply this materiality in designing the procedures and in evaluating the results obtained from those procedures. (Ref: Para. A70–A73)

44   The practitioner shall revise materiality for the financial statements as a whole in the event of becoming aware of information during the review that would have caused the practitioner to have determined a different amount initially. (Ref. Para. A74)

The Practitioner's Understanding

45   The practitioner shall obtain an understanding of the entity and its environment, and the applicable financial reporting framework, to identify areas in the financial statements where material misstatements are likely to arise and thereby provide a basis for designing procedures to address those areas. (Ref: Para. A75–A77)

46   The practitioner's understanding shall include the following: (Ref: Para. A78, A87, A89)

(a)   Relevant industry, regulatory, and other external factors including the applicable financial reporting framework;
(b)   The nature of the entity, including:
   (i)   Its operations;
   (ii)   Its ownership and governance structure;
   (iii)   The types of investments that the entity is making and plans to make;
   (iv)   The way that the entity is structured and how it is financed; and
   (v)   The entity's objectives and strategies;
(c)   The entity's accounting systems and accounting records; and
(d)   The entity's selection and application of accounting policies.

Designing and Performing Procedures

In obtaining sufficient appropriate evidence as the basis for a conclusion on the **47** financial statements as a whole, the practitioner shall design and perform inquiry and analytical procedures: (Ref: Para. A79–A83, A87, A89)

(a) To address all material items in the financial statements, including disclosures; and
(b) To focus on addressing areas in the financial statements where material misstatements are likely to arise.

The practitioner's inquiries of management and others within the entity, as appro- **48** priate, shall include the following: (Ref: Para. A84–A87)

(a) How management makes the significant accounting estimates required under the applicable financial reporting framework;
(b) The identification of related parties and related party transactions, including the purpose of those transactions;
(c) Whether there are significant, unusual or complex transactions, events or matters that have affected or may affect the entity's financial statements, including:
   (i) Significant changes in the entity's business activities or operations;
   (ii) Significant changes to the terms of contracts that materially affect the entity's financial statements, including terms of finance and debt contracts or covenants;
   (iii) Significant journal entries or other adjustments to the financial statements;
   (iv) Significant transactions occurring or recognized near the end of the reporting period;
   (v) The status of any uncorrected misstatements identified during previous engagements; and
   (vi) Effects or possible implications for the entity of transactions or relationships with related parties;
(d) The existence of any actual, suspected or alleged:
   (i) Fraud or illegal acts affecting the entity; and
   (ii) Non-compliance with provisions of laws and regulations that are generally recognized to have a direct effect on the determination of material amounts and disclosures in the financial statements, such as tax and pension laws and regulations;
(e) Whether management has identified and addressed events occurring between the date of the financial statements and the date of the practitioner's report that require adjustment of, or disclosure in, the financial statements;
(f) The basis for management's assessment of the entity's ability to continue as a going concern; (Ref: Para. A88)
(g) Whether there are events or conditions that appear to cast doubt on the entity's ability to continue as a going concern;
(h) Material commitments, contractual obligations or contingencies that have affected or may affect the entity's financial statements, including disclosures; and
(i) Material non-monetary transactions or transactions for no consideration in the financial reporting period under consideration.

In designing analytical procedures, the practitioner shall consider whether the data **49** from the entity's accounting system and accounting records are adequate for the purpose of performing the analytical procedures. (Ref: Para. A89–A91)

Procedures to Address Specific Circumstances

Related parties

50   During the review, the practitioner shall remain alert for arrangements or information that may indicate the existence of related party relationships or transactions that management has not previously identified or disclosed to the practitioner.

51   If the practitioner identifies significant transactions outside the entity's normal course of business in the course of performing the review, the practitioner shall inquire of management about:

(a)   The nature of those transactions;
(b)   Whether related parties could be involved; and
(c)   The business rationale (or lack thereof) of those transactions.

Fraud and non-compliance with laws or regulations

52   When there is an indication that fraud or non-compliance with laws or regulations, or suspected fraud or non-compliance with laws or regulations, has occurred in the entity, the practitioner shall:

(a)   Communicate that matter to the appropriate level of senior management or those charged with governance as appropriate;
(b)   Request management's assessment of the effect(s), if any, on the financial statements;
(c)   Consider the effect, if any, of management's assessment of the effects of fraud or non-compliance with laws or regulations communicated to the practitioner on the practitioner's conclusion on the financial statements and on the practitioner's report; and
(d)   Determine whether there is a responsibility to report the occurrence or suspicion of fraud or illegal acts to a party outside the entity. (Ref: Para. A92)

Going concern

53   A review of financial statements includes consideration of the entity's ability to continue as a going concern. In considering management's assessment of the entity's ability to continue as a going concern, the practitioner shall cover the same period as that used by management to make its assessment as required by the applicable financial reporting framework, or by law or regulation where a longer period is specified.

54   If, during the performance of the review, the practitioner becomes aware of events or conditions that may cast significant doubt about the entity's ability to continue as a going concern, the practitioner shall: (Ref: Para. A93)

(a)   Inquire of management about plans for future actions affecting the entity's ability to continue as a going concern and about the feasibility of those plans, and also whether management believes the outcome of those plans will improve the situation regarding the entity's ability to continue as a going concern;
(b)   Evaluate the results of those inquiries, to consider whether management's responses provide a sufficient basis to:
  (i)   Continue to present the financial statements on the going concern basis if the applicable financial reporting framework includes the assumption of an entity's continuance as a going concern; or

    (ii) Conclude whether the financial statements are materially misstated, or are otherwise misleading regarding the entity's ability to continue as a going concern; and

(c) Consider management's responses in light of all relevant information of which the practitioner is aware as a result of the review.

Use of work performed by others

In performing the review, it may be necessary for the practitioner to use work **55** performed by other practitioners, or the work of an individual or organization possessing expertise in a field other than accounting or assurance. If the practitioner uses work performed by another practitioner or an expert in the course of performing the review, the practitioner shall take appropriate steps to be satisfied that the work performed is adequate for the practitioner's purposes. (Ref: Para. A80)

Reconciling the Financial Statements to the Underlying Accounting Records

The practitioner shall obtain evidence that the financial statements agree with, or **56** reconcile to, the entity's underlying accounting records. (Ref: Para. A94)

Additional Procedures When the Practitioner Becomes Aware that the Financial Statements May Be Materially Misstated

If the practitioner becomes aware of a matter(s) that causes the practitioner to **57** believe the financial statements may be materially misstated, the practitioner shall design and perform additional procedures sufficient to enable the practitioner to: (Ref: Para. A95–A99)

(a) Conclude that the matter(s) is not likely to cause the financial statements as a whole to be materially misstated; or

(b) Determine that the matter(s) causes the financial statements as a whole to be materially misstated.

Subsequent Events

If the practitioner becomes aware of events occurring between the date of the **58** financial statements and the date of the practitioner's report that require adjustment of, or disclosure in, the financial statements, the practitioner shall request management to correct those misstatements.

The practitioner has no obligation to perform any procedures regarding the financial **59** statements after the date of the practitioner's report. However, if, after the date of the practitioner's report but before the date the financial statements are issued, a fact becomes known to the practitioner that, had it been known to the practitioner at the date of the practitioner's report, may have caused the practitioner to amend the report, the practitioner shall:

(a) Discuss the matter with management or those charged with governance, as appropriate;

(b) Determine whether the financial statements need amendment; and

(c) If so, inquire how management intends to address the matter in the financial statements.

If management does not amend the financial statements in circumstances where the **60** practitioner believes they need to be amended, and the practitioner's report has already been provided to the entity, the practitioner shall notify management and those charged with governance not to issue the financial statements to third parties before the necessary amendments have been made. If the financial statements are nevertheless subsequently issued without the necessary amendments, the practitioner shall take appropriate action to seek to prevent reliance on the practitioner's report.

Written Representations

61   The practitioner shall request management to provide a written representation that management has fulfilled its responsibilities described in the agreed terms of engagement. The written representation shall include that: (Ref: Para. A100–A102)

(a) Management has fulfilled its responsibility for the preparation of financial statements in accordance with the applicable financial reporting framework, including where relevant their fair presentation, and has provided the practitioner with all relevant information and access to information as agreed in the terms of the engagement; and

(b) All transactions have been recorded and are reflected in the financial statements.

If law or regulation requires management to make written public statements about its responsibilities, and the practitioner determines that such statements provide some or all of the representations required by subparagraphs (a)–(b), the relevant matters covered by such statements need not be included in the written representation.

62   The practitioner shall also request management's written representations that management has disclosed to the practitioner: (Ref: Para. A101)

(a) The identity of the entity's related parties and all the related party relationships and transactions of which management is aware;

(b) Significant facts relating to any frauds or suspected frauds known to management that may have affected the entity;

(c) Known actual or possible non-compliance with laws and regulations for which the effects of non-compliance affect the entity's financial statements;

(d) All information relevant to use of the going concern assumption in the financial statements;

(e) That all events occurring subsequent to the date of the financial statements and for which the applicable financial reporting framework requires adjustment or disclosure, have been adjusted or disclosed;

(f) Material commitments, contractual obligations or contingencies that have affected or may affect the entity's financial statements, including disclosures; and

(g) Material non-monetary transactions or transactions for no consideration undertaken by the entity in the financial reporting period under consideration.

63   If management does not provide one or more of the requested written representations, the practitioner shall: (Ref: Para. A100)

(a) Discuss the matter with management and those charged with governance, as appropriate;

(b) Re-evaluate the integrity of management, and evaluate the effect that this may have on the reliability of representations (oral or written) and evidence in general; and

(c) Take appropriate actions, including determining the possible effect on the conclusion in the practitioner's report in accordance with this ISRE.

The practitioner shall disclaim a conclusion on the financial statements, or withdraw **64** from the engagement if withdrawal is possible under applicable law or regulation, as appropriate, if:

(a) The practitioner concludes that there is sufficient doubt about the integrity of management such that the written representations are not reliable; or
(b) Management does not provide the required representations required by paragraph 61.

Date of and Period(s) Covered by Written Representations

The date of the written representations shall be as near as practicable to, but not **65** after, the date of the practitioner's report. The written representations shall be for all financial statements and period(s) referred to in the practitioner's report.

Evaluating Evidence Obtained from the Procedures Performed

The practitioner shall evaluate whether sufficient appropriate evidence has been **66** obtained from the procedures performed and, if not, the practitioner shall perform other procedures judged by the practitioner to be necessary in the circumstances to be able to form a conclusion on the financial statements. (Ref: Para. A103)

If the practitioner is not able to obtain sufficient appropriate evidence to form a **67** conclusion, the practitioner shall discuss with management and those charged with governance, as appropriate, the effects such limitations have on the scope of the review. (Ref: Para. A104–A105)

Evaluating the Effect on the Practitioner's Report

The practitioner shall evaluate the evidence obtained from the procedures performed **68** to determine the effect on the practitioner's report. (Ref: Para. A103)

Forming the Practitioner's Conclusion on the Financial Statements

Consideration of the Applicable Financial Reporting Framework in Relation to the Financial Statements

In forming the conclusion on the financial statements, the practitioner shall: **69**

(a) Evaluate whether the financial statements adequately refer to or describe the applicable financial reporting framework; (Ref: Para. A106–A107)
(b) Consider whether, in the context of the requirements of the applicable financial reporting framework and the results of procedures performed:
  (i) The terminology used in the financial statements, including the title of each financial statement, is appropriate;
  (ii) The financial statements adequately disclose the significant accounting policies selected and applied;
  (iii) The accounting policies selected and applied are consistent with the applicable financial reporting framework and are appropriate;
  (iv) Accounting estimates made by management appear reasonable;
  (v) The information presented in the financial statements appears relevant, reliable, comparable, and understandable; and
  (vi) The financial statements provide adequate disclosures to enable the intended users to understand the effects of material transactions and events on

the information conveyed in the financial statements. (Ref: Para. A108–A110)

70   The practitioner shall consider the impact of:

(a)   Uncorrected misstatements identified during the review, and in the previous year's review of the entity's financial statements, on the financial statements as a whole; and

(b)   Qualitative aspects of the entity's accounting practices, including indicators of possible bias in management's judgments. (Ref: Para. A111–A112)

71   If the financial statements are prepared using a fair presentation framework, the practitioner's consideration shall also include: (Ref: Para. A109)

(a)   The overall presentation, structure and content of the financial statements in accordance with the applicable framework; and

(b)   Whether the financial statements, including the related notes, appear to represent the underlying transactions and events in a manner that achieves fair presentation or gives a true and fair view, as appropriate, in the context of the financial statements as a whole.

Form of the Conclusion

72   The practitioner's conclusion on the financial statements, whether unmodified or modified, shall be expressed in the appropriate form in the context of the financial reporting framework applied in the financial statements.

Unmodified Conclusion

73   The practitioner shall express an unmodified conclusion in the practitioner's report on the financial statements as a whole when the practitioner has obtained limited assurance to be able to conclude that nothing has come to the practitioner's attention that causes the practitioner to believe that the financial statements are not prepared, in all material respects, in accordance with the applicable financial reporting framework.

74   When the practitioner expresses an unmodified conclusion, the practitioner shall, unless otherwise required by law or regulation, use one of the following phrases, as appropriate: (Ref: Para. A113–A114)

(a)   "Based on our review, nothing has come to our attention that causes us to believe that the financial statements do not present fairly, in all material respects (or do not give a true and fair view), ... in accordance with the applicable financial reporting framework," (for financial statements prepared using a fair presentation framework); or

(b)   "Based on our review, nothing has come to our attention that causes us to believe that the financial statements are not prepared, in all material respects, in accordance with the applicable financial reporting framework," (for financial statements prepared using a compliance framework).

Modified Conclusion

75   The practitioner shall express a modified conclusion in the practitioner's report on the financial statements as a whole when:

(a) The practitioner determines, based on the procedures performed and the evidence obtained, that the financial statements are materially misstated; or

(b) The practitioner is unable to obtain sufficient appropriate evidence in relation to one or more items in the financial statements that are material in relation to the financial statements as a whole.

When the practitioner modifies the conclusion expressed on the financial statements, **76** the practitioner shall:

(a) Use the heading "Qualified Conclusion," "Adverse Conclusion" or "Disclaimer of Conclusion," as appropriate, for the conclusion paragraph in the practitioner's report; and

(b) Provide a description of the matter giving rise to the modification, under an appropriate heading (for example, "Basis for Qualified Conclusion," "Basis for Adverse Conclusion" or "Basis for Disclaimer of Conclusion," as appropriate), in a separate paragraph in the practitioner's report immediately before the conclusion paragraph (referred to as the basis for conclusion paragraph).

Financial statements are materially misstated

If the practitioner determines that the financial statements are materially misstated, **77** the practitioner shall express:

(a) A qualified conclusion, when the practitioner concludes that the effects of the matter(s) giving rise to the modification are material, but not pervasive to the financial statements; or

(b) An adverse conclusion, when the effects of the matter(s) giving rise to the modification are both material and pervasive to the financial statements.

When the practitioner expresses a qualified conclusion on the financial statements **78** because of a material misstatement, the practitioner shall, unless otherwise required by law or regulation, use one of the following phrases, as appropriate:

(a) "Based on our review, except for the effects of the matter(s) described in the Basis for Qualified Conclusion paragraph, nothing has come to our attention that causes us to believe that the financial statements do not present fairly, in all material respects (or do not give a true and fair view), ... in accordance with the applicable financial reporting framework," (for financial statements prepared using a fair presentation framework); or

(b) "Based on our review, except for the effects of the matter(s) described in the Basis for Qualified Conclusion paragraph, nothing has come to our attention that causes us to believe that the financial statements are not prepared, in all material respects, in accordance with the applicable financial reporting framework," (for financial statements prepared using a compliance framework).

When the practitioner expresses an adverse conclusion on the financial statements, **79** the practitioner shall, unless otherwise required by law or regulation, use one of the following phrases, as appropriate:

(a) "Based on our review, due to the significance of the matter(s) described in the Basis for Adverse Conclusion paragraph, the financial statements do not present fairly, in all material respects (or do not give a true and fair view), ... in accordance with the applicable financial reporting framework," (for financial statements prepared using a fair presentation framework); or

(b) "Based on our review, due to the significance of the matter(s) described in the Basis for Adverse Conclusion paragraph, the financial statements are not prepared, in all material respects, in accordance with the applicable financial reporting framework," (for financial statements prepared using a compliance framework).

80   In the basis for conclusion paragraph, in relation to material misstatements that give rise to either a qualified conclusion or an adverse conclusion, the practitioner shall:

(a)   Describe and quantify the financial effects of the misstatement if the material misstatement relates to specific amounts in the financial statements (including quantitative disclosures), unless impracticable, in which case the practitioner shall so state;

(b)   Explain how disclosures are misstated if the material misstatement relates to narrative disclosures; or

(c)   Describe the nature of omitted information if the material misstatement relates to the non-disclosure of information required to be disclosed. Unless prohibited by law or regulation, the practitioner shall include the omitted disclosures where practicable to do so.

Inability to obtain sufficient appropriate evidence

81   If the practitioner is unable to form a conclusion on the financial statements due to inability to obtain sufficient appropriate evidence, the practitioner shall:

(a)   Express a qualified conclusion if the practitioner concludes that the possible effects on the financial statements of undetected misstatements, if any, could be material but not pervasive; or

(b)   Disclaim a conclusion if the practitioner concludes that the possible effects on the financial statements of undetected misstatements, if any, could be both material and pervasive.

82   The practitioner shall withdraw from the engagement if the following conditions are present: (Ref: Para. A115–A117)

(a)   Due to a limitation on the scope of the review imposed by management after the practitioner has accepted the engagement, the practitioner is unable to obtain sufficient appropriate evidence to form a conclusion on the financial statements;

(b)   The practitioner has determined that the possible effects on the financial statements of undetected misstatements are material and pervasive; and

(c)   Withdrawal is possible under applicable law or regulation.

83   When the practitioner expresses a qualified conclusion on the financial statements due to inability to obtain sufficient appropriate evidence, the practitioner shall, unless otherwise required by law or regulation, use one of the following phrases, as appropriate:

(a)   "Based on our review, except for the possible effects of the matter(s) described in the Basis for Qualified Conclusion paragraph, nothing has come to our attention that causes us to believe that the financial statements do not present fairly, in all material respects (or do not give a true and fair view), ... in accordance with the applicable financial reporting framework," (for financial statements prepared using a fair presentation framework); or

(b)   "Based on our review, except for the possible effects of the matter(s) described in the Basis for Qualified Conclusion paragraph, nothing has come to our attention that causes us to believe that the financial statements are not prepared, in all material respects, in accordance with the applicable financial reporting framework," (for financial statements prepared using a compliance framework).

When disclaiming a conclusion on the financial statements the practitioner shall state   **84**
in the conclusion paragraph that:

(a) Due to the significance of the matter(s) described in the Basis for Disclaimer of
     Conclusion paragraph, the practitioner is unable to obtain sufficient appro-
     priate evidence to form a conclusion on the financial statements; and
(b) Accordingly, the practitioner does not express a conclusion on the financial
     statements.

In the basis for conclusion paragraph, in relation to either the qualified conclusion   **85**
due to inability to obtain sufficient appropriate evidence or when the practitioner
disclaims a conclusion, the practitioner shall include the reason(s) for the inability to
obtain sufficient appropriate evidence.

The Practitioner's Report

The practitioner's report for the review engagement shall be in writing, and shall   **86**
contain the following elements: (Ref: Para. A118–A121, A142, A144)

(a) A title, which shall clearly indicate that it is the report of an independent
     practitioner for a review engagement;
(b) The addressee(s), as required by the circumstances of the engagement;
(c) An introductory paragraph that:
     (i)   Identifies the financial statements reviewed, including identification of the
           title of each of the statements contained in the set of financial statements
           and the date and period covered by each financial statement;
     (ii) Refers to the summary of significant accounting policies and other expla-
           natory information; and
     (iii) States that the financial statements have been reviewed;
(d) A description of the responsibility of management for the preparation of the
     financial statements, including an explanation that management is responsible
     for: (Ref: Para. A122–A125)
     (i)   Their preparation in accordance with the applicable financial reporting
           framework including, where relevant, their fair presentation;
     (ii) Such internal control as management determines is necessary to enable the
           preparation of financial statements that are free from material misstate-
           ment, whether due to fraud or error;
(e) If the financial statements are special purpose financial statements:
     (i)   A description of the purpose for which the financial statements are pre-
           pared and, if necessary, the intended users, or reference to a note in the
           special purpose financial statements that contains that information; and
     (ii) If management has a choice of financial reporting frameworks in the pre-
           paration of such financial statements, a reference within the explanation of
           management's responsibility for the financial statements to management's
           responsibility for determining that the applicable financial reporting fra-
           mework is acceptable in the circumstances;
(f) A description of the practitioner's responsibility to express a conclusion on the
     financial statements including reference to this ISRE and, where relevant,
     applicable law or regulation; (Ref: Para. A126–127, A143)
(g) A description of a review of financial statements and its limitations, and the
     following statements: (Ref: Para. A128)
     (i)   A review engagement under this ISRE is a limited assurance engagement;
     (ii) The practitioner performs procedures, primarily consisting of making
           inquiries of management and others within the entity, as appropriate, and
           applying analytical procedures, and evaluates the evidence obtained; and

(iii) The procedures performed in a review are substantially less than those performed in an audit conducted in accordance with International Standards on Auditing (ISAs), and, accordingly, the practitioner does not express an audit opinion on the financial statements;

(h) A paragraph under the heading "Conclusion" that contains:

   (i) The practitioner's conclusion on the financial statements as a whole in accordance with paragraphs 72–85, as appropriate; and

   (ii) A reference to the applicable financial reporting framework used to prepare the financial statements, including identification of the jurisdiction of origin of the financial reporting framework that is not International Financial Reporting Standards or International Financial Reporting Standard for Small and Medium-sized Entities issued by the International Accounting Standards Board, or International Public Sector Accounting Standards issued by the International Public Sector Accounting Standards Board; (Ref: Para. A129–A130)

(i) When the practitioner's conclusion on the financial statements is modified:

   (i) A paragraph under the appropriate heading that contains the practitioner's modified conclusion in accordance with paragraphs 72 and 75–85, as appropriate; and

   (ii) A paragraph, under an appropriate heading, that provides a description of the matter(s) giving rise to the modification; (Ref: Para. A131)

(j) A reference to the practitioner's obligation under this ISRE to comply with relevant ethical requirements;

(k) The date of the practitioner's report; (Ref: Para. A138–A141)

(l) The practitioner's signature; and (Ref: Para. A132)

(m) The location in the jurisdiction where the practitioner practices.

Emphasis of Matter and Other Matter Paragraphs in the Practitioner's Report

Emphasis of Matter Paragraphs

87   The practitioner may consider it necessary to draw users' attention to a matter presented or disclosed in the financial statements that, in the practitioner's judgment, is of such importance that it is fundamental to users' understanding of the financial statements. In such cases, the practitioner shall include an Emphasis of Matter paragraph in the practitioner's report, provided the practitioner has obtained sufficient appropriate evidence to conclude that the matter is not likely to be materially misstated as presented in the financial statements. Such paragraph shall refer only to information presented or disclosed in the financial statements.

88   The practitioner's report on special purpose financial statements shall include an Emphasis of Matter paragraph alerting users of the practitioner's report that the financial statements are prepared in accordance with a special purpose framework and that, as a result, the financial statements may not be suitable for another purpose. (Ref: Para. A133–A134)

89   The practitioner shall include an Emphasis of Matter paragraph immediately after the paragraph that contains the practitioner's conclusion on the financial statements under the heading "Emphasis of Matter," or other appropriate heading.

Other Matter Paragraphs

90   If the practitioner considers it necessary to communicate a matter other than those that are presented or disclosed in the financial statements that, in the practitioner's judgment, is relevant to users' understanding of the review, the practitioner's

responsibilities or the practitioner's report and this is not prohibited by law or regulation, the practitioner shall do so in a paragraph in the practitioner's report with the heading "Other Matter" or other appropriate heading.

Other Reporting Responsibilities

A practitioner may be requested to address other reporting responsibilities in the **91** practitioner's report on the financial statements that are in addition to the practitioner's responsibilities under this ISRE to report on the financial statements. In such situations, those other reporting responsibilities shall be addressed by the practitioner in a separate section in the practitioner's report headed "Report on Other Legal and Regulatory Requirements," or

otherwise as appropriate to the content of the section, following the section of the report headed "Report on the Financial Statements." (Ref: Para. A135–A137)

Date of the Practitioner's Report

The practitioner shall date the report no earlier than the date on which the practitioner has obtained sufficient appropriate evidence as the basis for the practitioner's **92** conclusion on the financial statements, including being satisfied that: (Ref: Para. A138–A141)

(a) All the statements that comprise the financial statements under the applicable financial reporting framework, including the related notes where applicable, have been prepared; and

(b) Those with the recognized authority have asserted that they have taken responsibility for those financial statements.

Documentation

The preparation of documentation for the review provides evidence that the review **93** was performed in accordance with this ISRE, and legal and regulatory requirements where relevant, and a sufficient and appropriate record of the basis for the practitioner's report. The practitioner shall document the following aspects of the engagement in a timely manner, sufficient to enable an experienced practitioner, having no previous connection with the engagement, to understand: (Ref: Para. A145)

(a) The nature, timing, and extent of the procedures performed to comply with this ISRE and applicable legal and regulatory requirements;

(b) Results obtained from the procedures, and the practitioner's conclusions formed on the basis of those results; and

(c) Significant matters arising during the engagement, the practitioner's conclusions reached thereon, and significant professional judgments made in reaching those conclusions.

In documenting the nature, timing and extent of procedures performed as required in **94** this ISRE, the practitioner shall record:

(a) Who performed the work and the date such work was completed; and

(b) Who reviewed the work performed for the purpose of quality control for the engagement, and the date and extent of the review.

95   The practitioner shall also document discussions with management, those charged with governance, and others as relevant to the performance of the review of significant matters arising during the engagement, including the nature of those matters.

96   If, in the course of the engagement, the practitioner identified information that is inconsistent with the practitioner's findings regarding significant matters affecting the financial statements, the practitioner shall document how the inconsistency was addressed.

***

Application and Other Explanatory Material

Scope of this ISRE (Ref: Para. 1–2)

A1   In performing a review of financial statements, the practitioner may be required to comply with legal or regulatory requirements, which may differ from the requirements established in this ISRE. While the practitioner may find aspects of this ISRE helpful in these circumstances, it is the responsibility of the practitioner to ensure compliance with all relevant legal, regulatory and professional obligations.

Reviews of Financial Information of Components in the Context of an Audit of the Financial Statements of a Group of Entities

A2   Review engagements in accordance with this ISRE may be requested for component entities by the auditor of the financial statements of a group of entities.[6] Such a review engagement performed in accordance with this ISRE may be accompanied by a request from the group auditor to undertake additional work or procedures as needed in the circumstances of the group audit engagement.

Relationship with ISQC 1 (Ref: Para. 4)

A3   ISQC 1 deals with the firm's responsibilities to establish and maintain its system of quality control for assurance engagements, including review engagements. Those responsibilities are directed at establishing the firm's:

- Quality control system; and
- Related policies designed to achieve the objective of the quality control system and the firm's procedures to implement and monitor compliance with those policies, including policies and procedures that address each of the following elements:
  - Leadership responsibilities for quality within the firm.
  - Relevant ethical requirements.
  - Acceptance and continuance of client relationships and specific engagements.
  - Human resources.
  - Engagement performance.
  - Monitoring.

A4   Under ISQC 1, the firm has an obligation to establish and maintain a system of quality control to provide it with reasonable assurance that:

---

[6] *ISA 600*, Special Considerations—Audits of Group Financial Statements (Including the Work of Component Auditors, *paragraph A52*.

(a) The firm and its personnel comply with professional standards and applicable legal and regulatory requirements; and

(b) Reports issued by the firm or engagement partners are appropriate in the circumstances.[7]

National requirements that deal with the firm's responsibilities to establish and maintain a system of quality control are at least as demanding as ISQC 1 when they address all the elements referred to in paragraph A3, and impose obligations on the firm that achieve the aims of the requirements set out in ISQC 1. **A5**

The Engagement to Review Historical Financial Statements
(Ref: Para. 5–8, 14)

Reviews of financial statements may be performed for a wide range of entities that vary by type or size, or by the level of complexity in their financial reporting. In some jurisdictions, the review of financial statements of certain types of entity may also be the subject of local laws or regulations and related reporting requirements. **A6**

Reviews may be performed in a variety of circumstances. For example, they may be required for entities that are exempt from requirements specified in law or regulation for mandatory audit. Reviews may also be requested on a voluntary basis, such as in connection with financial reporting undertaken for arrangements under the terms of a private contract, or to support funding arrangements. **A7**

Objectives (Ref: Para. 15)

This ISRE requires the practitioner to disclaim a conclusion on the financial statements if: **A8**

(a) The practitioner issues a report, or is required to issue a report for the engagement; and

(b) The practitioner is unable to form a conclusion on the financial statements due to inability to obtain sufficient appropriate evidence, and the practitioner concludes that the possible effects on the financial statements of undetected misstatements, if any, could be both material and pervasive.

The situation of being unable to obtain sufficient appropriate evidence in a review engagement (referred to as a scope limitation) may arise from: **A9**

(a) Circumstances beyond the control of the entity;

(b) Circumstances relating to the nature or timing of the practitioner's work; or

(c) Limitations imposed by management or those charged with governance of the entity.

This ISRE sets out requirements and guidance for the practitioner when the practitioner encounters a scope limitation, either prior to accepting a review engagement, or during the engagement. **A10**

---

[7] *ISQC 1, paragraph 11.*

Definitions (Ref: Para. 16)

Use of the Terms "Management" and "Those Charged with Governance"

A11   The respective responsibilities of management and those charged with governance will differ between jurisdictions, and between entities of various types. These differences affect the way the practitioner applies the requirements of this ISRE in relation to management or those charged with governance Accordingly, the phrase "management and, where appropriate, those charged with governance" used in various places throughout this ISRE is intended to alert the practitioner to the fact that different entity environments may have different management and governance structures and arrangements.

A12   Various responsibilities relating to preparation of financial information and external financial reporting will fall to either management or those charged with governance according to factors such as:

● The resources and structure of the entity; and
● The respective roles of management and those charged with governance within the entity as set out in relevant law or regulation or, if the entity is not regulated, in any formal governance or accountability arrangements established for the entity (for example, as recorded in contracts, a constitution or other type of establishment documents of the entity).

For example, in small entities there is often no separation of the management and governance roles. In larger entities, management is often responsible for execution of the business or activities of the entity and reporting thereon, while those charged with governance oversee management. In some jurisdictions, the responsibility for preparation of financial statements for an entity is the legal responsibility of those charged with governance, and in some other jurisdictions it is a management responsibility.

Limited Assurance – Use of the Term Sufficient Appropriate Evidence (Ref: Para. 17(f))

A13   Sufficient appropriate evidence is required to obtain limited assurance to support the practitioner's conclusion. Evidence is cumulative in nature and is primarily obtained from the procedures performed during the course of the review.

Conduct of a Review Engagement in Accordance with this ISRE (Ref: Para. 18)

A14   This ISRE does not override laws and regulations that govern a review of financial statements. In the event that those laws and regulations differ from the requirements of this ISRE, a review conducted only in accordance with laws and regulations will not automatically comply with this ISRE.

Ethical Requirements (Ref: Para. 21)

A15   Part A of the IESBA Code establishes the fundamental principles of professional ethics practitioners must comply with, and provides a conceptual framework for applying those principles. The fundamental principles are:

(a) Integrity;
(b) Objectivity;

(c) Professional competence and due care;
(d) Confidentiality; and
(e) Professional behavior.

Part B of the IESBA Code illustrates how the conceptual framework is to be applied in specific situations. In complying with the IESBA Code, threats to the practitioner's compliance with relevant ethical requirements are required to be identified and appropriately addressed.

In the case of an engagement to review financial statements, the IESBA Code **A16** requires that the practitioner be independent of the entity whose financial statements are reviewed. The IESBA Code describes independence as comprising both independence of mind and independence in appearance. The practitioner's independence safeguards the practitioner's ability to form a conclusion without being affected by influences that might otherwise compromise that conclusion. Independence enhances the practitioner's ability to act with integrity, to be objective and to maintain an attitude of professional skepticism.

Professional Skepticism and Professional Judgment

Professional Skepticism (Ref: Para. 22)

Professional skepticism is necessary for the critical assessment of evidence in a **A17** review. This includes questioning inconsistencies and investigating contradictory evidence, and questioning the reliability of responses to inquiries and other information obtained from management and those charged with governance. It also includes consideration of the sufficiency and appropriateness of evidence obtained in the light of the engagement circumstances.

Professional skepticism includes being alert to, for example: **A18**

- Evidence that is inconsistent with other evidence obtained.
- Information that calls into question the reliability of documents and responses to inquiries to be used as evidence.
- Conditions that may indicate possible fraud.
- Any other circumstances that suggest the need for additional procedures.

Maintaining professional skepticism throughout the review is necessary if the prac- **A19** titioner is to reduce the risks of:

- Overlooking unusual circumstances.
- Over-generalizing when drawing conclusions from evidence obtained.
- Using inappropriate assumptions in determining the nature, timing, and extent of the procedures performed in the review, and evaluating the results thereof.

The practitioner cannot be expected to disregard past experience of the honesty and **A20** integrity of the entity's management and those charged with governance. Nevertheless, a belief that management and those charged with governance are honest and have integrity does not relieve the practitioner of the need to maintain professional skepticism or allow the practitioner to be satisfied with evidence that is inadequate for the purpose of the review.

Professional Judgment (Ref: Para. 23)

A21   Professional judgment is essential to the proper conduct of a review engagement. This is because interpretation of relevant ethical requirements and the requirements of this ISRE, and the need for informed decisions throughout the performance of a review engagement, require the application of relevant knowledge and experience to the facts and circumstances of the engagement. Professional judgment is necessary, in particular:

- Regarding decisions about materiality, and the nature, timing, and extent of procedures used to meet the requirements of this ISRE, and to gather evidence.
- When evaluating whether the evidence obtained from the procedures performed reduces the engagement risk to a level that is acceptable in the engagement circumstances.
- When considering management's judgments in applying the entity's applicable financial reporting framework.
- When forming the conclusion on the financial statements based on the evidence obtained, including considering the reasonableness of the estimates made by management in preparing the financial statements.

A22   The distinguishing feature of the professional judgment expected of the practitioner is that it is exercised by a practitioner whose training, knowledge and experience, including in the use of assurance skills and techniques, have assisted in developing the necessary competencies to achieve reasonable judgments. Consultation on difficult or contentious matters during the course of the engagement, both within the engagement team and between the engagement team and others at the appropriate level within or outside the firm, assists the practitioner in making informed and reasonable judgments.

A23   The exercise of professional judgment in individual engagements is based on the facts and circumstances that are known by the practitioner throughout the engagement, including:

- Knowledge acquired from engagements carried out with respect to the entity's financial statements in prior periods, where applicable.
- The practitioner's understanding of the entity and its environment, including its accounting system, and of the application of the applicable financial reporting framework in the entity's industry.
- The extent to which the preparation and presentation of the financial statements require the exercise of management judgment.

A24   Professional judgment can be evaluated based on whether the judgment reached reflects a competent application of assurance and accounting principles, and is appropriate in the light of, and consistent with, the facts and circumstances that were known to the practitioner up to the date of the practitioner's report.

A25   Professional judgment needs to be exercised throughout the engagement. It also needs to be appropriately documented in accordance with the requirements of this ISRE. Professional judgment is not to be used as the justification for decisions that are not otherwise supported by the facts and circumstances of the engagement, or the evidence obtained.

Engagement Level Quality Control (Ref: Para. 24–25)

Assurance skills and techniques include: **A26**

- Applying professional skepticism and professional judgment to planning and performing an assurance engagement, including obtaining and evaluating evidence;
- Understanding information systems and the role and limitations of internal control;
- Linking the consideration of materiality and engagement risks to the nature, timing and extent of procedures for the review;
- Applying procedures as appropriate to the review engagement, which may include other types of procedures in addition to inquiry and analytical procedures (such as inspection, re-calculation, re-performance, observation and confirmation);
- Systematic documentation practices; and
- Application of skills and practices relevant for writing reports for assurance engagements.

Within the context of the firm's system of quality control, engagement teams have a   **A27**
responsibility to implement quality control procedures applicable to the engagement, and provide the firm with relevant information to enable the functioning of that part of the firm's system of quality control relating to independence.

The actions of the engagement partner and appropriate messages to the other   **A28**
members of the engagement team, in the context of the engagement partner taking responsibility for the overall quality on each review engagement, emphasize the fact that quality is essential in performing a review engagement, and the importance to the quality of the review engagement of:

(a) Performing work that complies with professional standards and regulatory and legal requirements.
(b) Complying with the firm's quality control policies and procedures as applicable.
(c) Issuing a report for the engagement that is appropriate in the circumstances.
(d) The engagement team's ability to raise concerns without fear of reprisals.

Unless information provided by the firm or other parties suggests otherwise, the   **A29**
engagement team is entitled to rely on the firm's system of quality control. For example, the engagement team may rely on the firm's system of quality control in relation to:

- Competence of personnel through their recruitment and formal training.
- Independence through the accumulation and communication of relevant independence information.
- Maintenance of client relationships through acceptance and continuance systems.
- Adherence to regulatory and legal requirements through the monitoring process.

In considering deficiencies identified in the firm's system of quality control that may affect the review engagement, the engagement partner may consider measures taken by the firm to rectify those deficiencies.

A deficiency in the firm's system of quality control does not necessarily indicate that   **A30**
a review engagement was not performed in accordance with professional standards and applicable legal and regulatory requirements, or that the practitioner's report was not appropriate.

Assignment of Engagement Teams (Ref: Para. 25(b))

A31 When considering the appropriate competence and capabilities expected of the engagement team as a whole, the engagement partner may take into consideration such matters as the team's:

- Understanding of, and practical experience with, review engagements of a similar nature and complexity through appropriate training and participation.
- Understanding of professional standards and applicable legal and regulatory requirements.
- Technical expertise, including expertise with relevant information technology and specialized areas of accounting or assurance.
- Knowledge of relevant industries in which the client operates.
- Ability to apply professional judgment.
- Understanding of the firm's quality control policies and procedures.

Acceptance and Continuance of Client Relationships and Review Engagements (Ref: Para. 25(d)(i))

A32 ISQC 1 requires the firm to obtain information as it considers necessary in the circumstances before accepting an engagement with a new client, when deciding whether to continue an existing engagement, and when considering acceptance of a new engagement with an existing client. Information that assists the engagement partner in determining whether acceptance and continuance of client relationships and review engagements are appropriate may include information concerning:

- The integrity of the principal owners, key management and those charged with governance; and
- Significant matters that have arisen during the current or a previous review engagement, and their implications for continuing the relationship.

A33 If the engagement partner has cause to doubt management's integrity to a degree that is likely to affect proper performance of the review, it is not appropriate under this ISRE to accept the engagement, unless required by law or regulation, as doing so may lead to the practitioner being associated with the entity's financial statements in an inappropriate manner.

Acceptance and Continuance of Client Relationships and Review Engagements (Ref: Para. 29)

A34 The practitioner's consideration of engagement continuance, and relevant ethical requirements, including independence, occurs throughout the engagement, as conditions and changes in circumstances occur. Performing initial procedures on engagement continuance and evaluation of relevant ethical requirements (including independence) at the beginning of an engagement informs the practitioner's decisions and actions prior to the performance of other significant activities for the engagement.

Factors Affecting Acceptance and Continuance of Client Relationships and Review Engagements (Ref: Para. 29)

Assurance engagements may only be accepted when the engagement exhibits certain characteristics[8] that are conducive to achieving the practitioner's objectives specified for the engagement.   **A35**

Rational Purpose (Ref: Para. 29(a)(i))

It may be unlikely that there is a rational purpose for the engagement if, for example: **A36**

(a) There is a significant limitation on the scope of the practitioner's work;
(b) The practitioner suspects the engaging party intends to associate the practitioner's name with the financial statements in an inappropriate manner; or
(c) The engagement is intended to meet compliance requirements of relevant law or regulation and such law or regulation requires the financial statements to be audited.

Review Engagement Is Appropriate (Ref: Para. 29(a)(ii))

When the practitioner's preliminary understanding of the engagement circumstances indicates that accepting a review engagement would not be appropriate, the practitioner may consider recommending that another type of engagement be undertaken. Depending on the circumstances, the practitioner may, for example, believe that performance of an audit engagement would be more appropriate than a review. In other cases, if the engagement circumstances preclude performance of an assurance engagement, the practitioner may recommend a compilation engagement, or other accounting services engagement, as appropriate.   **A37**

Information Needed to Perform the Review Engagement (Ref: Para. 29(c))

An example of where the practitioner may have cause to doubt that the information needed to perform the review will be available or reliable is where the accounting records necessary for purposes of performing analytical procedures are suspected to be substantially inaccurate or incomplete. This consideration is not directed at the need that sometimes arises in the course of a review engagement to assist management by recommending adjusting entries required to finalize the financial statements prepared by management.   **A38**

Preconditions for Accepting a Review Engagement (Ref: Para. 30)

This ISRE also requires the practitioner to ascertain certain matters, upon which it is necessary for the practitioner and the entity's management to agree, and which are within the control of the entity, prior to the practitioner accepting the engagement.   **A39**

---

[8] *Assurance Framework, paragraph 17.*

The Applicable Financial Reporting Framework (Ref: Para. 30(a))

A40   A condition for acceptance of an assurance engagement is that the criteria[9] referred to in the definition of an assurance engagement are suitable and available to intended users.[10] For purposes of this ISRE, the applicable financial reporting framework provides the criteria the practitioner uses to review the financial statements including, where relevant, the fair presentation of the financial statements. Some financial reporting frameworks are fair presentation frameworks, while others are compliance frameworks. The requirements of the applicable financial reporting framework determine the form and content of the financial statements, including what constitutes a complete set of financial statements.

Acceptability of the applicable financial reporting framework

A41   Without an acceptable financial reporting framework, management does not have an appropriate basis for the preparation of the financial statements and the practitioner does not have suitable criteria for the review of the financial statements.

A42   The practitioner's determination of the acceptability of the financial reporting framework applied in the financial statements is made in the context of the practitioner's understanding of who the intended users of the financial statements are. The intended users are the person, persons or group of persons for whom the practitioner prepares the report. The practitioner may not be able to identify all those who will read the assurance report, particularly where there is a large number of people who have access to it.

A43   In many cases, in the absence of any indications to the contrary, the practitioner may presume that the applicable financial reporting framework is acceptable (for example, a financial reporting framework that is prescribed by law or regulation in a jurisdiction to be used in the preparation of general purpose financial statements for certain types of entities).

A44   Factors that are relevant to the practitioner's determination of the acceptability of the financial reporting framework to be applied in the preparation of the financial statements include:

- The nature of the entity (for example, whether it is a business enterprise, a public sector entity or a not-for-profit organization).
- The purpose of the financial statements (for example, whether they are prepared to meet the common financial information needs of a wide range of users or the financial information needs of specific users).
- The nature of the financial statements (for example, whether the financial statements are a complete set of financial statements or a single financial statement).
- Whether the applicable financial reporting framework is prescribed in relevant law or regulation.

A45   If the financial reporting framework used to prepare the financial statements is not acceptable in view of the purpose of the financial statements and management will not agree to use of a financial reporting framework that is acceptable in the practitioner's view, the practitioner is required under this ISRE to decline the engagement.

---

[9] *Assurance Framework, paragraph 34.*

[10] *Assurance Framework, paragraph 17(b)(ii).*

Deficiencies in the applicable financial reporting framework that indicate that the **A46** framework is not acceptable may be encountered after the review engagement has been accepted. When use of that financial reporting framework is not prescribed by law or regulation, management may decide to adopt another framework that is acceptable. When management does so, the practitioner is required under this ISRE to agree the new terms of the review engagement with management to reflect the change in the applicable financial reporting framework.

Responsibilities of Management and Those Charged with Governance (Ref: Para. 30(b), 37(e))

The financial statements subject to review are those of the entity, prepared by **A47** management of the entity with oversight from those charged with governance. This ISRE does not impose responsibilities on management and those charged with governance, nor does it override laws and regulations that govern their respective responsibilities. However, a review in accordance with this ISRE is conducted on the premise that management, and those charged with governance as appropriate, have acknowledged certain responsibilities that are fundamental to the conduct of the review. The review of the financial statements does not relieve management and those charged with governance of their responsibilities.

As part of its responsibility for the preparation of the financial statements, man- **A48** agement is required to exercise judgment in making accounting estimates that are reasonable in the circumstances, and to select and apply appropriate accounting policies. These judgments are made in the context of the applicable financial reporting framework.

Because of the significance of the preconditions for undertaking a review of financial **A49** statements, the practitioner is required under this ISRE to obtain the agreement of management that it understands its responsibilities before accepting a review engagement. The practitioner may obtain management's agreement either orally or in writing. However, management's agreement is subsequently recorded within the written terms of the engagement.

If management, and those charged with governance where appropriate, do not or **A50** will not acknowledge their responsibilities in relation to the financial statements, it is not appropriate to accept the engagement unless law or regulation requires the practitioner to do so. In circumstances where the practitioner is required to accept the review engagement, the practitioner may need to explain to management and those charged with governance, where different, the importance of these matters and the implications for the engagement.

Additional Considerations When the Wording of the Practitioner's Report Is Prescribed by Law or Regulation (Ref: Para. 34–35)

This ISRE requires the practitioner to not represent compliance with this ISRE **A51** unless the practitioner has complied with all the requirements of this ISRE that are relevant to the review engagement. Law or regulation may prescribe matters in relation to an engagement that would ordinarily cause the practitioner to decline the engagement were it possible to do so, for example, if:

- The practitioner considers that the financial reporting framework prescribed by law or regulation is not acceptable; or

- The prescribed layout or wording of the practitioner's report is in a form or in terms that are significantly different from the layout or wording required by this ISRE.

Under this ISRE, a review conducted in these situations does not comply with this ISRE and the practitioner cannot represent compliance with this ISRE in the report issued for the engagement. Notwithstanding that the practitioner is not permitted to represent compliance with this ISRE, the practitioner is, however, encouraged to apply this ISRE, including the reporting requirements, to the extent practicable. When appropriate to avoid misunderstanding, the practitioner may consider including a statement in the report that the review is not conducted in accordance with this ISRE.

Agreeing the Terms of Engagement

Engagement Letter or Other Form of Written Agreement (Ref: Para. 37)

A52   It is in the interests of both management and those charged with governance, and the practitioner, that the practitioner sends an engagement letter prior to performing the review engagement, to help avoid misunderstandings with respect to the engagement.

Form and content of the engagement letter

A53   The form and content of the engagement letter may vary for each engagement. In addition to including the matters required by this ISRE, an engagement letter may make reference to, for example:

- Arrangements concerning the involvement of other practitioners and experts in the review engagement.
- Arrangements to be made with the predecessor practitioner, if any, in the case of an initial engagement.
- The fact that a review engagement will not satisfy any statutory or third party requirements for an audit.
- The expectation that management will provide written representations to the practitioner.
- The agreement of management to inform the practitioner of facts that may affect the financial statements of which management may become aware during the period from the date of the practitioner's report to the date the financial statements are issued.
- A request for management to acknowledge receipt of the engagement letter and to agree to the terms of the engagement outlined therein.

Review of components of groups of entities

A54   The auditor of the financial statements of a group of entities may request that a practitioner perform a review of the financial information of a component entity of the group. Depending on the instructions of the group auditor, a review of the financial information of a component may be performed in accordance with this ISRE. The group auditor may also specify additional procedures to supplement the work done for the review performed under this ISRE. Where the practitioner conducting the review is the auditor of the component entity's financial statements, the review is not performed in accordance with this ISRE.

Responsibilities of management prescribed by law or regulation (Ref: Para. 37(e))

If, in the circumstances of the engagement, the practitioner concludes that it is not **A55** necessary to record certain terms of the engagement in an engagement letter, the practitioner is still required to seek the written agreement from management, and those charged with governance where appropriate, required under this ISRE that they acknowledge and understand their responsibilities set out in this ISRE. This written agreement may use the wording of the law or regulation if the law or regulation establishes responsibilities for management that are equivalent in effect to those described in this ISRE.

Illustrative Engagement Letter (Ref: Para. 37)

An illustrative engagement letter for a review engagement is set out in Appendix 1 to **A56** this ISRE.

Recurring Engagements (Ref: Para. 38)

The practitioner may decide not to send a new engagement letter or other written **A57** agreement each period. However, the following factors may indicate that it is appropriate to revise the terms of the review engagement or to remind management and those charged with governance, as appropriate, of the existing terms of the engagement:

- Any indication that management misunderstands the objective and scope of the review.
- Any revised or special terms of the engagement.
- A recent change of senior management of the entity.
- A significant change in ownership of the entity.
- A significant change in nature or size of the entity's business.
- A change in legal or regulatory requirements affecting the entity.
- A change in the applicable financial reporting framework.

Acceptance of a Change in the Terms of the Review Engagement

Request to Change the Terms of the Review Engagement (Ref: Para. 39)

A request from the entity for the practitioner to change the terms of the review **A58** engagement may result from factors including:

- A change in circumstances affecting the need for the service.
- Misunderstanding as to the nature of a review engagement as originally requested.
- A restriction on the scope of the review engagement, whether imposed by management or caused by other circumstances.

A change in circumstances that affects the entity's requirements or a mis- **A59** understanding concerning the nature of the service originally requested may be considered a reasonable basis for requesting a change to the terms of the review engagement.

In contrast, a change may not be considered reasonable if it appears that the change **A60** relates to information that is incorrect, incomplete or otherwise unsatisfactory. An example might be where the practitioner is unable to obtain sufficient appropriate evidence for a material item in the financial statements, and management asks for the engagement to be changed to a related services engagement to avoid the expression of a modified conclusion by the practitioner.

Request to Change the Nature of the Engagement (Ref: Para. 40)

A61   Before agreeing to change a review engagement to another type of engagement or related service, a practitioner who was engaged to perform a review in accordance with this ISRE may need to assess, in addition to the matters referred to in this ISRE, any legal or contractual implications of the change.

A62   If the practitioner concludes that there is reasonable justification to change the review engagement to another type of engagement or related service, the work performed in the review engagement to the date of change may be relevant to the changed engagement; however, the work required to be performed and the report to be issued would be those appropriate to the revised engagement. In order to avoid confusing the reader, the report on the other engagement or related service would not include reference to:

   (a)   The original review engagement; or
   (b)   Any procedures that may have been performed in the original review engage-ment, except where the review engagement is changed to an engagement to perform agreed-upon procedures and thus reference to the procedures per-formed is a normal part of the report.

Communication with Management and Those Charged with Governance (Ref: Para. 42)

A63   In a review engagement, the practitioner's communications with management and those charged with governance take the form of:

   (a)   Inquiries the practitioner makes in the course of performing the procedures for the review; and
   (b)   Other communications, in the context of having effective two-way commu-nication to understand matters arising and to develop a constructive working relationship for the engagement.

A64   The appropriate timing for communications will vary with the circumstances of the engagement. Relevant factors include the significance and nature of the matter, and any action expected to be taken by management or those charged with governance. For example, it may be appropriate to communicate a significant difficulty encountered during the review as soon as practicable if management or those charged with governance are able to assist the practitioner to overcome the difficulty.

A65   Law or regulation may restrict the practitioner's communication of certain matters with those charged with governance. For example, law or regulation may specifically prohibit a communication, or other action, that might prejudice an investigation by an appropriate authority into an actual, or suspected, illegal act. In some circum-stances, potential conflicts between the practitioner's obligations of confidentiality and obligations to communicate may be complex. In such cases, the practitioner may consider obtaining legal advice.

Communicating Matters Concerning the Review

A66   Matters to be communicated to management or those charged with governance, as appropriate, under this ISRE may include:

- The practitioner's responsibilities in the review engagement, as included in the engagement letter or other suitable form of written agreement.
- Significant findings from the review, for example:
  - The practitioner's views about significant qualitative aspects of the entity's accounting practices, including accounting policies, accounting estimates and financial statement disclosures.
  - Significant findings from the performance of procedures, including situations where the practitioner considered performance of additional procedures necessary under this ISRE. The practitioner may need to confirm that those charged with governance have the same understanding of the facts and circumstances relevant to specific transactions or events.
  - Matters arising that may lead to modification of the practitioner's conclusion.
  - Significant difficulties, if any, encountered during the review; for example, unavailability of expected information; unexpected inability to obtain evidence that the practitioner considers necessary for the review; or restrictions imposed on the practitioner by management. In some circumstances, such difficulties may constitute a scope limitation that, if not addressed by management or those charged with governance, may lead to modification of the practitioner's conclusion or to the practitioner's withdrawal from the engagement in certain circumstances.

In some entities, different persons are responsible for the management and the governance of an entity. In these circumstances, management may have the responsibility to communicate matters of governance interest to those charged with governance. Communication by management with those charged with governance of matters that the practitioner is required to communicate does not relieve the practitioner of the responsibility to also communicate them to those charged with governance. However, communication of these matters by management may affect the form or timing of the practitioner's communication with those charged with governance. **A67**

Communication with Third Parties

In some jurisdictions, the practitioner may be required by law or regulation to, for example: **A68**

- Notify a regulatory or enforcement body of certain matters communicated with those charged with governance. For example, in some jurisdictions the practitioner has a duty to report misstatements to authorities where management and those charged with governance fail to take corrective action.
- Submit copies of certain reports prepared for those charged with governance to relevant regulatory or funding bodies or, in some cases, make such reports publicly available.

Unless required by law or regulation to provide a third party with a copy of the practitioner's written communications with those charged with governance, the practitioner may need the prior consent of management or those charged with governance before doing so. **A69**

Performing the Engagement

Materiality in a Review of Financial Statements (Ref: Para. 43)

A70   The practitioner's consideration of materiality is made in the context of the applicable financial reporting framework. Some financial reporting frameworks discuss the concept of materiality in the context of the preparation and presentation of financial statements. Although financial reporting frameworks may discuss materiality in different terms, they generally explain that:

- Misstatements, including omissions, are considered to be material if they, individually or in the aggregate, could reasonably be expected to influence the economic decisions of users taken on the basis of the financial statements;
- Judgments about materiality are made in light of surrounding circumstances, and are affected by the size or nature of a misstatement, or a combination of both; and
- Judgments about matters that are material to users of the financial statements are based on a consideration of the common financial information needs of users as a group. The possible effect of misstatements on specific individual users, whose needs may vary widely, is not considered.

A71   If present in the applicable financial reporting framework, a discussion of the concept of materiality provides a frame of reference for the practitioner in determining materiality for the review. If not present, the above considerations provide the practitioner with a frame of reference.

A72   The practitioner's determination of materiality is a matter of professional judgment, and is affected by the practitioner's perception of the needs of the intended users of the financial statements. In this context, it is reasonable for the practitioner to assume that users:

- Have a reasonable knowledge of business and economic activities and accounting, and a willingness to study the information in the financial statements with reasonable diligence;
- Understand that financial statements are prepared, presented and reviewed to levels of materiality;
- Recognize the uncertainties inherent in the measurement of amounts based on the use of estimates, judgment and the consideration of future events; and
- Make reasonable economic decisions on the basis of the information in the financial statements.

Further, unless the review engagement is undertaken for financial statements that are intended to meet the particular needs of specific users, the possible effect of misstatements on specific users, whose information needs may vary widely, is not ordinarily considered.

A73   The practitioner's judgment about what is material in relation to the financial statements as a whole is the same regardless of the level of assurance obtained by a practitioner as the basis for expressing the conclusion on the financial statements.

Revising Materiality (Ref: Para. 44)

A74   The practitioner's determination of materiality for the financial statements as a whole may need to be revised during the engagement as a result of:

- A change in the circumstances that occurred during the review (for example, a decision to dispose of a major part of the entity's business).

- New information, or a change in the practitioner's understanding of the entity and its environment as a result of performing procedures for the review in accordance with this ISRE (for example, if during the review it appears as though actual financial results are likely to be substantially different from the anticipated period-end financial results that were used initially to determine materiality for the financial statements as a whole).

The Practitioner's Understanding (Ref: Para. 45–46)

The practitioner uses professional judgment to determine the extent of the under- **A75**
standing of the entity and its environment required to perform the review of the entity's financial statements in accordance with this ISRE. The practitioner's primary consideration is whether the understanding obtained is sufficient to meet the practitioner's objectives for the engagement. The breadth and depth of the overall understanding that the practitioner obtains is less than that possessed by management.

Obtaining an understanding of the entity and its environment is a continual dynamic **A76**
process of gathering, updating and analyzing information throughout the review engagement. The practitioner's understanding is obtained and applied on an iterative basis throughout performance of the engagement, and is updated as changes in conditions and circumstances occur. Initial procedures for engagement acceptance and continuance at the time of commencement of a review engagement are based on the practitioner's preliminary understanding of the entity and of the engagement circumstances. In a continuing client relationship, the practitioner's understanding includes knowledge obtained from prior engagements performed by the practitioner in relation to the entity's financial statements and other financial information.

The understanding establishes a frame of reference within which the practitioner **A77**
plans and performs the review engagement, and exercises professional judgment throughout the engagement. Specifically, the understanding needs to be sufficient for the practitioner to be able to identify areas in the financial statements where material misstatements are likely to arise, to inform the practitioner's approach to designing and performing procedures to address those areas.

In obtaining an understanding of the entity and its environment, and of the **A78**
applicable financial reporting framework, the practitioner may also consider:

- Whether the entity is a component of a group of entities, or an associated entity of another entity.
- The complexity of the financial reporting framework.
- The entity's financial reporting obligations or requirements, and whether those obligations or requirements exist under applicable law or regulation or in the context of voluntary financial reporting arrangements established under formalized governance or accountability arrangements, for example, under contractual arrangements with third parties.
- Relevant provisions of laws and regulations that are generally recognized to have a direct effect on the determination of material amounts and disclosures in the financial statements, such as tax and pension laws and regulations.
- The level of development of the entity's management and governance structure regarding management and oversight of the entity's accounting records and financial reporting systems that underpin preparation of the financial statements. Smaller entities often have fewer employees, which may influence how management exercises oversight. For example, segregation of duties may not be practicable. However, in a small owner-managed entity, the owner-manager may be able to exercise more effective oversight than in a larger entity. This

oversight may compensate for the generally more limited opportunities for segregation of duties.

- The "tone at the top" and the entity's control environment through which the entity addresses risks relating to financial reporting and compliance with the entity's financial reporting obligations.
- The level of development and complexity of the entity's financial accounting and reporting systems and related controls through which the entity's accounting records and related information are maintained.
- The entity's procedures for recording, classifying and summarizing transactions, accumulating information for inclusion in the financial statements and related disclosures.
- The types of matters that required accounting adjustments in the entity's financial statements in prior periods.

Designing and Performing Procedures (Ref: Para. 47, 55)

A79 The planned nature, timing and extent of the procedures the practitioner considers are needed to obtain sufficient appropriate evidence as the basis for a conclusion on the financial statements as a whole are influenced by:

(a) The requirements of this ISRE; and

(b) Requirements established under applicable law or regulation, including additional reporting requirements contained in applicable laws or regulations.

A80 When the practitioner is engaged to review the financial statements of a group of entities, the planned nature, timing and extent of the procedures for the review are directed at achieving the practitioner's objectives for the review engagement stated in this ISRE, but in the context of the group financial statements.

A81 The requirements of this ISRE relating to designing and performing inquiry and analytical procedures, and procedures addressing specific circumstances, are designed to enable the practitioner to achieve the objectives specified in this ISRE. The circumstances of review engagements vary widely and, accordingly, there may be circumstances where the practitioner may consider it effective or efficient to design and perform other procedures. For example, if in the course of obtaining an understanding of the entity, the practitioner becomes aware of a significant contract the practitioner may choose to read the contract.

A82 The fact that the practitioner may deem it necessary to perform other procedures does not alter the practitioner's objective of obtaining limited assurance in relation to the financial statements as a whole.

Significant or Unusual Transactions

A83 The practitioner may consider, reviewing the accounting records with a view to identifying significant or unusual transactions that may require specific attention in the review.

Inquiry (Ref: Para. 46–48)

A84 In a review, inquiry includes seeking information of management and other persons within the entity, as the practitioner considers appropriate in the engagement circumstances. The practitioner may also extend inquiries to obtain non-financial data if appropriate. Evaluating the responses provided by management is integral to the inquiry process.

Depending on the engagement circumstances, inquiries may also include inquiries about:

- Actions taken at meetings of owners, those charged with governance and committees thereof, and proceedings at other meetings, if any, that affect the information and disclosures contained in the financial statements.
- Communications the entity has received, or expects to receive or obtain, from regulatory agencies.
- Matters arising in the course of applying other procedures. When performing further inquiries in relation to identified inconsistencies, the practitioner considers the reasonableness and consistency of management's responses in light of the results obtained from other procedures, and the practitioner's knowledge and understanding of the entity and the industry in which it operates.

A85

Evidence obtained through inquiry is often the principal source of evidence about management intent. However, information available to support management's intent may be limited. In that case, understanding management's past history of carrying out its stated intentions, management's stated reasons for choosing a particular course of action, and management's ability to pursue a specific course of action may provide relevant information to corroborate the evidence obtained through inquiry. Application of professional skepticism in evaluating responses provided by management is important to enable the practitioner to evaluate whether there are any matter(s) that would cause the practitioner to believe the financial statements may be materially misstated.

A86

Performing inquiry procedures assists the practitioner also in obtaining or updating the practitioner's understanding of the entity and its environment, to be able to identify areas where material misstatements are likely to arise in the financial statements.

A87

Inquiry about the entity's ability to continue as a going concern (Ref: Para. 48(f))

Often in smaller entities, management may not have prepared an assessment of the entity's ability to continue as a going concern, but instead may rely on knowledge of the business and anticipated future prospects. In these circumstances, it may be appropriate to discuss the medium and long-term prospects and financing of the entity with management, including consideration of whether management's contentions are not inconsistent with the practitioner's understanding of the entity.

A88

Analytical Procedures (Ref: Para. 46–47, 49)

In a review of financial statements, performing analytical procedures assists the practitioner in:

- Obtaining or updating the practitioner's understanding of the entity and its environment, including to be able to identify areas where material misstatements are likely to arise in the financial statements.
- Identifying inconsistencies or variances from expected trends, values or norms in the financial statements such as the level of congruence of the financial statements with key data, including key performance indicators.
- Providing corroborative evidence in relation to other inquiry or analytical procedures already performed.
- Serving as additional procedures when the practitioner becomes aware of matter(s) that cause the practitioner to believe that the financial statements may be materially misstated. An example of such an additional procedure is a comparative analysis of monthly revenue and cost figures across profit centers,

A89

branches or other components of the entity, to provide evidence about financial information contained in line items or disclosures contained in the financial statements.

A90 Various methods may be used to perform analytical procedures. These methods range from performing simple comparisons to performing complex analysis using statistical techniques. The practitioner may, for example, apply analytical procedures to evaluate the financial information underlying the financial statements through analysis of plausible relationships among both financial and non-financial data, and assessment of results for consistency with expected values with a view to identifying relationships and individual items that appear unusual, or that vary from expected trends or values. The practitioner would compare recorded amounts, or ratios developed from recorded amounts, to expectations developed by the practitioner from information obtained from relevant sources. Examples of sources of information the practitioner often uses to develop expectations, depending on the engagement circumstances, include:

- Financial information for comparable prior period(s), taking known changes into account.
- Information about expected operating and financial results, such as budgets or forecasts including extrapolations from interim or annual data.
- Relationships among elements of financial information within the period.
- Information regarding the industry in which the entity operates, such as gross margin information, or comparison of the entity's ratio of sales to accounts receivable with industry averages or with other entities of comparable size in the same industry.
- Relationships of financial information with relevant non-financial information, such as payroll costs to number of employees.

A91 The practitioner's consideration of whether data to be used for analytical procedures are satisfactory for the intended purpose(s) of those procedures is based on the practitioner's understanding of the entity and its environment, and is influenced by the nature and source of the data, and by the circumstances in which the data are obtained. The following considerations may be relevant:

- Source of the information available. For example, information may be more reliable when it is obtained from independent sources outside the entity;
- Comparability of the information available. For example, broad industry data may need to be supplemented or be adjusted to be comparable to data of an entity that produces and sells specialized products;
- Nature and relevance of the information available; for example, whether the entity's budgets are established as results to be expected rather than as goals to be achieved; and
- The knowledge and expertise involved in the preparation of the information, and related controls that are designed to ensure its completeness, accuracy and validity.

Such controls may include, for example, controls over the preparation, review and maintenance of budgetary information.

Procedures to Address Specific Circumstances

Fraud and non-compliance with laws or regulations (Ref: Para. 52(d))

A92 Under this ISRE, if the practitioner has identified or suspects fraud or illegal acts, the practitioner is required to determine whether there is a responsibility to report the occurrence or suspicion to a party outside the entity. Although the practitioner's professional duty to maintain the confidentiality of client information may preclude such reporting, the practitioner's legal responsibilities may override the duty of confidentiality in some circumstances.

Events or conditions that may cast doubt regarding use of the going concern assumption in the financial statements (Ref: Para. 54)

The list of factors below gives examples of events or conditions that, individually or collectively, may cast significant doubt about the going concern assumption. The list is not all-inclusive, and the existence of one or more of the items does not always signify that uncertainty exists about whether the entity can continue as a going concern.

A93

Financial

- Net liability or net current liability position
- Fixed-term borrowings approaching maturity without realistic prospects of renewal or repayment, or excessive reliance on short-term borrowings to finance long-term assets
- Indications of withdrawal of financial support by creditors
- Negative operating cash flows indicated by historical or prospective financial statements
- Adverse key financial ratios
- Substantial operating losses or significant deterioration in the value of assets used to generate cash flows
- Arrears or discontinuance of dividends
- Inability to pay creditors on due dates
- Inability to comply with the terms of loan agreements
- Change from credit to cash-on-delivery transactions with suppliers
- Inability to obtain financing for essential new product development or other essential investments

Operating

- Management intentions to liquidate the entity or to cease operations
- Loss of key management without replacement
- Loss of a major market, key customer(s), franchise, license, or principal supplier(s)
- Labor difficulties
- Shortages of important supplies
- Emergence of a highly successful competitor

Other

- Non-compliance with capital or other statutory requirements
- Pending legal or regulatory proceedings against the entity that may, if successful, result in claims that the entity is unlikely to be able to satisfy
- Changes in law or regulation or government policy expected to adversely affect the entity
- Uninsured or underinsured catastrophes when they occur

The significance of such events or conditions often can be mitigated by other factors. For example, the effect of an entity being unable to make its normal debt repayments may be counter-balanced by management's plans to maintain adequate cash flows by alternative means, such as by disposing of assets, rescheduling loan repayments, or obtaining additional capital. Similarly, the loss of a principal supplier may be mitigated by the availability of a suitable alternative source of supply.

Reconciling the Financial Statements to the Underlying Accounting Records (Ref: Para. 56)

A94   The practitioner ordinarily obtains evidence that the financial statements agree with, or reconcile to, the underlying accounting records by tracing the financial statement amounts and balances to the relevant accounting records such as the general ledger, or to a summary record or schedule that reflects the agreement or reconciliation of the financial statement amounts with the underlying accounting records (such as a trial balance).

Performing Additional Procedures (Ref: Para. 57)

A95   Additional procedures are required under this ISRE if the practitioner becomes aware of a matter that causes the practitioner to believe the financial statements may be materially misstated.

A96   The practitioner's response in undertaking additional procedures with respect to an item the practitioner has cause to believe may be materially misstated in the financial statements will vary, depending on the circumstances, and is a matter for the practitioner's professional judgment.

A97   The practitioner's judgment about the nature, timing and extent of additional procedures that are needed to obtain evidence to either conclude that a material misstatement is not likely, or determine that a material misstatement exists, is guided by:

- Information obtained from the practitioner's evaluation of the results of the procedures already performed;
- The practitioner's updated understanding of the entity and its environment obtained throughout the course of the engagement; and
- The practitioner's view on the persuasiveness of evidence needed to address the matter that causes the practitioner to believe that the financial statements may be materially misstated.

A98   Additional procedures focus on obtaining sufficient appropriate evidence to enable the practitioner to form a conclusion on matters that the practitioner believes may cause the financial statements to be materially misstated. The procedures may be:

- Additional inquiry or analytical procedures, for example, being performed in greater detail or being focused on the affected items (i.e. amounts or disclosures concerning the affected accounts or transactions as reflected in the financial statements); or
- Other types of procedures, for example, substantive test of details or external confirmations.

A99   The following example illustrates the practitioner's evaluation of the need to perform additional procedures, and the practitioner's response when the practitioner believes additional procedures are necessary.

- In the course of performing the inquiry and analytical procedures for the review, the practitioner's analysis of accounts receivable shows a material amount of past due accounts receivable, for which there is no allowance for bad or doubtful debts.

- This causes the practitioner to believe that the accounts receivable balance in the financial statements may be materially misstated. The practitioner then inquires of management whether there are uncollectible accounts receivable that would need to be shown as being impaired.
- Depending on management's response, the practitioner's evaluation of the response may:
  - (a) Enable the practitioner to conclude that the accounts receivable balance is not likely to be materially misstated. In that case, no further procedures are required.
  - (b) Enable the practitioner to determine that the matter causes the financial statements to be materially misstated. No further procedures are required, and the practitioner would form the conclusion that the financial statements as a whole are materially misstated.
  - (c) Lead the practitioner to continue to believe that the accounts receivable balance is likely to be materially misstated, while not providing sufficient appropriate evidence for the practitioner to determine that they are in fact misstated. In that case, the practitioner is required to perform additional procedures, for example, requesting from management an analysis of amounts received for those accounts after the balance sheet date to identify uncollectible accounts receivable. The evaluation of the results of the additional procedures may enable the practitioner to get to (a) or (b) above. If not, the practitioner is required to:
    - (i) Continue performing additional procedures until the practitioner reaches either (a) or (b) above; or
    - (ii) If the practitioner is not able to either conclude that the matter is not likely to cause the financial statements as a whole to be materially misstated, or to determine that the matter does cause the financial statements as a whole to be materially misstated, then a scope limitation exists and the practitioner is not able to form an unmodified conclusion on the financial statements.

Written Representations (Ref: Para. 61–63)

Written representations are an important source of evidence in a review engagement. If management modifies or does not provide the requested written representations, it may alert the practitioner to the possibility that one or more significant issues may exist. Further, a request for written, rather than oral, representations in many cases may prompt management to consider such matters more rigorously, thereby enhancing the quality of the representations. **A100**

In addition to the written representations required under this ISRE, the practitioner may consider it necessary to request other written representations about the financial statements. These may be needed, for example, to complete the practitioner's evidence with respect to certain items or disclosures reflected in the financial statements where the practitioner considers such representations to be important in forming a conclusion on the financial statements on either a modified or unmodified basis. **A101**

In some cases, management may include in the written representations qualifying language to the effect that representations are made to the best of management's knowledge and belief. It is reasonable for the practitioner to accept such wording if the practitioner is satisfied that the representations are being made by those with appropriate responsibilities and knowledge of the matters included in the representations. **A102**

Evaluating Evidence Obtained from the Procedures Performed (Ref: Para. 66–68)

A103   In some circumstances, the practitioner may not have obtained the evidence that the practitioner had expected to obtain through the design of primarily inquiry and analytical procedures and procedures addressing specific circumstances. In these circumstances, the practitioner considers that the evidence obtained from the procedures performed is not sufficient and appropriate to be able to form a conclusion on the financial statements. The practitioner may:

- Extend the work performed; or
- Perform other procedures judged by the practitioner to be necessary in the circumstances.

Where neither of these is practicable in the circumstances, the practitioner will not be able to obtain sufficient appropriate evidence to be able to form a conclusion and is required by this ISRE to determine the effect on the practitioner's report, or on the practitioner's ability to complete the engagement, for example, if a member of management is unavailable at the time of the review to respond to the practitioner's inquiries on significant matters. This situation may arise even though the practitioner has not become aware of a matter(s) that causes the practitioner to believe the financial statements may be materially misstated, as addressed in paragraph 57.

Scope Limitations

A104   Inability to perform a specific procedure does not constitute a limitation on the scope of the review if the practitioner is able to obtain sufficient appropriate evidence by performing other procedures.

A105   Limitations on the scope of the review imposed by management may have other implications for the review, such as for the practitioner's consideration of areas where the financial statements are likely to be materially misstated, and engagement continuance.

Forming the Practitioner's Conclusion on the Financial Statements

Description of the Applicable Financial Reporting Framework (Ref: Para. 69(a))

A106   The description of the applicable financial reporting framework in the financial statements is important because it advises users of the financial statements of the framework on which the financial statements are based. If the financial statements are special purpose financial statements, they may be prepared under a special purpose financial reporting framework that is available only to the engaging party and the practitioner. Description of the special purpose financial reporting framework used is important as the special purpose financial statements may not be appropriate for any use other than the intended use identified for the special purpose financial statements.

A107   A description of the applicable financial reporting framework that contains imprecise qualifying or limiting language (for example, "the financial statements are in substantial compliance with International Financial Reporting Standards") is not an adequate description of that framework as it may mislead users of the financial statements.

Disclosure of Effects of Material Transactions and Events on Information Conveyed in the Financial Statements (Ref: Para. 69(b)(vi), 71)

The practitioner is required under this ISRE to evaluate whether the financial statements provide adequate disclosures to enable the intended users to understand the effect of material transactions and events on the entity's financial position, financial performance and cash flows.   **A108**

In the case of financial statements prepared in accordance with the requirements of a fair presentation framework, management may need to include additional disclosures in the financial statements beyond those specifically required by the applicable financial reporting framework or, in extremely rare circumstances, to depart from a requirement in the framework, in order to achieve the fair presentation of the financial statements.   **A109**

Considerations When a Compliance Framework Is Used

It will be extremely rare for the practitioner to consider financial statements prepared in accordance with a compliance framework to be misleading if, in accordance with this ISRE, the practitioner has determined at the time of engagement acceptance that the framework is acceptable.   **A110**

Qualitative Aspects of the Entity's Accounting Practices (Ref: Para. 70(b))

In considering the qualitative aspects of the entity's accounting practices, the practitioner may become aware of possible bias in management's judgments. The practitioner may conclude that the cumulative effect of a lack of neutrality, together with the effect of apparent uncorrected misstatements, causes the financial statements as a whole to be materially misstated. Indicators of a lack of neutrality that may affect the practitioner's evaluation of whether the financial statements as a whole may be materially misstated include the following: **A111**

- The selective correction of apparent misstatements brought to management's attention during the review (for example, correcting misstatements with the effect of increasing reported earnings, but not correcting misstatements that have the effect of decreasing reported earnings).
- Possible management bias in the making of accounting estimates.

Indicators of possible management bias do not necessarily mean there are misstatements for purposes of drawing conclusions on the reasonableness of individual accounting estimates. They may, however, affect the practitioner's consideration of whether the financial statements as a whole may be materially misstated.   **A112**

Form of the Conclusion (Ref: Para. 74)

Description of the Information the Financial Statements Present

In the case of financial statements prepared in accordance with a fair presentation framework, the practitioner's conclusion states that nothing has come to the practitioner's attention that causes the practitioner to believe that the financial statements do not present fairly, in all material respects, ... (or do not give a true and fair view of ...) in accordance with [the applicable fair presentation framework]. In the case of many general purpose frameworks, for example, the financial statements are required to fairly present (or give a true and fair view of) the financial position of the entity as   **A113** at the end of a period, and the entity's financial performance and cash flows for that period.

"Present fairly, in all material respects" or "gives a true and fair view"

A114   Whether the phrase "present fairly, in all material respects," or the phrase "gives a true and fair view" is used in any particular jurisdiction is determined by the law or regulation governing the review of financial statements in that jurisdiction, or by generally accepted practice in that jurisdiction. Where law or regulation requires the use of different wording, this does not affect the requirement in this ISRE for the practitioner to evaluate the fair presentation of financial statements prepared in accordance with a fair presentation framework.

Inability to Form a Conclusion Due to a Management-Imposed Limitation on the Scope of the Review after Engagement Acceptance (Ref: Para. 15, 82)

A115   The practicality of withdrawing from the engagement may depend on the stage of completion of the engagement at the time that management imposes the scope limitation. If the practitioner has substantially completed the review, the practitioner may decide to complete the review to the extent possible, disclaim a conclusion and explain the scope limitation in the paragraph in the report that describes the basis for disclaiming a conclusion.

A116   In certain circumstances, withdrawal from the engagement may not be possible if the practitioner is required by law or regulation to continue the engagement. For example, this may be the case for a practitioner appointed to review the financial statements of a public sector entity. It may also be the case in jurisdictions where the practitioner is appointed to review the financial statements covering a specific period, or appointed for a specific period,

and is prohibited from withdrawing before the completion of the review of those financial statements or before the end of that period, respectively. The practitioner may also consider it necessary to include an Other Matter paragraph in the practitioner's report to explain why it is not possible for the practitioner to withdraw from the engagement.

Communication with Regulators or the Entity's Owners

A117   When the practitioner concludes that withdrawal from the engagement is necessary because of a scope limitation, there may be a professional, legal or regulatory requirement for the practitioner to communicate matters relating to the withdrawal from the engagement to regulators or the entity's owners.

The Practitioner's Report (Ref: Para. 86–92)

A118   The written report encompasses reports issued in hard copy format and those using an electronic medium.

Elements of the Practitioner's Report (Ref: Para. 86)

A119   A title indicating the report is the report of an independent practitioner, for example, "Independent Practitioner's Review Report," affirms that the practitioner has met all of the relevant ethical requirements regarding independence and, therefore, distinguishes the independent practitioner's report from reports issued by others.

Law or regulation may specify to whom the practitioner's report is to be addressed in that particular jurisdiction. The practitioner's report is normally addressed to those for whom the report is prepared, often either to the shareholders or to those charged with governance of the entity whose financial statements are being reviewed. **A120**

When the practitioner is aware that the financial statements that have been reviewed will be included in a document that contains other information, such as a financial report, the practitioner may consider, if the form of presentation allows, identifying the page numbers on which the financial statements that have been reviewed are presented. This helps users to identify the financial statements to which the practitioner's report relates. **A121**

Management's Responsibility for the Financial Statements (Ref: Para. 86(d))

The requirement of this ISRE that the practitioner must obtain management's agreement that it acknowledges and understands its responsibilities, both in relation to the preparation of the financial statements and in relation to the review engagement, is fundamental to performing the review and reporting on the engagement. The description of management's responsibilities in the practitioner's report provides context for readers of the practitioner's report about management's responsibilities, as they relate to the review engagement performed. **A122**

The practitioner's report need not refer specifically to "management" but instead may use the term that is appropriate in the context of the legal framework in the particular jurisdiction. In some jurisdictions, the appropriate reference is to those charged with governance of the entity. **A123**

There may be circumstances when it is appropriate for the practitioner to add to the description of management's responsibilities as described in this ISRE to reflect additional responsibilities that are relevant to the preparation of the financial statements in the context of a jurisdiction, or due to the type of entity. **A124**

In some jurisdictions, law or regulation prescribing management's responsibilities may specifically refer to a responsibility for the adequacy of the accounting books and records, or accounting system. As books, records and systems are an integral part of internal control, this ISRE does not use these descriptions or make any specific reference to them. **A125**

The Practitioner's Responsibility (Ref: Para. 86(f))

The practitioner's report states that the practitioner's responsibility is to express a conclusion on the financial statements based on the review performed, in order to contrast the practitioner's responsibility with management's responsibility for preparation of the financial statements. **A126**

Reference to standards (Ref: Para. 86(f))

The reference to the standards used by the practitioner for the review conveys to the users of the practitioner's report that the review has been conducted in accordance with established standards. **A127**

Communication of the Nature of a Review of Financial Statements (Ref: Para. 86(g))

A128   The description of the nature of a review engagement in the practitioner's report explains the scope and limitations of the engagement undertaken for the benefit of the readers of the report. This explanation clarifies, for avoidance of doubt, that the review is not an audit and that accordingly, the practitioner does not express an audit opinion on the financial statements.

Description of the Applicable Financial Reporting Framework and How It May Affect the Practitioner's Conclusion (Ref: Para. 86(i)(ii))

A129   The identification of the applicable financial reporting framework in the practitioner's conclusion is intended to advise users of the practitioner's report of the context in which that conclusion is expressed. It is not intended to limit the evaluation required in paragraph 30(a). The applicable financial reporting framework is identified in such terms as:

"... in accordance with International Financial Reporting Standards;" or

"... in accordance with accounting principles generally accepted in Jurisdiction X ..."

A130   When the applicable financial reporting framework encompasses financial reporting standards and legal or regulatory requirements, the framework is identified in such terms as "... in accordance with International Financial Reporting Standards and the requirements of Jurisdiction X Corporations Act."

Basis for Modification Paragraph When the Conclusion Is Modified (Ref: Para. 85(h)(ii))

A131   An adverse conclusion or a disclaimer of conclusion relating to a specific matter described in the basis for modification paragraph does not justify the omission of a description of other identified matters that would have otherwise required a modification of the practitioner's conclusion. In such cases, the disclosure of such other matters of which the practitioner is aware may be relevant to users of the financial statements.

Signature of the Practitioner (Ref: Para. 86(l))

A132   The practitioner's signature is either in the name of the practitioner's firm, the personal name of the individual practitioner, or both, as appropriate for the particular jurisdiction. In addition to the practitioner's signature, in certain jurisdictions, the practitioner may be required to make a declaration in the practitioner's report about professional designations or recognition by the appropriate licensing authority in that jurisdiction.

Alerting Readers that the Financial Statements Are Prepared in Accordance with a Special Purpose Framework (Ref: Para. 88)

A133   The special purpose financial statements may be used for purposes other than those for which they were intended. For example, a regulator may require certain entities to place the special purpose financial statements on public record. For avoidance of misunderstanding, it is important that the practitioner alert users of the practitioner's report that the financial statements are prepared in accordance with a special purpose framework and, therefore, may not be suitable for another purpose.

Restriction on Distribution or Use

In addition to the alert to the reader of the practitioner's report that is required by **A134** this ISRE when the financial statements are prepared using a special purpose framework, the practitioner may consider it appropriate to indicate that the practitioner's report is intended solely for the specific users. Depending on the law or regulation of the particular jurisdiction, this may be achieved by restricting the distribution or use of the practitioner's report. In these circumstances, the paragraph containing the alert about the use of a special purpose framework may be expanded to include these other matters, and the heading modified accordingly.

Other Reporting Responsibilities (Ref: Para. 91)

In some jurisdictions, the practitioner may have additional responsibilities to report **A135** on other matters that are supplementary to the practitioner's responsibility under this ISRE. For example, the practitioner may be asked to report certain matters if they come to the practitioner's attention during the course of the review of the financial statements. Alternatively, the practitioner may be asked to perform and report on additional specified procedures, or to express a conclusion on specific matters, such as the adequacy of accounting books and records. Standards on engagements to review financial statements in the specific jurisdiction may provide guidance on the practitioner's responsibilities with respect to specific additional reporting responsibilities in that jurisdiction.

In some cases, the relevant law or regulation may require or permit the practitioner **A136** to report on these other responsibilities within the practitioner's report on the financial statements. In other cases, the practitioner may be required or permitted to report on them in a separate report.

These other reporting responsibilities are addressed in a separate section of the **A137** practitioner's report, to clearly distinguish them from the practitioner's responsibility under this ISRE to report on the financial statements. Where relevant, this section may contain sub-heading(s) that describe(s) the content of the other reporting responsibility paragraph(s). In some jurisdictions, the additional reporting responsibilities may be addressed in a report that is separate from the practitioner's report provided for the review of the financial statements.

Date of the Practitioner's Report (Ref: Para. 86(k), 92)

The date of the practitioner's report informs the user of the practitioner's report that **A138** the practitioner has considered the effect of events and transactions of which the practitioner became aware and that occurred up to that date.

The practitioner's conclusion is provided on the financial statements and the **A139** financial statements are the responsibility of management. The practitioner is not in a position to conclude that sufficient appropriate evidence has been obtained until the practitioner is satisfied that all the statements that comprise the financial statements, including the related notes, have been prepared and management has accepted responsibility for them.

In some jurisdictions, law or regulation identifies the individuals or bodies (for **A140** example, the directors) that are responsible for concluding that all the statements that comprise the financial statements, including the related notes, have been prepared, and specifies the necessary approval process. In such cases, evidence is obtained of that approval before dating the report on the financial statements. In other jurisdictions, however, the approval process is not prescribed in law or regulation. In such cases, the procedures the entity follows in preparing and finalizing its financial statements in view of its management and governance structures are considered in order to identify the individuals or body with the authority to conclude that all the statements that comprise the financial statements, including the related notes, have been prepared. In some cases, law or regulation may identify the point in the financial statement reporting process at which the review is expected to be complete.

A141   In some jurisdictions, final approval of the financial statements by shareholders is required before the financial statements are issued publicly. In these jurisdictions, final approval by shareholders is not necessary for the practitioner to conclude on the financial statements. The date of approval of the financial statements for purposes of this ISRE is the earlier date on which those with the recognized authority determine that all the statements that comprise the financial statements, including the related notes, have been prepared and that those with the recognized authority have asserted that they have taken responsibility for them.

Practitioner's Report Prescribed by Law or Regulation (Ref: Para. 34–35, 86)

A142   Consistency in the practitioner's report, when the review has been conducted in accordance with this ISRE, promotes credibility in the global marketplace by making more readily identifiable those reviews of financial statements that have been conducted in accordance with globally recognized standards. The practitioner's report may refer to this ISRE when the differences between the legal or regulatory requirements and this ISRE relate only to the layout or wording of the practitioner's report and, at a minimum, the report complies with the requirements of paragraph 86 of this ISRE. Accordingly, in such circumstances the practitioner is considered to have complied with the requirements of this ISRE, even when the layout and wording used in the practitioner's report are specified by legal or regulatory reporting requirements. Where specific requirements in a particular jurisdiction do not conflict with this ISRE, adoption of the layout and wording used in this ISRE assists users of the practitioner's report to more readily recognize the practitioner's report as a report on a review of financial statements conducted in accordance with this ISRE. Circumstances where law or regulation prescribes the layout or wording of the practitioner's report in terms that are significantly different from the requirements of this ISRE are addressed in the requirements of this ISRE concerning acceptance of review engagements and continuance of client relationships.

Practitioner's Report for Reviews Conducted in Accordance with Both Relevant Standards of a Specific Jurisdiction and this ISRE (Ref: Para. 86(f))

A143   When, in addition to complying with the requirements of this ISRE, the practitioner also complies with relevant national standards, the report may refer to the review having been performed in accordance with both this ISRE and relevant national standards for engagements to review financial statements. However, a reference to both this ISRE and relevant national standards is not appropriate if there is a conflict between the requirements of this ISRE and those in the relevant national standards that would lead the practitioner to form a different conclusion or not to include an Emphasis of Matter paragraph that, in the particular circumstances, would be required by this ISRE. In such a case, the practitioner's report refers only to the relevant standards (either this ISRE or the relevant national standards) in accordance with which the practitioner's report has been prepared.

Illustrative Review Reports (Ref: Para. 86)

Appendix 2 to this ISRE contains illustrations of practitioners' reports for a review of financial statements incorporating the reporting requirements of this ISRE.   **A144**

Documentation

Timeliness of Engagement Documentation (Ref: Para. 93)

ISQC 1 requires the firm to establish time limits that reflect the need to complete the assembly of final engagement files on a timely basis.   **A145**

Appendix 1   (Ref: Para. A56)

Illustrative Engagement Letter for an Engagement to Review Historical Financial Statements

The following is an example of an engagement letter for a review of general purpose financial statements (prepared in accordance with International Financial Reporting Standards (IFRSs)), which illustrates the relevant requirements and guidance contained in this ISRE. This letter is not authoritative but is intended only to be a guide that may be used in conjunction with the considerations outlined in this ISRE. It will need to be varied according to individual requirements and circumstances. It is drafted to refer to the review of financial statements for a single reporting period and would require adaptation if intended or expected to apply to recurring reviews. It may be appropriate to seek legal advice that any proposed letter is suitable.

***

To the appropriate representative of management or those charged with governance of ABC Company:[11]

[*The objective and scope of the review*]

You[12] have requested that we review the general purpose financial statements of ABC Company, which comprise the statement of financial position as at December 31, 20X1, and the statement of comprehensive income, statement of changes in equity and cash flow statement for the year then ended, and a summary of significant accounting policies and other explanatory information. We are pleased to confirm our acceptance and our understanding of this review engagement by means of this letter.

Our review will be conducted with the objective of expressing our conclusion on the financial statements. Our conclusion, if unmodified, will be in the form "Based on our review, nothing has come to our attention that causes us to believe that these financial statements do not present fairly, in all material respects, (*or do not give a true and fair view of*) the financial position of the company as at [date] and (*of*) its

---

[11] *The addressees and references in the letter would be those that are appropriate in the circumstances of the engagement, including the relevant jurisdiction. It is important to refer to the appropriate persons—see paragraph 36 of this ISRE.*

[12] *Throughout this letter, references to "you," "we," "us," "management," "those charged with governance" and "practitioner" would be used or amended as appropriate in the circumstances.*

financial performance and cash flows for the year then ended in accordance with International Financial Reporting Standards (IFRSs)."

[*The practitioner's responsibilities*]

We will conduct our review in accordance with International Standard on Review Engagements (ISRE) 2400 (Revised), *Engagements to Review Historical Financial Statements*. ISRE 2400 (Revised) requires us to conclude whether anything has come to our attention that causes us to believe that the financial statements, taken as a whole, are not prepared in all material respects in accordance with the applicable financial reporting framework. ISRE 2400 also requires us to comply with relevant ethical requirements.

A review of financial statements in accordance with ISRE 2400 (Revised) is a limited assurance engagement. We will perform procedures, primarily consisting of making inquiries of management and others within the entity, as appropriate, and applying analytical procedures, and evaluate the evidence obtained. We will also perform additional procedures if we become aware of matters that cause us to believe the financial statements as a whole may be materially misstated. These procedures are performed to enable us to express our conclusion on the financial statements in accordance with ISRE 2400 (Revised). The procedures selected will depend on what we consider necessary applying our professional judgment, based on our under-standing of ABC Company and its environment, and our understanding of IFRSs and its application in the industry context.

A review is not an audit of the financial statements, therefore:

(a) There is a commensurate higher risk than there would be in an audit, that any material misstatements that exist in the financial statements reviewed may not be revealed by the review, even though the review is properly performed in accordance with ISRE 2400 (Revised).

(b) In expressing our conclusion from the review of the financial statements, our report on the financial statements will expressly disclaim any audit opinion on the financial statements.

[*The responsibilities of management and identification of the applicable financial reporting framework (for purposes of this example, it is assumed that the practitioner has not determined that the law or regulation prescribes those responsibilities in appropriate terms; the descriptions in paragraph 30(b) of this ISRE are therefore used).*]

Our review will be conducted on the basis that [management and, where appropriate, those charged with governance][13] acknowledge and understand that they have the responsibility:

(a) For preparation and fair presentation of the financial statements in accordance with IFRSs;[14]

(b) For such internal control as management determines is necessary to enable the preparation of financial statements that are free from material misstatement, whether due to fraud or error; and

(c) To provide us with:

[13] *Use terminology as appropriate in the circumstances.*

[14] *Or, if appropriate, "For the preparation of financial statements that give a true and fair view in accordance with IFRSs".*

(i)   Access to all information of which management is aware that is relevant to the preparation and fair presentation of the financial statements, such as records, documentation and other matters;

(ii) Additional information that we may request from management for the purpose of the review; and

(iii) Unrestricted access to persons within ABC Company from whom we determine it necessary to obtain evidence.

As part of our review, we will request from [management and, where appropriate, those charged with governance], written confirmation concerning representations made to us in connection with the review.

We look forward to full cooperation from your staff during our review.

[*Other relevant information*]

[*Insert other information, such as fee arrangements, billings and other specific terms, as appropriate.*]

[*Reporting*]

[*Insert appropriate reference to the expected form and content of the practitioner's report.*]

The form and content of our report may need to be amended in the light of our findings obtained from the review.

Please sign and return the attached copy of this letter to indicate your acknowledgement of, and agreement with, the arrangements for our review of the financial statements including our respective responsibilities.

XYZ & Co.

Acknowledged and agreed on behalf of ABC Company by

(signed)

....

Name and Title

Date

Appendix 2 (Ref: Para. A144)

Illustrative Practitioners' Review Reports

Review Reports on General Purpose Financial Statements
Illustrative Review Reports with Unmodified Conclusions

- Illustration 1: A practitioner's report on financial statements prepared in accordance with a fair presentation framework designed to meet the common financial information needs of a wide range of users (for example, the International Financial Reporting Standard for Small and Medium-sized Entities).

Illustrative Review Reports with Modified Conclusions

- Illustration 2: A practitioner's report containing a qualified conclusion due to an apparent material misstatement of the financial statements. Financial statements prepared in accordance with a compliance framework designed to meet the common information needs of a wide range of users. (Financial statements prepared using a compliance framework)
- Illustration 3: A practitioner's report containing a qualified conclusion due to the practitioner's inability to obtain sufficient appropriate evidence. (Financial statements prepared using a fair presentation framework—IFRSs)
- Illustration 4: A practitioner's report containing an adverse conclusion due to material misstatement of the financial statements. (Financial statements prepared using a fair presentation framework—IFRSs)
- Illustration 5: A practitioner's report containing a disclaimer of conclusion due to the practitioner's inability to obtain sufficient appropriate evidence about multiple elements of the financial statements—resulting in inability to complete the review. (Financial statements prepared using a fair presentation framework—IFRSs)

Review Reports on Special Purpose Financial Statements

- Illustration 6: A practitioner's report on financial statements prepared in accordance with the financial reporting provisions of a contract (for purposes of this illustration, a compliance framework).
- Illustration 7: A practitioner's report on a single financial statement prepared in accordance with the cash receipts and disbursements basis of accounting (for purposes of this illustration, a fair presentation framework).

Illustration 1

Circumstances include the following:

● Review of a complete set of financial statements.

● The financial statements are prepared for a general purpose by management of the entity in accordance with the International Financial Reporting Standard for Small and Medium-sized Entities.

● The terms of the review engagement reflect the description of management's responsibility for the financial statements in paragraph 30(b) of this ISRE.

● In addition to the review of the financial statements, the practitioner has other reporting responsibilities under local law.

INDEPENDENT PRACTITIONER'S REVIEW REPORT

[Appropriate Addressee]

Report on the Financial Statements[15]

We have reviewed the accompanying financial statements of ABC Company, which comprise the statement of financial position as at December 31, 20X1, and the statement of comprehensive income, statement of changes in equity and statement of cash flows for the year then ended, and a summary of significant accounting policies and other explanatory information.

Management's[16] *Responsibility for the Financial Statements*

Management is responsible for the preparation and fair presentation of these financial statements in accordance with the International Financial Reporting Standard for Small and Medium-sized Entities,[17] and for such internal control as management determines is necessary to enable the preparation of financial statements that are free from material misstatement, whether due to fraud or error.

Practitioner's Responsibility

Our responsibility is to express a conclusion on the accompanying financial statements. We conducted our review in accordance with International Standard on Review Engagements (ISRE) 2400 (Revised), *Engagements to Review Historical Financial Statements*. ISRE 2400 (Revised) requires us to conclude whether anything has come to our attention that causes us to believe that the financial statements, taken as a whole, are not prepared in all material respects in accordance with the applicable financial reporting framework. This Standard also requires us to comply with relevant ethical requirements.

---

[15] *The sub-title "Report on the Financial Statements" is unnecessary in circumstances when the second sub-title "Report on Other Legal and Regulatory Requirements" is not applicable.*

[16] *Or other term that is appropriate in the context of the legal framework in the particular jurisdiction.*

[17] *Where management's responsibility is to prepare financial statements that give a true and fair view, this may read: "Management is responsible for the preparation of financial statements that give a true and fair view in accordance with the International Financial Reporting Standard for Small and Medium-sized Entities, and for such ...".*

A review of financial statements in accordance with ISRE 2400 (Revised) is a limited assurance engagement. The practitioner performs procedures, primarily consisting of making inquiries of management and others within the entity, as appropriate, and applying analytical procedures, and evaluates the evidence obtained.

The procedures performed in a review are substantially less than those performed in an audit conducted in accordance with International Standards on Auditing. Accordingly, we do not express an audit opinion on these financial statements.

Conclusion

Based on our review, nothing has come to our attention that causes us to believe that these financial statements do not present fairly, in all material respects, (or *do not give a true and fair view of)* the financial position of ABC Company as at December 31, 20X1, and (*of)* its financial performance and cash flows for the year then ended, in accordance with the International Financial Reporting Standard for Small and Medium-sized Entities.

Report on Other Legal and Regulatory Requirements

[Form and content of this section of the practitioner's report will vary depending on the nature of the practitioner's other reporting responsibilities.]

[Practitioner's signature]

[Date of the practitioner's report]

[Practitioner's address]

Illustration 2

Circumstances include the following:

- Review of a complete set of financial statements required by law or regulation.

- The financial statements are prepared for a general purpose by management of the entity in accordance with the Financial Reporting Framework (XYZ Law) of Jurisdiction X (that is, a financial reporting framework, encompassing law or regulation, designed to meet the common financial information needs of a wide range of users, but which is not a fair presentation framework).

- The terms of the review engagement reflect the description of management's responsibility for the financial statements in paragraph 30(b) of this ISRE.

- Based on the review, inventories are misstated. The misstatement is material but not pervasive to the financial statements.

- In addition to the review of the financial statements, the practitioner has other reporting responsibilities under local law.

INDEPENDENT PRACTITIONER'S REVIEW REPORT

[Appropriate Addressee]

Report on the Financial Statements[18]

We have reviewed the accompanying financial statements of ABC Company, which comprise the statement of financial position as at December 31, 20X1, and the statement of comprehensive income, statement of changes in equity and statement of cash flows for the year then ended, and a summary of significant accounting policies and other explanatory information.

Management's[19] Responsibility for the Financial Statements

Management is responsible for the preparation of these financial statements in accordance with XYZ Law of Jurisdiction X, and for such internal control as management determines is necessary to enable the preparation of financial statements that are free from material misstatement, whether due to fraud or error.

Practitioner's Responsibility

Our responsibility is to express a conclusion on the accompanying financial statements. We conducted our review in accordance with International Standard on Review Engagements (ISRE) 2400 (Revised), *Engagements to Review Historical Financial Statements.* ISRE 2400 (Revised) requires us to conclude whether anything has come to our attention that causes us to believe that the financial statements, taken as a whole, are not prepared in all material respects in accordance with the applicable financial reporting framework. This Standard also requires us to comply with relevant ethical requirements.

---

[18] *The sub-title "Report on the Financial Statements" is unnecessary in circumstances when the second sub-title "Report on Other Legal and Regulatory Requirements" is not applicable.*

[19] *Or other term that is appropriate in the context of the legal framework in the particular jurisdiction.*

A review of financial statements in accordance with ISRE 2400 (Revised) is a limited assurance engagement. The practitioner performs procedures, primarily consisting of making inquiries of management and others within the entity, as appropriate, and applying analytical procedures, and evaluates the evidence obtained.

The procedures performed in a review are substantially less than those performed in an audit conducted in accordance with International Standards on Auditing. Accordingly, we do not express an audit opinion on these financial statements.

Basis for Qualified Conclusion

The company's inventories are carried in the statement of financial position at xxx. Management has not stated the inventories at the lower of cost and net realizable value but has stated them solely at cost, which constitutes a departure from the requirements of the Financial Reporting Framework (XYZ Law) of Jurisdiction X. The company's records indicate that, had management stated the inventories at the lower of cost and net realizable value, an amount of xxx would have been required to write the inventories down to their net realizable value. Accordingly, cost of sales would have been increased by xxx, and income tax, net income and shareholders' equity would have been reduced by xxx, xxx and xxx, respectively.

Qualified Conclusion

Based on our review, except for the effects of the matter described in the Basis for Qualified Conclusion paragraph, nothing has come to our attention that causes us to believe that the financial statements of ABC Company are not prepared, in all material respects, in accordance with the Financial Reporting Framework (XYZ Law) of Jurisdiction X.

Report on Other Legal and Regulatory Requirements

[Form and content of this section of the practitioner's report will vary depending on the nature of the practitioner's other reporting responsibilities.]

[Practitioner's signature]

[Date of the practitioner's report]

[Practitioner's address]

Illustration 3

Circumstances include the following:

- Review of a complete set of general purpose financial statements prepared by management of the entity in accordance with [a financial reporting framework designed to achieve fair presentation other than International Financial Reporting Standards].

- The terms of the review engagement reflect the description of management's responsibility for the financial statements in paragraph 30(b) of this ISRE.

- The practitioner was unable to obtain sufficient appropriate evidence regarding an investment in a foreign affiliate. The possible effects of the inability to obtain sufficient appropriate evidence are deemed to be material but not pervasive to the financial statements.

- The practitioner does not have other reporting responsibilities under local law in addition to the review of the consolidated financial statements.

INDEPENDENT PRACTITIONER'S REVIEW REPORT

[Appropriate Addressee]

We have reviewed the accompanying financial statements of ABC Company, which comprise the statement of financial position as at December 31, 20X1, and the statement of comprehensive income, statement of changes in equity and statement of cash flows for the year then ended, and a summary of significant accounting policies and other explanatory information.

Management's[20] Responsibility for the Financial Statements

Management is responsible for the preparation and fair presentation of these financial statements in accordance with [name of applicable financial reporting framework, including a reference to the jurisdiction or country of origin of the financial reporting framework when the financial reporting framework used is not International Financial Reporting Standards],[21] and for such internal control as management determines is necessary to enable the preparation of financial statements that are free from material misstatement, whether due to fraud or error.

Practitioner's Responsibility

Our responsibility is to express a conclusion on the accompanying financial statements. We conducted our review in accordance with International Standard on Review Engagements (ISRE) 2400 (Revised), *Engagements to Review Historical Financial Statements*. ISRE 2400 (Revised) requires us to conclude whether anything has come to our attention that causes us to believe that the financial statements, taken as a whole, are not prepared in all material respects in accordance with the

---

[20] *Or other term that is appropriate in the context of the legal framework in the particular jurisdiction.*

[21] *Where management's responsibility is to prepare financial statements that give a true and fair view, this may read: "Management is responsible for the preparation of financial statements that give a true and fair view in accordance with [name of applicable financial reporting framework, including a reference to the jurisdiction or country of origin of the financial reporting framework when the financial reporting framework used is not International Financial Reporting Standards], and for such ...".*

applicable financial reporting framework. This Standard also requires us to comply with relevant ethical requirements.

A review of financial statements in accordance with ISRE 2400 (Revised) is a limited assurance engagement. The practitioner performs procedures, primarily consisting of making inquiries of management and others within the entity, as appropriate, and applying analytical procedures, and evaluates the evidence obtained.

The procedures performed in a review are substantially less than those performed in an audit conducted in accordance with International Standards on Auditing. Accordingly, we do not express an audit opinion on these financial statements.

Basis for Qualified Conclusion

ABC Company's investment in XYZ Company, a foreign associate acquired during the year and accounted for by the equity method, is carried at xxx on the statement of financial position as at December 31, 20X1, and ABC's share of XYZ's net income of xxx is included in ABC's income for the year then ended. We were unable to obtain access to the relevant financial information of XYZ concerning the carrying amount of ABC's investment in XYZ as at December 31, 20X1 and ABC's share of XYZ's net income for the year. Consequently, we were unable to perform the procedures we considered necessary.

Qualified Conclusion

Based on our review, except for the possible effects of the matter described in the Basis for Qualified Conclusion paragraph, nothing has come to our attention that causes us to believe that the accompanying financial statements do not present fairly, in all material respects, (or *do not give a true and fair view of*) the financial position of ABC Company as at December 31, 20X1, and (*of*) its financial performance and cash flows for the year then ended in accordance with [name of applicable financial reporting framework, including a reference to the jurisdiction or country of origin of the financial reporting framework when the financial reporting framework used is not International Financial Reporting Standards].

[Practitioner's signature]

[Date of the practitioner's report]

[Practitioner's address]

Illustration 4

Circumstances include the following:

- Review of consolidated general purpose financial statements prepared by management of the parent in accordance with International Financial Reporting Standards.

- The terms of the review engagement reflect the description of management's responsibility for the financial statements in paragraph 30(b) of this ISRE.

- The financial statements are materially misstated due to the non-consolidation of a subsidiary. The material misstatement is deemed to be pervasive to the financial statements. The effects of the misstatement on the financial statements have not been determined because it was not practicable to do so.

- The practitioner does not have other reporting responsibilities under local law in addition to the review of the consolidated financial statements.

INDEPENDENT PRACTITIONER'S REVIEW REPORT

[Appropriate Addressee]

Report on the Consolidated Financial Statements[22]

We have reviewed the accompanying consolidated financial statements of ABC Company, which comprise the consolidated statement of financial position as at December 31, 20X1, and the consolidated statement of comprehensive income, statement of changes in equity and statement of cash flows for the year then ended, and a summary of significant accounting policies and other explanatory information.

Management's[23] Responsibility for the Financial Statements

Management is responsible for the preparation and fair presentation of these consolidated financial statements in accordance with International Financial Reporting Standards,[24] and for such internal control as management determines is necessary to enable the preparation of consolidated financial statements that are free from material misstatement, whether due to fraud or error.

Practitioner's Responsibility

Our responsibility is to express a conclusion on the accompanying consolidated financial statements. We conducted our review in accordance with International Standard on Review Engagements (ISRE) 2400 (Revised), *Engagements to Review Historical Financial Statements*. ISRE 2400 (Revised) requires us to conclude whether anything has come to our attention that causes us to believe that the consolidated financial statements, taken as a whole, are not prepared in all material

---

[22] *The sub-title "Report on the Consolidated Financial Statements" is unnecessary in circumstances when the second sub-title "Report on Other Legal and Regulatory Requirements" is not applicable.*

[23] *Or other term that is appropriate in the context of the legal framework in the particular jurisdiction.*

[24] *Where management's responsibility is to prepare financial statements that give a true and fair view, this may read: "Management is responsible for the preparation of financial statements that give a true and fair view in accordance with International Financial Reporting Standards, and for such ...".*

respects in accordance with the applicable financial reporting framework. This Standard also requires us to comply with relevant ethical requirements.

A review of consolidated financial statements in accordance with ISRE 2400 (Revised) is a limited assurance engagement. The practitioner performs procedures, primarily consisting of making inquiries of management and others within the entity, as appropriate, and applying analytical procedures, and evaluates the evidence obtained.

The procedures performed in a review are substantially less than those performed in an audit conducted in accordance with International Standards on Auditing. Accordingly, we do not express an audit opinion on these consolidated financial statements.

Basis for Adverse Conclusion

As explained in Note X, the company has not consolidated the financial statements of subsidiary XYZ Company it acquired during 20X1 because it has not yet been able to ascertain the fair values of certain of the subsidiary's material assets and liabilities at the acquisition date. This investment is therefore accounted for on a cost basis. Under International Financial Reporting Standards, the subsidiary should have been consolidated because it is controlled by the company. Had XYZ been consolidated, many elements in the accompanying financial statements would have been materially affected.

Adverse Conclusion

Based on our review, due to the significance of the matter discussed in the Basis for Adverse Conclusion paragraph, the consolidated financial statements do not present fairly (or *do not give a true and fair view of*) the financial position of ABC Company and its subsidiaries as at December 31, 20X1, and (*of*) their financial performance and cash flows for the year then ended in accordance with International Financial Reporting Standards.

Report on Other Legal and Regulatory Requirements

[Form and content of this section of the practitioner's report will vary depending on the nature of the practitioner's other reporting responsibilities.]

[Practitioner's signature]

[Date of the practitioner's report]

[Practitioner's address]

Illustration 5

Circumstances include the following:

- Review of a complete set of general purpose financial statements prepared by management of the entity in accordance with International Financial Reporting Standards.

- The terms of the review engagement reflect the description of management's responsibility for the financial statements in paragraph 30(b) of this ISRE.

- The practitioner was unable to form a conclusion on the financial statements, due to inability to obtain sufficient appropriate evidence about multiple elements of the financial statements, and the practitioner believes the effect is material and pervasive to the financial statements. Specifically, the practitioner was unable to obtain evidence about the entity's physical inventory and accounts receivable.

INDEPENDENT PRACTITIONER'S REVIEW REPORT

[Appropriate Addressee]

We were engaged to review the accompanying financial statements of ABC Company, which comprise the statement of financial position as at December 31, 20X1, and the statement of comprehensive income, statement of changes in equity and statement of cash flows for the year then ended, and a summary of significant accounting policies and other explanatory information.

Management's[25] Responsibility for the Financial Statements

Management is responsible for the preparation and fair presentation of these financial statements in accordance with International Financial Reporting Standards,[26] and for such internal control as management determines is necessary to enable the preparation of financial statements that are free from material misstatement, whether due to fraud or error.

Practitioner's Responsibility

Our responsibility is to express a conclusion on the accompanying financial statements. Because of the matter(s) described in the Basis for Disclaimer of Conclusion paragraph, however, we were not able to obtain sufficient appropriate evidence as a basis for expressing a conclusion on the financial statements.

Basis for Disclaimer of Conclusion

Management did not conduct a count of physical inventory on hand at the end of the year. We were unable to perform the procedures we considered necessary concerning the inventory quantities held at December 31, 20X1, which are stated at xxx in the statement of financial position at December 31, 20X1.

---

[25] *Or other term that is appropriate in the context of the legal framework in the particular jurisdiction.*

[26] *Where management's responsibility is to prepare financial statements that give a true and fair view, this may read: "Management is responsible for the preparation of financial statements that give a true and fair view in accordance with International Financial Reporting Standards, and for such ...".*

In addition, the introduction of a new computerized accounts receivable system in September 20X1 resulted in numerous errors in accounts receivable and inventory. As of the date of our report, management was still in the process of rectifying the system deficiencies and correcting the errors. As a result of these matters, we were unable to determine whether any adjustments might have been found necessary in respect of recorded or unrecorded inventories and accounts receivable, and the elements making up the statement of comprehensive income, statement of changes in equity and statement of cash flows.

Disclaimer of Conclusion

Due to the significance of the matters described in the Basis for Disclaimer of Conclusion paragraph, we were unable to obtain sufficient appropriate evidence to form a conclusion on the accompanying financial statements. Accordingly, we do not express a conclusion on these financial statements.

[Practitioner's signature]

[Date of the practitioner's report]

[Practitioner's address]

Illustration 6

Circumstances include the following:

- The financial statements have been prepared by management of the entity in accordance with the financial reporting provisions of a contract (that is, a special purpose framework), to comply with the provisions of the contract. Management does not have a choice of financial reporting frameworks.

- The applicable financial reporting framework is a compliance framework.

- The terms of the review engagement reflect the description of management's responsibility for the financial statements in paragraph 30(b) of this ISRE.

- Distribution or use of the practitioner's report is restricted.

INDEPENDENT PRACTITIONER'S REVIEW REPORT

[Appropriate Addressee]

We have reviewed the accompanying financial statements of ABC Company, which comprise the balance sheet as at December 31, 20X1, and the income statement, statement of changes in equity and cash flow statement for the year then ended, and a summary of significant accounting policies and other explanatory information. The financial statements have been prepared by management of ABC Company based on the financial reporting provisions of Section Z of the contract dated January 1, 20X1 between ABC Company and DEF Company ("the contract").

Management's[27] Responsibility for the Financial Statements

Management is responsible for the preparation of these financial statements in accordance with the financial reporting provisions of Section Z of the contract, and for such internal control as management determines is necessary to enable the preparation of financial statements that are free from material misstatement, whether due to fraud or error.

Practitioner's Responsibility

Our responsibility is to express a conclusion on the accompanying financial statements. We conducted our review in accordance with International Standard on Review Engagements (ISRE) 2400 (Revised), *Engagements to Review Historical Financial Statements*. ISRE 2400 (Revised) requires us to conclude whether anything has come to our attention that causes us to believe that the financial statements, taken as a whole, are not prepared in all material respects in accordance with the applicable financial reporting framework. This Standard also requires us to comply with relevant ethical requirements.

A review of financial statements in accordance with ISRE 2400 (Revised) is a limited assurance engagement. The practitioner performs procedures, primarily consisting of making inquiries of management and others within the entity, as appropriate, and applying analytical procedures, and evaluates the evidence obtained.

---

[27] *Or other term that is appropriate in the context of the legal framework in the particular jurisdiction.*

The procedures performed in a review are substantially less than those performed in an audit conducted in accordance with International Standards on Auditing. Accordingly, we do not express an audit opinion on these financial statements.

Conclusion

Based on our review, nothing has come to our attention that causes us to believe that these financial statements are not prepared, in all material respects, in accordance with the financial reporting provisions of Section Z of the contract.

Basis of Accounting, and Restriction on Distribution and Use

Without modifying our conclusion, we draw attention to Note X to the financial statements, which describes the basis of accounting. The financial statements are prepared to assist ABC Company to comply with the financial reporting provisions of the contract referred to above. As a result, the financial statements may not be suitable for another purpose. Our report is intended solely for ABC Company and DEF Company and should not be distributed to or used by parties other than ABC Company or DEF Company.

[Practitioner's signature]

[Date of the practitioner's report]

[Practitioner's address]

Illustration 7

Circumstances include the following:

● **Review of a statement of cash receipts and disbursements**

● **The financial statement has been prepared by management of the entity in accordance with the cash receipts and disbursements basis of accounting to respond to a request for cash flow information received from a creditor. The basis of accounting applied to prepare the financial statement has been agreed between the entity and the creditor.**

● **The applicable financial reporting framework is a fair presentation framework designed to meet the financial information needs of specific users.**

● **The practitioner has determined that it is appropriate to use the phrase "presents fairly, in all material respects," in the practitioner's conclusion.**

● **The terms of the review engagement reflect the description of management's responsibility for the financial statement in paragraph 30(b) of this ISRE.**

● **Distribution or use of the practitioner's report is not restricted.**

INDEPENDENT PRACTITIONER'S REVIEW REPORT

[Appropriate Addressee]

We have reviewed the accompanying statement of cash receipts and disbursements of ABC Company for the year ended December 31, 20X1, and a summary of significant accounting policies and other explanatory information (together "the financial statement"). The financial statement has been prepared by management of ABC Company using the cash receipts and disbursements basis of accounting described in Note X.

Management's[28] Responsibility for the Financial Statement

Management is responsible for the preparation and fair presentation of this financial statement in accordance with the cash receipts and disbursements basis of accounting described in Note X, and for such internal control as management determines is necessary to enable the preparation of the financial statement that is free from material misstatement, whether due to fraud or error.

Practitioner's Responsibility

Our responsibility is to express a conclusion on the accompanying financial statement. We conducted our review in accordance with International Standard on Review Engagements (ISRE) 2400 (Revised), *Engagements to Review Historical Financial Statements*. ISRE 2400 (Revised) requires us to conclude whether anything has come to our attention that causes us to believe that the financial statement is not prepared in all material respects in accordance with the applicable financial reporting framework. This Standard also requires us to comply with relevant ethical requirements.

A review of financial statements in accordance with ISRE 2400 (Revised) is a limited assurance engagement. The practitioner performs procedures, primarily consisting of

---

[28] *Or other term that is appropriate in the context of the legal framework in the particular jurisdiction.*

making inquiries of management and others within the entity, as appropriate, and applying analytical procedures, and evaluates the evidence obtained.

The procedures performed in a review are substantially less than those performed in an audit conducted in accordance with International Standards on Auditing. Accordingly, we do not express an audit opinion on this financial statement.

Conclusion

Based on our review, nothing has come to our attention that causes us to believe that the financial statement does not present fairly, in all material respects, (or *does not give a true and fair view of)* the cash receipts and disbursements of ABC Company for the year ended December 31, 20X1 in accordance with the cash receipts and disbursements basis of accounting described in Note X.

Basis of Accounting

Without modifying our conclusion, we draw attention to Note X to the financial statement, which describes the basis of accounting. The financial statement is prepared to provide information to XYZ Creditor. As a result, the financial statement may not be suitable for another purpose.

[Practitioner's signature]

[Date of the practitioner's report]

[Practitioner's address]

Part Five

*International Standards on Review Engagements
(UK & Ireland)*

International Standard on Review Engagements (UK and Ireland) 2410

Review of interim financial information performed by the independent auditor of the entity

(Effective for reviews of interim financial information for periods ending on or after 20 September 2007. Early adoption is permitted.)

Contents

International Standard on Review Engagements (UK and Ireland) (ISRE (UK and Ireland)) 2410, "Review of Interim Financial Information Performed by the Independent Auditor of the Entity" should be read in the context of the Statement "The Financial Reporting Council – Scope and Authority of Audit and Assurance Pronouncements." which sets out the application and authority of APB pronouncements.

ISRE (UK and Ireland) 2410 adopts the text of ISRE 2410 as issued by the International Auditing and Assurance Standards Board (IAASB) in July 2005. Supplementary material added by the APB is differentiated by the use of grey shading.

Introduction

The purpose of this International Standard on Review Engagements (UK and (Ireland) **1**
(ISRE (UK and Ireland)) is to establish standards and provide guidance on the auditor's
professional responsibilities when the auditor undertakes an engagement to review interim
financial information of an audit client, and on the form and content of the report. The
term 'auditor' is used throughout this ISRE (UK and Ireland), not because the auditor
is performing an audit function but because the scope of this ISRE (UK and Ireland) is
limited to a review of interim financial information performed by the independent auditor
of the financial statements of the entity.

This ISRE (UK and Ireland) uses the terms 'those charged with governance' and **1-1**
'management'. The term 'governance' describes the role of persons entrusted with
the supervision, control and direction of an entity. Ordinarily, those charged with
governance are accountable for ensuring that the entity achieves its objectives, and for
the quality of its financial reporting and reporting to interested parties. Those charged
with governance include management only when they perform such functions.

In the UK and Ireland, those charged with governance include the directors (executive **1-2**
and non-executive) of a company or other body, the members of an audit committee
where one exists, the partners, proprietors, committee of management or trustees of
other forms of entity, or equivalent persons responsible for directing the entity's affairs
and preparing its financial statements.

'Management' comprises those persons who perform senior managerial functions. **1-3**

In the UK and Ireland, depending on the nature and circumstances of the entity, **1-4**
management may include some or all of those charged with governance (e.g. executive
directors). Management will not normally include non-executive directors.

For purposes of this ISRE (UK and Ireland), interim financial information is financial **2**
information that is prepared and presented in accordance with an applicable financial
reporting framework[1] and comprises either a complete or a condensed set of financial
statements for a period that is shorter than the entity's financial year.

In the UK and Ireland, interim financial information usually comprises condensed **2-1**
financial information prepared for the first six months of the financial year. For entities
listed on the London Stock Exchange the applicable financial reporting framework
is established by the Disclosure and Transparency Rules of the Financial Services
Authority (FSA)[1a]. For entities listed on the Irish Stock Exchange the applicable
financial reporting framework is established by the Transparency (Directive 2004/109/
EC) Regulations 2007 and the Transparency Rules of the Financial Regulator[1b].

For entities listed on the London or Irish Stock Exchanges, issuers that are required to **2-2**
prepare consolidated annual accounts using International Financial Reporting Standards

---

[1] *For example, International Financial Reporting Standards as issued by the International Accounting Standards Board.*

[1a] *Disclosure and Transparency Rule (DTR) 4.2 'Half-yearly financial reports' applies to all issuers whose shares or debt securities are admitted to trading and whose home state is the UK, subject to the exemptions set out in DTR 4.4.*

[1b] *Requirements for half yearly financial reports are set out in regulations 6 to 8 of Part 2 of the Transparency (Directive 2004/109/EC) Regulations 2007, subject to the exemptions set out in Part 3. Further requirements applicable to half-yearly financial reports are set out in the Transparency Rules issued by The Financial Regulator in Ireland.*

(IFRS) are required to prepare half-yearly financial reports that include a condensed set of financial statements that comply with International Accounting Standard (IAS) 34, *Interim Financial Reporting*, as adopted by the European Union. The relatively few issuers that do not prepare consolidated accounts are required to comply with the minimum disclosure requirements set out in the relevant rules of the UK FSA and the Irish Transparency Regulations and rules of the Irish Financial Regulator as applicable. These rules and regulations also make clear that the persons making the required responsibility statements can satisfy the requirement to confirm that the condensed set of financial statements give a true and fair view by giving a statement that they have been prepared in accordance with IAS 34 as adopted by the European Union or, for UK or Irish issuers not using IFRS, pronouncements on interim reporting issued by the Accounting Standards Board[1c], provided always that such persons have reasonable grounds to be satisfied that the condensed set of financial statements is not misleading. Further information on the rules and regulations applicable to issuers is given in Appendix 9.

2-3   In the context of a review of consolidated interim financial information 'the entity,' as referred to in this ISRE (UK and Ireland), is the group.

3   **The auditor who is engaged to perform a review of interim financial information should perform the review in accordance with this ISRE (UK and Ireland).** Through performing the audit of the annual financial statements, the auditor obtains an understanding of the entity and its environment, including its internal control. When the auditor is engaged to review the interim financial information, this understanding is updated through inquiries made in the course of the review, and assists the auditor in focusing the inquiries to be made and the analytical and other review procedures to be applied. A practitioner who is engaged to perform a review of interim financial information, and who is not the auditor of the entity, performs the review in accordance with ISRE 2400, *Engagements to Review Financial Statements*.[1d] As the practitioner does not ordinarily have the same understanding of the entity and its environment, including its internal control, as the auditor of the entity, the practitioner needs to carry out different inquiries and procedures to meet the objective of the review.

3-1   In some cases the auditor may be asked to carry out specific agreed-upon procedures as an alternative to a review, or the auditor may be approached for advice and guidance on specific accounting and financial reporting issues such as the policies relating to asset impairment or the useful life of an intangible asset. In such circumstances the auditor first agrees the procedures to be carried out, and then reports within that context. Such engagements are outside the scope of this ISRE (UK and Ireland) and, in such circumstances, the auditor requests the entity to describe interim financial information as 'neither audited nor reviewed'[1e].

[1c] *For half-yearly periods ending on or after 20 September 2007, the relevant ASB pronouncement is the Statement 'Half-Yearly Financial Reports'.*

[1d] *ISRE 2400 has not been promulgated by the APB for application in the UK and Ireland.*

[1e] *The FSA's Disclosure and Transparency Rule 4.2.9(1), and the Irish Regulation 8(4)(a), requires that if the half-yearly financial report has been audited or reviewed by auditors pursuant to the Auditing Practices Board guidance on Review of Interim Financial Information, the audit report or review report must be reproduced in full.*

General Principles of a Review of Interim Financial Information

The auditor should comply with the ethical requirements relevant to the audit of   **4**
the annual financial statements of the entity[1f].These ethical requirements govern the
auditor's professional responsibilities in the following areas: independence, integrity,
objectivity, professional competence and due care, confidentiality, professional behavior,
and technical standards.

The auditor should implement quality control procedures that are applicable to the   **5**
individual engagement. The elements of quality control that are relevant to an individual
engagement include leadership responsibilities for quality on the engagement, ethical
requirements, acceptance and continuance of client relationships and specific engagements,
assignment of engagement teams, engagement performance, and monitoring.

The auditor should plan and perform the review with an attitude of professional   **6**
skepticism, recognizing that circumstances may exist that cause the interim financial
information to require a material adjustment for it to be prepared, in all material
respects, in accordance with the applicable financial reporting framework. An
attitude of professional skepticism means that the auditor makes a critical assessment,
with a questioning mind, of the validity of evidence obtained and is alert to evidence
that contradicts or brings into question the reliability of documents or representations by
management of the entity.

Objective of an Engagement to Review Interim Financial Information

The objective of an engagement to review interim financial information is to enable the   **7**
auditor to express a conclusion whether, on the basis of the review, anything has come
to the auditor's attention that causes the auditor to believe that the interim financial
information is not prepared, in all material respects, in accordance with an applicable
financial reporting framework. The auditor makes inquiries, and performs analytical and
other review procedures in order to reduce to a moderate level the risk of expressing an
inappropriate conclusion when the interim financial information is materially misstated.

The objective of a review of interim financial information differs significantly from   **8**
that of an audit conducted in accordance with International Standards on Auditing (UK
and Ireland) (ISAs (UK and Ireland)). A review of interim financial information does
not provide a basis for expressing an opinion whether the financial information gives a
true and fair view, or is presented fairly, in all material respects, in accordance with an
applicable financial reporting framework.

A review, in contrast to an audit, is not designed to obtain reasonable assurance that the   **9**
interim financial information is free from material misstatement. A review consists of
making inquiries, primarily of persons responsible for financial and accounting matters,
and applying analytical and other review procedures. A review may bring significant
matters affecting the interim financial information to the auditor's attention, but it does not
provide all of the evidence that would be required in an audit.

[1f] *In the UK and Ireland the relevant ethical pronouncements with which the auditor complies are the APB's Ethical Standards for Auditors and the ethical pronouncements relating to the work of auditors issued by the auditor's relevant professional body.*

Agreeing the Terms of the Engagement

10   The auditor and the client should agree on the terms of the engagement.

11   The agreed terms of the engagement are ordinarily recorded in an engagement letter. Such a communication helps to avoid misunderstandings regarding the nature of the engagement and, in particular, the objective and scope of the review, management's responsibilities, the extent of the auditor's responsibilities, the assurance obtained, and the nature and form of the report. The communication ordinarily covers the following matters:

- The objective of a review of interim financial information.
- The scope of the review.
- Management's responsibility for the interim financial information.
- The applicable financial reporting framework (e.g. IAS 34 as adopted by the European Union and/or, where applicable, rules and regulations of a listing/regulatory authority relating to the form and content of interim financial information).
- Management's responsibility for establishing and maintaining effective internal control relevant to the preparation of interim financial information.
- Management's responsibility for making all financial records and related information available to the auditor.
- Management's agreement to provide written representations to the auditor to confirm representations made orally during the review, as well as representations that are implicit in the entity's records.
- The anticipated form and content of the report to be issued, including the identity of the addressee of the report.
- Management's agreement that where any document containing interim financial information indicates that the interim financial information has been reviewed by the entity's auditor, the review report will also be included in the document.

An illustrative engagement letter is set out in Appendix 1 to this ISRE (UK and Ireland). The terms of engagement to review interim financial information can also be combined with the terms of engagement to audit the annual financial statements.

Procedures for a Review of Interim Financial Information

Understanding the Entity and its Environment, Including its Internal Control

12   The auditor should have an understanding of the entity and its environment, including its internal control, as it relates to the preparation of both annual and interim financial information, sufficient to plan and conduct the engagement so as to be able to:

(a)   Identify the types of potential material misstatement and consider the likelihood of their occurrence; and

(b)   Select the inquiries, analytical and other review procedures that will provide the auditor with a basis for reporting whether anything has come to the auditor's attention that causes the auditor to believe that the interim financial information is not prepared, in all material respects, in accordance with the applicable financial reporting framework.

13   As required by ISA (UK and Ireland) 315, *Understanding the Entity and its Environment and Assessing the Risks of Material Misstatement*, the auditor who has audited the entity's financial statements for one or more annual periods has obtained an understanding of the entity and its environment, including its internal control, as it relates to the preparation of annual financial information that was sufficient to conduct the audit. In planning a review of interim financial information, the auditor updates this understanding. The auditor also

obtains a sufficient understanding of internal control as it relates to the preparation of interim financial information as it may differ from internal control as it relates to annual financial information.

The auditor uses the understanding of the entity and its environment, including its **14** internal control, to determine the inquiries to be made and the analytical and other review procedures to be applied, and to identify the particular events, transactions or assertions to which inquiries may be directed or analytical or other review procedures applied.

The procedures performed by the auditor to update the understanding of the entity and its **15** environment, including its internal control, ordinarily include the following:

- Reading the documentation, to the extent necessary, of the preceding year's audit and reviews of prior interim period(s) of the current year and corresponding interim period(s) of the prior year, to enable the auditor to identify matters that may affect the current-period interim financial information.
- Considering any significant risks, including the risk of management override of controls, that were identified in the audit of the prior year's financial statements.
- Reading the most recent annual and comparable prior period interim financial information.
- Considering materiality with reference to the applicable financial reporting framework as it relates to interim financial information to assist in determining the nature and extent of the procedures to be performed and evaluating the effect of misstatements.
- Considering the nature of any corrected material misstatements and any identified uncorrected immaterial misstatements in the prior year's financial statements.
- Considering significant financial accounting and reporting matters that may be of continuing significance such as material weaknesses in internal control.
- Considering the results of any audit procedures performed with respect to the current year's financial statements.
- Considering the results of any internal audit performed and the subsequent actions taken by management.
- Reading management accounts and commentaries for the period.
- Considering any findings from prior periods relating to the quality and reliability of management accounts.
- Inquiring of management about the results of management's assessment of the risk that the interim financial information may be materially misstated as a result of fraud.
- Inquiring of management about the effect of changes in the entity's business activities.
- Inquiring of management about any significant changes in internal control and the potential effect of any such changes on the preparation of interim financial information.
- Inquiring of management of the process by which the interim financial information has been prepared and the reliability of the underlying accounting records to which the interim financial information is agreed or reconciled.

The auditor determines the nature of the review procedures, if any, to be performed for **16** components and, where applicable, communicates these matters to other auditors involved in the review. Factors to be considered include the materiality of, and risk of misstatement in, the interim financial information of components, and the auditor's understanding of the extent to which internal control over the preparation of such information is centralized or decentralized.

In order to plan and conduct a review of interim financial information, a recently **17** **appointed auditor, who has not yet performed an audit of the annual financial statements in accordance with ISAs (UK and Ireland), should obtain an understanding of the entity and its environment, including its internal control, as it relates to the preparation of both annual and interim financial information.**

18   This understanding enables the auditor to focus the inquiries made, and the analytical and other review procedures applied in performing a review of interim financial information in accordance with this ISRE (UK and Ireland). As part of obtaining this understanding, the auditor ordinarily makes inquiries of the predecessor auditor and, where practicable, reviews the predecessor auditor's documentation for the preceding annual audit, and for any prior interim periods in the current year that have been reviewed by the predecessor auditor. In doing so, the auditor considers the nature of any corrected misstatements, and any uncorrected misstatements aggregated by the predecessor auditor, any significant risks, including the risk of management override of controls, and significant accounting and any reporting matters that may be of continuing significance, such as material weaknesses in internal control.

Inquiries, Analytical and Other Review Procedures

19   **The auditor should make inquiries, primarily of persons responsible for financial and accounting matters, and perform analytical and other review procedures to enable the auditor to conclude whether, on the basis of the procedures performed, anything has come to the auditor's attention that causes the auditor to believe that the interim financial information is not prepared, in all material respects, in accordance with the applicable financial reporting framework.**

20   A review ordinarily does not require tests of the accounting records through inspection, observation or confirmation. Procedures for performing a review of interim financial information are ordinarily limited to making inquiries, primarily of persons responsible for financial and accounting matters, and applying analytical and other review procedures, rather than corroborating information obtained concerning significant accounting matters relating to the interim financial information. The auditor's understanding of the entity and its environment, including its internal control, the results of the risk assessments relating to the preceding audit and the auditor's consideration of materiality as it relates to the interim financial information, affects the nature and extent of the inquiries made, and analytical and other review procedures applied.

21   The auditor ordinarily performs the following procedures:

- Reading the minutes of the meetings of shareholders, those charged with governance, and other appropriate committees to identify matters that may affect the interim financial information, and inquiring about matters dealt with at meetings for which minutes are not available that may affect the interim financial information.
- Considering the effect, if any, of matters giving rise to a modification of the audit or review report, accounting adjustments or unadjusted misstatements, at the time of the previous audit or reviews.
- Communicating, where appropriate, with other auditors who are performing a review of the interim financial information of the reporting entity's significant components.
- Inquiring of members of management responsible for financial and accounting matters, and others as appropriate about the following:
  - Whether the interim financial information has been prepared and presented in accordance with the applicable financial reporting framework.
  - Whether there have been any changes in accounting principles or in the methods of applying them.
  - Whether any new transactions have necessitated the application of a new accounting principle.
  - Whether the interim financial information contains any known uncorrected misstatements.

- Unusual or complex situations that may have affected the interim financial information, such as a business combination or disposal of a segment of the business.
- Significant assumptions that are relevant to the fair value measurement or disclosures and management's intention and ability to carry out specific courses of action on behalf of the entity.
- Whether related party transactions have been appropriately accounted for and disclosed in the interim financial information.
- Significant changes in commitments and contractual obligations.
- Significant changes in contingent liabilities including litigation or claims.
- Compliance with debt covenants.
- Matters about which questions have arisen in the course of applying the review procedures.
- Significant transactions occurring in the last several days of the interim period or the first several days of the next interim period.
- Knowledge of any fraud or suspected fraud affecting the entity involving:
  o Management;
  o Employees who have significant roles in internal control; or
  o Others where the fraud could have a material effect on the interim financial information.
- Knowledge of any allegations of fraud, or suspected fraud, affecting the entity's interim financial information communicated by employees, former employees, analysts, regulators, or others.
- Knowledge of any actual or possible noncompliance with laws and regulations that could have a material effect on the interim financial information.

- For group interim financial information, reviewing consolidation adjustments for consistency with the preceding annual financial statements and enquiring into large or unusual adjustments, and into adjustments made in the preceding annual financial statements but not made in the financial information in the interim report.
- Reviewing correspondence with regulators where applicable.
- Applying analytical procedures to the interim financial information designed to identify relationships and individual items that appear to be unusual and that may reflect a material misstatement in the interim financial information. Analytical procedures may include ratio analysis and statistical techniques such as trend analysis or regression analysis and may be performed manually or with the use of computer-assisted techniques. Appendix 2 to this ISRE (UK and Ireland) contains examples of analytical procedures the auditor may consider when performing a review of interim financial information.
- Reading the interim financial information, and considering whether anything has come to the auditor's attention that causes the auditor to believe that the interim financial information is not prepared, in all material respects, in accordance with the applicable financial reporting framework.

22   The auditor may perform many of the review procedures before or simultaneously with the entity's preparation of the interim financial information. For example, it may be practicable to update the understanding of the entity and its environment, including its internal control, and begin reading applicable minutes before the end of the interim period. Performing some of the review procedures earlier in the interim period also permits early identification and consideration of significant accounting matters affecting the interim financial information.

23   The auditor performing the review of interim financial information is also engaged to perform an audit of the annual financial statements of the entity. For convenience and efficiency, the auditor may decide to perform certain audit procedures concurrently with the review of interim financial information. For example, information gained from reading

the minutes of meetings of the board of directors in connection with the review of the interim financial information also may be used for the annual audit. The auditor may also decide to perform, at the time of the interim review, auditing procedures that would need to be performed for the purpose of the audit of the annual financial statements, for example, performing audit procedures on significant or unusual transactions that occurred during the period, such as business combinations, restructurings, or significant revenue transactions.

24   A review of interim financial information ordinarily does not require corroborating the inquiries about litigation or claims. It is, therefore, ordinarily not necessary to send an inquiry letter to the entity's lawyer. Direct communication with the entity's lawyer with respect to litigation or claims may, however, be appropriate if a matter comes to the auditor's attention that causes the auditor to question whether the interim financial information is not prepared, in all material respects, in accordance with the applicable financial reporting framework, and the auditor believes the entity's lawyer may have pertinent information.

25   **The auditor should obtain evidence that the interim financial information agrees or reconciles with the underlying accounting records**. The auditor may obtain evidence that the interim financial information agrees or reconciles with the underlying accounting records by tracing the interim financial information to:

(a)   The accounting records, such as the general ledger, or a consolidating schedule that agrees or reconciles with the accounting records; and

(b)   Other supporting data in the entity's records as necessary.

25-1   For a review of consolidated group interim financial information, the auditor traces the financial information of group components to the consolidation schedules and records of significant consolidation journals and adjustments. The auditor is not required to check the financial information back to the accounting records of individual group components.

26   **The auditor should inquire whether management has identified all events up to the date of the review report that may require adjustment to or disclosure in the interim financial information.** It is not necessary for the auditor to perform other procedures to identify events occurring after the date of the review report.

27   **The auditor should inquire whether management has changed its assessment of the entity's ability to continue as a going concern. When, as a result of this inquiry or other review procedures, the auditor becomes aware of events or conditions that may cast significant doubt on the entity's ability to continue as a going concern, the auditor should:**

(a)   **Inquire of management as to its plans for future actions based on its going concern assessment, the feasibility of these plans, and whether management believes that the outcome of these plans will improve the situation; and**

(b)   **Consider the adequacy of the disclosure about such matters in the interim financial information.**

27-1   The guidance in *Going concern and financial reporting – guidance for directors of listed companies registered in the UK* issued in 1994 states 'Directors cannot be expected to consider going concern as fully at the interim, but they should undertake a review of their previous work.' Paragraph 57 of that guidance also states: 'They should look at the position at the previous year-end to see whether any of the significant factors which they had identified at that time have changed in the interim to such an extent as to affect the appropriateness of the going concern assumption.'

28   Events or conditions which may cast significant doubt on the entity's ability to continue as a going concern may have existed at the date of the annual financial statements or

may be identified as a result of inquiries of management or in the course of performing other review procedures. When such events or conditions come to the auditor's attention, the auditor inquires of management as to its plans for future action, such as its plans to liquidate assets, borrow money or restructure debt, reduce or delay expenditures, or increase capital. The auditor also inquires as to the feasibility of management's plans and whether management believes that the outcome of these plans will improve the situation. However, it is not ordinarily necessary for the auditor to corroborate the feasibility of management's plans and whether the outcome of these plans will improve the situation.

When a matter comes to the auditor's attention that leads the auditor to question   29
whether a material adjustment should be made for the interim financial information to be prepared, in all material respects, in accordance with the applicable financial reporting framework, the auditor should make additional inquiries or perform other procedures to enable the auditor to express a conclusion in the review report. For example, if the auditor's review procedures lead the auditor to question whether a significant sales transaction is recorded in accordance with the applicable financial reporting framework, the auditor performs additional procedures sufficient to resolve the auditor's questions, such as discussing the terms of the transaction with senior marketing and accounting personnel, or reading the sales contract.

Comparative Interim Financial Information

When comparative interim financial information is presented, the auditor should   29-1
consider whether:

(a) The accounting policies used for the comparative financial information are consistent with those of the current period and appropriate adjustments and disclosures have been made where this is not the case; and

(b) The comparative amounts agree with the amounts and other disclosures presented in the preceding interim financial report for the corresponding period or whether appropriate disclosures and adjustments have been made where this is not the case.

Evaluation of Misstatements

The auditor should evaluate, individually and in the aggregate, whether uncorrected   30
misstatements that have come to the auditor's attention are material to the interim financial information.

A review of interim financial information, in contrast to an audit engagement, is not   31
designed to obtain reasonable assurance that the interim financial information is free from material misstatement. However, misstatements which come to the auditor's attention, including inadequate disclosures, are evaluated individually and in the aggregate to determine whether a material adjustment is required to be made to the interim financial information for it to be prepared, in all material respects, in accordance with the applicable financial reporting framework.

The auditor exercises professional judgment in evaluating the materiality of any   32
misstatements that the entity has not corrected. The auditor considers matters such as the nature, cause and amount of the misstatements, whether the misstatements originated in the preceding year or interim period of the current year, and the potential effect of the misstatements on future interim or annual periods.

The auditor may designate an amount below which misstatements need not be aggregated,   33
because the auditor expects that the aggregation of such amounts clearly would not have

a material effect on the interim financial information. In so doing, the auditor considers the fact that the determination of materiality involves quantitative as well as qualitative considerations, and that misstatements of a relatively small amount could nevertheless have a material effect on the interim financial information.

33-1   The amount designated by the auditor, below which misstatements that have come to the auditors attention need not be aggregated, is the amount below which the auditor believes misstatements are clearly trivial[1g].

Management Representations

34   **The auditor should obtain written representation from management that:**

   (a)   **It acknowledges its responsibility for the design and implementation of internal control to prevent and detect fraud and error;**

   (b)   **The interim financial information is prepared and presented in accordance with the applicable financial reporting framework;**

   (c)   **It believes the effect of those uncorrected misstatements aggregated by the auditor during the review are immaterial, both individually and in the aggregate, to the interim financial information taken as a whole. A summary of such items is included in or attached to the written representations;**

   (d)   **It has disclosed to the auditor all significant facts relating to any frauds or suspected frauds known to management that may have affected the entity;**

   (e)   **It has disclosed to the auditor the results of its assessment of the risks that the interim financial information may be materially misstated as a result of fraud;[2]**

   (f)   **It has disclosed to the auditor all known actual or possible noncompliance with laws and regulations whose effects are to be considered when preparing the interim financial information; and**

   (g)   **It has disclosed to the auditor all significant events that have occurred subsequent to the balance sheet date and through to the date of the review report that may require adjustment to or disclosure in the interim financial information.**

35   The auditor obtains additional representations as are appropriate related to matters specific to the entity's business or industry. An illustrative management representation letter is set out in Appendix 3 to this ISRE (UK and Ireland).

Auditor's Responsibility for Accompanying Information[2a]

36   **The auditor should read the other information that accompanies the interim financial information to consider whether any such information is materially inconsistent with the interim financial information.** If the auditor identifies a material inconsistency, the

---

[1g] *This is not another expression for 'immaterial'. Matters which are 'clearly trivial' will be of an wholly different (smaller) order of magnitude than the materiality thresholds used in the review, and will be matters that are clearly inconsequential, whether taken individually or in aggregate and whether judged by any quantitative and/or qualitative criteria. Further, whenever there is any uncertainty about whether one or more items are 'clearly trivial' (in accordance with this definition), the presumption should be that the matter is not 'clearly trivial'.*

[2] *Paragraph 35 of ISA (UK and Ireland) 240,* The Auditor's Responsibility to Consider Fraud in an Audit of Financial Statements *explains that the nature, extent and frequency of such an assessment vary from entity to entity and that management may make a detailed assessment on an annual basis or as part of continuous monitoring. Accordingly, this representation, insofar as it relates to the interim financial information, is tailored to the entity's specific circumstances.*

[2a] *Other information in the half-yearly financial report of a listed entity includes the interim management report and the responsibility statements required by the rules and regulations of the listing/regulatory authorities. It may also include, for example, performance summaries, prospective information and a chairman's statement.*

auditor considers whether the interim financial information or the other information needs to be amended. If an amendment is necessary in the interim financial information and management refuses to make the amendment, the auditor considers the implications for the review report. If an amendment is necessary in the other information and management refuses to make the amendment, the auditor considers including in the review report an additional paragraph describing the material inconsistency, or taking other actions, such as withholding the issuance of the review report or withdrawing from the engagement. For example, management may present alternative measures of earnings that more positively portray financial performance than the interim financial information, and such alternative measures are given excessive prominence, are not clearly defined, or not clearly reconciled to the interim financial information such that they are confusing and potentially misleading[2b].

If a matter comes to the auditor's attention that causes the auditor to believe that   37
the other information appears to include a material misstatement of fact, the auditor should discuss the matter with the entity's management. While reading the other information for the purpose of identifying material inconsistencies, an apparent material misstatement of fact may come to the auditor's attention (i.e., information, not related to matters appearing in the interim financial information, that is incorrectly stated or presented). When discussing the matter with the entity's management, the auditor considers the validity of the other information and management's responses to the auditor's inquiries, whether valid differences of judgment or opinion exist and whether to request management to consult with a qualified third party to resolve the apparent misstatement of fact. If an amendment is necessary to correct a material misstatement of fact and management refuses to make the amendment, the auditor considers taking further action as appropriate, such as notifying those charged with governance and obtaining legal advice.

Communication

When, as a result of performing the review of interim financial information, a   38
matter comes to the auditor's attention that causes the auditor to believe that it is necessary to make a material adjustment to the interim financial information for it to be prepared, in all material respects, in accordance with the applicable financial reporting framework, the auditor should communicate this matter as soon as practicable to the appropriate level of management.

When, in the auditor's judgment, management does not respond appropriately   39
within a reasonable period of time, the auditor should inform those charged with

[2b] *The APB recognises that in some circumstances the presentation of alternative performance measures and associated narrative explanations may help shareholders understand better the financial performance of a company. However, the APB is concerned that in other circumstances such alternative performance measures have the potential to be misleading and shareholders may sometimes be misinformed by the manner in which alternative performance measures are presented. The APB believes that the potential for alternative performance measures to be misleading is considerable when they are given undue and inappropriate prominence, when there is no description of the basis on which the information was produced and, where appropriate, the adjusted numbers are not reconciled to the financial information that is presented in accordance with the applicable financial reporting framework.*

The APB's concerns are shared by the UK Listing Authority (UKLA). In its September 2005 newsletter, List!, the UKLA reminded issuers that they were free to disclose additional non-GAAP numbers in their interim accounts but, where they did, the UKLA said they should make clear the basis on which the numbers are calculated in order to avoid misleading investors. The UKLA also explained that it would not expect non-GAAP figures to be given greater prominence in interim announcements than any GAAP numbers. On 3 November 2005, the Committee of European Securities Regulators (CESR) published a recommendation on the use of alternative performance measures. In the February 2006 edition of List! the UKLA indicated that in its view the CESR recommendation represents best practice for the disclosure of alternative performance measures and encouraged issuers to follow the recommendation.

governance. The communication is made as soon as practicable, either orally or in writing. The auditor's decision whether to communicate orally or in writing is affected by factors such as the nature, sensitivity and significance of the matter to be communicated and the timing of such communications. If the information is communicated orally, the auditor documents the communication.

40 **When, in the auditor's judgment, those charged with governance do not respond appropriately within a reasonable period of time, the auditor should consider:**

(a) **Whether to modify the report; or**

(b) **The possibility of withdrawing from the engagement; and**

(c) **The possibility of resigning from the appointment to audit the annual financial statements.**

41 **When, as a result of performing the review of interim financial information, a matter comes to the auditor's attention that causes the auditor to believe in the existence of fraud or noncompliance by the entity with laws and regulations the auditor should communicate the matter as soon as practicable to the appropriate level of management.** The determination of which level of management is the appropriate one is affected by the likelihood of collusion or the involvement of a member of management. The auditor also considers the need to report such matters to those charged with governance and considers the implication for the review.

42 **The auditor should communicate relevant matters of governance interest arising from the review of interim financial information to those charged with governance.** As a result of performing the review of the interim financial information, the auditor may become aware of matters that in the opinion of the auditor are both important and relevant to those charged with governance in overseeing the financial reporting and disclosure process. The auditor communicates such matters to those charged with governance.

Reporting the Nature, Extent and Results of the Review of Interim Financial Information

43 **The auditor should issue a written report that contains the following:**

(a) **An appropriate title.**

(b) **An addressee, as required by the circumstances of the engagement.**

(c) **Identification of the interim financial information reviewed, including identification of the title of each of the statements contained in the complete or condensed set of financial statements and the date and period covered by the interim financial information.**

(d) **If the interim financial information comprises a complete set of general purpose financial statements prepared in accordance with a financial reporting framework designed to achieve fair presentation, a statement that management is responsible for the preparation and fair presentation of the interim financial information in accordance with the applicable financial reporting framework.**

(e) **In other circumstances, a statement that management is responsible for the preparation and presentation of the interim financial information in accordance with the applicable financial reporting framework.**

(f) **A statement that the auditor is responsible for expressing a conclusion on the interim financial information based on the review.**

(g) **A statement that the review of the interim financial information was conducted in accordance with International Standard on Review Engagements (UK and Ireland) (ISRE (UK and Ireland)) 2410, *Review of Interim Financial Information Performed by the Independent Auditor of the Entity*, and a statement that that such a review consists of making inquiries, primarily of persons responsible for financial and accounting matters, and applying analytical and other review procedures.**

(h)   A statement that a review is substantially less in scope than an audit conducted in accordance with International Standards on Auditing (UK and Ireland) and consequently does not enable the auditor to obtain assurance that the auditor would become aware of all significant matters that might be identified in an audit and that accordingly no audit opinion is expressed.

(i)   If the interim financial information comprises a complete set of general purpose financial statements prepared in accordance with a financial reporting framework designed to achieve fair presentation, a conclusion as to whether anything has come to the auditor's attention that causes the auditor to believe that the interim financial information does not give a true and fair view, or does not present fairly, in all material respects, in accordance with the applicable financial reporting framework (including a reference to the jurisdiction or country of origin of the financial reporting framework when the financial reporting framework used is not International Financial Reporting Standards); or

(j)   In other circumstances, a conclusion as to whether anything has come to the auditor's attention that causes the auditor to believe that the interim financial information is not prepared, in all material respects, in accordance with the applicable financial reporting framework (including a reference to the jurisdiction or country of origin of the financial reporting framework when the financial reporting framework used is not International Financial Reporting Standards).

(k)   The date of the report.

(l)   The location in the country or jurisdiction where the auditor practices.

(m)   The auditor's signature.

Illustrative review reports are set out in Appendix 4 to this ISRE (UK and Ireland).

An illustrative review report for a UK or Irish Company listed in the UK or Ireland and complying with IAS 34 as adopted by the European Union is set out in Appendix 8 to this ISRE (UK and Ireland).   **43-1**

In some jurisdictions, law or regulation governing the review of interim financial information may prescribe wording for the auditor's conclusion that is different from the wording described in paragraph 43(i) or (j). Although the auditor may be obliged to use the prescribed wording, the auditor's responsibilities as described in this ISRE (UK and Ireland) for coming to the conclusion remain the same.   **44**

Date of the Review Report

The date of the review report on an entity's financial information is the date on which the auditor signs the review report. The auditor should not date the review report earlier than the date on which the financial information is approved by management and those charged with governance.   **44-1**

Departure from the Applicable Financial Reporting Framework

The auditor should express a qualified or adverse conclusion when a matter has come to the auditor's attention that causes the auditor to believe that a material adjustment should be made to the interim financial information for it to be prepared, in all material respects, in accordance with the applicable financial reporting framework.   **45**

If matters have come to the auditor's attention that cause the auditor to believe that the interim financial information is or may be materially affected by a departure from the applicable financial reporting framework, and management does not correct the interim financial information, the auditor modifies the review report. The modification describes the nature of the departure and, if practicable, states the effects on the interim financial information. If the information that the auditor believes is necessary for adequate disclosure is not included in the interim financial information, the auditor modifies the review report and, if practicable, includes the necessary information in the review report.   **46**

The modification to the review report is ordinarily accomplished by adding an explanatory paragraph to the review report, and qualifying the conclusion. Illustrative review reports with a qualified conclusion are set out in Appendix 5 to this ISRE (UK and Ireland).

47   When the effect of the departure is so material and pervasive to the interim financial information that the auditor concludes a qualified conclusion is not adequate to disclose the misleading or incomplete nature of the interim financial information, the auditor expresses an adverse conclusion. Illustrative review reports with an adverse conclusion are set out in Appendix 7 to this ISRE (UK and Ireland).

Limitation on Scope

48   A limitation on scope ordinarily prevents the auditor from completing the review.

49   **When the auditor is unable to complete the review, the auditor should communicate, in writing, to the appropriate level of management and to those charged with governance the reason why the review cannot be completed, and consider whether it is appropriate to issue a report.**

Limitation on Scope Imposed by Management

50   The auditor does not accept an engagement to review the interim financial information if the auditor's preliminary knowledge of the engagement circumstances indicates that the auditor would be unable to complete the review because there will be a limitation on the scope of the auditor's review imposed by management of the entity.

51   If, after accepting the engagement, management imposes a limitation on the scope of the review, the auditor requests the removal of that limitation. If management refuses to do so, the auditor is unable to complete the review and express a conclusion. In such cases, the auditor communicates, in writing, to the appropriate level of management and those charged with governance the reason why the review cannot be completed. Nevertheless, if a matter comes to the auditor's attention that causes the auditor to believe that a material adjustment to the interim financial information is necessary for it to be prepared, in all material respects, in accordance with the applicable financial reporting framework, the auditor communicates such matters in accordance with the guidance in paragraphs 38-40.

52   The auditor also considers the legal and regulatory responsibilities, including whether there is a requirement for the auditor to issue a report. If there is such a requirement, the auditor disclaims a conclusion, and provides in the review report the reason why the review cannot be completed. However, if a matter comes to the auditor's attention that causes the auditor to believe that a material adjustment to the interim financial information is necessary for it to be prepared, in all material respects, in accordance with the applicable financial reporting framework, the auditor also communicates such a matter in the report.

Other Limitations on Scope

53   A limitation on scope may occur due to circumstances other than a limitation on scope imposed by management. In such circumstances, the auditor is ordinarily unable to complete the review and express a conclusion and is guided by paragraphs 51-52. There may be, however, some rare circumstances where the limitation on the scope of the auditor's work is clearly confined to one or more specific matters that, while material, are not in the auditor's judgment pervasive to the interim financial information. In such circumstances, the auditor modifies the review report by indicating that, except for the matter which is described in an explanatory paragraph to the review report, the review was conducted in accordance with this ISRE (UK and Ireland), and by qualifying the conclusion. Illustrative

review reports with a qualified conclusion are set out in Appendix 6 to this ISRE (UK and Ireland).

The auditor may have expressed a qualified opinion on the audit of the latest annual financial statements because of a limitation on the scope of that audit. The auditor considers whether that limitation on scope still exists and, if so, the implications for the review report. **54**

Going Concern and Significant Uncertainties

In certain circumstances, an emphasis of matter paragraph may be added to a review report, without affecting the auditor's conclusion, to highlight a matter that is included in a note to the interim financial information that more extensively discusses the matter. The paragraph would preferably be included after the conclusion paragraph and ordinarily refers to the fact that the conclusion is not qualified in this respect. **55**

If adequate disclosure is made in the interim financial information, the auditor should add an emphasis of matter paragraph to the review report to highlight a material uncertainty relating to an event or condition that may cast significant doubt on the entity's ability to continue as a going concern. **56**

The auditor may have modified a prior audit or review report by adding an emphasis of matter paragraph to highlight a material uncertainty relating to an event or condition that may cast significant doubt on the entity's ability to continue as a going concern. If the material uncertainty still exists and adequate disclosure is made in the interim financial information, the auditor modifies the review report on the current interim financial information by adding a paragraph to highlight the continued material uncertainty. **57**

If, as a result of inquiries or other review procedures, a material uncertainty relating to an event or condition comes to the auditor's attention that may cast significant doubt on the entity's ability to continue as a going concern, and adequate disclosure is made in the interim financial information the auditor modifies the review report by adding an emphasis of matter paragraph. **58**

If a material uncertainty that casts significant doubt about the entity's ability to continue as a going concern is not adequately disclosed in the interim financial information, the auditor should express a qualified or adverse conclusion, as appropriate. The report should include specific reference to the fact that there is such a material uncertainty. **59**

The auditor should consider modifying the review report by adding a paragraph to highlight a significant uncertainty (other than a going concern problem) that came to the auditor's attention, the resolution of which is dependent upon future events and which may affect the interim financial information. **60**

Requests to Discontinue an Interim Review Engagement

There may be rare circumstances in which the auditor indicates in advance to those charged with governance that the review report may be modified for one or more of the reasons set out in paragraphs 45 to 60 above. In these cases those charged with governance may choose to request the auditor to discontinue the review engagement rather than include a modified review report with the interim financial information. **60-1**

The auditor informs the audit committee, where one exists, of this situation as soon as practicable. If information is communicated orally, the auditor subsequently documents **60-2** the communication as appropriate. For a listed entity, if, in the auditor's judgment, the entity does not take appropriate action to address the auditor's concerns regarding the financial information to be published, the auditor considers requesting those charged with governance to discuss the matter with the entity's brokers, including whether the matter should be reported to the relevant regulatory authority. The auditor also evaluates whether to resign as the entity's auditor and include the auditor's reasons for resigning in a statement of circumstances as required by the Companies Act. The auditor may wish to take legal advice when considering resignation.

Other Considerations

61   The terms of the engagement include management's agreement that where any document containing interim financial information indicates that such information has been reviewed by the entity's auditor, the review report will also be included in the document. If management has not included the review report in the document, the auditor considers seeking legal advice to assist in determining the appropriate course of action in the circumstances.

62   If the auditor has issued a modified review report and management issues the interim financial information without including the modified review report in the document containing the interim financial information, the auditor considers seeking legal advice to assist in determining the appropriate course of action in the circumstances, and the possibility of resigning from the appointment to audit the annual financial statements.

63   Interim financial information consisting of a condensed set of financial statements does not necessarily include all the information that would be included in a complete set of financial statements, but may rather present an explanation of the events and changes that are significant to an understanding of the changes in the financial position and performance of the entity since the annual reporting date. This is because it is presumed that the users of the interim financial information will have access to the latest audited financial statements, such as is the case with listed entities. In other circumstances, the auditor discusses with management the need for such interim financial information to include a statement that it is to be read in conjunction with the latest audited financial statements. In the absence of such a statement, the auditor considers whether, without a reference to the latest audited financial statements, the interim financial information is misleading in the circumstances, and the implications for the review report.

Documentation

64   **The auditor should prepare review documentation that is sufficient and appropriate to provide a basis for the auditor's conclusion and to provide evidence that the review was performed in accordance with this ISRE (UK and Ireland) and applicable legal and regulatory requirements.** The documentation enables an experienced auditor having no previous connection with the engagement to understand the nature, timing and extent of the inquiries made, and analytical and other review procedures applied, information obtained, and any significant matters considered during the performance of the review, including the disposition of such matters.

Effective Date

65   This ISRE (UK and Ireland) is effective for reviews of interim financial information for periods ending on or after 20 September 2007. Early adoption is permitted.

Public Sector Perspective

Paragraph 10 requires that the auditor and the client agree on the terms of engagement. **1**
Paragraph 11 explains that an engagement letter helps to avoid misunderstandings regarding the nature of the engagement and, in particular, the objective and scope of the review, management's responsibilities, the extent of the auditor's responsibilities, the assurance obtained, and the nature and form of the report. Law or regulation governing review engagements in the public sector ordinarily mandates the appointment of the auditor. Consequently, engagement letters may not be a widespread practice in the public sector. Nevertheless, an engagement letter setting out the matters referred to in paragraph 11 may be useful to both the public sector auditor and the client. Public sector auditors, therefore, consider agreeing with the client the terms of a review engagement by way of an engagement letter.

In the public sector, the auditor's statutory audit obligation may extend to other work, **2**
such as a review of interim financial information. Where this is the case, the public sector auditor cannot avoid such an obligation and, consequently, may not be in a position not to accept (see paragraph 50) or to withdraw from a review engagement (see paragraphs 36 and 40(b)). The public sector auditor also may not be in the position to resign from the appointment to audit the annual financial statements (see paragraphs 40(c)) and 62).

Paragraph 41 discusses the auditor's responsibility when a matter comes to the auditor's **3**
attention that causes the auditor to believe in the existence of fraud or noncompliance by the entity with laws and regulations. In the public sector, the auditor may be subject to statutory or other regulatory requirements to report such a matter to regulatory or other public authorities.

Appendix 1

Example of an Engagement Letter for a Review of Interim Financial Information

The following letter is to be used as a guide in conjunction with the consideration outlined in paragraph 10 of this ISRE (UK and Ireland) and will need to be adapted according to individual requirements and circumstances.

For an engagement to review interim financial information prepared by a listed company in the UK or Ireland, the letter would ordinarily include paragraphs such as:

'As directors of XYZ PLC you are responsible under the [Companies Act 1985] [Companies Act 1990] for keeping proper accounting records. You are also responsible for presenting the half-yearly financial report in accordance with [International Accounting Standard 34, 'Interim Financial Reporting,' as adopted by the European Union] [the Accounting Standards Board Statement 'Half-Yearly Financial Reports'] and the requirements of the [Disclosure and Transparency Rules of the Financial Services Authority] [Transparency (Directive 2004/109/EC) Regulations 2007 and the Transparency Rules of the Financial Regulator].' [*The second sentence identifies the applicable financial reporting framework for the entity and should be amended as necessary.*]

'For the purpose of our review you will make available to us all of the company's accounting records and all other related information, including minutes of directors' shareholders', and audit committee meetings and of all relevant management meetings, that we consider necessary.'

To the Board of Directors (or the appropriate representative of senior management)

We are providing this letter to confirm our understanding of the terms and objectives of our engagement to review the entity's interim balance sheet as at June 30, 20X1 and the related statements of income, changes in equity and cash flows for the six-month period then ended.

Our review will be conducted in accordance with International Standard on Review Engagements (UK and Ireland) 2410, 'Review of Interim Financial Information Performed by the Independent Auditor of the Entity' issued by the Auditing Practices Board with the objective of providing us with a basis for reporting whether anything has come to our attention that causes us to believe that the interim financial information is not prepared, in all material respects, in accordance with the [indicate applicable financial reporting framework, including a reference to the jurisdiction or country of origin of the financial reporting when the financial reporting framework used is not International Financial Reporting Standards]. Such a review consists of making inquiries, primarily of persons responsible for financial and accounting matters, and applying analytical and other review procedures and does not, ordinarily, require corroboration of the information obtained. The scope of a review of interim financial information is substantially less than the scope of an audit conducted in accordance with International Standards on Auditing (UK and Ireland) whose objective is the expression of an opinion regarding the financial statements and, accordingly, we shall express no such opinion.

We expect to report on the interim financial information as follows:

[Include text of sample report]

Responsibility for the interim financial information, including adequate disclosure, is that of management of the entity. This includes designing, implementing and maintaining internal control relevant to the preparation and presentation of interim financial information that is free from material misstatement, whether due to fraud or error; selecting and applying appropriate accounting policies; and making accounting estimates that are reasonable in the circumstances. As part of our review, we will request written representations from management concerning assertions made in connection with the review. We will also request that where any document containing interim financial information indicates that the interim financial information has been reviewed, our report will also be included in the document.

A review of interim financial information does not provide assurance that we will become aware of all significant matters that might be identified in an audit. Further, our engagement cannot be relied upon to disclose whether fraud or errors, or illegal acts exist. However, we will inform you of any material matters that come to our attention.

We look forward to full cooperation with your staff ~~and we trust that they will make available to us whatever records, documentation and other information are requested in connection with our review.~~[2c]

[Insert additional information here regarding fee arrangements and billings, as appropriate.]

This letter will be effective for future years unless it is terminated, amended or superseded (if applicable).

[2c] *Rendered unnecessary by the alternative text presented in the shaded note immediately before this example letter.*

Please sign and return the attached copy of this letter to indicate that it is in accordance with your understanding of the arrangements for our review of the financial statements.

Acknowledged on behalf of ABC Entity by

(signed)

Name and Title

Date

Appendix 2

Analytical Procedures the Auditor may Consider When Performing a Review of Interim Financial Information

Examples of analytical procedures the auditor may consider when performing a review of interim financial information include the following:

- Comparing the interim financial information with the interim financial information of the immediately preceding interim period, with the interim financial information of the corresponding interim period of the preceding financial year, with the interim financial information that was expected by management for the current period, and with the most recent audited annual financial statements.
- Comparing current interim financial information with anticipated results, such as budgets or forecasts (for example, comparing tax balances and the relationship between the provision for income taxes to pretax income in the current interim financial information with corresponding information in (a) budgets, using expected rates, and (b) financial information for prior periods).
- Comparing current interim financial information with relevant non-financial information.
- Comparing the recorded amounts, or ratios developed from recorded amounts, to expectations developed by the auditor. The auditor develops such expectations by identifying and applying relationships that are reasonably expected to exist based on the auditor's understanding of the entity and of the industry in which the entity operates.
- Comparing ratios and indicators for the current interim period with those of entities in the same industry.
- Comparing relationships among elements in the current interim financial information with corresponding relationships in the interim financial information of prior periods, for example, expense by type as a percentage of sales, assets by type as a percentage of total assets, and percentage of change in sales to percentage of change in receivables.
- Comparing disaggregated data. The following are examples of how data may be disaggregated:
  - By period, for example, revenue or expense items disaggregated into quarterly, monthly, or weekly amounts.
  - By product line or source of revenue.
  - By location, for example, by component.
  - By attributes of the transaction, for example, revenue generated by designers, architects, or craftsmen.
  - By several attributes of the transaction, for example, sales by product and month.

Appendix 3

Example of a Management Representation Letter

The following letter is not intended to be a standard letter. Representations by management will vary from entity to entity and from one interim period to the next.

(Entity Letterhead)

(To Auditor)   (Date)

Opening paragraphs if interim financial information comprises condensed financial statements:

This representation letter is provided in connection with your review of the condensed balance sheet of ABC Entity as of March 31, 20X1 and the related condensed statements of income, changes in equity and cash flows for the three-month period then ended for the purposes of expressing a conclusion whether anything has come to your attention that causes you to believe that the interim financial information is not prepared, in all material respects, in accordance with [indicate applicable financial reporting framework, including a reference to the jurisdiction or country of origin of the financial reporting framework when the financial reporting framework used is not International Financial Reporting Standards].

We acknowledge our responsibility for the preparation and presentation of the interim financial information in accordance with [indicate applicable financial reporting framework].

Opening paragraphs if interim financial information comprises a complete set of general purpose financial statements prepared in accordance with a financial reporting framework designed to achieve fair presentation

This representation letter is provided in connection with your review of the balance sheet of ABC Entity as of March 31, 20X1 and the related statements of income, changes in equity and cash flows for the three-month period then ended and a summary of the significant accounting policies and other explanatory notes for the purposes of expressing a conclusion whether anything has come to your attention that causes you to believe that the interim financial information does not give a true and fair view of *(or 'does not present fairly, in all material respects,')* the financial position of ABC Entity as at March 31, 20X1, and of its financial performance and its cash flows in accordance with [indicate applicable financial reporting framework, including a reference to the jurisdiction or country of origin of the financial reporting framework when the financial reporting framework used is not International Financial Reporting Standards].

We acknowledge our responsibility for the fair presentation of the interim financial information in accordance with [indicate applicable financial reporting framework].

We confirm, to the best of our knowledge and belief, the following representations:

- The interim financial information referred to above has been prepared and presented in accordance with [indicate applicable financial reporting framework].
- We have made available to you all books of account and supporting documentation, and all minutes of meetings of shareholders and the board of directors (namely those held on [insert applicable dates]).

- There are no material transactions that have not been properly recorded in the accounting records underlying the interim financial information.
- There has been no known actual or possible noncompliance with laws and regulations that could have a material effect on the interim financial information in the event of noncompliance.
- We acknowledge responsibility for the design and implementation of internal control to prevent and detect fraud and error.
- We have disclosed to you all significant facts relating to any known frauds or suspected frauds that may have affected the entity.
- We have disclosed to you the results of our assessment of the risk that the interim financial information may be materially misstated as the result of fraud.
- We believe the effects of uncorrected misstatements summarized in the accompanying schedule are immaterial, both individually and in the aggregate, to the interim financial information taken as a whole.
- We confirm the completeness of the information provided to you regarding the identification of related parties.
- The following have been properly recorded and, when appropriate, adequately disclosed in the interim financial information:

  - Related party transactions, including sales, purchases, loans, transfers, leasing arrangements and guarantees, and amounts receivable from or payable to related parties;
  - Guarantees, whether written or oral, under which the entity is contingently liable; and
  - Agreements and options to buy back assets previously sold.

- The presentation and disclosure of the fair value measurements of assets and liabilities are in accordance with [indicate applicable financial reporting framework]. The assumptions used reflect our intent and ability to carry specific courses of action on behalf of the entity, where relevant to the fair value measurements or disclosure.
- We have no plans or intentions that may materially affect the carrying value or classification of assets and liabilities reflected in the interim financial information.
- We have no plans to abandon lines of product or other plans or intentions that will result in any excess or obsolete inventory, and no inventory is stated at an amount in excess of realizable value.
- The entity has satisfactory title to all assets and there are no liens or encumbrances on the entity's assets.
- We have recorded or disclosed, as appropriate, all liabilities, both actual and contingent.
- [Add any additional representations related to new accounting standards that are being implemented for the first time and consider any additional representations required by a new International Standard on Auditing (UK and Ireland) that are relevant to interim financial information.]

To the best of our knowledge and belief, no events have occurred subsequent to the balance sheet date and through the date of this letter that may require adjustment to or disclosure in the aforementioned interim financial information.

_____

(Senior Executive Officer)

_____

(Senior Financial Officer)

Appendix 4

Examples of Review Reports on Interim Financial Information

An example review report for a UK or Irish company listed in the UK or Ireland is set out in Appendix 8.

Complete set of General Purpose Financial Statements prepared in accordance with a Financial Reporting Framework designed to achieve fair presentation (see paragraph 43(i))

Report on review of interim financial information

(Appropriate addressee)

Introduction

We have reviewed the accompanying balance sheet of ABC Entity as of March 31, 20X1 and the related statements of income, changes in equity and cash flows for the threemonth period then ended, and a summary of significant accounting policies and other explanatory notes.[3] *Management is responsible for the preparation and fair presentation of this interim financial information in accordance with [indicate applicable financial reporting framework]. Our responsibility is to express a conclusion on this interim financial information based on our review.*

Scope of review

We conducted our review in accordance with International Standard on Review Engagements 2410, 'Review of Interim Financial Information Performed by the Independent Auditor of the Entity.' A review of interim financial information consists of making inquiries, primarily of persons responsible for financial and accounting matters, and applying analytical and other review procedures. A review is substantially less in scope than an audit conducted in accordance with International Standards on Auditing and consequently does not enable us to obtain assurance that we would become aware of all significant matters that might be identified in an audit. Accordingly, we do not express an audit opinion.

Conclusion

Based on our review, nothing has come to our attention that causes us to believe that the accompanying interim financial information does not give a true and fair view of (or 'does not present fairly, in all material respects,') the financial position of the entity as at March 31, 20X1, and of its financial performance and its cash flows for the threemonth period then ended in accordance with [applicable financial reporting framework, including a reference to the jurisdiction or country of origin of the financial reporting framework when the financial reporting framework used is not International Financial Reporting Standards].

AUDITOR

Date

Address

---

[3] The auditor may wish to specify the regulatory authority or equivalent with whom the interim financial information is filed.

Other Interim Financial Information (see paragraph 43(j))

Report on Review of Interim Financial Information

(Appropriate addressee)

Introduction

We have reviewed the accompanying [condensed] balance sheet of ABC Entity as of March 31, 20X1 and the related [condensed] statements of income, changes in equity and cash flows for the three-month period then ended.[4] Management is responsible for the preparation and presentation of this interim financial information in accordance with [indicate applicable financial reporting framework]. Our responsibility is to express a conclusion on this interim financial information based on our review.

Scope of review

We conducted our review in accordance with International Standard on Review Engagements 2410, 'Review of Interim Financial Information Performed by the Independent Auditor of the Entity.' A review of interim financial information consists of making inquiries, primarily of persons responsible for financial and accounting matters, and applying analytical and other review procedures. A review is substantially less in scope than an audit conducted in accordance with International Standards on Auditing and consequently does not enable us to obtain assurance that we would become aware of all significant matters that might be identified in an audit. Accordingly, we do not express an audit opinion.

Conclusion

Based on our review, nothing has come to our attention that causes us to believe that the accompanying interim financial information is not prepared, in all material respects, in accordance with [applicable financial reporting framework, including a reference to the jurisdiction or country of origin of the financial reporting framework when the financial reporting framework used is not International Financial Reporting Standards].

AUDITOR

Date

Address

---

[4] The auditor may wish to specify the regulatory authority or equivalent with whom the interim financial information is filed.

Appendix 5

Examples of Review Reports with a Qualified Conclusion for a Departure from the Applicable Financial Reporting Framework

An example unqualified review report for a UK or Irish company listed in the UK or Ireland is set out in Appendix 8 and can be tailored to give a report with a qualified conclusion when appropriate.

Complete set of General Purpose Financial Statements prepared in accordance with a Financial Reporting Framework designed to achieve fair presentation (see paragraph 43(i))

Report on review of interim financial information

(Appropriate addressee)

Introduction

We have reviewed the accompanying balance sheet of ABC Entity as of March 31, 20X1 and the related statements of income, changes in equity and cash flows for the three-month period then ended, and a summary of significant accounting policies and other explanatory notes.[5] Management is responsible for the preparation and fair presentation of this interim financial information in accordance with [indicate applicable financial reporting framework]. Our responsibility is to express a conclusion on this interim financial information based on our review.

Scope of review

We conducted our review in accordance with International Standard on Review Engagements 2410, 'Review of Interim Financial Information Performed by the Independent Auditor of the Entity.' A review of interim financial information consists of making inquiries, primarily of persons responsible for financial and accounting matters, and applying analytical and other review procedures. A review is substantially less in scope than an audit conducted in accordance with International Standards on Auditing and consequently does not enable us to obtain assurance that we would become aware of all significant matters that might be identified in an audit. Accordingly, we do not express an audit opinion.

Basis for qualified conclusion

Based on information provided to us by management, ABC Entity has excluded from property and long-term debt certain lease obligations that we believe should be capitalized to conform with [indicate applicable financial reporting framework]. This information indicates that if these lease obligations were capitalized at March 31, 20X1, property would be increased by $_____, long-term debt by $_____, and net income and earnings per share would be increased (decreased) by $_____, $_____, $_____, and $_____, respectively for the three-month period then ended.

---

[5] The auditor may wish to specify the regulatory authority or equivalent with whom the interim financial information is filed.

Qualified conclusion

Based on our review, with the exception of the matter described in the preceding paragraph, nothing has come to our attention that causes us to believe that the accompanying interim financial information does not give a true and fair view of (or 'does not present fairly, in all material respects,'*) the financial position of the entity as at March 31, 20X1, and of its financial performance and its cash flows for the threemonth period then ended in accordance with [indicate applicable financial reporting framework, including the reference to the jurisdiction or country of origin of the financial reporting framework when the financial reporting framework used is not International Financial Reporting Standards].*

AUDITOR

Date

Address

Other interim financial information (see paragraph 43(j))

Report on Review of Interim Financial Information

(Appropriate addressee)

Introduction

We have reviewed the accompanying [condensed] balance sheet of ABC Entity as of March 31, 20X1 and the related [condensed] statements of income, changes in equity and cash flows for the three-month period then ended.[6] Management is responsible for the preparation and presentation of this interim financial information in accordance with [indicate applicable financial reporting framework]. Our responsibility is to express a conclusion on this interim financial information based on our review.

Scope of review

We conducted our review in accordance with International Standard on Review Engagements 2410, 'Review of Interim Financial Information Performed by the Independent Auditor of the Entity.' A review of interim financial information consists of making inquiries, primarily of persons responsible for financial and accounting matters, and applying analytical and other review procedures. A review is substantially less in scope than an audit conducted in accordance with International Standards on Auditing and consequently does not enable us to obtain assurance that we would become aware of all significant matters that might be identified in an audit. Accordingly, we do not express an audit opinion.

Basis for qualified conclusion

Based on information provided to us by management, ABC Entity has excluded from property and long-term debt certain lease obligations that we believe should be capitalized to conform with [indicate applicable financial reporting framework]. This information indicates that if these lease obligations were capitalized at March 31, 20X1, property would be increased by $_____, long-term debt by $_____, and net income and earnings

---

[6] The auditor may wish to specify the regulatory authority or equivalent with whom the interim financial information is filed.

per share would be increased (decreased) by $_____, $_____, $_____, and $_____, respectively for the three-month period then ended.

Qualified conclusion

Based on our review, with the exception of the matter described in the preceding paragraph, nothing has come to our attention that causes us to believe that the accompanying interim financial information is not prepared, in all material respects, in accordance with [indicate applicable financial reporting framework, including a reference to the jurisdiction or country of origin of the financial reporting framework when the financial reporting framework used is not International Financial Reporting Standards].

AUDITOR

Date

Address

Appendix 6

Examples of Review Reports with a Qualified Conclusion for a Limitation on Scope Not Imposed By Management

An example unqualified review report for a UK or Irish company listed in the UK or Ireland is set out in Appendix 8 and can be tailored to give a report with a qualified conclusion when appropriate.

Complete set of General Purpose Financial Statements prepared in accordance with a Financial Reporting Framework designed to achieve fair presentation (see paragraph 43(i))

Report on Review of Interim Financial Information

(Appropriate addressee)

Introduction

We have reviewed the accompanying balance sheet of ABC Entity as of March 31, 20X1 and the related statements of income, changes in equity and cash flows for the three-month period then ended, and a summary of significant accounting policies and other explanatory notes.[7] Management is responsible for the preparation and fair presentation of this interim financial information in accordance with [indicate applicable financial reporting framework]. Our responsibility is to express a conclusion on this interim financial information based on our review.

Scope of review

Except as explained in the following paragraph, we conducted our review in accordance with International Standard on Review Engagements 2410, 'Review of Interim Financial Information Performed by the Independent Auditor of the Entity.' A review of interim financial information consists of making inquiries, primarily of persons responsible for

---

[7] The auditor may wish to specify the regulatory authority or equivalent with whom the interim financial information is filed.

financial and accounting matters, and applying analytical and other review procedures. A review is substantially less in scope than an audit conducted in accordance with International Standards on Auditing and consequently does not enable us to obtain assurance that we would become aware of all significant matters that might be identified in an audit. Accordingly, we do not express an audit opinion.

Basis for qualified conclusion

As a result of a fire in a branch office on (date) that destroyed its accounts receivable records, we were unable to complete our review of accounts receivable totaling $_____ included in the interim financial information. The entity is in the process of reconstructing these records and is uncertain as to whether these records will support the amount shown above and the related allowance for uncollectible accounts. Had we been able to complete our review of accounts receivable, matters might have come to our attention indicating that adjustments might be necessary to the interim financial information.

Qualified conclusion

Except for the adjustments to the interim financial information that we might have become aware of had it not been for the situation described above, based on our review, nothing has come to our attention that causes us to believe that the accompanying interim financial information does not give a true and fair view of (or 'does not present fairly, in all material respects,') the financial position of the entity as at March 31, 20X1, and of its financial performance and its cash flows for the three-month period then ended in accordance with [indicate applicable financial reporting framework, including a reference to the jurisdiction or country of origin of the financial reporting framework when the financial reporting framework used is not International Financial Reporting Standards].

AUDITOR

Date

Address

Other Interim Financial Information (see paragraph 43(j))

Report on Review of Interim Financial Information

(Appropriate addressee)

Introduction

We have reviewed the accompanying [condensed] balance sheet of ABC Entity as of March 31, 20X1 and the related [condensed] statements of income, changes in equity and cash flows for the three-month period then ended.[8] Management is responsible for the preparation and presentation of this interim financial information in accordance with [indicate applicable financial reporting framework]. Our responsibility is to express a conclusion on this interim financial information based on our review.

---

[8] The auditor may wish to specify the regulatory authority or equivalent with whom the interim financial information is filed.

Scope of review

Except as explained in the following paragraph, we conducted our review in accordance with International Standards on Review Engagements 2410, 'Review of Interim Financial Information Performed by the Auditor of the Entity.' A review of interim financial information consists of making inquiries, primarily of persons responsible for financial and accounting matters, and applying analytical and other review procedures. A review is substantially less in scope than an audit conducted in accordance with International Standards on Auditing and consequently does not enable us to obtain assurance that we would become aware of all significant matters that might be identified in an audit. Accordingly, we do not express an audit opinion.

Basis for qualified conclusion

As a result of a fire in a branch office on (date) that destroyed its accounts receivable records, we were unable to complete our review of accounts receivable totaling $_____ included in the interim financial information. The entity is in the process of reconstructing these records and is uncertain as to whether these records will support the amount shown above and the related allowance for uncollectible accounts. Had we been able to complete our review of accounts receivable, matters might have come to our attention indicating that adjustments might be necessary to the interim financial information.

Qualified conclusion

Except for the adjustments to the interim financial information that we might have become aware of had it not been for the situation described above, based on our review, nothing has come to our attention that causes us to believe that the accompanying interim financial information is not prepared, in all material respects, in accordance with [indicate applicable financial reporting framework, including a reference to the jurisdiction or country of origin of the financial reporting framework when the financial reporting framework used is not International Financial Reporting Standards].

AUDITOR

Date

Address

Appendix 7

Examples of Review Reports with an Adverse Conclusion for a Departure from the Applicable Financial Reporting Framework

An example unqualified review report for a UK or Irish company listed in the UK or Ireland is set out in Appendix 8 and can be tailored to give a report with an adverse conclusion when appropriate.

Complete set of General Purpose Financial Statements prepared in accordance with a Financial Reporting Framework designed to achieve fair presentation (see paragraph 43(i))

Report on Review of Interim Financial Information

(Appropriate addressee)

Introduction

We have reviewed the accompanying balance sheet of ABC Entity as of March 31, 20X1 and the related statements of income, changes in equity and cash flows for the three-month period then ended, and a summary of significant accounting policies and other explanatory notes.[9] Management is responsible for the preparation and fair presentation of this interim financial information in accordance with [indicate applicable financial reporting framework]. Our responsibility is to express a conclusion on this interim financial information based on our review.

Scope of review

We conducted our review in accordance with International Standard on Review Engagements 2410, 'Review of Interim Financial Information Performed by the Auditor of the Entity.' A review of interim financial information consists of making inquiries, primarily of persons responsible for financial and accounting matters, and applying analytical and other review procedures. A review is substantially less in scope than an audit conducted in accordance with International Standards on Auditing and consequently does not enable us to obtain assurance that we would become aware of all significant matters that might be identified in an audit. Accordingly, we do not express an audit opinion.

Basis for adverse conclusion

Commencing this period, management of the entity ceased to consolidate the financial statements of its subsidiary companies since management considers consolidation to be inappropriate because of the existence of new substantial non-controlling interests. This is not in accordance with [indicate applicable financial reporting framework, including a reference to the jurisdiction or country of origin of the financial reporting framework when the financial reporting framework used is not International Financial Reporting Standards]. Had consolidated financial statements been prepared, virtually every account in the interim financial information would have been materially different.

Adverse conclusion

Our review indicates that, because the entity's investment in subsidiary companies is not accounted for on a consolidated basis, as described in the preceding paragraph, this interim financial information does not give a true and fair view of (or 'does not present fairly, in all material respects,') the financial position of the entity as at March 31, 20X1, and of its financial performance and its cash flows for the three-month period then ended in accordance with [indicate applicable financial reporting framework, including a reference to the jurisdiction or country of origin of the financial reporting framework when the financial reporting framework used is not International Financial Reporting Standards].

AUDITOR

Date

Address

---

[9] The auditor may wish to specify the regulatory authority or equivalent with whom the interim financial information is filed.

Other Interim Financial Information (see paragraph 43(j))

Report on Review of Interim Financial Information

(Appropriate addressee)

Introduction

We have reviewed the accompanying [condensed] balance sheet of ABC Entity as of March 31, 20X1 and the related [condensed] statements of income, changes in equity and cash flows for the three-month period then ended.[10] Management is responsible for the preparation and presentation of this interim financial information in accordance with [indicate applicable financial reporting framework]. Our responsibility is to express a conclusion on this interim financial information based on our review.

Scope of review

We conducted our review in accordance with International Standard on Review Engagements 2410, 'Review of Interim Financial Information Performed by the Independence Auditor of the Entity.' A review of interim financial information consists of making inquiries, primarily of persons responsible for financial and accounting matters, and applying analytical and other review procedures. A review is substantially less in scope than an audit conducted in accordance with International Standards on Auditing and consequently does not enable us to obtain assurance that we would become aware of all significant matters that might be identified in an audit. Accordingly, we do not express an audit opinion.

Basis for adverse conclusion

Commencing this period, management of the entity ceased to consolidate the financial statements of its subsidiary companies since management considers consolidation to be inappropriate because of the existence of new substantial non-controlling interests. This is not in accordance with [indicate applicable financial reporting framework, including the reference to the jurisdiction or country of origin of the financial reporting framework when the financial reporting framework used is not International Financial Reporting Standards]. Had consolidated financial statements been prepared, virtually every account in the interim financial information would have been materially different.

Adverse conclusion

Our review indicates that, because the entity's investment in subsidiary companies is not accounted for on a consolidated basis, as described in the preceding paragraph, this interim financial information is not prepared, in all material respects, in accordance with [indicate applicable financial reporting framework, including a reference to the jurisdiction or country of origin of the financial reporting framework when the financial reporting framework used is not International Financial Reporting Standards].

AUDITOR

Date

Address

---

[10] The auditor may wish to specify the regulatory authority or equivalent with whom the interim financial information is filed.

Appendix 8

Example Review Report for a UK or Irish Company Listed in the UK or Ireland Preparing a Half-Yearly Financial Report in Compliance with IAS 34 as Adopted by the European Union

INDEPENDENT REVIEW REPORT TO XYZ PLC

Introduction

We have been engaged by the company to review the condensed set of financial statements in the half-yearly financial report for the six months ended ... which comprises [specify the primary financial statements and the related explanatory notes that have been reviewed].[10a] We have read the other information contained in the halfyearly financial report and considered whether it contains any apparent misstatements or material inconsistencies with the information in the condensed set of financial statements.

Directors' responsibilities

The half-yearly financial report is the responsibility of, and has been approved by, the directors. The directors are responsible for preparing the half-yearly financial report in accordance with the [Disclosure and Transparency Rules of the United Kingdom's Financial Services Authority] [Transparency (Directive 2004/109/EC) Regulations 2007 and the Transparency Rules of the Republic of Ireland's Financial Regulator].

As disclosed in note X, the annual financial statements of the [group/company] are prepared in accordance with IFRSs as adopted by the European Union. The condensed set of financial statements included in this half-yearly financial report has been prepared in accordance with International Accounting Standard 34, 'Interim Financial Reporting,' as adopted by the European Union.

Our responsibility

Our responsibility is to express to the Company a conclusion on the condensed set of financial statements in the half-yearly financial report based on our review.

Scope of review

We conducted our review in accordance with International Standard on Review Engagements (UK and Ireland) 2410, Review of Interim Financial Information Performed by the Independent Auditor of the Entity issued by the Auditing Practices Board for use in [the United Kingdom] [Ireland]. A review of interim financial information consists of making enquiries, primarily of persons responsible for financial and accounting matters, and applying analytical and other review procedures. A review is substantially less in scope than an audit conducted in accordance with International Standards on Auditing (UK and Ireland) and consequently does not enable us to obtain assurance that we would become aware of all significant matters that might be identified in an audit. Accordingly, we do not express an audit opinion.

[10a] Review reports of entities that do not publish their half-yearly reports on a web site or publish them using 'PDF' format may continue to refer to the pages of the half-yearly report.

Conclusion

Based on our review, nothing has come to our attention that causes us to believe that the condensed set of financial statements in the half-yearly financial report for the six months ended ... is not prepared, in all material respects, in accordance with International Accounting Standard 34 as adopted by the European Union and [the Disclosure and Transparency Rules of the United Kingdom's Financial Services Authority] [the Transparency (Directive 2004/109/EC) Regulations 2007 and the Transparency Rules of the Republic of Ireland's Financial Regulator].

AUDITOR

Date

Address

Appendix 9

Summary of Particular Requirements of Half-Yearly Reports Prepared by Listed Companies in the UK and Ireland

This Appendix sets out a summary of particular requirements of the FSA's Disclosure and Transparency Rules (DTRs) applicable to half-yearly financial reports prepared by an 'issuer' whose shares or debt securities are admitted to trading and whose home state is the United Kingdom, subject to the exemptions in DTR 4.4. Equivalent requirements are included in the Irish Transparency (Directive 2004/109/EC) Regulations 2007 (specifically Regulations 6 – 8 in Part 2, subject to the exemptions in Part 3) and Transparency Rules of the Financial Regulator in the Republic of Ireland (specifically Rule 6.2). It also gives a summary of Companies Act requirements relevant to the publication of non-statutory accounts. It does not set out in full all the applicable requirements and, therefore, is not intended to provide a substitute for the auditor reading the applicable Rules, Regulations and legislation to obtain an understanding of them.

FSA Disclosure and Transparency Rules

Rule 4.2.3 requires that an issuer publish a half-yearly financial report, containing:

(1)   a condensed set of financial statements;
(2)   an interim management report; and
(3)   responsibility statements.

Rule 4.2.4 requires that if an issuer is required to prepare consolidated accounts, the condensed set of financial statements must be prepared in accordance with International Accounting Standard 34 Interim Financial Reporting. (Under the FSA's definitions of 'International Accounting Standards' this will be IAS 34 as adopted by the European Union.)

If an issuer is not required to prepare consolidated accounts, the condensed set of financial information must contain, as a minimum, the following:

(a)   a condensed balance sheet;
(b)   a condensed profit and loss account; and
(c)   explanatory notes on these accounts.

Rule 4.2.5 requires that the condensed balance sheet and condensed profit and loss account referred to in (a) and (b) above must:

- follow the same principles for recognising and measuring as when preparing annual financial reports,
- show each of the headings and subtotals included in the most recent annual financial statements of the issuer. Additional line items must be included if, as a result of their omission, the half-yearly financial statements would give a misleading view of the assets, liabilities, financial position and profit or loss of the issuer.

For issuers not required to prepare consolidated accounts the Rules also set out further specific requirements in relation to comparative information and the content of the explanatory notes.

Rule 4.2.6 requires that the accounting policies and presentation applied to the halfyearly figures must be consistent with those applied in the latest published annual accounts except where:

(1)   the accounting policies and presentation are to be changed in the subsequent annual financial statements, in which case the new accounting policies and presentation should be followed, and the changes and the reasons for the changes should be disclosed in the half-yearly report; or
(2)   the FSA otherwise agrees.

Companies may choose to have the half-yearly financial report reviewed or audited by an auditor. Rule 4.2.9 requires that 'if the half-yearly financial report has been audited or reviewed by auditors pursuant to the Auditing Practices Board guidance on Review of Interim Financial Information, the audit report or review report must be reproduced in full.'

Responsibility Statements

Rule 4.2.10 requires that for each person making a responsibility statement, the statement must confirm that to the best of his or her knowledge, inter alia:

"the condensed set of financial statements, which has been prepared in accordance with the applicable set of accounting standards, gives a true and fair view of the assets, liabilities, financial position and profit or loss of the issuer, or the undertakings included in the consolidation as a whole ..."

However, Rule 4.2.10 also provides that:

"A person making a responsibility statement will satisfy the requirement ... to confirm that the condensed set of financial statements gives a true and fair view ... by including a statement that the condensed set of financial statements have been prepared in accordance with:

(a)   IAS 34; or
(b)   for UK issuers not using IFRS, pronouncements on interim reporting issued by the Accounting Standards Board[10b]; or
(c)   for all other issuers not using IFRS, a national accounting standard relating to interim reporting,

---

[10b] *For half-yearly periods ending on or after 20 September 2007, the relevant ASB pronouncement is the Statement 'Half-Yearly Financial Reports'.*

provided always that a person making such a statement has reasonable grounds to be satisfied that the condensed set of financial statements prepared in accordance with such a standard is not misleading."

Companies Act Requirements

United Kingdom

Financial statements included in half-yearly financial reports constitute non-statutory accounts under the provisions of the Companies Act[10c] and therefore must include a statement indicating:

(a) that they are not the statutory accounts;
(b) whether statutory accounts for any relevant financial year have been delivered to the registrar of companies;
(c) whether the auditors reported on the statutory accounts for any such year; and
(d) if so, whether it was qualified or unqualified, or included an emphasis of matter, or contained a statement by the auditor required under the Companies Act[10d] (accounting records or returns inadequate or accounts or directors' remuneration report not agreeing with records and returns, or failure to obtain necessary information and explanations).

Republic of Ireland

In the Republic of Ireland, financial statements included in a half-yearly report made by a single entity constitute abbreviated accounts under section 19 of the Companies (Amendment) Act, 1986. Financial statements included in a half-yearly report made by a group constitute abbreviated group accounts under regulation 40 of the European Communities (Companies: Group Accounts) Regulations, 1992. This states that where a parent undertaking publishes abbreviated group accounts relating to any financial year, it shall also publish a statement indicating:

(a) that the abbreviated group accounts are not the group accounts, copies of which are required by law to be annexed to the annual return,
(b) whether the copies of the group accounts so required to be annexed have in fact been so annexed,
(c) whether the auditors have made a report under section 193 of the Companies Act, 1990 in respect of the group accounts which relate to any financial year with which the abbreviated group accounts purport to deal, and
(d) whether the report of the auditors contained any qualifications.

The statement required for a single entity is similar.

[10c] *Relevant references are: for the Companies Act 1985 – section 240 (the equivalent legislation in Northern Ireland is Article 243(3) of the Companies (Northern Ireland) Order, 1986); for the Companies Act 2006 – section 435 (this also applies in Northern Ireland).*

[10d] *Relevant references are: for the Companies Act 1985 – section 237(2) and (3); for the Companies Act 2006 – section 498(2) and (3).*

Part Six

*International Standards on Assurance
Engagements (ISAEs)*

International Standard on Assurance Engagements 3000 (Revised December 2013)

Assurance engagements other than audits or reviews of historical financial information

(Effective for assurance reports dated on or after December 15, 2015)

Contents

International Standard on Assurance Engagements (ISAE) 3000 (Revised), *Assurance Engagements other than Audits or Reviews of Historical Financial Information*, should be read in conjunction with the *Preface to the International Standards on Quality Control, Auditing, Review, Other Assurance and Related Services Pronouncements.*

Introduction

This International Standard on Assurance Engagements (ISAE) deals with assurance engagements other than audits or reviews of historical financial information, which are dealt with in International Standards on Auditing (ISAs) and International Standards on Review Engagements (ISREs), respectively. (Ref: Para. A21–A22)

Assurance engagements include both attestation engagements, in which a party other than the practitioner measures or evaluates the underlying subject matter against the criteria, and direct engagements, in which the practitioner measures or evaluates the underlying subject matter against the criteria. This ISAE contains requirements and application and other explanatory material specific to reasonable and limited assurance attestation engagements. This ISAE may also be applied to reasonable and limited assurance direct engagements, adapted and supplemented as necessary in the engagement circumstances.

This ISAE is premised on the basis that:

(a) The members of the engagement team and the engagement quality control reviewer (for those engagements where one has been appointed) are subject to Parts A and B of the *Code of Ethics for Professional Accountants* issued by the International Ethics Standards Board for Accountants (IESBA Code) related to assurance engagements, or other professional requirements, or requirements in law or regulation, that are at least as demanding; and (Ref: Para. A30–A34)

(b) The practitioner who is performing the engagement is a member of a firm that is subject to ISQC 1,[1] or other professional requirements, or requirements in law or regulation, regarding the firm's responsibility for its system of quality control, that are at least as demanding as ISQC 1. (Ref: Para. A61–A66)

Quality control within firms that perform assurance engagements, and compliance with ethical principles, including independence requirements, are widely recognized as being in the public interest and an integral part of high-quality assurance engagements. Professional accountants in public practice will be familiar with such requirements. If a competent practitioner other than a professional accountant in public practice chooses to represent compliance with this or other ISAEs, it is important to recognize that this ISAE includes requirements that reflect the premise in the preceding paragraph.

Scope

This ISAE covers assurance engagements other than audits or reviews of historical financial information, as described in the *International Framework for Assurance Engagements* (Assurance Framework). Where a subject-matter specific ISAE is relevant to the subject matter of a particular engagement, that ISAE applies in addition to this ISAE. (Ref: Para. A21–A22)

Not all engagements performed by practitioners are assurance engagements. Other frequently performed engagements that are not assurance engagements, as defined by paragraph 12(a) (and therefore are not covered by the ISAEs) include:

---

[1] *International Standard on Quality Control (ISQC) 1, Quality Control for Firms that Perform Audits and Reviews of Financial Statements, and Other Assurance and Related Services Engagements.*

(a) Engagements covered by International Standards on Related Services (ISRS), such as agreed-upon procedure and compilation engagements;[2]

(b) The preparation of tax returns where no assurance conclusion is expressed; and

(c) Consulting (or advisory) engagements, such as management and tax consulting. (Ref: Para. A1)

7   An assurance engagement performed under the ISAEs may be part of a larger engagement. In such circumstances, the ISAEs are relevant only to the assurance portion of the engagement.

8   The following engagements, which may be consistent with the description in paragraph 12(a), are not considered assurance engagements in terms of the ISAEs:

(a) Engagements to testify in legal proceedings regarding accounting, auditing, taxation or other matters; and

(b) Engagements that include professional opinions, views or wording from which a user may derive some assurance, if all of the following apply:

   (i) Those opinions, views or wording are merely incidental to the overall engagement;

   (ii) Any written report issued is expressly restricted for use by only the intended users specified in the report;

   (iii) Under a written understanding with the specified intended users, the engagement is not intended to be an assurance engagement; and

   (iv) The engagement is not represented as an assurance engagement in the professional accountant's report.

Effective Date

9   This ISAE is effective for assurance engagements where the assurance report is dated on or after December 15, 2015.

Objectives

10   In conducting an assurance engagement, the objectives of the practitioner are:

(a) To obtain either reasonable assurance or limited assurance, as appropriate, about whether the subject matter information is free from material misstatement;

(b) To express a conclusion regarding the outcome of the measurement or evaluation of the underlying subject matter through a written report that conveys either a reasonable assurance or a limited assurance conclusion and describes the basis for the conclusion; (Ref: Para. A2) and

(c) To communicate further as required by this ISAE and any other relevant ISAEs.

11   In all cases when reasonable assurance or limited assurance, as appropriate, cannot be obtained and a qualified conclusion in the practitioner's assurance report is insufficient in the circumstances for purposes of reporting to the intended users, this ISAE requires that the practitioner disclaim a conclusion or withdraw (or resign) from the engagement, where withdrawal is possible under applicable law or regulation.

---

[2] *ISRS 4400, Engagements to Perform Agreed-Upon Procedures Regarding Financial Information, and ISRS 4410, Compilation Engagements.*

Definitions

For purposes of this ISAE and other ISAEs, unless indicated to the contrary, the fol-   **12**
lowing terms have the meanings attributed below. (Ref: Para. A27)

(a) Assurance engagement—An engagement in which a practitioner aims to obtain
sufficient appropriate evidence in order to express a conclusion designed to
enhance the degree of confidence of the intended users other than the responsible party about the subject matter information (that is, the outcome of the
measurement or evaluation of an underlying subject matter against criteria).
Each assurance engagement is classified on two dimensions: (Ref: Para. A3)

   (i) Either a reasonable assurance engagement or a limited assurance engagement:

       a. Reasonable assurance engagement—An assurance engagement in which
           the practitioner reduces engagement risk to an acceptably low level in the
           circumstances of the engagement as the basis for the practitioner's conclu-
           sion. The practitioner's conclusion is expressed in a form that conveys the
           practitioner's opinion on the outcome of the measurement or evaluation of
           the underlying subject matter against criteria.
       b. Limited assurance engagement—An assurance engagement in which the
           practitioner reduces engagement risk to a level that is acceptable in the
           circumstances of the engagement but where that risk is greater than for a
           reasonable assurance engagement as the basis for expressing a conclusion
           in a form that conveys whether, based on the procedures performed and
           evidence obtained, a matter(s) has come to the practitioner's attention to
           cause the practitioner to believe the subject matter information is materi-
           ally misstated. The nature, timing, and extent of procedures performed in a
           limited assurance engagement is limited compared with that necessary in
           a reasonable assurance engagement but is planned to obtain a level of as-
           surance that is, in the practitioner's professional judgment, meaningful. To
           be meaningful, the level of assurance obtained by the practitioner is likely
           to enhance the intended users' confidence about the subject matter infor-
           mation to a degree that is clearly more than inconsequential. (Ref: Para.
           A3–A7)

   (ii) Either an attestation engagement or a direct engagement: (Ref: Para. A8)

       a. Attestation engagement—An assurance engagement in which a party other
           than the practitioner measures or evaluates the underlying subject matter
           against the criteria. A party other than the practitioner also often pres-
           ents the resulting subject matter information in a report or statement. In
           some cases, however, the subject matter information may be presented by
           the practitioner in the assurance report. In an attestation engagement, the
           practitioner's conclusion addresses whether the subject matter information
           is free from material misstatement. The practitioner's conclusion may be
           phrased in terms of: (Ref: Para. A178, A180)
           (i) The underlying subject matter and the applicable criteria;
           (ii) The subject matter information and the applicable criteria; or
           (iii) A statement made by the appropriate party.
       b. Direct engagement—An assurance engagement in which the practitioner
           measures or evaluates the underlying subject matter against the applicable
           criteria and the practitioner presents the resulting subject matter informa-
           tion as part of, or accompanying, the assurance report. In a direct engage-
           ment, the practitioner's conclusion addresses the reported outcome of the
           measurement or evaluation of the underlying subject matter against the cri-
           teria.

(b) Assurance skills and techniques—Those planning, evidence gathering, evidence
evaluation, communication and reporting skills and techniques demonstrated

by an assurance practitioner that are distinct from expertise in the underlying subject matter of any particular assurance engagement or its measurement or evaluation. (Ref: Para. A9)

(c) Criteria—The benchmarks used to measure or evaluate the underlying subject matter. The "applicable criteria" are the criteria used for the particular engagement. (Ref: Para. A10)

(d) Engagement circumstances—The broad context defining the particular engagement, which includes: the terms of the engagement; whether it is a reasonable assurance engagement or a limited assurance engagement, the characteristics of the underlying subject matter; the measurement or evaluation criteria; the information needs of the intended users; relevant characteristics of the responsible party, the measurer or evaluator, and the engaging party and their environment; and other matters, for example events, transactions, conditions and practices, that may have a significant effect on the engagement.

(e) Engagement partner—The partner or other person in the firm who is responsible for the engagement and its performance, and for the assurance report that is issued on behalf of the firm, and who, where required, has the appropriate authority from a professional, legal or regulatory body. "Engagement partner" should be read as referring to its public sector equivalents where relevant.

(f) Engagement risk—The risk that the practitioner expresses an inappropriate conclusion when the subject matter information is materially misstated. (Ref: Para. A11–A14)

(g) Engaging party—The party(ies) that engages the practitioner to perform the assurance engagement. (Ref: Para. A15)

(h) Engagement team—All partners and staff performing the engagement, and any individuals engaged by the firm or a network firm who perform procedures on the engagement. This excludes a practitioner's external expert engaged by the firm or a network firm.

(i) Evidence—Information used by the practitioner in arriving at the practitioner's conclusion. Evidence includes both information contained in relevant information systems, if any, and other information. For purposes of the ISAEs: (Ref: Para. A146–A152)
   (i)   Sufficiency of evidence is the measure of the quantity of evidence.
   (ii) Appropriateness of evidence is the measure of the quality of evidence.

(j) Firm—A sole practitioner, partnership or corporation or other entity of individual practitioners. "Firm" should be read as referring to its public sector equivalents where relevant.

(k) Historical financial information—Information expressed in financial terms in relation to a particular entity, derived primarily from that entity's accounting system, about economic events occurring in past time periods or about economic conditions or circumstances at points in time in the past.

(l) Internal audit function – A function of an entity that performs assurance and consulting activities designed to evaluate and improve the effectiveness of the entity's governance, risk management and internal control processes.

(m) Intended users—The individual(s) or organization(s), or group(s) thereof that the practitioner expects will use the assurance report. In some cases, there may be intended users other than those to whom the assurance report is addressed. (Ref: Para. A16–A18, A37))

(n) Measurer or evaluator—The party(ies) who measures or evaluates the underlying subject matter against the criteria. The measurer or evaluator possesses expertise in the underlying subject matter. (Ref: Para. A37, A39)

(o) Misstatement—A difference between the subject matter information and the appropriate measurement or evaluation of the underlying subject matter in accordance with the criteria. Misstatements can be intentional or unintentional, qualitative or quantitative, and include omissions.

(p) Misstatement of fact (with respect to other information)—Other information that is unrelated to matters appearing in the subject matter information or the assurance report that is incorrectly stated or presented. A material misstatement of fact may undermine the credibility of the document containing the subject matter information.

(q) Other information—Information (other than the subject matter information and the assurance report thereon) which is included, either by law, regulation or custom, in a document containing the subject matter information and the assurance report thereon.

(r) Practitioner—The individual(s) conducting the engagement (usually the engagement partner or other members of the engagement team, or, as applicable, the firm). Where this ISAE expressly intends that a requirement or responsibility be fulfilled by the engagement partner, the term "engagement partner" rather than "practitioner" is used. (Ref: Para. A37)

(s) Practitioner's expert—An individual or organization possessing expertise in a field other than assurance, whose work in that field is used by the practitioner to assist the practitioner in obtaining sufficient appropriate evidence. A practitioner's expert may be either a practitioner's internal expert (who is a partner or staff, including temporary staff, of the practitioner's firm or a network firm), or a practitioner's external expert.

(t) Professional judgment—The application of relevant training, knowledge and experience, within the context provided by assurance and ethical standards, in making informed decisions about the courses of action that are appropriate in the circumstances of the engagement.

(u) Professional skepticism—An attitude that includes a questioning mind, being alert to conditions which may indicate possible misstatement, and a critical assessment of evidence.

(v) Responsible party—The party(ies) responsible for the underlying subject matter. (Ref: Para. A37)

(w) Risk of material misstatement—The risk that the subject matter information is materially misstated prior to the engagement.

(x) Subject matter information—The outcome of the measurement or evaluation of the underlying subject matter against the criteria, i.e., the information that results from applying the criteria to the underlying subject matter. (Ref: Para. A19)

(y) Underlying subject matter—The phenomenon that is measured or evaluated by applying criteria.

For the purposes of this ISAE and other ISAEs, references to "appropriate party(ies)" should be read hereafter as "the responsible party, the measurer or evaluator, or the engaging party, as appropriate." (Ref: Para. A20, A37)   **13**

Requirements

Conduct of an Assurance Engagement in Accordance with ISAEs

Complying with Standards that are Relevant to the Engagement

The practitioner shall comply with this ISAE and any subject matter-specific ISAEs relevant to the engagement.   **14**

The practitioner shall not represent compliance with this or any other ISAE unless the practitioner has complied with the requirements of this ISAE and any other ISAE relevant to the engagement. (Ref: Para. A21–A22, A170)   **15**

Text of an ISAE

16   The practitioner shall have an understanding of the entire text of an ISAE, including its application and other explanatory material, to understand its objectives and to apply its requirements properly. (Ref: Para. A23–A28)

Complying with Relevant Requirements

17   Subject to the following paragraph, the practitioner shall comply with each requirement of this ISAE and of any relevant subject matter-specific ISAE unless, in the circumstances of the engagement the requirement is not relevant because it is conditional and the condition does not exist. Requirements that apply to only limited assurance or reasonable assurance engagements have been presented in a columnar format with the letter "L" (limited assurance) or "R" (reasonable assurance) after the paragraph number. (Ref: Para. A29)

18   In exceptional circumstances, the practitioner may judge it necessary to depart from a relevant requirement in an ISAE. In such circumstances, the practitioner shall perform alternative procedures to achieve the aim of that requirement. The need for the practitioner to depart from a relevant requirement is expected to arise only where the requirement is for a specific procedure to be performed and, in the specific circumstances of the engagement, that procedure would be ineffective in achieving the aim of the requirement.

Failure to Achieve an Objective

19   If an objective in this ISAE or a relevant subject matter-specific ISAE cannot be achieved, the practitioner shall evaluate whether this requires the practitioner to modify the practitioner's conclusion or withdraw from the engagement (where withdrawal is possible under applicable law or regulation). Failure to achieve an objective in a relevant ISAE represents a significant matter requiring documentation in accordance with paragraph 79 of this ISAE.

Ethical Requirements

20   The practitioner shall comply with Parts A and B of the IESBA Code related to assurance engagements, or other professional requirements, or requirements imposed by law or regulation, that are at least as demanding. (Ref: Para. A30–A34, A60)

Acceptance and Continuance

21   The engagement partner shall be satisfied that appropriate procedures regarding the acceptance and continuance of client relationships and assurance engagements have been followed by the firm, and shall determine that conclusions reached in this regard are appropriate.

22   The practitioner shall accept or continue an assurance engagement only when: (Ref: Para. A30–A34)

(a) The practitioner has no reason to believe that relevant ethical requirements, including independence, will not be satisfied;

(b) The practitioner is satisfied that those persons who are to perform the engagement collectively have the appropriate competence and capabilities (see also paragraph 32); and

(c) The basis upon which the engagement is to be performed has been agreed, through:
   (i) Establishing that the preconditions for an assurance engagement are present (see also paragraphs 24–26); and
   (ii) Confirming that there is a common understanding between the practitioner and the engaging party of the terms of the engagement, including the practitioner's reporting responsibilities.

If the engagement partner obtains information that would have caused the firm to decline the engagement had that information been available earlier, the engagement partner shall communicate that information promptly to the firm, so that the firm and the engagement partner can take the necessary action.   **23**

Preconditions for the Assurance Engagement

In order to establish whether the preconditions for an assurance engagement are present, the practitioner shall, on the basis of a preliminary knowledge of the engagement circumstances and discussion with the appropriate party(ies), determine whether: (Ref: Para. A35–A36)   **24**

(a) The roles and responsibilities of the appropriate parties are suitable in the circumstances; and (Ref: Para. A37–A39)
(b) The engagement exhibits all of the following characteristics:
   (i)   The underlying subject matter is appropriate; (Ref: Para. A40–A44)
   (ii) The criteria that the practitioner expects to be applied in the preparation of the subject matter information are suitable for the engagement circumstances, including that they exhibit the following characteristics: (Ref: Para. A45–A50)
      a. Relevance.
      b. Completeness.
      c. Reliability.
      d. Neutrality.
      e. Understandability.
   (iii) The criteria that the practitioner expects to be applied in the preparation of the subject matter information will be available to the intended users. (Ref: Para. A51–A52)
   (iv) The practitioner expects to be able to obtain the evidence needed to support the practitioner's conclusion; (Ref: Para. A53–A55
   (v)   The practitioner's conclusion, in the form appropriate to either a reasonable assurance engagement or a limited assurance engagement, is to be contained in a written report; and
   (vi) A rational purpose including, in the case of a limited assurance engagement, that the practitioner expects to be able to obtain a meaningful level of assurance. (Ref: Para. A56)

If the preconditions for an assurance engagement are not present, the practitioner shall discuss the matter with the engaging party. If changes cannot be made to meet the preconditions, the practitioner shall not accept the engagement as an assurance engagement unless required by law or regulation to do so. However, an engagement conducted under such circumstances does not comply with ISAEs. Accordingly, the practitioner shall not include any reference within the assurance report to the engagement having been conducted in accordance with this ISAE or any other ISAE(s).   **25**

Limitation on Scope Prior to Acceptance of the Engagement

If the engaging party imposes a limitation on the scope of the practitioner's work in the terms of a proposed assurance engagement such that the practitioner believes   **26** the limitation will result in the practitioner disclaiming a conclusion on the subject matter information, the practitioner shall not accept such an engagement as an assurance engagement, unless required by law or regulation to do so. (Ref: Para. A155(c))

Agreeing on the Terms of the Engagement

27   The practitioner shall agree the terms of the engagement with the engaging party. The agreed terms of the engagement shall be specified in sufficient detail in an engagement letter or other suitable form of written agreement, written confirmation, or in law or regulation. (Ref: Para. A57–A58)

28   On recurring engagements, the practitioner shall assess whether circumstances require the terms of the engagement to be revised and whether there is a need to remind the engaging party of the existing terms of the engagement.

Acceptance of a Change in the Terms of the Engagement

29   The practitioner shall not agree to a change in the terms of the engagement where there is no reasonable justification for doing so. If such a change is made, the practitioner shall not disregard evidence that was obtained prior to the change. (Ref: Para. A59)

Assurance Report Prescribed by Law or Regulation

30   In some cases, law or regulation of the relevant jurisdiction prescribe the layout or wording of the assurance report. In these circumstances, the practitioner shall evaluate:

(a)   Whether intended users might misunderstand the assurance conclusion; and
(b)   If so, whether additional explanation in the assurance report can mitigate possible misunderstanding.

If the practitioner concludes that additional explanation in the assurance report cannot mitigate possible misunderstanding, the practitioner shall not accept the engagement, unless required by law or regulation to do so. An engagement conducted in accordance with such law or regulation does not comply with ISAEs. Accordingly, the practitioner shall not include any reference within the assurance report to the engagement having been conducted in accordance with this ISAE or any other ISAE(s) (see also paragraph 71).

Quality Control

Characteristics of the Engagement Partner

31   The engagement partner shall:

(a)   Be a member of a firm that applies ISQC 1, or other professional requirements, or requirements in law or regulation, that are at least as demanding as ISQC 1; (Ref: Para. A60–A66)
(b)   Have competence in assurance skills and techniques developed through extensive training and practical application; and (Ref: Para. A60)
(c)   Have sufficient competence in the underlying subject matter and its measurement or evaluation to accept responsibility for the assurance conclusion. (Ref: Para. A67–A68)

Assignment of the Team

The engagement partner shall: (Ref: Para. A69)   **32**

(a) Be satisfied that those persons who are to perform the engagement collectively have the appropriate competence and capabilities to: (Ref: Para. A70–A71)
   (i) Perform the engagement in accordance with relevant standards and applicable legal and regulatory requirements; and
   (ii) Enable an assurance report that is appropriate in the circumstances to be issued.
(b) Be satisfied that the practitioner will be able to be involved in the work of:
   (i) A practitioner's expert where the work of that expert is to be used; and (Ref: Para. A70–A71)
   (ii) Another practitioner, not part of the engagement team, where the assurance work of that practitioner is to be used, (Ref: Para. A72–A73)
   to an extent that is sufficient to accept responsibility for the assurance conclusion on the subject matter information.

Responsibilities of the Engagement Partner

The engagement partner shall take responsibility for the overall quality on the   **33** engagement. This includes responsibility for:

(a) Appropriate procedures being performed regarding the acceptance and continuance of client relationships and engagements;
(b) The engagement being planned and performed (including appropriate direction and supervision) to comply with professional standards and applicable legal and regulatory requirements;
(c) Reviews being performed in accordance with the firm's review policies and procedures, and reviewing the engagement documentation on or before the date of the assurance report; (Ref: Para. A74)
(d) Appropriate engagement documentation being maintained to provide evidence of achievement of the practitioner's objectives, and that the engagement was performed in accordance with relevant ISAEs and relevant legal and regulatory requirements; and
(e) Appropriate consultation being undertaken by the engagement team on difficult or contentious matters.

Throughout the engagement, the engagement partner shall remain alert, through   **34** observation and making inquiries as necessary, for evidence of non-compliance with relevant ethical requirements by members of the engagement team. If matters come to the engagement partner's attention through the firm's system of quality control or otherwise that indicate that members of the engagement team have not complied with relevant ethical requirements, the engagement partner, in consultation with others in the firm, shall determine the appropriate action.

The engagement partner shall consider the results of the firm's monitoring process   **35** as evidenced in the latest information circulated by the firm and, if applicable, other network firms and whether deficiencies noted in that information may affect the assurance engagement.

Engagement Quality Control Review

For those engagements, if any, for which a quality control review is required by law   **36** or regulation or for which the firm has determined that an engagement quality control review is required:

(a) The engagement partner shall take responsibility for discussing significant matters arising during the engagement with the engagement quality control reviewer, and not date the assurance report until completion of that review; and

(b) The engagement quality control reviewer shall perform an objective evaluation of the significant judgments made by the engagement team, and the conclusions reached in formulating the assurance report. This evaluation shall involve: (Ref: Para. A75)

   (i) Discussion of significant matters with the engagement partner;

   (ii) Review of the subject matter information and the proposed assurance report;

   (iii) Review of selected engagement documentation relating to the significant judgments the engagement team made and the conclusions it reached; and

   (iv) Evaluation of the conclusions reached in formulating the assurance report and consideration of whether the proposed assurance report is appropriate.

Professional Skepticism, Professional Judgment, and Assurance Skills and Techniques

37 The practitioner shall plan and perform an engagement with professional skepticism, recognizing that circumstances may exist that cause the subject matter information to be materiality misstated. (Ref: Para. A76–A80)

38 The practitioner shall exercise professional judgment in planning and performing an assurance engagement, including determining the nature, timing and extent of procedures. (Ref: Para. A81–A85)

39 The practitioner shall apply assurance skills and techniques as part of an iterative, systematic engagement process.

Planning and Performing the Engagement

Planning

40 The practitioner shall plan the engagement so that it will be performed in an effective manner, including setting the scope, timing and direction of the engagement, and determining the nature, timing and extent of planned procedures that are required to be carried out in order to achieve the objective of the practitioner. (Ref: Para. A86–A89)

41 The practitioner shall determine whether the criteria are suitable for the engagement circumstances, including that they exhibit the characteristics identified in paragraph 24(b)(ii).

42 If it is discovered after the engagement has been accepted that one or more preconditions for an assurance engagement is not present, the practitioner shall discuss the matter with the appropriate party(ies), and shall determine:

(a) Whether the matter can be resolved to the practitioner's satisfaction;

(b) Whether it is appropriate to continue with the engagement; and

(c) Whether and, if so, how to communicate the matter in the assurance report.

43 If it is discovered after the engagement has been accepted that some or all of the applicable criteria are unsuitable or some or all of the underlying subject matter is not appropriate for an assurance engagement, the practitioner shall consider withdrawing from the engagement, if withdrawal is possible under applicable law or regulation. If the practitioner continues with the engagement, the practitioner shall express a qualified or adverse conclusion, or disclaimer of conclusion, as appropriate in the circumstances. (Ref: Para. A90–A91)

Materiality

The practitioner shall consider materiality when: (Ref: Para. A92–A100)   **44**

(a) Planning and performing the assurance engagement, including when determining the nature, timing and extent of procedures; and
(b) Evaluating whether the subject matter information is free from material misstatement.

Understanding the Underlying Subject Matter and Other Engagement Circumstances

The practitioner shall make inquiries of the appropriate party(ies) regarding: **45**

(a) Whether they have knowledge of any actual, suspected or alleged intentional misstatement or non-compliance with laws and regulations affecting the subject matter information; (Ref: Para. A101)
(b) Whether the responsible party has an internal audit function and, if so, make further inquiries to obtain an understanding of the activities and main findings of the internal audit function with respect to the subject matter information; and
(c) Whether the responsible party has used any experts in the preparation of the subject matter information.

Limited Assurance	Reasonable Assurance
46L. The practitioner shall obtain an understanding of the underlying subject matter and other engagement circumstances sufficient to: (a) Enable the practitioner to identify areas where a material misstatement of the subject matter information is likely to arise; and (b) Thereby, provide a basis for designing and performing procedures to address the areas identified in paragraph 45L(a) and to obtain limited assurance to support the practitioner's conclusion. (Ref: Para. A101–A104, A107)	46R. The practitioner shall obtain an understanding of the underlying subject matter and other engagement circumstances sufficient to: (a) Enable the practitioner to identify and assess the risks of material misstatement in the subject matter information; and (b) Thereby, provide a basis for designing and performing procedures to respond to the assessed risks and to obtain reasonable assurance to support the practitioner's conclusion. (Ref: Para. A101–A103, A107)

47L. In obtaining an understanding of the underlying subject matter and other engagement circumstances under paragraph 46L, the practitioner shall consider the process used to prepare the subject matter information. (Ref: Para. A106)	47R. In obtaining an understanding of the underlying subject matter and other engagement circumstances under paragraph 46R, the practitioner shall obtain an understanding of internal control over the preparation of the subject matter information relevant to the engagement. This includes evaluating the design of those controls relevant to the engagement and determining whether they have been implemented by performing procedures in addition to inquiry of the personnel responsible for the subject matter information. (Ref: Para. A105)

Obtaining Evidence

Risk Consideration and Responses to Risks

Limited Assurance	Reasonable Assurance
48L. Based on the practitioner's understanding (see paragraph 46L), the practitioner shall: (Ref: Para. A108–A112) (a) Identify areas where a material misstatement of the subject matter information is likely to arise; (b) Design and perform procedures to address the areas identified in paragraph 48L(a) and to obtain limited assurance to support the practitioner's conclusion.	48R. Based on the practitioner's understanding (see paragraph 46R) the practitioner shall: (Ref: Para. A108–A110) (a) Identify and assess the risks of material misstatement in the subject matter information; and (b) Design and perform procedures to respond to the assessed risks and to obtain reasonable assurance to support the practitioner's conclusion. In addition to any other procedures on the subject matter information that are appropriate in the engagement circumstances, the practitioner's procedures shall include obtaining sufficient appropriate evidence as to the operating effectiveness of relevant controls over the subject matter information when:

Limited Assurance	Reasonable Assurance
	(i) The practitioner's assessment of the risks of material misstatement includes an expectation that controls are operating effectively, or (ii) Procedures other than testing of controls cannot alone provide sufficient appropriate evidence.
Determining Whether Additional Procedures Are Necessary in a Limited Assurance Engagement 49L. If the practitioner becomes aware of a matter(s) that causes the practitioner to believe that the subject matter information may be materially misstated, the practitioner shall design and perform additional procedures to obtain further evidence until the practitioner is able to: (Ref: Para. A112–A117) (a) Conclude that the matter is not likely to cause the subject matter information to be materially misstated; or (b) Determine that the matter(s) causes the subject matter information to be materially misstated.	**Revision of Risk Assessment in a Reasonable Assurance Engagement** 49R. The practitioner's assessment of the risks of material misstatement in the subject matter information may change during the course of the engagement as additional evidence is obtained. In circumstances where the practitioner obtains evidence which is inconsistent with the evidence on which the practitioner originally based the assessment of the risks of material misstatement, the practitioner shall revise the assessment and modify the planned procedures accordingly. (Ref: Para. A112)

When designing and performing procedures, the practitioner shall consider the relevance and reliability of the information to be used as evidence. If: **50**

(a) Evidence obtained from one source is inconsistent with that obtained from another; or
(b) The practitioner has doubts about the reliability of information to be used as evidence,

the practitioner shall determine what changes or additions to procedures are necessary to resolve the matter, and shall consider the effect of the matter, if any, on other aspects of the engagement.

The practitioner shall accumulate uncorrected misstatements identified during the   **51**
engagement other than those that are clearly trivial. (Ref: Para. A118–A119)

Work Performed by a Practitioner's Expert

52 When the work of a practitioner's expert is to be used, the practitioner shall also: (Ref: Para. A120–A124)

(a) Evaluate whether the practitioner's expert has the necessary competence, capabilities and objectivity for the practitioner's purposes. In the case of a practitioner's external expert, the evaluation of objectivity shall include inquiry regarding interests and relationships that may create a threat to that expert's objectivity; (Ref: Para. A125–A128)

(b) Obtain a sufficient understanding of the field of expertise of the practitioner's expert; (Ref: Para. A129–A130)

(c) Agree with the practitioner's expert on the nature, scope and objectives of that expert's work; and (Ref: Para. A131–A132)

(d) Evaluate the adequacy of the practitioner's expert's work for the practitioner's purposes. (Ref: Para. A133–A134)

Work Performed by Another Practitioner, a Responsible Party's or Measurer's or Evaluator's Expert, or an Internal Auditor (Ref: Para. A135)

53 When the work of another practitioner is to be used, the practitioner shall evaluate whether that work is adequate for the practitioner's purposes.

54 If information to be used as evidence has been prepared using the work of a responsible party's or a measurer's or evaluator's expert, the practitioner shall, to the extent necessary having regard to the significance of that expert's work for the practitioner's purposes:

(a) Evaluate the competence, capabilities and objectivity of that expert;

(b) Obtain an understanding of the work of that expert; and

(c) Evaluate the appropriateness of that expert's work as evidence.

55 If the practitioner plans to use the work of the internal audit function, the practitioner shall evaluate the following:

(a) The extent to which the internal audit function's organizational status and relevant policies and procedures support the objectivity of the internal auditors;

(b) The level of competence of the internal audit function;

(c) Whether the internal audit function applies a systematic and disciplined approach, including quality control; and

(d) Whether the work of the internal audit function is adequate for the purposes of the engagement.

Written Representations

56 The practitioner shall request from the appropriate party(ies) a written representation:

(a) That it has provided the practitioner with all information of which the appropriate party(ies) is aware that is relevant to the engagement. (Ref: Para. A54–A55 and A136–A138)

(b) Confirming the measurement or evaluation of the underlying subject matter against the applicable criteria, including that all relevant matters are reflected in the subject matter information.

If, in addition to required representations, the practitioner determines that it is nec- **57** essary to obtain one or more written representations to support other evidence relevant to the subject matter information, the practitioner shall request such other written representations.

When written representations relate to matters that are material to the subject matter **58** information, the practitioner shall:

(a) Evaluate their reasonableness and consistency with other evidence obtained, including other representations (oral or written); and
(b) Consider whether those making the representations can be expected to be well-informed on the particular matters.

The date of the written representations shall be as near as practicable to, but not **59** after, the date of the assurance report.

Requested Written Representations Not Provided or Not Reliable

If one or more of the requested written representations are not provided or the prac- **60** titioner concludes that there is sufficient doubt about the competence, integrity, ethical values, or diligence of those providing the written representations, or that the written representations are otherwise not reliable, the practitioner shall: (Ref: Para. A139)

(a) Discuss the matter with the appropriate party(ies);
(b) Reevaluate the integrity of those from whom the representations were requested or received and evaluate the effect that this may have on the reliability of representations (oral or written) and evidence in general; and
(c) Take appropriate actions, including determining the possible effect on the conclusion in the assurance report.

Subsequent Events

When relevant to the engagement, the practitioner shall consider the effect on the **61** subject matter information and on the assurance report of events up to the date of the assurance report, and shall respond appropriately to facts that become known to the practitioner after the date of the assurance report, that, had they been known to the practitioner at that date, may have caused the practitioner to amend the assurance report. The extent of consideration of subsequent events depends on the potential for such events to affect the subject matter information and to affect the appropriateness of the practitioner's conclusion. However, the practitioner has no responsibility to perform any procedures regarding the subject matter information after the date of the assurance report. (Ref: Para. A140–A141)

Other Information

When documents containing the subject matter information and the assurance report **62** thereon include other information, the practitioner shall read that other information to identify material inconsistencies, if any, with the subject matter information or the assurance report and, if on reading that other information, the practitioner: (Ref: Para. A142)

(a) Identifies a material inconsistency between that other information and the subject matter information or the assurance report; or

(b) Becomes aware of a material misstatement of fact in that other information that is unrelated to matters appearing in the subject matter information or the assurance report,

the practitioner shall discuss the matter with the appropriate party(ies) and take further action as appropriate.

Description of Applicable Criteria

63   The practitioner shall evaluate whether the subject matter information adequately refers to or describes the applicable criteria. (Ref: Para. A143–A145)

Forming the Assurance Conclusion

64   The practitioner shall evaluate the sufficiency and appropriateness of the evidence obtained in the context of the engagement and, if necessary in the circumstances, attempt to obtain further evidence. The practitioner shall consider all relevant evidence, regardless of whether it appears to corroborate or to contradict the measurement or evaluation of the underlying subject matter against the applicable criteria. If the practitioner is unable to obtain necessary further evidence, the practitioner shall consider the implications for the practitioner's conclusion in paragraph 65. (Ref: Para. A146–A152)

65   The practitioner shall form a conclusion about whether the subject matter information is free of material misstatement. In forming that conclusion, the practitioner shall consider the practitioner's conclusion in paragraph 64 regarding the sufficiency and appropriateness of evidence obtained and an evaluation of whether uncorrected misstatements are material, individually or in the aggregate. (Ref: Para. A3 and A153–A154)

66   If the practitioner is unable to obtain sufficient appropriate evidence, a scope limitation exists and the practitioner shall express a qualified conclusion, disclaim a conclusion, or withdraw from the engagement, where withdrawal is possible under applicable law or regulation, as appropriate. (Ref: Para. A155–A157)

Preparing the Assurance Report

67   The assurance report shall be in writing and shall contain a clear expression of the practitioner's conclusion about the subject matter information. (Ref: Para. A2, A158–A160)

68   The practitioner's conclusion shall be clearly separated from information or explanations that are not intended to affect the practitioner's conclusion, including any Emphasis of Matter, Other Matter, findings related to particular aspects of the engagements, recommendations or additional information included in the assurance report. The wording used shall make it clear that an Emphasis of Matter, Other Matter, findings, recommendations or additional information is not intended to detract from the practitioner's conclusion. (Ref: Para. A158–A160)

Assurance Report Content

The assurance report shall include at a minimum the following basic elements: **69**

(a) A title that clearly indicates the report is an independent assurance report. (Ref: Para. A161)
(b) An addressee. (Ref: Para. A162)
(c) An identification or description of the level of assurance obtained by the practitioner, the subject matter information and, when appropriate, the underlying subject matter. When the practitioner's conclusion is phrased in terms of a statement made by the appropriate party, that statement shall accompany the assurance report, be reproduced in the assurance report or be referenced therein to a source that is available to the intended users. (Ref: Para A163)
(d) Identification of the applicable criteria. (Ref: Para. A164)
(e) Where appropriate, a description of any significant inherent limitations associated with the measurement or evaluation of the underlying subject matter against the applicable criteria. (Ref: Para. A165)
(f) When the applicable criteria are designed for a specific purpose, a statement alerting readers to this fact and that, as a result, the subject matter information may not be suitable for another purpose. (Ref: Para. A166–A167)
(g) A statement to identify the responsible party and the measurer or evaluator if different, and to describe their responsibilities and the practitioner's responsibilities. (Ref: Para. A168)
(h) A statement that the engagement was performed in accordance with this ISAE or, where there is a subject-matter specific ISAE, that ISAE. (Ref: Para. A169–A170)
(i) A statement that the firm of which the practitioner is a member applies ISQC 1, or other professional requirements, or requirements in law or regulation, that are at least as demanding as ISQC 1. If the practitioner is not a professional accountant, the statement shall identify the professional requirements, or requirements in law or regulation, applied that are at least as demanding as ISQC 1. (Ref: Para. A171)
(j) A statement that the practitioner complies with the independence and other ethical requirements of the IESBA Code, or other professional requirements, or requirements imposed by law or regulation, that are at least as demanding as Parts A and B of the IESBA Code related to assurance engagements. If the practitioner is not a professional accountant, the statement shall identify the professional requirements, or requirements imposed by law or regulation, applied that are at least as demanding as Parts A and B of the IESBA Code related to assurance engagements. (Ref: Para. A172)
(k) An informative summary of the work performed as the basis for the practitioner's conclusion. In the case of a limited assurance engagement, an appreciation of the nature, timing, and extent of procedures performed is essential to understanding the practitioner's conclusion. In a limited assurance engagement, the summary of the work performed shall state that:
   (i) The procedures performed in a limited assurance engagement vary in nature and timing from, and are less in extent than for, a reasonable assurance engagement; and
   (ii) Consequently, the level of assurance obtained in a limited assurance engagement is substantially lower than the assurance that would have been obtained had a reasonable assurance engagement been performed. (Ref: Para. A6, A173–A177)
(l) The practitioner's conclusion: (Ref: Para. A2, A178–A180)
   (i) When appropriate, the conclusion shall inform the intended users of the context in which the practitioner's conclusion is to be read. (Ref: Para. A179)

(ii) In a reasonable assurance engagement, the conclusion shall be expressed in a positive form. (Ref: Para. A178)

(iii) In a limited assurance engagement, the conclusion shall be expressed in a form that conveys whether, based on the procedures performed and evidence obtained, a matter(s) has come to the practitioner's attention to cause the practitioner to believe that the subject matter information is materially misstated. (Ref: Para. A180)

(iv) The conclusion in (ii) or (iii) shall be phrased using appropriate words for the underlying subject matter and applicable criteria given the engagement circumstances and shall be phrased in terms of: (Ref: Para. A181)

    (a) The underlying subject matter and the applicable criteria;

    (b) The subject matter information and the applicable criteria; or

    (c) A statement made by the appropriate party.

(v) When the practitioner expresses a modified conclusion, the assurance report shall contain:

    a. A section that provides a description of the matter(s) giving rise to the modification; and

    b. A section that contains the practitioner's modified conclusion.(Ref: Para. A182)

(m) The practitioner's signature. (Ref: Para. A183)

(n) The date of the assurance report. The assurance report shall be dated no earlier than the date on which the practitioner has obtained the evidence on which the practitioner's conclusion is based, including evidence that those with the recognized authority have asserted that they have taken responsibility for the subject matter information.(Ref: Para. A184)

(o) The location in the jurisdiction where the practitioner practices.

Reference to the Practitioner's Expert in the Assurance Report

70 If the practitioner refers to the work of a practitioner's expert in the assurance report, the wording of that report shall not imply that the practitioner's responsibility for the conclusion expressed in that report is reduced because of the involvement of that expert. (Ref: Para. A185–A187)

Assurance Report Prescribed by Law or Regulation

71 If the practitioner is required by law or regulation to use a specific layout or wording of the assurance report, the assurance report shall refer to this or other ISAEs only if the assurance report includes, at a minimum, each of the elements identified in paragraph 69.

Unmodified and Modified Conclusions

72 The practitioner shall express an unmodified conclusion when the practitioner concludes:

(a) In the case of a reasonable assurance engagement, that the subject matter information is prepared, in all material respects, in accordance with the applicable criteria; or

(b) In the case of a limited assurance engagement, that, based on the procedures performed and evidence obtained, no matter(s) has come to the attention of the practitioner that causes the practitioner to believe that the subject matter information is not prepared, in all material respects, in accordance with the applicable criteria.

If the practitioner considers it necessary to: **73**

(a) Draw intended users' attention to a matter presented or disclosed in the subject matter information that, in the practitioner's judgment, is of such importance that it is fundamental to intended users' understanding of the subject matter information (an Emphasis of Matter paragraph); or

(b) Communicate a matter other than those that are presented or disclosed in the subject matter information that, in the practitioner's judgment, is relevant to intended users' understanding of the engagement, the practitioner's responsibilities or the assurance report (an Other Matter paragraph),

and this is not prohibited by law or regulation, the practitioner shall do so in a paragraph in the assurance report, with an appropriate heading, that clearly indicates the practitioner's conclusion is not modified in respect of the matter. In the case of an Emphasis of Matter paragraph, such a paragraph shall refer only to information presented or disclosed in the subject matter information.

The practitioner shall express a modified conclusion in the following circumstances: **74**

(a) When, in the practitioner's professional judgment, a scope limitation exists and the effect of the matter could be material (see paragraph 66). In such cases, the practitioner shall express a qualified conclusion or a disclaimer of conclusion.

(b) When, in the practitioner's professional judgment, the subject matter information is materially misstated. In such cases, the practitioner shall express a qualified conclusion or adverse conclusion. (Ref: Para. A190)

The practitioner shall express a qualified conclusion when, in the practitioner's professional judgment, the effects, or possible effects, of a matter are not so material and pervasive as to require an adverse conclusion or a disclaimer of conclusion. A qualified conclusion shall be expressed as being "except for" the effects, or possible effects, of the matter to which the qualification relates. (Ref: Para. A188–A189) **75**

If the practitioner expresses a modified conclusion because of a scope limitation but is also aware of a matter(s) that causes the subject matter information to be materially misstated, the practitioner shall include in the assurance report a clear description of both the scope limitation and the matter(s) that causes that the subject matter information to be materially misstated. **76**

When the statement made by the appropriate party has identified and properly described that the subject matter information is materially misstated, the practitioner shall either: **77**

(a) Express a qualified conclusion or adverse conclusion phrased in terms of the underlying subject matter and the applicable criteria; or

(b) If specifically required by the terms of the engagement to phrase the conclusion in terms of a statement made by the appropriate party, express an unqualified conclusion but include an Emphasis of Matter paragraph in the assurance report referring to the statement made by the appropriate party that identifies and properly describes that the subject matter information is materially misstated. (Ref: Para. A191)

(c) Other Communication Responsibilities

78   The practitioner shall consider whether, pursuant to the terms of the engagement and other engagement circumstances, any matter has come to the attention of the practitioner that is to be communicated with the responsible party, the measurer or evaluator, the engaging party, those charged with governance or others. (Ref: Para. A192)

Documentation

79   The practitioner shall prepare on a timely basis engagement documentation that provides a record of the basis for the assurance report that is sufficient and appropriate to enable an experienced practitioner, having no previous connection with the engagement, to understand: (Ref: Para. A193–A197)

    (a) The nature, timing and extent of the procedures performed to comply with relevant ISAEs and applicable legal and regulatory requirements;

    (b) The results of the procedures performed, and the evidence obtained; and

    (c) Significant matters arising during the engagement, the conclusions reached thereon, and significant professional judgments made in reaching those conclusions.

80   If the practitioner identifies information that is inconsistent with the practitioner's final conclusion regarding a significant matter, the practitioner shall document how the practitioner addressed the inconsistency.

81   The practitioner shall assemble the engagement documentation in an engagement file and complete the administrative process of assembling the final engagement file on a timely basis after the date of the assurance report. (Ref: Para. A198–A199)

82   After the assembly of the final engagement file has been completed, the practitioner shall not delete or discard engagement documentation of any nature before the end of its retention period. (Ref: Para. A200)

83   If the practitioner finds it necessary to amend existing engagement documentation or add new engagement documentation after the assembly of the final engagement file has been completed the practitioner shall, regardless of the nature of the amendments or additions, document:

    (a) The specific reasons for making the amendments or additions; and

    (b) When, and by whom, they were made and reviewed.

***

Application and Other Explanatory Material

Introduction (Ref: Para. 6)

A1   In a consulting engagement, the practitioner applies technical skills, education, observations, experiences, and knowledge. Consulting engagements involve an analytical process that typically involves some combination of activities relating to: objective-setting, fact-finding, definition of problems or opportunities, evaluation of alternatives, development of recommendations including actions, communication of results, and sometimes implementation and follow-up. Reports (if issued) are generally written in a narrative (or "long form") style. Generally the work performed is only for the use and benefit of the client. The nature and scope of work is determined by agreement between the practitioner and the client. Any service that meets the definition of an assurance engagement is not a consulting engagement but an assurance engagement.

Objectives

Engagements with Subject Matter Information Comprising a Number of Aspects (Ref: Para. 10, 65, 69(l))

Where the subject matter information is made up of a number of aspects, separate **A2** conclusions may be provided on each aspect. All such separate conclusions do not need to relate to the same level of assurance. Rather, each conclusion is expressed in the form that is appropriate to either a reasonable assurance engagement or a limited assurance engagement. References in this ISAE to the conclusion in the assurance report include each conclusion when separate conclusions are provided.

Definitions

The Nature, Timing and Extent of Procedures in Limited and Reasonable Assurance Engagements (Ref: Para. 12(a)(i))

Because the level of assurance obtained in a limited assurance engagement is lower **A3** than in a reasonable assurance engagement, the procedures the practitioner performs in a limited assurance engagement vary in nature and timing from, and are less in extent than for, a reasonable assurance engagement. The primary differences between the procedures for a reasonable assurance engagement and a limited assurance engagement include:

(a) The emphasis placed on the nature of various procedures as a source of evidence will likely differ, depending on the engagement circumstances. For example, the practitioner may judge it to be appropriate in the circumstances of a particular limited assurance engagement to place relatively greater emphasis on inquiries of the entity's personnel and analytical procedures, and relatively less emphasis, if any, on testing of controls and obtaining evidence from external sources than may be the case for a reasonable assurance engagement.
(b) In a limited assurance engagement the practitioner may:
- Select less items for examination; or
- Perform fewer procedures (for example, performing only analytical procedures in circumstances when, in a reasonable assurance engagement, both analytical procedures and other procedures would be performed).
(c) In a reasonable assurance engagement, analytical procedures performed in response to the engagement risk involve developing expectations that are sufficiently precise to identify material misstatements. In a limited assurance engagement, analytical procedures may be designed to support expectations regarding the direction of trends, relationships and ratios rather than to identify misstatements with the level of precision expected in a reasonable assurance engagement.
(d) Further, when significant fluctuations, relationships or differences are identified, appropriate evidence in a limited assurance engagement may be obtained

by making inquiries and considering responses received in the light of known engagement circumstances.

(e) In addition, when undertaking analytical procedures in a limited assurance engagement the practitioner may, for example use data that is more highly aggregated, such as quarterly data rather than monthly data, or use data that has not been subjected to separate procedures to test its reliability to the same extent as it would be for a reasonable assurance engagement.

A Level of Assurance that is Meaningful (Ref: Para. 12(a)(i)(b), 47L)

A4   The level of assurance the practitioner plans to obtain is not ordinarily susceptible to quantification, and whether it is meaningful is a matter of professional judgment for the practitioner to determine in the circumstances of the engagement. In a limited assurance engagement, the practitioner performs procedures that are limited compared with those necessary in a reasonable assurance engagement but are, nonetheless, planned to obtain a level of assurance that is meaningful. To be meaningful the level of assurance obtained by the practitioner is likely to enhance the intended users' confidence about the subject matter information to a degree that is clearly more than inconsequential (see also paragraphs A16–A18).

A5   Across the range of all limited assurance engagements, what is meaningful assurance can vary from just above assurance that is likely to enhance the intended users' confidence about the subject matter information to a degree that is clearly more than inconsequential to just below reasonable assurance. What is meaningful in a particular engagement represents a judgment within that range that depends on the engagement circumstances, including the information needs of intended users as a group, the criteria, and the underlying subject matter of the engagement.

A6   Because the level of assurance obtained by the practitioner in limited assurance engagements varies, the practitioner's report contains an informative summary of the procedures performed, recognizing that an appreciation of the nature, timing, and extent of procedures performed is essential to understanding the practitioner's conclusion (see paragraph 69(k) and A173–A177).

A7   Some of the factors that may be relevant in determining what constitutes meaningful assurance in a specific engagement include, for example:

- The characteristics of the underlying subject matter and the criteria, and whether there are any relevant subject matter-specific ISAEs.
- Instructions or other indications from the engaging party about the nature of the assurance the engaging party is seeking the practitioner to obtain. For example, the terms of the engagement may stipulate particular procedures that the engaging party considers necessary or particular aspects of the subject matter information on which the engaging party would like the practitioner to focus procedures. However, the practitioner may consider that other procedures are required to obtain sufficient appropriate evidence to obtain meaningful assurance.
- Generally accepted practice, if it exists, with respect to assurance engagements for the particular subject matter information, or similar or related subject matter information.
- The information needs of intended users as a group. Generally, the greater the consequence to intended users of receiving an inappropriate conclusion when the subject matter information is materially misstated, the greater the assurance that would be needed in order to be meaningful to them. For example, in some

cases, the consequence to intended users of receiving an inappropriate conclusion may be so great that a reasonable assurance engagement is needed for the practitioner to obtain assurance that is meaningful in the circumstances.
- The expectation by intended users that the practitioner will form the limited assurance conclusion on the subject matter information within a short time-frame and at a low cost.

Examples of Attestation Engagements (Ref: Para. 12(a)(ii)(a))

Examples of engagements that may be conducted under this ISAE include: **A8**

(a) Sustainability – An engagement on sustainability involves obtaining assurance on a report prepared by management or management's expert (the measurer or evaluator) on the sustainability performance of the entity.
(b) Compliance with law or regulation – An engagement on compliance with law or regulation involves obtaining assurance on a statement by another party (the measurer or evaluator) of compliance with the relevant law or regulation.
(c) Value for money – An engagement on value for money involves obtaining assurance on a measurement or evaluation of value for money by another party (the measurer or evaluator).

Assurance Skills and Techniques (Ref: Para. 12(b))

Assurance skills and techniques include: **A9**

- Application of professional skepticism and professional judgment;
- Planning and performing an assurance engagement, including obtaining and evaluating evidence;
- Understanding information systems and the role and limitations of internal control;
- Linking the consideration of materiality and engagement risks to the nature, timing and extent of procedures; and
- Applying procedures as appropriate to the engagement (which may include inquiry, inspection, re-calculation, re-performance, observation, confirmation, and analytical procedures); and
- Systematic documentation practices and assurance report-writing skills.

Criteria (Ref: Para. 12(c), Appendix)

Suitable criteria are required for reasonably consistent measurement or evaluation **A10**
of an underlying subject matter within the context of professional judgment. Without the frame of reference provided by suitable criteria, any conclusion is open to individual interpretation and misunderstanding. The suitability of criteria is context-sensitive, that is, it is determined in the context of the engagement circumstances. Even for the same underlying subject matter there can be different criteria, which will yield a different measurement or evaluation. For example, a measurer or evaluator might select, as one of the criteria for the underlying subject matter of customer satisfaction, the number of customer complaints resolved to the acknowledged satisfaction of the customer; another measurer or evaluator might select the number of repeat purchases in the three months following the initial purchase. The suitability of criteria is not affected by the level of assurance, that is, if criteria are unsuitable for a reasonable assurance engagement, they are also unsuitable for a limited assurance engagement, and vice versa. Suitable criteria include, when relevant, criteria for presentation and disclosure.

Engagement Risk (Ref: Para. 12(f))

A11   Engagement risk does not refer to, or include, the practitioner's business risks, such as loss from litigation, adverse publicity, or other events arising in connection with particular subject matter information.

A12   In general, engagement risk can be represented by the following components, although not all of these components will necessarily be present or significant for all assurance engagements:

(a)   Risks that the practitioner does not directly influence, which in turn consist of:
   (i)   The susceptibility of the subject matter information to a material misstatement before consideration of any related controls applied by the appropriate party(ies) (inherent risk); and
   (ii)   The risk that a material misstatement that occurs in the subject matter information will not be prevented, or detected and corrected, on a timely basis by the appropriate party(ies)'s internal control (control risk); and
(b)   The risk that the practitioner does directly influence, which is the risk that the procedures performed by the practitioner will not detect a material misstatement (detection risk).

A13   The degree to which each of these components is relevant to the engagement is affected by the engagement circumstances, in particular:

- The nature of the underlying subject matter and the subject matter information. For example, the concept of control risk may be more useful when the underlying subject matter relates to the preparation of information about an entity's performance than when it relates to information about the effectiveness of a control or the existence of a physical condition.
- Whether a reasonable assurance or a limited assurance engagement is being performed. For example, in limited assurance engagements the practitioner may often decide to obtain evidence by means other than testing of controls, in which case consideration of control risk may be less relevant than in a reasonable assurance engagement on the same subject matter information.

The consideration of risks is a matter of professional judgment, rather than a matter capable of precise measurement.

A14   Reducing engagement risk to zero is very rarely attainable or cost beneficial and, therefore, "reasonable assurance" is less than absolute assurance, as a result of factors such as the following:

- The use of selective testing.
- The inherent limitations of internal control.
- The fact that much of the evidence available to the practitioner is persuasive rather than conclusive.
- The use of professional judgment in gathering and evaluating evidence and forming conclusions based on that evidence.
- In some cases, the characteristics of the underlying subject matter when evaluated or measured against the criteria.

The Engaging Party (Ref: Para. 12(g), Appendix)

The engaging party may be, under different circumstances, management or those **A15** charged with governance of the responsible party, a legislature, the intended users, the measurer or evaluator, or a different third party.

Intended Users (Ref: Para. 12(m), Appendix)

In some cases there may be intended users other than those to whom the assurance **A16** report is addressed. The practitioner may not be able to identify all those who will read the assurance report, particularly where a large number of people have access to it. In such cases, particularly where possible users are likely to have a broad range of interests in the underlying subject matter, intended users may be limited to major stakeholders with significant and common interests. Intended users may be identified in different ways, for example, by agreement between the practitioner and the responsible party or engaging party, or by law or regulation.

Intended users or their representatives may be directly involved with the practitioner **A17** and the responsible party (and the engaging party if different) in determining the requirements of the engagement. Regardless of the involvement of others however, and unlike an agreed-upon procedures engagement (which involves reporting factual findings based upon procedures agreed with the engaging party and any appropriate third parties, rather than a conclusion):

(a) The practitioner is responsible for determining the nature, timing and extent of procedures; and
(b) The practitioner may need to perform additional procedures if information comes to the practitioner's attention that differs significantly from that on which the determination of planned procedures was based (see paragraphs A115–A117).

In some cases, intended users (for example, bankers and regulators) impose a **A18** requirement on, or request the appropriate party(ies) to arrange for an assurance engagement to be performed for a specific purpose. When engagements use criteria that are designed for a specific purpose, paragraph 69(f) requires a statement alerting readers to this fact. In addition, the practitioner may consider it appropriate to indicate that the assurance report is intended solely for specific users. Depending on the engagement circumstances, this may be achieved by restricting the distribution or use of the assurance report (see paragraphs A166–A167).

Subject Matter Information (Ref: Para. 12(x), Appendix)

In some cases, the subject matter information may be a statement that evaluates an **A19** aspect of a process, or of performance or compliance, in relation to the criteria. For example, "ABC's internal control operated effectively in terms of XYZ criteria during the period ...." or "ABC's governance structure conformed with XYZ criteria during the period ...".

The Appropriate Party(ies) (Ref: Para. 13, Appendix)

The roles played by the responsible party, the measurer or evaluator, and the engaging **A20** party can vary (see paragraph A36). Also, management and governance structures vary by jurisdiction and by entity, reflecting influences such as different cultural and legal backgrounds, and size and ownership characteristics. Such diversity means that it is not possible for ISAEs to specify for all engagements the person(s) with whom the practitioner is to inquire of, request representations from, or otherwise communicate with in all circumstances. In some cases, for example, when the appropriate party(ies) is only part of a complete legal entity, identifying the appropriate management personnel or those charged with governance with whom to communicate will require the exercise of professional judgment to determine which person(s) have the appropriate responsibilities for, and knowledge of, the matters concerned.

Conduct of an Assurance Engagement in Accordance with ISAEs

Complying with Standards that Are Relevant to the Engagement (Ref: Para. 1, 5, 15)

A21   This ISAE includes requirements that apply to assurance engagements[3] (other than audits or reviews of historical financial information), including engagements in accordance with a subject matter-specific ISAE. In some cases, a subject matter-specific ISAE is also relevant to the engagement. A subject matter-specific ISAE is relevant to the engagement when the ISAE is in effect, the subject matter of the ISAE is relevant to the engagement, and the circumstances addressed by the ISAE exist.

A22   The ISAs and ISREs have been written for assurance engagements other than audits and reviews of historical financial information, respectively, and do not apply to other assurance engagements. They may, however, provide guidance in relation to the engagement process generally for practitioners undertaking an assurance engagement in accordance with this ISAE.

Text of an ISAE (Ref: Para. 12, 16)

A23   ISAEs contain the objectives of the practitioner in following the ISAEs, and requirements designed to enable the practitioner to meet those objectives. In addition, they contain related guidance in the form of application and other explanatory material, introductory material that provides context relevant to a proper understanding of the ISAE, and definitions.

A24   The objectives in an ISAE provide the context in which the requirements of the ISAE are set, and are intended to assist in:

(a)   Understanding what is to be accomplished; and
(b)   Deciding whether more needs to be done to achieve the objectives.

The proper application of the requirements of an ISAE by the practitioner is expected to provide a sufficient basis for the practitioner's achievement of the objectives. However, because the circumstances of assurance engagements vary widely and all such circumstances cannot be anticipated in the ISAEs, the practitioner is responsible for determining the procedures necessary to fulfill the requirements of relevant ISAEs and to achieve the objectives stated therein. In the circumstances of an engagement, there may be particular matters that require the practitioner to perform

---

[3] *This ISAE contains requirements and application and other explanatory material specific to reasonable and limited assurance attestation engagements. This ISAE may also be applied to reasonable and limited assurance direct engagements, adapted and supplemented as necessary in the engagement circumstances.*

procedures in addition to those required by relevant ISAEs to meet the objectives specified in those ISAEs.

The requirements of ISAEs are expressed using "shall."   A25

Where necessary, the application and other explanatory material provides further   A26
explanation of the requirements and guidance for carrying them out. In particular, it may:

(a) Explain more precisely what a requirement means or is intended to cover; and
(b) Include examples that may be appropriate in the circumstances.

While such guidance does not in itself impose a requirement, it is relevant to the proper application of the requirements. The application and other explanatory material may also provide background information on matters addressed in an ISAE. Where appropriate, additional considerations specific to public sector audit organizations or smaller firms are included within the application and other explanatory material. These additional considerations assist in the application of the requirements in the ISAEs. They do not, however, limit or reduce the responsibility of the practitioner to apply and comply with the requirements in an ISAE.

Definitions are provided in the ISAEs to assist in the consistent application and   A27
interpretation of the ISAEs, and are not intended to override definitions that may be established for other purposes, whether by laws, regulations or otherwise.

Appendices form part of the application and other explanatory material. The purpose   A28
and intended use of an appendix are explained in the body of the related ISAE or within the title and introduction of the appendix itself.

Complying with Relevant Requirements (Ref: Para. 17)

Although some procedures are required only for reasonable assurance engagements,   A29
they may nonetheless be appropriate in some limited assurance engagements.

Ethical Requirements (Ref: Para. 3(a), 20, 22(a))

Part A of the IESBA Code establishes the following fundamental principles with   A30
which the practitioner is required to comply:

(a) Integrity;
(b) Objectivity;
(c) Professional competence and due care;
(d) Confidentiality; and
(e) Professional behavior.

Part A of the IESBA Code also provides a conceptual framework for professional   A31
accountants to apply to:

(a) Identify threats to compliance with the fundamental principles. Threats fall into
    one or more of the following categories:
    (i) Self-interest;
    (ii) Self-review;
    (iii) Advocacy;

    (iv) Familiarity; and

    (v) Intimidation;

(b) Evaluate the significance of the threats identified; and

(c) Apply safeguards, when necessary, to eliminate the threats or reduce them to an acceptable level. Safeguards are necessary when the professional accountant determines that the threats are not at a level at which a reasonable and informed third party would be likely to conclude, weighing all the specific facts and circumstances available to the professional accountant at that time, that compliance with the fundamental principles is not compromised.

A32   Part B of the IESBA Code describes how the conceptual framework in Part A applies in certain situations to professional accountants in public practice, including:

- Professional appointment;
- Conflicts of interest;
- Second opinions;
- Fees and other types of remuneration;
- Marketing professional services;
- Gifts and hospitality;
- Custody of client assets;
- Objectivity; and
- Independence.

A33   The IESBA Code defines independence as comprising both independence of mind and independence in appearance. Independence safeguards the ability to form an assurance conclusion without being affected by influences that might compromise that conclusion. Independence enhances the ability to act with integrity, to be objective and to maintain an attitude of professional skepticism. Matters addressed in the IESBA Code with respect to independence include:

- Financial interests;
- Loans and guarantees;
- Business relationships;
- Family and personal relationships;
- Employment with assurance clients;
- Recent service with an assurance client;
- Serving as a director or officer of an assurance client;
- Long association of senior personnel with assurance clients;
- Provision of non-assurance services to assurance clients;
- Fees (relative size, overdue, and contingent fees);
- Gifts and hospitality; and
- Actual or threatened litigation.

A34   Professional requirements, or requirements imposed by law or regulation, are at least as demanding as Parts A and B of the IESBA Code related to assurance engagements when they address all the matters referred to in paragraphs A30–A33 and impose obligations that achieve the aims of the requirements set out in Parts A and B of the IESBA Code related to assurance engagements.

Acceptance and Continuance

Preconditions for the Engagement (Ref: Para. 24)

In a public sector environment, some of the preconditions for an assurance engage-   **A35**
ment may be assumed to be present, for example:

(a) The roles and responsibilities of public sector audit organizations and the gov-
    ernment entities scoped into assurance engagements are assumed to be appro-
    priate because they are generally set out in legislation;
(b) Public sector audit organizations' right of access to the information necessary
    to perform the engagement is often set out in legislation;
(c) The practitioner's conclusion, in the form appropriate to either a reasonable
    assurance engagement or a limited assurance engagement, is generally required
    by legislation to be contained in a written report; and
(d) A rational purpose is generally present because the engagement is set out in
    legislation.

If suitable criteria are not available for all of the underlying subject matter but the   **A36**
practitioner can identify one or more aspects of the underlying subject matter for
which those criteria are suitable, then an assurance engagement can be performed
with respect to that aspect of the underlying subject matter in its own right. In such
cases, the assurance report may need to clarify that the report does not relate to the
original underlying subject matter in its entirety.

Roles and Responsibilities (Ref: Para. 12(m), 12(n), 12(r), 12(v), 13, 24(a),
Appendix)

All assurance engagements have at least three parties: the responsible party, the prac-   **A37**
titioner, and the intended users. In many attestation engagements, the responsible
party may also be the measurer or evaluator, and the engaging party. See the Appendix for a discussion of how each of these roles relate to an assurance engagement.

Evidence that the appropriate relationship exists with respect to responsibility for   **A38**
the underlying subject matter may be obtained through an acknowledgement provided by the responsible party. Such an acknowledgement also establishes a basis
for a common understanding of the responsibilities of the responsible party and the
practitioner. A written acknowledgement is the most appropriate form of documenting the responsible party's understanding. In the absence of a written acknowledgement of responsibility, it may still be appropriate for the practitioner to accept the
engagement if, for example, other sources, such as legislation or a contract, indicate responsibility. In other cases, it may be appropriate to decline the engagement
depending on the circumstances, or to disclose the circumstances in the assurance
report.

The measurer or evaluator is responsible for having a reasonable basis for the subject   **A39**
matter information. What constitutes a reasonable basis will depend on the nature of
the underlying subject matter and other engagement circumstances. In some cases, a
formal process with extensive internal controls may be needed to provide the measurer or evaluator with a reasonable basis that the subject matter information is free
from material misstatement. The fact that the practitioner will report on the subject
matter information is not a substitute for the measurer or evaluator's own processes
to have a reasonable basis for the subject matter information.

Appropriateness of the Underlying Subject Matter (Ref: Para. 24(b)(i))

A40   An appropriate underlying subject matter is identifiable and capable of consistent measurement or evaluation against the applicable criteria such that the resulting subject matter information can be subjected to procedures for obtaining sufficient appropriate evidence to support a reasonable assurance or limited assurance conclusion, as appropriate.

A41   The appropriateness of an underlying subject matter is not affected by the level of assurance, that is, if an underlying subject matter is not appropriate for a reasonable assurance engagement, it is also not appropriate for a limited assurance engagement, and vice versa.

A42   Different underlying subject matters have different characteristics, including the degree to which information about them is qualitative versus quantitative, objective versus subjective, historical versus prospective, and relates to a point in time or covers a period. Such characteristics affect the:

(a)   Precision with which the underlying subject matter can be measured or evaluated against criteria; and
(b)   The persuasiveness of available evidence.

A43   Identifying such characteristics and considering their effects assist the practitioner when assessing the appropriateness of the underlying subject matter and also in determining the content of the assurance report (see paragraph A163).

A44   In some cases, the assurance engagement may relate to only one part of a broader underlying subject matter. For example, the practitioner may be engaged to report on one aspect of an entity's contribution to sustainable development, such as a number of programs run by an entity that have positive environmental outcomes. In determining whether the engagement exhibits the characteristic of having an appropriate underlying subject matter in such cases, it may be appropriate for the practitioner to consider whether information about the aspect on which the practitioner is asked to report is likely to meet the information needs of intended users as a group, and also how the subject matter information will be presented and distributed, for example, whether there are more significant programs with less favorable outcomes that the entity is not reporting upon.

Suitability and Availability of the Criteria

Suitability of the criteria (Ref: Para. 24(b)(ii))

A45   Suitable criteria exhibit the following characteristics:

(a)   Relevance: Relevant criteria result in subject matter information that assists decision-making by the intended users.
(b)   Completeness: Criteria are complete when subject matter information prepared in accordance with them does not omit relevant factors that could reasonably be expected to affect decisions of the intended users made on the basis of that subject matter information. Complete criteria include, where relevant, benchmarks for presentation and disclosure.
(c)   Reliability: Reliable criteria allow reasonably consistent measurement or evaluation of the underlying subject matter including, where relevant, presentation and disclosure, when used in similar circumstances by different practitioners.

(d) Neutrality: Neutral criteria result in subject matter information that is free from bias as appropriate in the engagement circumstances.
(e) Understandability: Understandable criteria result in subject matter information that can be understood by the intended users.

Vague descriptions of expectations or judgments of an individual's experiences do not constitute suitable criteria.　　**A46**

The suitability of criteria for a particular engagement depends on whether they reflect the above characteristics. The relative importance of each characteristic to a particular engagement is a matter of professional judgment. Further, criteria may be suitable for a particular set of engagement circumstances, but may not be suitable for a different set of engagement circumstances. For example, reporting to governments or regulators may require the use of a particular set of criteria, but these criteria may not be suitable for a broader group of users.　　**A47**

Criteria can be selected or developed in a variety of ways, for example, they may be:　　**A48**

● Embodied in law or regulation.
● Issued by authorized or recognized bodies of experts that follow a transparent due process.
● Developed collectively by a group that does not follow a transparent due process.
● Published in scholarly journals or books.
● Developed for sale on a proprietary basis.
● Specifically designed for the purpose of preparing the subject matter information in the particular circumstances of the engagement.

How criteria are developed may affect the work that the practitioner carries out to assess their suitability.

In some cases, law or regulation prescribe the criteria to be used for the engagement. In the absence of indications to the contrary, such criteria are presumed to be suitable, as are criteria issued by authorized or recognized bodies of experts that follow a transparent due process if they are relevant to the intended users' information needs. Such criteria are known as established criteria. Even when established criteria exist for an underlying subject matter, specific users may agree to other criteria for their specific purposes. For example, various frameworks can be used as established criteria for evaluating the effectiveness of internal control. Specific users may, however, develop a more detailed set of criteria that meet their specific information needs in relation to, for example, prudential supervision. In such cases, the assurance report:　　**A49**

(a) Alerts readers that the subject matter information is prepared in accordance with special purpose criteria and that, as a result, the subject matter information may not be suitable for another purpose (see paragraph 69(f)); and
(b) May note, when it is relevant to the circumstances of the engagement, that the criteria are not embodied in law or regulation, or issued by authorized or recognized bodies of experts that follow a transparent due process.

If criteria are specifically designed for the purpose of preparing the subject matter information in the particular circumstances of the engagement, they are not suitable if they result in subject matter information or an assurance report that is misleading　　**A50** to the intended users. It is desirable for the intended users or the engaging party to acknowledge that specifically developed criteria are suitable for the intended users' purposes. The absence of such an acknowledgement may affect what is to be done to assess the suitability of the criteria, and the information provided about the criteria in the assurance report.

Availability of the criteria (Ref: Para. 24(b)(iii))

A51   Criteria need to be available to the intended users to allow them to understand how the underlying subject matter has been measured or evaluated. Criteria are made available to the intended users in one or more of the following ways:

(a)   Publicly.

(b)   Through inclusion in a clear manner in the presentation of the subject matter information.

(c)   Through inclusion in a clear manner in the assurance report (see paragraph A164).

(d)   By general understanding, for example the criterion for measuring time in hours and minutes.

A52   Criteria may also be available only to intended users, for example the terms of a contract, or criteria issued by an industry association that are available only to those in the industry because they are relevant only to a specific purpose. When this is the case, paragraph 69(f) requires a statement alerting readers to this fact. In addition, the practitioner may consider it appropriate to indicate that the assurance report is intended solely for specific users (see paragraph A166–A167).

Access to Evidence (Ref: Para. 24(b)(iv))

Quantity and quality of available evidence

A53   The quantity or quality of available evidence is affected by:

(a)   The characteristics of the underlying subject matter or the subject matter information. For example, less objective evidence might be expected when the subject matter information is future oriented rather than historical; and

(b)   Other circumstances, such as when evidence that could reasonably be expected to exist is not available because of, for example, the timing of the practitioner's appointment, an entity's document retention policy, inadequate information systems, or a restriction imposed by the responsible party.

Ordinarily, evidence will be persuasive rather than conclusive.

Access to records (Ref: Para. 56)

A54   Seeking the agreement of the appropriate party(ies) that it acknowledges and understands its responsibility to provide the practitioner with the following may assist the practitioner in determining whether the engagement exhibits the characteristic of access to evidence:

(a)   Access to all information of which the appropriate party(ies) is aware that is relevant to the preparation of the subject matter information such as records, documentation and other matters;

(b) Additional information that the practitioner may request from the appropriate party(ies) for the purpose of the engagement; and

(c) Unrestricted access to persons from the appropriate party(ies) from whom the practitioner determines it necessary to obtain evidence.

The nature of relationships between the responsible party, the measurer or evalua- **A55** tor, and the engaging party may affect the practitioner's ability to access to records, documentation and other information the practitioner may require as evidence to complete the engagement. The nature of such relationships may therefore be a relevant consideration when determining whether or not to accept the engagement. Examples of some circumstances in which the nature of these relationships may be problematic are included in paragraph A139.

A Rational Purpose (Ref: Para. 24(b)(vi))

In determining whether the engagement has a rational purpose, relevant consider- **A56** ations may include the following:

- The intended users of the subject matter information and the assurance report (particularly, when the criteria are designed for a special purpose). A further consideration is the likelihood that the subject matter information and the assurance report will be used or distributed more broadly than to intended users.
- Whether aspects of the subject matter information are expected to be excluded from the assurance engagement, and the reason for their exclusion.
- The characteristics of the relationships between the responsible party, the measurer or evaluator, and the engaging party, for example, when the measurer or evaluator is not the responsible party, whether the responsible party consents to the use to be made of the subject matter information and will have the opportunity to review the subject matter information before it is made available to intended users or to distribute comments with the subject matter information.
- Who selected the criteria to be applied to measure or evaluate the underlying subject matter, and what the degree of judgment and scope for bias is in applying them. The engagement is more likely to have a rational purpose if the intended users selected or were involved in selecting the criteria.
- Any significant limitations on the scope of the practitioner's work.
- Whether the practitioner believes the engaging party intends to associate the practitioner's name with the underlying subject matter or the subject matter information in an inappropriate manner.

Agreeing on the Terms of the Engagement (Ref: Para. 27)

It is in the interests of both the engaging party and the practitioner that the prac- **A57** titioner communicates in writing the agreed terms of the engagement before the commencement of the engagement to help avoid misunderstandings. The form and content of the written agreement or contract will vary with the engagement circumstances. For example, if law or regulation prescribe in sufficient detail the terms of the engagement, the practitioner need not record them in a written agreement, except for the fact that such law or regulation applies and that the appropriate party acknowledges and understands its responsibilities under such law or regulation.

Law or regulation, particularly in the public sector, may mandate the appointment of **A58** a practitioner and set out specific powers, such as the power to access an appropriate party(ies)'s records and other information, and responsibilities, such as requiring the practitioner to report directly to a minister, the legislature or the public if an appropriate party(ies) attempts to limit the scope of the engagement.

Acceptance of a Change in the Terms of the Engagement (Ref: Para. 29)

A59   A change in circumstances that affects the intended users' requirements, or a misunderstanding concerning the nature of the engagement, may justify a request for a change in the engagement, for example, from an assurance engagement to a non-assurance engagement, or from a reasonable assurance engagement to a limited assurance engagement. An inability to obtain sufficient appropriate evidence to form a reasonable assurance conclusion is not an acceptable reason to change from a reasonable assurance engagement to a limited assurance engagement.

Quality Control

Professional Accountants in Public Practice (Ref: Para. 20, 31(a)–(b))

A60   This ISAE has been written in the context of a range of measures taken to ensure the quality of assurance engagements undertaken by professional accountants in public practice, such as those taken by IFAC member bodies in accordance with IFAC's Member Body Compliance Program and Statements of Membership Obligations. Such measures include:

- Competency requirements, such as education and experience benchmarks for entry to membership, and ongoing continuing professional development as well as life-long learning requirements.
- Quality control policies and procedures implemented across the firm. ISQC 1 applies to all firms of professional accountants in respect of assurance and related services engagements.
- A comprehensive Code of Ethics, including detailed independence requirements, founded on fundamental principles of integrity, objectivity, professional competence and due care, confidentiality and professional behavior.

Firm Level Quality Control (Ref: Para. 3(b), 31(a))

A61   ISQC 1 deals with the firm's responsibilities to establish and maintain its system of quality control for assurance engagements. It sets out the responsibilities of the firm for establishing policies and procedures designed to provide it with reasonable assurance that the firm and its personnel comply with relevant ethical requirements, including those pertaining to independence. Compliance with ISQC 1 requires, among other things, that the firm establish and maintain a system of quality control that includes policies and procedures addressing each of the following elements, and that it documents its policies and procedures and communicates them to the firm's personnel:

(a) Leadership responsibilities for quality within the firm;
(b) Relevant ethical requirements;
(c) Acceptance and continuance of client relationships and specific engagements;
(d) Human resources;
(e) Engagement performance; and
(f) Monitoring.

Other professional requirements, or requirements in law or regulation that deal with **A62** the firm's responsibilities to establish and maintain a system of quality control, are at least as demanding as ISQC 1 when they address all the matters referred to in the preceding paragraph and impose obligations on the firm that achieve the aims of the requirements set out in ISQC 1.

The actions of the engagement partner, and appropriate messages to the other **A63** members of the engagement team, in the context of the engagement partner taking responsibility for the overall quality on each engagement, emphasize the fact that quality is essential in performing an assurance engagement, and the importance to the quality of the assurance engagement of:

(a) Performing work that complies with professional standards and regulatory and legal requirements.
(b) Complying with the firm's quality control policies and procedures as applicable.
(c) Issuing a report for the engagement that is appropriate in the circumstances.
(d) The engagement team's ability to raise concerns without fear of reprisals.

An effective system of quality control includes a monitoring process designed to **A64** provide the firm with reasonable assurance that its policies and procedures relating to the system of quality control are relevant, adequate and operating effectively.

Unless information provided by the firm or other parties suggests otherwise, the **A65** engagement team is entitled to rely on the firm's system of quality control. For example, the engagement team may rely on the firm's system of quality control in relation to:

(a) Competence of personnel through their recruitment and formal training.
(b) Independence through the accumulation and communication of relevant independence information.
(c) Maintenance of client relationships through acceptance and continuance systems.
(d) Adherence to regulatory and legal requirements through the monitoring process.

In considering deficiencies identified in the firm's system of quality control that may affect the assurance engagement, the engagement partner may consider measures taken by the firm to rectify those deficiencies.

A deficiency in the firm's system of quality control does not necessarily indicate **A66** that an assurance engagement was not performed in accordance with professional standards and applicable legal and regulatory requirements, or that the practitioner's report was not appropriate.

Skills, Knowledge and Experience with Respect to the Underlying Subject Matter and Its Measurement or Evaluation (Ref: Para. 31(c))

A practitioner may be requested to perform assurance engagements with respect to a **A67** wide range of underlying subject matter and subject matter information. Some may require specialized skills and knowledge beyond those ordinarily possessed by a particular individual.

The IESBA Code requires the professional accountant in public practice to agree **A68** to provide only those services that the professional accountant in public practice is competent to perform.[4] The practitioner has sole responsibility for the assurance conclusion expressed, and that responsibility is not reduced by the practitioner's use of the work of a practitioner's expert. Nonetheless, if the practitioner using the work of a practitioner's expert, having followed this ISAE, concludes that the work of that expert is adequate for the practitioner's purposes, the practitioner may accept that expert's findings or conclusions in the expert's field as appropriate evidence.

Assignment of the Team

Collective Competence and Capabilities (Ref: Para. 32)

A69   ISQC 1 requires the firm to establish policies and procedures for the acceptance and continuance of client relationships and specific engagements, designed to provide the firm with reasonable assurance that it will only undertake or continue relationships and engagements where the firm is competent to perform the engagement and has the capabilities, including time and resources, to do so.[5]

Practitioner's Expert (Ref: Para. 32(a), 32(b)(i))

A70   Some of the assurance work may be performed by a multi-disciplinary team that includes one or more practitioner's expert. For example, a practitioner's expert may be needed to assist the practitioner in obtaining an understanding of the underlying subject matter and other engagement circumstances or in one or more of the matters mentioned in paragraph 46R (in the case of a reasonable assurance engagement) or 46L (in the case of a limited assurance engagement).

A71   When the work of a practitioner's expert is to be used, it may be appropriate to perform some of the procedures required by paragraph 52 at the engagement acceptance or continuance stage.

Other Practitioners (Ref: Para. 32(b)(ii))

A72   The subject matter information may include information upon which another practitioner may have expressed a conclusion. The practitioner, in concluding on the subject matter information, may decide to use the evidence on which that other practitioner's conclusion is based to provide evidence regarding the subject matter information.

A73   The work of another practitioner may be used in relation to, for example, an underlying subject matter at a remote location or in a foreign jurisdiction. Such other practitioners are not part of the engagement team. Relevant considerations when the engagement team plans to use the work of another practitioner may include:

- Whether the other practitioner understands and complies with the ethical requirements that are relevant to the engagement and, in particular, is independent.
- The other practitioner's professional competence.
- The extent of the engagement team's involvement in the work of the other practitioner.

---

[4] *IESBA Code, paragraph 210.6.*

[5] *ISQC 1, paragraph 26.*

- Whether the other practitioner operates in a regulatory environment that actively oversees that practitioner.

Review Responsibilities (Ref: Para. 33(c))

Under ISQC 1, the firm's review responsibility policies and procedures are deter- **A74** mined on the basis that the work of less experienced team members is reviewed by more experienced team members.[6]

Engagement Quality Control Review (Ref: Para. 36(b))

Other matters that may be considered in an engagement quality control review **A75** include:

(a) The engagement team's evaluation of the firm's independence in relation to the engagement;
(b) Whether appropriate consultation has taken place on matters involving differences of opinion or other difficult or contentious matters, and the conclusions arising from those consultations; and
(c) Whether engagement documentation selected for review reflects the work performed in relation to the significant judgments and supports the conclusions reached.

Professional Skepticism and Professional Judgment

Professional Skepticism (Ref: Para. 37)

Professional skepticism is an attitude that includes being alert to, for example: **A76**

- Evidence that is inconsistent with other evidence obtained.
- Information that calls into question the reliability of documents and responses to inquiries to be used as evidence.
- Circumstances that suggest the need for procedures in addition to those required by relevant ISAEs.
- Conditions that may indicate likely misstatement.

Maintaining professional skepticism throughout the engagement is necessary if the **A77** practitioner is, for example, to reduce the risks of:

- Overlooking unusual circumstances.
- Overgeneralizing when drawing conclusions from observations.
- Using inappropriate assumptions in determining the nature, timing, and extent of the procedures, and evaluating the results thereof.

Professional skepticism is necessary to the critical assessment of evidence. This **A78** includes questioning inconsistent evidence and the reliability of documents and responses to inquiries. It also includes consideration of the sufficiency and appropriateness of evidence obtained in the light of the circumstances.

[6] *ISQC 1, paragraph 33*

A79   Unless the engagement involves assurance about whether documents are genuine, the practitioner may accept records and documents as genuine unless the practitioner has reason to believe the contrary. Nevertheless, the practitioner is required by paragraph 50 to consider the reliability of information to be used as evidence.

A80   The practitioner cannot be expected to disregard past experience of the honesty and integrity of those who provide evidence. Nevertheless, a belief that those who provide evidence are honest and have integrity does not relieve the practitioner of the need to maintain professional skepticism.

Professional Judgment (Ref: Para. 38)

A81   Professional judgment is essential to the proper conduct of an assurance engagement. This is because interpretation of relevant ethical requirements and relevant ISAEs and the informed decisions required throughout the engagement cannot be made without the application of relevant training, knowledge, and experience to the facts and circumstances. Professional judgment is necessary in particular regarding decisions about:

- Materiality and engagement risk.
- The nature, timing, and extent of procedures used to meet the requirements of relevant ISAEs and obtain evidence.
- Evaluating whether sufficient appropriate evidence has been obtained, and whether more needs to be done to achieve the objectives of this ISAE and any relevant subject matter specific ISAE. In particular, in the case of a limited assurance engagement, professional judgment is required in evaluating whether a meaningful level of assurance has been obtained.
- The appropriate conclusions to draw based on the evidence obtained.

A82   The distinguishing feature of the professional judgment expected of a practitioner is that it is exercised by a practitioner whose training, knowledge and experience have assisted in developing the necessary competencies to achieve reasonable judgments.

A83   The exercise of professional judgment in any particular case is based on the facts and circumstances that are known by the practitioner. Consultation on difficult or contentious matters during the course of the engagement, both within the engagement team and between the engagement team and others at the appropriate level within or outside the firm assist the practitioner in making informed and reasonable judgments, including the extent to which particular items in the subject matter information are affected by judgment of the appropriate party.

A84   Professional judgment can be evaluated based on whether the judgment reached reflects a competent application of assurance and measurement or evaluation principles and is appropriate in the light of, and consistent with, the facts and circumstances that were known to the practitioner up to the date of the practitioner's assurance report.

A85   Professional judgment needs to be exercised throughout the engagement. It also needs to be appropriately documented. In this regard, paragraph 79 requires the practitioner to prepare documentation sufficient to enable an experienced practitioner, having no previous connection with the engagement, to understand the significant professional judgments made in reaching conclusions on significant matters arising during the engagement. Professional judgment is not to be used as the justification for decisions that are not otherwise supported by the facts and circumstances of the engagement or sufficient appropriate evidence.

Planning and Performing the Engagement

Planning (Ref: Para. 40)

Planning involves the engagement partner, other key members of the engagement team, and any key practitioner's external experts developing an overall strategy for the scope, emphasis, timing and conduct of the engagement, and an engagement plan, consisting of a detailed approach for the nature, timing and extent of procedures to be performed, and the reasons for selecting them. Adequate planning helps to devote appropriate attention to important areas of the engagement, identify potential problems on a timely basis and properly organize and manage the engagement in order for it to be performed in an effective and efficient manner. Adequate planning also assists the practitioner to properly assign work to engagement team members, and facilitates the direction, supervision, and the review of their work. Further, it assists, where applicable, the coordination of work done by other practitioners and experts. The nature and extent of planning activities will vary with the engagement circumstances, for example the complexity of the underlying subject matter and criteria. Examples of the main matters that may be considered include:

- The characteristics of the engagement that define its scope, including the terms of the engagement and the characteristics of the underlying subject matter and the criteria.
- The expected timing and the nature of the communications required.
- The results of engagement acceptance activities and, where applicable, whether knowledge gained on other engagements performed by the engagement partner for the appropriate party(ies) is relevant.
- The engagement process.
- The practitioner's understanding of the appropriate party(ies) and their environment, including the risks that the subject matter information may be materially misstated.
- Identification of intended users and their information needs, and consideration of materiality and the components of engagement risk.
- The extent to which the risk of fraud is relevant to the engagement.
- The nature, timing and extent of resources necessary to perform the engagement, such as personnel and expertise requirements, including the nature and extent of experts' involvement.
- The impact of the internal audit function on the engagement.

A86

The practitioner may decide to discuss elements of planning with the appropriate party(ies) to facilitate the conduct and management of the engagement (for example, to coordinate some of the planned procedures with the work of the appropriate party(ies)'s personnel). Although these discussions often occur, the overall engagement strategy and the engagement plan remain the practitioner's responsibility. When discussing matters included in the overall engagement strategy or engagement plan, care is required in order not to compromise the effectiveness of the engagement. For example, discussing the nature and timing of detailed procedures with the appropriate party(ies) may compromise the effectiveness of the engagement by making the procedures too predictable.

A87

A88   Planning is not a discrete phase, but rather a continual and iterative process throughout the engagement. As a result of unexpected events, changes in conditions, or evidence obtained, the practitioner may need to revise the overall strategy and engagement plan, and thereby the resulting planned nature, timing and extent of procedures.

A89   In smaller or less complex engagements, the entire engagement may be conducted by a very small engagement team, possibly involving the engagement partner (who may be a sole practitioner) working without any other engagement team members. With a smaller team, co-ordination of, and communication between, team members is easier. Establishing the overall engagement strategy in such cases need not be a complex or time-consuming exercise; it varies according to the size of the entity, the complexity of the engagement, including the underlying subject matter and criteria, and the size of the engagement team. For example, in the case of a recurring engagement, a brief memorandum prepared at the completion of the previous period, based on a review of the working papers and highlighting issues identified in the engagement just completed, updated in the current period based on discussions with appropriate parties, can serve as the documented engagement strategy for the current engagement.

A90   If in the circumstances described in paragraph 43, the practitioner continues with the engagement:

(a)   When, in the practitioner's professional judgment, the unsuitable applicable criteria or inappropriate underlying subject matter is likely to mislead the intended users, a qualified conclusion or adverse conclusion would be appropriate in the circumstances depending on how material and pervasive the matter is.

(b)   In other cases, a qualified conclusion or a disclaimer of conclusion would be appropriate depending on, in the practitioner's professional judgment, how material and pervasive the matter is.

A91   For example, if after accepting the engagement, the practitioner discovers that the application of the applicable criteria leads to biased subject matter information, and the bias of the subject matter information is material and pervasive, then an adverse conclusion would be appropriate in the circumstances.

Materiality (Ref: Para. 44)

A92   Professional judgments about materiality are made in light of surrounding circumstances, but are not affected by the level of assurance, that is, for the same intended users and purpose, materiality for a reasonable assurance engagement is the same as for a limited assurance engagement because materiality is based on the information needs of intended users.

A93   The applicable criteria may discuss the concept of materiality in the context of the preparation and presentation of the subject matter information and thereby provide a frame of reference for the practitioner in considering materiality for the engagement. Although applicable criteria may discuss materiality in different terms, the concept of materiality generally includes the matters discussed in paragraphs A92–A100. If the applicable criteria do not include a discussion of the concept of materiality, these paragraphs provide the practitioner with a frame of reference.

A94   Misstatements, including omissions, are considered to be material if they, individually or in the aggregate, could reasonably be expected to influence relevant decisions of intended users taken on the basis of the subject matter information. The practitioner's consideration of materiality is a matter of professional judgment, and is affected by the practitioner's perception of the common information needs of intended users as a group. In this context, it is reasonable for the practitioner to assume that intended users:

(a) Have a reasonable knowledge of the underlying subject matter, and a willingness to study the subject matter information with reasonable diligence;
(b) Understand that the subject matter information is prepared and assured to appropriate levels of materiality, and have an understanding of any materiality concepts included in the applicable criteria;
(c) Understand any inherent uncertainties involved in the measuring or evaluating the underlying subject matter; and
(d) Make reasonable decisions on the basis of the subject matter information taken as a whole.

Unless the engagement has been designed to meet the particular information needs of specific users, the possible effect of misstatements on specific users, whose information needs may vary widely, is not ordinarily considered (see also paragraphs A16–A18).

Materiality is considered in the context of qualitative factors and, when applicable, quantitative factors. The relative importance of qualitative factors and quantitative factors when considering materiality in a particular engagement is a matter for the practitioner's professional judgment. **A95**

Qualitative factors may include such things as: **A96**

● The number of persons or entities affected by the subject matter.
● The interaction between, and relative importance of, various components of the subject matter information when it is made up of multiple components, such as a report that includes numerous performance indicators.
● The wording chosen with respect to subject matter information that is expressed in narrative form.
● The characteristics of the presentation adopted for the subject matter information when the applicable criteria allow for variations in that presentation.
● The nature of a misstatement, for example, the nature of observed deviations from a control when the subject matter information is a statement that the control is effective.
● Whether a misstatement affects compliance with law or regulation.
● In the case of periodic reporting on an underlying subject matter, the effect of an adjustment that affects past or current subject matter information or is likely to affect future subject matter information.
● Whether a misstatement is the result of an intentional act or is unintentional.
● Whether a misstatement is significant having regard to the practitioner's understanding of known previous communications to users, for example, in relation to the expected outcome of the measurement or evaluation of the underlying subject matter.
● Whether a misstatement relates to the relationship between the responsible party, the measurer or evaluator, or the engaging party or their relationship with other parties.
● When a threshold or benchmark value has been identified, whether the result of the procedure deviates from that value.

- When the underlying subject matter is a governmental program or public sector entity, whether a particular aspect of the program or entity is significant with regard to the nature, visibility and sensitivity of the program or entity.
- When the subject matter information relates to a conclusion on compliance with law or regulation, the seriousness of the consequences of non-compliance.

A97   Quantitative factors relate to the magnitude of misstatements relative to reported amounts for those aspects of the subject matter information, if any, that are:

- Expressed numerically; or
- Otherwise related to numerical values (for example, the number of observed deviations from a control may be a relevant quantitative factor when the subject matter information is a statement that the control is effective).

A98   When quantitative factors are applicable, planning the engagement solely to detect individually material misstatements overlooks the fact that the aggregate of uncorrected and undetected individually immaterial misstatements may cause the subject matter information to be materially misstated. It may therefore be appropriate when planning the nature, timing and extent of procedures for the practitioner to determine a quantity less than materiality as a basis for determining the nature, timing and extent of procedures.

A99   Materiality relates to the information covered by the assurance report. Therefore, when the engagement covers some, but not all, aspects of the information communicated about an underlying subject matter, materiality is considered in relation to only that portion that is covered by the engagement.

A100   Concluding on the materiality of the misstatements identified as a result of the procedures performed requires professional judgment. For example:

- The applicable criteria for a value for money engagement for a hospital's emergency department may include the speed of the services provided, the quality of the services, the number of patients treated during a shift, and benchmarking the cost of the services against other similar hospitals. If three of these applicable criteria are satisfied but one applicable criterion is not satisfied by a small margin, then professional judgment is needed to conclude whether the hospital's emergency department represents value for money as a whole.
- In a compliance engagement, the entity may have complied with nine provisions of the relevant law or regulation, but did not comply with one provision. Professional judgment is needed to conclude whether the entity complied with the relevant law or regulation as a whole. For example, the practitioner may consider the significance of the provision with which the entity did not comply, as well as the relationship of that provision to the remaining provisions of the relevant law or regulation.

Understanding the Engagement Circumstances (Ref: Para. 45–47R)

A101   Discussions between the engagement partner and other key members of the engagement team, and any key practitioner's external experts, about the susceptibility of the subject matter information to material misstatement, and the application of the applicable criteria to the facts and circumstances of the engagement, may assist the engagement team in planning and performing the engagement. It is also useful to communicate relevant matters to members of the engagement team, and to any practitioner's external experts not involved in the discussion.

Obtaining an understanding of the underlying subject matter and other engagement   **A102**
circumstances provides the practitioner with a frame of reference for exercising professional judgment throughout the engagement, for example when:

- Considering the characteristics of the underlying subject matter;
- Assessing the suitability of criteria;
- Considering the factors that, in the practitioner's professional judgment, are significant in directing the engagement team's efforts, including where special consideration may be necessary; for example, the need for specialized skills or the work of an expert;
- Establishing and evaluating the continued appropriateness of quantitative materiality levels (where appropriate), and considering qualitative materiality factors;
- Developing expectations for use when performing analytical procedures;
- Designing and performing procedures; and
- Evaluating evidence, including the reasonableness of the oral and written representations received by the practitioner.

The practitioner ordinarily has a lesser depth of understanding of the underlying   **A103**
subject matter and other engagement circumstances than the responsible party. The practitioner also ordinarily has a lesser depth of understanding of the underlying subject matter and other engagement circumstances for a limited assurance engagement than for a reasonable assurance engagement, for example, while in some limited assurance engagements the practitioner may obtain an understanding of internal control over the preparation of the subject matter information, this is often not the case.

In a limited assurance engagement, identifying the areas where a material misstate-   **A104**
ment of the subject matter information is likely to arise enables the practitioner to focus procedures on those areas. For example, in an engagement when the subject matter information is a sustainability report, the practitioner may focus on certain areas of the sustainability report. The practitioner may design and perform procedures over the entire subject matter information when the subject matter information consists of only a single area or when obtaining assurance over all areas of the subject matter information is necessary to obtain meaningful assurance.

In a reasonable assurance engagement, understanding internal control over the sub-   **A105**
ject matter information assists the practitioner in identifying the types of misstatements and factors that affect the risks of material misstatements in the subject matter information. The practitioner is required to evaluate the design of relevant controls and determines whether they have been implemented, by performing procedures in addition to inquiry of the responsible party. Professional judgment is needed to determine which controls are relevant in the engagement circumstances.

In a limited assurance engagement, considering the process used to prepare the sub-   **A106**
ject matter information assists the practitioner in designing and performing procedures that address the areas where a material misstatement of the subject matter information is likely to arise. In considering the process used, the practitioner uses professional judgment to determine which aspects of the process are relevant to the engagement, and may make inquiries of the appropriate party about those aspects.

In both a reasonable assurance and a limited assurance engagement, the results of   **A107**
the entity's risk assessment process may also assist the practitioner in obtaining an understanding of the underlying subject matter and other engagement circumstances.

Obtaining Evidence

The Nature, Timing and Extent of Procedures (Ref: Para. 48(L)–49(R))

A108   The practitioner chooses a combination of procedures to obtain reasonable assurance or limited assurance, as appropriate. The procedures listed below may be used, for example, for planning or performing the engagement, depending on the context in which they are applied by the practitioner:

- Inspection;
- Observation;
- Confirmation;
- Re-calculation;
- Re-performance;
- Analytical procedures; and
- Inquiry.

A109   Factors that may affect the practitioner's selection of procedures include the nature of the underlying subject matter; the level of assurance to be obtained; and the information needs of the intended users and the engaging party, including relevant time and cost constraints.

A110   In some cases, a subject matter-specific ISAE may include requirements that affect the nature, timing and extent of procedures. For example, a subject matter-specific ISAE may describe the nature or extent of particular procedures to be performed or the level of assurance expected to be obtained in a particular type of engagement. Even in such cases, determining the exact nature, timing and extent of procedures is a matter of professional judgment and will vary from one engagement to the next.

A111   In some engagements, the practitioner may not identify any areas where a material misstatement of the subject matter information is likely to arise. Irrespective of whether any such areas have been identified, the practitioner designs and performs procedures to obtain a meaningful level of assurance.

A112   An assurance engagement is an iterative process, and information may come to the practitioner's attention that differs significantly from that on which the determination of planned procedures was based. As the practitioner performs planned procedures, the evidence obtained may cause the practitioner to perform additional procedures. Such procedures may include asking the measurer or evaluator to examine the matter identified by the practitioner, and to make adjustments to the subject matter information if appropriate.

Determining Whether Additional Procedures Are Necessary in a Limited Assurance Engagement (Ref: Para. 49L)

A113   The practitioner may become aware of misstatements that are, after applying professional judgment, clearly not indicative of the existence of material misstatements. The following examples illustrate when additional procedures may not be needed because, in the practitioner's professional judgment, the identified misstatements are clearly not indicative of the existence of material misstatements:

- If materiality is 10,000 units, and the practitioner judges that a potential error of 100 units may exist, then additional procedures would not generally be required, unless there are other qualitative factors that need to be considered, because the risk of a material misstatement is likely to be acceptable in the engagement circumstances.

- If, in performing a set of procedures over an area where material misstatements are likely, a response to one inquiry among many was not as expected, additional procedures may not be needed if the risk of a material misstatement is, nevertheless, at a level that is acceptable in the circumstances of the engagement in light of the results of other procedures.

The practitioner may become aware of a matter(s) that causes the practitioner to believe that the subject matter information may be materially misstated. The following examples illustrate when additional procedures may be needed as the identified misstatements indicate that the subject matter information may be materially misstated: **A114**

- When performing analytical procedures, the practitioner may identify a fluctuation or relationship that is inconsistent with other relevant information or that differs significantly from expected amounts or ratios.
- The practitioner may become aware of a potential material misstatement from reviewing external sources.
- If the applicable criteria permit a 10% error rate and, based on a particular test, the practitioner discovered a 9% error rate, then additional procedures may be needed because the risk of a material misstatement may not be acceptable in the engagement circumstances.
- If the results of analytical procedures are within expectations but are, nevertheless, close to exceeding the expected value, then additional procedures may be needed because the risk of a material misstatement may not be acceptable in the engagement circumstances.

If, in the case of a limited assurance engagement, a matter(s) comes to the practitioner's attention that causes the practitioner to believe the subject matter information may be materially misstated, the practitioner is required by paragraph 49L to design and perform additional procedures. Additional procedures may include, for example, inquiring of the appropriate party(ies) or performing other procedures as appropriate in the circumstances.   **A115**

If, having performed the additional procedures required by paragraph 49L, the practitioner is not able to obtain sufficient appropriate evidence to either conclude that the matter(s) is not likely to cause the subject matter information to be materially misstated or determine that it does cause the subject matter information to be materially misstated, a scope limitation exists and paragraph 66 applies.   **A116**

The practitioner's judgment about the nature, timing and extent of additional procedures that are needed to obtain evidence to either conclude that a material misstatement is not likely, or determine that a material misstatement exists, is, for example, guided by: **A117**

- Information obtained from the practitioner's evaluation of the results of the procedures already performed;
- The practitioner's updated understanding of the underlying subject matter and other engagement circumstances obtained throughout the course of the engagement; and
- The practitioner's view on the persuasiveness of evidence needed to address the matter that causes the practitioner to believe that the subject matter information may be materially misstated.

Accumulating Uncorrected Misstatements (Ref: Para. 51, 65)

A118   Uncorrected misstatements are accumulated during the engagement (see paragraph 50) for the purpose of evaluating whether, individually or in aggregate, they are material when forming the practitioner's conclusion.

A119   The practitioner may designate an amount below which misstatements would be clearly trivial and would not need to be accumulated because the practitioner expects that the accumulation of such amounts clearly would not have a material effect on the subject matter information. "Clearly trivial" is not another expression for "not material." Matters that are clearly trivial will be of a wholly different (smaller) order of magnitude than materiality determined in accordance with paragraph 44, and will be matters that are clearly inconsequential, whether taken individually or in aggregate and whether judged by any criteria of size, nature or circumstances. When there is any uncertainty about whether one or more items are clearly trivial, the matter is considered not to be clearly trivial.

Considerations When a Practitioner's Expert Is Involved on the Engagement

Nature, Timing and Extent of Procedures (Ref: Para. 52)

A120   The following matters are often relevant when determining the nature, timing and extent of procedures with respect to the work of a practitioner's expert when some of the assurance work is performed by one or more practitioner's expert (see paragraph A70):

(a)   The significance of that expert's work in the context of the engagement (see also paragraphs A121–A122);
(b)   The nature of the matter to which that expert's work relates;
(c)   The risks of material misstatement in the matter to which that expert's work relates;
(d)   The practitioner's knowledge of and experience with previous work performed by that expert; and
(e)   Whether that expert is subject to the practitioner's firm's quality control policies and procedures (see also paragraphs A123–A124).

Integrating the work of a practitioner's expert

A121   Assurance engagements may be performed on a wide range of underlying subject matters that require specialized skills and knowledge beyond those possessed by the engagement partner and other members of the engagement team and for which the work of a practitioner's expert is used. In some situations, the practitioner's expert will be consulted to provide advice on an individual matter, but the greater the significance of the practitioner's expert's work in the context of the engagement, the more likely it is that expert will work as part of a multi-disciplinary team comprising subject matter experts and other assurance personnel. The more that expert's work is integrated in nature, timing and extent with the overall work effort, the more important effective two-way communication is between the practitioner's expert and other assurance personnel. Effective two-way communication facilitates the proper integration of the expert's work with the work of others on the engagement.

A122   As noted in paragraph A71, when the work of a practitioner's expert is to be used, it may be appropriate to perform some of the procedures required by paragraph 52 at the engagement acceptance or continuance stage. This is particularly so when the work of the practitioner's expert will be fully integrated with the work of other assurance personnel and when the work of the practitioner's expert is to be used in the early stages of the engagement, for example during initial planning and risk assessment.

The practitioner's firm's quality control policies and procedures

A practitioner's internal expert may be a partner or staff, including temporary **A123** staff, of the practitioner's firm, and therefore subject to the quality control policies and procedures of that firm in accordance with ISQC 1 or other professional requirements, or requirements in law or regulation, that are at least as demanding as ISQC 1. Alternatively, a practitioner's internal expert may be a partner or staff, including temporary staff, of a network firm, which may share common quality control policies and procedures with the practitioner's firm. A practitioner's external expert is not a member of the engagement team and is not subject to quality control policies and procedures in accordance with ISQC 1.

Engagement teams are entitled to rely on the firm's system of quality control, unless **A124** information provided by the firm or other parties suggests otherwise. The extent of that reliance will vary with the circumstances, and may affect the nature, timing and extent of the practitioner's procedures with respect to such matters as:

- Competence and capabilities, through recruitment and training programs.
- The practitioner's evaluation of the objectivity of the practitioner's expert. Practitioner's internal experts are subject to relevant ethical requirements, including those pertaining to independence.
- The practitioner's evaluation of the adequacy of the practitioner's expert's work. For example, the firm's training programs may provide the practitioner's internal experts with an appropriate understanding of the interrelationship of their expertise with the evidence gathering process. Reliance on such training and other firm processes, such as protocols for scoping the work of the practitioner's internal experts, may affect the nature, timing and extent of the practitioner's procedures to evaluate the adequacy of the practitioner's expert's work.
- Adherence to regulatory and legal requirements, through monitoring processes.
- Agreement with the practitioner's expert.
  Such reliance does not reduce the practitioner's responsibility to meet the requirements of this ISAE.

The Competence, Capabilities and Objectivity of the Practitioner's Expert
(Ref: Para. 52(a))

Information regarding the competence, capabilities and objectivity of a practitio- **A125** ner's expert may come from a variety of sources, such as:

- Personal experience with previous work of that expert.
- Discussions with that expert.
- Discussions with other practitioners or others who are familiar with that expert's work.
- Knowledge of that expert's qualifications, membership of a professional body or industry association, license to practice, or other forms of external recognition.
- Published papers or books written by that expert.
- The firm's quality control policies and procedures (see also paragraphs A123–A124).

A126   While practitioner's experts do not require the same proficiency as the practitioner in performing all aspects of an assurance engagement, a practitioner's expert whose work is used may need a sufficient understanding of relevant ISAEs to enable that expert to relate the work assigned to them to the engagement objective.

A127   The evaluation of the significance of threats to objectivity and of whether there is a need for safeguards may depend upon the role of the practitioner's expert and the significance of the expert's work in the context of the engagement. There may be some circumstances in which safeguards cannot reduce threats to an acceptable level, for example, if a proposed practitioner's expert is an individual who has played a significant role in preparing the subject matter information.

A128   When evaluating the objectivity of a practitioner's external expert, it may be relevant to:

- Inquire of the appropriate party(ies) about any known interests or relationships that the appropriate party(ies) has with the practitioner's external expert that may affect that expert's objectivity.
- Discuss with that expert any applicable safeguards, including any professional requirements that apply to that expert, and evaluate whether the safeguards are adequate to reduce threats to an acceptable level. Interests and relationships that it may be relevant to discuss with the practitioner's expert include:
  o   Financial interests.
  o   Business and personal relationships.
  o   Provision of other services by the expert, including by the organization in the case of an external expert that is an organization.

  In some cases, it may also be appropriate for the practitioner to obtain a written representation from the practitioner's external expert about any interests or relationships with the appropriate party(ies) of which that expert is aware.

Obtaining an Understanding of the Field of Expertise of the Practitioner's Expert (Ref: Para. 52(b))

A129   Having a sufficient understanding of the field of expertise of the practitioner's expert enables the practitioner to:

(a)   Agree with the practitioner's expert the nature, scope and objectives of that expert's work for the practitioner's purposes; and

(b)   Evaluate the adequacy of that work for the practitioner's purposes.

A130   Aspects of the practitioner's expert's field relevant to the practitioner's understanding may include:

- Whether that expert's field has areas of specialty within it that are relevant to the engagement.
- Whether any professional or other standards and regulatory or legal requirements apply.
- What assumptions and methods, including models where applicable, are used by the practitioner's expert, and whether they are generally accepted within that expert's field and appropriate in the circumstances of the engagement.
- The nature of internal and external data or information the practitioner's expert uses.

Agreement with the Practitioner's Expert (Ref: Para. 52(c))

It may be appropriate for the practitioner's agreement with the practitioner's expert **A131**
to also include matters such as the following:

(a) The respective roles and responsibilities of the practitioner and that expert;
(b) The nature, timing and extent of communication between the practitioner and
    that expert, including the form of any report to be provided by that expert; and
(c) The need for the practitioner's expert to observe confidentiality requirements.

The matters noted in paragraph A124 may affect the level of detail and formality **A132**
of the agreement between the practitioner and the practitioner's expert, including
whether it is appropriate that the agreement be in writing. The agreement between
the practitioner and a practitioner's external expert is often in the form of an engagement letter.

Evaluating the Adequacy of the Practitioner's Expert's Work (Ref: Para. 52(d))

The following matters may be relevant when evaluating the adequacy of the practi- **A133**
tioner's expert's work for the practitioner's purposes:

(a) The relevance and reasonableness of that expert's findings or conclusions, and
    their consistency with other evidence;
(b) If that expert's work involves use of significant assumptions and methods, the
    relevance and reasonableness of those assumptions and methods in the circum-
    stances; and
(c) If that expert's work involves the use of source data that is significant to that
    expert's work, the relevance, completeness, and accuracy of that source data.

If the practitioner determines that the work of the practitioner's expert is not ade- **A134**
quate for the practitioner's purposes, options available to the practitioner include:

(a) Agreeing with that expert on the nature and extent of further work to be per-
    formed by that expert; or
(b) Performing additional procedures appropriate to the circumstances.

Work Performed by Another Practitioner, a Responsible Party's or Measurer's or
Evaluator's Expert or an Internal Auditor (Ref: Para. 53–55)

While paragraphs A120–A134 have been written in the context of using work per- **A135**
formed by a practitioner's expert, they may also provide helpful guidance with
respect to using work performed by another practitioner, a responsible party's or
measurer's or evaluator's expert, or an internal auditor.

Written Representations (Ref: Para. 56)

Written confirmation of oral representations reduces the possibility of misunder- **A136**
standings between the practitioner and the appropriate party(ies). The person(s) from
whom the practitioner requests written representations will ordinarily be a member
of senior management or those charged with governance depending on, for example,
the management and governance structure of the appropriate party(ies), which may
vary by jurisdiction and by entity, reflecting influences such as different cultural and
legal backgrounds, and size and ownership characteristics.

A137   Other written representations requested may include the following:

- Whether the appropriate party(ies) believes the effects of uncorrected misstatements are immaterial, individually and in aggregate, to the subject matter information. A summary of such items is ordinarily included in or attached to the written representation;
- That significant assumptions used in making any material estimates are reasonable;
- That the appropriate party(ies) has communicated to the practitioner all deficiencies in internal control relevant to the engagement that are not clearly trivial and inconsequential of which the appropriate party(ies) is aware; and
- When the responsible party is different from the measurer or evaluator, that the responsible party acknowledges responsibility for the underlying subject matter.

A138   Representations by the appropriate party(ies) cannot replace other evidence the practitioner could reasonably expect to be available. Although written representations provide necessary evidence, they do not provide sufficient appropriate evidence on their own about any of the matters with which they deal. Furthermore, the fact that the practitioner has received reliable written representations does not affect the nature or extent of other evidence that the practitioner obtains.

Requested Written Representations Not Provided or Not Reliable (Ref: Para. 60)

A139   Circumstances in which the practitioner may not be able to obtain requested written representations include, for example, when:

- The responsible party contracts a third party to perform the relevant measurement or evaluation and later engages the practitioner to undertake an assurance engagement on the resultant subject matter information. In some such cases, for example where the responsible party has an ongoing relationship with the measurer or evaluator, the responsible party may be able to arrange for the measurer or evaluator to provide requested written representations, or the responsible party may be in a position to provide such representations if the responsible party has a reasonable basis for doing so, but in other cases this may not be so.
- An intended user engages the practitioner to undertake an assurance engagement on publicly available information but does not have a relationship with the responsible party of the kind necessary to ensure that party responds to the practitioner's request for a written representation.
- The assurance engagement is undertaken against the wishes of the measurer or evaluator. This may be the case when, for example, the engagement is undertaken pursuant to a court order, or a public sector practitioner is required by the legislature or other competent authority to undertake a particular engagement.

In these or similar circumstances, the practitioner may not have access to the evidence needed to support the practitioner's conclusion. If this is the case paragraph 66 of this ISAE applies.

Subsequent Events (Ref: Para. 61)

A140   Consideration of subsequent events in some assurance engagements may not be relevant because of the nature of the underlying subject matter. For example, when the engagement requires a conclusion about the accuracy of a statistical return at a point in time, events occurring between that point in time and the date of the assurance report may not affect the conclusion or require disclosure in the return or the assurance report.

As noted in paragraph 61, the practitioner has no responsibility to perform any procedures regarding the subject matter information after the date of the practitioner's report. However, if, after the date of the practitioner's report, a fact becomes known to the practitioner that, had it been known to the practitioner at the date of the practitioner's report, may have caused the practitioner to amend the report, the practitioner may need to discuss the matter with the appropriate party(ies) or take other action as appropriate in the circumstances.   **A141**

Other Information (Ref: Para. 62)

Further actions that may be appropriate if the practitioner identifies a material inconsistency or becomes aware of a material misstatement of fact include, for example: **A142**

- Requesting the appropriate party(ies) to consult with a qualified third party, such as the appropriate party(ies)'s legal counsel.
- Obtaining legal advice about the consequences of different courses of action.
- Communicating with third parties (for example, a regulator).
- Withholding the assurance report.
- Withdrawing from the engagement, where withdrawal is possible under applicable law or regulation.
- Describing the material inconsistency in the assurance report.

Description of Applicable Criteria (Ref: Para. 63)

The description of the applicable criteria advises intended users of the framework on which the subject matter information is based, and is particularly important when there are significant differences between various criteria regarding how particular matters may be treated in the subject matter information.   **A143**

A description that the subject matter information is prepared in accordance with particular applicable criteria is appropriate only if the subject matter information complies with all relevant requirements of those applicable criteria that are effective.   **A144**

A description of the applicable criteria that contains imprecise qualifying or limiting language (for example, "the subject matter information is in substantial compliance with the requirements of XYZ") is not an adequate description as it may mislead users of the subject matter information.   **A145**

Forming the Assurance Conclusion

Sufficiency and Appropriateness of Evidence (Ref: Para. 12(i), 64)

Evidence is necessary to support the practitioner's conclusion and assurance report. It is cumulative in nature and is primarily obtained from procedures performed during the course of the engagement. It may, however, also include information obtained from other sources such as previous engagements (provided the practitioner   **A146** has determined whether changes have occurred since the previous engagement that may affect its relevance to the current engagement) or a firm's quality control procedures for client acceptance and continuance. Evidence may come from sources inside and outside the appropriate party(ies). Also, information that may be used as evidence may have been prepared by an expert employed or engaged by the appropriate party(ies). Evidence comprises both information that supports and corroborates aspects of the subject matter information, and any information that contradicts aspects of the subject matter information. In addition, in some cases, the absence of information (for example, refusal by the appropriate party(ies) to provide a requested representation) is used by the practitioner, and therefore, also constitutes evidence. Most of the practitioner's work in forming the assurance conclusion consists of obtaining and evaluating evidence.

A147   The sufficiency and appropriateness of evidence are interrelated. Sufficiency is the measure of the quantity of evidence. The quantity of evidence needed is affected by the risks of the subject matter information being materially misstated (the higher the risks, the more evidence is likely to be required) and also by the quality of such evidence (the higher the quality, the less may be required). Obtaining more evidence, however, may not compensate for its poor quality.

A148   Appropriateness is the measure of the quality of evidence; that is, its relevance and its reliability in providing support for the practitioner's conclusion. The reliability of evidence is influenced by its source and by its nature, and is dependent on the individual circumstances under which it is obtained. Generalizations about the reliability of various kinds of evidence can be made; however, such generalizations are subject to important exceptions. Even when evidence is obtained from sources external to the appropriate party(ies), circumstances may exist that could affect its reliability. For example, evidence obtained from an external source may not be reliable if the source is not knowledgeable or objective. While recognizing that exceptions may exist, the following generalizations about the reliability of evidence may be useful:

- Evidence is more reliable when it is obtained from sources outside the appropriate party(ies).
- Evidence that is generated internally is more reliable when the related controls are effective.
- Evidence obtained directly by the practitioner (for example, observation of the application of a control) is more reliable than evidence obtained indirectly or by inference (for example, inquiry about the application of a control).
- Evidence is more reliable when it exists in documentary form, whether paper, electronic, or other media (for example, a contemporaneously written record of a meeting is ordinarily more reliable than a subsequent oral representation of what was discussed).

A149   The practitioner ordinarily obtains more assurance from consistent evidence obtained from different sources or of a different nature than from items of evidence considered individually. In addition, obtaining evidence from different sources or of a different nature may indicate that an individual item of evidence is not reliable. For example, corroborating information obtained from a source independent of the appropriate party(ies) may increase the assurance the practitioner obtains from a representation from the appropriate party(ies). Conversely, when evidence obtained from one source is inconsistent with that obtained from another, the practitioner determines what additional procedures are necessary to resolve the inconsistency.

In terms of obtaining sufficient appropriate evidence, it is generally more difficult **A150** to obtain assurance about subject matter information covering a period than about subject matter information at a point in time. In addition, conclusions provided on processes ordinarily are limited to the period covered by the engagement; the practitioner provides no conclusion about whether the process will continue to function in the specified manner in the future.

Whether sufficient appropriate evidence has been obtained on which to base the **A151** practitioner's conclusion is a matter of professional judgment.

In some circumstances, the practitioner may not have obtained the sufficiency or **A152** appropriateness of evidence that the practitioner had expected to obtain through the planned procedures. In these circumstances, the practitioner considers that the evidence obtained from the procedures performed is not sufficient and appropriate to be able to form a conclusion on the subject matter information. The practitioner may:

- Extend the work performed; or
- Perform other procedures judged by the practitioner to be necessary in the circumstances.

Where neither of these is practicable in the circumstances, the practitioner will not be able to obtain sufficient appropriate evidence to be able to form a conclusion. This situation may arise even though the practitioner has not become aware of a matter(s) that causes the practitioner to believe the subject matter information may be materially misstated, as addressed in paragraph 49L.

Evaluating the Sufficiency and Appropriateness of Evidence (Ref: Para. 65)

An assurance engagement is a cumulative and iterative process. As the practitioner **A153** performs planned procedures, the evidence obtained may cause the practitioner to change the nature, timing or extent of other planned procedures. Information may come to the practitioner's attention that differs significantly from that expected and upon which planned procedures were based. For example:

- The extent of misstatements that the practitioner identifies may alter the practitioner's professional judgment about the reliability of particular sources of information.
- The practitioner may become aware of discrepancies in relevant information, or inconsistent or missing evidence.
- If analytical procedures were performed towards the end of the engagement, the results of those procedures may indicate a previously unrecognized risk of material misstatement.

In such circumstances, the practitioner may need to reevaluate the planned procedures.

The practitioner's professional judgment as to what constitutes sufficient appropriate **A154** evidence is influenced by such factors as the following:

- Significance of a potential misstatement and the likelihood of its having a material effect, individually or when aggregated with other potential misstatements, on the subject matter information.
- Effectiveness of the appropriate party(ies)'s responses to address the known risk of material misstatement.

- Experience gained during previous assurance engagements with respect to similar potential misstatements.
- Results of procedures performed, including whether such procedures identified specific misstatements.
- Source and reliability of the available information.
- Persuasiveness of the evidence.
- Understanding of the appropriate party(ies) and its environment.

Scope Limitations (Ref: Para. 26, 66)

A155 A scope limitation may arise from:

(a) Circumstances beyond the control of the appropriate party(ies). For example, documentation the practitioner considers it necessary to inspect may have been accidentally destroyed;

(b) Circumstances relating to the nature or timing of the practitioner's work. For example, a physical process the practitioner considers it necessary to observe may have occurred before the practitioner's engagement; or

(c) Limitations imposed by the responsible party, the measurer or evaluator, or the engaging party on the practitioner who, for example, may prevent the practitioner from performing a procedure the practitioner considers to be necessary in the circumstances. Limitations of this kind may have other implications for the engagement, such as for the practitioner's consideration of engagement risk and engagement acceptance and continuance.

A156 An inability to perform a specific procedure does not constitute a scope limitation if the practitioner is able to obtain sufficient appropriate evidence by performing alternative procedures.

A157 The procedures performed in a limited assurance engagement are, by definition, limited compared with that necessary in a reasonable assurance engagement. Limitations known to exist prior to accepting a limited assurance engagement are a relevant consideration when establishing whether the preconditions for an assurance engagement are present, in particular, whether the engagement exhibits the characteristics of access to evidence (see paragraph 24b)(iv)) and a rational purpose (see paragraph 24(b)(vi)). If a further limitation is imposed by the appropriate party(ies) after a limited assurance engagement has been accepted, it may be appropriate to withdraw from the engagement, where withdrawal is possible under applicable law or regulation.

Preparing the Assurance Report

Form of Assurance Report (Ref: Para. 67–68)

A158 Oral and other forms of expressing conclusions can be misunderstood without the support of a written report. For this reason, the practitioner does not report orally or by use of symbols without also providing a written assurance report that is readily available whenever the oral report is provided or the symbol is used. For example, a symbol could be hyperlinked to a written assurance report on the Internet.

A159 This ISAE does not require a standardized format for reporting on all assurance engagements. Instead it identifies the basic elements the assurance report is to include. Assurance reports are tailored to the specific engagement circumstances. The practitioner may use headings, paragraph numbers, typographical devices, for example the bolding of text, and other mechanisms to enhance the clarity and readability of the assurance report.

The practitioner may choose a "short form" or "long form" style of reporting to facilitate effective communication to the intended users. "Short-form" reports ordinarily include only the basic elements. "Long-form" reports include other information and explanations that are not intended to affect the practitioner's conclusion. In addition to the basic elements, long-form reports may describe in detail the terms of the engagement, the applicable criteria being used, findings relating to particular aspects of the engagement, details of the qualifications and experience of the practitioner and others involved with the engagement, disclosure of materiality levels, and, in some cases, recommendations. The practitioner may find it helpful to consider the significance of providing such information to the information needs of the intended users. As required by paragraph 68, additional information is clearly separated from the practitioner's conclusion and phrased in such a manner so as make it clear that it is not intended to detract from that conclusion. **A160**

Assurance Report Content

Title (Ref: Para. 69(a))

An appropriate title helps to identify the nature of the assurance report, and to distinguish it from reports issued by others, such as those who do not have to comply with the same ethical requirements as the practitioner. **A161**

Addressee (Ref: Para. 69(b))

An addressee identifies the party or parties to whom the assurance report is directed. The assurance report is ordinarily addressed to the engaging party, but in some cases there may be other intended users. **A162**

Subject Matter Information and Underlying Subject Matter (Ref: Para. 69(c))

Identification and description of the subject matter information and, when appropriate, the underlying subject matter may include, for example: **A163**

- The point in time or period of time to which the measurement or evaluation of the underlying subject matter relates.
- Where applicable, the name of the responsible party or component of the responsible party to which the underlying subject matter relates.
- An explanation of those characteristics of the underlying subject matter or the subject matter information of which the intended users should be aware, and how such characteristics may influence the precision of the measurement or evaluation of the underlying subject matter against the applicable criteria, or the persuasiveness of available evidence. For example:
  - The degree to which the subject matter information is qualitative versus quantitative, objective versus subjective, or historical versus prospective.
  - Changes in the underlying subject matter or other engagement circumstances that affect the comparability of the subject matter information from one period to the next.

Applicable Criteria (Ref: Para. 69(d))

A164   The assurance report identifies the applicable criteria against which the underlying subject matter was measured or evaluated so the intended users can understand the basis for the practitioner's conclusion. The assurance report may include the applicable criteria, or refer to them if they are included in the subject matter information or if they are otherwise available from a readily accessible source. It may be relevant in the circumstances, to disclose:

- The source of the applicable criteria, and whether or not the applicable criteria are embodied in law or regulation, or issued by authorized or recognized bodies of experts that follow a transparent due process, that is, whether they are established criteria in the context of the underlying subject matter (and if they are not, a description of why they are considered suitable).
- Measurement or evaluation methods used when the applicable criteria allow for choice between a number of methods.
- Any significant interpretations made in applying the applicable criteria in the engagement circumstances.
- Whether there have been any changes in the measurement or evaluation methods used.

Inherent Limitations (Ref: Para. 69(e))

A165   While in some cases, inherent limitations can be expected to be well-understood by the intended users of an assurance report, in other cases it may be appropriate to make explicit reference to them in the assurance report. For example, in an assurance report related to the effectiveness of internal control, it may be appropriate to note that the historic evaluation of effectiveness is not relevant to future periods due to the risk that internal control may become inadequate because of changes in conditions, or that the degree of compliance with policies or procedures may deteriorate.

Specific Purpose (Ref: Para. 69(f))

A166   In some cases the applicable criteria used to measure or evaluate the underlying subject matter may be designed for a specific purpose. For example, a regulator may require certain entities to use particular applicable criteria designed for regulatory purposes. To avoid misunderstandings, the practitioner alerts readers of the assurance report to this fact and that, therefore, the subject matter information may not be suitable for another purpose.

A167   In addition to the alert required by paragraph 69(f), the practitioner may consider it appropriate to indicate that the assurance report is intended solely for specific users. Depending on the engagement circumstances, for example, the law or regulation of the particular jurisdiction, this may be achieved by restricting the distribution or use of the assurance report. While an assurance report may be restricted in this way, the absence of a restriction regarding a particular user or purpose does not itself indicate that a legal responsibility is owed by the practitioner in relation to that user or for that purpose. Whether a legal responsibility is owed will depend on the legal circumstances of each case and the relevant jurisdiction.

Relative Responsibilities (Ref: Para. 69(g))

Identifying relative responsibilities informs the intended users that the responsible party is responsible for the underlying subject matter, that the measurer or evaluator is responsible for the measurement or evaluation of the underlying subject matter against the applicable criteria, and that the practitioner's role is to independently express a conclusion about the subject matter information.

A168

Performance of the Engagement in Accordance with ISAE 3000 (Revised) and a Subject Matter Specific ISAE (Ref: Para. 69(h))

Where a subject matter specific ISAE applies to only part of the subject matter information, it may be appropriate to cite both that subject matter specific ISAE and this ISAE.

A169

A statement that contains imprecise qualifying or limiting language (for example "the engagement was performed by reference to ISAE 3000") may mislead users of assurance reports.

A170

Applicable Quality Control Requirements (Ref: Para. 69(i))

The following is an illustration of a statement in the assurance report regarding applicable quality control requirements:

A171

'The firm applies International Standard on Quality Control 1 and accordingly maintains a comprehensive system of quality control including documented policies and procedures regarding compliance with ethical requirements, professional standards and applicable legal and regulatory requirements.'

Compliance with Independence and Other Ethical Requirements (Ref: Para. 69(j))

The following is an illustration of a statement in the assurance report regarding compliance with ethical requirements:

A172

'We have complied with the independence and other ethical requirements of the *Code of Ethics for Professional Accountants* issued by the International Ethics Standards Board for Accountants, which is founded on fundamental principles of integrity, objectivity, professional competence and due care, confidentiality and professional behavior.'

Summary of the Work Performed (Ref: Para. A6, 69(k))

The summary of the work performed helps the intended users understand the practitioner's conclusion. For many assurance engagements, infinite variations in procedures are possible in theory. In practice, however, these are difficult to communicate clearly and unambiguously. Other authoritative pronouncements issued by the International Auditing and Assurance Standards Board may be useful to practitioners in preparing the summary.

A173

Where no specific ISAE provides guidance on procedures for a particular underlying subject matter, the summary might include a more detailed description of the work

A174

performed. It may be appropriate to include in the summary a statement that the work performed included evaluating the suitability of the applicable criteria.

A175   In a limited assurance engagement the summary of the work performed is ordinarily more detailed than for a reasonable assurance engagement and identifies the limitations on the nature, timing, and extent of procedures. This is because an appreciation of the nature, timing, and extent of procedures performed is essential to understanding a conclusion expressed in a form that conveys whether, based on the procedures performed, a material matter(s) has come to the practitioner's attention to cause the practitioner to believe the subject matter information is materially misstated. It also may be appropriate to indicate in the summary of the work performed certain procedures that were not performed that would ordinarily be expected to be performed in a reasonable assurance engagement. However, a complete identification of all such procedures may not be possible because the practitioner's required understanding and consideration of engagement risk is less than in a reasonable assurance engagement.

A176   Factors to consider in determining the level of detail to be provided in the summary of the work performed may include:

- Circumstances specific to the entity (e.g., the differing nature of the entity's activities compared to those typical in the sector).
- Specific engagement circumstances affecting the nature and extent of the procedures performed.
- The intended users' expectations of the level of detail to be provided in the report, based on market practice, or applicable law or regulation.

A177   It is important that the summary be written in an objective way that allows intended users to understand the work done as the basis for the practitioner's conclusion. In most cases, this will not involve detailing the entire work plan, but on the other hand it is important for it not to be so summarized as to be ambiguous, nor written in a way that is overstated or embellished.

The Practitioner's Conclusion (Ref: Para. 12(a)(i)(a), 69(l))

A178   Examples of conclusions expressed in a form appropriate for a reasonable assurance engagement include:

- When expressed in terms of the underlying subject matter and the applicable criteria, "In our opinion, the entity has complied, in all material respects, with XYZ law";
- When expressed in terms of the subject matter information and the applicable criteria, "In our opinion, the forecast of the entity's financial performance is properly prepared, in all material respects, based on XYZ criteria"; or
- When expressed in terms of a statement made by the appropriate party, "In our opinion, the [appropriate party's] statement that the entity has complied with XYZ law is, in all material respects, fairly stated," or "In our opinion, the [appropriate party's] statement that the key performance indicators are presented in accordance with XYZ criteria is, in all material respects, fairly stated".

A179   It may be appropriate to inform the intended users of the context in which the practitioner's conclusion is to be read when the assurance report includes an explanation of particular characteristics of the underlying subject matter of which the intended users should be aware. The practitioner's conclusion may, for example, include wording such as: "This conclusion has been formed on the basis of the matters outlined elsewhere in this independent assurance report."

Examples of conclusions expressed in a form appropriate for a limited assurance engagement include: **A180**

- When expressed in terms of the underlying subject matter and the applicable criteria, "Based on the procedures performed and evidence obtained, nothing has come to our attention that causes us to believe that [the entity] has not complied, in all material respects, with XYZ law."
- When expressed in terms of the subject matter information and the applicable criteria, "Based on the procedures performed and evidence obtained, we are not aware of any material amendments that need to be made to the assessment of key performance indicators for them to be in accordance with XYZ criteria."
- When expressed in terms of a statement made by the appropriate party, "Based on the procedures performed and evidence obtained, nothing has come to our attention that causes us to believe that the [appropriate party's] statement that [the entity] has complied with XYZ law, is not, in all material respects, fairly stated."

Forms of expression which may be useful for underlying subject matters include, for example, one, or a combination of, the following: **A181**

- For compliance engagements—"in compliance with" or "in accordance with."
- For engagements when the applicable criteria describe a process or methodology for the preparation or presentation of the subject matter information—"properly prepared."
- For engagement when the principles of fair presentation are embodied in the applicable criteria—"fairly stated."

Inclusion of a heading above paragraphs containing modified conclusions, and the matter(s) giving rise to the modification, aids the understandability of the practitioner's report. Examples of appropriate heading include "Qualified Conclusion," "Adverse Conclusion," or "Disclaimer of Conclusion" and "Basis for Qualified Conclusion," "Basis for Adverse Conclusion," as appropriate. **A182**

The Practitioner's Signature (Ref: Para. 69(m))

The practitioner's signature is either in the name of the practitioner's firm, the personal name of the individual practitioner or both, as appropriate for the particular jurisdiction. In addition to the practitioner's signature, in certain jurisdictions, the practitioner may be required to make a declaration in the practitioner's report about professional designations or recognition by the appropriate licensing authority in that jurisdiction. **A183**

Date (Ref: Para. 69(n))

Including the assurance report date informs the intended users that the practitioner has considered the effect on the subject matter information and on the assurance report of events that occurred up to that date. **A184**

Reference to the Practitioner's Expert in the Assurance Report (Ref: Para. 70)

A185 In some cases, law or regulation may require a reference to the work of a practitioner's expert in the assurance report, for example, for the purposes of transparency in the public sector. It may also be appropriate in others circumstances, for example, to explain the nature of a modification of the practitioner's conclusion, or when the work of an expert is integral to findings included in a long form report.

A186 Nonetheless, the practitioner has sole responsibility for the conclusion expressed, and that responsibility is not reduced by the practitioner's use of the work of a practitioner's expert. It is important therefore that if the assurance report refers to a practitioner's expert, that the wording of that report does not imply that the practitioner's responsibility for the conclusion expressed is reduced because of the involvement of that expert.

A187 A generic reference in a long form report to the engagement having been conducted by suitably qualified personnel including subject matter experts and assurance specialist is unlikely to be misunderstood as reduced responsibility. The potential for misunderstanding is higher, however, in the case of short form reports, where minimum contextual information is able to be presented, or when the practitioner's expert is referred to by name. Therefore, additional wording may be needed in such cases to prevent the assurance report implying that the practitioner's responsibility for the conclusion expressed is reduced because of the involvement of the expert.

Unmodified and Modified Conclusions (Ref: Para. 74–77, Appendix)

A188 The term 'pervasive' describes the effects on the subject matter information of misstatements or the possible effects on the subject matter information of misstatements, if any, that are undetected due to an inability to obtain sufficient appropriate evidence. Pervasive effects on the subject matter information are those that, in the practitioner's professional judgment:

(a) Are not confined to specific aspects of the subject matter information;

(b) If so confined, represent or could represent a substantial proportion of the subject matter information; or

(c) In relation to disclosures, are fundamental to the intended users' understanding of the subject matter information.

A189 The nature of the matter, and the practitioner's judgment about the pervasiveness of the effects or possible effects on the subject matter information, affects the type of conclusion to be expressed.

A190 Examples of qualified and adverse conclusions and a disclaimer of conclusion are:

- Qualified conclusion (an example for limited assurance engagements with a material misstatement) – "Based on the procedures performed and the evidence obtained, except for the effect of the matter described in the Basis for Qualified Conclusion section of our report, nothing has come to our attention that causes us to believe that the [appropriate party's] statement does not present fairly, in all material respects, the entity's compliance with XYZ law."
- Adverse conclusion (an example for a material and pervasive misstatement for both reasonable assurance and limited assurance engagements) – "Because of the significance of the matter described in the Basis for Adverse Conclusion

section of our report, the [appropriate party's] statement does not present fairly the entity's compliance with XYZ law."

- Disclaimer of conclusion (an example for a material and pervasive limitation of scope for both reasonable assurance and limited assurance engagements) – "Because of the significance of the matter described in the Basis for Disclaimer of Conclusion section of our report, we have not been able to obtain sufficient appropriate evidence to form a conclusion on the [appropriate party's] statement. Accordingly, we do not express a conclusion on that statement."

In some cases, the measurer or evaluator may identify and properly describe that the subject matter information is materially misstated. For example, in a compliance engagement the measurer or evaluator may correctly describe the instances of non-compliance. In such circumstances, paragraph 76 requires the practitioner to draw the intended users' attention to the description of the material misstatement, by either expressing a qualified or adverse conclusion or by expressing an unqualified conclusion but emphasizing the matter by specifically referring to it in the assurance report.   **A191**

Other Communication Responsibilities (Ref: Para. 78)

Matters that may be appropriate to communicate with the responsible party, the measurer or evaluator, the engaging party or others include fraud or suspected fraud, and bias in the preparation of the subject matter information.   **A192**

Documentation (Ref: Para. 79–83)

Documentation includes a record of the practitioner's reasoning on all significant matters that require the exercise of professional judgment, and related conclusions. When difficult questions of principle or professional judgment exist, documentation that includes the relevant facts that were known by the practitioner at the time the conclusion was reached may assist in demonstrating the practitioner's knowledge.   **A193**

It is neither necessary nor practical to document every matter considered, or professional judgment made, during an engagement. Further, it is unnecessary for the practitioner to document separately (as in a checklist, for example) compliance with matters for which compliance is demonstrated by documents included within the engagement file. Similarly, the practitioner need not include in engagement file superseded drafts of working papers, notes that reflect incomplete or preliminary thinking, previous copies of documents corrected for typographical or other errors, and duplicates of documents.   **A194**

In applying professional judgment to assessing the extent of documentation to be prepared and retained, the practitioner may consider what is necessary to provide an understanding of the work performed and the basis of the principal decisions taken (but not the detailed aspects of the engagement) to another practitioner who has no previous experience with the engagement. That other practitioner may only be able to obtain an understanding of detailed aspects of the engagement by discussing them with the practitioner who prepared the documentation.   **A195**

Documentation may include a record of, for example: **A196**

- The identifying characteristics of the specific items or matters tested;

- Who performed the engagement work and the date such work was completed; and
- Who reviewed the engagement work performed and the date and extent of such review.
- Discussions of significant matters with the appropriate party(ies) and others, including the nature of the significant matters discussed and when and with whom the discussions took place.

A197   Documentation may include a record of, for example:

- Issues identified with respect to compliance with relevant ethical requirements and how they were resolved.
- Conclusions on compliance with independence requirements that apply to the engagement, and any relevant discussions with the firm that support these conclusions.
- Conclusions reached regarding the acceptance and continuance of client relationships and assurance engagements.
- The nature and scope of, and conclusions resulting from, consultations undertaken during the course of the engagement.

Assembly of the Final Engagement File

A198   ISQC 1 (or other professional requirements, or requirements in law or regulation that are at least as demanding as ISQC 1) requires firms to establish policies and procedures for the timely completion of the assembly of engagement files.[7] An appropriate time limit within which to complete the assembly of the final engagement file is ordinarily not more than 60 days after the date of the assurance report.[8]

A199   The completion of the assembly of the final engagement file after the date of the assurance report is an administrative process that does not involve the performance of new procedures or the drawing of new conclusions. Changes may, however, be made to the documentation during the final assembly process if they are administrative in nature. Examples of such changes include:

- Deleting or discarding superseded documentation.
- Sorting, collating and cross-referencing working papers.
- Signing off on completion checklists relating to the file assembly process.
- Documenting evidence that the practitioner has obtained, discussed and agreed with the relevant members of the engagement team before the date of the assurance report.

A200   ISQC 1 (or national requirements that are at least as demanding as ISQC 1) requires firms to establish policies and procedures for the retention of engagement documentation.[9] The retention period for assurance engagements ordinarily is no shorter than five years from the date of the assurance report.[10]

---

[7] *ISQC 1, paragraph 45.*

[8] *ISQC 1, paragraph A54.*

Appendix

(Ref: Para. 2, A8, A11, A16, A36–A38)

Roles and Responsibilities

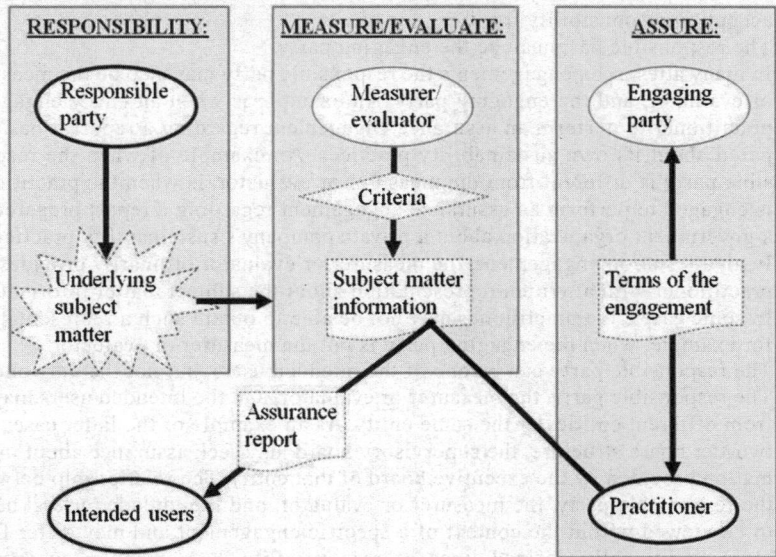

All assurance engagements have at least three parties: the responsible party, the **1** practitioner, and the intended users. Depending on the engagement circumstances, there may also be a separate role of measurer or evaluator, or engaging party.

The above diagram illustrates how the following roles relate to an assurance **2** engagement:

(a) The responsible party is responsible for the underlying subject matter.
(b) The measurer or evaluator uses the criteria to measure or evaluate the underlying subject matter resulting in the subject matter information.
(c) The engaging party agrees the terms of the engagement with the practitioner.
(d) The practitioner obtains sufficient appropriate evidence in order to express a conclusion designed to enhance the degree of confidence of the intended users other than the responsible party about the subject matter information.
(e) The intended users make decisions on the basis of the subject matter information. The intended users are the individual(s) or organization(s), or group(s) thereof that the practitioner expects will use the assurance report.

The following observations can be made about these roles: **3**

- Every assurance engagement has at least a responsible party and intended users, in addition to the practitioner.
- The practitioner cannot be the responsible party, the engaging party or an intended user.
- In a direct engagement, the practitioner is also the measurer or evaluator.

- In an attestation engagement, the responsible party, or someone else, but not the practitioner, can be the measurer or evaluator.
- When the practitioner has measured or evaluated the underlying subject matter against the criteria, the engagement is a direct engagement. The character of that engagement cannot be changed to an attestation engagement by another party assuming responsibility for the measurement or evaluation, for example, by the responsible party attaching a statement to the subject matter information accepting responsibility for it.
- The responsible party can be the engaging party.
- In many attestation engagements the responsible party may also be the measurer or evaluator, and the engaging party. An example is when an entity engages a practitioner to perform an assurance engagement regarding a report it has prepared about its own sustainability practices. An example of when the responsible party is different from the measurer or evaluator, is when the practitioner is engaged to perform an assurance engagement regarding a report prepared by a government organization about a private company's sustainability practices.
- In an attestation engagement, the measurer or evaluator ordinarily provides the practitioner with a written representation about the subject matter information. In some cases, the practitioner may not be able to obtain such a representation, for example, when the engaging party is not the measurer or evaluator.
- The responsible party can be one of the intended users, but not the only one.
- The responsible party, the measurer or evaluator, and the intended users may be from different entities or the same entity. As an example of the latter case, in a two-tier board structure, the supervisory board may seek assurance about information provided by the executive board of that entity. The relationship between the responsible party, the measurer or evaluator, and the intended users' needs to be viewed within the context of a specific engagement and may differ from more traditionally defined lines of responsibility. For example, an entity's senior management (an intended user) may engage a practitioner to perform an assurance engagement on a particular aspect of the entity's activities that is the immediate responsibility of a lower level of management (the responsible party), but for which senior management is ultimately responsible.
- An engaging party that is not also the responsible party can be the intended user.

4   The practitioner's conclusion may be phrased either in terms of:

- The underlying subject matter and the applicable criteria;
- The subject matter information and the applicable criteria; or
- A statement made by the appropriate party.

5   The practitioner and the responsible party may agree to apply the principles of the ISAEs to an engagement when there are no intended users other than the responsible party but where all other requirements of the ISAEs are met. In such cases, the practitioner's report includes a statement restricting the use of the report to the responsible party.

International Standard on Assurance Engagements 3400

(Previously ISA 810)

The examination of prospective financial information

(This Standard is effective)

Contents

International Standard on Assurance Engagements (ISAE) 3400, "The Examination of Prospective Financial Information" should be read in the context of the "Preface to the International Standards on Quality Control, Auditing, Review, Other Assurance and Related Services," which sets out the application and authority of ISAEs.

Introduction

The purpose of this International Standard on Assurance Engagements (ISAE) is to **1** establish standards and provide guidance on engagements to examine and report on prospective financial information including examination procedures for best-estimate and hypothetical assumptions. This ISAE does not apply to the examination of prospective financial information expressed in general or narrative terms, such as that found in management's discussion and analysis in an entity's annual report, though many of the procedures outlined herein may be suitable for such an examination.

In an engagement to examine prospective financial information, the auditor should **2** **obtain sufficient appropriate evidence as to whether:**

(a) **Management's best-estimate assumptions on which the prospective financial information is based are not unreasonable and, in the case of hypothetical assumptions, such assumptions are consistent with the purpose of the information;**
(b) **The prospective financial information is properly prepared on the basis of the assumptions;**
(c) **The prospective financial information is properly presented and all material assumptions are adequately disclosed, including a clear indication as to whether they are best-estimate assumptions or hypothetical assumptions; and**
(d) **The prospective financial information is prepared on a consistent basis with historical financial statements, using appropriate accounting principles.**

"Prospective financial information" means financial information based on assump- **3** tions about events that may occur in the future and possible actions by an entity. It is highly subjective in nature and its preparation requires the exercise of considerable judgment. Prospective financial information can be in the form of a forecast, a projection or a combination of both, for example, a one year forecast plus a five year projection.

A "forecast" means prospective financial information prepared on the basis of **4** assumptions as to future events which management expects to take place and the actions management expects to take as of the date the information is prepared (best-estimate assumptions).

A "projection" means prospective financial information prepared on the basis of: **5**

(a) Hypothetical assumptions about future events and management actions which are not necessarily expected to take place, such as when some entities are in a start-up phase or are considering a major change in the nature of operations; or
(b) A mixture of best-estimate and hypothetical assumptions.

Such information illustrates the possible consequences as of the date the information is prepared if the events and actions were to occur (a "what-if" scenario).

Prospective financial information can include financial statements or one or more **6** elements of financial statements and may be prepared:

(a) As an internal management tool, for example, to assist in evaluating a possible capital investment; or
(b) For distribution to third parties in, for example:
   - A prospectus to provide potential investors with information about future expectations.
   - An annual report to provide information to shareholders, regulatory bodies and other interested parties.

- A document for the information of lenders which may include, for example, cash flow forecasts.

7   Management is responsible for the preparation and presentation of the prospective financial information, including the identification and disclosure of the assumptions on which it is based. The auditor may be asked to examine and report on the prospective financial information to enhance its credibility whether it is intended for use by third parties or for internal purposes.

The Auditor's Assurance Regarding Prospective Financial Information

8   Prospective financial information relates to events and actions that have not yet occurred and may not occur. While evidence may be available to support the assumptions on which the prospective financial information is based, such evidence is itself generally future oriented and, therefore, speculative in nature, as distinct from the evidence ordinarily available in the audit of historical financial information. The auditor is, therefore, not in a position to express an opinion as to whether the results shown in the prospective financial information will be achieved.

9   Further, given the types of evidence available in assessing the assumptions on which the prospective financial information is based, it may be difficult for the auditor to obtain a level of satisfaction sufficient to provide a positive expression of opinion that the assumptions are free of material misstatement. Consequently, in this ISAE, when reporting on the reasonableness of management's assumptions the auditor provides only a moderate level of assurance. However, when in the auditor's judgment an appropriate level of satisfaction has been obtained, the auditor is not precluded from expressing positive assurance regarding the assumptions.

Acceptance of Engagement

10   Before accepting an engagement to examine prospective financial information, the auditor would consider, amongst other things:

- The intended use of the information;
- Whether the information will be for general or limited distribution;
- The nature of the assumptions, that is, whether they are best-estimate or hypothetical assumptions;
- The elements to be included in the information; and
- The period covered by the information.

11   **The auditor should not accept, or should withdraw from, an engagement when the assumptions are clearly unrealistic or when the auditor believes that the prospective financial information will be inappropriate for its intended use.**

12   **The auditor and the client should agree on the terms of the engagement.** It is in the interests of both entity and auditor that the auditor sends an engagement letter to help in avoiding misunderstandings regarding the engagement. An engagement letter would address the matters in paragraph 10 and set out management's responsibilities for the assumptions and for providing the auditor with all relevant information and source data used in developing the assumptions.

Knowledge of the Business

The auditor should obtain a sufficient level of knowledge of the business to be able to evaluate whether all significant assumptions required for the preparation of the prospective financial information have been identified.   The auditor would also need to become familiar with the entity's process for preparing prospective financial information, for example, by considering the following: **13**

- The internal controls over the system used to prepare prospective financial information and the expertise and experience of those persons preparing the prospective financial information.
- The nature of the documentation prepared by the entity supporting management's assumptions.
- The extent to which statistical, mathematical and computer-assisted techniques are used.
- The methods used to develop and apply assumptions.
- The accuracy of prospective financial information prepared in prior periods and the reasons for significant variances.

The auditor should consider the extent to which reliance on the entity's historical financial information is justified.   The auditor requires a knowledge of the entity's historical financial information to assess whether the prospective financial information has been prepared on a basis consistent with the historical financial information and to provide a historical yardstick for considering management's assumptions. The auditor will need to establish, for example, whether relevant historical information was audited or reviewed and whether acceptable accounting principles were used in its preparation.   **14**

If the audit or review report on prior period historical financial information was other than unmodified or if the entity is in a start-up phase, the auditor would consider the surrounding facts and the effect on the examination of the prospective financial information.   **15**

Period Covered

The auditor should consider the period of time covered by the prospective financial information. Since assumptions become more speculative as the length of the period covered increases, as that period lengthens, the ability of management to make best-estimate assumptions decreases. The period would not extend beyond the time for which management has a reasonable basis for the assumptions. The following are some of the factors that are relevant to the auditor's consideration of the period of time covered by the prospective financial information: **16**

- Operating cycle, for example, in the case of a major construction project the time required to complete the project may dictate the period covered.
- The degree of reliability of assumptions, for example, if the entity is introducing a new product the prospective period covered could be short and broken into small segments, such as weeks or months. Alternatively, if the entity's sole business is owning a property under long-term lease, a relatively long prospective period might be reasonable.
- The needs of users, for example, prospective financial information may be prepared in connection with an application for a loan for the period of time required to generate sufficient funds for repayment. Alternatively, the information may be prepared for investors in connection with the sale of debentures to illustrate the intended use of the proceeds in the subsequent period.

Examination Procedures

17   When determining the nature, timing and extent of examination procedures, the auditor's considerations should include:

    (a) **The likelihood of material misstatement;**
    (b) **The knowledge obtained during any previous engagements;**
    (c) **Management's competence regarding the preparation of prospective financial information;**
    (d) **The extent to which the prospective financial information is affected by the management's judgment; and**
    (e) **The adequacy and reliability of the underlying data.**

18   The auditor would assess the source and reliability of the evidence supporting management's best-estimate assumptions. Sufficient appropriate evidence supporting such assumptions would be obtained from internal and external sources including consideration of the assumptions in the light of historical information and an evaluation of whether they are based on plans that are within the entity's capacity.

19   The auditor would consider whether, when hypothetical assumptions are used, all significant implications of such assumptions have been taken into consideration. For example, if sales are assumed to grow beyond the entity's current plant capacity, the prospective financial information will need to include the necessary investment in the additional plant capacity or the costs of alternative means of meeting the anticipated sales, such as subcontracting production.

20   Although evidence supporting hypothetical assumptions need not be obtained, the auditor would need to be satisfied that they are consistent with the purpose of the prospective financial information and that there is no reason to believe they are clearly unrealistic.

21   The auditor will need to be satisfied that the prospective financial information is properly prepared from management's assumptions by, for example, making clerical checks such as recomputation and reviewing internal consistency, that is, the actions management intends to take are compatible with each other and there are no inconsistencies in the determination of the amounts that are based on common variables such as interest rates.

22   The auditor would focus on the extent to which those areas that are particularly sensitive to variation will have a material effect on the results shown in the prospective financial information. This will influence the extent to which the auditor will seek appropriate evidence. It will also influence the auditor's evaluation of the appropriateness and adequacy of disclosure.

23   When engaged to examine one or more elements of prospective financial information, such as an individual financial statement, it is important that the auditor consider the interrelationship of other components in the financial statements.

24   When any elapsed portion of the current period is included in the prospective financial information, the auditor would consider the extent to which procedures need to be applied to the historical information. Procedures will vary depending on the circumstances, for example, how much of the prospective period has elapsed.

25   **The auditor should obtain written representations from management regarding the intended use of the prospective financial information, the completeness of significant**

management assumptions and management's acceptance of its responsibility for the prospective financial information.

Presentation and Disclosure

When assessing the presentation and disclosure of the prospective financial infor-　**26** mation, in addition to the specific requirements of any relevant statutes, regulations or professional standards, the auditor will need to consider whether:

(a) The presentation of prospective financial information is informative and not misleading;

(b) The accounting policies are clearly disclosed in the notes to the prospective financial information;

(c) The assumptions are adequately disclosed in the notes to the prospective financial information. It needs to be clear whether assumptions represent management's best-estimates or are hypothetical and, when assumptions are made in areas that are material and are subject to a high degree of uncertainty, this uncertainty and the resulting sensitivity of results needs to be adequately disclosed;

(d) The date as of which the prospective financial information was prepared is disclosed. Management needs to confirm that the assumptions are appropriate as of this date, even though the underlying information may have been accumulated over a period of time;

(e) The basis of establishing points in a range is clearly indicated and the range is not selected in a biased or misleading manner when results shown in the prospective financial information are expressed in terms of a range; and

(f) Any change in accounting policy since the most recent historical financial statements is disclosed, along with the reason for the change and its effect on the prospective financial information.

Report on Examination of Prospective Financial Information

The report by an auditor on an examination of prospective financial information should　**27** contain the following:

(a) **Title;**

(b) **Addressee;**

(c) **Identification of the prospective financial information;**

(d) **A reference to the ISAE or relevant national standards or practices applicable to the examination of prospective financial information;**

(e) **A statement that management is responsible for the prospective financial information including the assumptions on which it is based;**

(f) **When applicable, a reference to the purpose and/or restricted distribution of the prospective financial information;**

(g) **A statement of negative assurance as to whether the assumptions provide a reasonable basis for the prospective financial information;**

(h) **An opinion as to whether the prospective financial information is properly prepared on the basis of the assumptions and is presented in accordance with the relevant financial reporting framework;**

(i) **Appropriate caveats concerning the achievability of the results indicated by the prospective financial information;**

(j) **Date of the report which should be the date procedures have been completed;**

(k) **Auditor's address; and**

(l) **Signature.**

28 Such a report would:

- State whether, based on the examination of the evidence supporting the assumptions, anything has come to the auditor's attention which causes the auditor to believe that the assumptions do not provide a reasonable basis for the prospective financial information.
- Express an opinion as to whether the prospective financial information is properly prepared on the basis of the assumptions and is presented in accordance with the relevant financial reporting framework.
- State that:
  - Actual results are likely to be different from the prospective financial information since anticipated events frequently do not occur as expected and the variation could be material. Likewise, when the prospective financial information is expressed as a range, it would be stated that there can be no assurance that actual results will fall within the range; and
  - In the case of a projection, the prospective financial information has been prepared for (state purpose), using a set of assumptions that include hypothetical assumptions about future events and management's actions that are not necessarily expected to occur. Consequently, readers are cautioned that the prospective financial information is not used for purposes other than that described.

29 The following is an example of an extract from an unmodified report on a forecast:

We have examined the forecast[1] in accordance with the International Standard on Assurance Engagements applicable to the examination of prospective financial information. Management is responsible for the forecast including the assumptions set out in Note X on which it is based.

Based on our examination of the evidence supporting the assumptions, nothing has come to our attention which causes us to believe that these assumptions do not provide a reasonable basis for the forecast. Further, in our opinion the forecast is properly prepared on the basis of the assumptions and is presented in accordance with ....[2]

Actual results are likely to be different from the forecast since anticipated events frequently do not occur as expected and the variation may be material.

30 The following is an example of an extract from an unmodified report on a projection:

We have examined the projection[3] in accordance with the International Standard on Assurance Engagements applicable to the examination of prospective financial information. Management is responsible for the projection including the assumptions set out in Note X on which it is based.

This projection has been prepared for (describe purpose). As the entity is in a start-up phase the projection has been prepared using a set of assumptions that include hypothetical assumptions about future events and management's actions that are not necessarily expected to occur. Consequently, readers are cautioned that this projection may not be appropriate for purposes other than that described above.

---

[1] *Include name of the entity, the period covered by the forecast and provide suitable identification, such as by reference to page numbers or by identifying the individual statements.*

[2] *Indicate the relevant financial reporting framework.*

[3] *Include name of the entity, the period covered by the projection and provide suitable identification, such as by reference to page numbers or by identifying the individual statements.*

Based on our examination of the evidence supporting the assumptions, nothing has come to our attention which causes us to believe that these assumptions do not provide a reasonable basis for the projection, assuming that (state or refer to the hypothetical assumptions). Further, in our opinion the projection is properly prepared on the basis of the assumptions and is presented in accordance with ....[4]

Even if the events anticipated under the hypothetical assumptions described above occur, actual results are still likely to be different from the projection since other anticipated events frequently do not occur as expected and the variation may be material.

When the auditor believes that the presentation and disclosure of the prospective financial information is not adequate, the auditor should express a qualified or adverse opinion in the report on the prospective financial information, or withdraw from the engagement as appropriate. An example would be where financial information fails to disclose adequately the consequences of any assumptions which are highly sensitive.

31

When the auditor believes that one or more significant assumptions do not provide a reasonable basis for the prospective financial information prepared on the basis of best-estimate assumptions or that one or more significant assumptions do not provide a reasonable basis for the prospective financial information given the hypothetical assumptions, the auditor should either express an adverse opinion in the report on the prospective financial information, or withdraw from the engagement.

32

When the examination is affected by conditions that preclude application of one or more procedures considered necessary in the circumstances, the auditor should either withdraw from the engagement or disclaim the opinion and describe the scope limitation in the report on the prospective financial information.

33

---

[4] *See footnote 2.*

International Standard on Assurance Engagements 3402
Assurance reports on controls at a service organization

(Effective for service auditors' assurance reports covering periods ending on or after June 15, 2011)

Contents

International Standard on Assurance Engagements (ISAE) 3402, "Assurance Reports on Controls at a Service Organization" should be read in conjunction with the "Preface to the International Standards on Quality Control, Auditing, Review, Other Assurance, and Related Services."

Introduction

Scope of this ISAE

1   This International Standard on Assurance Engagements (ISAE) deals with assurance engagements undertaken by a professional accountant in public practice[1] to provide a report for use by user entities and their auditors on the controls at a service organization that provides a service to user entities that is likely to be relevant to user entities' internal control as it relates to financial reporting. It complements ISA 402,[2] in that reports prepared in accordance with this ISAE are capable of providing appropriate evidence under ISA 402. (Ref: Para. A1)

2   The "International Framework for Assurance Engagements" (the Assurance Framework) states that an assurance engagement may be a "reasonable assurance" engagement or a "limited assurance" engagement; that an assurance engagement may be either an "assertion-based" engagement or a "direct reporting" engagement; and, that the assurance conclusion for an assertion-based engagement can be worded either in terms of the responsible party's assertion or directly in terms of the subject matter and the criteria.[3] This ISAE only deals with assertion-based engagements that convey reasonable assurance, with the assurance conclusion worded directly in terms of the subject matter and the criteria.[4]

3   This ISAE applies only when the service organization is responsible for, or otherwise able to make an assertion about, the suitable design of controls. This ISAE does not deal with assurance engagements:

(a)   To report only on whether controls at a service organization operated as described, or

(b)   To report on controls at a service organization other than those related to a service that is likely to be relevant to user entities' internal control as it relates to financial reporting (for example, controls that affect user entities' production or quality control).

This ISAE, however, provides some guidance for such engagements carried out under ISAE 3000.[5] (Ref: Para. A2)

4   In addition to issuing an assurance report on controls, a service auditor may also be engaged to provide reports such as the following, which are not dealt with in this ISAE:

(a)   A report on a user entity's transactions or balances maintained by a service organization; or

(b)   An agreed-upon procedures report on controls at a service organization.

---

[1]   *The* Code of Ethics for Professional Accountants *(IESBA Code), issued by the International Ethics Standards Board for Accountants, defines a professional accountant as "an individual who is a member of an IFAC member body," and a professional accountant in public practice as "a professional accountant, irrespective of functional classification (for example, audit, tax or consulting) in a firm that provides professional services. This term is also used to refer to a firm of professional accountants in public practice."*

[2]   *ISA 402,* Audit Considerations Relating to an Entity Using a Service Organization.

[3]   *Assurance Framework, paragraphs 10, 11 and 57.*

[4]   *Paragraphs 13 and 52(k) of this ISAE.*

[5]   *ISAE 3000,* Assurance Engagements Other than Audits or Reviews of Historical Financial Information.

Relationship with Other Professional Pronouncements

The performance of assurance engagements other than audits or reviews of historical 5
financial information requires the service auditor to comply with ISAE 3000. ISAE
3000 includes requirements in relation to such topics as engagement acceptance,
planning, evidence, and documentation that apply to all assurance engagements,
including engagements in accordance with this ISAE. This ISAE expands on how
ISAE 3000 is to be applied in a reasonable assurance engagement to report on
controls at a service organization. The Assurance Framework, which defines and
describes the elements and objectives of an assurance engagement, provides the
context for understanding this ISAE and ISAE 3000.

Compliance with ISAE 3000 requires, among other things, that the service auditor 6
comply with the International Ethics Standards Board for Accountants' *Code of
Ethics for Professional Accountants* (IESBA Code), and implement quality control
procedures that are applicable to the individual engagement.[6]

Effective Date

This ISAE is effective for service auditors' assurance reports covering periods ending 7
on or after June 15, 2011.

Objectives

The objectives of the service auditor are: 8

(a) To obtain reasonable assurance about whether, in all material respects, based on
    suitable criteria:
    (i)   The service organization's description of its system fairly presents the
          system as designed and implemented throughout the specified period (or in
          the case of a type 1 report, as at a specified date);
    (ii) The controls related to the control objectives stated in the service organi-
          zation's description of its system were suitably designed throughout the
          specified period (or in the case of a type 1 report, as at a specified date);
    (iii) Where included in the scope of the engagement, the controls operated
          effectively to provide reasonable assurance that the control objectives sta-
          ted in the service organization's description of its system were achieved
          throughout the specified period.
(b) To report on the matters in (a) above in accordance with the service auditor's
    findings.

Definitions

For purposes of this ISAE, the following terms have the meanings attributed below: 9

(a) Carve-out method – Method of dealing with the services provided by a sub-
    service organization, whereby the service organization's description of its system
    includes the nature of the services provided by a subservice organization, but
    that subservice organization's relevant control objectives and related controls
    are excluded from the service organization's description of its system and from
    the scope of the service auditor's engagement. The service organization's
    description of its system and the scope of the service auditor's engagement

---

[6] *ISAE 3000, paragraphs 4 and 6.*

include controls at the service organization to monitor the effectiveness of controls at the subservice organization, which may include the service organization's review of an assurance report on controls at the subservice organization.

(b) Complementary user entity controls – Controls that the service organization assumes, in the design of its service, will be implemented by user entities, and which, if necessary to achieve control objectives stated in the service organization's description of its system, are identified in that description.

(c) Control objective – The aim or purpose of a particular aspect of controls. Control objectives relate to risks that controls seek to mitigate.

(d) Controls at the service organization – Controls over the achievement of a control objective that is covered by the service auditor's assurance report. (Ref: Para. A3)

(e) Controls at a subservice organization – Controls at a subservice organization to provide reasonable assurance about the achievement of a control objective.

(f) Criteria – Benchmarks used to evaluate or measure a subject matter including, where relevant, benchmarks for presentation and disclosure.

(g) Inclusive method – Method of dealing with the services provided by a subservice organization, whereby the service organization's description of its system includes the nature of the services provided by a subservice organization, and that subservice organization's relevant control objectives and related controls are included in the service organization's description of its system and in the scope of the service auditor's engagement. (Ref: Para. A4)

(h) Internal audit function – An appraisal activity established or provided as a service to the service organization. Its functions include, amongst other things, examining, evaluating and monitoring the adequacy and effectiveness of internal control.

(i) Internal auditors – Those individuals who perform the activities of the internal audit function. Internal auditors may belong to an internal audit department or equivalent function.

(j) Report on the description and design of controls at a service organization (referred to in this ISAE as a "type 1 report") – A report that comprises:

  (i) The service organization's description of its system;

  (ii) A written assertion by the service organization that, in all material respects, and based on suitable criteria:

    a. The description fairly presents the service organization's system as designed and implemented as at the specified date;

    b. The controls related to the control objectives stated in the service organization's description of its system were suitably designed as at the specified date; and

  (iii) A service auditor's assurance report that conveys reasonable assurance about the matters in (ii)a.–b. above.

(k) Report on the description, design and operating effectiveness of controls at a service organization (referred to in this ISAE as a "type 2 report") – A report that comprises:

  (i) The service organization's description of its system;

  (ii) A written assertion by the service organization that, in all material respects, and based on suitable criteria:

    a. The description fairly presents the service organization's system as designed and implemented throughout the specified period;

    b. The controls related to the control objectives stated in the service organization's description of its system were suitably designed throughout the specified period; and

    c. The controls related to the control objectives stated in the service organization's description of its system operated effectively throughout the specified period; and

(iii) A service auditor's assurance report that:
    a.   Conveys reasonable assurance about the matters in (ii)a.–c. above; and
    b.   Includes a description of the tests of controls and the results thereof.

(l) Service auditor – A professional accountant in public practice who, at the request of the service organization, provides an assurance report on controls at a service organization.

(m) Service organization – A third-party organization (or segment of a third-party organization) that provides services to user entities that are likely to be relevant to user entities' internal control as it relates to financial reporting.

(n) Service organization's system (or the system) – The policies and procedures designed and implemented by the service organization to provide user entities with the services covered by the service auditor's assurance report. The service organization's description of its system includes identification of: the services covered; the period, or in the case of a type 1 report, the date, to which the description relates; control objectives; and related controls.

(o) Service organization's assertion – The written assertion about the matters referred to in paragraph 9(k)(ii) (or paragraph 9(j)(ii) in the case of a type 1 report).

(p) Subservice organization – A service organization used by another service organization to perform some of the services provided to user entities that are likely to be relevant to user entities' internal control as it relates to financial reporting.

(q) Test of controls – A procedure designed to evaluate the operating effectiveness of controls in achieving the control objectives stated in the service organization's description of its system.

(r) User auditor – An auditor who audits and reports on the financial statements of a user entity.[7]

(s) User entity – An entity that uses a service organization.

Requirements

ISAE 3000

The service auditor shall not represent compliance with this ISAE unless the service auditor has complied with the requirements of this ISAE and ISAE 3000. **10**

Ethical Requirements

The service auditor shall comply with relevant ethical requirements, including those pertaining to independence, relating to assurance engagements. (Ref: Para. A5) **11**

Management and Those Charged with Governance

Where this ISAE requires the service auditor to inquire of, request representations from, communicate with, or otherwise interact with the service organization, the service auditor shall determine the appropriate person(s) within the service organization's management or governance structure with whom to interact. This shall include consideration of which person(s) have the appropriate responsibilities for and knowledge of the matters concerned. (Ref: Para. A6) **12**

---

[7] *In the case of a subservice organization, the service auditor of a service organization that uses the services of the subservice organization is also a user auditor.*

Acceptance and Continuance

13   Before agreeing to accept, or continue, an engagement the service auditor shall:

(a) Determine whether:
   (i)   The service auditor has the capabilities and competence to perform the engagement; (Ref: Para. A7)
   (ii) The criteria to be applied by the service organization to prepare the description of its system will be suitable and available to user entities and their auditors; and
   (iii) The scope of the engagement and the service organization's description of its system will not be so limited that they are unlikely to be useful to user entities and their auditors.

(b) Obtain the agreement of the service organization that it acknowledges and understands its responsibility:
   (i)   For the preparation of the description of its system, and accompanying service organization's assertion, including the completeness, accuracy and method of presentation of that description and assertion; (Ref: Para. A8)
   (ii) To have a reasonable basis for the service organization's assertion accompanying the description of its system; (Ref: Para. A9)
   (ii) For stating in the service organization's assertion the criteria it used to prepare the description of its system;
   (iii) For stating in the description of its system:
      a.   The control objectives; and
      b.   Where they are specified by law or regulation, or another party (for example, a user group or a professional body), the party who specified them;
   (iv) For identifying the risks that threaten achievement of the control objectives stated in the description of its system, and designing and implementing controls to provide reasonable assurance that those risks will not prevent achievement of the control objectives stated in the description of its system, and therefore that the stated control objectives will be achieved; and (Ref: Para. A10)
   (v)   To provide the service auditor with:
      a.   Access to all information, such as records, documentation and other matters, including service level agreements, of which the service organization is aware that is relevant to the description of the service organization's system and the accompanying service organization's assertion;
      b.   Additional information that the service auditor may request from the service organization for the purpose of the assurance engagement; and
      c.   Unrestricted access to persons within the service organization from whom the service auditor determines it necessary to obtain evidence.

Acceptance of a Change in the Terms of the Engagement

14   If the service organization requests a change in the scope of the engagement before the completion of the engagement, the service auditor shall be satisfied that there is a reasonable justification for the change. (Ref: Para. A11–A12)

Assessing the Suitability of the Criteria

15   As required by ISAE 3000, the service auditor shall assess whether the service organization has used suitable criteria in preparing the description of its system, in

evaluating whether controls are suitably designed, and, in the case of a type 2 report, in evaluating whether controls are operating effectively.[8]

In assessing the suitability of the criteria to evaluate the service organization's **16** description of its system, the service auditor shall determine if the criteria encompass, at a minimum:

(a) Whether the description presents how the service organization's system was designed and implemented, including, as appropriate:
  (i) The types of services provided, including, as appropriate, classes of transactions processed;
  (ii) The procedures, within both information technology and manual systems, by which services are provided, including, as appropriate, procedures by which transactions are initiated, recorded, processed, corrected as necessary, and transferred to the reports and other information prepared for user entities;
  (iii) The related records and supporting information, including, as appropriate, accounting records, supporting information and specific accounts that are used to initiate, record, process and report transactions; this includes the correction of incorrect information and how information is transferred to the reports and other information prepared for user entities;
  (iv) How the service organization's system deals with significant events and conditions, other than transactions;
  (v) The process used to prepare reports and other information for user entities;
  (vi) The specified control objectives and controls designed to achieve those objectives;
  (vii) Complementary user entity controls contemplated in the design of the controls; and
  (viii) Other aspects of the service organization's control environment, risk assessment process, information system (including the related business processes) and communication, control activities and monitoring controls that are relevant to the services provided.
(b) In the case of a type 2 report, whether the description includes relevant details of changes to the service organization's system during the period covered by the description.
(c) Whether the description omits or distorts information relevant to the scope of the service organization's system being described, while acknowledging that the description is prepared to meet the common needs of a broad range of user entities and their auditors and may not, therefore, include every aspect of the service organization's system that each individual user entity and its auditor may consider important in its particular environment.

In assessing the suitability of the criteria to evaluate the design of controls, the **17** service auditor shall determine if the criteria encompass, at a minimum, whether:

(a) The service organization has identified the risks that threaten achievement of the control objectives stated in the description of its system; and
(b) The controls identified in that description would, if operated as described, provide reasonable assurance that those risks do not prevent the stated control objectives from being achieved.

In assessing the suitability of the criteria to evaluate the operating effectiveness of **18** controls in providing reasonable assurance that the stated control objectives identified in the description will be achieved, the service auditor shall determine if the criteria encompass, at a minimum, whether the controls were consistently applied as

---

[8] *ISAE 3000, paragraph 19.*

designed throughout the specified period. This includes whether manual controls were applied by individuals who have the appropriate competence and authority. (Ref: Para. A13–A15)

Materiality

19   When planning and performing the engagement, the service auditor shall consider materiality with respect to the fair presentation of the description, the suitability of the design of controls and, in the case of a type 2 report, the operating effectiveness of controls. (Ref: Para. A16–A18)

Obtaining an Understanding of the Service Organization's System

20   The service auditor shall obtain an understanding of the service organization's system, including controls that are included in the scope of the engagement. (Ref: Para. A19–A20)

Obtaining Evidence Regarding the Description

21   The service auditor shall obtain and read the service organization's description of its system, and shall evaluate whether those aspects of the description included in the scope of the engagement are fairly presented, including whether: (Ref: Para. A21–A22)

(a) Control objectives stated in the service organization's description of its system are reasonable in the circumstances; (Ref: Para. A23)
(b) Controls identified in that description were implemented;
(c) Complementary user entity controls, if any, are adequately described; and
(d) Services performed by a subservice organization, if any, are adequately described, including whether the inclusive method or the carve-out method has been used in relation to them.

22   The service auditor shall determine, through other procedures in combination with inquiries, whether the service organization's system has been implemented. Those other procedures shall include observation, and inspection of records and other documentation, of the manner in which the service organization's system operates and controls are applied. (Ref: Para. A24)

Obtaining Evidence Regarding Design of Controls

23   The service auditor shall determine which of the controls at the service organization are necessary to achieve the control objectives stated in the service organization's description of its system, and shall assess whether those controls were suitably designed. This determination shall include: (Ref: Para. A25–A27)

(a) Identifying the risks that threaten the achievement of the control objectives stated in the service organization's description of its system; and
(b) Evaluating the linkage of controls identified in the service organization's description of its system with those risks.

Obtaining Evidence Regarding Operating Effectiveness of Controls

24   When providing a type 2 report, the service auditor shall test those controls that the service auditor has determined are necessary to achieve the control objectives stated in the service organization's description of its system, and assess their operating effectiveness throughout the period. Evidence obtained in prior engagements about the satisfactory operation of controls in prior periods does not provide a basis for a reduction in testing, even if it is supplemented with evidence obtained during the current period. (Ref: Para. A28–A32)

When designing and performing tests of controls, the service auditor shall: **25**

(a) Perform other procedures in combination with inquiry to obtain evidence about:
   (i) How the control was applied;
   (ii) The consistency with which the control was applied; and
   (iii) By whom or by what means the control was applied;
(b) Determine whether controls to be tested depend upon other controls (indirect controls) and, if so, whether it is necessary to obtain evidence supporting the operating effectiveness of those indirect controls; and (Ref: Para. A33–A34)
(c) Determine means of selecting items for testing that are effective in meeting the objectives of the procedure. (Ref: Para. A35–A36)

When determining the extent of tests of controls, the service auditor shall consider **26** matters including the characteristics of the population to be tested, which includes the nature of controls, the frequency of their application (for example, monthly, daily, a number of times per day), and the expected rate of deviation.

Sampling

When the service auditor uses sampling, the service auditor shall: (Ref: Para. A35– **27** A36)

(a) Consider the purpose of the procedure and the characteristics of the population from which the sample will be drawn when designing the sample;
(b) Determine a sample size sufficient to reduce sampling risk to an appropriately low level;
(c) Select items for the sample in such a way that each sampling unit in the population has a chance of selection;
(d) If a designed procedure is not applicable to a selected item, perform the procedure on a replacement item; and
(e) If unable to apply the designed procedures, or suitable alternative procedures, to a selected item, treat that item as a deviation.

Nature and Cause of Deviations

The service auditor shall investigate the nature and cause of any deviations identified **28** and shall determine whether:

(a) Identified deviations are within the expected rate of deviation and are acceptable; therefore, the testing that has been performed provides an appropriate basis for concluding that the control is operating effectively throughout the specified period;
(b) Additional testing of the control or of other controls is necessary to reach a conclusion on whether the controls relative to a particular control objective are operating effectively throughout the specified period; or (Ref: Para. A25)
(c) The testing that has been performed provides an appropriate basis for concluding that the control did not operate effectively throughout the specified period.

29   In the extremely rare circumstances when the service auditor considers a deviation discovered in a sample to be an anomaly and no other controls have been identified that allow the service auditor to conclude that the relevant control objective is operating effectively throughout the specified period, the service auditor shall obtain a high degree of certainty that such deviation is not representative of the population. The service auditor shall obtain this degree of certainty by performing additional procedures to obtain sufficient appropriate evidence that the deviation does not affect the remainder of the population.

The Work of an Internal Audit Function[9]

Obtaining an Understanding of the Internal Audit Function

30   If the service organization has an internal audit function, the service auditor shall obtain an understanding of the nature of the responsibilities of the internal audit function and of the activities performed in order to determine whether the internal audit function is likely to be relevant to the engagement. (Ref: Para. A37)

Determining Whether and to What Extent to Use the Work of the Internal Auditors

31   The service auditor shall determine:

(a) Whether the work of the internal auditors is likely to be adequate for purposes of the engagement; and
(b) If so, the planned effect of the work of the internal auditors on the nature, timing or extent of the service auditor's procedures.

32   In determining whether the work of the internal auditors is likely to be adequate for purposes of the engagement, the service auditor shall evaluate:

(a) The objectivity of the internal audit function;
(b) The technical competence of the internal auditors;
(c) Whether the work of the internal auditors is likely to be carried out with due professional care; and
(d) Whether there is likely to be effective communication between the internal auditors and the service auditor.

33   In determining the planned effect of the work of the internal auditors on the nature, timing or extent of the service auditor's procedures, the service auditor shall consider: (Ref: Para. A38)

(a) The nature and scope of specific work performed, or to be performed, by the internal auditors;
(b) The significance of that work to the service auditor's conclusions; and
(c) The degree of subjectivity involved in the evaluation of the evidence gathered in support of those conclusions.

Using the Work of the Internal Audit Function

34   In order for the service auditor to use specific work of the internal auditors, the service auditor shall evaluate and perform procedures on that work to determine its adequacy for the service auditor's purposes. (Ref: Para. A39)

---

[9] *This ISAE does not deal with instances when individual internal auditors provide direct assistance to the service auditor in carrying out audit procedures.*

To determine the adequacy of specific work performed by the internal auditors for **35** the service auditor's purposes, the service auditor shall evaluate whether:

(a) The work was performed by internal auditors having adequate technical training and proficiency;
(b) The work was properly supervised, reviewed and documented;
(c) Adequate evidence has been obtained to enable the internal auditors to draw reasonable conclusions;
(d) Conclusions reached are appropriate in the circumstances and any reports prepared by the internal auditors are consistent with the results of the work performed; and
(e) Exceptions relevant to the engagement or unusual matters disclosed by the internal auditors are properly resolved.

Effect on the Service Auditor's Assurance Report

If the work of the internal audit function has been used, the service auditor shall **36** make no reference to that work in the section of the service auditor's assurance report that contains the service auditor's opinion. (Ref: Para. A40)

In the case of a type 2 report, if the work of the internal audit function has been used **37** in performing tests of controls, that part of the service auditor's assurance report that describes the service auditor's tests of controls and the results thereof shall include a description of the internal auditor's work and of the service auditor's procedures with respect to that work. (Ref: Para. A41)

Written Representations

The service auditor shall request the service organization to provide written repre- **38** sentations: (Ref: Para. A42)

(a) That reaffirm the assertion accompanying the description of the system;
(b) That it has provided the service auditor with all relevant information and access agreed to;[10] and
(c) That it has disclosed to the service auditor any of the following of which it is aware:
(i) Non-compliance with laws and regulations, fraud, or uncorrected deviations attributable to the service organization that may affect one or more user entities;
(ii) Design deficiencies in controls;
(iii) Instances where controls have not operated as described; and
(iv) Any events subsequent to the period covered by the service organization's description of its system up to the date of the service auditor's assurance report that could have a significant effect on the service auditor's assurance report.

The written representations shall be in the form of a representation letter addressed **39** to the service auditor. The date of the written representations shall be as near as practicable to, but not after, the date of the service auditor's assurance report.

If, having discussed the matter with the service auditor, the service organization does **40** not provide one or more of the written representations requested in accordance with paragraph 38(a) and (b) of this ISAE, the service auditor shall disclaim an opinion. (Ref: Para. A43)

---

[10] *Paragraph 13(b)(v) of this ISAE.*

Other Information

41   The service auditor shall read the other information, if any, included in a document containing the service organization's description of its system and the service auditor's assurance report, to identify material inconsistencies, if any, with that description. While reading the other information for the purpose of identifying material inconsistencies, the service auditor may become aware of an apparent misstatement of fact in that other information.

42   If the service auditor becomes aware of a material inconsistency or an apparent misstatement of fact in the other information, the service auditor shall discuss the matter with the service organization. If the service auditor concludes that there is a material inconsistency or a misstatement of fact in the other information that the service organization refuses to correct, the service auditor shall take further appropriate action. (Ref: Para. A44–A45)

Subsequent Events

43   The service auditor shall inquire whether the service organization is aware of any events subsequent to the period covered by the service organization's description of its system up to the date of the service auditor's assurance report that could have a significant effect on the service auditor's assurance report. If the service auditor is aware of such an event, and information about that event is not disclosed by the service organization, the service auditor shall disclose it in the service auditor's assurance report.

44   The service auditor has no obligation to perform any procedures regarding the description of the service organization's system, or the suitability of design or operating effectiveness of controls, after the date of the service auditor's assurance report.

Documentation

45   The service auditor shall prepare documentation that is sufficient to enable an experienced service auditor, having no previous connection with the engagement, to understand:

(a)   The nature, timing, and extent of the procedures performed to comply with this ISAE and applicable legal and regulatory requirements;

(b)   The results of the procedures performed, and the evidence obtained; and

(c)   Significant matters arising during the engagement, and the conclusions reached thereon and significant professional judgments made in reaching those conclusions.

46   In documenting the nature, timing and extent of procedures performed, the service auditor shall record:

(a)   The identifying characteristics of the specific items or matters being tested;

(b)   Who performed the work and the date such work was completed; and

(c)   Who reviewed the work performed and the date and extent of such review.

47   If the service auditor uses specific work of the internal auditors, the service auditor shall document the conclusions reached regarding the evaluation of the adequacy of the work of the internal auditors, and the procedures performed by the service auditor on that work.

The service auditor shall document discussions of significant matters with the service **48** organization and others including the nature of the significant matters discussed and when and with whom the discussions took place.

If the service auditor has identified information that is inconsistent with the service **49** auditor's final conclusion regarding a significant matter, the service auditor shall document how the service auditor addressed the inconsistency.

The service auditor shall assemble the documentation in an engagement file and **50** complete the administrative process of assembling the final engagement file on a timely basis after the date of the service auditor's assurance report.[11]

After the assembly of the final engagement file has been completed, the service **51** auditor shall not delete or discard documentation before the end of its retention period. (Ref: Para. A46)

If the service auditor finds it necessary to modify existing engagement documentation **52** or add new documentation after the assembly of the final engagement file has been completed and that documentation does not affect the service auditor's report, the service auditor shall, regardless of the nature of the modifications or additions, document:

(a) The specific reasons for making them; and
(b) When and by whom they were made and reviewed.

Preparing the Service Auditor's Assurance Report

Content of the Service Auditor's Assurance Report

The service auditor's assurance report shall include the following basic elements: **53** (Ref: Para. A47)

(a) A title that clearly indicates the report is an independent service auditor's assurance report.
(b) An addressee.
(c) Identification of:
  (i) The service organization's description of its system, and the service organization's assertion, which includes the matters described in paragraph 9(k)(ii) for a type 2 report, or paragraph 9(j)(ii) for a type 1 report.
  (ii) Those parts of the service organization's description of its system, if any, that are not covered by the service auditor's opinion.
  (iii) If the description refers to the need for complementary user entity controls, a statement that the service auditor has not evaluated the suitability of design or operating effectiveness of complementary user entity controls, and that the control objectives stated in the service organization's description of its system can be achieved only if complementary user entity controls are suitably designed or operating effectively, along with the controls at the service organization.
  (iv) If services are performed by a subservice organization, the nature of activities performed by the subservice organization as described in the service organization's description of its system and whether the inclusive method or the carve-out method has been used in relation to them. Where the carve-out method has been used, a statement that the service organization's description of its system excludes the control objectives and related

---

[11] *International Standard on Quality Control (ISQC) 1, paragraphs A54–A55, provide further guidance.*

controls at relevant subservice organizations, and that the service auditor's procedures do not extend to controls at the subservice organization. Where the inclusive method has been used, a statement that the service organization's description of its system includes control objectives and related controls at the subservice organization, and that the service auditor's procedures extended to controls at the subservice organization.

(d) Identification of the criteria, and the party specifying the control objectives.

(e) A statement that the report and, in the case of a type 2 report, the description of tests of controls are intended only for user entities and their auditors, who have a sufficient understanding to consider it, along with other information including information about controls operated by user entities themselves, when assessing the risks of material misstatements of user entities' financial statements. (Ref: Para. A48)

(f) A statement that the service organization is responsible for:
   (i) Preparing the description of its system, and the accompanying assertion, including the completeness, accuracy and method of presentation of that description and that assertion;
   (ii) Providing the services covered by the service organization's description of its system;
   (iii) Stating the control objectives (where not identified by law or regulation, or another party, for example, a user group or a professional body); and
   (iv) Designing and implementing controls to achieve the control objectives stated in the service organization's description of its system.

(g) A statement that the service auditor's responsibility is to express an opinion on the service organization's description, on the design of controls related to the control objectives stated in that description and, in the case of a type 2 report, on the operating effectiveness of those controls, based on the service auditor's procedures.

(h) A statement that the engagement was performed in accordance with ISAE 3402, "Assurance Reports on Controls at a Service Organization," which requires that the service auditor comply with ethical requirements and plan and perform procedures to obtain reasonable assurance about whether, in all material respects, the service organization's description of its system is fairly presented and the controls are suitably designed and, in the case of a type 2 report, are operating effectively.

(i) A summary of the service auditor's procedures to obtain reasonable assurance and a statement of the service auditor's belief that the evidence obtained is sufficient and appropriate to provide a basis for the service auditor's opinion, and, in the case of a type 1 report, a statement that the service auditor has not performed any procedures regarding the operating effectiveness of controls and therefore no opinion is expressed thereon.

(j) A statement of the limitations of controls and, in the case of a type 2 report, of the risk of projecting to future periods any evaluation of the operating effectiveness of controls.

(k) The service auditor's opinion, expressed in the positive form, on whether, in all material respects, based on suitable criteria:
   (i) In the case of a type 2 report:
       a. The description fairly presents the service organization's system that had been designed and implemented throughout the specified period;
       b. The controls related to the control objectives stated in the service organization's description of its system were suitably designed throughout the specified period; and
       c. The controls tested, which were those necessary to provide reasonable assurance that the control objectives stated in the description were achieved, operated effectively throughout the specified period.
   (ii) In the case of a type 1 report:

a. The description fairly presents the service organization's system that had been designed and implemented as at the specified date; and
b. The controls related to the control objectives stated in the service organization's description of its system were suitably designed as at the specified date.

(l) The date of the service auditor's assurance report, which shall be no earlier than the date on which the service auditor has obtained sufficient appropriate evidence on which to base the opinion.

(m) The name of the service auditor, and the location in the jurisdiction where the service auditor practices.

In the case of a type 2 report, the service auditor's assurance report shall include a **54** separate section after the opinion, or an attachment, that describes the tests of controls that were performed and the results of those tests. In describing the tests of controls, the service auditor shall clearly state which controls were tested, identify whether the items tested represent all or a selection of the items in the population, and indicate the nature of the tests in sufficient detail to enable user auditors to determine the effect of such tests on their risk assessments. If deviations have been identified, the service auditor shall include the extent of testing performed that led to identification of the deviations (including the sample size where sampling has been used), and the number and nature of the deviations noted. The service auditor shall report deviations even if, on the basis of tests performed, the service auditor has concluded that the related control objective was achieved. (Ref: Para. A18 and A49)

Modified Opinions

If the service auditor concludes that: (Ref: Para. A50–A52)   **55**

(a) The service organization's description does not fairly present, in all material respects, the system as designed and implemented;
(b) The controls related to the control objectives stated in the description were not suitably designed, in all material respects;
(c) In the case of a type 2 report, the controls tested, which were those necessary to provide reasonable assurance that the control objectives stated in the service organization's description of its system were achieved, did not operate effectively, in all material respects; or
(d) The service auditor is unable to obtain sufficient appropriate evidence,

the service auditor's opinion shall be modified, and the service auditor's assurance report shall contain a clear description of all the reasons for the modification.

Other Communication Responsibilities

If the service auditor becomes aware of non-compliance with laws and regulations, **56** fraud, or uncorrected errors attributable to the service organization that are not clearly trivial and may affect one or more user entities, the service auditor shall determine whether the matter has been communicated appropriately to affected user entities. If the matter has not been so communicated and the service organization is unwilling to do so, the service auditor shall take appropriate action. (Ref: Para. A53)

***

Application and Other Explanatory Material

Scope of this ISAE (Ref: Para. 1, 3)

A1   Internal control is a process designed to provide reasonable assurance regarding the achievement of objectives related to the reliability of financial reporting, effectiveness and efficiency of operations and compliance with applicable laws and regulations. Controls related to a service organization's operations and compliance objectives may be relevant to a user entity's internal control as it relates to financial reporting. Such controls may pertain to assertions about presentation and disclosure relating to account balances, classes of transactions or disclosures, or may pertain to evidence that the user auditor evaluates or uses in applying auditing procedures. For example, a payroll processing service organization's controls related to the timely remittance of payroll deductions to government authorities may be relevant to a user entity as late remittances could incur interest and penalties that would result in a liability for the user entity. Similarly, a service organization's controls over the acceptability of investment transactions from a regulatory perspective may be considered relevant to a user entity's presentation and disclosure of transactions and account balances in its financial statements. The determination of whether controls at a service organization related to operations and compliance are likely to be relevant to user entities' internal control as it relates to financial reporting is a matter of professional judgment, having regard to the control objectives set by the service organization and the suitability of the criteria.

A2   The service organization may not be able to assert that the system is suitably designed when, for example, the service organization is operating a system that has been designed by a user entity or is stipulated in a contract between a user entity and the service organization. Because of the inextricable link between the suitable design of controls and their operating effectiveness, the absence of an assertion with respect to the suitability of design will likely preclude the service auditor from concluding that the controls provide reasonable assurance that the control objectives have been met and thus from opining on the operating effectiveness of controls. As an alternative, the practitioner may choose to accept an agreed-upon procedures engagement to perform tests of controls, or an assurance engagement under ISAE 3000 to conclude on whether, based on tests of controls, the controls have operated as described.

Definitions (Ref: Para. 9(d), 9(g))

A3   The definition of "controls at the service organization" includes aspects of user entities' information systems maintained by the service organization, and may also include aspects of one or more of the other components of internal control at a service organization. For example, it may include aspects of a service organization's control environment, monitoring, and control activities when they relate to the services provided. It does not, however, include controls at a service organization that are not related to the achievement of the control objectives stated in the service organization's description of its system, for example, controls related to the preparation of the service organization's own financial statements.

A4   When the inclusive method is used, the requirements in this ISAE also apply to the services provided by the subservice organization, including obtaining agreement regarding the matters in paragraph 13(b)(i)–(v) as applied to the subservice organization rather than the service organization. Performing procedures at the subservice organization entails coordination and communication between the service organization, the subservice organization, and the service auditor. The inclusive method generally is feasible only if the service organization and the subservice organization are related, or if the contract between the service organization and the subservice organization provides for its use.

Ethical Requirements (Ref: Para. 11)

The service auditor is subject to relevant independence requirements, which ordi- **A5** narily comprise Parts A and B of the IESBA Code together with national requirements that are more restrictive. In performing an engagement in accordance with this ISAE, the IESBA Code does not require the service auditor to be independent from each user entity.

Management and Those Charged with Governance (Ref: Para. 12)

Management and governance structures vary by jurisdiction and by entity, reflecting **A6** influences such as different cultural and legal backgrounds, and size and ownership characteristics. Such diversity means that it is not possible for this ISAE to specify for all engagements the person(s) with whom the service auditor is to interact regarding particular matters. For example, the service organization may be a segment of a third-party organization and not a separate legal entity. In such cases, identifying the appropriate management personnel or those charged with governance from whom to request written representations may require the exercise of professional judgment.

Acceptance and Continuance

Capabilities and Competence to Perform the Engagement (Ref: Para. 13(a)(i))

Relevant capabilities and competence to perform the engagement include matters **A7** such as the following:

● Knowledge of the relevant industry;
● An understanding of information technology and systems;
● Experience in evaluating risks as they relate to the suitable design of controls; and
● Experience in the design and execution of tests of controls and the evaluation of the results.

Service Organization's Assertion (Ref: Para. 13(b)(i))

Refusal, by a service organization, to provide a written assertion, subsequent to an **A8** agreement by the service auditor to accept, or continue, an engagement, represents a scope limitation that causes the service auditor to withdraw from the engagement. If law or regulation does not allow the service auditor to withdraw from the engagement, the service auditor disclaims an opinion.

Reasonable Basis for Service Organization's Assertion (Ref: Para. 13(b)(ii))

In the case of a type 2 report, the service organization's assertion includes a state- **A9** ment that the controls related to the control objectives stated in the service organization's description of its system operated effectively throughout the specified period. This assertion may be based on the service organization's monitoring activities. Monitoring of controls is a process to assess the effectiveness of controls over time. It involves assessing the effectiveness of controls on a timely basis, identifying and reporting deficiencies to appropriate individuals within the service organization, and taking necessary corrective actions. The service organization accomplishes monitoring of controls through ongoing activities, separate evaluations, or a combination of both. The greater the degree and effectiveness of ongoing monitoring activities, the less need for separate evaluations. Ongoing monitoring activities are often built into the normal recurring activities of a service organization and include regular management and supervisory activities. Internal auditors or personnel performing similar functions may contribute to the monitoring of a service organization's activities. Monitoring activities may also include using information communicated by external parties, such as customer complaints and regulator comments, which may indicate problems or highlight areas in need of improvement. The fact that the service auditor will report on the operating effectiveness of controls is not a substitute for the service organization's own processes to provide a reasonable basis for its assertion.

Identification of Risks (Ref: Para. 13(b)(iv))

A10   As noted in paragraph 9(c), control objectives relate to risks that controls seek to mitigate. For example, the risk that a transaction is recorded at the wrong amount or in the wrong period can be expressed as a control objective that transactions are recorded at the correct amount and in the correct period. The service organization is responsible for identifying the risks that threaten achievement of the control objectives stated in the description of its system. The service organization may have a formal or informal process for identifying relevant risks. A formal process may include estimating the significance of identified risks, assessing the likelihood of their occurrence, and deciding about actions to address them. However, since control objectives relate to risks that controls seek to mitigate, thoughtful identification of control objectives when designing and implementing the service organization's system may itself comprise an informal process for identifying relevant risks.

Acceptance of a Change in the Terms of the Engagement (Ref: Para. 14)

A11   A request to change the scope of the engagement may not have a reasonable justification when, for example, the request is made to exclude certain control objectives from the scope of the engagement because of the likelihood that the service auditor's opinion would be modified; or the service organization will not provide the service auditor with a written assertion and the request is made to perform the engagement under ISAE 3000.

A12   A request to change the scope of the engagement may have a reasonable justification when, for example, the request is made to exclude from the engagement a subservice organization when the service organization cannot arrange for access by the service auditor, and the method used for dealing with the services provided by that subservice organization is changed from the inclusive method to the carve-out method.

Assessing the Suitability of the Criteria (Ref: Para. 15–18)

A13   Criteria need to be available to the intended users to allow them to understand the basis for the service organization's assertion about the fair presentation of its description of the system, the suitability of the design of controls and, in the case of a type 2 report, the operating effectiveness of the controls related to the control objectives.

ISAE 3000 requires the service auditor, among other things, to assess the suitability **A14** of criteria, and the appropriateness of the subject matter.[12] The subject matter is the underlying condition of interest to intended users of an assurance report. The following table identifies the subject matter and minimum criteria for each of the opinions in type 2 and type 1 reports.

	Subject matter	Criteria	Comment
Opinion about the fair presentation of the description of the service organization's system (type 1 and type 2 reports)	The service organization's system that is likely to be relevant to user entities' internal control as it relates to financial reporting and is covered by the service auditor's assurance report.	The description is fairly presented if it: (a) presents how the service organization's system was designed and implemented including, as appropriate, the matters identified in paragraph 16(a)(i)–(viii); (b) in the case of a type 2 report, includes relevant details of changes to the service organization's system during the period covered by the description; and (c) does not omit or distort information relevant to the scope of the service organization's system being described, while acknowledging that the description is prepared to meet the common needs of a broad range of user entities and may not, therefore, include every aspect of the service organization's system that each individual user entity may consider important in its own particular environment.	The specific wording of the criteria for this opinion may need to be tailored to be consistent with criteria established by, for example, law or regulation, user groups, or a professional body. Examples of criteria for this opinion are provided in the illustrative service organization's assertion in Appendix 1. Paragraphs A21–A24 offer further guidance on determining whether these criteria are met. (In terms of the requirements of ISAE 3000, the subject matter information[13] for this opinion is the service organization's description of its system and the service organization's assertion that the description is fairly presented.)

---

[12] *ISAE 3000, paragraphs 18–19.*

[13] *The "subject matter information" is the outcome of the evaluation or measurement of the subject matter that results from applying the criteria to the subject matter.*

	Subject matter	Criteria	Comment	
Opinion about suitability of design, and operating effectiveness (type 2 reports)	The suitability of the design and operating effectiveness of those controls that are necessary to achieve the control objectives stated in the service organization's description of its system.	The controls are suitably designed and operating effectively if: (a) the service organization has identified the risks that threaten achievement of the control objectives stated in the description of its system; (b) the controls identified in that description would, if operated as described, provide reasonable assurance that those risks do not prevent the stated control objectives from being achieved; and (c) the controls were consistently applied as designed throughout the specified period. This includes whether manual controls were applied by individuals who have the appropriate competence and authority.	When the criteria for this opinion are met, controls will have provided reasonable assurance that the related control objectives were achieved throughout the specified period. (In terms of the requirements of ISAE 3000, the subject matter information for this opinion is the service organization's assertion that controls are suitably designed and that they are operating effectively.)	The control objectives, which are stated in the service organization's description of its system, are part of the criteria for these opinions. The stated control objectives will differ from engagement to engagement. If, as part of forming the opinion on the description, the service auditor concludes the stated control objectives are not fairly presented then those control objectives would not be suitable as part of the criteria for forming an opinion on either the design or operating effectiveness of controls.
Opinion about suitability of design (type 1 reports)	The suitability of the design of those controls that are necessary to achieve the control objectives stated in the service organization's description of its system.	The controls are suitably designed if: (a) the service organization has identified the risks that threaten achievement of the control objectives stated in the description of its system; and (b) the controls identified in that description would, if operated as described, provide reasonable assurance that those risks do not prevent the stated control objectives from being achieved.	Meeting these criteria does not, of itself, provide any assurance that the related control objectives were achieved because no assurance has been obtained about the operation of controls. (In terms of the requirements of ISAE 3000, the subject matter information for this opinion is the service organization's assertion that controls are suitably designed.)	

Paragraph 16(a) identifies a number of elements that are included in the service **A15** organization's description of its system as appropriate. These elements may not be appropriate if the system being described is not a system that processes transactions, for example, if the system relates to general controls over the hosting of an IT application but not the controls embedded in the application itself.

Materiality (Ref: Para. 19, 54)

In an engagement to report on controls at a service organization, the concept of **A16** materiality relates to the system being reported on, not the financial statements of user entities. The service auditor plans and performs procedures to determine whether the service organization's description of its system is fairly presented in all material respects, whether controls at the service organization are suitably designed in all material respects and, in the case of a type 2 report, whether controls at the service organization are operating effectively in all material respects. The concept of materiality takes into account that the service auditor's assurance report provides information about the service organization's system to meet the common information needs of a broad range of user entities and their auditors who have an understanding of the manner in which that system has been used.

Materiality with respect to the fair presentation of the service organization's **A17** description of its system, and with respect to the design of controls, includes primarily the consideration of qualitative factors, for example: whether the description includes the significant aspects of processing significant transactions; whether the description omits or distorts relevant information; and the ability of controls, as designed, to provide reasonable assurance that control objectives would be achieved. Materiality with respect to the service auditor's opinion on the operating effectiveness of controls includes the consideration of both quantitative and qualitative factors, for example, the tolerable rate and observed rate of deviation (a quantitative matter), and the nature and cause of any observed deviation (a qualitative matter).

The concept of materiality is not applied when disclosing, in the description of the **A18** tests of controls, the results of those tests where deviations have been identified. This is because, in the particular circumstances of a specific user entity or user auditor, a deviation may have significance beyond whether or not, in the opinion of the service auditor, it prevents a control from operating effectively. For example, the control to which the deviation relates may be particularly significant in preventing a certain type of error that may be material in the particular circumstances of a user entity's financial statements.

Obtaining an Understanding of the Service Organization's System
(Ref: Para. 20)

Obtaining an understanding of the service organization's system, including controls, **A19** included in the scope of the engagement, assists the service auditor in:

- Identifying the boundaries of that system, and how it interfaces with other systems.
- Assessing whether the service organization's description fairly presents the system that has been designed and implemented.
- Determining which controls are necessary to achieve the control objectives stated in the service organization's description of its system.
- Assessing whether controls were suitably designed.
- Assessing, in the case of a type 2 report, whether controls were operating effectively.

A20 The service auditor's procedures to obtain this understanding may include:

- Inquiring of those within the service organization who, in the service auditor's judgment, may have relevant information.
- Observing operations and inspecting documents, reports, printed and electronic records of transaction processing.
- Inspecting a selection of agreements between the service organization and user entities to identify their common terms.
- Reperforming control procedures.

Obtaining Evidence Regarding the Description (Ref: Para. 21–22)

A21 Considering the following questions may assist the service auditor in determining whether those aspects of the description included in the scope of the engagement are fairly presented in all material respects:

- Does the description address the major aspects of the service provided (within the scope of the engagement) that could reasonably be expected to be relevant to the common needs of a broad range of user auditors in planning their audits of user entities' financial statements?
- Is the description prepared at a level of detail that could reasonably be expected to provide a broad range of user auditors with sufficient information to obtain an understanding of internal control in accordance with ISA 315?[14] The description need not address every aspect of the service organization's processing or the services provided to user entities, and need not be so detailed as to potentially allow a reader to compromise security or other controls at the service organization.
- Is the description prepared in a manner that does not omit or distort information that may affect the common needs of a broad range of user auditors' decisions, for example, does the description contain any significant omissions or inaccuracies in processing of which the service auditor is aware?
- Where some of the control objectives stated in the service organization's description of its system have been excluded from the scope of the engagement, does the description clearly identify the excluded objectives?
- Have the controls identified in the description been implemented?
- Are complementary user entity controls, if any, described adequately? In most cases, the description of control objectives is worded such that the control objectives are capable of being achieved through effective operation of controls implemented by the service organization alone. In some cases, however, the control objectives stated in the service organization's description of its system cannot be achieved by the service organization alone because their achievement requires particular controls to be implemented by user entities. This may be the case where, for example, the control objectives are specified by a regulatory authority. When the description does include complementary user entity controls, the description separately identifies those controls along with the specific control objectives that cannot be achieved by the service organization alone.
- If the inclusive method has been used, does the description separately identify controls at the service organization and controls at the subservice organization? If the carve-out method is used, does the description identify the functions that are performed by the subservice organization? When the carve-out method is used, the description need not describe the detailed processing or controls at the subservice organization.

---

[14] *ISA 315*, Identifying and Assessing Risks of Material Misstatement through Understanding the Entity and Its Environment.

The service auditor's procedures to evaluate the fair presentation of the description   **A22**
may include:

- Considering the nature of user entities and how the services provided by the service organization are likely to affect them, for example, whether user entities are from a particular industry and whether they are regulated by government agencies.
- Reading standard contracts, or standard terms of contracts, (if applicable) with user entities to gain an understanding of the service organization's contractual obligations.
- Observing procedures performed by service organization personnel.
- Reviewing the service organization's policy and procedure manuals and other systems documentation, for example, flowcharts and narratives.

Paragraph 21(a) requires the service auditor to evaluate whether the control objec-   **A23**
tives stated in the service organization's description of its system are reasonable in
the circumstances. Considering the following questions may assist the service auditor
in this evaluation:

- Have the stated control objectives been designated by the service organization or by outside parties such as a regulatory authority, a user group, or a professional body that follows a transparent due process?
- Where the stated control objectives have been specified by the service organization, do they relate to the types of assertions commonly embodied in the broad range of user entities' financial statements to which controls at the service organization could reasonably be expected to relate? Although the service auditor ordinarily will not be able to determine how controls at a service organization specifically relate to the assertions embodied in individual user entities' financial statements, the service auditor's understanding of the nature of the service organization's system, including controls, and services being provided is used to identify the types of assertions to which those controls are likely to relate.
- Where the stated control objectives have been specified by the service organization, are they complete? A complete set of control objectives can provide a broad range of user auditors with a framework to assess the effect of controls at the service organization on the assertions commonly embodied in user entities' financial statements.

The service auditor's procedures to determine whether the service organization's   **A24**
system has been implemented may be similar to, and performed in conjunction with,
procedures to obtain an understanding of that system. They may also include tracing
items through the service organization's system and, in the case of a type 2 report,
specific inquiries about changes in controls that were implemented during the period.
Changes that are significant to user entities or their auditors are included in the
description of the service organization's system.

Obtaining Evidence Regarding Design of Controls (Ref: Para. 23, 28(b))

From the viewpoint of a *user entity* or a *user auditor*, a control is suitably designed if,   **A25**
individually or in combination with other controls, it would, when complied with
satisfactorily, provide reasonable assurance that material misstatements are prevented, or detected and corrected. A *service organization* or a *service auditor*,
however, is not aware of the circumstances at individual user entities that would
determine whether or not a misstatement resulting from a control deviation is
material to those user entities. Therefore, from the viewpoint of a service auditor, a
control is suitably designed if, individually or in combination with other controls, it

would, when complied with satisfactorily, provide reasonable assurance that control objectives stated in the service organization's description of its system are achieved.

A26   A service auditor may consider using flowcharts, questionnaires, or decision tables to facilitate understanding the design of the controls.

A27   Controls may consist of a number of activities directed at the achievement of a control objective. Consequently, if the service auditor evaluates certain activities as being ineffective in achieving a particular control objective, the existence of other activities may allow the service auditor to conclude that controls related to the control objective are suitably designed.

Obtaining Evidence Regarding Operating Effectiveness of Controls

Assessing Operating Effectiveness (Ref: Para. 24)

A28   From the viewpoint of a *user entity* or a *user auditor*, a control is operating effectively if, individually or in combination with other controls, it provides reasonable assurance that material misstatements, whether due to fraud or error, are prevented, or detected and corrected. A *service organization* or a *service auditor*, however, is not aware of the circumstances at individual user entities that would determine whether a misstatement resulting from a control deviation had occurred and, if so, whether it is material. Therefore, from the viewpoint of a service auditor, a control is operating effectively if, individually or in combination with other controls, it provides reasonable assurance that control objectives stated in the service organization's description of its system are achieved. Similarly, a service organization or a service auditor is not in a position to determine whether any observed control deviation would result in a material misstatement from the viewpoint of an individual user entity.

A29   Obtaining an understanding of controls sufficient to opine on the suitability of their design is not sufficient evidence regarding their operating effectiveness, unless there is some automation that provides for the consistent operation of the controls as they were designed and implemented. For example, obtaining information about the implementation of a manual control at a point in time does not provide evidence about operation of the control at other times. However, because of the inherent consistency of IT processing, performing procedures to determine the design of an automated control, and whether it has been implemented, may serve as evidence of that control's operating effectiveness, depending on the service auditor's assessment and testing of other controls, such as those over program changes.

A30   To be useful to user auditors, a type 2 report ordinarily covers a minimum period of six months. If the period is less than six months, the service auditor may consider it appropriate to describe the reasons for the shorter period in the service auditor's assurance report. Circumstances that may result in a report covering a period of less than six months include when (a) the service auditor is engaged close to the date by which the report on controls is to be issued; (b) the service organization (or a particular system or application) has been in operation for less than six months; or (c) significant changes have been made to the controls and it is not practicable either to wait six months before issuing a report or to issue a report covering the system both before and after the changes.

A31   Certain control procedures may not leave evidence of their operation that can be tested at a later date and, accordingly, the service auditor may find it necessary to test the operating effectiveness of such control procedures at various times throughout the reporting period.

The service auditor provides an opinion on the operating effectiveness of controls **A32** throughout each period, therefore, sufficient appropriate evidence about the operation of controls during the current period is required for the service auditor to express that opinion. Knowledge of deviations observed in prior engagements may, however, lead the service auditor to increase the extent of testing during the current period.

Testing of Indirect Controls (Ref: Para. 25(b))

In some circumstances, it may be necessary to obtain evidence supporting the **A33** effective operation of indirect controls. For example, when the service auditor decides to test the effectiveness of a review of exception reports detailing sales in excess of authorized credit limits, the review and related follow up is the control that is directly of relevance to the service auditor. Controls over the accuracy of the information in the reports (for example, the general IT controls) are described as "indirect" controls.

Because of the inherent consistency of IT processing, evidence about the imple- **A34** mentation of an automated application control, when considered in combination with evidence about the operating effectiveness of the service organization's general controls (in particular, change controls), may also provide substantial evidence about its operating effectiveness.

Means of Selecting Items for Testing (Ref: Para. 25(c), 27)

The means of selecting items for testing available to the service auditor are: **A35**

(a) Selecting all items (100% examination). This may be appropriate for testing controls that are applied infrequently, for example, quarterly, or when evidence regarding application of the control makes 100% examination efficient;
(b) Selecting specific items. This may be appropriate where 100% examination would not be efficient and sampling would not be effective, such as testing controls that are not applied sufficiently frequently to render a large population for sampling, for example, controls that are applied monthly or weekly; and
(c) Sampling. This may be appropriate for testing controls that are applied frequently in a uniform manner and which leave documentary evidence of their application.

While selective examination of specific items will often be an efficient means of **A36** obtaining evidence, it does not constitute sampling. The results of procedures applied to items selected in this way cannot be projected to the entire population; accordingly, selective examination of specific items does not provide evidence concerning the remainder of the population. Sampling, on the other hand, is designed to enable conclusions to be drawn about an entire population on the basis of testing a sample drawn from it.

The Work of an Internal Audit Function

Obtaining an Understanding of the Internal Audit Function (Ref: Para. 30)

An internal audit function may be responsible for providing analyses, evaluations, **A37** assurances, recommendations, and other information to management and those charged with governance. An internal audit function at a service organization may perform activities related to the service organization's own system of internal control, or activities related to the services and systems, including controls, that the service organization is providing to user entities.

Determining Whether and to What Extent to Use the Work of the Internal Auditors (Ref: Para. 33)

A38   In determining the planned effect of the work of the internal auditors on the nature, timing or extent of the service auditor's procedures, the following factors may suggest the need for different or less extensive procedures than would otherwise be the case:

- The nature and scope of specific work performed, or to be performed, by the internal auditors is quite limited.
- The work of the internal auditors relates to controls that are less significant to the service auditor's conclusions.
- The work performed, or to be performed, by the internal auditors does not require subjective or complex judgments.

Using the Work of the Internal Audit Function (Ref: Para. 34)

A39   The nature, timing and extent of the service auditor's procedures on specific work of the internal auditors will depend on the service auditor's assessment of the significance of that work to the service auditor's conclusions (for example, the significance of the risks that the controls tested seek to mitigate), the evaluation of the internal audit function and the evaluation of the specific work of the internal auditors Such procedures may include:

- Examination of items already examined by the internal auditors;
- Examination of other similar items; and
- Observation of procedures performed by the internal auditors.

Effect on the Service Auditor's Assurance Report (Ref: Para. 36–37)

A40   Irrespective of the degree of autonomy and objectivity of the internal audit function, such function is not independent of the service organization as is required of the service auditor when performing the engagement. The service auditor has sole responsibility for the opinion expressed in the service auditor's assurance report, and that responsibility is not reduced by the service auditor's use of the work of the internal auditors.

A41   The service auditor's description of work performed by the internal audit function may be presented in a number of ways, for example:

- By including introductory material to the description of tests of controls indicating that certain work of the internal audit function was used in performing tests of controls.
- Attribution of individual tests to internal audit.

Written Representations (Ref: Para. 38, 40)

A42   The written representations required by paragraph 38 are separate from, and in addition to, the service organization's assertion, as defined at paragraph 9(o).

If the service organization does not provide the written representations requested in **A43** accordance with paragraph 38(c) of this ISAE, it may be appropriate for the service auditor's opinion to be modified in accordance with paragraph 55(d) of this ISAE.

Other Information (Ref: Para. 42)

The IESBA Code requires that a service auditor not be associated with information **A44** where the service auditor believes that the information:

(a) Contains a materially false or misleading statement;
(b) Contains statements or information furnished recklessly; or
(c) Omits or obscures information required to be included where such omission or obscurity would be misleading.[15]

If other information included in a document containing the service organization's description of its system and the service auditor's assurance report contains future-oriented information such as recovery or contingency plans, or plans for modifications to the system that will address deviations identified in the service auditor's assurance report, or claims of a promotional nature that cannot be reasonably substantiated, the service auditor may request that information be removed or restated.

If the service organization refuses to remove or restate the other information, further **A45** actions that may be appropriate include, for example:

● Requesting the service organization to consult with its legal counsel as to the appropriate course of action.
● Describing the material inconsistency or material misstatement of fact in the assurance report.
● Withholding the assurance report until the matter is resolved.
● Withdrawing from the engagement.

Documentation (Ref: Para. 51)

ISQC 1 (or national requirements that are at least as demanding) requires firms to **A46** establish policies and procedures for the timely completion of the assembly of engagement files.[16] An appropriate time limit within which to complete the assembly of the final engagement file is ordinarily not more than 60 days after the date of the service auditor's report.[17]

Preparing the Service Auditor's Assurance Report

Content of the Service Auditor's Assurance Report (Ref: Para. 53)

Illustrative examples of service auditors' assurance reports and related service **A47** organizations' assertions are contained in Appendices 1 and 2.

---

[15] *IESBA Code, paragraph 110.2.*

[16] *ISQC 1, paragraph 45.*

[17] *ISQC 1, paragraph A54.*

Intended Users and Purposes of the Service Auditor's Assurance Report (Ref: Para. 53(e))

A48   The criteria used for engagements to report on controls at a service organization are relevant only for the purposes of providing information about the service organization's system, including controls, to those who have an understanding of how the system has been used for financial reporting by user entities. Accordingly this is stated in the service auditor's assurance report. In addition, the service auditor may consider it appropriate to include wording that specifically restricts distribution of the assurance report other than to intended users, its use by others, or its use for other purposes.

Description of the Tests of Controls (Ref: Para. 54)

A49   In describing the nature of the tests of controls for a type 2 report, it assists readers of the service auditor's assurance report if the service auditor includes:

- The results of all tests where deviations have been identified, even if other controls have been identified that allow the service auditor to conclude that the relevant control objective has been achieved or the control tested has subsequently been removed from the service organization's description of its system.
- Information about causative factors for identified deviations, to the extent the service auditor has identified such factors.

Modified Opinions (Ref: Para. 55)

A50   Illustrative examples of elements of modified service auditor's assurance reports are contained in Appendix 3.

A51   Even if the service auditor has expressed an adverse opinion or disclaimed an opinion, it may be appropriate to describe in the basis for modification paragraph the reasons for any other matters of which the service auditor is aware that would have required a modification to the opinion, and the effects thereof.

A52   When expressing a disclaimer of opinion because of a scope limitation, it is not ordinarily appropriate to identify the procedures that were performed nor include statements describing the characteristics of a service auditor's engagement; to do so might overshadow the disclaimer of opinion.

Other Communication Responsibilities (Ref: Para. 56)

A53   Appropriate actions to respond to the circumstances identified in paragraph 56 may include:

- Obtaining legal advice about the consequences of different courses of action.
- Communicating with those charged with governance of the service organization.
- Communicating with third parties (for example, a regulator) when required to do so.
- Modifying the service auditor's opinion, or adding an Other Matter paragraph.
- Withdrawing from the engagement.

Appendix 1

Example Service Organization's Assertions

The following examples of service organization's assertions are for guidance only and are not intended to be exhaustive or applicable to all situations.

Example 1: Type 2 Service Organization's Assertion

Assertion by the Service Organization

The accompanying description has been prepared for customers who have used *[the type or name of]* system and their auditors who have a sufficient understanding to consider the description, along with other information including information about controls operated by customers themselves, when assessing the risks of material misstatements of customers' financial statements. *[Entity's name]* confirms that:

(a) The accompanying description at pages *[bb–cc]* fairly presents *[the type or name of]* system for processing customers' transactions throughout the period *[date]* to *[date]*. The criteria used in making this assertion were that the accompanying description:

   (i) Presents how the system was designed and implemented, including:

- The types of services provided, including, as appropriate, classes of transactions processed.
- The procedures, within both information technology and manual systems, by which those transactions were initiated, recorded, processed, corrected as necessary, and transferred to the reports prepared for customers.
- The related accounting records, supporting information and specific accounts that were used to initiate, record, process and report transactions; this includes the correction of incorrect information and how information was transferred to the reports prepared for customers.
- How the system dealt with significant events and conditions, other than transactions.
- The process used to prepare reports for customers.
- Relevant control objectives and controls designed to achieve those objectives.
- Controls that we assumed, in the design of the system, would be implemented by user entities, and which, if necessary to achieve control objectives stated in the accompanying description, are identified in the description along with the specific control objectives that cannot be achieved by ourselves alone.
- Other aspects of our control environment, risk assessment process, information system (including the related business processes) and communication, control activities and monitoring controls that were relevant to processing and reporting customers' transactions.

   (ii) Includes relevant details of changes to the service organization's system during the period *[date]* to *[date]*.

   (iii) Does not omit or distort information relevant to the scope of the system being described, while acknowledging that the description is prepared to meet the common needs of a broad range of customers and their auditors and may not, therefore, include every aspect of the system that each individual customer may consider important in its own particular environment.

(b) The controls related to the control objectives stated in the accompanying description were suitably designed and operated effectively throughout the period *[date]* to *[date]*. The criteria used in making this assertion were that:

   (i) The risks that threatened achievement of the control objectives stated in the description were identified;

   (ii) The identified controls would, if operated as described, provide reasonable assurance that those risks did not prevent the stated control objectives from being achieved; and

   (iii) The controls were consistently applied as designed, including that manual controls were applied by individuals who have the appropriate competence and authority, throughout the period *[date]* to *[date]*.

Example 2: Type 1 Service Organization's Assertion

The accompanying description has been prepared for customers who have used *[the type or name of]* system and their auditors who have a sufficient understanding to consider the description, along with other information including information about controls operated by customers themselves, when obtaining an understanding of customers' information systems relevant to financial reporting. *[Entity's name]* confirms that:

(a) The accompanying description at pages *[bb–cc]* fairly presents *[the type or name of]* system for processing customers' transactions as at *[date]*. The criteria used in making this assertion were that the accompanying description:

   (i) Presents how the system was designed and implemented, including:

- The types of services provided, including, as appropriate, classes of transactions processed.
- The procedures, within both information technology and manual systems, by which those transactions were initiated, recorded, processed, corrected as necessary, and transferred to the reports prepared for customers.
- The related accounting records, supporting information and specific accounts that were used to initiate, record, process and report transactions; this includes the correction of incorrect information and how information is transferred to the reports prepared customers.
- How the system dealt with significant events and conditions, other than transactions.
- The process used to prepare reports for customers.
- Relevant control objectives and controls designed to achieve those objectives.
- Controls that we assumed, in the design of the system, would be implemented by user entities, and which, if necessary to achieve control objectives stated in the accompanying description, are identified in the description along with the specific control objectives that cannot be achieved by ourselves alone.
- Other aspects of our control environment, risk assessment process, information system (including the related business processes) and communication, control activities and monitoring controls that were relevant to processing and reporting customers' transactions.

   (ii) Does not omit or distort information relevant to the scope of the system being described, while acknowledging that the description is prepared to meet the common needs of a broad range of customers and their auditors and may not, therefore, include every aspect of the system that each individual customer may consider important in its own particular environment.

(b) The controls related to the control objectives stated in the accompanying description were suitably designed as at *[date]*. The criteria used in making this assertion were that:
   (i) The risks that threatened achievement of the control objectives stated in the description were identified; and
   (ii) The identified controls would, if operated as described, provide reasonable assurance that those risks did not prevent the stated control objectives from being achieved.

Appendix 2 (Ref. Para. A47)

Illustrations of Service Auditor's Assurance Reports

The following illustrations of reports are for guidance only and are not intended to be exhaustive or applicable to all situations.

Illustration 1: Type 2 Service Auditor's Assurance Report

Independent Service Auditor's Assurance Report on the Description of Controls, their Design and Operating Effectiveness

To: XYZ Service Organization

Scope

We have been engaged to report on XYZ Service Organization's description at pages *[bb–cc]* of its *[type or name of]* system for processing customers' transactions throughout the period *[date]* to *[date]* (the description), and on the design and operation of controls related to the control objectives stated in the description.[18]

XYZ Service Organization's Responsibilities

XYZ Service Organization is responsible for: preparing the description and accompanying assertion at page *[aa]*, including the completeness, accuracy and method of presentation of the description and assertion; providing the services covered by the description; stating the control objectives; and designing, implementing and effectively operating controls to achieve the stated control objectives.

Service Auditor's Responsibilities

Our responsibility is to express an opinion on XYZ Service Organization's description and on the design and operation of controls related to the control objectives stated in that description, based on our procedures. We conducted our engagement in accordance with International Standard on Assurance Engagements 3402, "Assurance Reports on Controls at a Service Organization," issued by the International Auditing and Assurance Standards Board. That standard requires that we comply with ethical requirements and plan and perform our procedures to obtain reasonable assurance about whether, in all material respects, the description is fairly presented and the controls are suitably designed and operating effectively.

---

[18] *If some elements of the description are not included in the scope of the engagement, this is made clear in the assurance report.*

An assurance engagement to report on the description, design and operating effectiveness of controls at a service organization involves performing procedures to obtain evidence about the disclosures in the service organization's description of its system, and the design and operating effectiveness of controls. The procedures selected depend on the service auditor's judgment, including the assessment of the risks that the description is not fairly presented, and that controls are not suitably designed or operating effectively. Our procedures included testing the operating effectiveness of those controls that we consider necessary to provide reasonable assurance that the control objectives stated in the description were achieved. An assurance engagement of this type also includes evaluating the overall presentation of the description, the suitability of the objectives stated therein, and the suitability of the criteria specified by the service organization and described at page *[aa]*.

We believe that the evidence we have obtained is sufficient and appropriate to provide a basis for our opinion.

Limitations of Controls at a Service Organization

XYZ Service Organization's description is prepared to meet the common needs of a broad range of customers and their auditors and may not, therefore, include every aspect of the system that each individual customer may consider important in its own particular environment. Also, because of their nature, controls at a service organization may not prevent or detect all errors or omissions in processing or reporting transactions. Also, the projection of any evaluation of effectiveness to future periods is subject to the risk that controls at a service organization may become inadequate or fail.

Opinion

Our opinion has been formed on the basis of the matters outlined in this report. The criteria we used in forming our opinion are those described at page *[aa]*. In our opinion, in all material respects:

(a) The description fairly presents the *[the type or name of]* system as designed and implemented throughout the period from *[date]* to *[date]*;
(b) The controls related to the control objectives stated in the description were suitably designed throughout the period from *[date]* to *[date]*; and
(c) The controls tested, which were those necessary to provide reasonable assurance that the control objectives stated in the description were achieved, operated effectively throughout the period from *[date]* to *[date]*.

Description of Tests of Controls

The specific controls tested and the nature, timing and results of those tests are listed on pages *[yy–zz]*.

Intended Users and Purpose

This report and the description of tests of controls on pages *[yy–zz]* are intended only for customers who have used XYZ Service Organization's *[type or name of]* system, and their auditors, who have a sufficient understanding to consider it, along with other information including information about controls operated by customers themselves, when assessing the risks of material misstatements of customers' financial statements.

[*Service auditor's signature*]

[*Date of the service auditor's assurance report*]

[*Service auditor's address*]

Illustration 2: Type 1 Service Auditor's Assurance Report

Independent Service Auditor's Assurance Report on the Description of Controls and their Design

To: XYZ Service Organization

Scope

We have been engaged to report on XYZ Service Organization's description at pages [*bb–cc*] of its [*type or name of*] system for processing customers' transactions as at [*date*] (the description), and on the design of controls related to the control objectives stated in the description.[19]

We did not perform any procedures regarding the operating effectiveness of controls included in the description and, accordingly, do not express an opinion thereon.

XYZ Service Organization's Responsibilities

XYZ Service Organization is responsible for: preparing the description and accompanying assertion at page [*aa*], including the completeness, accuracy and method of presentation of the description and the assertion; providing the services covered by the description; stating the control objectives; and designing, implementing and effectively operating controls to achieve the stated control objectives.

Service Auditor's Responsibilities

Our responsibility is to express an opinion on XYZ Service Organization's description and on the design of controls related to the control objectives stated in that description, based on our procedures. We conducted our engagement in accordance with International Standard on Assurance Engagements 3402, "Assurance Reports on Controls at a Service Organization," issued by the International Auditing and Assurance Standards Board. That standard requires that we comply with ethical requirements and plan and perform our procedures to obtain reasonable assurance about whether, in all material respects, the description is fairly presented and the controls are suitably designed in all material respects.

An assurance engagement to report on the description and design of controls at a service organization involves performing procedures to obtain evidence about the disclosures in the service organization's description of its system, and the design of controls. The procedures selected depend on the service auditor's judgment, including the assessment that the description is not fairly presented, and that controls are not suitably designed. An assurance engagement of this type also includes evaluating the overall presentation of the description, the suitability of the control objectives stated therein, and the suitability of the criteria specified by the service organization and described at page [*aa*].

---

[19] *If some elements of the description are not included in the scope of the engagement, this is made clear in the assurance report.*

As noted above, we did not perform any procedures regarding the operating effectiveness of controls included in the description and, accordingly, do not express an opinion thereon.

We believe that the evidence we have obtained is sufficient and appropriate to provide a basis for our opinion.

Limitations of Controls at a Service Organization

XYZ Service Organization's description is prepared to meet the common needs of a broad range of customers and their auditors and may not, therefore, include every aspect of the system that each individual customer may consider important in its own particular environment. Also, because of their nature, controls at a service organization may not prevent or detect all errors or omissions in processing or reporting transactions.

Opinion

Our opinion has been formed on the basis of the matters outlined in this report. The criteria we used in forming our opinion are those described at page *[aa]*. In our opinion, in all material respects:

(a) The description fairly presents the *[the type or name of]* system as designed and implemented as at *[date]*; and
(b) The controls related to the control objectives stated in the description were suitably designed as at *[date]*.

Intended Users and Purpose

This report is intended only for customers who have used XYZ Service Organization's *[type or name of]* system, and their auditors, who have a sufficient understanding to consider it, along with other information including information about controls operated by customers themselves, when obtaining an understanding of customers' information systems relevant to financial reporting.

[Service auditor's signature]

[Date of the service auditor's assurance report]

[Service auditor's address]

Appendix 3   (Ref. Para. A50)

Illustrations of Modified Service Auditor's Assurance Reports

The following illustrations of modified reports are for guidance only and are not intended to be exhaustive or applicable to all situations. They are based on the illustrations of reports in Appendix 2.

Illustration 1: Qualified opinion – the service organization's description of the system is not fairly presented in all material respects

...

Service Auditor's Responsibilities

...

We believe that the evidence we have obtained is sufficient and appropriate to provide a basis for our qualified opinion.

Basis for Qualified Opinion

The accompanying description states at page *[mn]* that XYZ Service Organization uses operator identification numbers and passwords to prevent unauthorized access to the system. Based on our procedures, which included inquiries of staff personnel and observation of activities, we have determined that operator identification numbers and passwords are employed in Applications A and B but not in Applications C and D.

Qualified Opinion

Our opinion has been formed on the basis of the matters outlined in this report. The criteria we used in forming our opinion were those described in XYZ Service Organization's assertion at page *[aa]*. In our opinion, except for the matter described in the Basis for Qualified Opinion paragraph:

(a) ...

Illustration 2: Qualified opinion – the controls are not suitably designed to provide reasonable assurance that the control objectives stated in the service organization's description of its system will be achieved if the controls operate effectively

...

Service Auditor's Responsibilities

...

We believe that the evidence we have obtained is sufficient and appropriate to provide a basis for our qualified opinion.

Basis for Qualified Opinion

As discussed at page *[mn]* of the accompanying description, from time to time XYZ Service Organization makes changes in application programs to correct deficiencies or to enhance capabilities. The procedures followed in determining whether to make changes, in designing the changes and in implementing them, do not include review and approval by authorized individuals who are independent from those involved in making the changes. There are also no specified requirements to test such changes or provide test results to an authorized reviewer prior to implementing the changes.

Qualified Opinion

Our opinion has been formed on the basis of the matters outlined in this report. The criteria we used in forming our opinion were those described in XYZ Service

Organization's assertion at page *[aa]*. In our opinion, except for the matter described in the Basis for Qualified Opinion paragraph:

(a) ...

Illustration 3: Qualified opinion – the controls did not operate effectively throughout the specified period (type 2 report only)

...

Service Auditor's Responsibilities

...

We believe that the evidence we have obtained is sufficient and appropriate to provide a basis for our qualified opinion.

Basis for Qualified Opinion

XYZ Service Organization states in its description that it has automated controls in place to reconcile loan payments received with the output generated. However, as noted at page *[mn]* of the description, this control was not operating effectively during the period from *dd/mm/yyyy* to *dd/mm/yyyy* due to a programming error. This resulted in the non-achievement of the control objective "Controls provide reasonable assurance that loan payments received are properly recorded" during the period from *dd/mm/yyyy* to *dd/mm/yyyy*. XYZ implemented a change to the program performing the calculation as of *[date]*, and our tests indicate that it was operating effectively during the period from *dd/mm/yyyy* to *dd/mm/yyyy*.

Qualified Opinion

Our opinion has been formed on the basis of the matters outlined in this report. The criteria we used in forming our opinion were those described in XYZ Service Organization's assertion at page *[aa]*. In our opinion, except for the matter described in the Basis for Qualified Opinion paragraph:

...

Example 4: Qualified opinion – the service auditor is unable to obtain sufficient appropriate evidence

...

Service Auditor's Responsibilities

...

We believe that the evidence we have obtained is sufficient and appropriate to provide a basis for our qualified opinion.

Basis for Qualified Opinion

XYZ Service Organization states in its description that it has automated controls in place to reconcile loan payments received with the output generated. However, electronic records of the performance of this reconciliation for the period from *dd/mm/yyyy* to *dd/mm/yyyy* were deleted as a result of a computer processing error, and we were therefore unable to test the operation of this control for that period. Consequently, we were unable to determine whether the control objective "Controls provide reasonable assurance that loan payments received are properly recorded" operated effectively during the period from *dd/mm/yyyy* to *dd/mm/yyyy*.

Qualified Opinion

Our opinion has been formed on the basis of the matters outlined in this report. The criteria we used in forming our opinion were those described in XYZ Service Organization's assertion at page *[aa]*. In our opinion, except for the matter described in the Basis for Qualified Opinion paragraph:

(a) ...

13-21.]

International Standard on Assurance Engagements 3410
Assurance engagements on greenhouse gas statements

*(Effective for assurance reports covering periods
ending on or after September 30, 2013)*

Contents

International Standard on Assurance Engagements (ISAE) 3410, *Assurance Engagements on Greenhouse Gas Statements*, should be read in conjunction with the *Preface to the International Standards on Quality Control, Auditing, Review, Other Assurance and Related Services Pronouncements*.

Introduction

1   Given the link between greenhouse gas (GHG) emissions and climate change, many entities are quantifying their GHG emissions for internal management purposes, and many are also preparing a GHG statement:

    (a) As part of a regulatory disclosure regime;

    (b) As part of an emissions trading scheme; or

    (c) To inform investors and others on a voluntary basis. Voluntary disclosures may be, for example, published as a stand-alone document; included as part of a broader sustainability report or in an entity's annual report; or made to support inclusion in a "carbon register."

Scope of this ISAE

2   This International Standard on Assurance Engagements (ISAE) deals with assurance engagements to report on an entity's GHG statement.

3   The practitioner's conclusion in an assurance engagement may cover information in addition to a GHG statement, for example, when the practitioner is engaged to report on a sustainability report of which a GHG statement is only one part. In such cases: (Ref: Para. A1–A2)

    (a) This ISAE applies to assurance procedures performed with respect to the GHG statement other than when the GHG statement is a relatively minor part of the overall information subject to assurance; and

    (b) ISAE 3000[1] (or another ISAE dealing with a specific subject matter) applies to assurance procedures performed with respect to the remainder of the information covered by the practitioner's conclusion.

4   This ISAE does not deal with, or provide specific guidance for, assurance engagements to report on the following:

    (a) Statements of emissions other than GHG emissions, for example, nitrogen oxides (NOx) and sulfur dioxide (SO_2). This ISAE may nonetheless provide guidance for such engagements;[2]

    (b) Other GHG-related information, such as product lifecycle "footprints," hypothetical "baseline" information, and key performance indicators based on emissions data; or (Ref: Para. A3)

    (c) Instruments, processes or mechanisms, such as offset projects, used by other entities as emissions deductions. However, where an entity's GHG statement includes emissions deductions that are subject to assurance, the requirements of this ISAE apply in relation to those emissions deductions as appropriate (see paragraph 76(f)).

Assertion-Based and Direct Reporting Engagements

5   The *International Framework for Assurance Engagements* (the Assurance Framework) notes that an assurance engagement may be either an assertion-based

---

[1] *ISAE 3000*, Assurance Engagements Other than Audits or Reviews of Historical Financial Information. *ISAE 3000 is currently being revised by the IAASB. There may be conforming amendments to this ISAE as a result of changes to ISAE 3000.*

[2] *NOx (i.e., NO and NO_2, which differ from the GHG nitrous oxide, N_2O) and SO_2 are associated with "acid rain" rather than climate change.*

engagement or a direct reporting engagement. This ISAE deals only with assertion-based engagements.[3]

Procedures for Reasonable Assurance and Limited Assurance Engagements

The Assurance Framework notes that an assurance engagement may be either a **6** reasonable assurance engagement or a limited assurance engagement.[4] This ISAE deals with both reasonable and limited assurance engagements.

In both reasonable assurance and limited assurance engagements on a GHG state- **7** ment, the practitioner chooses a combination of assurance procedures, which can include: inspection; observation; confirmation; recalculation; reperformance; analytical procedures; and inquiry. Determining the assurance procedures to be performed on a particular engagement is a matter of professional judgment. Because GHG statements cover a wide range of circumstances, the nature, timing and extent of procedures are likely to vary considerably from engagement to engagement.

Unless otherwise stated, each requirement of this ISAE applies to both reasonable **8** and limited assurance engagements. Because the level of assurance obtained in a limited assurance engagement is lower than in a reasonable assurance engagement, the procedures the practitioner will perform in a limited assurance engagement will vary in nature from, and are less in extent than for, a reasonable assurance engagement.[5] Requirements that apply to only one or the other type of engagement have been presented in a columnar format with the letter "L" (limited assurance) or "R" (reasonable assurance) after the paragraph number. Although some procedures are required only for reasonable assurance engagements, they may nonetheless be appropriate in some limited assurance engagements (see also paragraph A90, which outlines the primary differences between the practitioner's further procedures for a reasonable assurance engagement and a limited assurance engagement on a GHG statement). (Ref: Para. A4, A90)

Relationship with ISAE 3000, Other Professional Pronouncements, and Other Requirements

The performance of assurance engagements other than audits or reviews of historical **9** financial information requires the practitioner to comply with ISAE 3000. ISAE 3000 includes requirements in relation to such topics as engagement acceptance, planning, evidence, and documentation that apply to all assurance engagements, including engagements in accordance with this ISAE. This ISAE expands on how ISAE 3000 is to be applied in an assurance engagement to report on an entity's GHG statement. The Assurance Framework, which defines and describes the elements and objectives of an assurance engagement, provides context for understanding this ISAE and ISAE 3000. (Ref: Para. A17)

Compliance with ISAE 3000 requires, among other things, that the practitioner **10** comply with the independence and other requirements of the *Code of Ethics for Professional Accountants* issued by the International Ethics Standards Board for

---

[3] *Assurance Framework, paragraph 10.*

[4] *Assurance Framework, paragraph 11.*

[5] *Assurance Framework, paragraph 53, and ISAE 3000, paragraph 37.*

Accountants (IESBA Code) and implement quality control procedures that are applicable to the individual engagement.[6] (Ref: Para. A5–A6)

11   Where the engagement is subject to local laws or regulations or the provisions of an emissions trading scheme, this ISAE does not override those laws, regulations or provisions. In the event that local laws or regulations or the provisions of an emissions trading scheme differ from this ISAE, an engagement conducted in accordance with local laws or regulations or the provisions of a particular scheme will not automatically comply with this ISAE. The practitioner is entitled to represent compliance with this ISAE in addition to compliance with local laws or regulations or the provisions of the emissions trading scheme only when all applicable requirements of this ISAE have been met. (Ref: Para. A7)

Effective Date

12   This ISAE is effective for assurance reports covering periods ending on or after September 30, 2013.

Objectives

13   The objectives of the practitioner are:

(a)   To obtain reasonable or limited assurance, as appropriate, about whether the GHG statement is free from material misstatement, whether due to fraud or error, thereby enabling the practitioner to express a conclusion conveying that level of assurance;

(b)   To report, in accordance with the practitioner's findings, about whether:

(i)   In the case of a reasonable assurance engagement, the GHG statement is prepared, in all material respects, in accordance with the applicable criteria; or

(ii)   In the case of a limited assurance engagement, anything has come to the practitioner's attention that causes the practitioner to believe, on the basis of the procedures performed and evidence obtained, that the GHG statement is not prepared, in all material respects, in accordance with the applicable criteria; and

(c)   To communicate as otherwise required by this ISAE, in accordance with the practitioner's findings.

Definitions

14   For purposes of this ISAE, the following terms have the meanings attributed below:[7]

(a)   Applicable criteria – The criteria used by the entity to quantify and report its emissions in the GHG statement.

(b)   Assertions – Representations by the entity, explicit or otherwise, that are embodied in the GHG statement, as used by the practitioner to consider the different types of potential misstatements that may occur.

(c)   Base year – A specific year or an average over multiple years against which an entity's emissions are compared over time.

---

[6] *ISAE 3000, paragraphs 4 and 6.*

[7] *The definitions in ISAE 3000 also apply to this ISAE.*

(d) Cap and trade – A system that sets overall emissions limits, allocates emissions allowances to participants, and allows them to trade allowances and emission credits with each other.

(e) Comparative information – The amounts and disclosures included in the GHG statement in respect of one or more prior periods.

(f) Emissions – The GHGs that, during the relevant period, have been emitted to the atmosphere or would have been emitted to the atmosphere had they not been captured and channeled to a sink. Emissions can be categorized as:

- Direct emissions (also known as Scope 1 emissions), which are emissions from sources that are owned or controlled by the entity. (Ref: Para. A8)
- Indirect emissions, which are emissions that are a consequence of the activities of the entity, but which occur at sources that are owned or controlled by another entity. Indirect emissions can be further categorized as:
  o Scope 2 emissions, which are emissions associated with energy that is transferred to and consumed by the entity. (Ref: Para. A9)
  o Scope 3 emissions, which are all other indirect emissions. (Ref: Para. A10) (g) Emissions deduction – Any item included in the entity's GHG statement that is deducted from the total reported emissions, but which is not a removal; it commonly includes purchased offsets, but can also include a variety of other instruments or mechanisms such as performance credits and allowances that are recognized by a regulatory or other scheme of which the entity is a part. (Ref: Para. A11– A12)

(h) Emissions factor – A mathematical factor or ratio for converting the measure of an activity (for example, liters of fuel consumed, kilometers travelled, the number of animals in husbandry, or tonnes of product produced) into an estimate of the quantity of GHGs associated with that activity.

(i) Emissions trading scheme – A market-based approach used to control greenhouse gases by providing economic incentives for achieving reductions in the emissions of such gases.

(j) Entity – The legal entity, economic entity, or the identifiable portion of a legal or economic entity (for example, a single factory or other form of facility, such as a land fill site), or combination of legal or other entities or portions of those entities (for example, a joint venture) to which the emissions in the GHG statement relate.

(k) Fraud – An intentional act by one or more individuals among management, those charged with governance, employees, or third parties, involving the use of deception to obtain an unjust or illegal advantage.

(l) Further procedures – Procedures performed in response to assessed risks of material misstatement, including tests of controls (if any), tests of details and analytical procedures.

(m) GHG statement – A statement setting out constituent elements and quantifying an entity's GHG emissions for a period (sometimes known as an emissions inventory) and, where applicable, comparative information and explanatory notes including a summary of significant quantification and reporting policies. An entity's GHG statement may also include a categorized listing of removals or emissions deductions. Where the engagement does not cover the entire GHG statement, the term "GHG statement" is to be read as that portion that is covered by the engagement. The GHG statement is the "subject matter information" of the engagement.[8]

(n) Greenhouse gases (GHGs) – Carbon dioxide (CO_2) and any other gases required by the applicable criteria to be included in the GHG statement, such as: methane; nitrous oxide; sulfur hexafluoride; hydrofluorocarbons;

---

[8] *Assurance Framework, paragraph 8.*

perfluorocarbons; and chlorofluorocarbons. Gases other than carbon dioxide are often expressed in terms of carbon dioxide equivalents (CO_2-e).

(o) Organizational boundary – The boundary that determines which operations to include in the entity's GHG statement.

(p) Performance materiality – The amount or amounts set by the practitioner at less than materiality for the GHG statement to reduce to an appropriately low level the probability that the aggregate of uncorrected and undetected misstatements exceeds materiality for the GHG statement. If applicable, performance materiality also refers to the amount or amounts set by the practitioner at less than the materiality level or levels for particular types of emissions or disclosures.

(q) Purchased offset – An emissions deduction in which the entity pays for the lowering of another entity's emissions (emissions reductions) or the increasing of another entity's removals (removal enhancements), compared to a hypothetical baseline. (Ref: Para. A13)

(r) Quantification – The process of determining the quantity of GHGs that relate to the entity, either directly or indirectly, as emitted (or removed) by particular sources (or sinks).

(s) Removal – The GHGs that the entity has, during the period, removed from the atmosphere, or that would have been emitted to the atmosphere had they not been captured and channeled to a sink. (Ref: Para. A14)

(t) Significant facility – A facility that is of individual significance due to the size of its emissions relative to the aggregate emissions included in the GHG statement or its specific nature or circumstances which give rise to particular risks of material misstatement. (Ref: Para. A15–A16)

(u) Sink – A physical unit or process that removes GHGs from the atmosphere.

(v) Source – A physical unit or process that releases GHGs into the atmosphere.

(w) Type of emission – A grouping of emissions based on, for example, source of emission, type of gas, region, or facility.

Requirements

ISAE 3000

15 The practitioner shall not represent compliance with this ISAE unless the practitioner has complied with the requirements of both this ISAE and ISAE 3000. (Ref: Para. A5–A6, A17, A21–A22, A37, A127)

Acceptance and Continuance of the Engagement

Skills, Knowledge and Experience

16 The engagement partner shall:

(a) Have sufficient assurance skills, knowledge and experience, and sufficient competence in the quantification and reporting of emissions, to accept responsibility for the assurance conclusion; and

(b) Be satisfied that the engagement team and any practitioner's external experts collectively possess the necessary professional competencies, including in the quantification and reporting of emissions and in assurance, to perform the assurance engagement in accordance with this ISAE. (Ref: Para. A18–A19)

Preconditions for the Engagement

In order to establish whether the preconditions for the engagement are present: **17**

(a) The engagement partner shall determine that both the GHG statement and the engagement have sufficient scope to be useful to intended users, considering, in particular: (Ref: Para. A20)

    (i) If the GHG statement is to exclude significant emissions that have been, or could readily be, quantified, whether such exclusions are reasonable in the circumstances;

    (ii) If the engagement is to exclude assurance with respect to significant emissions that are reported by the entity, whether such exclusions are reasonable in the circumstances; and

    (iii) If the engagement is to include assurance with respect to emissions deductions, whether the nature of the assurance the practitioner will obtain with respect to the deductions and the intended content of the assurance report with respect to them are clear, reasonable in the circumstances, and understood by the engaging party. (Ref: Para. A11-A12)

(b) When assessing the suitability of the applicable criteria, as required by ISAE 3000,[9] the practitioner shall determine whether the criteria encompass at a minimum: (Ref: Para. A23–A26)

    (i) The method for determining the entity's organizational boundary; (Ref: Para. A27–A28)

    (ii) The GHGs to be accounted for;

    (iii) Acceptable quantification methods, including methods for making adjustments to the base year (if applicable); and

    (iv) Adequate disclosures such that intended users can understand the significant judgments made in preparing the GHG statement. (Ref: Para. A29–A34)

(c) The practitioner shall obtain the agreement of the entity that it acknowledges and understands its responsibility:

    (i) For designing, implementing and maintaining such internal control as the entity determines is necessary to enable the preparation of a GHG statement that is free from material misstatement, whether due to fraud or error;

    (ii) For the preparation of its GHG statement in accordance with the applicable criteria; and (Ref: Para. A35)

    (iii) For referring to or describing in its GHG statement the applicable criteria it has used and, when it is not readily apparent from the engagement circumstances, who developed them. (Ref: Para. A36)

Agreement on Engagement Terms

The agreed terms of the engagement required by ISAE 3000[10] shall include: (Ref: **18** Para. A37)

(a) The objective and scope of the engagement;
(b) The responsibilities of the practitioner;
(c) The responsibilities of the entity, including those described in paragraph 17(c);
(d) Identification of the applicable criteria for the preparation of the GHG statement;

---

[9] *ISAE 3000, paragraph 19.*

[10] *ISAE 3000, paragraph 10.*

(e)   Reference to the expected form and content of any reports to be issued by the practitioner and a statement that there may be circumstances in which a report may differ from its expected form and content; and

(f)   An acknowledgement that the entity agrees to provide written representations at the conclusion of the engagement.

Planning

19   When planning the engagement as required by ISAE 3000,[11] the practitioner shall: (Ref: Para. A38–A41)

(a)   Identify the characteristics of the engagement that define its scope;

(b)   Ascertain the reporting objectives of the engagement to plan the timing of the engagement and the nature of the communications required;

(c)   Consider the factors that, in the practitioner's professional judgment, are significant in directing the engagement team's efforts;

(d)   Consider the results of engagement acceptance or continuance procedures and, where applicable, whether knowledge gained on other engagements performed by the engagement partner for the entity is relevant;

(e)   Ascertain the nature, timing and extent of resources necessary to perform the engagement, including the involvement of experts and of other practitioners; and (Ref: Para. A42– A43)

(f)   Determine the impact of the entity's internal audit function, if any, on the engagement.

Materiality in Planning and Performing the Engagement

Determining Materiality and Performance Materiality When Planning the Engagement

20   When establishing the overall engagement strategy, the practitioner shall determine materiality for the GHG statement. (Ref: Para. A44–A50)

21   The practitioner shall determine performance materiality for purposes of assessing the risks of material misstatement and determining the nature, timing and extent of further procedures.

Revision as the Engagement Progresses

22   The practitioner shall revise materiality for the GHG statement in the event of becoming aware of information during the engagement that would have caused the practitioner to have determined a different amount initially. (Ref: Para. A51)

Understanding the Entity and Its Environment, Including the Entity's Internal Control, and Identifying and Assessing Risks of Material Misstatement

Obtaining an Understanding of the Entity and Its Environment

23   The practitioner shall obtain an understanding of the following: (Ref: Para. A52–A53)

(a)   Relevant industry, regulatory, and other external factors including the applicable criteria.

---

[11] *ISAE 3000, paragraph 12.*

(b) The nature of the entity, including:
- (i) The nature of the operations included in the entity's organizational boundary, including: (Ref: Para. A27–A28)
  - a. The sources and completeness of emissions and, if any, sinks and emissions deductions;
  - b. The contribution of each to the entity's overall emissions; and
  - c. The uncertainties associated with the quantities reported in the GHG statement. (Ref: Para. A54–A59)
- (ii) Changes from the prior period in the nature or extent of operations, including whether there have been any mergers, acquisitions, or sales of emissions sources, or outsourcing of functions with significant emissions; and
- (iii) The frequency and nature of interruptions to operations. (Ref: Para. A60)
(c) The entity's selection and application of quantification methods and reporting policies, including the reasons for changes thereto and the potential for double-counting of emissions in the GHG statement.
(d) The requirements of the applicable criteria relevant to estimates, including related disclosures.
(e) The entity's climate change objective and strategy, if any, and associated economic, regulatory, physical and reputational risks. (Ref: Para. A61)
(f) The oversight of, and responsibility for, emissions information within the entity.
(g) Whether the entity has an internal audit function and, if so, its activities and main findings with respect to emissions.

Procedures to Obtain an Understanding and to Identify and Assess Risks of Material Misstatement

The procedures to obtain an understanding of the entity and its environment and to **24** identify and assess risks of material misstatement shall include the following: (Ref: Para. A52–A53, A62)

(a) Inquiries of those within the entity who, in the practitioner's judgment, have information that is likely to assist in identifying and assessing risks of material misstatement due to fraud or error.
(b) Analytical procedures. (Ref: Para. A63–A65)
(c) Observation and inspection. (Ref: Para. A66–A68)

Obtaining an Understanding of the Entity's Internal Control

Limited Assurance	Reasonable Assurance
25L. For internal control relevant to emissions quantification and reporting, as the basis for identifying and assessing the risks of material misstatement, the practitioner shall obtain an understanding, through inquiries, about: (Ref: Para. A52–A53, A69–A70)	25R. The practitioner shall obtain an understanding of the following components of the entity's internal control relevant to emissions quantification and reporting as the basis for identifying and assessing risks of material misstatement: (Ref: Para. A52–A53, A70)
(a) The control environment;	(a) The control environment;
(b) The information system, including the related business processes, and communication of	(b) The information system, including the related business processes, and communication of

Limited Assurance	Reasonable Assurance
emissions reporting roles and responsibilities and significant matters relating to emissions reporting; and (c) The results of the entity's risk assessment process.	emissions reporting roles and responsibilities and significant matters relating to emissions reporting; (c) The entity's risk assessment process; (d) Control activities relevant to the engagement, being those the practitioner judges it necessary to understand in order to assess the risks of material misstatement at the assertion level and design further procedures responsive to assessed risks. An assurance engagement does not require an understanding of all the control activities related to each significant type of emission and disclosure in the GHG statement or to every assertion relevant to them; and (Ref: Para. A71–A72) (e) Monitoring of controls.
	26R. When obtaining the understanding required by paragraph 25R, the practitioner shall evaluate the design of controls and determine whether they have been implemented by performing procedures in addition to inquiry of the entity's personnel. (Ref: Para. A52–A53)

Other Procedures to Obtain an Understanding and to Identify and Assess Risks of Material Misstatement

27   If the engagement partner has performed other engagements for the entity, the engagement partner shall consider whether information obtained is relevant to identifying and assessing risks of material misstatement. (Ref: Para. A73)

28   The practitioner shall make inquiries of management, and others within the entity as appropriate, to determine whether they have knowledge of any actual, suspected or alleged fraud or non-compliance with laws and regulations affecting the GHG statement. (Ref: Para. A84–A86)

29   The engagement partner and other key members of the engagement team, and any key practitioner's external experts, shall discuss the susceptibility of the entity's GHG statement to material misstatement whether due to fraud or error, and the

application of the applicable criteria to the entity's facts and circumstances. The engagement partner shall determine which matters are to be communicated to members of the engagement team, and to any practitioner's external experts not involved in the discussion.

The practitioner shall evaluate whether the entity's quantification methods and **30** reporting policies, including the determination of the entity's organizational boundary, are appropriate for its operations, and are consistent with the applicable criteria and quantification and reporting policies used in the relevant industry and in prior periods.

Performing Procedures on Location at the Entity's Facilities

The practitioner shall determine whether it is necessary in the circumstances of the **31** engagement to perform procedures on location at significant facilities. (Ref: Para. A15–A16, A74–A77)

Internal Audit

Where the entity has an internal audit function that is relevant to the engagement, **32** the practitioner shall: (Ref: Para. A78)

(a) Determine whether, and to what extent, to use specific work of the internal audit function; and

(b) If using the specific work of the internal audit function, determine whether that work is adequate for the purposes of the engagement.

Identifying and Assessing Risks of Material Misstatement

Limited Assurance	Reasonable Assurance
33L. The practitioner shall identify and assess risks of material misstatement: (a) At the GHG statement level; and (Ref: Para. A79–A80) (b) For material types of emissions and disclosures, (Ref: Para. A81) as the basis for designing and performing procedures whose nature, timing and extent: (c) Are responsive to assessed risks of material misstatement; and (d) Allow the practitioner to obtain limited assurance about whether the GHG statement is prepared, in all material respects, in accordance with the applicable criteria.	33R. The practitioner shall identify and assess risks of material misstatement: (a) At the GHG statement level; and (Ref: Para. A79–A80) (b) At the assertion level for material types of emissions and disclosures, (Ref: Para. A81–A82) as the basis for designing and performing procedures whose nature, timing and extent: (Ref: Para. A83) (c) Are responsive to assessed risks of material misstatement; and (d) Allow the practitioner to obtain reasonable assurance about whether the GHG statement is prepared, in all material respects, in accordance with the applicable criteria.

Causes of Risks of Material Misstatement

34   When performing the procedures required by paragraphs 33L or 33R, the practitioner shall consider at least the following factors: (Ref: Para. A84–A89)

(a)   The likelihood of intentional misstatement in the GHG statement; (Ref: Para. A84–A86)

(b)   The likelihood of non-compliance with the provisions of those laws and regulations generally recognized to have a direct effect on the content of the GHG statement; (Ref: Para. A87)

(c)   The likelihood of omission of a potentially significant emission; (Ref: Para. A88(a))

(d)   Significant economic or regulatory changes; (Ref: Para. A88(b))

(e)   The nature of operations; (Ref: Para. A88(c))

(f)   The nature of quantification methods; (Ref: Para. A88(d))

(g)   The degree of complexity in determining the organizational boundary and whether related parties are involved; (Ref: Para. A27–A28)

(h)   Whether there are significant emissions that are outside the normal course of business for the entity, or that otherwise appear to be unusual; (Ref: Para. A88(e))

(i)   The degree of subjectivity in the quantification of emissions; (Ref: Para. A88(e))

(j)   Whether Scope 3 emissions are included in the GHG statement; and (Ref: Para. A88(f))

(k)   How the entity makes significant estimates and the data on which they are based. (Ref: Para. A88(g))

Overall Responses to Assessed Risks of Material Misstatement and Further Procedures

35   The practitioner shall design and implement overall responses to address the assessed risks of material misstatement at the GHG statement level. (Ref: Para. A90–A93)

36   The practitioner shall design and perform further procedures whose nature, timing and extent are responsive to the assessed risks of material misstatement, having regard to the level of assurance, reasonable or limited, as appropriate. (Ref: Para. A90)

Limited Assurance	Reasonable Assurance
37L. In designing and performing the further procedures in accordance with paragraph 36, the practitioner shall: (Ref: Para. A90, A94)	37R. In designing and performing the further procedures in accordance with paragraph 36, the practitioner shall: (Ref: Para. A90, A94)
(a) Consider the reasons for the assessment given to the risks of material misstatement for material types of emissions and disclosures; and (Ref: Para. A95)	(a) Consider the reasons for the assessment given to the risks of material misstatement at the assertion level for material types of emissions and disclosures, including: (Ref: Para. A95)
(b) Obtain more persuasive evidence the higher the practitioner's assessment of risk. (Ref: Para. A97)	(i) The likelihood of material misstatement due to the particular

Limited Assurance	Reasonable Assurance
	characteristics of the relevant type of emission or disclosure (that is, the inherent risk); and
	(ii) Whether the practitioner intends to rely on the operating effectiveness of controls in determining the nature, timing and extent of other procedures; and (Ref: Para. A96)
	(b) Obtain more persuasive evidence the higher the practitioner's assessment of risk. (Ref: Para. A97)
	Tests of Controls
	38R. The practitioner shall design and perform tests of controls to obtain sufficient appropriate evidence as to the operating effectiveness of relevant controls if: (Ref: Para. A90(a))
	(a) The practitioner intends to rely on the operating effectiveness of controls in determining the nature, timing and extent of other procedures; or (Ref: Para. A96)
	(b) Procedures other than tests of controls cannot alone provide sufficient appropriate evidence at the assertion level. (Ref: Para. A98)
	39R. If deviations from controls upon which the practitioner intends to rely are detected, the practitioner shall make specific inquiries to understand these matters and their potential consequences, and shall determine whether: (Ref: Para. A90)
	(a) The tests of controls that have been performed provide an appropriate basis for reliance on the controls;

Limited Assurance	Reasonable Assurance
	(b) Additional tests of controls are necessary; or
	(c) The potential risks of material misstatement need to be addressed using other procedures.
	Procedures Other than Tests of Controls
	40R. Irrespective of the assessed risks of material misstatement, the practitioner shall design and perform tests of details or analytical procedures in addition to tests of controls, if any, for each material type of emission and disclosure. (Ref: Para. A90, A94)
	41R. The practitioner shall consider whether external confirmation procedures are to be performed. (Ref: Para.A90, A99)
Analytical Procedures Performed in Response to Assessed Risks of Material Misstatement	*Analytical Procedures Performed in Response to Assessed Risks of Material Misstatement*
42L. If designing and performing analytical procedures, the practitioner shall: (Ref: Para. A90(c), A100–A102)	42R. If designing and performing analytical procedures, the practitioner shall: (Ref: Para. A90(c), A100–A102)
(a) Determine the suitability of particular analytical procedures, taking account of the assessed risks of material misstatement and tests of details, if any;	(a) Determine the suitability of particular analytical procedures for given assertions, taking account of the assessed risks of material misstatement and tests of details, if any, for these assertions;
(b) Evaluate the reliability of data from which the practitioner's expectation of recorded quantities or ratios is developed, taking account of the source, comparability, and nature and relevance of information available, and controls over preparation; and	(b) Evaluate the reliability of data from which the practitioner's expectation of recorded quantities or ratios is developed, taking account of the source, comparability, and nature and relevance of information available, and controls over preparation; and
(c) Develop an expectation with respect to recorded quantities or ratios.	(c) Develop an expectation of recorded quantities or ratios which is sufficiently precise
43L. If analytical procedures identify fluctuations or relationships that are inconsistent with other	

Limited Assurance	Reasonable Assurance
relevant information or that differ significantly from expected quantities or ratios, the practitioner shall make inquiries of the entity about such differences. The practitioner shall consider the responses to these inquiries to determine whether other procedures are necessary in the circumstances. (Ref: Para. A90(c))	to identify possible material misstatements.
	43R. If analytical procedures identify fluctuations or relationships that are inconsistent with other relevant information or that differ significantly from expected quantities or ratios, the practitioner shall investigate such differences by: (Ref: Para. A90(c))
	(a) Inquiring of the entity and obtaining additional evidence relevant to the entity's responses; and
	(b) Performing other procedures as necessary in the circumstances.
Procedures Regarding Estimates	*Procedures Regarding Estimates*
44L. Based on the assessed risks of material misstatement, the practitioner shall: (Ref: Para. A103–A104)	44R. Based on the assessed risks of material misstatement, the practitioner shall evaluate whether: (Ref: Para. A103)
(a) Evaluate whether:	(a) The entity has appropriately applied the requirements of the applicable criteria relevant to estimates; and
(i) The entity has appropriately applied the requirements of the applicable criteria relevant to estimates; and	(b) The methods for making estimates are appropriate and have been applied consistently, and whether changes, if any, in reported estimates or in the method for making them from the prior period are appropriate in the circumstances.
(ii) The methods for making estimates are appropriate and have been applied consistently, and whether changes, if any, in reported estimates or in the method for making them from the prior period are appropriate in the circumstances; and	45R. In responding to an assessed risk of material misstatement, the practitioner shall undertake one or more of the following, taking account of the nature of estimates: (Ref: Para. A103)
(b) Consider whether other procedures are necessary in the circumstances.	(a) Test how the entity made the estimate and the data on which it is based. In doing so, the practitioner shall evaluate whether:
	(i) The method of quantification used is

Limited Assurance	Reasonable Assurance
	appropriate in the circumstances; and
	(ii) The assumptions used by the entity are reasonable.
	(b) Test the operating effectiveness of the controls over how the entity made the estimate, together with other appropriate procedures.
	(c) Develop a point estimate or a range to evaluate the entity's estimate. For this purpose:
	(i) If the practitioner uses assumptions or methods that differ from the entity's, the practitioner shall obtain an understanding of the entity's assumptions or methods sufficient to establish that the practitioner's point estimate or range takes into account relevant variables and to evaluate any significant differences from the entity's point estimate.
	(ii) If the practitioner concludes that it is appropriate to use a range, the practitioner shall narrow the range, based on evidence available, until all outcomes within the range are considered reasonable.

Sampling

46   If sampling is used, the practitioner shall, when designing the sample, consider the purpose of the procedure and the characteristics of the population from which the sample will be drawn. (Ref: Para. A90(b), A105)

Fraud, Laws and Regulations

The practitioner shall respond appropriately to fraud or suspected fraud and non-compliance or suspected non-compliance with laws and regulations identified during the engagement. (Ref: Para. A106–A107)   **47**

Limited Assurance	Reasonable Assurance
Procedures Regarding the GHG Statement Aggregation Process	*Procedures Regarding the GHG Statement Aggregation Process*
48L. The practitioner's procedures shall include the following procedures related to the GHG statement aggregation process: (Ref: Para. A108) (a) Agreeing or reconciling the GHG statement with the underlying records; and (b) Obtaining, through inquiry of the entity, an understanding of material adjustments made during the course of preparing the GHG statement and considering whether other procedures are necessary in the circumstances.	48R. The practitioner's procedures shall include the following procedures related to the GHG statement aggregation process: (Ref: Para. A108) (a) Agreeing or reconciling the GHG statement with the underlying records; and (b) Examining material adjustments made during the course of preparing the GHG statement.
Determining Whether Additional Procedures Are Necessary in a Limited Assurance Engagement	*Revision of Risk Assessment in a Reasonable Assurance Engagement*
49L. If the practitioner becomes aware of a matter(s) that causes the practitioner to believe the GHG statement may be materially misstated, the practitioner shall design and perform additional procedures sufficient to enable the practitioner to: (Ref: Para. A109–A110) (a) Conclude that the matter(s) is not likely to cause the GHG statement to be materially misstated; or (b) Determine that the matter(s) causes the GHG statement to be materially misstated. (Ref: Para. A111)	49R. The practitioner's assessment of the risks of material misstatement at the assertion level may change during the course of the engagement as additional evidence is obtained. In circumstances where the practitioner obtains evidence from performing further procedures, or if new information is obtained, either of which is inconsistent with the evidence on which the practitioner originally based the assessment, the practitioner shall revise the assessment and modify the planned procedures accordingly. (Ref: Para. A109)

Accumulation of Identified Misstatements

50   The practitioner shall accumulate misstatements identified during the engagement, other than those that are clearly trivial. (Ref: Para. A112)

Consideration of Identified Misstatements as the Engagement Progresses

51   The practitioner shall determine whether the overall engagement strategy and engagement plan need to be revised if:

(a)   The nature of identified misstatements and the circumstances of their occurrence indicate that other misstatements may exist that, when aggregated with misstatements accumulated during the engagement, could be material; or

(b)   The aggregate of misstatements accumulated during the engagement approaches materiality determined in accordance with paragraphs 20–22 of this ISAE.

52   If, at the practitioner's request, the entity has examined a type of emission or disclosure and corrected misstatements that were detected, the practitioner shall perform procedures with respect to the work performed by the entity to determine whether material misstatements remain.

Communication and Correction of Misstatements

53   The practitioner shall communicate on a timely basis all misstatements accumulated during the engagement with the appropriate level within the entity and shall request the entity to correct those misstatements.

54   If the entity refuses to correct some or all of the misstatements communicated by the practitioner, the practitioner shall obtain an understanding of the entity's reasons for not making the corrections and shall take that understanding into account when forming the practitioner's conclusion.

Evaluating the Effect of Uncorrected Misstatements

55   Prior to evaluating the effect of uncorrected misstatements, the practitioner shall reassess materiality determined in accordance with paragraphs 20–22 of this ISAE to confirm whether it remains appropriate in the context of the entity's actual emissions.

56   The practitioner shall determine whether uncorrected misstatements are material, individually or in the aggregate. In making this determination, the practitioner shall consider the size and nature of the misstatements, and the particular circumstances of their occurrence, in relation to particular types of emissions or disclosures and the GHG statement (see paragraph 72).

Using the Work of Other Practitioners

57   When the practitioner intends using the work of other practitioners, the practitioner shall:

(a)   Communicate clearly with those other practitioners about the scope and timing of their work and their findings; and (Ref: Para. A113–A114)

(b)   Evaluate the sufficiency and appropriateness of evidence obtained and the process for including related information in the GHG statement. (Ref: Para. A115)

Written Representations

The practitioner shall request written representations from a person(s) within the   **58**
entity with appropriate responsibilities for, and knowledge of, the matters concerned:
(Ref: Para. A116)

(a) That they have fulfilled their responsibility for the preparation of the GHG
    statement, including comparative information where appropriate, in accordance
    with the applicable criteria, as set out in the terms of the engagement;
(b) That they have provided the practitioner with all relevant information and
    access as agreed in the terms of the engagement and reflected all relevant matters
    in the GHG statement;
(c) Whether they believe the effects of uncorrected misstatements are immaterial,
    individually and in the aggregate, to the GHG statement. A summary of such
    items shall be included in, or attached to, the written representation;
(d) Whether they believe that significant assumptions used in making estimates are
    reasonable;
(e) That they have communicated to the practitioner all deficiencies in internal
    control relevant to the engagement that are not clearly trivial of which they are
    aware; and
(f) Whether they have disclosed to the practitioner their knowledge of actual,
    suspected or alleged fraud or non-compliance with laws and regulations where
    the fraud or non-compliance could have a material effect on the GHG
    statement.

The date of the written representations shall be as near as practicable to, but not   **59**
after, the date of the assurance report.

The practitioner shall disclaim a conclusion on the GHG statement or withdraw   **60**
from the engagement, where withdrawal is possible under applicable laws or regulations, if:

(a) The practitioner concludes that there is sufficient doubt about the integrity of
    the person(s) providing the written representations required by paragraphs 58(a)
    and (b) that written representations in these regards are not reliable; or
(b) The entity does not provide the written representations required by paragraphs
    58(a) and (b).

Subsequent Events

The practitioner shall: (Ref: Para. A117)   **61**

(a) Consider whether events occurring between the date of the GHG statement and
    the date of the assurance report require adjustment of, or disclosure in, the
    GHG statement, and evaluate the sufficiency and appropriateness of evidence
    obtained about whether such events are appropriately reflected in that GHG
    statement in accordance with the applicable criteria; and
(b) Respond appropriately to facts that become known to the practitioner after the
    date of the assurance report, that, had they been known to the practitioner at
    that date, may have caused the practitioner to amend the assurance report.

Comparative Information

When comparative information is presented with the current emissions information   **62**
and some or all of that comparative information is covered by the practitioner's

conclusion, the practitioner's procedures with respect to the comparative information shall include evaluating whether: (Ref: Para. A118–A121)

(a) The comparative information agrees with the amounts and other disclosures presented in the prior period or, when appropriate, has been properly restated and that restatement has been adequately disclosed; and (Ref Para. A121)

(b) The quantification policies reflected in the comparative information are consistent with those applied in the current period or, if there have been changes, whether they have been properly applied and adequately disclosed.

63   Irrespective of whether the practitioner's conclusion covers the comparative information, if the practitioner becomes aware that there may be a material misstatement in the comparative information presented the practitioner shall:

(a) Discuss the matter with those person(s) within the entity with appropriate responsibilities for, and knowledge of, the matters concerned and perform procedures appropriate in the circumstances; and (Ref: Para. A122–A123)

(b) Consider the effect on the assurance report. If the comparative information presented contains a material misstatement, and the comparative information has not been restated:

   (i) Where the practitioner's conclusion covers the comparative information, the practitioner shall express a qualified conclusion or an adverse conclusion in the assurance report; or

   (ii) Where the practitioner's conclusion does not cover the comparative information, the practitioner shall include an Other Matter paragraph in the assurance report describing the circumstances affecting the comparative information.

Other Information

64   The practitioner shall read other information included in documents containing the GHG statement and the assurance report thereon and, if, in the practitioner's judgment, that other information could undermine the credibility of the GHG statement and the assurance report, shall discuss the matter with the entity and take further action as appropriate. (Ref: Para. A124–A126)

Documentation

65   In documenting the nature, timing and extent of procedures performed, the practitioner shall record: (Ref: Para. A127)

(a) The identifying characteristics of the specific items or matters tested;

(b) Who performed the engagement work and the date such work was completed; and

(c) Who reviewed the engagement work performed and the date and extent of such review.

66   The practitioner shall document discussions of significant matters with the entity and others, including the nature of the significant matters discussed, and when and with whom the discussions took place. (Ref: Para. A127)

Quality Control

The practitioner shall include in the engagement documentation: 67

(a) Issues identified with respect to compliance with relevant ethical requirements and how they were resolved;
(b) Conclusions on compliance with independence requirements that apply to the engagement, and any relevant discussions with the firm that support these conclusions;
(c) Conclusions reached regarding the acceptance and continuance of client relationships and assurance engagements; and
(d) The nature and scope of, and conclusions resulting from, consultations undertaken during the course of the engagement.

Matters Arising after the Date of the Assurance Report

If, in exceptional circumstances, the practitioner performs new or additional pro-   68
cedures or draws new conclusions after the date of the assurance report, the practitioner shall document: (Ref: Para. A128)

(a) The circumstances encountered;
(b) The new or additional procedures performed, evidence obtained, and conclusions reached, and their effect on the assurance report; and
(c) When and by whom the resulting changes to engagement documentation were made and reviewed.

Assembly of the Final Engagement File

The practitioner shall assemble the engagement documentation in an engagement file   69
and complete the administrative process of assembling the final engagement file on a timely basis after the date of the assurance report. After the assembly of the final engagement file has been completed, the practitioner shall not delete or discard engagement documentation of any nature before the end of its retention period. (Ref: Para. A129)

In circumstances other than those envisaged in paragraph 68 where the practitioner   70
finds it necessary to modify existing engagement documentation or add new engagement documentation after the assembly of the final engagement file has been completed, the practitioner shall, regardless of the nature of the modifications or additions, document:

(a) The specific reasons for making them; and
(b) When and by whom they were made and reviewed.

Engagement Quality Control Review

For those engagements, if any, for which a quality control review is required by laws   71
or regulations or for which the firm has determined that an engagement quality control review is required, the engagement quality control reviewer shall perform an objective evaluation of the significant judgments made by the engagement team, and the conclusions reached in formulating the assurance report. This evaluation shall involve: (Ref: Para. A130)

(a) Discussion of significant matters with the engagement partner, including the engagement team's professional competencies with respect to the quantification and reporting of emissions and assurance;

(b) Review of the GHG statement and the proposed assurance report;

(c) Review of selected engagement documentation relating to the significant judgments the engagement team made and the conclusions it reached; and

(d) Evaluation of the conclusions reached in formulating the assurance report and consideration of whether the proposed assurance report is appropriate.

Forming the Assurance Conclusion

72   The practitioner shall conclude as to whether the practitioner has obtained reasonable or limited assurance, as appropriate, about the GHG statement. That conclusion shall take into account the requirements of paragraphs 56 and 73–75 of this ISAE.

Limited Assurance	Reasonable Assurance
73L. The practitioner shall evaluate whether anything has come to the practitioner's attention that causes the practitioner to believe that the GHG statement is not prepared, in all material respects, in accordance with the applicable criteria.	73R. The practitioner shall evaluate whether the GHG statement is prepared, in all material respects, in accordance with the applicable criteria.

74   This evaluation shall include consideration of the qualitative aspects of the entity's quantification methods and reporting practices, including indicators of possible bias in judgments and decisions in the making of estimates and in preparing the GHG statement,[12] and whether, in view of the applicable criteria:

(a) The quantification methods and reporting policies selected and applied are consistent with the applicable criteria and are appropriate;

(b) Estimates made in preparing the GHG statement are reasonable;

(c) The information presented in the GHG statement is relevant, reliable, complete, comparable and understandable;

(d) The GHG statement provides adequate disclosure of the applicable criteria, and other matters, including uncertainties, such that intended users can understand the significant judgments made in its preparation; and (Ref: Para. A29, A131–A133)

(e) The terminology used in the GHG statement is appropriate.

75   The evaluation required by paragraph 73 shall also include consideration of:

(a) The overall presentation, structure and content of the GHG statement; and

(b) When appropriate in the context of the criteria, the wording of the assurance conclusion, or other engagement circumstances, whether the GHG statement represents the underlying emissions in a manner that achieves fair presentation.

---

[12] *Indicators of possible bias do not themselves constitute misstatements for the purposes of drawing conclusions on the reasonableness of individual estimates.*

Assurance Report Content

The assurance report shall include the following basic elements: (Ref: Para. A134)   **76**

(a) A title that clearly indicates the report is an independent limited assurance or reasonable assurance report.
(b) The addressee of the assurance report.
(c) Identification of the GHG statement, including the period(s) it covers, and, if any information in that statement is not covered by the practitioner's conclusion, clear identification of the information subject to assurance as well as the excluded information, together with a statement that the practitioner has not performed any procedures with respect to the excluded information and, therefore, that no conclusion on it is expressed. (Ref: Para. A120, A135)
(d) A description of the entity's responsibilities. (Ref: Para. A35)
(e) A statement that GHG quantification is subject to inherent uncertainty. (Ref: Para. A54–A59)
(f) If the GHG statement includes emissions deductions that are covered by the practitioner's conclusion, identification of those emissions deductions, and a statement of the practitioner's responsibility with respect to them. (Ref: Para. A136–A139)
(g) Identification of the applicable criteria;
   (i) Identification of how those criteria can be accessed;
   (ii) If those criteria are available only to specific intended users, or are relevant only to a specific purpose, a statement restricting the use of the assurance report to those intended users or that purpose; and (Ref: Para. A140–A141)
   (iii) If established criteria need to be supplemented by disclosures in the explanatory notes to the GHG statement for those criteria to be suitable, identification of the relevant note(s). (Ref: Para. A131)
(h) A description of the practitioner's responsibility, including:
   (i) A statement that the engagement was performed in accordance with ISAE 3410, *Assurance Engagements on Greenhouse Gas Statements*; and
   (ii) A summary of the practitioner's procedures. In the case of a limited assurance engagement, this shall include a statement that the procedures performed in a limited assurance engagement vary in nature from, and are less in extent than for, a reasonable assurance engagement. As a result, the level of assurance obtained in a limited assurance engagement is substantially lower than the assurance that would have been obtained had a reasonable assurance engagement been performed. (Ref: Para. A142–A144)
(i) The practitioner's conclusion, expressed in the positive form in the case of a reasonable assurance engagement or in the negative form in the case of a limited assurance engagement, about whether the GHG statement is prepared, in all material respects, in accordance with the applicable criteria.
(j) If the practitioner expresses a conclusion that is modified, a clear description of all the reasons therefore.
(k) The practitioner's signature. (Ref: Para. A145)
(l) The date of the assurance report.
(m) The location in the jurisdiction where the practitioner practices.

Emphasis of Matter Paragraphs and Other Matter Paragraphs

If the practitioner considers it necessary to: (Ref: Para. A146–A152)   **77**

(a) Draw intended users' attention to a matter presented or disclosed in the GHG statement that, in the practitioner's judgment, is of such importance that it is fundamental to intended users' understanding of the GHG statement (an Emphasis of Matter paragraph); or

(b) Communicate a matter other than those that are presented or disclosed in the GHG statement that, in the practitioner's judgment, is relevant to intended users' understanding of the engagement, the practitioner's responsibilities or the assurance report (an Other Matter paragraph),

and this is not prohibited by laws or regulations, the practitioner shall do so in a paragraph in the assurance report, with an appropriate heading, that clearly indicates the practitioner's conclusion is not modified in respect of the matter.

Other Communication Requirements

78 The practitioner shall communicate to those person(s) with oversight responsibilities for the GHG statement the following matters that come to the practitioner's attention during the course of the engagement, and shall determine whether there is a responsibility to report them to another party within or outside the entity:

(a) Deficiencies in internal control that, in the practitioner's professional judgment, are of sufficient importance to merit attention;
(b) Identified or suspected fraud; and
(c) Matters involving non-compliance with laws and regulations, other than when the matters are clearly trivial. (Ref: Para. A87)

***

Application and Other Explanatory Material

Introduction

Assurance Engagements Covering Information in Addition to the GHG Statement (Ref: Para. 3)

A1 In some cases, the practitioner may perform an assurance engagement on a report that includes GHG information, but that GHG information does not comprise a GHG statement as defined in paragraph 14(m). In such cases, this ISAE may provide guidance for such an engagement.

A2 Where a GHG statement is a relatively minor part of the overall information that is covered by the practitioner's conclusion, the extent to which this ISAE is relevant is a matter for the practitioner's professional judgment in the circumstances of the engagement.

Key Performance Indicators Based on GHG Data (Ref: Para. 4(b))

A3 An example of a key performance indicator based on GHG data is the weighted average of emissions per kilometer of vehicles manufactured by an entity during a period, which is required to be calculated and disclosed by laws or regulations in some jurisdictions.

Procedures for Reasonable Assurance and Limited Assurance Engagements (Ref: Para. 8)

A4 Some procedures that are required only for reasonable assurance engagements may nonetheless be appropriate in some limited assurance engagements. For example, although obtaining an understanding of control activities is not required for limited assurance engagements, in some cases, such as when information is recorded, processed, or reported only in electronic form, the practitioner may nonetheless decide that testing controls, and therefore obtaining an understanding of relevant control activities, is necessary for a limited assurance engagement (see also paragraph A90).

Independence (Ref: Para. 10, 15)

The IESBA Code adopts a threats and safeguards approach to independence. **A5** Compliance with the fundamental principles may potentially be threatened by a broad range of circumstances. Many threats fall into the following categories:

- Self-interest, for example, undue dependence on total fees from the entity.
- Self-review, for example, performing another service for the entity that directly affects the GHG statement, such as involvement in the quantification of the entity's emissions.
- Advocacy, for example, acting as an advocate on behalf of the entity with respect to the interpretation of the applicable criteria.
- Familiarity, for example, a member of the engagement team having a long association, or close or immediate family relationship, with an employee of the entity who is in a position to exert direct and significant influence over the preparation of the GHG statement.
- Intimidation, for example, being pressured to reduce inappropriately the extent of work performed in order to lower fees, or being threatened with withdrawal of the practitioner's registration by a registering authority that is associated with the entity's industry group.

Safeguards created by the profession, laws or regulations, or safeguards in the work **A6** environment, may eliminate or reduce such threats to an acceptable level.

Local Laws and Regulations and the Provisions of an Emissions Trading Scheme (Ref: Para. 11)

Local laws or regulations or the provisions of an emissions trading scheme may: **A7** include requirements in addition to the requirements of this ISAE; require that specific procedures be undertaken on all engagements; or require that procedures be undertaken in a particular way. For example, local laws or regulations or the provisions of an emissions trading scheme may require the practitioner to report in a format that is not in compliance with this ISAE. When the law or regulation prescribes the layout or wording of the assurance report in a form or in terms that are significantly different from this ISAE, and the practitioner concludes that additional explanation in the assurance report cannot mitigate possible misunderstanding, the practitioner may consider including a statement in the report that the engagement is not conducted in accordance with this ISAE.

Definitions

Emissions (Ref: Para. 14(f), Appendix 1)

Scope 1 emissions may include stationary combustion (from fuel burned in the **A8** entity's stationary equipment, such as boilers, incinerators, engines, and flares), mobile combustion (from fuel burned in the entity's transport devices, such as trucks, trains, airplanes and boats), process emissions (from physical or chemical processes, such as cement manufacturing, petrochemical processing, and aluminum smelting), and fugitive emissions (intentional and unintentional releases, such as equipment leaks from joints and seals and emissions from wastewater treatment, pits, and cooling towers).

A9   Almost all entities purchase energy in a form such as electricity, heat or steam; therefore, almost all entities have Scope 2 emissions. Scope 2 emissions are indirect because the emissions associated with, for example, electricity that the entity purchases occur at the power station, which is outside the entity's organizational boundary.

A10   Scope 3 emissions may include emissions associated with, for example: employee business travel; outsourced activities; consumption of fossil fuel or electricity required to use the entity's products; extraction and production of materials purchased as inputs to the entity's processes; and transportation of purchased fuels. Scope 3 emissions are further discussed in paragraphs A31–A34.

Emissions Deductions (Ref: Para. 14(g), 17(a)(iii), Appendix 1)

A11   In some cases, emissions deductions include jurisdiction-specific credits and allowances for which there is no established link between the quantity of emissions allowed by the criteria to be deducted, and any lowering of emissions that may occur as a result of money paid or other action taken by the entity in order for it to claim the emissions deduction.

A12   Where an entity's GHG statement includes emissions deductions that are within the scope of the engagement, the requirements of this ISAE apply in relation to emissions deductions as appropriate (see also paragraphs A136-A139).

Purchased Offset (Ref: Para. 14(q), Appendix 1)

A13   When the entity purchases an offset from another entity, that other entity may spend the money it receives from the sale on emissions reduction projects (such as replacing energy generation using fossil fuels with renewable energy sources, or implementing energy efficiency measures), or on removing emissions from the atmosphere (for example, by planting and maintaining trees that would otherwise not have been planted or maintained), or the money may be compensation for not undertaking an action that would otherwise be undertaken (such as deforestation or forest degradation). In some jurisdictions, offsets can only be purchased if the emissions reduction or removal enhancement has already occurred.

Removal (Ref: Para. 14(s), Appendix 1)

A14   Removal may be achieved by storing GHGs in geological sinks (for example, underground) or biological sinks (for example, trees). Where the GHG statement includes the removal of GHGs that the entity would have otherwise emitted to the atmosphere, they are commonly reported in the GHG statement on a gross basis, that is, both the source and the sink are quantified in the GHG statement. Where removals are covered by the practitioner's conclusion, the requirements of this ISAE apply in relation to those removals as appropriate.

Significant Facility (Ref: Para. 14(t), 31)

A15   As the individual contribution of a facility to the aggregate emissions reported in the GHG statement increases, the risks of material misstatement to the GHG statement ordinarily increase. The practitioner may apply a percentage to a chosen benchmark as an aid to identify facilities that are of individual significance due to the size of their emissions relative to the aggregate emissions included in the GHG statement. Identifying a benchmark and determining a percentage to be applied to it involve the exercise of professional judgment. For example, the practitioner may consider that facilities exceeding 15% of total production volume are significant facilities. A higher or lower percentage may, however, be determined to be appropriate in the circumstances in the practitioner's professional judgment. This may be the case when, for example: there is a small number of facilities, none of which is less than 15% of total production volume, but in the practitioner's professional judgment not all the facilities are significant; or when there are a number of facilities that are marginally below 15% of total production volume which in the practitioner's professional judgment are significant.

The practitioner may also identify a facility as significant due to its specific nature or circumstances which give rise to particular risks of material misstatement. For example, a facility could be using different data gathering processes or quantification techniques from other facilities, require the use of particularly complex or specialized calculations, or involve particularly complex or specialized chemical or physical processes.   **A16**

ISAE 3000 (Ref: Para. 9, 15)

ISAE 3000 includes a number of requirements that apply to all assurance engagements, including engagements in accordance with this ISAE. In some cases, this ISAE may include additional requirements or application material in relation to those topics.   **A17**

Acceptance and Continuance of the Engagement

Competency (Ref: Para. 16(b))

GHG competencies may include: **A18**

- General understanding of climate science, including the scientific processes that relate GHGs to climate change.
- Understanding who the intended users of the information in the entity's GHG statement are, and how they are likely to use that information (see paragraph A47).
- Understanding emissions trading schemes and related market mechanisms, when relevant.
- Knowledge of applicable laws and regulations, if any, that affect how the entity should report its emissions, and may also, for example, impose a limit on the entity's emissions.
- GHG quantification and measurement methodologies, including the associated scientific and estimation uncertainties, and alternative methodologies available.
- Knowledge of the applicable criteria, including, for example:
  - Identifying appropriate emissions factors.
  - Identifying those aspects of the criteria that call for significant or sensitive estimates to be made, or for the application of considerable judgment.
  - Methods used for determining organizational boundaries, i.e., the entities whose emissions are to be included in the GHG statement.
  - Which emissions deductions are permitted to be included in the entity's GHG statement.

A19   The complexity of assurance engagements with respect to a GHG statement varies. In some cases, the engagement may be relatively straightforward, for instance, when an entity has no Scope 1 emissions and is reporting only Scope 2 emissions using an emissions factor specified in regulation, applied to electricity consumption at a single location. In this case, the engagement may focus largely on the system used to record and process electricity consumption figures identified on invoices, and arithmetical application of the specified emissions factor. When, however, the engagement is relatively complex, it is likely to require specialist competence in the quantification and reporting of emissions. Particular areas of expertise that may be relevant in such cases include:

Information systems expertise

- Understanding how emissions information is generated, including how data is initiated, recorded, processed, corrected as necessary, collated and reported in a GHG statement.

Scientific and engineering expertise

- Mapping the flow of materials through a production process, and the accompanying processes that create emissions, including identifying the relevant points at which source data is gathered. This may be particularly important in considering whether the entity's identification of emissions sources is complete.
- Analyzing chemical and physical relationships between inputs, processes and outputs, and relationships between emissions and other variables. The capacity to understand and analyze these relationships will often be important in designing analytical procedures.
- Identifying the effect of uncertainty on the GHG statement.
- Knowledge of the quality control policies and procedures implemented at testing laboratories, whether internal or external.
- Experience with specific industries and related emissions creation and removal processes. Procedures for Scope 1 emissions quantification vary greatly depending on the industries and processes involved, for example, the nature of electrolytic processes in aluminum production; combustion processes in the production of electricity using fossil fuels; and chemical processes in cement production are all different.
- The operation of physical sensors and other quantification methods, and the selection of appropriate emissions factors.

Scope of the GHG Statement and the Engagement (Ref: Para. 17(a))

A20   Examples of circumstances where the reasons for excluding known emissions sources from the GHG statement, or excluding disclosed emissions sources from the engagement, may not be reasonable in the circumstances include where:

- The entity has significant Scope 1 emissions but only includes Scope 2 emissions in the GHG statement.
- The entity is a part of a larger legal entity that has significant emissions that are not being reported on because of the way the organizational boundary has been determined when this is likely to mislead intended users.
- The emissions that the practitioner is reporting on are only a small proportion of the total emissions included in the GHG statement.

Assessing the Appropriateness of the Subject Matter (Ref: Para. 15)

ISAE 3000 requires the practitioner to assess the appropriateness of the subject **A21** matter.[13] In the case of a GHG statement, the entity's emissions (and removals and emissions deductions if applicable) are the subject matter of the engagement. That subject matter will be appropriate if, among other things, the entity's emissions are capable of consistent quantification using suitable criteria.[14]

GHG sources may be quantified by: **A22**

(a) Direct measurement (or direct monitoring) of GHG concentration and flow rates using continuous emissions monitoring or periodic sampling; or

(b) Measuring a surrogate activity, such as fuel consumption, and calculating emissions using, for example, mass balance equations,[15] entity-specific emissions factors, or average emissions factors for a region, source, industry or process.

Assessing the Suitability of the Criteria

Specifically Developed and Established Criteria (Ref: Para. 17(b))

Suitable criteria exhibit the following characteristics: relevance, completeness, **A23** reliability, neutrality, and understandability. Criteria may be "specifically developed" or they may be "established," that is, embodied in laws or regulations, or issued by authorized or recognized bodies of experts that follow a transparent due process.[16] Although criteria established by a regulator can be presumed to be relevant when that regulator is the intended user, some established criteria may be developed for a special purpose and be unsuitable for application in other circumstances. For example, criteria developed by a regulator that include emissions factors for a particular region may render misleading information if used for emissions in another region; or criteria that are designed to report only on particular regulatory aspects of emissions may be unsuitable for reporting to intended users other than the regulator that established the criteria.

Specifically developed criteria may be appropriate when, for example, the entity has **A24** very specialized machinery or is aggregating emissions information from different jurisdictions where the established criteria used in those jurisdictions differ. Special care may be necessary when assessing the neutrality and other characteristics of specifically developed criteria, particularly if they are not substantially based on established criteria generally used in the entity's industry or region, or are inconsistent with such criteria.

The applicable criteria may comprise established criteria supplemented by dis- **A25** closures, in the explanatory notes to the GHG statement, of specific boundaries, methods, assumptions, emissions factors, etc. In some cases, established criteria may not be suitable, even when supplemented by disclosures in the explanatory notes to the GHG statement, for example, when they do not encompass the matters noted in paragraph 17(b).

[13] *ISAE 3000, paragraph 18.*

[14] *Assurance Framework, paragraphs 34-38, and ISAE 3000, paragraphs 19–21.*

[15] *That is, equating the amount of a substance entering and exiting a defined boundary, for example, the amount of carbon in a hydrocarbon-based fuel entering a combustion device equals the amount of carbon exiting the device in the form of carbon dioxide.*

[16] *Assurance Framework, paragraphs 36–37.*

A26   It should be noted that the suitability of the applicable criteria is not affected by the level of assurance, that is, if they are not suitable for a reasonable assurance engagement, they are also not suitable for a limited assurance engagement, and vice versa.

Operations Included in the Entity's Organizational Boundary (Ref: Para. 17(b)(i), 23(b)(i), 34(g))

A27   Determining which operations owned or controlled by the entity to include in the entity's GHG statement is known as determining the entity's organizational boundary. In some cases, laws and regulations define the boundaries of the entity for reporting GHG emissions for regulatory purposes. In other cases, the applicable criteria may allow a choice between different methods for determining the entity's organizational boundary, for example, the criteria may allow a choice between an approach that aligns the entity's GHG statement with its financial statements and another approach that treats, for example, joint ventures or associates differently. Determining the entity's organizational boundary may require the analysis of complex organizational structures such as joint ventures, partnerships, and trusts, and complex or unusual contractual relationships. For example, a facility may be owned by one party, operated by another, and process materials solely for another party.

A28   Determining the entity's organizational boundary is different from what some criteria describe as determining the entity's "operational boundary." The operational boundary relates to which categories of Scope 1, 2 and 3 emissions will be included in the GHG statement, and is determined after setting the organizational boundary.

Adequate Disclosures (Ref: Para. 17(b)(iv), 74(d))

A29   In regulatory disclosure regimes, disclosures specified in the relevant laws or regulations are adequate for reporting to the regulator. Disclosure in the GHG statement of such matters as the following may be necessary in voluntary reporting situations for intended users to understand the significant judgments made in preparing the GHG statement:

(a)   Which operations are included in the entity's organizational boundary, and the method used for determining that boundary if the applicable criteria allow a choice between different methods (see paragraphs A27–A28);

(b)   Significant quantification methods and reporting policies selected, including:

    (i)   The method used to determine which Scope 1 and Scope 2 emissions have been included in the GHG statement (see paragraph A30);

    (ii)   Any significant interpretations made in applying the applicable criteria in the entity's circumstances, including data sources and, when choices between different methods are allowed, or entity-specific methods are used, disclosure of the method used and the rationale for doing so; and

    (iii)   How the entity determines whether previously reported emissions should be restated.

(c)   The categorization of emissions in the GHG statement. As noted in paragraph A14, where the GHG statement includes the removal of GHGs that the entity would have otherwise emitted to the atmosphere, both emissions and removals are commonly reported in the GHG statement on a gross basis, that is, both the source and the sink are quantified in the GHG statement;

(d)   A statement regarding the uncertainties relevant to the entity's quantification of its emissions, including: their causes; how they have been addressed; their effects on the GHG statement; and, where the GHG statement includes Scope 3 emissions, an explanation of: (see paragraphs A31–A34)

(i) The nature of Scope 3 emissions, including that it is not practicable for an entity to include all Scope 3 emissions in its GHG statement; and

(ii) The basis for selecting those Scope 3 emissions sources that have been included; and

(e) Changes, if any, in the matters mentioned in this paragraph or in other matters that materially affect the comparability of the GHG statement with a prior period(s) or base year.

Scope 1 and Scope 2 Emissions

Criteria commonly call for all material Scope 1, Scope 2, or both Scope 1 and Scope 2 emissions to be included in the GHG statement. Where some Scope 1 or Scope 2 emissions have been excluded, it is important that the explanatory notes to the GHG statement disclose the basis for determining which emissions are included and which are excluded, particularly if those that are included are not likely to be the largest for which the entity is responsible. **A30**

Scope 3 Emissions

While some criteria require the reporting of specific Scope 3 emissions, more commonly the inclusion of Scope 3 emissions is optional because it would be impracticable for nearly any entity to attempt to quantify the full extent of its indirect emissions as this includes all sources both up and down the entity's supply chain. For some entities, reporting particular categories of Scope 3 emissions provides important information for intended users, for example, where an entity's Scope 3 emissions are considerably larger than its Scope 1 and Scope 2 emissions, as may be the case with many service sector entities. In these cases, the practitioner may consider it inappropriate to undertake an assurance engagement if significant Scope 3 emissions are not included in the GHG statement. **A31**

Where some Scope 3 emissions sources have been included in the GHG statement, it is important that the basis for selecting which sources to include is reasonable, particularly if those included are not likely to be the largest sources for which the entity is responsible. **A32**

In some cases, the source data used to quantify Scope 3 emissions may be maintained by the entity. For example, the entity may keep detailed records as the basis for quantifying emissions associated with employee air travel. In some other cases, the source data used to quantify Scope 3 emissions may be maintained in a well-controlled and accessible source outside the entity. Where this is not the case, however, it may be unlikely that the practitioner will be able to obtain sufficient appropriate evidence with respect to such Scope 3 emissions. In such cases, it may be appropriate to exclude those Scope 3 emissions sources from the engagement. **A33**

It may also be appropriate to exclude Scope 3 emissions from the engagement where the quantification methods in use are heavily dependent on estimation and lead to a high degree of uncertainty in reported emissions. For example, various quantification methods for estimating the emissions associated with air travel can give widely varying quantifications even when identical source data is used. If such Scope 3 emissions sources are included in the engagement, it is important that the quantification methods used are selected **A34** objectively and that they are fully described along with the uncertainties associated with their use.

The Entity's Responsibility for the Preparation of the GHG Statement (Ref: Para. 17(c)(ii), 76(d))

A35   As noted in paragraph A70, for some engagements concerns about the condition and reliability of an entity's records may cause the practitioner to conclude that it is unlikely that sufficient appropriate evidence will be available to support an unmodified conclusion on the GHG statement. This may occur when the entity has little experience with the preparation of GHG statements. In such circumstances, it may be more appropriate for the quantification and reporting of emissions to be subject to an agreed-upon procedures engagement or a consulting engagement in preparation for an assurance engagement in a later period.

Who Developed the Criteria (Ref: Para. 17(c)(iii))

A36   When the GHG statement has been prepared for a regulatory disclosure regime or emissions trading scheme where the applicable criteria and form of reporting are prescribed, it is likely to be apparent from the engagement circumstances that it is the regulator or body in charge of the scheme that developed the criteria. In voluntary reporting situations, however, it may not be clear who developed the criteria unless it is stated in the explanatory notes to the GHG statement.

Changing the Terms of the Engagement (Ref: Para. 15, 18)

A37   ISAE 3000 requires that the practitioner not agree to a change in the terms of the engagement where there is no reasonable justification for doing so.[17] A request to change the scope of the engagement may not have a reasonable justification when, for example, the request is made to exclude certain emissions sources from the scope of the engagement because of the likelihood that the practitioner's conclusion would be modified.

Planning (Ref: Para. 19)

A38   When establishing the overall engagement strategy, it may be relevant to consider the emphasis given to different aspects of the design and implementation of the GHG information system. For example, in some cases the entity may have been particularly conscious of the need for adequate internal control to ensure the reliability of reported information, while in other cases the entity may have focused more on accurately determining the scientific, operational or technical characteristics of the information to be gathered.

A39   Smaller engagements or more straightforward engagements (see paragraph A19) may be conducted by a very small engagement team. With a smaller team, coordination of, and communication between, team members is easier. Establishing the overall engagement strategy for a smaller engagement, or for a more straightforward engagement, need not be a complex or time-consuming exercise. For example, a brief memorandum, based on discussions with the entity, may serve as the documented engagement strategy if it covers the matters noted in paragraph 19.

---

[17] *ISAE 3000, paragraph 11.*

The practitioner may decide to discuss elements of planning with the entity when **A40** determining the scope of the engagement or to facilitate the conduct and management of the engagement (for example, to coordinate some of the planned procedures with the work of the entity's personnel). Although these discussions often occur, the overall engagement strategy and the engagement plan remain the practitioner's responsibility. When discussing matters included in the overall engagement strategy or engagement plan, care is required in order not to compromise the effectiveness of the engagement. For example, discussing the nature and timing of detailed procedures with the entity may compromise the effectiveness of the engagement by making the procedures too predictable.

The performance of an assurance engagement is an iterative process. As the prac- **A41** titioner performs planned procedures, the evidence obtained may cause the practitioner to modify the nature, timing or extent of other planned procedures. In some cases, information may come to the practitioner's attention that differs significantly from that expected at an earlier stage of the engagement. For example, systematic errors discovered when performing procedures on location at selected facilities may indicate that it is necessary to visit additional facilities.

Planning to Use the Work of Experts or of Other Practitioners (Ref: Para. 19(e))

The engagement may be performed by a multidisciplinary team that includes one or **A42** more experts, particularly on relatively complex engagements when specialist competence in the quantification and reporting of emissions is likely to be required (see paragraph A19). ISAE 3000 contains a number of requirements with respect to using the work of an expert that may need to be considered at the planning stage when ascertaining the nature, timing and extent of resources necessary to perform the engagement.[18]

The work of another practitioner may be used in relation to, for example, a factory **A43** or other form of facility at a remote location; a subsidiary, division or branch in a foreign jurisdiction; or a joint venture or associate. Relevant considerations when the engagement team plans to request another practitioner to perform work on information to be included in the GHG statement may include:

- Whether the other practitioner understands and complies with the ethical requirements that are relevant to the engagement and, in particular, is independent.
- The other practitioner's professional competence.
- The extent of the engagement team's involvement in the work of the other practitioner.
- Whether the other practitioner operates in a regulatory environment that actively oversees that practitioner.

Materiality in Planning and Performing the Engagement

Determining Materiality When Planning the Engagement (Ref: Para. 20–21)

The criteria may discuss the concept of materiality in the context of the preparation **A44** and presentation of the GHG statement. Although criteria may discuss materiality in different terms, the concept of materiality generally includes that:

[18] *ISAE 3000, paragraphs 26–32.*

- Misstatements, including omissions, are considered to be material if they, individually or in the aggregate, could reasonably be expected to influence relevant decisions of users taken on the basis of the GHG statement;
- Judgments about materiality are made in light of surrounding circumstances, and are affected by the size or nature of a misstatement, or a combination of both; and
- Judgments about matters that are material to intended users of the GHG statement are based on a consideration of the common information needs of intended users as a group. The possible effect of misstatements on specific individual users, whose needs may vary widely, is not considered.

A45   Such a discussion, if present in the applicable criteria, provides a frame of reference to the practitioner in determining materiality for the engagement. If the applicable criteria do not include a discussion of the concept of materiality, the characteristics referred to above provide the practitioner with such a frame of reference.

A46   The practitioner's determination of materiality is a matter of professional judgment, and is affected by the practitioner's perception of the common information needs of intended users as a group. In this context, it is reasonable for the practitioner to assume that intended users:

(a)   Have a reasonable knowledge of GHG related activities, and a willingness to study the information in the GHG statement with reasonable diligence;

(b)   Understand that the GHG statement is prepared and assured to levels of materiality, and have an understanding of any materiality concepts included in the applicable criteria;

(c)   Understand that the quantification of emissions involves uncertainties (see paragraphs A54–A59); and

(d)   Make reasonable decisions on the basis of the information in the GHG statement.

A47   Intended users and their information needs may include, for example:

- Investors and other stakeholders such as suppliers, customers, employees, and the broader community in the case of voluntary disclosures. Their information needs may relate to decisions to buy or sell equity in the entity; lend to, trade with, or be employed by the entity; or make representations to the entity or others, for example, politicians.
- Market participants in the case of an emissions trading scheme, whose information needs may relate to decisions to trade negotiable instruments (such as permits, credits or allowances) created by the scheme, or impose fines or other penalties on the basis of excess emissions.
- Regulators and policy makers in the case of a regulatory disclosure regime. Their information needs may relate to monitoring compliance with the disclosure regime, and a broad range of government policy decisions related to climate change mitigation and adaptation, usually based on aggregated information.
- Management and those charged with governance of the entity who use information about emissions for strategic and operational decisions, such as choosing between alternative technologies and investment and divestment decisions, perhaps in anticipation of a regulatory disclosure regime or entering an emissions trading scheme.

The practitioner may not be able to identify all those who will read the assurance report, particularly where there are a large number of people who have access to it. In such cases, particularly where possible readers are likely to have a broad range of interests with respect to emissions, intended users may be limited to major stakeholders with significant and common interests. Intended users may be identified in different ways, for example, by agreement between the practitioner and the engaging party, or by laws or regulations.

Judgments about materiality are made in light of surrounding circumstances, and are affected by both quantitative and qualitative factors. It should be noted, however, that decisions regarding materiality are not affected by the level of assurance, that is, materiality for a reasonable assurance engagement is the same as for a limited assurance engagement. **A48**

A percentage is often applied to a chosen benchmark as a starting point in determining materiality. Factors that may affect the identification of an appropriate benchmark and percentage include: **A49**

- The elements included in the GHG statement (for example, Scope 1, Scope 2 and Scope 3 emissions, emissions deductions, and removals). A benchmark that may be appropriate, depending on the circumstances, is gross reported emissions, that is, the aggregate of reported Scope 1, Scope 2 and Scope 3 emissions before subtracting any emissions deductions or removals. Materiality relates to the emissions covered by the practitioner's conclusion. Therefore, when the practitioner's conclusion does not cover the entire GHG statement, materiality is set in relation to only that portion of the GHG statement that is covered by the practitioner's conclusion as if it were the GHG statement.
- The quantity of a particular type of emission or the nature of a particular disclosure. In some cases, there are particular types of emissions or disclosures for which misstatements of lesser or greater amounts than materiality for the GHG statement in its entirety are acceptable. For example, the practitioner may consider it appropriate to set a lower or greater materiality for emissions from a particular jurisdiction, or for a particular gas, scope or facility.
- How the GHG statement presents relevant information, for example, whether it includes a comparison of emissions with a prior period(s), a base year, or a "cap," in which case determining materiality in relation to the comparative information may be a relevant consideration. Where a "cap" is relevant, materiality may be set in relation to the entity's allocation of the cap if it is lower than reported emissions.
- The relative volatility of emissions. For example, if emissions vary significantly from period to period, it may be appropriate to set materiality relative to the lower end of the fluctuation range even if the current period is higher.
- The requirements of the applicable criteria. In some cases, the applicable criteria may set a threshold for accuracy and may refer to this as materiality. For example, the criteria may state an expectation that emissions are measured using a stipulated percentage as the "materiality threshold." Where this is the case, the threshold set by the criteria provides a frame of reference to the practitioner in determining materiality for the engagement.

Qualitative factors may include: **A50**

- The sources of emissions.
- The types of gases involved.
- The context in which the information in the GHG statement will be used (for example, whether the information is for use in an emissions trading scheme, is for submission to a regulator, or is for inclusion in a widely distributed sustainability report); and the types of decisions that intended users are likely to make.
- Whether there are one or more types of emissions or disclosures on which the attention of the intended users tends to be focused, for example, gases that, as well as contributing to climate change, are ozone depleting.

- The nature of the entity, its climate change strategies and progress toward related objectives.
- The industry and the economic and regulatory environment in which the entity operates.

Revision as the Engagement Progresses (Ref: Para. 22)

A51   Materiality may need to be revised as a result of a change in circumstances during the engagement (for example, the disposal of a major part of the entity's business), new information, or a change in the practitioner's understanding of the entity and its operations as a result of performing procedures. For example, it may become apparent during the engagement that actual emissions are likely to be substantially different from those used initially to determine materiality. If during the engagement the practitioner concludes that a lower materiality for the GHG statement (and, if applicable, materiality level or levels for particular types of emissions or disclosures) than that initially determined is appropriate, it may be necessary to revise performance materiality, and the nature, timing and extent of the further procedures.

Understanding the Entity and Its Environment, Including the Entity's Internal Control, and Identifying and Assessing Risks of Material Misstatement (Ref: Para. 23–26)

A52   The practitioner uses professional judgment to determine the extent of the understanding and the nature, timing and extent of procedures to identify and assess risks of material misstatement that are required to obtain reasonable or limited assurance, as appropriate. The practitioner's primary consideration is whether the understanding that has been obtained and the identification and assessment of risks are sufficient to meet the objective stated in this ISAE. The depth of the understanding that is required by the practitioner is less than that possessed by management in managing the entity, and both the depth of the understanding and the nature, timing and extent of procedures to identify and assess risks of material misstatement are less for a limited assurance engagement than for a reasonable assurance engagement.

A53   Obtaining an understanding and identifying and assessing risks of material misstatement is an iterative process. Procedures to obtain an understanding of the entity and its environment and to identify and assess risks of material misstatement by themselves do not provide sufficient appropriate evidence on which to base the assurance conclusion.

Uncertainty (Ref: Para: 23(b)(i)c, 76(e))

A54   The GHG quantification process can rarely be 100% accurate due to:

(a) *Scientific uncertainty*: This arises because of incomplete scientific knowledge about the measurement of GHGs. For example, the rate of GHG sequestration in biological sinks, and the "global warming potential" values used to combine emissions of different gases and report them as carbon dioxide equivalents, are subject to incomplete scientific knowledge. The degree to which scientific uncertainty affects the quantification of reported emissions is beyond the control of the entity. However, the potential for scientific uncertainty to result in unreasonable variations in reported emissions can be negated by the use of criteria that stipulate particular scientific assumptions to be used in preparing the GHG statement, or particular factors that embody those assumptions; and

(b) *Estimation (or measurement) uncertainty*: This results from the measurement and calculation processes used to quantify emissions within the bounds of existing scientific knowledge. Estimation uncertainty may relate to the data on which an estimate is based (for example, it may relate to uncertainty inherent in measurement instruments used), or the method, including where applicable the model, used in making the estimate (sometimes known as parameter and model uncertainty, respectively). The degree of estimation uncertainty is often controllable by the entity. Reducing the degree of estimation uncertainty may involve greater cost.

The fact that quantifying an entity's emissions is subject to uncertainty does not **A55** mean that an entity's emissions are inappropriate as a subject matter. For example, the applicable criteria may require Scope 2 emissions from electricity to be calculated by applying a prescribed emissions factor to the number of kilowatt hours consumed. The prescribed emissions factor will be based on assumptions and models that may not hold true in all circumstances. However, as long as the assumptions and models are reasonable in the circumstances and adequately disclosed, information in the GHG statement will ordinarily be capable of being assured.

The situation in paragraph A55 can be contrasted with quantification in accordance **A56** with criteria that use models and assumptions based on an entity's individual circumstances. Using entity-specific models and assumptions will likely result in more accurate quantification than using, for example, average emissions factors for an industry; it will also likely introduce additional risks of material misstatement with respect to how the entity-specific models and assumptions were arrived at. As noted in paragraph A55, as long as the assumptions and models are reasonable in the circumstances and adequately disclosed, information in the GHG statement will ordinarily be capable of being assured.

In some cases, however, the practitioner may decide that it is inappropriate to **A57** undertake an assurance engagement if the impact of uncertainty on information in the GHG statement is very high. This may be the case when, for example, a significant proportion of the entity's reported emissions are from fugitive sources (see paragraph A8) that are not monitored and estimation methods are not sufficiently sophisticated, or when a significant proportion of the entity's reported removals are attributable to biological sinks. It should be noted that decisions whether to undertake an assurance engagement in such circumstances are not affected by the level of assurance, that is, if it is not appropriate for a reasonable assurance engagement, it is also not appropriate for a limited assurance engagement, and vice versa.

A discussion in the explanatory notes to the GHG statement of the nature, causes, **A58** and effects of the uncertainties that affect the entity's GHG statement alerts intended users to the uncertainties associated with the quantification of emissions. This may be particularly important where the intended users did not determine the criteria to be used. For example, a GHG statement may be available to a broad range of intended users even though the criteria used were developed for a particular regulatory purpose.

Because uncertainty is a significant characteristic of all GHG statements, paragraph **A59** 76(e) requires it to be mentioned in the assurance report regardless of what, if any, disclosures are included in the explanatory notes to the GHG statement.[19]

---

[19] *See also ISAE 3000, paragraph 49(e).*

The Entity and Its Environment

Interruptions to Operations (Ref: Para. 23(b)(iii))

A60   Interruptions may include incidents such as shut downs, which may occur unexpectedly, or may be planned, for example, as part of a maintenance schedule. In some cases, the nature of operations may be intermittent, for example, when a facility is only used at peak periods.

Climate Change Objectives and Strategies (Ref: Para. 23(e))

A61   Consideration of the entity's climate change strategy, if any, and associated economic, regulatory, physical and reputational risks, may assist the practitioner to identify risks of material misstatement. For example, if the entity has made commitments to become carbon neutral, this may provide an incentive to understate emissions so the target will appear to be achieved within a declared timeframe. Conversely, if the entity is expecting to be subject to a regulated emissions trading scheme in the future, this may provide an incentive to overstate emissions in the meantime to increase the opportunity for it to receive a larger allowance at the outset of the scheme.

Procedures to Obtain an Understanding and to Identify and Assess Risks of Material Misstatement (Ref: Para. 24)

A62   Although the practitioner is required to perform all the procedures in paragraph 24 in the course of obtaining the required understanding of the entity, the practitioner is not required to perform all of them for each aspect of that understanding.

Analytical Procedures for Obtaining an Understanding of the Entity and Its Environment and Identifying and Assessing Risks of Material Misstatement (Ref: Para. 24(b))

A63   Analytical procedures performed to obtain an understanding of the entity and its environment and to identify and assess risks of material misstatement may identify aspects of the entity of which the practitioner was unaware and may assist in assessing the risks of material misstatement in order to provide a basis for designing and implementing responses to the assessed risks. Analytical procedures may include, for example, comparing GHG emissions from various facilities with production figures for those facilities.

A64   Analytical procedures may help identify the existence of unusual events, and amounts, ratios, and trends that might indicate matters that have implications for the engagement. Unusual or unexpected relationships that are identified may assist the practitioner in identifying risks of material misstatement.

A65   However, when such analytical procedures use data aggregated at a high level (which may be the situation with analytical procedures performed to obtain an understanding of the entity and its environment and to identify and assess risks of material misstatement), the results of those analytical procedures only provide a broad initial indication about whether a material misstatement may exist. Accordingly, in such cases, consideration of other evidence that has been gathered when identifying the risks of material misstatement together with the results of such analytical procedures may assist the practitioner in understanding and evaluating the results of the analytical procedures.

Observation and Inspection (Ref: Para. 24(c))

Observation consists of looking at a process or procedure being performed by others, for example, the practitioner's observation of monitoring devices being calibrated by the entity's personnel, or of the performance of control activities. Observation provides evidence about the performance of a process or procedure, but is limited to the point in time at which the observation takes place, and by the fact that the act of being observed may affect how the process or procedure is performed.   **A66**

Inspection involves: **A67**

(a) Examining records or documents, whether internal or external, in paper form, electronic form, or other media, for example, calibration records of a monitoring device. Inspection of records and documents provides evidence of varying degrees of reliability, depending on their nature and source and, in the case of internal records and documents, on the effectiveness of the controls over their production; or
(b) A physical examination of, for example, a calibrating device.

Observation and inspection may support inquiries of management and others, and may also provide information about the entity and its environment. Examples of such procedures include observation or inspection of the following: **A68**

- The entity's operations. Observing processes and equipment, including monitoring equipment, at facilities may be particularly relevant where significant Scope 1 emissions are included in the GHG statement.
- Documents (such as emissions mitigation plans and strategies), records (such as calibration records and results from testing laboratories), and manuals detailing information collection procedures and internal controls.
- Reports prepared for management or those charged with governance, such as internal or external reports with respect to the entity's environmental management systems.
- Reports prepared by management (such as quarterly management reports) and those charged with governance (such as minutes of board of directors' meetings).

Obtaining an Understanding of the Entity's Internal Control (Ref: Para. 25L–26R)

In a limited assurance engagement, the practitioner is not required to obtain an understanding of all of the components of the entity's internal control relevant to emissions quantification and reporting as is required in a reasonable assurance engagement. In addition, the practitioner is not required to evaluate the design of controls and determine whether they have been implemented. Therefore, in a limited assurance engagement, while it may often be appropriate to inquire of the entity about control activities and monitoring of controls relevant to the quantification and reporting of emissions, it will often not be necessary to obtain a detailed understanding of these components of the entity's internal control.   **A69**

The practitioner's understanding of relevant components of internal control may raise doubts about whether sufficient appropriate evidence is available for the practitioner to complete the engagement. For example (see also paragraphs A71–A72, A92–A93, and A96):   **A70**

- Concerns about the integrity of those preparing the GHG statement may be so serious as to cause the practitioner to conclude that the risk of management misrepresentation in the GHG statement is such that an engagement cannot be conducted.

- Concerns about the condition and reliability of an entity's records may cause the practitioner to conclude that it is unlikely that sufficient appropriate evidence will be available to support an unmodified conclusion on the GHG statement.

Control Activities Relevant to the Engagement (Ref: Para. 25R(d))

A71   The practitioner's judgment about whether particular control activities are relevant to the engagement may be affected by the level of sophistication, documentation and formality of the entity's information system, including the related business processes, relevant to reporting emissions. As reporting of emissions evolves, it can be expected that so too will the level of sophistication, documentation and formality of information systems and related control activities relevant to the quantification and reporting of emissions.

A72   In the case of very small entities or immature information systems, particular control activities are likely to be more rudimentary, less well-documented, and may only exist informally. When this is the case, it is less likely the practitioner will judge it necessary to understand particular control activities in order to assess the risks of material misstatement and design further procedures responsive to assessed risks. In some regulated schemes, on the other hand, the information system and control activities may be required to be formally documented and their design approved by the regulator. Even in some of these cases, however, not all relevant data flows and associated controls may be documented. For example, it may be more likely that control activities with respect to source data collection from continuous monitoring are sophisticated, well-documented, and more formal than control activities with respect to subsequent data processing and reporting (see also paragraphs A70, A92–A93, and A96).

Other Engagements Performed for the Entity (Ref: Para. 27)

A73   Information obtained from other engagements performed for the entity may relate to, for example, aspects of the entity's control environment.

Performing Procedures on Location at the Entity's Facilities (Ref: Para. 31)

A74   Performing observation and inspection, as well as other procedures, on location at a facility (often referred to as a "site visit") may be important in building on the understanding of the entity that the practitioner develops by performing procedures at head office. Because the practitioner's understanding of the entity and identification and assessment of risks of material misstatement can be expected to be more comprehensive for a reasonable assurance engagement than for a limited assurance engagement, the number of facilities at which procedures are performed on location in the case of a reasonable assurance engagement will ordinarily be greater than in the case of a limited assurance engagement.

A75   Performing procedures on location at a facility (or having another practitioner perform such procedures on behalf of the practitioner) may be done as part of planning, when performing procedures to identify and assess risks of material misstatement, or when responding to assessed risks of material misstatement. Performing procedures at significant facilities is often particularly important for an engagement being undertaken for the first time when considering the completeness of Scope 1 sources and of sinks included in the GHG statement, and when establishing whether the entity's data collection and processing systems, and its estimation techniques, are appropriate relative to the underlying physical processes and related uncertainties.

As noted in paragraph A74, performing procedures on location at a facility may be **A76** important in building on the understanding of the entity that the practitioner develops by performing procedures at head office. For many reasonable assurance engagements, the practitioner will also judge it necessary to perform procedures on location at each significant facility to respond to assessed risks of material mis-statement, particularly when the entity has significant facilities with Scope 1 emissions. For a limited assurance engagement where the entity has a number of significant facilities with Scope 1 emissions, a meaningful level of assurance may not be able to be obtained without the practitioner having performed procedures at a selection of significant facilities. Where the entity has significant facilities with Scope 1 emissions and the practitioner determines that effective and efficient procedures cannot be performed on location at the facility by the practitioner (or another practitioner on their behalf), alternative procedures may include one or more of the following:

- Reviewing source documents, energy flow diagrams, and material flow diagrams.
- Analyzing questionnaire responses from facility management.
- Inspecting satellite imagery of the facility.

To obtain adequate coverage of total emissions, particularly in a reasonable assur-   **A77** ance engagement, the practitioner may decide that it is appropriate to perform procedures on location at a selection of facilities that are not significant facilities. Factors that may be relevant to such a decision include:

- The nature of emissions at different facilities. For example, it is more likely that a practitioner may choose to visit a facility with Scope 1 emissions than a facility with only Scope 2 emissions. In the latter case, the examination of energy invoices at head office is more likely to be a primary source of evidence.
- The number and size of facilities, and their contribution to overall emissions.
- Whether facilities use different processes, or processes using different technol-ogies. Where this is the case, it may be appropriate to perform procedures on location at a selection of facilities using different processes or technologies.
- The methods used at different facilities to gather emissions information.
- The experience of relevant staff at different facilities.
- Varying the selection of facilities over time.

Internal Audit (Ref: Para. 32)

The entity's internal audit function is likely to be relevant to the engagement if the   **A78** nature of the internal audit function's responsibilities and activities are related to the quantification and reporting of emissions and the practitioner expects to use the work of the internal audit function to modify the nature or timing, or reduce the extent, of procedures to be performed.

Risks of Material Misstatement at the GHG Statement Level (Ref: Para. 33L(a)–33R(a))

Risks of material misstatement at the GHG statement level refer to risks that relate   **A79** pervasively to the GHG statement as a whole. Risks of this nature are not necessarily risks identifiable with a specific type of emission or disclosure level. Rather, they represent circumstances that may increase the risks of material misstatement more generally, for example, through management override of internal control. Risks of material misstatement at the GHG statement level may be especially relevant to the practitioner's consideration of the risks of material misstatement arising from fraud.

A80   Risks at the GHG statement level may derive in particular from a deficient control environment. For example, deficiencies such as management's lack of competence may have a pervasive effect on the GHG statement and may require an overall response by the practitioner. Other risks of material misstatement at the GHG statement level may include, for example:

- Inadequate, poorly controlled or poorly documented mechanisms for collecting data, quantifying emissions and preparing GHG statements.
- Lack of staff competence in collecting data, quantifying emissions and preparing GHG statements.
- Lack of management involvement in quantifying emissions and preparing GHG statements.
- Failure to identify accurately all sources of GHGs.
- Risk of fraud, for example, in connection with emissions trading markets.
- Presenting information covering prior periods that is not prepared on a consistent basis, for example, because of changed boundaries or changes in measurement methodologies.
- Misleading presentation of information in the GHG statement, for example, unduly highlighting particularly favorable data or trends.
- Inconsistent quantification methods and reporting policies, including different methods for determining the organizational boundary, at different facilities.
- Errors in unit conversion when consolidating information from facilities.
- Inadequate disclosure of scientific uncertainties and key assumptions in relation to estimates.

The Use of Assertions (Ref: Para. 33L(b–)33R(b))

A81   Assertions are used by the practitioner in a reasonable assurance engagement, and may be used in a limited assurance engagement, to consider the different types of potential misstatements that may occur.

A82   In representing that the GHG statement is in accordance with the applicable criteria, the entity implicitly or explicitly makes assertions regarding the quantification, presentation and disclosure of emissions. Assertions fall into the following categories and may take the following forms:

(a) Assertions about the quantification of emissions for the period subject to assurance:
  (i) Occurrence—emissions that have been recorded have occurred and pertain to the entity.
  (ii) Completeness—all emissions that should have been recorded have been recorded (see paragraphs A30–A34 for a discussion of completeness with respect to various Scopes).
  (iii) Accuracy—the quantification of emissions has been recorded appropriately.
  (iv) Cutoff—emissions have been recorded in the correct reporting period.
  (v) Classification—emissions have been recorded as the proper type.
(b) Assertions about presentation and disclosure:
  (i) Occurrence and responsibility—disclosed emissions and other matters have occurred and pertain to the entity.
  (ii) Completeness—all disclosures that should have been included in the GHG statement have been included.

(iii) Classification and understandability—emissions information is appropriately presented and described, and disclosures are clearly expressed.
(iv) Accuracy and quantification—emissions quantification and related information included in the GHG statement are appropriately disclosed.
(v) Consistency—quantification policies are consistent with those applied in the prior period, or changes are justified and have been properly applied and adequately disclosed; and comparative information, if any, is as reported in the prior period or has been appropriately restated.

Reliance on Internal Control (Ref: Para. 33R)

If the practitioner's assessment of risks of material misstatement at the assertion level **A83** includes an expectation that the controls are operating effectively (that is, the practitioner intends to rely on the operating effectiveness of controls in determining the nature, timing and extent of other procedures), the practitioner is required by paragraph 38R to design and perform tests of the operating effectiveness of those controls.

Causes of Risks of Material Misstatement (Ref: Para. 34)

Fraud (Ref: Para. 28, 34(a))

Misstatements in the GHG statement can arise from either fraud or error. The **A84** distinguishing factor between fraud and error is whether the underlying action that results in the misstatement of the GHG statement is intentional or unintentional.

Incentives for intentional misstatement of the GHG statement may arise if, for **A85** example, those who are directly involved with, or have the opportunity to influence, the emissions reporting process have a significant portion of their compensation contingent upon achieving aggressive GHG targets. As noted in paragraph A61, other incentives to either under or overstate emissions may result from the entity's climate change strategy, if any, and associated economic, regulatory, physical and reputational risks.

Although fraud is a broad legal concept, for the purposes of this ISAE, the practi- **A86** tioner is concerned with fraud that causes a material misstatement in the GHG statement. Although the practitioner may suspect or, in rare cases, identify the occurrence of fraud, the practitioner does not make legal determinations of whether fraud has actually occurred.

Non-Compliance with Laws and Regulations (Ref: Para. 34(b), 78(c))

This ISAE distinguishes the practitioner's responsibilities in relation to compliance **A87** with two different categories of laws and regulations as follows:

(a) The provisions of those laws and regulations generally recognized to have a direct effect on the determination of material amounts and disclosures in the GHG statement in that they determine the reported quantities and disclosures in an entity's GHG statement. Paragraph 34(b) requires the practitioner to consider the likelihood of material misstatement due to non-compliance with the provisions of such laws and regulations when performing the procedures required by paragraphs 33L or 33R; and
(b) Other laws and regulations that do not have a direct effect on the determination of the quantities and disclosures in the GHG statement, but compliance with which may be fundamental to the operating aspects of the business, to an

entity's ability to continue its business, or to avoid material penalties (for example, compliance with the terms of an operating license, or compliance with environmental regulations). Maintaining professional skepticism throughout the engagement, as required by ISAE 3000,[20] is important in the context of remaining alert to the possibility that procedures applied for the purpose of forming a conclusion on the GHG statement may bring instances of identified or suspected non-compliance with such laws and regulations to the practitioner's attention.

Other Causes of Risks of Material Misstatement (Ref: Para. 34)

A88   Examples of factors referred to in paragraph 34(c)–(k) include:

(a) Omission of one or more emissions sources is more likely for sources that are less obvious and may be overlooked, such as fugitive emissions.

(b) Significant economic or regulatory changes may include, for example, increases in renewable energy targets or significant price changes for allowances under an emissions trading scheme, which may lead to, for example, increased risk of misclassification of sources at an electricity generator.

(c) The nature of the entity's operations may be complex (for example, it may involve multiple and disparate facilities and processes), discontinuous (for example, peak load electricity generation), or result in few or weak relationships between the entity's emissions and other measurable activity levels (for example, a cobalt nickel plant). In such cases, the opportunity for meaningful analytical procedures may be significantly reduced.

Changes in operations or boundaries (for example, introduction of new processes, or the sale, acquisition or outsourcing of emissions sources or removal sinks) may also introduce risks of material misstatement (for example, through unfamiliarity with quantification or reporting procedures). Also, double counting of an emissions source or removals sink may occur due to inadequate coordination in the identification of sources and sinks at a complex installation.

(d) Selection of an inappropriate quantification method (for example, calculating Scope 1 emissions using an emissions factor when using a more accurate direct measurement method is available and would be more appropriate). Selecting an appropriate quantification method is particularly important when the method has been changed. This is because intended users are often interested in emissions trends over time, or relative to a base year. Some criteria may require that quantification methods are only changed when a more accurate method is to be used. Other factors related to the nature of quantification methods include:

- Incorrect application of a quantification method, such as not calibrating meters or not reading them sufficiently frequently, or use of an emissions factor that is inappropriate in the circumstances. For example, an emissions factor may be predicated on an assumption of continuous use and may not be appropriate to use after a shut down.

- Complexity in quantification methods, which will likely involve higher risk of material misstatement, for example: extensive or complex mathematical manipulation of source data (such as the use of complex mathematical models); extensive use of state conversion factors (such as those to convert measures of liquid to measures of gas); or extensive use of unit conversion factors (such as those to convert imperial measures to metric measures).

- Changes in quantification methods or input variables (for example, if the quantification method used is based on the carbon content of biomass, and the composition of the biomass used changes during the period).

---

[20] *ISAE 3000, paragraph 14.*

(e) Significant non-routine emissions or judgmental matters are a source of greater risk of material misstatement relative to routine, non-complex emissions that are subject to systematic quantification and reporting. Non-routine emissions are those that are unusual, in size or nature, and that therefore occur infrequently (for example, one-off events such as a plant malfunction or major leak). Judgmental matters may include the development of subjective estimates. Risks of material misstatement may be greater because of matters such as:
  - Greater management intervention to specify the quantification methods or reporting treatment.
  - Greater manual intervention for data collection and processing.
  - Complex calculations or quantification methods and reporting principles.
  - The nature of non-routine emissions, which may make it difficult for the entity to implement effective controls over the risks.
  - Quantification methods and reporting principles for estimates may be subject to differing interpretation.
  - Required judgments may be subjective or complex.

(f) The inclusion of Scope 3 emissions where the source data used in quantification are not maintained by the entity, or where quantification methods commonly in use are imprecise or lead to large variations in reported emissions (see paragraphs A31–A34).

(g) Matters that the practitioner may consider in obtaining an understanding of how the entity makes significant estimates and the data on which they are based include, for example:
  - An understanding of the data on which estimates are based;
  - The method, including where applicable the model, used in making estimates;
  - Relevant aspects of the control environment and information system;
  - Whether the entity has used an expert;
  - The assumptions underlying estimates;
  - Whether there has been or ought to have been a change from the prior period in the methods for making estimates and, if so, why; and
  - Whether and, if so, how the entity has assessed the effect of estimation uncertainty on the GHG statement, including:
    o Whether and, if so, how the entity has considered alternative assumptions or outcomes by, for example, performing a sensitivity analysis to determine the effect of changes in the assumptions on an estimate;
    o How the entity determines the estimate when analysis indicates a number of outcome scenarios; and
    o Whether the entity monitors the outcome of estimates made in the prior period, and whether it has appropriately responded to the outcome of that monitoring procedure.

Examples of other factors that may lead to risks of material misstatement include: **A89**

- Human error in the quantification of emissions, which may be more likely to occur if personnel are unfamiliar with, or not well-trained regarding, emissions processes or data recording.
- Undue reliance on a poorly designed information system, which may have few effective controls, for example, the use of spreadsheets without adequate controls.
- Manual adjustment of otherwise automatically recorded activity levels, for example, manual input may be required if a flare meter becomes overloaded.
- Significant external developments such as heightened public scrutiny of a particular facility.

Overall Responses to Assessed Risks of Material Misstatement and Further Procedures

Limited and Reasonable Assurance Engagements (Ref: Para. 8, 35–41R, 42L–43R, 46)

A90   Because the level of assurance obtained in a limited assurance engagement is lower than in a reasonable assurance engagement, the procedures the practitioner will perform in a limited assurance engagement will vary in nature from, and are less in extent than for, a reasonable assurance engagement. The primary differences between the practitioner's overall responses to address the assessed risks of material misstatement and further procedures for a reasonable assurance engagement and a limited assurance engagement on a GHG statement are as follows:

(a)   *The emphasis placed on the nature of various procedures*: The emphasis placed on the nature of various procedures as a source of evidence will likely differ, depending on the engagement circumstances. For example:

- The practitioner may judge it to be appropriate in the circumstances of a particular limited assurance engagement to place relatively greater emphasis on inquiries of the entity's personnel and analytical procedures, and relatively less emphasis, if any, on tests of controls and obtaining evidence from external sources than would be the case for a reasonable assurance engagement.

- Where the entity uses continuous measuring equipment to quantify emissions flows, the practitioner may decide in a limited assurance engagement to respond to an assessed risk of material misstatement by inquiring about the frequency with which the equipment is calibrated. In the same circumstances for a reasonable assurance engagement, the practitioner may decide to examine the entity's records of the equipment's calibration or independently test its calibration.

- Where the entity burns coal, the practitioner may decide in a reasonable assurance engagement to independently analyze the characteristics of the coal, but in a limited assurance engagement the practitioner may decide that reviewing the entity's records of laboratory test results is an adequate response to an assessed risk of material misstatement.

(b)   *The extent of further procedures*: The extent of further procedures performed in a limited assurance engagement is less than in a reasonable assurance engagement. This may involve:

- Reducing the number of items to be examined, for example, reducing sample sizes for tests of details;

- Performing fewer procedures (for example, performing only analytical procedures in circumstances when, in a reasonable assurance engagement, both analytical procedures and tests of detail would be performed); or

- Performing procedures on location at fewer facilities.

(c)   *The nature of analytical procedures*: In a reasonable assurance engagement, analytical procedures performed in response to assessed risks of material misstatement involve developing expectations of quantities or ratios that are sufficiently precise to identify material misstatements. In a limited assurance engagement, on the other hand, analytical procedures are often designed to support expectations regarding the direction of trends, relationships and ratios rather than to identify misstatements with the level of precision expected in a reasonable assurance engagement.[21]

Further, when significant fluctuations, relationships or differences are identified, appropriate evidence in a limited assurance engagement may often be obtained

---

[21] *This may not always be the case; for example, in some circumstances the practitioner may develop a precise expectation based on fixed physical or chemical relationships even in a limited assurance engagement.*

by making inquiries of the entity and considering responses received in the light of known engagement circumstances, without obtaining additional evidence as is required by paragraph 43R(a) in the case of a reasonable assurance engagement.

In addition, when undertaking analytical procedures in a limited assurance engagement the practitioner may, for example:

- Use data that is more highly aggregated, for example, data at a regional level rather than at a facility level, or monthly data rather than weekly data.
- Use data that has not been subjected to separate procedures to test its reliability to the same extent as it would be for a reasonable assurance engagement.

Overall Responses to Assessed Risks of Material Misstatement (Ref: Para. 35)

Overall responses to address the assessed risks of material misstatement at the GHG statement level may include:　　　　　　　　　　　　　　　　　　　　　　　**A91**

- Emphasizing to the assurance personnel the need to maintain professional skepticism.
- Assigning more experienced staff or those with special skills or using experts.
- Providing more supervision.
- Incorporating additional elements of unpredictability in the selection of further procedures to be performed.
- Making general changes to the nature, timing, or extent of procedures, for example: performing procedures at the period end instead of at an interim date; or modifying the nature of procedures to obtain more persuasive evidence.

The assessment of the risks of material misstatement at the GHG statement level,　**A92** and thereby the practitioner's overall responses, is affected by the practitioner's understanding of the control environment. An effective control environment may allow the practitioner to have more confidence in internal control and the reliability of evidence generated internally within the entity and thus, for example, allow the practitioner to conduct some procedures at an interim date rather than at the period end. Deficiencies in the control environment, however, have the opposite effect. For example, the practitioner may respond to an ineffective control environment by:

- Conducting more procedures as of the period end rather than at an interim date.
- Obtaining more extensive evidence from procedures other than tests of controls.
- Increasing sample sizes and the extent of procedures, such as the number of facilities at which procedures are performed.

Such considerations, therefore, have a significant bearing on the practitioner's gen-　**A93** eral approach, for example, the relative emphasis on tests of controls versus other procedures (see also paragraphs A70–A72, and A96).

Examples of Further Procedures (Ref: Para. 37L–37R, 40R)

Further procedures may include, for example:　　　　　　　　　　　　　　　　　　　**A94**

- Testing the operating effectiveness of controls over the collection and recording of activity data, such as kilowatt hours of electricity purchased.
- Agreeing emissions factors to appropriate sources (for example, government publications), and considering their applicability in the circumstances.
- Reviewing joint venture agreements and other contracts relevant to determining the entity's organizational boundary.

- Reconciling recorded data to, for example, odometers on vehicles owned by the entity.
- Reperforming calculations (for example, mass balance and energy balance calculations), and reconciling differences noted.
- Taking readings from continuous monitoring equipment.
- Observing or reperforming physical measurements, such as dipping oil tanks.
- Analyzing the soundness and appropriateness of unique measurement or quantification techniques, particularly complex methods that may involve, for example, recycle or feedback loops.
- Sampling and independently analyzing the characteristics of materials such as coal, or observing the entity's sampling techniques and reviewing records of laboratory test results.
- Checking the accuracy of calculations and the suitability of calculation methods used (for example, the conversion and aggregation of input measurements).
- Agreeing recorded data back to source documents, such as production records, fuel usage records, and invoices for purchased energy.

Factors that May Influence Assessed Risks of Material Misstatement (Ref: Para. 37L(a)–37R(a))

A95   Factors that may influence the assessed risks of material misstatement include:

- Inherent limitations on the capabilities of measurement instruments and the frequency of their calibration.
- The number, nature, geographical spread, and ownership characteristics of facilities from which data is collected.
- The number and nature of the various gases and emissions sources included in the GHG statement.
- Whether processes to which emissions relate are continuous or intermittent, and the risk of disruption to such processes.
- The complexity of methods for activity measurement and for calculating emissions, for example, some processes require unique measurement and calculation methods.
- The risk of unidentified fugitive emissions.
- The extent to which the quantity of emissions correlates with readily available input data.
- Whether personnel who perform data collection are trained in relevant methods, and the frequency of turnover of such personnel.
- The nature and level of automation used in data capture and manipulation.
- The quality control policies and procedures implemented at testing laboratories, whether internal or external.
- The complexity of criteria and of quantification and reporting policies, including how the organizational boundary is determined.

Operating Effectiveness of Controls (Ref: Para. 37R(a)(ii), 38R(a))

A96   In the case of very small entities or immature information systems, there may not be many control activities that could be identified by the practitioner, or the extent to which their existence or operation have been documented by the entity may be limited. In such cases, it may be more efficient for the practitioner to perform further procedures that are primarily other than tests of controls. In some rare cases, however, the absence of control activities or of other components of control may make it impossible to obtain sufficient appropriate evidence (see also paragraphsA70–A72, and A92–A93).

Persuasiveness of Evidence (Ref: Para. 37L(b)–37R(b))

To obtain more persuasive evidence because of a higher assessment of risk of material misstatement, the practitioner may increase the quantity of the evidence, or obtain evidence that is more relevant or reliable, for example, by obtaining corroborating evidence from a number of independent sources.

A97

Risks for Which Tests of Controls Are Necessary to Provide Sufficient Appropriate Evidence (Ref: 38R(b))

The quantification of emissions may include processes that are highly automated with little or no manual intervention, for example, where relevant information is recorded, processed, or reported only in electronic form such as in a continuous monitoring system, or when the processing of activity data is integrated with an information technology-based operational or financial reporting system. In such cases:

A98

- Evidence may be available only in electronic form, and its sufficiency and appropriateness dependent on the effectiveness of controls over its accuracy and completeness.
- The potential for improper initiation or alteration of information to occur and not be detected may be greater if appropriate controls are not operating effectively.

Confirmation Procedures (Ref: Para. 41R)

External confirmation procedures may provide relevant evidence about such information as:

A99

- Activity data collected by a third party, such as data about: employee air travel collated by a travel agent; the inflow of energy to a facility metered by a supplier; or kilometers travelled by entity-owned vehicles recorded by an external fleet manager.
- Industry benchmark data used in calculating emissions factors.
- The terms of agreements, contracts, or transactions between the entity and other parties, or information about whether other parties are, or are not, including particular emissions in their GHG statement, when considering the entity's organizational boundary.
- The results of laboratory analysis of samples (for example, the calorific value of input samples).

Analytical Procedures Performed in Response to Assessed Risks of Material Misstatement (Ref: Para. 42L–42R)

In many cases, the fixed nature of physical or chemical relationships between particular emissions and other measurable phenomena allows for the design of powerful analytical procedures (for example, the relationship between fuel consumption and carbon dioxide and nitrous oxide emissions).

A100

Similarly, a reasonably predictable relationship may exist between emissions and financial or operational information (for example, the relationship between Scope 2 emissions from electricity and the general ledger balance for electricity purchases or hours of operation). Other analytical procedures may involve comparisons of information about the entity's emissions with external data such as industry averages; or the analysis of trends during the period to identify anomalies for further

A101

investigation, and trends across periods for consistency with other circumstances such as the acquisition or disposal of facilities.

A102   Analytical procedures may be particularly effective when disaggregated data is readily available, or when the practitioner has reason to consider the data to be used is reliable, such as when it is extracted from a well-controlled source. In some cases, data to be used may be captured by the financial reporting information system, or may be entered in another information system in parallel with the entry of related financial data, and some common input controls applied. For example, the quantity of fuel purchased as recorded on suppliers' invoices may be input under the same conditions that relevant invoices are entered into an accounts payable system. In some cases, data to be used may be an integral input to operational decisions and therefore subject to increased scrutiny by operational personnel, or subject to separate external audit procedures (for example, as part of a joint venture agreement or oversight by a regulator).

Procedures Regarding Estimates (Ref: Para. 44L–45R)

A103   In some cases, it may be appropriate for the practitioner to evaluate how the entity has considered alternative assumptions or outcomes, and why it has rejected them.

A104   In some limited assurance engagements, it may be appropriate for the practitioner to undertake one or more of the procedures identified in paragraph 45R.

Sampling (Ref: Para. 46)

A105   Sampling involves:

(a)   Determining a sample size sufficient to reduce sampling risk to an acceptably low level. Because the acceptable level of assurance engagement risk is lower for a reasonable assurance engagement than for a limited assurance engagement, so too may be the level of sampling risk that is acceptable in the case of tests of details. Therefore, when sampling is used for tests of details in a reasonable assurance engagement, the sample size may be larger than when used in similar circumstances in a limited assurance engagement.

(b)   Selecting items for the sample in such a way that each sampling unit in the population has a chance of selection, and performing procedures, appropriate to the purpose, on each item selected. If the practitioner is unable to apply the designed procedures, or suitable alternative procedures, to a selected item, that item is treated as a deviation from the prescribed control, in the case of tests of controls, or a misstatement, in the case of tests of details.

(c)   Investigating the nature and cause of deviations or misstatements identified, and evaluating their possible effect on the purpose of the procedure and on other areas of the engagement.

(d)   Evaluating:

(i)   The results of the sample, including, for tests of details, projecting misstatements found in the sample to the population; and

(ii)   Whether the use of sampling has provided an appropriate basis for conclusions about the population that has been tested.

Fraud, Laws and Regulations (Ref: Para. 47)

A106   In responding to fraud or suspected fraud identified during the engagement, it may be appropriate for the practitioner to, for example:

- Discuss the matter with the entity.
- Request the entity to consult with an appropriately qualified third party, such as the entity's legal counsel or a regulator.
- Consider the implications of the matter in relation to other aspects of the engagement, including the practitioner's risk assessment and the reliability of written representations from the entity.
- Obtain legal advice about the consequences of different courses of action.
- Communicate with third parties (for example, a regulator).
- Withhold the assurance report.
- Withdraw from the engagement.

The actions noted in the paragraph A106 may be appropriate in responding to non-compliance or suspected non-compliance with laws and regulations identified during the engagement. It may also be appropriate to describe the matter in an Other Matter paragraph in the assurance report in accordance with paragraph 77 of this ISAE, unless the practitioner: **A107**

(a) Concludes that the non-compliance has a material effect on the GHG statement and has not been adequately reflected in the GHG statement; or
(b) Is precluded by the entity from obtaining sufficient appropriate evidence to evaluate whether non-compliance that may be material to the GHG statement has, or is likely to have, occurred, in which case paragraph 51 of ISAE 3000 applies.

Procedures Regarding the GHG Statement Aggregation Process (Ref: Para. 48L–48R)

As noted in paragraph A71, as reporting of emissions evolves, it can be expected that so too will the level of sophistication, documentation and formality of information systems relevant to the quantification and reporting of emissions. In immature information systems, the aggregation process may be very informal. In more sophisticated systems, the aggregation process may be more systematic and formally documented. The nature, and also the extent, of the practitioner's procedures with respect to adjustments and the manner in which the practitioner agrees or reconciles the GHG statement with the underlying records depends on the nature and complexity of the entity's quantifications and reporting process and the related risks of material misstatement.   **A108**

Additional Procedures (Ref: Para. 49L–49R)

An assurance engagement is an iterative process, and information may come to the practitioner's attention that differs significantly from that on which the determination of planned procedures was based. As the practitioner performs planned procedures, the evidence obtained may cause the practitioner to perform additional procedures. Such procedures may include asking the entity to examine the matter(s) identified by the practitioner, and to make adjustments to the GHG statement if appropriate.   **A109**

Determining Whether Additional Procedures Are Necessary in a Limited Assurance Engagement (Ref: Para. 49L, 49L(b))

The practitioner may become aware of a matter(s) that causes the practitioner to believe the GHG statement may be materially misstated. For example, when performing site visits, the practitioner may identify a potential source of emissions which does not appear to be included in the GHG statement. In such cases, the practitioner makes further inquiries as to whether the potential source has been incorporated into   **A110** the GHG statement. The extent of additional procedures performed, in accordance with paragraph 49L, will be a matter of professional judgment. The greater the likelihood of material misstatement the more persuasive the evidence the practitioner obtains.

A111   If, in the case of a limited assurance engagement, a matter(s) comes to the practitioner's attention that causes the practitioner to believe the GHG statement may be materially misstated, the practitioner is required by paragraph 49L to design and perform additional procedures. If having done so, however, the practitioner is not able to obtain sufficient appropriate evidence to either conclude that the matter(s) is not likely to cause the GHG statement to be materially misstated or determine that it does cause the GHG statement to be materially misstated, a scope limitation exists.

Accumulation of Identified Misstatements (Ref: Para. 50)

A112   The practitioner may designate an amount below which misstatements would be clearly trivial and would not need to be accumulated because the practitioner expects that the accumulation of such amounts clearly would not have a material effect on the GHG statement. "Clearly trivial" is not another expression for "not material." Matters that are clearly trivial will be of a wholly different (smaller) order of magnitude than materiality determined in accordance with this ISAE, and will be matters that are clearly inconsequential, whether taken individually or in the aggregate and whether judged by any criteria of size, nature or circumstances. When there is any uncertainty about whether one or more items are clearly trivial, the matter is considered not to be clearly trivial.

Using the Work of Other Practitioners

Communication to Other Practitioners (Ref: Para. 57(a))

A113   Relevant matters that the engagement team may communicate to other practitioners in respect of the work to be performed, the use to be made of that work, and the form and content of the other practitioner's communication with the engagement team may include:

- A request that the other practitioner, knowing the context in which the engagement team will use the work of the other practitioner, confirms that the other practitioner will cooperate with the engagement team.
- Performance materiality for the work of the other practitioner, which may be lower than performance materiality for the GHG statement (and, if applicable, the materiality level or levels for particular types of emissions or disclosures) and the threshold above which misstatements cannot be regarded as clearly trivial to the GHG statement.
- Identified risks of material misstatement of the GHG statement that are relevant to the work of the other practitioner; and a request that the other practitioner communicate on a timely basis any other risks identified during the engagement that may be material to the GHG statement, and the other practitioner's responses to such risks.

Communication from Other Practitioners (Ref: Para. 57(a))

A114   Relevant matters that the engagement team may request the other practitioner to communicate include:

- Whether the other practitioner has complied with ethical requirements that are relevant to the group engagement, including independence and professional competence.
- Whether the other practitioner has complied with the group engagement team's requirements.
- Information on instances of non-compliance with laws or regulations that could give rise to a material misstatement of the GHG statement.
- A list of uncorrected misstatements identified by the other practitioner during the engagement that are not clearly trivial.
- Indicators of possible bias in the preparation of relevant information.
- Description of any identified significant deficiencies in internal control identified by the other practitioner during the engagement.
- Other significant matters that the other practitioner has communicated or expects to communicate to the entity, including fraud or suspected fraud.
- Any other matters that may be relevant to the GHG statement, or that the other practitioner wishes to draw to the attention of the engagement team, including exceptions noted in any written representations that the other practitioner requested from the entity.
- The other practitioner's overall findings, conclusion or opinion.

Evidence (Ref: Para. 57(b))

Relevant considerations when obtaining evidence regarding the work of the other practitioner may include: **A115**

- Discussions with the other practitioner regarding business activities relevant to that other practitioner's work that are significant to the GHG statement.
- Discussions with the other practitioner regarding the susceptibility of relevant information to material misstatement.
- Reviewing the other practitioner's documentation of identified risks of material misstatement, responses to those risks, and conclusions.

Such documentation may take the form of a memorandum that reflects the other practitioner's conclusion with regard to the identified risks.

Written Representations (Ref: Para. 58)

In addition to the written representations required by paragraph 58, the practitioner may consider it necessary to request other written representations. The person(s) from whom the practitioner requests written representations will ordinarily be a member of senior management or those charged with governance. However, because management and governance structures vary by jurisdiction and by entity, reflecting influences such as different cultural and legal backgrounds, and size and ownership characteristics, it is not possible for this ISAE to specify for all engagements the appropriate person(s) from whom to request written representations. For example, the entity may be a facility that is not a separate legal entity in its own right. In such cases, identifying the appropriate management personnel or those charged with governance from whom to request written representations may require the exercise of professional judgment.   **A116**

Subsequent Events (Ref: Para. 61)

Subsequent events may include, for example, the publication of revised emissions factors by a body such as a government agency, changes to relevant legislation or regulations, improved scientific knowledge, significant structural changes in the   **A117** entity, the availability of more accurate quantification methods, or the discovery of a significant error.

Comparative Information (Ref: Para. 62–63, 76(c))

A118   Law or regulation, or the terms of the engagement, may specify the requirements in respect of presentation, reporting and assurance of the comparative information in a GHG statement. A key difference between financial statements and a GHG statement is that the amounts presented in a GHG statement measures emissions for a discrete period and are not based on cumulative amounts over time. As a result, the comparative information presented does not affect current year information unless emissions have been recorded in the wrong period and therefore the amounts may be based on the incorrect starting period for measurement.

A119   Where a GHG statement includes references to percentage reductions in emissions, or a similar comparison of period on period information, it is important that the practitioner consider the appropriateness of the comparisons. These may be inappropriate due to:

(a)   Significant changes in operations from the prior period;
(b)   Significant changes in conversion factors; or
(c)   Inconsistency of sources or methods of measurement.

A120   When comparative information is presented with the current emissions information but some or all of that comparative information is not covered by the practitioner's conclusion, it is important that the status of such information is clearly identified in both the GHG statement and the assurance report.

Restatements (Ref: Para. 62(a))

A121   The GHG quantities reported in a prior period may need to be restated in accordance with laws or regulations or the applicable criteria because of, for example, improved scientific knowledge, significant structural changes in the entity, the availability of more accurate quantification methods, or the discovery of a significant error.

Performing Procedures on Comparative Information (Ref: Para 63(a))

A122   In a limited assurance engagement that includes assurance on comparative information, if the practitioner becomes aware that there may be a material misstatement in the comparative information presented, the procedures to be performed are to be in accordance with the requirements of paragraph 49L. In the case of a reasonable assurance engagement, the procedures to be performed are to be sufficient to form an opinion on the comparative information.

A123   If the engagement does not include assurance on comparative information, the requirement to perform procedures in the circumstances addressed by paragraph 63(a) is to satisfy the practitioner's ethical obligation to not knowingly be associated with materially false or misleading information.

Other Information (Ref: Para. 64)

A124   A GHG statement may be published with other information that is not covered by the practitioner's conclusion, for example, a GHG statement may be included as part of an entity's annual report or sustainability report, or included with other climate change-specific information such as:

- A strategic analysis, including a statement about the impact climate change has on the entity's strategic objectives.
- An explanation and qualitative assessment of current and anticipated significant risks and opportunities associated with climate change.
- Disclosures about the entity's actions, including its long-term and short-term plan to address climate change-related risks, opportunities and impacts.
- Disclosures about future outlook, including trends and factors related to climate change that are likely to affect the entity's strategy or the timescale over which achievement of the strategy is planned.
- A description of governance processes and the entity's resources that have been assigned to the identification, management and oversight of climate change-related issues.

In some cases, the entity may publish emissions information that is calculated on a different basis from that used in preparing the GHG statement, for example, the other information may be prepared on a "like-for-like" basis whereby emissions are recalculated to omit the effect of non-recurring events, such as the commissioning of a new plant or the closing down of a facility. The practitioner may seek to have such information removed if the methods used to prepare it would be disallowed by the criteria used to prepare the GHG statement. The practitioner may also seek to have removed any narrative information that is inconsistent with the quantitative data included in the GHG statement or cannot be substantiated (for example, speculative projections or claims about future action). **A125**

Further actions that may be appropriate when other information could undermine the credibility of the GHG statement and the assurance report include, for example: **A126**

- Requesting the entity to consult with a qualified third party, such as the entity's legal counsel.
- Obtaining legal advice about the consequences of different courses of action.
- Communicating with third parties, for example, a regulator.
- Withholding the assurance report.
- Withdrawing from the engagement, where withdrawal is possible under applicable laws or regulations.
- Describing the matter in the assurance report.

Documentation

Documentation of the Procedures Performed and Evidence Obtained (Ref: Para. 15, 65–66)

ISAE 3000 requires the practitioner to document matters that are significant in providing evidence that supports the assurance report and that the engagement was performed in accordance with ISAEs.[22] The following are examples of matters that may be appropriate to include in the engagement documentation: **A127**

- Fraud: The risks of material misstatement and the nature, timing and extent of procedures with respect to fraud; and communications about fraud made to the entity, regulators and others.
- Laws and Regulations: Identified or suspected non-compliance with laws and regulations and the results of discussion with the entity and other parties outside the entity.

---

[22] *ISAE 3000, paragraph 42.*

- Planning: The overall engagement strategy, the engagement plan, and any significant changes made during the engagement, and the reasons for such changes.
- Materiality: The following amounts and the factors considered in their determination: materiality for the GHG statement; if applicable, the materiality level or levels for particular types of emissions or disclosures; performance materiality; and any revision of materiality as the engagement progresses.
- Risks of Material Misstatement: the discussion required by paragraph 29, and the significant decisions reached, key elements of the understanding obtained regarding each of the aspects of the entity and its environment specified in paragraph 23, and the risks of material misstatement for which in the practitioner's professional judgment further procedures were required.
- Further Procedures: the nature, timing and extent of the further procedures performed, the linkage of those further procedures with the risks of material misstatement, and the results of the procedures.
- Evaluation of Misstatements: The amount below which misstatements would be regarded as clearly trivial, misstatements accumulated during the engagement and whether they have been corrected, and the practitioner's conclusion as to whether uncorrected misstatements are material, individually or in the aggregate, and the basis for that conclusion.

Matters Arising after the Date of the Assurance Report (Ref: Para. 68)

A128   Examples of exceptional circumstances include facts which become known to the practitioner after the date of the assurance report but which existed at that date and which, if known at that date, might have caused the GHG statement to be amended or the practitioner to modify the conclusion in the assurance report, for example, the discovery of a significant uncorrected error. The resulting changes to the engagement documentation are reviewed in accordance with the firm's policies and procedures with respect to review responsibilities as required by ISQC 1, with the engagement partner taking final responsibility for the changes.[23]

Assembly of the Final Engagement File (Ref: Para. 69)

A129   ISQC 1 (or national requirements that are at least as demanding) requires firms to establish policies and procedures for the timely completion of the assembly of engagement files.[24] An appropriate time limit within which to complete the assembly of the final engagement file is ordinarily not more than 60 days after the date of the assurance report.[25]

Engagement Quality Control Review (Ref: Para. 71)

A130   Other matters that may be considered in an engagement quality control review include:

- The engagement team's evaluation of the firm's independence in relation to the engagement.

[23] *ISQC 1*, Quality Control for Firms that Perform Audits and Reviews of Financial Statements, and Other Assurance and Related Services Engagements, *paragraphs 32–33.*

[24] *ISQC 1, paragraph 45.*

[25] *ISQC 1, paragraph A54.*

- Whether appropriate consultation has taken place on matters involving differences of opinion or other difficult or contentious matters, and the conclusions arising from those consultations.
- Whether engagement documentation selected for review reflects the work performed in relation to the significant judgments and supports the conclusions reached.

Forming the Assurance Conclusion

Description of the Applicable Criteria (Ref: Para. 74(d), 76(g)(iv))

The preparation of the GHG statement by the entity requires the inclusion of an adequate description of the applicable criteria in the explanatory notes to the GHG statement. That description advises intended users of the framework on which the GHG statement is based, and is particularly important when there are significant differences between various criteria regarding how particular matters are treated in a GHG statement, for example: which emissions deductions are included, if any; how they have been quantified and what they represent; and the basis for selecting which Scope 3 emissions are included, and how they have been quantified.   **A131**

A description that the GHG statement is prepared in accordance with particular criteria is appropriate only if the GHG statement complies with all the requirements of those criteria that are effective during the period covered by the GHG statement.   **A132**

A description of the applicable criteria that contains imprecise qualifying or limiting language (for example, "the GHG statement is in substantial compliance with the requirements of XYZ") is not an adequate description as it may mislead users of the GHG statement.   **A133**

Assurance Report Content

Illustrative Assurance Reports (Ref: Para. 76)

Appendix 2 contains illustrations of assurance reports on GHG statements incorporating the elements set forth in paragraph 76.   **A134**

Information Not Covered by the Practitioner's Conclusion (Ref: Para. 76(c))

To avoid misunderstanding and undue reliance on information that has not been subject to assurance, where the GHG statement includes information, such as comparatives, that is not covered by the practitioner's conclusion, that information is ordinarily identified as such in the GHG statement and in the practitioner's assurance report.   **A135**

Emissions Deductions (Ref: Para. 76(f))

The wording of the statement to be included in the assurance report when the GHG statement includes emissions deductions may vary considerably depending on the circumstances.   **A136**

The availability of relevant and reliable information in relation to offsets and other emissions deductions varies greatly and, therefore, so does the evidence available to practitioners to support entities' claimed emissions deductions.   **A137**

A138   Because of the varied nature of emissions deductions and the often reduced number and nature of procedures that can be applied to emissions deductions by the practitioner, this ISAE requires identification in the assurance report of those emissions deductions, if any, that are covered by the practitioner's conclusion, and a statement of the practitioner's responsibility with respect to them.

A139   A statement of the practitioner's responsibility with respect to emissions deductions may be worded as follows when the emissions deductions are comprised of offsets: "The GHG statement includes a deduction from ABC's emissions for the year of yyy tonnes of CO_{2-e} relating to offsets. We have performed procedures as to whether these offsets were acquired during the year, and whether the description of them in the GHG statement is a reasonable summary of the relevant contracts and related documentation. We have not, however, performed any procedures regarding the external providers of these offsets, and express no opinion about whether the offsets have resulted, or will result, in a reduction of yyy tonnes of CO_{2-e}."

Use of the Assurance Report (Ref: Para. 76(g)(iii))

A140   As well as identifying the addressee of the assurance report, the practitioner may consider it appropriate to include wording in the body of the assurance report that specifies the purpose for which, or the intended users for whom, the report was prepared. For example, when the GHG statement will be lodged on the public record, it may be appropriate for the explanatory notes to the GHG statement and the assurance report to include a statement that the report is intended for users who have a reasonable knowledge of GHG related activities, and who have studied the information in the GHG statement with reasonable diligence and understand that the GHG statement is prepared and assured to appropriate levels of materiality.

A141   In addition, the practitioner may consider it appropriate to include wording that specifically restricts distribution of the assurance report other than to intended users, its use by others, or its use for other purposes.

Summary of the Practitioner's Procedures (Ref: Para. 76(h)(ii))

A142   The assurance report in a reasonable assurance engagement normally follows a standard wording and only briefly describes procedures performed. This is because, in a reasonable assurance engagement, describing in any level of detail the specific procedures performed would not assist users to understand that, in all cases where an unmodified report is issued, sufficient appropriate evidence has been obtained to enable the practitioner to express an opinion.

A143   In a limited assurance engagement, an appreciation of the nature, timing and extent of procedures performed is essential for the intended users to understand the conclusion expressed in a limited assurance report. The description of the practitioner's procedures in a limited assurance engagement is therefore ordinarily more detailed than in a reasonable assurance engagement. It also may be appropriate to include a description of procedures that were not performed that would ordinarily be performed in a reasonable assurance engagement. However, a complete identification of all such procedures may not be possible because the practitioner's required understanding and assessment of risks of material misstatement are less than in a reasonable assurance engagement.

Factors to consider in making that determination and the level of detail to be provided include:

- Circumstances specific to the entity (e.g., the differing nature of the entity's activities compared to those typical in the sector).
- Specific engagement circumstances affecting the nature and extent of the procedures performed.
- The intended users' expectations of the level of detail to be provided in the report, based on market practice, or applicable laws or regulations.

In describing the procedures performed in the limited assurance report, it is important that they are written in an objective way but are not summarized to the extent that they are ambiguous, nor written in a way that is overstated or embellished or that implies that reasonable assurance has been obtained. It is also important that the description of the procedures not give the impression that an agreed-upon procedures engagement has been undertaken, and in most cases will not detail the entire work plan.   **A144**

The Practitioner's Signature (Ref: Para. 76(k))

The practitioner's signature is either in the name of the practitioner's firm, the personal name of the practitioner, or both, as appropriate for the particular jurisdiction. In addition to the practitioner's signature, in certain jurisdictions, the practitioner may be required to declare in the assurance report the practitioner's professional designation or the fact that the practitioner or firm, as appropriate, has been recognized by the appropriate licensing authority in that jurisdiction.   **A145**

Emphasis of Matter Paragraphs and Other Matter Paragraphs (Ref: Para. 77)

A widespread use of Emphasis of Matter or Other Matter paragraphs diminishes the effectiveness of the practitioner's communication of such matters.   **A146**

An Emphasis of Matter paragraph may be appropriate when, for example, different criteria have been used or the criteria have been revised, updated or interpreted differently than in prior periods and this has had a fundamental effect on reported emissions, or a system breakdown for part of the period being accounted for means that extrapolation was used to estimate emissions for that time and this has been stated in the GHG statement.   **A147**

An Other Matter paragraph may be appropriate when, for example, the scope of the engagement has changed significantly from the prior period and this has not been stated in the GHG statement.   **A148**

The content of an Emphasis of Matter paragraph includes a clear reference to the matter being emphasized and to where relevant disclosures that fully describe the matter can be found in the GHG statement. It also indicates that the practitioner's conclusion is not modified in respect of the matter emphasized. (See also paragraph A125)   **A149**

The content of an Other Matter paragraph reflects clearly that such other matter is not required to be presented and disclosed in the GHG statement. Paragraph 77 limits the use of an Other Matter paragraph to matters relevant to users' understanding of the engagement, the practitioner's responsibilities or the assurance report, that the practitioner considers it necessary to communicate in the assurance report. (See also paragraph A124)   **A150**

Including the practitioner's recommendations on matters such as improvements to the entity's information system in the assurance report may imply that those matters   **A151** have not been appropriately dealt with in preparing the GHG statement. Such recommendations may be communicated, for example, in a management letter or in discussion with those charged with governance. Considerations relevant to deciding whether to include recommendations in the assurance report include whether their nature is relevant to the information needs of intended users, and whether they are worded appropriately to ensure they will not be misunderstood as a qualification of the practitioner's conclusion on the GHG statement.

A152　An Other Matter paragraph does not include information that the practitioner is prohibited from providing by laws, regulations or other professional standards, for example, ethical standards relating to confidentiality of information. An Other Matter paragraph also does not include information that is required to be provided by management.

Appendix 1   (Ref: Para. A8–A14)

Emissions, Removals and Emissions Deductions

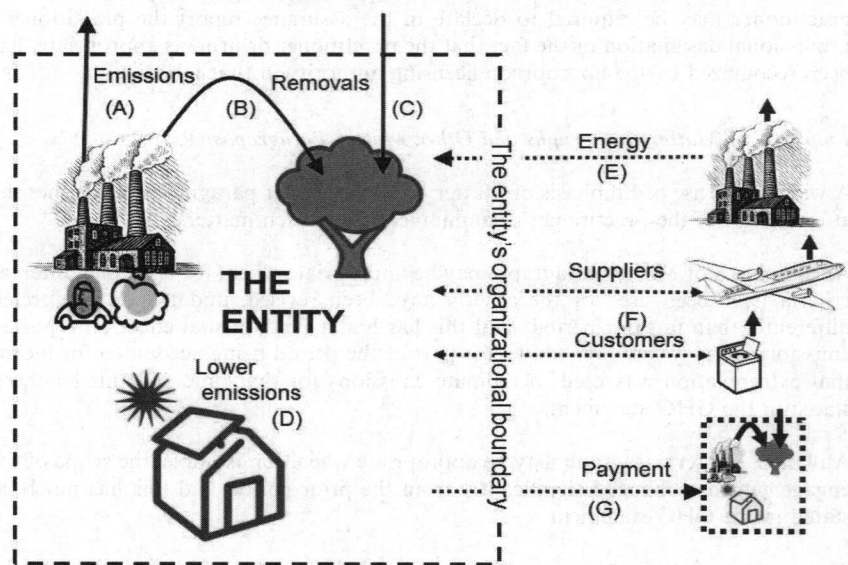

A = Direct, or Scope 1, emissions (see paragraph A8).

B = Removals (emissions that are generated within the entity's boundary but captured and stored within that boundary rather than released into the atmosphere. They are commonly accounted for on a gross basis, that is, as a Scope 1 emission and a removal) (see paragraph A14).

C = Removals (GHGs the entity has removed from the atmosphere) (see paragraph A14).

D = Actions the entity takes to lower its emissions. Such actions might reduce Scope 1 emissions (for example, using more fuel efficient vehicles), Scope 2 emissions (for example, installing solar panels to reduce the quantity of purchased electricity), or Scope 3 emissions (for example, reducing business travel or selling products that require less energy to use). The entity might discuss such actions in the explanatory notes to the GHG statement, but they only affect the quantification of emissions on the face of the entity's GHG statement to the extent that reported emissions are lower than they would otherwise be or they constitute an emissions deduction in accordance with the applicable criteria (see paragraph A11).

E = Scope 2 emissions (see paragraph A9).

F = Scope 3 emissions (see paragraph A10).

G = Emissions deductions, including purchased offsets (see paragraphs A11–A13).

Appendix 2 (Ref: Para. A134)

Illustrations of Assurance Reports on GHG Statements

Illustration 1:

Circumstances include the following:

- **Reasonable assurance engagement.**

- **The entity's GHG statement contains no Scope 3 emissions.**

- **The entity's GHG statement contains no emissions deductions.**

- **The GHG statement contains no comparative information.**

The following illustrative report is for guidance only and is not intended to be exhaustive or applicable to all situations.

INDEPENDENT PRACTITIONER'S REASONABLE ASSURANCE REPORT ON ABC'S GREENHOUSE GAS (GHG) STATEMENT

[Appropriate Addressee]

Report on GHG Statement (*this heading is not needed if this is the only section*)

We have undertaken a reasonable assurance engagement of the accompanying GHG statement of ABC for the year ended December 31, 20X1, comprising the Emissions Inventory and the Explanatory Notes on pages xx–yy. [This engagement was conducted by a multidisciplinary team including assurance practitioners, engineers and environmental scientists.][26]

ABC's Responsibility for the GHG Statement

ABC is responsible for the preparation of the GHG statement in accordance with [*applicable criteria*[27]], applied as explained in Note 1 to the GHG statement. This responsibility includes the design, implementation and maintenance of internal control relevant to the preparation of a GHG statement that is free from material misstatement, whether due to fraud or error.

---

[26] *The sentence should be deleted if it is not applicable to the engagement (for example, if the engagement was to report only on Scope 2 emissions and no other experts were used).*

[27] *[Applicable criteria]* are available for free download from www.######.org.

[As discussed in Note 1 to the GHG statement,][28] GHG quantification is subject to inherent uncertainty because of incomplete scientific knowledge used to determine emissions factors and the values needed to combine emissions of different gases.

Our Independence and Quality Control

We have complied with the *Code of Ethics for Professional Accountants* issued by the International Ethics Standards Board for Accountants, which includes independence and other requirements founded on fundamental principles of integrity, objectivity, professional competence and due care, confidentiality and professional behavior.

In accordance with International Standard on Quality Control 1,[29] *[name of firm]* maintains a comprehensive system of quality control including documented policies and procedures regarding compliance with ethical requirements, professional standards and applicable legal and regulatory requirements.

Our Responsibility

Our responsibility is to express an opinion on the GHG statement based on the evidence we have obtained. We conducted our reasonable assurance engagement in accordance with International Standard on Assurance Engagements 3410, *Assurance Engagements on Greenhouse Gas Statements* ("ISAE 3410"), issued by the International Auditing and Assurance Standards Board. That standard requires that we plan and perform this engagement to obtain reasonable assurance about whether the GHG statement is free from material misstatement.

A reasonable assurance engagement in accordance with ISAE 3410 involves performing procedures to obtain evidence about the quantification of emissions and related information in the GHG statement. The nature, timing and extent of procedures selected depend on the practitioner's judgment, including the assessment of the risks of material misstatement, whether due to fraud or error, in the GHG statement. In making those risk assessments, we considered internal control relevant to ABC's preparation of the GHG statement. A reasonable assurance engagement also includes:

- Assessing the suitability in the circumstances of ABC's use of *[applicable criteria]*, applied as explained in Note 1 to the GHG statement, as the basis for preparing the GHG statement;
- Evaluating the appropriateness of quantification methods and reporting policies used, and the reasonableness of estimates made by ABC; and
- Evaluating the overall presentation of the GHG statement.

We believe that the evidence we have obtained is sufficient and appropriate to provide a basis for our opinion.

Opinion

In our opinion, the GHG statement for the year ended December 31, 20X1 is prepared, in all material respects, in accordance with the *[applicable criteria]* applied as explained in Note 1 to the GHG statement.

---

[28] *Where there is no discussion of the inherent uncertainty in Note 1 to the GHG statement, this should be deleted.*

[29] ISQC 1, Quality Control for Firms that Perform Audits and Reviews of Financial Statements, and Other Assurance and Related Services Engagements.

Report on Other Legal and Regulatory Requirements *(applicable for some engagements only)*

[Form and content of this section of the assurance report will vary depending on the nature of the practitioner's other reporting responsibilities.]

[Practitioner's signature]

[Date of the assurance report]

[Practitioner's address]

Illustration 2:

Circumstances include the following:

- Limited assurance engagement.

- The entity's GHG statement contains no Scope 3 emissions.

- The entity's GHG statement contains no emissions deductions.

- The GHG statement contains no comparative information

The following illustrative report is for guidance only and is not intended to be exhaustive or applicable to all situations.

INDEPENDENT PRACTITIONER'S LIMITED ASSURANCE REPORT ON ABC'S GREENHOUSE GAS (GHG) STATEMENT

[Appropriate Addressee]

Report on GHG Statement (*this heading is not needed if this is the only section*)

We have undertaken a limited assurance engagement of the accompanying GHG statement of ABC for the year ended December 31, 20X1, comprising the Emissions Inventory [and the Explanatory Notes on pages xx–yy]. [This engagement was conducted by a multidisciplinary team including assurance practitioners, engineers and environmental scientists.][30]

ABC's Responsibility for the GHG Statement

ABC is responsible for the preparation of the GHG statement in accordance with [*applicable criteria*[31]], applied as explained in Note 1 to the GHG statement. This responsibility includes the design, implementation and maintenance of internal control relevant to the preparation of a GHG statement that is free from material misstatement, whether due to fraud or error.

[As discussed in Note 1 to the GHG statement,][32] GHG quantification is subject to inherent uncertainty because of incomplete scientific knowledge used to determine emissions factors and the values needed to combine emissions of different gases.

Our Independence and Quality Control

We have complied with the *Code of Ethics for Professional Accountants* issued by the International Ethics Standards Board for Accountants, which includes independence and other requirements founded on fundamental principles of integrity, objectivity, professional competence and due care, confidentiality and professional behavior.

---

[30] *The sentence should be deleted if it is not applicable to the engagement (for example, if the engagement was to report only on Scope 2 emissions and no other experts were used).*

[31] *[Applicable criteria]* are available for free download from www.######.org.

[32] *Where there is no discussion of the inherent uncertainty in Note 1 to the GHG statement, this should be deleted.*

In accordance with International Standard on Quality Control 1,[33] [*name of firm*] maintains a comprehensive system of quality control including documented policies and procedures regarding compliance with ethical requirements, professional standards and applicable legal and regulatory requirements.

Our Responsibility

Our responsibility is to express a limited assurance conclusion on the GHG statement based on the procedures we have performed and the evidence we have obtained. We conducted our limited assurance engagement in accordance with International Standard on Assurance Engagements 3410, *Assurance Engagements on Greenhouse Gas Statements* ("ISAE 3410"), issued by the International Auditing and Assurance Standards Board. That standard requires that we plan and perform this engagement to obtain limited assurance about whether the GHG statement is free from material misstatement.

A limited assurance engagement undertaken in accordance with ISAE 3410 involves assessing the suitability in the circumstances of ABC's use of [applicable criteria] as the basis for the preparation of the GHG statement, assessing the risks of material misstatement of the GHG statement whether due to fraud or error, responding to the assessed risks as necessary in the circumstances, and evaluating the overall presentation of the GHG statement. A limited assurance engagement is substantially less in scope than a reasonable assurance engagement in relation to both the risk assessment procedures, including an understanding of internal control, and the procedures performed in response to the assessed risks.

The procedures we performed were based on our professional judgment and included inquiries, observation of processes performed, inspection of documents, analytical procedures, evaluating the appropriateness of quantification methods and reporting policies, and agreeing or reconciling with underlying records.

> *[[The practitioner may insert a summary of the nature and extent of procedures performed that, in the practitioner's judgment, provides additional information that may be relevant to the users' understanding of the basis for the practitioner's conclusion.[34] The following section has been provided as guidance, and the example procedures are not an exhaustive list of either the type, or extent, of the procedures which may be important for the users' understanding of the work done.][35]*

Given the circumstances of the engagement, in performing the procedures listed above we:

- Through inquiries, obtained an understanding of ABC's control environment and information systems relevant to emissions quantification and reporting, but did not evaluate the design of particular control activities, obtain evidence about their implementation or test their operating effectiveness.
- Evaluated whether ABC's methods for developing estimates are appropriate and had been consistently applied. However, our procedures did not include

---

[33] *ISQC 1*, Quality Control for Firms that Perform Audits and Reviews of Financial Statements, and Other Assurance and Related Services Engagements.

[34] *The procedures are to be summarized but not to the extent that they are ambiguous, nor described in a way that is overstated or embellished or that implies that reasonable assurance has been obtained. It is important that the description of the procedures does not give the impression that an agreed-upon procedures engagement has been undertaken, and in most cases will not detail the entire work plan.*

[35] *In the final report, this explanatory paragraph will be deleted.*

testing the data on which the estimates are based or separately developing our own estimates against which to evaluate ABC's estimates.

- Undertook site visits [at three sites] to assess the completeness of the emissions sources, data collection methods, source data and relevant assumptions applicable to the sites. The sites selected for testing were chosen taking into consideration their emissions in relation to total emissions, emissions sources, and sites selected in prior periods. Our procedures [did/did not] include testing information systems to collect and aggregate facility data, or the controls at these sites.][36]

The procedures performed in a limited assurance engagement vary in nature from, and are less in extent than for, a reasonable assurance engagement. As a result, the level of assurance obtained in a limited assurance engagement is substantially lower than the assurance that would have been obtained had we performed a reasonable assurance engagement. Accordingly, we do not express a reasonable assurance opinion about whether ABC's GHG statement has been prepared, in all material respects, in accordance with the [*applicable criteria*] applied as explained in Note 1 to the GHG statement.

Limited Assurance Conclusion

Based on the procedures we have performed and the evidence we have obtained, nothing has come to our attention that causes us to believe that ABC's GHG statement for the year ended December 31, 20X1 is not prepared, in all material respects, in accordance with the [*applicable criteria*] applied as explained in Note 1 to the GHG statement.

Report on Other Legal and Regulatory Requirements *(applicable for some engagements only)*

[Form and content of this section of the assurance report will vary depending on the nature of the practitioner's other reporting responsibilities.]

[Practitioner's signature]

[Date of the assurance report]

[Practitioner's address]

---

[36] *This section should be deleted if the practitioner concludes that the expanded information on the procedures performed is not needed in the circumstances of the engagement.*

Part Seven

*International Standards on Related Services
(ISRSs)*

International Standard on Related Services 4400

(Previously ISA 920)

Engagements to perform agreed-upon procedures regarding financial information

(This Standard is effective)

Contents

International Standard on Related Services (ISRS) 4400, "Engagements to Perform Agreed-upon Procedures Regarding Financial Information" should be read in the context of the "Preface to the International Standards on Quality Control, Auditing, Review, Other Assurance and Related Services," which sets out the application and authority of ISRSs.

Introduction

1   The purpose of this International Standard on Related Services (ISRS) is to establish standards and provide guidance on the auditor's[1] professional responsibilities when an engagement to perform agreed-upon procedures regarding financial information is undertaken and on the form and content of the report that the auditor issues in connection with such an engagement.

2   This ISRS is directed toward engagements regarding financial information. However, it may provide useful guidance for engagements regarding non-financial information, provided the auditor has adequate knowledge of the subject matter in question and reasonable criteria exist on which to base findings. Guidance in the International Standards on Auditing (ISAs) may be useful to the auditor in applying this ISRS.

3   An engagement to perform agreed-upon procedures may involve the auditor in performing certain procedures concerning individual items of financial data (for example, accounts payable, accounts receivable, purchases from related parties and sales and profits of a segment of an entity), a financial statement (for example, a balance sheet) or even a complete set of financial statements.

Objective of an Agreed-Upon Procedures Engagement

4   **The objective of an agreed-upon procedures engagement is for the auditor to carry out procedures of an audit nature to which the auditor and the entity and any appropriate third parties have agreed and to report on factual findings.**

5   As the auditor simply provides a report of the factual findings of agreed-upon procedures, no assurance is expressed. Instead, users of the report assess for themselves the procedures and findings reported by the auditor and draw their own conclusions from the auditor's work.

6   The report is restricted to those parties that have agreed to the procedures to be performed since others, unaware of the reasons for the procedures, may misinterpret the results.

General Principles of an Agreed-Upon Procedures Engagement

7   **The auditor should comply with the *Code of Ethics for Professional Accountants* issued by the International Federation of Accountants.** Ethical principles governing the auditor's professional responsibilities for this type of engagement are:

(a)   Integrity;
(b)   Objectivity;
(c)   Professional competence and due care;
(d)   Confidentiality;
(e)   Professional behavior; and
(f)   Technical standards.

[1] *The term "auditor" is used throughout the pronouncements of the International Auditing and Assurance Standards Board when describing both audit, review, other assurance and related services that may be performed. Such reference is not intended to imply that a person performing review, other assurance or related services need be the auditor of the entity's financial statements.*

Independence is not a requirement for agreed-upon procedures engagements; however, the terms or objectives of an engagement or national standards may require the auditor to comply with the independence requirements of IFAC's *Code of Ethics for Professional Accountants*. Where the auditor is not independent, a statement to that effect would be made in the report of factual findings.

**The auditor should conduct an agreed-upon procedures engagement in accordance with   8
this ISRS and the terms of the engagement.**

Defining the Terms of the Engagement

**The auditor should ensure with representatives of the entity and, ordinarily, other   9
specified parties who will receive copies of the report of factual findings, that there is a
clear understanding regarding the agreed procedures and the conditions of the
engagement.** Matters to be agreed include the following:

* Nature of the engagement including the fact that the procedures performed will
  not constitute an audit or a review and that accordingly no assurance will be
  expressed.
* Stated purpose for the engagement.
* Identification of the financial information to which the agreed-upon procedures
  will be applied.
* Nature, timing and extent of the specific procedures to be applied.
* Anticipated form of the report of factual findings.
* Limitations on distribution of the report of factual findings. When such limitation would be in conflict with the legal requirements, if any, the auditor would
  not accept the engagement.

In certain circumstances, for example, when the procedures have been agreed to   10
between the regulator, industry representatives and representatives of the accounting
profession, the auditor may not be able to discuss the procedures with all the parties
who will receive the report. In such cases, the auditor may consider, for example,
discussing the procedures to be applied with appropriate representatives of the
parties involved, reviewing relevant correspondence from such parties or sending
them a draft of the type of report that will be issued.

It is in the interests of both the client and the auditor that the auditor sends an   11
engagement letter documenting the key terms of the appointment. An engagement
letter confirms the auditor's acceptance of the appointment and helps avoid misunderstanding regarding such matters as the objectives and scope of the engagement,
the extent of the auditor's responsibilities and the form of reports to be issued.

Matters that would be included in the engagement letter include the following: 12

* A listing of the procedures to be performed as agreed upon between the parties.
* A statement that the distribution of the report of factual findings would be
  restricted to the specified parties who have agreed to the procedures to be
  performed.

In addition, the auditor may consider attaching to the engagement letter a draft of
the type of report of factual findings that will be issued. An example of an engagement letter appears in Appendix 1 to this ISRS.

Planning

13   **The auditor should plan the work so that an effective engagement will be performed.**

Documentation

14   **The auditor should document matters which are important in providing evidence to support the report of factual findings, and evidence that the engagement was carried out in accordance with this ISRS and the terms of the engagement.**

Procedures and Evidence

15   **The auditor should carry out the procedures agreed upon and use the evidence obtained as the basis for the report of factual findings.**

16   The procedures applied in an engagement to perform agreed-upon procedures may include the following:

- Inquiry and analysis.
- Recomputation, comparison and other clerical accuracy checks.
- Observation.
- Inspection.
- Obtaining confirmations.

Appendix 2 to this ISRS is an example report which contains an illustrative list of procedures which may be used as one part of a typical agreed-upon procedures engagement.

Reporting

17   The report on an agreed-upon procedures engagement needs to describe the purpose and the agreed-upon procedures of the engagement in sufficient detail to enable the reader to understand the nature and the extent of the work performed.

18   **The report of factual findings should contain:**

(a)   **Title;**

(b)   **Addressee (ordinarily the client who engaged the auditor to perform the agreed-upon procedures);**

(c)   **Identification of specific financial or non-financial information to which the agreed-upon procedures have been applied;**

(d)   **A statement that the procedures performed were those agreed upon with the recipient;**

(e)   **A statement that the engagement was performed in accordance with the International Standard on Related Services applicable to agreed-upon procedures engagements, or with relevant national standards or practices;**

(f)   **When relevant a statement that the auditor is not independent of the entity;**

(g)   **Identification of the purpose for which the agreed-upon procedures were performed;**

(h)   **A listing of the specific procedures performed;**

(i)   **A description of the auditor's factual findings including sufficient details of errors and exceptions found;**

(j)   Statement that the procedures performed do not constitute either an audit or a review and, as such, no assurance is expressed;

(k)   A statement that had the auditor performed additional procedures, an audit or a review, other matters might have come to light that would have been reported;

(l)   A statement that the report is restricted to those parties that have agreed to the procedures to be performed;

(m) A statement (when applicable) that the report relates only to the elements, accounts, items or financial and non-financial information specified and that it does not extend to the entity's financial statements taken as a whole;

(n)   Date of the report;

(o)   Auditor's address; and

(p)   Auditor's signature.

Appendix 2 to this ISRS contains an example of a report of factual findings issued in connection with an engagement to perform agreed-upon procedures regarding financial information.

Public Sector Perspective

1.   *The report in a public sector engagement may not be restricted only to those parties that have agreed to the procedures to be performed, but made available also to a wider range of entities or people (for example, a parliamentary investigation about a specific public entity or governmental department).*

2.   *It also has to be noted that public sector mandates vary significantly and caution has to be taken to distinguish engagements that are truly "agreed-upon procedures" from engagements that are expected to be audits of financial information, such as performance reports.*

Appendix 1

Example of an Engagement Letter for an Agreed-Upon Procedures Engagement

The following letter is for use as a guide in conjunction with paragraph 9 of this ISRS and is not intended to be a standard letter. The engagement letter will need to be varied according to individual requirements and circumstances.

To the Board of Directors or other appropriate representatives of the client who engaged the auditor

This letter is to confirm our understanding of the terms and objectives of our engagement and the nature and limitations of the services that we will provide. Our engagement will be conducted in accordance with the International Standard on Related Services (or refer to relevant national standards or practices) applicable to agreed-upon procedures engagements and we will indicate so in our report.

We have agreed to perform the following procedures and report to you the factual findings resulting from our work:

(Describe the nature, timing and extent of the procedures to be performed, including specific reference, where applicable, to the identity of documents and records to be read, individuals to be contacted and parties from whom confirmations will be obtained.)

The procedures that we will perform are solely to assist you in (state purpose). Our report is not to be used for any other purpose and is solely for your information.

The procedures that we will perform will not constitute an audit or a review made in accordance with International Standards on Auditing or International Standards on Review Engagements (or refer to relevant national standards or practices) and, consequently, no assurance will be expressed.

We look forward to full cooperation with your staff and we trust that they will make available to us whatever records, documentation and other information requested in connection with our engagement.

Our fees, which will be billed as work progresses, are based on the time required by the individuals assigned to the engagement plus out-of-pocket expenses. Individual hourly rates vary according to the degree of responsibility involved and the experience and skill required.

Please sign and return the attached copy of this letter to indicate that it is in accordance with your understanding of the terms of the engagement including the specific procedures which we have agreed will be performed.

XYZ & Co

Acknowledged on behalf of ABC Company by

(signed)

Name and Title

Date

Appendix 2

Example of a Report of Factual Findings in Connection with Accounts Payable

REPORT OF FACTUAL FINDINGS

To (those who engaged the auditor)

We have performed the procedures agreed with you and enumerated below with respect to the accounts payable of ABC Company as at (date), set forth in the accompanying schedules (not shown in this example). Our engagement was undertaken in accordance with the International Standard on Related Services (or refer to relevant national standards or practices) applicable to agreed-upon procedures engagements. The procedures were performed solely to assist you in evaluating the validity of the accounts payable and are summarized as follows:

1. We obtained and checked the addition of the trial balance of accounts payable as at (date) prepared by ABC Company, and we compared the total to the balance in the related general ledger account.

2.   We compared the attached list (not shown in this example) of major suppliers and the amounts owing at (date) to the related names and amounts in the trial balance.

3.   We obtained suppliers' statements or requested suppliers to confirm balances owing at (date).

4.   We compared such statements or confirmations to the amounts referred to in 2. For amounts which did not agree, we obtained reconciliations from ABC Company. For reconciliations obtained, we identified and listed outstanding invoices, credit notes and outstanding checks, each of which was greater than xxx. We located and examined such invoices and credit notes subsequently received and checks subsequently paid and we ascertained that they should in fact have been listed as outstanding on the reconciliations.

We report our findings below:

(a)   With respect to item 1 we found the addition to be correct and the total amount to be in agreement.

(b)   With respect to item 2 we found the amounts compared to be in agreement.

(c)   With respect to item 3 we found there were suppliers' statements for all such suppliers.

(d)   With respect to item 4 we found the amounts agreed, or with respect to amounts which did not agree, we found ABC Company had prepared reconciliations and that the credit notes, invoices and outstanding checks over xxx were appropriately listed as reconciling items with the following exceptions:
(Detail the exceptions)

Because the above procedures do not constitute either an audit or a review made in accordance with International Standards on Auditing or International Standards on Review Engagements (or relevant national standards or practices), we do not express any assurance on the accounts payable as of (date).

Had we performed additional procedures or had we performed an audit or review of the financial statements in accordance with International Standards on Auditing or International Standards on Review Engagements (or relevant national standards or practices), other matters might have come to our attention that would have been reported to you.

Our report is solely for the purpose set forth in the first paragraph of this report and for your information and is not to be used for any other purpose or to be distributed to any other parties. This report relates only to the accounts and items specified above and does not extend to any financial statements of ABC Company, taken as a whole.

AUDITOR

Date
Address

International Standard on Related Services 4410 (Revised March 2012) Compilation Engagements

Basis for Conclusions

This Basis for Conclusions has been prepared by staff of the International Auditing and Assurance Standards Board (IAASB). It relates to, but does not form part of, International Standard on Related Services (ISRS) 4410 (Revised), *Compilation Engagements*, which was approved by the IAASB in December 2011, with the affirmative votes of 18 out of the 18 IAASB members.[1]

Background

1   The IAASB commenced the project to revise the extant ISRS 4410[2] in March 2009. This project was part of IAASB's strategic focus to explore standards for a range of services that are capable of meeting the unique needs of small- and medium-sized entities (SMEs), and the users of their financial information. In taking this initiative, the IAASB recognized the market demand for services, other than the financial statement audit, relevant to enhancing the credibility of the financial information of SMEs. This demand has been particularly apparent in jurisdictions where recent changes to law and regulation have resulted in a significant proportion of corporate entities no longer being required to have their financial statements subject to audit.

2   In undertaking the revision of extant ISRS 4410, the IAASB acknowledged the importance of compilation engagements for SMEs, both within jurisdictions where compilation engagements are already commonplace and those where use of these engagements is relatively new. It also was recognized that, in some jurisdictions, there may be existing types of services performed by professional accountants that, in some respects, are similar to the compilation engagement as described in the international standards, but that also differ in key areas.

3   An important consideration of the project has therefore been to make clear the key distinguishing features of a compilation engagement performed in accordance with ISRS 4410 (Revised), and the value of the engagement in enhancing the usefulness of an entity's financial information. Through the revision of this standard, the IAASB aims to help practitioners performing compilation engagements around the world converge to the use of a globally accepted benchmark for such engagements.

4   In October 2010, the IAASB exposed proposed revised ISRS 4410 (ED-4410). The comment period closed on March 31, 2011, with 49 comment letters from various respondents, including regulators and oversight authorities, national standard setters, IFAC member bodies and other professional bodies, firms and individuals. This Basis for Conclusions explains the more significant issues raised by respondents to the ED, and how the IAASB has addressed them.

---

[1] *See minutes of the December 5–9, 2011 IAASB meeting at www.ifac.org/auditing-assurance/meetings/los-angeles-california under the heading "Minutes."*

[2] *ISRS 4410*, Engagements to Compile Financial Statements.

The IAASB has discussed this project with its Consultative Advisory Group (CAG)   **5**
on six separate occasions.

Use and Applicability of the Standard

ED-4410 proposed that the standard be applicable when the practitioner is engaged   **6**
to compile historical financial information *and* provide a report for the engagement
in accordance with ISRS 4410. Accordingly, when a practitioner is engaged only to
compile financial information without providing a report in accordance with ISRS
4410 (Revised), the practitioner does not assert compliance with ISRS 4410
(Revised).

The majority of respondents to ED-4410 who expressly commented on this issue   **7**
agreed with this proposed scope. Several respondents, however, disagreed. Among
the respondents who disagreed, some were of the view that reporting should be
addressed only within the requirements of the standard, and should not be specified
as a part of the scope of the ISRS. The concern noted was that this formulation of
the scope of the standard could enable practitioners to opt out of using the ISRS by
merely agreeing to undertake an engagement to compile financial information
without providing the required report.

IAASB Decisions

The IAASB reaffirmed its view that ISRS 4410 (Revised) should address compilation   **8**
engagements that involve the issuance of a report on the engagement in accordance
with the ISRS, and that the matter of reporting should be explicitly acknowledged in
the scope of the standard. (See paragraph 1 of ISRS 4410 (Revised).)

The IAASB recognized that there are types of services performed by professional   **9**
accountants that, in some respects, are similar to the compilation engagement as
described in the international standards, but that also differ in some areas. One such
area is the need to report to users of the information on the nature of the engagement
performed. The IAASB believes that by specifying reporting as part of the scope of
the engagement, practitioners and others will be better able to determine whether
ISRS 4410 (Revised) applies in the circumstances. The IAASB is of the view that a
practitioner that performs an engagement in accordance with ISRS 4410 (Revised)
needs to communicate in a written report the nature of the practitioner's involvement
with the entity's financial information, and therefore the practitioner's association
with the compiled financial information.

The IAASB acknowledged that it cannot mandate application of the ISRS across all   **10**
types of compilation engagements. Mandatory application of the ISRS, however,
may be specified in jurisdictions for engagements where practitioners undertake
services relevant to the preparation and presentation of an entity's financial information. If mandatory application is not specified, by law, regulation, professional
standards or otherwise, the practitioner may nevertheless conclude that applying the
ISRS is appropriate in the circumstances. In finalizing ISRS 4410 (Revised), the
IAASB concluded that it is important to state, within the introductory section of the
ISRS, factors that indicate that it may be appropriate to apply the ISRS, including
reporting in accordance with the standard. These factors include whether:

- The financial information is required under provisions of applicable law or
  regulation, and whether it is required to be publicly filed.

- External parties other than the intended users of the compiled financial information are likely to associate the practitioner with the financial information, and there is a risk that the level of the practitioner's involvement with the information may be misunderstood, for example:
  - ○ If the financial information is intended for use by parties other than management or those charged with governance, or may be provided to, or obtained by, parties who are not the intended users of the information; and
  - ○ If the practitioner's name is identified with the financial information.

(See paragraph 3 of ISRS 4410 (Revised).)

Use of Technical Terms in ISRS 4410 (Revised)

The "Applicable Financial Reporting Framework"

11   ED-4410 focused the compilation engagement performed under ISRS 4410 (Revised) on assisting management with the preparation and presentation of financial information in accordance with an applicable financial reporting framework. In undertaking such engagements the practitioner contributes expertise in accounting and financial reporting, and in particular the practitioner's knowledge and understanding of the application of financial reporting frameworks for different financial reporting purposes.

12   A few respondents expressed the view that the term "applicable financial reporting framework" as used in ED-4410 could be interpreted as implying use of established financial reporting frameworks only, to the exclusion of other types of financial reporting frameworks. This was notwithstanding that ED-4410 also contained guidance explaining that the term is intended to encompass the full range of possible frameworks that can be used for financial reporting purposes (i.e., in the context of financial information prepared for either general or special purposes). Some respondents raised concerns that the intended meaning of the term was not sufficiently explained in ED-4410, and that the standard could be further enhanced through clearer guidance, including in relation to the particular circumstance where financial information is prepared for a special purpose.

IAASB Decisions

13   The IAASB reaffirmed its decision to use the term "applicable financial reporting framework" throughout the requirements and guidance of ISRS 4410 (Revised). The term is intended to be read in its most generic sense, recognizing that there is a wide variety of frameworks that can potentially be used, ranging from established financial reporting frameworks to frameworks developed on a customized basis to address the specific financial reporting needs of particular entities or types of entities. The term is defined in the IAASB's *Glossary of Terms* and is commonly understood by professional accountants using IAASB standards. The IAASB believes that introducing new terminology specific to ISRS 4410 would introduce unnecessary complexity in the standard.

14   However, the IAASB recognized that smaller entities typically use financial reporting frameworks that are less formal and that are often customized to their particular business reporting needs. These needs often reflect a variety of reporting situations for different types of users.(See paragraph 10 of ISRS 4410 (Revised).)

To make this clear, the IAASB agreed to amend ED-4410 to include in the standard, where appropriate, a reference to the alternative term "basis of accounting" , as a way to facilitate practitioners' understanding and interpretation of the requirements and guidance in ISRS 4410 (Revised). (See paragraph A16 and Appendix 2, Illustrative Reports 3–5, of ISRS 4410 (Revised).)

15

The Terms "Material Misstatement" and "Materially Misstated"

ED-4410 used the terms "material misstatement" and "materially misstated" in the requirements and guidance of the proposed standard for purposes of explaining the practitioner's responsibilities and required actions in the engagement. These requirements and guidance were focused on enabling the practitioner to comply with relevant ethical requirements, particularly in relation to the ethical principle of integrity, as explained in the International Ethics Standards Board for Accountants' *Code of Ethics for Professional Accountants* (the IESBA Code).

16

Some respondents expressed the view that use of this term would blur the distinction between a compilation engagement and an assurance engagement, because it would imply responsibilities for the practitioner, and associated work effort, that would not be applicable to a compilation engagement.

17

Several respondents also requested that ISRS 4410 include application guidance to guide practitioners on forming an assessment of materiality as relevant to performing the compilation engagement.

18

IAASB Decisions

The IAASB reaffirmed its decision to use the terms "material misstatement" and "materially misstated" within the requirements and guidance of ISRS 4410 (Revised), including in relation to the practitioner's compliance with relevant ethical obligations.

19

The IAASB took the view that, as "misstatement" is a term that practitioners are already very familiar with, ISRS 4410 (Revised) could be further enhanced by explaining the term's particular relevance in a compilation engagement, that is, in the context of the practitioner's ethical obligations under the IESBA Code, for example in respect of being knowingly associated with information that is materially false or misleading.

20

Therefore, to further enhance the clarity and understandability of the standard for practitioners, the IAASB decided to include a definition of the term "misstatement" within ISRS 4410 (Revised), aligned with the definition in the *Glossary of Terms* but adapted to the context of a compilation engagement. (See paragraph 17(e) of ISRS 4410 (Revised).)

21

In addition, the IAASB decided to include explanations about the concept of materiality within ISRS 4410 (Revised), to guide the practitioner's consideration of the need to take further action(s) in relation to the compiled financial information, for example, requesting management to amend the compiled financial information if necessary. (See paragraph 34 of ISRS 4410 (Revised).)

22

Practitioner's Responsibilities—The Applicable Financial Reporting Framework

23   ED-4410 was premised on the condition that the management of an entity is responsible for adopting a financial reporting framework for the preparation and presentation of the entity's financial information that is acceptable in view of the intended use of the financial information, and the needs of the intended users (as reflected also in the definition of the term "applicable financial reporting framework").

24   Further, ED-4410 recognized that, given the practitioner's expertise and in view of the practitioner's ethical obligations described above, the practitioner may provide assistance to management with identification of a financial reporting framework that is acceptable, including in the case where it becomes apparent to the practitioner in the course of performing the compilation engagement that the framework adopted by management is not acceptable in the context described above.

25   Several respondents believed that the requirements and guidance of ED-4410 regarding the practitioner's responsibilities for assisting management in these areas were unclear, and could be more simply stated in the ISRS. These respondents also pointed to the risk that these requirements could be seen as implying greater responsibility on the practitioner than is intended for a compilation engagement.

26   Several respondents also expressed a general concern that the requirements and guidance need to be as clear as possible that the practitioner's responsibilities in performing the compilation engagement are always framed in the context of assisting management with the preparation and presentation of an entity's financial information.

IAASB Decisions

27   The IAASB agreed that ISRS 4410 (Revised) could be enhanced by simplifying the requirements and guidance in respect of the practitioner's responsibilities. The IAASB determined that, to enhance the clarity and understandability of the standard, the context for the requirements should be clearly linked to achieving the practitioner's objectives for the engagement, including complying with relevant ethical requirements.

28   The IAASB accordingly included clearer explanations about the nature of the engagement in the introductory section of the standard, as context for the statement of the practitioner's objectives in a compilation engagement and the requirements of the ISRS designed to achieve those objectives. (See paragraphs 5 and 7 of ISRS 4410 (Revised)).

29   The IAASB also determined that a high-level explanation about the use of financial reporting frameworks in different financial reporting contexts, as part of management's responsibility for preparing the entity's financial information, would enhance understanding of the practitioner' responsibilities in a compilation engagement. Accordingly, the IAASB amended ED-4410 by moving such explanations from the application material into the introductory section of the standard. (See paragraph 10 of ISRS 4410 (Revised)).

30   To address the concern that there could be misunderstanding regarding the practitioner's responsibilities where the practitioner provides assistance to management with the identification of an acceptable financial reporting framework, the IAASB determined that the guidance for practitioners on proposing changes to the applicable financial reporting framework in the course of a compilation engagement should be deleted. The IAASB believes the practitioner's responsibility to comply with relevant ethical requirements would adequately guide the practitioner in that circumstance. (See paragraph 21 of ISRS 4410 (Revised).)

Practitioner's Responsibilities—Intentional Departures from the Applicable Financial Reporting Framework

ED-4410 included a requirement for the practitioner to withdraw from the compilation engagement if the compiled financial information contained departures from the applicable financial framework that the practitioner believed rendered the compiled information materially misstated or misleading, and management did not agree to amend the compiled financial information. This requirement was expressly supported by the majority of the respondents. **31**

However several respondents disagreed with the requirement. A few of these respondents believed the practitioner should be required to disclose intentional departures from the applicable financial reporting framework described in the compiled financial information, for the benefit of readers of the practitioner's report. Some other respondents were of the view that the practitioner should be permitted to include disclosure of such departures when the practitioner experiences a disagreement with management on the preparation and presentation of the compiled financial information in accordance with the applicable financial reporting framework and management refuses to amend the compiled financial information, as would be the case in an assurance engagement where qualification is possible. **32**

In contrast, some respondents who agreed with the requirement in ED-4410 expressly disagreed that the practitioner's report can be used for the purpose of disclosing such departures, or otherwise to draw them to the attention of readers of the report. These respondents cautioned against the risk that such disclosures by the practitioner could be misunderstood by readers, and be taken as a form of expression of an opinion or conclusion on the compiled financial information. Respondents were also concerned that the ISRS should not include provisions that could lead to the development of an expectations gap among users with respect to financial information compiled by practitioners under ISRS 4410 (Revised). **33**

IAASB Decisions

The IAASB reaffirmed its view that the practitioner, on becoming aware of circumstances that suggest that the compiled financial information is materially misstated or otherwise misleading (including in respect of disclosure of the applicable financial reporting framework actually applied to prepare and present the compiled financial information), should be required to request appropriate amendments to the compiled financial information, or withdraw from the engagement if management refuses to amend the information. (See paragraphs 35-36 of ISRS 4410 (Revised).) **34**

As to respondents who believed the practitioner's report could be used to make disclosures concerning the compiled financial information itself, the IAASB determined that ISRS 4410 (Revised) could be further strengthened in respect of communicating the purpose of the practitioner's report in a compilation engagement. Accordingly, to provide further context for the reporting requirements of the standard, the IAASB amended ED-4410 to expressly state that the practitioner's report is **35** not a vehicle to express an opinion or conclusion on the financial information in any form. (See paragraph 39 of ISRS 4410 (Revised).)

36   [Moved from below, redrafted] In view of the practice sometimes followed of using an established financial reporting framework with certain modifications, the IAASB determined that it is important to direct the practitioner's attention to the adequate disclosure of the applicable financial reporting framework in the compiled financial information. This would include situations where management elects to use an established framework with modifications, or when there are intentional departures from an established framework that are not disclosed within the compiled financial information itself. Accordingly, the IAASB has amended ED-4410 to emphasize that the description of the applicable financial reporting framework actually applied should be adequately referred to or described in the compiled financial information itself, and should not be otherwise misleading to the intended users of the financial information. (See paragraph 34 of ISRS 4410 (Revised)).

37   Further, the IAASB has clarified the requirements of the standard regarding actions the practitioner is required to take, and related considerations, if the practitioner becomes aware of material misstatements in the compiled financial information., This includes misstatements arising from intentional departures from the applicable financial reporting framework that are not adequately disclosed in the compiled financial information itself, on a transparent basis, for the benefit of users of the information. (See paragraph 34 of ISRS 4410 (Revised).)

Work Effort in Relation to Significant Judgments

38   ED-4410 proposed requiring the practitioner to discuss and agree with management significant judgments necessary to compile the financial information including, where applicable, the basis for significant accounting estimates and use of the going concern assumption.

39   Some respondents identified this requirement as an example of a type of procedure that could be misconstrued as one that is performed to gather evidence for the purpose of expressing an opinion or conclusion on the compiled financial information. These respondents expressed the concern that the requirement could be read as implying that the practitioner has obtained a level of understanding and assurance beyond that which is required for purposes of the compilation engagement. They pointed out the need to amend this requirement to avoid blurring the distinction between a compilation engagement and an assurance engagement.

40   In contrast, a respondent emphasized the importance of the practitioner devoting appropriate attention to significant judgments, particularly if the practitioner assists management in developing significant judgments required under the applicable financial reporting framework. It was argued that this would be particularly important as, in the case of many smaller entities, management may not be sufficiently knowledgeable about accounting or financial reporting matters to be able to make the necessary judgments without the practitioner's assistance and expertise.

41   Some respondents also pointed to the wider risk that, in assisting management, the practitioner may be perceived as having implicitly taken responsibility for judgments that are the responsibility of management. Some of these respondents suggested that, in order to address this, ED-4410 should require the practitioner to obtain management's acknowledgement of its responsibility for the final version of the compiled financial information.

IAASB Decisions

The IAASB reaffirmed its view that ISRS 4410 (Revised) should direct the practi-   **42**
tioner to devote appropriate attention to discussion with management, or those
charged with governance as appropriate, regarding significant judgments required to
compile the financial information in accordance with the applicable financial
reporting framework. However, the IAASB concluded that this requirement should
focus on the situation where the practitioner has provided assistance to management
in relation to making those judgments, in the course of compiling the financial
information. Doing so helps to focus the practitioner's work effort appropriately in
line with the practitioner's role in a compilation engagement, that is, to provide
assistance to management as opposed to gathering evidence for the purpose of
expressing an opinion or conclusion. (See paragraph 30 of ISRS 4410 (Revised).)

Further, in relation to respondents' comments on the risk that the practitioner could   **43**
be perceived as having taken responsibility for judgments that are management's
responsibility, the IAASB amended ED-4410 by explaining that when the compilation engagement involves assisting management in key areas affecting the
preparation and presentation of the entity's financial information, such assistance is
always provided on the basis that management understands, and accepts responsibility for, the significant judgments reflected in the compiled financial information.
(See paragraph A22 of ISRS 4410 (Revised).)

The IAASB also accepted respondents' suggestion that the standard could be further   **44**
enhanced by requiring the practitioner to obtain an acknowledgement from management or those charged with governance, as appropriate, that they have taken
responsibility for the final version of the compiled financial information including the
significant judgments reflected therein. The IAASB believes that requirement would
serve not only to emphasize management's responsibility for the compiled financial
information as finalized, including significant judgments reflected therein, but would
also clarify the completion of the compilation engagement by the practitioner. (See
paragraph 37 of ISRS 4410 (Revised).)

The Practitioner's Report—Illustrative Reports

ED-4410 proposed requirements addressing the elements of the practitioner's report,   **45**
and included several illustrative reports. The IAASB's objective in establishing these
reporting requirements was, among other things, to clearly distinguish the compilation engagement performed under ISRS 4410 (Revised) from an assurance
engagement, as a matter of public interest.

Broadly, the majority of respondents who commented on the proposed reporting   **46**
requirements and illustrative reports were of the view that these were clear and
appropriate. Many respondents, however, felt that the illustrative reports could
better distinguish the compilation engagement from other reporting engagements,
citing concerns in the following areas:

- The general appearance of the practitioner's report because of some similarities
  with an assurance report.
- The description of the engagement, including limitations.
- With respect to the circumstances when the compiled financial information is
  prepared for a special purpose, the use of an "alert to reader" sub-title in the
  practitioner's report. However it was noted that this alert could potentially be
  viewed by readers of the report as the practitioner expressing a form of opinion
  or conclusion on the compiled financial information.

IAASB Decisions

47 The IAASB determined that the primary consideration is a clear expression of the purpose of the practitioner's report in a compilation engagement. The IAASB concluded that ISRS 4410 (Revised) could be further strengthened in this regard. Accordingly, the IAASB introduced material within the requirements in the ISRS explaining that an important purpose of the practitioner's report is to clearly communicate the nature of the compilation engagement and the practitioner's role and responsibilities in the engagement. Importantly, the IAASB also clarified that the practitioner's report is not a vehicle to express an opinion or conclusion on the financial information in any form. (See paragraph 39 of ISRS 4410 (Revised).)

48 The IAASB agreed with respondents' view that the description of the compilation engagement could be further enhanced, in order to better explain the nature of the engagement for readers of the report. Accordingly, the IAASB modified the illustrative report to include a paragraph that more concisely describes the practitioner's involvement and also more clearly highlights the value contributed by the practitioner – an essential feature to distinguish the compilation engagement from other types of engagements, including assurance engagements. The illustrative practitioner's report now states that the practitioner has applied the practitioner's expertise in accounting and financial reporting to assist management in the preparation and presentation of the compiled financial information, and has complied with relevant ethical requirements, including principles of integrity, objectivity, professional competence and due care.

49 Similarly, the IAASB has included in a single paragraph in the illustrative practitioner's report the statements that address the limitations of the engagement. Further, it has redrafted the required statements by the practitioner to reduce the use of technical wording that may not be fully understood by the reader of the practitioner's report. This paragraph now states that since a compilation engagement is not an assurance engagement, the practitioner is not required to verify the accuracy or completeness of the information that management has provided to the practitioner to compile the financial information and, accordingly, the practitioner does not express an audit opinion or a review conclusion on whether the financial information is prepared in accordance with [the applicable financial reporting framework].

50 The IAASB agreed that while the purpose of the practitioner's report in a compilation engagement is different from that of a report issued in an assurance engagement, the visual appearance of the practitioner's report in a compilation engagement unavoidably bears a resemblance to the report issued for an assurance engagement. This is because there are some required reporting elements that are common to both types of engagements. Nevertheless, the IAASB agreed to amend the reporting requirements of ISRS 4410 (Revised), and the related guidance, to remove the impression that the practitioner is required to:

- Apply a specific sequencing in the report when presenting the required reporting elements, or
- Use headings to structure the content of the report (as is done in an assurance report, where the clear identification of the practitioner's opinion or conclusion is a key consideration in the presentation of the report).

Quality Control in a Compilation Engagement

ED-4410 included requirements pertaining to engagement level quality control on   **51**
the explicit premise that a firm providing compilation engagements under the standard is required to apply ISQC 1[3] or requirements that are at least as demanding.

Many respondents to ED-4410 supported this premise and noted that it would not   **52**
create implementation difficulties at a national level. Many respondents, however,
disagreed with the inclusion of this premise. Several of the respondents who disagreed cited perceived implementation difficulties surrounding ISQC 1 for firms
undertaking compilation engagements. It was noted in particular that the premise
will not hold in all cases, since ISQC 1 has not been adopted in all jurisdictions for
the purpose of related services engagements, including compilation engagements. A
few of these respondents believed that ISRS 4410 (Revised) should instead include,
as requirements, all the engagement level quality controls that are considered
necessary to achieve quality in individual compilation engagements, without reference to ISQC 1.

Several respondents further noted there may be difficulty in complying with ISQC 1   **53**
because some requirements of ISQC 1 are perceived as being too onerous for smaller
firms, or would require further interpretation for application to compilation
engagements. These respondents suggested that development of implementation
guidance that will assist smaller firms undertaking compilation engagements in
applying ISQC 1 would be helpful.

IAASB Decision

The IAASB concluded that reference to ISQC 1, or requirements that are at least as   **54**
demanding, should be retained as the premise underlying the provisions of ISRS
4410 (Revised) regarding quality control at the level of individual compilation
engagements. (See paragraph 4 of ISRS 4410 (Revised)).

The IAASB determined that it would not be in the public interest to exclude compilation engagements, or other related services, from relevant requirements directed   **55**
at quality control at the firm level, nor to limit the application of ISQC 1 thereto.
Firm-level quality control positively influences engagement level quality control, and
it would therefore be inappropriate to exclude consideration of the former. The
IAASB also noted that the premise is also sufficiently flexible to accommodate jurisdictions that have not adopted ISQC 1.

The IAASB considered, but did not support, the option of adding all quality control   **56**
provisions within the standard itself. To do so would add considerably to the length
of the ISRS while disproportionately affecting the overall balance of the requirements and guidance. This was seen as an outcome contrary to respondents' general
support for the development of an engagement standard for compilation engagements that is as concise and streamlined as possible.

The IAASB believed that if implementation of ISQC 1 by smaller firms needs to be   **57**
further addressed, it is preferable to address this through other appropriate means.
In this regard, the IAASB agreed to explore, as part of its *Strategy and Work
Program, 2012-2014*, the development of implementation support materials aimed at
promoting the proportionate implementation of ISQC 1 by smaller firms. It is

---

[3] *ISQC 1,* Quality Control for Firms that Perform Audits and Reviews of Financial Statements, and Other
Assurance and Related Services Engagements.

envisioned that such material would include guidance relevant to firms undertaking compilation engagements.

Relevant Ethical Requirements—Independence in a Compilation Engagement

58   ED-4410 proposed requiring the practitioner to comply with relevant ethical requirements as they relate to compilation engagements, and for the practitioner's report to include a description of the practitioner's responsibilities in compiling the financial information, including that the engagement was performed in accordance with relevant ethical requirements.

59   Several respondents to ED-4410 commented on the importance of the practitioner's communications with users of the compiled information in the area of independence, through the practitioner's report. Some of these respondents noted that ED-4410 did not include the requirements and guidance in extant ISRS 4410 stating that independence is not a requirement for a compilation engagement, and which require that, when relevant, if the practitioner is not independent, a statement to that effect be made in the practitioner's report.[4] These respondents believed that this material should be retained in ISRS 4410 (Revised), because information about the practitioner's independence is considered important for the users of the compiled financial information.

IAASB Decisions

60   The IAASB concluded that ISRS 4410 (Revised) should continue to require the practitioner to comply with relevant ethical requirements, and for the practitioner's report to describe the practitioner's responsibilities in compiling the financial information, including that the engagement was performed in accordance with relevant ethical requirements.

61   The IAASB also reaffirmed its view that it is not appropriate to retain the requirement in extant ISRS 4410 pertaining to a statement in the practitioner's report regarding independence. The IAASB is of the view that the practitioner implementing ISRS 4410 (Revised) would need to be guided as to the meaning of independence in the context of a compilation engagement in order to be able to comply with such a reporting requirement. The IAASB notes that the IESBA Code is silent with respect to the concept of independence in relation to a compilation engagement, as are some national standards. In light of this, the IAASB questioned how meaningful a reporting requirement would be in an international context.

62   Nevertheless, the IAASB included application material within ISRS 4410 to draw practitioners' attention to the fact that national ethical codes or laws or regulations may specify requirements or disclosure rules pertaining to independence (see paragraph A21 of ISRS 4410 (Revised)). The IAASB recognizes that in adopting ISRS 4410 (Revised) at national-level, the authorized national standard-setting body of a jurisdiction may elect to include further requirements or application material aimed at addressing this area if that is viewed as important in the national context.

---

[4] *Extant ISRS 4410, paragraph 5 read with paragraph 18(d).*

Part Eight

Quality Control

International Standard on Quality Control (UK) 1 (Revised June 2016) (Updated July 2017)

Quality control for firms that perform audits and reviews of financial statements, and other assurance and related services engagements

(Effective for engagements relating to financial periods commencing on or after 17 June 2016)[0]

Contents

International Standard on Quality Control (UK) (ISQC (UK)) 1 (Revised June 2016), *Quality Control for Firms that Perform Audits and Reviews of Financial Statements, and Other Assurance and Related Services Engagements*, should be read in conjunction with ISA (UK) 200 (Revised June 2016), *Overall Objectives of the Independent Auditor and the Conduct of an Audit in Accordance with International Standards on Auditing (UK)*.

[0] Conforming amendments to this standard as a result of ISA (UK) 250 (Revised July 2017), Section A— Consideration of Laws and Regulations in an Audit of Financial Statements, are included that are effective for audits of financial statements for periods commencing on or after 15 December 2017. Details of the amendments are given in the Annexure to ISA (UK) 250 (Revised December 2017) Section A.

Introduction

Scope of this ISQC (UK)

1   This International Standard on Quality Control (UK) (ISQC (UK)) deals with a firm's responsibilities for its system of quality control for audits and reviews of financial statements, and other assurance and related services engagements. This ISQC (UK) is to be read in conjunction with relevant ethical requirements.

1-1   In the UK, ISQC (UK) 1 (Revised June 2016) applies to firms that perform audits of financial statements and other public interest assurance engagements.[1a]

2   Other pronouncements of the International Auditing and Assurance Standards Board (IAASB) set out additional standards and guidance on the responsibilities of firm personnel regarding quality control procedures for specific types of engagements. ISA (UK) 220 (Revised June 2016),[1] for example, deals with quality control procedures for audits of financial statements.

3   A system of quality control consists of policies designed to achieve the objective set out in paragraph 11 and the procedures necessary to implement and monitor compliance with those policies.

Authority of this ISQC (UK)

4   This ISQC (UK) applies to all firms of professional accountants in respect of audits and reviews of financial statements, and other assurance and related services engagements. The nature and extent of the policies and procedures developed by an individual firm to comply with this ISQC (UK) will depend on various factors such as the size and operating characteristics of the firm, and whether it is part of a network.

5   This ISQC (UK) contains the objective of the firm in following the ISQC (UK), and requirements designed to enable the firm to meet that stated objective. In addition, it contains related guidance in the form of application and other explanatory material, as discussed further in paragraph 8, and introductory material that provides context relevant to a proper understanding of the ISQC (UK), and definitions.

6   The objective provides the context in which the requirements of this ISQC (UK) are set, and is intended to assist the firm in:

- Understanding what needs to be accomplished; and
- Deciding whether more needs to be done to achieve the objective.

7   The requirements of this ISQC (UK) are expressed using 'shall.'

[1a] *Audits of financial statements*[a] *undertaken in compliance with International Standards on Auditing (UK) and other engagements undertaken in compliance with performance standards issued by the FRC which, as of June 2016, comprise:*
- *Reporting accountants acting in connection with an investment circular (the Standards for Investment Reporting – 'SIRs');*
- *Review of interim financial information by the independent auditor of the entity (International Standard on Review Engagements (UK and Ireland) 2410); and*
- *Engagements to provide assurance on client assets to the Financial Conduct Authority (the CASS Standard).*

[a] *In the public sector the statutory scope of an audit can extend beyond the entity's financial statements to include reporting on an entity's arrangements for the proper conduct of its financial affairs, management of its performance or use of its resources.*

---

[1] ISA (UK) 220 (Revised June 2016), Quality Control for an Audit of Financial Statements.

Where necessary, the application and other explanatory material provides further   **8**
explanation of the requirements and guidance for carrying them out. In particular, it may:

- Explain more precisely what a requirement means or is intended to cover.
- Include examples of policies and procedures that may be appropriate in the circumstances.

While such guidance does not in itself impose a requirement, it is relevant to the proper
application of the requirements. The application and other explanatory material may
also provide background information on matters addressed in this ISQC (UK). Where
appropriate, additional considerations specific to public sector audit organizations or
smaller firms are included within the application and other explanatory material. These
additional considerations assist in the application of the requirements in this ISQC (UK).
They do not, however, limit or reduce the responsibility of the firm to apply and comply
with the requirements in this ISQC (UK).

This ISQC (UK) includes, under the heading 'Definitions,' a description of the meanings   **9**
attributed to certain terms for purposes of this ISQC (UK). These are provided to assist in
the consistent application and interpretation of this ISQC (UK), and are not intended to
override definitions that may be established for other purposes, whether in law, regulation
or otherwise. The Glossary of Terms[1b] relating to International Standards issued by the
IAASB in the *Handbook of International Quality Control, Auditing, Review, Other
Assurance, and Related Services* published by IFAC includes the terms defined in this
ISQC (UK). It also includes descriptions of other terms found in this ISQC (UK) to assist
in common and consistent interpretation and translation.

Effective Date

Systems of quality control in compliance with this ISQC (UK) are required to be established   **10**
for engagements relating to financial periods commencing on or after 17 June 2016.

Objective

The objective of the firm is to establish and maintain a system of quality control to provide   **11**
it with reasonable assurance that:
- (a) The firm and its personnel comply with professional standards and applicable legal and regulatory requirements; and
- (b) Reports issued by the firm or engagement partners are appropriate in the circumstances.

Definitions

In this ISQC (UK), the following terms have the meanings attributed below: **12**
- (a) Date of report – The date selected by the practitioner to date the report.
- (b) Engagement documentation – The record of work performed, results obtained, and conclusions the practitioner reached (terms such as 'working papers' or 'workpapers' are sometimes used).

> In the UK, engagement documentation shall include all documents, information, records and other data required by this ISQC (UK), ISAs (UK) and applicable legal and regulatory requirements.

[1b] *The FRC's Glossary of Terms defines terms used in the ISAs (UK). It is based on the Glossary of Terms issued by the IAASB supplemented by a small number of additional definitions.*

(c)   Engagement partner[2] – The partner or other person in the firm who is responsible for the engagement and its performance, and for the report that is issued on behalf of the firm, and who, where required, has the appropriate authority from a professional, legal or regulatory body.

(d)   Engagement quality control review – A process designed to provide an objective evaluation, on or before the date of the report, of the significant judgments the engagement team made and the conclusions it reached in formulating the report. The engagement quality control review process is for audits of financial statements of listed entities, and those other engagements, if any, for which the firm has determined an engagement quality control review is required.

(e)   Engagement quality control reviewer – A partner, other person in the firm, suitably qualified external person, or a team made up of such individuals, none of whom is part of the engagement team, with sufficient and appropriate experience and authority to objectively evaluate the significant judgments the engagement team made and the conclusions it reached in formulating the report.

(f)   Engagement team – All partners and staff performing the engagement, and any individuals engaged by the firm or a network firm who perform procedures on the engagement. This excludes an auditor's external expert engaged by the firm or by a network firm. The term 'engagement team' also excludes individuals within the client's internal audit function who provide direct assistance on an audit engagement when the external auditor complies with the requirements of ISA (UK) 610 (Revised June 2013).[3]

(g)   Firm – A sole practitioner, partnership or corporation or other entity of professional accountants.

(h)   Inspection – In relation to completed engagements, procedures designed to provide evidence of compliance by engagement teams with the firm's quality control policies and procedures.

(h)-1 Key audit partner – Is defined in UK legislation[3a] as:

(i)   The statutory auditor designated by an audit firm for a particular audit engagement as being primarily responsible for carrying out the statutory audit on behalf of the audit firm; or

(ii)   In the case of a group audit, the statutory auditor designated by an audit firm as being primarily responsible for carrying out the statutory audit at the level of the group and the statutory auditor designated at the level of material subsidiaries; or

(iii)   The statutory auditor who signs the audit report.

(i)   Listed entity – An entity whose shares, stock or debt are quoted or listed on a recognized stock exchange, or are marketed under the regulations of a recognized stock exchange or other equivalent body.

In the UK, this includes any company in which the public can trade shares, stock or debt on the open market, such as those listed on the London Stock Exchange (including those admitted to trading on the Alternative Investments Market) and

---

[2] *'Engagement partner,' 'partner,' and 'firm' should be read as referring to their public sector equivalents where relevant.*

[3] *ISA 610 (Revised June 2013),* Using the Work of Internal Auditors, *establishes limits on the use of direct assistance. It also acknowledges that the external auditor may be prohibited by law or regulation from obtaining direct assistance from internal auditors. Therefore, the use of direct assistance is restricted to situations where it is permitted. The use of internal auditors to provide direct assistance is prohibited in an audit conducted in accordance with ISAs (UK) – see ISA (UK) 610 (Revised June 2013), paragraph 5-1.*

[3a] *In the UK, Schedule 10 to the Companies Act 2006.*

ISDX Markets. It does not include entities whose quoted or listed shares, stock or debt are in substance not freely transferable or cannot be traded freely by the public or the entity.

(j)   Monitoring – A process comprising an ongoing consideration and evaluation of the firm's system of quality control, including a periodic inspection of a selection of completed engagements, designed to provide the firm with reasonable assurance that its system of quality control is operating effectively.

(k)   Network firm – A firm or entity that belongs to a network.

(l)   Network – A larger structure:
  (i)   That is aimed at cooperation, and
  (ii)   That is clearly aimed at profit or cost-sharing or shares common ownership, control or management, common quality control policies and procedures, common business strategy, the use of a common brand name, or a significant part of professional resources.

(m)   Partner – Any individual with authority to bind the firm with respect to the performance of a professional services engagement.

(n)   Personnel – Partners and staff.

(o)   Professional standards – IAASB Engagement Standards, as defined in the IAASB's *Preface to the International Standards on Quality Control, Auditing, Review, Other Assurance, and Related Services*, and relevant ethical requirements.

In the UK, professional standards in the context of ISQC (UK) 1 are the performance standards issued by the FRC.[1a]

(o)-1 Public interest entity – Is defined in UK legislation[3b] as:

  (i)   An issuer whose transferable securities are admitted to trading on a regulated market;[3c]
  (ii)   A credit institution within the meaning given by Article 4(1)(1) of Regulation (EU) No. 575/2013 of the European Parliament and of the Council, other than one listed in Article 2 of Directive 2013/36/EU of the European Parliament and of the Council on access to the activity of credit institutions and investment firms;
  (iii)   An insurance undertaking within the meaning given by Article 2(1) of Council Directive 1991/674/EEC of the European Parliament and of the Council on the annual accounts and consolidated accounts of insurance undertakings.

(p)   Reasonable assurance – In the context of this ISQC (UK), a high, but not absolute, level of assurance.

(q)   Relevant ethical requirements – Ethical requirements to which the engagement team and engagement quality control reviewer are subject, which ordinarily comprise Parts A and B of the International Ethics Standards Board for Accountants' *Code of Ethics for Professional Accountants* (IESBA Code) together with national requirements that are more restrictive.

In the UK, the firm and its personnel are subject to ethical requirements from two sources: the FRC's Ethical Standard concerning the integrity, objectivity and independence of the firm and its personnel, and the ethical pronouncements established by the auditor or assurance practitioner's relevant professional body.

[3b] *In the UK, Section 494A of the Companies Act 2006.*

[3c] *In the UK, 'issuer' and 'regulated market' have the same meaning as in Part 6 of the Financial Services and Markets Act 2000.*

(r) Staff – Professionals, other than partners, including any experts the firm employs.

(s) Suitably qualified external person – An individual outside the firm with the competence and capabilities to act as an engagement partner, for example a partner of another firm, or an employee (with appropriate experience) of either a professional accountancy body whose members may perform audits and reviews of historical financial information, or other assurance or related services engagements, or of an organization that provides relevant quality control services.

Requirements

Applying, and Complying with, Relevant Requirements

13 Personnel within the firm responsible for establishing and maintaining the firm's system of quality control shall have an understanding of the entire text of this ISQC (UK), including its application and other explanatory material, to understand its objective and to apply its requirements properly.

14 The firm shall comply with each requirement of this ISQC (UK) unless, in the circumstances of the firm, the requirement is not relevant to the services provided in respect of audits and reviews of financial statements, and other assurance and related services engagements. (Ref: Para. A1–A1-1)

15 The requirements are designed to enable the firm to achieve the objective stated in this ISQC (UK). The proper application of the requirements is therefore expected to provide a sufficient basis for the achievement of the objective. However, because circumstances vary widely and all such circumstances cannot be anticipated, the firm shall consider whether there are particular matters or circumstances that require the firm to establish policies and procedures in addition to those required by this ISQC (UK) to meet the stated objective.

15D-1 The firm shall:

(a) Take into consideration the scale and complexity of the firm's activities when complying with the requirements set out in paragraphs 16D-1, 16D-2, 20D-1, 21D-1, 29D-1, 29D-2, 32D-1 and 48D-1 of this ISQC (UK); and

(b) Be able to demonstrate to the competent authority[3d] that the firm's policies and procedures designed to achieve compliance with the applicable requirements of this ISQC (UK) are appropriate given the scale and complexity of the firm's activities.

Elements of a System of Quality Control

16 The firm shall establish and maintain a system of quality control that includes policies and procedures that address each of the following elements:

(a) Leadership responsibilities for quality within the firm.

(b) Relevant ethical requirements.

(c) Acceptance and continuance of client relationships and specific engagements.

(d) Human resources.

(e) Engagement performance.

(f) Monitoring.

[3d] *In the UK, the competent authority designated by law is the Financial Reporting Council or the Recognised Supervisory Body to whom the FRC has delegated regulatory tasks, as applicable.*

The firm shall establish appropriate policies and procedures to ensure that no partner, director, member or shareholder of the firm, or partner, director, member or shareholder any affiliate of the firm, intervenes in the carrying out of an engagement in any way which jeopardizes the firm's independence and objectivity in carrying out such work.   **16D-1**

The firm shall have: **16D-2**

(a)   Sound administrative and accounting procedures;
(b)   Internal quality control mechanisms which are designed to secure compliance with decisions and procedures at all levels of the firm's working structure;
(c)   Effective procedures for risk assessment; and
(d)   Effective control and safeguard arrangements for information processing systems.

The firm shall document its policies and procedures and communicate them to the firm's personnel. (Ref: Para. A2–A3)   **17**

Leadership Responsibilities for Quality within the Firm

The firm shall establish policies and procedures designed to promote an internal culture recognizing that quality is essential in performing engagements. Such policies and procedures shall require the firm's chief executive officer (or equivalent) or, if appropriate, the firm's managing board of partners (or equivalent) to assume ultimate responsibility for the firm's system of quality control. (Ref: Para. A4–A5)   **18**

The firm shall establish policies and procedures such that any person or persons assigned operational responsibility for the firm's system of quality control by the firm's chief executive officer or managing board of partners has sufficient and appropriate experience and ability, and the necessary authority, to assume that responsibility. (Ref: Para. A6)   **19**

Relevant Ethical Requirements

The firm shall establish policies and procedures designed to provide it with reasonable assurance that the firm and its personnel comply with relevant ethical requirements. (Ref: Para. A7–A10)   **20**

The firm shall establish appropriate and effective organizational and administrative arrangements for dealing with and recording incidents which have, or may have, serious consequences for the integrity of the firm's audit or other public interest assurance activities.   **20D-1**

Independence

The firm shall establish policies and procedures designed to provide it with reasonable assurance that the firm, its personnel and, where applicable, others subject to independence requirements (including network firm personnel) maintain independence where required by relevant ethical requirements. Such policies and procedures shall enable the firm to: (Ref: Para. A10)   **21**

(a)   Communicate its independence requirements to its personnel and, where applicable, others subject to them; and
(b)   Identify and evaluate circumstances and relationships that create threats to independence, and to take appropriate action to eliminate those threats or reduce

them to an acceptable level by applying safeguards, or, if considered appropriate, to withdraw from the engagement, where withdrawal is permitted by law or regulation.

21D-1   The firm shall establish appropriate and effective organizational and administrative arrangements to prevent, identify, eliminate or manage and disclose any threats to the firm's independence required by the FRC's Ethical Standard.

22   Such policies and procedures shall require: (Ref: Para. A10)

(a)   Engagement partners to provide the firm with relevant information about client engagements, including the scope of services, to enable the firm to evaluate the overall impact, if any, on independence requirements;

(b)   Personnel to promptly notify the firm of circumstances and relationships that create a threat to independence so that appropriate action can be taken; and

(c)   The accumulation and communication of relevant information to appropriate personnel so that:

(i)   The firm and its personnel can readily determine whether they satisfy independence requirements;

(ii)   The firm can maintain and update its records relating to independence; and

(iii)   The firm can take appropriate action regarding identified threats to independence that are not at an acceptable level.

23   The firm shall establish policies and procedures designed to provide it with reasonable assurance that it is notified of breaches of independence requirements, and to enable it to take appropriate actions to resolve such situations. The policies and procedures shall include requirements for: (Ref: Para. A10)

(a)   Personnel to promptly notify the firm of independence breaches of which they become aware;

(b)   The firm to promptly communicate identified breaches of these policies and procedures to:

(i)   The engagement partner who, with the firm, needs to address the breach; and

(ii)   Other relevant personnel in the firm and, where appropriate, the network, and those subject to the independence requirements who need to take appropriate action; and

(c)   Prompt communication to the firm, if necessary, by the engagement partner and the other individuals referred to in subparagraph (b)(ii) of the actions taken to resolve the matter, so that the firm can determine whether it should take further action.

24   At least annually, the firm shall obtain written confirmation of compliance with its policies and procedures on independence from all firm personnel required to be independent by relevant ethical requirements. (Ref: Para. A10–A11)

25   The firm shall establish policies and procedures:

(a)   Setting out criteria for determining the need for safeguards to reduce the familiarity threat to an acceptable level when using the same senior personnel on an assurance engagement over a long period of time; and

(b)   Requiring, for audits of financial statements of listed entities, the rotation of the engagement partner and the individuals responsible for engagement quality control review, and where applicable, others subject to rotation requirements, after a specified period in compliance with relevant ethical requirements. (Ref: Para. A10, A12–A17)

Acceptance and Continuance of Client Relationships and Specific Engagements

The firm shall establish policies and procedures for the acceptance and continuance of **26** client relationships and specific engagements, designed to provide the firm with reasonable assurance that it will only undertake or continue relationships and engagements where the firm:

(a)   Is competent to perform the engagement and has the capabilities, including time and resources, to do so; (Ref: Para. A18, A23)

(b)   Can comply with relevant ethical requirements; and

(c)   Has considered the integrity of the client, and does not have information that would lead it to conclude that the client lacks integrity. (Ref: Para. A19–A20, A23)

Such policies and procedures shall require: **27**

(a)   The firm to obtain such information as it considers necessary in the circumstances before accepting an engagement with a new client, when deciding whether to continue an existing engagement, and when considering acceptance of a new engagement with an existing client. (Ref: Para. A21, A23)

(b)   If a potential conflict of interest is identified in accepting an engagement from a new or an existing client, the firm to determine whether it is appropriate to accept the engagement.

(c)   If issues have been identified, and the firm decides to accept or continue the client relationship or a specific engagement, the firm to document how the issues were resolved.

Before accepting or continuing an audit engagement, the firm shall assess the following: **27D-1**

(a)   Whether the firm complies with relevant independence and objectivity requirements in the FRC's Ethical Standard;

(b)   Whether there are threats to the firm's independence, and the safeguards applied to mitigate those threats;

(c)   Whether the firm has the competent *personnel*, time and resources needed in order to carry out the audit in an appropriate manner; and

(d)   Whether the key audit partner is eligible for appointment as a statutory auditor.[3e]

Before accepting or continuing an engagement for an audit engagement of a public   **27R-2** interest entity, the firm shall also assess the following:

(a)   Whether the firm complies with the audit fees and the prohibition of the provision of non-audit services requirements in the FRC's Ethical Standard;

(b)   Whether the conditions for the duration of the audit engagement in accordance with the Audit Regulation[3f] are complied with; and

(c)   Without prejudice to UK anti-money laundering requirements,[3g] the integrity of the members of the supervisory, administrative and management bodies of the public interest entity.

[3e] *In the UK, eligibility for appointment as a statutory auditor is dealt with in sections 1212 to 1225 of the Companies Act 2006.*

[3f] *Regulation (EU) No 537/2014 of the European Parliament and of the Council of 16 April 2014.*

[3g] *Implemented pursuant to Directive 2005/60/EC of the European Parliament and of the Council of 26 October 2005.*

28   The firm shall establish policies and procedures on continuing an engagement and the client relationship, addressing the circumstances where the firm obtains information that would have caused it to decline the engagement had that information been available earlier. Such policies and procedures shall include consideration of:

(a)   The professional and legal responsibilities that apply to the circumstances, including whether there is a requirement for the firm to report to the person or persons who made the appointment or, in some cases, to regulatory authorities; and

(b)   The possibility of withdrawing from the engagement or from both the engagement and the client relationship. (Ref: Para. A22–A23)

28D-1   For audits of financial statements, where the auditor ceases to hold office as statutory auditor, or ceases to be eligible for appointment as a statutory auditor,[3e] the firm shall provide the successor statutory auditor with access to all relevant information concerning the entity, including information concerning the most recent audit.[3h] (Ref: Para. A22-1)

Human Resources

29   The firm shall establish policies and procedures designed to provide it with reasonable assurance that it has sufficient personnel with the competence, capabilities, and commitment to ethical principles necessary to:

(a)   Perform engagements in accordance with professional standards and applicable legal and regulatory requirements; and

(b)   Enable the firm or engagement partners to issue reports that are appropriate in the circumstances. (Ref: Para. A24–A29)

29D-1   For audits of financial statements, the firm shall:

(a)   Establish appropriate policies and procedures to ensure that the firm's personnel and any other individuals whose services are placed at the firm's disposal or under the firm's control, and who are directly involved in audit activities, have appropriate knowledge and experience for the duties assigned; and

(b)   Have in place adequate remuneration policies, including profit-sharing policies, providing sufficient performance incentives to secure audit quality, including provision that the amount of revenue that the firm derives from providing non-audit services to the audited entity shall not form part of the performance evaluation and remuneration of any person involved in, or able to influence the carrying out of, the audit.

Outsourcing

29D-2   For audits of financial statements, the firm shall establish appropriate policies and procedures to ensure that outsourcing of important audit functions is not undertaken in such a way as to impair the quality of the firm's internal quality control and the ability of the competent authority[3b] to supervise the firm's compliance with professional standards and applicable legal and regulatory requirements.

[3h] *In the UK, the relevant guidance on proposed communications with a predecessor auditor is provided by the pronouncements relating to the work of auditors issued by the auditor's relevant professional body.*

Assignment of Engagement Teams

The firm shall assign responsibility for each engagement to an engagement partner and shall establish policies and procedures requiring that: **30**

(a)   The identity and role of the engagement partner are communicated to key members of client management and those charged with governance;

(b)   The engagement partner has the appropriate competence, capabilities, and authority to perform the role; and

(c)   The responsibilities of the engagement partner are clearly defined and communicated to that partner. (Ref: Para. A30)

> For each audit of financial statements, the firm shall: **30D-1**
>
> (a)   Designate at least one key audit partner;[3i]
> (b)   Apply as its main criteria in selecting such a key audit partner the need to secure:
>   (i)   The quality of the audit; and
>   (ii)   The firm's independence and competence in carrying out the audit;
> (c)   Ensure the key audit partner is actively involved in carrying out of the audit.

The firm shall also establish policies and procedures to assign appropriate personnel with the necessary competence, and capabilities to: **31**

(a)   Perform engagements in accordance with professional standards and applicable legal and regulatory requirements; and

(b)   Enable the firm or engagement partners to issue reports that are appropriate in the circumstances. (Ref: Para. A31)

> For audits of financial statements, the firm shall provide the key audit partner(s) with sufficient resources and with personnel that have the necessary competence and capabilities to carry out the firm's duties appropriately.   **31D-1**

Engagement Performance

The firm shall establish policies and procedures designed to provide it with reasonable assurance that engagements are performed in accordance with professional standards and applicable legal and regulatory requirements, and that the firm or the engagement partner issue reports that are appropriate in the circumstances. Such policies and procedures shall include: **32**

(a)   Matters relevant to promoting consistency in the quality of engagement performance; (Ref: Para. A32–A33)

(b)   Supervision responsibilities; and (Ref: Para. A34)

(c)   Review responsibilities. (Ref: Para. A35)

> For audits of financial statements, the firm shall: **32D-1**
>
> (a)   Establish an internal quality control system to ensure the quality of the audit which covers at least the policies and procedures required by paragraph 32D-1(c);
> (b)   Ensure that responsibility for the internal quality control system lies with a person who is eligible for appointment as a statutory auditor;[3e]

[3i] *Key audit partner includes engagement partner.*

(c) Establish appropriate policies and procedures for carrying out audits, coaching, supervising and reviewing the activities of the firm's personnel and organizing the structure of the audit file;[3j] and

(d) Use appropriate systems, resources and procedures to ensure continuity and regularity in the carrying out of the firm's audit activities.

33   The firm's review responsibility policies and procedures shall be determined on the basis that work of less experienced team members is reviewed by more experienced engagement team members.

Consultation

34   The firm shall establish policies and procedures designed to provide it with reasonable assurance that:

(a) Appropriate consultation takes place on difficult or contentious matters;

(b) Sufficient resources are available to enable appropriate consultation to take place;

(c) The nature and scope of, and conclusions resulting from, such consultations are documented and are agreed by both the individual seeking consultation and the individual consulted; and

(d) Conclusions resulting from consultations are implemented. (Ref: Para. A36–A40)

Engagement Quality Control Review

35   The firm shall establish policies and procedures requiring, for appropriate engagements, an engagement quality control review that provides an objective evaluation of the significant judgments made by the engagement team and the conclusions reached in formulating the report. Such policies and procedures shall:

(a) Require an engagement quality control review for all audits of financial statements of listed entities;

(b) Set out criteria against which all other audits and reviews of historical financial information and other assurance and related services engagements shall be evaluated to determine whether an engagement quality control review should be performed; and (Ref: Para. A41)

(c) Require an engagement quality control review for all engagements, if any, meeting the criteria established in compliance with subparagraph (b).

36   The firm shall establish policies and procedures setting out the nature, timing and extent of an engagement quality control review. Such policies and procedures shall require that the engagement report not be dated until the completion of the engagement quality control review. (Ref: Para. A42–A43)

36R-1   For audits of financial statements of public interest entities, before the auditor's report and the additional report to the audit committee are issued,[3k] the firm shall require that an engagement quality control review shall be performed to assess whether the key audit partner(s) could reasonably have come to the opinion and conclusions expressed in the draft of those reports.

[3j] *ISA (UK) 230 (Revised June 2016),* Audit Documentation, *paragraph 14 sets out the requirement to assemble the audit documentation in an audit file. Paragraph 57D-1 of this ISQC (UK), paragraphs 24D-1(b) and 25R-2 of ISA (UK) 220 (Revised June 2016),* Quality Control for an Audit of Financial Statements, *paragraphs 8D-1 and 14D-1 of ISA (UK) 230 (Revised June 2016) and paragraph 23D-1 of ISA (UK) 260 (Revised June 2016),* Communication with Those Charged with Governance, *set out requirements in respect of documentation for audits.*

[3k] *ISA (UK) 260 (Revised June 2016), paragraph 16R-2 deals with the auditor's responsibilities to prepare an additional report to the audit committee.*

The firm shall establish policies and procedures to require the engagement quality control review to include:

(a) Discussion of significant matters with the engagement partner;
(b) Review of the financial statements or other subject matter information and the proposed report;
(c) Review of selected engagement documentation relating to significant judgments the engagement team made and the conclusions it reached; and
(d) Evaluation of the conclusions reached in formulating the report and consideration of whether the proposed report is appropriate. (Ref: Para. A44)

37

The firm shall establish policies and procedures to require the engagement quality control reviewer to: (Ref: Para. A44-1–A44-2)

(a) Consider the firm's compliance with the FRC's Ethical Standard in relation to the engagement;
(b) Form an independent opinion as to the appropriateness and adequacy of the safeguards applied; and
(c) Consider the adequacy of the documentation of the engagement partner's consideration of the objectivity and independence of the firm and its personnel.

37-1

For audits of financial statements of listed entities, the firm shall establish policies and procedures to require the engagement quality control review to also include consideration of the following:

(a) The engagement team's evaluation of the firm's independence in relation to the specific engagement;
(b) Whether appropriate consultation has taken place on matters involving differences of opinion or other difficult or contentious matters, and the conclusions arising from those consultations; and
(c) Whether documentation selected for review reflects the work performed in relation to the significant judgments and supports the conclusions reached. (Ref: Para. A45–A46)

38

Criteria for the Eligibility of Engagement Quality Control Reviewers

The firm shall establish policies and procedures to address the appointment of engagement quality control reviewers and establish their eligibility through:

(a) The technical qualifications required to perform the role, including the necessary experience and authority; and (Ref: Para. A47)
(b) The degree to which an engagement quality control reviewer can be consulted on the engagement without compromising the reviewer's objectivity. (Ref: Para. A48)

39

For audits of financial statements of public interest entities, the engagement quality control review shall be performed by an engagement quality control reviewer who shall:

(a) Be eligible for appointment as a statutory auditor;[3e] and
(b) Not be involved in the performance of the audit to which the engagement quality control review relates.

Where the audit is carried out by a firm and all the statutory auditors of that firm were involved in the carrying out of the audit, the firm shall arrange for another firm to perform an engagement quality control review. Documents or information disclosed to the engagement quality control reviewer for this purpose shall be subject to professional secrecy.

39R-1

40   The firm shall establish policies and procedures designed to maintain the objectivity of the engagement quality control reviewer. (Ref: Para. A49–A51)

41   The firm's policies and procedures shall provide for the replacement of the engagement quality control reviewer where the reviewer's ability to perform an objective review may be impaired.

Documentation of the Engagement Quality Control Review

42   The firm shall establish policies and procedures on documentation of the engagement quality control review which require documentation that:
  (a)   The procedures required by the firm's policies on engagement quality control review have been performed;
  (b)   The engagement quality control review has been completed on or before the date of the report; and
  (c)   The reviewer is not aware of any unresolved matters that would cause the reviewer to believe that the significant judgments the engagement team made and the conclusions it reached were not appropriate.

Differences of Opinion

43   The firm shall establish policies and procedures for dealing with and resolving differences of opinion within the engagement team, with those consulted and, where applicable, between the engagement partner and the engagement quality control reviewer. (Ref: Para. A52–A53)

43R-1   For statutory audits of financial statements of public interest entities, the firm shall also establish procedures for determining the manner in which any disagreement between the key audit partner(s) and the engagement quality control reviewer are to be resolved.

44   Such policies and procedures shall require that:
  (a)   Conclusions reached be documented and implemented; and
  (b)   The report not be dated until the matter is resolved.

Engagement Documentation

Completion of the Assembly of Final Engagement Files

45   The firm shall establish policies and procedures for engagement teams to complete the assembly of final engagement files on a timely basis after the engagement reports have been finalized. (Ref: Para. A54–A55)

Confidentiality, Safe Custody, Integrity, Accessibility and Retrievability of Engagement Documentation

46   The firm shall establish policies and procedures designed to maintain the confidentiality, safe custody, integrity, accessibility and retrievability of engagement documentation. (Ref: Para. A56–A59)

The firm shall establish policies and procedures designed to: **46D-1**

(a) Apply adequate provision on confidentiality and professional secrecy in relation to all information and documents to which the firm has access when carrying out an engagement; and
(b) Ensure that the firm complies with applicable legal and regulatory requirements relating to the confidentiality of information received in the course of the engagement.

Retention of Engagement Documentation

The firm shall establish policies and procedures for the retention of engagement   47
documentation for a period sufficient to meet the needs of the firm or as required by law or regulation. (Ref: Para. A60–A63)

Monitoring

Monitoring the Firm's Quality Control Policies and Procedures

The firm shall establish a monitoring process designed to provide it with reasonable   **48**
assurance that the policies and procedures relating to the system of quality control are relevant, adequate, and operating effectively. This process shall:

(a) Include an ongoing consideration and evaluation of the firm's system of quality control including, on a cyclical basis, inspection of at least one completed engagement for each engagement partner;
(b) Require responsibility for the monitoring process to be assigned to a partner or partners or other persons with sufficient and appropriate experience and authority in the firm to assume that responsibility; and
(c) Require that those performing the engagement or the engagement quality control review are not involved in inspecting the engagements. (Ref: Para. A64–A68)

For audits of financial statements, the firm shall: **48D-1**

(a) Monitor and evaluate the adequacy and effectiveness of the firm's systems, internal quality control mechanisms and arrangements established in accordance with this ISQC (UK) and take appropriate measures to address any deficiencies;
(b) Carry out an annual evaluation of the internal quality control system, referred to in paragraph 32D-1(a); and
(c) Keep records of the findings of the evaluation required by paragraph 48D-1(b) and any proposed measure to modify the internal quality control system.

External Monitoring of Group Audits

Where the firm is subject to a quality assurance review or an investigation concerning   **48D-2**
a group audit, the firm shall be responsible for complying with, and shall establish policies and procedures which require the group engagement team to comply with, any request by the competent authority:[3d]

(a) For relevant audit documentation retained by the group engagement team concerning the work performed by any component auditor for the purposes of the group audit (including any relevant component auditor's working papers relevant to the group audit);

(b)   To deliver any additional documentation of the work performed by any component auditor from a non-EEA member state for the purposes of the group audit, including that component auditor's working papers relevant to the group audit, where the competent authority is unable to obtain audit documentation of the work carried out by that component auditor.

48D-3   The firm shall establish policies and procedures, which require that, in order to comply with any request under paragraph 48D-2(b), the group engagement team shall either:

(a)   Retain copies of the documentation of the work carried out by the relevant component auditor for the purpose of the group audit (including the component auditor's working papers relevant to the group audit); or

(b)   Obtain the agreement of the relevant component auditor that the group engagement team shall have unrestricted access to such documentation on request; or

(c)   Retain documentation to show that the group engagement team has undertaken the appropriate procedures in order to gain access to the audit documentation, together with evidence supporting the existence of any impediments to such access; or

(d)   Take any other appropriate action.

Evaluating, Communicating and Remedying Identified Deficiencies

49   The firm shall evaluate the effect of deficiencies noted as a result of the monitoring process and determine whether they are either:

(a)   Instances that do not necessarily indicate that the firm's system of quality control is insufficient to provide it with reasonable assurance that it complies with professional standards and applicable legal and regulatory requirements, and that the reports issued by the firm or engagement partners are appropriate in the circumstances; or

(b)   Systemic, repetitive or other significant deficiencies that require prompt corrective action.

50   The firm shall communicate to relevant engagement partners and other appropriate personnel deficiencies noted as a result of the monitoring process and recommendations for appropriate remedial action. (Ref: Para. A69)

51   Recommendations for appropriate remedial actions for deficiencies noted shall include one or more of the following:

(a)   Taking appropriate remedial action in relation to an individual engagement or member of personnel;

(b)   The communication of the findings to those responsible for training and professional development;

(c)   Changes to the quality control policies and procedures; and

(d)   Disciplinary action against those who fail to comply with the policies and procedures of the firm, especially those who do so repeatedly.

52   The firm shall establish policies and procedures to address cases where the results of the monitoring procedures indicate that a report may be inappropriate or that procedures were omitted during the performance of the engagement. Such policies and procedures shall require the firm to determine what further action is appropriate to comply with relevant professional standards and legal and regulatory requirements and to consider whether to obtain legal advice.

The firm shall communicate at least annually the results of the monitoring of its system   **53**
of quality control to engagement partners and other appropriate individuals within the
firm, including the firm's chief executive officer or, if appropriate, its managing board of
partners. This communication shall be sufficient to enable the firm and these individuals to
take prompt and appropriate action where necessary in accordance with their defined roles
and responsibilities. Information communicated shall include the following:

(a)   A description of the monitoring procedures performed.
(b)   The conclusions drawn from the monitoring procedures.
(c)   Where relevant, a description of systemic, repetitive or other significant deficiencies
      and of the actions taken to resolve or amend those deficiencies.

Some firms operate as part of a network and, for consistency, may implement some of   **54**
their monitoring procedures on a network basis. Where firms within a network operate
under common monitoring policies and procedures designed to comply with this ISQC
(UK), and these firms place reliance on such a monitoring system, the firm's policies and
procedures shall require that:

(a)   At least annually, the network communicate the overall scope, extent and results of
      the monitoring process to appropriate individuals within the network firms; and
(b)   The network communicate promptly any identified deficiencies in the system of
      quality control to appropriate individuals within the relevant network firm or firms so
      that the necessary action can be taken,

in order that engagement partners in the network firms can rely on the results of the
monitoring process implemented within the network, unless the firms or the network
advise otherwise.

Complaints and Allegations

The firm shall establish policies and procedures designed to provide it with reasonable   **55**
assurance that it deals appropriately with:

(a)   Complaints and allegations that the work performed by the firm fails to comply with
      professional standards and applicable legal and regulatory requirements; and
(b)   Allegations of non-compliance with the firm's system of quality control.

As part of this process, the firm shall establish clearly defined channels for firm personnel
to raise any concerns in a manner that enables them to come forward without fear of
reprisals. (Ref: Para. A70)

For audits of financial statements, the firm shall keep records of any complaints made   **55D-1**
in writing about the performance of the audit engagements carried out.

If during the investigations into complaints and allegations, deficiencies in the design or   **56**
operation of the firm's quality control policies and procedures or non-compliance with the
firm's system of quality control by an individual or individuals are identified, the firm shall
take appropriate actions as set out in paragraph 51. (Ref: Para. A71–A72)

Documentation of the System of Quality Control

The firm shall establish policies and procedures requiring appropriate documentation to   **57**
provide evidence of the operation of each element of its system of quality control. (Ref:
Para. A73–A75)

57D-1 For audits of financial statements, the firm shall retain engagement documentation that is important for monitoring compliance with this ISQC (UK) and other applicable legal requirements.

57D-2 For audits of financial statements, the firm shall also document:

(a) Whether the firm complies with the independence and objectivity requirements in the FRC's Ethical Standard;

(b) Whether there are any threats to the firm's independence, and the safeguards applied to mitigate those threats;

(c) Whether the firm has the competent personnel, time and resources needed in order to carry out the audit in an appropriate manner; and

(d) Whether the key audit partner(s) is eligible to be appointed as a statutory auditor.[3e]

58 The firm shall establish policies and procedures that require retention of documentation for a period of time sufficient to permit those performing monitoring procedures to evaluate the firm's compliance with its system of quality control, or for a longer period if required by law or regulation.

58R-1 For audits of financial statements, the firm shall establish policies and procedures that require retention of audit documentation for a period that is not less than any period necessary to satisfy the requirements of any applicable laws or regulation relating to data protection and to meet the requirements for any applicable administrative and judicial proceedings, and that is in any case not less than six years from the date of the auditor's report.

59 The firm shall establish policies and procedures requiring documentation of complaints and allegations and the responses to them.

59D-1 For audits of financial statements, the firm shall:

(a) Keep records of any breaches (other than breaches which the firm reasonably considers to be minor breaches) of professional standards and applicable legal and regulatory requirements;

(b) Keep records of any consequences of any breach recorded in accordance with paragraph 59D-1(a), the measures taken to address such a breach and to modify the firm's internal quality control system; and

(c) Prepare an annual report containing an overview of any measures taken under paragraph 59D-1(b) and communicate that report internally.

59D-2 For audits of financial statements, the firm shall maintain a client account record which includes in respect of every audit:

(a) The audited entity's name, address and place of business;

(b) The name of the key audit partner or, where there is more than one key audit partner, the names of all the key audit partners; and

(c) The fees charged for carrying out the audit and for other services in any financial year.

***

Application and Other Explanatory Material

Applying, and Complying with, Relevant Requirements

Considerations Specific to Smaller Firms (Ref: Para. 14)

This ISQC (UK) does not call for compliance with requirements that are not relevant, for **A1** example, in the circumstances of a sole practitioner with no staff. Requirements in this ISQC (UK) such as those for policies and procedures for the assignment of appropriate personnel to the engagement team (see paragraph 31), for review responsibilities (see paragraph 33), and for the annual communication of the results of monitoring to engagement partners within the firm (see paragraph 53) are not relevant in the absence of staff.

Requirements for audits of financial statements that derive from the Audit Directive or **A1-1** the Audit Regulation are required by legislation to be complied with.[31]

Elements of a System of Quality Control (Ref: Para. 17)

In general, communication of quality control policies and procedures to firm personnel **A2** includes a description of the quality control policies and procedures and the objectives they are designed to achieve, and the message that each individual has a personal responsibility for quality and is expected to comply with these policies and procedures. Encouraging firm personnel to communicate their views or concerns on quality control matters recognizes the importance of obtaining feedback on the firm's system of quality control.

Considerations Specific to Smaller Firms

Documentation and communication of policies and procedures for smaller firms may be **A3** less formal and extensive than for larger firms.

Leadership Responsibilities for Quality within the Firm

Promoting an Internal Culture of Quality (Ref: Para. 18)

The firm's leadership and the examples it sets significantly influence the internal culture of **A4** the firm. The promotion of a quality-oriented internal culture depends on clear, consistent and frequent actions and messages from all levels of the firm's management that emphasize the firm's quality control policies and procedures, and the requirement to:
(a) Perform work that complies with professional standards and applicable legal and regulatory requirements; and
(b) Issue reports that are appropriate in the circumstances.

Such actions and messages encourage a culture that recognizes and rewards high quality work. These actions and messages may be communicated by, but are not limited to, training seminars, meetings, formal or informal dialogue, mission statements, newsletters, or briefing memoranda. They may be incorporated in the firm's internal documentation and training materials, and in partner and staff appraisal procedures such that they will support and reinforce the firm's view on the importance of quality and how, practically, it is to be achieved.

---

[31] *Directive 2006/43/EC of the European Parliament and of the Council of 17 May 2006 and Regulation (EU) No 537/2014 of the European Parliament and of the Council of 16 April 2014.*

A5   Of particular importance in promoting an internal culture based on quality is the need for the firm's leadership to recognize that the firm's business strategy is subject to the overriding requirement for the firm to achieve quality in all the engagements that the firm performs. Promoting such an internal culture includes:

    (a)   Establishment of policies and procedures that address performance evaluation, compensation, and promotion (including incentive systems) with regard to its personnel, in order to demonstrate the firm's overriding commitment to quality;

    (b)   Assignment of management responsibilities so that commercial considerations do not override the quality of work performed; and

    (c)   Provision of sufficient resources for the development, documentation and support of its quality control policies and procedures.

Assigning Operational Responsibility for the Firm's System of Quality Control
(Ref: Para. 19)

A6   Sufficient and appropriate experience and ability enables the person or persons responsible for the firm's system of quality control to identify and understand quality control issues and to develop appropriate policies and procedures. Necessary authority enables the person or persons to implement those policies and procedures.

Relevant Ethical Requirements

Compliance with Relevant Ethical Requirements (Ref: Para. 20)

A7   The IESBA Code[3m] establishes the fundamental principles of professional ethics, which include:

    (a)   Integrity;

    (b)   Objectivity;

    (c)   Professional competence and due care;

    (d)   Confidentiality; and

    (e)   Professional behavior.

A8   Part B of the IESBA Code[3m] illustrates how the conceptual framework is to be applied in specific situations. It provides examples of safeguards that may be appropriate to address threats to compliance with the fundamental principles and also provides examples of situations where safeguards are not available to address the threats.

A9   The fundamental principles are reinforced in particular by:

    •   The leadership of the firm;

    •   Education and training;

    •   Monitoring; and

    •   A process for dealing with non-compliance.

Definition of 'Firm,' 'Network' and 'Network Firm' (Ref: Para. 20–25)

A10   The definitions of 'firm,' 'network' or 'network firm' in relevant ethical requirements may differ from those set out in this ISQC (UK). For example, the IESBA Code defines the 'firm' as:

[3m] *See paragraph 12(q). Auditors and assurance practitioners in the UK are subject to ethical requirements from two sources: the FRC's Ethical Standard and the ethical pronouncements established by the auditor's relevant professional body.*

(i)   A sole practitioner, partnership or corporation of professional accountants;
(ii) An entity that controls such parties through ownership, management or other means; and
(iii) An entity controlled by such parties through ownership, management or other means.

The IESBA Code also provides guidance in relation to the terms 'network' and 'network firm.'

In complying with the requirements in paragraphs 20–25, the definitions used in the relevant ethical requirements apply in so far as is necessary to interpret those ethical requirements.

Written Confirmation (Ref: Para. 24)

Written confirmation may be in paper or electronic form. By obtaining confirmation and taking appropriate action on information indicating non-compliance, the firm demonstrates the importance that it attaches to independence and makes the issue current for, and visible to, its personnel.   **A11**

Familiarity Threat (Ref: Para. 25)

The IESBA Code[3m] discusses the familiarity threat that may be created by using the same senior personnel on an assurance engagement over a long period of time and the safeguards that might be appropriate to address such threats.   **A12**

Determining appropriate criteria to address familiarity threat may include matters such as: **A13**

- The nature of the engagement, including the extent to which it involves a matter of public interest; and
- The length of service of the senior personnel on the engagement.

Examples of safeguards include rotating the senior personnel or requiring an engagement quality control review.

The IESBA Code[3m] recognizes that the familiarity threat is particularly relevant in the context of financial statement audits of listed entities. For these audits, the IESBA Code requires the rotation of the key audit partner[4] after a pre-defined period, normally no more than seven years,[4a] and provides related standards and guidance. National requirements may establish shorter rotation periods.   **A14**

Considerations specific to public sector audit organizations

Statutory measures may provide safeguards for the independence of public sector auditors. However, threats to independence may still exist regardless of any statutory measures designed to protect it. Therefore, in establishing the policies and procedures required by paragraphs 20–25, the public sector auditor may have regard to the public sector mandate and address any threats to independence in that context.   **A15**

---

[4] *As defined in the IESBA Code.*
The IESBA definition of 'key audit partner' is not the same definition as applied in the FRC's ethical and auditing standards as the FRC's definition is derived from the Audit Directive. See paragraph 12(h)-1.

[4a] *The FRC's Ethical Standard, Section 3 – Long Association With Engagements and Entities Relevant to Engagements, specifies for the audits of public interest entities and listed companies the rotation periods for the audit engagement partner, the engagement quality control reviewer, and other key partners involved in the engagement.*

A16   Listed entities as referred to in paragraphs 25 and A14 are not common in the public sector. However, there may be other public sector entities that are significant due to size, complexity or public interest aspects, and which consequently have a wide range of stakeholders. Therefore, there may be instances when a firm determines, based on its quality control policies and procedures, that a public sector entity is significant for the purposes of expanded quality control procedures.

A17   In the public sector, legislation may establish the appointments and terms of office of the auditor with engagement partner responsibility. As a result, it may not be possible to comply strictly with the engagement partner rotation requirements envisaged for listed entities. Nonetheless, for public sector entities considered significant, as noted in paragraph A16, it may be in the public interest for public sector audit organizations to establish policies and procedures to promote compliance with the spirit of rotation of engagement partner responsibility.

Acceptance and Continuance of Client Relationships and Specific Engagements

Competence, Capabilities, and Resources (Ref: Para. 26(a))

A18   Consideration of whether the firm has the competence, capabilities, and resources to undertake a new engagement from a new or an existing client involves reviewing the specific requirements of the engagement and the existing partner and staff profiles at all relevant levels, and including whether:

- Firm personnel have knowledge of relevant industries or subject matters;
- Firm personnel have experience with relevant regulatory or reporting requirements, or the ability to gain the necessary skills and knowledge effectively;
- The firm has sufficient personnel with the necessary competence and capabilities;
- Experts are available, if needed;
- Individuals meeting the criteria and eligibility requirements to perform engagement quality control review are available, where applicable; and
- The firm is able to complete the engagement within the reporting deadline.

Integrity of Client (Ref: Para. 26(c))

A19   With regard to the integrity of a client, matters to consider include, for example:

- The identity and business reputation of the client's principal owners, key management, and those charged with its governance.
- The nature of the client's operations, including its business practices.
- Information concerning the attitude of the client's principal owners, key management and those charged with its governance towards such matters as aggressive interpretation of accounting standards and the internal control environment.
- Whether the client is aggressively concerned with maintaining the firm's fees as low as possible.
- Indications of an inappropriate limitation in the scope of work.
- Indications that the client might be involved in money laundering or other criminal activities.
- The reasons for the proposed appointment of the firm and non-reappointment of the previous firm.
- The identity and business reputation of related parties.

The extent of knowledge a firm will have regarding the integrity of a client will generally grow within the context of an ongoing relationship with that client.

Sources of information on such matters obtained by the firm may include the following: **A20**

- Communications with existing or previous providers of professional accountancy services to the client in accordance with relevant ethical requirements, and discussions with other third parties.
- Inquiry of other firm personnel or third parties such as bankers, legal counsel and industry peers.
- Background searches of relevant databases.

Continuance of Client Relationship (Ref: Para. 27(a))

Deciding whether to continue a client relationship includes consideration of significant   **A21** matters that have arisen during the current or previous engagements, and their implications for continuing the relationship. For example, a client may have started to expand its business operations into an area where the firm does not possess the necessary expertise.

Withdrawal (Ref: Para. 28)

Policies and procedures on withdrawal from an engagement or from both the engagement   **A22** and the client relationship address issues that include the following:

- Discussing with the appropriate level of the client's management and those charged with its governance the appropriate action that the firm might take based on the relevant facts and circumstances.
- If the firm determines that it is appropriate to withdraw, discussing with the appropriate level of the client's management and those charged with its governance withdrawal from the engagement or from both the engagement and the client relationship, and the reasons for the withdrawal.
- Considering whether there is a professional, legal or regulatory requirement for the firm to remain in place, or for the firm to report the withdrawal from the engagement, or from both the engagement and the client relationship, together with the reasons for the withdrawal, to regulatory authorities.
- Documenting significant matters, consultations, conclusions and the basis for the conclusions.

Statement by Auditor on Ceasing to Hold Office

The auditor of a company in the UK who ceases to hold office as auditor is required   **A22-1** to comply with the requirements of sections 519 and 521 of the Companies Act 2006 regarding the statement to be made by the auditor in relation to ceasing to hold office. In addition, the auditor may need to notify the appropriate audit authority in accordance with section 522 of the Companies Act 2006.

Considerations Specific to Public Sector Audit Organizations (Ref: Para. 26–28)

In the public sector, auditors may be appointed in accordance with statutory procedures.   **A23** Accordingly, certain of the requirements and considerations regarding the acceptance and continuance of client relationships and specific engagements as set out paragraphs 26–28 and A18–A22 may not be relevant. Nonetheless, establishing policies and procedures as described may provide valuable information to public sector auditors in performing risk assessments and in carrying out reporting responsibilities.

Human Resources (Ref: Para. 29)

A24   Personnel issues relevant to the firm's policies and procedures related to human resources include, for example:

- Recruitment.
- Performance evaluation.
- Capabilities, including time to perform assignments.
- Competence.
- Career development.
- Promotion.
- Compensation.
- The estimation of personnel needs.

Effective recruitment processes and procedures help the firm select individuals of integrity who have the capacity to develop the competence and capabilities necessary to perform the firm's work and possess the appropriate characteristics to enable them to perform competently.

A25   Competence can be developed through a variety of methods, including the following:

- Professional education.
- Continuing professional development, including training.
- Work experience.
- Coaching by more experienced staff, for example, other members of the engagement team.
- Independence education for personnel who are required to be independent.

A26   The continuing competence of the firm's personnel depends to a significant extent on an appropriate level of continuing professional development so that personnel maintain their knowledge and capabilities. Effective policies and procedures emphasize the need for continuing training for all levels of firm personnel, and provide the necessary training resources and assistance to enable personnel to develop and maintain the required competence and capabilities.

A27   The firm may use a suitably qualified external person, for example, when internal technical and training resources are unavailable.

A28   Performance evaluation, compensation and promotion procedures give due recognition and reward to the development and maintenance of competence and commitment to ethical principles. Steps a firm may take in developing and maintaining competence and commitment to ethical principles include:

- Making personnel aware of the firm's expectations regarding performance and ethical principles;
- Providing personnel with evaluation of, and counseling on, performance, progress and career development; and
- Helping personnel understand that advancement to positions of greater responsibility depends, among other things, upon performance quality and adherence to ethical principles, and that failure to comply with the firm's policies and procedures may result in disciplinary action.

Considerations Specific to Smaller Firms

The size and circumstances of the firm will influence the structure of the firm's performance   **A29**
evaluation process. Smaller firms, in particular, may employ less formal methods of
evaluating the performance of their personnel.

Assignment of Engagement Teams

Engagement Partners (Ref: Para. 30)

Policies and procedures may include systems to monitor the workload and availability of   **A30**
engagement partners so as to enable these individuals to have sufficient time to adequately
discharge their responsibilities.

Engagement Teams (Ref: Para. 31)

The firm's assignment of engagement teams and the determination of the level of   **A31**
supervision required, include for example, consideration of the engagement team's:

- Understanding of, and practical experience with, engagements of a similar nature and
  complexity through appropriate training and participation;
- Understanding of professional standards and legal and regulatory requirements;
- Technical knowledge and expertise, including knowledge of relevant information
  technology;
- Knowledge of relevant industries in which the clients operate;
- Ability to apply professional judgment; and
- Understanding of the firm's quality control policies and procedures.

Engagement Performance

Consistency in the Quality of Engagement Performance (Ref: Para. 32(a))

The firm promotes consistency in the quality of engagement performance through its   **A32**
policies and procedures. This is often accomplished through written or electronic manuals,
software tools or other forms of standardized documentation, and industry or subject
matter-specific guidance materials. Matters addressed may include:

- How engagement teams are briefed on the engagement to obtain an understanding of
  the objectives of their work.
- Processes for complying with applicable engagement standards.
- Processes of engagement supervision, staff training and coaching.
- Methods of reviewing the work performed, the significant judgments made and the
  form of report being issued.
- Appropriate documentation of the work performed and of the timing and extent of
  the review.
- Processes to keep all policies and procedures current.

Appropriate teamwork and training assist less experienced members of the engagement   **A33**
team to clearly understand the objectives of the assigned work.

Supervision (Ref: Para. 32(b))

A34   Engagement supervision includes the following:

- Tracking the progress of the engagement;
- Considering the competence and capabilities of individual members of the engagement team, whether they have sufficient time to carry out their work, whether they understand their instructions and whether the work is being carried out in accordance with the planned approach to the engagement;
- Addressing significant matters arising during the engagement, considering their significance and modifying the planned approach appropriately; and
- Identifying matters for consultation or consideration by more experienced engagement team members during the engagement.

Review (Ref: Para. 32(c))

A35   A review consists of consideration of whether:

- The work has been performed in accordance with professional standards and applicable legal and regulatory requirements;
- Significant matters have been raised for further consideration;
- Appropriate consultations have taken place and the resulting conclusions have been documented and implemented;
- There is a need to revise the nature, timing and extent of work performed;
- The work performed supports the conclusions reached and is appropriately documented;
- The evidence obtained is sufficient and appropriate to support the report; and
- The objectives of the engagement procedures have been achieved.

Consultation (Ref: Para. 34)

A36   Consultation includes discussion at the appropriate professional level, with individuals within or outside the firm who have specialized expertise.

A37   Consultation uses appropriate research resources as well as the collective experience and technical expertise of the firm. Consultation helps to promote quality and improves the application of professional judgment. Appropriate recognition of consultation in the firm's policies and procedures helps to promote a culture in which consultation is recognized as a strength and encourages personnel to consult on difficult or contentious matters.

A38   Effective consultation on significant technical, ethical and other matters within the firm, or where applicable, outside the firm can be achieved when those consulted:

- are given all the relevant facts that will enable them to provide informed advice; and
- have appropriate knowledge, seniority and experience,

and when conclusions resulting from consultations are appropriately documented and implemented.

A39   Documentation of consultations with other professionals that involve difficult or contentious matters that is sufficiently complete and detailed contributes to an understanding of:

- The issue on which consultation was sought; and
- The results of the consultation, including any decisions taken, the basis for those decisions and how they were implemented.

Considerations Specific to Smaller Firms

A firm needing to consult externally, for example, a firm without appropriate internal resources, may take advantage of advisory services provided by: **A40**

● Other firms;
● Professional and regulatory bodies; or
● Commercial organizations that provide relevant quality control services.

Before contracting for such services, consideration of the competence and capabilities of the external provider helps the firm to determine whether the external provider is suitably qualified for that purpose.

Engagement Quality Control Review

Criteria for an Engagement Quality Control Review (Ref: Para. 35(b))

Criteria for determining which engagements other than audits of financial statements of listed entities are to be subject to an engagement quality control review may include, for example: **A41**

● The nature of the engagement, including the extent to which it involves a matter of public interest.
● The identification of unusual circumstances or risks in an engagement or class of engagements.
● Whether laws or regulations require an engagement quality control review.

Nature, Timing and Extent of the Engagement Quality Control Review (Ref: Para. 36–37)

The engagement report is not dated until the completion of the engagement quality control review. However, documentation of the engagement quality control review may be completed after the date of the report.   **A42**

Conducting the engagement quality control review in a timely manner at appropriate stages during the engagement allows significant matters to be promptly resolved to the engagement quality control reviewer's satisfaction on or before the date of the report.   **A43**

The extent of the engagement quality control review may depend, among other things, on the complexity of the engagement, whether the entity is a listed entity, and the risk that the report might not be appropriate in the circumstances. The performance of an engagement quality control review does not reduce the responsibilities of the engagement partner.   **A44**

The firm's policies and procedures set out whether there are circumstances in which an engagement quality control review is performed for other audit or public interest assurance engagements as described in paragraph 35(b).   **A44-1**

Where the involvement of an engagement quality control reviewer provides a safeguard to reduce to an acceptable level those threats to independence that have been identified as potentially arising from the provision of non-audit or additional services, the engagement quality control review specifically addresses the related threat by ensuring that the work that was performed in the course of the non-audit or additional service engagement has been properly and effectively assessed in the context of the audit of the financial statements or other public interest assurance engagement.   **A44-2**

Engagement Quality Control Review of a Listed Entity (Ref: Para. 38)

A45   Other matters relevant to evaluating the significant judgments made by the engagement team that may be considered in an engagement quality control review of an audit of financial statements of a listed entity include:

- Significant risks identified during the engagement and the responses to those risks.
- Judgments made, particularly with respect to materiality and significant risks.
- The significance and disposition of corrected and uncorrected misstatements identified during the engagement.
- The matters to be communicated to management and those charged with governance and, where applicable, other parties such as regulatory bodies.

These other matters, depending on the circumstances, may also be applicable for engagement quality control reviews for audits of the financial statements of other entities as well as reviews of financial statements and other assurance and related services engagements.

Considerations specific to public sector audit organizations

A46   Although not referred to as listed entities, as described in paragraph A16, certain public sector entities may be of sufficient significance to warrant performance of an engagement quality control review.

Criteria for the Eligibility of Engagement Quality Control Reviewers

Sufficient and Appropriate Technical Expertise, Experience and Authority (Ref: Para. 39(a))

A47   What constitutes sufficient and appropriate technical expertise, experience and authority depends on the circumstances of the engagement. For example, the engagement quality control reviewer for an audit of the financial statements of a listed entity is likely to be an individual with sufficient and appropriate experience and authority to act as an audit engagement partner on audits of financial statements of listed entities.

Consultation with the Engagement Quality Control Reviewer (Ref: Para. 39(b))

A48   The engagement partner may consult the engagement quality control reviewer during the engagement, for example, to establish that a judgment made by the engagement partner will be acceptable to the engagement quality control reviewer. Such consultation avoids identification of differences of opinion at a late stage of the engagement and need not compromise the engagement quality control reviewer's eligibility to perform the role. Where the nature and extent of the consultations become significant the reviewer's objectivity may be compromised unless care is taken by both the engagement team and the reviewer to maintain the reviewer's objectivity. Where this is not possible, another individual within the firm or a suitably qualified external person may be appointed to take on the role of either the engagement quality control reviewer or the person to be consulted on the engagement.

Objectivity of the Engagement Quality Control Reviewer (Ref: Para. 40)

A49   The firm is required to establish policies and procedures designed to maintain objectivity of the engagement quality control reviewer. Accordingly, such policies and procedures provide that the engagement quality control reviewer:

- Where practicable, is not selected by the engagement partner;
- Does not otherwise participate in the engagement during the period of review;
- Does not make decisions for the engagement team; and
- Is not subject to other considerations that would threaten the reviewer's objectivity.

Considerations specific to smaller firms

It may not be practicable, in the case of firms with few partners, for the engagement **A50**
partner not to be involved in selecting the engagement quality control reviewer. Suitably
qualified external persons may be contracted where sole practitioners or small firms
identify engagements requiring engagement quality control reviews. Alternatively, some
sole practitioners or small firms may wish to use other firms to facilitate engagement
quality control reviews. Where the firm contracts suitably qualified external persons, the
requirements in paragraphs 39–41 and guidance in paragraphs A47–A48 apply.

Considerations specific to public sector audit organizations

In the public sector, a statutorily appointed auditor (for example, an Auditor General, or **A51**
other suitably qualified person appointed on behalf of the Auditor General) may act in a
role equivalent to that of engagement partner with overall responsibility for public sector
audits. In such circumstances, where applicable, the selection of the engagement quality
control reviewer includes consideration of the need for independence from the audited
entity and the ability of the engagement quality control reviewer to provide an objective
evaluation.

Differences of Opinion (Ref: Para. 43)

Effective procedures encourage identification of differences of opinion at an early stage, **A52**
provide clear guidelines as to the successive steps to be taken thereafter, and require
documentation regarding the resolution of the differences and the implementation of the
conclusions reached.

Procedures to resolve such differences may include consulting with another practitioner or **A53**
firm, or a professional or regulatory body.

Engagement Documentation

Completion of the Assembly of Final Engagement Files (Ref: Para. 45)

Law or regulation may prescribe the time limits by which the assembly of final engagement **A54**
files for specific types of engagement is to be completed. Where no such time limits are
prescribed in law or regulation, paragraph 45 requires the firm to establish time limits that
reflect the need to complete the assembly of final engagement files on a timely basis. In the
case of an audit, for example, such a time limit would ordinarily not be more than 60 days
after the date of the auditor's report.

Where two or more different reports are issued in respect of the same subject matter **A55**
information of an entity, the firm's policies and procedures relating to time limits for
the assembly of final engagement files address each report as if it were for a separate
engagement. This may, for example, be the case when the firm issues an auditor's report on
a component's financial information for group consolidation purposes and, at a subsequent
date, an auditor's report on the same financial information for statutory purposes.

Confidentiality, Safe Custody, Integrity, Accessibility and Retrievability of Engagement Documentation (Ref: Para. 46)

A56   Relevant ethical requirements establish an obligation for the firm's personnel to observe at all times the confidentiality of information contained in engagement documentation, unless specific client authority has been given to disclose information, or there are responsibilities under law, regulation or relevant ethical requirements.[5] Specific laws or regulations may impose additional obligations on the firm's personnel to maintain client confidentiality, particularly where data of a personal nature are concerned.

A57   Whether engagement documentation is in paper, electronic or other media, the integrity, accessibility or retrievability of the underlying data may be compromised if the documentation could be altered, added to or deleted without the firm's knowledge, or if it could be permanently lost or damaged. Accordingly, controls that the firm designs and implements to avoid unauthorized alteration or loss of engagement documentation may include those that:

- Enable the determination of when and by whom engagement documentation was created, changed or reviewed;
- Protect the integrity of the information at all stages of the engagement, especially when the information is shared within the engagement team or transmitted to other parties via the Internet;
- Prevent unauthorized changes to the engagement documentation; and
- Allow access to the engagement documentation by the engagement team and other authorized parties as necessary to properly discharge their responsibilities.

A58   Controls that the firm designs and implements to maintain the confidentiality, safe custody, integrity, accessibility and retrievability of engagement documentation may include the following:

- The use of a password among engagement team members to restrict access to electronic engagement documentation to authorized users.
- Appropriate back-up routines for electronic engagement documentation at appropriate stages during the engagement.
- Procedures for properly distributing engagement documentation to the team members at the start of the engagement, processing it during engagement, and collating it at the end of engagement.
- Procedures for restricting access to, and enabling proper distribution and confidential storage of, hardcopy engagement documentation.

A59   For practical reasons, original paper documentation may be electronically scanned for inclusion in engagement files. In such cases, the firm's procedures designed to maintain the integrity, accessibility, and retrievability of the documentation may include requiring the engagement teams to:

- Generate scanned copies that reflect the entire content of the original paper documentation, including manual signatures, cross-references and annotations;
- Integrate the scanned copies into the engagement files, including indexing and signing off on the scanned copies as necessary; and
- Enable the scanned copies to be retrieved and printed as necessary.

---

[5] *See, for example, Section 140.7 and Section 225.35 of the IESBA Code.*
In the UK, the auditor has regard to paragraph 46D-1 of this ISQC (UK) and any specific requirements of the auditor's relevant professional body.

There may be legal, regulatory or other reasons for a firm to retain original paper documentation that has been scanned.

Retention of Engagement Documentation (Ref: Para. 47)

The needs of the firm for retention of engagement documentation, and the period of such retention, will vary with the nature of the engagement and the firm's circumstances, for example, whether the engagement documentation is needed to provide a record of matters of continuing significance to future engagements. The retention period may also depend on other factors, such as whether local law or regulation prescribes specific retention periods for certain types of engagements, or whether there are generally accepted retention periods in the jurisdiction in the absence of specific legal or regulatory requirements. **A60**

In the specific case of audit engagements, the retention period would ordinarily be no shorter than five years from the date of the auditor's report, or, if later, the date of the group auditor's report. **A61**

In the UK, for statutory audits of financial statements, engagement documentation is retained in accordance with paragraph 58R-1. For other audit engagements, this requirement is applied having regard to specific requirements of the auditor's relevant professional body.

Procedures that the firm adopts for retention of engagement documentation include those that enable the requirements of paragraph 47 to be met during the retention period, for example to: **A62**

- Enable the retrieval of, and access to, the engagement documentation during the retention period, particularly in the case of electronic documentation since the underlying technology may be upgraded or changed over time;
- Provide, where necessary, a record of changes made to engagement documentation after the engagement files have been completed; and
- Enable authorized external parties to access and review specific engagement documentation for quality control or other purposes.

Ownership of engagement documentation

Unless otherwise specified by law or regulation, engagement documentation is the property of the firm. The firm may, at its discretion, make portions of, or extracts from, engagement documentation available to clients, provided such disclosure does not undermine the validity of the work performed, or, in the case of assurance engagements, the independence of the firm or its personnel. **A63**

Monitoring

Monitoring the Firm's Quality Control Policies and Procedures (Ref: Para. 48)

The purpose of monitoring compliance with quality control policies and procedures is to provide an evaluation of: **A64**

- Adherence to professional standards and legal and regulatory requirements;
- Whether the system of quality control has been appropriately designed and effectively implemented; and

- Whether the firm's quality control policies and procedures have been appropriately applied, so that reports that are issued by the firm or engagement partners are appropriate in the circumstances.

A65   Ongoing consideration and evaluation of the system of quality control include matters such as the following:

- Analysis of:
  - New developments in professional standards and legal and regulatory requirements, and how they are reflected in the firm's policies and procedures where appropriate;
  - Written confirmation of compliance with policies and procedures on independence;
  - Continuing professional development, including training; and
  - Decisions related to acceptance and continuance of client relationships and specific engagements.

- Determination of corrective actions to be taken and improvements to be made in the system, including the provision of feedback into the firm's policies and procedures relating to education and training.
- Communication to appropriate firm personnel of weaknesses identified in the system, in the level of understanding of the system, or compliance with it.
- Follow-up by appropriate firm personnel so that necessary modifications are promptly made to the quality control policies and procedures.

A66   Inspection cycle policies and procedures may, for example, specify a cycle that spans three years. The manner in which the inspection cycle is organized, including the timing of selection of individual engagements, depends on many factors, such as the following:

- The size of the firm.
- The number and geographical location of offices.
- The results of previous monitoring procedures.
- The degree of authority both personnel and offices have (for example, whether individual offices are authorized to conduct their own inspections or whether only the head office may conduct them).
- The nature and complexity of the firm's practice and organization.
- The risks associated with the firm's clients and specific engagements.

A67   The inspection process includes the selection of individual engagements, some of which may be selected without prior notification to the engagement team. In determining the scope of the inspections, the firm may take into account the scope or conclusions of an independent external inspection program. However, an independent external inspection program does not act as a substitute for the firm's own internal monitoring program.

Considerations Specific to Smaller Firms

A68   In the case of small firms, monitoring procedures may need to be performed by individuals who are responsible for design and implementation of the firm's quality control policies and procedures, or who may be involved in performing the engagement quality control review. A firm with a limited number of persons may choose to use a suitably qualified external person or another firm to carry out engagement inspections and other monitoring procedures. Alternatively, the firm may establish arrangements to share resources with other appropriate organizations to facilitate monitoring activities.

Communicating Deficiencies (Ref: Para. 50)

The reporting of identified deficiencies to individuals other than the relevant engagement **A69** partners need not include an identification of the specific engagements concerned, although there may be cases where such identification may be necessary for the proper discharge of the responsibilities of the individuals other than the engagement partners.

Complaints and Allegations

Source of Complaints and Allegations (Ref: Para. 55)

Complaints and allegations (which do not include those that are clearly frivolous) may **A70** originate from within or outside the firm. They may be made by firm personnel, clients or other third parties. They may be received by engagement team members or other firm personnel.

Investigation Policies and Procedures (Ref: Para. 56)

Policies and procedures established for the investigation of complaints and allegations **A71** may include for example, that the partner supervising the investigation:

- Has sufficient and appropriate experience;
- Has authority within the firm; and
- Is otherwise not involved in the engagement.

The partner supervising the investigation may involve legal counsel as necessary.

Considerations specific to smaller firms

It may not be practicable, in the case of firms with few partners, for the partner supervising **A72** the investigation not to be involved in the engagement. These small firms and sole practitioners may use the services of a suitably qualified external person or another firm to carry out the investigation into complaints and allegations.

Documentation of the System of Quality Control (Ref: Para. 57)

The form and content of documentation evidencing the operation of each of the elements **A73** of the system of quality control is a matter of judgment and depends on a number of factors, including the following:

- The size of the firm and the number of offices.
- The nature and complexity of the firm's practice and organization.

For example, large firms may use electronic databases to document matters such as independence confirmations, performance evaluations and the results of monitoring inspections.

Appropriate documentation relating to monitoring includes, for example: **A74**

- Monitoring procedures, including the procedure for selecting completed engagements to be inspected.
- A record of the evaluation of:

- o   Adherence to professional standards and applicable legal and regulatory requirements;
- o   Whether the system of quality control has been appropriately designed and effectively implemented; and
- o   Whether the firm's quality control policies and procedures have been appropriately applied, so that reports that are issued by the firm or engagement partners are appropriate in the circumstances.

- Identification of the deficiencies noted, an evaluation of their effect, and the basis for determining whether and what further action is necessary.

Considerations Specific to Smaller Firms

A75   Smaller firms may use more informal methods in the documentation of their systems of quality control such as manual notes, checklists and forms.

Part Nine

Other Guidance

Bulletin (October 2016): Compendium of illustrative auditor's reports on United Kingdom private sector financial statements for periods commencing on or after 17 June 2016

(October 2016)

Contents

Introduction

This Compendium of illustrative auditor's reports is applicable to United Kingdom private **1** sector financial statements for periods commencing on or after 17 June 2016. The auditor's reports set out in the Appendices support and illustrate how the requirements of ISA (UK) 700 (Revised June 2016)[1] and other reporting requirements of the ISAs (UK) can be applied. They also illustrate the requirements of the law and regulations applicable to the particular type of entity to which the illustration applies.

However, other approaches may be adopted provided that the form and content of **2** the auditor's report meets the requirements of ISA (UK) 700 (Revised June 2016), other relevant standards and applicable legal and regulatory requirements. The FRC supports profession-led innovation in auditor reporting which promotes audit quality and transparent and accessible auditor's reports for users of the audited financial statements.

The auditor's report is the key deliverable addressing the output of the audit process for **3** users of the audited financial statements. It is therefore important that the auditor's report is written in clear and unambiguous language.[2]

This Compendium replaces the guidance in: **4**

- Bulletin 2010/2 *Compendium of Illustrative Auditor's Reports on United Kingdom Private Sector Financial Statements for periods ended on or after 15 December 2010 (Revised)* (Updated March 2012); and
- Bulletin 4 *Recent Developments in Company Law, The Listing Rules and Auditing Standards that affect United Kingdom Auditor's Reports (Revised)* (Updated June 2015).

Describing the applicable financial reporting framework

In accordance with ISA (UK) 700 (Revised June 2016), the Opinion section of the auditor's **5** report shall make reference to the applicable financial reporting framework used to prepare the financial statements. In the UK, the applicable financial reporting framework is usually one of the following:

- International Financial Reporting Standards (IFRSs) as adopted by the European Union, and the national law that is applicable when using IFRSs and, in the case of consolidated financial statements of publicly traded companies,[3] Article 4 of the IAS Regulation (1606/2002/EC).

> The financial reporting framework that has been applied in their preparation is applicable law, and International Financial Reporting Standards (IFRSs) as adopted by the European Union.

- United Kingdom Generally Accepted Accounting Practice (UK GAAP), which comprises applicable UK law including one of the following UK Accounting Standards as issued by the FRC:

---

[1] *ISA (UK) 700 (Revised June 2016)* Forming an Opinion and Reporting on Financial Statements.

[2] *ISA (UK) 700 (Revised June 2016), paragraph 20-1.*

[3] *A publicly traded company is one whose securities are admitted to trading on a regulated market in any Member State in the European Union.*

    ○   Financial Reporting Standard 105,[4] where the financial statements are those of an entity that is eligible to apply FRS 105 and the entity opts to do so;[5]

    ○   Financial Reporting Standard 101,[6] where the financial statements are the individual financial statements of a qualifying entity, and the entity opts to do so;

    ○   Financial Reporting Standard 102.[7]

> The financial reporting framework that has been applied in their preparation is applicable law, and United Kingdom Accounting Standards, including [Financial Reporting Standard 101 *Reduced Disclosure Framework*] [Financial Reporting Standard 102 *The Financial Reporting Standard applicable in the UK and Republic of Ireland*] [Financial Reporting Standard 105 *The Financial Reporting Standard applicable to the Micro-entities Regime*] (United Kingdom Generally Accepted Accounting Practice).

Modifications to the auditor's opinion

6   Where the auditor:

- concludes that, based on the audit evidence obtained, the financial statements as a whole are not free from material misstatement; or
- is unable to obtain sufficient appropriate audit evidence to conclude that the financial statements as a whole are free from material misstatement,

the auditor is required to modify their opinion in the auditor's report in accordance with ISA (UK) 705 (Revised June 2016).[8]

7   The Appendix of ISA (UK) 705 (Revised June 2016) contains illustrations of auditor's reports with modifications to the opinion. Whilst these auditor's reports have not been tailored for the UK, they illustrate the requirements of the ISA (UK) where the auditor is required to modify or disclaim their opinion.

8   The auditor also considers the impact of any modified opinion on the financial statements on the auditor's other reporting responsibilities (including those on which they are required to report by exception). For example, if the auditor has been unable to obtain sufficient appropriate audit evidence to conclude that the financial statements as a whole are free from material misstatement, and issues a qualified or disclaimer of opinion arising from that limitation, the auditor considers whether a modified conclusion should be expressed on whether adequate accounting records have been maintained.[9]

---

[4] *Financial Reporting Standard 105* The Financial Reporting Standard applicable to the Micro-entities Regime *(FRS 105).*

[5] *Entities which prepare their annual financial statements in accordance with FRS 105 are not required by UK legislation to have an audit and it is anticipated that the entity will opt to have an audit only in rare circumstances. Further guidance on such matters is included in paragraph A36-1 and A36-2 of ISA (UK) 210 (Revised June 2016)* Agreeing the Terms of Audit Engagements.

[6] *Financial Reporting Standard 101* Reduced Disclosures Framework *(FRS 101).*

[7] *Financial Reporting Standard 102* The Financial Reporting Standard applicable in the UK and Republic of Ireland *(FRS 102).*

[8] *ISA (UK) 705 (Revised June 2016)* Modifications to the Opinion in the Independent Auditor's Report.

[9] *Similarly, paragraph A58-3 of ISA (UK) 700 (Revised June 2016) sets out the circumstances where a modified conclusion in respect of other reporting responsibilities (including those on which they are required to report by exception) leads to a modification of the auditor's opinion on the financial statements.*

Opinion in respect of an additional financial reporting framework

The financial statements of some companies may be prepared in accordance with two **9** financial reporting frameworks[10] (for example IFRSs as adopted by the European Union and IFRSs as issued by the IASB).

In such circumstances, each framework is considered separately when forming the auditor's **10** opinion on the financial statements and the auditor's opinion refers to both frameworks.

These opinions may be expressed separately or in a single sentence. Appendix 6 illustrates where **11** the opinion in respect of an additional financial reporting framework is expressed separately.

Going concern

ISA (UK) 570 (Revised June 2016)[11] sets out the reporting requirements in respect of **12** going concern.

This Compendium includes illustrative examples for the two most common scenarios when **13** reporting on going concern in an auditor's report as follows:

- Where the going concern basis of accounting is appropriate and no material uncertainty has been identified (see paragraph 15); and
- Where the going concern basis of accounting is appropriate and a material uncertainty has been identified and adequately disclosed in the financial statements (see paragraph 16).

For illustrative examples of auditor's reports with modified opinions relating to going concern, **14** see the Appendix in ISA (UK) 570 (Revised June 2016). Whilst these auditor's reports have not been tailored for the UK, they illustrate the requirements of the ISA (UK) where the auditor is required to modify their opinion or report that a material uncertainty exists.

No material uncertainty identified

Where the auditor concludes that management's use of the going concern basis of **15** accounting is appropriate in the circumstances and no material uncertainty has been identified, the auditor is required to report by exception on such matters.[12]

- Appendices 1, 2, 3, 5 and 7B illustrate reporting by exception under the heading Conclusions Relating to Going Concern.
- Appendices 6 and 7A provide alternative illustrations of these reporting requirements using an alternative heading.

Material uncertainty identified and adequately disclosed

Where the auditor concludes that a material uncertainty exists and management has **16** appropriately disclosed that fact in the financial statements, the auditor is required to express an unmodified opinion and include a separate section under the heading 'Material Uncertainty Related to Going Concern'.[13]

- Appendix 4 illustrates a Material Uncertainty Related to Going Concern section.

---

[10] *ISA (UK) 700 (Revised June 2016), paragraph A13.*

[11] *ISA (UK) 570 (Revised June 2016) Going Concern.*

[12] *ISA (UK) 570 (Revised June 2016), paragraph 21-2.*

[13] *ISA (UK) 570 (Revised June 2016), paragraph 22.*

Emphasis of matter and other matter paragraphs

17   ISA (UK) 706 (Revised June 2016)[14] deals with additional communication in the auditor's report when the auditor considers it necessary to:

- Draw users' attention to a matter or matters presented or disclosed in the financial statements that are of such importance that they are fundamental to users' understanding of the financial statements (known as an Emphasis of Matter); or
- Draw users' attention to any matter or matters other than those presented or disclosed in the financial statements that are relevant to users' understanding of the audit, the auditor's responsibilities or the auditor's report (known as an Other Matter).

18   Appendix 3 illustrates the inclusion of an emphasis of matter paragraph.

19   Appendices 4, 5, 6, 7A and 7B illustrate the inclusion of an other matter paragraph.

Other information

20   For entities that are required to prepare other information, as described in ISA (UK) 720 (Revised June 2016),[15] the auditor is required to report in the auditor's report on that other information in accordance with the ISA (UK). Appendices 1 to 7B include illustrative examples of Other Information sections.

21   The auditor's opinion on the financial statements does not cover the other information, nor is the auditor required to obtain audit evidence beyond that required to form an opinion on the financial statements, except in the circumstances:

- where the auditor is required to express an opinion, based on the work undertaken in the course of the audit, on the statutory other information[16] and state the nature of the work performed by the auditor; or
- otherwise in accordance with law or regulation.

22   Where statutory other information is not prepared, the auditor is required to include a statement that the auditor's opinion on the financial statements does not cover the other information. Where the entity has prepared statutory other information, the statement is amended as follows:

Where statutory other information is not prepared	Where statutory other information is prepared
Other information	**Other information**
Our opinion on the financial statements does not cover the other information and we do not express any form of assurance conclusion thereon.	Our opinion on the financial statements does not cover the other information and, except to the extent otherwise explicitly stated in our report, we do not express any form of assurance conclusion thereon.

---

[14] *ISA (UK) 706 (Revised June 2016)* Emphasis of Matter Paragraphs and Other Matter Paragraphs in the Independent Auditor's Report.

[15] *ISA (UK) 720 (Revised June 2016)* The Auditor's Responsibilities Relating to Other Information.

[16] *Statutory other information is defined in ISA (UK) 720 (Revised June 2016), paragraph 12(d). Where required to be prepared, this would include the directors' report, the strategic report and the separate corporate governance statement.*

Strategic report and directors' report

For entities which are required to prepare a directors' report or a strategic report,[17] the auditor is required to express an opinion on whether the information in the strategic report and the directors' report is consistent with the financial statements and whether those reports have been prepared in accordance with the applicable legal requirements. **23**

The table below sets out the wording to be included in the auditor's report: **24**

Where only a directors' report is prepared	Where both a directors' report and a strategic report are prepared
Opinions on other matters prescribed by the Companies Act 2006	**Opinions on other matters prescribed by the Companies Act 2006**
In our opinion, based on the work undertaken in the course of the audit: ● the information given in the directors' report for the financial year for which the financial statements are prepared is consistent with the financial statements; and ● the directors' report has been prepared in accordance with applicable legal requirements.	In our opinion, based on the work undertaken in the course of the audit: ● the information given in the strategic report and the directors' report for the financial year for which the financial statements are prepared is consistent with the financial statements; and ● the strategic report and the directors' report have been prepared in accordance with applicable legal requirements.
See: Appendix 1	*See: Appendices 2, 3, 4, 5, 6, 7A and 7B*

Where a directors' report or a strategic report is required to be prepared, the auditor is also required to state whether, in the light of the knowledge and understanding of the entity and its environment obtained in the course of the audit, the auditor has identified any material misstatements in those reports as follows: **25**

Where only a directors' report is prepared	Where both a directors' report and a strategic report are prepared
Matters on which we are required to report by exception	**Matters on which we are required to report by exception**
In the light of the knowledge and understanding of the company and its environment obtained in the course of the audit, we have not identified material misstatements in the directors' report.	In the light of the knowledge and understanding of the company and its environment obtained in the course of the audit, we have not identified material misstatements in the strategic report or the directors' report.
See: Appendix 1	*See: Appendices 2, 3, 4, 5, 6, 7A and 7B*

Where the directors of a company have taken advantage of the small companies exemptions in preparing the directors' report and to prepare a strategic report and in the auditor's opinion they were not entitled to do so, the auditor is required[18] to state that fact in the auditor's report. **26**

---

[17] *Section 496 of the Companies Act 2006 as amended by The Companies, Partnerships and Groups (Accounts and Reports) Regulations 2015 sets out this requirement.*

[18] *Subsection (5)(b) of Section 498 of The Companies Act 2006 sets out this requirement.*

> **Matters on which we are required to report by exception**
>
> We have nothing to report in respect of the following matters in relation to which the Companies Act 2006 requires us to report to you if, in our opinion:
> * …; or
> * the directors were not entitled to prepare the financial statements in accordance with the small companies regime and take advantage of the small companies' exemptions in preparing the directors' report and from the requirement to prepare a strategic report.

27   Appendix 1 includes an example of the statement to include in the matters to report by exception in respect of this requirement.

Corporate governance statement

28   Publically traded companies are required to include a corporate governance statement in their annual report[19] either:

* As a specific section of the directors' report (DTR 7.2.1R); or
* In a separate report which is either;
  * published together with, and in the same manner as, its annual report (DTR 7.2.9(1)R); or
  * by means of a cross reference in its directors' report to where such document is publicly available on the company's website (DTR 7.2.9(2)R).

Corporate governance statement included as a separate report

29   If the corporate governance statement is not included in the directors' report, the Companies Act 2006 imposes specific reporting responsibilities on the auditor with respect to the corporate governance statement.[20]

30   Section 497A of the Companies Act 2006 requires the auditor to report on whether certain information included in the corporate governance statement is consistent with the financial statements and has been prepared in accordance with applicable legal requirements, whether certain of the rules in the Disclosure Rules and Transparency Rules sourcebook made by the Financial Conduct Authority (the FCA Rules) have been complied with and whether the auditor has identified any material misstatements in this information.

31   The table below sets out illustrative wording to be included in the auditor's report in such circumstances:

> **Opinion on other matters prescribed by the Companies Act 2006**
>
> In our opinion, based on the work undertaken in the course of the audit:
> * the information about internal control and risk management systems in relation to financial reporting processes and about share capital structures, given in compliance with rules 7.2.5 and 7.2.6 in the Disclosure Rules and Transparency Rules sourcebook made by the Financial Conduct Authority (the FCA Rules), is consistent with the financial statements and has been prepared in accordance with applicable legal requirements; and
> * information about the company's corporate governance code and practices and about its administrative, management and supervisory bodies and their committees complies with rules 7.2.2, 7.2.3 and 7.2.7 of the FCA Rules.

---

[19] *The requirements relating to the content of the corporate governance statement are set out in Section 7.2 of the Disclosure and Transparency Rules (DTR) of the Financial Conduct Authority.*

[20] *Guidance on the auditor's responsibilities in respect of the corporate governance statement is set out more fully in Bulletin 2009/4* Developments in Corporate Governance Affecting the Responsibilities of Auditors of UK Companies.

> **Matters on which we are required to report by exception**
>
> In the light of the knowledge and understanding of the company and its environment obtained in the course of the audit, we have not identified material misstatements in:
> - the information about internal control and risk management systems in relation to financial reporting processes and about share capital structures, given in compliance with rules 7.2.5 and 7.2.6 of the FCA Rules.

Where the company is required to prepare a corporate governance statement, Section 498A of the Companies Act 2006 also requires the auditor to report on whether or not the company has prepared such a statement. In such cases, the auditor includes the following statement in the auditor's report: | **32**

> **Matters on which we are required to report by exception**
>
> We have nothing to report in respect of the following matters in relation to which the Companies Act 2006 requires us to report to you if, in our opinion:
> - ...; or
> - a corporate governance statement has not been prepared by the company.

Corporate governance statement is included in the directors' report or incorporated in the directors' report by cross reference

Where the corporate governance statement is included in the directors' report or incorporated in the directors' report by cross-reference, the reporting required by Sections 497A and 498A, and described in paragraphs 30 and 32, do not apply. | **33**

UK Corporate Governance Code reporting

For entities that are required, and those that choose voluntarily, to report on how they have applied the UK Corporate Governance Code the auditor also addresses specific elements of the other information in the auditor's report in accordance with paragraphs 22-3 and 22-4 of ISA (UK) 720 (Revised June 2016). These statements are included in Appendices 6 and 7A. | **34**

Reporting where the auditor has identified a material misstatement of the other information

Where the auditor concludes that there is an uncorrected material misstatement of the other information, the auditor is required to include a statement in the auditor's report that describes the material misstatement. ISA (UK) 720 (Revised June 2016) Appendix 2 includes such a statement in Illustrations 5, 6 and 7. Whilst these auditor's reports have not been tailored for the UK, they illustrate the requirements of the ISA (UK) where there is an uncorrected material misstatement of the other information. | **35**

Where the auditor concludes that there is an uncorrected material misstatement of the statutory other information, in addition to including the statement noted by paragraph 35, the auditor also considers the reporting implications for the specific opinions, conclusions or statements required by ISAs (UK), law or regulation. | **36**

The table below sets out example wording that the auditor includes in the auditor's report when a material misstatement of the other information, arising from an inconsistency between the other information and the financial statements, has been identified: | **37**

Other information

The other information comprises the information included in the annual report, other than the financial statements and our auditor's report thereon. The directors are responsible for the other information. Our opinion on the financial statements does not cover the other information and, except to the extent otherwise explicitly stated in our report, we do not express any form of assurance conclusion thereon.

In connection with our audit of the financial statements, our responsibility is to read the other information and, in doing so, consider whether the other information is materially inconsistent with the financial statements or our knowledge obtained in the audit or otherwise appears to be materially misstated. If we identify such material inconsistencies or apparent material misstatements, we are required to determine whether there is a material misstatement in the financial statements or a material misstatement of the other information.

If, based on the work we have performed, we conclude that there is a material misstatement of the other information, we are required to report that fact. As described in the Basis for qualified opinion on other matters prescribed by the Companies Act 2006 section of our report we have concluded that a material misstatement of the other information exists.

***

Qualified opinion on other matters prescribed by the Companies Act 2006

Except for the matter described in the Basis for qualified opinion on other matters prescribed by the Companies Act 2006 section of our report, in our opinion, based on the work undertaken in the course of the audit:

- the information given in the strategic report and the directors' report for the financial year for which the financial statements are prepared is consistent with the financial statements; and
- the strategic report and the directors' report have been prepared in accordance with applicable legal requirements.

Basis for qualified opinion on other matters prescribed by the Companies Act 2006

Based on the work undertaken in the course of the audit, the information given in the [*describe location*] of the [strategic / directors'] report is not consistent with the financial statements.

[*Description of material misstatement of statutory other information*]

***

Matters on which we are required to report by exception

Except for the material misstatement described in the Basis for qualified opinion on other matters prescribed by the Companies Act 2006 section of our report, in the light of the knowledge and understanding of the company and its environment obtained in the course of the audit, we have not identified material misstatements in the strategic report or the directors' report.

Location of the description of the auditor's responsibilities for the audit of the financial statements

ISA (UK) 700 (Revised June 2016)[21] permits the description of the auditor's responsibilities for the audit of the financial statements to be included either:

38

- Within the body of the auditor's report;
- Within an appendix to the auditor's report, in which case the auditor's report includes a reference to the location of the appendix; or
- By a specific reference within the auditor's report to the location of such a description on a website of an appropriate authority.[22]

In the illustrative auditor's reports these alternatives are shown as follows:

39

- Appendix 2 illustrates where the responsibilities are located within the body of the auditor's report.
- Appendix 6 illustrates where the responsibilities are located within an appendix to the auditor's report.
- Appendices 1, 3, 4, 5, 7A and 7B illustrate where a reference is included in the auditor's report to an appropriate website with a description of the responsibilities.

Further descriptions of the auditor's responsibilities are required to be included (either in the auditor's report, in an appendix or by cross-reference) when they are relevant to the circumstances of the particular audit as follows:

40

(a) When the financial statements are prepared in accordance with a fair presentation framework, the description of the auditor's responsibilities includes the responsibility to evaluate the overall presentation, structure and content of the financial statements, including the disclosures, and whether the financial statements represent the underlying transactions and events in a manner that achieves fair presentation. As noted in paragraph 5, the applicable financial reporting frameworks in the UK are either IFRSs as adopted by the EU or UK GAAP, both of which are fair presentation frameworks, hence this paragraph is usually required for audits of financial statements in the UK.

(b) When ISA (UK) 600 (Revised June 2016)[23] applies the following paragraph is included in the description of the auditor's responsibilities for the audit of the financial statements:

> **Auditor's responsibilities for the audit of the financial statements**
>
> We also:
> - Obtain sufficient appropriate audit evidence regarding the financial information of the entities or business activities within the group to express an opinion on the [consolidated] financial statements. We are responsible for the direction, supervision and performance of the group audit. We remain solely responsible for our audit opinion.

Appendices 2 and 6 include such a description of the auditor's responsibilities in a group audit engagement.

---

[21] *ISA (UK) 700 (Revised June 2016), paragraph 41.*

[22] *The website reference is www.frc.org.uk/auditorsresponsibilities.*

[23] *ISA (UK) 600 (Revised June 2016)* Special Considerations—Audits of Group Financial Statements (Including the Work of Component Auditors).

(c)   When the entity is listed[24] the following statement should be included in the auditor's report:

> **Auditor's responsibilities for the audit of the financial statements**
>
> We also provide those charged with governance with a statement that we have complied with relevant ethical requirements regarding independence, and to communicate with them all relationships and other matters that may reasonably be thought to bear on our independence, and where applicable, related safeguards.

Appendix 6 illustrates such a description.

(d)   When key audit matters are communicated in accordance with ISA (UK) 701[25] the following statement is included in the auditor's report:

> **Auditor's responsibilities for the audit of the financial statements**
>
> From the matters communicated with those charged with governance, we determine those matters that were of most significance in the audit of the consolidated financial statements of the current period and are therefore the key audit matters. We describe these matters in our auditor's report unless law or regulation precludes public disclosure about the matter or when, in extremely rare circumstances, we determine that a matter should not be communicated in our report because the adverse consequences of doing so would reasonably be expected to outweigh the public interest benefits of such communication.

Appendix 6 illustrates such a description.

Directors' remuneration report

41   Quoted companies[26] are required to prepare a directors' remuneration report[27] and the auditor has to report on certain aspects of that Report. Companies should describe clearly within the directors' remuneration report which disclosures have been audited.

42   Section 497 of the Companies Act 2006 requires the auditor to report to the company's members on whether the auditable part of the directors' remuneration report has been properly prepared in accordance with the Act. The auditor includes the following wording in the auditor's report:

> **Opinion on other matters prescribed by the Companies Act 2006**
>
> In our opinion the part of the directors' remuneration report to be audited has been properly prepared in accordance with the Companies Act 2006.

43   Section 498 of the Companies Act 2006 also requires the auditor to report on whether the auditable part of the directors' remuneration report is not in agreement with the accounting

---

[24] *'Listed entity' is defined in paragraph 7(g) of ISA (UK) 220 (Revised June 2016)* Quality Control for an Audit of Financial Statements.

[25] *ISA (UK) 701* Communicating Key Audit Matters in the Independent Auditor's Report.

[26] *The definition of 'quoted company' for the purposes of the directors' remuneration report is set out in Sections 385(1) and 385(2) of the Companies Act 2006. The definition of a quoted company differs from that of a publicly traded company. A publicly traded company may not necessarily meet the definition of a quoted company and a non-publicly traded company may be a quoted company.*

[27] *Part 3 of Schedule 8 to the Large and Medium-sized Companies and Groups (Accounts and Reports) Regulations 2008 (SI 2008 No. 410) sets out the information in the directors' remuneration report that is subject to audit.*

records and returns. The following underlined text is inserted into the matters on which the auditor is required to report by exception as follows:

> **Matters on which we are required to report by exception**
>
> We have nothing to report in respect of the following matters in relation to which the Companies Act 2006 requires us to report to you if, in our opinion:
> - …; or
> - the financial statements and the part of the directors' remuneration report to be audited are not in agreement with the accounting records and returns; or

Appendices 5, 6 and 7B illustrate the reporting requirements relating to the directors' remuneration report. **44**

Auditor's reports where consolidated financial statements are prepared

Omitting the parent company profit and loss account

Section 408 of the Companies Act 2006 allows a company that prepares group accounts to omit the parent company's profit and loss account from the company's financial statements provided that: **45**

- the notes to the parent company's balance sheet show the parent company's profit or loss for the financial year determined in accordance with the Companies Act 2006; and
- it is disclosed in the parent company's financial statements that the exemption applies.

The table below illustrates the difference in the wording that is required to be inserted where the Section 408 exemption has been taken in respect of the parent company's own profit and loss account and where it has not been taken. **46**

Where Section 408 exemption taken	Where Section 408 exemption not taken
Opinion	**Opinion**
We have audited the financial statements of [*name*] for the year ended [*date*] which comprise [*specify the titles of the primary statements*] and notes to the financial statements, including a summary of significant accounting policies. The financial reporting framework that has been applied in their preparation is applicable law and International Financial Reporting Standards (IFRSs) as adopted by the European Union and, as regards the parent company financial statements, as applied in accordance with the provisions of the Companies Act 2006.	We have audited the financial statements of [*name*] for the year ended [*date*] which comprise [*specify the titles of the primary statements*] and notes to the financial statements, including a summary of significant accounting policies. The financial reporting framework that has been applied in their preparation is applicable law and International Financial Reporting Standards (IFRSs) as adopted by the European Union.

Where Section 408 exemption taken	Where Section 408 exemption not taken
In our opinion: • the financial statements give a true and fair view of the state of the group's and of the parent company's affairs as at [*date*] and of the group's [profit / loss] for the year then ended; • the group financial statements have been properly prepared in accordance with IFRSs as adopted by the European Union; • the parent company financial statements have been properly prepared in accordance with IFRSs as adopted by the European Union and as applied in accordance with the provisions of the Companies Act 2006; and • the financial statements have been prepared in accordance with the requirements of the Companies Act 2006 and, as regards the group financial statements, Article 4 of the IAS Regulation.	In our opinion the financial statements: • give a true and fair view of the state of the group's and of the parent company's affairs as at [*date*] and of the group's and the parent company's [profit / loss] for the year then ended; • have been properly prepared in accordance with IFRSs as adopted by the European Union; and • have been prepared in accordance with the requirements of the Companies Act 2006 and, as regards the group financial statements, Article 4 of the IAS Regulation.

Alternative presentation options of the financial statements of a group

47   Group and parent company financial statements may be prepared in accordance with different financial reporting frameworks (for example IFRSs as adopted by the EU used for the group financial statements and UK GAAP used for the parent company financial statements).

48   Where the financial statements of the group and the parent company are presented in accordance with different financial reporting frameworks the financial statements might be presented separately within the annual report and in such circumstances separate auditor's reports might be provided.[28]

49   Where separate auditor's reports are provided on the group and parent company financial statements, the requirements of ISA (UK) 701 still apply to each separate auditor's report. Therefore, key audit matters and other audit planning and scoping matters are required to be communicated in respect of both the group and the parent company audits. The auditor may be able to avoid unnecessary duplication in respect of the auditor's reporting responsibilities by incorporating into the auditor's report by cross-reference the location of where such information can be accessed, so long as that cross-referenced material is readily accessible. However, there is certain information required by law or regulation that must be included in the auditor's report to which the financial statements relate.[29]

---

[28] *The Companies Act 2006 does not require the directors to sign the group balance sheet and thereby evidence their approval of it. Where separate financial statements are presented the auditor obtains evidence of the directors' approval of the group financial statements before signing the auditor's report on those group financial statements.*

[29] *ISA (UK) 701, paragraph A33-5.*

Appendices 2, 4 and 6 illustrate an auditor's reports where the report on the group financial statements and the report on the parent company financial statements are presented as a single auditor's report. **50**

Appendix 7 illustrates auditor's reports where the group and the parent company financial statements are presented separately. In such cases, the auditor might provide separate auditor's reports on the group financial statements (see Appendix 7A) and on the parent company financial statements (see Appendix 7B). **51**

Where separate auditor's reports are provided on the group and parent company financial statements the illustrative examples assume that: **52**

- The auditor's responsibilities with respect to the corporate governance statement are reported on in the auditor's report on the group financial statements;
- The auditor's responsibilities with respect to the UK Corporate Governance Code are reported on in the auditor's report on the group financial statements; and
- The directors' remuneration report is reported on in the auditor's report on the parent company financial statements.

However, other approaches may be adopted.

Appendices

- Appendix 1—Non-publicly traded company preparing financial statements under the small companies regime
- Appendix 2—Non-publicly traded company preparing group and parent company financial statements under UK GAAP
- Appendix 3—Publicly traded AIM listed company preparing financial statements under IFRSs with an emphasis of matter paragraph
- Appendix 4—Unlisted public interest entity preparing financial statements under UK GAAP with a material uncertainty related to going concern
- Appendix 5—Publicly traded standard listed company preparing group financial statements under IFRSs and parent company financial statements under UK GAAP
- Appendix 6—Publicly traded premium listed company preparing group and parent company financial statements under IFRSs
- Appendix 7A—Publicly traded premium listed company preparing group financial statements under IFRSs (reported on separately from the parent company financial statements)
- Appendix 7B—Publicly traded premium listed company preparing parent company financial statements under UK GAAP (reported on separately from the group financial statements)

Appendix 1—Non-publicly traded company preparing financial statements under the small companies regime

- Company qualifies as a small company and is not a public interest entity
- Financial statements are prepared in accordance with FRSs 100 and 102 (UK GAAP)
- Directors take advantage of the small companies' exemption in preparing the directors' report and from the requirement to prepare a strategic report
- Company does not prepare group financial statements or ISA (UK) 600 (Revised June 2016) does not otherwise apply
- Description of the auditor's responsibilities for the audit of the financial statements is included by reference to the location of such a description included on the FRC's website
- Auditor is not required, and has otherwise not decided, to communicate key audit matters in accordance with ISA (UK) 701

Independent auditor's report to the members of [XYZ Limited]

Opinion

We have audited the financial statements of [XYZ Limited] (the 'company') for the year ended [*date*] which comprise [*specify the titles of the primary statements*]³⁰ and notes to the financial statements, including a summary of significant accounting policies. The financial reporting framework that has been applied in their preparation is applicable law and United Kingdom Accounting Standards, including Financial Reporting Standard 102 *The Financial Reporting Standard applicable in the UK and Republic of Ireland* (United Kingdom Generally Accepted Accounting Practice).

In our opinion, the financial statements:

- give a true and fair view of the state of the company's affairs as at [*date*] and of its [profit/loss] for the year then ended;
- have been properly prepared in accordance with United Kingdom Generally Accepted Accounting Practice;
- have been prepared in accordance with the requirements of the Companies Act 2006.

Basis for opinion

We conducted our audit in accordance with International Standards on Auditing (UK) (ISAs (UK)) and applicable law. Our responsibilities under those standards are further described in the Auditor's responsibilities for the audit of the financial statements section of our report. We are independent of the company in accordance with the ethical requirements that are relevant to our audit of the financial statements in the UK, including the FRC's Ethical Standard[, and the provisions available for small entities, in the circumstances set out in note [X]³¹ to the financial statements]³², and we have fulfilled our other ethical

---

³⁰ *The terms used to describe the primary financial statements should be the same as those used by the directors.*

³¹ *Delete the words in square brackets if the relief and exemptions for audits of small entities provided by the FRC's Ethical Standard are not utilised.*

³² *As described in paragraph A35-4 of ISA (UK) 700 (Revised June 2016), the FRC's Ethical Standard* Section 6 Provisions available for audits of small entities, *paragraph 6.15 requires disclosure in the auditor's report where the audit firm has taken advantage of an exemption provided in paragraphs 6.11, 6.12 or 6.13 of the Ethical Standard.*

responsibilities in accordance with these requirements. We believe that the audit evidence we have obtained is sufficient and appropriate to provide a basis for our opinion.

Conclusions relating to going concern

We have nothing to report in respect of the following matters in relation to which the ISAs (UK) require us to report to you where:

- the directors' use of the going concern basis of accounting in the preparation of the financial statements is not appropriate; or
- the directors have not disclosed in the financial statements any identified material uncertainties that may cast significant doubt about the company's ability to continue to adopt the going concern basis of accounting for a period of at least twelve months from the date when the financial statements are authorised for issue.

Other information

The other information comprises the information included in the annual report,[33] other than the financial statements and our auditor's report thereon. The directors are responsible for the other information. Our opinion on the financial statements does not cover the other information and, except to the extent otherwise explicitly stated in our report, we do not express any form of assurance conclusion thereon. In connection with our audit of the financial statements, our responsibility is to read the other information and, in doing so, consider whether the other information is materially inconsistent with the financial statements or our knowledge obtained in the audit or otherwise appears to be materially misstated. If we identify such material inconsistencies or apparent material misstatements, we are required to determine whether there is a material misstatement in the financial statements or a material misstatement of the other information. If, based on the work we have performed, we conclude that there is a material misstatement of this other information, we are required to report that fact.

We have nothing to report in this regard.

Opinions on other matters prescribed by the Companies Act 2006

In our opinion, based on the work undertaken in the course of the audit:

- the information given in the directors' report for the financial year for which the financial statements are prepared is consistent with the financial statements; and
- the directors' report has been prepared in accordance with applicable legal requirements.

Matters on which we are required to report by exception

In the light of the knowledge and understanding of the company and its environment obtained in the course of the audit, we have not identified material misstatements in the directors' report.

We have nothing to report in respect of the following matters in relation to which the Companies Act 2006 requires us to report to you if, in our opinion:

---

[33] *The term used to describe the annual report should be the same as that used by the directors.*

- adequate accounting records have not been kept, or returns adequate for our audit have not been received from branches not visited by us; or
- the financial statements are not in agreement with the accounting records and returns; or
- certain disclosures of directors' remuneration specified by law are not made; or
- we have not received all the information and explanations we require for our audit; or
- the directors were not entitled to prepare the financial statements in accordance with the small companies regime and take advantage of the small companies' exemptions in preparing the directors' report and from the requirement to prepare a strategic report.

Responsibilities of directors

As explained more fully in the directors' responsibilities statement [set out on page ...], the directors are responsible for the preparation of the financial statements and for being satisfied that they give a true and fair view, and for such internal control as the directors determine is necessary to enable the preparation of financial statements that are free from material misstatement, whether due to fraud or error.

In preparing the financial statements, the directors are responsible for assessing the company's ability to continue as a going concern, disclosing, as applicable, matters related to going concern and using the going concern basis of accounting unless the directors either intend to liquidate the company or to cease operations, or have no realistic alternative but to do so.

Auditor's responsibilities for the audit of the financial statements

Our objectives are to obtain reasonable assurance about whether the financial statements as a whole are free from material misstatement, whether due to fraud or error, and to issue an auditor's report that includes our opinion. Reasonable assurance is a high level of assurance, but is not a guarantee that an audit conducted in accordance with ISAs (UK) will always detect a material misstatement when it exists. Misstatements can arise from fraud or error and are considered material if, individually or in the aggregate, they could reasonably be expected to influence the economic decisions of users taken on the basis of these financial statements.

A further description of our responsibilities for the audit of the financial statements is located on the Financial Reporting Council's website at: [*website link*].[34] This description forms part of our auditor's report.

[*Signature*]

John Smith (Senior Statutory Auditor)

For and on behalf of ABC LLP, Statutory Auditor

[*Address*]

[*Date*]

---

[34] *See paragraph 38 of this Compendium.*

Appendix 2—Non-publicly traded company preparing group and parent company financial statements under UK GAAP

- Company either does not qualify as a small company or qualifies as a small company but chooses not to prepare its financial statements under the small companies regime
- Company is not a public-interest entity
- Financial statements are prepared in accordance with FRSs 100 and 102 (UK GAAP)
- Company prepares group financial statements
- Section 408 exemption taken for parent company's own profit and loss account
- Description of the auditor's responsibilities for the audit of the financial statements is included within the body of the auditor's report
- Auditor is not required, and has otherwise not decided, to communicate key audit matters in accordance with ISA (UK) 701

Independent auditor's report to the members of [XYZ Limited]

Opinion

We have audited the financial statements of [XYZ Limited] (the 'parent company') and its subsidiaries (the 'group') for the year ended [*date*] which comprise [*specify the titles of the primary statements*][35] and notes to the financial statements, including a summary of significant accounting policies. The financial reporting framework that has been applied in their preparation is applicable law and United Kingdom Accounting Standards, including Financial Reporting Standard 102 *The Financial Reporting Standard applicable in the UK and Republic of Ireland* (United Kingdom Generally Accepted Accounting Practice).

In our opinion, the financial statements:

- give a true and fair view of the state of the group's and of the parent company's affairs as at [*date*] and of the group's [profit/loss] for the year then ended;
- have been properly prepared in accordance with United Kingdom Generally Accepted Accounting Practice;
- have been prepared in accordance with the requirements of the Companies Act 2006.

Basis for opinion

We conducted our audit in accordance with International Standards on Auditing (UK) (ISAs (UK)) and applicable law. Our responsibilities under those standards are further described in the Auditor's responsibilities for the audit of the financial statements section of our report. We are independent of the group in accordance with the ethical requirements that are relevant to our audit of the financial statements in the UK, including the FRC's Ethical Standard, and we have fulfilled our other ethical responsibilities in accordance with these requirements. We believe that the audit evidence we have obtained is sufficient and appropriate to provide a basis for our opinion.

---

[35] *The terms used to describe the primary financial statements should be the same as those used by the directors.*

Conclusions relating to going concern

We have nothing to report in respect of the following matters in relation to which the ISAs (UK) require us to report to you where:

* the directors' use of the going concern basis of accounting in the preparation of the financial statements is not appropriate; or
* the directors have not disclosed in the financial statements any identified material uncertainties that may cast significant doubt about the group's or the parent company's ability to continue to adopt the going concern basis of accounting for a period of at least twelve months from the date when the financial statements are authorised for issue.

Other information

The directors are responsible for the other information. The other information comprises the information included in the annual report,[36] other than the financial statements and our auditor's report thereon. Our opinion on the financial statements does not cover the other information and, except to the extent otherwise explicitly stated in our report, we do not express any form of assurance conclusion thereon.

In connection with our audit of the financial statements, our responsibility is to read the other information and, in doing so, consider whether the other information is materially inconsistent with the financial statements or our knowledge obtained in the audit or otherwise appears to be materially misstated. If we identify such material inconsistencies or apparent material misstatements, we are required to determine whether there is a material misstatement in the financial statements or a material misstatement of the other information. If, based on the work we have performed, we conclude that there is a material misstatement of this other information, we are required to report that fact.

We have nothing to report in this regard.

Opinions on other matters prescribed by the Companies Act 2006

In our opinion, based on the work undertaken in the course of the audit:

* the information given in the strategic report and the directors' report for the financial year for which the financial statements are prepared is consistent with the financial statements; and
* the strategic report and the directors' report have been prepared in accordance with applicable legal requirements.

Matters on which we are required to report by exception

In the light of the knowledge and understanding of the group and the parent company and its environment obtained in the course of the audit, we have not identified material misstatements in the strategic report or the directors' report.

We have nothing to report in respect of the following matters in relation to which the Companies Act 2006 requires us to report to you if, in our opinion:

---

[36] *The term used to describe the annual report should be the same as that used by the directors.*

- adequate accounting records have not been kept by the parent company, or returns adequate for our audit have not been received from branches not visited by us; or
- the parent company financial statements are not in agreement with the accounting records and returns; or
- certain disclosures of directors' remuneration specified by law are not made; or
- we have not received all the information and explanations we require for our audit.

Responsibilities of directors

As explained more fully in the directors' responsibilities statement [set out on page ...], the directors are responsible for the preparation of the financial statements and for being satisfied that they give a true and fair view, and for such internal control as the directors determine is necessary to enable the preparation of financial statements that are free from material misstatement, whether due to fraud or error.

In preparing the financial statements, the directors are responsible for assessing the group's and the parent company's ability to continue as a going concern, disclosing, as applicable, matters related to going concern and using the going concern basis of accounting unless the directors either intend to liquidate the group or the parent company or to cease operations, or have no realistic alternative but to do so.

Auditor's responsibilities for the audit of the financial statements

Our objectives are to obtain reasonable assurance about whether the financial statements as a whole are free from material misstatement, whether due to fraud or error, and to issue an auditor's report that includes our opinion. Reasonable assurance is a high level of assurance, but is not a guarantee that an audit conducted in accordance with ISAs (UK) will always detect a material misstatement when it exists. Misstatements can arise from fraud or error and are considered material if, individually or in the aggregate, they could reasonably be expected to influence the economic decisions of users taken on the basis of these financial statements.

As part of an audit in accordance with ISAs (UK), we exercise professional judgment and maintain professional scepticism throughout the audit. We also:

- Identify and assess the risks of material misstatement of the financial statements, whether due to fraud or error, design and perform audit procedures responsive to those risks, and obtain audit evidence that is sufficient and appropriate to provide a basis for our opinion. The risk of not detecting a material misstatement resulting from fraud is higher than for one resulting from error, as fraud may involve collusion, forgery, intentional omissions, misrepresentations, or the override of internal control.
- Obtain an understanding of internal control relevant to the audit in order to design audit procedures that are appropriate in the circumstances, but not for the purpose of expressing an opinion on the effectiveness of the group's internal control.
- Evaluate the appropriateness of accounting policies used and the reasonableness of accounting estimates and related disclosures made by the directors.
- Conclude on the appropriateness of the directors' use of the going concern basis of accounting and, based on the audit evidence obtained, whether a material uncertainty exists related to events or conditions that may cast significant doubt on the group's or the parent company's ability to continue as a going concern. If we conclude that a material uncertainty exists, we are required to draw attention in our auditor's report to the related disclosures in the financial statements or, if such disclosures are inadequate, to modify our opinion. Our conclusions are based on the audit evidence

obtained up to the date of our auditor's report. However, future events or conditions may cause the group or the parent company to cease to continue as a going concern.

- Evaluate the overall presentation, structure and content of the financial statements, including the disclosures, and whether the financial statements represent the underlying transactions and events in a manner that achieves fair presentation.

- Obtain sufficient appropriate audit evidence regarding the financial information of the entities or business activities within the group to express an opinion on the consolidated financial statements. We are responsible for the direction, supervision and performance of the group audit. We remain solely responsible for our audit opinion.[37]

We communicate with those charged with governance regarding, among other matters, the planned scope and timing of the audit and significant audit findings, including any significant deficiencies in internal control that we identify during our audit.

[*Signature*]

John Smith (Senior Statutory Auditor)

For and on behalf of ABC LLP, Statutory Auditor

[*Address*]

[*Date*]

---

[37] *This bullet point is only required where the company prepares group financial statements or ISA (UK) 600 (Revised June 2016) otherwise applies.*

Appendix 3—Publicly traded AIM listed company preparing financial statements under IFRSs with an emphasis of matter paragraph

- Company is an AIM-listed company, an unquoted company and not a public-interest entity
- Financial statements are prepared in accordance with IFRSs as adopted by the EU
- Company does not prepare group financial statements or ISA (UK) 600 (Revised June 2016) does not otherwise apply
- Description of the auditor's responsibilities for the audit of the financial statements is included by reference to the location of such a description included on the FRC's website
- Emphasis of matter paragraph is included in the auditor's report as in the auditor's judgment, the matter is of such importance that it is fundamental to users' understanding of the financial statements

Independent auditor's report to the members of [XYZ Limited]

Opinion

We have audited the financial statements of [XYZ Limited] (the 'company') for the year ended [*date*] which comprise [*specify the titles of the primary statements*][38] and notes to the financial statements, including a summary of significant accounting policies. The financial reporting framework that has been applied in their preparation is applicable law and International Financial Reporting Standards (IFRSs) as adopted by the European Union.

In our opinion, the financial statements:

- give a true and fair view of the state of the company's affairs as at [*date*] and of its [profit/loss] for the year then ended;
- have been properly prepared in accordance with IFRSs as adopted by the European Union; and
- have been prepared in accordance with the requirements of the Companies Act 2006.

Basis for opinion

We conducted our audit in accordance with International Standards on Auditing (UK) (ISAs (UK)) and applicable law. Our responsibilities under those standards are further described in the Auditor's responsibilities for the audit of the financial statements section of our report. We are independent of the company in accordance with the ethical requirements that are relevant to our audit of the financial statements in the UK, including the FRC's Ethical Standard as applied to listed entities,[39] and we have fulfilled our other ethical responsibilities in accordance with these requirements. We believe that the audit evidence we have obtained is sufficient and appropriate to provide a basis for our opinion.

---

[38] *The terms used to describe the primary financial statements should be the same as those used by the directors.*

[39] *The auditor uses 'as applied to SME listed entities' where the relief and exemptions for audits of SME listed entities provided by the FRC's Ethical Standard are utilised. See paragraph A35-3 of ISA (UK) 700 (Revised June 2016).*

Conclusions relating to going concern

We have nothing to report in respect of the following matters in relation to which the ISAs (UK) require us to report to you where:

- the directors' use of the going concern basis of accounting in the preparation of the financial statements is not appropriate; or
- the directors have not disclosed in the financial statements any identified material uncertainties that may cast significant doubt about the company's ability to continue to adopt the going concern basis of accounting for a period of at least twelve months from the date when the financial statements are authorised for issue.

Emphasis of matter[40]

We draw attention to note [X] of the financial statements, which describes [*brief summary of the matter*]. Our opinion is not modified in this respect.

Key audit matters

Key audit matters are those matters that, in our professional judgment, were of most significance in our audit of the financial statements of the current period and include the most significant assessed risks of material misstatement (whether or not due to fraud) we identified, including those which had the greatest effect on: the overall audit strategy, the allocation of resources in the audit; and directing the efforts of the engagement team. These matters were addressed in the context of our audit of the financial statements as a whole, and in forming our opinion thereon, and we do not provide a separate opinion on these matters.

[*Description of each key audit matter in accordance with ISA (UK) 701.*]

Our application of materiality

[*Explanation of how the auditor applied the concept of materiality in planning and performing the audit. This is required to include the threshold used by the auditor as being materiality for the financial statements as a whole but may include other relevant disclosures.*[41]]

An overview of the scope of our audit

[*Overview of the scope of the audit, including an explanation of how the scope addressed each key audit matter and was influenced by the auditor's application of materiality.*]

---

[40] *As noted in paragraph A16 of ISA (UK) 706 (Revised June 2016), an emphasis of matter paragraph may be presented either directly before or after the key audit matters section based on the auditor's judgment as to the relative significance of the information included in the emphasis of matter paragraph.*

[41] *ISA (UK) 701, paragraph A59-1 includes other disclosures relevant to an explanation of how the auditor applied the context of materiality in planning and performing the audit.*

Other information

The directors are responsible for the other information. The other information comprises the information included in the annual report,[42] other than the financial statements and our auditor's report thereon. Our opinion on the financial statements does not cover the other information and, except to the extent otherwise explicitly stated in our report, we do not express any form of assurance conclusion thereon.

In connection with our audit of the financial statements, our responsibility is to read the other information and, in doing so, consider whether the other information is materially inconsistent with the financial statements or our knowledge obtained in the audit or otherwise appears to be materially misstated. If we identify such material inconsistencies or apparent material misstatements, we are required to determine whether there is a material misstatement in the financial statements or a material misstatement of the other information. If, based on the work we have performed, we conclude that there is a material misstatement of this other information, we are required to report that fact. We have nothing to report in this regard.

Opinions on other matters prescribed by the Companies Act 2006

In our opinion, based on the work undertaken in the course of the audit:

- the information given in the strategic report and the directors' report for the financial year for which the financial statements are prepared is consistent with the financial statements; and
- the strategic report and the directors' report have been prepared in accordance with applicable legal requirements.

Matters on which we are required to report by exception

In the light of the knowledge and understanding of the company and its environment obtained in the course of the audit, we have not identified material misstatements in the strategic report or the directors' report.

We have nothing to report in respect of the following matters in relation to which the Companies Act 2006 requires us to report to you if, in our opinion:

- adequate accounting records have not been kept, or returns adequate for our audit have not been received from branches not visited by us; or
- the financial statements are not in agreement with the accounting records and returns; or
- certain disclosures of directors' remuneration specified by law are not made; or
- we have not received all the information and explanations we require for our audit.

Responsibilities of directors

As explained more fully in the directors' responsibilities statement [set out on page ...], the directors are responsible for the preparation of the financial statements and for being satisfied that they give a true and fair view, and for such internal control as the directors determine is necessary to enable the preparation of financial statements that are free from material misstatement, whether due to fraud or error.

---

[42] *The term used to describe the annual report should be the same as that used by the directors.*

In preparing the financial statements, the directors are responsible for assessing the company's ability to continue as a going concern, disclosing, as applicable, matters related to going concern and using the going concern basis of accounting unless the directors either intend to liquidate the company or to cease operations, or have no realistic alternative but to do so.

Auditor's responsibilities for the audit of the financial statements

Our objectives are to obtain reasonable assurance about whether the financial statements as a whole are free from material misstatement, whether due to fraud or error, and to issue an auditor's report that includes our opinion. Reasonable assurance is a high level of assurance, but is not a guarantee that an audit conducted in accordance with ISAs (UK) will always detect a material misstatement when it exists. Misstatements can arise from fraud or error and are considered material if, individually or in the aggregate, they could reasonably be expected to influence the economic decisions of users taken on the basis of these financial statements.

A further description of our responsibilities for the audit of the financial statements is located on the Financial Reporting Council's website at: [*website link*].[43] This description forms part of our auditor's report.

[*Signature*]

John Smith (Senior Statutory Auditor)

For and on behalf of ABC LLP, Statutory Auditor

[*Address*]

[*Date*]

---

[43] *See paragraph 38 of this Compendium.*

Appendix 4—Unlisted public interest entity preparing financial statements under UK GAAP with a material uncertainty related to going concern

- Company is a public interest entity
- Financial statements are prepared in accordance with FRSs 100 and 102 (UK GAAP)
- Company does not prepare group financial statements or ISA (UK) 600 (Revised June 2016) does not otherwise apply
- Based on the audit evidence obtained, the auditor has concluded that a material uncertainty exists related to events or conditions that may cast significant doubt on the company's ability to continue as a going concern. The disclosure of the material uncertainty in the financial statements is adequate.
- Description of the auditor's responsibilities for the audit of the financial statements is included by reference to the location of such a description included on the FRC's website

Independent auditor's report to the members of [XYZ Limited]

Opinion

We have audited the financial statements of [XYZ Limited] (the 'company') for the year ended [*date*] which comprise [*specify the titles of the primary statements*][44] and notes to the financial statements, including a summary of significant accounting policies. The financial reporting framework that has been applied in their preparation is applicable law and United Kingdom Accounting Standards, including Financial Reporting Standard 101 *Reduced Disclosure Framework* (United Kingdom Generally Accepted Accounting Practice).

In our opinion, the financial statements:

- give a true and fair view of the state of the company's affairs as at [*date*] and of its [profit/loss] for the year then ended;
- have been properly prepared in accordance with United Kingdom Generally Accepted Accounting Practice; and
- have been prepared in accordance with the requirements of the Companies Act 2006.

Basis for opinion

We conducted our audit in accordance with International Standards on Auditing (UK) (ISAs (UK)) and applicable law. Our responsibilities under those standards are further described in the Auditor's responsibilities for the audit of the financial statements section of our report. We are independent of the company in accordance with the ethical requirements that are relevant to our audit of the financial statements in the UK, including the FRC's Ethical Standard as applied to public interest entities, and we have fulfilled our other ethical responsibilities in accordance with these requirements. We believe that the audit evidence we have obtained is sufficient and appropriate to provide a basis for our opinion.

Material uncertainty related to going concern

We draw attention to note [X] in the financial statements, which indicates that [*brief description of events or conditions identified that may cast significant doubt on the entity's*

---

[44] *The terms used to describe the primary financial statements should be the same as those used by the directors.*

ability to continue as a going concern]. As stated in note [X], these events or conditions, along with the other matters as set forth in note [X], indicate that a material uncertainty exists that may cast significant doubt on the company's ability to continue as a going concern. Our opinion is not modified in respect of this matter.

Key audit matters

Key audit matters are those matters that, in our professional judgment, were of most significance in our audit of the financial statements of the current period and include the most significant assessed risks of material misstatement (whether or not due to fraud) we identified, including those which had the greatest effect on: the overall audit strategy, the allocation of resources in the audit; and directing the efforts of the engagement team. These matters were addressed in the context of our audit of the financial statements as a whole, and in forming our opinion thereon, and we do not provide a separate opinion on these matters.

[*Description of each key audit matter in accordance with ISA (UK) 701.*]

Our application of materiality

[*Explanation of how the auditor applied the concept of materiality in planning and performing the audit. This is required to include the threshold used by the auditor as being materiality for the financial statements as a whole but may include other relevant disclosures.*[45]]

An overview of the scope of our audit

[*Overview of the scope of the audit, including an explanation of how the scope addressed each key audit matter and was influenced by the auditor's application of materiality.*]

Other information

The directors are responsible for the other information. The other information comprises the information included in the annual report,[46] other than the financial statements and our auditor's report thereon. Our opinion on the financial statements does not cover the other information and, except to the extent otherwise explicitly stated in our report, we do not express any form of assurance conclusion thereon.

In connection with our audit of the financial statements, our responsibility is to read the other information and, in doing so, consider whether the other information is materially inconsistent with the financial statements or our knowledge obtained in the audit or otherwise appears to be materially misstated. If we identify such material inconsistencies or apparent material misstatements, we are required to determine whether there is a material misstatement in the financial statements or a material misstatement of the other information. If, based on the work we have performed, we conclude that there is a material misstatement of this other information, we are required to report that fact. We have nothing to report in this regard.

---

[45] *ISA (UK) 701, paragraph A59-1 includes other disclosures relevant to an explanation of how the auditor applied the context of materiality in planning and performing the audit.*

[46] *The term used to describe the annual report should be the same as that used by the directors.*

Opinions on other matters prescribed by the Companies Act 2006

In our opinion, based on the work undertaken in the course of the audit:

- the information given in the strategic report and the directors' report for the financial year for which the financial statements are prepared is consistent with the financial statements; and
- the strategic report and the directors' report have been prepared in accordance with applicable legal requirements.

Matters on which we are required to report by exception

In the light of the knowledge and understanding of the company and its environment obtained in the course of the audit, we have not identified material misstatements in the strategic report or the directors' report.

We have nothing to report in respect of the following matters in relation to which the Companies Act 2006 requires us to report to you if, in our opinion:

- adequate accounting records have not been kept, or returns adequate for our audit have not been received from branches not visited by us; or
- the financial statements are not in agreement with the accounting records and returns; or
- certain disclosures of directors' remuneration specified by law are not made; or
- we have not received all the information and explanations we require for our audit.

Responsibilities of directors

As explained more fully in the directors' responsibilities statement [set out on page ...], the directors are responsible for the preparation of the financial statements and for being satisfied that they give a true and fair view, and for such internal control as the directors determine is necessary to enable the preparation of financial statements that are free from material misstatement, whether due to fraud or error.

In preparing the financial statements, the directors are responsible for assessing the company's ability to continue as a going concern, disclosing, as applicable, matters related to going concern and using the going concern basis of accounting unless the directors either intend to liquidate the company or to cease operations, or have no realistic alternative but to do so.

Auditor's responsibilities for the audit of the financial statements

Our objectives are to obtain reasonable assurance about whether the financial statements as a whole are free from material misstatement, whether due to fraud or error, and to issue an auditor's report that includes our opinion. Reasonable assurance is a high level of assurance, but is not a guarantee that an audit conducted in accordance with ISAs (UK) will always detect a material misstatement when it exists. Misstatements can arise from fraud or error and are considered material if, individually or in the aggregate, they could reasonably be expected to influence the economic decisions of users taken on the basis of these financial statements.

[Explanation as to what extent the audit was considered capable of detecting irregularities, including fraud.]

A further description of our responsibilities for the audit of the financial statements is located on the Financial Reporting Council's website at: [*website link*].[47] This description forms part of our auditor's report.

Other matters which we are required to address

We were appointed by [*state by whom or which body the auditor(s) was appointed*] on [*date*]. The period of total uninterrupted engagement including previous renewals and reappointments of the firm is [X] years.

The non-audit services prohibited by the FRC's Ethical Standard were not provided to the company and we remain independent of the company in conducting our audit.

[*Indicate any services, in addition to the audit, which were provided by the firm to the company that have not been disclosed in the financial statements or elsewhere in the annual report.*]

Our audit opinion is consistent with the additional report to the audit committee.

[*Signature*]

John Smith (Senior Statutory Auditor)

For and on behalf of ABC LLP, Statutory Auditor

[*Address*]

[*Date*]

Appendix 5—Publicly traded standard listed company preparing group financial statements under IFRSs and parent company financial statements under UK GAAP

- Company is a standard listed company, a quoted company and a public-interest entity
- Company prepares group financial statements under IFRSs as adopted by the EU and parent company financial statements under UK GAAP (FRSs 100 and 101)
- Section 408 exemption taken in respect of parent company's own profit and loss account
- Corporate governance statement is incorporated into the directors' report either directly or by incorporation by reference
- Description of the auditor's responsibilities for the audit of the financial statements is included by reference to the location of such a description included on the FRC's website

Independent auditor's report to the members of [XYZ Plc]

Opinion

We have audited the financial statements of [XYZ Limited] (the 'parent company') and its subsidiaries (the 'group') for the year ended [*date*] which comprise [*specify the titles of the primary statements*][48] and notes to the financial statements, including a summary of significant accounting policies. The financial reporting framework that has been applied in the preparation of the group financial statements is applicable law and International Financial Reporting Standards (IFRSs) as adopted by the European Union. The financial reporting framework that has been applied in the preparation of the parent company financial statements is applicable law and United Kingdom Accounting Standards, including Financial Reporting Standard 101 *Reduced Disclosures Framework* (United Kingdom Generally Accepted Accounting Practice).

In our opinion:

- the financial statements give a true and fair view of the state of the group's and of the parent company's affairs as at [*date*] and of the group's [profit/loss] for the year then ended;
- the group financial statements have been properly prepared in accordance with IFRSs as adopted by the European Union;
- the parent company financial statements have been properly prepared in accordance with United Kingdom Generally Accepted Accounting Practice; and
- the financial statements have been prepared in accordance with the requirements of the Companies Act 2006; and, as regards the group financial statements, Article 4 of the IAS Regulation.

Basis for opinion

We conducted our audit in accordance with International Standards on Auditing (UK) (ISAs (UK)) and applicable law. Our responsibilities under those standards are further described in the Auditor's Responsibilities for the Audit of the Financial Statements section of our report. We are independent of the group and the parent company in accordance with

---

[48] *The terms used to describe the primary financial statements should be the same as those used by the directors.*

the ethical requirements that are relevant to our audit of the financial statements in the UK, including the FRC's Ethical Standard as applied to listed public interest entities, and we have fulfilled our other ethical responsibilities in accordance with these requirements. We believe that the audit evidence we have obtained is sufficient and appropriate to provide a basis for our opinion.

Conclusions relating to going concern

We have nothing to report in respect of the following matters in relation to which the ISAs (UK) require us to report to you where:

- the directors' use of the going concern basis of accounting in the preparation of the financial statements is not appropriate; or
- the directors have not disclosed in the financial statements any identified material uncertainties that may cast significant doubt about the group's or the parent company's ability to continue to adopt the going concern basis of accounting for a period of at least twelve months from the date when the financial statements are authorised for issue.

Key audit matters

Key audit matters are those matters that, in our professional judgment, were of most significance in our audit of the financial statements of the current period and include the most significant assessed risks of material misstatement (whether or not due to fraud) we identified, including those which had the greatest effect on: the overall audit strategy, the allocation of resources in the audit; and directing the efforts of the engagement team. These matters were addressed in the context of our audit of the financial statements as a whole, and in forming our opinion thereon, and we do not provide a separate opinion on these matters.

[*Description of each key audit matter in accordance with ISA (UK) 701.*]

Our application of materiality

[*Explanation of how the auditor applied the concept of materiality in planning and performing the group and parent company audit. This is required to include the threshold used by the auditor as being materiality for the group and parent company financial statements as a whole but may include other relevant disclosures.*[49]]

An overview of the scope of our audit

[*Overview of the scope of the group and parent company audit, including an explanation of how the scope addressed each key audit matter and was influenced by the auditor's application of materiality.*]

---

[49] *ISA (UK) 701, paragraph A59-1 includes other disclosures relevant to an explanation of how the auditor applied the context of materiality in planning and performing the audit.*

Other information

The directors are responsible for the other information. The other information comprises the information included in the annual report,[50] other than the financial statements and our auditor's report thereon. Our opinion on the financial statements does not cover the other information and, except to the extent otherwise explicitly stated in our report, we do not express any form of assurance conclusion thereon. In connection with our audit of the financial statements, our responsibility is to read the other information and, in doing so, consider whether the other information is materially inconsistent with the financial statements or our knowledge obtained in the audit or otherwise appears to be materially misstated. If we identify such material inconsistencies or apparent material misstatements, we are required to determine whether there is a material misstatement in the financial statements or a material misstatement of the other information. If, based on the work we have performed, we conclude that there is a material misstatement of this other information, we are required to report that fact. We have nothing to report in this regard.

Opinions on other matters prescribed by the Companies Act 2006

In our opinion the part of the directors' remuneration report to be audited has been properly prepared in accordance with the Companies Act 2006.

In our opinion, based on the work undertaken in the course of the audit:

- the information given in the strategic report and the directors' report for the financial year for which the financial statements are prepared is consistent with the financial statements; and
- the strategic report and the directors' report have been prepared in accordance with applicable legal requirements.

Matters on which we are required to report by exception

In the light of the knowledge and understanding of the group and the parent company and its environment obtained in the course of the audit, we have not identified material misstatements in the strategic report or the directors' report.

We have nothing to report in respect of the following matters in relation to which the Companies Act 2006 requires us to report to you if, in our opinion:

- adequate accounting records have not been kept by the parent company, or returns adequate for our audit have not been received from branches not visited by us; or
- the parent company financial statements and the part of the directors' remuneration report to be audited are not in agreement with the accounting records and returns; or
- certain disclosures of directors' remuneration specified by law are not made; or
- we have not received all the information and explanations we require for our audit.

Responsibilities of directors

As explained more fully in the directors' responsibilities statement [set out on page ...], the directors are responsible for the preparation of the financial statements and for being satisfied that they give a true and fair view, and for such internal control as the directors determine is necessary to enable the preparation of financial statements that are free from material misstatement, whether due to fraud or error.

---

[50] *The term used to describe the annual report should be the same as that used by the directors.*

In preparing the financial statements, the directors are responsible for assessing the group's and the parent company's ability to continue as a going concern, disclosing, as applicable, matters related to going concern and using the going concern basis of accounting unless the directors either intend to liquidate the group or the parent company or to cease operations, or have no realistic alternative but to do so.

Auditor's responsibilities for the audit of the financial statements

Our objectives are to obtain reasonable assurance about whether the financial statements as a whole are free from material misstatement, whether due to fraud or error, and to issue an auditor's report that includes our opinion. Reasonable assurance is a high level of assurance, but is not a guarantee that an audit conducted in accordance with ISAs (UK) will always detect a material misstatement when it exists. Misstatements can arise from fraud or error and are considered material if, individually or in the aggregate, they could reasonably be expected to influence the economic decisions of users taken on the basis of these financial statements.

[*Explanation as to what extent the audit was considered capable of detecting irregularities, including fraud.*]

A further description of our responsibilities for the audit of the financial statements is located on the Financial Reporting Council's website at: [*website link*].[51] This description forms part of our auditor's report.

Other matters which we are required to address

We were appointed by [*state by whom or which body the auditor was appointed*] on [*date*] to audit the financial statements for the period ending [*date*]. Our total uninterrupted period of engagement is [X] years, covering the periods ending [*date*] to [*date*].

The non-audit services prohibited by the FRC's Ethical Standard were not provided to the group or the parent company and we remain independent of the group and the parent company in conducting our audit.

[*Indicate any services, in addition to the audit, which were provided by the firm to the group that have not been disclosed in the financial statements or elsewhere in the annual report.*]

Our audit opinion is consistent with the additional report to the audit committee.

[*Signature*]

John Smith (Senior Statutory Auditor)

For and on behalf of ABC LLP, Statutory Auditor

[*Address*]

[*Date*]

---

[51] *See paragraph 38 of this Compendium.*

Appendix 6—Publicly traded premium listed company preparing group and parent company financial statements under IFRSs

- Company is a premium listed company, a quoted company and a public interest entity
- Financial statements are prepared in accordance with IFRSs as adopted by the EU and are also prepared in accordance with IFRSs as issued by the IAASB
- Company prepares group financial statements
- Section 408 exemption not taken in respect of parent company's own profit and loss account
- Corporate governance statement not incorporated into the strategic report or the directors' report, either directly or by incorporation by cross-reference
- Description of the auditor's responsibilities for the audit of the financial statements is included within an appendix to the auditor's report

Independent auditor's report to the members of [XYZ Plc]

Opinion

We have audited the financial statements of [XYZ Plc] (the 'parent company') and its subsidiaries (the 'group') for the year ended [*date*] which comprise [*specify the titles of the primary statements*][52] and notes to the financial statements, including a summary of significant accounting policies. The financial reporting framework that has been applied in their preparation is applicable law and International Financial Reporting Standards (IFRSs) as adopted by the European Union.

In our opinion the financial statements:

- give a true and fair view of the state of the group's and of the parent company's affairs as at [*date*] and of the group's and the parent company's [profit/loss] for the year then ended;
- have been properly prepared in accordance with [IFRSs as adopted by the European Union]; and
- have been prepared in accordance with the requirements of the Companies Act 2006 and, as regards the group financial statements, Article 4 of the IAS Regulation.

Separate opinion in relation to IFRSs as issued by the IASB

As explained in note [X] to the group financial statements, the group in addition to complying with its legal obligation to apply IFRSs as adopted by the European Union, has also applied IFRSs as issued by the International Accounting Standards Board (IASB).

In our opinion the group financial statements give a true and fair view of the consolidated financial position of the group as at [*date*] and of its consolidated financial performance and its consolidated cash flows for the year then ended in accordance with IFRSs as issued by the IASB.

---

[52] *The terms used to describe the primary financial statements should be the same as those used by the directors.*

Basis for opinion

We conducted our audit in accordance with International Standards on Auditing (UK) (ISAs (UK)) and applicable law. Our responsibilities under those standards are further described in the Auditor's responsibilities for the audit of the financial statements section of our report. We are independent of the group in accordance with the ethical requirements that are relevant to our audit of the financial statements in the UK, including the FRC's Ethical Standard as applied to listed public interest entities, and we have fulfilled our other ethical responsibilities in accordance with these requirements. We believe that the audit evidence we have obtained is sufficient and appropriate to provide a basis for our opinion.

Conclusions relating to principal risks, going concern and viability statement

We have nothing to report in respect of the following information in the annual report, in relation to which the ISAs (UK) require us to report to you whether we have anything material to add or draw attention to:

- the disclosures in the annual report[53] [set out on page ...] that describe the principal risks and explain how they are being managed or mitigated;
- the directors' confirmation [set out on page ...] in the annual report that they have carried out a robust assessment of the principal risks facing the group, including those that would threaten its business model, future performance, solvency or liquidity;
- the directors' statement [set out on page ...] in the financial statements about whether the directors considered it appropriate to adopt the going concern basis of accounting in preparing the financial statements and the directors' identification of any material uncertainties to the group and the parent company's ability to continue to do so over a period of at least twelve months from the date of approval of the financial statements;
- whether the directors' statement relating to going concern required under the Listing Rules in accordance with Listing Rule 9.8.6R(3) is materially inconsistent with our knowledge obtained in the audit; or
- the directors' explanation [set out on page ...] in the annual report as to how they have assessed the prospects of the group, over what period they have done so and why they consider that period to be appropriate, and their statement as to whether they have a reasonable expectation that the group will be able to continue in operation and meet its liabilities as they fall due over the period of their assessment, including any related disclosures drawing attention to any necessary qualifications or assumptions.

Key audit matters

Key audit matters are those matters that, in our professional judgment, were of most significance in our audit of the financial statements of the current period and include the most significant assessed risks of material misstatement (whether or not due to fraud) that we identified. These matters included those which had the greatest effect on: the overall audit strategy, the allocation of resources in the audit; and directing the efforts of the engagement team. These matters were addressed in the context of our audit of the financial statements as a whole, and in forming our opinion thereon, and we do not provide a separate opinion on these matters.

[Description of each key audit matter in accordance with ISA (UK) 701.]

---

[53] *The term used to describe the annual report should be the same as that used by the directors.*

Our application of materiality

[Explanation of how the auditor applied the concept of materiality in planning and performing the group and parent company audit. This is required to include the threshold used by the auditor as being materiality for the group and parent company financial statements as a whole but may include other relevant disclosures.[54]*]*

An overview of the scope of our audit

[Overview of the scope of the group and parent company audit, including an explanation of how the scope addressed each key audit matter and was influenced by the auditor's application of materiality.]

[Explanation as to what extent the audit was considered capable of detecting irregularities, including fraud.]

Other information

The other information comprises the information included in the annual report [set out on pages …][,including *[specify the titles of the other information]*[set out on pages …]], other than the financial statements and our auditor's report thereon. The directors are responsible for the other information. Our opinion on the financial statements does not cover the other information and, except to the extent otherwise explicitly stated in our report, we do not express any form of assurance conclusion thereon. In connection with our audit of the financial statements, our responsibility is to read the other information and, in doing so, consider whether the other information is materially inconsistent with the financial statements or our knowledge obtained in the audit or otherwise appears to be materially misstated. If we identify such material inconsistencies or apparent material misstatements, we are required to determine whether there is a material misstatement in the financial statements or a material misstatement of the other information. If, based on the work we have performed, we conclude that there is a material misstatement of the other information, we are required to report that fact.

We have nothing to report in this regard.

In this context, we also have nothing to report in regard to our responsibility to specifically address the following items in the other information and to report as uncorrected material misstatements of the other information where we conclude that those items meet the following conditions:

- **Fair, balanced and understandable [set out on page …]** – [the statement given / the explanation as to why the annual report does not include a statement] by the directors that they consider the annual report and financial statements taken as a whole is fair, balanced and understandable and provides the information necessary for shareholders to assess the group's performance, business model and strategy, is materially inconsistent with our knowledge obtained in the audit; or
- **Audit committee reporting [set out on page …]** – [the section describing the work of the audit committee does not appropriately address matters communicated by us to the audit committee / the explanation as to why the annual report does not include a section describing the work of the audit committee is materially inconsistent with our knowledge obtained in the audit]; or

---

[54] *ISA (UK) 701, paragraph A59-1 includes other disclosures relevant to an explanation of how the auditor applied the context of materiality in planning and performing the audit.*

- **Directors' statement of compliance with the UK Corporate Governance Code [set out on page ...]** – the parts of the directors' statement required under the Listing Rules relating to the company's compliance with the UK Corporate Governance Code containing provisions specified for review by the auditor in accordance with Listing Rule 9.8.10R(2) do not properly disclose a departure from a relevant provision of the UK Corporate Governance Code.

Opinions on other matters prescribed by the Companies Act 2006

In our opinion, the part of the directors' remuneration report to be audited has been properly prepared in accordance with the Companies Act 2006.

In our opinion, based on the work undertaken in the course of the audit:

- the information given in the strategic report and the directors' report for the financial year for which the financial statements are prepared is consistent with the financial statements and those reports have been prepared in accordance with applicable legal requirements;
- the information about internal control and risk management systems in relation to financial reporting processes and about share capital structures, given in compliance with rules 7.2.5 and 7.2.6 in the Disclosure Rules and Transparency Rules sourcebook made by the Financial Conduct Authority (the FCA Rules), is consistent with the financial statements and has been prepared in accordance with applicable legal requirements; and
- information about the company's corporate governance code and practices and about its administrative, management and supervisory bodies and their committees complies with rules 7.2.2, 7.2.3 and 7.2.7 of the FCA Rules.

Matters on which we are required to report by exception

In the light of the knowledge and understanding of the group and the parent company and its environment obtained in the course of the audit, we have not identified material misstatements in:

- the strategic report or the directors' report; or
- the information about internal control and risk management systems in relation to financial reporting processes and about share capital structures, given in compliance with rules 7.2.5 and 7.2.6 of the FCA Rules.

We have nothing to report in respect of the following matters in relation to which the Companies Act 2006 requires us to report to you if, in our opinion:

- adequate accounting records have not been kept by the parent company, or returns adequate for our audit have not been received from branches not visited by us; or
- the parent company financial statements and the part of the directors' remuneration report to be audited are not in agreement with the accounting records and returns; or
- certain disclosures of directors' remuneration specified by law are not made; or
- we have not received all the information and explanations we require for our audit; or
- a corporate governance statement has not been prepared by the parent company.

Responsibilities of directors

As explained more fully in the directors' responsibilities statement [set out on page ...], the directors are responsible for the preparation of the financial statements and for being satisfied that they give a true and fair view, and for such internal control as the directors determine is necessary to enable the preparation of financial statements that are free from material misstatement, whether due to fraud or error.

In preparing the financial statements, the directors are responsible for assessing the group's and the parent company's ability to continue as a going concern, disclosing, as applicable, matters related to going concern and using the going concern basis of accounting unless the directors either intend to liquidate the group or the parent company or to cease operations, or have no realistic alternative but to do so.

Auditor's responsibilities for the audit of the financial statements

Our objectives are to obtain reasonable assurance about whether the financial statements as a whole are free from material misstatement, whether due to fraud or error, and to issue an auditor's report that includes our opinion. Reasonable assurance is a high level of assurance, but is not a guarantee that an audit conducted in accordance with ISAs (UK) will always detect a material misstatement when it exists. Misstatements can arise from fraud or error and are considered material if, individually or in the aggregate, they could reasonably be expected to influence the economic decisions of users taken on the basis of these financial statements.

A further description of our responsibilities for the audit of the financial statements is included in appendix [X] of this auditor's report. This description, which is located at [*indicate page number of other specific reference to the location of the description*], forms part of our auditor's report.

Other matters which we are required to address

Following the recommendation of the audit committee, we were appointed by [*state by whom or which body the auditor was appointed*] on [*date*] to audit the financial statements for the year ending [*date*] and subsequent financial periods. The period of total uninterrupted engagement is [X] years, covering the years ending [*date*] to [*date*].

The non-audit services prohibited by the FRC's Ethical Standard were not provided to the group or the parent company and we remain independent of the group and the parent company in conducting our audit.

[*Indicate any services, in addition to the audit, which were provided by the firm to the group that have not been disclosed in the financial statements or elsewhere in the annual report.*]

Our audit opinion is consistent with the additional report to the audit committee.

[*Signature*]

John Smith (Senior Statutory Auditor)

For and on behalf of ABC LLP, Statutory Auditor

[*Address*]

[*Date*]

Appendix: Auditor's responsibilities for the audit of the financial statements

As part of an audit in accordance with ISAs (UK), we exercise professional judgment and maintain professional scepticism throughout the audit. We also:

- Identify and assess the risks of material misstatement of the financial statements, whether due to fraud or error, design and perform audit procedures responsive to those risks, and obtain audit evidence that is sufficient and appropriate to provide a basis for our opinion. The risk of not detecting a material misstatement resulting from fraud is higher than for one resulting from error, as fraud may involve collusion, forgery, intentional omissions, misrepresentations, or the override of internal control.
- Obtain an understanding of internal control relevant to the audit in order to design audit procedures that are appropriate in the circumstances, but not for the purpose of expressing an opinion on the effectiveness of the group's internal control.
- Evaluate the appropriateness of accounting policies used and the reasonableness of accounting estimates and related disclosures made by the directors.
- Conclude on the appropriateness of the directors' use of the going concern basis of accounting and, based on the audit evidence obtained, whether a material uncertainty exists related to events or conditions that may cast significant doubt on the group's or the parent company's ability to continue as a going concern. If we conclude that a material uncertainty exists, we are required to draw attention in our auditor's report to the related disclosures in the financial statements or, if such disclosures are inadequate, to modify our opinion. Our conclusions are based on the audit evidence obtained up to the date of our auditor's report. However, future events or conditions may cause the group or the parent company to cease to continue as a going concern.
- Evaluate the overall presentation, structure and content of the financial statements, including the disclosures, and whether the financial statements represent the underlying transactions and events in a manner that achieves fair presentation.
- Obtain sufficient appropriate audit evidence regarding the financial information of the entities or business activities within the group to express an opinion on the group financial statements. We are responsible for the direction, supervision and performance of the group audit. We remain solely responsible for our audit opinion.[55]

We communicate with those charged with governance regarding, among other matters, the planned scope and timing of the audit and significant audit findings, including any significant deficiencies in internal control that we identify during our audit.

We also provide those charged with governance with a statement that we have complied with relevant ethical requirements regarding independence, and to communicate with them all relationships and other matters that may reasonably be thought to bear on our independence, and where applicable, related safeguards.[56]

---

[55] *This bullet point is only required where the entity prepares group financial statements or ISA (UK) 600 (Revised June 2016) otherwise applies. See paragraph 40(b) of this Compendium.*

[56] *This bullet point is only required where the entity is a listed entity. See paragraph 40(c) of this Compendium.*

From the matters communicated with those charged with governance, we determine those matters that were of most significance in the audit of the consolidated financial statements of the current period and are therefore the key audit matters. We describe these matters in our auditor's report unless law or regulation precludes public disclosure about the matter or when, in extremely rare circumstances, we determine that a matter should not be communicated in our report because the adverse consequences of doing so would reasonably be expected to outweigh the public interest benefits of such communication.[57]

[57] *This bullet point is only required where the auditor is required, or has otherwise decided, to communicate key audit matters in accordance with ISA (UK) 701. See paragraph 40(d) of this Compendium.*

Appendix 7A—Publicly traded premium listed company preparing group financial statements under IFRSs (reported on separately from the parent company financial statements)

- Company is a premium listed company, a quoted company and a public interest entity
- Company prepares group financial statements
- Corporate governance statement incorporated into the directors' report, either directly or by incorporation by cross-reference and reported on in the auditor's report on the group financial statements
- UK Corporate Governance Code reported on in the auditor's report on the group financial statements
- Directors' Remuneration Report reported on in the auditor's report on the parent company financial statements
- Description of the auditor's responsibilities for the audit of the financial statements is included by reference to the location of such a description included on the FRC's website

Independent auditor's report to the members of [XYZ Plc]

Opinion

We have audited the group financial statements of [XYZ Plc] for the year ended [*date*] which comprise [*specify the titles of the primary statements*][58] and notes to the financial statements, including a summary of significant accounting policies. The financial reporting framework that has been applied in their preparation is applicable law and International Financial Reporting Standards (IFRSs) as adopted by the European Union.

In our opinion the group financial statements:

- give a true and fair view of the state of the group's affairs as at [*date*] and of its [profit/ loss] for the year then ended;
- have been properly prepared in accordance with IFRSs as adopted by the European Union; and
- have been prepared in accordance with the requirements of the Companies Act 2006 and Article 4 of the IAS Regulation.

Basis for opinion

We conducted our audit in accordance with International Standards on Auditing (UK) (ISAs (UK)) and applicable law. Our responsibilities under those standards are further described in the Auditor's Responsibilities for the audit of the group financial statements section of our report. We are independent of the group in accordance with the ethical requirements that are relevant to our audit of the financial statements in the UK, including the FRC's Ethical Standard as applied to listed public interest entities, and we have fulfilled our other ethical responsibilities in accordance with these requirements. We believe that the audit evidence we have obtained is sufficient and appropriate to provide a basis for our opinion.

---

[58] *The terms used to describe the primary financial statements should be the same as those used by the directors.*

Conclusions relating to principal risks, going concern and viability statement

We have nothing to report in respect of the following information in the annual report, in relation to which the ISAs (UK) require us to report to you whether we have anything material to add or draw attention to:

- the disclosures in the annual report[59] that describe the principal risks and explain how they are being managed or mitigated;
- the directors' confirmation in the annual report that they have carried out a robust assessment of the principal risks facing the group, including those that would threaten its business model, future performance, solvency or liquidity;
- the directors' statement in the financial statements about whether the directors considered it appropriate to adopt the going concern basis of accounting in preparing the financial statements and the directors' identification of any material uncertainties to the group's ability to continue to do so over a period of at least twelve months from the date of approval of the financial statements;
- whether the directors' statement relating to going concern required under the Listing Rules in accordance with Listing Rule 9.8.6R(3) is materially inconsistent with our knowledge obtained in the audit; or
- the directors' explanation in the annual report as to how they have assessed the prospects of the group, over what period they have done so and why they consider that period to be appropriate, and their statement as to whether they have a reasonable expectation that the group will be able to continue in operation and meet its liabilities as they fall due over the period of their assessment, including any related disclosures drawing attention to any necessary qualifications or assumptions.

Key audit matters

Key audit matters are those matters that, in our professional judgment, were of most significance in our audit of the group financial statements of the current period and include the most significant assessed risks of material misstatement (whether or not due to fraud) we identified, including those which had the greatest effect on: the overall audit strategy, the allocation of resources in the audit; and directing the efforts of the engagement team. These matters were addressed in the context of our audit of the group financial statements as a whole, and in forming our opinion thereon, and we do not provide a separate opinion on these matters.

[Description of each key audit matter in accordance with ISA (UK) 701.]

Our application of materiality

[Explanation of how the auditor applied the concept of materiality in planning and performing the group audit. This is required to include the threshold used by the auditor as being materiality for the group financial statements as a whole but may include other relevant disclosures.[60]]

---

[59] *The term used to describe the annual report should be the same as that used by the directors.*

[60] *ISA (UK) 701, paragraph A59-1 includes other disclosures relevant to an explanation of how the auditor applied the context of materiality in planning and performing the audit.*

An overview of the scope of our audit

[Overview of the scope of the group audit, including an explanation of how the scope addressed each key audit matter and was influenced by the auditor's application of materiality.]

Other information

The directors are responsible for the other information. The other information comprises the information included in the annual report, other than the financial statements and our auditor's report thereon. Our opinion on the financial statements does not cover the other information and, except to the extent otherwise explicitly stated in our report, we do not express any form of assurance conclusion thereon.

In connection with our audit of the group financial statements, our responsibility is to read the other information and, in doing so, consider whether the other information is materially inconsistent with the group financial statements or our knowledge obtained in the audit or otherwise appears to be materially misstated. If we identify such material inconsistencies or apparent material misstatements, we are required to determine whether there is a material misstatement of the group financial statements or a material misstatement of the other information. If, based on the work we have performed, we conclude that there is a material misstatement of this other information, we are required to report that fact. We have nothing to report in this regard.

In this context, we also have nothing to report in regard to our responsibility to specifically address the following items in the other information and to report as uncorrected material misstatements of the other information where we conclude that those items meet the following conditions:

- **Fair, balanced and understandable** – [the statement given / the explanation as to why the annual report does not include a statement] by the directors that they consider the annual report and financial statements taken as a whole is fair, balanced and understandable and provides the information necessary for shareholders to assess the group's performance, business model and strategy, is materially inconsistent with our knowledge obtained in the audit; or
- **Audit committee reporting** – [the section describing the work of the audit committee does not appropriately address matters communicated by us to the audit committee / the explanation as to why the annual report does not include a section describing the work of the audit committee is materially inconsistent with our knowledge obtained in the audit]; or
- **Directors' statement of compliance with the UK Corporate Governance Code** – the parts of the directors' statement required under the Listing Rules relating to the company's compliance with the UK Corporate Governance Code containing provisions specified for review by the auditor in accordance with Listing Rule 9.8.10R(2) do not properly disclose a departure from a relevant provision of the UK Corporate Governance Code.

Opinions on other matters prescribed by the Companies Act 2006

In our opinion, based on the work undertaken in the course of the audit:

- the information given in the strategic report and the directors' report for the financial year for which the group financial statements are prepared is consistent with the financial statements; and

- the strategic report and the directors' report have been prepared in accordance with applicable legal requirements.

Matters on which we are required to report by exception

In the light of the knowledge and understanding of the group and its environment obtained in the course of the audit, we have not identified material misstatements in the strategic report or the directors' report.

We have nothing to report in respect of the following matters in relation to which the Companies Act 2006 requires us to report to you if, in our opinion:

- certain disclosures of directors' remuneration specified by law are not made; or
- we have not received all the information and explanations we require for our audit.

Responsibilities of directors

As explained more fully in the directors' responsibilities statement [set out on page ...], the directors are responsible for the preparation of the group financial statements and for being satisfied that they give a true and fair view, and for such internal control as the directors determine is necessary to enable the preparation of group financial statements that are free from material misstatement, whether due to fraud or error.

In preparing the group financial statements, the directors are responsible for assessing the group's ability to continue as a going concern, disclosing, as applicable, matters related to going concern and using the going concern basis of accounting unless the directors either intend to liquidate the group or to cease operations, or have no realistic alternative but to do so.

Auditor's responsibilities for the audit of the group financial statements

Our objectives are to obtain reasonable assurance about whether the group financial statements as a whole are free from material misstatement, whether due to fraud or error, and to issue an auditor's report that includes our opinion. Reasonable assurance is a high level of assurance, but is not a guarantee that an audit conducted in accordance with ISAs (UK) will always detect a material misstatement when it exists. Misstatements can arise from fraud or error and are considered material if, individually or in the aggregate, they could reasonably be expected to influence the economic decisions of users taken on the basis of these group financial statements.

[*Explanation as to what extent the audit was considered capable of detecting irregularities, including fraud.*]

A further description of our responsibilities for the audit of the financial statements is located on the Financial Reporting Council's website at: [*website link*].[61] This description forms part of our auditor's report.

Other matters which we are required to address

We were appointed by [*state by whom or which body the auditor was appointed*] on [*date*]. The period of total uninterrupted engagement including previous renewals and reappointments of the firm is [X] years.

---

[61] *See paragraph 38 of this Compendium.*

The non-audit services prohibited by the FRC's Ethical Standard were not provided to the group and we remain independent of the group in conducting our audit.

[*Indicate any services, in addition to the audit, which were provided by the firm to the group that have not been disclosed in the financial statements or elsewhere in the annual report.*]

Our audit opinion is consistent with the additional report to the audit committee.

We have reported separately on the parent company financial statements of [XYZ Plc] for the year ended [*date*]. [That report includes details of the parent company key audit matters; how we applied the concept of materiality in planning and performing our audit; and an overview of the scope of our audit.[62]] [That report includes a statement on a material uncertainty related to going concern.] [That report includes an emphasis of matter.] [The opinion in that report is [qualified / an adverse opinion / a disclaimer of opinion].]

[*Signature*]

John Smith (Senior Statutory Auditor)

For and on behalf of ABC LLP, Statutory Auditor

[*Address*]

[*Date*]

---

[62] *See paragraph 49 of this Compendium.*

Appendix 7B—Publicly traded premium listed company preparing parent company financial statements under UK GAAP (reported on separately from the group financial statements)

- Company is a premium listed company, a quoted company and a public-interest entity
- Company prepares group financial statements
- Corporate governance statement incorporated into the directors' report, either directly or by incorporation by cross-reference and reported on in the auditor's report on the group financial statements
- UK Corporate Governance Code reported on in the auditor's report on the group financial statements
- Directors' remuneration report reported on in the auditor's report on the parent company financial statements
- Description of the auditor's responsibilities for the audit of the financial statements is included by reference to the location of such a description included on the FRC's website

Independent auditor's report to the members of [XYZ Plc]

Opinion

We have audited the parent company financial statements of [XYZ Plc] for the year ended [*date*] which comprise [*specify the titles of the primary statements*][63] and notes to the financial statements, including a summary of significant accounting policies. The financial reporting framework that has been applied in their preparation is applicable law and United Kingdom Accounting Standards, including Financial Reporting Standard 102 *The Financial Reporting Standard applicable in the UK and Republic of Ireland* (United Kingdom Generally Accepted Accounting Practice).

In our opinion the parent company financial statements:

- give a true and fair view of the state of the parent company's affairs as at [*date*] [and of its [profit/loss] for the year then ended];[64]
- have been properly prepared in accordance with United Kingdom Generally Accepted Accounting Practice; and
- have been prepared in accordance with the requirements of the Companies Act 2006.

Basis for opinion

We conducted our audit in accordance with International Standards on Auditing (UK) (ISAs (UK)) and applicable law. Our responsibilities under those standards are further described in the Auditor's Responsibilities for the audit of the parent company financial statements section of our report. We are independent of the parent company in accordance with the ethical requirements that are relevant to our audit of the parent company financial statements in the UK, including the FRC's Ethical Standard as applied to listed public interest entities, and we have fulfilled our other ethical responsibilities in accordance

---

[63] *The terms used to describe the primary financial statements should be the same as those used by the directors.*

[64] *The words 'and of its profit (or loss) for the year then ended' are included only where Section 408 exemption is not taken in respect of the parent company's own profit and loss account.*

with these requirements. We believe that the audit evidence we have obtained is sufficient and appropriate to provide a basis for our opinion.

Conclusions relating to going concern

We have nothing to report in respect of the following matter in relation to which the ISAs (UK) require us to report to you whether we have anything material to add or draw attention to in relation to:

- the directors' statement in the parent company financial statements about whether the directors considered it appropriate to adopt the going concern basis of accounting in preparing the parent company financial statements and the directors' identification of any material uncertainties to the parent company's ability to continue to do so over a period of at least twelve months from the date of approval of the parent company financial statements.

Key audit matters[65]

Key audit matters are those matters that, in our professional judgment, were of most significance in our audit of the parent company financial statements of the current period and include the most significant assessed risks of material misstatement (whether or not due to fraud) we identified, including those which had the greatest effect on: the overall audit strategy, the allocation of resources in the audit; and directing the efforts of the engagement team. These matters were addressed in the context of our audit of the parent company financial statements as a whole, and in forming our opinion thereon, and we do not provide a separate opinion on these matters.

[Description of each key audit matter in accordance with ISA (UK) 701.]

Our application of materiality[66]

[Explanation of how the auditor applied the concept of materiality in planning and performing the parent company audit. This is required to include the threshold used by the auditor as being materiality for the parent company financial statements as a whole but may include other relevant disclosures.[67]]

An overview of the scope of our audit[68]

[Overview of the scope of the parent company audit, including an explanation of how the scope addressed each key audit matter and was influenced by the auditor's application of materiality for the parent company financial statements as a whole.]

---

[65] *Key audit matters that relate solely to the parent company must be included within the auditor's report on the parent company financial statements for public interest entities and cannot be cross-referred to the auditor's report on the group financial statements.*

[66] *As noted in paragraph 49 of this Compendium, the explanation of how the auditor applied the concept of materiality in planning and performing the parent company audit may be presented either in the auditor's report on the parent company financial statements or separately identified in the auditor's report on the group financial statements via a cross-reference from the Other Matter paragraph.*

[67] *ISA (UK) 701, paragraph A59-1 includes other disclosures relevant to an explanation of how the auditor applied the context of materiality in planning and performing the audit.*

[68] *As noted in paragraph 49 of this Compendium, the overview of the scope of the parent company audit may be presented either in the auditor's report on the parent company financial statements or separately identified in the auditor's report on the group financial statements via a cross-reference from the Other Matter paragraph.*

Other information

The directors are responsible for the other information. The other information comprises the information included in the annual report,[69] other than the financial statements and our auditor's report thereon. Our opinion on the financial statements does not cover the other information and, except to the extent otherwise explicitly stated in our report, we do not express any form of assurance conclusion thereon.

In connection with our audit of the parent company financial statements, our responsibility is to read the other information and, in doing so, consider whether the other information is materially inconsistent with the parent company financial statements or our knowledge obtained in the audit or otherwise appears to be materially misstated. If we identify such material inconsistencies or apparent material misstatements, we are required to determine whether there is a material misstatement of the parent company financial statements or a material misstatement of the other information.

If, based on the work we have performed, we conclude that there is a material misstatement of this other information, we are required to report that fact. We have nothing to report in this regard.

Opinion on other matters prescribed by the Companies Act 2006

In our opinion, the part of the directors' remuneration report to be audited has been properly prepared in accordance with the Companies Act 2006.

In our opinion, based on the work undertaken in the course of the audit:

- the information given in the strategic report and the directors' report for the financial year for which the parent company financial statements are prepared is consistent with the financial statements; and
- the strategic report and the directors' report have been prepared in accordance with applicable legal requirements.

In the light of the knowledge and understanding of the parent company and its environment obtained in the course of the audit, we have not identified material misstatements in the strategic report or the directors' report.

Matters on which we are required to report by exception

We have nothing to report in respect of the following matters in relation to which the Companies Act 2006 requires us to report to you if, in our opinion:

- adequate accounting records have not been kept by the parent company, or returns adequate for our audit have not been received from branches not visited by us; or
- the parent company financial statements and the part of the directors' remuneration report to be audited are not in agreement with the accounting records and returns; or
- certain disclosures of directors' remuneration specified by law are not made; or
- we have not received all the information and explanations we require for our audit.

---

[69] *The term used to describe the annual report should be the same as that used by the directors.*

Responsibilities of directors

As explained more fully in the directors' responsibilities statement [set out on page ...], the directors are responsible for the preparation of the parent company financial statements and for being satisfied that they give a true and fair view, and for such internal control as the directors determine is necessary to enable the preparation of parent company financial statements that are free from material misstatement, whether due to fraud or error.

In preparing the parent company financial statements, the directors are responsible for assessing the parent company's ability to continue as a going concern, disclosing, as applicable, matters related to going concern and using the going concern basis of accounting unless the directors either intend to liquidate the parent company or to cease operations, or have no realistic alternative but to do so.

Auditor's responsibilities for the audit of the parent company financial statements

Our objectives are to obtain reasonable assurance about whether the parent company financial statements as a whole are free from material misstatement, whether due to fraud or error, and to issue an auditor's report that includes our opinion. Reasonable assurance is a high level of assurance, but is not a guarantee that an audit conducted in accordance with ISAs (UK) will always detect a material misstatement when it exists. Misstatements can arise from fraud or error and are considered material if, individually or in the aggregate, they could reasonably be expected to influence the economic decisions of users taken on the basis of these parent company financial statements.

[*Explanation as to what extent the audit was considered capable of detecting irregularities, including fraud.*]

A further description of our responsibilities for the audit of the parent company financial statements is located on the Financial Reporting Council's website at: [*website link*].[70] This description forms part of our auditor's report.

Other matters which we are required to address

We were appointed by [*state by whom or which body the auditor was appointed*] on [*date*]. The period of total uninterrupted engagement including previous renewals and reappointments of the firm is [X] years.

The non-audit services prohibited by the FRC's Ethical Standard were not provided to the parent company and its controlled undertakings and we remain independent of the parent company and its controlled undertakings in conducting our audit.

[*Indicate any services, in addition to the audit, which were provided by the firm to the parent company and its controlled undertaking(s) that have not been disclosed in the financial statements or elsewhere in the annual report.*]

Our audit opinion is consistent with the additional report to the audit committee.

We have reported separately on the group financial statements of [XYZ Plc] for the year ended [*date*]. [That report includes details of the group key audit matters; how we applied the concept of materiality in planning and performing our audit; and an overview of the

---

[70] *See paragraph 38 of this Compendium.*

scope of our audit.[71]] [That report includes a statement on a material uncertainty related to going concern.] [That report includes an emphasis of matter.] [The opinion in that report is [qualified / an adverse opinion / a disclaimer of opinion].]

[*Signature*]

John Smith (Senior Statutory Auditor)

For and on behalf of ABC LLP, Statutory Auditor

[*Address*]

[*Date*]

Briefing Paper

Professional scepticism – Establishing a common understanding and reaffirming its central role in delivering audit quality

Contents

Section 1 – Introduction

This paper sets out the APB's considered views on the nature of auditor scepticism and its role in the audit. Given the significance of scepticism to the quality of individual audits, and to the value of audit more generally, we believe that this document is an important point of reference on this topic and one which we hope all auditors will consider with great care.

It is written in an unusual format for an APB document, being much more discursive than is customary and drawing analogies from a diverse group of areas. This is because we believe that what is meant by scepticism needs to be more broadly understood and that drawing these analogies will assist in broadening that understanding. We are also keen to stimulate and provide input to an international debate on the issue of scepticism and believe that this broader and more discursive approach will provide a valuable input to that debate.

This document builds on the APB Discussion Paper published in August 2010 'Auditor Scepticism: Raising the Bar' and the subsequent Feedback Paper published in March 2011, which summarised the comments received and outlined the actions that the APB, and other parts of the FRC, intended to take in light of the responses received.

The Feedback Paper noted the following[1]:

- Responses suggested a wide range of views about what the initial mindset should be and raised concerns for the APB that there is a lack of consensus about the nature of professional scepticism and its role in the conduct of an audit.
- The APB did not accept that the auditor's role is limited to ensuring that management have appropriate evidence to support its assertions if this means accepting the evidence management present without subjecting it to robust challenge and comparison to alternative sources of evidence.
- The APB questioned whether a 'neutral mindset', or indeed just an 'inquiring mind', is appropriate for an auditor. The auditor's mindset is applied during audit planning to assess the risk of misstatement of the financial statements and such risk assessments determine the nature and extent of audit evidence to be obtained. It is also applied in assessing the validity of accounting estimates that are subject both to significant uncertainties and to considerable management judgment.

The first of the areas in which the APB proposed to undertake further work was ensuring that there is a consistent understanding of the nature of professional scepticism and its role in the conduct of an audit.

Section 2 considers the philosophical origins of scepticism in ancient Greece and how it later influenced scepticism in the scientific method that began to flourish in the 17th Century. The relationship between scepticism and the disposition to believe or disbelieve is explored as well as the influences of evidence and behaviours on that disposition.

Section 3 seeks to provide insight into the mind-set required to develop the audit strategy and plan and to evaluate the audit evidence obtained, by demonstrating how another learning – science – has developed a sceptical approach that now commands respect.

---

[1] See 'Auditor scepticism: Raising the bar: Feedback Statement' – March 2011 http://www.frc.org.uk/apb/publications/pub2343.html.

Section 4 seeks to provide further insight into the mindset of the auditor by considering the nature of the agency relationships, and the resultant need for assurance, that gave rise to early auditing traditions in manorial households from the 14th Century.

Section 5 sets out the APB's conclusions from the foregoing analysis as to what a sceptical audit looks like. It suggests that professional scepticism is the cornerstone of audit quality – it defines the quality of each audit judgment and through these the overall effectiveness of the audit in meeting the needs of shareholders and other stakeholders.

Section 6 sets out the APB's views about the conditions that are necessary for auditors to demonstrate the appropriate degree of professional scepticism. It highlights the APB's expectations of individual auditors, engagement teams, audit firms and of the supporting role that can be played by audit committees, management and others.

Finally, Section 7 sets out how the APB proposes to take these matters forward.

Section 2 – Exploring the roots of scepticism and identifying lessons for its role in the conduct of an audit

Scepticism is derived from the Greek word "σκέψις" (skepsis), meaning[2]: *examination, inquiry into, hesitation or doubt, especially of the Sceptics or Pyrrhone philosophers.* Greek philosophical Scepticism was a school of thought from the 5th Century BC that doubted the certainty of knowledge. From this developed the philosophical viewpoint that it is not possible to gain certain knowledge (truth) about the natural world.

Scepticism in Greek philosophy

Beyond understanding the etymological basis for the modern term "scepticism", what more can we learn from early Greek philosophical scepticism?

- First, the essence of scepticism is doubt and that doubt stimulates informed challenge and inquiry. The sceptics' doubts arose from the many conflicting views that persisted about fundamental issues. Their doubt stimulated them to challenge conventional wisdom and to inquire after a better understanding of the nature of knowledge.
- Second, in the face of doubt they would suspend their judgment about the truth.
- Third, in its extreme forms scepticism is not pragmatic as it may lead to the conclusion that no judgments about the truth can be made[3].

The disposition to believe or disbelieve and its conditioning influences

Today, scepticism commonly means 'doubt as to the truth of some assertion or supposed fact'[4]. Doubt is unbelief, whose antonyms include belief and trust[5]. Neither doubt nor trust need be absolute. Each has expression in different degrees. Uncertainty lies between them and absolute trust (belief) and absolute distrust (disbelief) are at their extremes. Doubt, trust and uncertainty are passive concepts – states of mind. They describe an individual's disposition to believe or disbelieve an assertion.

The actual level of doubt or trust in the state of mind conditions the individual's response. When the levels of both trust and doubt are low, there is uncertainty which either may result in a passive response – the indefinite suspension of judgment – or may stimulate an active inquiry to pursue the truth or falseness of the assertion. The results of that inquiry will further condition the state of mind and the process may be repeated. Only if and when a state of mind of trust or doubt is sufficiently high will the active response – acceptance or rejection of belief in the assertion – ensue.

---

[2] *Liddell & Scott Greek-English Lexicon.*

[3] *Bertrand Russell, in his 1958 book: "The Will to Doubt" illustrates such "heroic" scepticism by retelling the following: "A story is told of Pyrrho, the founder of Pyrrhonism (which was the old name for scepticism). He maintained that we never know enough to be sure that one course of action is wiser than another. In his youth, when he was taking his constitutional one afternoon, he saw his teacher in philosophy (from whom he had imbibed his principles) with his head stuck in a ditch, unable to get out. After contemplating him for some time, he walked on, maintaining that there was no sufficient ground for thinking he would do any good by pulling the man out. Others, less sceptical, effected a rescue, and blamed Pyrrho for his heartlessness. But his teacher, true to his principles, praised him for his consistency.*

[4] *The Shorter Oxford English Dictionary.*

[5] *See Roget's Thesaurus of synonyms and antonyms: categories 484 (Belief) and 485 (Unbelief; Doubt).*

The disposition to believe or disbelieve an assertion may be conditioned by many influences. These include not only the results of inquiry but also potentially the biases of the individual (whether conscious or sub-conscious) and the individual's perceptions and assessments of their self-interest. These other conditioning influences must be filtered out if objective truth is to be attained.

In the context of audit judgments, it may be helpful to understand the implications of the behavioural rules ('heuristics') underlying human decision-making and judgment processes. A number of heuristics have been proposed to help explain these processes, especially in the face of complex problems or incomplete information. It is also thought that they may, in some circumstances, introduce systematic errors or biases into these processes.

One illustration of these ideas may be found in a recent academic paper[6], which shows that people are less likely to adjust their beliefs in response to evidence that contradicts their optimistic beliefs than to evidence that contradicts their pessimistic beliefs.

What is needed to counteract this is a mechanism to encourage a structured consideration of the alternative point of view. One example of such a mechanism being applied in a financial services context is 'reverse stress testing'. In this form of stress testing, the directors consider what it would take to make the entity fail and then assess the evidence as to the likelihood of those circumstances arising.

Evidence based theories of knowledge and scientific scepticism

Later Sceptics were more pragmatic, arguing that there were ways of approaching (even if not quite attaining) the absolute truth. The Empirical school of thought proposed that the only or primary source of knowledge is experience gained through the senses. It therefore emphasised the role of empirical (observed) evidence in inducing knowledge rather than deducing knowledge from innate ideas and traditions.

Empiricism was highly influential in the development of science and the scientific method in the 17th Century. Scientific scepticism doubts the veracity of assertions that are not supported by empirical evidence that is reproducible and therefore seeks to exclude other influences from the scientific search for truth.

Evidence, trust and agency in the audit process

An audit is an evidence-based process to assess and report on the truth and fairness of the financial statements prepared by the directors to whom capital resources are entrusted by the shareholders. The audit is entrusted to another agent of the shareholders – the auditor.

This description refers to two features of an audit which are relevant to scepticism – the evidence-based nature of the audit and the entrustment and agency relationships

[6] *See:* How unrealistic optimism is maintained in the face of reality, *by Sharot, Korn and Dolan, in Nature Neuroscience, Nov 2011. This and earlier research considering the impact of new evidence on existing beliefs is discussed in a recent Research Paper from Societe Generale:* In defence of the doom merchants: when hearing isn't listening, *Jan 2012 at: http://www.frc.org.uk/images/uploaded/documents/Societe%20Generale%20 Research%20Paper%20January%202012.pdf. The Paper suggests that people have a natural tendency to take note of the evidence which backs their own theories and to ignore evidence which contradicts them. If anything, this tendency is exacerbated when they are exhorted to try harder.*

inherent in the audit. The role of scepticism in relation to each of these is explored further below. The evidence-based nature of the process suggests some parallels with, and is explored in the context of, the scientific method and scientific scepticism in Section 3. In Section 4, lessons about the expression of professional scepticism are also identified by considering the nature of the entrustment and agency relationships and the need for assurance that gave rise to the tradition of auditing servants in the manorial estates of the fourteenth century in the origins of the modern audit in the UK.

Section 3 – Scientific scepticism and the scientific method

The scientific method seeks to understand the causes and effects of natural processes by:

- *Empirical observation* of their behaviours in different conditions;
- Postulating how they work (*constructing theories* of cause and effect that are consistent with the observations) – an approach that relies on inductive logic.
- Predicting effects that would necessarily follow from the truth of a theory in specific conditions (*constructing hypotheses*) – an approach that relies on deductive logic.
- *Testing* those hypotheses by considering not only what evidence would support them but also what evidence would falsify them – accordingly, experiments are designed and performed to find such evidence.
- Each step of the process is *transparent and repeatable*, subject to the critical review of other scientists and capable of being challenged and retested by them.
- In the development of scientific knowledge in a new area, there may be several competing theories, each of which has survived hypothesis testing. The advancement of a theory to the status of accepted scientific knowledge requires a *'critical experiment'*, one capable of providing evidence that will prove the superiority of one theory over all the other competing theories.

This process can disprove a postulated theory but cannot absolutely prove it. If testing falsifies a hypothesis, then theories are reassessed in light of the new observations and if necessary new ones are postulated. A theory that survives rigorous testing remains plausible, for the time being. Scientific knowledge is therefore dynamic and constantly subject to challenge.

Prior to the development of the scientific method, knowledge of the natural world was largely based on accepted ancient wisdom (axiomatic truths) and advanced by developing consequential "knowledge" by logical deduction (the deductive method). A critical development in the evolution of the scientific method was the acceptance that there are no axiomatic truths that can be observed and that there is a continuing need to question and challenge all matters that may appear to be so.

Robert Boyle is widely recognised as the father of modern chemistry and an early proponent of the scientific method. His treatise on the new approach is aptly called 'The Sceptical Chymist'[7].

Scepticism in the scientific method can be described as a <u>systematic form of continual informed questioning</u> that requires the scientist:

- To <u>critically appraise</u> existing theories, actively looking for alternative plausible mechanisms of cause and effect that are consistent with their rigorous assessment of the empirical (observed) evidence;
- To undertake experiments that are repeatable and transparent, to look for <u>evidence that contradicts rather than supports</u> the validity of any given theory; and
- To <u>suspend judgment</u> about the validity of any given theory (ie to defer making an active decision to believe or disbelieve it) until it has both survived destructive testing and has been subjected to critical experiments the evidence from which makes it is possible to conclude that one theory is superior to all other current plausible theories.

---

[7] *Robert Boyle, 1661: The Sceptical Chymist: or Chymico-Physical Doubts & Paradoxes Touching the Spagyrist's Principles Commonly call'd Hypostatical As they are wont to be Propos'd and Defended by the Generality of Alchemists.*

There are many parallels between the scientific method and the audit and, whilst this analogy should, of course, not be taken too far, at a certain level there is much to learn from a consideration of the nature of scientific scepticism and the role it plays in the conduct of the scientific method. Scientific scepticism is the backbone of the scientific method, influencing every judgment in the process of learning and ultimately supporting the whole body of scientific knowledge.

However, the subject matters of scientific and audit inquiry are different in nature. The subject matter of Science is knowledge of the natural world, which experience shows to ordinarily behave in a systematic way. The subject matter of auditing is the outputs from the business performance and reporting systems of the entity, which though usually intended to operate systematically often do not as they are subject to the vagaries of external influences, as well as human error and fraud.

In science, the potential variables are identified and can be controlled and varied individually under laboratory conditions. In the audit, they cannot and the outputs of the business performance and reporting systems of the entity must be observed in real world (multivariate) conditions.

Notwithstanding these limitations to the analogy between the audit and the scientific method, elements of the scientific method suggest critical audit activities which will underpin appropriate scepticism in the audit:

- Empirical observation *suggests* developing a good understanding of the business of the audited entity and of the environment;
- Constructing falsifiable hypotheses *suggests* actively considering that material misstatements may exist and designing audit tests to identify them, rather than only considering how well the evidence obtained by management supports their conclusion that there are none; and
- Transparency and repeatability *suggest* the importance of documentation in underpinning transparency and repeatability of the audit work to internal reviewers and to external inspectors.

The comparison says less about how far the auditor should go in pursuing these activities:

- When should the active search for risks of material misstatement stop?
- How far should the auditor's understanding be pursued?
- How much testing and stress testing should the auditor undertake?
- When is the evidence sufficient?

The scientific analogy suggests there is no absolute level to which such matters should be pursued. Scientific scepticism is pursued up to the point where other similarly objective scientists would want to go before they accept or reject a hypothesis. In the scientific field, acceptance of a hypothesis only occurs when the level of trust in that hypothesis is approaching virtual certainty. This may not be the most appropriate point to which professional scepticism should be pursued in the audit. This is considered further in the next section in the context of the historical origins of the modern audit in the UK.

Section 4 – The origins of the modern audit

The origins of the modern audit can be seen in the tradition of auditing household servants in manorial estates that developed from the fourteenth century[8]. The auditor was the most trusted servant in the household and all other servants were required to account to the auditor for the resources entrusted to them.

In its simplest form, an account was required from each household servant of all money and other assets entrusted to them – they were "charged" with the assets when placed in their care and "discharged" when the auditor had heard and accepted their account.

When free incorporation joint stock companies were established in the Joint Stock Companies Act of 1844, there were default provisions for auditors to be appointed, that built on these traditions. Under the default provisions, at least one of the auditors should be appointed by the shareholders, their fees should be paid by the company but set by a government agency (the Commissioners of the Treasury) as they saw fit, and their report should be made publicly available. The auditor was neither required to be a shareholder nor a professional accountant but often was a shareholder and frequently employed professional accountants to assist them.

The Joint Stock Companies Act of 1856 enhanced the earlier default provisions to specifically allow the auditor to employ accountants to assist them at the company's expense and to prohibit the auditor from being a director or an officer of the company and from having any interest in any transaction of the company other than as a shareholder. The absolute requirement that companies should have an audit (initially just for joint stock banks but later extended to all companies) as opposed to optional default provisions, originated in the 1879 Companies Act following the collapse of the City Bank of Glasgow. In time, the practice of appointing share-holders as auditors fell away and public accountants were employed to undertake the role directly.

Looking back, it would seem that, in its origin, the audit was essentially a check, carried out on behalf of a principal by their trusted associate or agent, on the fidelity of other agents to whom the principal's resources were entrusted. The trust that existed between principal and auditor was a critical ingredient, if not the critical ingredient of the audit. The importance of professional skills only came later. The whole rationale for the audit was that the principal could not assume, and therefore sought assurance about, the fidelity of those to whom their assets were entrusted.

This may suggest how far the auditor should pursue professional scepticism in the audit. The strong bond of trust between the principal and the auditor and the principal's need for assurance about the fidelity of those to whom they had entrusted their assets would have determined the mindset of the auditor. That would have guided the appropriate degree of scepticism in the auditor when holding a hearing to question those entrusted with the principal's assets and to assess whether they had given a proper account of their handling of those assets. They would have asked the questions they would expect their principal to ask, they would have challenged where they would expect their principal to challenge and they would have pursued matters until they were satisfied that the evidence would satisfy their principal.

---

[8] *See* Be careful what you wish for: How accountants and Congress created the problem of auditor independence, 2004, Sean M. O'Connor at: http://www.bc.edu/dam/files/schools/law/lawreviews/journals/bclawr/45_4/01_FMS.htm.

This is perhaps a fair lens through which to understand the necessary degree of scepticism in the modern audit. What would the shareholders (and other stakeholders) expect the auditor to ask, what matters would they expect them to challenge and what evidence would they need to satisfy those challenges?

Whilst fidelity may have been the issue in the 19th Century and much of the 20th Century (and remains an issue in the 21st Century), the development and increased complexity of business activity, and the increased size and reach of such businesses, combined with the arrival of the technological age mean that there are many other areas in relation to which shareholders (and other users) seek information and reassurance. For example, misalignment of their personal interests may simply lead to misalignment of risk taking appetite between the directors and shareholders.

This suggests that whilst the sceptical mindset is a constant, the degree of action taken by a sceptical auditor (by way of inquiry, challenge and testing) is responsive both to the expectations of shareholders (and other stakeholders) and to what emerges as the audit proceeds. This is the 'sliding scale' that was referred to in *Auditor Scepticism: Raising the Bar.*

Because of the need to consider their expectations, the perspective of shareholders and other stakeholders (as users) is embedded in the auditing standards in relation to materiality, and scepticism should embed that perspective in the making of all audit judgments. Against this background, the APB believes that when undertaking a modern audit the following factors accentuate the need for the auditor to be especially vigilant and aware of his or her responsibilities for the exercise of professional scepticism:

- There is potential for auditors not to be sceptical or thought not to be sceptical because they are engaged and paid by the company in a way that is relatively detached from shareholders. In addition, they have little, if any, direct contact with shareholders throughout the audit process; as a result, shareholders have no way of observing, and thereby gaining trust in, the audit process. This emphasises the need for strong governance generally and, in particular, the importance of the responsibility that audit committees have in both assessing and communicating to investors whether the auditors have executed a high quality, sceptical audit;
- Auditors necessarily have strong working relationships with management and audit committees, which may lead them to develop trust that may lead to either a lack of, or reduced, scepticism; and
- The audit firms' business models encourage a culture of building strong relationships with audited entities. This introduces the moral hazard of the auditor putting his or her interests ahead of those of shareholders and could lead the audit firm and the auditor to develop trust or self-interest motivations that may compromise either their objectivity or willingness to challenge management to the extent required.

It is perhaps not surprising that auditors often refer to the audited entity as the 'client', given the strength of these relationships and the all but formal appointment of the auditor by the directors and not by the shareholders. However, trust in management may compromise the auditor's exercise of scepticism because that trust may colour his/her judgement as to when and where a sceptical approach is required. It is important to lean against unjustified trust developing, just as it is important to address threats to the auditor's objectivity that may arise from the provision of non-audit services – it is interesting to note in this context that the auditor originally was not permitted to have any interest in any transaction with the company.

The factors described above are widely recognised to pose challenges to the reality and perception of auditors' professional integrity (including their objectivity and independence). The need to address these challenges gives rise to a variety of responses that seek to lean against them, including the responsibilities, liabilities and disclosures relating to the audit and the auditor established in the law and professional standards, including the Ethical Standards. This is also one of the principal reasons for the need for the application and demonstration of appropriate professional scepticism in the audit.

Despite the increasing role of audit committees as independent non-executive directors in monitoring and challenging the entity's financial information and controls (in effect as the representatives of the shareholders), there is also a risk that audit committees' views may be seen too readily by the auditor as a surrogate for those of the shareholders. Just addressing the concerns of the audit committee does not necessarily amount to meeting the expectations of shareholders (and other stakeholders).

For all of these reasons, the rigorous assessment of when, and the degree to which, professional scepticism is required is fundamental to an effective audit.

Section 5 – Conclusions about professional scepticism in the audit

In the growth and development of a living thing, the expression of its DNA in the formation of its cells defines its essence and its effectiveness in meeting the challenges of its environment. In the words of Richard Dawkins[9]:

DNA neither cares nor knows. DNA just is. And we dance to its music.

In the same way, the expression of professional scepticism by the audit team defines the essence of the particular audit. It defines the quality of each audit judgment and, through these, the overall effectiveness of the audit in addressing the challenges it faces in meeting the needs of shareholders (and other stakeholders) who rely on it. The reality and perception of the expression of professional scepticism define and underpin the confidence that others place in the audit and in turn the confidence they place in the audited financial statements.

The preceding analysis suggests that the appropriate application of professional scepticism in the audit requires a mindset which rigorously questions and challenges management's assertions with a degree of doubt that reflects the expectations of shareholders (and other stakeholders) for whose benefit it is performed. All judgments made in the course of the audit should be founded on the perspective of the shareholders (and other stakeholders). That mindset demands the sort of hard evidence – to back each audit judgment and, ultimately, the board's assertion that the financial statements give a true and fair view – that would be convincing and persuasive to shareholders (and other stakeholders), given the auditor's risk assessment.

The analysis suggests that in an appropriately sceptical audit:

- The auditor's risk assessment process should involve a critical appraisal of management's assertions, actively looking for risks of material misstatement. These may arise due to fraud or error and may reflect weaknesses in the design or the operation of management's system for controlling and reporting the entity's financial position and performance (such that relevant matters are not identified, or are not adequately controlled or reported, or that the design has not been implemented and operated effectively[10]).
- The auditor develops a high degree of knowledge of the audited entity's business and the environment in which it operates, sufficient to enable it to make its risk assessment through its own fresh and independent eyes rather than through the eyes of management.
- This enables the auditor to make informed challenge of consensus views and to consider the possible incidence of low probability high impact events. The alternative would give rise to the risk of what is known in science as "hypothesis bias" which is an example of "group-think". The challenges in acquiring sufficient knowledge and experience should not be underestimated, especially in relation to complex business models. The traditional pyramid structure of the audit team may not always be appropriate and different models may need to be explored, such as including experienced business people on the team.
- The auditor designs audit procedures to consider actively if there is any evidence that would contradict management assertions not only to consider the extent to which management has identified evidence that is consistent with them. The

---

[9] *Richard Dawkins: River Out of Eden: A Darwinian View of Life (1995), 133.*

[10] *This is not to suggest that the auditor must always test the operating effectiveness of the financial reporting system, rather than taking a substantive approach and testing the outputs from that system.*

opposite of a sceptical audit might be one in which the auditor merely ratio-nalises and documents management's assertions.

- The auditor has strong skills in making evidence-based judgments and suspends judgment about whether the financial statements do or do not give a true and fair view until satisfied that:
  - There has been sufficient inquiry and challenge;
  - Sufficient testing of management's assertions has been undertaken;
  - The quality of the resulting evidence obtained has been critically appraised and judged by the auditor to be sufficiently persuasive; and
  - Where there are plausible alternative treatments of an item in the financial statements (such as different valuation bases), an assessment has been made as to whether one is superior and whether sufficient disclosure of the alternatives has been given, in order to give a true and fair view.
- The auditor approaches and documents audit judgments and audit review processes in a manner that facilitates challenge and demonstrates the rigour of that challenge.

The auditor's documentation of audit judgments is conclusive rather than conclu-sionary and therefore always sets out not only the auditor's conclusion but also their rationale for the conclusion, relating it to the nature of the challenges raised in the underlying work and reviews, the strength of the evidence obtained and the per-spective of shareholders (and other stakeholders). The auditor needs strong skills in logical argument to do this effectively.

Section 6 – Fostering conditions necessary for auditors to demonstrate the appropriate degree of professional scepticism

The application of an appropriate degree of professional scepticism is a crucial skill for auditors. Unless auditors are prepared to challenge management's assertions they will not be able to confirm with confidence that a company's financial statements present a true and fair view.

The APB believes that in order to demonstrate the value of the audit, the auditor should perform a sceptical audit, evidence the exercise of appropriate scepticism in the audit documentation and convince audit committees and ultimately the shareholders (and other stakeholders) that it has done so.

The challenge for firms is to identify, develop and retain people with the necessary skills and to deploy them appropriately. It also involves nurturing the conditions that allow professional scepticism to flourish.

The prospects for a sceptical audit are likely to be enhanced if the environment in which the auditor operates also recognises and supports the important role that scepticism plays in the audit.

The APB considers that the conditions necessary for auditors to demonstrate the appropriate degree of professional scepticism are likely to include the following.

Individual auditors

- Develop a good understanding of the entity and its business.
- Have a questioning mind and are willing to challenge management assertions.
- Assess critically the information and explanations obtained in the course of their work and corroborate them.
- Seek to understand management motivations for possible misstatement of the financial statements.
- Investigate the nature and cause of deviations or misstatements identified and avoid jumping to conclusions without appropriate audit evidence.
- Are alert for evidence that is inconsistent with other evidence obtained or calls into question the reliability of documents and responses to inquiries.
- Have the confidence to challenge management and the persistence to follow things through to a conclusion – even if predisposed to agree with management's assertion, the auditor should actively consider the alternative views and challenge management to demonstrate that they are not more appropriate.

Engagement teams

- Have good business knowledge and experience.
- Actively consider in what circumstances management numbers may be misstated, whether due to fraud or error, and the possible sources of misstatement, notwithstanding existing knowledge and relationships.
- Develop a good understanding of the entity and its business in order to provide a basis for identifying unusual events or transactions and share information on a regular basis.
- Partners and managers are actively involved in assessing risk and planning the audit procedures to be performed – they think about the changes that are taking place in the entity and its environment and plan audit tests that are responsive to them.

- Partners and managers actively lead and participate in audit team planning meetings to discuss the susceptibility of the entity's financial statements to material misstatement including through fraud and the misuse of related parties.
- Partners and managers are accessible to other staff during the audit and encourage them to consult with them on a timely basis.
- Engagement teams document their key audit judgments and conclusions, especially those reported to the audit committee, in a way that clearly demonstrates that they have exercised an appropriate degree of challenge to management and professional scepticism. In particular, the reasons why the audit team concurs with management's assertions are clearly articulated in a way that, where appropriate, discusses the appropriateness of reasonably credible alternative views and the reasons why they have not been adopted.
- Partners and managers bring additional scepticism to the audit through taking the steps necessary to carry out, face to face where appropriate, a diligent challenge and review of the audit work performed, and the adequacy of the documentation prepared, by other members of the engagement team.

Audit firms

- The culture within the firm emphasises the importance of:
  - understanding and pursuing the perspective of the shareholders (and other stakeholders) of the audited entity in making audit judgments;
  - coaching less experienced staff to foster appropriate scepticism;
  - sharing experiences about difficult audit judgments within the firm;
  - consultation with others about difficult audit judgments; and
  - supporting audit partners when they need to take and communicate difficult audit judgements.
- Scepticism is embedded in the firm's training and competency frameworks used for evaluating and rewarding partner and staff performance.
- The firm requires rigorous engagement quality control reviews that challenge engagement teams' judgments and conclusions.
- Firm methodologies and review processes emphasise the importance of, and provide practical support for auditors in:
  - developing a thorough understanding of the entity's business and its environment, sufficient to enable the auditor to carry out a robust risk assessment through their own fresh eyes;
  - identifying issues early in the planning cycle to allow adequate time for them to be investigated and resolved;
  - rigorously taking such steps as are appropriate to the scale and complexity of the financial reporting systems, to identify unusual transactions;
  - changing risk assessments, materiality and the audit plan in response to audit findings;
  - documenting audit judgments in a conclusive rather than a conclusionary manner and therefore setting out not only the conclusion but also the rationale for the conclusion, relating it to the nature of the challenges
  - raised in the underlying work and reviews, the strength of the evidence obtained and the perspective of shareholders (and other stakeholders);
  - raising matters with the Audit Committee (or those charged with governance) in relation to which the auditor believes the perspective of shareholders (and other stakeholders) about the treatment or disclosure of the matter in the financial statements or related narrative reports could well be different from that adopted by the entity; and
  - ensuring that the disclosures relating to such matters are carefully assessed to ensure that those of relevance to shareholders (and other stakeholders)

are sufficient and appropriate in the circumstances, having regard to the auditor's consideration of the true and fair view[11].

The role of Audit Committees and management

Whilst it is the responsibility of the auditor to ensure that an appropriate degree of professional scepticism is applied in an audit, the Audit Committee and management can have a significant influencing role.

The Audit Committee's role includes overseeing the integrity of financial reporting and the related processes (including internal financial controls, the independence and objectivity of the external auditor and the effectiveness of the audit process). In this role, the APB believes that Audit Committees should seek to foster appropriate professional scepticism in the external audit, for example, through:

- Promoting the development of a culture within the entity which elicits a constructive response from management and staff to auditor challenge;
- Challenging whether the auditor has developed an adequate understanding of the business and its environment and provided an appropriately informed fresh perspective in making its risk assessment;
- Ensuring that, where management and auditor have resolved either contentious issues or issues that involve significant judgment, these are brought to the audit committee's attention; and
- Seeking to understand in relation to issues brought to their attention (including issues where management and auditor agree the position) whether or not an appropriate degree of challenge was exercised by the auditor – for example, by demanding an explanation of the auditor's rationale for particular conclusions, what alternatives were considered and why the specific judgment was considered to be the most appropriate of the alternatives.

The APB believes that this is consistent with the FRC's *Effective Company Stewardship* proposals[12], under which it is proposed that Audit Committees should produce fuller reports for the Board, in particular setting out their advice on the integrity of the Annual Report and explaining how they discharged their responsibilities for this and other aspects of their remit (such as their oversight of the external audit process and appointment of external auditors). Taken together with the proposal for Boards to discuss these matters in the Annual Report, the effect should be to ensure that the Annual Report demonstrates that the audit addressed those matters of most interest to shareholders and other stakeholders with appropriate challenge and scepticism.

---

[11] *See the FRC document:* True and Fair – July 2011 *at: http://www.frc.org.uk/images/uploaded/documents/ Paper%20True%20and%20Fair1.pdf.*

[12] *See http://www.frc.org.uk/about/effcompsteward.cfm.*

Section 7 – Taking these matters forward

The main purpose of this document is to explain the APB's views on professional scepticism and to encourage auditors to apply its principles in executing high quality sceptical audits and in documenting and demonstrating that they have done so. The APB has also considered the definition of professional scepticism and the extent and manner in which it has been dealt with in the ISAs (UK & I) and in ISQC 1 (UK &I), in light of the conclusions drawn in this Paper.

Although these standards contain many elements[13] that support the understanding of professional scepticism developed in this Paper, it is also possible for an auditor to follow the 'letter' of the standards without conducting a truly sceptical audit. The APB acknowledges that these standards may well need to be improved further to reflect better some of the conclusions reflected in this Paper and to be clearer about the performance, documentation and communication of professional scepticism.

Accordingly, whilst it has concluded that in taking these matters forward, the immediate emphasis should be on encouraging auditors and others to deliver a step change in behaviours that will achieve consistency in the manner in which professional scepticism is exercised in the conduct of their audits, it also intends to seek to influence the IAASB to enhance the auditing standards in due course.

The APB therefore proposes to:

- Stimulate debate and acceptance by stakeholders of the conclusions set out in this Paper about the nature and role of professional scepticism in the audit;
- Encourage the auditing profession and the audit firms to consider the implications of these conclusions for their business models and culture and for their approach to audits and to implement such changes as are necessary to respond to the challenges they identify – including the need to reflect the perspective of shareholders (and other stakeholders) in exercising their professional judgment;
- Promote these conclusions with Audit Committee members and management to encourage them to recognise and act on the important contribution that they can make to support the appropriate exercise of professional scepticism;
- Promote with those preparing the financial statements and Annual Report the benefits of open communication and consideration of the key judgments involved in doing so and in responding to the challenges raised in the audit; and
- Promote the conclusions set out in this Paper internationally, with a view to identifying ways in which the International Standards on Auditing might be developed to better reflect these conclusions, as part of the post Clarity ISA implementation review.

---

[13] *See IAASB Staff Questions and Answers on* 'Professional Skepticism in an audit of Financial Statements' *at:* http://www.ifac.org/sites/default/files/publications/files/IAASB%20Professional%20Skepticism%20QandA-final. pdf.

Part Ten

IESBA and ICAEW Codes of Ethics

Handbook of the Code of Ethics for Professional Accountants

2016 EDITION

Contents

Handbook of the Code of Ethics for Professional Accountants

Table of Contents

Introduction to the International Ethics Standards Board for Accountants®

The International Ethics Standards Board for Accountants® (IESBA®) is an independent standard-setting body that develops an internationally appropriate *Code of Ethics for Professional Accountants*[[amptrade]] (the Code).

The objective of the IESBA, as outlined in its Terms of Reference, is to serve the public interest by setting high-quality ethics standards for professional accountants. The IESBA's long-term objective is convergence of the Code's ethical standards for professional accountants, including auditor independence standards, with those issued by regulators and national standard setters. Convergence to a single set of standards can enhance the quality and consistency of services provided by professional accountants throughout the world and can improve the efficiency of global capital markets.

The IESBA consists of 18 board members from around the world, of whom no more than 9 are practitioners and no fewer than 3 are public members (individuals who are expected to reflect, and are seen to reflect, the wider public interest). Members are appointed by the IFAC Board, based on recommendations from the IFAC Nominating Committee and with the approval of the Public Interest Oversight Board (PIOB), which oversees the activities of the IESBA.

The standard-setting process of the IESBA includes the involvement of the PIOB and the IESBA's Consultative Advisory Group (CAG), which provides public interest input into the development of the IESBA's standards and guidance.

In developing its standards, the IESBA is required to be transparent in its activities, and to adhere to due process as approved by the PIOB. Board meetings, including meetings by teleconference, are open to the public, and agenda papers are available on its website.

Please visit www.ethicsboard.org for more information.

The International Federation of Accountants' Role

The International Federation of Accountants (IFAC) serves the public interest by contributing to the development of strong and sustainable organizations, markets, and economies. It advocates for transparency, accountability, and comparability of financial reporting; helps develop the accountancy profession; and communicates the importance and value of accountants to the global financial infrastructure. Founded in 1977, IFAC is currently comprised of more than 175 members and associates in more than 130 countries and jurisdictions, representing almost 3 million accountants in public practice, education, government service, industry, and commerce.

As part of its public interest mandate, IFAC contributes to the development, adoption, and implementation of high-quality international ethics standards for accountants, primarily through its support of the IESBA. IFAC provides human resources, facilities management, communications support, and funding to this independent standard-setting board, and facilitates the nominations and selection process for board members.

The IESBA sets its own agendas and approves its publications in accordance with its due process and without IFAC's involvement. IFAC has no ability to influence the agendas or publications. IFAC publishes the handbooks, standards, and other publications and owns the copyrights.

The IESBA's independence is safeguarded in a number of ways:

- formal, independent public interest oversight for standard setting by the PIOB (see www.ipiob.org for more information), which includes a rigorous due process involving public consultation
- a public call for nominations, and formal, independent oversight of the nominations/ selection process by the PIOB
- full transparency, both in terms of due process for standard setting, as well as public access to agenda materials, meetings, and a published basis for conclusions with each final standard
- the involvement of a Consultative Advisory Group and observers in the standard-setting process, and
- the requirement that IESBA members, as well as nominating/employing organizations, commit to the board's independence, integrity, and public interest mission.

Visit the IFAC website at www.ifac.org for further information.

Scope of this Handbook 2016 Edition

This handbook brings together for continuing reference information about the role of IFAC and the official text of the *Code of Ethics for Professional Accountants* (the Code) issued by the IESBA.

Changes of Substance from 2015 Edition

Code of Ethics for Professional Accountants

This handbook replaces the 2015 edition of the *Handbook of the Code of Ethics for Professional Accountants*.

Changes

The 2016 edition of the handbook contains new Sections 225 and 360 addressing professional accountants' responsibilities when they become aware of non-compliance or suspected non-compliance with laws and regulations committed by a client or employer.

Consequential and conforming changes have been made to Sections 100, 140, 150, 210, and 270 of the Code.

The changes will be effective on July 15, 2017. Early adoption is permitted.

The changes were published on the IESBA website in July 2016.

Changes to the Code Issued Subsequent to July 2016 and Exposure Drafts

For information on recent developments and to obtain final pronouncements issued subsequent to July 2016, or outstanding Exposure Drafts, visit the IESBA's website at www.ethicsboard.org.

Preface

The IESBA develops and issues, under its own authority, the *Code of Ethics for Professional Accountants* (the Code) for use by professional accountants around the world.

A member body of IFAC or firm shall not apply less stringent standards than those stated in this Code. However, if a member body or firm is prohibited from complying with certain parts of this Code by law or regulation, they shall comply with all other parts of this Code.

Some jurisdictions may have requirements and guidance that differ from those contained in this Code. Professional accountants in those jurisdictions need to be aware of those differences and comply with the more stringent requirements and guidance unless prohibited by law or regulation.

Part A—General application of the Code

Section 100

Introduction and Fundamental Principles

100.1   A distinguishing mark of the accountancy profession is its acceptance of the responsibility to act in the public interest. Therefore, a professional accountant's responsibility is not exclusively to satisfy the needs of an individual client or employer. In acting in the public interest, a professional accountant shall observe and comply with this Code. If a professional accountant is prohibited from complying with certain parts of this Code by law or regulation, the professional accountant shall comply with all other parts of this Code.

100.2   This Code contains three parts. Part A establishes the fundamental principles of professional ethics for professional accountants and provides a conceptual framework that professional accountants shall apply to:

(a)   Identify threats to compliance with the fundamental principles;

(b)   Evaluate the significance of the threats identified; and

(c)   Apply safeguards, when necessary, to eliminate the threats or reduce them to an acceptable level. Safeguards are necessary when the professional accountant determines that the threats are not at a level at which a reasonable and informed third party would be likely to conclude, weighing all the specific facts and circumstances available to the professional accountant at that time, that compliance with the fundamental principles is not compromised.

A professional accountant shall use professional judgment in applying this conceptual framework.

100.3   Parts B and C describe how the conceptual framework applies in certain situations. They provide examples of safeguards that may be appropriate to address threats to compliance with the fundamental principles. They also describe situations where safeguards are not available to address the threats, and consequently, the circumstance or relationship creating the threats shall be avoided. Part B applies to professional accountants in public practice. Part C applies to professional accountants in business. Professional accountants in public practice may also find Part C relevant to their particular circumstances.

100.4   The use of the word 'shall' in this Code imposes a requirement on the professional accountant or firm to comply with the specific provision in which 'shall' has been used. Compliance is required unless an exception is permitted by this Code.

Fundamental Principles

100.5   A professional accountant shall comply with the following fundamental principles:

(a)   Integrity – to be straightforward and honest in all professional and business relationships.

(b)   Objectivity – to not allow bias, conflict of interest or undue influence of others to override professional or business judgments.

(c)   Professional Competence and Due Care – to maintain professional knowledge and skill at the level required to ensure that a client or employer receives competent professional service based on current developments in practice, legislation and techniques and act diligently and in accordance with applicable technical and professional standards.

(d)   Confidentiality – to respect the confidentiality of information acquired as a result of professional and business relationships and, therefore, not disclose any such information to third parties without proper and specific authority, unless there is a legal or professional right or duty to disclose, nor use the information for the personal advantage of the professional accountant or third parties.

(e) Professional Behavior – to comply with relevant laws and regulations and avoid any action that discredits the profession.

Each of these fundamental principles is discussed in more detail in Sections 110–150.

Conceptual Framework Approach

The circumstances in which professional accountants operate may create specific threats to compliance with the fundamental principles. It is impossible to define every situation that creates threats to compliance with the fundamental principles and specify the appropriate action. In addition, the nature of engagements and work assignments may differ and, consequently, different threats may be created, requiring the application of different safeguards. Therefore, this Code establishes a conceptual framework that requires a professional accountant to identify, evaluate, and address threats to compliance with the fundamental principles. The conceptual framework approach assists professional accountants in complying with the ethical requirements of this Code and meeting their responsibility to act in the public interest. It accommodates many variations in circumstances that create threats to compliance with the fundamental principles and can deter a professional accountant from concluding that a situation is permitted if it is not specifically prohibited.

100.6

When a professional accountant identifies threats to compliance with the fundamental principles and, based on an evaluation of those threats, determines that they are not at an acceptable level, the professional accountant shall determine whether appropriate safeguards are available and can be applied to eliminate the threats or reduce them to an acceptable level. In making that determination, the professional accountant shall exercise professional judgment and take into account whether a reasonable and informed third party, weighing all the specific facts and circumstances available to the professional accountant at the time, would be likely to conclude that the threats would be eliminated or reduced to an acceptable level by the application of the safeguards, such that compliance with the fundamental principles is not compromised.

100.7

A professional accountant shall evaluate any threats to compliance with the fundamental principles when the professional accountant knows, or could reasonably be expected to know, of circumstances or relationships that may compromise compliance with the fundamental principles.

100.8

A professional accountant shall take qualitative as well as quantitative factors into account when evaluating the significance of a threat. When applying the conceptual framework, a professional accountant may encounter situations in which threats cannot be eliminated or reduced to an acceptable level, either because the threat is too significant or because appropriate safeguards are not available or cannot be applied. In such situations, the professional accountant shall decline or discontinue the specific professional activity or service involved or, when necessary, resign from the engagement (in the case of a professional accountant in public practice) or the employing organization (in the case of a professional accountant in business).

100.9

Sections 290 and 291 contain provisions with which a professional accountant shall comply if the professional accountant identifies a breach of an independence provision of the Code. If a professional accountant identifies a breach of any other provision of this Code, the professional accountant shall evaluate the significance of the breach and its impact on the accountant's ability to comply with the fundamental principles. The accountant shall take whatever actions that may be available, as soon as possible, to satisfactorily address the

100.10

consequences of the breach. The accountant shall determine whether to report the breach, for example, to those who may have been affected by the breach, a member body, relevant regulator or oversight authority.

100.11   When a professional accountant encounters unusual circumstances in which the application of a specific requirement of the Code would result in a disproportionate outcome or an outcome that may not be in the public interest, it is recommended that the professional accountant consult with a member body or the relevant regulator.

Threats and Safeguards

100.12   Threats may be created by a broad range of relationships and circumstances. When a relationship or circumstance creates a threat, such a threat could compromise, or could be perceived to compromise, a professional accountant's compliance with the fundamental principles. A circumstance or relationship may create more than one threat, and a threat may affect compliance with more than one fundamental principle. Threats fall into one or more of the following categories:

(a)   Self-interest threat – the threat that a financial or other interest will inappropriately influence the professional accountant's judgment or behavior;

(b)   Self-review threat – the threat that a professional accountant will not appropriately evaluate the results of a previous judgment made, or activity or service performed by the professional accountant, or by another individual within the professional accountant's firm or employing organization, on which the accountant will rely when forming a judgment as part of performing a current activity or providing a current service;

(c)   Advocacy threat – the threat that a professional accountant will promote a client's or employer's position to the point that the professional accountant's objectivity is compromised;

(d)   Familiarity threat [[ampboxh]] the threat that due to a long or close relationship with a client or employer, a professional accountant will be too sympathetic to their interests or too accepting of their work; and

(e)   Intimidation threat – the threat that a professional accountant will be deterred from acting objectively because of actual or perceived pressures, including attempts to exercise undue influence over the professional accountant.

Parts B and C of this Code explain how these categories of threats may be created for professional accountants in public practice and professional accountants in business, respectively. Professional accountants in public practice may also find Part C relevant to their particular circumstances.

100.13   Safeguards are actions or other measures that may eliminate threats or reduce them to an acceptable level. They fall into two broad categories:

(a)   Safeguards created by the profession, legislation or regulation; and

(b)   Safeguards in the work environment.

100.14   Safeguards created by the profession, legislation or regulation include:

- Educational, training and experience requirements for entry into the profession.
- Continuing professional development requirements.
- Corporate governance regulations.
- Professional standards.
- Professional or regulatory monitoring and disciplinary procedures.
- External review by a legally empowered third party of the reports, returns, communications or information produced by a professional accountant.

Parts B and C of this Code discuss safeguards in the work environment for professional accountants in public practice and professional accountants in business, respectively. **100.15**

Certain safeguards may increase the likelihood of identifying or deterring unethical behavior. Such safeguards, which may be created by the accounting profession, legislation, regulation, or an employing organization, include: **100.16**

- Effective, well-publicized complaint systems operated by the employing organization, the profession or a regulator, which enable colleagues, employers and members of the public to draw attention to unprofessional or unethical behavior.
- An explicitly stated duty to report breaches of ethical requirements.

Conflicts of Interest

A professional accountant may be faced with a conflict of interest when undertaking a professional activity. A conflict of interest creates a threat to objectivity and may create threats to the other fundamental principles. Such threats may be created when: **100.17**

- The professional accountant undertakes a professional activity related to a particular matter for two or more parties whose interests with respect to that matter are in conflict; or
- The interests of the professional accountant with respect to a particular matter and the interests of a party for whom the professional accountant undertakes a professional activity related to that matter are in conflict.

Parts B and C of this Code discuss conflicts of interest for professional accountants in public practice and professional accountants in business, respectively. **100.18**

Ethical Conflict Resolution

A professional accountant may be required to resolve a conflict in complying with the fundamental principles. **100.19**

When initiating either a formal or informal conflict resolution process, the following factors, either individually or together with other factors, may be relevant to the resolution process: **100.20**

(a) Relevant facts;
(b) Ethical issues involved;
(c) Fundamental principles related to the matter in question;
(d) Established internal procedures; and
(e) Alternative courses of action.

Having considered the relevant factors, a professional accountant shall determine the appropriate course of action, weighing the consequences of each possible course of action. If the matter remains unresolved, the professional accountant may wish to consult with other appropriate persons within the firm or employing organization for help in obtaining resolution.

Where a matter involves a conflict with, or within, an organization, a professional accountant shall determine whether to consult with those charged with governance of the organization, such as the board of directors or the audit committee. **100.21**

It may be in the best interests of the professional accountant to document the substance of the issue, the details of any discussions held, and the decisions made concerning that issue. **100.22**

100.23   If a significant conflict cannot be resolved, a professional accountant may consider obtaining professional advice from the relevant professional body or from legal advisors. The professional accountant generally can obtain guidance on ethical issues without breaching the fundamental principle of confidentiality if the matter is discussed with the relevant professional body on an anonymous basis or with a legal advisor under the protection of legal privilege. Instances in which the professional accountant may consider obtaining legal advice vary. For example, a professional accountant may have encountered a fraud, the reporting of which could breach the professional accountant's responsibility to respect confidentiality. The professional accountant may consider obtaining legal advice in that instance to determine whether there is a requirement to report.

100.24   If, after exhausting all relevant possibilities, the ethical conflict remains unresolved, a professional accountant shall, where possible, refuse to remain associated with the matter creating the conflict. The professional accountant shall determine whether, in the circumstances, it is appropriate to withdraw from the engagement team or specific assignment, or to resign altogether from the engagement, the firm or the employing organization.

Communicating with Those Charged with Governance

100.25   When communicating with those charged with governance in accordance with the provisions of this Code, the professional accountant or firm shall determine, having regard to the nature and importance of the particular circumstances and matter to be communicated, the appropriate person(s) within the entity's governance structure with whom to communicate. If the professional accountant or firm communicates with a subgroup of those charged with governance, for example, an audit committee or an individual, the professional accountant or firm shall determine whether communication with all of those charged with governance is also necessary so that they are adequately informed.

Section 110

Integrity

The principle of integrity imposes an obligation on all professional accountants to be straightforward and honest in all professional and business relationships. Integrity also implies fair dealing and truthfulness. **110.1**

A professional accountant shall not knowingly be associated with reports, returns, communications or other information where the professional accountant believes that the information: **110.2**

(a) Contains a materially false or misleading statement;
(b) Contains statements or information furnished recklessly; or
(c) Omits or obscures information required to be included where such omission or obscurity would be misleading.

When a professional accountant becomes aware that the accountant has been associated with such information, the accountant shall take steps to be disassociated from that information.

A professional accountant will be deemed not to be in breach of paragraph 110.2 if the professional accountant provides a modified report in respect of a matter contained in paragraph 110.2. **110.3**

Section 120

Objectivity

120.1   The principle of objectivity imposes an obligation on all professional accountants not to compromise their professional or business judgment because of bias, conflict of interest or the undue influence of others.

120.2   A professional accountant may be exposed to situations that may impair objectivity. It is impracticable to define and prescribe all such situations. A professional accountant shall not perform a professional activity or service if a circumstance or relationship biases or unduly influences the accountant's professional judgment with respect to that service.

Section 130

Professional Competence and Due Care

The principle of professional competence and due care imposes the following obligations on all professional accountants: **130.1**

(a) To maintain professional knowledge and skill at the level required to ensure that clients or employers receive competent professional service; and
(b) To act diligently in accordance with applicable technical and professional standards when performing professional activities or providing professional services.

Competent professional service requires the exercise of sound judgment in applying professional knowledge and skill in the performance of such service. Professional competence may be divided into two separate phases: **130.2**

(a) Attainment of professional competence; and
(b) Maintenance of professional competence.

The maintenance of professional competence requires a continuing awareness and an understanding of relevant technical, professional and business developments. Continuing professional development enables a professional accountant to develop and maintain the capabilities to perform competently within the professional environment. **130.3**

Diligence encompasses the responsibility to act in accordance with the requirements of an assignment, carefully, thoroughly and on a timely basis. **130.4**

A professional accountant shall take reasonable steps to ensure that those working under the professional accountant's authority in a professional capacity have appropriate training and supervision. **130.5**

Where appropriate, a professional accountant shall make clients, employers or other users of the accountant's professional services or activities aware of the limitations inherent in the services or activities. **130.6**

Section 140

Confidentiality

140.1   The principle of confidentiality imposes an obligation on all professional accountants to refrain from:

(a)   Disclosing outside the firm or employing organization confidential information acquired as a result of professional and business relationships without proper and specific authority or unless there is a legal or professional right or duty to disclose; and

(b)   Using confidential information acquired as a result of professional and business relationships to their personal advantage or the advantage of third parties.

140.2   A professional accountant shall maintain confidentiality, including in a social environment, being alert to the possibility of inadvertent disclosure, particularly to a close business associate or a close or immediate family member.

140.3   A professional accountant shall maintain confidentiality of information disclosed by a prospective client or employer.

140.4   A professional accountant shall maintain confidentiality of information within the firm or employing organization.

140.5   A professional accountant shall take reasonable steps to ensure that staff under the professional accountant's control and persons from whom advice and assistance is obtained respect the professional accountant's duty of confidentiality.

140.6   The need to comply with the principle of confidentiality continues even after the end of relationships between a professional accountant and a client or employer. When a professional accountant changes employment or acquires a new client, the professional accountant is entitled to use prior experience. The professional accountant shall not, however, use or disclose any confidential information either acquired or received as a result of a professional or business relationship.

140.7   The following are circumstances where professional accountants are or may be required to disclose confidential information or when such disclosure may be appropriate:

(a)   Disclosure is permitted by law and is authorized by the client or the employer;

(b)   Disclosure is required by law, for example:

(i)   Production of documents or other provision of evidence in the course of legal proceedings; or

(ii)   Disclosure to the appropriate public authorities of infringements of the law that come to light; and

(c)   There is a professional duty or right to disclose, when not prohibited by law:

(i)   To comply with the quality review of a member body or professional body;

(ii)   To respond to an inquiry or investigation by a member body or regulatory body;

(iii)   To protect the professional interests of a professional accountant in legal proceedings; or

(iv)   To comply with technical standards and ethics requirements.

140.8   In deciding whether to disclose confidential information, relevant factors to consider include:

- Whether the interests of all parties, including third parties whose interests may be affected, could be harmed if the client or employer consents to the disclosure of information by the professional accountant.

- Whether all the relevant information is known and substantiated, to the extent it is practicable; when the situation involves unsubstantiated facts, incomplete information or unsubstantiated conclusions, professional judgment shall be used in determining the type of disclosure to be made, if any.
- The type of communication that is expected and to whom it is addressed.
- Whether the parties to whom the communication is addressed are appropriate recipients.

Section 150

Professional Behavior

150.1   The principle of professional behavior imposes an obligation on all professional accountants to comply with relevant laws and regulations and avoid any action that the professional accountant knows or should know may discredit the profession. This includes actions that a reasonable and informed third party, weighing all the specific facts and circumstances available to the professional accountant at that time, would be likely to conclude adversely affects the good reputation of the profession.

150.2   In marketing and promoting themselves and their work, professional accountants shall not bring the profession into disrepute. Professional accountants shall be honest and truthful and not:

(a)   Make exaggerated claims for the services they are able to offer, the qualifications they possess, or experience they have gained; or

(b)   Make disparaging references or unsubstantiated comparisons to the work of others.

Part B—Professional accountants in public practice

Section 200

Introduction

200.1   This Part of the Code describes how the conceptual framework contained in Part A applies in certain situations to professional accountants in public practice. This Part does not describe all of the circumstances and relationships that could be encountered by a professional accountant in public practice that create or may create threats to compliance with the fundamental principles. Therefore, the professional accountant in public practice is encouraged to be alert for such circumstances and relationships.

200.2   A professional accountant in public practice shall not knowingly engage in any business, occupation, or activity that impairs or might impair integrity, objectivity or the good reputation of the profession and as a result would be incompatible with the fundamental principles.

Threats and Safeguards

200.3   Compliance with the fundamental principles may potentially be threatened by a broad range of circumstances and relationships. The nature and significance of the threats may differ depending on whether they arise in relation to the provision of services to an audit client and whether the audit client is a public interest entity, to an assurance client that is not an audit client, or to a non-assurance client.

Threats fall into one or more of the following categories:

(a) Self-interest;
(b) Self-review;
(c) Advocacy;
(d) Familiarity; and
(e) Intimidation.

These threats are discussed further in Part A of this Code.

200.4   Examples of circumstances that create self-interest threats for a professional accountant in public practice include:

- A member of the assurance team having a direct financial interest in the assurance client.
- A firm having undue dependence on total fees from a client.
- A member of the assurance team having a significant close business relationship with an assurance client.
- A firm being concerned about the possibility of losing a significant client.
- A member of the audit team entering into employment negotiations with the audit client.
- A firm entering into a contingent fee arrangement relating to an assurance engagement.
- A professional accountant discovering a significant error when evaluating the results of a previous professional service performed by a member of the professional accountant's firm.

200.5   Examples of circumstances that create self-review threats for a professional accountant in public practice include:

- A firm issuing an assurance report on the effectiveness of the operation of financial systems after designing or implementing the systems.

- A firm having prepared the original data used to generate records that are the subject matter of the assurance engagement.
- A member of the assurance team being, or having recently been, a director or officer of the client.
- A member of the assurance team being, or having recently been, employed by the client in a position to exert significant influence over the subject matter of the engagement.
- The firm performing a service for an assurance client that directly affects the subject matter information of the assurance engagement.

Examples of circumstances that create advocacy threats for a professional accountant in public practice include: **200.6**

- The firm promoting shares in an audit client.
- A professional accountant acting as an advocate on behalf of an audit client in litigation or disputes with third parties.

Examples of circumstances that create familiarity threats for a professional accountant in public practice include: **200.7**

- A member of the engagement team having a close or immediate family member who is a director or officer of the client.
- A member of the engagement team having a close or immediate family member who is an employee of the client who is in a position to exert significant influence over the subject matter of the engagement.
- A director or officer of the client or an employee in a position to exert significant influence over the subject matter of the engagement having recently served as the engagement partner.
- A professional accountant accepting gifts or preferential treatment from a client, unless the value is trivial or inconsequential.
- Senior personnel having a long association with the assurance client.

Examples of circumstances that create intimidation threats for a professional accountant in public practice include: **200.8**

- A firm being threatened with dismissal from a client engagement.
- An audit client indicating that it will not award a planned non-assurance contract to the firm if the firm continues to disagree with the client's accounting treatment for a particular transaction.
- A firm being threatened with litigation by the client.
- A firm being pressured to reduce inappropriately the extent of work performed in order to reduce fees.
- A professional accountant feeling pressured to agree with the judgment of a client employee because the employee has more expertise on the matter in question.
- A professional accountant being informed by a partner of the firm that a planned promotion will not occur unless the accountant agrees with an audit client's inappropriate accounting treatment.

Safeguards that may eliminate or reduce threats to an acceptable level fall into two broad categories: **200.9**

(a) Safeguards created by the profession, legislation or regulation; and
(b) Safeguards in the work environment.

Examples of safeguards created by the profession, legislation or regulation are described in paragraph 100.14 of Part A of this Code.

200.10   A professional accountant in public practice shall exercise judgment to determine how best to deal with threats that are not at an acceptable level, whether by applying safeguards to eliminate the threat or reduce it to an acceptable level or by terminating or declining the relevant engagement. In exercising this judgment, a professional accountant in public practice shall consider whether a reasonable and informed third party, weighing all the specific facts and circumstances available to the professional accountant at that time, would be likely to conclude that the threats would be eliminated or reduced to an acceptable level by the application of safeguards, such that compliance with the fundamental principles is not compromised. This consideration will be affected by matters such as the significance of the threat, the nature of the engagement and the structure of the firm.

200.11   In the work environment, the relevant safeguards will vary depending on the circumstances. Work environment safeguards comprise firm-wide safeguards and engagement-specific safeguards.

200.12   Examples of firm-wide safeguards in the work environment include:
- Leadership of the firm that stresses the importance of compliance with the fundamental principles.
- Leadership of the firm that establishes the expectation that members of an assurance team will act in the public interest.
- Policies and procedures to implement and monitor quality control of engagements.
- Documented policies regarding the need to identify threats to compliance with the fundamental principles, evaluate the significance of those threats, and apply safeguards to eliminate or reduce the threats to an acceptable level or, when appropriate safeguards are not available or cannot be applied, terminate or decline the relevant engagement.
- Documented internal policies and procedures requiring compliance with the fundamental principles.
- Policies and procedures that will enable the identification of interests or relationships between the firm or members of engagement teams and clients.
- Policies and procedures to monitor and, if necessary, manage the reliance on revenue received from a single client.
- Using different partners and engagement teams with separate reporting lines for the provision of non-assurance services to an assurance client.
- Policies and procedures to prohibit individuals who are not members of an engagement team from inappropriately influencing the outcome of the engagement.
- Timely communication of a firm's policies and procedures, including any changes to them, to all partners and professional staff, and appropriate training and education on such policies and procedures.
- Designating a member of senior management to be responsible for overseeing the adequate functioning of the firm's quality control system.
- Advising partners and professional staff of assurance clients and related entities from which independence is required.
- A disciplinary mechanism to promote compliance with policies and procedures.
- Published policies and procedures to encourage and empower staff to communicate to senior levels within the firm any issue relating to compliance with the fundamental principles that concerns them.

200.13   Examples of engagement-specific safeguards in the work environment include:
- Having a professional accountant who was not involved with the non-assurance service review the non-assurance work performed or otherwise advise as necessary.
- Having a professional accountant who was not a member of the assurance team review the assurance work performed or otherwise advise as necessary.

- Consulting an independent third party, such as a committee of independent directors, a professional regulatory body or another professional accountant.
- Discussing ethical issues with those charged with governance of the client.
- Disclosing to those charged with governance of the client the nature of services provided and extent of fees charged.
- Involving another firm to perform or re-perform part of the engagement.
- Rotating senior assurance team personnel.

Depending on the nature of the engagement, a professional accountant in public practice may also be able to rely on safeguards that the client has implemented. However it is not possible to rely solely on such safeguards to reduce threats to an acceptable level.

200.14

Examples of safeguards within the client's systems and procedures include:

200.15

- The client requires persons other than management to ratify or approve the appointment of a firm to perform an engagement.
- The client has competent employees with experience and seniority to make managerial decisions.
- The client has implemented internal procedures that ensure objective choices in commissioning non-assurance engagements.
- The client has a corporate governance structure that provides appropriate oversight and communications regarding the firm's services.

Section 210

Professional Appointment

Client Acceptance

210.1   Before accepting a new client relationship, a professional accountant in public practice shall determine whether acceptance would create any threats to compliance with the fundamental principles. Potential threats to integrity or professional behavior may be created from, for example, questionable issues associated with the client (its owners, management or activities).

210.2   Client issues that, if known, could threaten compliance with the fundamental principles include, for example, client involvement in illegal activities (such as money laundering), dishonesty or questionable financial reporting practices.

210.3   A professional accountant in public practice shall evaluate the significance of any threats and apply safeguards when necessary to eliminate them or reduce them to an acceptable level.

Examples of such safeguards include:

- Obtaining knowledge and understanding of the client, its owners, managers and those responsible for its governance and business activities; or
- Securing the client's commitment to improve corporate governance practices or internal controls.

210.4   Where it is not possible to reduce the threats to an acceptable level, the professional accountant in public practice shall decline to enter into the client relationship.

210.5   It is recommended that a professional accountant in public practice periodically review acceptance decisions for recurring client engagements.

Engagement Acceptance

210.6   The fundamental principle of professional competence and due care imposes an obligation on a professional accountant in public practice to provide only those services that the professional accountant in public practice is competent to perform. Before accepting a specific client engagement, a professional accountant in public practice shall determine whether acceptance would create any threats to compliance with the fundamental principles. For example, a self-interest threat to professional competence and due care is created if the engagement team does not possess, or cannot acquire, the competencies necessary to properly carry out the engagement.

210.7   A professional accountant in public practice shall evaluate the significance of threats and apply safeguards, when necessary, to eliminate them or reduce them to an acceptable level. Examples of such safeguards include:

- Acquiring an appropriate understanding of the nature of the client's business, the complexity of its operations, the specific requirements of the engagement and the purpose, nature and scope of the work to be performed;
- Acquiring knowledge of relevant industries or subject matters;
- Possessing or obtaining experience with relevant regulatory or reporting requirements;
- Assigning sufficient staff with the necessary competencies;
- Using experts where necessary;

- Agreeing on a realistic time frame for the performance of the engagement; or
- Complying with quality control policies and procedures designed to provide reasonable assurance that specific engagements are accepted only when they can be performed competently.

When a professional accountant in public practice intends to rely on the advice or work of an expert, the professional accountant in public practice shall determine whether such reliance is warranted. Factors to consider include: reputation, expertise, resources available and applicable professional and ethical standards. Such information may be gained from prior association with the expert or from consulting others.   **210.8**

Changes in a Professional Appointment

A professional accountant in public practice who is asked to replace another professional accountant in public practice, or who is considering tendering for an engagement currently held by another professional accountant in public practice, shall determine whether there are any reasons, professional or otherwise, for not accepting the engagement, such as circumstances that create threats to compliance with the fundamental principles that cannot be eliminated or reduced to an acceptable level by the application of safeguards. For example, there may be a threat to professional competence and due care if a professional accountant in public practice accepts the engagement before knowing all the pertinent facts.   **210.9**

A professional accountant in public practice shall evaluate the significance of any threats. Depending on the nature of the engagement, this may require direct communication with the existing accountant to establish the facts and circumstances regarding the proposed change so that the professional accountant in public practice can decide whether it would be appropriate to accept the engagement. For example, the apparent reasons for the change in appointment may not fully reflect the facts and may indicate disagreements with the existing accountant that may influence the decision to accept the appointment.   **210.10**

Safeguards shall be applied when necessary to eliminate any threats or reduce them to an acceptable level. Examples of such safeguards include: **210.11**

- When replying to requests to submit tenders, stating in the tender that, before accepting the engagement, contact with the existing accountant will be requested so that inquiries may be made as to whether there are any professional or other reasons why the appointment should not be accepted;
- Asking the existing accountant to provide known information on any facts or circumstances that, in the existing accountant's opinion, the proposed accountant needs to be aware of before deciding whether to accept the engagement; or
- Obtaining necessary information from other sources.

When the threats cannot be eliminated or reduced to an acceptable level through the application of safeguards, a professional accountant in public practice shall, unless there is satisfaction as to necessary facts by other means, decline the engagement.

A professional accountant in public practice may be asked to undertake work that is complementary or additional to the work of the existing accountant. Such circumstances may create threats to professional competence and due care resulting from, for example, a lack of or incomplete information. The significance of any threats shall be evaluated and safeguards applied when necessary to eliminate the threat or reduce it to an acceptable level. An example of such a safeguard is notifying the existing accountant of the proposed work, which would give the existing accountant the opportunity to provide any relevant information needed for the proper conduct of the work.   **210.12**

210.13   An existing accountant is bound by confidentiality. Whether that professional accountant is permitted or required to discuss the affairs of a client with a proposed accountant will depend on the nature of the engagement and on:

(a)   Whether the client's permission to do so has been obtained; or

(b)   The legal or ethical requirements relating to such communications and disclosure, which may vary by jurisdiction.

Circumstances where the professional accountant is or may be required to disclose confidential information or where such disclosure may otherwise be appropriate are set out in Section 140 of Part A of this Code.

210.14   A professional accountant in public practice will generally need to obtain the client's permission, preferably in writing, to initiate discussion with an existing accountant. Once that permission is obtained, the existing accountant shall comply with relevant legal and other regulations governing such requests. Where the existing accountant provides information, it shall be provided honestly and unambiguously. If the proposed accountant is unable to communicate with the existing accountant, the proposed accountant shall take reasonable steps to obtain information about any possible threats by other means, such as through inquiries of third parties or background investigations of senior management or those charged with governance of the client.

Section 220

Conflicts of Interest

A professional accountant in public practice may be faced with a conflict of interest when performing a professional service. A conflict of interest creates a threat to objectivity and may create threats to the other fundamental principles. Such threats may be created when: **220.1**

- The professional accountant provides a professional service related to a particular matter for two or more clients whose interests with respect to that matter are in conflict; or
- The interests of the professional accountant with respect to a particular matter and the interests of the client for whom the professional accountant provides a professional service related to that matter are in conflict.

A professional accountant shall not allow a conflict of interest to compromise professional or business judgment.

When the professional service is an assurance service, compliance with the fundamental principle of objectivity also requires being independent of assurance clients in accordance with Sections 290 or 291 as appropriate.

Examples of situations in which conflicts of interest may arise include: **220.2**

- Providing a transaction advisory service to a client seeking to acquire an audit client of the firm, where the firm has obtained confidential information during the course of the audit that may be relevant to the transaction.
- Advising two clients at the same time who are competing to acquire the same company where the advice might be relevant to the parties' competitive positions.
- Providing services to both a vendor and a purchaser in relation to the same transaction.
- Preparing valuations of assets for two parties who are in an adversarial position with respect to the assets.
- Representing two clients regarding the same matter who are in a legal dispute with each other, such as during divorce proceedings or the dissolution of a partnership.
- Providing an assurance report for a licensor on royalties due under a license agreement when at the same time advising the licensee of the correctness of the amounts payable.
- Advising a client to invest in a business in which, for example, the spouse of the professional accountant in public practice has a financial interest.
- Providing strategic advice to a client on its competitive position while having a joint venture or similar interest with a major competitor of the client.
- Advising a client on the acquisition of a business which the firm is also interested in acquiring.
- Advising a client on the purchase of a product or service while having a royalty or commission agreement with one of the potential vendors of that product or service.

When identifying and evaluating the interests and relationships that might create a conflict of interest and implementing safeguards, when necessary, to eliminate or reduce any threat to compliance with the fundamental principles to an acceptable level, a professional accountant in public practice shall exercise professional judgment and take into account whether a reasonable and informed third party, weighing all the specific facts and circumstances available to the professional accountant at the time, would be likely to conclude that compliance with the fundamental principles is not compromised. **220.3**

220.4   When addressing conflicts of interest, including making disclosures or sharing information within the firm or network and seeking guidance of third parties, the professional accountant in public practice shall remain alert to the fundamental principle of confidentiality.

220.5   If the threat created by a conflict of interest is not at an acceptable level, the professional accountant in public practice shall apply safeguards to eliminate the threat or reduce it to an acceptable level. If safeguards cannot reduce the threat to an acceptable level, the professional accountant shall decline to perform or shall discontinue professional services that would result in the conflict of interest; or shall terminate relevant relationships or dispose of relevant interests to eliminate the threat or reduce it to an acceptable level.

220.6   Before accepting a new client relationship, engagement, or business relationship, a professional accountant in public practice shall take reasonable steps to identify circumstances that might create a conflict of interest, including identification of:

- The nature of the relevant interests and relationships between the parties involved; and
- The nature of the service and its implication for relevant parties.

The nature of the services and the relevant interests and relationships may change during the course of the engagement. This is particularly true when a professional accountant is asked to conduct an engagement in a situation that may become adversarial, even though the parties who engage the professional accountant may not initially be involved in a dispute. The professional accountant shall remain alert to such changes for the purpose of identifying circumstances that might create a conflict of interest.

220.7   For the purpose of identifying interests and relationships that might create a conflict of interest, having an effective conflict identification process assists a professional accountant in public practice to identify actual or potential conflicts of interest prior to determining whether to accept an engagement and throughout an engagement. This includes matters identified by external parties, for example clients or potential clients. The earlier an actual or potential conflict of interest is identified, the greater the likelihood of the professional accountant being able to apply safeguards, when necessary, to eliminate the threat to objectivity and any threat to compliance with other fundamental principles or reduce it to an acceptable level. The process to identify actual or potential conflicts of interest will depend on such factors as:

- The nature of the professional services provided.
- The size of the firm.
- The size and nature of the client base.
- The structure of the firm, for example, the number and geographic location of offices.

220.8   If the firm is a member of a network, conflict identification shall include any conflicts of interest that the professional accountant in public practice has reason to believe may exist or might arise due to interests and relationships of a network firm. Reasonable steps to identify such interests and relationships involving a network firm will depend on factors such as the nature of the professional services provided, the clients served by the network and the geographic locations of all relevant parties.

220.9   If a conflict of interest is identified, the professional accountant in public practice shall evaluate:

- The significance of relevant interests or relationships; and
- The significance of the threats created by performing the professional service or services. In general, the more direct the connection between the professional service

and the matter on which the parties' interests are in conflict, the more significant the threat to objectivity and compliance with the other fundamental principles will be.

The professional accountant in public practice shall apply safeguards, when necessary, to eliminate the threats to compliance with the fundamental principles created by the conflict of interest or reduce them to an acceptable level. Examples of safeguards include: **220.10**

- Implementing mechanisms to prevent unauthorized disclosure of confidential information when performing professional services related to a particular matter for two or more clients whose interests with respect to that matter are in conflict. This could include:
    - o Using separate engagement teams who are provided with clear policies and procedures on maintaining confidentiality.
    - o Creating separate areas of practice for specialty functions within the firm, which may act as a barrier to the passing of confidential client information from one practice area to another within a firm.
    - o Establishing policies and procedures to limit access to client files, the use of confidentiality agreements signed by employees and partners of the firm and/or the physical and electronic separation of confidential information.
- Regular review of the application of safeguards by a senior individual not involved with the client engagement or engagements.
- Having a professional accountant who is not involved in providing the service or otherwise affected by the conflict, review the work performed to assess whether the key judgments and conclusions are appropriate.
- Consulting with third parties, such as a professional body, legal counsel or another professional accountant.

In addition, it is generally necessary to disclose the nature of the conflict of interest and the related safeguards, if any, to clients affected by the conflict and, when safeguards are required to reduce the threat to an acceptable level, to obtain their consent to the professional accountant in public practice performing the professional services. Disclosure and consent may take different forms, for example: **220.11**

- General disclosure to clients of circumstances where the professional accountant, in keeping with common commercial practice, does not provide services exclusively for any one client (for example, in a particular service in a particular market sector) in order for the client to provide general consent accordingly. Such disclosure might, for example, be made in the professional accountant's standard terms and conditions for the engagement.
- Specific disclosure to affected clients of the circumstances of the particular conflict, including a detailed presentation of the situation and a comprehensive explanation of any planned safeguards and the risks involved, sufficient to enable the client to make an informed decision with respect to the matter and to provide explicit consent accordingly.
- In certain circumstances, consent may be implied by the client's conduct where the professional accountant has sufficient evidence to conclude that clients know the circumstances at the outset and have accepted the conflict of interest if they do not raise an objection to the existence of the conflict.

The professional accountant shall determine whether the nature and significance of the conflict of interest is such that specific disclosure and explicit consent is necessary. For this purpose, the professional accountant shall exercise professional judgment in weighing the outcome of the evaluation of the circumstances that create a conflict of interest, including the parties that might be affected, the nature of the issues that might arise and the potential for the particular matter to develop in an unexpected manner.

220.12　Where a professional accountant in public practice has requested explicit consent from a client and that consent has been refused by the client, the professional accountant shall decline to perform or shall discontinue professional services that would result in the conflict of interest; or shall terminate relevant relationships or dispose of relevant interests to eliminate the threat or reduce it to an acceptable level, such that consent can be obtained, after applying any additional safeguards if necessary.

220.13　When disclosure is verbal, or consent is verbal or implied, the professional accountant in public practice is encouraged to document the nature of the circumstances giving rise to the conflict of interest, the safeguards applied to reduce the threats to an acceptable level and the consent obtained.

220.14　In certain circumstances, making specific disclosure for the purpose of obtaining explicit consent would result in a breach of confidentiality. Examples of such circumstances may include:

- Performing a transaction-related service for a client in connection with a hostile takeover of another client of the firm.
- Performing a forensic investigation for a client in connection with a suspected fraudulent act where the firm has confidential information obtained through having performed a professional service for another client who might be involved in the fraud.

The firm shall not accept or continue an engagement under such circumstances unless the following conditions are met:

- The firm does not act in an advocacy role for one client where this requires the firm to assume an adversarial position against the other client with respect to the same matter;
- Specific mechanisms are in place to prevent disclosure of confidential information between the engagement teams serving the two clients; and
- The firm is satisfied that a reasonable and informed third party, weighing all the specific facts and circumstances available to the professional accountant in public practice at the time, would be likely to conclude that it is appropriate for the firm to accept or continue the engagement because a restriction on the firm's ability to provide the service would produce a disproportionate adverse outcome for the clients or other relevant third parties.

The professional accountant shall document the nature of the circumstances, including the role that the professional accountant is to undertake, the specific mechanisms in place to prevent disclosure of information between the engagement teams serving the two clients and the rationale for the conclusion that it is appropriate to accept the engagement.

Section 230

Second Opinions

Situations where a professional accountant in public practice is asked to provide a second opinion on the application of accounting, auditing, reporting or other standards or principles to specific circumstances or transactions by or on behalf of a company or an entity that is not an existing client may create threats to compliance with the fundamental principles. For example, there may be a threat to professional competence and due care in circumstances where the second opinion is not based on the same set of facts that were made available to the existing accountant or is based on inadequate evidence. The existence and significance of any threat will depend on the circumstances of the request and all the other available facts and assumptions relevant to the expression of a professional judgment. **230.1**

When asked to provide such an opinion, a professional accountant in public practice shall evaluate the significance of any threats and apply safeguards when necessary to eliminate them or reduce them to an acceptable level. Examples of such safeguards include seeking client permission to contact the existing accountant, describing the limitations surrounding any opinion in communications with the client and providing the existing accountant with a copy of the opinion. **230.2**

If the company or entity seeking the opinion will not permit communication with the existing accountant, a professional accountant in public practice shall determine whether, taking all the circumstances into account, it is appropriate to provide the opinion sought. **230.3**

Section 240

Fees and Other Types of Remuneration

240.1   When entering into negotiations regarding professional services, a professional accountant in public practice may quote whatever fee is deemed appropriate. The fact that one professional accountant in public practice may quote a fee lower than another is not in itself unethical. Nevertheless, there may be threats to compliance with the fundamental principles arising from the level of fees quoted. For example, a self-interest threat to professional competence and due care is created if the fee quoted is so low that it may be difficult to perform the engagement in accordance with applicable technical and professional standards for that price.

240.2   The existence and significance of any threats created will depend on factors such as the level of fee quoted and the services to which it applies. The significance of any threat shall be evaluated and safeguards applied when necessary to eliminate the threat or reduce it to an acceptable level. Examples of such safeguards include:

- Making the client aware of the terms of the engagement and, in particular, the basis on which fees are charged and which services are covered by the quoted fee; or
- Assigning appropriate time and qualified staff to the task.

240.3   Contingent fees are widely used for certain types of non-assurance engagements.[1] They may, however, create threats to compliance with the fundamental principles in certain circumstances. They may create a self-interest threat to objectivity. The existence and significance of such threats will depend on factors including:

- The nature of the engagement.
- The range of possible fee amounts.
- The basis for determining the fee.
- Whether the outcome or result of the transaction is to be reviewed by an independent third party.

240.4   The significance of any such threats shall be evaluated and safeguards applied when necessary to eliminate or reduce them to an acceptable level. Examples of such safeguards include:

- An advance written agreement with the client as to the basis of remuneration;
- Disclosure to intended users of the work performed by the professional accountant in public practice and the basis of remuneration;
- Quality control policies and procedures; or
- Review by an independent third party of the work performed by the professional accountant in public practice.

240.5   In certain circumstances, a professional accountant in public practice may receive a referral fee or commission relating to a client. For example, where the professional accountant in public practice does not provide the specific service required, a fee may be received for referring a continuing client to another professional accountant in public practice or other expert. A professional accountant in public practice may receive a commission from a third party (for example, a software vendor) in connection with the sale of goods or services to a client. Accepting such a referral fee or commission creates a self-interest threat to objectivity and professional competence and due care.

---

[1] *Contingent fees for non-assurance services provided to audit clients and other assurance clients are discussed in Sections 290 and 291 of this Code.*

A professional accountant in public practice may also pay a referral fee to obtain a client, for example, where the client continues as a client of another professional accountant in public practice but requires specialist services not offered by the existing accountant. The payment of such a referral fee also creates a self-interest threat to objectivity and professional competence and due care.   **240.6**

The significance of the threat shall be evaluated and safeguards applied when necessary to eliminate the threat or reduce it to an acceptable level. Examples of such safeguards include: **240.7**

- Disclosing to the client any arrangements to pay a referral fee to another professional accountant for the work referred;
- Disclosing to the client any arrangements to receive a referral fee for referring the client to another professional accountant in public practice; or
- Obtaining advance agreement from the client for commission arrangements in connection with the sale by a third party of goods or services to the client.

A professional accountant in public practice may purchase all or part of another firm on the basis that payments will be made to individuals formerly owning the firm or to their heirs or estates. Such payments are not regarded as commissions or referral fees for the purpose of paragraphs 240.5–240.7 above.   **240.8**

Section 250

Marketing Professional Services

250.1   When a professional accountant in public practice solicits new work through advertising or other forms of marketing, there may be a threat to compliance with the fundamental principles. For example, a self-interest threat to compliance with the principle of professional behavior is created if services, achievements, or products are marketed in a way that is inconsistent with that principle.

250.2   A professional accountant in public practice shall not bring the profession into disrepute when marketing professional services. The professional accountant in public practice shall be honest and truthful, and not:

(a)   Make exaggerated claims for services offered, qualifications possessed, or experience gained; or

(b)   Make disparaging references or unsubstantiated comparisons to the work of another.

If the professional accountant in public practice is in doubt about whether a proposed form of advertising or marketing is appropriate, the professional accountant in public practice shall consider consulting with the relevant professional body.

Section 260

Gifts and Hospitality

A professional accountant in public practice, or an immediate or close family member, **260.1** may be offered gifts and hospitality from a client. Such an offer may create threats to compliance with the fundamental principles. For example, a self-interest or familiarity threat to objectivity may be created if a gift from a client is accepted; an intimidation threat to objectivity may result from the possibility of such offers being made public.

The existence and significance of any threat will depend on the nature, value, and intent **260.2** of the offer. Where gifts or hospitality are offered that a reasonable and informed third party, weighing all the specific facts and circumstances, would consider trivial and inconsequential, a professional accountant in public practice may conclude that the offer is made in the normal course of business without the specific intent to influence decision making or to obtain information. In such cases, the professional accountant in public practice may generally conclude that any threat to compliance with the fundamental principles is at an acceptable level.

A professional accountant in public practice shall evaluate the significance of any threats **260.3** and apply safeguards when necessary to eliminate the threats or reduce them to an acceptable level. When the threats cannot be eliminated or reduced to an acceptable level through the application of safeguards, a professional accountant in public practice shall not accept such an offer.

Section 270

Custody of Client Assets

270.1   A professional accountant in public practice shall not assume custody of client monies or other assets unless permitted to do so by law and, if so, in compliance with any additional legal duties imposed on a professional accountant in public practice holding such assets.

270.2   The holding of client assets creates threats to compliance with the fundamental principles; for example, there is a self-interest threat to professional behavior and may be a self-interest threat to objectivity arising from holding client assets. A professional accountant in public practice entrusted with money (or other assets) belonging to others shall therefore:

(a)   Keep such assets separately from personal or firm assets;

(b)   Use such assets only for the purpose for which they are intended;

(c)   At all times be ready to account for those assets and any income, dividends, or gains generated, to any persons entitled to such accounting; and

(d)   Comply with all relevant laws and regulations relevant to the holding of and accounting for such assets.

270.3   As part of client and engagement acceptance procedures for services that may involve the holding of client assets, a professional accountant in public practice shall make appropriate inquiries about the source of such assets and consider legal and regulatory obligations. For example, if the assets were derived from illegal activities, such as money laundering, a threat to compliance with the fundamental principles would be created. In such situations, the professional accountant may consider seeking legal advice.

Section 280

Objectivity–All Services

A professional accountant in public practice shall determine when providing any **280.1** professional service whether there are threats to compliance with the fundamental principle of objectivity resulting from having interests in, or relationships with, a client or its directors, officers or employees. For example, a familiarity threat to objectivity may be created from a family or close personal or business relationship.

A professional accountant in public practice who provides an assurance service shall be **280.2** independent of the assurance client. Independence of mind and in appearance is necessary to enable the professional accountant in public practice to express a conclusion, and be seen to express a conclusion, without bias, conflict of interest, or undue influence of others. Sections 290 and 291 provide specific guidance on independence requirements for professional accountants in public practice when performing assurance engagements.

The existence of threats to objectivity when providing any professional service will depend **280.3** upon the particular circumstances of the engagement and the nature of the work that the professional accountant in public practice is performing.

A professional accountant in public practice shall evaluate the significance of any threats **280.4** and apply safeguards when necessary to eliminate them or reduce them to an acceptable level. Examples of such safeguards include:

- Withdrawing from the engagement team;
- Supervisory procedures;
- Terminating the financial or business relationship giving rise to the threat;
- Discussing the issue with higher levels of management within the firm; or
- Discussing the issue with those charged with governance of the client.

If safeguards cannot eliminate or reduce the threat to an acceptable level, the professional accountant shall decline or terminate the relevant engagement.

Section 290

Independence—Audit and review engagements

Contents

Section 290

Structure of Section

290.1   This section addresses the independence requirements for audit engagements and review engagements, which are assurance engagements in which a professional accountant in public practice expresses a conclusion on financial statements. Such engagements comprise audit and review engagements to report on a complete set of financial statements and a single financial statement. Independence requirements for assurance engagements that are not audit or review engagements are addressed in Section 291.

290.2   In certain circumstances involving audit engagements where the audit report includes a restriction on use and distribution and provided certain conditions are met, the independence requirements in this section may be modified as provided in paragraphs 290.500 to 290.514. The modifications are not permitted in the case of an audit of financial statements required by law or regulation.

290.3   In this section, the term(s):

(a)   'Audit,' 'audit team,' 'audit engagement,' 'audit client' and 'audit report' includes review, review team, review engagement, review client and review report; and

(b)   'Firm' includes network firm, except where otherwise stated.

A Conceptual Framework Approach to Independence

290.4   In the case of audit engagements, it is in the public interest and, therefore, required by this Code, that members of audit teams, firms and network firms shall be independent of audit clients.

290.5   The objective of this section is to assist firms and members of audit teams in applying the conceptual framework approach described below to achieving and maintaining independence.

290.6   Independence comprises:

- Independence of Mind
  The state of mind that permits the expression of a conclusion without being affected by influences that compromise professional judgment, thereby allowing an individual to act with integrity and exercise objectivity and professional skepticism.

- Independence in Appearance
  The avoidance of facts and circumstances that are so significant that a reasonable and informed third party would be likely to conclude, weighing all the specific facts and circumstances, that a firm's, or a member of the audit team's, integrity, objectivity or professional skepticism has been compromised.

290.7   The conceptual framework approach shall be applied by professional accountants to:

(a)   Identify threats to independence;

(b)   Evaluate the significance of the threats identified; and

(c)   Apply safeguards, when necessary, to eliminate the threats or reduce them to an acceptable level.

When the professional accountant determines that appropriate safeguards are not available or cannot be applied to eliminate the threats or reduce them to an acceptable level, the professional accountant shall eliminate the circumstance or relationship creating the threats or decline or terminate the audit engagement.

A professional accountant shall use professional judgment in applying this conceptual framework.

Many different circumstances, or combinations of circumstances, may be relevant in assessing threats to independence. It is impossible to define every situation that creates threats to independence and to specify the appropriate action. Therefore, this Code establishes a conceptual framework that requires firms and members of audit teams to identify, evaluate, and address threats to independence. The conceptual framework approach assists professional accountants in practice in complying with the ethical requirements in this Code. It accommodates many variations in circumstances that create threats to independence and can deter a professional accountant from concluding that a situation is permitted if it is not specifically prohibited.

290.8

Paragraphs 290.100 and onwards describe how the conceptual framework approach to independence is to be applied. These paragraphs do not address all the circumstances and relationships that create or may create threats to independence.

290.9

In deciding whether to accept or continue an engagement, or whether a particular individual may be a member of the audit team, a firm shall identify and evaluate threats to independence. If the threats are not at an acceptable level, and the decision is whether to accept an engagement or include a particular individual on the audit team, the firm shall determine whether safeguards are available to eliminate the threats or reduce them to an acceptable level. If the decision is whether to continue an engagement, the firm shall determine whether any existing safeguards will continue to be effective to eliminate the threats or reduce them to an acceptable level or whether other safeguards will need to be applied or whether the engagement needs to be terminated. Whenever new information about a threat to independence comes to the attention of the firm during the engagement, the firm shall evaluate the significance of the threat in accordance with the conceptual framework approach.

290.10

Throughout this section, reference is made to the significance of threats to independence. In evaluating the significance of a threat, qualitative as well as quantitative factors shall be taken into account.

290.11

This section does not, in most cases, prescribe the specific responsibility of individuals within the firm for actions related to independence because responsibility may differ depending on the size, structure and organization of a firm. The firm is required by International Standards on Quality Control (ISQCs) to establish policies and procedures designed to provide it with reasonable assurance that independence is maintained when required by relevant ethical requirements. In addition, International Standards on Auditing (ISAs) require the engagement partner to form a conclusion on compliance with the independence requirements that apply to the engagement.

290.12

Networks and Network Firms

If a firm is deemed to be a network firm, the firm shall be independent of the audit clients of the other firms within the network (unless otherwise stated in this Code). The independence requirements in this section that apply to a network firm apply to any entity, such as a consulting practice or professional law practice, that meets the definition of a network firm irrespective of whether the entity itself meets the definition of a firm.

290.13

To enhance their ability to provide professional services, firms frequently form larger structures with other firms and entities. Whether these larger structures create a network depends on the particular facts and circumstances and does not depend on whether the firms and entities are legally separate and distinct. For example, a larger structure may be aimed

290.14

only at facilitating the referral of work, which in itself does not meet the criteria necessary to constitute a network. Alternatively, a larger structure might be such that it is aimed at co-operation and the firms share a common brand name, a common system of quality control, or significant professional resources and consequently is deemed to be a network.

290.15   The judgment as to whether the larger structure is a network shall be made in light of whether a reasonable and informed third party would be likely to conclude, weighing all the specific facts and circumstances, that the entities are associated in such a way that a network exists. This judgment shall be applied consistently throughout the network.

290.16   Where the larger structure is aimed at co-operation and it is clearly aimed at profit or cost sharing among the entities within the structure, it is deemed to be a network. However, the sharing of immaterial costs does not in itself create a network. In addition, if the sharing of costs is limited only to those costs related to the development of audit methodologies, manuals, or training courses, this would not in itself create a network. Further, an association between a firm and an otherwise unrelated entity to jointly provide a service or develop a product does not in itself create a network.

290.17   Where the larger structure is aimed at cooperation and the entities within the structure share common ownership, control or management, it is deemed to be a network. This could be achieved by contract or other means.

290.18   Where the larger structure is aimed at co-operation and the entities within the structure share common quality control policies and procedures, it is deemed to be a network. For this purpose, common quality control policies and procedures are those designed, implemented and monitored across the larger structure.

290.19   Where the larger structure is aimed at co-operation and the entities within the structure share a common business strategy, it is deemed to be a network. Sharing a common business strategy involves an agreement by the entities to achieve common strategic objectives. An entity is not deemed to be a network firm merely because it co-operates with another entity solely to respond jointly to a request for a proposal for the provision of a professional service.

290.20   Where the larger structure is aimed at co-operation and the entities within the structure share the use of a common brand name, it is deemed to be a network. A common brand name includes common initials or a common name. A firm is deemed to be using a common brand name if it includes, for example, the common brand name as part of, or along with, its firm name, when a partner of the firm signs an audit report.

290.21   Even though a firm does not belong to a network and does not use a common brand name as part of its firm name, it may give the appearance that it belongs to a network if it makes reference in its stationery or promotional materials to being a member of an association of firms. Accordingly, if care is not taken in how a firm describes such memberships, a perception may be created that the firm belongs to a network.

290.22   If a firm sells a component of its practice, the sales agreement sometimes provides that, for a limited period of time, the component may continue to use the name of the firm, or an element of the name, even though it is no longer connected to the firm. In such circumstances, while the two entities may be practicing under a common name, the facts are such that they do not belong to a larger structure aimed at co-operation and are, therefore, not network firms. Those entities shall determine how to disclose that they are not network firms when presenting themselves to outside parties.

Where the larger structure is aimed at co-operation and the entities within the structure share a significant part of professional resources, it is deemed to be a network. Professional resources include:

- Common systems that enable firms to exchange information such as client data, billing and time records;
- Partners and staff;
- Technical departments that consult on technical or industry specific issues, transactions or events for assurance engagements;
- Audit methodology or audit manuals; and
- Training courses and facilities.

290.23

The determination of whether the professional resources shared are significant, and therefore the firms are network firms, shall be made based on the relevant facts and circumstances. Where the shared resources are limited to common audit methodology or audit manuals, with no exchange of personnel or client or market information, it is unlikely that the shared resources would be significant. The same applies to a common training endeavor. Where, however, the shared resources involve the exchange of people or information, such as where staff are drawn from a shared pool, or a common technical department is created within the larger structure to provide participating firms with technical advice that the firms are required to follow, a reasonable and informed third party is more likely to conclude that the shared resources are significant.

290.24

Public Interest Entities

Section 290 contains additional provisions that reflect the extent of public interest in certain entities. For the purpose of this section, public interest entities are:

290.25

(a) All listed entities; and
(b) Any entity:
    (i) Defined by regulation or legislation as a public interest entity; or
    (ii) For which the audit is required by regulation or legislation to be conducted in compliance with the same independence requirements that apply to the audit of listed entities. Such regulation may be promulgated by any relevant regulator, including an audit regulator.

Firms and member bodies are encouraged to determine whether to treat additional entities, or certain categories of entities, as public interest entities because they have a large number and wide range of stakeholders. Factors to be considered include:

290.26

- The nature of the business, such as the holding of assets in a fiduciary capacity for a large number of stakeholders. Examples may include financial institutions, such as banks and insurance companies, and pension funds;
- Size; and
- Number of employees.

Related Entities

In the case of an audit client that is a listed entity, references to an audit client in this section include related entities of the client (unless otherwise stated). For all other audit clients, references to an audit client in this section include related entities over which the client has direct or indirect control. When the audit team knows or has reason to believe that a relationship or circumstance involving another related entity of the client is relevant to the evaluation of the firm's independence from the client, the audit team shall include

290.27

that related entity when identifying and evaluating threats to independence and applying appropriate safeguards.

Those Charged with Governance

290.28   Even when not required by the Code, applicable auditing standards, law or regulation, regular communication is encouraged between the firm and those charged with governance of the audit client regarding relationships and other matters that might, in the firm's opinion, reasonably bear on independence. Such communication enables those charged with governance to:

(a)   Consider the firm's judgments in identifying and evaluating threats to independence;
(b)   Consider the appropriateness of safeguards applied to eliminate them or reduce them to an acceptable level; and
(c)   Take appropriate action.

Such an approach can be particularly helpful with respect to intimidation and familiarity threats.

In complying with requirements in this section to communicate with those charged with governance, the firm shall determine, having regard to the nature and importance of the particular circumstances and matter to be communicated, the appropriate person(s) within the entity's governance structure with whom to communicate. If the firm communicates with a subgroup of those charged with governance, for example, an audit committee or an individual, the firm shall determine whether communication with all of those charged with governance is also necessary so that they are adequately informed.

Documentation

290.29   Documentation provides evidence of the professional accountant's judgments in forming conclusions regarding compliance with independence requirements. The absence of documentation is not a determinant of whether a firm considered a particular matter nor whether it is independent.

The professional accountant shall document conclusions regarding compliance with independence requirements, and the substance of any relevant discussions that support those conclusions. Accordingly:

(a)   When safeguards are required to reduce a threat to an acceptable level, the professional accountant shall document the nature of the threat and the safeguards in place or applied that reduce the threat to an acceptable level; and
(b)   When a threat required significant analysis to determine whether safeguards were necessary and the professional accountant concluded that they were not because the threat was already at an acceptable level, the professional accountant shall document the nature of the threat and the rationale for the conclusion.

Engagement Period

290.30   Independence from the audit client is required both during the engagement period and the period covered by the financial statements. The engagement period starts when the audit team begins to perform audit services. The engagement period ends when the audit report is issued. When the engagement is of a recurring nature, it ends at the later of the notification by either party that the professional relationship has terminated or the issuance of the final audit report.

When an entity becomes an audit client during or after the period covered by the financial statements on which the firm will express an opinion, the firm shall determine whether any threats to independence are created by:

290.31

(a) Financial or business relationships with the audit client during or after the period covered by the financial statements but before accepting the audit engagement; or

(b) Previous services provided to the audit client.

If a non-assurance service was provided to the audit client during or after the period covered by the financial statements but before the audit team begins to perform audit services and the service would not be permitted during the period of the audit engagement, the firm shall evaluate any threat to independence created by the service. If a threat is not at an acceptable level, the audit engagement shall only be accepted if safeguards are applied to eliminate any threats or reduce them to an acceptable level. Examples of such safeguards include:

290.32

● Not including personnel who provided the non-assurance service as members of the audit team;

● Having a professional accountant review the audit and non-assurance work as appropriate; or

● Engaging another firm to evaluate the results of the non-assurance service or having another firm re-perform the non-assurance service to the extent necessary to enable it to take responsibility for the service.

Mergers and Acquisitions

When, as a result of a merger or acquisition, an entity becomes a related entity of an audit client, the firm shall identify and evaluate previous and current interests and relationships with the related entity that, taking into account available safeguards, could affect its independence and therefore its ability to continue the audit engagement after the effective date of the merger or acquisition.

290.33

The firm shall take steps necessary to terminate, by the effective date of the merger or acquisition, any current interests or relationships that are not permitted under this Code. However, if such a current interest or relationship cannot reasonably be terminated by the effective date of the merger or acquisition, for example, because the related entity is unable by the effective date to effect an orderly transition to another service provider of a non-assurance service provided by the firm, the firm shall evaluate the threat that is created by such interest or relationship. The more significant the threat, the more likely the firm's objectivity will be compromised and it will be unable to continue as auditor. The significance of the threat will depend upon factors such as:

290.34

● The nature and significance of the interest or relationship;

● The nature and significance of the related entity relationship (for example, whether the related entity is a subsidiary or parent); and

● The length of time until the interest or relationship can reasonably be terminated.

The firm shall discuss with those charged with governance the reasons why the interest or relationship cannot reasonably be terminated by the effective date of the merger or acquisition and the evaluation of the significance of the threat.

If those charged with governance request the firm to continue as auditor, the firm shall do so only if:

290.35

(a) The interest or relationship will be terminated as soon as reasonably possible and in all cases within six months of the effective date of the merger or acquisition;

(b)   Any individual who has such an interest or relationship, including one that has arisen through performing a non-assurance service that would not be permitted under this section, will not be a member of the engagement team for the audit or the individual responsible for the engagement quality control review; and

(c)   Appropriate transitional measures will be applied, as necessary, and discussed with those charged with governance. Examples of transitional measures include:

- Having a professional accountant review the audit or non-assurance work as appropriate;
- Having a professional accountant, who is not a member of the firm expressing the opinion on the financial statements, perform a review that is equivalent to an engagement quality control review; or
- Engaging another firm to evaluate the results of the non-assurance service or having another firm re-perform the non-assurance service to the extent necessary to enable it to take responsibility for the service.

290.36   The firm may have completed a significant amount of work on the audit prior to the effective date of the merger or acquisition and may be able to complete the remaining audit procedures within a short period of time. In such circumstances, if those charged with governance request the firm to complete the audit while continuing with an interest or relationship identified in paragraph 290.33, the firm shall do so only if it:

(a)   Has evaluated the significance of the threat created by such interest or relationship and discussed the evaluation with those charged with governance;

(b)   Complies with the requirements of paragraph 290.35(b)–(c); and

(c)   Ceases to be the auditor no later than the issuance of the audit report.

290.37   When addressing previous and current interests and relationships covered by paragraphs 290.33 to 290.36, the firm shall determine whether, even if all the requirements could be met, the interests and relationships create threats that would remain so significant that objectivity would be compromised and, if so, the firm shall cease to be the auditor.

290.38   The professional accountant shall document any interests or relationships covered by paragraphs 290.34 and 36 that will not be terminated by the effective date of the merger or acquisition and the reasons why they will not be terminated, the transitional measures applied, the results of the discussion with those charged with governance, and the rationale as to why the previous and current interests and relationships do not create threats that would remain so significant that objectivity would be compromised.

Breach of a Provision of this Section

290.39   A breach of a provision of this section may occur despite the firm having policies and procedures designed to provide it with reasonable assurance that independence is maintained. A consequence of a breach may be that termination of the audit engagement is necessary.

290.40   When the firm concludes that a breach has occurred, the firm shall terminate, suspend or eliminate the interest or relationship that caused the breach and address the consequences of the breach.

290.41   When a breach is identified, the firm shall consider whether there are any legal or regulatory requirements that apply with respect to the breach and, if so, shall comply with those requirements. The firm shall consider reporting the breach to a member body, relevant regulator or oversight authority if such reporting is common practice or is expected in the particular jurisdiction.

When a breach is identified, the firm shall, in accordance with its policies and procedures, promptly communicate the breach to the engagement partner, those with responsibility for the policies and procedures relating to independence, other relevant personnel in the firm, and, where appropriate, the network, and those subject to the independence requirements who need to take appropriate action. The firm shall evaluate the significance of that breach and its impact on the firm's objectivity and ability to issue an audit report. The significance of the breach will depend on factors such as: **290.42**

- The nature and duration of the breach;
- The number and nature of any previous breaches with respect to the current audit engagement;
- Whether a member of the audit team had knowledge of the interest or relationship that caused the breach;
- Whether the individual who caused the breach is a member of the audit team or another individual for whom there are independence requirements;
- If the breach relates to a member of the audit team, the role of that individual;
- If the breach was caused by the provision of a professional service, the impact of that service, if any, on the accounting records or the amounts recorded in the financial statements on which the firm will express an opinion; and
- The extent of the self-interest, advocacy, intimidation or other threats created by the breach.

Depending upon the significance of the breach, it may be necessary to terminate the audit engagement or it may be possible to take action that satisfactorily addresses the consequences of the breach. The firm shall determine whether such action can be taken and is appropriate in the circumstances. In making this determination, the firm shall exercise professional judgment and take into account whether a reasonable and informed third party, weighing the significance of the breach, the action to be taken and all the specific facts and circumstances available to the professional accountant at that time, would be likely to conclude that the firm's objectivity would be compromised and therefore the firm is unable to issue an audit report. **290.43**

Examples of actions that the firm may consider include: **290.44**

- Removing the relevant individual from the audit team;
- Conducting an additional review of the affected audit work or re-performing that work to the extent necessary, in either case using different personnel;
- Recommending that the audit client engage another firm to review or re-perform the affected audit work to the extent necessary; and
- Where the breach relates to a non-assurance service that affects the accounting records or an amount that is recorded in the financial statements, engaging another firm to evaluate the results of the non-assurance service or having another firm re-perform the non-assurance service to the extent necessary to enable it to take responsibility for the service.

If the firm determines that action cannot be taken to satisfactorily address the consequences of the breach, the firm shall inform those charged with governance as soon as possible and take the steps necessary to terminate the audit engagement in compliance with any applicable legal or regulatory requirements relevant to terminating the audit engagement. Where termination is not permitted by law or regulation, the firm shall comply with any reporting or disclosure requirements. **290.45**

If the firm determines that action can be taken to satisfactorily address the consequences of the breach, the firm shall discuss the breach and the action it has taken or proposes to take with those charged with governance. The firm shall discuss the breach and the action as soon as possible, unless those charged with governance have specified an alternative timing for reporting less significant breaches. The matters to be discussed shall include: **290.46**

- The significance of the breach, including its nature and duration;
- How the breach occurred and how it was identified;
- The action taken or proposed to be taken and the firm's rationale for why the action will satisfactorily address the consequences of the breach and enable it to issue an audit report;
- The conclusion that, in the firm's professional judgment, objectivity has not been compromised and the rationale for that conclusion; and
- Any steps that the firm has taken or proposes to take to reduce or avoid the risk of further breaches occurring.

290.47 The firm shall communicate in writing with those charged with governance all matters discussed in accordance with paragraph 290.46 and obtain the concurrence of those charged with governance that action can be, or has been, taken to satisfactorily address the consequences of the breach. The communication shall include a description of the firm's policies and procedures relevant to the breach designed to provide it with reasonable assurance that independence is maintained and any steps that the firm has taken, or proposes to take, to reduce or avoid the risk of further breaches occurring. If those charged with governance do not concur that the action satisfactorily addresses the consequences of the breach, the firm shall take the steps necessary to terminate the audit engagement, where permitted by law or regulation, in compliance with any applicable legal or regulatory requirements relevant to terminating the audit engagement. Where termination is not permitted by law or regulation, the firm shall comply with any reporting or disclosure requirements.

290.48 If the breach occurred prior to the issuance of the previous audit report, the firm shall comply with this section in evaluating the significance of the breach and its impact on the firm's objectivity and its ability to issue an audit report in the current period. The firm shall also consider the impact of the breach, if any, on the firm's objectivity in relation to any previously issued audit reports, and the possibility of withdrawing such audit reports, and discuss the matter with those charged with governance.

290.49 The firm shall document the breach, the action taken, key decisions made and all the matters discussed with those charged with governance and any discussions with a member body, relevant regulator or oversight authority. When the firm continues with the audit engagement, the matters to be documented shall also include the conclusion that, in the firm's professional judgment, objectivity has not been compromised and the rationale for why the action taken satisfactorily addressed the consequences of the breach such that the firm could issue an audit report.

Paragraphs 290.50 to 290.99 are intentionally left blank.

Application of the Conceptual Framework Approach to Independence

290.100 Paragraphs 290.102 to 290.226 describe specific circumstances and relationships that create or may create threats to independence. The paragraphs describe the potential threats and the types of safeguards that may be appropriate to eliminate the threats or reduce them to an acceptable level and identify certain situations where no safeguards could reduce the threats to an acceptable level. The paragraphs do not describe all of the circumstances and relationships that create or may create a threat to independence. The firm and the members of the audit team shall evaluate the implications of similar, but different, circumstances and relationships and determine whether safeguards, including the safeguards in paragraphs 200.12 to 200.15, can be applied when necessary to eliminate the threats to independence or reduce them to an acceptable level.

Paragraphs 290.102 to 290.125 contain references to the materiality of a financial interest, **290.101**
loan, or guarantee, or the significance of a business relationship. For the purpose of
determining whether such an interest is material to an individual, the combined net worth of
the individual and the individual's immediate family members may be taken into account.

Financial Interests

Holding a financial interest in an audit client may create a self-interest threat. The existence **290.102**
and significance of any threat created depends on:

(a)   The role of the person holding the financial interest,
(b)   Whether the financial interest is direct or indirect, and
(c)   The materiality of the financial interest.

Financial interests may be held through an intermediary (for example, a collective **290.103**
investment vehicle, estate or trust). The determination of whether such financial interests
are direct or indirect will depend upon whether the beneficial owner has control over
the investment vehicle or the ability to influence its investment decisions. When control
over the investment vehicle or the ability to influence investment decisions exists, this
Code defines that financial interest to be a direct financial interest. Conversely, when the
beneficial owner of the financial interest has no control over the investment vehicle or
ability to influence its investment decisions, this Code defines that financial interest to be
an indirect financial interest.

If a member of the audit team, a member of that individual's immediate family, or a firm **290.104**
has a direct financial interest or a material indirect financial interest in the audit client,
the self-interest threat created would be so significant that no safeguards could reduce the
threat to an acceptable level. Therefore, none of the following shall have a direct financial
interest or a material indirect financial interest in the client: a member of the audit team;
a member of that individual's immediate family; or the firm.

When a member of the audit team has a close family member who the audit team member **290.105**
knows has a direct financial interest or a material indirect financial interest in the audit
client, a self-interest threat is created. The significance of the threat will depend on factors
such as:

●   The nature of the relationship between the member of the audit team and the close
    family member; and
●   The materiality of the financial interest to the close family member.

The significance of the threat shall be evaluated and safeguards applied when necessary
to eliminate the threat or reduce it to an acceptable level. Examples of such safeguards
include:

●   The close family member disposing, as soon as practicable, of all of the financial
    interest or disposing of a sufficient portion of an indirect financial interest so that the
    remaining interest is no longer material;
●   Having a professional accountant review the work of the member of the audit team; or
●   Removing the individual from the audit team.

If a member of the audit team, a member of that individual's immediate family, or a firm **290.106**
has a direct or material indirect financial interest in an entity that has a controlling interest
in the audit client, and the client is material to the entity, the self-interest threat created
would be so significant that no safeguards could reduce the threat to an acceptable level.
Therefore, none of the following shall have such a financial interest: a member of the audit
team; a member of that individual's immediate family; and the firm.

290.107   The holding by a firm's retirement benefit plan of a direct or material indirect financial interest in an audit client creates a self-interest threat. The significance of the threat shall be evaluated and safeguards applied when necessary to eliminate the threat or reduce it to an acceptable level.

290.108   If other partners in the office in which the engagement partner practices in connection with the audit engagement, or their immediate family members, hold a direct financial interest or a material indirect financial interest in that audit client, the self-interest threat created would be so significant that no safeguards could reduce the threat to an acceptable level. Therefore, neither such partners nor their immediate family members shall hold any such financial interests in such an audit client.

290.109   The office in which the engagement partner practices in connection with the audit engagement is not necessarily the office to which that partner is assigned. Accordingly, when the engagement partner is located in a different office from that of the other members of the audit team, professional judgment shall be used to determine in which office the partner practices in connection with that engagement.

290.110   If other partners and managerial employees who provide non-audit services to the audit client, except those whose involvement is minimal, or their immediate family members, hold a direct financial interest or a material indirect financial interest in the audit client, the self-interest threat created would be so significant that no safeguards could reduce the threat to an acceptable level. Accordingly, neither such personnel nor their immediate family members shall hold any such financial interests in such an audit client.

290.111   Despite paragraphs 290.108 and 290.110, the holding of a financial interest in an audit client by an immediate family member of:

(a)   A partner located in the office in which the engagement partner practices in connection with the audit engagement; or

(b)   A partner or managerial employee who provides non-audit services to the audit client

is deemed not to compromise independence if the financial interest is received as a result of the immediate family member's employment rights (for example, through pension or share option plans) and, when necessary, safeguards are applied to eliminate any threat to independence or reduce it to an acceptable level.

However, when the immediate family member has or obtains the right to dispose of the financial interest or, in the case of a stock option, the right to exercise the option, the financial interest shall be disposed of or forfeited as soon as practicable.

290.112   A self-interest threat may be created if the firm or a member of the audit team, or a member of that individual's immediate family, has a financial interest in an entity and an audit client also has a financial interest in that entity. However, independence is deemed not to be compromised if these interests are immaterial and the audit client cannot exercise significant influence over the entity. If such interest is material to any party, and the audit client can exercise significant influence over the other entity, no safeguards could reduce the threat to an acceptable level. Accordingly, the firm shall not have such an interest and any individual with such an interest shall, before becoming a member of the audit team, either:

(a)   Dispose of the interest; or

(b)   Dispose of a sufficient amount of the interest so that the remaining interest is no longer material.

A self-interest, familiarity or intimidation threat may be created if a member of the audit   **290.113**
team, or a member of that individual's immediate family, or the firm, has a financial interest
in an entity when a director, officer or controlling owner of the audit client is also known
to have a financial interest in that entity. The existence and significance of any threat will
depend upon factors such as:

- The role of the professional on the audit team;
- Whether ownership of the entity is closely or widely held;
- Whether the interest gives the investor the ability to control or significantly influence
  the entity; and
- The materiality of the financial interest.

The significance of any threat shall be evaluated and safeguards applied when necessary
to eliminate the threat or reduce it to an acceptable level. Examples of such safeguards
include:

- Removing the member of the audit team with the financial interest from the audit
  team; or
- Having a professional accountant review the work of the member of the audit team.

The holding by a firm, or a member of the audit team, or a member of that individual's   **290.114**
immediate family, of a direct financial interest or a material indirect financial interest in
the audit client as a trustee creates a self-interest threat. Similarly, a self-interest threat is
created when:

(a) A partner in the office in which the engagement partner practices in connection with
    the audit;
(b) Other partners and managerial employees who provide non-assurance services to the
    audit client, except those whose involvement is minimal; or
(c) Their immediate family members, hold a direct financial interest or a material indirect
    financial interest in the audit client as trustee.

Such an interest shall not be held unless:

(a) Neither the trustee, nor an immediate family member of the trustee, nor the firm are
    beneficiaries of the trust;
(b) The interest in the audit client held by the trust is not material to the trust;
(c) The trust is not able to exercise significant influence over the audit client; and
(d) The trustee, an immediate family member of the trustee, or the firm cannot significantly
    influence any investment decision involving a financial interest in the audit client.

Members of the audit team shall determine whether a self-interest threat is created by any   **290.115**
known financial interests in the audit client held by other individuals including:

(a) Partners and professional employees of the firm, other than those referred to above,
    or their immediate family members; and
(b) Individuals with a close personal relationship with a member of the audit team.

Whether these interests create a self-interest threat will depend on factors such as:

- The firm's organizational, operating and reporting structure; and
- The nature of the relationship between the individual and the member of the audit
  team.

The significance of any threat shall be evaluated and safeguards applied when necessary
to eliminate the threat or reduce it to an acceptable level. Examples of such safeguards
include:

- Removing the member of the audit team with the personal relationship from the audit team;
- Excluding the member of the audit team from any significant decision-making concerning the audit engagement; or
- Having a professional accountant review the work of the member of the audit team.

290.116   If a firm or a partner or employee of the firm, or a member of that individual's immediate family, receives a direct financial interest or a material indirect financial interest in an audit client, for example, by way of an inheritance, gift or as a result of a merger and such interest would not be permitted to be held under this section, then:

(a)   If the interest is received by the firm, the financial interest shall be disposed of immediately, or a sufficient amount of an indirect financial interest shall be disposed of so that the remaining interest is no longer material;

(b)   If the interest is received by a member of the audit team, or a member of that individual's immediate family, the individual who received the financial interest shall immediately dispose of the financial interest, or dispose of a sufficient amount of an indirect financial interest so that the remaining interest is no longer material; or

(c)   If the interest is received by an individual who is not a member of the audit team, or by an immediate family member of the individual, the financial interest shall be disposed of as soon as possible, or a sufficient amount of an indirect financial interest shall be disposed of so that the remaining interest is no longer material. Pending the disposal of the financial interest, a determination shall be made as to whether any safeguards are necessary.

Loans and Guarantees

290.117   A loan, or a guarantee of a loan, to a member of the audit team, or a member of that individual's immediate family, or the firm from an audit client that is a bank or a similar institution may create a threat to independence. If the loan or guarantee is not made under normal lending procedures, terms and conditions, a self-interest threat would be created that would be so significant that no safeguards could reduce the threat to an acceptable level. Accordingly, neither a member of the audit team, a member of that individual's immediate family, nor a firm shall accept such a loan or guarantee.

290.118   If a loan to a firm from an audit client that is a bank or similar institution is made under normal lending procedures, terms and conditions and it is material to the audit client or firm receiving the loan, it may be possible to apply safeguards to reduce the self-interest threat to an acceptable level. An example of such a safeguard is having the work reviewed by a professional accountant from a network firm that is neither involved with the audit nor received the loan.

290.119   A loan, or a guarantee of a loan, from an audit client that is a bank or a similar institution to a member of the audit team, or a member of that individual's immediate family, does not create a threat to independence if the loan or guarantee is made under normal lending procedures, terms and conditions. Examples of such loans include home mortgages, bank overdrafts, car loans and credit card balances.

290.120   If the firm or a member of the audit team, or a member of that individual's immediate family, accepts a loan from, or has a borrowing guaranteed by, an audit client that is not a bank or similar institution, the self-interest threat created would be so significant that no safeguards could reduce the threat to an acceptable level, unless the loan or guarantee is immaterial to both (a) the firm or the member of the audit team and the immediate family member, and (b) the client.

Similarly, if the firm or a member of the audit team, or a member of that individual's **290.121**
immediate family, makes or guarantees a loan to an audit client, the self-interest threat
created would be so significant that no safeguards could reduce the threat to an acceptable
level, unless the loan or guarantee is immaterial to both (a) the firm or the member of the
audit team and the immediate family member, and (b) the client.

If a firm or a member of the audit team, or a member of that individual's immediate family, **290.122**
has deposits or a brokerage account with an audit client that is a bank, broker or similar
institution, a threat to independence is not created if the deposit or account is held under
normal commercial terms.

Business Relationships

A close business relationship between a firm, or a member of the audit team, or a member **290.123**
of that individual's immediate family, and the audit client or its management, arises from
a commercial relationship or common financial interest and may create self-interest or
intimidation threats. Examples of such relationships include:

- Having a financial interest in a joint venture with either the client or a controlling
  owner, director, officer or other individual who performs senior managerial activities
  for that client.
- Arrangements to combine one or more services or products of the firm with one or
  more services or products of the client and to market the package with reference to
  both parties.
- Distribution or marketing arrangements under which the firm distributes or markets
  the client's products or services, or the client distributes or markets the firm's products
  or services.

Unless any financial interest is immaterial and the business relationship is insignificant
to the firm and the client or its management, the threat created would be so significant
that no safeguards could reduce the threat to an acceptable level. Therefore, unless the
financial interest is immaterial and the business relationship is insignificant, the business
relationship shall not be entered into, or it shall be reduced to an insignificant level or
terminated.

In the case of a member of the audit team, unless any such financial interest is immaterial
and the relationship is insignificant to that member, the individual shall be removed from
the audit team.

If the business relationship is between an immediate family member of a member of the
audit team and the audit client or its management, the significance of any threat shall be
evaluated and safeguards applied when necessary to eliminate the threat or reduce it to an
acceptable level.

A business relationship involving the holding of an interest by the firm, or a member of **290.124**
the audit team, or a member of that individual's immediate family, in a closely-held entity
when the audit client or a director or officer of the client, or any group thereof, also holds
an interest in that entity does not create threats to independence if:

(a) The business relationship is insignificant to the firm, the member of the audit team
    and the immediate family member, and the client;
(b) The financial interest is immaterial to the investor or group of investors; and
(c) The financial interest does not give the investor, or group of investors, the ability to
    control the closely-held entity.

290.125   The purchase of goods and services from an audit client by the firm, or a member of the audit team, or a member of that individual's immediate family, does not generally create a threat to independence if the transaction is in the normal course of business and at arm's length. However, such transactions may be of such a nature or magnitude that they create a self-interest threat. The significance of any threat shall be evaluated and safeguards applied when necessary to eliminate the threat or reduce it to an acceptable level. Examples of such safeguards include:

- Eliminating or reducing the magnitude of the transaction; or
- Removing the individual from the audit team.

Family and Personal Relationships

290.126   Family and personal relationships between a member of the audit team and a director or officer or certain employees (depending on their role) of the audit client may create self-interest, familiarity or intimidation threats. The existence and significance of any threats will depend on a number of factors, including the individual's responsibilities on the audit team, the role of the family member or other individual within the client and the closeness of the relationship.

290.127   When an immediate family member of a member of the audit team is:

(a) a director or officer of the audit client; or
(b) an employee in a position to exert significant influence over the preparation of the client's accounting records or the financial statements on which the firm will express an opinion,

or was in such a position during any period covered by the engagement or the financial statements, the threats to independence can only be reduced to an acceptable level by removing the individual from the audit team. The closeness of the relationship is such that no other safeguards could reduce the threat to an acceptable level. Accordingly, no individual who has such a relationship shall be a member of the audit team.

290.128   Threats to independence are created when an immediate family member of a member of the audit team is an employee in a position to exert significant influence over the client's financial position, financial performance or cash flows. The significance of the threats will depend on factors such as:

- The position held by the immediate family member; and
- The role of the professional on the audit team.

The significance of the threat shall be evaluated and safeguards applied when necessary to eliminate the threat or reduce it to an acceptable level. Examples of such safeguards include:

- Removing the individual from the audit team; or
- Structuring the responsibilities of the audit team so that the professional does not deal with matters that are within the responsibility of the immediate family member.

290.129   Threats to independence are created when a close family member of a member of the audit team is:

(a) A director or officer of the audit client; or
(b) An employee in a position to exert significant influence over the preparation of the client's accounting records or the financial statements on which the firm will express an opinion.

The significance of the threats will depend on factors such as:

- The nature of the relationship between the member of the audit team and the close family member;
- The position held by the close family member; and
- The role of the professional on the audit team.

The significance of the threat shall be evaluated and safeguards applied when necessary to eliminate the threat or reduce it to an acceptable level. Examples of such safeguards include:

- Removing the individual from the audit team; or
- Structuring the responsibilities of the audit team so that the professional does not deal with matters that are within the responsibility of the close family member.

Threats to independence are created when a member of the audit team has a close relationship with a person who is not an immediate or close family member, but who is a director or officer or an employee in a position to exert significant influence over the preparation of the client's accounting records or the financial statements on which the firm will express an opinion. A member of the audit team who has such a relationship shall consult in accordance with firm policies and procedures. The significance of the threats will depend on factors such as: **290.130**

- The nature of the relationship between the individual and the member of the audit team;
- The position the individual holds with the client; and
- The role of the professional on the audit team.

The significance of the threats shall be evaluated and safeguards applied when necessary to eliminate the threats or reduce them to an acceptable level. Examples of such safeguards include:

- Removing the professional from the audit team; or
- Structuring the responsibilities of the audit team so that the professional does not deal with matters that are within the responsibility of the individual with whom the professional has a close relationship.

Self-interest, familiarity or intimidation threats may be created by a personal or family relationship between (a) a partner or employee of the firm who is not a member of the audit team and (b) a director or officer of the audit client or an employee in a position to exert significant influence over the preparation of the client's accounting records or the financial statements on which the firm will express an opinion. Partners and employees of the firm who are aware of such relationships shall consult in accordance with firm policies and procedures. The existence and significance of any threat will depend on factors such as: **290.131**

- The nature of the relationship between the partner or employee of the firm and the director or officer or employee of the client;
- The interaction of the partner or employee of the firm with the audit team;
- The position of the partner or employee within the firm; and
- The position the individual holds with the client.

The significance of any threat shall be evaluated and safeguards applied when necessary to eliminate the threat or reduce it to an acceptable level. Examples of such safeguards include:

- Structuring the partner's or employee's responsibilities to reduce any potential influence over the audit engagement; or
- Having a professional accountant review the relevant audit work performed.

Employment with an Audit Client

290.132   Familiarity or intimidation threats may be created if a director or officer of the audit client, or an employee in a position to exert significant influence over the preparation of the client's accounting records or the financial statements on which the firm will express an opinion, has been a member of the audit team or partner of the firm.

290.133   If a former member of the audit team or partner of the firm has joined the audit client in such a position and a significant connection remains between the firm and the individual, the threat would be so significant that no safeguards could reduce the threat to an acceptable level. Therefore, independence would be deemed to be compromised if a former member of the audit team or partner joins the audit client as a director or officer, or as an employee in a position to exert significant influence over the preparation of the client's accounting records or the financial statements on which the firm will express an opinion, unless:

(a)   The individual is not entitled to any benefits or payments from the firm, unless made in accordance with fixed pre-determined arrangements, and any amount owed to the individual is not material to the firm; and

(b)   The individual does not continue to participate or appear to participate in the firm's business or professional activities.

290.134   If a former member of the audit team or partner of the firm has joined the audit client in such a position, and no significant connection remains between the firm and the individual, the existence and significance of any familiarity or intimidation threats will depend on factors such as:

- The position the individual has taken at the client;
- Any involvement the individual will have with the audit team;
- The length of time since the individual was a member of the audit team or partner of the firm; and
- The former position of the individual within the audit team or firm, for example, whether the individual was responsible for maintaining regular contact with the client's management or those charged with governance.

The significance of any threats created shall be evaluated and safeguards applied when necessary to eliminate the threats or reduce them to an acceptable level. Examples of such safeguards include:

- Modifying the audit plan;
- Assigning individuals to the audit team who have sufficient experience in relation to the individual who has joined the client; or
- Having a professional accountant review the work of the former member of the audit team.

290.135   If a former partner of the firm has previously joined an entity in such a position and the entity subsequently becomes an audit client of the firm, the significance of any threat to independence shall be evaluated and safeguards applied when necessary to eliminate the threat or reduce it to an acceptable level.

290.136   A self-interest threat is created when a member of the audit team participates in the audit engagement while knowing that the member of the audit team will, or may, join the client some time in the future. Firm policies and procedures shall require members of an audit team to notify the firm when entering employment negotiations with the client. On receiving such notification, the significance of the threat shall be evaluated and safeguards applied when necessary to eliminate the threat or reduce it to an acceptable level. Examples of such safeguards include:

- Removing the individual from the audit team; or
- A review of any significant judgments made by that individual while on the team.

Audit Clients that are Public Interest Entities

Familiarity or intimidation threats are created when a key audit partner joins the audit client that is a public interest entity as: **290.137**

(a) A director or officer of the entity; or
(b) An employee in a position to exert significant influence over the preparation of the client's accounting records or the financial statements on which the firm will express an opinion.

Independence would be deemed to be compromised unless, subsequent to the partner ceasing to be a key audit partner, the public interest entity had issued audited financial statements covering a period of not less than twelve months and the partner was not a member of the audit team with respect to the audit of those financial statements.

An intimidation threat is created when the individual who was the firm's Senior or Managing Partner (Chief Executive or equivalent) joins an audit client that is a public interest entity as: **290.138**

(a) An employee in a position to exert significant influence over the preparation of the entity's accounting records or its financial statements; or
(b) A director or officer of the entity.

Independence would be deemed to be compromised unless twelve months have passed since the individual was the Senior or Managing Partner (Chief Executive or equivalent) of the firm.

Independence is deemed not to be compromised if, as a result of a business combination, a former key audit partner or the individual who was the firm's former Senior or Managing Partner is in a position as described in paragraphs 290.137 and 290.138, and: **290.139**

(a) The position was not taken in contemplation of the business combination;
(b) Any benefits or payments due to the former partner from the firm have been settled in full, unless made in accordance with fixed pre-determined arrangements and any amount owed to the partner is not material to the firm;
(c) The former partner does not continue to participate or appear to participate in the firm's business or professional activities; and;
(d) The position held by the former partner with the audit client is discussed with those charged with governance.

Temporary Staff Assignments

The lending of staff by a firm to an audit client may create a self-review threat. Such assistance may be given, but only for a short period of time and the firm's personnel shall not be involved in: **290.140**

(a) Providing non-assurance services that would not be permitted under this section; or
(b) Assuming management responsibilities.

In all circumstances, the audit client shall be responsible for directing and supervising the activities of the loaned staff.

The significance of any threat shall be evaluated and safeguards applied when necessary to eliminate the threat or reduce it to an acceptable level. Examples of such safeguards include:

- Conducting an additional review of the work performed by the loaned staff;
- Not giving the loaned staff audit responsibility for any function or activity that the staff performed during the temporary staff assignment; or
- Not including the loaned staff as a member of the audit team.

Recent Service with an Audit Client

290.141   Self-interest, self-review or familiarity threats may be created if a member of the audit team has recently served as a director, officer, or employee of the audit client. This would be the case when, for example, a member of the audit team has to evaluate elements of the financial statements for which the member of the audit team had prepared the accounting records while with the client.

290.142   If, during the period covered by the audit report, a member of the audit team had served as a director or officer of the audit client, or was an employee in a position to exert significant influence over the preparation of the client's accounting records or the financial statements on which the firm will express an opinion, the threat created would be so significant that no safeguards could reduce the threat to an acceptable level. Consequently, such individuals shall not be assigned to the audit team.

290.143   Self-interest, self-review or familiarity threats may be created if, before the period covered by the audit report, a member of the audit team had served as a director or officer of the audit client, or was an employee in a position to exert significant influence over the preparation of the client's accounting records or financial statements on which the firm will express an opinion. For example, such threats would be created if a decision made or work performed by the individual in the prior period, while employed by the client, is to be evaluated in the current period as part of the current audit engagement. The existence and significance of any threats will depend on factors such as:

- The position the individual held with the client;
- The length of time since the individual left the client; and
- The role of the professional on the audit team.

The significance of any threat shall be evaluated and safeguards applied when necessary to reduce the threat to an acceptable level. An example of such a safeguard is conducting a review of the work performed by the individual as a member of the audit team.

Serving as a Director or Officer of an Audit Client

290.144   If a partner or employee of the firm serves as a director or officer of an audit client, the self-review and self-interest threats created would be so significant that no safeguards could reduce the threats to an acceptable level. Accordingly, no partner or employee shall serve as a director or officer of an audit client.

290.145   The position of Company Secretary has different implications in different jurisdictions. Duties may range from administrative duties, such as personnel management and the maintenance of company records and registers, to duties as diverse as ensuring that the company complies with regulations or providing advice on corporate governance matters. Generally, this position is seen to imply a close association with the entity.

290.146

If a partner or employee of the firm serves as Company Secretary for an audit client, self-review and advocacy threats are created that would generally be so significant that no safeguards could reduce the threats to an acceptable level. Despite paragraph 290.144, when this practice is specifically permitted under local law, professional rules or practice, and provided management makes all relevant decisions, the duties and activities shall be limited to those of a routine and administrative nature, such as preparing minutes and maintaining statutory returns. In those circumstances, the significance of any threats shall be evaluated and safeguards applied when necessary to eliminate the threats or reduce them to an acceptable level.

290.147

Performing routine administrative services to support a company secretarial function or providing advice in relation to company secretarial administration matters does not generally create threats to independence, as long as client management makes all relevant decisions.

Long Association of Senior Personnel (Including Partner Rotation) with an Audit Client

General Provisions

290.148

Familiarity and self-interest threats are created by using the same senior personnel on an audit engagement over a long period of time. The significance of the threats will depend on factors such as:

- How long the individual has been a member of the audit team;
- The role of the individual on the audit team;
- The structure of the firm;
- The nature of the audit engagement;
- Whether the client's management team has changed; and
- Whether the nature or complexity of the client's accounting and reporting issues has changed.

The significance of the threats shall be evaluated and safeguards applied when necessary to eliminate the threats or reduce them to an acceptable level. Examples of such safeguards include:

- Rotating the senior personnel off the audit team;
- Having a professional accountant who was not a member of the audit team review the work of the senior personnel; or
- Regular independent internal or external quality reviews of the engagement.

Audit Clients that are Public Interest Entities

290.149

In respect of an audit of a public interest entity, an individual shall not be a key audit partner for more than seven years. After such time, the individual shall not be a member of the engagement team or be a key audit partner for the client for two years. During that period, the individual shall not participate in the audit of the entity, provide quality control for the engagement, consult with the engagement team or the client regarding technical or industry-specific issues, transactions or events or otherwise directly influence the outcome of the engagement.

290.150 Despite paragraph 290.149, key audit partners whose continuity is especially important to audit quality may, in rare cases due to unforeseen circumstances outside the firm's control, be permitted an additional year on the audit team as long as the threat to independence can be eliminated or reduced to an acceptable level by applying safeguards. For example, a key audit partner may remain on the audit team for up to one additional year in circumstances where, due to unforeseen events, a required rotation was not possible, as might be the case due to serious illness of the intended engagement partner.

290.151 The long association of other partners with an audit client that is a public interest entity creates familiarity and self-interest threats. The significance of the threats will depend on factors such as:

- How long any such partner has been associated with the audit client;
- The role, if any, of the individual on the audit team; and
- The nature, frequency and extent of the individual's interactions with the client's management or those charged with governance.

The significance of the threats shall be evaluated and safeguards applied when necessary to eliminate the threats or reduce them to an acceptable level. Examples of such safeguards include:

- Rotating the partner off the audit team or otherwise ending the partner's association with the audit client; or
- Regular independent internal or external quality reviews of the engagement.

290.152 When an audit client becomes a public interest entity, the length of time the individual has served the audit client as a key audit partner before the client becomes a public interest entity shall be taken into account in determining the timing of the rotation. If the individual has served the audit client as a key audit partner for five years or less when the client becomes a public interest entity, the number of years the individual may continue to serve the client in that capacity before rotating off the engagement is seven years less the number of years already served. If the individual has served the audit client as a key audit partner for six or more years when the client becomes a public interest entity, the partner may continue to serve in that capacity for a maximum of two additional years before rotating off the engagement.

290.153 When a firm has only a few people with the necessary knowledge and experience to serve as a key audit partner on the audit of a public interest entity, rotation of key audit partners may not be an available safeguard. If an independent regulator in the relevant jurisdiction has provided an exemption from partner rotation in such circumstances, an individual may remain a key audit partner for more than seven years, in accordance with such regulation, provided that the independent regulator has specified alternative safeguards which are applied, such as a regular independent external review.

Provision of Non-assurance Services to an Audit Client

290.154 Firms have traditionally provided to their audit clients a range of non-assurance services that are consistent with their skills and expertise. Providing non-assurance services may, however, create threats to the independence of the firm or members of the audit team. The threats created are most often self-review, self-interest and advocacy threats.

290.155 New developments in business, the evolution of financial markets and changes in information technology make it impossible to draw up an all-inclusive list of non-assurance services that might be provided to an audit client. When specific guidance on a particular non-assurance service is not included in this section, the conceptual framework shall be applied when evaluating the particular circumstances.

Before the firm accepts an engagement to provide a non-assurance service to an audit client, a determination shall be made as to whether providing such a service would create a threat to independence. In evaluating the significance of any threat created by a particular non-assurance service, consideration shall be given to any threat that the audit team has reason to believe is created by providing other related non-assurance services. If a threat is created that cannot be reduced to an acceptable level by the application of safeguards, the non-assurance service shall not be provided.   **290.156**

A firm may provide non-assurance services that would otherwise be restricted under this section to the following related entities of the audit client: **290.157**

(a) An entity, which is not an audit client, that has direct or indirect control over the audit client;
(b) An entity, which is not an audit client, with a direct financial interest in the client if that entity has significant influence over the client and the interest in the client is material to such entity; or
(c) An entity, which is not an audit client, that is under common control with the audit client,

if it is reasonable to conclude that (a) the services do not create a self-review threat because the results of the services will not be subject to audit procedures and (b) any threats that are created by the provision of such services are eliminated or reduced to an acceptable level by the application of safeguards.

A non-assurance service provided to an audit client does not compromise the firm's independence when the client becomes a public interest entity if: **290.158**

(a) The previous non-assurance service complies with the provisions of this section that relate to audit clients that are not public interest entities;
(b) Services that are not permitted under this section for audit clients that are public interest entities are terminated before or as soon as practicable after the client becomes a public interest entity; and
(c) The firm applies safeguards when necessary to eliminate or reduce to an acceptable level any threats to independence arising from the service.

Management Responsibilities

Management responsibilities involve controlling, leading and directing an entity, including making decisions regarding the acquisition, deployment and control of human, financial, technological, physical and intangible resources.   **290.159**

Determining whether an activity is a management responsibility depends on the circumstances and requires the exercise of judgment. Examples of activities that would be considered a management responsibility include: **290.160**

- Setting policies and strategic direction.
- Hiring or dismissing employees.
- Directing and taking responsibility for the actions of employees in relation to the employees' work for the entity.
- Authorizing transactions.
- Controlling or managing of bank accounts or investments.
- Deciding which recommendations of the firm or other third parties to implement.
- Reporting to those charged with governance on behalf of management.

- Taking responsibility for the preparation and fair presentation of financial statements in accordance with the applicable financial reporting framework.
- Taking responsibility for designing, implementing, monitoring or maintaining internal controls.

290.161   A firm shall not assume a management responsibility for an audit client. The threats created would be so significant that no safeguards could reduce the threats to an acceptable level. For example, deciding which recommendations of the firm to implement will create self-review and self-interest threats. Further, assuming a management responsibility creates a familiarity threat because the firm becomes too closely aligned with the views and interests of management. Subject to compliance with paragraph 290.162, providing advice and recommendations to assist management in discharging its responsibilities is not assuming a management responsibility.

290.162   To avoid the risk of assuming a management responsibility when providing non-assurance services to an audit client, the firm shall be satisfied that client management makes all judgments and decisions that are the responsibility of management. This includes ensuring that the client's management:

- Designates an individual who possesses suitable skill, knowledge and experience to be responsible at all times for the client's decisions and to oversee the services. Such an individual, preferably within senior management, would understand the objectives, nature and results of the services and the respective client and firm responsibilities. However, the individual is not required to possess the expertise to perform or re-perform the services;
- Provides oversight of the services and evaluates the adequacy of the results of the services performed for the client's purpose; and
- Accepts responsibility for the actions, if any, to be taken arising from the results of the services.

Administrative Services

290.163   Administrative services involve assisting clients with their routine or mechanical tasks within the normal course of operations. Such services require little to no professional judgment and are clerical in nature. Examples of administrative services include word processing services, preparing administrative or statutory forms for client approval, submitting such forms as instructed by the client, monitoring statutory filing dates, and advising an audit client of those dates. Providing such services does not generally create a threat to independence. However, the significance of any threat created shall be evaluated and safeguards applied when necessary to eliminate the threat or reduce it to an acceptable level.

Preparing Accounting Records and Financial Statements

General Provisions

290.164   Management is responsible for the preparation and fair presentation of the financial statements in accordance with the applicable financial reporting framework. These responsibilities include:

- Determining accounting policies and the accounting treatment within those policies.
- Preparing or changing source documents or originating data, in electronic or other form, evidencing the occurrence of a transaction (for example, purchase orders, payroll time records, and customer orders).

- Originating or changing journal entries, or determining or approving the account classifications of transactions.

Providing an audit client with accounting and bookkeeping services, such as preparing accounting records or financial statements, creates a self-review threat when the firm subsequently audits the financial statements. **290.165**

The audit process, however, necessitates dialogue between the firm and management of the audit client, which may involve: **290.166**

- The application of accounting standards or policies and financial statement disclosure requirements;
- The appropriateness of financial and accounting control and the methods used in determining the stated amounts of assets and liabilities; or
- Proposing adjusting journal entries.

These activities are considered to be a normal part of the audit process and do not, generally, create threats to independence so long as the client is responsible for making decisions in the preparation of the accounting records and financial statements.

Similarly, the client may request technical assistance from the firm on matters such as resolving account reconciliation problems or analyzing and accumulating information for regulatory reporting. In addition, the client may request technical advice on accounting issues such as the conversion of existing financial statements from one financial reporting framework to another (for example, to comply with group accounting policies or to transition to a different financial reporting framework such as International Financial Reporting Standards). Such services do not, generally, create threats to independence provided the firm does not assume a management responsibility for the client. **290.167**

Audit clients that are not public interest entities

The firm may provide services related to the preparation of accounting records and financial statements to an audit client that is not a public interest entity where the services are of a routine or mechanical nature, so long as any self-review threat created is reduced to an acceptable level. Services that are routine or mechanical in nature require little to no professional judgment from the professional accountant. Some examples of such services are: **290.168**

- Preparing payroll calculations or reports based on client-originated data for approval and payment by the client.
- Recording recurring transactions for which amounts are easily determinable from source documents or originating data, such as a utility bill where the client has determined or approved the appropriate account classification.
- Recording a transaction for which the client has already determined the amount to be recorded, even though the transaction involves a significant degree of subjectivity.
- Calculating depreciation on fixed assets when the client determines the accounting policy and estimates of useful life and residual values.
- Posting client-approved entries to the trial balance.
- Preparing financial statements based on information in the client-approved trial balance and preparing the related notes based on client-approved records.

In all cases, the significance of any threat created shall be evaluated and safeguards applied when necessary to eliminate the threat or reduce it to an acceptable level. Examples of such safeguards include:

- Arranging for such services to be performed by an individual who is not a member of the audit team; or
- If such services are performed by a member of the audit team, using a partner or senior staff member with appropriate expertise who is not a member of the audit team to review the work performed.

Audit clients that are public interest entities

290.169   A firm shall not provide to an audit client that is a public interest entity accounting and bookkeeping services, including payroll services, or prepare financial statements on which the firm will express an opinion or financial information which forms the basis of the financial statements.

290.170   Despite paragraph 290.169, a firm may provide accounting and bookkeeping services, including payroll services and the preparation of financial statements or other financial information, of a routine or mechanical nature for divisions or related entities of an audit client that is a public interest entity if the personnel providing the services are not members of the audit team and:

(a)   The divisions or related entities for which the service is provided are collectively immaterial to the financial statements on which the firm will express an opinion; or

(b)   The services relate to matters that are collectively immaterial to the financial statements of the division or related entity.

Valuation Services

General Provisions

290.171   A valuation comprises the making of assumptions with regard to future developments, the application of appropriate methodologies and techniques, and the combination of both to compute a certain value, or range of values, for an asset, a liability or for a business as a whole.

290.172   Performing valuation services for an audit client may create a self-review threat. The existence and significance of any threat will depend on factors such as:

- Whether the valuation will have a material effect on the financial statements.
- The extent of the client's involvement in determining and approving the valuation methodology and other significant matters of judgment.
- The availability of established methodologies and professional guidelines.
- For valuations involving standard or established methodologies, the degree of subjectivity inherent in the item.
- The reliability and extent of the underlying data.
- The degree of dependence on future events of a nature that could create significant volatility inherent in the amounts involved.
- The extent and clarity of the disclosures in the financial statements.

The significance of any threat created shall be evaluated and safeguards applied when necessary to eliminate the threat or reduce it to an acceptable level. Examples of such safeguards include:

- Having a professional who was not involved in providing the valuation service review the audit or valuation work performed; or
- Making arrangements so that personnel providing such services do not participate in the audit engagement.

Certain valuations do not involve a significant degree of subjectivity. This is likely the case where the underlying assumptions are either established by law or regulation, or are widely accepted and when the techniques and methodologies to be used are based on generally accepted standards or prescribed by law or regulation. In such circumstances, the results of a valuation performed by two or more parties are not likely to be materially different.   **290.173**

If a firm is requested to perform a valuation to assist an audit client with its tax reporting obligations or for tax planning purposes and the results of the valuation will not have a direct effect on the financial statements, the provisions included in paragraph 290.186 apply.   **290.174**

Audit clients that are not public interest entities

In the case of an audit client that is not a public interest entity, if the valuation service has a material effect on the financial statements on which the firm will express an opinion and the valuation involves a significant degree of subjectivity, no safeguards could reduce the self-review threat to an acceptable level. Accordingly a firm shall not provide such a valuation service to an audit client.   **290.175**

Audit clients that are public interest entities

A firm shall not provide valuation services to an audit client that is a public interest entity if the valuations would have a material effect, separately or in the aggregate, on the financial statements on which the firm will express an opinion.   **290.176**

Taxation Services

Taxation services comprise a broad range of services, including: **290.177**

- Tax return preparation;
- Tax calculations for the purpose of preparing the accounting entries;
- Tax planning and other tax advisory services; and
- Assistance in the resolution of tax disputes.

While taxation services provided by a firm to an audit client are addressed separately under each of these broad headings; in practice, these activities are often interrelated.

Performing certain tax services creates self-review and advocacy threats. The existence and significance of any threats will depend on factors such as: **290.178**

- The system by which the tax authorities assess and administer the tax in question and the role of the firm in that process;
- The complexity of the relevant tax regime and the degree of judgment necessary in applying it;
- The particular characteristics of the engagement; and
- The level of tax expertise of the client's employees.

Tax Return Preparation

Tax return preparation services involve assisting clients with their tax reporting obligations by drafting and completing information, including the amount of tax due (usually on standardized forms) required to be submitted to the applicable tax authorities. Such services also include advising on the tax return treatment of past transactions and responding on   **290.179** behalf of the audit client to the tax authorities' requests for additional information and analysis (including providing explanations of and technical support for the approach being taken). Tax return preparation services are generally based on historical information and principally involve analysis and presentation of such historical information under existing tax law, including precedents and established practice. Further, the tax returns are subject to whatever review or approval process the tax authority deems appropriate. Accordingly, providing such services does not generally create a threat to independence if management takes responsibility for the returns including any significant judgments made.

Tax Calculations for the Purpose of Preparing Accounting Entries

Audit clients that are not public interest entities

290.180   Preparing calculations of current and deferred tax liabilities (or assets) for an audit client for the purpose of preparing accounting entries that will be subsequently audited by the firm creates a self-review threat. The significance of the threat will depend on:

(a)   The complexity of the relevant tax law and regulation and the degree of judgment necessary in applying them;

(b)   The level of tax expertise of the client's personnel; and

(c)   The materiality of the amounts to the financial statements.

Safeguards shall be applied when necessary to eliminate the threat or reduce it to an acceptable level. Examples of such safeguards include:

●   Using professionals who are not members of the audit team to perform the service;

●   If the service is performed by a member of the audit team, using a partner or senior staff member with appropriate expertise who is not a member of the audit team to review the tax calculations; or

●   Obtaining advice on the service from an external tax professional.

Audit clients that are public interest entities

290.181   In the case of an audit client that is a public interest entity, a firm shall not prepare tax calculations of current and deferred tax liabilities (or assets) for the purpose of preparing accounting entries that are material to the financial statements on which the firm will express an opinion.

Tax Planning and Other Tax Advisory Services

290.182   Tax planning or other tax advisory services comprise a broad range of services, such as advising the client how to structure its affairs in a tax efficient manner or advising on the application of a new tax law or regulation.

290.183   A self-review threat may be created where the advice will affect matters to be reflected in the financial statements. The existence and significance of any threat will depend on factors such as:

●   The degree of subjectivity involved in determining the appropriate treatment for the tax advice in the financial statements;

●   The extent to which the outcome of the tax advice will have a material effect on the financial statements;

●   Whether the effectiveness of the tax advice depends on the accounting treatment or presentation in the financial statements and there is doubt as to the appropriateness

of the accounting treatment or presentation under the relevant financial reporting framework;
- The level of tax expertise of the client's employees;
- The extent to which the advice is supported by tax law or regulation, other precedent or established practice; and
- Whether the tax treatment is supported by a private ruling or has otherwise been cleared by the tax authority before the preparation of the financial statements.

For example, providing tax planning and other tax advisory services where the advice is clearly supported by tax authority or other precedent, by established practice or has a basis in tax law that is likely to prevail does not generally create a threat to independence.

The significance of any threat shall be evaluated and safeguards applied when necessary to eliminate the threat or reduce it to an acceptable level. Examples of such safeguards include: **290.184**

- Using professionals who are not members of the audit team to perform the service;
- Having a tax professional, who was not involved in providing the tax service, advise the audit team on the service and review the financial statement treatment;
- Obtaining advice on the service from an external tax professional; or
- Obtaining pre-clearance or advice from the tax authorities.

Where the effectiveness of the tax advice depends on a particular accounting treatment or presentation in the financial statements and: **290.185**

(a) The audit team has reasonable doubt as to the appropriateness of the related accounting treatment or presentation under the relevant financial reporting framework; and
(b) The outcome or consequences of the tax advice will have a material effect on the financial statements on which the firm will express an opinion;

The self-review threat would be so significant that no safeguards could reduce the threat to an acceptable level. Accordingly, a firm shall not provide such tax advice to an audit client.

In providing tax services to an audit client, a firm may be requested to perform a valuation to assist the client with its tax reporting obligations or for tax planning purposes. Where the result of the valuation will have a direct effect on the financial statements, the provisions included in paragraphs 290.171 to 290.176 relating to valuation services are applicable. Where the valuation is performed for tax purposes only and the result of the valuation will not have a direct effect on the financial statements (that is, the financial statements are only affected through accounting entries related to tax), this would not generally create threats to independence if such effect on the financial statements is immaterial or if the valuation is subject to external review by a tax authority or similar regulatory authority. If the valuation is not subject to such an external review and the effect is material to the financial statements, the existence and significance of any threat created will depend upon factors such as: **290.186**

- The extent to which the valuation methodology is supported by tax law or regulation, other precedent or established practice and the degree of subjectivity inherent in the valuation.
- The reliability and extent of the underlying data.

The significance of any threat created shall be evaluated and safeguards applied when necessary to eliminate the threat or reduce it to an acceptable level. Examples of such safeguards include:

- Using professionals who are not members of the audit team to perform the service;

- Having a professional review the audit work or the result of the tax service; or
- Obtaining pre-clearance or advice from the tax authorities.

Assistance in the Resolution of Tax Disputes

290.187   An advocacy or self-review threat may be created when the firm represents an audit client in the resolution of a tax dispute once the tax authorities have notified the client that they have rejected the client's arguments on a particular issue and either the tax authority or the client is referring the matter for determination in a formal proceeding, for example before a tribunal or court. The existence and significance of any threat will depend on factors such as:

- Whether the firm has provided the advice which is the subject of the tax dispute;
- The extent to which the outcome of the dispute will have a material effect on the financial statements on which the firm will express an opinion;
- The extent to which the matter is supported by tax law or regulation, other precedent, or established practice;
- Whether the proceedings are conducted in public; and
- The role management plays in the resolution of the dispute.

The significance of any threat created shall be evaluated and safeguards applied when necessary to eliminate the threat or reduce it to an acceptable level. Examples of such safeguards include:

- Using professionals who are not members of the audit team to perform the service;
- Having a tax professional, who was not involved in providing the tax service, advise the audit team on the services and review the financial statement treatment; or
- Obtaining advice on the service from an external tax professional.

290.188   Where the taxation services involve acting as an advocate for an audit client before a public tribunal or court in the resolution of a tax matter and the amounts involved are material to the financial statements on which the firm will express an opinion, the advocacy threat created would be so significant that no safeguards could eliminate or reduce the threat to an acceptable level. Therefore, the firm shall not perform this type of service for an audit client. What constitutes a 'public tribunal or court' shall be determined according to how tax proceedings are heard in the particular jurisdiction.

290.189   The firm is not, however, precluded from having a continuing advisory role (for example, responding to specific requests for information, providing factual accounts or testimony about the work performed or assisting the client in analyzing the tax issues) for the audit client in relation to the matter that is being heard before a public tribunal or court.

Internal Audit Services

General Provisions

290.190   The scope and objectives of internal audit activities vary widely and depend on the size and structure of the entity and the requirements of management and those charged with governance. Internal audit activities may include:

- Monitoring of internal control – reviewing controls, monitoring their operation and recommending improvements thereto;
- Examination of financial and operating information – reviewing the means used to identify, measure, classify and report financial and operating information, and

specific inquiry into individual items including detailed testing of transactions, balances and procedures;

● Review of the economy, efficiency and effectiveness of operating activities including non-financial activities of an entity; and

● Review of compliance with laws, regulations and other external requirements, and with management policies and directives and other internal requirements.

Internal audit services involve assisting the audit client in the performance of its internal audit activities. The provision of internal audit services to an audit client creates a self-review threat to independence if the firm uses the internal audit work in the course of a subsequent external audit. Performing a significant part of the client's internal audit activities increases the possibility that firm personnel providing internal audit services will assume a management responsibility. If the firm's personnel assume a management responsibility when providing internal audit services to an audit client, the threat created would be so significant that no safeguards could reduce the threat to an acceptable level. Accordingly, a firm's personnel shall not assume a management responsibility when providing internal audit services to an audit client.   **290.191**

Examples of internal audit services that involve assuming management responsibilities include: **290.192**

(a) Setting internal audit policies or the strategic direction of internal audit activities;
(b) Directing and taking responsibility for the actions of the entity's internal audit employees;
(c) Deciding which recommendations resulting from internal audit activities shall be implemented;
(d) Reporting the results of the internal audit activities to those charged with governance on behalf of management;
(e) Performing procedures that form part of the internal control, such as reviewing and approving changes to employee data access privileges;
(f) Taking responsibility for designing, implementing and maintaining internal control; and
(g) Performing outsourced internal audit services, comprising all or a substantial portion of the internal audit function, where the firm is responsible for determining the scope of the internal audit work and may have responsibility for one or more of the matters noted in (a)–(f).

To avoid assuming a management responsibility, the firm shall only provide internal audit services to an audit client if it is satisfied that: **290.193**

(a) The client designates an appropriate and competent resource, preferably within senior management, to be responsible at all times for internal audit activities and to acknowledge responsibility for designing, implementing, and maintaining internal control;
(b) The client's management or those charged with governance reviews, assesses and approves the scope, risk and frequency of the internal audit services;
(c) The client's management evaluates the adequacy of the internal audit services and the findings resulting from their performance;
(d) The client's management evaluates and determines which recommendations resulting from internal audit services to implement and manages the implementation process; and
(e) The client's management reports to those charged with governance the significant findings and recommendations resulting from the internal audit services.

When a firm uses the work of an internal audit function, ISAs require the performance of procedures to evaluate the adequacy of that work. When a firm accepts an engagement to   **290.194** provide internal audit services to an audit client, and the results of those services will be used in conducting the external audit, a self-review threat is created because of the possibility that the audit team will use the results of the internal audit service without appropriately evaluating those results or exercising the same level of professional skepticism as would be exercised when the internal audit work is performed by individuals who are not members of the firm. The significance of the threat will depend on factors such as:

- The materiality of the related financial statement amounts;
- The risk of misstatement of the assertions related to those financial statement amounts; and
- The degree of reliance that will be placed on the internal audit service.

The significance of the threat shall be evaluated and safeguards applied when necessary to eliminate the threat or reduce it to an acceptable level. An example of such a safeguard is using professionals who are not members of the audit team to perform the internal audit service.

Audit clients that are public interest entities

290.195   In the case of an audit client that is a public interest entity, a firm shall not provide internal audit services that relate to:

(a) A significant part of the internal controls over financial reporting;

(b) Financial accounting systems that generate information that is, separately or in the aggregate, significant to the client's accounting records or financial statements on which the firm will express an opinion; or

(c) Amounts or disclosures that are, separately or in the aggregate, material to the financial statements on which the firm will express an opinion.

IT Systems Services

General Provisions

290.196   Services related to information technology (IT) systems include the design or implementation of hardware or software systems. The systems may aggregate source data, form part of the internal control over financial reporting or generate information that affects the accounting records or financial statements, or the systems may be unrelated to the audit client's accounting records, the internal control over financial reporting or financial statements. Providing systems services may create a self-review threat depending on the nature of the services and the IT systems.

290.197   The following IT systems services are deemed not to create a threat to independence as long as the firm's personnel do not assume a management responsibility:

(a) Design or implementation of IT systems that are unrelated to internal control over financial reporting;

(b) Design or implementation of IT systems that do not generate information forming a significant part of the accounting records or financial statements;

(c) Implementation of 'off-the-shelf' accounting or financial information reporting software that was not developed by the firm if the customization required to meet the client's needs is not significant; and

(d) Evaluating and making recommendations with respect to a system designed, implemented or operated by another service provider or the client.

Audit clients that are not public interest entities

Providing services to an audit client that is not a public interest entity involving the design **290.198** or implementation of IT systems that (a) form a significant part of the internal control over financial reporting or (b) generate information that is significant to the client's accounting records or financial statements on which the firm will express an opinion creates a self-review threat.

The self-review threat is too significant to permit such services unless appropriate **290.199** safeguards are put in place ensuring that:

(a)   The client acknowledges its responsibility for establishing and monitoring a system of internal controls;
(b)   The client assigns the responsibility to make all management decisions with respect to the design and implementation of the hardware or software system to a competent employee, preferably within senior management;
(c)   The client makes all management decisions with respect to the design and implementation process;
(d)   The client evaluates the adequacy and results of the design and implementation of the system; and
(e)   The client is responsible for operating the system (hardware or software) and for the data it uses or generates.

Depending on the degree of reliance that will be placed on the particular IT systems as part **290.200** of the audit, a determination shall be made as to whether to provide such non-assurance services only with personnel who are not members of the audit team and who have different reporting lines within the firm. The significance of any remaining threat shall be evaluated and safeguards applied when necessary to eliminate the threat or reduce it to an acceptable level. An example of such a safeguard is having a professional accountant review the audit or non-assurance work.

Audit clients that are public interest entities

In the case of an audit client that is a public interest entity, a firm shall not provide services **290.201** involving the design or implementation of IT systems that (a) form a significant part of the internal control over financial reporting or (b) generate information that is significant to the client's accounting records or financial statements on which the firm will express an opinion.

Litigation Support Services

Litigation support services may include activities such as acting as an expert witness, **290.202** calculating estimated damages or other amounts that might become receivable or payable as the result of litigation or other legal dispute, and assistance with document management and retrieval. These services may create a self-review or advocacy threat.

If the firm provides a litigation support service to an audit client and the service involves **290.203** estimating damages or other amounts that affect the financial statements on which the firm will express an opinion, the valuation service provisions included in paragraphs 290.171 to 290.176 shall be followed. In the case of other litigation support services, the significance of any threat created shall be evaluated and safeguards applied when necessary to eliminate the threat or reduce it to an acceptable level.

Legal Services

290.204   For the purpose of this section, legal services are defined as any services for which the person providing the services must either be admitted to practice law before the courts of the jurisdiction in which such services are to be provided or have the required legal training to practice law. Such legal services may include, depending on the jurisdiction, a wide and diversified range of areas including both corporate and commercial services to clients, such as contract support, litigation, mergers and acquisition legal advice and support and assistance to clients' internal legal departments. Providing legal services to an entity that is an audit client may create both self-review and advocacy threats.

290.205   Legal services that support an audit client in executing a transaction (for example, contract support, legal advice, legal due diligence and restructuring) may create self-review threats. The existence and significance of any threat will depend on factors such as:

- The nature of the service;
- Whether the service is provided by a member of the audit team; and
- The materiality of any matter in relation to the client's financial statements.

The significance of any threat created shall be evaluated and safeguards applied when necessary to eliminate the threat or reduce it to an acceptable level. Examples of such safeguards include:

- Using professionals who are not members of the audit team to perform the service; or
- Having a professional who was not involved in providing the legal services provide advice to the audit team on the service and review any financial statement treatment.

290.206   Acting in an advocacy role for an audit client in resolving a dispute or litigation when the amounts involved are material to the financial statements on which the firm will express an opinion would create advocacy and self-review threats so significant that no safeguards could reduce the threat to an acceptable level. Therefore, the firm shall not perform this type of service for an audit client.

290.207   When a firm is asked to act in an advocacy role for an audit client in resolving a dispute or litigation when the amounts involved are not material to the financial statements on which the firm will express an opinion, the firm shall evaluate the significance of any advocacy and self-review threats created and apply safeguards when necessary to eliminate the threat or reduce it to an acceptable level. Examples of such safeguards include:

- Using professionals who are not members of the audit team to perform the service; or
- Having a professional who was not involved in providing the legal services advise the audit team on the service and review any financial statement treatment.

290.208   The appointment of a partner or an employee of the firm as General Counsel for legal affairs of an audit client would create self-review and advocacy threats that are so significant that no safeguards could reduce the threats to an acceptable level. The position of General Counsel is generally a senior management position with broad responsibility for the legal affairs of a company, and consequently, no member of the firm shall accept such an appointment for an audit client.

Recruiting Services

General Provisions

Providing recruiting services to an audit client may create self-interest, familiarity or intimidation threats. The existence and significance of any threat will depend on factors such as: **290.209**

- The nature of the requested assistance; and
- The role of the person to be recruited.

The significance of any threat created shall be evaluated and safeguards applied when necessary to eliminate the threat or reduce it to an acceptable level. In all cases, the firm shall not assume management responsibilities, including acting as a negotiator on the client's behalf, and the hiring decision shall be left to the client.

The firm may generally provide such services as reviewing the professional qualifications of a number of applicants and providing advice on their suitability for the post. In addition, the firm may interview candidates and advise on a candidate's competence for financial accounting, administrative or control positions.

Audit clients that are public interest entities

A firm shall not provide the following recruiting services to an audit client that is a public interest entity with respect to a director or officer of the entity or senior management in a position to exert significant influence over the preparation of the client's accounting records or the financial statements on which the firm will express an opinion: **290.210**

- Searching for or seeking out candidates for such positions; and
- Undertaking reference checks of prospective candidates for such positions.

Corporate Finance Services

Providing corporate finance services such as: **290.211**

- Assisting an audit client in developing corporate strategies;
- Identifying possible targets for the audit client to acquire;
- Advising on disposal transactions;
- Assisting finance raising transactions; and
- Providing structuring advice,

may create advocacy and self-review threats. The significance of any threat shall be evaluated and safeguards applied when necessary to eliminate the threat or reduce it to an acceptable level. Examples of such safeguards include:

- Using professionals who are not members of the audit team to provide the services; or
- Having a professional who was not involved in providing the corporate finance service advise the audit team on the service and review the accounting treatment and any financial statement treatment.

Providing a corporate finance service, for example advice on the structuring of a corporate finance transaction or on financing arrangements that will directly affect amounts that will be reported in the financial statements on which the firm will provide an opinion may create a self-review threat. The existence and significance of any threat will depend on factors such as: **290.212**

- The degree of subjectivity involved in determining the appropriate treatment for the outcome or consequences of the corporate finance advice in the financial statements;
- The extent to which the outcome of the corporate finance advice will directly affect amounts recorded in the financial statements and the extent to which the amounts are material to the financial statements; and
- Whether the effectiveness of the corporate finance advice depends on a particular accounting treatment or presentation in the financial statements and there is doubt as to the appropriateness of the related accounting treatment or presentation under the relevant financial reporting framework.

The significance of any threat shall be evaluated and safeguards applied when necessary to eliminate the threat or reduce it to an acceptable level. Examples of such safeguards include:

- Using professionals who are not members of the audit team to perform the service; or
- Having a professional who was not involved in providing the corporate finance service to the client advise the audit team on the service and review the accounting treatment and any financial statement treatment.

290.213 Where the effectiveness of corporate finance advice depends on a particular accounting treatment or presentation in the financial statements and:

(a) The audit team has reasonable doubt as to the appropriateness of the related accounting treatment or presentation under the relevant financial reporting framework; and

(b) The outcome or consequences of the corporate finance advice will have a material effect on the financial statements on which the firm will express an opinion.

The self-review threat would be so significant that no safeguards could reduce the threat to an acceptable level, in which case the corporate finance advice shall not be provided.

290.214 Providing corporate finance services involving promoting, dealing in, or underwriting an audit client's shares would create an advocacy or self-review threat that is so significant that no safeguards could reduce the threat to an acceptable level. Accordingly, a firm shall not provide such services to an audit client.

Fees

Fees—Relative Size

290.215 When the total fees from an audit client represent a large proportion of the total fees of the firm expressing the audit opinion, the dependence on that client and concern about losing the client creates a self-interest or intimidation threat. The significance of the threat will depend on factors such as:

- The operating structure of the firm;
- Whether the firm is well established or new; and
- The significance of the client qualitatively and/or quantitatively to the firm.

The significance of the threat shall be evaluated and safeguards applied when necessary to eliminate the threat or reduce it to an acceptable level. Examples of such safeguards include:

- Reducing the dependency on the client;
- External quality control reviews; or
- Consulting a third party, such as a professional regulatory body or a professional accountant, on key audit judgments.

A self-interest or intimidation threat is also created when the fees generated from an audit client represent a large proportion of the revenue from an individual partner's clients or a large proportion of the revenue of an individual office of the firm. The significance of the threat will depend upon factors such as:

290.216

- The significance of the client qualitatively and/or quantitatively to the partner or office; and
- The extent to which the remuneration of the partner, or the partners in the office, is dependent upon the fees generated from the client.

The significance of the threat shall be evaluated and safeguards applied when necessary to eliminate the threat or reduce it to an acceptable level. Examples of such safeguards include:

- Reducing the dependency on the audit client;
- Having a professional accountant review the work or otherwise advise as necessary; or
- Regular independent internal or external quality reviews of the engagement.

Audit Clients that are Public Interest Entities

Where an audit client is a public interest entity and, for two consecutive years, the total fees from the client and its related entities (subject to the considerations in paragraph 290.27) represent more than 15% of the total fees received by the firm expressing the opinion on the financial statements of the client, the firm shall disclose to those charged with governance of the audit client the fact that the total of such fees represents more than 15% of the total fees received by the firm, and discuss which of the safeguards below it will apply to reduce the threat to an acceptable level, and apply the selected safeguard:

290.217

- Prior to the issuance of the audit opinion on the second year's financial statements, a professional accountant, who is not a member of the firm expressing the opinion on the financial statements, performs an engagement quality control review of that engagement or a professional regulatory body performs a review of that engagement that is equivalent to an engagement quality control review ('a pre-issuance review'); or
- After the audit opinion on the second year's financial statements has been issued, and before the issuance of the audit opinion on the third year's financial statements, a professional accountant, who is not a member of the firm expressing the opinion on the financial statements, or a professional regulatory body performs a review of the second year's audit that is equivalent to an engagement quality control review ('a post-issuance review').

When the total fees significantly exceed 15%, the firm shall determine whether the significance of the threat is such that a post-issuance review would not reduce the threat to an acceptable level and, therefore, a pre-issuance review is required. In such circumstances a pre-issuance review shall be performed.

Thereafter, when the fees continue to exceed 15% each year, the disclosure to and discussion with those charged with governance shall occur and one of the above safeguards shall be applied. If the fees significantly exceed 15%, the firm shall determine whether the significance of the threat is such that a post-issuance review would not reduce the threat to an acceptable level and, therefore, a pre-issuance review is required. In such circumstances a pre-issuance review shall be performed.

Fees–Overdue

290.218　A self-interest threat may be created if fees due from an audit client remain unpaid for a long time, especially if a significant part is not paid before the issue of the audit report for the following year. Generally the firm is expected to require payment of such fees before such audit report is issued. If fees remain unpaid after the report has been issued, the existence and significance of any threat shall be evaluated and safeguards applied when necessary to eliminate the threat or reduce it to an acceptable level. An example of such a safeguard is having an additional professional accountant who did not take part in the audit engagement provide advice or review the work performed. The firm shall determine whether the overdue fees might be regarded as being equivalent to a loan to the client and whether, because of the significance of the overdue fees, it is appropriate for the firm to be re-appointed or continue the audit engagement.

Contingent Fees

290.219　Contingent fees are fees calculated on a predetermined basis relating to the outcome of a transaction or the result of the services performed by the firm. For the purposes of this section, a fee is not regarded as being contingent if established by a court or other public authority.

290.220　A contingent fee charged directly or indirectly, for example through an intermediary, by a firm in respect of an audit engagement creates a self-interest threat that is so significant that no safeguards could reduce the threat to an acceptable level. Accordingly, a firm shall not enter into any such fee arrangement.

290.221　A contingent fee charged directly or indirectly, for example through an intermediary, by a firm in respect of a non-assurance service provided to an audit client may also create a self-interest threat. The threat created would be so significant that no safeguards could reduce the threat to an acceptable level if:

(a)　The fee is charged by the firm expressing the opinion on the financial statements and the fee is material or expected to be material to that firm;

(b)　The fee is charged by a network firm that participates in a significant part of the audit and the fee is material or expected to be material to that firm; or

(c)　The outcome of the non-assurance service, and therefore the amount of the fee, is dependent on a future or contemporary judgment related to the audit of a material amount in the financial statements.

Accordingly, such arrangements shall not be accepted.

290.222　For other contingent fee arrangements charged by a firm for a non-assurance service to an audit client, the existence and significance of any threats will depend on factors such as:

● The range of possible fee amounts;

● Whether an appropriate authority determines the outcome of the matter upon which the contingent fee will be determined;

● The nature of the service; and

● The effect of the event or transaction on the financial statements.

The significance of any threats shall be evaluated and safeguards applied when necessary to eliminate the threats or reduce them to an acceptable level. Examples of such safeguards include:

● Having a professional accountant review the relevant audit work or otherwise advise as necessary; or

- Using professionals who are not members of the audit team to perform the non-assurance service.

Compensation and Evaluation Policies

A self-interest threat is created when a member of the audit team is evaluated on or compensated for selling non-assurance services to that audit client. The significance of the threat will depend on: **290.223**

- The proportion of the individual's compensation or performance evaluation that is based on the sale of such services;
- The role of the individual on the audit team; and
- Whether promotion decisions are influenced by the sale of such services.

The significance of the threat shall be evaluated and, if the threat is not at an acceptable level, the firm shall either revise the compensation plan or evaluation process for that individual or apply safeguards to eliminate the threat or reduce it to an acceptable level. Examples of such safeguards include:

- Removing such members from the audit team; or
- Having a professional accountant review the work of the member of the audit team.

A key audit partner shall not be evaluated on or compensated based on that partner's success in selling non-assurance services to the partner's audit client. This is not intended to prohibit normal profit-sharing arrangements between partners of a firm. **290.224**

Gifts and Hospitality

Accepting gifts or hospitality from an audit client may create self-interest and familiarity threats. If a firm or a member of the audit team accepts gifts or hospitality, unless the value is trivial and inconsequential, the threats created would be so significant that no safeguards could reduce the threats to an acceptable level. Consequently, a firm or a member of the audit team shall not accept such gifts or hospitality. **290.225**

Actual or Threatened Litigation

When litigation takes place, or appears likely, between the firm or a member of the audit team and the audit client, self-interest and intimidation threats are created. The relationship between client management and the members of the audit team must be characterized by complete candor and full disclosure regarding all aspects of a client's business operations. When the firm and the client's management are placed in adversarial positions by actual or threatened litigation, affecting management's willingness to make complete disclosures, self-interest and intimidation threats are created. The significance of the threats created will depend on such factors as: **290.226**

- The materiality of the litigation; and
- Whether the litigation relates to a prior audit engagement.

The significance of the threats shall be evaluated and safeguards applied when necessary to eliminate the threats or reduce them to an acceptable level. Examples of such safeguards include:

- If the litigation involves a member of the audit team, removing that individual from the audit team; or
- Having a professional review the work performed.

If such safeguards do not reduce the threats to an acceptable level, the only appropriate action is to withdraw from, or decline, the audit engagement.

Paragraphs 290.227 to 290.499 are intentionally left blank.

Reports that Include a Restriction on Use and Distribution

Introduction

290.500   The independence requirements in Section 290 apply to all audit engagements. However, in certain circumstances involving audit engagements where the report includes a restriction on use and distribution, and provided the conditions described in paragraphs 290.501 to 290.502 are met, the independence requirements in this section may be modified as provided in paragraphs 290.505 to 290.514. These paragraphs are only applicable to an audit engagement on special purpose financial statements (a) that is intended to provide a conclusion in positive or negative form that the financial statements are prepared in all material respects, in accordance with the applicable financial reporting framework, including, in the case of a fair presentation framework, that the financial statements give a true and fair view or are presented fairly, in all material respects, in accordance with the applicable financial reporting framework, and (b) where the audit report includes a restriction on use and distribution. The modifications are not permitted in the case of an audit of financial statements required by law or regulation.

290.501   The modifications to the requirements of Section 290 are permitted if the intended users of the report (a) are knowledgeable as to the purpose and limitations of the report, and (b) explicitly agree to the application of the modified independence requirements. Knowledge as to the purpose and limitations of the report may be obtained by the intended users through their participation, either directly or indirectly through their representative who has the authority to act for the intended users, in establishing the nature and scope of the engagement. Such participation enhances the ability of the firm to communicate with intended users about independence matters, including the circumstances that are relevant to the evaluation of the threats to independence and the applicable safeguards necessary to eliminate the threats or reduce them to an acceptable level, and to obtain their agreement to the modified independence requirements that are to be applied.

290.502   The firm shall communicate (for example, in an engagement letter) with the intended users regarding the independence requirements that are to be applied with respect to the provision of the audit engagement. Where the intended users are a class of users (for example, lenders in a syndicated loan arrangement) who are not specifically identifiable by name at the time the engagement terms are established, such users shall subsequently be made aware of the independence requirements agreed to by the representative (for example, by the representative making the firm's engagement letter available to all users).

290.503   If the firm also issues an audit report that does not include a restriction on use and distribution for the same client, the provisions of paragraphs 290.500 to 290.514 do not change the requirement to apply the provisions of paragraphs 290.1 to 290.226 to that audit engagement.

290.504   The modifications to the requirements of Section 290 that are permitted in the circumstances set out above are described in paragraphs 290.505 to 290.514. Compliance in all other respects with the provisions of Section 290 is required.

Public Interest Entities

When the conditions set out in paragraphs 290.500 to 290.502 are met, it is not necessary to apply the additional requirements in paragraphs 290.100 to 290.226 that apply to audit engagements for public interest entities.

290.505

Related Entities

When the conditions set out in paragraphs 290.500 to 290.502 are met, references to audit client do not include its related entities. However, when the audit team knows or has reason to believe that a relationship or circumstance involving a related entity of the client is relevant to the evaluation of the firm's independence of the client, the audit team shall include that related entity when identifying and evaluating threats to independence and applying appropriate safeguards.

290.506

Networks and Network Firms

When the conditions set out in paragraphs 290.500 to 290.502 are met, reference to the firm does not include network firms. However, when the firm knows or has reason to believe that threats are created by any interests and relationships of a network firm, they shall be included in the evaluation of threats to independence.

290.507

Financial Interests, Loans and Guarantees, Close Business Relationships and Family and Personal Relationships

When the conditions set out in paragraphs 290.500 to 290.502 are met, the relevant provisions set out in paragraphs 290.102 to 290.143 apply only to the members of the engagement team, their immediate family members and close family members.

290.508

In addition, a determination shall be made as to whether threats to independence are created by interests and relationships, as described in paragraphs 290.102 to 290.143, between the audit client and the following members of the audit team:

290.509

(a) Those who provide consultation regarding technical or industry specific issues, transactions or events; and

(b) Those who provide quality control for the engagement, including those who perform the engagement quality control review.

An evaluation shall be made of the significance of any threats that the engagement team has reason to believe are created by interests and relationships between the audit client and others within the firm who can directly influence the outcome of the audit engagement, including those who recommend the compensation of, or who provide direct supervisory, management or other oversight of the audit engagement partner in connection with the performance of the audit engagement (including those at all successively senior levels above the engagement partner through to the individual who is the firm's Senior or Managing Partner (Chief Executive or equivalent)).

An evaluation shall also be made of the significance of any threats that the engagement team has reason to believe are created by financial interests in the audit client held by individuals, as described in paragraphs 290.108 to 290.111 and paragraphs 290.113 to 290.115.

290.510

Where a threat to independence is not at an acceptable level, safeguards shall be applied to eliminate the threat or reduce it to an acceptable level.

290.511

290.512   In applying the provisions set out in paragraphs 290.106 and 290.115 to interests of the firm, if the firm has a material financial interest, whether direct or indirect, in the audit client, the self-interest threat created would be so significant that no safeguards could reduce the threat to an acceptable level. Accordingly, the firm shall not have such a financial interest.

Employment with an Audit Client

290.513   An evaluation shall be made of the significance of any threats from any employment relationships as described in paragraphs 290.132 to 290.136. Where a threat exists that is not at an acceptable level, safeguards shall be applied to eliminate the threat or reduce it to an acceptable level. Examples of safeguards that might be appropriate include those set out in paragraph 290.134.

Provision of Non-Assurance Services

290.514   If the firm conducts an engagement to issue a restricted use and distribution report for an audit client and provides a non-assurance service to the audit client, the provisions of paragraphs 290.154 to 290.226 shall be complied with, subject to paragraphs 290.504 to 290.507.

Section 291

Independence—Other assurance engagements

Contents

Section 291 – Independence – Other Assurance Engagements

Structure of Section

This section addresses independence requirements for assurance engagements that are not audit or review engagements. Independence requirements for audit and review engagements are addressed in Section 290. If the assurance client is also an audit or review client, the requirements in Section 290 also apply to the firm, network firms and members of the audit or review team. In certain circumstances involving assurance engagements where the assurance report includes a restriction on use and distribution and provided certain conditions are met, the independence requirements in this section may be modified as provided in paragraphs 291.21 to 291.27.   **291.1**

Assurance engagements are designed to enhance intended users' degree of confidence about the outcome of the evaluation or measurement of a subject matter against criteria. The International Framework for Assurance Engagements (the Assurance Framework) issued by the International Auditing and Assurance Standards Board describes the elements and objectives of an assurance engagement and identifies engagements to which International Standards on Assurance Engagements (ISAEs) apply. For a description of the elements and objectives of an assurance engagement, refer to the Assurance Framework.   **291.2**

Compliance with the fundamental principle of objectivity requires being independent of assurance clients. In the case of assurance engagements, it is in the public interest and, therefore, required by this Code of Ethics, that members of assurance teams and firms be independent of assurance clients and that any threats that the firm has reason to believe are created by a network firm's interests and relationships be evaluated. In addition, when the assurance team knows or has reason to believe that a relationship or circumstance involving a related entity of the assurance client is relevant to the evaluation of the firm's independence from the client, the assurance team shall include that related entity when identifying and evaluating threats to independence and applying appropriate safeguards.   **291.3**

A Conceptual Framework Approach to Independence

The objective of this section is to assist firms and members of assurance teams in applying the conceptual framework approach described below to achieving and maintaining independence.   **291.4**

Independence comprises: **291.5**

(a) Independence of Mind
The state of mind that permits the expression of a conclusion without being affected by influences that compromise professional judgment, thereby allowing an individual to act with integrity and exercise objectivity and professional skepticism.
(b) Independence in Appearance
The avoidance of facts and circumstances that are so significant that a reasonable and informed third party would be likely to conclude, weighing all the specific facts and circumstances, that a firm's, or a member of the assurance team's, integrity, objectivity or professional skepticism has been compromised.

The conceptual framework approach shall be applied by professional accountants to: **291.6**

(a) Identify threats to independence;
(b) Evaluate the significance of the threats identified; and
(c) Apply safeguards when necessary to eliminate the threats or reduce them to an acceptable level.

When the professional accountant determines that appropriate safeguards are not available or cannot be applied to eliminate the threats or reduce them to an acceptable level, the professional accountant shall eliminate the circumstance or relationship creating the threats or decline or terminate the assurance engagement.

A professional accountant shall use professional judgment in applying this conceptual framework.

291.7 Many different circumstances, or combinations of circumstances, may be relevant in assessing threats to independence. It is impossible to define every situation that creates threats to independence and to specify the appropriate action. Therefore, this Code establishes a conceptual framework that requires firms and members of assurance teams to identify, evaluate, and address threats to independence. The conceptual framework approach assists professional accountants in public practice in complying with the ethical requirements in this Code. It accommodates many variations in circumstances that create threats to independence and can deter a professional accountant from concluding that a situation is permitted if it is not specifically prohibited.

291.8 Paragraphs 291.100 and onwards describe how the conceptual framework approach to independence is to be applied. These paragraphs do not address all the circumstances and relationships that create or may create threats to independence.

291.9 In deciding whether to accept or continue an engagement, or whether a particular individual may be a member of the assurance team, a firm shall identify and evaluate any threats to independence. If the threats are not at an acceptable level, and the decision is whether to accept an engagement or include a particular individual on the assurance team, the firm shall determine whether safeguards are available to eliminate the threats or reduce them to an acceptable level. If the decision is whether to continue an engagement, the firm shall determine whether any existing safeguards will continue to be effective to eliminate the threats or reduce them to an acceptable level or whether other safeguards will need to be applied or whether the engagement needs to be terminated. Whenever new information about a threat comes to the attention of the firm during the engagement, the firm shall evaluate the significance of the threat in accordance with the conceptual framework approach.

291.10 Throughout this section, reference is made to the significance of threats to independence. In evaluating the significance of a threat, qualitative as well as quantitative factors shall be taken into account.

291.11 This section does not, in most cases, prescribe the specific responsibility of individuals within the firm for actions related to independence because responsibility may differ depending on the size, structure and organization of a firm. The firm is required by ISQCs to establish policies and procedures designed to provide it with reasonable assurance that independence is maintained when required by relevant ethical standards.

Assurance Engagements

291.12 As further explained in the Assurance Framework, in an assurance engagement the professional accountant in public practice expresses a conclusion designed to enhance the degree of confidence of the intended users (other than the responsible party) about the outcome of the evaluation or measurement of a subject matter against criteria.

291.13 The outcome of the evaluation or measurement of a subject matter is the information that results from applying the criteria to the subject matter. The term 'subject matter information' is used to mean the outcome of the evaluation or measurement of a subject matter. For example, the Framework states that an assertion about the effectiveness of internal control (subject matter information) results from applying a framework for evaluating the effectiveness of internal control, such as COSO[1] or CoCo[2] (criteria), to internal control, a process (subject matter).

Assurance engagements may be assertion-based or direct reporting. In either case, they involve three separate parties: a professional accountant in public practice, a responsible party and intended users. 291.14

In an assertion-based assurance engagement, the evaluation or measurement of the subject matter is performed by the responsible party, and the subject matter information is in the form of an assertion by the responsible party that is made available to the intended users. 291.15

In a direct reporting assurance engagement, the professional accountant in public practice either directly performs the evaluation or measurement of the subject matter, or obtains a representation from the responsible party that has performed the evaluation or measurement that is not available to the intended users. The subject matter information is provided to the intended users in the assurance report. 291.16

Assertion-Based Assurance Engagements

In an assertion-based assurance engagement, the members of the assurance team and the firm shall be independent of the assurance client (the party responsible for the subject matter information, and which may be responsible for the subject matter). Such independence requirements prohibit certain relationships between members of the assurance team and (a) directors or officers, and (b) individuals at the client in a position to exert significant influence over the subject matter information. Also, a determination shall be made as to whether threats to independence are created by relationships with individuals at the client in a position to exert significant influence over the subject matter of the engagement. An evaluation shall be made of the significance of any threats that the firm has reason to believe are created by network firm[3] interests and relationships. 291.17

In the majority of assertion-based assurance engagements, the responsible party is responsible for both the subject matter information and the subject matter. However, in some engagements, the responsible party may not be responsible for the subject matter. For example, when a professional accountant in public practice is engaged to perform an assurance engagement regarding a report that an environmental consultant has prepared about a company's sustainability practices for distribution to intended users, the environmental consultant is the responsible party for the subject matter information but the company is responsible for the subject matter (the sustainability practices). 291.18

In assertion-based assurance engagements where the responsible party is responsible for the subject matter information but not the subject matter, the members of the assurance team and the firm shall be independent of the party responsible for the subject matter information (the assurance client). In addition, an evaluation shall be made of any threats the firm has reason to believe are created by interests and relationships between a member of the assurance team, the firm, a network firm and the party responsible for the subject matter. 291.19

---

[1] *'Internal Control Integrated Framework' The Committee of Sponsoring Organizations of the Treadway Commission.*

[2] *'Guidance on Assessing Control The CoCo Principles' Criteria of Control Board, The Canadian Institute of Chartered Accountants.*

[3] *See paragraphs 290.13 to 290.24 for guidance on what constitutes a network firm.*

Direct Reporting Assurance Engagements

291.20   In a direct reporting assurance engagement, the members of the assurance team and the firm shall be independent of the assurance client (the party responsible for the subject matter). An evaluation shall also be made of any threats the firm has reason to believe are created by network firm interests and relationships.

Reports that Include a Restriction on Use and Distribution

291.21   In certain circumstances where the assurance report includes a restriction on use and distribution, and provided the conditions in this paragraph and in paragraph 291.22 are met, the independence requirements in this section may be modified. The modifications to the requirements of Section 291 are permitted if the intended users of the report (a) are knowledgeable as to the purpose, subject matter information and limitations of the report and (b) explicitly agree to the application of the modified independence requirements. Knowledge as to the purpose, subject matter information, and limitations of the report may be obtained by the intended users through their participation, either directly or indirectly through their representative who has the authority to act for the intended users, in establishing the nature and scope of the engagement. Such participation enhances the ability of the firm to communicate with intended users about independence matters, including the circumstances that are relevant to the evaluation of the threats to independence and the applicable safeguards necessary to eliminate the threats or reduce them to an acceptable level, and to obtain their agreement to the modified independence requirements that are to be applied.

291.22   The firm shall communicate (for example, in an engagement letter) with the intended users regarding the independence requirements that are to be applied with respect to the provision of the assurance engagement. Where the intended users are a class of users (for example, lenders in a syndicated loan arrangement) who are not specifically identifiable by name at the time the engagement terms are established, such users shall subsequently be made aware of the independence requirements agreed to by the representative (for example, by the representative making the firm's engagement letter available to all users).

291.23   If the firm also issues an assurance report that does not include a restriction on use and distribution for the same client, the provisions of paragraphs 291.25 to 291.27 do not change the requirement to apply the provisions of paragraphs 291.1 to 291.156 to that assurance engagement. If the firm also issues an audit report, whether or not it includes a restriction on use and distribution, for the same client, the provisions of Section 290 shall apply to that audit engagement.

291.24   The modifications to the requirements of Section 291 that are permitted in the circumstances set out above are described in paragraphs 291.25 to 291.27. Compliance in all other respects with the provisions of Section 291 is required.

291.25   When the conditions set out in paragraphs 291.21 and 291.22 are met, the relevant provisions set out in paragraphs 291.104 to 291.132 apply to all members of the engagement team, and their immediate and close family members. In addition, a determination shall be made as to whether threats to independence are created by interests and relationships between the assurance client and the following other members of the assurance team:

(a)   Those who provide consultation regarding technical or industry specific issues, transactions or events; and

(b)   Those who provide quality control for the engagement, including those who perform the engagement quality control review.

An evaluation shall also be made, by reference to the provisions set out in paragraphs 291.104 to 291.132, of any threats that the engagement team has reason to believe are created by interests and relationships between the assurance client and others within the firm who can directly influence the outcome of the assurance engagement, including those who recommend the compensation, or who provide direct supervisory, management or other oversight, of the assurance engagement partner in connection with the performance of the assurance engagement.

Even though the conditions set out in paragraphs 291.21 to 291.22 are met, if the firm had a material financial interest, whether direct or indirect, in the assurance client, the self-interest threat created would be so significant that no safeguards could reduce the threat to an acceptable level. Accordingly, the firm shall not have such a financial interest. In addition, the firm shall comply with the other applicable provisions of this section described in paragraphs 291.112 to 291.156.   **291.26**

An evaluation shall also be made of any threats that the firm has reason to believe are created by network firm interests and relationships.   **291.27**

Multiple Responsible Parties

In some assurance engagements, whether assertion-based or direct reporting, there might be several responsible parties. In determining whether it is necessary to apply the provisions in this section to each responsible party in such engagements, the firm may take into account whether an interest or relationship between the firm, or a member of the assurance team, and a particular responsible party would create a threat to independence that is not trivial and inconsequential in the context of the subject matter information. This will take into account factors such as: **291.28**

- The materiality of the subject matter information (or of the subject matter) for which the particular responsible party is responsible; and
- The degree of public interest associated with the engagement.

If the firm determines that the threat to independence created by any such interest or relationship with a particular responsible party would be trivial and inconsequential, it may not be necessary to apply all of the provisions of this section to that responsible party.

Documentation

Documentation provides evidence of the professional accountant's judgments in forming conclusions regarding compliance with independence requirements. The absence of documentation is not a determinant of whether a firm considered a particular matter nor whether it is independent.   **291.29**

The professional accountant shall document conclusions regarding compliance with independence requirements, and the substance of any relevant discussions that support those conclusions. Accordingly:

(a) When safeguards are required to reduce a threat to an acceptable level, the professional accountant shall document the nature of the threat and the safeguards in place or applied that reduce the threat to an acceptable level; and
(b) When a threat required significant analysis to determine whether safeguards were necessary and the professional accountant concluded that they were not because the threat was already at an acceptable level, the professional accountant shall document the nature of the threat and the rationale for the conclusion.

Engagement Period

291.30   Independence from the assurance client is required both during the engagement period and the period covered by the subject matter information. The engagement period starts when the assurance team begins to perform assurance services with respect to the particular engagement. The engagement period ends when the assurance report is issued. When the engagement is of a recurring nature, it ends at the later of the notification by either party that the professional relationship has terminated or the issuance of the final assurance report.

291.31   When an entity becomes an assurance client during or after the period covered by the subject matter information on which the firm will express a conclusion, the firm shall determine whether any threats to independence are created by:

(a)   Financial or business relationships with the assurance client during or after the period covered by the subject matter information but before accepting the assurance engagement; or

(b)   Previous services provided to the assurance client.

291.32   If a non-assurance service was provided to the assurance client during or after the period covered by the subject matter information but before the assurance team begins to perform assurance services and the service would not be permitted during the period of the assurance engagement, the firm shall evaluate any threat to independence created by the service. If any threat is not at an acceptable level, the assurance engagement shall only be accepted if safeguards are applied to eliminate any threats or reduce them to an acceptable level. Examples of such safeguards include:

- Not including personnel who provided the non-assurance service as members of the assurance team;
- Having a professional accountant review the assurance and non-assurance work as appropriate; or
- Engaging another firm to evaluate the results of the non-assurance service or having another firm re-perform the non-assurance service to the extent necessary to enable it to take responsibility for the service.

However, if the non-assurance service has not been completed and it is not practical to complete or terminate the service before the commencement of professional services in connection with the assurance engagement, the firm shall only accept the assurance engagement if it is satisfied:

(a)   The non-assurance service will be completed within a short period of time; or

(b)   The client has arrangements in place to transition the service to another provider within a short period of time.

During the service period, safeguards shall be applied when necessary. In addition, the matter shall be discussed with those charged with governance.

Breach of a Provision of this Section

291.33   When a breach of a provision of this section is identified, the firm shall terminate, suspend or eliminate the interest or relationship that caused the breach, and shall evaluate the significance of that breach and its impact on the firm's objectivity and ability to issue an assurance report. The firm shall determine whether action can be taken that satisfactorily addresses the consequences of the breach. In making this determination, the firm shall exercise professional judgment and take into account whether a reasonable and informed third party, weighing the significance of the breach, the action to be taken and all the specific facts and circumstances available to the professional accountant at that time, would be likely to conclude that the firm's objectivity would be compromised such that the firm is unable to issue an assurance report.

If the firm determines that action cannot be taken to satisfactorily address the consequences of the breach, the firm shall, as soon as possible, inform the party that engaged the firm or those charged with governance, as appropriate, and take the steps necessary to terminate the assurance engagement in compliance with any applicable legal or regulatory requirements relevant to terminating the assurance engagement. **291.34**

If the firm determines that action can be taken to satisfactorily address the consequences of the breach, the firm shall discuss the breach and the action it has taken or proposes to take with the party that engaged the firm or those charged with governance, as appropriate. The firm shall discuss the breach and the proposed action on a timely basis, taking into account the circumstances of the engagement and the breach. **291.35**

If the party that engaged the firm or those charged with governance, as appropriate, do not concur that the action satisfactorily addresses the consequences of the breach, the firm shall take the steps necessary to terminate the assurance engagement in compliance with any applicable legal or regulatory requirements relevant to terminating the assurance engagement. **291.36**

The firm shall document the breach, the actions taken, key decisions made and all the matters discussed with the party that engaged the firm or those charged with governance. When the firm continues with the assurance engagement, the matters to be documented shall also include the conclusion that, in the firm's professional judgment, objectivity has not been compromised and the rationale for why the action taken satisfactorily addressed the consequences of the breach such that the firm could issue an assurance report. **291.37**

Paragraphs 291.38 to 291.99 are intentionally left blank.

Application of the Conceptual Framework Approach to Independence

Paragraphs 291.104 to 291.156 describe specific circumstances and relationships that create or may create threats to independence. The paragraphs describe the potential threats and the types of safeguards that may be appropriate to eliminate the threats or reduce them to an acceptable level and identify certain situations where no safeguards could reduce the threats to an acceptable level. The paragraphs do not describe all of the circumstances and relationships that create or may create a threat to independence. The firm and the members of the assurance team shall evaluate the implications of similar, but different, circumstances and relationships and determine whether safeguards, including the safeguards in paragraphs 200.11 to 200.14 can be applied when necessary to eliminate the threats to independence or reduce them to an acceptable level. **291.100**

The paragraphs demonstrate how the conceptual framework approach applies to assurance engagements and are to be read in conjunction with paragraph 291.28 which explains that, in the majority of assurance engagements, there is one responsible party and that responsible party is the assurance client. However, in some assurance engagements there are two or more responsible parties. In such circumstances, an evaluation shall be made of any threats the firm has reason to believe are created by interests and relationships between a member of the assurance team, the firm, a network firm and the party responsible for the subject matter. For assurance reports that include a restriction on use and distribution, the paragraphs are to be read in the context of paragraphs 291.21 to 291.27. **291.101**

291.102   Interpretation 2005–01 provides further guidance on applying the independence requirements contained in this section to assurance engagements.

291.103   Paragraphs 291.104 to 291.119 contain references to the materiality of a financial interest, loan, or guarantee, or the significance of a business relationship. For the purpose of determining whether such an interest is material to an individual, the combined net worth of the individual and the individual's immediate family members may be taken into account.

Financial Interests

291.104   Holding a financial interest in an assurance client may create a self-interest threat. The existence and significance of any threat created depends on:

(a)   The role of the person holding the financial interest,

(b)   Whether the financial interest is direct or indirect, and

(c)   The materiality of the financial interest.

291.105   Financial interests may be held through an intermediary (for example, a collective investment vehicle, estate or trust). The determination of whether such financial interests are direct or indirect will depend upon whether the beneficial owner has control over the investment vehicle or the ability to influence its investment decisions. When control over the investment vehicle or the ability to influence investment decisions exists, this Code defines that financial interest to be a direct financial interest. Conversely, when the beneficial owner of the financial interest has no control over the investment vehicle or ability to influence its investment decisions, this Code defines that financial interest to be an indirect financial interest.

291.106   If a member of the assurance team, a member of that individual's immediate family, or a firm has a direct financial interest or a material indirect financial interest in the assurance client, the self-interest threat created would be so significant that no safeguards could reduce the threat to an acceptable level. Therefore, none of the following shall have a direct financial interest or a material indirect financial interest in the client: a member of the assurance team; a member of that individual's immediate family member; or the firm.

291.107   When a member of the assurance team has a close family member who the assurance team member knows has a direct financial interest or a material indirect financial interest in the assurance client, a self-interest threat is created. The significance of the threat will depend on factors such as

- The nature of the relationship between the member of the assurance team and the close family member; and
- The materiality of the financial interest to the close family member.

The significance of the threat shall be evaluated and safeguards applied when necessary to eliminate the threat or reduce it to an acceptable level. Examples of such safeguards include:

- The close family member disposing, as soon as practicable, of all of the financial interest or disposing of a sufficient portion of an indirect financial interest so that the remaining interest is no longer material;
- Having a professional accountant review the work of the member of the assurance team; or
- Removing the individual from the assurance team.

291.108   If a member of the assurance team, a member of that individual's immediate family, or a firm has a direct or material indirect financial interest in an entity that has a controlling interest in the assurance client, and the client is material to the entity, the self-interest threat created would be so significant that no safeguards could reduce the threat to an acceptable level. Therefore, none of the following shall have such a financial interest: a member of the assurance team; a member of that individual's immediate family; and the firm.

The holding by a firm or a member of the assurance team, or a member of that individual's **291.109** immediate family, of a direct financial interest or a material indirect financial interest in the assurance client as a trustee creates a self-interest threat. Such an interest shall not be held unless:

(a) Neither the trustee, nor an immediate family member of the trustee, nor the firm are beneficiaries of the trust;
(b) The interest in the assurance client held by the trust is not material to the trust;
(c) The trust is not able to exercise significant influence over the assurance client; and
(d) The trustee, an immediate family member of the trustee, or the firm cannot significantly influence any investment decision involving a financial interest in the assurance client.

Members of the assurance team shall determine whether a self-interest threat is created by **291.110** any known financial interests in the assurance client held by other individuals including:

- Partners and professional employees of the firm, other than those referred to above, or their immediate family members; and
- Individuals with a close personal relationship with a member of the assurance team.

Whether these interests create a self-interest threat will depend on factors such as:

- The firm's organizational, operating and reporting structure; and
- The nature of the relationship between the individual and the member of the assurance team.

The significance of any threat shall be evaluated and safeguards applied when necessary to eliminate the threat or reduce it to an acceptable level. Examples of such safeguards include:

- Removing the member of the assurance team with the personal relationship from the assurance team;
- Excluding the member of the assurance team from any significant decision-making concerning the assurance engagement; or
- Having a professional accountant review the work of the member of the assurance team.

If a firm, a member of the assurance team, or an immediate family member of the **291.111** individual, receives a direct financial interest or a material indirect financial interest in an assurance client, for example, by way of an inheritance, gift or as a result of a merger, and such interest would not be permitted to be held under this section, then:

(a) If the interest is received by the firm, the financial interest shall be disposed of immediately, or a sufficient amount of an indirect financial interest shall be disposed of so that the remaining interest is no longer material, or
(b) If the interest is received by a member of the assurance team, or a member of that individual's immediate family, the individual who received the financial interest shall immediately dispose of the financial interest, or dispose of a sufficient amount of an indirect financial interest so that the remaining interest is no longer material.

Loans and Guarantees

291.112   A loan, or a guarantee of a loan, to a member of the assurance team, or a member of that individual's immediate family, or the firm from an assurance client that is a bank or a similar institution, may create a threat to independence. If the loan or guarantee is not made under normal lending procedures, terms and conditions, a self-interest threat would be created that would be so significant that no safeguards could reduce the threat to an acceptable level. Accordingly, neither a member of the assurance team, a member of that individual's immediate family, nor a firm shall accept such a loan or guarantee.

291.113   If a loan to a firm from an assurance client that is a bank or similar institution is made under normal lending procedures, terms and conditions and it is material to the assurance client or firm receiving the loan, it may be possible to apply safeguards to reduce the self-interest threat to an acceptable level. An example of such a safeguard is having the work reviewed by a professional accountant from a network firm that is neither involved with the assurance engagement nor received the loan.

291.114   A loan, or a guarantee of a loan, from an assurance client that is a bank or a similar institution to a member of the assurance team, or a member of that individual's immediate family, does not create a threat to independence if the loan or guarantee is made under normal lending procedures, terms and conditions. Examples of such loans include home mortgages, bank overdrafts, car loans and credit card balances.

291.115   If the firm or a member of the assurance team, or a member of that individual's immediate family, accepts a loan from, or has a borrowing guaranteed by, an assurance client that is not a bank or similar institution, the self-interest threat created would be so significant that no safeguards could reduce the threat to an acceptable level, unless the loan or guarantee is immaterial to both the firm, or the member of the assurance team and the immediate family member, and the client.

291.116   Similarly, if the firm, or a member of the assurance team, or a member of that individual's immediate family, makes or guarantees a loan to an assurance client, the self-interest threat created would be so significant that no safeguards could reduce the threat to an acceptable level, unless the loan or guarantee is immaterial to both the firm, or the member of the assurance team and the immediate family member, and the client.

291.117   If a firm or a member of the assurance team, or a member of that individual's immediate family, has deposits or a brokerage account with an assurance client that is a bank, broker, or similar institution, a threat to independence is not created if the deposit or account is held under normal commercial terms.

Business Relationships

291.118   A close business relationship between a firm, or a member of the assurance team, or a member of that individual's immediate family, and the assurance client or its management arises from a commercial relationship or common financial interest and may create self-interest or intimidation threats. Examples of such relationships include:

- Having a financial interest in a joint venture with either the client or a controlling owner, director or officer or other individual who performs senior managerial activities for that client.
- Arrangements to combine one or more services or products of the firm with one or more services or products of the client and to market the package with reference to both parties.

- Distribution or marketing arrangements under which the firm distributes or markets the client's products or services, or the client distributes or markets the firm's products or services.

Unless any financial interest is immaterial and the business relationship is insignificant to the firm and the client or its management, the threat created would be so significant that no safeguards could reduce the threat to an acceptable level. Therefore, unless the financial interest is immaterial and the business relationship is insignificant, the business relationship shall not be entered into, or shall be reduced to an insignificant level or terminated.

In the case of a member of the assurance team, unless any such financial interest is immaterial and the relationship is insignificant to that member, the individual shall be removed from the assurance team.

If the business relationship is between an immediate family member of a member of the assurance team and the assurance client or its management, the significance of any threat shall be evaluated and safeguards applied when necessary to eliminate the threat or reduce it to an acceptable level.

The purchase of goods and services from an assurance client by the firm, or a member of the assurance team, or a member of that individual's immediate family, does not generally create a threat to independence if the transaction is in the normal course of business and at arm's length. However, such transactions may be of such a nature or magnitude that they create a self-interest threat. The significance of any threat shall be evaluated and safeguards applied when necessary to eliminate the threat or reduce it to an acceptable level. Examples of such safeguards include: **291.119**

- Eliminating or reducing the magnitude of the transaction; or
- Removing the individual from the assurance team.

Family and Personal Relationships

Family and personal relationships between a member of the assurance team and a director or officer or certain employees (depending on their role) of the assurance client, may create self-interest, familiarity or intimidation threats. The existence and significance of any threats will depend on a number of factors, including the individual's responsibilities on the assurance team, the role of the family member or other individual within the client, and the closeness of the relationship.   **291.120**

When an immediate family member of a member of the assurance team is: **291.121**

(a) A director or officer of the assurance client, or
(b) An employee in a position to exert significant influence over the subject matter information of the assurance engagement,

or was in such a position during any period covered by the engagement or the subject matter information, the threats to independence can only be reduced to an acceptable level by removing the individual from the assurance team. The closeness of the relationship is such that no other safeguards could reduce the threat to an acceptable level. Accordingly, no individual who has such a relationship shall be a member of the assurance team.

Threats to independence are created when an immediate family member of a member of the assurance team is an employee in a position to exert significant influence over the subject matter of the engagement. The significance of the threats will depend on factors such as: **291.122**

- The position held by the immediate family member; and
- The role of the professional on the assurance team.

The significance of the threat shall be evaluated and safeguards applied when necessary to eliminate the threat or reduce it to an acceptable level. Examples of such safeguards include:

- Removing the individual from the assurance team; or
- Structuring the responsibilities of the assurance team so that the professional does not deal with matters that are within the responsibility of the immediate family member.

291.123   Threats to independence are created when a close family member of a member of the assurance team is:

- A director or officer of the assurance client; or
- An employee in a position to exert significant influence over the subject matter information of the assurance engagement.

The significance of the threats will depend on factors such as:

- The nature of the relationship between the member of the assurance team and the close family member;
- The position held by the close family member; and
- The role of the professional on the assurance team.

The significance of the threat shall be evaluated and safeguards applied when necessary to eliminate the threat or reduce it to an acceptable level. Examples of such safeguards include:

- Removing the individual from the assurance team; or
- Structuring the responsibilities of the assurance team so that the professional does not deal with matters that are within the responsibility of the close family member.

291.124   Threats to independence are created when a member of the assurance team has a close relationship with a person who is not an immediate or close family member, but who is a director or officer or an employee in a position to exert significant influence over the subject matter information of the assurance engagement. A member of the assurance team who has such a relationship shall consult in accordance with firm policies and procedures. The significance of the threats will depend on factors such as:

- The nature of the relationship between the individual and the member of the assurance team;
- The position the individual holds with the client; and
- The role of the professional on the assurance team.

The significance of the threats shall be evaluated and safeguards applied when necessary to eliminate the threats or reduce them to an acceptable level. Examples of such safeguards include:

- Removing the professional from the assurance team; or
- Structuring the responsibilities of the assurance team so that the professional does not deal with matters that are within the responsibility of the individual with whom the professional has a close relationship.

291.125   Self-interest, familiarity or intimidation threats may be created by a personal or family relationship between (a) a partner or employee of the firm who is not a member of the assurance team and (b) a director or officer of the assurance client or an employee in a position to exert significant influence over the subject matter information of the assurance engagement. The existence and significance of any threat will depend on factors such as:

- The nature of the relationship between the partner or employee of the firm and the director or officer or employee of the client;
- The interaction of the partner or employee of the firm with the assurance team;
- The position of the partner or employee within the firm; and
- The role of the individual within the client.

The significance of any threat shall be evaluated and safeguards applied when necessary to eliminate the threat or reduce it to an acceptable level. Examples of such safeguards include:

- Structuring the partner's or employee's responsibilities to reduce any potential influence over the assurance engagement; or
- Having a professional accountant review the relevant assurance work performed.

Employment with an Assurance Client

Familiarity or intimidation threats may be created if a director or officer of the assurance client, or an employee who is in a position to exert significant influence over the subject matter information of the assurance engagement, has been a member of the assurance team or partner of the firm.   **291.126**

If a former member of the assurance team or partner of the firm has joined the assurance client in such a position, the existence and significance of any familiarity or intimidation threats will depend on factors such as: **291.127**

- The position the individual has taken at the client;
- Any involvement the individual will have with the assurance team;
- The length of time since the individual was a member of the assurance team or partner of the firm; and
- The former position of the individual within the assurance team or firm, for example, whether the individual was responsible for maintaining regular contact with the client's management or those charged with governance.

In all cases the individual shall not continue to participate in the firm's business or professional activities.

The significance of any threats created shall be evaluated and safeguards applied when necessary to eliminate the threats or reduce them to an acceptable level. Examples of such safeguards include:

- Making arrangements such that the individual is not entitled to any benefits or payments from the firm, unless made in accordance with fixed pre-determined arrangements.
- Making arrangements such that any amount owed to the individual is not material to the firm;
- Modifying the plan for the assurance engagement;
- Assigning individuals to the assurance team who have sufficient experience in relation to the individual who has joined the client; or
- Having a professional accountant review the work of the former member of the assurance team.

291.128   If a former partner of the firm has previously joined an entity in such a position and the entity subsequently becomes an assurance client of the firm, the significance of any threats to independence shall be evaluated and safeguards applied when necessary, to eliminate the threat or reduce it to an acceptable level.

291.129   A self-interest threat is created when a member of the assurance team participates in the assurance engagement while knowing that the member of the assurance team will, or may, join the client some time in the future. Firm policies and procedures shall require members of an assurance team to notify the firm when entering employment negotiations with the client. On receiving such notification, the significance of the threat shall be evaluated and safeguards applied when necessary to eliminate the threat or reduce it to an acceptable level. Examples of such safeguards include:

- Removing the individual from the assurance team; or
- A review of any significant judgments made by that individual while on the team.

Recent Service with an Assurance Client

291.130   Self-interest, self-review or familiarity threats may be created if a member of the assurance team has recently served as a director, officer, or employee of the assurance client. This would be the case when, for example, a member of the assurance team has to evaluate elements of the subject matter information the member of the assurance team had prepared while with the client.

291.131   If, during the period covered by the assurance report, a member of the assurance team had served as director or officer of the assurance client, or was an employee in a position to exert significant influence over the subject matter information of the assurance engagement, the threat created would be so significant that no safeguards could reduce the threat to an acceptable level. Consequently, such individuals shall not be assigned to the assurance team.

291.132   Self-interest, self-review or familiarity threats may be created if, before the period covered by the assurance report, a member of the assurance team had served as director or officer of the assurance client, or was an employee in a position to exert significant influence over the subject matter information of the assurance engagement. For example, such threats would be created if a decision made or work performed by the individual in the prior period, while employed by the client, is to be evaluated in the current period as part of the current assurance engagement. The existence and significance of any threats will depend on factors such as:

- The position the individual held with the client;
- The length of time since the individual left the client; and
- The role of the professional on the assurance team.

The significance of any threat shall be evaluated and safeguards applied when necessary to reduce the threat to an acceptable level. An example of such a safeguard is conducting a review of the work performed by the individual as part of the assurance team.

Serving as a Director or Officer of an Assurance Client

291.133   If a partner or employee of the firm serves a director or officer of an assurance client, the self-review and self-interest threats would be so significant that no safeguards could reduce the threats to an acceptable level. Accordingly, no partner or employee shall serve as a director or officer of an assurance client.

The position of Company Secretary has different implications in different jurisdictions. Duties may range from administrative duties, such as personnel management and the maintenance of company records and registers, to duties as diverse as ensuring that the company complies with regulation or providing advice on corporate governance matters. Generally, this position is seen to imply a close association with the entity.   **291.134**

If a partner or employee of the firm serves as Company Secretary for an assurance client, self-review and advocacy threats are created that would generally be so significant that no safeguards could reduce the threats to an acceptable level. Despite paragraph 291.133, when this practice is specifically permitted under local law, professional rules or practice, and provided management makes all relevant decisions, the duties and activities shall be limited to those of a routine and administrative nature, such as preparing minutes and maintaining statutory returns. In those circumstances, the significance of any threats shall be evaluated and safeguards applied when necessary to eliminate the threats or reduce them to an acceptable level.   **291.135**

Performing routine administrative services to support a company secretarial function or providing advice in relation to company secretarial administration matters does not generally create threats to independence, as long as client management makes all relevant decisions.   **291.136**

Long Association of Senior Personnel with an Assurance Client

Familiarity and self-interest threats are created by using the same senior personnel on an assurance engagement over a long period of time. The significance of the threats will depend on factors such as: **291.137**

- How long the individual has been a member of the assurance team;
- The role of the individual on the assurance team;
- The structure of the firm;
- The nature of the assurance engagement;
- Whether the client's management team has changed; and
- Whether the nature or complexity of the subject matter information has changed.

The significance of the threats shall be evaluated and safeguards applied when necessary to eliminate the threats or reduce them to an acceptable level. Examples of such safeguards include:

- Rotating the senior personnel off the assurance team;
- Having a professional accountant who was not a member of the assurance team review the work of the senior personnel; or
- Regular independent internal or external quality reviews of the engagement.

Provision of Non-assurance Services to an Assurance Client

Firms have traditionally provided to their assurance clients a range of non-assurance services that are consistent with their skills and expertise. Providing non-assurance services may, however, create threats to the independence of the firm or members of the assurance team. The threats created are most often self-review, self-interest and advocacy threats.   **291.138**

When specific guidance on a particular non-assurance service is not included in this section, the conceptual framework shall be applied when evaluating the particular circumstances.   **291.139**

Before the firm accepts an engagement to provide a non-assurance service to an assurance client, a determination shall be made as to whether providing such a service would create   **291.140** a threat to independence. In evaluating the significance of any threat created by a particular non-assurance service, consideration shall be given to any threat that the assurance team has reason to believe is created by providing other related non-assurance services. If a threat is created that cannot be reduced to an acceptable level by the application of safeguards the non-assurance service shall not be provided.

Management Responsibilities

291.141 Management responsibilities involve controlling, leading and directing an entity, including making decisions regarding the acquisition, deployment and control of human, financial, technological, physical and intangible resources.

291.142 Determining whether an activity is a management responsibility depends on the circumstances and requires the exercise of judgment. Examples of activities that would be considered a management responsibility include:

- Setting policies and strategic direction.
- Hiring or dismissing employees.
- Directing and taking responsibility for the actions of employees in relation to the employees' work for the entity.
- Authorizing transactions.
- Control or management of bank accounts or investments.
- Deciding which recommendations of the firm or other third parties to implement.
- Reporting to those charged with governance on behalf of management.
- Taking responsibility for designing, implementing, monitoring or maintaining internal controls.

291.143 In providing assurance services to an assurance client, a firm shall not assume a management responsibility as part of the assurance service. If the firm were to assume a management responsibility as part of the assurance service, the threats created would be so significant that no safeguards could reduce the threats to an acceptable level. If the firm assumes a management responsibility as part of any other services provided to the assurance client, the firm shall ensure that the responsibility is not related to the subject matter or subject matter information of the assurance engagement provided by the firm.

291.144 When providing services that are related to the subject matter or subject matter information of an assurance engagement provided by the firm, the firm shall be satisfied that client management makes all judgments and decisions relating to the subject matter or subject matter information of the assurance engagement that are the responsibility of management. This includes ensuring that the client's management:

- Designates an individual who possesses suitable skill, knowledge and experience to be responsible at all times for the client's decisions and to oversee the services. Such an individual, preferably within senior management, would understand the objectives, nature and results of the services and the respective client and firm responsibilities. However, the individual is not required to possess the expertise to perform or re-perform the services;
- Provides oversight of the services and evaluates the adequacy of the results of the services performed for the client's purpose; and
- Accepts responsibility for the actions, if any, to be taken arising from the results of the services.

Other Considerations

Threats to independence may be created when a firm provides a non-assurance service **291.145** related to the subject matter information of an assurance engagement. In such cases, an evaluation of the significance of the firm's involvement with the subject matter information of the engagement shall be made, and a determination shall be made of whether any self-review threats that are not at an acceptable level can be reduced to an acceptable level by the application of safeguards.

A self-review threat may be created if the firm is involved in the preparation of subject **291.146** matter information which is subsequently the subject matter information of an assurance engagement. For example, a self-review threat would be created if the firm developed and prepared prospective financial information and subsequently provided assurance on this information. Consequently, the firm shall evaluate the significance of any self-review threat created by the provision of such services and apply safeguards when necessary to eliminate the threat or reduce it to an acceptable level.

When a firm performs a valuation that forms part of the subject matter information of an **291.147** assurance engagement, the firm shall evaluate the significance of any self-review threat and apply safeguards when necessary to eliminate the threat or reduce it to an acceptable level.

Fees

Fees—Relative Size

When the total fees from an assurance client represent a large proportion of the total fees of **291.148** the firm expressing the conclusion, the dependence on that client and concern about losing the client creates a self-interest or intimidation threat. The significance of the threat will depend on factors such as:

- The operating structure of the firm;
- Whether the firm is well established or new; and
- The significance of the client qualitatively and/or quantitatively to the firm.

The significance of the threat shall be evaluated and safeguards applied when necessary to eliminate the threat or reduce it to an acceptable level. Examples of such safeguards include:

- Reducing the dependency on the client;
- External quality control reviews; or
- Consulting a third party, such as a professional regulatory body or a professional accountant, on key assurance judgments.

A self-interest or intimidation threat is also created when the fees generated from an **291.149** assurance client represent a large proportion of the revenue from an individual partner's clients. The significance of the threat shall be evaluated and safeguards applied when necessary to eliminate the threat or reduce it to an acceptable level. An example of such a safeguard is having an additional professional accountant who was not a member of the assurance team review the work or otherwise advise as necessary.

Fees—Overdue

A self-interest threat may be created if fees due from an assurance client remain unpaid **291.150** for a long time, especially if a significant part is not paid before the issue of the assurance report, if any, for the following period. Generally the firm is expected to require payment of such fees before any such report is issued. If fees remain unpaid after the report has been issued, the existence and significance of any threat shall be evaluated and safeguards applied when necessary to eliminate the threat or reduce it to an acceptable level. An example of such a safeguard is having another professional accountant who did not take part in the assurance engagement provide advice or review the work performed. The firm shall determine whether the overdue fees might be regarded as being equivalent to a loan to the client and whether, because of the significance of the overdue fees, it is appropriate for the firm to be re-appointed or continue the assurance engagement.

Contingent Fees

291.151   Contingent fees are fees calculated on a predetermined basis relating to the outcome of a transaction or the result of the services performed by the firm. For the purposes of this section, fees are not regarded as being contingent if established by a court or other public authority.

291.152   A contingent fee charged directly or indirectly, for example through an intermediary, by a firm in respect of an assurance engagement creates a self-interest threat that is so significant that no safeguards could reduce the threat to an acceptable level. Accordingly, a firm shall not enter into any such fee arrangement.

291.153   A contingent fee charged directly or indirectly, for example through an intermediary, by a firm in respect of a non-assurance service provided to an assurance client may also create a self-interest threat. If the outcome of the non-assurance service, and therefore, the amount of the fee, is dependent on a future or contemporary judgment related to a matter that is material to the subject matter information of the assurance engagement, no safeguards could reduce the threat to an acceptable level. Accordingly, such arrangements shall not be accepted.

291.154   For other contingent fee arrangements charged by a firm for a non-assurance service to an assurance client, the existence and significance of any threats will depend on factors such as:

- The range of possible fee amounts;
- Whether an appropriate authority determines the outcome of the matter upon which the contingent fee will be determined;
- The nature of the service; and
- The effect of the event or transaction on the subject matter information.

The significance of any threats shall be evaluated and safeguards applied when necessary to eliminate the threats or reduce them to an acceptable level. Examples of such safeguards include:

- Having a professional accountant review the relevant assurance work or otherwise advise as necessary; or
- Using professionals who are not members of the assurance team to perform the non-assurance service.

Gifts and Hospitality

291.155   Accepting gifts or hospitality from an assurance client may create self-interest and familiarity threats. If a firm or a member of the assurance team accepts gifts or hospitality, unless the value is trivial and inconsequential, the threats created would be so significant that no safeguards could reduce the threats to an acceptable level. Consequently, a firm or a member of the assurance team shall not accept such gifts or hospitality.

Actual or Threatened Litigation

When litigation takes place, or appears likely, between the firm or a member of the assurance team and the assurance client, self-interest and intimidation threats are created. The relationship between client management and the members of the assurance team must be characterized by complete candor and full disclosure regarding all aspects of a client's business operations. When the firm and the client's management are placed in adversarial positions by actual or threatened litigation, affecting management's willingness to make complete disclosures self-interest and intimidation threats are created. The significance of the threats created will depend on such factors as:

291.156

- The materiality of the litigation; and
- Whether the litigation relates to a prior assurance engagement.

The significance of the threats shall be evaluated and safeguards applied when necessary to eliminate the threats or reduce them to an acceptable level. Examples of such safeguards include:

- If the litigation involves a member of the assurance team, removing that individual from the assurance team; or
- Having a professional review the work performed.

If such safeguards do not reduce the threats to an acceptable level, the only appropriate action is to withdraw from, or decline, the assurance engagement.

Interpretation 2005–01 (Revised July 2009 to conform to changes resulting from the IESBA's project to improve the clarity of the Code)

Application of Section 291 to Assurance Engagements that are Not Financial Statement Audit Engagements

This interpretation provides guidance on the application of the independence requirements contained in Section 291 to assurance engagements that are not financial statement audit engagements.

This interpretation focuses on the application issues that are particular to assurance engagements that are not financial statement audit engagements. There are other matters noted in Section 291 that are relevant in the consideration of independence requirements for all assurance engagements. For example, paragraph 291.3 states that an evaluation shall be made of any threats the firm has reason to believe are created by a network firm's interests and relationships. It also states that when the assurance team has reason to believe that a related entity of such an assurance client is relevant to the evaluation of the firm's independence of the client, the assurance team shall include the related entity when evaluating threats to independence and when necessary applying safeguards. These matters are not specifically addressed in this interpretation.

As explained in the International Framework for Assurance Engagements issued by the International Auditing and Assurance Standards Board, in an assurance engagement, the professional accountant in public practice expresses a conclusion designed to enhance the degree of confidence of the intended users other than the responsible party about the outcome of the evaluation or measurement of a subject matter against criteria.

Assertion-Based Assurance Engagements

In an assertion-based assurance engagement, the evaluation or measurement of the subject matter is performed by the responsible party, and the subject matter information is in the form of an assertion by the responsible party that is made available to the intended users.

In an assertion-based assurance engagement independence is required from the responsible party, which is responsible for the subject matter information and may be responsible for the subject matter.

In those assertion-based assurance engagements where the responsible party is responsible for the subject matter information but not the subject matter, independence is required from the responsible party. In addition, an evaluation shall be made of any threats the firm has reason to believe are created by interests and relationships between a member of the assurance team, the firm, a network firm and the party responsible for the subject matter.

Direct Reporting Assurance Engagements

In a direct reporting assurance engagement, the professional accountant in public practice either directly performs the evaluation or measurement of the subject matter, or obtains a representation from the responsible party that has performed the evaluation or measurement that is not available to the intended users. The subject matter information is provided to the intended users in the assurance report.

In a direct reporting assurance engagement independence is required from the responsible party, which is responsible for the subject matter.

Multiple Responsible Parties

In both assertion-based assurance engagements and direct reporting assurance engagements there may be several responsible parties. For example, a public accountant in public practice may be asked to provide assurance on the monthly circulation statistics of a number of independently owned newspapers. The assignment could be an assertion based assurance engagement where each newspaper measures its circulation and the statistics are presented in an assertion that is available to the intended users. Alternatively, the assignment could be a direct reporting assurance engagement, where there is no assertion and there may or may not be a written representation from the newspapers.

In such engagements, when determining whether it is necessary to apply the provisions in Section 291 to each responsible party, the firm may take into account whether an interest or relationship between the firm, or a member of the assurance team, and a particular responsible party would create a threat to independence that is not trivial and inconsequential in the context of the subject matter information. This will take into account:

(a) The materiality of the subject matter information (or the subject matter) for which the particular responsible party is responsible; and
(b) The degree of public interest that is associated with the engagement.

If the firm determines that the threat to independence created by any such relationships with a particular responsible party would be trivial and inconsequential it may not be necessary to apply all of the provisions of this section to that responsible party.

Example

The following example has been developed to demonstrate the application of Section 291. It is assumed that the client is not also a financial statement audit client of the firm, or a network firm.

A firm is engaged to provide assurance on the total proven oil reserves of 10 independent companies. Each company has conducted geographical and engineering surveys to determine their reserves (subject matter). There are established criteria to determine when a reserve may be considered to be proven which the professional accountant in public practice determines to be suitable criteria for the engagement. The proven reserves for each company as at December 31, 20X0 were as follows:

	Proven oil reserves thousands of barrels
Company 1	5,200
Company 2	725
Company 3	3,260
Company 4	15,000
Company 5	6,700
Company 6	39,126
Company 7	345
Company 8	175
Company 9	24,135
Company 10	9,635
Total	**104,301**

The engagement could be structured in differing ways:

Assertion-Based Engagements

A1   Each company measures its reserves and provides an assertion to the firm and to intended users.

A2   An entity other than the companies measures the reserves and provides an assertion to the firm and to intended users.

Direct Reporting Engagements

D1   Each company measures the reserves and provides the firm with a written representation that measures its reserves against the established criteria for measuring proven reserves. The representation is not available to the intended users.

D2   The firm directly measures the reserves of some of the companies.

Application of Approach

A1   Each company measures its reserves and provides an assertion to the firm and to intended users.

There are several responsible parties in this engagement (Companies 1–10). When determining whether it is necessary to apply the independence provisions to all of the companies, the firm may take into account whether an interest or relationship with a particular company would create a threat to independence that is not at an acceptable level. This will take into account factors such as:

- The materiality of the company's proven reserves in relation to the total reserves to be reported on; and
- The degree of public interest associated with the engagement (paragraph 291.28).

For example Company 8 accounts for 0.17% of the total reserves, therefore a business relationship or interest with Company 8 would create less of a threat than a similar relationship with Company 6, which accounts for approximately 37.5% of the reserves.

Having determined those companies to which the independence requirements apply, the assurance team and the firm are required to be independent of those responsible parties that would be considered to be the assurance client (paragraph 291.28).

A2   An entity other than the companies measures the reserves and provides an assertion to the firm and to intended users.

The firm shall be independent of the entity that measures the reserves and provides an assertion to the firm and to intended users (paragraph 291.19). That entity is not responsible for the subject matter and so an evaluation shall be made of any threats the firm has reason to believe are created by interests/relationships with the party responsible for the subject matter (paragraph 291.19). There are several parties responsible for the subject matter in this engagement (Companies 1–10). As discussed in example A1 above, the firm may take into account whether an interest or relationship with a particular company would create a threat to independence that is not at an acceptable level.

D1   Each company provides the firm with a representation that measures its reserves against the established criteria for measuring proven reserves. The representation is not available to the intended users.

There are several responsible parties in this engagement (Companies 1–10). When determining whether it is necessary to apply the independence provisions to all of the companies, the firm may take into account whether an interest or relationship with a particular company would create a threat to independence that is not at an acceptable level. This will take into account factors such as:

- The materiality of the company's proven reserves in relation to the total reserves to be reported on; and
- The degree of public interest associated with the engagement (paragraph 291.28).

For example, Company 8 accounts for 0.17% of the reserves, therefore a business relationship or interest with Company 8 would create less of a threat than a similar relationship with Company 6 that accounts for approximately 37.5% of the reserves.

Having determined those companies to which the independence requirements apply, the assurance team and the firm shall be independent of those responsible parties that would be considered to be the assurance client (paragraph 291.28).

D2   The firm directly measures the reserves of some of the companies.

The application is the same as in example D1.

Part C—Professional accountants in business

Section 300

Introduction

This Part of the Code describes how the conceptual framework contained in Part A applies in certain situations to professional accountants in business. This Part does not describe all of the circumstances and relationships that could be encountered by a professional accountant in business that create or may create threats to compliance with the fundamental principles. Therefore, the professional accountant in business is encouraged to be alert for such circumstances and relationships. **300.1**

Investors, creditors, employers and other sectors of the business community, as well as governments and the public at large, all may rely on the work of professional accountants in business. Professional accountants in business may be solely or jointly responsible for the preparation and reporting of financial and other information, which both their employing organizations and third parties may rely on. They may also be responsible for providing effective financial management and competent advice on a variety of business-related matters. **300.2**

A professional accountant in business may be a salaried employee, a partner, director (whether executive or non-executive), an owner manager, a volunteer or another working for one or more employing organization. The legal form of the relationship with the employing organization, if any, has no bearing on the ethical responsibilities incumbent on the professional accountant in business. **300.3**

A professional accountant in business has a responsibility to further the legitimate aims of the accountant's employing organization. This Code does not seek to hinder a professional accountant in business from properly fulfilling that responsibility, but addresses circumstances in which compliance with the fundamental principles may be compromised. **300.4**

A professional accountant in business may hold a senior position within an organization. The more senior the position, the greater will be the ability and opportunity to influence events, practices and attitudes. A professional accountant in business is expected, therefore, to encourage an ethics-based culture in an employing organization that emphasizes the importance that senior management places on ethical behavior. **300.5**

A professional accountant in business shall not knowingly engage in any business, occupation, or activity that impairs or might impair integrity, objectivity or the good reputation of the profession and as a result would be incompatible with the fundamental principles. **300.6**

Compliance with the fundamental principles may potentially be threatened by a broad range of circumstances and relationships. Threats fall into one or more of the following categories: **300.7**

(a) Self-interest;
(b) Self-review;
(c) Advocacy;
(d) Familiarity; and
(e) Intimidation.

These threats are discussed further in Part A of this Code.

Examples of circumstances that may create self-interest threats for a professional accountant in business include: **300.8**

- Holding a financial interest in, or receiving a loan or guarantee from the employing organization.
- Participating in incentive compensation arrangements offered by the employing organization.
- Inappropriate personal use of corporate assets.
- Concern over employment security.
- Commercial pressure from outside the employing organization.

300.9   An example of a circumstance that creates a self-review threat for a professional accountant in business is determining the appropriate accounting treatment for a business combination after performing the feasibility study that supported the acquisition decision.

300.10   When furthering the legitimate goals and objectives of their employing organizations, professional accountants in business may promote the organization's position, provided any statements made are neither false nor misleading. Such actions generally would not create an advocacy threat.

300.11   Examples of circumstances that may create familiarity threats for a professional accountant in business include:

- Being responsible for the employing organization's financial reporting when an immediate or close family member employed by the entity makes decisions that affect the entity's financial reporting.
- Long association with business contacts influencing business decisions.
- Accepting a gift or preferential treatment, unless the value is trivial and inconsequential.

300.12   Examples of circumstances that may create intimidation threats for a professional accountant in business include:

- Threat of dismissal or replacement of the professional accountant in business or a close or immediate family member over a disagreement about the application of an accounting principle or the way in which financial information is to be reported.
- A dominant personality attempting to influence the decision making process, for example with regard to the awarding of contracts or the application of an accounting principle.

300.13   Safeguards that may eliminate or reduce threats to an acceptable level fall into two broad categories:

(a) Safeguards created by the profession, legislation or regulation; and
(b) Safeguards in the work environment.

Examples of safeguards created by the profession, legislation or regulation are detailed in paragraph 100.14 of Part A of this Code.

300.14   Safeguards in the work environment include:

- The employing organization's systems of corporate oversight or other oversight structures.
- The employing organization's ethics and conduct programs.
- Recruitment procedures in the employing organization emphasizing the importance of employing high caliber competent staff.
- Strong internal controls.
- Appropriate disciplinary processes.
- Leadership that stresses the importance of ethical behavior and the expectation that employees will act in an ethical manner.

- Policies and procedures to implement and monitor the quality of employee performance.
- Timely communication of the employing organization's policies and procedures, including any changes to them, to all employees and appropriate training and education on such policies and procedures.
- Policies and procedures to empower and encourage employees to communicate to senior levels within the employing organization any ethical issues that concern them without fear of retribution.
- Consultation with another appropriate professional accountant.

In circumstances where a professional accountant in business believes that unethical behavior or actions by others will continue to occur within the employing organization, the professional accountant in business may consider obtaining legal advice. In those extreme situations where all available safeguards have been exhausted and it is not possible to reduce the threat to an acceptable level, a professional accountant in business may conclude that it is appropriate to resign from the employing organization. **300.15**

Section 310

Conflicts of Interest

310.1   A professional accountant in business may be faced with a conflict of interest when undertaking a professional activity. A conflict of interest creates a threat to objectivity and may create threats to the other fundamental principles. Such threats may be created when:

- The professional accountant undertakes a professional activity related to a particular matter for two or more parties whose interests with respect to that matter are in conflict; or
- The interests of the professional accountant with respect to a particular matter and the interests of a party for whom the professional accountant undertakes a professional activity related to that matter are in conflict.

A party may include an employing organization, a vendor, a customer, a lender, a shareholder, or another party.

A professional accountant shall not allow a conflict of interest to compromise professional or business judgment.

310.2   Examples of situations in which conflicts of interest may arise include:

- Serving in a management or governance position for two employing organizations and acquiring confidential information from one employing organization that could be used by the professional accountant to the advantage or disadvantage of the other employing organization.
- Undertaking a professional activity for each of two parties in a partnership employing the professional accountant to assist them to dissolve their partnership.
- Preparing financial information for certain members of management of the entity employing the professional accountant who are seeking to undertake a management buy-out.
- Being responsible for selecting a vendor for the accountant's employing organization when an immediate family member of the professional accountant could benefit financially from the transaction.
- Serving in a governance capacity in an employing organization that is approving certain investments for the company where one of those specific investments will increase the value of the personal investment portfolio of the professional accountant or an immediate family member.

310.3   When identifying and evaluating the interests and relationships that might create a conflict of interest and implementing safeguards, when necessary, to eliminate or reduce any threat to compliance with the fundamental principles to an acceptable level, a professional accountant in business shall exercise professional judgment and be alert to all interests and relationships that a reasonable and informed third party, weighing all the specific facts and circumstances available to the professional accountant at the time, would be likely to conclude might compromise compliance with the fundamental principles.

310.4   When addressing a conflict of interest, a professional accountant in business is encouraged to seek guidance from within the employing organization or from others, such as a professional body, legal counsel or another professional accountant. When making disclosures or sharing information within the employing organization and seeking guidance of third parties, the professional accountant shall remain alert to the fundamental principle of confidentiality.

If the threat created by a conflict of interest is not at an acceptable level, the professional accountant in business shall apply safeguards to eliminate the threat or reduce it to an acceptable level. If safeguards cannot reduce the threat to an acceptable level, the professional accountant shall decline to undertake or discontinue the professional activity that would result in the conflict of interest; or shall terminate the relevant relationships or dispose of relevant interests to eliminate the threat or reduce it to an acceptable level.

310.5

In identifying whether a conflict of interest exists or may be created, a professional accountant in business shall take reasonable steps to determine:

310.6

- The nature of the relevant interests and relationships between the parties involved; and
- The nature of the activity and its implication for relevant parties.

The nature of the activities and the relevant interests and relationships may change over time. The professional accountant shall remain alert to such changes for the purposes of identifying circumstances that might create a conflict of interest.

If a conflict of interest is identified, the professional accountant in business shall evaluate:

310.7

- The significance of relevant interests or relationships; and
- The significance of the threats created by undertaking the professional activity or activities. In general, the more direct the connection between the professional activity and the matter on which the parties' interests are in conflict, the more significant the threat to objectivity and compliance with the other fundamental principles will be.

The professional accountant in business shall apply safeguards, when necessary, to eliminate the threats to compliance with the fundamental principles created by the conflict of interest or reduce them to an acceptable level. Depending on the circumstances giving rise to the conflict of interest, application of one or more of the following safeguards may be appropriate:

310.8

- Restructuring or segregating certain responsibilities and duties.
- Obtaining appropriate oversight, for example, acting under the supervision of an executive or non-executive director.
- Withdrawing from the decision-making process related to the matter giving rise to the conflict of interest.
- Consulting with third parties, such as a professional body, legal counsel or another professional accountant.

In addition, it is generally necessary to disclose the nature of the conflict to the relevant parties, including to the appropriate levels within the employing organization and, when safeguards are required to reduce the threat to an acceptable level, to obtain their consent to the professional accountant in business undertaking the professional activity. In certain circumstances, consent may be implied by a party's conduct where the professional accountant has sufficient evidence to conclude that parties know the circumstances at the outset and have accepted the conflict of interest if they do not raise an objection to the existence of the conflict.

310.9

When disclosure is verbal, or consent is verbal or implied, the professional accountant in business is encouraged to document the nature of the circumstances giving rise to the conflict of interest, the safeguards applied to reduce the threats to an acceptable level and the consent obtained.

`310.10

A professional accountant in business may encounter other threats to compliance with the fundamental principles. This may occur, for example, when preparing or reporting financial

310.11

information as a result of undue pressure from others within the employing organization or financial, business or personal relationships that close or immediate family members of the professional accountant have with the employing organization. Guidance on managing such threats is covered by Sections 320 and 340 of the Code.

Section 320

Preparation and Reporting of Information

Professional accountants in business are often involved in the preparation and reporting **320.1** of information that may be either made public or used by others inside or outside the employing organization. Such information may include financial or management information, for example, forecasts and budgets, financial statements, management's discussion and analysis, and the management letter of representation provided to the auditors during the audit of the entity's financial statements. A professional accountant in business shall prepare or present such information fairly, honestly and in accordance with relevant professional standards so that the information will be understood in its context.

A professional accountant in business who has responsibility for the preparation or **320.2** approval of the general purpose financial statements of an employing organization shall be satisfied that those financial statements are presented in accordance with the applicable financial reporting standards.

A professional accountant in business shall take reasonable steps to maintain information **320.3** for which the professional accountant in business is responsible in a manner that:

(a) Describes clearly the true nature of business transactions, assets, or liabilities;
(b) Classifies and records information in a timely and proper manner; and
(c) Represents the facts accurately and completely in all material respects.

Threats to compliance with the fundamental principles, for example, self-interest or **320.4** intimidation threats to integrity, objectivity or professional competence and due care, are created where a professional accountant in business is pressured (either externally or by the possibility of personal gain) to prepare or report information in a misleading way or to become associated with misleading information through the actions of others.

The significance of such threats will depend on factors such as the source of the pressure **320.5** and the corporate culture within the employing organization. The professional accountant in business shall be alert to the principle of integrity, which imposes an obligation on all professional accountants to be straightforward and honest in all professional and business relationships. Where the threats arise from compensation and incentive arrangements, the guidance in section 340 is relevant.

The significance of any threat shall be evaluated and safeguards applied when necessary to **320.6** eliminate the threat or reduce it to an acceptable level. Such safeguards include consultation with superiors within the employing organization, the audit committee or those charged with governance of the organization, or with a relevant professional body.

Where it is not possible to reduce the threat to an acceptable level, a professional accountant **320.7** in business shall refuse to be or remain associated with information the professional accountant determines is misleading. A professional accountant in business may have been unknowingly associated with misleading information. Upon becoming aware of this, the professional accountant in business shall take steps to be disassociated from that information. In determining whether there is a requirement to report the circumstances outside the organization, the professional accountant in business may consider obtaining legal advice. In addition, the professional accountant may consider whether to resign.

Section 330

Acting with Sufficient Expertise

330.1   The fundamental principle of professional competence and due care requires that a professional accountant in business only undertake significant tasks for which the professional accountant in business has, or can obtain, sufficient specific training or experience. A professional accountant in business shall not intentionally mislead an employer as to the level of expertise or experience possessed, nor shall a professional accountant in business fail to seek appropriate expert advice and assistance when required.

330.2   Circumstances that create a threat to a professional accountant in business performing duties with the appropriate degree of professional competence and due care include having:

- Insufficient time for properly performing or completing the relevant duties.
- Incomplete, restricted or otherwise inadequate information for performing the duties properly.
- Insufficient experience, training and/or education.
- Inadequate resources for the proper performance of the duties.

330.3   The significance of the threat will depend on factors such as the extent to which the professional accountant in business is working with others, relative seniority in the business, and the level of supervision and review applied to the work. The significance of the threat shall be evaluated and safeguards applied when necessary to eliminate the threat or reduce it to an acceptable level. Examples of such safeguards include:

- Obtaining additional advice or training.
- Ensuring that there is adequate time available for performing the relevant duties.
- Obtaining assistance from someone with the necessary expertise.
- Consulting, where appropriate, with:
  - Superiors within the employing organization;
  - Independent experts; or
  - A relevant professional body.

330.4   When threats cannot be eliminated or reduced to an acceptable level, professional accountants in business shall determine whether to refuse to perform the duties in question. If the professional accountant in business determines that refusal is appropriate, the reasons for doing so shall be clearly communicated.

Section 340

Financial Interests, Compensation and Incentives Linked to Financial Reporting and Decision Making

Professional accountants in business may have financial interests, including those arising **340.1**
from compensation or incentive arrangements, or may know of financial interests of
immediate or close family members, that, in certain circumstances, may create threats
to compliance with the fundamental principles. For example, self-interest threats to
objectivity or confidentiality may be created through the existence of the motive and
opportunity to manipulate price-sensitive information in order to gain financially.
Examples of circumstances that may create self-interest threats include situations where
the professional accountant in business or an immediate or close family member:

- Holds a direct or indirect financial interest in the employing organization and the
  value of that financial interest could be directly affected by decisions made by the
  professional accountant in business.
- Is eligible for a profit-related bonus and the value of that bonus could be directly
  affected by decisions made by the professional accountant in business.
- Holds, directly or indirectly, deferred bonus share entitlements or share options in the
  employing organization, the value of which could be directly affected by decisions
  made by the professional accountant in business.
- Otherwise participates in compensation arrangements which provide incentives
  to achieve performance targets or to support efforts to maximize the value of the
  employing organization's shares, for example, through participation in long-term
  incentive plans which are linked to certain performance conditions being met.

Self-interest threats arising from compensation or incentive arrangements may be **340.2**
further compounded by pressure from superiors or peers in the employing organization
who participate in the same arrangements. For example, such arrangements often entitle
participants to be awarded shares in the employing organization at little or no cost to
the employee provided certain performance criteria are met. In some cases, the value of
the shares awarded may be significantly greater than the base salary of the professional
accountant in business.

A professional accountant in business shall not manipulate information or use confidential **340.3**
information for personal gain or for the financial gain of others. The more senior the position
that the professional accountant in business holds, the greater the ability and opportunity
to influence financial reporting and decision making and the greater the pressure there
might be from superiors and peers to manipulate information. In such situations, the
professional accountant in business shall be particularly alert to the principle of integrity,
which imposes an obligation on all professional accountants to be straightforward and
honest in all professional and business relationships.

The significance of any threat created by financial interests, shall be evaluated and **340.4**
safeguards applied, when necessary, to eliminate the threat or reduce it to an acceptable
level. In evaluating the significance of any threat, and, when necessary, determining the
appropriate safeguards to be applied, a professional accountant in business shall evaluate
the nature of the interest. This includes evaluating the significance of the interest. What
constitutes a significant interest will depend on personal circumstances. Examples of such
safeguards include:

- Policies and procedures for a committee independent of management to determine the
  level or form of remuneration of senior management.

- Disclosure of all relevant interests, and of any plans to exercise entitlements or trade in relevant shares, to those charged with the governance of the employing organization, in accordance with any internal policies.
- Consultation, where appropriate, with superiors within the employing organization.
- Consultation, where appropriate, with those charged with the governance of the employing organization or relevant professional bodies.
- Internal and external audit procedures.
- Up-to-date education on ethical issues and on the legal restrictions and other regulations around potential insider trading.

Section 350

Inducements

Receiving Offers

A professional accountant in business or an immediate or close family member may be offered an inducement. Inducements may take various forms, including gifts, hospitality, preferential treatment, and inappropriate appeals to friendship or loyalty.   **350.1**

Offers of inducements may create threats to compliance with the fundamental principles. When a professional accountant in business or an immediate or close family member is offered an inducement, the situation shall be evaluated. Self-interest threats to objectivity or confidentiality are created when an inducement is made in an attempt to unduly influence actions or decisions, encourage illegal or dishonest behavior, or obtain confidential information. Intimidation threats to objectivity or confidentiality are created if such an inducement is accepted and it is followed by threats to make that offer public and damage the reputation of either the professional accountant in business or an immediate or close family member.   **350.2**

The existence and significance of any threats will depend on the nature, value and intent behind the offer. If a reasonable and informed third party, weighing all the specific facts and circumstances, would consider the inducement insignificant and not intended to encourage unethical behavior, then a professional accountant in business may conclude that the offer is made in the normal course of business and may generally conclude that there is no significant threat to compliance with the fundamental principles.   **350.3**

The significance of any threats shall be evaluated and safeguards applied when necessary to eliminate them or reduce them to an acceptable level. When the threats cannot be eliminated or reduced to an acceptable level through the application of safeguards, a professional accountant in business shall not accept the inducement. As the real or apparent threats to compliance with the fundamental principles do not merely arise from acceptance of an inducement but, sometimes, merely from the fact of the offer having been made, additional safeguards shall be adopted. A professional accountant in business shall evaluate any threats created by such offers and determine whether to take one or more of the following actions: **350.4**

(a) Informing higher levels of management or those charged with governance of the employing organization immediately when such offers have been made;
(b) Informing third parties of the offer – for example, a professional body or the employer of the individual who made the offer; a professional accountant in business may however, consider seeking legal advice before taking such a step; and
(c) Advising immediate or close family members of relevant threats and safeguards where they are potentially in positions that might result in offers of inducements, for example, as a result of their employment situation; and
(d) Informing higher levels of management or those charged with governance of the employing organization where immediate or close family members are employed by competitors or potential suppliers of that organization.

Making Offers

A professional accountant in business may be in a situation where the professional accountant in business is expected, or is under other pressure, to offer inducements to influence the judgment or decision-making process of an individual or organization, or obtain confidential information.   **350.5**

350.6   Such pressure may come from within the employing organization, for example, from a colleague or superior. It may also come from an external individual or organization suggesting actions or business decisions that would be advantageous to the employing organization, possibly influencing the professional accountant in business improperly.

350.7   A professional accountant in business shall not offer an inducement to improperly influence professional judgment of a third party.

350.8   Where the pressure to offer an unethical inducement comes from within the employing organization, the professional accountant shall follow the principles and guidance regarding ethical conflict resolution set out in Part A of this Code.

Definitions

In this *Code of Ethics for Professional Accountants*, the following expressions have the following meanings assigned to them:

Acceptable level	A level at which a reasonable and informed third party would be likely to conclude, weighing all the specific facts and circumstances available to the professional accountant at that time, that compliance with the fundamental principles is not compromised.
Advertising	The communication to the public of information as to the services or skills provided by professional accountants in public practice with a view to procuring professional business.
Assurance client	The responsible party that is the person (or persons) who:

(a) In a direct reporting engagement, is responsible for the subject matter; or

(b) In an assertion-based engagement, is responsible for the subject matter information and may be responsible for the subject matter.

Assurance engagement

An engagement in which a professional accountant in public practice expresses a conclusion designed to enhance the degree of confidence of the intended users other than the responsible party about the outcome of the evaluation or measurement of a subject matter against criteria.

(For guidance on assurance engagements see the International Framework for Assurance Engagements issued by the International Auditing and Assurance Standards Board which describes the elements and objectives of an assurance engagement and identifies engagements to which International Standards on Auditing (ISAs), International Standards on Review Engagements (ISREs) and International Standards on Assurance Engagements (ISAEs) apply.)

Assurance team

(a) All members of the engagement team for the assurance engagement;

(b) All others within a firm who can directly influence the outcome of the assurance engagement, including:

(i) Those who recommend the compensation of, or who provide direct supervisory, management or other oversight of the assurance engagement partner in connection with the performance of the assurance engagement;

(ii) Those who provide consultation regarding technical or industry specific issues, transactions or events for the assurance engagement; and

(iii) Those who provide quality control for the assurance engagement, including those who perform the engagement quality control review for the assurance engagement.

Audit client

An entity in respect of which a firm conducts an audit engagement. When the client is a listed entity, audit client will always include its related entities. When the audit client is not a listed entity, audit client includes those related entities over which the client has direct or indirect control.

Audit engagement	A reasonable assurance engagement in which a professional accountant in public practice expresses an opinion whether financial statements are prepared, in all material respects (or give a true and fair view or are presented fairly, in all material respects,), in accordance with an applicable financial reporting framework, such as an engagement conducted in accordance with International Standards on Auditing. This includes a Statutory Audit, which is an audit required by legislation or other regulation.

Audit team

(a)   All members of the engagement team for the audit engagement;

(b)   All others within a firm who can directly influence the outcome of the audit engagement, including:

    (i)   Those who recommend the compensation of, or who provide direct supervisory, management or other oversight of the engagement partner in connection with the performance of the audit engagement including those at all successively senior levels above the engagement partner through to the individual who is the firm's Senior or Managing Partner (Chief Executive or equivalent);

    (ii)   Those who provide consultation regarding technical or industry-specific issues, transactions or events for the engagement; and

    (iii)   Those who provide quality control for the engagement, including those who perform the engagement quality control review for the engagement; and

(c)   All those within a network firm who can directly influence the outcome of the audit engagement.

Close family	A parent, child or sibling who is not an immediate family member.
Contingent fee	A fee calculated on a predetermined basis relating to the outcome of a transaction or the result of the services performed by the firm. A fee that is established by a court or other public authority is not a contingent fee.

Direct financial interest

A financial interest:

(a)   Owned directly by and under the control of an individual or entity (including those managed on a discretionary basis by others); or

(b)   Beneficially owned through a collective investment vehicle, estate, trust or other intermediary over which the individual or entity has control, or the ability to influence investment decisions.

Director or officer	Those charged with the governance of an entity, or acting in an equivalent capacity, regardless of their title, which may vary from jurisdiction to jurisdiction.
Engagement partner	The partner or other person in the firm who is responsible for the engagement and its performance, and for the report that is issued on behalf of the firm, and who, where required, has the appropriate authority from a professional, legal or regulatory body.
Engagement quality control review	A process designed to provide an objective evaluation, on or before the report is issued, of the significant judgments the engagement team made and the conclusions it reached in formulating the report.

Engagement team	All partners and staff performing the engagement, and any individuals engaged by the firm or a network firm who perform assurance procedures on the engagement. This excludes external experts engaged by the firm or by a network firm. The term 'engagement team' also excludes individuals within the client's internal audit function who provide direct assistance on an audit engagement when the external auditor complies with the requirements of ISA 610 (Revised 2013), *Using the Work of Internal Auditors*.*
Existing accountant	A professional accountant in public practice currently holding an audit appointment or carrying out accounting, taxation, consulting or similar professional services for a client.
External expert	An individual (who is not a partner or a member of the professional staff, including temporary staff, of the firm or a network firm) or organization possessing skills, knowledge and experience in a field other than accounting or auditing, whose work in that field is used to assist the professional accountant in obtaining sufficient appropriate evidence.
Financial interest	An interest in an equity or other security, debenture, loan or other debt instrument of an entity, including rights and obligations to acquire such an interest and derivatives directly related to such interest.
Financial statements	A structured representation of historical financial information, including related notes, intended to communicate an entity's economic resources or obligations at a point in time or the changes therein for a period of time in accordance with a financial reporting framework. The related notes ordinarily comprise a summary of significant accounting policies and other explanatory information. The term can relate to a complete set of financial statements, but it can also refer to a single financial statement, for example, a balance sheet, or a statement of revenues and expenses, and related explanatory notes.
Financial statements on which the firm will express an opinion	In the case of a single entity, the financial statements of that entity. In the case of consolidated financial statements, also referred to as group financial statements, the consolidated financial statements.
Firm	(a) A sole practitioner, partnership or corporation of professional accountants; (b) An entity that controls such parties, through ownership, management or other means; and (c) An entity controlled by such parties, through ownership, management or other means.
Historical financial information	Information expressed in financial terms in relation to a particular entity, derived primarily from that entity's accounting system, about economic events occurring in past time periods or about economic conditions or circumstances at points in time in the past.
Immediate family	A spouse (or equivalent) or dependent.

---

* ISA 610 (Revised 2013) establishes limits on the use of direct assistance. It also acknowledges that the external auditor may be prohibited by law or regulation from obtaining direct assistance from internal auditors. Therefore, the use of direct assistance is restricted to situations where it is permitted.

Independence	Independence is: (a) Independence of mind – the state of mind that permits the expression of a conclusion without being affected by influences that compromise professional judgment, thereby allowing an individual to act with integrity, and exercise objectivity and professional skepticism. (b) Independence in appearance – the avoidance of facts and circumstances that are so significant that a reasonable and informed third party would be likely to conclude, weighing all the specific facts and circumstances, that a firm's, or a member of the audit or assurance team's, integrity, objectivity or professional skepticism has been compromised.
Indirect financial interest	A financial interest beneficially owned through a collective investment vehicle, estate, trust or other intermediary over which the individual or entity has no control or ability to influence investment decisions.
Key audit partner	The engagement partner, the individual responsible for the engagement quality control review, and other audit partners, if any, on the engagement team who make key decisions or judgments on significant matters with respect to the audit of the financial statements on which the firm will express an opinion. Depending upon the circumstances and the role of the individuals on the audit, 'other audit partners' may include, for example, audit partners responsible for significant subsidiaries or divisions.
Listed entity	An entity whose shares, stock or debt are quoted or listed on a recognized stock exchange, or are marketed under the regulations of a recognized stock exchange or other equivalent body.
Network	A larger structure: (a) That is aimed at co-operation; and (b) That is clearly aimed at profit or cost sharing or shares common ownership, control or management, common quality control policies and procedures, common business strategy, the use of a common brand-name, or a significant part of professional resources.
Network firm	A firm or entity that belongs to a network.
Office	A distinct sub-group, whether organized on geographical or practice lines.
Professional accountant	An individual who is a member of an IFAC member body.
Professional accountant in business	A professional accountant employed or engaged in an executive or non-executive capacity in such areas as commerce, industry, service, the public sector, education, the not for profit sector, regulatory bodies or professional bodies, or a professional accountant contracted by such entities.
Professional accountant in public practice	A professional accountant, irrespective of functional classification (for example, audit, tax or consulting) in a firm that provides professional services. This term is also used to refer to a firm of professional accountants in public practice.
Professional activity	An activity requiring accountancy or related skills undertaken by a professional accountant, including accounting, auditing, taxation, management consulting, and financial management.

Professional services	Professional activities performed for clients.

Public interest entity	(a) A listed entity; and
	(b) An entity:
	    (i) Defined by regulation or legislation as a public interest entity; or
	    (ii) For which the audit is required by regulation or legislation to be conducted in compliance with the same independence requirements that apply to the audit of listed entities. Such regulation may be promulgated by any relevant regulator, including an audit regulator.

Related entity	An entity that has any of the following relationships with the client: (a) An entity that has direct or indirect control over the client if the client is material to such entity; (b) An entity with a direct financial interest in the client if that entity has significant influence over the client and the interest in the client is material to such entity; (c) An entity over which the client has direct or indirect control; (d) An entity in which the client, or an entity related to the client under (c) above, has a direct financial interest that gives it significant influence over such entity and the interest is material to the client and its related entity in (c); and (e) An entity which is under common control with the client (a 'sister entity') if the sister entity and the client are both material to the entity that controls both the client and sister entity.
Review client	An entity in respect of which a firm conducts a review engagement.
Review engagement	An assurance engagement, conducted in accordance with International Standards on Review Engagements or equivalent, in which a professional accountant in public practice expresses a conclusion on whether, on the basis of the procedures which do not provide all the evidence that would be required in an audit, anything has come to the accountant's attention that causes the accountant to believe that the financial statements are not prepared, in all material respects, in accordance with an applicable financial reporting framework.

Review team	(a) All members of the engagement team for the review engagement; and
	(b) All others within a firm who can directly influence the outcome of the review engagement, including:
	    (i) Those who recommend the compensation of, or who provide direct supervisory, management or other oversight of the engagement partner in connection with the performance of the review engagement including those at all successively senior levels above the engagement partner through to the individual who is the firm's Senior or Managing Partner (Chief Executive or equivalent);
	    (ii) Those who provide consultation regarding technical or industry specific issues, transactions or events for the engagement; and
	    (iii) Those who provide quality control for the engagement, including those who perform the engagement quality control review for the engagement; and
	(c) All those within a network firm who can directly influence the outcome of the review engagement.

| Special purpose financial statements | Financial statements prepared in accordance with a financial reporting framework designed to meet the financial information needs of specified users. |
| Those charged with governance | The person(s) or organization(s) (for example, a corporate trustee) with responsibility for overseeing the strategic direction of the entity and obligations related to the accountability of the entity. This includes overseeing the financial reporting process. For some entities in some jurisdictions, those charged with governance may include management personnel, for example, executive members of a governance board of a private or public sector entity, or an owner-manager. |

Effective Date

The Code is effective.

Changes to the code—Certain non-assurance services provisions for audit and assurance clients

Contents

Section 225

Responding to Non-Compliance with Laws and Regulations
Purpose

A professional accountant in public practice may encounter or be made aware of non-compliance or suspected non-compliance with laws and regulations in the course of providing a professional service to a client. The purpose of this section is to set out the professional accountant's responsibilities when encountering such non-compliance or suspected non-compliance, and guide the professional accountant in assessing the implications of the matter and the possible courses of action when responding to it. This section applies regardless of the nature of the client, including whether or not it is a public interest entity. **225.1**

Non-compliance with laws and regulations ('non-compliance') comprises acts of omission or commission, intentional or unintentional, committed by a client, or by those charged with governance, by management or by other individuals working for or under the direction of a client which are contrary to the prevailing laws or regulations. **225.2**

In some jurisdictions, there are legal or regulatory provisions governing how professional accountants should address non-compliance or suspected non-compliance which may differ from or go beyond this section. When encountering such non-compliance or suspected non-compliance, the professional accountant has a responsibility to obtain an understanding of those provisions and comply with them, including any requirement to report the matter to an appropriate authority and any prohibition on alerting the client prior to making any disclosure, for example, pursuant to anti-money laundering legislation. **225.3**

A distinguishing mark of the accountancy profession is its acceptance of the responsibility to act in the public interest. When responding to non-compliance or suspected non-compliance, the objectives of the professional accountant are: **225.4**

(a)   To comply with the fundamental principles of integrity and professional behavior;
(b)   By alerting management or, where appropriate, those charged with governance of the client, to seek to:
   (i)   Enable them to rectify, remediate or mitigate the consequences of the identified or suspected non-compliance; or
   (ii)   Deter the commission of the non-compliance where it has not yet occurred; and
(c)   To take such further action as appropriate in the public interest.

Scope

This section sets out the approach to be taken by a professional accountant who encounters or is made aware of non-compliance or suspected non-compliance with: **225.5**

(a)   Laws and regulations generally recognized to have a direct effect on the determination of material amounts and disclosures in the client's financial statements; and
(b)   Other laws and regulations that do not have a direct effect on the determination of the amounts and disclosures in the client's financial statements, but compliance with which may be fundamental to the operating aspects of the client's business, to its ability to continue its business, or to avoid material penalties.

Examples of laws and regulations which this section addresses include those that deal with: **225.6**

- Fraud, corruption and bribery.
- Money laundering, terrorist financing and proceeds of crime.
- Securities markets and trading.

- Banking and other financial products and services.
- Data protection.
- Tax and pension liabilities and payments.
- Environmental protection.
- Public health and safety.

225.7   Non-compliance may result in fines, litigation or other consequences for the client that may have a material effect on its financial statements. Importantly, such non-compliance may have wider public interest implications in terms of potentially substantial harm to investors, creditors, employees or the general public. For the purposes of this section, an act that causes substantial harm is one that results in serious adverse consequences to any of these parties in financial or non-financial terms. Examples include the perpetration of a fraud resulting in significant financial losses to investors, and breaches of environmental laws and regulations endangering the health or safety of employees or the public.

225.8   A professional accountant who encounters or is made aware of matters that are clearly inconsequential, judged by their nature and their impact, financial or otherwise, on the client, its stakeholders and the general public, is not required to comply with this section with respect to such matters.

225.9   This section does not address:

(a)   Personal misconduct unrelated to the business activities of the client; and

(b)   Non-compliance other than by the client or those charged with governance, management or other individuals working for or under the direction of the client. This includes, for example, circumstances where a professional accountant has been engaged by a client to perform a due diligence assignment on a third party entity and the identified or suspected non-compliance has been committed by that third party.

The professional accountant may nevertheless find the guidance in this section helpful in considering how to respond in these situations.

Responsibilities of the Client's Management and Those Charged with Governance

225.10   It is the responsibility of the client's management, with the oversight of those charged with governance, to ensure that the client's business activities are conducted in accordance with laws and regulations. It is also the responsibility of management and those charged with governance to identify and address any non-compliance by the client, by an individual charged with governance of the entity, by a member of management, or by other individuals working for or under the direction of the client.

Responsibilities of Professional Accountants in Public Practice

225.11   Where a professional accountant becomes aware of a matter to which this section applies, the steps that the professional accountant takes to comply with this section shall be taken on a timely basis, having regard to the professional accountant's understanding of the nature of the matter and the potential harm to the interests of the entity, investors, creditors, employees or the general public.

Audits of Financial Statements

Obtaining an Understanding of the Matter

225.12   If a professional accountant engaged to perform an audit of financial statements becomes aware of information concerning an instance of non-compliance or suspected non-compliance, whether in the course of performing the engagement or through information provided by other parties, the professional accountant shall obtain an understanding of the matter, including the nature of the act and the circumstances in which it has occurred or may occur.

The professional accountant is expected to apply knowledge, professional judgment and expertise, but is not expected to have a level of knowledge of laws and regulations that is greater than that which is required to undertake the engagement. Whether an act constitutes non-compliance is ultimately a matter to be determined by a court or other appropriate adjudicative body. Depending on the nature and significance of the matter, the professional accountant may consult on a confidential basis with others within the firm, a network firm or a professional body, or with legal counsel.   **225.13**

If the professional accountant identifies or suspects that non-compliance has occurred or may occur, the professional accountant shall discuss the matter with the appropriate level of management and, where appropriate, those charged with governance.   **225.14**

Such discussion serves to clarify the professional accountant's understanding of the facts and circumstances relevant to the matter and its potential consequences. The discussion also may prompt management or those charged with governance to investigate the matter.   **225.15**

The appropriate level of management with whom to discuss the matter is a question of professional judgment. Relevant factors to consider include: **225.16**

- The nature and circumstances of the matter.
- The individuals actually or potentially involved.
- The likelihood of collusion.
- The potential consequences of the matter.
- Whether that level of management is able to investigate the matter and take appropriate action.

The appropriate level of management is generally at least one level above the person or persons involved or potentially involved in the matter. If the professional accountant believes that management is involved in the non-compliance or suspected non-compliance, the professional accountant shall discuss the matter with those charged with governance. The professional accountant may also consider discussing the matter with internal auditors, where applicable. In the context of a group, the appropriate level may be management at an entity that controls the client.   **225.17**

Addressing the Matter

In discussing the non-compliance or suspected non-compliance with management and, where appropriate, those charged with governance, the professional accountant shall advise them to take appropriate and timely actions, if they have not already done so, to: **225.18**

(a) Rectify, remediate or mitigate the consequences of the non-compliance;
(b) Deter the commission of the non-compliance where it has not yet occurred; or
(c) Disclose the matter to an appropriate authority where required by law or regulation or where considered necessary in the public interest.

The professional accountant shall consider whether the client's management and those charged with governance understand their legal or regulatory responsibilities with respect to the non-compliance or suspected non-compliance. If not, the professional accountant may suggest appropriate sources of information or recommend that they obtain legal advice.   **225.19**

225.20   The professional accountant shall comply with applicable:

(a)   Laws and regulations, including legal or regulatory provisions governing the reporting of non-compliance or suspected non-compliance to an appropriate authority. In this regard, some laws and regulations may stipulate a period within which reports are to be made; and

(b)   Requirements under auditing standards, including those relating to:
  - Identifying and responding to non-compliance, including fraud.
  - Communicating with those charged with governance.
  - Considering the implications of the non-compliance or suspected non-compliance for the auditor's report.

Communication with Respect to Groups

225.21   A professional accountant may:

- For purposes of an audit of group financial statements, be requested by the group engagement team to perform work on financial information related to a component of the group; or
- Be engaged to perform an audit of a component's financial statements for purposes other than the group audit, for example, a statutory audit.

Where the professional accountant becomes aware of non-compliance or suspected non-compliance in relation to the component in either situation, the professional accountant shall, in addition to responding to the matter in accordance with the provisions of this section, communicate it to the group engagement partner unless prohibited from doing so by law or regulation. This is to enable the group engagement partner to be informed about the matter and to determine, in the context of the group audit, whether and, if so, how it should be addressed in accordance with the provisions in this section.

225.22   Where the group engagement partner becomes aware of non-compliance or suspected non-compliance in the course of an audit of group financial statements, including as a result of being informed of such a matter in accordance with paragraph 225.21, the group engagement partner shall, in addition to responding to the matter in the context of the group audit in accordance with the provisions of this section, consider whether the matter may be relevant to one or more components:

(a)   Whose financial information is subject to work for purposes of the audit of the group financial statements; or

(b)   Whose financial statements are subject to audit for purposes other than the group audit, for example, a statutory audit.

If so, the group engagement partner shall take steps to have the non-compliance or suspected non-compliance communicated to those performing work at components where the matter may be relevant, unless prohibited from doing so by law or regulation. If necessary in relation to subparagraph (b), appropriate inquiries shall be made (either of management or from publicly available information) as to whether the relevant component(s) is subject to audit and, if so, to ascertain to the extent practicable the identity of the auditor. The communication is to enable those responsible for work at such components to be informed about the matter and to determine whether and, if so, how it should be addressed in accordance with the provisions in this section.

Determining Whether Further Action Is Needed

The professional accountant shall assess the appropriateness of the response of management and, where applicable, those charged with governance.   **225.23**

Relevant factors to consider in assessing the appropriateness of the response of management and, where applicable, those charged with governance include whether: **225.24**

- The response is timely.
- The non-compliance or suspected non-compliance has been adequately investigated.
- Action has been, or is being, taken to rectify, remediate or mitigate the consequences of any non-compliance.
- Action has been, or is being, taken to deter the commission of any non-compliance where it has not yet occurred.
- Appropriate steps have been, or are being, taken to reduce the risk of re-occurrence, for example, additional controls or training.
- The non-compliance or suspected non-compliance has been disclosed to an appropriate authority where appropriate and, if so, whether the disclosure appears adequate.

In light of the response of management and, where applicable, those charged with governance, the professional accountant shall determine if further action is needed in the public interest.   **225.25**

The determination of whether further action is needed, and the nature and extent of it, will depend on various factors, including: **225.26**

- The legal and regulatory framework.
- The urgency of the matter.
- The pervasiveness of the matter throughout the client.
- Whether the professional accountant continues to have confidence in the integrity of management and, where applicable, those charged with governance.
- Whether the non-compliance or suspected non-compliance is likely to recur.
- Whether there is credible evidence of actual or potential substantial harm to the interests of the entity, investors, creditors, employees or the general public.

Examples of circumstances that may cause the professional accountant no longer to have confidence in the integrity of management and, where applicable, those charged with governance include situations where: **225.27**

- The professional accountant suspects or has evidence of their involvement or intended involvement in any non-compliance.
- The professional accountant is aware that they have knowledge of such non-compliance and, contrary to legal or regulatory requirements, have not reported, or authorized the reporting of, the matter to an appropriate authority within a reasonable period.

In determining the need for, and nature and extent of, further action, the professional accountant shall exercise professional judgment and take into account whether a reasonable and informed third party, weighing all the specific facts and circumstances available to the professional accountant at the time, would be likely to conclude that the professional accountant has acted appropriately in the public interest.   **225.28**

Further action by the professional accountant may include: **225.29**

- Disclosing the matter to an appropriate authority even when there is no legal or regulatory requirement to do so.

- Withdrawing from the engagement and the professional relationship where permitted by law or regulation.

225.30 Where the professional accountant determines that withdrawing from the engagement and the professional relationship would be appropriate, doing so would not be a substitute for taking other actions that may be needed to achieve the professional accountant's objectives under this section. In some jurisdictions, however, there may be limitations as to the further actions available to the professional accountant and withdrawal may be the only available course of action.

225.31 Where the professional accountant has withdrawn from the professional relationship pursuant to paragraphs 225.25 and 225.29, the professional accountant shall, on request by the proposed successor accountant, provide all such facts and other information concerning the identified or suspected non-compliance that, in the predecessor accountant's opinion, the proposed successor accountant needs to be aware of before deciding whether to accept the audit appointment. The predecessor accountant shall do so despite paragraph 210.14, unless prohibited by law or regulation. If the proposed successor accountant is unable to communicate with the predecessor accountant, the proposed successor accountant shall take reasonable steps to obtain information about the circumstances of the change of appointment by other means, such as through inquiries of third parties or background investigations of management or those charged with governance.

225.32 As consideration of the matter may involve complex analysis and judgments, the professional accountant may consider consulting internally, obtaining legal advice to understand the professional accountant's options and the professional or legal implications of taking any particular course of action, or consulting on a confidential basis with a regulator or professional body.

Determining Whether to Disclose the Matter to an Appropriate Authority

225.33 Disclosure of the matter to an appropriate authority would be precluded if doing so would be contrary to law or regulation. Otherwise, the purpose of making disclosure is to enable an appropriate authority to cause the matter to be investigated and action to be taken in the public interest.

225.34 The determination of whether to make such a disclosure depends in particular on the nature and extent of the actual or potential harm that is or may be caused by the matter to investors, creditors, employees or the general public. For example, the professional accountant may determine that disclosure of the matter to an appropriate authority is an appropriate course of action if:

- The entity is engaged in bribery (for example, of local or foreign government officials for purposes of securing large contracts).
- The entity is regulated and the matter is of such significance as to threaten its license to operate.
- The entity is listed on a securities exchange and the matter could result in adverse consequences to the fair and orderly market in the entity's securities or pose a systemic risk to the financial markets.
- Products that are harmful to public health or safety would likely be sold by the entity.
- The entity is promoting a scheme to its clients to assist them in evading taxes.

The determination of whether to make such a disclosure will also depend on external factors such as:

- Whether there is an appropriate authority that is able to receive the information, and cause the matter to be investigated and action to be taken. The appropriate authority will depend on the nature of the matter, for example, a securities regulator in the case of fraudulent financial reporting or an environmental protection agency in the case of a breach of environmental laws and regulations.
- Whether there exists robust and credible protection from civil, criminal or professional liability or retaliation afforded by legislation or regulation, such as under whistle-blowing legislation or regulation.
- Whether there are actual or potential threats to the physical safety of the professional accountant or other individuals.

If the professional accountant determines that disclosure of the non-compliance or suspected non-compliance to an appropriate authority is an appropriate course of action in the circumstances, this will not be considered a breach of the duty of confidentiality under Section 140 of this Code. When making such disclosure, the professional accountant shall act in good faith and exercise caution when making statements and assertions. The professional accountant shall also consider whether it is appropriate to inform the client of the professional accountant's intentions before disclosing the matter. **225.35**

In exceptional circumstances, the professional accountant may become aware of actual or intended conduct that the professional accountant has reason to believe would constitute an imminent breach of a law or regulation that would cause substantial harm to investors, creditors, employees or the general public. Having considered whether it would be appropriate to discuss the matter with management or those charged with governance of the entity, the professional accountant shall exercise professional judgment and may immediately disclose the matter to an appropriate authority in order to prevent or mitigate the consequences of such imminent breach of law or regulation. Such disclosure will not be considered a breach of the duty of confidentiality under Section 140 of this Code. **225.36**

Documentation

In relation to an identified or suspected act of non-compliance that falls within the scope of this section, the professional accountant shall, in addition to complying with the documentation requirements under applicable auditing standards, document: **225.37**

- How management and, where applicable, those charged with governance have responded to the matter.
- The courses of action the professional accountant considered, the judgments made and the decisions that were taken, having regard to the reasonable and informed third party perspective.
- How the professional accountant is satisfied that the professional accountant has fulfilled the responsibility set out in paragraph 225.25.

International Standards on Auditing (ISAs), for example, require a professional accountant performing an audit of financial statements to: **225.38**

- Prepare documentation sufficient to enable an understanding of significant matters arising during the audit, the conclusions reached, and significant professional judgments made in reaching those conclusions;
- Document discussions of significant matters with management, those charged with governance, and others, including the nature of the significant matters discussed and when and with whom the discussions took place; and
- Document identified or suspected non-compliance, and the results of discussion with management and, where applicable, those charged with governance and other parties outside the entity.

Professional Services Other Than Audits of Financial Statements

Obtaining an Understanding of the Matter and Addressing It with Management and Those Charged with Governance

225.39   If a professional accountant engaged to provide a professional service other than an audit of financial statements becomes aware of information concerning an instance of non-compliance or suspected non-compliance, the professional accountant shall seek to obtain an understanding of the matter, including the nature of the act and the circumstances in which it has occurred or may be about to occur.

225.40   The professional accountant is expected to apply knowledge, professional judgment and expertise, but is not expected to have a level of understanding of laws and regulations beyond that which is required for the professional service for which the accountant was engaged. Whether an act constitutes actual non-compliance is ultimately a matter to be determined by a court or other appropriate adjudicative body. Depending on the nature and significance of the matter, the professional accountant may consult on a confidential basis with others within the firm, a network firm or a professional body, or with legal counsel.

225.41   If the professional accountant identifies or suspects that non-compliance has occurred or may occur, the professional accountant shall discuss the matter with the appropriate level of management and, if the professional accountant has access to them and where appropriate, those charged with governance.

225.42   Such discussion serves to clarify the professional accountant's understanding of the facts and circumstances relevant to the matter and its potential consequences. The discussion also may prompt management or those charged with governance to investigate the matter.

225.43   The appropriate level of management with whom to discuss the matter is a question of professional judgment. Relevant factors to consider include:

- The nature and circumstances of the matter.
- The individuals actually or potentially involved.
- The likelihood of collusion.
- The potential consequences of the matter.
- Whether that level of management is able to investigate the matter and take appropriate action.

Communicating the Matter to the Entity's External Auditor

225.44   If the professional accountant is performing a non-audit service for an audit client of the firm, or a component of an audit client of the firm, the professional accountant shall communicate the non-compliance or suspected non-compliance within the firm, unless prohibited from doing so by law or regulation. The communication shall be made in accordance with the firm's protocols or procedures or, in the absence of such protocols and procedures, directly to the audit engagement partner.

225.45   If the professional accountant is performing a non-audit service for an audit client of a network firm, or a component of an audit client of a network firm, the professional accountant shall consider whether to communicate the non-compliance or suspected non-compliance to the network firm. Where the communication is made, it shall be made in accordance with the network's protocols or procedures or, in the absence of such protocols and procedures, directly to the audit engagement partner.

225.46   If the professional accountant is performing a non-audit service for a client that is not:

(a)   An audit client of the firm or a network firm; or

(b)   A component of an audit client of the firm or a network firm,

the professional accountant shall consider whether to communicate the non-compliance or suspected non-compliance to the firm that is the client's external auditor, if any.

Factors relevant to considering the communication in accordance with paragraphs 225.45 and 225.46 include: 225.47

- Whether doing so would be contrary to law or regulation.
- Whether there are restrictions about disclosure imposed by a regulatory agency or prosecutor in an ongoing investigation into the non-compliance or suspected non-compliance.
- Whether the purpose of the engagement is to investigate potential non-compliance within the entity to enable it to take appropriate action.
- Whether management or those charged with governance have already informed the entity's external auditor about the matter.
- The likely materiality of the matter to the audit of the client's financial statements or, where the matter relates to a component of a group, its likely materiality to the audit of the group financial statements.

In all cases, the communication is to enable the audit engagement partner to be informed about the non-compliance or suspected non-compliance and to determine whether and, if so, how it should be addressed in accordance with the provisions of this section.   225.48

Considering Whether Further Action Is Needed

The professional accountant shall also consider whether further action is needed in the public interest.   225.49

Whether further action is needed, and the nature and extent of it, will depend on factors such as: 225.50

- The legal and regulatory framework.
- The appropriateness and timeliness of the response of management and, where applicable, those charged with governance.
- The urgency of the matter.
- The involvement of management or those charged with governance in the matter.
- The likelihood of substantial harm to the interests of the client, investors, creditors, employees or the general public.

Further action by the professional accountant may include: 225.51

- Disclosing the matter to an appropriate authority even when there is no legal or regulatory requirement to do so.
- Withdrawing from the engagement and the professional relationship where permitted by law or regulation.

In considering whether to disclose to an appropriate authority, relevant factors to take into account include: 225.52

- Whether doing so would be contrary to law or regulation.
- Whether there are restrictions about disclosure imposed by a regulatory agency or prosecutor in an ongoing investigation into the non-compliance or suspected non-compliance.

- Whether the purpose of the engagement is to investigate potential non-compliance within the entity to enable it to take appropriate action.

225.53   If the professional accountant determines that disclosure of the non-compliance or suspected non-compliance to an appropriate authority is an appropriate course of action in the circumstances, this will not be considered a breach of the duty of confidentiality under Section 140 of this Code. When making such disclosure, the professional accountant shall act in good faith and exercise caution when making statements and assertions. The professional accountant shall also consider whether it is appropriate to inform the client of the professional accountant's intentions before disclosing the matter.

225.54   In exceptional circumstances, the professional accountant may become aware of actual or intended conduct that the professional accountant has reason to believe would constitute an imminent breach of a law or regulation that would cause substantial harm to investors, creditors, employees or the general public. Having considered whether it would be appropriate to discuss the matter with management or those charged with governance of the entity, the professional accountant shall exercise professional judgment and may immediately disclose the matter to an appropriate authority in order to prevent or mitigate the consequences of such imminent breach of law or regulation. Such disclosure will not be considered a breach of the duty of confidentiality under Section 140 of this Code.

225.55   The professional accountant may consider consulting internally, obtaining legal advice to understand the professional or legal implications of taking any particular course of action, or consulting on a confidential basis with a regulator or professional body.

Documentation

225.56   In relation to an identified or suspected act of non-compliance that falls within the scope of this section, the professional accountant is encouraged to document:

- The matter.
- The results of discussion with management and, where applicable, those charged with governance and other parties.
- How management and, where applicable, those charged with governance have responded to the matter.
- The courses of action the professional accountant considered, the judgments made and the decisions that were taken.
- How the professional accountant is satisfied that the professional accountant has fulfilled the responsibility set out in paragraph 225.49.

Section 360

Responding to Non-Compliance with Laws and Regulations

Purpose

A professional accountant in business may encounter or be made aware of non-compliance **360.1** or suspected non-compliance with laws and regulations in the course of carrying out professional activities. The purpose of this section is to set out the professional accountant's responsibilities when encountering such non-compliance or suspected non-compliance, and guide the professional accountant in assessing the implications of the matter and the possible courses of action when responding to it. This section applies regardless of the nature of the employing organization, including whether or not it is a public interest entity.

A professional accountant in business may encounter or be made aware of non-compliance **360.2** or suspected non-compliance with laws and regulations in the course of carrying out professional activities. The purpose of this section is to set out the professional accountant's responsibilities when encountering such non-compliance or suspected non-compliance, and guide the professional accountant in assessing the implications of the matter and the possible courses of action when responding to it. This section applies regardless of the nature of the employing organization, including whether or not it is a public interest entity.

In some jurisdictions, there are legal or regulatory provisions governing how professional **360.3** accountants should address non-compliance or suspected non-compliance which may differ from or go beyond this section. When encountering such non-compliance or suspected non-compliance, the professional accountant has a responsibility to obtain an understanding of those provisions and comply with them, including any requirement to report the matter to an appropriate authority and any prohibition on alerting the relevant party prior to making any disclosure, for example, pursuant to anti-money laundering legislation.

A distinguishing mark of the accountancy profession is its acceptance of the responsibility **360.4** to act in the public interest. When responding to non-compliance or suspected non-compliance, the objectives of the professional accountant are:

(a)   To comply with the fundamental principles of integrity and professional behavior;
(b)   By alerting management or, where appropriate, those charged with governance of the employing organization, to seek to:
  (i)   Enable them to rectify, remediate or mitigate the consequences of the identified or suspected non-compliance; or
  (ii)   Deter the commission of the non-compliance where it has not yet occurred; and
(c)   To take such further action as appropriate in the public interest.

Scope

This section sets out the approach to be taken by a professional accountant who encounters **360.5** or is made aware of non-compliance or suspected non-compliance with:

(a)   Laws and regulations generally recognized to have a direct effect on the determination of material amounts and disclosures in the employing organization's financial statements; and
(b)   Other laws and regulations that do not have a direct effect on the determination of the amounts and disclosures in the employing organization's financial statements, but compliance with which may be fundamental to the operating aspects of the employing

organization's business, to its ability to continue its business, or to avoid material penalties.

360.6 Examples of laws and regulations which this section addresses include those that deal with:

- Fraud, corruption and bribery.
- Money laundering, terrorist financing and proceeds of crime.
- Securities markets and trading.
- Banking and other financial products and services.
- Data protection.
- Tax and pension liabilities and payments.
- Environmental protection.
- Public health and safety.

360.7 Non-compliance may result in fines, litigation or other consequences for the employing organization that may have a material effect on its financial statements. Importantly, such non-compliance may have wider public interest implications in terms of potentially substantial harm to investors, creditors, employees or the general public. For the purposes of this section, an act that causes substantial harm is one that results in serious adverse consequences to any of these parties in financial or non-financial terms. Examples include the perpetration of a fraud resulting in significant financial losses to investors, and breaches of environmental laws and regulations endangering the health or safety of employees or the public.

360.8 A professional accountant who encounters or is made aware of matters that are clearly inconsequential, judged by their nature and their impact, financial or otherwise, on the employing organization, its stakeholders and the general public, is not required to comply with this section with respect to such matters.

360.9 This section does not address:

(a) Personal misconduct unrelated to the business activities of the employing organization; and

(b) Non-compliance other than by the employing organization or those charged with governance, management, or other individuals working for or under the direction of the employing organization.

The professional accountant may nevertheless find the guidance in this section helpful in considering how to respond in these situations.

Responsibilities of the Employing Organization's Management and Those Charged with Governance

360.10 It is the responsibility of the employing organization's management, with the oversight of those charged with governance, to ensure that the employing organization's business activities are conducted in accordance with laws and regulations. It is also the responsibility of management and those charged with governance to identify and address any non-compliance by the employing organization or by an individual charged with governance of the entity, by a member of management, or by other individuals working for or under the direction of the employing organization.

Responsibilities of Professional Accountants in Business

360.11 Many employing organizations have established protocols and procedures (for example, an ethics policy or internal whistle-blowing mechanism) regarding how non-compliance or suspected non-compliance by the employing organization should be raised internally. Such protocols and procedures may allow for matters to be reported anonymously through designated channels. If these protocols and procedures exist within the professional accountant's employing organization, the professional accountant shall consider them in determining how to respond to such non-compliance.

Where a professional accountant becomes aware of a matter to which this section applies, **360.12** the steps that the professional accountant takes to comply with this section shall be taken on a timely basis, having regard to the professional accountant's understanding of the nature of the matter and the potential harm to the interests of the employing organization, investors, creditors, employees or the general public.

Responsibilities of Senior Professional Accountants in Business

Senior professional accountants in business ('senior professional accountants') are directors, **360.13** officers or senior employees able to exert significant influence over, and make decisions regarding, the acquisition, deployment and control of the employing organization's human, financial, technological, physical and intangible resources. Because of their roles, positions and spheres of influence within the employing organization, there is a greater expectation for them to take whatever action is appropriate in the public interest to respond to non-compliance or suspected non-compliance than other professional accountants within the employing organization.

Obtaining an Understanding of the Matter

If, in the course of carrying out professional activities, a senior professional accountant **360.14** becomes aware of information concerning an instance of non-compliance or suspected non-compliance, the professional accountant shall obtain an understanding of the matter, including:

(a)   The nature of the act and the circumstances in which it has occurred or may occur;
(b)   The application of the relevant laws and regulations to the circumstances; and
(c)   The potential consequences to the employing organization, investors, creditors, employees or the wider public.

A senior professional accountant is expected to apply knowledge, professional judgment **360.15** and expertise, but is not expected to have a level of understanding of laws and regulations beyond that which is required for the professional accountant's role within the employing organization. Whether an act constitutes non-compliance is ultimately a matter to be determined by a court or other appropriate adjudicative body. Depending on the nature and significance of the matter, the professional accountant may cause, or take appropriate steps to cause, the matter to be investigated internally. The professional accountant may also consult on a confidential basis with others within the employing organization or a professional body, or with legal counsel.

Addressing the Matter

If the senior professional accountant identifies or suspects that non-compliance has **360.16** occurred or may occur, the professional accountant shall, subject to paragraph 360.11, discuss the matter with the professional accountant's immediate superior, if any, to enable a determination to be made as to how the matter should be addressed. If the professional accountant's immediate superior appears to be involved in the matter, the professional accountant shall discuss the matter with the next higher level of authority within the employing organization.

360.17 The senior professional accountant shall also take appropriate steps to:

    (a) Have the matter communicated to those charged with governance to obtain their concurrence regarding appropriate actions to take to respond to the matter and to enable them to fulfill their responsibilities;

    (b) Comply with applicable laws and regulations, including legal or regulatory provisions governing the reporting of non-compliance or suspected non-compliance to an appropriate authority;

    (c) Have the consequences of the non-compliance or suspected non-compliance rectified, remediated or mitigated;

    (d) Reduce the risk of re-occurrence; and

    (e) Seek to deter the commission of the non-compliance if it has not yet occurred.

360.18 In addition to responding to the matter in accordance with the provisions of this section, the senior professional accountant shall determine whether disclosure of the matter to the employing organization's external auditor, if any, is needed pursuant to the professional accountant's duty or legal obligation to provide all information necessary to enable the auditor to perform the audit.

Determining Whether Further Action Is Needed

360.19 The senior professional accountant shall assess the appropriateness of the response of the professional accountant's superiors, if any, and those charged with governance.

360.20 Relevant factors to consider in assessing the appropriateness of the response of the senior professional accountant's superiors, if any, and those charged with governance include whether:

- The response is timely.
- They have taken or authorized appropriate action to seek to rectify, remediate or mitigate the consequences of the non-compliance, or to avert the non-compliance if it has not yet occurred.
- The matter has been disclosed to an appropriate authority where appropriate and, if so, whether the disclosure appears adequate.

360.21 In light of the response of the senior professional accountant's superiors, if any, and those charged with governance, the professional accountant shall determine if further action is needed in the public interest.

360.22 The determination of whether further action is needed, and the nature and extent of it, will depend on various factors, including:

- The legal and regulatory framework.
- The urgency of the matter.
- The pervasiveness of the matter throughout the employing organization.
- Whether the senior professional accountant continues to have confidence in the integrity of the professional accountant's superiors and those charged with governance.
- Whether the non-compliance or suspected non-compliance is likely to recur.
- Whether there is credible evidence of actual or potential substantial harm to the interests of the employing organization, investors, creditors, employees or the general public.

360.23 Examples of circumstances that may cause the senior professional accountant no longer to have confidence in the integrity of the professional accountant's superiors and those charged with governance include situations where:

- The professional accountant suspects or has evidence of their involvement or intended involvement in any non-compliance.
- Contrary to legal or regulatory requirements, they have not reported the matter, or authorized the matter to be reported, to an appropriate authority within a reasonable period.

In determining the need for, and nature and extent of any further action needed, the senior professional accountant shall exercise professional judgment and take into account whether a reasonable and informed third party, weighing all the specific facts and circumstances available to the professional accountant at the time, would be likely to conclude that the professional accountant has acted appropriately in the public interest. **360.24**

Further action by the professional accountant may include: **360.25**

- Informing the management of the parent entity of the matter if the employing organization is a member of a group.
- Disclosing the matter to an appropriate authority even when there is no legal or regulatory requirement to do so.
- Resigning from the employing organization.

Where the senior professional accountant determines that resigning from the employing organization would be appropriate, doing so would not be a substitute for taking other actions that may be needed to achieve the professional accountant's objectives under this section. In some jurisdictions, however, there may be limitations as to the further actions available to the professional accountant and resignation may be the only available course of action. **360.26**

As consideration of the matter may involve complex analysis and judgments, the senior professional accountant may consider consulting internally, obtaining legal advice to understand the professional accountant's options and the professional or legal implications of taking any particular course of action, or consulting on a confidential basis with a regulator or professional body. **360.27**

Determining Whether to Disclose the Matter to an Appropriate Authority

Disclosure of the matter to an appropriate authority would be precluded if doing so would be contrary to law or regulation. Otherwise, the purpose of making disclosure is to enable an appropriate authority to cause the matter to be investigated and action to be taken in the public interest. **360.28**

The determination of whether to make such a disclosure depends in particular on the nature and extent of the actual or potential harm that is or may be caused by the matter to investors, creditors, employees or the general public. For example, the senior professional accountant may determine that disclosure of the matter to an appropriate authority is an appropriate course of action if: **360.29**

- The employing organization is engaged in bribery (for example, of local or foreign government officials for purposes of securing large contracts).
- The employing organization is a regulated entity and the matter is of such significance as to threaten its license to operate.
- The employing organization is listed on a securities exchange and the matter could result in adverse consequences to the fair and orderly market in the employing organization's securities or pose a systemic risk to the financial markets.
- Products that are harmful to public health or safety would likely be sold by the employing organization.

- The employing organization is promoting a scheme to its clients to assist them in evading taxes.

The determination of whether to make such a disclosure will also depend on external factors such as:

- Whether there is an appropriate authority that is able to receive the information, and cause the matter to be investigated and action to be taken. The appropriate authority will depend upon the nature of the matter, for example, a securities regulator in the case of fraudulent financial reporting or an environmental protection agency in the case of a breach of environmental laws and regulations.
- Whether there exists robust and credible protection from civil, criminal or professional liability or retaliation afforded by legislation or regulation, such as under whistle-blowing legislation or regulation.
- Whether there are actual or potential threats to the physical safety of the professional accountant or other individuals.

360.30 If the senior professional accountant determines that disclosure of the matter to an appropriate authority is an appropriate course of action in the circumstances, this will not be considered a breach of the duty of confidentiality under Section 140 of this Code. When making such disclosure, the professional accountant shall act in good faith and exercise caution when making statements and assertions.

360.31 In exceptional circumstances, the senior professional accountant may become aware of actual or intended conduct that the professional accountant has reason to believe would constitute an imminent breach of a law or regulation that would cause substantial harm to investors, creditors, employees or the general public. Having considered whether it would be appropriate to discuss the matter with management or those charged with governance of the entity, the professional accountant shall exercise professional judgment and may immediately disclose the matter to an appropriate authority in order to prevent or mitigate the consequences of such imminent breach of law or regulation. Such disclosure will not be considered a breach of the duty of confidentiality under Section 140 of this Code.

Documentation

360.32 In relation to an identified or suspected act of non-compliance that falls within the scope of this section, the senior professional accountant is encouraged to have the following matters documented:

- The matter.
- The results of discussions with the professional accountant's superiors, if any, and those charged with governance and other parties.
- How the professional accountant's superiors, if any, and those charged with governance have responded to the matter.
- The courses of action the professional accountant considered, the judgments made and the decisions that were taken.
- How the professional accountant is satisfied that the professional accountant has fulfilled the responsibility set out in paragraph 360.21.

Responsibilities of Professional Accountants Other Than Senior Professional Accountants in Business

360.33 If, in the course of carrying out professional activities, a professional accountant becomes aware of information concerning an instance of non-compliance or suspected non-compliance, the professional accountant shall seek to obtain an understanding of the matter, including the nature of the act and the circumstances in which it has occurred or may occur.

The professional accountant is expected to apply knowledge, professional judgment and expertise, but is not expected to have a level of understanding of laws and regulations beyond that which is required for the professional accountant's role within the employing organization. Whether an act constitutes non-compliance is ultimately a matter to be determined by a court or other appropriate adjudicative body. Depending on the nature and significance of the matter, the professional accountant may consult on a confidential basis with others within the employing organization or a professional body, or with legal counsel.

360.34

If the professional accountant identifies or suspects that non-compliance has occurred or may occur, the professional accountant shall, subject to paragraph 360.11, inform an immediate superior to enable the superior to take appropriate action. If the professional accountant's immediate superior appears to be involved in the matter, the professional accountant shall inform the next higher level of authority within the employing organization.

360.35

In exceptional circumstances, the professional accountant may decide that disclosure of the matter to an appropriate authority is an appropriate course of action. If the professional accountant does so pursuant to paragraph 360.29, this will not be considered a breach of the duty of confidentiality under Section 140 of this Code. When making such disclosure, the professional accountant shall act in good faith and exercise caution when making statements and assertions.

360.36

Documentation

In relation to an identified or suspected act of non-compliance that falls within the scope of this section, the professional accountant is encouraged to have the following matters documented:

360.37

- The matter.
- The results of discussions with the professional accountant's superior, management and, where applicable, those charged with governance and other parties.
- How the professional accountant's superior has responded to the matter.
- The courses of action the professional accountant considered, the judgments made and the decisions that were taken.

Section 100

Introduction and Fundamental Principles

...

Fundamental Principles

[Bullet point (e) in extant paragraph 100.5 will be replaced by bullet point (e) below.]

...

(e)   Professional Behavior – to comply with relevant laws and regulations and avoid any conduct that discredits the profession.

...

Conflicts of Interest

...

Ethical Conflict Resolution

...

[Extant paragraphs 100.23 and 100.24 will be replaced by paragraphs 100.23 and 100.24 below.]

100.23   If a significant conflict cannot be resolved, a professional accountant may consider obtaining professional advice from the relevant professional body or from legal advisors. The professional accountant generally can obtain guidance on ethical issues without breaching the fundamental principle of confidentiality if the matter is discussed with the relevant professional body on an anonymous basis or with a legal advisor under the protection of legal privilege.

100.24   If, after exhausting all relevant possibilities, the ethical conflict remains unresolved, a professional accountant shall, unless prohibited by law, refuse to remain associated with the matter creating the conflict. The professional accountant shall determine whether, in the circumstances, it is appropriate to withdraw from the engagement team or specific assignment, or to resign altogether from the engagement, the firm or the employing organization.

[Paragraph 100.26 below will be added after extant paragraph 100.25.]

100.26   In some cases, all of those charged with governance are involved in managing the entity, for example, a small business where a single owner manages the entity and no one else has a governance role. In these cases, if matters are communicated with person(s) with management responsibilities, and those person(s) also have governance responsibilities, the matters need not be communicated again with those same person(s) in their governance role. The professional accountant or firm shall nonetheless be satisfied that communication with person(s) with management responsibilities adequately informs all of those with whom the professional accountant or firm would otherwise communicate in their governance capacity.

Section 140

Confidentiality

[Extant paragraph 140.7 will be replaced by paragraph 140.7 below.]

As a fundamental principle, confidentiality serves the public interest because it facilitates **140.7** the free flow of information from the professional accountant's client or employing organization to the professional accountant. Nevertheless, the following are circumstances where professional accountants are or may be required to disclose confidential information or when such disclosure may be appropriate:

(a) Disclosure is permitted by law and is authorized by the client or the employer;

(b) Disclosure is required by law, for example:
  (i) Production of documents or other provision of evidence in the course of legal proceedings; or
  (ii) Disclosure to the appropriate public authorities of infringements of the law that come to light; and

(c) There is a professional duty or right to disclose, when not prohibited by law:
  (i) To comply with the quality review of a member body or professional body;
  (ii) To respond to an inquiry or investigation by a member body or regulatory body;
  (iii) To protect the professional interests of a professional accountant in legal proceedings; or
  (iv) To comply with technical and professional standards, including ethical requirements.

Section 150

Professional Behavior

[Extant paragraph 150.1 will be replaced by paragraph 150.1 below.]

150.1 The principle of professional behavior imposes an obligation on all professional accountants to comply with relevant laws and regulations and avoid any conduct that the professional accountant knows or should know may discredit the profession. This includes conduct that a reasonable and informed third party, weighing all the specific facts and circumstances available to the professional accountant at that time, would be likely to conclude adversely affects the good reputation of the profession.

Section 210

Professional Appointment

[Paragraphs 210.1 to 210.4 together with the heading below will replace extant paragraphs 210.1 to 210.5 and the heading above extant paragraph 210.1.]

Client Acceptance and Continuance

Before accepting a new client relationship, a professional accountant in public practice shall determine whether acceptance would create any threats to compliance with the fundamental principles. Potential threats to integrity or professional behavior may be created from, for example, issues associated with the client (its owners, management or activities) that, if known, could threaten compliance with the fundamental principles. These include, for example, client involvement in illegal activities (such as money laundering), dishonesty, questionable financial reporting practices or other unethical behavior. **210.1**

A professional accountant in public practice shall evaluate the significance of any threats and apply safeguards when necessary to eliminate them or reduce them to an acceptable level. **210.2**

Examples of such safeguards include:

- Obtaining knowledge and understanding of the client, its owners, managers and those responsible for its governance and business activities; or
- Securing the client's commitment to address the questionable issues, for example, through improving corporate governance practices or internal controls.

Where it is not possible to reduce the threats to an acceptable level, the professional accountant in public practice shall decline to enter into the client relationship. **210.3**

Potential threats to compliance with the fundamental principles may have been created after acceptance that would have caused the professional accountant to decline the engagement had that information been available earlier. A professional accountant in public practice shall, therefore, periodically review whether to continue with a recurring client engagement. For example, a threat to compliance with the fundamental principles may be created by a client's unethical behavior such as improper earnings management or balance sheet valuations. If a professional accountant in public practice identifies a threat to compliance with the fundamental principles, the professional accountant shall evaluate the significance of the threats and apply safeguards when necessary to eliminate the threat or reduce it to an acceptable level. Where it is not possible to reduce the threat to an acceptable level, the professional accountant in public practice shall consider terminating the client relationship where termination is not prohibited by law or regulation. **210.4**

[Extant paragraphs 210.6 to 210.9 will be renumbered paragraphs 210.5 to 210.8 respectively.]

[Extant paragraphs 210.10 and 210.11 will be replaced by paragraph 210.9 below.]

A professional accountant in public practice shall evaluate the significance of any threats. Safeguards shall be applied when necessary to eliminate any threats or reduce them to an acceptable level. Examples of such safeguards include: **210.9**

- When replying to requests to submit tenders, stating in the tender that, before accepting the engagement, contact with the existing or predecessor accountant will be requested so that inquiries may be made as to whether there are any professional or other reasons why the appointment should not be accepted;

- Asking the predecessor accountant to provide known information on any facts or circumstances that, in the predecessor accountant's opinion, the proposed successor accountant needs to be aware of before deciding whether to accept the engagement. For example, the apparent reasons for the change in appointment may not fully reflect the facts and may indicate disagreements with the predecessor accountant that may influence the decision to accept the appointment; or
- Obtaining necessary information from other sources.

210.10   When the threats cannot be eliminated or reduced to an acceptable level through the application of safeguards, a professional accountant in public practice shall, unless there is satisfaction as to necessary facts by other means, decline the engagement.

[Extant paragraph 210.12 will be renumbered paragraph 210.11.]

[Extant paragraphs 210.13 and 210.14 will be replaced by paragraphs 210.12 and 210.13 below.]

210.12   An existing or predecessor accountant is bound by confidentiality. Whether that professional accountant is permitted or required to discuss the affairs of a client with a proposed accountant will depend on the nature of the engagement and on:

(a)   Whether the client's permission to do so has been obtained; or
(b)   The legal or ethical requirements relating to such communications and disclosure, which may vary by jurisdiction.

Circumstances where the professional accountant is or may be required to disclose confidential information or where such disclosure may otherwise be appropriate are set out in Section 140 of Part A of this Code.

210.13   A professional accountant in public practice will generally need to obtain the client's permission, preferably in writing, to initiate discussion with an existing or predecessor accountant. Once that permission is obtained, the existing or predecessor accountant shall comply with relevant laws and regulations governing such requests. Where the existing or predecessor accountant provides information, it shall be provided honestly and unambiguously. If the proposed accountant is unable to communicate with the existing or predecessor accountant, the proposed accountant shall take reasonable steps to obtain information about any possible threats by other means, such as through inquiries of third parties or background investigations of senior management or those charged with governance of the client.

[Paragraph 210.14 below will be added after paragraph 210.13.]

210.14   In the case of an audit of financial statements, a professional accountant shall request the predecessor accountant to provide known information regarding any facts or other information that, in the predecessor accountant's opinion, the proposed successor accountant needs to be aware of before deciding whether to accept the engagement. Except for the circumstances involving identified or suspected non-compliance with laws and regulations set out in paragraph 225.31:

(a)   If the client consents to the predecessor accountant disclosing any such facts or other information, the predecessor accountant shall provide the information honestly and unambiguously; and

(b) If the client fails or refuses to grant the predecessor accountant permission to discuss the client's affairs with the proposed successor accountant, the predecessor accountant shall disclose this fact to the proposed successor accountant, who shall carefully consider such failure or refusal when determining whether or not to accept the appointment.

Section 270

Custody of Client Assets

[Extant paragraph 270.3 will be replaced by paragraph 270.3 below.]

270.3   As part of client and engagement acceptance procedures for services that may involve the holding of client assets, a professional accountant in public practice shall make appropriate inquiries about the source of such assets and consider legal and regulatory obligations. For example, if the assets were derived from illegal activities, such as money laundering, a threat to compliance with the fundamental principles would be created. In such situations, the professional accountant shall comply with the provisions of section 225.

Effective Date

The changes will be effective on July 15, 2017. Early adoption is permitted.

ICAEW Code of Ethics

Contents

Effective from 1 January 2011. Where guidance relates to projects or engagements commencing prior to that date, previous guidance may be applied up to completion of the project or engagement. Transitional arrangements are available in respect of Independence – Audit and Review Engagements (section 290).

Approach, scope and authority

- **Introduction**
- **Approach**
- **Scope**
- **Authority**
- **Relationship with other ethical requirements**
- **Sources of guidance**

Introduction

1.1 One of the principal objects of the Royal Charter is to maintain a high standard of efficiency and professional conduct by member firms where relevant. These are referred to in the remainder of this Code as professional accountants.

1.2 Professional accountants have a responsibility to take into consideration the public interest (considered in more detail in paragraph 100.1) and to maintain the reputation of the accountancy profession. Personal self-interest must not prevail over those duties. This Code helps professional accountants to meet these obligations by providing them with ethical guidance. Failure to follow this Code may lead to a professional accountant becoming liable to disciplinary action as outlined in the Disciplinary Bye-laws 4, 5, 6 and 6A.

Approach

1.3 Guidance is given in the form of fundamental principles and illustrations of how they are to be applied in specific situations. These are available at www.icaew.com/ethics. The fundamental principles are drawn from the duties owed by professional accountants, whether in practice or not, and from the requirements of the Royal Charter. They are framed in broad and general terms and constitute basic requirements of professional behaviour. The illustrations provide guidance on what is expected of professional accountants in relation to particular situations that commonly arise either in practice or in business. The value of this principles-based approach is that it avoids excessive legalism by not having to anticipate every contingency, whilst at the same time being helpful in giving examples of problem situations. In some instances, prohibitions or mandatory actions arise from the analysis of threats: these are considered further in paragraph 100.12.

Scope

1.4 Professional accountants shall follow the guidance contained in the fundamental principles in all of their professional and business activities whether carried out with or without reward and in other circumstances where to fail to do so would bring discredit to the profession. This Code also includes a number of specific requirements, which are shown by use of the word 'shall'. This means that a professional accountant shall follow the requirements, including prohibitions or mandatory actions, where circumstances are the same as, or analogous to, those addressed by those requirements. Failure to follow such guidance may be justified in those rare circumstances where to follow a precise prohibition or mandated action would result in failure to adhere to the fundamental principles.

For convenience, the illustrations in this Code are grouped into parts applicable principally to professional accountants working in public practice, business and insolvency respectively, but professional accountants may find any of them of use in relevant circumstances.   **1.5**

Professional accountants shall be guided not merely by the terms but also by the spirit of this Code and the fact that particular conduct does not appear among a list of examples does not prevent it amounting to misconduct.   **1.6**

Professional accountants shall ensure that work for which they are responsible, which is undertaken by others on their behalf, is carried out in accordance with the requirements of this Code.   **1.7**

Member firms are reminded that this Code applies to their employees, whether members or not, and that they are responsible for applying this requirement.   **1.8**

Certain areas of work are reserved by statute to professional accountants who are in practice, whether or not with other persons, namely investment business, insolvency and audit. In these areas professional accountants may be subject to rules laid down by laws and regulation, breach of which can give rise to disciplinary proceedings against the professional accountant.   **1.9**

If the advice in this Code conflicts with laws and regulations, professional accountants are bound to follow the laws and regulations.   **1.10**

Professional accountants working overseas shall comply with this Code unless to do so would breach local laws and regulations.   **1.11**

Authority

In determining whether or not a complaint is proved, the Investigation and Disciplinary Committees may have regard to any code of practice, ethical or technical, and to any regulations affecting professional accountants, laid down or approved by the ICAEW's Council.   **1.12**

Paragraph 100.2 notes that safeguards are required to be put into place to eliminate or reduce the threats to an acceptable level. In the event of a complaint, the Investigation and Disciplinary Committees will consider the matter, including whether a reasonable and informed third party would conclude, weighing all the specific facts and circumstances available to the professional accountant at that time, that compliance with the fundamental principles is compromised.   **1.13**

Relationship with other ethical requirements

Except as noted below, this Code has been derived from the International Ethics Standards Board of Accountants (IESBA) Code of Ethics issued in July 2009 by the International Federation of Accountants. Accordingly, compliance with the remainder of this Code will ensure compliance with the principles of the IESBA   **1.14**

Code. Paragraph numbering in the rest of this Code replicates that used in the IESBA Code of Ethics, except in respect of:

- Sections 221, 241 and Part D which have no direct equivalent in the IESBA Code of Ethics;
- Text framed in grey in parts A, B and C is where ICAEW's Council considers additional discussion and/or requirements to be useful or necessary.
- The fact that wording is or is not framed in grey does not indicate any difference in the degree of importance that should be attached to it.
- A direct link has been retained to paragraph numbering in the IESBA Code of Ethics. However, as a result of the additional discussion and requirements noted above, and deletion of material that is not applicable to the professional accountants of the ICAEW, the paragraph referencing in this Code is not necessarily consecutive.

1.15   In accordance with UK legislation, ICAEW has adopted, as regards auditor audit engagements in accordance with ISAs (UK and Ireland), professional accountants shall comply with the requirements of the APB's Ethical Standards for Auditors, including Provisions Available for Small Entities (ES-PASE). For other audit and assurance engagements ICAEW's Code may apply (see 1.17 below).

1.16   The APB has stated, in ISA (UK and Ireland) 200, that it is not aware of any significant instances where the relevant parts of IESBA Code of Ethics are more restrictive than the APB's Ethical Standards.

1.17   The independence requirements to be adopted for different types of assurance engagement, are set out below:

Type of assurance engagement	Independence requirements to be followed
Audit engagements in accordance with ISAs (UK and Ireland)	APB's Ethical Standards for Auditors
Audit engagements performed in accordance with other standards	Section 290 of this Code or if more convenient to apply, the independence requirements of the APB's Ethical Standards for Auditors.
Review engagements (see appendix to section 290)	Section 290 of this Code or if more convenient to apply, the independence requirements of the APB's Ethical Standards for Auditors.
Other types of assurance engagements	Section 291 of this Code.

1.18   Note that the Statements of Investment Circular Reporting Standards (SIRS), issued by the APB require compliance with the APB's Ethical Standard for Reporting Accountants (ESRA). Accordingly, any professional accountant in public practice issuing a report that states that the work has been carried out in accordance with the SIRS will need to comply with the independence requirements of the ESRA.

Sources of guidance

1.19   Professional accountants who are in doubt as to their ethical position may seek advice from the following sources, available to all members of ICAEW:

- ICAEW's Technical Advisory Services by email: ethics@icaew.com or phone +44 (0)1908 248250. This service is confidential and the advisors are free from the duty to report professional misconduct within ICAEW. Further information on the Technical Advisory Services can be found at www.icaew.com/ethicsadvice, along with helpsheets and answers to a number of frequently asked questions.
- The Support Members Scheme. This is wider in scope than the Technical Advisory Services. The Support Members Scheme is run by volunteer members of the ICAEW from a wide range of backgrounds. It is a confidential, free service exempt from the duty to report misconduct and provides advice and help to members in difficulties. A member can contact the Support Members Scheme by phone on +44 (0) 800 917 3526.

Seeking advice from the Technical Advisory Services does not discharge a professional accountant's duty to report misconduct, including their own misconduct (see 'The duty to report misconduct'). **1.20**

A professional accountant is encouraged to consider taking legal advice to resolve issues arising from the application of laws and regulations to particular situations relating to confidentiality, disclosure, privilege, self-incrimination and other areas. **1.21**

Additional information on ethics, including case studies is available at www. icaew.com/ethics. These case studies provide practical guidance for resolving ethical dilemmas on topics such as conflicts of interest, confidentiality and questionable accounting and business practices. **1.22**

Code of Ethics A

Effective from 1st January 2011. This section establishes the fundamental principles of professional ethics for professional accountants and provides a conceptual framework that professional accountants can follow.

Except as noted below, this Code has been derived from the International Ethics Standards Board of Accountants' (IESBA) Code of Ethics issued in July 2009 by the International Federation of Accountants. Accordingly, compliance with the remainder of this Code will ensure compliance with the principles of the IESBA Code. Paragraph numbering in the rest of this Code replicates that used in the IESBA Code of Ethics, except in respect of Sections 221, 241 and Part D which have no direct equivalent in the IESBA Code of Ethics.

Wording replicates the IESBA Code of Ethics.

Text framed in grey is where ICAEW's Council considers additional discussion and/ or requirements to be useful or necessary.

The fact that wording is or is not framed in grey does not indicate any difference in the degree of importance that should be attached to it.

- **100 Introduction and fundamental principles**
  - ○ Fundamental principles
  - ○ Conceptual framework approach
  - ○ Threats and safeguards
  - ○ Ethical conflict resolution
- **110 Integrity**
- **120 Objectivity**
- **130 Professional competence and due care**
- **140 Confidentiality**
  - ○ The principle of confidentiality
  - ○ Disclosure of confidential information
- **150 Professional behaviour**
- **Appendix**

100 Introduction and fundamental principles

100.1   A distinguishing mark of the accountancy profession is its acceptance of the responsibility to act in the public interest.

Acting in the public interest involves having regard to the legitimate interests of clients, government, financial institutions, employers, employees, investors, the business and financial community and others who rely upon the objectivity and integrity of the accounting profession to support the propriety and orderly functioning of commerce. This reliance imposes a public interest responsibility on the profession. Professional accountants shall take into consideration the public interest and reasonable and informed public perception in deciding whether to accept or continue with an engagement or appointment, bearing in mind that the level of the public interest will be greater in larger entities and entities which are in the public eye.

Therefore, a professional accountant's responsibility is not exclusively to satisfy the needs of an individual client or employer. In acting in the public interest, a professional accountant shall observe and comply with this Code. If a professional accountant is prohibited from complying with certain parts of this Code by law or regulation, the professional accountant shall comply with all other parts of this Code.

This Code contains four parts. Part A establishes the fundamental principles of professional ethics for professional accountants and provides a conceptual framework that professional accountants shall apply to: **100.2**

- Identify threats to compliance with the fundamental principles;
- Evaluate the significance of the threats identified; and
- Apply safeguards, when necessary, to eliminate the threats or reduce them to an acceptable level. Safeguards are necessary when the professional accountant determines that the threats are not at a level at which a reasonable and informed third party would be likely to conclude, weighing all the specific facts and circumstances available to the professional accountant at that time, that compliance with the fundamental principles is not compromised.

A professional accountant shall use professional judgment in applying this conceptual framework.

Where a professional accountant decides to accept or continue an engagement, appointment, task or employment in a situation where a significant threat to the fundamental principles has been identified, the professional accountant is expected to be able to demonstrate that the availability and effectiveness of safeguards has been considered and that it was reasonable to conclude that those safeguards will adequately preserve their compliance with the fundamental principles. It may be useful to document the reasoning and other evidence which supports the evaluation of threats and safeguards to such an extent that it enables a reasonable and informed third party to conclude that the decisions are acceptable.

Parts B and C describe how the conceptual framework applies in certain situations. They provide examples of safeguards that may be appropriate to address threats to compliance with the fundamental principles. They also describe situations where safeguards are not available to address the threats, and consequently, the circumstance or relationship creating the threats shall be avoided. Part B applies to professional accountants in public practice. Part C applies to professional accountants in business. Professional accountants in public practice may also find Part C relevant to their particular circumstances. **100.3**

Part D deals with professional accountants undertaking insolvency work.

The use of the word "shall" in this Code imposes a requirement on the professional accountant or firm to comply with the specific provision in which "shall" has been used. Compliance is required unless an exception is permitted by this Code. (See Code of Ethics 1.4) **100.4**

Fundamental principles

A professional accountant shall comply with the following fundamental principles: **100.5**

- **Integrity** – to be straightforward and honest in all professional and business relationships.
- **Objectivity** – to not allow bias, conflict of interest or undue influence of others to override professional or business judgments.
- **Professional competence and due care** – to maintain professional knowledge and skill at the level required to ensure that a client or employer receives competent

professional services based on current developments in practice, legislation and techniques and act diligently and in accordance with applicable technical and professional standards.

- **Confidentiality** – to respect the confidentiality of information acquired as a result of professional and business relationships and, therefore, not disclose any such information to third parties without proper and specific authority, unless there is a legal or professional right or duty to disclose, nor use the information for the personal advantage of the professional accountant or third parties.
- **Professional behaviour** – to comply with relevant laws and regulations and avoid any action that discredits the profession.

Each of these fundamental principles is discussed in more detail in sections 110-150.

Conceptual framework approach

100.6 The circumstances in which professional accountants operate may create specific threats to compliance with the fundamental principles. It is impossible to define every situation that creates threats to compliance with the fundamental principles and specify the appropriate action. In addition, the nature of engagements and work assignments may differ and, consequently, different threats may be created, requiring the application of different safeguards. Therefore, this Code establishes a conceptual framework that requires a professional accountant to identify, evaluate, and address threats to compliance with the fundamental principles. The conceptual framework approach assists professional accountants in complying with the ethical requirements of this Code and meeting their responsibility to act in the public interest. It accommodates many variations in circumstances that create threats to compliance with the fundamental principles and can deter a professional accountant from concluding that a situation is permitted if it is not specifically prohibited.

100.7 When a professional accountant identifies threats to compliance with the fundamental principles and, based on an evaluation of those threats, determines that they are not at an acceptable level, the professional accountant shall determine whether appropriate safeguards are available and can be applied to eliminate the threats or reduce them to an acceptable level. In making that determination, the professional accountant shall exercise professional judgment and take into account whether a reasonable and informed third party, weighing all the specific facts and circumstances available to the professional accountant at the time, would be likely to conclude that the threats would be eliminated or reduced to an acceptable level by the application of the safeguards, such that compliance with the fundamental principles is not compromised.

100.8 A professional accountant shall evaluate any threats to compliance with the fundamental principles when the professional accountant knows, or could reasonably be expected to know, of circumstances or relationships that may compromise compliance with the fundamental principles.

100.9 A professional accountant shall take qualitative as well as quantitative factors into account when evaluating the significance of a threat. When applying the conceptual framework, a professional accountant may encounter situations in which threats cannot be eliminated or reduced to an acceptable level, either because the threat is too significant or because appropriate safeguards are not available or cannot be applied. In such situations, the professional accountant shall decline or discontinue the specific professional service involved or, when necessary, resign from the engagement (in the case of a professional accountant in public practice) or the employing organisation (in the case of a professional accountant in business).

A professional accountant may inadvertently violate a provision of this Code. **100.10**
Depending on the nature and significance of the matter, such an inadvertent violation may be deemed not to compromise compliance with the fundamental principles
provided, once the violation is discovered, the violation is corrected promptly and
any necessary safeguards are applied.

When a professional accountant encounters unusual circumstances in which the **100.11**
application of a specific requirement of the Code would result in a disproportionate
outcome or an outcome that may not be in the public interest, it is recommended that
the professional accountant consult with ICAEW (see Sources of Guidance in section
1 of this Code) or the relevant regulator.

Threats may be created by a broad range of relationships and circumstances. When a **100.12**
relationship or circumstance creates a threat, such a threat could compromise, or
could be perceived to compromise, a professional accountant's compliance with the
fundamental principles. A circumstance or relationship may create more than one
threat, and a threat may affect compliance with more than one fundamental principle. Threats fall into one or more of the following categories:

- Self-interest threat – the threat that a financial or other interest will inappropriately influence the professional accountant's judgment or behaviour;
- Self-review threat – the threat that a professional accountant will not appropriately evaluate the results of a previous judgment made or service performed
  by the professional accountant, or by another individual within the professional
  accountant's firm or employing organisation, on which the accountant will rely
  when forming a judgment as part of providing a current service;
- Advocacy threat – the threat that a professional accountant will promote a
  client's or employer's position to the point that the professional accountant's
  objectivity is compromised;
- Familiarity threat – the threat that due to a long or close relationship with a
  client or employer, a professional accountant will be too sympathetic to their
  interests or too accepting of their work; and
- Intimidation threat – the threat that a professional accountant will be deterred
  from acting objectively because of actual or perceived pressures, including
  attempts to exercise undue influence over the professional accountant.

Parts B and C of this Code explain how these categories of threats may be created for
professional accountants in public practice and professional accountants in business,
respectively. Professional accountants in public practice may also find Part C relevant to their particular circumstances.

Code of Ethics Part D deals with professional accountants undertaking insolvency
work.

Professional accountants shall note that each of the categories of threat discussed
above may arise in relation to the professional accountant's own person or in relation to connected persons such as members of their family or partners or persons
who are close to the professional accountants for some other reason, for instance by
reason of a past or present association, obligation or indebtedness.

Threats and safeguards

Safeguards are actions or other measures that may eliminate threats or reduce them **100.13**
to an acceptable level. They fall into two broad categories:

- Safeguards created by the profession, legislation or regulation; and

●   Safeguards in the work environment.

100.14   Safeguards created by the profession, legislation or regulation include:

●   Educational, training and experience requirements for entry into the profession.
●   Continuing professional development requirements.
●   Corporate governance regulations.
●   Professional standards.
●   Professional or regulatory monitoring and disciplinary procedures.
●   External review by a legally empowered third party of the reports, returns, communications or information produced by a professional accountant.

100.15   Parts B and C of this Code discuss safeguards in the work environment for professional accountants in public practice and professional accountants in business, respectively.

100.16   Certain safeguards may increase the likelihood of identifying or deterring unethical behaviour. Such safeguards, which may be created by the accounting profession, legislation, regulation, or an employing organisation, include:

●   Effective, well-publicised complaint systems operated by the employing organisation, the profession or a regulator, which enable colleagues, employers and members of the public to draw attention to unprofessional or unethical behaviour.
●   An explicitly stated duty to report breaches of ethical requirements.

Ethical conflict resolution

100.17   A professional accountant may be required to resolve a conflict in complying with the fundamental principles.

100.18   When initiating either a formal or informal conflict resolution process, the following factors, either individually or together with other factors, may be relevant to the resolution process:

●   Relevant facts;
●   Relevant parties;
●   Ethical issues involved;
●   Fundamental principles related to the matter in question;
●   Established internal procedures; and
●   Alternative courses of action.

Having considered the relevant factors, a professional accountant shall determine the appropriate course of action, weighing the consequences of each possible course of action. If the matter remains unresolved, the professional accountant may wish to consult with other appropriate persons within the firm or employing organisation for help in obtaining resolution.

It will generally be preferable for the ethical conflict to be resolved within the employing organisation before consulting individuals outside the employing organisation.

100.19   Where a matter involves a conflict with, or within, an organisation, a professional accountant shall determine whether to consult with those charged with governance of the organisation, such as the board of directors or the audit committee.

It may be in the best interests of the professional accountant to document the sub- **100.20** stance of the issue, the details of any discussions held, and the decisions made concerning that issue.

If a significant conflict cannot be resolved, a professional accountant may consider **100.21** obtaining professional advice from ICAEW or from legal advisors. The professional accountant generally can obtain guidance on ethical issues without breaching the fundamental principle of confidentiality if the matter is discussed with ICAEW's ethics helpline or with a legal advisor under the protection of legal privilege. Instances in which the professional accountant may consider obtaining legal advice vary. For example, a professional accountant may have encountered a fraud, the reporting of which could breach the professional accountant's responsibility to respect confidentiality. The professional accountant may consider obtaining legal advice in that instance to determine whether there is a requirement to report.

Further information on sources of guidance is available in section 1.

If, after exhausting all relevant possibilities, the ethical conflict remains unresolved, a **100.22** professional accountant shall, where possible, refuse to remain associated with the matter creating the conflict. The professional accountant shall determine whether, in the circumstances, it is appropriate to withdraw from the engagement team or specific assignment, or to resign altogether from the engagement, the firm or the employing organisation.

More detailed guidance on the ethical conflict resolution process is available in the Appendix to Part A.

110 Integrity

The principle of integrity imposes an obligation on all professional accountants to be **110.1** straightforward and honest in all professional and business relationships. Integrity also implies fair dealing and truthfulness.

It follows that a professional accountant's advice and work must be uncorrupted by self-interest and not be influenced by the interests of other parties.

A professional accountant shall not knowingly be associated with reports, returns, **110.2** communications or other information where the professional accountant believes that the information:

- Contains a materially false or misleading statement;
- Contains statements or information furnished recklessly; or
- Omits or obscures information required to be included where such omission or obscurity would be misleading.

When a professional accountant becomes aware that the accountant has been associated with such information, the accountant shall take steps to be disassociated from that information.

A professional accountant will be deemed not to be in breach of paragraph 110.2 if **110.3** the professional accountant provides a modified report in respect of a matter contained in paragraph 110.2.

Further discussion on integrity, which is not part of the Code requirements, is available at www.icaew.com/ethics.

120 Objectivity

120.1   The principle of objectivity imposes an obligation on all professional accountants not to compromise their professional or business judgment because of bias, conflict of interest or the undue influence of others.

Objectivity is the state of mind which has regard to all considerations relevant to the task in hand but no other.

120.2   A professional accountant may be exposed to situations that may impair objectivity. It is impracticable to define and prescribe all such situations. A professional accountant shall not perform a professional service if a circumstance or relationship biases or unduly influences the accountant's professional judgment with respect to that service.

130 Professional competence and due care

130.1   The principle of professional competence and due care imposes the following obligations on all professional accountants:

- To maintain professional knowledge and skill at the level required to ensure that clients or employers receive competent professional service; and
- To act diligently in accordance with applicable technical and professional standards when providing professional services.

130.2   Competent professional service requires the exercise of sound judgment in applying professional knowledge and skill in the performance of such service. Professional competence may be divided into two separate phases:

- Attainment of professional competence; and
- Maintenance of professional competence.

130.3   The maintenance of professional competence requires a continuing awareness and an understanding of relevant technical, professional and business developments. Continuing professional development enables a professional accountant to develop and maintain the capabilities to perform competently within the professional environment.

Further guidance on continuing professional development is available at www.icaew. com/cpd and in the Regulations relating to learning and professional development which are available at www.icaew.com/regulations.

130.4   Diligence encompasses the responsibility to act in accordance with the requirements of an assignment, carefully, thoroughly and on a timely basis.

130.5   A professional accountant shall take reasonable steps to ensure that those working under the professional accountant's authority in a professional capacity have appropriate training and supervision.

130.6   Where appropriate, a professional accountant shall make clients, employers or other users of the accountant's professional services aware of the limitations inherent in the services.

140 Confidentiality

The principle of confidentiality

The principle of confidentiality is not only to keep information confidential, but also to take all reasonable steps to preserve confidentiality. Whether information is confidential or not will depend on its nature. A safe and proper approach for professional accountants to adopt is to assume that all unpublished information about a client's or employer's affairs, however gained, is confidential. Some clients or employers may regard the mere fact of their relationship with a professional accountant as being confidential. **140.0**

The principle of confidentiality imposes an obligation on all professional accountants to refrain from: **140.1**

- Disclosing outside the firm or employing organisation confidential information acquired as a result of professional and business relationships without proper and specific authority or unless there is a legal or professional right or duty to disclose; and
- Using confidential information acquired as a result of professional and business relationships to their personal advantage or the advantage of third parties.

Professional accountants in public practice must not disclose confidential information to a client even though the information is relevant to an engagement for, or would be beneficial to, that client.

Where professional accountants in public practice have confidential information which affects an assurance report, or other report which requires a professional accountant to state their opinion, the professional accountant cannot provide an opinion which they already know, from whatever source, to be untrue. If the professional accountant in public practice is to continue the engagement, the professional accountant must resolve this disparity. In order to do so, the professional accountant is entitled to apply normal procedures and to make such enquiries in order to enable the professional accountant to obtain that same information but from another source. Under no circumstances, however, shall there be any disclosure of confidential information outside the firm.

A professional accountant shall maintain confidentiality, including in a social environment, being alert to the possibility of inadvertent disclosure, particularly to a close business associate or a close or immediate family member. **140.2**

A professional accountant shall maintain confidentiality of information disclosed by a prospective client or employer. **140.3**

This requirement extends not only to clients, past and present, but also to third parties from or about whom information has been received in confidence. The principle of confidentiality clearly does not prevent an employee from using the skills acquired while working with a former employer in undertaking a new role with a different organisation. Professional accountants shall neither use nor appear to use special knowledge which could only have been acquired with access to confidential information. It is a matter of judgement as to the dividing line which separates experience gained from special knowledge acquired.

A professional accountant shall maintain confidentiality of information within the firm or employing organisation. **140.4**

140.5   A professional accountant shall take reasonable steps to ensure that staff under the professional accountant's control and persons from whom advice and assistance is obtained respect the professional accountant's duty of confidentiality.

Member firms shall ensure that all who work on their behalf are trained in, and understand:

- The importance of confidentiality;
- The importance of identifying any conflicts of interest and confidentiality issues between clients, or between themselves or the firm and a client, in relation to a current or prospective engagement; and
- The procedures the firm has in place for the recognition and consideration of possible conflicts of interest and confidentiality issues.

140.6   The need to comply with the principle of confidentiality continues even after the end of relationships between a professional accountant and a client or employer. When a professional accountant changes employment or acquires a new client, the professional accountant is entitled to use prior experience. The professional accountant shall not, however, use or disclose any confidential information either acquired or received as a result of a professional or business relationship.

140.6a   Detailed guidance on conflicts of interest, including situations where such conflicts may result in threats (or perceived threats) to preservation of confidentiality, are included in section 220.

Disclosure of confidential information

140.7   The following are circumstances where professional accountants are or may be required to disclose confidential information or when such disclosure may be appropriate:

- Disclosure is permitted by law and is authorised by the client or the employer;
- Disclosure is required by law, for example:
  - Production of documents or other provision of evidence in the course of legal proceedings; or
  - Disclosure to the appropriate public authorities of infringements of the law that come to light; and

  Where required by law or regulations to disclose confidential information, for example as a result of anti-money laundering or anti-terrorist legislation, or in connection with legal proceedings involving either themselves or their employing organisation, professional accountants shall always disclose that information in compliance with relevant legal requirements. Professional accountants shall take care when communicating relevant facts to others relating to known or suspected money laundering or terrorist activities. Under the UK Money Laundering Regulations 2007, the Terrorism Act 2000 and the Terrorism Act 2006, it is a criminal offence to 'tip off' a money launderer or terrorist. For further discussion, please refer to the money laundering legislation and guidance available at www.icaew.com/moneylaundering.
- There is a professional duty or right to disclose, when not prohibited by law:
  - To comply with the quality review of ICAEW or professional regulator or professional body;
  - To respond to an inquiry or investigation by ICAEW a regulatory body or regulatory body;
  - To protect the professional interests of a professional accountant in legal proceedings; or
  - To comply with technical standards and ethics requirements.

A professional accountant may disclose confidential information to third parties, when not obliged to do so by law or regulations, if the disclosure can be justified in the public interest and is not contrary to laws and regulations. Before making such disclosure, professional accountants are encouraged to obtain legal or professional advice regarding their duties and obligations in the context of their professional and business relationships, and possible protection under the UK Public Interest Disclosure Act 1998. Further guidance on disclosure in the public interest is available in *Professional conduct and disclosure in relation to defaults or unlawful acts*.

Confidentiality and privilege is a complex area. For example, information which is confidential may not be privileged and, therefore, may be admissible in court proceedings. Privilege is a difficult area, quite distinct from confidentiality, and it is recommended that further advice be taken if a professional accountant is in doubt as to the action to be taken.

Guidance on money laundering reporting requirements in privileged circumstances is included in Technical Release 02/06, available at www.icaew.com/technical.

In deciding whether to disclose confidential information, relevant factors to consider include: **140.8**

- Whether the interests of all parties, including third parties whose interests may be affected, could be harmed if the client or employer consents to the disclosure of information by the professional accountant;
- Whether all the relevant information is known and substantiated, to the extent it is practicable; when the situation involves unsubstantiated facts, incomplete information or unsubstantiated conclusions, professional judgment shall be used in determining the type of disclosure to be made, if any;
- The type of communication that is expected and to whom it is addressed; and
- Whether the parties to whom the communication is addressed are appropriate recipients.
- Whether or not the information is privileged, either under Legal Professional Privilege or in Privileged Circumstances under section 330 of the UK Proceeds of Crime Act 2002 (see Technical Release 02/06); and
- The legal and regulatory obligations and the possible implications of disclosure for the professional accountant.

The paragraphs above deal with professional accountants' treatment of confidential information belonging to a client or employer. There is another context in which professional accountants will be given or may obtain information which they must handle sensitively. Professional accountants may be approached in confidence with information about alleged illegal or improper actions on the part of employees or management of the business for which the informant works or with which the informant has some other relationship. Professional accountants may receive that information because of being trusted by the informant, or may receive it in connection with work their firm is carrying out for the informant's employer. Whatever the circumstances in which the information comes to professional accountants, the professional accountants shall: **140.9**

- Advise informants to pass the information to their employer through the medium of the employer's own internal procedures (if they exist);
- Use their best endeavours to protect the identity of the informant, taking care not to mislead the informant as to the extent to which this can be done, and shall only cause the employer to be made aware of the informant's identity where this cannot be avoided; and
- Take care in determining the quality of the information and how best to use it, if at all.

140.10   For a more detailed explanation of the operation of the provisions of the UK Public Interest Disclosure Act 1998, professional accountants are referred to ICAEW Technical Releases 16/99 'Receipt of Information in Confidence by Auditors' and 17/99 'Public Interest Disclosure Act 1998' (www.icaew.com/technicalreleases).

150 Professional behaviour

150.1   The principle of professional behaviour imposes an obligation on all professional accountants to comply with relevant laws and regulations and avoid any action that the professional accountant knows or should know may discredit the profession. This includes actions that a reasonable and informed third party, weighing all the specific facts and circumstances available to the professional accountant at that time, would be likely to conclude adversely affects the good reputation of the profession.

Professional accountants shall conduct themselves with courtesy and consideration towards all with whom they come into contact when performing their work.

150.2   In marketing and promoting themselves and their work, professional accountants shall not bring the profession into disrepute. Professional accountants shall be honest and truthful and not:

- Make exaggerated claims for the services they are able to offer, the qualifications they possess, or experience they have gained; or
- Make disparaging references or unsubstantiated comparisons to the work of others.

Appendix to Part A – further guidance on ethical conflict resolution

Further guidance on the matters discussed in paragraph 100.18:

(a) Relevant facts

Seek to establish the known facts of the situation and any limitations. It may not be possible to obtain all relevant facts but the professional accountant may be able to obtain more background information to address the limitations by:

- Referring to the organisation's policy, procedures, code of conduct and previous history;
- Discussing the matter with parties internal and external to the organisation. For example trusted managers and colleagues.

(b) Relevant parties

Consider affected parties ranging from individuals, organisations to society. The parties to be considered include, but are not limited to, employees, employers, shareholders, consumers/clients, investors, government and the community at large.

(c) Ethical issues involved

Analyse the professional, organisational and personal ethical issues of the matter.

(d) Fundamental principles related to the matter in question

Refer to the guidance contained in this Code in order to establish which fundamental principles are affected by the situation.

(e) Established internal procedures

Refer to the employing organisation's internal procedures and also consider which parties ought to be involved in the ethical conflict resolution process, in what role and at what stage. For example, the professional accountant needs to consider when it would be appropriate to refer to external sources for help, such as ICAEW (see paragraphs 1.19 to 1.22 of this Code for sources of advice and guidance).

Professional accountants may find it useful to discuss the ethical conflict issue within the organisation with the following parties:

- Immediate superior;
- The next level of management;
- A corporate governance body, for example, the audit committee;
- Other departments in the organisation which include, but are not limited to, legal, audit and human resources departments.

(f) Alternative courses of action

In considering courses of action, the professional accountant is encouraged to consider the following:

When evaluating the suggested course of action, a professional accountant is expected to test the adequacy of the suggested course of action by considering the following:

- The organisation's policies, procedures and guidelines;
- Applicable laws and regulations;
- Universal values and principles adopted by society;
- Long term and short term consequences;
- Symbolic consequences;
- Private and public consequences.

When evaluating the suggested course of action, a professional accountant is expected to test the adequacy of the suggested course of action by considering the following:

- Have all consequences associated with the course of action been discussed and evaluated?
- Is there any reason why the suggested course of action will not stand the test of time?
- Would a similar course of action be undertaken in a similar situation?
- Would the suggested course of action stand scrutiny from peers, family and friends?

Code of Ethics B

Effective from 1st January 2011. This part of the Code describes how the conceptual framework contained in General Application applies in certain situations to professional accountants in public practice.

Except as noted below, this Code has been derived from the International Ethics Standards Board of Accountants' (IESBA) Code of Ethics issued in July 2009 by the International Federation of Accountants. Accordingly, compliance with the remainder of this Code will ensure compliance with the principles of the IESBA Code. Paragraph numbering in the rest of this Code replicates that used in the IESBA Code of Ethics, except in respect of Sections 221, 241 and Part D which have no direct equivalent in the IESBA Code of Ethics.

Wording replicates the IESBA Code of Ethics.

Text framed in grey is where ICAEW's Council considers additional discussion and/ or requirements to be useful or necessary.

The fact that wording is or is not framed in grey does not indicate any difference in the degree of importance that should be attached to it.

- **200 Introduction**
  - ○ Fundamental principles
  - ○ Threats and safeguards
- **210 Professional appointment**
  - ○ Client acceptance
  - ○ Engagement acceptance
  - ○ Changes in a professional appointment
  - ○ Transfer of records
- **Section 210 Appendix – Changes in professional appointment procedures**
  - ○ Prospective accountants
  - ○ Existing accountants
  - ○ Further information
- **220 Conflicts of interest**
- **221 Corporate finance advice**
  - ○ Introduction
  - ○ Categories of corporate finance activity
  - ○ General principles applicable to all professional accountants
  - ○ General corporate cinance advice applicable to professional accountants in public practice
  - ○ Takeovers and mergers
  - ○ Underwriting and marketing of shares
  - ○ Sponsors, nominated advisers and corporate advisers
  - ○ Appendix 1 to Section 221 – Corporate finance advice
  - ○ Appendix 2 to Section 221 – Corporate finance advice
  - ○ Appendix 3 to Section 221 – Corporate Finance Advice
- **230 Second opinions**

200 Introduction

200.1　This Part of the Code describes how the conceptual framework contained in Part A applies in certain situations to professional accountants in public practice. This Part does not describe all of the circumstances and relationships that could be encountered by a professional accountant in public practice that create or may create threats to compliance with the fundamental principles. Therefore, the professional accountant in public practice is encouraged to be alert for such circumstances and relationships.

A professional accountant in public practice shall not knowingly engage in any business, occupation, or activity that impairs or might impair integrity, objectivity or the good reputation of the profession and as a result would be incompatible with the fundamental principles. **200.2**

Fundamental principles

A professional accountant shall comply with the following fundamental principles: **200.2a**

- **Integrity** – to be straightforward and honest in all professional and business relationships
- **Objectivity** – to not allow bias, conflict of interest or undue influence of others to override professional or business judgments.
- **Professional Competence and Due Care** – to maintain professional knowledge and skill at the level required to ensure that a client or employer receives competent professional services based on current developments in practice, legislation and techniques and act diligently and in accordance with applicable technical and professional standards.
- **Confidentiality** – to respect the confidentiality of information acquired as a result of professional and business relationships and, therefore, not disclose any such information to third parties without proper and specific authority, unless there is a legal or professional right or duty to disclose, nor use the information for the personal advantage of the professional accountant or third parties.
- **Professional** – to comply with relevant laws and regulations and avoid any action that discredits the profession.

Threats and safeguards

Compliance with the fundamental principles may potentially be threatened by a broad range of circumstances and relationships. The nature and significance of the threats may differ depending on whether they arise in relation to the provision of services to an audit client and whether the audit client is a public interest entity, to an assurance client that is not an audit client, or to a non-assurance client. Threats fall into one or more of the following categories: **200.3**

- Self-interest;
- Self-review;
- Advocacy;
- Familiarity; and;
- Intimidation.

These threats are discussed further in Part A of this Code.

The paragraphs below set out examples of the circumstances that may result in threat and the types of safeguards that may be applicable, depending on the particular circumstances. They are not an exhaustive list nor do they imply that such circumstances will always create a significant threat. Regard should be had to the specific requirements in sections 210 to 291, when the circumstances are the same as, or analogous to, those addressed by them.

200.4   Examples of circumstances that create self-interest threats for a professional accountant in public practice include:

- A member of the assurance team having a direct financial interest in the assurance client.
- A firm having undue dependence on total fees from a client.
- A member of the assurance team having a significant close business relationship with an assurance client.
- A firm being concerned about the possibility of losing a significant client.
- A member of the audit team entering into employment negotiations with the audit client.
- A firm entering into a contingent fee arrangement relating to an assurance engagement.
- A professional accountant discovering a significant error when evaluating the results of a previous professional service performed by a member of the professional accountant's firm.

200.5   Examples of circumstances that create self-review threats for a professional accountant in public practice include:

- A firm issuing an assurance report on the effectiveness of the operation of financial systems after designing or implementing the systems.
- A firm having prepared the original data used to generate records that are the subject matter of the assurance engagement.
- A member of the assurance team being, or having recently been, a director or officer of the client.
- A member of the assurance team being, or having recently been, employed by the client in a position to exert significant influence over the subject matter of the engagement.
- The firm performing a service for an assurance client that directly affects the subject matter information of the assurance engagement.

200.6   Examples of circumstances that create advocacy threats for a professional accountant in public practice include:

- The firm promoting shares in an audit client.
- A professional accountant acting as an advocate on behalf of an audit client in litigation or disputes with third parties.

200.7   Examples of circumstances that create familiarity threats for a professional accountant in public practice include:

- A member of the engagement team having a close or immediate family member who is a director or officer of the client.
- A member of the engagement team having a close or immediate family member who is an employee of the client who is in a position to exert significant influence over the subject matter of the engagement.
- A director or officer of the client or an employee in a position to exert significant influence over the subject matter of the engagement having recently served as the engagement partner.
- A professional accountant accepting gifts or preferential treatment from a client, unless the value is trivial or inconsequential.
- Senior personnel having a long association with the assurance client.

200.8   Examples of circumstances that create intimidation threats for a professional accountant in public practice include:

- A firm being threatened with dismissal from a client engagement.

- An audit client indicating that it will not award a planned non-assurance contract to the firm if the firm continues to disagree with the client's accounting treatment for a particular transaction.
- A firm being threatened with litigation by the client.
- A firm being pressured to reduce inappropriately the extent of work performed in order to reduce fees.
- A professional accountant feeling pressured to agree with the judgment of a client employee because the employee has more expertise on the matter in question.
- A professional accountant being informed by a partner of the firm that a planned promotion will not occur unless the accountant agrees with an audit client's inappropriate accounting treatment.

Safeguards that may eliminate or reduce threats to an acceptable level fall into two broad categories: **200.9**

- Safeguards created by the profession, legislation or regulation; and
- Safeguards in the work environment.

Examples of safeguards created by the profession, legislation or regulation are described in paragraph 100.14 of Part A of this Code.

A professional accountant in public practice shall exercise judgment to determine **200.10** how best to deal with threats that are not at an acceptable level, whether by applying safeguards to eliminate the threat or reduce it to an acceptable level or by terminating or declining the relevant engagement. In exercising this judgment, a professional accountant in public practice shall consider whether a reasonable and informed third party, weighing all the specific facts and circumstances available to the professional accountant at that time, would be likely to conclude that the threats would be eliminated or reduced to an acceptable level by the application of safeguards, such that compliance with the fundamental principles is not compromised. This consideration will be affected by matters such as the significance of the threat, the nature of the engagement and the structure of the firm.

In the work environment, the relevant safeguards will vary depending on the circumstances. Work environment safeguards comprise firm-wide safeguards and engagement-specific safeguards. **200.11**

Examples of firm-wide safeguards in the work environment include: **200.12**

- Leadership of the firm that stresses the importance of compliance with the fundamental principles.
- Leadership of the firm that establishes the expectation that members of an assurance team will act in the public interest.
- Policies and procedures to implement and monitor quality control of engagements.
- Documented policies regarding the need to identify threats to compliance with the fundamental principles, evaluate the significance of those threats, and apply safeguards to eliminate or reduce the threats to an acceptable level or, when appropriate safeguards are not available or cannot be applied, terminate or decline the relevant engagement.
- Documented internal policies and procedures requiring compliance with the fundamental principles.
- Policies and procedures that will enable the identification of interests or relationships between the firm or members of engagement teams and clients.
- Policies and procedures to monitor and, if necessary, manage the reliance on revenue received from a single client.

- Using different partners and engagement teams with separate reporting lines for the provision of non-assurance services to an assurance client.
- Policies and procedures to prohibit individuals who are not members of an engagement team from inappropriately influencing the outcome of the engagement.
- Timely communication of a firm's policies and procedures, including any changes to them, to all partners and professional staff, and appropriate training and education on such policies and procedures.
- Designating a member of senior management to be responsible for overseeing the adequate functioning of the firm's quality control system.
- Advising partners and professional staff of assurance clients and related entities from which independence is required.
- A disciplinary mechanism to promote compliance with policies and procedures.
- Published policies and procedures to encourage and empower staff to communicate to senior levels within the firm any issue relating to compliance with the fundamental principles that concerns them.

200.13   Examples of engagement-specific safeguards in the work environment include:

- Having a professional accountant who was not involved with the non-assurance service review the non-assurance work performed or otherwise advise as necessary.
- Having a professional accountant who was not a member of the assurance team review the assurance work performed or otherwise advise as necessary.
- Consulting an independent third party, such as a committee of independent directors, a professional regulatory body or another professional accountant.
- Discussing ethical issues with those charged with governance of the client.
- Disclosing to those charged with governance of the client the nature of services provided and extent of fees charged.
- Involving another firm to perform or re-perform part of the engagement.
- Rotating senior assurance team personnel.

200.14   Depending on the nature of the engagement, a professional accountant in public practice may also be able to rely on safeguards that the client has implemented. However it is not possible to rely solely on such safeguards to reduce threats to an acceptable level.

200.15   Examples of safeguards within the client's systems and procedures include:

- The client requires persons other than management to ratify or approve the appointment of a firm to perform an engagement.
- The client has competent employees with experience and seniority to make managerial decisions.
- The client has implemented internal procedures that ensure objective choices in commissioning non-assurance engagements.
- The client has a corporate governance structure that provides appropriate oversight and communications regarding the firm's services.

200.16   Professional accountants who are in doubt as to their ethical position may seek advice from the ICAEW's Technical Advisory Services by email: ethics@icaew.com or phone +44 (0)1908 248 250. Further information on guidance is available in section 1, paragraphs 1.19 to 1.22.

210 Professional Appointment

Clients have the right to choose their accountants, whether as auditors or professional advisers, and to change their accountants if they so desire. Professional accountants have the right to choose for whom they act. **210.0**

Client Acceptance

Before accepting a new client relationship, a professional accountant in public practice shall determine whether acceptance would create any threats to compliance with the fundamental principles. Potential threats to integrity or professional behaviour may be created from, for example, questionable issues associated with the client (its owners, management or activities). **210.1**

Client issues that, if known, could threaten compliance with the fundamental principles include, for example, client involvement in illegal activities (such as money laundering), dishonesty or questionable financial reporting practices. **210.2**

Further information relating to money laundering legislation and guidance is included in paragraph 210.13.

A professional accountant in public practice shall evaluate the significance of any threats and apply safeguards when necessary to eliminate them or reduce them to an acceptable level. Examples of such safeguards include: **210.3**

- Obtaining knowledge and understanding of the client, its owners, managers and those responsible for its governance and business activities; or
- Securing the client's commitment to improve corporate governance practices or internal controls.

Where it is not possible to reduce the threats to an acceptable level, the professional accountant in public practice shall decline to enter into the client relationship. **210.4**

It is recommended that a professional accountant in public practice periodically review acceptance decisions for recurring client engagements. **210.5**

Engagement Acceptance

The fundamental principle of professional competence and due care imposes an obligation on a professional accountant in public practice to provide only those services that the professional accountant in public practice is competent to perform. Before accepting a specific client engagement, a professional accountant in public practice shall determine whether acceptance would create any threats to compliance with the fundamental principles. For example, a self-interest threat to professional competence and due care is created if the engagement team does not possess, or cannot acquire, the competencies necessary to properly carry out the engagement. **210.6**

A professional accountant in public practice shall evaluate the significance of threats and apply safeguards, when necessary, to eliminate them or reduce them to an acceptable level. Examples of such safeguards include: **210.7**

- Acquiring an appropriate understanding of the nature of the client's business, the complexity of its operations, the specific requirements of the engagement and the purpose, nature and scope of the work to be performed.
- Acquiring knowledge of relevant industries or subject matters.

- Possessing or obtaining experience with relevant regulatory or reporting requirements.
- Assigning sufficient staff with the necessary competencies.
- Using experts where necessary.
- Agreeing on a realistic time frame for the performance of the engagement.
- Complying with quality control policies and procedures designed to provide reasonable assurance that specific engagements are accepted only when they can be performed competently.

210.8   When a professional accountant in public practice intends to rely on the advice or work of an expert, the professional accountant in public practice shall determine whether such reliance is warranted. Factors to consider include: reputation, expertise, resources available and applicable professional and ethical standards. Such information may be gained from prior association with the expert or from consulting others.

Changes in a Professional appointment

210.9   A professional accountant in public practice who is asked to replace another professional accountant in public practice, or who is considering tendering for an engagement currently held by another professional accountant in public practice, shall determine whether there are any reasons, professional or otherwise, for not accepting the engagement, such as circumstances that create threats to compliance with the fundamental principles that cannot be eliminated or reduced to an acceptable level by the application of safeguards. For example, there may be a threat to professional competence and due care if a professional accountant in public practice accepts the engagement before knowing all the pertinent facts.

Upon being asked to accept an appointment, professional accountants shall undertake the same procedures with all accountants, irrespective of whether the accountant works in public practice or not

210.10   A professional accountant in public practice shall evaluate the significance of any threats. Depending on the nature of the engagement, this may require direct communication with the existing accountant to establish the facts and circumstances regarding the proposed change so that the professional accountant in public practice can decide whether it would be appropriate to accept the engagement. For example, the apparent reasons for the change in appointment may not fully reflect the facts and may indicate disagreements with the existing accountant that may influence the decision to accept the appointment.

Having been asked to accept an appointment, the professional accountant in public practice shall at least seek to contact the existing accountant. The appropriate procedures are considered further in the Appendix to this Section.

210.11   Safeguards shall be applied when necessary to eliminate any threats or reduce them to an acceptable level. Examples of such safeguards include:

- When replying to requests to submit tenders, stating in the tender that, before accepting the engagement, contact with the existing accountant will be requested so that inquiries may be made as to whether there are any professional or other reasons why the appointment shall not be accepted;
- Asking the existing accountant to provide known information on any facts or circumstances that, in the existing accountant's opinion, the proposed accountant needs to be aware of before deciding whether to accept the engagement; or
- Obtaining necessary information from other sources.

When the threats cannot be eliminated or reduced to an acceptable level through the application of safeguards, a professional accountant in public practice shall, unless there is satisfaction as to necessary facts by other means, decline the engagement.

Counsel has advised that as far as UK law is concerned, an existing accountant who communicates to a prospective accountant matters damaging to the client or to any individuals concerned with the client's business will have a strong measure of protection were any action for defamation to be brought against the existing accountant in that the communication will be protected by qualified privilege. This means that the existing accountant shall not be liable to pay damages for defamatory statements even if they turn out to be untrue, provided that they are made without malice. There is little likelihood of an existing accountant being held to have acted maliciously provided that:

- Only what is sincerely believed to be true is stated; and
- Reckless imputations are not made against a client or connected individuals for which there can be no reason to believe they are true.

A professional accountant in public practice may be asked to undertake work that is complementary or additional to the work of the existing accountant. Such circumstances may create threats to professional competence and due care resulting from, for example, a lack of or incomplete information. The significance of any threats shall be evaluated and safeguards applied when necessary to eliminate the threat or reduce it to an acceptable level. An example of such a safeguard is notifying the existing accountant of the proposed work, which would give the existing accountant the opportunity to provide any relevant information needed for the proper conduct of the work. **210.12**

In circumstances where the professional accountant is asked to undertake work which is relevant to the work of the existing accountant, the professional accountant shall notify the existing accountant of the proposed work, unless the client provides acceptable reasons why the existing accountant cannot be informed. The professional accountant ought to be aware of the risks of undertaking such work without the advantage of communicating with the other accountant. Further guidance on providing second opinions is available in section 230 of this Code.

An existing accountant is bound by confidentiality. Whether that professional accountant is permitted or required to discuss the affairs of a client with a proposed accountant will depend on the nature of the engagement and on: **210.13**

- Whether the client's permission to do so has been obtained; or
- The legal or ethical requirements relating to such communications and disclosure, which may vary by jurisdiction.

Circumstances where the professional accountant is or may be required to disclose confidential information or where such disclosure may otherwise be appropriate are set out in section 140 of Part A of this Code.

However, care must be taken when communicating all relevant facts to a professional accountant in situations where the existing accountant knows or suspects that their client is involved in money laundering or a terrorist activity. Under the UK Money Laundering regulations 2007, the Terrorism Act 2000 and the Terrorism Act 2006, it is a criminal offence to 'tip off' a money launderer or terrorist. Accordingly:

- The prospective accountant shall not specifically enquire whether the existing accountant has reported suspicions of money laundering or terrorism. Such questions place the existing accountant in a difficult position and are likely not to be answered. In addition, the prospective accountant shall not ask the existing accountant whether client identification or 'knowing your client' procedures have been carried out under anti-money laundering legislation. The prospective accountant has responsibility for obtaining information for client identification and 'knowing your client' and this cannot be delegated to the existing accountant.

- Disclosure of money laundering or terrorist suspicion reporting by the existing accountant to the potential successor shall be avoided because this information may be discussed with the client or former client.

For further discussion, please refer to the money laundering legislation and guidance and the ICAEW's Ethics Advisory helpsheet on 'changes in professional appointments'.

210.14   A professional accountant in public practice will generally need to obtain the client's permission, preferably in writing, to initiate discussion with an existing accountant. Once that permission is obtained, the existing accountant shall comply with relevant legal and other regulations governing such requests. Where the existing accountant provides information, it shall be provided honestly and unambiguously. If the proposed accountant is unable to communicate with the existing accountant, the proposed accountant shall take reasonable steps to obtain information about any possible threats by other means, such as through inquiries of third parties or background investigations of senior management or those charged with governance of the client.

If the client fails or refuses to grant the existing accountant permission to discuss the client's affairs with the proposed successor, the existing accountant shall report this fact to the prospective accountant who shall consider carefully the reason for such failure or refusal when determining whether or not to accept nomination/appointment.

210.15   Guidance on appropriate procedures to be adopted by professional accountants relating to changes in professional appointments is included as an Appendix to this Section.

Transfer of Records

210.16   An existing accountant shall deal promptly with any reasonable request for the transfer of records and may have the right of particular lien if there are unpaid fees (see section 240 of this Code and 'Documents and records: ownership, lien and right of access' at (icaew.com/regulations). The courts have held that no lien can exist over books or documents of a registered company which, either by statute or by articles of association of the company, have to be available for public inspection (see 'Documents and records: ownership, lien and rights of access' at (icaew.com/regulations). It may be necessary for professional accountants to obtain legal advice prior to the exercise of a lien.

If the existing accountant has fees outstanding from a client they are entitled to mention this to the potential successor. However, if this is as a result of genuine reservations by the client, this may not be a reason to withhold cooperation with a successor. It may be useful to consider the section on fee disputes in 'Duty on firms to investigate complaints – guidance on how to handle or avoid them' at (icaew.com/regulations).

The prospective accountant often asks the existing accountant for information as to the client's affairs. If the client is unable to provide the information and lack thereof might prejudice the client's interests, such information shall be promptly given. In such circumstances, no charge shall normally be made unless there is good reason to the contrary. An example of such a reason would be that a significant amount of work is involved. Where a charge is made, the arrangements shall comply with section 240 of this Code.

210.17

Attention is drawn to Chapter 3 of the Audit regulations and Guidance relating to access to all relevant information held by the existing accountant in respect of the last audit report and Technical Release AAF 01/08 Access to Information by Successor Auditors.

210.18

Appendix to Section 210 – Changes in Professional Appointments Procedures

Prospective Accountants

In the majority of cases, the appropriate procedures for any professional accountant who is invited to act in succession to another, whether the changeover is at the insistence of the client or of the existing accountant, is to:

1

- Explain to the prospective client that there is a professional duty to communicate with the existing accountant; and
- Request the client (i) to confirm the proposed change in accountant to the existing accountant and (ii) to authorise the existing accountant to co-operate with the prospective accountant; and
- Write to the existing accountant regarding the prospective involvement with the client and request disclosure of any issue or circumstance which might be relevant to the successor's decision to accept or decline the appointment (making oral enquiry if no written reply is forthcoming).

When these procedural steps have been taken, the prospective accountant shall consider, in light of the information received from the existing accountant, or any other factors, including conclusions reached following discussion with the client, whether:

2

- To accept the engagement, or
- Accept it only after having addressed any factors arising from the information received from the existing accountant (this may include imposing conditions on acceptance), or
- Decline it.

The prospective accountant shall ordinarily treat in confidence any information provided by the existing accountant, unless it is needed to be disclosed to perform the role required (such as making investigations into matters which need the perspective of the client's officers or senior employees).

3

In circumstances where the enquiries referred to above are not answered, the prospective accountant shall write to the existing accountant by recorded delivery service stating an intention to accept the engagement in the absence of a reply within a specific and reasonable period. The prospective accountant is entitled to assume that the existing accountant's silence implies there was no adverse comment to be made, although this does not obviate the requirement in 210.9 to consider all appropriate circumstances.

4

5 A professional accountant who is nominated as a joint auditor shall communicate with all existing auditors and be guided by similar principles to those set out in relation to nomination as an auditor. Where it is proposed that a joint audit appointment becomes a sole appointment, the surviving auditor shall communicate formally with the other joint auditor as though for a new appointment.

6 A professional accountant invited to accept nomination on the death of a sole practitioner shall endeavour to obtain such information as may be needed from the latter's alternate (where appropriate), the administrators of the estate, or other source.

7 If the prospective accountant accepts the engagement, the prospective accountant shall comply with the relevant legal and regulatory requirements as indicated in paragraph 13.

Existing accountants

8 The appropriate procedure for any professional accountant who receives any communication in terms of the above paragraphs, whether or not the professional accountant is still in office, is to:

- Answer promptly any communication from the potential successor about the client's affairs; and
- Confirm whether there are any matters about those affairs which the prospective accountant ought to know, explaining them meaningfully, or confirm there are no such matters.

9 If the existing accountant has made one or more suspicious activity reports relating to money laundering or terrorism, the existing accountant shall not disclose that fact to the prospective accountant, or make other disclosures that could amount to tipping off. However, the existing accountant's legal and professional obligations remain. In order to meet these obligations, the existing accountant can undertake one or more of the following actions:

- Contact the relevant investigating authority, for example, the Serious Organised Crime Agency (SOCA), to ascertain if appropriate wording can be agreed in a communication;
- Include a factual reference to the irregularities; (further discussion is included in the ICAEW's Ethics Advisory Services Helpsheet on Changes in Professional Appointments);
- Consider seeking legal advice.

Guidance on money laundering reporting requirements in privileged circumstances is included in Technical Release 02/06.

10 The above actions are also relevant when the existing accountant is preparing the required statement of circumstances in accordance with Section 519 of the UK Companies Act 2006, or other similar statutory provisions, of matters connected with ceasing to hold office which, the auditor believes, shall be brought to the notice of the professional accountants, shareholders or creditors of the client or under the relevant professional and other regulatory bodies. Further guidance can be found in Chapter 3 of the 2008 Audit regulations and Guidance.

11 It is best practice for the prospective accountant and the existing accountant to record in writing such discussions as are referred to in the paragraphs above.

Where the professional accountant decides to accept nomination/appointment **12** having been given notice of any matters which are the subject of contention between the existing accountant and the client, the professional accountant shall be prepared, if requested to do so, to demonstrate to the professional and regulatory investigating authorities that proper consideration has been given to those matters and the relevant legal, regulatory and ethical requirements have been met.

Further Information

Professional accountants' attention is drawn to additional guidance as follows: **13**

- Chapter 3 of the 2008 Audit regulations and Guidance, in particular technical standards relating to changes in professional appointments and access to relevant information relating to the signed audit report.
- ISQC (UK & Ireland) – quality control for firms that perform audits and reviews of historical financial information, and other assurance and related services engagements (frc.org.uk/apb/publications).
- Statement of Auditing Standards frc.org.uk/apb/publications:
- ISA 240 (UK and Ireland) – The auditor's responsibility to consider fraud in an audit of financial statements;
- ISA 250 (UK and Ireland) – Consideration of laws and regulations in an audit of financial statements;
- ISA 510 (UK and Ireland) Initial engagements – opening balances and continuing engagements – opening balances.
- Practice Note 12 (Revised) 'Money laundering' frc.org.uk/apb/publications.
- Anti-money laundering for the Accountancy Sector at icaew.com/regulations.
- Technical Release 02/06 – 'Guidance on changes to the money laundering reporting requirements: the exemption from reporting knowledge or suspicion of money laundering formed in privileged circumstances' (icaew.com/technical).
- Practice Helpsheet – Changes in a professional appointment (icaew.com/ethicsadvice).

220 Conflicts of Interest

A professional accountant in public practice shall take reasonable steps to identify **220.1** circumstances that could pose a conflict of interest. Such circumstances may create threats to compliance with the fundamental principles. For example, a threat to objectivity may be created when a professional accountant in public practice competes directly with a client or has a joint venture or similar arrangement with a major competitor of a client. A threat to objectivity or confidentiality may also be created when a professional accountant in public practice performs services for clients whose interests are in conflict or the clients are in dispute with each other in relation to the matter or transaction in question.

Subject to the specific provisions, there is, however, nothing improper in a professional accountant in public practice having two clients whose interests are in conflict.

A professional accountant in public practice shall evaluate the significance of any **220.2** threats and apply safeguards when necessary to eliminate the threats or reduce them to an acceptable level. Before accepting or continuing a client relationship or specific engagement, the professional accountant in public practice shall evaluate the significance of any threats created by business interests or relationships with the client or a third party.

A test is whether a reasonable and informed observer would perceive that the objectivity of professional accountants or their firms is likely to be impaired. The professional accountants or their firms shall be able to satisfy themselves and the client that any conflict can be managed with available safeguards. Attention is also drawn to the ethical conflict resolution process in Part A.

220.3   Depending upon the circumstances giving rise to the conflict, application of one of the following safeguards is generally necessary:

- Notifying the client of the firm's business interest or activities that may represent a conflict of interest and obtaining their consent to act in such circumstances; or
- Notifying all known relevant parties that the professional accountant in public practice is acting for two or more parties in respect of a matter where their respective interests are in conflict and obtaining their consent to so act; or
- Notifying the client that the professional accountant in public practice does not act exclusively for any one client in the provision of proposed services (for example, in a particular market sector or with respect to a specific service) and obtaining their consent to so act.

Professional accountants' attention is drawn to section 240 Fees and other types of remuneration and section 241 Agencies and referrals which provide additional guidance on the ethical and legal considerations relating to these areas, including fiduciary relationships and accounting for commission and other benefits.

220.4   The professional accountant shall also determine whether to apply one or more of the following additional safeguards:

- The use of separate engagement teams;
- Procedures to prevent access to information (e.g., strict physical separation of such teams, confidential and secure data filing);
- Clear guidelines for members of the engagement team on issues of security and confidentiality;
- The use of confidentiality agreements signed by employees and partners of the firm; and
- regular review of the application of safeguards by a senior individual not involved with relevant client engagements.

220.4a   Where a conflict of interest arises, the preservation of confidentiality, and the perception thereof will be of paramount importance. Therefore firms shall deploy safeguards, which generally will take the form of information barriers. These information barriers may include the following features:

- Ensuring that there is, and continues to be, no overlap between the teams servicing the relevant clients and that each has separate internal reporting lines;
- Physically separating, and restricting access to, departments providing different professional services, or creating such divisions within departments if necessary, so that confidential information about one client is not accessible by anyone providing services to another client where their interests conflict;
- Setting strict and carefully defined procedures for dealing with any apparent need to disseminate information beyond a barrier and for maintaining proper records where this occurs.

The professional accountant shall ensure that the adequacy and effectiveness of the barriers are closely and independently monitored and that appropriate disciplinary sanctions are applied for breaches of them. The overall arrangements shall regularly be reviewed by a designated senior partner.

Professional accountants shall note that it has been suggested by the courts that in some circumstances information barriers must be constructed as part of the organisational structure of the firm to be effective, rather than on an ad hoc basis.

If client service issues render it impracticable to put in place such safeguards or suitable alternatives, it is important that relevant parties, who have conflicts of interest which may result in threats to preservation of confidentiality, are made aware of and agree to the professional accountant continuing to act for them.   **220.4b**

Where a conflict of interest creates a threat to one or more of the fundamental principles, including objectivity, confidentiality, or professional behaviour, that cannot be eliminated or reduced to an acceptable level through the application of safeguards, the professional accountant in public practice shall not accept a specific engagement or shall resign from one or more conflicting engagements.   **220.5**

Where a professional accountant in public practice has requested consent from a client to act for another party (which may or may not be an existing client) in respect of a matter where the respective interests are in conflict and that consent has been refused by the client, the professional accountant in public practice shall not continue to act for one of the parties in the matter giving rise to the conflict of interest.   **220.6**

Professional accountants' attention is drawn to section 221, Corporate Finance Advice, section 290, Independence Audit and review engagements, section 400, Code of Ethics for Insolvency Practitioners, for guidance on issues arising from certain corporate finance activities, reporting assignments, and insolvency appointments.

221 Corporate Finance Advice

(Updated as regards to changes in legislation as at 1 April 2010)

Introduction

The nature of corporate finance activities is wide ranging. Therefore, the threats to a professional accountant's objectivity, integrity and independence will depend on the nature of the corporate finance activities being provided and the particular circumstances and relationships involved.   **221.0**

Categories of Corporate Finance Activity

Categories of activity covered by this section are as follows: **221.1**

* general corporate finance advice;
* acting as adviser in relation to takeovers and mergers;
* underwriting and marketing or placing securities on behalf of a client; and
* acting as sponsor, nominated adviser or corporate adviser under the Listing Rules, the AIM Rules and the PLUS Rules respectively.

Professional accountants shall note that the guidance given in relation to general corporate finance advice is applicable to all categories of activity.   **221.2**

General Principles applicable to all Professional accountants

Statutory and other regulatory requirements

221.3 Professional accountants must be aware of and comply with legislative and regulatory measures and professional guidance governing corporate finance assignments. As a guide, a list of legislative and regulatory measures current at 1 April 2010 is given in Appendix 1 to this section but professional accountants shall ensure that they are aware of the most up-to-date legislative and regulatory requirements.

221.4 Professional accountants are required to comply with the City Code on Takeovers and Mergers ('the City Code') (see Appendix 2 to this Section) in respect of all relevant takeover transactions involving companies governed by the City Code and shall treat the general principles of the City Code as best practice guidance in respect of other takeover transactions.

221.5 Professional accountants proposing to provide corporate finance advice to a client or his employer shall at the outset draw attention to the legislative and regulatory responsibilities which will apply to the client or his employer. The professional accountant shall make clear to the client or his employer that, where necessary, legal advice shall be taken. The professional accountant shall also draw attention to his own responsibilities outlined in this Code and if appropriate, the Auditing Practices Board's Ethical Standards for Auditors and the Auditing Practices Board's Ethical Standards for Reporting Accountants.

Acquisition searches

221.6 It may be appropriate for a professional accountant to conduct an acquisition search which could identify another client or his employer as a target provided the search is based solely on information which is not confidential to that client.

Interests of Shareholders and Owners

221.7 Professional accountants shall remain aware when giving advice that they shall have regard to the interests of all shareholders and owners unless they are specifically acting for a single or defined group thereof. This is particularly so when advising on a proposal which is stated to be agreed by directors and/or majority shareholders or owners.

Preparation of documents

221.8 Any document shall be prepared in accordance with normal professional standards of integrity and objectivity and with a proper degree of care. All statements or observations therein must be capable, taken individually or as a whole, of being justified on an objective examination of the available facts.

221.9 In order to differentiate the roles and responsibilities of the various advisers, professional accountants shall ensure that these roles and responsibilities are clearly described in all public documents and circulars and that each adviser is named.

221.10 Professional accountants intending to comment on published audited accounts shall act in accordance with paragraphs 221.20-22 below.

Overseas transactions

This section has been drafted with regard to the situation in the UK and the Republic of Ireland. Professional accountants shall apply the spirit of the guidance, subject to local legislation and regulation, to overseas transactions of a similar nature. | **221.11**

General corporate finance advice applicable to professional accountants in public practice

The nature of corporate finance activities is so wide ranging that all the threats to the fundamental principles identified in section 100 and section 200, can arise when professional accountants in public practice provide corporate finance advice to both assurance clients and non-assurance clients: the self-interest threat, the self-review threat, the advocacy threat, the familiarity threat and the intimidation threat. | **221.12**

When advising a non-assurance client there can be no objection to a professional accountant in public practice accepting an engagement which is designed primarily with a view to advancing that client's case, though the professional accountant in public practice shall be aware that the self-interest threat could arise. Where a non-assurance client has received advice over a period of time on a series of related or unrelated transactions it is likely that, additionally, the familiarity threat may exist. But where a professional accountant in public practice advises an assurance client which is subject to a takeover bid or where a professional accountant in public practice acts as sponsor nominated adviser or corporate adviser to an assurance client involved in the issue of securities, the self-interest threat will become more acute and the advocacy threat will arise.

Some corporate finance activities such as marketing or underwriting of securities contain so strong an element of advocacy as to be incompatible with the objectivity required for the reporting roles of an auditor or reporting accountant. Even where the activities of an auditor or reporting accountant are restricted to ensuring their clients' compliance with the Listing Roles, the AIM Roles or the PLUS Roles it is likely that a self-review threat could arise.

It may be in the best interests of a company for corporate finance advice to be provided by its auditor and there is nothing improper in the professional accountant in public practice supporting an assurance client in this way. | **221.13**

A professional accountant in public practice's objectivity may be seriously threatened if their role involves undertaking the management responsibilities of an assurance client. Co-ordination tasks, such as initiating and organising meetings, issuing timetables and reporting progress, are unlikely to threaten reporting objectivity. When involved in negotiations on behalf of an assurance client, the professional accountant in public practice shall ensure that he does not assume the role of taking decisions for a client which would prejudice reporting objectivity. Accordingly, the professional accountant in public practice shall ensure that the client takes foll responsibility for the final decisions arising from any such negotiations. | **221.14**

Conflict of Interest

Professional accountants in public practice shall be aware of the danger of a conflict of interest arising. All reasonable steps shall be taken to ascertain whether a conflict of interest exists or is likely to arise in the future between a professional accountant | **221.15** in public practice and his clients, both with regard to new clients and to the changing circumstances of existing clients, and including any implications arising from the possession of confidential information.

221.16   The attention of professional accountants in public practice is directed to section 220, 'Conflicts of interest' and to the safeguards indicated in paragraphs 220.3 and 220.4 of that section. Where there appears to be a conflict of interest between clients but after careful consideration the professional accountant in public practice believes that either the conflict is not material or is unlikely seriously to prejudice the interests of any of those clients and that its safeguards are sufficient, the professional accountant in public practice may accept or continue the engagement. Unless client confidentiality considerations dictate otherwise it would be advisable, if appropriate, to seek the clients' consent. Considerations that lead to a conclusion to accept or continue the engagement shall be explicitly recorded.

221.17   Where a professional accountant in public practice acts or continues to act for two or more clients having obtained consent, if appropriate, in accordance with the previous paragraphs, safeguards will need to be implemented to manage any conflict which arises. The safeguards may include:

- the use of different partners and teams for different clients, each having separate internal reporting lines;
- all necessary steps being taken to prevent the leakage of confidential information between different teams and sections within the firm;
- regular review of the situation by a senior partner or compliance officer not personally involved with either client; and
- advising the clients to seek additional independent advice, where it is appropriate.

Any decision on the part of a sole practitioner shall take account of the fact that the safeguards at (a) to (c) of the above paragraph will not be available to him or her. Similar considerations apply to small firms where the number of partners is insufficient to spread the work as indicated above.

221.18   Where a conflict of interest is so fundamental that it cannot be managed effectively by the implementation of appropriate safeguards and is likely seriously to prejudice the interests of a client, the engagement shall not be accepted or continued even if all relevant clients consent to the engagement.

221.19   Where a professional accountant in public practice is required for any reason to disengage from an existing client, the professional accountant in public practice shall do so as speedily as practicable having regard to the interest of the client.

Documents for client and public use

221.20   In the case of a document prepared solely for the client and its professional advisers, it shall be a condition of the engagement that the document shall not be disclosed to any third party without the firm's prior written consent.

221.21   A professional accountant in public practice is, in the absence of any indication to the contrary, entitled to assume that a company's published financial information that has been reported on by a professional accountant in public practice has been prepared properly and in accordance with all relevant Accounting Standards. If a professional accountant in public practice is commenting in a public document on such financial information and where scope for alternative accounting treatment exists, and the accuracy of the comment or observation is dependent on an assumption as to the actual accounting treatment chosen, that assumption must be stated, together with any other assumptions material to the commentary. Where the professional accountant in public practice is not in possession of sufficient information to warrant a clear opinion this shall be declared in the document.

A professional accountant in public practice must take responsibility for anything **221.22** published under his name, provided he consented to such publication, and the published document shall make clear the client for whom the professional accountant in public practice is acting. To prevent misleading or out-of-context quotations, it shall be a condition of the engagement that, if anything less than the foll document is to be published, the text and its context shall be expressly agreed with the professional accountant in public practice.

Takeovers and Mergers

City code transactions

Professional accountants in public practice are reminded that, if in doubt as to the **221.23** propriety of any aspect of a City Code transaction with which they are involved, they shall consult the Panel on Takeovers and Mergers ('the Takeover Panel'). (See Appendix 2 of this section).

Where a professional accountant in public practice finds itself acting as auditor or **221.24** reporting accountant for two or more parties involved in a transaction subject to the City Code, a perceived conflict of interest may arise. In such circumstances (subject to paragraph 221.26 below) a professional accountant in public practice may act for more than one party, including both offeror and offeree companies as auditor, as reporting accountants, and in the provision of incidental advice consistent with these roles but must implement adequate safeguards (see paragraph 221.17 above).

Lead advisers in city code transactions

For the purposes of this Section, a 'lead adviser' is the professional accountant in **221.25** public practice primarily responsible for advising on, organising and presenting an offer or the response to an offer. This definition would include an 'independent financial adviser' required under Role 3 of the City Code.

In no circumstances shall a professional accountant in public practice be a lead **221.26** adviser to more than one party involved in a transaction subject to the City Code. Where a professional accountant in public practice finds itself acting in an auditor or reporting accountant role for any party involved in a transaction subject to the City Code, the professional accountant in public practice shall not act as lead adviser for any party involved, save in the circumstances set out below in paragraphs 221.27-221.29.

A professional accountant in public practice who is auditor to a target company may **221.27** be requested to act as lead adviser to a bidder on an offer subject to the City Code. Where the bid is hostile, it is likely that the professional accountant in public practice's objectivity will be perceived to be prejudiced by its possession of material confidential information on the target and it will not therefore be able to advise on the offer. However, if the bid is agreed, the professional accountant in public practice may be able to act or continue to act as lead adviser to the bidder with the agreement of the target and subject to the prior approval of the Takeover Panel. The professional accountant in public practice shall obtain confirmation from its clients that their interests would not be prejudiced if the professional accountant in public practice were to act or continue to act in both capacities.

221.28   Where a professional accountant in public practice is acting as lead adviser to a company which is involved in a bid subject to the City Code, conflicts of interest for the professional accountant in public practice may arise due to an existing relationship with a second or subsequent bidder. Providing that the relationship with the second or subsequent bidder is confined to that of auditor or reporting accountant, and subject to the prior approval of the Takeover Panel, the professional accountant in public practice may continue to act as lead adviser, providing that it is satisfied that the implementation of safeguards (see paragraph 221.27 above) provides the necessary level of protection to each of the clients involved.

221.29   Where a professional accountant in public practice is requested to act as lead adviser to a target company in relation to a bid which is subject to the City Code from a company which is an existing assurance client, they may act as lead adviser to the target company only with the prior approval of the Takeover Panel.

The ethical guidance for professional accountants in public practice seeking to act for more than one party in a takeover transaction subject to the City Code is summarised in Appendix 3 to this section. Appendix 3 has been prepared only as a useful reference and is not intended to form part of this section.

Transactions not subject to the city code

221.30   Where a takeover is not subject to the City Code, and there is no substantial public interest involved, a professional accountant in public practice may, subject to the implementation of appropriate safeguards (see paragraphs 221.16 and 221.17 above), provide financial advice to both sides or to competing bidders. However, the professional accountant in public practice shall not act as lead adviser to both the target and a bidder in respect of such a transaction. The professional accountant in public practice shall be alive to the possibility of conflicts of interest arising in relation to minority interests and shall ensure that any such conflicts are addressed. Where appropriate, the advisory client and minority interests shall be advised as to the desirability of the minority interests appointing a wholly independent adviser.

Underwriting and marketing of shares

221.31   A professional accountant in public practice who is an auditor or reporting accountant shall not deal in, underwrite or promote shares for their client (see also APB's Ethical Standard 5 and APB's Ethical Standard for Reporting Accountants). Involvement of this kind would give rise to an advocacy threat, self-review threat and self-interest threat such that the professional accountant in public practice's objectivity and independence would be threatened.

221.32   It may be appropriate:

- for an auditor or reporting accountant otherwise to assist a client in raising capital; or
- for an auditor or reporting accountant otherwise to provide independent advice to a client, or its professional advisers, in connection with the issue or sale of shares or securities to the public; or
- for an auditor or reporting accountant otherwise to provide advice as sponsor, as an AIM nominated adviser or as a PLUS corporate adviser to a company as set out below.

In these situations the professional accountant in public practice shall adopt steps similar to those described in paragraph 220.3 and 220.4 of section 220 and, additionally, set up procedures to review and identify any potential conflicts of interest which could compromise the professional accountant in public practice's objectivity.

Sponsors, nominated advisers and corporate advisers

The attention of professional accountants in public practice is drawn to: **221.33**

- the UK Listing Authority's Listing Rules when a firm accepts the responsibilities of a sponsor;
- the London Stock Exchange's Alternative Investment Market ('AIM') Roles and, AIM Rules for Nominated Advisers (which include the Eligibility Criteria for Nominated Advisers.) AIM's requirement is that for AIM companies to maintain their trading facility they shall have a nominated adviser at all times. In this context professional accountants in public practice shall have in place procedures to enable them to identify whether any conflicts exist or are likely to arise in the future before acting as a nominated adviser. Professional accountants in public practice shall note the policy of the London Stock Exchange that it will not normally allow a nominated adviser to be the reporting accountant to the issuer unless appropriate safeguards are in place as set out in paragraph 221.17 above. Furthermore, professional accountants in public practice shall note that the London Stock Exchange does not permit a nominated adviser to act for any other party to a transaction or takeover other than its AIM client company. In cases of doubt, professional accountants in public practice shall consult the London Stock Exchange.
- the PLUS Rules and in particular the PLUS Corporate Advisers Handbook when acting as a Corporate Adviser defined by the PLUS Rules. PLUS's requirement is that for PLUS companies to maintain their trading facility they shall have a corporate adviser at all times. In this context professional accountants in public practice shall have in place procedures to enable them to identify whether any conflicts exist or are likely to arise in the future before acting as a corporate adviser. Professional accountants in public practice shall note that PLUS does not permit a corporate adviser to act for any other party to a transaction or takeover other than its PLUS client company. In cases of doubt, professional accountants in public practice shall consult PLUS.

Considerable care needs to be taken if a professional accountant in public practice is **221.34** also to act as sponsor, nominated adviser or corporate adviser to an assurance client. A threat to the objectivity of the auditor or reporting accountant can arise as the duties of a sponsor, nominated adviser or corporate adviser are different from those of an auditor or reporting accountant and are owed to a different party. Although it is quite possible that no conflict will arise between the two roles, professional accountants in public practice need to recognise the possibility of conflicts arising, particularly if the role of sponsor, nominated adviser or corporate adviser is to include any advocacy of the directors' views or if the transaction is to involve any issue of securities. To comply with the requirements of paragraph 221.31 above, where there is an issue of securities associated with such a transaction, a separate broker shall be appointed to take responsibility for any underwriting or marketing of the company's shares.

Appendix 1 to Section 221 – Corporate finance advice

Information on statutory and other regulatory and professional requirements

For the assistance of professional accountants a list of the relevant legislative and regulatory measures and professional guidance is set out below. This reflects the position as at **1 April 2010**. Professional accountants shall be aware that this list may be subject to variation in the future and when undertaking corporate finance assignments professional accountants shall ensure they are aware of the current status of the list.

1   The Financial Services and Markets Act 2000, the Companies Act 1985 as amended, the Companies Act 2006, Part V of the Criminal Justice Act 1993 and, where applicable, the requirements of the Financial Services Authority's Handbook (fsa.-gov.uk/Pages/handbook) or the ICAEW's Designated Professional Body Handbook (icaew.com/dpb).

2   The City Code on Takeovers and Mergers (the 'City Code').

3   The Financial Services Authority Handbook which includes:
    * the Listing Rules;
    * the Prospectus Rules;
    * the Disclosure and Transparency Rules; and
    * the London Stock Exchange's AIM Rules and AIM Rules for Nominated Advisers (which include the Eligibility Criteria for Nominated Advisers)

4   The PLUS Market Corporate Adviser Handbook.

5   The Admission and Disclosure Standards of the London Stock Exchange.

6   The Auditing Practices Board's Ethical Standards, in particular ES 5 Non-Audit Services Provided to Audit clients and the Ethical Standard for Reporting Accountants (frc.org.uk/apb/publications).

And in the Republic of Ireland:

7   Investment Intermediaries Act, 1995 as amended by the Investor Compensation Act, 1998 and the Insurance Act, 2000 ('IIA'), and where applicable the requirements of the Central Bank of Ireland's Role Book or the ICAEW's Investment Business regulations and Guidance.

8   Irish Takeover Panel Act, 1997.

9   The Listing Rules of the Irish Stock Exchange: the IEX Roles.

10 Code of Conduct issued by the Central Bank of Ireland under Section 37 of the IIA, as amended by S. 30 of the Insurance Act 2000.

11 European Communities (Takeover Bids (Directive 2004/25/EC) regulations 2006 (RoI).

12 Investment Funds, Companies and Miscellaneous Provisions Act, 2005 (RoI).

13 Market Abuse (Directive 2003/6/EC) regulations 2005 (RoI).

14 Prospectus (Directive 2003/71/EC) regulations 2005.

Appendix 2 to Section 221 – Corporate finance advice

A professional accountant in public practice who provides takeover services for **1** clients is required to comply with the City Code and with all rulings made and guidance issued under it by the Panel on Takeovers and Mergers ('the Takeover Panel').

Accordingly a professional accountant in public practice proposing to provide **2** takeover services to a client shall at the outset:

• explain that these responsibilities will apply; and
• include in the terms of the engagement recognition of the professional accountant in public practice's obligation to comply with the City Code including any steps which the professional accountant in public practice may be obliged to take in performing those responsibilities. A specimen clause for the engagement letter is set out in paragraph 3 below.

Specimen clause for engagement letters

The client agrees and acknowledges that where the services provided by the pro- **3** fessional accountant in public practice relate to a transaction within the scope of the City Code, the client and the professional accountant in public practice will comply with the provisions of the City Code and will observe the terms of the Guidance Note published by the Institutes of Chartered Accountants relevant to such services or transactions. In particular, the client acknowledges that:

• if the client or its advisers or agents fail to comply with the City Code then the professional accountant in public practice may withdraw from acting for the client; and
• the professional accountant in public practice is obliged to supply to the Takeover Panel any information, books, documents or other records concerning the services or transaction which the Takeover Panel may require.

Scope of takeover services

Takeover services' means any professional services provided by a professional **4** accountant in public practice to a client in connection with a transaction to which the City Code applies.

The kinds of activities most commonly relevant for this purpose include: **5**

• acting as financial adviser to one of the parties (for example, as 'Role 3 adviser' to the offeree company);
• reporting on profit forecasts and/or valuations for the purposes of takeover documents;
• conducting acquisition searches for clients, and introducing clients to other parties with a view to effecting transactions;
• advising in relation to acquisitions and disposals of securities of companies which are subject to City Code.
• acting as a reporting accountant where both the City Code and the Listing Rules or Take Over Roles apply.

Whilst the City Code does not define precisely the range of activities and transactions **6** within its scope, paragraph 3 of the Introduction to the City Code describes the companies and transactions which are subject to the City Code. In practice, those engaged in providing takeover services rarely experience difficulty in determining whether the City Code is or may be relevant to the activities proposed to be undertaken for any particular client. In cases of any doubt the Takeover Panel shall be consulted.

Special responsibilities

7   A professional accountant in public practice who has provided or is providing takeover services to a client shall:

- supply to the Takeover Panel any information, books, documents or other records concerning the relevant transaction or arrangement which the Takeover Panel may properly require and which are in the possession or under the control of the professional accountant in public practice; and
- otherwise render all such assistance as the professional accountant in public practice is reasonably able to give to the Takeover Panel, provided that in each case the relevant information, books, documents or other records were acquired by the professional accountant in public practice in the course of providing the relevant takeover services.

8   Except with the consent of the Takeover Panel, a professional accountant in public practice shall not provide or continue to provide any takeover services to any person if the Takeover Panel has stated that it considers that such a person is not likely to comply with the standards of conduct for the time being expected in the United Kingdom concerning the practices of those involved in takeovers, mergers or substantial acquisitions of shares and the Takeover Panel has not subsequently indicated a change in this view. A person to whom this paragraph applies will normally have been named in a statement published by the Takeover Panel, inter alia, for the purposes of Role 4.3.1 of the Financial Services Authority's Handbook on Market Conduct.

9   If professional accountants in public practice have included in the engagement letter agreed with the client a provision as outlined in paragraph 3 above, they will be able to discharge their responsibilities under paragraph 7 and/or 8 above, without any breach of confidentiality or duty to the client. While professional accountants in public practice shall include such a provision, it is recognised that, on occasion, compliance with such responsibilities may still involve a breach of confidentiality to a third party or a breach of some other duty owed to the client. In such circumstances this Appendix is not applicable.

The Financial Services and Markets Act 2000

10   The provision of corporate finance services may require authorisation by the Financial Services Authority or a licence under the Designated Professional Body arrangements. However, this Guidance Note applies to all professional accountants in public practice whether authorised/licensed or not.

Appendix 3 to Section 221 – Corporate Finance Advice

Guidance for firms seeking to act for more than one party in a takeover subject to the City Code

This table is intended for illustrative purposes only and shall be read in conjunction with section 221, Corporate Finance Advice.

	Bid Situation	Target	Bidder	Subsequent Bidder	Comments
A	Agreed – relationship with one bidder	Ass	Ass	–	Permitted – see paragraph 221.24
B		Adv	Ass	–	Permitted by agreement with the Takeover Panel – see paragraph 221.29
C		Ass	Adv	–	Permitted with conditions – see paragraph 221.27
D		Adv	Adv	–	Prohibited – see paragraph 221.26
E	Hostile one bidder	Ass	Ass	–	Permitted with conditions – see paragraph 221.24
F		Adv	Ass		Permitted by agreement with the Takeover Panel – see paragraph 221.29
G		Ass	Adv		Prohibited – see paragraph 221.26 and 221.27
H		Adv	Adv		Prohibited – see paragraph 221.26
I	Subsequent bidder emerges	Ass	Ass	Ass	Permitted – see paragraph 221.24
J		Ass		Ass	Permitted see paragraph 221.24
K		Adv		Ass	Permitted – see paragraph 221.28
L		Ass		Adv	Prohibited – see paragraph 221.26

M		Adv		Adv	Prohibited – see paragraph 221.26
N	Acting for rival bidders		Ass	Ass	Permitted – see paragraph 221.24
O			Adv	Ass	Permitted – see paragraph 221.28
P			Ass	Adv	Prohibited – see paragraph 221.26
Q			Adv	Adv	Prohibited – see paragraph 221.26

In all of the above cases where professional accountants in public practice may be permitted to act for more than one party, the professional accountants in public practice must consider the potential threats and put in place the appropriate safeguards as set out in paragraph 221.33. Furthermore, where stated, permission for the professional accountant in public practice to act for more than one party shall be obtained from the Takeover Panel.

Key

Adv   Professional accountant in public practice acts as lead adviser (see paragraph 221.17)

Ass   Professional accountant in public practice acts as auditor or reporting accountant.

As regards the application of this guidance to non-audit assurance engagements, professional accountant in public practice's attention is drawn to the explanatory note contained in the Definitions to Parts A, B and C.

Notes

1.   This matrix does not address a reverse takeover situation, where the offeror is required by the City Code to appoint advisers.
2.   The matrix does not cover the takeover of private companies, except those which are subject to the City Code. Private companies are subject to the general requirements of this Code.

230 Second Opinions

230.0   Opinions expressed informally by a professional accountant may be acted on, and professional accountants shall bear in mind the potential consequences of those opinions. Oral opinions shall as a matter of good practice, because of legal implications, be confirmed in writing as soon as practicable after giving the opinion. If a professional accountant is asked for a 'general opinion' (one relative to a hypothetical situation not related to specific entities or circumstances), whether written or oral, the professional accountant shall ensure that the recipient of the opinion understands that it has been given in the context of that particular hypothetical situation only.

Situations where a professional accountant in public practice is asked to provide a   **230.1**
second opinion on the application of accounting, auditing, reporting or other standards or principles to specific circumstances or transactions by or on behalf of a company or an entity that is not an existing client may create threats to compliance with the fundamental principles. For example, there may be a threat to professional competence and due care in circumstances where the second opinion is not based on the same set of facts that were made available to the existing accountant or is based on inadequate evidence. The existence and significance of any threat will depend on the circumstances of the request and all the other available facts and assumptions relevant to the expression of a professional judgment.

This section does not apply to expert evidence assignments, opinions pursuant to litigation and opinions provided to other firms and their clients jointly.

When asked to provide such an opinion, a professional accountant in public practice   **230.2**
shall evaluate the significance of any threats and apply safeguards when necessary to eliminate them or reduce them to an acceptable level. Examples of such safeguards include seeking client permission to contact the existing accountant, describing the limitations surrounding any opinion in communications with the client and providing the existing accountant with a copy of the opinion.

Professional accountant providing a second opinion will normally need to seek contact with the existing accountant (particularly if the existing accountant is engaged as auditor) and the client in order to:

- Ascertain the circumstances in which the consultation has been made; and
- Be apprised of all the facts relevant to the issue at the time the opinion is given.

If the company or entity seeking the opinion will not permit communication with the   **230.3**
existing accountant, a professional accountant in public practice shall determine whether, taking all the circumstances into account, it is appropriate to provide the opinion sought.

If the client will not allow the opinion-giver to carry out any of the steps referred to above, the opinion-giver must normally decline to act (particularly if the existing accountant is engaged as auditor).

240 Fees and other types of remuneration

ICAEW does not set charge-out rates or otherwise prescribe the basis for calculating   **240.0**
fees, nor does it ordinarily investigate complaints relating solely to the quantum of fees charged. However, professional accountants in public practice have certain professional responsibilities in relation to fees as set out in the following paragraphs.

When entering into negotiations regarding professional services, a professional   **240.1**
accountant in public practice may quote whatever fee is deemed appropriate. The fact that one professional accountant in public practice may quote a fee lower than another is not in itself unethical. Nevertheless, there may be threats to compliance with the fundamental principles arising from the level of fees quoted. For example, a self-interest threat to professional competence and due care is created if the fee quoted is so low that it may be difficult to perform the engagement in accordance with applicable technical and professional standards for that price.

240.2　The existence and significance of any threats created will depend on factors such as the level of fee quoted and the services to which it applies. The significance of any threat shall be evaluated and safeguards applied when necessary to eliminate the threat or reduce it to an acceptable level. Examples of such safeguards include:

- Making the client aware of the terms of the engagement and, in particular, the basis on which fees are charged and which services are covered by the quoted fee.
- Assigning appropriate time and qualified staff to the task.

240.2a　The basis on which fees will be calculated shall be discussed and explained at the earliest opportunity together with, where practicable, the estimated initial fee. Fees shall be determined by reference to:

- The seniority and professional expertise of the persons necessarily engaged on the work;
- The time expended by each;
- The degree of risk and responsibility which the work entails;
- The nature of the client's business, the complexity of its operation and the work to be performed;
- The priority and importance of the work to the client;
- Expenses properly incurred.

240.2b　The arrangements agreed shall be confirmed in writing prior to the commencement of any engagement, normally in an engagement letter, including a confirmation of any estimate, quotation or other indication, and where the basis of future fees will differ from that of initial fees, the basis on which such fees will be rendered. Where there is no engagement letter the professional accountant in public practice shall confirm the initial discussion in writing to the client as soon as practicable.

240.2c　In the case of assurance work, and in particular audit work, professional accountants in public practice who obtain work having quoted levels of fees which they have reason to believe are significantly lower than existing fees or, for example, those quoted by other tendering firms, shall be aware that their objectivity and the quality of their work may appear to be threatened by self-interest in securing the client. Such professional accountants in public practice shall ensure that their work complies with relevant standards, guidelines and regulations and, in particular, quality control procedures.

240.2d　In the event of a complaint being made to ICAEW where fees were a feature in obtaining or retaining the work, professional accountants in public practice shall demonstrate that:

- The work done was in accordance with relevant standards; and
- The client was not misled as to the basis on which fees for the current and/or subsequent years are to be determined.

240.3　Contingent fees are widely used for certain types of non-assurance engagements.[1] They may, however, create threats to compliance with the fundamental principles in certain circumstances. They may create a self-interest threat to objectivity. The existence and significance of such threats will depend on factors including:

- The nature of the engagement.
- The range of possible fee amounts.
- The basis for determining the fee.
- Whether the outcome or result of the transaction is to be reviewed by an independent third party.

The significance of any such threats shall be evaluated and safeguards applied when necessary to eliminate or reduce them to an acceptable level. Examples of such safeguards include: **240.4**

- An advance written agreement with the client as to the basis of remuneration.
- Disclosure to intended users of the work performed by the professional accountant in public practice and the basis of remuneration.
- Quality control policies and procedures.
- Review by an independent third party of the work performed by the professional accountant in public practice.

In some formal appointments under insolvency legislation, in particular bankruptcies, liquidations and administrations, the remuneration of the professional accountant in public practice may, by statute, be based on a percentage of: **240.4a**

- Realisations or the value of the property with which the professional accountant in public practice has to deal; and/or
- Distributions.

Consequently, it may not be possible to base the fee on the principle in paragraph 240.4 above.

In some circumstances, such as advising on a management buy-in or buy-out, the raising of venture capital, acquisition searches or sales mandates, where no professional opinion is given, it may not be appropriate to charge fees save on a contingent fee basis: to require otherwise might deprive potential clients of professional assistance, for example where the capacity of the client to pay is dependent upon the success or failure of the venture. **240.4b**

Due diligence assignments, particularly those performed in relation to a prospective transaction, typically involve a high level of risk and responsibility. A higher fee may be charged for such work in respect of a completed transaction than for the same transaction if it is not completed, for whatever reason, provided that the difference reflects any additional risk and responsibility. **240.4c**

Fee information and disputes

A professional accountant in public practice shall furnish, either in the fee account or subsequently on request, and without further charge, such details as are reasonable to enable the client to understand the basis on which the fee account has been prepared. **240.4d**

Where fees rendered without prior agreement exceed, by more than a reasonable amount, a quotation or estimate or indication of fees given by a professional accountant in public practice, the professional accountant in public practice shall be prepared to provide the client with a full and detailed explanation of the excess and to take steps to resolve speedily any dispute which arises. **240.4e**

A professional accountant in public practice whose fees have not been paid may be entitled to retain certain books and papers of a client by exercising a lien and may refuse to pass on information to the client or the successor accountant until those fees are paid (but see section 210, 'Professional appointment'). However, a professional accountant in public practice who so acts shall be prepared to take reasonable and prompt steps to resolve any dispute relating to the amount of that fee. In respect of any fee dispute, a professional accountant in public practice shall be aware of the fee arbitration services offered by the Institute. **240.4f**

240.4g   Overdue fees may give rise to a perceived or real self-interest threat (see section 280). Similar considerations apply to work-in-progress for a client if billing is unduly deferred.

Referrals and commissions

240.5   In certain circumstances, a professional accountant in public practice may receive a referral fee or commission relating to a client. For example, where the professional accountant in public practice does not provide the specific service required, a fee may be received for referring a continuing client to another professional accountant in public practice or other expert. A professional accountant in public practice may receive a commission from a third party (e.g., a software vendor) in connection with the sale of goods or services to a client. Accepting such a referral fee or commission creates a self-interest threat to objectivity and professional competence and due care.

240.6   A professional accountant in public practice may also pay a referral fee to obtain a client, for example, where the client continues as a client of another professional accountant in public practice but requires specialist services not offered by the existing accountant. The payment of such a referral fee also creates a self-interest threat to objectivity and professional competence and due care.

240.7   The significance of the threat shall be evaluated and safeguards applied when necessary to eliminate the threat or reduce it to an acceptable level. Examples of such safeguards include:

- Disclosing to the client any arrangements to pay a referral fee to another professional accountant for the work referred.
- Disclosing to the client any arrangements to receive a referral fee for referring the client to another professional accountant in public practice.
- Obtaining advance agreement from the client for commission arrangements in connection with the sale by a third party of goods or services to the client.

Remuneration of employees would not normally be included within the scope of the payments addressed above.

240.7a   A fiduciary relationship between a professional accountant in public practice and his or her client will arise where the accountant acts as the client's agent; and/or where the accountant gives professional advice to the client so as to give rise to a relationship which the law would regard as one of 'trust and confidence'. Where a fiduciary relationship exists at the time between a professional accountant in public practice and a client, the professional accountant in public practice is legally bound to account to the client for any commission, fee or other benefit received from a third party at any time. ICAEW is advised that the effect is that a professional accountant in public practice will require the informed consent of the client if the professional accountant in public practice is to retain the commission, fee or other benefit or any part of it. If professional accountants in public practice are in doubt as to whether the circumstances give rise to a fiduciary relationship, they are recommended to seek appropriate legal advice.

240.7b   Under the general law, professional accountants must adopt one of the following courses in respect of commission receivable[2] :

- Account to the client for the commission or other benefit. This could be effected:
  - By payment of the whole commission or benefit to the client, or
  - By deducting the amount received from the fees otherwise chargeable to the client and by showing such deduction on the face of the bill.

- Obtain the client's advance consent to each receipt of commission
  This involves obtaining consent before the commission is received and the firm must disclose, in advance, the actual amount of the commission (or its basis of calculation) and the terms and timing of its payment.
- Obtain the client's advance general consent to the member's retaining commission.
  This could be by way of the engagement letter, or by a supplementary agreement, containing explicit wording permitting such retention, such as the following:
  'In some circumstances, commissions or other benefits may become payable to us [or to one of our associates] in respect of transactions we [or such associates] arrange for you, in which case you will be notified in writing of the amount and terms of payment. [The fees that would otherwise be payable by you as described above will [or will not] be abated by such amounts.] You consent to such commission or other benefits being retained by us [or, as the case may be, by our associates,] without our, [or their,] being liable to account to you for any such amounts.'
  Note:
  o   Before the client agrees to any such provision, examples must be given of likely commissions that may be received and the likely amounts, and it shall be emphasised that these are only examples and may not cover all receipts in the future. If, in the future, abnormally large commissions are received which were not envisaged when the engagement letter was signed, it would be advisable to obtain specific consent to the retention of those commissions in order to meet any assertion that retention of such commission was not authorised by the engagement letter.
  o   Any further provision which indicated likely levels of commission, and then continued 'Commissions of less than £X will be retained by us, and commissions of more than £X will be divided equally between yourselves and ourselves' might be effective. Members are advised, however, to consult with their lawyers before including such a provision.
  o   Where an existing client of the member is to sign a new engagement letter containing such a provision as is referred to above, the firm shall explain that, in the absence of the signed engagement letter, the firm could retain the commission only if the client gave full and informed consent on each occasion after receiving full disclosure of the amount involved, whereas, once the letter is signed, the firm can keep the commission.
- Obtain the client's subsequent consent
  If the member does not obtain the client's consent in one of the ways referred to in paragraph 240.7b above, the commission may still be able to be retained if the client subsequently expressly consents to such retention (on the basis of foll disclosure of the amount, terms and timing of payment).

Alternatively professional accountants will be able to retain the commission if the client (with knowledge of all relevant facts) impliedly consents by acquiescing in such retention, for instance by deciding to proceed with the transaction having been notified both of the fact that the firm will receive commission and of the foll details of that commission. **240.7c**

Even where a fiduciary relationship does not exist, where a professional accountant in public practice becomes aware that any commission, fee or other benefit may be received (directly or indirectly), there shall be disclosed to the client in writing: **240.7d**

- That commission or benefit will result or is likely to result, and
- When the fact is known, that such commission or benefit will be received, and

- As early as possible, the amount and terms of the benefit to the professional accountant in public practice.

240.7e   As regards payments of referral fees, professional accountants in public practice have a responsibility to ascertain that a referral manner is in accordance with this Code because professional accountants in public practice must not do, or be seen to do, through others what they may not do themselves. To this end, professional accountants in public practice shall consider whether there are any indications that the work or client has been initially procured in an unprofessional manner. In addition, where needed to complete a referred engagement properly, professional accountants in public practice shall:

- Satisfy themselves as to the competence and professional standards of staff within their firm whose work on the engagement it would be their duty to review; and
- Ensure their right of direct access to the client and, in appropriate circumstances, render their own fee account to the client.

240.7f   In the case of insolvency work, Insolvency Practitioners shall have regard to Part D of this Code.

240.7g   Where an invitation to conduct a statutory audit comes other than directly from the client, the professional accountant in public practice shall first ensure that the audit appointment has properly been made in accordance with statute. It shall be made clear to all interested parties on all relevant documents that the professional accountant in public practice is acting as principal, with all that that function implies. In those circumstances, professional accountants in public practice shall deal directly with the client and shall render their own fee account in addition to complying with the other requirements above.

240.8   A professional accountant in public practice may purchase all or part of another firm on the basis that payments will be made to individuals formerly owning the firm or to their heirs or estates. Such payments are not regarded as commissions or referral fees for the purpose of paragraphs 240.5-240.7 above.

Attention is drawn to additional requirements in respect of agency and referral arrangements, in section 241.

241 Agencies and referrals

241.1   When referring or receiving referred work or when establishing agency arrangements, which are in effect permanent arrangements for making referrals, professional accountants in public practice are required to assess threats to compliance with the fundamental principles and to apply safeguards. A referral covers a formal request made in the course of a professional relationship for advice on the selection of a potential professional adviser and may also cover an informal request, regardless of whether there is an existing relationship.

Attention is drawn to additional requirements in respect of referral fee arrangements, in section 240.

Duty of care

In making a referral, a duty of care may arise. The extent of a duty of care varies **241.2**
according to the circumstances, including whether the exchange or provision of
information was solicited or not. A greater duty of care will arise for matters which
are reasonably expected to be within a professional accountant in public practice's
knowledge or where a fee is charged. A professional accountant in public practice
needs to look at this from the client's or enquirer's point of view and what their
expectations would be of what a professional accountant in public practice would be
expected to know:

- Where a referral fee is received, or where the service referred is in a professional
  or finance-related sphere, the client (or enquirer) can reasonably presume
  knowledge by the professional accountant in public practice. Any limitation of
  knowledge would clearly need to be explained.
- Where the enquiry relates to a service outside the normal sphere of expertise of
  an accountant and no referral fee is contemplated, then it is reasonable to
  presume that the enquiry is being made in a personal capacity, unless circumstances suggest otherwise. It is still advisable to express any limitations of
  knowledge and to clarify, in case of doubt, that any opinion is based on personal
  experience rather than in a professional capacity.

When making a referral, disclosure of relevant knowledge limitations shall be con- **241.3**
sidered. Professional accountants in public practice shall consider whether it would
be in their interest for such knowledge limitations to be disclosed in writing,
according to the circumstances. Factors that a professional accountant in public
practice shall consider when making such a decision include:

- The nature of the professional relationship with the enquirer (an existing client,
  someone who could reasonably be considered to be making the enquiry as a
  prospective client or a casual enquiry).
- The context in which the enquiry is made. Is it professional or personal, casual
  or formal?
- The nature of the personal relationship. Does the enquirer know the professional accountant in public practice is a Chartered Accountant and are they
  consulting them as a respected professional?
- The scope of enquiry and whether a referral fee is contemplated, as considered
  in section 240.
- The enquirer's expectations.

A referral arises typically, when the professional accountant in public practice does **241.4**
not have the expertise and/or resource in house to undertake the potential engagement. It follows that the professional accountant in public practice will not
necessarily know enough to be able to completely assess whether the third party is
the optimum choice or not. This is an inevitable limitation in most referrals, and
what the referral is based on will vary. However, the professional accountant in
public practice shall consider the fitness for purpose of the third party to address the
client's needs.

In making that consideration, the professional accountant in public practice: **241.5**

- Can take account of the professional or regulatory status of the prospective
  referee;
- Is not normally expected to have to make additional enquiries about the prospective referee and can make the assessment based on what is already known.

241.6   A referral shall not normally be made to a third party even with a disclaimer, when, taking into account known factors, the professional accountant in public practice knows of a better alternative. If the client or enquirer insists on being referred to a particular third party and the professional accountant in public practice believes there is a better alternative, the reference may be made but the client or enquirer shall be made aware of the professional accountant in public practice's concerns. Where the referral relates to an end product or service, rather than an intermediary, and the professional accountant in public practice knows there are other alternatives but does not know if they are better, this shall be explained.

241.7   If there is a relationship with the third party, for example a family connection or an automatic referral arrangement, there are clear self-interest or familiarity threats and the connection shall be disclosed. This is particularly important where a professional accountant in public practice is considering recommending the products of another supplier with which there is an agency, and/or a principal or employee of the professional accountant in public practice's firm is a principal or officer of the other supplier. If in substance there is a one-to-one relationship between the professional accountant in public practice and the third party (for example, the professional accountant in public practice is the only accountant in the area and the third party is the only solicitor), which implies automatic referral, this shall also be disclosed.

241.8   In summary, professional accountants in public practice shall:

- Consider any factors they are aware of that would indicate the proposed third party is not fit for purpose in terms of the potential engagement. The professional accountant in public practice shall take into account what a reasonable person might expect a Chartered Accountant to know;
- Make clients (or enquirers), that are proposed to be referred, aware of limitations in knowledge;
- Disclose any referral arrangement;
- Ensure that any contractual arrangement does not override the needs of an individual client.

Establishing Agencies

241.9   The guidance which follows is intended to assist professional accountants in public practice in their arrangements with other suppliers of services and products.

241.10   This section addresses agreements that in effect provide for permanent arrangements for referrals. The issues are considered to be similar to those above for referrals in general except that an agency contract will usually bind the agent in terms of whom it can refer to for particular types of work. When professional accountants in public practice are considering the establishment of an agency, the terms of the agency contract (actual or implied) shall not require exclusive referral of all clients regardless of suitability. For example, professional accountants in public practice shall not be party to an agency by which they are constrained to channel all funds received by it for investment into a single bank/building society. Such a clause would make important safeguards inoperable.

241.11   Before accepting appointment as auditor of another entity of which they are an agent, professional accountants in public practice shall consider whether the agency constitutes a material business relationship. See section 290, 'Independence – audit and review engagements.'

241.12   Professional accountants in public practice shall not, because of the self-interest threat, enter into any financial arrangements with another supplier either personally or through their firm which would prejudice the objectivity of themselves or their firm.

Before accepting or continuing an agency with another supplier, professional accountants in public practice shall satisfy themselves that their ability to discharge their professional obligations to their clients is not compromised.   **241.13**

A professional accountant in public practice shall not in any circumstances conduct its practice in such a manner as to give the impression that the professional accountant is a principal rather than an agent. This would include considering signs on premises and any other outward signs or literature used. This would relate in particular to agencies with entities such as banks and building societies, where confusion as to status can arise (see also 'The names and letterheads of practising firms' at (icaew.com/regulations).   **241.14**

Firms in the Republic of Ireland must be authorised under the Investment Intermediaries Act, 1995 to hold an agency with a building society and that arrangement shall relate solely to deposit taking and not for example relate to products of a particular insurance company or unit trust organisation for which the building society is an appointed representative. Firms holding building society agencies must ensure that their agency agreement contains no obligation which would cause, or would be perceived to cause, them to breach the provisions of either the Act or the Institute of Chartered Accountants in Ireland's Investment Business regulations and Guidance. Firms cannot hold agencies with banks.   **241.15**

Investment business agencies and introductions

When considering referrals of investment business ('introductions') or the establishment of investment business agencies, professional accountants in public practice shall apply the general principles and requirements set out in the previous Sections. However, they will also need to consider: **241.16**

● Whether the introduction or agency is permitted by regulation; and
● Whether the status of the third party investment business provider is compatible with the requirement to give objective advice.

Regulated activities under the Financial Services and Markets Act 2000 (United Kingdom)

In order to make a decision about whether an introduction is a regulated activity, the professional accountant in public practice must look at how the introduction is made and also what type of investment the client is considering (such as life assurance and pensions, unit trusts, shares, mortgages or general insurance). A regulated introduction can only be made under the terms of the Act by a firm which is licensed by ICAEW as a Designated Professional Body ('DPB') (a licensed firm) or a firm which is authorised by the Financial Services Authority ('authorised'). Unauthorised / unlicensed firms are restricted in that they can only make introductions for general financial advice where no specific type of investment is referred to, or for a restricted range of investments, such as shares and unit trusts. Such introductions can only be made to those authorised firms who can give independent advice. However, unauthorised / unlicensed firms can provide information to a client about a third party provided no recommendation is made.   **241.17**

Further guidance on the difference between a regulated introduction and the provision of information in respect of insurance business, and the regulatory   **241.18** consequences thereof, is set out in Schedule 6 to Part 3 of the DPB Handbook, available at icaew.com/dpb.

241.19   Having established that an introduction can be made in compliance with regulatory requirements, professional accountants in public practice shall bear in mind the need to provide their clients with objective advice, in compliance with these ethical standards.

241.20   Professional accountants in public practice can become appointed representatives of another authorised firm. When selecting which authorised firm to become an appointed representative of, professional accountants in public practice shall again bear in mind the need to provide their clients with objective advice.

Regulated Activities under the Investment Intermediaries Act, 1995 (Republic of Ireland)

241.21   Professional accountants in public practice may only make an introduction or refer clients to another authorised firm if they are themselves authorised to conduct investment business under the Investment Intermediaries Act 1995 and where required hold an appropriate letter of appointment.

241.22   Professional accountants in public practice when selecting an authorised firm shall bear in mind the need to provide their clients with objective advice.

Status of investment business providers

241.23   Authorised firms can fall into the following categories:

Type of firm	What the firm can recommend	Can there generally be introductions to this type of firm?
Independent	Recommend products from the whole market and offer clients the ability to pay by fee. Only these firms can describe themselves as independent financial advisers. The client may be able to elect for the adviser to be paid by commission	Yes (241.24 below)
Whole of market (UK only)	Recommend products from the whole market but do not offer clients the ability to pay by fee. The firm is remunerated by commission.	Yes (241.25 below)
Multi-tied (Multi-agency in RoI)	Recommend the products of more than one product provider with whom the firm has agreements, but recommends on less than the whole market.	Depends on scope of choice (241.26 below)
Tied	Recommend the products of one product provider.	No (241.27 below)

An introduction to an independent firm would be likely to meet the requirement to give objective advice but professional accountants in public practice are reminded of the general requirements above. **241.24**

Professional accountants in public practice may also regard 'whole of market' authorised firms as equivalent to independent firms as the method by which the authorised firm is remunerated (which is the difference between independent and whole of market) is not relevant for the purposes of compliance with this statement. **241.25**

Professional accountants in public practice may in some situations be able to introduce to multi-tied firms and still comply with the ethical requirements (however, see paragraphs 241.16-241.18 above as to whether the introduction can only be made by a DPB licensed firm or an FSA authorised firm, if it is a 'regulated' activity). Clearly the principal threat is that clients might not be offered the most appropriate choice. The professional accountant in public practice will need to assess the client's requirements and whether the multi-tied firm places business with the product providers who account for a large majority of the relevant market or offer the sector of the market which is most suitable for the client's needs. However, members must ensure that in making such an assessment, they are not effectively making their own recommendation unless they are able to do so under the terms of a licence or authorisation. The professional accountant in public practice may decide that this does not restrict the client's access to the range of product providers to an extent where there is any potential detriment. The professional accountant in public practice shall make the client aware of restrictions in the range of investments offered by the firm to which the client is being referred. **241.26**

An introduction to a tied firm restricts the client's ability to obtain independent advice and would therefore not be objective. **241.27**

Similar considerations to those noted above apply to whether a professional accountant in public practice shall become an appointed representative under the Financial Services and Markets Act 2000. Thus, for example, a professional firm cannot become an appointed representative for regulated investment business, of a tied firm as the agency agreement would probably oblige the firm to make referrals to the principal in all circumstances and the firm would be unable to provide objective advice. **241.28**

250 Marketing Professional services

When a professional accountant in public practice solicits new work through advertising or other forms of marketing, there may be a threat to compliance with the fundamental principles. For example, a self-interest threat to compliance with the principle of professional behaviour is created if services, achievements, or products are marketed in a way that is inconsistent with that principle. **250.1**

A professional accountant in public practice shall not bring the profession into disrepute when marketing professional services. The professional accountant in public practice shall be honest and truthful and not: **250.2**

- Make exaggerated claims for services offered, qualifications possessed, or experience gained; or
- Make disparaging references or unsubstantiated comparisons to the work of another.

In particular, where professional accountants in public practice seek to make comparisons of their promotional material between their practices or services and those of others, great care will be required. In particular, they shall ensure that such comparisons:

- Are objective and not misleading,
- Relate to the same services,
- Are factual and verifiable, and
- Do not discredit or denigrate the practice or services of others.

particular care is needed in unclear or subjective claims of size or quality. For example, it is impossible to know whether a claim to be 'the largest firm' in an area is a reference to the number of partners or staff, the number of offices or the amount of fee income. A claim to be 'the best firm' is unlikely to be able to be substantiated.

If the professional accountant in public practice is in doubt about whether a proposed form of advertising or marketing is appropriate, the professional accountant in public practice shall consider consulting with ICAEW.

250.3   A professional accountant in public practice shall ensure that all advertisements, including letterheads, invoices and other practice documents, comply with the law and conform with the requirements of the relevant Advertising Standards Authority (for example, the British Code of Advertising) notably, as to legality, decency, clarity, honesty and truthfulness.

250.4   If reference is made in promotional material to fees, the basis on which the fees are calculated, or to hourly or other charging rates, the greatest care shall be taken to ensure that such reference does not mislead as to the precise range of services and the time commitment that the reference is intended to cover. Professional accountants in public practice are unlikely to be able to comply with the requirements of 250.2 if making a comparison in such material between their fees and the fees of another accounting practice, whether members or not. A professional accountant in public practice may offer a free consultation at which fees are discussed.

250.5   Professional accountants in public practice shall never promote or seek to promote their services, or the services of other professional accountants in public practice, in such a way, or to such an extent, as to amount to harassment of a potential client.

It shall be noted that special roles apply in relation to the conduct of Insolvency Practice and licensed practitioners shall have regard to the relevant legislation and to Part D. Similarly professional accountants in public practice whose firm is registered for the conduct of investment business shall have recourse to the relevant Investment Business regulations.

250.6   Further guidance on marketing professional services is available to members in a helpsheet from the Ethics Advisory Services (icaew.com/ethicsadvice). See also sections 210, 'Professional appointment' and 230, 'Second opinions'.

260 Gifts and hospitality

260.1   A professional accountant in public practice, or an immediate or close family member, may be offered gifts and hospitality from a client. Such an offer may create threats to compliance with the fundamental principles. For example, a self-interest or familiarity threat to objectivity may be created if a gift from a client is accepted; an intimidation threat to objectivity may result from the possibility of such offers being made public.

The existence and significance of any threat will depend on the nature, value, and intent of the offer. Where gifts or hospitality are offered that a reasonable and informed third party, weighing all the specific facts and circumstances, would consider trivial and inconsequential, a professional accountant in public practice may conclude that the offer is made in the normal course of business without the specific intent to influence decision making or to obtain information. In such cases, the professional accountant in public practice may generally conclude that any threat to compliance with the fundamental principles is at an acceptable level.

260.2

A professional accountant in public practice shall evaluate the significance of any threats and apply safeguards when necessary to eliminate the threats or reduce them to an acceptable level. When the threats cannot be eliminated or reduced to an acceptable level through the application of safeguards, a professional accountant in public practice shall not accept such an offer.

260.3

Further guidance on dealing with gifts and hospitality in an assurance engagement is available in paragraph 290.230.

260.4

270 Custody of client assets

A professional accountant in public practice shall not assume custody of client monies or other assets unless permitted to do so by law and, if so, in compliance with any additional legal duties imposed on a professional accountant in public practice holding such assets.

270.1

The holding of client assets creates threats to compliance with the fundamental principles; for example, there is a self-interest threat to professional behaviour and may be a self interest threat to objectivity arising from holding client assets. A professional accountant in public practice entrusted with money (or other assets) belonging to others shall therefore:

270.2

- Keep such assets separately from personal or firm assets;
- Use such assets only for the purpose for which they are intended;
- At all times be ready to account for those assets and any income, dividends, or gains generated, to any persons entitled to such accounting; and
- Comply with all relevant laws and regulations relevant to the holding of and accounting for such assets.

regulations on the procedures required to be adopted by professional accountants holding client monies are available at 'Clients' money regulations'. For firms licensed by ICAEW under the Designated Professional Bodies arrangements, additional requirements are included in Chapter 4 of the Designated Professional Bodies Handbook.

As part of client and engagement acceptance procedures for services that may involve the holding of client assets, a professional accountant in public practice shall make appropriate inquiries about the source of such assets and consider legal and regulatory obligations. For example, if the assets were derived from illegal activities, such as money laundering, a threat to compliance with the fundamental principles would be created. In such situations, the professional accountant may consider seeking legal advice.

270.3

Further guidance on money laundering regulation and legislation is available in 'Anti-money laundering guidance for the accountancy sector'.

See also 'Document and records: ownership, lien and rights of access'.

280 Objectivity – all services

280.1   A professional accountant in public practice shall determine when providing any professional service whether there are threats to compliance with the fundamental principle of objectivity resulting from having interests in, or relationships with, a client or its directors, officers or employees. For example, a familiarity threat to objectivity may be created from a family or close personal or business relationship.

280.2   A professional accountant in public practice who provides an assurance service shall be independent of the assurance client. Independence of mind and in appearance is necessary to enable the professional accountant in public practice to express a conclusion, and be seen to express a conclusion, without bias, conflict of interest, or undue influence of others. Sections 290 and 291 provide specific guidance on independence requirements for professional accountants in public practice when performing assurance engagements.

280.3   The existence of threats to objectivity when providing any professional service will depend upon the particular circumstances of the engagement and the nature of the work that the professional accountant in public practice is performing.

280.4   A professional accountant in public practice shall evaluate the significance of any threats and apply safeguards when necessary to eliminate them or reduce them to an acceptable level. Examples of such safeguards include:

- Withdrawing from the engagement team.
- Supervisory procedures.
- Terminating the financial or business relationship giving rise to the threat.
- Discussing the issue with higher levels of management within the firm.
- Discussing the issue with those charged with governance of the client.

If safeguards cannot eliminate or reduce the threat to an acceptable level, the professional accountant shall decline or terminate the relevant engagement.

290 Independence – audit and review engagements

Introduction

290.0a   In accordance with UK legislation, ICAEW has adopted, as regards auditor independence requirements, the Ethical Standards for Auditors, issued by the Auditing Practices Board ('APB'). Therefore, when conducting audit engagements in accordance with ISAs (UK and Ireland), professional accountants shall comply with the requirements of the APB's Ethical Standards for Auditors, including Provisions Available for Small Entities (ES-PASE). For other audit and assurance engagements ICAEW's Code may apply (see 290.0c below).

290.0b   The APB has stated, in ISA (UK and Ireland) 200, that it is not aware of any significant instances where the relevant parts of the IESBA Code of Ethics are more restrictive than the APB's Ethical Standards.

The independence requirements to be adopted for different types of assurance engagement, are set out below: **290.0c**

Type of assurance engagement	Independence requirements to be followed
Audit engagements in accordance with ISAs (UK and Ireland)	The APB's Ethical Standards for Auditors
Audit engagements performed in accordance with other standards	Section 290 of this Code or if more convenient to apply, the independence requirements of the APB's Ethical Standards for Auditors.
Review engagements (see appendix to section 290)	Section 290 of this Code or if more convenient to apply, the independence requirements of the APB's Ethical Standards for Auditors.
Other types of assurance engagements	Section 291 of this Code.

Note that the Statements of Investment Circular Reporting Standards (SIRS), issued by the APB require compliance with the APB's Ethical Standard for Reporting Accountants (ESRA). Accordingly, any professional accountant in public practice issuing a report that states that the work has been carried out in accordance with the SIRS will need to comply with the independence requirements of the ESRA.   **290.0d**

Structure of section

This section addresses the independence requirements for audit engagements and review engagements, which are assurance engagements in which a professional accountant in public practice expresses a conclusion on financial statements. Such engagements comprise audit and review engagements to report on a complete set of financial statements and a single financial statement. Independence requirements for assurance engagements that are not audit or review engagements are addressed in section 291.   **290.1**

In certain circumstances involving audit engagements where the audit report includes a restriction on use and distribution and provided certain conditions are met, the independence requirements in this section may be modified as provided in paragraphs 290.500 to 290.514. The modifications are not permitted in the case of an audit of financial statements required by law or regulation.   **290.2**

In this section, the term(s):   **290.3**

- "Audit," "audit team," "audit engagement," "audit client" and "audit report" includes review, review team, review engagement, review client and review report; and
- "Firm" includes network firm, except where otherwise stated.

A conceptual framework approach to independence

In the case of audit engagements, it is in the public interest and, therefore, required by this Code of Ethics, that members of audit teams, firms and network firms shall be independent of audit clients.   **290.4**

290.5   The objective of this section is to assist firms and members of audit teams in applying the conceptual framework approach described below to achieving and maintaining independence.

290.6   Independence comprises:

- independence of Mind
  The state of mind that permits the expression of a conclusion without being affected by influences that compromise professional judgment, thereby allowing an individual to act with integrity and exercise objectivity and professional scepticism.
- independence in Appearance
  The avoidance of facts and circumstances that are so significant that a reasonable and informed third party would be likely to conclude, weighing all the specific facts and circumstances, that a firm's, or a member of the audit team's, integrity, objectivity or professional scepticism has been compromised.

290.7   The conceptual framework approach shall be applied by professional accountants to:

- Identify threats to independence;
- Evaluate the significance of the threats identified; and
- Apply safeguards, when necessary, to eliminate the threats or reduce them to an acceptable level.

When the professional accountant determines that appropriate safeguards are not available or cannot be applied to eliminate the threats or reduce them to an acceptable level, the professional accountant shall eliminate the circumstance or relationship creating the threats or decline or terminate the audit engagement.

A professional accountant shall use professional judgment in applying this conceptual framework.

290.8   Many different circumstances, or combinations of circumstances, may be relevant in assessing threats to independence. It is impossible to define every situation that creates threats to independence and to specify the appropriate action. Therefore, this Code establishes a conceptual framework that requires firms and members of audit teams to identify, evaluate, and address threats to independence. The conceptual framework approach assists professional accountants in practice in complying with the ethical requirements in this Code. It accommodates many variations in circumstances that create threats to independence and can deter a professional accountant from concluding that a situation is permitted if it is not specifically prohibited.

290.9   Paragraphs 290.100 and onwards describe how the conceptual framework approach to independence is to be applied. These paragraphs do not address all the circumstances and relationships that create or may create threats to independence.

290.10   In deciding whether to accept or continue an engagement, or whether a particular individual may be a member of the audit team, a firm shall identify and evaluate threats to independence. If the threats are not at an acceptable level, and the decision is whether to accept an engagement or include a particular individual on the audit team, the firm shall determine whether safeguards are available to eliminate the threats or reduce them to an acceptable level. If the decision is whether to continue an engagement, the firm shall determine whether any existing safeguards will continue to be effective to eliminate the threats or reduce them to an acceptable level or whether other safeguards will need to be applied or whether the engagement needs to be terminated. Whenever new information about a threat to independence comes to the attention of the firm during the engagement, the firm shall evaluate the significance of the threat in accordance with the conceptual framework approach.

Throughout this section, reference is made to the significance of threats to independence. In evaluating the significance of a threat, qualitative as well as quantitative factors shall be taken into account.

290.11

This section does not, in most cases, prescribe the specific responsibility of individuals within the firm for actions related to independence because responsibility may differ depending on the size, structure and organisation of a firm. The firm is required by International Standards on Quality Control to establish policies and procedures designed to provide it with reasonable assurance that independence is maintained when required by relevant ethical requirements. In addition, International Standards on Auditing require the engagement partner to form a conclusion on compliance with the independence requirements that apply to the engagement.

290.12

Networks and network firms

If a firm is deemed to be a network firm, the firm shall be independent of the audit clients of the other firms within the network (unless otherwise stated in this Code). The independence requirements in this section that apply to a network firm apply to any entity, such as a consulting practice or professional law practice, that meets the definition of a network firm irrespective of whether the entity itself meets the definition of a firm.

290.13

To enhance their ability to provide professional services, firms frequently form larger structures with other firms and entities. Whether these larger structures create a network depends on the particular facts and circumstances and does not depend on whether the firms and entities are legally separate and distinct. For example, a larger structure may be aimed only at facilitating the referral of work, which in itself does not meet the criteria necessary to constitute a network. Alternatively, a larger structure might be such that it is aimed at co-operation and the firms share a common brand name, a common system of quality control, or significant professional resources and consequently is deemed to be a network.

290.14

The judgment as to whether the larger structure is a network shall be made in light of whether a reasonable and informed third party would be likely to conclude, weighing all the specific facts and circumstances, that the entities are associated in such a way that a network exists. This judgment shall be applied consistently throughout the network.

290.15

Where the larger structure is aimed at co-operation and it is clearly aimed at profit or cost sharing among the entities within the structure, it is deemed to be a network. However, the sharing of immaterial costs does not in itself create a network. In addition, if the sharing of costs is limited only to those costs related to the development of audit methodologies, manuals, or training courses, this would not in itself create a network. Further, an association between a firm and an otherwise unrelated entity to jointly provide a service or develop a product does not in itself create a network.

290.16

Where the larger structure is aimed at cooperation and the entities within the structure share common ownership, control or management, it is deemed to be a network. This could be achieved by contract or other means.

290.17

290.18   Where the larger structure is aimed at co-operation and the entities within the structure share common quality control policies and procedures, it is deemed to be a network. For this purpose, common quality control policies and procedures are those designed, implemented and monitored across the larger structure.

290.19   Where the larger structure is aimed at co-operation and the entities within the structure share a common business strategy, it is deemed to be a network. Sharing a common business strategy involves an agreement by the entities to achieve common strategic objectives. An entity is not deemed to be a network firm merely because it co-operates with another entity solely to respond jointly to a request for a proposal for the provision of a professional service.

290.20   Where the larger structure is aimed at co-operation and the entities within the structure share the use of a common brand name, it is deemed to be a network. A common brand name includes common initials or a common name. A firm is deemed to be using a common brand name if it includes, for example, the common brand name as part of, or along with, its firm name, when a partner of the firm signs an audit report.

290.21   Even though a firm does not belong to a network and does not use a common brand name as part of its firm name, it may give the appearance that it belongs to a network if it makes reference in its stationery or promotional materials to being a member of an association of firms. Accordingly, if care is not taken in how a firm describes such memberships, a perception may be created that the firm belongs to a network.

290.22   If a firm sells a component of its practice, the sales agreement sometimes provides that, for a limited period of time, the component may continue to use the name of the firm, or an element of the name, even though it is no longer connected to the firm. In such circumstances, while the two entities may be practising under a common name, the facts are such that they do not belong to a larger structure aimed at co-operation and are, therefore, not network firms. Those entities shall determine how to disclose that they are not network firms when presenting themselves to outside parties.

290.23   Where the larger structure is aimed at co-operation and the entities within the structure share a significant part of professional resources, it is deemed to be a network. Professional resources include:

- Common systems that enable firms to exchange information such as client data, billing and time records;
- Partners and staff;
- Technical departments that consult on technical or industry specific issues, transactions or events for assurance engagements;
- Audit methodology or audit manuals; and
- Training courses and facilities.

290.24   The determination of whether the professional resources shared are significant, and therefore the firms are network firms, shall be made based on the relevant facts and circumstances. Where the shared resources are limited to common audit methodology or audit manuals, with no exchange of personnel or client or market information, it is unlikely that the shared resources would be significant. The same applies to a common training endeavour. Where, however, the shared resources involve the exchange of people or information, such as where staff are drawn from a shared pool, or a common technical department is created within the larger structure to provide participating firms with technical advice that the firms are required to follow, a reasonable and informed third party is more likely to conclude that the shared resources are significant.

Public interest entities

Section 290 contains additional provisions that reflect the extent of public interest in certain entities. For the purpose of this section, public interest entities are: **290.25**

- All listed entities; and
- Any entity:
  - Defined by regulation or legislation as a public interest entity or
  - For which the audit is required by regulation or legislation to be conducted in compliance with the same independence requirements that apply to the audit of listed entities. Such regulation may be promulgated by any relevant regulator, including an audit regulator.

Firms are encouraged to determine whether to treat additional entities, or certain categories of entities, as public interest entities because they have a large number and wide range of stakeholders. Factors to be considered include: **290.26**

- The nature of the business, such as the holding of assets in a fiduciary capacity for a large number of stakeholders. Examples may include financial institutions, such as banks and insurance companies, and pension funds;
- Size; and
- Number of employees.

Related Entities

In the case of an audit client that is a listed entity, references to an audit client in this section include related entities of the client (unless otherwise stated). For all other audit clients, references to an audit client in this section include related entities over which the client has direct or indirect control. When the audit team knows or has reason to believe that a relationship or circumstance involving another related entity of the client is relevant to the evaluation of the firm's independence from the client, the audit team shall include that related entity when identifying and evaluating threats to independence and applying appropriate safeguards. **290.27**

Those charged with governance

Even when not required by the Code, applicable auditing standards, law or regulation, regular communication is encouraged between the firm and those charged with governance of the audit client regarding relationships and other matters that might, in the firm's opinion, reasonably bear on independence. Such communication enables those charged with governance to: **290.28**

- consider the firm's judgments in identifying and evaluating threats to independence,
- consider the appropriateness of safeguards applied to eliminate them or reduce them to an acceptable level, and
- take appropriate action. Such an approach can be particularly helpful with respect to intimidation and familiarity threats.

Documentation

Documentation provides evidence of the professional accountant's judgments in forming conclusions regarding compliance with independence requirements. The absence of documentation is not a determinant of whether a firm considered a particular matter nor whether it is independent. The professional accountant shall document conclusions regarding compliance with independence requirements, and **290.29** the substance of any relevant discussions that support those conclusions. Accordingly:

- When safeguards are required to reduce a threat to an acceptable level, the professional accountant shall document the nature of the threat and the safeguards in place or applied that reduce the threat to an acceptable level; and
- When a threat required significant analysis to determine whether safeguards were necessary and the professional accountant concluded that they were not because the threat was already at an acceptable level, the professional accountant shall document the nature of the threat and the rationale for the conclusion.

Engagement Period

290.30 Independence from the audit client is required both during the engagement period and the period covered by the financial statements. The engagement period starts when the audit team begins to perform audit services. The engagement period ends when the audit report is issued. When the engagement is of a recurring nature, it ends at the later of the notification by either party that the professional relationship has terminated or the issuance of the final audit report.

290.31 When an entity becomes an audit client during or after the period covered by the financial statements on which the firm will express an opinion, the firm shall determine whether any threats to independence are created by:

- Financial or business relationships with the audit client during or after the period covered by the financial statements but before accepting the audit engagement; or
- Previous services provided to the audit client.

290.32 If a non-assurance service was provided to the audit client during or after the period covered by the financial statements but before the audit team begins to perform audit services and the service would not be permitted during the period of the audit engagement, the firm shall evaluate any threat to independence created by the service. If a threat is not at an acceptable level, the audit engagement shall only be accepted if safeguards are applied to eliminate any threats or reduce them to an acceptable level. Examples of such safeguards include:

- Not including personnel who provided the non-assurance service as members of the audit team;
- Having a professional accountant review the audit and non-assurance work as appropriate; or
- Engaging another firm to evaluate the results of the non-assurance service or having another firm re-perform the non-assurance service to the extent necessary to enable it to take responsibility for the service.

Mergers and Acquisitions

290.33 When, as a result of a merger or acquisition, an entity becomes a related entity of an audit client, the firm shall identify and evaluate previous and current interests and relationships with the related entity that, taking into account available safeguards, could affect its independence and therefore its ability to continue the audit engagement after the effective date of the merger or acquisition.

290.34 The firm shall take steps necessary to terminate, by the effective date of the merger or acquisition, any current interests or relationships that are not permitted under this Code. However, if such a current interest or relationship cannot reasonably be terminated by the effective date of the merger or acquisition, for example, because the related entity is unable by the effective date to effect an orderly transition to another service provider of a non-assurance service provided by the firm, the firm shall evaluate the threat that is created by such interest or relationship. The more significant the threat, the more likely the firm's objectivity will be compromised and it will be unable to continue as auditor. The significance of the threat will depend upon factors such as:

- The nature and significance of the interest or relationship;
- The nature and significance of the related entity relationship (for example, whether the related entity is a subsidiary or parent); and
- The length of time until the interest or relationship can reasonably be terminated.

The firm shall discuss with those charged with governance the reasons why the interest or relationship cannot reasonably be terminated by the effective date of the merger or acquisition and the evaluation of the significance of the threat.

If those charged with governance request the firm to continue as auditor, the firm shall do so only if: **290.35**

- the interest or relationship will be terminated as soon as reasonably possible and in all cases within six months of the effective date of the merger or acquisition;
- any individual who has such an interest or relationship, including one that has arisen through performing a non-assurance service that would not be permitted under this section, will not be a member of the engagement team for the audit or the individual responsible for the engagement quality control review; and
- appropriate transitional measures will be applied, as necessary, and discussed with those charged with governance. Examples of transitional measures include:
  o Having a professional accountant review the audit or non-assurance work as appropriate;
  o Having a professional accountant, who is not a member of the firm expressing the opinion on the financial statements, perform a review that is equivalent to an engagement quality control review; or
  o Engaging another firm to evaluate the results of the non-assurance service or having another firm re-perform the non-assurance service to the extent necessary to enable it to take responsibility for the service.

The firm may have completed a significant amount of work on the audit prior to the effective date of the merger or acquisition and may be able to complete the remaining audit procedures within a short period of time. In such circumstances, if those charged with governance request the firm to complete the audit while continuing with an interest or relationship identified in 290.33, the firm shall do so only if it: **290.36**

- Has evaluated the significance of the threat created by such interest or relationship and discussed the evaluation with those charged with governance;
- Complies with the requirements of paragraph 290.35(b)-(c); and
- Ceases to be the auditor no later than the issuance of the audit report.

When addressing previous and current interests and relationships covered by paragraphs 290.33 to 290.36, the firm shall determine whether, even if all the requirements could be met, the interests and relationships create threats that would remain so significant that objectivity would be compromised and, if so, the firm shall cease to be the auditor. **290.37**

The professional accountant shall document any interests or relationships covered by paragraphs 290.34 and 36 that will not be terminated by the effective date of the **290.38** merger or acquisition and the reasons why they will not be terminated, the transitional measures applied, the results of the discussion with those charged with governance, and the rationale as to why the previous and current interests and relationships do not create threats that would remain so significant that objectivity would be compromised.

Other considerations

290.39   There may be occasions when there is an inadvertent violation of this section. If such an inadvertent violation occurs, it generally will be deemed not to compromise independence provided the firm has appropriate quality control policies and procedures in place, equivalent to those required by International Standards on Quality Control, to maintain independence and, once discovered, the violation is corrected promptly and any necessary safeguards are applied to eliminate any threat or reduce it to an acceptable level. The firm shall determine whether to discuss the matter with those charged with governance.

Paragraphs 290.40 to 290.99 are intentionally left blank.

Application of the conceptual framework approach to independence

290.100   Paragraphs 290.102 to 290.231 describe specific circumstances and relationships that create or may create threats to independence. The paragraphs describe the potential threats and the types of safeguards that may be appropriate to eliminate the threats or reduce them to an acceptable level and identify certain situations where no safeguards could reduce the threats to an acceptable level. The paragraphs do not describe all of the circumstances and relationships that create or may create a threat to independence. The firm and the members of the audit team shall evaluate the implications of similar, but different, circumstances and relationships and determine whether safeguards, including the safeguards in paragraphs 200.12 to 200.15, can be applied when necessary to eliminate the threats to independence or reduce them to an acceptable level.

290.101   Paragraphs 290.102 to 290.126 contain references to the materiality of a financial interest, loan, or guarantee, or the significance of a business relationship. For the purpose of determining whether such an interest is material to an individual, the combined net worth of the individual and the individual's immediate family members may be taken into account.

Financial interests

290.102   Holding a financial interest in an audit client may create a self-interest threat. The existence and significance of any threat created depends on:

- the role of the person holding the financial interest,
- whether the financial interest is direct or indirect, and
- the materiality of the financial interest.

290.103   Financial interests may be held through an intermediary (e.g. a collective investment vehicle, estate or trust). The determination of whether such financial interests are direct or indirect will depend upon whether the beneficial owner has control over the investment vehicle or the ability to influence its investment decisions. When control over the investment vehicle or the ability to influence investment decisions exists, this Code defines that financial interest to be a direct financial interest. Conversely, when the beneficial owner of the financial interest has no control over the investment vehicle or ability to influence its investment decisions, this Code defines that financial interest to be an indirect financial interest.

If a member of the audit team, a member of that individual's immediate family or a **290.104** firm has a direct financial interest or a material indirect financial interest in the audit client, the self-interest threat created would be so significant that no safeguards could reduce the threat to an acceptable level. Therefore, none of the following shall have a direct financial interest or a material indirect financial interest in the client: a member of the audit team; a member of that individual's immediate family; or the firm.

When a member of the audit team has a close family member who the audit team **290.105** member knows has a direct financial interest or a material indirect financial interest in the audit client, a self-interest threat is created. The significance of the threat will depend on factors such as:

- The nature of the relationship between the member of the audit team and the close family member; and
- The materiality of the financial interest to the close family member.

The significance of the threat shall be evaluated and safeguards applied when necessary to eliminate the threat or reduce it to an acceptable level. Examples of such safeguards include:

- The close family member disposing, as soon as practicable, of all of the financial interest or disposing of a sufficient portion of an indirect financial interest so that the remaining interest is no longer material;
- Having a professional accountant review the work of the member of the audit team; or
- Removing the individual from the audit team.

If a member of the audit team, a member of that individual's immediate family, or a **290.106** firm has a direct or material indirect financial interest in an entity that has a controlling interest in the audit client, and the client is material to the entity, the self-interest threat created would be so significant that no safeguards could reduce the threat to an acceptable level. Therefore, none of the following shall have such a financial interest: a member of the audit team; a member of that individual's immediate family; and the firm.

The holding by a firm's retirement benefit plan of a direct or material indirect **290.107** financial interest in an audit client creates a self-interest threat. The significance of the threat shall be evaluated and safeguards applied when necessary to eliminate the threat or reduce it to an acceptable level.

If other partners in the office in which the engagement partner practices in con- **290.108** nection with the audit engagement, or their immediate family members, hold a direct financial interest or a material indirect financial interest in that audit client, the self-interest threat created would be so significant that no safeguards could reduce the threat to an acceptable level. Therefore, neither such partners nor their immediate family members shall hold any such financial interests in such an audit client.

The office in which the engagement partner practices in connection with the audit **290.109** engagement is not necessarily the office to which that partner is assigned. Accordingly, when the engagement partner is located in a different office from that of the other members of the audit team, professional judgment shall be used to determine in which office the partner practices in connection with that engagement.

290.110   If other partners and managerial employees who provide non-audit services to the audit client, except those whose involvement is minimal, or their immediate family members, hold a direct financial interest or a material indirect financial interest in the audit client, the self-interest threat created would be so significant that no safeguards could reduce the threat to an acceptable level. Accordingly, neither such personnel nor their immediate family members shall hold any such financial interests in such an audit client.

290.111   Despite paragraphs 290.108 and 290.110, the holding of a financial interest in an audit client by an immediate family member of :

- a partner located in the office in which the engagement partner practices in connection with the audit engagement, or
- a partner or managerial employee who provides non-audit services to the audit client, is deemed not to compromise independence if the financial interest is received as a result of the immediate family member's employment rights (e.g., through pension or share option plans) and, when necessary, safeguards are applied to eliminate any threat to independence or reduce it to an acceptable level.

However, when the immediate family member has or obtains the right to dispose of the financial interest or, in the case of a stock option, the right to exercise the option, the financial interest shall be disposed of or forfeited as soon as practicable.

290.112   A self-interest threat may be created if the firm or a member of the audit team, or a member of that individual's immediate family, has a financial interest in an entity and an audit client also has a financial interest in that entity. However, independence is deemed not to be compromised if these interests are immaterial and the audit client cannot exercise significant influence over the entity. If such interest is material to any party, and the audit client can exercise significant influence over the other entity, no safeguards could reduce the threat to an acceptable level. Accordingly, the firm shall not have such an interest and any individual with such an interest shall, before becoming a member of the audit team, either:

- Dispose of the interest; or
- Dispose of a sufficient amount of the interest so that the remaining interest is no longer material.

290.113   A self-interest, familiarity or intimidation threat may be created if a member of the audit team, or a member of that individual's immediate family, or the firm, has a financial interest in an entity when a director, officer or controlling owner of the audit client is also known to have a financial interest in that entity. The existence and significance of any threat will depend upon factors such as:

- The role of the professional on the audit team;
- Whether ownership of the entity is closely or widely held;
- Whether the interest gives the investor the ability to control or significantly influence the entity; and
- The materiality of the financial interest.

The significance of any threat shall be evaluated and safeguards applied when necessary to eliminate the threat or reduce it to an acceptable level. Examples of such safeguards include:

- Removing the member of the audit team with the financial interest from the audit team; or
- Having a professional accountant review the work of the member of the audit team.

The holding by a firm, or a member of the audit team, or a member of that individual's immediate family, of a direct financial interest or a material indirect financial interest in the audit client as a trustee creates a self-interest threat. Similarly, a self-interest threat is created when:

290.114

- a partner in the office in which the engagement partner practices in connection with the audit,
- other partners and managerial employees who provide non-assurance services to the audit client, except those whose involvement is minimal, or
- their immediate family members, hold a direct financial interest or a material indirect financial interest in the audit client as trustee.

Such an interest shall not be held unless:

- Neither the trustee, nor an immediate family member of the trustee, nor the firm are beneficiaries of the trust;
- The interest in the audit client held by the trust is not material to the trust;
- The trust is not able to exercise significant influence over the audit client; and
- The trustee, an immediate family member of the trustee, or the firm cannot significantly influence any investment decision involving a financial interest in the audit client.

Members of the audit team shall determine whether a self-interest threat is created by any known financial interests in the audit client held by other individuals including:

290.115

- Partners and professional employees of the firm, other than those referred to above, or their immediate family members; and
- Individuals with a close personal relationship with a member of the audit team.

Whether these interests create a self-interest threat will depend on factors such as:

- The firm's organisational, operating and reporting structure; and
- The nature of the relationship between the individual and the member of the audit team.

The significance of any threat shall be evaluated and safeguards applied when necessary to eliminate the threat or reduce it to an acceptable level. Examples of such safeguards include:

- Removing the member of the audit team with the personal relationship from the audit team;
- Excluding the member of the audit team from any significant decision-making concerning the audit engagement; or
- Having a professional accountant review the work of the member of the audit team.

If a firm or a partner or employee of the firm, or a member of that individual's immediate family, receives a direct financial interest or a material indirect financial interest in an audit client, for example, by way of an inheritance, gift or as a result of a merger and such interest would not be permitted to be held under this section, then:

290.116

- If the interest is received by the firm, the financial interest shall be disposed of immediately, or a sufficient amount of an indirect financial interest shall be disposed of so that the remaining interest is no longer material;
- If the interest is received by a member of the audit team, or a member of that individual's immediate family, the individual who received the financial interest shall immediately dispose of the financial interest, or dispose of a sufficient amount of an indirect financial interest so that the remaining interest is no longer material; or

- If the interest is received by an individual who is not a member of the audit team, or by an immediate family member of the individual, the financial interest shall be disposed of as soon as possible, or a sufficient amount of an indirect financial interest shall be disposed of so that the remaining interest is no longer material. Pending the disposal of the financial interest, a determination shall be made as to whether any safeguards are necessary.

290.117   When an inadvertent violation of this section as it relates to a financial interest in an audit client occurs, it is deemed not to compromise independence if:

- The firm has established policies and procedures that require prompt notification to the firm of any breaches resulting from the purchase, inheritance or other acquisition of a financial interest in the audit client;
- The actions in paragraph 290.116 (a)-(c) are taken as applicable; and
- The firm applies other safeguards when necessary to reduce any remaining threat to an acceptable level. Examples of such safeguards include:
  - Having a professional accountant review the work of the member of the audit team; or
  - Excluding the individual from any significant decision-making concerning the audit engagement.
- The firm shall determine whether to discuss the matter with those charged with governance.

Loans and Guarantees

290.118   A loan or a guarantee of a loan, to a member of the audit team, or a member of that individual's immediate family, or the firm from an audit client that is a bank or a similar institution may create a threat to independence. If the loan or guarantee is not made under normal lending procedures, terms and conditions, a self-interest threat would be created that would be so significant that no safeguards could reduce the threat to an acceptable level. Accordingly, neither a member of the audit team, a member of that individual's immediate family, nor a firm shall accept such a loan or guarantee.

290.119   If a loan to a firm from an audit client that is a bank or similar institution is made under normal lending procedures, terms and conditions and it is material to the audit client or firm receiving the loan, it may be possible to apply safeguards to reduce the self-interest threat to an acceptable level. An example of such a safeguard is having the work reviewed by a professional accountant from a network firm that is neither involved with the audit nor received the loan.

290.120   A loan, or a guarantee of a loan, from an audit client that is a bank or a similar institution to a member of the audit team, or a member of that individual's immediate family, does not create a threat to independence if the loan or guarantee is made under normal lending procedures, terms and conditions. Examples of such loans include home mortgages, bank overdrafts, car loans and credit card balances.

290.121   If the firm or a member of the audit team, or a member of that individual's immediate family, accepts a loan from, or has a borrowing guaranteed by, an audit client that is not a bank or similar institution, the self-interest threat created would be so significant that no safeguards could reduce the threat to an acceptable level, unless the loan or guarantee is immaterial to both (a) the firm or the member of the audit team and the immediate family member, and (b) the client.

290.122   Similarly, if the firm or a member of the audit team, or a member of that individual's immediate family, makes or guarantees a loan to an audit client, the self-interest threat created would be so significant that no safeguards could reduce the threat to an acceptable level, unless the loan or guarantee is immaterial to both (a) the firm or the member of the audit team and the immediate family member, and (b) the client.

If a firm or a member of the audit team, or a member of that individual's immediate family, has deposits or a brokerage account with an audit client that is a bank, broker or similar institution, a threat to independence is not created if the deposit or account is held under normal commercial terms.   **290.123**

Business relationships

A close business relationship between a firm, or a member of the audit team, or a   **290.124**
member of that individual's immediate family, and the audit client or its management, arises from a commercial relationship or common financial interest and may
create self-interest or intimidation threats. Examples of such relationships include:

- Having a financial interest in a joint venture with either the client or a controlling owner, director, officer or other individual who performs senior
  managerial activities for that client.
- Arrangements to combine one or more services or products of the firm with one
  or more services or products of the client and to market the package with
  reference to both parties.
- Distribution or marketing arrangements under which the firm distributes or
  markets the client's products or services, or the client distributes or markets the
  firm's products or services.

Unless any financial interest is immaterial and the business relationship is insignificant to the firm and the client or its management, the threat created would be so
significant that no safeguards could reduce the threat to an acceptable level.
Therefore, unless the financial interest is immaterial and the business relationship is
insignificant, the business relationship shall not be entered into, or it shall be reduced
to an insignificant level or terminated.

In the case of a member of the audit team, unless any such financial interest is
immaterial and the relationship is insignificant to that member, the individual shall
be removed from the audit team.

If the business relationship is between an immediate family member of a member of
the audit team and the audit client or its management, the significance of any threat
shall be evaluated and safeguards applied when necessary to eliminate the threat or
reduce it to an acceptable level.

A business relationship involving the holding of an interest by the firm, or a member   **290.125**
of the audit team, or a member of that individual's immediate family, in a closely-
held entity when the audit client or a director or officer of the client, or any group
thereof, also holds an interest in that entity does not create threats to independence
if:

- The business relationship is insignificant to the firm, the member of the audit
  team and the immediate family member, and the client;
- The financial interest is immaterial to the investor or group of investors; and
- The financial interest does not give the investor, or group of investors, the ability
  to control the closely-held entity.

The purchase of goods and services from an audit client by the firm, or a member of   **290.126**
the audit team, or a member of that individual's immediate family, does not

generally create a threat to independence if the transaction is in the normal course of business and at arm's length. However, such transactions may be of such a nature or magnitude that they create a self-interest threat. The significance of any threat shall be evaluated and safeguards applied when necessary to eliminate the threat or reduce it to an acceptable level. Examples of such safeguards include:

- Eliminating or reducing the magnitude of the transaction; or
- Removing the individual from the audit team.

Family and Personal Relationships

290.127   Family and personal relationships between a member of the audit team and a director or officer or certain employees (depending on their role) of the audit client may create self-interest, familiarity or intimidation threats. The existence and significance of any threats will depend on a number of factors, including the individual's responsibilities on the audit team, the role of the family member or other individual within the client and the closeness of the relationship.

290.128   When an immediate family member of a member of the audit team is:

- A director or officer of the audit client; or
- An employee in a position to exert significant influence over the preparation of the client's accounting records or the financial statements on which the firm will express an opinion,

or was in such a position during any period covered by the engagement or the financial statements, the threats to independence can only be reduced to an acceptable level by removing the individual from the audit team. The closeness of the relationship is such that no other safeguards could reduce the threat to an acceptable level. Accordingly, no individual who has such a relationship shall be a member of the audit team.

290.129   Threats to independence are created when an immediate family member of a member of the audit team is an employee in a position to exert significant influence over the client's financial position, financial performance or cash flows. The significance of the threats will depend on factors such as:

- The position held by the immediate family member; and
- The role of the professional on the audit team.

The significance of the threat shall be evaluated and safeguards applied when necessary to eliminate the threat or reduce it to an acceptable level. Examples of such safeguards include:

- Removing the individual from the audit team; or
- Structuring the responsibilities of the audit team so that the professional does not deal with matters that are within the responsibility of the immediate family member.

290.130   Threats to independence are created when a close family member of a member of the audit team is:

- A director or officer of the audit client; or
- An employee in a position to exert significant influence over the preparation of the client's accounting records or the financial statements on which the firm will express an opinion.

The significance of the threats will depend on factors such as:

- The nature of the relationship between the member of the audit team and the close family member;
- The position held by the close family member; and
- The role of the professional on the audit team.

The significance of the threat shall be evaluated and safeguards applied when necessary to eliminate the threat or reduce it to an acceptable level. Examples of such safeguards include:

- Removing the individual from the audit team; or
- Structuring the responsibilities of the audit team so that the professional does not deal with matters that are within the responsibility of the close family member.

Threats to independence are created when a member of the audit team has a close relationship with a person who is not an immediate or close family member, but who is a director or officer or an employee in a position to exert significant influence over the preparation of the client's accounting records or the financial statements on which the firm will express an opinion. A member of the audit team who has such a relationship shall consult in accordance with firm policies and procedures. The significance of the threats will depend on factors such as:

290.131

- The nature of the relationship between the individual and the member of the audit team;
- The position the individual holds with the client; and
- The role of the professional on the audit team.

The significance of the threats shall be evaluated and safeguards applied when necessary to eliminate the threats or reduce them to an acceptable level. Examples of such safeguards include:

- Removing the professional from the audit team; or
- Structuring the responsibilities of the audit team so that the professional does not deal with matters that are within the responsibility of the individual with whom the professional has a close relationship.

Self-interest, familiarity or intimidation threats may be created by a personal or family relationship between (a) a partner or employee of the firm who is not a member of the audit team and (b) a director or officer of the audit client or an employee in a position to exert significant influence over the preparation of the client's accounting records or the financial statements on which the firm will express an opinion. Partners and employees of the firm who are aware of such relationships shall consult in accordance with firm policies and procedures. The existence and significance of any threat will depend on factors such as:

290.132

- The nature of the relationship between the partner or employee of the firm and the director or officer or employee of the client;
- The interaction of the partner or employee of the firm with the audit team;
- The position of the partner or employee within the firm; and
- The position the individual holds with the client.

The significance of any threat shall be evaluated and safeguards applied when necessary to eliminate the threat or reduce it to an acceptable level. Examples of such safeguards include:

- Structuring the partner's or employee's responsibilities to reduce any potential influence over the audit engagement; or
- Having a professional accountant review the relevant audit work performed.

290.133   When an inadvertent violation of this section as it relates to family and personal relationships occurs, it is deemed not to compromise independence if:

- The firm has established policies and procedures that require prompt notification to the firm of any breaches resulting from changes in the employment status of their immediate or close family members or other personal relationships that create threats to independence;
- The inadvertent violation relates to an immediate family member of a member of the audit team becoming a director or officer of the audit client or being in a position to exert significant influence over the preparation of the client's accounting records or the financial statements on which the firm will express an opinion, and the relevant professional is removed from the audit team; and
- The firm applies other safeguards when necessary to reduce any remaining threat to an acceptable level. Examples of such safeguards include:
  - Having a professional accountant review the work of the member of the audit team; or
  - Excluding the relevant professional from any significant decision-making concerning the engagement.

The firm shall determine whether to discuss the matter with those charged with governance.

Employment with an audit client

290.134   Familiarity or intimidation threats may be created if a director or officer of the audit client, or an employee in a position to exert significant influence over the preparation of the client's accounting records or the financial statements on which the firm will express an opinion, has been a member of the audit team or partner of the firm.

290.135   If a former member of the audit team or partner of the firm has joined the audit client in such a position and a significant connection remains between the firm and the individual, the threat would be so significant that no safeguards could reduce the threat to an acceptable level. Therefore, independence would be deemed to be compromised if a former member of the audit team or partner joins the audit client as a director or officer, or as an employee in a position to exert significant influence over the preparation of the client's accounting records or the financial statements on which the firm will express an opinion, unless:

- The individual is not entitled to any benefits or payments from the firm, unless made in accordance with fixed pre-determined arrangements, and any amount owed to the individual is not material to the firm; and
- The individual does not continue to participate or appear to participate in the firm's business or professional activities.

290.136   If a former member of the audit team or partner of the firm has joined the audit client in such a position, and no significant connection remains between the firm and the individual, the existence and significance of any familiarity or intimidation threats will depend on factors such as:

- The position the individual has taken at the client;
- Any involvement the individual will have with the audit team;
- The length of time since the individual was a member of the audit team or partner of the firm; and
- The former position of the individual within the audit team or firm, for example, whether the individual was responsible for maintaining regular contact with the client's management or those charged with governance.

The significance of any threats created shall be evaluated and safeguards applied when necessary to eliminate the threats or reduce them to an acceptable level. Examples of such safeguards include:

- Modifying the audit plan;
- Assigning individuals to the audit team who have sufficient experience in relation to the individual who has joined the client; or
- Having a professional accountant review the work of the former member of the audit team.

If a former partner of the firm has previously joined an entity in such a position and the entity subsequently becomes an audit client of the firm, the significance of any threat to independence shall be evaluated and safeguards applied when necessary to eliminate the threat or reduce it to an acceptable level. **290.137**

A self-interest threat is created when a member of the audit team participates in the audit engagement while knowing that the member of the audit team will, or may, join the client some time in the future. Firm policies and procedures shall require members of an audit team to notify the firm when entering employment negotiations with the client. On receiving such notification, the significance of the threat shall be evaluated and safeguards applied when necessary to eliminate the threat or reduce it to an acceptable level. Examples of such safeguards include: **290.138**

- Removing the individual from the audit team; or
- A review of any significant judgments made by that individual while on the team.

Audit clients that are public interest entities

Familiarity or intimidation threats are created when a key audit partner joins the audit client that is a public interest entity as: **290.139**

- A director or officer of the entity; or
- An employee in a position to exert significant influence over the preparation of the client's accounting records or the financial statements on which the firm will express an opinion.

Independence would be deemed to be compromised unless, subsequent to the partner ceasing to be a key audit partner, the public interest entity had issued audited financial statements covering a period of not less than twelve months and the partner was not a member of the audit team with respect to the audit of those financial statements.

An intimidation threat is created when the individual who was the firm's Senior or Managing Partner (Chief Executive or equivalent) joins an audit client that is a public interest entity as: **290.140**

- an employee in a position to exert significant influence over the preparation of the entity's accounting records or its financial statements; or
- a director or officer of the entity. Independence would be deemed to be compromised unless twelve months have passed since the individual was the Senior or Managing Partner (Chief Executive or equivalent) of the firm.

Independence is deemed not to be compromised if, as a result of a business combination, a former key audit partner or the individual who was the firm's former Senior or Managing Partner is in a position as described in paragraphs 290.139 and 290.140, and: **290.141**

- The position was not taken in contemplation of the business combination;
- Any benefits or payments due to the former partner from the firm have been settled in full, unless made in accordance with fixed pre-determined arrangements and any amount owed to the partner is not material to the firm;
- The former partner does not continue to participate or appear to participate in the firm's business or professional activities; and
- The position held by the former partner with the audit client is discussed with those charged with governance.

Temporary staff assignments

290.142   The lending of staff by a firm to an audit client may create a self-review threat. Such assistance may be given, but only for a short period of time and the firm's personnel shall not be involved in:

- Providing non-assurance services that would not be permitted under this section; or
- Assuming management responsibilities.

In all circumstances, the audit client shall be responsible for directing and supervising the activities of the loaned staff. The significance of any threat shall be evaluated and safeguards applied when necessary to eliminate the threat or reduce it to an acceptable level. Examples of such safeguards include:

- Conducting an additional review of the work performed by the loaned staff;
- Not giving the loaned staff audit responsibility for any function or activity that the staff performed during the temporary staff assignment; or
- Not including the loaned staff as a member of the audit team.

Recent service with an audit client

290.143   Self-interest, self-review or familiarity threats may be created if a member of the audit team has recently served as a director, officer, or employee of the audit client. This would be the case when, for example, a member of the audit team has to evaluate elements of the financial statements for which the member of the audit team had prepared the accounting records while with the client.

290.144   If, during the period covered by the audit report, a member of the audit team had served as a director or officer of the audit client, or was an employee in a position to exert significant influence over the preparation of the client's accounting records or the financial statements on which the firm will express an opinion, the threat created would be so significant that no safeguards could reduce the threat to an acceptable level. Consequently, such individuals shall not be assigned to the audit team.

290.145   Self-interest, self-review or familiarity threats may be created if, before the period covered by the audit report, a member of the audit team had served as a director or officer of the audit client, or was an employee in a position to exert significant influence over the preparation of the client's accounting records or financial statements on which the firm will express an opinion. For example, such threats would be created if a decision made or work performed by the individual in the prior period, while employed by the client, is to be evaluated in the current period as part of the current audit engagement. The existence and significance of any threats will depend on factors such as:

- The position the individual held with the client;
- The length of time since the individual left the client; and

- The role of the professional on the audit team.

The significance of any threat shall be evaluated and safeguards applied when necessary to reduce the threat to an acceptable level. An example of such a safeguard is conducting a review of the work performed by the individual as a member of the audit team.

Serving as a Director or Officer of an audit client

If a partner or employee of the firm serves as a director or officer of an audit client, the self-review and self-interest threats created would be so significant that no safeguards could reduce the threats to an acceptable level. Accordingly, no partner or employee shall serve as a director or officer of an audit client.   **290.146**

The position of Company Secretary has different implications in different jurisdictions. Duties may range from administrative duties, such as personnel management and the maintenance of company records and registers, to duties as diverse as ensuring that the company complies with regulations or providing advice on corporate governance matters. Generally, this position is seen to imply a close association with the entity.   **290.147**

If a partner or employee of the firm serves as Company Secretary for an audit client, self-review and advocacy threats are created that would generally be so significant that no safeguards could reduce the threats to an acceptable level. Despite paragraph 290.146, when this practice is specifically permitted under local law, professional roles or practice, and provided management makes all relevant decisions, the duties and activities shall be limited to those of a routine and administrative nature, such as preparing minutes and maintaining statutory returns. In those circumstances, the significance of any threats shall be evaluated and safeguards applied when necessary to eliminate the threats or reduce them to an acceptable level.   **290.148**

Performing routine administrative services to support a company secretarial function or providing advice in relation to company secretarial administration matters does not generally create threats to independence, as long as client management makes all relevant decisions.   **290.149**

Long association of senior personnel (including partner rotation) with an audit client

General provisions

Familiarity and self-interest threats are created by using the same senior personnel on an audit engagement over a long period of time. The significance of the threats will depend on factors such as: **290.150**

- How long the individual has been a member of the audit team;
- The role of the individual on the audit team;
- The structure of the firm;
- The nature of the audit engagement;
- Whether the client's management team has changed; and
- Whether the nature or complexity of the client's accounting and reporting issues has changed.

The significance of the threats shall be evaluated and safeguards applied when necessary to eliminate the threats or reduce them to an acceptable level. Examples of such safeguards include:

- Rotating the senior personnel off the audit team;
- Having a professional accountant who was not a member of the audit team review the work of the senior personnel; or
- regular independent internal or external quality reviews of the engagement.

Audit clients that are public interest entities

290.151 In respect of an audit of a public interest entity, an individual shall not be a key audit partner for more than seven years. After such time, the individual shall not be a member of the engagement team or be a key audit partner for the client for two years. During that period, the individual shall not participate in the audit of the entity, provide quality control for the engagement, consult with the engagement team or the client regarding technical or industry-specific issues, transactions or events or otherwise directly influence the outcome of the engagement.

290.152 Despite paragraph 290.151, key audit partners whose continuity is especially important to audit quality may, in rare cases due to unforeseen circumstances outside the firm's control, be permitted an additional year on the audit team as long as the threat to independence can be eliminated or reduced to an acceptable level by applying safeguards. For example, a key audit partner may remain on the audit team for up to one additional year in circumstances where, due to unforeseen events, a required rotation was not possible, as might be the case due to serious illness of the intended engagement partner.

290.153 The long association of other partners with an audit client that is a public interest entity creates familiarity and self-interest threats. The significance of the threats will depend on factors such as:

- How long any such partner has been associated with the audit client;
- The role, if any, of the individual on the audit team; and
- The nature, frequency and extent of the individual's interactions with the client's management or those charged with governance.

The significance of the threats shall be evaluated and safeguards applied when necessary to eliminate the threats or reduce them to an acceptable level. Examples of such safeguards include:

- Rotating the partner off the audit team or otherwise ending the partner's association with the audit client; or
- regular independent internal or external quality reviews of the engagement.

290.154 When an audit client becomes a public interest entity, the length of time the individual has served the audit client as a key audit partner before the client becomes a public interest entity shall be taken into account in determining the timing of the rotation. If the individual has served the audit client as a key audit partner for five years or less when the client becomes a public interest entity, the number of years the individual may continue to serve the client in that capacity before rotating off the engagement is seven years less the number of years already served. If the individual has served the audit client as a key audit partner for six or more years when the client becomes a public interest entity, the partner may continue to serve in that capacity for a maximum of two additional years before rotating off the engagement.

290.155 When a firm has only a few people with the necessary knowledge and experience to serve as a key audit partner on the audit of a public interest entity, rotation of key audit partners may not be an available safeguard. If an independent regulator in the relevant jurisdiction has provided an exemption from partner rotation in such circumstances, an individual may remain a key audit partner for more than seven years, in accordance with such regulation, provided that the independent regulator has specified alternative safeguards which are applied, such as a regular independent external review.

Provision of Non-assurance Services to Audit clients

Firms have traditionally provided to their audit clients a range of non-assurance services that are consistent with their skills and expertise. Providing non-assurance services may, however, create threats to the independence of the firm or members of the audit team. The threats created are most often self-review, self-interest and advocacy threats.   **290.156**

New developments in business, the evolution of financial markets and changes in information technology make it impossible to draw up an all-inclusive list of non-assurance services that might be provided to an audit client. When specific guidance on a particular non-assurance service is not included in this section, the conceptual framework shall be applied when evaluating the particular circumstances.   **290.157**

Before the firm accepts an engagement to provide a non-assurance service to an audit client, a determination shall be made as to whether providing such a service would create a threat to independence. In evaluating the significance of any threat created by a particular non-assurance service, consideration shall be given to any threat that the audit team has reason to believe is created by providing other related non-assurance services. If a threat is created that cannot be reduced to an acceptable level by the application of safeguards, the non-assurance service shall not be provided.   **290.158**

Providing certain non-assurance services to an audit client may create a threat to independence so significant that no safeguards could reduce the threat to an acceptable level. However, the inadvertent provision of such a service to a related entity, division or in respect of a discrete financial statement item of such a client will be deemed not to compromise independence if any threats have been reduced to an acceptable level by arrangements for that related entity, division or discrete financial statement item to be audited by another firm or when another firm re-performs the non-assurance service to the extent necessary to enable it to take responsibility for that service.   **290.159**

A firm may provide non-assurance services that would otherwise be restricted under this section to the following related entities of the audit client: **290.160**

- An entity, which is not an audit client, that has direct or indirect control over the audit client;
- An entity, which is not an audit client, with a direct financial interest in the client if that entity has significant influence over the client and the interest in the client is material to such entity; or
- An entity, which is not an audit client, that is under common control with the audit client.

If it is reasonable to conclude that (a) the services do not create a self-review threat because the results of the services will not be subject to audit procedures and (b) any threats that are created by the provision of such services are eliminated or reduced to an acceptable level by the application of safeguards.

A non-assurance service provided to an audit client does not compromise the firm's independence when the client becomes a public interest entity if: **290.161**

- The previous non-assurance service complies with the provisions of this section that relate to audit clients that are not public interest entities;
- Services that are not permitted under this section for audit clients that are public interest entities are terminated before or as soon as practicable after the client becomes a public interest entity; and
- The firm applies safeguards when necessary to eliminate or reduce to an acceptable level any threats to independence arising from the service.

Management responsibilities

290.162   Management of an entity performs many activities in managing the entity in the best interests of stakeholders of the entity. It is not possible to specify every activity that is a management responsibility. However, management responsibilities involve leading and directing an entity, including making significant decisions regarding the acquisition, deployment and control of human, financial, physical and intangible resources.

290.163   Whether an activity is a management responsibility depends on the circumstances and requires the exercise of judgment. Examples of activities that would generally be considered a management responsibility include:

- Setting policies and strategic direction;
- Directing and taking responsibility for the actions of the entity's employees;
- Authorising transactions;
- Deciding which recommendations of the firm or other third parties to implement;
- Taking responsibility for the preparation and fair presentation of the financial statements in accordance with the applicable financial reporting framework; and
- Taking responsibility for designing, implementing and maintaining internal control.

290.164   Activities that are routine and administrative, or involve matters that are insignificant, generally are deemed not to be a management responsibility. For example, executing an insignificant transaction that has been authorised by management or monitoring the dates for filing statutory returns and advising an audit client of those dates is deemed not to be a management responsibility. Further, providing advice and recommendations to assist management in discharging its responsibilities is not assuming a management responsibility.

290.165   If a firm were to assume a management responsibility for an audit client, the threats created would be so significant that no safeguards could reduce the threats to an acceptable level. For example, deciding which recommendations of the firm to implement will create self-review and self-interest threats. Further, assuming a management responsibility creates a familiarity threat because the firm becomes too closely aligned with the views and interests of management. Therefore, the firm shall not assume a management responsibility for an audit client.

290.166   To avoid the risk of assuming a management responsibility when providing non-assurance services to an audit client, the firm shall be satisfied that a member of management is responsible for making the significant judgments and decisions that are the proper responsibility of management, evaluating the results of the service and accepting responsibility for the actions to be taken arising from the results of the service. This reduces the risk of the firm inadvertently making any significant judgments or decisions on behalf of management. The risk is further reduced when the firm gives the client the opportunity to make judgments and decisions based on an objective and transparent analysis and presentation of the issues.

Preparing Accounting Records and Financial statements

General provisions

Management is responsible for the preparation and fair presentation of the financial statements in accordance with the applicable financial reporting framework. These responsibilities include: **290.167**

- Originating or changing journal entries, or determining the account classifications of transactions; and
- Preparing or changing source documents or originating data, in electronic or other form, evidencing the occurrence of a transaction (for example, purchase orders, payroll time records, and customer orders).

Providing an audit client with accounting and bookkeeping services, such as preparing accounting records or financial statements, creates a self-review threat when the firm subsequently audits the financial statements. **290.168**

The audit process, however, necessitates dialogue between the firm and management of the audit client, which may involve: **290.169**

- the application of accounting standards or policies and financial statement disclosure requirements,
- the appropriateness of financial and accounting control and the methods used in determining the stated amounts of assets and liabilities, or
- proposing adjusting journal entries. These activities are considered to be a normal part of the audit process and do not, generally, create threats to independence.

Similarly, the client may request technical assistance from the firm on matters such as resolving account reconciliation problems or analysing and accumolating information for regulatory reporting. In addition, the client may request technical advice on accounting issues such as the conversion of existing financial statements from one financial reporting framework to another (for example, to comply with group accounting policies or to transition to a different financial reporting framework such as International Financial Reporting Standards). Such services do not, generally, create threats to independence provided the firm does not assume a management responsibility for the client. **290.170**

Audit clients that are not public interest entities

The firm may provide services related to the preparation of accounting records and financial statements to an audit client that is not a public interest entity where the services are of a routine or mechanical nature, so long as any self-review threat created is reduced to an acceptable level. Examples of such services include: **290.171**

- Providing payroll services based on client-originated data;
- Recording transactions for which the client has determined or approved the appropriate account classification;
- Posting transactions coded by the client to the general ledger;
- Posting client-approved entries to the trial balance; and
- Preparing financial statements based on information in the trial balance.

In all cases, the significance of any threat created shall be evaluated and safeguards applied when necessary to eliminate the threat or reduce it to an acceptable level. Examples of such safeguards include:

- Arranging for such services to be performed by an individual who is not a member of the audit team; or
- If such services are performed by a member of the audit team, using a partner or senior staff member with appropriate expertise who is not a member of the audit team to review the work performed.

Audit clients that are public interest entities

290.172   Except in emergency situations, a firm shall not provide to an audit client that is a public interest entity accounting and bookkeeping services, including payroll services, or prepare financial statements on which the firm will express an opinion or financial information which forms the basis of the financial statements.

290.173   Despite paragraph 290.172, a firm may provide accounting and bookkeeping services, including payroll services and the preparation of financial statements or other financial information, of a routine or mechanical nature for divisions or related entities of an audit client that is a public interest entity if the personnel providing the services are not members of the audit team and:

- The divisions or related entities for which the service is provided are collectively immaterial to the financial statements on which the firm will express an opinion; or
- The services relate to matters that are collectively immaterial to the financial statements of the division or related entity.

Emergency situations

290.174   Accounting and bookkeeping services, which would otherwise not be permitted under this section, may be provided to audit clients in emergency or other unusual situations when it is impractical for the audit client to make other arrangements. This may be the case when (a) only the firm has the resources and necessary knowledge of the client's systems and procedures to assist the client in the timely preparation of its accounting records and financial statements, and (b) a restriction on the firm's ability to provide the services would result in significant difficulties for the client (for example, as might result from a failure to meet regulatory reporting requirements). In such situations, the following conditions shall be met:

- Those who provide the services are not members of the audit team;
- The services are provided for only a short period of time and are not expected to recur; and
- The situation is discussed with those charged with governance.

Valuation services

General provision

290.175   A valuation comprises the making of assumptions with regard to future developments, the application of appropriate methodologies and techniques, and the combination of both to compute a certain value, or range of values, for an asset, a liability or for a business as a whole.

290.176   A Performing valuation services for an audit client may create a self-review threat. The existence and significance of any threat will depend on factors such as:

- Whether the valuation will have a material effect on the financial statements.

- The extent of the client's involvement in determining and approving the valuation methodology and other significant matters of judgment.
- The availability of established methodologies and professional guidelines.
- For valuations involving standard or established methodologies, the degree of subjectivity inherent in the item.
- The reliability and extent of the underlying data.
- The degree of dependence on future events of a nature that could create significant volatility inherent in the amounts involved.
- The extent and clarity of the disclosures in the financial statements.

The significance of any threat created shall be evaluated and safeguards applied when necessary to eliminate the threat or reduce it to an acceptable level. Examples of such safeguards include:

- Having a professional who was not involved in providing the valuation service review the audit or valuation work performed; or
- Making arrangements so that personnel providing such services do not participate in the audit engagement.

Certain valuations do not involve a significant degree of subjectivity. This is likely the case where the underlying assumptions are either established by law or regulation, or are widely accepted and when the techniques and methodologies to be used are based on generally accepted standards or prescribed by law or regulation. In such circumstances, the results of a valuation performed by two or more parties are not likely to be materially different.   **290.177**

If a firm is requested to perform a valuation to assist an audit client with its tax reporting obligations or for tax planning purposes and the results of the valuation will not have a direct effect on the financial statements, the provisions included in paragraph 290.191 apply.   **290.178**

Audit clients that are not public interest entities

In the case of an audit client that is not a public interest entity, if the valuation service has a material effect on the financial statements on which the firm will express an opinion and the valuation involves a significant degree of subjectivity, no safeguards could reduce the self-review threat to an acceptable level. Accordingly a firm shall not provide such a valuation service to an audit client.   **290.179**

Audit clients that are public interest entities

A firm shall not provide valuation services to an audit client that is a public interest entity if the valuations would have a material effect, separately or in the aggregate, on the financial statements on which the firm will express an opinion.   **290.180**

Taxation Services

Taxation services comprise a broad range of services, including: **290.181**

- Tax return preparation;
- Tax calculations for the purpose of preparing the accounting entries;
- Tax planning and other tax advisory services; and
- Assistance in the resulution of tax disputes.

While taxation services provided by a firm to an audit client are addressed separately under each of these broad headings; in practice, these activities are often interrelated.

290.182   Performing certain tax services creates self-review and advocacy threats. The existence and significance of any threats will depend on factors such as (a) the system by which the tax authorities assess and administer the tax in question and the role of the firm in that process, (b) the complexity of the relevant tax regime and the degree of judgment necessary in applying it, (c) the particular characteristics of the engagement, and (d) the level of tax expertise of the client's employees.

Tax return preparation

290.183   Tax return preparation services involve assisting clients with their tax reporting obligations by drafting and completing information, including the amount of tax due (usually on standardised forms) required to be submitted to the applicable tax authorities. Such services also include advising on the tax return treatment of past transactions and responding on behalf of the audit client to the tax authorities' requests for additional information and analysis (including providing explanations of and technical support for the approach being taken). Tax return preparation services are generally based on historical information and principally involve analysis and presentation of such historical information under existing tax law, including precedents and established practice. Further, the tax returns are subject to whatever review or approval process the tax authority deems appropriate. Accordingly, providing such services does not generally create a threat to independence if management takes responsibility for the returns including any significant judgments made.

Tax calculations for the purpose of preparing accounting entries

Audit clients that are not public interest entities

290.184   Preparing calculations of current and deferred tax liabilities (or assets) for an audit client for the purpose of preparing accounting entries that will be subsequently audited by the firm creates a self-review threat. The significance of the threat will depend on (a) the complexity of the relevant tax law and regulation and the degree of judgment necessary in applying them, (b) the level of tax expertise of the client's personnel, and (c) the materiality of the amounts to the financial statements. Safeguards shall be applied when necessary to eliminate the threat or reduce it to an acceptable level. Examples of such safeguards include:

- Using professionals who are not members of the audit team to perform the service;
- If the service is performed by a member of the audit team, using a partner or senior staff member with appropriate expertise who is not a member of the audit team to review the tax calculations; or
- Obtaining advice on the service from an external tax professional.

Audit clients that are public interest entities

290.185   Except in emergency situations, in the case of an audit client that is a public interest entity, a firm shall not prepare tax calculations of current and deferred tax liabilities (or assets) for the purpose of preparing accounting entries that are material to the financial statements on which the firm will express an opinion.

The preparation of calculations of current and deferred tax liabilities (or assets) for   **290.186**
an audit client for the purpose of the preparation of accounting entries, which would
otherwise not be permitted under this section, may be provided to audit clients in
emergency or other unusual situations when it is impractical for the audit client to
make other arrangements. This may be the case when (a) only the firm has the
resources and necessary knowledge of the client's business to assist the client in the
timely preparation of its calculations of current and deferred tax liabilities (or assets),
and (b) a restriction on the firm's ability to provide the services would result in
significant difficulties for the client (for example, as might result from a failure to
meet regulatory reporting requirements). In such situations, the following conditions
shall be met:

- Those who provide the services are not members of the audit team;
- The services are provided for only a short period of time and are not expected to
  recur; and
- The situation is discussed with those charged with governance.

Tax planning and other tax advisory services

Tax planning or other tax advisory services comprise a broad range of services, such   **290.187**
as advising the client how to structure its affairs in a tax efficient manner or advising
on the application of a new tax law or regulation.

A self-review threat may be created where the advice will affect matters to be   **290.188**
reflected in the financial statements. The existence and significance of any threat will
depend on factors such as:

- The degree of subjectivity involved in determining the appropriate treatment for
  the tax advice in the financial statements;
- The extent to which the outcome of the tax advice will have a material effect on
  the financial statements;
- Whether the effectiveness of the tax advice depends on the accounting treatment
  or presentation in the financial statements and there is doubt as to the appropriateness of the accounting treatment or presentation under the relevant
  financial reporting framework;
- The level of tax expertise of the client's employees;
- The extent to which the advice is supported by tax law or regulation, other
  precedent or established practice; and
- Whether the tax treatment is supported by a private ruling or has otherwise been
  cleared by the tax authority before the preparation of the financial statements.

For example, providing tax planning and other tax advisory services where the
advice is clearly supported by tax authority or other precedent, by established
practice or has a basis in tax law that is likely to prevail does not generally create a
threat to independence.

The significance of any threat shall be evaluated and safeguards applied when   **290.189**
necessary to eliminate the threat or reduce it to an acceptable level. Examples of such
safeguards include:

- Using professionals who are not members of the audit team to perform the
  service;
- Having a tax professional, who was not involved in providing the tax service,
  advise the audit team on the service and review the financial statement
  treatment;
- Obtaining advice on the service from an external tax professional; or
- Obtaining pre-clearance or advice from the tax authorities.

290.190   Where the effectiveness of the tax advice depends on a particular accounting treatment or presentation in the financial statements and:

- The audit team has reasonable doubt as to the appropriateness of the related accounting treatment or presentation under the relevant financial reporting framework; and
- The outcome or consequences of the tax advice will have a material effect on the financial statements on which the firm will express an opinion;

The self-review threat would be so significant that no safeguards could reduce the threat to an acceptable level. Accordingly, a firm shall not provide such tax advice to an audit client.

290.191   In providing tax services to an audit client, a firm may be requested to perform a valuation to assist the client with its tax reporting obligations or for tax planning purposes. Where the result of the valuation will have a direct effect on the financial statements, the provisions included in paragraphs 290.175 to 290.180 relating to valuation services are applicable. Where the valuation is performed for tax purposes only and the result of the valuation will not have a direct effect on the financial statements (i.e. the financial statements are only affected through accounting entries related to tax), this would not generally create threats to independence if such effect on the financial statements is immaterial or if the valuation is subject to external review by a tax authority or similar regulatory authority. If the valuation is not subject to such an external review and the effect is material to the financial statements, the existence and significance of any threat created will depend upon factors such as:

- The extent to which the valuation methodology is supported by tax law or regulation, other precedent or established practice and the degree of subjectivity inherent in the valuation.
- The reliability and extent of the underlying data.

The significance of any threat created shall be evaluated and safeguards applied when necessary to eliminate the threat or reduce it to an acceptable level. Examples of such safeguards include:

- Using professionals who are not members of the audit team to perform the service;
- Having a professional review the audit work or the result of the tax service; or
- Obtaining pre-clearance or advice from the tax authorities.

Assistance in the resolution of tax disputes

290.192   An advocacy or self-review threat may be created when the firm represents an audit client in the resolution of a tax dispute once the tax authorities have notified the client that they have rejected the client's arguments on a particular issue and either the tax authority or the client is referring the matter for determination in a formal proceeding, for example before a tribunal or court. The existence and significance of any threat will depend on factors such as:

- Whether the firm has provided the advice which is the subject of the tax dispute;
- The extent to which the outcome of the dispute will have a material effect on the financial statements on which the firm will express an opinion;
- The extent to which the matter is supported by tax law or regulation, other precedent, or established practice;
- Whether the proceedings are conducted in public; and
- The role management plays in the resolution of the dispute.

The significance of any threat created shall be evaluated and safeguards applied when necessary to eliminate the threat or reduce it to an acceptable level. Examples of such safeguards include:

- Using professionals who are not members of the audit team to perform the service;
- Having a tax professional, who was not involved in providing the tax service, advise the audit team on the services and review the financial statement treatment; or
- Obtaining advice on the service from an external tax professional.

Where the taxation services involve acting as an advocate for an audit client before a **290.193** public tribunal or court in the resolution of a tax matter and the amounts involved are material to the financial statements on which the firm will express an opinion, the advocacy threat created would be so significant that no safeguards could eliminate or reduce the threat to an acceptable level. Therefore, the firm shall not perform this type of service for an audit client. What constitutes a "public tribunal or court" shall be determined according to how tax proceedings are heard in the particular jurisdiction.

The firm is not, however, precluded from having a continuing advisory role (for **290.194** example, responding to specific requests for information, providing factual accounts or testimony about the work performed or assisting the client in analysing the tax issues) for the audit client in relation to the matter that is being heard before a public tribunal or court.

Internal audit services

General provisions

The scope and objectives of internal audit activities vary widely and depend on the **290.195** size and structure of the entity and the requirements of management and those charged with governance. Internal audit activities may include:

- Monitoring of internal control-reviewing controls, monitoring their operation and recommending improvements thereto;
- Examination of financial and operating information-reviewing the means used to identify, measure, classify and report financial and operating information, and specific inquiry into individual items including detailed testing of transactions, balances and procedures;
- Review of the economy, efficiency and effectiveness of operating activities including non-financial activities of an entity; and
- Review of compliance with laws, regulations and other external requirements, and with management policies and directives and other internal requirements.

Internal audit services involve assisting the audit client in the performance of its **290.196** internal audit activities. The provision of internal audit services to an audit client creates a self-review threat to independence if the firm uses the internal audit work in the course of a subsequent external audit. Performing a significant part of the client's internal audit activities increases the possibility that firm personnel providing internal audit services will assume a management responsibility. If the firm's personnel assume a management responsibility when providing internal audit services to an audit client, the threat created would be so significant that no safeguards could reduce the threat to an acceptable level. Accordingly, a firm's personnel shall not assume a management responsibility when providing internal audit services to an audit client.

290.197   Examples of internal audit services that involve assuming management responsibilities include:

- Setting internal audit policies or the strategic direction of internal audit activities;
- Directing and taking responsibility for the actions of the entity's internal audit employees;
- Deciding which recommendations resulting from internal audit activities shall be implemented;
- Reporting the results of the internal audit activities to those charged with governance on behalf of management;
- Performing procedures that form part of the internal control, such as reviewing and approving changes to employee data access privileges;
- Taking responsibility for designing, implementing and maintaining internal control; and
- Performing outsourced internal audit services, comprising all or a substantial portion of the internal audit function, where the firm is responsible for determining the scope of the internal audit work and may have responsibility for one or more of the matters noted in (a)-(f).

290.198   To avoid assuming a management responsibility, the firm shall only provide internal audit services to an audit client if it is satisfied that:

- The client designates an appropriate and competent resource, preferably within senior management, to be responsible at all times for internal audit activities and to acknowledge responsibility for designing, implementing, and maintaining internal control;
- The client's management or those charged with governance reviews, assesses and approves the scope, risk and frequency of the internal audit services;
- The client's management evaluates the adequacy of the internal audit services and the findings resulting from their performance;
- The client's management evaluates and determines which recommendations resulting from internal audit services to implement and manages the implementation process; and
- The client's management reports to those charged with governance the significant findings and recommendations resulting from the internal audit services.

290.199   When a firm uses the work of an internal audit function, International Standards on Auditing require the performance of procedures to evaluate the adequacy of that work. When a firm accepts an engagement to provide internal audit services to an audit client, and the results of those services will be used in conducting the external audit, a self-review threat is created because of the possibility that the audit team will use the results of the internal audit service without appropriately evaluating those results or exercising the same level of professional scepticism as would be exercised when the internal audit work is performed by individuals who are not members of the firm. The significance of the threat will depend on factors such as:

- The materiality of the related financial statement amounts;
- The risk of misstatement of the assertions related to those financial statement amounts; and
- The degree of reliance that will be placed on the internal audit service.

The significance of the threat shall be evaluated and safeguards applied when necessary to eliminate the threat or reduce it to an acceptable level. An example of such a safeguard is using professionals who are not members of the audit team to perform the internal audit service.

Audit clients that are public interest entities

In the case of an audit client that is a public interest entity, a firm shall not provide internal audit services that relate to: **290.200**

- A significant part of the internal controls over financial reporting;
- Financial accounting systems that generate information that is, separately or in the aggregate, significant to the client's accounting records or financial statements on which the firm will express an opinion; or
- Amounts or disclosures that are, separately or in the aggregate, material to the financial statements on which the firm will express an opinion.

IT Systems Services

General Provisions

Services related to information technology ("IT") systems include the design or implementation of hardware or software systems. The systems may aggregate source data, form part of the internal control over financial reporting or generate information that affects the accounting records or financial statements, or the systems may be unrelated to the audit client's accounting records, the internal control over financial reporting or financial statements. Providing systems services may create a self-review threat depending on the nature of the services and the IT systems. **290.201**

The following IT systems services are deemed not to create a threat to independence as long as the firm's personnel do not assume a management responsibility: **290.202**

- Design or implementation of IT systems that are unrelated to internal control over financial reporting;
- Design or implementation of IT systems that do not generate information forming a significant part of the accounting records or financial statements;
- Implementation of "off-the-shelf" accounting or financial information reporting software that was not developed by the firm if the customisation required to meet the client's needs is not significant; and
- Evaluating and making recommendations with respect to a system designed, implemented or operated by another service provider or the client.

Audit clients that are not public interest entities

Providing services to an audit client that is not a public interest entity involving the design or implementation of IT systems that (a) form a significant part of the internal control over financial reporting or (b) generate information that is significant to the client's accounting records or financial statements on which the firm will express an opinion creates a self-review threat. **290.203**

The self-review threat is too significant to permit such services unless appropriate safeguards are put in place ensuring that: **290.204**

- The client acknowledges its responsibility for establishing and monitoring a system of internal controls;
- The client assigns the responsibility to make all management decisions with respect to the design and implementation of the hardware or software system to a competent employee, preferably within senior management;
- The client makes all management decisions with respect to the design and implementation process;

- The client evaluates the adequacy and results of the design and implementation of the system; and
- The client is responsible for operating the system (hardware or software) and for the data it uses or generates.

290.205   Depending on the degree of reliance that will be placed on the particular IT systems as part of the audit, a determination shall be made as to whether to provide such non-assurance services only with personnel who are not members of the audit team and who have different reporting lines within the firm. The significance of any remaining threat shall be evaluated and safeguards applied when necessary to eliminate the threat or reduce it to an acceptable level. An example of such a safeguard is having a professional accountant review the audit or non-assurance work.

Audit clients that are public interest entities

290.206   In the case of an audit client that is a public interest entity, a firm shall not provide services involving the design or implementation of IT systems that (a) form a significant part of the internal control over financial reporting or (b) generate information that is significant to the client's accounting records or financial statements on which the firm will express an opinion.

Litigation Support Services

290.207   Litigation support services may include activities such as acting as an expert witness, calculating estimated damages or other amounts that might become receivable or payable as the result of litigation or other legal dispute, and assistance with document management and retrieval. These services may create a self-review or advocacy threat.

290.208   If the firm provides a litigation support service to an audit client and the service involves estimating damages or other amounts that affect the financial statements on which the firm will express an opinion, the valuation service provisions included in paragraphs 290.175 to 290.180 shall be followed. In the case of other litigation support services, the significance of any threat created shall be evaluated and safeguards applied when necessary to eliminate the threat or reduce it to an acceptable level.

Legal Services

290.209   For the purpose of this section, legal services are defined as any services for which the person providing the services must either be admitted to practice law before the courts of the jurisdiction in which such services are to be provided or have the required legal training to practice law. Such legal services may include, depending on the jurisdiction, a wide and diversified range of areas including both corporate and commercial services to clients, such as contract support, litigation, mergers and acquisition legal advice and support and assistance to clients' internal legal departments. Providing legal services to an entity that is an audit client may create both self-review and advocacy threats.

290.210   Legal services that support an audit client in executing a transaction (e.g., contract support, legal advice, legal due diligence and restructuring) may create self-review threats. The existence and significance of any threat will depend on factors such as:

- The nature of the service;
- Whether the service is provided by a member of the audit team; and

- The materiality of any matter in relation to the client's financial statements.

The significance of any threat created shall be evaluated and safeguards applied when necessary to eliminate the threat or reduce it to an acceptable level. Examples of such safeguards include:

- Using professionals who are not members of the audit team to perform the service; or
- Having a professional who was not involved in providing the legal services provide advice to the audit team on the service and review any financial statement treatment.

Acting in an advocacy role for an audit client in resolving a dispute or litigation when the amounts involved are material to the financial statements on which the firm will express an opinion would create advocacy and self-review threats so significant that no safeguards could reduce the threat to an acceptable level. Therefore, the firm shall not perform this type of service for an audit client. **290.211**

When a firm is asked to act in an advocacy role for an audit client in resolving a dispute or litigation when the amounts involved are not material to the financial statements on which the firm will express an opinion, the firm shall evaluate the significance of any advocacy and self-review threats created and apply safeguards when necessary to eliminate the threat or reduce it to an acceptable level. Examples of such safeguards include: **290.212**

- Using professionals who are not members of the audit team to perform the service; or
- Having a professional who was not involved in providing the legal services advise the audit team on the service and review any financial statement treatment.

The appointment of a partner or an employee of the firm as General Counsel for legal affairs of an audit client would create self-review and advocacy threats that are so significant that no safeguards could reduce the threats to an acceptable level. The position of General Counsel is generally a senior management position with broad responsibility for the legal affairs of a company, and consequently, no member of the firm shall accept such an appointment for an audit client. **290.213**

Recruiting Services

General provisions

Providing recruiting services to an audit client may create self-interest, familiarity or intimidation threats. The existence and significance of any threat will depend on factors such as: **290.214**

- The nature of the requested assistance; and
- The role of the person to be recruited.

The significance of any threat created shall be evaluated and safeguards applied when necessary to eliminate the threat or reduce it to an acceptable level. In all cases, the firm shall not assume management responsibilities, including acting as a negotiator on the client's behalf, and the hiring decision shall be left to the client.

The firm may generally provide such services as reviewing the professional qualifications of a number of applicants and providing advice on their suitability for the post. In addition, the firm may interview candidates and advise on a candidate's competence for financial accounting, administrative or control positions.

Audit clients that are public interest entities

290.215   A firm shall not provide the following recruiting services to an audit client that is a public interest entity with respect to a director or officer of the entity or senior management in a position to exert significant influence over the preparation of the client's accounting records or the financial statements on which the firm will express an opinion:

- Searching for or seeking out candidates for such positions; and
- Undertaking reference checks of prospective candidates for such positions.

Corporate Finance Services

290.216   Providing corporate finance services such as:

- assisting an audit client in developing corporate strategies,
- identifying possible targets for the audit client to acquire,
- advising on disposal transactions,
- assisting finance raising transactions, and
- providing structuring advice

may create advocacy and self-review threats. The significance of any threat shall be evaluated and safeguards applied when necessary to eliminate the threat or reduce it to an acceptable level. Examples of such safeguards include:

- Using professionals who are not members of the audit team to provide the services; or
- Having a professional who was not involved in providing the corporate finance service advise the audit team on the service and review the accounting treatment and any financial statement treatment.

290.217   Providing a corporate finance service, for example advice on the structuring of a corporate finance transaction or on financing arrangements that will directly affect amounts that will be reported in the financial statements on which the firm will provide an opinion may create a self-review threat. The existence and significance of any threat will depend on factors such as:

- The degree of subjectivity involved in determining the appropriate treatment for the outcome or consequences of the corporate finance advice in the financial statements;
- The extent to which the outcome of the corporate finance advice will directly affect amounts recorded in the financial statements and the extent to which the amounts are material to the financial statements; and
- Whether the effectiveness of the corporate finance advice depends on a particular accounting treatment or presentation in the financial statements and there is doubt as to the appropriateness of the related accounting treatment or presentation under the relevant financial reporting framework.

The significance of any threat shall be evaluated and safeguards applied when necessary to eliminate the threat or reduce it to an acceptable level. Examples of such safeguards include:

- Using professionals who are not members of the audit team to perform the service; or

- Having a professional who was not involved in providing the corporate finance service to the client advise the audit team on the service and review the accounting treatment and any financial statement treatment.

Where the effectiveness of corporate finance advice depends on a particular accounting treatment or presentation in the financial statements and: **290.218**

- The audit team has reasonable doubt as to the appropriateness of the related accounting treatment or presentation under the relevant financial reporting framework; and
- The outcome or consequences of the corporate finance advice will have a material effect on the financial statements on which the firm will express an opinion;

The self-review threat would be so significant that no safeguards could reduce the threat to an acceptable level, in which case the corporate finance advice shall not be provided.

Providing corporate finance services involving promoting, dealing in, or under-writing an audit client's shares would create an advocacy or self-review threat that is so significant that no safeguards could reduce the threat to an acceptable level. Accordingly, a firm shall not provide such services to an audit client.   **290.219**

Fees

Fees – relative size

When the total fees from an audit client represent a large proportion of the total fees of the firm expressing the audit opinion, the dependence on that client and concern about losing the client creates a self-interest or intimidation threat. The significance of the threat will depend on factors such as: **290.220**

- The operating structure of the firm;
- Whether the firm is well established or new; and
- The significance of the client qualitatively and/or quantitatively to the firm.

The significance of the threat shall be evaluated and safeguards applied when necessary to eliminate the threat or reduce it to an acceptable level. Examples of such safeguards include:

- Reducing the dependency on the client;
- External quality control reviews; or
- Consulting a third party, such as a professional regulatory body or a professional accountant, on key audit judgments.

A self-interest or intimidation threat is also created when the fees generated from an audit client represent a large proportion of the revenue from an individual partner's clients or a large proportion of the revenue of an individual office of the firm. The significance of the threat will depend upon factors such as: **290.221**

- The significance of the client qualitatively and/or quantitatively to the partner or office; and
- The extent to which the remuneration of the partner, or the partners in the office, is dependent upon the fees generated from the client.

The significance of the threat shall be evaluated and safeguards applied when necessary to eliminate the threat or reduce it to an acceptable level. Examples of such safeguards include:

- Reducing the dependency on the audit client;
- Having a professional accountant review the work or otherwise advise as necessary; or
- regular independent internal or external quality reviews of the engagement.

Audit clients that are public interest entities

290.222   Where an audit client is a public interest entity and, for two consecutive years, the total fees from the client and its related entities (subject to the considerations in paragraph 290.27) represent more than 15% of the total fees received by the firm expressing the opinion on the financial statements of the client, the firm shall disclose to those charged with governance of the audit client the fact that the total of such fees represents more than 15% of the total fees received by the firm, and discuss which of the safeguards below it will apply to reduce the threat to an acceptable level, and apply the selected safeguard:

- Prior to the issuance of the audit opinion on the second year's financial statements, a professional accountant, who is not a member of the firm expressing the opinion on the financial statements, performs an engagement quality control review of that engagement or a professional regulatory body performs a review of that engagement that is equivalent to an engagement quality control review ("a pre-issuance review"); or
- After the audit opinion on the second year's financial statements has been issued, and before the issuance of the audit opinion on the third year's financial statements, a professional accountant, who is not a member of the firm expressing the opinion on the financial statements, or a professional regulatory body performs a review of the second year's audit that is equivalent to an engagement quality control review ("a post-issuance review").

When the total fees significantly exceed 15%, the firm shall determine whether the significance of the threat is such that a post-issuance review would not reduce the threat to an acceptable level and, therefore, a pre-issuance review is required. In such circumstances a pre-issuance review shall be performed.

Thereafter, when the fees continue to exceed 15% each year, the disclosure to and discussion with those charged with governance shall occur and one of the above safeguards shall be applied. If the fees significantly exceed 15%, the firm shall determine whether the significance of the threat is such that a post-issuance review would not reduce the threat to an acceptable level and, therefore, a pre-issuance review is required. In such circumstances a pre-issuance review shall be performed.

Fees – overdue

290.223   A self-interest threat may be created if fees due from an audit client remain unpaid for a long time, especially if a significant part is not paid before the issue of the audit report for the following year. Generally the firm is expected to require payment of such fees before such audit report is issued. If fees remain unpaid after the report has been issued, the existence and significance of any threat shall be evaluated and safeguards applied when necessary to eliminate the threat or reduce it to an acceptable level. An example of such a safeguard is having an additional professional accountant who did not take part in the audit engagement provide advice or review the work performed. The firm shall determine whether the overdue fees might be regarded as being equivalent to a loan to the client and whether, because of the significance of the overdue fees, it is appropriate for the firm to be re-appointed or continue the audit engagement.

Contingent fees

Contingent fees are fees calculated on a predetermined basis relating to the outcome of a transaction or the result of the services performed by the firm. For the purposes of this section, a fee is not regarded as being contingent if established by a court or other public authority.

290.224

A contingent fee charged directly or indirectly, for example through an intermediary, by a firm in respect of an audit engagement creates a self-interest threat that is so significant that no safeguards could reduce the threat to an acceptable level. Accordingly, a firm shall not enter into any such fee arrangement.

290.225

A contingent fee charged directly or indirectly, for example through an intermediary, by a firm in respect of a non-assurance service provided to an audit client may also create a self-interest threat. The threat created would be so significant that no safeguards could reduce the threat to an acceptable level if:

290.226

- The fee is charged by the firm expressing the opinion on the financial statements and the fee is material or expected to be material to that firm;
- The fee is charged by a network firm that participates in a significant part of the audit and the fee is material or expected to be material to that firm; or
- The outcome of the non-assurance service, and therefore the amount of the fee, is dependent on a future or contemporary judgment related to the audit of a material amount in the financial statements.

Accordingly, such arrangements shall not be accepted.

For other contingent fee arrangements charged by a firm for a non-assurance service to an audit client, the existence and significance of any threats will depend on factors such as:

290.227

- The range of possible fee amounts;
- Whether an appropriate authority determines the outcome of the matter upon which the contingent fee will be determined;
- The nature of the service; and
- The effect of the event or transaction on the financial statements.

The significance of any threats shall be evaluated and safeguards applied when necessary to eliminate the threats or reduce them to an acceptable level. Examples of such safeguards include:

- Having a professional accountant review the relevant audit work or otherwise advise as necessary; or
- Using professionals who are not members of the audit team to perform the non-assurance service.

Compensation and evaluation policies

A self-interest threat is created when a member of the audit team is evaluated on or compensated for selling non-assurance services to that audit client. The significance of the threat will depend on:

290.228

- The proportion of the individual's compensation or performance evaluation that is based on the sale of such services;
- The role of the individual on the audit team; and
- Whether promotion decisions are influenced by the sale of such services.

The significance of the threat shall be evaluated and, if the threat is not at an acceptable level, the firm shall either revise the compensation plan or evaluation process for that individual or apply safeguards to eliminate the threat or reduce it to an acceptable level. Examples of such safeguards include:

- Removing such members from the audit team; or
- Having a professional accountant review the work of the member of the audit team.

290.229   A key audit partner shall not be evaluated on or compensated based on that partner's success in selling non-assurance services to the partner's audit client. This is not intended to prohibit normal profit-sharing arrangements between partners of a firm.

Gifts and hospitality

290.230   Accepting gifts or hospitality from an audit client may create self-interest and familiarity threats. If a firm or a member of the audit team accepts gifts or hospitality, unless the value is trivial and inconsequential, the threats created would be so significant that no safeguards could reduce the threats to an acceptable level. Consequently, a firm or a member of the audit team shall not accept such gifts or hospitality.

Actual or threatened litigation

290.231   When litigation takes place, or appears likely, between the firm or a member of the audit team and the audit client, self-interest and intimidation threats are created. The relationship between client management and the members of the audit team must be characterised by complete candour and foll disclosure regarding all aspects of a client's business operations. When the firm and the client's management are placed in adversarial positions by actual or threatened litigation, affecting management's willingness to make complete disclosures, self-interest and intimidation threats are created. The significance of the threats created will depend on such factors as:

- The materiality of the litigation; and
- Whether the litigation relates to a prior audit engagement.

The significance of the threats shall be evaluated and safeguards applied when necessary to eliminate the threats or reduce them to an acceptable level. Examples of such safeguards include:

- If the litigation involves a member of the audit team, removing that individual from the audit team; or
- Having a professional review the work performed.

If such safeguards do not reduce the threats to an acceptable level, the only appropriate action is to withdraw from, or decline, the audit engagement.

Paragraphs 290.232 to 290.499 are intentionally left blank.

Reports that Include a Restriction on Use and Distribution

Introduction

The independence requirements in section 290 apply to all audit engagements. However, in certain circumstances involving audit engagements where the report includes a restriction on use and distribution, and provided the conditions described in 290.501 to 290.502 are met, the independence requirements in this section may be modified as provided in paragraphs 290.505 to 290.514. These paragraphs are only applicable to an audit engagement on special purpose financial statements (a) that is intended to provide a conclusion in positive or negative form that the financial statements are prepared in all material respects, in accordance with the applicable financial reporting framework, including, in the case of a fair presentation framework, that the financial statements give a true and fair view or are presented fairly, in all material respects, in accordance with the applicable financial reporting framework, and (b) where the audit report includes a restriction on use and distribution. The modifications are not permitted in the case of an audit of financial statements required by law or regulation. **290.500**

The modifications to the requirements of section 290 are permitted if the intended users of the report (a) are knowledgeable as to the purpose and limitations of the report, and (b) explicitly agree to the application of the modified independence requirements. Knowledge as to the purpose and limitations of the report may be obtained by the intended users through their participation, either directly or indirectly through their representative who has the authority to act for the intended users, in establishing the nature and scope of the engagement. Such participation enhances the ability of the firm to communicate with intended users about independence matters, including the circumstances that are relevant to the evaluation of the threats to independence and the applicable safeguards necessary to eliminate the threats or reduce them to an acceptable level, and to obtain their agreement to the modified independence requirements that are to be applied. **290.501**

The firm shall communicate (for example, in an engagement letter) with the intended users regarding the independence requirements that are to be applied with respect to the provision of the audit engagement. Where the intended users are a class of users (for example, lenders in a syndicated loan arrangement) who are not specifically identifiable by name at the time the engagement terms are established, such users shall subsequently be made aware of the independence requirements agreed to by the representative (for example, by the representative making the firm's engagement letter available to all users). **290.502**

If the firm also issues an audit report that does not include a restriction on use and distribution for the same client, the provisions of paragraphs 290.500 to 290.514 do not change the requirement to apply the provisions of paragraphs 290.1 to 290.232 to that audit engagement. **290.503**

The modifications to the requirements of section 290 that are permitted in the circumstances set out above are described in paragraphs 290.505 to 290.514. Compliance in all other respects with the provisions of section 290 is required. **290.504**

Public interest entities

When the conditions set out in paragraphs 290.500 to 290.502 are met, it is not necessary to apply the additional requirements in paragraphs 290.100 to 290.232 that apply to audit engagements for public interest entities. **290.505**

Related Entities

290.506   When the conditions set out in paragraphs 290.500 to 290.502 are met, references to audit client do not include its related entities. However, when the audit team knows or has reason to believe that a relationship or circumstance involving a related entity of the client is relevant to the evaluation of the firm's independence of the client, the audit team shall include that related entity when identifying and evaluating threats to independence and applying appropriate safeguards.

Networks and network firms

290.507   When the conditions set out in paragraphs 290.500 to 290.502 are met, reference to the firm does not include network firms. However, when the firm knows or has reason to believe that threats are created by any interests and relationships of a network firm, they shall be included in the evaluation of threats to independence.

Financial interests, loans and guarantees, close business relationships and family and personal relationships

290.508   When the conditions set out in paragraphs 290.500 to 290.502 are met, the relevant provisions set out in paragraphs 290.102 to 290.145 apply only to the members of the engagement team, their immediate family members and close family members.

290.509   In addition, a determination shall be made as to whether threats to independence are created by interests and relationships, as described in paragraphs 290.102 to 290.145, between the audit client and the following members of the audit team:

- Those who provide consultation regarding technical or industry specific issues, transactions or events; and
- Those who provide quality control for the engagement, including those who perform the engagement quality control review.

An evaluation shall be made of the significance of any threats that the engagement team has reason to believe are created by interests and relationships between the audit client and others within the firm who can directly influence the outcome of the audit engagement, including those who recommend the compensation of, or who provide direct supervisory, management or other oversight of the audit engagement partner in connection with the performance of the audit engagement (including those at all successively senior levels above the engagement partner through to the individual who is the firm's Senior or Managing Partner (Chief Executive or equivalent)).

290.510   An evaluation shall also be made of the significance of any threats that the engagement team has reason to believe are created by financial interests in the audit client held by individuals, as described in paragraphs 290.108 to 290.111 and paragraphs 290.113 to 290.115.

290.511   Where a threat to independence is not at an acceptable level, safeguards shall be applied to eliminate the threat or reduce it to an acceptable level.

290.512   In applying the provisions set out in paragraphs 290.106 and 290.115 to interests of the firm, if the firm has a material financial interest, whether direct or indirect, in the audit client, the self-interest threat created would be so significant that no safeguards could reduce the threat to an acceptable level. Accordingly, the firm shall not have such a financial interest.

Employment with an audit client

An evaluation shall be made of the significance of any threats from any employment **290.513**
relationships as described in paragraphs 290.134 to 290.138. Where a threat exists
that is not at an acceptable level, safeguards shall be applied to eliminate the threat
or reduce it to an acceptable level. Examples of safeguards that might be appropriate
include those set out in paragraph 290.136.

Provision of non-assurance services

If the firm conducts an engagement to issue a restricted use and distribution report **290.514**
for an audit client and provides a non-assurance service to the audit client, the
provisions of paragraphs 290.156 to 290.232 shall be complied with, subject to
paragraphs 290.504 to 290.507.

Appendix to Section 290 – nature of assurance engagements

The IESBA and ICAEW Codes include two different sets of requirements to ensure **1**
independence is maintained in assurance engagements. If the engagement is an audit
engagement, or a review engagement, the requirements of section 290 apply (or the
APB Ethical Standards – see 290.0c). For other assurance engagements, section 291
applies.

To assist professional accountants in public practice determine which section to **2**
apply, set out below are a number of examples of engagements typically undertaken
and an indication of whether they would normally be regarded as audit or review
(thus section 290 or APB) or other assurance (thus section 291).

As individual engagements can vary, even within categories, professional accoun- **3**
tants in public practice should consider the examples as indicative rather than
definitive and should have regard to the nature of the conclusion to be given. In
particular they should have regard to the definitions of 'review engagement' and
'financial statements' in the IESBA and ICAEW Codes, which are:

"Review engagement – An assurance engagement, conducted in accordance with
International Standards on Review Engagements or equivalent, in which a professional accountant in public practice expresses a conclusion on whether, on the basis
of the procedures which do not provide all the evidence that would be required in an
audit, anything has come to the accountant's attention that causes the accountant to
believe that the financial statements are not prepared, in all material respects, in
accordance with an applicable financial reporting framework."

"Financial statements – A structured representation of historical financial information, including related notes, intended to communicate an entity's economic
resources or obligations at a point in time or the changes therein for a period of time
in accordance with a financial reporting framework. The related notes ordinarily
comprise a summary of significant accounting policies and other explanatory
information. The term can relate to a complete set of financial statements, but it can
also refer to a single financial statement, for example, a balance sheet, or a statement
of revenues and expenses, and related explanatory notes."

Taken together, the key elements in determining that an assurance engagement is a **4**
review engagement are:

- the subject matter: historical financial information, and
- the nature of the report: limited procedures but nothing has come to attention to indicate the information is not prepared in accordance with applicable financial reporting framework.

Examples of engagements that would normally be considered to be audit or review engagements (section 290 or APB)

- Statutory or other audits, or engagements possessing the characteristics of an audit (i.e. involving a 'true and fair' or 'fairly presents' conclusion).
- Review in accordance with ISRE 2410 (UK and Ireland): review of interim financial information performed by independent auditor of the entity, or ISRE 2400: engagements to review financial statements
- Review in accordance with the ICAEW Assurance Service.
- Independent Examination of Charities: again historical financial information and a negative opinion indicating no evidence of non compliance with a specified framework
- Public sector year-end audits
- Special report on the abbreviated accounts of a small company (the report must be prepared by the auditors, who as such, should apply section 290/APB).

Examples of engagements that would normally be considered to be other assurance engagements (section 291)

- Assurance reports on internal controls of service organisations, conducted in accordance with, for example, AAF 01/06.
- Assurance reports on the outsourced provision of information services and information processing services, conducted in accordance with, for example, ITF 01/07.
- Any assurance conducted based on AAF 02/07 A framework for assurance reports on third party operations.
- Any assurance engagements on prospective financial or non-financial information.
- Any other assurance engagements based on ISAE 3000 including narrative information, greenhouse gas and sustainability reports if conducted outside the scope of annual accounts.
- Independent accountant's report on grant claims, conducted in accordance with, for example, AAF 01/10.

Note that for all of the above and any other engagements, if the professional accountant in public practice is also the auditor of the entity, section 290/ APB Ethical standards will already have to be followed. No additional compliance with section 291 is necessary in such circumstances.

TRANSITIONAL PROVISIONS

Effective date

This Code is effective on January 1, 2011; early adoption is permitted. This Code is subject to the following transitional provisions:

Public interest entities

1   Section 290 of the Code contains additional independence provisions when the audit or review client is a public interest entity. The additional provisions that are applicable because of the new definition of a public interest entity or the guidance in

paragraph 290.26 are effective on January 1, 2012. For partner rotation require-ments, the transitional provisions contained in paragraphs 2 and 3 below apply.

Partner rotation

For a partner who is subject to the rotation provisions in paragraph 290.151 because **2** the partner meets the definition of the new term "key audit partner," and the partner is neither the engagement partner nor the individual responsible for the engagement quality control review, the rotation provisions are effective for the audits or reviews of financial statements for years beginning on or after December 15, 2011. For example, in the case of an audit client with a calendar year-end, a key audit partner, who is neither the engagement partner nor the individual responsible for the engagement quality control review, who had served as a key audit partner for seven or more years (i.e., the audits of 2003-2010), would be required to rotate after serving for one more year as a key audit partner (i.e., after completing the 2011 audit).

For an engagement partner or an individual responsible for the engagement quality **3** control review who immediately prior to assuming either of these roles served in another key audit partner role for the client, and who, at the beginning of the first fiscal year beginning on or after December 15, 2010, had served as the engagement partner or individual responsible for the engagement quality control review for six or fewer years, the rotation provisions are effective for the audits or reviews of financial statements for years beginning on or after December 15, 2011. For example, in the case of an audit client with a calendar year-end, a partner who had served the client in another key audit partner role for four years (i.e., the audits of 2002-2005) and subsequently as the engagement partner for five years (i.e., the audits of 2006-2010) would be required to rotate after serving for one more year as the engagement partner (i.e., after completing the 2011 audit).

Non-assurance services

Paragraphs 290.156-290.219 address the provision of non-assurance services to an **4** audit or review client. If, at the effective date of the Code, services are being provided to an audit or review client and the services were permissible under the June 2005 Code (revised July 2006) but are either prohibited or subject to restrictions under the revised Code, the firm may continue providing such services only if they were con-tracted for and commenced prior to January 1, 2011, and are completed before July 1, 2011.

Fees – relative size

Paragraph 290.222 provides that, in respect of an audit or review client that is a **5** public interest entity, when the total fees from that client and its related entities (subject to the considerations in paragraph 290.27) for two consecutive years represent more than 15% of the total fees of the firm expressing the opinion on the financial statements, a pre- or post-issuance review (as described in paragraph 290.222) of the second year's audit shall be performed. This requirement is effective for audits or reviews of financial statements covering years that begin on or after December 15, 2010. For example, in the case of an audit client with a calendar year end, if the total fees from the client exceeded the 15% threshold for 2011 and 2012, the pre- or post-issuance review would be applied with respect to the audit of the 2012 financial statements.

Compensation and evaluation policies

6   Paragraph 290.229 provides that a key audit partner shall not be evaluated or compensated based on that partner's success in selling non-assurance services to the partner's audit client. This requirement is effective on January 1, 2012. A key audit partner may, however, receive compensation after January 1, 2012 based on an evaluation made prior to January 1, 2012 of that partner's success in selling non-assurance services to the audit client.

291 Independence – other assurance engagements

Structure of section

291.1   This section addresses independence requirements for assurance engagements that are not audit or review engagements. As indicated in paragraphs 1.14 to 1.17 independence requirements for audit and review engagements are addressed in section 290. If the assurance client is also an audit or review client, the requirements in section 290 also apply to the firm, network firms and members of the audit or review team. In certain circumstances involving assurance engagements where the assurance report includes a restriction on use and distribution and provided certain conditions are met, the independence requirements in this section may be modified as provided in 291.21 to 291.27.

291.2   Assurance engagements are designed to enhance intended users' degree of confidence about the outcome of the evaluation or measurement of a subject matter against criteria. The International Framework for Assurance engagements (the Assurance Framework) issued by the International Auditing and Assurance Standards Board describes the elements and objectives of an assurance engagement and identifies engagements to which International Standards on Assurance engagements (ISAEs) apply. For a description of the elements and objectives of an assurance engagement, refer to the Assurance Framework.

291.3   Compliance with the fundamental principle of objectivity requires being independent of assurance clients. In the case of assurance engagements, it is in the public interest and, therefore, required by this Code of Ethics, that members of assurance teams and firms be independent of assurance clients and that any threats that the firm has reason to believe are created by a network firm's interests and relationships be evaluated. In addition, when the assurance team knows or has reason to believe that a relationship or circumstance involving a related entity of the assurance client is relevant to the evaluation of the firm's independence from the client, the assurance team shall include that related entity when identifying and evaluating threats to independence and applying appropriate safeguards.

A conceptual framework approach to independence

291.4   The objective of this section is to assist firms and members of assurance teams in applying the conceptual framework approach described below to achieving and maintaining independence.

291.5   Independence comprises:

- Independence of Mind
  The state of mind that permits the expression of a conclusion without being affected by influences that compromise professional judgment, thereby allowing

an individual to act with integrity and exercise objectivity and professional scepticism.
- Independence in Appearance
  The avoidance of facts and circumstances that are so significant that a reasonable and informed third party would be likely to conclude, weighing all the specific facts and circumstances, that a firm's, or a member of the assurance team's, integrity, objectivity or professional scepticism has been compromised.

The conceptual framework approach shall be applied by professional accountants to: **291.6**

- Identify threats to independence;
- Evaluate the significance of the threats identified; and
- Apply safeguards when necessary to eliminate the threats or reduce them to an acceptable level.

When the professional accountant determines that appropriate safeguards are not available or cannot be applied to eliminate the threats or reduce them to an acceptable level, the professional accountant shall eliminate the circumstance or relationship creating the threats or decline or terminate the assurance engagement.

A professional accountant shall use professional judgment in applying this conceptual framework.

Many different circumstances, or combinations of circumstances, may be relevant in **291.7** assessing threats to independence. It is impossible to define every situation that creates threats to independence and to specify the appropriate action. Therefore, this Code establishes a conceptual framework that requires firms and members of assurance teams to identify, evaluate, and address threats to independence. The conceptual framework approach assists professional accountants in public practice in complying with the ethical requirements in this Code. It accommodates many variations in circumstances that create threats to independence and can deter a professional accountant from concluding that a situation is permitted if it is not specifically prohibited.

Paragraphs 291.100 and onwards describe how the conceptual framework approach **291.8** to independence is to be applied. These paragraphs do not address all the circumstances and relationships that create or may create threats to independence.

In deciding whether to accept or continue an engagement, or whether a particular **291.9** individual may be a member of the assurance team, a firm shall identify and evaluate any threats to independence. If the threats are not at an acceptable level, and the decision is whether to accept an engagement or include a particular individual on the assurance team, the firm shall determine whether safeguards are available to eliminate the threats or reduce them to an acceptable level. If the decision is whether to continue an engagement, the firm shall determine whether any existing safeguards will continue to be effective to eliminate the threats or reduce them to an acceptable level or whether other safeguards will need to be applied or whether the engagement needs to be terminated. Whenever new information about a threat comes to the attention of the firm during the engagement, the firm shall evaluate the significance of the threat in accordance with the conceptual framework approach.

Throughout this section, reference is made to the significance of threats to inde- **291.10** pendence. In evaluating the significance of a threat, qualitative as well as quantitative factors shall be taken into account.

291.11   This section does not, in most cases, prescribe the specific responsibility of individuals within the firm for actions related to independence because responsibility may differ depending on the size, structure and organisation of a firm. The firm is required by International Standards on Quality Control to establish policies and procedures designed to provide it with reasonable assurance that independence is maintained when required by relevant ethical standards.

Assurance engagements

291.12   As further explained in the Assurance Framework, in an assurance engagement the professional accountant in public practice expresses a conclusion designed to enhance the degree of confidence of the intended users (other than the responsible party) about the outcome of the evaluation or measurement of a subject matter against criteria.

291.13   The outcome of the evaluation or measurement of a subject matter is the information that results from applying the criteria to the subject matter. The term "subject matter information" is used to mean the outcome of the evaluation or measurement of a subject matter. For example, the Framework states that an assertion about the effectiveness of internal control (subject matter information) results from applying a framework for evaluating the effectiveness of internal control, such as COSO or CoCo (criteria), to internal control, a process (subject matter).

291.14   Assurance engagements may be assertion-based or direct reporting. In either case, they involve three separate parties: a professional accountant in public practice, a responsible party and intended users.

291.15   In an assertion-based assurance engagement, the evaluation or measurement of the subject matter is performed by the responsible party, and the subject matter information is in the form of an assertion by the responsible party that is made available to the intended users.

291.16   In a direct reporting assurance engagement, the professional accountant in public practice either directly performs the evaluation or measurement of the subject matter, or obtains a representation from the responsible party that has performed the evaluation or measurement that is not available to the intended users. The subject matter information is provided to the intended users in the assurance report.

Assertion-based assurance engagements

291.17   In an assertion-based assurance engagement, the members of the assurance team and the firm shall be independent of the assurance client (the party responsible for the subject matter information, and which may be responsible for the subject matter). Such independence requirements prohibit certain relationships between members of the assurance team and (a) directors or officers, and (b) individuals at the client in a position to exert significant influence over the subject matter information. Also, a determination shall be made as to whether threats to independence are created by relationships with individuals at the client in a position to exert significant influence over the subject matter of the engagement. An evaluation shall be made of the significance of any threats that the firm has reason to believe are created by network firm interests and relationships.

291.18   In the majority of assertion-based assurance engagements, the responsible party is responsible for both the subject matter information and the subject matter. However, in some engagements, the responsible party may not be responsible for the subject matter. For example, when a professional accountant in public practice is engaged to perform an assurance engagement regarding a report that an environmental consultant has prepared about a company's sustainability practices for distribution to intended users, the environmental consultant is the responsible party for the subject matter information but the company is responsible for the subject matter (the sustainability practices).

In assertion-based assurance engagements where the responsible party is responsible **291.19** for the subject matter information but not the subject matter, the members of the assurance team and the firm shall be independent of the party responsible for the subject matter information (the assurance client). In addition, an evaluation shall be made of any threats the firm has reason to believe are created by interests and relationships between a member of the assurance team, the firm, a network firm and the party responsible for the subject matter.

Direct reporting assurance engagements

In a direct reporting assurance engagement, the members of the assurance team and **291.20** the firm shall be independent of the assurance client (the party responsible for the subject matter). An evaluation shall also be made of any threats the firm has reason to believe are created by network firm interests and relationships.

Reports that include a restriction on use and distribution

In certain circumstances where the assurance report includes a restriction on use and **291.21** distribution, and provided the conditions in this paragraph and in 291.22 are met, the independence requirements in this section may be modified. The modifications to the requirements of section 291 are permitted if the intended users of the report (a) are knowledgeable as to the purpose, subject matter information and limitations of the report and (b) explicitly agree to the application of the modified independence requirements. Knowledge as to the purpose, subject matter information, and limitations of the report may be obtained by the intended users through their participation, either directly or indirectly through their representative who has the authority to act for the intended users, in establishing the nature and scope of the engagement. Such participation enhances the ability of the firm to communicate with intended users about independence matters, including the circumstances that are relevant to the evaluation of the threats to independence and the applicable safeguards necessary to eliminate the threats or reduce them to an acceptable level, and to obtain their agreement to the modified independence requirements that are to be applied.

The firm shall communicate (for example, in an engagement letter) with the intended **291.22** users regarding the independence requirements that are to be applied with respect to the provision of the assurance engagement. Where the intended users are a class of users (for example, lenders in a syndicated loan arrangement) who are not specifically identifiable by name at the time the engagement terms are established, such users shall subsequently be made aware of the independence requirements agreed to by the representative (for example, by the representative making the firm's engagement letter available to all users).

If the firm also issues an assurance report that does not include a restriction on use **291.23** and distribution for the same client, the provisions of paragraphs 291.25 to 291.27 do not change the requirement to apply the provisions of paragraphs 291.1 to 291.159 to that assurance engagement. If the firm also issues an audit report, whether or not it includes a restriction on use and distribution, for the same client, the provisions of section 290 shall apply to that audit engagement.

291.24   The modifications to the requirements of section 291 that are permitted in the circumstances set out above are described in paragraphs 291.25 to 291.27. Compliance in all other respects with the provisions of section 291 is required.

291.25   When the conditions set out in paragraphs 291.21 and 291.22 are met, the relevant provisions set out in paragraphs 291.104 to 291.134 apply to all members of the engagement team, and their immediate and close family members. In addition, a determination shall be made as to whether threats to independence are created by interests and relationships between the assurance client and the following other members of the assurance team:

- Those who provide consultation regarding technical or industry specific issues, transactions or events; and
- Those who provide quality control for the engagement, including those who perform the engagement quality control review.

An evaluation shall also be made, by reference to the provisions set out in paragraphs 291.104 to 291.134, of any threats that the engagement team has reason to believe are created by interests and relationships between the assurance client and others within the firm who can directly influence the outcome of the assurance engagement, including those who recommend the compensation, or who provide direct supervisory, management or other oversight, of the assurance engagement partner in connection with the performance of the assurance engagement.

291.26   Even though the conditions set out in paragraphs 291.21 to 291.22 are met, if the firm had a material financial interest, whether direct or indirect, in the assurance client, the self-interest threat created would be so significant that no safeguards could reduce the threat to an acceptable level. Accordingly, the firm shall not have such a financial interest. In addition, the firm shall comply with the other applicable provisions of this section described in paragraphs 291.113 to 291.159.

291.27   An evaluation shall also be made of any threats that the firm has reason to believe are created by network firm interests and relationships.

Multiple responsible parties

291.28   In some assurance engagements, whether assertion-based or direct reporting, there might be several responsible parties. In determining whether it is necessary to apply the provisions in this section to each responsible party in such engagements, the firm may take into account whether an interest or relationship between the firm, or a member of the assurance team, and a particular responsible party would create a threat to independence that is not trivial and inconsequential in the context of the subject matter information. This will take into account factors such as:

- The materiality of the subject matter information (or of the subject matter) for which the particular responsible party is responsible; and
- The degree of public interest associated with the engagement.

If the firm determines that the threat to independence created by any such interest or relationship with a particular responsible party would be trivial and inconsequential, it may not be necessary to apply all of the provisions of this section to that responsible party.

Documentation

Documentation provides evidence of the professional accountant's judgments in forming conclusions regarding compliance with independence requirements. The absence of documentation is not a determinant of whether a firm considered a particular matter nor whether it is independent. The professional accountant shall document conclusions regarding compliance with independence requirements, and the substance of any relevant discussions that support those conclusions. Accordingly:

291.29

- When safeguards are required to reduce a threat to an acceptable level, the professional accountant shall document the nature of the threat and the safeguards in place or applied that reduce the threat to an acceptable level; and
- When a threat required significant analysis to determine whether safeguards were necessary and the professional accountant concluded that they were not because the threat was already at an acceptable level, the professional accountant shall document the nature of the threat and the rationale for the conclusion.

Engagement period

Independence from the assurance client is required both during the engagement period and the period covered by the subject matter information. The engagement period starts when the assurance team begins to perform assurance services with respect to the particular engagement. The engagement period ends when the assurance report is issued. When the engagement is of a recurring nature, it ends at the later of the notification by either party that the professional relationship has terminated or the issuance of the final assurance report.

291.30

When an entity becomes an assurance client during or after the period covered by the subject matter information on which the firm will express a conclusion, the firm shall determine whether any threats to independence are created by:

291.31

- Financial or business relationships with the assurance client during or after the period covered by the subject matter information but before accepting the assurance engagement; or
- Previous services provided to the assurance client.

If a non-assurance service was provided to the assurance client during or after the period covered by the subject matter information but before the assurance team begins to perform assurance services and the service would not be permitted during the period of the assurance engagement, the firm shall evaluate any threat to independence created by the service. If any threat is not at an acceptable level, the assurance engagement shall only be accepted if safeguards are applied to eliminate any threats or reduce them to an acceptable level. Examples of such safeguards include:

291.32

- Not including personnel who provided the non-assurance service as members of the assurance team;
- Having a professional accountant review the assurance and non-assurance work as appropriate; or
- Engaging another firm to evaluate the results of the non-assurance service or having another firm re-perform the non-assurance service to the extent necessary to enable it to take responsibility for the service.

However, if the non-assurance service has not been completed and it is not practical to complete or terminate the service before the commencement of professional services in connection with the assurance engagement, the firm shall only accept the assurance engagement if it is satisfied:

- The non-assurance service will be completed within a short period of time; or
- The client has arrangements in place to transition the service to another provider within a short period of time.

During the service period, safeguards shall be applied when necessary. In addition, the matter shall be discussed with those charged with governance.

Other considerations

291.33   There may be occasions when there is an inadvertent violation of this section. If such an inadvertent violation occurs, it generally will be deemed not to compromise independence provided the firm has appropriate quality control policies and procedures in place equivalent to those required by International Standards on Quality Control to maintain independence and, once discovered, the violation is corrected promptly and any necessary safeguards are applied to eliminate any threat or reduce it to an acceptable level. The firm shall determine whether to discuss the matter with those charged with governance.

Paragraphs 291.34 to 291.99 are intentionally left blank.

Application of the conceptual framework approach to independence

291.100   Paragraphs 291.104 to 291.159 describe specific circumstances and relationships that create or may create threats to independence. The paragraphs describe the potential threats and the types of safeguards that may be appropriate to eliminate the threats or reduce them to an acceptable level and identify certain situations where no safeguards could reduce the threats to an acceptable level. The paragraphs do not describe all of the circumstances and relationships that create or may create a threat to independence. The firm and the members of the assurance team shall evaluate the implications of similar, but different, circumstances and relationships and determine whether safeguards, including the safeguards in paragraphs 200.11 to 200.14 can be applied when necessary to eliminate the threats to independence or reduce them to an acceptable level.

291.101   The paragraphs demonstrate how the conceptual framework approach applies to assurance engagements and are to be read in conjunction with paragraph 291.28 which explains that, in the majority of assurance engagements, there is one responsible party and that responsible party is the assurance client. However, in some assurance engagements there are two or more responsible parties. In such circumstances, an evaluation shall be made of any threats the firm has reason to believe are created by interests and relationships between a member of the assurance team, the firm, a network firm and the party responsible for the subject matter. For assurance reports that include a restriction on use and distribution, the paragraphs are to be read in the context of paragraphs 291.21 to 291.27.

291.102   Interpretation 2005-01 provides further guidance on applying the independence requirements contained in this section to assurance engagements.

291.103   Paragraphs 291.104 to 291.120 contain references to the materiality of a financial interest, loan, or guarantee, or the significance of a business relationship. For the purpose of determining whether such an interest is material to an individual, the combined net worth of the individual and the individual's immediate family members may be taken into account.

Financial interests

Holding a financial interest in an assurance client may create a self-interest threat. The existence and significance of any threat created depends on:

291.104

- the role of the person holding the financial interest,
- whether the financial interest is direct or indirect, and
- the materiality of the financial interest.

Financial interests may be held through an intermediary (e.g. a collective investment vehicle, estate or trust). The determination of whether such financial interests are direct or indirect will depend upon whether the beneficial owner has control over the investment vehicle or the ability to influence its investment decisions. When control over the investment vehicle or the ability to influence investment decisions exists, this Code defines that financial interest to be a direct financial interest. Conversely, when the beneficial owner of the financial interest has no control over the investment vehicle or ability to influence its investment decisions, this Code defines that financial interest to be an indirect financial interest.

291.105

If a member of the assurance team, a member of that individual's immediate family or a firm has a direct financial interest or a material indirect financial interest in the assurance client, the self-interest threat created would be so significant that no safeguards could reduce the threat to an acceptable level. Therefore, none of the following shall have a direct financial interest or a material indirect financial interest in the client: a member of the assurance team; a member of that individual's immediate family member; or the firm.

291.106

When a member of the assurance team has a close family member who the assurance team member knows has a direct financial interest or a material indirect financial interest in the assurance client, a self-interest threat is created. The significance of the threat will depend on factors such as

291.107

- The nature of the relationship between the member of the assurance team and the close family member; and
- The materiality of the financial interest to the close family member.

The significance of the threat shall be evaluated and safeguards applied when necessary to eliminate the threat or reduce it to an acceptable level. Examples of such safeguards include:

- The close family member disposing, as soon as practicable, of all of the financial interest or disposing of a sufficient portion of an indirect financial interest so that the remaining interest is no longer material;
- Having a professional accountant review the work of the member of the assurance team; or
- Removing the individual from the assurance team.

If a member of the assurance team, a member of that individual's immediate family, or a firm has a direct or material indirect financial interest in an entity that has a controlling interest in the assurance client, and the client is material to the entity, the self-interest threat created would be so significant that no safeguards could reduce the threat to an acceptable level. Therefore, none of the following shall have such a financial interest: a member of the assurance team; a member of that individual's immediate family; and the firm.

291.108

291.109   The holding by a firm or a member of the assurance team, or a member of that individual's immediate family, of a direct financial interest or a material indirect financial interest in the assurance client as a trustee creates a self-interest threat. Such an interest shall not be held unless:

- Neither the trustee, nor an immediate family member of the trustee, nor the firm are beneficiaries of the trust;
- The interest in the assurance client held by the trust is not material to the trust;
- The trust is not able to exercise significant influence over the assurance client; and
- The trustee, an immediate family member of the trustee, or the firm cannot significantly influence any investment decision involving a financial interest in the assurance client.

291.110   Members of the assurance team shall determine whether a self-interest threat is created by any known financial interests in the assurance client held by other individuals including:

- Partners and professional employees of the firm, other than those referred to above, or their immediate family members; and
- Individuals with a close personal relationship with a member of the assurance team.

Whether these interests create a self-interest threat will depend on factors such as:

- The firm's organisational, operating and reporting structure; and
- The nature of the relationship between the individual and the member of the assurance team.

The significance of any threat shall be evaluated and safeguards applied when necessary to eliminate the threat or reduce it to an acceptable level. Examples of such safeguards include:

- Removing the member of the assurance team with the personal relationship from the assurance team;
- Excluding the member of the assurance team from any significant decision-making concerning the assurance engagement; or
- Having a professional accountant review the work of the member of the assurance team.

291.111   If a firm, a member of the assurance team, or an immediate family member of the individual, receives a direct financial interest or a material indirect financial interest in an assurance client, for example, by way of an inheritance, gift or as a result of a merger, and such interest would not be permitted to be held under this section, then:

- If the interest is received by the firm, the financial interest shall be disposed of immediately, or a sufficient amount of an indirect financial interest shall be disposed of so that the remaining interest is no longer material, or
- If the interest is received by a member of the assurance team, or a member of that individual's immediate family, the individual who received the financial interest shall immediately dispose of the financial interest, or dispose of a sufficient amount of an indirect financial interest so that the remaining interest is no longer material.

291.112   When an inadvertent violation of this section as it relates to a financial interest in an assurance client occurs, it is deemed not to compromise independence if:

- The firm has established policies and procedures that require prompt notification to the firm of any breaches resulting from the purchase, inheritance or other acquisition of a financial interest in the assurance client;
- The actions taken in paragraph 291.111(a) – (b) are taken as applicable; and
- The firm applies other safeguards when necessary to reduce any remaining threat to an acceptable level. Examples of such safeguards include:
  - ○ Having a professional accountant review the work of the member of the assurance team; or
  - ○ Excluding the individual from any significant decision-making concerning the assurance engagement.

The firm shall determine whether to discuss the matter with those charged with governance.

Loans and guarantees

A loan, or a guarantee of a loan, to a member of the assurance team, or a member of **291.113** that individual's immediate family, or the firm from an assurance client that is a bank or a similar institution, may create a threat to independence. If the loan or guarantee is not made under normal lending procedures, terms and conditions, a self-interest threat would be created that would be so significant that no safeguards could reduce the threat to an acceptable level. Accordingly, neither a member of the assurance team, a member of that individual's immediate family, nor a firm shall accept such a loan or guarantee.

If a loan to a firm from an assurance client that is a bank or similar institution is **291.114** made under normal lending procedures, terms and conditions and it is material to the assurance client or firm receiving the loan, it may be possible to apply safeguards to reduce the self-interest threat to an acceptable level. An example of such a safeguard is having the work reviewed by a professional accountant from a network firm that is neither involved with the assurance engagement nor received the loan.

A loan, or a guarantee of a loan, from an assurance client that is a bank or a similar **291.115** institution to a member of the assurance team, or a member of that individual's immediate family, does not create a threat to independence if the loan or guarantee is made under normal lending procedures, terms and conditions. Examples of such loans include home mortgages, bank overdrafts, car loans and credit card balances.

If the firm or a member of the assurance team, or a member of that individual's **291.116** immediate family, accepts a loan from, or has a borrowing guaranteed by, an assurance client that is not a bank or similar institution, the self-interest threat created would be so significant that no safeguards could reduce the threat to an acceptable level, unless the loan or guarantee is immaterial to both the firm, or the member of the assurance team and the immediate family member, and the client.

Similarly, if the firm, or a member of the assurance team, or a member of that **291.117** individual's immediate family, makes or guarantees a loan to an assurance client, the self-interest threat created would be so significant that no safeguards could reduce the threat to an acceptable level, unless the loan or guarantee is immaterial to both the firm, or the member of the assurance team and the immediate family member, and the client.

If a firm or a member of the assurance team, or a member of that individual's **291.118** immediate family, has deposits or a brokerage account with an assurance client that is a bank, broker, or similar institution, a threat to independence is not created if the deposit or account is held under normal commercial terms.

Business relationships

291.119   A close business relationship between a firm, or a member of the assurance team, or a member of that individual's immediate family, and the assurance client or its management arises from a commercial relationship or common financial interest and may create self-interest or intimidation threats. Examples of such relationships include:

- Having a financial interest in a joint venture with either the client or a controlling owner, director or officer or other individual who performs senior managerial activities for that client.
- Arrangements to combine one or more services or products of the firm with one or more services or products of the client and to market the package with reference to both parties.
- Distribution or marketing arrangements under which the firm distributes or markets the client's products or services, or the client distributes or markets the firm's products or services.

Unless any financial interest is immaterial and the business relationship is insignificant to the firm and the client or its management, the threat created would be so significant that no safeguards could reduce the threat to an acceptable level. Therefore, unless the financial interest is immaterial and the business relationship is insignificant, the business relationship shall not be entered into, or shall be reduced to an insignificant level or terminated.

In the case of a member of the assurance team, unless any such financial interest is immaterial and the relationship is insignificant to that member, the individual shall be removed from the assurance team.

If the business relationship is between an immediate family member of a member of the assurance team and the assurance client or its management, the significance of any threat shall be evaluated and safeguards applied when necessary to eliminate the threat or reduce it to an acceptable level.

291.120   The purchase of goods and services from an assurance client by the firm, or a member of the assurance team, or a member of that individual's immediate family, does not generally create a threat to independence if the transaction is in the normal course of business and at arm's length. However, such transactions may be of such a nature or magnitude that they create a self-interest threat. The significance of any threat shall be evaluated and safeguards applied when necessary to eliminate the threat or reduce it to an acceptable level. Examples of such safeguards include:

- Eliminating or reducing the magnitude of the transaction; or
- Removing the individual from the assurance team.

Family and personal relationships

291.121   Family and personal relationships between a member of the assurance team and a director or officer or certain employees (depending on their role) of the assurance client, may create self-interest, familiarity or intimidation threats. The existence and significance of any threats will depend on a number of factors, including the individual's responsibilities on the assurance team, the role of the family member or other individual within the client, and the closeness of the relationship.

When an immediate family member of a member of the assurance team is: **291.122**

- A director or officer of the assurance client, or
- An employee in a position to exert significant influence over the subject matter information of the assurance engagement,

or was in such a position during any period covered by the engagement or the subject matter information, the threats to independence can only be reduced to an acceptable level by removing the individual from the assurance team. The closeness of the relationship is such that no other safeguards could reduce the threat to an acceptable level. Accordingly, no individual who has such a relationship shall be a member of the assurance team.

Threats to independence are created when an immediate family member of a member **291.123** of the assurance team is an employee in a position to exert significant influence over the subject matter of the engagement. The significance of the threats will depend on factors such as:

- The position held by the immediate family member; and
- The role of the professional on the assurance team.

The significance of the threat shall be evaluated and safeguards applied when necessary to eliminate the threat or reduce it to an acceptable level. Examples of such safeguards include:

- Removing the individual from the assurance team; or
- Structuring the responsibilities of the assurance team so that the professional does not deal with matters that are within the responsibility of the immediate family member.

Threats to independence are created when a close family member of a member of the **291.124** assurance team is:

- A director or officer of the assurance client; or
- An employee in a position to exert significant influence over the subject matter information of the assurance engagement.

The significance of the threats will depend on factors such as:

- The nature of the relationship between the member of the assurance team and the close family member;
- The position held by the close family member; and
- The role of the professional on the assurance team.

The significance of the threat shall be evaluated and safeguards applied when necessary to eliminate the threat or reduce it to an acceptable level. Examples of such safeguards include:

- Removing the individual from the assurance team; or
- Structuring the responsibilities of the assurance team so that the professional does not deal with matters that are within the responsibility of the close family member.

Threats to independence are created when a member of the assurance team has a **291.125** close relationship with a person who is not an immediate or close family member, but who is a director or officer or an employee in a position to exert significant influence over the subject matter information of the assurance engagement. A member of the assurance team who has such a relationship shall consult in accordance with firm policies and procedures. The significance of the threats will depend on factors such as:

- The nature of the relationship between the individual and the member of the assurance team;
- The position the individual holds with the client; and
- The role of the professional on the assurance team.

The significance of the threats shall be evaluated and safeguards applied when necessary to eliminate the threats or reduce them to an acceptable level. Examples of such safeguards include:

- Removing the professional from the assurance team; or
- Structuring the responsibilities of the assurance team so that the professional does not deal with matters that are within the responsibility of the individual with whom the professional has a close relationship.

291.126   Self-interest, familiarity or intimidation threats may be created by a personal or family relationship between (a) a partner or employee of the firm who is not a member of the assurance team and (b) a director or officer of the assurance client or an employee in a position to exert significant influence over the subject matter information of the assurance engagement. The existence and significance of any threat will depend on factors such as:

- The nature of the relationship between the partner or employee of the firm and the director or officer or employee of the client;
- The interaction of the partner or employee of the firm with the assurance team;
- The position of the partner or employee within the firm; and
- The role of the individual within the client.

The significance of any threat shall be evaluated and safeguards applied when necessary to eliminate the threat or reduce it to an acceptable level. Examples of such safeguards include:

- Structuring the partner's or employee's responsibilities to reduce any potential influence over the assurance engagement; or
- Having a professional accountant review the relevant assurance work performed.

291.127   When an inadvertent violation of this section as it relates to family and personal relationships occurs, it is deemed not to compromise independence if:

- The firm has established policies and procedures that require prompt notification to the firm of any breaches resulting from changes in the employment status of their immediate or close family members or other personal relationships that create threats to independence;
- The inadvertent violation relates to an immediate family member of a member of the assurance team becoming a director or officer of the assurance client or being in a position to exert significant influence over the subject matter information of the assurance engagement, and the relevant professional is removed from the assurance team; and
- The firm applies other safeguards when necessary to reduce any remaining threat to an acceptable level. Examples of such safeguards include:
  - Having a professional accountant review the work of the member of the assurance team; or
  - Excluding the relevant professional from any significant decision-making concerning the engagement.

The firm shall determine whether to discuss the matter with those charged with governance.

Employment with assurance clients

Familiarity or intimidation threats may be created if a director or officer of the assurance client, or an employee who is in a position to exert significant influence over the subject matter information of the assurance engagement, has been a member of the assurance team or partner of the firm. **291.128**

If a former member of the assurance team or partner of the firm has joined the assurance client in such a position, the existence and significance of any familiarity or intimidation threats will depend on factors such as: **291.129**

- The position the individual has taken at the client;
- Any involvement the individual will have with the assurance team;
- The length of time since the individual was a member of the assurance team or partner of the firm; and
- The former position of the individual within the assurance team or firm, for example, whether the individual was responsible for maintaining regular contact with the client's management or those charged with governance.

In all cases the individual shall not continue to participate in the firm's business or professional activities. The significance of any threats created shall be evaluated and safeguards applied when necessary to eliminate the threats or reduce them to an acceptable level. Examples of such safeguards include:

- Making arrangements such that the individual is not entitled to any benefits or payments from the firm, unless made in accordance with fixed pre-determined arrangements.
- Making arrangements such that any amount owed to the individual is not material to the firm;
- Modifying the plan for the assurance engagement;
- Assigning individuals to the assurance team who have sufficient experience in relation to the individual who has joined the client; or
- Having a professional accountant review the work of the former member of the assurance team.

If a former partner of the firm has previously joined an entity in such a position and the entity subsequently becomes an assurance client of the firm, the significance of any threats to independence shall be evaluated and safeguards applied when necessary, to eliminate the threat or reduce it to an acceptable level. **291.130**

A self-interest threat is created when a member of the assurance team participates in the assurance engagement while knowing that the member of the assurance team will, or may, join the client some time in the future. Firm policies and procedures shall require members of an assurance team to notify the firm when entering employment negotiations with the client. On receiving such notification, the significance of the threat shall be evaluated and safeguards applied when necessary to eliminate the threat or reduce it to an acceptable level. Examples of such safeguards include: **291.131**

- Removing the individual from the assurance team; or
- A review of any significant judgments made by that individual while on the team.

Recent service with an assurance client

291.132   Self-interest, self-review or familiarity threats may be created if a member of the assurance team has recently served as a director, officer, or employee of the assurance client. This would be the case when, for example, a member of the assurance team has to evaluate elements of the subject matter information the member of the assurance team had prepared while with the client.

291.133   If, during the period covered by the assurance report, a member of the assurance team had served as director or officer of the assurance client, or was an employee in a position to exert significant influence over the subject matter information of the assurance engagement, the threat created would be so significant that no safeguards could reduce the threat to an acceptable level. Consequently, such individuals shall not be assigned to the assurance team.

291.134   Self-interest, self-review or familiarity threats may be created if, before the period covered by the assurance report, a member of the assurance team had served as director or officer of the assurance client, or was an employee in a position to exert significant influence over the subject matter information of the assurance engagement. For example, such threats would be created if a decision made or work performed by the individual in the prior period, while employed by the client, is to be evaluated in the current period as part of the current assurance engagement. The existence and significance of any threats will depend on factors such as:

- The position the individual held with the client;
- The length of time since the individual left the client; and
- The role of the professional on the assurance team.

The significance of any threat shall be evaluated and safeguards applied when necessary to reduce the threat to an acceptable level. An example of such a safeguard is conducting a review of the work performed by the individual as part of the assurance team.

Serving as a Director or Officer of an assurance client

291.135   If a partner or employee of the firm serves a director or officer of an assurance client, the self-review and self-interest threats would be so significant that no safeguards could reduce the threats to an acceptable level. Accordingly, no partner or employee shall serve as a director or officer of an assurance client.

291.136   The position of Company Secretary has different implications in different jurisdictions. Duties may range from administrative duties, such as personnel management and the maintenance of company records and registers, to duties as diverse as ensuring that the company complies with regulation or providing advice on corporate governance matters. Generally, this position is seen to imply a close association with the entity.

291.137   If a partner or employee of the firm serves as Company Secretary for an assurance client, self-review and advocacy threats are created that would generally be so significant that no safeguards could reduce the threats to an acceptable level. Despite paragraph 291.135, when this practice is specifically permitted under local law, professional roles or practice, and provided management makes all relevant decisions, the duties and activities shall be limited to those of a routine and administrative nature, such as preparing minutes and maintaining statutory returns. In those circumstances, the significance of any threats shall be evaluated and safeguards applied when necessary to eliminate the threats or reduce them to an acceptable level.

Performing routine administrative services to support a company secretarial function **291.138** or providing advice in relation to company secretarial administration matters does not generally create threats to independence, as long as client management makes all relevant decisions.

Long association of senior personnel with assurance clients

Familiarity and self-interest threats are created by using the same senior personnel **291.139** on an assurance engagement over a long period of time. The significance of the threats will depend on factors such as:

- How long the individual has been a member of the assurance team;
- The role of the individual on the assurance team;
- The structure of the firm;
- The nature of the assurance engagement;
- Whether the client's management team has changed; and
- Whether the nature or complexity of the subject matter information has changed.

The significance of the threats shall be evaluated and safeguards applied when necessary to eliminate the threats or reduce them to an acceptable level. Examples of such safeguards include:

- Rotating the senior personnel off the assurance team;
- Having a professional accountant who was not a member of the assurance team review the work of the senior personnel; or
- regular independent internal or external quality reviews of the engagement.

Provision of non-assurance services to assurance clients

Firms have traditionally provided to their assurance clients a range of non-assurance **291.140** services that are consistent with their skills and expertise. Providing non-assurance services may, however, create threats to the independence of the firm or members of the assurance team. The threats created are most often self-review, self-interest and advocacy threats.

When specific guidance on a particular non-assurance service is not included in this **291.141** section, the conceptual framework shall be applied when evaluating the particular circumstances.

Before the firm accepts an engagement to provide a non-assurance service to an **291.142** assurance client, a determination shall be made as to whether providing such a service would create a threat to independence. In evaluating the significance of any threat created by a particular non-assurance service, consideration shall be given to any threat that the assurance team has reason to believe is created by providing other related non-assurance services. If a threat is created that cannot be reduced to an acceptable level by the application of safeguards the non-assurance service shall not be provided.

Management responsibilities

291.143   Management of an entity performs many activities in managing the entity in the best interests of stakeholders of the entity. It is not possible to specify every activity that is a management responsibility. However, management responsibilities involve leading and directing an entity, including making significant decisions regarding the acquisition, deployment and control of human, financial, physical and intangible resources.

291.144   Whether an activity is a management responsibility depends on the circumstances and requires the exercise of judgment. Examples of activities that would generally be considered a management responsibility include:

- Setting policies and strategic direction;
- Directing and taking responsibility for the actions of the entity's employees;
- Authorising transactions;
- Deciding which recommendations of the firm or other third parties to implement; and
- Taking responsibility for designing, implementing and maintaining internal control.

291.145   Activities that are routine and administrative, or involve matters that are insignificant, generally are deemed not to be a management responsibility. For example, executing an insignificant transaction that has been authorised by management or monitoring the dates for filing statutory returns and advising an assurance client of those dates is deemed not to be a management responsibility. Further, providing advice and recommendations to assist management in discharging its responsibilities is not assuming a management responsibility.

291.146   Assuming a management responsibility for an assurance client may create threats to independence. If a firm were to assume a management responsibility as part of the assurance service, the threats created would be so significant that no safeguards could reduce the threats to an acceptable level. Accordingly, in providing assurance services to an assurance client, a firm shall not assume a management responsibility as part of the assurance service. If the firm assumes a management responsibility as part of any other services provided to the assurance client, it shall ensure that the responsibility is not related to the subject matter and subject matter information of an assurance engagement provided by the firm.

291.147   To avoid the risk of assuming a management responsibility related to the subject matter or subject matter information of the assurance engagement, the firm shall be satisfied that a member of management is responsible for making the significant judgments and decisions that are the proper responsibility of management, evaluating the results of the service and accepting responsibility for the actions to be taken arising from the results of the service. This reduces the risk of the firm inadvertently making any significant judgments or decisions on behalf of management. This risk is further reduced when the firm gives the client the opportunity to make judgments and decisions based on an objective and transparent analysis and presentation of the issues.

Other considerations

291.148   Threats to independence may be created when a firm provides a non-assurance service related to the subject matter information of an assurance engagement. In such cases, an evaluation of the significance of the firm's involvement with the subject matter information of the engagement shall be made, and a determination shall be made of whether any self-review threats that are not at an acceptable level can be reduced to an acceptable level by the application of safeguards.

A self-review threat may be created if the firm is involved in the preparation of subject matter information which is subsequently the subject matter information of an assurance engagement. For example, a self-review threat would be created if the firm developed and prepared prospective financial information and subsequently provided assurance on this information. Consequently, the firm shall evaluate the significance of any self-review threat created by the provision of such services and apply safeguards when necessary to eliminate the threat or reduce it to an acceptable level.

291.149

When a firm performs a valuation that forms part of the subject matter information of an assurance engagement, the firm shall evaluate the significance of any self-review threat and apply safeguards when necessary to eliminate the threat or reduce it to an acceptable level.

291.150

Fees

Fees – relative size

When the total fees from an assurance client represent a large proportion of the total fees of the firm expressing the conclusion, the dependence on that client and concern about losing the client creates a self-interest or intimidation threat. The significance of the threat will depend on factors such as:

291.151

- The operating structure of the firm;
- Whether the firm is well established or new; and
- The significance of the client qualitatively and/or quantitatively to the firm.

The significance of the threat shall be evaluated and safeguards applied when necessary to eliminate the threat or reduce it to an acceptable level. Examples of such safeguards include:

- Reducing the dependency on the client;
- External quality control reviews; or
- Consulting a third party, such as a professional regulatory body or a professional accountant, on key assurance judgments.

A self-interest or intimidation threat is also created when the fees generated from an assurance client represent a large proportion of the revenue from an individual partner's clients. The significance of the threat shall be evaluated and safeguards applied when necessary to eliminate the threat or reduce it to an acceptable level. An example of such a safeguard is having an additional professional accountant who was not a member of the assurance team review the work or otherwise advise as necessary.

291.152

Fees – overdue

A self-interest threat may be created if fees due from an assurance client remain unpaid for a long time, especially if a significant part is not paid before the issue of the assurance report, if any, for the following period. Generally the firm is expected to require payment of such fees before any such report is issued. If fees remain unpaid after the report has been issued, the existence and significance of any threat shall be evaluated and safeguards applied when necessary to eliminate the threat or reduce it to an acceptable level. An example of such a safeguard is having another

291.153

professional accountant who did not take part in the assurance engagement provide advice or review the work performed. The firm shall determine whether the overdue fees might be regarded as being equivalent to a loan to the client and whether, because of the significance of the overdue fees, it is appropriate for the firm to be re-appointed or continue the assurance engagement.

Contingent fees

291.154   Contingent fees are fees calculated on a predetermined basis relating to the outcome of a transaction or the result of the services performed by the firm. For the purposes of this section, fees are not regarded as being contingent if established by a court or other public authority.

291.155   A contingent fee charged directly or indirectly, for example through an intermediary, by a firm in respect of an assurance engagement creates a self-interest threat that is so significant that no safeguards could reduce the threat to an acceptable level. Accordingly, a firm shall not enter into any such fee arrangement.

291.156   A contingent fee charged directly or indirectly, for example through an intermediary, by a firm in respect of a non-assurance service provided to an assurance client may also create a self-interest threat. If the outcome of the non-assurance service, and therefore, the amount of the fee, is dependent on a future or contemporary judgment related to a matter that is material to the subject matter information of the assurance engagement, no safeguards could reduce the threat to an acceptable level. Accordingly, such arrangements shall not be accepted.

291.157   For other contingent fee arrangements charged by a firm for a non-assurance service to an assurance client, the existence and significance of any threats will depend on factors such as:

- The range of possible fee amounts;
- Whether an appropriate authority determines the outcome of the matter upon which the contingent fee will be determined;
- The nature of the service; and
- The effect of the event or transaction on the subject matter information.

The significance of any threats shall be evaluated and safeguards applied when necessary to eliminate the threats or reduce them to an acceptable level. Examples of such safeguards include:

- Having a professional accountant review the relevant assurance work or otherwise advise as necessary; or
- Using professionals who are not members of the assurance team to perform the non-assurance service.

Gifts and hospitality

291.158   Accepting gifts or hospitality from an assurance client may create self-interest and familiarity threats. If a firm or a member of the assurance team accepts gifts or hospitality, unless the value is trivial and inconsequential, the threats created would be so significant that no safeguards could reduce the threats to an acceptable level. Consequently, a firm or a member of the assurance team shall not accept such gifts or hospitality.

Actual or threatened litigation

When litigation takes place, or appears likely, between the firm or a member of the **291.159** assurance team and the assurance client, self-interest and intimidation threats are created. The relationship between client management and the members of the assurance team must be characterised by complete candour and full disclosure regarding all aspects of a client's business operations. When the firm and the client's management are placed in adversarial positions by actual or threatened litigation, affecting management's willingness to make complete disclosures self-interest and intimidation threats are created. The significance of the threats created will depend on such factors as:

- The materiality of the litigation; and
- Whether the litigation relates to a prior assurance engagement.

The significance of the threats shall be evaluated and safeguards applied when necessary to eliminate the threats or reduce them to an acceptable level. Examples of such safeguards include:

- If the litigation involves a member of the assurance team, removing that individual from the assurance team; or
- Having a professional review of the work performed.

If such safeguards do not reduce the threats to an acceptable level, the only appropriate action is to withdraw from, or decline, the assurance engagement.

Interpretation 2005-01 (Revised July 2009 to conform to changes resulting from the IESBA's project to improve the clarity of the Code)

Application of section 291 to Assurance engagements that are not Financial statement Audit engagements

This interpretation provides guidance on the application of the independence requirements contained in section 291 to assurance engagements that are not financial statement audit engagements.

This interpretation focuses on the application issues that are particular to assurance engagements that are not financial statement audit engagements. There are other matters noted in section 291 that are relevant in the consideration of independence requirements for all assurance engagements. For example, paragraph 291.3 states that an evaluation shall be made of any threats the firm has reason to believe are created by a network firm's interests and relationships. It also states that when the assurance team has reason to believe that a related entity of such an assurance client is relevant to the evaluation of the firm's independence of the client, the assurance team shall include the related entity when evaluating threats to independence and when necessary applying safeguards. These matters are not specifically addressed in this interpretation.

As explained in the International Framework for Assurance engagements issued by the International Auditing and Assurance Standards Board, in an assurance engagement, the professional accountant in public practice expresses a conclusion designed to enhance the degree of confidence of the intended users other than the responsible party about the outcome of the evaluation or measurement of a subject matter against criteria.

Assertion-Based Assurance engagements

In an assertion-based assurance engagement, the evaluation or measurement of the subject matter is performed by the responsible party, and the subject matter information is in the form of an assertion by the responsible party that is made available to the intended users.

In an assertion-based assurance engagement independence is required from the responsible party, which is responsible for the subject matter information and may be responsible for the subject matter.

In those assertion-based assurance engagements where the responsible party is responsible for the subject matter information but not the subject matter, independence is required from the responsible party. In addition, an evaluation shall be made of any threats the firm has reason to believe are created by interests and relationships between a member of the assurance team, the firm, a network firm and the party responsible for the subject matter.

Direct Reporting Assurance engagements

In a direct reporting assurance engagement, the professional accountant in public practice either directly performs the evaluation or measurement of the subject matter, or obtains a representation from the responsible party that has performed the evaluation or measurement that is not available to the intended users. The subject matter information is provided to the intended users in the assurance report.

In a direct reporting assurance engagement independence is required from the responsible party, which is responsible for the subject matter.

Multiple Responsible Parties

In both assertion-based assurance engagements and direct reporting assurance engagements there may be several responsible parties. For example, a public accountant in public practice may be asked to provide assurance on the monthly circulation statistics of a number of independently owned newspapers. The assignment could be an assertion based assurance engagement where each newspaper measures its circulation and the statistics are presented in an assertion that is available to the intended users. Alternatively, the assignment could be a direct reporting assurance engagement, where there is no assertion and there may or may not be a written representation from the newspapers.

In such engagements, when determining whether it is necessary to apply the provisions in section 291 to each responsible party, the firm may take into account whether an interest or relationship between the firm, or a member of the assurance team, and a particular responsible party would create a threat to independence that is not trivial and inconsequential in the context of the subject matter information. This will take into account:

- The materiality of the subject matter information (or the subject matter) for which the particular responsible party is responsible; and
- The degree of public interest that is associated with the engagement.

If the firm determines that the threat to independence created by any such relationships with a particular responsible party would be trivial and inconsequential it may not be necessary to apply all of the provisions of this section to that responsible party.

Example

The following example has been developed to demonstrate the application of section 291. It is assumed that the client is not also a financial statement audit client of the firm, or a network firm.

A firm is engaged to provide assurance on the total proven oil reserves of 10 independent companies. Each company has conducted geographical and engineering surveys to determine their reserves (subject matter). There are established criteria to determine when a reserve may be considered to be proven which the professional accountant in public practice determines to be suitable criteria for the engagement.

The proven reserves for each company as at December 31, 20X0 were as follows:

	Proven oil reserves thousands of barrels
Company 1	5,200
Company 2	725
Company 3	3,260
Company 4	15,000
Company 5	6,700
Company 6	39,126
Company 7	345
Company 8	175
Company 9	24,135
Company 10	9,635
Total	**104,301**

The engagement could be structured in differing ways:

Assertion-Based Engagements

A1 Each company measures its reserves and provides an assertion to the firm and to intended users.
A2 An entity other than the companies measures the reserves and provides an assertion to the firm and to intended users.

Direct Reporting Engagements

D1 Each company measures the reserves and provides the firm with a written representation that measures its reserves against the established criteria for measuring proven reserves. The representation is not available to the intended users.
D2 The firm directly measures the reserves of some of the companies.

Application of Approach

A1   Each company measures its reserves and provides an assertion to the firm and to intended users.

There are several responsible parties in this engagement (companies 1-10). When determining whether it is necessary to apply the independence provisions to all of the companies, the firm may take into account whether an interest or relationship with a particular company would create a threat to independence that is not at an acceptable level. This will take into account factors such as:

- The materiality of the company's proven reserves in relation to the total reserves to be reported on; and
- The degree of public interest associated with the engagement (paragraph 291.28).

For example Company 8 accounts for 0.17% of the total reserves, therefore a business relationship or interest with Company 8 would create less of a threat than a similar relationship with Company 6, which accounts for approximately 37.5% of the reserves.

Having determined those companies to which the independence requirements apply, the assurance team and the firm are required to be independent of those responsible parties that would be considered to be the assurance client (paragraph 291.28).

A2   An entity other than the companies measures the reserves and provides an assertion to the firm and to intended users.

The firm shall be independent of the entity that measures the reserves and provides an assertion to the firm and to intended users (paragraph 291.19). That entity is not responsible for the subject matter and so an evaluation shall be made of any threats the firm has reason to believe are created by interests/relationships with the party responsible for the subject matter (paragraph 291.19). There are several parties responsible for the subject matter in this engagement (Companies 1-10). As discussed in example A1 above, the firm may take into account whether an interest or relationship with a particular company would create a threat to independence that is not at an acceptable level.

D1   Each company provides the firm with a representation that measures its reserves against the established criteria for measuring proven reserves. The representation is not available to the intended users.

There are several responsible parties in this engagement (Companies 1-10). When determining whether it is necessary to apply the independence provisions to all of the companies, the firm may take into account whether an interest or relationship with a particular company would create a threat to independence that is not at an acceptable level. This will take into account factors such as:

- The materiality of the company's proven reserves in relation to the total reserves to be reported on; and
- The degree of public interest associated with the engagement. (Paragraph 291.28).

For example, Company 8 accounts for 0.17% of the reserves, therefore a business relationship or interest with Company 8 would create less of a threat than a similar relationship with Company 6 that accounts for approximately 37.5% of the reserves.

Having determined those companies to which the independence requirements apply, the assurance team and the firm shall be independent of those responsible parties that would be considered to be the assurance client (paragraph 291.28).

D2 The firm directly measures the reserves of some of the companies.

The application is the same as in example D1.

References

Contingent fees for non-assurance services provided to a audit clients and other assurance clients are discussed in sections 290 and 291 of this Part of the Code. **1**

Professional accountants are reminded that where detailed regulatory requirements cover the same issues as this Code, the regulatory requirements prevail where these are more onerous. **2**

"Internal Control – Integrated Framework" The Committee of Sponsoring Organisations of the Treadway Commission. **3**

"Guidance on Assessing Control – The CoCo Principles" Criteria of Control Board, The Canadian Institute of Chartered Accountants. **4**

See paragraphs 290.13 to 290.24 for guidance on what constitutes a network firm. **5**

Code of Ethics C

- **Introduction**
- **Potential conflicts**
- **Preparation and reporting of information**
- **Acting with sufficient expertise**
- **Financial interests**
- **Inducements**

Introduction

300.1 This Part of the Code describes how the conceptual framework contained in Part A applies in certain situations to professional accountants in business. This Part does not describe all of the circumstances and relationships that could be encountered by a professional accountant in business that create or may create threats to compliance with the fundamental principles. Therefore, the professional accountant in business is encouraged to be alert for such circumstances and relationships.

Professional accountants in business shall also read Part A which sets out the fundamental principles and conceptual framework that professional accountants are required to adhere to. It may also be helpful for professional accountants in business to refer to other parts of this Code in relevant circumstances: for example, sections 221, 'Corporate finance advice', and 241, 'Agencies and referrals'.

300.2 Investors, creditors, employers and other sectors of the business community, as well as governments and the public at large, all may rely on the work of professional accountants in business. Professional accountants in business may be solely or jointly responsible for the preparation and reporting of financial and other information, which both their employing organisations and third parties may rely on. They may also be responsible for providing effective financial management and competent advice on a variety of business-related matters.

Professional accountants in business are engaged in an executive or non-executive capacity in such areas as commerce, industry, the public and service sectors (including public sector bodies), education, the not for profit sector, regulatory bodies or professional bodies.

300.3 A professional accountant in business may be a salaried employee, a partner, director (whether executive or non-executive), an owner manager, a volunteer or another working for one or more employing organisation. The legal form of the relationship with the employing organisation, if any, has no bearing on the ethical responsibilities incumbent on the professional accountant in business.

Professional accountants are reminded that this Code applies to all their professional and business activities, with and without reward.

300.4 A professional accountant in business has a responsibility to further the legitimate aims of the accountant's employing organisation. This Code does not seek to hinder a professional accountant in business from properly fulfilling that responsibility, but addresses circumstances in which compliance with the fundamental principles may be compromised.

300.5 A professional accountant in business may hold a senior position within an organisation. The more senior the position, the greater will be the ability and opportunity to influence events, practices and attitudes. A professional accountant in business is expected, therefore, to encourage an ethics-based culture in an employing organisation that emphasises the importance that senior management places on ethical behaviour.

A professional accountant in business shall not knowingly engage in any business, occupation, or activity that impairs or might impair integrity, objectivity or the good reputation of the profession and as a result would be incompatible with the fundamental principles. **300.6**

Fundamental principles

A professional accountant shall comply with the following fundamental principles: **300.6a**

- **Integrity** – to be straightforward and honest in all professional and business relationships.
- **Objectivity** – to not allow bias, conflict of interest or undue influence of others to override professional or business judgments
- **Professional Competence and Due Care** – to maintain professional knowledge and skill at the level required to ensure that a client or employer receives competent professional services based on current developments in practice, legislation and techniques and act diligently and in accordance with applicable technical and professional standards.
- **Confidentiality** – to respect the confidentiality of information acquired as a result of professional and business relationships and, therefore, not disclose any such information to third parties without proper and specific authority, unless there is a legal or professional right or duty to disclose, nor use the information for the personal advantage of the professional accountant or third parties.
- **Professional Behaviour** – to comply with relevant laws and regulations and avoid any action that discredits the profession.

Compliance with the fundamental principles may potentially be threatened by a broad range of circumstances and relationships. Threats fall into one or more of the following categories: **300.7**

- self-interest
- self-review
- advocacy
- familiarity
- intimidation.

These threats are discussed further in Part A of this Code.

Examples of circumstances that may create self-interest threats for a professional accountant in business include: **300.8**

- Holding a financial interest in, or receiving a loan or guarantee from the employing organisation.
- Participating in incentive compensation arrangements offered by the employing organisation.
- Inappropriate personal use of corporate assets.
- Concern over employment security.
- Commercial pressure from outside the employing organisation.

An example of a circumstance that creates a self-review threat for a professional accountant in business is determining the appropriate accounting treatment for a **300.9** business combination after performing the feasibility study that supported the acquisition decision.

300.10   When furthering the legitimate goals and objectives of their employing organisations, professional accountants in business may promote the organisation's position, provided any statements made are neither false nor misleading. Such actions generally would not create an advocacy threat.

300.11   Examples of circumstances that may create familiarity threats for a professional accountant in business include:

- Being responsible for the employing organisation's financial reporting when an immediate or close family member employed by the entity makes decisions that affect the entity's financial reporting.
- Long association with business contacts influencing business decisions.
- Accepting a gift or preferential treatment, unless the value is trivial and inconsequential.

300.12   Examples of circumstances that may create intimidation threats for a professional accountant in business include:

- Threat of dismissal or replacement of the professional accountant in business or a close or immediate family member over a disagreement about the application of an accounting principle or the way in which financial information is to be reported.
- A dominant personality attempting to influence the decision making process, for example with regard to the awarding of contracts or the application of an accounting principle.

300.13   Safeguards that may eliminate or reduce threats to an acceptable level fall into two broad categories:

- Safeguards created by the profession, legislation or regulation; and
- Safeguards in the work environment.

Examples of safeguards created by the profession, legislation or regulation are detailed in paragraph 100.14 of Part A of this Code.

300.14   Safeguards in the work environment include:

- The employing organisation's systems of corporate oversight or other oversight structures.
- The employing organisation's ethics and conduct programs.
- Recruitment procedures in the employing organisation emphasizing the importance of employing high calibre competent staff.
- Strong internal controls.
- Appropriate disciplinary processes.
- Leadership that stresses the importance of ethical behaviour and the expectation that employees will act in an ethical manner.
- Policies and procedures to implement and monitor the quality of employee performance.
- Timely communication of the employing organisation's policies and procedures, including any changes to them, to all employees and appropriate training and education on such policies and procedures.
- Policies and procedures to empower and encourage employees to communicate to senior levels within the employing organisation any ethical issues that concern them without fear of retribution.
- Consultation with another appropriate professional accountant.

In circumstances where a professional accountant in business believes that unethical behaviour or actions by others will continue to occur within the employing organisation, the professional accountant in business may consider obtaining legal advice. In those extreme situations where all available safeguards have been exhausted and it is not possible to reduce the threat to an acceptable level, a professional accountant in business may conclude that it is appropriate to disassociate from the task and/or resign from the employing organisation. **300.15**

To assist professional accountants to determine an appropriate course of action when faced with a situation which could threaten their compliance with the fundamental principles the following sections (preparing and reporting of information; acting with sufficient expertise; financial information; inducements and disclosing confidential information) give examples of specific areas of activity which could give rise to ethical dilemmas and the action which could be taken in response. This is not a comprehensive list of examples but aims to cover the key areas most likely to be encountered by professional accountants. Illustrative case studies of how the guidance might be applied in example situations are available at www.icaew.com/ethics. **300.16**

Professional accountants who are in doubt as to their ethical position may seek advice from the ICAEW's Technical Advisory Services by email: ethics@icaew.com or phone +44 (0)1908 248 250. Further guidance on sources of advice is available in section 1. **300.17**

Potential conflicts

A professional accountant in business shall comply with the fundamental principles. There may be times, however, when a professional accountant's responsibilities to an employing organisation and professional obligations to comply with the fundamental principles are in conflict. A professional accountant in business is expected to support the legitimate and ethical objectives established by the employer and the rules and procedures drawn up in support of those objectives. Nevertheless, where a relationship or circumstance creates a threat to compliance with the fundamental principles, a professional accountant in business shall apply the conceptual framework approach described in section 100 to determine a response to the threat. **310.1**

As a consequence of responsibilities to an employing organisation, a professional accountant in business may be under pressure to act or behave in ways that could create threats to compliance with the fundamental principles. Such pressure may be explicit or implicit; it may come from a supervisor, manager, director or another individual within the employing organisation. A professional accountant in business may face pressure to: **310.2**

- Act contrary to law or regulation.
- Act contrary to technical or professional standards.
- Facilitate unethical or illegal earnings management strategies.
- Lie to others, or otherwise intentionally mislead (including misleading by remaining silent) others, in particular:
  – The auditors of the employing organisation; or
  – Regulators.
- Issue, or otherwise be associated with, a financial or non-financial report that materially misrepresents the facts, including statements in connection with, for example:
  – The financial statements;
  – Tax compliance;

– Legal compliance; or
– Reports required by securities regulators.

310.3   The significance of any threats arising from such pressures, such as intimidation threats, shall be evaluated and safeguards applied when necessary to eliminate them or reduce them to an acceptable level. Examples of such safeguards include:

- Obtaining advice, where appropriate, from within the employing organisation, an independent professional advisor or ICAEW (see section 1 of this Code).
- Using a formal dispute resolution process within the employing organisation.
- Seeking legal advice.

Informal discussions with fellow professional accountants in business or in practice may assist in clarifying the steps needed to be taken.

Preparation and reporting of information

320.1   Professional accountants in business are often involved in the preparation and reporting of information that may either be made public or used by others inside or outside the employing organisation. Such information may include financial or management information, for example, forecasts and budgets, financial statements, management's discussion and analysis, and the management letter of representation provided to the auditors during the audit of the entity's financial statements. A professional accountant in business shall prepare or present such information fairly, honestly and in accordance with relevant professional standards so that the information will be understood in its context.

320.2   A professional accountant in business who has responsibility for the preparation or approval of the general purpose financial statements of an employing organisation shall be satisfied that those financial statements are presented in accordance with the applicable financial reporting standards.

320.3   A professional accountant in business shall take reasonable steps to maintain information for which the professional accountant in business is responsible in a manner that:

- Describes clearly the true nature of business transactions, assets, or liabilities;
- Classifies and records information in a timely and proper manner; and
- Represents the facts accurately and completely in all material respects.

320.4   Threats to compliance with the fundamental principles, for example, self-interest or intimidation threats to objectivity or professional competence and due care, are created where a professional accountant in business is pressured (either externally or by the possibility of personal gain) to become associated with misleading information or to become associated with misleading information through the actions of others.

Accordingly, professional accountants shall not be associated with reports, returns, communications or other information where they believe that the information:

- Contains a materially false or misleading statement;
- Contains statements or information furnished recklessly;
- Omits or obscures information required to be included where such omission or obscurity would be misleading.

320.5   The significance of such threats will depend on factors such as the source of the pressure and the degree to which the information is, or may be, misleading. The significance of the threats shall be evaluated and safeguards applied when necessary to eliminate them or reduce them to an acceptable level. Such safeguards include consultation with superiors within the employing organisation, the audit committee or those charged with governance of the organisation, or with ICAEW.

Where it is not possible to reduce the threat to an acceptable level, a professional accountant in business shall refuse to be or remain associated with information the professional accountant determines is misleading. A professional accountant in business may have been unknowingly associated with misleading information. Upon becoming aware of this, the professional accountant in business shall take steps to be disassociated from that information. In determining whether there is a requirement to report, the professional accountant in business may consider obtaining legal advice. In addition, the professional accountant may consider whether to resign. **320.6**

Acting with sufficient expertise

The fundamental principle of professional competence and due care requires that a professional accountant in business only undertake significant tasks for which the professional accountant in business has, or can obtain, sufficient specific training or experience. A professional accountant in business shall not intentionally mislead an employer as to the level of expertise or experience possessed, nor shall a professional accountant in business fail to seek appropriate expert advice and assistance when required. **330.1**

Circumstances that create a threat to a professional accountant in business performing duties with the appropriate degree of professional competence and due care include having: **330.2**

- Insufficient time for properly performing or completing the relevant duties.
- Incomplete, restricted or otherwise inadequate information for performing the duties properly.
- Insufficient experience, training and/or education.
- Inadequate resources for the proper performance of the duties.

The significance of the threat will depend on factors such as the extent to which the professional accountant in business is working with others, relative seniority in the business, and the level of supervision and review applied to the work. The significance of the threat shall be evaluated and safeguards applied when necessary to eliminate the threat or reduce it to an acceptable level. Examples of such safeguards include: **330.3**

- Obtaining additional advice or training.
- Ensuring that there is adequate time available for performing the relevant duties.
- Obtaining assistance from someone with the necessary expertise.
- Consulting, where appropriate, with:
- Superiors within the employing organisation;
- Independent experts; or
- ICAEW

When threats cannot be eliminated or reduced to an acceptable level, professional accountants in business shall determine whether to refuse to perform the duties in question. If the professional accountant in business determines that refusal is appropriate, the reasons for doing so shall be clearly communicated. **330.4**

Financial interests

340.1   Professional accountants in business may have financial interests, or may know of financial interests of immediate or close family members, that, in certain circumstances, may create threats to compliance with the fundamental principles. For example, self-interest threats to objectivity or confidentiality may be created through the existence of the motive and opportunity to manipulate price sensitive information in order to gain financially. Examples of circumstances that may create self-interest threats include situations where the professional accountant in business or an immediate or close family member:

- Holds a direct or indirect financial interest in the employing organisation and the value of that financial interest could be directly affected by decisions made by the professional accountant in business;
- Is eligible for a profit related bonus and the value of that bonus could be directly affected by decisions made by the professional accountant in business;
- Holds, directly or indirectly, share options in the employing organisation, the value of which could be directly affected by decisions made by the professional accountant in business;
- Holds, directly or indirectly, share options in the employing organisation which are, or will soon be, eligible for conversion; or
- May qualify for share options in the employing organisation or performance related bonuses if certain targets are achieved.

340.2   The significance of any threat shall be evaluated and safeguards applied when necessary to eliminate the threat or reduce it to an acceptable level. In evaluating the significance of any threat, and, when necessary, determining the appropriate safeguards to be applied to eliminate the threat or reduce it to an acceptable level, a professional accountant in business shall evaluate the nature of the financial interest. This includes evaluating the significance of the financial interest and determining whether it is direct or indirect. What constitutes a significant or valuable stake in an organisation will vary from individual to individual, depending on personal circumstances. Examples of such safeguards include:

- Policies and procedures for a committee independent of management to determine the level or form of remuneration of senior management.
- Disclosure of all relevant interests and of any plans to trade in relevant shares to those charged with the governance of the employing organisation, in accordance with any internal policies.
- Consultation, where appropriate, with superiors within the employing organisation.
- Consultation, where appropriate, with those charged with the governance of the employing organisation or relevant professional bodies.
- Internal and external audit procedures.
- Up-to-date education on ethical issues and on the legal restrictions and other regulations around potential insider trading.

340.3   A professional accountant in business shall neither manipulate information nor use confidential information for personal gain.

Inducements

Receiving offers

A professional accountant in business or an immediate or close family member may be offered an inducement. Inducements may take various forms, including gifts, hospitality, preferential treatment, and inappropriate appeals to friendship or loyalty. **350.1**

Offers of inducements may create threats to compliance with the fundamental principles. When a professional accountant in business or an immediate or close family member is offered an inducement, the situation shall be evaluated. Self-interest threats to objectivity or confidentiality are created when an inducement is made in an attempt to unduly influence actions or decisions, encourage illegal or dishonest behaviour, or obtain confidential information. Intimidation threats to objectivity or confidentiality are created if such an inducement is accepted and it is followed by threats to make that offer public and damage the reputation of either the professional accountant in business or an immediate or close family member. **350.2**

The existence and significance of any threats will depend on the nature, value and intent behind the offer. If a reasonable and informed third party, weighing all the specific facts and circumstances, would consider the inducement insignificant and not intended to encourage unethical behaviour, then a professional accountant in business may conclude that the offer is made in the normal course of business and may generally conclude that there is no significant threat to compliance with the fundamental principles. **350.3**

The significance of any threats shall be evaluated and safeguards applied when necessary to eliminate them or reduce them to an acceptable level. When the threats cannot be eliminated or reduced to an acceptable level through the application of safeguards, a professional accountant in business shall not accept the inducement. As the real or apparent threats to compliance with the fundamental principles do not merely arise from acceptance of an inducement but, sometimes, merely from the fact of the offer having been made, additional safeguards shall be adopted. A professional accountant in business shall evaluate any threats created by such offers and determine whether to take one or more of the following actions: **350.4**

- Informing higher levels of management or those charged with governance of the employing organisation immediately when such offers have been made;
- Informing third parties of the offer – for example, ICAEW or the employer of the individual who made the offer; a professional accountant in business may however, consider seeking legal advice before taking such a step; and
- Advising immediate or close family members of relevant threats and safeguards where they are potentially in positions that might result in offers of inducements, for example, as a result of their employment situation; and
- Informing higher levels of management or those charged with governance of the employing organisation where immediate or close family members are employed by competitors or potential suppliers of that organisation.

Making offers

A professional accountant in business may be in a situation where the professional accountant in business is expected, or is under other pressure, to offer inducements to influence the judgment or decision-making process of an individual or organisation, or obtain confidential information. **350.5**

350.6   Such pressure may come from within the employing organisation, for example, from a colleague or superior. It may also come from an external individual or organisation suggesting actions or business decisions that would be advantageous to the employing organisation, possibly influencing the professional accountant in business improperly.

350.7   A professional accountant in business shall not offer an inducement to improperly influence professional judgment of a third party.

350.8   Where the pressure to offer an unethical inducement comes from within the employing organisation, the professional accountant shall follow the principles and guidance regarding ethical conflict resolution set out in Part A of this Code.

Code of Ethics ABC definitions

Acceptable level

A level at which a reasonable and informed third party would be likely to conclude, weighing all the specific facts and circumstances available to the professional accountant at that time, that compliance with the fundamental principles is not compromised.

Advertising

The communication to the public of information as to the services or skills provided by professional accountants in public practice with a view to procuring professional business.

Affiliates

A person granted affiliate status by ICAEW under its regulations.

Assurance client

The responsible party that is the person (or persons) who:

- In a direct reporting engagement, is responsible for the subject matter; or
- In an assertion-based engagement, is responsible for the subject matter information and may be responsible for the subject matter.

Assurance engagement

An engagement in which a professional accountant in public practice expresses a conclusion designed to enhance the degree of confidence of the intended users other than the responsible party about the outcome of the evaluation or measurement of a subject matter against criteria.

(For guidance on assurance engagements see the International Framework for Assurance engagements issued by the International Auditing and Assurance Standards Board which describes the elements and objectives of an assurance engagement and identifies engagements to which International Standards on Auditing (ISAs), International Standards on Review engagements (ISREs) and International

Standards on Assurance engagements (ISAEs) apply.) www.ifac.org/IAASB/Pronouncements.php

Assurance team

- All members of the engagement team for the assurance engagement;
- All others within a firm who can directly influence the outcome of the assurance engagement, including:
  - those who recommend the compensation of, or who provide direct supervisory, management or other oversight of the assurance engagement partner in connection with the performance of the assurance engagement;
  - those who provide consultation regarding technical or industry specific issues, transactions or events for the assurance engagement; and
  - those who provide quality control for the assurance engagement, including those who perform the engagement quality control review for the assurance engagement.

Audit client

An entity in respect of which a firm conducts an audit engagement. When the client is a listed entity, audit client will always include its related entities. When the audit client is not a listed entity, audit client includes those related entities over which the client has direct or indirect control.

Audit committee

Those charged with governance. This may be a separate committee or the full Board.

Audit engagement

A reasonable assurance engagement in which a professional accountant in public practice expresses an opinion whether financial statements are prepared, in all material respects (or give a true and fair view or are presented fairly, in all material respects), in accordance with an applicable financial reporting framework, such as an engagement conducted in accordance with International Standards on Auditing. This includes a Statutory Audit, which is an audit required by legislation or other regulation.

Audit team

- All members of the engagement team for the audit engagement;
- All others within a firm who can directly influence the outcome of the audit engagement, including:
  - Those who recommend the compensation of, or who provide direct supervisory, management or other oversight of the engagement partner in connection with the performance of the audit engagement including those at all successively senior levels above the engagement partner through to the individual who is the firm's Senior or Managing Partner (Chief Executive or equivalent);
  - Those who provide consultation regarding technical or industry-specific issues, transactions or events for the engagement; and

    ○   Those who provide quality control for the engagement, including those who perform the engagement quality control review for the engagement; and

    ○   All those within a network firm who can directly influence the outcome of the audit engagement.

Close family

A parent, child or sibling who is not an immediate family member.

Contingent fee

A fee calculated on a predetermined basis relating to the outcome of a transaction or the result of the services performed by the firm. A fee that is established by a court or other public authority is not a contingent fee.

Direct financial interest

A financial interest:

- Owned directly by and under the control of an individual or entity (including those managed on a discretionary basis by others); or
- Beneficially owned through a collective investment vehicle, estate, trust or other intermediary over which the individual or entity has control, or the ability to influence investment decisions.

Director or officer

Those charged with the governance of an entity, or acting in an equivalent capacity, regardless of their title, which may vary from jurisdiction to jurisdiction.

Engagement partner

The partner or other person in the firm who is responsible for the engagement and its performance, and for the report that is issued on behalf of the firm, and who, where required, has the appropriate authority from a professional, legal or regulatory body.

Engagement quality control review

A process designed to provide an objective evaluation, on or before the report is issued, of the significant judgments the engagement team made and the conclusions it reached in formulating the report.

Engagement team

All partners and staff performing the engagement, and any individuals engaged by the firm or a network firm who perform assurance procedures on the engagement. This excludes external experts engaged by the firm or a network firm.

Existing accountant

A professional accountant in public practice currently holding an audit appointment or carrying out accounting, taxation, consulting or similar professional services for a client.

External expert

An individual (who is not a partner or a member of the professional staff, including temporary staff, of the firm or a network firm) or organisation possessing skills, knowledge and experience in a field other than accounting or auditing, whose work in that field is used to assist the professional accountant in obtaining sufficient appropriate evidence.

Financial interest

An interest in equity or other security, debenture, loan or other debt instrument of an entity, including rights and obligations to acquire such an interest and derivatives directly related to such interest.

Financial statements

A structured representation of historical financial information, including related notes, intended to communicate an entity's economic resources or obligations at a point in time or the changes therein for a period of time in accordance with a financial reporting framework. The related notes ordinarily comprise a summary of significant accounting policies and other explanatory information. The term can relate to a complete set of financial statements, but it can also refer to a single financial statement, for example, a balance sheet, or a statement of revenues and expenses, and related explanatory notes.

Financial statements on which the firm will express an opinion

In the case of a single entity, the financial statements of that entity. In the case of consolidated financial statements, also referred to as group financial statements, the consolidated financial statements.

Firm

- A member firm;
- An entity that controls a member firm, through ownership, management or other means; and
- An entity controlled by a member firm, through ownership, management or other means.

Historical financial information

Information expressed in financial terms in relation to a particular entity, derived primarily from that entity's accounting system, about economic events occurring in past time periods or about economic conditions or circumstances at points in time in the past.

Immediate family

A spouse (or equivalent) or dependent. Independence

- independence of mind – the state of mind that permits the expression of a conclusion without being affected by influences that compromise professional judgment, thereby allowing an individual to act with integrity, and exercise objectivity and professional scepticism
- independence in appearance – the avoidance of facts and circumstances that are so significant that a reasonable and informed third party would be likely to conclude, weighing all the specific facts and circumstances, that a firm's, or a member of the audit or assurance team's, integrity, objectivity or professional scepticism has been compromised.

Indirect financial interest

A financial interest beneficially owned through a collective investment vehicle, estate, trust or other intermediary over which the individual or entity has no control or ability to influence investment decisions.

Key audit partner

The engagement partner, the individual responsible for the engagement quality control review, and other audit partners, if any, on the engagement team who make key decisions or judgments on significant matters with respect to the audit of the financial statements on which the firm will express an opinion. Depending upon the circumstances and the role of the individuals on the audit, "other audit partners" may include, for example, audit partners responsible for significant subsidiaries or divisions.

Listed entity

An entity whose shares, stock or debt are quoted or listed on a recognised stock exchange, or are marketed under the regulations of a recognised stock exchange or other equivalent body.

Loan

A sum of money lent, whether direct or through a third party, with the intention that it will be repaid with or without interest.

Member

A member of ICAEW, an affiliate, an employee of a member firm or affiliate, or a provisional member.

Member firm

This means, for the purposes of this Code:

- A member engaged in public practice as a sole practitioner, or
- A partnership engaged in public practice of which more than 50 per cent of the right to vote on all, or substantially all, matters of substance at meetings of the partnership is held by members; or

- A limited liability partnership engaged in public practice of which more than 50 per cent of the rights to vote on all, or substantially all, matters of substance at meetings of the partnership is held by members; or
- Any body corporate (other than a limited liability partnership) engaged in public practice of which:
- 50 per cent or more of the directors are members; and
- More than 50 per cent of the nominal value of the voting shares is held by members; and
- More than 50 per cent of the aggregate in nominal value of the voting and non-voting shares is held by members.

Network

A larger structure:

- That is aimed at co-operation; and
- That is clearly aimed at profit or cost sharing or shares common ownership, control or management, common quality control policies and procedures, common business strategy, the use of a common brand-name, or a significant part of professional resources.

Network firm

A firm or entity that belongs to a network.

Office

A distinct sub-group, whether organised on geographical or practice lines.

Officer

Those charged with the governance of an entity, or acting in an equivalent capacity, regardless of their title, which may vary from jurisdiction to jurisdiction.

Partner or principal

References to a partner or principal of a firm include the following:

- A partner/principal;
- A sole-practitioner;
- A director of a corporate firm;
- A member of a limited liability partnership;
- An employee of a corporate firm who is:
  - A responsible individual within the meaning of the Audit Regulations;
  - A licensed insolvency practitioner;
  - Defined as such in circumstances determined by Council

Professional accountant

An individual who is a member of an IFAC member body.

Professional accountant in business

A professional accountant employed or engaged in an executive or non-executive capacity in such areas as commerce, industry, service, the public sector, education, the not for profit sector, regulatory bodies or professional bodies, or a professional accountant contracted by such entities.

A professional accountant in business may be a salaried employee, a partner, director (whether executive or non-executive), an owner manager, a volunteer, or another working for one or more employing organisations. The legal form of the relationship with the employing organisation, if any, has no bearing on the ethical responsibilities incumbent on the professional accountant in business.

Professional accountant in public practice

A professional accountant, irrespective of functional classification (e.g., audit, tax or consulting) in a firm that provides professional services. This term is also used to refer to a firm of professional accountants in public practice.

Professional service

Services requiring accountancy or related skills performed by a professional accountant including accounting, auditing, taxation, management consulting and financial management services.

Provisional member

A person:
- who is training under a training agreement; or has registered their period of approved training
- who has trained under such agreement or period of approved training and is eligible either to sit for the ACA examinations of ICAEW or, having successfully sat those examinations, to apply for membership;

and for the purposes only of this definition an order under bye-law 22(7) (d) of the Disciplinary Bye-laws (concerning eligibility to sit examinations) shall be disregarded.

Public interest entity

- A listed entity; and
- An entity (a) defined by regulation or legislation as a public interest entity or (b) for which the audit is required by regulation or legislation to be conducted in compliance with the same independence requirements that apply to the audit of listed entities. Such regulation may be promulgated by any relevant regulator, including an audit regulator.

Related entity

An entity that has any of the following relationships with the client:
- An entity that has direct or indirect control over the client if the client is material to such entity;

- An entity with a direct financial interest in the client if that entity has significant influence over the client and the interest in the client is material to such entity;
- An entity over which the client has direct or indirect control;
- An entity in which the client, or an entity related to the client under (c) above, has a direct financial interest that gives it significant influence over such entity and the interest is material to the client and its related entity (c); and
- An entity which is under common control with the client (a "sister entity") if the sister entity and the client are both material to the entity that controls both the client and sister entity.

Review client

An entity in respect of which a firm conducts a review engagement.

Review engagement

An assurance engagement, conducted in accordance with International Standards on Review engagements or equivalent, in which a professional accountant in public practice expresses a conclusion on whether, on the basis of the procedures which do not provide all the evidence that would be required in an audit, anything has come to the accountant's attention that causes the accountant to believe that the financial statements are not prepared, in all material respects, in accordance with an applicable financial reporting framework.

Review team

- All members of the engagement team for the review engagement; and
- All others within a firm who can directly influence the outcome of the review engagement, including:
  - Those who recommend the compensation of, or who provide direct supervisory, management or other oversight of the engagement partner in connection with the performance of the review engagement including those at all successively senior levels above the engagement partner through to the individual who is the firm's Senior or Managing Partner (Chief Executive or equivalent);
  - Those who provide consultation regarding technical or industry specific issues, transactions or events for the engagement; and
  - Those who provide quality control for the engagement, including those who perform the engagement quality control review for the engagement; and
- All those within a network firm who can directly influence the outcome of the review engagement.

Code of Ethics D

- **General application of the code**
  - Practice of insolvency
  - Identification of threats to the fundamental principles
  - Framework of approach
  - Evaluation of threats
  - Possible safeguards
- **Specific application of the code**
  - Insolvency appointments
  - Conflicts of interest
  - Practice mergers
  - Transparency
  - Professional competence and due care
  - Professional and personal relationships
  - Identifying relationships
  - Is the relationship significant to the conduct of the insolvency appointment?
  - Dealing with the assets of an entity
  - Obtaining specialist advice and services
- **Fees and other types of remuneration**
  - Prior to accepting an insolvency appointments
  - After accepting an insolvency appointments
  - Obtaining insolvency appointments
  - Gifts and hospitality
  - Record keeping
- **The application of the framework to specific situations**
  - Introduction to specific situation
  - Examples that do not relate to a previous of existing insolvency appointment
  - Examples that relate to previous or existing insolvency appointments
  - Examples in respect of cases conducted under Scottish law
- **Definitions**

General application of the code

Practice of insolvency

400.1   This Code is intended to assist Insolvency Practitioners meet the obligations expected of them by providing professional and ethical guidance.

400.2   This Code applies to all Insolvency Practitioners. Insolvency Practitioners should take steps to ensure that the Code is applied in all professional work relating to an insolvency appointment, and to any professional work that may lead to such an insolvency appointment. Although an insolvency appointment will be of the Insolvency practitioner personally rather than his practice, he should ensure that the standards set out in this Code are applied to all members of the insolvency team.

400.3   It is this Code, and the spirit that underlies it, that governs the conduct of Insolvency Practitioners. Failure to observe this Code may not, of itself, constitute professional misconduct, but will be taken into account in assessing the conduct of an Insolvency practitioner.

Fundamental principles

An Insolvency practitioner is required to comply with the following fundamental **400.4**
principles:

- Integrity
  An Insolvency practitioner should be straightforward and honest in all professional and business relationships.
- Objectivity
  An Insolvency practitioner should not allow bias, conflict of interest or undue
  influence of others to override professional or business judgements.
- Professional competence and due care
  An Insolvency practitioner has a continuing duty to maintain professional
  knowledge and skill at the level required to ensure that a client or employer
  receives competent professional service based on current developments in
  practice, legislation and techniques. An Insolvency practitioner should act
  diligently and in accordance with applicable technical and professional standards when providing professional services.
- Confidentiality
  An Insolvency practitioner should respect the confidentiality of information
  acquired as a result of professional and business relationships and should not
  disclose any such information to third parties without proper and specific
  authority unless there is a legal or professional right or duty to disclose. Confidential information acquired as a result of professional and business
  relationships should not be used for the personal advantage of the Insolvency
  practitioner or third parties.
- Professional behaviour
  An Insolvency practitioner should comply with relevant laws and regulations
  and should avoid any action that discredits the profession. Insolvency Practitioners should conduct themselves with courtesy and consideration towards all
  with whom they come into contact when performing their work.

Framework approach

The framework approach is amethod which Insolvency Practitioners can use to **400.5**
identify actual or potential threats to the fundamental principles and determine
whether there are any safeguards that might be available to offset them. The framework approach requires an Insolvency practitioner to:

- take reasonable steps to identify any threats to compliance with the fundamental
  principles;
- evaluate any such threats; and
- respond in an appropriate manner to those threats.

Throughout this Code there are examples of threats and possible safeguards. These **400.6**
examples are illustrative and should not be considered as exhaustive lists of all
relevant threats or safeguards. It is impossible to define every situation that creates a
threat to compliance with the fundamental principles or to specify the safeguards
that may be available.

Identification of threats to the fundamental principles

An Insolvency practitioner should take reasonable steps to identify the existence of **400.7**
any threats to compliance with the fundamental principles which arise during the
course of his professional work.

400.8   An Insolvency practitioner should take particular care to identify the existence of threats which exist prior to or at the time of taking an insolvency appointment or which, at that stage, it may reasonably be expected might arise during the course of such an insolvency appointment. Sections insolvency appointments and professional and personal relationships below contain particular factors an Insolvency practitioner should take into account when deciding whether to accept an insolvency appointment.

400.9   In identifying the existence of any threats, an Insolvency practitioner should have regard to relationships whereby the practice is held out as being part of a national or an international association.

400.10   Many threats fall into one or more of five categories:

- **Self-interest threats:** which may occur as a result of the financial or other interests of a practice or an Insolvency practitioner or of a close or immediate family member of an individual within the practice;
- **Self-review threats:** which may occur when a previous judgement made by an individual within the practice needs to be re-evaluated by the Insolvency practitioner;
- **Advocacy threats:** which may occur when an individual within the practice promotes a position or opinion to the point that subsequent objectivity may be compromised;
- **Familiarity threats:** which may occur when, because of a close relationship, an individual within the practice becomes too sympathetic or antagonistic to the interests of others; and
- **Intimidation threats:** which may occur when an Insolvency practitioner may be deterred from acting objectively by threats, actual or perceived.

400.11   The following paragraphs give examples of the possible threats that an Insolvency practitioner may face.

400.12   Examples of circumstances that may create self-interest threats for an Insolvency practitioner include:

- An individual within the practice having an interest in a creditor or potential creditor with a claim which requires subjective adjudication.
- Concern about the possibility of damaging a business relationship.
- Concerns about potential future employment.

400.13   Examples of circumstances that may create self-review threats include:

- The acceptance of an insolvency appointment in respect of an entity where an individual within the practice has recently been employed by or seconded to that entity.
- An Insolvency practitioner or the practice has carried out professional work of any description, including sequential insolvency appointments, for that entity.

Such self-review threats may diminish over the passage of time.

400.14   Examples of circumstances that may create advocacy threats include:

- Acting in an advisory capacity for a creditor of an entity.
- Acting as an advocate for a client in litigation or dispute with an entity.

400.15   Examples of circumstances that may create familiarity threats include:

- An individual within the practice having a close relationship with any individual having a financial interest in the insolvent entity.
- An individual within the practice having a close relationship with a potential purchaser of an insolvent's assets and/or business.

In this regard a close relationship includes both a close professional relationship and a close personal relationship.

Examples of circumstances that may create intimidation threats include: **400.16**

- The threat of dismissal or replacement being used to:
  - Apply pressure not to follow regulations, this Code, any other applicable code, technical or professional standards.
  - Exert influence over an insolvency appointment where the Insolvency practitioner is an employee rather than a principal of the practice.
- Being threatened with litigation.
- The threat of a complaint being made to the Insolvency practitioner's authorising body.

Evaluation of threats

An Insolvency practitioner should take reasonable steps to evaluate any threats to compliance with the fundamental principles that he has identified. **400.17**

In particular, an Insolvency practitioner should consider what a reasonable and informed third party, having knowledge of all relevant information, including the significance of the threat, would conclude to be acceptable. **400.18**

Possible safeguards

Having identified and evaluated a threat to the fundamental principles an Insolvency practitioner should consider whether there any safeguards that may be available to reduce the threat to an acceptable level. The relevant safeguards will vary depending on the circumstances. Generally safeguards fall into two broad categories. Firstly, safeguards created by the profession, legislation or regulation. Secondly, safeguards in the work environment. In the insolvency context safeguards in the work environment can include safeguards specific to an insolvency appointment. These are considered in section insolvency appointments below. In addition, safeguards can be introduced across the practice. These safeguards seek to create a work environment in which threats are identified and the introduction of appropriate safeguards is encouraged. Some examples include: **400.19**

- Leadership that stresses the importance of compliance with the fundamental principles.
- Policies and procedures to implement and monitor quality control of engagements.
- Documented policies regarding the identification of threats to compliance with the fundamental principles, the evaluation of the significance of these threats and the identification and the application of safeguards to eliminate or reduce the threats, other than those that are trivial, to an acceptable level.
- Documented internal policies and procedures requiring compliance with the fundamental principles.
- Policies and procedures to consider the fundamental principles of this Code before the acceptance of an insolvency appointment.
- Policies and procedures regarding the identification of interests or relationships between individuals within the practice and third parties.

- Policies and procedures to prohibit individuals who are not members of the insolvency team from inappropriately influencing the outcome of an insolvency appointment.
- Timely communication of a practice's policies and procedures, including any changes to them, to all individuals within the practice, and appropriate training and education on such policies and procedures.
- Designating a member of senior management to be responsible for overseeing the adequate functioning of the safeguarding system.
- A disciplinary mechanism to promote compliance with policies and procedures.
- Published policies and procedures to encourage and empower individuals within the practice to communicate to senior levels within the practice and/or the Insolvency practitioner any issue relating to compliance with the fundamental principles that concerns them.

Part 2 Specific application of the code

Insolvency appointments

400.20   The practice of insolvency is principally governed by statute and secondary legislation and in many cases is subject ultimately to the control of the Court. Where circumstances are dealt with by statute or secondary legislation, an Insolvency practitioner must comply with such provisions. An Insolvency practitioner must also comply with any relevant judicial authority relating to his conduct and any directions given by the Court.

400.21   An Insolvency practitioner should act in a manner appropriate to his position as an officer of the Court (where applicable) and in accordance with any quasi-judicial, fiduciary or other duties that he may be under.

400.22   Before agreeing to accept any insolvency appointment (including a joint appointment), an Insolvency practitioner should consider whether acceptance would create any threats to compliance with the fundamental principles. Of particular importance will be any threats to the fundamental principle of objectivity created by conflicts of interest or by any significant professional or personal relationships. These are considered in more detail below.

400.23   In considering whether objectivity or integrity may be threatened, an Insolvency practitioner should identify and evaluate any professional or personal relationship (see section dealing with the assets of an entity below) which may affect compliance with the fundamental principles. The appropriate response to the threats arising from any such relationships should then be considered, together with the introduction of any possible safeguards.

400.24   Generally, it will be inappropriate for an Insolvency practitioner to accept an insolvency appointment where a threat to the fundamental principles exists or may reasonably be expected might arise during the course of the insolvency appointment unless:

- disclosure is made, prior to the insolvency appointment, of the existence of such a threat to the Court or to the creditors on whose behalf the Insolvency practitioner would be appointed to act and no objection is made to the Insolvency practitioner being appointed; and
- safeguards are or will be available to eliminate or reduce that threat to an acceptable level. If the threat is other than trivial, safeguards should be

considered and applied as necessary to reduce them to an acceptable level, where possible.

The following safeguards may be considered: **400.25**

- Involving and/or consulting another Insolvency practitioner from within the practice to review the work done.
- Consulting an independent third party, such as a committee of creditors, an authorising body or another Insolvency practitioner.
- Involving another Insolvency practitioner to perform part of the work, which may include another Insolvency practitioner taking a joint appointment where the conflict arises during the course of the insolvency appointment.
- Obtaining legal advice from a solicitor or barrister with appropriate experience and expertise.
- Changing the members of the insolvency team.
- The use of separate Insolvency Practitioners and/or staff.
- Procedures to prevent access to information by the use of information barriers (e.g. strict physical separation of such teams, confidential and secure data filing).
- Clear guidelines for individuals within the practice on issues of security and confidentiality.
- The use of confidentiality agreements signed by individuals within the practice.
- Regular review of the application of safeguards by a senior individual within the practice not involved with the insolvency appointment.
- Terminating the financial or business relationship that gives rise to the threat.
- Seeking directions from the court.

As regards joint appointments, where an Insolvency practitioner is specifically pre- **400.26** cluded by this Code from accepting an insolvency appointment as an individual, a joint appointment will not be an appropriate safeguard and will not make accepting the insolvency appointment appropriate.

In deciding whether to take an insolvency appointment in circumstances where a **400.27** threat to the fundamental principles has been identified, the Insolvency practitioner should consider whether the interests of those on whose behalf he would be appointed to act would best be served by the appointment of another Insolvency practitioner who did not face the same threat and, if so, whether any such appro- priately qualified and experienced other Insolvency practitioner is likely to be available to be appointed.

An Insolvency practitioner will encounter situations where no safeguards can reduce **400.28** a threat to acceptable level. Where this is the case, an Insolvency practitioner should conclude that it is not appropriate to accept an insolvency appointment.

Following acceptance, any threats should continue to be kept under appropriate **400.29** review and an Insolvency practitioner should be mindful that other threats may come to light or arise. There may be occasions when the Insolvency practitioner is no longer in compliance with this Code because of changed circumstances or something which has been inadvertently overlooked. This would generally not be an issue provided the Insolvency practitioner has appropriate quality control policies and procedures in place to deal with such matters and, once discovered, the matter is corrected promptly and any necessary safeguards are applied. In deciding whether to continue an insolvency appointment the Insolvency practitioner may take into account the wishes of the creditors, who after full disclosure has been made have the right to retain or replace the Insolvency practitioner.

400.30   In all cases an Insolvency practitioner will need to exercise his judgment to determine how best to deal with an identified threat. In exercising his judgment, an Insolvency practitioner should consider what a reasonable and informed third party, having knowledge of all relevant information, including the significance of the threat and the safeguards applied, would conclude to be acceptable. This consideration will be affected by matters such as the significance of the threat, the nature of the work and the structure of the practice.

Conflicts of interest

400.31   An Insolvency practitioner should take reasonable steps to identify circumstances that could pose a conflict of interest. Such circumstances may give rise to threats to compliance with the fundamental principles. Examples of where a conflict of interest may arise are where:

- An Insolvency practitioner has to deal with claims between the separate and conflicting interests of entities over whom he is appointed.
- There are a succession of or sequential insolvency appointments (see section on the application of the framework to specific situations).
- A significant relationship has existed with the entity or someone connected with the entity (see also section on professional and personal relationships)

400.32   Some of the safeguards listed at 400.25 may be applied to reduce the threats created by a conflict of interest to an acceptable level. Where a conflict of interest arises, the preservation of confidentiality will be of paramount importance; therefore, the safeguards used should generally include the use of effective information barriers.

Practice mergers

400.33   Where practices merge, they should subsequently be treated as one for the purposes of assessing threats to the fundamental principles. At the time of the merger, existing insolvency appointments should be reviewed and any threats identified. Principals and employees of the merged practice become subject to common ethical constraints in relation to accepting new insolvency appointments to clients of either of the former practices. However, existing insolvency appointments which are rendered in apparent breach of the Code by such a merger need not be determined automatically, provided that a considered review of the situation by the practice discloses no obvious and immediate ethical conflict.

400.34   Where an individual within the practice has, in any former practice, undertaken work upon the affairs of an entity in a capacity that is incompatible with an insolvency appointment of the new practice, the individual should not work or be employed on that assignment.

Transparency

400.35   Both before and during an insolvency appointment an Insolvency practitioner may acquire personal information that is not directly relevant to the insolvency or confidential commercial information relating to the affairs of third parties. The information may be such that others might expect that confidentiality would be maintained.

400.36   Nevertheless an Insolvency practitioner in the role as office holder has a professional duty to report openly to those with an interest in the outcome of the insolvency. An Insolvency practitioner should always report on his acts and dealings as fully as possible given the circumstances of the case, in a way that is transparent and understandable. An Insolvency practitioner should bear in mind the expectations of others and what a reasonable and informed third party would consider appropriate.

Professional competence and due care

Prior to accepting an insolvency appointment the Insolvency practitioner should ensure that he is satisfied that the following matters have been considered:

400.37

- Obtaining knowledge and understanding of the entity, its owners, managers and those responsible for its governance and business activities.
- Acquiring an appropriate understanding of the nature of the entity's business, the complexity of its operations, the specific requirements of the engagement and the purpose, nature and scope of the work to be performed.
- Acquiring knowledge of relevant industries or subject matters.
- Possessing or obtaining experience with relevant regulatory or reporting requirements.
- Assigning sufficient staff with the necessary competencies.
- Using experts where necessary.
- Complying with quality control policies and procedures designed to provide reasonable assurance that specific engagements are accepted only when they can be performed competently.

The fundamental principle of professional competence and due care requires that an Insolvency practitioner should only accept an insolvency appointment when the Insolvency practitioner has sufficient expertise. For example, a self interest threat to the fundamental principle of professional competence and due care is created if the Insolvency practitioner or the insolvency team does not possess or cannot acquire the competencies necessary to carry out the insolvency appointment. Expertise will include appropriate training, technical knowledge, knowledge of the entity and the business with which the entity is concerned.

400.38

Maintaining and acquiring professional competence requires a continuing awareness and understanding of relevant technical and professional developments, including:

400.39

- Developments in insolvency legislation.
- Statements of Insolvency Practice.
- The regulations of their authorising body, including any continuing professional development requirements.
- Guidance issued by their authorising body or the Insolvency Service.
- Technical issues being discussed within the profession.

Professional and personal relationships

The environment in which Insolvency Practitioners work and the relationships formed in their professional and personal lives can lead to threats to the fundamental principle of objectivity.

400.40

Identifying relationships

In particular, the principle of objectivity may be threatened if any individual within the practice, the close or immediate family of an individual within the practice or the practice itself, has or has had a professional or personal relationship which relates to the insolvency appointment being considered.

400.41

400.42   Professional or personal relationships may include (but are not restricted to) relationships with:

- the entity
- any director or shadow director or former director or shadow director of the entity
- shareholders of the entity
- any principal or employee of the entity
- business partners of the entity
- companies or entities controlled by the entity
- companies which are under common control;
- creditors (including debenture holders) of the entity
- debtors of the entity
- close or immediate family of the entity (if an individual) or its officers (if a corporate body);
- others with commercial relationships with the practice.

400.43   Safeguards within the practice should include policies and procedures to identify relationships between individuals within the practice and third parties in a way that is proportionate and reasonable in relation to the insolvency appointment being considered.

Is the relationship significant to the conduct of the insolvency appointment?

400.44   Where a professional or personal relationship of the type described in paragraph 400.41 has been identified the Insolvency practitioner should evaluate the impact of the relationship in the context of the insolvency appointment being sought or considered. Issues to consider in evaluating whether a relationship creates a threat to the fundamental principles may include the following:

- The nature of the previous duties undertaken by a practice during an earlier relationship with the entity.
- The impact of the work conducted by the practice on the financial state and/or the financial stability of the entity in respect of which the insolvency appointment is being considered.
- Whether the fee received for the work by the practice is or was significant to the practice itself or is or was substantial.
- How recently any professional work was carried out. It is likely that greater threats will arise (or may be seen to arise) where work has been carried out within the previous three years. However, there may still be instances where, in respect of non-audit work, any threat is at an acceptable level. Conversely, there may be situations whereby the nature of the work carried out was such that a considerably longer period should elapse before any threat can be reduced to an acceptable level.
- Whether the insolvency appointment being considered involves consideration of any work previously undertaken by the practice for that entity.
- The nature of any personal relationship and the proximity of the Insolvency practitioner to the individual with whom the relationship exists and, where appropriate, the proximity of that individual to the entity in relation to which the insolvency appointment relates.
- Whether any reporting obligations will arise in respect of the relevant individual with whom the relationship exists (e.g. an obligation to report on the conduct of directors and shadow directors of a company to which the insolvency appointment relates).
- The nature of any previous duties undertaken by an individual within the practice during any earlier relationship with the entity.

- The extent of the insolvency team's familiarity with the individuals connected with the entity.

Having identified and evaluated a relationship that may create a threat to the fundamental principles, the Insolvency practitioner should consider his response including the introduction of any possible safeguards to reduce the threat to an acceptable level.

400.45

Some of the safeguards which may be considered to reduce the threat created by a professional or personal relationship to an acceptable level are considered in paragraph 400.25. Other safeguards may include:

400.46

- Withdrawing from the insolvency team.
- Terminating (where possible) the financial or business relationship giving rise to the threat.
- Disclosure of the relationship and any financial benefit received by the practice (whether directly or indirectly) to the entity or to those on whose behalf the Insolvency practitioner would be appointed to act.

An Insolvency practitioner may encounter situations in which no or no reasonable safeguards can be introduced to eliminate a threat arising from a professional or personal relationship, or to reduce it to an acceptable level. In such situations, the relationship in question will constitute a significant professional relationship ('Significant Professional Relationship') or a significant personal relationship ('Significant Personal Relationship'). Where this is case the Insolvency practitioner should conclude that it is not appropriate to take the insolvency appointment.

400.47

Consideration should always be given to the perception of others when deciding whether to accept an insolvency appointment. Whilst an Insolvency practitioner may regard a relationship as not being significant to the insolvency appointment, the perception of others may differ and this may in some circumstances be sufficient to make the relationship significant.

400.48

Dealing with the assets of an entity

Actual or perceived threats (for example self interest threats) to the fundamental principles may arise when during an insolvency appointment, an Insolvency practitioner realises assets.

400.49

Save in circumstances which clearly do not impair the Insolvency Practitioner's objectivity, Insolvency Practitioners appointed to any insolvency appointment in relation to an entity, should not themselves acquire, directly or indirectly, any of the assets of an entity, nor knowingly permit any individual within the practice, or any close or immediate family member of the Insolvency practitioner or of an individual within the practice, directly or indirectly, to do so.

400.50

Where the assets and business of an insolvent company are sold by an Insolvency practitioner shortly after appointment on pre-agreed terms, this could lead to an actual or perceived threat to objectivity. The sale may also be seen as a threat to objectivity by creditors or others not involved in the prior agreement. The threat to objectivity may be eliminated or reduced to an acceptable level by safeguards such as obtaining an independent valuation of the assets or business being sold, or the consideration of other potential purchasers.

400.51

It is also particularly important for an Insolvency practitioner to take care to ensure (where to do so does not conflict with any legal or professional obligation) that his

400.52

decision making processes are transparent, understandable and readily identifiable to all third parties who may be affected by the sale or proposed sale.

Obtaining specialist advice and services

400.53 When an Insolvency practitioner intends to rely on the advice or work of another, the Insolvency practitioner should evaluate whether such reliance is warranted. The Insolvency practitioner should consider factors such as reputation, expertise, resources available and applicable professional and ethical standards. Any payment to the third party should reflect the value of the work undertaken.

400.54 Threats to the fundamental principles (for example familiarity threats and self interest threats) can arise if services are provided by a regular source independent of the practice.

400.55 Safeguards should be introduced to reduce such threats to an acceptable level. These safeguards should ensure that a proper business relationship is maintained between the parties and that such relationships are reviewed periodically to ensure that best value and service is being obtained in relation to each insolvency appointment. Additional safeguards may include clear guidelines and policies within the practice on such relationships. An Insolvency practitioner should also consider disclosure of the existence of such business relationships to the general body of creditors or the creditor's committee if one exists.

400.56 Threats to the fundamental principles can also arise where services are provided from within the practice or by a party with whom the practice, or an individual within the practice, has a business or personal relationship. An Insolvency practitioner should take particular care in such circumstances to ensure that the best value and service is being provided.

Fees and other types of remuneration

Prior to accepting an insolvency appointment

400.57 Where an engagement may lead to an insolvency appointment, an Insolvency practitioner should make any party to the work aware of the terms of the work and, in particular, the basis on which any fees are charged and which services are covered by those fees.

400.58 Where an engagement may lead to an insolvency appointment, Insolvency Practitioners should not accept referral fees or commissions unless they have established safeguards to reduce the threats created by such fees or commissions to an acceptable level.

400.59 Safeguards may include disclosure in advance of any arrangements. If after receiving any such payments, an Insolvency practitioner accepts an insolvency appointment, the amount and source of any fees or commissions received should be disclosed to creditors.

After accepting an insolvency appointment

During an insolvency appointment, accepting referral fees or commissions represents a significant threat to objectivity. Such fees or commissions should not therefore be accepted other than where to do so is for the benefit of the insolvent estate.   **400.60**

If such fees or commissions are accepted they should only be accepted for the benefit of the estate; not for the benefit of the Insolvency practitioner or the practice.   **400.61**

Further, where such fees or commissions are accepted an Insolvency practitioner should consider making disclosure to creditors.   **400.62**

Obtaining insolvency appointments

The special nature of insolvency appointments makes the payment or offer of any commission for or the furnishing of any valuable consideration towards, the introduction of insolvency appointments inappropriate. This does not, however, preclude an arrangement between an Insolvency practitioner and an employee whereby the employee's remuneration is based in whole or in part on introductions obtained for the Insolvency practitioner through the efforts of the employee.   **400.63**

When an Insolvency practitioner seeks an insolvency appointment or work that may lead to an insolvency appointment through advertising or other forms of marketing, there may be threats to compliance with the fundamental principles.   **400.64**

When considering whether to accept an insolvency appointment an Insolvency practitioner should satisfy himself that any advertising or other form of marketing pursuant to which the insolvency appointment may have been obtained is or has been: **400.65**

● Fair and not misleading.
● Avoids unsubstantiated or disparaging statements.
● Complies with relevant codes of practice and guidance in relation to advertising.

Advertisements and other forms of marketing should be clearly distinguishable as such and be legal, decent, honest and truthful.   **400.66**

If reference is made in advertisements or other forms of marketing to fees or to the cost of the services to be provided, the basis of calculation and the range of services that the reference is intended to cover should be provided. Care should be taken to ensure that such references do not mislead as to the precise range of services and the time commitment that the reference is intended to cover.   **400.67**

An Insolvency practitioner should never promote or seek to promote his services, or the services of another Insolvency practitioner, in such a way, or to such an extent as to amount to harassment.   **400.68**

Where an Insolvency practitioner or the practice advertises for work via a third party, the Insolvency practitioner is responsible for ensuring that the third party follows the above guidance.   **400.69**

Gifts and hospitality

An Insolvency practitioner, or a close or immediate family member, may be offered gifts and hospitality. In relation to an insolvency appointment, such an offer will give   **400.70** rise to threats to compliance with the fundamental principles. For example, self-interest threats may arise if a gift is accepted and intimidation threats may arise from the possibility of such offers being made public.

400.71   The significance of such threats will depend on the nature, value and intent behind the offer. In deciding whether to accept any offer of a gift or hospitality the Insolvency practitioner should have regard to what a reasonable and informed third party having knowledge of all relevant information would consider to be appropriate. Where such a reasonable and informed third party would consider the gift to be made in the normal course of business without the specific intent to influence decision making or obtain information the Insolvency practitioner may generally conclude that there is no significant threat to compliance with the fundamental principles.

400.72   Where appropriate, safeguards should be considered and applied as necessary to eliminate any threats to the fundamental principles or reduce them to an acceptable level. If an Insolvency practitioner encounters a situation in which no or no reasonable safeguards can be introduced to reduce a threat arising from offers of gifts or hospitality to an acceptable level he should conclude that it is not appropriate to accept the offer.

400.73   An Insolvency practitioner should also not offer or provide gifts or hospitality where this would give rise to an unacceptable threat to compliance with the fundamental principles.

Record keeping

400.74   It will always be for the Insolvency practitioner to justify his actions. An Insolvency practitioner will be expected to be able to demonstrate the steps that he took and the conclusions that he reached in identifying, evaluating and responding to any threats, both leading up to and during an insolvency appointment, by reference to written contemporaneous records.

400.75   The records an Insolvency practitioner maintains, in relation to the steps that he took and the conclusions that he reached, should be sufficient to enable a reasonable and informed third party to reach a view on the appropriateness of his actions.

The application of the framework to specific situations

Introduction to specific situations

400.76   The following examples describe specific circumstances and relationships that will create threats to compliance with the fundamental principles. The examples may assist an Insolvency practitioner and the members of the insolvency team to assess the implications of similar, but different, circumstances and relationships.

400.77   The examples are divided into three parts. Part 1 contains examples which do not relate to a previous or existing insolvency appointment. Part 2 contains examples that do relate to a previous or existing insolvency appointment. Part 3 contains some examples under Scottish law. The examples are not intended to be exhaustive.

Part 1 – Examples that do not relate to a previous or existing insolvency appointment

The following situations involve a professional relationship which does not consist of a previous insolvency appointment.

400.78

Insolvency appointment following audit related work

400.79

Relationship: The practice or an individual within the practice has previously carried out audit related work within the previous 3 years.

Response: A Significant Professional Relationship will arise: an Insolvency practitioner should conclude that it is not appropriate to take the insolvency appointment.

Where audit related work was carried out more than three years before the proposed date of the appointment of the Insolvency practitioner a threat to compliance with the fundamental principles may still arise. The Insolvency practitioner should evaluate any such threat and consider whether the threat can be eliminated or reduced to an acceptable level by the existence or introduction of safeguards.

This restriction does not apply where the insolvency appointment is in a members' voluntary liquidation; an Insolvency practitioner may normally take an appointment as liquidator. However, the Insolvency practitioner should consider whether there are any other circumstances that give rise to an unacceptable threat to compliance with the fundamental principles. Further, the Insolvency practitioner should satisfy himself that the directors' declaration of solvency is likely to be substantiated by events.

Appointment as Investigating Accountant at the instigation of a creditor

400.80

Previous relationship: The practice or an individual within the practice was instructed by, or at the instigation of, a creditor or other party having a financial interest in an entity, to investigate, monitor or advise on its affairs.

Response: A Significant Professional Relationship would not normally arise in these circumstances provided that:-

- there has not been a direct involvement by an individual within the practice in the management of the entity; and
- the practice had its principal client relationship with the creditor or other party, rather than with the company or proprietor of the business; and
- the entity was aware of this.

An Insolvency practitioner should however consider all the circumstances before accepting an insolvency appointment, including the effect of any discussions or lack of discussions about the financial affairs of the company with its directors, and whether such circumstances give rise to an unacceptable threat to compliance with the fundamental principles.

Where such an investigation was conducted at the request of, or at the instigation of, a secured creditor who then requests an Insolvency practitioner to accept an insolvency appointment as an administrator or administrative receiver, the Insolvency practitioner should satisfy himself that the company, acting by its board of directors, does not object to him taking such an insolvency appointment. If the secured creditor does not give prior warning of the insolvency appointment to the company or if such warning is given and the company objects but the secured creditor still wishes to appoint the Insolvency practitioner, he should consider whether the circumstances give rise to an unacceptable threat to compliance with the fundamental principles.

Part 2 – Examples relating to previous or existing insolvency appointments

400.81   The following situations involve a prior professional relationship that involves a previous or existing insolvency appointment:-

400.82   *Insolvency appointment following an appointment as Administrative or other Receiver*

Previous appointment: An individual within the practice has been administrative or other receiver.

Proposed appointment: Any insolvency appointment.

Response: An Insolvency practitioner should not accept any insolvency appointment.

This restriction does not, however, apply where the individual within the practice was appointed a receiver by the Court. In such circumstances, the Insolvency practitioner should however consider whether any other circumstances which give rise to an unacceptable threat to compliance with the fundamental principles.

400.83   *Administration or Liquidation following appointment as Supervisor of a Voluntary Arrangement*

Previous appointment: An individual within the practice has been supervisor of a company voluntary arrangement.

Proposed appointment : Administrator or liquidator.

Response: An Insolvency practitioner may normally accept an appointment as administrator or liquidator. However the Insolvency practitioner should consider whether there are any circumstances that give rise to an unacceptable threat to compliance with the fundamental principles.

400.84   *Liquidation following appointment as Administrator*

Previous Appointment: An individual within the practice has been administrator.

Proposed Appointment: Liquidator.

Response: An Insolvency practitioner may normally accept an appointment as liquidator provided he has complied with the relevant legislative requirements. However, the Insolvency practitioner should also consider whether there are any circumstances that give rise to an unacceptable threat to compliance with the fundamental principles.

400.85   *Conversion of Members' Voluntary Liquation into Creditors' Voluntary Liquidation*

Previous appointment: An individual within the practice has been the liquidator of a company in a members' voluntary liquidation.

Proposed appointment: Liquidator in a creditors' voluntary liquidation, where it has been necessary to convene a creditors' meeting.

Response: Where there has been a Significant Professional Relationship, an Insolvency practitioner may continue or accept an appointment (subject to creditors' approval) only if he concludes that the company will eventually be able to pay its debts in full, together with interest.

However, the Insolvency practitioner should consider whether there are any other circumstances that give rise to an unacceptable threat to compliance with the fundamental principles.

Bankruptcy following appointment as Supervisor of an Individual Voluntary Arrangement **400.86**

Previous appointment: An individual within the practice has been supervisor of an individual voluntary arrangement.

Proposed Appointment: Trustee in bankruptcy.

Response: An Insolvency practitioner may normally accept an appointment as trustee in bankruptcy. However, the Insolvency practitioner should consider whether there are any circumstances that give rise to an unacceptable threat to compliance with the fundamental principles.

Part 3 – Examples in respect of cases conducted under Scottish Law

Sequestration following appointment as Trustee under a Trust Deed for creditors **400.87**

Previous appointment: An individual within the practice has been trustee under a trust deed for creditors.

Proposed appointment: Interim trustee or trustee in sequestration.

Response An Insolvency practitioner may normally accept an appointment as an interim trustee or trustee in sequestration. However, the Insolvency practitioner should consider whether there are any circumstances that give rise to an unacceptable threat to compliance with the fundamental principles.

Sequestration where the Accountant in Bankruptcy is Trustee following appointment as **400.88**
Trustee under a Trust Deed for creditors

Previous appointment: An individual within the practice has been trustee under a trust deed for creditors.

Proposed appointment: Agent for the Accountant in Bankruptcy in sequestration.

Response: An Insolvency practitioner may normally accept an appointment as agent for the Accountant in Bankruptcy. However, the Insolvency practitioner should consider whether there are any circumstances that give rise to an unacceptable threat to compliance with the fundamental principles.

Definitions

Authorising body	A body declared to be a recognised professional body or a competent authority under any legislation governing the administration of insolvency in the United Kingdom.
Close or immediate family	A spouse (or equivalent), dependant, parent, child or sibling.
Entity	Any natural or legal person or any group of such persons, including a partnership.
He/she	In this Code, he is to be read as including she.
Individual within the practice	The Insolvency practitioner, any principals in the practice and any employees within the practice.
Insolvency appointment	A formal appointment:

- which, under the terms of legislation must be undertaken by an Insolvency Practitioner; or
- as a nominee or supervisor of a voluntary arrangement.

Insolvency Practitioner	An individual who is authorised or recognised to act as an Insolvency Practitioner in the United Kingdom by an authorising body. For the purpose of the application of this Code only, the term Insolvency Practitioner also includes an individual who acts as a nominee or supervisor of a voluntary arrangement.
Insolvency team	Any person under the control or direction of an Insolvency Practitioner.
Practice	The organisation in which the Insolvency practitioner practices.
Principal	In respect of a practice:

- which is a company: a director;
- which is a partnership: a partner;
- which is a limited liability partnership: a member;
- which is comprised of a sole practitioner: that person;

Alternatively any person within the practice who is held out as being a director, partner or member.

Part Eleven

FRC Revised Ethical Standard (2016) and Glossary

Revised Ethical Standard

(June 2016)

Integrity, objectivity and independence

Contents

PREFACE

The FRC's Ethical Standard applies in the audit of financial statements and other *public interest assurance engagements*. It is read in the context of the Statement 'The Financial Reporting Council – Scope and Authority of Audit and Assurance Pronouncements' which sets out the application and authority of the FRC's Ethical Standard.

The terms used in the FRC's Ethical Standard are explained in the Glossary on the FRC's website.

The FRC's Ethical Standard applies to audits of financial statements and other *public interest assurance engagements* in both the private and the public sectors.

Introduction

Scope of this Ethical Standard

I1   This Ethical Standard applies to *audit engagements* and other *public interest assurance engagements*[1]. The term *'engagement'* is used in this Ethical Standard specifically to mean an *audit engagement* or *other public interest assurance engagement*, or both where the context permits, unless stated otherwise. A fundamental objective of any such *engagement* is that the intended users trust and have confidence that the audit or assurance opinion is professionally sound and objective. This in turn should enhance the credibility for users of the information the opinion covers (the *'subject matter information'*[2] – e.g. in the case of an audit engagement, the financial statements). It should also enhance the intended users' understanding of the underlying *'subject matter'* (e.g. in the case of an *audit engagement*, the historical financial position and performance of the entity).

I2   Users are neither responsible for the *subject matter information* nor for the underlying *subject matter* of the *engagement*. Their interest in the *engagement* usually arises because they have an actual or prospective stake in an *entity relevant to the engagement* but do not have direct access to the *subject matter*.

I3   Although auditors and assurance practitioners are reporting to users, they are generally engaged to do so by the entity whose information they are reporting on. Accordingly their contractual 'client' (the entity) is different to their beneficial 'client' (the users). These principal-agent relationships (where the users are the principals and the directors and auditors of the entity their agents) give rise to the potential for conflicts of interests that need to be addressed if the user is to have trust and confidence in the audit/assurance process, the *subject matter information* and the directors of the entity itself. Regulation

---

[1] *Audits of financial statements*[(*)] *undertaken in compliance with International Standards on Auditing (ISAs) (UK) and other engagements undertaken in compliance with performance standards issued by the FRC which, as of 17 June 2016, comprise:*

  a.   Reporting accountants *acting in connection with an* investment circular *(the Standards for Investment Reporting – 'SIRs');*

  b.   *Review of interim financial information by the independent auditor of the entity (International Standard on Review Engagements (UK and Ireland) 2410); and*

  c.   *Engagements to provide assurance on client assets to the Financial Conduct Authority (the CASS Standard).*

[(*)] *In the public sector the statutory scope of an audit can extend beyond the entity's financial statements to include reporting on an entity's arrangements for the proper conduct of its financial affairs, management of its performance or use of its resources.*

[2] *'Subject matter information' is the outcome that results from the evaluation or measurement of 'subject matter' against suitable criteria. More full definitions are given in the Glossary of Terms.*

and oversight of audit and assurance practitioners, including professional and ethical codes and standards, addresses the need for trust and confidence between users and practitioners. The *engagement* then addresses the need for trust and confidence between the users and the directors of the entity.

In the context of an *engagement*, such conflicts of interest create a potential risk (threat) **I4** that the practitioner's judgment or actions in conducting or determining the outcome of the *engagement* may be unduly influenced by interests other than those of the intended user (the beneficial 'client' under the *engagement*). Such other interests are potentially wide-ranging and will usually be legitimate in themselves (though they may also not be so). However, they would be objectionable in the circumstances if the practitioner is unduly influenced by them, because this may prejudice the interests of the intended users, which should be paramount.

Users do not have all the information necessary for judging whether the *firm*, its partners **I5** and *staff* and any other *covered persons* are, in fact, acting with integrity and objectivity. Although the *firm* may be satisfied that the integrity, objectivity and independence of the *firm* or such persons will not in fact be compromised by a particular condition or relationship, an objective, reasonable and informed third party may reach a different conclusion. For example, if such a third party were aware that the *firm*, its partners or *staff* and/or any other covered persons had certain financial, employment, business or personal relationships with an *entity relevant to the engagement*, that third party might reasonably conclude that the *firm* and such persons could be subject to undue influence from the directors of the entity or would not be impartial or unbiased. Public confidence in the integrity, objectivity and independence of the *firm* or such persons could therefore suffer as a result of this perception, irrespective of whether there is any actual impairment.

Other regulators or competent authorities may specify compliance with this Ethical **I6** Standard in relation to other types of work.

Ethical guidance on other matters, together with statements of fundamental ethical **I7** principles governing the work of all professional accountants, are issued by professional accountancy bodies. These also provide a basis for enhancing the trust and confidence of intended users that the *engagement* is professionally sound.

Investment Circular Reporting Engagements

Because investment circulars may relate to transactions that are price sensitive and **I8** therefore confidential, the fact that a *firm* has been engaged to undertake an *investment circular reporting engagement* is likely to be known by only a limited number of individuals within the *firm*. For this reason, for such engagements, the supporting ethical provisions and requirements of this Ethical Standard apply only to.

(a)   persons with actual knowledge of the engagement as described in the definition of *covered persons* applicable to an *investment circular reporting engagement*; and

(b)   where required by this Ethical Standard, the *firm*.

Meeting the Ethical Outcomes Established by the Overarching Principles, Supporting Ethical Provisions and Specific Requirements

Part A of this Ethical Standard sets out the overarching principles of integrity, objectivity **I9** and independence, together with supporting ethical provisions. Together, these establish a framework, of ethical outcomes that are required to be met by the auditor or assurance practitioner, to provide a basis for user trust and confidence in the integrity and objectivity of the practitioner in performing the *engagement*.

I10 Part B sets out specific requirements relevant to certain circumstances that may arise in audit and other *public interest assurance engagements*. These specific requirements are designed to assist in meeting the ethical outcomes required by the overarching principles and supporting ethical provisions. However, circumstances relating to *engagements* vary widely and meeting the ethical outcomes required by the overarching principles and supporting ethical provisions is paramount. Compliance with the specific requirements may not always be sufficient to achieve this as Part B does not, nor is it practicable for it to, address all possible circumstances that may exist. Accordingly practitioners need to be alert for, and respond appropriately to, other circumstances that create threats to meeting the ethical outcomes required by the overarching principles and supporting ethical provisions.

I11 The *firm* and persons required to meet the outcomes of the overarching principles and supporting ethical provisions are required to be able to demonstrate that they have, where applicable, identified and addressed relevant conditions and circumstances, including that they have:

- implemented, maintained and/or complied with effective systems and processes to enable them to do so;
- established and operated effective safeguards;
- evaluated the threats and safeguards appropriately; and
- taken any additional steps that are necessary to meet the ethical outcomes required by the overarching principles and supporting ethical provisions.

I12 The FRC believes that stakeholders (users of practitioner's reports issued under *engagements*) expect an equivalent standard of independence for *firms*, their partners and other *covered persons*, whether performing audit or other *public interest assurance engagements*. *Firms*, their partners and *staff*, and other persons where identified, are required to meet the ethical outcomes required by the overarching principles and supporting ethical provisions and to comply with the requirements unless the circumstances to which they apply do not exist.

I13 When a statement or examples are given in this Ethical Standard to help clarify or illustrate a position in relation to particular circumstances, this is not intended to, and should not be interpreted as, indicating that in other circumstances the same position necessarily either is or is not intended. Whether the ethical outcomes required by the overarching principles and supporting ethical provisions are achieved is always paramount and is a matter to be determined exercising professional judgment.

The 'Third Party Test'

I14 Importantly, consideration of whether the ethical outcomes required by the overarching principles and supporting ethical provisions have been met should be evaluated by reference to the perspective of an objective, reasonable and informed third party (see the definition of *independence*).

I15 The *firm*, as well as each *covered person*, is required to be independent in the performance (conduct and determination of the outcome) of the *engagement*. Complete freedom from threats to integrity and objectivity, even taking into account safeguards, is not feasible, for example, as a result of the influence that the directors and management of a responsible entity have over the appointment and remuneration of the *firm* where (as in the case of an audit) that entity is the engaging party. Accordingly, independence not being compromised (which is the test to be applied in evaluating the likely consequences of conditions and relationships that may create threats to integrity and objectivity) is not whether the *firm* considers that the integrity and objectivity of the *firm*, its partners and *staff* and any other *covered persons* is impaired, but is whether there is freedom from threats to integrity and objectivity, taking into account safeguards applied, at a level where it is probable (more likely than not) that an objective, reasonable and informed third party would not conclude that integrity or objectivity (and therefore independence) is compromised. This is identified more concisely in Parts A and B of this Ethical Standard as a 'level at which independence is not compromised'.

Threats to Integrity, Objectivity and Independence

When the threats that exist mean that independence is, or is perceived to be, compromised, an objective, reasonable and informed third party would not have sufficient trust and confidence in the practitioner to perform or continue to perform the *engagement*. Consequently, in those circumstances actions have to be taken: to remove or reduce the threats; or to apply additional safeguards; or, where the threats relate to individuals rather than the *firm*, to exclude those individuals from any role which would put them in a position as a *covered person* to exert influence on the *engagement*. These actions must be taken individually or collectively to such an extent that it is probable that an objective, reasonable and informed third party would no longer conclude that integrity or objectivity (and therefore independence) are compromised. Otherwise, the *firm* is not permitted to accept, or if already engaged is required to withdraw from, the *engagement* unless not permitted to do so by legislation. **I16**

Conditions and relationships that affect the *firm* or its *network firms* and their partners and *staff* and any other *covered persons* are relevant in the context of identifying conflicts of interest that may give rise to threats to integrity or objectivity in the performance of the *engagement*. Individuals who perform an *engagement* do so in the context of the *firm*'s cultural and ethical values, and its governance and management arrangements (including its quality control systems). In turn, the *firm* operates in the context of its wider network, if any. Accordingly, such conditions and relationships that are relevant in the context of an engagement may arise within the *firm* or its network or externally. **I17**

Relevant internal conditions would include, for example, the culture, governance and management arrangements within the *firm* and its *network firms*, and their policies and practices with respect to performance, pay and promotion. These internal conditions are expressed, in the context of those responsible for the performance of the *engagement*, through the formal and informal relationships of influence they have with other persons within the *firm*, and potentially within the *firm*'s network, and in turn any such relationships that those other persons may have internally. Such other persons within the *firm* may therefore be *covered persons* in a position to influence the conduct or outcome of the engagement. **I18**

Relevant external relationships would include, for example: family and personal relationships of *covered persons*; financial, business and employment relationships of the *firm* or such individuals (or closely connected persons) with an *entity relevant to the engagement* and potentially with other entities; and relationships with an entity relevant to the *engagement* that arise in the performance of the *engagement* or other services provided to those entities. Relevant external conditions may include, for example: the culture, governance and management of the entity; long association of those performing the *engagement* with an *entity relevant to the engagement*; and economic dependence on an *entity relevant to the engagement*. **I19**

The EU Audit Directive and Regulation

I20   In April 2014 the European Commission published a Directive[3] amending the Statutory Audit Directive[4] and a new Audit Regulation[5]. The Audit Directive establishes specific requirements concerning the *statutory audit* of annual and consolidated financial statements. The Audit Regulation establishes further specific requirements regarding the *statutory audit* of '*public interest entities*' as defined by the Audit Directive (see the definitions below).

I21   The Audit Regulation has the direct effect of law and Member States are required to adopt appropriate provisions to ensure its effective application. The Audit Directive does not have a direct effect in law and Member States are required to adopt and publish the measures necessary to comply with it. Articles in both the Audit Directive and Audit Regulation establish provisions that relate to matters that are the subject of this Ethical Standard. In relation to a number of these provisions there are Member State options that have been implemented in this Ethical Standard.

I22   The overarching principles, supporting ethical provisions and requirements in this Ethical Standard reflect the Audit Directive and Regulation where relevant. These requirements are highlighted with shading and 'D' (for the Directive) or 'R' (for the Regulation) added to the paragraph number as applicable.

Definitions

I23   Particular terms used in the FRC's Ethical Standard are explained in the Glossary which is available on the FRC website. Defined terms are presented in italicised text.

Integrity, Objectivity and Independence

Integrity – being trustworthy, straightforward, honest, fair and candid; complying with the spirit as well as the letter of applicable ethical principles, laws and regulations; behaving so as to maintain the public's trust in the auditing profession; and respecting confidentiality except where disclosure is in the public interest or is required to adhere to legal and professional responsibilities.

Objectivity – acting and making decisions and judgments impartially, fairly and on merit (having regard to all considerations relevant to the task in hand but no other), without discrimination, bias, or compromise because of commercial or personal self-interest, conflicts of interest or the undue influence of others, and having given due consideration to the best available evidence.

The need for objectivity in performing the engagement arises from, among other things, the fact that many of the important issues involved in the performance of the engagement, including those arising in the preparation of the subject matter information, do not relate to questions of fact but rather to questions of judgment. For example, with regard to financial statements, there are choices to be made by the board of directors in deciding on the accounting policies to be adopted by the entity: the directors have to select the ones that they consider most appropriate and this decision can have a material impact on the financial statements. Furthermore, many items included in the financial statements cannot

---

[3] *Directive 2014/56/EU.*

[4] *Directive 2006/43/EC.*

[5] *Regulation 537/2014.*

be measured with absolute precision and certainty. In many cases, estimates have to be made and the directors may have to choose one value from a range of possible outcomes. When exercising discretion in these areas, the directors have regard to the applicable financial reporting framework.

Independence – freedom from conditions and relationships which, in the context of an *engagement*, would compromise the integrity or objectivity of the *firm* or *covered persons*.

Integrity or objectivity (and therefore independence) would be compromised if it is probable (more likely than not) that an objective, reasonable and informed third party would conclude that the threats, arising from any conditions or relationships that exist (taking into account any conflicts of interest that they may cause, or generally be perceived to cause, or otherwise, and having regard to any safeguards implemented), would impair integrity or objectivity to such an extent that it would be inappropriate for the firm to accept or continue to perform the audit or other public interest assurance engagement unless the threats were eliminated or further reduced or unless more, or more effective, safeguards were implemented.

Part A – Overarching Principles and Supporting Ethical Provisions

The overarching principles of integrity, objectivity and independence established by this Ethical Standard are set out below together with the related supporting ethical provisions. Cross references are given to the Sections in Part B of this Ethical Standard that establish related requirements and/or guidance.

Integrity and Objectivity

Overarching Principle

The *firm*, its partners[6] and all *staff*[7] shall behave with integrity and objectivity in all professional and business activities and relationships.   **1.**

Supporting Ethical Provisions

The senior management of the *firm* and those with direct responsibility for the management of the *firm*'s audit and other public interest assurance business shall instil the necessary culture and behaviours respectively throughout the *firm* and that business, so as to ensure that meeting the ethical outcomes of the overarching principles and supporting ethical provisions is paramount and overrides all commercial interests of the *firm*.	1.1 – 1.25 Compliance	**1.1**
The *firm* shall establish and apply confidential whistle-blowing policies and procedures across the *firm* which enable partners and *staff* to report, without fear, concerns about the *firm*'s commitment to quality work and professional judgement and values in a way that properly takes the public interest into consideration.	1.11(h)	**1.2**

---

[6] *The term 'partner' includes any individual with authority to bind the* firm *with respect to the performance of a professional services engagement.*

[7] *The term 'staff' includes any natural persons whose services are placed at the disposal or under the control of the* firm.

Independence

Overarching Principle

2.   **In relation to each *engagement*, the *firm*, and each *covered person*, shall ensure (in the case of a *covered person*, insofar as they are able to do so) that the *firm* and each *covered person* is free from conditions and relationships which would make it probable that an objective, reasonable and informed third party would conclude the independence of the *firm* or any *covered person* is compromised.**

Supporting Ethical Provisions

2.1D   The *firm* and each *covered person*, shall ensure (in the case of a *covered person*, insofar as they are able to do so) that the independence of the *firm* and each *covered person* is not compromised with respect to each *entity relevant to the engagement*. This includes ensuring that the *firm* and each covered person is not involved in the decision-taking of any such entity. The period during which independence shall not be compromised is:

(a) In the case of an audit, at least throughout the period covered by the financial statements to be audited and throughout any subsequent period until the audit has been completed;

(b) In the case of an other *public interest assurance engagement*, other than an *investment circular reporting engagement*, at least throughout any period over which, or from the time as at which, the *subject matter* is measured or evaluated in connection with the engagement and throughout any subsequent period until the *engagement* has been completed;

(c) In the case of an investment circular reporting engagement, the period during which the engagement is undertaken and any additional period before that but subsequent to the balance sheet date of the most recent audited financial statements of the *entity relevant to the engagement*. [AD 22.1]

2.2D   The *firm* shall take all reasonable steps to ensure that, when carrying out an *engagement*, the integrity, objectivity and independence of the *firm* and each *covered person* is not affected by any existing or potential conflict of interest or any business or other direct or indirect relationship involving:

1.26 – 1.44
Identification and
Assessment of Threats

(i) the *firm*; or where applicable any members of its network;

(ii) any of the *firm*'s partners or *staff*; or

1.45 – 1.52
Identification and
Assessment of
Safeguards

(iii) the *firm*'s owners, shareholders or any other person directly or indirectly linked to the *firm* by control. [AD 22.1]

1.53 – 1.55
Other Firms

The *firm* shall not accept, continue or carry out an *engagement*:

(i) if there is any threat of self-review, self-interest, advocacy, familiarity or intimidation created by financial, personal, business, employment or other relationships between:

    (a) *the firm, any of its network firms, or any covered person, and*

    (b) *any entity (relevant to the engagement; or*

(ii) unless required by law or regulation to do so, if any other condition or relationship exists;

which would compromise the independence of the *firm* or any *covered person*. [AD 22.1]

For each *engagement*, the *firm* and the *engagement partner* (in the case of the *engagement partner* insofar as they are able to do so) shall ensure that the *firm*'s independence is not compromised as a result of conditions or relationships that would compromise the independence of a *network firm* (whether or not its work is used in the conduct of engagement) or a third party *firm* whose work is used in the conduct of the engagement, having regard to the ethical requirements that are relevant to the engagement as applicable to such other *firm*, which are as follows:

(a) For each such other *firm*, the extant version of the IES-BA Code[8]; and

(b) In the case of a *network firm* whose work is used in the conduct of an *engagement* where any *entity relevant to the engagement* is a *public interest entity*, this Ethical Standard.

In evaluating whether or not a condition or relationship would compromise independence, it is the responsibility of (i) the *firm*, and (ii) each *covered person* and any other person with responsibility to behave with integrity and objectivity and to maintain their independence (or to ensure that others do so); to be able to demonstrate that any conditions or relationships that exist, taking account of any safeguards implemented, would not compromise the independence of the *firm* or any *covered person*.

---

[8] *The Code of Ethics for Professional Accountants issued by the International Ethics Standards Board for Accountants*

2.6	All partners and *staff* of the *firm* and all other *covered persons* shall remain alert to conditions or relationships which could compromise the independence of the *firm* or any *covered person*.	1.26 – 1.44 Identification and Assessment of Threats

2.7   All partners and *staff* of the *firm* and all other *covered persons* who become aware of any condition or relationship which could impair the independence of the *firm* or any *covered person* shall report the matter to the *engagement partner* (if known) or (failing that) to the *firm's Ethics Partner*/Function, where applicable, or otherwise to the senior management of the *firm* or those with direct responsibility for the management of the *firm's* audit and other public interest assurance business, at the earliest opportunity.

2.8	The *firm* shall have policies and procedures designed to ensure that action is taken promptly: to investigate any condition or relationship reported in accordance with supporting ethical provision 2.7, to assess whether the independence of the *firm* or any *covered person* would be compromised and, if so, to eliminate the condition or relationship or apply sufficient safeguards, to reduce threats to a level where the independence of the *firm* and *covered persons* is not compromised, or to withdraw from the *engagement*.	1.45 – 1.52 Identification and Assessment of Safeguards 1.57 – 1.60 Overall Conclusion
2.9	In relation to an *engagement*, a *firm* shall not: • agree a basis for determining fees, or • have remuneration and evaluation policies for partners and *staff*, which would compromise the independence of the *firm* or of any *covered person*.	Section 4 (4.1 – 4.55) Section 4 (4.56D – 4.60)
2.10	The *firm*, its partners and staff and any other *covered person*, and *persons closely associated* with *covered persons*, shall not provide or accept gifts and hospitality in relation to an *engagement* unless it is probable that an objective, reasonable and informed third party would consider the value thereof to be trivial or inconsequential.	Section 4 (4.61D – 4.65)
2.11	The *firm* shall not accept or continue an *engagement* for an entity, unless required by law to do so, where litigation in relation to any *engagement* between the *firm* its partners or any *covered person* and the entity or its *affiliates* is already in progress, or where the *engagement partner* considers such litigation to be probable, and which would compromise the independence of the *firm* or any *covered person*.	Section 4 (4.66 – 4.68)
2.12	The *firm* shall not provide any *non-audit / additional services* to an *entity relevant to an engagement*, where such provision would compromise the independence of the *firm* or any *covered person*.	Section 5

2.13   Failure to comply with a requirement of this Ethical Standard shall be deemed to compromise independence unless such failure has been addressed in accordance with paragraphs 1.22 and 1.23 of Section 1 of Part B of this Ethical Standard.

Part B

Section 1 – General Requirements and Guidance

Compliance

The *firm* shall establish appropriate policies and procedures to ensure that its owners or shareholders, as well as the members of the administrative, management and supervisory bodies of the *firm*, or of an *affiliate firm*, do not intervene in the carrying-out of an *engagement* in any way which jeopardises the integrity, objectivity or independence of the *firm* or *covered persons*; [AD 24a.1(a)]   1.1D

The *firm* shall establish appropriate and effective organisational and administrative arrangements: 1.2D
(a) that are designed to prevent, identify, eliminate or manage and disclose any threats to its independence; [AD 24a.1(e)]
(b) for dealing with and recording incidents which have, or may have, serious consequences for the integrity of its audit or other public interest assurance activities; [AD24a.1(i)]

The *firm* shall take into consideration the scale and complexity of its activities when complying with the requirements set out in paragraphs 1.1D and 1.2D. [AD 24a.2]   1.3D

The *firm* shall be able to demonstrate to the FRC (or the Recognised Supervisory Body to whom the FRC has delegated regulatory tasks, where applicable) that the policies and procedures designed to achieve such compliance with the requirements in paragraphs 1.1D and 1.2D are appropriate given the scale and complexity of activities of the *firm*. [AD 24a.2]   1.4D

The *firm*, its partners and *staff* shall, in so far as they are required to meet the ethical outcomes of the overarching principles and supporting ethical provisions in this Ethical Standard, be able to demonstrate that they have done so. This shall include, in so far as applicable to their roles, being able to demonstrate that they have: 1.5

- implemented and maintained, and/or complied with, effective systems and processes to enable meeting those outcomes;
- identified and reported relevant conditions and circumstances that threaten meeting those outcomes;
- established and operated effective safeguards;
- evaluated the threats and safeguards appropriately;
- taken any additional steps that are appropriate in the circumstances to meet those outcomes.

The specific requirements in Sections 1 – 5 of Part B of this Ethical Standard are designed to assist in meeting the ethical outcomes of the overarching principles and supporting ethical provisions. However, circumstances relating to *engagements* vary widely and meeting these ethical outcomes is paramount. Compliance with the specific requirements may not be sufficient to do so as they do not address all possible circumstances.   1.6

When a statement or examples are given in this Ethical Standard to help clarify or illustrate a position in relation to particular circumstances, this is not intended to, and should not be interpreted as, indicating that in other circumstances the same position necessarily either is or is not intended. Whether the ethical outcomes of the overarching principles and   1.7

supporting ethical provisions are met is always paramount and is a matter to be determined exercising professional judgment.

1.8 Meeting the ethical outcomes of the overarching principles and supporting ethical provisions, and complying with the specific requirements, regarding integrity, objectivity and independence is a responsibility of both the *firm* and of individual partners and *staff*. The *firm* establishes policies and procedures, appropriate to the size and nature of the *firm*, to promote and monitor meeting the ethical outcomes of the overarching principles and supporting ethical provisions, and compliance with the specific requirements, by the *firm*, its partners and its staff.9,

1.9 Supporting ethical provision 1.1 establishes that the senior management of the *firm*, and those with direct responsibility for the management of the *firm*'s audit and other public interest assurance business, instil the necessary culture and behaviours throughout the *firm* so as to ensure that meeting the ethical outcomes of the overarching principles and supporting ethical provisions is paramount and supersedes all commercial interests of the *firm*. The senior management of the *firm* influences the internal culture of the *firm* by its actions and by its example ('the tone at the top'). Achieving a robust control environment requires that the senior management give clear, consistent and frequent messages, backed up by appropriate actions, which emphasise the importance of meeting the ethical outcomes of the overarching principles and supporting ethical provisions for *audit* and other *public interest assurance engagements* by all parts of the *firm*, including those parts that are not involved in providing audit and other public interest assurance services.

1.10 **The senior management of the *firm*, and those with direct responsibility for the management of the *firm*'s audit and other public interest assurance business, shall establish appropriate policies, procedures and quality control and monitoring systems; dedicate appropriate resources and leadership to compliance with supporting ethical provision 1.1; and make appropriate arrangements with *network firms* to ensure compliance as necessary across the network. The *firm* shall ensure that such appropriate policies, procedures and quality control and monitoring systems are implemented and operated effectively.**

1.11 In order to promote a strong control environment, the *firm* establishes policies and procedures that include:

(a) requirements for its partners and *staff* to report where applicable in relation to an *entity relevant to an engagement* by the *firm*:

- family and other personal relationships involving such an entity;
- financial interests in such an entity;
- decisions to join such an entity.

(b) monitoring of compliance with the *firm*'s policies and procedures relating to integrity, objectivity and independence. Such monitoring procedures include, on a test basis, periodic review of the *engagement partners'* documentation of the consideration of the integrity, objectivity and independence of the *firm*, its partners and *staff*, addressing, for example:

- financial interests in *entities relevant to an engagement* by the *firm*;
- economic dependence on *entities relevant to an engagement* by the *firm*;
- the performance of *non-audit / additional services*;
- *engagement partner* rotation;

---

⁹ *Monitoring of compliance with ethical requirements will often be performed as part of a broader quality control process.* ISQC (UK) 1 Quality Control for Firms that Perform Audits and Reviews of Financial Statements and other Assurance and Related Services Engagements *establishes requirements in relation to a firm's responsibilities for its system of quality control for audits.*

(c)   identification of the entities which partners and *staff*, and, where applicable, *persons closely associated* with them, need to be independent from;

(d)   arrangements for prompt communication of possible or actual breaches of the *firm*'s policies and procedures to the relevant *engagement partners*;

(e)   evaluation by *engagement partners* of the implications of any identified possible or actual breaches of the *firm*'s policies and procedures that are reported to them;

(f)   reporting by *engagement partners* of particular circumstances or relationships as required by this Ethical Standard;

(g)   operation of an enforcement mechanism to promote compliance with policies and procedures;

(h)   empowerment of its *staff* to communicate without fear to senior levels within the *firm* any concerns about the *firm*'s commitment to quality work and professional judgment and values, including issues of integrity, objectivity or independence that concerns them; this includes establishing confidential communication channels open to *staff*, encouraging *staff* to use these channels and ensuring that *staff* who use these channels are not discriminated against and are not subject to disciplinary proceedings as a result.

Ethics Partner

The senior management of the *firm* shall designate a partner in the *firm* possessing the necessary seniority, relevant experience, authority and leadership levels (the 'Ethics Partner') as having responsibility for ensuring the *firm*'s compliance with supporting ethical provision 1.1. The *Ethics Partner* is supported, where appropriate, by other persons with relevant experience in the *firm*, comprising an 'Ethics Function'. The *Ethics Partner* shall have direct reporting lines to the *firm*'s leadership Board and to the *firm*'s independent non-executives, where applicable.   **1.12**

Save where the circumstances contemplated in paragraph 1.20 apply, the responsibilities of the *Ethics Partner* shall include: **1.13**

(a)   the adequacy of the *firm*'s policies and procedures relating to integrity, objectivity and independence, meeting the ethical outcomes required by the overarching principals and supporting ethical provisions, and compliance with the requirements of this Ethical Standard, and the effectiveness of its communication to its partners and *staff* on these matters within the *firm*; and

(b)   providing related guidance to individual partners and *staff* with a view to achieving a consistent approach to the application of this Ethical Standard.

If differences of opinion arise between the *Ethics Partner* and persons consulting him or her, the *firm*'s policies and procedures for dealing with and resolving differences of opinion shall be followed[10].   **1.14**

The *Ethics Partner* is an individual with seniority and authority at leadership levels within the *firm*, possessing relevant experience, and whose decisions and advice on ethical matters will be respected by persons at all levels within the *firm*, including by any more senior partners. Experience of audit and/or other *public interest assurance engagements* would be useful.   **1.15**

The *Ethics Partner* shall not undertake another role within the *firm* which conflicts with their responsibilities as Ethics Partner.   **1.16**

---

[10] *ISQC (UK) 1, paragraph 43, requires firms to establish policies and procedures for dealing with and resolving differences of opinion with those consulted.*

1.17   Where the *Ethics Partner* undertakes this role together with a role such as Compliance or Risk Management he or she ensures that the responsibilities of the *Ethics Partner* take precedence over the responsibilities of other functions. Where the *Ethics Partner* is supported by an Ethics Function, the *Ethics Partner* retains overall responsibility for operation of that function and the decisions made and advice given by it.

1.18   In the case of *firms* that undertake *engagements* for *public interest entities* (PIEs) or other *listed entities*, the *Ethics Partner* has direct access to the *firm*'s independent non-executives where such roles are introduced in the *firm*[11] or, alternatively, to the *firm*'s most senior governance body.

1.19   In assessing the effectiveness of the *firm*'s communication of its policies and procedures relating to integrity, objectivity and independence, the *Ethics Partner* considers whether ethics are covered properly in the *firm*'s induction programmes, professional training and continuing professional development for all partners and *staff. Ethics Partners* also provide guidance on matters referred to them and on matters, which they otherwise become aware of, where a difficult and objective judgment needs to be made or a consistent position reached. The *Ethics Partner* is proactive in considering the ethical implications of developments in the business of the *firm* and the environment in which it operates and in providing advice and guidance to partners and *staff* where appropriate.

1.20   In *firms* with three or fewer partners who are 'Responsible Individuals'[12], it may not be practicable for an *Ethics Partner* to be designated. In these circumstances all partners will regularly discuss ethical issues amongst themselves, so ensuring that they act in a consistent manner and observe the overarching principles and supporting ethical provisions set out in this Ethical Standard. In the case of a sole practitioner, advice on matters where a difficult and objective judgment needs to be made is obtained through the ethics helpline of the practitioner's professional body, or through discussion with a practitioner from another *firm*. In all cases, it is important that such discussions are documented.

1.21   **To be able to discharge his or her responsibilities, the *Ethics Partner* shall be provided with sufficient staff support and other resources (the Ethics Function), commensurate with the size of the *firm*. Alternative arrangements shall be established to allow for:**

- **the provision of guidance on those audits or other *public interest assurance engagements* where the *Ethics Partner* is the *engagement partner*; and**
- **situations where the *Ethics Partner* is unavailable, for example due to illness or holidays.**

Where such support is shared with other functions such as Compliance or Risk Management, the *Ethics Partner* shall establish policies and procedures to ensure that:

- **matters delegated to the Ethics Function by the *Ethics Partner*, whether directly or indirectly through the operation of delegation policies established by the *Ethics Partner*, are clearly identified in internal documentation as relating to the *Ethics Partner* role and are addressed and supervised in a manner consistent with the *Ethics Partner* role, avoiding conflicts with other objectives; and**

---

[11] Firms *that comply with the Audit Firm Governance Code will have appointed independent non-executives who should have the majority on a body that oversees public interest matters. Other firms may also have independent non-executives.*

[12] *A 'Responsible Individual' is a partner or employee of the* firm *who is responsible for audit work and designated as such under the audit regulations of a Recognised Supervisory Body.*

- **all matters required to be communicated to, consulted upon with, or approved by the *Ethics Partner* are communicated to him or her or an authorised delegate personally, on a timely basis.**

Breaches

Whenever a possible or actual breach of this Ethical Standard, or of policies and procedures established pursuant to the overarching principles and supporting ethical provisions and requirements established in it, is identified, the *engagement partner*, in the first instance, and the *Ethics Partner*, where appropriate, assesses the implications of the breach, determines whether there are safeguards that can be put in place or other actions that can be taken to address any potential adverse consequences and considers whether there is a need to resign or withdraw from the *engagement*. **1.22**

An inadvertent violation of this Ethical Standard does not necessarily call into question the *firm*'s ability to give an audit or other public interest assurance opinion, provided that: **1.23**

(a) the *firm* has established policies and procedures that require all partners, *staff* and other *covered persons* to report any breach promptly to the *engagement partner* or to the *Ethics Partner*, as appropriate;
(b) the *engagement partner* or *Ethics Partner* promptly notifies the relevant partner, member of *staff* or other *covered person* that any matter which has given rise to a breach is to be addressed as soon as possible and ensures that such action is taken;
(c) safeguards, where appropriate, are applied, (for example, having another partner review the work done by the relevant partner, member of *staff* or other *covered person* or removing him or her from the *engagement team* or from otherwise being a *covered person*; and
(d) the actions taken and the rationale for them are documented.

Non-involvement in Management Decision-taking

Supporting ethical provision 2.1D requires that the *firm* and each *covered person* is not involved in the decision-taking of an *entity relevant to the engagement*. Paragraph 5.167R of Section 5 of Part B of this Ethical Standard requires in accordance with the EU Audit Regulation that, in the case of a *statutory audit* of a *public interest entity*, *non-audit services* shall not be provided that involve playing any part in the management or decision-making of an *audited entity*. **1.24**

It is not possible to specify all types of decision that are the responsibility of management, but they typically involve leading and directing the entity, including making significant judgments and taking decisions regarding the acquisition, deployment and control of human, financial, physical and intangible resources. Examples of judgments and decisions that should not be made by the *firm* or a *covered person* include: **1.25**

- Setting policies and strategic direction;
- Directing and taking responsibility for the actions of the entity's employees;
- Authorising transactions;
- Deciding which recommendations of the *firm* or other third parties should be implemented;
- Taking responsibility for the preparation and fair presentation of financial statements in accordance with the applicable financial reporting framework;
- Taking responsibility for the preparation and presentation of *subject matter information* in the case of an other *public interest assurance engagement*; and
- Taking responsibility for designing, implementing and maintaining internal control.

Identification and Assessment of Threats

1.26 The *engagement partner* identifies and assesses the circumstances which could adversely affect the integrity or objectivity of the *firm* or of *covered persons* ('threats'), including any that could impair independence, and applies procedures ('safeguards'), which will either:

(a) eliminate the threat (for example, by eliminating the circumstances, such as removing an individual from the *engagement team* or disposing of a financial interest in the entity); or

(b) reduce the threat to level at which independence is not compromised.

1.27D **If, during the period covered by the financial statements or by an other *public interest assurance engagement*, an *entity relevant to the engagement* is acquired by, merges with, or acquires another entity, the *firm* and each relevant engagement partner shall identify and evaluate any current or recent interests or relationships, including any *non-audit / additional services* provided to that entity, which, taking into account available safeguards, could compromise the integrity, objectivity or independence of the *firm* or *covered persons* and the ability to continue with the *engagement* after the effective date of the merger or acquisition. As soon as possible, and in any event within three months, the *firm* and each relevant *engagement partner* shall take all such steps as may be necessary to terminate any current interests or relationships that would compromise integrity, objectivity or independence and shall, where possible, adopt safeguards to eliminate or reduce any threat to integrity or objectivity, including any threats that could impair independence, arising from prior and current interests and relationships, to a level where independence is not compromised. [AD 22.6]**

Threats to Integrity, Objectivity and Independence

1.28 When complying with supporting ethical provisions 2.1D – 2.3D, conditions and relationship that could give rise to threats to the integrity, objectivity or independence of the *firm* or *covered persons* are communicated to the appropriate person, having regard to the nature of the threats and to the part of the *firm* and the identity of any person involved. The consideration of all threats on an individual and cumulative[13] basis and the action taken is documented. If the *engagement partner* is personally involved in the threat, or is unsure about the action to be taken, the matter is resolved through consultation with the *Ethics Partner* / Function who should be provided with all facts relevant to consideration of the issue.

1.29 The principal types of threats to the integrity, objectivity and independence of the *firm* and *covered persons* are:

- **self-interest threat**
  A self-interest threat arises when any of the *firm*, its partners, *staff* or other *covered persons*, has financial or other interests which might cause the *firm* or any *covered person* to be, or perceived to be, reluctant to take actions in connection with the engagement that would be adverse to such interests of the *firm* or any *such person*. For example, such interests may include holding an investment in the entity, seeking to provide additional services to the entity or needing to recover long-outstanding fees from the entity. In relation to *non-audit / additional services*, the main self-interest threats concern fees and economic dependence and these are addressed in Section 4 of this Ethical Standard.

---

[13] *For this purpose, 'cumulative' means all current relationships and any past completed relationships that may be expected to have a continuing relevance to the auditor's independence and consideration of the threats that might exist.*

- **self-review threat**

  A self-review threat arises when the results of *non-audit / additional services*, or where the *subject matter* of such services, whether performed by the *firm*, the *engagement team* or others within the *firm*, are addressed in the *engagement* or reflected in the amounts included or disclosed in the financial statements or other *subject matter information* of the *engagement*. For example, a self-review threat may arise where the *firm* has been involved in maintaining the accounting records, or undertaking valuations that are incorporated in financial statements that the *firm* audits or reports on in relation to an initial public offering. In the course of the *engagement*, the persons conducting the *engagement* may need to re-evaluate the work performed in the *non-audit / additional service*. As, by virtue of providing the *non-audit / additional service*, the *firm* is associated with aspects of the preparation of the financial statements or other *subject matter* or *subject matter information* relating to the *non-audit / additional services*, the *firm* or *covered person* may be, or may be perceived to be, unable to take an impartial view of relevant aspects of those financial statements or other *subject matter information*.

  In assessing the significance of the self-review threat, the persons conducting the *engagement* consider the extent to which the *non-audit / additional service* will:

  o   involve a significant degree of subjective judgment; and
  o   have a material effect on the preparation and presentation of the financial statements or other *subject matter information* or *subject matter* of the *engagement*. [ES 5.33]

  Where a significant degree of judgment is involved in a *non-audit / additional service* relating to the financial statements, or other *subject matter information*, or to the *subject matter* of an *engagement*, the persons conducting the *engagement* may be inhibited from questioning that judgment in the course of the *engagement*. Whether a significant degree of subjective judgment is involved will depend upon whether the *non-audit / additional service* involves the application of well-established principles and procedures, and whether reliable information is available. If such circumstances do not exist because the *non-audit / additional service* is based on concepts, methodologies or assumptions that require judgment and are not established by the entity or by authoritative guidance, the integrity and objectivity of the *firm* and *covered persons* and their independence could be compromised. Where the provision of a proposed *non-audit / additional service* would also have a material effect on the financial statements, or other *subject matter information*, or on the *subject matter* of an *engagement*, it is unlikely that any safeguard can eliminate or reduce the self-review threat to a level where independence is not compromised.

  In relation to an *investment circular reporting engagement*, there is, for example, a self-review threat where a *firm* prepares an accountant's report on historical financial information which has been included in, or formed part of, financial statements which have already been subject to audit by the same *firm*. In such situations, where the two engagement teams are not independent of each other, the *engagement partner* evaluates the significance of the self-review threat created. If this is other than clearly insignificant, safeguards are applied, such as the appointment of an *engagement quality control reviewer* who has not been involved in the audit.

- **management threat**

  Supporting ethical provision 2.1D requires that the *firm* and each *covered person* is not involved in the decision-taking of an *entity relevant to the engagement*. Paragraph 5.167R of Section 5 of Part B of this Ethical Standard requires in accordance with the EU Audit Regulation that, in the case of a *statutory audit* of a *public interest entity, non-audit services* shall not be provided that involve playing any part in the management or decision-making of an *audited entity*. Some activities that may be undertaken by the *firm* or its *staff* may give rise to a threat of being involved in making decisions that are the responsibility of management. A threat to integrity, objectivity and independence also arises where the *firm* provides *non-audit / additional services* and, based on that work, management are required to make judgments and take decisions. The persons conducting the service may become closely aligned with the views and interests of management and this may erode the distinction between the entity and the *firm*, in turn, impairing or calling into question the ability of the persons conducting an *engagement* to apply a proper degree of professional scepticism. The integrity and objectivity of the *firm* and *covered persons could be adversely affected* and their independence could be compromised.

In determining whether a *non-audit / additional service* does or does not give rise to a management threat, the persons conducting the engagement consider whether there is '*informed management*'. *Informed management* exists when:

○   a member of management (or senior employee of the entity) has been designated by the entity to receive the results of the *non-audit / additional service* and has been given the authority to make any judgments and decisions of the type set out in paragraphs 1.24 and 1.25 that are needed;

○   that member of management has the capability to make independent management judgments and decisions on the basis of the information provided; and

○   the results of the *non-audit / additional service* are communicated to the entity and, where judgments or decisions are to be made by management they are supported by an objective analysis of the issues to consider and the entity is given the opportunity to decide between reasonable alternatives.

In the absence of such *informed management* it is unlikely that any other safeguards can eliminate a management threat or reduce it to a level where independence is not compromised.

> In relation to an *investment circular reporting engagement*, a management threat arises, for example, when the *firm* undertakes work that involves making judgments and taking decisions, which are the responsibility of the management of the party responsible for issuing the *investment circular* containing the financial information or the party on whose financial information the *firm* is reporting in relation to:
>
> ○   the transaction (for example, where it has been working closely with a company in developing a divestment strategy); or
>
> ○   the financial information that is the subject of the *investment circular reporting engagement* (for example, deciding on the assumptions to be used in a profit forecast).

● **advocacy threat**

An advocacy threat arises when the *firm* undertakes work that involves acting as an advocate for an *entity relevant to an engagement*, and supporting a position taken by management in an adversarial or promotional context (for example, by acting as a legal advocate for the entity in litigation or a regulatory investigation, or undertaking an active responsibility for the marketing of an entity's shares). In order to act in an advocacy role, the *firm* has to adopt a position closely aligned to that of management. This creates both actual and perceived threats to the integrity, objectivity and independence of the *firm* and *covered persons*. For example, where the *firm*, acting as advocate, has supported a particular contention of management, it may be difficult for the persons conducting the *engagement* to take an impartial view of this in the context of an audit of the financial statements.

Where the provision of a *non-audit / additional service* would require the *firm*, its partners or staff to act as an advocate for the entity in relation to matters that are material to the financial statements or other *subject matter information*, or to the *subject matter* of an *engagement*, it is unlikely that any safeguards can eliminate or reduce the advocacy threat to a level where independence would not be compromised.

- **familiarity (or trust) threat**
  A familiarity (or trust) threat arises when the *firm* or a *covered person* predisposed to accept, or is insufficiently questioning of, the point of view of an *entity relevant to the engagement. Such threats may arise*, for example, where close personal relationships are developed with such an entity's personnel through long association with the entity.
- **intimidation threat**
  An intimidation threat arises when the conduct of the *firm* or a *covered person* is influenced by fear or threats (for example, where the persons conducting the *engagement* encounter an aggressive and / or dominating individual).

These categories of threat may not be entirely distinct and certain circumstances may give rise to more than one type of threat. For example, where a *firm* wishes to retain the fee income from a large *entity relevant to an engagement*, but encounters an aggressive or dominating individual, there may be a self-interest threat as well as an intimidation threat. Furthermore, relationships with *connected parties* of the entity (such as an *affiliate*) may give rise to similar threats.

Threats to the integrity and objectivity of the *firm* and *covered persons*, including threats **1.30** that could compromise independence, may, for example, arise where the *firm* is appointed to provide *non-audit / additional services* for an entity not relevant to an *engagement* by the *firm*, but where an entity that is relevant to an *engagement* by the *firm* makes this decision. In such cases, even if the entity not relevant to an *engagement* by the *firm* pays the fee for the *non-audit / additional service* services, the *firm* considers the implication of the threats (especially the self-interest threat) that arise from the appointment.

Threats to the integrity or objectivity of the *firm* and *covered persons*, including threats that **1.31** could compromise independence, may also arise where a *non-audit / additional service* is provided by the *firm* to a third party which is connected (through a relationship) to an *entity relevant to an engagement* by the *firm*, and the outcome of that service has a material impact on the financial statements of the entity or other *subject matter, information*, or on the *subject matter* of the *engagement*. For example, such threats may arise if the *firm* provides actuarial services to the pension scheme of an audited entity, which is in deficit and the *firm* subsequently gives an opinion on financial statements that include judgments given in connection with that service.

Similarly threats may arise where the *firm* or any *covered person* has a relationship with **1.32** any *connected party* of the entity. Where any member of the *engagement team* is aware of such relationships, an assessment is made of whether independence is compromised (see also paragraph 1.37).

The *firm* shall establish policies and procedures to require the *engagement partner* 1.33 to identify and assess the significance of threats to the integrity and objectivity of the *firm* and *covered persons* on an individual and cumulative[10] basis, including any threats that may compromise independence:

(a) **when considering whether to accept or retain an *engagement*;**
(b) **when planning the *engagement*;**

(c) **when forming an opinion and signing the report on the financial statements or other *subject matter information*;**[14]

(d) **when considering whether to accept or continue to provide non-audit / additional services to an *engagement* by the *firm*; and**

(e) **when potential threats are reported to him or her.**

1.34 An initial assessment of the threats to integrity, objectivity and independence is required when the *engagement partner* is considering whether to accept or retain an *engagement*. That assessment is reviewed and updated at the planning stage of each *engagement*. If consideration of whether to accept or retain an *engagement* does not arise, for example where responsibility for the *engagement* is assigned by legislation (e.g. for certain bodies in the public sector), an assessment of the threats to integrity, objectivity and independence is still undertaken. At the end of the *engagement* process, when forming an opinion on the financial statements or other *subject matter information* but before issuing the report, the *engagement partner* draws an overall conclusion as to whether all threats to integrity or objectivity including any that may compromise independence have been properly addressed on an individual and cumulative basis in accordance with this Ethical Standard. If, at any time, the *firm* is invited to provide *non-audit / additional services*, the *engagement partner* considers the impact this may have on the integrity, objectivity and independence of the *firm*, its partners or *staff*.

1.35 **When identifying and assessing threats to the integrity or objectivity of the *firm* or any *covered persons*, including any that may compromise independence, the *engagement partner* shall take into account current relationships with the entity (including *non-audit / additional services* provided and known relationships with *connected parties* of the entity) and with other parties in certain circumstances (see paragraph 1.37), that existed prior to the current *engagement* and any known to be in prospect following the current *engagement*.**

> **For an *investment circular reporting engagement*, the *relevant period* for consideration covers the period during which the engagement is undertaken and any additional period before that but subsequent to the balance sheet date of the most recent audited financial statements**[15] **of the *entity relevant to the engagement*. A *firm*'s procedures will include reference to records of past and current services / engagements whenever a new *investment circular reporting engagement* is proposed.**

1.36 The requirement in paragraph 1.35 is because those prior and subsequent relationships may be perceived as likely to influence the *firm* or *covered persons* in the performance of the *engagement* or as otherwise compromising the integrity, objectivity or independence of the *firm* or *covered persons*.

1.37 Threats to the integrity or objectivity of the *firm* and *covered persons*, including those that may compromise independence, may arise where a service is provided by the *firm* to a third party which is connected (through a relationship) to an *entity relevant to an engagement* by the *firm*, and the outcome of that service has a material impact on the financial statements or other *subject matter information* of the entity. For example, if the *firm* provides actuarial services to the pension scheme of an *audited entity*, which is in deficit, and the *firm* subsequently gives an opinion on financial statements that include judgments given in connection with that service.

---

[14] *In the case of listed entities, the auditor also assesses whether there is any threat to the auditor's integrity, objectivity or independence when discharging responsibilities in relation to preliminary announcements and when reporting on interim results.*

[15] *In the case of newly incorporated clients (not part of an established group of companies), where there has been no financial statement audit, this period is from the date of incorporation.*

Where the entity *relevant to an engagement* or a third party calls into question the integrity, objectivity or independence of the *firm* in relation to a particular entity, the *Ethics Partner* shall carry out such investigations as may be appropriate and determine what action, if any, is needed.

1.38

Investment Circular Reporting Engagements

When identifying threats to integrity or objectivity including any that could impair independence, *reporting accountants* consider circumstances and relationships with a number of different parties. For example, the *entities relevant to the engagement* may constitute one or more parties, dependent on the circumstances of the transaction which is the subject of the *investment circular*[16]. Where the party responsible for issuing the *investment circular* is different from the party whose financial information is included in the *investment circular*, the *reporting accountant* makes an assessment of independence with respect to each of these parties, applying the alternative procedures set out in paragraph 1.40 as necessary.

1.39

Where either:

1.40

- an *investment circular reporting engagement* is undertaken to provide a report on the financial information relating to an entity audited by the *firm* but the *reporting accountant's* report is to be published in an *investment circular* issued by another entity that is not an entity audited by the *firm*; or
- the *reporting accountant's* report is to be published in an *investment circular* issued by an entity audited by the *firm* but the *reporting accountant's* report is on financial information relating to another entity that is not an entity audited by the *firm*,

it may not be practicable in the time available to identify all relationships and other services or engagements recently undertaken by the *firm* for the non-audit *entity relevant to the engagement* and its *significant affiliates*. In such instances the *reporting accountant* undertakes those enquiries[17] that are practical in the time available into the relationships and other services / engagements that the *firm* has with the non-audit *entity relevant to the engagement* and, having regard to its obligations to maintain confidentiality, addresses any identified threats. Having done so, the *reporting accountant* discloses to those charged with governance of the issuing *entity relevant to the engagement* that a consideration of all known threats has been undertaken and, where appropriate, safeguards applied, but that this does not constitute a full evaluation of all relationships and other services provided to the non-audit *entity relevant to the engagement*.

In addition to considering independence with respect to each *entity relevant to the engagement*, the *reporting accountant* shall also consider relationships with other parties who are connected with the *investment circular*. These parties shall include the sponsor or nominated advisor, other parties from whom, in accordance with the engagement letter, the *reporting accountant* takes instructions and other entities directly involved in the transaction which is the subject of the *investment circular*.[18]

1.41

---

[16] *For example, where a report on a target company's financial statements is prepared by that company's auditors for inclusion in the acquiring company's* investment circular.

[17] *For example, these enquiries are likely to include reviewing the list of engagements recorded in the* firm's *accounting systems and an enquiry of individuals within the* firm *who are responsible for maintaining such systems as to whether any confidentially coded engagements could be relevant.*

[18] *Where such entities are part of a complex group or corporate structure, the* reporting accountant *considers issues relating to the wider group and not just the entity directly involved in the transaction.*

1.42   The *reporting accountant* considers the circumstances involved and uses judgment to assess whether it is probable that an objective, reasonable and informed third party would conclude that the *reporting accountant's* integrity or objectivity is impaired and independence is compromised as a result of relationships held with any of these parties.

1.43   In the case of established financial institutions or advisers, the *reporting accountant* may have extensive relationships with these parties, including for the provision of other services or the purchase of goods and services in the ordinary course of business that are not material to any *entity relevant to the engagement*. These relationships will not generally give rise to a significant threat to the *reporting accountant's* integrity or objectivity.

1.44   Relationships with other parties who are connected with the *investment circular* which are outside the ordinary course of business or which are material to any *entity relevant to the engagement* are more likely to give rise to a significant threat to the *reporting accountant's* integrity or objectivity. Consideration of the threats to the *reporting accountant's* integrity or objectivity in relation to other entities will primarily be concerned with matters that could give rise to self-interest and intimidation threats, for example:
- where there is financial dependence on the relationship with the other party arising from fees (including any contingent element) for *investment circular reporting engagements* undertaken by the *firm* as a result of connections with the other parties;
- joint ventures or similar relationships with the other party or with a senior member of their management;
- significant purchases of goods or services which are not in the ordinary course of business or are not on an arm's length basis;
- personal relationships between *engagement team* members and individuals in senior positions within the other party; or
- large direct financial interests in, or loans made by, the other party.

Identification and Assessment of Safeguards

1.45   **If the *engagement partner* identifies threats to the integrity or objectivity of the *firm* or *covered persons*, including any that could compromise independence, he or she shall identify and assess the effectiveness of the available safeguards and apply such safeguards as are sufficient to eliminate the threats or reduce them to a level where independence would not be compromised.**

1.46   The nature and extent of safeguards to be applied depend on the significance of the threats. Where a threat is clearly insignificant, no safeguards are needed.

1.47   Other sections of this Ethical Standard address specific circumstances that can create threats to integrity or objectivity or could impair the independence of the *firm* or *covered persons*. They give examples of safeguards that can, in some circumstances, eliminate the threat or reduce it to level where it would not compromise independence. In some circumstances, the *firm* either does not accept or withdraws from the *engagement* as appropriate or, in the case of threats arising from the provision of *non-audit / additional services*, does not undertake or withdraws from the *non-audit / additional service*.

1.48   This Ethical Standard contains certain additional requirements or prohibitions that apply only in the case of *engagements* for *public interest entities* (PIEs) or *listed entities or in both cases*:

- *Public interest entities* only: paragraphs 1.75R, 2.39(b)(i), 3.10R, 3.18R, 3.19R, 4.34R, 5.167R, 5.168R, 5.170R, 5.171R, 5.172R, 5.173R
- *Listed entities* only (including such entities that are PIEs) other than SME listed entities: paragraphs 5.67(a), 5.74(a), 5.85(a), 5.92, 5.104(a), 5.111, 5.148, 5.155(a)
- *Listed entities* only (including *SME listed entities* and *listed entities* that are PIEs): paragraphs 3.11, 5.47
- *Listed entities* (including *SME listed entities*) and *public interest entities*: paragraphs 1.66, 3.20, 3.21, 4.25, 4.37, 4.42, 4.47

These additional requirements also apply where regulation or legislation requires that the *engagement* for an entity is conducted in accordance with the standards or ethical requirements that are applicable to *engagements* for *public interest entities* or other *listed entities*.

The *firm* shall establish policies and procedures which set out the circumstances in which those additional requirements listed in paragraph 1.48 that apply to *public interest entities* or to *listed entities* or both are applied to other *engagements*. Where such requirements are applied to a *public interest entity* or to a *listed entity* or both, or to an other entity under such policies and procedures, the *engagement partner* shall ensure that fact is communicated to those charged with governance.   1.49

Such policies and procedures take into consideration any additional criteria set by the *firm*, such as the nature of the entity's business, its size, the number of its employees and the range of its stakeholders. For example, a *firm* may decide to extend the additional requirements to *engagements* for certain large private sector entities.   1.50

The *engagement partner* shall not accept or shall not continue an *engagement* if he or she concludes that any threats to the integrity or objectivity of the *firm* or *covered persons* cannot be reduced to a level where independence would not be compromised.   1.51

Where an objective, reasonable and informed third party would regard ceasing to act as the provider of an *engagement* as detrimental to the shareholders of the *audited entity* (or equivalent intended users of the audit or other assurance engagement report) of, or would otherwise be contrary to the public interest, then resignation may not be immediate. However, the *firm* discloses full details of the position to those charged with governance of the entity and, if applicable (e.g. for an *investment circular reporting engagement*), other entities and persons the *firm* is instructed to advise, and establishes appropriate safeguards.   1.52

Other Firms Involved Engagements

In order to use the work of another *firm* (including *network firms*) for the purpose of an *engagement*, the lead *firm* for the *engagement* has to be satisfied that such another *firm* is independent of each *entity relevant to the engagement* in accordance with supporting ethical provision 2.4 of this Ethical Standard.   1.53

The *engagement partner* obtains sufficient appropriate evidence[19] as necessary to be satisfied that *network firms* (whether or not involved in the *engagement*), and third party *firms* whose work is used in the conduct of the *engagement*, are independent of each *entity relevant to the engagement* in accordance with supporting ethical provision 2.4. If   1.54

---

[19] *For an audit, ISA (UK) 600* 'Special Considerations – Audits of Group Financial Statements (Including the Work of Component Auditors)' *requires that the group engagement team shall obtain an understanding of whether the component auditor understands and will comply with the ethical requirements that are relevant to the group audit and, in particular, is independent.*

the *engagement partner* is not able to obtain such evidence, or obtains evidence that the other *firm* does not meet the relevant independence requirements, the *engagement team* cannot use the work of that other *firm* for the purpose of the *engagement*. Work for the purpose of the *engagement* may be undertaken, where possible, by partners and *staff* from the *firm* performing the *engagement* or by another *firm* which is independent of each *entity relevant to the engagement* as required.

1.55   In the case of a *public interest entity* or an other *listed entity*, the *engagement partner* establishes that the *entity relevant to the engagement* has communicated its policy[20] on the use of *firms* to supply *non-audit / additional services* to its *affiliates* and obtains confirmation that the other *firms* involved in the engagement will comply with this policy.

Engagement Quality Control Review

1.56   Requirements for engagement quality control review are established in ISQC (UK) 1.

Overall Conclusion

1.57   **At the end of the *engagement* process, when forming an opinion to be reported, or otherwise reporting on the work undertaken, but before issuing the report, the *engagement partner* shall reach an overall conclusion that any threats to integrity or objectivity including any that could impair independence on an individual and cumulative basis have been properly addressed in accordance with this Ethical Standard. If the *engagement partner* cannot make such a conclusion, he or she shall not report and the *firm* shall resign or otherwise withdraw from the *engagement* unless not permitted to do so by law or regulation.**

1.58   In addition to assessing individual threats to integrity or objectivity including any that could impair independence of the *firm* or *covered persons*, the *engagement partner* assesses the cumulative impact of all the threats identified so as to reach a conclusion that the threats identified, when viewed individually and cumulatively, have been eliminated or reduced to a level where independence would not be compromised.

1.59   If the *engagement partner* remains unable to conclude that any individual threats to integrity or objectivity including any that could impair independence, or that all such threats viewed on a cumulative basis, have been eliminated or reduced to a level where independence would not be compromised, or if there is a disagreement between the *engagement partner* and the *engagement quality control reviewer*, he or she consults the *Ethics Partner / Function*.

1.60   In concluding on these matters, the *engagement partner* is entitled to rely on the completeness and accuracy of the data developed by the *firm*'s systems relating to independence (for example, in relation to the reporting of financial interests by *staff*), unless informed otherwise by the *firm*. In this context 'data' does not include any judgments made about specific matters identified as the responsibility of the *engagement partner* in this Ethical Standard.

Communication with Those Charged with Governance

1.61   **The *engagement partner* shall ensure that those charged with governance of each *entity relevant to an engagement*, and, in the case of an *investment circular reporting***

---

[20] *The UK Corporate Governance Code requires audit committees to develop the company's policy on the engagement of the external auditor to supply* non-audit services.

engagement, any other persons or entities the *firm* is instructed to advise, are appropriately informed on a timely basis of all significant facts and matters that may bear upon the integrity, objectivity and independence of the *firm* or *covered persons.*

The audit committee, where one exists, is usually responsible for oversight of the relationship of an *entity relevant to the engagement* with the *firm* and of the conduct and outcome of the *engagement*. It therefore has a particular interest in being informed about the *firm*'s ability to express an objective opinion on the financial statements or other *subject matter information* or on the *subject matter* of the *engagement*. Where there is no audit committee, or where its responsibilities do not extend to other *public interest assurance engagements*, this role may be undertaken by another body with equivalent responsibilities or by the board of directors.[21]   **1.62**

The aim of these communications is to ensure full and fair disclosure by the *firm* to those charged with governance of each *entity relevant to the engagement* on matters in which they have an interest. These matters will generally include the key elements of the *engagement partner's* consideration of integrity, objectivity and independence, such as: **1.63**

- the principal threats, if any, to integrity or objectivity including any that could impair independence identified by the *firm*, including consideration of all relationships between the entity, its *affiliates* and directors and the *firm*;
- any safeguards adopted and the reasons why they are considered to be effective, including any independent partner review;
- the overall assessment of threats and safeguards;
- information about the general policies and processes within the *firm* for maintaining integrity, objectivity and independence.

For an *investment circular reporting engagement*, if applicable, communications are made also to those from whom, in accordance with the engagement letter, the *firm* takes instructions on matters in which they have an interest. It may be that all of the parties to the engagement letter wish to be informed about all significant facts and matters that bear upon the integrity, objectivity and independence of the *firm* and *covered persons*. In other cases, however, the parties to the engagement letter (other than an *entity relevant to the engagement*) may not wish to be directly involved and may appoint one or more of their number to review these matters on their behalf. At the time of appointment, the *engagement partner* ensures that it is clear in the engagement letter to whom these communications are provided. If no such provision is included in the engagement letter, disclosures will be made to all those from whom, in accordance with the engagement letter, the *firm* takes instructions.   **1.64**

Communications between the *firm* and those charged with the governance of each *entity relevant to the engagement* and, in the case of an *investment circular reporting engagement*, any other persons the *firm* may be instructed to advise, will be needed at the planning stage and whenever significant judgments are made about threats to integrity, objectivity and independence and the appropriateness of safeguards put in place, for example, when accepting to provide *non-audit / additional services*.   **1.65**

In the case of *public interest entities*, and *listed entities*, relevant to an engagement <u>other than an investment circular reporting engagement</u>, the *engagement partner* shall ensure that the audit committee is provided with: **1.66**

(a) a written disclosure of relationships (including the provision of *non-audit / additional services*) that may bear on the integrity, objectivity or independence

---

[21] *Where there is no audit committee or equivalent body, references in this Ethical Standard to communication with the audit committee are to be construed as including communication with the board of directors.*

of the *firm* or *covered persons*. This shall have regard to relationships with the entity, its directors and senior management, its *affiliates*, and its *connected parties*, and the threats to integrity or objectivity, including those that could compromise independence, that these create. It shall also detail any safeguards that have been put in place and why they address such threats, together with any other information necessary to enable the integrity, objectivity and independence of the *firm* and each *covered person* to be assessed;

(b) details of *non-audit / additional services* provided and the fees charged in relation thereto;

(c) written confirmation that the *firm* and each *covered person* is independent;

(d) details of any inconsistencies between this Ethical Standard and the policy of the *entity* for the provision of *non-audit / additional services* by the *firm* and any apparent breach of that policy.

(e) an opportunity to discuss independence issues.

1.67   For an *investment circular reporting engagement*, the *engagement partner* shall ensure those charged with governance of each *entity relevant to the engagement*, and any other persons or entities the *firm* is instructed to advise are provided in writing with:

(i) details of all relationships that the *reporting accountant* considers may reasonably be thought to bear on the integrity, objectivity and independence of the *reporting accountant*, having regard to its relationships with each *entity relevant to the engagement*, its directors and senior management and its *affiliates*. This shall include significant services previously provided by the *firm* and *network firms* involved in the *investment circular reporting engagement* to each *entity relevant to the engagement* and its *significant affiliates*.

(ii) disclosure of:

- all relationships that give rise to a threat to integrity or objectivity between the *reporting accountant* and:

  ○ the sponsor and such other parties from whom the *reporting accountant* takes instructions. Where a party to the engagement letter is an established financial institution or adviser, a generic disclosure that the *firm* has extensive relationships entered into in the ordinary course of business with these parties is sufficient with specific disclosure only being made in the case of relationships which are outside the ordinary course of business or which are material to any party;

  ○ other entities directly involved in the transaction which is the subject of the *investment circular*;

- whether the total amount of fees that the *reporting accountant* is likely to charge an *entity relevant to the engagement* and its *significant affiliates* for the provision of services relating to the transaction which is the subject of the *investment circular* during the *relevant period* is greater than 5% of the fee income of the *firm* in the *relevant period* or the part of the *firm* by reference to which the *engagement partner's* profit share is calculated during the *relevant period*; and

- the related safeguards that are in place and why they are considered effective;

(iii) confirmation that the *firm* and each *covered person* is independent and, where relevant, the circumstances contemplated in paragraph 1.40 exist and that a consideration of all known threats and safeguards has been undertaken, but this does not constitute a full evaluation of all business relationships and other services provided to the entity.

The most appropriate time for these final written confirmations of independence is usually at the conclusion of the *engagement*.   **1.68**

The disclosure in writing of all relationships with the *entity relevant to the engagement*, and its directors and senior management and its *affiliates*, includes all services provided by the *firm* and its network to the entity, its directors and senior management and its *affiliates*, and other services provided to other known *connected parties* that may reasonably be thought to bear on the integrity, objectivity or independence of the *firm* or *covered persons* and the related safeguards that are in place.   **1.69**

For an *audit engagement*, the *engagement partner* ensures that the total amount of fees that the *firm* and its *network firms* have charged to the *audited entity* and its *affiliates* for the provision of services during the reporting period, analysed into appropriate categories are disclosed. The Appendix to this Ethical Standard contains an illustrative template for the provision of such information to an audit committee[22]. Separately, the auditor provides information on any contingent fee arrangements[23], the amounts of any future services which have been contracted, and details of any written proposal to provide *non-audit services* that has been submitted.   **1.70**

The written confirmation that the *firm* and each *covered person* is independent indicates that the *firm* considers that it complies with this Ethical Standard and that, in the *engagement partner's* professional judgment, the integrity, objectivity and independence of the *firm* and each *covered person* is not compromised. If it is not possible to make such a confirmation, the communication will include any concerns that the integrity, objectivity or independence of the *firm* or any *covered person* may be compromised (including instances where the *engagement partner* considers that the independence of an other *firm* involved in the *engagement* is compromised) and an explanation of the actions which necessarily follow from this.   **1.71**

Documentation

The *firm* shall document in the *engagement* working papers all significant threats to the integrity or objectivity, including any that could impair independence, of the *firm* and all *covered persons* as well as the safeguards applied to mitigate those threats and why they mitigate the threats. [AD 22.3]   **1.72D**

The *engagement partner* shall ensure that his or her consideration of the integrity, objectivity and independence of the *firm* and *covered persons* is appropriately documented on a timely basis.   **1.73**

Before accepting or continuing an *engagement*, the *firm* shall assess and document the following: **1.74D**

- **whether it meets the ethical outcomes of the overarching principles and supporting ethical provisions, and complies with the requirements, of this Ethical Standard;**
- **whether there are threats to its integrity, objectivity or independence and the safeguards applied to mitigate those threats and why they mitigate the threats;** [AD 22b.1)

---

[22] *When considering how to present this analysis of fees, the auditor takes account of any applicable legislation.*

[23] *Paragraph 4.25 of Section 4 of Part B of this Ethical Standard requires the engagement partner to disclose to the audit committee, in writing, any contingent fee arrangements for* non-audit / additional services *provided by the* firm *or its* network firms.

1.75R Before accepting or continuing an engagement for a *statutory audit* of a *public interest entity, ~~a statutory auditor or~~* an *audit firm* shall assess and document, in addition to the provisions of ~~Article 22b of Directive 2006/43/EC~~ paragraph 1.74D above, the following:

(a) whether ~~he, she or~~ it complies with the requirements of Articles 424 and 525 of ~~this~~ the EU Audit Regulation;

(b) whether the conditions of Article 1726 of ~~this~~ the EU Audit Regulation are complied with;

(c) ~~without prejudice to Directive 2005/60/EC,~~ the integrity of the members of the supervisory, administrative and management bodies of the *public interest entity.* [AR 6.1]

1.76 The requirement to document these issues contributes to the clarity and rigour of the *engagement partner's* thinking and the quality of his or her judgments. In addition, such documentation provides evidence that the *engagement partner's* consideration of the integrity, objectivity and independence of the *firm* and *covered person* was properly performed and, for *public interest entities* and other *listed entities* and where otherwise applicable, provides the basis for review by the *engagement quality control reviewer*.

1.77 Matters to be documented[27] include all key elements of the process and any significant judgments concerning:

- threats identified, other than those which are clearly insignificant, and the process used in identifying them.

> For an *investment circular reporting engagement* this includes threats in relation to each *entity relevant to the engagement*, those from whom, in accordance with the engagement letter, the *reporting accountant* takes instructions and other entities directly involved in the transaction which is the subject of the *investment circular*;

- safeguards adopted and the reasons why they are considered to be effective;
- review by an *engagement quality control reviewer* or an independent partner;
- overall assessment of threats and safeguards on an individual and cumulative basis, and
- communication with those charged with governance and, where applicable, any other persons or entities the *firm* is instructed to advise.

Effective Date

1.78 This Ethical Standard becomes effective on 17 June 2016.

1.79 *Firms* may complete *engagements* relating to periods commencing before 17 June 2016 in accordance with existing ethical standards, putting in place any necessary changes in the subsequent engagement period.

---

[24] *See Section 4, paragraphs 4.6R, 4.7R and 4.34R – 4.36R, of Part B of this Ethical Standard.*

[25] *See Section 5, paragraphs 5.167R – 5.173R, of Part B of this Ethical Standard.*

[26] *See Section 3, paragraphs 3.9, 3.10R, 3.18R, 3.19R, of Part B of this Ethical Standard.*

[27] *The necessary working papers can be combined with those prepared pursuant to paragraph 24 of ISA (UK) 220* Quality Control for an Audit of Financial Statements, *which requires that: 'The auditor shall include in the audit documentation conclusions on compliance with independence requirements that apply to the* audit engagement, *and any relevant discussions with the* firm *that support these conclusions.'*

Engagements to provide tax services wholly or partly on a *contingent fee basis* to a *listed* **1.80**
entity relevant to an engagement that is not an *SME listed entity* (see paragraph 5.85 of
Section 5 of Part B of this Ethical Standard), or a *significant affiliate* of such an entity,
entered into before 17 June 2016 may continue until currently active services are completed
in accordance with the engagement terms as long as:

- the engagement was permitted under the existing ethical standards; and
- safeguards established continue to be applied

A 'currently active service' is one where the entity has already asked the *firm* for advice in
relation to a particular matter and the *firm* has commenced work in relation to that matter.
It does not include advice on future matters that may, for example, be provided for in an
open ended engagement/contract.

Section 2 – Financial, Business, Employment and Personal Relationships

Financial Relationships

General Considerations

A financial interest in an entity is an interest in a *financial instrument* issued, guaranteed   **2.1**
or otherwise supported by an entity, including rights and obligations to acquire such an
interest and derivatives directly related to such an interest.

A financial interest may be: **2.2**

(a) a 'direct financial interest', held by way of

   (i)   direct ownership of the *financial instrument*; or
   (ii) a 'direct beneficial interest' – i.e. an interest held through an intermediary which
         is controlled by that person holding the financial interest or where that person
         has the ability to influence the intermediary's investment policy.

         For example, a direct beneficial interest may exist by virtue of the person being
         an identified potential beneficiary under a trust, or under a will relating to an
         estate, where the trust or estate holds an underlying direct financial interest and
         the person has such control or influence over the trust or estate; or

(b) an 'indirect financial interest', held through an intermediary (other than an
     intermediary over which the person holding the financial interest has control or
     influence as described in (a)).

For example, an indirect financial interest may be held through a diversified collective
investment scheme, such as an authorised unit or investment trust, an open ended
investment company, managed funds such as pensions or life insurance or other similar
investment schemes with diversified investments, diversified investors and independent
investment managers.

For an *engagement* *other than an investment circular reporting engagement*, save   **2.3D**
where otherwise required when the circumstances contemplated in paragraphs 2.7,
2.9, 2.12, 2.18 and 2.20 apply, and always subject to the prohibitions on holding
financial interests set out in paragraph 2.4D, the *firm*, each partner in the *firm*,
each *covered person* and any *persons closely associated* with any such partner or
***covered person*, shall not hold:**
(a) any direct financial interest in an *entity relevant to the engagement* or an entity
**   that is an *affiliate* of such an entity; or**

(b) any indirect financial interest in an *entity relevant to the engagement* or any entity that is an *affiliate* of such an entity, that is material to the *firm*, or the person or the intermediary; or

(c) any other indirect financial interest in an *entity relevant to the engagement* or an entity that is an *affiliate* of such an entity, where the person holding it has both:

    (i) the ability to influence the investment decisions of the intermediary; and

    (ii) actual knowledge of the existence of the underlying holding of a direct financial interest by the intermediary. [AD22.4]

2.4D The *firm*, each of the *firm's key audit partners* and each of the *firm's directly involved covered persons* for any *engagement* other than an *investment circular reporting engagement*, and any *persons closely associated* with the *firm* or any such partner or *covered person*, shall not:

(a) hold any material *financial interest* (other than an indirect financial interest held through a diversified collective investment scheme) in, or engage in any transaction in, any *financial instrument* of any *entity relevant to an engagement* in the *area* of *activity*[28] in which they (or in the case of a *person closely associated*, the *area of activity* in which the *firm*, *key audit partner* or *covered person* with whom they are closely associated) are involved relating to *engagements* other than *investment circular reporting engagements*; or

(b) hold any financial interest, other than an indirect financial interest held through a diversified collective investment scheme, in:

    (i) any *entity relevant to an engagement* other than an *investment circular reporting engagement* for which they are a *directly involved covered person*; or

    (ii) an entity which is an *affiliate* of such an entity; or

    (iii) any other entity otherwise related to such an entity in circumstances where holding such a financial interest may cause, or may be generally perceived as causing, a conflict of interest;

or, if a person holds such a financial interest they shall be excluded from any role by virtue of which they would be a *covered person* for any such engagement. [AD 22.2]

2.5 For an *investment circular reporting engagement*, the *firm* and each *covered person*, and *persons closely associated with them*, shall not hold during the engagement period:

(a) a direct financial interest; or

(b) an indirect financial interest that is material to the *firm* or to the individual or to the intermediary; or

(c) any other indirect financial interest where the person holding it has both (i) the ability to influence the investment decisions of the intermediary, and (ii) actual knowledge of the of the existence of the underlying investment;

in any *entity relevant to the engagement* or in an entity that is an *affiliate* of, or otherwise related to, such an entity.

---

[28] *In relation to a* key audit partner *or other* covered person, *or a* person closely associated *with such a partner or* covered person, *any* engagements *for which the* covered person *is a* directly involved covered person *and any other* engagements, *in relation to which the* engagement partner *practices in the same office or business unit as the* covered person.

The requirements in paragraphs 2.3D to 2.5 have been established because threats to   **2.6**
integrity, objectivity and independence in relation to *engagements*, where the *firm* or
other persons have direct or indirect financial interests in an *entity relevant to an engagement*
in the circumstances referred to in those paragraphs, are such that it is considered that no
safeguards can eliminate them or reduce them to a level where they would not compromise
independence, and they are therefore precluded.

Except where prohibited in accordance with paragraph 2.4D, where a *person closely*   **2.7**
associated with a partner in the *firm* who is not a *covered person* for an *engagement* of the
firm, has a financial interest in any *entity relevant to the engagement*, or in any *affiliate* of
such an entity, as a consequence of:

- the compensation arrangements of that closely associated person (for example, a
  share option scheme, where the shares have not vested); or
- a decision made, or a transaction undertaken, by an entity with whom that closely
  associated person has a contractual business or employment arrangement (for
  example, a partnership agreement);

such financial interests are not generally considered to threaten integrity or objectivity or
to compromise independence in relation to the *engagement*. However, where such interests
are significant or the relevant partner or other person referred to in paragraph 2.4D has
close working contacts with the *engagement team*, the *Ethics Partner*/Function considers
whether any safeguards need to be put in place.

For the purposes of paragraph 2.3D, where financial interests in a diversified collective   **2.8**
investment scheme that is an *entity relevant to an engagement* of the *firm*, or an *affiliate* of
such an entity, are held by a partner in the *firm*, or by a *person closely associated* with such
a partner and that partner is not a *covered person* for such an *engagement*, such interests are
to be treated as indirect financial interests. Such interests can therefore be held as long as:

(a) they are not material to the individual; and
(b) the individual has no influence over the investment decisions of the entity.

Except where prohibited in accordance with paragraph 2.4D, for the purposes of   **2.9**
paragraph 2.3D, where a person who is a *covered person*, or any *person closely associated*
with them, is a member or shareholder of any *entity that is relevant to an engagement*, as
a result of the entity's membership or equivalent requirements, the *firm* should ensure that
no more than the minimum number of shares necessary to comply with the requirement are
held and should assess whether this financial interest is material to either the entity or the
person holding the interest. Disclosure of such interests should be made to those charged
with governance of such an entity, in accordance with paragraph 1.61 of Section 1 of Part
B of this Ethical Standard.

Where the *firm*, a partner or a *covered person* holds any financial interests that they would   **2.10**
not be permitted to hold, or engages in any transaction in *financial instruments* that they
would not be permitted to engage in, in breach of the requirements in paragraphs 2.3D,
2.4D(a) or 2.5 in circumstances other than those contemplated in paragraphs 2.11 or 2.12,
either: the entire financial interest is disposed of; or, where only a material holding is not
permitted, a sufficient amount of the financial interest is disposed of so that the remaining
interest is no longer material. In addition, in the case of a person, they are excluded from
any role by virtue of which they would be a *covered person*; and, where the holding or
transaction is not permitted in accordance with paragraph 2.4D(a) they are excluded from
any role by virtue of which they would be operating in their area of *activity relating to
engagements* other than *investment circular reporting engagements* that encompasses any
engagements for entities in which the financial interests were held, or in whose *financial*

instruments the person engaged in transactions. In addition, in the case of a *firm*, the *firm* does not accept (or withdraws from) the *engagement*.

2.11   In relation to an *investment circular reporting engagement*, if the existence of the transaction which is connected with the *investment circular* is price sensitive information then disposal of any financial interest in accordance with paragraph 2.10 may not be possible and the *firm* either does not accept the *engagement* or the relevant individuals are not included in the *engagement team*. Where a person holding the financial interests specified would otherwise be a *covered person*, that person is excluded from any role by virtue of which they would be a *covered person* for the purposes of the particular *investment circular reporting engagement*.

2.12   Where a person who is joining the *firm* as a partner or *staff* member, or any *person closely associated* with them, has any financial interests acquired before the person joined the *firm* that they would not be permitted to hold in accordance with the requirements in paragraphs 2.3D or 2.4D, they should:

(i)   Where they would not be permitted to hold the financial interests in accordance with paragraph 2.4D, dispose of those financial interests prior to the person joining the *firm*;

(ii)   Where they would not be permitted to hold the financial interests in accordance with paragraph 2.3D, disposed of those financial interests prior to, or immediately when, the person joins the *firm*, unless:

(a)   the person joining the *firm* is not able to influence the affairs of any *entity relevant to an engagement* in which the interests are held; and

(b)   either there is no market for such interests, or the individual does not have the power to sell or to direct the sale of the interest; and

(c)   the financial interests are not held in an *entity relevant to an engagement* in relation to which the person joining the *firm*:
- is a *covered person*; or
- works in the same part of the *firm* as the *engagement partner* for any such *engagement*; or
- is involved in the provision of a *non-audit / additional service* to any such entity or in an entity that is an *affiliate* of such an entity;

(d)   Where not disposed of prior to, or immediately when, the person joins the *firm*, financial interests that the person would not be permitted to hold in accordance with paragraph 2.3D must be disposed of as soon as possible after the individual holding them becomes able to make a disposal. The *firm* ensures that:

(a)   the deferral of the disposal of such financial interests is approved by the *Ethics Partner*/Function;

(b)   a record is maintained of such individuals and interests, including a description of the circumstances; and

(c)   this information is communicated to the relevant *engagement partner*.

2.13   Where any financial interest specified in paragraph 2.3D is acquired unintentionally, as a result of an external event (for example, inheritance, gift, or merger of *firms* or companies), the disposal of the financial interest is required immediately, or as soon as possible after the relevant person has actual knowledge of, and the right to dispose of, the interest. More specific requirements are set out in paragraph 1.27D of Section 1 of Part B of this Ethical Standard, that apply in circumstances where during the period covered by the financial statements an *audited entity* is acquired by, merges with, or acquires another entity.

2.14   Where the disposal of a financial interest in accordance with paragraphs 2.4D(b), 2.10, 2.11, 2.12 or 2.13 does not take place immediately, the *firm* should adopt safeguards to preserve integrity, objectivity and independence until the financial interest is disposed of. These may include the temporary exclusion of a *covered person* from any role by virtue of which they would be a *covered person* for the *engagement*, or (where continued participation in the *engagement* is not otherwise precluded in accordance with paragraphs 2.3D or 2.4D) a review of the relevant person's work by a partner having sufficient experience and authority to fulfil the role who is not involved in the *engagement*.

Where the *firm* or one of the individuals specified in paragraph 2.3D or 2.5 holds an indirect financial interest but does not have both: **2.15**

(a) the ability to influence the investment decisions of the intermediary; and

(b) actual knowledge of the existence of the underlying investment in the *entity relevant to the engagement*;

there may not be a significant threat to integrity or objectivity and independence. For example, where the indirect financial interest takes the form of an investment in a pension fund, the composition of the funds and the size and nature of any underlying investment in the entity may be known but there is unlikely to be any influence on investment decisions, as the fund will generally be managed independently on a discretionary basis. In the case of an 'index tracker' fund, the investment in the entity is determined by the composition of the relevant index and there may be no threat to integrity or objectivity. As long as the person holding the indirect interest is not directly involved in an *engagement* involving the intermediary, nor able to influence the individual investment decisions of the intermediary, any threat to integrity or objectivity and any impairment of independence may be regarded as clearly insignificant.

Where the *firm* or one of the individuals specified in paragraph 2.4D or 2.5 holds a beneficial interest in a properly operated 'blind' trust, they are (by definition) completely unaware of the identity of the underlying investments. If these include an investment in the entity, this means that they are unaware of the existence of an indirect financial interest. In these circumstances, any threat to integrity or objectivity and any impairment of independence may be regarded as clearly insignificant.   **2.16**

Where a partner in the *firm* or a *covered person* becomes aware that a *close family* member holds any financial interest specified in paragraphs 2.3D, 2.4D or 2.5, that person shall report the matter to the *engagement partner* to take appropriate action. If it is a *close family* member of the *engagement partner*, or if the *engagement partner* is in doubt as to the action to be taken, the *engagement partner* shall resolve the matter through consultation with the *Ethics Partner*/Function.   **2.17**

Financial Interests Held as Trustee

Where a direct or an indirect financial interest in an *entity relevant to the engagement* or in any *affiliate* of such an entity is held in a trustee capacity by a *covered person*, or by a *person closely associated* with them, a self-interest threat may be created because either the existence of the trustee interest may influence the conduct or outcome of the *engagement* or the trust may influence the actions of the entity. Accordingly, such a trustee interest is not held when: **2.18**

●   the relevant person is an identified potential beneficiary of the trust; or

●   the financial interest held by the trust in the entity is material to the trust; or

●   the trust is able to exercise significant influence over the entity or an *affiliate* of the entity; or

●   the relevant person has significant influence over the investment decisions made by the trust, in so far as they relate to the financial interest in the entity; or

●   such a holding is otherwise precluded by the requirements in paragraph 2.4D.

2.19   Where it is not clear whether the financial interest in the entity held by the trust is material to the trust or whether the trust is able to exercise significant influence over the entity, the financial interest is reported to the *Ethics Partner*/Function, so that a decision can be made as to the steps that need to be taken.

2.20   A direct or an indirect financial interest in the entity or its *affiliates* held in a trustee capacity by the *firm* or by a partner in the *firm* who is not a *covered person* or a *person closely associated* with them, cannot be held when the *firm* or relevant person is an identified potential beneficiary of the trust.

Financial Interests Held by Firm Pension Schemes

2.21   Where the pension scheme of a *firm* has a financial interest in an *entity relevant to an engagement*, or in the entity's *affiliates*, and the *firm* has any influence over the trustees' investment decisions (other than indirect strategic and policy decisions), the self-interest threat created is such that no safeguards can eliminate it or reduce it to a level where independence is not compromised. In other cases (for example, where the pension scheme invests through a collective investment scheme and the *firm*'s influence is limited to investment policy decisions, such as the allocation between different categories of investment), the *Ethics Partner* considers the acceptability of the position, having regard to the materiality of the financial interest to the pension scheme.

Loans and Guarantees

2.22   Where *firms, covered persons* or *persons closely associated* with them:

(a)   accept a loan[29] or a guarantee of their borrowings from an *entity relevant to the engagement*; or

(b)   make a loan to or guarantee the borrowings of an *entity relevant to the engagement*,

a self-interest threat and an intimidation threat to integrity or objectivity can be created and independence may be compromised. In a number of situations, as in the case of those addressed in paragraphs 2.23, 2.24 and 2.25, it is considered that no safeguards can eliminate these threats or reduce them to a level where independence is not compromised and accepting and making loans in those circumstances is therefore precluded.

2.23   *Firms, covered persons* **and** *persons closely associated* **with them shall not make a loan to, or guarantee the borrowings of, an** *entity relevant to the engagement*, **or the** *affiliates* **of such an entity, unless this represents a deposit made with a bank or similar deposit taking institution in the ordinary course of business and on normal business terms.**

2.24   *Firms* **shall not accept a loan from, or have their borrowings guaranteed by an** *entity relevant to an engagement*, **or the** *affiliates* **of such an entity, unless:**

(a)   **the entity is a bank or similar deposit taking institution; and**

(b)   **the loan or guarantee is made in the ordinary course of business on normal business terms; and**

(c)   **the loan or guarantee is not material to both the** *firm* **and the entity.**

2.25   *Covered persons* **and** *persons closely associated* **with them shall not accept a loan from, or have their borrowings guaranteed by, the** *entity relevant to the engagement*, **or the** *affiliates* **of such an entity, unless:**

---

[29] *For the purpose of this Ethical Standard, the term 'loan' does not include ordinary trade credit arrangements or deposits placed for goods or services, unless they are material to either party (see paragraph 2.29).*

(a) **the entity is a bank or similar deposit taking institution; and**

(b) **the loan or guarantee is made in the ordinary course of business on normal business terms; and**

(c) **the loan or guarantee is not material to the entity.**

Loans by an *entity relevant to an engagement* that is a bank or similar institution to a **2.26**
covered person, or to *persons closely associated* with them (for example, home mortgages,
bank overdrafts or car loans), do not create an unacceptable threat to integrity or objectivity
that compromises independence, provided that normal business terms apply. However,
where such loans are in arrears by a significant amount, this creates an intimidation threat
that compromises independence. Where such a situation arises, the *covered person* reports
the matter to the *engagement partner* or to the *Ethics Partner*/Function, as appropriate and
ceases to have any involvement with the *engagement*. The *engagement partner* or, where
appropriate, the *Ethics Partner*/Function considers whether any *engagement* work is to be
reperformed.

Business Relationships

A business relationship between: **2.27**

(a) the *firm* or a *covered person*, or *persons closely associated* with them; and

(b) any *entity relevant to the engagement*, or the entity's *affiliates* or its management;

involves the two parties having a common commercial interest. Business relationships
may create self-interest, advocacy or intimidation threats to integrity or objectivity and
independence may be compromised. Examples include:

- joint ventures with the entity or with a director, officer or other individual who
  performs a management role for the entity;
- arrangements to combine one or more services or products of the *firm* with one or
  more services or products of the entity and to market the package with reference to
  both parties;
- distribution or marketing arrangements under which the *firm* acts as a distributor or
  marketer of any of the entity's products or services, or the entity acts as the distributor
  or marketer of any of the products or services of the *firm*;
- other commercial transactions, such as the *firm* leasing its office space from or to the
  entity.

Subject to the alternative procedures outlined in paragraph 1.40 of Section 1 of Part B of
this Ethical standard that may be relevant to an *investment circular reporting engagement*,
a *firm* will identify all business relationships entered into by the *firm, covered persons*, or
persons closely associated with them.

Persons or *firms* referred to in paragraph 2.4D shall not have a business **2.28D**
or other relationship with any *entity relevant to an engagement* within the
period referred in supporting ethical provision 2.1D that would compromise
independence; or, if a person has such a business or other relationship they shall
be excluded from any role by virtue of which they would be a *covered person* for
such an *engagement*. [AD 22.4]

***Firms, covered persons* and *persons closely associated* with them shall not enter into** **2.29**
business relationships with any *entity relevant to the engagement*, or its management
or its *affiliates* except where those relationships:

- involve the purchase of goods or services from the *firm* or the entity in the ordinary course of business and on an arm's length basis and which are not material to either party; or
- would be inconsequential to either party in the view of an objective, reasonable and informed third party.

> For an *investment circular reporting engagement*, the requirement in paragraph 2.29 shall apply during the *relevant period* – the engagement period and any additional period before the engagement period but subsequent to the balance sheet date of the most recent audited financial statements of the entity.

2.30   Where there are doubts about whether a relationship would be inconsequential to either party in the view of and objective, reasonable and informed third party, then the relationship is not regarded as inconsequential.

2.31   Where a business relationship exists, that is not permitted under paragraph 2.29, and has been entered into by:

(a)   *the firm:* either the relationship is terminated or the *firm* does not accept (or withdraws from) the *engagement*;

(b)   *a covered person:* either the relationship is terminated or that person is excluded from any role in which they would be a *covered person*;

(c)   a *person closely associated* with a *covered person:* either the relationship is terminated or the *covered person* is excluded from any role in which they would be a *covered person*.

> In the case of an *investment circular reporting engagement*, where termination of the relationship is necessary it is undertaken before the start of the *relevant period*. If the existence of the transaction which is connected with the *investment circular* is price sensitive information then termination of the business relationship may not be possible and the *firm* either does not accept the *engagement* or the relevant individuals are not included in the *engagement team*. Where a partner with one of the business relationships specified normally has direct supervisory or management responsibility over the *engagement team*, he or she is excluded from this responsibility for the purposes of the particular *investment circular reporting engagement*.

For an *engagement* other than an *investment circular reporting engagement*, where there is an unavoidable delay in the termination of a business relationship, the *firm* adopts safeguards to preserve integrity and objectivity in relation to any relevant *engagements* until the relationship is terminated. These may include a review of the relevant person's *engagement* work or a temporary exclusion of the relevant person from any role in which they would be a *covered person*.

2.32   Compliance with paragraph 2.29 is not intended to prevent a *firm* giving advice in accordance with regulatory requirements[30] to a third party in relation to investment products or services, including those supplied by an *entity relevant to an engagement*. In such circumstances, the *firm* considers the advocacy and self-interest threats that might be created by the provision of this advice where it gives rise to commission or similar payments by the entity to the *firm* and assesses whether any safeguards are required.

2.33   **Where a *covered person* becomes aware that a *close family* member has entered into one of the business relationships specified in paragraph 2.27, or any other business relationship that could impair independence, that person shall report the matter to**

---

[30] Firms *providing such services will be authorised either by the Financial Conduct Authority or by their professional accountancy body acting as a Designated Professional Body.*

the *engagement partner* to take appropriate action. If it is a *close family* member of the *engagement partner* or if the *engagement partner* is in doubt as to the action to be taken, the *engagement partner* shall resolve the matter through consultation with the *Ethics Partner*/Function.

Where there are doubts as to whether a transaction or series of transactions are either in the ordinary course of business and on an arm's length basis or of such materiality that they constitute a threat to the integrity, objectivity or independence of the *firm* or *covered persons*, the *engagement partner* reports the issue: 2.34

- to the *Ethics Partner*/Function, so that a decision can be made as to the appropriate action that needs to be taken to ensure that the matter is resolved; and
- in the case of an *engagement* other than an *investment circular reporting engagement*, to those charged with governance of the entity, together with other significant facts and matters that bear upon the integrity, objectivity or independence of the *firm* and *covered persons*, to obtain their views on the matter.

A *firm* shall not provide an *engagement* to any entity or person where that entity or person is in a position to influence the affairs of the *firm* or the performance of any *engagement* of the *firm*. 2.35

This prohibition applies to: 2.36

(a) any entity that owns any significant part of the *firm*, or is an *affiliate* of such an entity; or

(b) any shareholder, director or other person in a position to direct the affairs of such an entity or its *affiliate*.

A significant ownership is one that carries the ability to influence materially the policy of an entity.[31]

Employment Relationships

Persons or *firms* referred to in paragraph 2.4D shall not have an employment relationship with an *entity relevant to the engagement*, or an *affiliate* of such an entity, within the period referred in supporting ethical provision 2.1D that would compromise independence; or, if a person has such an employment relationship they shall be excluded from any role by virtue of which they would be a *covered person* for such an *engagement*. [AD 22.4] 2.37D

Management Role with an Entity Relevant to an Engagement

A *firm* shall not admit to the partnership, or employ a person in a position as a *covered person*, if that person is also employed by any *entity relevant to the engagement*, or by any *affiliate* of such an entity ('dual employment'). 2.38

Loan Staff Assignments

A *firm* shall not enter into an agreement with an *entity relevant to an engagement* other than an *investment circular reporting engagement*, or with the *affiliates* of such an entity, or otherwise, to provide any partner or employee ('loan staff') to work for 2.39

---

[31] *For companies, competition authorities have generally treated a 15% shareholding as sufficient to provide a material ability to influence policy.*

a temporary period as if that individual were an employee of any such entity or its *affiliates* (a 'loan staff assignment') unless:

(a) the agreement is for a short period of time and does not involve employees or partners performing *non-audit / additional services* that would not be permitted under this Ethical Standard; and

(b) the entity:

    (i) agrees that any individual loan staff concerned will not hold a management position, will not be involved in the decision-taking of the entity and, in the case of an *audited entity* that is a *public interest entity*, will not play any part in the management of the entity; and

    (ii) acknowledges its responsibility for directing and supervising the work to be performed, which will not include such matters as:

       ● making management decisions; or

       ● exercising discretionary authority to commit the entity to a particular position or accounting treatment.

2.40

> A *firm* shall not enter into an agreement with an *entity relevant to an investment circular reporting engagement* to provide any partner or employee ('loan staff') to work for a temporary period as if that individual were an employee of any such entity or its *affiliates* (a 'loan staff assignment') during the *relevant period* or for a period of one year before it unless:
>
> (a) the agreement is for a short period of time and does not involve employees or partners performing *additional services* that would not be permitted under this Ethical Standard; and
>
> (b) the entity:
>
>   (i) agrees that any individual loan staff concerned will not hold a management position in relation to the transaction or the financial information that is the subject of the *investment circular reporting engagement,*; and
>
>   (ii) acknowledges its responsibility for directing and supervising the work to be performed, which will not include such matters as:
>
>   ● making management decisions; or
>
>   ● exercising discretionary authority to commit the entity to a particular position or accounting treatment.

2.41 Where a *firm* agrees to assist an *entity relevant to an engagement* by providing loan staff, threats to objectivity and independence may be created. A management threat may arise if the employee undertakes work that involves making judgments and taking decisions that are properly the responsibility of management. In the context of applying the requirement in paragraph 2.39(a) and 2.40(a), a short period of time is generally expected to be no more than a small number of months.

2.42 A self-review threat may also arise if the individual, during the loan staff assignment, is in a position to influence the preparation of the entity's financial statements or other *subject matter information* or *subject matter* of an *engagement*, and then, on completion of that assignment, is assigned to the *engagement team* for that entity, with responsibility to report on matters for which he or she was responsible whilst on that loan staff assignment.

2.43 Where a partner or employee returns to the *firm* on completion of a loan staff assignment, that individual shall not be given any role on any *engagement* involving any function or activity that he or she performed or supervised during that assignment.

2.44 In considering for how long this restriction is to be observed, the need to realise the potential value to the effectiveness of the *engagement* of the increased knowledge of the entity's business gained through the assignment has to be weighed against the potential threats to integrity or objectivity and the potential for independence to be compromised. Those threats increase with the length of the assignment and with the intended level of responsibility of the individual within the *engagement team*. As a minimum, this restriction will apply to at least the period until the first *engagement* has been completed following the completion of the loan staff assignment.

Partners and Engagement Team Members Joining an Entity Relevant to an Engagement

Where a former partner in the *firm* joins an *entity relevant to an engagement*, the *firm* shall take action as quickly as possible – and, in any event, before any further work is done by the *firm* in connection with any such *engagement* – to ensure that no significant connections remain between the *firm* and the individual, or to withdraw from the *engagement*.   **2.45**

Ensuring that no significant connections remain between the *firm* and the individual requires that: **2.46**

- all capital balances and similar financial interests be fully settled (including retirement benefits) unless these are made in accordance with pre-determined arrangements that cannot be influenced by any remaining connections between the individual and the *firm*; and
- the individual does not participate or appear to participate in the *firm's* business or professional activities by way of employment, consultancy or other contractual arrangement, or in any other way.

***Firms* shall establish policies and procedures that require in relation to any *entity relevant to an engagement* in which an individual is, or was at any time over the previous year (two years in the case of a partner), directly involved:**   **2.47**

(a) for all such *engagements:*
   (i) senior members of the *engagement team* to notify the *firm* of any situation involving their potential employment with any such entity; and
   (ii) other members of the *engagement team* to notify the *firm* of any situation involving their probable employment with any such entity;
(b) for an *engagement* <u>other than an</u> *investment circular reporting engagement*:
   (i) all partners in the *firm* to notify the *firm* of any situation involving their potential employment with any such entity; and
   (ii) any other employee of the *firm* and any other natural person whose services are placed at the disposal of or under the control of the *firm*, where such employee or other person is personally approved as a *statutory auditor* under relevant legislation within the European Union, to notify the *firm* of any situation involving their probable employment with any such entity;
(c) anyone who has given such notice to be removed from the *engagement team*; and
(d) a review of the *engagement* work performed by any resigning or former *engagement team* member in the current and, where appropriate, the most recent *engagement*.

Integrity, objectivity and independence may be threatened where a director, an officer or an employee of any *entity relevant to an engagement* who is in a position to exert direct and significant influence over the preparation of the financial statements or other *subject matter information* or *subject matter* of an *engagement*, has recently been a partner in the *firm*, a member of the *engagement team* or another employee or person whose services are at the disposal or under the control of the *firm*, where such employee or person is personally approved as a *statutory auditor* within the European Union. Such circumstances   **2.48** may create self-interest, familiarity and intimidation threats, particularly when significant connections remain between the individual and the *firm*. Similarly, integrity or objectivity may be threatened and independence compromised when an individual knows, or has reason to believe, that he or she will or may be joining the entity at some time in the future.

2.49   Where a partner in the *firm* or a member of an *engagement team* for an *entity relevant to an engagement* or another person who is personally approved as a *statutory auditor* as described in paragraph 2.48 has left the *firm* and taken up employment with such an entity, the significance of the self-interest, familiarity and intimidation threats is assessed and normally depends on such factors as:

- the position that individual had in the *engagement team* or *firm*;
- the position that individual has taken at the entity;
- the amount of involvement that individual will have with the *engagement team* (especially where it includes former colleagues with whom he or she worked);
- the length of time since that individual was a member of the *engagement team* or employed by the *firm*.

Following the assessment of any such threats, appropriate safeguards are applied where necessary to reduce such threats to a level where the independence of the *firm* or *covered persons* would not be compromised.

2.50   Any review of *engagement* work is performed by a more senior *engagement* professional. If the individual joining the entity is a partner, the review is performed by a partner who is not involved in the *engagement*. Where, due to its size, the *firm* does not have a partner who was not involved in the *engagement*, it seeks either a review by another *firm* or advice from its professional body.

2.51   **As required by legislation[32], a natural person appointed as a *statutory auditor* or *key audit partner* for an entity subject to a *statutory audit* shall not take up:**

(a)   any *key management position*;
(b)   membership of the entity's audit committee;
(c)   membership of any body performing equivalent functions to an audit committee in relation to the entity;
(d)   any other position as director of the entity or, where the entity's affairs are managed by a management body or other committee, membership of that management body or committee;

before the end of:

(a)   in the case of a *public interest entity*, two years; and
(b)   in any other case, one year;

beginning with the day on which the person ceased to be the entity's *statutory auditor* or *key audit partner* in connection with the *statutory audit* of the entity.

2.52   The requirements set out in paragraph 2.51 above reflect legal restrictions imposed on particular individuals who may wish to join an entity subject to a *statutory audit*. Should a partner or other *covered person* join an *entity relevant to an engagement*, threats to integrity, objectivity and independence may arise that a *firm* will need to address. Such threats may also exist where a former partner or other *covered person* is employed by an entity that the *firm* is considering accepting an *engagement* for.

---

[32] *SI 2016/649 The Statutory Auditors and Third Country Auditors Regulations 2016, Schedule 1, paragraph 7.*

Where a partner[33], or another person (including a person whose services are at the disposal or under the control of the *firm*) who is personally approved as a *statutory auditor* as described in paragraph 2.48, is appointed as a director (including as a non-executive director), a member of the audit committee or body performing equivalent functions, or to a *key management position* with an *entity relevant to an engagement*, having previously been a covered person: 2.53

(a) in the case of a partner, at any time during the two years prior to such appointment; or

(b) in the case of another person, at any time during the year prior to such appointment;

the *firm* shall resign from the *engagement* where possible under applicable law or regulation.[34] The *firm* shall not accept an other engagement for the entity until:

(i)   in the case of a partner, a two-year period; or

(ii)   in the case of another person, a one year period;

commencing when the person ceased to be a *covered person*, has elapsed or until the person ceases employment with the entity, whichever is the sooner.

In the circumstances covered by paragraph 2.53, where the responsibility for the *engagement* is assigned by legislation or regulation and the auditor cannot resign from the *engagement* (e.g. in the case of certain public sector bodies) the *firm* shall consider alternative safeguards that can be put in place to reduce threats to integrity or objectivity to a level where independence would not be compromised.   2.54

Where a person who is either a partner or another person (including a person whose services are at the disposal or under the control of the *firm*) who is personally approved as a *statutory auditor* as described in paragraph 2.48 (other than someone covered by paragraph 2.53) or was a former member of an *engagement team*, joins the entity as a director (including as a non-executive director), a member of the audit committee or body performing equivalent functions, or in a *key management position*, within two years of ceasing to be a *covered person* for the entity, the *firm* shall ensure that no significant connections remain between the *firm* and the individual and consider whether the composition of the *engagement team* is appropriate (paragraph 2.45 also applies in the case of a former partner).   2.55

The *firm* evaluates the appropriateness of the composition of the *engagement team* by reference to the factors listed in paragraph 2.49 and alters or strengthens the *engagement team* to address any threat to the integrity, objectivity or independence of the *firm* or *covered persons* that may be identified.   2.56

If a former partner of the *firm*, or another person personally approved as a *statutory auditor* as described in paragraph 2.48 formerly employed by or otherwise at the disposal of or under the control of the *firm*, has joined an entity as a director (including as a non-executive director), a member of the audit committee or body performing equivalent functions, or in a *key management position*, the *firm* shall not accept an *engagement* for the entity where the person had, prior to leaving the *firm* and: 2.57

(a) in the case of a partner, within two years before acceptance of the *engagement*; or

(b) in the case of another person, within one year before acceptance of the *engagement*;

---

[33] *'Partner' includes any individual with authority to bind the* firm *with respect to the performance of a professional services engagement.*

[34] *The timing of the* audit firm's *resignation as auditor is determined in accordance with paragraph 1.52 of Section 1 of Part B of this Ethical Standard.*

been a *covered person* for any *engagement* involving any partner of the *firm* who would be a member of the *engagement team*, or would be the *engagement quality control reviewer*, for the *engagement* were it to be accepted.

2.58 Where a former partner, or person (including a person whose services are at the disposal or under the control of the *firm*) personally approved as a *statutory auditor* as described in paragraph 2.48, left, or ceased to be at the disposal or under the control of, the *firm* earlier than the beginning of the periods specified in paragraph 2.57(a) or (b), the *firm* shall evaluate the significance of any threats to integrity or objectivity and whether independence would be compromised before accepting such an *engagement* for the entity. The *firm* shall not accept the *engagement* unless any threats identified can be reduced to a level where independence would not be compromised.

Family Members Employed by an Entity Relevant to an Engagement

2.59 Where a *covered person*, or any partner in the *firm*, becomes aware that a *person closely associated* with them, or a *close family* member who is not a *person closely associated* with them, is employed by an *entity relevant to the engagement* and that person is in a position to exercise influence on the accounting records or financial statements or other *subject matter information* or *subject matter* of such an *engagement*, that *covered person* or that partner shall either:

(a) in the case of a *person closely associated* with them being employed by the entity in such a position, be excluded from any role in which they would be a *covered person*; or

(b) in the case of a *close family* member of a *covered person* who is not a *person closely associated with them*, or, <u>for an engagement other than an *investment circular reporting engagement*</u>, any *close family* member of any partner in the *firm* who is not a *person closely associated* with them, report the matter to the *engagement partner* to take appropriate action. If it is a *close family* member of the *engagement partner* or if the *engagement partner* is in doubt as to the action to be taken, the *engagement partner* shall resolve the matter in consultation with the *Ethics Partner*/Function.

Governance Role with an Entity Relevant to an Engagement

2.60 Paragraphs 2.61 to 2.63 are supplementary to certain statutory or regulatory provisions that prohibit directors of entities from being appointed as their auditor.[35]

2.61 The *firm* or a partner or member of *staff* of the *firm* shall not accept appointment or perform a role:

(a) as an officer[36] or member of the board of directors of an *entity relevant to an engagement* of the *firm*;

(b) as a member of any subcommittee of that board; or

(c) in such a position in an entity which holds directly or indirectly more than 20% of the voting rights in the *entity relevant to an engagement*, or in an entity in which the *entity relevant to such an engagement* holds directly or indirectly more than 20% of the voting rights.

---

[35] *For example, in the case of limited companies and certain other organisations, section 1214 of the Companies Act 2006 contains detailed provisions. Amongst other things, these state that:*
'...A person may not act as statutory auditor of an audited person if [he] is (a) an officer or employee of the audited person, or (b) a partner or employee of such a person, or a partnership of which such a person is a partner.'

[36] *As defined in Section 1173 of the Companies Act 2006 as including a director, manager or secretary.*

> Where the *firm* is undertaking an *investment circular reporting engagement*, the requirements in this paragraph shall apply during the period of the *engagement*.

Where a *covered person* becomes aware that a *person closely associated* with them, or a **2.62** *close family* member who is not a *person closely associated* with them, holds a position described in paragraph 2.61, the *firm* shall take appropriate steps to ensure that the relevant person is excluded from any role in which they would be a *covered person*.

Where a partner or member of *staff* of the *firm*, but who is not a *covered person*, becomes **2.63** aware that a *person closely associated* with them, or a *close family* member who is not a *person closely associated* with them, holds a position described in paragraph 2.61, that individual shall report that fact to the *engagement partner*, who shall evaluate whether the relationship would compromise independence. If the *engagement partner* concludes that independence may be compromised, they shall consult with the *Ethics Partner*/Function to determine whether appropriate safeguards exist. If no such safeguards exist, the *firm* shall withdraw from the *engagement*.

Employment with the Firm

Integrity and objectivity may be threatened and independence may be compromised where **2.64** a former director or employee of an *entity relevant to an engagement* of the *firm* becomes a member of the *engagement team* or is otherwise a *covered person*. Self-interest, self-review and familiarity threats may be created where a member of the *engagement team* has to report on, for example, financial statements which he or she prepared, or other information for which he or she had responsibility, while with the entity.

Where a former director or a former employee of an *entity relevant to an engagement*, **2.65** who was in a position to exert significant influence over the preparation of the financial statements or other *subject matter information* or *subject matter* of such an *engagement*, joins the *firm*, that individual shall be excluded from any role in which they would be a *covered person* relevant to that entity or its *affiliates* for a period of two years following the date of leaving the entity.

Recusal from responsibilities of any particular role with respect to influencing particular **2.66** matters cannot remove the individual from being in a position to do so. In certain circumstances, a longer period of exclusion from being a *covered person* may be appropriate. For example, threats to integrity, objectivity and independence may exist in relation to an *engagement* for any period where the financial statements or other *subject matter information* or other *subject matter* of such an *engagement*, are materially affected by the work of that person whilst occupying his or her former position of influence with the entity. The significance of these threats depends on factors such as:

- the position the individual held with the entity;
- the length of time since the individual left the entity;
- the position the individual holds in the *engagement team* or the *firm*.

Family and Other Personal Relationships

A relationship between a *covered person* and a party other than those referred to elsewhere **2.67** in this Section does not generally affect the consideration of integrity and objectivity and the evaluation of whether independence is compromised. However, if it is a relationship with a family member, and if the family member also has a financial, business or employment relationship with any *entity relevant to the engagement*, then this may create self-interest, familiarity or intimidation threats to integrity and objectivity and may impair independence. The significance of any such threats depends on such factors as:

- the relevant person's involvement in the *engagement*;
- the nature of the relationship between the relevant person and his or her family member;
- the family member's relationship with the entity.

2.68 A distinction is made between relationships with '*persons closely associated*' (which include *immediate family* members – a spouse or equivalent and dependents), and other *close family* relationships (which additionally comprise any other parents, non-dependent children and siblings who are not '*persons closely associated*'). While an individual can usually be presumed to be aware of matters concerning *persons closely associated* with them and to be able to influence their behaviour, it is generally recognised that the same levels of knowledge and influence do not exist in the case of *close family* members who are not a *person closely associated* with them.

2.69 When considering family relationships, it needs to be acknowledged that the concept of what constitutes a family is evolving and relationships between individuals which have no status formally recognised by law may nevertheless be considered as significant as those which do. It may therefore be appropriate to regard certain other personal relationships, particularly those that would be considered close personal relationships, as if they are family relationships.

2.70 The *firm* shall establish policies and procedures that require:

    (a) partners and professional *staff* members to report to the *firm* any *persons closely associated* with them, any *close family* who are not a *person closely associated with them*, and other personal relationships, where any of those persons is involved with an *entity relevant to an engagement* of the *firm*, where the partner or professional *staff* member considers that the relationship might create a threat to integrity or objectivity or may compromise independence;

    (b) the relevant *engagement partners* to be notified promptly of any information reported by partners and other professional *staff* members as required by paragraph (a).

2.71 The *engagement partner* shall:

    (a) assess the threats to integrity and objectivity and evaluate whether independence would be compromised, on the basis of the information reported to the *firm* by partners and other professional *staff* members as required by paragraph 2.70;

    (b) apply appropriate safeguards to eliminate any threats or to reduce them to a level where independence would not be compromised; and

    (c) where there are unresolved matters or the need for clarification, consult with the *Ethics Partner*/Function.

2.72 Where such matters are identified or reported, the *engagement partner* or the *Ethics Partner*/Function assesses the information available and the potential for there to be a threat to integrity or objectivity and for independence to be compromised, treating any personal relationship as if it were a family relationship.

External Consultants Involved in an Engagement

2.73 *Firms* may employ external consultants as experts as part of their *engagement*, for example, in an *audit engagement*, in order to obtain sufficient appropriate audit evidence regarding certain financial statement assertions.[37] There may be threats to an expert's integrity or

---

[37] *ISA (UK) 620* 'Using the Work of an Auditor's Expert' *requires that the auditor shall evaluate whether the expert has the necessary objectivity.*

objectivity and their independence may be compromised if the expert is related to any *entity relevant to the engagement*, for example by being financially dependent upon or having an investment in, the entity.

The *engagement partner* shall be satisfied that any external consultant involved in the   **2.74**
engagement will act with integrity and objectivity with respect to the *engagement* and
shall document the rationale for that conclusion.

The *engagement partner* obtains information from the external consultant as to the   **2.75**
existence of any connections that they have with the entity including:

- financial interests;
- business relationships;
- employment (past, present and future);
- family and other personal relationships.

Section 3 – Long Association with Engagements and With Entities Relevant to Engagements

General Requirements

The *firm* shall establish policies and procedures to monitor the length of time and   **3.1**
extent of involvement that partners and *staff* in senior positions, including those
from other disciplines, serve as members of the *engagement team(s)* for recurring
engagements for particular entities.

Where partners and *staff* in senior positions have a long association or extensive   **3.2**
involvement with an *entity relevant to the engagement*, the *firm* shall assess the threats
to integrity, objectivity and independence of the *firm* and *covered persons* and shall:

- **apply safeguards to reduce the threats to a level where independence would not**
  be compromised; and
- **disclose the *engagements* previously undertaken by the *firm* for an *entity relevant***
  ***to the engagement* to those charged with governance and, where applicable, any**
  other persons or entities the *firm* is instructed to advise.

Where appropriate safeguards cannot be applied, the *firm* shall not accept the
engagement, shall resign from the *engagement* or not stand for reappointment, as
appropriate. Where the responsibility for the *engagement* is assigned by legislation or
regulation and the *firm* cannot resign from the *engagement* (e.g. in the case of certain
public sector bodies) the *firm* shall consider alternative safeguards that can be put in
place.

Where partners and *staff* in senior positions have a long association or extensive involvement   **3.3**
with an *entity relevant to the engagement*, self-interest, self-review and familiarity threats to
the integrity or objectivity of any person performing the *engagement* may arise. Similarly,
such circumstances may impair, and could compromise, independence. The significance
of such threats depends upon factors such as:

- the role of the individual in the *engagement team(s)*;
- the proportion of time that the entity contributes to the individual's annual billable
  hours;
- the length of time that the individual has been associated with an *entity relevant to
  the engagement*;

- whether the individual is employed exclusively or principally on an *engagement* that extends for a significant period of time;
- whether the individual is remunerated on the basis of the performance of a part of the *firm* which is substantially dependent on fees from that entity.

3.4   For an *investment circular reporting engagement*, the *firm* gives careful consideration to which individual is appointed as the *engagement partner* on such an *engagement*. This consideration will reflect the need for relevant expertise[38] as well as factors such as:
- the nature of the *investment circular reporting engagement* and whether it will involve the reappraisal of previously audited financial information;
- the length of time that the *engagement partner* for the *audit engagement* has been associated with the *audit engagement*;
- the length of time that other partners have acted for the entity on corporate finance and other transaction related engagements;
- whether the objectivity of the *engagement partner* on a subsequent *engagement* could be adversely affected by an opinion on a profit forecast included in the investment circular; and
- the scope of the engagement quality control review.

3.5   In order to address threats that are identified, *firms* apply safeguards. Appropriate safeguards may include:

- appointing a partner who has no previous involvement with the entity as the *engagement partner*;
- removing ('rotating') the partners and the other senior members of the *engagement team* after a pre-determined number of years;
- involving an additional partner, who is not and has not recently been a member of the *engagement team*, to review the work done by the partners and the other senior members of the *engagement team* and to advise as necessary;
- arranging an engagement quality control review of the *engagement* in question.

3.6   Where applicable, once an *engagement partner* has held this role for a continuous period of ten years, careful consideration is given as to whether it is probable that an objective, reasonable and informed third party would conclude the integrity, objectivity or independence of the *firm* or *covered persons* are compromised. Where the individual concerned is not rotated after ten years, it is important that:

(a) safeguards other than rotation, such as those noted in paragraph 3.5, are applied; or

(b) (i)   the reasoning as to why the individual continues to participate in the *engagement* without any safeguards is documented; and

    (ii)   the facts are communicated to those charged with governance of the entity in accordance with paragraphs 1.61 – 1.71 of Section 1 of Part B of this Ethical Standard.

3.7   The *firm's* policies and procedures set out whether there are circumstances in which the *engagement partners, engagement quality control reviewers* and other key partners involved in recurring *engagements* for non-listed entities that are not *public interest entities* are subject to accelerated rotation requirements, such as those set out in paragraph 3.11, as described in paragraph 1.49 of Section 1 of Part B of this Ethical Standard.

---

[38] *Paragraph 25 of SIR 1000 requires that a partner with appropriate experience should be involved in the conduct of the work.*

Any scheme of rotation of partners and other senior members of the *engagement team* needs to take into account the factors which affect the quality of the *engagement work*, including the experience and continuity of members of the *engagement team* and the need to ensure appropriate succession planning.

3.8

Public Interest Entities and Other Listed Entities

> The requirements and guidance in paragraphs 3.9 – 3.23 are relevant to recurring *engagements* that are undertaken for an entity over periods of five or more years.

Audit Firm Rotation

The requirements for *audit firm* rotation, implementing the relevant provisions of Article 17 of the EU Audit Regulation, are set out in legislation[39]. The *firm* shall ensure that it does not accept or continue an *audit engagement* that would cause those requirements to not be complied with.

3.9

Key Audit Partners and Engagement Partners[40]

Save where the circumstances in paragraphs 3.14 and 3.15 apply, the *key audit partners* responsible for carrying out a *statutory audit* of a *public interest entity* shall cease their participation in the *statutory audit* of the *audited entity* not later than ~~seven~~ five[41] years from the date of their appointment. They shall not participate again in the *statutory audit* of the *audited entity* before ~~three~~ five years have elapsed following that cessation. [AR 17.7]

3.10R

In the case of *listed entities*, save where the circumstances contemplated in paragraph 3.14 and 3.15 apply, the *firm* shall establish policies and procedures to ensure in respect of a recurring *engagement* that:

3.11

(a) no one shall act as *engagement partner* for more than five years; and

(b) anyone who has acted as the *engagement partner* for a particular entity for a period of five years, shall not subsequently participate in the *engagement* until a further period of five years has elapsed.

The roles that constitute participating in an *engagement* for the purposes of paragraph 3.11(b), include providing quality control for the *engagement*, advising or consulting with the *engagement team* or the entity regarding technical or industry specific issues, transactions or events, or otherwise directly influencing the conduct or outcome of the *engagement*. This does not include responding to queries in relation to any completed *engagement*. This is not intended to preclude partners whose primary responsibility within a *firm* is to be consulted on technical or industry specific issues from providing such consultation to the *engagement team* or entity after a period of two years has elapsed from their ceasing to act as *engagement partner*, provided that such consultation is in respect of new issues or new types of transactions or events that were not previously required to be considered by that individual in the course of acting as *engagement partner*.

3.12

Where an *engagement partner* continues in a non-engagement role having been rotated off the *engagement team*, the new *engagement partner* and the individual concerned ensure that

3.13

---

[39] *Sections 487 and 489 of the Companies Act 2006.*

[40] *For an audit, the* engagement partner *is a* key audit partner.

[41] *The FRC has exercised the Member State option in the second sub-paragraph of Article 17.7 to set a shorter period than the default seven year period.*

that person, while acting in this new role, does not exert any influence on the *engagement*. Positions in which an individual is responsible for the *firm's* client relationship with the particular entity would not be an acceptable non-engagement role.

3.14   When an entity becomes a *public interest entity* or an other *listed entity*, the length of time the *engagement partner* has served the entity in that capacity is taken into account in calculating the period before the *engagement partner* is rotated off the *engagement team*. However, where the *engagement partner* has already served for four or more years, that individual may continue to serve as the *engagement partner* for not more than two years after the entity becomes such a *public interest entity* or an other *listed entity*.

3.15   In circumstances where the audit committee (or equivalent) of an entity that is a *public interest entity* or an other *listed entity* decide that a degree of flexibility over the timing of rotation is necessary to safeguard the quality of the *engagement* and the *firm* agrees, the *engagement partner* may continue in this position for an additional period of up to two years, so that no longer than seven years in total is spent in the position of *engagement partner*. An audit committee and the *firm* may consider that such flexibility safeguards the quality of the *engagement*, for example, where:

- substantial change has recently been made or will soon be made to the nature or structure of the entity's business; or
- there are unexpected changes in the senior management of the entity; or
- the *firm*, having taken all reasonable succession planning steps, has no other partners with the necessary knowledge and experience who are able to take over as *engagement partner*.

In these circumstances alternative safeguards are applied to reduce any threats to a level where it is not probable that an objective, reasonable and informed third party would conclude the integrity, objectivity or independence of the *firm* or *covered persons* are compromised. Such safeguards may include ensuring that an expanded review of the *engagement* work is undertaken by the *engagement quality control reviewer* or a partner with relevant expertise, who is not involved in the *engagement*.

3.16   For an *audit engagement*, where it has been determined that the *engagement partner* may act for a further period (not to exceed two years) in the interests of audit quality, this fact and the reasons for it, are to be disclosed to the *audited entity's* shareholders as early as practicable and in each of the additional years. If the *audited entity* is not prepared to make such a disclosure, the *audit firm* does not permit the *engagement partner* to continue in this role.

3.17   In the case of joint audit arrangements for *public interest entities* and for other *listed entities*, *audit firms* will make arrangements for changes of *engagement partners* over a five-year period so that the familiarity threat is avoided, whilst also taking into consideration factors that affect the quality of the audit work.

Engagement Quality Control Reviewers and Other Key Partners Involved in the Engagement

3.18R   For an audit of a *public interest entity*, the statutory auditor or the *audit firm* shall establish an appropriate gradual rotation mechanism with regard to the most senior personnel involved in the *statutory audit*, including at least the persons who are registered as *statutory auditors*. The gradual rotation mechanism shall be applied in phases on the basis of individuals rather than of the entire *engagement team*. It shall be proportionate in view of the scale and the complexity of the activity of the statutory auditor or the *audit firm*. [AR 17.7]

<u>*For an audit of a public interest entity,*</u> the ~~statutory auditor or the~~ *audit firm* shall   **3.19R**
be able to demonstrate to the competent authority[42] that such mechanism is
effectively applied and adapted to the scale and the complexity of the activity of
the ~~statutory auditor or the~~ *audit firm.* [AR 17.7]

In the case of *public interest entities* and other *listed entities*, the *firm* shall establish   **3.20**
policies and procedures to ensure in respect of a recurring *engagement* that:

(a)   no one shall act as the *engagement quality control reviewer* or a *key partner
      involved in the engagement* for a period longer than seven years;
(b)   where an *engagement quality control reviewer* or a *key partner involved in the
      engagement* becomes the *engagement partner*, the combined period of service in
      these positions shall not exceed seven years; and
(c)   anyone who has acted:
      (i)   as an *engagement quality control reviewer* for a particular entity for a period
             of seven years, whether continuously or in aggregate, shall not participate in
             the *engagement* until a further period of five years has elapsed;
      (ii)   as a *key partner involved in the engagement* for a particular entity for a period
             of seven years, whether continuously or in aggregate, shall not participate in
             the *engagement* until a further period of two years has elapsed;
      (iii) in a combination of roles as:

             ● the *engagement quality control reviewer,*
             ● a *key partner involved in the engagement,* or
             ● the *engagement partner*
             for a particular entity for a period of seven years, whether continuously or
             in aggregate, shall not participate in the *engagement* until a further period
             of five years has elapsed.

Other Partners and Staff Involved in the Engagement in Senior Positions

In the case of *public interest entities* and other *listed entities*, the *engagement partner*   **3.21**
shall review the safeguards put in place to address the threats to the objectivity and
independence of the person or persons conducting the *engagement* arising where
partners and *staff* have been involved in the *engagement* in senior positions for a
continuous period longer than seven years and shall discuss those situations with
the *engagement quality control reviewer.* Any unresolved problems or issues shall be
referred to the Ethics Function / Partner.

The significance of the threats arising where partners and *staff* have been involved in   **3.22**
the *engagement* in senior positions for a continuous period longer than seven years will
depend on:

● the total period of time that the individual has been involved in the *engagement*;
● changes in the nature of the work and the role performed by the individual during
  that period; and

the portion of time the individual has spent on any engagements with the entity during
that period.

Following the assessment of any such threats, appropriate safeguards are applied where   **3.23**
necessary. Safeguards that address these threats might include:

---

[42] *The FRC or the Recognised Supervisory Body to whom the FRC has delegated regulatory tasks, as applicable.*

- changes in the roles within the *engagement team*;
- an additional review of the work done by the individual by the *engagement partner* or other partners in the *engagement team*;
- additional procedures carried out as part of the engagement quality control review.

If such safeguards do not reduce the threats to a level where independence is not compromised, the partner or member of *staff* is removed from the *engagement team*.

Section 4 – Fees, Remuneration and Evaluation Policies, Gifts and Hospitality, Litigation

Fees

4.1   **The *engagement partner* shall be satisfied and able to demonstrate that the *engagement* has assigned to it sufficient partners and *staff* with appropriate time and skill to perform the *engagement* in accordance with all applicable Engagement and Ethical Standards, irrespective of the *engagement* fee to be charged.**

4.2   Paragraph 4.1 is not intended to prescribe the approach to be taken by *firms* to the setting of *engagement* fees, but rather to emphasise that there are no circumstances where the amount of the *engagement* fee can justify any lack of appropriate resource or time taken to perform a proper engagement in accordance with applicable Engagement and Ethical Standards.

4.3D   **Fees for *engagements* shall not be influenced or determined by the provision of *non-audit / additional services* to an *entity relevant to the engagement*.** [AD 25, ES 4.7]

4.4   The *engagement* fee ordinarily reflects the time spent, the skills and experience of the personnel performing the *engagement* in accordance with all the relevant requirements, and the competitive situation in the market. Paragraph 4.3D is intended to prevent any relationship between the appropriate cost of the *engagement* and the actual or potential provision of *non-audit / additional services*.

4.5   Paragraph 4.3D is not intended to prohibit proper cost savings that can be achieved as a result of providing *non-audit / additional services* in accordance with Section 5 of this Ethical Standard to the entity, for example, where information gained through undertaking a *non-audit service* is referred to by audit staff when carrying out the audit of the financial statements.

4.6R   **Fees for the provision of ~~statutory audits~~ engagements ~~to public-interest entities~~ shall not be contingent fees.** [AR 4.1]

4.7R   ~~Without prejudice to Article 25 of Directive 2006/43/EC, for the purposes of the first subparagraph, c~~Contingent fees means fees ~~for audit engagements~~ calculated on a predetermined basis relating to the outcome or result of a transaction, or other event, or the result of the work performed. Fees shall not be regarded as being contingent if a court, ~~or a~~ competent authority, or other public authority has established them. [AR 4.1]

A *contingent fee basis* includes any arrangement made at the outset of an *engagement* under   **4.8**
which a specified commission on or percentage of any consideration or saving is payable
to the *firm* upon the happening of a specified event or the achievement of an outcome
(or alternative outcomes). Differential hourly fee rates, or arrangements under which the
fee payable will be negotiated after the completion of the *engagement*, or increased to
cover additional work identified as necessary during the *engagement*, do not constitute
contingent fee arrangements.

Contingent fee arrangements in respect of *engagements* create self-interest threats to the   **4.9**
integrity and objectivity of the *firm* and *covered persons* that are so significant that they
cannot be eliminated or reduced to a level where independence would not be compromised.

The fee for an *engagement* does not depend on whether the *firm's* report on the financial   **4.10**
statements, or on *subject matter information* or other *subject matter* of such an *engagement*,
is qualified or unqualified. The basis for the calculation of the fee is agreed with the entity
before significant *engagement* work is undertaken and ordinarily reflects the time spent
and the skills and experience of the personnel performing the *engagement* in accordance
with all the relevant requirements. For recurring *engagements*, such as an audit, the fee is
agreed before each recurrence. Arrangements under which estimated fees are agreed with
the entity on terms where the fees may be varied based on the level of *engagement* work
required do not constitute contingent fee arrangements.

Investigations into possible acquisitions or disposals ('due diligence engagements'), particularly those performed in relation to a prospective transaction, typically involve a high level of risk and responsibility. A *firm* carrying out a due diligence engagement may charge a higher fee for work relating to a completed transaction than for the same transaction if it is not completed, for whatever reason, provided that the difference is related to such additional risk and responsibility and not the outcome of the due diligence engagement.

4.11

In relation to *investment circular reporting engagements*, where the *firm* is aware that an *entity relevant to the engagement* has a record of seeking substantial discounts to the fee payable where a transaction is unsuccessful or abortive, the *engagement partner* discusses the position with the *Ethics Partner*. An appropriate safeguard may involve arranging an engagement quality control review of the *investment circular reporting engagement*.

4.12

Contingent fee arrangements in respect of *non-audit / additional services* provided by   **4.13**
the *firm* in respect of an entity can create significant self-interest threats to the integrity,
objectivity and independence of the *firm* and *covered persons*, as they may have, or may
appear to have, an interest in the outcome of the *non-audit / additional service*.

**The *firm* shall not provide *non-audit / additional services*, in respect of an *entity*   4.14
relevant to an engagement*, wholly or partly on a *contingent fee basis* where:**

(a) **the contingent fee is material to the *firm*, or that part of the *firm* by reference to
    which the *engagement partner's* profit share is calculated; or**
(b) **the amount of the fee is dependent on an outcome or result of those *non-audit /
    additional services* that is relevant to a future or contemporary judgment
    relating to a material matter in the financial statements or other *subject matter
    information* or *subject matter* of the *engagement*.**

In relation to tax services, the requirements of paragraph 5.85 of Section 5 of Part B of this Ethical Standard also apply.

4.15   Where *non-audit / additional services* are provided on a *contingent fee basis*, there may be a perception that the *firm's* interests are so closely aligned with the entity that the integrity, objectivity and independence of the *firm* and *covered persons* could be, or be seen to be, compromised.

4.16   The significance of the self-interest threat is likely to be, or be seen to be, influenced by the materiality of the contingent fee to the *firm* or to the part of the *firm* by reference to which the *engagement partner's* profit share is calculated – any contingent fee that is material to the *firm*, or that part of the *firm* by reference to which the *engagement partner's* profit share is calculated, will create a self-interest threat that cannot be eliminated or reduced to a level where independence is not compromised and the *firm* does not undertake such a service at the same time as an *audit engagement* or other *public interest assurance engagement*.

4.17   In addition, where the contingent fee is dependent on an outcome or result of the *non-audit / additional service* that is relevant to a future or contemporary audit or assurance judgment relating to a material matter that is included in the audited financial statements, in the case of an *entity relevant to an engagement*, the self-interest threat cannot be eliminated or reduced to a level where independence is not compromised.

4.18   Paragraph 4.14 is not intended to prohibit a *firm* from charging a lower fee where the service relates to a transaction or engagement that was either aborted or prematurely terminated for whatever reason and where the rationale for the lower fee is to take account of either the reduced risk and responsibility involved or the fact that less work was undertaken than had been anticipated.

4.19   For *non-audit / additional services* provided on a *contingent fee basis*, other than those prohibited under paragraph 4.14, the *engagement partner* assesses the significance of the self-interest threat and considers whether there are safeguards that could be applied which would be effective to eliminate the threat or reduce it to a level where independence is not compromised. The significance of the self-interest threat will depend on factors such as:

- the range of possible fee amounts;
- the nature of the *non-audit / additional service*;
- for an audit, the effect of the outcome of the additional *non-audit service* on the financial statements of the *audited entity*;
- for an other *public interest assurance engagement*, the effect of the outcome of the additional service on the *subject matter information* or *subject matter* of the *engagement*.

4.20   Examples of safeguards that might be applied to reduce any self-interest threats arising from the provision of *non-audit / additional services* on a *contingent fee basis* (other than those set out in paragraph 4.14 above) to a level where independence is not compromised include:

- the provision of such *non-audit / additional services* by partners and *staff* who have no involvement in the *engagement*;
- review of the *engagement* by a partner with relevant expertise who is not involved in the *engagement* to ensure that the *subject matter* of the *non-audit / additional service* has been properly and effectively addressed in the context of the *engagement*.

For an *investment circular reporting engagement*, in situations where a *reporting accountant* can see at the outset of the *investment circular reporting engagement* that there is likely to be a judgment that will be made in relation to a material aspect of the *investment circular reporting engagement* which could adversely affect the successful completion of the transaction to which the investment circular relates, the *firm* will not agree to undertake any corporate finance services in relation to the transaction on a *contingent fee basis*, or will not accept the *investment circular reporting engagement*. Where corporate finance services are entered into on a *contingent fee basis* and a judgment needs to be made in relation to a material aspect of the *investment circular reporting engagement* during the course of an *investment circular reporting engagement*, then the *firm* changes the terms of the corporate finance service so that it no longer involves a contingent fee or withdraws from either the relevant corporate finance service or the *investment circular reporting engagement*.
4.21

Where the *firm* provides a range of corporate finance services to an *entity relevant to the engagement*, including acting as a Sponsor or Nominated Advisor, on terms that involve a contingent fee, and that *firm* also undertakes a public reporting engagement for an *entity relevant to the engagement*, the self-interest threat caused by contingent fee arrangements may be reduced to a level where independence is not compromised by the application of safeguards, such as the corporate finance services being provided by partners and *staff* who have no involvement in the *investment circular reporting engagement*. In such circumstances the *reporting accountant* ensures that the situation is fully disclosed to the Financial Conduct Authority (FCA), or the London Stock Exchange and any related regulatory requirements have been complied with.
4.22

The *firm* shall establish policies and procedures to ensure that the *engagement partner* and the *Ethics Partner*/Function are notified where others within the *firm* propose to adopt contingent fee arrangements in relation to the provision of *non-audit / additional services* to the *entity relevant to the engagement* or its *affiliates*.
4.23

Contingent fee arrangements in respect of *non-audit / additional services* provided by the *firm* may create a threat to the integrity, objectivity or independence of the *firm* and *covered persons*. The circumstances in which such fee arrangements are not permitted for *non-audit / additional services* are dealt with in paragraph 4.14 of this Section.
4.24

In the case of *public interest entities* and of other *listed entities relevant to an engagement*, the *engagement partner* shall disclose to the audit committee, in writing, any contingent fee arrangements for *non-audit / additional services* provided by the *firm* or its *network firms*.
4.25

In the case of a group *engagement* of a *public interest entity* or of an other *listed entity*, which involves other *firms*, the letter of instruction sent by the group *engagement partner* to the other *firms* requests disclosure of any contingent fees for *non-audit / additional services* charged or proposed to be charged by the other *firms*.
4.26

For a recurring *engagement*, the actual amount of the *engagement* fee for the previous *engagement* and the arrangements for its payment shall be agreed with the entity before the *firm* formally accepts appointment for the *engagement* in respect of the following period.
4.27

Ordinarily, any outstanding fees for the previous engagement period are paid before the *firm* commences any new *engagement* work. Where they are not, it is important for the *engagement partner* to understand the nature of any disagreement or other issue.
4.28

4.29   Where fees for professional services from an entity are overdue and the amount cannot be regarded as trivial, the *engagement partner*, in consultation with the *Ethics Partner/ Function*, shall consider whether the *firm* can accept or continue an *engagement* for the entity or whether it is necessary to resign.

4.30   Where fees due from an entity, whether for *an audit engagement, other public interest assurance engagements*, or for other professional services, remain unpaid for a long time – and, in particular, where a significant part is not paid before the *firm's* audit report on the financial statements for the following year, or report on other *subject matter information* or *subject matter* in the case of an other *public interest assurance engagement* for a subsequent *engagement*, is due to be issued – a self-interest threat to the integrity, objectivity and independence of the *firm* and *covered persons* is created because the issue of an unqualified report may enhance the *firm's* prospects of securing payment of such overdue fees.

4.31   Where the outstanding fees are in dispute and the amount involved is significant, the threats to the integrity and objectivity of the *firm* and *covered persons* may be such that they cannot be reduced to a level where independence would not be compromised. The *engagement partner* therefore considers whether the *firm* can continue with the *engagement*.

4.32   Where the outstanding fees are unpaid because of exceptional circumstances (including financial distress), the *engagement partner* considers whether the entity will be able to resolve its difficulties. In deciding what action to take, the *engagement partner* weighs the threats to the integrity, objectivity and independence of the *firm* and *covered persons*, if the *firm* were to remain appointed to provide the *engagement*, against the difficulties the entity would be likely to face in finding a successor, and therefore the public interest considerations, if the *firm* were to resign or withdraw from the *engagement*.

4.33   In any case where the *firm* does not resign from the *engagement*, the *engagement partner* applies appropriate safeguards (such as a review by a partner with relevant expertise who is not involved in the *engagement*) and notifies the *Ethics Partner* of the facts concerning the overdue fees.

4.34R   When the ~~statutory auditor or the~~ *audit firm*, <u>or a member of its network,</u> provides to ~~the audited~~ *a public interest* entity <u>that it audits</u>, its parent undertaking or its controlled undertakings, ~~for a period of three or more consecutive financial years,~~ non-audit services other than those referred to in Article 5(1)[43] of ~~this~~ <u>the EU Audit</u> Regulation:

    (a) the total fees for such services <u>provided to the audited entity and its controlled undertakings</u> shall be limited to no more than 70% of the average of the fees paid in the last three consecutive financial years[44] for the ~~statutory~~ audit(s) of the audited entity and ~~of its parent undertaking,~~ of its controlled undertakings and of the consolidated financial statements of that group of undertakings; <u>and</u>

    (b) the total fees for such services <u>provided by the *audit firm*</u> shall be limited to no more than 70% of the average of the fees paid <u>to the *audit firm*</u> in the last three consecutive financial years[44] for the ~~statutory~~ audit(s) of the audited entity and, where applicable, of its parent undertaking, of its controlled undertakings and of the consolidated financial statements of that group of undertakings. [AR 4.2]

---

[43] *See paragraph 5.167R of Section 5 of Part B of this Ethical Standard.*

[44] *This requirement does not apply retrospectively. The cap is based on average audit fees for the three consecutive financial periods commencing on or after 17 June 2016. Following the appointment of a new auditor after that date the cap will apply from the fourth financial period of that engagement.*

For the purposes of the limits specified in ~~the first subparagraph~~ paragraph 4.34R, non-audit services, other than those referred to in Article 5(1) of the EU Audit Regulation, required by Union or national legislation shall be excluded. *[AR 4.2]*   4.35R

Upon a request by the ~~statutory auditor or the~~ *audit firm*, on an exceptional basis, the competent authority[45] may allow that ~~statutory auditor or~~ *audit firm* to be exempt from the requirements in ~~the first sub-paragraph~~ paragraph 4.34R in respect of an *audited entity* for a period not exceeding two financial years. [AR 4.2]   4.36R

In the case of *public interest entities* and of other *listed entities*, where: 4.37

(a)   the fees charged by the *firm* and members of its *network* in aggregate: or

(b)   the fees charged by the *firm* or by any member of its *network* whose work is used in the conduct of the *engagement*;

for *non-audit / additional services*, and for services provided to *connected parties* that may bear on independence, for a financial year are expected to be greater than the aggregate (or the individual firm's) annual fees for the *engagement*, the *engagement partner* shall provide details of the circumstances to the *Ethics Partner*/Function and discuss them with him or her. The *engagement partner* shall determine whether the threats to independence of the *firm* or any such member of its network are at a level where independence is not compromised or, if necessary, put in place appropriate safeguards such that independence is not compromised, which may include the *firm* or member of its network not providing the *non-audit / additional* service.

Where the *firm* and/or members of its network provide services to a group, the requirement in paragraph 4.37 shall apply on a group basis for all services provided by the *firm* and its *network firms* to all entities in the group and to their *connected parties*.   4.38

Where substantial fees are regularly generated from the provision of *non-audit / additional services* and the fees for *non-audit / additional services* are greater than the annual fees for recurring *engagements* for an entity, the *engagement partner* has regard to the possibility that there may be perceived to be a loss of independence resulting from the expected or actual level of fees for *non-audit / additional services*. The *engagement partner* determines whether there is any risk that there will be an actual loss of integrity, objectivity or independence by the *firm* or *covered persons*. In making that assessment, the *engagement partner* considers matters such as whether the *non-audit / additional services* were: **4.39**

●   audit related services;

●   provided on a *contingent fee basis*;

●   consistent with the services undertaken and fees received on a consistent basis in previous years;

●   in the case of a group, disproportionate in relation to any individual group entity;

●   unusual in size but unlikely to recur; and/or

●   of such a size and nature that an objective, reasonable and informed third party would be concerned at the effect that such services would have on the integrity, objectivity and independence of the *firm* or *covered persons*.

Having made that assessment, the *engagement partner* determines whether the threats to independence from the level of fees for *non-audit / additional services* are at a level where independence is not compromised (or can be reduced to such a level by putting in place appropriate safeguards) and appropriately informs the audit committee or those charged

---

[45] *The competent authority for this purpose is the Financial Reporting Council.*

with governance of the position on a timely basis in accordance with paragraphs 1.61, 1.66 and 1.67 of Section 1 of Part B of this Ethical Standard.

4.40   Discussing the level of fees for *non-audit / additional services* with the *Ethics Partner/* Function ensures that appropriate attention is paid to the issue by the *firm*. The *firm's* policies and procedures will set out whether there are circumstances in which the *engagement partner* responsible for the *engagement* discusses the level of *non-audit / additional service* fees with the *Ethics Partner*/Function for non-listed entities, that are not *public interest entities*, as described in paragraph 1.49 of Section 1 of Part B of this Ethical Standard.

4.41   Paragraphs 4.42 to 4.52 below do not apply to *engagements* of entities where the responsibility for the *engagement* is assigned by legislation and the *firm* cannot resign from the *engagement*, irrespective of considerations of economic dependence (e.g. for certain public sector bodies).

4.42   **Where it is expected that the total fees for services receivable from a *public interest entity* or other *listed entity* and its subsidiaries relevant to a recurring *engagement* by the *firm*[46] will regularly exceed 10% of the annual fee income of the *firm*[47] or, where profits are not shared on a *firm*-wide basis, of the part of the *firm* by reference to which the *engagement partner's* profit share is calculated, the *firm* shall not act as the provider of the *engagement* for that entity and shall either resign or not stand for reappointment, as appropriate.**

4.43   The requirements in paragraph 4.42 are applied in place of the less stringent requirements in Article 4.3 of the EU Audit Regulation, as permitted by Article 4.4 of the EU Audit regulation.

4.44   **Where it is expected that the total fees for services receivable from a non-listed entity that is not a *public interest entity* and its subsidiaries relevant to a recurring *engagement* by the *firm* will regularly exceed 15% of the annual fee income of the *firm* or, where profits are not shared on a *firm*-wide basis, of the part of the *firm* by reference to which the *engagement partner's* profit share is calculated, the *firm* shall not act as the provider of the *engagement* for that entity and shall either resign or not stand for reappointment, as appropriate.**

4.45   Where it is expected that the total fees for services receivable from an entity and its subsidiaries relevant to a recurring *engagement* by the *firm* will regularly exceed 10%, in the case of *public interest entities* or other *listed entities*, and 15%, in the case of non-listed entities that are not *public interest entities*, of the annual fee income of the part of the *firm* by reference to which the *engagement partner's* profit share is calculated, it may be possible to assign the *engagement* to another part of the *firm*.

4.46   Paragraphs 4.42 and 4.44 are not intended to require the *firm* to resign as provider of a recurring *engagement*, or not stand for reappointment, as a result of an individual event or *engagement*, the nature or size of which was unpredictable and where an objective, reasonable and informed third party would regard ceasing to act as detrimental to the shareholders (or equivalent) of the entity or otherwise contrary to the public interest. However, in such circumstances, the *engagement partner* discloses full details of the position to the *Ethics Partner*/Function and to those charged with governance of the entity,

---

[46] *Total fees will include those billed by others where the* firm *is entitled to the fees, but will not include fees billed by the* firm *where it is acting as agent for another party.*

[47] *In the case of a sole practitioner, annual fee income of the* firm *includes all earned income received by the individual.*

including the audit committee where there is one, and discusses with both the threats to the integrity, objectivity and independence of the *firm* and *covered persons* and the safeguards applied to eliminate or reduce those threats to a level where independence would not be compromised.

Where it is expected that the total fees services receivable from a *public interest entity*   **4.47**
or other *listed entity* and its subsidiaries relevant to a recurring *engagement* by the *firm*
will regularly exceed 5% of the annual fee income of the *firm* or the part of the *firm*
by reference to which the *engagement partner's* profit share is calculated, but will not
regularly exceed 10%, the *engagement partner* shall disclose that expectation to the
***Ethics Partner*/Function and to those charged with governance of the entity, including**
the audit committee where there is one, and discusses with both the threat to integrity,
objectivity and independence of the *firm* and *covered persons* and whether safeguards
need to be applied to eliminate or reduce the threat to a level where independence
would not be compromised.

It is fundamental to the integrity and objectivity of the *firm* and *covered persons* that they   **4.48**
be willing and able, if necessary, to disagree with the directors and management, regardless
of the consequences to the *firm's* own position. Where the *firm* is, to any significant extent,
economically dependent on the entity, this may inhibit the willingness or constrain the
firm's ability to express a qualified opinion on the financial statements or other *subject*
matter information or *subject matter* of an *engagement*, since this could be viewed as
likely to lead to the *firm* losing the *engagement* and the entity as a client.

A *firm* is deemed to be economically dependent on a *public interest entity* or other *listed*   **4.49**
entity if the total fees for all other services from that entity and its subsidiaries relevant to a
recurring *engagement* represent 10% of the total fees of the *firm* or the part of the *firm* by
reference to which the *engagement partner's* profit share is calculated. Where such fees are
between 5% and 10%, the *engagement partner* and the *Ethics Partner*/Function consider
the significance of the threat and the need for appropriate safeguards.

Such safeguards might include: **4.50**

- taking steps to reduce the other work to be undertaken and therefore the fees earned
  from the entity;
- applying independent internal quality control reviews.

Where it is expected that the total fees for services receivable from a non-listed entity,   **4.51**
that is not a *public interest entity*, and its subsidiaries relevant to a recurring *engagement*
will regularly exceed 10% of the annual fee income of the *firm* or the part of the *firm*
by reference to which the *engagement partner's* profit share is calculated, but will not
regularly exceed 15%, the *engagement partner* shall disclose that expectation to the
***Ethics Partner*/Function and to those charged with governance of the entity and the**
firm* shall arrange an external independent quality control review of the *engagement
to be undertaken before the *firm's* report is finalised.

A quality control review involves discussion with the *engagement partner*, a review of the   **4.52**
financial statements or other *subject matter information* or *subject matter* of an *engagement*
and the *firm's* report thereon, and consideration of whether the report is appropriate. It
also involves a review of selected working papers relating to the significant judgments
the *engagement team* has made and the conclusions they have reached. The extent of the
review depends on the complexity of the *engagement* and the risk that the report might
not be appropriate in the circumstances. The review includes considering the following:

- Significant risks identified during the *engagement* and the responses to those risks.
- Judgments made, particularly with respect to materiality and significant risks.
- The *engagement team's* consideration of the entity's compliance with applicable laws and regulations.
- Whether appropriate consultation has taken place on matters involving differences of opinion or other difficult or contentious matters, and the conclusions arising from those consultations.
- The significance and disposition of corrected and uncorrected misstatements identified during the *engagement*.
- The appropriateness of the report to be issued.

Where the quality control reviewer makes recommendations that the *engagement partner* does not accept and the matter is not resolved to the reviewer's satisfaction, the report is not issued until the matter is resolved by following the *firm's* procedures for dealing with differences of opinion.

4.53   A new *firm* seeking to establish itself may find the requirements relating to economic dependence difficult to comply with in the short term. In these circumstances, such *firms* would:

(a)   not undertake any *engagements* of *public interest entities* or other *listed entities*, where fees from such an entity would represent 10% or more of the annual fee income of the *firm*; and

(b)   for a period not exceeding two years, require external independent quality control reviews of those of non-listed entities, that are not *public interest entities*, that represent more than 15% of the annual fee income before the *engagement* report/opinion is issued.

The *firm* might also develop its practice by accepting work from entities not relevant to an *engagement* by the *firm* so as to bring the fees payable by each entity which is relevant to an *engagement* below 15%.

4.54   A self-interest threat may also be created where a partner in the *engagement team*:

- is employed exclusively or principally on that *engagement*; and
- is remunerated on the basis of the performance of part of the *firm* which is substantially dependent on fees from that entity.

4.55   Where the circumstances described in paragraph 4.54 arise, the *firm* assesses the significance of the threat and applies safeguards to reduce the threat to a level where independence would not be compromised. Such safeguards might include:

- reducing the dependence of the office, partner or other *covered person* by reallocating the work within the practice;
- a review by an *engagement partner* with relevant expertise who is not involved with the *engagement* to ensure that the integrity, objectivity or independence of the *firm* and *covered persons* is not affected by the self-interest threat.

Remuneration and Evaluation Policies

4.56D   A *firm* shall have in place adequate remuneration policies, including profit-sharing policies, providing sufficient performance incentives to secure *engagement* quality. In particular, the amount of revenue that the *firm* derives from providing *non-audit / additional services* to the entity shall not form part of the performance evaluation and remuneration of any *covered person* involved in, or able to influence the carrying out of, an *engagement*. [AD 24a.1(j)]

The *firm* shall establish policies and procedures to ensure that each of the following is true in relation to each *entity relevant to an engagement* by the *firm*:   **4.57**

(a) a primary criterion for evaluating the performance or promotion of members of the *engagement team* is how they have contributed to the quality of *engagements* undertaken;

(b) the objectives of the members of the *engagement team* do not include selling *non-audit / additional services* to the entity;

(c) the criteria for evaluating the performance or promotion of members of the *engagement team* do not include success in selling *non-audit / additional services* to the entity; and

(d) no specific element of the remuneration of a member of the *engagement team* is based on his or her success in selling *non-audit / additional services* to the entity.

This requirement does not apply to those members of the *engagement team* from specialist practice areas where the nature and extent of their involvement in the *engagement* is clearly insignificant.

Where the *firm*, its partners or *staff* identify areas for possible improvement in an *entity*   **4.58**
relevant to an engagement, they may provide general business advice, which might include suggested solutions to problems. Before discussing any *non-audit / additional service* that might be provided by the *firm* or effecting any introductions to colleagues from outside the *engagement team*, the *engagement partner* considers the threats that such a service would have on the *engagement*, in line with the requirements in Section 5 of this Ethical Standard, and whether it is probable that an objective, reasonable and informed third party would conclude the integrity, objectivity or independence of the *firm* or *covered persons* are compromised.

The last sentence of paragraph 4.57 recognises the fact that an *engagement team* may   **4.59**
include personnel from specialist practice areas and that it would be inappropriate to limit the business development activities of such persons where their involvement in the *engagement* is clearly insignificant.

The policies and procedures required for compliance with paragraph 4.57 are not intended   **4.60**
to inhibit normal profit-sharing arrangements. However, such policies and procedures are central to the ability of a *firm* that provides *engagement* services to demonstrate the integrity, objectivity and independence of the *firm* and *covered persons*, and to rebut any suggestion that an *engagement* that it has undertaken and the report/opinion that it has given are influenced by the nature and extent of any *non-audit / additional services* that it has provided to that entity. The *Ethics Partner*/Function pays particular attention to the actual implementation of those policies and procedures and is available for consultation when needed.

Gifts and Hospitality

A *firm*, its partners and any *covered person*, and *persons closely associated* with   **4.61D**
them, shall not solicit or accept pecuniary and non-pecuniary gifts or favours, including hospitality, from an *entity relevant to the engagement*, or any other entity related to that entity, unless an objective, reasonable and informed third party would consider the value thereof as trivial or inconsequential. [AD 22.5]

Where gifts, favours or hospitality are accepted from an *entity relevant to an engagement*,   **4.62**
or from other entities related to that entity, self-interest and familiarity threats to the integrity, objectivity and independence of the *firm*, its partners and any other *covered*

person are created. Familiarity threats also arise where gifts, favours or hospitality are offered to an *entity relevant to an engagement*, its partners or any other *covered person*.

4.63   **The *firm* shall establish policies on the nature and value of gifts, favours and hospitality that may be accepted from and offered to an *entity relevant to an engagement*, or any other entity related to that entity, their directors, officers and employees, and shall issue guidance to assist partners and *staff* to comply with such policies.**

4.64   Where gifts, favours and hospitality are accepted or offered more than once, the view of an objective, reasonable and informed third party of the cumulative effect is considered.

4.65   Where there is any doubt as to the acceptability of gifts, favours or hospitality offered by the entity, members of the *engagement team* discuss the position with the *engagement partner*. If there is any doubt as to the acceptability of gifts, favours or hospitality offered to the *engagement partner*, or if the *engagement partner* has any residual doubt about the acceptability of gifts, favours or hospitality to other individuals, the *engagement partner* reports the facts to the *Ethics Partner*/Function, for further consideration regarding any action to be taken.

Threatened and Actual Litigation

4.66   Paragraphs 4.67 and 4.68 below, which support Supporting Ethical Provision 2.11, do not apply to the *engagements* of those entities where the responsibility for the *engagement* is assigned by legislation and the *firm* cannot resign from the *engagement*. In these circumstances the *firm* reports significant litigation to the relevant legislative authority.

4.67   Where litigation (in relation to any services) actually takes place between the *firm*, its partners, or any *covered person*, and the entity or its *affiliates*, or where such litigation is considered probable, self-interest, advocacy and intimidation threats to the integrity, objectivity and independence of the *firm* and *covered persons* are created because the *firm's* interest will be the achievement of an outcome to the dispute or litigation that is favourable to itself. In addition, an effective *engagement* process requires complete candour and full disclosure between the entity's management and the *engagement team*: such disputes or litigation may place the two parties in opposing adversarial positions and may affect management's willingness to make complete disclosure of relevant information. Where the *firm* can foresee that such a threat may arise and independence compromised, the *firm* informs the audit committee of its intention to resign or, where there is no audit committee, the board of directors. Where applicable, the *firm* also informs any other persons or entities the *firm* is instructed to advise of its intention to withdraw from the *engagement*.

4.68   The *firm* is not required to resign immediately in circumstances where an objective, reasonable and informed third party would not regard it as being in the interests of the shareholders (or equivalent) or otherwise contrary to the public interest. Such circumstances might arise, for example, where:

- the litigation was commenced as the *engagement* was about to be completed, and shareholder (or other stakeholder) interests would be adversely affected by a delay in the *engagement*;
- on appropriate legal advice, the *firm* deems that the threatened or actual litigation is vexatious or designed solely to bring pressure to bear on the opinion to be expressed by the *firm*.

Section 5 – Non-audit / Additional Services

General Approach to Non-audit / Additional Services

Investment Circular Reporting Engagements

In relation to an *investment circular reporting engagement*, this Section applies only to those *additional services* provided by the *firm* to an *entity relevant to the engagement* during the '*relevant period*'. The *relevant period* covers the period during which the *investment circular reporting engagement* is undertaken and any additional period subsequent to the date of the most recent audited financial statements. Other services provided prior to that date are unlikely to create threats to integrity or objectivity because:

5.1

- where the *reporting accountant* undertook the last audit of the financial statements of an *entity relevant to the engagement* and complied with the FRC's Ethical Standard, the requirements applicable to the provision of other services will have been observed; or
- where the last audit of the financial statements of an *entity relevant to the engagement* was undertaken by a different *firm*, the work done by the *reporting accountant* in providing other services will have been the subject of independent review in the course of the audit.

Paragraphs 5.3 to 5.39 of this Section set out the general approach to be adopted by *firms* in relation to the provision of *non-audit services* to entities audited by them and *additional services* to entities which they may not audit but for which they undertake other public interest assurance services. This approach is applicable irrespective of the nature of the *non-audit / additional services*, which may be in question in a given case. (Paragraphs 5.44 to 5.164 of this Section illustrate the application of the general approach to a number of common *non-audit / additional services*.)

5.2

ISAs (UK) require that auditors exercise professional judgment and maintain professional scepticism throughout the planning and performance of the audit and, among other things:

5.3

- Identify and assess risks of material misstatement, whether due to fraud or error, based on an understanding of the entity and its environment, including the entity's internal control.
- Obtain sufficient appropriate audit evidence about whether material misstatements exist, through designing and implementing appropriate responses to the assessed risks.
- Form an opinion on the financial statements based on conclusions drawn from the audit evidence obtained[48].

Judgments regarding the nature and extent of evidence necessary to support an audit opinion or opinion given in respect of an other *public interest assurance engagement* are a matter for the *firm* but will include:

5.4

- Identifying, evaluating and testing, where appropriate, those internal control systems the effectiveness of which is necessary for the *engagement* and where, if any control weaknesses are identified, extended testing will be required; and
- additional work undertaken to respond to risks identified by management or the audit committee that the *firm* considers could impact the *firm's* opinion on financial statements or on other *subject matter information* or *subject matter* of the *engagement*.

---

[48] *ISA (UK) 200* Overall Objectives of the Independent Auditor and the Conduct of an Audit in Accordance with International Standards on Auditing (UK) *paragraph 7.*

5.5   Other work undertaken by the *engagement team* at the request of management or those charged with governance will not be categorised as part of the *engagement* irrespective of whether it forms part of the *engagement* proposal or *engagement*, unless it is clear that the predominant rationale for the performance of the work in question is to enable a soundly based opinion on the financial statements, or on other *subject matter information* or *subject matter* of the *engagement*, to be expressed. Therefore, an *engagement* does not include work where:

- The objective of that work is not to gather evidence to support the *firm's* opinion on the financial statements or on other *subject matter information* or *subject matter* of the *engagement*; or
- The nature and extent of testing is not determined by the *firm*, or in the case of a group, the work of other *firms* in relation to group components, in the context of expressing an opinion on the financial statements or on other *subject matter information* or *subject matter* of the *engagement*; or
- The principal terms and conditions for the work differ from that of the *engagement*.

5.6   In the context of an *audit engagement*, if additional work on financial information49 and/or financial controls is authorised by those charged with governance, but the objective of that work is not to enable the auditor to provide an audit opinion on the entity's financial statements, it will be considered as an 'audit related service' (see paragraph 5.40) for the purpose of this Ethical Standard provided that it:

- is integrated with the work performed in the audit and performed largely by the existing *audit team*; and
- is performed on the same principal terms and conditions as the audit.

As a consequence of these factors, any threats to auditor independence arising from the performance of such additional work are considered to be clearly insignificant.

5.7   For entities audited by the *firm*, other additional work that:

- does not relate to financial information and/or financial controls; or
- is not integrated with the work performed in the audit, or is not performed largely by the existing *audit team*, or
- is not on the same principal terms and conditions as the audit;

will be regarded as an 'other *non-audit service*' for the purpose of this Ethical Standard.

5.8   '*Non-audit services*' comprise any engagement in which a *firm*, or a member of its network, provides professional services to:

- an *audited entity*;
- an *audited entity's affiliates*; or
- another entity where the subject matter of the *engagement* includes the *audited entity*[50] and/or its *significant affiliates*;

other than the audit of financial statements of the *audited entity*.

5.9   For a *public interest assurance engagement* other than an audit, '*additional services*' comprise any engagement in which a *firm*, or a member of its *network*, provides professional services to an *entity relevant to the engagement* other than pursuant to:

---

[49] *This does not include* accounting services.

[50] *For example, where an engagement is undertaken to assist in the preparation of listing particulars for a company acquiring the* audited entity.

(a) any other *public interest assurance engagement*;

(b) the audit of financial statements; and

(c) those other roles which legislation or regulation specify can be performed by the auditor of the entity (for example, considering the preliminary announcements of listed companies, complying with the procedural and reporting requirements of regulators, such as requirements relating to the audit of the client's internal controls and reports in accordance with Section 714 of the Companies Act 2006).

Where the *entity relevant to the engagement* is a member of a group, *additional services* for the purposes of this Ethical Standard include:

– services provided by the *firm* to the parent entity or to any of its *significant affiliates*; and

– services provided by a *network firm* which is involved in the *engagement* to the *entity relevant to the engagement* or any of its *significant affiliates*.

There may be circumstances where the *firm* is engaged to provide a *non-audit / additional service* and where that service and its scope are determined by an entity which is not audited or relevant to an other *public interest assurance engagement* by the *firm*. However, it might be contemplated that an entity relevant to an *engagement*, may gain some benefit from that *non-audit / additional service*[51]. In some circumstances, there may be no threat to the integrity, objectivity and independence of the *firm* and *covered persons* at the time of appointment. However, the *firm* considers how the *non-audit / additional service* may be expected to develop, whether there are any threats that the *firm* may be subject to if additional relevant parties which are *entities relevant to an engagement*, are identified, and whether any safeguards need to be put in place. For example, when the results of such a *non-audit / additional service* performed by the *firm* are reflected in the financial statements or other *subject matter information* or *subject matter* of an *engagement*; or where the fees earned from such a *non-audit / additional service* performed by the *firm* could be perceived as compromising independence for an *engagement* by the *firm*. **5.10**

The *firm* shall establish policies and procedures that require others within the *firm*, when considering whether to provide a *non-audit / additional service* to an *entity relevant to an engagement*, other than an _investment circular reporting engagement_, or to any of its *affiliates*, to communicate details of the proposed *non-audit / additional service* to the *engagement partner*. **5.11**

The *firm* establishes appropriate channels of internal communication to ensure that, in relation to an *entity relevant to an engagement*, the *engagement partner* (or their delegate) is informed about any proposed *non-audit / additional service* to the entity or any of its *affiliates* and that he or she considers the implications for the integrity, objectivity and independence of the *firm* and *covered persons* before provision of the *non-audit / additional service* is accepted. Additionally, when addressing services provided to another entity in respect of an *entity relevant to an engagement*, the procedures address any requirement to preserve client confidentiality. **5.12**

In the case of a group audit of a *public interest entity* or an other *listed entity* the group *engagement partner* establishes that the entity has communicated its policy on the engagement of the external auditor to supply *non-audit services* to its *affiliates* and obtains confirmation that the auditors of the *affiliates* will comply with this policy.[52] The group **5.13**

---

[51] *For example, in a vendor due diligence engagement, the engagement is initiated and scoped by the vendor before the purchaser is identified. If an entity audited by the* firm *undertaking the due diligence engagement is the purchaser, that audited entity may gain the benefit of the report issued by its auditor, it may be a party to the engagement letter and it may pay an element of the fee.*

[52] *The UK Corporate Governance Code requires audit committees to develop the company's policy on the engagement of the external auditor to supply* non-audit services.

engagement partner also requires that relevant information on *non-audit services* provided by *network firms* is communicated on a timely basis.

5.14   **In relation to *investment circular reporting engagements*, the *firm* should establish policies and procedures, including the alternative procedures outlined in paragraph 1.40 of Section 1 of Part B of this Ethical Standard, that enable it to identify circumstances where others within the *firm* and *network firms* involved in the *investment circular reporting engagement* have undertaken to provide during the *relevant period*, an *additional service* to an *entity relevant to the engagement* or any of that entity's *significant affiliates*.**

5.15   The *firm* establishes appropriate policies and procedures to ensure that, in relation to an *entity relevant to an investment circular reporting engagement*, any undertaking to provide an *additional service* to the entity, or any of its *significant affiliates*, during the *relevant period* is identified, so that the *engagement partner* can consider the implications for integrity, objectivity and independence of the *firm* and *covered persons* before the *investment circular reporting engagement* is accepted. Such policies and procedures are likely to involve:

(i)   enquiries of each *entity relevant to the engagement*;

(ii)   reference to records of past and current *additional services* provided by the *firm*;

(iii)   enquiries of *network firms* involved in the *investment circular reporting engagement* as to whether they have provided any *additional services* to an *entity relevant to the engagement* or any of its *significant affiliates* during the *relevant period*.

Such enquiries are undertaken in a manner which seeks to protect confidentiality.

Identification and Assessment of Threats and Safeguards

5.16   **For an *engagement* other than an <u>*investment circular reporting engagement*</u>, before the *firm* accepts to provide a *non-audit / additional service* to an *entity relevant to the engagement*, the *engagement partner* shall:**

(a)   **identify and assess the significance of any related threats to the integrity or objectivity of the *firm* and *covered persons*, including whether independence would be compromised; and**

(b)   **identify and assess the effectiveness of the available safeguards to eliminate the threats or reduce them to a level where independence would not be compromised; and**

(c)   **consider whether it is probable that an objective, reasonable and informed third party, having regard to the threats and safeguards, would conclude that that the proposed *non-audit / additional service* would not impair integrity or objectivity and compromise the independence of the *firm* or *covered persons*.**

5.17   When assessing the significance of threats to the integrity, objectivity and independence of the *firm* and *covered persons*, the *engagement partner* considers the following factors:

- The likely relevance and impact of the *non-audit / additional service* on the financial statements, or on *subject matter information* or *subject matter* of the *engagement*;
- The extent to which performance of the proposed *non-audit / additional service* will involve the exercise of professional judgment;
- The size of the *non-audit / additional service* and the associated fee;
- The basis on which the fee is to be calculated;

- The *staff* who would be carrying out the *non-audit / additional service*[53];
- The staff from the *entity relevant to the engagement* who would be involved in the *non-audit / additional service*[54].

To ensure that this assessment is made with a proper understanding of the nature of the *non-audit / additional service*, it may be necessary to refer to a draft engagement letter in respect of the proposed *non-audit / additional service* or to discuss the service with the partner involved.

The assessment of the threats to the integrity, objectivity and independence of the *firm*   **5.18** and *covered persons* arising from any particular *non-audit / additional service* is a matter for the *engagement partner* responsible for the *engagement*. The *engagement partner* may decide to delegate some information gathering activities to senior personnel on the *engagement team* and may allow such personnel to make decisions in relation to routine *non-audit / additional services*. If this is the case, the *engagement partner* will:

- provide specific criteria for such decisions that reflect both the requirements of this Ethical Standard and the entity's policy for the purchase of *non-audit / additional services*; and
- monitor the decisions being made on a regular basis.

Where the *engagement partner* is not able to undertake the assessment of the significance   **5.19** of threats in relation to a proposed *non-audit / additional service* to an *entity relevant to an engagement*, for example due to illness or holidays, alternative arrangements are established (for example, by authorising the *engagement quality control reviewer* to consider the proposed service).

For an *engagement* other than an *investment circular reporting engagement*, where it is   **5.20**
probable that an objective, reasonable and informed third party would conclude that
the proposed *non-audit / additional service* would impair integrity or objectivity and
compromise the independence of the *firm* or *covered persons*, the *firm* shall either:

(a) not undertake the *non-audit / additional service*; or
(b) not accept or shall withdraw from the *engagement* as appropriate.

> **For an *investment circular reporting engagement*, where the *engagement partner***   **5.21**
> **considers that it is probable that a reasonable and informed third party would**
> **regard the objectives of an additional service[55] undertaken during the *relevant***
> ***period* as being inconsistent with the objectives of the *investment circular reporting***
> ***engagement*, the *firm* shall not accept or shall withdraw from the *investment***
> ***circular reporting engagement* as appropriate.**

The objectives of *non-audit / additional services* vary and depend on the specific terms   **5.22** of the service. In some cases these objectives may be inconsistent with those of an *audit engagement* or other *public interest assurance engagement* provided by the *firm* and, in

---

[53] *For example, where those handling the* non-audit service *are particularly expert so that the* audit team *(or persons advising it) may have difficulty in reviewing effectively the advice given or the work undertaken by the* non-audit service team *in the course of conducting a subsequent audit, with the result that the effectiveness of the audit might be compromised.*

[54] *For example, the safeguards necessary to address any self-review threat will require careful consideration where those involved are particularly senior and can be expected to be actively involved in any audit discussion as this may also create an intimidation threat.*

[55] *This includes consideration of any private reporting engagements associated with the transaction which is the subject of the* investment circular *that were undertaken before the* investment circular *was contemplated.*

such cases, this may give rise to a threat to the integrity or objectivity of the *firm* and *covered persons* and to the appearance of their independence.

5.23 Similarly, in relation to a possible appointment as provider of an *audit engagement* or other *public interest assurance engagement* to an entity that the *firm* has not provided such an *engagement* before, consideration needs to be given to recent, current and potential *non-audit / additional services* provided by the *firm* to the entity. The *firm* does not accept appointment to undertake such an *engagement* unless it is probable that an objective, reasonable and informed third party, taking into account safeguards applied, would conclude that the independence of the *firm* or *covered persons* are not compromised.

5.24 The passage of time since a service was provided, and audit or review of the outcome of the service by another *firm*, may help mitigate actual and perceived threats to independence. However, it is still necessary for an assessment of the threats to be undertaken in accordance with paragraph 1.33 of Section 1 of Part B of this Ethical Standard before an *engagement* is accepted. Such an assessment takes account of the nature of the service and significance of the outcome provided to the proposed *engagement* and whether an objective, reasonable and informed third party, taking into account safeguards applied, would conclude that the independence of the *firm* or *covered persons* are not compromised.

5.25 When tendering for a new *investment circular reporting engagement* or, in the case of *public interest entities* and other *listed entities*, when tendering for a new *audit engagement* or other *public interest assurance engagement*, the *firm* ensures that relevant information on recent *non-audit / additional services* is drawn to the attention of the audit committee (or those charged with governance if the entity does not have an audit committee) and, where applicable, any other persons or entities the *firm* is instructed to advise, including:

- when recent *non-audit / additional services* were provided;
- the materiality of those *non-audit / additional services* to the proposed *engagement*;
- whether those *non-audit / additional services* would have been prohibited if the entity had been an *entity relevant to an engagement* by the *firm* at the time when they were undertaken; and
- the extent to which the outcomes of *non-audit / additional services* have been audited or reviewed by another *firm*.

Threats to Objectivity and Independence

5.26 As identified in Section 1, the principal types of threats to the integrity, objectivity and independence of the *firm* and *covered persons* are:

- self-interest threat;
- self-review threat;
- management threat;
- advocacy threat;
- familiarity (or trust) threat; and
- intimidation threat.

The *firm*, its partners and *staff* remain alert to the possibility that any of these threats may occur in connection with *non-audit / additional services*. However, the threats most commonly associated with *non-audit / additional services* are self-interest threat, self-review threat, management threat and advocacy threat (see paragraph 1.29 of Section 1 of Part B of this Ethical Standard).

Safeguards

Where any threat to the integrity and objectivity of the *firm* or any *covered person* and **5.27**
the appearance of their independence is identified, the *engagement partner* assesses
the significance of that threat and considers whether there are safeguards that could be
applied and which would be effective to eliminate the threat or reduce it to a level where
independence is not compromised. If such safeguards can be identified and are applied, the
non-audit / additional service may be provided. However, where no such safeguards are
applied, the only course is for the *firm* either not to undertake the *non-audit / additional
service* in question or not to accept or to withdraw from the *engagement*.

When considering what safeguards, if any, would be effective in reducing the threats to **5.28**
integrity, objectivity and independence to a level where independence is not compromised,
the *engagement partner* has regard to the following safeguards which, individually or in
combination, may be effective, depending on the circumstances:

(a) The *non-audit / additional services* are provided by a separate team from the
engagement team, and:
- if circumstances require, to address the threat identified, there is effective
physical and electronic segregation of the individuals in each team, and of their
documentation, at all times during the provision of the *engagement* and *non-
audit / additional services*; and/or
- the team providing the *non-audit / additional services* avoids taking any action
or making any statement that compromises the integrity or objectivity and
independence of the *engagement team*, for example, expressing any opinion about
the approach that the *engagement team* might take or the conclusion it might reach
when considering the appropriateness of accounting or other judgments.
The *Ethics Partner* establishes policies and procedures to ensure that, where safeguards
of this nature are considered appropriate, the arrangements put in place are effective
at all times. This will involve the *Ethics Partner*/Function being satisfied that there
are effective arrangements in place for each member of the *non-audit / additional
services* team to acknowledge their responsibilities and for each member of the
engagement team to notify him or her of any breach of this requirement that the team
member becomes aware of. Where notified of a breach, the *Ethics Partner*/Function
considers together with the *engagement partner* the significance of the breach and the
implications for the integrity, objectivity and independence of the *engagement team*,
including whether any further safeguards are necessary and whether the matter should
be reported to those charged with governance of the entity;
(b) The *engagement quality control reviewer*, or another partner of sufficient relevant
experience and seniority who is, and is seen to be, an effective challenge to both
the *engagement partner* and the partner leading the *non-audit / additional services*,
reviews the work and conclusions of the *engagement team*. The review includes
consideration of the judgments of the persons conducting the *engagement*, if any,
relating to the *subject matter* of the *non-audit / additional service*, having regard to
the self-review threat identified, and determines and documents his or her conclusions
as to whether the work is sufficient and the conclusions of the *engagement team* are
appropriate. Where the review partner has concerns, the *engagement partner* does
not sign the engagement opinion/report until those concerns have been subject to
full consultation, including escalation through any processes required by the *firm's*
policies. Where this safeguard is considered appropriate, the *Ethics Partner*/Function
is satisfied that the review partner undertaking this role is appropriate, that the
review partner is aware of the circumstances leading to the conclusion that there is a
significant self-review threat and that any concerns raised by the review partner have
been satisfactorily resolved before signature of the opinion.

5.29   For an *engagement* other than an *investment circular reporting engagement*, where the *engagement partner* concludes, with respect to threats to the integrity or objectivity of the *firm* or *covered persons*, including any threats that could compromise independence, related to a proposed *non-audit / additional service* to an *entity relevant to the engagement*, that no appropriate safeguards are available to eliminate or reduce such threats to a level where independence would not be compromised, he or she shall inform the others concerned within the *firm* of that conclusion and the *firm* shall either:

(a) not undertake the *non-audit / additional service*; or

(b) not accept or shall withdraw from the *engagement* as appropriate.

If the *engagement partner* is in doubt as to the appropriate action to be taken, he or she shall resolve the matter through consultation with the *Ethics Partner*/Function.

5.30   An initial assessment of the threats to integrity, objectivity and independence and the safeguards to be applied is required when the *engagement partner* is considering the acceptance of a *non-audit / additional service*. The assessment of the threats and the safeguards applied is reviewed whenever the scope and objectives of the *non-audit / additional service* change significantly. If such a review suggests that safeguards cannot reduce the threat to a level where independence would not be compromised, the *firm* withdraws from the *non-audit / additional service*, or does not accept or withdraws from the *engagement* as appropriate.

5.31   Where both an *investment circular reporting engagement* and an engagement to undertake other services are provided concurrently, the initial assessment of the threats to objectivity and independence and the safeguards to be applied shall be reviewed whenever the scope and objectives of the other service or the *investment circular reporting engagement* change significantly. If such a review suggests that safeguards cannot reduce the threat to a level where independence is not compromised, the *firm* shall withdraw from the other service, or withdraw from the *investment circular reporting engagement*.

5.32   Where there is doubt as to the appropriate action to be taken, consultation with the *Ethics Partner*/Function ensures that an objective judgment is made and the *firm's* position is consistent.

Communication with Those Charged With Governance

5.33   Transparency is a key element in addressing the issues raised by the provision of *non-audit / additional services* by *firms* to the entities audited by them or for which other public interest assurance services are provided. Paragraphs 1.61, 1.66 and 1.67 of Section 1 of part B of this Ethical Standard establish requirements to communicate to those charged with governance, and other persons where appropriate, significant facts and matters that may bear upon the integrity, objectivity and independence of the *firm*. These include relevant facts and matters related to the provision of *non-audit / additional services*.

5.34   In the case of *public interest entities* and other *listed entities*, and entities that may be seeking a listing, ensuring that the audit committee is properly informed about the issues associated with the provision of *non-audit services* will assist them to comply with the provisions of the UK Corporate Governance Code relating to reviewing and monitoring the external auditor's independence and objectivity and to developing a policy on the use of the external auditor to supply *non-audit services*. This will include discussion of any inconsistencies between the entity's policy and this Ethical Standard and ensuring that the policy is communicated to *affiliates*.

Communications with those charged with governance regarding the impact on the integrity, objectivity or independence of the *firm* and *covered persons* of *non-audit / additional services* are likely to be facilitated if disclosure of such *non-audit / additional services* distinguishes between 'audit related services' (see paragraphs 5.40 – 5.43) and other *non-audit / additional services* (see paragraphs 5.8 and 5.9). **5.35**

Documentation

For an *engagement* <u>**other than an**</u> *<u>investment circular reporting engagement</u>***, the** *engagement partner* **shall ensure that the reasoning for a decision to provide** *non-audit / additional services***, and any safeguards adopted and why they are effective, is appropriately documented.** **5.36**

Matters to be documented include any significant judgments concerning: **5.37**

● threats identified;
● safeguards adopted and the reasons why they are considered to be effective; and
● communication with those charged with governance.

In situations where a management threat is identified in connection with the provision of *non-audit / additional services*, this documentation will include the assessment of the persons conducting the *engagement* of whether there is *informed management*. The documentation of communications with the entity where judgments and decisions are made by management may take a variety of forms, for example an informal meeting note covering the matters discussed. **5.38**

> For an *investment circular reporting engagement* the *engagement partner*, in accordance with paragraph 1.73 of Section 1 of Part B of this Ethical Standard, ensures that his or her consideration of the integrity, objectivity and independence of the *firm* and *covered persons* is appropriately documented on a timely basis. This includes consideration of non-audit/additional services provided during the *relevant period*. **5.39**

Audit Related Services

Audit related services are those *non-audit services* specified in this Ethical Standard that are largely carried out by members of the *audit engagement team*, and where the work involved is closely related to the work performed in the audit and the threats to auditor independence are clearly insignificant and, as a consequence, safeguards need not be applied. However, such services provided to *public interest entities*, other than those required by Union or national legislation, are still subject to the 70% cap (see paragraphs 4.34R and 4.35R of Section 4 of Part B of this Ethical Standard) and still require approval by the audit committee. **5.40**

Audit related services are: **5.41**

● Reporting required by law or regulation to be provided by the auditor;
● Reviews of interim financial information;
● Reporting on regulatory returns;
● Reporting to a regulator on client assets:
● Reporting on government grants;
● Reporting on internal financial controls when required by law or regulation;

- Extended audit work that is authorised by those charged with governance performed on financial information[56] and/or financial controls where this work is integrated with the audit work and is performed on the same principal terms and conditions.

5.42   **The *engagement partner* shall ensure that only those *non-audit services* listed in paragraph 5.41 are described as audit related services in communications with those charged with governance of the *audited entity*.**

5.43   In the UK, legislation requires large companies to disclose fees receivable by their auditors and their auditors' associates (see the Appendix to this Ethical Standard). The specified categories of disclosure include 'audit related assurance services', which will only include those services which are identified as audit related services in paragraph 5.41 above.

Evaluation of Specific Non-audit Services and Additional Services

5.44   There are services other than 'audit related services' (see paragraphs 5.40 – 5.43) for which it is generally accepted that the auditor of the entity is an appropriate provider. However the threats to independence arising from such services are not necessarily clearly insignificant and the *firm* considers whether such services give rise to threats to independence and, where appropriate, the need to apply safeguards. Such services include:

- Reports, that are not 'audit related services', required by the competent authorities / regulators supervising the *audited entity*, where the authority / regulator has either specified the auditor to provide the service or identified to the entity that the auditor would be an appropriate choice for service provider. These might include, for example:
  - ○   in relation to entities regulated under the Financial Services and Markets Act 2000 (FSMA), reports under s166 and s340 of FSMA; and
  - ○   other reports provided for under the rules of a competent authority / regulator.
- Audit and other services provided as auditor of the entity, or as *reporting accountant*, in relation to information of the *audited entity* for which it is probable that an objective, reasonable and informed third party would conclude that the understanding of the entity obtained by the auditor for the audit of the financial statements is relevant to the service, and where the nature of the service would not compromise independence. These might include, for example:
  - ○   audit and other services relating to public reporting as *reporting accountant* on financial or other information of the *audited entity* in a prospectus or circular (including reports that may be required by the Prospectus Rules, the Listing Rules and the Take Over Code);
  - ○   services, including private reporting, that are customarily performed by the *reporting accountant* to support statements made by the directors, disclosures in a prospectus or circular or, in the case of premium listed issuers, to support confirmations provided by the sponsor to the FCA;
  - ○   audit and other assurance services relating to public reporting on other information issued by the entity, such as reports on information in the front of annual reports not covered by the auditor's report on the financial statements.

The above list is not intended to be fully comprehensive and does not preclude other services being provided. Such services provided to *public interest entities*, other than those required by Union or national legislation, are still subject to the 70% cap (see paragraphs 4.34R and 4.35R of Section 4 of Part B of this Ethical Standard) and still require approval by the audit committee.

---

[56] *This does not include* accounting services.

In evaluating threats to compliance with the overarching principles of integrity, objectivity and independence arising from the provision of *non-audit / additional services*, the requirements and guidance below apply to all entities as indicated *relevant to an engagement*. This includes for *public interest entities* and their *significant affiliates* where applicable. Where a more stringent requirement for an audited *public interest entity* is established in paragraph 5.167R below, that more stringent requirement must be complied with.   **5.45**

For example, with regards to valuation services, paragraph 5.67 requires that the *firm* shall not provide such services to a *listed entity* that is not an *SME listed entity*, or a *significant affiliate* of such an entity, where the valuation would have a material effect on the *listed entity's* financial statements being audited, or on other *subject matter information* or *subject matter* of the *engagement* in the case of an other *public interest assurance engagement*, either separately or in aggregate with other valuations provided. Where the listed entity is also a *public interest entity* audited by the *firm*, paragraph 5.167R prohibits the provision of valuation services, subject to the derogation in paragraph 5.168R, including that the service has no direct or, in the view of an objective, reasonable and informed third party, would have an inconsequential effect, separately or in the aggregate on the audited financial statements of the *public interest entity*.   **5.46**

For the purpose of the requirements below, an '*SME listed entity*' is: **5.47**

   (a) **An entity whose equity *financial instruments* had an average market capitalisation of less than €200m on the basis of year end quotes for the previous three calendar years; or**

   (b) **An entity that issues exclusively non-equity *financial instruments* if:**
      (i) **the total nominal amount of the non-equity *financial instruments* issued and outstanding does not exceed €200m; or**
      (ii) **according to the last annual or consolidated accounts, meets at least two of the following criteria:**
         • **an average number of employee during the financial year of less than 250;**
         • **a total balance sheet not exceeding €43m;**
         • **an annual net turnover not exceeding €50m.**

An entity whose equity *financial instruments* have been admitted to trading for less than three years shall be deemed an SME if its market capitalisation is below €200m based on:

   (a) **the closing share price of the first day of trading, if its shares have been admitted to trading for less than one year;**

   (b) **the last closing share price of the first year of trading, if its *financial instruments* have been admitted to trading for more than one year but less than two years; or**

   (c) **the average of the last closing share prices of each of the first two years of trading, if its *financial instruments* have been admitted to trading for more than two years but less than three years.**

Internal Audit Services

The range of 'internal audit services' is wide and they may not be termed as such by an *entity relevant to an engagement*. For example, the *firm* may undertake: **5.48**

• to outsource the entity's entire internal audit function; or
• to supplement the entity's internal audit function in specific areas (for example, by providing specialised technical services or resources in particular locations); or
• to provide occasional internal audit services to the entity on an ad hoc basis.

All such services would fall within the term 'internal audit services'.

5.49   The nature of possible internal audit services is also wide. While the internal audit remit will vary from entity to entity, it often involves compliance and assurance activities designed to assess the design and operating effectiveness of existing or proposed systems or controls and advisory activities where advice is given to an entity on the design and implementation of risk management, control and governance processes.

5.50   The nature and extent of the threats to the *firm's* independence when undertaking internal audit services vary depending on the nature of the services provided. The main threats to the integrity, objectivity and independence of the *firm* and *covered persons* arising from the provision of internal audit services are the self-review threat and the management threat. Generally these will be lower for activities that are primarily designed to provide assurance to those charged with governance, for example that internal controls are operating effectively, than for advisory activities designed to assist the entity in improving the effectiveness of its risk management, control and governance processes.

5.51   Internal audit services – other than those prohibited in paragraph 5.53 – may be undertaken, provided that the *firm* is satisfied that there is *informed management* (see paragraph 1.29 of Section 1 of Part B of this Ethical Standard) and appropriate safeguards are applied to reduce the self-review threat to a level where independence is not compromised.

5.52   Examples of safeguards that may be appropriate when internal audit services are provided to an *entity relevant to an engagement* include ensuring that:

- internal audit projects undertaken by the *firm* are performed by partners and *staff* who have no involvement in the *engagement*;
- the *engagement* is reviewed by partner with relevant expertise who is not involved in the *engagement*, to ensure that the internal audit work performed by the *firm* has been properly and effectively assessed in the context of the *engagement*.

5.53   **The *firm* shall not provide internal audit services to an *entity relevant to an engagement* where it is reasonably foreseeable that:**

(a)   **for the purposes of the *engagement*, the *firm* would place significant reliance on the internal audit work performed by the *firm*; or**

(b)   **where the *firm* is undertaking an *engagement* <u>other than an *investment circular reporting engagement*</u>, for the purposes of the internal audit services, the *firm* would undertake part of the role of management; or**

(c)   **where the *firm* is undertaking an *investment circular reporting engagement*, for the purposes of the internal audit services, the *firm* would undertake part of the role of management in relation to the transaction or the financial information that is the subject of the *investment circular reporting engagement*.**

> For audits of *public interest entities* the prohibition established in paragraph 5.167R(h) must also be complied with.

5.54   The self-review threat is unacceptably high where substantially all of the internal audit activity is outsourced to the *firm* and this is significant to the entity or the *firm* cannot perform the *engagement* without placing significant reliance on the work performed for the purposes of the internal audit service. In the case of *listed entities* that are not SME *listed entities*, the provision of internal audit services in relation to the following examples is likely to be unacceptable as the *engagement team* is likely to place significant reliance on the work performed by the internal audit team in relation to the entity's internal financial controls:

- a significant part of the internal controls over financial reporting;
- financial accounting systems which generate information that is significant to the entity's accounting records;
- amounts or disclosures that are material to the financial statements of the entity or to other *subject matter information* or *subject matter* of the *engagement*.

> Where the *firm* is undertaking an *investment circular reporting engagement*, the above examples are relevant where they involve the *firm* taking decisions in relation to the transaction or the financial information that is the *subject matter* of the *investment circular reporting engagement*.

5.55 The management threat is unacceptably high where the *firm* provides internal audit services that involve *firm* personnel taking decisions or making judgments, which are properly the responsibility of management. For example, such situations arise where the internal audit function is outsourced to the *firm* and this is significant to the entity or where the nature of the internal audit work involves:

- Taking decisions on the scope and nature of the internal audit services to be provided to the entity;
- Designing internal controls or implementing changes thereto;
- Taking responsibility for risk management decisions;
- Undertaking work to evaluate the cost effectiveness of activities, systems and controls;
- Undertaking pre-implementation work on non-financial systems.

> Where the *firm* is undertaking an *investment circular reporting engagement*, the above examples are relevant where they involve the *firm* taking decisions in relation to the transaction or the financial information that is the *subject matter* of the *investment circular reporting engagement*.

5.56 During the course of the *engagement*, the persons conducting the *engagement* may evaluate the design and test the operating effectiveness of some of the entity's internal financial controls, and the operation of any relevant internal audit function, and provide management with observations on matters that have come to their attention, including comments on weaknesses in the internal control systems and/or the internal audit function together with suggestions for addressing them. This work is a by-product of the *engagement* rather than the result of a separate undertaking to provide *non-audit services* and therefore does not constitute internal audit services for the purposes of this Ethical Standard.

5.57 In some circumstances, additional work is undertaken to respond to risks identified by management or those charged with governance. Where the persons conducting the *engagement* consider that such risks could impact their opinion on the financial statements, or on other *subject matter information* or *subject matter* of the *engagement*, such work is considered to be *engagement* work for the purposes of this Ethical Standard (see paragraphs 5.6 and 5.7). Where the risks do not impact the opinion, whether it is appropriate for such work to be undertaken by the *firm* will depend on the extent to which it gives rise to a threat to the integrity, objectivity or independence of the *firm* and *covered persons*. The *engagement partner* reviews the scope of the objectives of the proposed work and assesses the threats to which it gives rise and the safeguards available.

5.58 If extended audit work on financial information and/or financial controls is authorised by those charged with governance, it will be considered as an 'audit related service' (see paragraphs 5.40 – 5.43) provided that it is integrated with the work performed in the audit and performed largely by the existing *audit team*, and is performed on the same principal terms and conditions as the audit.

5.59   Additional work will not be considered an 'audit related service' if it:

- does not relate to financial information and/or financial controls; or
- is not authorised by those charged with governance; or
- is not integrated with the work performed in the audit, or is not performed largely by the existing *audit team*; or
- is not on the same principal terms and conditions as the audit.

In such circumstances the threats and the safeguards will be communicated to those charged with governance. The *engagement partner* reviews the scope and objectives of the proposed work and assesses the threats to which it gives rise and the safeguards available. Whether it is appropriate for this work to be undertaken by the *audit firm* will depend on the extent to which it gives rise to threats to the auditor's integrity, objectivity or independence.

Information Technology Services

5.60   Design, provision and implementation of information technology (including financial information technology) systems by *firms* for an *entity relevant to an engagement* creates threats to the integrity, objectivity and independence of the *firm* and *covered persons*. The principal threats are the self-review threat and the management threat.

5.61   Design, provision or implementation of information technology systems that are not important to any significant part of the accounting system or to the production of the financial statements audited by the *firm*, or other *subject matter information* or *subject matter* of the *engagement* in the case of an other *public interest assurance engagement*, and do not have significant reliance placed on them by the persons conducting the *engagement*, may be undertaken, provided that there is *informed management* (see paragraph 1.29 of Section 1 of Part B of this Ethical Standard) and appropriate safeguards are applied to reduce the self-review threat to a level where independence is not compromised.

5.62   Examples of safeguards that may be appropriate when information technology services are provided to an *entity relevant to an engagement* include ensuring that:

- information technology projects undertaken by the *firm* are performed by partners and *staff* who have no involvement in the *engagement*;
- the work undertaken in the course of the *engagement* is reviewed by a partner with relevant expertise who is not involved in the *engagement* to ensure that the information technology work performed has been properly and effectively assessed in the context of the *engagement*.

5.63   The *firm* shall not design, provide or implement information technology systems for an *entity relevant to an engagement* where:

(a)   the systems concerned would be important to any significant part of the accounting system or to the production of the financial statements audited by the *firm*, or of other *subject matter information* or *subject matter* of the *engagement* in the case of an other *public interest assurance engagement*, and the persons conducting the *engagement* would place significant reliance upon them as part of the *engagement*; or

(b)   where the *firm* is undertaking an *engagement* other than an *investment circular reporting engagement*, for the purposes of the information technology services, the *firm* would undertake part of the role of management; or

(c)   where the *firm* is undertaking an *investment circular reporting engagement*, for the purposes of the information technology services, the *firm* would undertake part of the role of management in relation to the transaction or the financial information that is the subject of the *investment circular reporting engagement*.

For audits of *public interest entities* the prohibition established in paragraph 5.167R(e) must also be complied with.

Where it is reasonably apparent that, having regard to the activities and size of the entity and the range and complexity of the proposed system, management lacks the expertise required to take responsibility for the systems concerned, it is unlikely that any safeguards would be sufficient to eliminate these threats or to reduce them to a level where independence is not compromised. In particular, formal acceptance by management of the systems designed and installed by the *firm* is unlikely to be an effective safeguard when, in substance, the *firm* has been retained by management as experts and makes important decisions in relation to the design or implementation of systems of internal control and financial reporting that is the subject of the *engagement*. **5.64**

The provision and installation of information technology services associated with a standard 'off the shelf accounting package' (including basic set-up procedures to make the package operate on the entity's existing platform and peripherals, setting up the chart of accounts and the entry of standard data such as the entity's product names and prices) is unlikely to create a level of threat to the integrity, objectivity and independence of the *firm* and *covered persons* that cannot be addressed through applying appropriate safeguards. **5.65**

Valuation Services

A valuation comprises the making of assumptions with regard to future developments, the application of appropriate methodologies and techniques, and the combination of both to compute a certain value, or range of values, for an asset, a liability or for a business as a whole. **5.66**

The *firm* shall not provide a valuation service to: **5.67**

(a) a *listed entity relevant to an engagement* that is not an *SME listed entity* (see paragraph 5.47), or a *significant affiliate* of such an entity, where the valuation would have a material effect on the *listed entity's* financial statements, or other *subject matter information* or *subject matter* of the *engagement*, either separately or in aggregate with other valuations provided; or

(b) any other *entity relevant to an engagement*, where the valuation would both involve a significant degree of subjective judgment and have a material effect on the financial statements or other *subject matter information* or *subject matter* of the *engagement*, either separately or in aggregate with other valuations provided.

For audits of *public interest entities* the prohibition established in paragraph 5.167R(f) must also be complied with, subject to the derogation provided for in paragraph 5.168R.

The main threats to the integrity, objectivity and independence of the *firm* and *covered persons* arising from the provision of valuation services are the self-review threat and the management threat. In all cases, the self-review threat is considered too high to allow the provision of valuation services which involve the valuation of amounts with a significant degree of subjectivity and that may have a material effect on financial statements subject to an *audit engagement*, or on other *subject matter information* or *subject matter* of the *engagement* in the case of an other *public interest assurance engagement*. **5.68**

For *listed entities* that are not SME *listed entities*, or *significant affiliates* of such entities, the threats to integrity, objectivity and independence that would be perceived to be created are too high to allow the *firm* to undertake any valuation that has a material effect on the *listed entity's* financial statements being audited, or on other *subject matter information* **5.69** or *subject matter* of the *engagement* in the case of an other *public interest assurance engagement*.

5.70   The *firm's* policies and procedures will set out whether there are circumstances in which valuation services are not undertaken for non-listed entities as described in paragraph 1.49 of Section 1 of Part B of this Ethical Standard.

5.71   In circumstances where the *firm* is designated by legislation or regulation as being required to carry out a valuation the restrictions in paragraph 5.67 do not apply. In such circumstances, the *engagement partner* applies appropriate safeguards to reduce threats to integrity, objectivity and independence to a level where independence is not compromised.

5.72   It is usual for the persons conducting an *audit engagement* or *investment circular reporting engagement* (and in some cases other *public interest assurance engagements*) to provide management with accounting advice in relation to valuation matters that have come to the attention of persons conducting the *engagement* during the course of the *engagement*. Such matters might typically include:

- comments on valuation assumptions and their appropriateness;
- errors identified in a valuation calculation and suggestions for correcting them;
- advice on accounting policies and any valuation methodologies used in their application.

Advice on such matters does not constitute valuation services for the purpose of this Ethical Standard.

5.73   Where the *firm* is engaged to collect and verify the accuracy of data to be used in a valuation to be performed by others, such engagements do not constitute valuation services under this Ethical Standard.

Actuarial Valuation Services

5.74   **The *firm* shall not provide actuarial valuation services to:**

(a)   **a *listed entity relevant to an engagement* that is not an *SME listed entity* (see paragraph 5.47), or a *significant affiliate* of such an entity, unless the *firm* is satisfied that the valuation has no material effect on the *listed entity's* financial statements, or other *subject matter information* or *subject matter* of the *engagement*, either separately or in aggregate with other valuations provided; or**

(b)   **any other *entity relevant to an engagement*, unless the *firm* is satisfied that either all significant judgments, including the assumptions, are made by *informed management* or the valuation has no material effect on the financial statements, or other *subject matter information* or *subject matter* of the *engagement*, either separately or in aggregate with other valuations provided.**

> For audits of *public interest entities* the prohibition established in paragraph 5.167R(f) must also be complied with, subject to the derogation provided for in paragraph 5.168R.

5.75   Actuarial valuation services are subject to the same general principles as other valuation services. In all cases, where they involve the *firm* in making a subjective judgment and have a material effect on the financial statements subject to an audit, or other *subject matter information* or *subject matter* of the *engagement* in the case of an other *public interest assurance engagement*, actuarial valuations give rise to an unacceptable level of self-review threat and so may not be performed by *firms* for *entities relevant to an engagement*.

In the case of non-listed entities that are not *public interest entities*, where all significant **5.76**
judgments concerning the assumptions, methodology and data for the actuarial valuation
are made by '*informed management*' and the *firm's* role is limited to applying proven
methodologies using the given data, for which the management takes responsibility, it
may be possible to establish effective safeguards to protect the integrity, objectivity and
independence of the *firm* and *covered persons*.

For *listed entities* that are not *SME listed entities*, or *significant affiliates* of such entities, **5.77**
the threats to integrity, objectivity and independence that would be perceived to be created
are too high to allow the *firm* to undertake any actuarial valuation unless the *firm* is
satisfied that the valuation has no material effect on the *listed entity's* financial statements
being audited, or other *subject matter information* or *subject matter* of the *engagement* in
the case of an other *public interest assurance engagement.*

The *firm's* policies and procedures will set out whether there are circumstances in which **5.78**
actuarial valuation services are not undertaken for non-listed entities as described in
paragraph 1.49 of Section 1 of Part B of this Ethical Standard.

Tax Services

The range of activities encompassed by the term 'tax services' is wide. They include where **5.79**
the *firm*:

(a) provides advice to the entity on one or more specific matters at the request of the
     entity; or
(b) undertakes a substantial proportion of the tax planning or compliance work for the
     entity; or
(c) promotes tax structures or products to the entity, the effectiveness of which is likely
     to be influenced by the manner in which they are accounted for in the financial
     statements, or in other *subject matter information.*

Whilst it is possible to consider tax services under broad headings, such as tax planning
or compliance, in practice these services are often interrelated and it is impracticable to
analyse services in this way for the purposes of attempting to identify generically the threats
to which specific tax services give rise. As a result, *firms* need to identify and assess, on
a case-by-case basis, the potential threats to the integrity, objectivity and independence of
the *firm* and *covered persons* before deciding whether to provide tax services to an entity
relevant to an engagement.

The provision of tax services by *firms* to *entities relevant to an engagement* may give **5.80**
rise to a number of threats to the integrity, objectivity and independence of the *firm* and
covered persons, including the self-interest threat, the management threat, the advocacy
threat and, where the work involves a significant degree of subjective judgment and has
a material effect on the financial statements, or on other *subject matter information* or
subject matter of an *engagement*, the self-review threat.

Where the *firm* provides advice to an *entity relevant to an engagement* on one or more **5.81**
specific matters at the request of the entity, a self-review threat may be created. This self-
review threat is more significant where the *firm* undertakes a substantial proportion of the
tax planning and compliance work for the entity. However, the *firm* may be able to provide
such services, provided that there is *informed management* and appropriate safeguards are
applied to reduce the self-review threat to a level where independence is not compromised.

Examples of such safeguards that may be appropriate when tax services are provided to an **5.82**
entity relevant to an engagement include ensuring that:

- the tax services are provided by partners and *staff* who have no involvement in the *engagement*;
- the tax services are reviewed by an independent tax partner, or other senior tax employee;
- external independent advice is obtained on the tax work;
- tax computations prepared by the *engagement team* are reviewed by a partner or senior *staff* member with relevant expertise who is not a member of the *engagement team*; or
- a partner with relevant expertise not involved in the *engagement* reviews whether the tax work has been properly and effectively addressed in the context of the *engagement*.

5.83   **The *firm* shall not promote tax structures or products or provide tax advice to an *entity relevant to an engagement* where the *engagement partner* has, or ought to have, reasonable doubt as to whether the related accounting treatment involved is based on well-established interpretations or is appropriate, having regard to the relevant financial reporting framework, including, where applicable, the requirement for financial statements to give a true and fair view.**

> For audits of *public interest entities* the prohibition established in paragraph 5.167R(a)(vii) must also be complied with, subject to the derogation provided for in paragraph 5.168R.

5.84   Where the *firm* promotes tax structures or products or provides tax advice to an *entity relevant to an engagement*, it may be necessary to adopt an accounting treatment that is not based on well-established interpretations or may not be appropriate, in order to achieve the desired result. A self-review threat arises in the course of an *engagement* because the *firm* may be unable to form an impartial view of the accounting treatment to be adopted for the purposes of the proposed arrangements. Accordingly, this Ethical Standard does not permit the promotion of tax structures or products by *firms* to an *entity relevant to an engagement* where, in the view of the *engagement partner*, after such consultation as is appropriate, there is reasonable doubt as to whether the effectiveness of the tax structure or product depends on an accounting treatment that is well-established and appropriate.

5.85   **The *firm* shall not provide tax services wholly or partly on a *contingent fee basis* to:**

(a) **a *listed entity relevant to an engagement* that is not an *SME listed entity* (see paragraph 5.47), or a *significant affiliate* of such an entity; or**

(b) **or any other *entity relevant to an engagement*, where not otherwise prohibited by paragraph 4.14 of Section 4 of Part B of this Ethical Standard, for which the tax outcome in respect of the services (and, therefore, the amount of the fee) is uncertain, dependent on the proposed application of tax law, and may be material to present or future financial statements or other *subject matter information* or *subject matter* of the *engagement*.**

> For audits of *public interest entities* the prohibitions established in paragraph 5.167R(a) must also be complied with, subject to the derogations provided for in paragraph 5.168R.

5.86   Paragraph 4.14 of Section 4 of Part B of this Ethical Standard establishes conditions that preclude providing *non-audit / additional services* on a *contingent fee basis*.

5.87   Where tax services, such as advising on corporate structures, structuring transactions to achieve a particular effect, or otherwise with an objective of reducing tax charges are undertaken on a *contingent fee basis* for an *entity relevant to an engagement*, self-interest threats to the integrity, objectivity and independence of the *firm* or *covered persons* may arise. The *firm* may have, or may appear to have, an interest in the success of the tax services, causing the *firm* to make a judgment about which there is reasonable doubt as to its appropriateness. For an *entity relevant to an engagement* that is a *listed entity* that is not an SME *listed entity*, or a *significant affiliate* of such an entity, the self-interest threat cannot be eliminated or reduced to a level where independence is not compromised by the application of any safeguards.

For other *entities relevant to an engagement*, the self-interest threat cannot be eliminated 5.88 or reduced to a level where independence is not compromised by the application of any safeguards where the outcome in respect of the services (and, therefore, the amount of the contingent fee) is uncertain, dependent on the proposed application of tax law, and where the tax implications are, or may be, material to present or future financial statements or other *subject matter information* or *subject matter* of the *engagement*.

The *firm* shall not provide tax services to an *entity relevant to an engagement* other than 5.89 an *investment circular reporting engagement* where the service would involve the *firm* undertaking a management role.

> For audits of *public interest entities* the prohibition established in paragraph 5.167R(b) must also be complied with.

> The *firm* shall not provide tax services to an *entity relevant to an investment circular* 5.90 *reporting engagement* where the service would involve the *firm* undertaking a management role in relation to the transaction or the financial information that is the subject of the *investment circular reporting engagement*.

When providing tax services to an *entity relevant to an engagement*, there is a risk 5.91 that the *firm* undertakes a management role, unless the *firm* is working with '*informed management*'.

Where an *entity relevant to the engagement* is a *listed entity* that is not an *SME listed* 5.92 *entity* (see paragraph 5.47), or a *significant affiliate* of such an entity, the *firm* shall not provide a service to prepare current or deferred tax calculations that are or may reasonably be expected to be used by the entity when preparing accounting entries that are material to the financial statements or other *subject matter information* or *subject matter of the engagement*.

> For audits of *public interest entities* the prohibition established in paragraph 5.167R(a) (vi) must also be complied with, subject to the derogation provided for in paragraph 5.168R.

For *listed entities* that are not *SME listed entities*, or *significant affiliates* of such entities, 5.93 the threats to integrity, objectivity and independence that would be created are too high to allow the *firm* to provide a service to prepare calculations of current or deferred tax liabilities or assets for the purpose of preparing accounting entries that are material to the financial statements or other *subject matter information* or *subject matter* of the 5.94 *engagement*, together with associated disclosure notes.

Paragraph 5.92 is not intended to prevent a *firm* preparing tax calculations after the completion of the *engagement* for the purpose of submitting tax returns.

For entities other than *public interest entities* and other *listed entities* that are not *SME* 5.95 *listed entities*, or *significant affiliates* of *listed entities* that are not *SME listed entities*, the *firm* may provide a service to prepare current or deferred tax calculations for the purpose of preparing accounting entries, provided that:

(a) such services:
  (i)   do not involve initiating transactions or taking management decisions; and
  (ii)   are of a technical, mechanical or an informative nature; and
(b) appropriate safeguards are applied.

5.96 The *firm's* policies and procedures will set out whether there are circumstances in which current or deferred tax calculations for the purpose of preparing accounting entries are not prepared for non-listed entities as described in paragraph 1.49 of Section 1of Part B of this Ethical Standard.

5.97 **The *firm* shall not provide tax services to an *entity relevant to an engagement* where this would involve acting as an advocate for the entity in the resolution of an issue:**

  (a) that is material to the entity's present or future financial statements, or the *subject matter information* or *subject matter* of the *engagement*; or
  (b) where the outcome of the tax issue is dependent on a future or contemporary judgment by the *firm* in relation to the financial statements, or other *subject matter information* or *subject matter* of the *engagement*.

> For audits of *public interest entities* the prohibition established in paragraph 5.167R(a)(v) must also be complied with, subject to the derogation provided for in paragraph 5.168R.

5.98 Supporting ethical provision 2.3D, which embodies legal requirements for *statutory audits*, requires, inter alia, that a *firm* does not accept, continue or carry out an *engagement* if there is any threat of advocacy which would compromise the independence of the *firm* or *covered persons*. Where the tax services to be provided by the *firm* include representing the entity in any negotiations or proceedings involving the tax authorities, advocacy threats to the integrity, objectivity and independence of the *firm* and *covered persons* may arise.

5.99 The meaning of an 'advocacy threat' is described in paragraph 1.29 of Section 1 of Part B of this Ethical Standard. It includes supporting a position taken by management in an adversarial context, where the *firm* has to adopt a position closely aligned to that of management.

5.100 The *firm* is not acting as an advocate where the tax services involve the provision of information to the tax authorities (including an explanation of the approach being taken and the arguments being advanced by the entity). In such circumstances effective safeguards may exist and the tax authorities will undertake their own review of the issues.

5.101 Where the *firm* has been providing assistance in dealing with tax authorities and those tax authorities indicate that they are minded to reject the entity's arguments on a particular issue and the matter is likely to be determined by an appeals tribunal or court, the *firm* may become so closely identified with management's arguments that the *firm* is inhibited from forming an impartial view of the treatment of the issue in the financial statements, or in other *subject matter information* or *subject matter* of the *engagement* in the case of an other *public interest assurance engagement*. In such circumstances, if the issue is material to the financial statements, or other *subject matter information* or *subject matter* of the *engagement*, or is dependent on a future or contemporary judgment by the *firm* in relation to the *engagement*, the advocacy threat will be such that no safeguards can reduce it to a level where independence is not compromised. Accordingly, in such circumstances, the *firm* discusses the matter with the entity and makes it clear that it will have to withdraw from providing tax services that require it to act as advocate for the entity, or resign from the *engagement* from the time when the matter is formally listed for hearing before the appeals tribunal.

If the *firm* withdraws from providing tax services for the reasons described in paragraph 5.101, the *firm* is not precluded from having a continuing role (for example, responding to specific requests for information) for the entity in relation to the appeal, providing that the continuing role does not give rise to an advocacy threat that would compromise the independence of the *firm* or *covered persons*. The *firm* also assesses the threat associated with any continuing role in accordance with paragraphs 5.103 to 5.105 of this Section.

5.102

Litigation Support Services

Although management and advocacy threats may arise in litigation support services, such as acting as an expert witness, the primary issue is that a self-review threat will arise in all cases where such services involve a subjective estimation of the likely outcome of a matter that is material to the amounts to be included or the disclosures to be made in the financial statements.

5.103

The *firm* shall not provide litigation support services to:

5.104

(a) **a *listed entity relevant to an engagement* that is not an *SME listed entity* (see paragraph 5.47), or a *significant affiliate* of such an entity, where this would involve the estimation by the *firm* of the likely outcome of a pending legal matter that could be material to the amounts to be included or the disclosures to be made in the *listed entity's* financial statements, or in other *subject matter information* or *subject matter* of the *engagement*, either separately or in aggregate with other estimates and valuations provided; or**

(b) **any other *entity relevant to an engagement*, where this would involve the estimation by the *firm* of the likely outcome of a pending legal matter that could be material to the amounts to be included or the disclosures to be made in the entity's financial statements, or in other *subject matter information* or *subject matter* of the *engagement*, either separately or in aggregate with other estimates and valuations provided and there is a significant degree of subjectivity involved.**

> For audits of *public interest entities* the prohibition established in paragraph 5.167R(f) must also be complied with, subject to the derogation provided for in paragraph 5.168R.

In the case of non-listed entities, litigation support services that do not involve such subjective estimations are not prohibited, provided that the *firm* has carefully considered the implications of any threats and established safeguards to reduce those threats to a level where independence is not compromised.

5.105

The *firm*'s policies and procedures will set out whether there are circumstances in which litigation support services are not undertaken for non-listed entities as described in paragraph 1.49 of Section 1 of Part B of this Ethical Standard.

5.106

Legal Services

The *firm* shall not provide legal services to an *entity relevant to an engagement*, where this would involve acting as the solicitor formally nominated to represent the entity in the resolution of a dispute or litigation which is material to the amounts to be included or the disclosures to be made in the financial statements, or in other *subject matter information* or *subject matter* of the *engagement*.

5.107

> For audits of *public interest entities* the prohibition established in paragraph 5.167R(g) must also be complied with.

5.108   Although the provision by the *firm* of certain types of legal services to an *entity relevant to an engagement* may create advocacy, self-review and management threats, this Ethical Standard does not impose a general prohibition on the provision of legal services. However, in view of the degree of advocacy involved in litigation or other types of dispute resolution procedures and the potential importance of any assessment by the *firm* of the merits of the entity's position when undertaking an *engagement*, this Ethical Standard prohibits a *firm* from acting as the formally nominated representative for an *entity relevant to an engagement* in the resolution of a dispute or litigation which is material to the amounts recognised or disclosed the financial statements or other *subject matter information* or *subject matter* of the *engagement*.

Recruitment and Remuneration Services

5.109   **The *firm* shall not provide recruitment services to an *entity relevant to an engagement*, that would involve the *firm* taking responsibility for the appointment of any director or:**

  (a)   **where the *firm* is undertaking an *engagement* other than an *investment circular reporting engagement*, any employee of the entity; or**

  (b)   **where the *firm* is undertaking an *investment circular reporting engagement*, any employee of the entity who will be involved in an area that is directly concerned with the transaction which is the subject of the *investment circular*.**

> For audits of *public interest entities* the prohibitions established in paragraphs 5.167R(b) and (k) must also be complied with.

5.110   A management threat arises where *firm* personnel take responsibility for any decision as to who is appointed by the entity.

5.111   **For a *listed entity*, that is not an *SME listed entity* (see paragraph 5.47), *relevant to an engagement*, the *firm* shall not provide recruitment services in relation to a *key management position* of the entity, or a *significant affiliate* of such an entity.**

> For audits of *public interest entities* the prohibition established in paragraph 5.167R(k) must also be complied with.

5.112   A familiarity threat arises if the *firm* plays a significant role in relation to the identification and recruitment of senior members of management within the entity, as the *engagement team* may be less likely to be critical of the information or explanations provided by such individuals than might otherwise be the case. Accordingly, for a *listed entity relevant to an engagement*, other than an *investment circular reporting engagement*, that is not an *SME listed entity*, and for *significant affiliates* of such entities, the *firm* does not provide services that involve the recruitment of individuals for *key management positions*.

5.113   The *firm's* policies and procedures will set out whether there are circumstances in which recruitment services are not undertaken for non-listed entities as described in paragraph 1.49 of Section 1 of Part B of this Ethical Standard.

5.114
> Where the *firm* providing an *investment circular reporting engagement* has played a significant role in relation to the identification and recruitment of a senior member of management within the entity, including all directors, prior to the '*relevant period*', the *engagement partner* considers whether a familiarity threat exists, taking account of factors such as:

- the closeness of personal relationships between the *firm's* partners, *staff* and other *covered persons*, and the entity's personnel;
- the length of time since the recruitment of the individual in question;
- the position held by the individual at the entity;
- the extent of involvement that the individual will have with the transaction that is the subject of the *investment circular*;
- whether the individual is in a position to exercise influence on the accounting records or financial information.

Following the assessment of any such threats, appropriate safeguards are applied where necessary, such as ensuring that the *engagement team* does not include individuals with a close relationship to the senior member of management or who were involved in the recruitment exercise.

Recruitment services involve a specifically identifiable, and separately remunerated, **5.115** engagement. *Firms* and *engagement teams* may contribute to an entity's recruitment process in less formal ways. The prohibitions set out in paragraphs 5.109 and 5.111 do not extend to:

- senior members of an *engagement team* interviewing prospective directors or employees of the entity and advising on the candidate's technical financial competence; or
- the entity using information gathered by the *firm*, including that relating to salary surveys.

The *firm* shall not provide advice on the quantum of the remuneration package or **5.116**
the measurement criteria on which the quantum is calculated, for a director or *key*
***management position* of an *entity relevant to an engagement*.**

For audits of *public interest entities* the prohibition established in paragraph 5.167R(k) must also be complied with.

The provision of advice on remuneration packages (including bonus arrangements, **5.117** incentive plans and other benefits) to existing or prospective employees of the entity gives rise to familiarity threats. The significance of the familiarity threat is considered too high to allow advice on the overall amounts to be paid or on the quantitative measurement criteria included in remuneration packages for directors and *key management positions*.

For other employees, these threats can be adequately addressed by the application **5.118** of safeguards, such as the advice being provided by partners and *staff* who have no involvement in the *engagement*.

In cases where all significant judgments concerning the assumptions, methodology and **5.119** data for the calculation of remuneration packages for directors and key management are made by '*informed management*' or a third party and the *firm's* role is limited to applying proven methodologies using the given data, for which the management takes responsibility, it may be possible to establish effective safeguards to protect the integrity, objectivity and independence of the *firm* and *covered persons*.

Advice on tax, pensions and interpretation of accounting standards relating to remuneration **5.120** packages for directors and key management can be provided by the *firm*, provided they are not prohibited by the requirements of this Ethical Standard relating to tax, actuarial valuations and *accounting services*. Disclosure of the provision of any such advice would be made to those charged with governance of the entity (see Section 1 of this Ethical Standard, paragraphs 1.61 to 1.71 of Section 1 of part B of this Ethical Standard).

Corporate Finance Services

5.121   The range of services encompassed by the term 'corporate finance services' is wide. For example, the *firm* may undertake:

- to identify possible purchasers for parts of the entity's business and provide advisory services in the course of such sales; or
- to identify possible 'targets' for the entity to acquire; or
- to advise the entity on how to fund its financing requirements; or
- to act as sponsor on admission to listing on the London Stock Exchange, as Nominated Advisor on the admission of the entity on the Alternative Investments Market (AIM); or
- to act as financial adviser to entity offerors or offerees in connection with public takeovers.

5.122   The potential for the integrity, objectivity and independence of the *firm* and *covered persons* to be compromised through the provision of corporate finance services varies considerably depending on the precise nature of the service provided. The main threats to integrity, objectivity and independence arising from the provision of corporate finance services are the self-review, management and advocacy threats. Self-interest threats may also arise, especially in situations where the *firm* is paid on a *contingent fee basis*.

5.123   When providing corporate finance services to an *entity relevant to an engagement*, there is a risk that the *firm* undertakes a management role, unless the *firm* is working with '*informed management*'. In addition, appropriate safeguards are applied to reduce any self-review threat to a level where independence is not compromised.

5.124   Examples of safeguards that may be appropriate when corporate finance services are provided to an *entity relevant to an engagement*, include ensuring that:

- the corporate finance advice is provided by partners and *staff* who have no involvement in the *engagement*;
- any advice provided is reviewed by an independent corporate finance partner within the *firm*;
- external independent advice on the corporate finance work is obtained;
- a partner who is not involved in the engagement reviews the *engagement* work performed in relation to the *subject matter* of the corporate finance services provided to ensure that such *engagement* work has been properly and effectively reviewed and assessed in the context of the *engagement*.

5.125   Where the *firm* provides corporate finance services to an *entity relevant to an engagement* in connection with conducting the sale or purchase of a material part of the entity's business, the *engagement partner* informs the audit committee (or equivalent) and, where applicable, any other person or entity the *firm* is instructed to advise, about the corporate finance service, as set out in paragraphs 1.61 to 1.71 of Section 1 of Part B of this Ethical Standard.

5.126   **The *firm* shall not provide corporate finance services in respect of an *entity relevant to an engagement*, where:**

(a)   **the service would involve the *firm* taking responsibility for dealing in, underwriting, or promoting shares; or**

(b)   **the *engagement partner* has, or ought to have, reasonable doubt as to whether an accounting treatment that is subject to a contemporary or future judgment by the *firm* relating to a material matter in the financial statements or in other *subject matter information* or *subject matter* of the engagement, and upon which the success of the related transaction depends:**

(i)   is based on well-established interpretations; or

(ii)   is appropriate;

having regard to the requirements of the relevant reporting framework, including where applicable for financial statements to give a true and fair view; or

(c)   the *firm* is undertaking an *engagement other than an investment circular reporting engagement*, and the service would involve undertaking a management role in the entity; or

(d)   the *firm* is undertaking an *investment circular reporting engagement*, and the service would involve undertaking a management role in the entity in relation to the transaction or the *subject matter information* or *subject matter* of the *investment circular reporting engagement*.

For audits of *public interest entities* the prohibitions established in paragraphs 5.167R(b), (i) and (j) must also be complied with.

An unacceptable advocacy threat arises where, in the course of providing a corporate finance service, the *firm* promotes the interests of the entity by taking responsibility for dealing in, underwriting, or promoting shares.   **5.127**

Where the *firm* acts as a sponsor under the Listing Rules[57], or as Nominated Adviser on the admission of the entity to the AIM, the *firm* is required to confirm that the entity has satisfied all applicable conditions for listing and other relevant requirements of the listing (or AIM or ESM) rules. Where there is, or there ought to be, reasonable doubt that the *firm* will be able to give that confirmation, it does not enter into providing such service.   **5.128**

A self-review threat arises where the outcome or consequences of the corporate finance service provided by the *firm* may be material to the financial statements or other *subject matter information* or *subject matter*, which are, or will be, subject to an *engagement* by the same *firm*. Where the *firm* provides corporate finance services, for example advice to the entity on financing arrangements, it may be necessary to adopt an accounting treatment that is not based on well-established interpretations or which may not be appropriate, in order to achieve the desired result. A self-review threat is created because the *firm* may be unable to form an impartial view of the accounting treatment to be adopted for the purposes of the proposed arrangements. Accordingly, this Ethical Standard does not permit the provision of such services by *firms* in respect of an *entity relevant to an engagement* by them where there is or ought to be reasonable doubt as to whether an accounting treatment that is subject to a contemporary or future judgment by the *firm* relating to a material matter in the financial statements, or in other *subject matter information* or *subject matter*, of the entity and on which the success of a transaction depends is well-established and appropriate.   **5.129**

Advice to entities on funding issues and banking arrangements, where there is no reasonable doubt as to the appropriateness of the accounting treatment, is not prohibited provided this does not involve the *firm* in taking decisions or making judgments which are properly the responsibility of management.   **5.130**

These restrictions do not apply in circumstances where the *firm* is designated by legislation or regulation as being required to carry out a particular service. In such circumstances, the *engagement partner* establishes appropriate safeguards.   **5.131**

---

[57] *In the United Kingdom, the UK Listing Authority's publication the 'Listing Rules'.*

Transaction Related Services

5.132 In addition to corporate finance services, there are other services associated with transactions that a *firm* may undertake for an *entity relevant to an engagement*. For example:

- investigations into possible acquisitions or disposals ('due diligence' investigations); or
- investigations into the tax affairs of possible acquisitions or disposals; or
- the provision of information to management or sponsors in relation to prospectuses and other *investment circulars* (for example, long form reports, comfort letters on the adequacy of working capital); or
- agreed-upon procedures or reports provided to management in relation to particular transactions (for example, securitisations).

5.133 When providing transaction related services to an *entity relevant to an engagement*, there is a risk that the *firm* may face a management threat, unless the *firm* is working with *informed management*. In addition, appropriate safeguards are applied to reduce any self-review threat to a level where independence is not compromised.

5.134 Examples of safeguards that may be appropriate when threats are identified in relation to transaction related services provided to an *entity relevant to an engagement* include ensuring that:

- the transaction related advice is provided by partners and *staff* who have no involvement in the *engagement*;
- any advice provided is reviewed by an independent transactions partner within the *firm*;
- external independent advice on the transaction related work is obtained;
- a partner with relevant expertise who is not involved in the *engagement* reviews the *engagement* work performed in relation to the *subject matter* of the transaction related service provided to ensure that such work has been properly and effectively reviewed and assessed in the context of the *engagement*.

5.135 **The *firm* shall not provide transaction related services in respect of an *entity relevant to an engagement*, where:**

(a) the *engagement partner* has, or ought to have, reasonable doubt as to whether an accounting treatment that is subject to a contemporary or future judgment by the *firm* relating to a material matter in the financial statements, or other *subject matter information* or *subject matter* of the *engagement*, and upon which the success of the related transaction depends;

(i)   is based on well-established interpretations; or

(ii)   is appropriate;

having regard to the requirements of the relevant reporting framework, including where applicable for financial statements to give a true and fair view; or

(b) the *firm* is undertaking an *engagement* <u>other than an *investment circular reporting engagement*</u>, and the service would involve undertaking a management role in the entity; or

(c) the *firm* is undertaking an *investment circular reporting engagement*, and the service would involve undertaking a management role in the entity in relation to the transaction or the *subject matter information* or *subject matter* of the *investment circular reporting engagement*.

> For audits of *public interest entities* the prohibition established in paragraphs 5.167R(b) and (i) must also be complied with.

A self-review threat arises where the outcome of the transaction related services undertaken **5.136** by the *firm* may be material to the financial statements or other *subject matter information* or *subject matter* of the entity which are, or will be, subject to an *engagement* by the same *firm*. Where the entity proposes to undertake a transaction, it may be necessary to adopt an accounting treatment that is not based on well-established interpretations or may not be appropriate, in order to achieve the desired result of the transaction (for example, to take assets off the balance sheet). A self-review threat is created if the *firm* undertakes transaction related services in connection with such a transaction. Accordingly, this Ethical Standard does not permit the provision of services by *firms* in respect of an *entity relevant to an engagement* by them where there is or ought to be reasonable doubt as to whether an accounting treatment, that is subject to a contemporary or future judgment by the *firm* relating to a material matter in the financial statements, or in other *subject matter information* or *subject matter* of the entity and on which the success of a related transaction depends, is well-established and appropriate.

These restrictions do not apply in circumstances where the *firm* is designated by legislation **5.137** or regulation as being required to carry out a particular service. In such circumstances, the *engagement partner* establishes appropriate safeguards.

Restructuring Services

Restructuring services are any *non-audit services* provided to an entity in connection with **5.138** the entity's development or implementation of a transaction or package of transactions (a 'restructuring plan') designed to change its equity or debt financing structure, its corporate structure, or its operating structure. There are a variety of possible purposes for developing a restructuring plan, for example to address financial or operating difficulties, to support tax planning, to improve operating efficiency, or to improve the cost of capital. The range of *non-audit / additional services* that may be regarded as 'Restructuring Services' is extensive, and the nature of those services may encompass many of the other types of *non-audit / additional services* discussed in this Ethical Standard. Where applicable, the related requirements and guidance covered elsewhere in this Ethical Standard apply to Restructuring Services.

The restructuring services that an entity may use a *firm* to provide may vary considerably **5.139** and may range from the incidental and routine to advice that is fundamental to the efficacy of the restructuring plan. Consequently, where such services are provided by a *firm* that that provides an *engagement* for the entity, the *engagement partner*:

- the threats that the restructuring services may present to the *firm's* ability to conduct any contemporary or future *engagement* with integrity, objectivity and independence; and
- the probability that an objective, reasonable and informed third party would conclude that the independence of the *firm* or *covered persons* would be compromised.

The *firm* shall not provide restructuring services in respect of an *entity relevant to an* **5.140** ***engagement*, where:**

(a) the service would involve the firm undertaking a management role in or on behalf of the entity; or

(b) the service would require the *firm* to act as an advocate for the entity in relation to matters that are material to the financial statements, or other *subject matter information* or *subject matter* of the *engagement*.

For audits of *public interest entities* the prohibition established in paragraphs 5.167R(b) and (i) must also be complied with.

5.141   The potential for the integrity, objectivity and independence of the *firm* or *covered persons* to be compromised through the provision of restructuring services varies depending on the nature of the service provided. Two of the main threats to integrity, objectivity and independence arising from the provision of restructuring services arise where the *firm* undertakes a management or advocacy role:

- A *firm* undertakes a management role if the entity does not have '*informed management*' capable of taking responsibility for the decisions to be made.
- To avoid undertaking an advocacy role on behalf of the entity, the *firm* takes particular care not to assume (or seen to be assuming) responsibility for the entity's proposals or being regarded as negotiating on behalf of the entity or advocating the appropriateness of the proposals such that its independence would be compromised. This is particularly important when the *firm* attends meetings with the entity's bank or other interested parties.

If the *firm* undertakes a management role or acts as advocate for the entity, the threats to integrity, objectivity and independence of the *firm* and *covered persons* are such that no safeguards can reduce the threat to a level where independence is not compromised[58].

5.142   **The *firm* shall not provide restructuring services in respect of an *entity relevant to engagement*, where that service may give rise to a self-review threat in the course of a contemporary or future *engagement* unless it is satisfied that such threats can be reduced by appropriate safeguards to a level where independence is not compromised and that such safeguards have been put in place.**

> For audits of *public interest entities* the prohibition established in paragraph 5.167R(i) must also be complied with.

5.143   The provision of restructuring services gives rise to a self-review threat where the restructuring services to be provided involve advice or judgments which are likely to be material to a contemporary or future judgment of the *firm* in relation to an *engagement*.

5.144   Examples of restructuring services that the *firm* may be requested to undertake and which may give rise to a self-review threat include:

- Providing preliminary general advice on the options and choices available to management or stakeholders of an entity facing urgent financial or other difficulties.
- Undertaking a review of the business of the entity with a view to advising the entity on liquidity management or operational restructuring options.
- Advising on the development of forecasts or projections, for presentation to lenders and other stakeholders, including assumptions.
- Advising the entity on how to fund its financing requirements, including equity and debt restructuring programmes.
- Participating in the design or implementation of an overall restructuring plan including, for example, participating in the preparation of cash flow and other forecasts and financial models underpinning the overall restructuring plan.

5.145   The self-review threat arising from the provision of such services is particularly significant where, in relation to an *audit engagement*, it has potential to impact the *firm's* assessment of whether it is appropriate to prepare the entity's financial statements on a going concern basis. Where the *firm* has been involved in aspects of the preparation of a cash flow, a forecast or a financial model, it is probable that an objective, reasonable and informed

---

[58] '*ES – Provisions Available for Small Entities (Revised)*' provides exemptions relating to informed management *and the advocacy threat for auditors of small entities.*

third party would conclude that the *firm* would have a significant self-review threat in considering the going concern assumption.

The self-review threat arising from the provision of such services is also particularly **5.146** significant where the restructuring services are provided in respect of an *audited entity* and involve developing or implementing a restructuring plan to address the actual or anticipated financial or operational difficulties that threaten the survival of that entity as a going concern (an '*audited entity in distress*').

The *firm* puts in place those safeguards that it regards as appropriate to reduce the threats to **5.147** the integrity and objectivity of the *firm* and *covered persons* to a level where independence is not compromised. If the *firm* concludes that the threats arising from some or all of the restructuring services involved cannot be addressed by putting appropriate safeguards in place, it declines providing the service, or those parts of the service affected by those threats that cannot be adequately addressed.

Where an *entity in distress relevant to an engagement*, is a listed entity that is not an **5.148** **SME listed entity (see paragraph 5.47), or a *significant affiliate* of such a *listed entity*,** **the restructuring services provided by the *firm* shall be limited to providing:**

(a) preliminary general advice to an *entity in distress*;
(b) assistance with the implementation of elements of an overall restructuring plan, **such as the sale of a non-significant component business, provided those elements** **are not material to the overall restructuring plan;**
(c) challenging, but in no circumstances developing, the projections and assumptions **within a financial model that has been produced by the *entity in distress*;**
(d) reporting on a restructuring plan, or aspects of it, in connection with the proposed **issue of an *investment circular*; and**
(e) where specifically permitted by a regulatory body with oversight of the *entity in* **distress.**

> For audits of *public interest entities* the prohibition established in paragraph 5.167R(i) must also be complied with.

Except to the extent identified in paragraph 5.148, the significance of the self-review threat **5.149** is too high to permit the provision of other restructuring services to an *entity in distress* that is a *listed entity* that is not an *SME listed entity*, or a *significant affiliate* of such a *listed entity*, because there are no safeguards that would be sufficient to reduce the resultant threats to a level where independence is not compromised.

The *firm's* policies and procedures will set out whether there are circumstances in which **5.150** restructuring services are not undertaken for non-listed entities in distress as described in paragraph 1.49 of Section 1 of Part B of this Ethical Standard.

Accounting Services

For the purpose of this Ethical Standard, the term '*accounting services*' is defined as the **5.151** provision of services that involve the maintenance of accounting records or the preparation of financial statements or other *subject matter information* or *subject matter* that are then subject to audit or an other *public interest assurance engagement*. Advice on the implementation of current and proposed accounting standards is not included in the term *accounting services*.

The range of activities encompassed by the term *accounting services* is wide. In some **5.152** cases, the entity may ask the *firm* to provide a complete accounting service including maintaining all of the accounting records and the preparation of the financial statements. Other common situations are:

- the *firm* may take over the provision of a specific accounting function on an outsourced basis (for example, payroll);
- the entity maintains the accounting records, undertakes basic bookkeeping and prepares a year-end trial balance and asks the *firm* to assist with the preparation of the necessary adjustments and the financial statements.

5.153   The provision of *accounting services* by the *firm* to an *entity relevant to an engagement* creates threats to the integrity, objectivity and independence of the *firm* and *covered persons*, principally self-review and management threats, the significance of which depends on the nature and extent of the *accounting services* in question and upon the level of public interest in the entity.

5.154   When providing *accounting services* to an entity relevant to an audit or other *public interest assurance engagement* by the *firm*, unless the *firm* is working with *informed management*, there is a risk that the *firm* undertakes a management role.

5.155   **The *firm* shall not provide *accounting services* to an *entity relevant to an engagement* other than an *investment circular reporting engagement* where:**

(a) the entity is a *listed entity* that is not an *SME listed entity* (see paragraph 5.47), *relevant to an engagement* by the *firm*, or a *significant affiliate* of such an entity; or

(b) for any other entity:

- **those *accounting services* would involve the *firm* undertaking part of the role of management; or**
- **the financial information is the subject of an *investment circular reporting engagement*.**

> For audits of *public interest entities* the prohibitions established in paragraphs 5.167R(a)(i)–(a)(iii), (b), (c) and (d) must also be complied with, subject to the derogation provided for in paragraph 5.168R regarding 5.167R(a)(i).

5.156   **The *firm* shall not provide *accounting services* in relation to the financial information that is the subject of an *investment circular reporting engagement* by the *firm*.**

5.157   Even where there is no undertaking to provide any *accounting services*, it is usual for the *firm* to provide the management with accounting advice on matters that have come to its attention during the course of an *engagement*. Such matters might typically include:

- comments on weaknesses in the accounting records and suggestions for addressing them;
- errors identified in the accounting records and in the financial statements, or other *subject matter information* or *subject matter*, and suggestions for correcting them;
- advice on the accounting policies in use and on the application of current and proposed accounting standards.

This advice is a by-product of the *engagement* rather than the result of any undertaking to provide *non-audit / additional services*. Consequently, as it is part of the *engagement*, such advice is not regarded as giving rise to any threat to the integrity, objectivity and independence of the *firm* and *covered persons*.

For *listed entities* that are not *SME listed entities relevant to an engagement* ~~other than~~ ~~an *investment circular reporting engagement*~~, or *significant affiliates* of such entities, the threats to integrity, objectivity and independence that would be created are too high to allow the *firm* to provide any *accounting services*.   **5.158**

> The threats to the *reporting accountant's* integrity, objectivity and independence that would be created are too high to allow the *firm* to provide any *accounting services* in relation to the financial information that is the subject of an *investment circular reporting engagement* by the *firm*.   **5.159**

The *firm's* policies and procedures will set out whether there are circumstances in which *accounting services* are not undertaken for non-listed entities as described in paragraph 1.49 of Section 1 of Part B of this Ethical Standard.   **5.160**

For entities other than *listed entities* that are not *SME listed entities* relevant to an *engagement* ~~other than an *investment circular reporting engagement*~~, or *significant affiliates* of such *listed entities*, the *firm* may provide *accounting services*, provided that: **5.161**

(a)   such services:
   (i)   do not involve initiating transactions or taking management decisions; and
   (ii)   are of a technical, mechanical or an informative nature; and
(b)   appropriate safeguards are applied to reduce the self-review threat to a level where independence is not compromised.

The maintenance of the accounting records and the preparation of the financial statements are the responsibility of the management of the entity. Accordingly, in any undertaking to provide the entity with *accounting services*, the *firm* does not initiate any transactions or take any decisions or make any judgments, which are properly the responsibility of the management. These include: **5.162**

● authorising or approving transactions;
● preparing originating data (including valuation assumptions);
● determining or changing journal entries, or the classifications for accounts or transactions, or other accounting records without management approval.

Examples of *accounting services* of a technical or mechanical nature or of an informative nature include: **5.163**

● recording transactions for which management has determined the appropriate account classification, posting coded transactions to the general ledger, posting entries approved by management to the trial balance or providing certain data-processing services (for example, payroll);
● assistance with the preparation of the financial statements where management takes all decisions on issues requiring the exercise of judgment and has prepared the underlying accounting records.

Examples of safeguards that may be appropriate when *accounting services* are provided to an *entity relevant to an engagement*, include: **5.164**

● *accounting services* provided by the *firm* are performed by partners and staff who have no involvement in the *engagement*;
● the *accounting services* are reviewed by a partner or other senior *staff* member with relevant expertise who is not a member of the *engagement team*;
● the *engagement* is reviewed by a partner with relevant expertise who is not involved in the *engagement* to ensure that the *accounting services* performed have been properly and effectively assessed in the context of the *engagement*.

Prohibited Non-audit Services for Public Interest Entities

5.165   The requirements in paragraph 5.167R below set out prohibited *non-audit services* for *public interest entities*, as established in the EU Audit Regulation. These prohibitions are applied more widely than the EU where necessary to achieve the ethical outcome of independence, having regard to supporting ethical provision 2.4. Where the work of a *network firm* is used in the conduct of an *engagement*, supporting ethical provision 2.4 stipulates that the ethical requirements that are relevant to the *engagement* are:

> " (b)   In the case of a *network firm* whose work is used in the conduct of an *engagement* where any *entity relevant to the engagement* is a *public interest entity*, this Ethical Standard."

Accordingly, such *network firms*, whether or not within the Union, are also subject to the prohibitions in paragraph 5.167R for an *audit engagement* where any *entity relevant to the engagement* is a *public interest entity*.

5.166   The *audit firm's* policies and procedures will set out whether there are circumstances in which the services specified in paragraph 5.167R are undertaken for entities that are not *public interest entities* as described in paragraph 1.49 of Section 1 of Part B of this Ethical Standard.

5.167R   A statutory auditor or An *audit firm* carrying out the *statutory audit* of a *public interest entity*, or any member of the network to which the statutory auditor or the *audit firm* belongs, shall not directly or indirectly provide to the *audited entity*, to its parent undertaking or to its controlled undertakings within the Union any prohibited non-audit services in:
(a)   the period between the beginning of the period audited and the issuing of the audit report; and
(b)   the financial year immediately preceding the period referred to in point (a) in relation to the services listed in point (e) of the second subparagraph.

For these purposes of this Article, prohibited non-audit services shall mean:
(a)   tax services relating to:
   (i)   preparation of tax forms;
   (ii)   payroll tax;
   (iii) customs duties;
   (iv)   identification of public subsidies and tax incentives unless support from the statutory auditor or the *audit firm* in respect of such services is required by law;
   (v)   support regarding tax inspections by tax authorities unless support from the statutory auditor or the *audit firm* in respect of such inspections is required by law;
   (vi)   calculation of direct and indirect tax and deferred tax;
   (vii) provision of tax advice;
(b)   services that involve playing any part in the management or decision-making of the *audited entity*;
(c)   bookkeeping and preparing accounting records and financial statements;
(d)   payroll services;
(e)   designing and implementing internal control or risk management procedures related to the preparation and/or control of financial information or designing and implementing financial information technology systems;
(f)   valuation services, including valuations performed in connection with actuarial services or litigation support services;

(g) legal services, with respect to:
    (i)   the provision of general counsel;
    (ii) negotiating on behalf of the *audited entity*; and
    (iii) acting in an advocacy role in the resolution of litigation;
(h) services related to the *audited entity's* internal audit function;
(i) services linked to the financing, capital structure and allocation, and investment strategy of the *audited entity*, except providing assurance services in relation to the financial statements, such as the issuing of comfort letters in connection with prospectuses issued by the *audited entity*;
(j) promoting, dealing in, or underwriting shares in the *audited entity*;
(k) human resources services, with respect to:
    (i)   management in a position to exert significant influence over the preparation of the accounting records or financial statements which are the subject of the *statutory audit*, where such services involve:
       – searching for or seeking out candidates for such position; or
       – undertaking reference checks of candidates for such positions;
    (ii) structuring the organisation design; and
    (iii) cost control. [AR 5.1]

By way of derogation from the second subparagraph of paragraph ~~1~~ 5.167R, the services referred to in points (a)(i), (a)(iv) to (a)(vii) and (f), may be provided if the following requirements are complied with: **5.168R**
(a) they have no direct or, <u>in the view of an objective, reasonable and informed third party, would</u> have ~~immaterial~~ <u>an inconsequential</u> effect, separately or in the aggregate on the audited financial statements;
(b) the estimation of the effect on the audited financial statements is comprehensively documented and explained in the additional report to the audit committee ~~referred to in Article 11~~; ~~and~~
(c) the principles of independence laid down in <u>Section 1 of this Ethical Standard</u> ~~the EU Audit Directive 2006/43/EC~~ are complied with ~~by the statutory auditor or the audit *firm*~~; <u>and</u> [AR 5.3]
(d) <u>for the purposes of the *statutory audit* of the financial statements, the *audit firm* would not place significant reliance on the work performed by the *audit firm* in performing these services.</u>

Where there are doubts about whether a service would have an inconsequential effect on the audited financial statements in the view of and objective, reasonable and informed third party, then the effect is not regarded as inconsequential.   **5.169**

~~A statutory auditor or~~ An audit firm carrying out statutory audits of public interest entities and, where ~~the statutory auditor or~~ the audit firm belongs to a network, any member of such network, may provide to the audited entity, to its parent undertaking or to its controlled undertakings non-audit services other than the prohibited non-audit services referred to in paragraph~~s 1 and 2~~ 5.167R subject to the approval of the audit committee after it has properly assessed threats to independence and the safeguards applied in accordance with <u>this Ethical Standard</u> ~~Article 22b of the EU Audit Directive 2006/43/EC~~. <u>The Audit Regulation requires that</u> the audit committee shall, where applicable, issue guidelines with regard to the services referred to in paragraph ~~3~~ 5.168R. [AR 5.4]   **5.170R**

When a member of a network to which ~~the statutory auditor or~~ the *audit firm* carrying out a *statutory audit* of a *public interest entity* belongs provides any of the non-audit services, referred to in paragraph~~s 1 and 2~~ 5.167R ~~of this Article~~, to an undertaking incorporated in a third country which is controlled by the audited   **5.171R**

public interest entity, ~~the statutory auditor or~~ the *audit firm* concerned shall assess whether ~~his, her or~~ its independence would be compromised by such provision of services by the member of the network. [AR 5.5]

5.172R   If ~~his, her or~~ its independence is affected, ~~the statutory auditor or~~ the *audit firm* shall apply safeguards where applicable in order to mitigate the threats caused by such provision of services in a third country. ~~The statutory auditor or~~ The *audit firm* may continue to carry out the *statutory audit* of the *public interest entity* only if ~~he, she or~~ it can justify, in accordance with Article 6 of ~~this~~ the EU Audit Regulation and Article 22b59 of the EU Audit Directive ~~2006/43/EC~~, that such provision of services does not affect ~~his, her or~~ its professional judgement and the audit report. [AR 5.5]

5.173R   For the purposes of ~~this paragraph~~ the requirements in paragraph 5.171R and 5.172R:
   (a)   being involved in the decision-taking of the *audited entity* and the provision of the services referred to in points (b), (c) and (e) of the second subparagraph of paragraph ~~1~~ 5.167R shall be deemed to affect such independence in all cases and to be incapable of mitigation by any safeguards.
   (b)   provision of the services referred to in the second subparagraph of paragraph ~~1~~ 5.167R other than points (b), (c) and (e) thereof shall be deemed to affect such independence and therefore to require safeguards to mitigate the threats caused thereby. [AR 5.5]

Section 6 – Provisions Available for Audits of Small Entities

Introduction

> This Section does not apply for the audit of *'public interest entities'*.

6.1   This Ethical Standard sets out the overarching principles, supporting ethical provisions and specific requirements, that auditors are required to comply with in order to discharge their responsibilities in respect of their integrity, objectivity and independence. It addresses such matters as:

- How *audit firms* set policies and procedures to ensure that, in relation to each audit, the *audit firm* and all those who are *covered persons* act with integrity, objectivity and independence;
- Financial, business, employment and personal relationships;
- Long association with the *audit engagement*;
- Fees, remuneration and evaluation policies, litigation, gifts and hospitality;
- *Non-audit services* provided to audited entities.

This Ethical Standard applies to all *audit firms* and to all audits and must be read in order to understand the alternative provisions and exemptions contained in this Section of it.

6.2   The FRC is aware that a limited number of the requirements in Sections 1 to 5 of the Ethical Standard are difficult for certain *audit firms* to comply with, particularly when auditing a small entity. Whilst the FRC is clear that Sections 1 to 5 are appropriate in the interests of establishing the integrity, objectivity and independence of auditors, it accepts that certain dispensations, as set out in this Section, are appropriate to facilitate the cost effective audit of the financial statements of Small Entities (as defined below) that are not *'public interest entities'*.

---

[59]   *See paragraph 1.74D of Section 1 of Part B of this Ethical Standard.*

This Section provides alternative provisions for auditors of Small Entities, that are **6.3** not '*public interest entities*', to apply in respect of the threats arising from economic dependence and where tax or *accounting services* are provided and allows the option of taking advantage of exemptions from certain of the requirements in Sections 1 to 5 for a Small Entity *audit engagement*. Where an *audit firm* takes advantage of the exemptions within this Section, it is required to:

(a) take the steps described in this Section; and
(b) disclose in the audit report the fact that the *firm* has applied the FRC's Ethical Standard – Provisions Available for Audits of Small Entities.

(i) In this Standard, for the UK a 'Small Entity' is:

   (a) any company, which is not a UK listed company or an *affiliate* thereof, that qualifies as a small company under Section 382 of the Companies Act 2006;
   (b) where group accounts are produced, any group that qualifies as small under Section 383 of the Companies Act 2006;
   (c) any charity with an income of less than the turnover threshold applicable to small companies as identified in Section 382 of the Companies Act 2006;
   (d) any pension fund with less than 100 members (including active, deferred and pensioner members)[60];
   (e) any *firm* regulated by the FCA, which is not required to appoint an auditor in accordance with rule SUP 3.3.2R of the FCA Handbook;
   (f) any credit union which is a mutually owned financial co-operative established under the Credit Unions Act 1979 and the Industrial and Provident Societies Act 1965 (or equivalent legislation), which meets the criteria set out in (a) above;
   (g) any entity registered under the Industrial and Provident Societies Act 1965, incorporated under the Friendly Societies Act 1992 or registered under the Friendly Societies Act 1974 (or equivalent legislation), which meets the criteria set out in (a) above;
   (h) any registered social landlord with less than 250 units; and
   (i) any other entity, such as a club, which would be a Small Entity if it were a company.

Where an entity falls into more than one of the above categories, it is only regarded as a **6.4** 'Small Entity' if it meets the criteria of all relevant categories.

Alternative Provisions

Economic Dependence

When auditing the financial statements of a Small Entity, an *audit firm* is not required **6.5** **to comply with the requirement in paragraph 4.51 of Section 4 of Part B of this Ethical Standard that an external independent quality control review is performed.**

Although an external independent quality control review is not required, nevertheless **6.6** the *engagement partner* discloses the expectation that fees will amount to between 10% and 15% of the *firm's* annual fee income to the *Ethics Partner* and to those charged with governance of the *audited entity*.

---

[60] *In cases where a scheme with more than 100 members has been in wind-up over a number of years, such a scheme does not qualify as a Small Entity, even where the remaining number of members falls below 100.*

Self-review Threat – Non-audit Services

6.7   **When undertaking *non-audit services* for a Small Entity *audited entity*, the *audit firm* is not required to apply safeguards to address a self-review threat provided:**

    (a)   **the *audited entity* has '*informed management*'; and**

    (b)   **the *audit firm* extends the cyclical inspection of completed *audit engagements* that is performed for quality control purposes.**

6.8   The *audit firm* extends the number of *audit engagements* inspected under the requirements of ISQC (UK) 1 '*Quality Control for Firms that Perform Audits and Reviews of Financial Statements, and other Assurance and Related Services Engagements*'[61] to include a random selection of audit engagements where *non-audit services* have been provided. Particular attention is given to ensuring that there is documentary evidence that '*informed management*' has made such judgments and decisions that are needed in relation to the presentation and disclosure of information in the financial statements.

6.9   Those inspecting the *audit engagements* are not involved in performing the *audit engagement*. Small *audit firms* may wish to use a suitably qualified external person or another *firm* to carry out *audit engagement* inspections.

6.10   In addition to the documentation requirements of ISQC (UK) 1, those inspecting the *audit engagements* document their evaluation of whether the documentary evidence that '*informed management*' made such judgments and decisions that were needed in relation to the presentation and disclosure of information in the financial statements.

Exemptions

Management Threat – Non-audit Services

6.11   **When undertaking *non-audit services* for Small Entity audited entities, the *audit firm* is not required to adhere to the prohibitions in Section 5 of Part B of this Ethical Standard relating to providing *non-audit services* that involve the *audit firm* undertaking part of the role of management, provided that:**

    (a)   **it discusses objectivity and independence issues related to the provision of *non-audit services* with those charged with governance, confirming that management accept responsibility for any decisions taken; and**

    (b)   **it discloses the fact that it has applied the FRC's Ethical Standard – Provisions Available for Audits of Small Entities, in accordance with paragraph 6.15.**

Advocacy Threat – Non-audit Services

6.12   **The *audit firm* of a Small Entity is not required to comply with paragraphs 5.97 (tax services that involve acting as an advocate) and 5.140(b) (restructuring services that involve acting as an advocate) of Section 5 of Part B of this Ethical Standard, provided that it discloses the fact that it has applied the FRC's Ethical Standard – Provisions Available for Audits of Small Entities, in accordance with paragraph 6.15.**

---

[61] *ISQC (UK) 1 requires* audit firms *to establish policies and procedures which include a periodic inspection of a selection of completed engagements. Engagements selected for inspection include at least one engagement for each engagement partner over the inspection cycle, which ordinarily spans no more than three years.*

Partners and Other Persons Approved as a Statutory Auditor Joining an Audited Entity

The *audit firm* of a Small Entity is not required to comply with paragraphs 2.53 and 2.57 of Section 2 of Part B of this Ethical Standard, provided that: **6.13**

(a) **it takes appropriate steps to determine that there is no significant threat to the *audit team's* integrity, objectivity and independence; and**

(b) **it discloses the fact that it has applied the FRC's Ethical Standard – Provisions Available for Audits of Small Entities, in accordance with paragraph 6.15.**

An *audit firm* takes appropriate steps to determine that there is no significant threat to the   **6.14**
audit team's integrity, objectivity and independence as a result of the employment of a former partner, or other person approved as a *statutory auditor*, by an *audited entity* that is a Small Entity by:

(a) assessing the significance of the self-interest, familiarity or intimidation threats, having regard to the following factors:
  ● the position the individual has taken at the *audited entity*;
  ● the nature and amount of any involvement the individual will have with the *audit team* or the audit process;
  ● the length of time that has passed since the individual was a member of the *audit team* or *firm*; and
  ● the former position of the individual within the *audit team* or *firm*, and

(b) if the threat is other than clearly insignificant, applying alternative procedures such as:
  ● considering the appropriateness or necessity of modifying the audit plan for the *audit engagement*;
  ● assigning an *audit team* to the subsequent *audit engagement* that is of sufficient experience in relation to the individual who has joined the *audited entity*;
  ● involving an audit partner or senior *staff* member with appropriate expertise, who, where the *firm* already audits the entity, was not a member of the *audit team*, to review the work done or otherwise advise as necessary; or
  ● undertaking an engagement quality control review of the *audit engagement*.

Disclosure Requirements

Where the *audit firm* has taken advantage of an exemption provided in paragraphs 6.11, 6.12 or 6.13, the *engagement partner* shall ensure that: **6.15**

(a) **the auditors' report discloses this fact, and**

(b) **either the financial statements, or the auditors' report, discloses the type of *non-audit services* provided to the *audited entity* or the fact that a former *engagement partner*, or other person personally approved as a *statutory auditor*, has joined the *audited entity*.**

The fact that an *audit firm* has taken advantage of an exemption provided by the FRC's   **6.16**
Ethical Standard – Provisions Available for Small Entities is set out in a separate paragraph of the audit report. It does not affect the Opinion paragraph.

The *engagement partner* ensures that within the financial statements reference is made   **6.17**
to the type of *non-audit services* provided to the *audited entity* or the fact that a former partner or other person personally approved as a *statutory auditor* has joined the *audited entity*. Where such a disclosure is not made within the financial statements it is included in the auditors' report.

APPENDIX: Illustrative template for communicating information on audit and non-audit services provided to the group

	Current year £m	Prior year £m
Audit of company	X	X
Audit of subsidiaries	X	X
Total audit	X	X
Audit related assurance services[62]	X	X
Other assurance services[63] [64]	X	X
Total assurance services	X	X
Tax compliance services (i.e. related to assistance with corporate tax returns)	X	X
Tax advisory services	X	X
Services relating to taxation	X	X
Internal audit services	X	X
Services related to corporate finance transactions not covered above	X	X
Other non-audit services not covered above	X	X
Total other non-audit services	X	X
Total non-audit services	X	X
Total fees	X	X
Occupational pension scheme audits	X	X
Non-audit services in respect of the audited entity provided to a third party[65].	X	X

Disclosure of contingent fee arrangements under paragraph 4.25 of Section 4 of Part B of this Ethical Standard can also be facilitated through the use of a footnote to this template.

Disclosures required under UK company legislation[66] are indicated by those categories in bold type above. Fuller information can be provided by companies if desired.

[62] *This will, and will only, include those services which are identified as audit related services in paragraph 5.41 of Section 5 of Part B of this Ethical Standard.*

[63] *This will not include any tax or internal audit services, all of which should be disclosed under those headings.*

[64] *The definition of an assurance engagement is provided in the Glossary of Terms on the FRC's website. Services provided under such engagements will include assurance engagements such as those which involve reporting on historical financial information which are included in an investment circular in accordance with the Standards for Investment Reporting 2000 (Revised): Investment reporting standards applicable to public reporting engagements on historical financial information.*

[65] *For the purposes of this Ethical Standard, non-audit services include services provided to another entity in respect of the audited entity, for example, where the audit firm provides transaction related services, in respect of an audited entity's financial information, to a prospective acquirer of the audited entity (see paragraph 5.8 of Section 5 of Part B of this Ethical Standard).*

[66] *SI 2011/2198 'The Companies (Disclosure of Auditor Remuneration and Liability Limitation Agreements) (Amendment) Regulations 2011'.*

Glossary of Terms
Ethics and auditing (2018)

Glossary of Terms[1]

(March 2018)

This Glossary defines terms used in the ISAs (UK), the ISQC (UK) and the FRC's Ethical Standard. It is based on the International Auditing and Assurance Standards Board (IAASB) glossary of terms, with supplemental definitions used in the FRC standards shown in grey highlighted text.

Access controls—Procedures designed to restrict access to on-line terminal devices, programs and data. Access controls consist of 'user authentication' and 'user authorization.' 'User authentication' typically attempts to identify a user through unique logon identifications, passwords, access cards or biometric data. 'User authorization' consists of access rules to determine the computer resources each user may access. Specifically, such procedures are designed to prevent or detect:

- Unauthorized access to on-line terminal devices, programs and data;
- Entry of unauthorized transactions;
- Unauthorized changes to data files;
- The use of computer programs by unauthorized personnel; and
- The use of computer programs that have not been authorized.

Accounting estimate—An approximation of a monetary amount in the absence of a precise means of measurement. This term is used for an amount measured at fair value where there is estimation uncertainty, as well as for other amounts that require estimation. Where ISA (UK) 540 (Revised June 2016)[2] addresses only accounting estimates involving measurement at fair value, the term 'fair value accounting estimates' is used.

Accounting records—The records of initial accounting entries and supporting records, such as checks and records of electronic fund transfers; invoices; contracts; the general and subsidiary ledgers, journal entries and other adjustments to the financial statements that are not reflected in formal journal entries; and records such as work sheets and spreadsheets supporting cost allocations, computations, reconciliations and disclosures.

Accounting services—The provision of services that involve the maintenance of accounting records or the preparation of financial statements or other subject matter information or subject matter that are then subject to audit or an other public interest assurance engagement.

Additional services—For a public interest assurance engagement other than an audit, 'additional services' comprise any engagement in which a firm, or a member of its network, provides professional services to an entity relevant to the engagement other than pursuant to:

(a) Any other public interest assurance engagement;
(b) The audit of financial statements; and
(c) Those other roles which legislation or regulation specify can be performed by the auditor of the entity (for example, considering the preliminary announcements

---

[1] *In the case of public sector engagements, the terms in this glossary should be read as referring to their public sector equivalents.*

Where accounting terms have not been defined in the pronouncements of the International Auditing and Assurance Standards Board, reference should be made to the Glossary of Terms published by the International Accounting Standards Board.

[2] *ISA (UK) 540 (Revised June 2016),* Auditing Accounting Estimates, Including Fair Value Accounting Estimates, and Related Disclosures.

of listed companies, complying with the procedural and reporting requirements of regulators, such as requirements relating to the audit of the client's internal controls and reports in accordance with Section 714 of the Companies Act 2006).

Where the entity relevant to the engagement is a member of a group, additional services for the purposes of the FRC's Ethical Standard include:

– Services provided by the *firm* to the parent entity or to any of its significant affiliates; and
– Services provided by a network firm which is involved in the engagement to the entity relevant to the engagement or any of its significant affiliates.

Affiliate firm—Any undertaking, regardless of its legal form, which is connected to a firm by means of common ownership, control or management.

Affiliate (of an entity)–

For investment circular reporting engagement, an affiliate is any undertaking which is connected to another by means of common ownership, control or management.

For a public interest assurance engagement other than an investment circular reporting engagement, an affiliate is an entity that has any of the following relationships with an entity relevant to the engagement:

(a) An entity that has direct or indirect control over the entity relevant to the engagement if the entity relevant to the engagement is material, quantitatively or qualitatively, to such entity;
(b) An entity with a direct financial interest in the entity relevant to the engagement if that entity has significant influence over the entity relevant to the engagement and the interest in the entity relevant to the engagement is material, quantitatively or qualitatively, to such entity;
(c) An entity over which the entity relevant to the engagement has direct or indirect control;
(d) An entity in which the entity relevant to the engagement, or an affiliate of the entity relevant to the engagement under (c) above, has a direct financial interest that gives it significant influence over such entity and the interest is material, quantitatively or qualitatively, to the entity relevant to the engagement and its affiliate in (c); and
(e) An entity which is under common control with the entity relevant to the engagement (a 'sister entity') if the sister entity and the entity relevant to the engagement are both material, quantitatively or qualitatively, to the entity that controls both the entity relevant to the engagement and sister entity.

Factors that may be relevant in determining whether an entity or an interest in an entity is material to another entity include:

● The extent and nature of the relationships between the entity relevant to the engagement and the other entity and the impact these have on the relationships of either entity with the firm, and
● The extent and nature of the relationship(s) between the firm and the other entity and the impact that this has on independence.

Agreed-upon procedures engagement—An engagement in which an auditor or reporting accountant is engaged to carry out those procedures of an audit or assurance nature to which the auditor or reporting accountant and the entity and any appropriate third parties have agreed and to report on factual findings. The recipients of the report form their own conclusions from the report by the auditor or reporting accountant. The report is restricted to those parties that have agreed to the procedures to be performed since others, unaware of the reasons for the procedures, may misinterpret the results.

Analytical procedures—Evaluations of financial information through analysis of plausible relationships among both financial and non-financial data. Analytical procedures also encompass such investigation as is necessary of identified fluctuations or relationships that are inconsistent with other relevant information or that differ from expected values by a significant amount.

Annual report—A document, or combination of documents, prepared typically on an annual basis by management or those charged with governance in accordance with law, regulation or custom, the purpose of which is to provide owners (or similar stakeholders) with information on the entity's operations and the entity's financial results and financial position as set out in the financial statements. An annual report contains or accompanies the financial statements and the auditor's report thereon and usually includes information about the entity's developments, its future outlook and risks and uncertainties, a statement by the entity's governing body, and reports covering governance matters.

In the UK an annual report includes at least:
(i)   The statutory other information; and
(ii) Any other documents that are incorporated by cross-reference in, or distributed to shareholders with, statutory other information either voluntarily or pursuant to law or regulation or the requirements of a stock exchange listing.

Anomaly—A misstatement or deviation that is demonstrably not representative of misstatements or deviations in a population.

Applicable financial reporting framework—The financial reporting framework adopted by management and, where appropriate, those charged with governance in the preparation of the financial statements that is acceptable in view of the nature of the entity and the objective of the financial statements, or that is required by law or regulation.

The term 'fair presentation framework' is used to refer to a financial reporting framework that requires compliance with the requirements of the framework and:
(a)   Acknowledges explicitly or implicitly that, to achieve fair presentation of the financial statements, it may be necessary for management to provide disclosures beyond those specifically required by the framework; or
(b)   Acknowledges explicitly that it may be necessary for management to depart from a requirement of the framework to achieve fair presentation of the financial statements. Such departures are expected to be necessary only in extremely rare circumstances.

The term 'compliance framework' is used to refer to a financial reporting framework that requires compliance with the requirements of the framework, but does not contain the acknowledgements in (a) or (b) above.

In the UK the applicable financial reporting framework includes the requirements of applicable law.

Application controls in information technology—Manual or automated procedures that typically operate at a business process level. Application controls can be preventative or detective in nature and are designed to ensure the integrity of the accounting records. Accordingly, application controls relate to procedures used to initiate, record, process and report transactions or other financial data.

Appropriateness (of audit evidence)—The measure of the quality of audit evidence; that is, its relevance and its reliability in providing support for the conclusions on which the auditor's opinion is based.

Area of activity (relating to engagements)—In relation to a key audit partner or other covered person, or a person closely associated with such a partner or covered person, any engagements for which the covered person is a directly involved covered person and any other engagements, in relation to which the engagement partner practices in the same office or business unit as the covered person.

Arm's length transaction—A transaction conducted on such terms and conditions as between a willing buyer and a willing seller who are unrelated and are acting independently of each other and pursuing their own best interests.

Assertions—Representations by management, explicit or otherwise, that are embodied in the financial statements, as used by the auditor to consider the different types of potential misstatements that may occur.

Assess—Analyze identified risks of to conclude on their significance. 'Assess,' by convention, is used only in relation to risk. (also see *Evaluate*)

Association—(see *Auditor association with financial information*)

Assurance—(see *Reasonable assurance*)

Assurance engagement—An engagement in which a practitioner aims to obtain sufficient appropriate audit evidence in order to express a conclusion designed to enhance the degree of confidence of the intended users other than the responsible party about the subject matter information (that is, the outcome of the measurement or evaluation of an underlying subject matter against criteria).

    Reasonable assurance engagement—An assurance engagement in which the practitioner reduces engagement risk to an acceptably low level in the circumstances of the engagement as the basis for the practitioner's conclusion. The practitioner's conclusion is expressed in a form that conveys the practitioner's opinion on the outcome of the measurement or evaluation of the underlying subject matter against criteria.

    Limited assurance engagement—An assurance engagement in which the practitioner reduces engagement risk to a level that is acceptable in the circumstances of the engagement, but where that risk is greater than for a reasonable assurance engagement, as the basis for expressing a conclusion in a form that conveys whether, based on the procedures performed and evidence obtained, a matter(s) has come to the practitioner's attention to cause the practitioner to believe that the subject matter information is materially misstated. The nature, timing and extent of procedures performed in a limited assurance engagement is limited compared with that necessary in a reasonable assurance engagement but is planned to obtain a level of assurance that is, in the practitioner's professional judgement, meaningful. To be meaningful, the level of assurance obtained by the practitioner is likely to enhance the intended users' confidence about the subject matter information to a degree that is clearly more than inconsequential.

Assurance engagement risk—The risk that the practitioner expresses an inappropriate conclusion when the subject matter information is materially misstated.

Audit documentation—The record of audit procedures performed, relevant audit evidence obtained, and conclusions the auditor reached (terms such as 'working papers' or 'workpapers' are also sometimes used).

In the UK audit documentation includes all document, information, records and other data required by ISQC (UK) 1, ISAs (UK) and applicable legal and regulatory requirements.

Audit engagement—An engagement to perform an audit in accordance with the ISAs (UK) and, where applicable, relevant legislation. It includes a statutory audit performed pursuant to the EU Audit Directive and Regulation or otherwise designated by national law as a statutory audit.

Audit evidence—Information used by the auditor in arriving at the conclusions on which the auditor's opinion is based. Audit evidence includes both information contained in the accounting records underlying the financial statements and information obtained from other sources. (See *Sufficiency of audit evidence* and *Appropriateness of audit evidence*.)

Audit file—One or more folders or other storage media, in physical or electronic form, containing the records that comprise the audit documentation for a specific engagement.

Audit firm—The sole practitioner, partnership, limited liability partnership or other corporate entity engaged in the provision of audit services. For the purpose of the FRC's Ethical Standard, audit firm includes network firms in the UK which are controlled by the audit firm or its partners.

Audit opinion—(see *Modified opinion and Unmodified opinion*)

Audit risk—The risk that the auditor expresses an inappropriate audit opinion when the financial statements are materially misstated. Audit risk is a function of the risks of material misstatement and detection risk.

Audit sampling (sampling)—The application of audit procedures to less than 100% of items within a population of audit relevance such that all sampling units have a chance of selection in order to provide the auditor with a reasonable basis on which to draw conclusions about the entire population.

Audit team—All audit professionals who, regardless of their legal relationship with the auditor or audit firm, are assigned to a particular audit engagement in order to perform the audit task (e.g. audit partner(s), audit manager(s) and audit staff).

Audited entity—The entity whose financial statements are subject to audit by the audit firm.

Auditor—'Auditor' is used to refer to the person or persons conducting the audit, usually the engagement partner[3] or other members of the engagement team, or, as applicable, the firm. Where an ISA (UK) expressly intends that a requirement or responsibility be fulfilled by the engagement partner, the term 'engagement partner' rather than 'auditor' is used. 'Engagement partner' and 'firm' are to be read as referring to their public sector equivalents where relevant.

---

[3] *In the UK, this includes the key audit partner.*

Auditor association with financial information—An auditor is associated with financial information when the auditor attaches a report to that information or consents to the use of the auditor's name in a professional connection.

Auditor's expert—An individual or organization possessing expertise in a field other than accounting or auditing, whose work in that field is used by the auditor to assist the auditor in obtaining sufficient appropriate audit evidence. An auditor's expert may be either an auditor's internal expert (who is a partner[4] or staff, including temporary staff, of the auditor's firm or a network firm), or an auditor's external expert.

Auditor's point estimate or auditor's range—The amount, or range of amounts, respectively, derived from audit evidence for use in evaluating management's point estimate.

Auditor's range—(see *Auditor's point estimate*)

Business risk—A risk resulting from significant conditions, events, circumstances, actions or inactions that could adversely affect an entity's ability to achieve its objectives and execute its strategies, or from the setting of inappropriate objectives and strategies.

Close family—A non-dependent parent, child or sibling.

Comparative financial statements—Comparative information where amounts and other disclosures for the prior period are included for comparison with the financial statements of the current period but, if audited, are referred to in the auditor's opinion. The level of information included in those comparative financial statements is comparable with that of the financial statements of the current period.

Comparative information—The amounts and disclosures included in the financial statements in respect of one or more prior periods in accordance with the applicable financial reporting framework.

Compilation engagement—An engagement in which accounting expertise, as opposed to auditing expertise, is used to collect, classify and summarize financial information.

Complementary user entity controls—Controls that the service organization assumes, in the design of its service, will be implemented by user entities, and which, if necessary to achieve control objectives, are identified in the description of its system.

Compliance framework—(see *Applicable financial reporting framework* and *General purpose framework*)

Component—An entity or business activity for which group or component management prepares financial information that should be included in the group financial statements.

Component auditor—An auditor who, at the request of the group engagement team, performs work on financial information related to a component for the group audit.

Component management—Management responsible for the preparation of the financial information of a component.

Component materiality—The materiality for a component determined by the group engagement team.

---

[4] *'Partner' and 'firm' should be read as referring to their public sector equivalents where relevant.*

Computer-assisted audit techniques—Applications of auditing procedures using the computer as an audit tool (also known as CAATs).

Connected parties—An entity's connected parties are:

(a) Its affiliates;

(b) Key members of management (including but not limited to directors and those charged with governance) of the entity and its significant affiliates, individually or collectively; and

(c) Any person or entity with an ability to influence (other than in the capacity of professional advisors), whether directly or indirectly, key members of management or those charged with governance of the entity and its significant affiliates, individually or collectively, in relation to their responsibility for or approach to any matter or judgment that is material to the entity's financial statements or other subject matter information or subject matter.

Contingent fee basis—Any arrangement made under which a fee is calculated on a predetermined basis relating to the outcome or result of a transaction, or other event, or the result of the work performed. A fee that is established by a court, competent authority or other public authority is not a contingent fee.

Differential hourly fee rates, or arrangements under which the fee payable will be negotiated after the completion of the engagement, or increased to cover additional work identified as necessary during the engagement, do not constitute contingent fee arrangements.

Control activities—Those policies and procedures that help ensure that management directives are carried out. Control activities are a component of internal control.

Control environment—Includes the governance and management functions and the attitudes, awareness and actions of those charged with governance and management concerning the entity's internal control and its importance in the entity. The control environment is a component of internal control.

Control risk—(see *Risk of material misstatement*)

Corporate governance—(see *Governance*)

Corresponding figures—Comparative information where amounts and other disclosures for the prior period are included as an integral part of the current period financial statements, and are intended to be read only in relation to the amounts and other disclosures relating to the current period (referred to as 'current period figures'). The level of detail presented in the corresponding amounts and disclosures is dictated primarily by its relevance to the current period figures.

Covered person—A person in a position to influence the conduct or outcome of the engagement.

For an audit engagement and for an other public interest assurance engagement other than an investment circular reporting engagement:

(a)(i) Each member of the engagement team with responsibilities for managing the performance of the engagement (including the person(s) responsible for 'day to day' direction and supervision on site at the entity, and all more senior members of the engagement team above them) and persons who provide engagement quality control review for the engagement;

(a)(ii) All other members of the engagement team;

(b)   Any other natural person whose services are placed at the disposal or under the control of the firm and who is involved in the audit or other public interest assurance engagement, including for example any individual who is, or whose services are provided by, any external expert of the firm;

(c)   Any person in the firm with supervisory, management or other oversight responsibility over:

   (i)   The engagement or the engagement partner or other key partners involved in the engagement; or

   (ii)   The conduct of audit or other public interest assurance engagements performed by the firm.

   This includes each partner, principal, shareholder and other person in the firm:

   (a)   At each level of firm management, supervision or oversight relating to the audit or other public interest assurance engagement, up to and including individuals who have ultimate responsibility for the management or governance of the firm[5]; or

   (b)   Who is in a position to prepare or approve the performance appraisal and/or remuneration of any individual defined in (a)(i), (b), (c)(i) and (c)(ii); and

(d)   Any other person within the firm or a network firm who, due to any other circumstances, is in a position to influence the conduct or outcome of the audit or other public interest assurance engagement.

It does not include any independent non-executive individuals on a supervisory or equivalent board.

For an investment circular reporting engagement:

(a)   Each member of the engagement team and persons who provide engagement quality control review for the engagement;

(b)   Any other natural person whose services are placed at the disposal or under the control of the firm and who is directly involved in the engagement, including for example any individual who is, or whose services are provided by, any external expert of the firm; and

(c)   Any other person within the firm or a network firm, with actual knowledge of the engagement, who, due to any other circumstances, is in a position to influence the conduct or outcome of the engagement, including for example: those with actual knowledge of the engagement who are in such a position as a result of:

   (i)   Their professional or personal relationships with the engagement partner or other key members of the engagement team; or

   (ii)   The scope and nature of their responsibilities within the firm's network.

It does not include any independent non-executive individuals on a supervisory or equivalent board.

Criteria—The benchmarks use to measure or evaluate the underlying subject matter. The 'applicable criteria' are the criteria used for the particular engagement.

Date of approval of the financial statements—The date on which all the statements that comprise the financial statements, including the related notes, have been prepared and

---

[5] *Senior or managing partner, chief executive or equivalent, and other members of the firm's management and supervisory bodies.*

those with the recognized authority have asserted that they have taken responsibility for those financial statements.

Date of report (in relation to quality control)—The date selected by the practitioner to date the report.

Date of the auditor's report—The date the auditor dates the report on the financial statements in accordance with ISA (UK) 700[6].

Date of the financial statements—The date of the end of the latest period covered by the financial statements.

Date the financial statements are issued—The date that the auditor's report and audited financial statements are made available to third parties.

Deficiency in internal control—This exists when:
(a) A control is designed, implemented or operated in such a way that it is unable to prevent, or detect and correct, misstatements in the financial statements on a timely basis; or
(b) A control necessary to prevent, or detect and correct, misstatements in the financial statements on a timely basis is missing.

Detection risk—The risk that the procedures performed by the auditor to reduce audit risk to an acceptably low level will not detect a misstatement that exists and that could be material, either individually or when aggregated with other misstatements.

Direct assistance—The use of internal auditors to perform audit procedures under the direction, supervisions and review of the external auditor.

The use of internal auditors to provide direct assistance is prohibited in an audit conducted in accordance with ISAs (UK). See paragraph 5-1 of ISA (UK) 610 (Revised June 2013), 'Using the Work of Internal Auditors'.

Directly involved covered person—In relation to an engagement, a covered person for the engagement that falls within the scope of paragraphs (a) or (b) of the definition of a covered person.

Emphasis of Matter paragraph—A paragraph included in the auditor's report that refers to a matter appropriately presented or disclosed in the financial statements that, in the auditor's judgment, is of such importance that it is fundamental to users' understanding of the financial statements.

Engagement—In the FRC's Ethical Standard, an audit engagement or an other public interest assurance engagement, or both where the context permits.

Engagement documentation—The record of work performed, results obtained, and conclusions the practitioner reached (terms such as 'working papers' or 'workpapers' are sometimes used).

Engagement letter—Written terms of an engagement in the form of a letter.

---

[6] *ISA (UK) 700 (Revised June 2016), Forming an Opinion and Reporting on Financial Statements.*

Engagement partner[7]—The partner or other person in the firm who is responsible for the engagement and its performance, and for the report that is issued on behalf of the firm, and who, where required, has the appropriate authority from a professional, legal or regulatory body.

> For an audit, the engagement partner is a key audit partner.

> *Engagement period*—For an investment circular reporting engagement, the engagement period starts when the firm accepts the investment circular reporting engagement and ends on the date of the report

Engagement quality control review—A process designed to provide an objective evaluation, on or before the date of the report, of the significant judgments the engagement team made and the conclusions it reached in formulating the report. The engagement quality control review process is for audits of financial statements of listed entities and those other engagements, if any, for which the firm has determined an engagement quality control review is required.

Engagement quality control reviewer—A partner, other person in the firm, suitably qualified external person, or a team made up of such individuals, none of whom is part of the engagement team, with sufficient and appropriate experience and authority to objectively evaluate the significant judgments the engagement team made and the conclusions it reached in formulating the report.

Engagement risk—The risk that the practitioner expresses an inappropriate conclusion when the subject matter information is materially misstated.

Engagement team—All partners and staff performing the engagement, and any individuals engaged by the firm or a network firm who perform procedures on the engagement. This excludes external experts engaged by the firm or a network firm.

> For the purposes of the FRC's Ethical Standard, engagement team comprises all persons who are directly involved in the acceptance and performance of a particular audit or other public interest assurance engagement. This includes the audit / assurance team, professional personnel from other disciplines involved in the engagement and those who provide quality control (other than the engagement quality control reviewer) or direct oversight of the audit engagement, but it does not include any external experts contracted by the firm.

> *Entity in distress*—An entity with actual or anticipated financial or operational difficulties that threaten the survival of that entity as a going concern.

> *Entity relevant to the engagement*—An entity with respect to which the firm and covered persons are required to be independent. In the case of an audit engagement, the entity relevant to the engagement is the audited entity which is responsible for the audited financial statements reported on by the firm. In the case of an other public interest assurance engagement, an entity relevant to the engagement is any entity responsible for the subject matter information of the engagement (except when the responsible entity is the assurance practitioner) or the subject matter of the engagement, reported on by the firm, or (where applicable) both.

---

[7] *'Engagement partner,' 'partner,' and 'firm' should be read as referring to their public sector equivalents where relevant.*

In relation to an investment circular reporting engagement, entities relevant to the engagement include the entity responsible for issuing the investment circular containing the financial information (the issuing engagement entity) and, if different, the entity on whose financial information the firm is reporting.

Entity's risk assessment process—A component of internal control that is the entity's process for identifying business risks relevant to financial reporting objectives and deciding about actions to address those risks, and the results thereof.

Error—An unintentional misstatement in financial statements, including the omission of an amount or a disclosure.

Estimation uncertainty—The susceptibility of an accounting estimate and related disclosures to an inherent lack of precision in its measurement.

Ethics Partner—The partner in the firm having responsibility for the adequacy of the firm's policies and procedures relating to integrity, objectivity and independence, their compliance with the FRC's Ethical Standard and the effectiveness of their communication to partners and staff within the firm and providing related guidance to individual partners.

Evaluate—Identify and analyze the relevant issues, including performing further procedures as necessary, to come to a specific conclusion on a matter. 'Evaluation,' by convention, is used only in relation to a range of matters, including evidence, the results of procedures and the effectiveness of management's response to a risk. (also see *Assess*)

Exception—A response that indicates a difference between information requested to be confirmed, or contained in the entity's records, and information provided by the confirming party.

Experienced auditor—An individual (whether internal or external to the firm) who has practical audit experience, and a reasonable understanding of:
(a) Audit processes;
(b) ISAs (UK) and applicable legal and regulatory requirements;
(c) The business environment in which the entity operates; and
(d) Auditing and financial reporting issues relevant to the entity's industry.

Expert—(see *Auditor's expert* and *Management's expert*)

Expertise—Skills, knowledge and experience in a particular field.

External confirmation—Audit evidence obtained as a direct written response to the auditor from a third party (the confirming party), in paper form, or by electronic or other medium.

Fair presentation framework—(see *Applicable financial reporting framework* and *General purpose framework*)

Financial instruments—These are defined in EU Directive 2014/65/EU, on markets in financial instruments, as:

(1) Transferable securities;
(2) Money-market instruments;

(3)   Units in collective investment undertakings;
(4)   Options, futures, swaps, forward rate agreements and any other derivative contracts relating to securities, currencies, interest rates or yields, emission allowances or other derivatives instruments, financial indices or financial measures which may be settled physically or in cash;
(5)   Options, futures, swaps, forwards and any other derivative contracts relating to commodities that must be settled in cash or may be settled in cash at the option of one of the parties other than by reason of default or other termination event;
(6)   Options, futures, swaps, and any other derivative contract relating to commodities that can be physically settled provided that they are traded on a regulated market, a Multilateral Trading Facility (MTF), or an Organised Trading Facility (OTF), except for wholesale energy products traded on an OTF that must be physically settled;
(7)   Options, futures, swaps, forwards and any other derivative contracts relating to commodities, that can be physically settled not otherwise mentioned in point 6 of this Section and not being for commercial purposes, which have the characteristics of other derivative financial instruments;
(8)   Derivative instruments for the transfer of credit risk;
(9)   Financial contracts for differences;
(10)   Options, futures, swaps, forward rate agreements and any other derivative contracts relating to climatic variables, freight rates or inflation rates or other official economic statistics that must be settled in cash or may be settled in cash at the option of one of the parties other than by reason of default or other termination event, as well as any other derivative contracts relating to assets, rights, obligations, indices and measures not otherwise mentioned in this Section, which have the characteristics of other derivative financial instruments, having regard to whether, inter alia, they are traded on a regulated market, OTF, or an MTF;
(11)   Emission allowances consisting of any units recognised for compliance with the requirements of Directive 2003/87/EC (Emissions Trading Scheme).

Financial statements—A structured representation of historical financial information, including disclosures, intended to communicate an entity's economic resources or obligations at a point in time or the changes therein for a period of time in accordance with a financial reporting framework. The term 'financial statements' ordinarily refers to a complete set of financial statements as determined by the requirements of the applicable financial reporting framework, but it can also refer to a single financial statement. Disclosures comprise explanatory or descriptive information, set out as required, expressly permitted or otherwise allowed by the applicable financial reporting framework, on the face of a financial statement, or in the notes, or incorporated therein by cross reference.

Firm—A sole practitioner, partnership, limited liability partnership, or corporation or other entity of professional accountants engaged in the provision of engagements. 'Firm' should be read as referring to its public sector equivalents where relevant.

In the case of an audit engagement, this includes a 'statutory auditor' who is a natural person; and a legal person or any other entity, regardless of its legal form, with the appropriate approval to carry out statutory audits. For the purpose of the FRC's Ethical Standard, 'firm' also includes network firms in the UK and Ireland which are controlled by the firm or its partners.

Forecast—Prospective financial information prepared on the basis of assumptions as to future events which management expects to take place and the actions management expects to take as of the date the information is prepared (best-estimate assumptions).

Fraud—An intentional act by one or more individuals among management, those charged with governance, employees, or third parties, involving the use of deception to obtain an unjust or illegal advantage.

Fraud risk factors—Events or conditions that indicate an incentive or pressure to commit fraud or provide an opportunity to commit fraud.

Fraudulent financial reporting—Involves intentional misstatements, including omissions of amounts or disclosures in financial statements, to deceive financial statement users.

Further procedures—Procedures performed in response to assessed risks of material misstatement, including tests of controls (if any), tests of details and analytical procedures.

General IT-controls—Policies and procedures that relate to many applications and support the effective functioning of application controls by helping to ensure the continued proper operation of information systems. General IT-controls commonly include controls over data center and network operations; system software acquisition, change and maintenance; access security; and application system acquisition, development, and maintenance.

General purpose financial statements—Financial statements prepared in accordance with a general purpose framework.

General purpose framework—A financial reporting framework designed to meet the common financial information needs of a wide range of users. The financial reporting framework may be a fair presentation framework or a compliance framework.

The term 'fair presentation framework' is used to refer to a financial reporting framework that requires compliance with the requirements of the framework and:
(a) Acknowledges explicitly or implicitly that, to achieve fair presentation of the financial statements, it may be necessary for management to provide disclosures beyond those specifically required by the framework; or
(b) Acknowledges explicitly that it may be necessary for management to depart from a requirement of the framework to achieve fair presentation of the financial statements. Such departures are expected to be necessary only in extremely rare circumstances.

The term 'compliance framework' is used to refer to a financial reporting framework that requires compliance with the requirements of the framework, but does not contain the acknowledgements in (a) or (b) above.[8]

Governance—Describes the role of person(s) or organization(s) with responsibility for overseeing the strategic direction of the entity and obligations related to the accountability of the entity.

Group—All the components whose financial information is included in the group financial statements. A group always has more than one component.

Group audit—The audit of group financial statements.

---

[8] *ISA (UK) 200 (Revised June 2016)*, Overall Objectives of the Independent Auditor and the Conduct of an Audit in Accordance with International Standards on Auditing (UK), *paragraph 13(a)*.

Group audit opinion—The audit opinion on the group financial statements.

Group engagement partner—The partner or other person in the firm who is responsible for the group audit engagement and its performance, and for the auditor's report on the group financial statements that is issued on behalf of the firm. Where joint auditors conduct the group audit, the joint engagement partners and their engagement teams collectively constitute the group engagement partner and the group engagement team.

Group engagement team—Partners, including the group engagement partner, and staff who establish the overall group audit strategy, communicate with component auditors, perform work on the consolidation process, and evaluate the conclusions drawn from the audit evidence as the basis for forming an opinion on the group financial statements.

Group financial statements—Financial statements that include the financial information of more than one component. The term 'group financial statements' also refers to combined financial statements aggregating the financial information prepared by components that have no parent but are under common control.

Group management—Management responsible for the preparation of the group financial statements.

Group-wide controls—Controls designed, implemented and maintained by group management over group financial reporting.

Historical financial information—Information expressed in financial terms in relation to a particular entity, derived primarily from that entity's accounting system, about economic events occurring in past time periods or about economic conditions or circumstances at points in time in the past.

Immediate family—A spouse (or equivalent) or dependent.

Independence–

Freedom from conditions and relationships which, in the context of an engagement, would compromise the integrity or objectivity of the firm or covered persons.

> *Integrity or objectivity (and therefore independence) would be compromised if it is probable (more likely than not) that an objective, reasonable and informed third party would conclude that the threats, arising from any conditions or relationships that exist (taking into account any conflicts of interest that they may cause, or generally be perceived to cause, or otherwise, and having regard to any safeguards implemented), would impair integrity or objectivity to such an extent that it would be inappropriate for the firm to accept or continue to perform the audit or other public interest assurance engagement unless the threats were eliminated or further reduced or unless more, or more effective, safeguards were implemented.*

Information system relevant to financial reporting—A component of internal control that includes the financial reporting system, and consists of the procedures and records established to initiate, record, process and report entity transactions (as well as events and conditions) and to maintain accountability for the related assets, liabilities and equity.

Informed management—Member of management (or senior employee) of the entity relevant to the engagement who has the authority and capability to make independent management judgments and decisions in relation to non-audit / additional services on the basis of information provided by the firm.

Inherent risk—(see *Risk of material misstatement*)

Initial audit engagement—An engagement in which either:
(a) The financial statements for the prior period were not audited; or
(b) The financial statements for the prior period were audited by a predecessor auditor.

Inquiry—Inquiry consists of seeking information of knowledgeable persons, both financial and non-financial, within the entity or outside the entity.

Inspection (as an audit procedure)—Examining records or documents, whether internal or external, in paper form, electronic form, or other media, or a physical examination of an asset.

Inspection (in relation to quality control)—In relation to completed engagements, procedures designed to provide evidence of compliance by engagement teams with the firm's quality control policies and procedures.

Integrity—Being trustworthy, straightforward, honest, fair and candid; complying with the spirit as well as the letter of applicable ethical principles, laws and regulations; behaving so as to maintain the public's trust in the auditing profession; and respecting confidentiality except where disclosure is in the public interest or is required to adhere to legal and professional responsibilities.

Interim financial information or statements—Financial information (which may be less than a complete set of financial statements as defined above) issued at interim dates (usually half-yearly or quarterly) in respect of a financial period.

Internal audit function—A function of an entity that performs assurance and consulting activities designed to evaluate and improve the effectiveness of the entity's governance, risk management and internal control processes.

Internal auditors—Those individuals who perform the activities of the internal audit function. Internal auditors may belong to an internal audit department or equivalent function.

Internal control—The process designed, implemented and maintained by those charged with governance, management and other personnel to provide reasonable assurance about the achievement of an entity's objectives with regard to reliability of financial reporting, effectiveness and efficiency of operations, and compliance with applicable laws and regulations. The term 'controls' refers to any aspects of one or more of the components of internal control.

International Financial Reporting Standards—The International Financial Reporting Standards issued by the International Accounting Standards Board.

Investigate—Inquire into matters arising from other procedures to resolve them.

Investment circular—An investment circular is a document issued by an entity pursuant to statutory or regulatory requirements relating to securities on which it is intended that a third party should make an investment decision, including a prospectus, listing particulars, a circular to shareholders or similar document.

Investment circular reporting engagement—Any public or private reporting engagement in connection with an investment circular where the engagement is undertaken in accordance with Standards for Investment Reporting (SIRs).

IT environment—The policies and procedures that the entity implements and the IT infrastructure (hardware, operating systems, etc.) and application software that it uses to support business operations and achieve business strategies.

Key audit matters—Those matters that, in the auditor's professional judgment, were of most significance in the audit of the financial statements of the current period. Key audit matters are selected from matters communicated with those charged with governance.

Key audit partner–
(i)   The statutory auditor designated by an audit firm for a particular audit engagement as being primarily responsible for carrying out the statutory audit on behalf of the audit firm; or
(ii) In the case of a group audit, the statutory auditor designated by an audit firm as being primarily responsible for carrying out the statutory audit at the level of the group and the statutory auditor designated at the level of material subsidiaries; or
(iii) The statutory auditor who signs the audit report.

Key management position—Any position at an entity relevant to an engagement which involves the responsibility for fundamental management decisions at the entity (e.g. as a CEO or CFO), including an ability to influence the accounting policies and the preparation of the financial statements of the entity. A key management position also arises where there are contractual and factual arrangements which in substance allow an individual to participate in exercising such a management function in a different way (e.g. via a consulting contract).

Key partner involved in the engagement—A partner, or other person in the engagement team (other than the engagement partner or engagement quality control reviewer) who either:
● Is involved at the group level and is responsible for key aspects of the engagement, including decisions or judgments on significant matters or risk factors that relate to the engagement for that entity, or
● Is primarily responsible for the engagement work in respect of a significant affiliate, division or function of the entity.

Limited assurance engagement—(see *Assurance engagement*)

Listed entity—An entity whose shares, stock or debt are quoted or listed on a recognized stock exchange, or are marketed under the regulations of a recognized stock exchange or other equivalent body.

This includes any company in which the public can trade shares, stock or debt on the open market, such as those listed on the London Stock Exchange (including those admitted to trading on the Alternative Investment Market), and ISDX Markets. It does not include entities whose quoted or listed shares, stock or debt are in substance not freely transferable or cannot be traded freely by the public or the entity.

Management—The person(s) with executive responsibility for the conduct of the entity's operations. For some entities in some jurisdictions, management includes some or all of those charged with governance, for example, executive members of a governance board, or an owner-manager.

In the UK, management will not normally include non-executive directors.

Management bias—A lack of neutrality by management in the preparation of information.

Management's expert—An individual or organization possessing expertise in a field other than accounting or auditing, whose work in that field is used by the entity to assist the entity in preparing the financial statements.

Management's point estimate—The amount selected by management for recognition or disclosure in the financial statements as an accounting estimate.

Misappropriation of assets—Involves the theft of an entity's assets and is often perpetrated by employees in relatively small and immaterial amounts. However, it can also involve management who are usually more capable of disguising or concealing misappropriations in ways that are difficult to detect.

Misstatement—A difference between the reported amount, classification, presentation, or disclosure of a financial statement item and the amount, classification, presentation, or disclosure that is required for the item to be in accordance with the applicable financial reporting framework. Misstatements can arise from error or fraud. Where the auditor expresses an opinion on whether the financial statements are presented fairly, in all material respects, or give a true and fair view, misstatements also include those adjustments of amounts, classifications, presentation, or disclosures that, in the auditor's judgment, are necessary for the financial statements to be presented fairly, in all material respects, or to give a true and fair view.

Misstatement of the other information—A misstatement of the other information exists when the other information is incorrectly stated or otherwise misleading (including because it omits or obscures information necessary for a proper understanding of a matter disclosed in the other information).

In the UK, a misstatement of the other information also exists when the statutory other information has not been prepared in accordance with the legal and regulatory requirements applicable to the statutory other information.

Modified opinion—A qualified opinion, an adverse opinion or a disclaimer of opinion.

Monitoring (in relation to quality control)—A process comprising an ongoing consideration and evaluation of the firm's system of quality control, including a periodic inspection of a selection of completed engagements, designed to provide the firm with reasonable assurance that its system of quality control is operating effectively.

Monitoring of controls—A process to assess the effectiveness of internal control performance over time. It includes assessing the design and operation of controls on a timely basis and taking necessary corrective actions modified for changes in conditions. Monitoring of controls is a component of internal control.

Negative confirmation request—A request that the confirming party respond directly to the auditor only if the confirming party disagrees with the information provided in the request.

Network—A larger structure:
(a)   That is aimed at cooperation, and
(b)   That is clearly aimed at profit or cost-sharing or shares common ownership, control or management, common quality control policies and procedures, common business strategy, the use of a common brand name, or a significant part of professional resources.

Network firm—A firm or entity that belongs to a network.

A network firm is any entity which is part of a larger structure that is aimed at co-operation and which is:
(i)   Controlled by the firm; or
(ii)   Under common control, ownership or management; or
(iii)   Part of a larger structure that is clearly aimed at profit or cost sharing; or
(iv)   Otherwise affiliated or associated with the audit firm through common quality control policies and procedures, common business strategy, the use of a common name or through the sharing of significant common professional resources.

Non-audit services—Any engagement in which an audit firm provides professional services to an audited entity, its affiliates or another entity where the subject matter of the engagement includes the audited entity and/or its significant affiliates other than the audit of financial statements of the audited entity.

Non-compliance (in the context of ISA (UK) 250[9])—Acts of omission or commission by the entity, either intentional or unintentional, which are contrary to the prevailing laws or regulations. Such acts include transactions entered into by, or in the name of, the entity, or on its behalf, by those charged with governance, management or employees. Noncompliance does not include personal misconduct (unrelated to the business activities of the entity) by those charged with governance, management or employees of the entity.

Non-response—A failure of the confirming party to respond, or fully respond, to a positive confirmation request, or a confirmation request returned undelivered.

Non-sampling risk—The risk that the auditor reaches an erroneous conclusion for any reason not related to sampling risk.

Objectivity—Acting and making decisions and judgments impartially, fairly and on merit (having regard to all considerations relevant to the task in hand but no other), without discrimination, bias, or compromise because of commercial or personal self-interest, conflicts of interest or the undue influence of others, and having given due consideration to the best available evidence.

---

[9] *ISA (UK) 250 (Revised December 2017)* Section A – Consideration of Laws and Regulations in an Audit of Financial Statements, *and ISA (UK) 250 (Revised June 2016),* Section B – The Auditor's Statutory Right and Duty to Report to Regulators of Public Interest Entities and Regulators of Other Entities in the Financial Sector.

> *The need for objectivity in performing the engagement arises from, among other things, the fact that many of the important issues involved in the performance of the engagement, including those arising in the preparation of the subject matter information, do not relate to questions of fact but rather to questions of judgment. For example, with regard to financial statements, there are choices to be made by the board of directors in deciding on the accounting policies to be adopted by the entity: the directors have to select the ones that they consider most appropriate and this decision can have a material impact on the financial statements. Furthermore, many items included in the financial statements cannot be measured with absolute precision and certainty. In many cases, estimates have to be made and the directors may have to choose one value from a range of possible outcomes. When exercising discretion in these areas, the directors have regard to the applicable financial reporting framework.*

Observation—Consists of looking at a process or procedure being performed by others, for example, the auditor's observation of inventory counting by the entity's personnel, or of the performance of control activities.

Opening balances—Those account balances that exist at the beginning of the period. Opening balances are based upon the closing balances of the prior period and reflect the effects of transactions and events of prior periods and accounting policies applied in the prior period. Opening balances also include matters requiring disclosure that existed at the beginning of the period, such as contingencies and commitments.

Other information—Financial and non-financial information (other than the financial statements and the auditor's report thereon) included in an entity's annual report.

Other Matter paragraph—A paragraph included in the auditor's report that refers to a matter other than those presented or disclosed in the financial statements that, in the auditor's judgment, is relevant to users' understanding of the audit, the auditor's responsibilities or the auditor's report.

Outcome of an accounting estimate—The actual monetary amount which results from the resolution of the underlying transaction(s), event(s) or condition(s) addressed by the accounting estimate.

Overall audit strategy—Sets the scope, timing and direction of the audit, and guides the development of the more detailed audit plan.

Partner—Any individual with authority to bind the firm with respect to the performance of a professional services engagement.

Performance materiality—The amount or amounts set by the auditor at less than materiality for the financial statements as a whole to reduce to an appropriately low level the probability that the aggregate of uncorrected and undetected misstatements exceeds materiality for the financial statements as a whole. If applicable, performance materiality also refers to the amount or amounts set by the auditor at less than the materiality level or levels for particular classes of transactions, account balances or disclosures.

Personnel—Partners and staff.

> *Persons closely associated*[10] – A 'person closely associated' is:
>
> (a) A spouse, or a partner considered to be equivalent to a spouse in accordance with national law;
> (b) A dependent child, in accordance with national law;
> (c) A relative who (at any time in the period from the start of the financial period in respect of which the engagement is being conducted to the date on which the engagement report is signed) has lived in the same household as the person with whom they are associated for at least one year;
> (d) A firm whose managerial responsibilities are discharged by, or which is directly or indirectly controlled by, the firm/person with whom they are associated, or by any person mentioned in (a), (b) or (c) or in which the *firm* or any such person has a beneficial or other substantially equivalent economic interest;
> (e) A trust whose managerial responsibilities are discharged by, or which is directly or indirectly controlled by, or which is set up for the benefit of, or whose economic interests are substantially equivalent to, the firm/person with whom they are associated or any person mentioned in (a), (b) or (c).

Pervasive—A term used, in the context of misstatements, to describe the effects on the financial statements of misstatements or the possible effects on the financial statements of misstatements, if any, that are undetected due to an inability to obtain sufficient appropriate audit evidence. Pervasive effects on the financial statements are those that, in the auditor's judgment:

(a) Are not confined to specific elements, accounts or items of the financial statements;
(b) If so confined, represent or could represent a substantial proportion of the financial statements; or
(c) In relation to disclosures, are fundamental to users' understanding of the financial statements.

Population—The entire set of data from which a sample is selected and about which the auditor wishes to draw conclusions.

Positive confirmation request—A request that the confirming party respond directly to the auditor indicating whether the confirming party agrees or disagrees with the information in the request, or providing the requested information.

Practitioner—A professional accountant in public practice.

Preconditions for an audit—The use by management of an acceptable financial reporting framework in the preparation of the financial statements and the agreement of management and, where appropriate, those charged with governance to the premise[11] on which an audit is conducted.

Predecessor auditor—The auditor from a different audit firm, who audited the financial

---

[10] *This definition covers that required by the EU Audit Directive, and persons identified in paragraphs 5(i)(a) and 5(2)(b)(c) and (d) of paragraph 5 of Schedule 1 of SI 2016/649, 'The Statutory Auditors and Third Country Auditors Regulations 2016'. The EU Audit Directive defines a 'person closely associated' as within the meaning in Commission Directive 2004/72/EC. However, Regulation 596/2014 on market abuse (market abuse regulation) repeals and replaces, inter alia, Commission Directive 2004/72/EC with effect from 3 July 2016.*

[11] *ISA (UK) 200 (Revised June 2016), paragraph 13.*

statements of an entity in the prior period and who has been replaced by the current auditor.

Premise, relating to the responsibilities of management and, where appropriate, those charged with governance, on which an audit is conducted—That management and, where appropriate, those charged with governance have acknowledged and understand that they have the following responsibilities that are fundamental to the conduct of an audit in accordance with ISAs (UK). That is, responsibility:

(a) For the preparation of the financial statements in accordance with the applicable financial reporting framework, including where relevant their fair presentation;

(b) For such internal control as management and, where appropriate, those charged with governance determine is necessary to enable the preparation of financial statements that are free from material misstatement, whether due to fraud or error; and

(c) To provide the auditor with:

    (i) Access to all information of which management and, where appropriate, those charged with governance are aware that is relevant to the preparation of the financial statements such as records, documentation and other matters;

    (ii) Additional information that the auditor may request from management and, where appropriate, those charged with governance for the purpose of the audit; and

    (iii) Unrestricted access to persons within the entity from whom the auditor determines it necessary to obtain audit evidence.

In the case of a fair presentation framework, (a) above may be restated as 'for the preparation and fair presentation of the financial statements in accordance with the financial reporting framework,' or 'for the preparation of financial statements that give a true and fair view in accordance with the financial reporting framework.'

The 'premise, relating to the responsibilities of management and, where appropriate, those charged with governance, on which an audit is conducted' may also be referred to as the 'premise.'

Private reporting engagement—An engagement, in connection with an investment circular, in which a reporting accountant does not express a conclusion that is published in an investment circular.

Professional accountant—

For the purpose of the ISAs (UK) and the FRC's Ethical Standard, *Professional accountants* are those persons who are members of a professional accountancy body, whether in public practice (including a sole practitioner, partnership or corporate body), industry, commerce, the public sector or education.

Professional accountant in public practice—A professional accountant, irrespective of functional classification (for example, audit, tax or consulting) in a firm that provides professional services. This term is also used to refer to a firm of professional accountants in public practice.

Professional judgment—The application of relevant training, knowledge and experience, within the context provided by auditing, accounting and ethical standards, in making informed decisions about the courses of action that are appropriate in the circumstances of the audit engagement.

Professional skepticism—An attitude that includes a questioning mind, being alert to conditions which may indicate possible misstatement due to error or fraud, and a critical assessment of evidence.

Professional standards—International Standards on Auditing (ISAs) (UK) and relevant ethical requirements.

In the UK, professional standards in the context of ISQC (UK) 1 (Revised June 2016)[12] are the Ethical and Engagement Standards described in the Statement 'The Financial Reporting Council – Scope and Authority of Audit and Assurance Pronouncements.'

Projection—Prospective financial information prepared on the basis of:
(a)   Hypothetical assumptions about future events and management actions which are not necessarily expected to take place, such as when some entities are in a startup phase or are considering a major change in the nature of operations; or
(b)   A mixture of best-estimate and hypothetical assumptions.

Prospective financial information—Financial information based on assumptions about events that may occur in the future and possible actions by an entity. Prospective financial information can be in the form of a forecast, a projection or a combination of both. (see Forecast and Projection)

Public interest assurance engagement—Audits of financial statements[13] undertaken in compliance with International Standards on Auditing (ISAs) (UK) and other engagements undertaken in compliance with performance standards issued by the FRC which, as of June 2016, comprise:

(a)   Reporting accountants acting in connection with an investment circular (the Standards for Investment Reporting – 'SIRs');
(b)   Review of interim financial information by the independent auditor of the entity (International Standard on Review Engagements (UK and Ireland) 2410); and
(c)   Engagements to provide assurance on client assets to the Financial Conduct Authority (the CASS Standard).

Public interest entity—These are:

(a)   An issuer whose transferable securities are admitted to trading on a regulated market[14];
(b)   A credit institution within the meaning of Article 4(1)(1) of Regulation (EU) No 575/2013 of the European Parliament and of the Council[15], other than those listed in Article 2 of Directive 2013/36/EU of the European Parliament and of the Council on access to the activity of credit institutions and investment firms;

---

[12] *ISQC (UK) 1 (Revised June 2016)*, Quality Control for Firms that Perform Audits and Reviews of Financial Statements, and Other Assurance and Related Services Engagements.

[13] *In the public sector the statutory scope of an audit can extend beyond the entity's financial statements to include reporting on an entity's arrangements for the proper conduct of its financial affairs, management of its performance or use of its resources.*

[14] *'issuer' and 'regulated market' have the same meaning as in Part 6 of Financial Services and Markets Act 2000. 'Transferable securities' means anything which is a transferable security for the purposes of Directive 2004/39/EC of the European Parliament and of the Council on markets in financial instruments.*

[15] *Regulation (EU) 575/2013 of the European Parliament and of the Council of 26 June 2013 on prudential requirements for credit institutions and investment firms and amending Regulation (EU) No 648/2012.*

(c) An insurance undertaking within the meaning given by Article 2(1) of Council Directive 1991/674/EEC of the European Parliament and of the Council on the annual accounts and consolidated accounts of insurance undertaking.

No other entities have been specifically designated in law in the UK as 'public interest entities'.

Public reporting engagement—An engagement in which a reporting accountant expresses a conclusion that is published in an investment circular and which is designed to enhance the degree of confidence of the intended users of the report about the 'outcome' of the directors' evaluation or measurement of 'subject matter' (usually financial information) against suitable criteria.

Public sector—National governments, regional (for example, state, provincial, territorial) governments, local (for example, city, town) governments and related governmental entities (for example, agencies, boards, commissions and enterprises).

Reasonable assurance (in the context of assurance engagements and in quality control)—A high, but not absolute, level of assurance.

Reasonable assurance engagement—(see *Assurance engagement*)

Recalculation—Consists of checking the mathematical accuracy of documents or records.

Related party—A party that is either:
(a) A related party as defined in the applicable financial reporting framework; or
(b) Where the applicable financial reporting framework establishes minimal or no related party requirements:
  (i)   A person or other entity that has control or significant influence, directly or indirectly through one or more intermediaries, over the reporting entity;
  (ii) Another entity over which the reporting entity has control or significant influence, directly or indirectly through one or more intermediaries; or
  (iii) Another entity that is under common control with the reporting entity through having:
    (a) Common controlling ownership;
    (b) Owners who are close family members; or
    (c) Common key management.
  However, entities that are under common control by a state (that is, a national, regional or local government) are not considered related unless they engage in significant transactions or share resources to a significant extent with one another.

In the UK relevant definitions of 'related party' are set out in the applicable financial reporting frameworks (for example, the definitions in International Accounting Standard 24, *Related Party Disclosures*, or FRS 102, *The Financial Reporting Standard applicable in the UK and the Republic of Ireland*).

Related services—Comprise agreed-upon procedures and compilations.

Relevant ethical requirements–

In the UK the firm and its personnel are subject to ethical requirements from two sources: the FRC's Ethical Standard concerning the integrity, objectivity and independence of the firm and its personnel, and the ethical established by the auditor or assurance practitioner's relevant professional.

Relevant period—The engagement period and any additional period before the engagement period but subsequent to the balance sheet date of the most recent audited financial statements of the engagement client.

Reperformance—The auditor's independent execution of procedures or controls that were originally performed as part of the entity's internal controls.

Report on the description and design of controls at a service organization (referred to in ISA (UK) 402[16] *as a type 1 report)*—A report that comprises:

(a) A description, prepared by management of the service organization, of the service organization's system, control objectives and related controls that have been designed and implemented as at a specified date; and

(b) A report by the service auditor with the objective of conveying reasonable assurance that includes the service auditor's opinion on the description of the service organization's system, control objectives and related controls and the suitability of the design of the controls to achieve the specified control objectives.

Report on the description, design, and operating effectiveness of controls at a service organization (referred to in ISA (UK) 402 as a type 2 report)—A report that comprises:

(a) A description, prepared by management of the service organization, of the service organization's system, control objectives and related controls, their design and implementation as at a specified date or throughout a specified period and, in some cases, their operating effectiveness throughout a specified period; and

(b) A report by the service auditor with the objective of conveying reasonable assurance that includes:

   (i) The service auditor's opinion on the description of the service organization's system, control objectives and related controls, the suitability of the design of the controls to achieve the specified control objectives, and the operating effectiveness of the controls; and

   (ii) A description of the service auditor's tests of the controls and the results thereof.

Reporting accountant—An accountant engaged to prepare a report for inclusion in, or in connection with, an investment circular. The reporting accountant may or may not be the auditor of the entity issuing the investment circular. The term 'reporting accountant' is used to describe either the engagement partner or the engagement partner's firm[17]. The reporting accountant could be a limited company or a principal employed by the company.

---

[16] *ISA (UK) 402*, Audit Considerations Relating to an Entity Using a Service Organization.

[17] *Where the term applies to the engagement partner, it describes the responsibilities or obligations of the engagement partner. Such obligations or responsibilities may be fulfilled by either the engagement partner or another member of the engagement team.*

Review (in relation to quality control)—Appraising the quality of the work performed and conclusions reached by others.

Review engagement—The objective of a review engagement is to enable an auditor to state whether, on the basis of procedures which do not provide all the evidence that would be required in an audit, anything has come to the auditor's attention that causes the auditor to believe that the financial statements are not prepared, in all material respects, in accordance with an applicable financial reporting framework.

Review procedures—The procedures deemed necessary to meet the objective of a review engagement, primarily inquiries of entity personnel and analytical procedures applied to financial data.

Risk assessment procedures—The audit procedures performed to obtain an understanding of the entity and its environment, including the entity's internal control, to identify and assess the risks of material misstatement, whether due to fraud or error, at the financial statement and assertion levels.

Risk of material misstatement—The risk that the financial statements are materially misstated prior to audit. This consists of two components, described as follows at the assertion level:
(a) Inherent risk—The susceptibility of an assertion about a class of transaction, account balance or disclosure to a misstatement that could be material, either individually or when aggregated with other misstatements, before consideration of any related controls.
(b) Control risk—The risk that a misstatement that could occur in an assertion about a class of transaction, account balance or disclosure and that could be material, either individually or when aggregated with other misstatements, will not be prevented, or detected and corrected, on a timely basis by the entity's internal control.

Sampling—(see *Audit sampling*)

Sampling risk—The risk that the auditor's conclusion based on a sample may be different from the conclusion if the entire population were subjected to the same audit procedure. Sampling risk can lead to two types of erroneous conclusions:
(a) In the case of a test of controls, that controls are more effective than they actually are, or in the case of a test of details, that a material misstatement does not exist when in fact it does. The auditor is primarily concerned with this type of erroneous conclusion because it affects audit effectiveness and is more likely to lead to an inappropriate audit opinion.
(b) In the case of a test of controls, that controls are less effective than they actually are, or in the case of a test of details, that a material misstatement exists when in fact it does not. This type of erroneous conclusion affects audit efficiency as it would usually lead to additional work to establish that initial conclusions were incorrect.

Sampling unit—The individual items constituting a population.

Scope of a review—The review procedures deemed necessary in the circumstances to achieve the objective of the review.

Service auditor—An auditor who, at the request of the service organization, provides an assurance report on the controls of a service organization.

Service organization—A third-party organization (or segment of a third-party organization) that provides services to user entities that are part of those entities' information systems relevant to financial reporting.

Service organization's system—The policies and procedures designed, implemented and maintained by the service organization to provide user entities with the services covered by the service auditor's report.

Significance—The relative importance of a matter, taken in context. The significance of a matter is judged by the practitioner in the context in which it is being considered. This might include, for example, the reasonable prospect of its changing or influencing the decisions of intended users of the practitioner's report; or, as another example, where the context is a judgment about whether to report a matter to those charged with governance, whether the matter would be regarded as important by them in relation to their duties. Significance can be considered in the context of quantitative and qualitative factors, such as relative magnitude, the nature and effect on the subject matter and the expressed interests of intended users or recipients.

Significant affiliate—An affiliate identified by the group engagement team:
(i) That is of individual financial significance to the group, or
(ii) That, due to its specific nature or circumstances, is likely to include significant risks of material misstatement of the group financial statements.

Significant component—A component identified by the group engagement team (i) that is of individual financial significance to the group, or (ii) that, due to its specific nature or circumstances, is likely to include significant risks of material misstatement of the group financial statements.

Significant deficiency in internal control—A deficiency or combination of deficiencies in internal control that, in the auditor's professional judgment, is of sufficient importance to merit the attention of those charged with governance.

Significant risk—An identified and assessed risk of material misstatement that, in the auditor's judgment, requires special audit consideration.

Smaller entity—An entity which typically possesses qualitative characteristics such as:
(a) Concentration of ownership and management in a small number of individuals (often a single individual – either a natural person or another enterprise that owns the entity provided the owner exhibits the relevant qualitative characteristics); and
(b) One or more of the following:
   (i)   Straightforward or uncomplicated transactions;
   (ii) Simple record-keeping;
   (iii) Few lines of business and few products within business lines;
   (iv) Few internal controls;
   (v)   Few levels of management with responsibility for a broad range of controls; or
   (vi) Few personnel, many having a wide range of duties.

These qualitative characteristics are not exhaustive, they are not exclusive to smaller entities, and smaller entities do not necessarily display all of these characteristics.

In the UK, company law provides a lighter reporting regime for companies that are defined, by legislation, as small. A company qualifies as 'small' if it meets particular thresholds in respect of turnover, balance sheet total/gross assets and number of employees and certain other criteria. The thresholds and other criteria are subject to change and reference to the relevant legislation should be made to determine what they are in respect of a particular accounting period.

For the purpose of the FRC's Ethical Standard, a small entity is defined in Section 6 of Part B of that standard.

SME listed entity–

(a) An entity whose equity financial instruments had an average market capitalisation of less than €200m on the basis of year end quotes for the previous three calendar years; or
(b) An entity that issues exclusively non-equity financial instruments if:
    (i) The total nominal amount of the non-equity financial instruments issued and outstanding does not exceed €200m; or
    (ii) According to the last annual or consolidated accounts, meets at least two of the following criteria:
- An average number of employee during the financial year of less than 250;
- A total balance sheet not exceeding €43m;
- An annual net turnover not exceeding €50m.

An entity whose equity financial instruments have been admitted to trading for less than three years shall be deemed an SME if its market capitalisation is below €200m based on:

(a) The closing share price of the first day of trading, if its shares have been admitted to trading for less than one year;
(b) The last closing share price of the first year of trading, if its financial instruments have been admitted to trading for more than one year but less than two years; or
(c) The average of the last closing share prices of each of the first two years of trading, if its financial instruments have been admitted to trading for more than two years but less than three years.

Special purpose financial statements—Financial statements prepared in accordance with a special purpose framework.

Special purpose framework—A financial reporting framework designed to meet the financial information needs of specific users. The financial reporting framework may be a fair presentation framework or a compliance framework.[18]

Staff—Professionals, other than partners, including any experts the firm employs.

For the FRC's Ethical Standard, 'staff' are the firm's, managers, auditors, employees and any other natural persons whose services are placed at the disposal or under the control of the firm.

Statistical sampling—An approach to sampling that has the following characteristics:
(a) Random selection of the sample items; and
(b) The use of probability theory to evaluate sample results, including measurement of sampling risk.

A sampling approach that does not have characteristics (a) and (b) is considered non-statistical sampling.

---

[18] *ISA (UK) 200 (Revised June 2016), paragraph 13(a).*

Statutory audit—An audit performed pursuant to the EU Audit Directive and Regulation or otherwise designated by national law as a statutory audit.

Statutory auditor[19]—A natural person with the appropriate approval to carry out statutory audits.

Statutory other information—For statutory audits of financial statements, Those documents or reports that are required to be prepared and issued by the entity (including any reports or documents that are incorporated by cross reference) in relation to which the auditor is required to report publicly in accordance with law or regulation.

In the UK, the statutory other information includes, where required to be prepared:
(i)   The directors' report;
(ii)   The strategic report;
(iii) The separate corporate governance statement.[20]

Stratification—The process of dividing a population into sub-populations, each of which is a group of sampling units which have similar characteristics (often monetary value).

Subject matter—The underlying object of the engagement, the outcome of the evaluation or measurement of which against the criteria comprises the subject matter information.

> *Subject matter varies widely in assurance engagements but in public interest assurance engagements is often one or more financial or non-financial aspects of an entity of interest to the intended users of the assurance report. The entity responsible for the subject matter is therefore usually the entity whose underlying subject matter is being addressed in such engagements. In some engagements, there can be more than one entity responsible for the subject matter.*

Subject matter information—The outcome of the evaluation or measurement of the subject matter against the criteria,

> *The entity responsible for the subject matter information is therefore the entity responsible for the measurement or evaluation of the subject matter against the criteria. In many attestation assurance engagements, this is the same as the entity responsible for the subject matter (as is also the case in an audit engagement). However, there may be a separate evaluator or measurer of the subject matter. In direct assurance engagements (such as the CASS audit213), the evaluation or measurement is performed by the assurance practitioner. When the entity responsible for the subject matter information is the assurance practitioner, it is not an entity relevant to the engagement. In some engagements, there can be more than one entity responsible for the subject matter information.*

---

[19] *In the EU Audit Directive and Regulation the term 'statutory auditor' is used in the context of a natural person. In the UK Companies Act 2006, the term 'statutory auditor' is used for both natural and legal persons.*

[20] *When the required information is not included within or incorporated by cross reference to the directors' report.*

[21] *Engagements to provide assurance on client assets to the Financial Conduct Authority.*

Subsequent events—Events occurring between the date of the financial statements and the date of the auditor's report, and facts that become known to the auditor after the date of the auditor's report.

Subservice organization—A service organization used by another service organization to perform some of the services provided to user entities that are part of those user entities' information systems relevant to financial reporting.

Substantive procedure—An audit procedure designed to detect material misstatements at the assertion level. Substantive procedures comprise:

(a) Tests of details (of classes of transactions, account balances, and disclosures); and
(b) Substantive analytical procedures.

Sufficiency (of audit evidence)—The measure of the quantity of audit evidence. The quantity of the audit evidence needed is affected by the auditor's assessment of the risks of material misstatement and also by the quality of such audit evidence.

Suitably qualified external person—An individual outside the firm with the competence and capabilities to act as an engagement partner, for example a partner of another firm, or an employee (with appropriate experience) of either a professional accountancy body whose members may perform audits and reviews of historical financial information, or other assurance or related services engagements, or of an organization that provides relevant quality control services.

Supplementary information—Information that is presented together with the financial statements that is not required by the applicable financial reporting framework used to prepare the financial statements, normally presented in either supplementary schedules or as additional notes.

Test—The application of procedures to some or all items in a population.

Tests of controls—An audit procedure designed to evaluate the operating effectiveness of controls in preventing, or detecting and correcting, material misstatements at the assertion level.

Those charged with governance—The person(s) or organization(s) (e.g., a corporate trustee) with responsibility for overseeing the strategic direction of the entity and obligations related to the accountability of the entity. This includes overseeing the financial reporting process. For some entities in some jurisdictions, those charged with governance may include management personnel, for example, executive members of a governance board of a private or public sector entity, or an owner-manager.[22]

> In the UK, those charged with governance include the directors (executive and non-executive) of a company and the members of an audit committee where one exists. For other types of entity it usually includes equivalent persons such as the partners, proprietors, committee of management or trustees.

---

[22] *For discussion of the diversity of governance structures, see paragraphs A1–A8 of ISA (UK) 260 (Revised June 2016)*, Communication with Those Charged with Governance.

Tolerable misstatement—A monetary amount set by the auditor in respect of which the auditor seeks to obtain an appropriate level of assurance that the monetary amount set by the auditor is not exceeded by the actual misstatement in the population.

Tolerable rate of deviation—A rate of deviation from prescribed internal control procedures set by the auditor in respect of which the auditor seeks to obtain an appropriate level of assurance that the rate of deviation set by the auditor is not exceeded by the actual rate of deviation in the population.

Uncertainty—A matter whose outcome depends on future actions or events not under the direct control of the entity but that may affect the financial statements.

Uncorrected misstatements—Misstatements that the auditor has accumulated during the audit and that have not been corrected.

Unmodified opinion—The opinion expressed by the auditor when the auditor concludes that the financial statements are prepared, in all material respects, in accordance with the applicable financial reporting framework.

User auditor—An auditor who audits and reports on the financial statements of a user entity.

User entity—An entity that uses a service organization and whose financial statements are being audited.

Walk-through test—Involves tracing a few transactions through the financial reporting system.

Written representation—A written statement by management provided to the auditor to confirm certain matters or to support other audit evidence. Written representations in this context do not include financial statements, the assertions therein, or supporting books and records.